SAAB 900

16 VALVE

Official Service Manual
1985, 1986, 1987, 1988, 1989, 1990, 1991, 1992, 1993

B BentleyPublishers .com

Selected Books and Repair Information From Bentley Publishers

Engineering

Bosch Fuel Injection and Engine Management *Charles O. Probst, SAE*
ISBN 0-8376-0300-5

Maximum Boost: Designing, Testing, and Installing Turbocharger Systems
Corky Bell ISBN 0-8376-0160-6

Race Car Aerodynamics *Joseph Katz*
ISBN 0-8376-0142-8

Scientific Design of Exhaust and Intake Systems *Phillip H. Smith & John C. Morrison* ISBN 0-8376-0309-9

Audi Repair Manuals (paper)

Audi A4 Service Manual: 1996-2001, 1.8L Turbo, 2.8L, including Avant and quattro *Bentley Publishers*
ISBN 0-8376-0371-4

Audi TT Service Manual: 2000-2006, 1.8L turbo, 3.2 L, including Roadster and quattro *Bentley Publishers*
ISBN 0-8376-1500-3

Audi A6 (C5 platform) Service Manual: 1998-2004, includes A6, allroad quattro, S6, RS6 *Bentley Publishers*
ISBN 0-8376-1499-6

Audi Repair Manuals (electronic)

Audi A3: 2006 Repair Manual on CD-ROM *Audi of America*
ISBN 0-8376-1363-9

Audi A6: 2005-2006 Repair Manual on CD-ROM *Audi of America*
ISBN 0-8376-1362-0

Audi A4/S4: 1996-2002 Manual on DVD-ROM *Audi of America*
ISBN 0-8376-1255-1

Audi TT Coupe: 2000-2006, Roadster: 2001-2006 Repair Manual on CD-ROM *Audi of America*
ISBN 0-8376-1261-6

BMW Repair Manuals (paper only)

BMW 7 Series (E38) Service Manual: 1995-2001, 740i, 740iL, 750iL
Bentley Publishers
ISBN 0-8376-1531-3

BMW 3 Series (E46) Service Manual: 1999-2005 *Bentley Publishers*
ISBN 0-8376-1277-2

BMW Z3 (E36/7)Service Manual: 1996-2002 *Bentley Publishers*
ISBN 0-8376-1250-0

BMW 5 Series (E39) Service Manual: 1997-2002 *Bentley Publishers*
ISBN 0-8376-0317-X

BMW 3 Series (E36) Service Manual: 1992-1998 *Bentley Publishers*
ISBN 0-8376-0326-9

BMW 5 Series (E34) Service Manual: 1989-1995 *Bentley Publishers*
ISBN 0-8376-0319-6

BMW 7 Series (E32) Service Manual: 1988-1994 *Bentley Publishers*
ISBN 0-8376-0328-5

BMW 3 Series (E30) Service Manual: 1984-1990 *Bentley Publishers*
ISBN 0-8376-0325-0

Porsche Repair Manuals (paper only)

Porsche Boxster Service Manual: 1997-2004 *Bentley Publishers*
ISBN 0-8376-1333-7

Porsche 911 Carrera Service Manual: 1984-1989 *Bentley Publishers*
ISBN 0-8376-0291-2

Porsche 911 SC Service Manual: 1987-1983 *Bentley Publishers*
ISBN 0-8376-0290-4

Volkswagen Repair Manuals (paper)

Volkswagen Jetta Service Manual: 2005-2006 *Bentley Publishers*
ISBN 0-8376-1335-3

Volkswagen Jetta, Golf, GTI Service Manual: 1999-2005 *Bentley Publishers*
ISBN 0-8376-1251-9

Volkswagen Passat Service Manual: 1998-2005 *Bentley Publishers*
ISBN 0-8376-1483-X

Volkswagen Jetta, Golf, GTI: 1993-1999 Cabrio: 1995-2002 Service Manual *Bentley Publishers*
ISBN 0-8376-0366-8

Volkswagen GTI, Golf, Jetta Service Manual: 1985-1992 *Bentley Publishers*
ISBN 0-8376-0342-0

Volkswagen Vanagon Repair Manual: 1980-1991 *Volkswagen of America*
ISBN 0-8376-0336-6

Volkswagen Corrado Repair Manual: 1990-1994 *Volkswagen of America*
ISBN 0-8376-0387-0

Volkswagen Rabbit, Scirocco, Jetta Service Manual: 1980-1984 Gasoline Models *Bentley Publishers*
ISBN 0-8376-0183-5

Volkswagen Super Beetle, Beetle and Karmann Ghia Service Manual Type 1: 1970-1979 *Volkswagen of America*
ISBN 0-8376-0096-0

Volkswagen Repair Manuals (electronic)

Volkswagen Jetta: 2005-2007 Repair Manual on DVD-ROM *Volkswagen of America* ISBN 0-8376-1360-4

Volkswagen Golf, GTI: 1999-2006, Jetta: 1999-2005, Jetta Wagon: 2001-2006 Repair Manual on DVD-ROM
Volkswagen of America
ISBN 0-8376-1264-0

Volkswagen Passat, Passat Wagon: 1998-2005 Repair Manual on DVD-ROM
Volkswagen of America
ISBN 0-8376-1267-5

Volkswagen Passat, Passat Wagon: 1995-1997 Repair Manual on DVD-ROM
Volkswagen of America
ISBN 0-8376-1266-7

Volkswagen New Beetle: 1998-2006, New Beetle Convertible 2003-2006 Repair Manual on DVD-ROM
Volkswagen of America
ISBN 0-8376-1265-9

[B] BentleyPublishers™ .com

Automotive Reference

Bentley Publishers has published service manuals and automobile books since 1950. For more information, please contact Bentley Publishers at 1734 Massachusetts Avenue, Cambridge, MA 02138, visit our web site at **www.BentleyPublishers.com** or call 1-800-423-4595 for a free copy of our complete catalog.

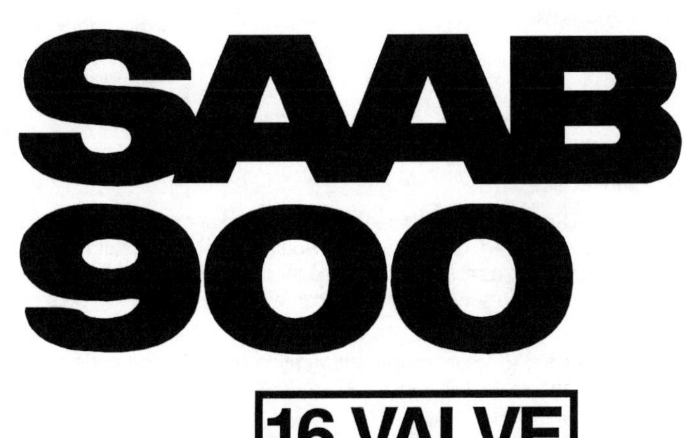

16 VALVE

Official Service Manual
1985, 1986, 1987, 1988, 1989, 1990, 1991, 1992, 1993

B BentleyPublishers.com

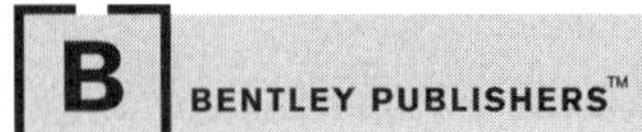

Bentley Publishers, a division of Robert Bentley, Inc.
1734 Massachusetts Avenue
Cambridge, MA 02138 USA
800-423-4595 / 617-547-4170

Information that makes the difference®

BentleyPublishers.com

Technical Contact Information

We welcome your constructive feedback on this book. Please submit any corrections, updates and additions to this book that may be of use to other enthusiasts to our technical discussion forum at:

`http://www.BentleyPublishers.com`

Errata Information

We will evaluate submissions and post appropriate editorial changes online as text errata or tech discussion. Appropriate errata will be incorporated with the book text in following printings. Read errata for this book before beginning work on your vehicle. See the following web page for further information:

`http://www.BentleyPublishers.com/errata/`

WARNING—Important Safety Notice

Do not use this manual unless you are familiar with basic automotive repair procedures and safe workshop practices. This manual illustrates the workshop procedures required for most service work; it is not a substitute for full and up-to-date information from the vehicle manufacturer or for proper training as an automotive technician. Note that it is not possible for us to anticipate all of the ways or conditions under which vehicles may be serviced or to provide warnings and cautions as to all of the possible hazards that may result.

The vehicle manufacturer will continue to issue service information updates and parts retrofits after the editorial closing of this manual. Some of these updates and retrofits will apply to procedures and specifications in this manual. We regret that we cannot supply updates to purchasers of this manual.

We have endeavored to ensure the accuracy of the information in this manual. Please note, however, that considering the vast quantity and the complexity of the service information involved, we cannot warrant the accuracy or completeness of the information contained in this manual.

FOR THESE REASONS, NEITHER THE PUBLISHER NOR THE AUTHOR MAKES ANY WARRANTIES, EXPRESS OR IMPLIED, THAT THE INFORMATION IN THIS BOOK IS FREE OF ERRORS OR OMISSIONS AND WE EXPRESSLY DISCLAIM THE IMPLIED WARRANTIES OF MERCHANTABILITY AND OF FITNESS FOR A PARTICULAR PURPOSE, EVEN IF THE PUBLISHER OR AUTHOR HAVE BEEN ADVISED OF A PARTICULAR PURPOSE, AND EVEN IF A PARTICULAR PURPOSE IS INDICATED IN THE MANUAL. THE PUBLISHER AND AUTHOR ALSO DISCLAIM ALL LIABILITY FOR DIRECT, INDIRECT, INCIDENTAL OR CONSEQUENTIAL DAMAGES THAT RESULT FROM ANY USE OF THE EXAMPLES, INSTRUCTIONS OR OTHER INFORMATION IN THIS BOOK. IN NO EVENT SHALL OUR LIABILITY WHETHER IN TORT, CONTRACT OR OTHERWISE EXCEED THE COST OF THIS MANUAL.

Your common sense and good judgment are crucial to safe and successful service work. Read procedures through before starting them. Think about whether the condition of your car, your level of mechanical skill, or your level of reading comprehension might result in or contribute in some way to an occurrence which might cause you injury, damage your car, or result in an unsafe repair. If you have doubts for these or other reasons about your ability to perform safe repair work on your car, have the work done at an authorized Saab dealer or other qualified shop.

This Do-It-Yourself repair manual is only intended for persons who have a great deal of experience in repairing automobiles and who are seeking specific information about the Saab 900 model. It is not for those who are looking for general information on automobile repair. REPAIR OF AUTOMOBILES IS DANGEROUS UNLESS UNDERTAKEN WITH FULL KNOWLEDGE OF THE CONSEQUENCES.

The information in this manual is based on product information available from Saab Automobile AB and Saab Cars USA, Inc. at the time of editorial closing. Saab has not reviewed and does not warrant the accuracy or completeness of the technical specifications and procedures described in this manual. Neither Saab Automobile AB nor Saab Cars USA, Inc. shall be responsible for new developments or information developed after the printing of this manual. Contact Bentley Publishers for any new developments and information that may become available after the publication of this manual.

Part numbers listed in this manual are for identification purposes only, not for ordering. Always check with your authorized Saab dealer to verify part numbers and availability before beginning service work that may require new parts.

Before attempting any work on your Saab, read the warnings and cautions on pages ix and x and any warning or caution that accompanies a procedure in the service manual. Review the warnings and cautions on pages ix and x each time you prepare to work on your Saab.

Special tools required to perform certain service operations are identified in the manual and are recommended for use. Use of tools other than those recommended in this service manual may be detrimental to the car's safe operation as well as the safety of the person servicing the car.

Copies of this manual may be purchased from authorized Saab dealers, most automotive accessories and parts dealers specializing in Saabs, from selected booksellers, or directly from the publisher. The publisher encourages comments from the reader of this manual. These communications have been and will be considered in the preparation of this and other manuals. Please contact Bentley Publishers at the address listed on the top of this page.

This manual was published by Bentley Publishers.

Library of Congress Catalog Card No. 93-70727
ISBN 0-8376-0313-7
Bentley Stock No. S993
Saab P/N 02 16 861

Editorial closing 06/93

Printing Code: S993-12 0712

The paper used in this publication is acid free and meets the requirements of the National Standard for Information Sciences- Permanence of Paper for Printed Library Materials. ∞

Foreword

This Saab 900 16 Valve Service Manual covers all1985 through 1993 900 models with 16 valve engines and is specifically designed to cover these models built for sale in the United States only.

All Saab 900 16 valve models:

1985-1993	Turbo, including Turbo SPG (all)
1987-1993	Convertible (all)
1986-1993	900S (all)
1989-1992	900 (all)

This manual has been organized using the Saab Official numbered indexing system. This numbered system will be primarily helpful to Saab factory-trained technicians experienced with the multi-volume Official Saab 900 Service Manual binder set, but we hope it will also facilitate information retrieval for all other users of the manual.

Saab uses an internal code for the various engines used in the 900 models. All 16 valve engines used in the 900 models are grouped under the B202 or B212 heading. The letter "B" designates the fuel type, or gasoline (benzine). The first two numbers designate the engine size, e.g. 2.0 or 2.1 liter. The last number designates the number of camshafts. All 16 valve engines are of the twin overhead camshaft design. The single overhead camshaft Saab 2.0 liter 8 valve engine has an engine code of B201. This information is primarily used internally by Saab, but may be helpful if you have access to Saab technical information.

For the Saab owner with automobile repair skills and training, this manual gives detailed maintenance and repair information. In addition, the Saab owner who has no intention of working on his or her own car will find that owning and reading this manual will make it possible to be better informed and to discuss repairs more intelligently with a professional technician. This manual has been prepared from the repair information that Saab provides to its factory-trained technicians and has been developed primarily with the experienced do-it-yourself Saab owner in mind. The aim throughout has been clarity and understanding with practical functional descriptions, step-by-step procedures, and accurate specifications.

The Saab owner intending to do maintenance and repair should have a set of tools including a set of metric wrenches and sockets, screwdrivers, a torque wrench, and feeler gauges, since these basic tools will be used to do the majority of the maintenance and repair procedures described in this manual. This manual includes detailed information on these basic tools and other tips for the beginner in the first section of the manual, entitled 100 Fundamentals for the Do-it-yourself Owner. For some of the repairs described in this manual, Saab technicians use special tools. The text will note when a repair requires these special tools and, where possible, will recommend practical alternatives.

We have endeavored to ensure the accuracy of the information in this manual . When the vast array of data presented in the manual is taken into account, however, no claim to infallibility can be made. The publisher therefore cannot be responsible for the result of any errors that may have crept into the text. The publisher encourages comments from the readers of this manual in regard to any errors and, also, suggestions for improvement in the presentation of technical material. These communications have been and will be carefully considered in the preparation of future printings of this and other manuals. Please write to Robert Bentley, Inc., Cambridge, Massachusetts 02138.

Saab offers extensive warranties, especially on components of the fuel delivery and emissions control systems. Therefore, before deciding to repair a Saab that may still be covered wholly or in part by any warranties issued by Saab Cars USA Inc., consult your authorized Saab dealer. You may find that he can make the repair either free or at minimum cost.

Regardless of its age and whether or not it is still protected by warranty, your Saab is both an easy car to service and an easy car to get serviced. So, if at any time a repair is needed that you feel is too difficult or dangerous to do yourself, a trained Saab technician is ready to do the job for you. Each authorized Saab dealer service department has made a significant investment in service and diagnostic test equipment, specials tools, and Saab original parts. He is also the best source of the most up-to-date repair and service techniques, which includes factory training and technical literature. Servicing your Saab through an authorized Saab dealer will insure that your investment will be protected while maintaining the highest degree of service standards.

Robert Bentley, Inc.

Please read these warnings and cautions before proceeding with maintenance and repair work.

WARNING—

- Some repairs may be beyond your capability. If you lack the skills, tools and equipment, or a suitable workplace for any procedure described in this manual, we suggest you leave such repairs to an authorized Saab dealer service department, or other qualified shop.

- Saab is constantly improving its cars. Sometimes these changes, both in parts and specifications, are made applicable to earlier models. Therefore, before starting any major jobs or repairs to components on which passenger safety may depend, consult your authorized Saab dealer about Technical Bulletins that may have been issued since the editorial closing of this manual.

- Do not re-use any fasteners that are worn or deformed in normal use. Many fasteners are designed to be used only once and become unreliable and may fail when used a second time. This includes, but is not limited to, nuts, bolts, washers, self-locking nuts or bolts, circlips and cotter pins. Always replace these fasteners with new parts.

- Never work under a lifted car unless it is solidly supported on stands designed for the purpose. Do not support a car on cinder blocks, hollow tiles or other props that may crumble under continuous load. Never work under a car that is supported solely by a jack. Never work under the car while the engine is running.

- If you are going to work under a car on the ground, make sure that the ground is level. Block the wheels to keep the car from rolling. Disconnect the battery negative (–) terminal (Ground strap) to prevent others from starting the car while you are under it.

- Never run the engine unless the work area is well ventilated. Carbon monoxide kills.

- Finger rings, bracelets and other jewelry should be removed so that they cannot cause electrical shorts, get caught in running machinery, or be crushed by heavy parts.

- Tie long hair behind your head. Do not wear a necktie, a scarf, loose clothing, or a necklace when you work near machine tools or running engines. If your hair, clothing, or jewelry were to get caught in the machinery, severe injury could result.

- Do not attempt to work on your car if you do not feel well. You increase the danger of injury to yourself and others if you are tired, upset or have taken medication or any other substance that may keep you from being fully alert.

- Illuminate your work area adequately but safely. Use a portable safety light for working inside or under the car. Make sure the bulb is enclosed by a wire cage. The hot filament of an accidentally broken bulb can ignite spilled fuel or oil.

- Catch draining fuel, oil, or brake fluid in suitable containers. Do not use food or beverage containers that might mislead someone into drinking from them. Store flammable fluids away from fire hazards. Wipe up spills at once, but do not store the oily rags, which can ignite and burn spontaneously.

- Always observe good workshop practices. Wear goggles when you operate machine tools or work with battery acid. Gloves or other protective clothing should be worn whenever the job requires working with harmful substances.

- Friction materials such as brake or clutch discs may contain asbestos fibers. Do not create dust by grinding, sanding, or by cleaning with compressed air. Avoid breathing asbestos fibers and asbestos dust. Breathing asbestos can cause serious diseases such as asbestosis or cancer, and may result in death.

- Disconnect the battery negative (–) terminal (Ground strap) whenever you work on the fuel system or the electrical system. Do not smoke or work near heaters or other fire hazards. Keep an approved fire extinguisher handy.

- Batteries give off explosive hydrogen gas during charging. Keep sparks, lighted matches and open flame away from the top of the battery. If hydrogen gas escaping from the cap vents is ignited, it will ignite gas trapped in the cells and cause the battery to explode.

- Connect and disconnect battery cables, jumper cables or a battery charger only with the ignition switched off, to prevent sparks. Do not disconnect the battery while the engine is running.

- Do not quick-charge the battery (for boost starting) for longer than one minute. Wait at least one minute before boosting the battery a second time.

- Do not allow battery charging voltage to exceed 15.0 volts. If the battery begins producing gas or boiling violently, reduce the charging rate. Boosting a sulfated battery at a high charging rate can cause an explosion.

- The air-conditioning system is filled with chemical refrigerant, which is hazardous. The A/C system should be serviced only by trained technicians using approved refrigerant recovery/recycling equipment, trained in related safety precautions, and familiar with regulations governing the discharging and disposal of automotive chemical refrigerants.

- Do not expose any part of the A/C system to high temperatures such as open flame. Excessive heat will increase system pressure and may cause the system to burst.

- Some aerosol tire inflators are highly flammable. Be extremely cautious when repairing a tire that may have been inflated using an aerosol tire inflator. Keep sparks, open flame or other sources of ignition away from the tire repair area. Inflate and deflate the tire at least four times before breaking the bead from the rim. Completely remove the tire from the rim before attempting any repair.

- Some cars covered by this manual are equipped with a supplemental restraint system (SRS), that automatically deploys an airbag in the event of a frontal impact. The airbag is inflated by an explosive device. Handled improperly or without adequate safeguards, it can be accidently activated and cause serious injury.

- To prevent personal injury or airbag system failure, **only trained Saab dealer service technicians** should test, disassemble or service the airbag system.

- The airbag unit should not be removed, nor should any other work be performed on the airbag system, until at least 20 minutes after the battery is disconnected.

continued on next page

Please read these warnings and cautions before proceeding with maintenance and repair work.

WARNING (continued) —

- On airbag-equipped cars, never apply stickers or any other type of covering on the steering wheel. Do not let chemical cleaners, oil or grease come into contact with the vinyl covering of the airbag unit.

- Never open or otherwise attempt to repair airbag system parts. Always use new parts. Never leave airbag parts or the partially disassembled airbag system unattended.

- Do not expose the airbag unit to temperature above 194°F (90°C), even for brief periods. Keep clear of heat sources such as hot plates, soldering irons, heat lamps and welding equipment.

- When driving or riding in an airbag-equipped vehicle never hold test equipment in your hands or lap while the vehicle is in motion. Objects between you and the airbag can increase the risk of injury in an accident.

- On cars equipped with anti-lock brakes (ABS), the ABS modular assembly is capable of "self-pressuring" up to 210 bar (3045 psi). Serious injury may result if the unit is not properly depressurized before servicing the system.

- Greases, lubricants and other automotive chemicals contain toxic substances, many of which are absorbed directly through the skin. Read manufacturer's instructions and warnings carefully. Use hand and eye protection. Avoid direct skin contact.

CAUTION—

- If you lack the skills, tools and equipment, or a suitable workshop for any procedure described in this manual, we suggest you leave such repairs to an authorized Saab dealer or other qualified shop.

- Saab offers extensive warranties, especially on components of fuel delivery and emission control systems. Therefore, before deciding to repair a Saab that may still be covered wholly or in part by any warranties issued by Saab Cars USA, Inc., consult your authorized Saab dealer. You may find that he can make the repair for free, or at minimal cost.

- Saab part numbers listed in this manual are for identification purposes only, not for ordering. Always check with your authorized Saab dealer to verify part numbers and availability before beginning service work that may require new parts.

- Before starting a job, make certain that you have all the necessary tools and parts on hand. Read all the instructions thoroughly, do not attempt shortcuts. Use tools appropriate to the work and use only replacement parts meeting Saab specifications. Makeshift tools, parts and procedures will not make good repairs.

- Use pneumatic and electric tools only to loosen threaded parts and fasteners. Never use these tools to tighten fasteners, especially on light alloy parts. Always use a torque wrench to tighten fasteners to the tightening torque specification listed.

- Be mindful of the environment and ecology. Before you drain the crankcase, find out the proper way to dispose of the oil. Do not pour oil onto the ground, down a drain, or into a stream, pond or lake. Consult local ordinances that govern the disposal of wastes.

- On cars equipped with the anti-lock brakes (ABS), the ABS control unit cannot withstand temperatures from a paint-drying booth or a heat lamp in excess of 203°F (95°C) and should not be subjected to temperatures in excess of 185°F (85°C) for more than two hours.

- Before doing any electrical welding on cars equipped with ABS, disconnect the battery negative (–) terminal (Ground strap) and the ABS control unit connector.

- On cars equipped with anti-theft radios, make sure you know the correct radio activation code before disconnecting the battery or removing the radio. If the wrong code is entered into the radio when power is restored, that radio may lock up and be rendered inoperable, even if the correct code is then entered.

- Connect and disconnect a battery charger only with the battery charger switched off.

- Do not quick-charge the battery (for boost starting) for longer than one minute. Wait at least one minute before boosting the battery a second time.

- Sealed or "maintenance free" batteries should be slow-charged only, at an amperage rate that is approximately 10% of the battery's ampere-hour (Ah) rating.

- Do not allow battery charging voltage to exceed 15.0 volts. If the battery begins producing gas or boiling violently, reduce the charging rate. Boosting a sulfated battery at a high charging rate can cause an explosion.

010 Technical Data—General

TECHNICAL DATA—GENERAL

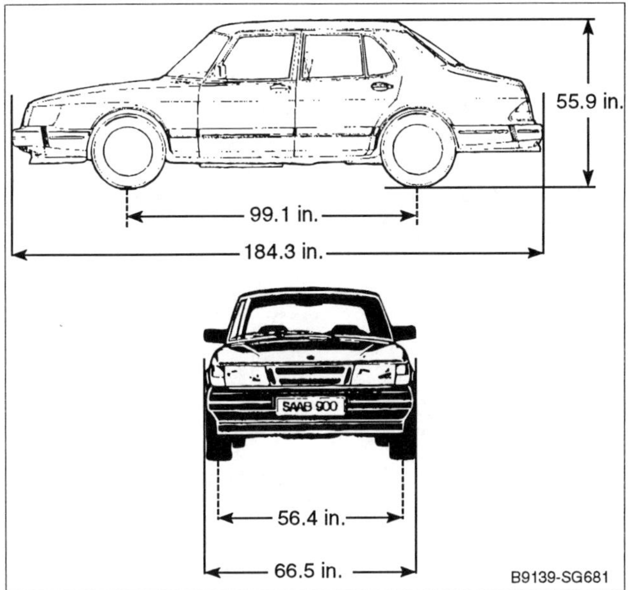

General	mm	in.
Overall length (sedans, convertibles)	4680	184.3
Overall length (hatchback)	4687	184.5
Overall width	1690	66.5
Overall height (at curb weight)	1419	55.9
Overall height with convertible at highest point	2230	87.8
Road clearance (full load)		
SPG models	120	4.7
all other models	137	5.4
Track (front)		
alloy wheels	1430	56.4
steel wheels	1437	56.6

	mm	in.
Track (rear)	1440	56.7
Wheelbase	2517	99.1
Turning radius	5600	220.5
	kg.	**lb.**
Curb weight (depending on equipment)	1252-1411	2755-3105
Gross vehicle weight (depending on equipment)	1677-1768	3690-3890
Weight distribution		
at curb weight	59-62% front	
at gross weight	52-55% front	
Vehicle capacity weight—ex. conv. (five people, 180 lb. luggage)	422	930
Maximum roof rack load—ex. conv.	100	220
Maximum trailer weight:		
trailer with brakes	900	2000
trailer without brakes	450	1000
Maximum trailer tongue weight	75	165
Trunk volume (SAE)		
hatchback		14.9 cu.ft.
hatchback, parcel shelf removed		19.1 cu.ft.
sedan		14.2 cu.ft.
convertible		10.7 cu.ft.

Engine Specifications

Model	Year	Displacement cc (cu. in.)	Compression ratio	Horsepower @ rpm SAE net	Torque lb-ft @ rpm SAE net	Fuel system
900/900S/Convertible	1986-1987	1985 (121)	10.1:1	125 @ 5500	128 @ 3000	Bosch LH 2.2
	1988	1985 (121)	10.1:1	128 @ 6000	128 @ 3000	Bosch LH 2.4
	1989-1990	1985 (121)	10.1:1	128 @ 6000	128 @ 3000	Bosch LH 2.4
	1991-1993	2118 (129)	10.1:1	140 @ 6000	133 @ 2900	Bosch LH 2.4.2
900 Turbo/Turbo Convertible	1985-1988	1985 (121)	9.0:1	160 @ 5500	188 @ 3000	Bosch LH 2.2
	1989-1993	1985 (121)	9.0:1	160 @ 5500	188 @ 3000	Bosch LH 2.4
900 SPG	1985-1986	1985 (121)	9.0:1	160 @ 5500	188 @ 3000	Bosch LH 2.2
	1987-1988	1985 (121)	9:0:1	165 @ 5500	195 @ 3000	Bosch LH 2.2
	1989	1985 (121)	9.0:1	165 @ 5500	195 @ 3000	Bosch LH 2.4
	1990-1991	1985 (121)	9.0:1	175 @ 5500	195 @ 3000	Bosch LH 2.4

LUBRICATION AND MAINTENANCE—QUICK DATA

Engine Oil Change	
Saab recommended engine oil	SAE 10W-30, API Service Rating SG or SF/CD
Alternate for extremely hot climates	15W-40, API Service Rating SG or SF/CD
Engine oil drain plug tightening torque (13 mm or 19mm wrench size)	29-39 Nm (21-29 ft-lb)
Engine Oil Capacity (including filter)	4.2 quarts (4.0 liters)

Ignition System Applications	
1985-1992 turbo models	basic Hall ignition
1986-1992 non-turbo models	EZK ignition —Hall-effect with knock sensor

Spark Plug Applications	
Model	**Spark Plug**
1986-1988 Normally aspirated	NGK BCP 6ES
alternate	NGK BCP 6EV
1989-1993 Normally-aspirated	NGK BCP 5ES

Spark Plug Applications	
Model	**Spark Plug**
1985-1993 Turbo	
normal driving	NGK BCP 7EV
alternate	NGK BCP 7ES
city driving	NGK BCP 6EV
alternate	NGK BCP 6ES
Spark plug electrode gap	0.024-0.028 in. (0.6-0.7 mm)
Tightening torque—sparkplugs	25 to 29 Nm (18 to 21 ft-lb)

Ignition Timing	
Distributor vacuum hose disconnected and plugged, where applicable	
Turbo models	16°BTDC @ 850 rpm
Normally aspirated models	14°BTDC @ 850 rpm

Cooling System	
Capacity (50/50 mixture anti-freeze and water)	10.5 quarts (10 liters)

Engine Drive Belt Tensions (measure using special belt tensioning gauge)		
Drive belt tension	**N**	**(lb)**
Alternator		
checking (minimum)		
one belt	200	(45)
two belts	420	(95)
adjusting, used belts		
one belt	310±20	(70±5)
two belts	645±20	(145±5)
adjusting, new belts		
one belt	535±45	(120±10)
A/C compressor		
checking (minimum)	245	(55)
adjusting, used belt	355±20	(80±5)
adjusting, new belt	535±45	(120±10)
Power steering		
checking (minimum)	220	(50)
adjusting, used belt	310±20	(70±5)
adjusting, new belt	445±45	(100±10)

Manual Transmission	
Grade of oil	SAE 10W-30 SF/CC, SF/CD, SG
Alternate grade of oil	SAE EP 75 API-GL-4 or API-GL-5
Oil capacity	3.1 quarts (3.0 liters)

Automatic Transmission	
ATF	Ford Specification M2C-33F (alternate: Ford Specification G)
ATF capacity	8.5 quarts (8.0 liters)
A/T final drive grade of oil	SAE EP 80 or 75 API-GL-4 or API-GL-5
Alternate grade of oil	10W-30 engine oil
A/T final drive capacity	1.3 quarts (1.25 liters)
ATF drain plug tightening torque	5-8 Nm (48-72 in-lb)
A/T final drive drain or filler plug tightening torque	39-59 Nm (28-44 ft-lb)

Brake System	
Brake Fluid Grade	SAE Dot 4
Brake Pad Wear Limit	
1985-1987 models	1.0 mm (0.04 in.)
1988 and later models	4.0 mm (0.16 in.)

WARNING
Do not use SAE DOT 5 brake fluid. Brake system failure may result.

Steering and Wheel Alignment	
Power Steering Fluid	GM Power Steering Fluid (GM 9985010), Texaco TL4634 or equivalent

022 Engine—Technical Data

ENGINE TIGHTENING TORQUES

B9081

Tightening Torques	Nm	ft-lb (in-lb)
Camshaft sprocket to camshaft	63	46
Camshaft bearing caps to cylinder head	15	11
Camshaft timing chain tensioner to timing case	63	46
Clutch slave cylinder to transmission case	6–14	(53–124 in-lb)
Coolant drain plug to engine block	15	11
Coolant temperature sensor (LH sensor)	20	15
Connecting rod cap to connecting rod	55	41
Crankshaft pulley to crankshaft		
1985-1990	190	140
1991 and later	175	129

continued

Tightening Torques	Nm	ft-lb (in-lb)
Cylinder block end plate to engine (flywheel end)	20	15
Cylinder head to cylinder block		
stage 1	60	44
stage 2	80 plus and additional 90° (1/4 turn)	59 plus and additional 90° (1/4 turn)
Engine to transmission		
automatic transmission	33–39	24–29
manual transmission	25±3	18±2.2
Engine oil cooler line to oil filter housing	7–10	(62–89 in-lb)
Engine oil drain plug to case	29–39	21–29
EGR valve to cylinder head	8	(71 in-lb)
Exhaust manifold to cylinder head		
turbo models	25	18
normally aspirated models	20	15
Flywheel to crankshaft (17 mm bolt head)	60	44
Flywheel to crankshaft (19 mm bolt head)	85	63
Fuel pump to fuel tank (threaded collar)—1990 and later	55	41
Ignition distributor to cylinder head	20	15
Intake manifold to cylinder head	22	16

continued on next page

Tightening Torques	Nm	ft-lb (in-lb)
Main bearing caps to cylinder block	110	81
Oil filter to oil filter housing	10	7.4
Oil pressure switch to oil filter housing		
small (1/4"-18 NPTF)	10	(89 in-lb)
large (M14X1.5)	30	22
Oil pump to timing chain cover	8	(71 in-lb)
Oxygen sensor	40	30
Spark plugs to cylinder head	28	21
Thermostat housing to cylinder head	18	13
Timing chain cover to engine block and cylinder head	20	15
Timing chain tensioner to cylinder head	63	46
Valve cover to cylinder head	15	11
All other fasteners		
M5 bolt	5	(44 in-lb)
M6 bolt	10	(89 in-lb)
M8 bolt	20	15
M10 bolt	40	30

CONNECTING RODS AND PISTON PINS

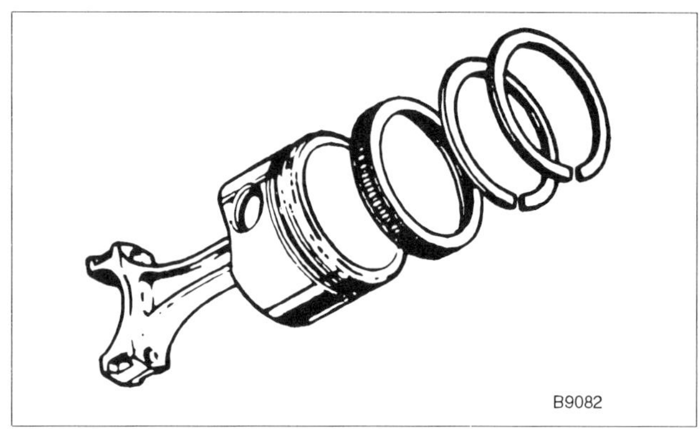
B9082

Connecting rods	mm	in.
Diameter of big end (bearing shells removed)	56.000–56.019	2.2047–2.2055
Diameter of small end (bushing installed)	24.005–24.010	0.9451–0.9453
Big-end clearance	0.026–0.062	0.0010–0.0024
Maximum permissible weight variation per set	9 g (0.32 oz.)	

Piston pins	mm	in.
Piston pin diameter	23.996–24.000	0.9447–0.9449
Piston pin to connecting rod clearance		
B202 engine	0.005–0.014	0.0002–0.0006
B212 engine	0.002–0.011	0.00008–0.0004

PISTON RINGS

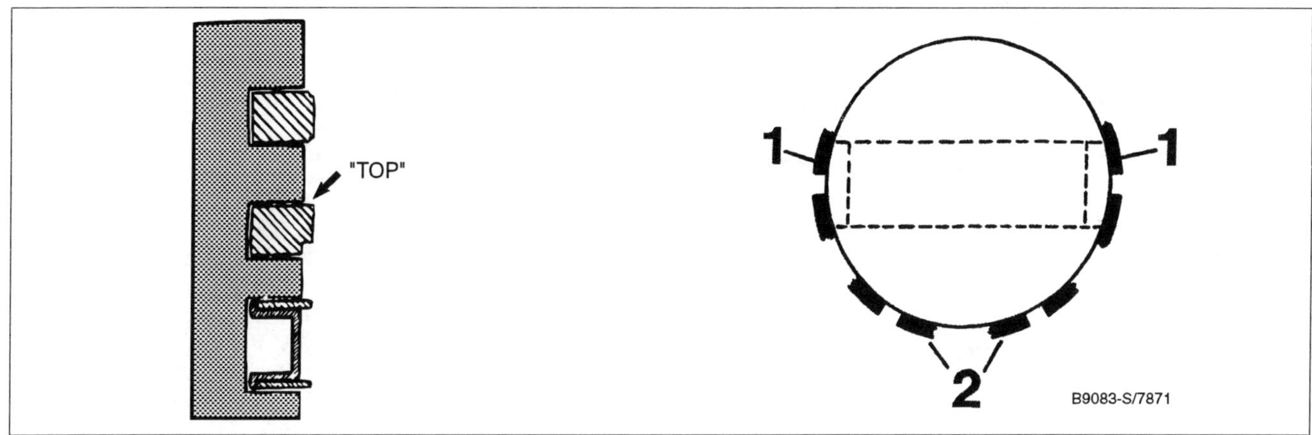

Piston Ring	Top compression ring	Second compression ring	Oil scraper ring
End gap	0.35–0.55 mm 0.0138–0.0217 in.	0.30–0.45 mm 0.0118–0.0177 in.	0.38–1.40 mm 0.0150–0.0551 in.*
Width (thickness)	1.73–1.75 mm 0.0681–0.0689 in.	1.98–1.99 mm 0.0780–0.0783 in.	2.63–2.73 mm 0.1035–0.1075 in.**
Side clearance in piston groove	0.05–0.09 mm 0.0020–0.0035 in.	0.04–0.07 mm 0.0016–0.0028 in.	—

*Applies to segment part of ring

**Oil scraper ring segment width (thickness) 0.58–0.64 mm 0.0028–0.02552 in.

PISTONS

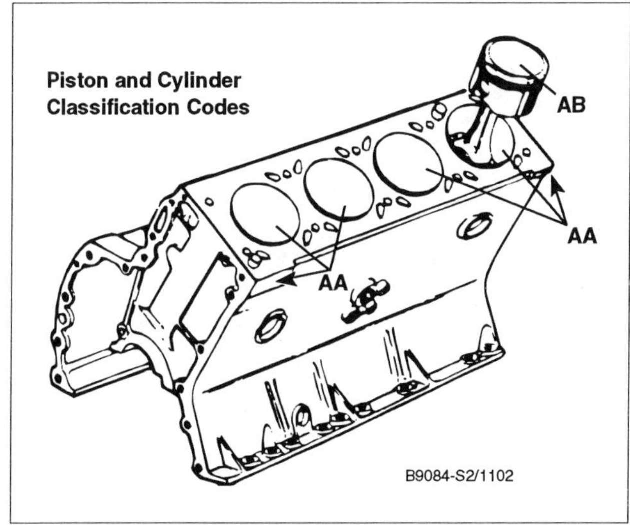

Piston diameter	mm	in.
Turbo engine with Mahle pistons		
standard A	89.960–89.970	3.5417–3.5421
standard AB	89.970–89.978	3.5421–3.5424
standard B	89.978–89.986	3.5424–3.5427
standard C	89.986–90.002	3.5427–3.5434

continued

Piston diameter	mm	in.
Turbo engine with Mahle pistons (cont'd)		
first oversize (0.5 mm)	90.460–90.475	3.5614–3.5620
second oversize (1.0 mm)	90.960–89.975	3.5811–3.5817
Normally aspirated engine with Mahle or KS pistons (ex. B212 engine)		
standard A	89.978–89.988	3.5424–3.5428
standard AB	89.988–89.996	3.5428–3.5431
standard B	89.996–90.004	3.5431–3.5435
standard C	90.004–90.020	3.5435–3.5441
first oversize (0.5 mm)	90.482–90.497	3.5623–3.5629
second oversize (1.0 mm)	90.982–89.997	3.5820–3.5826
Normally aspirated engine with Hepolite pistons (ex. B212 engine)		
standard A	89.977–89.985	3.5424–3.5427
standard AB	89.985–89.991	3.5427–3.5430
standard B	89.991–89.999	3.5430–3.5433
standard C	89.999–90.015	3.5433–3.5439
Normally aspirated engine with Hepolite pistons (ex. B212 engine)		
first oversize (0.5 mm)	90.477–90.492	3.5621–3.5627
second oversize (1.0 mm)	90.977–89.992	3.5818–3.5824

continued on next page

Piston diameter	mm	in.
B212 engine (2.1 liter engine)		
standard A	92.982–92.992	3.6607–3.6611
standard B	92.993–93.002	3.6611–3.6615
standard B	93.003–93.012	3.6615–3.6619
first oversize (0.5 mm)	93.482–93.492	3.6804–3.6808
second oversize (1.0 mm)	93.982–93.992	3.7001–3.7005
nominal piston clearance	0.009–0.035	0.00035–0.00137

Piston-to-Cylinder Clearance (mm)

piston/ cylinder classification	non-turbo (KS)	turbo	non-turbo (Hepolite)
B202 engine (2.0 L)			
A/A	0.012–0.032	0.030–0.050	0.015–0.033
AB/A	0.004–0.022	0.022–0.040	0.009–0.025
AB/B	0.014–0.032	0.032–0.050	0.019–0.035
B/A	—	0.014–0.032	0.001–0.019
B/B	0.006–0.024	0.024–0.042	0.011–0.029
C/B	—	0.008–0.034	—
B212 engine (2.1 L)			
A/A	—	—	0.008–0.028
B/B	—	—	0.009–0.027
B /B	—	—	0.009–0.027

CYLINDER HEAD AND VALVE MECHANISM

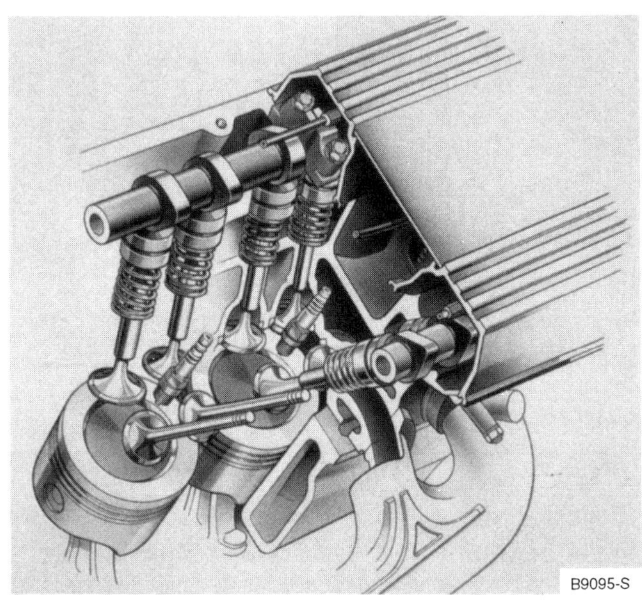

B9095-S

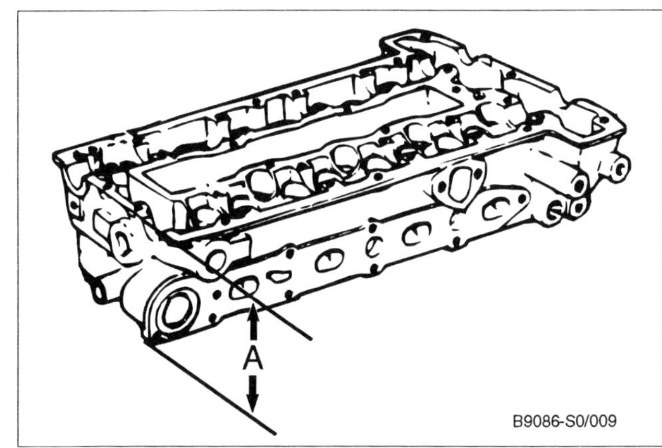

B9086-S0/009

Cylinder head height (dimension A)	mm	in.
New	140.5±0.1	5.533±0.004
After machining	140.1±0.05	5.516±0.004
Machining limit	0.4	0.0016

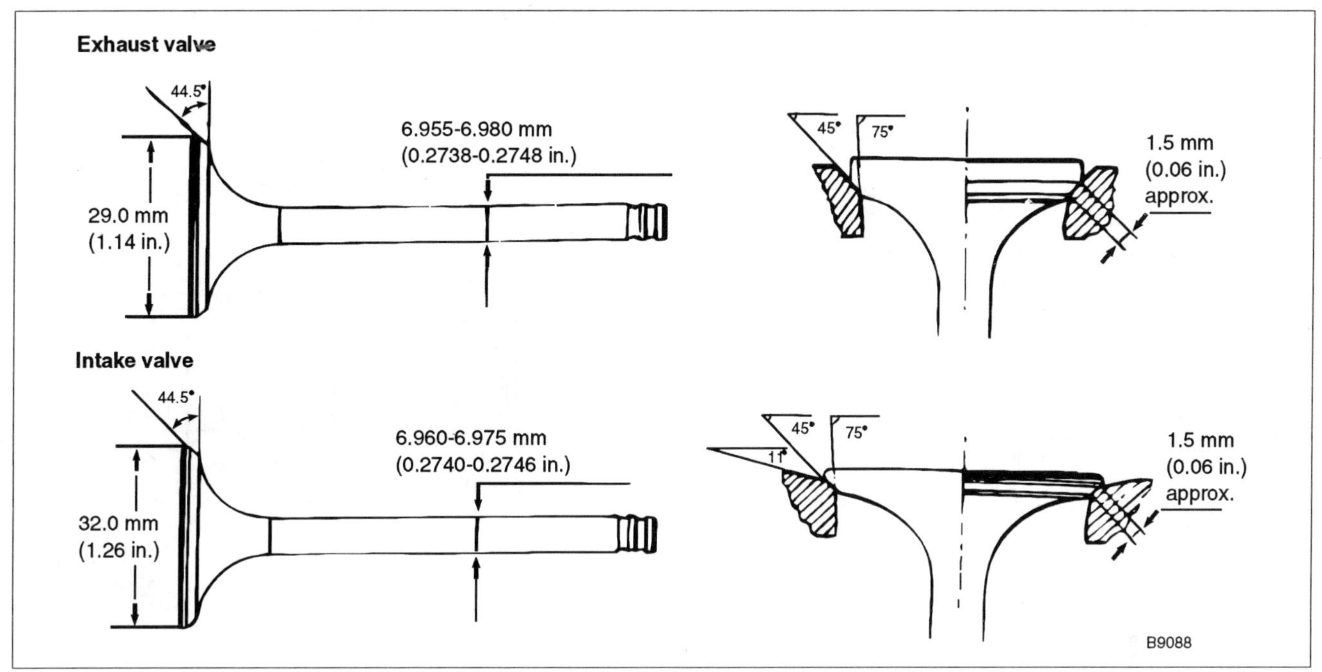

Valves	mm	in.
Valve clearance	non-adjustable	
Valve guides		
valve guide wear (clearance between valve guide and valve stem)		
maximum permissible	0.5	0.02
length	49.00	1.929
outside diameter	12.039–12.050	0.4740–0.4744
bore for valve guide in cylinder head	12.000–12.018	0.4724–0.4731
Valve Springs		
out-of-square (maximum)	1.75	0.07
free height	45.0±1.5	1.77±0.06
installed height	37.0	1.46
height when compressed with pressure of 131–141 lbs.	28.4	1.12

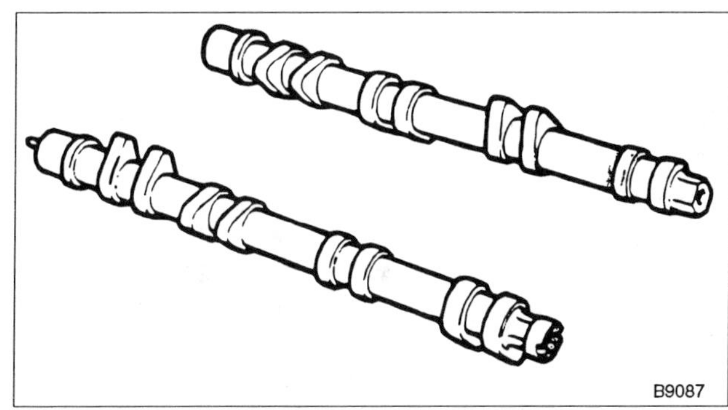

Camshaft	mm	in.
Bearing diameter	28.922–28.935	1.1387–1.1392
Axial play (maximum permissible)	0.08–0.35	0.0031–0.0138

Cam followers	mm	in.
Diameter	32.96–32.98	1.2976–1.2984
Height	26	1.02
Bore for cam followers in camshaft bridge	33.000–33.016	1.2992–1.2998

CRANKSHAFT

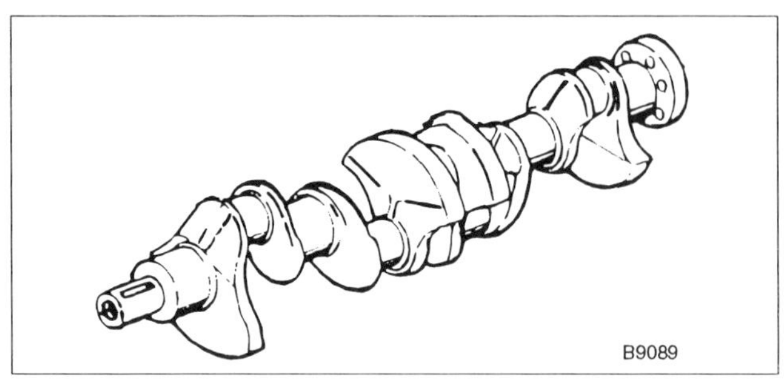
B9089

Crankshaft	mm	in.
Maximum variation in straightness (runout)	0.10	0.004
Axial play (end float)	0.08–0.28	0.003–0.011
Maximum out-of-round of journals	0.05	0.002
Radius of main journal fillet	2.2–2.5	0.09–0.10
Main bearing oil clearance	0.020–0.062	0.0008–0.0024
Big-end bearing oil clearance	0.026–0.062	0.0010–0.0024
Crankpin diameter		
standard	51.981–52.000	2.0465–2.0472
first undersize	51.731–51.750	2.0367–2.0374
second undersize	51.481–51.500	2.0268–2.0276
third undersize	51.237–51.250	2.0172–2.0177
fourth undersize	50.987–51.000	2.0074–2.0079
Main journal diameter		
standard	57.981–58.000	2.2827–2.2835
first undersize	57.731–57.750	2.2729–2.2736
second undersize	57.481–57.500	2.2630–2.2638
third undersize	57.237–57.250	2.2534–2.2539
fourth undersize	56.987–57.000	2.2436–2.2441

Color markings, main and big-end bearing shells		
standard	first oversize	second oversize
thin-red	thin-yellow	thin-white
thick-blue	thick-green	thick-brown

LUBRICATION SYSTEM

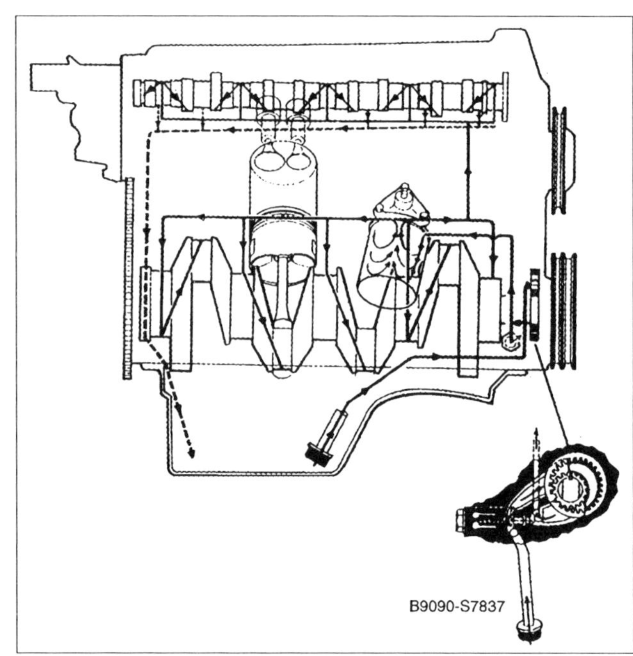
B9090-S7837

Lubrication System		
Oil pressure at 2000 rpm, engine temp. 80°C (176°F)	at least 2.7 bar	(39 psi)
Oil pressure relief valve opening pressure	3.6–5.3 bar	(52–77 psi)
Warning light on pressure	below 0.3–0.5 bar	(4.4–7.3 psi)
Oil pump end float	0.03–0.08 mm	(0.0012–0.0031 in.)

LH FUEL INJECTION

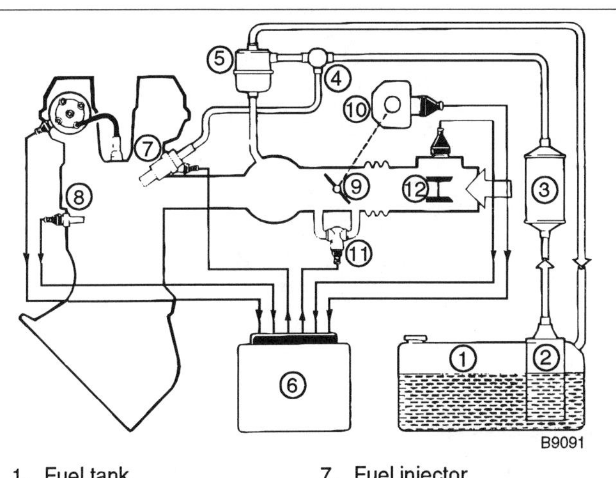

1. Fuel tank
2. Fuel pump
3. Fuel filter
4. Fuel distribution
5. Pressure regulator
6. LH control unit
7. Fuel injector
8. Coolant temperature sensor
9. Throttle plate
10. Throttle switch
11. AIC valve
12. Air mass meter

System	Year/Model	Identification
LH 2.2	1985–1988 turbo 1986–1987 normally aspirated	Three wire AIC idle valve, metal air mass meter with sealed mixture adjustment screw
LH 2.4	1989 and later turbo 1988–1990 normally aspirated	Two wire AIC idle valve, plastic air mass meter without mixture adjustment
LH 2.4.2	1991 and later normally aspirated	Three wire AIC idle valve, similar plastic air mass meter without mixture adjustment

Fuel Pump	
Fuel Pump Delivery Volume (minimum)	900 ml (30 oz.) in 30 seconds
Fuel system pressure — fuel pump running, engine off	
normally aspirated models	3.0 bar (43.5 psi)
turbo models	2.5±0.05 bar (36.3±0.7 psi)
Fuel system pressure — engine idling	
normally aspirated models	2.4 bar (34.8 psi)
turbo models	1.9 bar (27.6 psi)
Residual fuel pressure	
all models	0.1–0.2 bar (1.5–3.0 psi) below system pressure, minimum after 10 minutes

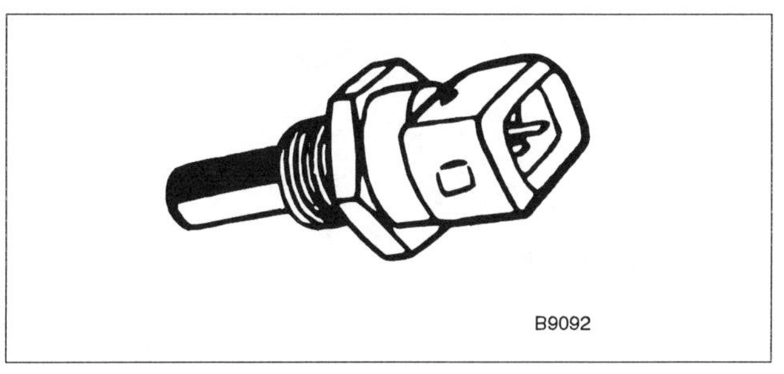

Fuel Injection	
LH Coolant Temperature Sensor Resistance	
Temperature	**Resistance (Ohms, ±10%)**
–4°F (–20°C)	14,000
14°F (–10°C)	9,000
32°F (0°C)	5,800
50°F (10°C)	3,800
58°F (15°C)	3,000
68°F (20°C)	2,600
76°F (25°C)	2,000
86°F (30°C)	1,700
176°F (80°C)	320

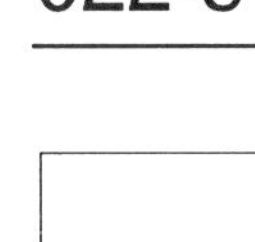

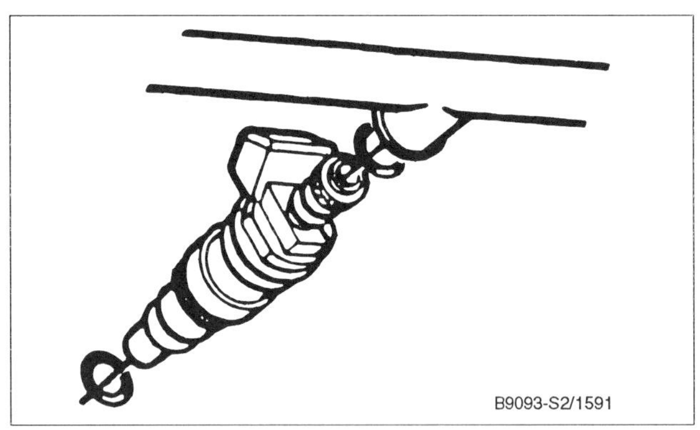

Fuel Injection		
Fuel injector resistance	16 Ohms at 68°F (20°C)	
Oxygen Sensor Specifications		
Oxygen sensor voltage at idle (engine warm)	0.4–1 volt	
Oxygen sensor preheater resistance	approx. 4 Ohms	
AIC Valve Resistance		
Fuel System	Test terminals	Resistance (Ohms)
LH 2.2	1 and 2	20±2
	2 and 3	20±2
	1 and 3	40±4
LH 2.4	1 and 2	8±2
LH 2.4.2	1 and 2	10–15
	2 and 3	10–15
Idle speed (adjustable only on LH 2.2 injection)		850±50 rpm
Idle %CO (adjustable only on LH 2.2 injection)		
normally aspirated	0.5–1.5%	
turbo	0.9–1.6%	
Dashpot Adjustment Specifications (LH 2.2)	speed at which dashpot rod touches throttle lever	
normally aspirated	2500±100 rpm	
turbo	2600±100 rpm	

COOLING SYSTEM

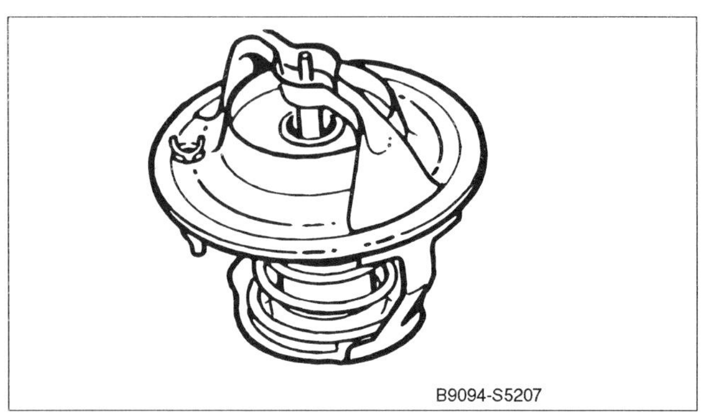

Cooling System	
Cooling system capacity	10 liters (10.5 qts.)
Permissible coolant leakage	1 qt. over 60,000 miles (1 liter/100,000 km)
Coolant thermoswitch closing temperature	194–203°F (90–95°C)
Coolant thermoswitch opening temperature	185–194°F (85–90°C)
Coolant type	Phosphate-free 50% mixture anti-freeze 50% water
Coolant temperature sender resistance	51.2±4.3 Ohms at 90°C (194°F)
Cooling system test pressure (maximum)	1.2 bar (17.4 psi.)

TURBOCHARGER

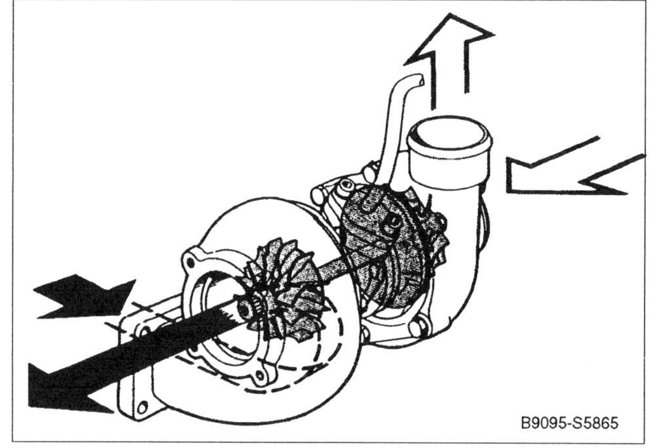

Turbocharger basic boost pressure	bar	psi
All except 1987 and later SPG models	0.35±0.03	5.0±0.4
1987 and later SPG models	0.40±0.03	5.8±0.4

023 Electrical System—Technical Data

ELECTRICAL SYSTEM

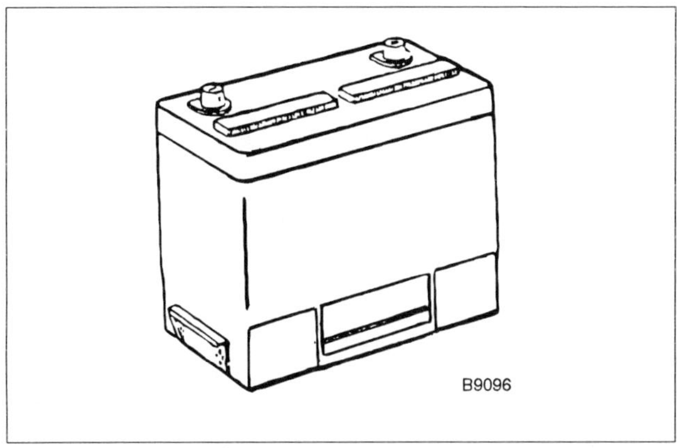

Tightening Torques	Nm	ft-lb (in-lb)
Ignition distributor hold-down bolt	15	11
Knock sensor to engine block	20	15
Solenoid to starter	4.5–5.5	(40–49 in-lb)
Starter field winding strap and battery cable to solenoid	7–9	(62–80 in-lb)
all other fasteners		
M5 bolt	5	(44 in-lb)
M6 bolt	10	(89 in-lb)
M8 bolt	20	15
M10 bolt	40	30

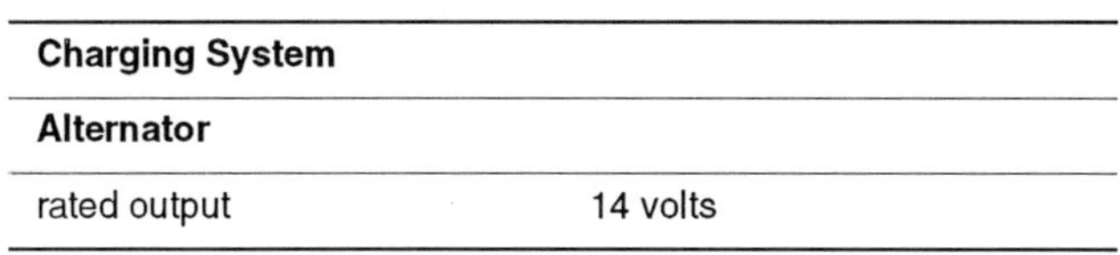

Charging System	
Alternator	
rated output	14 volts

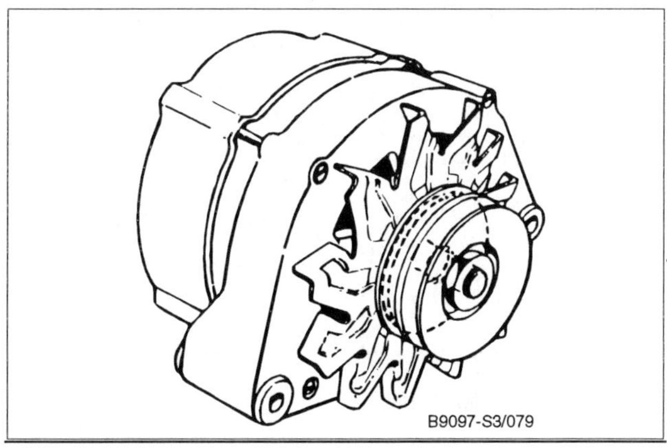

Charging System	
Alternator	
rated speed	1900 rpm
minimum brush length	5 mm (0.2 in.)
Output test values	
36 amps	@ 1500 rpm
54 amps	@ 1900 rpm
80 amps	@ 6000 rpm

Ignition System	
Ignition system type	

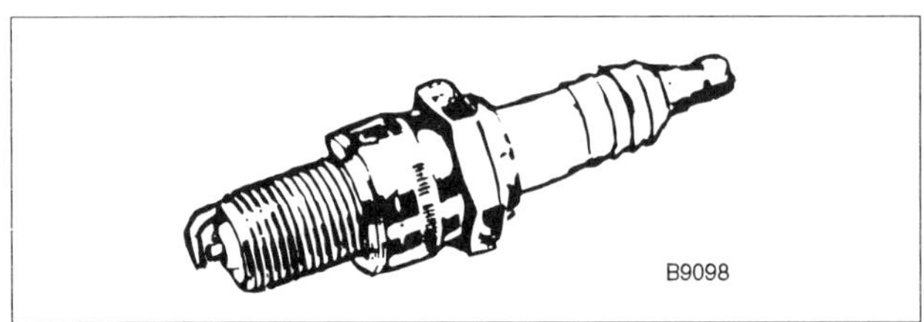

Ignition System	
1985 and later, turbo	basic Hall ignition
1986 and later, non-turbo	EZK ignition-Hall-effect with knock sensor
Ignition firing order	1-3-4-2 (no. 1 cylinder next to firewall)
Ignition timing (vacuum hose disconnected)	
Turbo	16°BTDC @ 850 rpm
Non-turbo	14°BTDC @ 850 rpm
Ignition coil	
primary winding resistance*	0.5–0.9 Ohms
secondary winding resistance*	7200–8200 Ohms
Spark plug wires and rotor	
ignition rotor resistance	1000 Ohms
coil high tension lead resistance (complete with end connectors)	500-1500 Ohms
spark plug lead resistance (complete with end connectors)	2000-4000 Ohms

*Measure with all wires disconnected from coil. See **340 Ignition System** for testing information

024 Transmission—Technical Data

TRANSMISSION

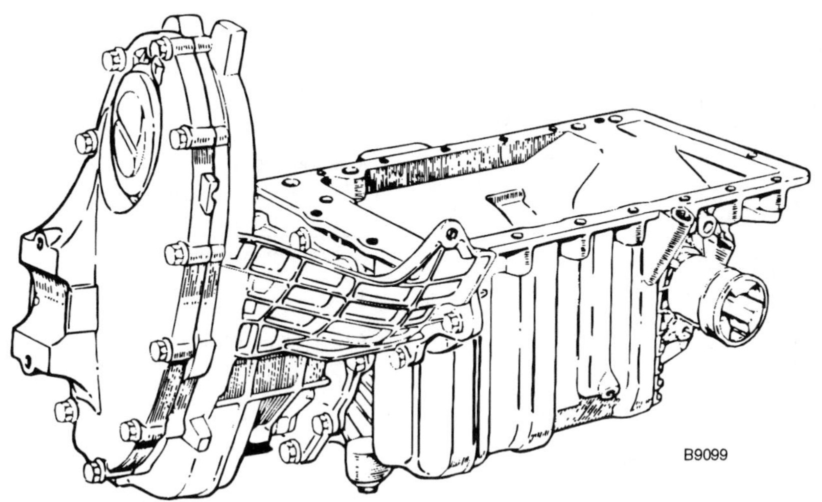

Tightening Torques	Nm	ft-lb (in-lb)
ATF pressure tap (automatic transmission)	5–7	(44–62 in-lb)
ATF sump pan bolts (automatic transmission)	8–12	(71–106 in-lb)
ATF sump pan drain plug (automatic transmission)	5–8	(44–71 in-lb)
ATF cooler connection nut (automatic transmission)	13–16	10–12
Clutch slave cylinder mounting screws	6–14	(53–124 in-lb)
Gearbox drain plug (manual transmission)	39–59	29–44
Selector cable setscrew tightening torque (automatic transmission)	2.5	(22 in-lb)

Tightening Torques	Nm	ft-lb (in-lb)
Shift rod clamp bolt (manual transmission)	30–35	22–26
All other fasteners		
M5 bolt	5	(44 in-lb)
M6 bolt	10	(89 in-lb)
M8 bolt	20	15
M10 bolt	40	30

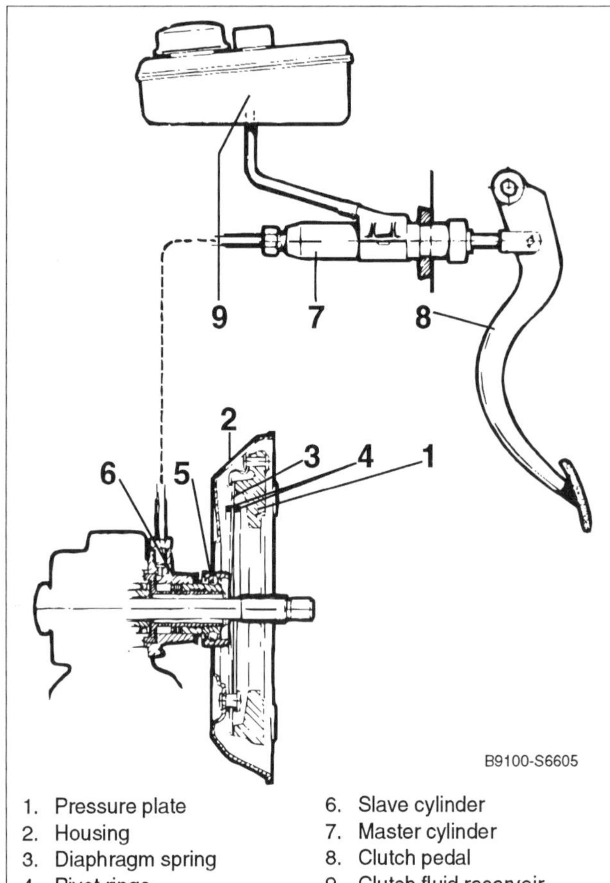

1. Pressure plate
2. Housing
3. Diaphragm spring
4. Pivot rings
5. Release bearing
6. Slave cylinder
7. Master cylinder
8. Clutch pedal
9. Clutch fluid reservoir

Manual Transmission	
Clutch type	Fichtel & Sachs
Clutch diameter	
non-turbo	204 mm (8 in.)
turbo	216 mm (8.5 in.)
Clutch adjustment	automatic (non-adjustable)
Manual transmission oil capacity	3.0 l (3.5 U.S. qts.)
Grade of oil	SAE 10W-30 SF/CC, SF/CD, SG
Alternate grade of oil	SAE EP 75 API-GL-4 or API GL-5
Clutch/brake master cylinder fluid	DOT 4 brake fluid

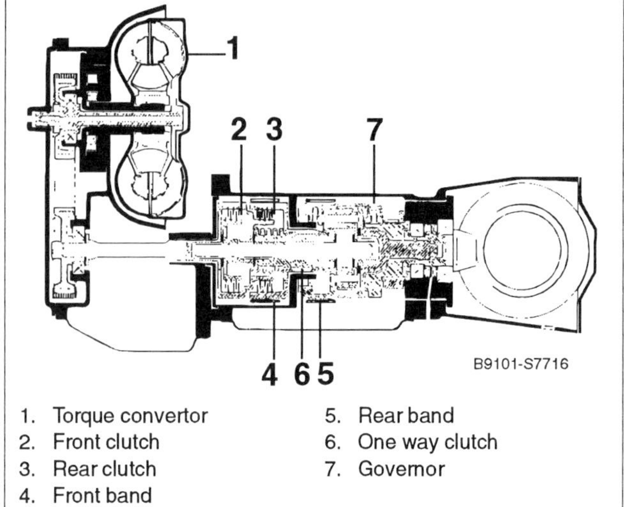

1. Torque convertor
2. Front clutch
3. Rear clutch
4. Front band
5. Rear band
6. One way clutch
7. Governor

Automatic Transmission	
Type	Borg Warner 37
ATF volume (transmission)	8.0 l (8.5 U.S. qts.)
ATF	Ford specification M2C-33F (alternate Ford specification G)
A/T final drive capacity	1.25 l (1.3 U.S. qts.)
A/T final drive grade of oil	SAE EP80 or 75 API-GL-4 or AP I-GL5
Alternate grade	SAE 10W-30 engine oil
General stall speed (APC solenoid unplugged)	2250–2700 rpm
Line pressure at idle (gear selector in D)	4.2–4.9 bar (61–71 psi)

025 Brakes—Technical Data

BRAKES

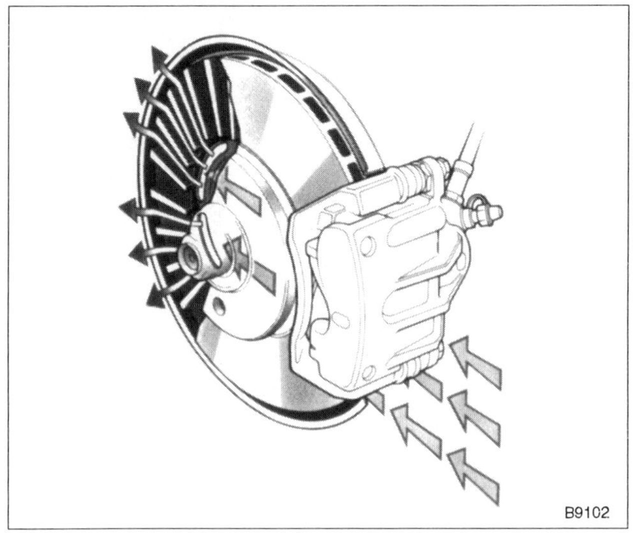

Tightening Torques	Nm	ft-lb (in-lb)
ABS hydraulic unit to bulkhead	26±4	19±3
Front caliper mounting bolt to guide pin (1988 models and later)	30–35	22–26
Front caliper to steering member (1985 to 1987)	110–130	81–96
Front pad carrier to steering member (1988 models and later)	70–110	52–81
Rear caliper to axle (1985 to 1987)	70–90	52–66
Rear caliper to pad carrier (pins) (1988 models and later)	25–30	18–22
Rear pad carrier to axle (1988 models and later)	40–54	30–40
All other fasteners		
M5 bolt	5	(44 in-lb)
M6 bolt	10	(89 in-lb)
M8 bolt	20	15
M10 bolt	40	30

Front Brake Disc Applications	
Model year and Model	**Disc type**
1985 through 1987 900	Solid
1985 and 1986 900s	Solid
1985 Turbo	Solid
1987 900s	Ventilated
1986 through 1987 Turbo, including convertible	Ventilated
1988 and later	All Ventilated

Front Brake Disc	Solid disc	Ventilated disc (1986-1987)	Ventilated disc (1988 and later)
Thickness (new)	12.7 mm (0.50 in.)	20 mm (0.787 in.)	23.5 mm (0.93 in.)
Thickness (wear limit)	11.2 mm (0.441 in.)	18 mm (0.709 in.)	21.5 mm (0.85 in.)
Brake surface lateral runout (maximum)	0.1 mm (0.004 in.)	0.1 mm (0.004 in.)	0.08 mm (0.003 in.)

Rear Brake Disc	
Thickness (new)	9.0 mm (0.354 in.)
Thickness (wear limit)	7.0 mm (0.276 in.)
Brake surface lateral runout (maximum)	0.1 mm (0.004 in.)

ABS Specification	
ABS wheel speed sensor air gap	0.65 mm (0.026 in.)

026 Steering and Wheel Alignment—Technical Data

STEERING AND WHEEL ALIGNMENT

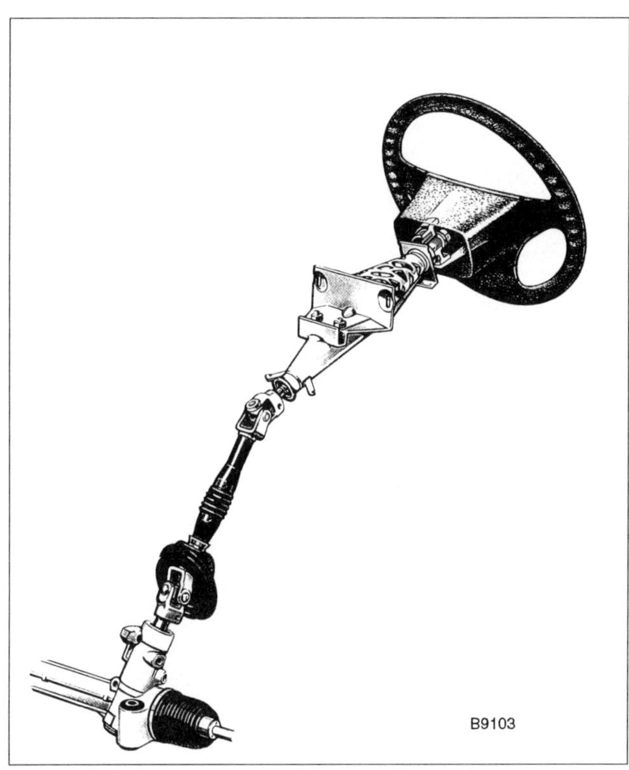

Tightening Torques	Nm	ft-lb (in-lb)
Ball joint to control arm (upper or lower)	40–55	29–41
Ball joint to control arm bolts (self-locking nuts)	40–55	29–41
Ball joint to steering swivel member (self-locking nut)	35–50	26–37
Bearing bracket to control arm (locknut and lock washer)		
lower control arm bracket to control arm	75–90	55–66
upper control arm bracket to control arm	55–70	41–52
Coil spring seat to control arm	55–110	41–81

Tightening Torques	Nm	ft-lb (in-lb)
Lower control arm bearing bracket (front or rear) to body		
M12 dry joint	70–95	52–70
M12 lubricated joint (waxed nut)	45–55	33–41
Lower control arm bracket to body	25–35	18–26
Power steering rack to body	60–80	44–59
Road wheel to wheel hub		
lug nuts	90–110	66–81
lug bolts	105–125	77–92
Steering column to steering rack (clamping bolt, self-locking nut)	20–27	15–20
Steering column to body (bolts, use with Loctite)	20–27	15–20
Steering wheel to steering column (self-locking nut)	25–28	18–21
Universal joint to pinion shaft (clamping bolt and self-locking nut)	25–34	18–25
Power steering hose fittings	20–34	15–25
Tie rod end to tie rod	60–80	44–59
Upper control arm bearing bracket (front or rear) to body	40–55	30–41
All other fasteners		
M5 bolt	5	(44 in-lb)
M6 bolt	10	(89 in-lb)
M8 bolt	20	15
M10 bolt	40	30

Steering and Wheel Alignment Specifications	
Chassis Ride Height (measured between top of wheel rim and fender/hood gap)	
Except sport chassis	243 mm (9.56 in.)
Sport chassis	
with 15 in. wheel	230 mm (9.06 in.)
with 16 in. wheel	217 mm (8.54 in.)

Wheel Alignment Specifications		
Measurement	**Model**	
	except sport chassis	sport chassis
Front		
caster	2°±0.5	2°±0.25
camber	0.5°±0.5	0.25°±0.25
toe-in	2±1 mm (0.08±0.04 in.)	1.5±0.5 mm (0.06±0.02 in)
Swivel pin inclination	11.5°±1	11.5°±1
Steering angle—outer wheel	20°	20°
Steering angle—inner wheel	20.75°±0.50	20.75°±0.50
Rear wheels (non-adjustable)		
toe-in	4±1 mm (0.16±0.04 in.)	4±1 mm (0.16±0.04 in.)
camber	-0.5°±0.25	-0.5°±0.25
Ball joint wear limit		
maximum radial play	1 mm	0.040 in.
maximum axial play	2 mm	0.078 in.
Power Steering Fluid		
GM power steering fluid (GM 9985010), Texaco TL4634 or equivalent	75 cl	0.8 qt

027 Suspension—Technical Data

SUSPENSION

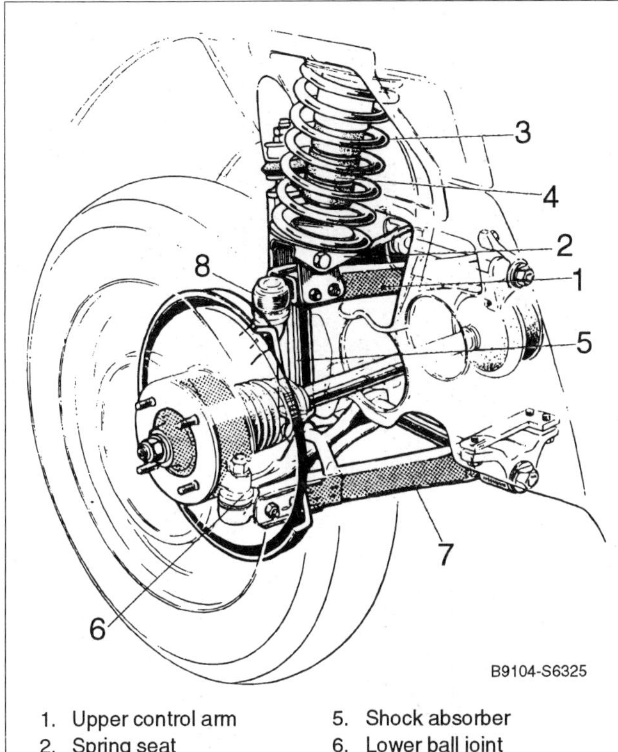

1. Upper control arm
2. Spring seat
3. Coil spring
4. Bump stop
5. Shock absorber
6. Lower ball joint
7. Lower control arm
8. Upper ball joint

Tightening Torques	Nm	ft-lb (in-lb)
Front shock absorber to lower control arm	90–100	66–74
Front suspension coil spring seat to control arm	55–110	41–81
Anti-roll bar bracket to lower control arm	40–55	30–41
Power steering rack to body	60–80	44–59
Spring link front mount to body	70–90	52–66

Tightening Torques	Nm	ft-lb (in-lb)
Panhard rod to body or rear axle	40–70	30–52
Torque arm to body or rear axle		
lubricated bushings	21–35	15–26
dry bushings	40–70	30–52
Wheel hubs to drive axle (locking nut)	290–310	214–229
Wheel lug bolts	105–125	77–92
Wheel lug nuts	90–110	66–81
All other fasteners		
M5 bolt	5	(44 in-lb)
M6 bolt	10	(89 in-lb)
M8 bolt	20	15
M10 bolt	40	30

Front Coil Spring Specifications		
Spring color codes	**Spring free length**	
Standard chassis		
green, light green, black, or white	373 mm	14.7 in.
yellow or red	380 mm	15.0 in.
pink or brown	388 mm	15.3 in.
blue or light blue	372 mm	14.6 in.
Sport chassis		
silver or bronze	301 mm	11.8 in.

Rear Coil Spring Specifications		
Spring color codes	**Spring free length**	
Standard chassis		
black or white (left spring)	311 mm	12.24 in.
green or light green (right spring)	308 mm	12.12 in.
Sport chassis		
silver or bronze	293 mm	11.5 in.

028 Body—Technical Data

BODY

Tightening Torques	Nm	ft-lb (in-lb)
A/C system tightening torques		
A/C compressor-to-evaporator hose		
connection at compressor (pad-type)	22–27	16–20
hose fitting at evaporator	28–39	21–29
A/C compressor-to-condensor hose		
connection at compressor (pad-type)	22–27	16–20
hose fitting at condensor	21–28	15–21
A/C condensor-to-receiver/dryer hose		
hose fitting at condensor	14–20	10–15
hose fitting at receiver/dryer	14–20	10–15
A/C evaporator-to-receiver/dryer hose		
hose fitting at evaporator	14–20	10–15
hose fitting at receiver/dryer	14–20	10–15
A/C expansion valve to evaporator	21–27	15–20
A/C expansion valve pressure equalization fitting to evaporator	7–10	(62–89 in-lb)
Oil fill plug to A/C compressor	8–12	(71–106 in-lb)
Convertible top hydraulic hose fittings	5.1–6.2	(45–55 in-lb)
Seatbelt guide bolt to body (convertible models)	24–40	18–30
All other seat belt mounting bolts	45±10	33±7
All other fasteners		
M5 bolt	5	(44 in-lb)
M6 bolt	10	(89 in-lb)
M8 bolt	20	15
M10 bolt	40	30

continued

Body Specifications		
Convertible pump hydraulic fluid	Aeroshell Fluid 4/Shell Code 60 421 (Saab part no. 30 18 694	
Convertible top hydraulic pump minimum working pressure	25 bar	365 psi

A/C System Specifications		
Refrigerant oil capacity (compressor replacement)	1.75 dl	4.9 oz.
Refrigerant oil capacity per component (due to sudden leakage)		
evaporator	0.5 dl	1.4 oz.
receiver/dryer	0.2 dl	0.57 oz.
condenser	0.2 dl	0.57 oz.
hose	0.2 dl	0.57 oz.
A/C refrigerant pressure switch (low gas pressure)		
opening pressure	2.9 bar	41 psi
A/C Coolant temperature switch		
opening temperature	115°C	239°F
A/C Anti-frost switch		
switch closed	4.0–6.2°C	39.2–43.1°F
switch open	0.4–2.6°C	33–36.6°F

100 Fundamentals for the Do-it-yourself Owner

TABLES

GENERAL

Although the Saab 900 is a sophisticated and complex machine, nearly all basic maintenance and most repairs can be accomplished by any interested owner with basic mechanical skills and the right information. While some of the repairs covered in this manual are complicated and require special knowledge and equipment, most of the care that is required in the lifetime of the average Saab is well within the capabilities of the do-it-yourselfer.

CAUTION

Do not use this manual unless you are familiar with basic automotive repair procedures and safe workshop practices. This manual illustrates the workshop procedures required for most service work; it is not a substitute for full and up-to-date information from the vehicle manufacturer or for proper training as an automotive technician. Note that it is not possible for us to anticipate all of the ways or conditions under which vehicles may be serviced or to provide cautions as to all of the possible hazards that may result.

CAUTION
Your common sense and good judgment are crucial to safe and successful service work. Read procedures through before starting them. Think about whether the condition of your car, your level of mechanical skill, or your level of reading comprehension might result in or contribute in some way to an occurrence which might cause you injury, damage your car, or result in an unsafe repair. If you have doubts for these or other reasons about your ability to perform safe repair work on your car, have the work done at an authorized Saab dealer or other qualified shop.

This section of the manual is intended to help the beginner get started smartly and safely with Saab maintenance and repair. The section begins with **Form and Function,** a general description of the car and its individual systems, followed by a discussion on **How To Use This Manual.**

Tips on mechanic's skills and workshop practices that can help the beginner do a faster, complete, and more thorough job can be found under **Getting Started. Tools** describes the basic tools needed to do most of the procedures in this manual.

The section ends with a quick reference guide to emergencies—what to do when the car won't start or when a warning light comes on, including basic troubleshooting and information on how to gauge the seriousness of a problem.

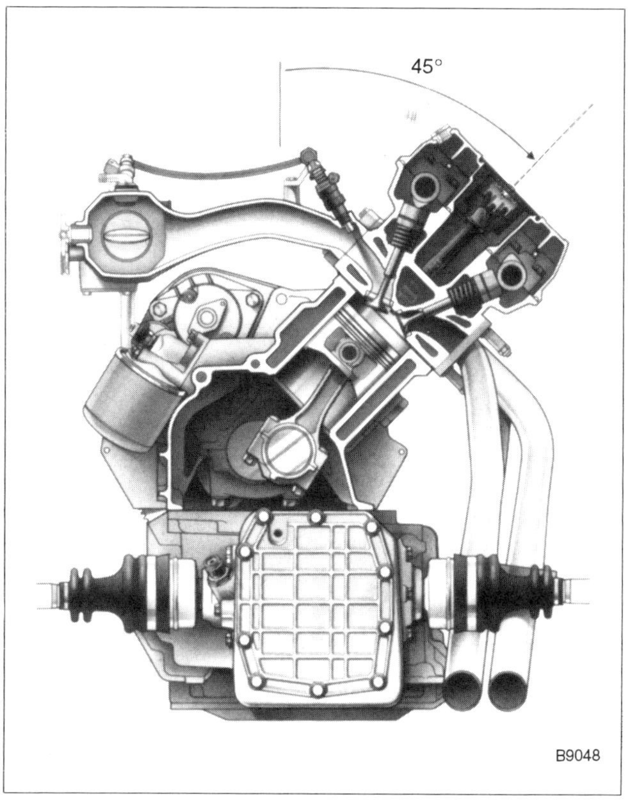

Fig. 1. Cutaway of Saab 900 16 valve overhead camshaft engine. The engine is sloped at 45% to lower the car's center of gravity and to allow for a low hood line. The transmission is bolted to the bottom of the engine.

FORM AND FUNCTION

While the complexity of the Saab 900 may at first seem overwhelming to the do-it-yourself owner, it can be simplified and more easily understood by viewing the car as an assembly of simpler systems, each performing its own independent functions.

Engine

The Saab 900 models covered by this manual are powered by a liquid-cooled, four-cylinder, 16-valve, in-line engine. The power train is integrated with the clutch, transmission, and differential in a compact, lightweight power unit that occupies very little space. See Fig. 1.

The 16 valve cylinder head uses self-adjusting hydraulic cam followers to actuate the valves. Each valve has a large flow area to allow the engine to breath efficiently. Because the cylinder head has four valves per cylinder instead of two, individual valves are subject to far less demanding working conditions. See Fig. 2.

Fig. 2. Cutaway view of valve train.

Saab Turbo with APC

In addition to the naturally aspirated engine family, the 900 is available with a turbocharged engine. See Fig. 3. The turbo engine delivers extra power at low engine speeds when demanded, but during normal driving it is as economical as the naturally aspirated engine. The turbocharged engine offers the same acceleration as many six-cylinder and eight-cylinder engines, but without the well-known disadvantages of excessive weight, unwieldy bulk with too many moving parts, and high fuel consumption.

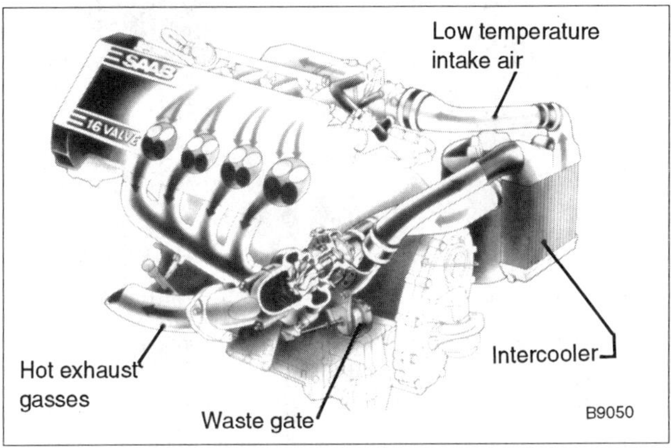

Fig. 3. Cutaway of turbocharger system. The intake air is compressed by the exhaust-driven turbocharger. It is then cooled by as much as 110°F in the intercooler before it enters the engine. The intercooler increases power and reduces the thermal stresses in the engine.

Safety margins must be built into the design of an internal combustion engine to allow for manufacturing tolerances, changes in the condition of the engine, and varying climatic conditions and fuel quality. As a result, the energy content of the fuel cannot be fully utilized. To answer this problem, the Saab APC system was designed to ensure maximum utilization of the energy in the fuel at all times. The boost pressure delivered by the turbocharger is continually adjusted to suit the knocking limit of the air/fuel mixture in the cylinders. Therefore, the engine adjusts itself automatically to the fuel being used. The higher the octane, the higher the maximum engine power. See Fig. 4.

NOTE

On Saab Turbo SPG models, premium unleaded fuel is required at all times.

The APC system consists of simple electronics. A knock sensor on the engine block senses the onset and degree of engine knock and transmits an electrical signal to the control unit. The control unit also receives signals from the intake manifold pressure sensor and the ignition system (engine rpm). The data is processed by the control unit, which transmits a signal to the APC solenoid valve to regulate the boost pressure (via the wastegate) of the turbocharger. Therefore, maximum operating boost pressure under full engine load is electronically governed. In the event of an APC system malfunction, the wastegate is mechanically adjusted to provide a safe, low boost pressure limit.

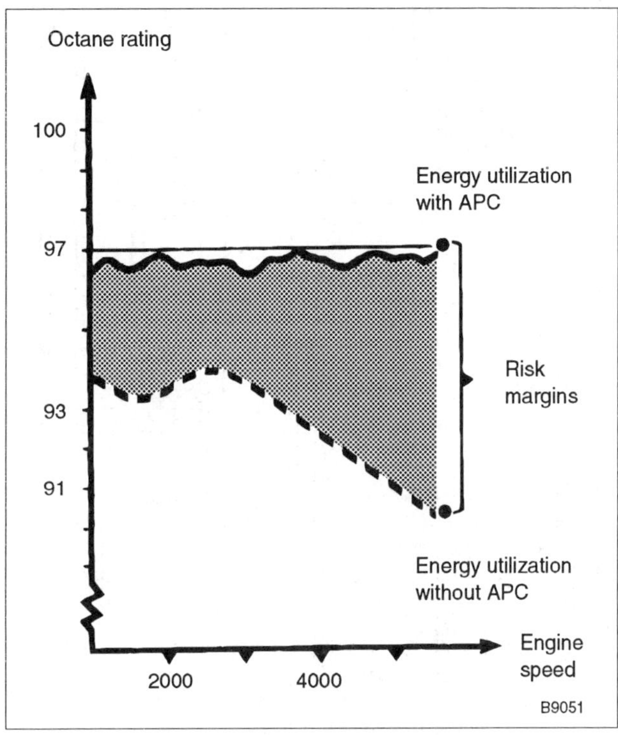

Fig. 4. A conventional engine must incorporate safety margins for engine tolerances, various climatic conditions, and variations in fuel grades available. The Saab APC turbo engine adjusts itself automatically to suit the operating conditions.

Fuel Injection

All Saab 900 16-valve models use an electronically controlled Bosch LH-Jetronic fuel injection system. See Fig. 5. LH is a German acronym for hot wire, or "Luft masse messen mit hitzdraht". Hot wire refers to the operation of the air mass meter, which is used to measure the air entering the engine.

The intake air flows across an electrically heated platinum wire in the tubular air meter. See Fig. 6. The control unit then measures the electrical energy necessary to maintain the wire at a constant temperature as a measure of the air mass. At the same time the control unit senses the engine speed and the engine temperature, which enables it to meter the correct quantity of fuel to suit the requirements of the engine at all times.

Fuel is delivered to the engine through the fuel injectors. The intake manifold is equipped with one fuel injector per cylinder. Each injector is fitted upstream of the corresponding intake valves and actuated electro-magnetically by signals from the electronic control unit. The control unit calculates the opening time for the injectors so that the quantity of the fuel injected will be correct in relation to the quantity of air flowing to the engine. See Fig. 7.

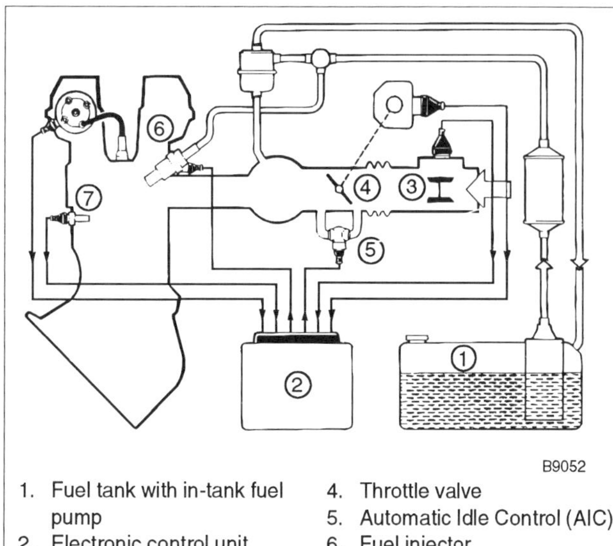

Fig. 5. Schematic of LH-Jetronic fuel injection system used on all Saab 16 valve engines.

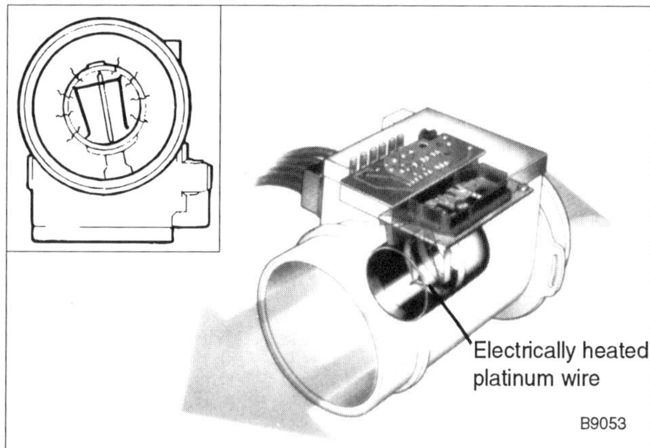

Fig. 6. View of LH (hot wire) air mass meter. The platinum heated wire is maintained at a constant temperature and measures the mass of the air flow going into the engine. It uses solid-state circuitry and has no moving parts to wear out. The inset shows a front view of air mass meter.

Ignition System

The electronic ignition system creates the high-voltage spark necessary to ignite the combustible air/fuel mixture in the cylinders. The ignition coil boosts the voltage so that the spark will be hot enough to ignite the air/fuel mixture. The timing of the spark is controlled by the ignition control unit.

The ignition distributor, synchronized to the rotation of the engine, delivers the spark to the right cylinder at precisely the right time. Since each cylinder has to have a spark once for every two revolutions of the crankshaft, the distributor turns at one-half crankshaft speed. The basic system is shown schematically in Fig. 8.

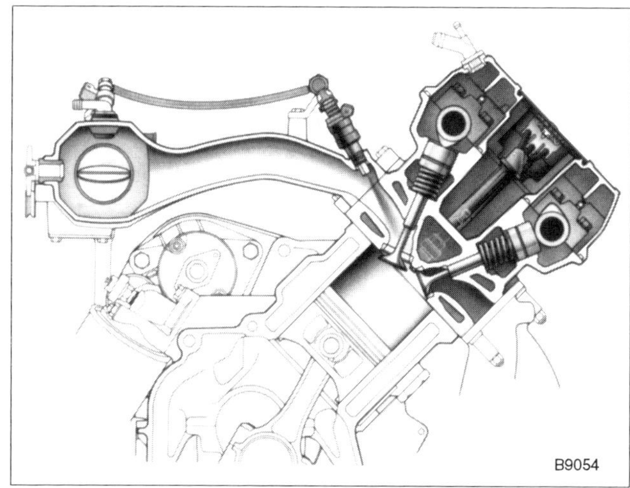

Fig. 7. Cutaway view of engine showing operation of the electromagnetic fuel injector. The injectors are mounted in the intake manifold, one for each cylinder.

Electrical System

Many components, and all electrical accessories, are powered by the car's electrical system. The electrical system uses a battery to store energy, an engine-driven alternator to generate electricity and recharge the battery, and various wiring harnesses and other circuits to distribute electric power to the rest of the car. The electrical system is represented in Fig. 9.

The flow of electricity depends upon a closed-loop path—a complete circuit. Electrical current flows through wires to the consumer, a light bulb for example, and back to the battery in a complete circuit. The electrical route back to the source, which completes the circuit, is called a path to ground. Every consumer of electrical power in the car must have a source of power and a path to ground in order to operate.

Commonly, the electrically conductive metal structure of the automobile is used as a ground path. The negative (–) terminal of the battery connects to the car body, and all of the electrical consumers in the car make a ground connection to the car body, thus eliminating the need for many feet of additional wire.

Electrical components near the engine are often grounded directly to the engine, which is then grounded to the body. Some components are grounded through their housings which are bolted to a ground. Electrically, the effect is the same.

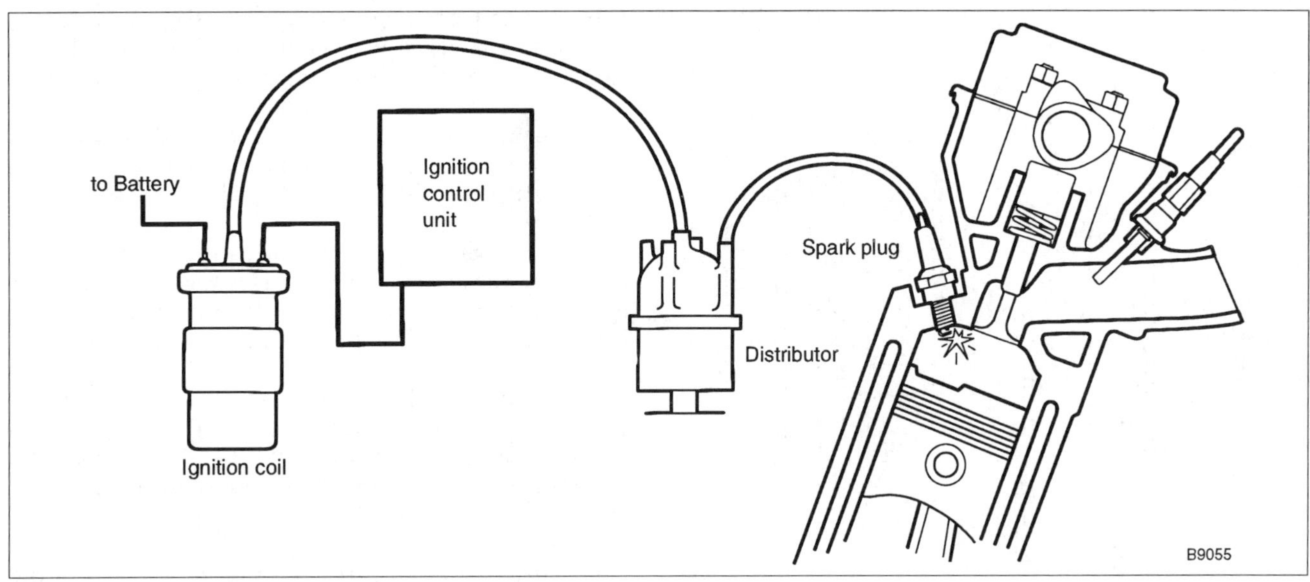

Fig. 8. Schematic of typical ignition system.

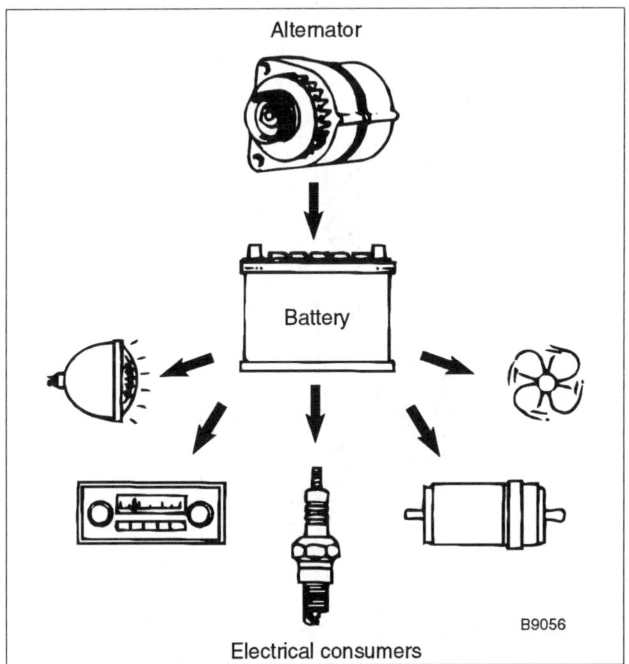

Fig. 9. The alternator generates electricity to recharge battery and power other electrical consumers.

Transmission and Drive Train

The transmission is mounted beneath the engine and is arranged in a housing together with the final drive. See Fig. 10. The transmission is chain driven off the engine via the clutch.

Although the Saab engine develops a substantial amount of power, it does so best at relatively high revolutions per minute (rpm). To handle all driving conditions, it is necessary to use gearing to change the ratio of engine rpm to vehicle speed. See Fig. 11.

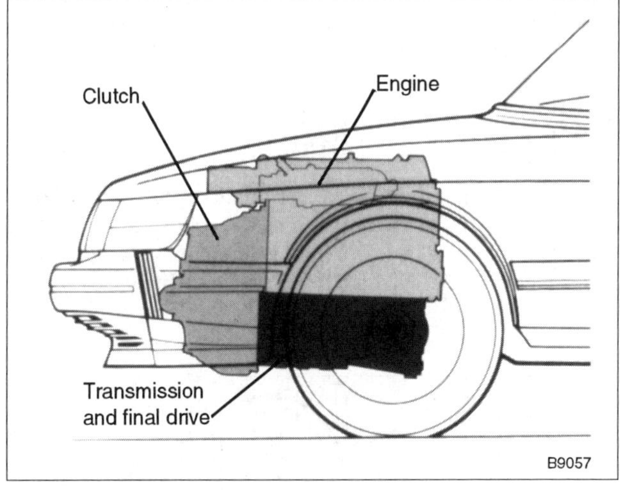

Fig. 10. The transmission and final drive are mounted beneath engine.

A manual transmission arranges several sets of gears in a common housing. A set of two gears determines a gear ratio, each suited to a particular range of driving speeds. A shifting mechanism allows the driver to change from one gear ratio to the next to match vehicle speed.

In an automatic transmission, hydraulic fluid under pressure in a complex network of passages, valves and control mechanisms engage and disengage constantly meshed planetary gear sets. Hydraulic controls responding to vehicle speed, engine load, throttle position and gear shift position select the appropriate gear ratio.

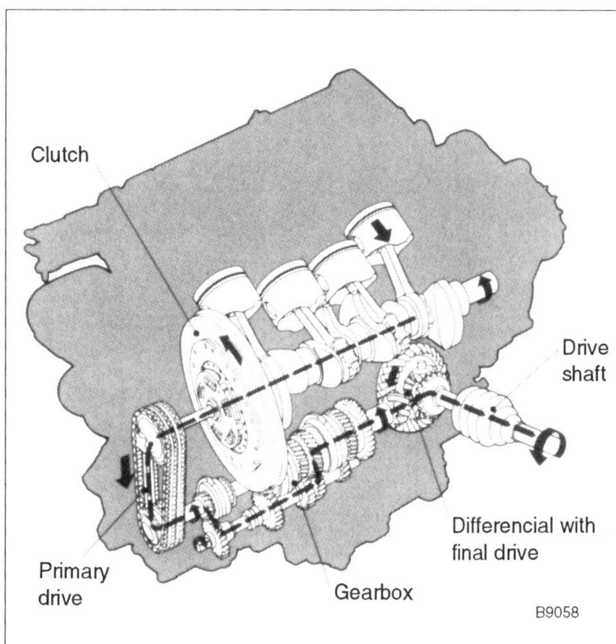

Fig. 11. The gear reduction between the engine and the driven wheels takes place in three stages: the primary chain drive, the transmission gears, and the final drive.

Brakes

All of the Saab models covered in this manual feature disc brakes at all four wheels. A disc brake squeezes pads lined with friction material against both sides of a flat, round brake disc, called a rotor. A typical disc brake assembly is shown in Fig. 12.

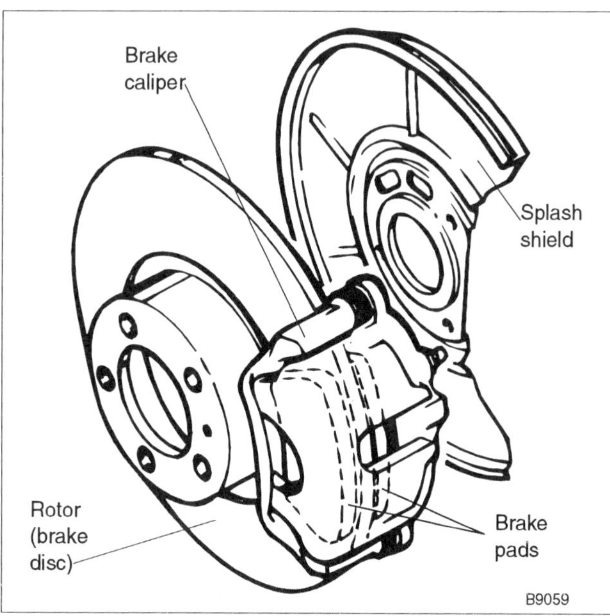

Fig. 12. Disc brake assembly showing disc, caliper, and splash shield. Caliper assembly holds pads with friction material.

The brakes act to slow or stop the car by causing friction. Since cars are relatively heavy, the friction required to stop safely and effectively is quite high, and generating this friction requires considerable force. The cars covered by this manual use either an engine vacuum boost system or hydraulic boost system (cars with ABS) to multiply the force applied to the brake pedal and to distribute it uniformly to the wheels.

The brake pedal is connected by a mechanical linkage to the master cylinder, mounted on the firewall at the back of the engine compartment. A piston in the master cylinder creates hydraulic pressure in the brake lines going to the wheels.

At each wheel, the hydraulic pressure acts on the brake caliper to cause friction and slow the wheel. The sizes of the hydraulic components are such that the driver's force applied to the brake pedal is multiplied many times by the time it reaches the wheels.

1990 and later 900 models are equipped with an anti-lock braking system (ABS). As the name implies, the purpose of this system is to prevent the wheels from locking during hard braking. Speed sensors at each wheel sense when the wheel is about to lock, and an electronic system modulates the braking force to that wheel. See Fig. 13.

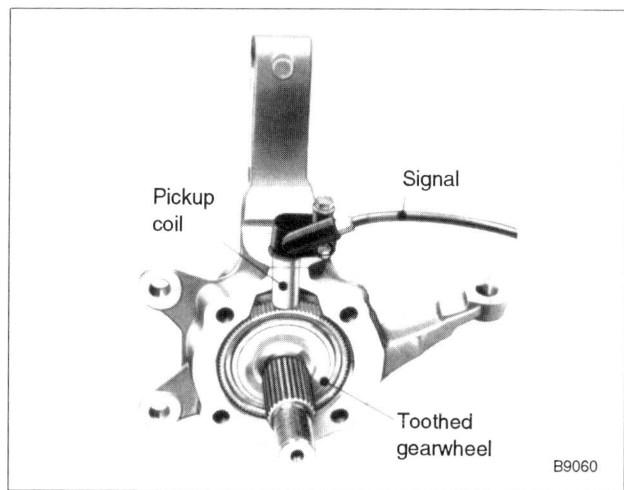

Fig. 13. A moisture-proof sensor senses the rolling speed of each wheel. The sensor is inductive in that an electric current is induced in the pickup coil every time a tooth on the gearwheel passes the sensor.

Steering and Suspension

The suspension and steering systems are what allow the wheels to move and turn for a smooth ride, stability and directional control. See Fig. 14. The suspension system is the combination of springs, shock absorbers, and other stabilizing devices that support the weight of the car and cushion the effects of bumps. On some models, stabilizer bars aid stability by transferring some of the cornering force acting on the suspension.

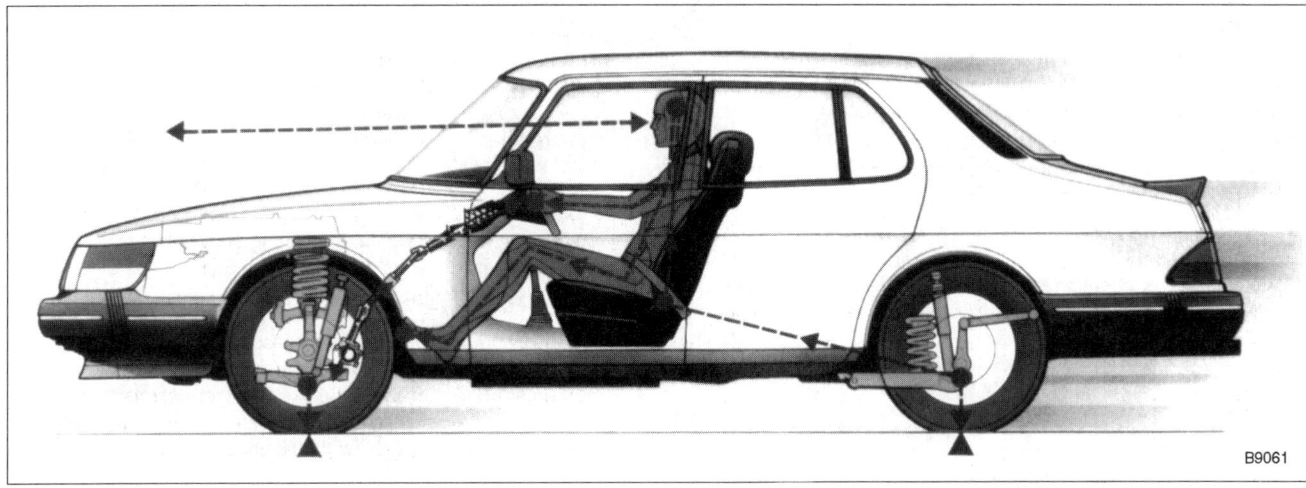

Fig. 14. The suspension and steering system gives the driver control over the car by supplying constant feedback on the car's reactions.

The steering system consists of the steering rack mechanisms, linkages, and a belt-driven hydraulic pump. Power-assisted steering uses hydraulic fluid under pressure to do some of the work normally done by the driver turning the steering wheel.

Body

The body is the basic building block. All of the Saab models covered in this manual feature unitized body construction, meaning that they do not have a separate frame. A complex body shell is the main structural platform to which all the other systems are attached. Subassemblies attach engine, drivetrain, suspension, and steering systems to the basic body structure.

The doors, the instrument panel, the seats, and other interior trim pieces are also added to the body shell. Other parts of the body shell function as mounting points for the other major and minor subsystems.

HOW TO USE THIS MANUAL

The manual is divided into 9 sections:

0 TECHNICAL DATA
1 LUBRICATION AND MAINTENANCE
2 ENGINE
3 ELECTRICAL SYSTEM
4 TRANSMISSION
5 BRAKES
6 STEERING AND WHEEL ALIGNMENT
7 SUSPENSION
8 BODY AND STEERING

0 TECHNICAL DATA lists all of the specifications used throughout the manual and is intended to be used as a quick reference guide for the more experienced technician familiar with Saab 900 cars. **1 LUBRICATION AND MAINTENANCE** covers the maintenance schedules and service procedures needed to do all of the Saab recommended scheduled maintenance work.

The remaining seven sections (2 through 8) are repair oriented and are divided into multiple repair groups. For clarity and ease of use, each major section begins with a **General** repair group, e.g. **200 Engine—General.** These "00" (double zero) groups are mostly descriptive in nature, covering topics such as theory of operation and troubleshooting. The remainder of the repair groups contain the more involved and more detailed system repair information.

A master listing of the 9 sections and the corresponding 69 individual repair groups can be found at the beginning of each section. Thumb tabs on the first page of each repair group page help locate the groups quickly.

Each repair group has its own Table of Contents listing the major subject headings within the group, and the pages on which they begin. Page numbers throughout the manual are organized according to the repair group system. For example, you can expect to find information on the turbocharger (Repair Group 291) beginning on page 291-1. A comprehensive index is found at the back of the manual.

Warnings, Cautions and Notes

Throughout this manual are many passages with the headings **WARNING**, **CAUTION**, or **NOTE**. These very important headings have different meanings.

WARNING
A warning is the most serious of the three. It warns of unsafe practices that are very likely to cause injury, either by direct threat to the person(s) doing the work or by increased risk of accident or mechanical failure while driving.

CAUTION
A caution calls attention to important precautions to be observed during the repair work that will help prevent accidentally damaging the car or its parts.

NOTE
A note contains helpful information, tips that will help in doing a better job and completing it more easily.

Please read every **WARNING**, **CAUTION**, and **NOTE** at the front of the manual and as they appear in repair procedures. They are very important. Read them before you begin any maintenance or repair job.

Some **WARNING**s and **CAUTION**s are repeated wherever they apply. Read them all. Do not skip any. These messages are important, even to the owner who never intends to work on the car.

GETTING STARTED

Most of the necessary maintenance and minor repair that a Saab will need can be done with ordinary tools, even by owners with little or no experience in car repair. Below is some important information on how to work safely, a discussion of what tools will be needed and how to use them, and a series of mechanic's tips on methods and workmanship.

Safety

Although an automobile presents many hazards, common sense and good equipment can ensure safety. Accidents happen because of carelessness. Pay attention and stick to these few important safety rules.

WARNING
- Never run the engine in the work area unless it is well-ventilated. The exhaust should be vented to the outside. Carbon Monoxide (CO) in the exhaust kills.

- Remove all neckties, scarfs, loose clothing, or jewelry when working near running engines or power tools. Tuck in shirts. Tie long hair and secure it under a cap. Severe injury can result from these things being caught in rotating parts.

WARNING
- Remove rings, watches, and bracelets. Aside from the dangers of moving parts, metallic jewelry conducts electricity and may cause shorts, sparks, burns, or damage to the electrical system when accidentally contacting the battery or other electrical terminals.

- Disconnect the battery negative (–) cable whenever working on or near the fuel system or anything that is electrically powered. Accidental electrical contact may damage the electrical system or cause fire.

- Never work under a lifted car unless it is solidly supported on jack stands that are intended for that purpose. Do not support a car on cinder blocks, bricks, or other objects that may shift or crumble under continuous load. Never work under a car that is supported only by the lifting jack.

- The fuel system is designed to retain pressure even when the ignition is off. When working with the fuel system, loosen the fuel lines very slowly to allow the residual pressure to dissipate gradually. Avoid spraying fuel.

- Fuel is highly flammable. When working around fuel, do not smoke or work near heaters or other fire hazards. Keep an approved fire extinguisher handy.

- Illuminate the work area adequately and safely. Use a portable safety light for working inside or under the car. A fluorescent type light is best because it gives off less heat. If using a light with a normal incandescent bulb, use rough service bulbs to avoid breakage. The hot filament of an accidentally broken bulb can ignite spilled fuel or oil.

- Keep sparks, lighted matches, and open flame away from the top of the battery. Hydrogen gas emitted by the battery is highly flammable. Any nearby source of ignition may cause the battery to explode.

- Never lay tools or parts in the engine compartment or on top of the battery. They may fall into confined spaces and be difficult to retrieve, become caught in belts or other rotating parts when the engine is started, or cause electrical shorts and damage to the electrical system.

- Some of the cars covered by this manual are equipped with a Supplemental Restraint System (SRS) that automatically deploys an airbag. The airbag unit uses an explosive device to electrically ignite a powerful gas. On cars so equipped, any work involving the steering wheel should only be performed by an authorized Saab dealer. Performing repairs without disarming the SRS may cause serious personal injury.

Lifting the Car

For those repairs that require raising the car, the proper jacking points should be used to raise the car safely and avoid damage. There are six jacking points from which the car can be safely raised. The jack supplied with the car by Saab can only be used at the four side points—just behind the front wheel or just in front of the rear wheel. In addition to the four side points, there are front and rear center jacking points that can be used to lift one end. See Fig. 15.

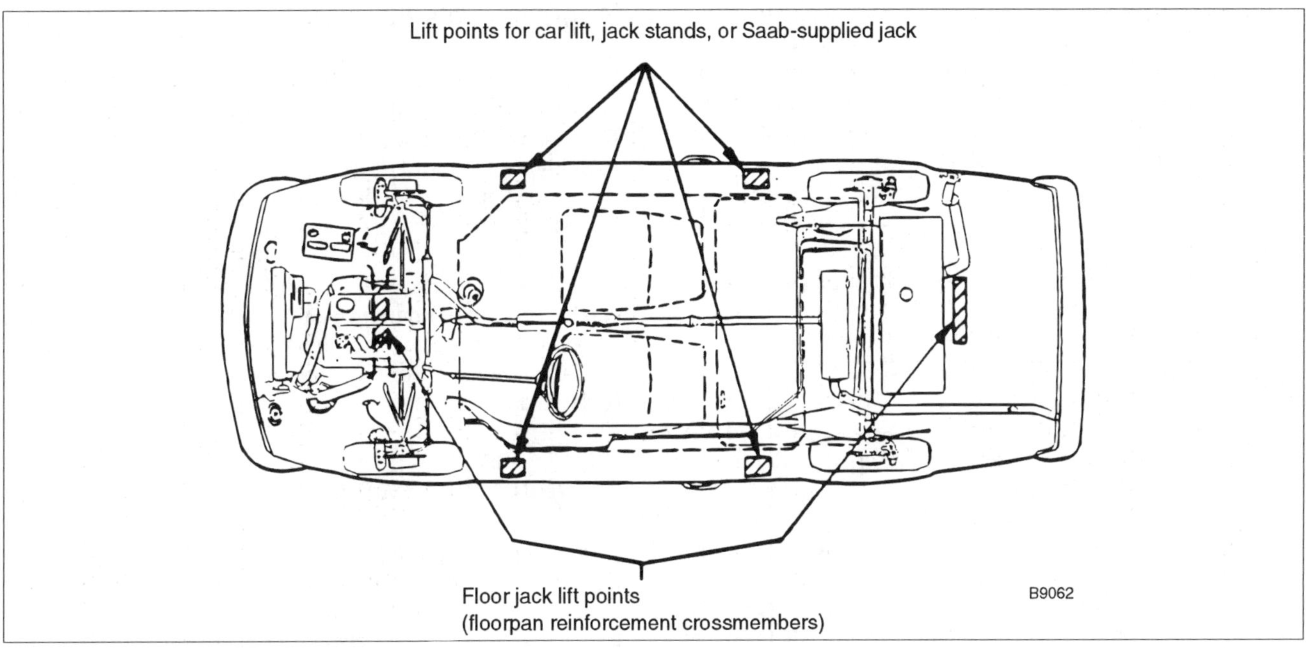

Fig. 15. Saab jacking points.

CAUTION

When raising the car using a floor jack or a hydraulic lift, carefully position the jack pad so that it does not damage the body. A suitable liner (wood, rubber. etc.) should be placed between the jack and the car so that the underbody will not be damaged.

To raise car safely

1. Park the car on a flat, level surface.
2. Place the jack in position. See Fig. 16. Make sure the jack is resting on flat, solid ground. Use a board or other support to provide a firm surface for the jack, if necessary.

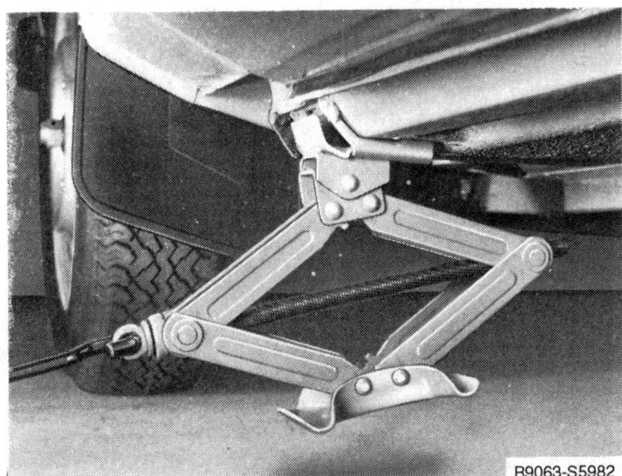

Fig. 16. Saab-supplied jack correctly installed at front left jacking point.

3. Raise the car slowly.

WARNING

Watch the jack closely. Make it stays stable and does not shift or tilt. As the car is raised, the car will want to roll slightly and the jack will want to shift.

---

4. Once the car is raised, block the wheel that is opposite and farthest from the jack to prevent the car from unexpectedly rolling.

WARNING

Do not rely on the transmission or the emergency brake to keep the car from rolling. While they will help, they are not a substitute for positively blocking the opposite wheel.

Never work under a car that is supported only by a jack. Use jack stands that are properly designed to support the car. See **Tools**.

To work safely under a car

1. Disconnect the battery negative (–) cable so that no one else can start the car. Let others know what you will be doing.
2. Raise the car slowly as described above.

3. Use at least two jack stands to support the car. A jack is a temporary lifting device and should not be used alone to support the car while you are under it. Use positively locking jack stands that are designed for the purpose of supporting a car. For more information on jack stands, see **Tools** below.

WARNING

Do not use wood, concrete blocks, or bricks to support a car. Wood may split. Blocks or bricks, while strong, are not designed for that kind of load, and may break or collapse.

---

4. Place jack stands on a firm, solid surface, just like the jack. If necessary, use a flat board or similar solid object to provide a firm footing.

5. After placing the jack stands, lower the car slowly until its weight is fully supported by the jack stands. Watch to make sure that the jack stands do not tip or lean as the car settles on them, and that they are placed solidly and will not move.

6. Observe all jacking precautions again when raising the car to remove the jack stands.

GENERAL ADVICE FOR THE BEGINNER

The tips in the paragraphs that follow are general advice to help any do-it-yourself Saab owner perform repairs and maintenance tasks more easily and more professionally.

Planning Ahead

Most of the repairs and maintenance tasks described in this manual can be successfully completed by anyone with basic tools and abilities. Some cannot. To prevent getting in too deep, know what the whole job requires before starting. Read the procedure thoroughly, from beginning to end, in order to know just what to expect and what parts will have to be replaced.

Cleanliness

Keeping things organized, neat, and clean is essential to doing a good job, and a more satisfying way to work. When working under the hood, fender covers will protect the finish from scratches and other damage. Make sure the car is relatively clean so that dirt under the cover does not scratch.

Avoid getting tools or clothing near the battery. Battery electrolyte is a corrosive acid. Be careful with brake fluid, as it can cause permanent damage to the car's paint. Finally, keep rubber parts such as hoses and belts free from oil or gasoline, as they will cause the material to soften and fail prematurely.

Non-reusable Fasteners

Many fasteners used on the cars covered by this manual must be replaced with new ones when they are removed. These include but are not limited to: bolts, nuts (self-locking, nylock etc.), cotter pins, studs, brake fittings, roll pins, pins, clips and washers. Genuine Saab parts should only be used for this purpose.

Some bolts, for example, are designed to stretch during assembly and are permanently altered rendering them unusable again. Always replace fasteners where instructed to do so. See an authorized Saab dealer for applications and ordering information.

Tightening Fasteners

When tightening the bolts or nuts that attach a component, it is always good practice to tighten the bolts gradually and evenly to avoid misalignment or over stressing any one portion of the component. For components sealed with gaskets, this method helps to ensure that the gasket will seal properly and completely.

Where there are several fasteners, tighten them in a sequence alternating between opposite sides of the component. Fig. 17 shows such a sequence for tightening six bolts attaching a typical component. Repeat the sequence until all the bolts are evenly tightened to the proper specification.

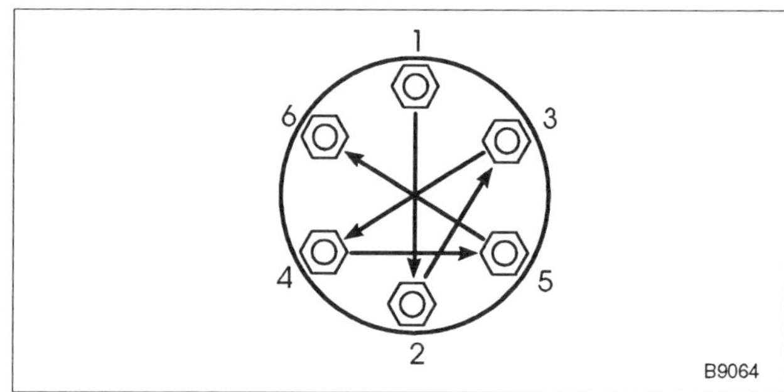

Fig. 17. Sequence for alternately tightening multiple fasteners.

For some repairs a specific tightening sequence is necessary, or a particular order of assembly is required. Such special conditions are noted in the text, and the necessary sequence is described or illustrated.

Bolt Torque

Tightening fasteners to a specified torque value using a torque wrench is a good way to ensure that bolts are correctly tightened. If a torque wrench is not used there is a danger of going too far and damaging the fastener or the threads in the mating part.

Too little torque on a fastener can also cause problems. Vibration of assembled parts can subject fasteners to stress alternating in opposite directions that will eventually cause them to loosen. To counter this loosening, fasteners are tightened more and actually stretched a small amount.

When special tightening torques are required, they are listed in the text where the fastener is being installed. If there is no torque listed for a specific fastener, use **Table a** as a general guide. The sizes listed are for the bolt thread diameter, not the size of the wrench. **Table b** lists the most common wrench sizes for the bolts used on the cars covered by this manual.

Table a. General Tightening Torques (unless noted otherwise in text)

Bolt diameter	Nm	ft-lb
M5	5	3.5 (44 in-lb)
M6	10	7.5 (89 in-lb)
M8	20	15
M10	40	30

Table b. Bolt Diameter and Wrench Size

Bolt diameter	Most Common Wrench Size
M5	8 mm
M6	10 mm
M8	12mm or 13mm
M10	17mm
M12	19mm
M14	22mm

Gaskets

The smoothest metal mating surfaces still have imperfections that can allow leakage. To prevent leakage at critical joints, gaskets of soft, form-fitting material are used to fill in the imperfections.

To be most effective, gaskets are designed to crush and become thinner as the mating parts are bolted together. Once a gasket has been used and crushed, it is no longer capable of making as good a seal as when new, and is much more likely to leak. For this reason, gaskets should not be reused. Always plan to use new gaskets for any reassembly. Some gaskets — such as headgaskets are directional. Make sure that these are being installed correctly. This same logic applies to any part used for sealing, including rubber O-rings and copper sealing washers.

Seals

In places where a shaft must pass through a housing, flexible lip seals are used to keep the lubricating oil or grease from leaking out past the rotating shaft.

Seals are designed to be installed in the housing only once and should never be reused. As long as they are not removed from the housing and not leaking, they need not be replaced. Seals, however, do age and deteriorate, and there is no easier time to replace them than when the car is already apart for some other repair.

When doing repairs that require removing a seal, be very careful not to scratch or otherwise damage the metal surfaces. Even minor damage to sealing surfaces can cause seal damage and leakage.

The key to seal installation is to get the seal in straight without damaging it. Use an object that is the same diameter as the seal housing to gently and evenly drive it into place. If a proper size seal driver is not available, a socket of the right size will do.

Coat the entire seal with oil to help it go in more easily. Seals are directional. Make sure that it is being installed with the lip facing the correct way. Normally the lip faces the inside. Notice the installation direction of the old seal before removing it.

Cleaning

Any repair job will be less troublesome if the parts are clean. For cleaning old parts, there are any number of solvents and parts cleaners available commercially.

For cleaning parts prior to assembly, commercially available aerosol cans of carburetor cleaner or brake cleaner are handy to use, and the cleaner will evaporate completely, leaving no residue.

WARNING

Virtually all solvents used for cleaning parts are highly flammable, especially in aerosol form. Use with extreme care. Do not smoke. Do not use these products near any source of sparks or flame.

Let any solvent or cleaning product dry completely. Low-pressure, dry compressed air is helpful if available. Also, use only lint-free rags for cleaning and drying.

Electrical Testing

A great many electrical problems can be understood and solved with only a little fundamental knowledge of how electrical circuits function.

Electric current only flows in a complete circuit. To operate, every electrical device in the car requires a complete circuit including a voltage source and a path to ground. The positive (+) side of the battery is the original voltage source, and ground is any return path to the negative (–) side of the battery, whether through the wiring harness or the car body. Except for portions of the charging system, all electrical current in the car is direct current (DC) and flows from positive (+) to negative (–).

Switches are used to turn components on or off by completing or interrupting the circuit. A switch is "open" when the circuit is interrupted, and "closed" when the circuit is completed. Fig. 18 shows a complete circuit schematically. See **3 ELECTRICAL SYSTEM** for electrical troubleshooting.

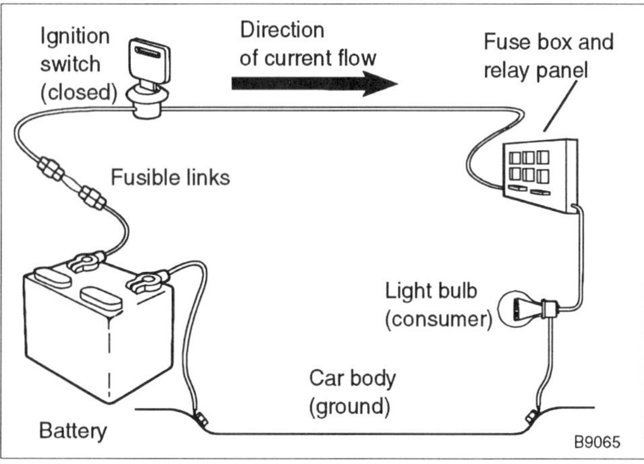

Fig. 18. Schematic representation of simple circuit for light bulb. Switch is shown closed, making circuit complete.

Wire Repairs

Repairs to a wiring harness to reconnect broken wires or correct shorts to ground deserve special care to make the repair permanent. The wire ends must be clean. If frayed or otherwise damaged, cut off the end. If the wire is too short, splice in a new piece of wire of the same size and make two connections.

Use connectors that are designed for the purpose. Crimped-on or soldered-on connectors are best. Crimp connectors and special crimping pliers are widely available. If soldering, use a needlenose pliers to hold the wire near the solder joint and create a "heat dam". This keeps the heat and the solder from traveling up the wire. Always use a solder made specifically for electrical work.

NOTE
Twisting wires together is really only a temporary repair, since corrosion and vibration will eventually spoil the connection.

Insulate the finished connection. Electronics stores can supply heat-shrinkable insulating tubing that can be placed onto the wire before connecting, slid over the finished joint, and shrunk to a tight fit with a heat gun or hair dryer. The next best alternative is electrical tape. Make sure the wire is clean and free of solder flux or other contamination. Wrap the joint tightly and completely to seal out moisture.

BUYING PARTS

Many of the maintenance and repair tasks in this manual call for the installation of new parts, or the use of new gaskets and other materials when reinstalling parts. Most often, the parts that will be needed should be on hand before beginning the job. Read the introductory text and the complete procedure to determine which parts will be needed.

NOTE
For some bigger jobs, partial disassembly and inspection are required to determine a complete parts list. Read the procedure carefully and, if necessary, make other arrangements to get the necessary parts while your car is disassembled.

Information You Need To Know

Fig. 19 shows the locations of the important information that may be necessary to have on hand when buying parts or having work done on the car.

Genuine Saab Parts

Genuine Saab replacement parts from an authorized Saab dealer are designed and manufactured to the same high standards as the original parts. They will be the correct material, manufactured to the same specifications, and guaranteed to fit and work as intended by the engineers who designed the car. Some genuine Saab parts have a limited warranty.

Many independent repair shops make a point of using genuine Saab parts, even though they may at times be more expensive. They know the value of doing the job right with the right parts. Parts from other sources can be as good, particularly if manufactured by one of Saabs original equipment suppliers, but it is often difficult to know.

Saab is constantly updating and improving their cars, often making improvements during a given model year. Saab may recommend a newer, improved part as a replacement, and your authorized dealer's parts department will know about it and provide it. The Saab parts organization is best equipped to deal with any Saab parts needs.

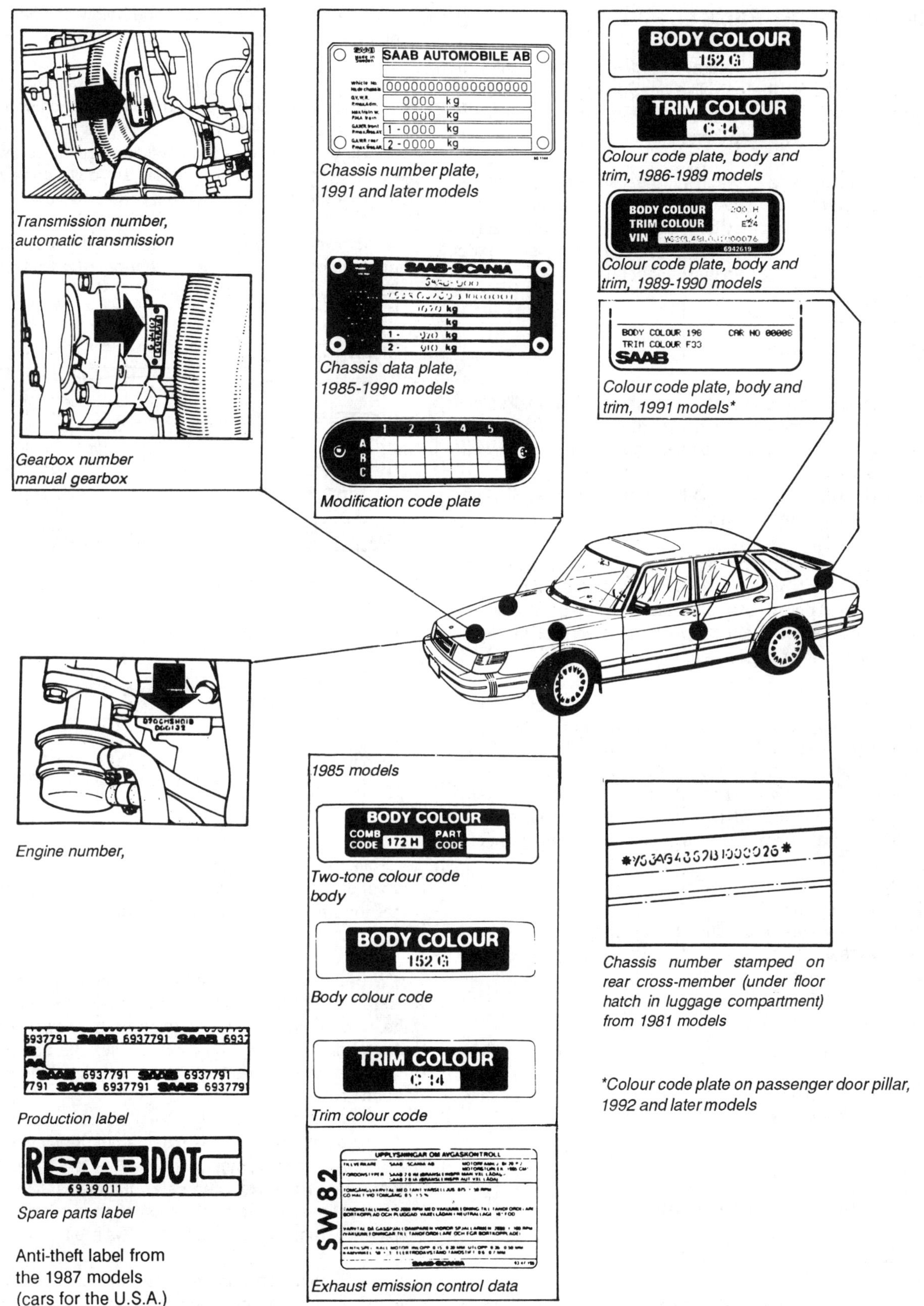

Transmission number, automatic transmission
Gearbox number manual gearbox
SAAB AUTOMOBILE AB
0000 kg
1 - 0000 kg
2 - 0000 kg
Chassis number plate, 1991 and later models
SAAB-SCANIA
Chassis data plate, 1985-1990 models
A
B
C
1 2 3 4 5
Modification code plate
BODY COLOUR
152 G
TRIM COLOUR
C 14
Colour code plate, body and trim, 1986-1989 models
BODY COLOUR
TRIM COLOUR
VIN
Colour code plate, body and trim, 1989-1990 models
BODY COLOUR 198
TRIM COLOUR F33
SAAB
Colour code plate, body and trim, 1991 models*
Engine number,
1985 models
BODY COLOUR
COMB CODE 172 H
PART CODE
Two-tone colour code body
BODY COLOUR
152 G
Body colour code
TRIM COLOUR
C 14
Trim colour code
Chassis number stamped on rear cross-member (under floor hatch in luggage compartment) from 1981 models
*Colour code plate on passenger door pillar, 1992 and later models
6937791 SAAB 6937791
Production label
R SAAB DOT
6939011
Spare parts label
Anti-theft label from the 1987 models (cars for the U.S.A.)
SW 82
UPPLYSNINGAR OM AVGASKONTROLL
Exhaust emission control data

Fig. 19. Locations of important information that may be required when buying parts.

Non-returnable Parts

Some parts cannot be returned for credit, even if they are the wrong parts for the car. The best example is electrical parts, which are almost universally considered non-returnable because they are so easily damaged internally.

Buy electrical parts carefully, and be as sure as possible that a replacement is needed, especially for expensive parts such as control units. It may be wise to let an authorized Saab dealer or other qualified shop confirm your diagnosis before replacing an expensive part that cannot be returned.

TOOLS

Most maintenance can be accomplished with a small selection of the right tools. Tools range in quality from inexpensive junk, which may break at first use, to very expensive and well-made tools which, to the professional, are worth every bit of their high cost. The best tools for most do-it-yourself Saab owners lie somewhere in between.

Cheap tools are not a bargain. They often do not hold up to even casual use, and they present a greater risk of personal injury. If they fit poorly, they can actually damage the fasteners they are intended to remove, making it that much harder to use a good tool the next time around.

Many reputable tool manufacturers offer good quality, moderately priced tools with a lifetime guarantee. A broken tool can be exchanged for a new one, for the life of the tool. These are your best buy. They cost a little more, but they are good quality tools that will do what is expected of them. Sears' Craftsman® line is one such source of good quality, reasonably priced, and guaranteed tools. Other sources of special tools are:

Schley Products Inc.
5350 E. Hunter Ave., Anaheim Hills, CA 92807
(714) 693-7666

Baum Tools Unltd. Inc.
P.O. Box 87, Longboat Key, FL 34228
(800) 848-6657

Assenmacher Specialty Tools
6440 Odell Place, Boulder, CO 80301
(303) 530-2424

Basic Tool Requirements

NOTE
Saabs are delivered with a tool kit mounted to the underside of the trunk lid. The kit contains a basic selection of tools that may fulfill some of the requirements listed in this section.

The basic hand tools described below can be used to accomplish most of the simple maintenance and repair tasks.

Screwdrivers. Three types, the common flat-blade type, the Phillips type will handle almost all screws used on Saabs. Two or three different sizes of each type will be best, since a screwdriver of the wrong size will damage the screw head. On late models Saabs, Torx® screw are quite common. A T25 size Torx driver will handle most of these screws.

A complete set of screwdrivers can often be purchased for about the same money as the four or six individual ones that are really necessary. See Fig. 20.

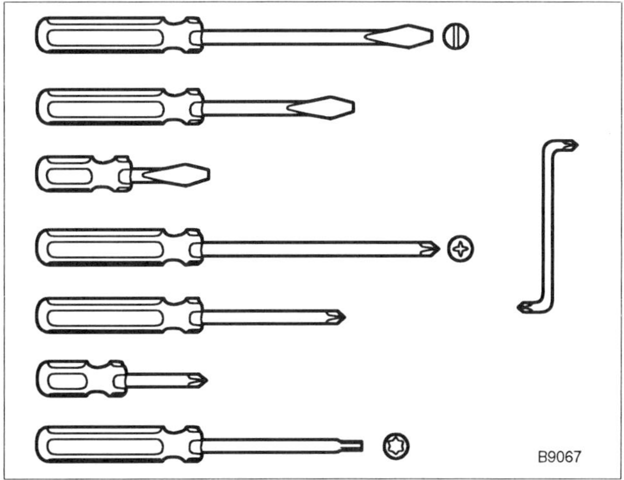

Fig. 20. Common flat-blade (top), Phillips (middle) and Torx® (bottom) screwdrivers. Offset screwdriver (right) is used for screws with limited access.

For a more complete tool box, include "stubby" screwdrivers or offset screwdrivers for use in tight spots where a normal length screwdriver will not easily fit and Torx®head screwdrivers.

Wrenches. Wrenches come in different styles for different uses. Fig. 21 shows several. The basic open-end wrench is the most widely used, but grips on only two sides. It can spread apart and slip off more easily. The box-end wrench has better grip, on all six sides of a nut or bolt, and is much less prone to slip.

A 12-point box-end can loosen a nut or bolt where there is less room for movement, while a 6-point box-end provides better grip. For hex fasteners on fluid lines, like brake lines and fuel lines, a flare-nut wrench offers the advantages of a box-end wrench with a slot that allows it to fit over the line.

The combination wrench, shown in Fig. 22, is the most universal. It has one open-end and one 12-point box-end. For Saabs, 10mm and 13mm wrenches are the most common sizes needed. On most models, a 19mm wrench is needed to loosen and tighten the engine oil drain plug. A complete set should also include 6mm, 7mm, 8mm, 9mm, 11mm, 12mm, 14mm, and 15mm.

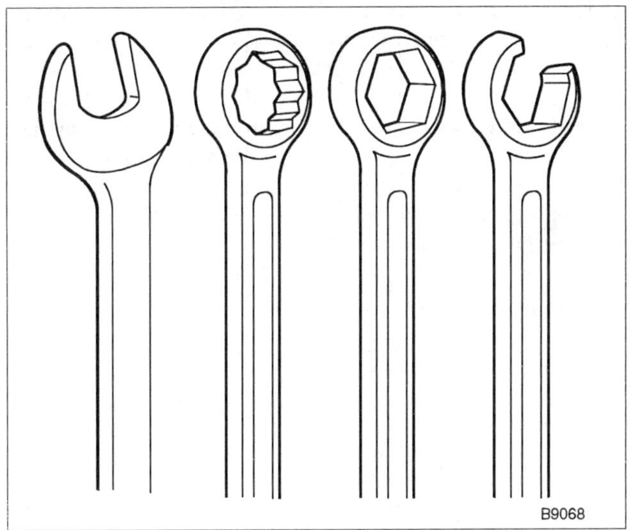

Fig. 21. Types of wrench heads. From left, open-end, 12-point box-end, 6-point box-end, flare nut.

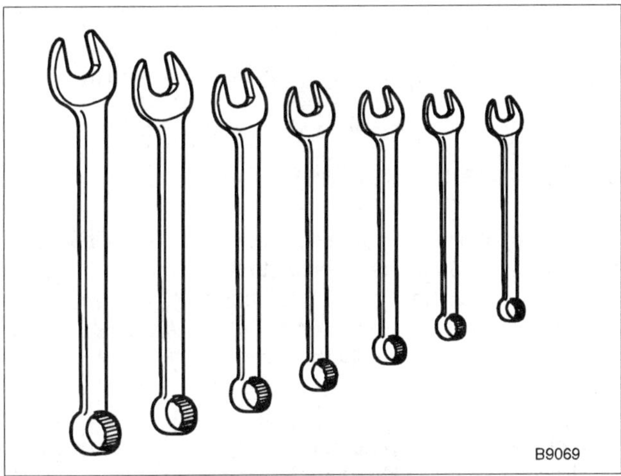

Fig. 22. Combination wrenches with one open-end and one 12-point box-end.

Sockets. Sockets perform the same job as box-end wrenches, but offer greater flexibility. They are normally used with a ratchet handle for speed and convenience, and can be combined with extensions to reach fasteners more easily.

Standard sockets come in 6-point and 12-point styles. For use with a ratchet the 6-point offers a better grip on tight nuts and bolts. As with wrenches, 6mm to 15mm, 17mm, and 19mm are the most needed sizes. See Fig. 23.

Sockets come with different size connections to drive handles or extensions, called the drive size. The most common drive sizes are 1/4 in., 3/8 in., and 1/2 in.

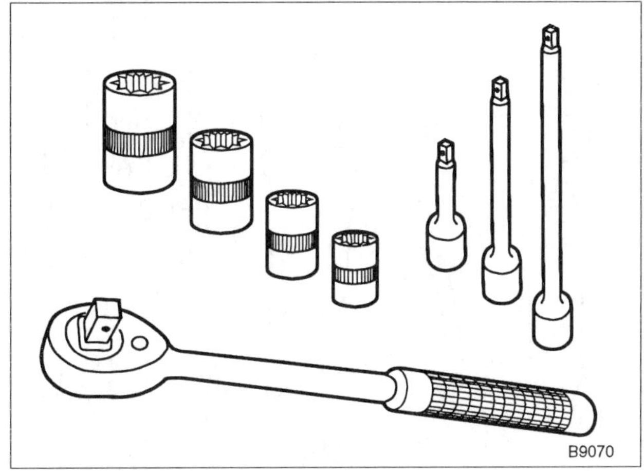

Fig. 23. Sockets, extensions, and a ratchet handle.

As a start, 6-point sockets with a 3/8 in. square drive, two or three 3/8 in. extensions of different lengths, and a 3/8 in. drive ratchet handle will be suitable for most jobs.

For a more complete tool box, add deep sockets and a greater variety of handles and extensions. A universal joint extension can allow access from an angle where a straight extension will not quite fit.

Spark Plug Socket. A special socket for spark plugs is the correct size, is deep enough to accommodate a spark plug's length, and includes a rubber insert to both protect the spark plug from damage and grip it for easier removal. The spark plugs used in Saab engines require a 5/8 in. socket. See Fig. 24.

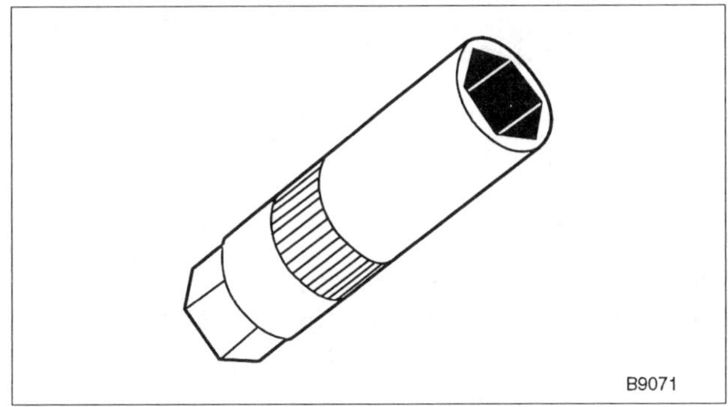

Fig. 24. Spark plug socket (5/8 in.).

Pliers. A few of the many types of pliers are shown in Fig. 25. Most are used for holding irregular objects, bending, or crimping. Some have special applications.

A needlenose plier is used for gripping small and poorly accessible objects, and is useful for wiring and other electrical work. A locking plier such as the well-known Vise-Grip® is useful because of its tight grip.

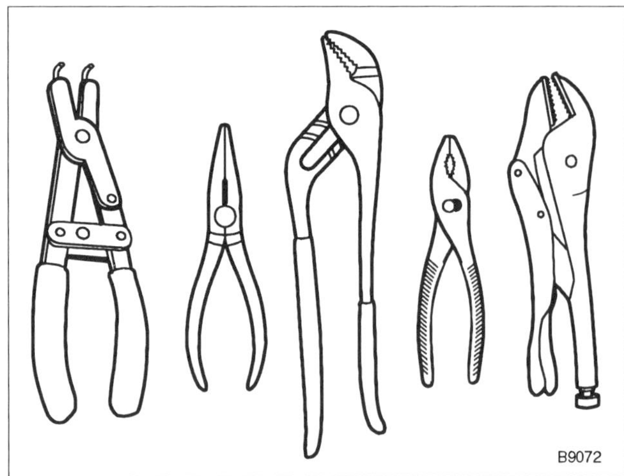

Fig. 25. Pliers. From left, snap-ring, needlenose, Channel-lock®, common, locking.

Snap-ring and circlip pliers with special tipped jaws are used to remove and install snap-rings or circlips. A Channel-lock® or water pump plier has adjustable jaws that can be quickly changed to match the size of the object being held to give greater leverage.

Adjustable wrench can be a useful addition to a small tool kit. See Fig. 26. It can substitute in a pinch, if two wrenches of the same size are needed to remove a nut and bolt. Use extra care with adjustable wrenches, as they especially tend to loosen, slip, and damage fasteners.

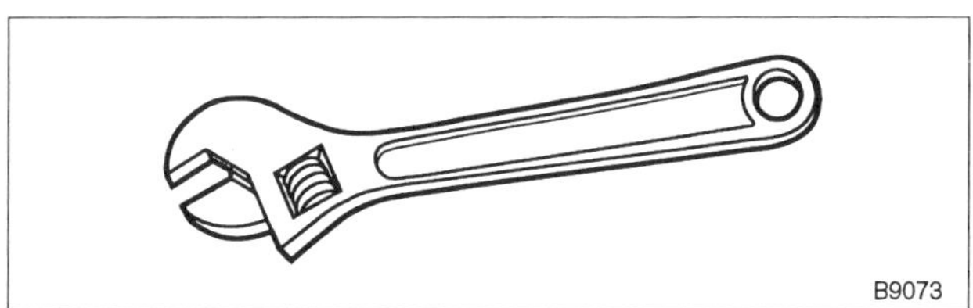

Fig. 26. Adjustable wrench.

Compared to a wrench of the correct size, an adjustable wrench is always second best. They should only be used when the correct size wrench is not available. Choose one of average size range, about 6 to 8 inches in length.

Jack Stands

Strong jack stands are extremely important for any work that is done under the car. Jacks are designed only for short term use and are not solid enough to support the car for a long period. A jack should never be used alone to support the car while working underneath.

Use only jack stands that are designed for the purpose. Blocks of wood, concrete, bricks, etc. are not safe or suitable substitutes.

Jack stands are available in several styles. A typical jack stand is shown in Fig. 27. The best ones are made of heavy material for strength, have a wide base for stability, and are equipped to positively lock in their raised positions. Get the best ones available.

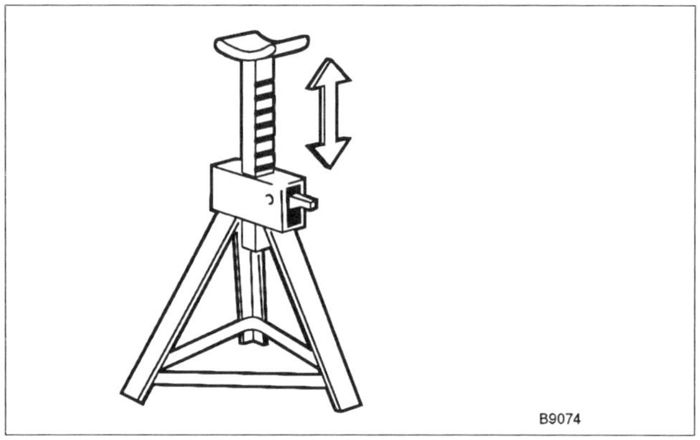

Fig. 27. Jack stand for safely supporting car to work underneath.

Oil Change Equipment

Changing engine oil requires a box-end wrench or socket to loosen and tighten the drain plug 19mm (13mm on 1991 and later cars), a drain pan (at least 7 qt. capacity), and an oil filter wrench. These items are shown in Fig. 28. A wide, low drain pan will fit more easily under the car. Use a funnel to pour the new oil into the engine.

An oil filter wrench is needed for some models to remove the oil filter. Be sure to get a filter wrench that will grip the Saab oil filter tightly.

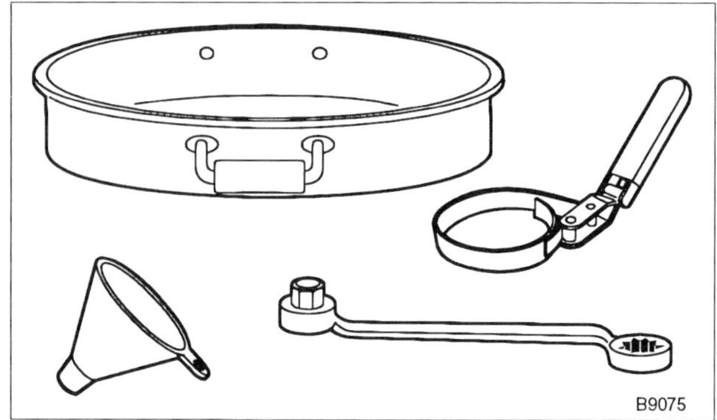

Fig. 28. Oil change equipment includes drain plug wrench (19mm or 13mm), 7 qt. drain pan, oil filter wrench, and funnel.

Torque Wrench

A torque wrench is used to precisely tighten threaded fasteners to a predetermined value. Nearly all of the repair procedures in this manual include Saab-specified torque values in Newton-meters (Nm) and the equivalent values in foot-pounds (ft-lb).

Several types of torque wrenches are widely available. They all do the same job, but offer different convenience features at different prices. Two typical torque wrenches are shown in Fig. 29. The most convenient ones have a built-in ratchet, and can be preset to indicate when a specific torque value has been reached. Follow the wrench manufacturer's directions for use to achieve the greatest accuracy.

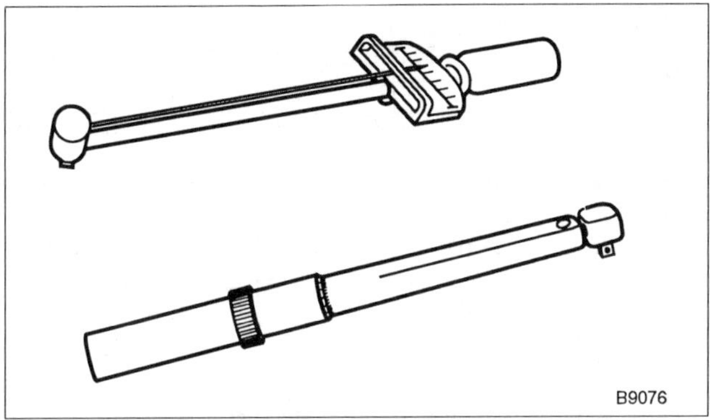

Fig. 29. Torque wrenches. Inexpensive beam-type (top) is adequate but must be read visually. Ratchet-type (bottom) can be preset to indicate when torque value has been reached.

A torque wrench with a range up to about 250 Nm (185 ft-lb) has adequate capacity for most of the repairs covered in this manual. For recommended torque values of 10 Nm or below, the English system equivalent is given in inch-pounds (in-lb). These small values may be most easily reached using a torque wrench calibrated in inch-pounds. To convert foot-pounds to inch-pounds, multiply by 12. To convert inch-pounds to foot-pounds, divide by 12.

Feeler Gauges

Feeler gauges are thin metal strips of precise thickness, used to measure small clearances. They are normally available as a set, covering a range of sizes. For Saabs, metric feeler gauges (in millimeters) are the best choice. Fig. 30 shows a set of feeler gauges.

Volt-Ohm Meter (VOM) or Multimeter

Many of the electrical tests in this manual call for the measurement of resistance (ohms) or voltage values. For safe and accurate tests of ignition, fuel injection, and emission control systems, the multimeter, shown in Fig. 31, should be digital, with high (at least 10,000 ohms) input impedance. Some

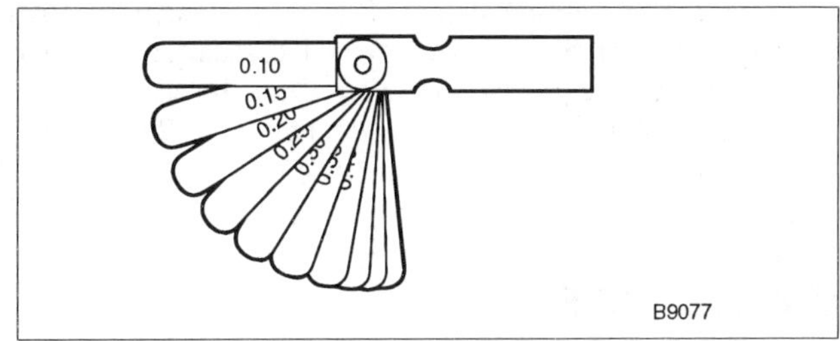

Fig. 30. Feeler gauge set, used for precise measurement of clearances between parts.

meters have automotive functions such as dwell and pulse width that are useful for troubleshooting ignition and fuel injection problems.

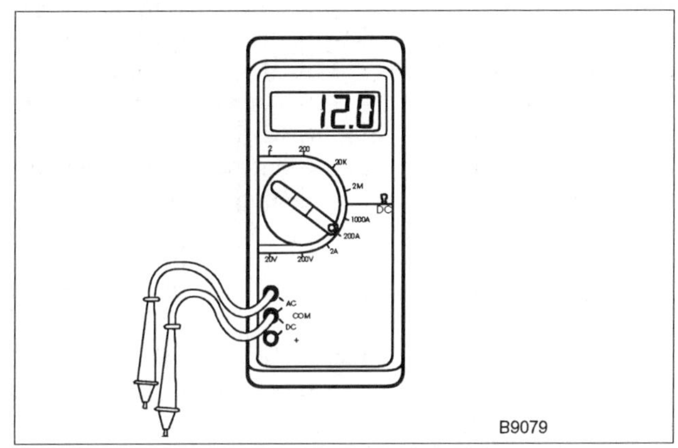

Fig. 31. Multimeter with test probes.

CAUTION

Ignition, fuel injection, emission controls and other electronic systems may be damaged by the high current draw of a test light with a normal incandescent bulb. As a general rule, use a high impedance digital multimeter or an LED test light for all electrical testing.

Saab Special Tools

Some of the more challenging repairs covered in this manual call for the use of Saab special tools. This, however, does not automatically mean that the job is too complicated or out of reach of the novice.

Many of the Saab special tools mentioned in this manual are inexpensive and are simply the best thing to use to do the job correctly. In these cases, the tool is identified with a Saab part number. See your authorized Saab dealer parts department for information on how to order special tools.

There are some jobs for which expensive special tools are essential, and not a cost-effective purchase for one-time repair by the do-it-yourself owner. This manual includes such repairs for the benefit of those with the necessary experience and access to tools. For the do-it-yourselfer, the need for special tools is noted in the text, and whether or not Saab dealer service is recommended.

EMERGENCIES

Changing a Tire

If a tire goes flat while driving, pull well off the road. Changing a tire on a busy street or highway is very dangerous. If necessary, drive a short distance on the flat tire to get to a safe place. It is much better to ruin a tire or rim than to risk being hit.

Stop the car on as flat a surface as possible, in a place where you can be easily seen by other drivers. Avoid stopping just over the crest of a hill. Turn on the emergency flashers, and set out flares or emergency markers well behind the car. Passengers should get out of the car and stand well away from the road. Take the jack, tools, and spare wheel from the trunk. Chock the wheel diagonally opposite to the one being changed.

Loosen the wheel bolts while the car is on the ground, but leave them a little snug. Place the jack under in the lifting point nearest the wheel being changed (lifting points are shown above in Fig. 15). Use a board to provide a firm footing for the jack if the ground is soft. Raise the car only far enough so that the wheel is off the ground, and then remove the wheel bolts and the wheel. Remove the lug bolts or nuts and remove the tire.

Install the spare wheel. Install the wheel bolts or nuts and tighten them by hand, then lower the car. With all wheels on the ground, fully tighten the bolts in a cross-wise pattern. Torque the wheel bolts when installing the wheel.

Tightening torques
- wheel lug bolts . . . . . . 105 to 125 Nm (77 to 92 ft-lb)
- wheel lug nuts . . . . 90 to 110 Nm (66 to 81 ft-lb)

If torquing the wheel fasteners is not possible, tighten them as much as possible, then loosen and retorque the bolts to the proper specification at the earliest opportunity. Check the inflation pressure of the spare tire.

Car Will Not Start

If the engine turns over slowly or not at all, especially on cold mornings, the battery may not be sufficiently charged. Jump-starting the battery from another car may help. Jump-starting is described below.

NOTE
Be sure to read the cautions under **Jump Starting** prior to jump starting a low battery. Failure to follow the cautions may result in damage to the electronic components in the car.

Push starting (or tow starting) a car with an insufficiently charged battery is another option. To push start the car, turn on the ignition, put the car in second or third gear and push in the clutch pedal. Push or tow the car. When the car is moving at a fair speed (10 to 15 mph), release the clutch pedal. After the engine has started, push the clutch pedal back in and allow the engine to idle. Rev the engine for a few minutes to help restore the charge to the battery.

WARNING
Use extreme caution when push starting a car. Be aware of other traffic. Use the emergency flashers.

NOTE
On cars with automatic transmissions, the design of the transmission makes it impossible to start the engine by pushing the car.

If the engine is turning over at normal speed with the starter motor, the battery and starter are fine. Check to make sure that there is fuel in the tank. Don't rely on the fuel gauge, it may be faulty. Instead, remove the gas filler cap and rock the car. If there is gas in the tank, you should hear a sloshing sound at the filler neck. If so, turn the ignition on and listen for the sound of the fuel pump. It should run for a few seconds, then stop. If it doesn't, fuel may not be reaching the engine.

The engine also may have difficulty starting because it has too much fuel, because the fuel system is vapor-locked on a hot day, or because the ignition system is wet on a very damp day. There will probably be a strong smell of gas if the engine has too much fuel (referred to as "flooded").

Try holding the accelerator pedal fully to the floor while starting. This electrically turns off the fuel injectors. If the engine stills does not start, wait for a few minutes and then try starting the engine again. If you suspect vapor-lock, raise the hood, let the engine cool, and then try to start the engine.

On damp days, check the distributor cap and spark plug wires for condensation. If they are wet, remove and replace the wires one at a time and dry them off with a clean dry cloth, then remove the distributor cap and wipe it dry inside and out.

Jump-Starting

Cars with partially discharged or completely dead batteries can be jump-started using the good battery from another car.

When jump-starting the engine, always heed the following warnings and cautions.

WARNING

• Battery acid (electrolyte) can cause severe burns, and will damage the car and clothing. If electrolyte is spilled, wash the surface with large quantities of water. If it gets into eyes, flush them with water for several minutes and call a doctor.

• Batteries produce explosive and noxious gasses. Keep sparks and flames away. Do not smoke near batteries.

• Do not jump-start the engine if you suspect that the battery is frozen. Trapped gas may explode. Allow the battery to thaw first.

• Do not quick-charge the battery (for boost starting) for longer than one minute, and do not exceed 15 volts at the battery with the boosting cables attached. Wait at least one minute before boosting the battery a second time.

To jump-start the engine, place the cars close together, but do not allow them to touch. Turn off the engine of the car with the good battery. Connect the jumper cables as shown in Fig. 32.

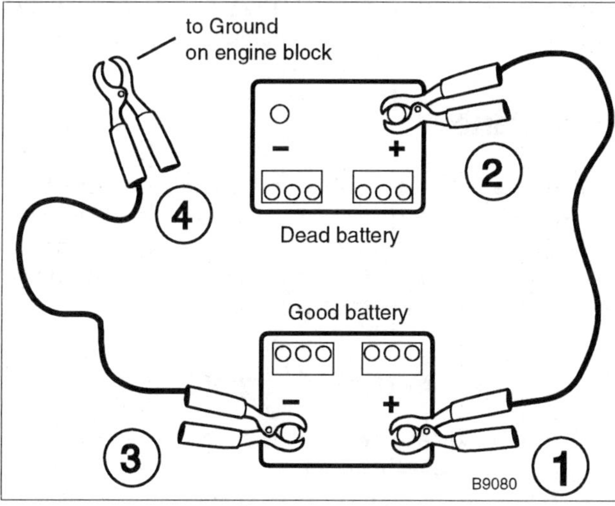

Fig. 32. Battery jumper cables connections. Numbers indicate correct sequence for cable attachment.

The battery is mounted in the front right corner of the engine compartment. Connect the end of one cable to the positive post of the good battery, and the other end of the same cable to the positive post of the dead battery. The positive post is marked with a plus (+) sign.

Connect one end of the other cable to the negative (–) post of the good battery, and connect the other end of the same cable to the engine block of the car with the dead battery. Make the connection as far away from the battery as possible, as there may be sparks.

Have a helper start the car with the good battery and race the engine slightly, then start the car with the dead battery. Leave the cars running and disconnect the cables in the reverse order in which they were installed. The car with the dead battery will need to run for about a 1/2 hour to recharge the battery.

Overheating

If the coolant temperature is too high, find a safe place to stop and turn the engine off. Open the hood and allow the engine to cool until the temperature gauge needle is at the lower third of the scale. Continuing to drive an overheated car can cause expensive engine damage.

WARNING

Do not remove the coolant reservoir or radiator cap with the engine hot. Undoing either could spray hot coolant, and cause burns, or damage the engine.

NOTE

If the engine cannot be safely turned off, make sure the air conditioner is off and turn the heater to high. This will help cool the engine until a safe stopping place can be reached.

Overheating may be caused by low coolant level or a damaged V-belt. Visually check the coolant level and V-belts as described in **110 Maintenance Program**. If coolant is lost, check the filler cap, hoses, clamps and radiator for signs of leakage. Check for leaks at the water pump on the rear of the engine.

If no leaks are found, add coolant after the engine has cooled. The car can be driven, but have the cooling system thoroughly checked as soon as possible. If replacement coolant is not available, then plain water can be used, but the coolant should later be drained and refilled with the proper mixture of anti-freeze and water.

CAUTION

Do not add cold water or coolant to a hot engine. Severe engine damage could result from the sudden temperature change.

If steam is coming from the engine compartment then there is most likely a burst coolant hose or a large leak in the cooling system. To find the leak, look for signs of coolant leakage on hoses, at hose connections, or on the radiator. Let the engine cool thoroughly, then add coolant or water to fill the system and start the engine. If a great deal of water or coolant flows out of the hole, then the car should not be driven until repairs are made. If there is a slight seepage, then it may be possible to drive a short distance, adding coolant as needed.

Oil Pressure Warning Light

If the oil pressure warning light does not go out immediately after the engine starts, or if it comes on while driving the car, stop the engine immediately to prevent severe engine damage.

Check the oil level as described in **110 Maintenance Program**. If the level is low, add oil to the correct level and start the engine. If the light is still on, do not run the car at all. Have it towed.

Brake Fluid Level Warning Light

The red brake fluid level warning light is an indicator of brake fluid loss. Problems with the brake system should be checked and repaired immediately. See **5 BRAKES** for more information.

Anti-Lock Brake System Warning Indicator

If the anti-lock brake system warning indicator comes on at normal driving speeds, the anti-lock braking system is out of service. Under normal conditions, there will be no change in the effectiveness of the brakes. In an emergency situation, however, the normal anti-lock function is lost and the brakes could lock. Check the system as described in **5 BRAKES**.

Dim Lights

Headlights that are dim or gradually getting dimmer generally indicate a problem with the battery or charging system. The battery charge indicator light may come on as the lights are dimming. In either case, the engine and accessories are running off of the battery alone, and will soon discharge it altogether.

If possible, do not stop the engine unless you have the capability to jump start it. There may not be enough power in the starting system to restart the engine. Instead, turn off as many electrical consumers as possible. This will reduce the current drain and will allow the car to be driven farther before you lose all battery power.

With the engine and ignition off, check to see if the battery cables are firmly attached, or if there are any loose wires leading to the battery or to the alternator. Look for heavily corroded (covered by fluffy white deposits) wires and connectors.

Disconnecting, cleaning, and reinstalling corroded wires and connectors may solve the problem. Also check V-belt tension as described in **110 Maintenance Program.**

Towing

The cars covered by this manual should be towed with a tow truck using wheel lift or flat bed equipment. Do not tow the car on all four wheels except for very short distances to move it to a safe place. If flat-towing the car, use the towing eyes at the front of the car under the bumper. Set the transmission in neutral.

When towing the car from the rear with the front wheels on the ground, a maximum distance of 30 miles is acceptable. If the car needs to be towed further, have the front wheels placed on dollies.

NOTE

Do not tow with sling-type equipment. The front spoilers and the bumpers may sustain damage.

Towing a Saab with an automatic transmission with the front wheels on the ground can result in transmission damage due to lack of lubrication. Always tow the car with the transmission lever in “N” (neutral) and the key in position “1”. Saab recommends that cars with automatic transmission be towed with the rear wheels on the ground for no more than 30 miles (50 km), at no more than 25 mph (40 km/h). Be sure the transmission fluid has been topped off before starting the tow.

Spare Parts Kit

Carrying a basic set of spare parts can prevent a minor breakdown from turning into a major annoyance. Many of the following items won’t allow you to do major repair work on the car, but they will help in the event of the failure of something that can disable the car or compromise its safety.

Spare Parts Kit - Basic Contents:

- V-belts for the alternator and water pump
- one or two quarts of engine oil
- a gallon container of engine coolant (premixed 50/50 anti-freeze and water)
- spare fuel pump relay, also spare main relay
- a new, unopened bottle of brake fluid (DOT 4 specifications)
- 10 amp, 15 amp, and 20 amp fuses
- upper and lower radiator hoses

Spare Parts Kit - Additional Contents

- replacement headlight (sealed beam or bulb)
- brake light, turn signal light, and tail light bulbs
- wiper blades
- distributor cap and rotor

110 Maintenance Program

TABLES

GENERAL

The useful life of any car depends on the kind of maintenance it receives. The procedures described in this section of the manual include all of the routine checks and maintenance steps that are both required by Saab under the terms of their warranty protection and recommended by Saab to ensure long and reliable operation of your car. Also included are some instructions and recommendations for more basic car care.

Some maintenance procedures, such as oil change service, require no special tools and can be carried out by almost any interested Saab owner, regardless of his or her previous mechanical experience. Certain other maintenance tasks require special tools and equipment. Idle speed and ignition timing adjustments are some examples. If you lack the tools or a suitable workplace for doing any of the maintenance described in this section, we suggest you leave this work to an authorized Saab dealer or other qualified shop. We especially urge you to consult an authorized Saab dealer before beginning any repairs on a car still covered by the manufacturer's warranty.

All of the maintenance work described here is important and should be carried out at the correct time or mileage interval. Your Saab should not be thought of as a maintenance-free machine. Correct care will protect your investment and help you to get many years of driving reliability and enjoyment from your Saab.

Saab is constantly updating their recommended maintenance procedures and requirements. The information contained here is as accurate as possible at the time of publication. If there is any doubt about what procedures apply to a specific model or model year, or what intervals should be followed, remember that an authorized Saab dealer always has the latest information on factory-recommended maintenance.

SAAB RECOMMENDED MAINTENANCE PROGRAM

Table a and **Table b** list the maintenance tasks specified by Saab that should be done at specified mileage intervals to ensure the proper function, safety and durability of the Saab automobile under normal use. The schedules are divided into two parts; **Oil Change/Safety Inspection** and **Major Service.**

NOTE
Aside from keeping your car in the best possible condition, proper maintenance plays a role in maintaining full protection under Saab's new-car warranty coverage. If in doubt about the terms and conditions of your car's warranty, an authorized Saab dealer should be able to explain them.

The **Oil Change/Safety Inspection** covers the most basic level of routine maintenance. Saab's required Oil Change/-Safety Inspection specifies changing the engine oil and oil filter, rotating the tires, and checking other systems and their fluids. This service should be made at 7,500 mile intervals on all models except 1992 nad later, models. On 1992 and later models, the service should be made at 10,000 mile intervals, beginning at 15,000 miles.

NOTE
On 1992 and later, Saab specifies a one-time 5,000 mile "First Service", which should be done by an authorized dealer. There is no charge for this service. For more information on the Saab maintenance system, see your glove box information or an authorized Saab dealer.

The **Major Service** interval signals the need for more comprehensive maintenance and inspection. This service should be performed every 30,000 miles.

NOTE
On 1992 and later models, the first Major Service should be done at 35,000 miles, then at 30,000 mile intervals thereafter.

Except where noted, the maintenance items listed apply to all models covered by this manual. The columns on the right side of each table give quick-reference information about the job—whether tools are needed, whether the procedure requires new parts, whether the car should be warmed-up to normal operating temperature and, in some cases, a recommendation that the job be turned over to an authorized Saab dealer because of the need for special equipment or expertise.

Following the Saab recommended maintenance tables are detailed descriptions of all of the tasks, in the order in which they appear in the tables.

Table a. Oil Service/Safety Inspection
1985-1991: every 7,500 miles
1992 and later: every 10,000 miles

Maintenance item	Tools required	New parts required	Warm engine required	Dealer service recommended
Engine maintenance				
Change oil and oil filter	*	*	*	
Check engine coolant level and add as required. Check coolant freezing point. Inspect coolant hoses and hose clamps	*	*		
Check engine drive belt (V-belt) condition and tension	*			
Inspect exhaust system				
Inspect fuel system components, fuel lines, and vacuum hoses				
Electrical System Maintenance				
Check battery terminal connections and electrolyte level. Clean terminals if necessary				
Check for proper function of exterior and interior lights				

continued on next page

Table a. Oil Service/Safety Inspection (continued)
1985-1991: every 7,500 miles
1992 and later: every 10,000 miles

Maintenance item	Tools required	New parts required	Warm engine required	Dealer service recommended
Transmission Maintenance				
Check manual transmission oil level and add as required		*		
Check automatic transmission fluid level and add as required		*		
Check automatic transmission final drive oil level and add as required	*	*		
Inspect rubber boots for inner and outer drive axle joints				
Chassis Maintenance				
Inspect brake system for damaged hoses and lines, leaks or damage				
Check brake pad wear (road wheels removed)	*			
Check brake (and clutch) fluid level and add as required		*		
Check parking brake operation				
Check power steering fluid level and add as required		*		
Check windshield washer fluid level and add as required				
Check shock absorber bushings and shock function				
Inspect rubber boots for ball joints, tie-rod ends, and steering rack				
Check tire pressure, including spare	*			
Rotate tires. Inspect tires for uneven wear	*			
Check front wheel toe-in alignment (1985-1991 models only)	*		*	*
Body Maintenance				
Check operation of doors. Lubricate door hinges, stops, and locks				
Road Test				
Check engine, transmission, clutch, steering, and brake performance. Check cruise control control and ventilation system. Check for any noises (brake squeal, rattle, etc.)				

Table b. Major Service
(every 30,000 miles*)

Maintenance item	Tools required	New parts required	Warm engine required	Dealer service recommended
Engine Maintenance				
Change oil and oil filter	*	*	*	
Flush and replace engine coolant (maximum 2-year intervals)	*	*		
Inspect coolant hoses and hose clamps	*			
Check engine drive belt (V-belt) condition and tension*	*			
Replace distributor cap and rotor**	*	*		
Replace and gap spark plugs	*	*		
Inspect and check resistance of spark plug wires***	*			
Check and adjust ignition timing** (all except models with crankshaft mounted EZK Ignition Hall Sender. See **340 Ignition System** for application information)	*		*	*
Check and adjust idle speed (cars with LH 2.2 Fuel Injection only, see **240 Fuel Injection** for application information)	*		*	*
Check and adjust deceleration system** (cars with LH 2.2 Fuel Injection only, see **240 Fuel Injection** for application information)	*		*	*
Check turbo overpressure safety switch (1985-1988 Turbo models only)	*	*	*	*
Replace oxygen sensor** (cars with LH 2.2 Fuel Injection only, see **240 Fuel Injection** for application information)	*	*		
Inspect crankcase ventilation system***				
Inspect Evaporative Loss Control Device (ELCD) system***				
Replace charcoal canister (1985-1990 models)**	*	*		
Replace air filter element		*		
Inspect fuel system components, fuel lines, and vacuum hoses				
Lubricate accelerator and throttle linkage				
Replace fuel filter	*	*		
Inspect exhaust system				
Electrical System Maintenance				
Check battery terminal connections and electrolyte level. Clean terminals if necessary				
Check for proper function of exterior and interior lights				
Check headlight aim	*			*
Transmission Maintenance				
Check manual transmission oil level and add as required	*	*		
Drain and refill automatic transmission fluid. Remove front pan and clean transmission filter****	*	*	*	*
Check automatic transmission final drive oil level and add as required	*	*		
Inspect rubber boots for inner and outer drive axle joints				

continued on next page

Table b. Major Service (continued)
(every 30,000 miles*)

Maintenance item	Tools required	New parts required	Warm engine required	Dealer service recommended
Chassis Maintenance				
Inspect brake system for damaged hoses and lines, leaks or damage				
Check brake pad wear (road wheels removed)	*			
Replace brake fluid and flush and bleed brake system	*	*		*
Check parking brake operation				
Check power steering fluid level				
Check windshield washer fluid level				
Check shock absorber bushings and shock function				
Inspect rubber boots for ball joints, tie-rod ends, and steering rack				
Check tire pressure, including spare	*			
Rotate tires. Inspect tires for uneven wear	*			
Check front wheel alignment (camber, caster, toe-in)	*	*		*
Body Maintenance				
Check operation of doors. Lubricate door hinges, stops, and locks				
Check and lubricate convertible top latches				
Road Test				
Check engine, transmission, clutch, steering, and brake performance. Check function of instruments, controls, horn, windshield wipers, cruise control control and ventilation system. Check for any noises (brake squeal, rattle, etc.)				

* Every 12 months or 30,000 miles, which ever comes first only
**Every 60,000 miles
***At the first 60,000 miles, then every 12 months thereafter
****An automatic transmission service is recommended every 15,000 miles if the vehicle is under the severe service conditions of trailer towing, extensive city driving or driving in hot climates.

ENGINE MAINTENANCE

Engine Oil and Oil Filter

The engine oil level is checked with a dipstick located on the in the engine block on the side of the intake manifold. See Fig. 1. Make sure the car is on level ground. If the engine has been run, allow it to cool for about 3 minutes for the most accurate check.

Check the level by pulling out the dipstick and wiping it clean. Reinsert it all the way and withdraw it again. The oil level is correct if it is between the maximum and minimum marks on the end of the stick. The distance between the marks corresponds to approximately one quart of oil.

Top up the oil through the dipstick tube. Add only the amount needed to bring the level to the maximum mark on the dipstick, using an oil of the correct viscosity and grade as listed below. Too much oil can be just as harmful as too little. Make sure the dipstick is screwed down properly after use.

CAUTION
The use of fluids or lubricants that do not meet Saab's specifications may impair performance and reliability, and may void warranty coverage.

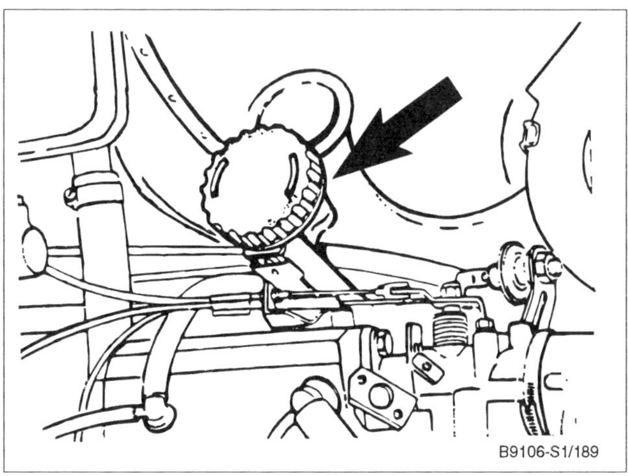

Fig. 1. Location of oil filler cap with dipstick (arrow). Remove and install by turning.

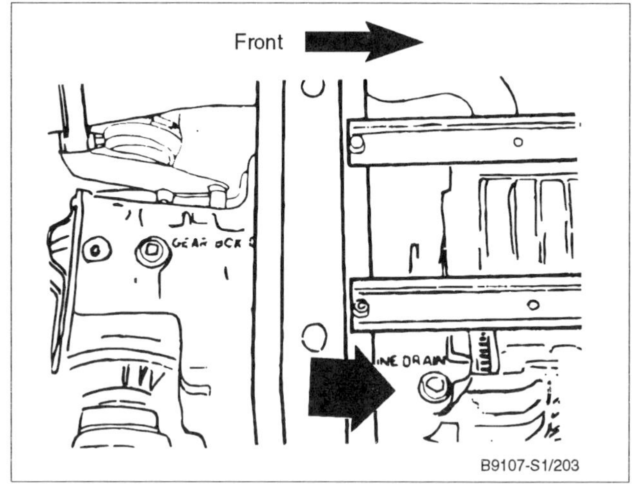

Fig. 2. Engine oil drain plug (arrow) in oil pan underneath engine.

Saab Recommended Engine Oil

- SAE 10W-30, API Service Rating SG or SF/CD
- Alternate for extremely hot climates:
  15W-40, API Service Rating SG or SF/CD

NOTE

The amount of oil that needs to be added between oil changes varies from one engine to another. Generally, a new engine or an engine operated routinely at high speeds will consume more oil. It is helpful to become familiar with the rate at which a particular engine requires oil. A sudden increase may be an early warning of engine mechanical problems.

If the car is used primarily for short trips in slow moving traffic, or routinely operated aggressively, the oil should be changed at more frequent intervals (twice as often) to promote longer engine life.

A complete oil change requires new oil, a new oil filter, and a new drain plug sealing washer. The tools needed are a drain plug socket or box wrench (19 or 13 mm), a drain pan of at least 6 US qt. (5.6 L) capacity, and an oil filter wrench.

To change oil and filter

1. Run the car for a few minutes to slightly warm the engine and the oil, then shut the engine off.

2. With the car on level ground, place a drain pan under the oil drain plug shown in Fig. 2.

NOTE

The car will not need to be raised if a shallow drain pan is used.

---

3. Using a socket or box wrench, loosen the drain plug. By hand, remove the plug and let the oil drain into the pan.

WARNING

Pull the loose plug away from the hole quickly to avoid being burned by the hot oil. If possible, use gloves to protect your hands.

---

4. When the oil flow has diminished to an occasional drip, reinstall the drain plug with a new sealing washer and torque the plug.

CAUTION

If using a "fast-lube" service facility for oil changes, make sure the technician hand-starts and torques the engine oil drain plug using only hand-tools. Using power tools can strip the threads of the plug and the oil pan.

Tightening torque

- engine oil drain plug (13 mm
  or 19mm wrench size) . . . . . . 29-39 Nm (21-29 ft-lb)

NOTE

On mid-1991 and later cars with manual transmission, the engine oil drain plug was changed from a 19mm wrench size to a 13mm wrench size. The plugs are identical except for the bolt head size. This change was made to reduce the possibility of overtightening the larger head drain plug and cracking the transmission case. If replacing the larger drain plug with the smaller plug, be sure to use a new steel washer with the rubber bonded to the perimeter. Do not use the old design copper drain plug gasket with the larger head bolt.

---

5. Position the drain pan directly under the oil filter. Using an oil filter wrench, loosen it in a counterclockwise direction, then remove it by hand. See Fig. 3.

Fig. 3. Engine oil filter on left-hand (driver's) side of engine.

6. After the oil stops dripping, wipe clean the oil filter gasket surface on the filter mounting flange. Lubricate the rubber gasket of the new oil filter with a light coating of clean engine oil.

7. Install the filter by hand until the gasket contacts the mounting flange, then turn the filter another 1/2 turn to tighten it.

CAUTION

Overtightening the oil filter will make the next change much more difficult.

---

8. Refill the crankcase with oil. Use the dipstick to check for the correct oil level.

Engine Oil Capacity (including filter)

- 4.2 quarts (4.0 liters)

Saab Recommended Engine Oil

- SAE 10W-30, API Service Rating SG or SF/CD
- Alternate for extremely hot climates: 15W-40, API Service Rating SG or SF/CD

---

9. Start the engine and check that the oil pressure warning light immediately goes out. Allow the engine to run for a few minutes to circulate the new oil, then check for leaks at the drain plug and around the oil filter. Stop the engine and recheck the oil level.

NOTE

Dispose of the used oil properly. Use tight-sealing containers and mark them clearly. Check with the place of purchase about disposal.

Coolant (Antifreeze) and Cooling System

Cooling system maintenance consists of maintaining the coolant level and its freezing point as well inspecting the hoses. Because the coolant's anti-corrosion and anti-freeze additives gradually lose their effectiveness, replacement of the coolant is recommended every 30,000 miles or 2 years, whichever comes first. Drain and refill the coolant as described in **261 Radiator and Cooling System.**

Cooling System Capacity

- 10.5 quarts (10 liters)

CAUTION

Use only Saab original anti-freeze when filling the cooling system. Use of any other anti-freeze may be harmful to the cooling system. If Saab original anti-freeze is not used, Saab recommends changing the coolant every 12 months.

A translucent expansion tank, or overflow reservoir, provides easy monitoring of coolant level without opening the system. The coolant level should always be checked when the engine is cold. The coolant level should be between the maximum and the minimum mark on the expansion tank, as shown in Fig. 4.

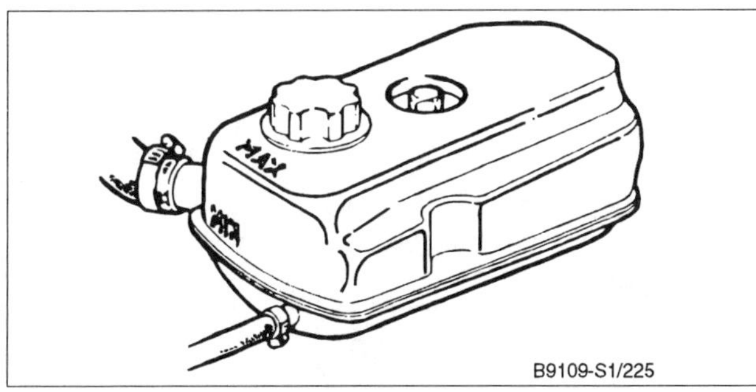

Fig. 4. Fill mark on coolant expansion tank. Coolant level should be between MAX and MIN marks.

Inspect the hose by first checking that all connections are tight and dry. Coolant seepage indicates either that the hose clamp is loose, that the hose is damaged, or that the connection is dirty or corroded. Dried coolant has a chalky appearance. Check the hose condition by pinching them. Hoses should be firm and springy. Replace any hose that is cracked, that has become soft and limp, or has been contaminated by oil. See Fig. 5.

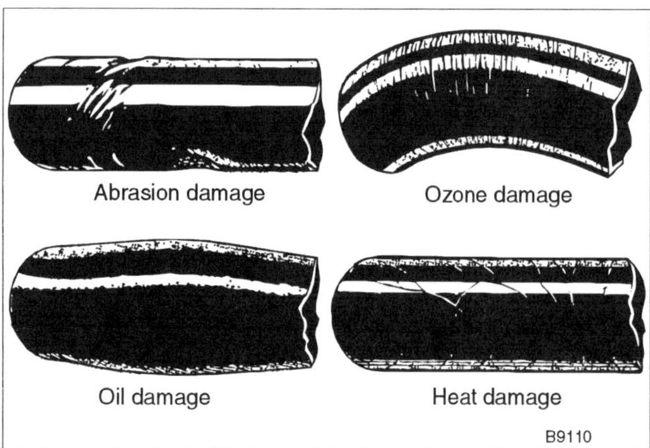

Fig. 5. Examples of damaged coolant hoses. Any of conditions shown is cause for replacement. Courtesy of Gates Rubber Inc.

To check the freezing point of the coolant, use a hydrometer. With the engine cold, remove the cap from the expansion tank and draw up some coolant with the hydrometer. Saab recommends using a 50/50 mixture of anti-freeze and water, which has a freezing point of -35°F (-38°C). If the freezing point is too high, drain a small amount of coolant from the system and add new anti-freeze until the proper protection level is obtained.

Drive Belts

Drive belts (or V-belts) and pulleys transfer power from the engine crankshaft to various accessories. Cars covered by this manual have four drive belts. The alternator and coolant pump are driven by two belts, side by side. See Fig. 6.

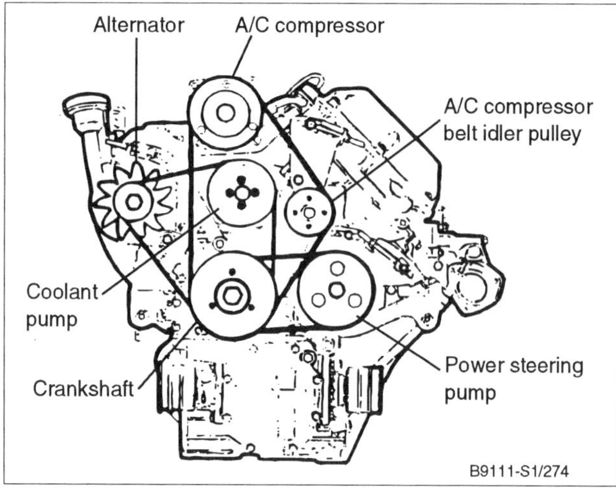

Fig. 6. Drive belt configuration.

Incorrect drive belt tension can decrease the life of the belt and the component it drives. Inspect belts with the engine off. Twist the belt to inspect its sidewalls and bottom. Belt structural damage, glazed or shiny sidewalls caused by a loose belt, or separation caused by oil contamination are all reasons to replace a belt. Some of these faults are illustrated in Fig. 7.

NOTE

Always replace both alternator belts as a matched set.

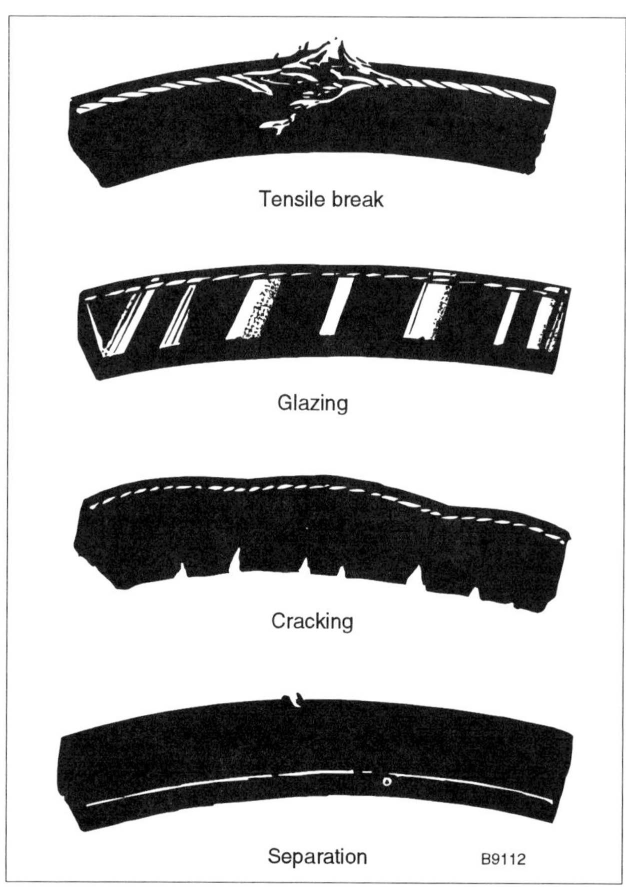

Fig. 7. Examples of belt failure. Courtesy of Gates Rubber Inc.

Drive belt squealing is normally caused by incorrect belt tension (too loose) or by a worn belt. Extremely loud squealing may only be corrected by replacing the belt. To accurately tension the drive belts, a special drive belt tensioning tool should be used. Correct belt tensions are listed in **Table c.**

Table c. Drive Belt Tensions (measure using special belt tensioning gauge)

Drive belt	Tension N (lb)
Alternator	
checking (minimum)	
one belt	200 (45)
two belts	420 (95)
adjusting, used belts	
one belt	310±20 (70±5)
two belts	645±20 (145±5)
adjusting, new belts	
one belt	535±45 (120±10)
A/C compressor	
checking (minimum)	245 (55)
adjusting, used belt	355±20 (80±5)
adjusting, new belt	535±45 (120±10)
Power steering	
checking (minimum)	220 (50)
adjusting, used belt	310±20 (70±5)
adjusting, new belt	445±45 (100±10)

Adjust the alternator belt by first disconnecting the negative (–) battery cable. Loosen the lower (pivot) mounting bolt and then adjust the belt tension through the adjusting nut. See Fig. 8. When the belt is correctly tensioned, there should be approximately 0.2 in (5 mm) of deflection in either direction at the midpoint of the belt. For the most accurate check, use a belt tensioning gauge.

Fig. 8. Alternator drive belt tension being adjusted.

The A/C compressor drive belt is adjusted through the belt's idler pulley. See Fig. 7 above. To adjust the A/C compressor belt, simply loosen the idler pulley mounting bolts, adjust the position of the pulley until the belt tension is correct, and tighten the mounting bolts. Check the belt tension using a drive belt tensioning gauge.

To adjust the power steering drive belt, first loosen the pump's mounting bolts. Then adjust the belt tension by turning the adjusting nut. See Fig. 9. Check the belt tension using a drive belt tensioning gauge.

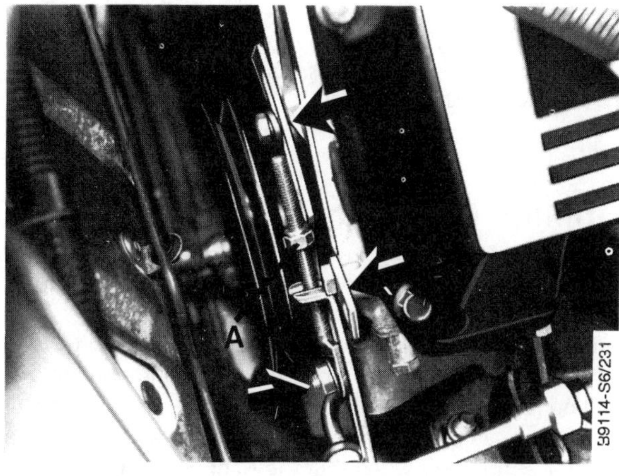

Fig. 9. To adjust power steering drive belt, loosen pump mounting bolts (arrows), and then turn adjusting nut (**A**).

To reduce the chance of drive belt failure while driving, replacement of the belts every four years is recommended. Loosen the mounting and belt adjusting bolts and adjust until the belt tension is as loose as possible, then remove the belt by slipping it over the pulleys. In some cases it may be necessary to remove one drive belt to get to another. Cross section and length determine belt size. Use the old belt for comparison, or make sure that the new belt fits into the pulley groove as shown in Fig. 10.

NOTE

When belts are replaced with new ones, keep the old set in the luggage compartment by the spare tire for emergency use.

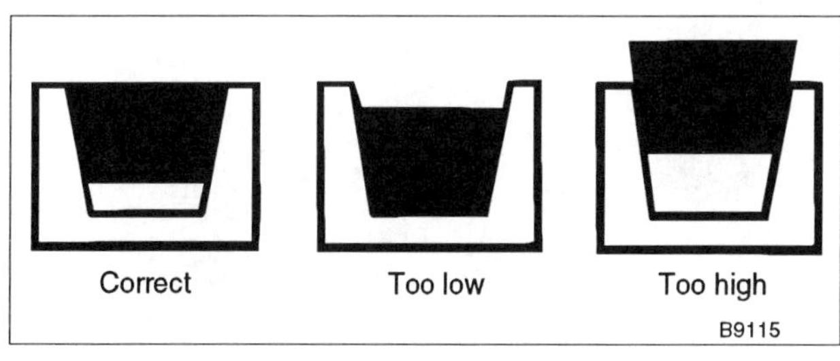

Fig. 10. Cross-section of correct drive belt position in pulley. Courtesy of Gates Rubber Inc.

With the belt off, clean the pulleys using a suitable solvent. Inspect the pulleys for wear or damage that may cause early failure of the new belt. This is also a good opportunity to inspect the belt-driven accessory, checking for bearing wear and excess play, for example. When installing the new belt, gently pry it over the pulleys. Too much force may damage the belt or the accessory. Tension the belt(s), run the engine for a few minutes (at least 1500 rpm), then recheck the belt tension.

CAUTION

Do not overtighten the drive belts. Overtightening will cause the bearings to fail prematurely.

Distributor Cap, Rotor, and Spark Plugs

The distributor cap, the rotor, and the spark plug wires deliver a high-voltage spark to the spark plugs. See Fig. 11. They are subject to insulation breakdown, corrosion fouling, and electrode wear and damage. The cap, rotor and spark plugs should be replaced at the specified intervals to ensure maximum ignition system efficiency. There is no replacement intervals for spark plug wires, but they should be periodically tested and inspected. Guidelines for visual inspection and testing, and instructions for distributor cap and rotor replacement are found in **340 Ignition System**.

WARNING

Lethal voltages are present at the distributor, ignition coil, spark plug wires, and spark plugs when the key is turned on or the engine is running.

NOTE

When removing the spark plug wires, label their positions so that they can be reinstalled in the proper places. If the wires get mixed up, see **340 Ignition System** for more information on the firing order.

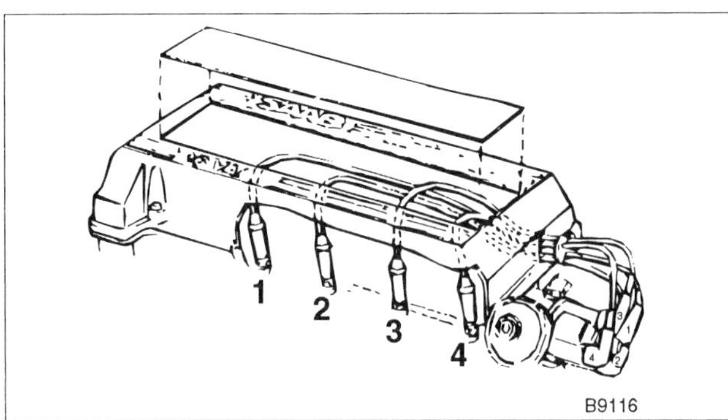

Fig. 11. Ignition system.

To replace the spark plugs, first remove the center cover above the plugs. Gently remove the spark plug wire by pulling on the protective boot, and blow or brush away any dirt from around the base of the plug to prevent it from entering the engine when the plug is removed.

Use a 5/8 in. spark plug socket to remove spark plugs. See Fig. 12. The correct spark plugs for the different engines covered by this manual are listed in **Table d.** Use a spark plug gap gauge to check the gap. If necessary, bend the outer electrode slightly to adjust the gap to meet the specification. Do not bend or file the center electrode. See Fig. 13.

Fig. 12. Spark plug being removed.

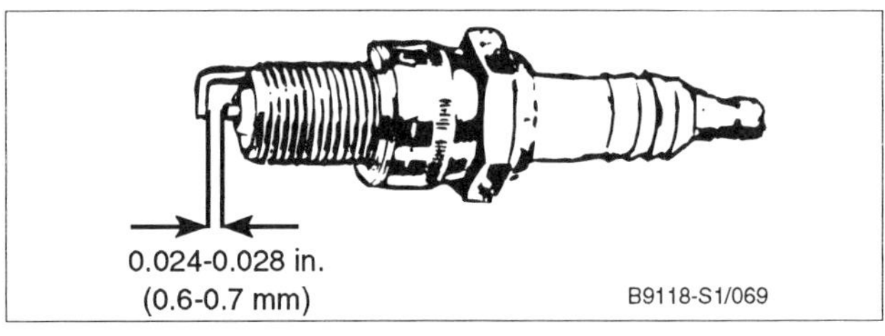

Fig. 13. Spark plug electrode gap.

Spark Plug Electrode Gap

• All . . . . 0.024-0.028 in. (0.6-0.7 mm)

Table d. Spark Plug Applications

Model	Spark Plug
1986 and later, Non-turbo	NGK BCP 6ES
alternate	NGK BCP 6EV
1989 and later, Non-turbo	NGK BCP 5ES
1985 and later, Turbo	
normal driving	NGK BCP 7EV
alternate	NGK BCP 7ES
city driving*	NGK BCP 6EV
alternate	NGK BCP 6ES

* On 1985 through 1987 turbo models, the Saab recommended spark plug replacement interval for city driving is 15,000 miles. On 1988 and later turbo, this interval is 30,000 miles.

Lightly lubricate the new spark plug threads with a little oil. Thread the plugs into the cylinder head by hand to prevent cross-threading. Torque the spark plugs.

Tightening torque

- sparkplugs . . . . .25 to 29 Nm (18 to 22 ft-lb)

Ignition Timing, Idle Speed, Deceleration System

Ignition timing should be checked every 60,000 miles on all cars with distributor-mounted Hall sensors. See **340 Ignition System** for Hall sensor applications and procedures for checking and adjusting ignition timing. It is not necessary to check/adjust ignition timing on cars with a crankshaft-mounted Hall sensor.

Ignition Timing (distributor vacuum hose disconnected and plug, where applicable)

- Turbo models. . . . . 16°BTDC @ 850 rpm
- Normally aspirated models . . . 14°BTDC @ 850 rpm

On all cars covered by this manual, the idle speed is electronically controlled by the Automatic Idle Control (AIC) System. On cars with LH 2.2 Fuel Injection, the idle speed should be checked and adjusted through the AIC system at the specified mileage interval as described in **240 Fuel Injection.**

NOTE

It is not necessary to check the idle speed on cars with LH 2.4 or LH 2.4.2 Fuel Injection, as the idle speed is fully adaptive (self-correcting) through the LH control unit.

On cars with LH 2.2 Fuel injection and automatic transmission, a mechanical deceleration dashpot is mounted to the throttle housing to hold the throttle open for a short period when the throttle is quickly closed. The dashpot plunger should be adjusted to touch the throttle lever at a specified engine speed. See **240 Fuel Injection** for dashpot adjustment procedures and specifications.

Turbo Overpressure Safety Switch (1985-1998 Turbo models)

The turbo overpressure safety switch turns the fuel pump off when the manifold pressure reaches a higher than normal level. This is a safety feature in the event the turbocharger wastegate malfunctions. Checking the switch requires a hand-held pressure/vacuum pump and an accurate pressure gauge. This procedure is described in detail in **234 Fuel Pump and Fuel Tank.**

Oxygen Sensor

The oxygen sensor monitors engine combustion efficiency by measuring the oxygen content of the exhaust gasses. That information in turn is used to control the fuel injection system and reduce exhaust emissions. Any problems with the oxygen sensor will directly affect exhaust emissions and the way the engine runs.

Replacement of the oxygen sensor at the specified interval ensures that the engine and emission control system will continue to operate as designed. The sensor is mounted in the front exhaust pipe, ahead of the catalytic convertor.

NOTE

On 1991 and later models, there is no recommended replacement interval for the oxygen sensor. When the sensor is no longer operating correctly the Check Engine light will come on signaling the need for the sensor's replacement.

The sensor is threaded into place and has wires extending from the tip. Trace the sensor wiring back from the sensor and disconnect the electrical connector. When installing a new sensor, apply a light coat of anti-seize compound to the sensor threads. Torque the sensor and reconnect the wiring.

Tightening torque

- oxygen sensor to exhaust pipe . . . . 40 Nm (30 ft-lb)

CAUTION

Do not get any anti-seize compound on the sensor tip or in the sensor slits. The anti-seize compound will quickly foul the sensor element and render the sensor inoperative.

NOTE

Special sockets for replacing the oxygen sensor are available from most automotive parts stores to allow the sensor to be installed without damaging the wiring.

Crankcase Ventilation and Vacuum Hoses

The rubber vacuum hoses for the crankcase ventilation system should be carefully inspected for cracks or deterioration. Gently bend the hoses at all connecting points to check for cracks. Fig. 14 shows a typical hose routing diagram.

Evaporative Loss Control Device (ELCD)

The ELCD system collect fuel vapors from the fuel tank. Check all of the rubber vapor hoses for cracks or deteriora-

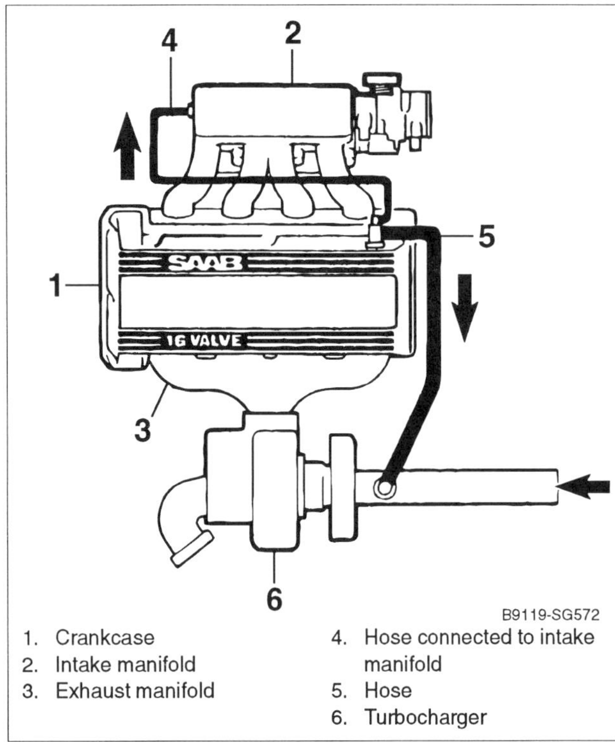

1. Crankcase
2. Intake manifold
3. Exhaust manifold
4. Hose connected to intake manifold
5. Hose
6. Turbocharger

Fig. 14. Hose routing for typical crankcase ventilation system.

tion. On all models up to 1990, the charcoal canister should be replaced at 60,000 mile intervals. The canister is mounted in the left-front corner of the engine compartment and is easily removed. Fig. 15 shows the canister. For more information on the ELCD system, see **254 Exhaust Emission Control.**

> **NOTE**
> On 1991 and later models, there is no recommended replacement interval for the charcoal canister.

Fuel System

A fuel system safety inspection should be made at the specified mileage intervals listed in the maintenance program tables given earlier. Inspect the fuel tank, fuel lines and hoses, and fuel system for damage or leaks. If fuel odors are detected in the passenger compartment, the fuel pump seal (beneath the luggage compartment) may be faulty. Also check the ELCD vapor hoses that run overhead through the headliner. See **234 Fuel Tank and Fuel Pump** for replacement of the fuel pump seal. Inspect all electrical connections for corrosion or damage or loose connections.

Air Filter Element

The specified replacement interval (30,000 miles) for the air filter element is based on normal use. If the car is operated primarily in dusty conditions, the air filter should be serviced more frequently. A dirty air filter starves the engine for air, reducing power output and increasing fuel consumption. Fig. 16 shows the typical air filter housing for the engines covered by this manual.

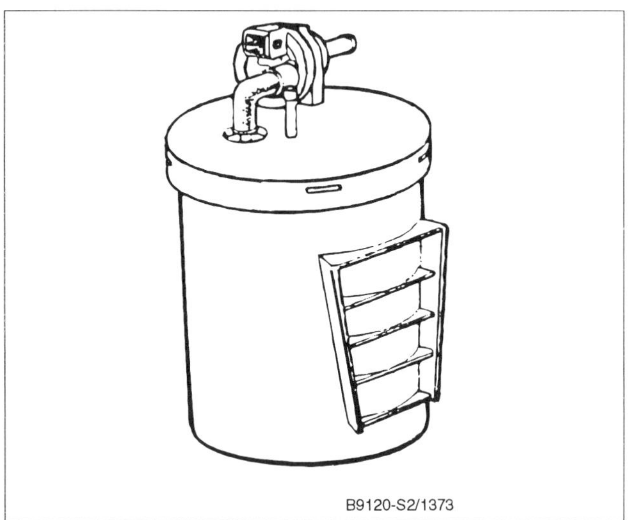

Fig. 15. Charcoal canister for ELCD system.

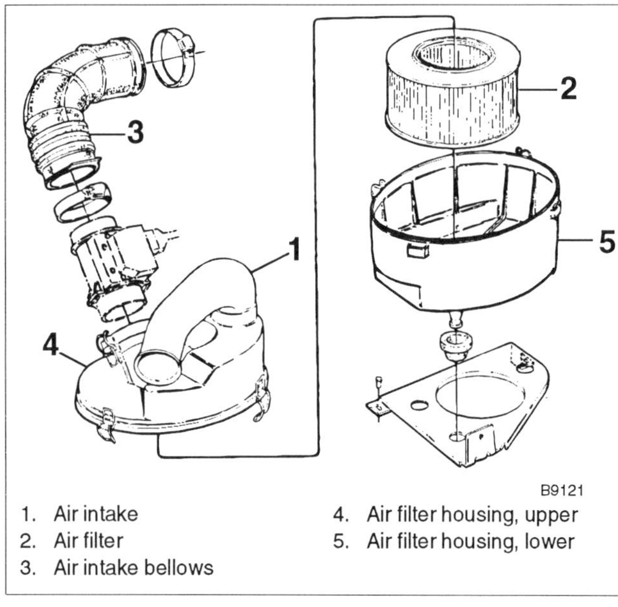

1. Air intake
2. Air filter
3. Air intake bellows
4. Air filter housing, upper
5. Air filter housing, lower

Fig. 16. Typical air filter housing in front left corner of engine compartment.

The upper and lower parts of the air filter housing are fastened together with spring clips around the outside edge. To replace the air filter element, unfasten the clips and separate the upper air filter housing from the lower housing just enough to remove the filter element. Take note of the filter's installed position. Wipe the inside of the air filter housing using a lint-free cloth and install the new filter and housing.

Fuel Filter

Because of varying quality of gasoline, the fuel filter may become contaminated or clogged enough to restrict fuel flow. To prevent any such problems, and to guarantee continued good performance, the filter should be replaced every 30,000 miles. The fuel filter is located beneath the right rear of the car, just in front of the gas tank.

When replacing the fuel filter, disconnect the battery negative (–) cable and clamp the filter inlet and outlet hoses to lessen fuel spillage. Loosen the center mounting bracket and the two banjo fittings on either end of the filter. See Fig. 17. Note the arrow or markings indicating direction of flow on the new filter. Install the filter and using new sealing washers at the banjo fitting.

WARNING
Fuel will be expelled when the filter is removed. Do not smoke or work near heaters or other fire hazards. Keep a fire extinguisher handy.

CAUTION
Clean thoroughly around the filter connections before removing them, and make sure that no dirt gets into the fuel lines.

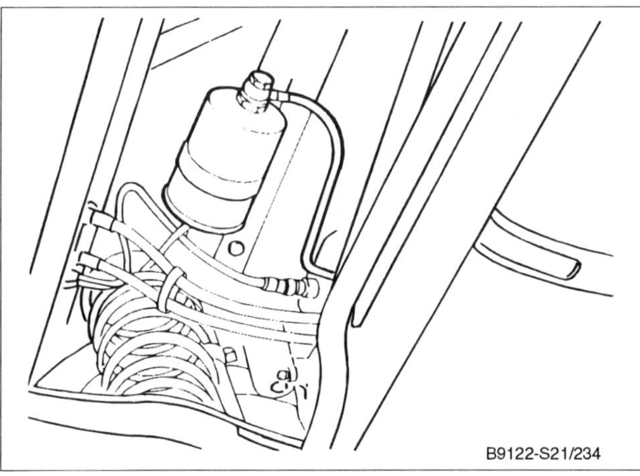

Fig. 17. Fuel filter beneath car near right rear wheel. Direction of flow is indicated by arrow or markings on filter housing.

Accelerator and Throttle Linkage

The accelerator and throttle linkage should be lubricated at the intervals specified in the tables given earlier. Use a general purpose oil on the joints and bearings of the linkage. Use a multipurpose grease on the bearing points of the throttle plate.

Exhaust System

Scheduled maintenance of the exhaust system is limited to inspection. Check for restrictions due to dents or kinks. Check for weakness or perforation due to rust. Check to see that all the hangers are in place and properly supporting the system and that the system does not strike the body. Alignment of the system and the location of the hangers are described in **252 Exhaust System**.

Exhaust system life varies widely according to driving habits and environmental conditions. If short-distance driving predominates, the moisture and condensation in the system will not fully dry out. This will lead to early corrosion damage and more frequent replacement.

ELECTRICAL SYSTEM AND BATTERY SERVICE

Electrical System Functional Check

Electrical system service includes checking that all electrical components, including interior and exterior lighting, are working correctly. Replace any faulty bulbs found. If more involved electrical work is required, refer to **3 ELECTRICAL SYSTEM** for system troubleshooting and wiring diagrams.

Battery Service

Battery maintenance includes keeping the battery and terminals clean and keeping the connections tight. See Fig. 18. Even a thin layer of dust containing conductive acid salts can cause the battery to slowly discharge. Inspect the battery cables for chafing and deterioration of the insulation caused by high heat. For a more detailed discussion of the battery, including testing and charging, see **311 Battery**.

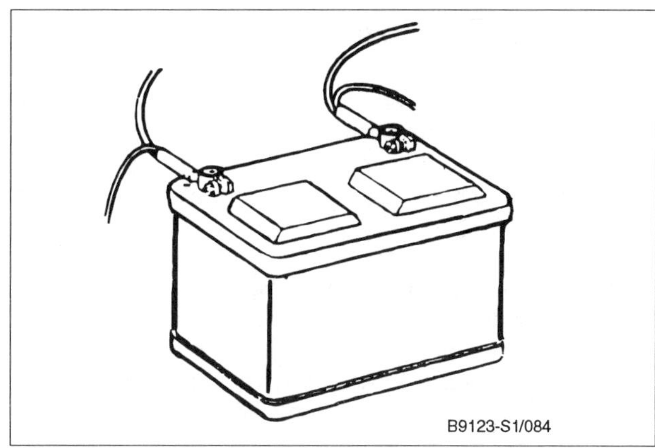

Fig. 18. Battery.

To remove battery corrosion, begin by disconnecting the cables. Disconnect the negative (–) cable first. Clean the terminal posts and the cable clamps with a wire brush. Clean the main chassis ground terminal on the opposite end of the negative (–) cable.

Corrosion can be washed away with a baking soda and water solution that will neutralize the acid. Apply the solution carefully, though, since it will also neutralize the acid inside the battery. Avoid getting the solution into the battery cells through vent holes. Reconnect the cable clamps, positive (+) cable first. Lightly coat the outsides of the terminals, hold down screw, and clamps with petroleum jelly, grease, or a commercial battery terminal corrosion inhibitor.

WARNING
Battery acid is extremely dangerous. Take care to keep it from contacting eyes, skin, or clothing. Wear eye protection. Extinguish all smoking materials and do not work near any open flames.

CAUTION
Disconnecting the battery cables with the engine running, or reconnecting the cables to the incorrect posts will damage the electrical system.

Battery electrolyte should be maintained at the correct level just above the battery plates and their separators. The correct level is approximately 5 mm (1/4 in.) above the top of battery plates or to the top of the indicator marks (if applicable). The battery plates and the indicator marks can be seen once the filler caps are removed. If the electrolyte level is low, replenish it by adding distilled water only.

TRANSMISSION SERVICE

Automatic Transmission

Many automatic transmission problems can be traced to an incorrect fluid level, incorrect type of fluid, a clogged ATF filter, or contaminated fluid. With regular preventative maintenance, expensive and unnecessary automatic transmission repair may be avoided.

Before checking the ATF level, inspect for leaks. ATF leaks are most likely to be seen around the ATF oil pan gaskets. Leaks should be promptly corrected to avoid costly repairs. If necessary, replace a leaky ATF oil pan gasket as described in **472 Automatic Transmission Seals and Gaskets.**

CAUTION
Extreme cleanliness is important when working on the automatic transmission. Use lint-free rags to check the level, and use a clean funnel when adding fluid.

The location of the dipstick for checking the ATF is shown in Fig. 19. The area between the **MIN** mark and the **MAX** mark on the dipstick represents approximately 1 pint (1/2 liter) of ATF.

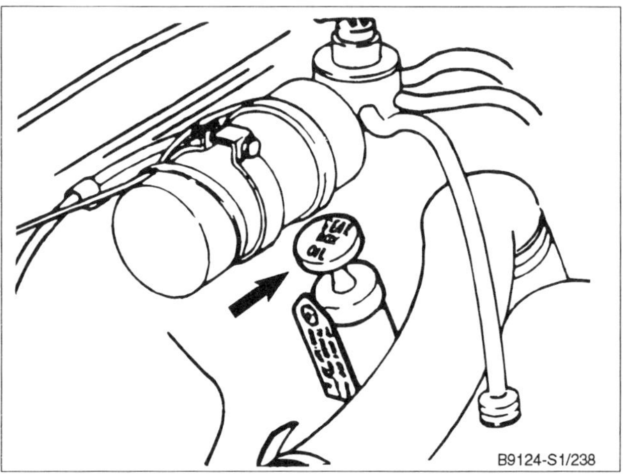

Fig. 19. ATF dipstick location (arrow).

The ATF level should be checked with the car on a level surface with the engine idling and the transmission fully warmed. Firmly set the parking brake and place the transmission selector lever in park or neutral and remove the ATF dipstick. The ATF level is correct if it is between the **MIN** and **MAX** marks. See Fig. 20.

NOTE
Driving the car for five to ten minutes around town, or approximately 12 miles (20 km) on the highway will ensure a fully warmed transmission.

If the level is too low, use a clean funnel to add ATF through the dipstick/filler tube until the fluid level is correct.

Automatic Transmission Fluid (ATF)

- Ford Specification M2C-33F (alternate: Ford Specification G)

Check the condition of the ATF by rubbing some between your fingers and sniffing it. The ATF should not be foamy, gritty, or have a burnt odor. Contaminated ATF should be drained

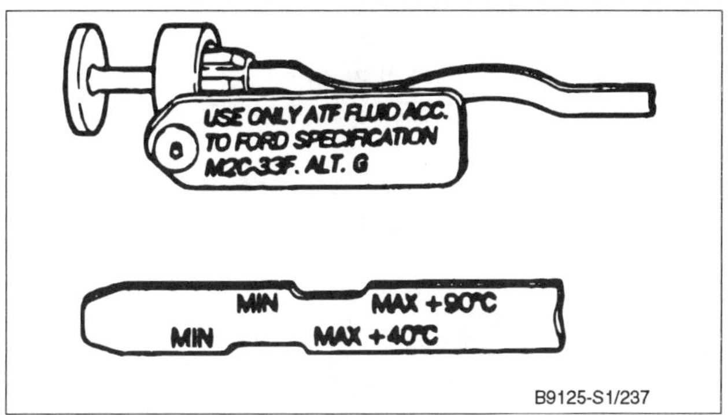

Fig. 20. ATF dipstick and fluid level marks.

Fig. 21. Automatic transmission fluid drain plug (**1**). Final drive drain plug is shown at **2**.

and replaced to prevent further damage, but doing so will not repair any internal transmission damage that has already occurred.

NOTE

Because ATF is a red/brown color that discolors to black/-brown during normal use, ATF color may not be a good indicator of its condition.

To replace ATF and clean ATF filter

The ATF should be changed and the filter cleaned every 30,000 miles under normal conditions. If the car is operated under severe service conditions of trailer towing, extensive city driving or driving in hot climates Saab recommends that the fluid be changed every 15,000 miles.

CAUTION

Towing the car or running the engine without ATF in the transmission will severely damage the transmission. See **100 Fundamentals for the Do-it-yourself Owner** for towing instructions.

---

1. Raise the car and support it on jackstands.

2. Remove the support member or protective plate from beneath the transmission.

3. Place a drain pan of at least 10 quarts (10 liters) capacity under the transmission and remove the transmission drain plug. See Fig. 21.

4. Clean the front transmission pan (sump) and surrounding areas. Remove the front pan mounting bolts and remove the pan from the transmission.

5. Remove the filter mounting bolts and remove the filter. See Fig. 22. Clean the filter using a suitable solvent or fresh ATF.

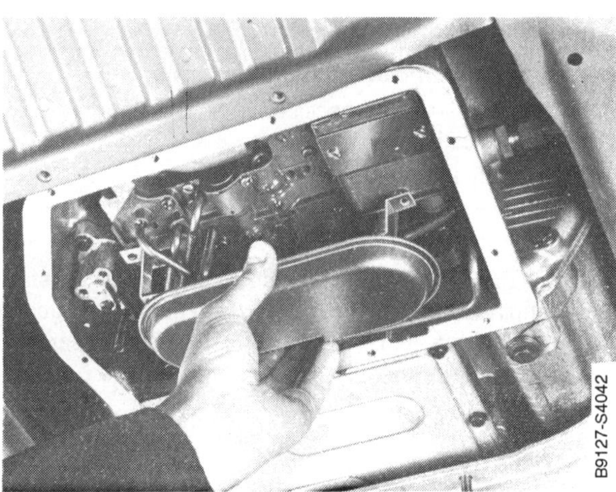

Fig. 22. ATF filter being removed.

6. Remove and clean the magnet in the oil pan. Note the position of the magnet.

7. Clean the oil pan and install the pan magnet. See Fig. 23. Make sure the pan is completely dry. Remount the filter using a new O-ring and tighten the mounting bolts.

8. Using a new pan gasket without any sealer, install the front pan. Install the ATF drain plug. Tighten the bolts and the plug to the torque listed below.

Tightening torques

- ATF pan mounting bolts. . . . . 8-12 Nm (71-106 in-lb)
- ATF drain plug . . . . 5-8 Nm (44-71 in-lb)

---

9. Install the support member or protective plate.

10. Refill the transmission with fluid according to the type and amount specified below.

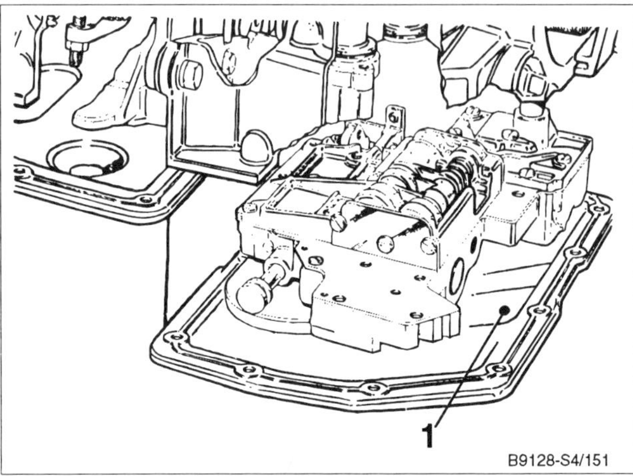

Fig. 23. Correct location of pan magnet (**1**) in front pan.

Automatic Transmissions Specifications
- Grade of ATF — Ford Specification M2C-33F (alternate: Ford Specification G)
- ATF capacity 8.5 quarts (8.0 liters)

11. Lower the car. Firmly apply the handbrake, then start the engine and shift the transmission through all gears to circulate the fluid. Check the fluid level as described earlier. Check for leaks.

Automatic Transmission Final Drive

The final drive on cars with automatic transmission is lubricated with a separate gear oil. Final drive service consists of checking the gear oil level and inspecting for leaks.

The final drive gear oil level should be checked regularly, although there is no specified replacement interval specified by Saab. The final drive oil drain plug is shown earlier in Fig. 20.

Check the lubricant level with the car level. Remove the oil filler plug, shown in Fig. 24. The level is correct when the fluid just reaches the edge of the filler hole. If the oil level is low, Add oil through the filler plug until it begins to run out of the filler hole. Install and torque the filler plug.

Tightening torque
- final drive drain or filler plug. . 39-59 Nm (29-44 ft-lb)

Final Drive Specifications (automatic transmission only)
- Grade of oil — SAE EP 80 or 75 API-GL-4 or API-GL-5
- alternate grade of oil — 10W-30 engine oil
- Fluid capacity — 1.3 quarts (1.25 liters)

Fig. 24. Final drive fill plug (arrow).

Manual Transmission

Manual transmission service consists of checking the gear oil level and inspecting for leaks. The gear oil level should be checked regularly, although there is no specified replacement interval specified by Saab. In addition, 1990 and later models do not have a drain plug. Two types of manual transmission oil dipsticks are used on the cars covered by this manual.

On 1985 through 1990 models, the dipstick is similar to the engine oil dipstick. See Fig. 25. On 1991 and later cars, the manual transmission oil dipstick is shown in Fig. 26.

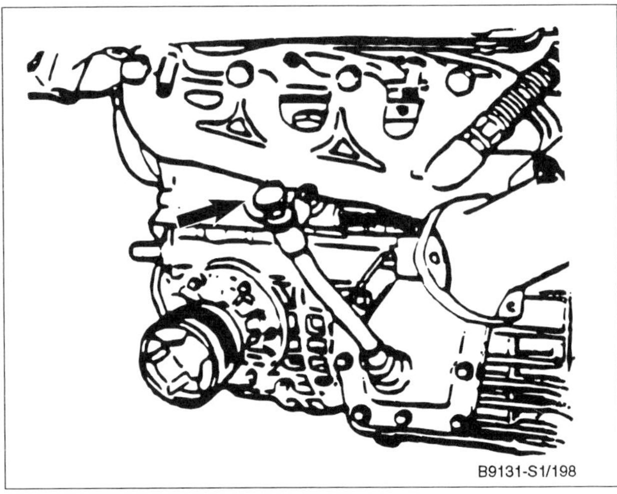

Fig. 25. Manual transmission oil dipstick (arrow) used on 1985-1990 models.

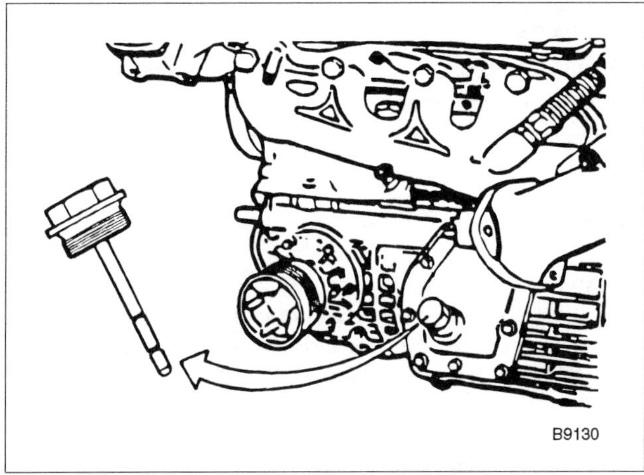

Fig. 26. Manual transmission oil dipstick (arrow) used on 1991 and later cars.

Check and fill the transmission with the car on a level surface. Remove the dipstick from the side of the transmission wipe the stick clean. Then reinsert it fully and remove it. On 1985 through 1990 models, the oil level should be between the MAX and MIN marks. On 1991 and later models, the oil level should be between the two grooves cut on the dipstick. Add oil as necessary.

Manual Transmission Oil Specifications

- Grade of oil — SAE 10W-30 SF/CC, SF/CD, SG
- alternate grade of oil — SAE EP 75 API-GL-4 or API-GL-5
- Oil capacity — 3.1 quarts (3.0 liters)

Drive Axle Joint Boots

The inner and outer boots on the front drive axles should be closely inspected for cracks and any other damage that will allow contaminants to get into the joint. See Fig. 27. If the rubber boots fail, water and dirt can enter the joint and quickly damage it. Replacement of the drive axle joint boots and inspection of the joints are described in **774 Wheel Bearings and Drive Axles.**

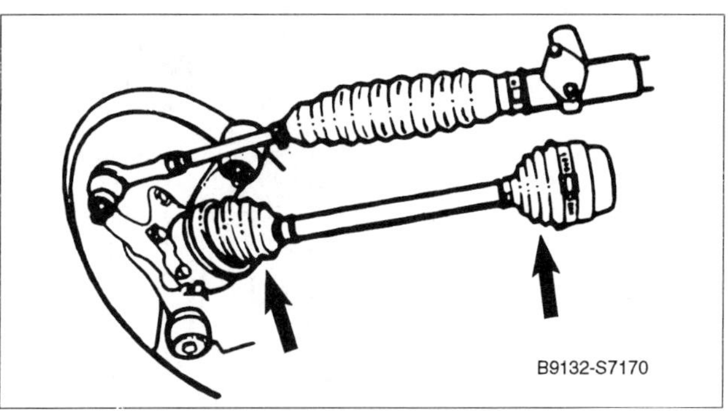

Fig. 27. Drive axle joint boots (inner and outer) should be inspected for tears and cracks. Also check that the boot clamps are tight and in good condition.

CHASSIS SERVICE

Brakes

Routine maintenance of the brake system includes maintaining an adequate level of brake fluid in the reservoir, checking brake pads for wear, checking hand brake function, and inspecting the system for fluid leaks or other damage.

WARNING

- Friction materials such as brake linings may contain asbestos fibers. Do not create dust by grinding, sanding, or cleaning the pads with compressed air. Avoid breathing asbestos fibers and asbestos dust, as it may result in serious diseases such as asbestosis and cancer, or in death.

- Brake fluid is poisonous. Do not siphon brake fluid by mouth. Wear gloves when working with brake fluid or brake pads to prevent contamination of cuts.

The level of the brake fluid will drop slightly as the brakes wear. Check the fluid level at the brake fluid reservoir, located on the driver's side, near the firewall. See Fig. 28. When filling the reservoir, use only new brake fluid from previously unopened containers.

Brake Fluid Grade

- SAE DOT 4

WARNING

Do not use SAE DOT 5 brake fluid. Brake system failure may result.

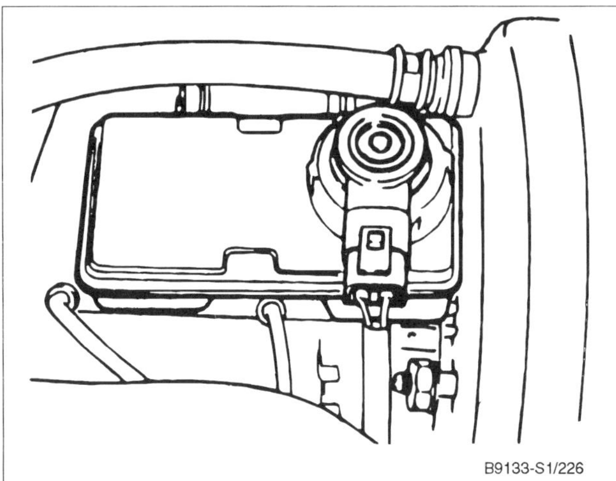

Fig. 28. Brake fluid reservoir on driver's side of engine compartment, at the firewall. Reservoir has MAX and MIN marks molded into its side.

To inspect brake hoses, gently bend them to check for cracks. Check that all hoses are correctly routed to avoid chafing or kinking. Inspect the unions and the brake calipers for signs of fluid leaks. Inspect the lines for corrosion, dents, or other damage. Replace faulty hoses or lines and bleed the brake system as described in **520 Brake Fluid and Brake Bleeding**.

WARNING

Incorrect installation or overtightening hoses, lines, and unions may cause chafing or leakage. This can lead to partial or complete brake system failure.

Brake pad thickness should be regularly checked. Brake pad thickness can be inspected by looking through an opening in the caliper after removing the wheel. See Fig. 29. For information on replacing worn pads, see **517 Brake Pads.**

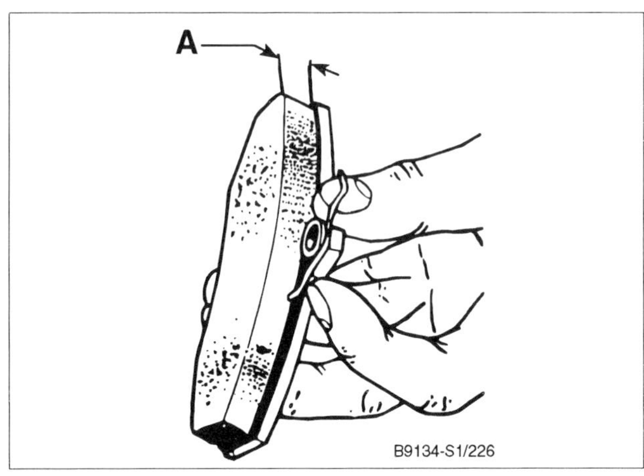

Fig. 29. Brake pad thickness (**A**)

Brake Pad Wear Limit (dimension A)

- 1985-1987 models . . . . 1.0 mm (0.04 in.)
- 1988 and later models . . . . 4.0 mm (0.16 in.)

Brake Fluid

Saab strictly recommends replacing the brake fluid every two years. Doing this will help protect against corrosion and the effects of moisture in the fluid. The procedure is described in detail in **520 Brake Fluid and Brake Bleeding.**

Parking Brake

The parking brake system is independent of the main braking system and does not require any periodic adjustment, although the function of the parking brake should be checked regularly. Check that the cable moves freely in its housing. A complete description of the parking brake is described in **551 Parking Brake.**

Power Steering Fluid

The only maintenance of the power steering system is to check the power steering fluid and add as necessary. The power steering fluid level can be easily checked through the translucent reservoir on the right side wheel housing in the engine compartment. See Fig. 30. When the car is at normal operating temperature, the fluid level should be between the HOT and COLD marks. If the level is checked when the car is cold, it should be between the COLD mark and the ADD mark.

Power Steering Fluid

- GM Power Steering Fluid (GM 9985010), Texaco TL4634 or equivalent

---

Windshield Washer Fluid

Check and add windshield washer fluid as necessary. The fluid reservoir in the front right wheel housing, directly behind the corner parking light assembly.

Ball Joints, Steering Joints (Tie Rod Ends)

The control arm ball joints and steering rack tie rod ends should be carefully checked for play with the front of the car raised. Also inspect the joint's rubber boots for damage. If the boots are torn open, water and dirt can enter the joint and quickly damage it. If the ball joint or tie rod boots are damaged, the complete joint will need to be replaced.

Fig. 30. Power steering fluid reservoir.

Replacement of the control arm ball joints is covered in **631 Ball Joints**. Replacement of the steering rack tie rod ends is covered in **643 Tie Rod Ends.**

Shock Absorbers and Bushings

Inspect the shock absorber bushings carefully, especially checking the lower bushing. See Fig. 31. If the lower bushing is worn, there is usually a constant clunking sound when traveling over rough road surfaces. The shock absorber's function should also be periodically checked. See **731 Front Suspension** for a quick check of the shock absorber condition.

NOTE

Individual shock absorber bushings are available through an authorized Saab dealer.

Tires

For stability and car control, the wheels and tires must be of the correct size and in good condition. Tires must be inflated to the recommended air pressures and the wheels must be in proper alignment. For maximum safety and best all-around handling, always install replacement radial tires having the same specifications. When possible, all four tires should be replaced at once, or at least in pairs on the front or rear. New tires do not provide maximum traction, and should be broken in gently for the first 100 miles (160 kilometers) or so.

NOTE

Be sure to also check the compact spare tire condition and inflation pressure. Keep the spare inflated to 60 psi.

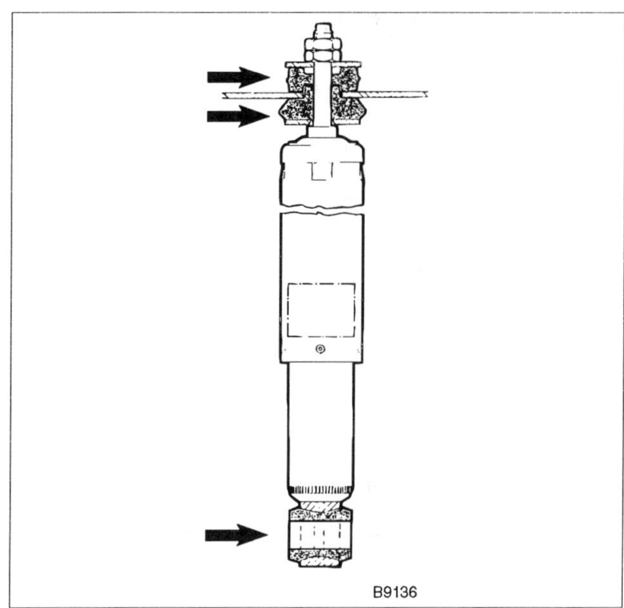

Fig. 31. Shock absorber bushings should be inspected (arrows).

Correct tire inflation pressures are important to handling and stability, fuel economy, and tire wear. Tire pressures change with temperature. Pressures should be checked often during seasonal temperature changes. The correct inflation pressures for cars covered by this manual are listed in the glovebox owner's manual. Tire pressures are also listed on a sticker located on one of the door jambs. Notice that the pressures should be higher when the car is more heavily loaded.

All inflation pressures are for cold inflation. That is, when the car has not been driven for at least three hours, or for more than one mile after sitting for at least three hours.

WARNING

Do not inflate any tire to a higher pressure than the tire's maximum inflation pressure listed on the sidewall. Use care when adding air to warm tires. Warm tire pressures can increase as much as 4 psi (0.3 bar) over their cold pressures.

To promote even wear and maximum tire life, Saab recommends rotating the tires from the front to the rear on the same side at the specified intervals listed earlier. Owing to the car's suspension design, the front tires begin to wear first at the outer shoulder and the rear tires begin to wear first at the middle of the tread or inner shoulder.

Tightening torques

- wheel lug nuts . . . . 90-110 Nm (66-81 ft-lb)
- wheel lug bolts. . . . . 105-125 Nm (77-92 ft-lb)

Front Wheel Alignment

Saab recommends checking the front and rear wheel alignment at the specified interval or whenever new tires are installed. Only the front wheel alignment is adjustable. See **601 Wheel Alignment** for a more detailed discussion of alignment requirements and specifications.

BODY MAINTENANCE

Maintenance of the body includes lubricating various hinges, locks and slides.

Lubricate the seat runners with multipurpose grease. Do not apply any oil to rubber parts. Lubricate the sunroof guide rails with silicone spray. If door weatherstrips are sticking, lubricate them with silicone spray or talcum powder. The hood release cable should be lubricated as well. The radio antenna mast should be cleaned and lubricated with a product such as WD-40.

The door locks, hinges and lock cylinders can be lubricated with an oil that contains graphite. The body and door hinges, the hood latch, and the door check rods should be lubricated with SAE 30 or SAE 40 engine oil. See Fig. 32.

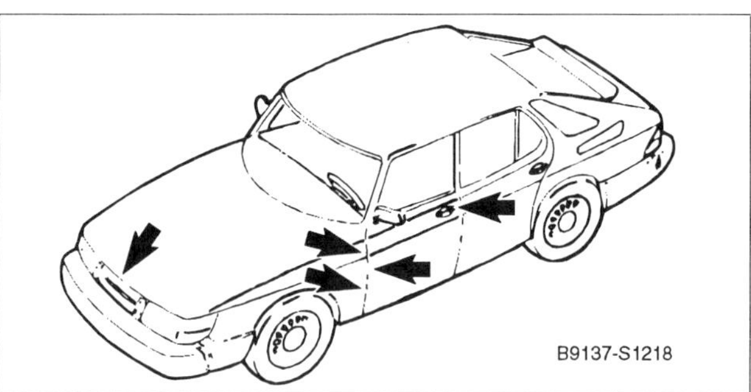

Fig. 32. Exterior body lubrication points.

Air Bag System

The air bag should be replaced every 10 years. See an authorized Saab dealer for all service relating to the SRS air bag system.

WARNING

On cars equipped with an SRS airbag system, do not attempt to service the air bag, the wiring in the steering wheel, the steering column assembly, or the airbag control unit. The airbag may ignite causing injury. See an authorized Saab dealer for all service and repairs to the SRS airbag system.

ROAD TEST

As a final check, the car should be taken for a test drive. Check the overall condition of the various systems, noting especially the function of the brakes, clutch, general engine performance and driving comfort. Check that the cruise control system and the air conditioning system are functioning correctly. See Fig. 33.

Fig. 33. Road test.

200 Engine—General

TABLES

General

Engine Assembly

Two basic engine configurations are used in the 16-valve cars covered by this manual. On all 1985 through 1990 models and on 1991 and later turbo models, a 2.0 liter engine is used. On 1991 and later non–turbo models, a 2.1 liter engine is used. See **Table a** for complete specifications.

Cylinder Head, Camshaft and Valve Train

The twin-overhead-cam cylinder head assembly is a light aluminum alloy casting. Bolts hold the cylinder head to the cylinder block. Replaceable valve guides are press-fit into the cylinder head.

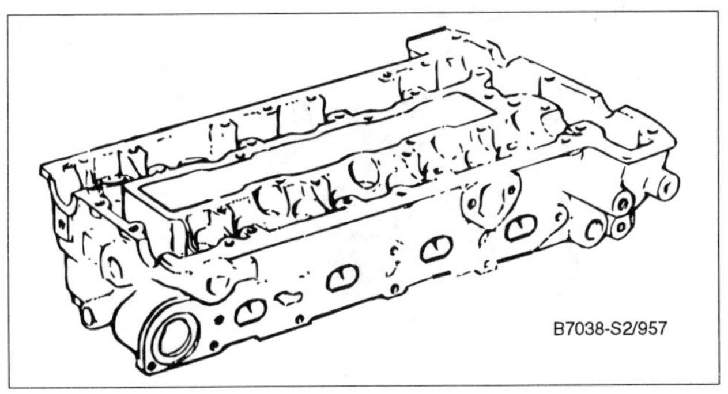

Fig. 1. Cylinder Head.

The camshafts are driven by a single chain and operate directly on the valves via hydraulic cam followers. The valves are made of steel and have chromium plated stems. The intake valve heads are induction-hardened and the exhaust valve heads are coated with stellite.

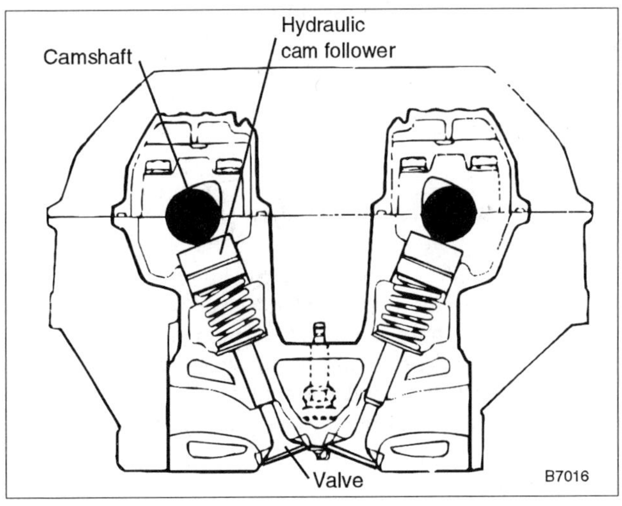

Fig. 2. Valve train.

Table a. Engine Specifications

Model	Year	Displacement cc (cu. in.)	Compression ratio	Horsepower @rpm SAE net	Torque lb-ft @rpm SAE net	Fuel System
900 900S Convertible	1986-1987	1985 (121)	10.1:1	125 @5500	128 @3000	Bosch LH 2.2
	1988	1985 (121)	10.1:1	128 @6000	128 @3000	Bosch LH 2.4
	1989-1990	1985 (121)	10.1:1	128 @6000	128 @3000	Bosch LH 2.4
	1991-on	2118 (129)	10.1:1	140 @6000	140 @2900	Bosch LH 2.4.2
900 Turbo Turbo Convertible	1985-1988	1985 (121)	9.0:1	160 @5500	188 @3000	Bosch LH 2.2
	1989-on	1985 (121)	9.0:1	160 @5500	188 @3000	Bosch LH 2.4
900 Turbo SPG	1985-1986	1985 (121)	9.0:1	160@5500	188@3000	Bosch LH 2.2
	1987-1988	1985 (121)	9.0:1	165 @5500	195 @3000	Bosch LH 2.2
	1989	1985 (121)	9.0:1	165 @5500	195 @3000	Bosch LH 2.4
	1990-1991	1985 (121)	9.0:1	175 @5500	195 @3000	Bosch LH 2.4

Cylinder Block

The cylinder block is made of cast iron. The cylinder bores are drilled straight out of the block and are surrounded by cooling jackets. The block also contains oilways, or channels, for the lubrication system.

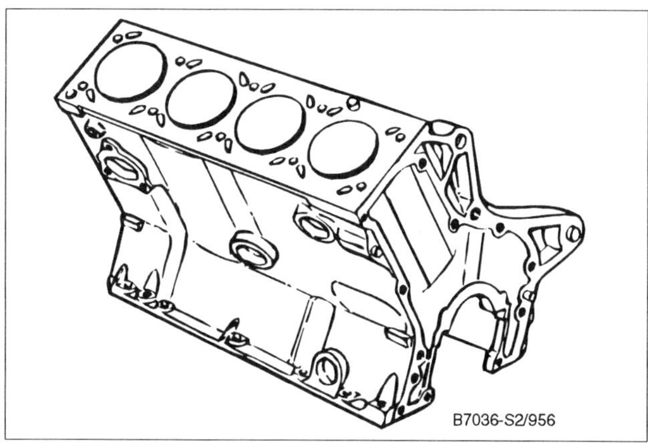

Fig. 3. Cylinder block.

Crankshaft and Bearings

The crankshaft is a steel forging. The crankshaft journals are ground, hardened, and treated with a "Tenifer" treatment. This provides a hard, non-metallic surface to help prevent bearing seizure. The crankshaft is supported by five main bearings. End float, or thrust, is controlled at the center bearing. Oilways are drilled into the shaft for bearing lubrication.

Lubrication System

The lubrication system has forced-flow circulation. The oil pressure is generated by a separate gear-type oil pump driven directly off the crankshaft. The oil is forced through a spin-on replaceable oil filter and into the engine oil passages. All models covered by this manual have a low-oil-pressure warning system. Turbo models use an engine oil cooler to help moderate engine oil temperature.

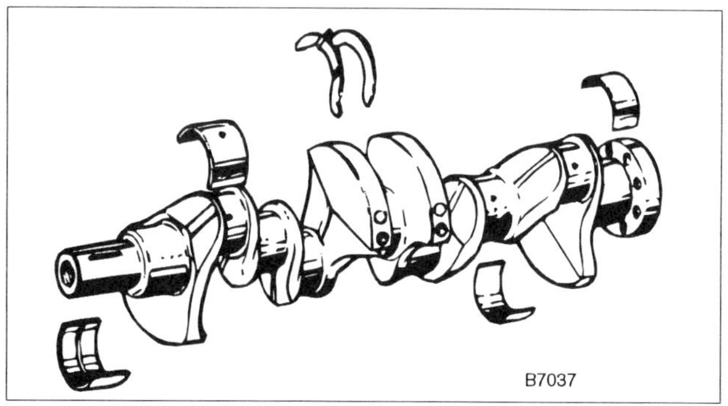

Fig. 4. Crankshaft and bearings.

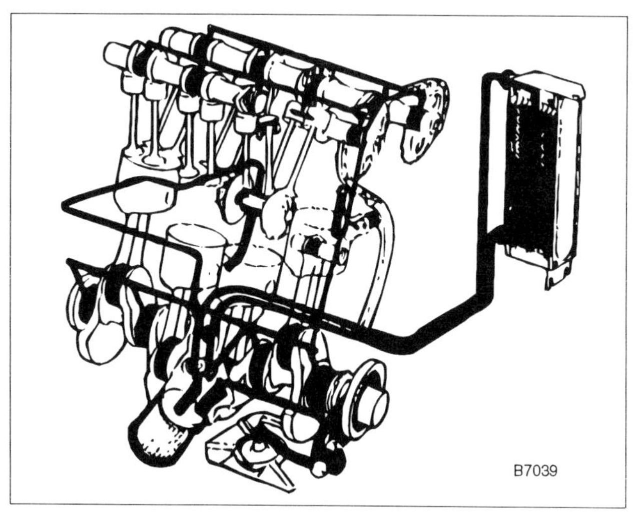

Fig. 5. Lubrication system.

Fuel Supply and Fuel Injection

The fuel supply system stores the fuel and provides the fuel injection system with a constant flow of pressurized, clean fuel. While there is some variation in components, all Saab 900 models have an electric, in-tank fuel pump and an in-line fuel filter. The injection-molded plastic fuel tank is located beneath the car, behind the rear seat. The fuel gauge sending unit and the electric fuel pump are mounted in the top of the tank.

All Saab 900 16-valve models use a Bosch LH fuel injection system. LH fuel injection is completely electronic in operation. Air flow is measured electronically, and a proportional amount of fuel is metered by electrically opening and closing the fuel injectors.

In LH fuel injection, many sensors supply information about engine operating conditions to a central electronic control unit. The control unit then calculates the amount of fuel needed for the correct air-fuel ratio and opens the fuel injectors, once for each engine revolution. The amount of fuel metered to the engine is determined solely by how long the injectors are open.

Cooling System

The engine cooling system relies on a closed system of circulating coolant to maintain an even engine temperature and help transfer heat away. The closed system becomes pressurized at normal engine operating temperature. Under pressure, the boiling point of the coolant is increased, allowing the engine and cooling system to operate at higher temperatures without boiling the coolant.

The coolant pump is driven mechanically by the engine using a V-belt. Coolant circulates through the engine to the radiator and heater core, and from the radiator back to the pump. Before the engine is up to normal operating temperature, the flow of coolant is controlled by a thermostat. When closed, the thermostat forces coolant to bypass the radiator and return directly to the coolant pump. This retains as much heat as possible until the engine is warm.

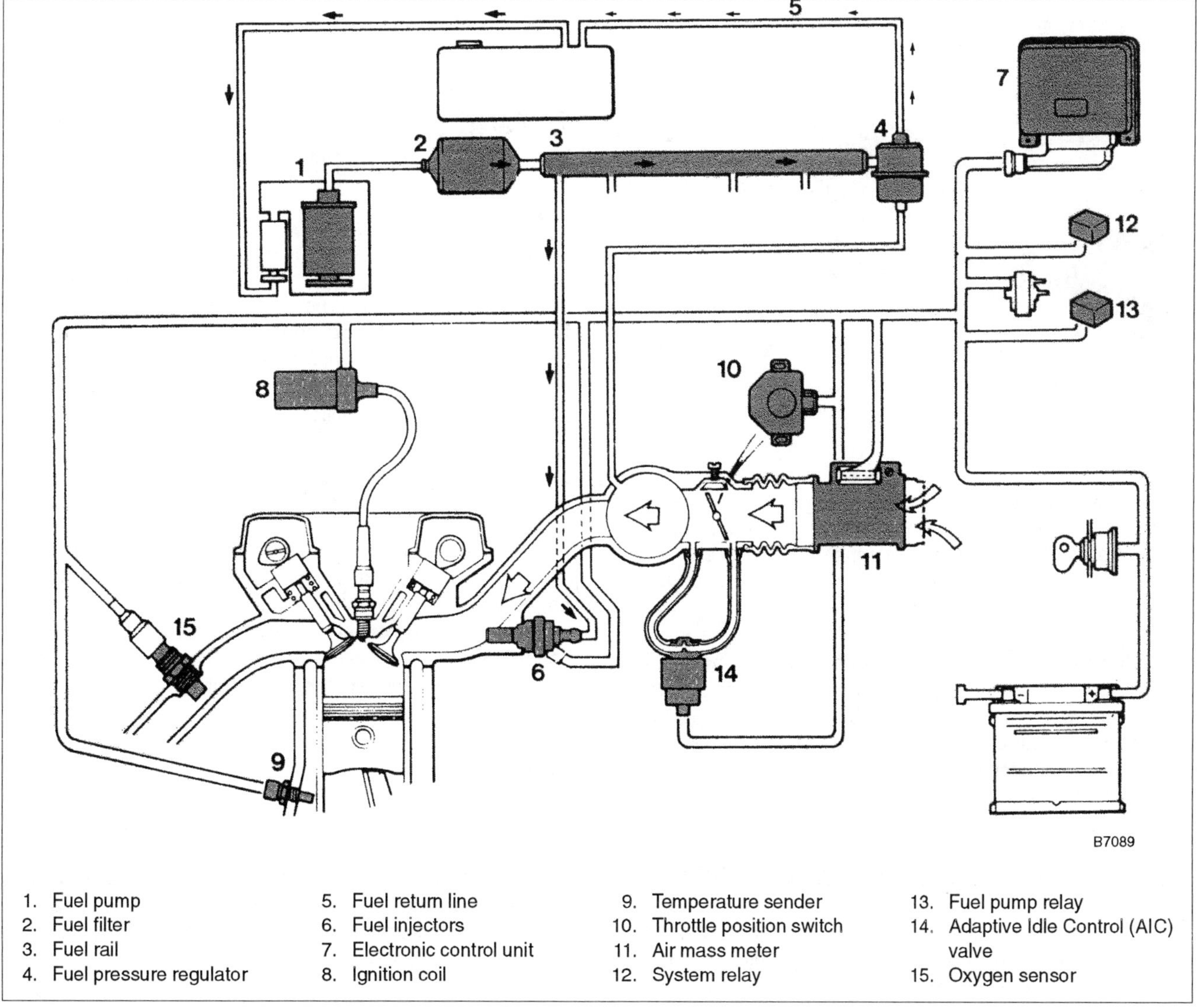

1. Fuel pump
2. Fuel filter
3. Fuel rail
4. Fuel pressure regulator
5. Fuel return line
6. Fuel injectors
7. Electronic control unit
8. Ignition coil
9. Temperature sender
10. Throttle position switch
11. Air mass meter
12. System relay
13. Fuel pump relay
14. Adaptive Idle Control (AIC) valve
15. Oxygen sensor

Fig. 6. LH fuel injection system.

An electric cooling fan, located behind the radiator, is thermostatically controlled so that it runs only when the coolant has reached a certain temperature. An auxiliary electric cooling fan is located next to the main cooling fan and operates in addition to the first fan when necessary or when the air conditioning system is on.

Turbocharger

The turbocharger is an exhaust-driven pump that forces air into the cylinders at higher than atmospheric pressure. This allows the engine to burn more fuel and therefore produce more power.

The turbocharger unit consists of two wheels mounted on a common rotating shaft. One of the wheels, called the turbine, is driven by the exhaust gas. The other wheel, called the compressor, is located in the intake air stream and compresses the intake air.

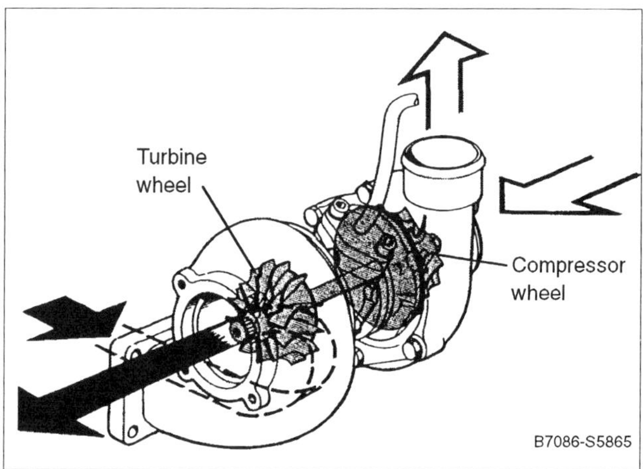

Fig. 7. Turbocharger, showing exhaust gas flow (black arrows) and intake air flow (white arrows).

The turbine is equipped with a waste gate—a pressure controlled valve that automatically bleeds off any excess pressure. If the boost pressure exceeds the predetermined value, in spite of the waste gate, a pressure switch will temporarily interrupt the fuel supply to the engine.

When the intake air is compressed by the turbocharger, its temperature rises and its density decreases. To ensure that the air is as cool and dense as possible to burn the most fuel, the compressed air is routed through an intercooler before it enters the combustion chamber. The intercooler can cool the air by as much as 110°F.

Automatic Performance Control (APC)

The APC system is used on all 16-valve turbo cars. The APC system continually monitors engine detonation or knock and adjusts the turbocharger boost pressure accordingly.

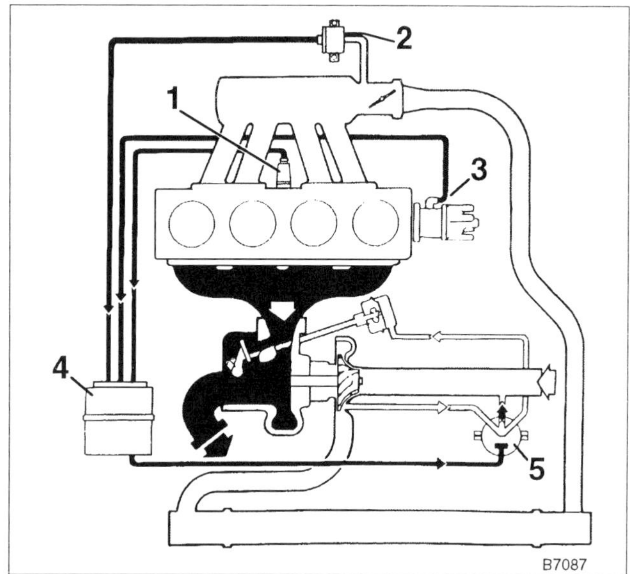

Fig. 8. The APC system control unit (**4**) receives input signals from three components: the ignition distributor (**3**), the knock sensor (**1**), and the pressure sensor (**2**). The control unit controls boost pressure via the solenoid valve (**5**).

Engine Mechanical Troubleshooting

This troubleshooting section applies to problems affecting the basic engine assembly, including the cylinder block, cylinder head, and their internal moving parts. For problems relating to how the engine runs and its overall driveability, see **Driveability Troubleshooting** below. For troubleshooting specific cooling system, ignition system, fuel system, or turbocharger/APC system problems, see the appropriate main repair group under **2 ENGINE**.

Troubleshooting Basics

Only a few basic functions are required of the engine. The block, cylinder head, and their moving parts must fit together properly, operate smoothly, seal well enough to create and maintain compression, and keep pistons, valve train, and ignition properly timed. The problems discussed below are those that affect one or more of these functions.

Noise

In order to run smoothly under harsh conditions, the internal engine parts are made to precise dimensions, assembled with precision clearances, and lubricated by a pressurized oiling system. Most unidentified engine noises result from clearances that have become too large due to worn parts, lack of adequate lubrication, or both.

Rumbling or groaning from the engine compartment may not indicate engine problems at all, but rather a worn bearing or bushing in an engine-driven accessory. They include the coolant pump, the alternator, the power steering pump, and the air conditioning compressor. To check these, run the engine briefly with the drive belt disconnected and see if the noise has stopped. Once the drive belt is removed, turning the pulley and shaft by hand may also reveal a bad bearing or bushing. A properly functioning accessory should turn smoothly.

Fluid Leaks

Fluid leaking from the engine is most likely either oil, coolant, brake fluid, or power steering fluid. Look for wet spots on the engine to help pinpoint the source. It may be helpful to start by cleaning the suspected area.

The most common areas of engine oil leaks are the timing chain cover, the engine end plate (flywheel end), the crankshaft oil seals, the cylinder head cover gasket, the transmission-to-engine mating surface, and the oil filter seal.

A pressure test of the cooling system is the best way to discover and pinpoint coolant leaks. Coolant is a mixture of water and anti-freeze, yellow-green in color or perhaps brown if the coolant is old. See **261 Radiator and Cooling System** for more information.

The brake system and power steering system are other sources of leaks near the engine. Brake fluid is clear, perhaps slightly purple, and a little slippery. Look for wet spots around the master cylinder or brake lines. Especially check the flexible hoses near the wheels. See **5 BRAKES** for repair information.

Smoking

Smoke that is visible at the tailpipe is usually either blue-gray smoke from burning oil, or white steam from the cooling system. The color of the smoke identifies the contaminant.

Blue-gray oil smoke in the exhaust usually indicates general engine wear. If smoking is most obvious under high engine vacuum, such as while coasting at high rpm, valve guide oil seals or worn valve guides are the most likely cause.

NOTE

- See **291 Turbocharger** for additional troubleshooting where applicable.

- Oil smoke or steam appearing suddenly in the exhaust, along with low compression pressure in one or more cylinders, is probably due to a failed cylinder head gasket. Look for bubbles in the coolant or coolant loss, oil in the radiator, or water in the oil (that turns the oil an opaque, creamy brown).

- Black smoke is caused by the engine getting too much fuel. See **240 Fuel Injection** for more troubleshooting information.

Excessive Oil Consumption

Some oil consumption is normal. This is why the oil level must be checked, and occasionally corrected, between oil changes. Aside from leaks, increased oil consumption will usually be accompanied by some smoking, however slight. The causes of excessive oil consumption are the same as those for oil smoke in the exhaust. As with smoking symptoms, gradual increases are caused by worn piston rings, valve guides or a failed turbocharger, where applicable. Sudden high oil consumption suggests broken piston rings.

Poor Fuel Consumption and Low Power

Poor fuel consumption and low power can suggest problems with the fuel, ignition, or turbocharger systems, particularly on a low-mileage engine. On an engine with high mileage, engine wear and low compression may be the cause. Normal wear of the valves, piston rings, and cylinder walls decreases their ability to make a good seal. The engine becomes less efficient and has to work harder, using more fuel to produce the same amount of power.

All 16-valve naturally-aspirated engines are equipped with Bosch EZK ignition. All 16-valve turbo models are equipped with an Automatic Performance Control (APC) system. These systems continuously monitor engine detonation to adjust either ignition timing (EZK) or turbocharger boost pressure (APC) to achieve maximum engine performance.

If either the EZK or APC system detects a fault, a set of predetermined values are used to prevent engine damage caused by detonation. This means the engine is slightly detuned to safely run on all gasoline octane ratings. If low power is experienced, be sure to check the operation of these systems. The EZK system is covered in **340 Ignition System.** The APC system is covered in **291 Turbocharger.**

NOTE

- In order for the EZK and APC system to operate most efficiently, the engine is allowed to knock occasionally. A limited amount of knock is considered normal.

- The EZK control unit has built-in diagnostic capabilities. A fault will show up as a series of pulses on the "**CHECK ENGINE**" light. These pulses will continually repeat themselves with a brief pause between sequences. For more information on EZK on-board diagnostics, see **340 Ignition System.**

Engine Not Running

An engine problem that affects ignition or valve timing may prevent the engine from starting or running. The camshaft timing chain and sprockets are responsible for correctly timing the actions of the valves and the ignition system. A worn timing chain may jump teeth, throwing off all the engine's timing functions, and still appear to be perfectly normal. To accurately check camshaft timing, see **215 Camshaft Timing Chain**.

Table b lists additional symptoms of engine mechanical problems, their probable causes and suggested corrective actions. The boldface numbers in the corrective action column indicate the heading in this section of the manual where the applicable test and repair procedures can be found.

DRIVEABILITY TROUBLESHOOTING

This heading covers general engine management principles and the basic requirements that allow an engine to run smoothly. Therefore, effective troubleshooting of specific running conditions can only take place after all of the common problem areas listed below have been eliminated as a source of trouble.

Most driveability problems are complex in nature. Therefore, a logical method needs to be used to isolate the trouble area. Always begin with the simplest and most fundamental engine management basics. Jumping to conclusions or

Table b. Engine Mechanical Troubleshooting

Symptom	Probable cause and corrective action
1. Pinging or rattling noise under load, uphill or accelerating, especially from low speeds. Indicates detonation or pre-ignition	**a.** Fuel octane level too low, use higher octane fuel **b.** Engine running too hot, overheating. Check for cooling system faults. See **261 Radiator and Cooling System** **c.** Spark plugs damaged or wrong plug type installed. Replace plugs. See **340 Ignition System** **d.** Air-fuel mixture too lean due to air leaks or low fuel pressure. See **240 Fuel Injection**
2. Light metallic tapping noise, varies directly with engine speed. Oil warning light **not** illuminated	**a.** Low oil pressure, defective warning light circuit. See **220 Lubrication System** **b.** Faulty hydraulic cam follower. See **214 Cylinder Head and Valve Mechanism**
3. Light metallic knock, varies directly with engine speed. Oil warning light blinking or fully illuminated (may be most noticeable on hard stops or cornering)	**a.** Low oil level, correct if necessary **b.** Oil flow restricted. Replace oil filter. See **1 LUBRICATION AND MAINTENANCE** **c.** Low oil pressure. Check oil pressure. See **220 Lubrication System**
4. Blue-gray exhaust smoke, oil fouled spark plugs. Indicates oil burning in combustion chamber	**a.** Faulty valve stem oil seals or valve guides. See **211 Cylinder Head Removal and Installation** **b.** Worn, broken, or incorrectly installed pistons or piston rings. See **212 Pistons, Connecting Rods, Cylinder Bores**
5. White steam in exhaust	**a.** Failed cylinder head gasket or warped cylinder head (probably accompanied by low compression). Replace or resurface cylinder head and gasket as necessary. See **211 Cylinder Head Removal and Installation** **b.** Cracked cylinder block. Replace engine or short block. See **212 Pistons, Connecting Rods, Cylinder Bores**
6. Black exhaust smoke	**a.** Air-fuel mixture too rich due to faulty fuel injection component. See **240 Fuel Injection**
7. Screeching or squealing noise under load. Goes away when coasting. Indicates slipping V-belt	**a.** Loose, worn, or damaged V-belt(s). Inspect, replace, or tighten belt(s). See **1 LUBRICATION AND MAINTENANCE**
8. Growling or rumbling, varies with engine rpm. Bad bearing or bushing in an engine-driven accessory	**a.** Remove belt from engine driven accessory and check for play, bearing roughness, or loose mountings
9. Check engine light illuminated or flashing	**a.** EZK ignition system on-board diagnostics fault detected. Check fault codes. See **340 Ignition System** **b.** LH fuel injection control on-board diagnostics fault detected. Check fault codes. See **240 Fuel Injection.**
10. Engine will not start or run. Starter operates, engine turns over at normal speed	**a.** No spark to spark plugs. Check ignition system. See **340 Ignition System** **b.** Incorrect valve timing. Check camshaft timing chain for wear. See **215 Camshaft Timing Chain** **c.** No fuel being delivered to engine. See **240 Fuel Injection**

searching aimlessly for the problem can be time consuming and frustrating.

NOTE

Models with EZK ignition and models with 2.4 LH and 2.4.2 LH fuel injection have built-in diagnostic capabilities which will light the "**CHECK ENGINE**" light. For more information on EZK diagnostics, see **340 Ignition System.** For more information on LH fuel injection diagnostics, see **240 Fuel Injection.**

As with any troubleshooting, careful observation of symptoms is the key to identifying and isolating driveability problems. A test drive can help by demonstrating when the problem is most pronounced, such as a hesitation that occurs only when the engine is cold, or a steady miss at high speed.

How has the symptom developed? A symptom that develops quickly is probably caused by a problem that can be corrected by simple maintenance or repair. A symptom that has developed gradually over time, especially after sixty or seventy thousand miles is more likely an indication of general wear and the need for more comprehensive work.

Warnings and Cautions

For general safety, and to protect the sensitive electronic components, the following warnings and cautions should be adhered to during any troubleshooting, maintenance, or repair work. Always follow the proper repair and working procedures in the sections that are referenced.

WARNING

- The ignition systems used on the cars covered by this manual are high-energy systems operating in a dangerous voltage range. Exposure to terminals or live parts could prove to be fatal. Use extreme caution when working on a car with the ignition on or the engine running.

- Do not touch or disconnect any of the high tension cables from the coil, distributor, or spark plugs while the engine is running or being cranked by the starter.

- Connect and disconnect ignition system wires, multiple connectors, and ignition test equipment leads only while the ignition is switched off.

- Before operating the starter without starting the engine, disable the ignition. See **340 Ignition System.** Do not disconnect terminal 4 (center terminal) from the coil or remove the distributor cap as a means of disabling the ignition.

- During any test where fuel is discharged, do not smoke or work near heaters or other fire hazards. Have a fire extinguisher handy.

CAUTION

- Do not connect test instruments with a 12-volt power supply to terminal 15 (+) of the ignition coil. The current flow will damage the ignition control unit. In general, make test connections only as specified by Saab, as described in this manual, or as described by the test instrument's manufacturer.

- Do not disconnect the battery while the engine is running.

- Do not exceed 16 volts at the battery with boosting cables attached, and do not quick-charge the battery (for boost starting) for longer than one minute. Wait at least one minute before boosting the battery a second time.

- Do not connect terminal 1 (-) of the ignition coil to ground as a means of preventing the engine from starting.

- Running the engine with a spark plug wire disconnected may damage the catalytic converter.

- Cleanliness is essential when working with fuel circuit components. Before disconnecting any fuel lines, thoroughly clean the unions. Use clean tools.

Mechanical Condition

Before troubleshooting a poorly running engine or an engine that will not start, determine the general condition of the engine, especially if it has high mileage. If the engine is severely worn or has mechanical problems, the only remedy is overhaul or repair. If a tune-up or scheduled maintenance is due, it should be done before proceeding further with troubleshooting.

Only a few basic functions are required of the engine. The parts must fit together properly, operate smoothly, and seal well enough to create and maintain compression, and keep pistons, valve train, and ignition properly timed. General engine condition can be easily assessed by performing a compression test.

NOTE

Saab does not give specific compression pressure specifications. In addition, a compression test requires special equipment. If the equipment is not available, most automotive repair shops can do these tests quickly and at a reasonable cost.

Carbon Deposits

Carbon deposits on the fuel injectors and the intake valves will affect the way the engine idles and runs. See Fig. 9. Even a ten percent decrease in the amount of fuel that the injectors deliver will cause driveability problems. These deposits normally form during the "hot soak" period immediately after the engine is turned off, at which point the engine temperature rises slightly for a short period.

Fig. 9. Examples of carbon deposits on fuel injector (left) and intake valve (right). Carbon deposits can cause a rough idle, hard cold starting, and overall poor performance.

Driving style may be the main contributor to the problem. A car that is predominantly driven on short trips around town or in city traffic seems to increase the likelihood of deposits forming.

Carbon deposits on the intake valves and injectors should be removed prior to troubleshooting driveability problems. Special fuel injector test equipment is required to accurately check for clogged injectors. If the injectors are severely clogged, they can be removed and visually inspected. Inspecting the intake valves is more difficult because the intake manifold must be removed. Check with an authorized Saab dealer for the latest information on carbon deposits and the best methods to remove them.

CAUTION

Always follow the manufacturer's directions when using fuel additives designed to remove carbon deposits and clean injectors. As a general rule, high detergency fuels should not be used together with fuel additives. The additional cleaner in the fuel can dilute engine oil and accelerate engine wear.

Tune-up and Preventive Maintenance

A tune-up is regular maintenance of the ignition and fuel system components for normal wear and contamination. The condition of the tune-up and emission control components can affect engine performance and driveability. The ignition components all carry high voltage to deliver a precisely timed spark to ignite the air-fuel mixture. If any of these components are faulty or worn, the intensity and timing of the spark will be affected. Dirt contamination of fuel system and emission control components can adversely affect fuel delivery, air-fuel mixture, and exhaust emissions.

When experiencing driveability problems, a good starting point is to do a tune-up. Many driveability problems are eliminated by simply replacing these components.

Replacement schedules and procedures for the spark plugs, spark plug wires, distributor cap, ignition rotor, fuel filter, air filter, oxygen sensor, and oil and oil filter are given in **1 LUBRICATION AND MAINTENANCE.**

NOTE

For information on inspecting ignition components, see **340 Ignition System.** For information on checking the oxygen sensor, see **254 Exhaust Emission Control.**

Basic Adjustments

In addition to tune-up component replacement, it is important that all of the basic adjustments that can be made are correctly set. Check idle speed, idle mixture (%CO), and ignition timing to be sure they are all within the specified limits. See **1 LUBRICATION AND MAINTENANCE.**

NOTE

All of the basic adjustments require the use of specialized test equipment. If any of the test equipment is not available, it is recommended that the adjustments be done by an authorized Saab dealer or other qualified repair shop. These adjustments can be made quickly and at a reasonable cost.

The systems that adapt the idle mixture (Lambda system), idle speed (AIC system), ignition timing (EZK system, where applicable), and turbo boost pressure (APC system) can only correct engine operation within a limited range. Once these limits are exceeded, driveability problems will become noticeable. For example, the oxygen (Lambda) sensor can adapt idle mixture for things such as a small vacuum leak or minor engine wear. A large vacuum leak or a severely worn engine may exceed the operating range of the sensor, causing the engine to run lean. If large adjustments are necessary, the faults that are causing these incorrect settings should be corrected prior to making any adjustments.

Oxygen Sensor

The oxygen sensor, also called the Lambda sensor, affects the air-fuel mixture by sending a varying voltage signal to the fuel injection control unit. The sensor is positioned in the exhaust stream and actually measures the amount of oxygen in the exhaust gas so that the fuel injection system can correctly adjust the air-fuel mixture. See Fig. 10. A high concentration of oxygen in the exhaust gas indicates a lean mixture and a low content indicates a rich mixture.

NOTE

The control unit ignores the signal from the oxygen sensor until the engine reaches a specified temperature. Therefore, when troubleshooting cold engine driveability problems, the oxygen sensor can be ruled out as a possible cause.

Fig. 10. Oxygen sensor reacts to oxygen content in exhaust gas to constantly monitor air-fuel mixture.

As the sensor ages, it loses its ability to react quickly to changing conditions. It may eventually cease to produce any signal at all. When this happens, idle speed may fluctuate and fuel consumption may increase. The oxygen sensor should be replaced at the specified mileage interval as described in **1 LUBRICATION AND MAINTENANCE.**

Air Flow Measurement and Vacuum Leaks

The Bosch LH fuel injection system uses an air mass meter to precisely measure incoming air. The air mass meter sends an electrical signal to the LH control unit proportional to the amount of air passing through the meter. This is the main input used to determine the amount of fuel delivered to the engine.

Because proper fuel metering depends on accurately metering the intake air, any unmeasured air entering the system will cause a lean fuel mixture and poor running. To see how air leaks can affect engine running, remove the oil filler cap while the engine is running.

There are many possible places for unmeasured air to enter the engine. Carefully inspect for cracks or looseness all hoses, fittings, duct work, and seals and gaskets. See Fig. 11. For a thorough inspection, it may be necessary to remove hoses and ducts that cannot be completely checked in their installed positions. Check that the throttle mounting nuts are tight and that the throttle plate is closed.

Use a vacuum gauge connected downstream of the throttle plate to check engine vacuum. Start the engine and let it idle. If the system is operating correctly, engine vacuum should be within the range listed below.

Engine Vacuum

• at idle (850±50 rpm) . . 12 to 23 in. Hg (-.4 to -.8 bar)

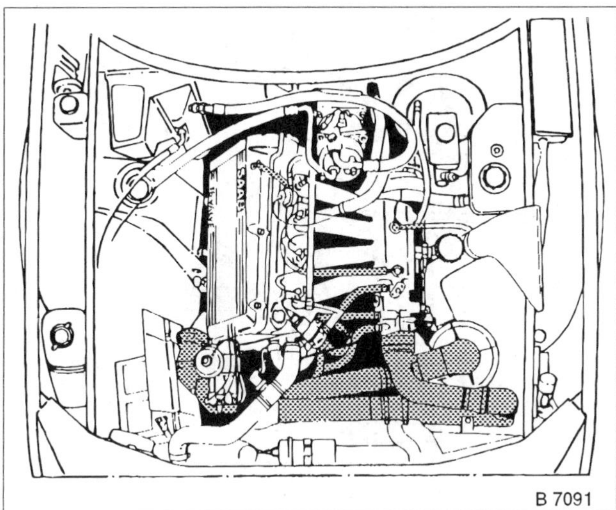

Fig. 11. Common places to check for intake air leaks (shaded areas). Intake air leaks can cause rough running, especially at idle.

In addition to air leaks, an air restriction can cause driveability problems. Remove the air filter and check that it is clean. Hold the filter up to a strong light source. If the light cannot be seen through the filter it should be replaced. Remove the air bellows from the throttle housing and check for residue around the throttle plate. Large amounts of residue on the throttle plate can cause an erratic idle. Clean the throttle housing with a carburetor cleaner and reinstall the bellows. Check the AIC idle setting as described in **240 Fuel Injection**.

NOTE

• On turbo models, be sure to check the hoses and plastic hose clamps on the turbo bypass valve. The valve is located on the compressor side of the turbocharger. See Fig. 12. If the car exhibits minor driveability problems and no other vacuum leaks can be found, check the operation of the bypass valve as described in **291 Turbocharger.** The valve may be faulty and leaking internally.

• Some early 1985 models may not have a turbo bypass valve.

Electrical System

All the cars covered by this manual use fuel injection and ignition systems that rely on precise electrical signals for proper operation. If any of these signals are distorted, incorrect, or missing, the car can develop major driveability problems.

Battery Voltage

One of the most fundamental requirements in troubleshooting engine performance problems is to make sure the battery is fully charged and in good condition. Many of the sophisticat-

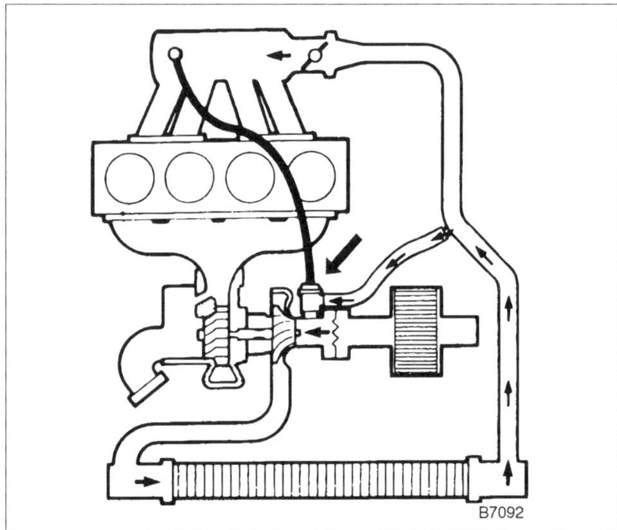

Fig. 12. Leaking turbo bypass valve (arrow) can be the source of minor driveability problems.

ed electronics used on the cars covered by this manual require a specific operating voltage to function correctly.

Battery voltage can be measured across its terminals with all cables attached. Do not eliminate the battery as a possible source of trouble until a load test has been performed, especially if starting problems are encountered. See **300 Electrical—General** for battery testing information.

NOTE

A digital voltmeter should be used to measure battery voltage. A fully charged battery will measure 12.6 volts, or more, as compared to a battery only 25% charged that measures 12.15 volts. Using an analog meter may result in inaccurate results.

For the battery to maintain its proper voltage level, the charging system must be functioning correctly. If in doubt about the condition of the charging system, have the system checked. Most automotive repair shops can test the system quickly and at a reasonable cost.

Wiring and Harness Connectors

The cars covered by this manual are equipped with electronic fuel injection and ignition systems that are controlled by central electronic control units. Many of the circuits operate on very low current and are sensitive to increased resistance due to faulty or corroded wiring or connectors.

NOTE

In most cases, faulty electronic control units are not the cause of driveability problems. These units are extremely durable and reliable. Actual failures are very rare. Driveability problems are more often caused by missing or incorrect signals to the control unit, or other faulty components.

The electrical system is subject to corrosion, vibration, roadway elements and general wear. Because of this, the integrity and freedom from corrosion in the connections, wires, and switches, including all ground connections, is one of the most important conditions for trouble-free operation of the fuel injection and ignition systems.

Always make a thorough visual inspection of all wires and connectors, switches and fuses. Loose or damaged connectors can cause intermittent problems, especially at the small terminals in each control unit connector. In most cases, a visual inspection will detect any faults. If a connector shows no visible faults, but is still suspect, perform a voltage drop test at the connector. Even a small amount of corrosion in a connector can cause a large voltage drop to the circuit's load. See **300 Electrical—General** for more electrical troubleshooting information.

Ground Connections

For any electrical circuit to work, it must make a complete path, beginning at the negative (-) battery terminal and ending at the positive (+) terminal. The negative (-) battery cable runs directly to the car's chassis. Therefore, connecting a wire to the chassis or any metal part bolted to the chassis provides a good ground source or path back to the negative (-) side of the battery.

Poor ground connections are one of the major sources of driveability problems. There are only a few main ground connections or points for the fuel injection and ignition systems. If any of these ground points are faulty, the voltage to the circuit will be reduced or even eliminated. Be sure to carefully check the main ground(s) for the LH system at the engine lifting bracket on the intake manifold. Also check the ground for the fuel pump at the center crossmember in the luggage compartment.

When checking ground wires, ground points, or ground straps, begin with a thorough visual inspection. Ground connections and wires can corrode, become loose, or break in areas that are not visible. To thoroughly check a circuit ground, check the voltage drop between the connector and a good ground source. Large voltage drops indicate too much resistance. The connection is corroded, dirty or otherwise damaged. Clean or repair the connection and retest. Also check both battery terminals and all ground straps between the engine and the body for voltage drops.

NOTE

For voltage drop tests and other general electrical troubleshooting information, see **300 Electrical—General.**

Fuel System

For the engine to start quickly when cold or hot, run correctly throughout all operating conditions, and accelerate smoothly without hesitation, the fuel system must deliver a precise amount of fuel in relation to the amount of air that is drawn in by the engine.

Fuel Supply

To start and run, the engine needs an adequate supply of fuel. Fuel from the tank is supplied to the engine via an electric fuel pump, a fuel filter, and the connecting fuel lines. If either the filter or a fuel line is restricted, the engine may not run properly. If the restriction is severe, or the main fuel pump is faulty, the engine may not start at all. If fuel delivery problems are suspected, check the fuel pump and pump relay as described in **234 Fuel Pump and Fuel Tank**.

NOTE

On some turbo models, a faulty turbocharger over-pressure switch can cause a no-start condition. The turbocharger over-pressure switch is designed to turn off the fuel pump during overboost conditions. Test this switch as described in **291 Turbocharger.**

The fuel injection system has the main function of delivering the correct amount of fuel for all engine operating conditions. Basic fuel delivery is dependent on fuel pressure and the correctly functioning injectors. Fuel pressure is often overlooked when diagnosing driveability problems.

The fuel pressure from the fuel pump is controlled by a pressure regulator. This regulator returns surplus fuel to the fuel tank. The amount of fuel delivered to the engine is varied by changing the amount of time the electric pulsed-type fuel injectors remain open. A change in fuel pressure results in a change in the amount of fuel (or fuel mixture) delivered to the engine. Fuel pressure and fuel pressure regulator tests are described in **240 Fuel Injection.**

NOTE

Fuel pressure tests require the use of a pressure gauge. If this equipment is not available, fuel pressure tests can be performed by an authorized Saab dealer or other qualified shop.

Correctly operating fuel injectors play a major role in fuel delivery. The injectors are switched on and off at the ground side of the connector. Positive (+) battery voltage is always present at the connector when the car is running. An injector can become clogged, it can completely fail or lose power and refuse to open, or it can short to ground and remain open whenever the engine is running. Checking if an injector is fundamentally working can be accomplished easily; checking an injector's spray pattern is more difficult. See **240 Fuel Injection** for additional information.

NOTE

High or low fuel pressure or a faulty injector will result in an incorrect fuel mixture and overall poor driveability. A lean mixture (too little fuel) can cause the engine to run poorly when cold or stumble upon acceleration. A rich mixture (too much fuel) can dilute the engine oil, foul the spark plugs, and cause a rough idle.

Table c lists some of the more common driveability symptoms, causes and corrective actions. The boldface type indicates the repair group where the applicable tests and repair procedures can be found.

Table c. Engine Management—Driveability Troubleshooting

SYMPTOMS

a. Engine fails to start
b. Engine starts but stops immediately
c. Erratic idling
d. Poor response on acceleration
e. Engine erratic in all speed ranges
f. Excessive fuel consumption
g. Engine fails to rev up (no power)
h. CO content too low
i. CO content too high

a	b	c	d	e	f	g	h	i	CAUSES	CHECK/REMEDY
a									Fuel pump not running	Test fuel pump. **234**
a	b								Ignition system faulty	Test ignition system components **340**
a	b								System relay faulty	Test system relay. **240**
a	b								Fuel pump relay faulty	Check fuel pump relay. **234**
a	b	c							AIC idle valve faulty	Test AIC valve. **240**
		c							EGR valve sticking or faulty	Test and clean EGR valve. **254**
	b				f				Throttle position sensor faulty or out of adjustment	Test throttle position sensor and adjust if necessary. **240**
		c	d	e	f	g		i	Air mass meter faulty	Test air mass meter. **240**
a	b	c	d	e		g	h		Induction (intake) system leaking	Checks for air leaks. Make a vacuum gauge test. **200**
a		c	d	e		g	h	i	Fuel pressure too low	Measure fuel pressure. **240**
					f			i	Fuel pressure too high	Measure fuel pressure. **240**
			d	e		g	h		Fuel pump output too low	Make fuel delivery test. **234**
a	b	c	d	e	f	g	h	i	Coolant temperature sensor faulty	Test sensor resistance, replace if necessary. **240**
		c	d	e	f				Oxygen sensor faulty	Test oxygen sensor output signal. Replace sensor if mileage interval exceeded. **254**
		c		e	f			i	Fuel injectors leaking	Check fuel injectors for leaks. Replace leaky injectors. **240**
					f	g			Binding throttle plate, or throttle plate incorrectly adjusted	Check throttle plate and adjust if necessary. **240**
a	b	c	d	e	f	g	h	i	Electrical connection(s) loose, broken, or corroded	Visually inspect electrical connectors and correct any faults found. **300**
a	b	c	d	e	f	g	h	i	Ground point(s) loose, broken, or corroded	Visually inspect ground points and correct any faults found. **300**
	b	c			f				CO content too high	Test air mass meter. **240**
	b	c	d						CO content too low	Test air mass meter. **240**
a	b	c	d	e	f	g	h	i	Input(s) signals to LH control unit missing	Make electrical tests at control unit connector. **240**
						g			Turbocharger APC system faulty	Test APC system components. **291**
a	b	c	d	e	f	g	h	i	LH control unit faulty	Test inputs to control unit. If all inputs are correct, replace control unit. **240**

201 Engine Removal and Installation

REMOVING AND INSTALLING ENGINE

The engine is removed together with the transmission as a complete assembly. The removal and installation procedure described below applies specifically to 1988 turbocharged models with manual transmission. Minor departures from the procedures may be necessary depending on model year, engine and transmission.

To remove engine and transmission assembly

1. Open the hood and disconnect the windshield washer hoses. Remove the hood hinge mounting bolts and carefully lift off the hood. See Fig. 1.

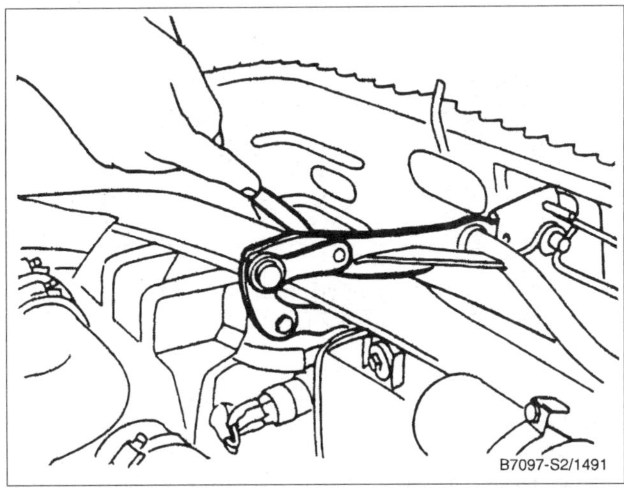

Fig. 1. Hood hinge bolt being removed.

2. Using the steering wheel, turn the right-hand wheel to its full right-lock position. Then insert Saab special tool no. 83 93 209 between the upper control arm and the body as shown in Fig. 2.

NOTE
The Saab special tool is used to hold the suspension control arm in its loaded position while the car is raised. This aids in disconnecting the drive axle inner joint from the transmission as the engine is pulled.

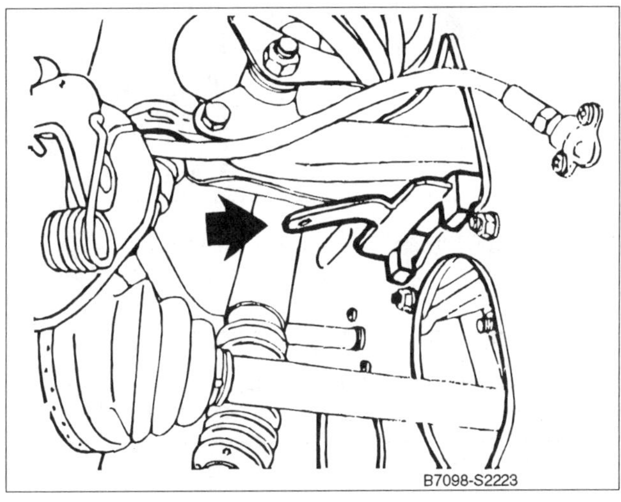

Fig. 2. Special tool (arrow) inserted between body and suspension control arm to limit suspension travel.

3. Disconnect the battery leads and remove the battery.

4. Disconnect the exhaust pipe from the exhaust manifold. See **252 Exhaust System.**

5. Loosen the right-hand wheel lug bolts.

6. Drain the power steering fluid reservoir. See **644 Power Steering.**

7. Raise the car enough to work safely under it and support it securely on jackstands.

WARNING
Never work under a lifted car unless it solidly supported on stands designed for the purpose. Do not work under a car supported solely by a jack.

8. Remove the nut from the shift selector rod taper pin and tap the pin out of the rod. See Fig. 3. Disconnect the rod from the shift linkage.

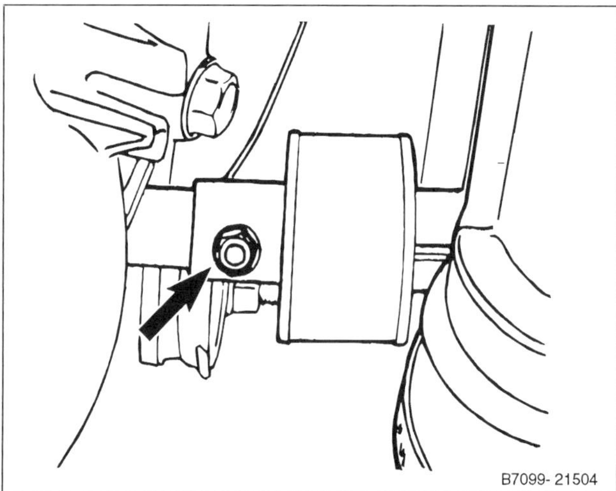

Fig. 3. Manual shift selector rod taper pin retaining nut (arrow).

NOTE
For removal of the shift cable on models with automatic transmission see **444 Automatic Transmission Controls**.

9. Thoroughly clean the area around the speedometer cable at the left-hand differential-bearing housing. Unscrew the speedometer cable from the housing. See Fig. 4.

10. Remove the mounting bolts holding the front exhaust pipe bracket to the transmission. See Fig. 5.

11. Remove the large clamps holding the inner drive axle joint boots to the drive axle drivers. Pull the boots off the drivers.

12. Remove the right-hand road wheel. Remove the two through-bolts from the lower ball joint. Separate the ball joint from the control arm and remove the inner drive axle joint from its driver. See Fig. 6. Push the drive axle assembly forward and rest it on the control arm.

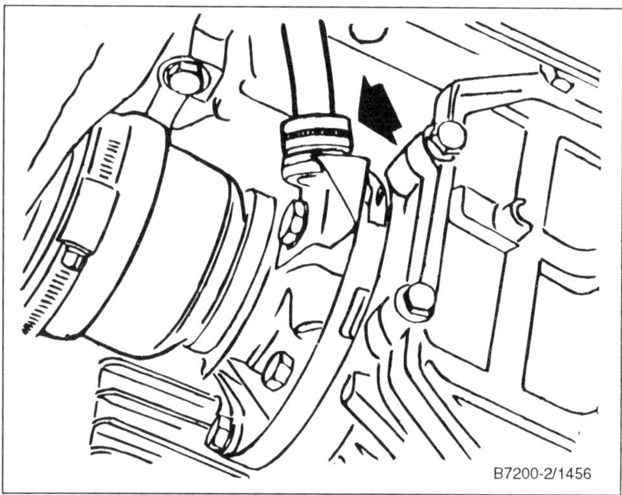

Fig. 4. Unscrew speedometer cable retaining collar (arrow) and pull cable from bearing housing.

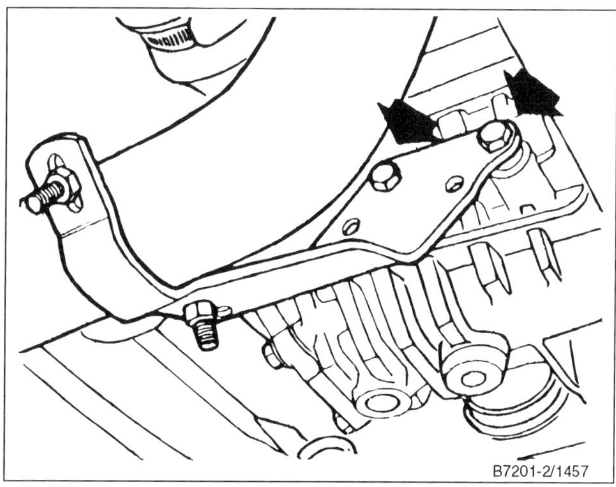

Fig. 5. Front exhaust pipe mounting bracket. Remove bracket bolts (arrows) from transmission.

CAUTION
Cleanliness is essential when working on drive axle joints. Even a small amount of sand or dirt will appreciably shorten the service life of the joint. Cover or wrap the joint and inner drivers on the transmission.

13. Disconnect the power steering pump pressure line union on the exhaust side of the engine. See Fig. 7.

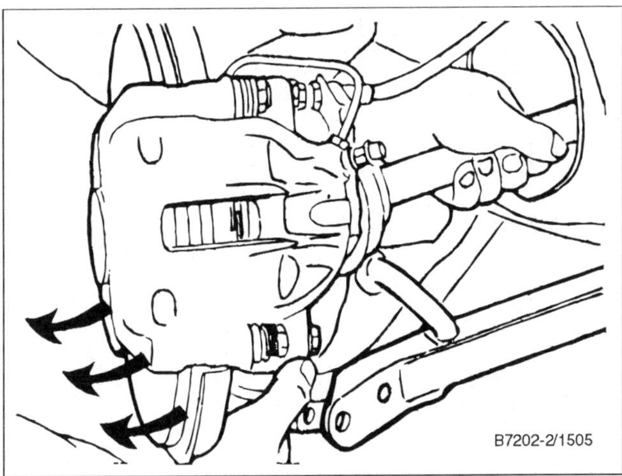

Fig. 6. Hub assembly and drive axle being pulled out to remove inner joint from drive axle driver. Rest drive axle on control arm.

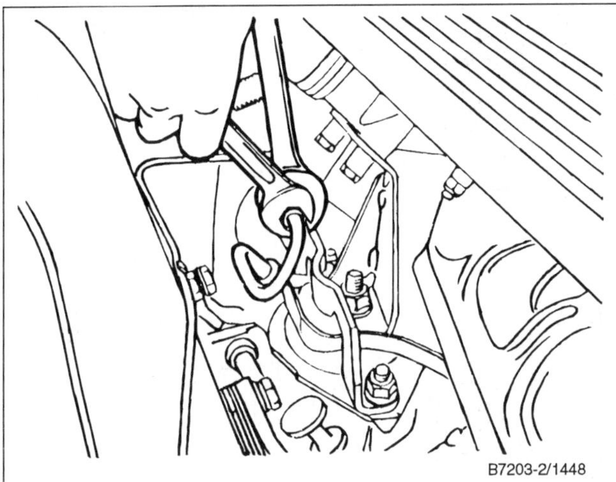

Fig. 7. Power steering pump pressure line union being disconnected.

14. Drain the coolant from the radiator and block as as described in **261 Radiator and Cooling System.** Disconnect the coolant hoses shown in Fig. 8.

15. Disconnect the wiring connectors and ground wires shown in Fig. 9. Lift the wiring loom out of the engine compartment and rest it on the A/C evaporator housing. Position all other disconnected wires and connectors so that they will not interfere with the engine's removal.

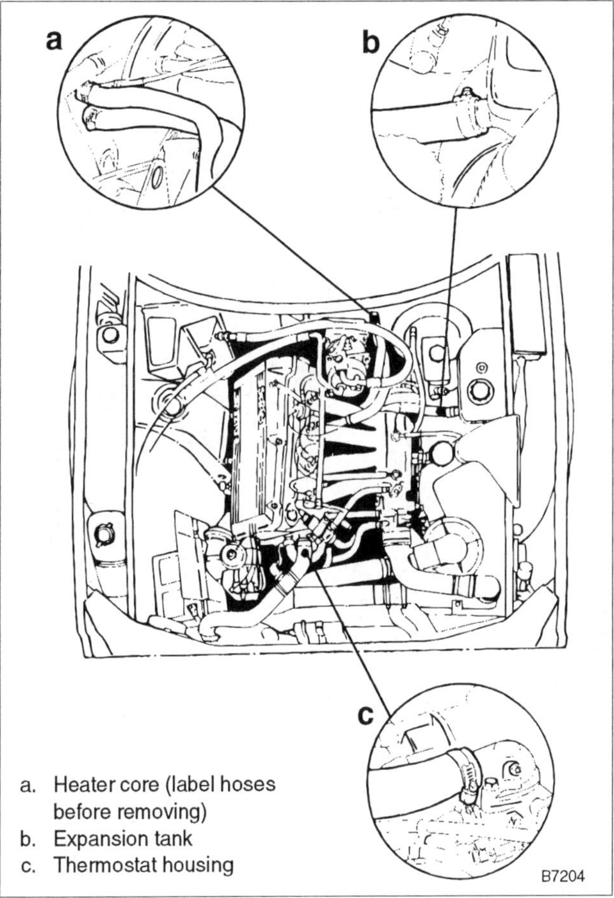

Fig. 8. Coolant hoses to be disconnected.

NOTE

Use a small screwdriver to remove the connector retaining clips where necessary.

---

16. On turbo models, disconnect the turbocharger discharge pipe.

17. Remove the air mass meter with its rubber socket connector.

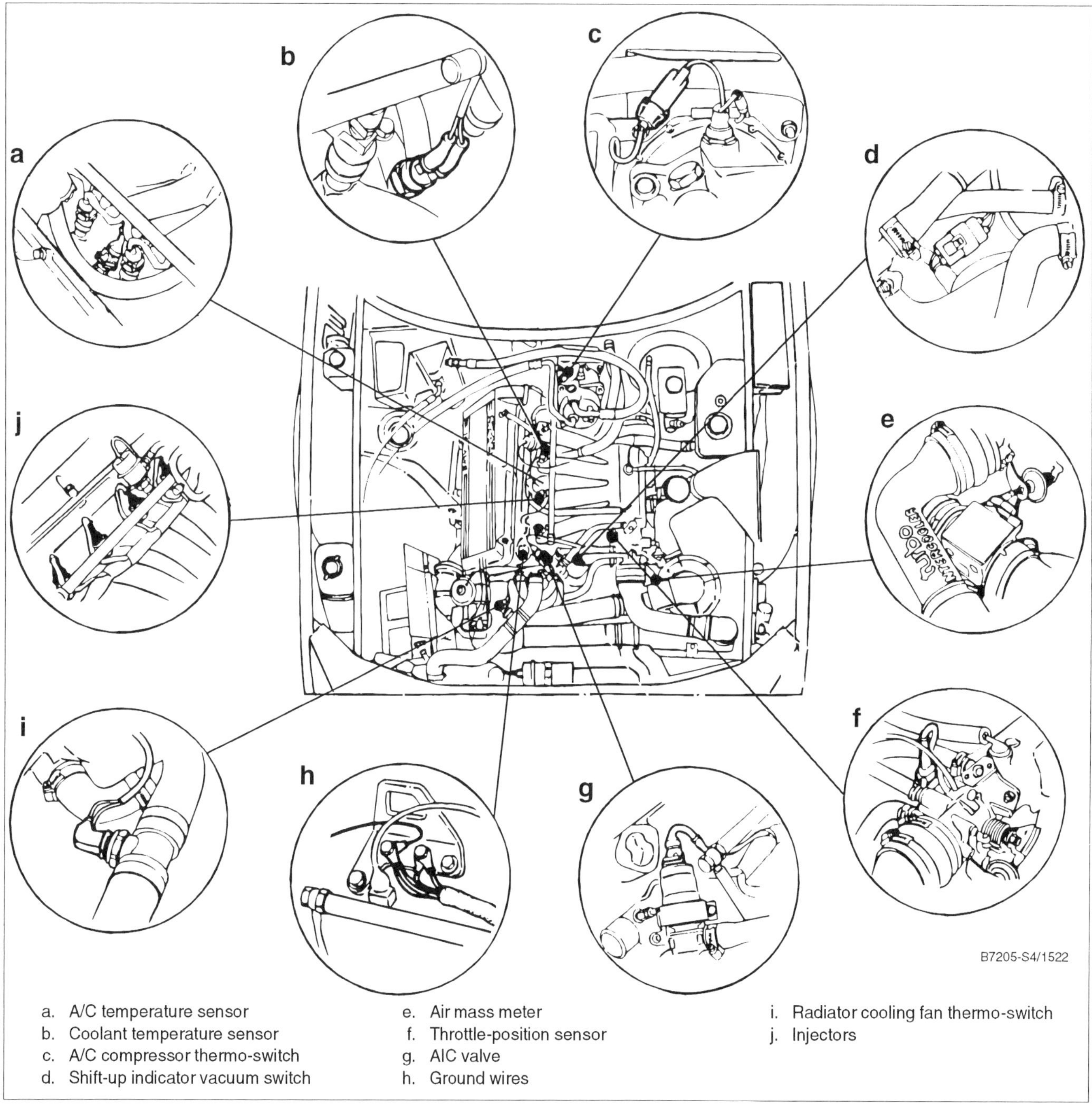

a. A/C temperature sensor
b. Coolant temperature sensor
c. A/C compressor thermo-switch
d. Shift-up indicator vacuum switch
e. Air mass meter
f. Throttle-position sensor
g. AIC valve
h. Ground wires
i. Radiator cooling fan thermo-switch
j. Injectors

Fig. 9. Wiring connectors and ground wires to be removed.

18. Remove the air cleaner together with the intake air pipe. See Fig. 10.

19. Remove the intercooler together with the air pipe. See Fig. 11. Cover or cap the inlet to the turbocharger.

20. Remove the intercooler side baffle plate and top cover. See Fig. 12.

21. Remove and label the wires at the ignition coil. Remove the coil from its bracket.

22. Remove the A/C radiator cooling fan. See **261 Radiator and Cooling System.**

23. Disconnect the lower radiator hose from the radiator.

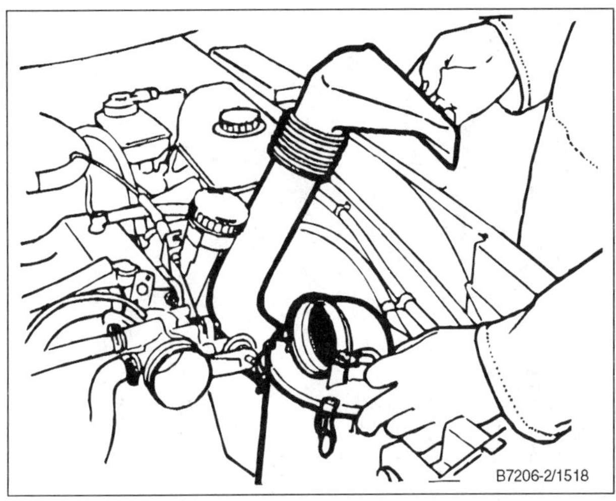

Fig. 10. Air cleaner assembly and intake air pipe being removed.

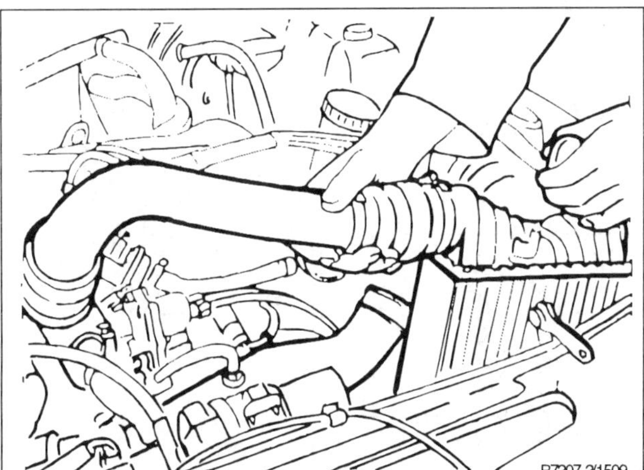

Fig. 11. Intercooler and air pipe being removed.

24. Disconnect the harness connector and hoses from the turbocharger APC solenoid. See Fig. 13. Label the hoses before removing them.

25. Disconnect the accelerator cable from the throttle housing and its bracket.

26. Disconnect the vacuum hoses for the brake booster and the charcoal canister at the intake manifold and throttle housing.

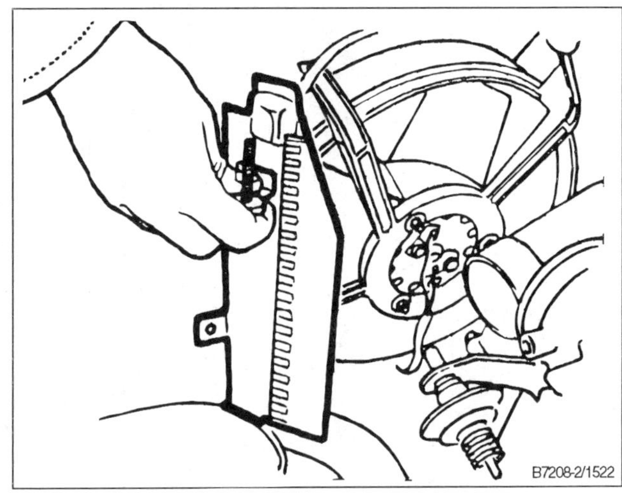

Fig. 12. Intercooler side baffle plate being removed.

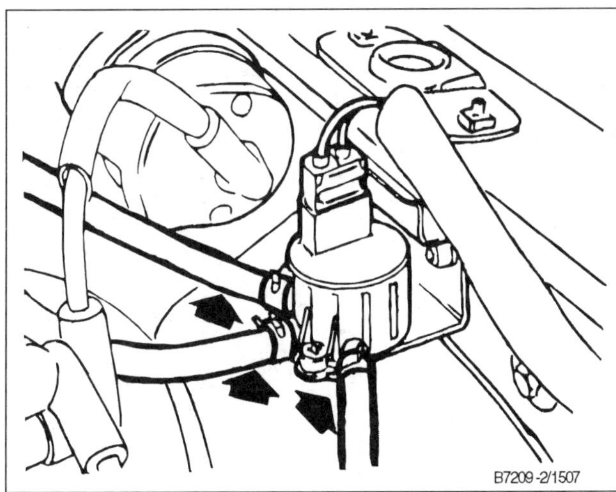

Fig. 13. APC solenoid. Remove harness connector and hoses (arrows). Label hoses before removal.

27. Disconnect the wiring connectors and wires shown in Fig. 14. Cut any wiring ties and lift the wiring loom out of the engine compartment and set aside. Position all other disconnected wires and connectors so that they will not interfere with the engine's removal.

NOTE

Use a small screwdriver to remove the connector retaining clips where necessary.

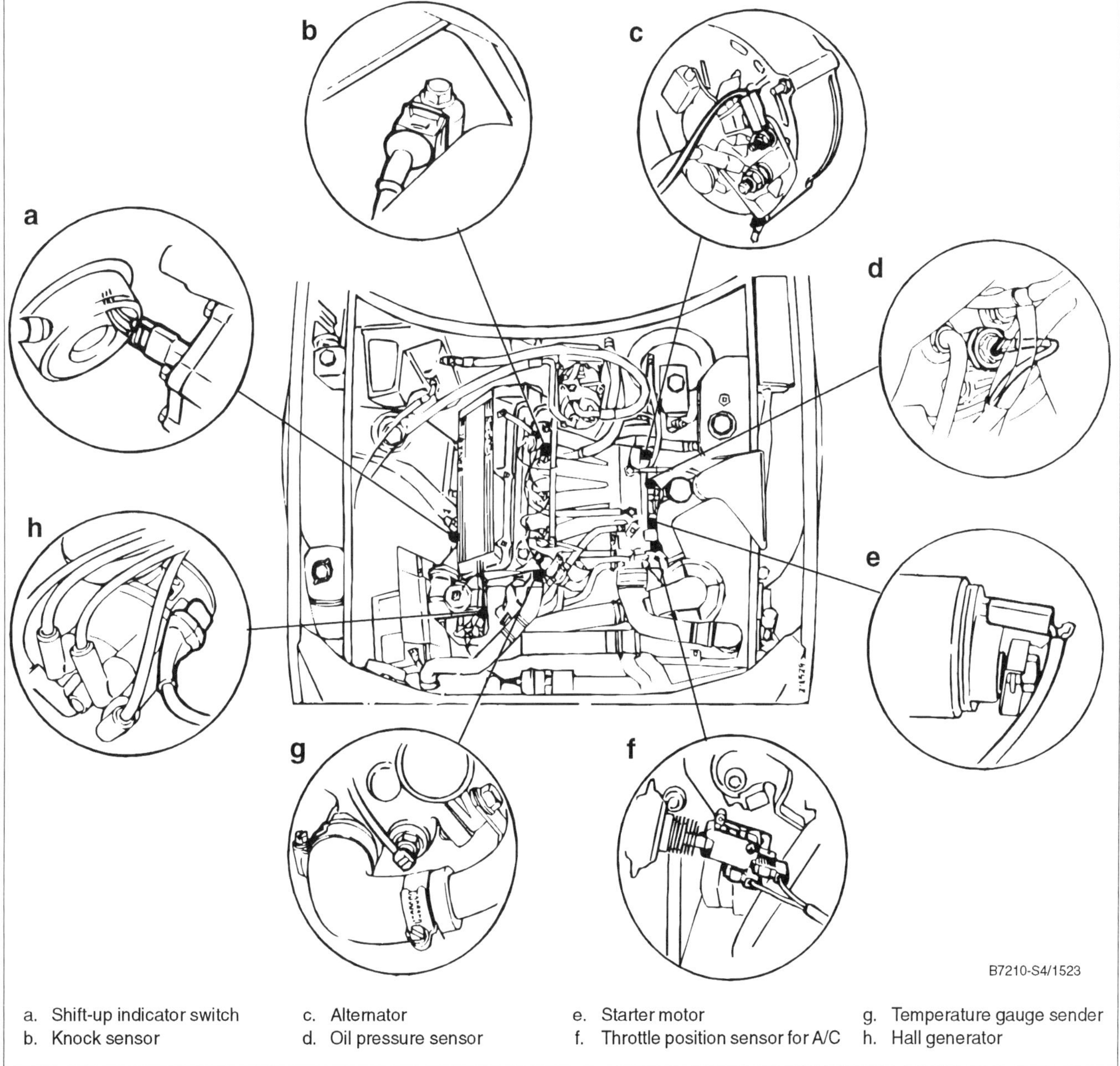

Fig. 14. Wiring connectors and ground wires to be removed.

28. Remove the positive battery cable from it brackets on the engine and on the starter motor. Set the cable on the battery tray.

29. Disconnect the ground wire at the timing chain cover and the transmission.

30. Unplug the oxygen sensor connector above the right-hand wheel well. Unhook the wiring harness from the fender and set it on the engine.

31. Disconnect the hydraulic line from the clutch slave cylinder. See Fig. 15.

32. Disconnect the fuel supply line and return line from the fuel rail and fuel pressure regulator.

33. Unbolt the A/C compressor (4 bolts) and carefully place the compressor on the A/C evaporator housing without disconnecting or loosening any refrigerant hoses.

WARNING

Loosening or disconnecting refrigerant hoses will allow the refrigerant to be discharged under high pressure, possibly causing personal injury. Recharging a discharged A/C system requires special equipment and knowledge.

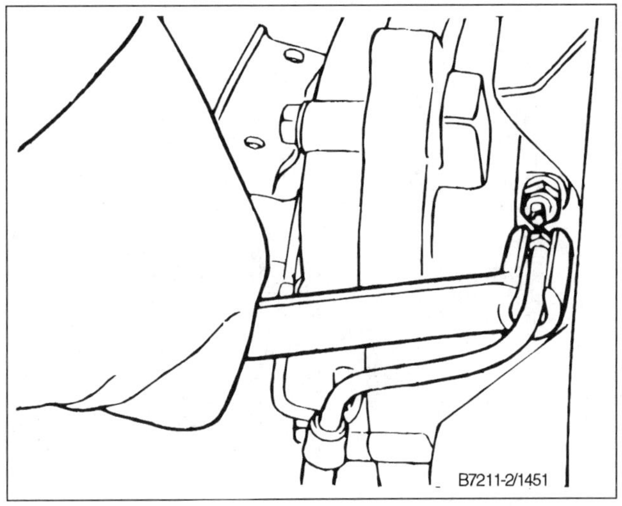

Fig. 15. Clutch slave cylinder hydraulic line being removed.

34. Attach an engine hoist to the engine. The front lifting point is at the intake manifold. The rear lifting point is at the A/C bracket. Raise the engine slightly.

NOTE

The A/C bracket has a lifting eye, which is used to attach the lifting hoist hook. If the bracket has been removed, bolt a separate lifting eye to the coolant pump cover using the existing mounting bolts.

---

35. Remove the bolts from the three engine mounts (front, left, and right). Remove the bump stop on the front and right-hand mounts. The left-hand mount is a through bolt with a spacer. See Fig. 16, Fig. 17, and Fig. 18.

Fig. 16. Front engine mount and bump stop assembly.

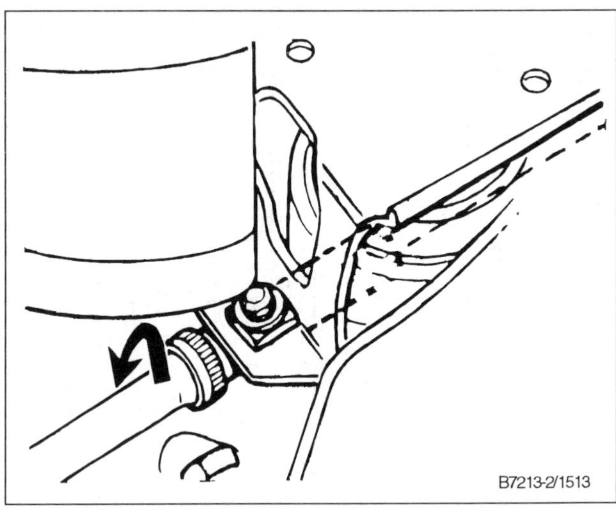

Fig. 17. Left-hand engine mount being loosened. Spacer sleeve is hidden behind bracket (dotted line).

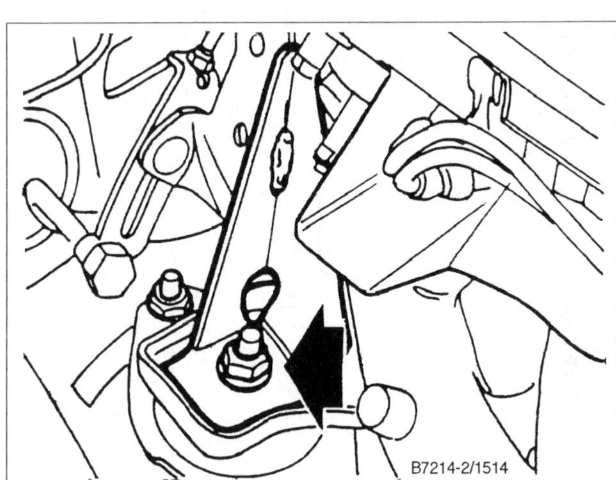

Fig. 18. Right-hand engine mount.

36. Raise the engine just enough to separate the left-hand inner drive axle joint from the driver. See Fig. 19.

CAUTION

Cleanliness is essential when working on drive axle joints. Even a small amount of sand or dirt will appreciably shorten the service life of the joint. Cover or wrap the joint and inner drivers on the transmission.

---

37. Disconnect the power steering pump return line from the bottom of the power steering pump.

38. Remove the oil pressure sensor connector and disconnect the oil cooler lines from the oil filter housing. See Fig. 20.

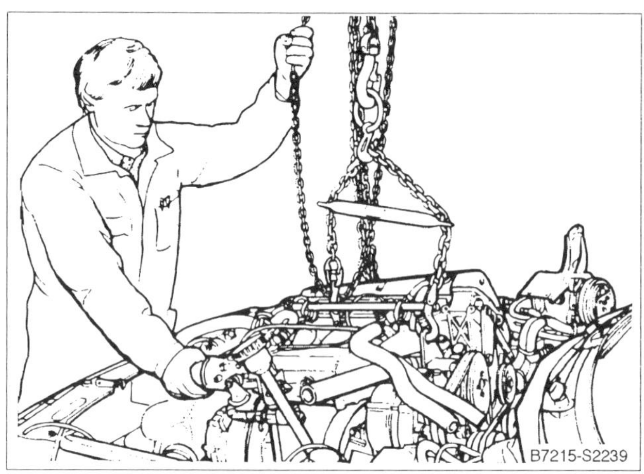

Fig. 19. Engine being raised just enough to separate inner drive axle joint from driver.

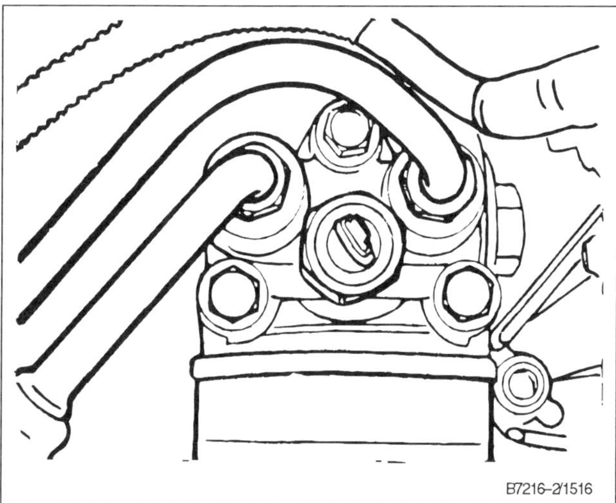

Fig. 20. Top view of oil filter housing showing oil pressure sensor and oil cooler lines.

39. Raise the engine and transmission assembly out of the car. Be careful not to damage the radiator or APC solenoid valve.

Before installing the engine make sure the drive axle drivers are packed with grease. See **774 Wheel Bearings and Drive Axles**. Install any coolant drain plugs removed earlier. When lowering the engine into the engine compartment, incline the engine slightly down in the front. See Fig. 21.

Lower the engine into position just enough to install the power steering pump return line and oil cooler lines. Align the left-hand drive axle joint and the engine mounts and lower the engine into its final position. Be sure to install the spacer sleeve on the left-hand engine mount. Reconnect all hoses, connectors and ground wires. Be sure to replace any wire ties

Fig. 21. Engine being lowered into engine compartment. Note engine tilted down in front during installation.

cut off during the removal procedure. Use new self-locking nuts when reinstalling the lower ball joint to the control arm.

WARNING

Always replace self-locking nuts and bolts. These fasteners are designed to be used only once. They may become unreliable and fail when used a second time.

Refill the engine with engine oil and coolant, and refill the power steering system. If applicable bleed the clutch slave cylinder as described in **412 Clutch Control.** The remainder of installation is the reverse of removal.

Tightening torques

- clutch slave cylinder to transmission case. . . . . . 6 to 10 Nm (53 to 89 in-lb)
- coolant drain plug to engine block . . 15 Nm (11 ft-lb)
- oil cooler line to oil filter housing. . . . . 7 to 10 Nm (62 to 89 in-lb)
- lower ball joint to lower control arm . . . . . . 40 to 55 Nm (30 to 41 ft-lb)
- road wheel to wheel bearing hub
  - lug nuts . . . . 90 to 110 Nm (66 to 81 ft-lb)
  - lug bolts . . . . 105 to 125 Nm (77 to 92 ft-lb)
- power steering line union. . . . . 20 to 34 Nm (15 to 25 ft-lb)
- all other fasteners
  - M5 bolt. . . . . 5 Nm (44 in-lb)
  - M6 bolt. . . . . 10 Nm (89 in-lb)
  - M8 bolt. . . . . 20 Nm (15 ft-lb)
  - M10 bolt. 40 Nm (30 ft-lb)

SEPARATING ENGINE FROM TRANSMISSION

The engine must be first removed from the car to separate the transmission from the engine.

To separate engine from transmission (manual transmission)

1. Thoroughly clean the external surfaces of the engine and transmission.
2. Drain the engine oil and remove the EGR pipe, if applicable.
3. Remove the plastic clutch cover from over the flywheel.
4. Remove the transmission oil dipstick tube.
5. On turbo models, disconnect the oil return line from the turbocharger.
6. Remove the starter motor and unscrew the starter motor stay plate.
7. Remove the transmission input shaft. Remove the clutch slave cylinder mounting bolts. See **411 Clutch.**
8. Remove all of the engine to transmission mounting bolts. Remove the bracket for the oil filler pipe at the throttle housing.
9. Carefully lift the engine away from the transmission. See Fig. 22. Guide off the clutch release-bearing sleeve and slave cylinder as the engine is lifted off.

Fig. 22. Engine being lifted off transmission together with clutch release-bearing sleeve and slave cylinder.

CAUTION
If the engine does not immediately lift off the transmission, do not attempt to pry them apart until making sure that all fasteners have been removed.

---

10. Remove all old traces of oil and dirt from the flanges.
11. Before refitting the engine to the transmission, make sure the two guide sleeves are fitted in the transmission flange. Place a new gasket onto the transmission flange and apply a sealing compound (Permatex Ultrablue) to the slots shown in Fig. 23.
12. Apply a thread sealing compound (Loctite 45, Saab Part No. 3009081) to the six bolt holes shown in Fig. 24.

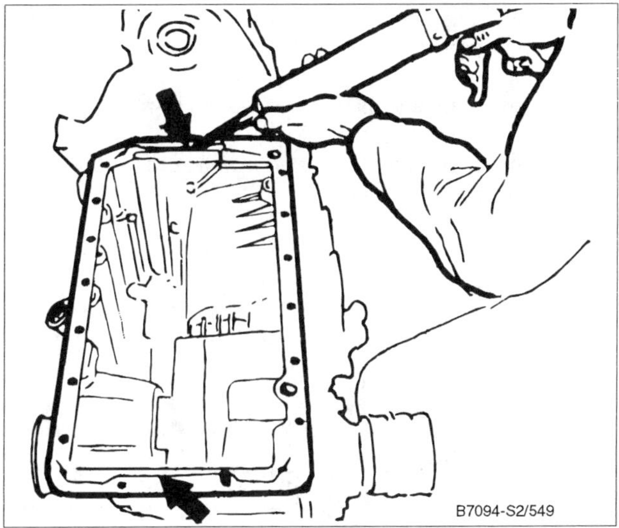

Fig. 23. Sealing compound being installed to slots (arrows) on transmission flange.

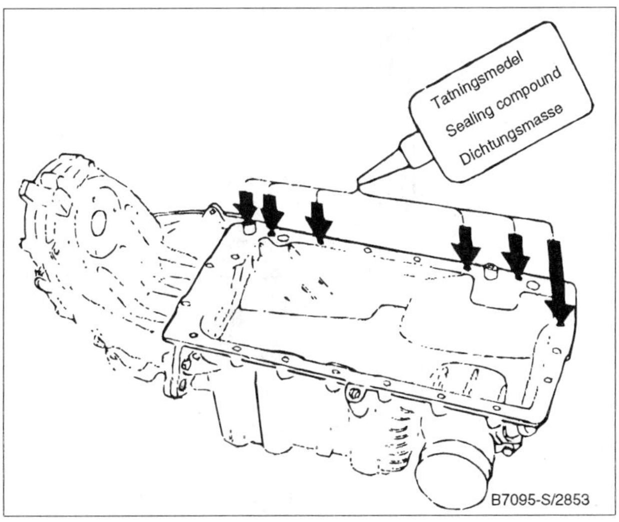

Fig. 24. Bolt holes in transmission case requiring thread sealer.

The remainder of the procedure is the reverse of removal. Fig. 25 shows engine-to-transmission bolt identification and location.

Tightening torques
- engine to transmission .... 25 Nm (18 ft-lb)
- all other fasteners
  - M5 bolt .... 5 Nm (44 in-lb)
  - M6 bolt .... 10 Nm (89 in-lb)
  - M8 bolt .... 20 Nm (15 ft-lb)
  - M10 bolt .... 40 Nm (30 ft-lb)

To separate engine from transmission (automatic transmission)

1. Thoroughly clean the external surfaces of the engine and transmission.
2. Drain the engine oil and remove the oil filler pipe.
3. Remove the plastic cover from above the drive plate and torque converter.
4. Disconnect the throttle (kick-down) cable at the throttle housing.
5. On turbo models, remove the turbocharger support.
6. Remove all of the engine to transmission mounting bolts. Remove the ATF cooler lines from the transmission.
7. Remove the 8 bolts holding the drive plate to the torque converter. When all bolts are removed, position the drive plate so that the two brackets on the drive plate perimeter are horizontal.

NOTE
To best access the bolts, spin the drive plate until the bolts are accessible from above.

8. Carefully lift the engine straight off the transmission. See Fig. 22 above for reference.

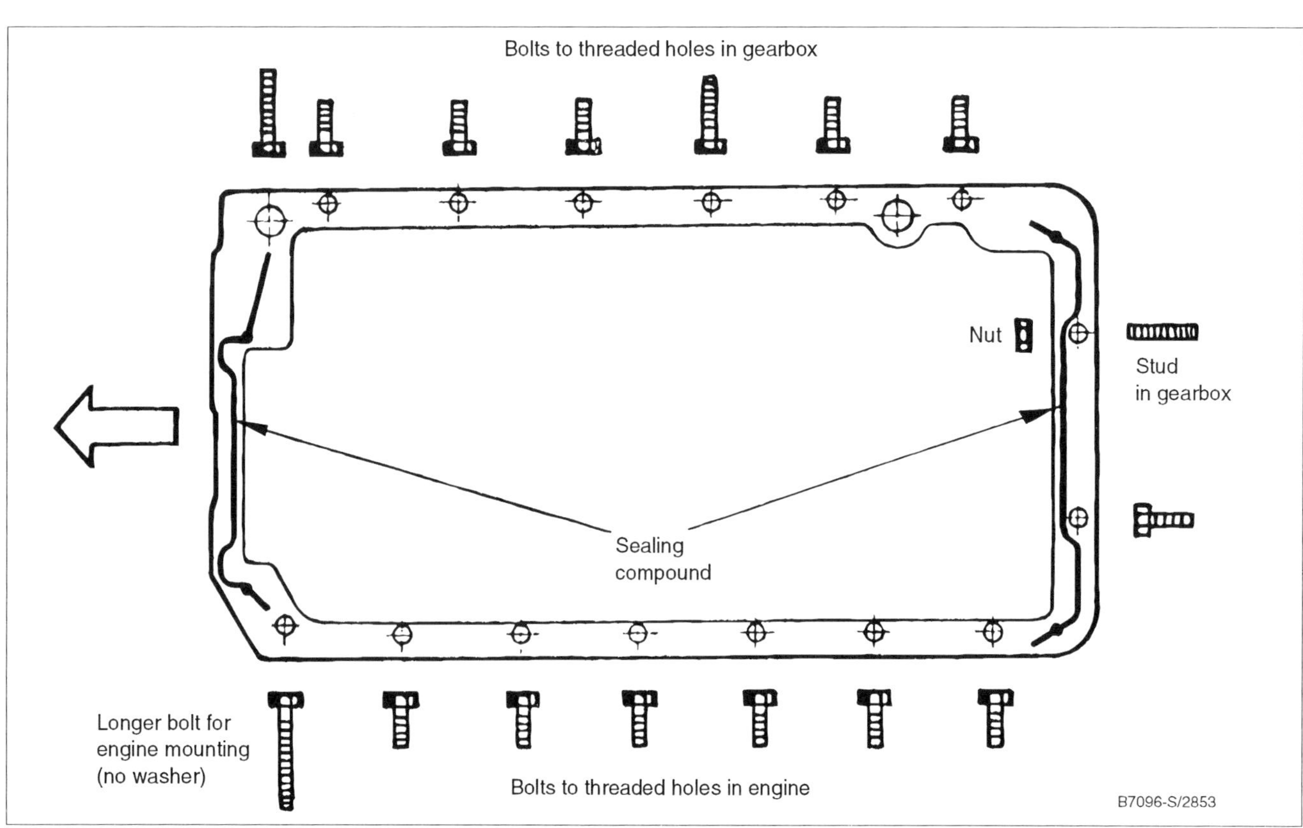

Fig. 25. Engine-to-transmission mounting bolt identification for manual transmission.

CAUTION

If the engine does not immediately lift off the transmission, do not attempt to pry them apart until making sure that all fasteners have been removed.

NOTE

Use Saab special tool 87 90 255 to support the torque converter once the engine is removed from the transmission. See Fig. 26. If the torque converter is left unsupported, the torque converter oil seal may be damaged. As an alternative, remove the torque converter and store it in its normally installed position.

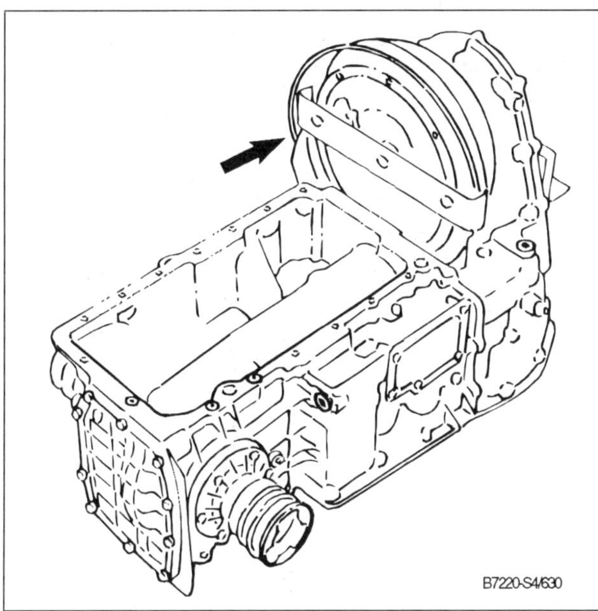

Fig. 26. Torque converter support bracket (arrow).

9. Remove all old traces of oil and dirt from the flanges.

NOTE

When cleaning the removed transmission, plug all of the openings shown in Fig. 27.

---

10. Before refitting the engine to the transmission, carefully inspect the drive plate for cracks. Make sure both mating surfaces are completely clean. Make sure the two brackets on the drive plate perimeter are horizontal.

11. Place a new gasket onto the transmission flange and apply a sealing compound (Permatex Ultra-blue) to the slots shown in Fig. 28.

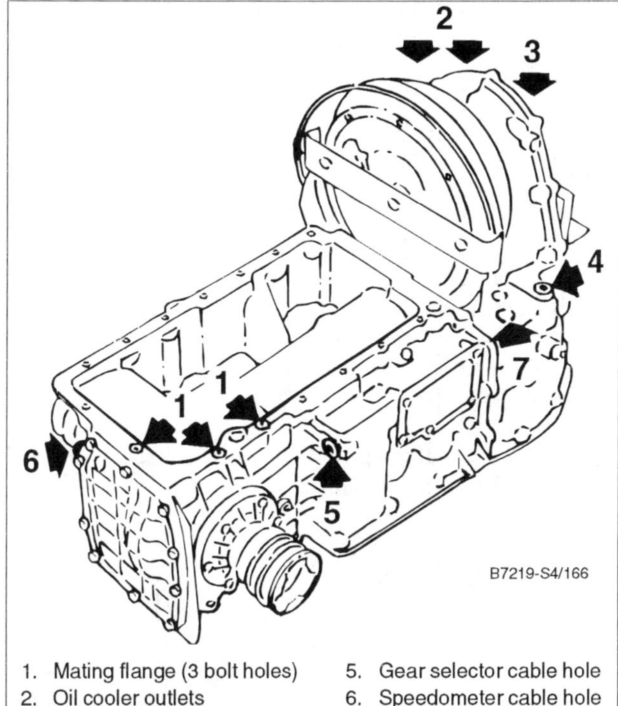

1. Mating flange (3 bolt holes)
2. Oil cooler outlets
3. Primary drive cover
4. Oil filler hole
5. Gear selector cable hole
6. Speedometer cable hole
7. Reverse gear switch hole

Fig. 27. Areas of automatic transmission which must be plugged prior to cleaning.

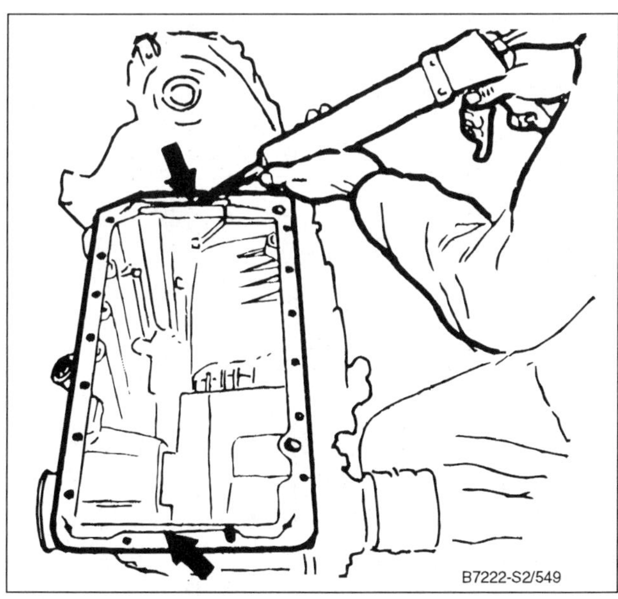

Fig. 28. Sealing compound being installed to slots (arrows) on transmission flange.

12. Apply a thread sealing compound (Loctite 45, Saab Part No. 45 3009081) to the three bolts holes shown in Fig. 29.

CAUTION

Saab part numbers are for reference only. Consult an authorized Saab dealer for the most up-to-date parts information.

---

13. Install the engine to the transmission. Take care not to damage the torque converter centering pin when lowering the engine onto the transmission. Tighten mounting bolts in stages.

The remainder of the procedure is the reverse of removal. Be sure to fill the engine with oil.

Tightening torques

- engine to transmission . . . . 25 Nm (18 ft-lb)
- all other fasteners
  - M5 bolt . . . . .5 Nm (44 in-lb)
  - M6 bolt . . . . .10 Nm (89 in-lb)
  - M8 bolt . . . . 20 Nm (15 ft-lb)
  - M10 bolt . . . . 40 Nm (30 ft-lb)

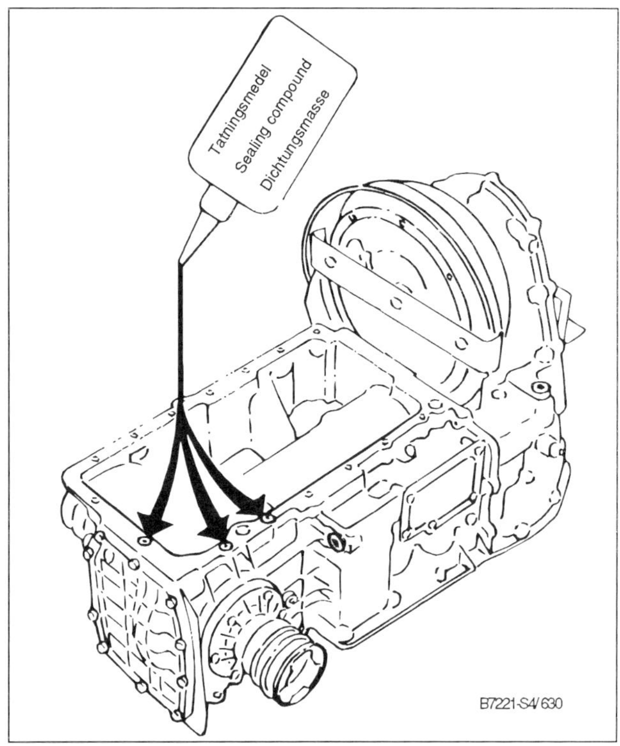

Fig. 29. Bolt holes in transmission case requiring thread sealer.

210 Engine Disassembly and Assembly

GENERAL

Fig. 1 shows the complete engine assembly. This repair group covers disassembly and assembly of the engine cylinder block only. Cylinder block reconditioning procedures and specifications can be found in **212 Pistons, Connecting Rods, Cylinder Bores**, and in **216 Crankshaft.**

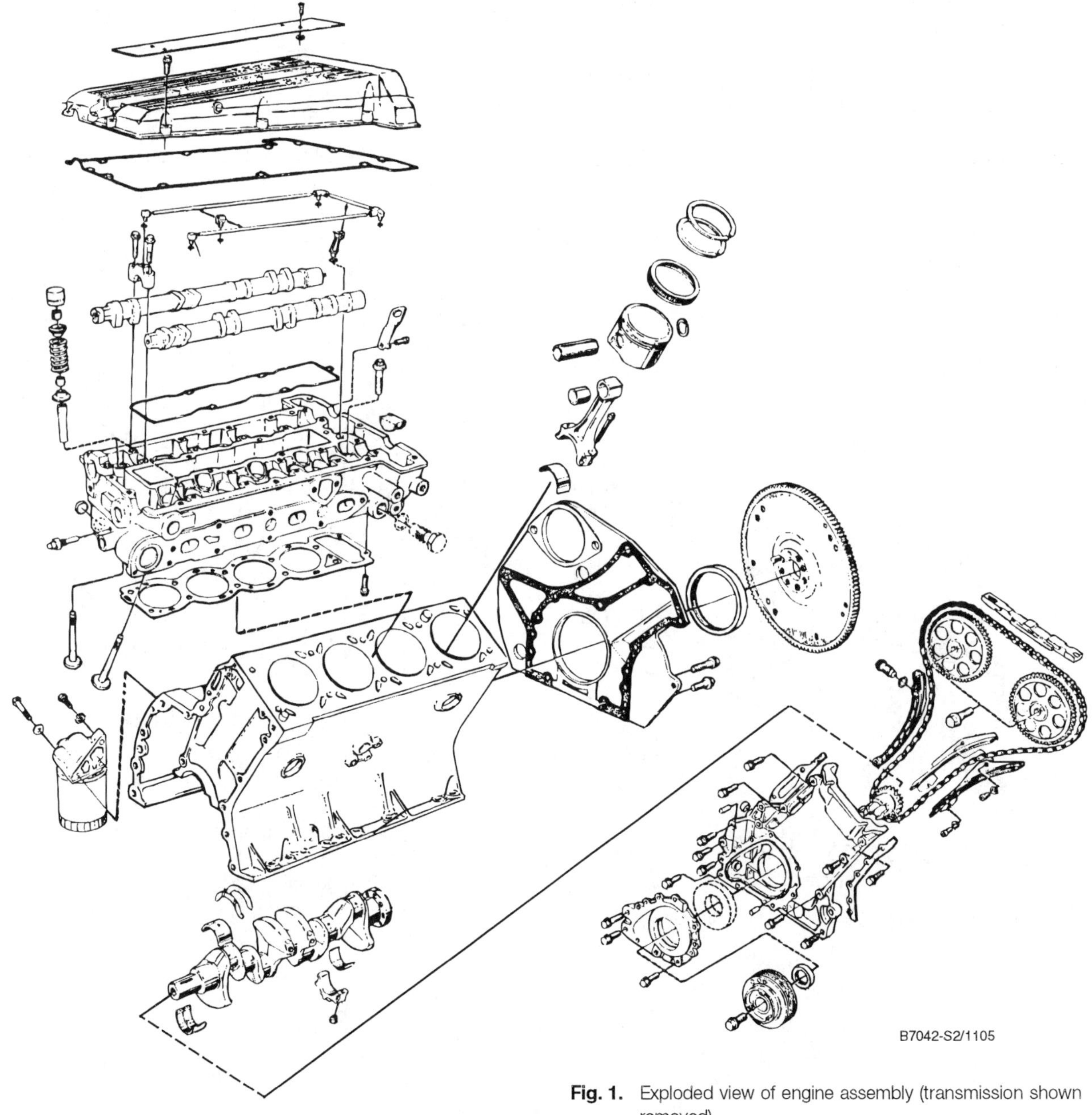

Fig. 1. Exploded view of engine assembly (transmission shown removed).

Disassembling and Assembling Cylinder Block

Disassembly and assembly procedures for the Saab cylinder block are similar to those of most other water-cooled engines.

Thoroughly mark the position and orientation of all parts as they are removed. Connecting rods, rod caps, rod bearings, pistons, main bearing caps and main bearings are assembled in an exact location and orientation. This "assembly code" is critical to proper engine operation if any of the parts are going to be reused.

To disassemble cylinder block

1. Remove the engine from the car and separate the transmission from the engine as described in **201 Engine Removal and Installation.**

2. Remove the cylinder head as described in **211 Cylinder Head Removal and Installation.**

3. Remove the plastic clutch cover from above the flywheel.

4. With the alternator V-belt installed and tensioned, loosen the bolts from the coolant pump pulley.

5. Remove the alternator V-belt.

6. Immobilize the flywheel with a holding fixture. See Fig. 2.

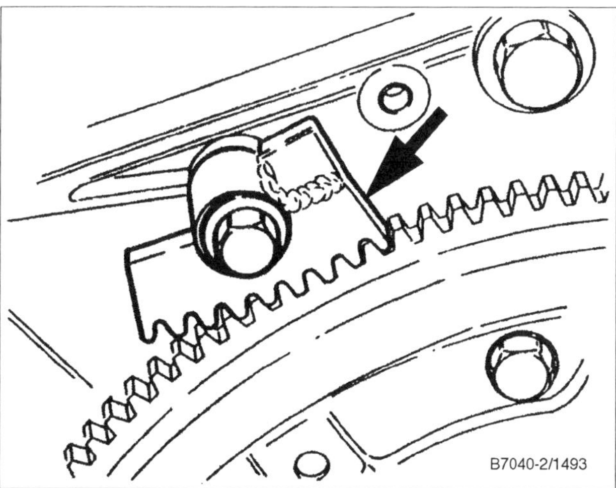

Fig. 2. Flywheel being immobilized using holding fixture (arrow).

7. Remove the center bolt from the crankshaft pulley. See Fig. 3. Remove the pulley from the crankshaft.

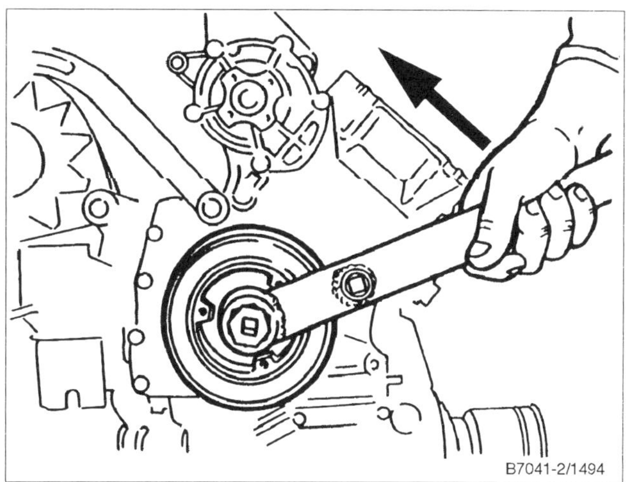

Fig. 3. Crankshaft pulley mounting bolt being removed.

8. Remove the oil pump mounting bolts and remove the pump from the timing chain cover. See Fig. 4.

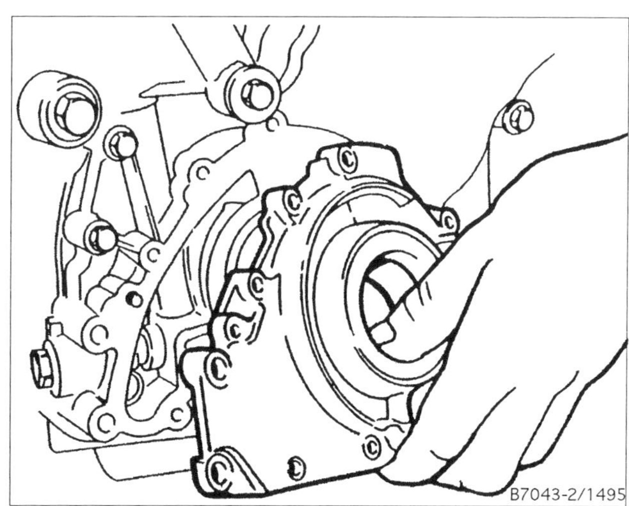

Fig. 4. Oil pump being removed from timing chain cover.

9. Disconnect the lower hose from the coolant pump.

10. Remove the alternator together with its stabilizer bar.

11. Remove the mounting bolts from the timing chain cover and remove the cover together with the water pump and hoses. See Fig. 5.

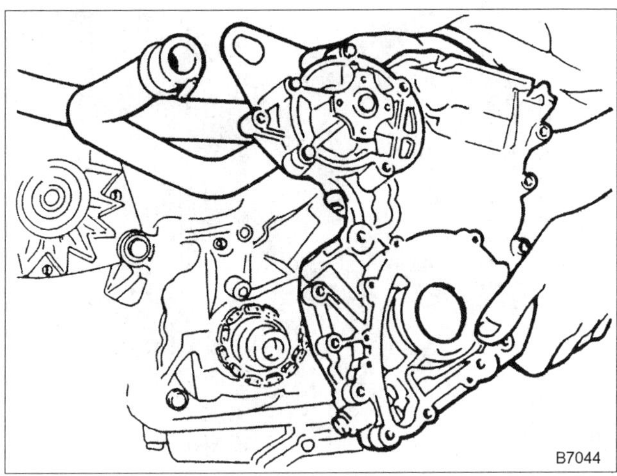

Fig. 5. Timing chain cover with coolant pump and hoses being removed.

12. Remove the pivoting timing chain guide. See Fig. 6.

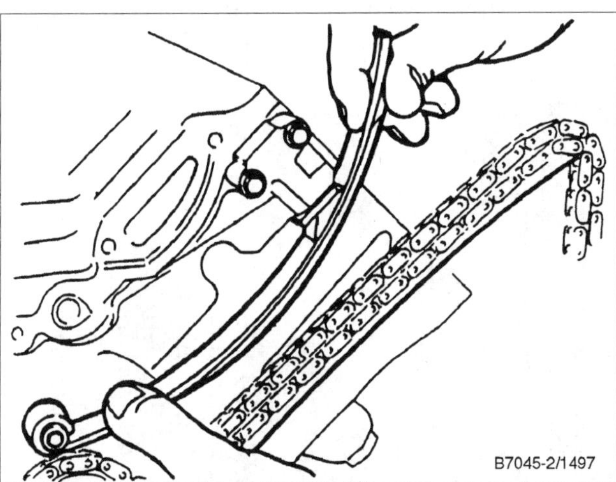

Fig. 6. Pivoting camshaft timing chain guide being removed.

13. Pull off the crankshaft sprocket with the timing chain. See Fig. 7. Remove the key from the keyway in the crankshaft.

14. Remove the fixed timing chain guide. See Fig. 8

15. Unscrew the oil filter and unbolt the oil filter housing from the cylinder block.

16. Mark the cylinder number on the top of each piston. Remove the piston and connecting rod assemblies.

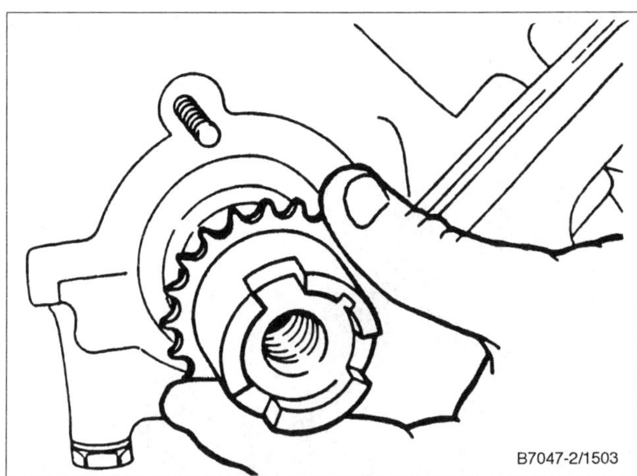

Fig. 7. Crankshaft sprocket being removed.

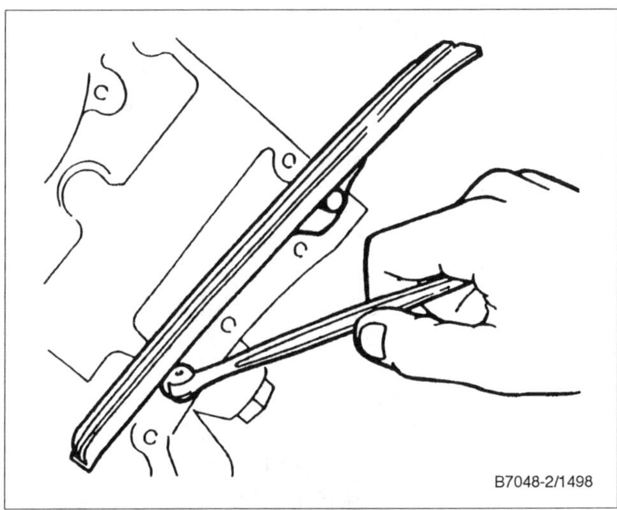

Fig. 8. Fixed timing chain guide being removed.

CAUTION

Before removing the pistons from the cylinders, remove any ridge or carbon deposits from the top of the cylinder. Install small lengths of rubber hose over the connecting rod studs to protect the cylinders during piston removal.

NOTE

Observe the markings on the connecting rod big-ends. Where necessary, mark all parts so that they can be reinstalled in their exact positions. This includes noting which bearing shells are in the upper positions and which ones are in the lower positions.

---

17. Turn the engine block on its end so that the flywheel is facing up and remove the flywheel. See Fig. 9.

Fig. 9. Flywheel being removed.

18. Remove the cylinder block end plate. See Fig. 10.

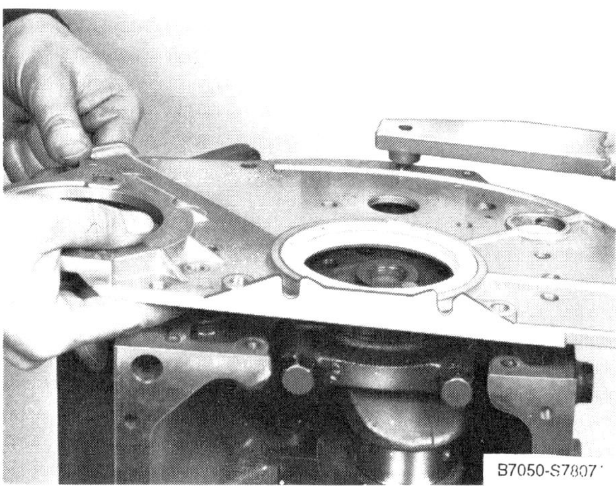

Fig. 10. Cylinder block end cover being removed.

19. Remove the crankshaft bearing caps and remove the crankshaft. See Fig. 11.

NOTE
Note the main bearing cap markings and locations for reinstallation.

To assemble cylinder block

NOTE
When reusing old parts, make sure that they are installed in their original positions.

Fig. 11. Crankshaft being removed.

1. Lubricate the bearing shell saddles and install the upper shells into position. Carefully install the crankshaft.

2. Fit the center thrust washers to the crankshaft. See Fig. 12. Check that the crankshaft end float is within specification as described in **216 Crankshaft.**

Fig. 12. Crankshaft thrust washer being installed.

3. Lubricate the lower bearing shells and install the shells and main bearing caps in their original locations.

Tightening torque
- main bearing caps to cylinder block . . . . 110 Nm (81 ft-lb)

NOTE
Note the markings on the bearing caps. See Fig. 13.

Fig. 13. Main bearing cap markings.

4. Apply a small amount of grease to hold the new end-plate gasket to the cylinder block. Install the plate, being careful not to damage the crankshaft oil seal. If necessary, trim the gasket at the transmission-to-engine flange. See Fig. 14.

CAUTION

- To prevent oil leaks, the crankshaft seal should be perfectly centered around the crankshaft . A special guide (Saab tool no. 83 92 540) fits over the crankshaft to center the end plate and seal. The tool also protects the crankshaft seal during the installation of the end plate.
- Do not use an adhesive sealer on the gasket.

NOTE

For procedures on replacing the crankshaft oil seal, see **216 Crankshaft.**

Tightening torque

- cylinder block end plate to engine (flywheel end) . . . . 20 Nm (15 ft-lb)

---

5. Install the flywheel using a sealant on the mounting bolts. Be sure the old bolts are cleaned before applying the fresh sealant.

Tightening torques

- flywheel to crankshaft
  17 mm bolt head . . . . 60 Nm (44 ft-lb)
  19 mm bolt head . . . . 85 Nm (63 ft-lb)

Fig. 14. Cylinder block end plate gasket being trimmed at transmission gasket surface.

6. Align the compression rings so that their end gaps are approximately aligned over the wrist pin. Make sure the double oil scraper ring joints do not align. See Fig. 15.

NOTE

When installing the second compression ring, make sure the **"TOP"** marking on the ring is facing up.

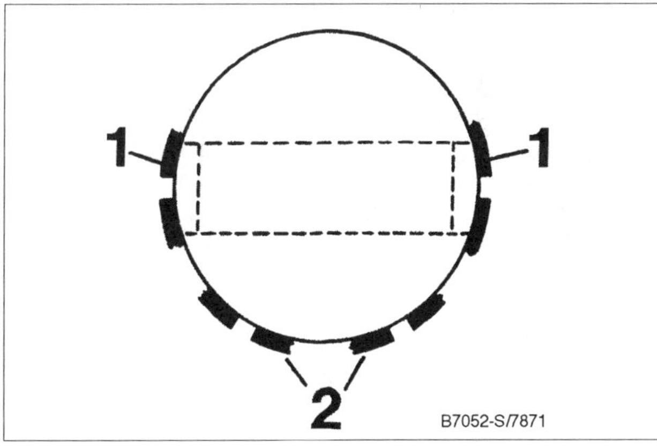

Fig. 15. Piston ring end gaps correctly aligned. Compression rings shown at **1** and double oil scraper ring shown at **2**.

7. Lightly lubricate the pistons and rings with engine oil. Install the pistons so that the notch in the top of the piston faces the camshaft timing chain and the numbers on the connecting rod big-end face the exhaust side of the engine. See Fig. 16. Install and tighten the connecting rod caps.

NOTE

Make sure the flange on the connecting rod cap nut is towards the rod cap, facing the piston.

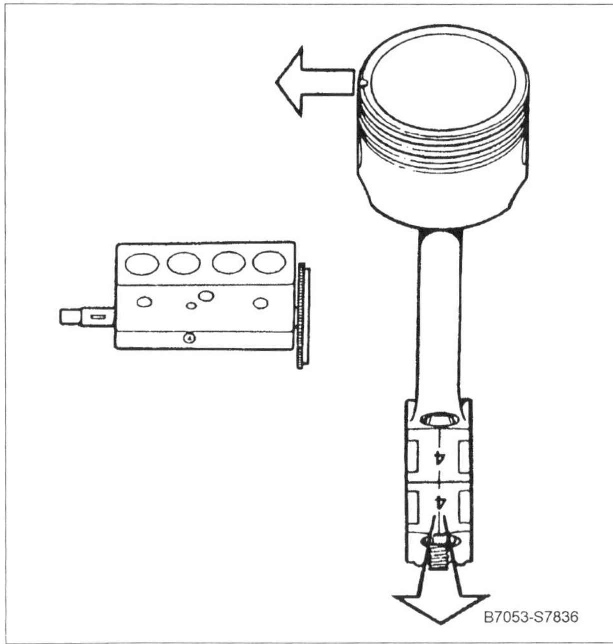

Fig. 16. Install piston so that top notch faces camshaft timing chain and connecting rod big-end numbers face the exhaust side of the block.

Tightening torque
- connecting rod cap to connecting rod. . . . . 55 Nm (41 ft-lb)

8. Install the timing chain sprocket and the timing chain guides. Hang the timing chain on the sprocket.

9. Install the timing chain cover using a new gasket. Do not use sealer on this gasket.

Tightening torque
- timing chain cover to engine block . . 20 Nm (15 ft-lb)

10. Install the oil pump using a new O-ring.

Tightening torque
- oil pump to timing chain cover . . . . . . 8 Nm (71 in-lb)

11. Using engine oil, prime the cavity between the oil filter housing and the oil pump. See Fig. 17. Then install the oil filter housing and a new oil filter.

Tightening torque
- oil filter to oil filter housing . . . . 10 Nm (89 in-lb)

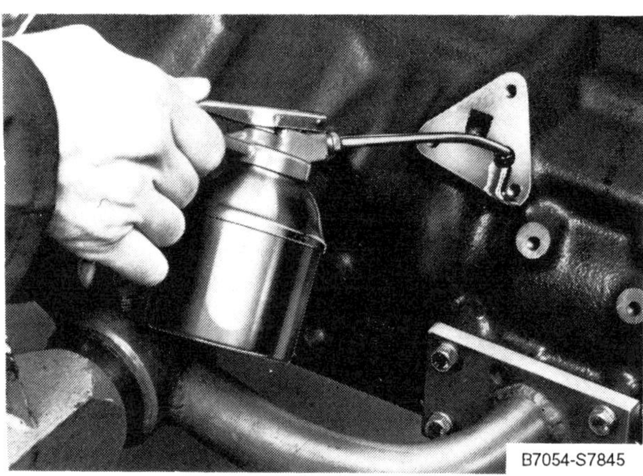

Fig. 17. Oil pump being primed through oil filter housing hole.

12. Install the crankshaft pulley with its key. While holding the flywheel stationary, tighten the mounting bolt.

Tightening torque
- crankshaft pulley to crankshaft
  1985-1990 . . . . 190 Nm (140 ft-lb)
  1991and later. . . . . 175 Nm (129 ft-lb)

13. The remainder of the assembly is the reverse of removal.

Tightening torques
- all other fasteners
  M5 bolt. . . . . 5 Nm (44 in-lb)
  M6 bolt. . . . . 10 Nm (89 in-lb)
  M8 bolt. . . . . 20 Nm (15 ft-lb)
  M10 bolt. . . . . 40 Nm (30 ft-lb)

211 Cylinder Head Removal and Installation

GENERAL

This section covers only cylinder head removal and installation. For complete cylinder head, camshaft, and valve train repair information, see **214 Cylinder Head and Valve Mechanism.** For camshaft timing chain repair information, see **215 Camshaft Timing Chain.**

CYLINDER HEAD REMOVAL AND INSTALLATION

To remove cylinder head

1. Raise the hood and remove the hood hinge mounting bolts. See Fig. 1. Carefully remove the hood from the car.

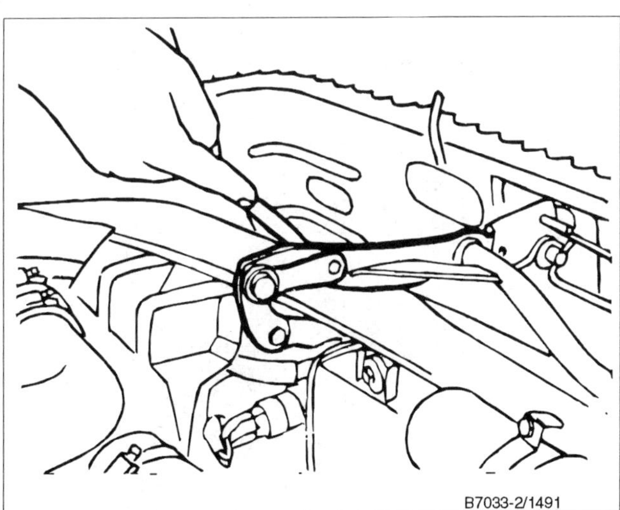

Fig. 1. Hood hinge mounting bolt being removed.

2. Disconnect the battery terminals and remove the battery from the car.

3. Drain the coolant from the radiator and from the engine block. See **261 Radiator and Cooling System.**

4. Remove the exhaust manifold.

5. If applicable, remove the turbocharger as described in **291 Turbocharger.**

6. Remove the air conditioning compressor belt and tensioning pulley.

7. Loosen the power steering pump pivot bolts. Remove the power steering pump V-belt and push the power steering pump out of the way.

8. Remove the center cover from above the spark plugs. Disconnect the spark wires from the spark plugs and remove the distributor cap with the spark plug wire assembly.

9. Remove the valve cover and the valve cover split rubber plugs as described in **214 Cylinder Head and Valve Mechanism.**

10. Remove the two bolts holding the timing chain cover to the bottom of cylinder head. See Fig. 2.

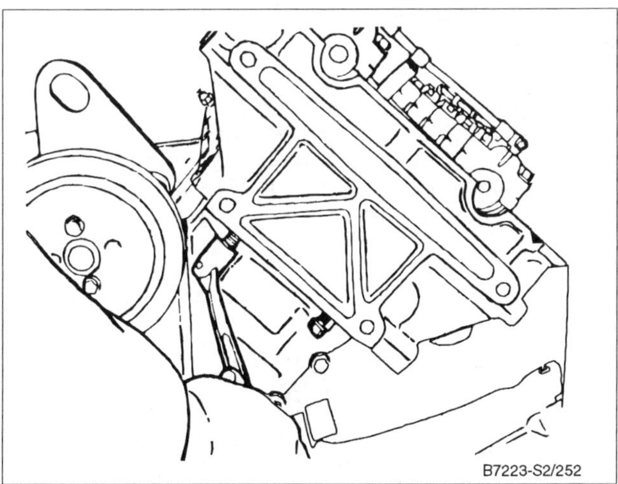

Fig. 2. Camshaft timing chain cover to cylinder head mounting bolt being removed.

11. Working from below, jack up the engine just enough to relieve the weight on the right-hand engine mount (exhaust side of engine). Then remove mounting bolts (and spacer sleeve) that are screwed into the cylinder head.

12. Disconnect the coolant hose from the thermostat housing.

13. Unbolt the fuel pressure regulator complete with bracket from the cylinder head. See Fig. 3. Do not disconnect fuel hoses.

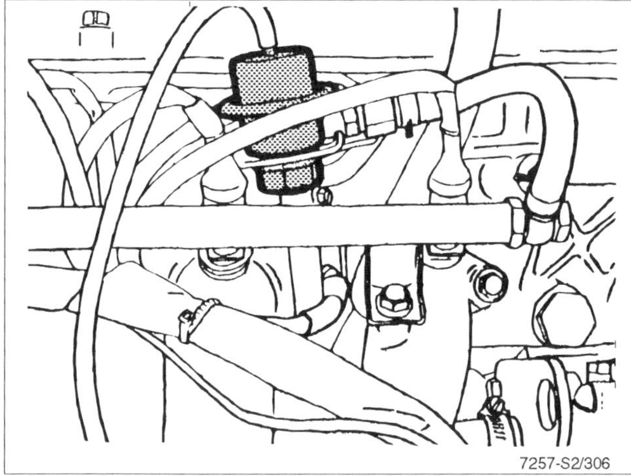

Fig. 3. Fuel pressure regulator.

14. Disconnect the fuel injection system ground wires from the cylinder head.

15. Unbolt the A/C bracket from the cylinder head.

16. Unbolt the intake manifold, complete with fuel injectors and fuel rail and set aside. See Fig. 4.

CAUTION
Cleanliness is essential when working with fuel injection components. Before removing the intake manifold, thoroughly clean the area around the injectors, the fuel rail, and the intake manifold. If possible, blow the area clean using compressed air.

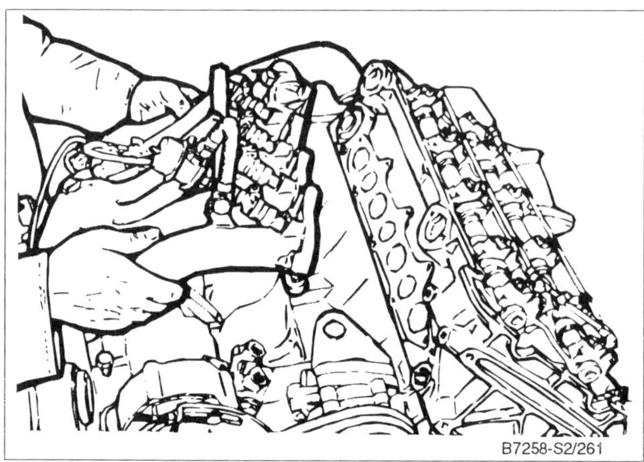

Fig. 4. Intake manifold with fuel injectors and fuel rail being removed.

17. Disconnect the wires from the temperature sensor.

18. Set the engine to TDC by rotating the crankshaft in normal engine rotation until the "0" mark on the flywheel is aligned with the timing mark on the end plate. Check that the timing marks on the camshaft are also aligned. See Fig. 5 and Fig. 6.

CAUTION
Do not turn the engine over using the camshafts. The camshafts are not designed to take this type of load. Use a wrench on the crankshaft pulley center bolt to turn the engine over.

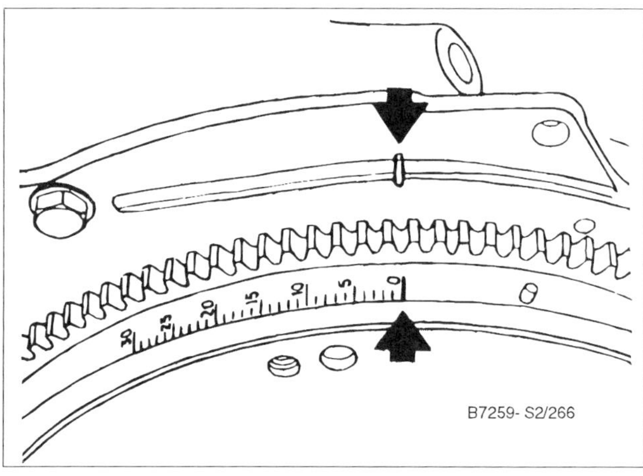

Fig. 5. Flywheel 0° TDC mark aligned with timing mark on engine end plate (arrows).

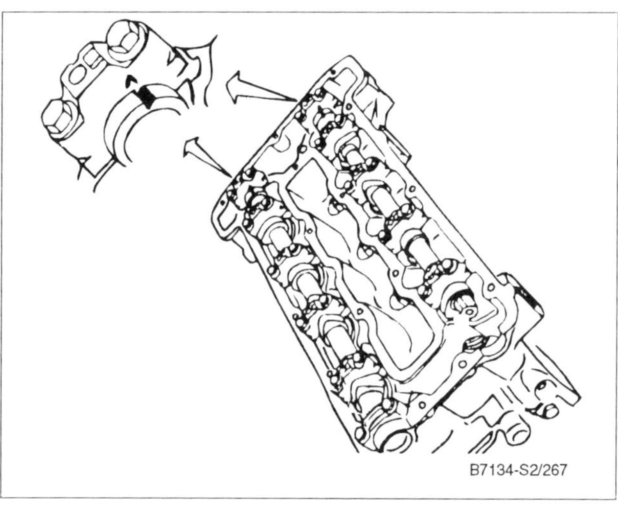

Fig. 6. Camshaft timing mark aligned with mark on camshaft bearing cap.

19. Loosen, but do not remove, the camshaft sprocket center mounting bolts. Hold the camshaft flats with an open-end wrench while loosening the bolts. See Fig. 7.

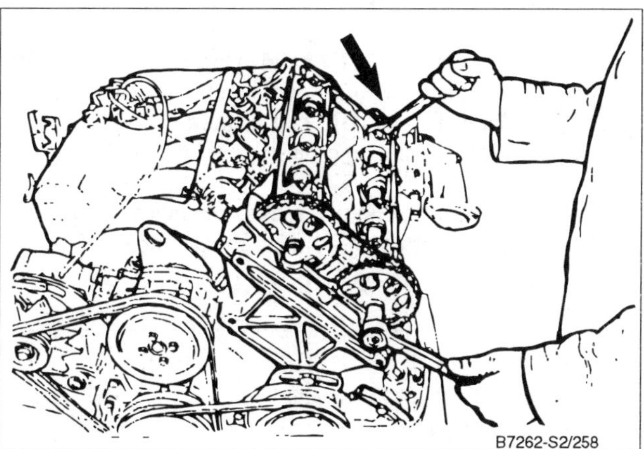

Fig. 7. Camshaft sprocket mounting bolt being loosened. Hold camshaft on flats (arrow) when loosening bolts.

20. Remove the camshaft timing chain tensioner. See Fig. 8.

Fig. 8. Camshaft timing chain tensioner being removed from side of cylinder head.

CAUTION
Do not rotate the engine if the camshaft timing chain tension is relieved. The pistons can hit the valves and damage them.

---

21. Remove the camshaft sprockets.

NOTE
Insert a stiff wire through the chain to prevent it from falling into the timing chain cover area.

---

22. Siphon off any excess oil from the inside of the cylinder head. Then remove the cylinder head bolts in stages, working towards the center of the head starting with the outer-most bolts first.

23. Insert a threaded guide pin (Saab tool no. 83 92 128) into one of the cylinder head bolt holes. Position the timing chain and its pivoting guide so that it does not interfere with the removal of the cylinder head. Carefully lift the cylinder head off, pivoting the head as it passes the timing chain guide. See Fig. 9.

NOTE
As an alternative to the special guide pin, a wooden dowel can be used. The guide pins are used to align the head during removal. If the guide pin or dowel is not used, there is risk of damaging the chain guide when the head is lifted off.

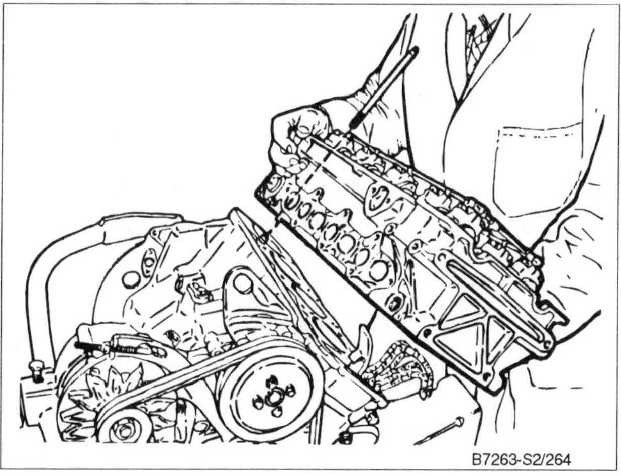

Fig. 9. Cylinder head being removed.

24. Place the cylinder head on wooden blocks to prevent damaging the open valves.

To install cylinder head

1. Check to make sure the camshafts and the crankshaft are correctly set to 0°TDC as shown above in Fig. 5 and Fig. 6.

2. Place a new cylinder head gasket onto the cylinder block.

3. Fit the guide pin (or dowel) to the cylinder block and position the timing chain and pivoting chain guide as shown in Fig. 10.

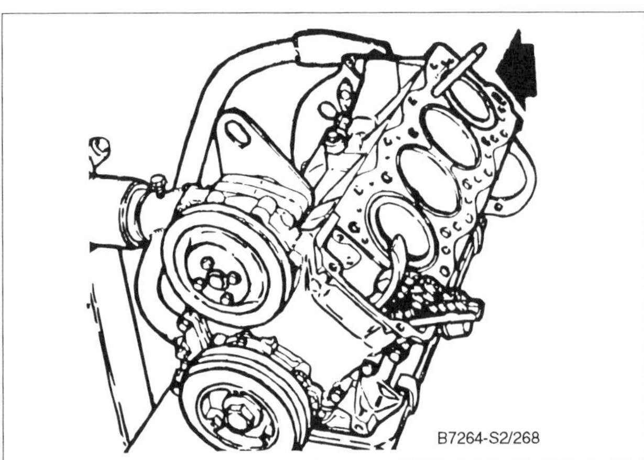

Fig. 10. Guide pin installed in cylinder block (arrow), and timing chain and chain guide correctly positioned for installation of cylinder head.

4. Slide the cylinder head into position, using the guide pin as a pivot when lowering the cylinder head over the chain guide. Install and torque the cylinder head bolts. See Fig. 11.

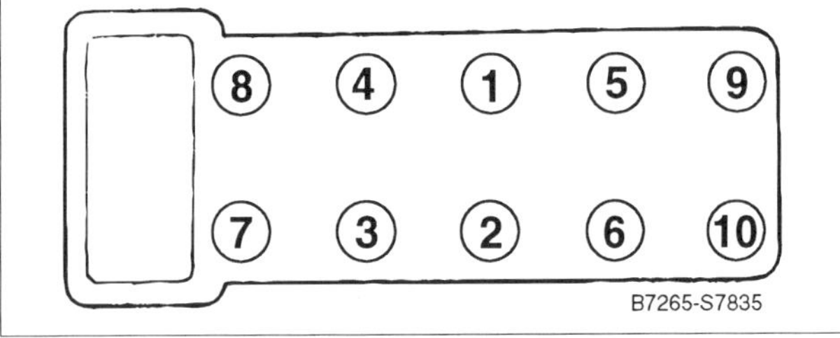

Fig. 11. Cylinder head bolt tightening sequence.

Tightening torques
- cylinder head to cylinder block
  stage 1 . . . . 60 Nm (44 ft-lb)
  stage 2 . . . . 80 Nm (59 ft-lb)
  plus and additional 90° (1/4 turn)

5. Install the two M8 bolts into the underside of the cylinder head as shown above in Fig. 2.

6. With all TDC (timing) marks aligned, install the exhaust-side camshaft sprocket, making sure there is no chain slack between the cam sprocket and crankshaft sprocket.

7. Install the intake-side camshaft sprocket, keeping the chain tight between the two sprockets. Hand tighten the sprocket mounting bolts. Install the timing chain tensioner.

Tightening torque
- timing chain tensioner
  to cylinder head . . . . 63 Nm (47 ft-lb)

8. Rotate the crankshaft by hand in the direction of normal engine rotation two full revolutions. Recheck that the TDC marks are all correctly aligned. If any faults are found reset the timing chain.

9. Tighten the camshaft sprocket mounting bolts while holding the camshafts stationary as shown earlier in Fig. 7.

Tightening torque
- camshaft sprocket to camshaft . . . . . 63 Nm (47 ft-lb)

10. Install the valve cover as described in **214 Cylinder Head and Valve Mechanism.**

11. Install the distributor cap, the spark plug wires, and the center cover above the spark plugs.

12. Using new nuts, install the exhaust manifold, and if applicable, the EGR pipe. Install the intake manifold.

Tightening torques
- exhaust manifold to cylinder head
  turbo engines. . . . . 25 Nm (18 ft-lb)
  all other engines . . . . 20 Nm (15 ft-lb)
- intake manifold to cylinder head . . . . 22 Nm (16 ft-lb)
- EGR valve to cylinder head . . . . 8 Nm (71 in. lb)

13. If applicable, install the turbocharger. Connect the turbo discharge pipe, the oil supply pipe and the oil return pipe.

14. The remainder of installation is the reverse of removal.

NOTE
Upon first start up, the hydraulic lifters will most likely be noisy. Avoid racing the engine above 3,000 rpm until the noise has dissipated.See **214 Cylinder Head and Valve Mechanism** for more information on hydraulic cam followers .

Tightening torques
- all other fasteners
  M5 bolt . . . . 5 Nm (44 in-lb)
  M6 bolt . . . . 10 Nm (89 in-lb)
  M8 bolt . . . . 20 Nm (15 ft-lb)
  M10 bolt . . . . 40 Nm (30 ft-lb)

212 Pistons, Connecting Rods, Cylinder Bores

TABLES

212

GENERAL

This repair group provides the specifications and special reconditioning information necessary to repair the Saab short block. The information contained here is intended to be used as a reconditioning guide for the professional or experienced automotive mechanic. Many of the operations described below require precision measuring equipment. If you lack the skills, tools, or a suitable workplace for reconditioning, we suggest you leave these repairs to an authorized Saab dealer or other qualified shop.

Be sure to carefully mark the position and orientation of all parts as they are removed. Connecting rods, rod caps, rod bearings, pistons, main bearing caps and main bearings are assembled in an exact location and orientation.

NOTE

Cylinder block disassembly and assembly is covered in **210 Engine Disassembly and Assembly.**

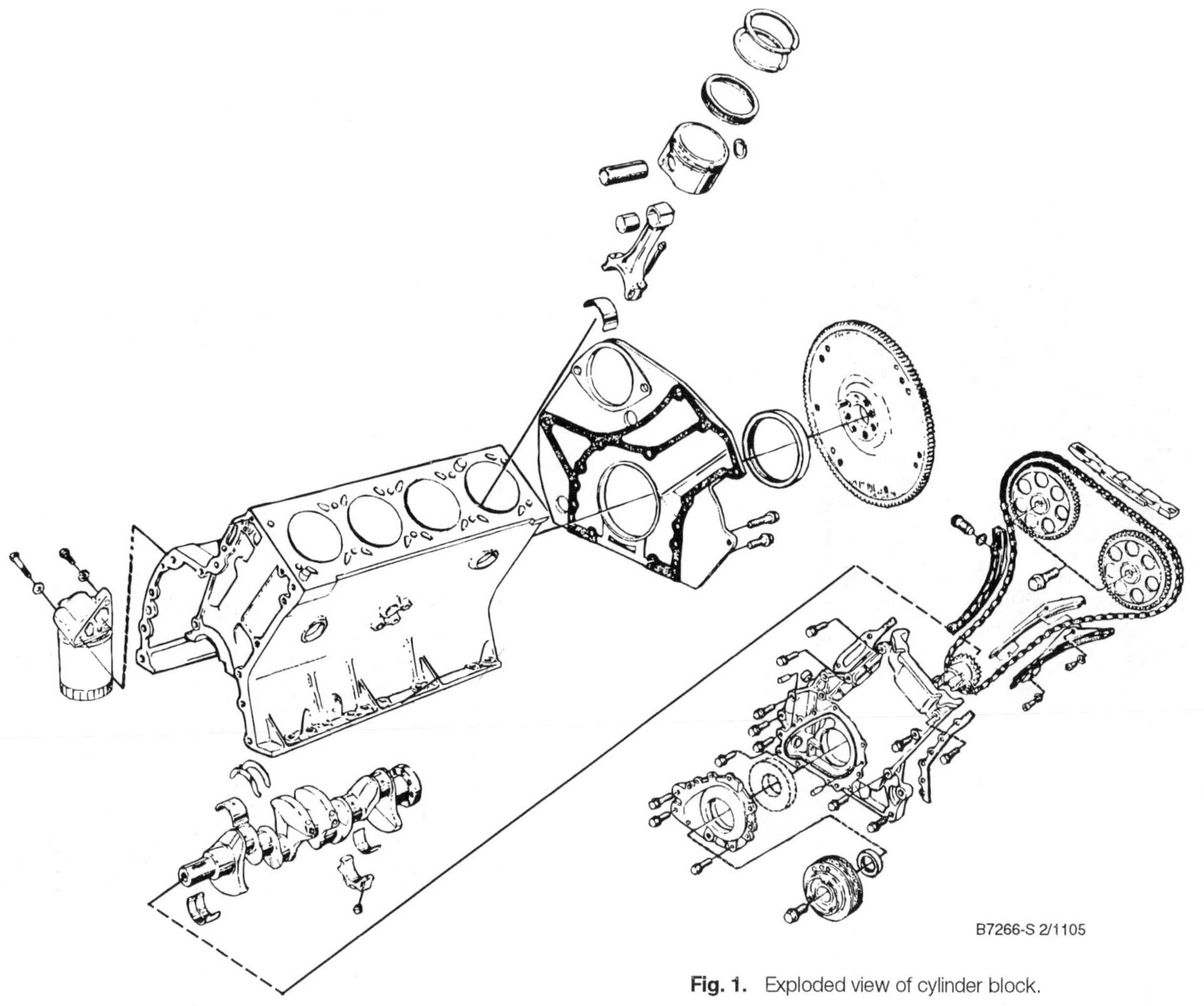

Fig. 1. Exploded view of cylinder block.

CYLINDER BLOCK AND PISTON RECONDITIONING

All of the disassembled parts should be thoroughly cleaned before inspection.

Connecting Rods and Pistons

If pistons, piston pins, piston rings, connecting rods, and bearings are to be reused, they should always be reinstalled in their exact positions. Used parts should never be interchanged between cylinders.

The piston pin should fit without any play. The fit can be quickly checked by pushing the pin through the rod by hand. There should be slight resistance as the pin moves through the rod. A more accurate check can be made using a micrometer.

Each connecting rod is matched to its cap and identified by a number. See Fig. 2. Connecting rods should be checked for bend, twist and bearing bore out-of-roundness using connecting rod alignment and measuring equipment.

CAUTION
The pistons, piston rings, and connecting rods must be installed according to their markings. See **210 Engine Disassembly and Assembly.**

Fig. 2. Connecting rod big-end and cap matching numbers. Always install connecting rod nuts with flange on nut facing piston.

Tightening torque
- connecting rod cap to connecting rod . . . . 55 Nm (41 ft-lb)

Piston pins, connecting rod bushings, and connecting rods are all available as individual replacement parts. The piston pin circlips should be replaced with new circlips any time they are removed. **Table a** lists connecting rod and piston pin specifications.

Table a. Connecting Rod and Piston Pin Specifications

Connecting rods	
big end diameter	56.000-56.019 mm (2.2047-2.2055 in.)
small end diameter, bushing installed	24.005-24.010 mm (0.9451-0.9453 in.)
big-end oil clearance	0.026-0.062 mm (0.0010-0.0024 in.)*
maximum permissible weight variation per set	9 g (0.32 oz.)
piston pin diameter	23.996-24.000 mm (0.9447-0.9449 in.)
Piston pin to connecting rod oil clearance	
B202 engine	0.005-0.014 mm (0.0002-0.0006 in.)
B212 engine	0.002-0.011 mm (0.00008-0.0004 in.)

* See **216 Crankshaft** for more information on connecting rod big-end clearances and bearing shell color codes.

Saab supplies pistons in size ranges or classifications. These are "A", "B" and "C." The cylinder bores and the pistons are individually coded. The piston codes are on the piston domes and the cylinder block codes are stamped into the cylinder block. See Fig. 3. The Saab block is originally fitted with either an "A" class piston or a "B" class piston, depending on the final size of the bore. It is possible to find both classes in one cylinder block. Other piston classes are available as standard and oversize replacements when servicing the engine.

Small amounts of wear in the cylinders can usually be corrected by installing a larger standard piston. If the cylinder is excessively worn, it may require boring to fit an oversized piston. Piston diameters and their corresponding classifications are listed in **0 TECHNICAL DATA.**

CAUTION
When replacing pistons, use only pistons from the same manufacturer. Saab engines can be fitted with pistons from one of three manufacturers—Mahle, KS (Karl Schmidt), or Hepolite. The manufacturer's stamp is found on the inside of the piston.

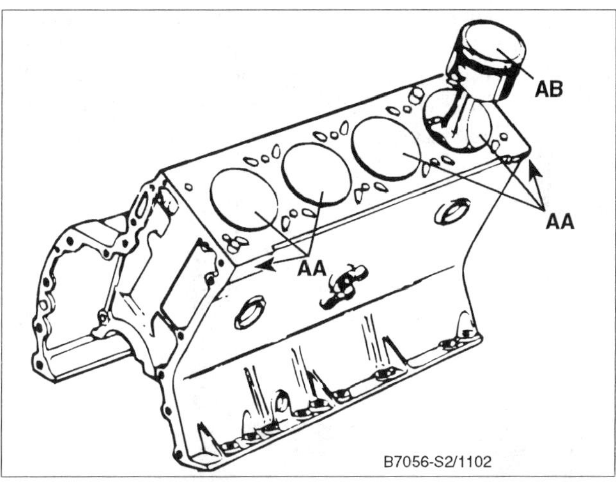

Fig. 3. Piston and cylinder classification locations.

NOTE

- The classifications for standard replacements pistons are AB, B, and C (B on B212 engines), with the C or B class pistons being the largest and most commonly used replacement piston on high-mileage engines.

- Standard piston class A is not available as a replacement part.

When measuring the piston diameter, make measurements at right angles (90°) to the wrist pin and at the height indicated in Fig. 4.

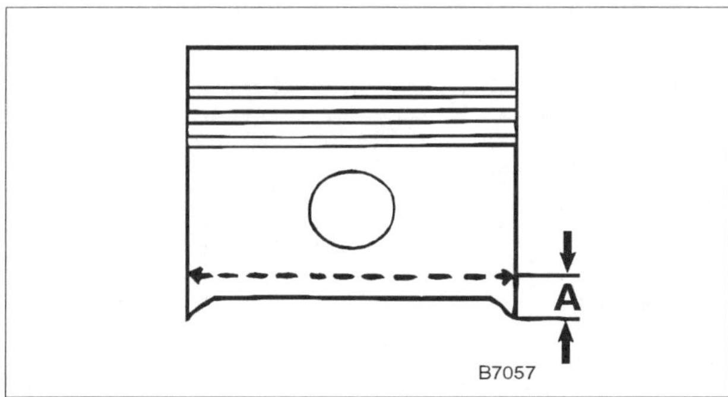

Fig. 4. Piston measuring point (**dotted line**) used when checking piston diameter. Distance varies depending on piston manu-

---

Piston measuring point (distance A)

- Manufacturer

Mahle	16 mm (5/8 in.)
KS	22 mm (7/8 in.)

Cylinders

When checking the piston-to-cylinder clearance, a set of feeler gauges with a 1/2 inch wide blade and a spring scale are needed to perform the procedure described below. A conventional piston-to-cylinder clearance measuring procedure can be used (micrometer and bore gauge), although the method described below is simpler and is the one recommended by Saab.

To check piston-to-cylinder clearance

1. Lightly oil the cylinder and the piston.

2. Insert a feeler gauge blade into the cylinder and then install the piston (piston rings removed) upside down into its matching cylinder. Select a feeler gauge that fits snugly.

NOTE

- The 1/2 in. wide feeler gauge blade is critical to accurate results.

- The feeler gauge blade should be inserted at right angles to the wrist pin.

---

3. Connect the spring scale to the feeler gauge and pull on the scale. See Fig. 5. Note the amount of force required to start the gauge moving out of the cylinder.

NOTE

Repeat the above step at several depths in the cylinder.

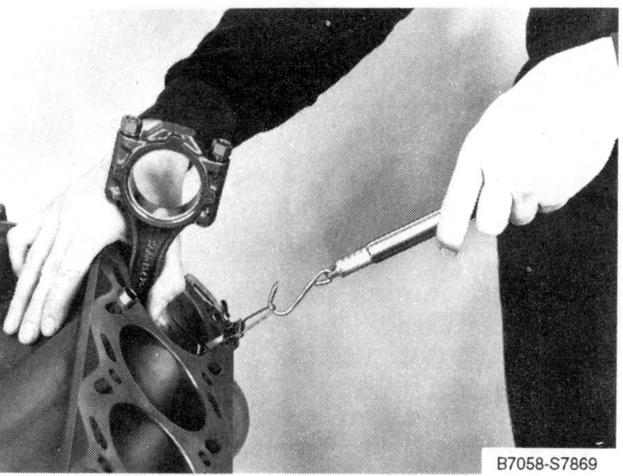

Fig. 5. Piston-to-cylinder clearance being checked using spring scale and feeler gauge with 1/2 inch blade.

4. Continue to try different feeler gauges until the pulling force is within the specified limits listed below.

Correct spring scale force
- 8-12 N (1.7-2.6 lb-ft)

CAUTION
When replacing pistons, do not mix pistons from different manufacturers. Pistons can be individually replaced, although they must be from the same manufacturer.

NOTE
- The thickness of the correct feeler gauge equals the piston-to-cylinder clearance. Piston-to-cylinder clearances vary depending on the piston manufacturer and piston/cylinder classifications. See **Table b**.
- If the piston-to-cylinder clearance is excessive, the piston should be replaced with a larger standard piston. Excessively worn cylinders can be bored to accept oversized pistons. See **0 TECHNICAL DATA** for piston classifications and diameters.

Piston Rings

Check piston ring end gaps, ring side clearances in the piston, and ring thicknesses. Piston ring end gaps are checked with the piston rings inserted one at a time into the cylinders. See Fig. 6. Use an inverted piston to position the rings squarely in the bore. Be sure to check the end gap at the bottom of the piston's travel when checking rings in a worn cylinder. Piston ring specifications are listed in **Table c**. The end gap should be checked after the final cylinder hone, if applicable.

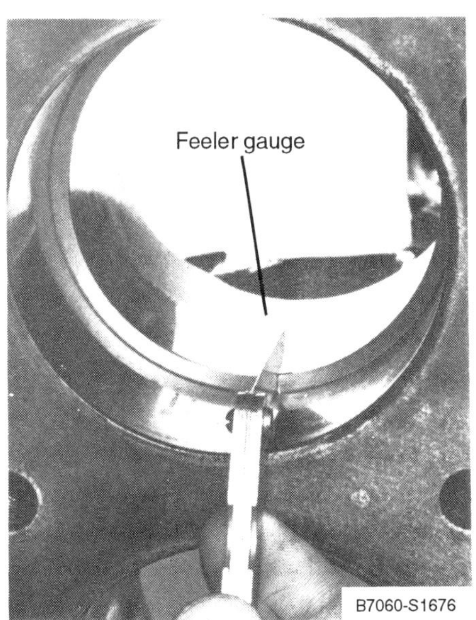

Fig. 6. Piston ring end gap being checked in cylinder block using feeler gauge.

Table b. Piston-to-Cylinder Clearances

Piston/cylinder classification	Non-turbo (KS)	Turbo	Non-turbo (Hepolite)
B202 engine (2.0 L)			
A/A	0.012-0.032 mm	0.030-0.050 mm	0.015-0.033 mm
AB/A	0.004-0.022 mm	0.022-0.040 mm	0.009-0.025 mm
AB/B	0.014-0.032 mm	0.032-0.050 mm	0.019-0.035 mm
B/A	—	0.014-0.032 mm	0.001-0.019 mm
B/B	0.006-0.024 mm	0.024-0.042 mm	0.011-0.029 mm
C/B	—	0.008-0.034 mm	—
B212 engine (2.1 L)			
A/A	—	—	0.008-0.028 mm
B/B	—	—	0.009-0.027 mm
B+/B+	—	—	0.009-0.027 mm

Table c. Piston Ring Specifications

	Top compression ring	Second compression ring	Oil scraper ring
end gap	0.35-0.55 mm (0.0138-0.0217 in.)	0.30-0.45 mm (0.0118-0.0177 in.)	0.38-1.40 mm (0.0150-0.0551 in.)*
width (thickness)	1.73-1.75 mm (0.0681-0.0689 in.)	1.98-1.99 mm (0.0780-0.0783 in.)	2.63-2.73 mm (0.1035-0.1075 in.)**
side clearance in piston groove	0.05-0.09 mm (0.0020-0.0035 in.)	0.04-0.07 mm (0.0016-0.0028 in.)	—

*Applies to segment part of ring
**Oil scraper ring segment width (thickness): 0.58-0.64 mm (0.022-0.025 in.)

When installing the rings, install the second compression ring so that the word "TOP" found on the ring faces up. See Fig. 7. Make sure the ring end gaps are offset as shown in Fig. 8. Lightly coat the cylinders and the rings with engine oil before installation.

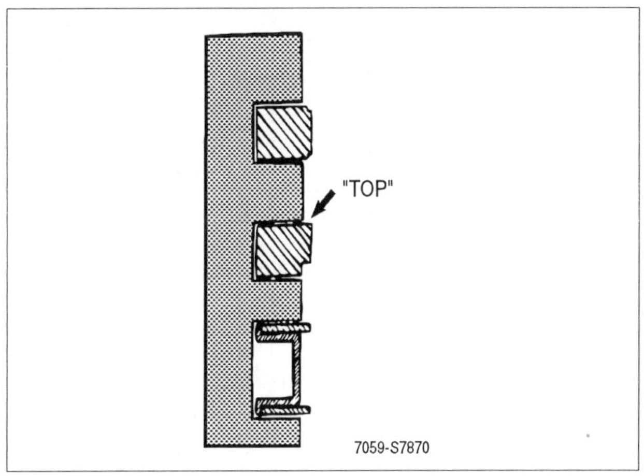

Fig. 7. "TOP" marking on second compression ring correctly installed.

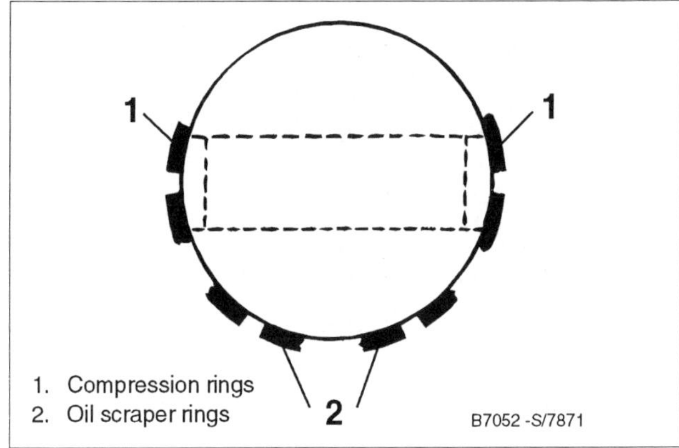

Fig. 8. Position compression ring end gaps 180° apart and directly above piston pin. Position scraper ring end gaps evenly around piston and not in line with each other.

214 Cylinder Head and Valve Mechanism

GENERAL

Some special tools may be required to disassemble and repair the valve mechanism owing to the cylinder head design. Read the procedures carefully before starting the job to determine what tools and equipment will be needed.

HYDRAULIC CAM FOLLOWERS

The valve gear mechanism uses hydraulic cam followers to keep the valve clearances within a limited working range of 2.055 mm (0.081 in.). See Fig. 1. The cam followers are sealed units and require no maintenance or adjustment.

Under some circumstances, such as removal and installation of the cylinder head, the cam followers may become noisy. Hydraulic cam follower noise usually makes a tapping or chattering sound. In most instances, this is considered normal as long as the noise goes away after a few minutes (maximum of 30 minutes). If the noise does not go away, either the follower is faulty, the oil pressure to the follower is too low, or there is trapped air in the system. Some of the common conditions that can cause follower noise are listed below.

1. Starting the engine after an oil change. If the noise was not present before the oil change, it should go away as soon as the oil pressure is restored.

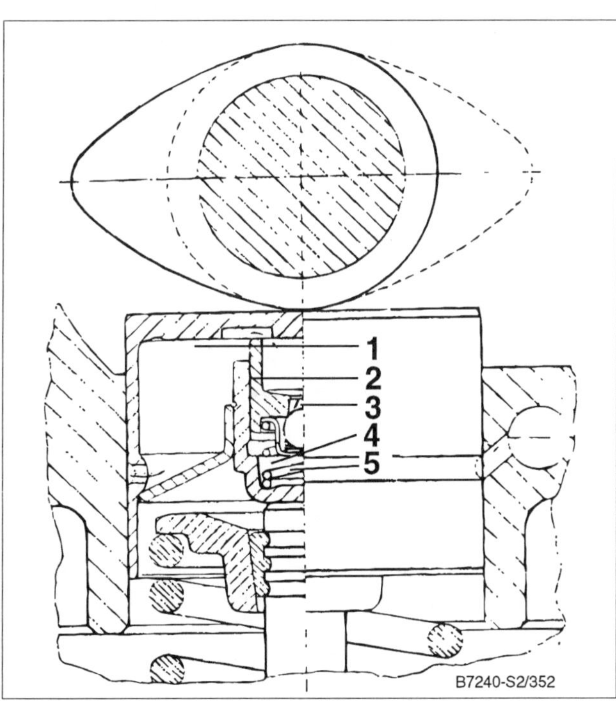

Fig. 1. Cutaway of hydraulic cam follower. Each cam follower consists of two adjacent storage chambers (**1**), a leakage passage (**2**), a check valve (**3**), a high pressure chamber (**4**), and a spring (**5**).

2. Starting a cold engine or starting an engine that has been sitting for long periods. This noise is normal and should disappear as soon as the oil reaches normal operating pressure.

3. After doing work that required cranking the engine by hand or by the starter motor. This can cause the oil in the follower to be forced out. Again, the noise should go away as soon as the oil pressure is restored. Under severe conditions where the follower has been totally drained, it may take as long as 30 minutes at engine speeds between 2,000 and 3,000 rpm to fully expel the air from the follower.

CAUTION

When trying to restore oil pressure to a hydraulic lifter, do not raise the engine speed above 3,000 rpm, as cam follower damage may result.

---

4. After installing a new replacement cam follower. The oil in a new follower may drain out if the follower is incorrectly stored. This situation is the same as the drained follower described above.

5. After a short period of idling (engine hot). Run the engine at 1,500 rpm or above. The noise should disappear. The noise is due to low oil pressure in the hydraulic cam followers when the engine is idling. Check the external oil feed pipe connectors and O-rings in the top of the cylinder head, where applicable.

NOTE

On cylinder heads used on mid-1988 and later models, the external supply pipes were discontinued owing to a new cylinder head design. The oil to the followers is now supplied via internal oil passages.

---

6. Only at high engine speeds. Noise goes away at idle. This is due to excessive amounts of air in the oil at high engine speeds. The intake of air into the lubrication system is most likely caused by a leak on the suction side of the oil pump. Check the oil pump's suction pipe O-ring and the suction pipe itself for damage.

NOTE

The oil pump suction pipe is in the engine oil sump of the transmission. To reach the suction pipe, the engine and transmission assembly needs to be removed and the engine separated from the transmission. See **201 Engine Removal and Installation.**

---

7. Noise at all times, regardless of engine speed or temperature. A noisy follower at all times usually means that the follower is faulty and should be replaced.

NOTE

On cylinder heads introduced on mid-1988 models, with internal oil passages, it is possible for air to become trapped in the system, causing cam follower noise. If more than one follower is exhibiting noise, try bleeding the lubrication system before checking and/or replacing noisy cam followers as described below.

Checking and Replacing Hydraulic Cam Followers

To check for a faulty cam follower, run the engine briefly to build up oil pressure. Then turn the engine off and remove the valve cover as described below under **Valve Mechanism.** Using a wooden stick, press down on the top of the follower. If the follower feels spongy or can be pressed down at all, it is most likely faulty and should be replaced. A faulty cam follower can be easily removed after removing the camshaft as described below. Use a magnetic tool to remove the cam followers.

NOTE

- Keep in mind that a damaged or poorly sealed oil passageway to the follower may be the cause of the noise rather than the follower itself.

- Do not mix up cam followers between cylinders. Used cam followers should always be installed in their original positions.

- Be sure to inspect the cam follower lobe for scoring or wear when replacing a faulty lifter. Camshaft specifications can found below under **Valve Mechanism Reconditioning.**

Bleeding Air Trapped in Cylinder Head (from Mid-1988 models—engine no. J082586—and later)

The cylinder head introduced on mid-1988 and later models uses small drilled oil passages to supply oil to the camshaft and cam followers. In some cases, it is possible for air to become trapped due to the tight tolerances of the passages. If more than one follower is noisy even after running the engine for more than a half-hour, try bleeding the lubrication system as described below.

NOTE

- On earlier cylinder heads (up to engine no. J082585), oil to the followers is supplied via oil pipes. Trapped air has not been a problem on cylinder heads with external oil pipes.
- See **100 Fundamentals for the Do-it-yourself Owner** for engine number location.

To bleed lubrication system

1. Remove the valve cover as described below in **Valve Mechanism**.
2. Loosen (three or four turns) the black bolt on the no. 5 intake camshaft bearing cap. See Fig. 2.

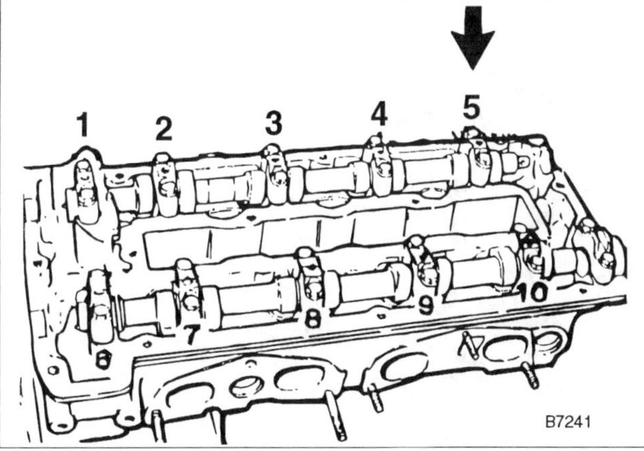

Fig. 2. Black bolt on no. 5 intake camshaft bearing cap (arrow).

3. Install the valve cover using at least one top bolt and one bottom bolt.

NOTE

Place some clean shop towels in the spark plug recesses to catch any spilled oil.

---

4. Disable the ignition by removing the harness connector from the EZK amplifier (normally-aspirated models) or the ignition control unit (turbo models).

NOTE

The EZK amplifier and the ignition control unit are mounted on the left-hand (driver's) side fender. See **340 Ignition System** for exact component location.

---

5. Make sure the car is in neutral. Then crank the starter motor for 15 seconds. Wait about 30 seconds. Repeat this procedure two or three times.
6. Remove the valve cover and inspect the loosened camshaft bearing cap bolt. There should be evidence that oil has been forced passed the bolt. Tighten the bolt.

Tightening torque

- camshaft bearing cap to cylinder head. . . . . 15 Nm (11 ft-lb)

---

7. Remove the shop towels from the spark plug area and clean up any spilled oil.
8. Thoroughly clean the valve cover gasket surface and reinstall the valve cover using a high-temperature silicone sealer as described below in **Valve Mechanism**.
9. Start the engine. The noise should go away within a few minutes.

NOTE

If the cam follower noise does not go away, it is most likely faulty and should be replaced as described earlier.

Valve Mechanism

Fig. 3 is an exploded view of the valve mechanism and cylinder head assembly.

To remove and install valve cover

1. Remove the two screws and center cover from above the spark plugs. See Fig. 4.

2. Remove the spark plug wires from the spark plugs and remove the wires with the grommet from the valve cover.

3. Remove the outer and inner valve cover mounting bolts and remove the cover and two cover gaskets.

4. Thoroughly clean the gasket surfaces of the cover and cylinder head. Install the new gaskets to the cylinder head. Then apply a 1/8 in. bead of high-temperature silicone sealer (Bostik Silicone 2680 or equivalent) at the three split plugs and above the distributor. See Fig. 5.

5. The remainder of installation is the reverse of removal. Tighten the mounting bolts in stages until the final torque is reached.

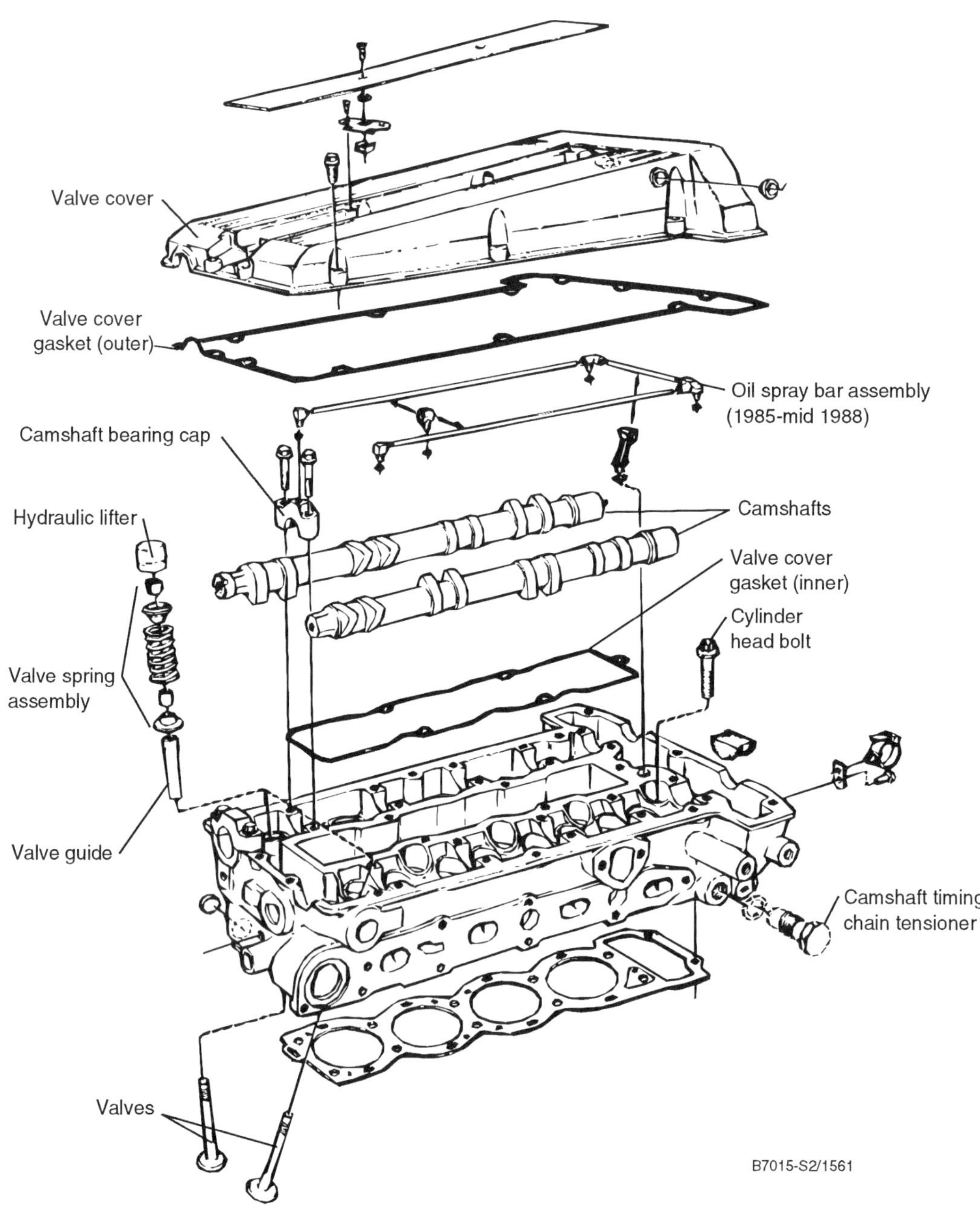

Fig. 3. Exploded view of valve mechanism and cylinder head.

Fig. 4. Center spark plug cover being removed.

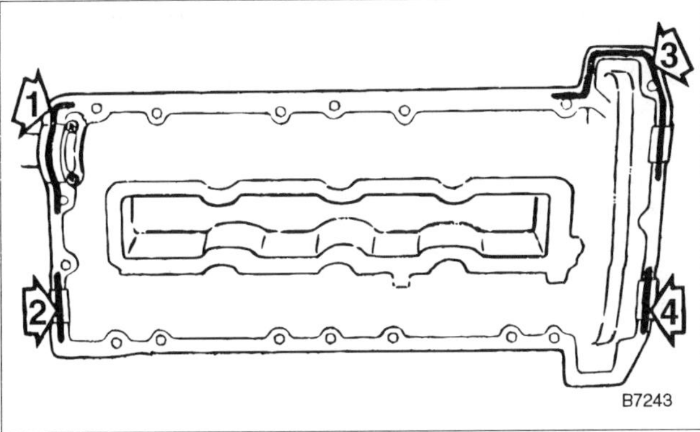

Fig. 5. Areas of valve cover gasket requiring high-temperature silicone sealer.

Tightening Torque
- valve cover to cylinder head . . . . 15 Nm (11 ft-lb)

To remove and install camshafts (cylinder head installed)

1. Remove the valve cover as described above.

2. Set the engine to TDC by rotating the crankshaft in normal engine rotation until the "0°" mark on the flywheel is aligned with the timing mark on the end plate. See Fig. 6.

NOTE
Check also that the marks on the camshafts are aligned with their matching marks on the bearing caps. See Fig. 7. If the marks are not aligned, turn the engine over an additional 360° (1 revolution).

CAUTION
If the camshaft timing marks shown below are not exactly aligned, the timing chain or one of the sprockets may be severely worn or the timing chain may have jumped out of position. See **215 Camshaft Timing Chain.** for additional information.

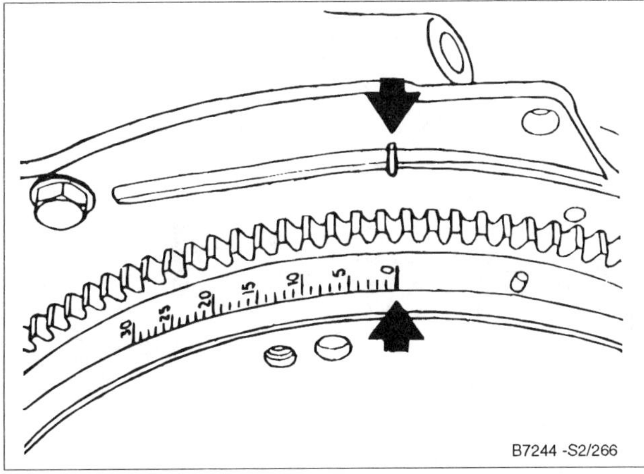

Fig. 6. Flywheel 0° TDC mark aligned with timing mark on engine end plate (arrows).

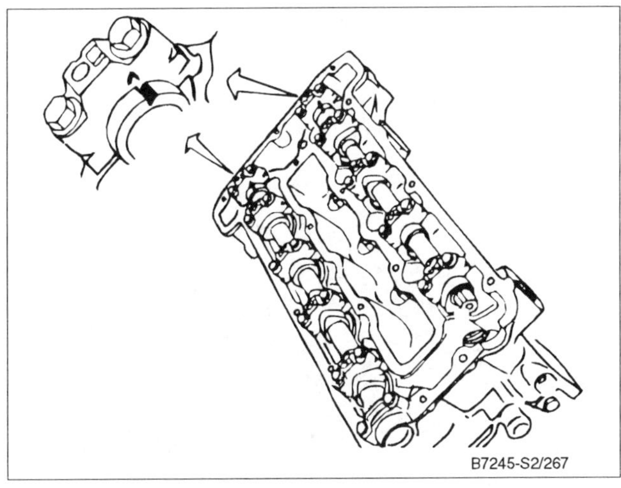

Fig. 7. Camshaft timing mark aligned with mark on camshaft bearing cap.

3. Remove the ignition distributor as described in **340 Ignition System.**

4. Remove the external oil supply pipes from the cylinder head, if applicable. See Fig. 8

CAUTION
Do not twist the pipes when removing them. This may damage the sealing surfaces between the pipes and the fittings.

NOTE
Beginning in mid-1988, a new cylinder head was used and the external oil supply pipes were discontinued.

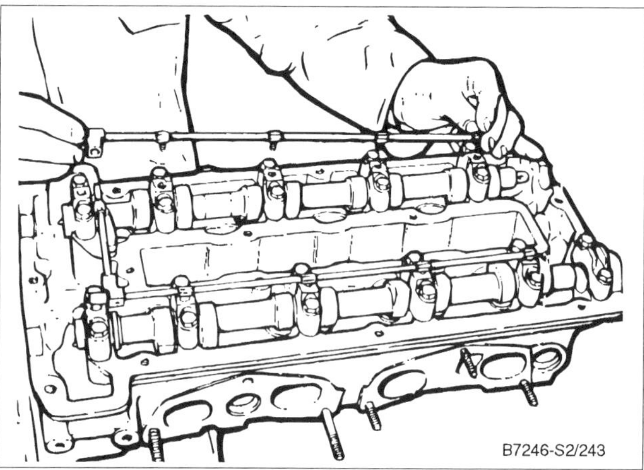

Fig. 8. Oil supply pipes for hydraulic cam followers being removed on mid-1988 and earlier cars.

5. Working from the side of the cylinder head, remove the camshaft timing chain tensioner. See Fig. 9.

Fig. 9. Camshaft timing chain tensioner being removed.

6. Carefully unbolt the camshaft bearing caps evenly until all valve spring pressure is relieved. Remove the camshaft by lifting the chain off the sprocket.

CAUTION
Do not rotate the engine if the camshaft timing chain is removed from either camshaft. The pistons can hit the valves and damage them.

NOTE
If removing both camshafts, insert a stiff wire through the chain to prevent it from falling into the timing chain cover area.

Installation is the reverse of removal. If removed, be sure to refit the hydraulic cam followers in their original positions. Make sure the flywheel is set at the TDC mark (shown in Fig. 6 above). Install the camshafts such that the timing marks are correctly aligned (shown in Fig. 7 above) before tightening the camshaft bearing caps. When installing the camshaft bearing caps, make sure all numbers on the caps align with their numbers on the cylinder head, if applicable. Install the black camshaft bearing cap bolts on the spark plug side of the cap. See Fig. 10. Make sure the oil spray bar is correctly aligned with the bar's fittings (see Fig. 22 given later).

CAUTION
The black camshaft bearing cap bolts are drilled to provide oil passages to the hydraulic cam followers and must always be installed on the spark plug side of the cap..

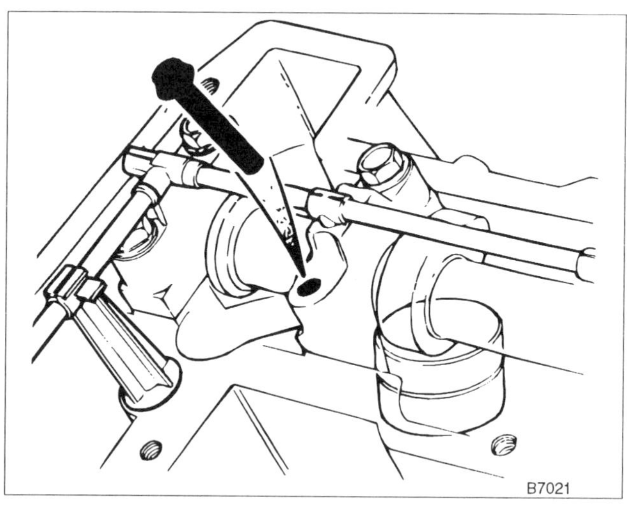

Fig. 10. Special black camshaft bearing cap bolts must be installed on spark plug side of cap.

NOTE
Bearing caps marked with numbers 1 through 5 are used on the intake camshaft and 6 through 10 are used on the exhaust camshaft.

Make sure all of the timing chain slack is on the tensioner side of the chain and install the chain tensioner. Turn the engine over several revolutions in the direction of normal rotation and bring it back to TDC. Double check all timing marks. If necessary, remove the tensioner and reposition the chain on the sprockets. Install the valve cover using new gaskets and sealer as described earlier. Install the distributor and ignition wires as described in **340 Ignition System.**

CAUTION
Correct camshaft timing is critical. If the timing chain is off by as little as two teeth on the sprocket, the pistons can contact the valves. Always check and recheck camshaft timing by turning the engine over by hand.

Tightening Torques
- camshaft bearing caps to cylinder head . . . . 15 Nm (11 ft-lb)
- camshaft timing chain tensioner to timing case . . . . 63 Nm (46 ft-lb)
- valve cover to cylinder head . . . . 15 Nm (11 ft-lb)

To replace valve stem oil seals (cylinder head installed)

The procedure below covers valve stem oil seal replacement with the cylinder head installed, using Saab special tools and a source of compressed air. The oil seals can also be replaced as part of the disassembly/assembly procedure described later under this repair group.

1. Set the engine to TDC and remove the camshafts as described earlier.

2. Using a magnetic tool, extract the cam followers. Label each follower so that they can be reinstalled in their original positions. See Fig. 11

CAUTION
The cam follower bores create a sealing surface for the cam followers. These surfaces must not be scratched or scored. Special plastic protector sleeves are available from an authorized Saab dealer (special tool no. 83 93 746). See Fig. 12.

3. Remove a spark plug from the cylinder head. Thread an appropriate adapter into the spark plug hole and connect the compressed air line to the adapter. Raise the air pressure in the cylinder.

Fig. 11. Cam follower being removed from cylinder head.

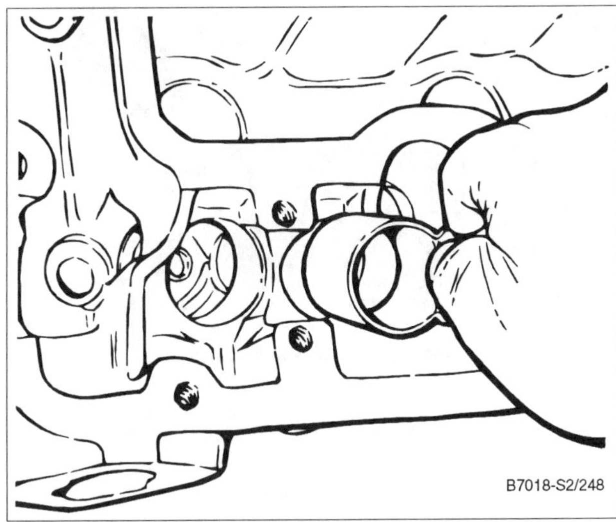

Fig. 12. Plastic sleeves being installed in cylinder head to protect cam follower bores.

NOTE
The spark plug hole adapter is available under Saab special tool no. 83 92 326.

4. Place Saab special tool 83 94 181 on top of the valve spring retainer. See Fig. 13.

5. Firmly tap the tool so that the valve spring keepers come free and follow the tool out. See Fig. 14.

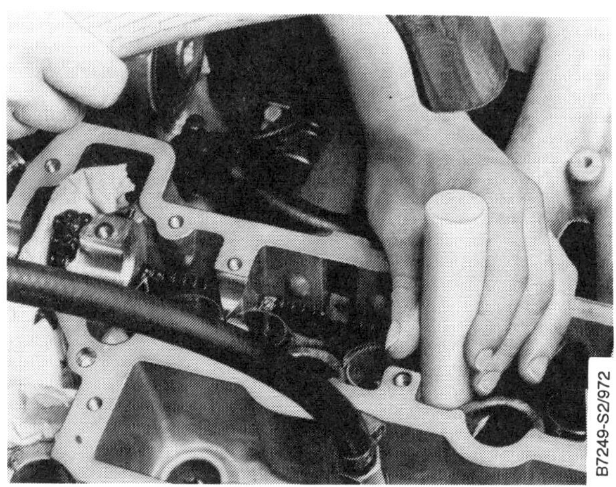

Fig. 13. Special Saab tool installed on top of valve spring retainer.

Fig. 14. Removed valve spring keepers in special tool.

6. Lift out the valve spring retainer and the spring. Then using valve stem oil seal removal pliers, remove the seal. See Fig. 15.

7. Using Saab special tool 83 93 803, insert the new valve stem oil seal into the tool. See Fig. 16.

8. Fit the seal into position and gently tap on the tool until the seal is firmly seated. See Fig. 17.

9. Install the spring and the spring retainer. Fit the valve keepers into position on the valve spring retainer.

10. Place Saab special tools 83 94 181 and 83 94 207 onto the valve spring retainer and tap the tool firmly to seat the keepers in the keeper grooves. See Fig. 18.

11. Repeat the above procedures for the remaining valve stem oil seals.

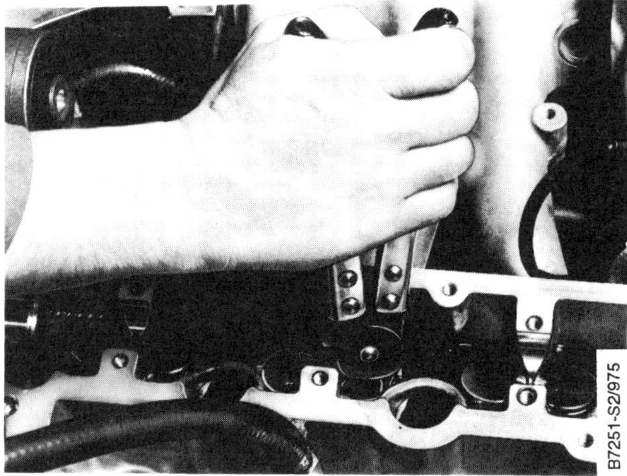

Fig. 15. Valve stem oil seal removed with special pliers.

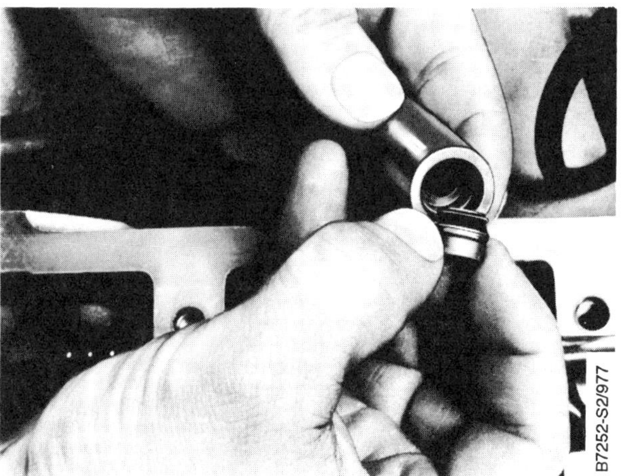

Fig. 16. Valve stem oil seal being installed into special tool.

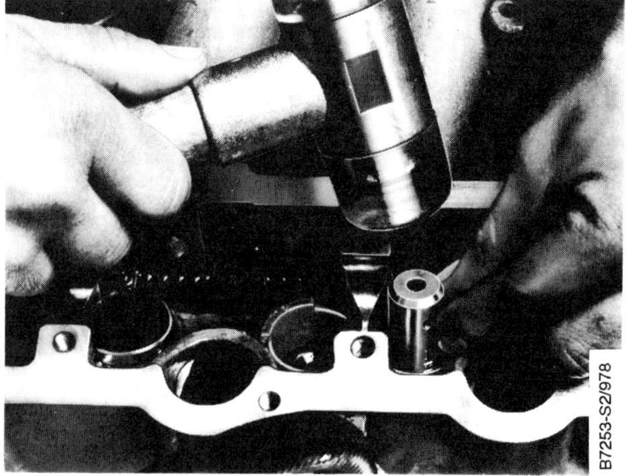

Fig. 17. Valve stem oil seal being installed on valve guide.

Fig. 18. Hammer and special tools being used to install valve spring keepers.

12. Remove the plastic sleeves and fit the cam followers into their original positions. Install the camshafts and valve cover as described above.

To disassemble valve mechanism (cylinder head removed)

NOTE

Cylinder head removal and installation is covered under **211 Cylinder Head Removal and Installation.**

---

1. Remove the ignition distributor as described in **340 Ignition System.**

2. Remove the intake and exhaust manifolds from the cylinder head.

3. If applicable, pull the oil spray bar assembly from the top of the cylinder head.

CAUTION

Do not twist the spray bars during removal. This can cause damage to the mating surfaces between the bars and the fittings.

---

4. Remove the camshaft bearing caps. Label each cap so that they can be reinstalled in their original positions. Remove the camshafts.

5. Using a magnetic tool, extract the cam followers. Label each follower so that they can be reinstalled in their original positions.

CAUTION

The cam follower bores create a sealing surface for the cam followers. These surfaces must not be scratched or scored. Special plastic protector sleeves are available from an authorized Saab dealer (special tool no. 83 93 746). See Fig. 12 given earlier.

---

6. Remove the valves, the valve spring retainers, the valve springs, and the spring seats. Label each complete assembly as it is removed.

NOTE

A valve spring compressor adaptor or a special valve spring compressor is needed to depress the valve springs. Saab special valve spring compressor (Saab tool no. 83 93 761 or KD tool no. 308) and special anvil (tool no. 83 93 779) are shown below in Fig. 19.

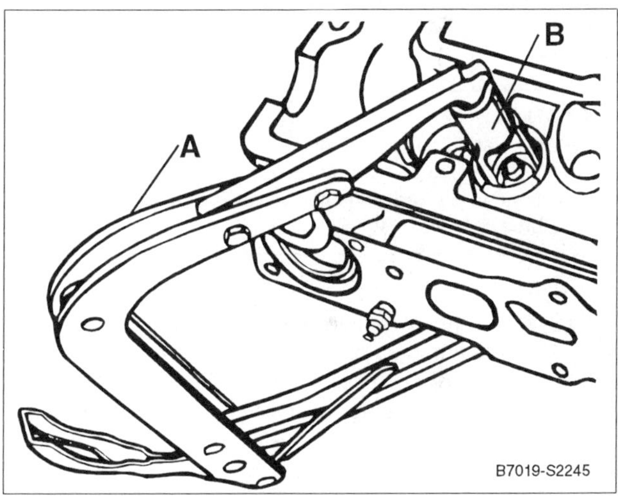

Fig. 19. Special valve spring compressor (**A**) and anvil (**B**) being used to remove valve.

WARNING

The valve springs are under considerable pressure. Use extreme care when removing the valves. Wear hand and eye protection.

---

7. Remove the valve stem oils seals using valve stem oil seal removal pliers. See Fig. 20.

Cylinder head assembly is the reverse of disassambly. Prior to installation, inspect all components for wear as described below. Be sure all parts are installed in their original positions. Lubricate the camshaft, the valve stems, and the valve stem oil seals prior to installation. Always use new valve

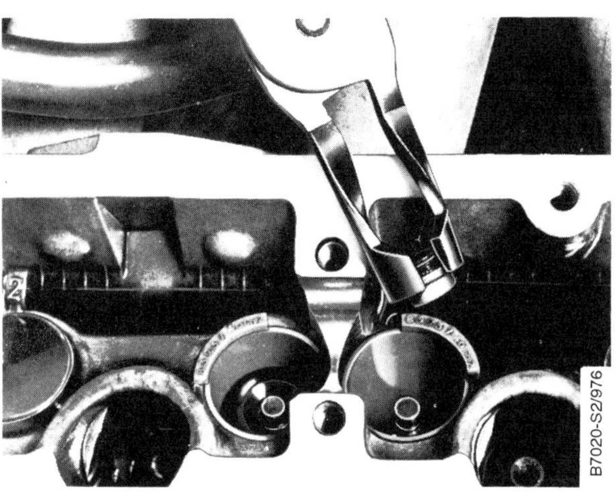

Fig. 20. Valve stem oil seals being removed using special pliers.

stem oil seals, tapping them in using an appropriate drift and a plastic hammer. Be sure to install the lower valve spring seat before installing the valve stem oil seals.

CAUTION

When installing the camshafts, place the cylinder head on wooden blocks to prevent damaging the valves as the camshaft bearing caps are tightened down. Tighten all caps evenly in three or four stages.

Always refit the cam followers in their original positions. Make sure the numbers on the camshaft bearing caps align with their numbers on the cylinder head, if applicable. Install the black camshaft bearing cap bolts on the spark plug side of the cap.

CAUTION

The black camshaft bearing cap bolts must always be fitted to the spark plug side of the bearing cap. These bolts are drilled to provide oil passages to the hydraulic cam followers. See Fig. 21.

NOTE

Bearing caps marked with numbers 1 through 5 are used on the intake camshaft and 6 through 10 are used on the exhaust camshaft.

If applicable, replace any worn or faulty O-rings for the oil spray bar fittings. To ensure proper lubrication, make sure the holes in the spray bars align with the holes in the fittings. See Fig. 22.

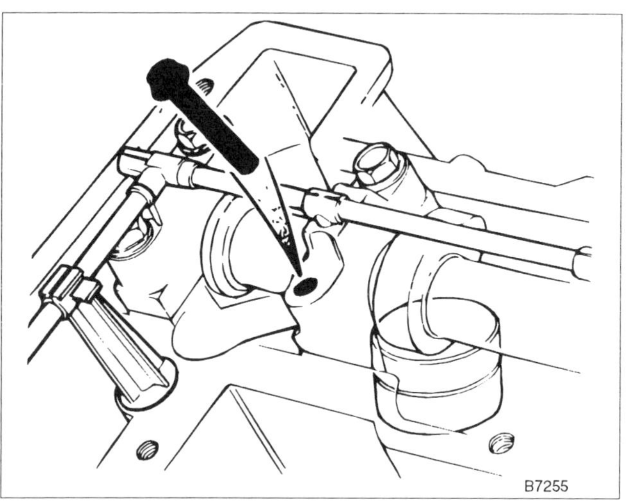

Fig. 21. Black camshaft bearing cap bolts are specially drilled and must always be installed on the spark plug side of the cap.

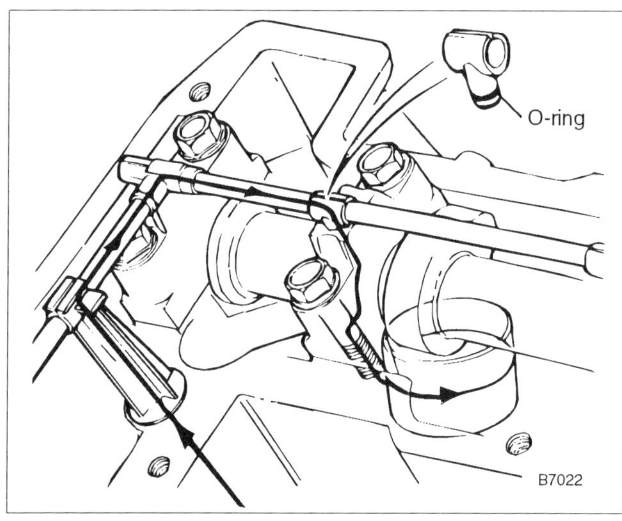

Fig. 22. Oil spray bar fittings correctly installed for proper lubrication to the camshafts and cam followers.

Tightening Torques

- camshaft bearing caps
  to cylinder head . . . . 15 Nm (11 ft-lb)
- spark plugs to cylinder head . . . . 28 Nm (21 ft-lb)
- camshaft sprocket to camshaft . . . . . 63 Nm (46 ft-lb)
- intake manifold to cylinder head . . . . 18 Nm (13 ft-lb)
- exhaust manifold to cylinder head
  turbo models . . . . 25 Nm (18 ft-lb)
  normally-aspirated models . . . . 20 Nm (15 ft-lb)
- timing chain cover
  to cylinder head . . . . 20 Nm (15 ft-lb)
- valve cover to cylinder head . . . . 15 Nm (11 ft-lb)
- ignition distributor to cylinder head . . 20 Nm (15 ft-lb)

VALVE MECHANISM RECONDITIONING

For anyone with the proper equipment and basic experience in cylinder head reconditioning, this section provides the necessary specifications and special reconditioning information.

Cylinder Head Assembly

The disassembled cylinder head should be carefully inspected for warpage, cracks, and wear. Check the valve guides and valve seats for wear as described below under **Valve Guides** and **Valves and Valve Seats.**

Always decarbonize and clean the head before inspecting it. A high quality straight edge can be used to check for warpage. Visually inspect the cylinder head for cracks. If a cracked cylinder head is suspected and no cracks are detected through the visual inspection, have the head further tested for cracks by an authorized Saab dealer or a qualified machine shop. A cracked cylinder head should be replaced.

A warped cylinder head can be machined provided the minimum cylinder head height is not exceeded. If further machining is required, the head should be replaced. Removing more than this amount will reduce the size of the combustion chamber and adversely affect engine performance.

CAUTION
If the cylinder head has been machined, make sure all sharp edges and burrs are removed from the combustion chamber. Lightly smooth the edges all around the combustion chamber and remove any imperfections.

Always check the total height of the cylinder head prior to machining. See Fig. 23. A maximum amount of 0.4 mm (0.016 in.) can be removed from a new cylinder head. If the cylinder head has been previously machined, it probably cannot be machined again. Cylinder head dimensions and minimum resurfacing height specifications are listed below.

Cylinder Head Height (dimension A)
- new . . . . 140.5±0.1 mm (5.531±0.004 in.)
- after machining . . . . 140.1±0.1 mm (5.516±0.004 in.)
- machining limit . . . . 0.4 mm (0.0016 in.)

Check the camshaft followers and the follower bores for wear. Replace the cam followers or the cylinder head if any signs of wear are visible or if any part does not meet the specifications listed below.

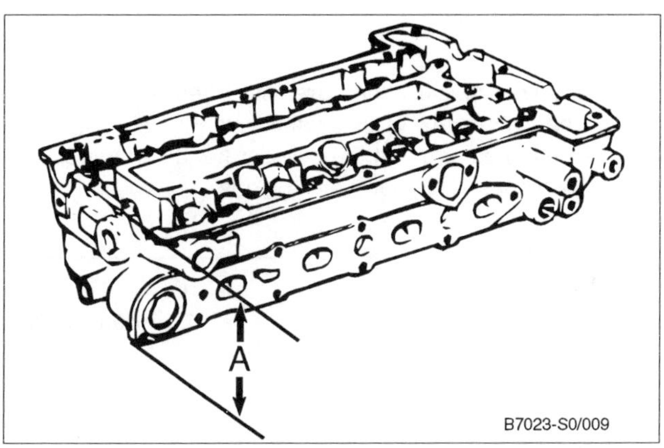

Fig. 23. Front view of cylinder head showing minimum resurfacing dimension (**A**). Measure between valve cover gasket surface and cylinder head gasket surface.

Cam followers
- diameter . . . . 32.96-32.98 mm (1.2976-1.2984 in.)
- height. . . . . .26 mm (1.02 in.)
- bore in cylinder head. . . . . 33.000-33.016 mm (1.2992-1.2998 in.)

Camshafts

Camshaft wear is usually caused by insufficient lubrication. Engine oil dilution, extended oil drain intervals, or high mileage are all additional causes of camshaft wear. Checking the camshaft for wear and runout requires precision measuring equipment.

Visually inspect the camshaft lobes and journals for wear. Lightly lubricate the camshafts and place them in the cylinder head. Install and tighten the bearing caps. Check that the camshaft turns smoothly. Using a feeler gauge, check the camshaft axial play (end float) between the camshaft flange and the thrust surface on the front of the cylinder head.

Camshaft
- axial play (end float)
  maximum permissible . . . . 0.08 to 0.35 mm (0.0031 to 0.0138 in.)
- camshaft bearing diameter . . . . . 28.922-28.935 mm (1.1387-1.1392 in.)

Valve Guides

Valve guide specifications are listed below. Check valve guide wear with a new valve as shown in Fig. 24. Inspect the valve seats to ensure that the cylinder head can be reconditioned before installing new valve guides.

Valve Guides

- length .... 49.00 mm (1.929 in.)
- outside diameter .... 12.039-12.050 mm (0.4740-0.4744 in.)
- bore for valve guide in cylinder head .... 12.000-12.018 mm (0.4724-0.4731 in.)

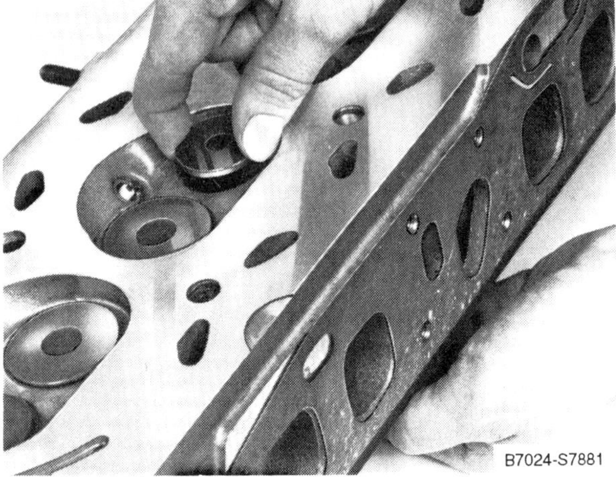

Fig. 24. Valve guide wear being checked. Raise valve 3 mm (0.12 in.) from its seat and rock the valve head to check for play. (Saab 8-valve cylinder head shown.)

Valve guide wear (clearance between valve guide and valve stem)

- maximum permissible .... 0.5 mm (0.02 in.)

Saab special tools should be used to replace worn valve guides. See Fig. 25. Always finish replacement valve guides using a 7.0 mm (H7) reamer.

NOTE

The Saab special tools are recommended to replace the valve guides, although conventional methods can also be used.

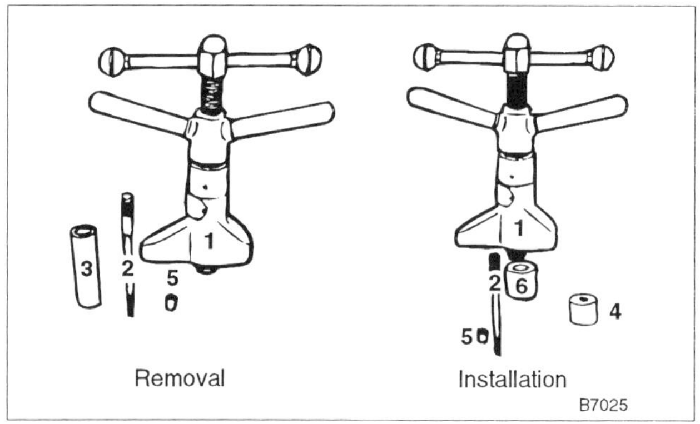

Fig. 25. Saab special tools for removing and installing valve guides.

Valve guide removal/installation special tools

- jack screw (**1**) .... tool no. 83 90 494
- pull rod (**2**). .... tool no. 83 93 811
- spacer sleeve (**3**) .... tool no. 83 93 829
- stop (**4**) .... tool no. 83 93 837
- special nut(**5**) .... tool no. 83 93 845
- mandrel (**6**) .... tool no. 83 90 379

To replace valve guides

1. Flush the cylinder head with hot water.

CAUTION

Always heat the head with hot water prior to removing and installing the valve guides. Failure to the heat the head may result in damage to the cylinder head casting.

2. Working from the camshaft side of the cylinder head, insert the special tools. See Fig. 26 and Fig. 27. Withdraw the valve guide by turning the jack screw.

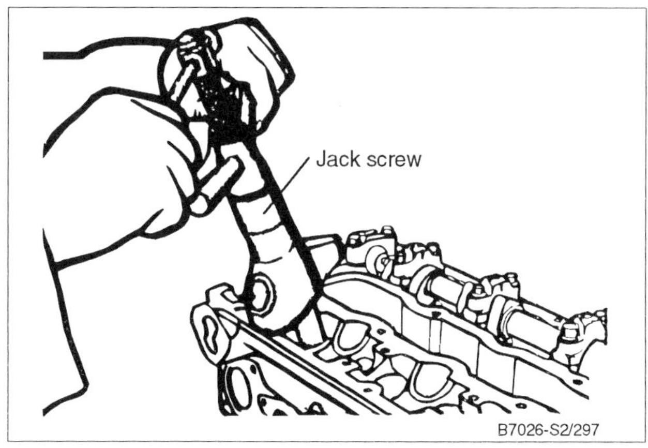

Fig. 26. Valve guide being removed using special tools.

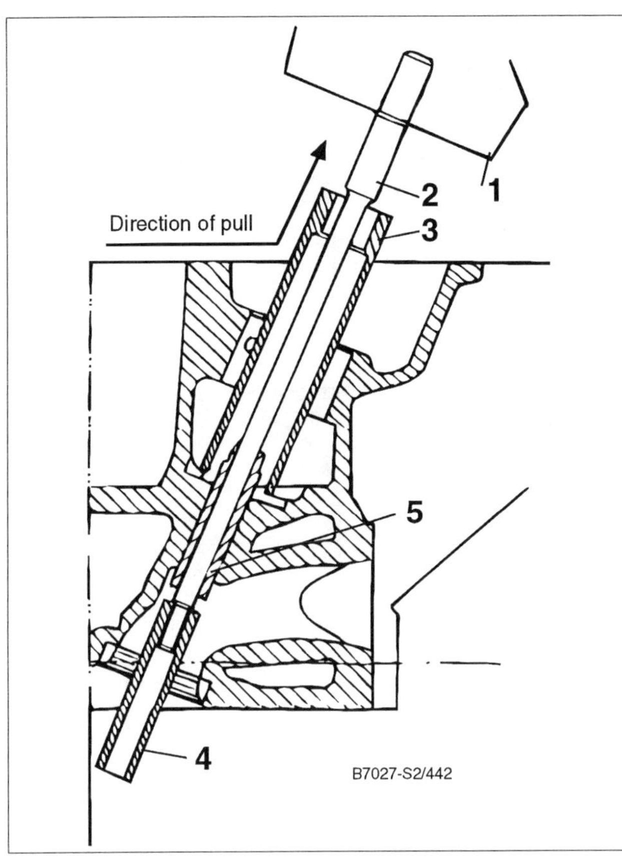

Fig. 27. Cutaway view of special valve guide removal tools. Withdraw valve guide (**5**) using jack screw (**1**), pull rod (**2**), spacer sleeve (**3**), and special nut (**4**)

3. Flush the new guide with cold water and fit the guide into the cylinder head. Working from the combustion chamber side of the cylinder head, insert the special tools. See Fig. 28. Draw the valve guide into the head until the stop is fully seated.

4. Finish the guide using a 7.0 mm undersize reamer (Saab tool no. 83 93 944). Then Follow up with a 7.0 mm H7 valve guide reamer.

Valves and Valve Seats

Valve and valve seat specifications vary between turbo and non-turbo models. Exhaust valves are sodium-filled and stellite-coated and should be hand-lapped only. Refacing exhaust valves by grinding will remove this coating and render the valve useless. Valve and valve seat dimensions are shown below in Fig. 29.

Whenever work is done on the valves or valve seats, the valve stem height must be checked. This measurement is critical to proper hydraulic cam follower operation. A special tool (Saab tool no. 83 93 753) is available to make the measurement, although precision measuring equipment can be substituted.

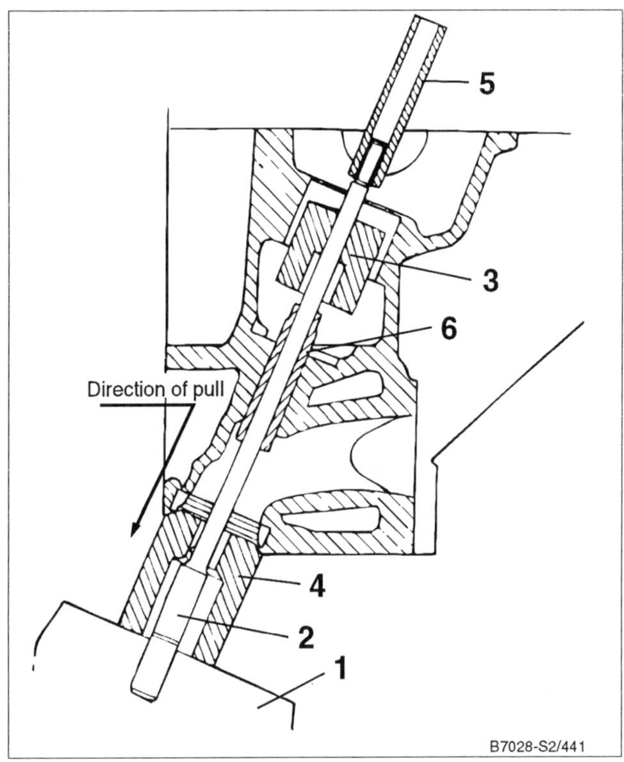

Fig. 28. Cutaway view of special tools used to install valve guide. Draw valve guide (**6**) in using jack screw (**1**), pull rod (**2**), stop (**3**), centering mandrel (**4**), and special nut (**5**).

With the valves installed and the camshafts and cam followers removed, measure the distance between the end of the valve stem and lowest part of the camshaft bearing surface as shown in Fig. 30.

NOTE

When using the special Saab stepped tool, lay the tool across the camshaft bearings so that the long and short legs are directly above the end of the valve stem. See Fig. 31. Check that the shorter step does not touch the valve (maximum valve height) and that the longer step raises the tool off the bearing surface (minimum valve height).

If any fault is found, either grind the end of the valve stem (valve stem too high) or machine the valve seat (valve stem too low). If the valve stem is worn, replacing the valve is also an alternative to valve seat grinding.

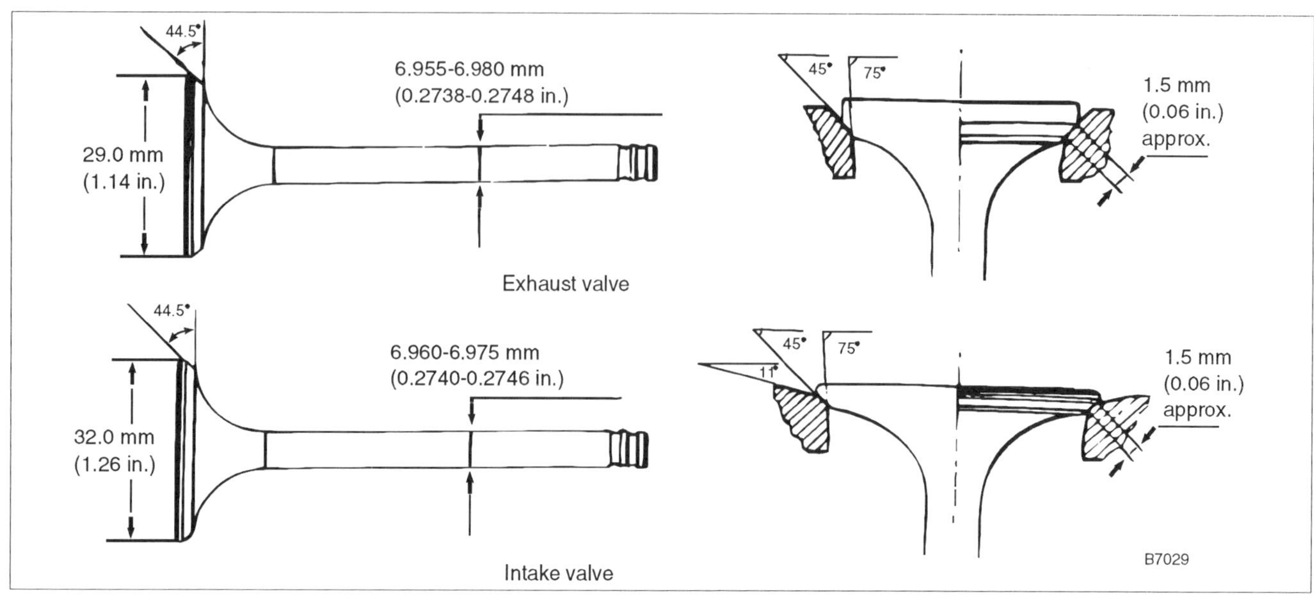

Fig. 29. Valve and valve seat dimensions.

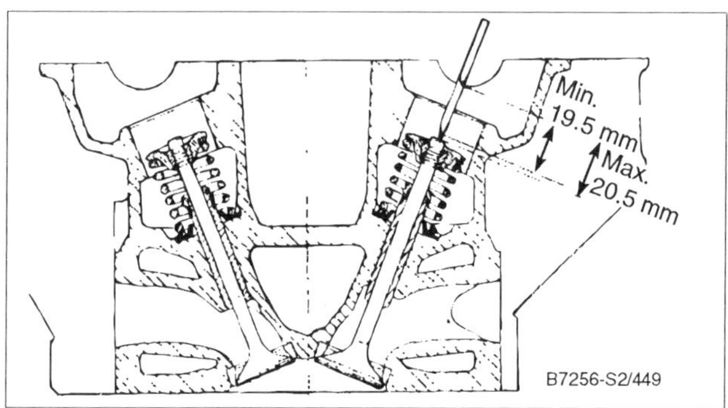

Fig. 30. Working range of hydraulic cam follower (valve stem height).

Scrapping Sodium Filled Valves

All of the fuel injected cars covered by this manual use sodium-filled exhaust valves. The sodium contained in the hollow stems of the valves is considered Hazardous Waste under the resource Conservation and Recovery Act. Disposal of used sodium-filled valves must be done in accordance with local, state, and federal regulations.

WARNING
Discarded sodium-filled exhaust valves should never, under any circumstances, be mixed with normal scrap metal as they are liable to explode when melted down.

To scrap sodium-filled exhaust valves

1. Drill a hole through the center of the valve and into the sodium compound. See Fig. 32.

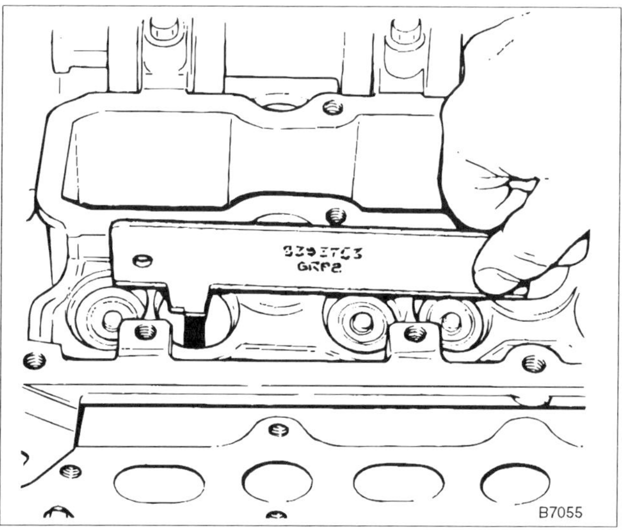

Fig. 31. Valve stem height being checked using Saab special tool no. 83 93 753.

2. Drill another hole into the stem or cut off the stem approximately 25 mm (1.0 in.) from the end of the stem.

WARNING
When drilling or cutting, keep clear of any water to avoid an explosion.

---

3. Throw the valve into a bucket of water and quickly move at least 10 feet away. See Fig. 33.

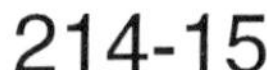

Fig. 32. Hole being drilled into sodium-filled exhaust valve.

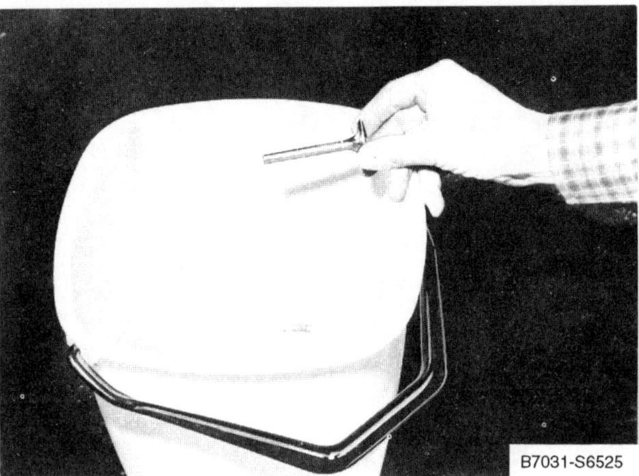

Fig. 33. Sodium-filled valve being dropped into bucket of water to neutralize sodium.

4. After about two minutes, the reaction should die down. Remove the valve from the bucket and dispose of the valve in the normal way.

Valve Springs

Valve springs should be checked for squareness and fatigue. Accurately checking for worn springs requires special spring testing equipment to compress the valve under a specified pressure. Always replace a spring that fails to meet any specification.

To quickly check the springs, line them all up in a row. Place a straight edge across the top of the springs. Any spring that is significantly shorter than the others (more than 1/16 in.) is worn and should be replaced. As a final check, measure the free height of the spring. Spring specifications are listed below.

Use a high-quality square to check the springs maximum out-of-square. Place the spring against the square and turn the spring one full rotation to obtain the largest gap. Measure the gap between the spring and the square. See Fig. 34.

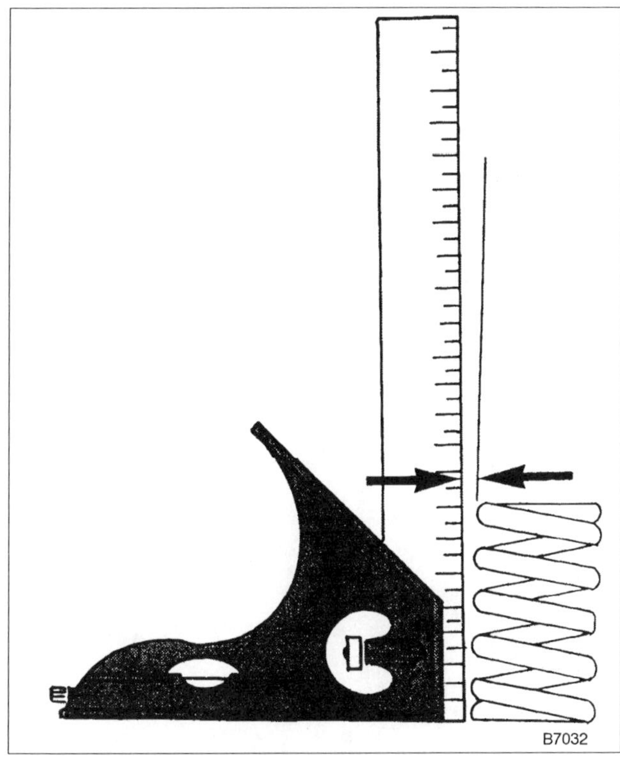

Fig. 34. Valve spring being checked for out-of-square. Make measurement at arrows.

Valve Springs	
• out-of-square (maximum)	1.75 mm (0.07 in.)
• free height	45.0±1.5 mm (1.77±0.06 in.)
• height when compressed with pressure of 131-141 lbs.	28.4 mm (1.12 in.)

215 Camshaft Timing Chain

GENERAL

The overhead camshafts are driven by a single row chain. The chain is tensioned using a hydraulic chain tensioner system, which is mounted in the side of the cylinder head. See Fig. 1. The timing chain and its related components normally do not require maintenance. If either the chain, the lower guides or the crankshaft sprocket are worn and need to be replaced, the engine will have to be removed from the car.

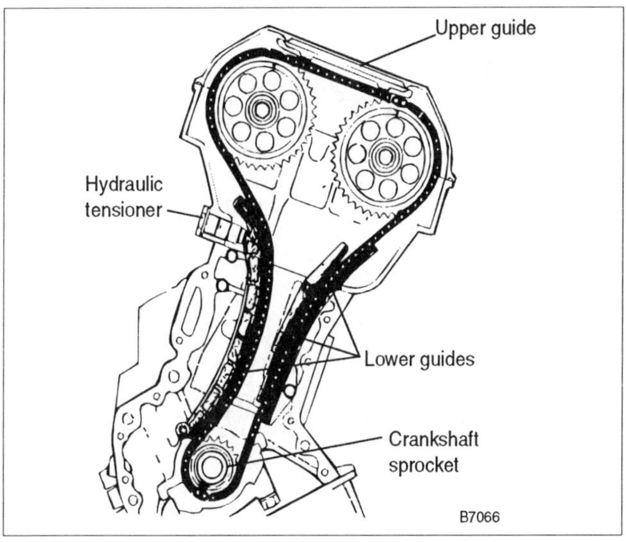

Fig. 1. Timing chain and related components used on 16-valve engines.

CAMSHAFT TIMING CHAIN

Checking Camshaft Timing Chain

The camshaft timing chain and its components can be quickly checked to determine if the chain, sprockets, or guides are worn or if the chain is incorrectly positioned on it sprockets.

CAUTION

The camshafts must always be properly timed to the crankshaft or the pistons may contact the valve heads resulting in engine damage. Do not alter the position of the crankshaft or camshafts once the timing chain is removed from its sprockets.

To check the timing chain and its components, remove the valve cover as described in **214 Cylinder Head and Valve Mechanism.** Then using a wrench on the crankshaft pulley mounting bolt, turn the engine over in the direction of normal engine rotation until the camshafts and the flywheel are set to TDC (0°TDC). See Fig. 2.

CAUTION

Do not turn the engine over using the flats on the camshaft.

NOTE

Normal engine rotation is counterclockwise when viewing the engine from the front of the car.

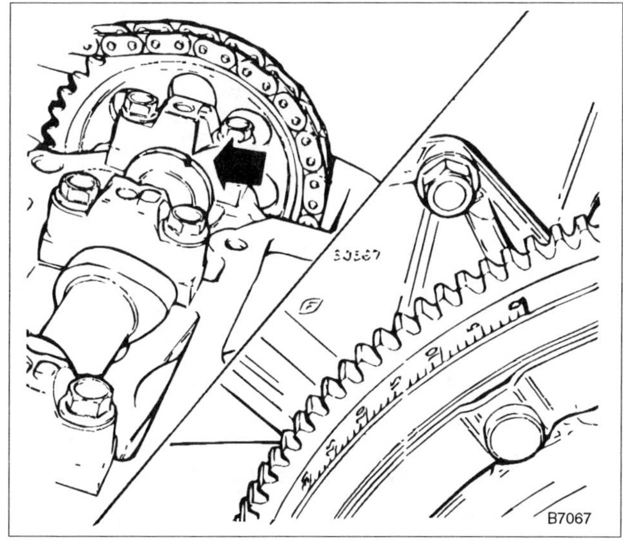

Fig. 2. Camshaft sprocket and crankshaft TDC marks set at 0°TDC. Both camshaft marks and the flywheel mark should be exactly aligned.

If all three marks are not perfectly aligned, either the timing chain is severely worn or the chain is incorrectly installed. See Fig. 3 for camshaft sprocket diagnosis. Remove and install the chain as described to below.

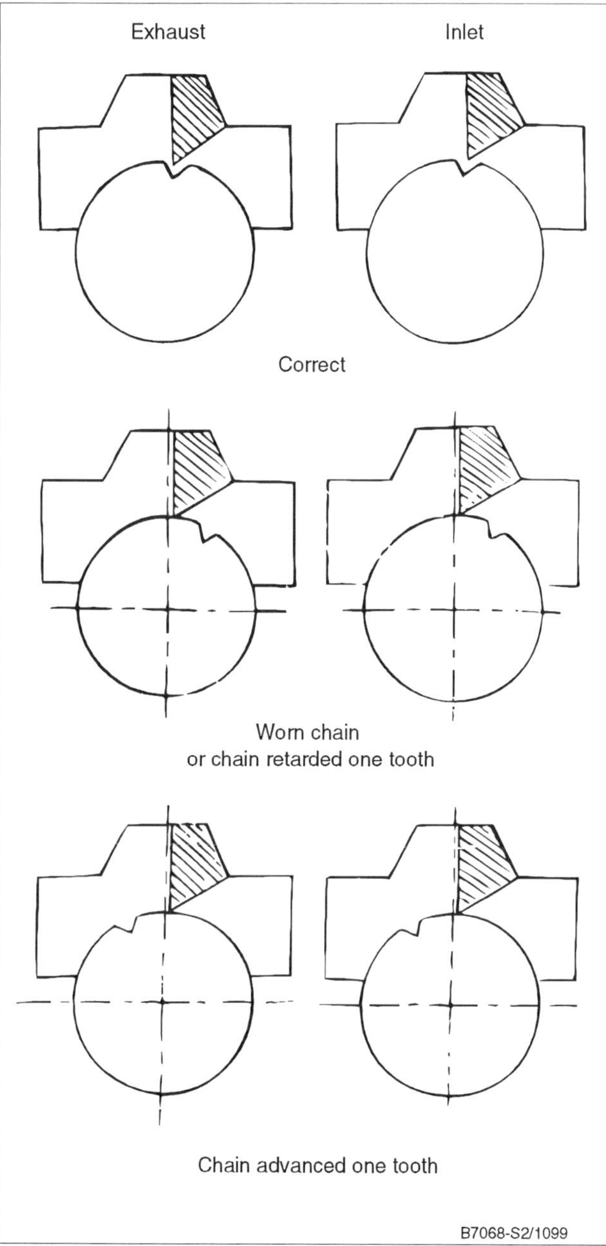

Fig. 3. Camshaft alignment marks.

Replacing Camshaft Timing Chain and Tensioner

Replacing the timing chain or any of the components behind the timing chain cover will require that the engine assembly be removed from the car. The camshaft timing chain cover cannot be properly removed with the engine installed. The camshaft sprockets, the chain tensioner, and the upper chain guide can all be replaced with the engine installed.

To replace camshaft timing chain

1. Remove the engine as described in **201 Engine Removal and Installation.**
2. Remove the valve cover and align the camshaft and the flywheel at TDC as shown above.
3. Remove the oil pump from the timing chain cover as described in **220 Lubrication System.**
4. Disconnect the lower hose from the coolant pump.
5. Remove the alternator with its support bracket.
6. Remove the bolts from the timing chain cover and remove the cover from the engine. See Fig. 4.

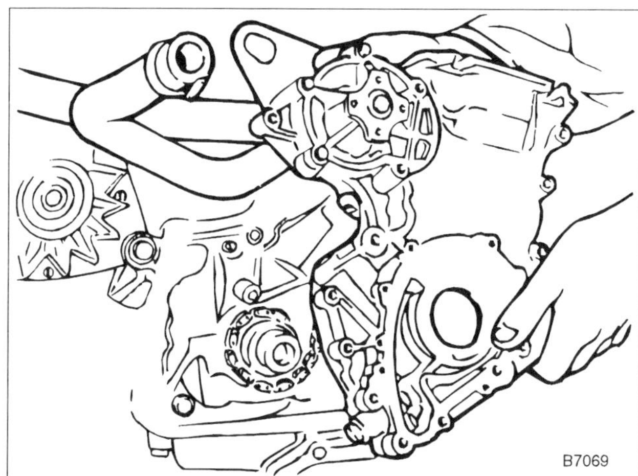

Fig. 4. Camshaft timing chain cover being removed.

7. Remove the upper chain guide from above the camshaft sprockets.
8. While holding the camshaft stationary, loosen the two camshaft sprocket mounting bolts. Use a 19 mm wrench on the camshaft flats to hold the camshaft. See Fig. 5.
9. Remove the chain tensioner from the side of the cylinder head. See Fig. 6.
10. Remove the camshaft sprockets and the chain. See Fig. 7.

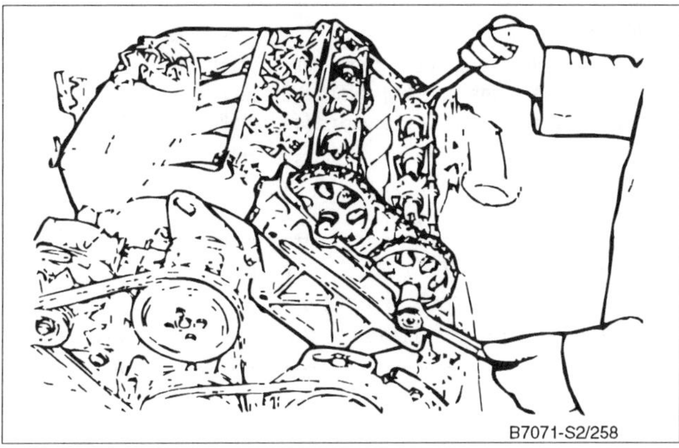

Fig. 5. Camshaft sprocket mounting bolt being loosened while camshaft is held stationary.

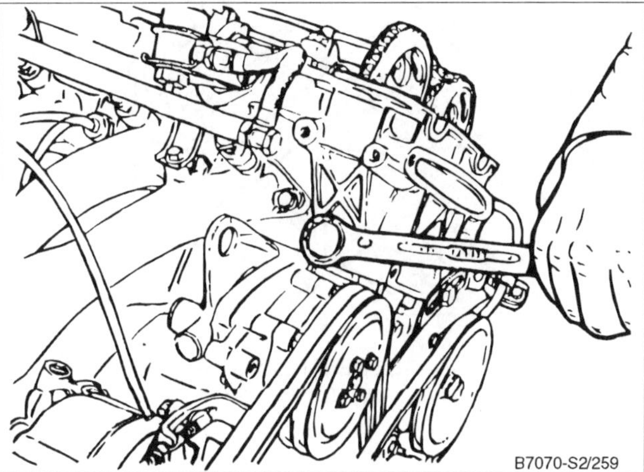

Fig. 6. Camshaft timing chain tensioner being removed.

CAUTION

The camshafts must always be correctly timed to the crankshaft or the pistons may contact the valve heads resulting in engine damage. Do not alter the position of the crankshaft or camshafts once the timing chain is removed from its sprockets.

---

11. Inspect the chain sprockets, the chain guides, and the chain tensioners. Replace any sprocket that is visibly worn. Replace any guide that is deeply scored.

12. With all TDC (timing) marks aligned, install the timing chain and the exhaust-side camshaft sprocket, making sure there is no chain slack between the cam sprocket and crankshaft sprocket.

13. Install the intake-side camshaft sprocket, keeping the chain tight between the sprockets. Hand tighten the sprocket mounting bolts.

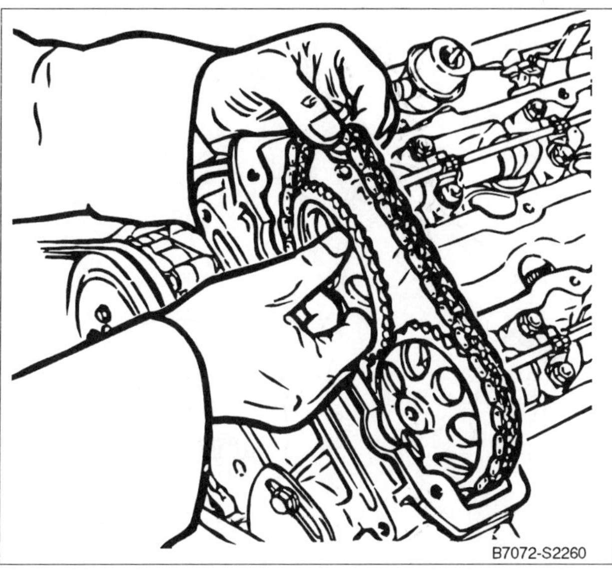

Fig. 7. Camshaft sprocket being removed from camshaft.

CAUTION

Make sure that the chain is centered on the guides.

---

14. Preset the tensioner so that it will not tension the chain when installed. Then install and tighten the tensioner to the cylinder head.

NOTE

- Two types of tensioners are used on 16-valve engines and are preset differently. The early-style tensioner can be preset by fully pressing the spring-loaded piston in and turning it until it locks. The late-style tensioner, which has a ratcheting mechanism, can be preset by removing the small bolt and spring in the end of the tensioner. Lift up on the ratcheting pawl and push the lever all the way in. See Fig. 8.

- The late-type ratcheting tensioner can be retrofitted on all 16-valve cars with the early-style tensioner.

Tightening torque

- timing chain tensioner to cylinder head. . . . . .63 Nm (47 ft-lb)

---

15. Tension the camshaft timing chain by either installing the center bolt and spring (late-style tensioner) or by releasing the tensioner piston by pressing on the guide rail. See Fig. 9.

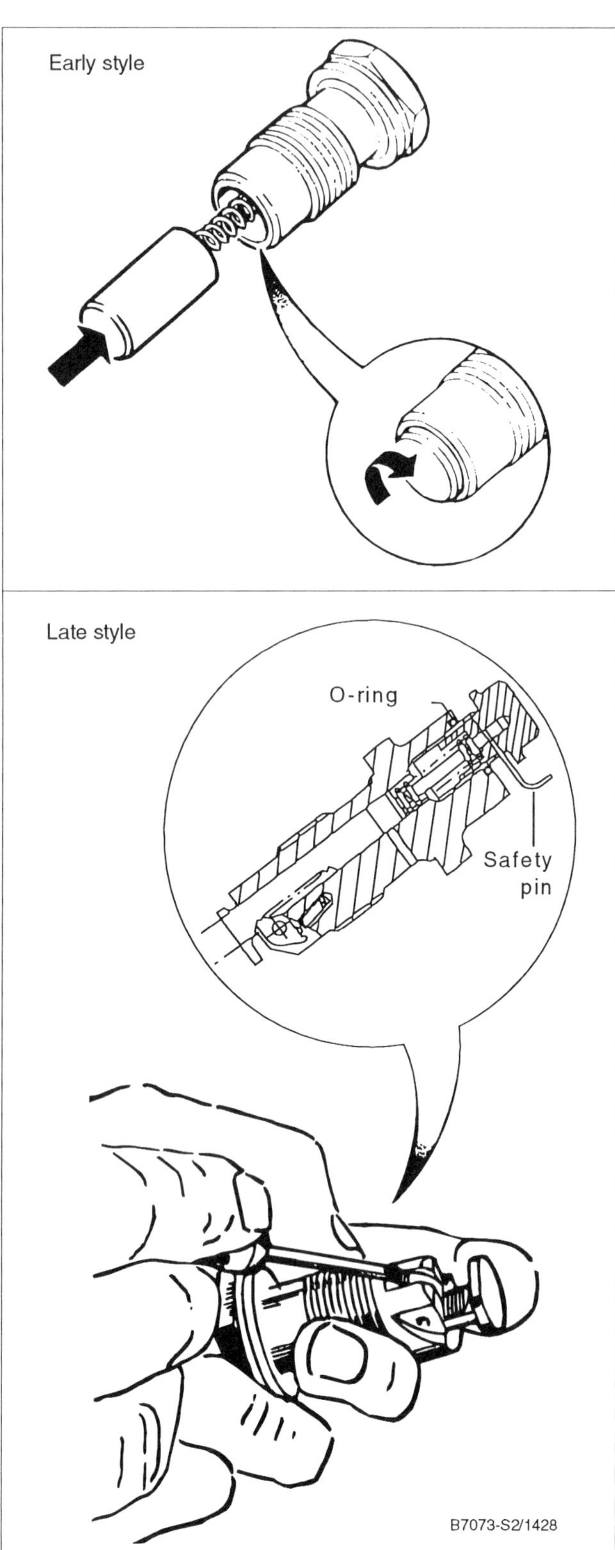

Fig. 8. Early and late style camshaft timing chain tensioners being preset prior to installation.

NOTE

New late-style tensioners come with a safety pin installed. Removing the safety pin will release the tensioner arm. Do not remove the pin until the tensioner is installed.

Tightening torque

- camshaft timing chain center tensioner plug (bolt) to tensioner . . . 22 Nm (16 ft-lb)

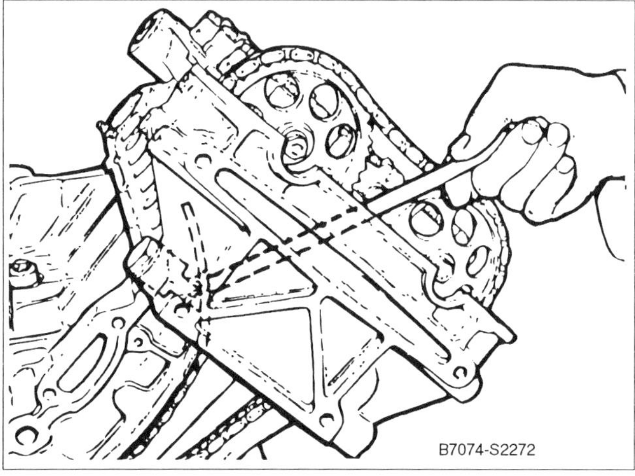

Fig. 9. Early-style camshaft timing chain tensioner being released by pressing on guide rail with blunt object.

16. Rotate the crankshaft by hand in the direction of normal engine rotation two full revolutions. Recheck that the TDC marks are all correctly aligned. If any faults are found reset the timing chain.

CAUTION

Recheck all timing marks carefully. It is very easy to be off one tooth.

---

17. Remove the camshaft sprocket bolts one at a time, coat them with Loctite, and reinstall. Tighten the bolts while holding the camshaft stationary as shown in Fig. 10.

CAUTION

Hold the camshaft steady using a 19 mm wrench on the camshaft flats when tightening the camshaft sprocket bolts. Do not allow the tensioner or the chain to take this load.

Tightening torque
- camshaft sprocket to camshaft . . . . . 63 Nm (47 ft-lb)

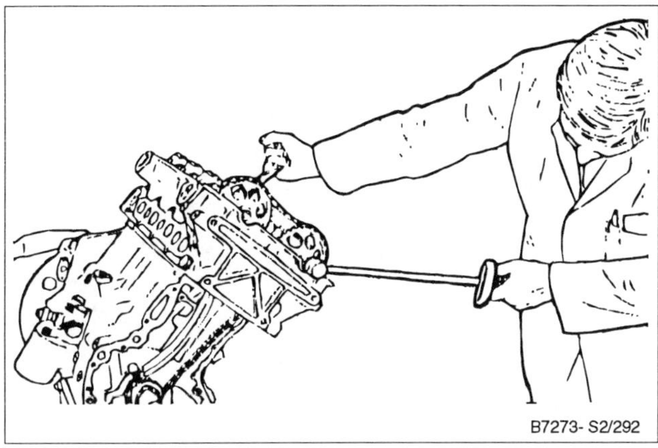

Fig. 10. Camshaft sprocket bolt being tightened.

18. Install the camshaft timing chain cover, the oil pump, and crankshaft sprocket.

CAUTION
Be careful not to damage the crankshaft oil seal when installing the oil pump.

Tightening torques
- timing chain cover to engine block and cylinder head. . . . . .20 Nm (15 ft-lb)
- oil pump to timing chain cover. . . . . . 8 Nm (71 in-lb)
- crankshaft pulley to crankshaft
  - 1985-1990 . . . . 190 Nm (140 ft-lb)
  - 1991and later . . . . .175 Nm (129 ft-lb)

19. Install the valve cover as described in **214 Cylinder Head and Valve Mechanism.**

Tightening torque
- valve cover to cylinder head . . . . 15 Nm (11 ft-lb)

20. Install the alternator as described in **321 Alternator and Charging System.**

Tightening torques
- all other fasteners
  - M5 bolt . . . . 5 Nm (44 in-lb)
  - M6 bolt . . . . 10 Nm (89 in-lb)
  - M8 bolt . . . . .20 Nm (15 ft-lb)
  - M10 bolt . . . . .40 Nm (30 ft-lb)

216 Crankshaft

TABLES

CRANKSHAFT

Crankshaft main bearing caps and used bearing shells should only be installed in their original positions. Label all parts carefully.

NOTE

Crankshaft removal and installation is part of the engine disassembly procedure covered in **210 Engine Disassembly and Assembly.**

To inspect crankshaft

1. Thoroughly clean the removed crankshaft, the crankshaft bearings, and the bearing surfaces in the cylinder block. Make all parts being measured are dry and oil-free.

2. Carefully place the upper bearing shells in the cylinder block and set the crankshaft into the block. Install the center thrust washers. See Fig. 1.

Fig. 1. Crankshaft thrust washers being installed.

3. Using a dial indicator, measure the crankshaft end float by gently levering the crankshaft back and forth using a screwdriver. See Fig. 2.

Crankshaft
- end float allowable. . . . . 0.08-0.28 mm (0.003-0.011 in.)

Fig. 2. Crankshaft end float being checked with dial indicator (arrow). Move the crankshaft back and forth with screwdriver to obtain readings.

4. Remove the crankshaft from the cylinder block and place the crankshaft in two V-blocks. Using a dial indicator at the center main journal, measure the crankshaft radial play by rolling the crankshaft in the V-blocks.

Crankshaft radial play (runout)
- maximum allowable. . . . . 0.10 mm (0.004 in.)

5. Measure the main journal and crankpin diameters using a micrometer. Make the measurements at several points to check for out-of-roundness. Journal diameters are listed in **Table a.**

Crankshaft journal out-of-round
- maximum allowable . . . . 0.05 mm (0.002 in.)

Table a. Crankshaft Main Journal and Crankpin Diameters

Main journals	diameter mm (in)
standard	57.981-58.000 (2.2827-2.2835)
first undersize	57.731-57.750 (2.2729-2.2736)
second undersize	57.481-57.500 (2.2630-2.2638)
third undersize	57.237-57.250 (2.2534-2.2539)
fourth undersize	56.987-57.000 (2.2436-2.2441)
Crankpin	**diameter mm (in)**
standard	51.981-52.000 (2.0465-2.0472)
first undersize	51.731-51.750 (2.0367-2.0374)
second undersize	51.481-51.500 (2.0268-2.0276)
third undersize	51.237-51.250 (2.0172-2.0177)
fourth undersize	50.987-51.000 (2.0074-2.0079)

NOTE
The crankshaft can be ground down to one undersize without affecting its hardened surface. If any more material needs to be removed, the crankshaft should be rehardened using a "Tenifer" hardening treatment. Contact your authorized Saab dealer for information on crankshaft hardening and replacement crankshafts.

6. Measure the main bearing oil clearances by placing the bearing shells and the crankshaft in the cylinder block.

7. Place a strip of plastigage about 6mm (1/4 in.) to one side of the journal's center-line. See Fig. 3. Install the bearing cap, tighten the bolts and then remove the cap.

NOTE
Plastigage comes in three thicknesses. Use the green type (PG-1) to make the measurements described here. Keep the crankshaft stationary when measuring oil clearances.

Tightening torque
- main bearing caps to cylinder block . . . . 110 Nm (81 ft-lb)

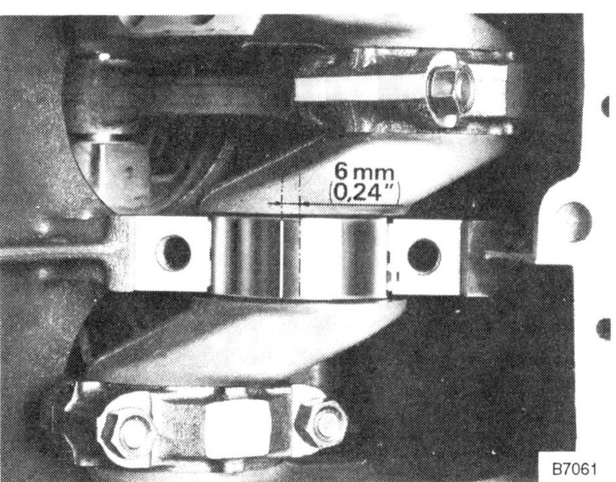

Fig. 3. Plastigage correctly positioned on crankshaft journal.

8. Measure the strip of plastigage at the widest point. Repeat the procedure for the remaining main bearings.

Crankshaft main bearing
- oil clearance . . .0.020-0.062 mm (0.0008-0.0024 in.)

9. To measure the big-end oil clearances, install the piston and connecting rod assemblies into their respective cylinders. Rotate the crankshaft so that the piston is at approximately 60° BTDC. Place a strip of plastigage about 6mm (1/4 in.) to one side of the crankpin's center-line as shown above. Install the connecting rod cap, tighten the nuts and then remove the cap.

Tightening torque
- connecting rod cap to connecting rod . . . . .55 Nm (41 ft-lb)

10. Measure the strip of plastigage at the widest point. Repeat the procedure for the remaining big-end bearings.

Connecting rod big-end bearing
- oil clearance . . .0.026-0.062 mm (0.0010-0.0024 in.)

Replacement bearing shells come in the standard size and four undersizes. Standard, first undersize, and second undersize shells are available in two thicknesses and are marked with a colored paint dot code, indicating the size and thickness classification.

Crankshaft Bearing Shell Color Codes
- main and big-end bearing shells
  - standard
    - thin-red
    - thick-blue
  - first undersize
    - thin-yellow
    - thick-green
  - second undersize
    - thin-white
    - thick-brown

The proper way of fitting bearing shells is as follows: Begin by fitting two thin shells and measure the oil clearance using plastigage as described above. If the clearance is too big, attempt to reduce it by combining a thick and thin shell or two thick shells. If the clearance is still too large with two thick shells, the crankshaft will have to be machined to accept undersized bearing shells. See **Table a** above.

FLYWHEEL AND DRIVE PLATE

Replacement of the flywheel or the drive plate are similar operations. When removing the mounting bolts, hold the ring gear stationary using a holding fixture such as Saab tool no 83 92 987. The flywheel or driveplate should be inspected for wear and excessive runout using a dial indicator. Replace the driveplate or flywheel if it is warped, cracked, or deeply scored.

NOTE
Saab does not list wear specifications for the flywheel or drive plate.

Before installing the flywheel, check the transmission clutch shaft bearing and replace it if there is any play or if it does not roll smoothly. See Fig. 4.

Installation of the flywheel and the drive plate is the reverse of removal. Be sure all old thread sealer is cleaned from the bolts and their holes. Use a thread sealer when reinstalling the bolts and tighten them in a alternating pattern.

Tightening torques
- flywheel to crankshaft
  - 17 mm bolt head . . . . 60 Nm (44 ft-lb)
  - 19 mm bolt head . . . . 85 Nm (63 ft-lb)

CYLINDER BLOCK OIL SEALS

The cylinder block oil seal(s) at the timing chain end of the engine can be replaced with the engine removed or installed. On cars with manual transmission, the oil seal at the flywheel end of the engine can be replaced with the engine installed, but the clutch and flywheel must first be removed.

Fig. 4. Clutch shaft bearing in flywheel being removed. Special drift (Saab tool no. 83 91 997) shown.

NOTE
On cars with automatic transmission, the oil seal at the drive plate end of the engine can only be replaced after removing the transmission torque converter. Removing the torque converter requires that the transmission be separated from the engine as described in **201 Engine Removal and Installation.**

To replace crankshaft oil seal at flywheel end (cars with manual transmission only)

1. Remove the clutch and pressure plate as described in **411 Clutch.**

2. While holding the flywheel stationary, remove the flywheel mounting bolts and remove the flywheel.

NOTE
The flywheel can be held stationary using a locking tool such as Saab tool no. 83 92 987.

3. Carefully pry out the old oil seal using a screwdriver.

4. Lubricate the new seal with oil. Fit the new seal so that the spring ring side of the seal is towards the crankshaft.

5. Using a suitable seal driver install the seal. See Fig. 5.

NOTE
The old seal was originally installed flush to the cover surface. The new seal should be installed slightly deeper so that it does not ride on the same area of the shaft. This will allow for a good seal despite any wear.

Fig. 5. Crankshaft oil seal at flywheel end of engine being installed. (Saab special tool no. 83 92 540 shown).

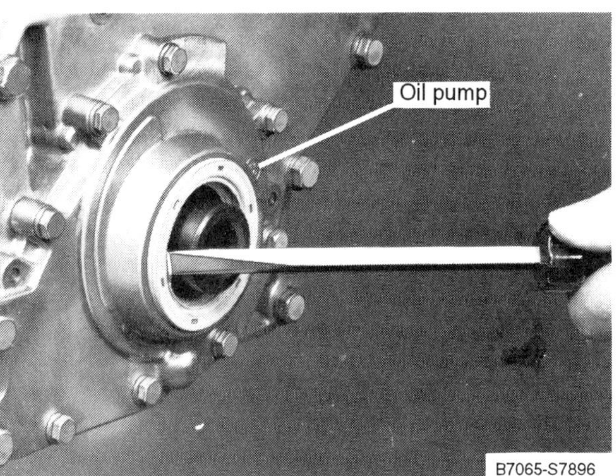

Fig. 7. Crankshaft oil seal at timing chain end of engine being removed.

To replace crankshaft oil seal at timing chain end

1. If necessary, remove the alternator and A/C V-belts as described **1 LUBRICATION AND MAINTENANCE.**

2. While holding the flywheel stationary, remove the crankshaft pulley mounting bolt and the pulley with its woodruff key. See Fig. 6.

Fig. 6. Crankshaft pulley being removed.

3. Pry out the old oil seal using a screwdriver. See Fig. 7.

4. Lubricate the new seal with oil. Fit the new seal and install it using the special sleeve (Saab tool no. 83 94 215), the pulley center bolt, and special wrench (Saab tool no. 33 92 185). See Fig. 8.

Fig. 8. Crankshaft oil seal at timing chain end of engine being installed using sleeve **A** (Saab tool no 8394 215) and **B** wrench (Saab tool no. 83 92 185).

NOTE
The old seal was originally installed flush to the cover surface. The new seal should be installed slightly deeper so that it does not ride on the same area of the shaft. This will allow for a good seal despite any wear.

---

5. Install the crankshaft pulley with its woodruff key. Install and tension the engine V-belts as described in **1 LUBRICATION AND MAINTENANCE.**

Tightening torque
- Crankshaft pulley to crankshaft
  1985-1990 .... 190 Nm (140 ft-lb)
  1991 and later .... 175 Nm (129 ft-lb)

---

220 Lubrication System

GENERAL

This section covers inspection and repair of the lubrication system, which includes the oil pump, the oil pressure warning system, and the oil cooler.

Oil pressure is generated by a gear-type pump mounted externally to the front of the cylinder block. The pump is driven directly by the crankshaft. When the engine is running, oil is drawn from the oil pickup tube in the oil sump and circulated through the engine, the turbocharger and the oil cooler (where applicable).See Fig. 1.

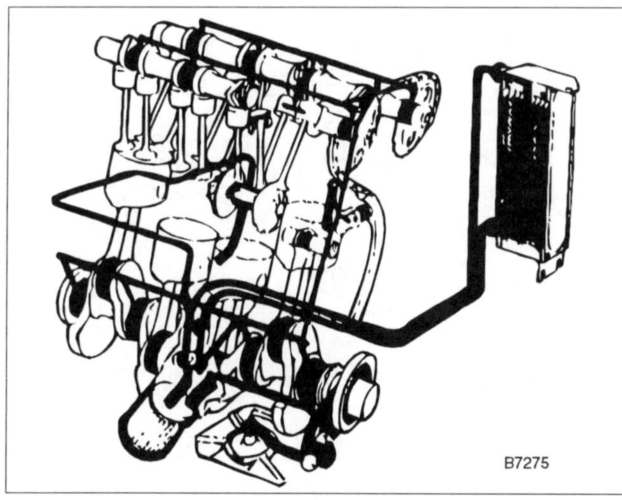

Fig. 1. Schematic of lubrication system.

The oil sump is an integral part of the transmission housing, although the engine oil and the transmission oil are separated from each other.

NOTE
Oil and oil filter change are covered in **1 LUBRICATION AND MAINTENANCE.**

All engines covered by this manual have an oil pressure warning system that warns the driver of insufficient oil pressure immediately after startup. Other safety features include a filter bypass, to guard against bursting the filter due to over pressure, and an oil pump pressure relief valve to prevent excessive system pressure.

OIL PUMP AND OIL PICKUP TUBE

There is normally no need to remove the oil pump or pickup tube unless oil pressure is inadequate. Check the oil pressure as described below under **Oil Pressure Warning Systems**.

The oil pump can be removed with the engine installed or removed. Removal of the oil pickup tube requires that the engine be removed and separated from the transmission.

To remove, inspect, and install oil pump

1. Remove the V-belts from the crankshaft pulley and drain the engine oil as described in **1 LUBRICATION AND MAINTENANCE.**

2. While holding the flywheel steady, remove the crankshaft pulley mounting bolt and remove the pulley from the crankshaft. See Fig. 2.

NOTE
Immobilize the crankshaft by locking the flywheel using a locking tool, such as Saab special tool no. 83 92 987.

---

3. Thoroughly clean the area around the oil pump.

Fig. 2. Crankshaft sprocket mounting bolt being removed.

4. Remove the oil pump mounting bolts and remove the pump. See Fig. 3.

NOTE

Before removing the pump, inspect for any signs of oil around the crankshaft oil seal in the oil pump housing. If the seal is leaking, it should be replaced at this time as described in **216 Crankshaft** .

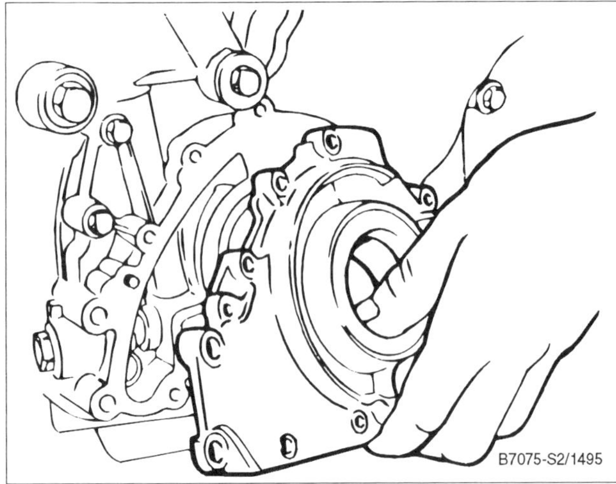

Fig. 3. Oil pump being removed.

5. Disassemble and clean the oil pump gears. Inspect the inside of the oil pump housing for scoring or wear. Inspect the oil pump O-ring and the crankshaft seal. Replace any worn or faulty parts

6. Reassemble the pump making sure the small punch mark in the outer gear is facing up. See Fig. 4.

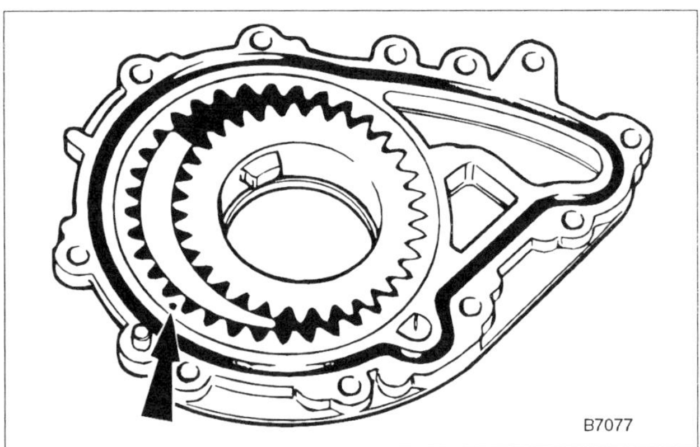

Fig. 4. Oil pump outer gear correctly installed with punch mark facing up (arrow).

7. Using a straight edge and a feeler gauge, check the end float between the pump body and the gear wheel. See Fig. 5.

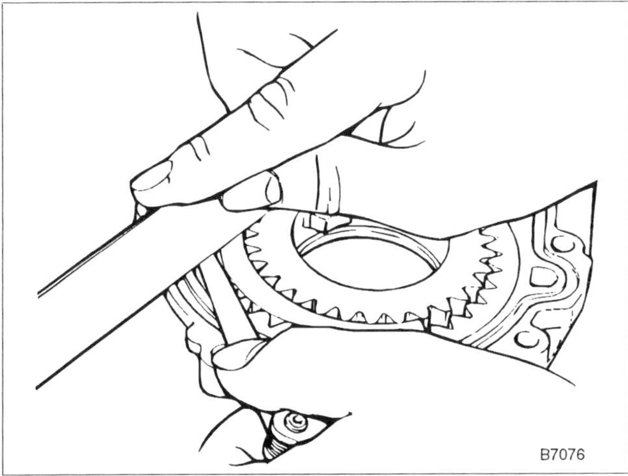

Fig. 5. Oil pump being checked for wear (end-float).

Oil pump end float

- 0.03-0.08 mm (0.0012-0.0031 in.)

---

8. Fit the O-ring in the oil pump groove. Lubricate the crankshaft oil seal and the pump gears with engine oil.

9. Pull the inner gear out of the pump slightly and install the pump, making sure that the dog on pump gear engages the slot on the crankshaft hub. Push the pump on while aligning the dowel. See Fig. 6.

Fig. 6. Oil pump being installed. Pull gear out of housing to align dog on gear with slot on crankshaft hub.

NOTE

The oil pump locating dowel aids in centering the pump to the crankshaft. Some models may not be equipped with the dowel. If the dowel is missing, a special tool (Saab tool no. 83 93 589) is available to center the pump and protect the oil seal during oil pump installation. See Fig. 7.

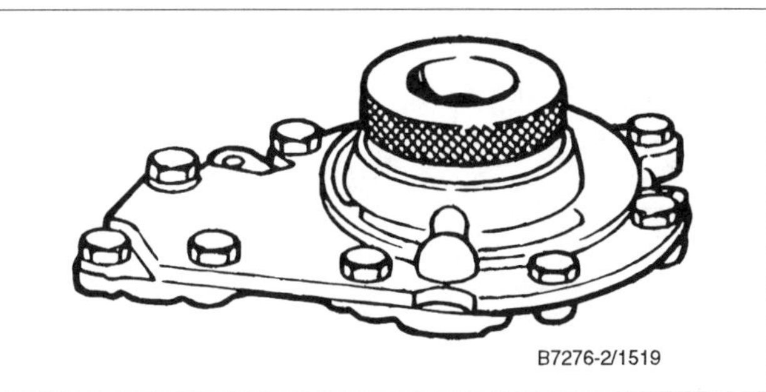

Fig. 7. Saab special tool installed in oil pump prior to pump installation.

10. Install and tighten the pump mounting bolts in an alternating pattern. Carefully install the crankshaft pulley and tighten the mounting bolt. Install the V-belts.

CAUTION

Be careful not to damage the crankshaft oil seal when installing the crankshaft pulley. Thoroughly clean and oil the pulley flange before installation.

Tightening torques

- oil pump to timing chain cover. . . . . . 8 Nm (71 in-lb)
- crankshaft pulley to crankshaft
  - 1985-1990 . . . . .190 Nm (140 ft-lb)
  - 1991 and later . . . . .175 Nm (129 ft-lb)

---

11. Remove the oil filter housing from the cylinder block. Then fill the oil pump pressure cavity with clean engine oil to prime the pump. See Fig. 8.

CAUTION

The oil pump must be primed any time it is removed.

Fig. 8. Oil pump being primed through oil pump pressure cavity.

12. Using a new gasket, install the filter housing and refill the engine with oil.

Oil Pump Pickup Tube

The oil pickup tube is mounted to bottom of the engine block. Because the oil sump is an integral part of the transmission case, the engine needs to be removed and the transmission separated from the engine to reach the pickup tube. See **201 Engine Removal and Installation** for these procedures.

CAUTION

Different oil pickup tubes are used depending on the type of transmission installed. Cars with manual transmission use a longer tube than cars with automatic transmission. If the wrong tube is installed, inadequate lubrication and engine damage can result.

OIL PRESSURE WARNING SYSTEMS

When diagnosing the cause of an illuminated oil pressure warning light, certain basic checks should be made before assuming that engine damage has occurred.

CAUTION

If the oil pressure warning indicator stays on after the engine is started, or flashes on while driving, always assume that low oil pressure is the cause.

First, check that the warning light electrical circuit is functioning correctly by making the quick checks described below in **Oil Pressure Warning Circuit**. Check that the engine oil level and oil type is correct.

Second, if the engine has been run for any length of time with the warning light on, it should be determined if any engine damaged has occurred. If abnormal noises are heard with engine running, turn the engine off and remove the valve cover and the camshaft bearing cap from the no. 4 cylinder (cylinder closest to the radiator). This is the cylinder farthest from the oil pump. Inspect the bearings surface for damage. If the surfaces are badly worn, chances are that other parts of the engine are also damaged.

Third, check the oil pressure as described below. If the oil pressure is below the specification listed, remove and clean the oil pressure relief valve (also described below). Then prime the oil system (see Fig. 8 above) and reinstall the oil pressure relief valve. Recheck the oil pressure and the oil pressure warning light.

NOTE

Occasionally, a small particle of metal or other contaminant may become lodged in the valve, causing it to stick open. In some cases when the valve is removed for inspection, the oil that runs out of the bore carries the contaminants away, leaving the impression that the valve was not the cause of the low pressure. Do not disassemble the engine until first cleaning the pressure relief valve. If this corrects the problem, be sure to change the oil and the filter to remove any additional debris.

Testing Oil Pressure

Test the oil pressure by removing the pressure switch and installing a pressure gauge. See Fig. 9. Run the engine just long enough to get an accurate reading. If testing shows that the oil pressure is too low or too high, either the oil pump is worn or faulty, the relief valve is stuck, or the engine is severely worn. If the pressure is as specified and the warning light still stays on, check the light's electrical circuit as described below in **Oil Pressure Waring Circuit**.

NOTE

For the most accurate pressure readings, change the oil and the oil filter before making the pressure test.

Fig. 9. Oil pressure switch (arrow).

Lubrication system test pressures

- oil pressure
  at 2000 rpm,
  engine temp. 80°C (176°F) . . . . at least 2.7 (39 psi)
- oil pressure relief valve
  opening pressure . . . . 3.6-5.2 bar (52-75 psi)
- warning light
  on pressure. . . . . below 0.3-0.5 bar (4.4-7.2 psi)

Tightening torque

- oil pressure switch
  (1/4"-18 NPTF) . . . . 10 Nm (89 in-lb)

Oil Pressure Relief Valve

The oil pressure relief valve is located in the side of the camshaft timing chain cover. See Fig. 10. The valve is designed to open and route oil back to the inlet side of the oil pump when the oil pressure exceeds a predetermined level. If the pressure is abnormally high or low, remove and clean the valve. Change the oil and the oil filter and recheck the oil pressure. If the pressure is still low, remove and inspect the oil pump as described above in **Oil Pump and Oil Pickup Tube**.

NOTE

Low oil pressure can also be caused by general engine wear, such as worn engine bearings on a high-mileage car.

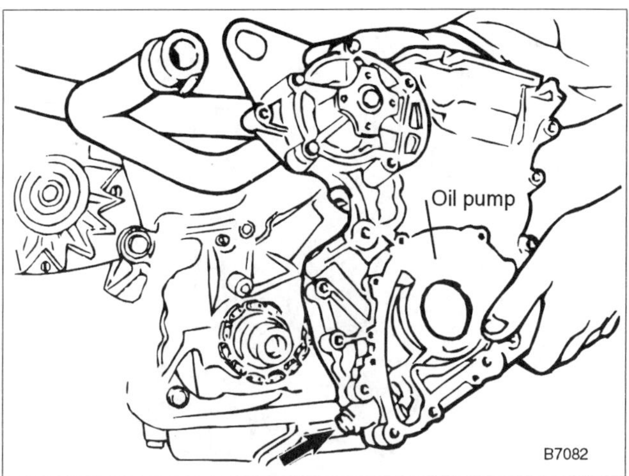

Fig. 10. Oil pressure relief valve (arrow).

Oil Pressure Warning Circuit

The oil pressure warning electrical circuit consists of an oil pressure switch mounted in the oil circuit and an instrument panel warning light. When the ignition switch is turned on, a warning light comes on. When the engine is started and the oil pressure rises, the oil pressure switch opens and the warning light goes out. If the light doesn't come on at all or stays on all the time, check to make sure the oil level and the oil pressure are correct before doing the tests listed below.

NOTE

For information on center console gauges (oil pressure and oil temperature gauges), see **3 ELECTRICAL SYSTEM.**

To test oil pressure warning system

1. Turn the ignition switch on. The warning light on the instrument panel should light up. Remove the wire from the oil pressure switch (See Fig. 9 above). The light should go out.

NOTE

If the light does not go out, the wiring to the switch is most likely shorted to ground between the terminal and the warning light. See **3 ELECTRICAL SYSTEM** for electrical wiring troubleshooting information.

---

2. If the warning light does not light when the ignition is on, remove the terminal from the oil pressure switch and ground the wire to a clean metal surface.

NOTE

If the warning light comes on, check the switch as described in the next step. If the warning light does not come on, the wiring circuit to the dash light or the light itself is faulty.

---

3. To test the switch, connect an ohmmeter between the switch terminal and ground. With the engine off, there should be continuity. With the engine running there should be no continuity. If any faults are found, the switch is faulty and should be replaced.

Tightening torque

- oil pressure switch to oil filter housing
  small (1/4"-18 NPTF) . . . . 10 Nm (89 in-lb)
  large (M14X1.5) . . . . .30 Nm (22 ft-lb)

CAUTION

If the oil pressure switch is not faulty and the light remains on while the engine is running, the oil pressure may be dangerously low. Do not operate the engine until the problem is corrected. The engine may be severely damaged.

OIL COOLER (TURBO MODELS ONLY)

Turbocharged engines uses an oil-to-air cooler to aid in engine oil cooling. A thermostat in the oil filter housing prevents oil flow to the cooler until the oil temperature reaches 167°F (75°C).

The engine oil cooler is fitted beneath the front left-hand head light. The oil cooler thermostat is screwed into the side of the oil filter housing. Fig. 11 shows the oil cooler and its hoses.

To remove oil cooler

1. Remove the left-hand turn signal/parking light assembly.
2. Remove the baffle plate from behind the light assembly.
3. Remove the left-hand headlight.
4. Working from below, remove the spoiler grille from beneath the car.
5. Working from in the engine compartment, remove the oil cooler mounting nut from the radiator member. See Fig. 12.

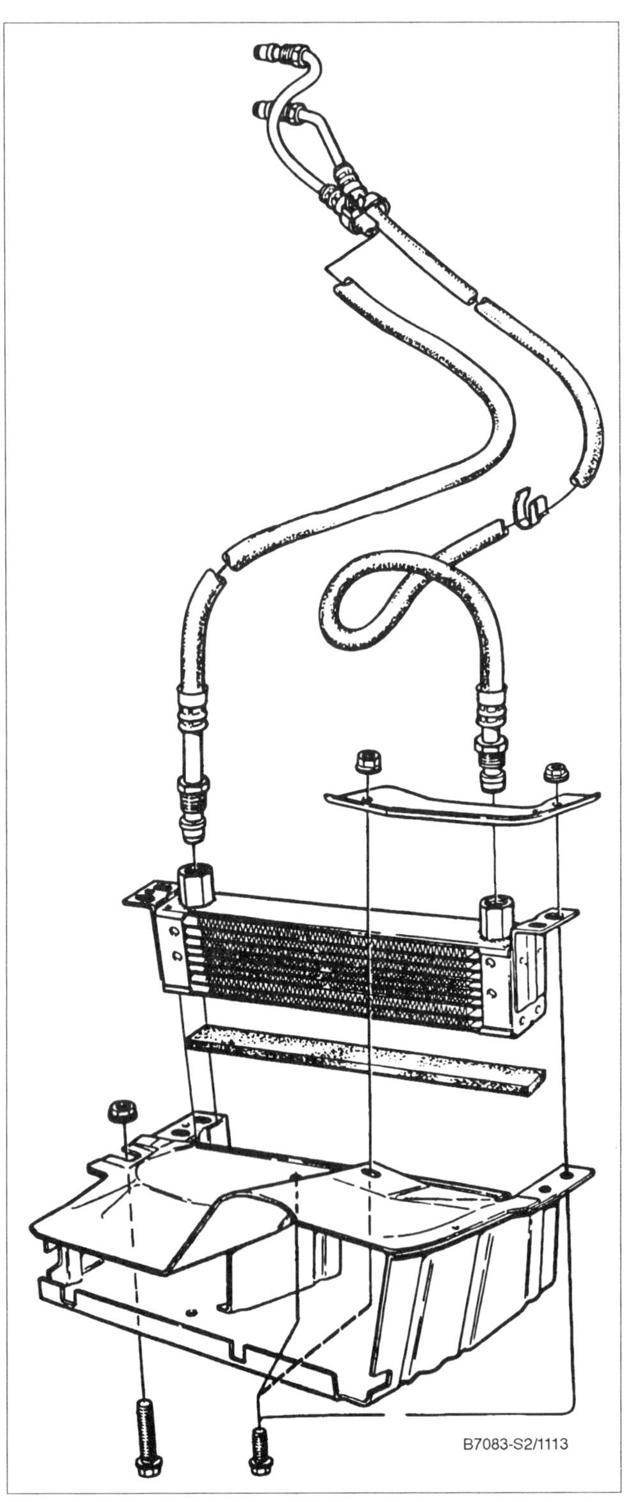

Fig. 11. Oil cooler and related components for turbo engines.

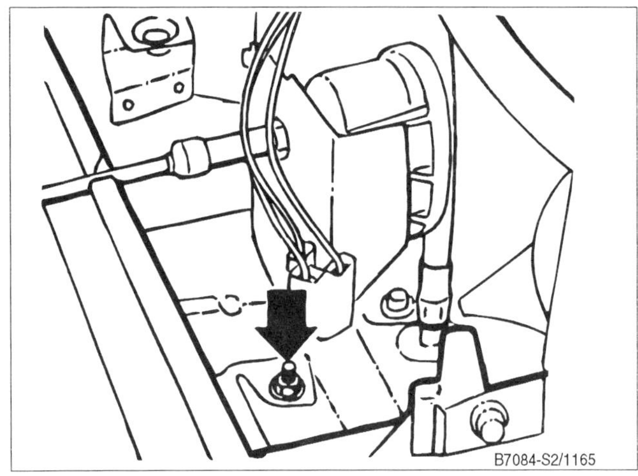

Fig. 12. Oil cooler mounting nut in engine compartment near radiator.

6. Unbolt the cooler together with its shroud from below. Carefully pull the cooler and shroud down. See Fig. 13. Unbolt the shroud from the cooler and remove the lines from the cooler.

Installation is the reverse of removal.

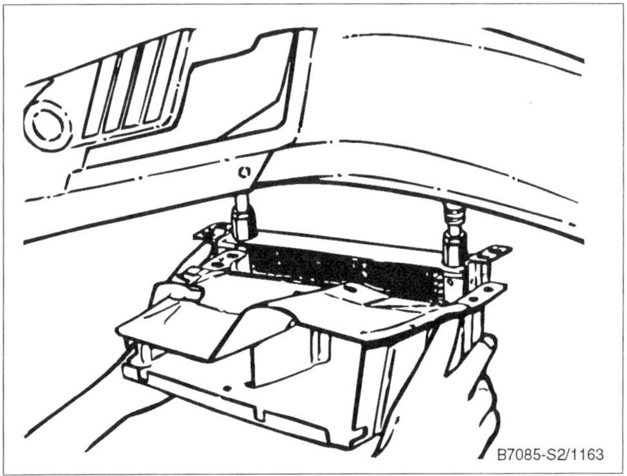

Fig. 13. Oil cooler being removed from recess behind headlight.

234 Fuel Pump and Fuel Tank

TABLES

GENERAL

The injection-molded plastic fuel tank is located beneath the car, behind the rear seat. The fuel gauge sender and the electric fuel pump are mounted in the top of the tank. See Fig. 1. The fuel tank is designed to prevent overfilling and allow for fuel expansion. The filler cap contains a valve to prevent a vacuum from occurring in the tank. To prevent a backflow of fuel from the tank when the car is stopped, there is a check valve in the fuel return line from the fuel injection system.

The fuel pump is an electric rotary pump mounted inside the fuel tank. The fuel pump constantly circulates fuel throughout the system. Fuel is drawn from the tank, filtered, routed to the fuel injectors, regulated to maintain a constant pressure, and then recirculated back into the fuel tank.

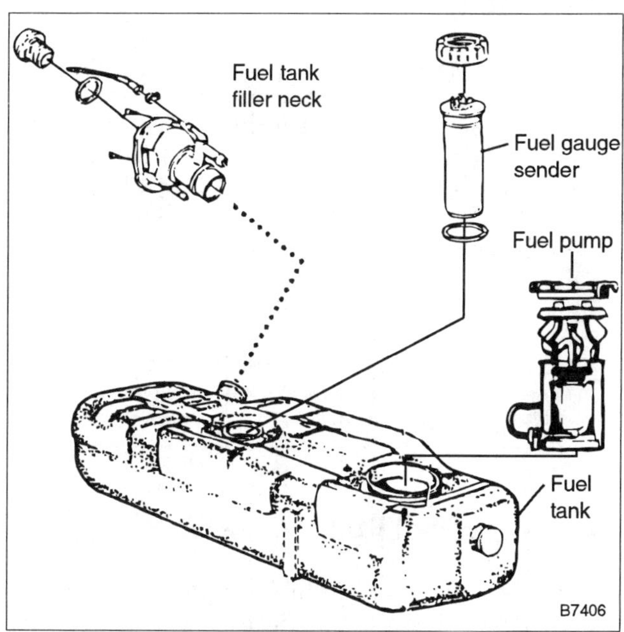

Fig. 1. Fuel tank and related components.

NOTE

Fuel filter replacement is covered in **1 LUBRICATION AND MAINTENANCE.**

Fuel flows through the pump and over the pump's electric motor. This helps cool the pump during normal operation. An inlet strainer helps prevent pump clogging. The main pump is mounted in a reservoir to help prevent fuel starvation. The fuel pump contains a bypass valve to prevent high pressure from damaging the system if there is a kinked or blocked fuel line. Also, there is a check valve at the pump outlet to hold pressure in the system after the pump is turned off.

The electrical current that operates the fuel pump is controlled by a relay. This ensures that the pump will not flood the engine, or continue running in the event of an accident or if the engine stalls. Turbo models have an additional pump safety feature that turns the pump off during overboost situations.

Two different fuel pump combinations and mountings are installed on Saab 900 models depending on the model year. See **Table a.** The two pump types are not interchangeable, owing to a different fuel tank design.

Table a. Fuel Pump Applications

Model	Pump type
1986-1988 Non-turbo *	Roller
1985-1989 Turbo models*	
1989- and later Non-turbo	Rotor
1990 and later, Turbo	

*Some early models may be equipped with a special replacement rotor-type fuel pump. This dealer-installed service pump was designed to eliminate a complaint of poor driveability or noisy pump operation and can be identified by its rubber mounting collar—other rotor-type pumps are mounted with a threaded plastic collar.

Roller-type Fuel Pump Assembly with Supply Pump

Fig. 2 shows the roller-type fuel pump assembly. The pump is mounted in a fuel reservoir that is fed with fuel by the electric supply pump. In addition, the fuel return from the fuel injection system also feeds the fuel reservoir. This design helps prevent fuel starvation during hard cornering. The reservoir has a safety valve that opens at 0.1 bar (1.4 psi). The pump is mounted to the tank by a rubber collar.

NOTE

It may require at least two gallons of fuel to prime the pump if the car ran out of gas. If the car is not on level ground, additional fuel may need to be added.

Rotor-type Fuel Pump Assembly

Fig. 3 shows the rotor-type "ejector-style" fuel pump. The rotor-type pump is similar to the roller-type pump, although the separate supply pump is not used. The ejector picks up additional fuel from the bottom of the tank and forces it into the reservoir.

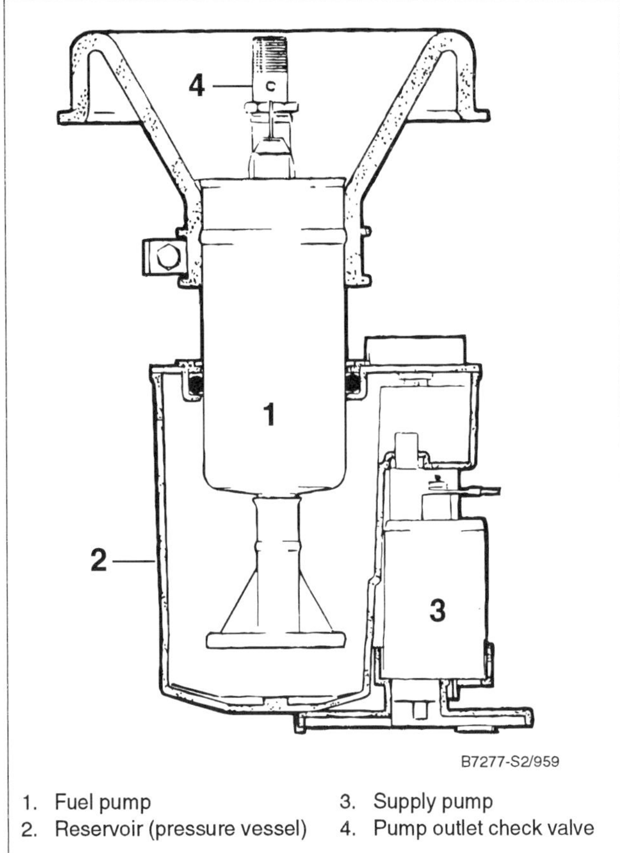

1. Fuel pump
2. Reservoir (pressure vessel)
3. Supply pump
4. Pump outlet check valve

Fig. 2. Roller-type fuel pump assembly.

Safety Precautions

Please read the following warnings before doing any work the fuel pump, fuel tank or fuel lines.

WARNING

- Always disconnect the negative (–) battery terminal and cover the terminal with an insulated material whenever working on any fuel related component.
- Gasoline is dangerous to your health. Wear hand and skin protection when working on the fuel system. Do not breathe fuel vapors and always work in a well-ventilated area.
- Fuel and fuel vapors will be present during many of the operations described in this repair group. Do not smoke or create sparks. Have an approved fire extinguisher handy.
- The fuel injection system is designed to maintain pressure in the system after the engine is turned off. Fuel will be expelled under pressure as fuel lines are disconnected. This can be a fire hazard, especially if the engine is warm. Always wrap a clean shop rag around the fitting before loosening or disconnecting any fuel line.

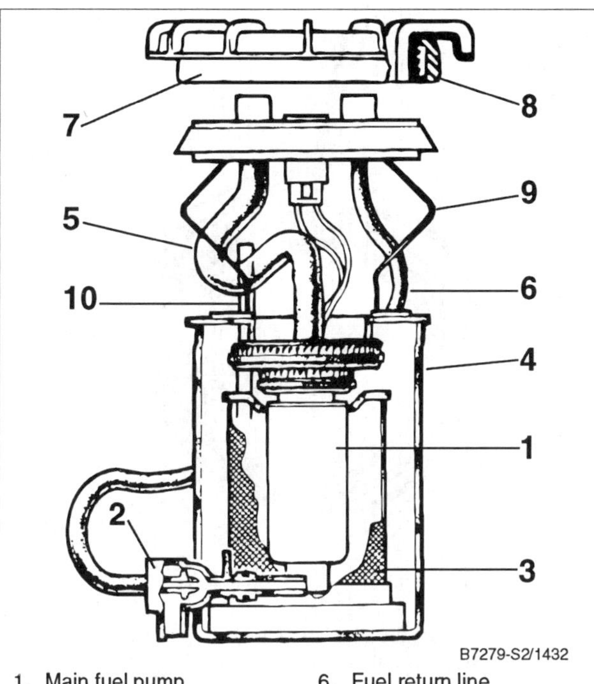

1. Main fuel pump
2. Ejector pump
3. Filter
4. Reservoir
5. Fuel delivery line
6. Fuel return line
7. Threaded retaining collar
8. Seal
9. Spring
10. Filter breather pipe

Fig. 3. Rotor-type fuel pump assembly.

FUEL PUMP TROUBLESHOOTING

The fuel supply system is an integral part of the operation of the fuel injection system. Problems such as a no-start condition, hesitation or stalling may be due to poor fuel delivery. There are some preliminary tests to quickly determine if the fuel pump or its electrical circuit are causing the problem. Some of the tests described below require special test equipment, such as a fuel pressure gauge.

NOTE
General engine management and driveability troubleshooting should begin by consulting **200 Engine—General.**

Cleanliness is essential when working with the fuel system. Even a tiny particle of dirt can cause trouble if it reaches an injector.

CAUTION
- Thoroughly clean fuel line unions before loosening or disconnecting them. Use only clean tools.
- Keep removed components clean, and seal or cover them with a clean, lint-free cloth, especially if the repair cannot be finished immediately.

CAUTION
- Avoid the use of compressed air nearby, and do not move the car while the fuel system is open.
- When replacing parts, install only new, clean components. Seals and O-rings should always be replaced rather than reused.

NOTE
To help prevent poor fuel delivery due to pump cavitation, Saab recommends avoiding the use of alcohol-enhanced fuel above ambient temperatures of 75°F (24°C).

Basic Troubleshooting Principles

The basic function of the fuel pump is to deliver an adequate amount pressurized fuel. Problems caused by a fault with fuel pump range from a no-start condition to intermittent poor performance and driveability. These problems can be the result of a fault in the pump electrical circuit or a worn or faulty pump.

Begin troubleshooting with a simple check of the fuel pump electrical circuit. The pump should run while cranking the engine with the starter. If necessary, remove the access cover under the trunk floor and listen or feel to see whether the pump is running. If the pump does not run, see **Fuel Pump Electrical Tests** below.

If fuel delivery problems are suspected, begin troubleshooting with a check of the fuel pump delivery rate. See **Fuel Pump Delivery Rate.** The test will indicate whether further tests are necessary. This is especially important on high-mileage cars, where normal pump wear may decrease delivery volume.

Also check for correct pump installation, a clogged pump strainer, or a bad supply/ejector pump. Any combination of these may cause the problems listed above.

NOTE
- On Turbo models, a faulty over-pressure switch may cause momentary fuel pump cut-out or a no-start condition. See **Testing Turbo Over-pressure Switch (1985-1988 models only)** for more information.
- On models with rotor-type pumps, poor performance may be caused by a ruptured or ballooned delivery hose in the pump assembly. This hose is available as a replacement part. See **Replacing Rotor-type Pump** for additional information.
- Poor driveability or performance on 1988 and some 1989 models with roller-type or rotor-type pumps may be due to a blocked return line check valve at the fuel tank, causing excessive line pressure. The problem is covered under Saab's vehicle warranty. For more information see an authorized Saab dealer.

NOTE

During 1990 model production, a modified rotor-type pump was installed as a running change. The new design helps eliminate pump cavitation, pump noise, and pump overheating. The new pump can be retrofitted to earlier models with the rotor-type (threaded collar) pump.

Fuel Pump Noise

Fuel pump noise does not always indicate a bad pump. The amount of noise that is transmitted to the passenger compartment varies with the car. Humming or buzzing at various levels is generally considered normal, while clicking, ratcheting or grinding may signal imminent pump failure.

On roller-type pumps, improper pump or fuel tank installation can increase pump noise, as can a faulty supply pump. On rotor-type pumps, a clogged ejector pump can often cause noise. Many times the main fuel pump is replaced needlessly when the supply or ejector pump is at fault.

NOTE

Supply pump test procedures are covered below under **Supply Pump Quick Check (roller-type pump only)**.

Operating Fuel Pump for Tests

The electric fuel pump only runs when the cars is running or being started. This is to prevent running the fuel pump indefinitely if the engine stalls. Testing the fuel pump and the fuel injection system requires running the pump with the engine off.

The procedure for operating the pump uses a temporary wiring connection on the fuse/relay panel to bypass the fuel pump relay. The preferred method is to use a remote switch, such as the Saab special tool, Part No. 83 93 886, but you can accomplish the same thing with a homemade jumper wire and an in-line switch. See Fig. 4.

CAUTION

- A homemade jumper wire with a switch should be at least 1.5 mm metric wire size (14 gauge-AWG) and, for safety, should include a 20 amp in-line fuse.
- Avoid damaging the fuse sockets. The ends of the jumper wire should be flat-blade connectors that are the same size as the sockets in the fuse panel.
- Connect and disconnect the remote switch or jumper wire only with the switch in the off position.

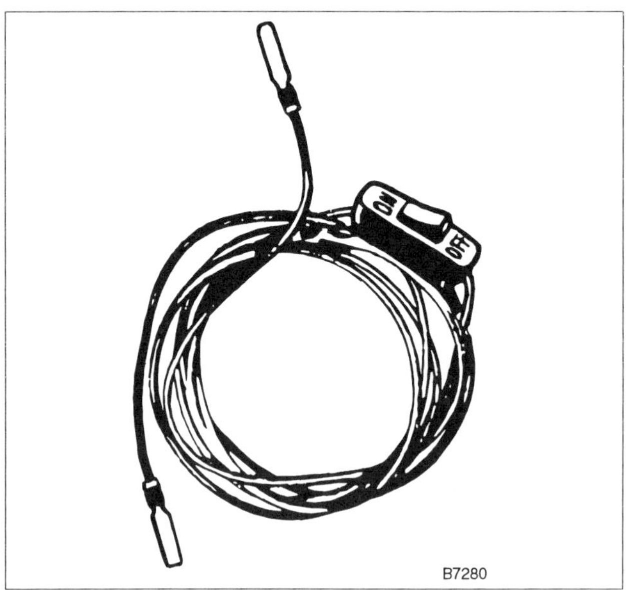

Fig. 4. Jumper wire with flat-blade connectors and switch for running fuel pump without running engine.

To run the pump, remove fuses number 27 and 30. With the ignition off, connect the jumper wire and switch as shown in Fig. 5. Turn the switch ON to run the pump.

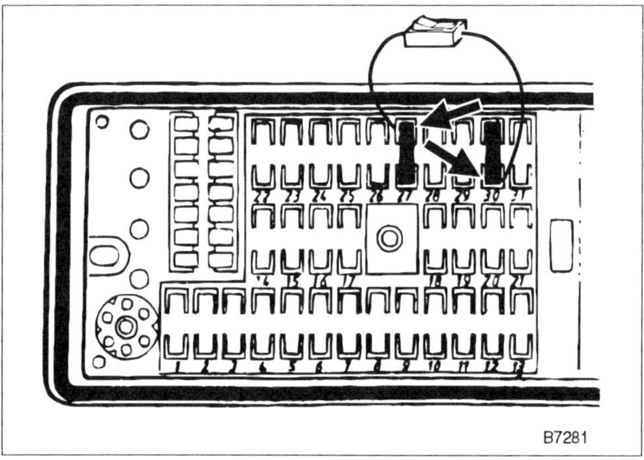

Fig. 5. Schematic view of jumper wire and switch connected at fuse sockets (fuses removed) for running fuel pump. Fuse/relay panel is in engine compartment, on top of left fender.

NOTE

If the pump runs only when the jumper is connected, the relay or wiring is faulty. If the pump doesn't run with the jumper installed, the problem is in the wiring to the pump or the pump itself. See **Fuel Pump Electrical Tests** for more information

Supply Pump Quick Check
(roller-type pump only)

The following test will help determine whether a faulty supply pump is the cause of fuel delivery problems. A faulty supply pump usually manifests itself through a noisy fuel pump.

WARNING
- The fuel tank must be no more than 3/4 full when making this check or fuel may be spilled.
- Fuel will be expelled. Do not disconnect wires that could cause sparks. Have a fire extinguisher handy. Perform the test outside if possible. Have a supply of rags handy to clean up any spills.

To test roller-type supply pump

1. Working in the trunk, remove the pump access cover. Disconnect the main pump terminals and slacken and remove the mounting boot clamp. See Fig. 6.

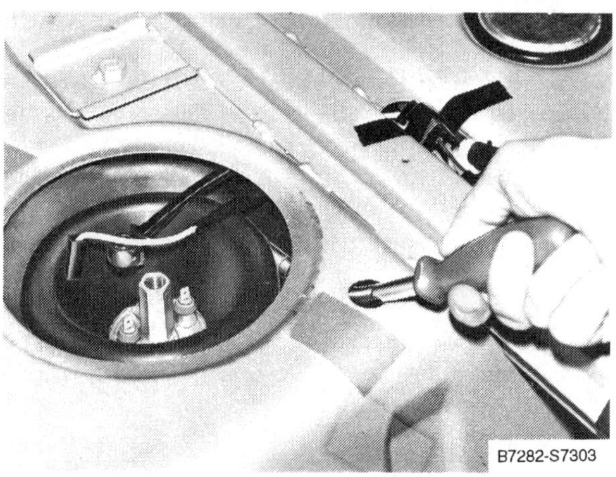

Fig. 6. Fuel pump mounting boot clamp being loosened using flexible socket driver.

2. Carefully peel back the pump mounting boot so that the top of the fuel pump reservoir is visible.

3. Run the fuel pump as described above under **Operating Fuel Pump for Tests** As the supply pump runs, fuel should be forced out of the reservoir relief valve. See Fig. 7.

WARNING
The fuel forced out of the relief valve will be partially vaporized and is extremely flammable. Do not smoke or create sparks. Have an approved fire extinguisher handy.

NOTE
If fuel comes out of the relief valve, the supply pump is working correctly. If no fuel comes out, the supply pump is most likely faulty and should be replaced. The supply pump is available as a replacement part. See **Replacing Roller-type Pump** below.

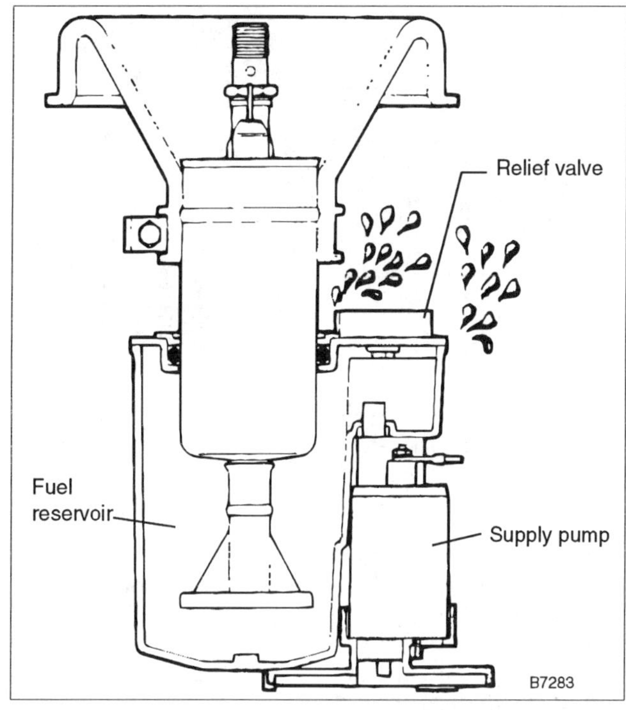

Fig. 7. Cutaway view of roller-type fuel pump showing fuel forced out of relief valve as supply pump operates.

4. When finished, clean up all spilled fuel and reinstall the pump mounting boot.

Fuel Pump

Fuel Pump Delivery Rate

This test checks the fuel pump output. Insufficient fuel delivery can result in poor performance, hard starts, hesitation, and stalling.

To test pump delivery

1. Working in the engine compartment, disconnect the fuel return line from the pressure regulator. See Fig. 8. Attach a length of fuel line to the pressure regulator and place the hose into a 2 liter (2 quart) container.

WARNING
Fuel will be expelled as the line is disconnected.

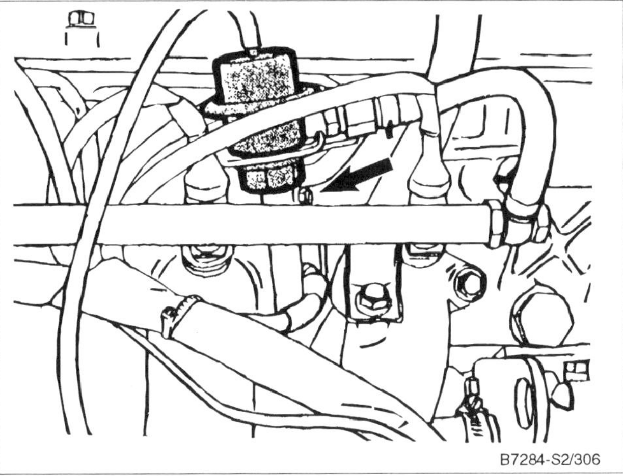

Fig. 8. Disconnect fuel return line at pressure regulator (arrow). Attach length of hose to regulator and place hose end into container.

2. Install the switched jumper (see Fig. 5) and run the fuel pump for exactly 30 seconds. Check the amount of fuel in the container.

Fuel Pump Delivery Volume
- minimum of 900 ml (30 oz.) in 30 seconds

Causes of insufficient delivery:
- system pressure incorrect. Check fuel pressure as described in **240 Fuel Injection**
- clogged pump strainer/fuel filter/supply line
- voltage at fuel pump incorrect. See **Fuel Pump Electrical Tests**
- worn fuel pump

If fuel delivery volume is low, reconnect the fuel return line to the pressure regulator. Install a pressure gauge as described in **240 Fuel Injection**. Run the fuel pump and slowly clamp shut the fuel return line at the pressure regulator. Immediately release the pinched hose as soon as the pressure approaches 6 bar (83 psi). When the return line is clamped shut, the gauge needle should rapidly rise to about 6 bar (83 psi). If not then the pump is probably faulty.

CAUTION
Allow the fuel pressure to rise slowly. Do not allow the pressure to exceed 6 bar (83 psi). Damage to the fuel pump or lines can result.

Fuel Pump Electrical Tests

The fuel pump electrical circuit is relay controlled, which means that power to the pump must pass through the relay before the pump can run. The LH control unit controls the relay.To keep the relay closed and the pump running, the LH control unit must get a signal that the engine is turning over. This pulse signal comes from the ignition system. 1985 through 1988 Turbo models use an additional over-pressure switch to prevent engine damage as a result of turbocharger wastegate malfunction. The over-pressure switch cuts off power to the fuel pump relay whenever boost pressure is above a safe level.

NOTE
- Testing of the turbo over-pressure switch is covered below.
- An additional engine over-rev protection feature turns off the fuel injectors if the engine speed goes above 6,000 rpm. This feature is handled by the LH control unit.

If the pump fails to run at all when the starter is cranked, the problem can be due to one of the following: the fuel pump relay, the electrical circuit, the LH control unit, or the pump itself.

Always check the fuel pump fuse first. This is especially true in cold weather when moisture in the fuel may freeze in the pump, overloading the circuit and blowing the fuse.

CAUTION
- Do not bypass a failed fuse to power the circuit directly until finding out why the fuse has failed.
- Repeated fuse failures indicate an electrical problem, usually a short to ground or an overloaded circuit. A circuit overload can be caused by a faulty component, such as a jammed pump.

NOTE
For the best troubleshooting results, perform all tests listed below in the sequence in which they appear.

Testing Fuel Pump Circuit

Check the circuit that powers the pump by bypassing the relay to run the pump. Remove the fuel pump relay, shown in Fig. 9. Install a jumper wire between sockets 30 and 87b in the relay panel. The pump should run.

If the pump runs with the relay bypassed, you can assume that the pump and the wiring to the pump is OK. It is either the relay, or the circuit that controls the relay that is faulty. See **Testing Relay Circuit** below.

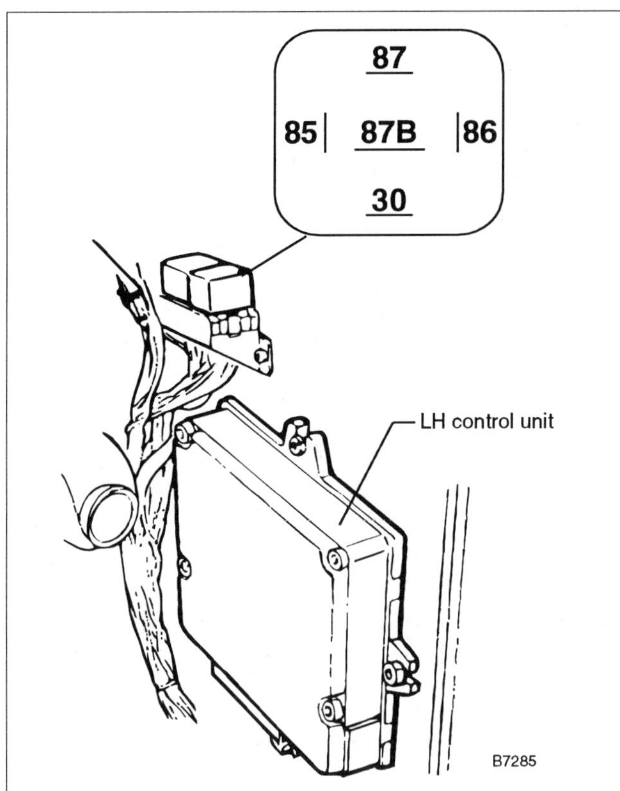

Fig. 9. Fuel pump relay and LH control unit located behind right side trim panel in front passenger footwell. Inset shows relay terminal designations on relay panel with relay removed.

If the pump does not run with the relay bypassed, then there is a fault in the fuel pump circuit. Power may not be getting from the relay panel to the pump, or even from the battery to the relay panel. Use the wiring diagrams in **371 Wiring Diagrams, Fuses and Relays** to check power and ground in the circuit.

To test fuel pump relay control circuit

1. Remove the fuel pump relay. See Fig. 9 above.

2. Turn the ignition on and check for power at terminal 86 of the fuel pump relay socket. If there is no power then either the fuel-injection main relay or the wiring from the main relay to socket 86 of the fuel pump relay panel is faulty.

NOTE
See **240 Fuel Injection** for information on checking the LH main relay. See **371 Wiring Diagrams, Fuses and Relays** for all LH wiring diagrams.

---

3. Connect a voltmeter across relay socket terminals 86 (+) and 85 (–). Briefly crank the starter and check that there is battery voltage. If not, the ground signal from the LH control unit to the fuel pump relay is not present.

CAUTION
Use only a digital voltmeter with high input impedance when testing solid-state components.

NOTE
The LH control unit must get an ignition pulse telling it that the engine is being cranked or running. This signal comes from the ignition system. If this signal is not present at the LH control unit, the fuel pump relay will not operate. See **240 Fuel Injection** for LH control unit electrical tests.

---

4. If there is power at relay sockets as described above, test the relay itself. When battery power is applied to terminals 85 (–) and 86 (+), the relay should click closed (pull-down) and there should be continuity between terminals 30 and 87 and between 30 and 87b. If not, the relay is faulty.

NOTE
The above test in step 4 does not guarantee that the relay is working correctly under all operating conditions. Sometimes the relay may work intermittently only when it has been operating for some time.

Checking for Voltage at the Fuel Pump

This test checks to see if the correct voltage is reaching the pump. To make the test, remove the pump access cover in the floor of the luggage compartment. With the engine off, run the fuel pump as described above under **Operating Fuel Pump for Tests.** Then measure the voltage across the pump terminals. See Fig. 10.

Voltage at fuel pump with pump running
- at least 11.5 volts

If the voltage is below 11.5 volts, check all wiring connections in the circuit for looseness or corrosion. Clean or tighten as necessary. If there is no voltage at the pump, check the wire between the pump and the relay and the ground wire from the pump to the center crossmember in the trunk.

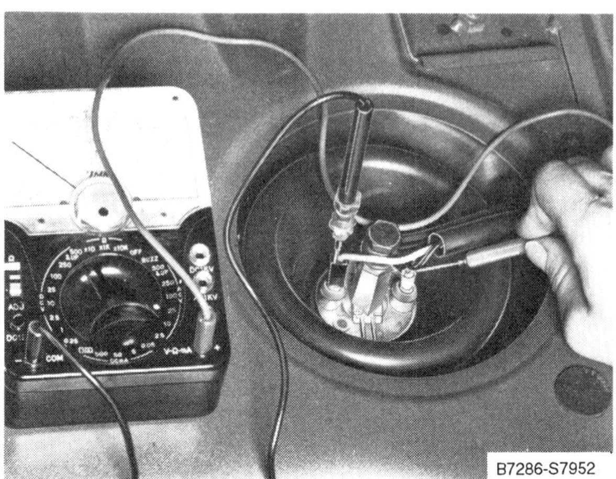

Fig. 10. Checking for voltage across fuel pump terminals with pump running and engine off. Roller-type pump shown. On models with rotor-type pump probe from back of wiring connector.

Testing Turbo Over-pressure Switch
(1985-1988 models only)

The over-pressure switch is mounted under the instrument panel to the left of the steering wheel, just behind the fuse/relay panel. Fig. 11 shows the switch. The switch is used as a backup safety device in the event the turbocharger wastegate malfunctions. If the turbocharger boost pressure exceeds a safe level, the over-pressure switch interrupts power to the fuel pump. The tests described below require the use of hand-held vacuum/pressure pump.

NOTE

All 1989 and later Turbo models also have an over-pressure safety feature, although it is handled by the 2.4 LH control unit instead of a separate pressure switch.

To test turbo over-pressure switch

1. Working beneath the left-hand side of the instrument panel, disconnect the vacuum hose from the switch and plug the hose. Attach the pump to the switch using the piece of hose.

2. With the engine running, slowly increase pressure. The engine should shut off when the pressure reaches approximately 1 bar (14.5 psi).

3. If the engine does not shut off, turn off the engine and disconnect the harness connectors from the switch. Connect an ohmmeter across switch terminals 1 and 2. With no pressure applied to the switch, there should be continuity. With 1 bar (14.5 psi) of pressure applied to the switch, there should be no continuity. If any faults are found, replace the switch.

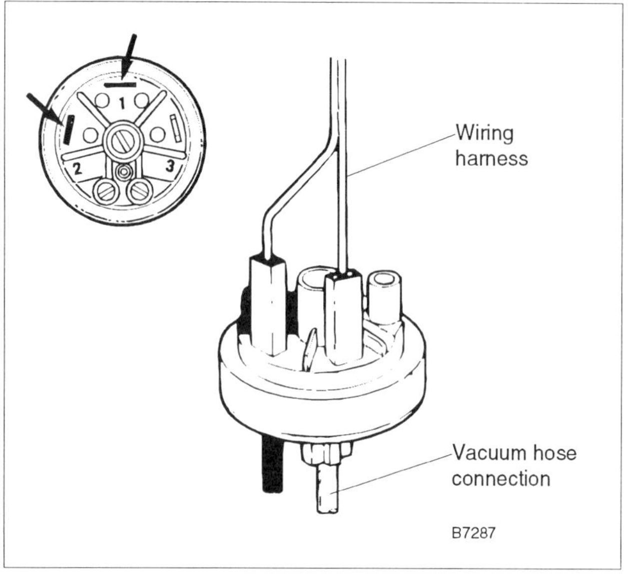

Fig. 11. Turbo over-pressure switch used on 1985-1988 Turbo models. Be sure to connect switch wires to terminals 1 and 2, as shown at arrows.

Replacing Roller-type Pump

When replacing a roller-type pump, pay close attention to the installed height and orientation of the pump. Incorrect installation can lead to fuel starvation or pump failure. Be sure to have new fuel line sealing washers on hand.

To replace roller-type pump assembly

1. Disconnect the battery negative (–) cable and cover the terminal pole on the battery. Remove the fuel pump access cover in floor of luggage compartment. Disconnect the pump wiring.

NOTE

On cars with LH 2.4 fuel injection, disconnecting the battery will erase the control unit's adaptive memory. When the engine is restarted it may operate erratically. The engine must be driven for at least 30 minutes for the adaptive memory to be reset.

---

2. Disconnect the fuel line from the pump. Using an open-ended wrench, hold the pump still while removing the dome nut. See Fig. 12.

WARNING

Fuel will be expelled when the fuel lines are disconnected and the pump is removed. Do not smoke or create sparks. Have an approved fire extinguisher handy.

CAUTION
Be careful not to damage the fuel pump terminals when loosening the center banjo bolt. If a terminal is broken off it is not repairable and the entire pump must be replaced. A special wrench is available to reduce the possibility of breaking a pump terminal. The wrench is Saab Part No. 83 94 330

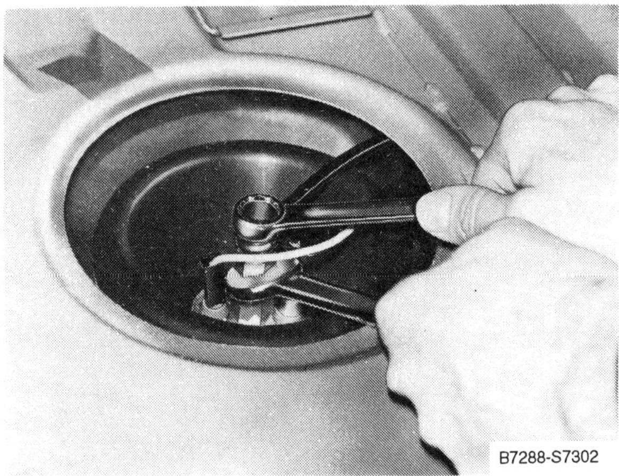

Fig. 12. Fuel line being removed from fuel pump.

3. Lift the pump up just enough to disconnect the fuel return line from the fuel reservoir and the wiring from the supply pump.

4. Using a flexible nut driver, loosen the collar mounting strap. See Fig. 13. Carefully lift out the pump.

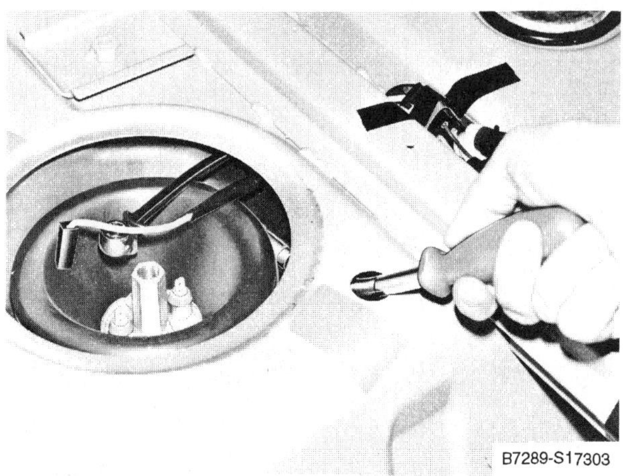

Fig. 13. Fuel pump mounting collar strap being loosened.

5. To disassemble the pump, pull the main pump out of the reservoir. The supply pump is held with a bracket and two screws.

6. To assemble the pump, install the wiring to the supply pump and install the supply pump into the reservoir, pressing it against the stop.

NOTE
On the supply pump, the white wire goes to the positive (+) terminal and the black wire to the negative (–) terminal.

7. Install the main pump into the collar and adjust it to the height shown in Fig. 14. Install the pump with collar into the reservoir and adjust the total height of the pump assembly to the specification shown in the figure.

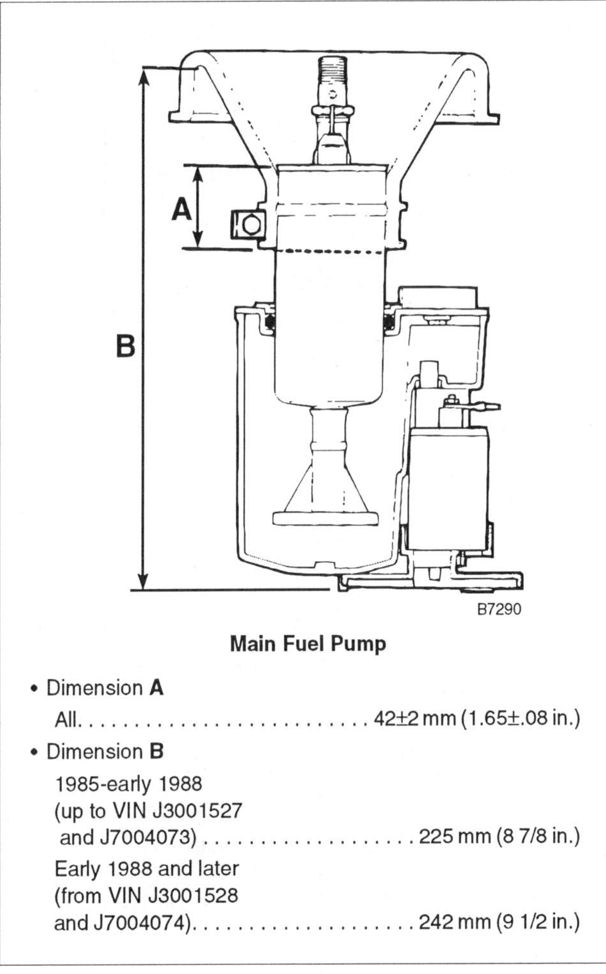

Main Fuel Pump

- Dimension **A**
  All. . . . . 42±2 mm (1.65±.08 in.)
- Dimension **B**
  1985-early 1988
  (up to VIN J3001527
  and J7004073) . . . . 225 mm (8 7/8 in.)
  Early 1988 and later
  (from VIN J3001528
  and J7004074). 242 mm (9 1/2 in.)

Fig. 14. Assembled dimension of main fuel pump in reservoir and rubber collar.

NOTE

- Proper pump height and pump orientation in the tank is very important. Scribe a mark 42 mm (1 21/32 or 1.65 in.) from the top of the pump to accurately position the collar to the pump during assembly.
- See **1 LUBRICATION AND MAINTENANCE** for information on VIN numbers and their locations.
- The supply pump on some early models may be equipped with a "bow-tie" style strainer. For better fuel pick-up and delivery, a modified strainer should be installed. See Fig. 15. The new strainer is Saab Part No. 93 86 491.

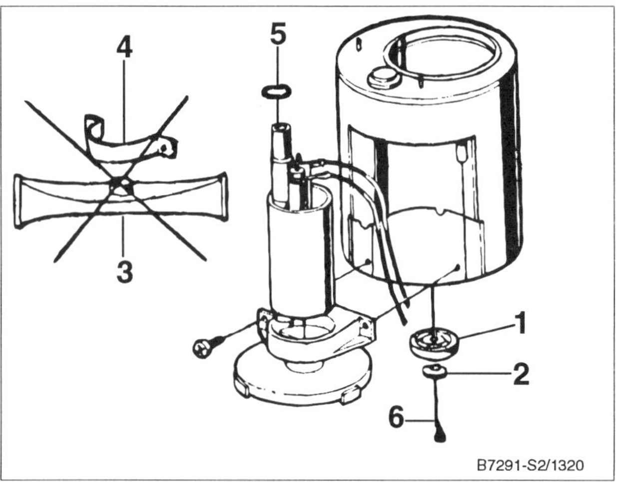

Fig. 15. Where installed, always replace bow-tie strainer (**3**) with modified strainer shown. Replace supports (**1** and **2**), clamp (**4**), and O-ring (**5**) when using new strainer. Screw (**6**) must be reinstalled for proper pressurization of reservoir.

8. Install the pump into the tank, making sure to reconnect the supply pump connector and the fuel return line before fully installing the pump. Orient the pump as shown in Fig. 16 or Fig. 17. Tighten the mounting collar clamp.
9. Using new sealing washers, reinstall the fuel line and banjo bolt/dome nut. Reconnect the wiring.

NOTE

The direction of pump rotation is determined by the polarity of the wiring, so + and – signs are cast in the pump housing to ensure proper wiring connection.

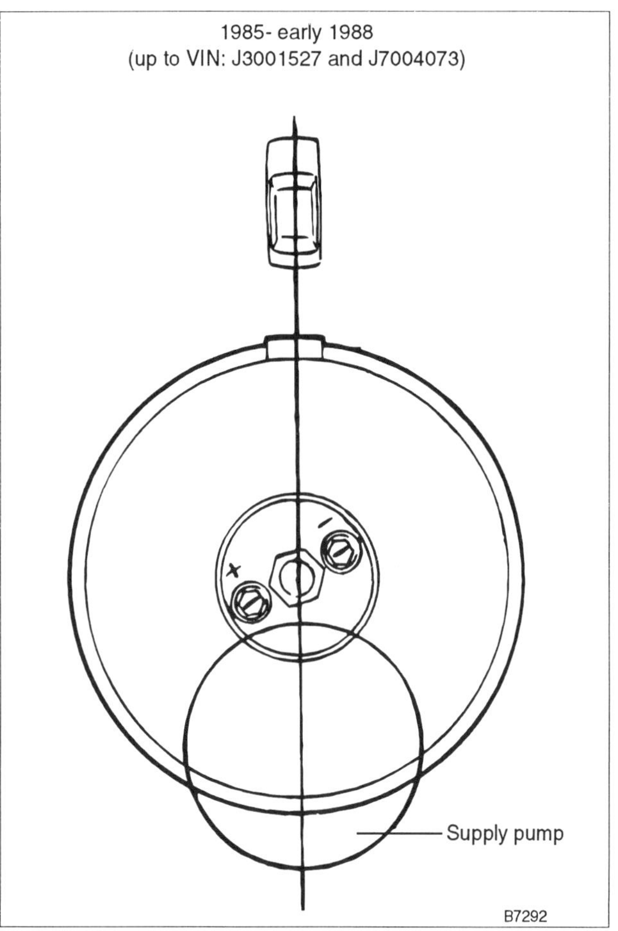

Fig. 16. 1985 to early 1988 fuel pump orientation relative to car.

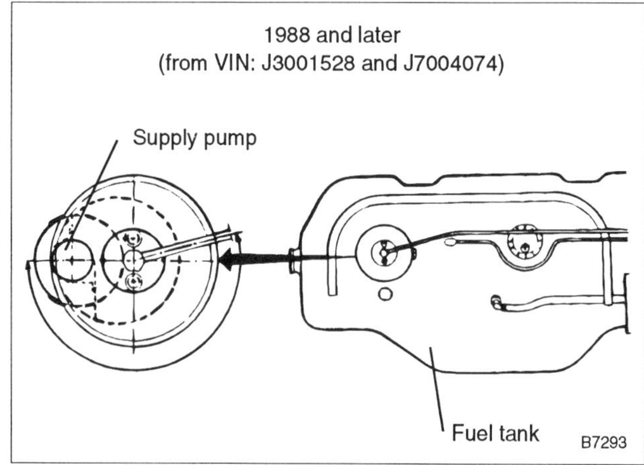

Fig. 17. Early 1988 and later fuel pump orientation relative to fuel tank.

Replacing Rotor-type Pump

When removing and installing the rotor-type fuel pump, always replace the O-rings that seal the fuel lines and the pump to the tank. This is especially important on 1990 and later models because the O-rings are designed to swell when exposed to fuel vapor. These O-rings cannot be reinstalled unless they are completely dry.

There were two styles of rotor-type pumps installed. The early version had the supply check valve installed in the pump assembly. The later pump (identified by the internal T-fitting in the pump's supply line) had the supply check valve fitted in the supply line fitting. If the early pump is replaced, a new check valve must be inserted into the end of the supply line using special tools, as the early-style pump is no longer available. See **Replacing Fuel Pump Check Valve** below for replacement procedures.

To replace rotor-type pump assembly

1. Disconnect the battery negative (–) cable and cover the terminal pole on the battery.

NOTE

On cars with LH 2.4 fuel injection, disconnecting the battery cable will erase the control unit's adaptive memory. When the engine is restarted it may operate erratically for up to 30 minutes.

---

2. Working in the luggage compartment, remove the access panel from above the pump.

3. Remove the clamp that secures the fuel lines and wiring. See Fig. 18. Disconnect the wiring from the pump.

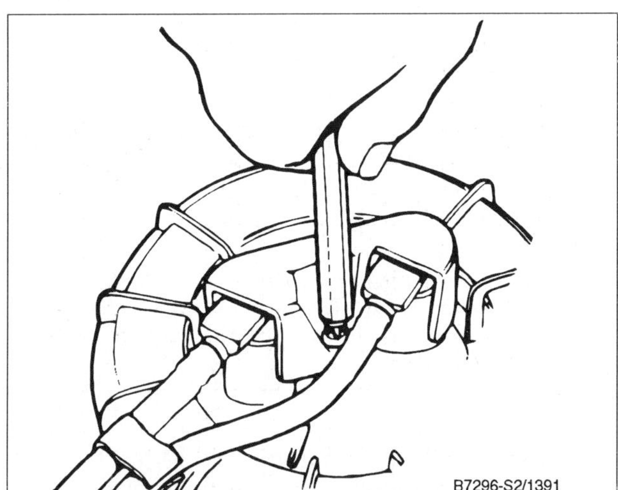

Fig. 18. Fuel line and pump wiring hold-down clamp.

4. Using a round-jawed pliers, disconnect the fuel lines by pulling them straight up. See Fig. 19. Tie the fuel lines back.

WARNING

Fuel will be expelled under pressure. Wrap clean rags around the fuel line fittings before removing them from the pump.

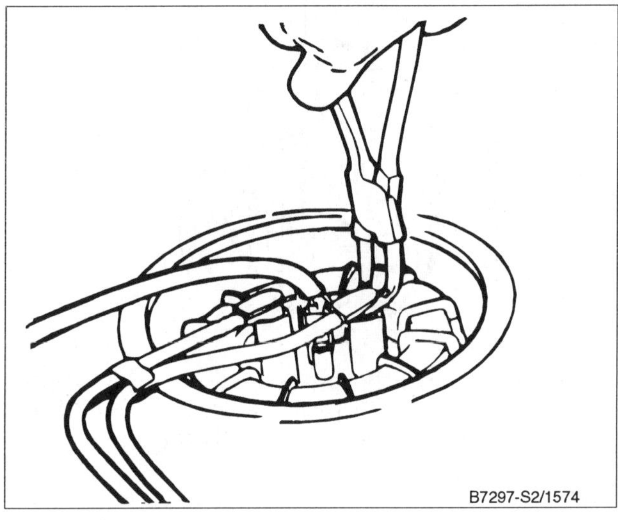

Fig. 19. Fuel lines being removed.

5. Loosen the large threaded retaining collar while holding the pump stationary.

CAUTION

The pump must not turn when loosening the retaining collar or the ejector assembly could be damaged. A special tool is available to hold the pump stationary as the collar is loosened. See Fig. 20.

---

6. Lift the pump assembly up to allow excess fuel to drain, then tilt it slightly to remove it from the tank. Place it in a receptacle to catch any remaining fuel.

NOTE

Carefully inspect the fuel delivery line . If the hose is distorted or ballooned, it should be replaced. This hose is available as a replacement part through and authorized Saab dealer. Be sure to check the fuel system pressure if the hose is distorted. Excessive fuel pressure due to a blocked check valve will cause the new hose to balloon.

---

7. Carefully insert the new pump assembly (ejector pump side first) into the tank so that the fuel line fittings on the pump are parallel with the length of the car and that the matching mark on the pump is aligned with the mark on the tank. See Fig. 21.

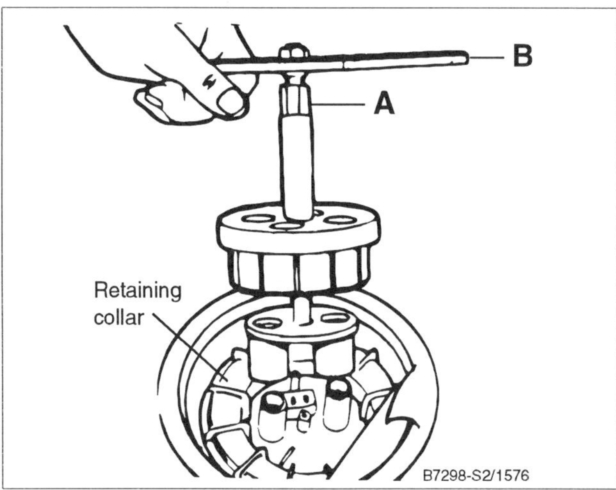

Fig. 20. Special tool for fuel pump removal. Loosen collar by turning outer part of tool with open-end wrench at **A** while holding pump stationary with handle (**B**) on inner tool.

NOTE

Make sure that the pump fits between the locating ribs in the bottom of the tank and that the matching marks on the pump and tank are exactly aligned.

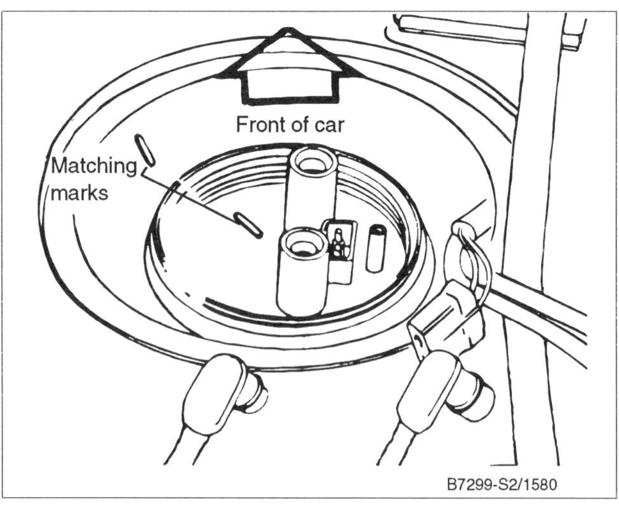

Fig. 21. Correct alignment of pump assembly relative to tank.

8. On 1989 models, lubricate the new collar seal with petroleum jelly (Vaseline) and insert it into the retaining collar. Install the collar while aligning the matching marks. See Fig. 22. Press down firmly on the collar until it engages the tank. Tighten the collar until it stops.

CAUTION

Do not allow the pump assembly to turn when tightening the collar. Otherwise the ejector assembly may be damaged.

NOTE

The locating marks on the retaining collar must be within 30° to either side of the marks on pump and tank.

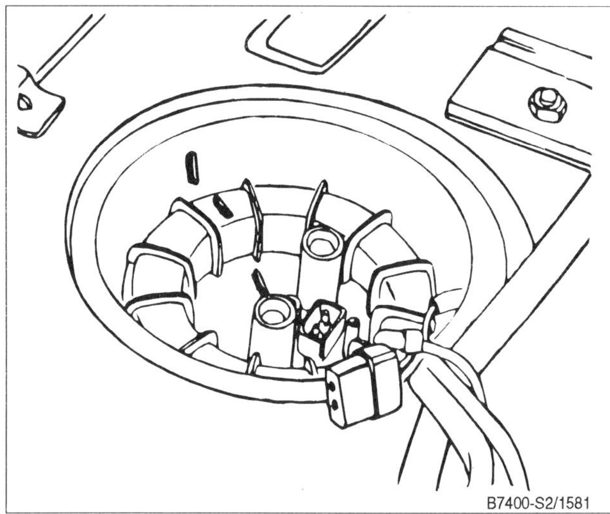

Fig. 22. Matching marks on retaining collar and fuel tank correctly aligned.

9. On 1990 and later models, fit the new collar seal in the groove in the fuel tank. Install the retaining collar, tightening it using Saab special tool no. 83 94 462 or an equivalent. See Fig. 23.

Tightening torque

- Fuel pump to fuel tank (threaded collar)
  1990 and later . . . . 55 Nm (40 ft-lb)

CAUTION

Do not allow the pump assembly to turn when tightening the collar. Otherwise the ejector assembly may be damaged. Check that the locating marks on the pump and tank are still aligned after tighening.

---

10. Using new O-rings, reconnect the fuel lines. The return line (with check-valve) attaches to the outlet nearest the front of the car. The supply line attaches to the rear outlet. Reconnect the wiring and fit the clamp.

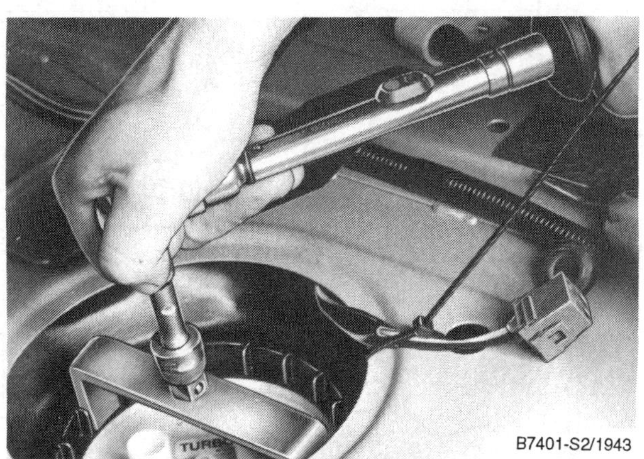

Fig. 23. Threaded collar being tightened using Saab special tool no. 83 94 462 on 1990 and later models.

NOTE

During 1990 production, the supply line check valve was moved from the supply-line socket in the pump to the end of the supply line itself. Make sure you identify each fuel line correctly before connecting it.

To replace fuel pump screen (models with rotor-type pump only)

1. Carefully ease back the lugs that secure the ejector pump, turn the ejector 90° (1/4 turn) clockwise and remove it from the reservoir. See Fig. 24.

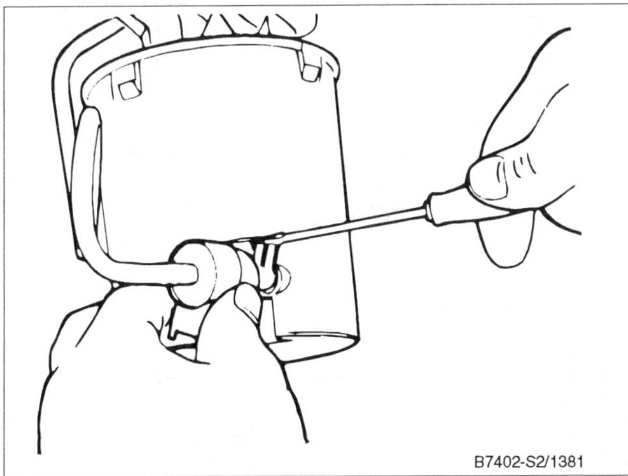

Fig. 24. Ejector pump retaining lugs being eased back. Turn ejector 1/4 turn and remove from reservoir assembly.

2. Separate the reservoir and filter unit from the top section. See Fig. 25.

3. Install the new reservoir and filter assembly to the pump upper part using a new O-ring.

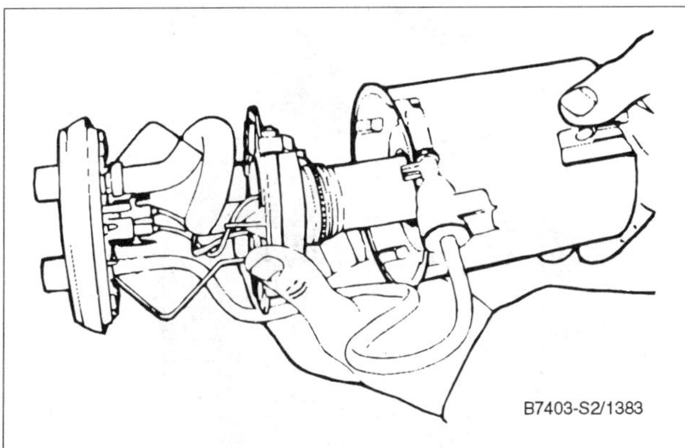

Fig. 25. Reservoir and filter unit being separated from pump top section.

4. Fit a new O-ring to the ejector pump and reinstall it into the reservoir, turning it 90° counter-clockwise to lock it to the dog on the reservoir.

NOTE

Check that the ejector pump is clean. If necessary blow through using compressed air to remove any foreign material.

Replacing Fuel Pump Check Valve

A one-way check valve is used at the fuel pump supply line to hold fuel pressure in the system after the pump shuts off. A faulty valve can cause longer engine cranking on restart because of the loss of fuel system rest pressure. The check valve is tested as part of a fuel system pressure test as described **240 Fuel Injection**

WARNING

- Fuel under pressure will be expelled. Wipe up any spilled fuel immediately. Wrap fuel lines with a clean rag before removing them. Do not smoke or create sparks. Have an approved fire extinguisher handy.

- Always remove the battery negative (–) cable before doing any work on any fuel system component.

To replace the check valve on models with roller-type pump, remove the banjo fitting while holding the pump steady. Then carefully remove the check valve from the pump. Install the new check valve and the banjo fitting, using new sealing washers. See Fig. 26.

CAUTION

Do not grip the check valve too tightly, as it may become damaged.

Fig. 26. Fuel pump check valve shown removed from roller-type fuel pump.

On models with the rotor-type pump, two types of check valves were used on the cars covered by this manual. On 1989 models, the return line check valve was part of the fuel pump. On 1990 and later models, the check valve was integrated into the supply line fitting (elbow). If a 1989 pump is being replaced with the newer superseded pump or if the new style check valve is faulty, installation of a new check valve will require the use of a special tool.

To install the check valve in the supply line, first cut the old fitting from the end of the line as close as possible to the fitting. Using the special tool (Saab tool no. 83 94 546) and a channel-lock pliers, carefully press the new check valve fitting into the fuel supply line. See Fig. 27. Use new O-rings when reconnecting the fuel supply line to the pump.

NOTE

Do not cut more than 12–14 mm (1/2 in.) of the supply line when removing the fitting/check valve. If more than this is removed, a new fuel-pump-to-fuel-filter fuel line will have to be installed.

FUEL TANK AND LINES

Fuel Tank

The fuel tank is held in place with two straps. Removal and installation is fairly straightforward as long as the rear of the car can be raised and supported securely. The following information is a general guide to the necessary steps for tank removal and installation.

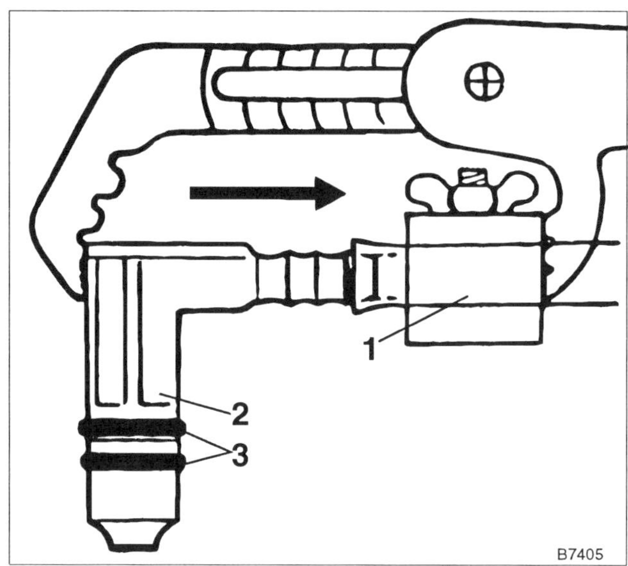

Fig. 27. New supply line check valve (**2**) being installed with Saab special tool (**1**). Always use new O-rings (**3**).

WARNING

Fuel will be expelled when the fuel lines are disconnected. Do not smoke or create sparks. Have an approved fire extinguisher handy.

To remove and install fuel tank

1. Drain the fuel tank using the fuel pump. Run a hose from the pump outlet on the tank into a suitable container. See Fig. 28. Then run the fuel pump without running the engine as described earlier under **Fuel Pump Troubleshooting.**

NOTE

The fuel tank is not equipped with a drain plug.

---

2. Disconnect the battery negative (–) cable.

NOTE

On cars with LH 2.4 fuel injection, disconnecting the battery cable will erase the control unit's adaptive memory. The engine must be driven for about 30 minutes for the adaptive memory to be reset.

---

3. Working from the luggage compartment, remove the floor covers and disconnect the electrical leads from the pump and fuel gauge sender.

4. Raise the rear of the car and support it securely.

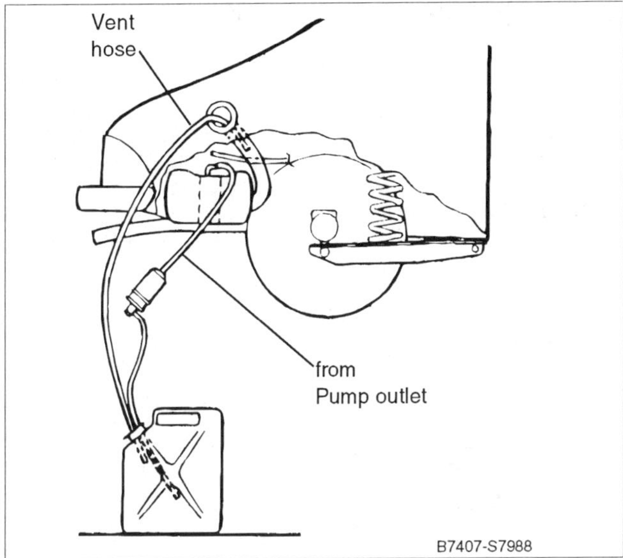

Fig. 28. Setup used to drain fuel tank. A vent hose should be used to prevent emission of hydrocarbons.

5. Disconnect the filler pipe, breather lines, and fuel return line from the tank. Undo the fuel line clips.

6. Remove the strap nuts and lower the tank.

NOTE

Before installing the tank, check that the rubber seal around the fuel sender opening is positioned correctly and undamaged. Cover the tank openings with tape.

---

7. Raise the tank into position and support it with the straps. Adjust the tank's lateral position, then tighten the straps and remove the tape.

8. Reconnect the filler pipe, making sure the rubber grommet is in position.

9. Reconnect all fuel lines, clips, and electrical connections.

10. Lower the car and reconnect the battery negative (–) cable.

To remove and install fuel gauge sender unit

WARNING

Fuel will be exposed. Do not smoke or create sparks. Have an approved fire extinguisher handy.

NOTE

There are different fuel sender gaskets depending on the sender installed. For the most correct replacement, bring the old gasket to an authorized Saab dealer to match up with the replacement gasket.

---

1. Disconnect the battery negative (–) cable. Cover the battery terminal.

2. Remove the cover from above the sender in the luggage compartment. Disconnect the sender wiring.

3. Remove the sender's threaded retaining ring.

NOTE

A Saab special tool (tool no. 83 93 365) is available to remove and install the threaded retaining ring. See Fig. 29.

Fig. 29. Fuel gauge sender retaining ring being removed using socket wrench and Saab special tool no. 83 93 365. (Saab Part No. 83 93 365).

4. Withdraw the sender and let it drain. Remove the old seal and discard.

5. Fit a new sender seal, insert the sender into the tank, and tighten the retaining ring. Reconnect the wiring and fit the cover.

NOTE

New senders are shipped with a retaining wire at the bottom to prevent float damage. Remove the wire before installing the sender, or else the gauge will only read EMPTY.

To replace fuel tank rollover valve

1. Working in the luggage compartment, remove the trim from the right-hand side.

2. Remove the rollover valve mounting screws and pull the valve into the luggage compartment. See Fig. 30.

Fig. 30. Rollover valve in luggage compartment being removed.

3. Disconnect the hose from the valve and remove the valve.

Installation is the reverse of removal. Make sure the long outlet on the valve is facing up when installing.

Fuel Lines

The fuel lines that run from the fuel tank to the engine compartment are routed along the left-hand sill inside the car.

To replace fuel lines inside car

1. Remove the left-hand sill scuff plate and roll the carpet back.

2. Peel back the tape holding the fuel lines to the body.

3. Carefully remove the insulation felt from the bulkhead.

4. Disconnect the fuel return and supply lines in the engine compartment and pull the lines through the bulkhead grommets and into the passenger compartment.

5. Release the lines from the retaining clips at the fuel tank and remove the lines from the car.

Installation is the reverse of removal. Clean the fuel lines using low pressure compressed air. Tape the open ends before reinstalling them. Always replace fuel fitting sealing washers and any crimp-type hose clamps.

To replace banjo fitting on fuel line

WARNING
The procedure below requires the use of a soldering iron with a knife tip. Completely remove the hose and its fitting from the car. Move a safe distance away from the car and any open fuel when making the repair.

1. Using a soldering iron, melt a notch into the into the end of the line. See Fig. 31.

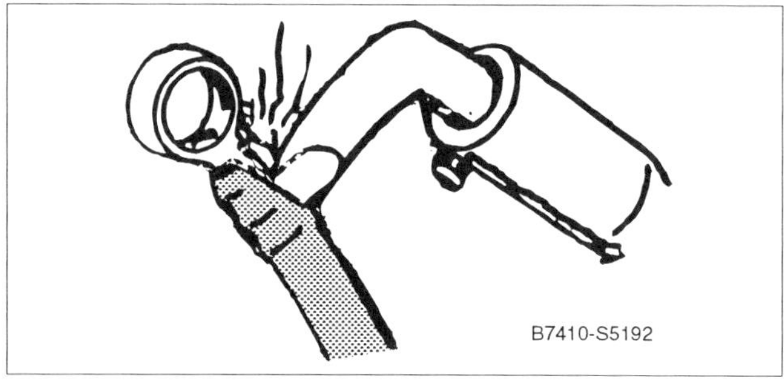

Fig. 31. Soldering iron being used to melt notch in fuel line.

2. Pull the fitting out of the fuel line. Cut the fuel line back just enough to remove the melted notch made earlier.

3. Using a section of thick rubber hose, slice it open and place it over the fuel line. Place the fuel line in a vice. Allow the end of the line to overhang the vise jaws slightly. See Fig. 32.

NOTE
As a better alternative to the split rubber hose, use Saab special tool no. 83 94 546 and a channel-lock pliers to install the fitting to the fuel line. See Fig. 27 shown earlier.

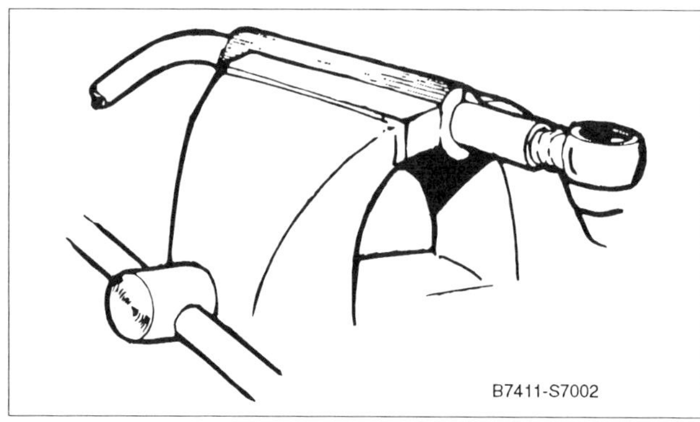

Fig. 32. Fuel line (protected with rubber hose) installed in vice.

4. Tap the fitting into the fuel line until it is fully seated.

240 Fuel Injection

TABLES

GENERAL

All Saab 16-valve models feature Bosch LH Fuel Injection as standard equipment. This system is also know as Hot-wire fuel injection, owing to the operation of the air mass meter, which uses a heated wire to help measure the incoming air.

Fuel injection component troubleshooting and repair are covered in detail within this repair group. Special equipment may be necessary for some of the procedures included here. If you do not have the equipment or the experience required to accurately do the job, we suggest leaving those tests or repairs to an authorized Saab dealer. The Saab dealer is equipped with special diagnostic test equipment; the ISAT (Intelligent Saab Tester) and the LH Tester. Both of these electronic tools are capable of quickly pinpointing hard-to-find LH fuel injection problems.

NOTE

- Fuel supply—the system that pressurizes the fuel and delivers it to the injection system—is covered in **234 Fuel Pump and Fuel Tank**.
- Exhaust emission systems, such as Evaporative Loss Control (ELCD), and Exhaust Gas Recirculation (EGR) are covered separately in **254 Exhaust Emission Control.**

Principle of Operation

Bosch LH fuel injection is completely electronic in operation. Air flow is measured electronically, and a proportional amount of fuel is metered by electrically opening and closing the fuel injectors.

In LH fuel injection, many sensors supply information about engine operating conditions to a central electronic control unit (ECU). The control unit then calculates the amount of fuel needed for the correct air-fuel ratio and opens the fuel injectors, once for each engine revolution. The amount of fuel metered to the engine is determined solely by how long the injectors are open.

There are three versions of LH fuel injection on 16-valve models. Each has the same basic components and operating principles. The differences among the three are mainly in refinements of certain operations and additional functions, introduced on newer models. See **Table a.**

Air Intake. All air entering the engine passes through a pleated paper air filter in the air cleaner. Air flow is controlled by the throttle valve in the throttle housing. Along with the throttle valve, the housing contains idle air passages, connec-

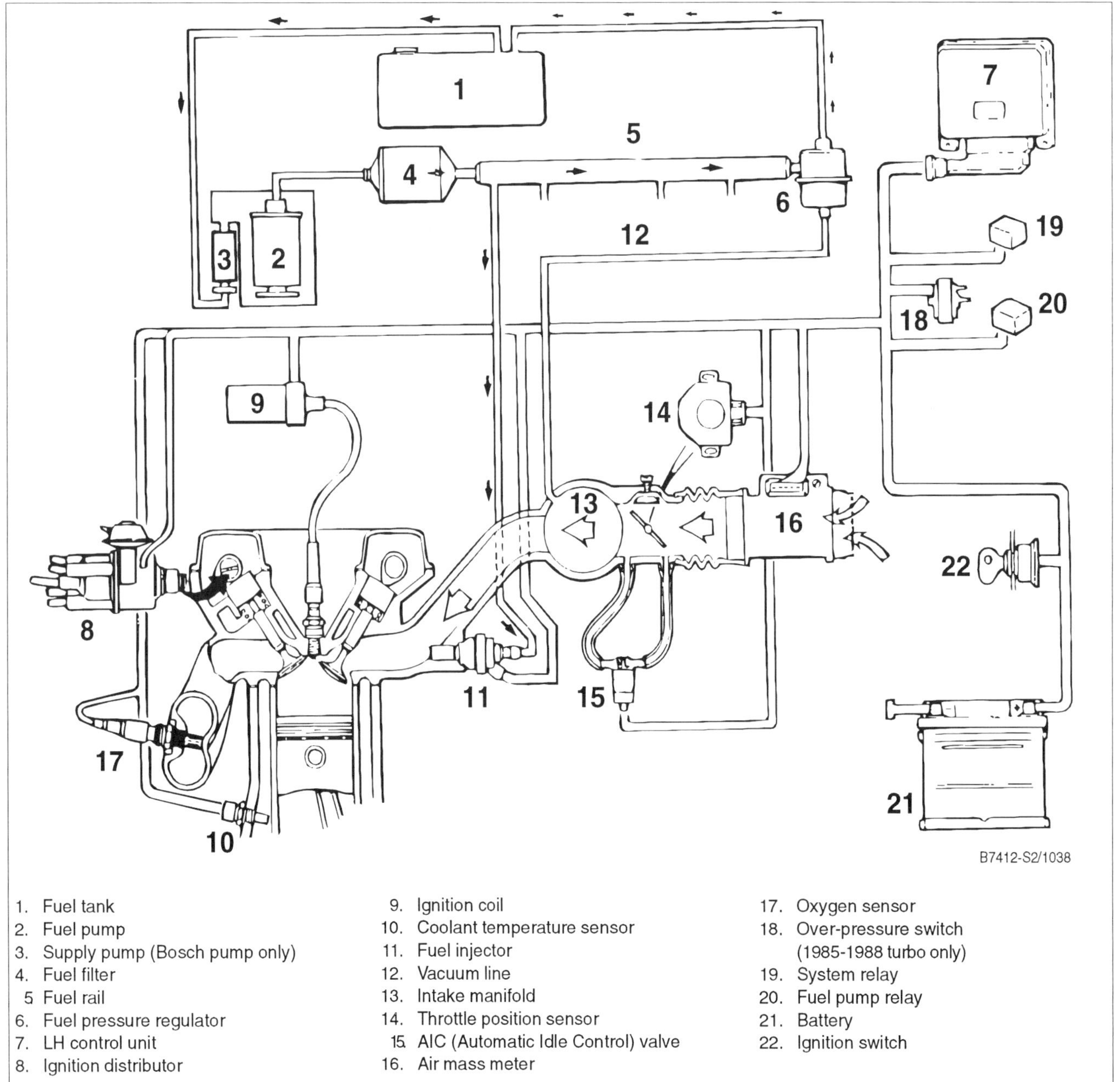

Fig. 1. Schematic view of LH fuel injection.

Table a. LH Fuel Injection Variants

System	Year/Model	Identification
LH 2.2	1985-1988 Turbo	Three-wire AIC idle valve, metal air mass meter with a sealed mixture adjustment screw, and a throttle dashpot
	1986-1987 Non-turbo	
LH 2.4	1989-1992 Turbo	Two-wire AIC idle valve, plastic air mass meter without a mixture adjustment screw
	1988-1990 Non-turbo	
LH 2.4.2	1991and later Non-turbo	Three-wire AIC idle valve, similar plastic air mass meter without a mixture adjustment screw, and a throttle potentiometer.

tions for the Adaptive Idle Control (AIC) valve, and vacuum connections. The housing is connected to the hot-wire air mass meter by flexible rubber ducts. Air entering the engine is measured by the air mass meter. The meter has no moving parts. Instead, the meter measures air flow electronically and generates a voltage signal. This signal is then used by the control unit to determine how much fuel to inject.

Fuel Metering. The control unit meters fuel by changing the opening time (pulse time) of the fuel injectors. To ensure that injector pulse time is the only factor that determines fuel metering, fuel pressure is precisely controlled by a fuel pressure regulator. The injectors are mounted to a common fuel supply called the fuel rail. The control unit monitors engine speed (ignition pulse) to determine the rate of injector openings. Other signals to the control unit help determine injector pulse time for different operating conditions. A temperature sensor signals engine temperature for cold-start and warm-up enrichment. A throttle position sensor signals throttle position for full-throttle and idle. An oxygen sensor signals information about combustion efficiency for control of the air-fuel mixture.

Automatic Idle Control (AIC). Idle speed is electronically controlled. The LH control unit controls an idle valve that allows air to bypass the closed throttle valve. This bypass control is known as the AIC system. The control unit makes continual changes to the valve opening to adjust idle speed based on engine operating conditions. The bypass air passage is upstream of the air mass meter, so mixture is not affected by changing the idle speed.

LH 2.4 Fuel Injection. Both the AIC and mixture control systems are adaptive on this system. That means that each system compensates automatically for changes in the engine due to age or small problems. As a result, idle speed and mixture do not need to be adjusted. A deceleration fuel shut-off function in the LH 2.4 control unit replaces the deceleration dashpot used on LH 2.2. An integrated Evaporative Loss Control Device (ELCD) system is used on LH 2.4. Operation of the ELCD valve is controlled by the LH control unit. Another main feature of the LH 2.4 system is that it has on-board diagnostics. See **On-board Diagnostics** for more information.

LH 2.4.2 Fuel Injection This fuel injection system is used only on 900 models with the 2.1 liter engine. LH 2.4.2 has all of the features of the earlier LH 2.4 system, plus additional refinements. The system uses a new AIC valve. A throttle potentiometer replaces the throttle switch, and the control unit has been reprogrammed to modify the control of many other functions, including additional diagnostic codes.

NOTE

Unless otherwise noted, all procedures and specifications in this chapter apply to all LH fuel injection variants. Where distinction is important, the systems will be referred to by their alpha-numeric codes—LH 2.2, LH 2.4, LH 2.4.2.

Safety Precautions

The following warnings and caution should be adhered to whenever doing work on the fuel injection system.

WARNING

- Fuel will be discharged during many fuel system test procedures. Do not smoke or work near heaters or other fire hazards. Have a fire extinguisher handy. Work only in a well-ventilated area.

- Wear suitable hand protection, as prolonged contact with fuel can cause illnesses and skin disorders.

CAUTION

- Connect and disconnect wires and test equipment only with the ignition off.

- Before making any electrical tests that require the engine to be cranked using the starter, disable the ignition system as described in **340 Ignition System**

- On models with LH 2.4 and LH 2.4.2, always wait at least 40 seconds after turning off the ignition before removing the control unit connector. If the connector is removed before this time, residual power in the system relay may damage the control unit.

- Cleanliness is essential when working with parts of the fuel system open. Thoroughly clean fuel line connections and surrounding areas before loosening. Avoid the use of compressed air, and avoid moving the car. Only install clean parts.

CAUTION

Fuel system cleaners and other chemical additives other than those specifically recommended by Saab may seriously damage the catalytic converter, the oxygen sensor and the plastic gas tank.

FAULT DIAGNOSIS

The management of engine functions is controlled by a number of systems—ignition, fuel injection, and emission control. Because these functions are interrelated, it is difficult if not impossible to isolate general driveability problems by examining components of the fuel injection system alone. For this reason, engine management and driveability troubleshooting information can found in **200 Engine—General.** This information is organized to help isolate problems and suggest more specific troubleshooting steps by taking all of the interrelated systems into consideration.

Fig. 2 shows an overall view of the engine compartment to help you identify component locations for testing and replacement.

Basics Requirements for LH Fuel Injection

The following list contains basic checks that should be made when experiencing fuel injection problems. Again, if in doubt of whether the fault is caused by the fuel system or

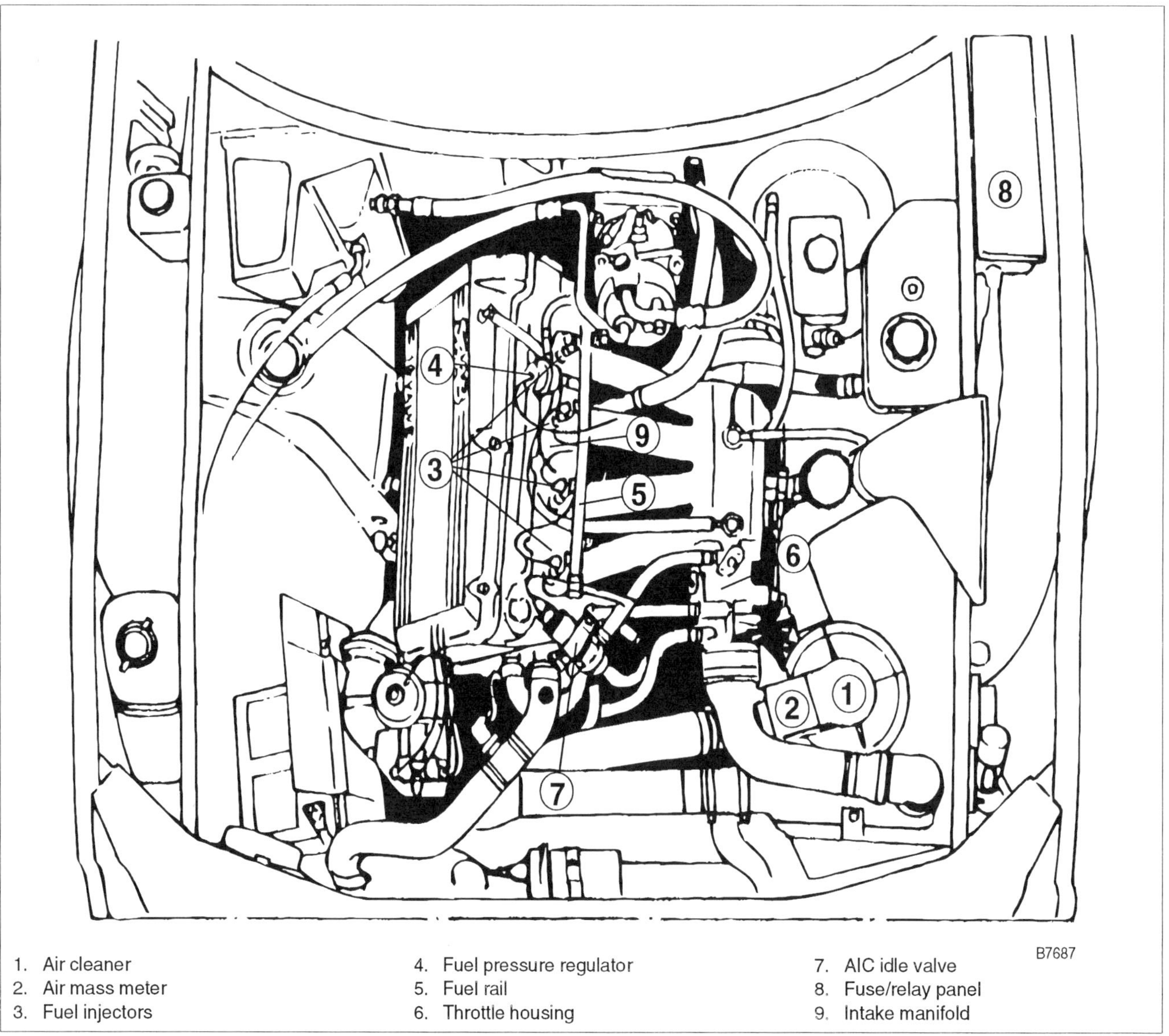

1. Air cleaner
2. Air mass meter
3. Fuel injectors
4. Fuel pressure regulator
5. Fuel rail
6. Throttle housing
7. AIC idle valve
8. Fuse/relay panel
9. Intake manifold

Fig. 2. Typical view of engine compartment from front of car.

some other system such as the ignition system, consult **200 Engine—General** first.

1. Check the intake (induction) system for leaks. Check for cracked, loose, or disconnected hoses and duct work. Check that all hose clamps are tight. On Turbo cars, be sure to check the hoses and hose clamps at the turbocharger by-pass valve. See **291 Turbocharger.**

NOTE

An air leak allows unmeasured air to enter the engine, often resulting in an in overly lean fuel mixture and causing driveability problems.

---

2. Check that the battery is in good condition. Check that the battery cables are tight and free of corrosion. Check that all related ground points are firmly connected and in good condition. Don't forget to check the main ground at the battery. Check all of the harness connectors for damage and corrosion. Check for power and ground at the LH control unit. See **371 Wiring Diagrams, Fuses and Relays.**

3. Check the fuses.

4. Check for sufficient fuel in the tank. If the engine ran out of fuel it takes up to two gallons to prime the pump. See **234 Fuel Pump and Fuel Tank.**

5. Check for spark at the spark plugs. If the tachometer needle bounces while the engine is cranked by the starter then the ignition system is probably working correctly. See **340 Ignition System.**

6. On cars with LH 2.4 and LH 2.4.2, check for any faults through the on-board diagnostics system (LH 2.4 and LH 2.4.2 only) as described below.

On-board Diagnostics (LH 2.4 and LH 2.4.2 only)

LH 2.4 and LH 2.4.2 fuel injection systems feature built-in diagnostic circuitry that detects and stores coded fault information in the LH control unit's memory. When the system compensates for values that are outside the permitted limits, a fault code is generated. The fault codes can be "read-out" through the **Check Engine** light.

The system has the ability to store up to three fault codes, including intermittent faults. The system also has a built-in test cycle that can actively test all major fuel injection components and their signals.

NOTE

- As a general rule, a steady-on Check Engine light means the LH control unit has detected a fault. A flashing Check Engine light means that the EZK Ignition system has detected a fault. As an exception to the rule, the check engine light on 1992 models does not flash. Therefore, a steady-on Check Engine light on these models could be either an EZK system or an LH system fault.

- LH 2.2 is not equipped with LH on-board diagnostics. Although these models are equipped with a check engine light, it is primarily used for EZK ignition system fault detection. On LH 2.2, the Check Engine light will come on in the event of an air mass meter fault and the engine will go into a "limp-home" mode.

The fault code display is triggered by grounding a pin at the LH control unit test connector. A special Saab test harness (tool no. 83 93 886), available from an authorized Saab dealer, should be used to make the test. As an alternative, a switched test lead can be constructed using simple electrical components. Be sure to make the lead long enough to reach the driver's seat.

The following on-board diagnostic codes are broken into two parts—one for LH faults and the other for component and signal testing.

To display LH fault codes

1. With the ignition key off and the test lead switch off, connect one end of the lead to ground and the other end to the connector terminal shown in Fig. 3.

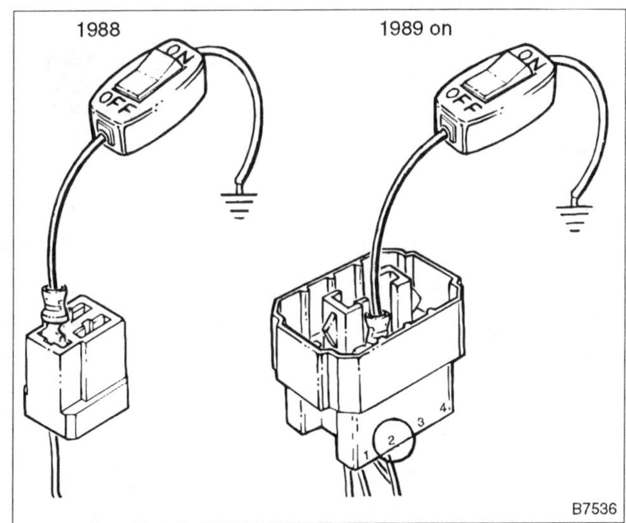

Fig. 3. Switch lead shown connected to test connector. On 1988 models the 3-pin connector is in the engine compartment, near the fresh air intake. On 1989 and later sedan models the 10-pin connector is beneath the rear seat. On 1989 and later convertible models, the 10-pin connector is under the bellows ahead of the shifter.

CAUTION

Carry out the tests exactly as shown. An extra few seconds at the wrong time can clear the fault memory.

2. With the engine off and the test lead switch OFF, turn the ignition key to the ON position.

3. When the Check Engine light comes on, turn the test lead switch ON. The light should immediately go out.

4. Wait until the Check Engine light flashes once and then immediately turn the test lead switch OFF.

5. A fault code (if present) will begin to flash through the Check Engine light. There is a long flash at the beginning and end of each code. The code itself is a series of short flashes. Once the code is fully displayed it will begin to repeat itself until the next code is called up. **Table b** lists fault codes, their probable faults, and corrective actions.

Table b. Fuel Injection On-board Diagnostic Fault Codes (LH 2.4, LH 2.4.2 only)

Error code	Check Engine light in normal driving	Probable fault	Corrective action, first check
12231	Off	No rpm signal (this code will always be present if the test is run with the engine off). Crank the engine for 5 seconds. If the code disappears, the rpm signal is O.K.	Check fuse no. 3. Check the ignition system input at pin 1 of the LH control unit
12221	On	No signal from air mass meter (LH system is in limp-home mode)	Check air mass meter connections. Check for air mass meter burn-off. (Do not interchange air mass meter from LH 2.2—component damage may result)
12214	On	Coolant temperature signal incorrect (temperature signal out of range: below -90°C or above 160°C)	Test coolant temperature sensor. Make resistance test at pin 13 of LH control unit and ground. (Resistance should be approx. 2280-2720 ohms at 68°F (20°C) and 290-365 ohms at 176°F (80°C))
12211	Off	Incorrect battery voltage (below 10 volts or over 16 volts with engine running)	Check charging system, battery connections, grounds, etc.
12225	On	Incorrect oxygen sensor output. Sensor pre-heater circuit may be open. (Engine temp. must be above 176°F for 1988 model, or above 158°F for 1989 and later model)	Check oxygen sensor output voltage (voltage fluctuating between 0 and 1.0 volt). Check oxygen sensor pre-heater circuit and fuse
12223	On	Air-fuel mixture too lean	Tighten all boot clamps and carefully check all hose connections. Check injector O-rings. Check ELCD valve.Check fuel pressure. (Also see fault code 12225 above)
12241	On	Air-fuel mixture fault	
12224	On	Air-fuel mixture too rich	
12233	On	LH control unit fault (ROM mixture fault)	Replace LH control unit
12242	On	Air mass meter burn-off function fault	Check air mass meter wiring and burn-off function
12243	Off	No signal from road speed sensor	Check signal output from road speed sensor on speedometer. Check for power and ground supply at sensor
12244	Off	A/T "Drive" signal faulty. (signal absent while driving or constantly present even when stopped)	Check the fuse for the reverse lights, the reverse light switch, the wiring connections, etc
12245	On	EGR temperature too low (where applicable)	Check function of EGR system. See **254 Exhaust Emission Control**
12232	Off	Memory voltage below 1 volt	Check for battery voltage at pin 4 of the LH control unit with the ignition off
12212	Off	Idle contacts in throttle position switch shorted, closed throttle switch while driving (LH 2.4 only)	Check and adjust throttle position switch. Check wiring harness for short to ground

continued on next page

Table b. Fuel Injection On-board Diagnostic Fault Codes (LH 2.4, LH 2.4.2 only) (continued)

Error code	Check Engine light in normal driving	Probable fault	Corrective action, first check
12251	Off	Incorrect or missing signal from throttle potentiometer (LH 2.4.2 only)	Check throttle potentiometer function (harness disconnected at potentiometer)
12213	Off	Full throttle contacts in throttle position switch shorted, full throttle signal at idle (LH 2.4 only)	Check and adjust throttle position switch. Check wiring harness for short to ground
12222	Off	AIC valve circuit fault	Check electrical connections between LH control unit and AIC valve
12111	Off	Oxygen sensor self-compensating circuit problem (incorrect air-fuel ratio while driving)	Check for air fuel leaks. Check the oxygen sensor pre-heater circuit and sensor output. Check ELCD system. Check fuel pressures
12112	Off	Oxygen sensor self-compensating circuit problem (incorrect air-fuel ratio at idle)	
12113	Off	AIC self-compensating circuit problem (system unable to reduce idle speed to correct level)	Check throttle stop screw setting. Check throttle plate for an over-center condition. Check for vacuum leaks
12114	Off	AIC self-compensating fault. (system unable to increase idle to an acceptable level)	Check for binding AIC valve. Check for a mechanical engine problem causing low idle problem
00000	Off	No more faults	No corrective action necessary. This code must be present before fault memory can be erased

NOTE
As an example, if the test is run with the engine off, the first code displayed would be for "no RPM signal" (fault code 1-2-2-3-1). This would be viewed as a long flash followed by a single flash, two flashes, two flashes, three flashes, and ending with a single flash. The light would then come one for a long flash and the code would begin to repeat itself. See Fig. 4.

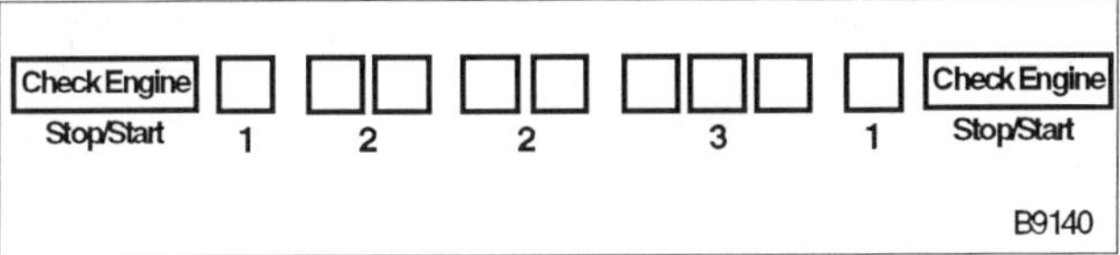

Fig. 4. Graphic representation of flashing Check Engine light.

6. To cycle to the next fault code, simply turn the test lead switch ON, wait until the Check Engine light flashes once, and then turn the switch OFF. Any new codes will begin to flash.

NOTE
The test sequence can be restarted by allowing the Check Engine light to flash twice before turning the switch OFF. Do not let the light flash three times, as this can cancel the fault memory.

To erase fault code memory

Before erasing the memory, the error code 00000 ("no more faults") listed in **Table b** must be present.

NOTE
After making repairs, it takes a certain amount of time for the LH system to re-adapt or compensate for the new conditions. Usually ten minutes of driving, allowing the engine to reach operating temperature, should be sufficient. Recheck for the "no more faults" code only after making a test drive to prevent the same error codes from reoccurring.

1. With the engine off, the test lead switch OFF, and no faults codes present as described above, turn the ignition key to the on position.
2. As soon as the Check Engine light comes on, turn the test lead switch ON. The light should immediately go out.
3. Wait until the Check Engine light flashes three times and then turn the test lead switch OFF. The fault memory will now be erased.

To test components and signals

The LH 2.4 and LH 2.4.2 control unit has a built-in component test that actively tests all major fuel injection components. The test will also display a code through the Check Engine light.

1. On cars with automatic transmission, place the transmission in "D".

2. With the ignition key off and the test lead switch off, connect the switched test lead as shown above in Fig. 3.

3. Turn the test lead switch ON.

4. Turn the ignition key ON and wait for a short flash of the Check Engine light, then immediately turn the test lead switch OFF.

NOTE

As soon as the check engine light flashes, the fuel pump should run briefly (provided the pump is functioning correctly). This is the first component tested, verifying that the component and signal diagnosis program has been accessed. The Check Engine light will not flash a test code during the fuel pump test.

---

5. To move on to the next component test (and test code), turn the test lead switch on. After a short flash, turn the switch OFF. The fuel injectors should be clicking on and off.

6. Proceed through the remaining tests using the same procedure of turning the test lead switch on, waiting for a short flash and turning the switch OFF. **Table c** lists the test sequence, the test code, the signal or component being tested, and the operational check being made.

FUEL PRESSURE TESTS

Checking the fuel pressure is a fundamental part of troubleshooting and diagnosing the system. An accurate fuel pressure gauge will be needed to make the tests described below.

There are two significant fuel pressure values: 1) System pressure—created by the main fuel pump and maintained by the pressure regulator, and 2) Residual pressure—the pressure maintained in the closed system after the engine (and fuel pump) are shut off.

Relieving Fuel Pressure and Connecting Fuel Pressure Gauge

Much of the work on fuel injection requires the disconnecting of fuel lines. To prevent fuel from spraying all over, especially on a hot engine, it is a good idea to relieve the pressure in the lines before fully disconnecting them.

One basic method of relieving the pressure is to remove the fuses for the fuel pump and then run the engine until it stalls. Another method is to connect a hand vacuum pump to the vacuum connection on the fuel pressure regulator. When vacuum is applied to the regulator it will open and dump fuel back to the tank.

WARNING

Fuel will be discharged during many fuel system tests described below. Do not smoke or work near heaters or other fire hazards. Have a fire extinguisher handy.

Basic system troubleshooting requires a pressure gauge to measure fuel pressure under different operating conditions. To install the pressure gauge, remove the banjo bolt holding the fuel supply line to the fuel rail. See Fig. 5. Then reinstall the supply line and the gauge fitting.

NOTE

Use Saab pressure gauge Part No. 83 93 852, or an equivalent that has a range of at least 0 to 5 bar (approximately 0 to 100 psi). Always use new sealing washers when making connections.

Table c. Fuel Injection Component Test (LH 2.4, LH 2.4.2 only)

Test sequence	Test Code	Component/signal being checked	Operational check
1	No light display	Fuel pump circuit	Listen for pump running or fuel flow in the engine compartment
2	12411	Injector circuit	Listen for clicking injectors
3	12412	AIC actuator circuit	AIC valve will audibly cycle between open and closed once a second
4	12413	ELCD (charcoal canister purge valve)	ELCD valve audibly clicks once a second
5	12421	Automatic transmission drive position signal	Flashing stops when shifting from drive to neutral
6	12424	Closed throttle signal from throttle position switch	Flashing stops when throttle is opened
7	12431	Full throttle signal from throttle position switch	Flashing stops as accelerator pedal approaches full throttle

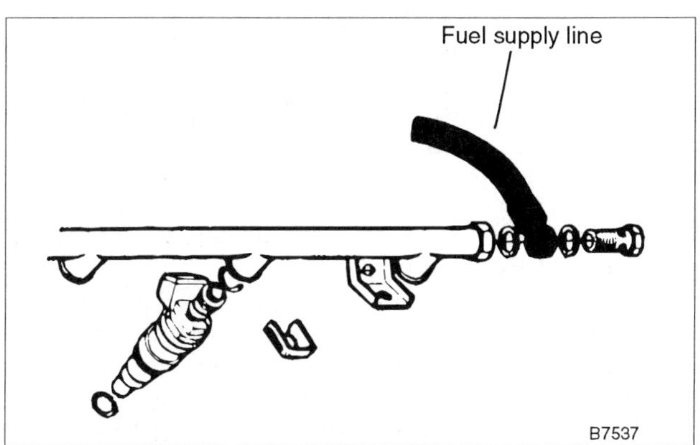

Fig. 5. Fuel pressure gauge installation location at fuel supply line on front of fuel rail.

CAUTION
Absolute cleanliness is essential when working with fuel circuit components. Even a minute particle of dirt can cause trouble if it reaches an injector. Thoroughly clean the unions before disconnecting any fuel lines. Use clean tools.

Fuel Pressure Regulator

The fuel pressure regulator is mounted to the end of the fuel rail and is spring operated. See Fig.6 and Fig. 7. Fuel pump pressure presses on the regulator valve diaphragm. The valve opens at a set pressure and returns excess fuel to the tank. When the pump shuts off, the regulator valve closes, holding residual pressure in the fuel system. This helps prevent fuel vaporization in the lines and possible vapor lock.

The pressure regulator is connected to the intake manifold through a vacuum hose. As manifold pressure changes, it

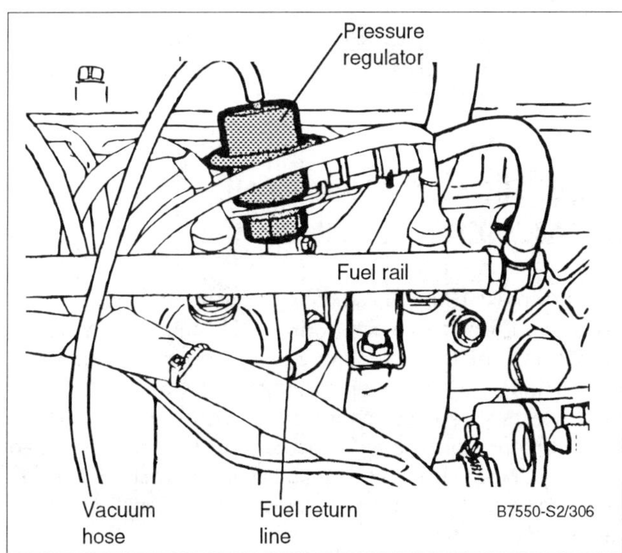

Fig. 6. Fuel pressure regulator.

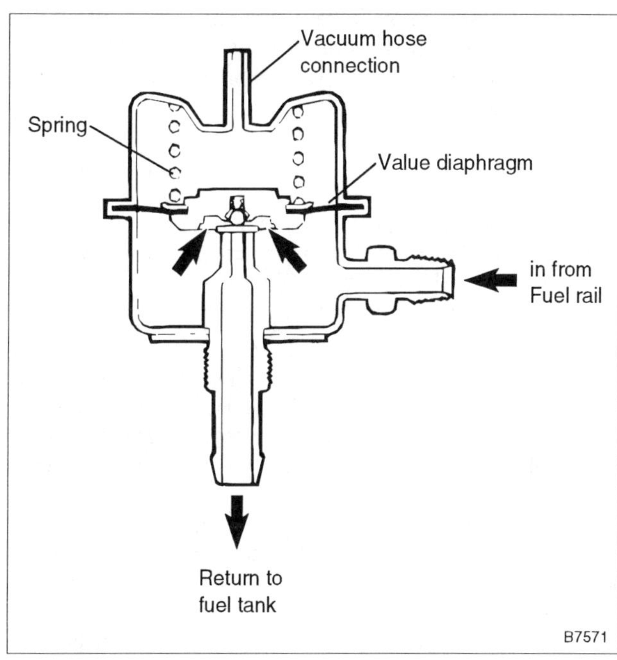

Fig. 7. Cutaway view of LH fuel pressure regulator.

acts on the pressure regulator diaphragm to increase or decrease fuel pressure in the same ratio. Thus the pressure differential between fuel pressure in the system and manifold pressure is constant. This ensures that the amount of fuel injected is influenced only by injector opening time, and not by intake manifold pressure.

Checking System Line Pressure

System pressure is checked in two steps. The first step checks basic operation of the pressure regulator. The second step checks the regulator's response to manifold pressure.

With the fuel gauge connected as described above and the engine off, run the fuel pump by bypassing the fuel pump relay as described in **234 Fuel Pump and Fuel Tank.** System pressure specifications are given in **Table d**.

Table d. System Pressure — Fuel Pump Running, Engine Off

Model	Fuel Pressure
Non-Turbo models	3.0 bar (43.5 psi)
Turbo models	25±.05 bar (36.3±0.7 psi)

NOTE
Pressure specifications give fuel pressure relative to normal atmospheric pressure (1 bar/14.5 psi) in the intake manifold.

If system pressure is too high, first check for a blocked or damaged fuel return line from the pressure regulator. Also check the return line check valve. If there are no obstructions, replace the pressure regulator.

NOTE

The fuel return line check valve is either near the fuel tank or in the top of the fuel tank depending on the type of tank installed. See **234 Fuel Pump and Fuel Tank.**

If system pressure is too low, first check for fuel leaks. Test the fuel pump as described in **234 Fuel Pump and Fuel Tank.** A restricted fuel filter or a damaged fuel line are also potential causes. If there are no other faults, replace the pressure regulator.

To check pressure regulator response to manifold pressure, reinstall the fuel pump fuse and then start the engine. With the engine idling, system pressure should be slightly lower than with the engine off. See **Table e**. If not, check the regulator vacuum hose and its connection to the intake manifold. If there are no faults, the regulator is faulty and should be replaced.

Table e. System Pressure — Engine Idling

Model	Fuel Pressure
Non-Turbo models	2.4 bar (34.8 psi)
Turbo models	1.9 bar (27.6 psi)

NOTE

- These pressures are approximate, and based on a manifold pressure of –0.6 bar (–8.7 psi) at idle. Allowances should be made for altitude and other factors influencing manifold pressure.
- The most accurate test of pressure regulator response is made by using a hand vacuum pump and pressure pump (Turbo models) to apply vacuum/pressure to the regulator with the fuel pump running. Fuel pressure should always be lesser/greater than system pressure by the same amount of vacuum/pressure that is applied.

Checking Residual Pressure

Hot-start problems are usually the only reason to suspect a residual pressure problem, but it deserves a routine check as long as the gauge is connected.

With the engine off, run the fuel pump for about 30 seconds or so to pressurize the system. Turn the pump off and watch the pressure gauge. **Table f** gives the specification.

Table f. Residual Pressure

All models	0.1–0.2 bar (1.5–3 psi) below system pressure, maximum after 10 minutes

If pressure drops beyond specification, check for leaks in the fuel lines, at the fuel pump, and at the fuel injectors. If there are no leaks, then either the pressure regulator or the fuel pump check valve is faulty.

To determine which, turn the pump on and off again, then immediately clamp shut the fuel return line at the pressure regulator. If pressure still drops, then the fuel pump check valve is faulty. See **234 Fuel Pump and Fuel Tank** for replacement. If residual pressure is now OK, then the pressure regulator is faulty.

Checking Fuel Pump Delivery Pressure

The fuel pump is capable of developing a much higher pressure than that regulated by the pressure regulator. The fuel pump has an internal check-valve that will not allow the system pressure to exceed 6.0 bar (87 psi).

To check fuel pump delivery pressure, run the fuel pump with the engine off. Then briefly pinch shut the return line at the pressure regulator. The fuel pressure should quickly rise. If the pressure does not respond quickly, and no leaks can be found, the fuel pump is worn and should be replaced.

CAUTION

In the event the fuel pump check valve is faulty (stuck closed), make sure the fuel pressure does not rise above 6.0 bar (87 psi). Damage to the fuel lines or fuel system components could result.

NOTE

Additional fuel pump tests, including testing the fuel pump relay, are covered in **234 Fuel Pump and Fuel Tank.**

ELECTRICAL CHECKS AND COMPONENT TESTING

Before making any electrical checks or tests, disconnect the main harness connector from the LH control unit and from the air mass meter. The control unit is behind the side kick panel in the front passenger compartment. See Fig. 8. When making tests at harness connectors, probe from the rear of the connector only, as the small delicate pins in the connector can be easily spread apart, causing faulty or intermittent signals. Peel back rubber boots and remove seals to gain access to the rear of the connector.

CAUTION

• Avoid damaging harness connectors or relay panel sockets. Jumper wires should end with flat-blade connectors that are the same size as the connector or relay terminals.

• Always switch a meter to the appropriate function and range before making test connections.

• Connect and disconnect test equipment only with the ignition switched off.

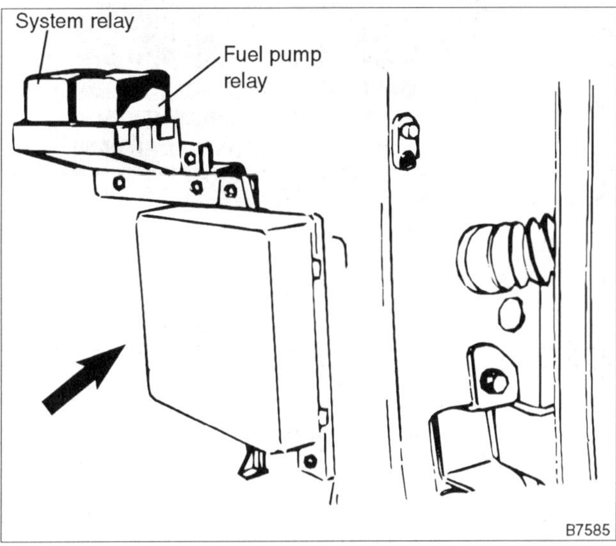

Fig. 8. LH control unit (arrow) behind kick panel in passenger compartment ahead of front door.

System Relay

The system relay supplies power to the LH control unit and the fuel pump relay when the ignition key is in the run position. On later models with LH 2.4, the system relay also supplies power to the fuel injectors, the air mass meter, the AIC idle valve, and the charcoal canister purge valve (ELCD). If this relay is faulty the engine will not start.

To test system relay

1. With the ignition key off, remove the harness connector from the air mass meter and the LH control unit.

2. Working at the LH control unit connector, check for ground at pin 11 on LH 2.2 or at pin 17 on LH 2.4 and LH 2.4.2. Repair any wiring faults using the appropriate wiring diagram shown in **371 Wiring Diagrams, Fuses and Relays.**

CAUTION

On models with LH 2.4 and LH 2.4.2, always wait at least 40 seconds after turning off the ignition before removing the control unit connector. If the connector is removed before this time, residual power in the system relay may damage the control unit.

3. Connect pin 21 in the LH control unit connector to ground. Turn the ignition key on and check for voltage at pin 9 of the LH control unit connector. See Fig. 9. Check for voltage at the air mass meter connector; on cars with LH 2.2 check for voltage at pin 2 and on LH 2.4 and LH 2.4.2, check for voltage at pin 5.

NOTE

If no faults are found, the system relay is working correctly. If the voltage is not as specified, continue testing as described below.

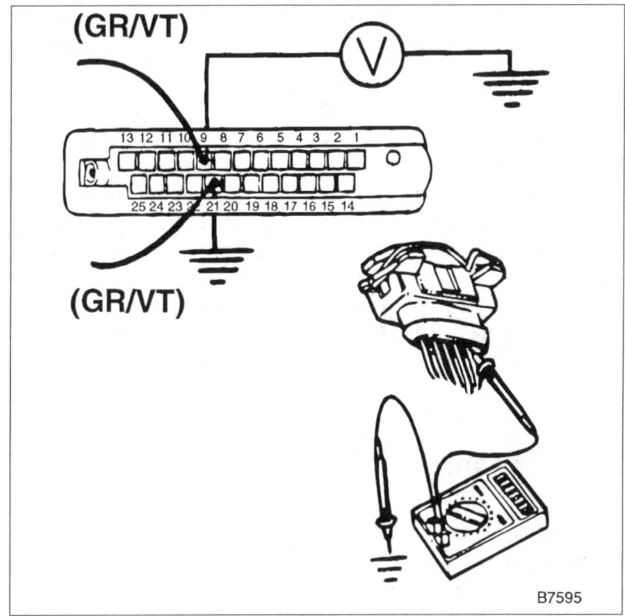

Fig. 9. Voltage being measured at air mass meter connector (pin 2 on LH 2.2 or pin 5 on LH 2.4 and LH 2.4.2) and LH control unit connector (pin 9).

4. Remove the system relay and check for voltage at terminal 30 and terminal 86 of the relay socket. See Fig. 10. If any faults are found, check the wiring between the battery and the relay sockets using the appropriate wiring diagram.

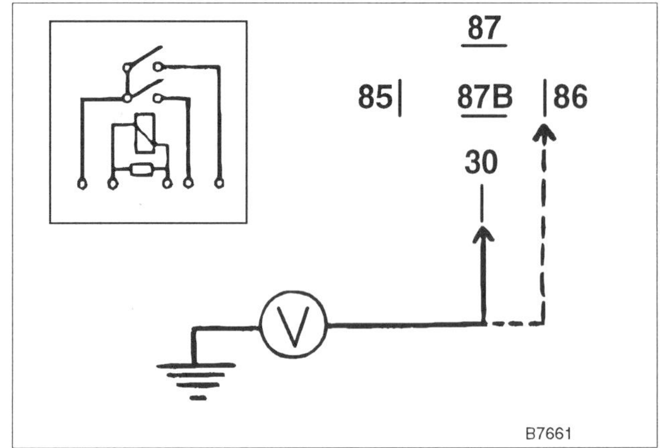

Fig. 10. Voltage being checked at system relay terminals 30 and 86.

5. If voltage is as specified in step 3, check the wiring between the system relay sockets and the following components; the LH control unit connector (pin 21 and pin 9), the air mass meter connector (pin 2 on LH 2.2 or pin 5 on all others), and the fuel pump relay (terminal 86). If no wiring faults can be found, the system relay is probably faulty.

NOTE

On 1985 through 1988 turbo models, a turbo over-pressure switch interrupts power to the fuel pump relay (terminal 86) when the turbocharger's boost pressure gets too high. Check for continuity in the wire between terminal 87 of the system relay socket and terminal 86 of the fuel pump relay socket. If there is no continuity, test the turbo over-pressure switch as described in **234 Fuel Pump and Fuel Tank.**

Coolant Temperature Sensor

The coolant temperature sensor sends continuous engine temperature information to the LH control unit. If there is break in the signal from the temperature sensor, the ECU will simulate a fixed signal, and the system will continue to operate based on an engine temperature of 68°F (20°C) on cars with LH 2.2 or 113°F (45°C) on cars with LH 2.4 and LH 2.4.2.

The sensor is mounted in the intake manifold. See Fig. 11. It projects into the cylinder head to measure engine coolant temperature. The sensor has a negative temperature coefficient (NTC), which means that its resistance goes down as its temperature goes up.

To check the sensor, disconnect the harness connector and check the resistance across the sensor terminals. **Table g** lists sensor resistances based on engine temperature. If any faults are found, the sensor should be replaced as described later under **Component Replacement.**

Fig. 11. Coolant temperature sensor.

NOTE

A faulty coolant temperature sensor will cause a noticeable increase in idle speed, as well as possibly affecting driveability. On LH 2.4 and LH 2.4.2 the Check Engine light should illuminate.

Table g. Coolant Temperature Sensor Resistance

Temperature	Resistance (ohms, ±10%)
–4°F (–20°C)	14,000
14°F (–10°C)	9,000
32°F (0°C)	5,800
50°F (10°C)	3,800
58°F (15°C)	3,000
68°F (20°C)	2,600
76°F (25°C)	2,000
86°F (30 °C)	1,700
176°F (80°C)	320

Throttle Position Sensor

The throttle position sensor is mounted on the side of the throttle housing and is directly connected to the throttle valve shaft. See Fig. 12. The sensor provides a signal to the control unit based on the position of the throttle valve.

On models with LH 2.2 and LH 2.4 fuel injection, there are two switches in the housing that provide a ground signal whenever the throttle is fully closed or fully open.

On models with LH 2.4.2 fuel injection, there is a potentiometer in the housing that changes resistance as the throttle moves. The control unit sends a voltage signal to the position sensor and monitors the voltage that comes back. Resistance decreases (voltage increases) as the throttle opens.

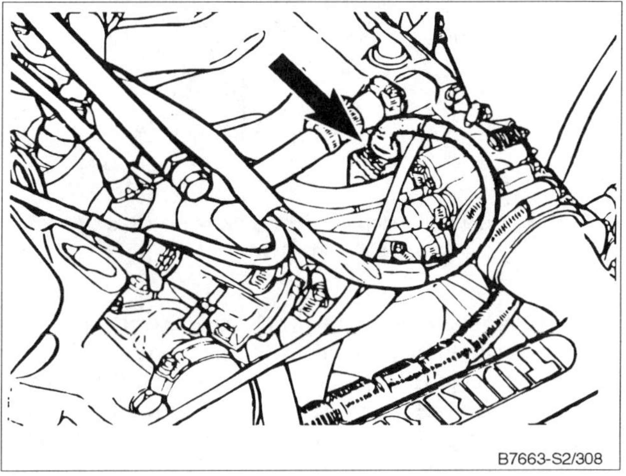

Fig. 12. Throttle position sensor (arrow) mounted to side of throttle housing.

Check throttle position sensor function by disconnecting the harness connector and checking continuity across the terminals while changing the throttle position. See Fig. 13. **Table h** and **Table i** list the correct test results. If the results are incorrect, check sensor adjustment as described below under **LH Fuel Injection Adjustments.** If adjustment does not correct the problem, replace the throttle position sensor.

NOTE

On models with LH 2.4.2, the throttle potentiometer is non-adjustable. If test results are incorrect, replace the throttle position sensor.

Table h. Throttle Position Sensor Tests—LH 2.2 and LH 2.4

Throttle position	Terminals checked	Test results
closed	1 and 2	continuity
	2 and 3	no continuity
half open	1 and 2	no continuity
	2 and 3	no continuity
wide open	1 and 2	no continuity
	2 and 3	continuity

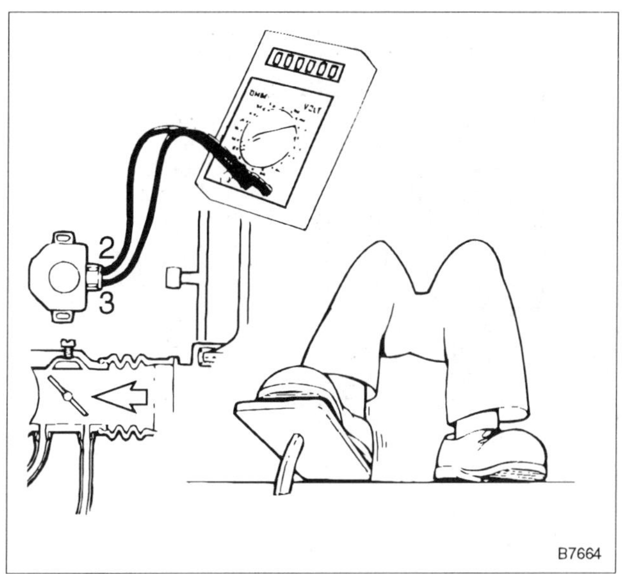

Fig. 13. Throttle position sensor being checked on cars with LH 2.2 and LH 2.4.

Table i. Throttle Position Sensor Tests—LH 2.4.2

Throttle position	Terminals checked	Test results
closed	1 and 3	2600–3000 ohms
wide open	1 and 3	1100–1500 ohms
between closed and wide open	1 and 3	continuously variable between 1100–3000 ohms, with no dropouts

Air Mass Meter

The heart of the LH fuel injection system is the air mass meter. It is located between the air filter and the intake manifold. The air mass meter electronically measures the air entering the engine. The air mass meter has no moving parts.

When the engine is running, a current is used to heat a thin wire in the center of the meter. See Fig. 14. The current flowing through the wire is regulated to maintain a wire temperature that is always 100°C more than that of the cooler air passing over it. The current used to heat the wire is then electronically converted into a precise voltage measurement corresponding to the air entering the engine.

Because the hot wire measures air mass, no other inputs to the control unit are needed for air temperature or altitude. A screen across the meter intake helps protect the wire and also breaks up air flow for more accurate measurements. To keep the wire free from dirt, it is heated to a temperature of about 1000°C (1830°F) for one second. This "burn-off" cycle takes place automatically, four seconds after the engine is turned off.

If the hot wire breaks or if there is no output from the air mass meter, the control unit automatically switches to a "limp-home" mode and turns on the Check Engine light. The engine

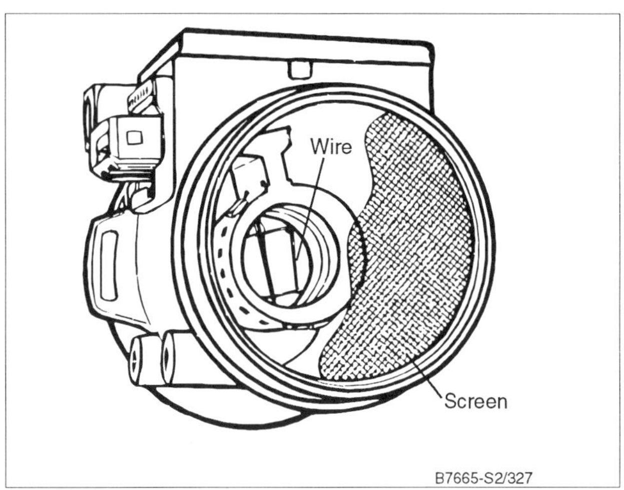

Fig. 14. Air mass meter.

can usually be started and driven. The air mass meter has no internal moving parts and cannot be serviced.

To test air mass meter

1. Disconnect the air mass meter from the air cleaner only. Leave it connected to the duct leading to the intake manifold and leave the wiring harness connected.

2. Start engine and run it to normal operating temperature

3. Rev the engine to at least 2500 rpm, then shut it off. Look through the front of the meter at the hot wire. After approximately four seconds the wire should glow brightly for about one second.

NOTE

If the wire glows as specified, then the air mass meter and control unit are probably operating correctly. If the wire does not glow, continue testing.

---

4. Remove the air mass meter and look through it to see if the wire is broken. It's very small, so check carefully. If the wire is broken, the meter will have to be replaced as described below. If the wire is intact, continue testing.

5. Reinstall the air mass meter and the harness connector. Peel back the rubber boot from the harness connector. Working from the rear of the connector, connect a digital voltmeter across terminals 1 and 4. See Fig. 15.

CAUTION

Use only a digital voltmeter for the above test. An analog meter can damage the air mass meter.

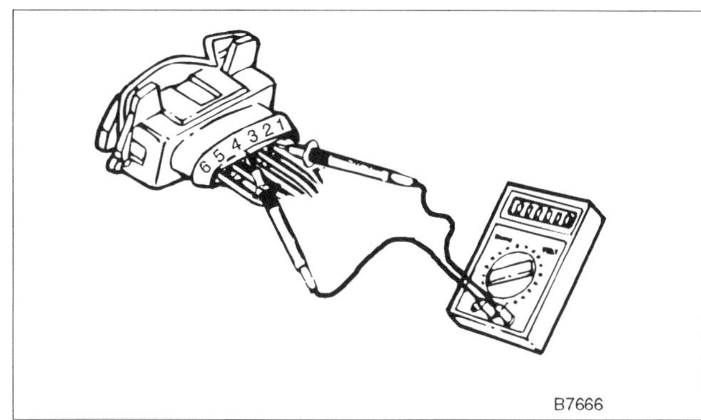

Fig. 15. Voltmeter connected to air mass meter terminals 1 (–) and 4 (+) to check for meter burn-off voltage.

6. Start and rev the engine to at least 2500 rpm, then shut it off. After about 4 seconds, the voltage should rise to about 4 volts for a duration of one second. If the voltage is as specified, but the wire does not glow as described in step 3 above, the air mass meter is faulty and should be replaced.

NOTE

- On models with LH 2.2, a new replacement air mass meter should be adjusted as described below under **LH Fuel Injection Adjustments.** Air mass meters used on LH 2.4 and 2.4.2 do not require any adjustments.

- The air mass meter used on LH 2.2 (aluminum body) is not the same meter used on LH 2.4 and LH 2.4.2 (black plastic body). **Do not interchange these meters.**

---

7. If voltage is not present in step 6, turn the ignition key on and check for voltage and ground at the meter's connector. There should be ground at pin 4. There should be positive (+) battery voltage at pin 2 (LH 2.2) or at pin 5 (LH 2.2, LH2.4.2).

If any faults are found, check for wiring breaks between the air mass meter and the LH control unit and between the air mass meter and the system relay. Also check the operation of the system relay as described above.

Fuel Injectors

The fuel injectors are electrically operated solenoid valves. They are switched on and off (open and closed) by the LH control unit. The injectors are connected to a common fuel supply, called the fuel rail. See Fig. 16.

There are a couple of common injector problems. Carbon deposits that form at the tips of injectors will clog them and reduce fuel flow. This often causes rough running, stalling, and power loss. This problem can usually be reduced and controlled through the use of quality gasolines containing deter-

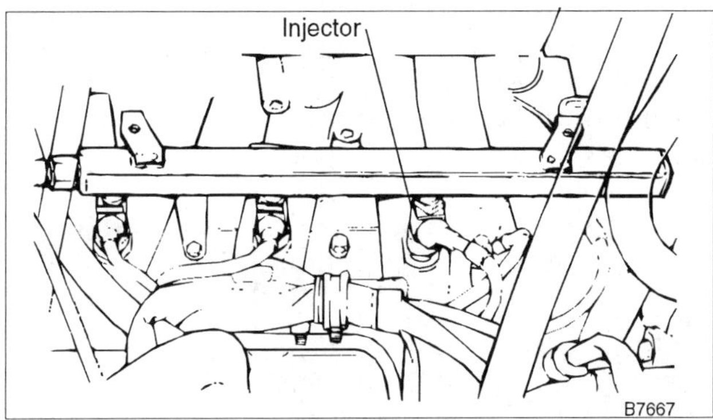

Fig. 16. Fuel rail is common fuel supply and mounting for all four injectors.

gents. If the problem is serious, a Saab dealer or other qualified repair shop has specialized injector cleaning equipment.

A second problem is old and cracked O-rings. They allow unmeasured air to enter the engine. Since the air is unmeasured, additional fuel is not injected and the mixture is leaned. The LH control unit will usually adapt itself to this extra air, but a symptom of this problem is increased fuel consumption. The injectors must be removed as later described under **Component Replacement.**

NOTE

Damaged injector O-rings are just one of many possible causes of increased fuel consumption. For more information see **200 Engine—General.**

To test injectors

NOTE

The information below is an electrical test only. The test does not check the spray patterns or fuel supply to the injectors. A Saab dealer or other qualified repair shop can perform such a test as part of the injector cleaning procedure.

---

1. Disconnect a harness connector from an injector and connect to it an LED test light, an injector tester, or a digital voltmeter across the connector. See Fig. 17. When the engine is cranked, the LED should flash or the following voltage should be present:

Injector cranking voltage (approximate VDC)

- engine temp. 32°F .... 1 volt
- engine temp. 68°F .... 0.6 volt
- engine temp. 176°F .... 0.3 volt

CAUTION

Use only a digital voltmeter, an LED test light or an LED injector tester. Use of an analog VOM or incandescent test light may damage the control unit.

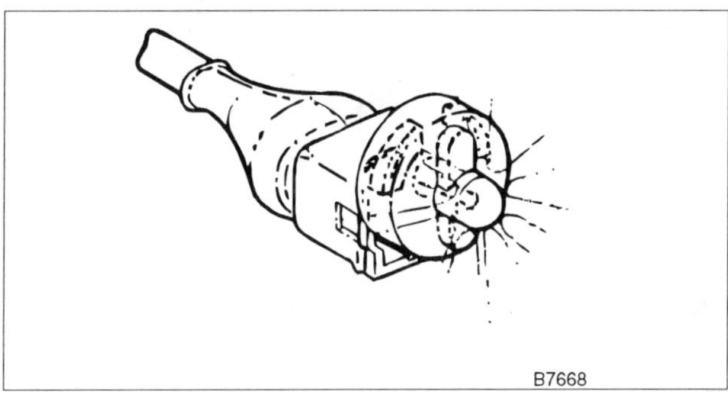

Fig. 17. Special LED test light connected across fuel injector connector for voltage test. Simple LED test light or digital VOM can also be used.

NOTE

If the engine runs but you think one injector is bad, place a screwdriver or an automotive stethoscope on the injector. There should be a buzzing or vibration as the engine runs. If the injector is not buzzing, check for voltage to the injector and check its resistance as described below. If the injector is buzzing, very briefly unplug the harness connector from the injector with the engine running. If the injector is working correctly, there should be a noticeable rpm drop.

---

2. If the light doesn't flash or there is no voltage, check for power to the injector. There should be battery voltage (+) at the blue/red wire of each injector connector with the ignition key on. See Fig. 18. If not, check the wiring to the injector using the wiring diagrams listed in **371 Wiring Diagrams, Fuses and Relays.**

NOTE

If there is positive (+) battery voltage as described in step 2, but there was no response through the LED or voltmeter in step 1, check the wire from the control unit to the injectors. If no wiring faults can be found, the ground signal from the control unit is missing. See **Electrical Checks and Component Testing** for additional electrical tests.

---

3. If power is present as described in the above step, unplug the injector connectors and check the injector resistance. Replace the injector if the resistance is incorrect.

Injectors

- resistance .... 16 ohms at 68°F (20°C)

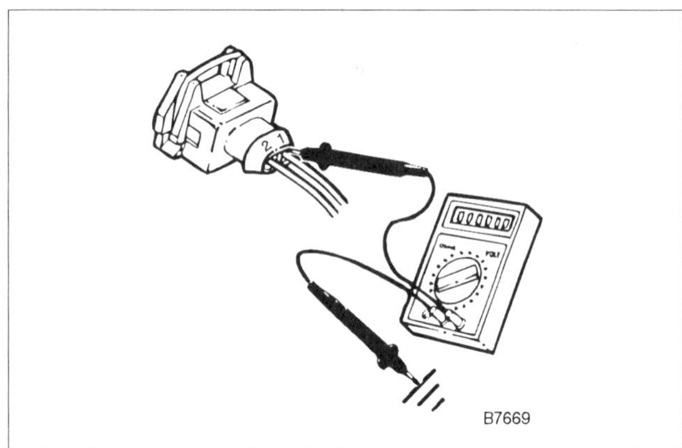

Fig. 18. Checking power to injector with ignition on. Check at red-blue wire of connector.

> **NOTE**
> Injector resistance will vary slightly depending on temperature. In general, the range should be between 10 and 20 ohms.

4. If no faults are found up to this point, check the pulse-time regulation function of the control unit. Peel back the rubber boot from the injector connector and connect a voltmeter to the wires in the connector. Start the engine. Check that the voltage decreases as the engine warms up. The values given below are approximate.

Injector warm-up enrichment voltage (VDC)
- engine temp. 32°F .... 1 volt
- engine temp. 68°F .... 0.6 volt
- engine temp. 176°F .... 0.3 volt

If the voltage readings are incorrect, check the temperature sensor as described above. Also check the CO reading and the air mass meter burn off function. If these are OK, then either the wiring to the control unit or the control unit itself is faulty. Check the control unit inputs and wiring by making the electrical checks described below under **LH Control Unit.**

Oxygen Sensor

The oxygen sensor monitors the exhaust gas and provides the LH control unit with feedback about the air-fuel ratio and combustion efficiency. Using this information, the control unit continuously adjusts the air-fuel mixture to ensure optimum driveability and exhaust emissions.

The oxygen sensor is mounted in the exhaust system. See Fig. 19. The oxygen sensor produces a small voltage (0-1 volt) based on the oxygen content in the exhaust gas as compared to the oxygen outside the exhaust pipe. The bigger the differential, the greater the output voltage. When the mixture is rich, there is very little oxygen in the exhaust (high output voltage). When the mixture is lean, there is an excess of oxygen in the exhaust (low output voltage).

Fig. 19. Location of oxygen sensor (arrow) on turbo model (in exhaust manifold). On non-turbo model, the oxygen sensor is mounted in the front exhaust pipe, near the steering rack.

The oxygen sensor must be at a temperature of at least 600°F to generate voltage, so it is electrically heated to help it reach operating temperature more quickly. The oxygen sensor is checked by seeing if it generates a voltage when the engine is idling at normal operating temperature.

To test oxygen sensor

1. Disconnect the sensor's single black wire (sensor signal wire). See Fig. 20.

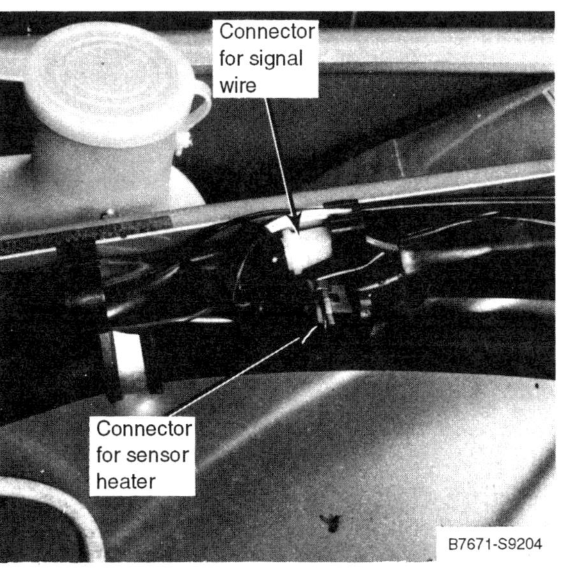

Fig. 20. Oxygen sensor wiring connectors are located on right (passenger) inner fender well, just above battery.

2. Connect the positive lead of a voltmeter to the black wire coming from the sensor and connect the negative meter lead to chassis ground. See Fig. 21. Start the car and let it idle. The oxygen sensor should start to produce a fluctuating voltage within a short period.

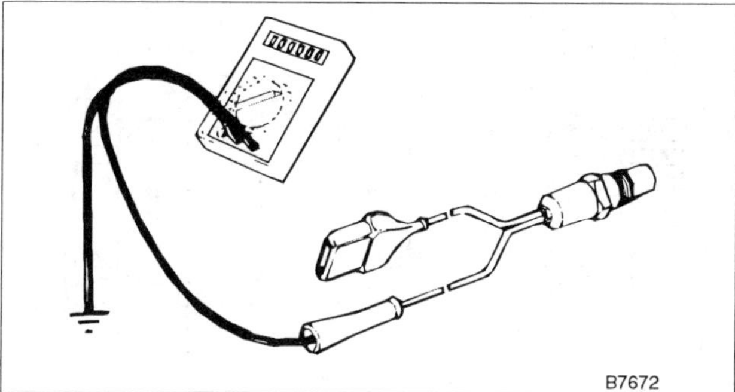

Fig. 21. Oxygen sensor output voltage being checked (shown schematically). Sensor should be installed and the engine should be running.

Oxygen sensor
- voltage at idle . . . . .0.4 to 1 volt

NOTE
To further check sensor response to lean and rich mixtures, slightly open the oil filler cap to create an air leak, or pull the vacuum hose off of the fuel pressure regulator to increase fuel pressure.

---

3. If the sensor does not emit a fluctuating voltage, turn the engine off and check the sensor's preheater circuit. Disconnect the two-wire connector and check for battery voltage at the connector with the engine running. If voltage is not present, check the wiring to the preheater and check the preheater fuse. If voltage is present, check the preheater coil resistance. See Fig. 22. If any faults are found, replace the sensor.

NOTE
On 1986 through 1988 models, the preheater fuse is in-line, in the engine compartment on the right-hand side fender. On 1989 and later cars, the fuse is in the main fuse/relay panel (position no. 1). On 1985 models, the preheater is not fuse protected.

Oxygen sensor
- preheater resistance . . . . .approx. 4 ohms

---

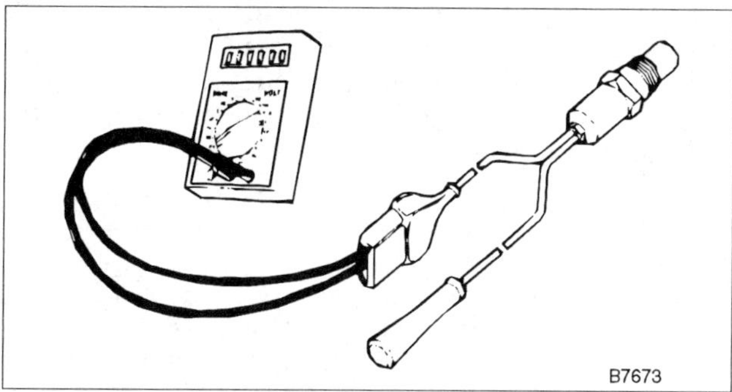

Fig. 22. Oxygen sensor heating coil resistance being measured (shown schematically).

If the oxygen sensor doesn't produce voltage, and the preheater circuit is OK, replace the sensor.

Tightening Torque
- Oxygen sensor . . . . 40 Nm (29 ft-lb)

NOTE
Coat the oxygen sensor threads with an anti-seize compound before installation. Do not get the compound on the sensor tip. This can damage the sensor.

Automatic Idle Control (AIC) System

The AIC system maintains idle speed through the AIC idle control valve. See Fig. 23. The system compensates for engine load and engine operating conditions, so periodic adjustment of the idle speed is unnecessary. The AIC valve is controlled by the LH control unit.

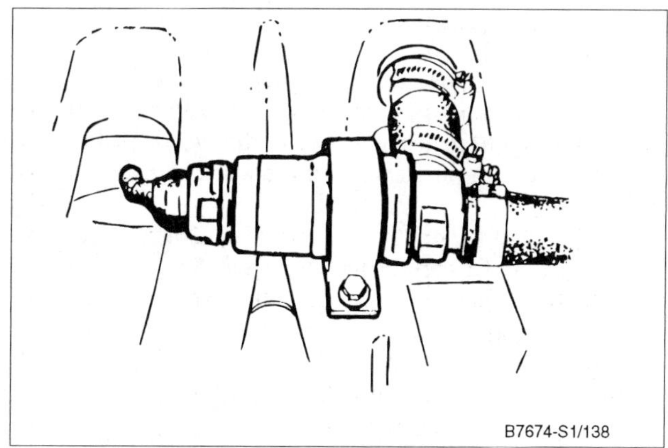

Fig. 23. AIC valve.

The LH control unit monitors engine rpm and other operating conditions such as air conditioning and automatic transmission loads, and then sends an electrical signal to open or close the valve. This changes the amount of air that bypasses the closed throttle valve.

NOTE

There are three different idle control valves used on the cars covered by this manual, depending on the fuel system. These valves operate differently and are not interchangeable between fuel systems.

On LH 2.4 and LH 2.4.2 fuel injection, the AIC function is completely adaptive. The control unit remembers how far the valve was open the last time the engine was at idle and reverts to this as a base setting. In addition, the valves used on these models have a limp-home feature that maintains a fixed idle speed in the event of an AIC valve failure. This idle speed is approximately 1,200 rpm on cars with LH 2.4 and 850 rpm on cars with LH 2.4.2.

Before proceeding with troubleshooting an idle problem, check that the throttle position sensor is working correctly as described earlier under **Throttle Position Sensor**. On cars with high mileage, enough residue and dirt may collect on the throttle valve plate and bore to restrict air flow and affect the AIC system. remove the AIC valve and the air intake duct from the throttle housing. Clean both the AIC valve and the throttle plate and bore. Reinstall the valve and duct and run the engine to check idle.

NOTE

On models with LH 2.2 fuel injection, the base idle may need to be reset after this procedure. See **LH Fuel Injection Adjustments** as described below.

To test AIC system

1. With the engine running, check that the idle control valve is buzzing. On cars with air conditioning (A/C) or automatic transmission, turn on the A/C or shift the car into drive. Idle should remain steady or increase slightly.

2. If the valve is not buzzing, or if idle decreases, stop the engine and disconnect the harness connector from the valve. Check the resistance of the valve across its terminals. Fig. 24 shows the valve terminals. **Table j** lists the test terminals and results. If resistance is incorrect, replace the valve. If resistance is OK, test for power to the valve as described below.

NOTE

If you suspect an intermittent fault, lightly tap the valve while you are testing resistance.

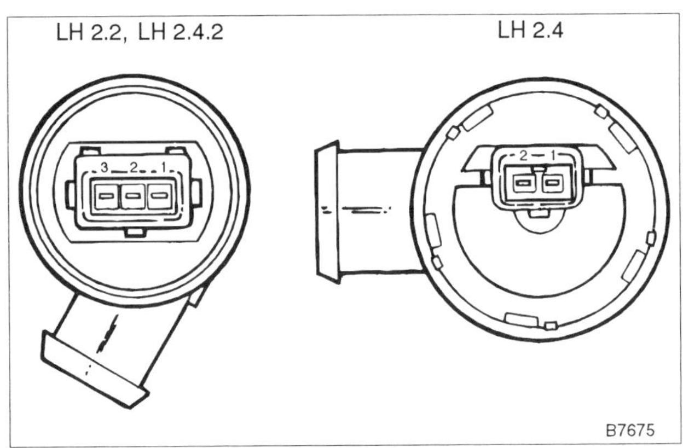

Fig. 24. Idle control valve terminals.

Table j. AIC Valve Resistance

Fuel System	Test terminals	Resistance (ohms)
LH 2.2	1 and 2	20±2
	2 and 3	20±2
	1 and 3	40±4
LH 2.4	1 and 2	8±2
LH 2.4.2	1 and 2	10–15
	2 and 3	10–15

3. With the valve's harness connector disconnected, check for voltage at the blue/red wire in the connector. When the ignition is turned on there should be approximately battery voltage.

NOTE

On models with LH 2.2 fuel injection, the voltage will be momentary—only for as long as the fuel pump relay is closed. To get a constant voltage supply, run the engine.

---

4. If there is no voltage at the connector, check the wiring to the valve's connector. See **371 Wiring Diagrams, Fuses and Relays.**

NOTE

On LH 2.2, the AIC valve receives positive (+) battery voltage from the fuel pump relay. On LH 2.4 and LH 2.4.2, the valve receives voltage from the system relay.

---

5. If voltage is present as described in step 3, check the wiring between the control unit and the valve and fix any breaks. If no wiring faults are found, check the LH control unit signal to the AIC valve. If the signal to the valve is as specified, the AIC valve is probably faulty and should be replaced.

NOTE

- On cars with LH 2.2, the AIC valve control signal can be checked using a duty cycle meter (or dwell meter) as described below under **LH Fuel Injection Adjustments.**

- On cars with LH 2.4 and LH 2.4.2, the AIC valve control signal can be checked by making the electrical tests outline below under **LH Control Unit.**

There are some additional inputs to the control unit that affect idle speed (i.e. throttle position, A/C-on signals, and A/T Drive position). To check these signals, make the electrical tests described below under **LH Control Unit.**

LH Control Unit

The following voltage and continuity tests will help determine whether there are faults in the wiring or components that provide information to the LH control unit. If all inputs and wiring are OK but operational problems still exist, the control unit itself may be faulty.

Generally, a complete absence of voltage or continuity means there is a wiring or connector problem. See **371 Wiring Diagrams, Fuses and Relays** for help in diagnosis. Test results with different values than those specified do not necessarily mean that a component is faulty. Check for loose connections or connections that are inadequate due to corrosion or contamination. If the results are still incorrect, test the component itself.

Make these tests at the LH control unit connector using a digital VOM. The control unit is mounted in the passenger compartment, in the passenger-side footwell. See Fig. 8 given earlier. Remove the control unit, unplug the connector, and make tests from the back of the connector to avoid damaging connector terminals. See Fig. 25. Control unit connector terminals are shown in Fig. 26. **Table k** and **Table l** list the tests and correct test results.

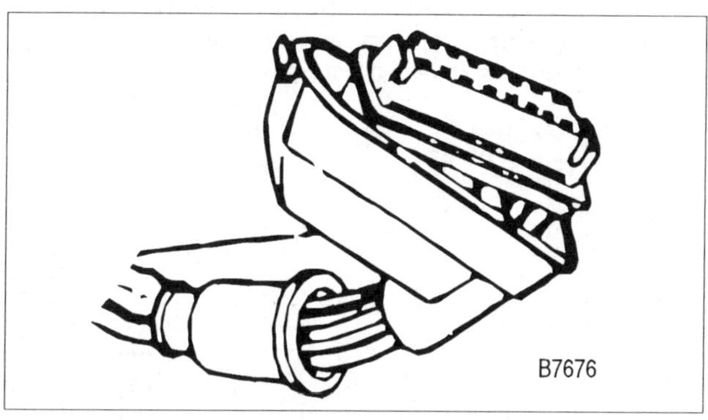

Fig. 25. For access to back of connector terminals when testing, disconnect connector and remove rubber gasket.

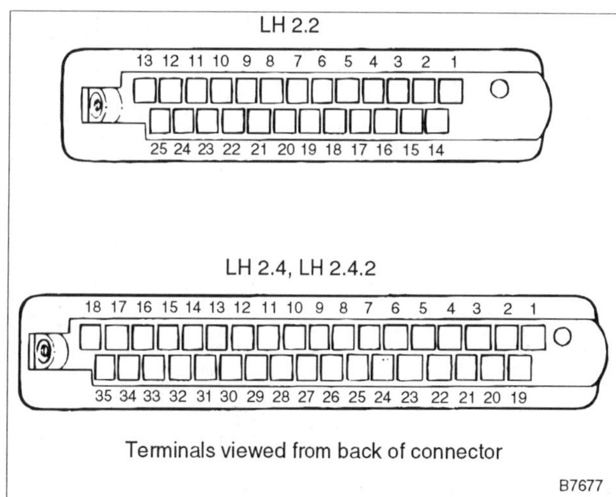

Fig. 26. Terminal identification for LH fuel injection control unit connectors. Take care not to damage connector terminals with test probes.

CAUTION

• Always connect or disconnect the control unit connector and meter probes with the ignition off to avoid damage to electronic components.

• On models with LH 2.4 and LH 2.4.2, always wait at least 40 seconds after turning off the ignition before removing the control unit connector. If the connector is removed before this time, residual power in the system relay may damage the control unit.

NOTE

• On cars with LH 2.4 and LH 2.4.2 fuel injection, disconnecting the control unit connector will erase the control unit's adaptive and diagnostic memory. When the engine is restarted it may operate erratically. The engine must be driven for at least 30 minutes for the adaptive memory to be reset.

• The electrical tests below call for measuring voltage, current or resistance using a digital volt-ohm meter (DVOM) or a multimeter. Using an analog meter may damage the control unit or other solid state components

Table k. LH 2.2 Electrical Tests

Component or circuit	Test terminals (Test conditions at LH connector unless otherwise noted)	Test conditions	Test value
Control unit power (switched), fuse 22	18 and ground	Ignition on	Approximately 12 volts (battery voltage)
Control unit grounds	18 and 5, 18 and 11, 18 and 25	Ignition on	Approximately 12 volts (battery voltage)
System relay	Jumper terminals 5 and 21		System relay closes, power to pin 9, power to pin 2 of air mass meter
Fuel pump relay (see **234 Fuel Pump and Fuel Tank**)	Jumper terminals 5 and 17, and 21 and 25		Fuel pump runs, power to oxygen sensor preheater (blue/red wire), power to fuel injectors (blue/red wire)
Ignition pulse signal	1 and 25	Crank engine	2–3 volts (VAC)
Coolant temperature sensor	2 and 25		Resistance according to **Table g** shown earlier
Throttle position sensor	3 and ground	Throttle closed	Continuity
		Throttle 1/2 open	No continuity
	12 and ground	Throttle wide open	Continuity
Automatic transmission switch (see **444 Automatic Transmission Controls**)	4 and 25	Ignition on, transmission in Drive	Approximately 12 volts (battery voltage)
AIC valve	10 and 23		40±4 ohms
Fuel injectors	13 and socket 87 of fuel pump relay		4 ohms
Air conditioning ON signal	12 and 16	Jumper sockets 16 and TK of A/C compressor relay	Continuity
Oxygen sensor	20 and 25	Oxygen sensor connected	No continuity
		Separate connector and connect green wire to ground	Continuity
Signal to EZK ignition system (ex. turbo models) (see **340 Ignition System**)	3 and 24	Disconnect EZK control unit connector, bridge terminals 7 and 8 of connector	Continuity

Table I. LH 2.4 and LH 2.4.2 Electrical Tests

Component or circuit	Test terminals (at disconnected LH connector unless otherwise noted)	Test conditions	Test value
Control unit power (switched), fuse 22	35 and ground	Ignition on	Approximately 12 volts (battery voltage)
Control unit power (constant)	4 and ground		Approximately 12 volts (battery voltage)
Control unit grounds	4 and 5, 4 and 17		Approximately 12 volts (battery voltage)
System relay	Jumper terminals 17 and 21		Relay closes, power to pin 9, power to pin 5 of air mass meter, power to fuel injectors (blue/red wire)
Fuel pump relay (see **234 Fuel Pump and Fuel Tank**), power from system relay, oxygen sensor heater power	Jumper terminals 5 and 20, and 17 and 21		Fuel pump runs, power to blue-red wire at oxygen sensor connector
Ignition pulse signal (LH 2.4)	1 and 17	Crank engine	2–3 volts (VAC)
Ignition pulse signal (LH 2.4.2)	1 and 17	Crank engine	6.5 volts (VAC)
Coolant temperature sensor	13 and 17		Resistance according to **Table g** shown earlier
Throttle position sensor (LH 2.4)	2 and ground	Throttle closed	Continuity
		Throttle 1/2 open	No continuity
	3 and ground	Throttle wide open	Continuity
Throttle potentiometer (LH 2.4.2)	2 and 10		Resistance according to **Table i** shown earlier
Automatic transmission switch. (see **444 Automatic Transmission Controls)**	30 and 17	Ignition on, transmission in Drive	Approximately 12 volts (battery voltage)
AIC valve (LH 2.4)	33 and 17	LH control unit connector connected, engine running, probe terminals from rear of connector	Approximately 8 volts at idle. Voltage should drop as load increases
AIC valve (LH 2.4.2)	33 and 17	LH control unit connector connected, engine running, probe terminals from rear of connector	Approximately 7 volts at idle. Voltage should drop as load increases
Fuel injectors	18 and socket 87 of system relay		4 ohms
Air conditioning ON signal (LH 2.4)	14 and ground	LH control unit connector connected, engine running, probe terminals from rear of connector	less than 0.1 volt with A/C off and battery voltage with A/C on.
Air conditioning ON signal (LH 2.4)	14 and ground11 and ground	LH control unit connector connected, engine running, probe terminals from rear of connector	less than 0.1 volt with A/C off and battery voltage with A/C on.
Oxygen sensor	24 and 17	Oxygen sensor connected	No continuity
		Separate connector and connect green wire to ground	Continuity
EGR modulating valve (where applicable—see **254 Exhaust Emission Control)**	19 and 17	Ignition on	Approximately 12 volts (battery voltage)

continued on next page

Table I. LH 2.4 and LH 2.4.2 Electrical Tests (continued)

Component or circuit	Test terminals (at disconnected LH connector unless otherwise noted)	Test conditions	Test value
EGR valve temperature sensor (where applicable—see **254 Exhaust Emission Control**)	23 and 17	Run engine at operating temperature. Turn off engine and disconnect control unit connector (after waiting 45 seconds)	Resistance should measure several megohms
Charcoal canister purge valve(ELCD) (see **254 Exhaust Emission Control**)	27 and 17	Ignition on	Approximately 12 volts (battery voltage)
Vehicle speed sensor	34 and ground	Ignition on, raise front of car and rotate front left wheel slowly	Voltage alternates between 0.5 and 5.0 volts
Upshift light	Jumper 26 and 17	Ignition on	Light illuminates
Check Engine light	Jumper 22 and 17	Ignition on	Light illuminates

COMPONENT REPLACEMENT

To remove LH control unit

1. Disconnect the negative (–) battery cable.
2. Remove the door sill plate from the passenger side of the car. Peel up the lower front edge of the door weather stripping.
3. Remove the trim plate holding the carpet to the front side panel and peel the carpet until the control unit and relays are visible.
4. Unplug the control unit harness connector by releasing the fastener and then pivoting the connector up and off of the unit.
5. Remove the mounting screws holding the control unit to the body.

Installation is the reverse of removal.

To remove coolant temperature sensor

1. Detach the crankcase ventilation hose from the valve cover.
2. Unbolt the fuel pressure regulator and its mounting bracket from the cylinder head and push it to one side.

NOTE
On some models, it may be necessary to remove the regulator completely for access to the temperature sensor.

3. Drain approximately 4 quarts of coolant from the cooling system. This is so that coolant will not leak out when the sensor is removed. See **261 Radiator and Cooling System.**
4. Disconnect the sensor wiring and remove the sensor using a 3/4 in. deep-well socket.
5. Before installing the new sensor, check the mating surface on the intake manifold. Use a new copper sealing washer.

Tightening torque
- Coolant temperature sensor. . . . . . . 20 Nm (15 ft-lb)

Installation is the reverse of removal. Refit the pressure regulator and crankcase ventilation hose. Make sure the LH system grounds are properly replaced on the pressure regulator mounting.

To remove throttle position sensor

1. Unplug the harness connector from the sensor. See Fig. 12 given earlier.
2. Remove the mounting screws holding the sensor to the side of the throttle housing.

Installation is the reverse of removal. On LH 2.2 and LH 2.4, the switch must be adjusted as described below under **LH Fuel Injection Adjustments.**

To remove air mass meter

1. Loosen the large hose clamp securing the rubber duct to the air mass meter.

2. Disconnect the harness connector from the meter.

3. Release the two spring clip fasteners from the air cleaner housing cover. See Fig. 27. Remove the air mass meter from the duct and cover.

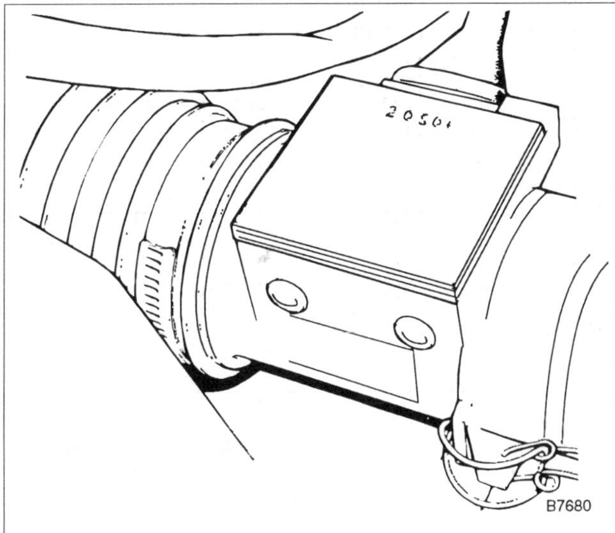

Fig. 27. Air mass meter and spring clip.

Installation is the reverse of removal. Where applicable, make sure the ridge in the air mass meter and the recess in the air cleaner cover are aligned before fastening the spring clips.

To remove fuel injectors

WARNING
Fuel will be expelled when fuel lines are disconnected. Do not smoke or work near heaters or other fire hazards. Keep a fire extinguisher handy.

CAUTION
Absolute cleanliness is essential when working with fuel circuit components. Even a minute particle of dirt can cause trouble if it reaches an injector. Thoroughly clean the unions before disconnecting any fuel lines. Use clean tools.

1. Detach the crankcase ventilation hose from the valve cover.

2. Unplug the wiring harness connectors from the injectors. Free the wiring harness from the fuel rail by undoing the clips. Carefully pull the harness to the side.

3. Disconnect the fuel inlet and outlet hoses on the fuel rail by removing the banjo bolts. See Fig. 28.

WARNING
Wrap a clean shop towel around the banjo bolts before loosening them.

CAUTION
To prevent damaging the fuel rail assembly, use an open-end wrench on the flats on the rail to hold it steady while loosening the fuel lines.

Fig. 28. Fuel rail assembly and fuel lines (arrows).

4. Remove the bolts that hold the fuel rail to the intake manifold and pull the fuel rail away complete with injectors.

5. To remove the injectors from the fuel rail, pry off the retaining clips, then twist the injectors slightly and pull them off.

When installing the injectors, fit new O-rings to the injectors. For ease of installation, lightly lubricate the O-rings with petroleum jelly. Install the injectors to the fuel rail but do not install the retaining clips. Position the fuel rail and injectors on the intake manifold. Make sure that injectors and the fuel rail are fully seated and then install the retaining clips and mounting bolts. Reconnect the fuel hoses to the fuel rail. Reconnect the crankcase ventilation hose.

To remove fuel pressure regulator

WARNING
Fuel under pressure will be expelled when fuel lines are disconnected. Do not smoke or work near heaters or other fire hazards. Keep a fire extinguisher handy.

1. Disconnect the vacuum hose from the regulator.

2. Disconnect from the regulator the fuel hose coming from the fuel rail.

3. Remove the fuel pressure regulator mounting bolts and lift out the regulator and its bracket. Disconnect the fuel return hose from the regulator. Remove the regulator from the bracket.

Installation is the reverse of removal. Remember to reconnect the ground wires to the fuel pressure regulator mounting bolt.

To remove AIC valve

1. Disconnect the harness connector from the AIC valve.

2. Loosen the valve's hose clamps and disconnect the hoses from the valve. See Fig. 29.

Fig. 29. AIC valve hose clamp being loosened.

3. Remove the valve bracket mounting bolt and remove the valve from the bracket.

Installation is reverse of removal. On models with LH 2.2, adjust the base setting of the valve as described below.

LH FUEL INJECTION ADJUSTMENTS

Except for the adjustment of the throttle position sensor, all of the adjustment described below are for cars with LH 2.2 only. Cars with LH 2.4 and LH 2.4.2 are fully adaptive and do not require any adjustments.

Setting the base idle speed ensures that the AIC idle control valve is operating in about the middle of its range under normal conditions. Base idle speed is set at the factory and does not normally need to be checked or adjusted, unless repairs are made to the throttle valve or housing.

Base idle speed is set by reading the control unit signal to the valve. This signal is known as the duty cycle. It is the ratio of on-time to off-time of voltage and is expressed as a percentage. It is measured using a duty cycle or dwell meter.

NOTE

- Remember that 100% on a duty cycle meter corresponds to 90° on a dwell meter.
- The test meter must be a quality digital dwell meter, with an accuracy of at least 0.5%. Using an inexpensive analog meter that has an error of 2° would result in a setting 25% out of calibration.

To adjust AIC valve and basic idle speed (LH 2.2)

NOTE

For the most accurate adjustment, the engine should be at operating temperature, the ignition timing and idle mixture should be checked and adjusted if necessary.

---

1. Back off the dashpot so that the plunger no longer contacts the throttle lever. See Fig. 30. Check that there is slack in the accelerator cable. If necessary, loosen the cable.

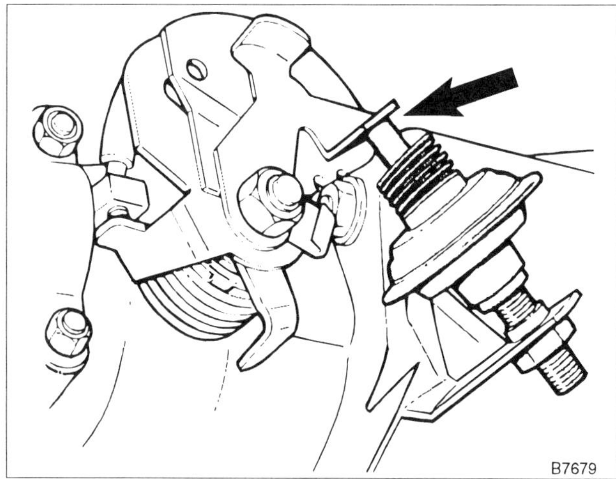

Fig. 30. Dashpot plunger should be backed off throttle lever (arrow).

2. Loosen the screws for the throttle position sensor so that it doesn't affect the throttle valve. Disconnect the sensor harness connector and connect a jumper wire as shown in Fig. 31. This will simulate a closed-throttle signal.

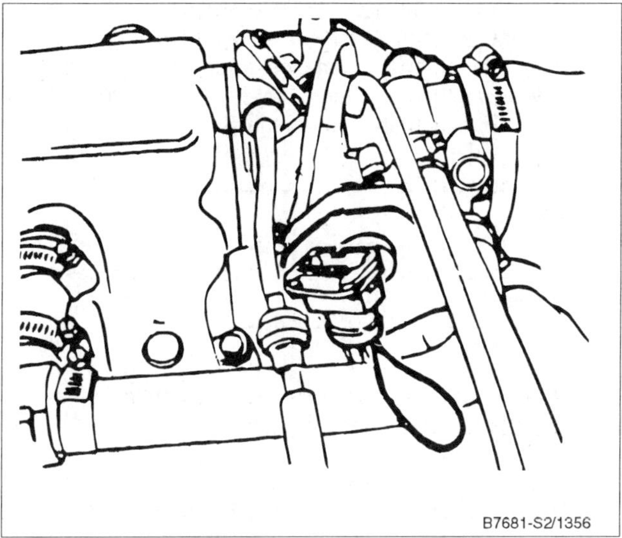

Fig. 31. Jumper terminals 1 (gray wire) and 2 (black-white wire) of throttle position sensor connector. Connect wire from back of connector to prevent damage to terminals.

3. Loosen the throttle stop screw locknut and back out the screw until it is no longer contacting the throttle lever. See Fig. 32. Thread the screw in until it touches the lever then turn it an additional 3/4 turn. Tighten the locknut.

Fig. 32. Throttle stop screw and locknut (arrow).

4. Working from the rear of the AIC valve's harness connector, connect the dwell meter to terminals 2 and 3. See Fig. 33. Connect the tachometer.

5. Start the engine and let it run until the radiator fan cycles at least once.

Fig. 33. Meter leads connected to idle control valve terminals 2 and 3 (valve terminal 4 and 5).

NOTE

Make sure all other electrical accessories on the car are off. Make all adjustments to idle only when the fan is off.

---

6. Depending on the throttle housing, turn either the throttle valve stop screw (Fig. 32) or the throttle valve air bleed screw (Fig. 34) out until the duty cycle is 38% (34° dwell).

NOTE

If the correct reading cannot be obtained, check for intake air leaks or other engine problems.

Fig. 34. Throttle valve air bleed screw (arrow) used on early models. Later models with LH 2.2 do not have this screw.

7. Next, turn the screw back in until the meter reading is as specified in the table below.

NOTE
When the correct reading is obtained, the base idle speed should be 850±50 rpm. If it isn't, check for intake air leaks or other engine problems.

Base Idle Speed (at 850±50 rpm)
- **Duty cycle** 33%
- **Dwell** . . . . 30°

8. Lock the adjusting screw and recheck the reading.

9. Turn off the engine and remove all test equipment. Reset the dashpot and throttle switch as described below

To adjust throttle position sensor (LH 2.2 and LH 2.4)

The throttle position sensor has two switches in the housing that provide a ground signal whenever the throttle is fully closed or fully open.

1. Loosen the switch mounting screws.

2. Attach a VOM to terminals 1 and 2 of the switch to measure continuity. See Fig. 35.

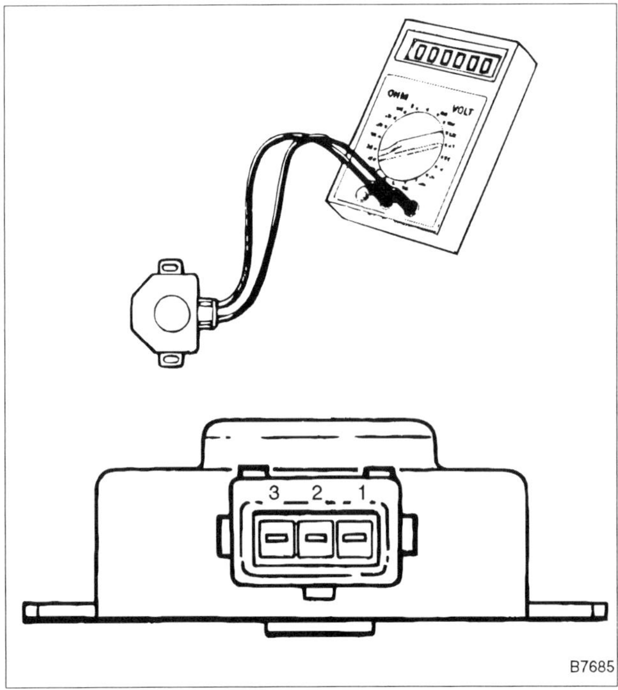

Fig. 35. Ohmmeter shown connected to throttle position sensor.

3. Rotate the switch so that the switch is just open (no continuity), then rotate the switch in the opposite direction until the switch just closes (continuity). Rotate the switch a bit further (approximately.5 mm/.020 in.) in the same direction and tighten the screws.

NOTE
Rotation of the throttle position sensor too far can cause the switch to hold the throttle open. This may lead to excessive idle speed.

---

4. Check that the switch opens (no continuity) as the throttle is just opened from idle.

5. Connect the ohmmeter to terminals 2 and 3 to check the full throttle switch contacts. There should be no continuity until the switch is almost fully open. At 72° of open throttle, the switch should close (continuity). If the contacts do not close, the switch should be replaced.

To check basic setting of fuel injection system (LH 2.2)

The procedure below should only be carried out when the engine function has been disturbed, such as for the replacement of the air mass meter or after major engine work has been completed. Saab does not recommend any specified interval for this check. For the most accurate results, a high-quality digital multimeter should be used.

1. Run the engine until it reaches operating temperature.

2. Connect the positive lead of a voltmeter to the black wire coming from the oxygen sensor. Connect the negative lead to chassis ground.

NOTE
Do not disconnect the wires from the oxygen sensor.

---

3. With the engine running, check the voltage signal coming from the oxygen sensor. The voltage should be fluctuating around the middle of its operating range.

Oxygen sensor
- voltage at idle, engine fully warmed . . . . approx. 0.5 volts (fluctuating)

NOTE
If the sensor is not putting out a signal or if the signal is not fluctuating, make sure the oxygen sensor system is functioning correctly as described earlier under **Oxygen Sensor.**

4. If the voltage is too high or too low, turn the engine off and remove the harness connector from the air mass meter. Connect a digital ohmmeter across terminals 3 and 6 of the meter and measure the resistance.

Air Mass Meter Base Setting

- resistance measured at meter terminals 3 and 6. 380 ohms

---

5. If the resistance reading is incorrect, remove the anti-tamper plug from the side of the air mass meter. See Fig. 36. Turn the screw until the correct reading is obtained.

NOTE

If a reading of 380 ohms cannot be obtained, the air mass meter is faulty and should be replaced.

Fig. 36. Air mass meter anti-tamper plug (arrow).

6. Reconnect the harness connector and start the car. Recheck the voltage signal at the oxygen sensor as described above. The voltage should now be fluctuating around the middle of its operating range (approximately 0.5 volts)

7. If the sensor voltage is incorrect, adjust the screw in the side of the air mass meter until the oxygen sensor voltage is correct.

8. Install a new anti-tamper plug anti-tamper plug from the side of the air mass meter.

If the correct oxygen sensor reading still cannot be obtained, check the wiring between the air mass meter and the control unit. Test the oxygen sensor and its circuit. Try substituting a known good air mass meter or oxygen sensor. If no faults can be found, the LH control unit may be faulty.

To adjust dashpot (LH 2.2)

The dashpot is mounted to the throttle housing and holds the throttle valve open for a moment when the throttle is closed suddenly. This helps reduce the exhaust emission of unburned fuel. A defective or misadjusted dashpot may be the cause of a high idle or the cause of an idle that takes a long time to return to normal when the throttle is released.

NOTE

Before making the adjustment below, check that the basic throttle adjustment is correct.

---

1. With the engine at operating temperature, rev the engine up to at least 3000 rpm, then release the throttle and check that the engine speed returns to normal within 3 to 6 seconds. If the dashpot fails this test, proceed with dashpot adjustment.

2. Loosen the dashpot locknut and turn the dashpot so that its operating rod moves away from the throttle lever. See Fig. 29 above.

3. Rev the engine up to the speed given below and hold the engine speed steady. Turn the dashpot in until its rod just touches the throttle lever. See **Table n**.Tighten the locknut.

Table n. Dashpot Adjustment Specifications

Model	Speed at which dashpot rod touches throttle lever
Non-turbo	2500±100 rpm
Turbo	2600±100 rpm

4. Recheck dashpot operation. If it still fails the test, replace it.

252 Exhaust System

GENERAL

Fig. 1 and Fig. 2 are exploded views of the exhaust systems used on the cars covered by this manual. Proper exhaust and emission system functions depend on each component being free from holes, with air-tight seals at all joints. Exhaust systems components are subjected to vibration, extreme temperatures and road hazards. Although the exhaust system is designed to be maintenance free, regular inspection is warranted due to these harsh operating conditions.

The catalytic converter is similar in appearance to a small muffler and is mounted to the front pipe. Its chemically-reactive core contains surfaces coated with precious metal catalysts. These catalysts promote chemical reactions in the exhaust gases to reduce the quantity of harmful pollutants in the gases. Under normal conditions, the catalytic converter does not require replacement unless it damaged.

The catalytic converter reduces emissions most efficiently when the percentage of oxygen in the exhaust system falls within a narrow range. The oxygen sensor monitors the exhaust gas and provides feedback about combustion efficiency to the fuel injection control unit. For information on testing and removing the oxygen sensor, see **240 Fuel Injection.** For information on testing other emission control systems, including the EGR system, see **254 Exhaust Emission Control**.

WARNING

Toxic exhaust gases are colorless and odorless. Do not run the engine in a non-ventilated area. Repair any structural damaged to the body that would allow the entrance of exhaust gases.

EXHAUST SYSTEM

To remove and install exhaust system

New fasteners, rubber hangers and clamps are always recommended. Gaskets should be replaced whenever the flanged joints are disconnected.

1. Raise the car to a safe level.

WARNING

Never work under a lifted car unless it is solidly supported on stands designed for the purpose. Do not work on a car that is supported solely by a jack.

---

2. Remove the bolts securing the front exhaust pipe to the exhaust manifold or turbocharger.

3. Loosen all clamps and flange bolts.

4. On turbo models, remove the front pipe-to-transmission bracket.

5. Detach the rubber mountings. Separate and remove the pipes and mufflers as necessary. Be sure to inspect the heats shields while the system is removed.

CAUTION

Inspect the heat shields carefully whenever the exhaust system is removed, especially the front heat shields. See Fig. 3. The front shields protect the ignition switch wiring harness from the heat of the hot catalytic converter. If these shields are deteriorated or damaged, they should be replaced

---

Installation is the reverse of removal. Loosely install and assemble the complete system. Then evenly tighten the clamps and mounting bolts. Make sure that no part of the exhaust system contacts any part of the body.

Make sure the rear retaining rings are slightly preloaded toward the front of the car. See Fig. 4. Install the clamps 9 mm (1/3 in.) from the ends of the pipes. See Fig. 5. When installation is complete, start the engine and check for leaks by briefly placing a clean rag over the tailpipe and listening for hissing sounds. If any leaks are present, loosen the system fasteners and readjust the system. Check the system alignment by driving the car over rough road surfaces to check if the system contacts the underbody.

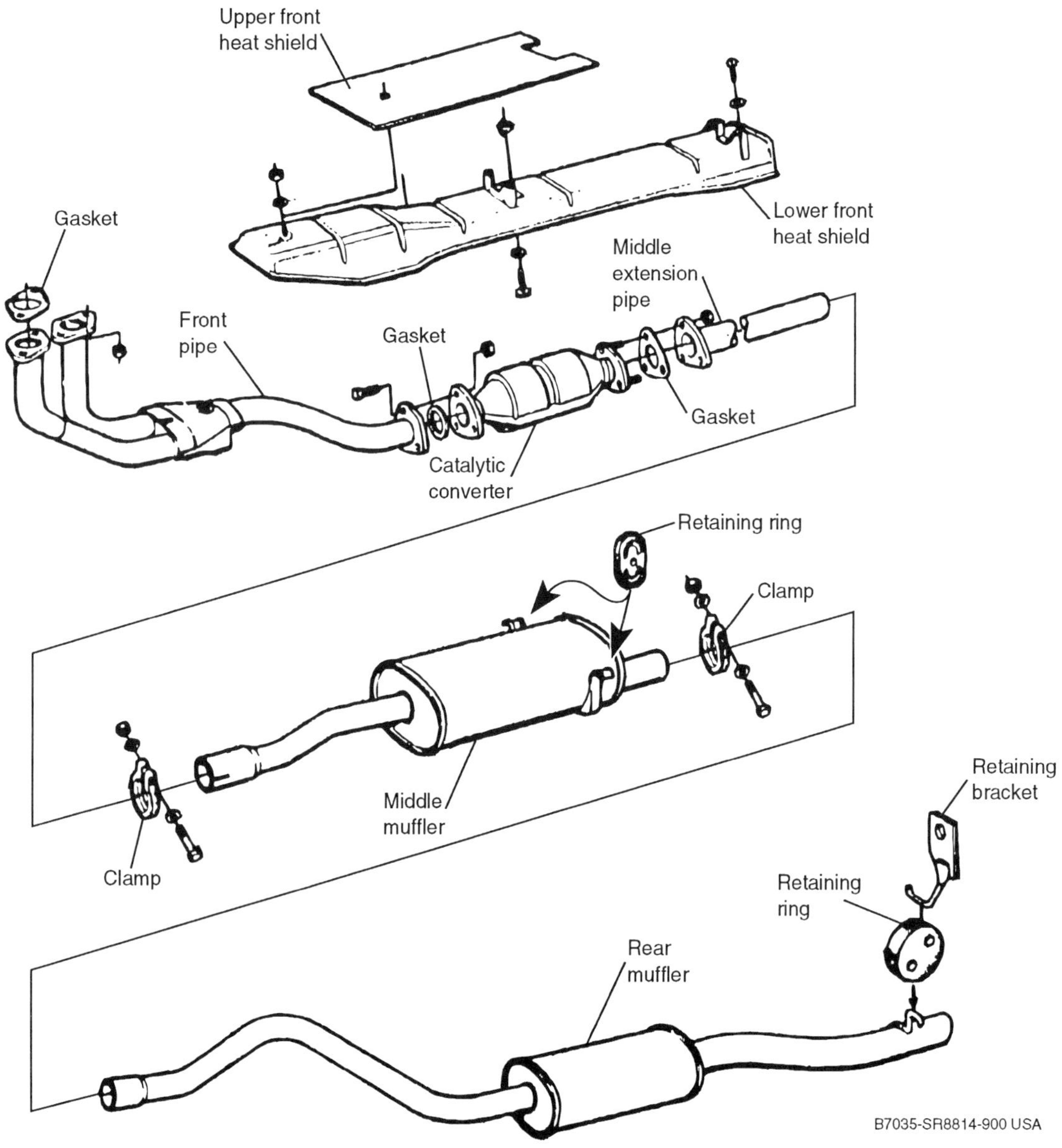

Fig. 1. Exploded view of exhaust system used on cars with normally-aspirated engines.

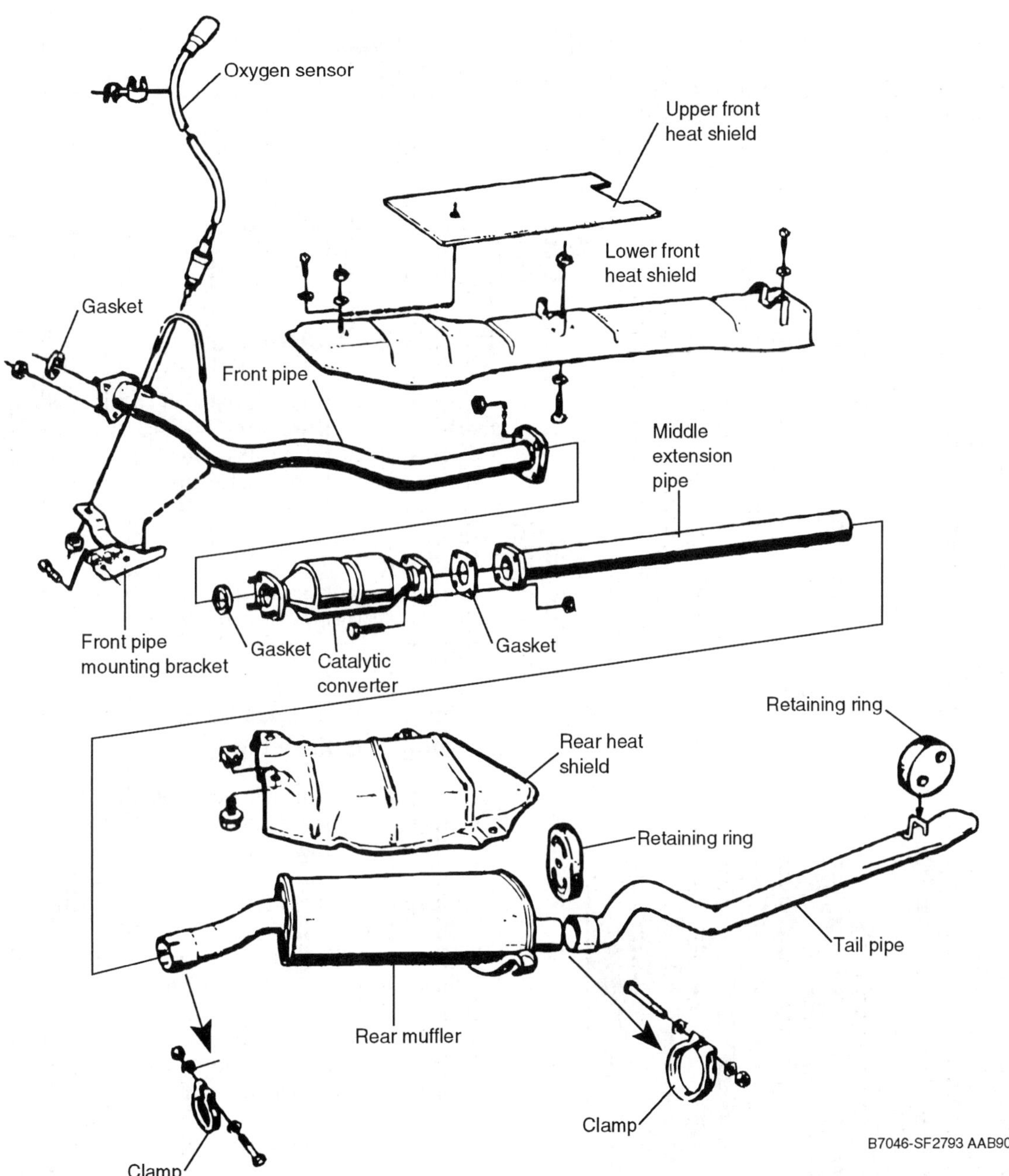

Fig. 2. Exploded view of exhaust system used on cars with turbo-charged engines.

NOTE
Anti-seize compound used on threaded fasteners and exhaust pipe joints will make future replacement easier.

CAUTION
Do not let anti-seize compound or penetrating oil come in contact with the slit portion of the oxygen sensor body. The oxygen sensor will be destroyed.

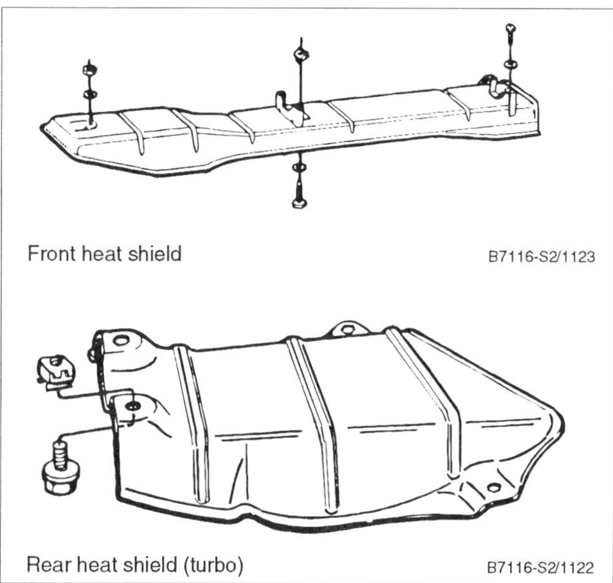

Fig. 3. Exhaust system heat shields.

Fig. 4. Rear muffler retaining ring shown preloaded for exhaust system expansion.

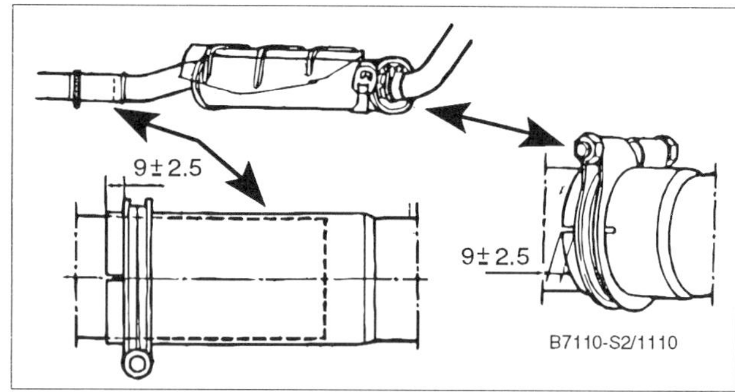

Fig. 5. Exhaust system clamps should be installed 9 mm (1/3 in.) from end of pipe.

EXHAUST MANIFOLD

The exhaust manifold is made of cast iron. Normally-aspirated models use a two-piece manifold assembly. Turbo models use a one-piece manifold. See Fig. 6. Always use a new manifold gasket when installing the manifold.

CAUTION
Do not let cold water come in contact with a hot exhaust manifold or turbocharger. The manifold could crack as a result.

To remove and install exhaust manifold (normally-aspirated engine)

1. On cars with manual transmission, remove the oil filler pipe from the side of the transmission. Plug the opening in the transmission.

2. Separate the front exhaust pipe from the manifold.

3. Remove the mounting bolts from the center manifold and remove it from the cylinder head.

4. Remove the upper-left manifold mounting stud from the cylinder head by locking two nuts on the stud. Use the inner nut to thread the stud out.

5. Remove the remaining mounting bolts from the outer manifold. Remove the manifold by pivoting the front end up while lifting it off the studs. See Fig. 7.

Installation is the reverse of removal. Use new mounting nuts, tightening them evenly to their specified tightening torque.

Tightening torque
normally-aspirated engine
- exhaust manifold to cylinder head . . 20 Nm (15 ft-lb)

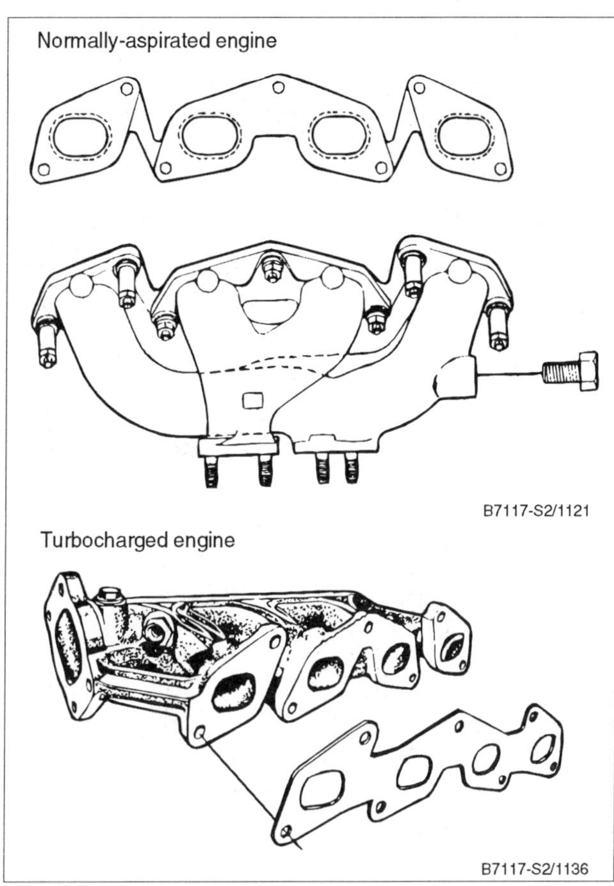

Fig. 6. Exhaust manifolds.

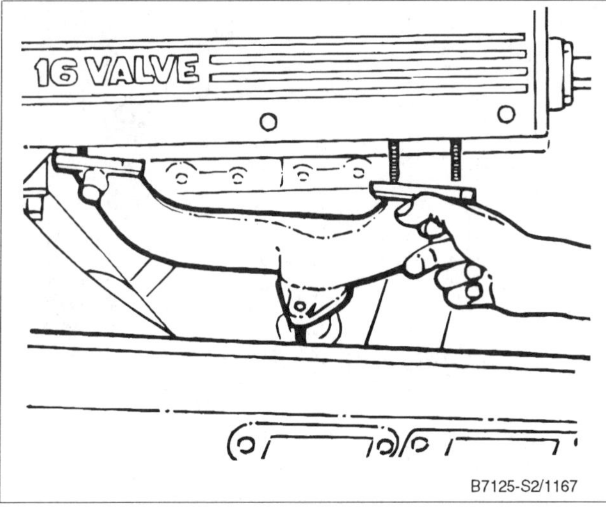

Fig. 7. Exhaust manifold being removed.

To remove and install exhaust manifold (turbo engine)

1. Remove the battery from the car.
2. Remove the ignition distributor as described in **340 Ignition System.**
3. Remove the distributor heat shield from the cylinder head.
4. Disconnect the turbocharger air intake pipe, air outlet pipe and oil supply pipe from the turbocharger. Disconnect the turbocharger oil supply pipe from the engine.
5. On 1988 and later models, drain the cooling system as described in **261 Radiator and Cooling System.** Then remove the coolant lines from the turbocharger.
6. Remove and label the small pressure hoses from the APC solenoid on the radiator crossmember.
7. Where applicable, disconnect the EGR pipe from the exhaust manifold and from the EGR valve.
8. Remove the mounting bolts from the turbo unit bracket at the transmission.
9. On cars with manual transmission, remove the oil filler tube from the side of the transmission. Plug the opening in the transmission.
10. Disconnect the oil return pipe from the turbocharger.
11. Unbolt the front exhaust pipe from the turbocharger.
12. Remove the exhaust manifold mounting nuts, spacers, and washers. Slide the manifold with turbocharger off the studs and out of the car. Separate the turbocharger from the exhaust manifold, if necessary.

Installation is the reverse of removal. Use new mounting nuts, tightening them evenly to their specified tightening torque. Replace the manifold gasket. Replace all turbocharger oil line seals and gaskets. For additional information on the turbocharger see **291 Turbocharger**.

Tightening torque
turbo engine
• exhaust manifold to cylinder head . . 25 Nm (18 ft-lb)

254 Exhaust Emission Control

GENERAL

This repair groups covers only the Evaporative Loss Control Device (ELCD) and the Exhaust Gas Recirculation (EGR) system. For repair and troubleshooting information of other emissions-related systems, such as the oxygen sensor system, the throttle dashpot, and the Automatic Idle Control (AIC) system, see **240 Fuel Injection.**

For proper exhaust emissions, a number of engine systems (ignition, fuel injection, and emission controls) must be functioning correctly. Because of the interrelation of these systems, it is difficult to isolate general driveability problems by examining a single emission control system. For this reason, engine management and driveability troubleshooting information can found in **200 Engine—General.** This information is organized to help isolate problems and suggest more specific troubleshooting steps by taking all of the interrelated systems into consideration.

NOTE

Cars with LH 2.4 and LH 2.4.2 fuel injection systems feature built-in diagnostic circuitry that detects and stores system faults in the LH control unit's memory, including emissions-related faults. When a system compensates for values that are outside the permitted limits, a fault code is generated in the control unit's memory. It is highly recommended that checking for any faults codes be the first step in diagnosing an emissions-related fault. See **240 Fuel Injection** for instructions on viewing the fault codes.

EVAPORATIVE LOSS CONTROL DEVICE (ELCD)

All 900 models use a charcoal-filter canister to absorb vapors from the fuel tank. This system is known as the Evaporative Loss Control Device (ELCD). See Fig. 1. The fuel tank is vented to the canister and the canister is in turn vented to the intake manifold via the ELCD valve. When the engine is running, the accumulated vapors in the canister are drawn through the open ELCD valve and into the engine to be burned. The charcoal canister is mounted in the driver's side wheel well, behind the headlight. The ELCD valve is mounted to the top of the canister. Two types of ELCD systems are used, depending on the fuel system installed. See **Table a.**

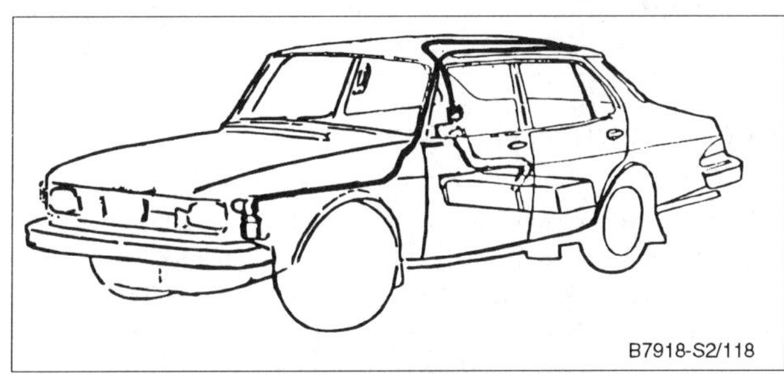

Fig. 1. Evaporative Loss Control Device (ELCD) system. Note how hoses run through headliner.

Table a. ELCD Systems Applications

Fuel Injection Systems*	ELCD System
LH 2.2	Vacuum operated
LH 2.4, LH 2.4.2	Electronically controlled

*see 240 Fuel Injection for system identification

The ELCD valve controls the amount of fuel vapors drawn into the engine and therefore can affect the fuel mixture and exhaust emissions. A fault in the ELCD system can often result in an overly lean or an overly rich mixture, causing driveability problems, especially at idle.

NOTE

On most models, charcoal canister replacement is a maintenance procedure scheduled at a specified mileage interval. See **1 LUBRICATION AND MAINTENANCE** for the recommended service interval.

On models with LH 2.2 fuel injection, a vacuum-operated diaphragm valve on the canister controls when fuel vapors are drawn into the engine. See Fig. 2. Vacuum from the intake manifold opens the valve during cruising.

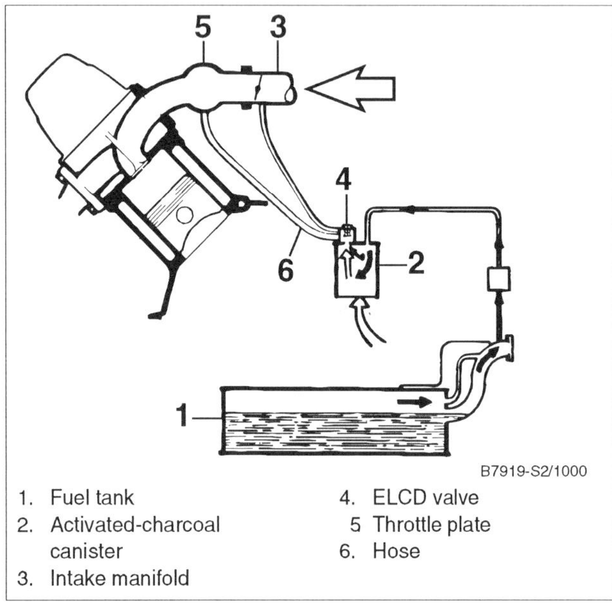

1. Fuel tank
2. Activated-charcoal canister
3. Intake manifold
4. ELCD valve
5. Throttle plate
6. Hose

Fig. 2. Schematic view of ELCD system.

To test the vacuum-operated ELCD valve, disconnect the vacuum hoses from the valve. If necessary, remove the canister from the car. Blow into the lower (larger) hose fitting on the valve. Air should not pass through the valve. Connect a hand-held vacuum pump to the top hose fitting on the valve. With vacuum applied to the top fitting, air should now pass through the lower fitting. See Fig. 3. If any faults are found, the valve is faulty and should be replaced.

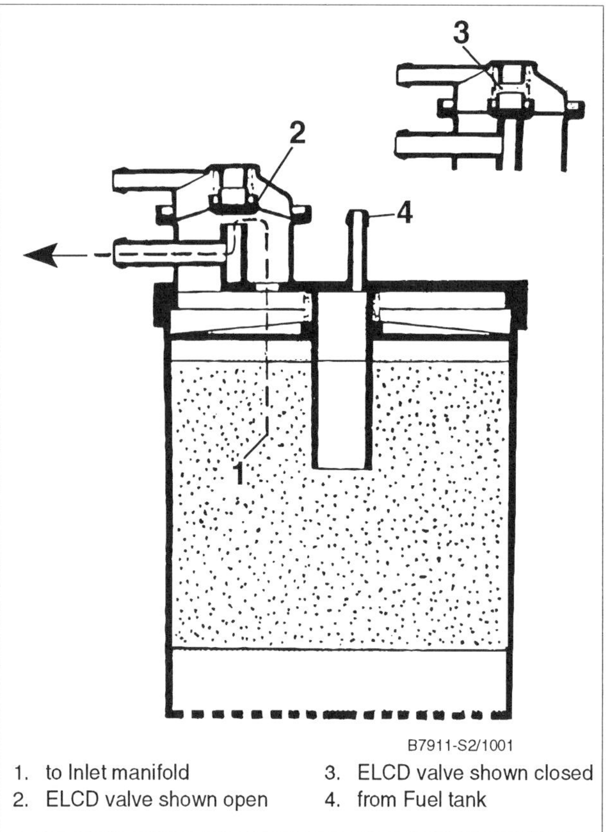

1. to Inlet manifold
2. ELCD valve shown open
3. ELCD valve shown closed
4. from Fuel tank

Fig. 3. Vacuum-operated ELCD valve and charcoal canister.

ELCD valve

• valve resistance . . . . 40 to 60 ohms

On models with LH 2.4 and LH 2.4.2 fuel injection, an electric solenoid valve controls canister purge. The valve is opened and closed electronically by the LH control unit. With the engine running, the valve should be audibly buzzing, and the buzzing noise should vary in intensity depending on engine speed.

The electric ELCD valve can be tested by disconnecting its harness connector and supplying battery voltage to the valve terminals. The valve should click open when voltage is supplied. If no faults are found, check for voltage to the valve's connector with the ignition in the run position. There should be battery voltage between the gray/white wire and ground. If voltage is not present, check for faults using the appropriate wiring diagram shown in **371 Wiring Diagrams, Fuses and Relays**. If voltage is present, check the electrical resistance of the valve. See Fig. 4. If the resistance is not as specified, the valve should be replaced.

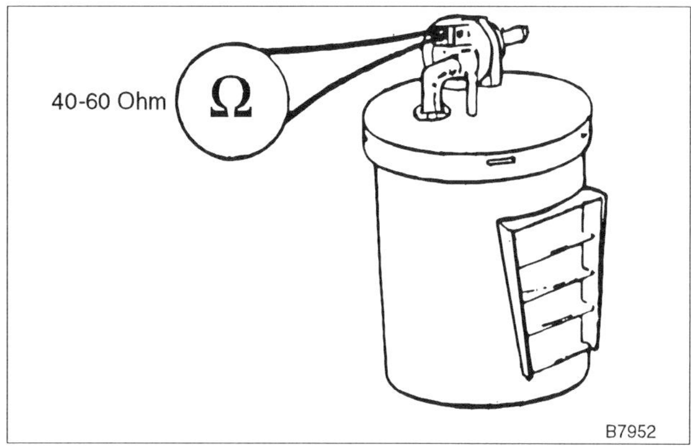

Fig. 4. Electric ELCD valve resistance being measured (shown schematically).

EXHAUST GAS RECIRCULATION SYSTEM (EGR)

The exhaust gas recirculation system functions to recirculate a small amount of the exhaust gases into the intake manifold. This lowers combustion chamber temperatures and reduces exhaust emissions.

Electronic EGR System (1990 and later Californian and SPG models only)

This electronic system is controlled by the LH control unit and uses engine temperature, engine load, and road speed inputs to determine the optimum amount of EGR needed. The main components of the system are the valve, the temperature sensor, and the modulating valve. See Fig. 5

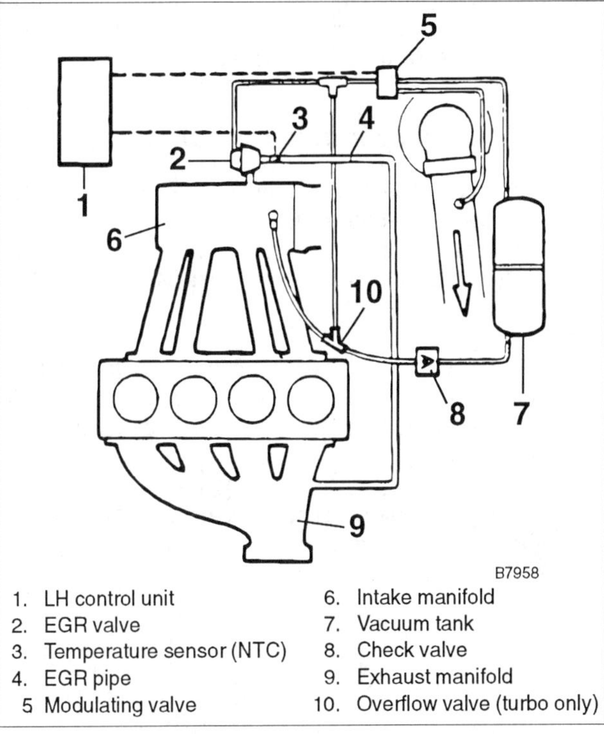

1. LH control unit
2. EGR valve
3. Temperature sensor (NTC)
4. EGR pipe
5. Modulating valve
6. Intake manifold
7. Vacuum tank
8. Check valve
9. Exhaust manifold
10. Overflow valve (turbo only)

Fig. 5. Schematic of Electronic EGR system and hose routing.

The LH control unit sends a signal to the modulating valve, which allows engine vacuum to open the EGR valve. The temperature sensor, which is mounted to the EGR valve, monitors when the valve is open and closed. When troubleshooting the EGR system, check that all hoses are properly connected. Check the hoses for cracks or deterioration. Check the wiring to the EGR modulating valve and the temperature sensor for any visible damage.

NOTE

- If a fault occurs in the EGR system, the Check Engine light will come on and a fault code will be stored in the memory of the LH control unit.

- On cars equipped with the electronic EGR system, the Check Engine light may come on intermittently, even though there are no emissions or fuel system-related faults. To remedy this problem, a special wiring harness has been made. See an authorized Saab dealer for additional information.

To test EGR valve

The EGR valve is shown in Fig. 6.

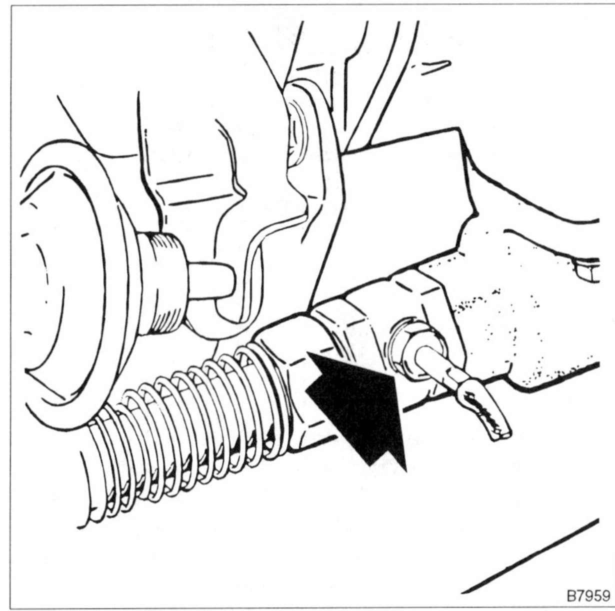

Fig. 6. EGR valve on underside of intake manifold. Temperature sensor shown at arrow.

1. Start and run the engine until it is at operating temperature. Disconnect the hose leading to the EGR valve.

2. Apply vacuum to the disconnected hose. Use a hand-held vacuum pump or suck on the end of the hose to create the vacuum. The engine idle speed should drop noticeably, and the engine may even stall. Reconnect the hose to the EGR valve.

If any faults are found, remove and clean the EGR valve. Be sure to also clean the EGR valve opening in the bottom of the intake manifold. Install the EGR valve and recheck. If any faults are found, the EGR valve should be replaced.

To test modulating valve and signal to modulating valve

The EGR modulating valve is mounted to the driver's side of the fender. See Fig. 7.

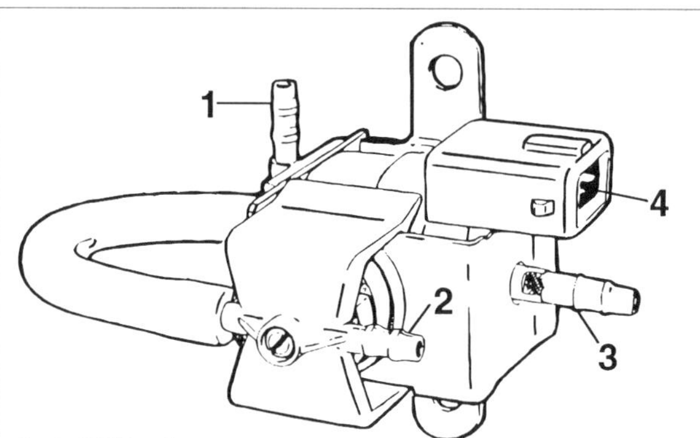

1. to EGR valve
2. to Intake manifold via vacuum tank
3. Turbo: to air hose between air mass meter and turbocharger Non-turbo: to air hose between air mass meter and throttle housing
4. Two pin connector (signal from LH control unit)

Fig. 7. EGR modulating valve.

1. Disconnect the connector from the modulating valve. Check the electrical resistance of the valve with an ohmmeter or apply battery voltage to the valve's terminals. The valve should audibly click when voltage is applied. If the resistance is not as specified or the valve doesn't click, it should be replaced.

EGR modulating valve

• valve resistance . . . . approximately 30 ohms

NOTE

It may be easier to apply voltage to the valve by first removing it from its mountings.

---

2. Connect an LED test light or a fuel injector test light to the valve's harness connector. See Fig. 8.

3. Start and run the engine until it is at operating temperature.

4. Raise the idle speed above 2500 rpm. The LED should flicker.

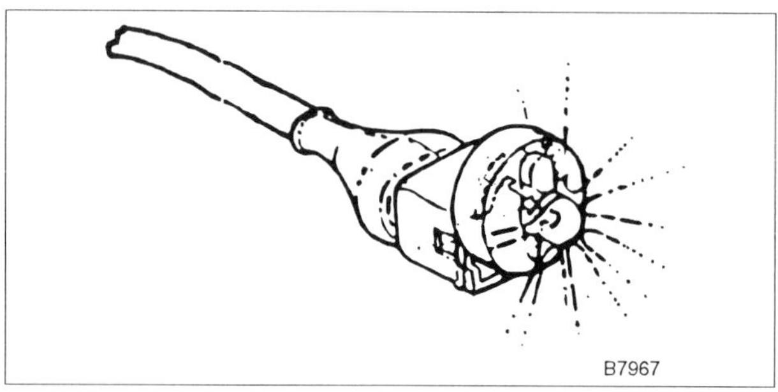

Fig. 8. LED test light connected to modulating valve connector.

If the light does not flicker as described above, turn the engine off and check for power at pin 1 of the connector with the ignition key on. If battery voltage is not present, check for wiring faults to the valve using the appropriate wiring diagram shown in **371 Wiring Diagrams, Fuses and Relays.** If battery voltage is present, check for continuity in the wire between the valve and the LH control unit (pin 19). If no wiring faults can be found, the LH control unit may be faulty.

To test EGR temperature sensor

1. With the engine cold, disconnect the 2-pin connector from the temperature sensor on the EGR valve (see Fig. 6 shown above). Connect an ohmmeter to the sensor terminals. Check that there are several megohms of resistance.

2. Run the engine at speeds above 2500 rpm. After a short period, the sensor's resistance should gradually drop to several thousand ohms or less as the EGR valve heats up.

If the EGR temperature sensor does not respond as specified, it should be replaced. Be sure to check for a good ground at pin 2 (black wire) of the sensor.

261 Radiator and Cooling System

GENERAL

This section covers repairs and troubleshooting information for the engine cooling system only. For heater core and related heating and air conditioning components, see **854 Heating and Air Conditioning.** For information on the engine oil cooler used on turbo models, see **220 Lubrication System**. For information on the ATF cooler used on models with automatic transmission, see **4 TRANSMISSION.**

Additional cooling system components and accessories, such as a winter thermostat for extremely cold climates, an air diverter for extra air flow across the radiator for warm climates, and engine block heaters for easier winter starting, are available through an authorized Saab dealer. Check with your authorized dealer for application and availability information.

Fig. 1 is a schematic view of the cooling system.

Coolant Pump and Thermostat

The coolant pump is crankshaft-driven by a V-belt. A three-stage thermostat controls the flow of coolant. When the engine is cold the thermostat is closed and coolant bypasses the radiator to circulate coolant through the engine and heater core only. When the engine warms up, the thermostat opens and coolant circulates through the complete system. When the engine reaches full operating temperature, the thermostat closes off the lower outlet in the thermostat housing to substantially reduce the coolant flow through the heater core. See Fig. 2.

NOTE

On certain 1985 through 1989 models, the heater core may not receive sufficient coolant flow at low engine speeds during stop-and-go driving in cold weather. If low heater output is experienced during these conditions only, see **854 Heating and Air Conditioning** for information on installing a special circulation pump.

Radiator and Expansion Tank

The radiator is a crossflow design. A translucent expansion tank, or overflow reservoir provides for coolant expansion at higher temperatures and easy monitoring of coolant level.

Radiator Cooling Fans

The cooling fans are mounted to the radiator and are electrically operated. The main fan is switched on and off via a coolant thermoswitch. The main fan also runs whenever the A/C

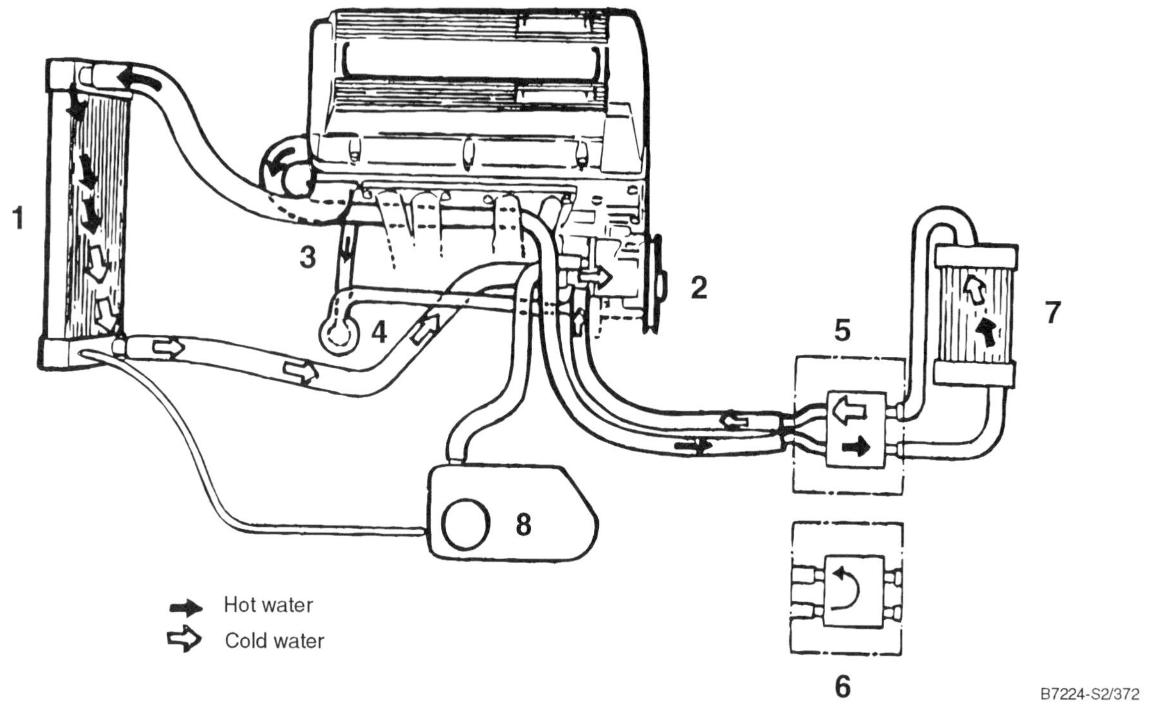

Hot water
Cold water

B7224-S2/372

1. Radiator
2. Coolant pump
3. Thermostat housing
4. Preheater, intake manifold
5. Heater valve in open position
6. Heater valve in closed position
7. Heater core
8. Coolant expansion tank

Fig. 1. Schematic view of cooling system.

switch is on. The auxiliary cooling fan runs anytime the A/C compressor is cycling.

Warnings and Cautions

The following warnings and cautions should be followed when working on the cooling system.

WARNING

- At normal operating temperature the cooling system is pressurized. Allow the system to cool as long as possible before opening—a minimum of an hour—then release the cap very slowly to allow safe release of pressure.

- Releasing the cooling system pressure lowers the coolant's boiling point, and the coolant may boil suddenly. Use heavy gloves and wear eye and face protection to guard against scalding.

- Use extreme care when draining and disposing of engine coolant. Coolant is poisonous and lethal to pets. Pets are attracted to coolant because of its sweet smell and taste. See a veterinarian immediately if any amount of coolant is ingested by the animal.

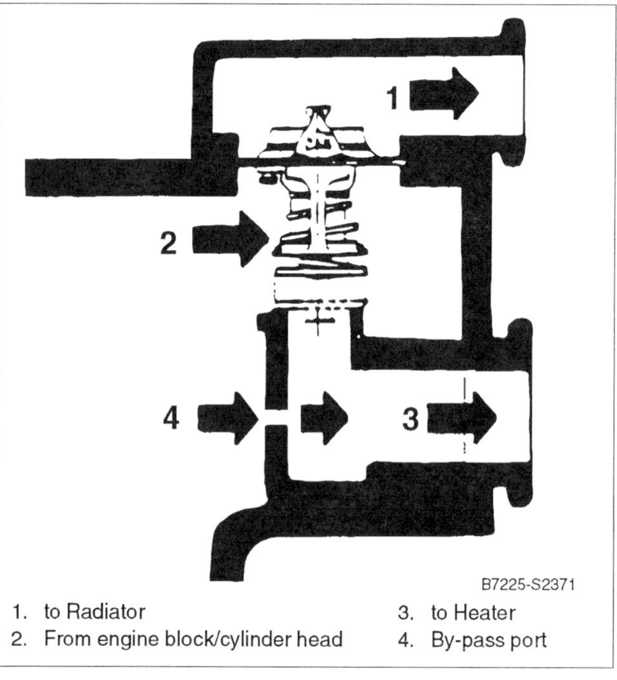

1. to Radiator
2. From engine block/cylinder head
3. to Heater
4. By-pass port

Fig. 2. Schematic view of three-way thermostat.

CAUTION
Avoid adding cold water to the coolant while the engine is hot or overheated. If it is necessary to add coolant to a hot system, do so only with the engine running and coolant pump turning.

TROUBLESHOOTING

When investigating the cause of overheating or coolant loss, begin with a visual inspection of the system. Carefully check for a broken or loose coolant pump V-belt. Check the coolant level and check for evidence of coolant leaks.

Check that the radiator fins are not blocked with dirt or debris. Clean the radiator fins using low-pressure water or compressed air. Blow from the engine side out.

Inspect the coolant pump by first removing the V-belt from the pump. Firmly grasp opposite sides of the pulley and check for play in all directions. Rotate the pulley and check that the shaft runs smoothly. If any faults are found the pump should be replaced.

NOTE
The coolant provides some lubrication for the pump shaft, so an occasional drop of coolant leaking from the pump is acceptable. If coolant drips from the vent hole, the pump should be replaced.

Most cooling system faults can be grouped into one of three main categories: 1) cooling system leaks, 2) poor coolant circulation, or 3) radiator cooling fan electrical faults.

The cooling system becomes pressurized at normal operating temperature, which raises the boiling point of the coolant. Leaks may prevent the system from becoming pressurized, allowing the coolant to boil at a lower temperature. If visual evidence is inconclusive, a cooling system pressure test, as described below, will help to pin point hard to find leaks.

If the cooling system is full of coolant and holds pressure, the next most probable cause of overheating is the result of poor coolant circulation due to a failed thermostat or coolant pump, a pinched or restricted hose, or a clogged system.

To quickly check if the thermostat is opening and if coolant is circulating through the radiator, allow a cold engine to reach operating temperature (temperature gauge needle approximately centered). Feel the radiator hoses. If the hoses are hot to the touch, the coolant is probably circulating correctly. If there are any cool areas in the hoses or radiator, coolant flow to the radiator is restricted. Check for a faulty thermostat or a plugged radiator.

WARNING
Be careful when working near the cooling fans when the engine is hot. The fan can come on at anytime—even if the ignition key is off.

NOTE
A thermostat that is stuck open will cause the engine to warm up slowly and run below normal temperature at highway speed. A thermostat that is stuck closed will restrict coolant flow to the radiator and cause overheating.

An otherwise sound cooling system will overheat if the electric cooling fans are not operating correctly. The fans should switch on and off according to engine coolant temperature or whenever the A/C is on. Below are a few quick checks to help diagnose cooling system faults.

If the engine overheats and no other cooling system tests indicate trouble, the radiator may have some plugged passages that are restricting coolant flow. This does not necessarily mean that the radiator must be replaced. In many cases the radiator can be chemically cleaned by a qualified radiator repair shop.

Pressure Test

A pressure test uses a special tester to pressurize the system and simulate normal running conditions. If the system is unable to hold pressure, the engine will overheat more easily. Aside from locating external leaks, a pressure test can be used to check for internal leaks. Some of the common sources of internal leaks are a faulty cylinder head gasket, a cracked cylinder head, or a cracked cylinder block.

Requirements:
- cooling system pressure tester
- engine warm

With the engine at normal operating temperature, pressurize the system. See Fig. 3. Loss of pressure indicates leaks that may also be detected by the seepage of coolant. If the pressure drops rapidly and there is no sign of coolant leakage, the cylinder head gasket may be faulty. See **211 Cylinder Head Removal and Installation** for gasket replacement procedures.

The screw-on type expansion tank cap should also be tested using a pressure tester and the correct tester adapter. Carefully inspect the cap for damage. A faulty cap or a damaged cap gasket should be replaced.

Cooling system test pressures
- Maximum system pressure . . . . . . 1.2 bar (17.5 psi)
- Expansion tank cap opening pressure . . . . 0.9 to 1.2 bar (13 to 17.5 psi)

CAUTION
Exceeding the specified test pressure could damage the radiator or other cooling system components.

Fig. 3. Cooling system being checked for leaks using pressure tester.

Temperature Gauge Quick-Check

A quick-check of the coolant temperature sender can be made to determine the cause of a faulty coolant temperature gauge. The checks should be made at the coolant temperature sender on the front of the cylinder head, below the distributor. See Fig. 4.

Disconnect the wire from the sender and hold it to ground. Turn the ignition on. If the gauge needle moves upward, the sending unit is faulty. If the gauge does not respond, the wiring to the gauge is broken (open circuit) or the gauge itself is faulty. To check the resistance of the sender measure between ground and the sender terminal with the wire disconnected.

Coolant temperature sender specification
- sender resistance at 90°C (194°F) . . . 51.2±4.3 ohms

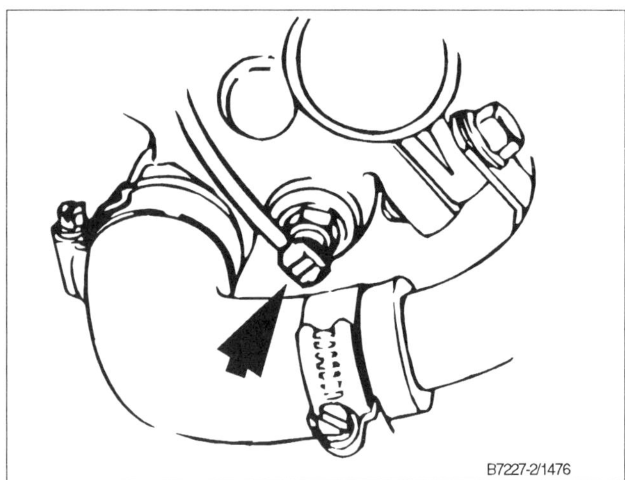

Fig. 4. Coolant temperature sender (arrow) below distributor on front of cylinder head.

When replacing a faulty coolant temperature sender, drain the cooling system down below the level of the sender and then unscrew the sender.

Radiator Fan Quick-Check

If the main fan does not come on, a quick-check can be made to determine whether the fault is in the fan, the thermoswitch, or the fan's electrical circuit. Be sure to check fuse no. 25 (30 amp) and fuse no. 6 (30 amp) before making any tests.

To test the fan, turn the ignition on and remove the rubber boot from the fan's thermoswitch on the left side of the radiator. Using a screwdriver, short the two switch terminals together and check that the fan runs. See Fig. 5.

Fig. 5. Main cooling fan thermoswitch being shorted using screwdriver.

If the fan runs only when the switch is bypassed, the thermoswitch is faulty and should be replaced. If the fan does not run, check for battery voltage between the green wire and ground at the thermoswitch. If voltage is present, the fan is faulty and should be replaced. If voltage is not present, check the wiring and the fan relay using the diagrams shown in **371 Wiring Digrams, Fuses and Relays.** Additional information on replacing the thermoswitch and the radiator cooling fan is given below.

NOTE

The auxiliary fan located beside the main fan on the radiator is part of the A/C system. See **8 BODY** for additional information on this fan.

Thermostat Quick-Check

To quickly check if the thermostat is opening and if coolant is circulating through the radiator, allow a cold engine to reach operating temperature (temperature gauge needle approximately centered). Feel the radiator hoses. If the hoses are hot to the touch, the coolant is circulating. If the hoses are not hot, coolant flow to the radiator is restricted. Check for a faulty thermostat or a plugged radiator.

COOLANT AND HOSES

To drain and fill cooling system

1. Disconnect the negative (–) battery cable, remove the expansion tank cap, and set the temperature control knob in the passenger compartment to warm.

2. Loosen the radiator drain plug at the bottom of the radiator next to the battery. See Fig. 6.

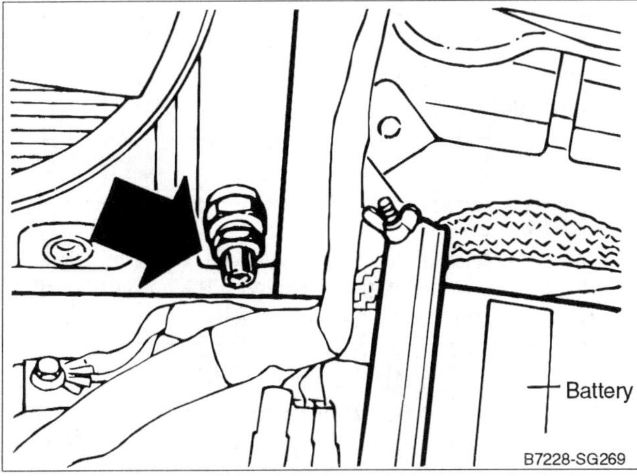

Fig. 6. Radiator drain plug (arrow).

3. Remove the engine block drain plug. See Fig. 7. The drain plug is located behind the exhaust manifold.

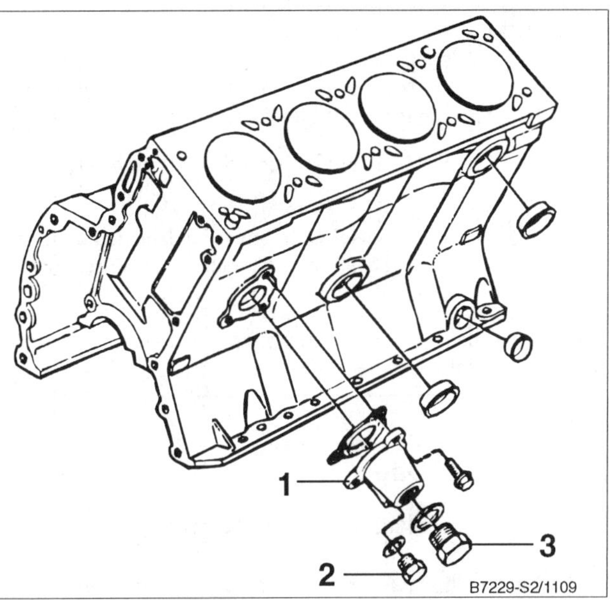

Fig. 7. Cylinder block showing location of coolant drain plug **2**. Do not remove cover **1** or plug **3**.

4. Reinstall the drain plugs using new gaskets.

Tightening torque

- Engine block drain plug (with new gasket) .... 15 Nm (11 ft-lb)

---

5. With the engine off, open the bleeder screw on the thermostat housing. See Fig. 8. Using a coolant mixture of 50% anti-freeze and 50% water, fill the expansion tank slowly so that air is allowed to escape. Close the bleeder screw when coolant begins to come out of the bleeder. Run the engine and check for leaks.

Cooling system capacity

- 10 liters (10.5 qts.)

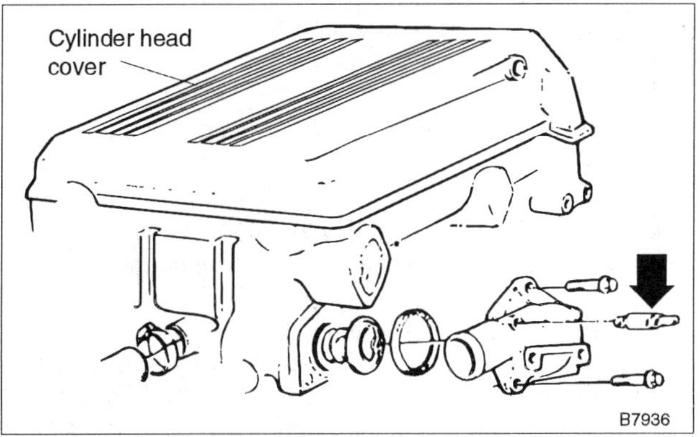

Fig. 8. Exploded veiw of thermostat housing and bleeder screw (arrow). 16 valve model shown.

CAUTION
- Always use Saab original coolant to avoid the formation of harmful, clogging deposits in the cooling system. Use of other anti-freeze solutions may be harmful to the cooling system.
- The final coolant level is best checked when the cooling system is fully cold.
- Do not reuse the coolant when replacing damaged engine parts. Contaminated coolant may damage the engine or cooling system.
- If coolant comes in contact with paint or bodywork rinse with water. Coolant will damage paint.

To replace a hose

1. Drain the coolant as described above.
2. Remove the hose. Using a screwdriver, loosen each hose clamp and slide the clamps away from the hose ends.

NOTE
If a radiator hose is stuck to the radiator connection, cut the old hose off the connection as shown in Fig. 9. Prying the hose loose may damage the connection or the radiator.

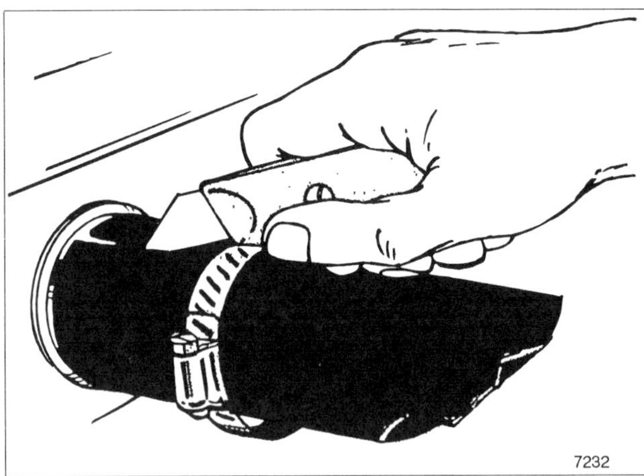

Fig. 9. Stuck hose being removed by cutting.

3. Clean the hose connections and remove any bits of old hose and sealer.
4. Install the new hose. Slide the loose clamps over the hose and slide the hose ends over the connections.
5. Position and tighten the clamps. Place the clamp as near the bead as possible and at least 4 mm (5/32 in.) from the hose end, as shown in Fig. 10. Tighten the clamps enough to compress the hose firmly around the connections.

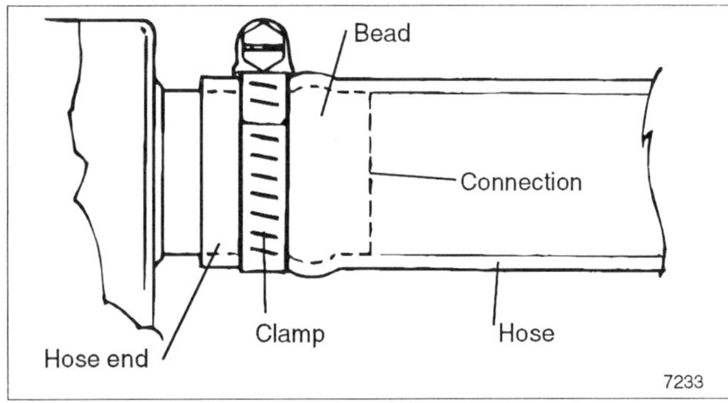

Fig. 10. Hose clamp correctly installed on hose end.

CAUTION
Do not overtighten clamps. Tighten just enough to seal. Over-tightening may damage the hose and cause premature failure.

6. Refill and bleed the radiator as described above. Run the engine until warm. Check for leaks.

THERMOSTAT

To replace thermostat

1. Drain the coolant as described above.
2. Remove the thermostat housing bolts. Remove the housing and thermostat. See Fig. 8 above.
3. Position the new thermostat and gasket in the outlet. Install the thermostat housing.

Tightening torque
- thermostat housing to cylinder head . . . . 18 Nm (13 ft-lb)

CAUTION
Saab uses a special three stage thermostat. When replacing, be sure to use only an original Saab part. The engine should not be operated without a thermostat.

4. Refill and bleed the cooling system.

COOLANT PUMP

Fig. 11 is an exploded view of the coolant pump. Always plan to replace gaskets and seals and to have them on hand before beginning repairs.

To replace coolant pump

1. Disconnect the negative (–) battery cable.
2. Drain the cooling system as described above.

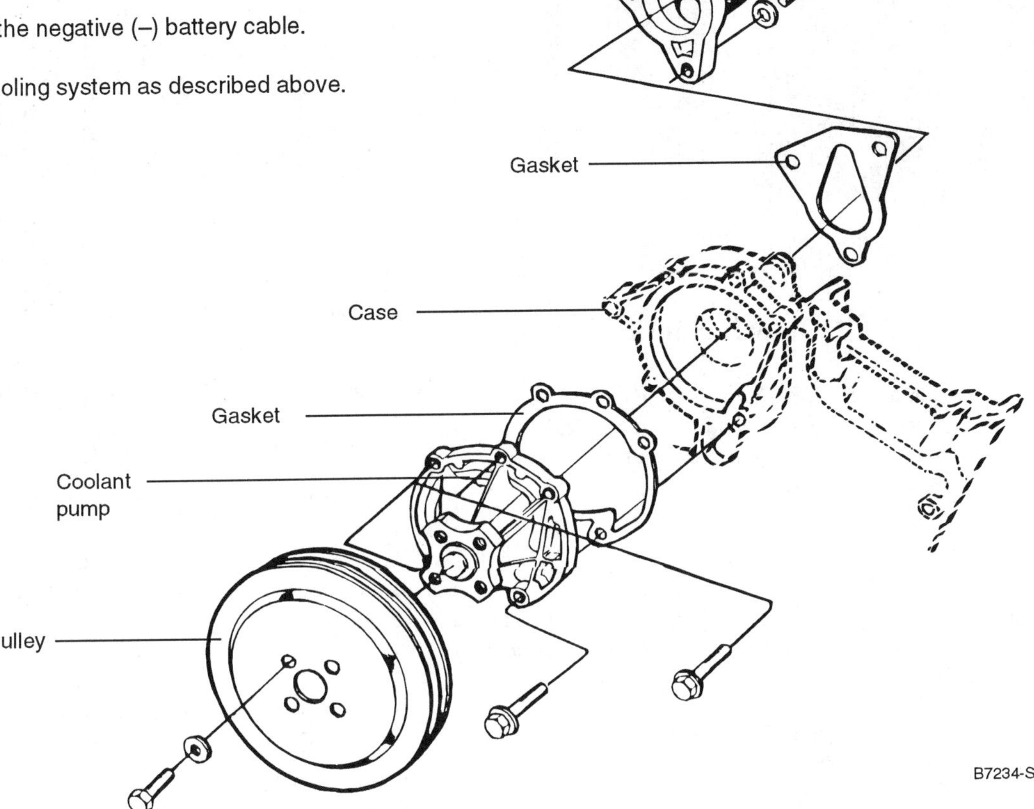

Fig. 11. Coolant pump exploded view.

3. Loosen the four bolts securing the pulley to the pump.
4. Remove the V-belts from the pump as described in **1 LUBRICATION AND MAINTENANCE**. Then remove the pulley mounting bolts and the pulley. See Fig. 12.
5. Remove the coolant pump bolts and remove the coolant pump from the case. See Fig. 13. Note the position of the two longer bolts.

Installation is the reverse of removal. Clean the pump mating surface before installing a new gasket. Install the V-belts as described in **1 LUBRICATION AND MAINTENANCE**. Fill and bleed the cooling system as described above. Start the engine and check for leaks.

Fig. 12. Coolant pump pulley being removed.

Fig. 13. Coolant pump being removed.

RADIATOR AND COOLING FANS

Replacement radiators from Saab may not fit into some of 1989 and early cars without installing a special radiator mounting kit and making some minor modifications. See your Saab dealer for details.

To remove radiator

1. Disconnect the negative (–) battery cable. Disconnect the harness connectors from the fans, the ground straps, and the thermoswitch wires.
2. Drain the cooling system as described above. Disconnect all coolant hoses from the radiator.
3. Remove the air filter intake shroud and the distributor cap.
4. Remove the two bolts securing the radiator and remove the radiator and cooling fans as an assembly. See Fig. 14.
5. Working at the bench, remove the fan assemblies and any other hardware.

Installation is the reverse of removal. Inspect the rubber lower radiator mountings and replace any that are damaged. Fill and bleed the cooling system as described above.

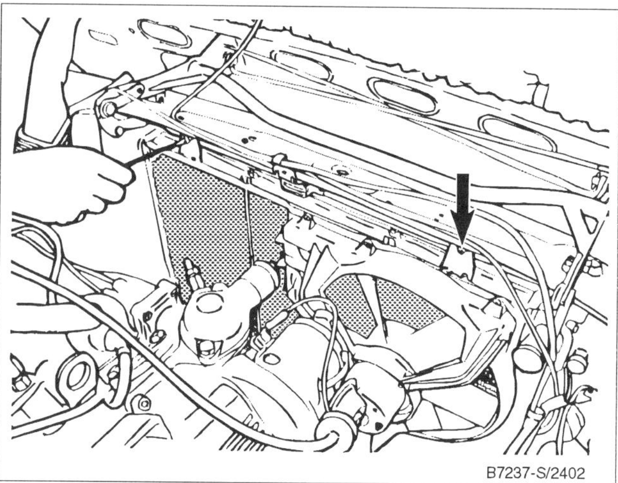

Fig. 14. Radiator mounting screw being removed. Also remove screw (arrow) on other side. Tilt radiator back to remove.

To replace radiator cooling fan thermoswitch

1. Disconnect the negative (–) battery cable.
2. Drain the cooling system as described earlier.
3. Disconnect the wires from the thermoswitch and unscrew the switch. Install the new switch. See Fig. 15.

NOTE

- Always the replace the sealing ring when installing a new thermoswitch.
- To test the thermoswitch, heat it in a pan of water with an ohmmeter connected to it terminals. Check the temperature of the water when the switch closes.

Radiator Cooling Fan Thermoswitch

- closes (fan on) . . . . 194–203°F (90–95°C)
- opens (fan off). . . . . 185–194°F (85–90°C)

---

4. Fill and bleed the cooling system. Start the engine and check for leaks. Always verify that both fans operate by allowing the engine to run at temperature and by switching on the A/C.

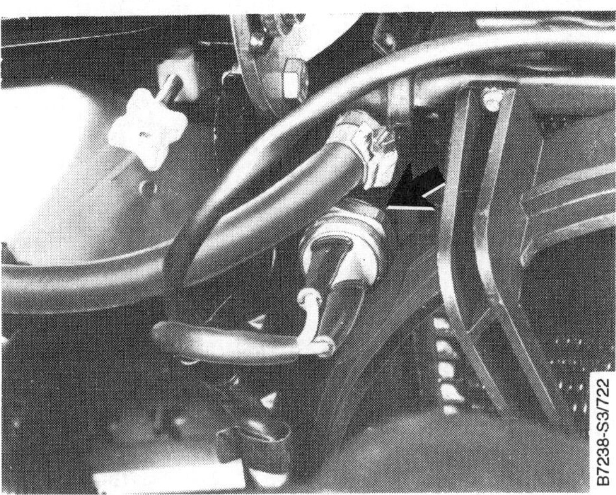

Fig. 15. Main cooling fan thermoswitch in left-side of radiator (arrow).

Fig. 16. Fan and shroud assembly being removed.

To remove radiator cooling fans

1. Disconnect the negative (–) battery cable. Disconnect the fan harness connector and the ground strap.

2. Remove the screws securing the fan shroud to the radiator. Remove the fan and shroud as a unit. See Fig. 16.

3. Working at the bench, remove the screws or nuts holding the fan motor to the shroud assembly.

Installation is reverse of removal. Use a thread locking compound such as Loctite® on the screws or nuts that secure the fan motor to the shroud. Always test fan operation after reinstalling the fan/shroud assembly.

NOTE

- If the engine overheats even though the fan cycles on and off as specified, the fan may be running in reverse. Check that the fan is drawing air through the radiator and not blowing air out. Some fans were wired improperly at the connector. The wires in the fan connector should mate with the same color wires in the harness connector.

- Always check the tightness of the fan to the shroud. These fasteners can vibrate loose. Use a thread locking compound on all screws or nuts.

291 Turbocharger

TABLES

GENERAL

This section covers turbocharger and Automatic Performance Control (APC) system service and repair. Special test equipment is required for some of the test procedures. If this equipment is not available, the tests should be left to an authorized Saab dealer.

Turbocharger

A schematic of the turbocharger with intercooler is shown in Fig. 1. The exhaust-driven turbocharger rotates at very high speeds and is precisely balanced. The turbocharger is cooled and lubricated with engine oil. On 1988 and later models, the turbocharger is also water-cooled. The turbocharger's boost pressure is limited by a mechanical wastegate. When the boost pressure exceeds a predetermined level, the wastegate opens to bypass some of the exhaust gases around the turbine.

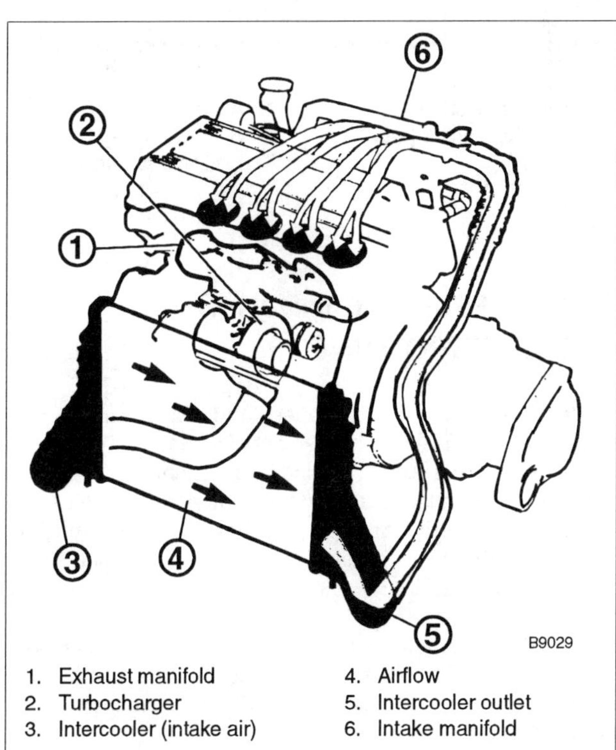

1. Exhaust manifold
2. Turbocharger
3. Intercooler (intake air)
4. Airflow
5. Intercooler outlet
6. Intake manifold

Fig. 1. Turbocharger system.

Automatic Performance Control (APC)

The Automatic Performance Control (APC) system enables the engine to achieve optimum performance and good fuel economy, regardless of the grade of fuel being used at any given time. The APC system consists of simple electronic components. See Fig. 2.

A knock sensor on the engine block senses the onset and degree of engine knock and transmits an electronic signal to the control unit. The control unit also receives intake manifold pressure information from a pressure sensor and engine speed information from the ignition system. Using this information, the APC control unit electrically modulates the APC solenoid valve to regulate boost pressure via the wastegate.

Through the APC system, the boost pressure is allowed to increase (up to a limit) until the engine begins to knock. It does this by venting some of the manifold pressure away from the wastegate and in effect "tricking" the wastegate that the boost pressure is lower than it really is. When the engine begins to knock, the solenoid valve closes and true boost pressure is applied to the wastegate diaphragm and the wastegate valve is pushed off its seat.

NOTE

In the event the APC system or the wastegate malfunction, allowing the boost pressure to exceed a safe level, the fuel pump will be turned off. On cars with LH 2.2, this feature is handled by an overpressure switch. On 1989 and later cars with LH 2.4, the LH control unit handles this feature. See **234 Fuel Pump and Fuel Tank** for more information on the overpressure switch.

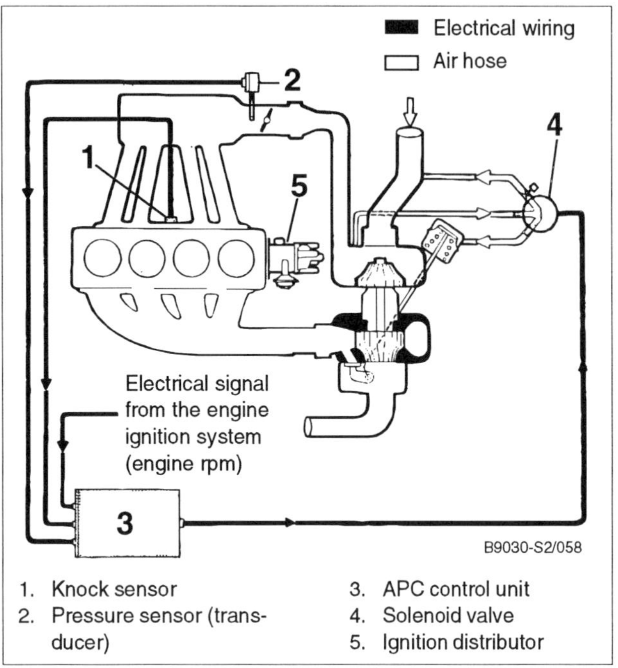

1. Knock sensor
2. Pressure sensor (transducer)
3. APC control unit
4. Solenoid valve
5. Ignition distributor

Fig. 2. Schematic of APC system.

TURBOCHARGER AND APC TROUBLESHOOTING

Due to the extremely high speeds and temperatures, proper lubrication of the turbocharger is critical. Small oil passages are drilled into the turbo housing and bearings. Piston-type sealing rings are placed around the shaft at each end to prevent oil from entering the compressor and turbine housing. There is a high rate of flow of oil to ensure the shaft floats on a film of oil. See Fig. 3.

When the turbo bearings and seals become worn, the lubricating oil can slip past the seals and into the combustion chamber. The result is blue-gray oil smoke exiting through the tailpipe. When the bearings become severely worn, the turbocharger compressor and turbine impeller may contact the turbocharger housing, making loud screeching or thumping noises.

The major cause of turbocharger bearing and seal failure is due to carbon deposits caused by "coking" or baking of the oil in the turbocharger's oil passages. During operation, the temperature of the turbocharger housing can exceed the boiling point of the oil running through it. Because the oil is constantly circulating, it stays cool enough to prevent coking. If the oil pipes are clogged or if the engine is turned off before the turbocharger has had time to cool down, the oil can quickly coke. When coking deposits form, the oil flow to the turbocharger is reduced. In addition, this substance is abrasive and can wear the seals and bearings prematurely.

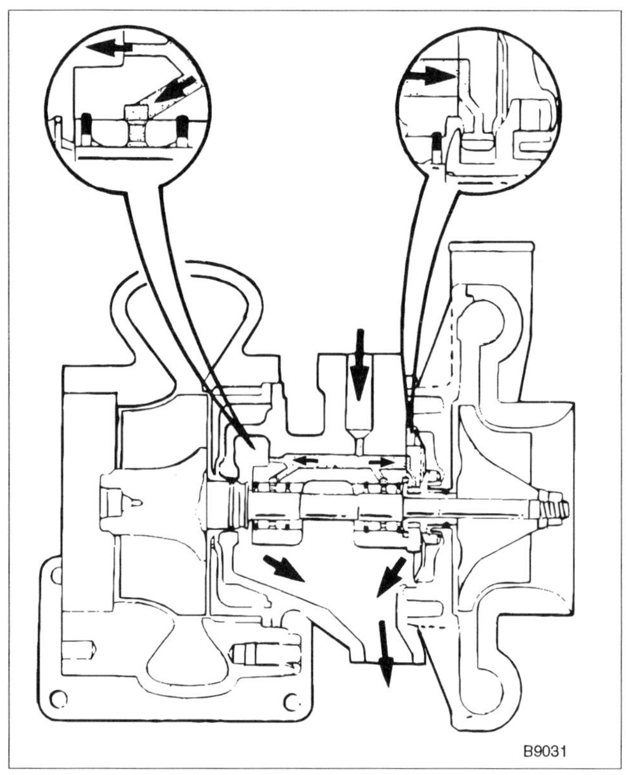

Fig. 3. Cutaway view of turbocharger showing lubrication circuit.

If none of the above faults are present, but engine performance and the turbocharger's output is low, first check for any loose or broken hoses. Check the small vacuum/pressure hoses as well as the larger intake air hoses. Be sure to check the hoses at the turbo bypass valve, which is directly below the turbocharger. Check the electrical connectors to the APC control unit (under rear seat on 1985 cars; at driver's side wheel housing on all 1986 and later cars), the solenoid valve (at radiator crossmember) and the pressure sensor (under left-hand side of instrument panel). If there are any faults in the APC system, the boost pressure will only boost to the "basic" pressure as described below.

In addition to the APC system components, there are two other components that can reduce the turbocharger's boost pressure. The cruise control vacuum switch and the brake light switch (1986 and later cars) will revert the system to the "basic" boost setting automatically whenever the brakes are applied or the cruise control system is activated. If either one of these components is faulty, the wastegate will open at a low boost level. Testing and adjusting information for the brake light switch is given in **364 Electric Controls and Switches.** Testing information for the cruise control vacuum switch is given in **368 Cruise Control.**

Besides low boost pressure, the boost pressure can also be too high, and this can result in complete engine failure. **Table a** lists turbocharger and APC system faults, their probable causes, and corrective actions.

NOTE
It is a good idea to measure the boost pressure as a first step in turbocharger and APC troubleshooting.

Turbo Boost Pressure

There are two boost pressure measurements that should be made to check the performance of the turbocharger and to check that the APC system is operating.

The first part of the pressure check measures basic boost. The basic boost pressure is the base or "basic" setting of the wastegate and is adjustable. This pressure setting is a safety feature to prevent engine damage caused by detonation. In the event of an APC component malfunction, the system reverts to the basic setting of the wastegate. The basic setting is also selected whenever the cruise control system is selected or the brake pedal is depressed (1986 and later models only).

The second part of the pressure check measures the efficiency of the turbocharger and also checks the operation of the APC system. This setting is not adjustable and is regulated based on the quality of the fuel in the tank. The better the quality of fuel in the tank, the higher the boost level.

Table a. Turbocharger and APC Troubleshooting

Symptom	Probable cause	Corrective action
1. Noise or vibration from turbo unit	**a.** Insufficient lubrication to turbo shaft and bearing	**a.** Remove and check the turbo oil supply pipe for clogging or deposits. Check the oil pressure and oil flow to the turbocharger
	b. Leakage in the intake or exhaust system	**b.** Check for leaking seals (O-rings) or pipe connections. Tighten all connections and replace defective seals
	c. Turbo shaft unbalanced	**c.** Replace turbo unit
2. Boost pressure too low	**a.** Leakage between compressor and cylinder head or turbine and exhaust system	**a.** Check for leaking pipe connections. Tighten all connections
	b. Incorrectly adjusted charge pressure	**b.** Check and adjust basic boost and maximum boost
	c. Wastegate sticking open	**c.** Clean and lubricate wastegate. Replace the wastegate assembly if it cannot be made to move freely
	d. Partially clogged exhaust system	**d.** Check exhaust system for blockage, especially in the catalytic converter. Replace faulty exhaust components
	e. Clogged air cleaner	**e.** Replace air cleaner
	f. Binding turbo shaft	**f.** Replace turbo unit
	g. Faulty brake light switch (1986 and later) or faulty cruise control vacuum switch	**g.** Test switches and replace if faulty
	h. Faulty APC component	**h.** Test the knock sensor, the pressure sensor, and the solenoid valve. If no faults are found, the APC control unit may be faulty
3. Boost pressure too high	**a.** Leak in hose at APC solenoid valve or faulty solenoid valve	**a.** Check for leaks and replace any faulty hoses. Test the APC solenoid and replace if faulty
	b. Leaky wastegate diaphragm unit	**b.** Replace diaphragm unit
	c. Leaking hose to pressure sensor or faulty pressure sensor	**c.** Check for leaks and replace any faulty hoses. Test the pressure sensor and replace if faulty
	d. Wastegate sticking closed or binding	**d.** Clean and lubricate wastegate. Replace the wastegate assembly if it cannot be made to move freely
	e. Incorrectly adjusted charge pressure	**e.** Check and adjust basic boost and maximum boost
	f. Faulty pressure sensor or APC control unit	**f.** Test pressure sensor. If no faults are found the APC control unit may be faulty
4. Normal boost pressure despite intensive knocking	**a.** APC system not working	**a.** Test APC system components
	b. Knock sensor or wiring to knock deter faulty	**b.** Test knock sensor and replace if faulty
	c. Knock sensor not correctly tightened to block	**c.** Check that sensor is torqued to 14 Nm (10 ft-lb)
	d. Wastegate sticking closed	**d.** Clean and lubricate wastegate. Replace the wastegate assembly if it can not be made to move freely

CAUTION

Do not measure the maximum turbocharger boost pressure by eliminating the knock sensor from the APC system. Although the system is designed to limit boost pressure based on the input from the pressure sensor (and at even higher levels, the fuel pump is turned off), the pressure at which this occurs may be too high if the fuel quality is low, resulting in engine failure.

To check and adjust boost pressure

An accurate vacuum/pressure gauge with a long extension hose is required to measure the boost pressure. See Fig. 4. Hang the gauge from the rear view mirror for ease of viewing to obtain the most accurate results. In addition, a helper is required to make the test described below.

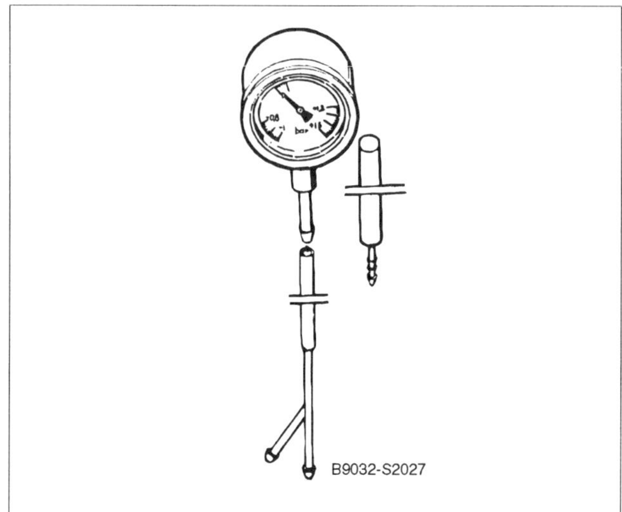

Fig. 4. Vacuum/pressure gauge (Saab tool no. 83 93 514) for measuring turbo boost pressure and for testing APC components.

WARNING

The following test requires that the car be driven on the road while checking the boost pressure on the gauge. This should always be done using a helper. Do not make the test if a helper is not available to read and record the gauge results.

CAUTION

It is recommended that the highest octane-rated fuel available be used when making this test. Otherwise the engine may knock continually during the test, possibly causing engine damage.

1. Run the engine until it is fully warmed up.

2. Working at the radiator crossmember, unplug the wiring connectors from the solenoid valve. See Fig. 5.

Fig. 5. APC solenoid valve wiring connectors being disconnected.

NOTE

When using Saab tool no. 83 94 074, the APC solenoid valve can be isolated from the system by turning the solenoid-valve switch off. Make sure the knock detector switch is also off. See Fig. 6.

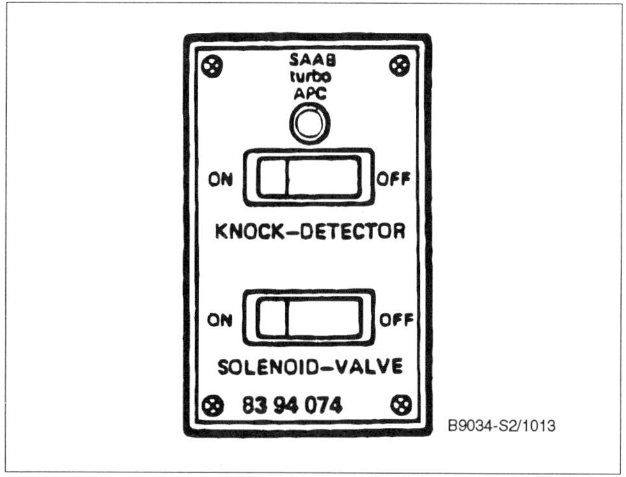

Fig. 6. Optional Saab APC test box (Saab tool no. 83 94 074). Switches should be set to off position.

3. Using a pressure/vacuum gauge with a long hose, connect the gauge hose between the fitting on the intake manifold and the hose leading to the pressure sensor. See Fig. 7. Place the gauge in the passenger compartment, preferably hanging vertically from the rear view mirror.

4. While driving the car on a long open stretch of road, place the transmission in 3rd gear with the engine speed at or below 1,500 rpm.

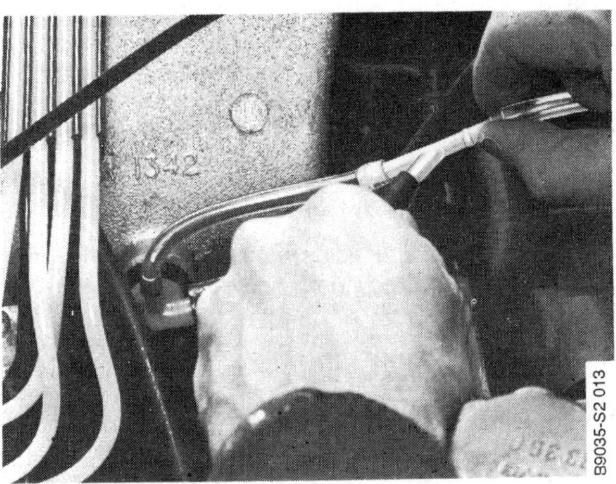

Fig. 7. Pressure/vacuum gauge hose being connected to fitting on intake manifold. Use a long hose so gauge can reach into passenger compartment.

NOTE

On cars with automatic transmission, place the transmission in the "1" drive position.

---

5. Depress the accelerator pedal to the floor until the engine speed approaches 3,000 rpm. Apply the brakes hard as necessary to keep rpm at 3,000 while continuing to hold the accelerator pedal to the floor. Within a short time, the gauge reading will stabilize. Have the helper record the gauge reading at this point.

CAUTION

Make the test as quickly as possible (within three to five seconds) to avoid overheating the brakes. If the test is to be made a second time, drive the car about one mile before repeating the test to allow the brakes to cool.

Turbocharger Basic Boost Pressure

- All ex. 1987 and later SPG models .... 0.35±0.03 bar (5.0±0.4 psi)
- 1987 and later SPG models .... 0.40±0.03 bar (5.8±0.4 psi)

---

6. If the basic boost setting is incorrect, allow the turbocharger to cool. Then remove the anti-tamper seal (if installed) and the circlip from the end of the wastegate actuator rod. Remove the rod from the wastegate lever. See Fig. 8.

CAUTION

Use extreme care when working near a hot turbocharger.

NOTE

Some late models may not have the wastegate seal installed, as the seal has been discontinued in production and does not need to be reinstalled.

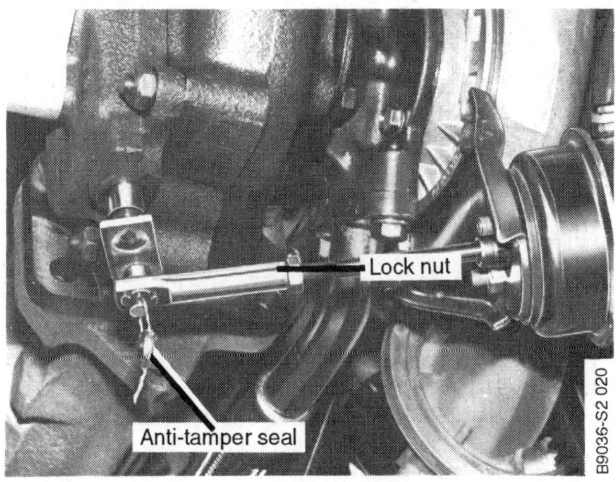

Fig. 8. Wastegate actuator (diaphragm) rod.

7. While holding the rod stationary, loosen the locknut and thread the end piece in or out to readjust the length of the rod. See Fig. 9. Then tighten the locknut. Reinstall the rod to the lever. Recheck the basic boost pressure as described above. If necessary, readjust the length of the rod.

CAUTION

Do not allow the wastegate actuator rod to turn the diaphragm or the diaphragm may be damaged.

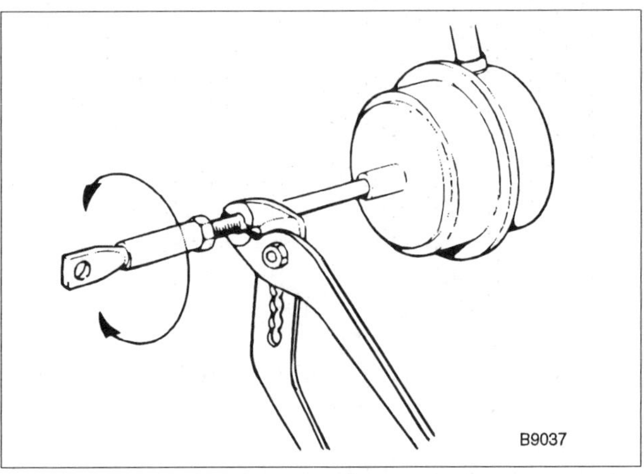

Fig. 9. Hold wastegate actuator rod stationary with pliers when adjusting the end piece or tightening the locknut.

NOTE

If the charging pressure is too low, turn the end piece clockwise to shorten the rod. If the pressure is too high, turn the end piece counter clockwise to lengthen the rod. Adjust the rod in small increments. One complete turn of the end piece roughly equates to a 0.04 bar (0.6 psi) pressure change.

---

8. When the basic boost pressure setting is correct, reconnect the wiring connectors to the solenoid valve. Keep the vacuum/ pressure gauge connected.

9. On 1986 and later cars, disconnect the white wire from the brake light switch above the brake pedal.

NOTE

On 1986 and later cars, a voltage signal via the brake light switch (white wire) is applied to the APC control unit when the brakes are applied. This reduces the maximum boost pressure to the basic boost setting of the wastegate.

---

10. Again, drive the car on a long open stretch of road and repeat the above test. In a short time, the gauge reading should stabilize. Have the helper record the reading at this point.

CAUTION

Make the test as quickly as possible. (in three to five seconds) to avoid overheating the brakes. If the test needs to be made a second time, drive the car about one mile before repeating the test to allow the brakes to cool.

NOTE

The specifications listed below should be used only as a guide. Do not expect the gauge reading to reach this level, as this maximum pressure is controlled by the signal from the knock sensor. When engine knocks, the wastegate will open, resulting in gauge reading considerably lower than that specified.

Turbocharger Maximum Boost Pressure

- All ex. 1987 and later
  SPG models . . . . 0.75±0.05 bar (10.9±0.7 psi)
- 1987 and later
  SPG models . . . . 0.85±0.05 bar (12.3±0.7 psi)

---

11. If the pressure stabilizes at the basic setting or goes above the maximum setting, test the turbocharger APC components as described below. If the pressure reading is only slightly above the basic setting even though the gas is of high-quality, the turbocharger may be faulty. See the troubleshooting table given earlier.

CAUTION

Do not attempt to adjust the maximum boost pressure through the wastegate actuator rod. This will not increase the boost pressure or engine performance, as maximum boost pressure is controlled by the APC system.

---

12. When the pressure test is complete, remove the pressure gauge and reconnect the wiring at the brake light switch, if applicable.

APC COMPONENT TESTING

To test APC solenoid valve

The APC solenoid valve is mounted in the engine compartment, at the radiator crossmember. Based on the signal from the APC control unit, the valve regulates the control pressure to the wastegate. See Fig. 10. When the solenoid is closed (connection between port C and W only), the wastegate will open at a low (basic) boost pressure. When the solenoid is open (all three ports open), there is not enough pressure to open the wastegate and the boost pressure is allowed to increase until engine knock is detected.

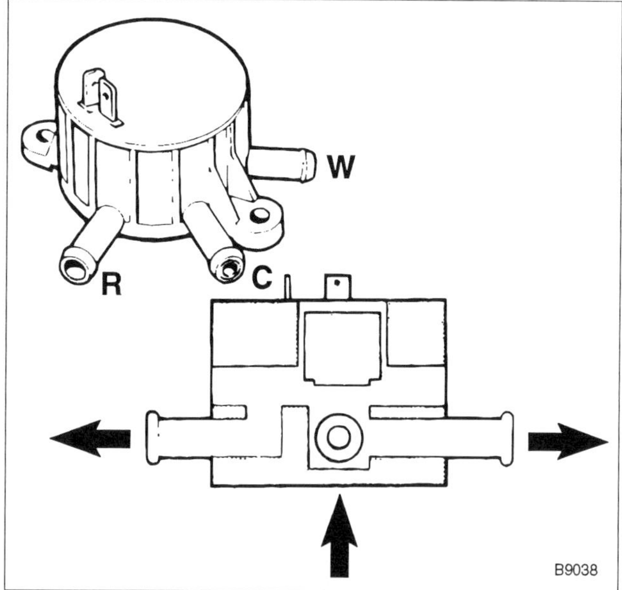

Fig. 10. APC solenoid valve. Port **C** is the pressure line from the turbo compressor (true manifold pressure), **W** is the pressure line to the wastegate, and **R** is a bleed or return line back to the turbo compressor.

1. Disconnect the electrical connectors from the APC solenoid valve. See Fig. 5 given above.

2. Disconnect the hose between the turbo compressor inlet and the connection marked “R” on the solenoid.

3. Using jumper wires, connect battery voltage to the solenoid terminals. Blow through the disconnected hose (port R) and check that air passes freely through the valve. See Fig. 11.

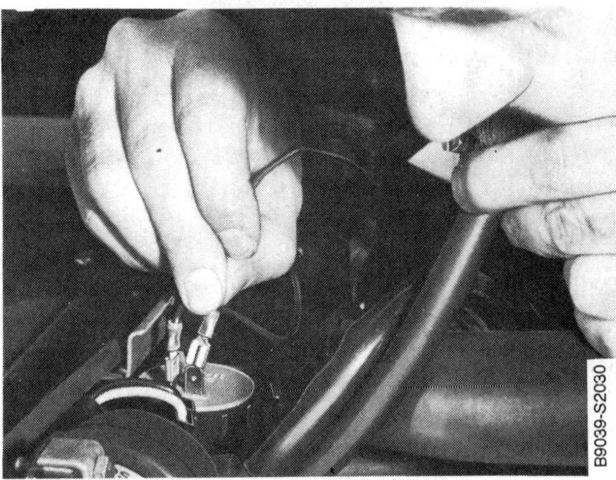

Fig. 11. APC solenoid being tested. When battery voltage is applied to terminals, air should pass through valve.

4. Remove the voltage and check air does not pass through the valve. If any faults are found, the valve is faulty and should be replaced.

To test APC knock sensor

The knock sensor is mounted to the engine block between cylinders no. 2 and 3, below the intake manifold. See Fig. 12. The sensor functions like a microphone and is able to convert mechanical vibration (knock) into a small AC voltage signal. The APC control unit is programmed to react to the signals whose frequencies are characteristic of combustion chamber noise.

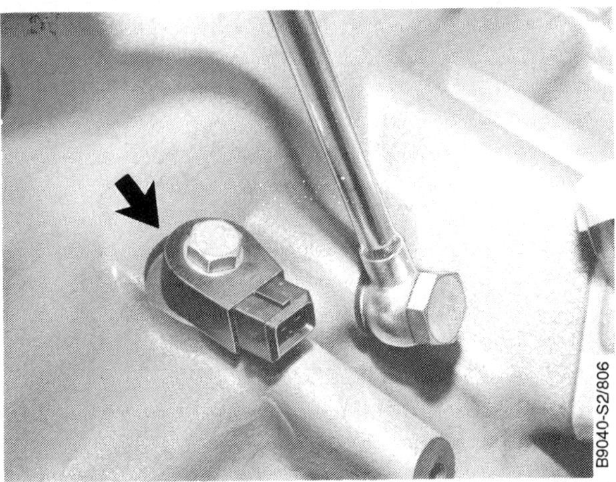

Fig. 12. APC knock sensor (arrow). Sensor is bolted to engine block beneath intake manifold.

1. Disconnect the harness connector from the APC control unit. Using a digital voltmeter (set to VAC scale), connect it to control unit terminals 2 and 3 on 1985 models or 16 and 17 on all 1986 and later models. See Fig. 13.

NOTE

On 1985 models, the APC control unit is under the rear seat. On 1986 and later models, the control is mounted to the left-hand side wheel well in the engine compartment.

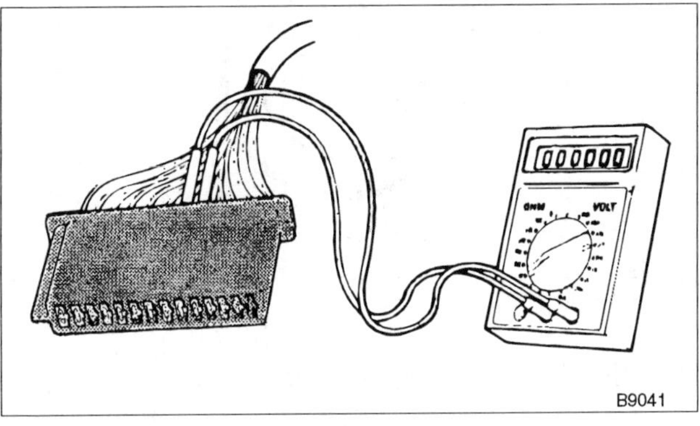

Fig. 13. Voltmeter connected to knock sensor terminals in APC control unit connector. Back-probe connector to prevent damaging connector terminals.

2. Gently tap on the knock sensor mounting bolt. The voltmeter should register a small voltage and the reading should vary depending on the intensity of the tap.

3. If the knock sensor does not respond to the tapping, remove the sensor from the engine. Then connect the voltmeter directly to the sensor terminals and repeat the above tapping test. If the sensor now tests good, check the wiring from the sensor connector to the control unit.

If the sensor does not respond as specified, it is faulty and should be replaced. When replacing the sensor, thoroughly clean the mounting surface on the engine and the threads on the mounting bolt. Install the new sensor with the electrical connector towards the front, offset to the left about 20°. See Fig. 14. Torque the bolt to the specification given below while holding the sensor steady.

Tightening torque

- APC knock sensor
  to engine block . . . . 14 Nm (10 ft-lb)

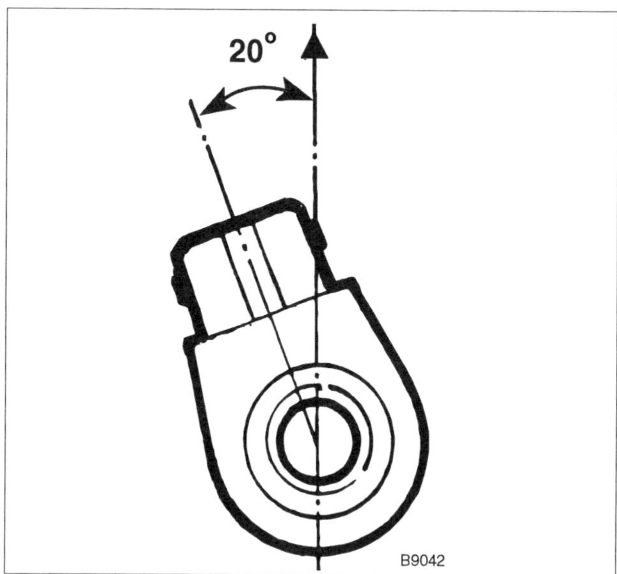

Fig. 14. Knock sensor installation angle. Hold sensor steady when tightening bolt.

To test APC pressure sensor

The sensor monitors the turbo boost pressure in the manifold downstream of the throttle. The pressure is converted into an electrical resistance signal and is monitored by the control unit.

The pressure sensor is mounted beneath the left-hand (driver's) side of the dashboard. A hand-pump and pressure gauge is required to accurately check the sensor.

1. Disconnect the harness connector from the APC control unit. Using a digital voltmeter (set to resistance scale), connect it to control unit terminals 8 and 9 on 1985 models or 10 and 23 on all 1986 and later models. Check the sensor's resistance. If any faults are found, the sensor should be replaced.

Pressure Sensor Test Specifications
- resistance at atmospheric pressure . . . . 5 to 13 ohms

NOTE
On 1985 models, the APC control unit is under the rear seat. On 1986 and later models, the control is mounted to the left-hand side wheel well in the engine compartment.

2. Remove the center storage console and the lower dashboard pad as described in **853 Dashboard and Consoles.**

3. Unscrew the pressure sensor mounting bracket from the relay panel member to access the sensor. See Fig. 15.

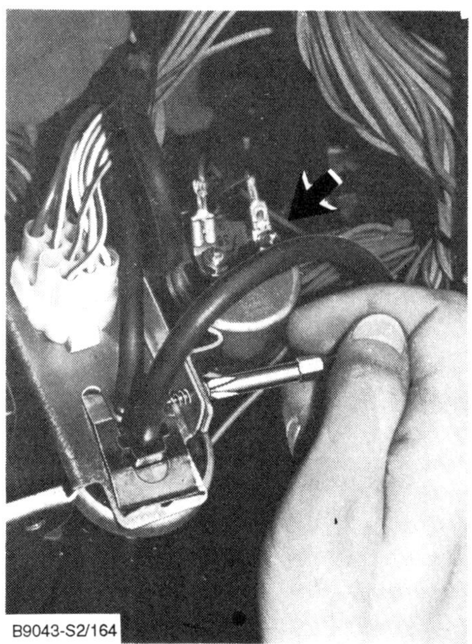

Fig. 15. Pressure sensor mounting bracket beneath left hand side of dashboard. Pressure sensor shown at arrow.

4. Disconnect the hose leading to the sensor and connect a pressure gauge and hand-pump. See Fig. 16. Pump the pressure up to 1 bar (14.5 psi), then reduce the pressure to 0.6 bar (8.7 psi) while tapping lightly on the side of the sensor. Check the sensor's resistance. If any faults are found, the sensor should be replaced.

Pressure Sensor Test Specifications
- resistance at 0.6 bar (8.7 psi) pressure . . . . 83 to 92 ohms

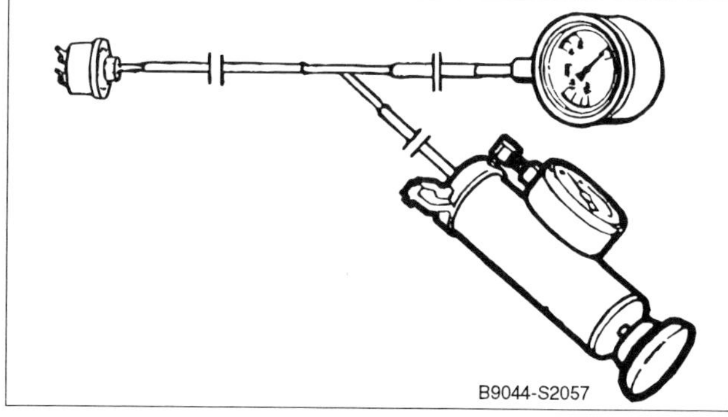

Fig. 16. Pressure gauge and pressure pump connected to pressure sensor (shown schematically).

To test APC bypass valve

The vacuum controlled bypass valve redirects turbocharger output (boost) to the suction side of the compressor when the throttle is snapped shut. This dampens the distribution of intake air flow that results when full boost is suddenly bounced off the closed throttle plate. See Fig. 17.

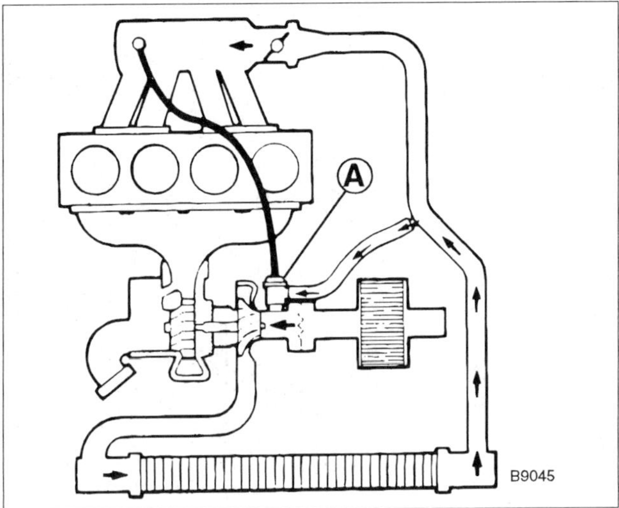

Fig. 17. Schematic of APC system showing the operation of the bypass valve (**A**).

The symptoms of a faulty bypass valve are usually minor driveability problems (slight surging when opening the throttle on cars with manual transmission), and noises (hooting sounds). The bypass valve is mounted below the center of the turbocharger. Use a hand-held vacuum pump to accurately test the valve.

NOTE
Some early 1985 models with automatic transmission may not have a bypass valve.

1. With the engine cold, remove the bypass valve below the turbocharger.

WARNING
Do not remove the bypass valve when the engine is hot. The turbocharger operates at very high temperatures.

2. Using a hand-pump, apply vacuum to the fitting on the valve and check that it lifts off its seat. See Fig. 18. With the vacuum applied, check that the valve stays open. If the valve slowly closes, the diaphragm is leaking and the valve should be replaced.

NOTE
Inspect the hose clamps on the bypass valve. If the old style plastic clamps are installed, they should be replaced with metal screw-type clamps. The plastic clamps are known to break easily, allowing the pressure from the turbocharger to blow the hoses off the valve.

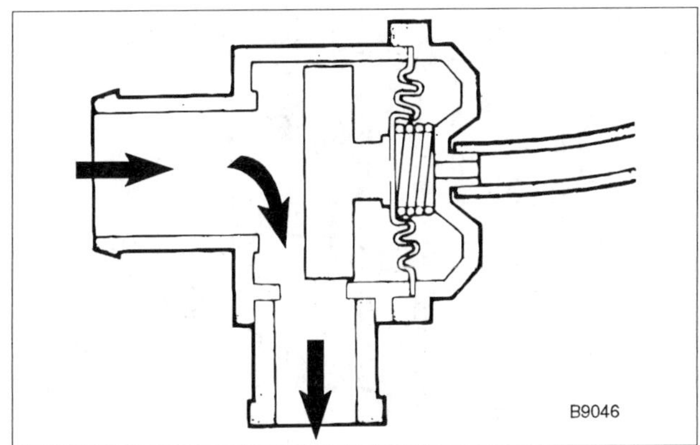

Fig. 18. APC bypass valve shown with vacuum applied to diaphragm. The valve diaphragm should hold valve stay off its seat.

Replacing Turbocharger

Turbocharger removal and installation is done by first removing the exhaust manifold with the turbocharger as a complete unit. with the manifold removed, unbolt the turbocharger from the manifold. See **252 Exhaust System** for removal and installation of the exhaust manifold.

NOTE
The turbocharger-to-exhaust manifold mounting nuts are self-locking and should always be replaced.

When replacing the turbocharger, the oil return and supply pipes should be removed and thoroughly cleaned using a stiff brush and solvent. See Fig. 19. If the pipes cannot be completely cleaned, they should be replaced. The engine oil and oil filter should also be changed.

NOTE
If the turbocharger is being replaced because of excessive exhaust smoke, there will be some oil remaining in the exhaust system that will most likely cause smoking upon start-up. Be sure to test drive the car long enough to clear the leftover oil from the exhaust system before suspecting that the replacement turbocharger is faulty.

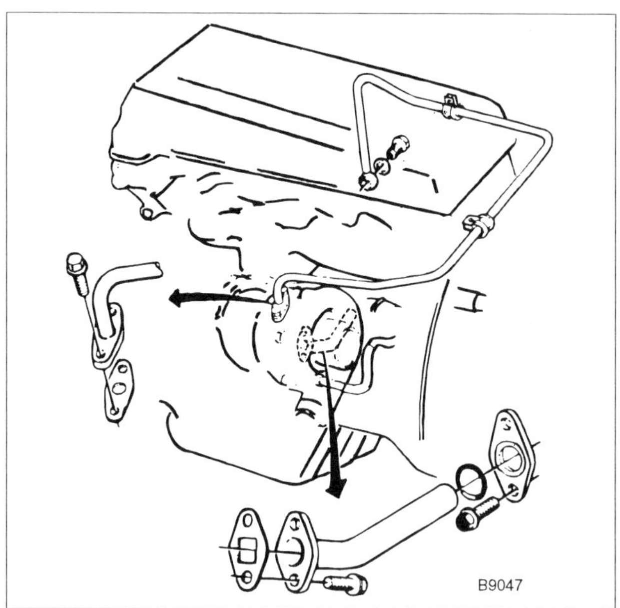

Fig. 19. Turbocharger oil supply and return pipes.

300 Electrical System —General

TABLES

300

GENERAL

A brief description of the principal parts of the electrical system is presented here. Also covered here are general electrical system troubleshooting tips as well as instructions on using the Saab wiring diagrams.

Voltage and Polarity

Saab electrical systems are 12-volt direct current (DC) negative-ground systems. A voltage regulator controls the system voltage at approximately the 12-volt rating of the battery. All circuits are grounded by direct or indirect connection to the negative (–) terminal of the battery. A number of ground connections throughout the car connect the wiring harness to chassis ground. These circuits are completed by the battery cable or ground strap between the body and the battery negative (–) terminal.

Wiring, Fuses, and Relays

Nearly all parts of the wiring harness connect to components of the electrical system with keyed, push-on connectors that lock into place. Notable exceptions are the heavy battery cables and the alternator wiring. The wiring is color-coded for circuit identification.

With the exception of the battery charging system, all electrical power is routed from the ignition switch or the battery through the fuse/relay panel, located in the right side of the engine compartment. Fuses prevent excessive current from damaging components and wiring. Fuses are color coded to indicate their different current capacities.

Fuse rating and color

Red	10 amp
Blue	15 amp
Yellow	20 amp
Green	30 amp

The relays are electromagnetic switches that operate on low current to switch a high-current circuit on and off. Many of the relays are mounted on the fuse/relay panel in the engine compartment, although later models are equipped with additional auxiliary relay panels. For information on relay and fuse locations, see **371 Wiring Diagrams, Fuses and Relays.**

Electrical System Safety Precautions

Please read the following warnings and cautions before doing any work on your electrical system.

WARNING

- Some of the cars covered by this manual are equipped with a Supplemental Restraint System (SRS) that automatically deploys an airbag. The airbag unit uses an explosive device to electrically ignite a powerful gas. On cars so equipped, any work involving the steering wheel and SRS system should only be performed by an authorized Saab dealer. Performing repairs without disarming the SRS may cause serious personal injury.

- On cars equipped with SRS (airbag) the ignition switch must be in the lock position before replacing fuses. If fuse no. 7 is removed with the ignition switch on, an SRS fault will be detected. If the SRS warning light comes on, see an authorized Saab dealer.

WARNING

- The ignition system of the car operates at lethal voltages. People with pacemakers or weak hearts should not expose themselves to the ignition system. Extra caution must be taken when working on the ignition system or when servicing the engine while it is running or the key is on. See **340 Ignition System** for additional ignition system warnings and cautions.
- Before operating the starter without starting the engine (as when making a compression test), disable the ignition system as described in **340 Ignition System.**
- Keep hands, clothing and other objects clear of the radiator cooling fan when working on a warm engine. The fan may start at any time, even when the ignition is switched off.

CAUTION

- Always turn off the engine and remove the negative (–) battery cable before removing any electrical components.
- Connect and disconnect ignition system wires, multiple connectors, and ignition test equipment leads only while the ignition is off.
- Do not disconnect the battery while the engine is running.
- Do not quick-charge the battery (for boost starting) for longer than one minute, and do not exceed 16.5 volts at the battery with the boosting cables attached. Wait at least one minute before boosting the battery a second time.
- Do not use a test lamp that has a normal incandescent bulb to test circuits containing electronic components. The high electrical consumption of these test lamps may damage the components.
- Many of the solid-state modules are static sensitive. Static discharge will permanently damage them. Always handle the modules using proper static prevention equipment and techniques.
- To avoid damaging harness connectors or relay panel sockets, use jumper wires with flat-blade connectors that are the same size as the connector or relay terminals.
- Always switch a test meter to the appropriate function and range before making test connections.
- Do not try to start the engine of a car which has been heated above 176°F (80°C), (for example, in a paint drying booth) until allowing it to cool to normal temperature.
- Disconnect the battery before doing any electric welding on the car.
- Do not tow a car suspected of having a defective ignition system without first disconnecting the ignition control unit.
- Do not wash the engine while it is running, or anytime the ignition is switched on.

Electrical Test Equipment

Many of the electrical tests described in this manual call for measuring voltage, current or resistance using a digital multimeter (DMM). Digital meters are preferred for precise measurements and for electronics work because they are generally more accurate than analog meters. The numerical display is also less likely to be misread, since there is no needle position to be misinterpreted by reading at an angle.

An LED test light is a safe, inexpensive tool that can be used to perform many simple electrical tests that would otherwise require a multimeter. The LED indicates when voltage is present between any two test-points in a circuit.

CAUTION

- Choose test equipment carefully. Use a meter with at least 10 megohm input impedance, or an LED test light. An analog meter (swing-needle) or a test light with a normal incandescent bulb may draw enough current to damage sensitive electronic components.
- An ohmmeter must not be used to measure resistance on solid state components such as control units or time delay relays.
- Always disconnect the battery before making resistance (ohm) measurements on the circuit.

WIRING DIAGRAMS

The wiring diagrams shown in **371 Wiring Diagrams, Fuses and Relays** have been specially designed to enable quick and efficient diagnosis and troubleshooting of electrical malfunctions.

Each electrical sub-system, such as the ignition system, the hazard warning lights, etc., is described individually and a separate wiring diagram is shown for each sub-system on the car. Each wiring sub-system consists of a spread that includes a brief description of the circuit operation, fault tracing, a list of all the components used in the circuit along with their location in the car, and the wiring diagram(s) applicable to that circuit.

Wiring Codes and Abbreviations

A tremendous amount of information is included in each wiring diagram if you know how to read them. For example, you will notice that all electrical components, connectors, fuses, and ground locations are identified using a unique number. Each of these numbers corresponds to a particular part in the circuit. A complete listing of these component numbers, their identifications and locations is given in **371 Wiring Diagrams, Fuses and Relays.**

All wire colors in the diagrams are abbreviated. Combined color codes indicate a multi-colored wire. For example the code BL/RD indicates a Blue wire with a Red stripe. Wire color abbreviation are listed below. Immediately following the wire color is the nominal cross-sectional area of the wire given in mm^2.

NOTE

Sometimes the color of an installed wire may be different than the one on the wiring diagram. Don't be concerned, just be sure to confirm that the wire connects to the proper terminals.

Wire color codes

BL or BU . . . . Blue
BR or BN. . . . . Brown
GL or YE. . . . . Yellow
GN . . . . Green
GR or GY . . . . Gray
OG . . . . Orange
RA or PK. . . . . Pink
RD. . . . . Red
SV or BK. . . . . Black
VL . . . . Violet
VT or WH . . . . White

Most terminals are identified by numbers on the components and harness connectors. The terminal numbers for major electrical connections are shown in the diagrams. Though many terminal numbers appear only once, several other numbers appear in numerous places throughout the electrical system and identify certain types of circuits. Several of the most common circuit numbers are listed below in **Table a.**

Table a. Terminal and Circuit Numbers

Number	Circuit description
1	Low voltage switched (1) terminal of coil
4	High voltage center terminal of coil
+X	Originates at ignition switch. Supplies power when the ignition switch is in the PARK, RUN, or START position
S	Originates at ignition switch. Supplies power whenever the key is in the ignition switch. (power in LOCK, PARK, RUN, or START position)
15 or +15	Originates at ignition switch. Supplies power when ignition switch is in RUN or START position
30 or +30	Battery positive (+) voltage. Supplies power whenever battery is connected. (Not dependent on ignition switch position, unfused)
31	Ground, battery negative (–) terminal

continued

Table a. Terminal and Circuit Numbers (continued)

Number	Circuit description
50 or +50	Supplies power from battery to starter solenoid when ignition switch is in START position only
+54	Originates at ignition switch. Supplies power when ignition switch is in the RUN position only
85	Ground side (–) of relay coil
86	Power-in side (+) of relay coil
87	Relay change-over contact
D	Alternator warning light and field energizing circuit

Additional abbreviations shown in the wiring diagrams are given below.

Abbreviations

ABS. . . . . antilock brakes
AC . . . . air conditioning
AIC . . . . automatic idle control
APC. . . . . automatic performance control (turbo models)
AUT . . . . automatic transmission
CAB. . . . . cabriolet (convertible)
CC . . . . cruise control
CONV . . . . convertible
ECU . . . . electronic control unit
EZK . . . . electronic ignition with knock control
I. . . . . fuel injection engine
LH . . . . fuel injection system
LHD. . . . . left hand drive
LHF. . . . . left hand, front
LHR. . . . . left hand, rear
LHS. . . . . left hand, side
M__ . . . . designation for model year, i.e. M89 for 1989 model
MAN . . . . manual transmission
P . . . . passenger
RHD. . . . . right hand drive
RHF. . . . . right hand, front
RHR. . . . . right hand, rear
RHS. . . . . right hand, side
SRS . . . . supplemental restraint system Airbag (see warnings in text)
T . . . . turbo
TSI . . . . timing service instrument (test socket)
2-D . . . . 2-door sedan
3-D . . . . 3-door hatchback
4-D . . . . 4-door sedan
US . . . . Cars for sale in the United States
CA. . . . . Cars for sale in Canada
UC . . . . Cars for sale in California

CAUTION
Many of the wiring diagrams are applicable to cars delivered to other world markets served by Saab. At times, there may be certain parts of the diagram that are applicable only to these markets. This manual covers only Saab cars delivered to the United States (US), California (UC), and Canada (CA). Abbreviations other than US, UC, and CA found on a particular diagram should be ignored. For example the abbreviation "ME" is for cars sold in the Middle East. **Table b** is a complete list of the market codes.

Table b. Market Codes

Market codes	Market	Market codes	Market
AT	Austria	FR	France
AU	Australia	GB	Great Britain
BE	Belgium	GR	Greece
CA	Canada	IS	Iceland
CH	Switzerland	IT	Italy
DE	Germany	JP	Japan
DK	Denmark	ME	Middle East
ES	Spain	NL	Netherlands
EU	Europe	NO	Norway
FE	Far East	SE	Sweden
FI	Finland	US	USA

Using the Wiring Diagrams

An example of a wiring diagram is shown below together with an explanation of the symbols used in the diagram. See Fig. 1.

NOTE
- Unless specified otherwise, switches and relays are shown in the rest or de-energized position.

- Throughout the wiring diagrams, a fuse is shown together with the designation **22A.** This 22A code is the component number for the fuse holder in the fuse/relay panel and should not be confused with the fuse rating or the fuse position.

- Designations such as **+30**, **+15**, **+54** are positive voltage supplies, usually found at the top of each circuit. Each number represents when voltage is present in the circuit. For example, +30 is live at all times (unfused) and +15 is live when the key is in the run or start position. See above for a listing of the common terminal and circuit numbers.

ELECTRICAL TROUBLESHOOTING

Four things are required for current to flow in any electrical circuit: a voltage source, wires or connections to transport the voltage, a consumer or device that uses the electricity, and a connection to ground. Most problems can be found using only a digital multimeter (volt/ohm/amp meter) to check for voltage supply, for breaks in the wiring (infinite resistance/no continuity), or for a path to ground that completes the circuit.

Electric current is logical in its flow, always moving from the voltage source toward ground. Keeping this in mind, electrical faults can be located through a process of elimination. When troubleshooting a complex circuit, separate the circuit into smaller parts. The general tests outlined below may be helpful in finding electrical problems. The information is most helpful when used with the wiring diagrams.

Be sure to analyze the problem. Use the wiring diagrams to determine the most likely cause of the problem. Get an understanding of how the circuit works by following the circuit from ground back to the power source.

You will find the problem if you follow a simple and logical step-by-step procedure. Test portions of the circuit at one time, starting with the area or component most likely to be at fault. Test first at points that you can reach most easily. When you find the cause of the problem, make the repair. Use appropriate tools and procedures. As a final check, test the functions of the circuit that you worked on.

When making test connections at connectors and components, use care to avoid spreading or damaging the connectors or terminals. Some electrical tests may require jumper wires to temporarily bypass components or connections in the wiring harness. When connecting jumper wires, use blade connectors at the wire ends that match the size of the terminal being tested. The delicate internal contacts are easily spread apart, and this can cause intermittent or faulty connections that can lead to more problems.

Checking for Voltage and Ground

Checking for the presence of voltage or ground is usually the first step in troubleshooting a problem circuit. When checking for voltage, a digital voltmeter or LED test light should be used. for example, if a parking light does not work, check for voltage at the bulb socket will quickly determine if the circuit is functioning properly or if the bulb itself is faulty. If voltage and ground are found at the socket, then the bulb is most likely faulty.

Another valuable troubleshooting technique is a voltage drop test. This is a good test to make if current is flowing through the circuit, but the circuit is not operating correctly. Sluggish wipers or dim headlights are examples of this. A voltage drop test will help to pinpoint a corroded ground strap or a faulty switch. Normally, there should be less than 1 volt drop across most wires or closed switches. A voltage drop across a connector or short cable should not exceed 0.5 volts.

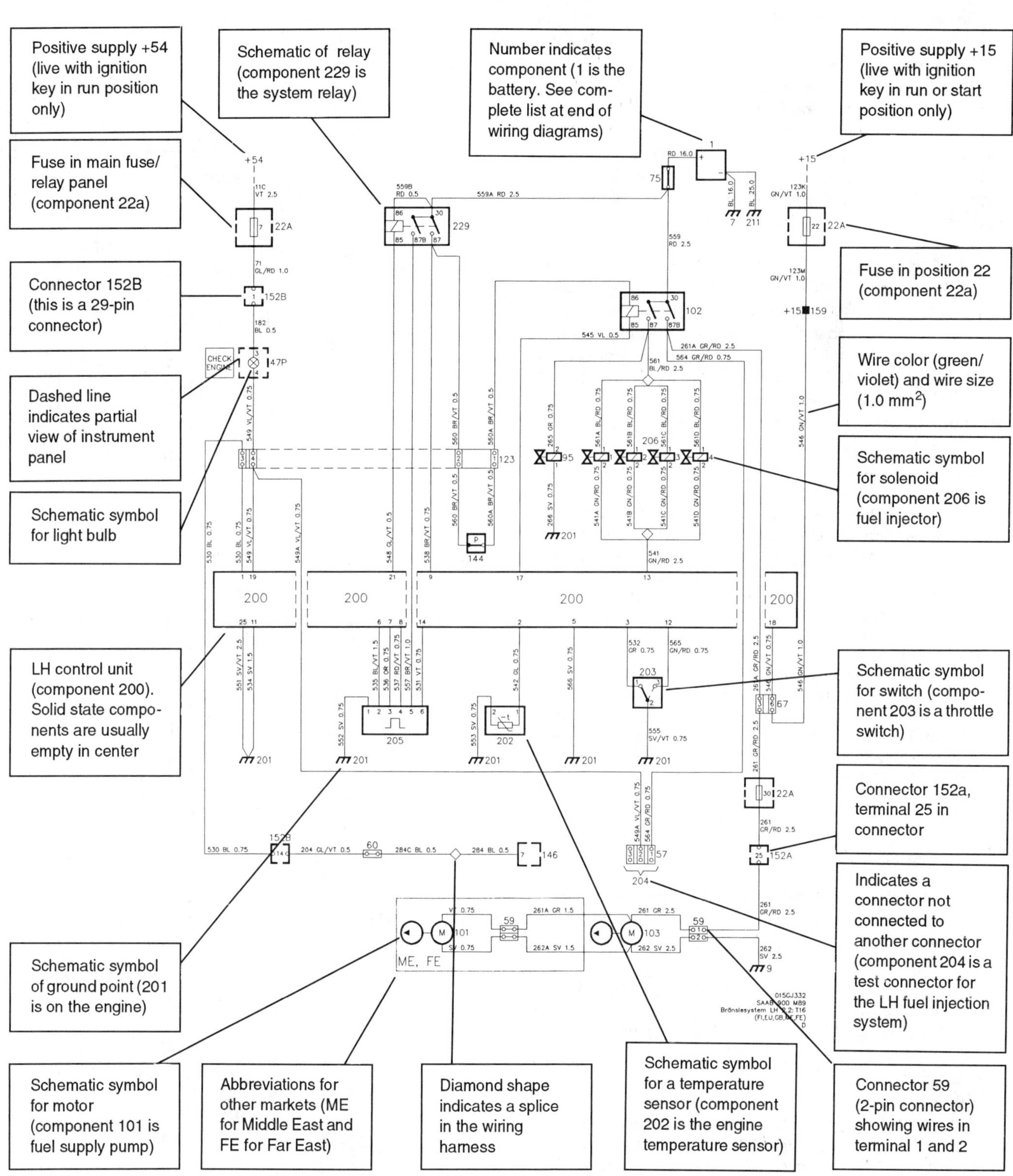

Fig. 1. Example of how to read Saab wiring diagrams.

The wires, connectors, and switches that carry current are designed with very low resistance so that current flows with a minimum loss of voltage. A voltage drop is caused by higher than normal resistance in a circuit. This additional resistance actually decreases or stops the flow of current. A voltage drop can be noticed by problems ranging from dim headlights to sluggish wipers. Some common sources of voltage drops are faulty wires or switches, dirty or corroded connections or contacts, and loose or corroded ground wires and ground connections.

Voltage drop can only be checked when current is running through the circuit, such as by operating the starter motor or turning on the headlights. Making a voltage drop test requires measuring the voltage in the circuit and comparing it to what the voltage should be. Since these measurements are usually small, a digital voltmeter should be used to ensure accurate readings. If a voltage drop is suspected, turn the circuit on and measure the voltage at the circuit's load.

NOTE

- A voltage drop test is generally more accurate than a simple resistance check because the resistances involved are often too small to measure with most ohmmeters. For example, a resistance as small as 0.02 ohms would results in a 3 Volt drop in a typical 150 amp starter circuit. (150 amps x 0.02 ohms =3 volts).
- Keep in mind that voltage with the key on and voltage with the engine running are not the same. With the ignition on and the engine off (battery voltage), voltage should be approximately 12.6 volts. With the engine running (charging voltage), voltage should be approximately 14.0 volts. Measure voltage at the battery with the ignition on and then with the engine running to get exact measurements.

To measure voltage

1. Connect the voltmeter negative lead to a reliable ground point on the car. The negative (–) battery terminal is always a good a ground point.
2. Connect the voltmeter positive lead to the point in the circuit you wish to measure. See Fig. 2. If a reading is obtained, current is flowing through the circuit.

NOTE

The voltage reading should not deviate more than 1 volt less than the voltage at the battery. If the voltage is less than this, there is probably a fault in the circuit, such as a corroded connector or a loose ground wire.

To check for a voltage drop

1. Connect the voltmeter positive lead to the positive (+) battery terminal or a positive power supply close to the battery source.

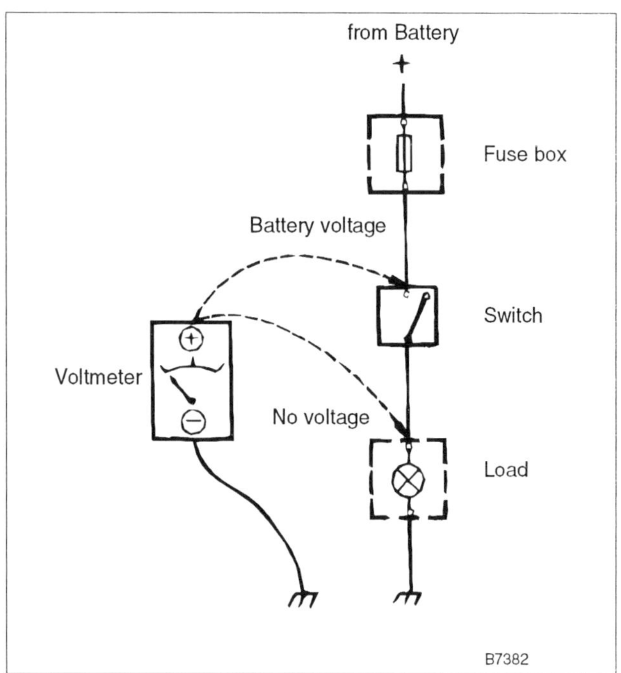

Fig. 2. Voltmeter being used to check for voltage.

2. Connect the voltmeter negative lead to the other end of the cable or switch being tested. See Fig. 3.

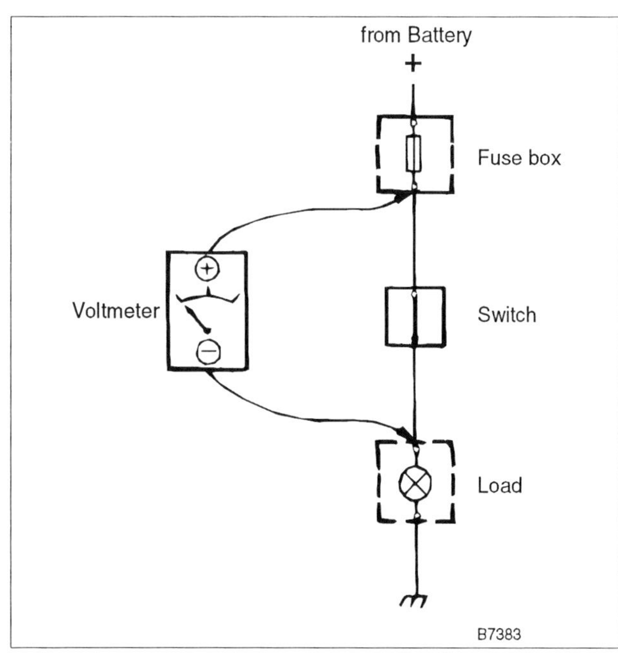

Fig. 3. Voltmeter being used to check for voltage drop.

3. With the power on and the circuit working, the meter shows the voltage drop (the difference between the two points). This value should not exceed 1 volt.

NOTE

The maximum voltage drop in an automotive circuit, as recommended by the Society of Automotive Engineers (SAE), is as follows: 0 Volts for small wire connections; 0.1 Volts for high current connections; 0.2 Volts for high current cables; and 0.3 Volts for switch or solenoid contacts. On longer wires or cables, the drop may be slightly higher. In any case, a voltage drop of more than 1.0 Volt usually indicates a problem.

Checking for Continuity

The continuity test can be used to check a circuit or switch. Because most automotive circuits are designed to have little or no resistance, a circuit or part of a circuit can be easily checked for faults using an ohmmeter. An open circuit or a circuit with high resistance will not allow current to flow. A circuit with little or no resistance allows current to flow easily.

CAUTION

Do not use an analog (swing-needle) ohmmeter to check circuit resistance or continuity on any electronic (solid-state) components. The internal power source used in most analog meters can damage solid state components. Use only a high quality digital ohmmeter having high input impedance when checking electronic components.

When checking continuity, the ignition should be off. On circuits that are powered at all times, the battery should be disconnected. Using the appropriate wiring diagram, a circuit can be easily tested for faulty connections, wires, switches, relays, and engine sensors by checking for continuity. Fig. 4 shows continuity test being made on a brake light switch.

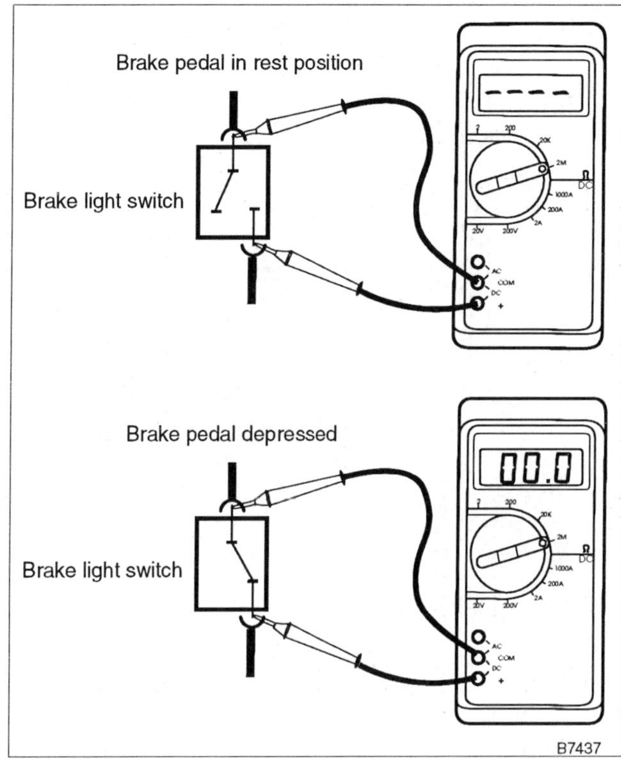

Fig. 4. Brake light switch being tested for continuity. With brake pedal in rest position (switch open) there is no continuity (infinite ohms). With the pedal depressed (switch closed) there is continuity (zero ohms).

Checking for Short Circuits

A short circuit is exactly what the name implies. The circuit takes a shorter path than it was designed to take. The most common short that causes problems is a short to ground where the insulation on a positive (+) wire wears away and the metal wire is exposed. When the wire rubs against a metal part of the car or other ground source, the circuit is shorted to ground. If the exposed wire is live (positive battery voltage), a fuse will blow and the circuit may possibly be damaged.

Shorts to ground can be located with an ohmmeter or a voltmeter. Short circuits are often difficult to locate and may vary in nature. Short circuits can be found using a logical approach based on the current path.

CAUTION

- On circuits protected with large fuses (25 amp and greater), the wires or circuit components may be damaged before the fuse blows. Always check for damage before replacing fuses of this rating.

- When replacing blown fuses, use only fuses having the correct rating. Always confirm the correct fuse rating printed on the fuse/relay panel cover.

To check for a short circuit using an ohmmeter

1. Remove the blown fuse from the circuit and disconnect the cables from the battery.

2. Disconnect the harness connector from the circuit's load or consumer.

3. Using an ohmmeter, connect one test lead to the load side of the fuse terminal (terminal leading to the circuit) and the other test lead to ground. See Fig. 5.

4. If there is continuity to ground, there is a short to ground.

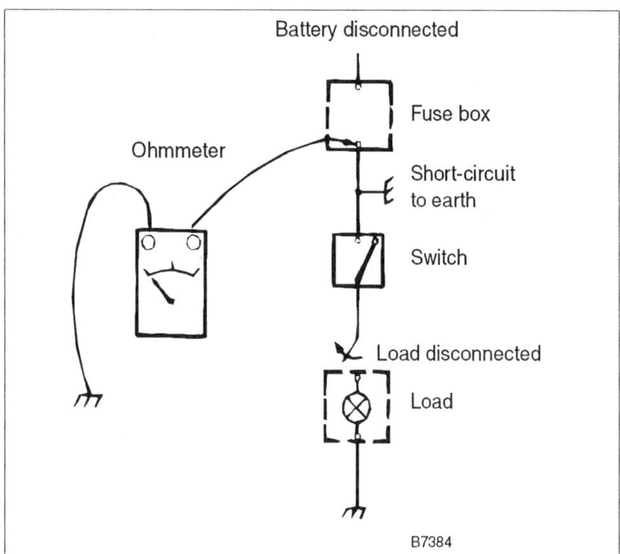

Fig. 5. Ohmmeter being used to find short circuit.

5. If there is no continuity, work from the wire harness nearest to the fuse/relay panel and move or wiggle the wires while observing the meter. Continue to move down the harness until the meter displays a reading. This is the location of the short to ground.

Visually inspect the wire harness at this point for any faults. If no faults are visible, carefully slice open the harness cover or the wire insulation for further inspection. Repair any faults found.

To check for a short circuit using a voltmeter

1. Remove the blown fuse from the circuit.
2. Disconnect the harness connector from the circuit's load or consumer.
3. Using a voltmeter, connect the test leads across the fuse terminals. See Fig. 6. Make sure power is present in the circuit, if necessary turn the key on.

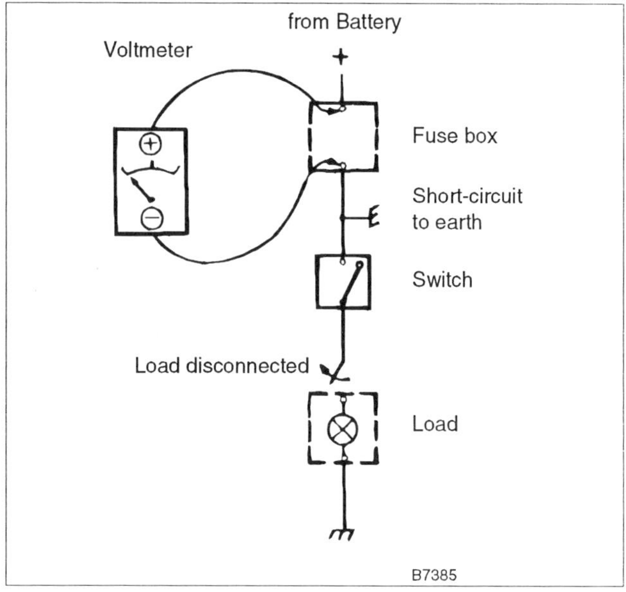

Fig. 6. Voltmeter being used to find short circuit.

4. If voltage is present at the voltmeter, there is a short to ground.
5. If voltage is not present, work from the wire harness nearest to the fuse/relay panel and move or wiggle the wires while observing the meter. Continue to move down the harness until the meter displays a reading. This is the location of the short to ground.

Visually inspect the wire harness at this point for any faults. If no faults are visible, carefully slice open the harness cover or the wire insulation for further inspection. Repair any faults found.

311 Battery

TABLES

GENERAL

The six-cell, 12-volt lead-acid battery capacity is rated by ampere/hours (Ah) and cold cranking amps (CCA). The Ah rating is determined by the average amount of current the battery can deliver over time without dropping below a specified voltage. The CCA rating is determined by the battery's ability to deliver starting current at 0° (–18°C). The original battery installed is rated at 62 Ah and is located in the engine compartment, behind the right headlight assembly.

Maintenance consists of keeping the battery and terminals clean and keeping the connections tight. After cleaning, a light coating of petroleum jelly should be spread on the terminals. Inspect the battery cables for chafing and deterioration of the insulation due to high heat.

For general information on troubleshooting electrical systems see **300 Electrical System—General**. For information on battery wiring see **371 Wiring Diagrams, Fuses and Relays**.

WARNING

- Wear goggles, rubber gloves, and a rubber apron when working with battery electrolyte. Electrolyte contains sulfuric acid and can cause skin irritation and burning. If electrolyte is spilled on your skin or clothing, flush the area at once with large quantities of water. If electrolyte gets into your eyes, bathe them with large quantities of clean water for several minutes and call a physician.

- Batteries that are being charged or are fully charged give off explosive hydrogen gas. Keep sparks and open flames away. Do not smoke.

CAUTION

- Do not disconnect the battery when the engine is running. The alternator will be damaged.

- Replace batteries if the case is cracked or leaking. Electrolyte can damage the car. If electrolyte is spilled, clean the area with a solution of baking soda and water.

- Always allow a frozen battery to thaw before attempting to recharge it.

- Always disconnect the battery terminals during battery recharging. This will prevent damage to solid-state components.

CAUTION

- Do not quick-charge the battery (for boost starting) for longer than one minute, and do not exceed 16.5 volts at the battery with the boosting cables attached. Wait at least one minute before boosting the battery a second time.

- Always disconnect the negative (–) battery cable first and reconnect it last. Cover the battery post with an insulating material whenever the terminal is removed.

- When boost starting the car using jumper cables, be careful not to reverse the battery connections. Even a momentary connection will damage the alternator.

BATTERY TESTING

Battery testing determines the state of battery charge. The most common methods are open-circuit and load voltage testing. Batteries that have filler caps can also be tested by checking the specific gravity of the electrolyte. The specific gravity test checks the amount of acid in the electrolyte as an indication of battery charge. Inexpensive specific gravity testers are available at most auto supply stores.

Open-Circuit Voltage Test

An open-circuit voltage test checks battery voltage by connecting an accurate digital voltmeter to the battery posts after disconnecting the battery ground cable. Before making an open-circuit voltage test on a battery, first load the battery with 15 amps for one minute, for example by turning on the headlights without the engine running. Open-circuit voltage levels and their corresponding percentages of charge are in **Table a.**

Table a. Open-Circuit Voltage and Battery Charge

Open-circuit voltage	State of charge
12.6 V or more	Fully charged
12.4 V	75% charged
12.2 V	50% charged
12.0 V	25% charged
11.7 V or less	Fully discharged

The battery is in satisfactory condition if the open-circuit voltage is at least 12.4 volts. If the open-circuit voltage is at this level or above, but the battery still lacks power for starting, make a load voltage test to determine the battery's service condition. If the open-circuit voltage is below 12.4 volts, recharge the battery. If the battery cannot be recharged to at least 75%, it should be replaced.

Load Voltage Testing

A load voltage battery test is made by connecting a specific resistive load to the battery terminals and then measuring voltage. The test requires a special tester and can generally be performed quickly and inexpensively by an authorized Saab dealer or qualified repair facility. The battery should be fully charged for the most accurate results. If the equipment is available, disconnect the negative (-) battery cable. Then apply a 200 Amp load for 15 seconds and measure the battery's voltage. If the voltage is below that listed, the battery should be replaced.

WARNING

Always wear protective goggles and clothing when performing a load test.

Battery load test minimum voltage

- (200 amp load for 15 seconds)
  - 9.6 V at 80°F (27°C)
  - 9.5 V at 60°F (16°C)
  - 9.3 V at 40°F (4°C)
  - 8.9 V at 20°F (-7°C)
  - 8.5 V at 0°F (-18°C)

If the battery quickly becomes discharged, there may be a fault in the charging system or in the electrical system. See **321 Alternator and Charging System** for charging system tests. On all models, be certain that the appropriate heat shields are securely attached to the battery.

NOTE

If the key is left in the ignition switch, a battery draw of about 40 milliamps will discharge the battery over a period of time.

BATTERY CHARGING

Discharged batteries can be recharged using a battery charger, but a battery can never be charged to a voltage in excess of that which it is capable of producing electro-chemically. Prolonged charging causes gassing that will evaporate the electrolyte to a level that can damage the battery.

Always read and follow the instructions provided by the battery charger's manufacturer. Do not use a charger if the instructions are not available. **Table b** lists charging rates and times that should be followed when charging batteries.

WARNING

The gasses given off by the battery during charging are explosive. Do not smoke. Keep open flames away from the top of the battery, and prevent electrical sparks by turning off the battery charger before connecting or disconnecting it.

CAUTION

Always disconnect a battery cable when using a battery charger. This will prevent damage to solid-state components.

Table b. Battery Charging Specifications

Charging rate (low-maintenance batteries)	Specific gravity	Approximate charging time
Fast charge (at 80% to 90% of battery's capacity, example: 44 to 50 amperes for a 55-ampere hour battery)	1.150 or less	1 hour
	1.150 to 1.175	3/4 hour
	1.175 to 1.200	1/2 hour
	1.200 to 1.225	1/4 hour
Slow charge (at 10% of battery's capacity, example: 5.5 amperes for a 55-ampere hour battery)	Above 1.225	Slow charge only, to a specific gravity of 1.250 to 1.265

321 Alternator and Charging System

GENERAL

The charging system consists of a belt-driven 14-volt alternator and a voltage regulator. The voltage regulator, which is mounted on the alternator, also serves as the alternator brush holder. The charging system provides the current necessary to keep the battery charged and to operate the car electrical accessories.

To prevent damage to the alternator or regulator when making tests or repairs, make all connections with negative (–) to negative, and positive (+) to positive. Even momentary contact with a conductor of the wrong polarity can damage the alternator's diodes.

Please read the following cautions before doing any work on the charging system or alternator.

CAUTION

- Never operate the engine with the battery disconnected. Never operate the alternator with its output terminal (B+ or 30) disconnected and the other terminals connected. Never short, bridge, or ground any terminals of the charging system.
- Always disconnect the negative (–) battery cable before removing the alternator. This will prevent an accidental short from one of the alternator terminals.
- Do not reverse the polarity of the battery. Damage to the alternator will result.
- Always disconnect both battery cables before doing any electric (arc) welding to the car.

CHARGING SYSTEM TROUBLESHOOTING

Charging system trouble is indicated by an illuminated alternator warning light on the instrument panel, or by an under- or overcharged battery.

The alternator generates electrical current by electrical induction. When the engine is running, part of the current it produces energizes its electromagnetic field. When starting, some other current must be provided to initially energize the field and begin the current generating process. This current is provided by the battery through the alternator warning light in the instrument cluster. If the lamp burns out, the alternator will not charge the battery properly.

Charging System Quick-check

As a quick-check, measure the voltage across the battery terminal with the key off and then again with the engine running. The battery voltage should be approximately 12.6 with key off and 14.0 with the engine running. If the voltage does not increase when the engine is running, there is fault in the charging system.

To test charging system

1. Inspect the V-belts and make sure they are tight. Make sure the battery is fully charged, as described in **311 Battery.**

2. Check the charge warning lamp. On 1987 and later cars, check that the ignition switch relay closes when the key is turned on. See **371 Wiring Diagrams, Fuses and Relays** for a complete listing of fuse and relay locations.

NOTE

- The charging system warning light should come on when the key is on and go out when the car is started. Turning the key on is a test that checks the warning light circuit to the alternator. If the light does not come on when the key is turned on, check the light bulb and the wiring to the bulb using the appropriate wiring diagram before making any more tests. Wiring diagrams can be found in **371 Wiring Diagrams, Fuses and Relays.**
- When replacing the charging system warning bulb, be sure to use the correct 2.0 watt replacement bulb. A similar 1.2 watt bulb (with black socket base) will also fit in this location. If the smaller bulb is installed, the battery will not charge correctly at idle. The light will also go out at a higher rpm. See an authorized Saab parts department for additional information.

321

3. Check for battery voltage between ground and terminal **B+** at the back of the alternator. Then check for battery voltage between terminal **D+** and ground with the ignition key on.

NOTE
If the voltage is not present at either terminal, check the alternator wiring and electrical circuit using the appropriate wiring diagram.

---

4. With the engine running, carefully measure the voltage between terminal D+ and ground and then between B+ and ground. The difference should not exceed 0.7 volts.

NOTE
If battery voltage was present at terminal D+ and B+ as described in step 3, but the voltage difference in step 4 is not as specified, the alternator is faulty and should be replaced.

---

5. If no faults are found up to this point, the alternator should be tested using special test equipment, such as the Sun VAT40. Alternator test specifications are shown below.

Alternator output specifications
• Bosch 80 Amp . . . . .54 Amps @ 1900 rpm

NOTE
If a load tester is not available, an output test can be done by running the engine at 1900 rpm and turning on all electrical loads such as fans, lights and heated window. Voltage at the battery should be approximately 12 volts or higher.

To remove and install alternator

1. Disconnect the negative (–) battery cable.
2. Loosen the alternator mounting bolts, pivot the alternator and remove the alternator V-belts.
3. Disconnect the wires from the rear of the alternator.
4. Remove the alternator mounting bolts and the alternator. See Fig. 1

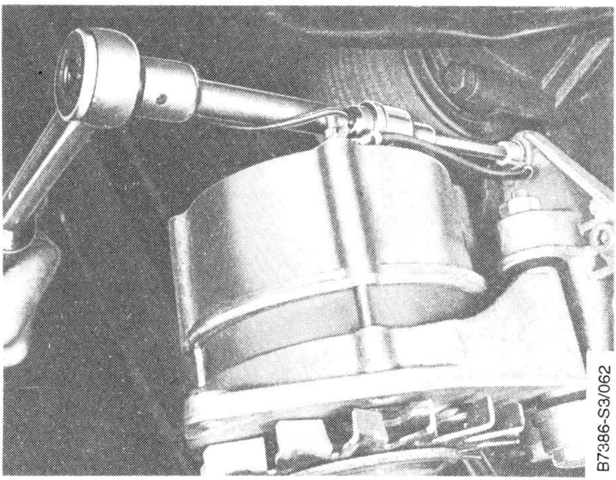

Fig. 1. Alternator mounting bolt being removed.

5. Install the new alternator, leaving the mounting bolts slightly loose. Install the V-belt and tension it as described in **1 LUBRICATION AND MAINTENANCE.**

CAUTION
V-belt tension is critical to the life of alternator and proper alternator operation. A loose belt will cause undercharging (and often a loud screeching sound). A tight belt will quickly destroy the alternator bearings and the bearings of other component driven off the same belt.

---

6. Tighten all mounting bolts. Install the wiring to the alternator. Reconnect the battery terminal and check the operation of the charging system warning lamp.

NOTE
Be sure to reinstall the insulating boots to the wire terminals on the back of the alternator.

Regulator/Brush Assembly

The voltage regulator is easily removed from the back of the alternator by removing the two mounting screws. See Fig. 2. The regulator is available as replacement part. In addition, the carbon brushes can also be separately replaced.

With the regulator removed measure the brush length. See Fig. 3. If the brush length is less than the minimum length specified in the figure, they should be replaced. Replacing the brushes requires a soldering iron and electric/electronic solder.

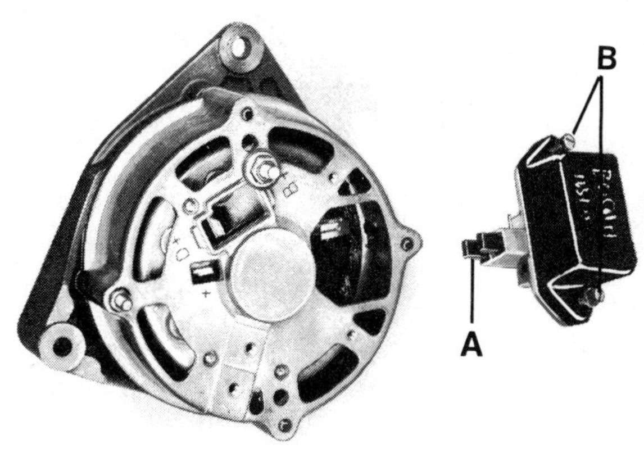

Fig. 2. Voltage regulator and brush holder removed from back of alternator. The brushes are at **A**. Remove the holder screws at **B**.

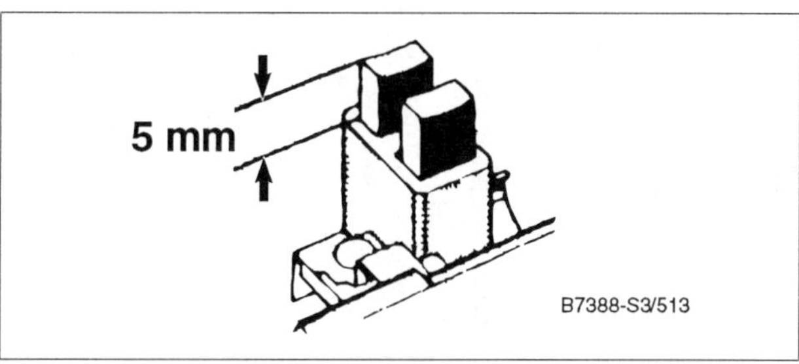

Fig. 3. Minimum regulator brush length. If brushes are shorter than 5 mm (0.2 in.), they should be replaced.

To replace regulator brushes

1. Remove the voltage regulator from the alternator.

2. Carefully unsolder the brush lead from the brush holder terminal, withdrawing the brush from the holder at the same time.

CAUTION

Work quickly to prevent overheating the solid state regulator.

---

3. Remove any traces of solder from the brush holder terminal.

4. Fit the new brush into the holder, insert the brush lead into the terminal, and solder it into place.

5. Reinstall the regulator.

331 Starter

STARTING SYSTEM

The starter is an electric motor that drives a ring gear on the flywheel via a pinion on the end of the starter. When the ignition key is turned to the start position, a solenoid moves the pinion into engagement with the ring gear. The solenoid then closes the main electrical contacts to the starter motor and the motor turns to start the car.

When the engine has started, the ring gear speed exceeds that of the pinion, and the pinion is disengaged from the pinion shaft. When the key is released from the start position, a spring returns the pinion to the rest position. Fig. 1 shows the starter components.

The starter is located at the front of the engine under the intake manifold. The starter and solenoid are removed together as an assembly. The solenoid can be separated from the starter motor once removed. Although the starter is generally replaced as an exchanged unit, the solenoid and other parts are available from an authorized Saab dealer.

Starter Troubleshooting

Before troubleshooting the starter, make sure the battery is fully charged and the battery cables and ground connections are free of corrosion and in good condition. Troubleshooting information for the starting system appear in **Table a.**

> **NOTE**
> - For information on starter wiring and component location see **371 Wiring Diagrams, Fuses and Relays**.
> - Starter efficiency is affected by engine oil viscosity. This is especially true in cold weather. Make sure the correct oil is in the engine. See **1 LUBRICATION AND MAINTENANCE.**

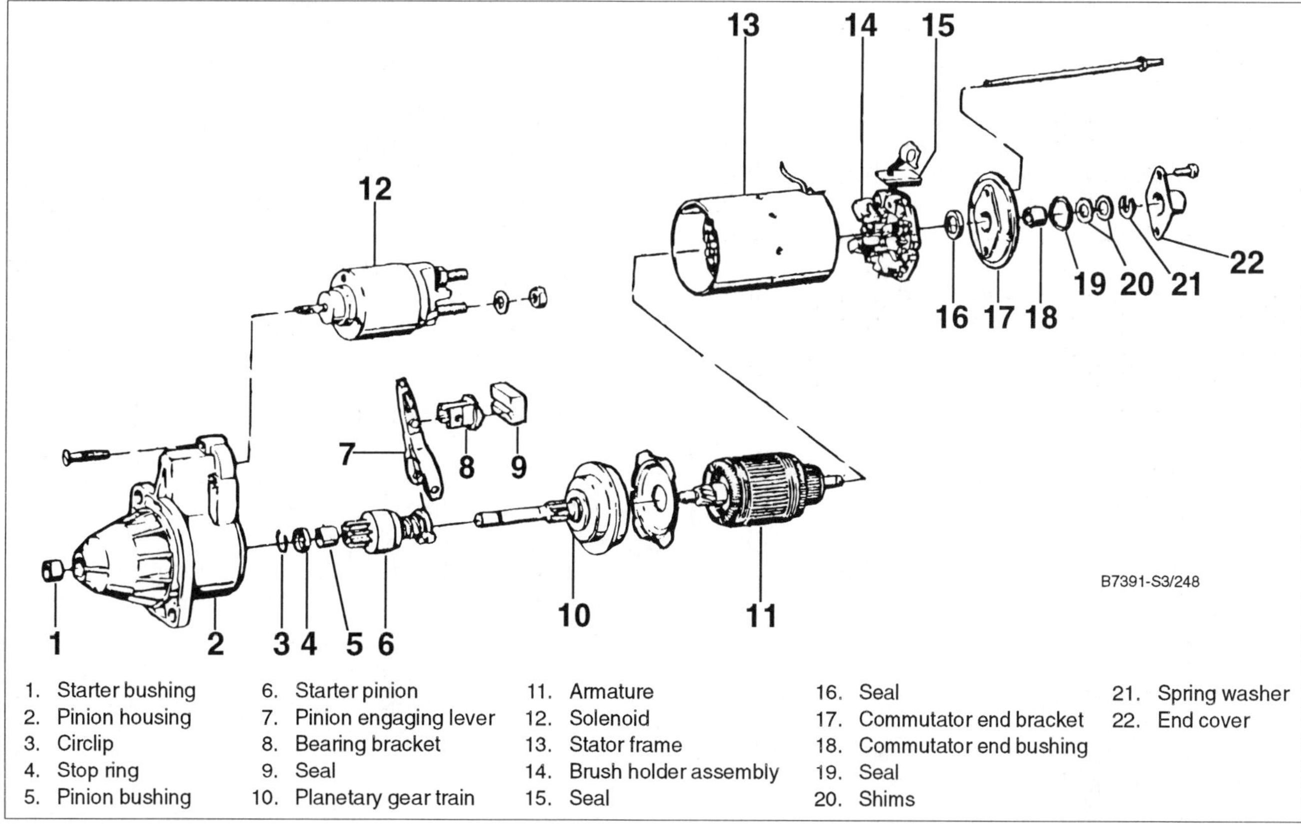

1. Starter bushing
2. Pinion housing
3. Circlip
4. Stop ring
5. Pinion bushing
6. Starter pinion
7. Pinion engaging lever
8. Bearing bracket
9. Seal
10. Planetary gear train
11. Armature
12. Solenoid
13. Stator frame
14. Brush holder assembly
15. Seal
16. Seal
17. Commutator end bracket
18. Commutator end bushing
19. Seal
20. Shims
21. Spring washer
22. End cover

Fig. 1. Exploded view of starter motor.

Table a. Battery, Starter and Charging System Troubleshooting

Symptom	Probable cause	Corrective action
1. Starter does not operate when ignition switch is turned to START	**a.** Ignition switch or wire leading from ignition switch to solenoid faulty (less than 8 volts to solenoid switch)	**a.** Test for voltage at terminal 50 of solenoid switch with ignition switch at START. If not at least 8 volts, test for voltage at terminal 50 of ignition switch with switch at START. Replace ignition switch (See **432 Manual Transmission Control**) or eliminate open circuit between ignition switch and solenoid switch
	b. Solenoid switch faulty (less than 8 volts to starter motor)	**b.** Test for voltage at field-winding strap with ignition at START. If not at least 8 volts, replace solenoid
	c. Starter motor faulty	**c.** Test for voltage at field-winding strap with ignition at START. If 8 volts or more, repair or replace starter motor
	d. Automatic transmission neutral safety switch faulty (models with automatic transmission only)	**d.** Test switch. See **371 Wiring Diagrams, Fuses and Relays**. See **364 Electric Controls and Switches** for switch adjustment
2. Starter turns slowly or fails to turn engine	**a.** Dirty, loose, or corroded starter connections	**a.** Remove, clean, and tighten connections
	b. Dirty, loose, or corroded ground strap between engine and body	**b.** Remove and clean or replace strap
	c. Starter worn or faulty	**c.** Repair or replace starter
3. Starter makes unusual noise, turns erratically, or fails to turn	**a.** Drive pinion defective	**a.** Repair or replace starter
	b. Flywheel or driveplate ring gear damaged	**b.** Replace flywheel or driveplate. See **216 Crankshaft**
4. Starter operates, but does not turn engine	**a.** Starter drive pinion or armature shaft faulty	**a.** Repair or replace starter
	b. Solenoid switch mechanism faulty	**b.** Replace starter solenoid switch

To remove starter

1. Disconnect the negative (–) battery cable. Remove any hoses that may be in the way, such as the air intake pipe.

2. Disconnect the large battery cable and the wire at terminal 50 from the starter motor.

NOTE

Terminal 50 has a small wire leading into the terminal. Terminal 30 has a large cable coming from the battery. The field-winding strap is a braided wire running from the solenoid to the starter housing.

---

3. Remove the two bolts holding the starter to the engine end plate and remove the starter.

Installation is the reverse of removal.

To replace solenoid

1. Remove the starter.

2. Remove the nut from the field-winding strap and disconnect the strap from the solenoid.

3. Remove the solenoid retaining screws and withdraw the solenoid, lifting it off the pinion engaging lever.

NOTE

The mounting screws are tightly fitted and may be difficult to remove. To help loosen the screws, use an impact driver with a slotted bit.

---

4. Install the new solenoid, hooking it over the pinion engaging lever. Make sure the terminals are correctly orientated and install the retaining screws and the field-winding strap.

5. Install the starter motor.

Tightening torques
- field-winding strap and battery cable to solenoid . . . . . . 7-9 nm (62-80 in-lb)
- solenoid to starter. . . . . 4.5-5.5 Nm (40-49 in-lb)

---

340 Ignition System

GENERAL

Two versions of Hall-effect electronic ignition systems are used on the cars covered by this manual. The term Hall-effect refers to the Hall Sensor, an electronic device in the distributor that replaces conventional mechanical breaker points.

Ignition System Applications
- 1985 and later Turbo . . . . . basic Hall-effect ignition
- 1986 and later Non-turbo . . . . EZK ignition— Hall-effect with knock sensor

Basic Hall Ignition System (1985 and later Turbo)

Fig. 1 shows a schematic of the basic Hall-effect ignition system. The firing of the spark is triggered by the Hall sensor in the distributor. The Hall sensor produces a voltage, which provides the ignition control unit with information about engine speed and crankshaft position. With this input, the control unit operates the ignition coil secondary circuit to precisely time the firing of the spark plugs.

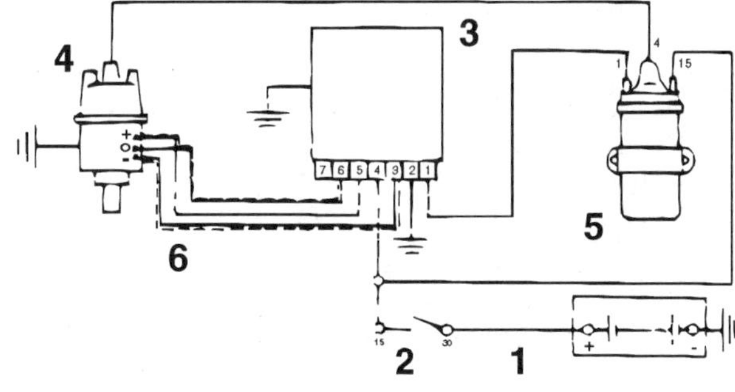

1. Battery
2. Ignition switch
3. Ignition control unit
4. Ignition distributor
5. Ignition coil
6. Shielded cable

Fig. 1. Schematic of basic Hall-effect ignition system.

EZK Ignition System (1986 and later Non-Turbo)

Fig. 2 shows a schematic of the EZK ignition system. This system is more sophisticated than the basic Hall system in that it includes a knock sensor to monitor and control ignition knock or ping. A knock sensor functions like a microphone and is able to convert mechanical vibration (knock) into electrical signals. The EZK control unit is programmed to react to the signals whose frequencies are characteristic of combustion chamber noise and change ignition timing accordingly.

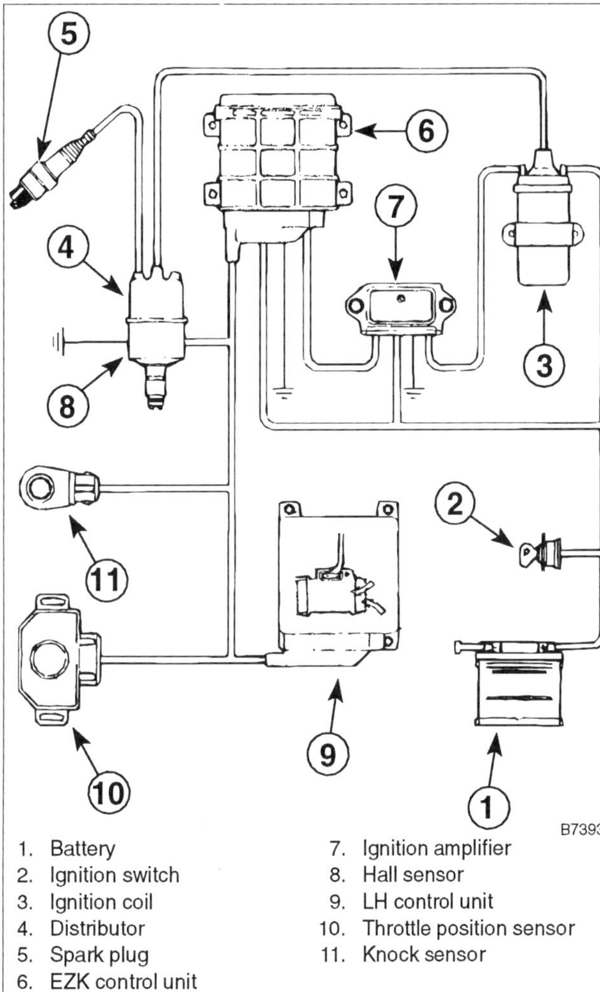

Fig. 2. Schematic of EZK ignition system with knock sensor.

The throttle switch (also used in the LH fuel injection system) signals the EZK control unit when the engine is idling. This allows the EZK control unit to set a base timing when the throttle is closed. The EZK control unit also receives an "engine load signal" from the LH control unit.

NOTE

- For more information on the throttle switch, including adjusting and testing procedures, see **240 Fuel Injection.**

- Turbo models also use a knock sensor to detect ignition knock as part of the APC (Automatic Performance Control) system. For more information, see **291 Turbocharger.**

EZK Knock Sensor Operation and Ignition Timing

During cranking, the ignition timing is locked at 5°BTDC. This setting will be held until engine speed exceeds 700 rpm. The timing will then change to a fixed 14°BTDC setting until the throttle is opened.

When the throttle is opened, the knock sensing system takes over and adjusts ignition timing according to engine conditions. The timing can vary from 5° to 22° BTDC in response to engine speed, engine load, or detonation. If engine knock occurs, the ECU determines which cylinder(s) are knocking and retards just the affected cylinder by 3°. If the knocking continues, the timing is further retarded in steps of 3°. The timing position will be maintained for a short period and will then begin to advance the timing by 1/3° increments until normal ignition is resumed.

NOTE

An occasional knocking may be heard on engines with EZK. This is normal and is necessary for proper operation of the EZK system.

IGNITION SYSTEM TROUBLESHOOTING

Poor driveability may have a variety of causes. The fault may lie with the ignition system, the fuel system, parts of the emission control system, or a combination of the three. Because of the interrelated functions of these systems, it is often difficult to know where to begin looking for problems. For this reason, effective troubleshooting should always consider these systems in unison, as one major system.

A complete failure of the ignition system to produce spark at the spark plugs is self-evident. For other problems such as rough idle, misfiring, or poor starting, however, the cause is not so clear. For troubleshooting engine management and the way the car runs, see **200 Engine—General.**

Ignition system service and repair work must be carried out carefully. The ignition system contains sensitive electronic components. To protect the system, and for general safety, the following warnings should be observed during any ignition system troubleshooting, maintenance, or repair work.

WARNING

- The ignition systems installed on the cars covered by this manual are high-energy systems operating in a dangerous voltage range which could prove to be fatal if exposed terminals or live parts are contacted. Use extreme caution when working on a vehicle with the ignition on or the engine running.

WARNING

• Connect and disconnect ignition system wires, multiple connectors, and ignition test equipment leads only while the ignition is off. Do not touch or disconnect any of the high tension cables from the coil, distributor, or spark plugs while the engine is running or being cranked by the starter.

• Before operating the starter without starting the engine (as when making a compression test), always disable the ignition as described below.

• Inefficient combustion can overload the catalytic converter with raw fuel, leading to converter overheating or plugging. An overheated catalytic converter can be a fire hazard.

CAUTION

• Do not conduct ignition system tests with a test lamp that uses a normal incandescent bulb. The high electrical consumption of these test lamps may damage the electronic components.

• Do not connect test instruments with a 12-volt supply to terminal 15 (+) of the ignition coil. The voltage backflow can damage the ignition control unit.

• Do not connect terminal 1 of the coil to ground as a means of preventing the engine from starting (for example, when installing or servicing anti-theft devices).

• Do not disconnect terminal 4 (center terminal) from the coil or remove the distributor cap to disable the ignition.

• Do not disconnect the battery while the engine is running.

On-board Diagnostics (EZK ignition only)

The EZK ignition system features built-in diagnostic circuitry that detects and stores in memory coded information about system faults. These fault codes can be "read-out" through flashes of the **Check Engine** light. Before troubleshooting an EZK fault and a flashing Check Engine light, check for broken or loose engine mounts or brackets.

NOTE

• As a general rule, a steady-on Check Engine light means the LH control unit has detected a fault. A flashing Check Engine light means that the EZK Ignition system has detected a fault. As an exception to the rule, the Check Engine light on 1992 models does not flash. Therefore, a steady-on Check Engine light on these models could be either a EZK system fault or an LH fuel system fault.

• On 1989 models with EZK only, the Check Engine light may flash intermittently due to a faulty EZK control unit. Check for a control unit date code of "945" or lower (see Fig. 13 for control unit location). The date code is stamped on the unit next to the connector housing. If the control unit is within these dates codes, see an authorized Saab dealer for additional information on correcting this fault.

On 1986-1991 models, start the engine and allow it to reach operating temperature. Briefly raise engine speed above 2000 rpm. Count the number of times the check engine light flashes before repeating the flashing code. The number of times the Check Engine light flashes determines the fault in the system.

EZK Check Engine light fault diagnosis

- three flashes—EZK control unit internal fault*
- four flashes — fault in the knock sensor, sensor wiring, or EZK control unit
- five flashes — faulty input signal from LH control unit.

*This code is applicable to 1989 and later models only.

NOTE

If the wiring harness to the EZK knock sensor is defective, a replacement wire harness is available from an authorized Saab dealer. This harness eliminates the need to replace the entire engine harness.

Test Equipment

Many of the tests of ignition system components require the use of high-impedance test equipment to prevent damage to the electrical components. A high-impedance digital multimeter should be used for all voltage and resistance tests. An LED test light should be used in place of an incandescent-type test lamp.

Many tests require checking for voltage, continuity, or resistance at the terminals of the components' harness connectors. The blunt tips of a multimeter's probes can spread open the small connector terminals and cause poor connections. To prevent damage, use flat male connectors to probe the harness connector terminals.

Disabling Ignition System

To prevent the engine from starting and to prevent the presence of dangerous voltages, the ignition system should be disabled anytime work is done on the ignition system. The ignition system should also be disabled any time work is being done in the engine compartment with the ignition key on or if the starter needs to be operated without running the engine, such as when making an engine compression test.

Disabling the ignition system is easily accomplished by disconnecting the Hall sensor connector. On all 1985-1988 models and 1989 and later Turbo models, disconnect the Hall sensor connector from the side of the distributor. On 1989 and later models with EZK ignition, the Hall sensor is mounted behind the crankshaft pulley. To disconnect the sensor connector, follow the wiring harness up from the sensor until you reach the connector in the engine compartment. See Fig. 3.

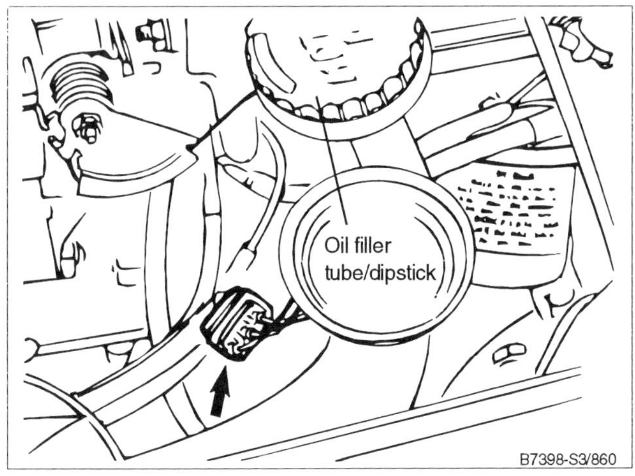

Fig. 3. Hall sensor connector on 1989 and later cars with EZK ignition. The sensor on these cars is mounted behind crankshaft pulley.

Basic Troubleshooting Principles

An engine that starts and runs indicates that the ignition system is fundamentally working—delivering voltage to the spark plugs. A hard-starting or poor-running engine, however, may indicate a problem with how well the spark is delivered. A faulty coil or control unit, cracked or deteriorated spark plug wires, a worn or cracked distributor cap or rotor, and worn or fouled spark plugs are all causes of reduced spark intensity and inefficient combustion.

An engine that has good cranking speed but will not start may indicate a complete failure of the system to produce spark. Inspect the ignition system visually. Make sure the spark plug wires have not been interchanged. Ignition firing order is described below under **Firing Order.**

If no visual faults are located, make a basic quick-check to see if spark is being produced as described below. This will be the most important first troubleshooting step. If a strong spark is observed, then the failure to start is due to another cause, perhaps no fuel being delivered to the engine.

Quick-Check of Ignition System

The first step in troubleshooting a no-start condition is to determine whether the problem is caused by the ignition system or some other system, such as a fuel delivery problem. This done by checking that the spark plugs are firing. If no spark is present, then more detailed testing of the ignition system is necessary.

To make the check, turn the ignition off and remove a spark plug wire from a spark plug. Connect to the plug wire a spark-tester or a known good spark plug gapped to 4 mm (0.16 or 5/32 in.) Position the plug so that the outer electrode is grounded on the engine.

NOTE

For the most accurate test results, the battery should be fully charged.

While a helper actuates the starter, look and listen for spark in the spark plug gap. A bright blue spark indicates a healthy ignition system. A yellow-orange spark is weaker and indicates that, while spark is present and the system is functioning, it is not operating at peak efficiency. Check the condition of the ignition system components as described below **Visual Inspection.** If there is no spark, test the system components as described below under **Electrical Tests and Fault Tracing**.

WARNING

- Do not hold the spark plug or its connector, even if using insulated pliers.

- If ignition system failure is not the problem, the engine may start during this test. Be prepared to turn off the ignition immediately. Running the engine with a spark plug wire disconnected may damage the catalytic converter.

If no faults have been detected up to this point but there is still no spark or a weak spark, refer to **Table a** for more troubleshooting information. If a strong spark is observed but the engine still will not start, refer to **200 Engine—General** for more troubleshooting information.

Firing Order

The firing order of the cylinders is 1-3-4-2. Cylinder no. 1 is next to the V-belts by the firewall and cylinder no. 4 is at the front of the car. The engine rotates counter-clockwise when viewed from the front of the car. See Fig. 4.

Table a. Ignition System Troubleshooting

Symptom	Probable cause	Corrective action
1. No spark or weak spark observed during spark test	a. Wet or damp distributor cap and/or spark plug wires	a. Remove cap and wires. Dry and reinstall
	b. Faulty wires or connectors (primary circuit).	b. Test and replace as needed
	c. Weak or faulty coil	c. Test and replace as needed
	d. Defective spark plug wires	d. Test and replace as needed
	e. Worn or fouled spark plugs	e. Replace spark plugs. See **1 LUBRICATION AND MAINTENANCE**
	f. Faulty Hall sensor	f. Test and replace as needed
	g. Faulty ignition control unit or amplifier	g. Test and replace as needed

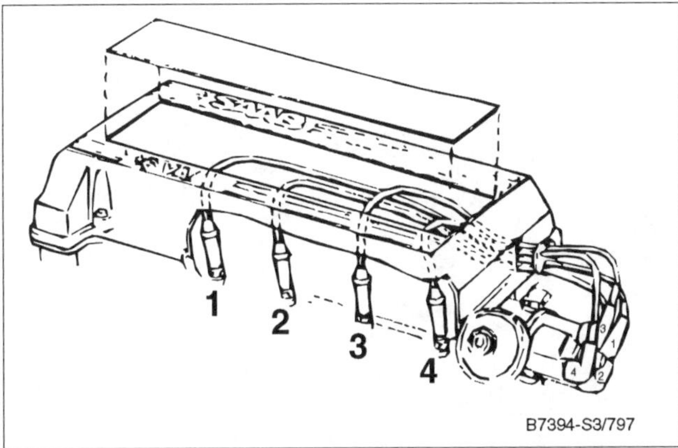

Fig. 4. Firing order and proper orientation of high tension leads.

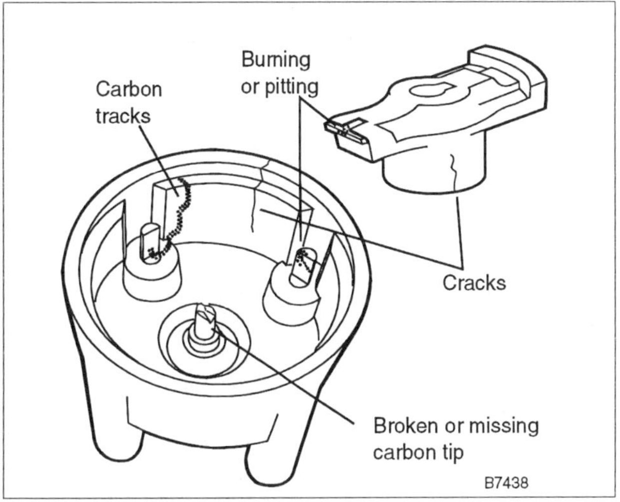

Fig. 5. Distributor cap and rotor. Inspect cap and rotor at contact points.

Visual Inspection

The spark plug wires, the distributor cap, and the distributor rotor are subject to wear and electrical breakdown, which will impair their ability to deliver a crisply timed and powerful spark. Dirt and moisture on any of these components are also potential causes of poor spark at the spark plugs.

To inspect the distributor cap and rotor, first unclip and remove the cap. Inspect the contacts inside the distributor cap and at the tip of the rotor for carbon tracks, wear, or pitting. See Fig. 5. Cracks or carbon tracks in the distributor cap may cause shorts to ground. The cracks may be fine and difficult to see. Check that the center black carbon brush inside the cap springs back when compressed. If any faults are found, replace the cap and/or rotor.

To visually check the spark plug wires, gently bend them in several places. This will expose cracks in the insulation which may cause spark "leaks". Peel back the rubber boots and check them for pliancy and the ability to seal out dirt and moisture. Wires that are cracked, oil-soaked or dry and brittle should be replaced.

The coil should be closely examined for cracks, burns, carbon tracks, or any leaking fluid. The coil tower, center terminal 4, should be clean and dry. If necessary, remove the coil for cleaning and closer examination. Check that the wiring at the coil top is not contacting the metal coil housing. Loosen the nuts and reposition the wires if necessary.

Inspect all primary wires and connections for any corrosion or damage. Clean or repair any faults found. In these sensitive electronic ignition systems, corroded or loose connections may interfere with the ignition function.

Electrical Tests and Fault Tracing

The following electrical test should be done in the sequence given. Review the information given earlier before making the tests described here. On cars with EZK ignition, be sure to check for any EZK fault codes as described earlier.

For the most accurate test results, check that the battery is fully charged, there is fuel in the tank, and that engine and ambient temperature are between 32°F and 104°F (0°C and 40°C).

CAUTION
Do not unplug components or disconnect grounds when the ignition key is on. Damage to electronic components could result.

To test basic Hall ignition system (turbo models only)

1. **Check the basic components subject to wear and electrical breakdown.** Test the condition of the spark plug wires and the ignition rotor by testing the resistance of each component.

Spark Plug Wire and Rotor Resistances
- Ignition rotor .... 1,000 Ohms
- Coil high tension lead (complete with end connectors) .. 500-1,500 Ohms
- Spark plug leads (complete with end connectors) .... 2,000-4,000 Ohms

2. **Check for power to the Hall sensor.** Unplug the wiring connector from the side of the distributor. Connect a voltmeter between the two outer terminals in the connector. See Fig. 6. Turn the ignition on. The voltmeter should read at least 10 volts (VDC). Turn the ignition off and reconnect the connector. If no faults are found, proceed to the next step. If voltage is not present, check the wires between the distributor connector and the control unit. Repair any wiring faults before proceeding.

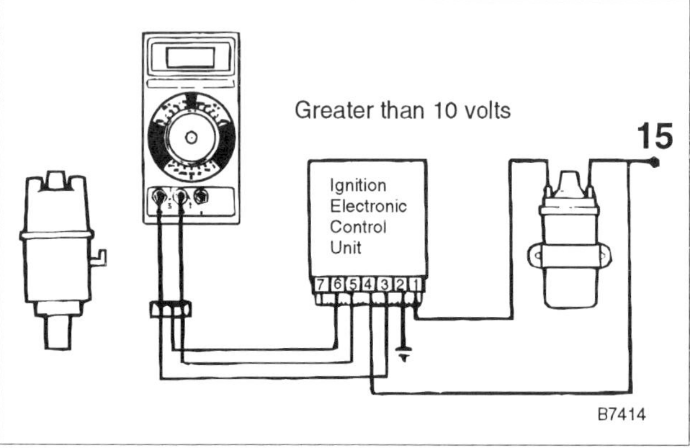

Fig. 6. Voltmeter being used to check for voltage to Hall sensor.

3. **Check for power to the ignition control unit.** Disconnect the connector from the ignition control unit. See Fig. 7. Connect a voltmeter to terminal 4 (+) and terminal 2 (–) of the control unit connector. See Fig. 8. Turn the ignition on and check that the voltage is at least 10 volts (DC). Turn the ignition off and reconnect the connector. If voltage is as specified, proceed to the next step. If voltage is not present, use the diagrams shown in **371 Wiring Diagrams, Fuses and Relays** to check for wiring faults.

NOTE
It may be necessary to remove the control unit from its mountings to gain access to the connector.

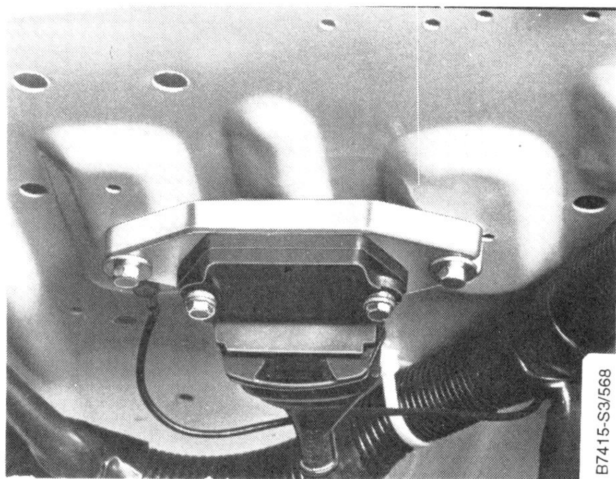

Fig. 7. Ignition control unit in left front (driver's side) fender well.

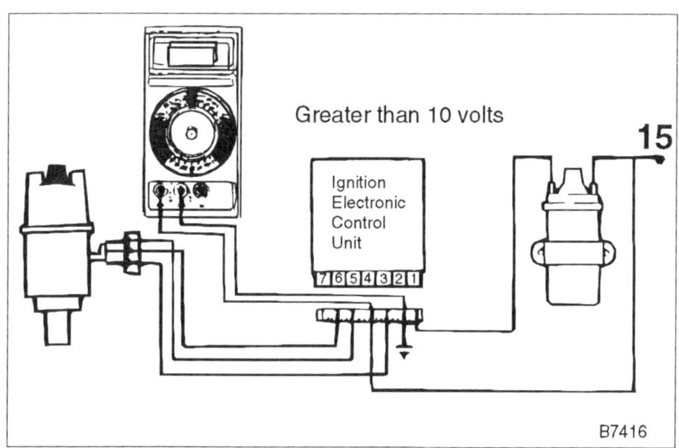

Fig. 8. Voltmeter being used to check for voltage to control unit.

4. **Check the Hall sensor output signal.** Peel back the rubber boot on the control unit connector. Connect a voltmeter between terminal 6 and 3, working from rear of the connector. See Fig. 9. Turn the ignition on and slowly turn the engine over by hand. The voltage should oscillate between 0.4 (DC)volts (or less) and 3.0 volts (or higher). If no faults are found, proceed to the next step. If any faults are found, check the wires between the control unit and the Hall sensor. If no wiring faults are found, the Hall sensor is faulty and should be replaced.

CAUTION

Turn the engine over only in the direction of normal rotation. Otherwise damage to the timing chain and its components may result. To determine normal rotation, put the car in gear and rock the car forward, noting the rotation of the ignition rotor, the flywheel, or a belt-driven component. As an alternative, briefly operate the starter.

NOTE

The engine can be turned over using a wrench on the crankshaft pulley.

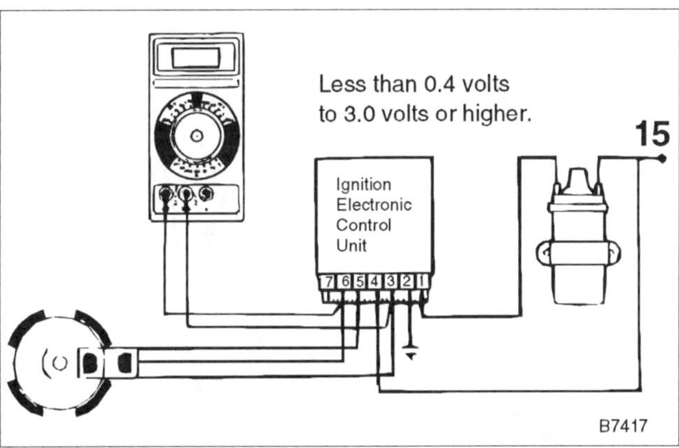

Fig. 9. Voltmeter being used to check Hall sensor operation.

5. **Check for power to the coil.** Connect a voltmeter between terminal 15 (+) of the coil and ground. Turn the ignition on and check that the voltage is at least 10 volts (DC). Turn the ignition off. If voltage is as specified, proceed to the next step. If voltage is not present, use the diagrams shown in **371 Wiring Diagrams, Fuses and Relays** to check for wiring faults.

6. **Check the coil primary and secondary circuit resistance.** Remove all wires from the coil. Measure the coil primary and secondary circuit resistance as shown below in Fig. 10. Reconnect the wires to the coil. If the coil resistance is not as specified, the coil is faulty and should be replaced. If no faults are found, proceed to the next step.

Ignition coil resistance*

- between terminal 1 and 15 .... 0.5 to 0.9 Ohms
- between terminal 1 and center tower .... 7200 to 8200 Ohms

---

* measure with all wires disconnected from coil

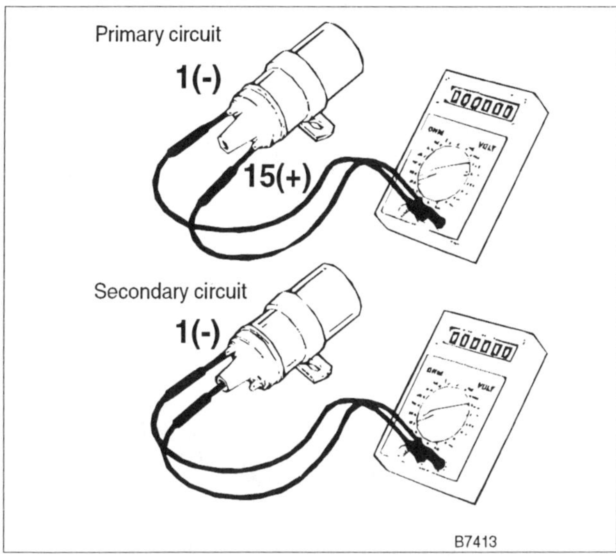

Fig. 10. Coil circuits being tested using ohmmeter. Coil terminal numbers are found on coil.

7. **Check the ignition control unit switching function to the coil.** Disconnect the Hall sensor connector from the distributor. Connect the voltmeter between coil terminals 15 and 1. See Fig. 11. Turn the ignition on. The voltage should rise to about 5 volts (DC) and then drop to 0 volts within 1 to 2 seconds. Reconnect the connector. If any faults are found, the control unit is faulty and should be replaced. If no faults are found, the ignition system is functioning correctly.

NOTE

If on 1986 and 1987 models, all electrical checks are as specified but the car still does not start, check the ignition pulse amplifier on the main fuse relay panel. See Fig. 12. This relay-like amplifier is designed to "amplify" the tachometer signal for more reliable control of electronic components affected by the ignition system (LH fuel injection, fuel pump control, etc.). To check the amplifier, simply remove it from its socket. Then using a jumper wire, jumper the fuse/relay panel sockets corresponding to relay terminals TD-I and TD-O. Try to start the engine. If the engine now runs, replace the amplifier.

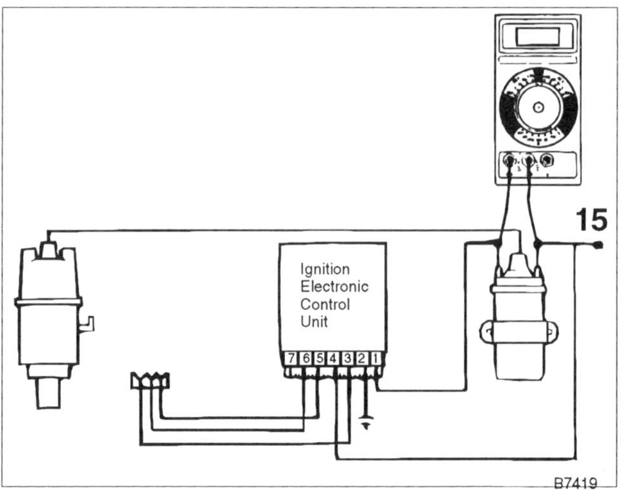

Fig. 11. Voltmeter being used to check control unit switching function.

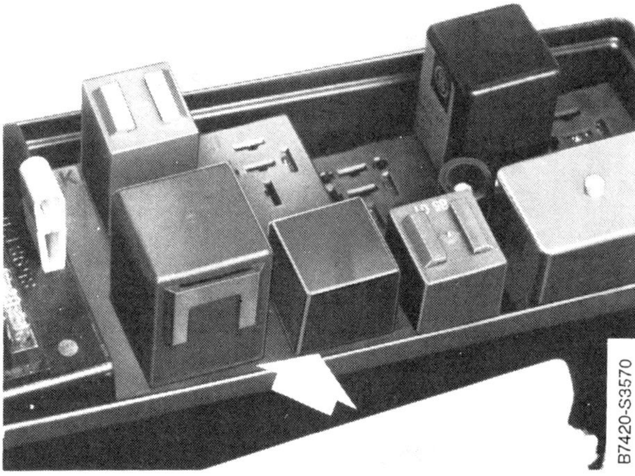

Fig. 12. Ignition pulse amplifier used on 1986 and 1987 models. A faulty pulse amplifier will cause a no-start condition.

To test EZK ignition system (non-turbo models only)

1. **Check the basic components subject to wear and electrical breakdown.** Test the condition of the spark plug wires and the ignition rotor by testing the resistance of each component.

Spark Plug Wire and Rotor Resistances

- Ignition rotor . . . . 1,000 ohms
- Coil high tension lead (complete with end connectors) . . . 500-1,500 ohms
- Spark plug leads (complete with end connectors) . . . . 2,000-3,000 ohms

---

2. **Test the knock sensor output signal.** Remove the harness connector from the EZK control unit. See Fig. 13. Using a digital voltmeter (set to VAC scale), connect it to terminal 12 and 13 of the control unit connector. Gently tap on the knock sensor mounting bolt. The voltmeter should register a small voltage and the reading should vary depending on the intensity of the tap.

NOTE

- The knock sensor is mounted to the engine block between cylinders no. 2 and 3, below the intake manifold.
- Procedure step 1 checks both the knock sensor and the wiring to the control unit. If the knock sensor does not respond to the tapping, remove the sensor and its connector. Then connect the voltmeter directly to the sensor terminals and repeat the above test. If the sensor now tests good, check the wiring from the sensor connector to the EZK control unit. If the sensor does not respond, it is faulty and should be replaced.

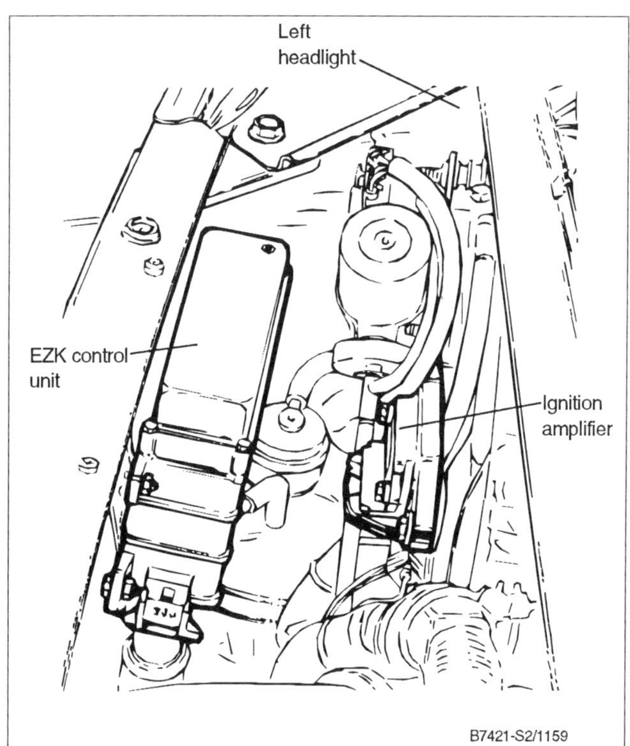

Fig. 13. EZK control unit and amplifier locations in left (driver's) side fender well. On 1988 and 1989 cars, amplifier is on side of ignition coil.

NOTE

On all cars except 1988 and 1989 models with EZK ignition, a conventional coil with a separate amplifier is used. On 1988 and 1989 cars with EZK ignition, a special coil with integrated amplifier is used. See Fig. 14. Testing procedures and replacement parts vary depending on coil style.

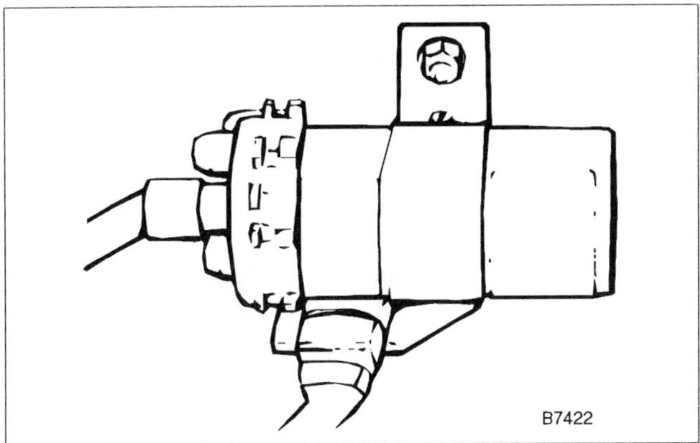

Fig. 14. Ignition coil with integrated amplifier (power stage) used on 1988 and 1989 cars. Coil is mounted on right-hand side of engine compartment, near the battery.

3. **Check for power to the EZK control unit.** Unplug the connector from the EZK control unit and connect a voltmeter (VDC scale) between terminal 6 (+) and 20 (–) of the connector. With the ignition on, there should be battery voltage. Turn the ignition off and reconnect the connector. If no faults are found proceed to the next step. If voltage is not present, use the diagrams shown in **371 Wiring Diagrams, Fuses and Relays** to check for wiring faults.

4. **Check for power to the amplifier.** Peel back the boot on the amplifier harness connector. Connect a voltmeter between the terminal 4 (+) and 2 (–) on fender-mounted amplifiers (Fig. 15) or between terminals 3 (+) and 2 (–) on coil-mounted amplifiers. With the ignition on, there should be battery voltage. If no faults are found proceed to the next step. If voltage is not present, use the wiring diagrams to check for wiring faults from the ignition switch.

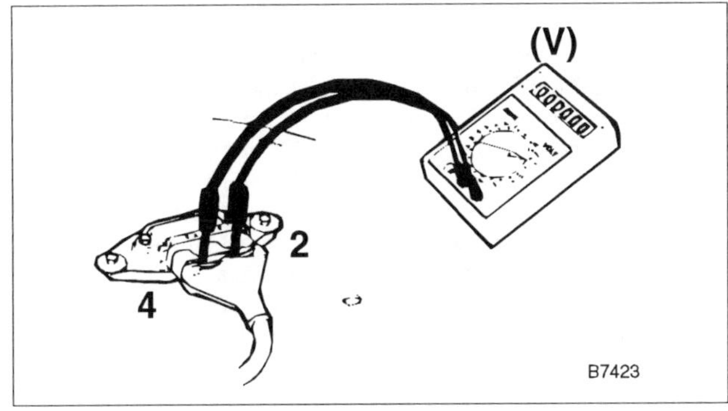

Fig. 15. Voltmeter being used to check for voltage to EZK amplifier (fender-mounter amplifier shown).

NOTE

On fender-mounted amplifiers, the amplifier should be removed from its mountings to access the harness connector.

---

5. **Check for power to the coil.** Connect a voltmeter between terminal 15 and ground on conventional coils or between terminal 3 and ground on coils with amplifier. With the ignition on, there should be battery voltage. If no faults are found proceed to the next step. If voltage is not present, use the wiring diagrams to check for wiring faults from the ignition switch.

6. **Check the coil primary and secondary circuit resistance.** With the ignition off, remove all wires from the coil. Measure the resistance of the coil circuits as shown in Fig. 16. If any faults are found the coil is faulty and should be replaced. If no faults are found, proceed to the next step. Reconnect the wires to the coil.

Ignition coil resistance*

Model	Test terminals and resistance
except 1988-1989	1 and 15 — 0.5 to 0.9 Ohms 1 and center tower — 7200 to 8200
1988-1989	4 and 3 — 0.5 to 0.9 Ohms 4 and center tower — 7200 to 8200 Ohms

* measure with all wires disconnected from coil

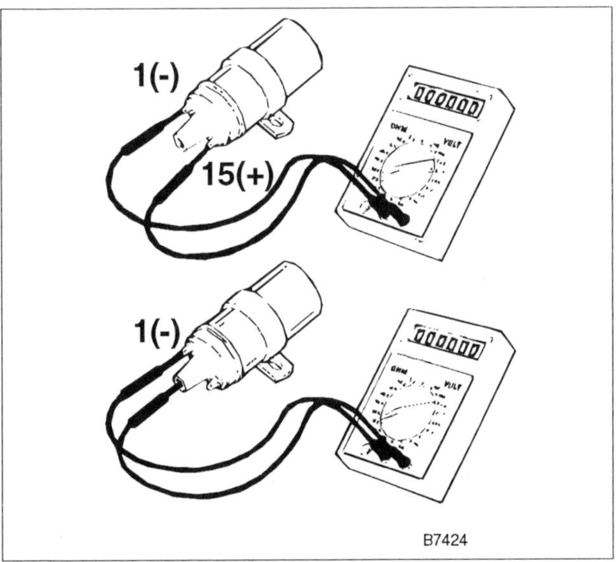

Fig. 16. Coil circuits being tested using ohmmeter (conventional coil shown).

7. **Check the amplifier switching function.** Connect the voltmeter between coil terminals 15 (+) and 1 (–) on conventional coils or between terminal 3 (+) and 4 (–) on coils with integrated amplifier. Turn the ignition on. The voltage should rise to about 6 volts (DC) and then drop to 0 volts within 1 to 2 seconds. If any faults are found, replace the amplifier. If no faults are found proceed to the next step.

8. **Check the pulse signal from the EZK control unit to the amplifier.** Peel back the rubber boot on the control unit connector. Connect a voltmeter between the terminals 5 (+) and 2 (–) on fender-mounted amplifiers or between terminals 4 (+) and 2 (–) on coil mounted amplifiers. While operating the starter, there should be an oscillating voltage (pulses between 0 and 8 volts (DC), average of 2.8 volts). If no faults are found, the amplifier is faulty and should be replaced. If there is no pulse, proceed to the next step.

9. **Check the Hall sensor signal to the EZK control unit.** Peel back the rubber boot on the EZK control unit connector. Connect a voltmeter between terminal 24 (+) and 20 (–). See Fig. 17. Turn the ignition on and slowly turn the engine over by hand. The voltage should oscillate between 0.4 volts (DC) (or less) and 3.0 volts (or higher). If no faults are found, the EZK control unit is probably faulty and should be replaced. If any faults are found, proceed to the next step.

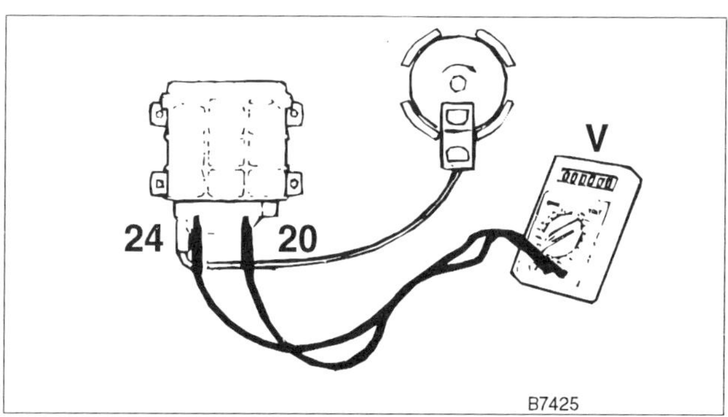

Fig. 17. Voltmeter being used to check Hall sensor operation at EZK control unit.

CAUTION

Turn the engine over only in the direction of normal rotation. Otherwise damage to the timing chain and its components may result. To determine normal rotation, put the car in gear and rock the car forward, noting the rotation of the ignition rotor, the flywheel, or a belt-driven component. As an alternative, briefly operate the starter.

NOTE

The engine can be turned over using a wrench on the crankshaft pulley.

---

10. **Check for voltage to the Hall sensor.** Working from the rear of the EZK control unit connector, connect a voltmeter between terminal 4 (+) and 10 (–). See Fig. 18. With the ignition on, there should be battery voltage. If no faults are found, the Hall sensor is faulty and should be replaced. If voltage is not present, the EZK control unit is faulty.

NOTE

On all 1986-1988 cars, the Hall sensor is in the distributor. On 1989 and later cars, the Hall sensor is mounted behind the crankshaft pulley. Hall sensor replacement procedures are described below.

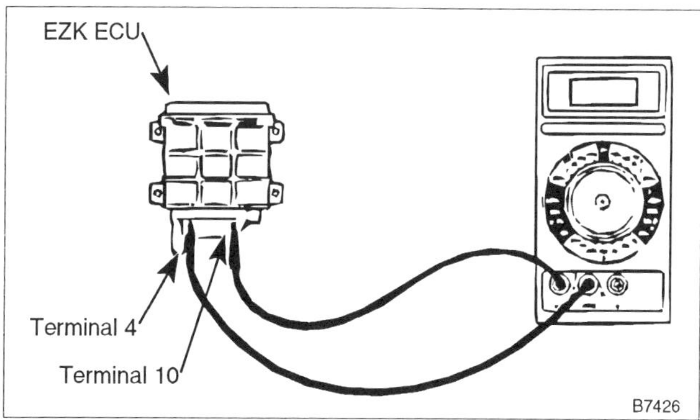

Fig. 18. Voltmeter being used to check for voltage supply to Hall sensor from EZK control unit.

NOTE

If on 1986 and 1987 models, all electrical checks are as specified but the car still does not start, check the ignition pulse amplifier on the main fuse relay panel. See Fig. 12 above. This relay-like amplifier is designed to "amplify" the tachometer signal for more reliable control of electronic components affected by the ignition system (LH fuel injection, fuel pump control, etc.). To check the amplifier, simply remove it from its socket. Then using a jumper wire, jumper the fuse/relay panel sockets corresponding to relay terminals TD-I and TD-O. Try to start the engine. If the engine now runs, replace the pulse amplifier.

COMPONENT REMOVAL AND REPLACEMENT

NOTE
Spark plug replacement is covered in **1 LUBRICATION AND MAINTENANCE.** Spark plugs are replaced at regular intervals and should not be cleaned or regapped.

To replace distributor cap and rotor

1. Unhook the spring clips from the distributor cap and pull off the cap. Leave the wires in the cap.

2. Remove the rotor by cracking it off the distributor shaft using a slip-joint pliers. See Fig. 19.

NOTE
Replacement rotors may not always be glued in place. Check to see if the rotor can be pulled off first.

Fig. 19. Ignition rotor being crushed to remove it from shaft.

3. Install a new rotor with a locking compound (Loctite 601 locking compound or equivalent).

4. To replace the distributor cap, clip the new cap into position. Then transfer one ignition wire at a time to maintain proper firing order of the spark plugs.

To remove and install distributor

1. Make matching marks on the base of the distributor and the cylinder head.

2. Unhook the spring clips from the distributor cap and pull off the cap. Leave the wires in the cap.

3. Remove the vacuum hose from the vacuum diaphragm and the harness connector from the Hall sensor, where applicable.

NOTE
Turbo models have no mechanical advance in the distributor. Models with EZK have no vacuum or mechanical advance.

4. Remove the distributor clamp-down bolt and bracket. See Fig. 20.

Fig. 20. Distributor clamp-down bolt being removed.

5. Pull the distributor from the cylinder head. Inspect the O-ring on the distributor shaft and replace if faulty.

6. Install the distributor into the cylinder head while rotating the rotor until the dog on the shaft engages the offset cutout in the camshaft. See Fig. 21.

7. Install the clamp-down bracket and its mounting bolt. Do not fully tighten the bolt.

8. Rotate the distributor housing until the matching marks made earlier are aligned. Check and adjust ignition timing as described below.

Tightening torque
- Ignition distributor hold-down bolt . . 15 Nm (11 ft-lb)

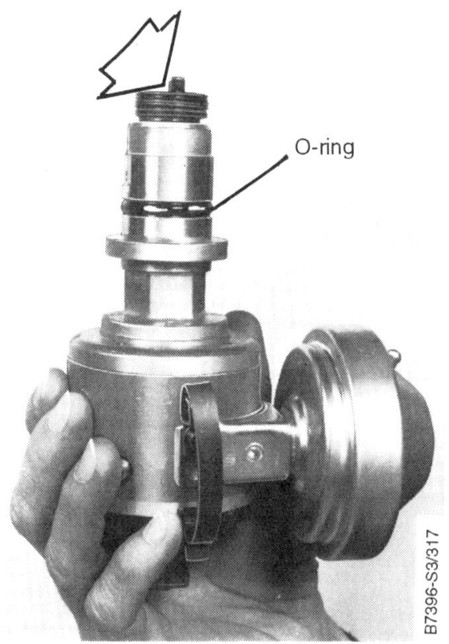

Fig. 21. Offset dog on distributor shaft (arrow) must engage cutout in camshaft.

Hall Sensor

Two different Hall sensors are used in the cars covered by this manual. Replacement procedures vary between styles.

Hall sensor location	
1986-1988 Non-Turbo	in distributor
1985 and later Turbo	
1989-and later Non-turbo	behind crankshaft

NOTE
Distributor replacement parts, including the a rebuild kit for the distributor-mounted Hall sensor, are available from an authorized Saab dealer.

To replace Hall sensor (distributor-mounted sensor)

1. Remove the distributor as described above.
2. Thoroughly clean the distributor shaft, removing any glue or other residues from the shaft.
3. Remove the field rotor circlip. See Fig. 22.
4. Using a small 2-jaw puller, carefully remove the field rotor. See Fig. 23. Remove and save the field rotor locating pin. See Fig. 24.

Fig. 22. Field rotor circlip being removed.

Fig. 23. Hall sensor field rotor being removed.

Fig. 24. Field rotor locating pin (arrow).

5. Remove from the distributor shaft the two circlips and spacer from above the Hall sensor. Remove the plastic cover.

6. Carefully pry off the plastic connector housing from the side of the distributor. See Fig. 25. Lift the sensor out of the distributor.

NOTE

Make sure the spacer underneath the Hall sensor does not come out with the sensor.

Fig. 25. Hall sensor connector housing being removed.

7. Install the new sensor into the distributor. Where applicable, make sure the locating pin on the sensor engages the hole in the diaphragm arm. See Fig. 26.

8. The remainder of installation is the reverse of removal. Be sure to install the field rotor locating pin (see Fig. 24).

Fig. 26. When installing sensor, engage pin on sensor with hole in vacuum diaphragm arm (arrows).

To replace Hall sensor (crankshaft-mounted sensor)

1. Disconnect the negative (–) battery cable.

2. Remove all the V-belts from the crankshaft pulley. See **1 LUBRICATION AND MAINTENANCE** for more information on removing V-belts.

3. While holding the flywheel stationary, remove the crankshaft pulley center mounting bolt. Remove the pulley and its woodruff key.

NOTE

A special flywheel holding fixture (Saab tool no. 83 92 987) is available from an authorized Saab dealer.

---

4. If necessary remove the Hall sensor field rotor from the pulley by removing the three bolts. See Fig. 27.

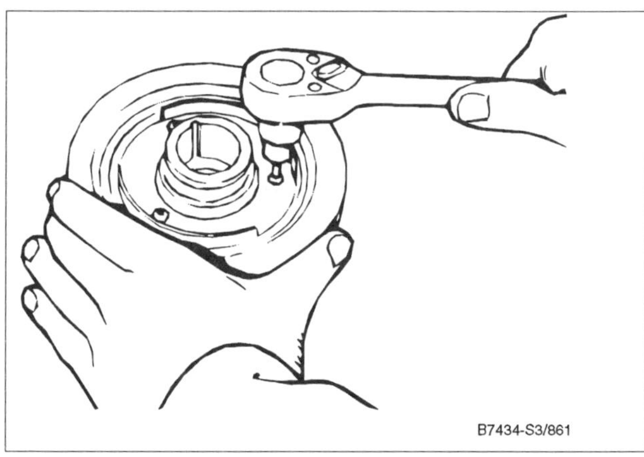

Fig. 27. Ignition field rotor being removed from rear of crankshaft pulley.

5. Disconnect the Hall sensor connector. The connector is located below the oil dipstick tube. See Fig. 28.

6. Remove the Hall sensor bolts and remove the sensor. See Fig. 29.

Installation is the reverse of removal. Use Loctite® 270 on the sensor mounting bolts. Reinstall the pulley and woodruff key. Tighten the bolt while holding the flywheel steady.

Tightening torque

- crankshaft pulley bolt to crankshaft
  - 1989 . . . . 190 Nm (140 ft-lb)
  - 1991and later . . . . 175 Nm (128 ft-lb)

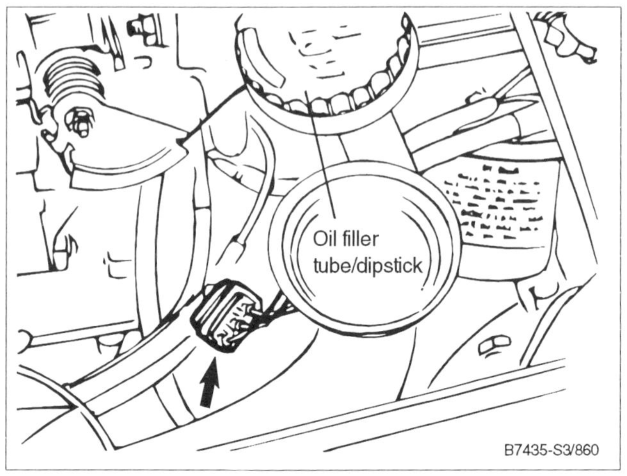

Fig. 28. Hall sensor harness connector (arrow).

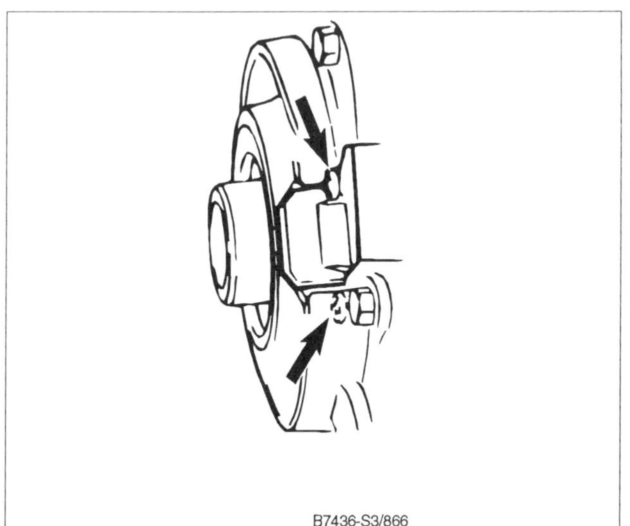

Fig. 29. Hall sensor mounting bolts (arrows).

To replace knock sensor (EZK ignition only)

1. Disconnect the knock sensor harness from the sensor. See Fig. 30.

NOTE

The knock sensor is mounted to the engine block between cylinders no. 2 and 3, below the intake manifold.

---

2. Remove the knock sensor mounting bolt and remove the sensor. See Fig. 31.

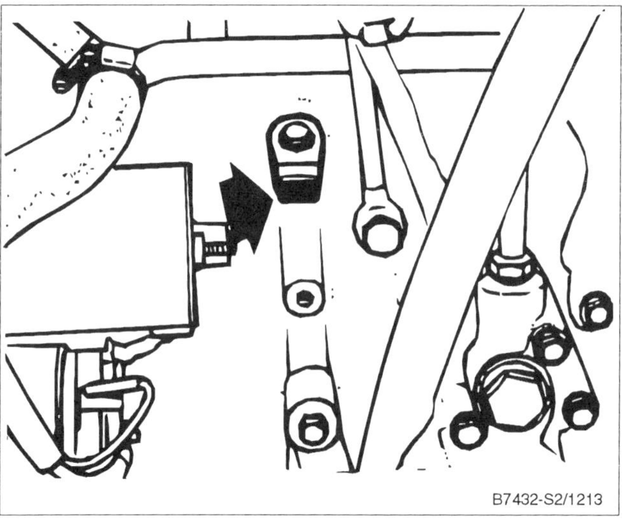

Fig. 30. Knock sensor connector removed from sensor (arrow).

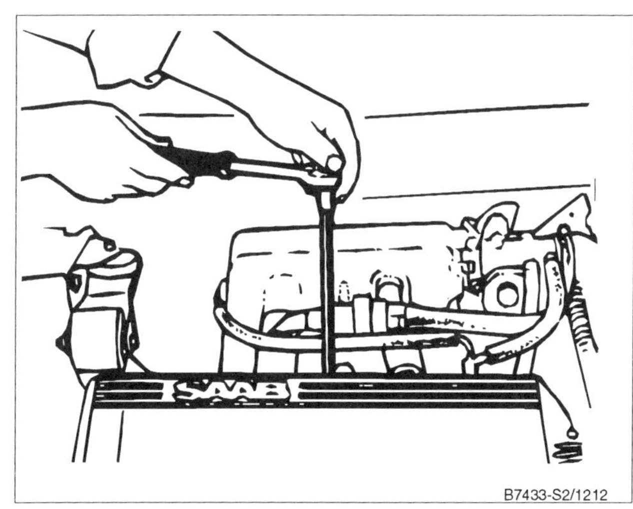

Fig. 31. Knock sensor being removed.

3. Thoroughly clean the knock sensor mounting surface on the engine. Clean the mounting bolt threads. Hold the sensor steady and install and torque the bolt. Reconnect the harness connector.

Tightening torque

- Knock sensor to engine block . . . . . 20 Nm (15 ft-lb)

IGNITION TIMING

On most models, ignition timing should be checked at regular service intervals as listed in **1 LUBRICATION AND MAINTENANCE.** Timing should also be checked any time the distributor position has been altered.

NOTE
On 1989 and later models with a crankshaft-mounted sensor, checking and adjusting ignition timing at regular intervals is no longer necessary.

To check and adjust ignition timing

WARNING
The ignition systems installed on the cars covered by this manual are high-energy systems operating in a dangerous voltage range which could prove to be fatal if exposed terminals or live parts are contacted. Use extreme caution when working on a vehicle with the ignition on or the engine running.

---

1. Connect a timing light and a tachometer according to the manufacturer's instructions. Start the engine and allow it to reach operating temperature.

2. If applicable, disconnect the vacuum advance hose from the throttle housing. Check that the idle speed is as specified. See Fig. 32. If idle speed is incorrect, adjust it as described in **240 Fuel Injection.**

3. While pointing the timing light at the flywheel, check that the timing marks are correctly aligned. See Fig. 33. If the marks are not aligned, loosen the distributor clamp-down bolt and slowly rotate the distributor until the marks are aligned. Tighten the bolt.

Ignition Timing
- Turbo models (vacuum hose disconnected) . . . . 16°BTDC @ 850 rpm
- Non-turbo models . . . . 14°BTDC @ 850 rpm

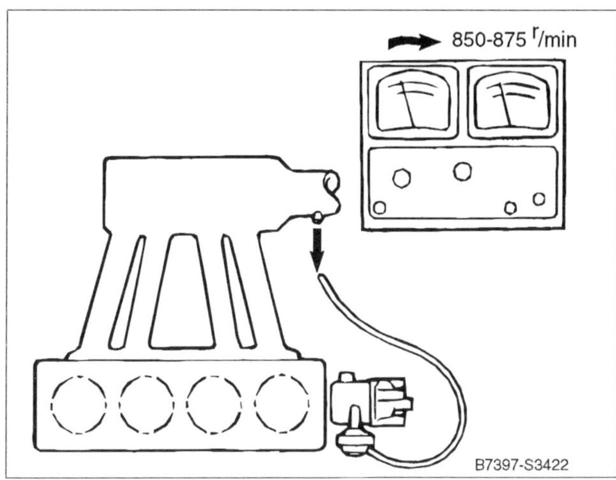

Fig. 32. When checking timing, idle speed must correct. Where applicable, disconnect the vacuum hose (arrow).

Fig. 33. Ignition timing marks on flywheel and clutch cover (arrows). Clutch cover is in front of engine.

Tightening torque
- Ignition distributor hold-down bolt . . . 15 Nm (11ft-lb)

---

4. Turn the engine off. Disconnect the test equipment. Reconnect the vacuum hose, if applicable.

351 Lighting

GENERAL

This repair group covers procedures for replacing exterior and interior bulbs.

NOTE

Also see **853 Dashboard and Consoles** for additional cluster bulb replacement information.

Lighting faults can usually be traced by observing whether one light is out, or other lights on the same circuit are out. If only one bulb is out, chances are the bulb has failed. If more than one bulb is out, there is probably an electrical fault in the circuit, such as a poor ground connection. Always begin by checking fuses and connectors. For wiring diagrams and additional lighting information, see **371 Wiring Diagrams, Fuses and Relays.**

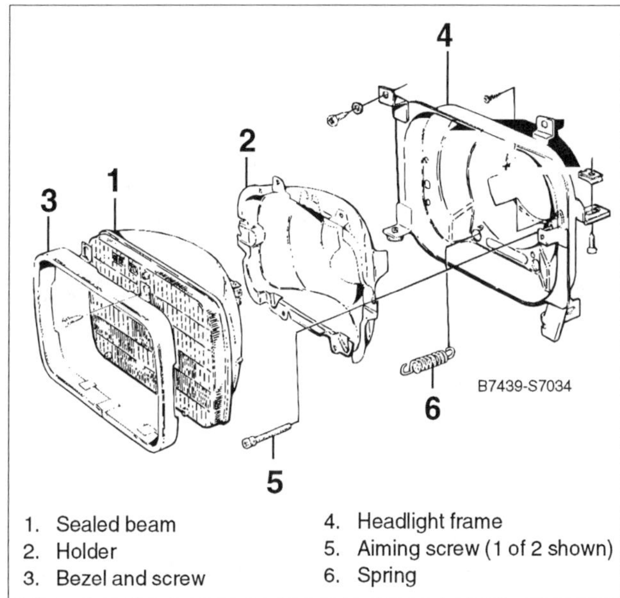

Fig. 1. Sealed beam headlight on 1985 and 1986 models.

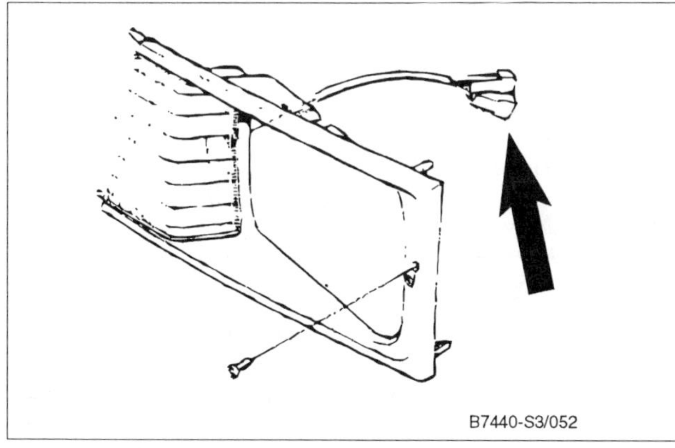

Fig. 2. Headlight trim with integrate park light. Disconnect connector for inner park light (arrow).

To replace sealed beam headlight (1985 and 1986 models)

1. Remove the headlight trim mounting screws. Remove the trim and disconnect the wiring harness for the park light. See Fig. 2.

CAUTION

Do not disturb the headlight aiming screws when changing the bulb. If the headlight aim is changed, special adjusting equipment will be required to correctly re-aim the headlights.

---

2. Remove the four sheet metal screws holding the sealed beam bezel to the headlight frame.

3. Lift out the headlight and disconnect the harness connector.

Installation is the reverse of removal. Be sure to install the new sealed beam so that the glass tabs on the beam correctly engage the cutouts of the headlight holder.

To replace headlight bulb (1987 and later models)

1. Open the hood and remove the bulb holder from behind by turning the locking ring counterclockwise. See Fig. 3 Remove the bulb.

CAUTION

Do not disturb the headlight aiming screws when changing the bulb. If the headlight aim is changed, special adjusting equipment will be required to correctly re-aim the headlights.

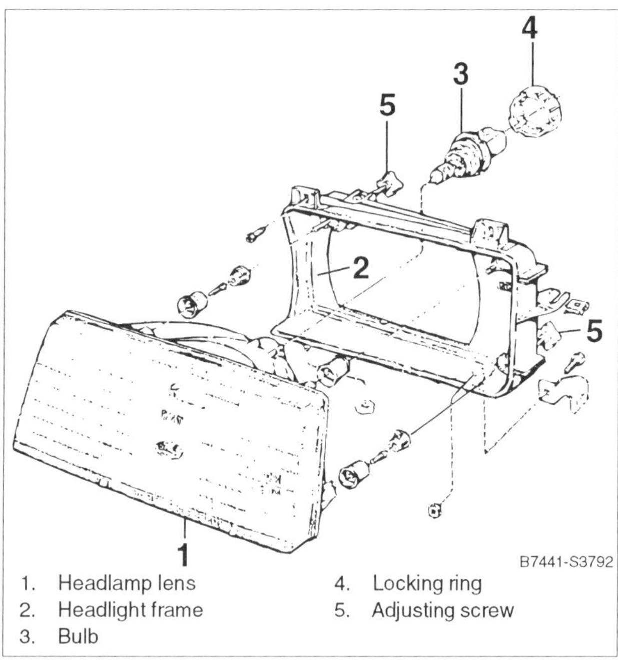

Fig. 3. Headlight with replaceable bulb on 1987 and later models.

2. Disconnect the harness connector from the bulb.

CAUTION

Do not touch the bulb glass with your hands. If the bulb was handled, use a clean rag to clean it. Finger prints can cause hot spots on the bulb, shortening its life.

---

3. Connect the harness connector to the new bulb and install it into its holder. See Fig. 4. Make sure the bulb is squarely seated. Install and tighten the locking ring.

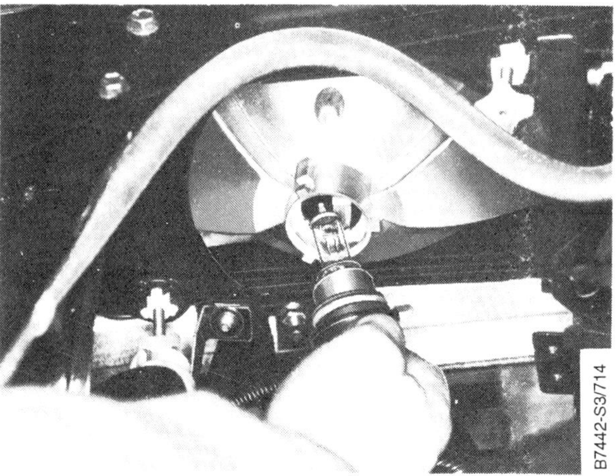

Fig. 4. Headlight bulb being installed on 1987 and later models

To replace headlight lens assembly (1987 and later models)

1. Open the hood and remove the side light assembly mounting screws. See Fig. 5. Pull the front edge of the light assembly out slightly, disconnect the harness connector and remove the assembly.

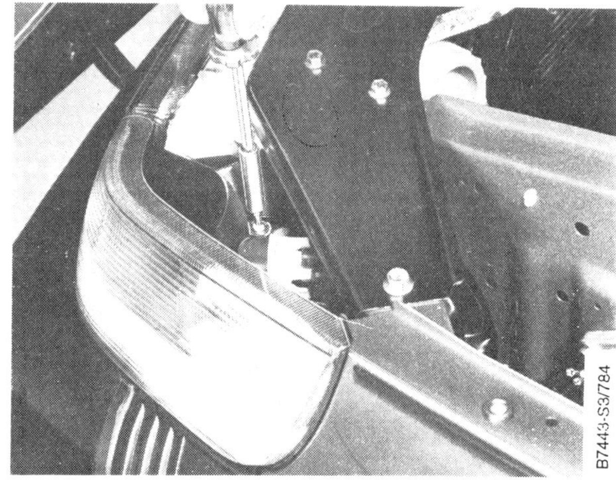

Fig. 5. Front side light assembly mounting screw being removed.

2. Remove the three headlight assembly mounting screws and the remove the assembly. Two screws are removed from the front. See Fig. 6. One screw is removed from the rear, lower corner.

3. Carefully pry the headlight lens assembly out of the headlight frame. See Fig. 7.

4. Installation is the reverse of removal. Be sure to have the headlight aim checked after replacing the lens assembly.

Fig. 6. Headlight mounting screw being removed. One mounting screw is removed from rear of assembly.

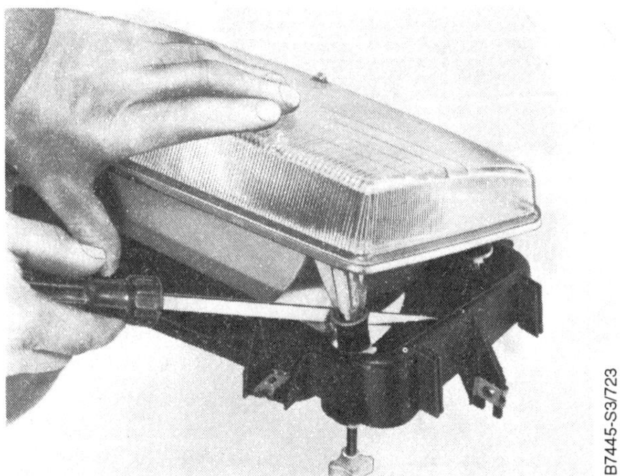

Fig. 7. Headlight lens assembly being removed from headlight holder.

Replacing front park, direction indicator, stop, side marker and side reversing light bulbs

On all 1985 and 1986 models, the bulbs in the front corner cluster are accessed after removing the lens from the front of the cluster. See Fig. 8. On 1987 and later models, the bayonet-mounted bulbs are removed from the rear of the cluster. See Fig. 9.

To replace the parking light bulb in the headlight trim (inner side) first remove the trim frame as shown above in Fig. 2. Then remove the bulb holder from the rear of the light. Replace the bulb, reinstall the bulb holder and the headlight trim.

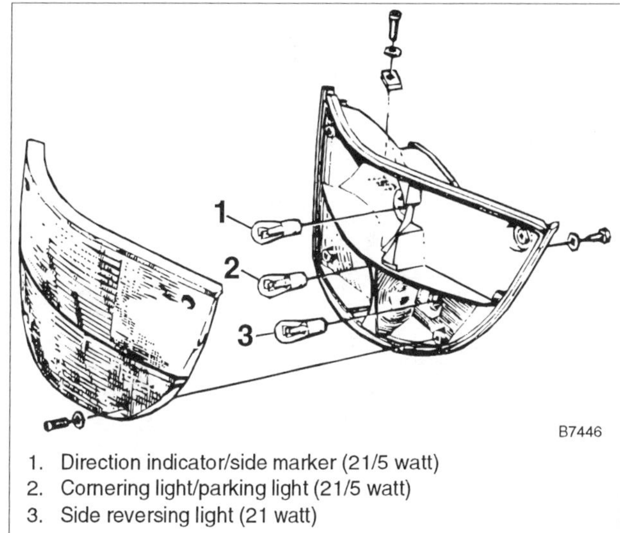

1. Direction indicator/side marker (21/5 watt)
2. Cornering light/parking light (21/5 watt)
3. Side reversing light (21 watt)

Fig. 8. Front lamp cluster on 1985 and 1986 models.

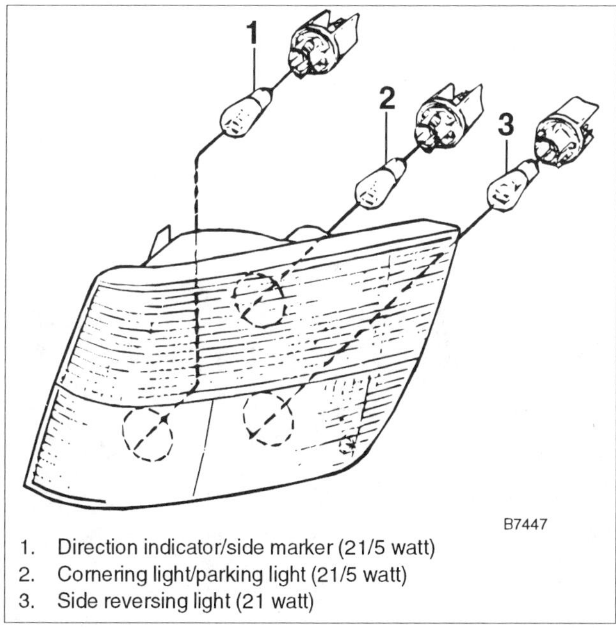

1. Direction indicator/side marker (21/5 watt)
2. Cornering light/parking light (21/5 watt)
3. Side reversing light (21 watt)

Fig. 9. Front lamp cluster on 1987 and later models.

To replace the fender-mounted direction indicator bulbs (1986 and later models), slide the light assembly toward the rear of the car while carefully prying it out. See Fig. 10. Replace the bulb and reinstall the light.

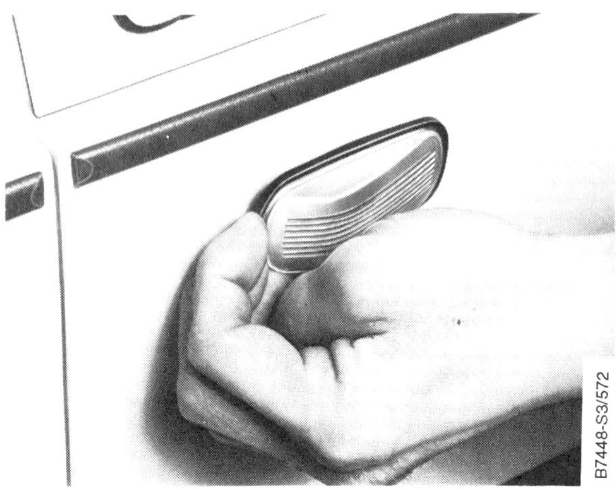

Fig. 10. Fender-mounted direction indicator lens being removed.

Replacing rear park, direction indicator, stop, reversing light, and license plate illumination bulbs

On all 3-door hatchback models, the bulbs in the rear light cluster are accessed after removing the lens from the front of the cluster. See Fig. 11. On all sedan models, the bulbs are accessed through the luggage compartment. Remove the bulb holder by depressing the plastic locking tab and swinging the assembly out. See Fig. 12.

1. Direction indicator (21 watt)
2. Backup light (21 watt)
3. Parking light/brake light (5/21 watt)
4. Brake light (21 watt)
5. Parking light (5 watt)

Fig. 11. Rear light cluster on hatchback models.

To replace the center (3rd) brake light bulb, remove the brake light cover by squeezing the two ribbed markings on the cover while sliding the cover off. Replace the bulb and reinstall the cover. To access the center brake light bulbs on convertible models, remove the two screws and remove the lens. See Fig. 13.

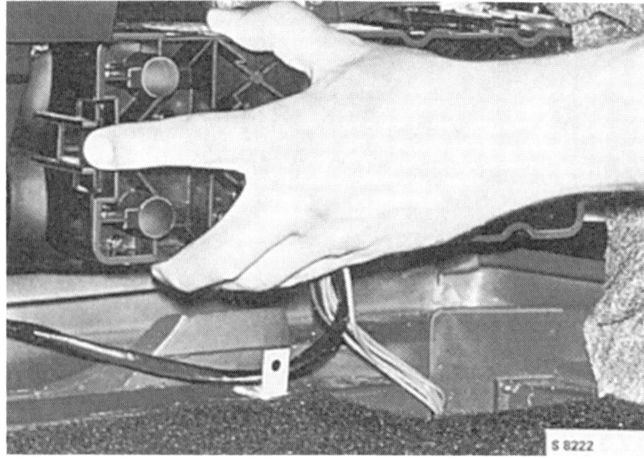

Fig. 12. Rear light cluster on sedan models being removed.

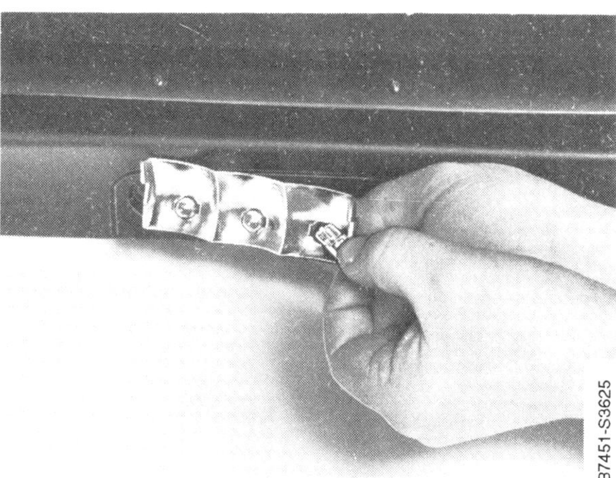

Fig. 13. Center brake light bulb being removed on convertible model.

The license plate illumination bulbs can be replaced after removing the light assembly see Fig. 14.

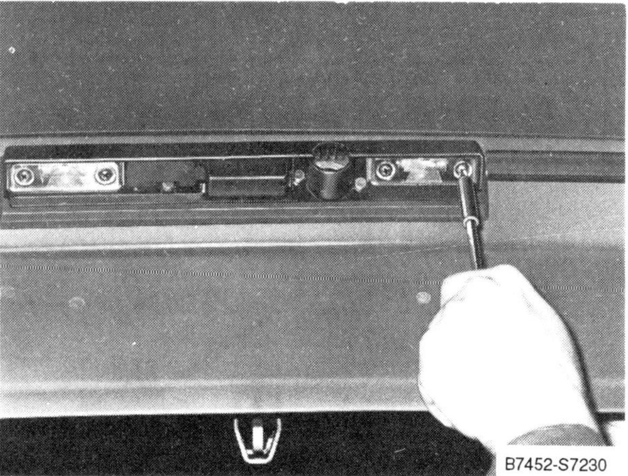

Fig. 14. License plate light assembly being removed.

Replacing Interior Bulbs

The interior dome lights and the glovebox light can be changed by carefully prying away the clear plastic cover. Some models have a time delay feature controlled by the time-delay relay. This relay is located under the back seat on the left side.

The ignition key light can be changed by peeling away the shift lever boot on cars with manual transmission or removing the plastic trim piece around the shift lever on cars with automatic. Then remove the front console and rear console screws (rear screws are behind rear passenger ashtray). Carefully lift up the console and pull the bulb from its holder.

NOTE

Remove the ignition key before attempting to remove the console.

All instrument cluster lamps, except the fuel level warning lamp, can be replaced without removing the cluster. These bulbs can be accessed after removing the left-front speaker grille. See Fig. 15.

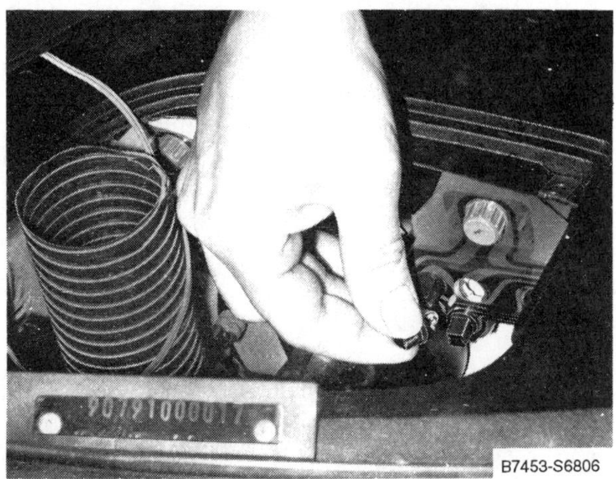

Fig. 15. Instrument cluster illumination bulbs being replaced through left speaker grille access hole.

On most 1985 dash-mounted switches, the illumination bulbs can be replaced once the switch is carefully pried out of the dashboard. On 1986 and later models, the switch illumination is integral with the switch and the bulbs cannot be separately replaced.

363 Wipers and Washers

WINDSHIELD WIPERS AND WASHERS

The windshield wiper assembly is located in the engine compartment on the firewall. The wiper motor and the linkage assembly are removed as a complete assembly. See Fig. 1. Windshield wiper wiring diagrams can be found **371 Wiring Diagrams, Fuses and Relays**.

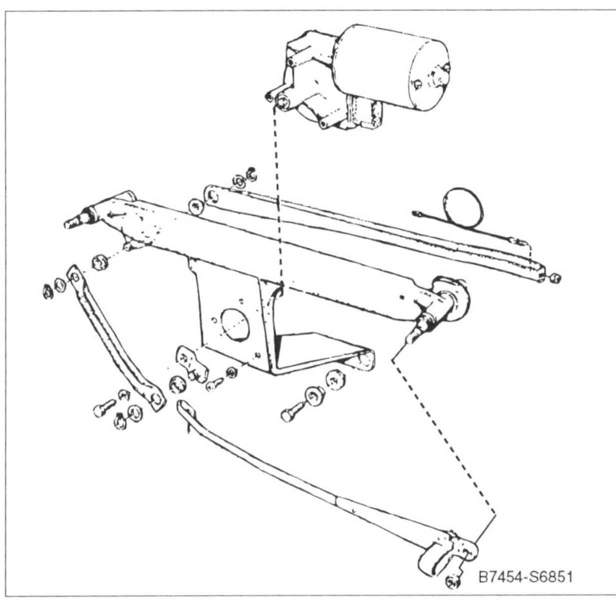

Fig. 1. Exploded view of windshield wiper assembly.

The windshield washer pump is located under the washer fluid reservoir next to the battery. To remove the washer pump, remove the reservoir bottle hold-down bracket and lift up while disconnecting the fluid hose and the pump wiring. Pull the washer pump out of the bottle. Replace the O-ring when installing a new pump.

CAUTION

Do not operate the pump unless there is fluid in the bottle. Damage to the pump may result.

To remove the windshield wiper assembly

1. Disconnect the negative (–) battery cable.

2. Lift the wiper arms off the glass. Pry up the retaining nut cover and remove the retaining nut. See Fig. 2.

NOTE

Before removing the wiper arms, note the parked position of the arms on the glass.

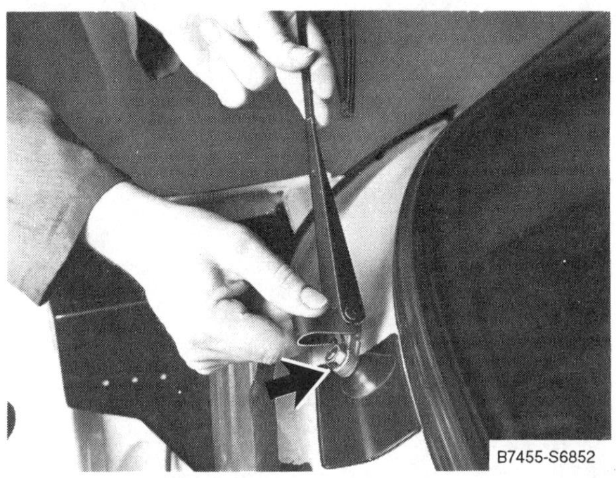

Fig. 2. Wiper arm cover being lifted to expose arm mounting nut (arrow).

3. Remove the rubber grommets covering the wiper shafts.

4. Remove the four bolts holding the wiper assembly in position. Disconnect the wiring and remove the assembly from the car. See Fig. 3.

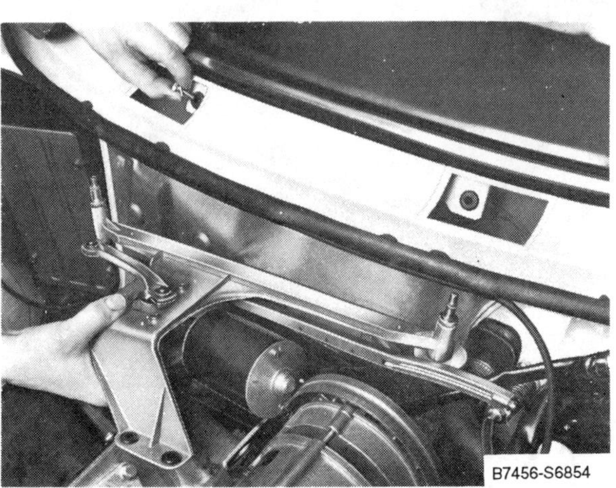

Fig. 3. Wiper assembly being removed.

Installation is the reverse of removal. To make sure the wiper motor is stopped in the park position, operate the motor through several cycles before reattaching the wiper arms.

Headlight Wipers and Washers (1991 and Later Models)

All 1991 and later models covered by this manual are equipped with headlight wipers. The headlight wipers and washer pump will operate if the stalk switch is pulled toward the steering wheel. After five cycles, the wipers will park.

To remove headlight wiper motor

1. Disconnect the negative (–) battery cable.

2. Lift the wiper arm off the headlight. Pry up the retaining nut cover and remove the retaining nut. See Fig. 4.

NOTE

Before removing the wiper arms, note the parked position of the arms on the headlight.

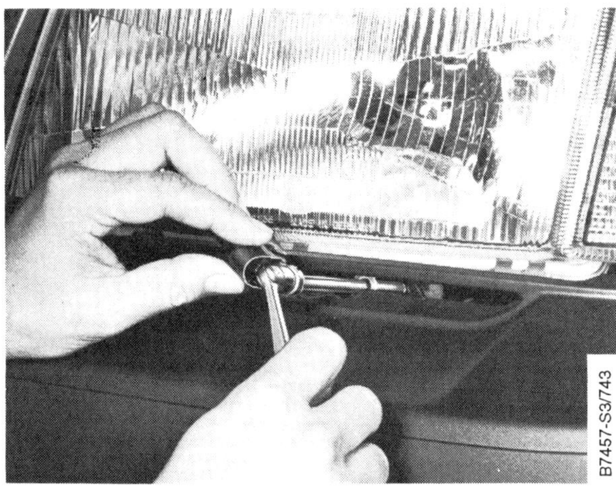

Fig. 4. Headlight wiper arm nut being removed.

3. Remove the headlight assembly as described in **351 Lighting**. Remove the bolts holding the wiper motor assembly to the body. See Fig. 5.

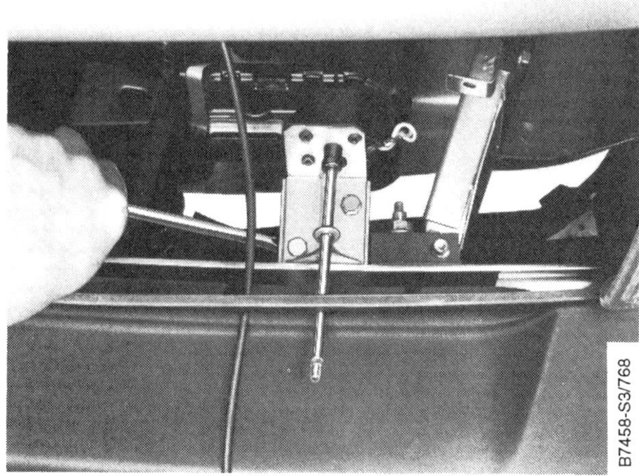

Fig. 5. Headlight wiper motor being removed.

Installation is the reverse of removal. To make sure the wiper motor is stopped in the park position, operate the motor through several cycles before reattaching the wiper arms.

364 Electric Controls and Switches

GENERAL

This repair group covers mainly the switches and controls used throughout the car's interior. Some engine control switches and instruments are also covered here. For switch testing, use the wiring diagram schematics found under **371 Wiring Diagrams, Fuses and Relays.**

WARNING
1990 and later models are equipped with an airbag or SRS system. The airbag is a explosive device. Do not attempt to remove the steering wheel or service the wiring in the steering column assembly. You could accidentally ignite the airbag, causing serious personal injury. See an authorized Saab dealer for any repairs to the SRS system or to disarm the system prior to removing the steering wheel.

SWITCHES AND CONTROLS

Replacing switches is straightforward and easy to do. Some switches may need to be adjusted for proper operation after they are installed. Usually the switches needing adjustment have a threaded body or have mounting screw adjusting holes. Some of the fasteners are Torx-type bolts and screws. Plan to have Torx drivers on hand before starting the job. If you are replacing a switch with many wires, it helps to draw a picture of the terminals and wire colors. This will prevent hooking up the wires improperly during installation. See **371 Wiring Diagrams, Fuses and Relays** for more information on identifying components and their locations.

WARNING
Always check the function of the circuit after replacing a switch to verify proper and safe operation.

CAUTION
Always disconnect the negative (–) battery cable before replacing any switches.

Instrument Panel Switches

Most of the switches located in the instrument panel can be replaced without removing the instrument panel. An exception to this is the air distribution switch, the heater control knob, and the extra dimmer switch (rheostat)—which all require removal of the instrument panel as described below.

Fig. 1 shows the headlight switch being removed . After removing the switch, disconnect the wires as shown. The panel switches can be carefully pried away from the panel. See Fig. 2.

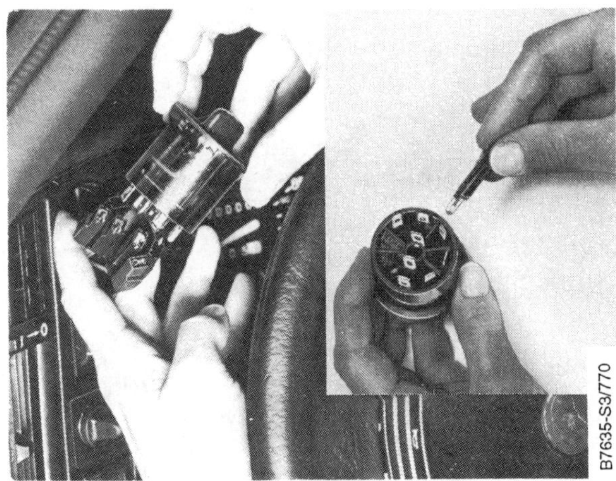

Fig. 1. Headlight switch being replaced. Inset shows bulb in back of switch being removed.

364

Fig. 2. A/C switch being removed. All square switches pull away from the instrument panel.

To remove instrument panel (1985-1989 models only)

1. Disconnect the negative (–) battery cable.

2. Remove the steering wheel as described in **641 Steering Column.**

3. Working from below the instrument panel, remove and label the four long mounting screws. See Fig. 3. and Fig. 4.

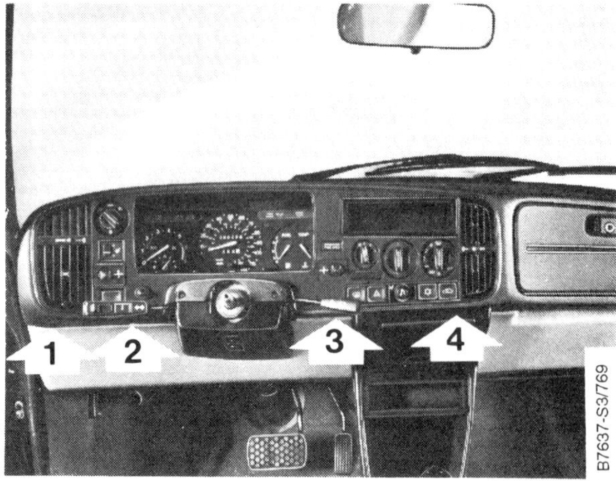

Fig. 3. Instrument panel mounting screw locations (arrows).

4. Carefully pull the panel out. Label any vacuum hoses or wires before removing them. Disconnect the control rod to the heater knob.

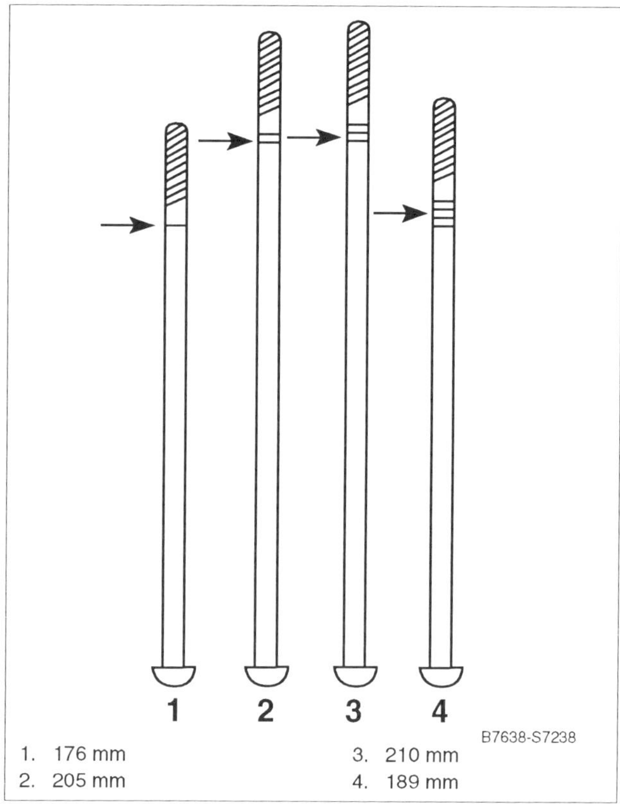

Fig. 4. Each instrument panel screw is a different length and marked accordingly.

NOTE

The extra rheostat for instrument panel lighting is removed after removing the knob and locking nut from the front of the panel. The air distribution switch and the heater control knob can be removed after removing the mounting screws from the rear of the panel. See Fig. 5.

Fig. 5. Air distribution switch mounting screw being removed. Switch is held in place with two screws (arrows). Heater control knob removal is similar.

Installation is the reverse of removal. Be sure the panel mounting screws are installed in their correct positions. If the screws are interchanged, the padded dashboard could be damaged.

Steering Column Stalk Switches and Horn Switch (1985-1989 models)

The direction indicator and windshield washer switches are mounted to the steering column. To replace a switch, remove the lower steering column trim. Then remove the screws holding the switch and disconnect the electrical connector. See Fig. 6.

WARNING
1990 and later models are equipped with an airbag or SRS system. The airbag is an explosive device. Do not attempt to remove the steering wheel or service the wiring in the steering column assembly. You could accidentally ignite the airbag, causing serious personal injury. See an authorized Saab dealer for any repairs to the SRS system or to disarm the system prior to removing the steering wheel, stalk switches, or steering column wiring.

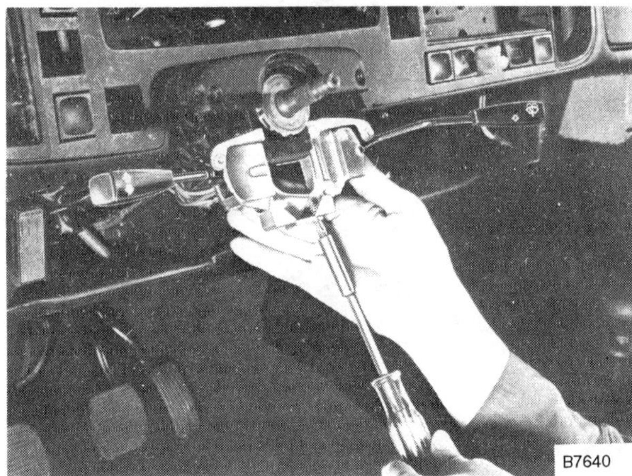

Fig. 6. Steering column stalk switches being removed.

To remove the horn switches, carefully pry them away from the steering wheel. See Fig. 7.

Interior Switches

On 1985 through 1990 models, the power window switches, sunroof switch, and interior light switch can all be changed by carefully prying the assembly from the center console. See Fig. 8.

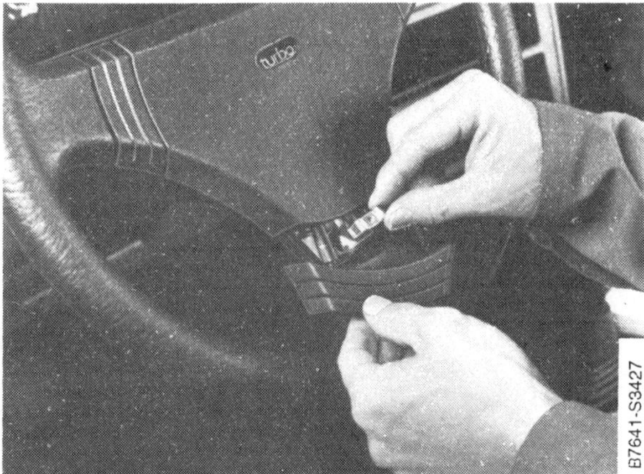

Fig. 7. Horn button switch being removed. Turbo model shown, other models are similar.

Fig. 8. Power window switch assembly in center console being pried up with a screwdriver.

NOTE
- On 1985 through 1990 models, the individual switches in the switch assembly can be separately replaced.
- On 1991 and later models, the entire power window/sunroof switch assembly must be replaced if a single switch is faulty. The bulb for the switch assembly can be replaced by turning the bulb holder 90° and removing the bulb. See Fig. 9.

The brake light switch is located on the upper part of the brake pedal assembly. See Fig. 10. Adjust the switch so the brake lights come on as soon as the pedal is depressed and go out when the pedal is in the rest position. For the most accurate adjustment, use the specification shown below.

Brake light switch adjustment
- brake lights come on when brake pedal is depressed. . . . . 0.4 in. (10 mm)

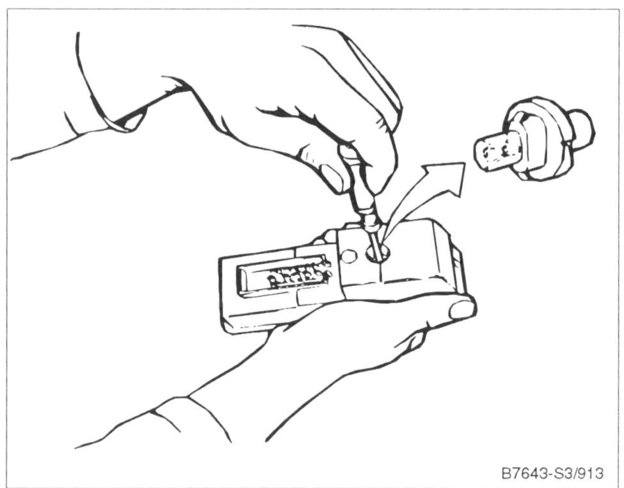

Fig. 9. Power window switch light bulb being replaced.

Fig. 10. Brake light switch (arrow) on brake pedal cluster. Switch should always be adjusted after installation.

NOTE
The cruise control brake switch and clutch switch are covered in **368 Cruise Control.**

The back-up light switch, used only on cars with manual transmission, screws into the left side of gear shift housing. See Fig. 11. To access the switch, remove the center console as described in **432 Manual Transmission Controls.**

On models with automatic transmission, the back-up light switch is part of the neutral/safety (start inhibit) switch. To adjust this switch, move the lever to N (neutral) then loosen the screws on the side and rotate the switch until the mark on the switch aligns with the shift lever. See Fig. 12.

The handbrake warning lamp switch is located between the seats under the handbrake bracket. Remove the center console as described in **432 Manual Transmission Controls** then remove the switch. See Fig. 13.

Fig. 11. Back-up light switch (arrow) on gear shift housing (manual transmission). Gear shift lever shown at top.

Fig. 12. Back-up light switch on models with automatic transmission being adjusted. With shift lever in **N**, align mark on switch with lever (arrows).

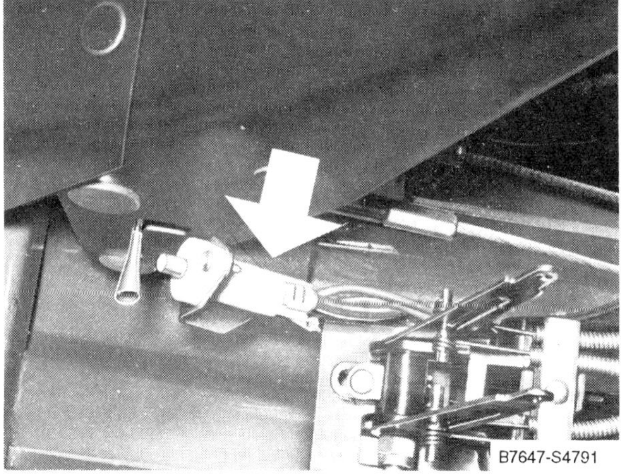

Fig. 13. Handbrake warning lamp switch (arrow) can be removed after removing center console.

The mercury switch on convertible models is used to prevent the rear window defogger from turning on when the roof is in the down position. The switch can be removed after removing the screws. See Fig. 14. The switch is located at the top of the frame member for the convertible top.

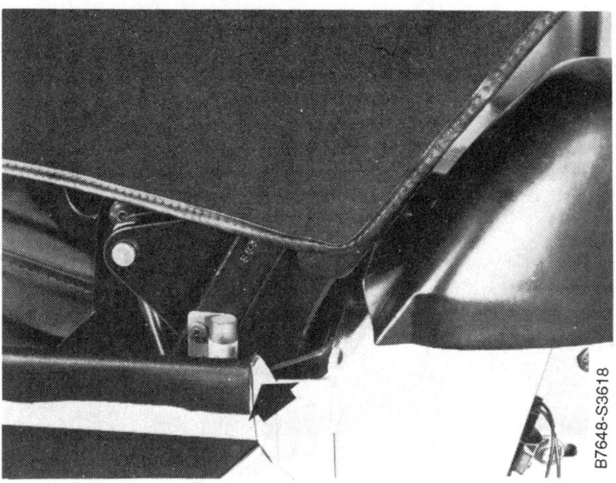

14. Mercury switch (arrow) interrupts power to heated rear window when convertible top is down.

Engine Compartment Switches

Most of the switches located in the engine compartment are used to monitor engine conditions and are covered in the various repair groups under **2 ENGINE.**

The temperature switch for the shift-up indicator prevents the shift-up system from operating until the engine reaches a certain temperature. The switch screws into the intake manifold. See Fig. 15.

Fig. 15. Temperature switch (arrow) for shift-up indicator on intake manifold. Saab 8-valve engine shown.

The fifth-gear lockout switch for shift-up indicator is shown in Fig. 16.

Fig. 16. 5th gear lockout switch (arrow) for shift-up indicator. Switch screws into right front transmission side cover, near battery.

The throttle switch for the shift-up indicator is used on cars with LH 2.2 Fuel Injection. On these models, a throttle dashpot holds the throttle open for a short period of time. The throttle switch is used to tell the shift-up relay that the accelerator pedal is released, even though the engine speed is still high. This switch is mounted on the throttle housing. See Fig. 17. To remove the switch, simply remove the screws.

Fig. 17. Throttle switch (arrow) for shift-up indicator on throttle housing.

The brake fluid warning lamp switch is part of the fluid reservoir cap. A float switch turns on the lamp when the fluid is low. To replace the switch, remove the connector and unscrew the cap. See Fig. 18.

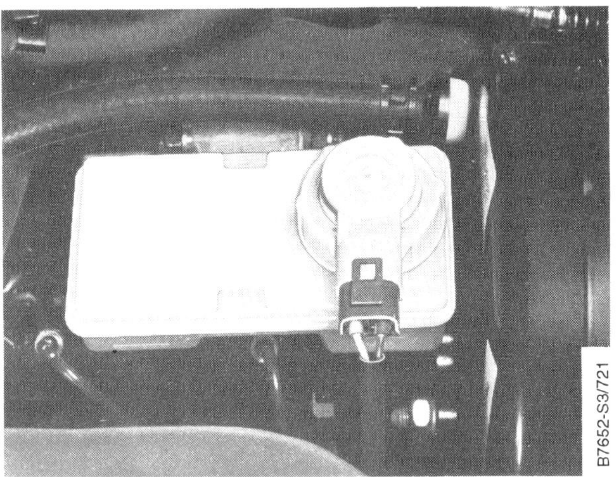

Fig. 18. Location of brake fluid level warning lamp switch on master cylinder.

Extra Gauges

Extra gauges, available from Saab, can be located in the center console storage area. See Fig. 19. When installing new gauges, always follow the instructions that come with the instrument. The wiring shown in Fig. 20, Fig. 21, Fig. 22, and Fig. 23 can be used as a guide in installing the gauges. All of the gauges require a 52 mm diameter space in the console.

The outside temperature gauge can be adjusted as shown in Fig. 24. To calibrate the gauge, use a good quality temperature probe such as the Fluke® 80 multimeter.

NOTE

The calibration of the outside temperature gauge should be done over a period of 20 minutes to prevent misleading temperature readings.

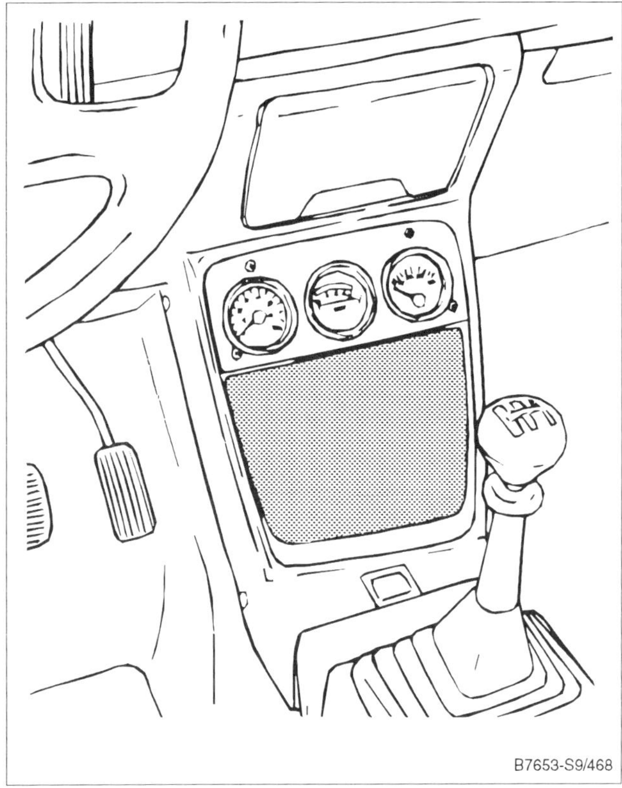

Fig. 19. Extra gauges in center console.

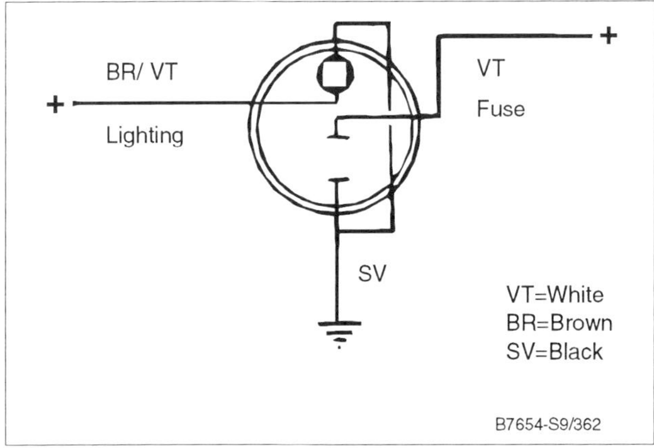

Fig. 20. Wiring diagram for extra voltmeter.

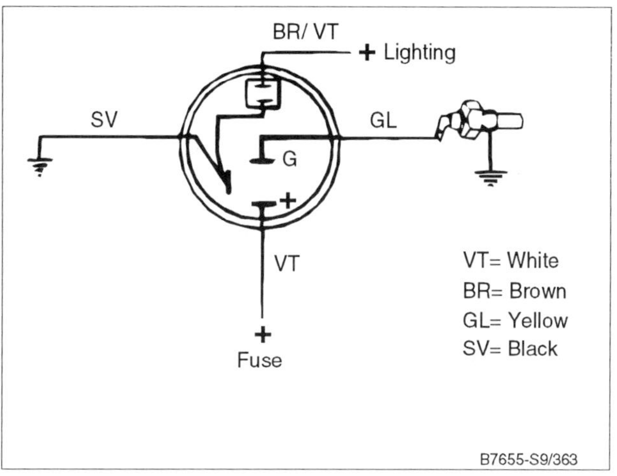

Fig. 21. Wiring diagram for extra oil temperature gauge.

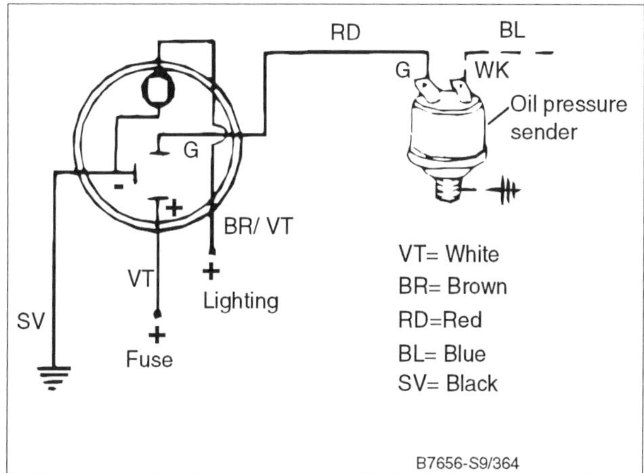

Fig. 22. Wiring diagram for extra oil pressure gauge.

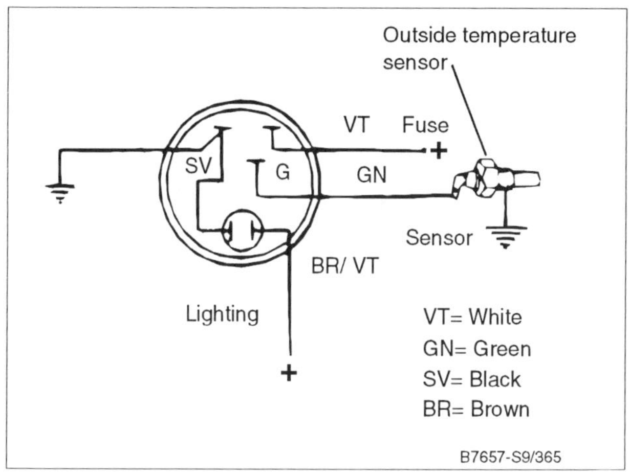

Fig. 23. Wiring diagram for extra outside temperature gauge.

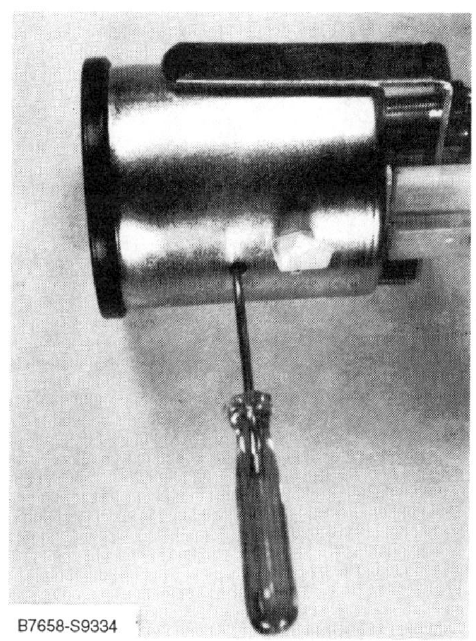

Fig. 24. Outside temperature gauge being calibrated.

368 Cruise Control

TABLES

GENERAL

WARNING
1990 and later models are equipped with an airbag or SRS system. The airbag is a explosive device. Do not attempt to remove the steering wheel or service the wiring in the steering column assembly. You could accidentally ignite the airbag, causing serious personal injury. See an authorized Saab dealer for any repairs to the SRS system or to disarm the system prior to removing the steering wheel.

The cruise control system enables the driver to select a cruising speed that will be maintained without the use of the accelerator pedal. The system can be turned on and off at the steering column stalk switch. The system will automatically disengage when either the clutch pedal or the brake pedal is depressed. Fig. 1 shows the components of the cruise control system.

When the Set button is depressed and the road speed is above 23 mph, the speed transmitter sends an electronic road-speed signal to the control unit. The control unit then operates the vacuum pump to increase or reduce vacuum to the vacuum regulator, changing the position of the accelerator pedal and throttle plate.

When the system is in operation, temporary acceleration can be accomplished by depressing the accelerator pedal. As soon as the pressure on the pedal is released, the car will resume the preselected cruising speed.

When the brake pedal or the clutch pedal is depressed, the pedal switch releases vacuum in systems, allowing the throttle plate to return to the idle position. The vacuum pump is also switched off.

Provided the road speed has not fallen below 23 mph, the previously selected road speed can be resumed using the Resume function at the control switch. If the road speed has gone below 23 mph, if the stalk switch is moved to the off position, or if the ignition is turned off, this memory function is canceled.

On turbo models, engaging the cruise control system causes the vacuum switch to interrupt power to the APC solenoid. This automatically drops the turbocharger boost pressure to a safe preset value. On 1989 and later models, an instrument cluster lamp is fitted that lights up when the cruise control is engaged.

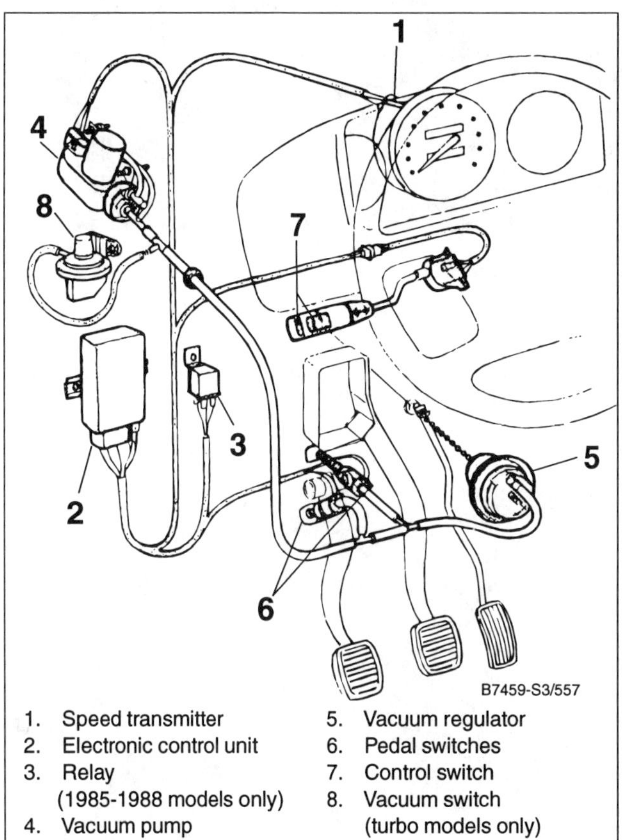

Fig. 1. Schematic view of cruise control system.

NOTE
Replacement of the cruise control indicator lamp on 1989 and later models is covered in **351 Lighting.**

COMPONENT LOCATIONS

The cruise control switch is located on the steering column. For information on removing the switch, see **364 Electric Controls and Switches.**

The speed transmitter is fitted behind the speedometer. The transmitter can be accessed through left speaker grille access hole. See Fig. 2.

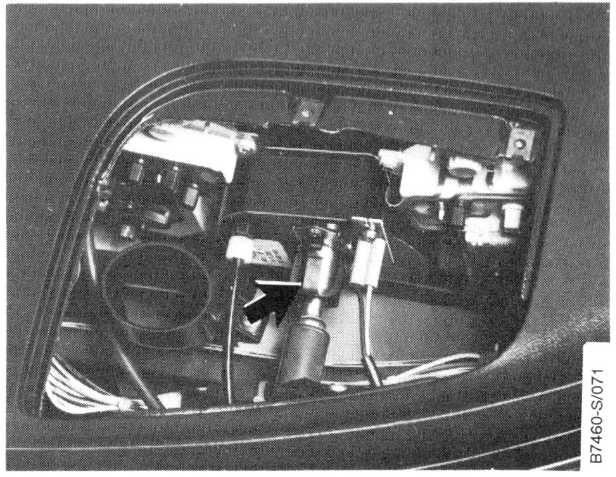

Fig. 2. Speed transmitter (arrow) on rear of speedometer. Access transmitter through left speaker grille.

The electronic control unit and the cruise control relay (where applicable) are located under the left-hand side of the dashboard. See Fig. 3.

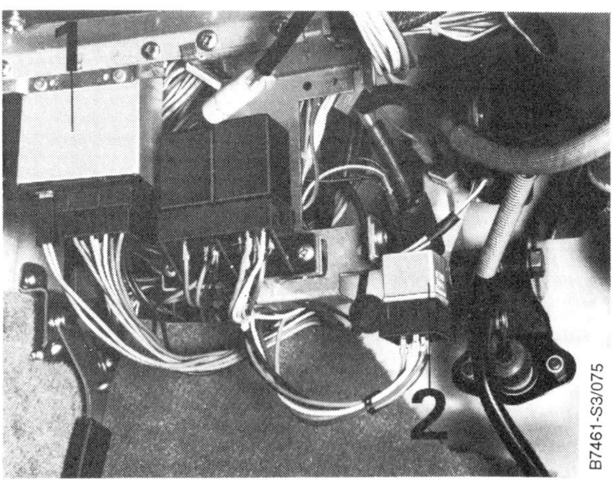

Fig. 3. Cruise control electronic control unit (**1**) and relay (**2**) as viewed from underneath left-hand side of dashboard (lower trim panel removed).

The vacuum regulator is mounted on a bracket in the heater housing area, under the center of the dashboard. The brake switch and the clutch switch (manual transmission only) are mounted above the pedals. See Fig. 4.

The vacuum pump is mounted in the engine compartment, forward of the left-hand wheel housing. On turbo models, the vacuum switch is mounted in the engine compartment on the left front fender.

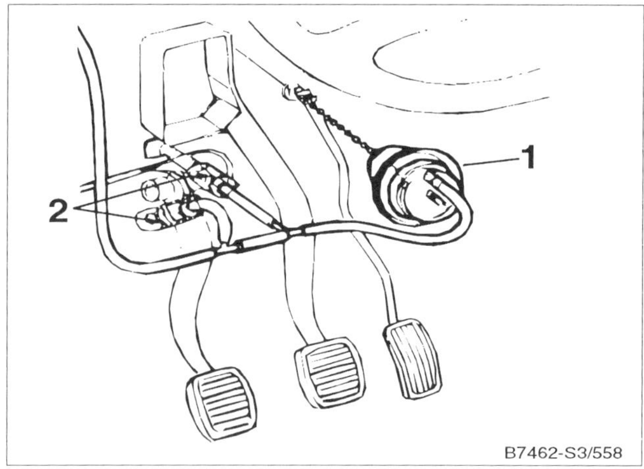

Fig. 4. Cruise control vacuum regulator (**1**) and pedal switches (**2**). Remove lower trim panel to reach components.

ELECTRICAL TESTS AND FAULT TRACING

There are some basic fault tracing and electrical tests that can be made to test the cruise control components. Be sure to check the fuses. If the brake light bulbs are burned out, the system will not engage. Complete cruise control wiring diagrams are shown in **371 Wiring Diagrams, Fuses and Relays.**

Checking Pedal Switches

If the system is not working correctly, the first thing to check is the vacuum lines at the pedal switches. Remove the lower trim and inspect the hoses for cracks or deterioration. If no faults are found, disconnect the vacuum hose at the switch and connect in its place a length of rubber hose. While blowing through the hose with the pedal in the rest position, air should not pass through the switch. When the pedal is depressed, air should pass through the switch.

NOTE

The brake pedal switch is not the same switch used for the brake lights. On 1989 and later models, the brake light switch is also used in the cruise control circuit. Be sure to check that the brake lights are operating correctly. If necessary, adjust the brake light switch as described in **364 Electric Controls and Switches.**

To check the electrical part of the switch, disconnect the wires from the switch and connect an ohmmeter across the switch terminals. With pedal in the rest position, there should be continuity. There should be no continuity when the pedal is depressed.

If any faults are found, check that the switch is correctly adjusted as shown in Fig. 5. If no faults are found, the switch is faulty and should be replaced.

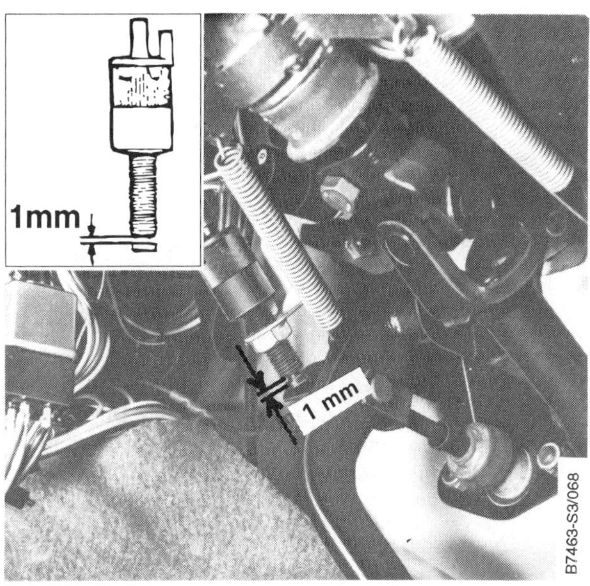

Fig. 5. Pedal switch adjustment. Adjust switch so that plunger is exposed 1 mm (0.04 in.) as shown in inset

Checking Vacuum Pump and Regulator

Remove the Harness connector from the vacuum pump. Connect a 12-volt source to terminal 3 (+) of the pump connector. Connect terminals 1 and 2 to ground. See Fig. 6. The vacuum pump should run and draw the vacuum regulator in. Check that the accelerator throttle plate is open.

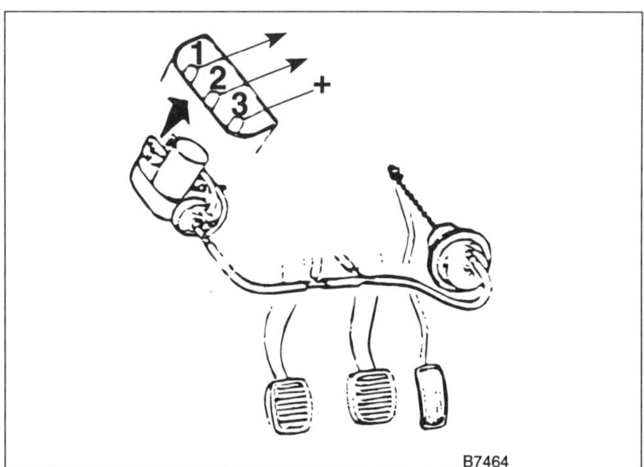

Fig. 6. Vacuum pump and terminal designation.

If the pump does not run, it is faulty and should be replaced. If the pump runs, but the accelerator does not pull in and open the throttle, check that the ball chain on the regulator is connected to the accelerator linkage. Check for vacuum to the regulator with the pump running. If the pump operates as specified and the regulator does not respond correctly, the regulator is faulty and should be replaced.

Remove the ground wire from terminal 2 only. The pump should stop and the accelerator should remain in the open position. If the accelerator slowly returns the rest position, either the regulator is leaking or the pump is faulty. To check for a leaking regulator, connect to it a length of hose. Suck on the hose and then block off then end. If the regulator slowly returns to its rest position, it is leaking and should be replaced.

Remove the wire from terminal 1 and check that the regulator returns to its rest position. If any faults are found, the pump is faulty and should be replaced.

NOTE

When replacing the regulator, use care not to damage the rubber diaphragm during installation. Install the chain so that it is as tight as possible without tensioning the accelerator.

Checking Cruise Control Switch

WARNING

1990 and later models are equipped with an airbag or SRS system. The airbag is a explosive device. Do not attempt to remove the steering wheel or service the wiring in the steering column assembly. You could accidentally ignite the airbag, causing serious personal injury. See an authorized Saab dealer for any repairs to the SRS system or to disarm the system prior to removing the steering wheel.

Remove the lower steering column trim and disconnect the switch's 4-pin harness connector. Cut any wire ties if necessary. Fig. 7 shows the connector terminals. Test the switch by making the checks listed in **Table a.** If any faults are found, the switch is faulty and should be replaced as described in **364 Electric Controls and Switches.**

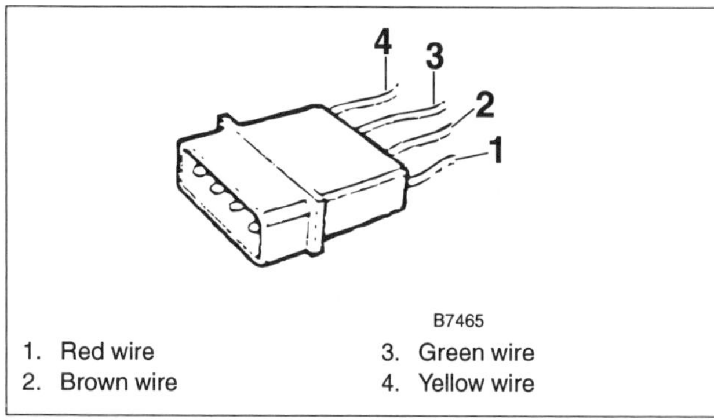

1. Red wire
2. Brown wire
3. Green wire
4. Yellow wire

Fig. 7. Cruise control switch harness connector used on 1985 through 1988 cars. Connector used on 1989 and later cars is different, although wire colors and their respective terminals numbers are the same.

Table a. Cruise Control Switch Continuity Test

Switch position	1985–1987 (up to chassis no. H2013308	1987 (from chassis no. H2013309) 1988	1989 and later
OFF	no continuity between any terminals	2 and 3	no continuity between any terminals
ON	1 and 2	1 and 2	1 and 2
RESUME	1 and 2, 2 and 4	1 and 2, 2 and 4	1 and 2, 2 and 4
SET SPEED ON	2 and 3	2 and 4 (continuity between 2 and 3 is removed when button is depressed)	2 and 3

NOTE

On 1985 through 1988 models, the original design cruise control switch is no longer available. The superceded switch kit requires replacing the harness connector to match the connector on the new switch, removing and discarding the cruise control relay and splicing the green wire of the relay connector (terminal 86) into the red/white wire in the relay connector
(terminal 30).

If no faults are found up to this point, use the wiring diagram to check for power and ground to the control unit. On 1989 and later models, check for power and ground to the speed transmitter on the rear of the speedometer. If no faults are found the problem may lie in the circuit wiring, the control unit, or the speed sensor. Use the appropriate wiring diagram to check for wiring faults.

371 Wiring Diagrams, Fuses and Relays

TABLES

MAIN FUSE AND RELAY LOCATIONS

With the exception of the battery charging system, all electrical power is routed from the ignition switch or the battery through the fuse/relay panel.

The main fuse/relay panel is located in the engine compartment, on the driver's side wheel housing. See Fig. 1. Always check the cover on the panel for exact descriptions of fuses and relays. Three main connectors run from the fuse/relay panel to the interior of the car. These connectors are accessible from inside the car, behind the instrument panel. Note that the connectors vary depending on model variant. See Fig. 2.

CAUTION
On cars equipped with SRS (airbag) the ignition switch must be in the lock position before replacing any fuses. If fuse no. 7 is removed with the ignition switch in the drive or accessory position, an SRS fault will register causing the SRS warning light to come on. Only an authorized Saab dealer can erase the fault and turn off the light.

Main Fuse Positions

Fuses prevent excessive current from damaging components and wiring. Fuses are color coded to indicate their different current capacities. **Table a** through **Table d** list the fuse positions in the main fuse/relay panel.

371

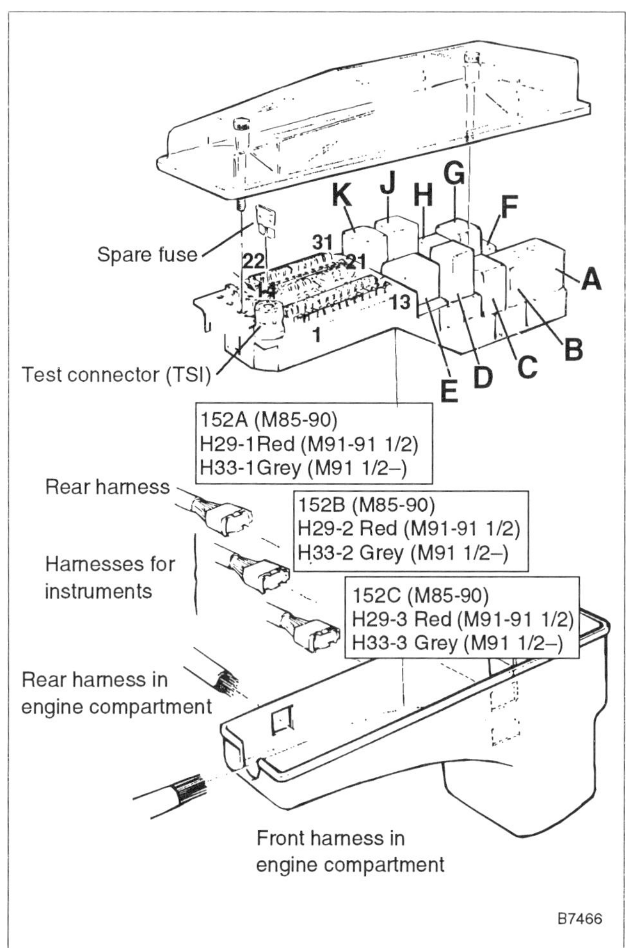

Fig. 1. Exploded view of main fuse/relay panel. Main connectors vary between years.

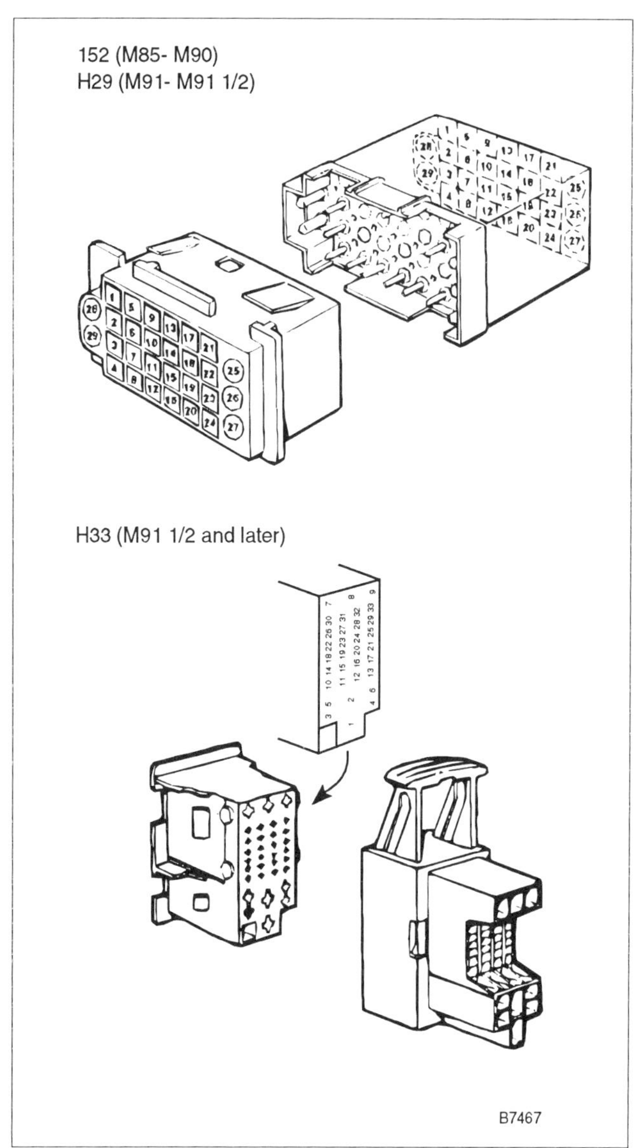

Fig. 2. Terminal identification for main bulkhead connectors at side of fuse/relay panel.

Fuse color and rating	
• Red	10 amp
• Blue	15 amp
• Yellow	20 amp
• Transparent	25 amp
• Green	30 amp

Table a. 1985 and 1986 Fuse positions—main fuse/relay panel

Position	Rating	Function
1	—	spare
2	—	spare
3	—	spare
4	10 A	shift-up indicator
5	15 A	brake fluid warning, wipers, seatbelt warning, exhaust warning (where applicable)
6	30 A	Air conditioner (A/C)
7	15 A	direction indicators , tachometer (1986 models), alternator warning light (1986 models)
8	10 A	power mirrors, cruise control
9	30 A	blower fan
10	10 A	APC system (turbo models)
11	30 A	power windows, sunroof
12	15 A	heated seats, time-delay for interior lights
13	20 A	backup lights, cigarette lighter
14	15 A	right high beam
15	15 A	left high beam, high beam warning
16	15 A	right low beam
17	15 A	left low beam
18	10 A	right front park and right rear lights, license plate light, glovebox and ashtray lights, instrument lights
19	10 A	left front park and left rear lights, burglar alarm (where applicable)
20	15 A	radio, front cornering lights
21	15 A	—
22	10 A	fuel system, ignition system, temperature gauge, handbrake warning light, tachometer (1985 models), alternator warning light (1985 models)
23	—	spare
24	10 A	central locking
25	30 A	radiator fan
26	25 A	horn
27	15 A	hazard warning lights
28	15 A	interior lighting, clock, radio, power antenna
29	20 A	heated rear window
30	20 A	fuel pump
31	15 A	brake lights

Table b. 1987 and 1988 Fuse positions—main fuse/relay panel

Position	Rating	Function
1	—	spare
2	30 A	rear windows (convertible) (1988 models)
3	30 A	rear windows (convertible) (1987 models)
4	10 A	shift-up indicator
5	15 A	brake fluid warning, wipers, seatbelt warning, exhaust warning
6	30 A	Air conditioner (A/C)
7	15 A	direction indicators, tachometer, alternator warning light
8	10 A	power mirrors, cruise control
9	30 A	blower fan
10	10 A	APC system, lighting for controls and glovebox
11	30 A	power windows, sunroof
12	20 A	heated seats, time-delay for interior lights
13	20 A	backup lights, cigarette lighter
14	15 A	right high beam
15	15 A	left high beam, high beam warning light
16	15 A	right low beam
17	15 A	left low beam
18	10 A	right front park and right rear light, license plate light
19	10 A	left front park and left rear light, burglar alarm (where applicable)
20	15 A	radio, front cornering lights
21	15 A	extra fog lights
22	10 A	fuel system, ignition system, temperature gauge, handbrake warning light
23	—	spare
24	10 A	central locking
25	30 A	radiator fan
26	25 A	horn
27	15 A	hazard warning lights
28	15 A	interior lighting, clock, radio, power antenna
29	20 A	heated rear window
30	20 A	fuel pump
31	15 A	brake lights

Table c. 1989 and 1990 Fuse positions—main fuse/relay panel

Position	Rating	Function
1	10 A	lambda sensor preheater
2	30 A	rear windows (convertible)
3	15 A	ignition system
4	20 A	daytime driving lights (Canada only)
5	15 A	wipers, seatbelt reminder lamp
6	30 A	Air conditioner (A/C)
7	15 A	direction indicators, tachometer, warning lights for alternator, check engine, oil pressure, and SRS airbag (1990 models)
8	10 A	power mirrors, cruise control
9	30 A	blower fan
10	10 A	APC system, ABS (where applicable)
11	30 A	power windows, sunroof
12	20 A	heated seats, time-delay for interior lights, convertible top actuation, seatbelt warning buzzer
13	20 A	backup lights, cigarette lighter, passive seatbelts (1989 models)
14	15 A	right high beam
15	15 A	left high beam, high beam warning light
16	15 A	right low beam
17	15 A	left low beam
18	10 A	right front park, sidemarker lights, right rear lights, license plate light
19	10 A	left front park, sidemarker lights, left rear lights, burglar alarm (ex. convertible models)
20	15 A	radio, cornering lights, burglar alarm (ex. 1989 sedan models)
21	15 A	extra fog lights
22	10 A	fuel system, temperature gauge, fuel level gauge, speed sensor (cruise control), warning lights for handbrake, ABS and footbrake
23	10 A	lighting for controls and glovebox
24	10 A	central locking, burglar alarm
25	30 A	radiator fan
26	25 A	horn
27	15 A	hazard warning lights
28	15 A	interior lighting, clock, radio, antenna, luggage compartment light
29	20 A	heated rear window
30	20 A	fuel pump
31	15 A	brake lights, ABS (1990 models)

Table d. 1991-1993 Fuse positions—main fuse/relay panel

Position	Rating	Function
1	10 A	lambda sensor preheater
2	30 A	rear windows (convertible)
3	15 A	ignition system, EGR modulating valve (California only)
4	20 A	daytime driving lights (Canada only)
5	15 A	wipers, seatbelt reminder light
6	30 A	Air conditioner (A/C)
7	15 A	direction indicators, tachometer, warning lights for alternator, check engine, oil pressure and SRS airbag, shift-up indicator
8	10 A	headlight wipers, power mirrors, cruise control, EZK test connector
9	30 A	blower fan
10	10 A	APC system
11	—	spare
12	—	spare
13	20 A	backup lights, cigarette lighter
14	15 A	right high beam
15	15 A	left high beam, high beam warning light
16	15 A	right low beam
17	15 A	left low beam
18	10 A	right front park, sidemarker lights right rear lights, license plate light
19	10 A	left front park, sidemarker lights, left rear lights
20	15 A	cornering lights
21	15 A	extra fog lights
22	10 A	fuel system, temperature gauge, fuel level gauge, speed sensor (cruise control), warning lights for handbrake, ABS and footbrake
23	10 A	lighting for controls and glovebox
24	—	spare
25	30 A	radiator fan
26	25 A	horn
27	15 A	hazard warning lights
28	15 A	clock
29	—	spare
30	20 A	fuel pump
31	15 A	brake lights, ABS

Main Relay Positions

The relays are electromagnetic switches that operate on low current to switch a high-current circuit on and off. Many of the relays are mounted on the main fuse/relay panel in the engine compartment (see in Fig. 1), although later models are equipped with additional auxiliary relay panels. **Table e** through **Table g** list the relay positions in the main fuse/relay panel.

CAUTION

- Relays positions are subject to change and can vary from car to car, depending on options and new equipment installed. If questions arise, consult the appropriate wiring diagrams. Please remember that an authorized Saab dealer is the best source for the most accurate and up-to-date information.

- Most relays incorporate several different electrical functions. Although another relay may plug into the same panel position, do not interchange relays.

Table e. 1985 Relay positions—main fuse/relay panel

Position	Function
A/B	headlights
C	heated rear window
D	A/C compressor
E	ignition switch
F	—
G	—
H	—
J	A/C radiator fan
K	horn

Table f. 1986–1988 Relay positions—main fuse/relay panel

Position	Function
A/B	headlights
C	heated rear window
D	ignition pulse amplifier (1986-1987 models)
E	ignition switch
F	shift up indicator
G	extra fog lights
H	A/C compressor
J	A/C radiator fan
K	horn

Table g. 1989-1993 Relay positions—main fuse/relay panel

Position	Function
A/B	headlights
C	heated rear window (1989-1990)
D	extra fog lights
E	ignition switch
F	daytime driving lights (Canada only)
G	radiator cooling fan
H	A/C compressor
J	A/C radiator fan
K	horn

Additional Fuse and Relay Locations

Several other fuse and relay locations are used depending on model year and equipment.

On 1989 models, the ABS relay panel is located in the engine compartment on the driver's side wheel housing. On 1990 and later models, the ABS relay panel is located in the engine compartment on the passenger side wheel housing by the door hinge. Fig. 3 shows the fuse/relay panel used for ABS functions.

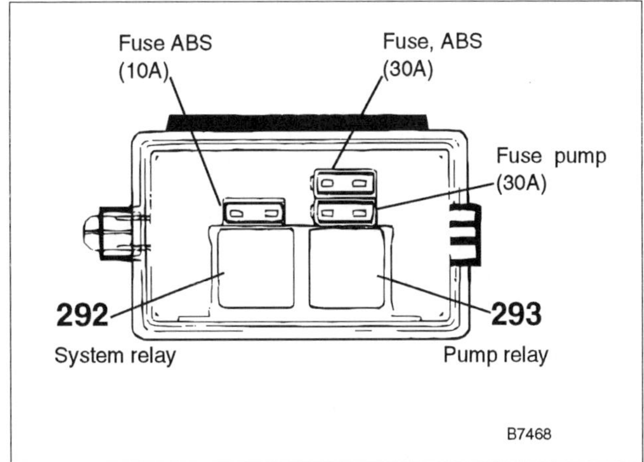

Fig. 3. ABS fuse/relay panel located in engine compartment.

On models with motorized passive seat belts, the fuses and relays for the seatbelt system are located under the rear seat on the driver side.

On 1989 and 1990 convertible models and all 1991 and later models, an extra fuse/relay panel (component 401A) can be found under the rear seat. See Fig. 4. **Table h** gives a list of fuse and relay functions for this fuse/relay panel.

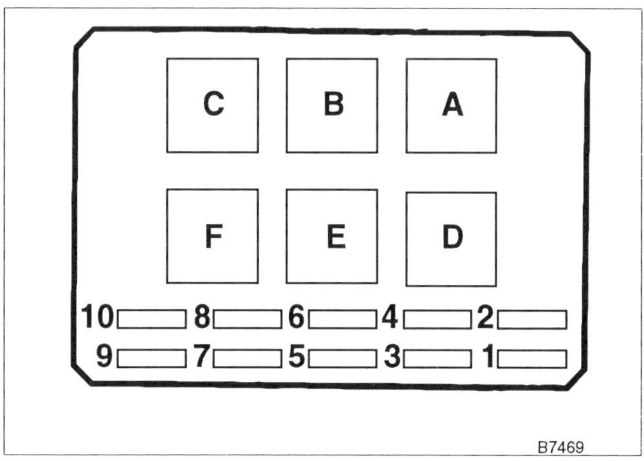

Fig. 4. Extra fuse/relay panel under rear seat used on 1989 and 1990 convertible and all 1991 and later models.

NOTE

Always check the panel cover for correct fuse ratings and relay functions. The fuses are numbered 1 through 10. The relays are lettered A through F.

NOTE

On some convertible models, there are in-line fuses located in the engine compartment for raising and lowering the convertible top. These fuses are on the passenger side bulkhead near the exhaust manifold.

Components, Connectors and Ground Locations

All of the components, connectors, and ground locations are uniquely numbered throughout the wiring diagrams. Each number corresponds to a specific component, connector, or ground point. As a general rule, the first page of each wiring topic contains a complete list of component, connector, and ground locations.

NOTE

A complete listing of component, connector, and ground locations can also be found at the end of this repair group. This master list is presented twice; first in a numerical order and then alphabetically.

Ground points are an important part of the electrical system. There are only a small number of main ground locations used throughout the car. See Fig. 5.

Table h. Fuse/relay panel under rear seat

Position	Rating	1989-1990 Convertibles	All 1991 and later models
1	20 A		convertible top
2	20 A		heated seats, interior lighting, seatbelt and key warning
3	25 A		heated rear window, power mirrors
4	10 A (15 A 1992 convertible)		interior lighting, burglar alarm, central locking on convertible
5	20 A		radio, burglar alarm
6	20 A		power antenna
7	30 A		power windows (front)
8	30 A		power windows (rear), sunroof
9	30 A		power seats (driver's side)
10	30 A		power seats (passenger's side)
A	—	relay for power windows (convertible models)	relay for seatbelt warning
B	—	relay for interior lighting time delay	relay for heated rear window
C	—	relay for raising convertible top	relay for raising convertible top
D	—	relay for lowering convertible top	relay for lowering convertible top
E	—	relay for seatbelt warning	relay for interior lighting time delay
F	—	relay for burglar alarm	relay for ignition switch

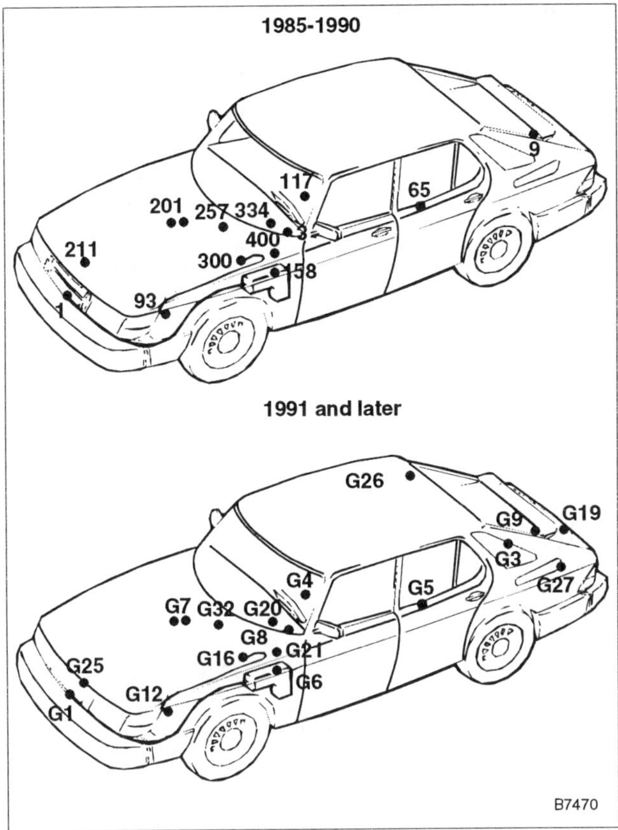

Fig. 5. Main chassis ground distribution.

Ignition Switch and Positive Supply

With the exception of the battery charging system, all electrical power is routed from the ignition switch or the battery through the main fuse/relay panel.

Battery voltage supplied directly to components is designated terminal **30** in the wiring diagrams. This supply is always live. All switched battery voltage is supplied via ignition switch terminals **15**, **50**, **X** and **54**, depending on the position of the ignition key. Additionally, as long as the key is in the ignition switch, terminal **S** of the switch will be live to the warning relay. See Fig. 6.

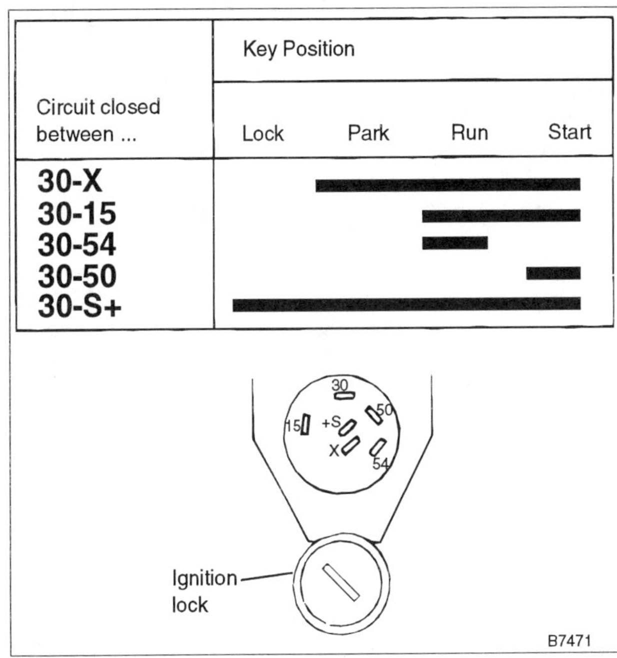

Circuit closed between ...	Key Position			
	Lock	Park	Run	Start
30-X		■	■	■
30-15			■	■
30-54			■	
30-50				■
30-S+	■	■	■	■

Fig. 6. Ignition switch terminals and terminal distribution.

Wiring Diagrams

The following wiring diagrams have been specially designed to enable quick and efficient diagnosis and troubleshooting of electrical malfunctions. Each wiring sub-system or topic, such as Ignition System, or Power Mirrors, is described individually. Most sub-systems include a brief circuit operation description, fault tracing, a list of component, connector and ground locations, and the wiring diagram(s).

NOTE

Many of the wiring diagrams are applicable to cars delivered to other world markets served by Saab. At times, there may be certain parts of the diagram that are applicable only to these markets. This manual covers only Saab cars delivered to the United States (US), California (UC), and Canada (CA). Abbreviations other than US, UC, and CA found on a particular diagram should be ignored. For example the abbreviation "ME" is for cars sold in the Middle East.

Anti-lock Braking System (ABS)

Operation

The Anti-lock Braking System or ABS is controlled and monitored electrically. For information on the mechanical components of the braking system see **5 BRAKES**.

A sensor at each wheel supplies the ABS control unit with information on the wheel rotation speed. If any of the wheels should begin to lock, the control unit will adjust the braking pressure to the wheel(s). ABS braking on the front wheels is individually controlled, whereas on the rear wheels it is controlled jointly.

A hydraulic pump (component 297) controls the servo action of the brakes. The hydraulic fluid pressure is controlled at the required value by means of a pressure switch (component 294) which controls the pump motor.

The ANTI-LOCK and the BRAKE FLUID warning lamps in the instrument cluster monitor the system. The ANTI-LOCK warning lamp will light up if a problem or fault occurs in the Anti-lock Braking System. The BRAKE FLUID warning lamp will light up if the brake fluid level in the reservoir falls too low.

WARNING

If either the ANTI-LOCK or the BRAKE FLUID warning lamp should come on, the car must not be driven. Brake failure may occur. Have the problem corrected promptly by an authorized Saab dealer.

Fault Tracing

The following fault tracing should be used as a guide only. Comprehensive fault tracing is best carried out using special ABS test equipment available through an authorized Saab dealer.

1. Check the fuses. The control unit (component 291), the system relay (component 292), and the pump relay (component 293) are all protected by fuses. These fuses are located in the ABS electrical distribution box (component 302).
2. Test the components shown in the table using a DMM (digital multi-meter). Use the wiring diagram(s) for terminal identification.

ABS component	Test value	Comments
wheel sensors	800 to 1400 ohms	
wheel sensors	at least 0.1 VAC	with wheel rotating at 1 revolution per second
master valve	2 to 5 ohms	measure between terminals 1 and 2 at master valve (295) on hydraulic unit
inlet valves	5 to 7 ohms	measure inlet valve coil resistances (IFL, IFR, IR) at ABS valve block (296)
outlet valves	3 to 5 ohms	measure outlet valve coil resistances (OFL, OFR, OR) at ABS valve block (296)
brake fluid level sensor	10 ohms at contacts 1 and 2	contacts closed, float at bottom
brake fluid level sensor	1 ohm at contacts 3 and 4	contacts closed, float at top

Component Locations

20 ignition switch in center console
21A Ignition switch relay, in relay panel
22A main fuse/relay panel in left wheel housing
29 brake light switch at brake pedal
47F brake warning light in instrument cluster
47Q ABS warning lamp in instrument cluster
47T SRS airbag warning lamp in instrument cluster. See SRS warnings
158 negative distribution in main fuse/relay panel
291 ABS control unit (1989) at ABS distribution box, engine compartment left wheel housing
291 ABS control unit (1990 and later), under rear seat, right side
292 ABS system relay (1989) in ABS distribution box, engine compartment left wheel housing
292 ABS system relay (1990 and later) in ABS distribution box, behind right wheel housing
293 ABS pump relay (1989) at ABS distribution box, left wheel housing
293 ABS pump relay (1990 and later) in ABS distribution box, behind right wheel housing
294 ABS pressure switch on the ABS hydraulic unit
295 ABS master valve on the hydraulic unit
296 ABS valve block in front of left wheel housing
297 ABS hydraulic pump motor in engine compartment at hydraulic unit
298A ABS wheel sensor in left front wheel
298B ABS wheel sensor in right front wheel
298C ABS wheel sensor in left rear wheel
298D ABS wheel sensor in right rear wheel
299 ABS brake fluid level sensor in brake fluid reservoir
302 ABS electrical distribution box (1989) engine compartment, left wheel housing
302 ABS electrical distribution box (1990 and later) behind right wheel housing
302A ABS fuse holder (1989) engine compartment, left wheel housing
302A ABS fuse holder (1990-and later) behind right wheel housing
303B ABS diode (1989) engine compartment, left wheel housing
303B ABS diode (1990 and later) behind right wheel housing
397 ABS diagnostic 2-pin test socket near the hydraulic unit (in wiring harness)

Anti-lock Braking System (ABS)

Connector Locations

1989-1990 models

57 3-pin connector in right front wheel sensor
57 3-pin connector in left front wheel sensor
58 12-pin connector behind instrument panel, to left of steering column
59 2-pin connector at the main fuse/relay panel (22)
59 2-pin connector under rear seat (1990 models)
59 2-pin connector at the ABS hydraulic unit in engine compartment
59 2-pin connector in engine compartment at right side of the bulkhead partition
60 1-pin connector in main fuse/relay panel (1990 models)
98 10-pin connector at the ABS control unit
98 10-pin connector behind the instrument panel to the left of the steering column
123 4-pin connector (2) at the ABS control unit
123 4-pin connector (black) left wheel sensor
123 4-pin connector (gray) right wheel sensor
152A 29-pin bulkhead connector in main fuse/relay panel
152B 29-pin bulkhead connector in main fuse/relay panel
152C 29-pin bulkhead connector in main fuse/relay panel

1991and later

H2-12 2-pin connector under rear seat, left side
H2-22 2-pin connector in engine compartment near ABS hydraulic unit
H2-23 2-pin connector in engine compartment right side partition
H2-24 2-pin connector under rear seat, left side
H2-25 2-pin connector under rear seat, right side
H2-27 2-pin connector in main fuse/relay panel
H3-4 3-pin connector in main fuse/relay panel
H29-1 29-pin bulkhead connector behind main fuse/relay panel (1991-1991 1/2)
H29-3 29-pin bulkhead connector behind main fuse/relay panel (1991-1991 1/2)
H33-1 33-pin bulkhead connector behind main fuse/relay panel (1991 1/2 and later)
H33-3 33-pin bulkhead connector behind main fuse/relay panel (1991 1/2 and later)

Ground Locations

1990

3 ground point behind instrument panel
65 ground point at the handbrake
93 ground point at left wheel housing
211 ground point at gearbox
257 ground point at alternator bracket
300 ABS ground point at the front of the hydraulic unit

1991 and later

G1 ground point at radiator cross member
G5 ground point under rear seat
G8 ground point behind instrument panel
G12 ground point at left wheel housing
G16 ground point in front of the ABS hydraulic unit
G25 ground point on gearbox

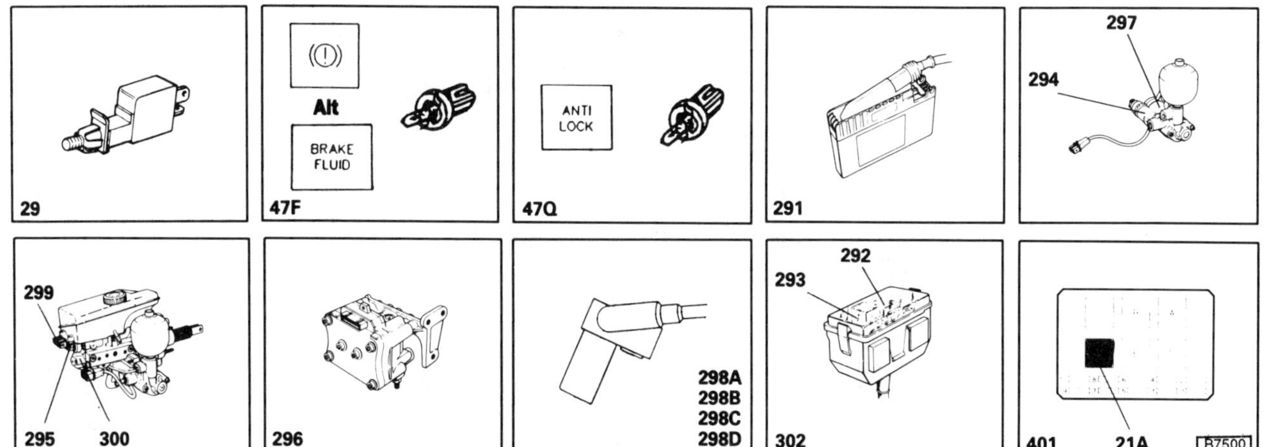

Anti-lock Braking System (ABS)

1989-1990

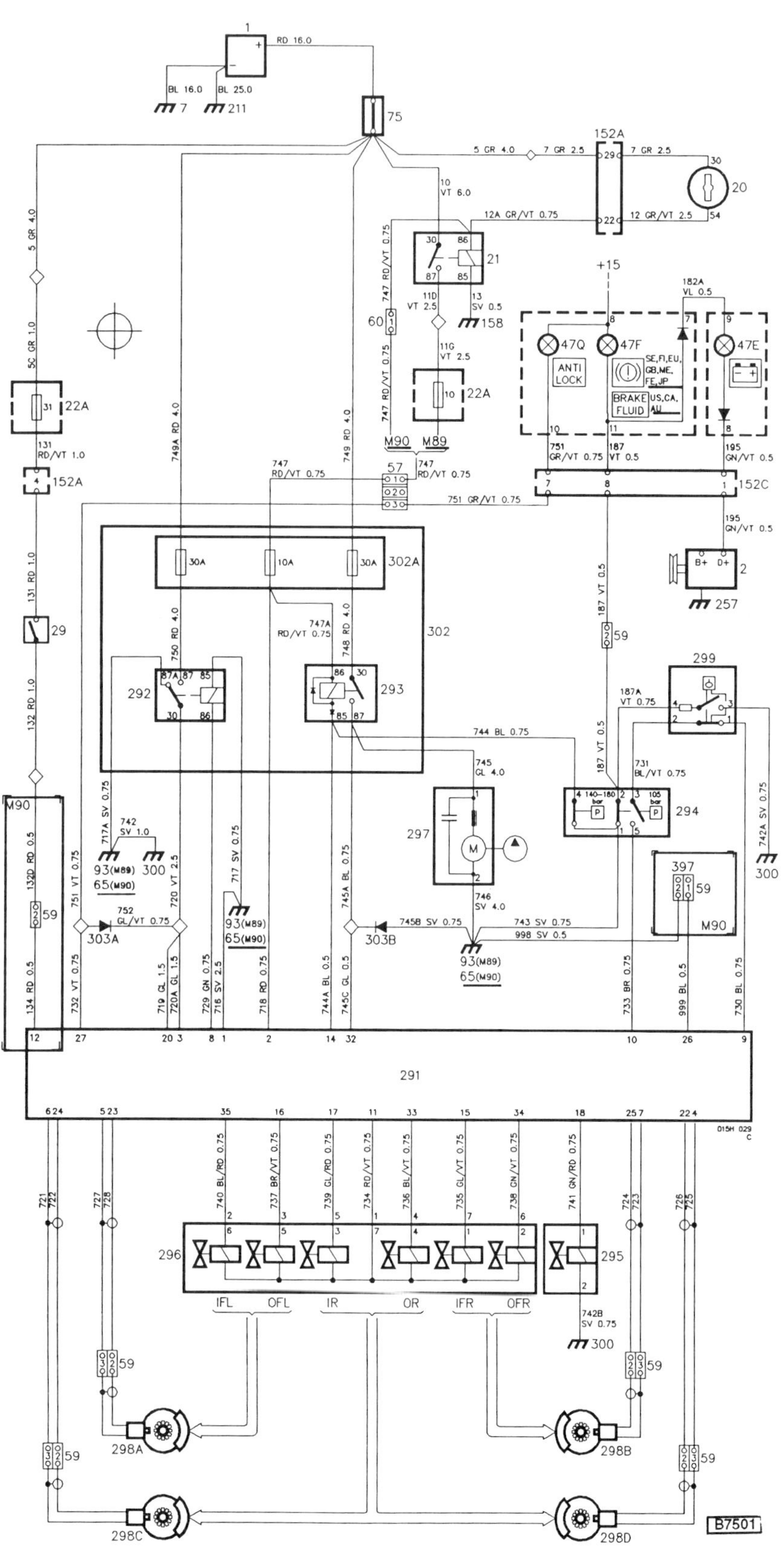

Anti-lock Braking System (ABS)

1991-1993 (page 1 of 2)

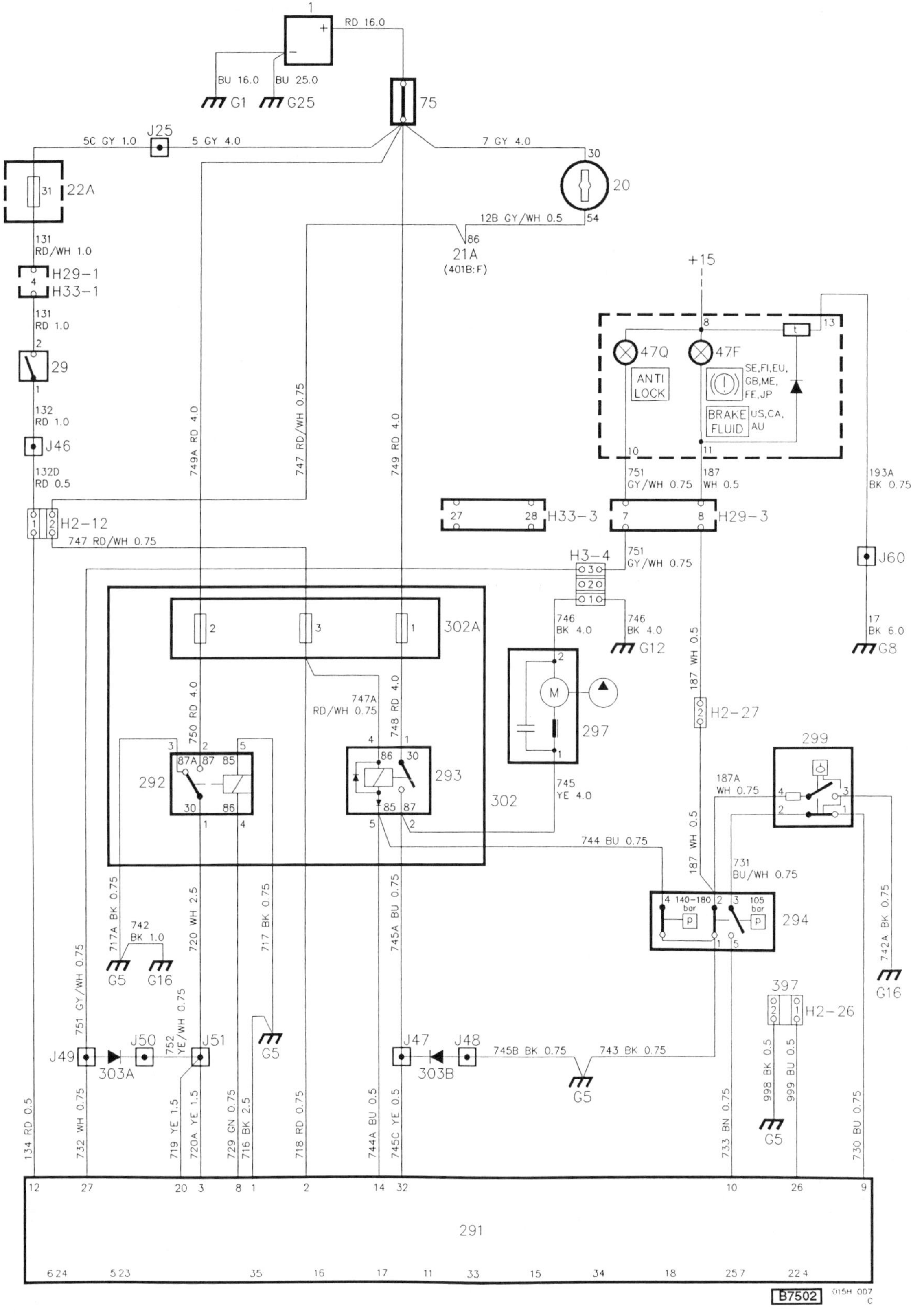

Anti-lock Braking System (ABS)

1991-1993 (page 2 of 2)

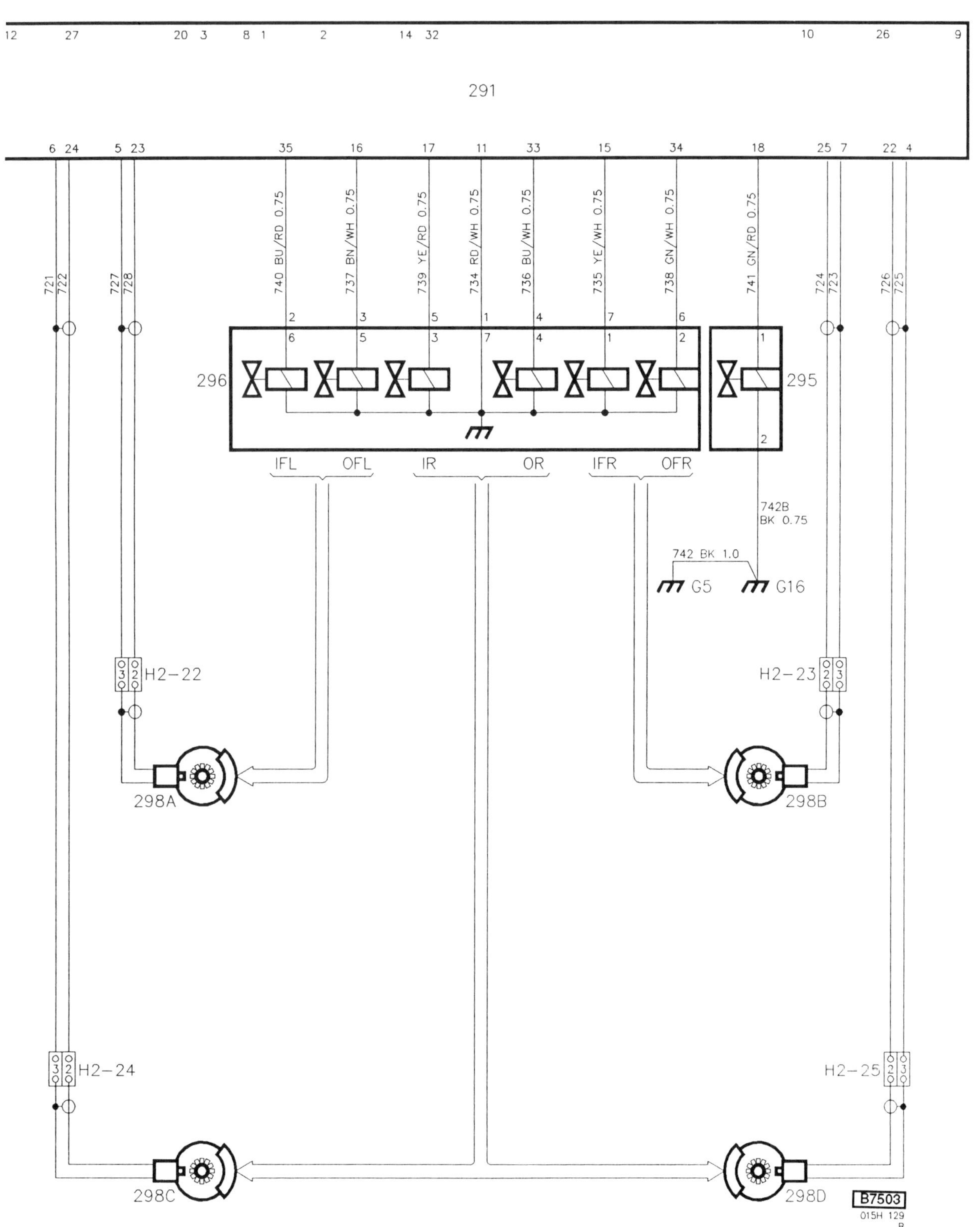

Air Conditioner (A/C)

Operation

The air conditioner is controlled by the A/C switch (component 169) and the recirculation switch (component 143) on the instrument panel. The A/C compressor (component 170) and evaporator are protected by pressure and temperature safety switches. The system also has an A/C cooling fan (component 172) behind the radiator. Idle speed compensation is done by the AIC valve.

For A/C repair information see **854 Heating and Air Conditioning**. For repair information on the cooling system see **261 Radiator and Cooling System**.

WARNING

Air conditioner repair and service requires special tools and knowledge. Pressures in excess of 300 psi are created in the system. The refrigerant (R12) can be poisonous and can immediately freeze anything it contacts including eyes and skin. Always wear eye protection and gloves when working on the A/C system.

Fault Tracing

1. Check the fuse(s).
2. Listen for an audible click of the compressor clutch when pushing the A/C switch on with the key on.
3. Check for voltage at the A/C compressor (component 170) and the A/C cooling fan (172).

Component Locations

20 ignition switch
22A main fuse/relay panel in left wheel housing
35 ventilation fan switch in instrument panel
37 radiator cooling fan motor behind radiator
38 recirculation valve (solenoid)
1985–1987 in engine compartment, right wheel housing
1988 and later– behind instrument panel, near right side A pillar
74 resistor pack for ventilation fan under the left speaker grille
143 recirculation switch in dashboard
149 main switch for ventilation fan integrated in the air distribution switch
150 air distribution switch in instrument panel
155 relay for A/C cooling fan in main fuse/relay panel
156 A/C compressor relay in main fuse/relay panel
158 negative distribution in main fuse/relay panel
166 A/C pressure switch for cooling fan in receiver/dryer unit, near battery
167 A/C throttle switch in throttle housing
168 A/C coolant temperature switch in radiator hose near distributor
169 A/C switch in instrument panel
170 A/C compressor at top of engine near firewall
171 A/C antifreeze thermostat in instrument panel, right side ahead of A pillar
172 A/C cooling fan behind radiator
173 A/C compressor diode in engine wiring harness, rear of valve cover
200 LH control unit, forward of right front, door behind trim
203 throttle angle transmitter on throttle housing
396 radiator fan relay in main fuse/relay panel

Connector Locations

1985-1990

59 2-pin connector next to radiator cooling fan
59 2-pin connector next to A/C cooling fan
60 1-pin connector at A/C compressor, top rear of engine
67 6-pin connector in engine compartment near fresh air intake
152A 29-pin bulkhead connector in main fuse/relay panel
152B 29-pin bulkhead connector in main fuse/relay panel
152C 29-pin bulkhead connector in main fuse/relay panel

1991 and later

H1-10 1-pin connector near A/C compressor in engine compartment
H2-1 2-pin connector at the radiator fan motor
H2-2 2-pin connector next to A/C cooling fan (172)
H2-10 2-pin connector behind cigarette lighter
H6-2 6-pin connector in engine compartment right wheel housing
H29-3 29-pin bulkhead connector behind main fuse/relay panel (1991-1991 1/2)
H33-3 33-pin bulkhead connector behind main fuse/relay panel (1991 1/2 and later)

Ground Locations

1985-1990

3 ground point behind instrument panel
7 ground point at radiator cross member
201 ground point for fuel injection at engine lifting lug, 2 points

1991 and later

G1 ground point at radiator cross member
G6 ground distribution in main fuse/relay panel
G7 ground point in engine lifting lug
G8 ground point behind instrument panel

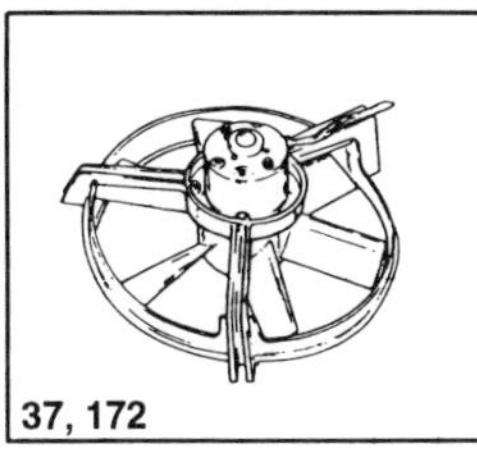
37, 172

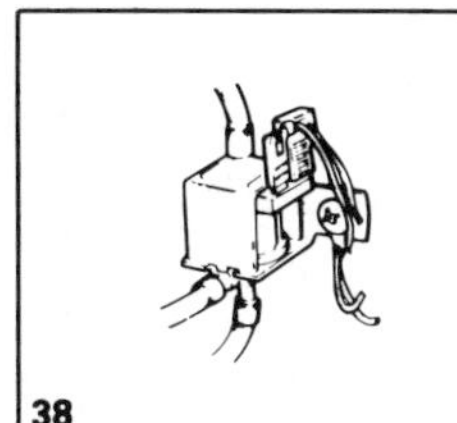
38

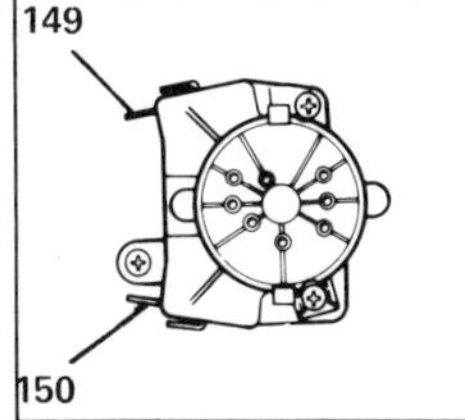

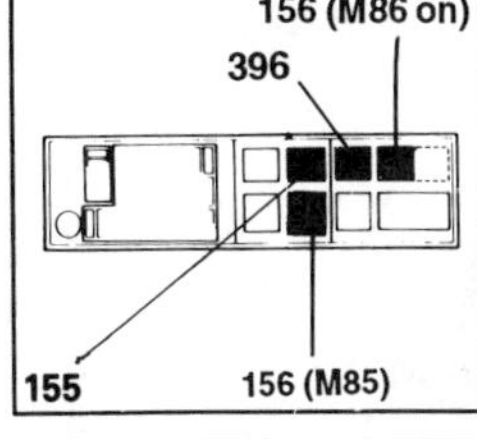

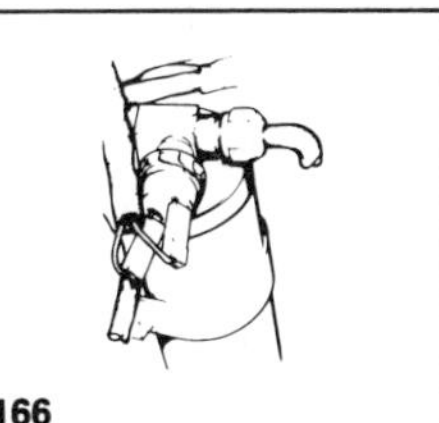
166

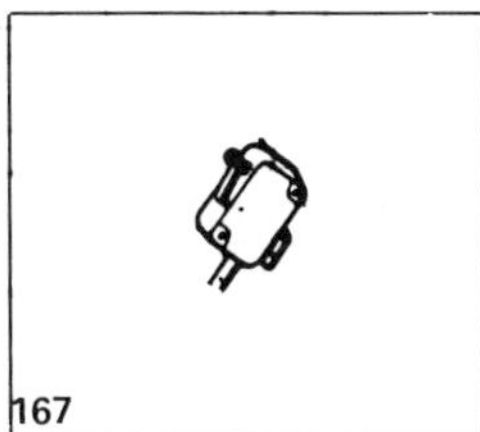
167

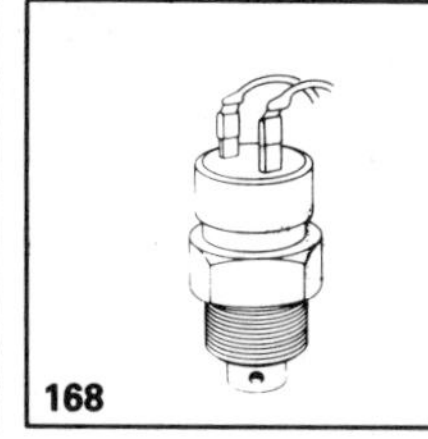
168

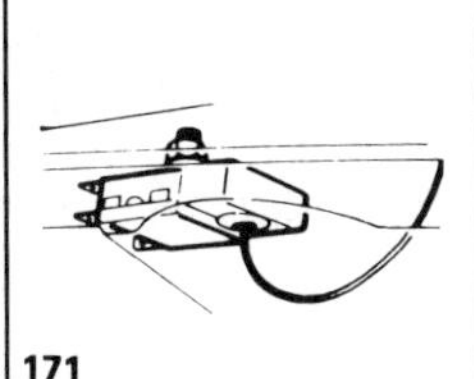
171

200

203 (EZK, LH 2.4) B7504

Air Conditioner (A/C)

1985

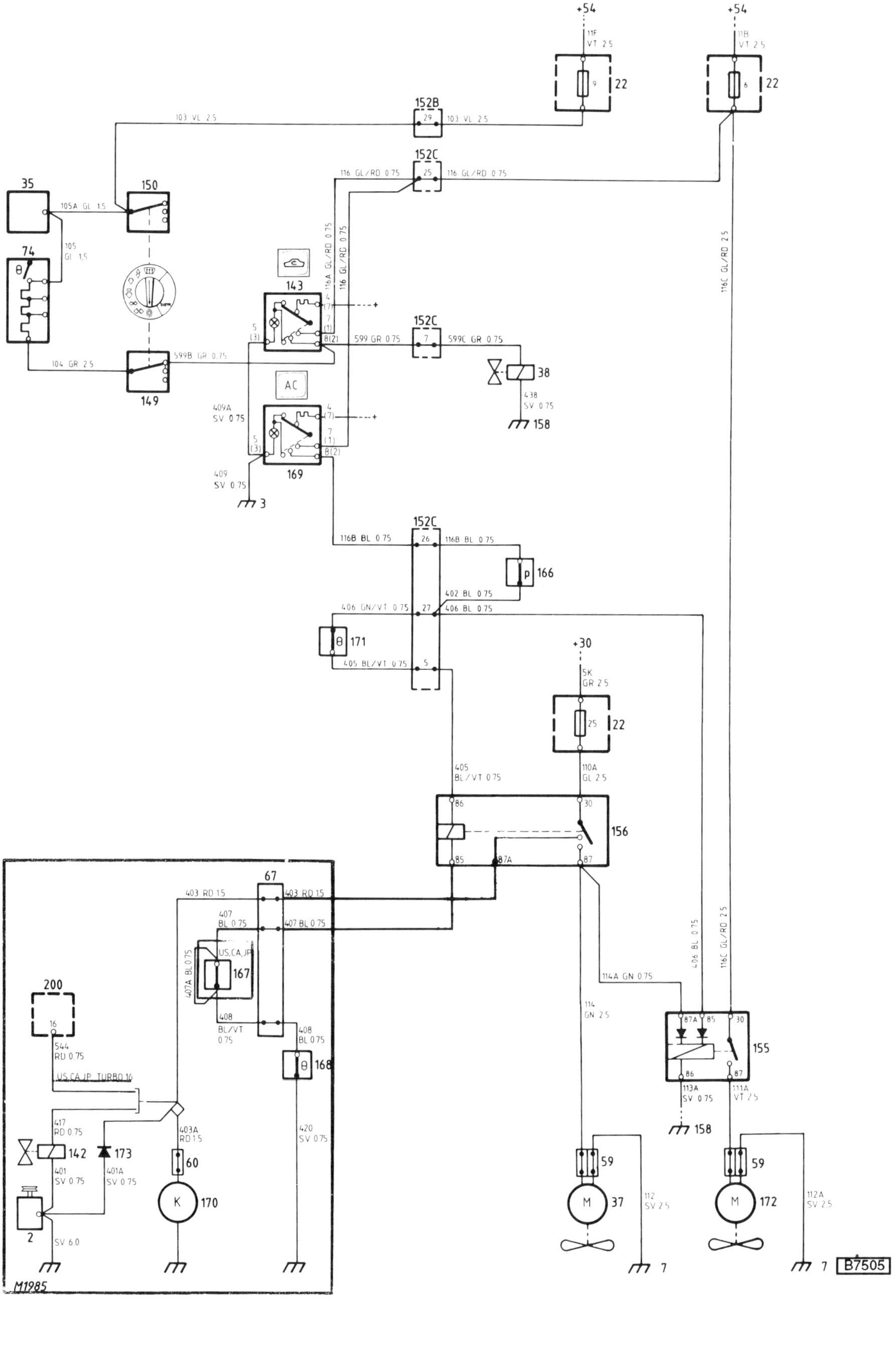

Air Conditioner (A/C)

1986-1988

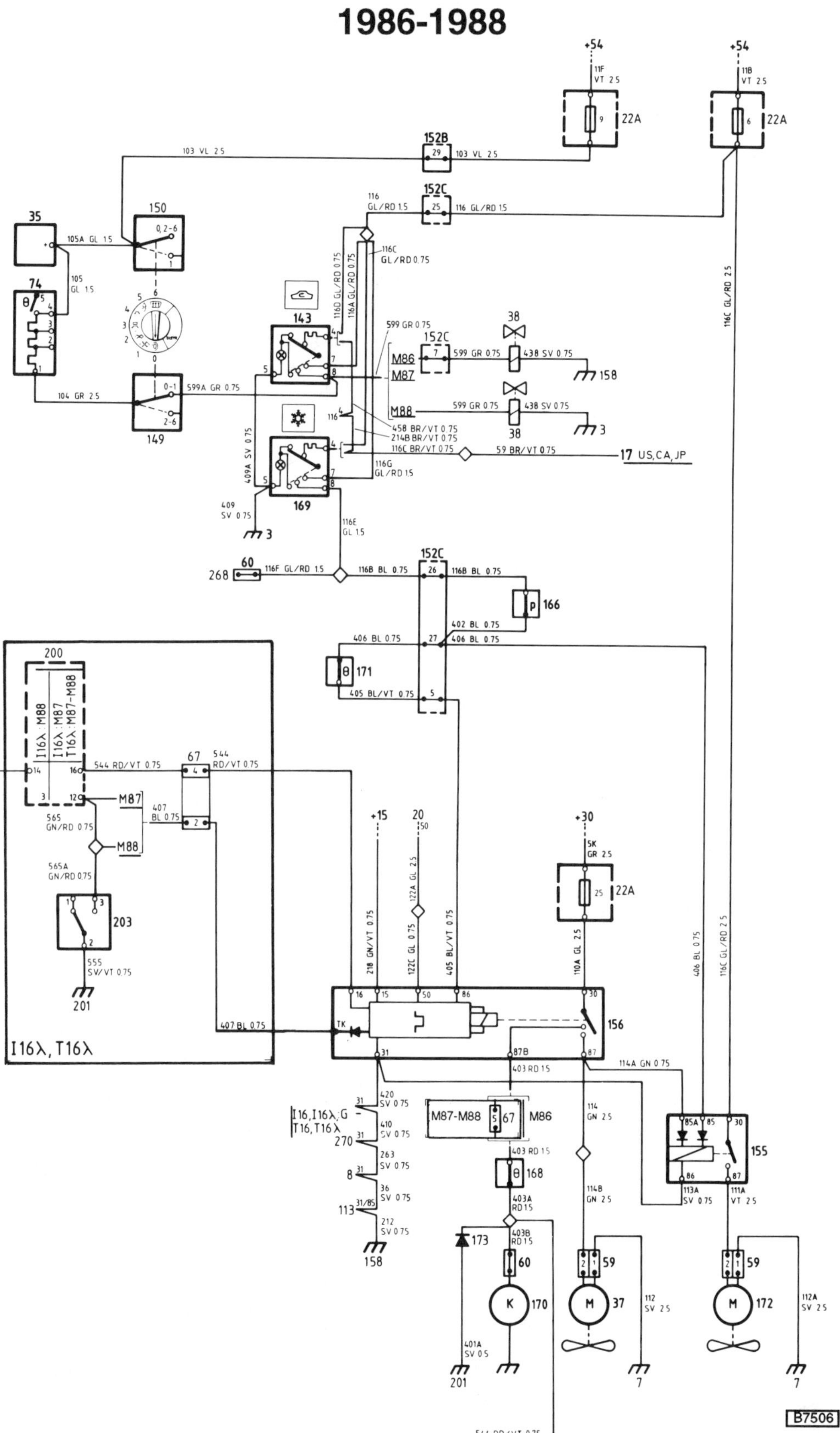

Air Conditioner (A/C)

1989-1990

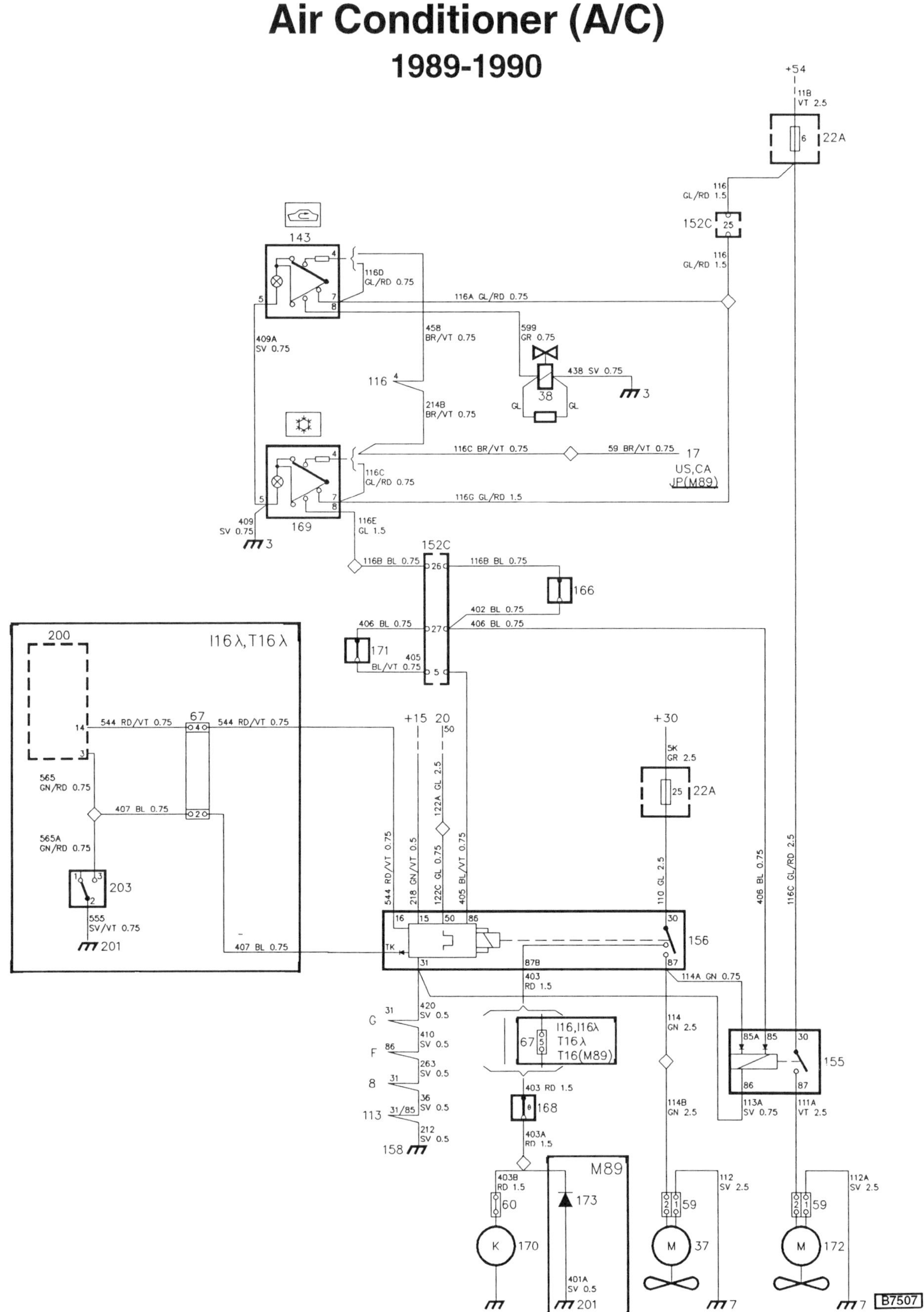

Air Conditioner (A/C)

1991-1993 non-turbo

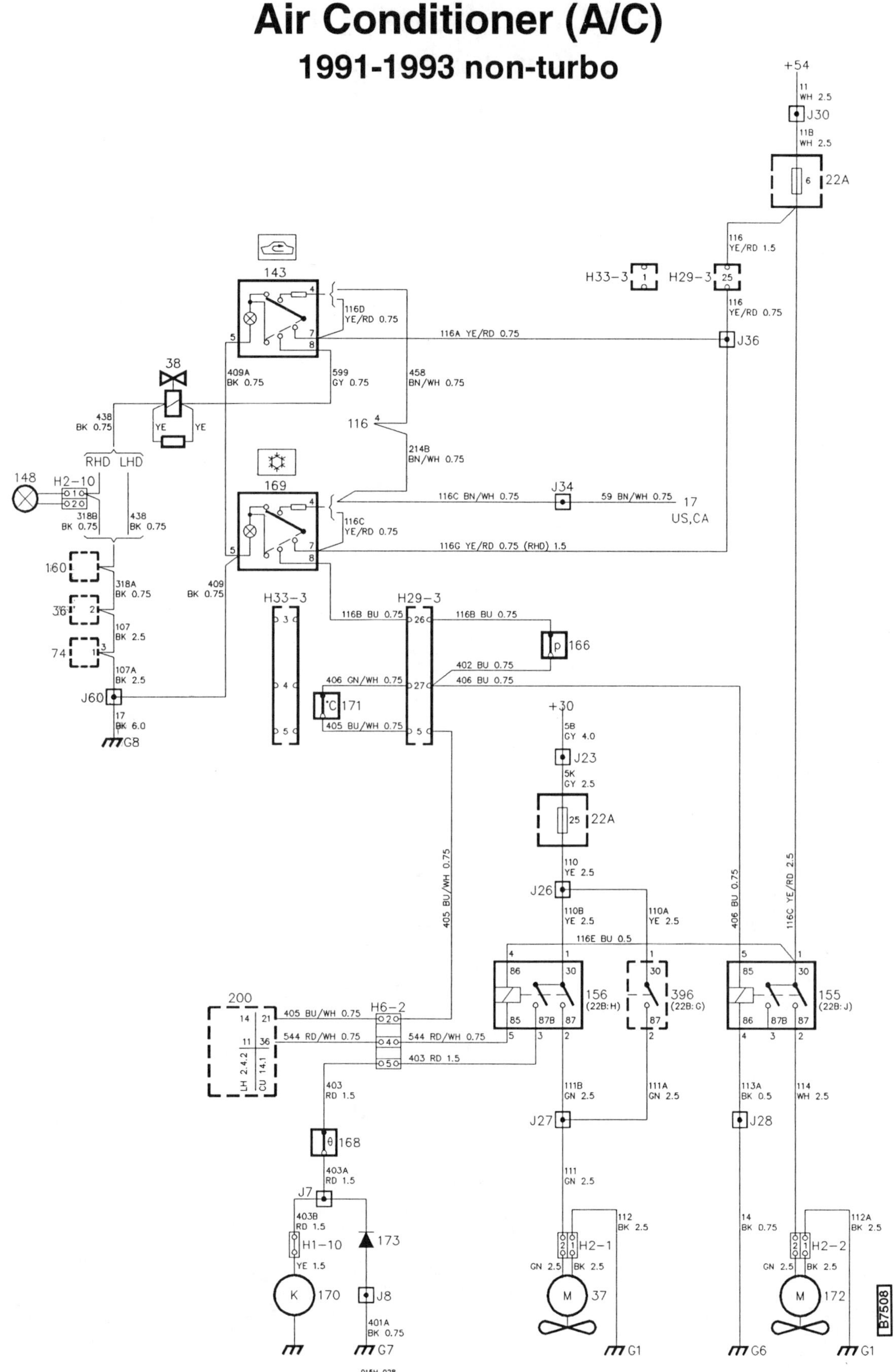

Air Conditioner (A/C)
1991-1993 turbo

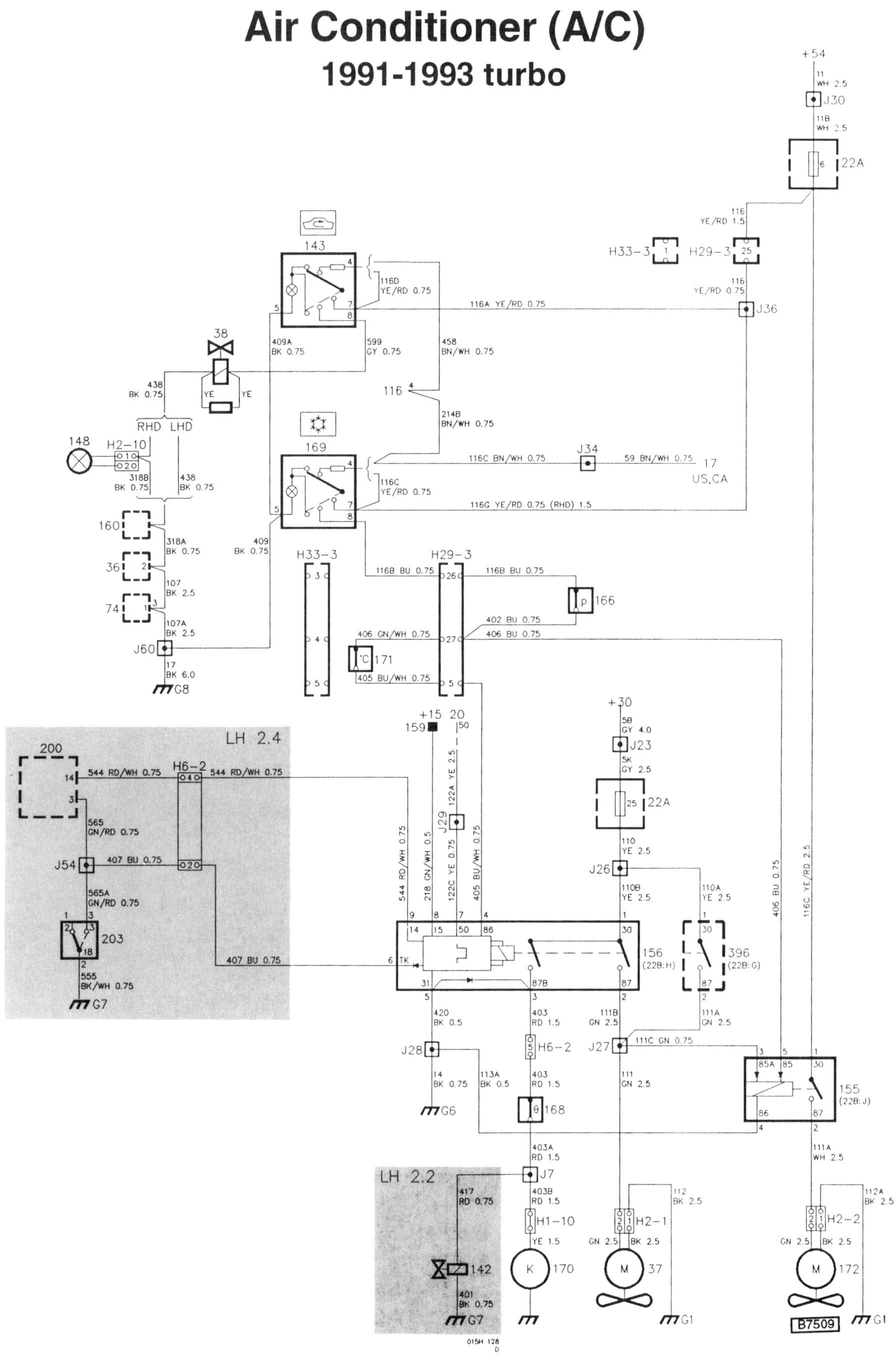

Alternator and Charging System

Operation

The alternator supplies the electrical components and recharges the battery. The alternator is not fused. Voltage regulation is controlled internally by a regulator. The alternator circuit includes a warning lamp in the instrument cluster. If the lamp burns out, the alternator will not charge the battery properly. See **853 Dashboard and Consoles** and **351 Lighting** for information on changing the lamp.

See **321 Alternator and Charging System** for alternator and charging system repair information and additional fault tracing.

CAUTION

- Do not disconnect the battery or any wire when the engine is running. Do not reverse the polarity of the battery. Do not ground any alternator terminals. This will damage the alternator.
- Always disconnect the negative (–) battery cable before removing the alternator. Unfused battery voltage is always present at the rear of the alternator.
- Always disconnect the negative (–) battery cable and all wires to the alternator before doing any electric (arc) welding to the car.

Fault Tracing

1. Inspect the V-belts and make sure they are tight. Test for a fully charged battery as described in **311 Battery**.
2. Check for faulty connections and broken wires.
3. If no visible faults can be found, test the alternator output using an alternator load tester.

Alternator output specification

- Bosch type 80 A . . . . .54 Amps @ 1900 rpm

NOTE

If a load tester is not available, an output test can be done by running the engine at 2000 rpm and turning on all electrical loads such as fans, lights and heated window. Voltage at the battery should be approximately 12 volts or higher.

Component Locations

1	battery
2	alternator in back of engine compartment
4	starter motor under intake manifold
21	ignition switch relay in main fuse/relay panel
22A	main fuse/relay panel in left wheel housing
47E	charging lamp in instrument cluster
75	distribution block in right wheel housing
159	+15 distribution in main fuse/relay panel

Connector Locations

1985-1990

59	2-pin connector in main fuse/relay panel
152A	29-pin bulkhead connector behind main fuse/relay panel
152B	29-pin bulkhead connector behind main fuse/relay panel
152C	29-pin bulkhead connector behind main fuse/relay panel

1991 and later

H29-1	29-pin bulkhead connector behind main fuse/relay pane l (1991-1991 1/2)
H29-2	29-pin bulkhead connector behind main fuse/relay panel (1991-1991 1/2)
H29-3	29-pin bulkhead connector behind main fuse/relay panel (1991-1991 1/2)
H33-1	33-pin bulkhead connector behind main fuse/relay panel (1991 1/2 and later)
H33-2	33-pin bulkhead connector behind main fuse/relay panel (1991 1/2 and later)
H33-3	33-pin bulkhead connector behind main fuse/relay panel (1991 1/2 and later)

Ground Locations

1985-1990

7	ground point at radiator cross member
158	ground distribution in main fuse/relay panel
211	ground point on gearbox

1991 and later

G1	ground point at radiator cross member
G6	ground distribution in main fuse/relay panel
G25	ground point on gearbox

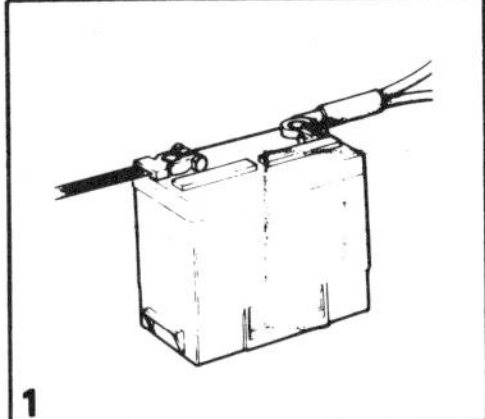
1

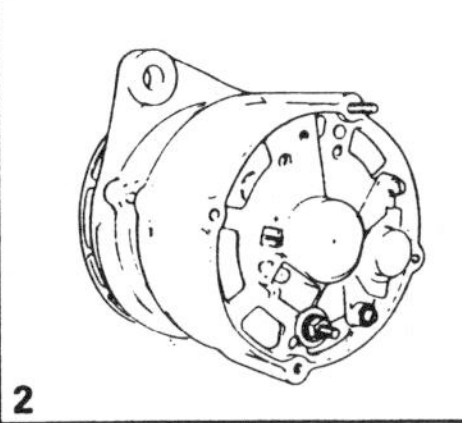
2

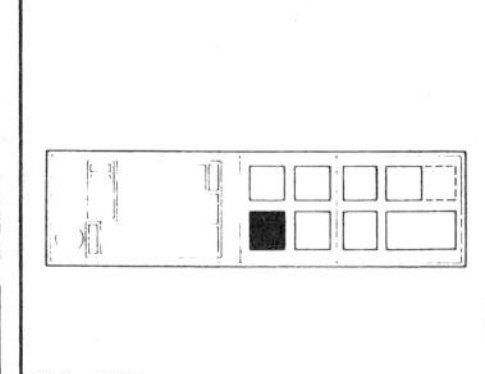
21, 22a

47E, 110

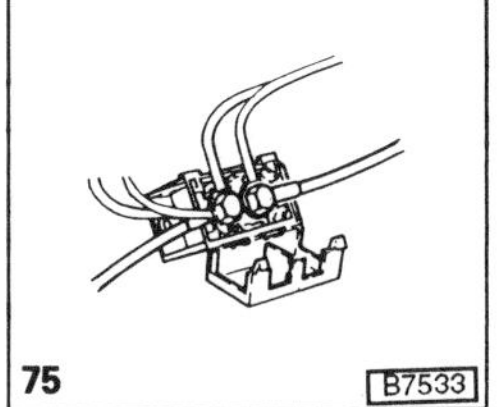
75

B7533

Alternator and Charging System

1985-1986

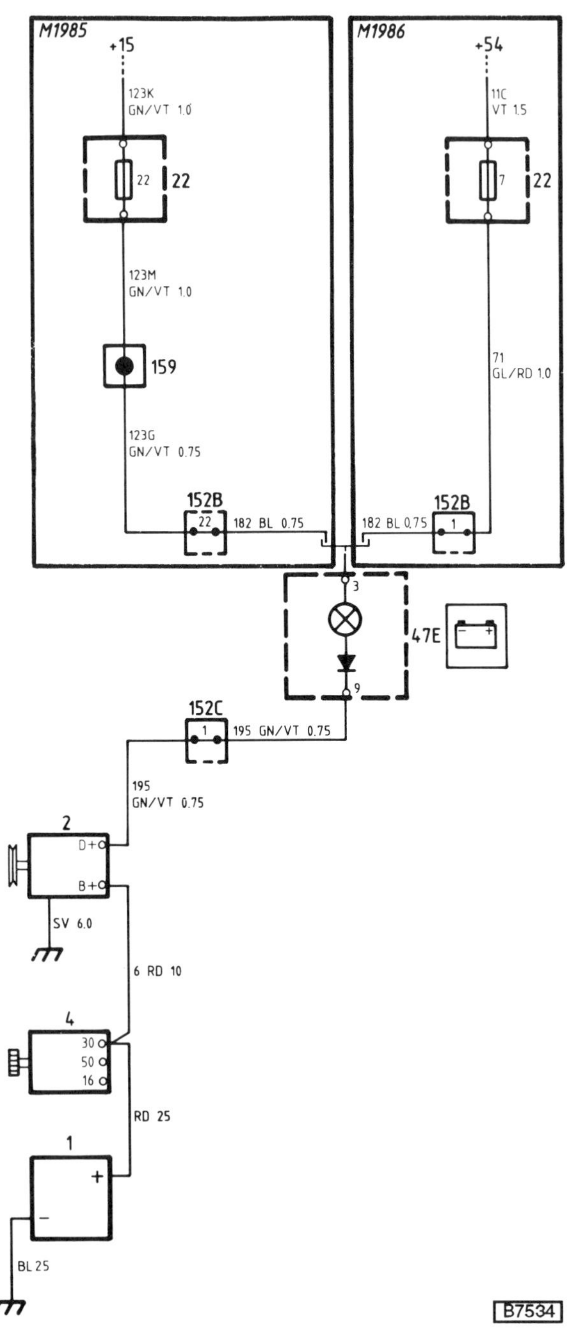

Alternator and Charging System

1987-1990

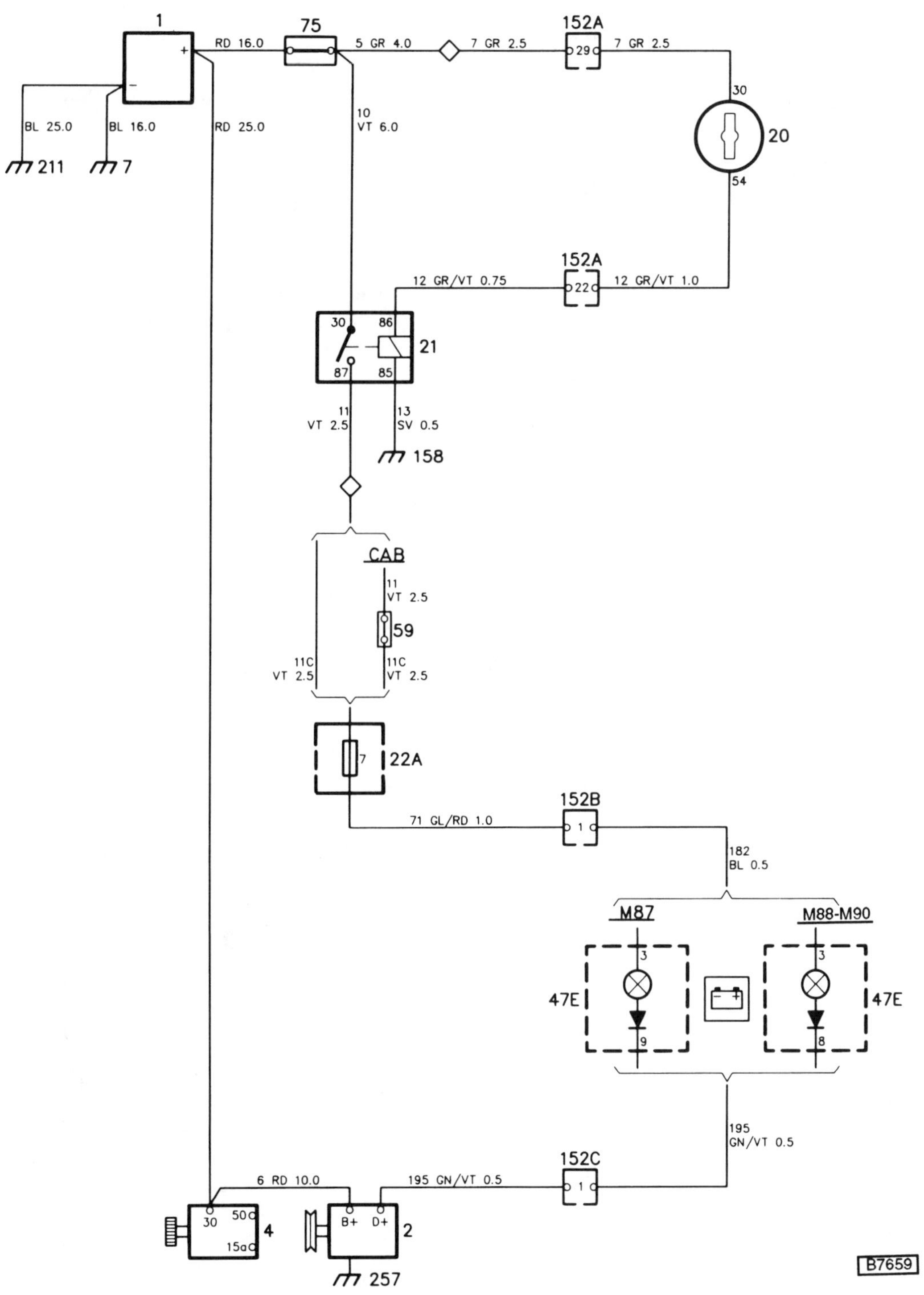

Alternator and Charging System

1991-1993

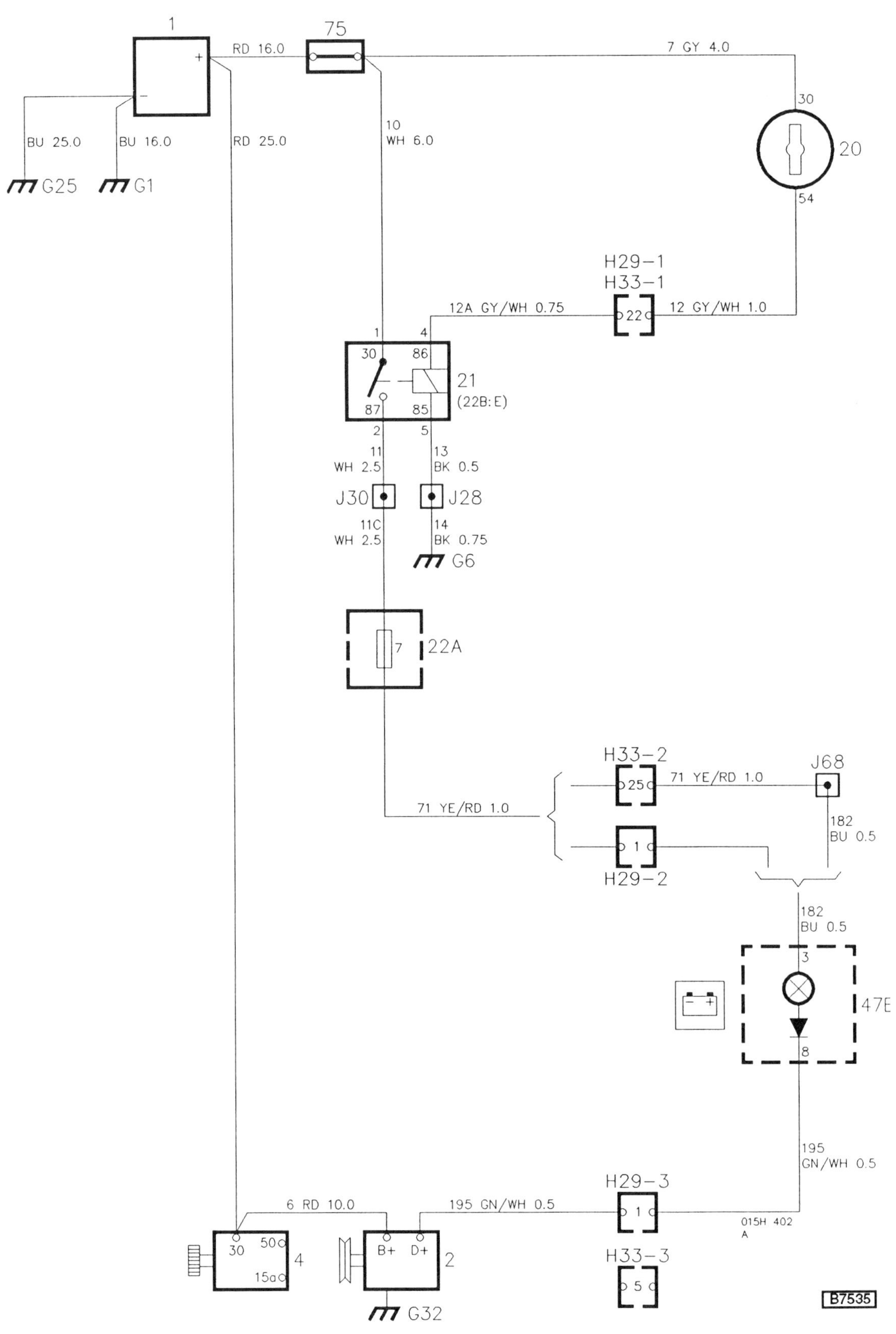

APC System

Operation

APC or Automatic Performance Control is used on turbo models only. The APC system continuously monitors engine detonation and adjusts the turbocharger boost pressure accordingly. This allows the engine to be run at a higher compression ratio for better fuel economy and throttle response. See **291 Turbocharger** for a complete system description and repair information.

Fault Tracing

1. Check fuse 10 and fuse 31 (where applicable).
2. On 1986 and later models, check that the brake light switch is functioning correctly.

NOTE

On 1986 and later cars, the brake light switch cancels the APC system when the brakes are applied, allowing the system to operate at a reduced boost pressure.

---

3. Measure the resistance at the intake manifold pressure sensor connector.

Intake manifold pressure sensor (180)

• resistance . . . . .5 to 13 ohms

Component Locations

5 ignition coil on radiator
29 brake light switch at the brake pedal
73 TSI connector at main fuse/relay panel
146 ignition amplifier in engine compartment, left bulkhead
147 ignition pulse amplifier in main fuse/relay panel (1986-1987)
177 APC control unit under back seat (1985), ahead of left wheel housing (1986 and later)
178 knock sensor on engine block, below intake manifold
179 pressure boost solenoid valve on the radiator fan casing
180 boost pressure sensor behind instrument panel to the left of the steering column
187 vacuum pump for cruise control
233 vacuum switch in engine compartment, left wheel housing

Connector Locations

1985-1990

59 2-pin connector in the engine compartment left wheel housing
60 1-pin connector in the engine compartment
152A 29 pole white bulkhead connector
152C 29 pole black bulkhead connector

1991 and later

H2-34 2-pin connector on the left wheel housing
H29-1 29-pin white bulkhead connector (1991-1991 1/2)
H29-3 29-pin black bulkhead connector (1991-1991 1/2)
H33-1 33-pin black bulkhead connector (1991 1/2 and later)
H33-3 33-pin blue bulkhead connector (1991 1/2 and later)

Ground Locations

1985-1990

7 ground point at radiator cross member
9 ground point in luggage compartment
93 ground point in left wheel housing

1991 and later

G1 ground point at radiator cross member
G6 ground distribution in main fuse/relay panel
G12 ground point in left wheel housing

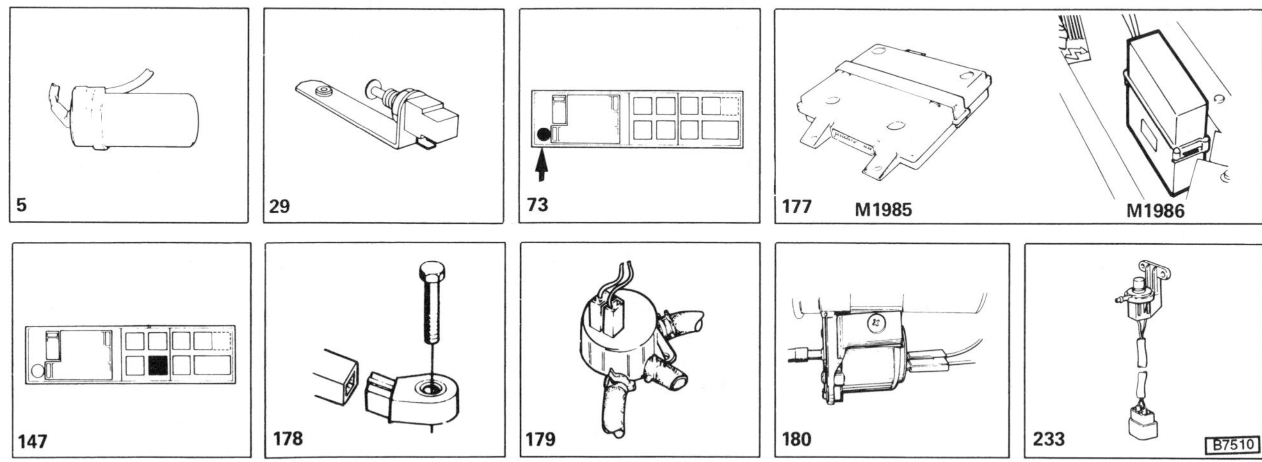

APC System

1985

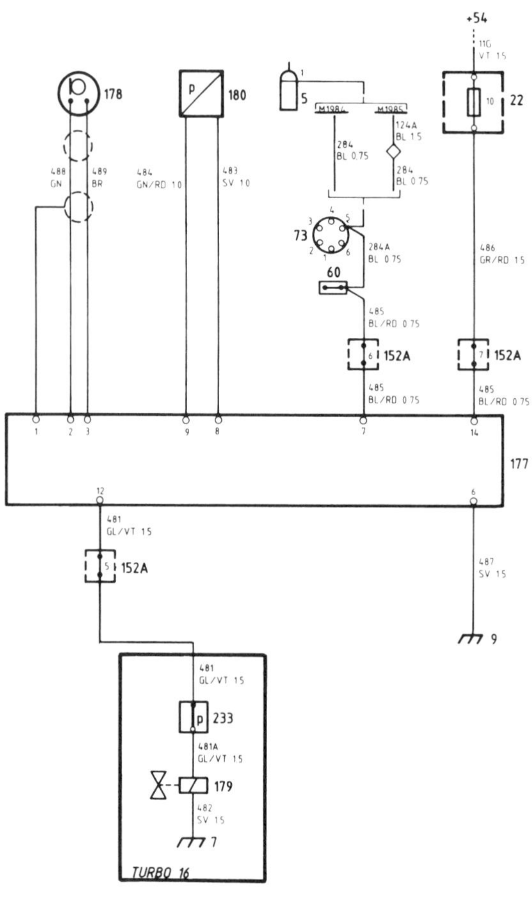

1986

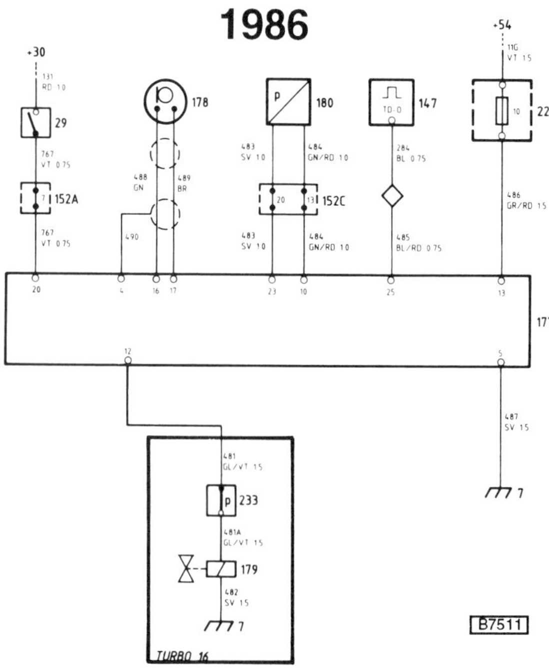

APC System

1987-1993

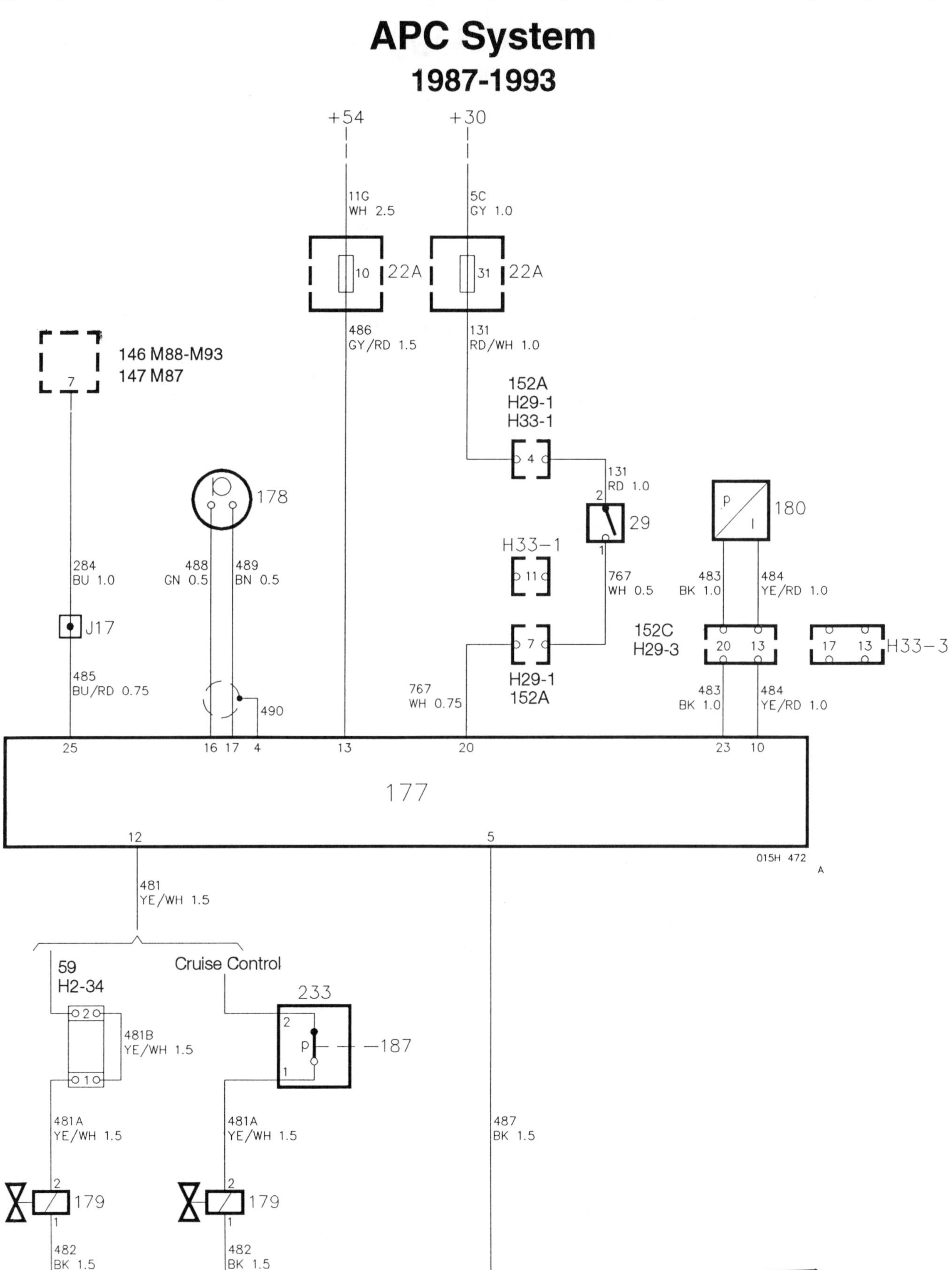

Backup Lights

Operation

Voltage is supplied to the backup light switch whenever the key is on. When the transmission is in reverse and the key is on, the switch closes to supply voltage to the backup lights.

Models with automatic transmission have a selector lever switch that can be adjusted as described in **364 Electric Controls and Switches.** Models with manual transmission have a non-adjustable switch that screws into the side of the shift-lever housing. See **432 Manual Transmission Controls**.

Fault Tracing

1. Check fuse 13.
2. With the ignition key in the off position, check for resistance across the switch terminals. There should be continuity with the transmission in reverse and no continuity when the transmission is taken out of reverse.
3. Check for voltage at the reverse lights with transmission in reverse and the key on.

Component Locations

22 main fuse/relay panel
31 backup light switch under the center console
32 backup lights in rear light cluster
119 side reversing lights in the front light cluster

Connector Locations

1985-1990

152A 29-pin bulkhead connector in main fuse/relay panel

1991 and later

H29-1 29-pin bulkhead connector behind main fuse/relay panel (1991-1991 1/2)
H33-1 33-pin bulkhead connector behind main fuse/relay panel (1991 1/2 and later)

Ground Locations

1985-1990

7 ground point at radiator cross member
9 ground point in luggage compartment
93 ground point at left wheel housing

1991 and later

G1 ground point at radiator cross member
G3 ground point in luggage compartment
G12 ground point at left wheel housing

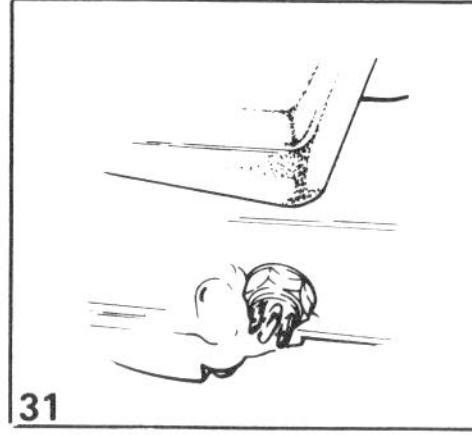
31

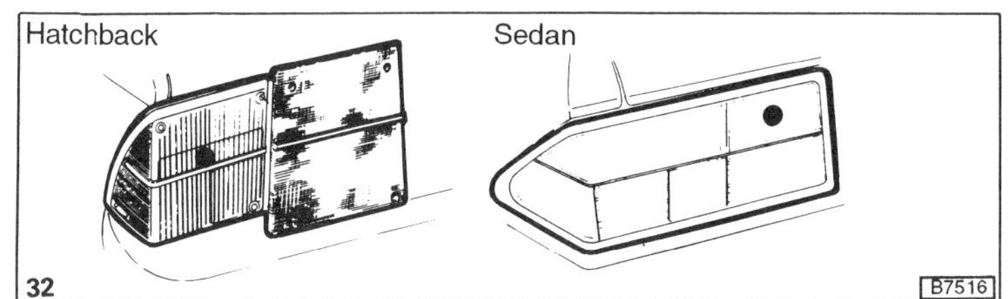

32

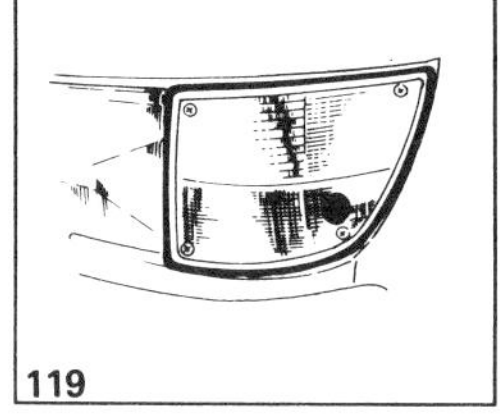
119

Backup Lights

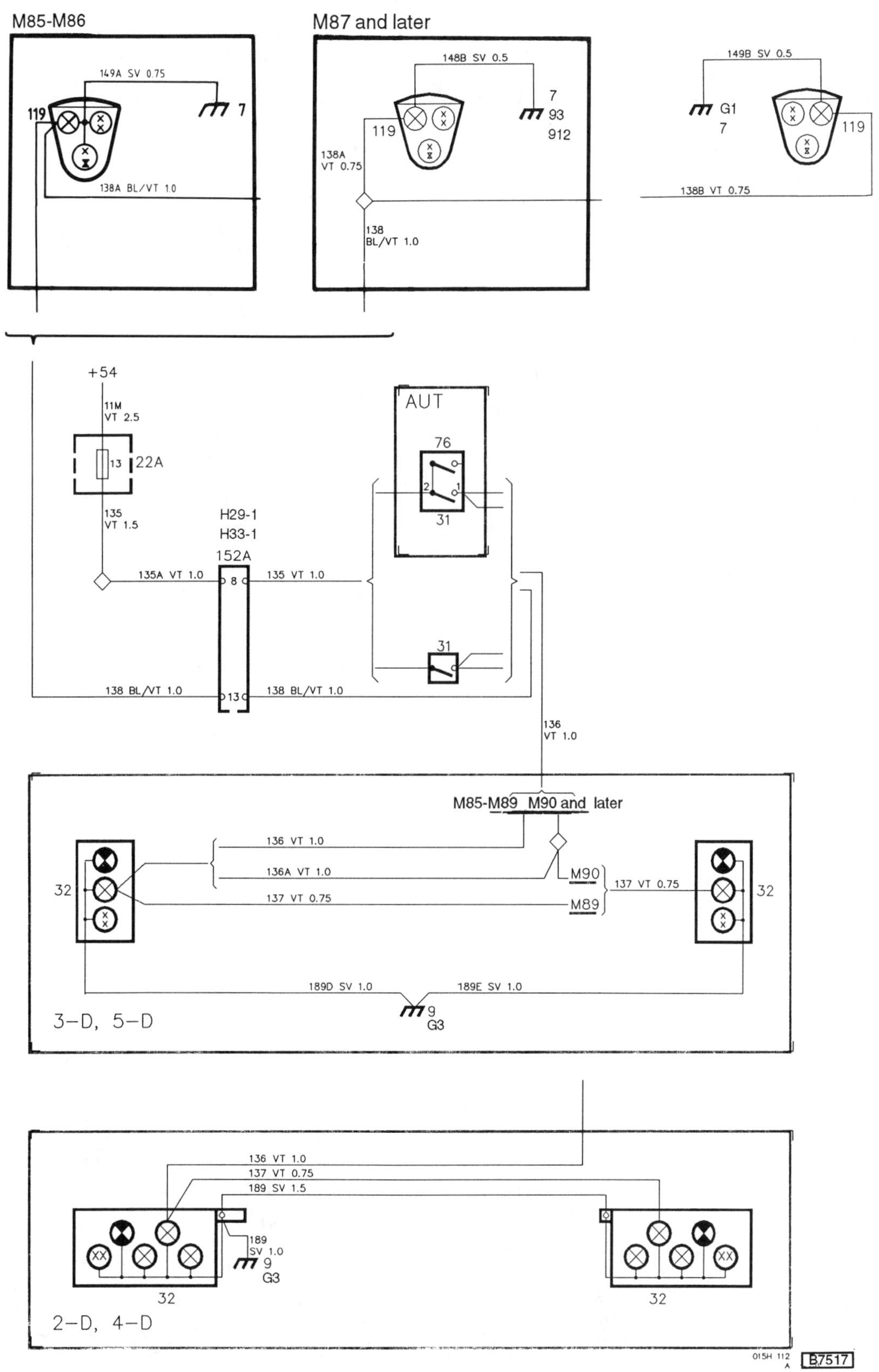

Brake Lights

Operation

The brake lights are supplied voltage through the brake light switch (29). When the brake pedal is depressed, the brake light switch closes and completes the circuit to the brake lights. The brake switch is mounted on the upper part of the brake pedal and is adjustable. On 1986 and later models, a center brake light is used. See **351 Lighting** for information on changing bulbs. For troubleshooting information on the ABS warning lights see the **Anti-lock Braking System (ABS)** wiring diagram.

Fault Tracing

1. Check fuse 31.
2. Check for voltage at the brake light switch. Check for voltage at the brake light sockets when the brake pedal is depressed.

NOTE

A wooden rod can be used to hold the brake pedal down during troubleshooting.

---

3. Check the adjustment of the brake light switch. The brake lights should come on when the brake pedal is depressed 10 mm (0.4 in.) or more. If necessary, adjust the switch as described in **364 Electric Controls and Switches.**

Component Locations

- 22 main fuse/relay panel
- 29 brake light switch at the brake pedal
- 30 brake lights in the rear clusters
- 109 third (center) brake light

Connector Locations

1985-1990

- 57 3-pin connector (hatchback only) in the luggage compartment
- 59 2-pin connector in the luggage compartment
- 60 1-pin connector in luggage compartment at the rear light
- 123 4-pin connector at hatchback, left side
- 152A 29-pin bulkhead connector at main fuse/relay panel

1991 and later

- H2-17 2-pin connector at hatchback left side, or on sedan under parcel shelf
- H2-18 2-pin connector at hatchback, left side
- H2-42 2-pin connector at luggage compartment lid
- H2-43 2-pin connector at left hinge, convertible
- H3-13 3-pin connector in luggage compartment, left air outlet
- H4-12 4-pin connector in trunk lid, left air outlet
- H29-1 29-pin bulkhead connector behind main fuse/relay panel (1991-1991 1/2)
- H33-1 33-pin bulkhead connector behind main fuse/relay panel (1991 1/2 and later)

Ground Locations

1985-1990

- 9 ground point in luggage compartment

1991and later

- G3 ground point in luggage compartment
- G5 ground point under the rear seat
- G9 ground point in luggage compartment
- G19 ground point in hatchback

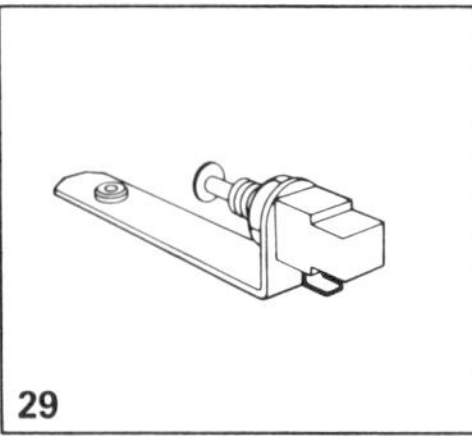
29

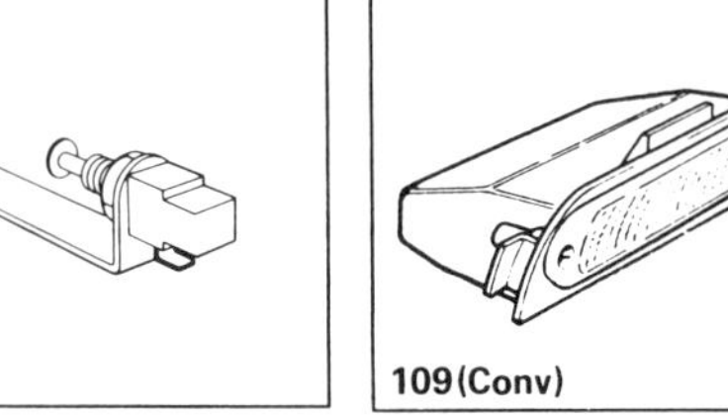
109(Conv)

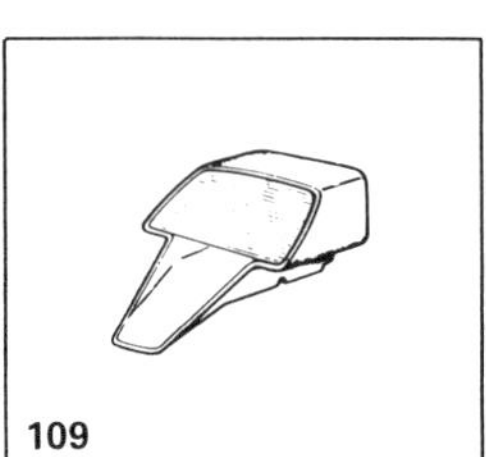
109

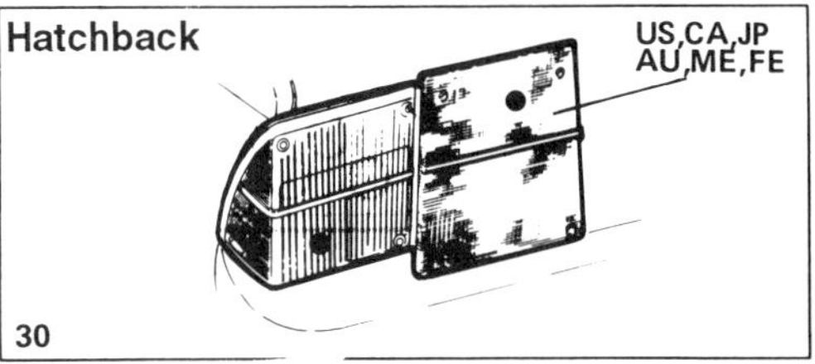

30

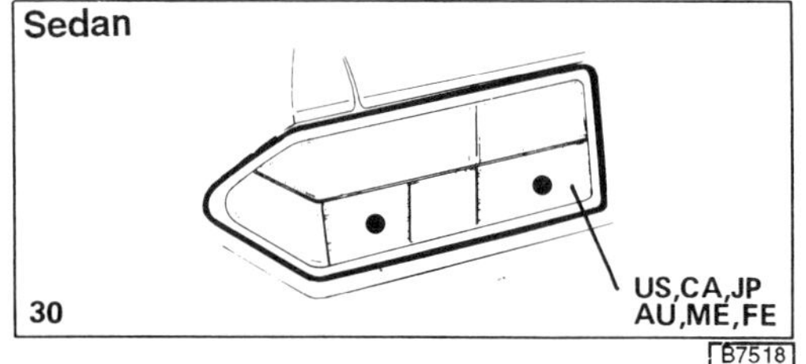

30

B7518

Brake Lights

1985-1989

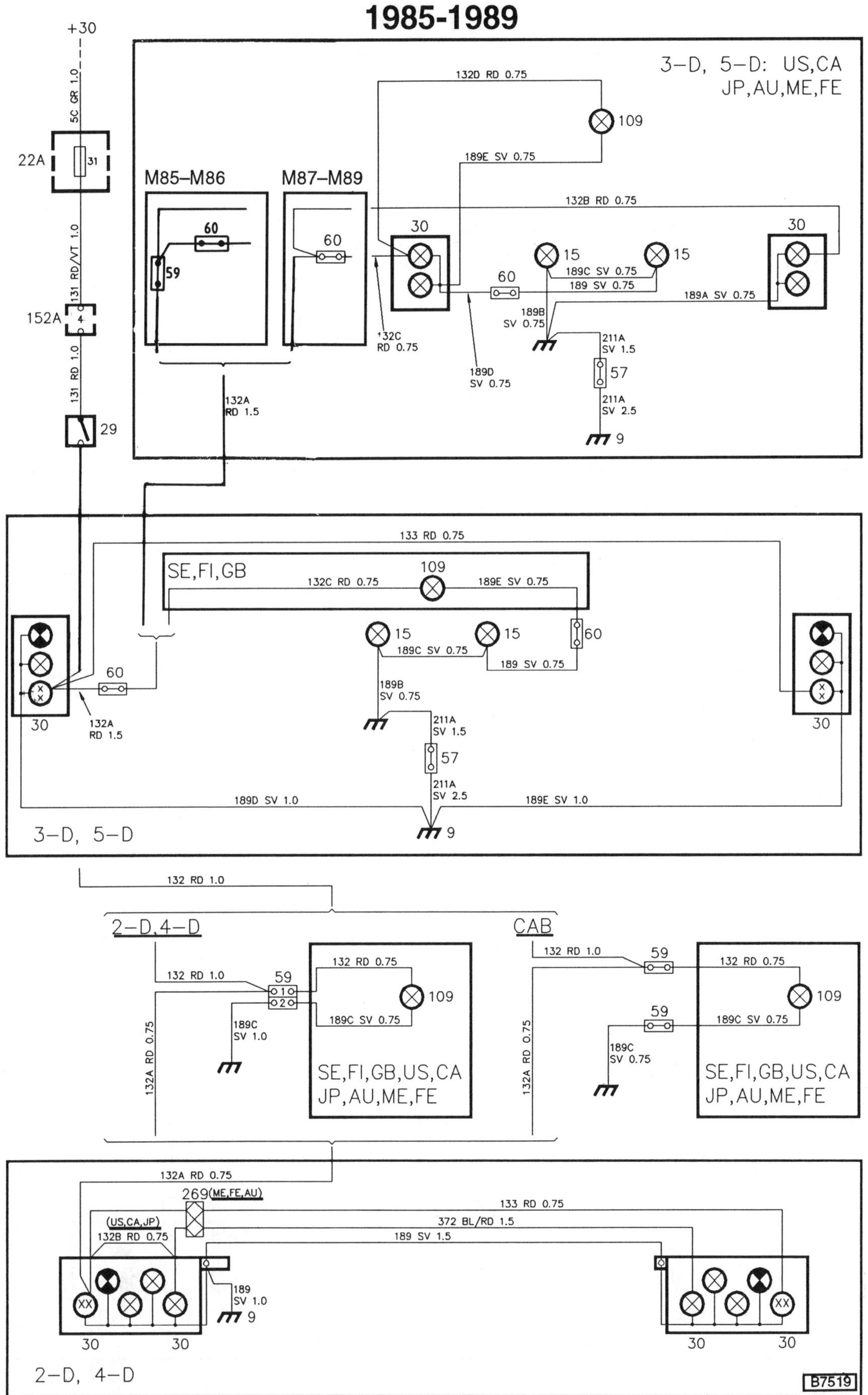

Brake Lights

1990-1993

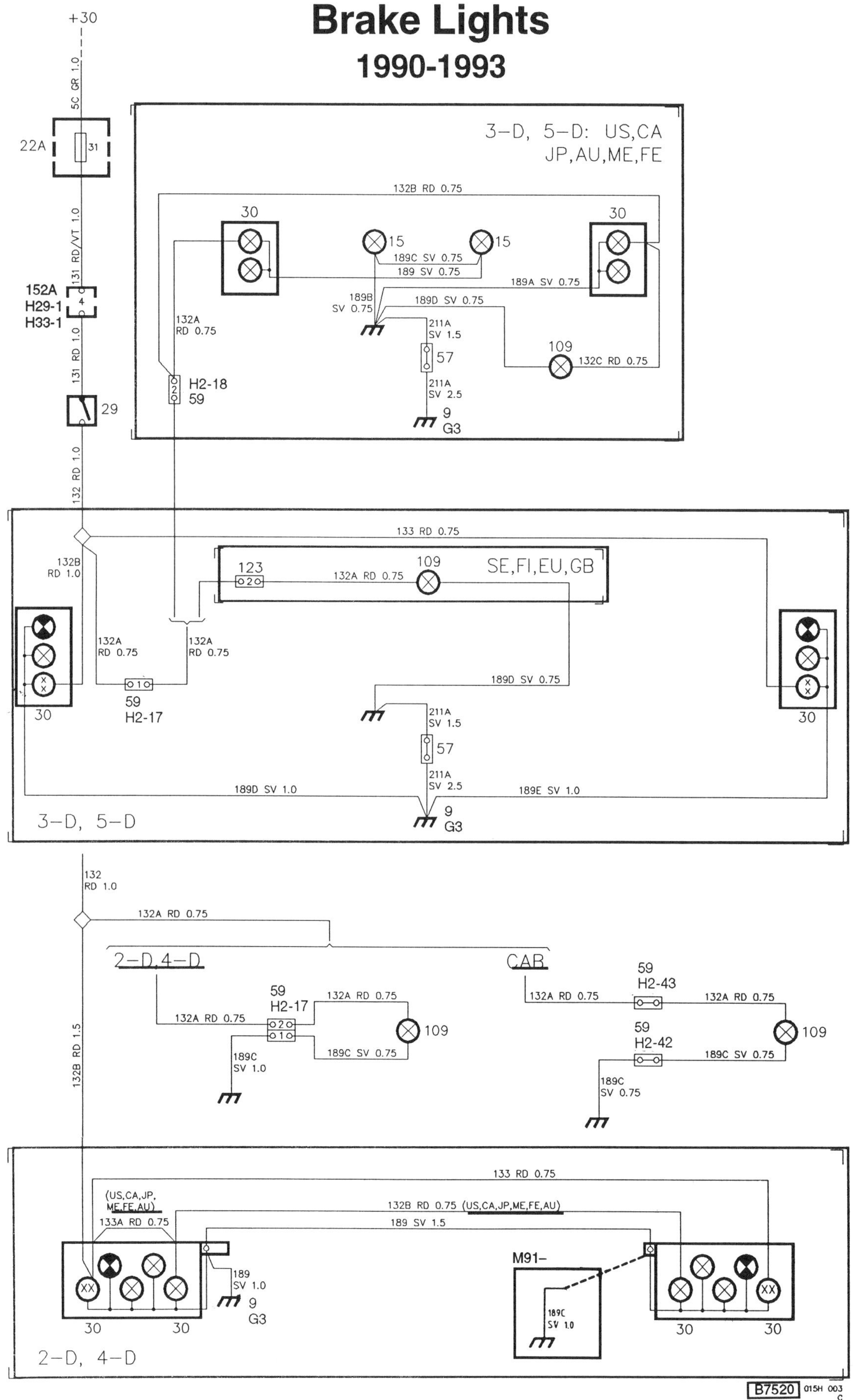

Burglar Alarm

Operation

The burglar alarm consists of a control unit, a main switch, a siren, switches in the doors, hood, and luggage compartment, and a remote control unit. On some later models, a motion detector, a glass breakage detector, a service-mode switch, and a rear seat switch are used. The alarm system is integrated with the central locking system. See the **Central Locking** wiring diagram found later in this repair group.

Fault Tracing

1. Check the fuses.
2. Check that the batteries in the remote control unit are good condition. Replace the batteries if in doubt.
3. Check the function of the LED on the left speaker grille.
4. Check all switches for proper operation.

Component Locations

1 battery at right front of engine compartment
4 starter motor under intake manifold
20 ignition switch
22A main fuse/relay panel in left wheel housing
27 left-hand direction indicator lamps
28 right-hand direction indicator lamps
53 interior light switch in center console
54 door switches on the door jamb
55 luggage compartment light in storage area
56 luggage compartment light switch in storage area
77 neutral/safety switch (automatics only) at gear selector lever
82 seatbelt warning relay under the rear seat
151 interior lighting time delay relay under the rear seat
274 fuse for burglar alarm under rear seat
275 alarm siren in engine compartment near right headlamp
276 alarm hood switch under the hood at front of wheel housing
288 alarm switch at center console
289 alarm control unit under the rear seat
304 alarm motion detector under the rear seat
305 alarm LED at left speaker grille
313 alarm relay under the rear seat
314 alarm seat switch in driver seat
315 alarm seat switch in passenger seat
316 alarm diode under the rear seat in the wiring harness
401 auxiliary fuse/relay panel under rear seat
412 alarm service mode switch under left side passenger seat
413 alarm glass breakage detector under passenger seat
423 alarm start interlock relay (convertible) under rear seat
424 alarm hazard warning light relay (convertible) under rear seat at the control unit
425 door lock switch in center console
426 switch for rear seat under the rear seat

Connector Locations

1985-1990

57A 3-pin white connector
57B 3-pin red connector
57D 3-pin green connector
57E 3-pin blue connector
58 12-pin connector behind instrument panel to the left of the steering column
59 2-pin connector in luggage compartment near left hinge
60 1-pin connector (3) one for the alarm siren in engine compartment, two under left speaker grille for the LEDs
122 8-pin connector for alarm under the rear seat
123 4-pin connector one in each B pillar
152A 29-pin bulkhead connector at main fuse/relay panel

1991 and later

H1-18 1-pin connector under center console
H1-21 1-pin connector for LED, under left speaker grille
H1-22 1-pin connector for LED, under left speaker grille
H1-28 1-pin connector under rear seat
H2-40 2-pin connector for the alarm siren, behind headlamp
H2-41 2-pin connector under passenger seat, right side
H2-42 2-pin connector in trunk lid
H2-43 2-pin connector at left hinge, convertible
H2-53 2-pin connector under the rear seat
H8-3 8-pin connector under the rear seat
H10-8 10-pin connector under rear seat at alarm control unit
H12-1 12-pin connector behind instrument panel, left of steering column
H33-1 33-pin bulkhead connector behind main fuse/relay panel (1991 1/2 and later

Ground Locations

1985-1990

117 ground point at the handbrake

1991 and later

G1 ground point at radiator cross member
G4 ground point between ignition switch and handbrake
G5 ground point under the rear seat
G5 ground point under the rear seat
G25 ground point at the gearbox

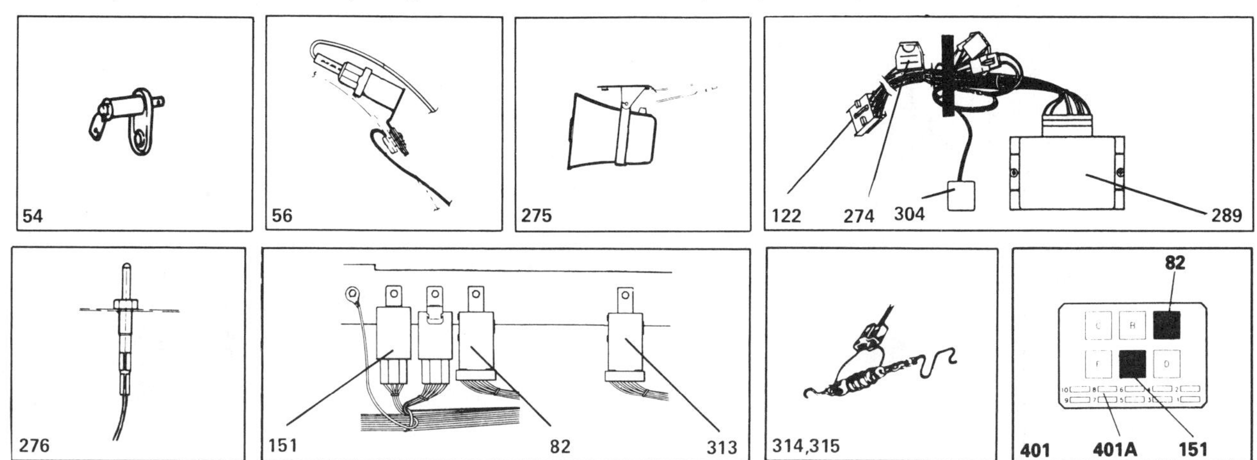

Burglar Alarm—ex. Convertible

1985-1986

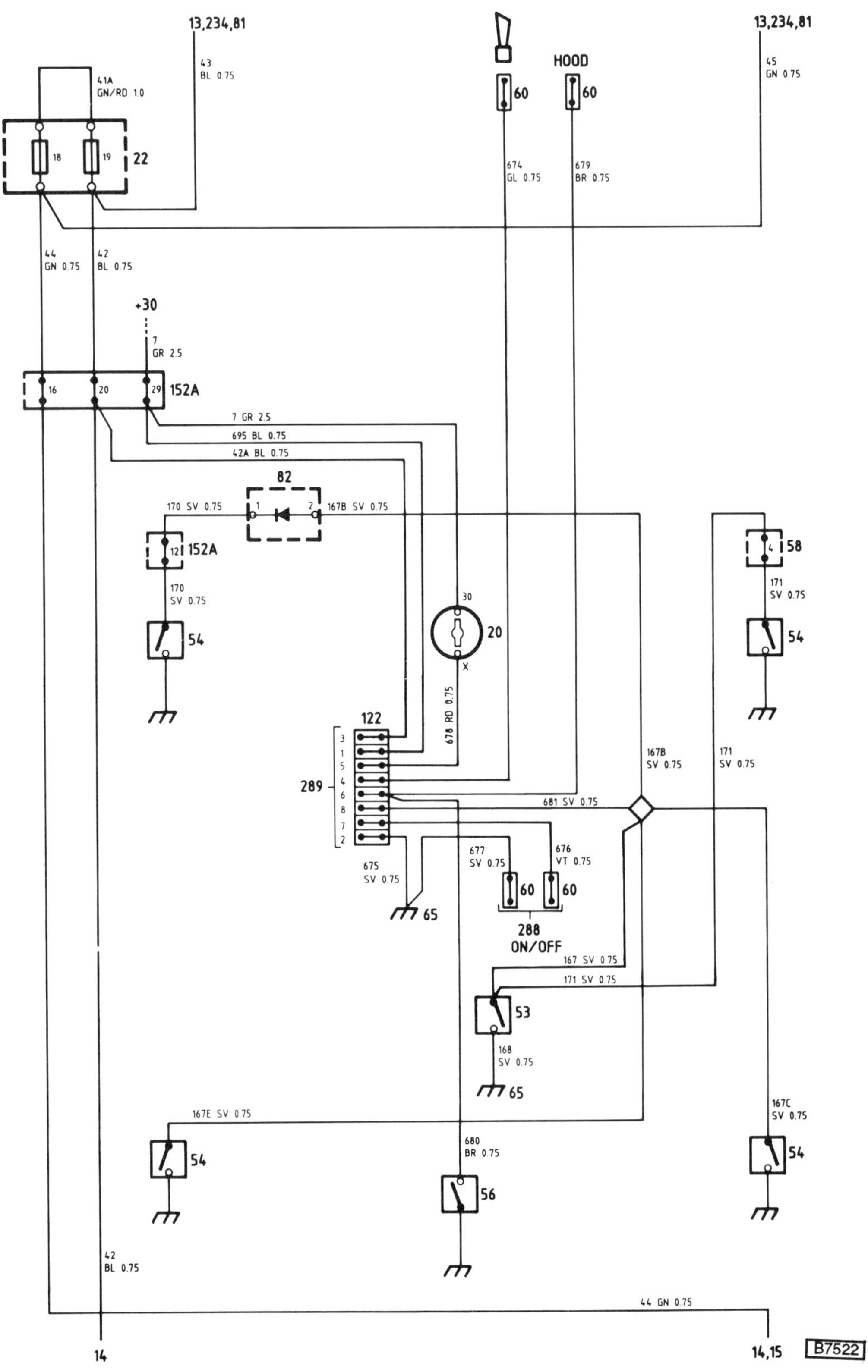

Burglar Alarm—ex. Convertible

1987-1990

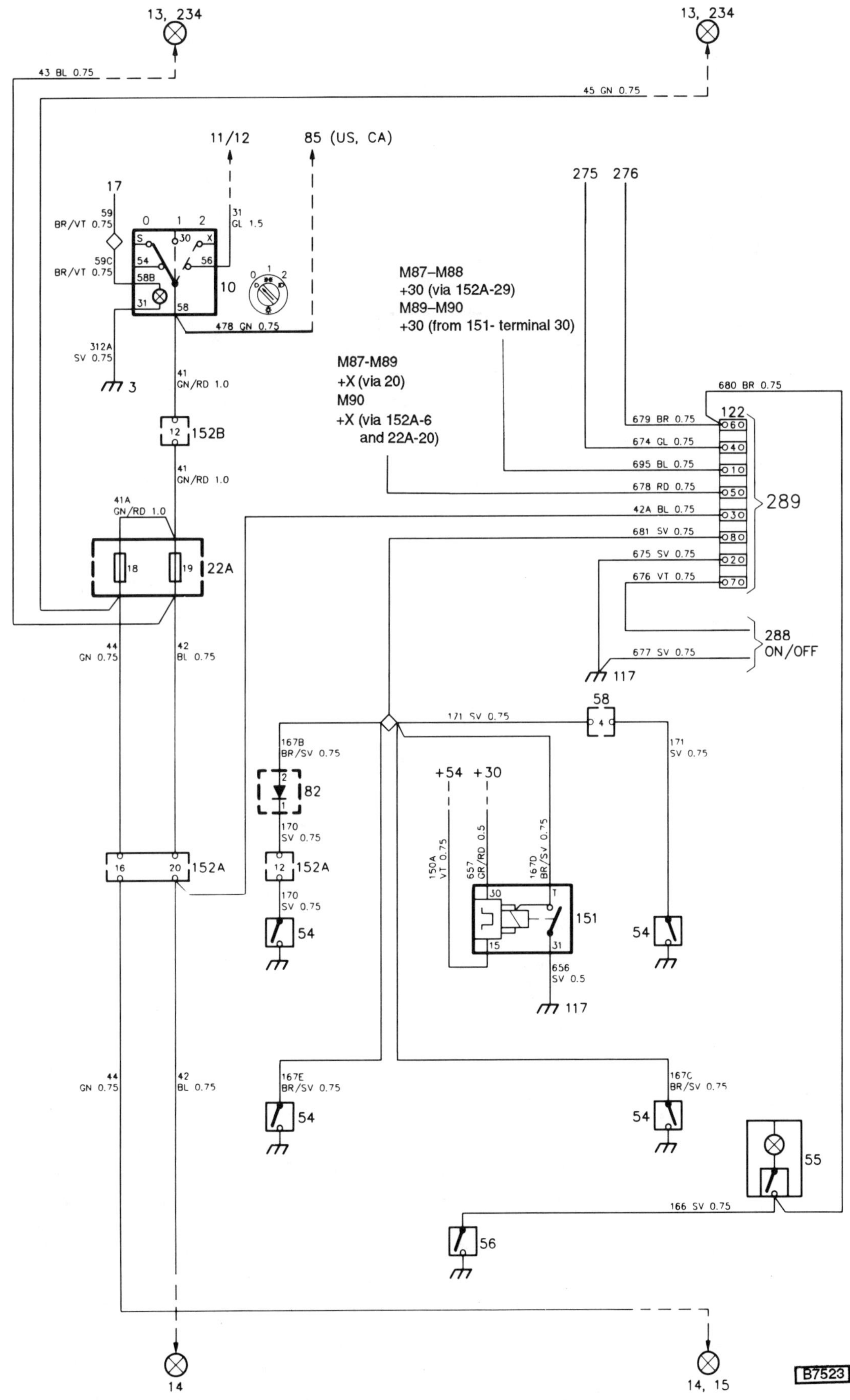

Burglar Alarm—ex. Convertible

1991-1993

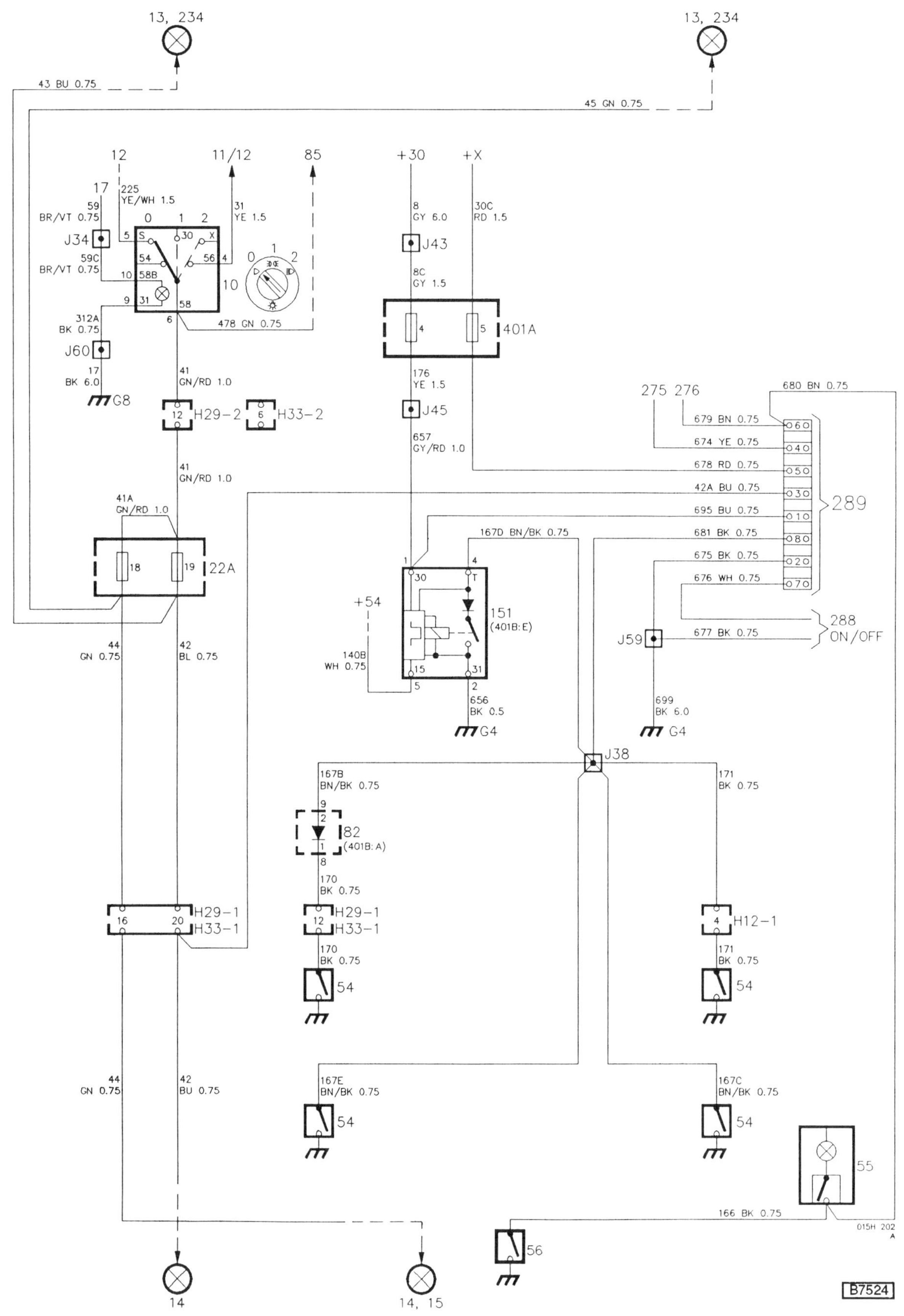

Burglar Alarm—Convertible

1987-1988

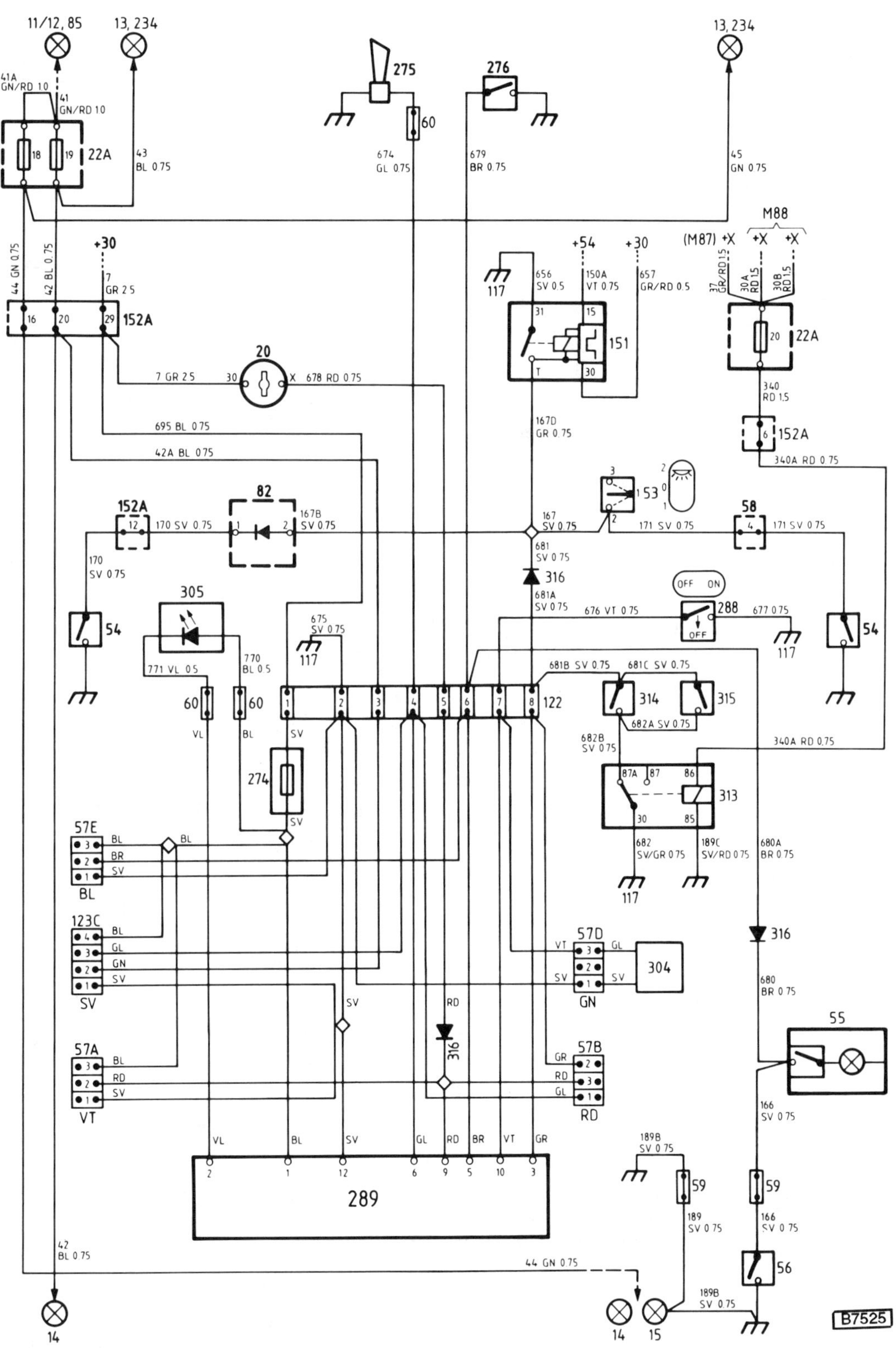

B7525

Burglar Alarm—Convertible

1989

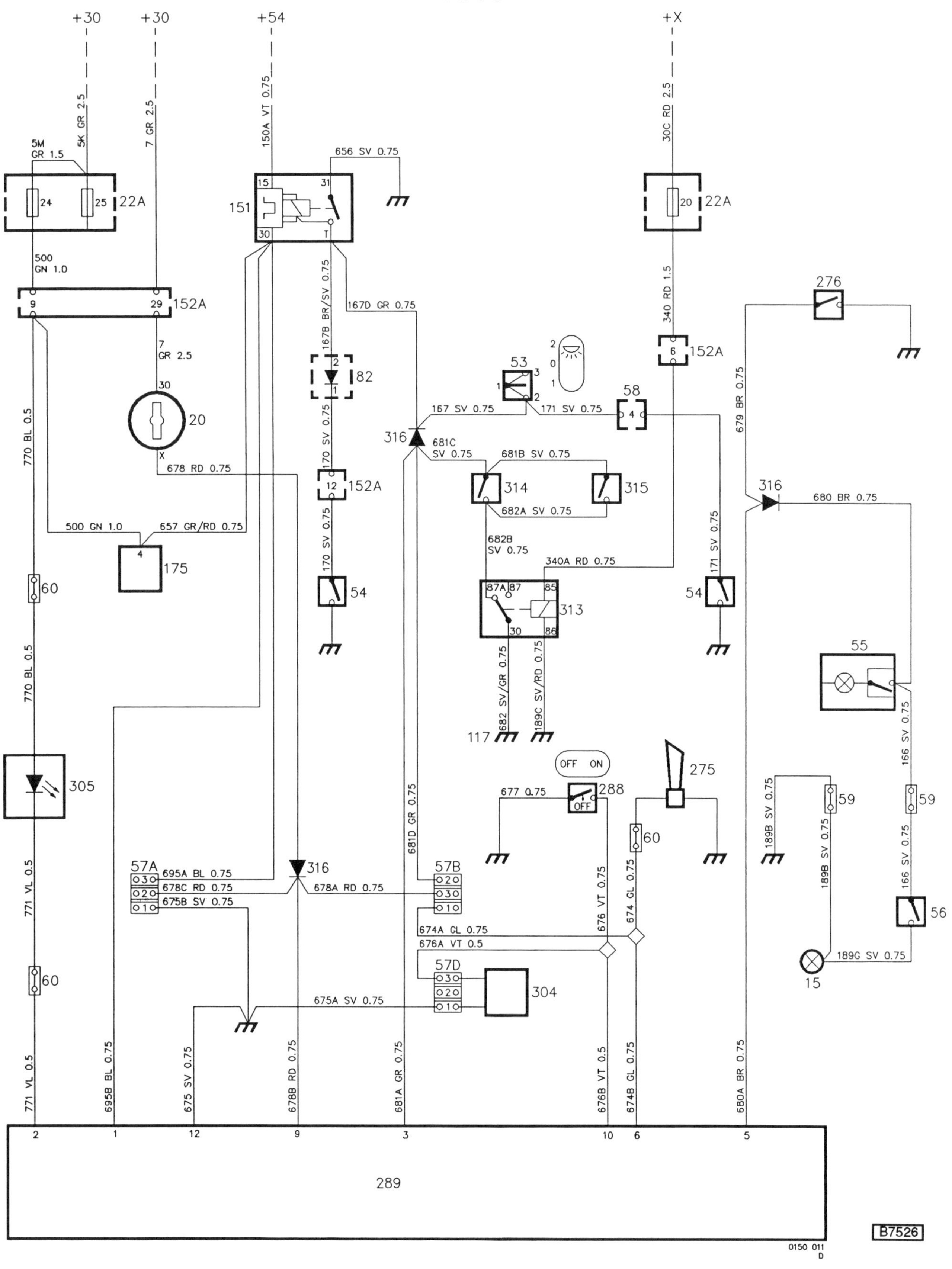

Burglar Alarm—Convertible

1990

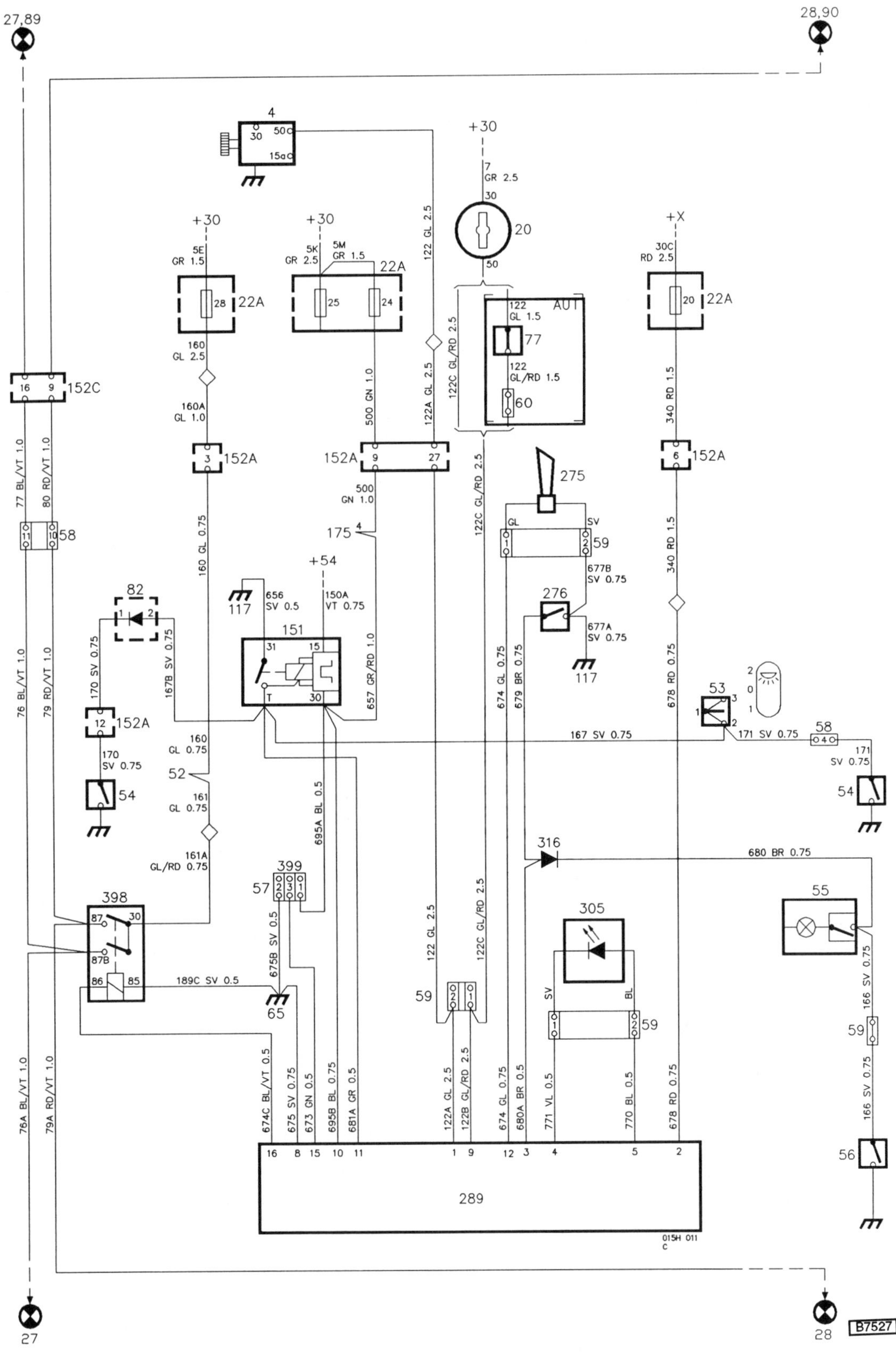

B7527

Burglar Alarm—Convertible

1991

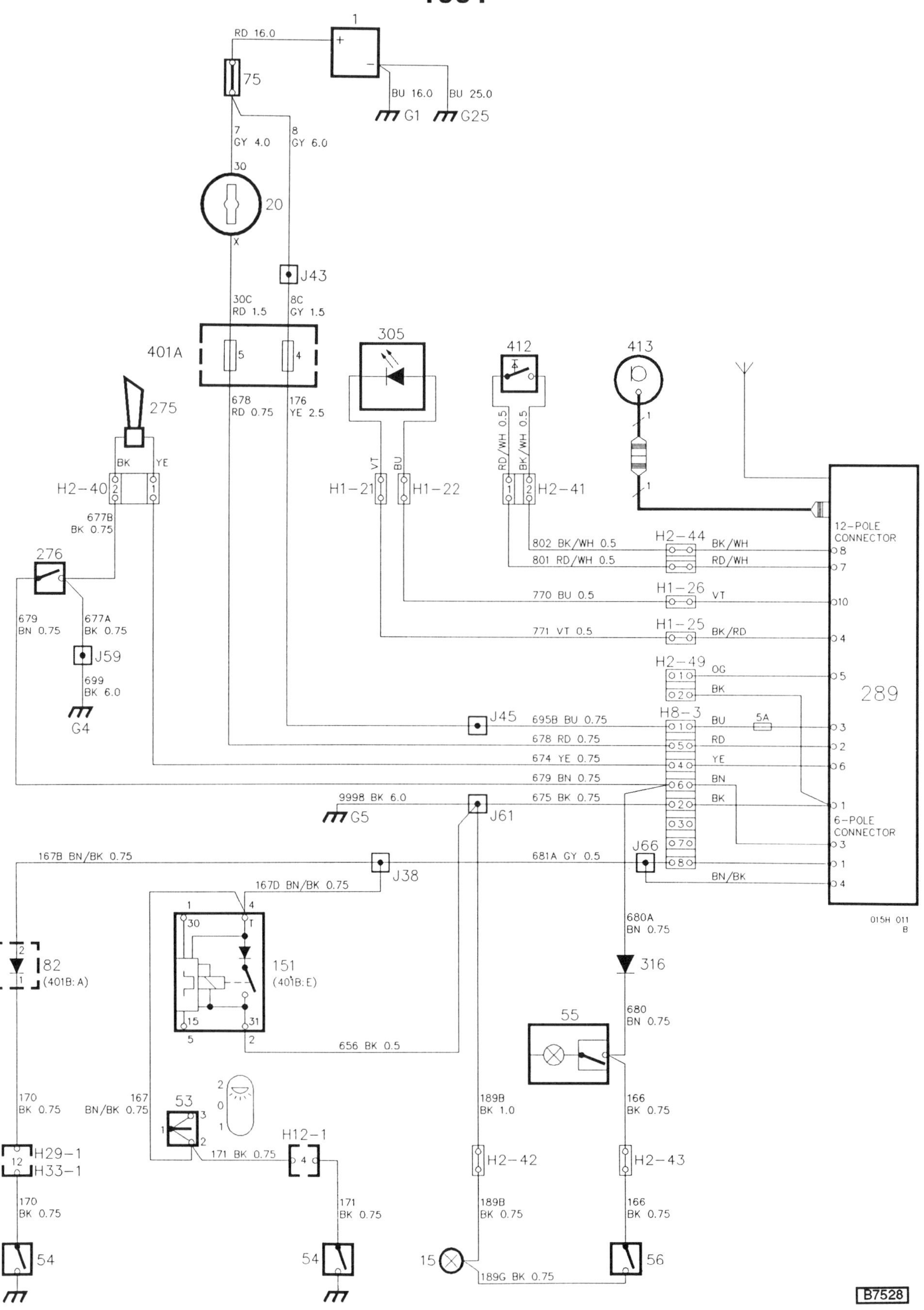

Burglar Alarm—Convertible

1992 and later

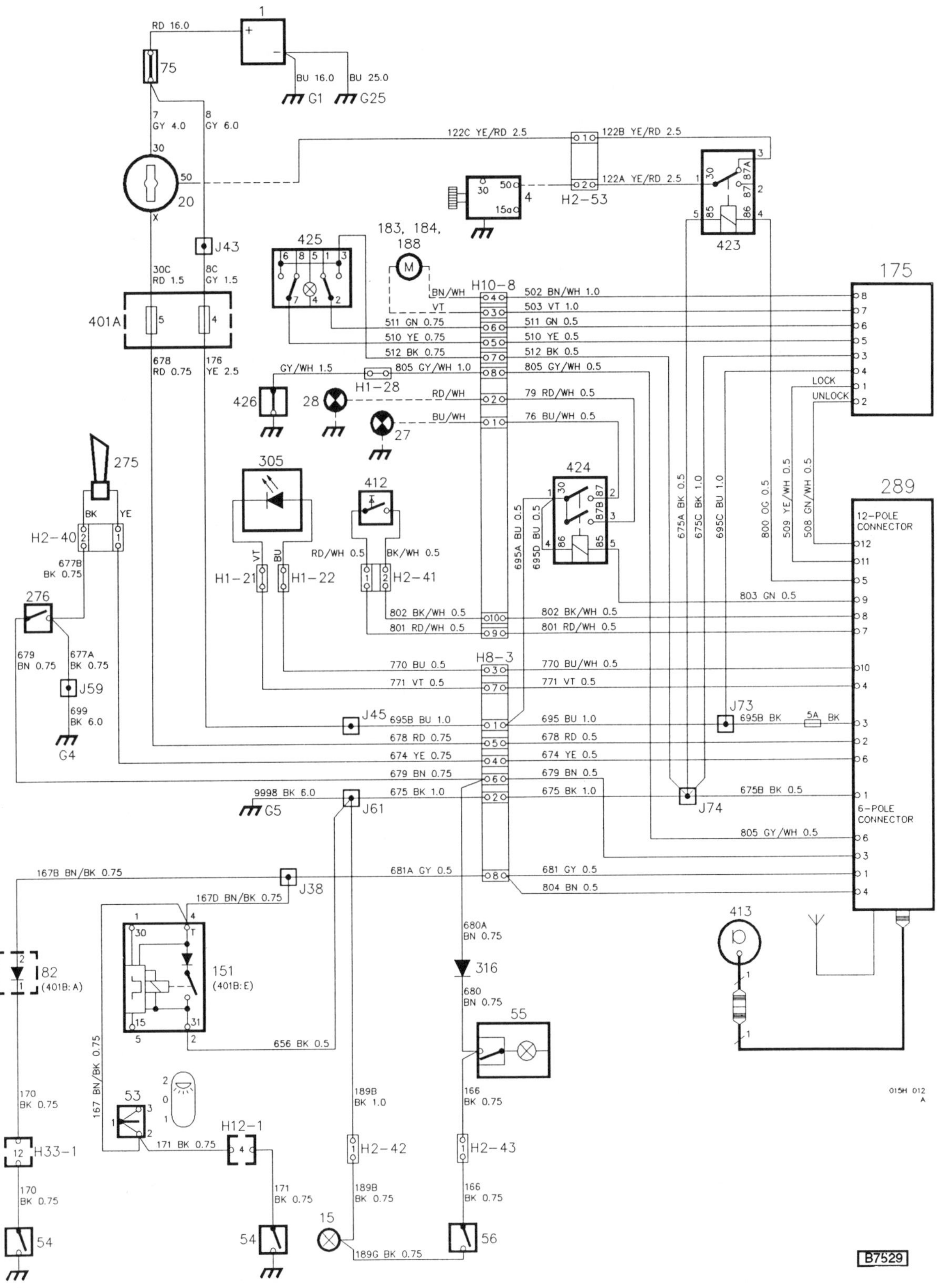

Central Locking

Operation

All of the door locks and the luggage compartment lid are locked or unlocked when the key is turned in the driver's door. The central locking control unit (175) actuates all of the lock motors via pin 7 and pin 8.

See **830 Doors, Windows, and Lids** for more information on removing the lock motors and other door components.

Fault Tracing

1. Check the fuses. Check the voltage supply to control unit (175) pin 4. This pin should always be live.
2. Check that pin 7 of the control unit (175) is live when the door key is in the unlock position. Check that pin 8 of the control unit (175) is live when the key is in the unlock position.

CAUTION

The lock motors should only be tested through pin 7 and pin 8 of the control unit (175). Do not 'bench test' the lock motors using any other power supply sources as this may overload and damage the motors.

NOTE

When testing pin 7 and pin 8, the supply will only be live for approximately 1 second.

Component Locations

- 22A main fuse/relay panel at left wheel housing
- 75 distribution block at right wheel housing
- 175 central locking control unit behind instrument panel right side
- 183 key switch for the driver's central door locking in driver door
- 184 central door lock motor in passenger door
- 185 central door lock motor in right rear door
- 186 central door lock motor in left rear door
- 188 central door lock motor in tailgate lock
- 401 auxiliary fuse/relay panel under rear seat

Connector Locations

1985-1990

- 57 3-pin connector (2) in driver door and in engine compartment near left door hinge
- 59 2-pin connector (5) right front door, engine compartment near right door hinge, left rear door, right rear door, luggage compartment near central lock motor
- 123 4-pin connector (2) one in each B pillar
- 152A 29-pin bulkhead connector at main fuse/relay panel

1991 and later

- H2-4 2-pin connector at engine compartment near right door hinge
- H2-8 2-pin connector at engine compartment near right door hinge
- H2-20 2-pin connector in luggage compartment, left wheel housing
- H2-30 2-pin connector in left rear door
- H2-31 2-pin connector in right rear door
- H2-32 2-pin connector in luggage compartment near the central lock motor
- H3-7 3-pin connector in engine compartment near left door hinge
- H3-15 3-pin connector in the driver door
- H4-4 4-pin connector at right B pillar behind trim
- H4-5 4-pin connector at left B pillar behind trim
- H10-1 10-pin connector behind instrument panel, left of steering column
- H12-1 12-pin connector behind instrument panel, left of steering column
- H29-2 29-pin bulkhead connector behind main fuse/relay panel (1991-1991 1/2)
- H33-2 33-pin bulkhead connector behind main fuse/relay panel (1991 1/2 and later)

Ground Locations

1985-1990

- 65 ground point at the handbrake
- 117 ground point at the handbrake

1991 and later

- G1 ground point at radiator cross member
- G8 ground point behind instrument panel
- G25 ground point at gearbox

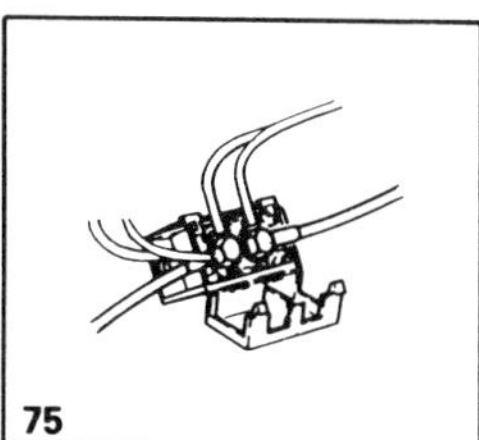

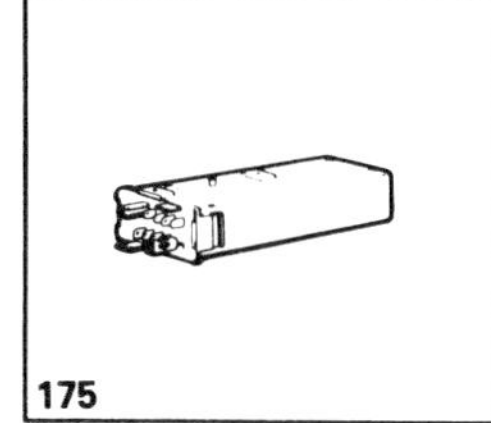

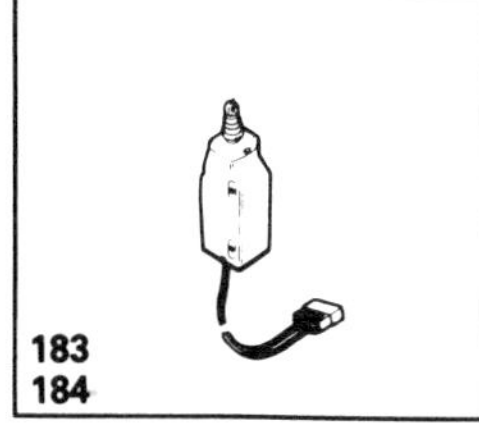

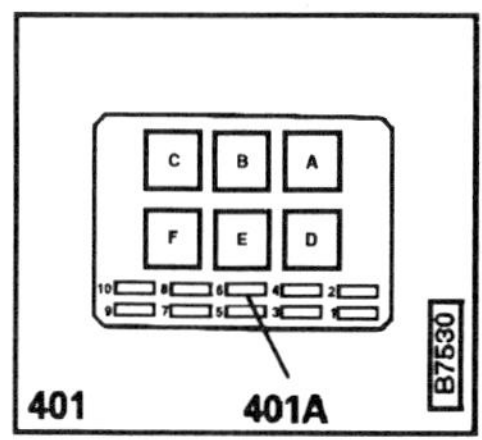

Central Locking

1985-1990

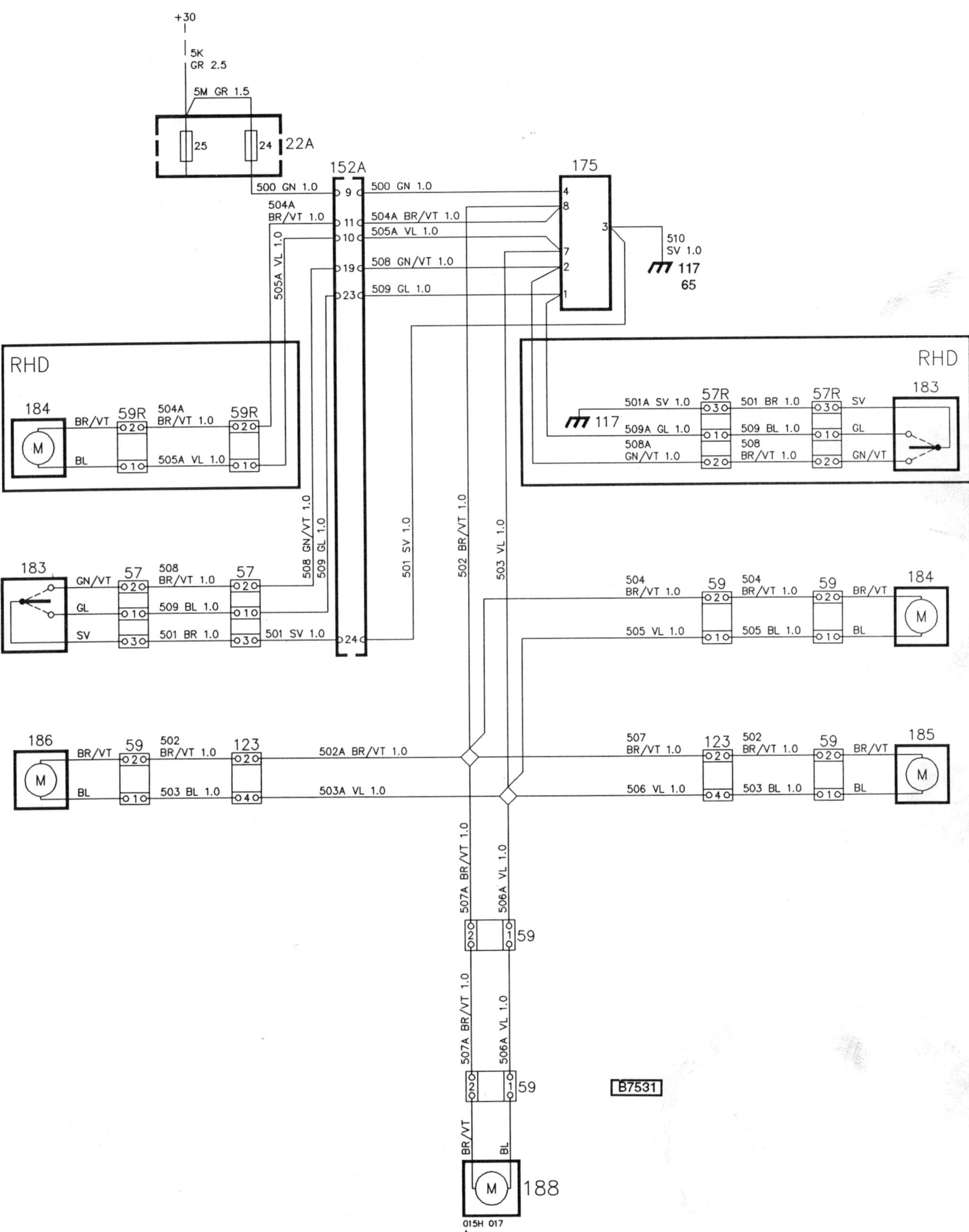

Central Locking

1991 and later (ex. 1992 and later convertible)

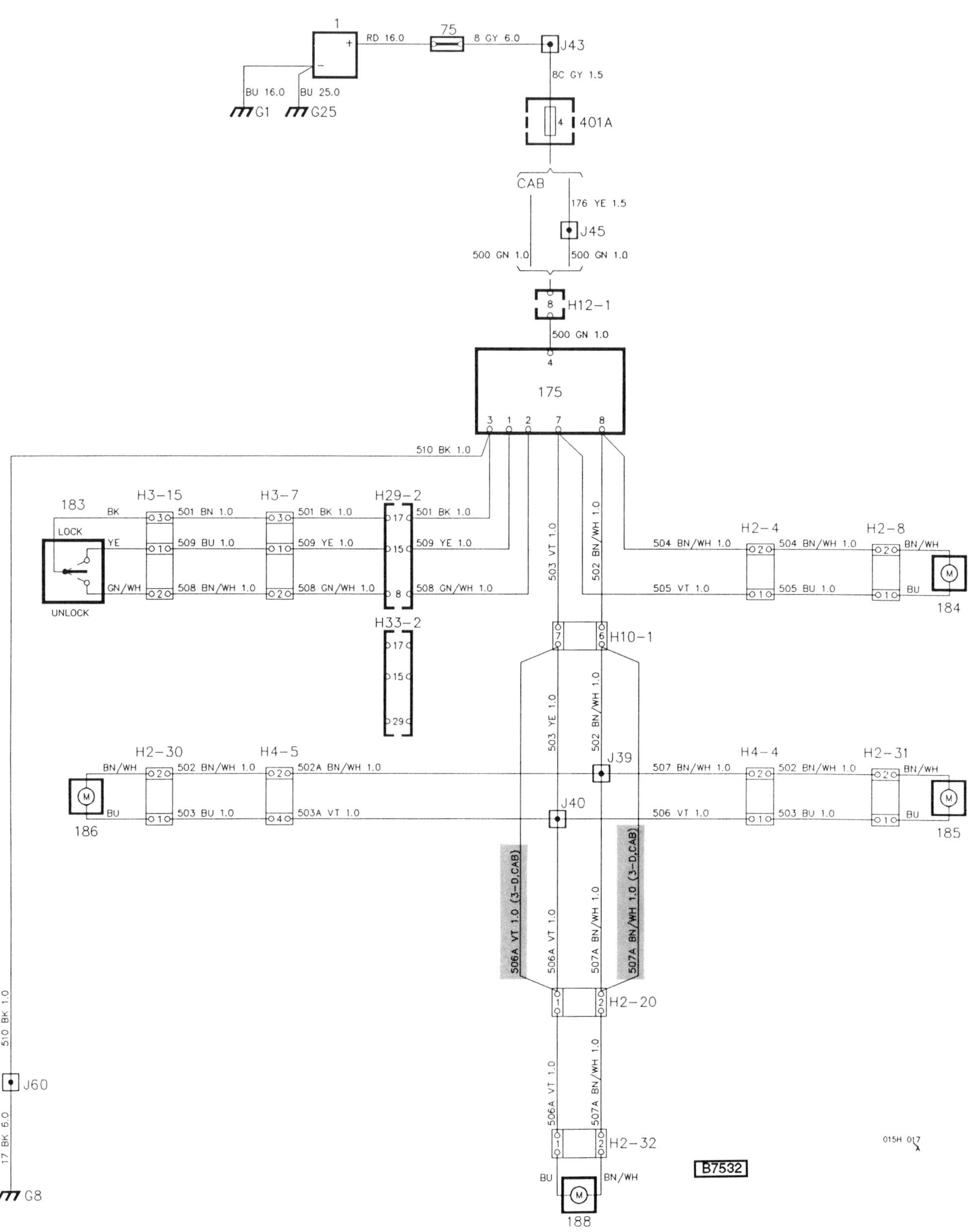

Central Locking

1992 and later Convertible

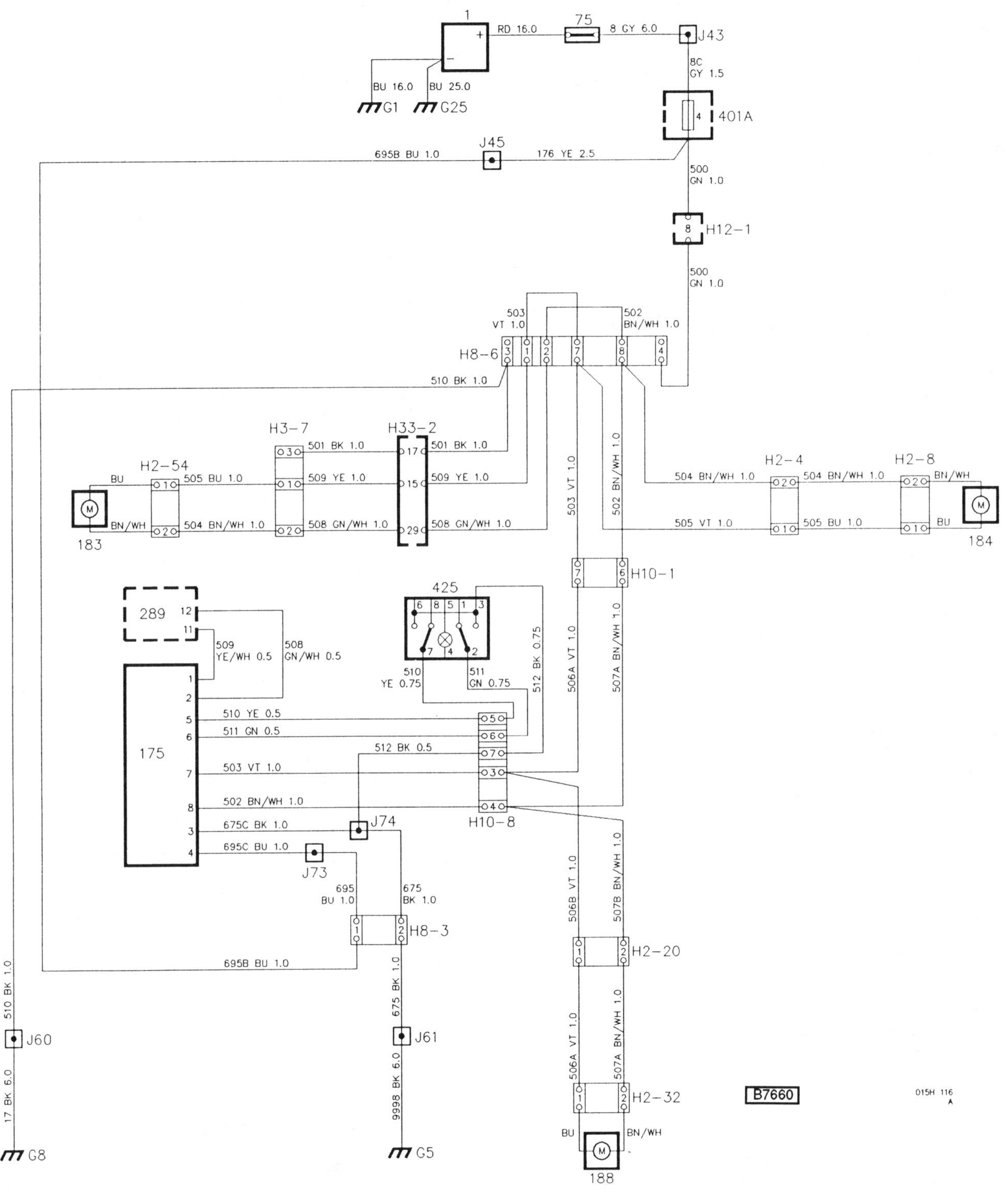

Combined Instruments

Operation

The combined instruments, or instrument cluster, monitors various operating functions. See **853 Dashboard and Consoles** for more information on removing and testing the instrument cluster and instrument panel. Additional test and repair information on sensors related to instrument warnings can be found in **364 Electric Controls and Switches** or in the section pertaining to the warning function such as **5 BRAKES** or **2 ENGINE**.

Fault Tracing

1. Check the fuses.
2. Check for power and ground to the instrument cluster.

Component Locations

2 alternator at back of engine compartment
8 lighting relay
10 lighting switch
16 rheostat for instrument cluster
18 instrument lighting
20 ignition switch
21 ignition switch relay in main fuse/relay panel
22A main fuse/relay panel at left wheel housing
25 hazard warning switch
42 brake fluid level switch in brake fluid reservoir
43 handbrake switch under the handbrake lever
44 oil pressure switch at left side of engine, above oil filter
45 coolant temperature transmitter at front of engine near thermostat housing
46 fuel level transmitter in the fuel tank, accessible in luggage compartment
47 instrument cluster
47A fuel level gauge
47B fuel warning light
47C coolant temperature gauge
47D oil pressure warning light
47E charging lamp
47F brake warning light
47G high beam warning light
47H left-hand direction indicator warning lamp
47I right-hand direction indicator warning lamp
47J rear window heater warning lamp
47K shift-up indicator
47M handbrake warning lamp
47N rear fog light warning lamp
47P CHECK ENGINE light
47Q ABS warning lamp
47S passive seatbelt warning lamp
47T SRS airbag warning lamp (see SRS warnings)
47U cruise control warning lamp
49 clock
75 distribution block at right wheel housing
110 tachometer
116 rear heated window switch
132 speed transmitter at the rear of the instrument cluster
141 selector for cruise control at direction indicator stalk
146 ignition amplifier in front of left wheel housing
148 ashtray lighting
153 cigarette lighter lamp
154 heater control lighting
158 negative distribution in main fuse/relay panel
159 +15 distribution in main fuse/relay panel
161 rear fog light switch
176 EZK control unit at inner left fender
200 LH control unit forward of the right front door, behind trim
291 ABS control unit (1989) in engine compartment, left wheel housing
291 ABS control unit (1990 and later) under rear seat, right side
306 logic box for passive seatbelts under rear seat, left side
331 SRS airbag control unit behind instrument panel, left grille.

Connector Locations

1985-1990

57 3-pin connector (2) Under spare tire cover, under rear seat, left side
58 12-pin connector behind instrument panel to left of steering column
59 2-pin connector at main fuse/relay panel, convertibles
60 1-pin connector under center console
98 10-pin connector behind instrument panel to left of steering column
123 4-pin connector at hatchback, left side
152A 29-pin bulkhead connector at main fuse/relay panel
152B 29-pin bulkhead connector at main fuse/relay panel
152C 29-pin bulkhead connector at main fuse/relay panel
267 radio connector in instrument panel

1991 and later

H2-3 2-pin connector behind the instrument cluster
H2-6 2-pin connector behind instrument cluster,left of steering column
H2-7 2-pin connector in instrument panel at light switch
H2-10 2-pin connector behind cigarette lighter
H2-27 2-pin connector at main fuse/relay panel
H3-4 3-pin connector at main fuse/relay panel
H4-6 4-pin connector in instrument panel left side
H4-7 4-pin connector at the LH control unit, forward of right front door
H4-15 4-pin connector under rear seat, next to fuse/relay panel 401
H10-2 10-pin connector at the SRS airbag control unit, left speaker grille
H29-1 29-pin bulkhead connector at main fuse/relay panel (1991–1991 1/2)
H29-2 29-pin bulkhead connector at main fuse/relay panel (1991–1991 1/2)
H29-3 29-pin bulkhead connector at main fuse/relay panel (1991–1991 1/2)
H33-1 33-pin bulkhead connector at main fuse/relay panel (1991 1/2 –on)
H33-2 33-pin bulkhead connector at main fuse/relay panel (1991 1/2 –on)
H33-3 33-pin bulkhead connector at main fuse/relay panel (1991 1/2 –on)

Ground Locations

3/G8 ground point behind instrument panel
7/G1 ground point at radiator cross member
9/G3 ground point in luggage compartment
G6 ground distribution at main fuse/relay panel
117 ground point under the handbrake
211/G25 ground point at the gearbox
257/G32 ground point at alternator bracket

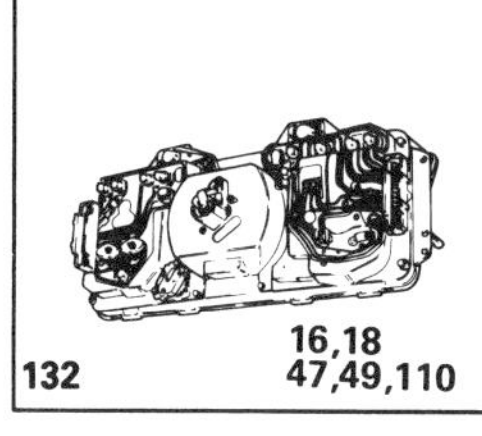

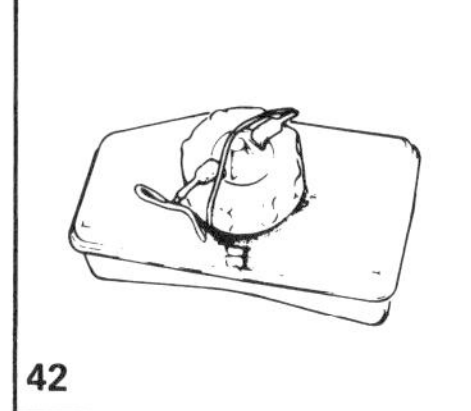

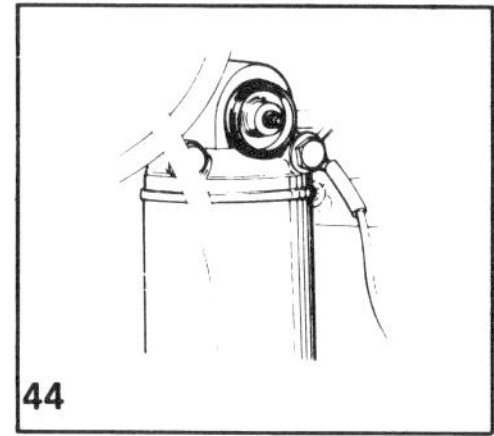

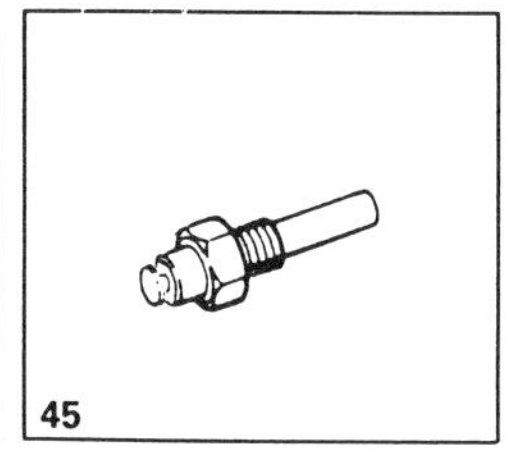

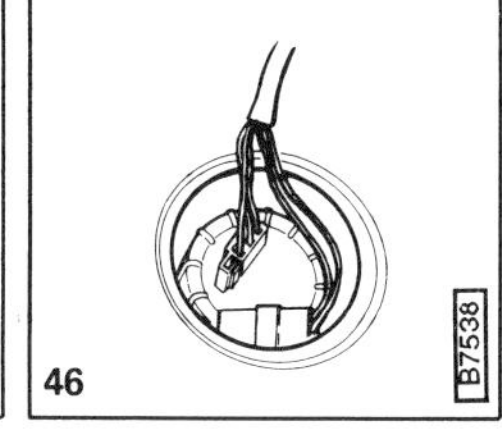

Combined Instruments
1985-1987

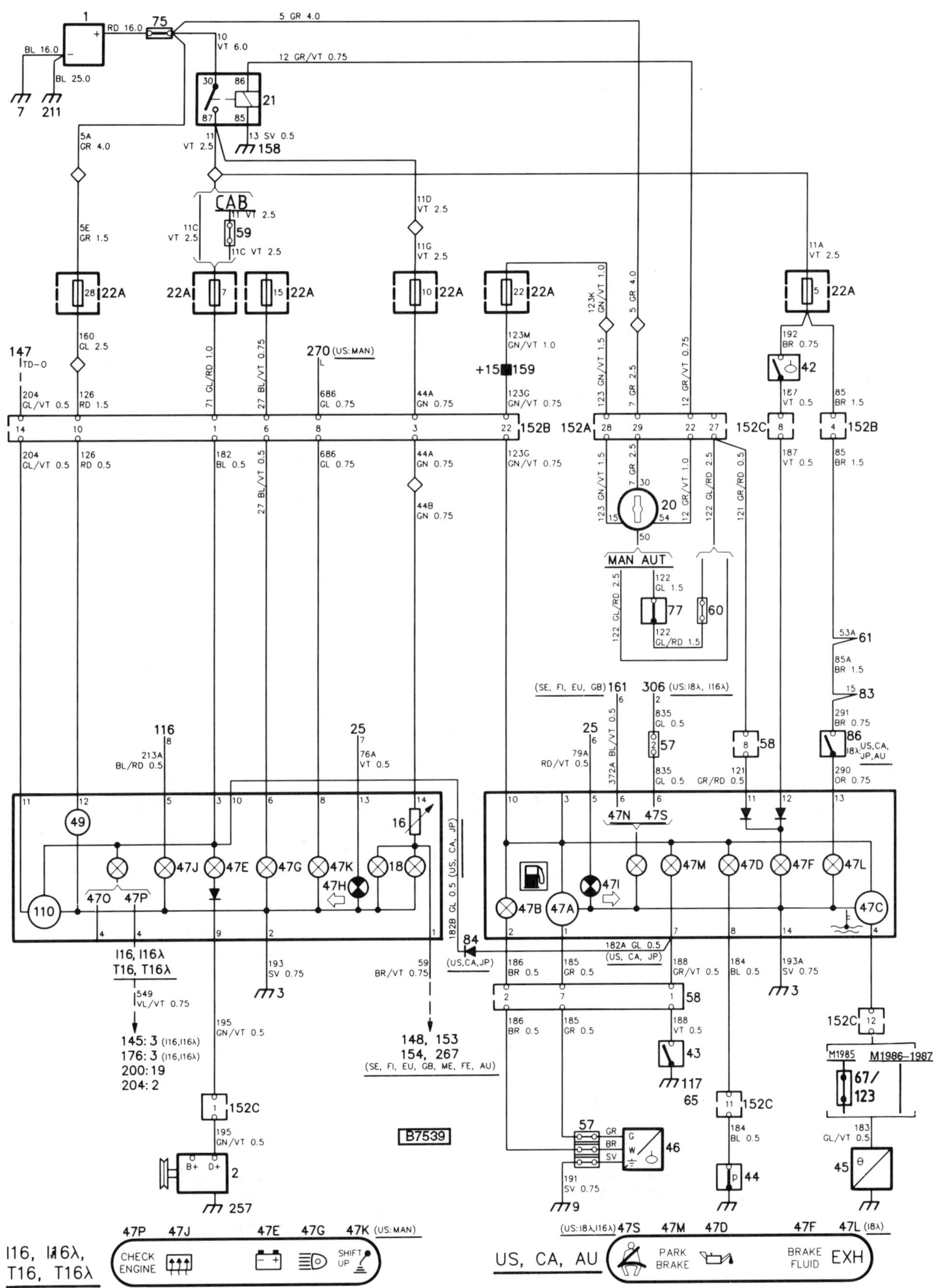

Combined Instruments

1988

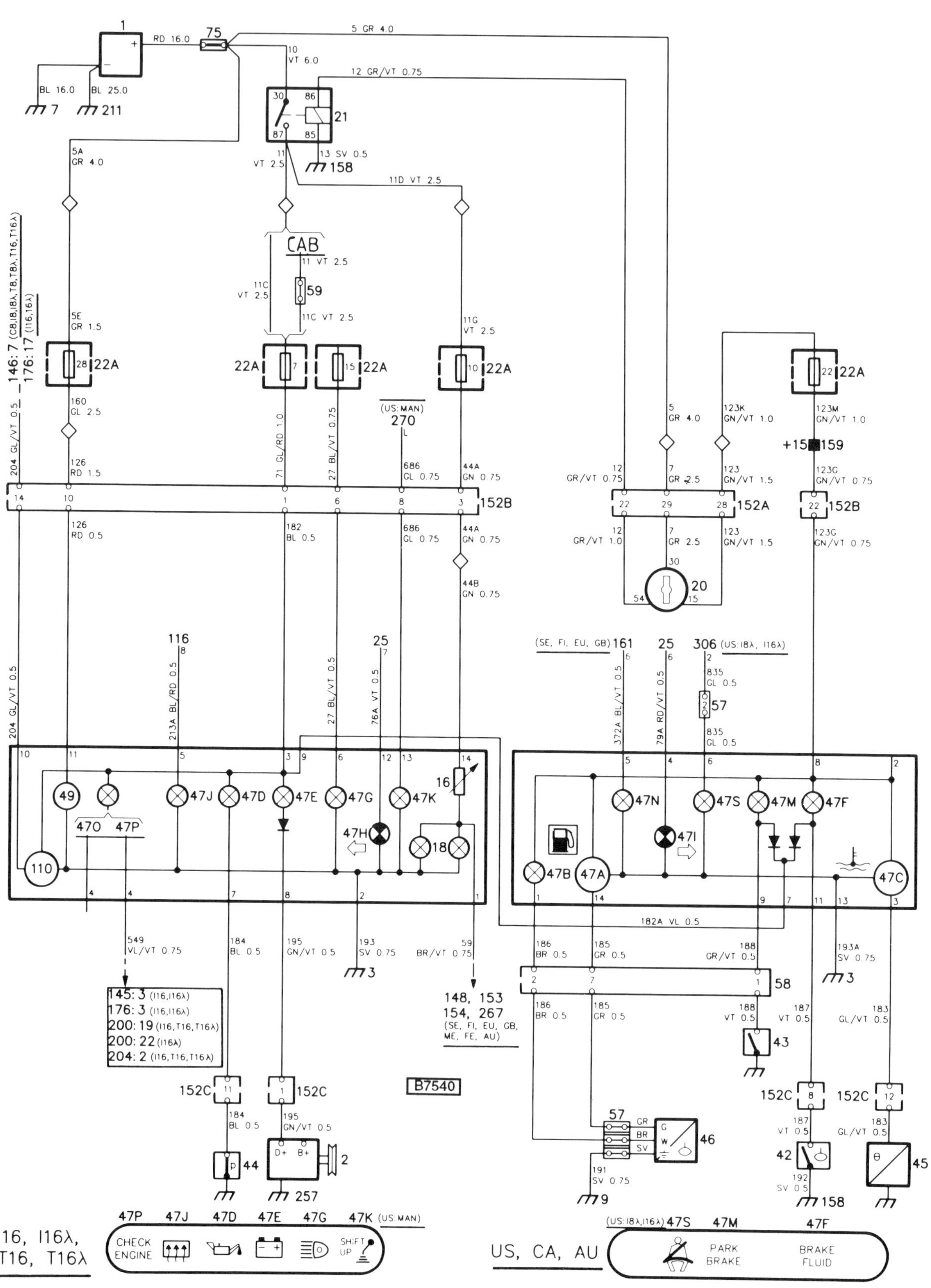

Combined Instruments

1989-1990

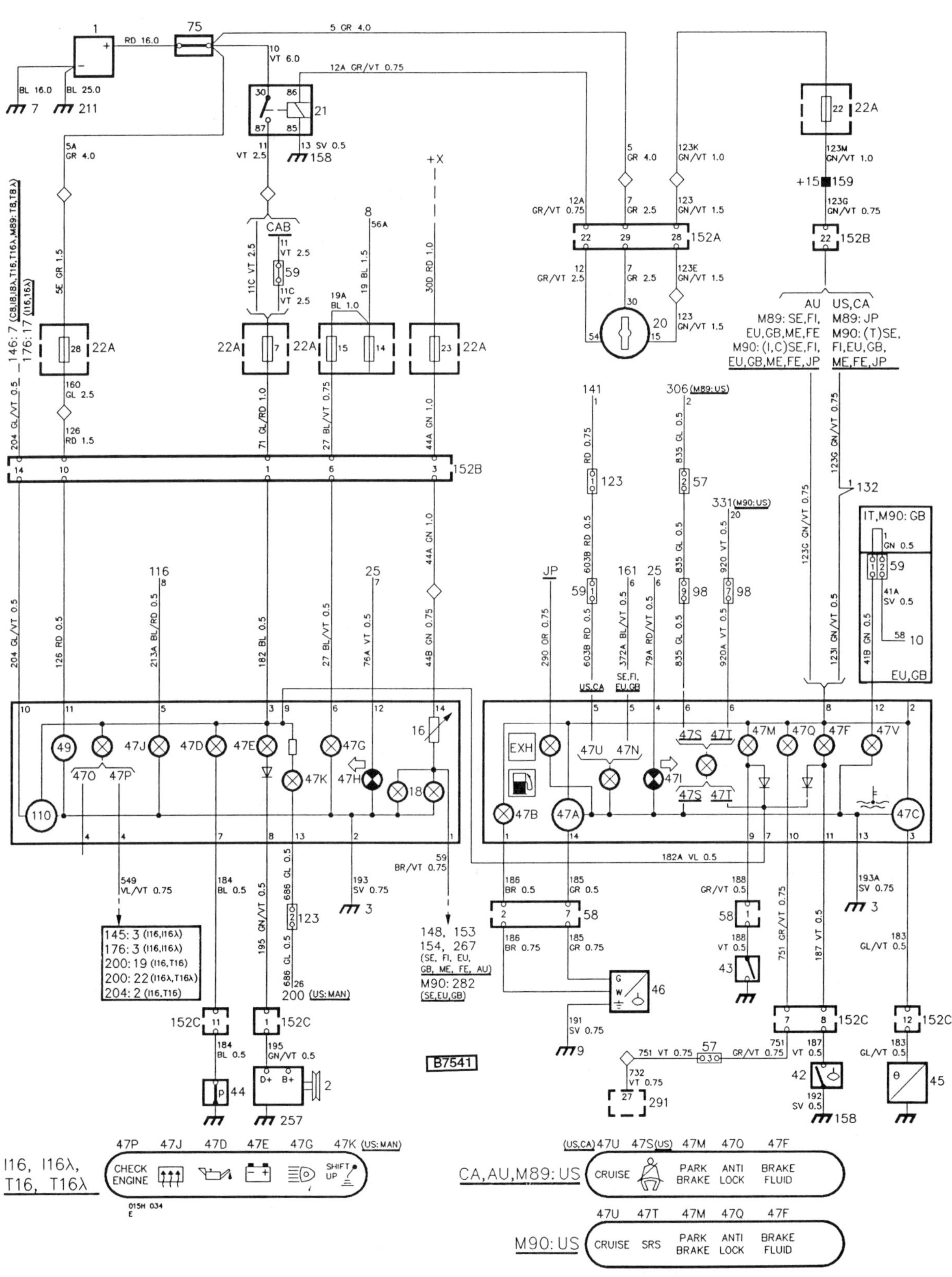

Combined Instruments

1991 and later

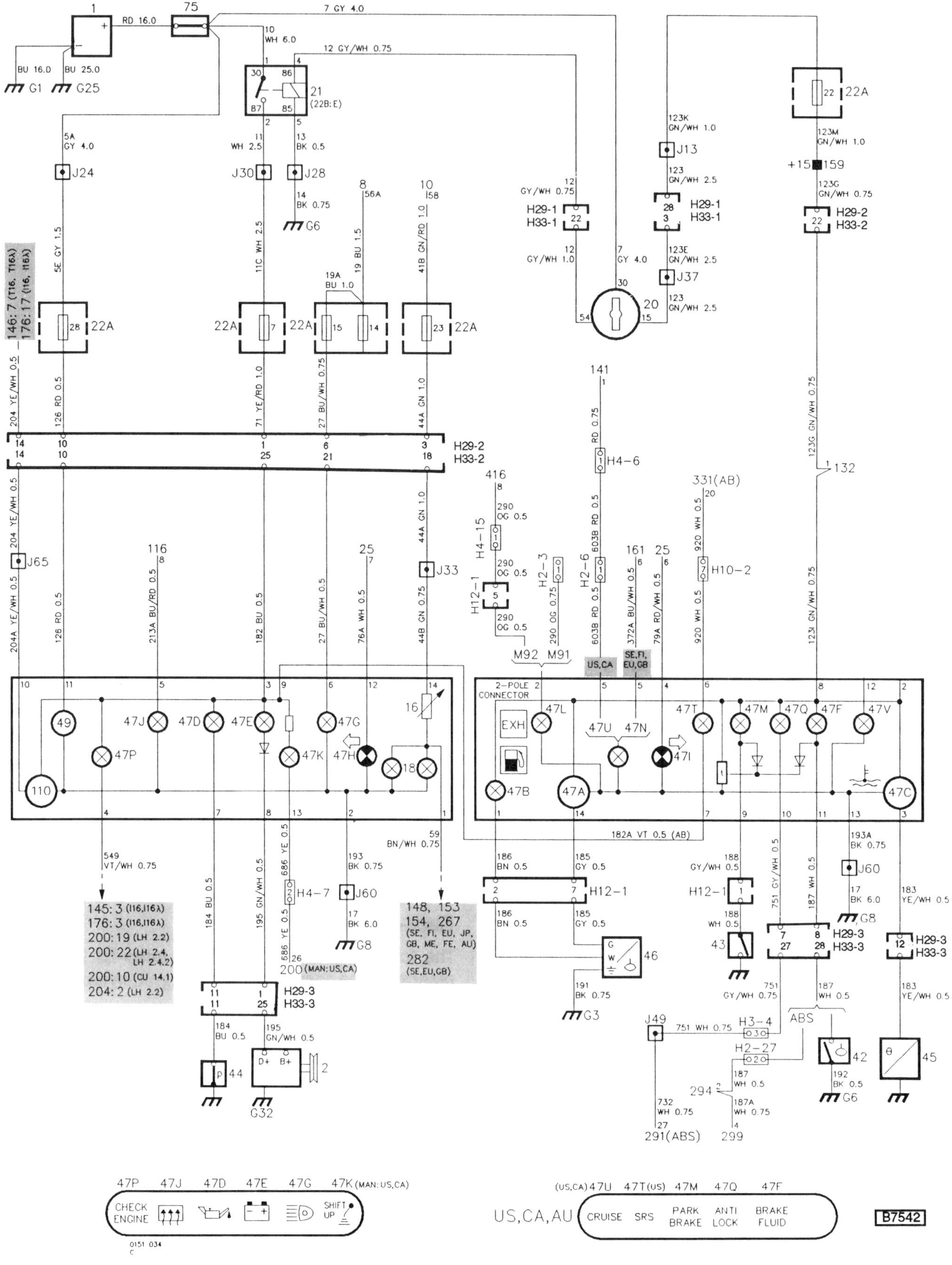

Convertible Top

Operation

The convertible top is raised and lowered through two hydraulic cylinders actuated by an electric pump. The handbrake must be applied before the top can be operated. When lowering the top, relay (278) is energized and current flows to the motor. When raising the top, relay (277) is energized and current flows in the opposite direction to the motor. See **812 Convertible Top** for repair information on the convertible top.

Fault Tracing

1. Check the fuses. Check the voltage supply to the main switch.
2. Check the operation of both relays.
3. Check for voltage at the electric pumps when the switch is actuated. Check that the voltage polarity changes when the switch is toggled the opposite way.

Component Locations

- 1 battery at right front of engine compartment
- 22A main fuse/relay panel in left wheel housing
- 43 handbrake switch under the handbrake
- 75 distribution block at right wheel housing
- 181 power sunroof or convertible switch in center console
- 273 motor for the convertible hydraulic pump under rear seat, right side
- 277 relay for raising the convertible top (1987-1988) under the rear seat on the bulkhead
- 277 relay for raising the convertible top (1989 on) under the rear seat in fuse/relay panel 401
- 278 relay for lowering the convertible top (1987-1988) under the rear seat on the bulkhead
- 278 relay for lowering the convertible top (1989 on) under the rear seat in fuse/relay panel 401
- 283 diodes for convertible top (1987-1988) under rear seat in the wiring harness
- 290 fuse for the convertible top in engine compartment, next to distribution block 75
- 290A fuse for the convertible top in engine compartment, next to distribution block 75
- 290B fuse for the convertible top in engine compartment, next to distribution block 75
- 401 auxiliary fuse/relay panel under rear seat

Connector Locations

1987-1990

- 58 12-pin connector behind instrument panel to left of steering column
- 60 1-pin connector (2) under the center console
- 98 10-pin connector behind instrument panel to left of steering column
- 152B 29-pin bulkhead connector at main fuse/relay panel

1991 and later

- H1-17 1-pin connector under center console
- H1-27 1-pin connector in engine compartment, next to distribution block 75
- H1-27 1-pin connector in engine compartment, next to distribution block 75
- H2-48 2-pin connector at the convertible top motor
- H12-1 12-pin connector behind instrument panel, left of steering column
- H29-2 29-pin bulkhead connector behind main fuse/relay panel (1991-1991 1/2)
- H33-2 33-pin bulkhead connector behind main fuse/relay panel (1991 1/2 and later)

Ground Locations

1987-1990

- 117 ground point at the handbrake
- 211 ground point at the gearbox

1991 and later

- G1 ground point at radiator cross member
- G4 ground point between ignition switch and handbrake
- G5 ground point under the rear seat
- G25 ground point at the gearbox

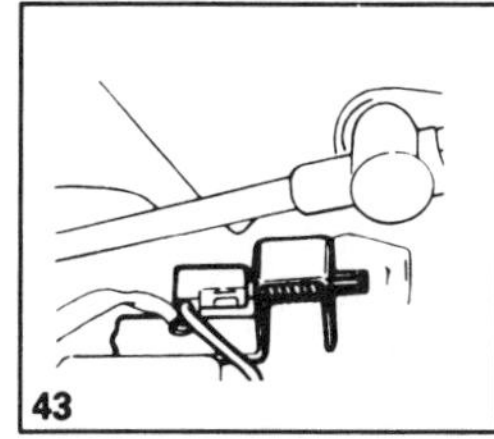

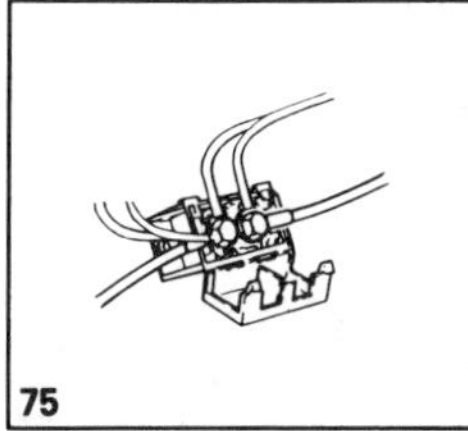

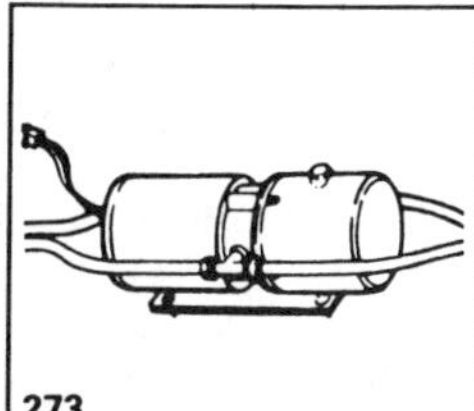

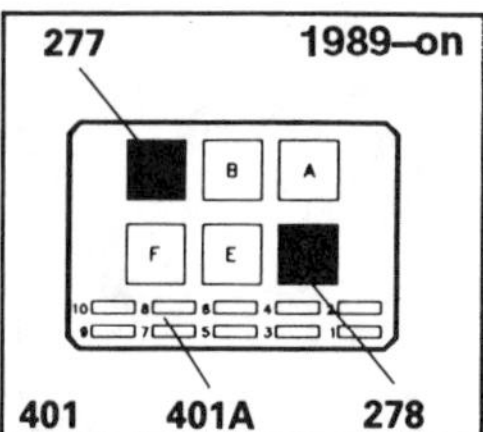

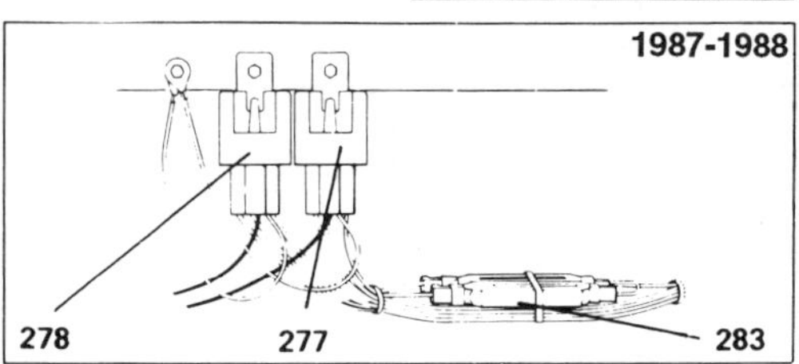

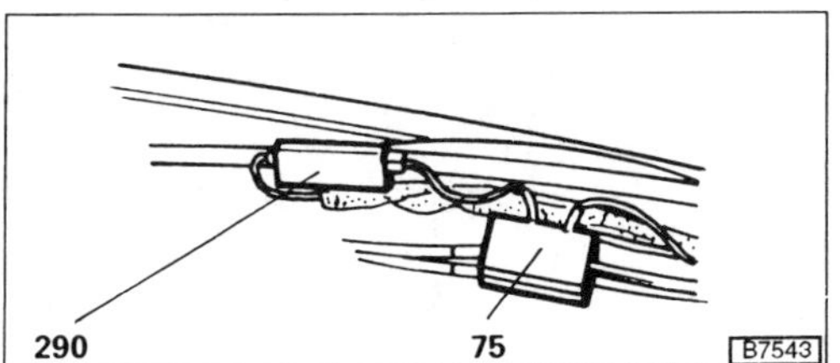

Convertible Top

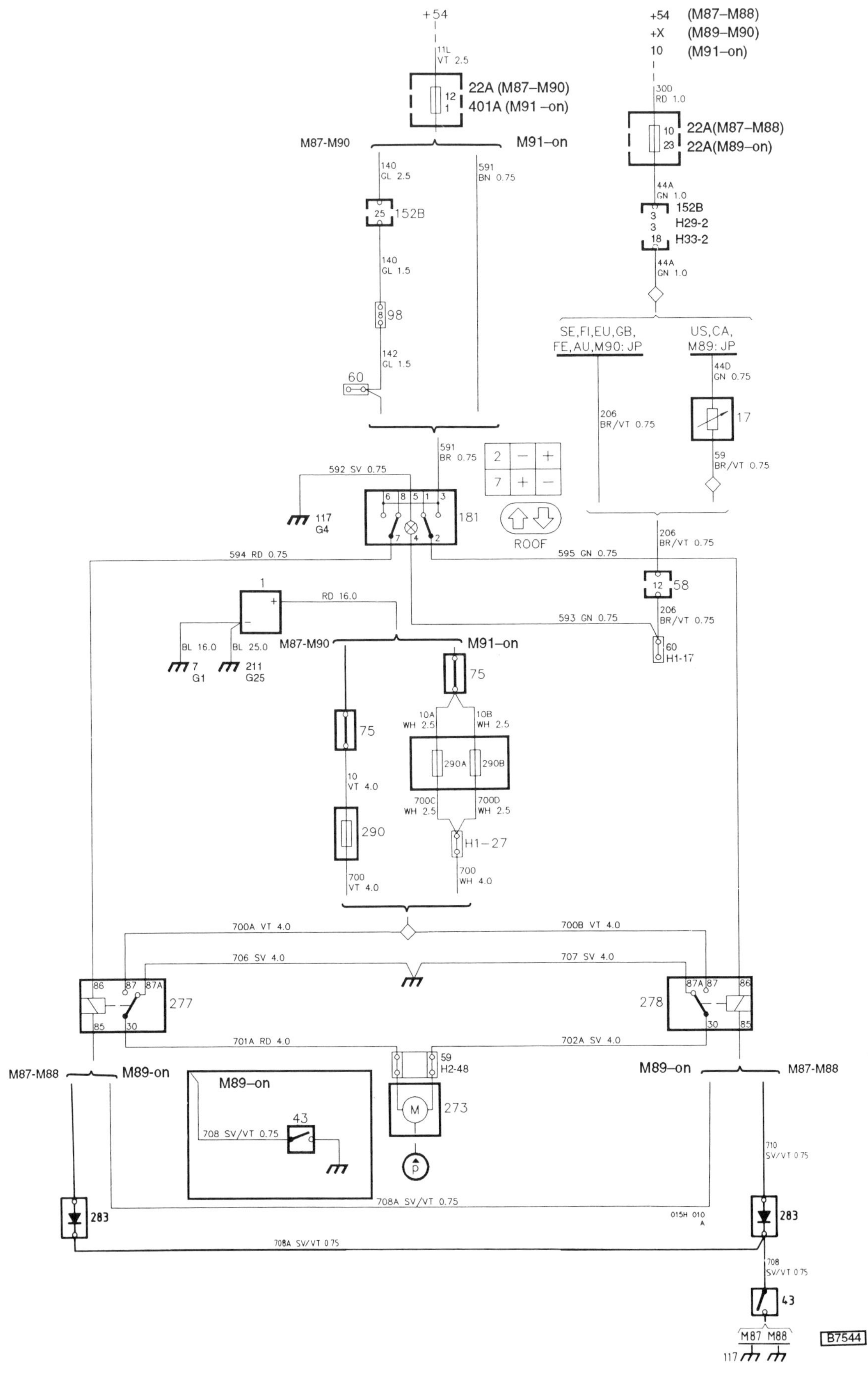

Cruise Control

Operation

Cruise control is an electro-mechanical system that uses a vacuum pump and vacuum actuator to control the accelerator linkage. The speed of the car is electronically sensed by a speedometer-mounted sensor. A clutch switch (cars with manual transmission) and a brake switch disable the system if either pedal is depressed. Disabling the system, via these two switches, is done electrically by opening the circuit to ground, and pneumatically by releasing the vacuum to the actuator. See **368 Cruise Control** for additional information, including repair information.

Fault Tracing

1. Check the fuses.
2. Check the voltage supply to selector switch (141) and cruise control unit (131) with the ignition key in the run position.
3. On 1989 and later cars, check for voltage to the speed transmitter (132) at the back of the instrument cluster.

WARNING
After completing cruise control electrical tests, the cruise control system should be road tested. Particular attention should be paid to the brake and clutch canceling functions. Be sure any faults found are repaired before driving the car.

Component Locations

22A main fuse/relay panel at left wheel housing
29 brake light switch at brake pedal cluster
31 backup light switch in gear selector housing
47U cruise control warning lamp
76 switch for raising idle speed (automatic transmission) under center console at shift lever
128 speed control relay behind instrument panel, left side
131 control unit for cruise control behind instrument panel, left side
132 speed transmitter at the rear of the instrument cluster
133 clutch switch for cruise control at the clutch pedal
134 brake switch for cruise control at the brake pedal
141 selector for cruise control at direction indicator stalk
159 +15 distribution in main fuse/relay panel
177 APC control unit at left wheel housing
179 APC solenoid valve above radiator fan on radiator
187 cruise control vacuum pump in engine compartment left wheel housing
233 cruise control vacuum switch in engine compartment left wheel housing

Connector Locations

1985-1990 models

59 2-pin connector behind instrument panel, left side
60 1-pin connector (2) left side near bulkhead connectors
98 10-pin connector behind instrument panel to the left of the steering column
123 4-pin connector behind instrument panel, left side
152A 29-pin bulkhead connector at main fuse/relay panel
152B 29-pin bulkhead connector at main fuse/relay panel
152C 29-pin bulkhead connector at main fuse/relay panel

1991 and later

H1-2 1-pin connector next to bulkhead connectors, left side behind instrument panel
H1-5 1-pin connector behind instrument panel to the left of the steering column
H1-8 1-pin connector behind instrument panel to the left of the steering column
H1-16 1-pin connector under center console next to shift selector (automatics)
H1-16 1-pin connector under center console next to shift selector (automatic)
H2-6 2-pin connector behind instrument cluster, left of steering column
H4-6 4-pin connector at instrument panel left side
H4-16 4-pin connector behind instrument panel to the left of the steering column
H10-1 10-pin connector behind instrument panel, left of steering column
H29-1 29-pin bulkhead connector behind main fuse/relay panel (1991-1991 1/2)
H29-2 29-pin bulkhead connector behind main fuse/relay panel (1991-1991 1/2)
H29-3 29-pin bulkhead connector behind main fuse/relay panel (1991-1991 1/2)
H33-1 33-pin bulkhead connector behind main fuse/relay panel (1991 1/2 –on)
H33-2 33-pin bulkhead connector behind main fuse/relay panel (1991 1/2 –on)
H33-3 33-pin bulkhead connector behind main fuse/relay panel (1991 1/2 –on)

Ground Locations

1985-1990 models

3 ground point behind instrument panel
7 ground point at radiator cross member

1991 and later models

G1 ground point at radiator cross member
G3 ground point in luggage compartment
G8 ground point behind instrument panell;

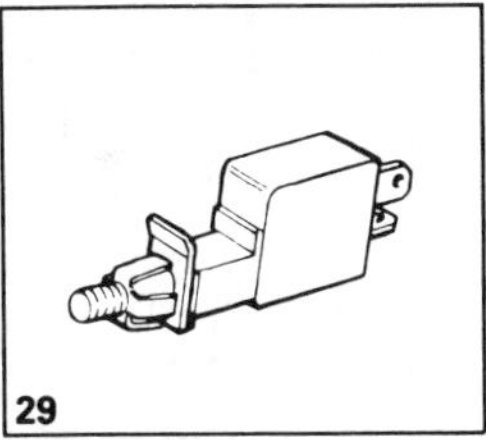
29

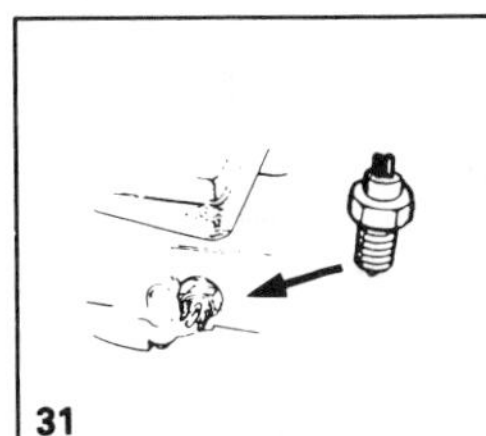
31

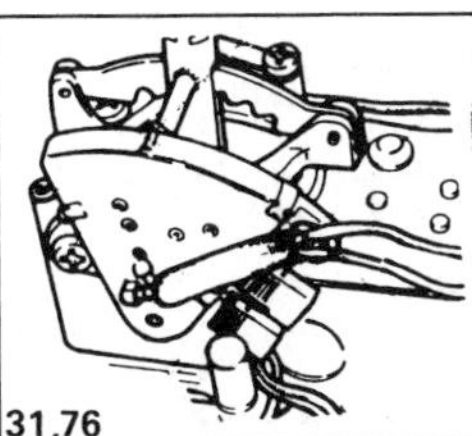
31,76

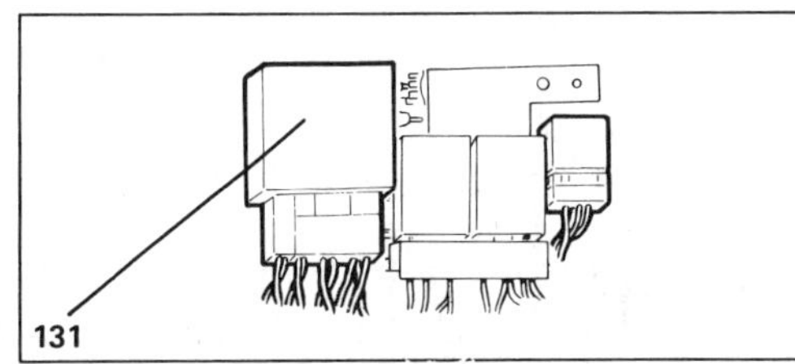
131

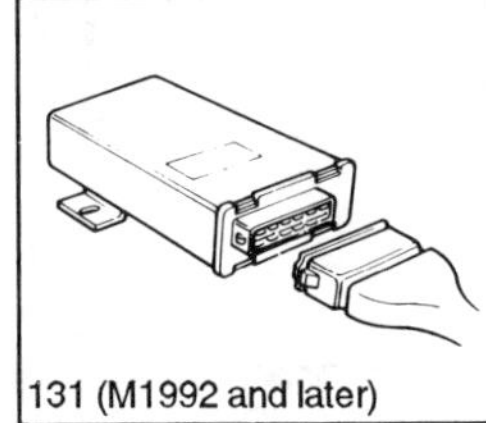
131 (M1992 and later)

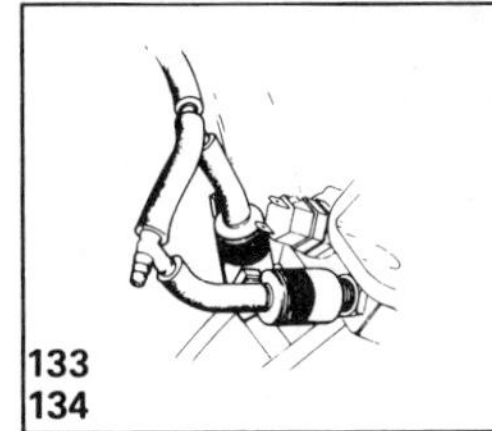
133
134

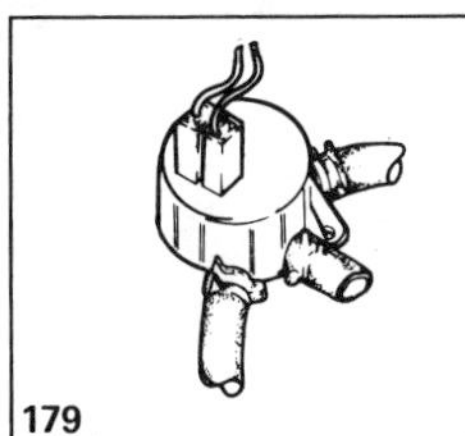
179

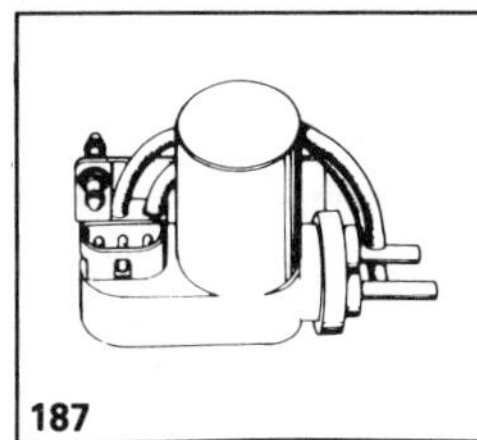
187

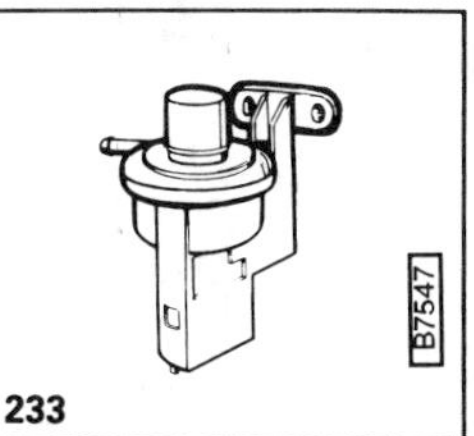

233

Cruise Control
1985-1988

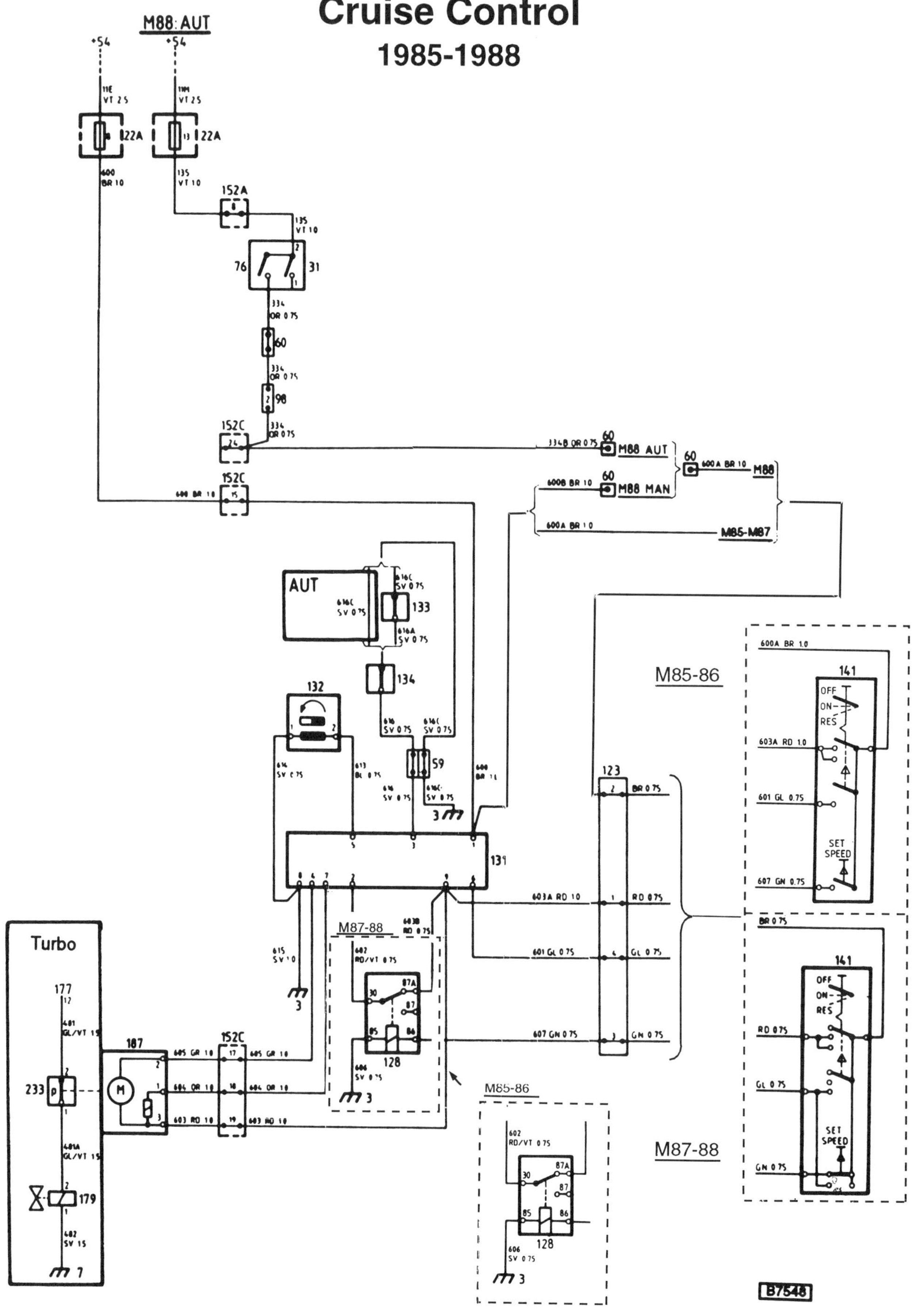

Cruise Control

1989-1991

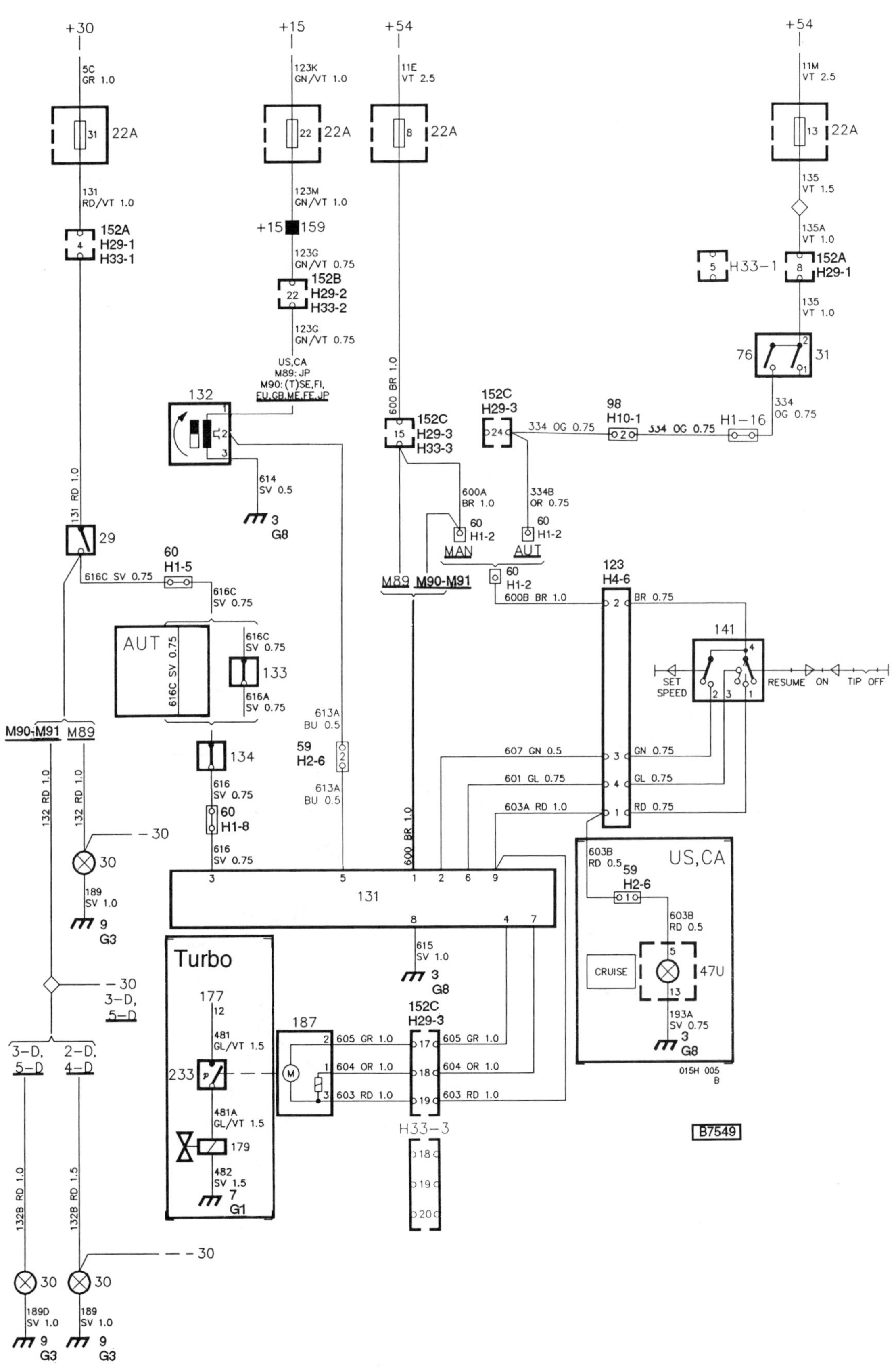

Cruise Control

1992 and later

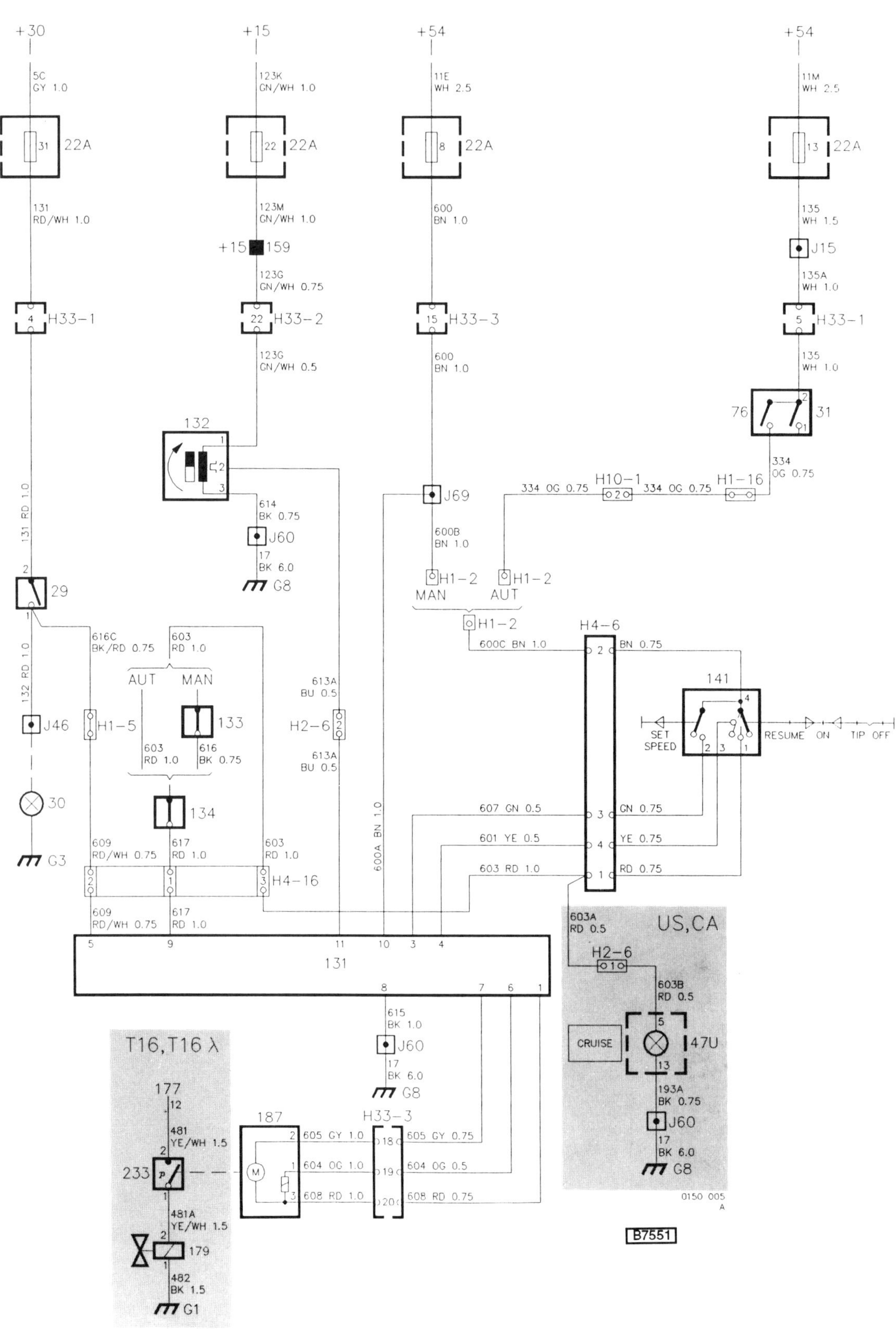

Direction Indicators and Hazard Warning Lights

Operation

The direction indicator stalk (24) switch connects either the left or right direction lights to the flasher relay (23). This creates a load at terminal 49a of the flasher relay (23). With the load connected, the flasher relay (23) begins cycling on and off. The direction indicator stalk (24) also supplies constant voltage to the cornering light (118) in the front cluster when signaling left or right. For information on changing bulbs see **351 Lighting**.

NOTE
- If the direction indicators on one side operate correctly, the flasher relay (23) is OK and can be ruled out as a problem.
- The direction indicators will operate erratically if a bulb is burned out or the wrong type of bulb is installed.

Fault Tracing

1. Check for voltage to the direction indicator switch terminal 1 and the flasher relay terminal 49 whenever the key is in the run position.
2. Check for ground at the flasher relay (23), terminal 31.

Component Locations

22A main fuse/relay panel
23 flasher relay under instrument panel, left side
24 direction indicator switch on steering column
25 hazard warning switch in instrument panel
27 direction indicator lights at left clusters
28 direction indicator lights at right clusters
47H left direction indicator in instrument cluster
47I right direction indicator in instrument cluster
89 side direction indicator in left fender (1986 and later)
90 side direction indicator in right fender (1986 and later)
118 cornering lights in the front clusters
158 negative distribution in main fuse/relay panel

Connector Locations

1985-1990

58 12-pin connector behind the instrument panel to left of steering column
152B 29-pin bulkhead connector at main fuse/relay panel
152C 29-pin bulkhead connector at main fuse/relay panel

1991 and later

H12-1 12-pin behind instrument panel, left of steering column
H29-2 29-pin bulkhead connector behind main fuse/relay panel (1991-1991 1/2)
H29-3 29-pin bulkhead connector behind main fuse/relay panel (1991-1991 1/2)
H33-2 33-pin bulkhead connector behind main fuse/relay panel (1991 1/2 and later)
H33-3 33-pin bulkhead connector behind main fuse/relay panel (1991 1/2 and later)

Ground Locations

1985-1990

3 ground point behind instrument panel
7 ground point at radiator cross member
9 ground point in luggage compartment
93 ground point at left wheel housing

1991 and later

G1 ground point at radiator cross member
G3 ground point in luggage compartment
G6 ground distribution at main fuse/relay panel
G8 ground point behind instrument panel
G12 ground point at left wheel housing

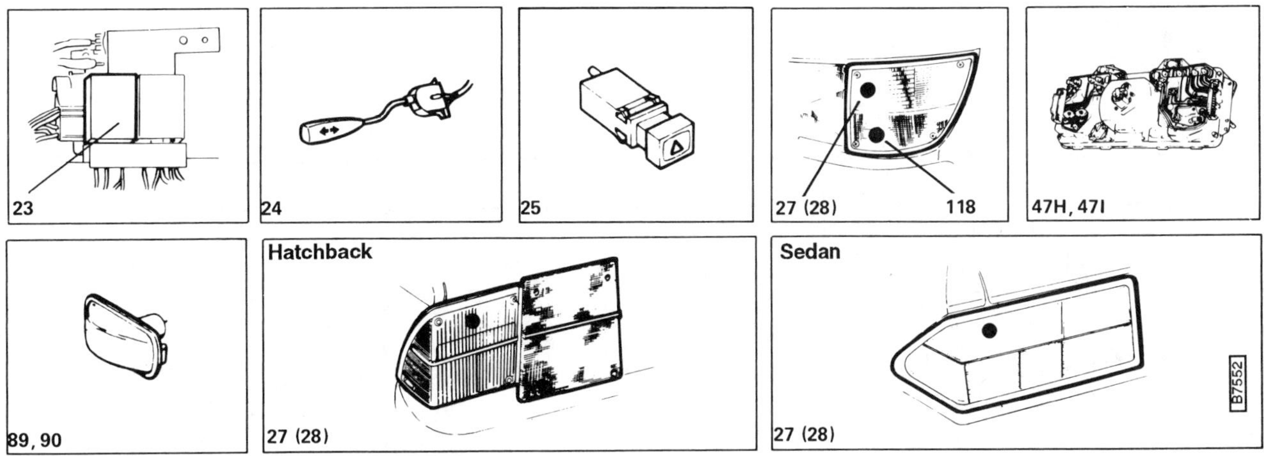

Direction Indicators and Hazard Warning Lights

1985-1990

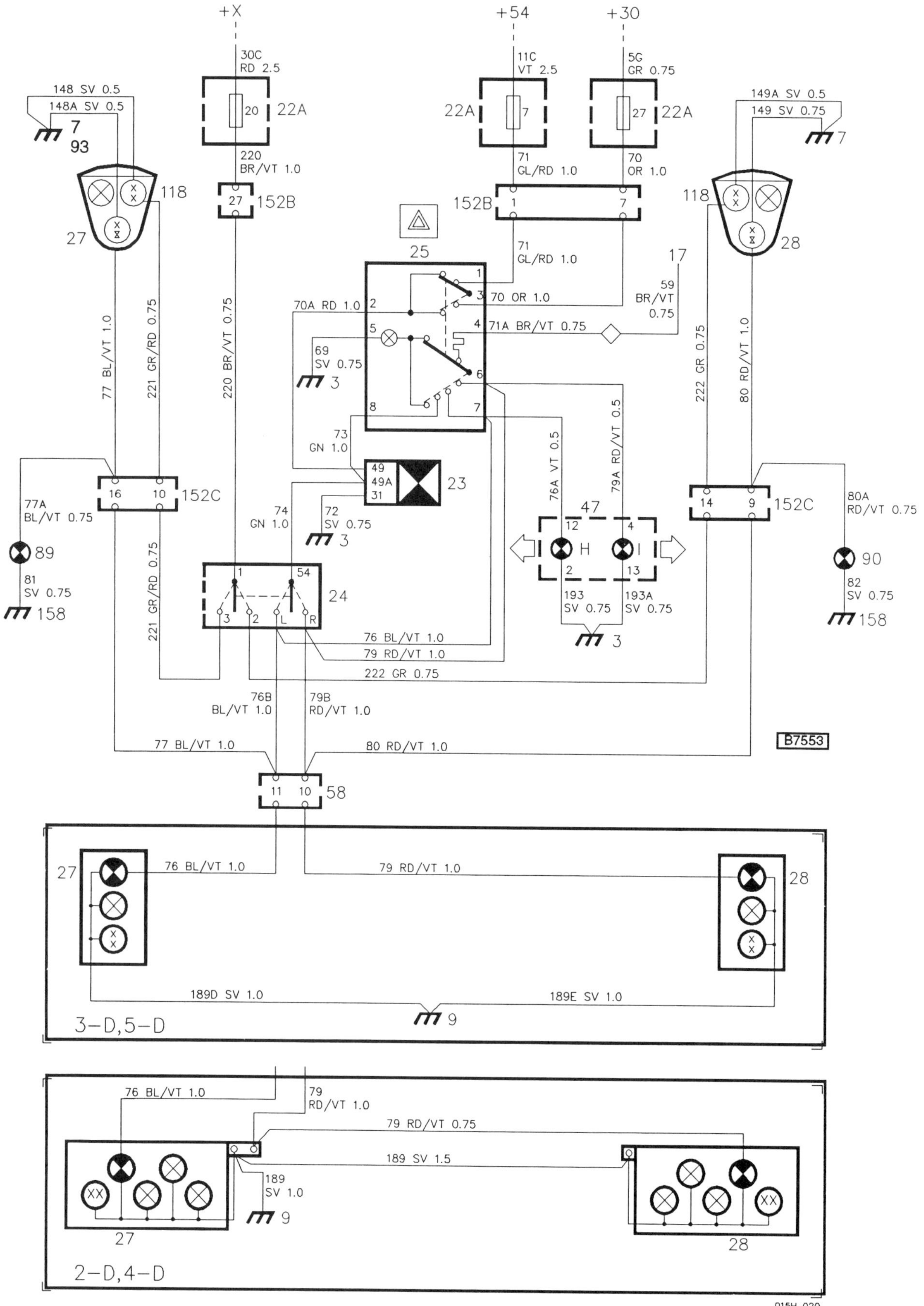

Direction Indicators and Hazard Warning Lights

1991 and later

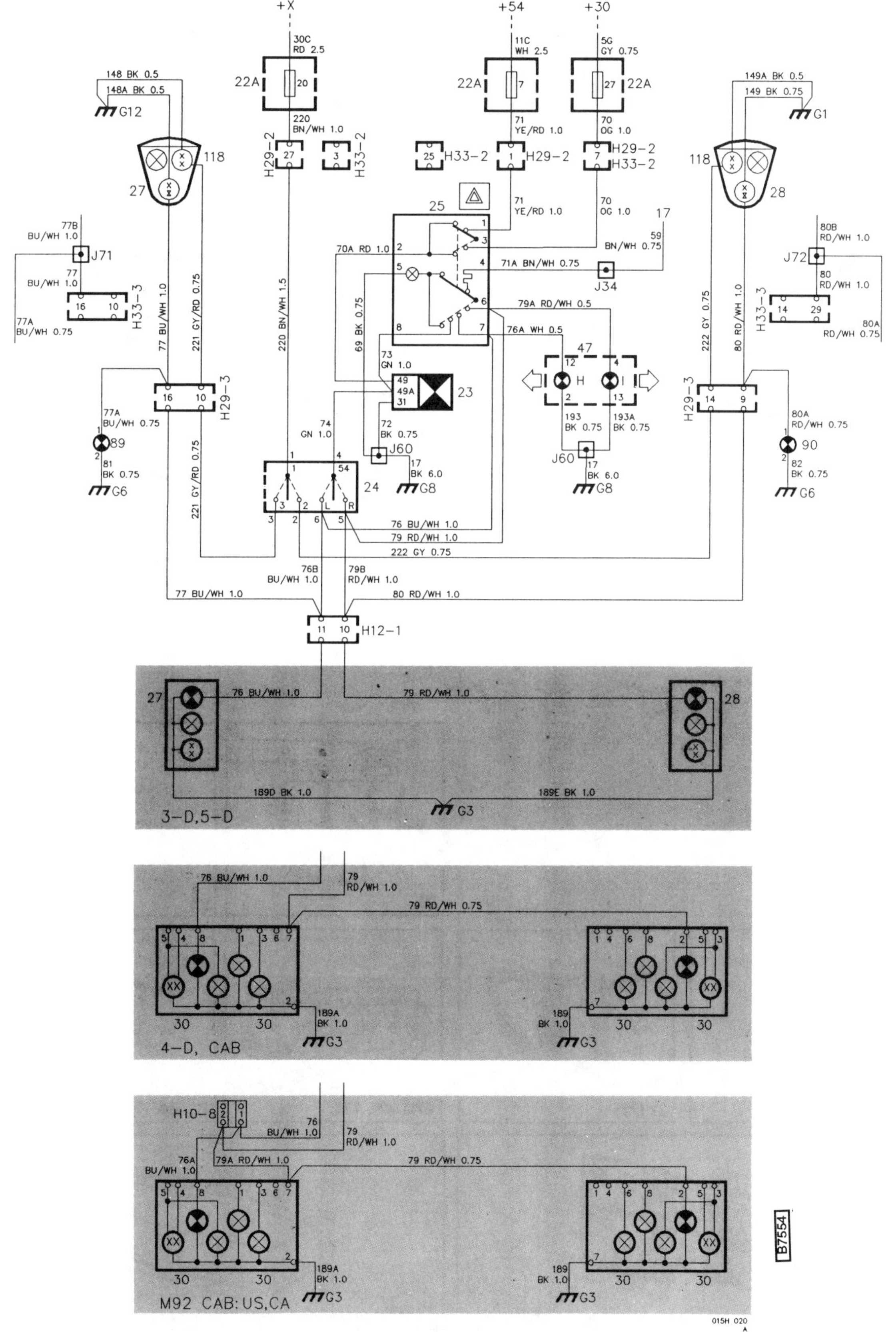

Foglamps

Operation

Foglamps come on only when the park or low beam headlights are on. Voltage to control the foglamp relay (107) is supplied by the foglamp switch (88), and ground is supplied by the high beam headlight filaments. When the high beams are switched on, the foglamp relay (107) is de-energized because there is voltage at both terminals 85 and 86.

Fault Tracing

1. Check fuse 21. Check that the highbeam headlights are not blown.
2. Turn the headlight switch (10) to the park position and turn the foglamp switch (88) on. Check for ground at terminal 85 of the fog lamp relay (107), and check for voltage at terminal 86.

Component Locations

10 lighting switch in instrument panel
22A main fuse/relay panel at left wheel housing
85 foglamps under front bumper
88 switch for foglamps in instrument panel
107 relay for foglamps in main fuse/relay panel
174 relay for daytime driving lights

Connector Locations

1985-1990

152B 29-pin bulkhead connector at main fuse/relay panel
152C 29-pin bulkhead connector at main fuse/relay panel

1991 and later

H29-2 29-pin bulkhead connector behind main fuse/relay panel (1991-1991 1/2)
H29-3 29-pin bulkhead connector behind main fuse/relay panel (1991-1991 1/2)
H33-2 33-pin bulkhead connector behind main fuse/relay panel (1991 1/2 and later)
H33-3 33-pin bulkhead connector behind main fuse/relay panel (1991 1/2 and later)

Ground Locations

1985-1990

3 ground point behind instrument panel
7 ground point at radiator cross member

1991 and later

G1 ground point at radiator cross member
G8 ground point behind instrument panel

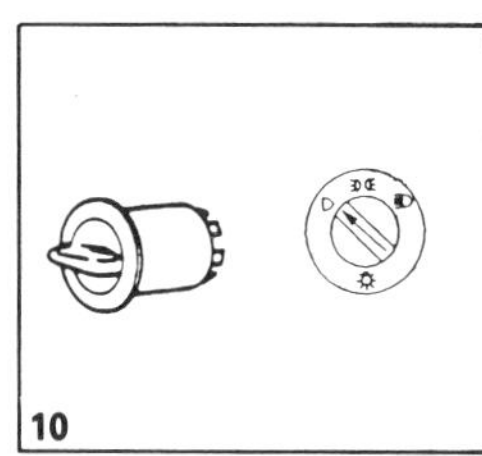

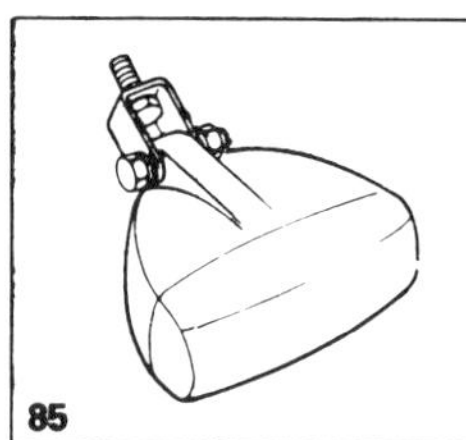

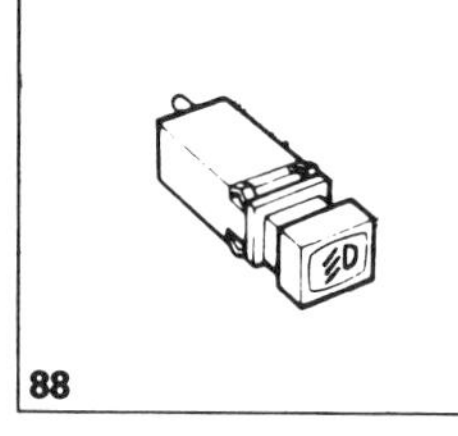

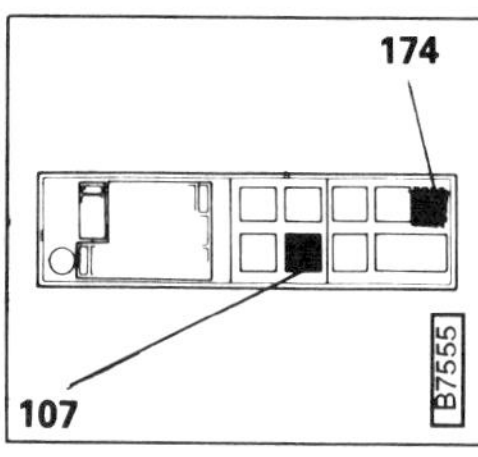

Foglamps

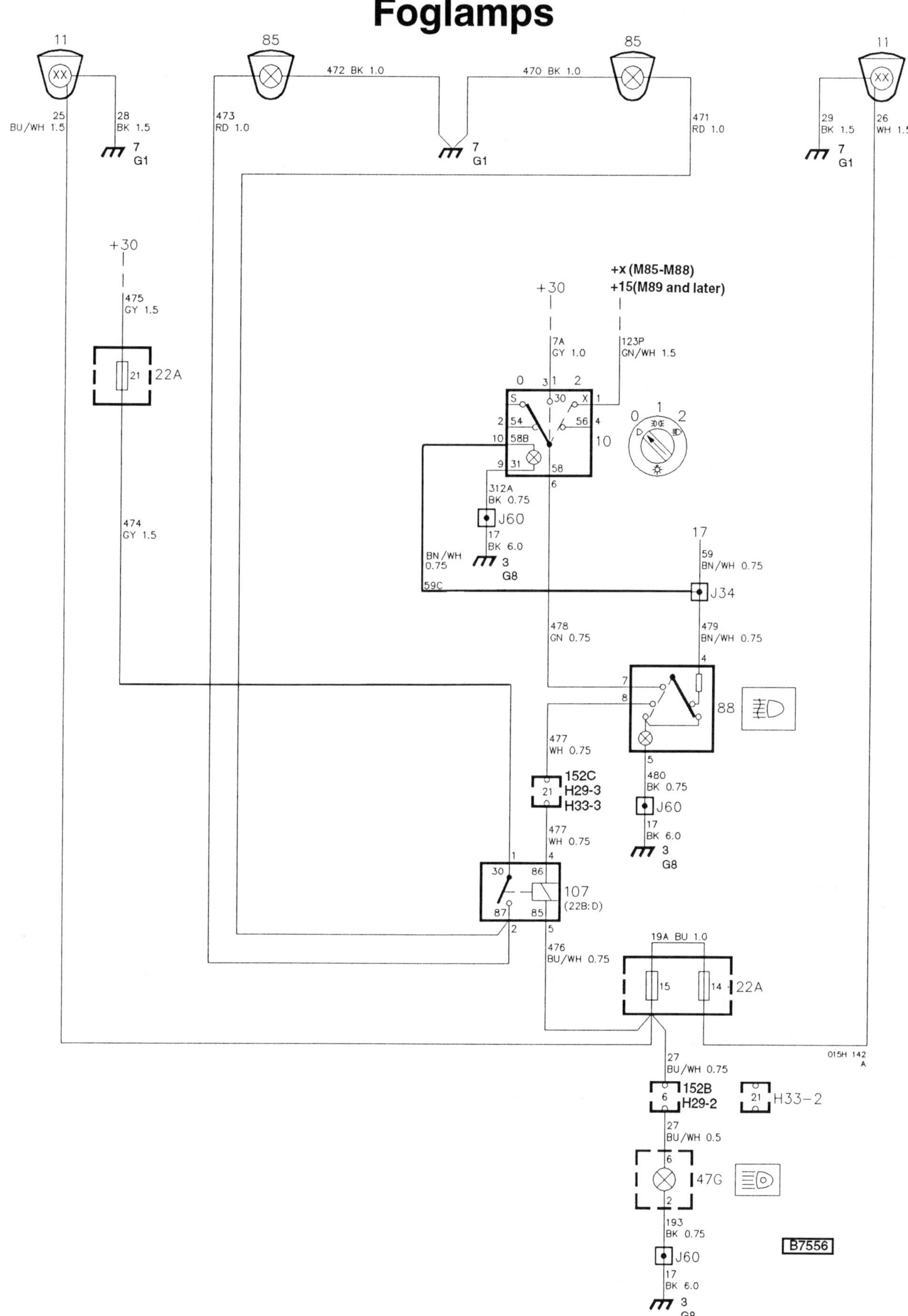
11
85
472 BK 1.0
470 BK 1.0
85
11
25
BU/WH 1.5
28
BK 1.5
7
G1
473
RD 1.0
7
G1
471
RD 1.0
29
BK 1.5
26
WH 1.5
7
G1
+30
475
GY 1.5
21
22A
+x (M85-M88)
+15(M89 and later)
+30
7A
GY 1.0
123P
GN/WH 1.5
10
312A
BK 0.75
J60
17
BK 6.0
3
G8
474
GY 1.5
BN/WH
0.75
59C
17
59
BN/WH 0.75
J34
478
GN 0.75
479
BN/WH 0.75
88
477
WH 0.75
152C
H29-3
H33-3
480
BK 0.75
J60
17
BK 6.0
3
G8
477
WH 0.75
107
(22B:D)
19A BU 1.0
476
BU/WH 0.75
22A
015H 142
A
27
BU/WH 0.75
152B
H29-2
H33-2
27
BU/WH 0.5
47G
193
BK 0.75
J60
17
BK 6.0
3
G8
B7556

Fuel System

Operation

All the cars covered by this manual have a variant of the Bosch LH fuel injection system. **Table a** shows the applications for the LH system. This is a pulsed, electronic system.

This section covers only the electrical fault tracing, component location, and wiring. Information on troubleshooting the fuel injection system can be found in **240 Fuel Injection**.

Table a. LH Fuel Injection Variants

System	Year/Model	Identification
LH 2.2	1985-1988 Turbo 1986-1987 Non-Turbo	Three-wire AIC idle valve, metal air mass meter with a sealed mixture adjustment screw, and a throttle dashpot
LH 2.4	1989 and later Turbo 1988-1990 Non-Turbo	Two-wire AIC idle valve, plastic air mass meter without a mixture adjustment screw
LH 2.4.2	1991and later Non-Turbo	Three-wire AIC idle valve, similar plastic air mass meter without a mixture adjustment screw, and a throttle potentiometer

Fault Tracing

CAUTION

- Before making electrical tests on the fuel system, please read and understand the warnings given at the beginning of **300 Electrical—General**.
- Always wait at least 40 seconds before disconnecting the main connector at the LH control unit (200). The main fuel injection relay has a timing feature that maintains power for about 30 seconds. Damage to the control unit will result if the connector is removed too soon.
- On models with LH 2.4 and LH 2.4.2, activate and read any stored fault codes before disconnecting the LH control unit (200) connector. The LH diagnostic memory will be erased if the battery is disconnected or if the control unit connector is removed. See **240 Fuel Injection** for information on LH fault diagnosis.
- Use only a digital multimeter (DMM) or LED test light when making electrical checks/tests on the LH fuel system circuit.
- Where possible, probe the rear of connectors when making electrical checks. Otherwise the small contacts in the connectors may be damaged causing faulty or intermittent operation.

1. Check the fuses. Check the ground wires at the cylinder head lifting lug.
2. Using an LED test light, check for a pulsed signal between pin 1 of the LH control unit (200) and ground while cranking the engine. This is the tach signal from the ignition system.
3. Using an LED test light, check for a pulsed signal at the fuel injector connectors while cranking the engine. Positive (+) battery voltage is always present at the connectors and the LH control unit switches the ground side of the circuit to turn the injectors on and off.

Component Locations

22 main fuse/relay panel in engine compartment
47 combined instruments
47P CHECK ENGINE light
75 voltage distribution block in engine compartment right bulkhead
76 switch for raising idle speed (automatic transmission) at center console at shift lever
94 starting injector in throttle housing
101 supply fuel pump in the fuel tank
102 fuel pump relay at the LH control unit 200, forward of r.f. door
103 main fuel pump in the fuel tank
132 speed transmitter at the rear of the instrument cluster
136 lambda (oxygen) exhaust sensor in the exhaust manifold
144 boost pressure switch (turbo)
146 ignition amplifier/control unit in engine compartment, left bulkhead
147 ignition pulse amplifier at main fuse/relay panel, position D
156 A/C compressor relay at main fuse/relay panel, engine compartment
159 +15 distribution terminal in main fuse/relay panel, engine compartment
166 A/C pressure switch for cooling fan at receiver/dryer unit, engine compartment
176 EZK control unit in engine compartment, left bulkhead
200 LH control unit forward of the right front door, behind trim
202 engine temperature transmitter at intake manifold flange, between cylinders 2 and 3
203 throttle angle transmitter on throttle housing
204 LH diagnostic connector, in engeine compartment, behind right-hand wheel housing
205 LH air mass meter in the throttle intake hose
206 fuel injectors at intake manifold
229 fuel injection main relay at the LH control unit 200, forward of r.f. door
271 lambda preheater (integral with lambda sensor)
272 AIC valve (idle speed motor) at front left side of cylinder head
285 fuse for lambda sensor in engine compartment, next to fresh air intake
321 charcoal canister valve (ELCD) in engine compartment, ahead of left wheel housing
323 fuel pump in fuel tank
347 LH diagnostic connector, under rear seat, right side
389 NTC resistor under intake manifold (1990 and later)
390 EGR modulating valve ahead of left wheel housing (1990 and later)

Fuel System

Connector Locations

1985-1990

204 LH test connector in engine compartment, behind right wheel housing
322 coding connector at the LH control unit 200, forward of r.f. door
347 diagnostic test connector under rear seat, right side

1991 and later

H1-9 1-pin connector near lambda sensor, right wheel housing
H1-12 1-pin connector in engine compartment, right side near air intake
H1-16 1-pin connector under center console next to shift selector (automatic)
H1-19 1-pin connector near LH control unit, behind right A pillar trim
H2-13 2-pin connector at the fuel pump in the storage area
H2-33 2-pin connector near the lambda sensor in the engine compartment
H3-14 3-pin connector near LH control unit, behind right A pillar trim
H4-7 4-pin connector at the LH control unit, forward of right front door
H6-1 6-pin connector in engine compartment right wheel housing
H6-2 6-pin connector in engine compartment right wheel housing
H29-1 29-pin bulkhead connector behind main fuse/relay panel (1991-1991 1/2)
H29-2 29-pin bulkhead connector behind main fuse/relay panel (1991-1991 1/2)
H29-3 29-pin bulkhead connector behind main fuse/relay panel (1991-1991 1/2)
H33-1 33-pin bulkhead connector behind main fuse/relay panel (1991 1/2 and later)
H33-2 33-pin bulkhead connector behind main fuse/relay panel (1991 1/2 and later)
H33-3 33-pin bulkhead connector behind main fuse/relay panel (1991 1/2 and later)

Ground Locations

1985-1990

201 ground point for fuel injection at engine lifting lug, 2 points

1991 and later

G1 ground point at radiator cross member
G3 ground point in luggage compartment
G7 ground point at engine lifting lug
G25 ground point at gearbox

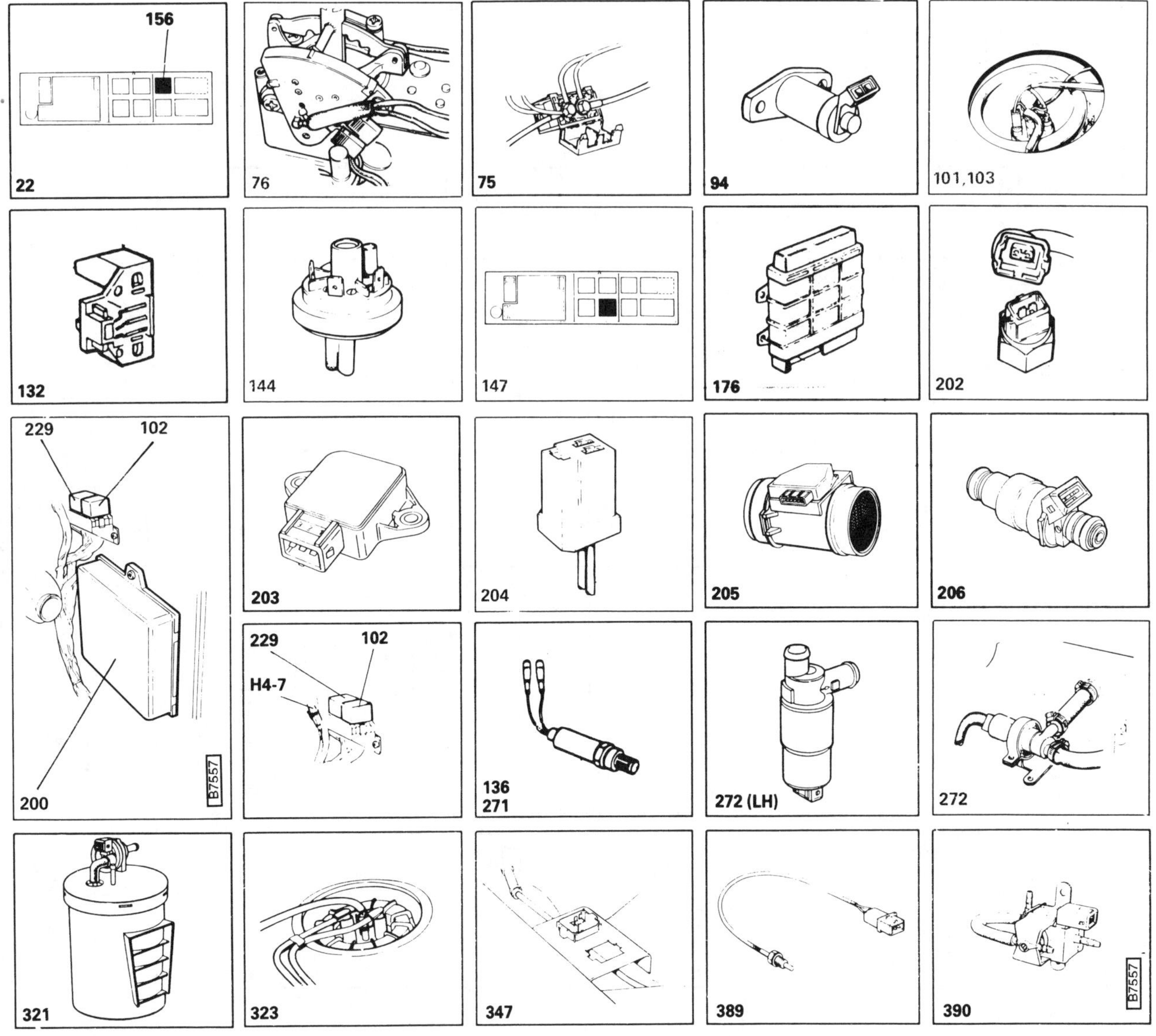

LH 2.2 Fuel System

1985-1986 (all)

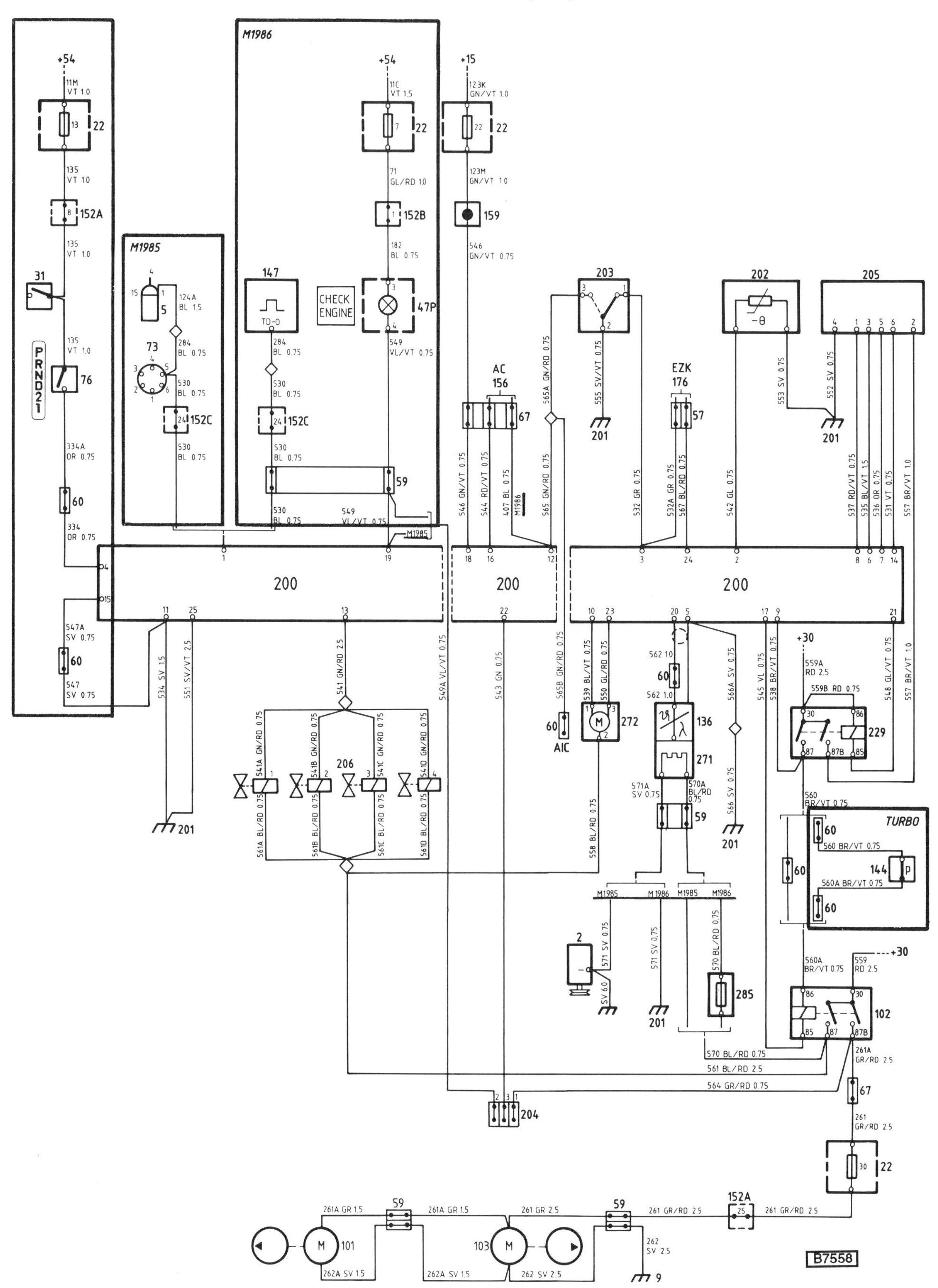

LH 2.2 Fuel System

1987-1988 turbo

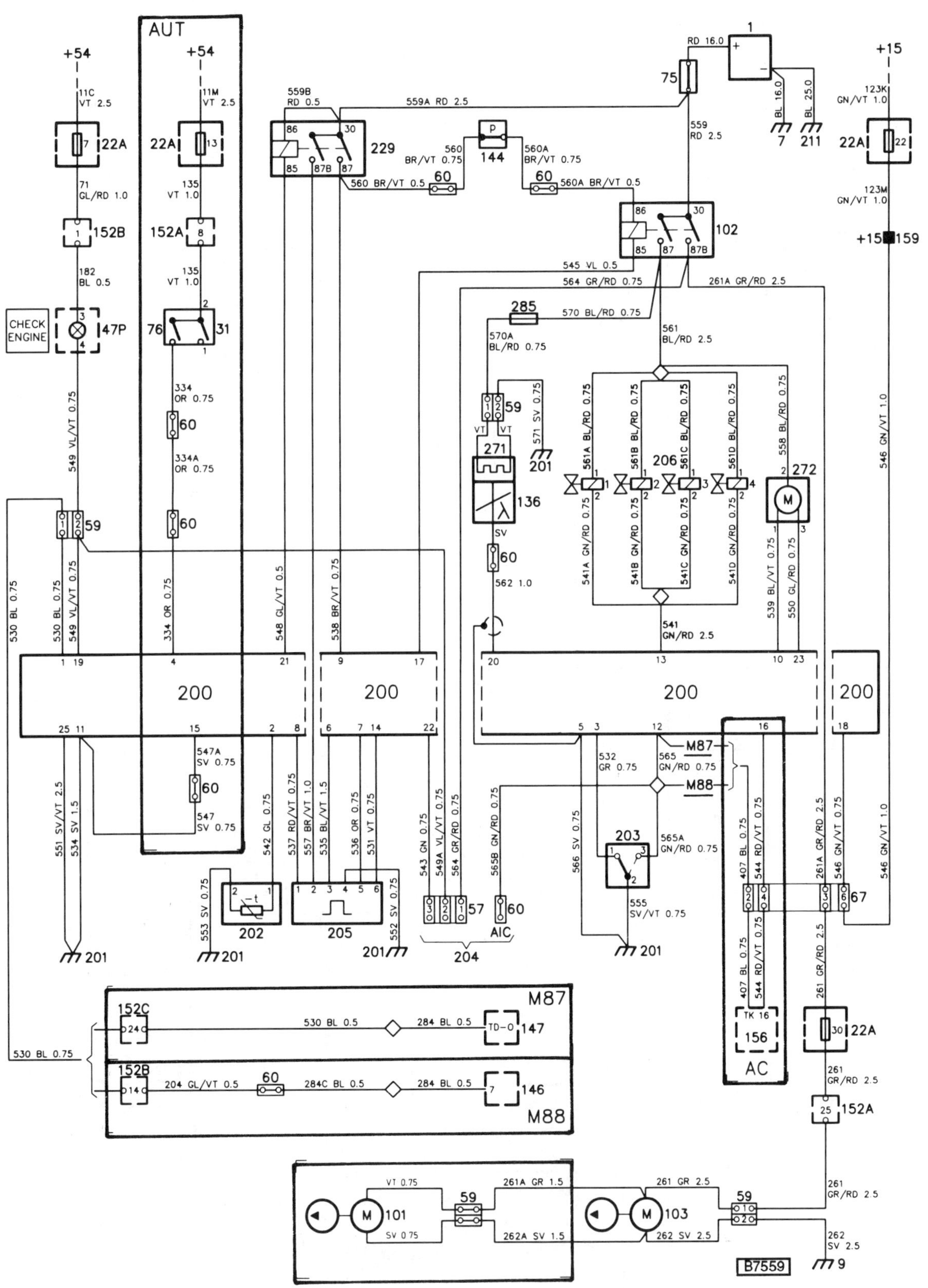

LH 2.2 Fuel System

1987 non-turbo

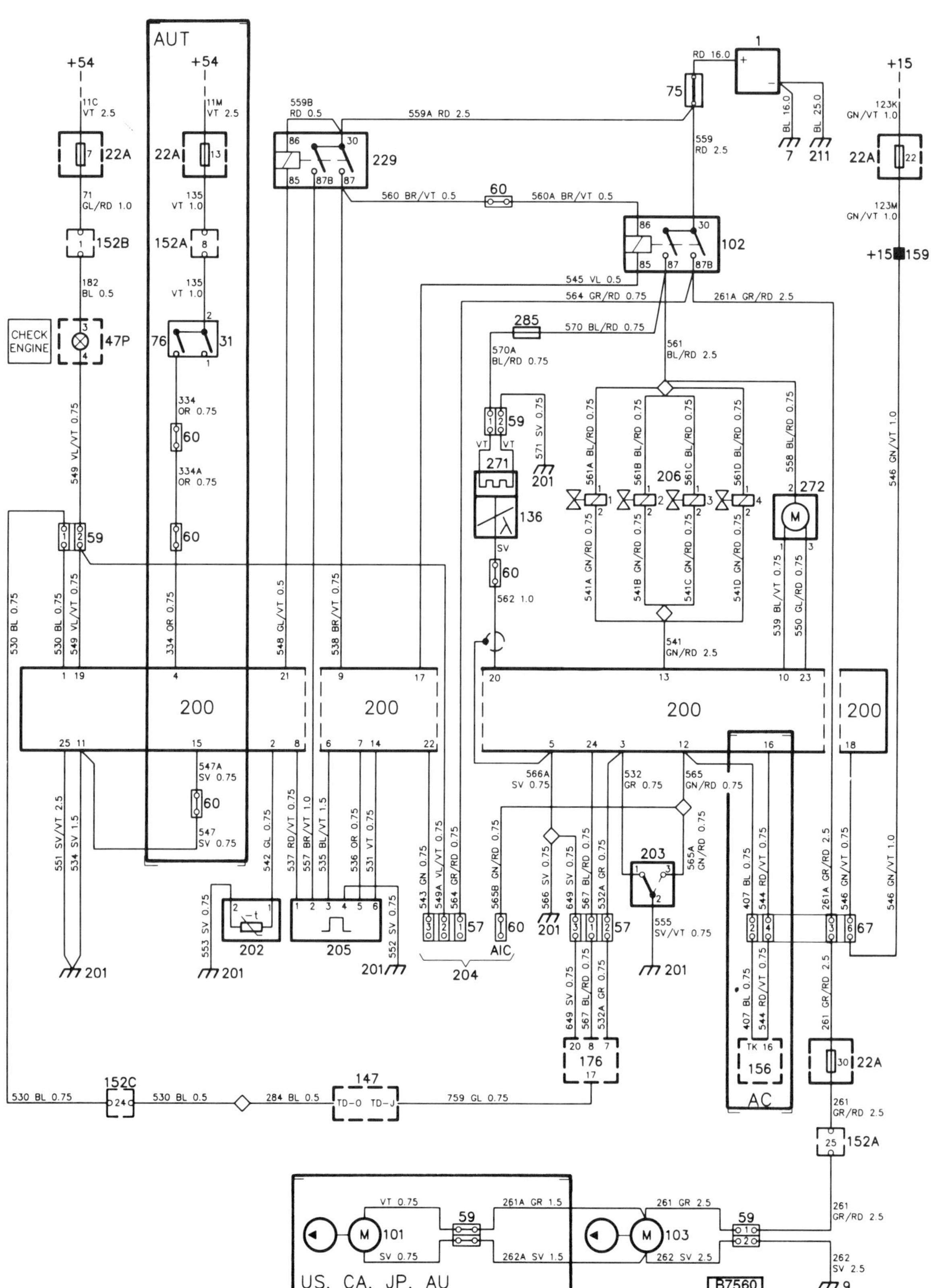

LH 2.4 Fuel System

1988 non-turbo

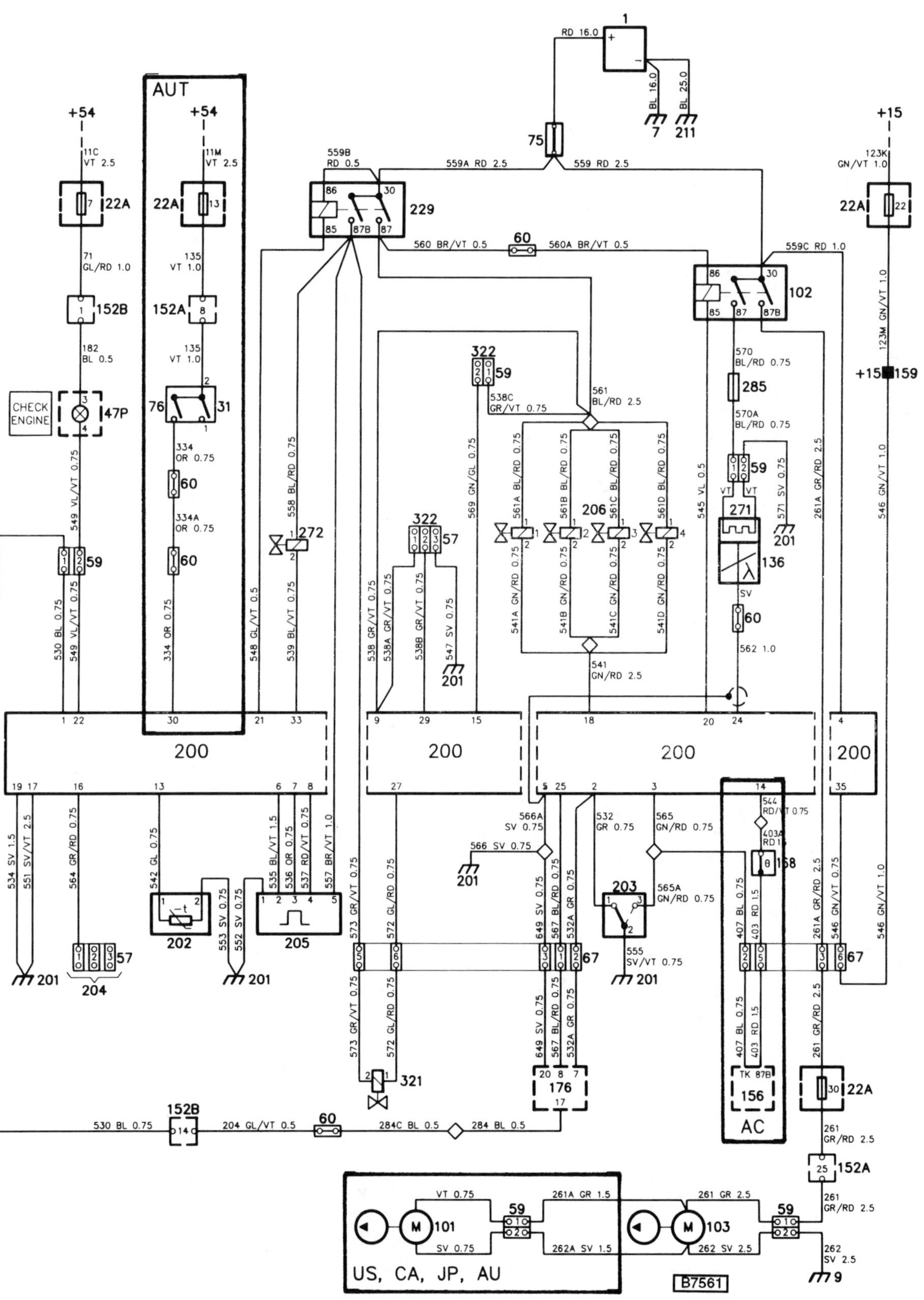

LH 2.4 Fuel System

1989-1990 (all)

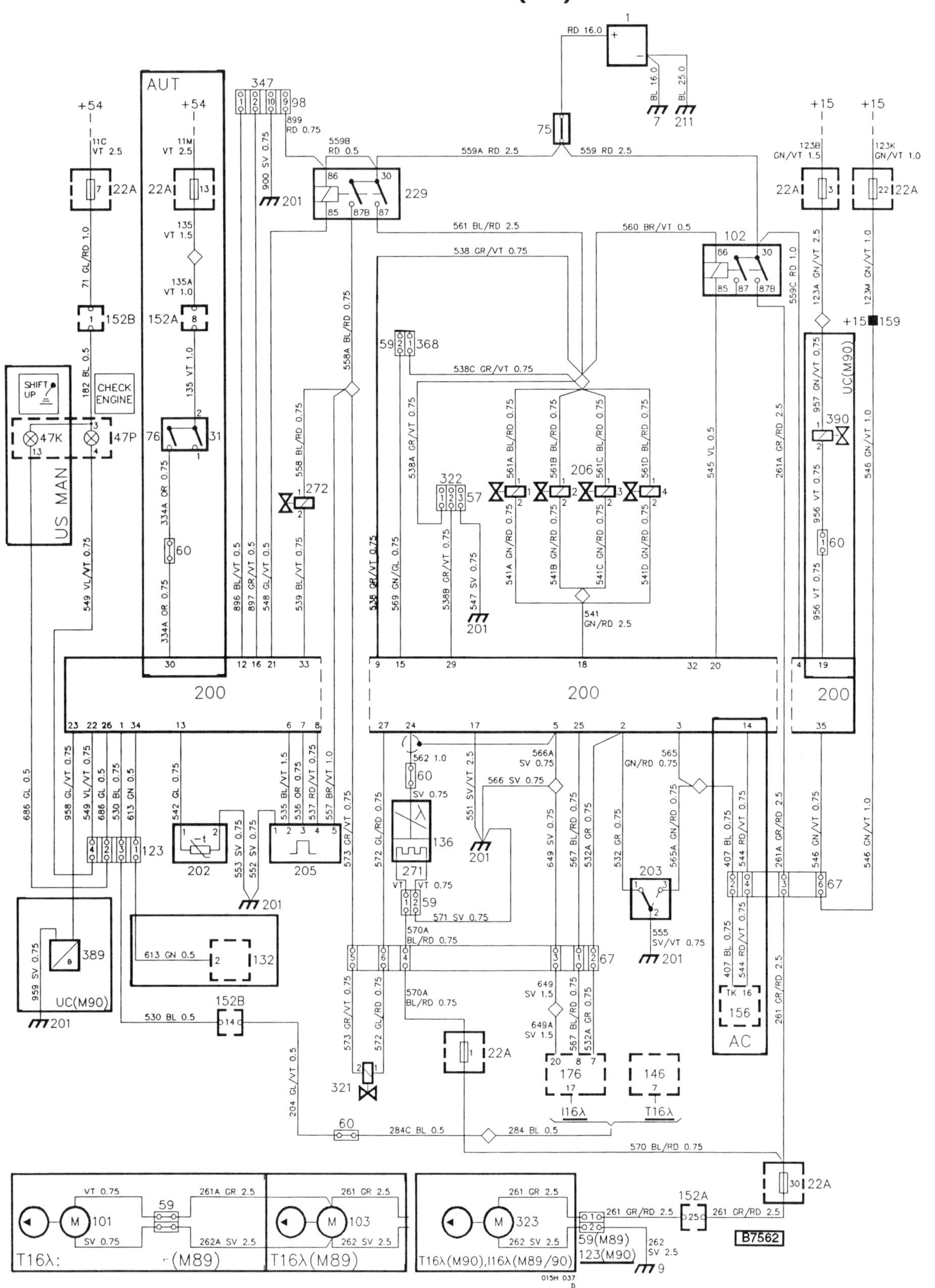

LH 2.4 Fuel System with 29-pin connector

1991-1992 turbo

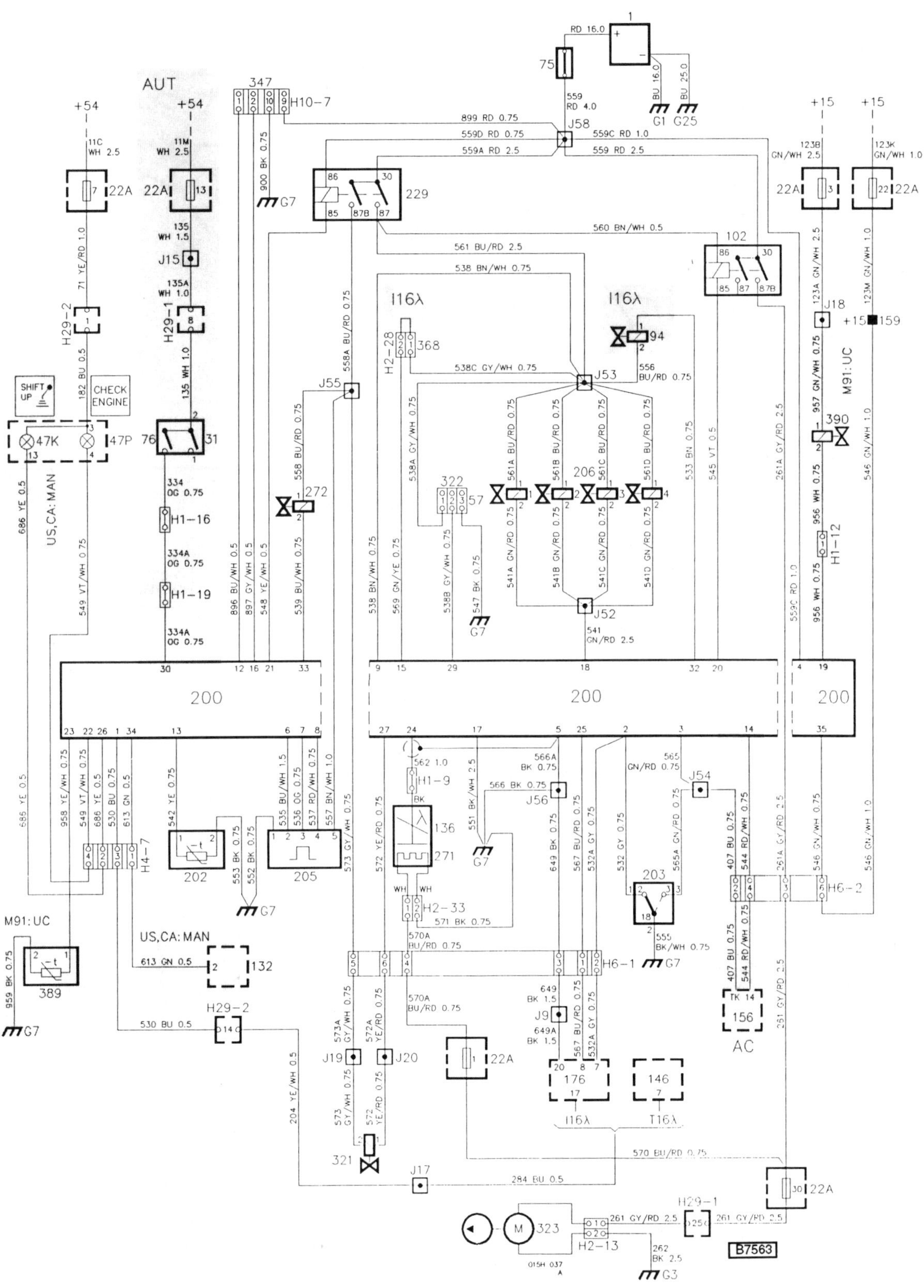

LH 2.4 Fuel System with 33-pin connector

1991 and later Turbo

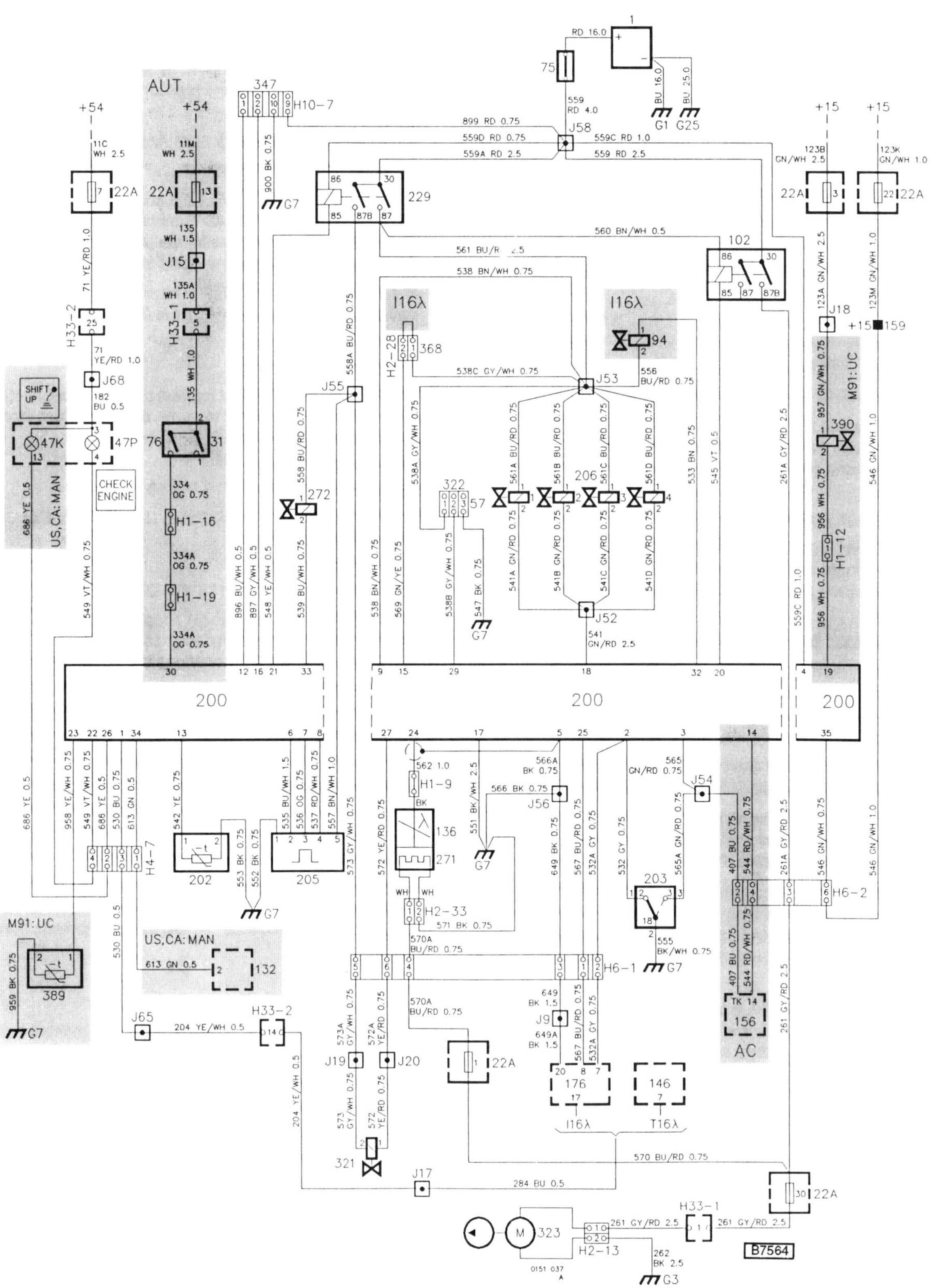

LH 2.4.2 Fuel System with 29-pin connector

1991-1992 non-turbo

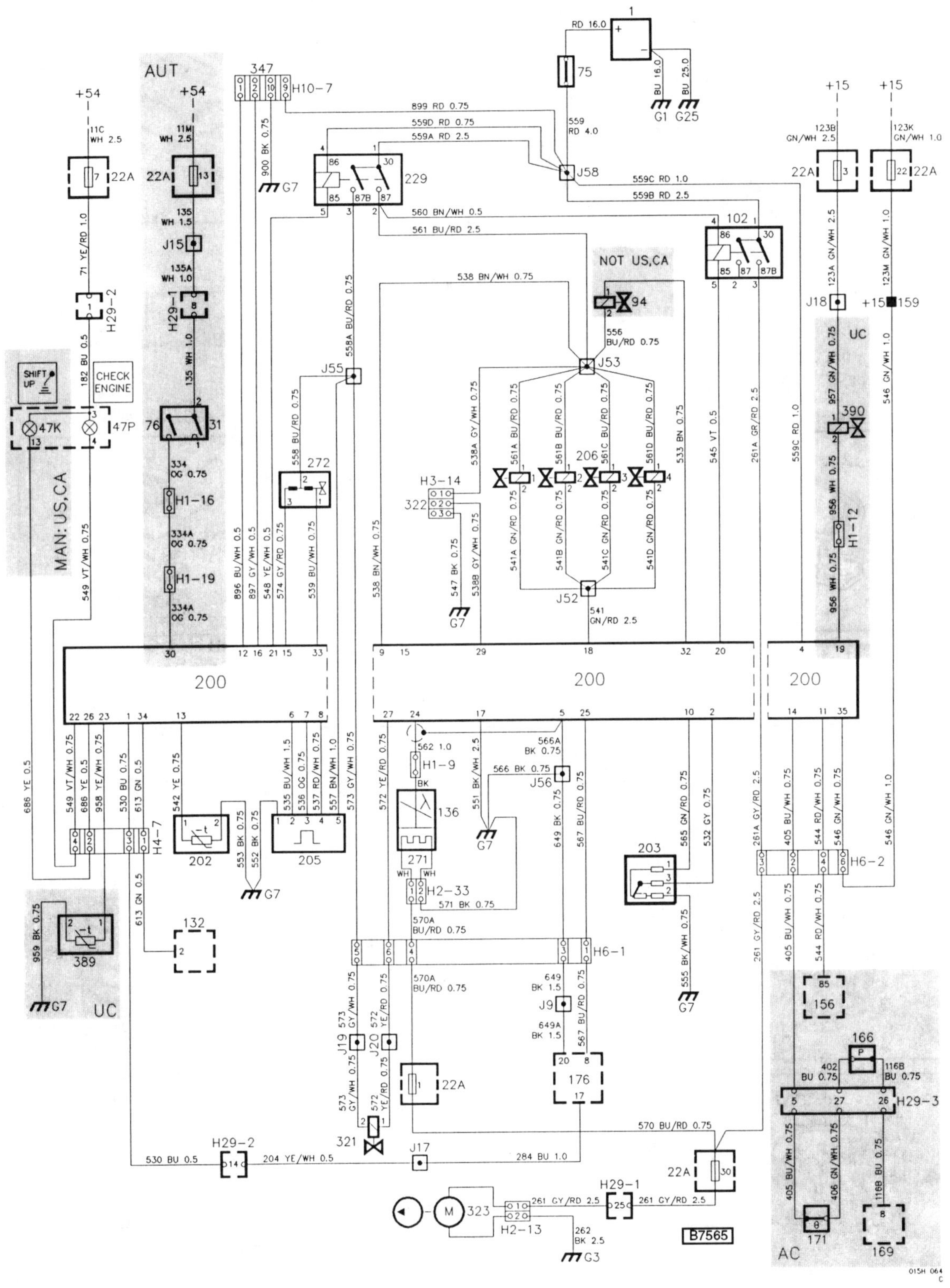

LH 2.4.2 Fuel System with 33-pin connector

1991 and later Non-turbo

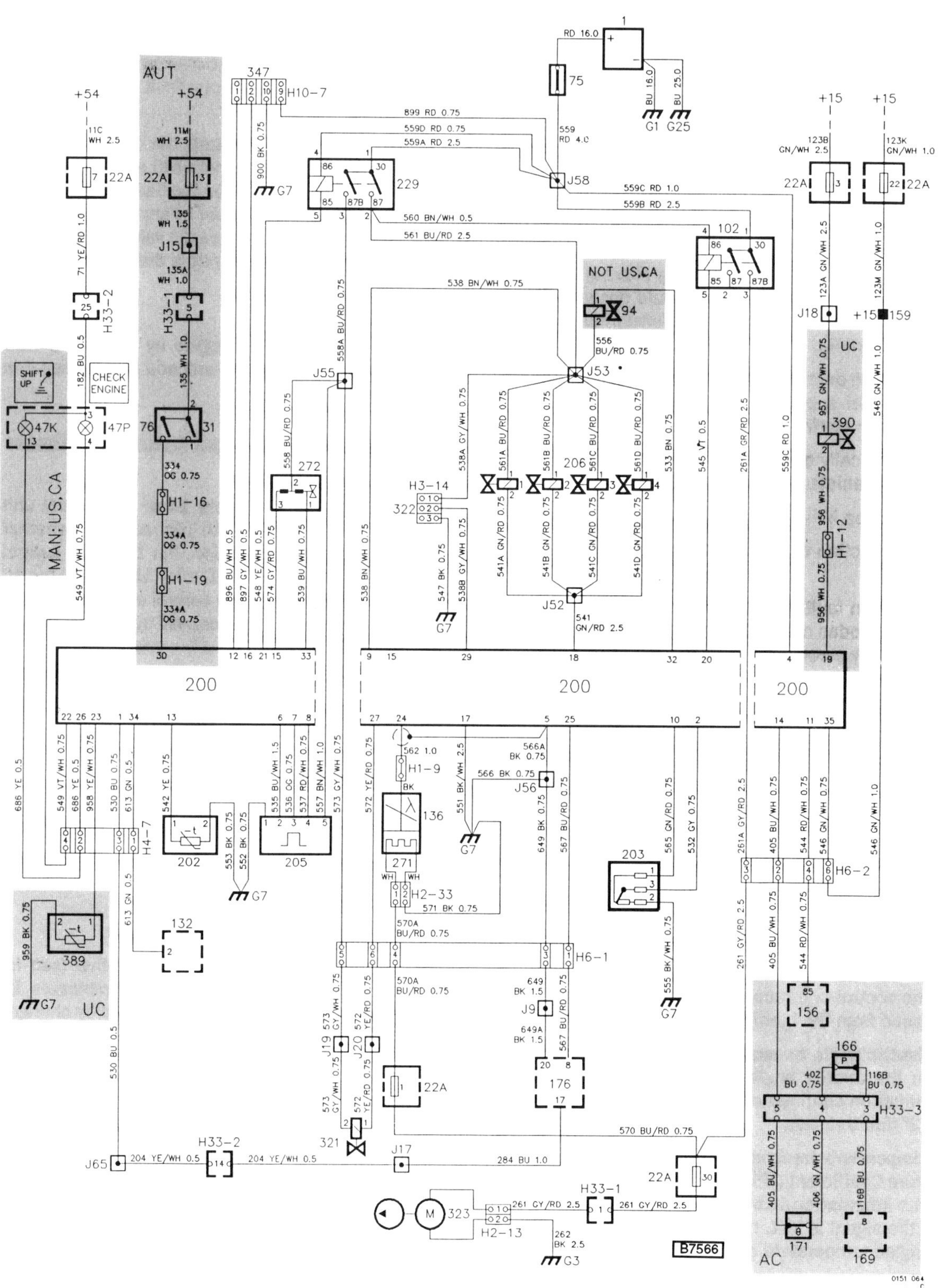

Glovebox Lighting

Operation

The glovebox light (19) is controlled by the glovebox switch (160). With the glovebox door open, the switch is closed lighting up the lamp. To change the bulb, pry off the lens.

Fault Tracing

1. Check the fuse. Check for voltage at the lamp assembly whenever the key is in the run position and the headlight switch is in the on position.
2. Check for continuity to ground to the left of the steering wheel behind the instrument panel.

Component Locations

10 light switch in instrument panel
19 glovebox light in glovebox
22 main fuse/relay panel
160 glovebox light switch in side of glovebox

Connector Locations

1985-1990

152B 29-pin bulkhead connector at main fuse/relay panel

1991 and later

H29-2 29-pin bulkhead connector behind main fuse/relay panel (1991-1991 1/2)
H33-2 33-pin bulkhead connector behind main fuse/relay panel (1991 1/2 and later)

Ground Locations

1985-1990

3 ground point behind instrument panel

1991 and later

G8 ground point behind instrument panel

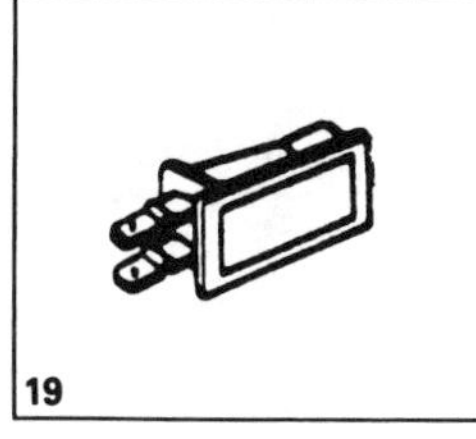
19

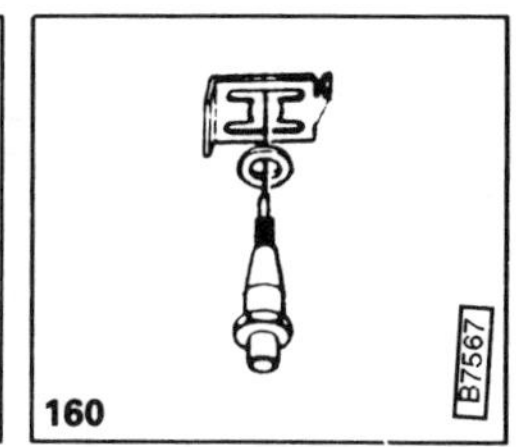
160

B7567

Glovebox Lighting

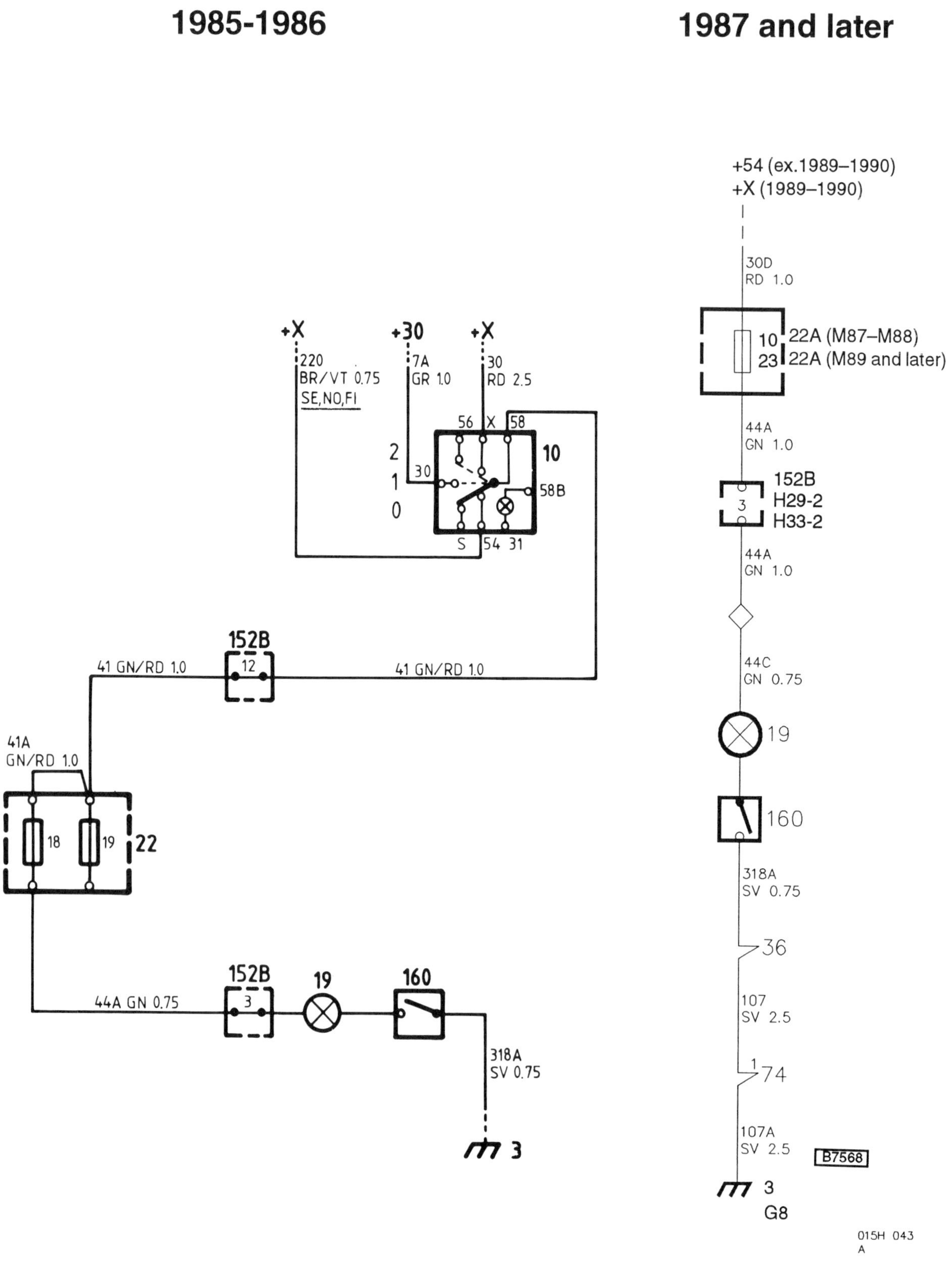

1985-1986
1987 and later
+X
+30
+X
220
BR/VT 0.75
SE,NO,FI
7A
GR 1.0
30
RD 2.5
56
X
58
10
2
1
0
30
58B
S
54
31
152B
12
41 GN/RD 1.0
41 GN/RD 1.0
41A
GN/RD 1.0
18
19
22
152B
3
19
160
44A GN 0.75
318A
SV 0.75
3
+54 (ex.1989–1990)
+X (1989–1990)
30D
RD 1.0
10
23
22A (M87–M88)
22A (M89 and later)
44A
GN 1.0
152B
H29-2
H33-2
44A
GN 1.0
44C
GN 0.75
19
160
318A
SV 0.75
36
107
SV 2.5
74
107A
SV 2.5
3
G8
B7568
015H 043
A

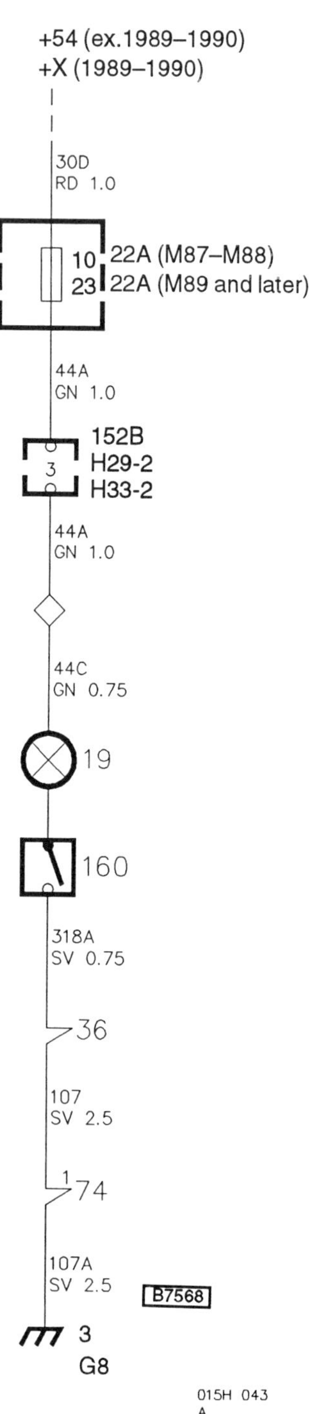

Headlights

Operation

The headlights receive power from the headlight switch whenever the key is in the run position. All power to the headlights must pass through the headlight relay and four separate fuses. Each beam (i.e. left low beam) is protected by a separate fuse. Two types of headlights are used on the cars covered by this manual. On 1985 and 1986 models, a sealed beam is used. On 1987 and later cars, a replaceable headlight bulb is used.

Fault tracing

Always begin by checking fuses and connectors. Check and tighten all grounds. See **351 Lighting** for repair information, including changing bulbs.

Component Location

- 8 lighting relay in main fuse/relay panel
- 10 lighting switch in instrument panel
- 11 headlight high beam
- 12 headlight low beam
- 47G headlight high beam warning light in instrument cluster
- 75 terminal distribution in right bulkhead near exhaust manifold
- 158 negative distribution terminal in main fuse/relay panel
- 215 dip switch

Connector Locations

1985-1990

- 58 12-pin connector behind instrument panel to left of steering column
- 60 1-pin connector behind instrument panel to left of steering column
- 152A 29-pin bulkhead connector
- 152B 29-pin bulkhead connector

1991 and later

- H2-7 2-pin connector at the light switch
- H12-1 12-pin connector in left side of instrument panel
- H29-2 29-pin red bulkhead connector (1991–1991 1/2)
- H33-3 33-pin gray bulkhead connector (1991 and later)

Ground Locations

1985-1990

- 3 ground point behind instrument panel
- 7 ground point at radiator cross member

1991 and later

- G1 ground point at radiator cross member
- G6 ground distribution in main fuse/relay panel
- G8 ground point behind instrument panel
- G25 ground point on gearbox

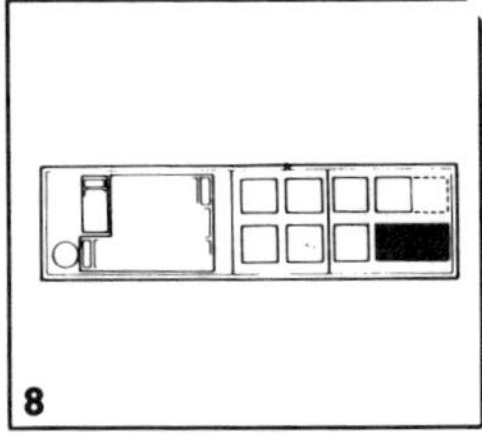
8

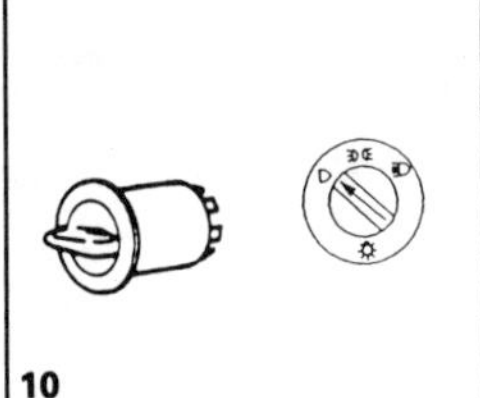
10

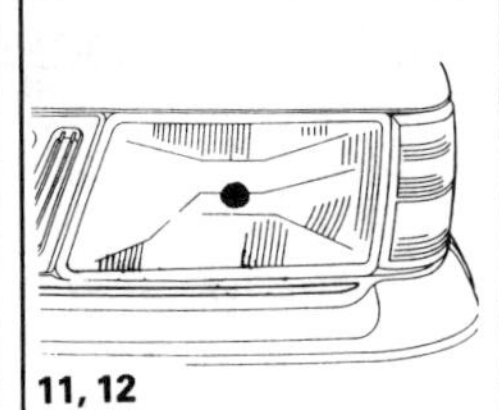
11, 12

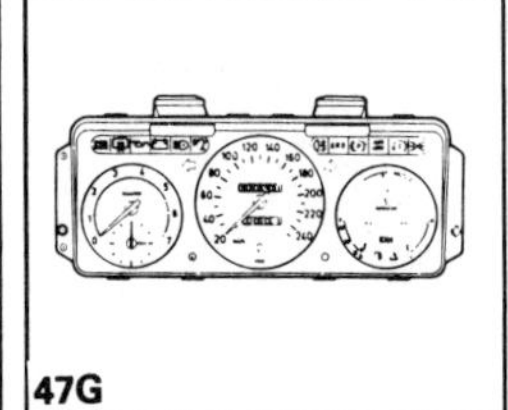
47G

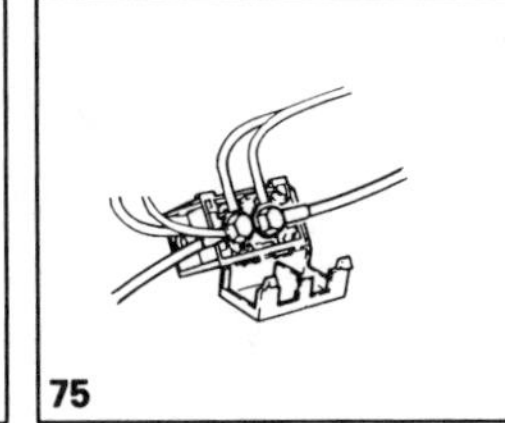
75

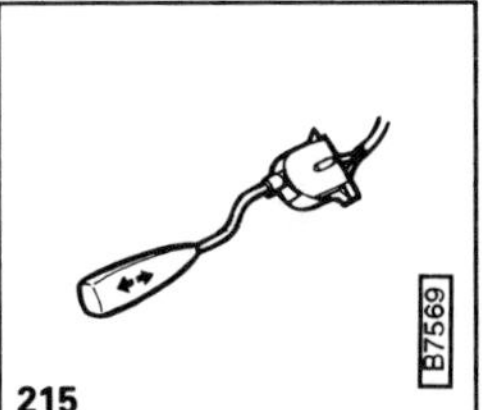

215

Headlights

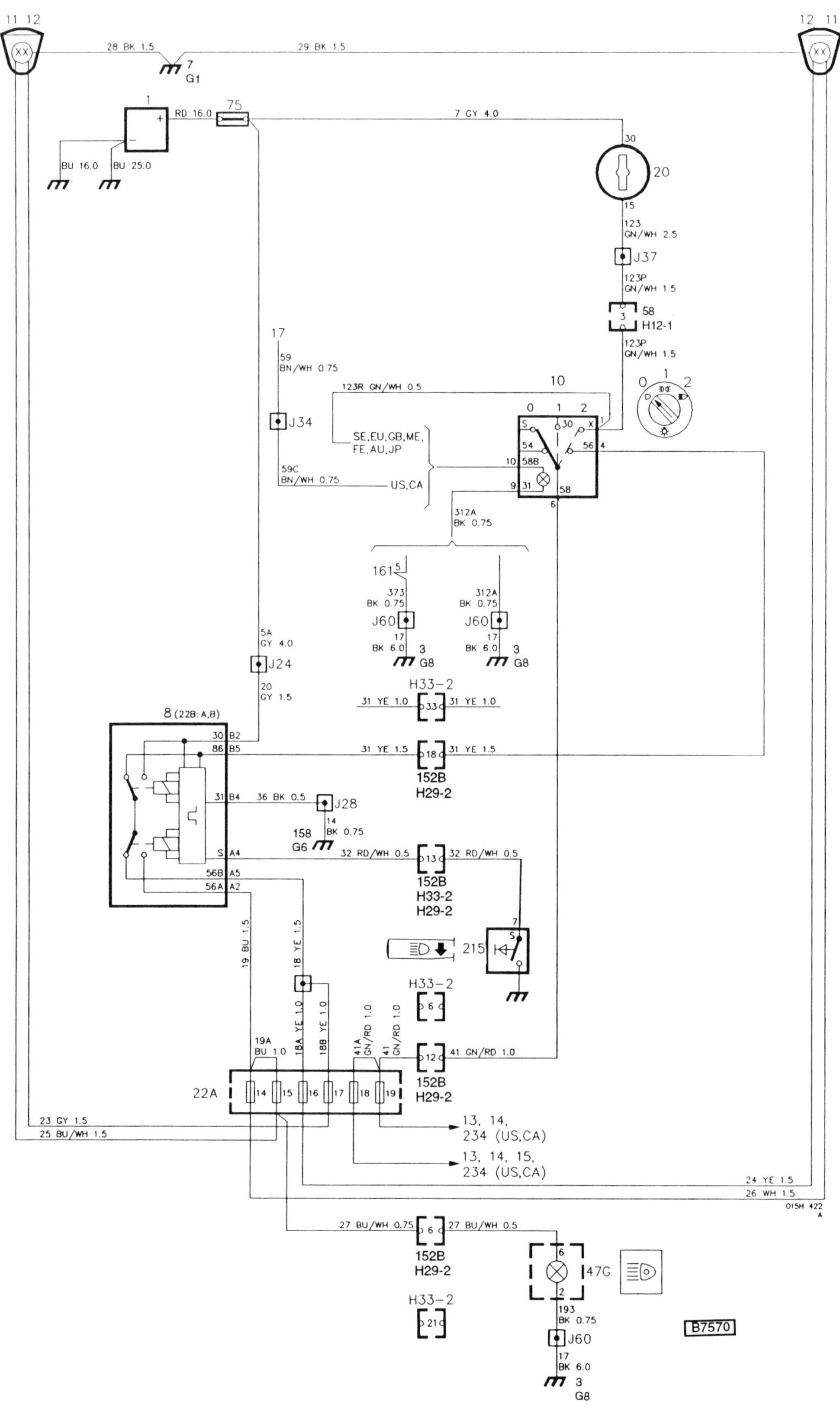

Heated Rear Window and Cigarette Lighter

Heated Rear Window Operation

The heated rear window element (115) is activated by the switch (116) on the instrument panel. A rear window heater warning light (47J) will light up in the instrument cluster. The circuit has a time delay relay (113) that will turn off the supply to the heating element after about 10 minutes. Convertible models have a mercury switch (279) that deactivates the circuit if the convertible top is down.

Heated Rear Window Fault Tracing

1. Check the fuse.
2. Check for voltage at the heating element. Check the continuity of the heating element to find breaks in the rear window grid.
3. Check for voltage at time delay relay (113) terminal 30 and terminal 87.

Cigarette Lighter Operation

The cigarette lighter works after it is pushed in only with the key in the run position.

Cigarette Lighter Fault Tracing

1. Check the fuse.
2. Remove the cigarette lighter element and carefully check for voltage between the center contact and ground with the key on.
3. Inspect the heating element for breaks. Check the continuity of the heating element.

Component Locations

20 ignition switch
22A main fuse/relay panel at left wheel housing
47 instrument cluster
47J rear window heater warning lamp
48 cigarette lighter
113 time delay relay for heated rear window under rear seat, auxiliary fuse/relay panel
115 rear window heater element
116 rear window heater switch
158 negative distribution in main fuse/relay panel
159 +15 distribution in main fuse/relay panel
207 heated rear view mirrors on front doors
279 mercury switch for convertible heated rear window at left side top mounting
401 auxiliary fuse/relay panel under rear seat

Connector Locations

1985-1990

57 3-pin connector in luggage compartment, left air outlet
59 2-pin connector in luggage compartment, left air outlet
152A 29-pin bulkhead connector at main fuse/relay panel
152B 29-pin bulkhead connector at main fuse/relay panel

1991 and later

H2-10 2-pin connector behind cigarette lighter
H3-13 3-pin connector in luggage compartment, left air outlet
H10-1 10-pin connector behind instrument panel, left of steering column
H29-2 29-pin bulkhead connector behind main fuse/relay panel (1991-1991 1/2)
H33-2 33-pin bulkhead connector behind main fuse/relay panel (1991 1/2 and later)

Ground Locations

1985-1990

3 ground point behind instrument panel

1991 and later

G3 ground point in luggage compartment
G5 ground point under the rear seat
G8 ground point behind instrument panel
G19 ground point at hatchback
G26 ground point at right C pillar on sedans

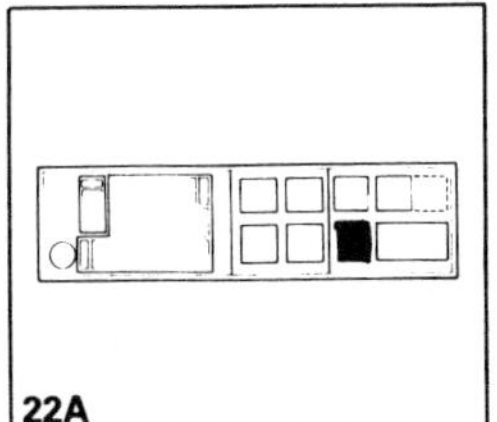
22A

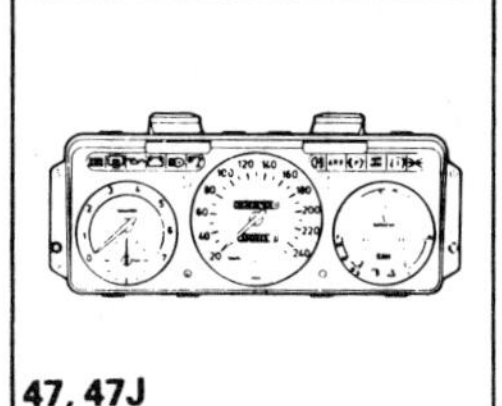
47, 47J

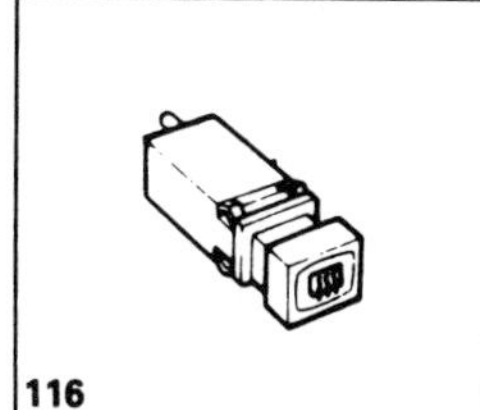
116

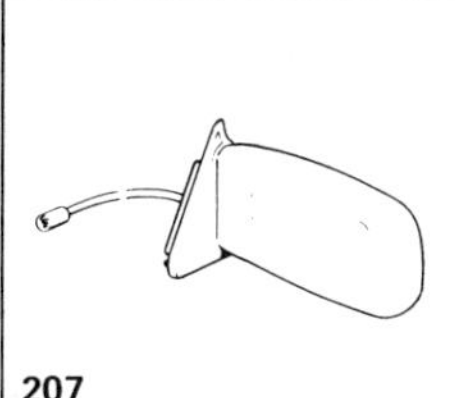
207

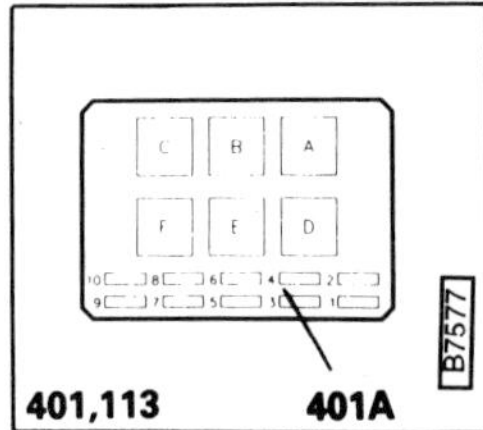

401,113 401A

Heated Rear Window and Cigarette Lighter

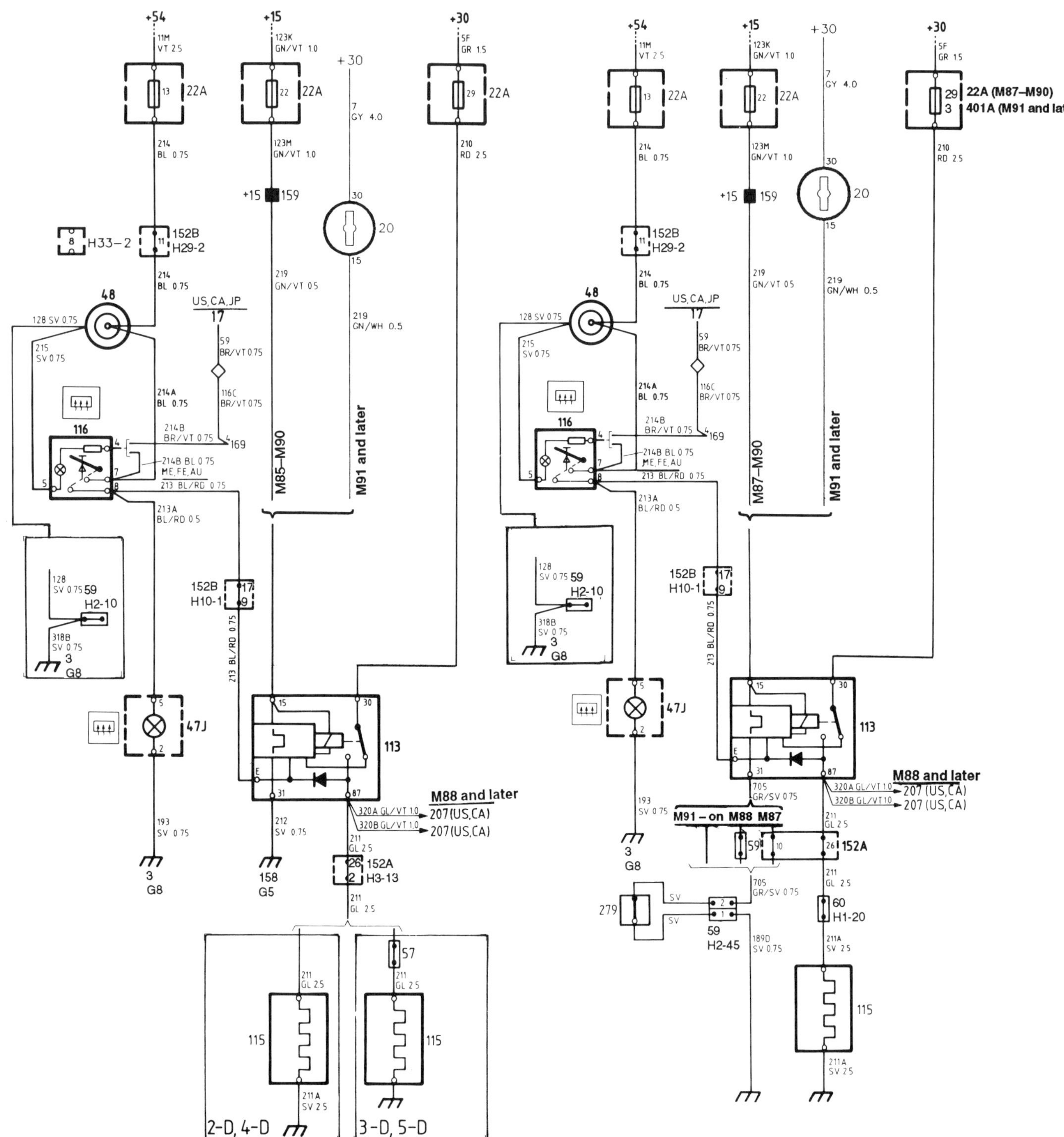

Heated Seats

Operation

The front heated seats are thermostatically controlled. Some models have a rheostat (252) on the instrument panel for temperature control. The heating element is located under the bottom seat cover and the seat back. A thermostatic button under the bottom cover turns the heating element on and off. The passenger seat switch (121) prevents the heater from turning on if the passenger seat is not occupied.

For information on removing the seats and seat covers, see **851 Interior Trim and Upholstery**.

Fault Tracing

1. Check the fuse. On 1991 and later models, the fuse is located in the fuse/relay panel (401) under the rear seat.
2. Check for voltage at the seat heating pad element (64) and check for continuity through the element.
3. Check the seat switch (121) under the passenger seat. This switch should be closed (continuity through switch) when a passenger is in the seat.
4. Check the thermostat button under the bottom seat cover. The thermostat should be closed (continuity) or open (no continuity) depending on the temperature of the switch.

Heated seat thermostat

- switch closed. . . . . below 54°F (12°C)
- switch open . . . . above 82°F (28°C)

NOTE

A commercial aerosol freeze spray can be sprayed on the thermostat button to simulate cold temperatures for testing. Always check compatibility of the spray with components and upholstery before using.

Component Locations

22A main fuse/relay panel at left wheel housing
64 heated seat pad with thermostat in the seat cushion and backrest
121 passenger seat switch for heated seats under the passenger seat
252 driver heated seat rheostat in instrument panel
254 driver seat temperature transmitter in driver seat
401 auxiliary fuse/relay panel under rear seat

Connector Locations

1985-1990

59 2-pin connector under each front seat
60 1-pin connector under the center console
98 10-pin connector to the left of the steering column
152A 29-pin bulkhead connector at main fuse/relay panel
152B 29-pin bulkhead connector at main fuse/relay panel

1991 and later

H8-1 8-pin connector under the passenger seat
H8-2 8-pin connector under the driver seat
H10-1 10-pin connector behind instrument panel, left of steering column
H10-6 10-pin connector at the auxiliary fuse/relay panel under rear seat

Ground Locations

1985-1990

65 ground point at the handbrake
117 ground point at the handbrake

1991 and later

G4 ground point between ignition switch and handbrake

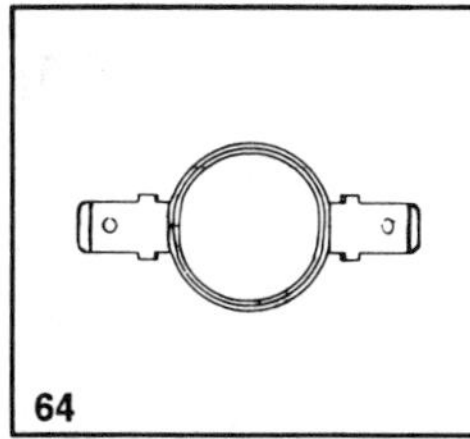

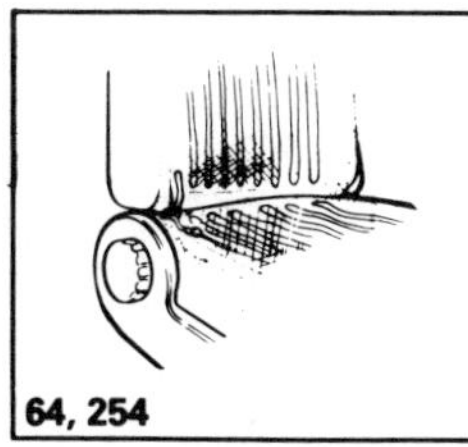

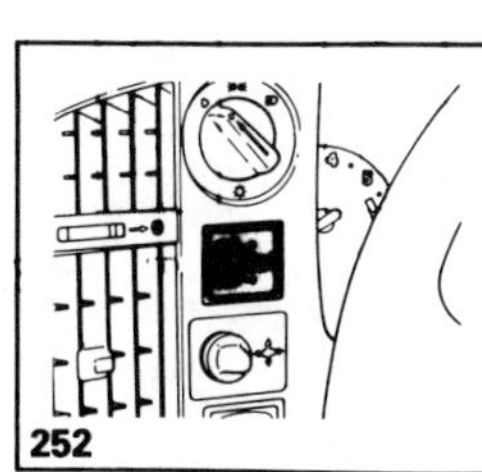

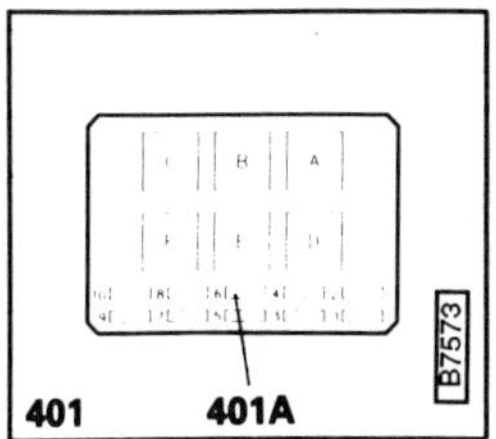

Heated Front Seats without Rheostat

1985-1988

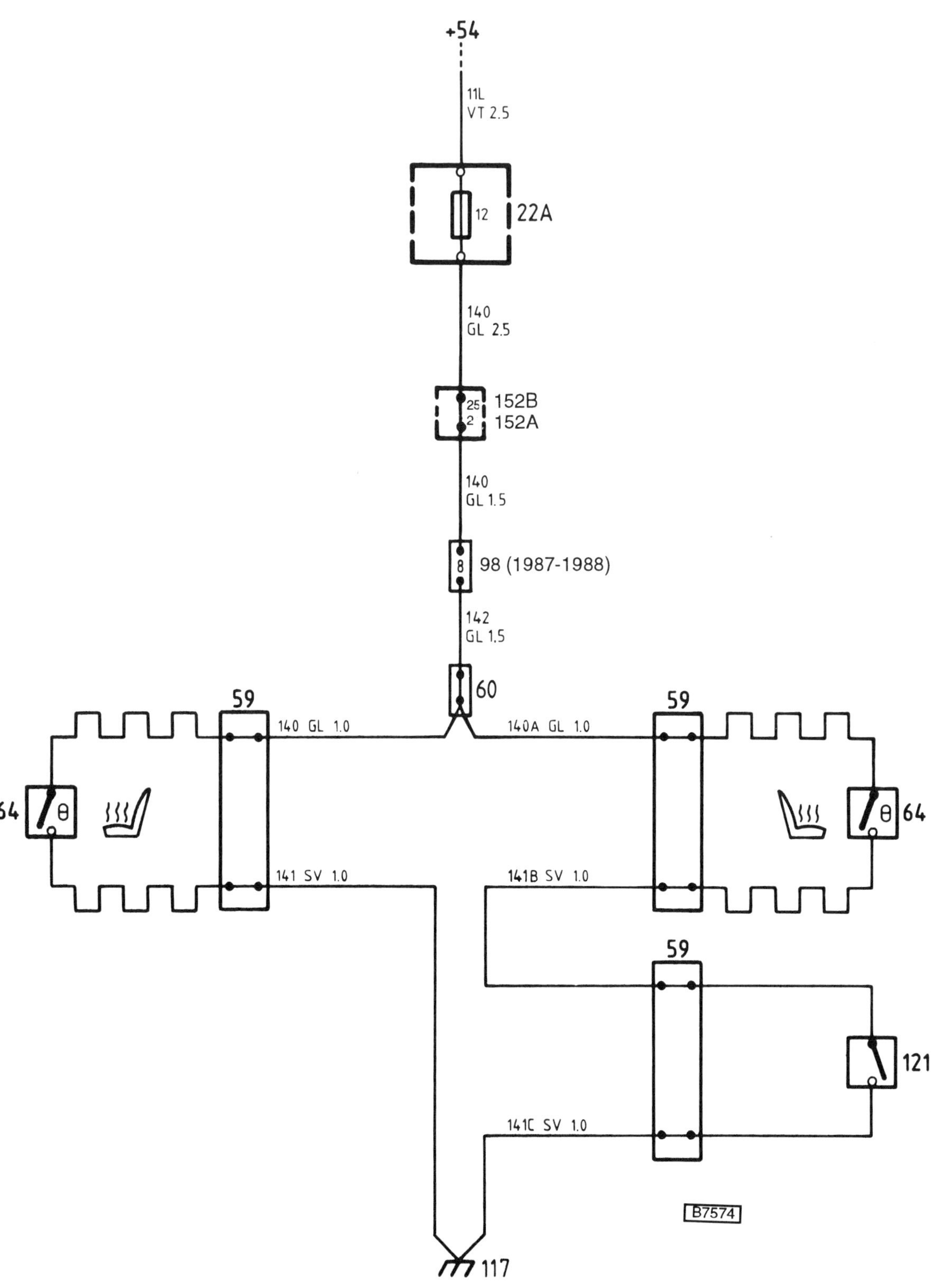

Heated Front Seats with Rheostat

1987-1990

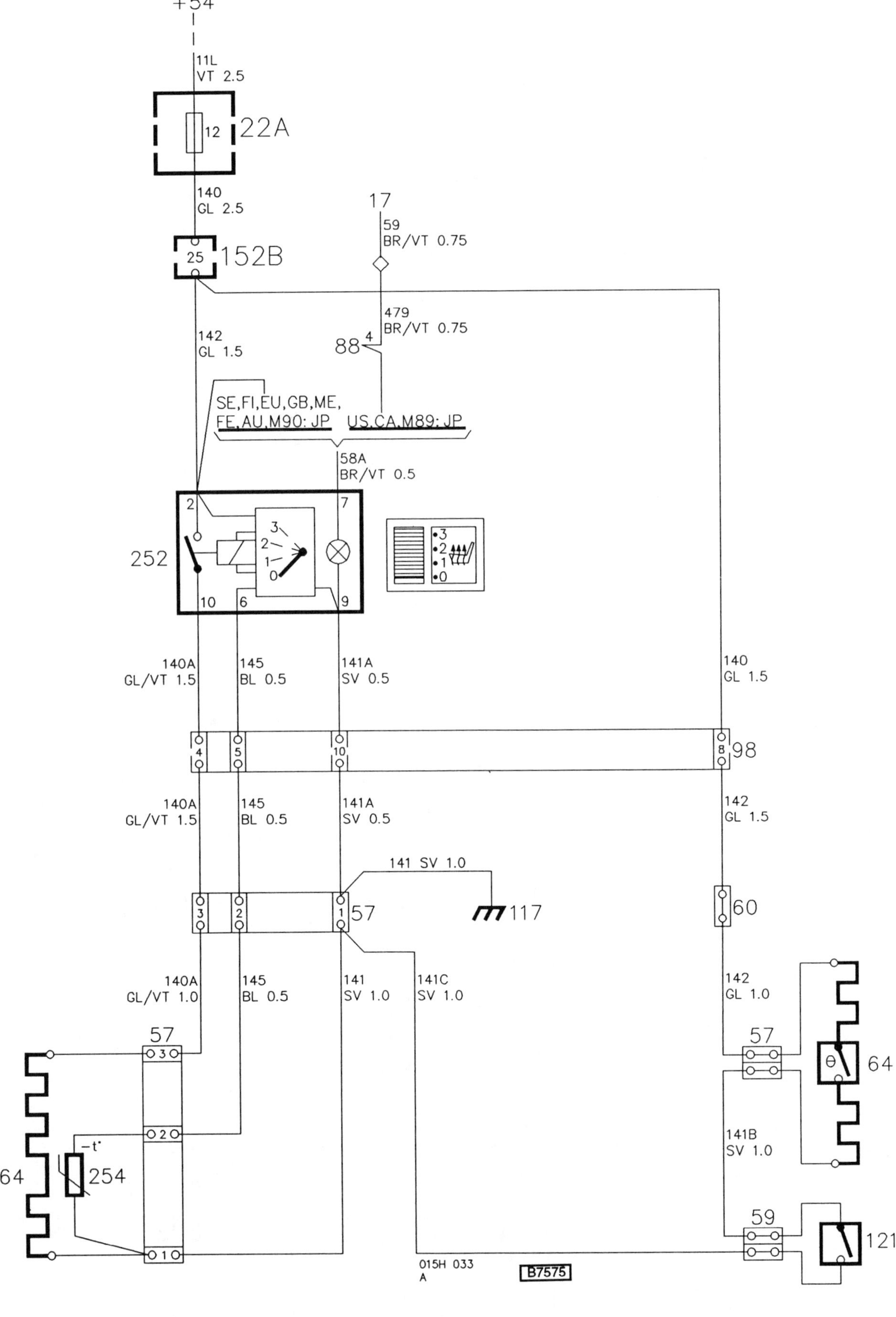

Heated Front Seats with Rheostat

1991 and later

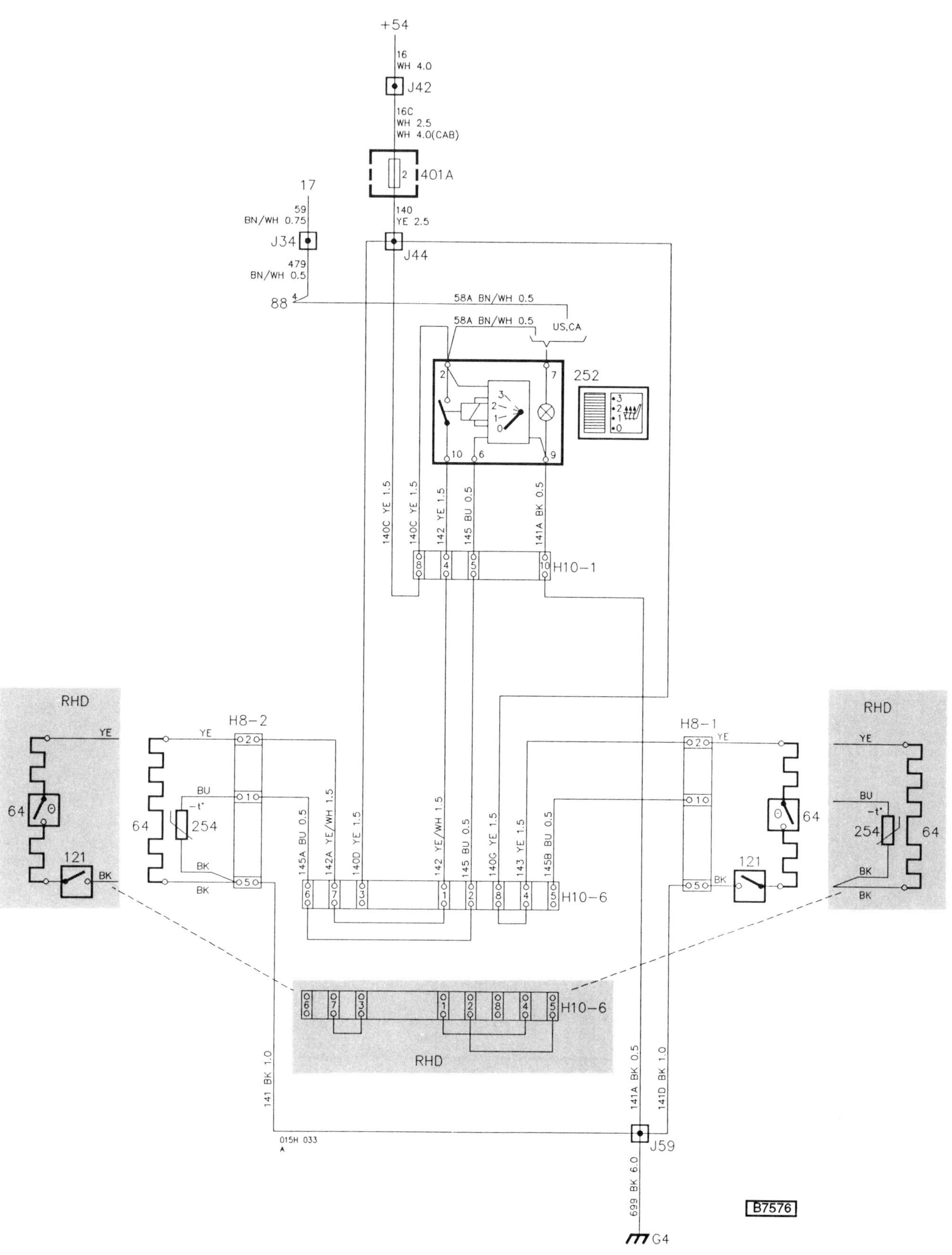

Horns

Operation

The horns can be sounded with the key in the run position. The buttons on the steering pad (41) complete the circuit to ground through the slip ring assembly (352/336) in the steering wheel and the horn relay (68).

WARNING

Some cars covered by this manual are equipped with an explosive SRS airbag device. Do not attempt to service the wiring in the steering wheel or steering column assembly. The airbag may accidentally ignite, causing personal injury. See an authorized Saab dealer for any repairs necessary to the SRS wiring or components.

For information on removing and repairing the steering wheel see **641 Steering Column.**

Fault Tracing

1. Check that the fuse is okay.
2. Remove the horn relay (68) and jumper pins 30 and 87, the horn should sound. If not, there is a problem between the fuse and the horns.
3. Check for ground at pin 85 of the horn relay when the horn button is depressed. If ground is not present, check the slip ring assembly.
4. Check for positive (+) battery voltage at pin 86 of the horn relay when the key is in the run position. If there is no voltage check the wiring from the ignition switch (20) through the ignition switch relay (21).

Component Locations

20 ignition switch in center console
21 ignition switch relay in main fuse/relay panel
22A main fuse/relay panel
40A horns located on right side behind headlight
41 horn switch in steering wheel pad
68 horn relay in main fuse/relay panel
75 distribution block at right wheel housing
158 negative distribution in main fuse/relay panel
289 burglar alarm control unit (convertible) under rear seat
336 slip ring contact behind steering wheel (cars with SRS Airbag)
352 slip ring switch behind steering wheel

Connector Locations

1985-1990

152A 29-pin bulkhead connector behind main fuse/relay panel
152B 29-pin bulkhead connector behind main fuse/relay panel

1991 and later

H29-1 29-pin bulkhead connector behind main fuse/relay panel (1991-1991 1/2)
H29-2 29-pin bulkhead connector behind main fuse/relay panel (1991-1991 1/2)
H33-1 33-pin bulkhead connector behind main fuse/relay panel (1991 1/2 and later)
H33-2 33-pin bulkhead connector behind main fuse/relay panel (1991 1/2 and later)

Ground Locations

1985-1990

7 ground point at radiator cross member
211 ground point at gearbox

1991 and later

G1 ground point at radiator cross member
G6 ground distribution at main fuse/relay panel
G25 ground point at gearbox

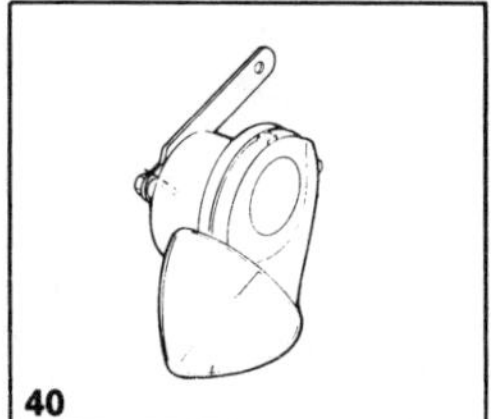

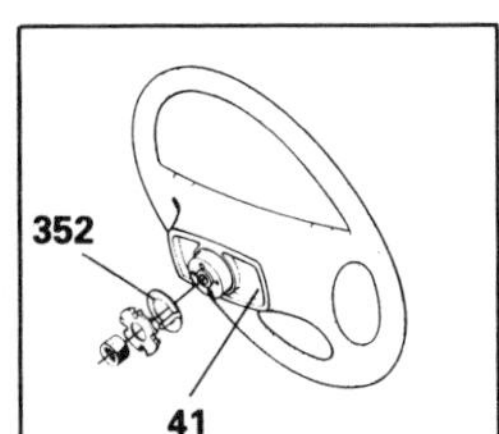

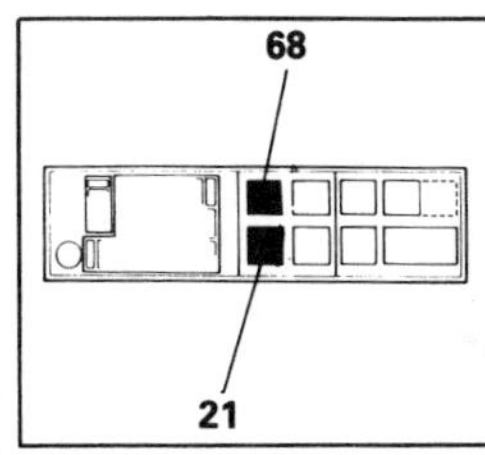

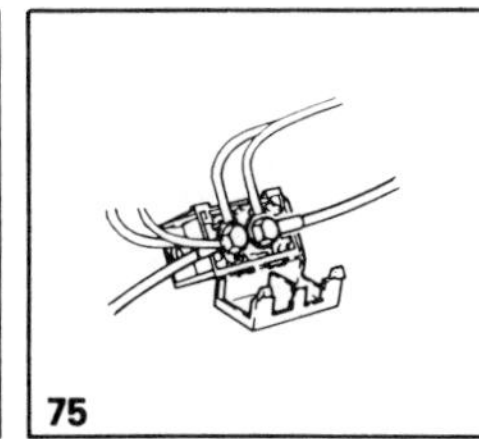

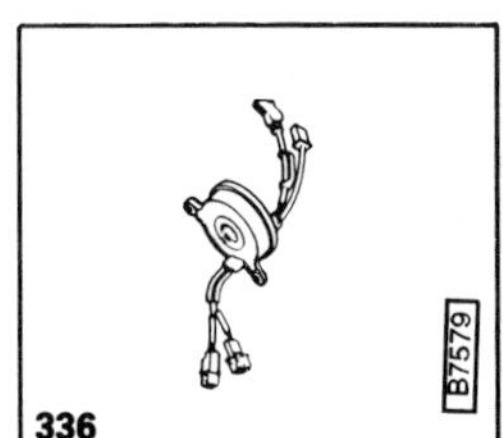

Horns

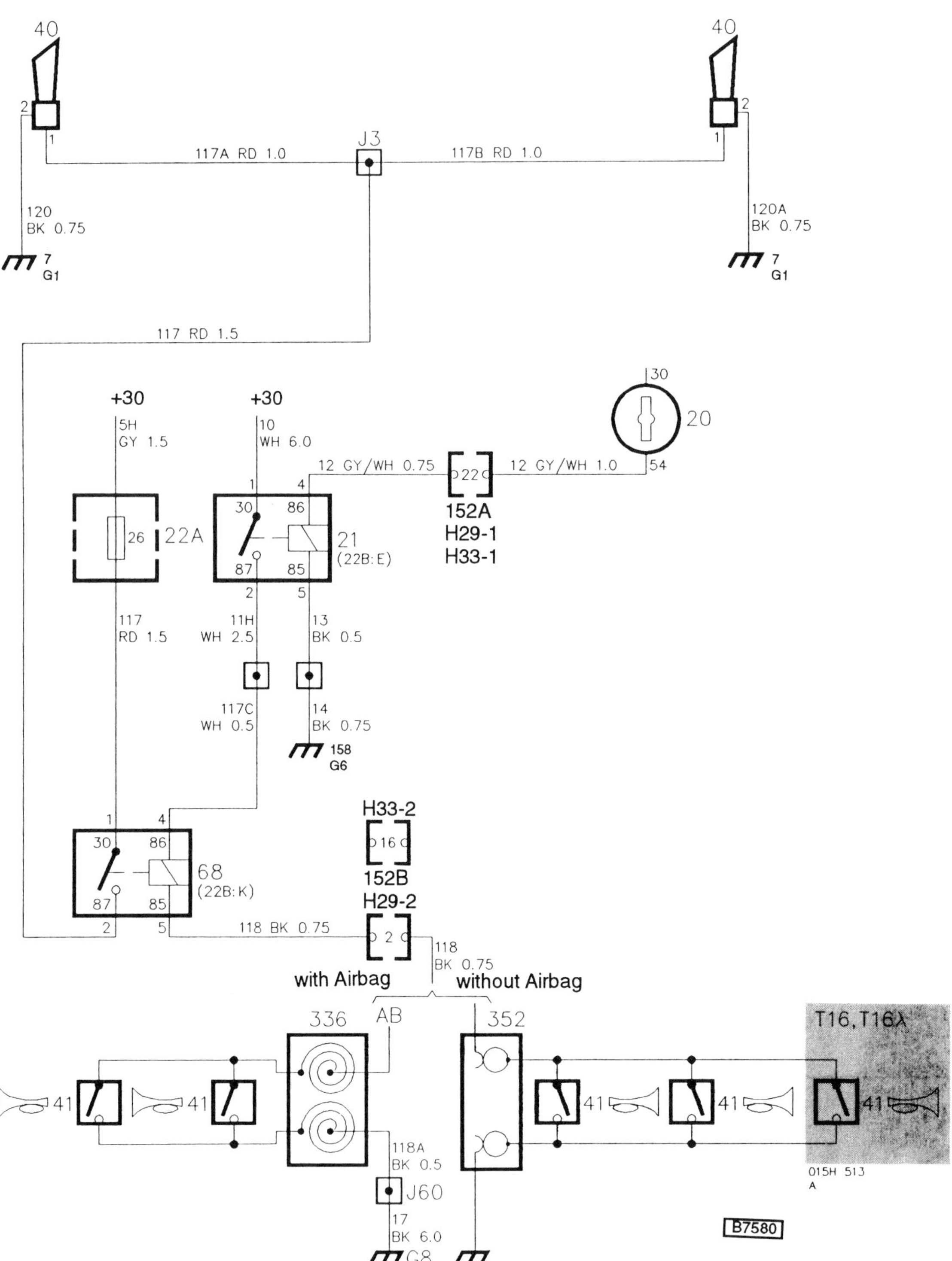
40
40
2
1
J3
117A RD 1.0
117B RD 1.0
120
BK 0.75
120A
BK 0.75
7
G1
117 RD 1.5
+30
+30
30
20
5H
GY 1.5
10
WH 6.0
12 GY/WH 0.75
22
12 GY/WH 1.0
54
26
22A
30
86
87
85
21
(22B:E)
152A
H29-1
H33-1
117
RD 1.5
11H
WH 2.5
13
BK 0.5
117C
WH 0.5
14
BK 0.75
158
G6
H33-2
16
152B
H29-2
68
(22B:K)
118 BK 0.75
2
118
BK 0.75
with Airbag
without Airbag
336
AB
352
T16, T16λ
41
118A
BK 0.5
J60
17
BK 6.0
G8
015H 513
A
B7580

Ignition System

Operation

The ignition system creates and regulates the high voltage pulses that fire the spark plugs. Two versions of a Hall-effect electronic ignition system are used on the cars covered by this manual. Complete ignition system repair information is covered under **340 Ignition System.**

Ignition System Applications

- Turbo models — basic Hall ignition
- Non-turbo models — EZK ignition (with knock sensor)

WARNING

Any time work is being done on the ignition system it should first be disabled as described in **340 Ignition System**. The ignition system operates at lethal voltages. People with pacemakers or weak hearts should not expose themselves to the ignition system. Extra caution must be taken when working on or servicing the engine while it is running or if the key is on.

Fault Tracing

Read and understand the warnings and cautions given in **300 Electrical—General** before working on the ignition system. See **340 Ignition System** for fault tracing.

Component Locations

5 ignition coil on top of radiator
6 distributor at end of cylinder head
47P Check Engine light
73 TSI socket in main fuse/relay panel
110 Tachometer in instrument cluster
145 EZK test connector next to main fuse/relay panel
146 Ignition Control Unit (non-EZK ignition)
Ignition amplifier (EZK ignition)(in front of left wheel housing)
147 Ignition pulse amplifier main fuse/relay panel, position D (1986-1987)
158 ground (–) distribution in main fuse/relay panel
159 +15 distribution in main fuse/relay panel
176 EZK control unit on inner left fender
178 EZK knock sensor on engine block, below intake manifold
200 LH control unit behind passenger side A pillar trim
203 throttle angle transmitter on throttle housing
320 ignition coil with integrated amplifier on inner right fender, near battery (1988-1989)
345 EZK crankshaft sensor behind crank pulley (1989 and later)

Connector Locations

1985-1990

57 3-pin connector in engine compartment right side
59 2-pin connector in engine compartment right side
60 1-pin connector near main fuse/relay panel
67 6-pin connector in engine compartment right side

1991 and later

H1-18 1-pin connector under center console
H2-53 2-pin connector under the rear seat
H3-3 3-pin connector to left of starter motor
H3-5 3-pin connector in engine compartment, left of air intake
H4-1 4-pin connector at left wheel housing
H4-1 4-pin connector behind instrument panel right side behind trim
H6-1 6-pin connector in engine compartment right wheel housing
H6-2 6-pin connector in engine compartment right wheel housing
H29-1 29-pin bulkhead connector behind main fuse/relay panel (1991-1991 1/2)
H29-2 29-pin bulkhead connector behind main fuse/relay panel (1991-1991 1/2)
H33-1 33-pin bulkhead connector behind main fuse/relay panel (1991 1/2 and later)
H33-2 33-pin bulkhead connector behind main fuse/relay panel (1991 1/2 and later)

Ground Locations

1985-1990

7 ground point at radiator cross member
158 ground (–) distribution in main fuse/relay panel
211 ground point at gearbox

1991 and later

G1 ground point at radiator cross member
G6 ground distribution at main fuse/relay panel
G7 ground point at engine lifting lug
G8 ground point behind instrument panel
G12 ground point at left wheel housing
G25 ground point at gearbox

Ignition System—turbo
1985

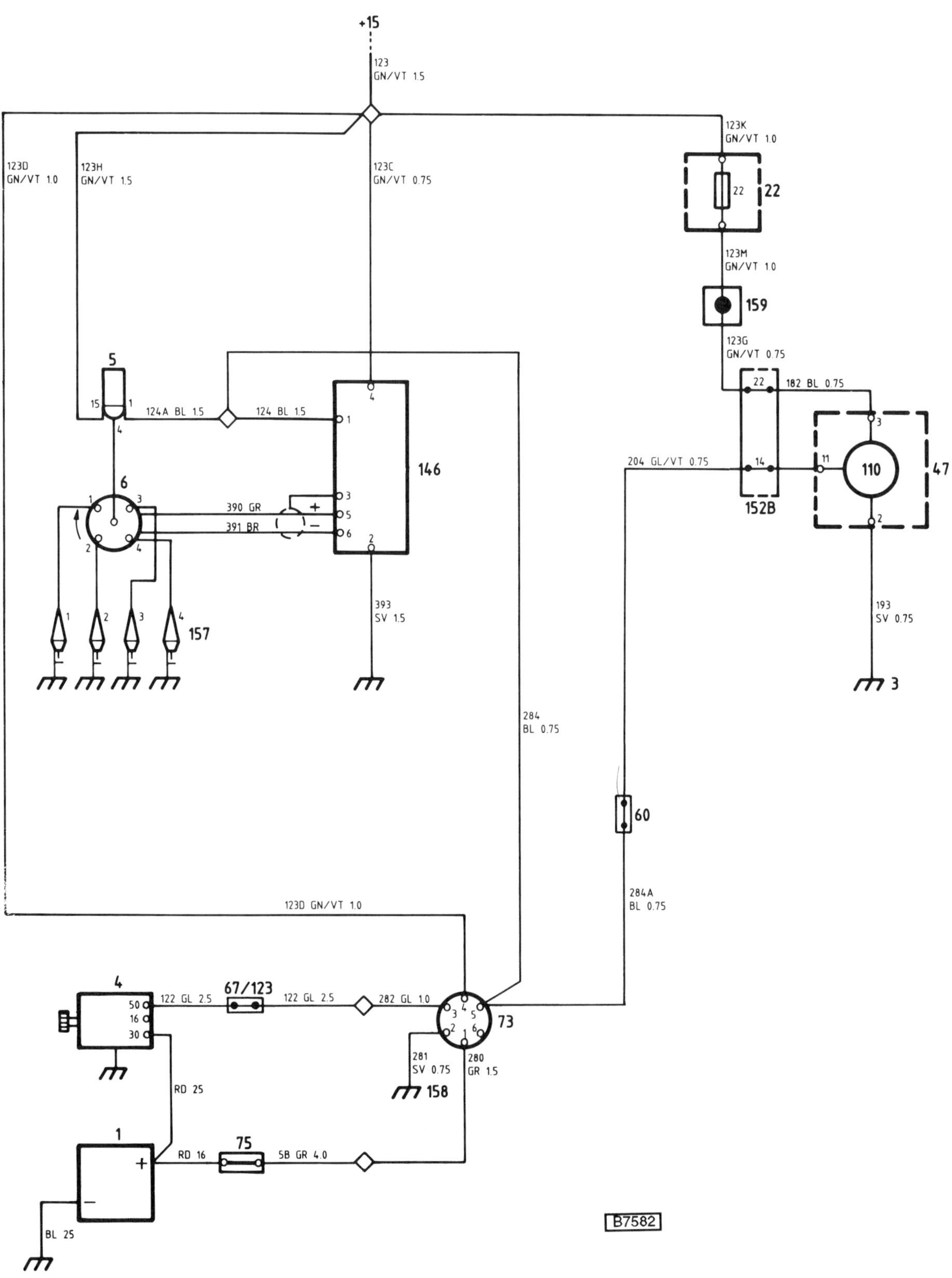

Ignition System—turbo

1986-1987

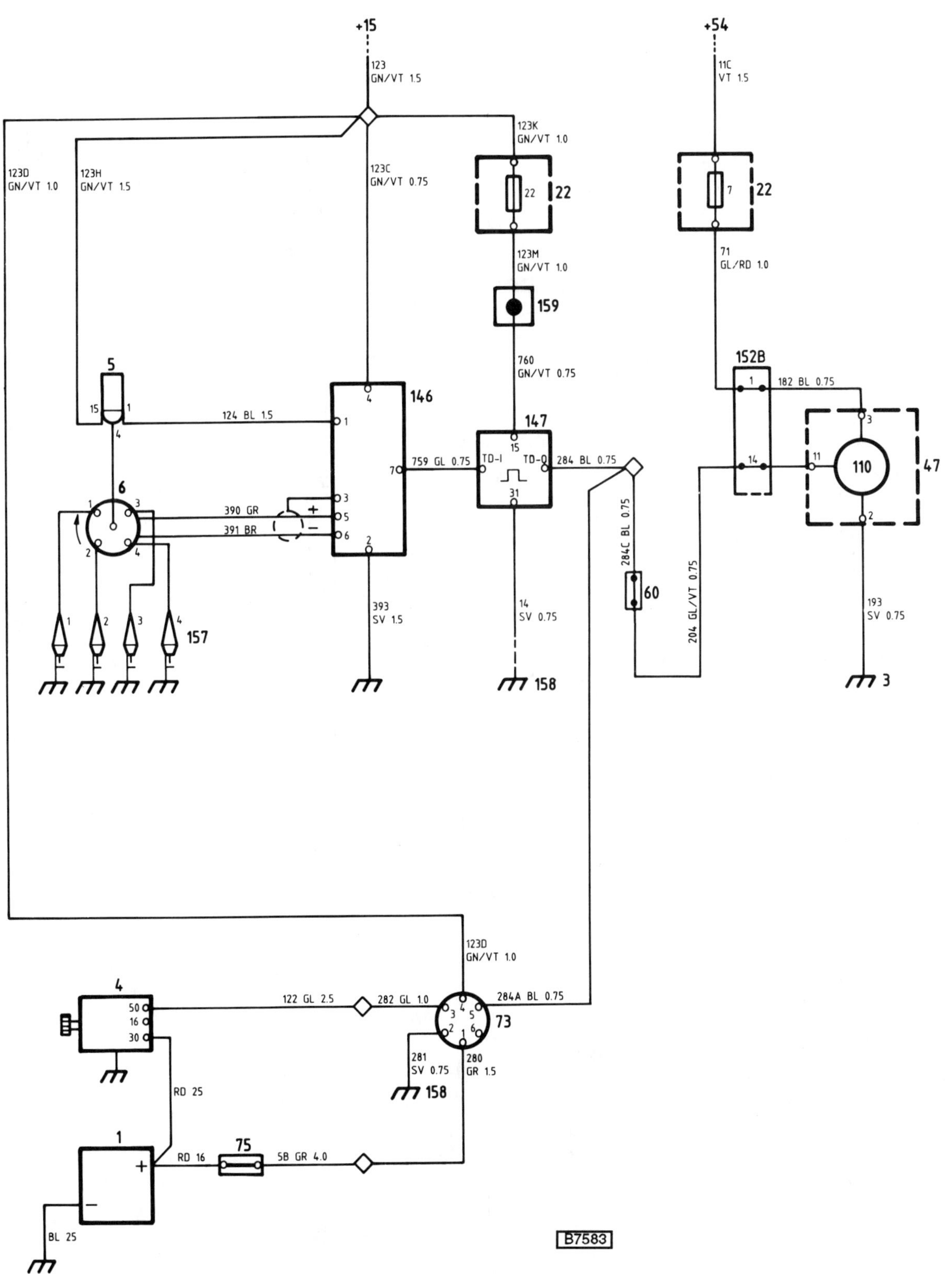

Ignition System—turbo

1988 and later

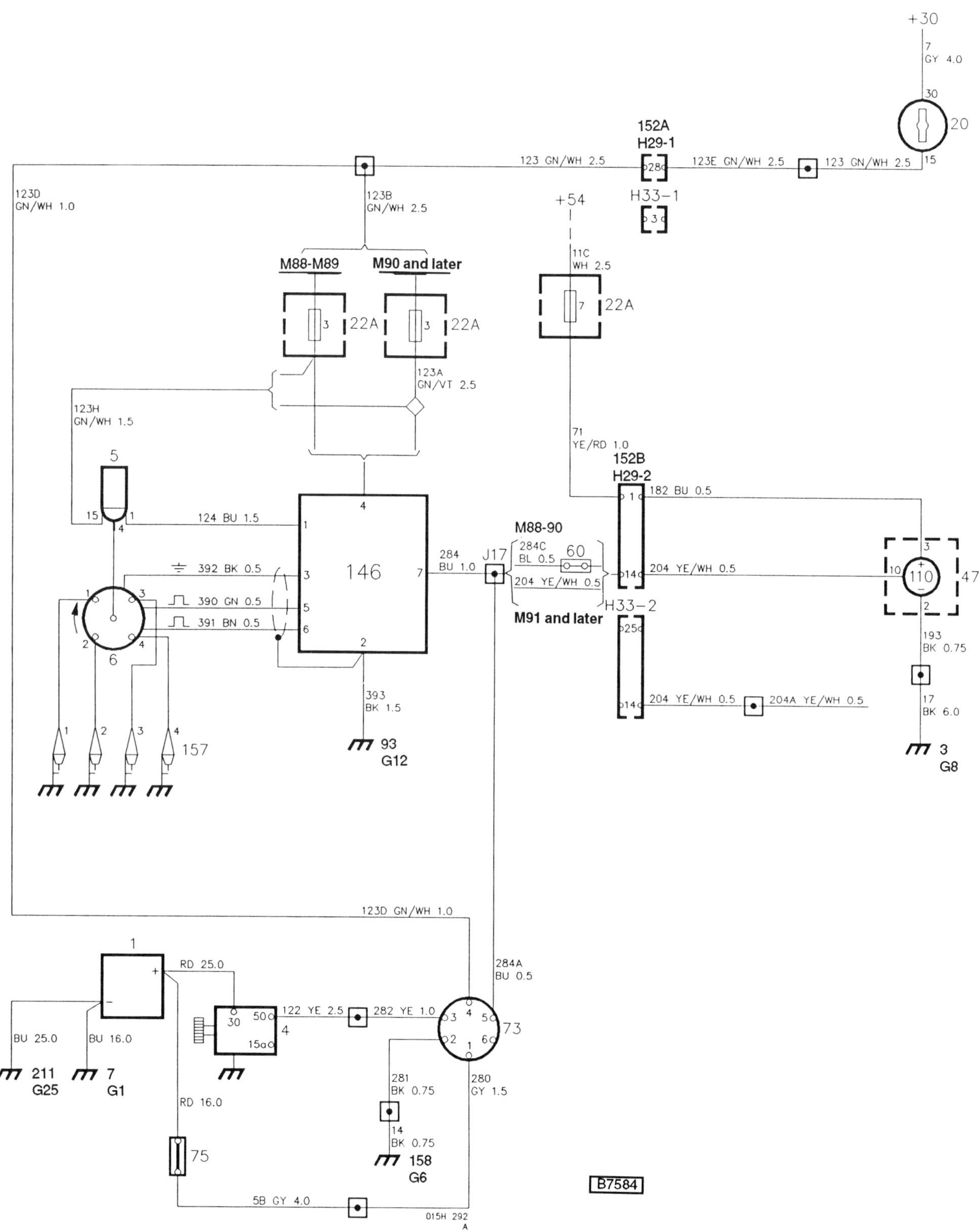

EZK Ignition System—non-turbo

1986-1987

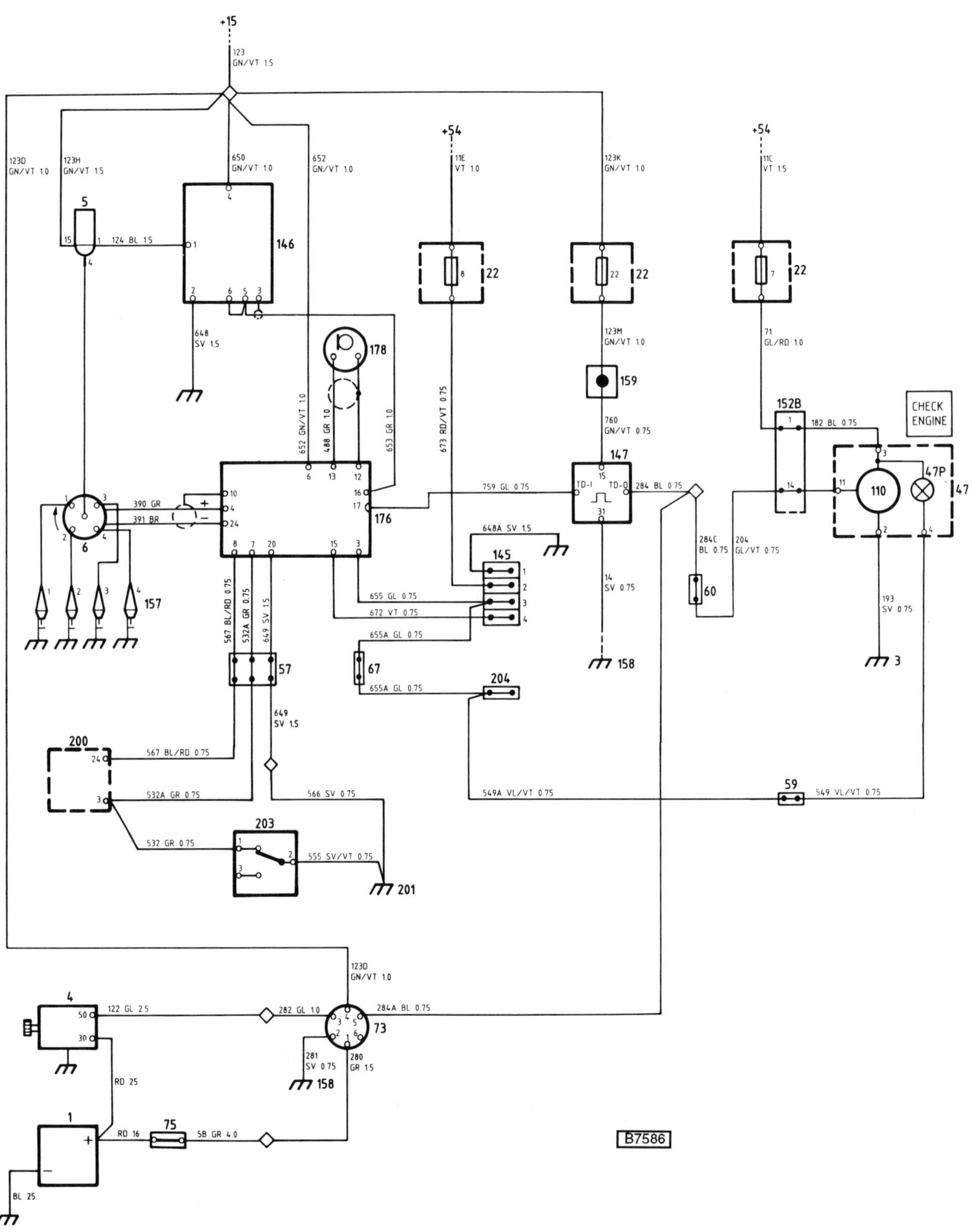

EZK Ignition System—non-turbo

1988

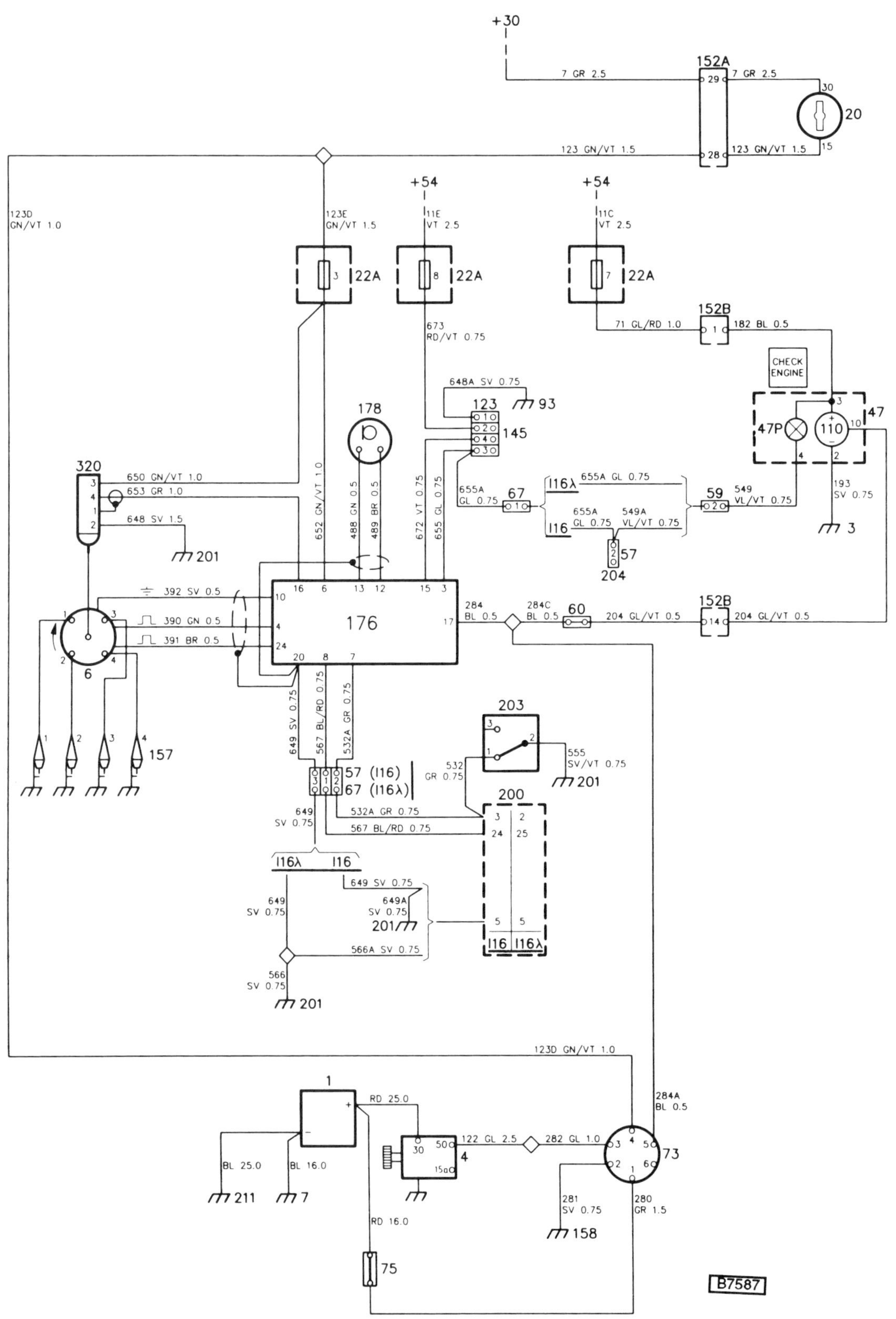

EZK Ignition System—non-turbo
1989

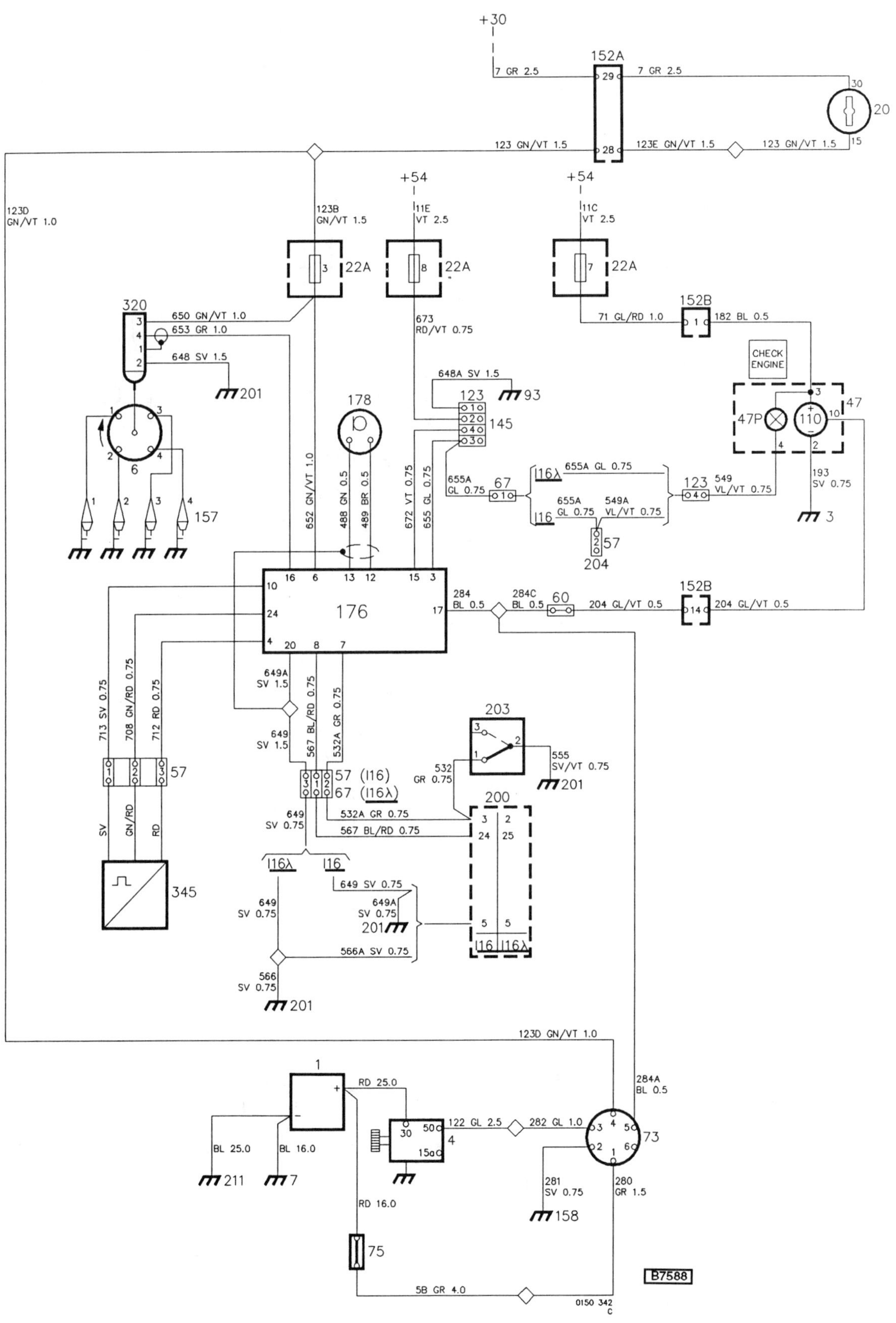

EZK Ignition System—non-turbo

1990

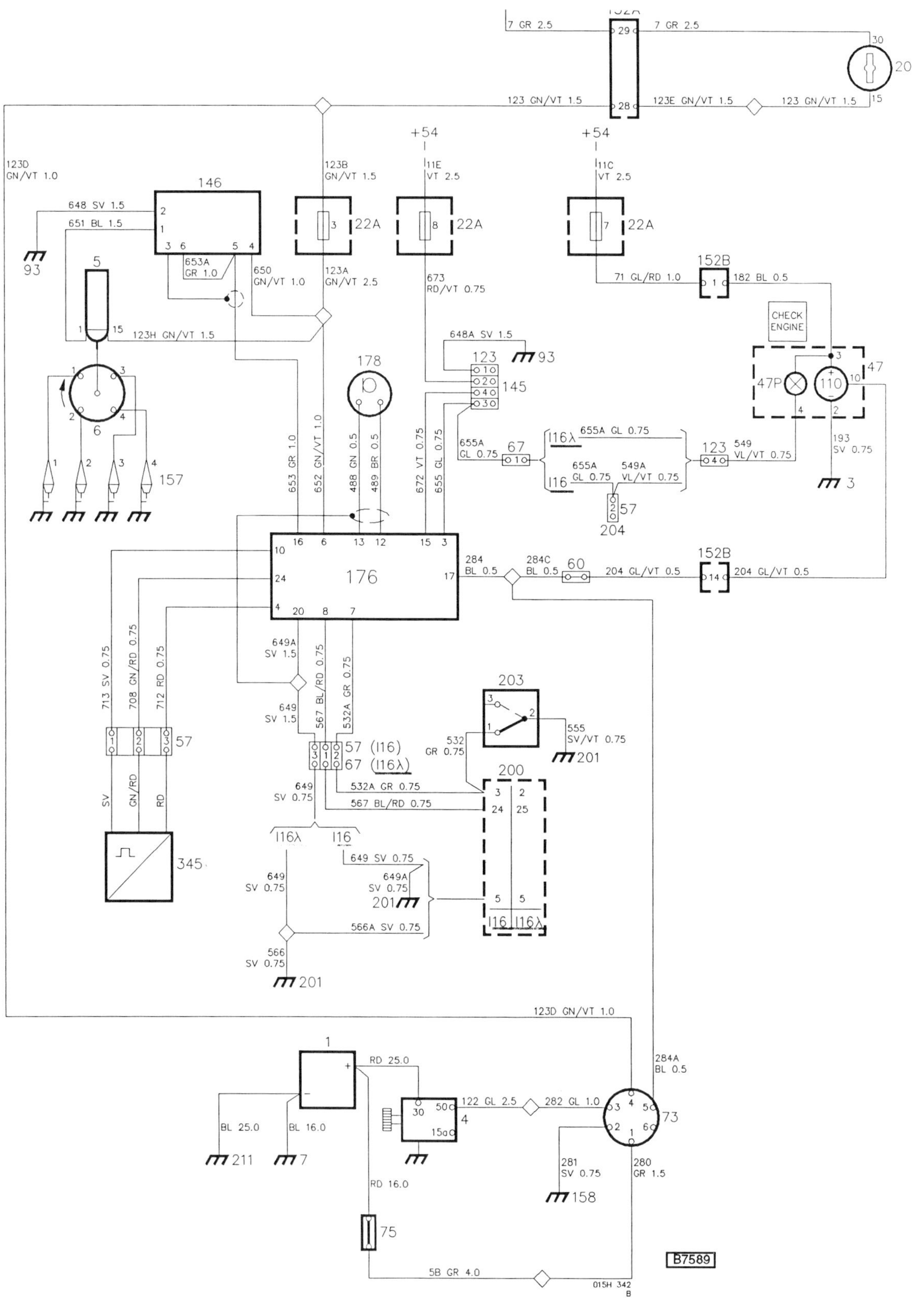

EZK Ignition System—non-turbo

1991 and later

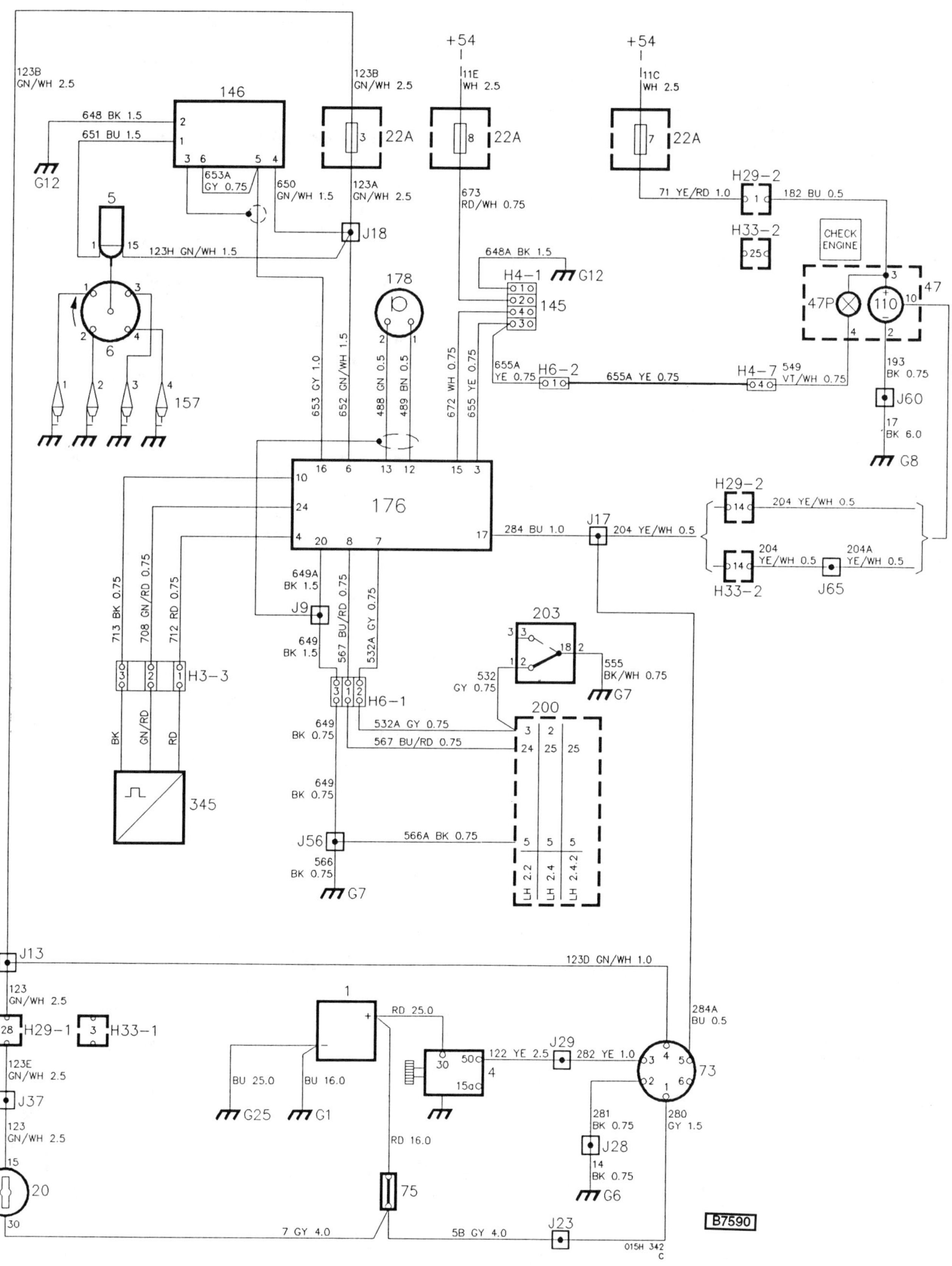

Interior Lighting

Operation

The interior lighting is controlled by the door switches on the door jambs. The door switches can be overridden by the center console switch or the combination roof light/switch (except convertible). A time delay relay is located under the back seat. On hatchback models, a cargo area light is controlled by a switch located below the lock striker plate .

The roof light bulbs or switches can be removed after removing the screws (where applicable) and carefully prying away the lens. The ignition switch light can be pulled straight down out of its holder after carefully peeling up the shift lever boot and reaching under the console. See **432 Manual Transmission Controls** for information on removing the center console.

Fault Tracing

1. Check the fuse. Check for battery voltage at the lamp assembly at all times.
2. Check for ground at the lamp assembly whenever a door is opened or when the center console switch is toggled.
3. Check door switches for a good ground through the chassis screw or switch assembly. Check the wiring to each door switch.

Component Locations

22 main fuse/relay panel
50 roof lamp/switch in the headliner
51 front roof lamp at rear view mirror
52 ignition switch light next to ignition switch, center console
53 interior light switch in center console
54 door switches on the door jamb
82 seat belt warning relay under the rear seat
151 time delay relay under the rear seat
175 central locking control unit behind instrument panel right side
225 reading lamp at rear seat
289 burglar alarm control unit under the rear seat
316 diode for the burglar alarm
401 auxiliary fuse/relay panel under rear seat

Connector Locations

1985-1990

57 3-pin connector under center console
58 12-pin connector behind instrument panel, left of steering column
59 2-pin connector in luggage compartment, left wheel housing
59 2-pin connector under roof lining at rear view mirror
59 2-pin connector at reading lamps (convertible)
60 1-pin connector under center console
98 10-pin connector to left of steering column
123 4-pin connector at hatchback, left side
152A 29-pin bulkhead connector at main fuse/relay panel
152B 29-pin bulkhead connector at main fuse/relay panel

1991 and later

H2-21 2-pin connector in luggage compartment, left wheel housing
H2-35 2-pin connector above roof lining at the rear view mirror
H2-46 2-pin connector at left reading lamp, convertible
H2-47 2-pin connector at right reading lamp, convertible
H12-1 12-pin connector behind instrument panel, left of steering column
H29-1 29-pin bulkhead connector behind main fuse/relay panel (1991-1991 1/2)
H33-1 33-pin bulkhead connector behind main fuse/relay panel (1991 1/2 and later)

Ground Locations

1985-1990

65 ground point under the handbrake
117 ground point under the handbrake

1991 and later

G4 ground point between ignition switch and handbrake
G5 ground point under the rear seat

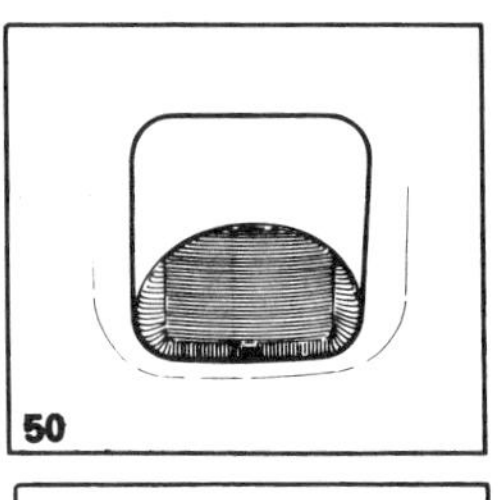

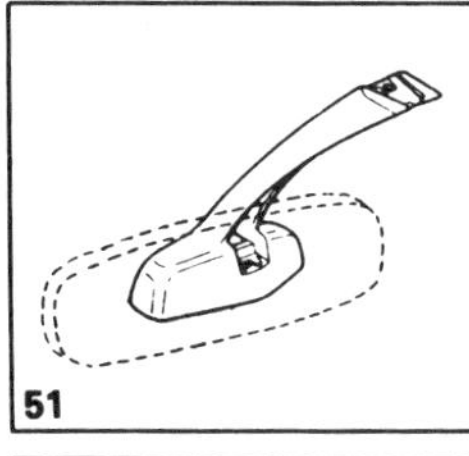

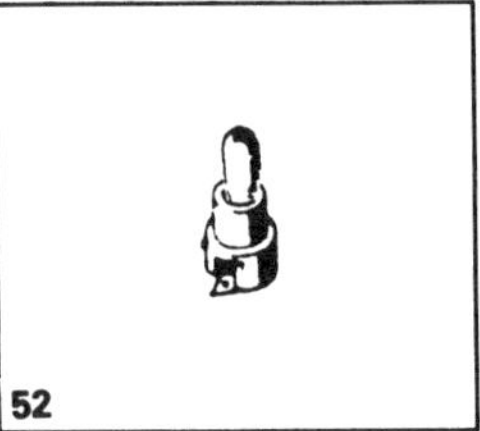

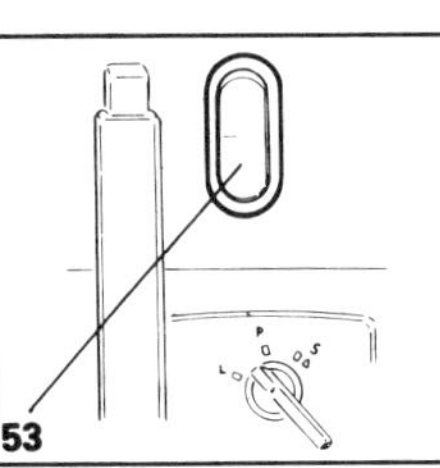

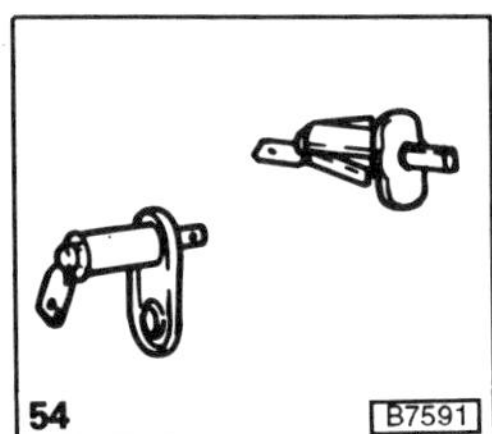

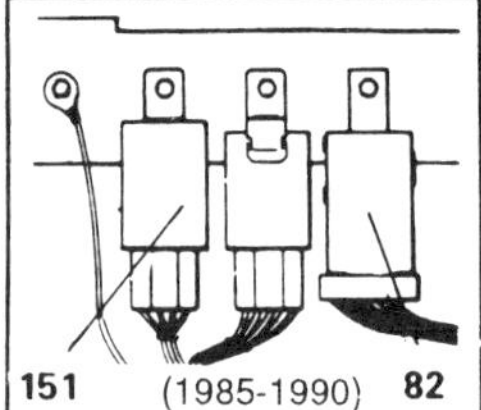

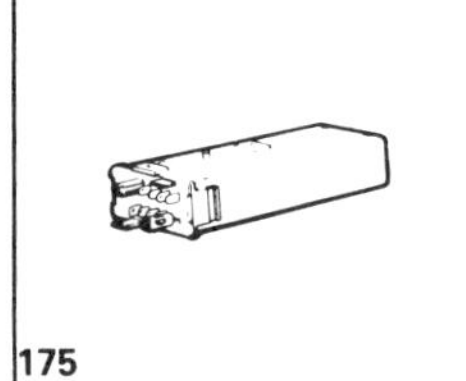

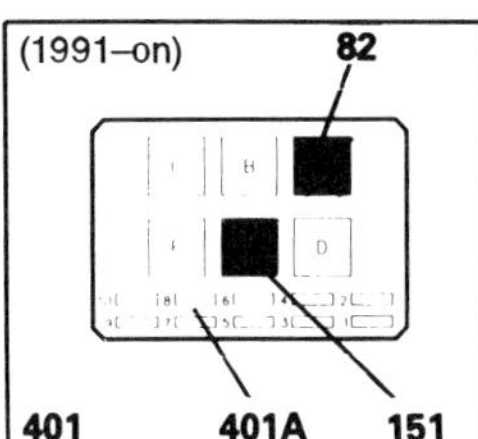

Interior Lighting—ex. Convertible

1985-1986

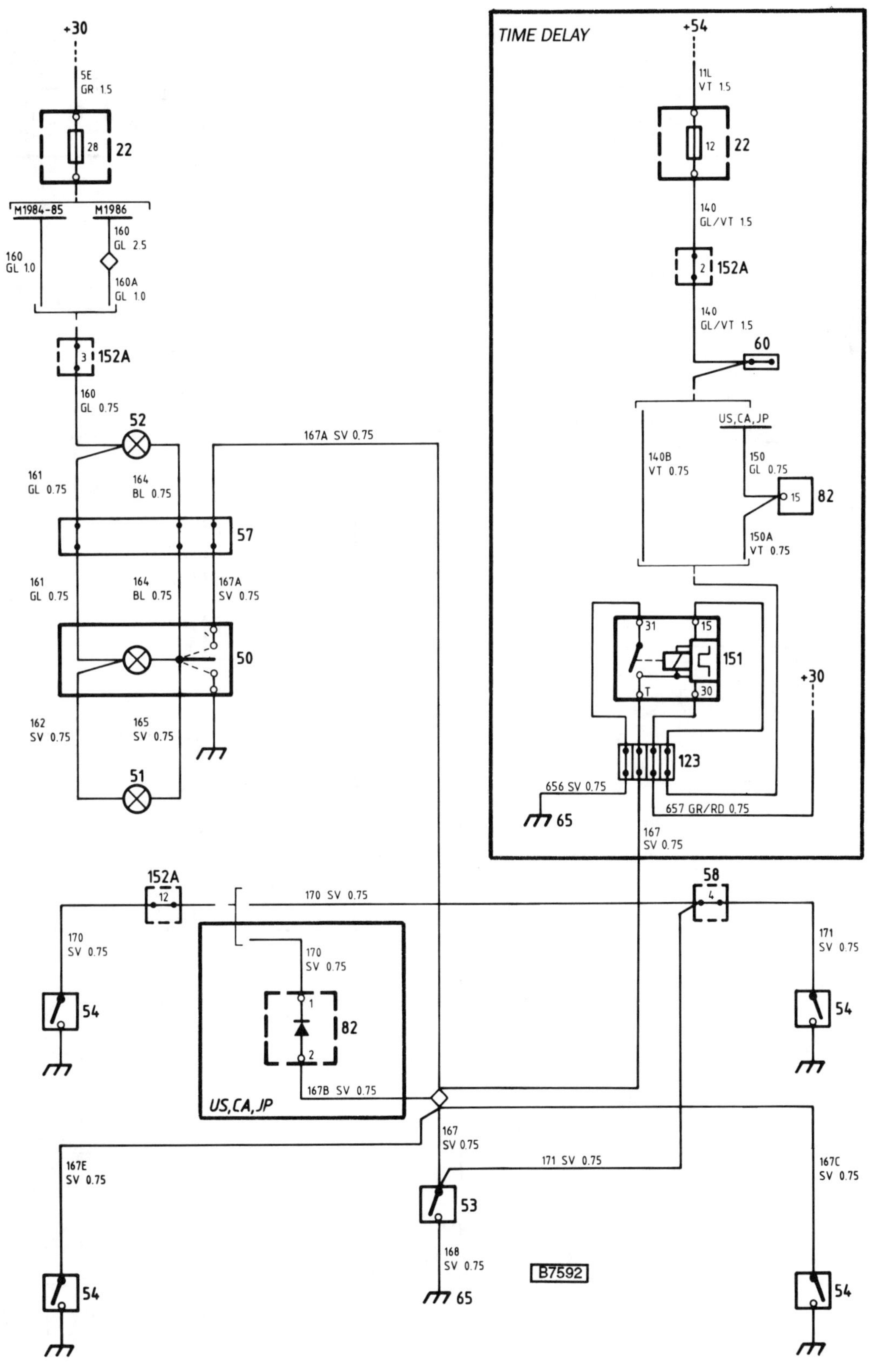

Interior Lighting—ex. Convertible

1987-1990

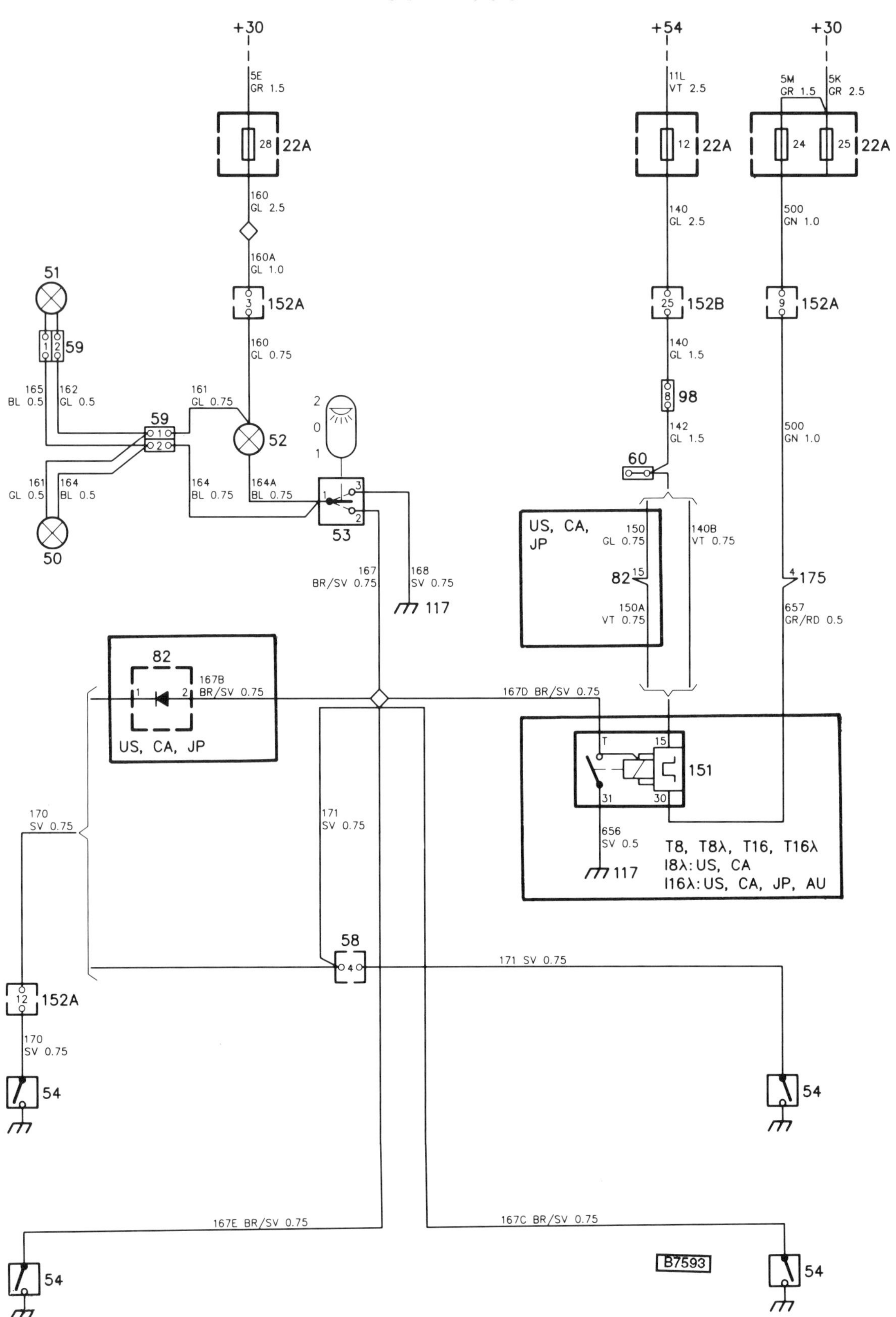

Interior Lighting—ex. Convertible

1991 and later

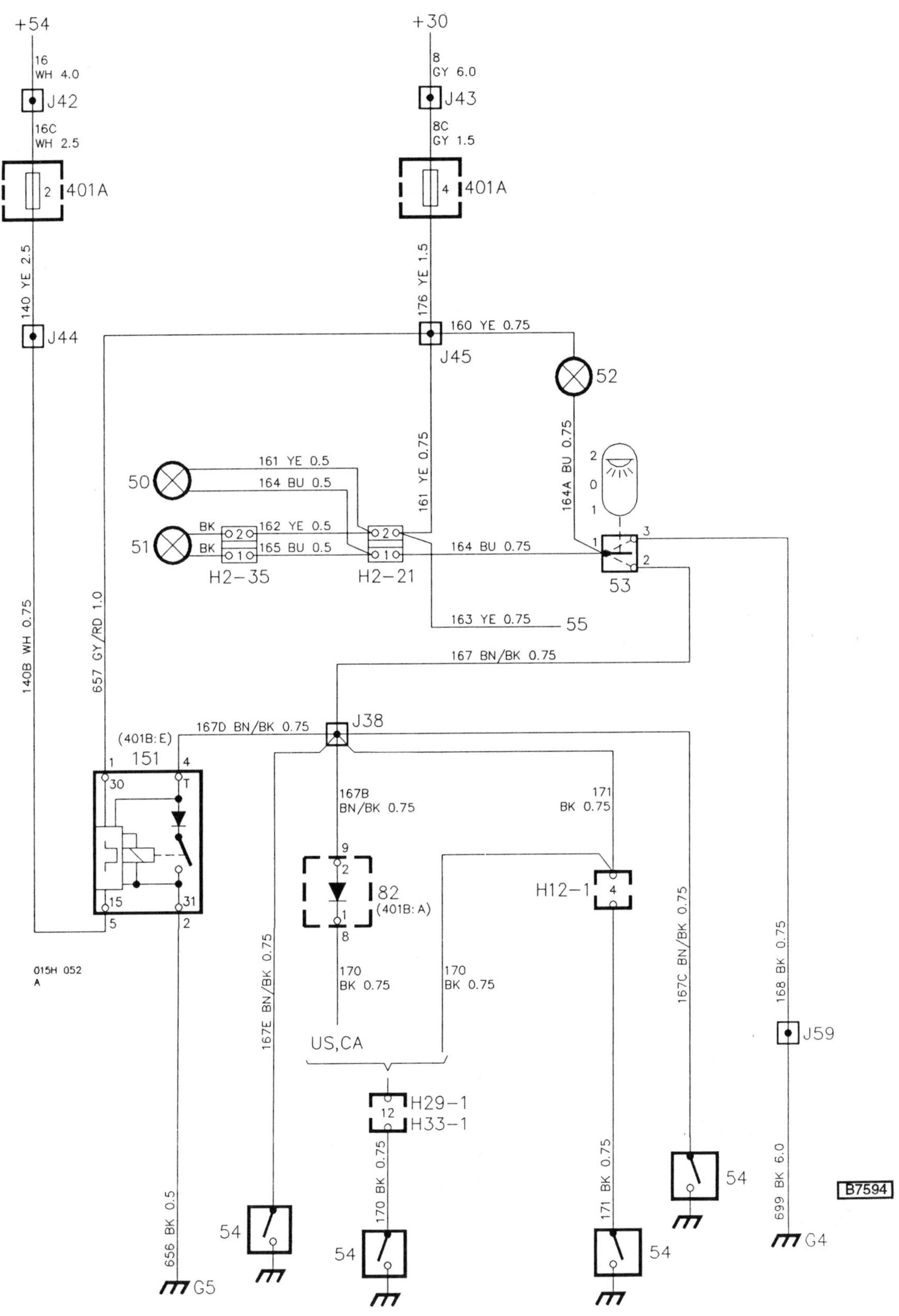

Interior Lighting — Convertible

1987-1990

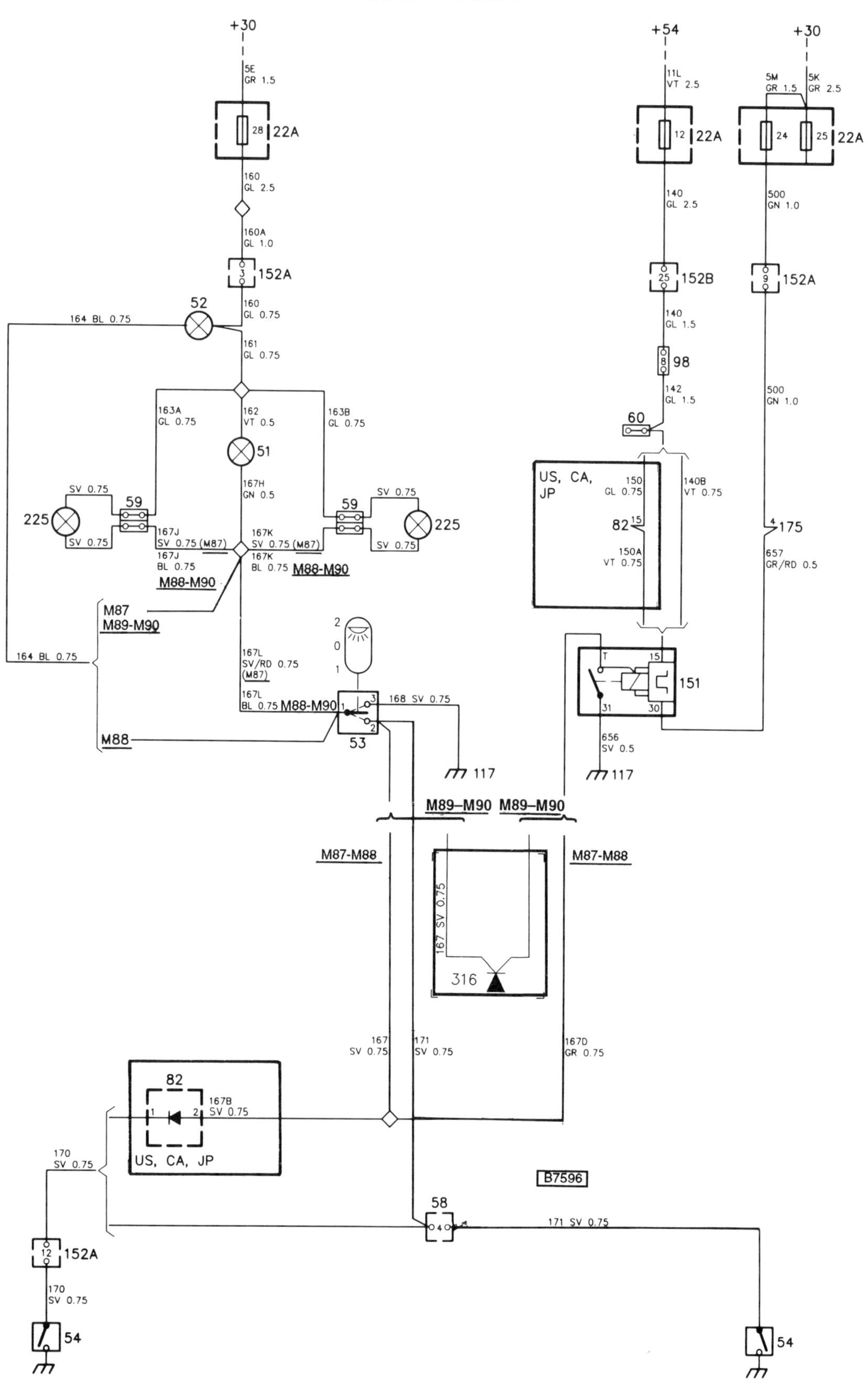

Interior Lighting — Convertible

1991 and later

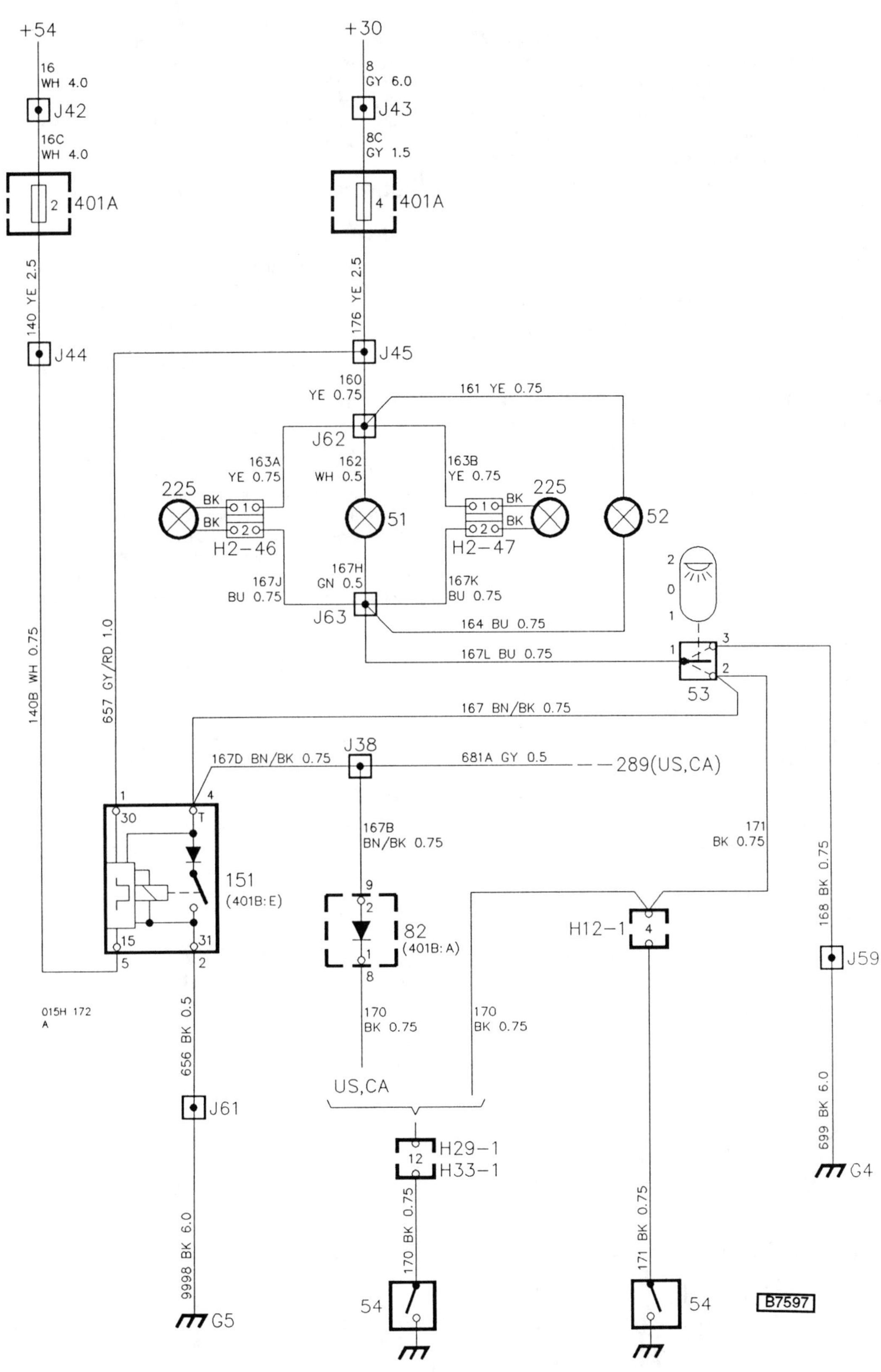

Lighting for Controls

Operation

The Lighting for Controls wiring diagrams cover instrument panel and switch illumination. Some of the switches have replaceable bulbs. See **364 Electric Controls and Switches** for information on replacing switch bulbs. See **853 Dashboard and Consoles** for information on removing the instrument cluster. See **432 Manual Transmission Controls** or **444 Automatic Transmission Controls** for details on removing the center console.

Fault Tracing

1. Check the fuses and check for voltage at rheostat (16) and rheostat (17) with the key in the run position.
2. Check that the rheostats are fully clockwise.
3. Check the ground point to the left of the steering column behind the instrument panel, and the ground point under the center console at the handbrake lever.

Component Locations

- 10 light switch in instrument panel
- 16 rheostat in instrument cluster
- 17 rheostat in instrument panel
- 18 combined instrument lighting
- 22 main fuse/relay panel, left wheel housing
- 25 hazard warning light switch in instrument panel
- 47 cigarette lighter
- 48 instrument cluster
- 88 fog lamp switch in instrument panel
- 91 gear position light (automatic) in center console
- 116 heated rear window switch in instrument panel
- 143 A/C recirculation switch in instrument panel
- 148 ashtray light in instrument panel
- 153 cigarette light in instrument panel
- 154 heater control lights in instrument panel
- 162 driver power window switch light in center console
- 163 passenger power window switch light in center console
- 169 A/C switch in instrument panel
- 181 sunroof switch light in center console
- 189 lockout switch for rear power windows in center console
- 190 left rear power window switch in center console
- 191 right rear power window switch in center console
- 252 driver seat rheostat light in instrument panel
- 386 switch for power windows and sunroof in center console
- 425 power door lock switch in center console

Connector Locations

1985-1990

- 57 3-pin connector (3) one behind left B pillar trim, one behind right B pillar trim, one under driver's seat
- 58 12-pin connector behind instrument panel, to left of steering column
- 59 2-pin connector in instrument panel, behind cigarette lighter
- 60 1-pin connector (3) one in each rear door, one under center console
- 98 10-pin connector behind instrument panel, for radio

1991 and later

- H1-6 1-pin connector at right B pillar, behind trim
- H1-7 1-pin connector at left B pillar, behind trim
- H1-17 1-pin connector under center console
- H2-10 2-pin connector behind cigarette lighter
- H3-10 3-pin connector at right B pillar, behind trim
- H3-11 3-pin connector at left B pillar, behind trim
- H10-1 10-pin connector behind instrument panel, left of steering column
- H12-1 12-pin connector behind instrument panel, left of steering column
- H29-2 29-pin bulkhead connector behind main fuse/relay panel (1991-1991 1/2)
- H33-2 33-pin bulkhead connector behind main fuse/relay panel (1991 1/2–on)

Ground Locations

1985-1990

- 3 ground point behind instrument panel
- 117 ground point under the handbrake

1991 and later

- G4 ground point between ignition switch and handbrake
- G8 ground point behind instrument panel

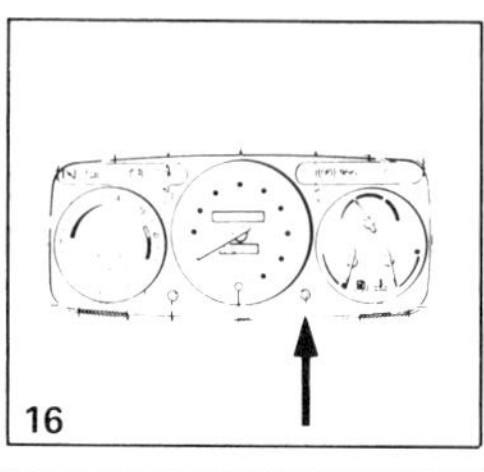
16

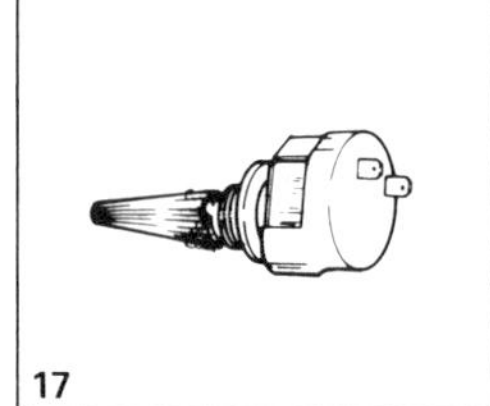
17

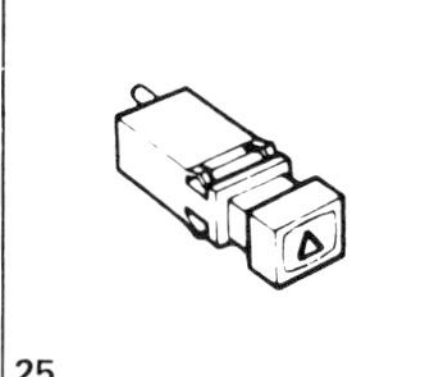
25

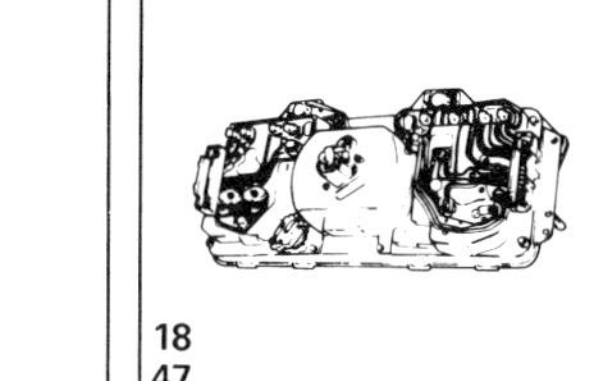
18
47

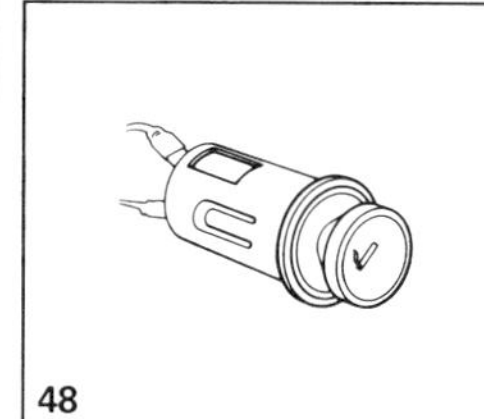
48

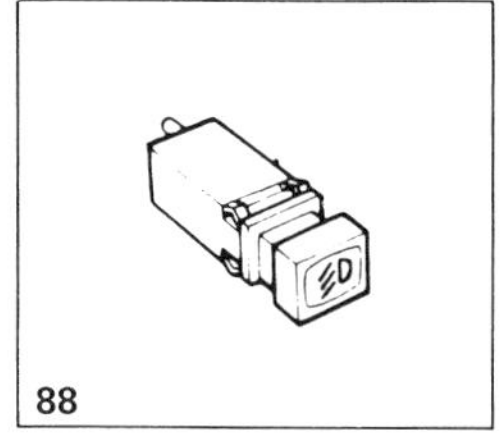
88

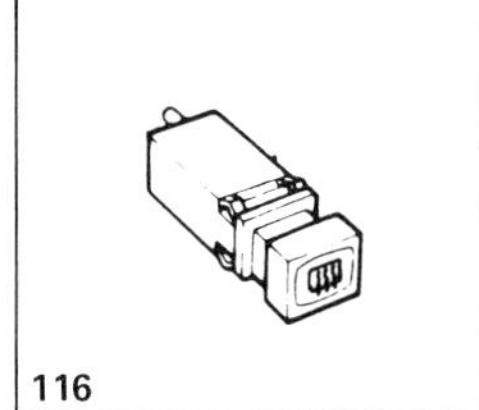
116

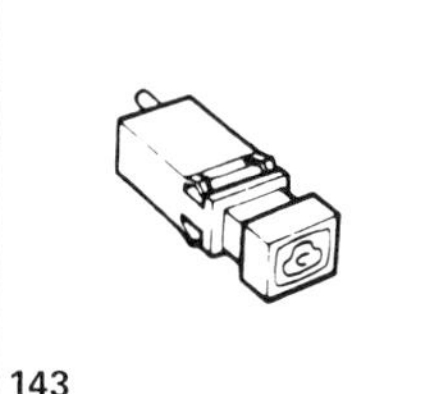
143

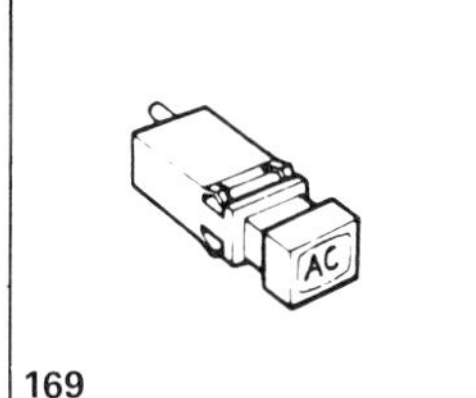

169

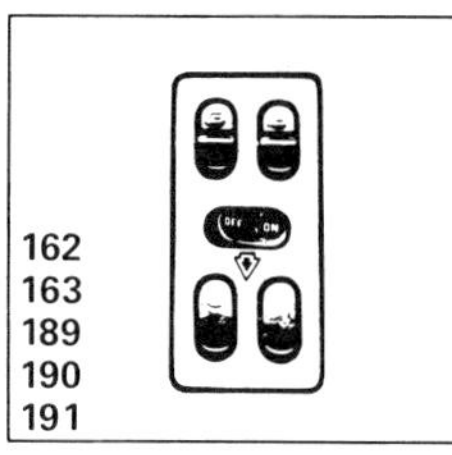
162
163
189
190
191

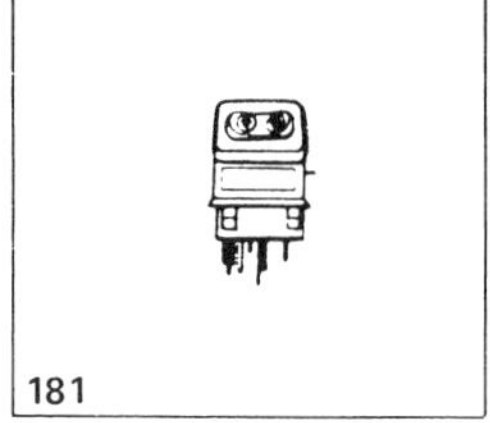
181

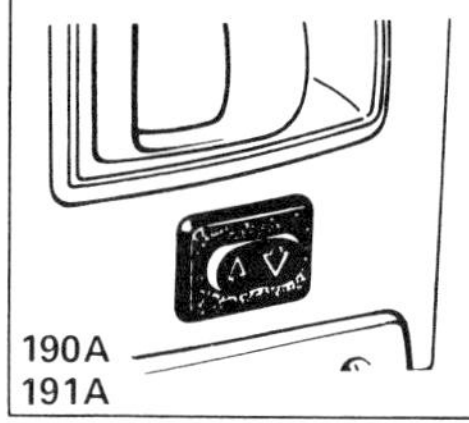
190A
191A

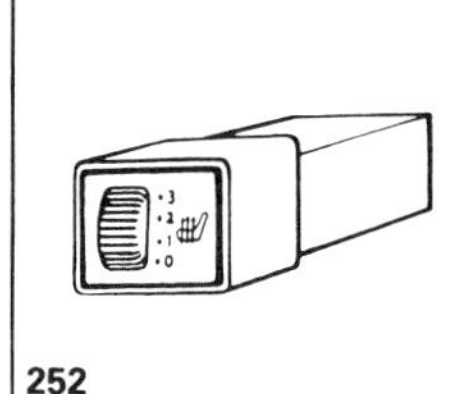
252

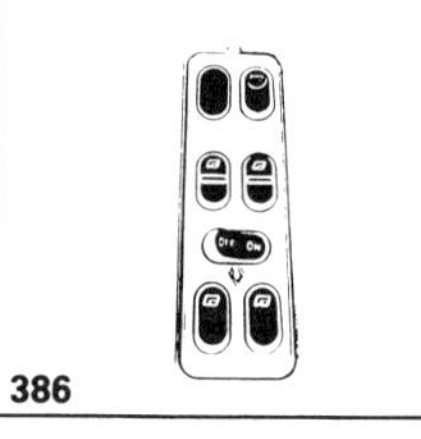
386

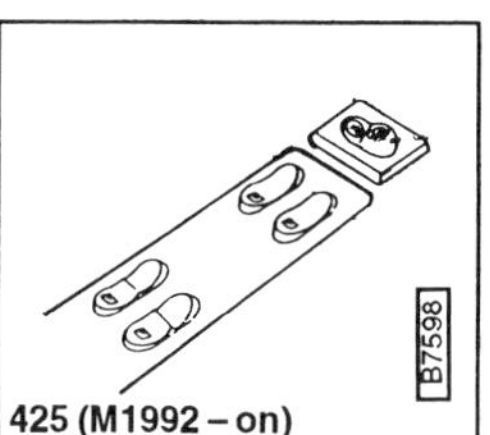

425 (M1992 – on)

Lighting for Controls

1985-1986

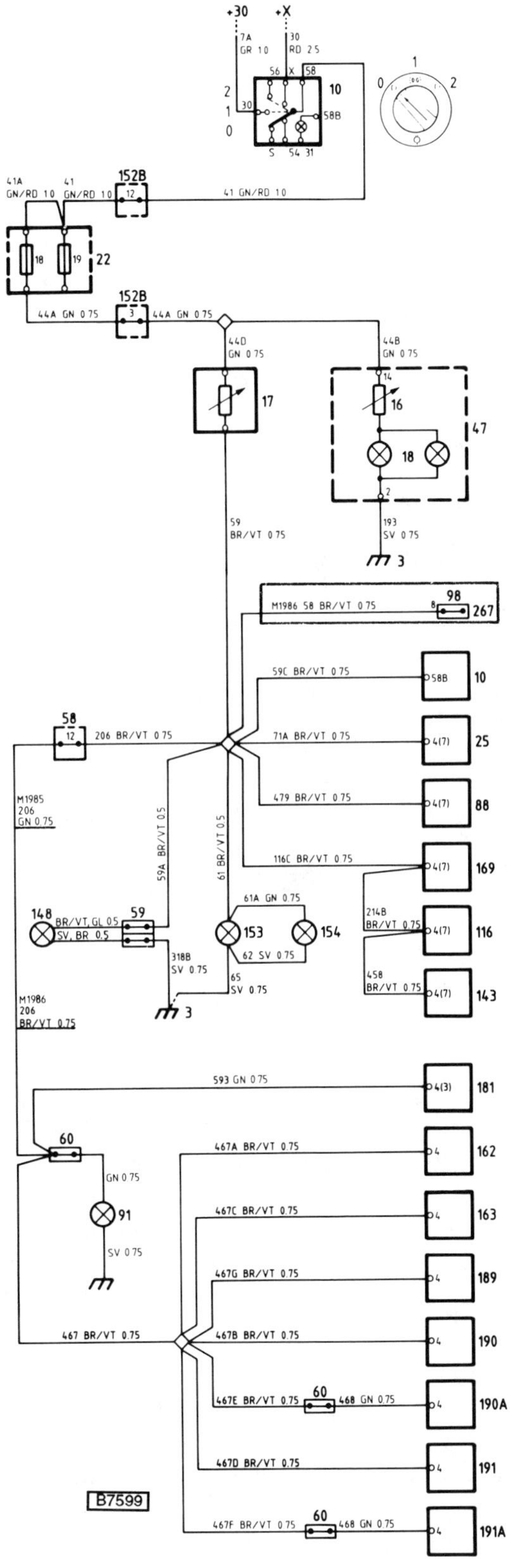

Lighting for Controls

1987-1990

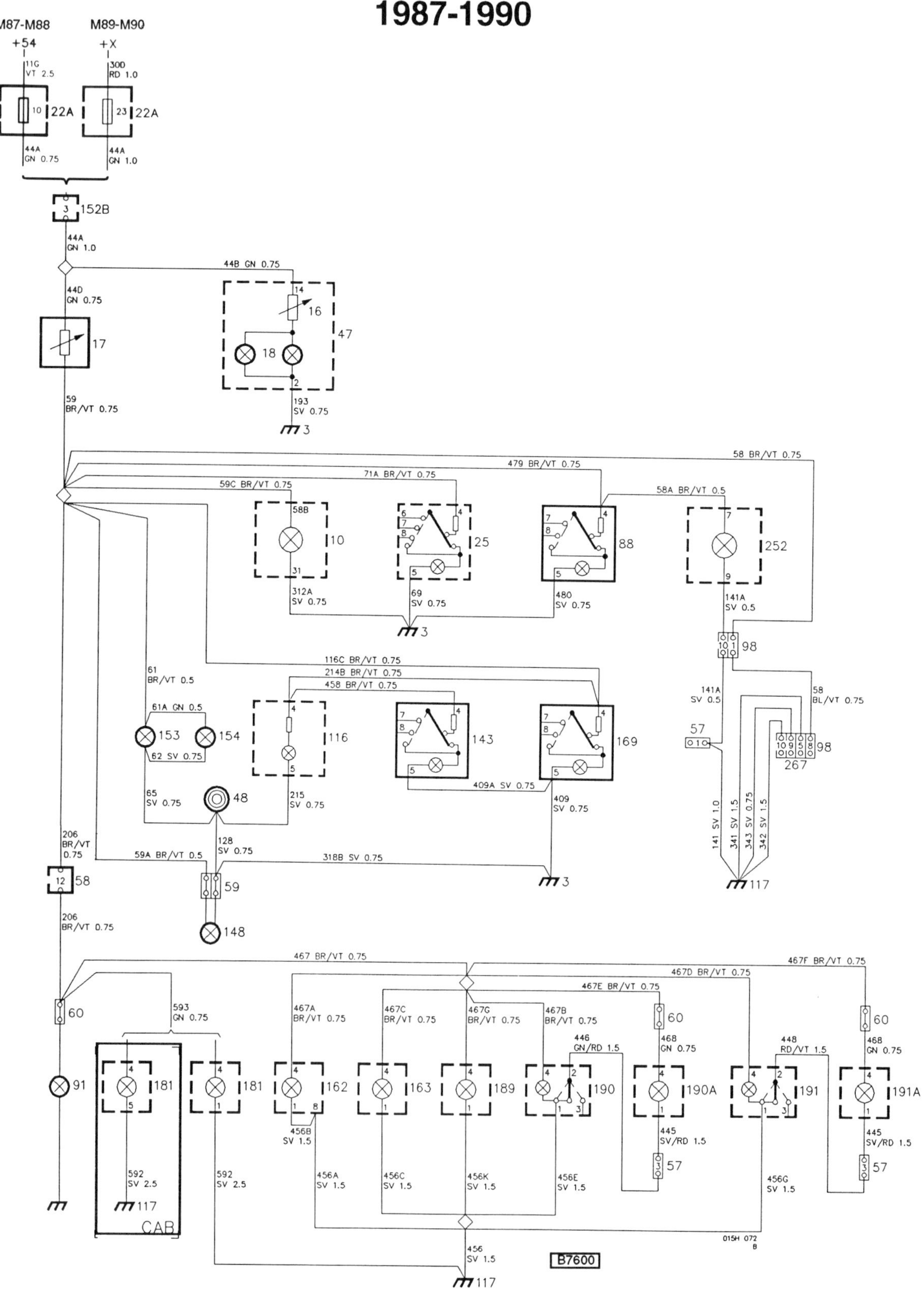

Lighting for Controls

1991 and later

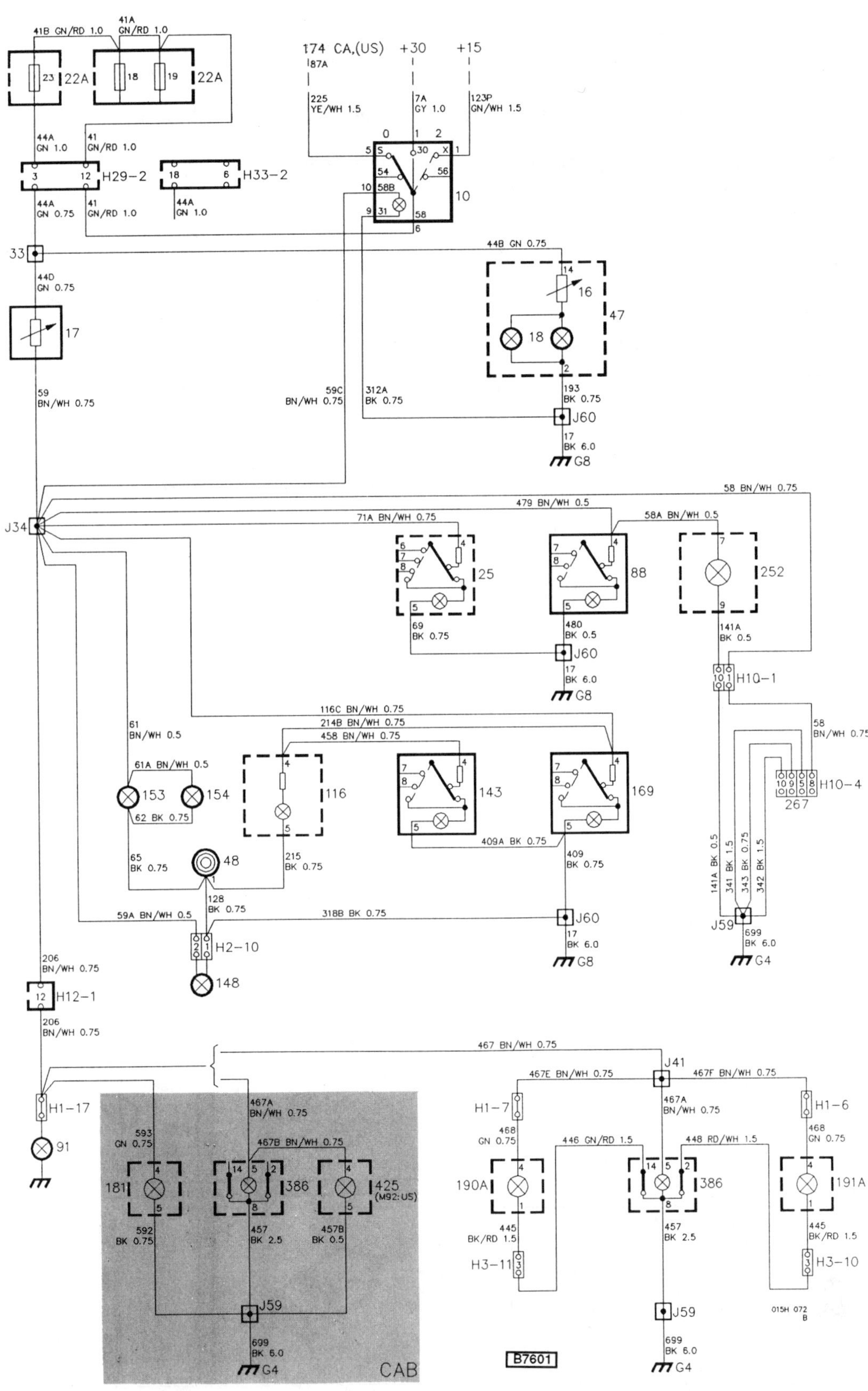

Luggage Compartment Lighting

Operation

The luggage compartment light (55) is controlled by a luggage compartment light switch located behind the left trunk hinge on sedans and beneath the striker plate on hatchbacks. With the trunk open, the switch is closed to light the lamp. The luggage compartment light (55) also has a switch to disable the light at all times. To change the bulb, pry off the lens. Convertible models use a mercury switch (position sensitive) rather than a mechanical switch.

Fault Tracing

1. Check the fuse.
2. Check for battery voltage at the lamp assembly.
3. Check for ground at the light switch.

Component Locations

1 battery
15 license plate light on the rear sill (convertible only)
22A main fuse/relay panel
52 ignition switch light in center console
55 luggage compartment light in storage area
56 luggage compartment light switch in storage area
75 terminal block at right engine bulkhead
401 auxiliary fuse/relay panel under rear seat

Connector Locations

1985-1990

57 3-pin connector at left side of luggage compartment (1985-1986)
59 2-pin connector at left side of luggage compartment (1987-1990)
152A 29-pin bulkhead connector at main fuse/relay panel

1991 and later

H2-21 2-pin connector in luggage compartment, left wheel housing
H2-43 2-pin connector at left hinge, convertible
H2-42 2-pin connector in trunk lid

Ground Locations

1991 and later

G1 ground point at radiator cross member
G5 ground point under the rear seat
G25 ground point at gearbox

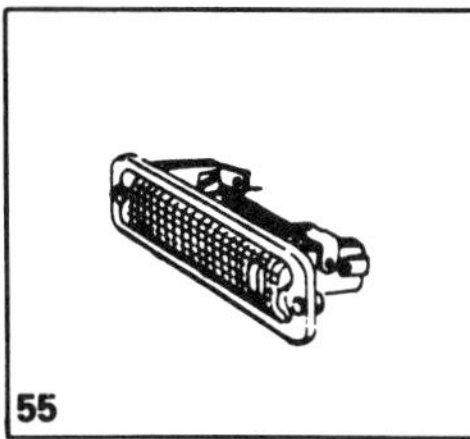
55

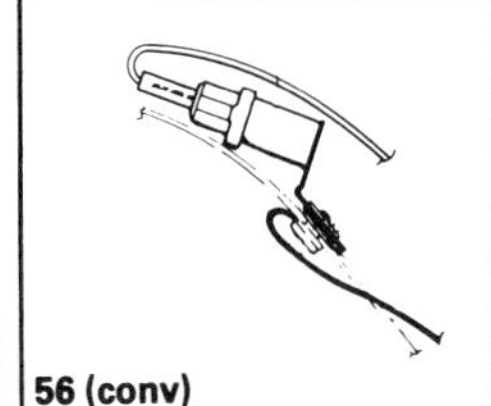
56 (conv)

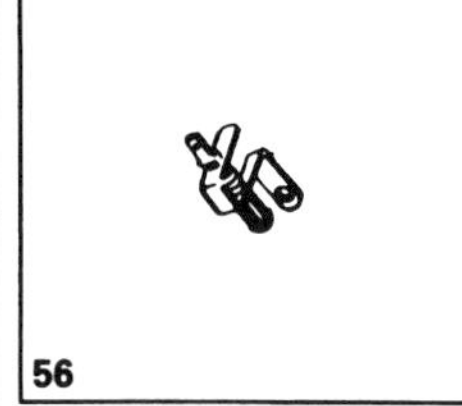
56

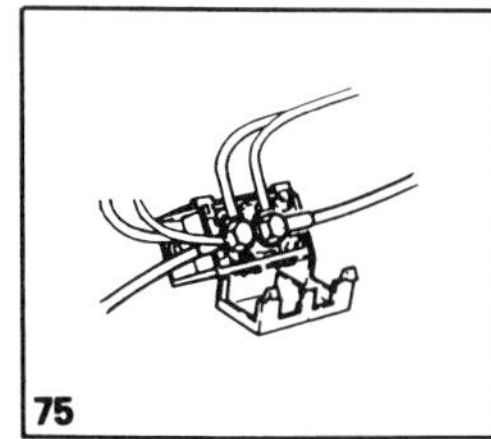
75

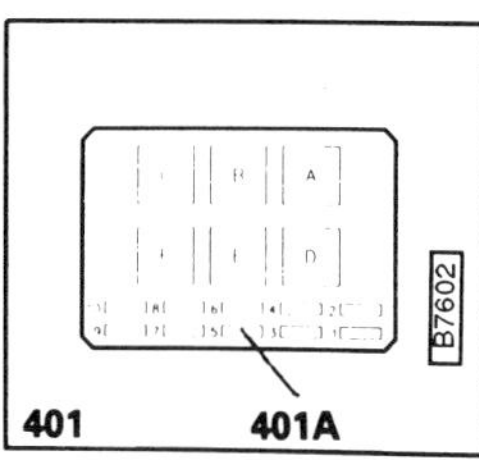

401 401A

Luggage Compartment Lighting

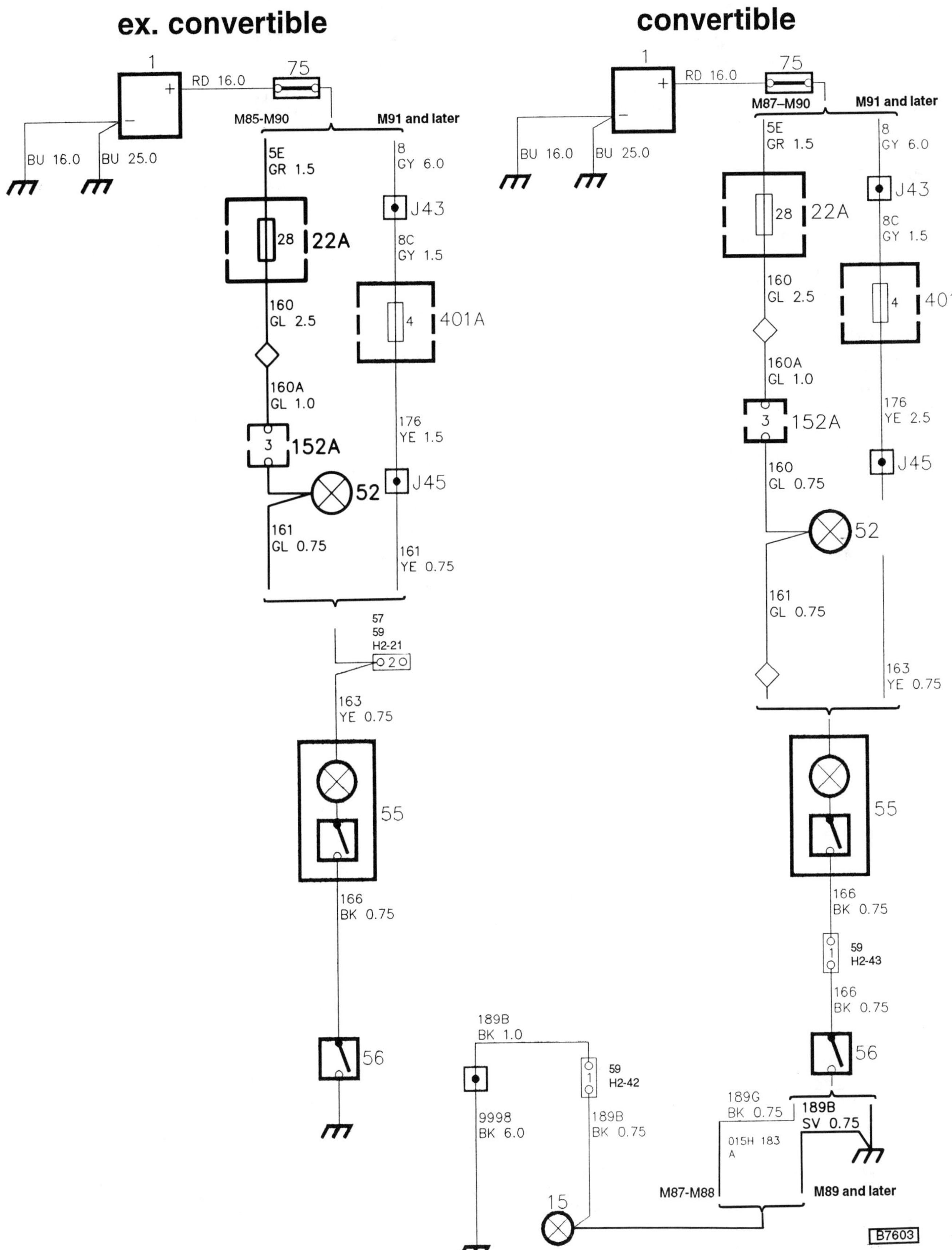

Parking Lights

Operation

When the light switch (10) is in position 1, battery voltage powers the parking lights and the side marker lights. See **351 Lighting** for repair information and information on replacing bulbs.

Fault Tracing

1. Check for battery voltage at terminal 3 (30) of the light switch (10). Check fuses 18 and 19.

Component Locations

- 10 light switch in instrument panel
- 13 park lights
- 14 rear lights
- 15 license plate lights
- 22 main fuse/relay panel in engine compartment
- 234 side marker lights in the front cluster

Connector Locations

1985-1990

- 57 3-pin connector in luggage compartment, near air outlet
- 59 2-pin connector in luggage compartment
- 81 driving lights, below front bumper
- 152A 29-pin bulkhead connector at main fuse/relay panel
- 152B 29-pin bulkhead connector at main fuse/relay panel

1991 and later

- H2-7 2-pin connector behind instrument panel
- H2-18 2-pin connector at hatchback, left side
- H2-19 2-pin connector in trunk lid
- H3-13 3-pin connector in luggage compartment, left air outlet
- H4-12 4-pin connector in trunk lid, left air outlet
- H29-1 29-pin bulkhead connector behind main fuse/relay panel (1991-1991 1/2)
- H29-2 29-pin bulkhead connector behind main fuse/relay panel (1991-1991 1/2)
- H33-1 33-pin bulkhead connector behind main fuse/relay panel (1991 1/2 and later)
- H33-2 33-pin bulkhead connector behind main fuse/relay panel (1991 1/2 and later)

Ground Locations

1985-1990

- 3 ground point behind instrument panel
- 7 ground point at radiator cross member
- 9 ground point in luggage compartment
- 93 ground point at left wheel housing (1989-1990)

1991 and later

- G1 ground point at radiator cross member
- G3 ground point in luggage compartment
- G8 ground point behind instrument panel
- G9 ground point in luggage compartment
- G12 ground point at left wheel housing
- G19 ground point at hatchback

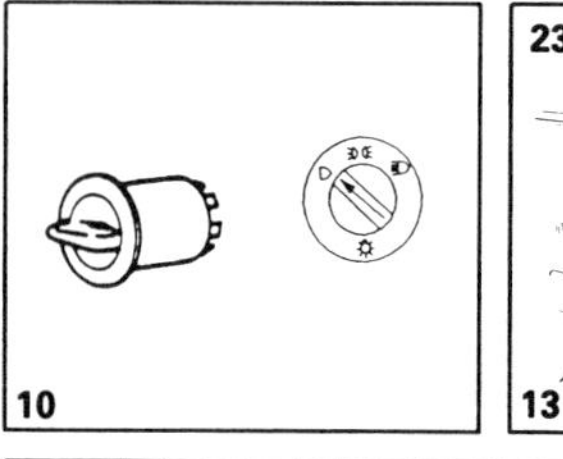

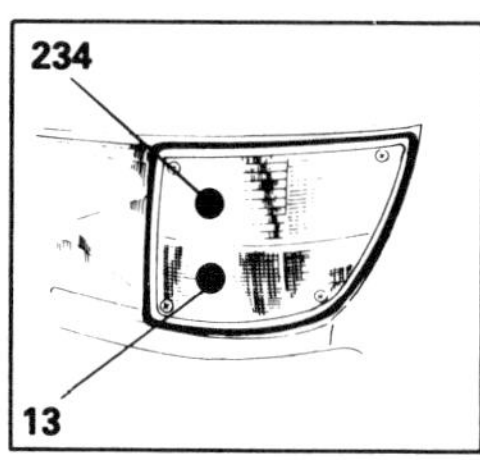

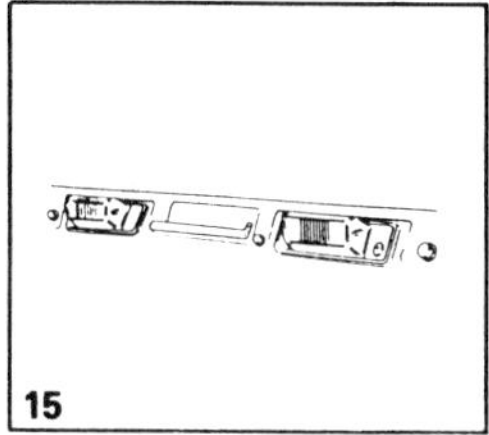

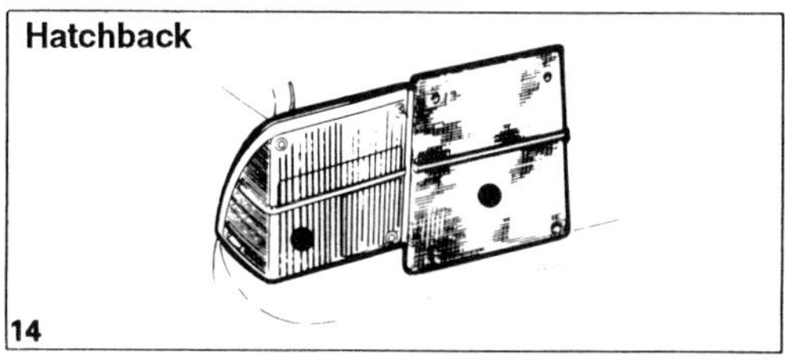

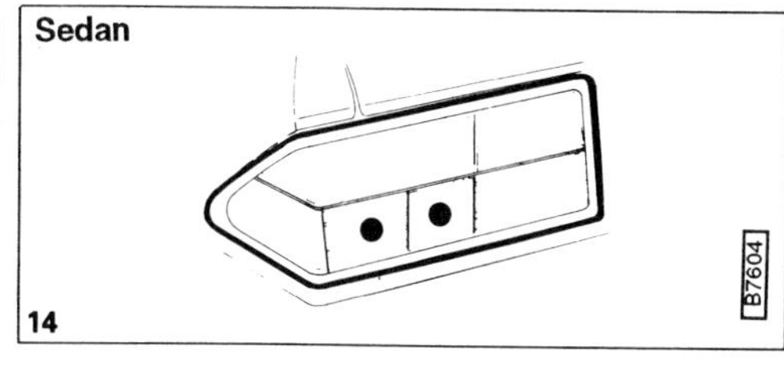

Parking Lights

1985-1986

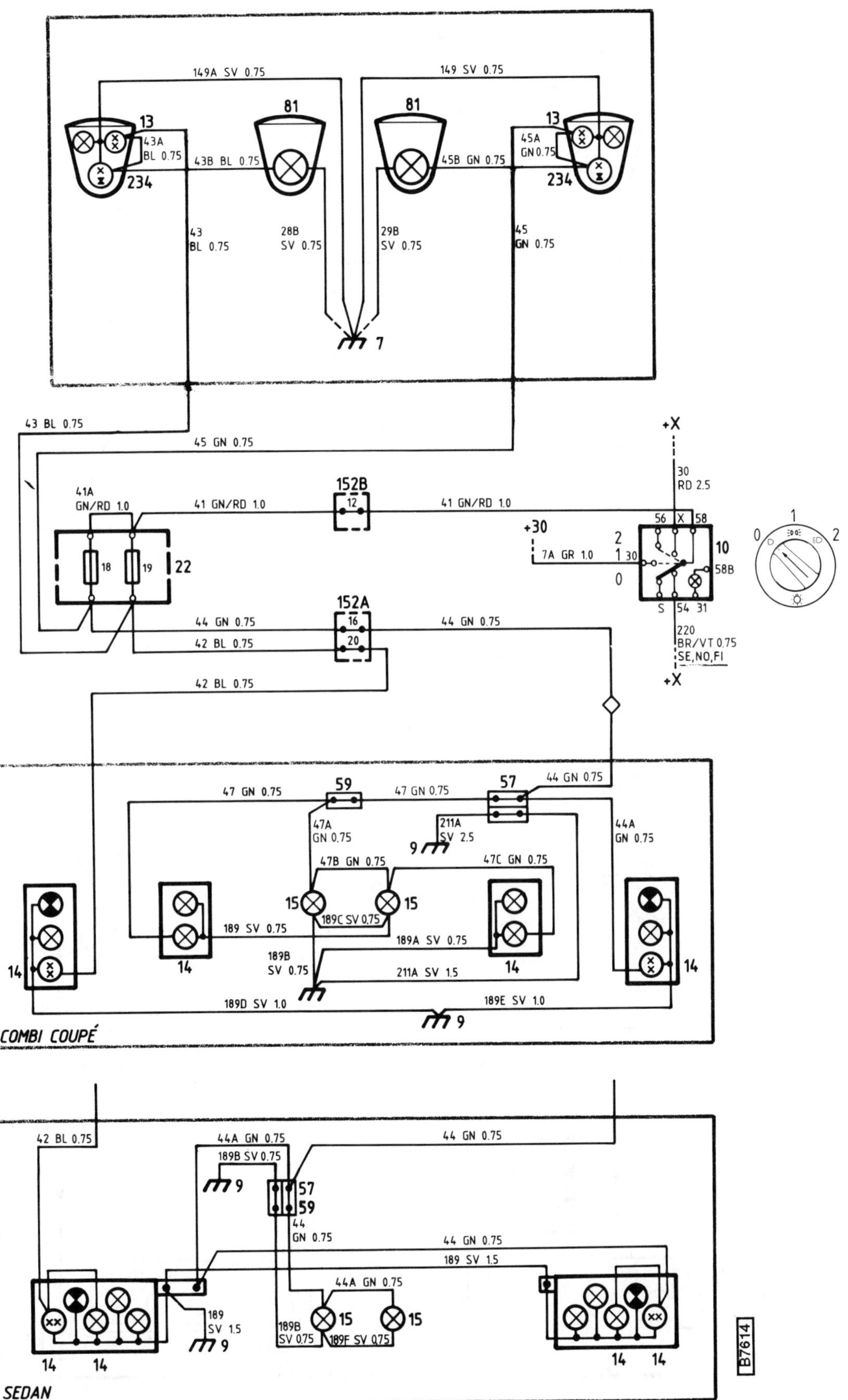

Parking Lights
1987 and later

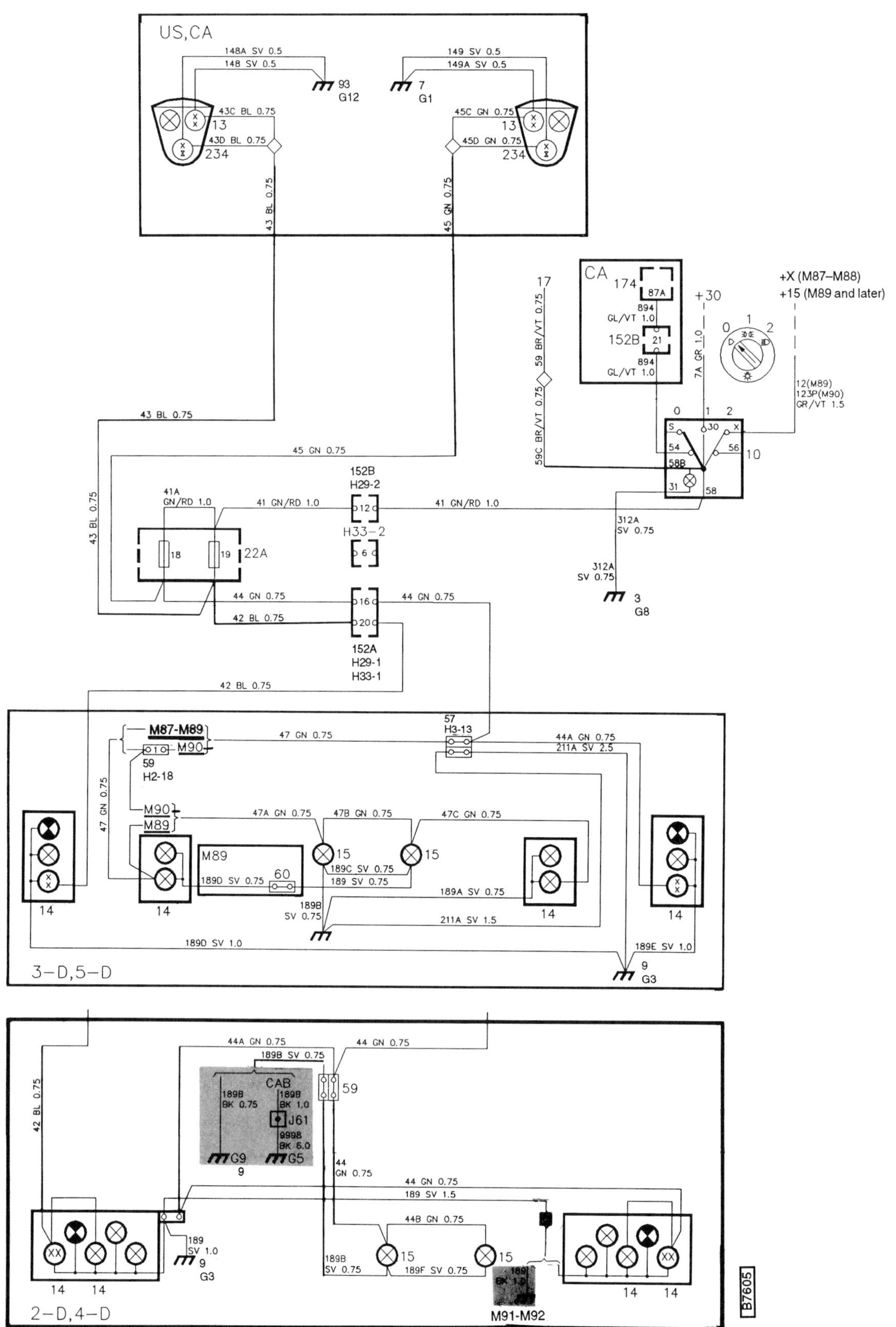

Passive Seat Belts

Operation

The passive seat belt consists of a motor-driven, two-point diagonal strap and manual lap belt. The diagonal strap is controlled and monitored by the logic box (306). The belt travel is controlled by two limit switches at the A pillar and at the B pillar. A warning lamp on the dash (47S) will flash or remain continuously lit if a fault is detected in the seat belt travel. The passive seat belt fuses, relays, and logic box are located under the rear seat on the driver's side.

WARNING
If the seat belt warning lamp on the instrument cluster lights up at any time, do not drive the car. Have an authorized Saab dealer inspect and correct any faults in the system before the car is driven.

Fault Tracing

CAUTION
Always disconnect the connector to the logic box (306) before making any measurements.

1. Check the fuses under the rear seat. Also check fuses 5, 12, and 13 in the main fuse relay panel (22).
2. Using a voltmeter, check for battery voltage between the disconnected logic box connector terminals and ground with the key in the run position. See **Table a.**

Table a. Passive Seat Belt Logic Box Connector Test Voltage

Logic box connector terminal	Comments
11	reverse gear engaged
12	ignition switch in run position
18	via the relay coil (312P)
19	via the relay coil (311P)
22	via the relay coil (312D)
23	via the relay coil (311D)
25	via the g sensor (309)

3. Using an ohmmeter, check for continuity between the specified logic box connector terminal and ground with the key off. See **Table b.**

Table b. Passive Seat Belt Continuity Checks

Logic box connector terminal	Resistance (ohms)	Comments
1	0	belt in the carriage
2	approx. 13	bulb resistance
4	approx. 22	coil resistance
5	open circuit	carriage at A pillar
6	0	—
7	0	passenger door open
8	approx. 22	coil resistance
9	open circuit	carriage at A pillar
10	0	—
13	0	—
14	0	belt in the carriage
17	open circuit	—
20	0	lap strap not fastened
21	open circuit	—
24	0	driver door open

Component Locations

20 ignition switch
22A main fuse/relay panel at left wheel housing
31 backup light switch
47S passive seat belt warning lamp
70 seat belt switch, driver side between driver and passenger seat
72 seat belt warning light in center of instrument panel
76 switch for raising idle speed (automatic transmission) in center console at shift lever
82 seat belt warning relay under the rear seat
208D passive seat belt door switch in driver door
208P passive seat belt door switch in passenger door
306 logic box for passive seat belts under rear seat, left side
307D passive seat belt belt reel at driver seat
307P passive seat belt belt reel at passenger seat
308D passive seat belt motor with limit switches at driver seat
308P passive seat belt motor with limit switches at passenger seat
309 passive seat belt g sensor under the rear seat, left side
310D passive seat belt fuse for driver seat under rear seat
310P passive seat belt fuse for passenger seat under rear seat
311D passive seat belt motor relay for driver seat under rear seat
311P passive seat belt motor relay for passenger seat under rear seat
312D passive seat belt motor relay for driver seat under rear seat
312P passive seat belt motor relay for passenger seat under rear seat

Passive Seat Belts

Connector Locations

57 3-pin connector behind instrument panel, to left of steering column
58 12-pin connector behind instrument panel, to left of steering column
59 2-pin connector (2) in engine compartment, one at top left hinge, one at top right hinge
60 1-pin connector (4) two in each door, behind door trim
98 10-pin connector behind instrument panel to left of steering column
122 8-pin connector for burglar alarm under the rear seat
152A 29-pin bulkhead connector in main fuse/relay panel
152B 29-pin bulkhead connector in main fuse/relay panel

Ground Locations

3 ground point behind instrument panel
65 ground point at handbrake
117 ground point at handbrake

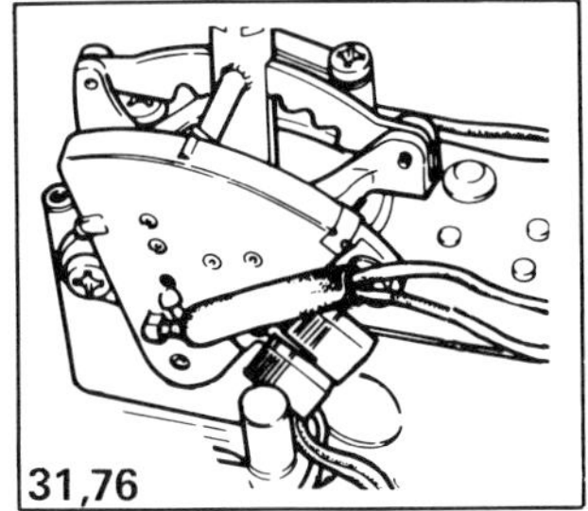

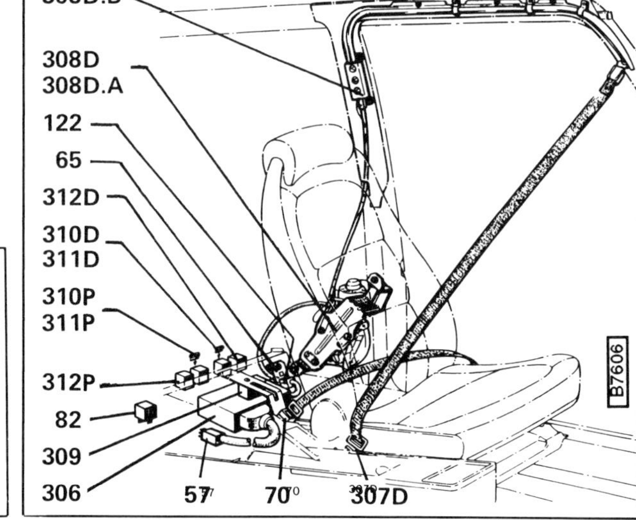

Passive Seat Belts

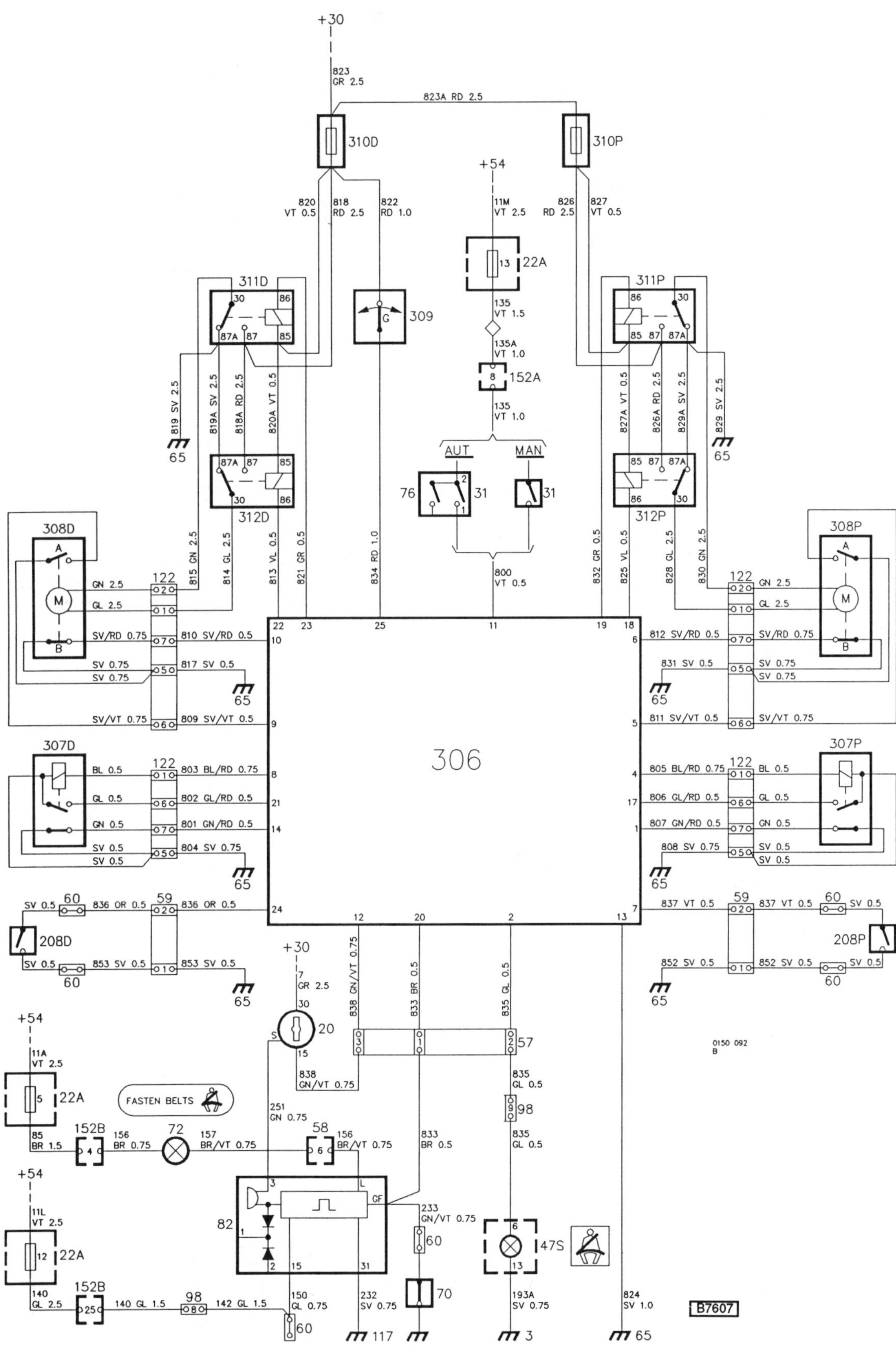

Power Mirrors

Operation

Each power mirror is controlled by a four-way switch. Horizontal mirror movement is controlled by a motor in the mirror assembly. Vertical movement is also controlled by the same motor and a solenoid. On 1988 and later models, the mirror glass is electrically heated and is controlled by the heated rear window circuit. See **Heated Rear Window** elsewhere in this section.

See **830 Doors, Windows, and Lids** for more information on removing the power mirrors and switches.

Fault Tracing

1. Check the fuses. Check the power supply to the switch with the key on.
2. Use the table below and the wiring diagram to test for ground and positive power at the mirror.

Left mirror			
Switch Position	**+ at motor**	**– at motor**	**+ at solenoid**
left	316 grey-red	317 green-white	
right	317 green-white	316 grey-red	
up	316 grey-red	317 green-white	315 white
down	317 green-white	316 grey-red	315 white
Right mirror			
Switch Position	**+ at motor**	**– at motor**	**+ at solenoid**
left	321 grey-red	320 green-white	
right	320 green-white	321 grey-red	
up	321 grey-red	320 green-white	319 white
down	320 green-white	321 grey-red	319 white

Component Locations

22A main fuse/relay panel at left wheel housing
113 time delay relay for heated rear window under rear seat, auxiliary fuse/relay panel
124 left power mirror switch in instrument panel
125 right power mirror switch in instrument panel
126 left power mirror motor and solenoid in the left mirror
127 right power mirror motor and solenoid in the right mirror
158 negative distribution in main fuse/relay panel
207 heated rear view mirrors on front doors

Connector Locations

1985-1990

152B 29-pin bulkhead connector at main fuse/relay panel

1991 and later

H1-1 1-pin connector in engine compartment, upper left door hinge
H1-3 1-pin connector in engine compartment, upper right door hinge
H1-14 1-pin connector in the left front door
H1-15 1-pin connector in the right front door
H4-2 4-pin connector in engine compartment, near top left door hinge
H4-3 4-pin connector in engine compartment, near top right door hinge
H4-8 4-pin connector in the left front door
H4-9 4-pin connector in the right front door
H29-1 29-pin bulkhead connector behind main fuse/relay panel (1991-1991 1/2)
H29-2 29-pin bulkhead connector behind main fuse/relay panel (1991-1991 1/2)
H33-1 33-pin bulkhead connector behind main fuse/relay panel (1991 1/2 and later)
H33-2 33-pin bulkhead connector behind main fuse/relay panel (1991 1/2 and later)

Ground Locations

1985-1990

3 ground point behind instrument panel

1991 and later

G6 ground distribution at main fuse/relay panel
G8 ground point behind instrument panel

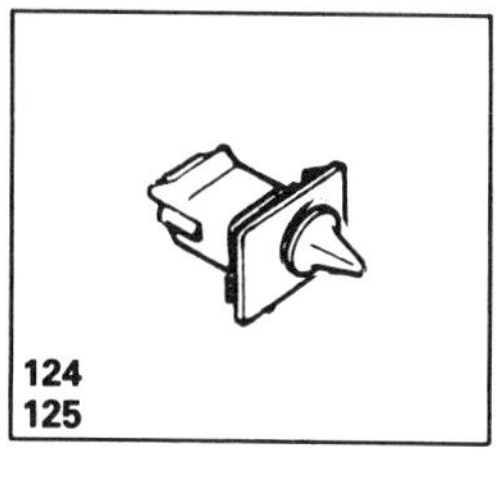

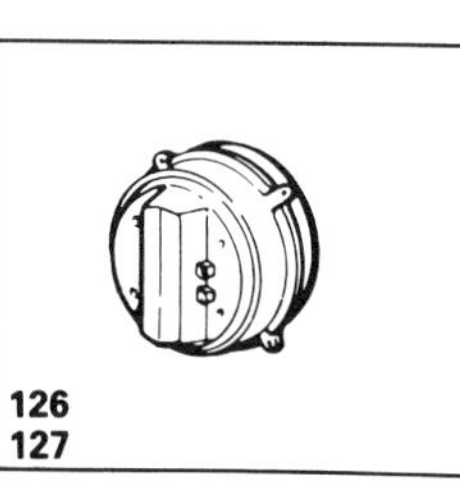

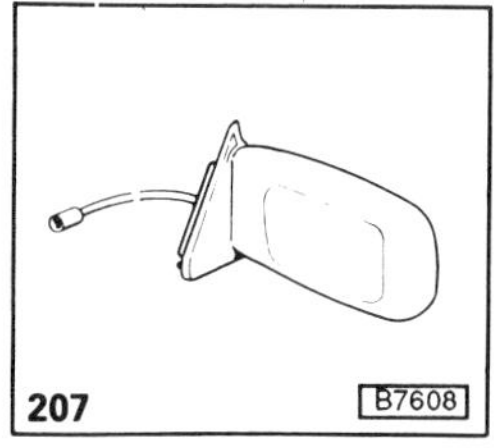

Power Mirrors

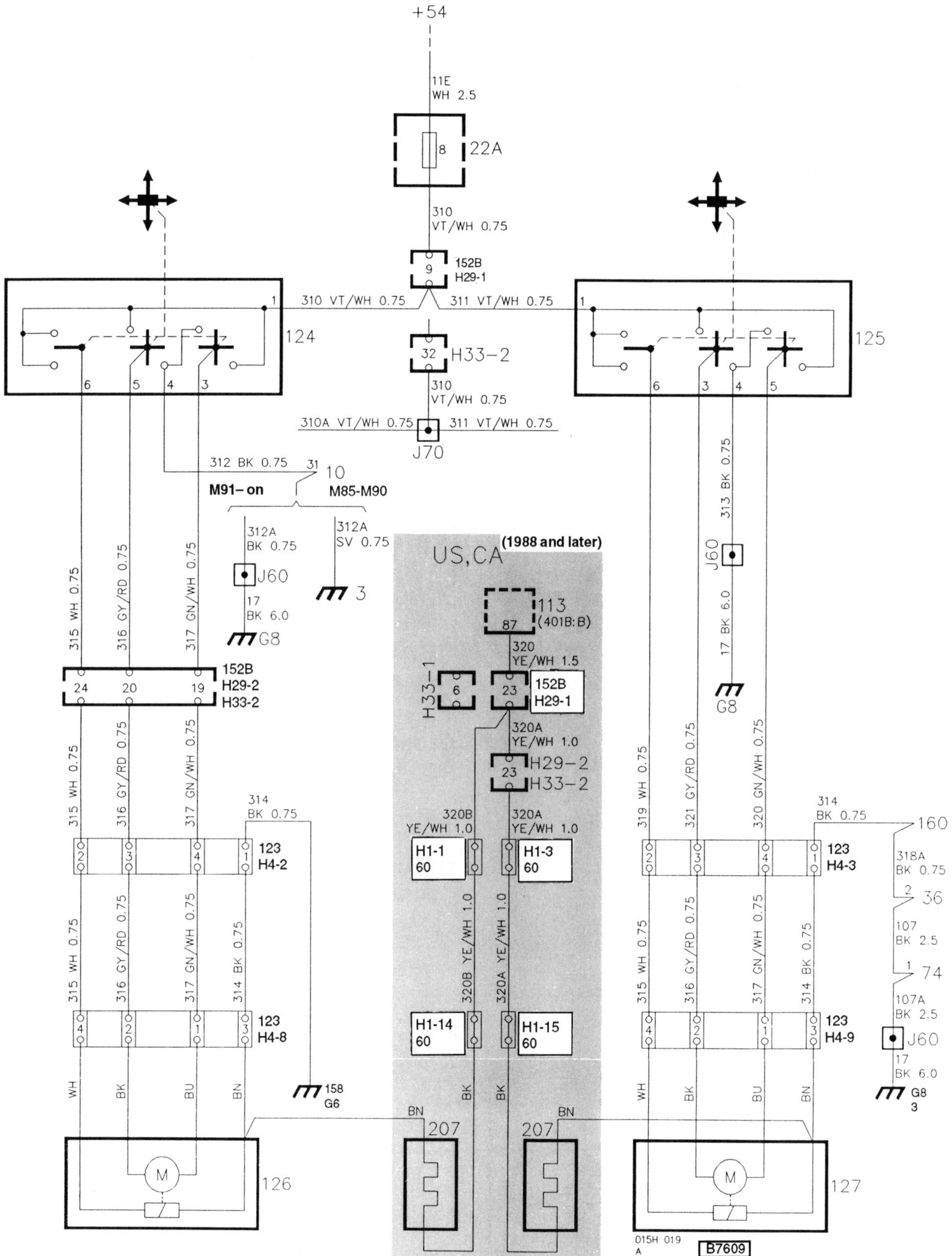

Power Windows

Operation

The power windows are controlled by console switches, and, if applicable, door-mounted switches. Electric motors in each door raise and lower the window. Motor direction is controlled by changing the voltage polarity at the motor. On 4-door cars, a lockout switch—labelled ON/OFF allows the driver to disable operation of the rear power windows.

NOTE

The console switch assembly (386) on 1991 and later models also contains the relays for the automatic window down feature. These relays cannot be replaced separately.

See **830 Doors, Windows, and Lids** for information on removing the window motors and glass. Additional information can be found in **364 Electric Controls and Switches** for replacing the switch and switch illumination bulbs.

Fault Tracing

1. Check the fuses. Check the power supply to the switch.
2. At the window motor, check for battery voltage with the switch pushed in one direction. Reverse the test leads and push the switch in the other direction. There should again be battery voltage.

Component Locations

22A main fuse/relay panel at left wheel housing
162 switch for driver power window in center console
163 switch for passenger power window in center console
164 power window motor in left front door
165 power window motor in right front door
189 lockout switch for rear power windows
190 switch for left rear power window in center console
190a switch for left rear power window in left rear door
191 switch for right rear power window in center console
191a switch for right rear power window in right rear door
193 power window motor in left rear
194 power window motor in right rear
287 power window relay for automatic control
1989-1990 Convertible under rear seat in fuse/relay panel. 401
1989-1990 ex. Convertible under rear seat, left-hand side
386 switch assembly for power windows and sunroof (where applicable) in center console
401 auxiliary fuse/relay panel under rear seat

Connector Locations

1985-1990

57 3-pin connector behind trim at left or right B pillar
58 12-pin connector behind instrument panel, left of steering column
59 2-pin connector at top left front door hinge or top right front door hinge, (2) in the main fuse/relay panel, (2) under center console
60 1-pin connector under center console
152A 29-pin bulkhead connector at main fuse/relay panel
152B 29-pin bulkhead connector at main fuse/relay panel

1991 and later

H1-6 1-pin connector at right B pillar, behind trim
H1-7 1-pin connector at left B pillar, behind trim
H1-17 1-pin connector under center console
H2-5 2-pin connector in engine compartment, near top left door hinge
H2-11 2-pin connector in engine compartment, near top right door hinge
H3-10 3-pin connector at right B pillar, behind trim
H3-11 3-pin connector at left B pillar, behind trim
H12-1 12-pin connector behind instrument panel, left of steering column
H29-1 29-pin bulkhead connector behind main fuse/relay panel (1991-1991 1/2)
H29-2 29-pin bulkhead connector behind main fuse/relay panel (1991-1991 1/2)
H33-1 33-pin bulkhead connector behind main fuse/relay panel (1991 1/2 and later)
H33-2 33-pin bulkhead connector behind main fuse/relay panel (1991 1/2 and later)

Ground Locations

1985-1990

65 ground point at handbrake
117 ground point at handbrake

1991 and later

G4 ground point between ignition switch and handbrake

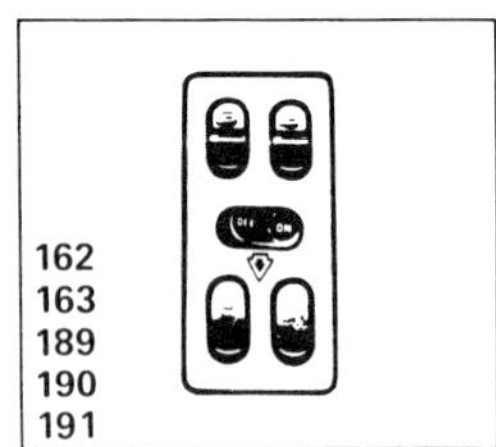

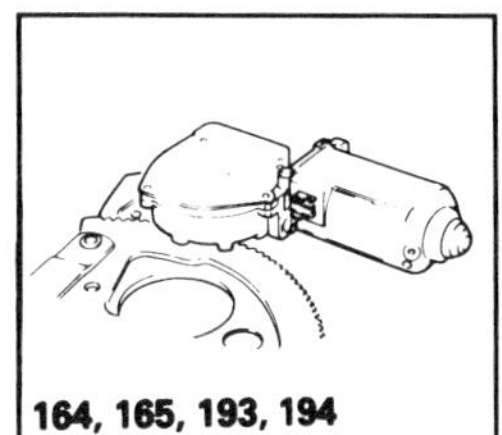

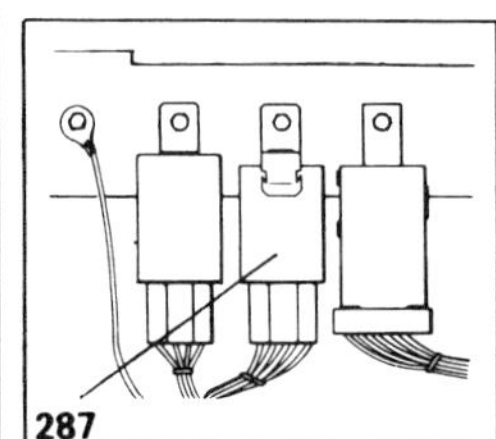

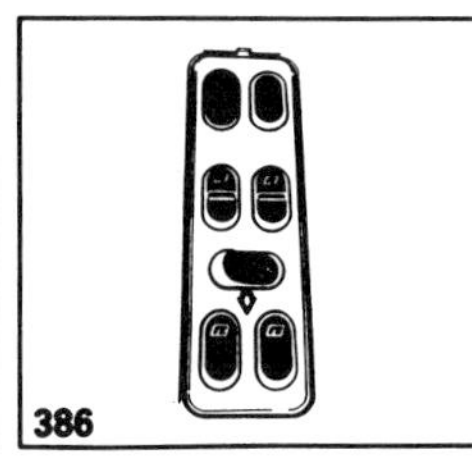

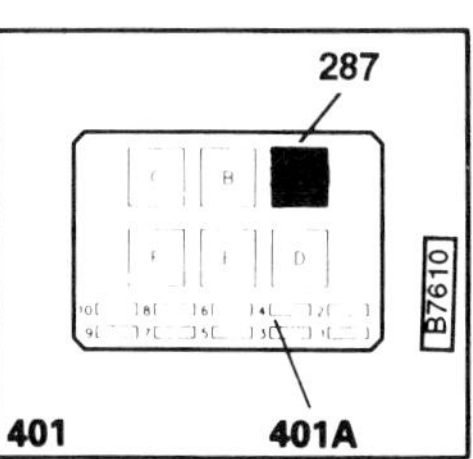

Power Windows
1985

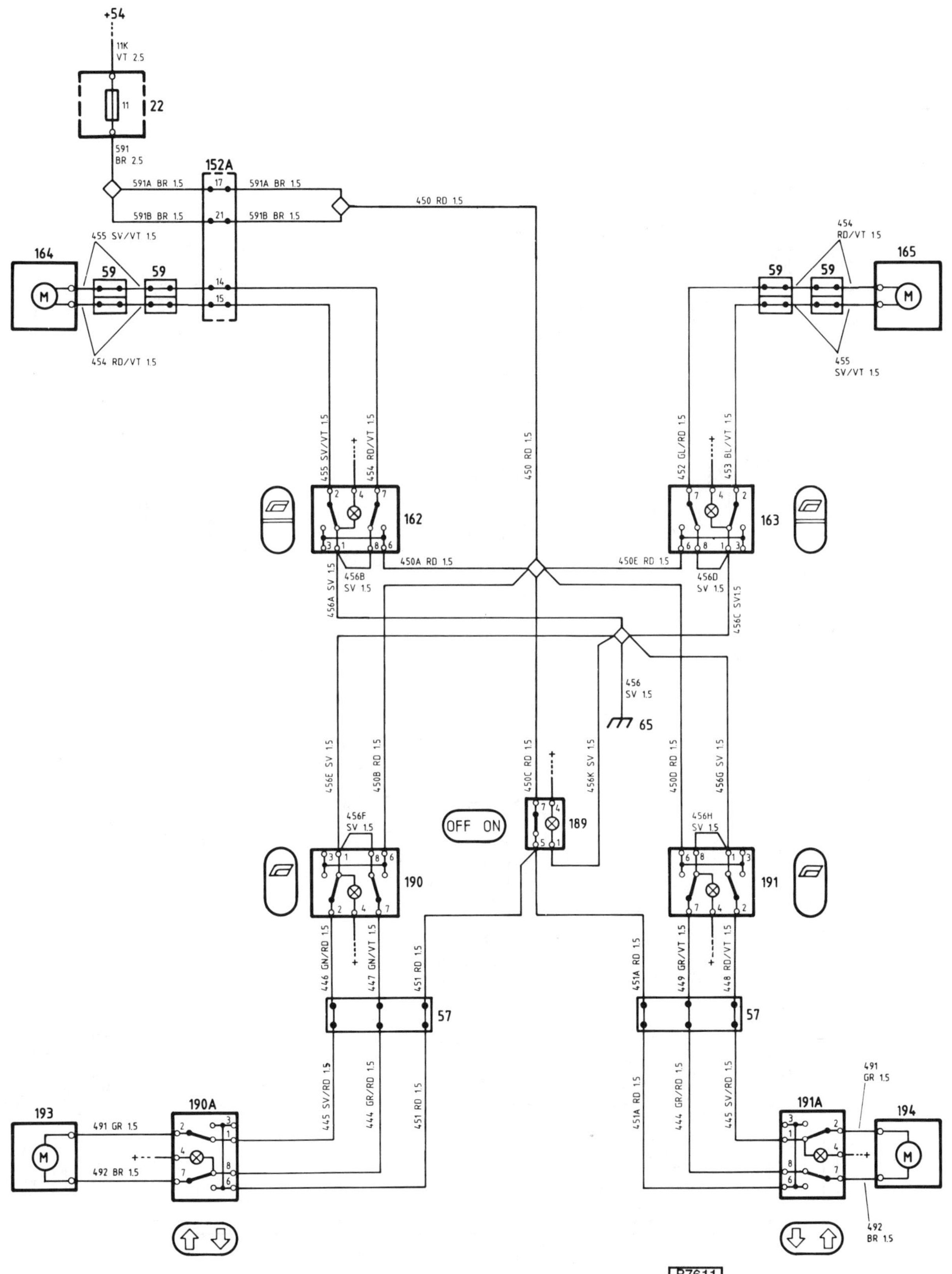

Power Windows

1986-1990

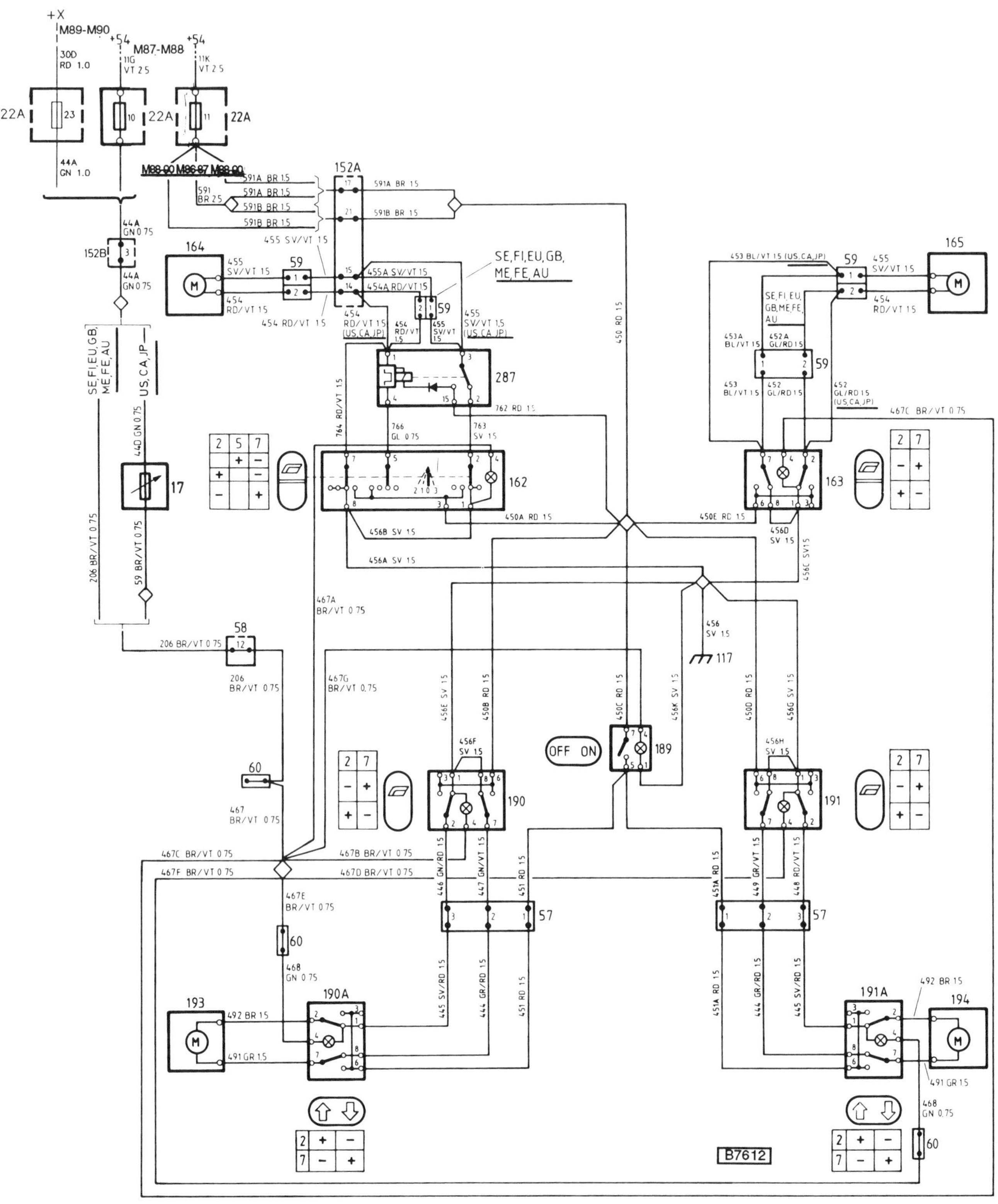

Power Windows

1991 and later

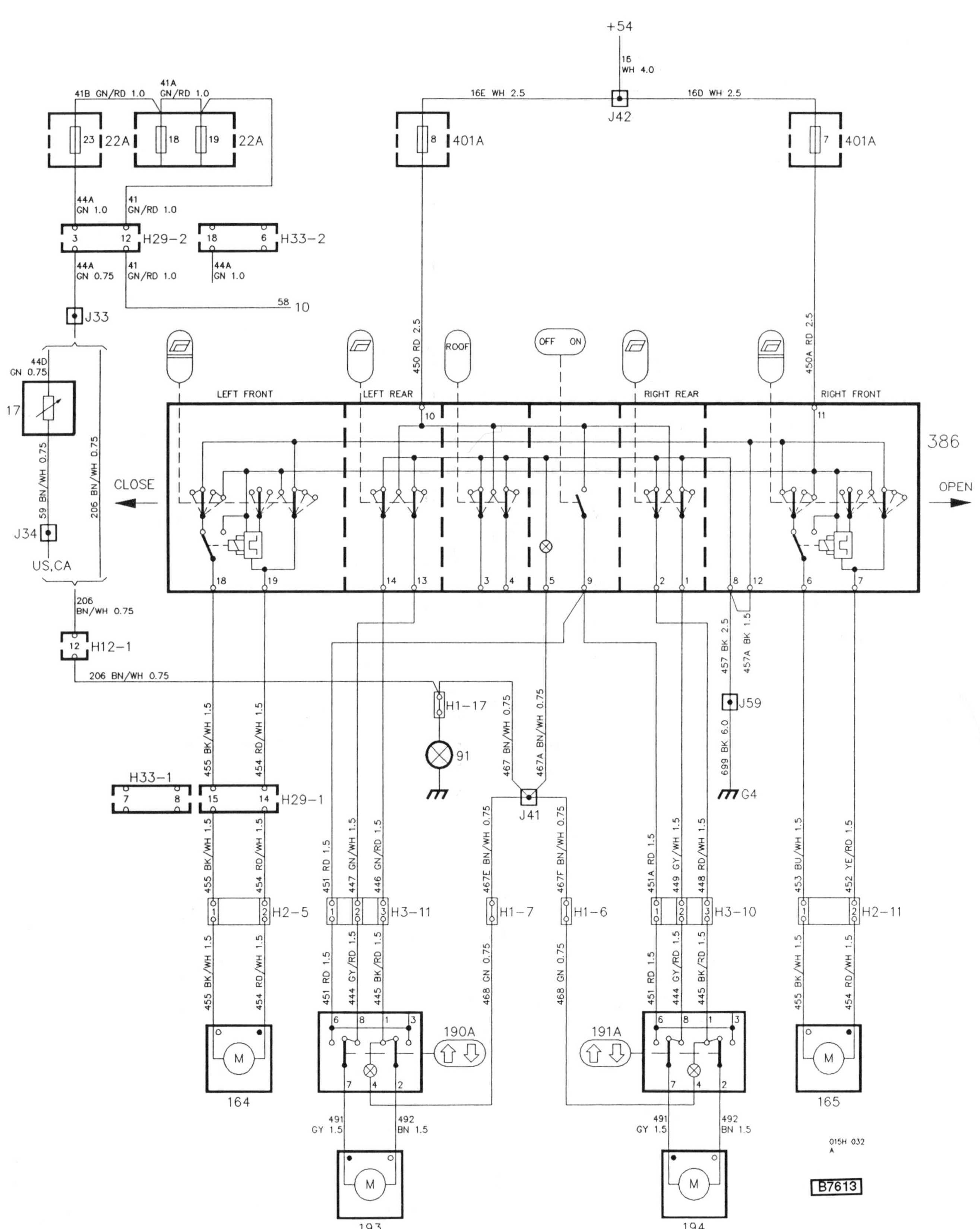

Power Windows—Convertible

1987-1990

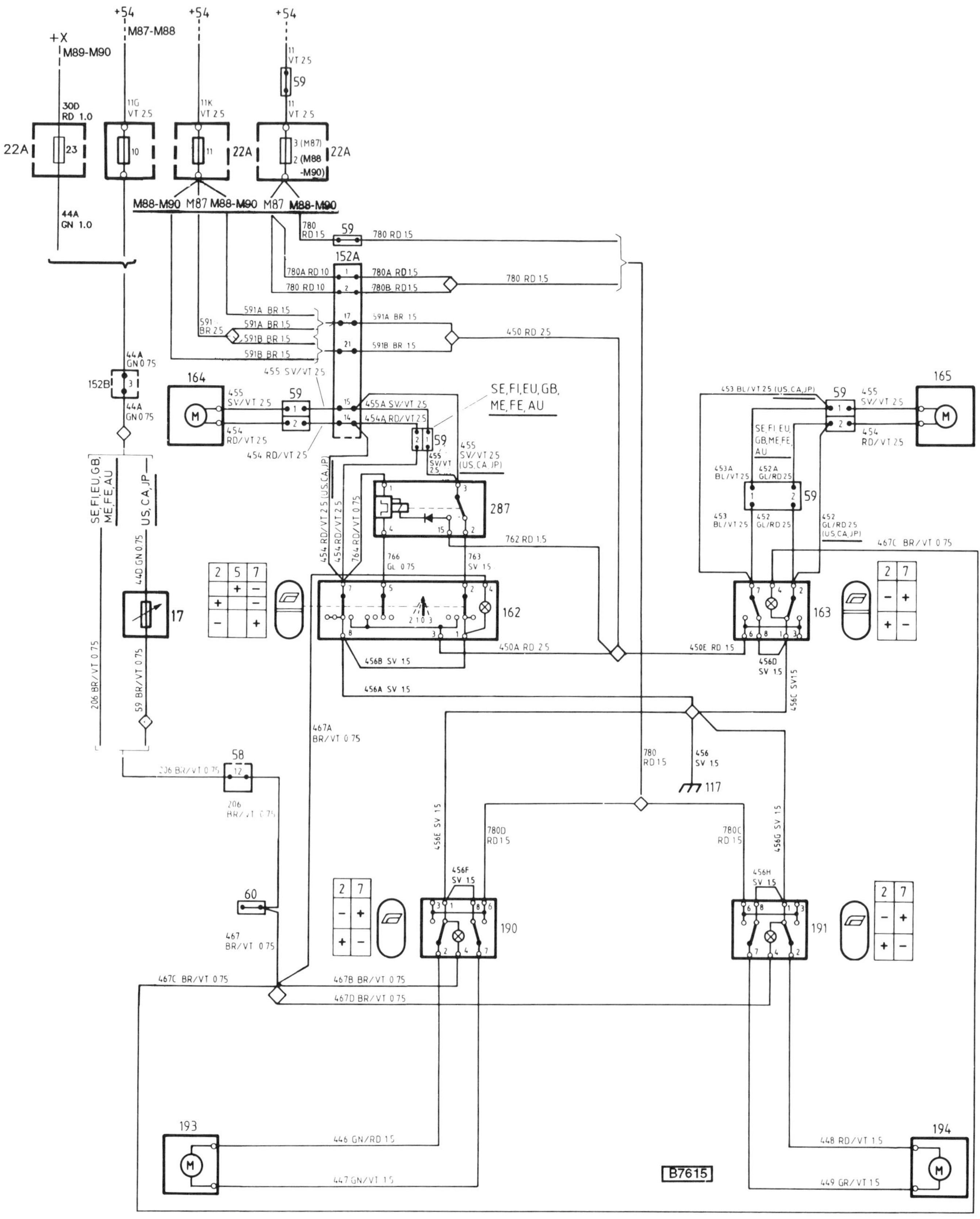

Power Windows—Convertible

1991 and later

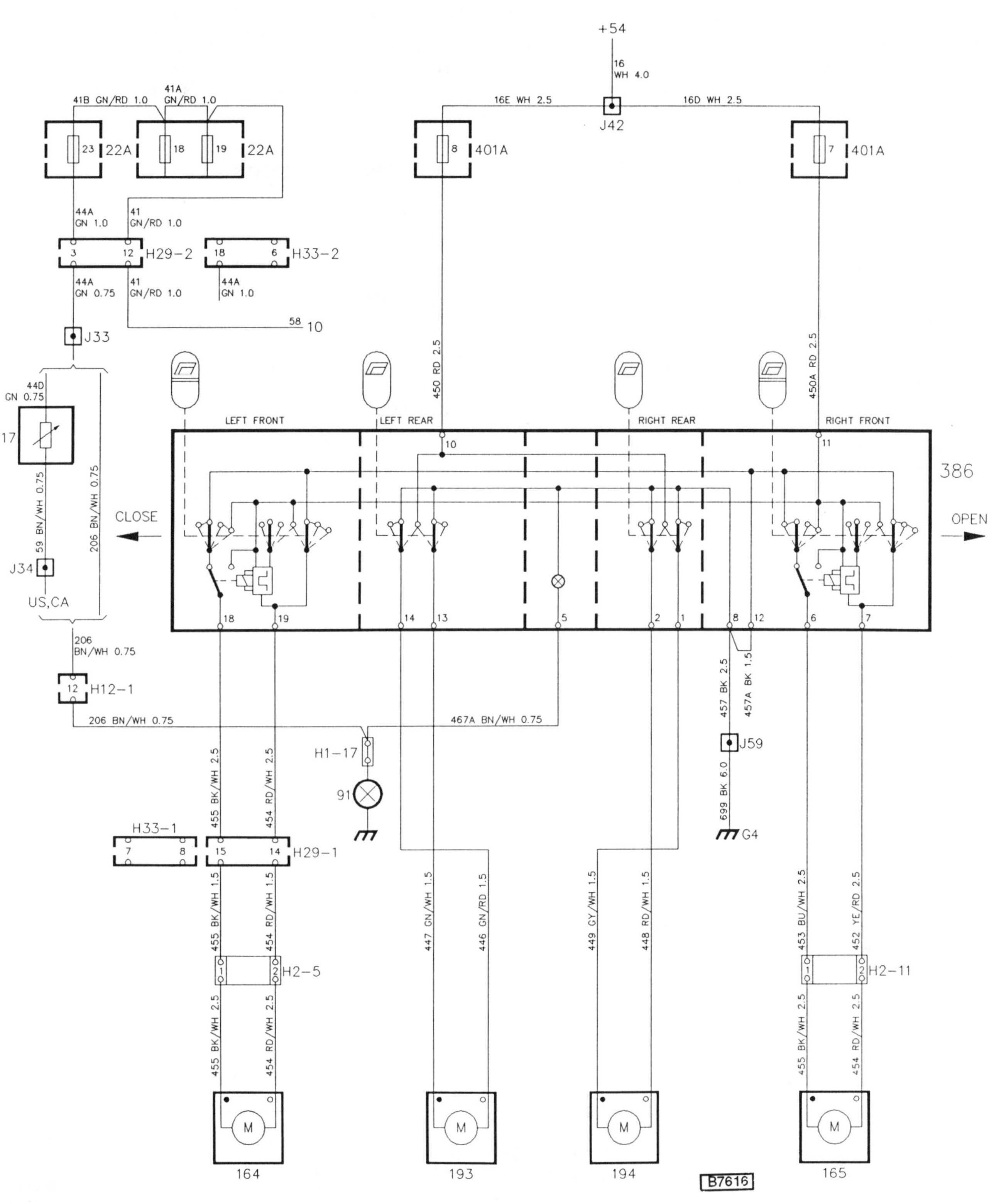

Radiator Cooling Fan

Operation

The cooling fan, located behind the radiator, is thermostatically controlled by the coolant temperature switch (39) located at the top left of the radiator. A coolant fan time delay relay (26) or radiator fan relay (396) is used depending on model year.

For information on the electric radiator cooling fan for the air conditioner, see **Air Conditioner** elsewhere in this section. For cooling system repair information, see **261 Radiator and Cooling System**.

Fault Tracing

1. Check the fuses.
2. Check the coolant fan time delay relay (26) by checking for voltage at the relay panel sockets (terminals 30 and 87).
3. Check the coolant temperature switch by jumpering the switch terminals with the key on. The fan should now run.

Component Locations

22A main fuse/relay panel at left wheel housing
26 coolant fan time delay relay at front left wheel housing
37 radiator cooling fan motor behind radiator
39 coolant fan temperature switch at upper left corner of radiator
156 A/C compressor relay at main fuse/relay panel, engine compartment
159 +15 distribution in main fuse/relay panel
396 radiator fan relay at main fuse/relay panel

Connector Locations

1985-1990

59 2-pin connector at radiator fan motor
60 1-pin connector behind radiator

1991 and later

H2-1 2-pin connector at radiator fan motor

Ground Locations

1985-1990

7 ground point at radiator cross member

1991 and later

G1 ground point at radiator cross member
G6 ground distribution at main fuse/relay panel

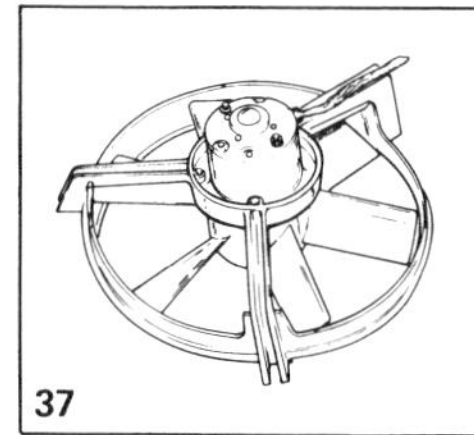

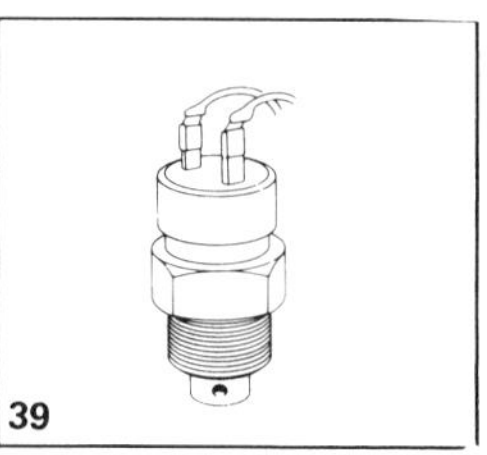

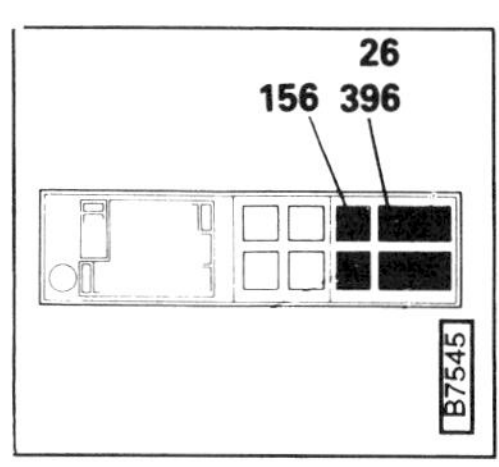

Radiator Cooling Fan

1985-1989 1990 1991 and later

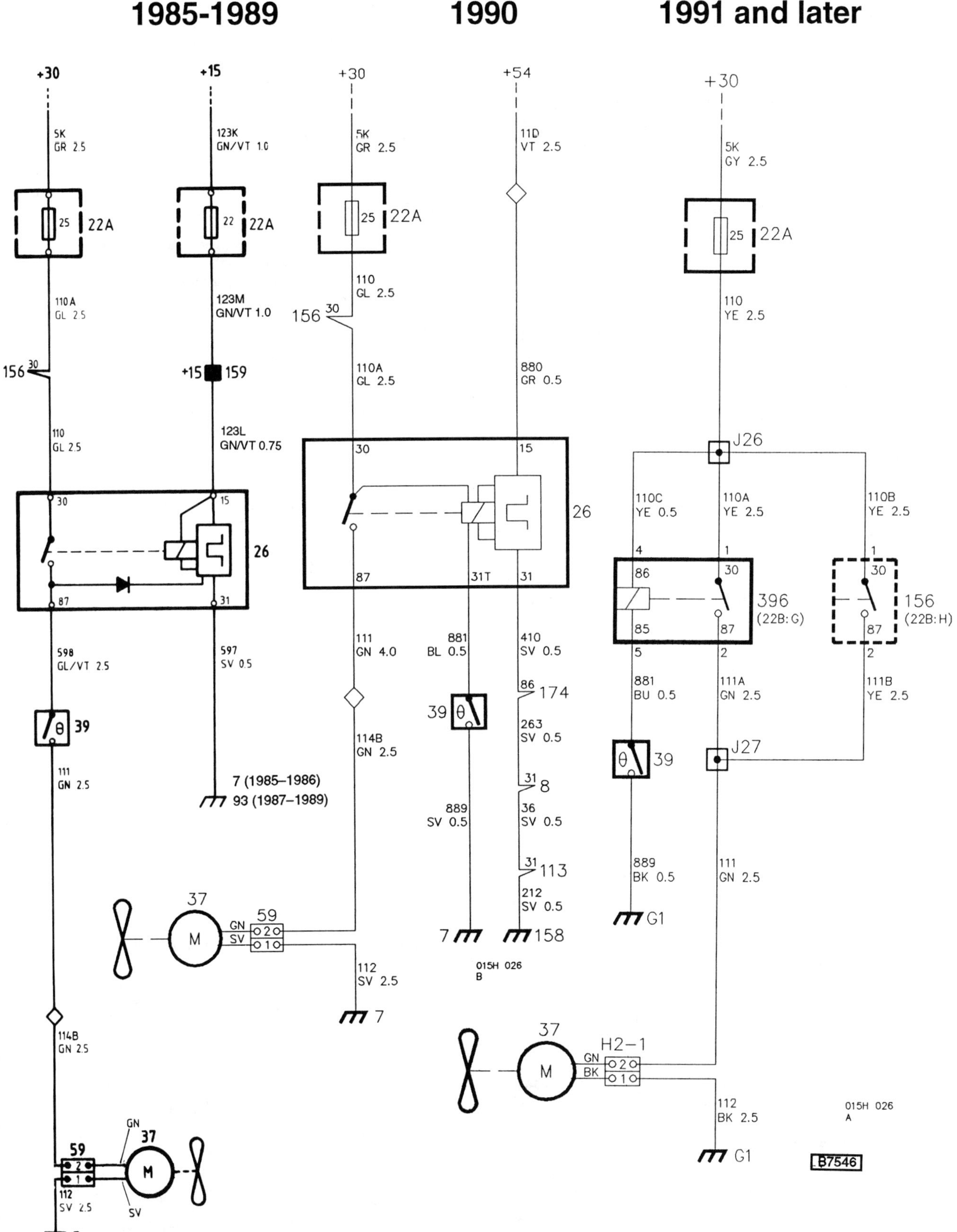

Radio

Operation

Radio wiring is provided to the opening in the instrument panel on all models. Some models have wiring for a graphic equalizer and compact disc player in the center console. An electric antenna is available on some models. A coaxial antenna cable is installed from the left rear up to the instrument panel.

See **853 Dashboard and Consoles** for information on removing the radio. See **851 Interior Trim and Upholstery** for information on removing the antenna.

Fault Tracing

1. Check the fuses, including the ones in the back of the instrument panel opening. See **Component Locations** below.
2. To check the coaxial cable with an ohmmeter, unplug the cable at both ends. There should be no continuity (open circuit) between the center and outer conductors. There should be no continuity (open circuit) between either conductor and chassis ground.
3. To check the coaxial cable for internal continuity, unplug the cable at both ends. Short the conductors together at one end of the cable with a piece of wire. Test for approximately 0 ohms (short circuit) at the other end of the cable between the conductors.

Component Locations

22A main fuse/relay panel at left wheel housing
265 electric radio antenna in left rear body panel
266 radio speakers (4) two in front, two in rear
349 radio contact box with amplifier in instrument panel
350 contact box for CD player or equalizer in center console top compartment
351 audio amplifier under rear seat below ABS control unit (291)
401 auxiliary fuse/relay panel under rear seat

Connector Locations

1985-1990

59 2-pin connector near electric antenna
60 1-pin connector near each speaker
98 10-pin connector in instrument panel, radio compartment
123 4-pin connector in instrument panel, (2) in radio compartment
152A 29-pin bulkhead connector in main fuse/relay panel
267 radio connector in instrument panel

1991 and later

H2-14 2-pin connector in left rear wheel housing in luggage compartment
H2-51 2-pin connector for left rear speaker
H2-52 2-pin connector for right rear speaker
H6-4 6-pin connector behind instrument panel
H8-7 8-pin connector behind instrument panel
H8-8 8-pin connector behind instrument panel
H10-1 10-pin connector behind instrument panel, left of steering column
H10-5 10-pin connector behind instrument panel
H12-3 12-pin connector behind instrument panel
H12-4 12-pin connector behind instrument panel

Ground Locations

1985-1990

3 ground point behind instrument panel

1991 and later

G4 ground point between ignition switch and handbrake
G5 ground point under rear seat
G27 ground point for electric antenna

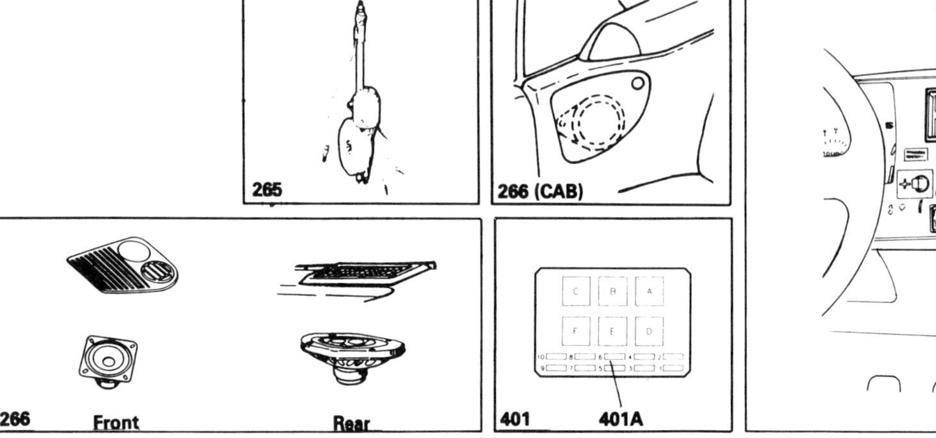

Radio

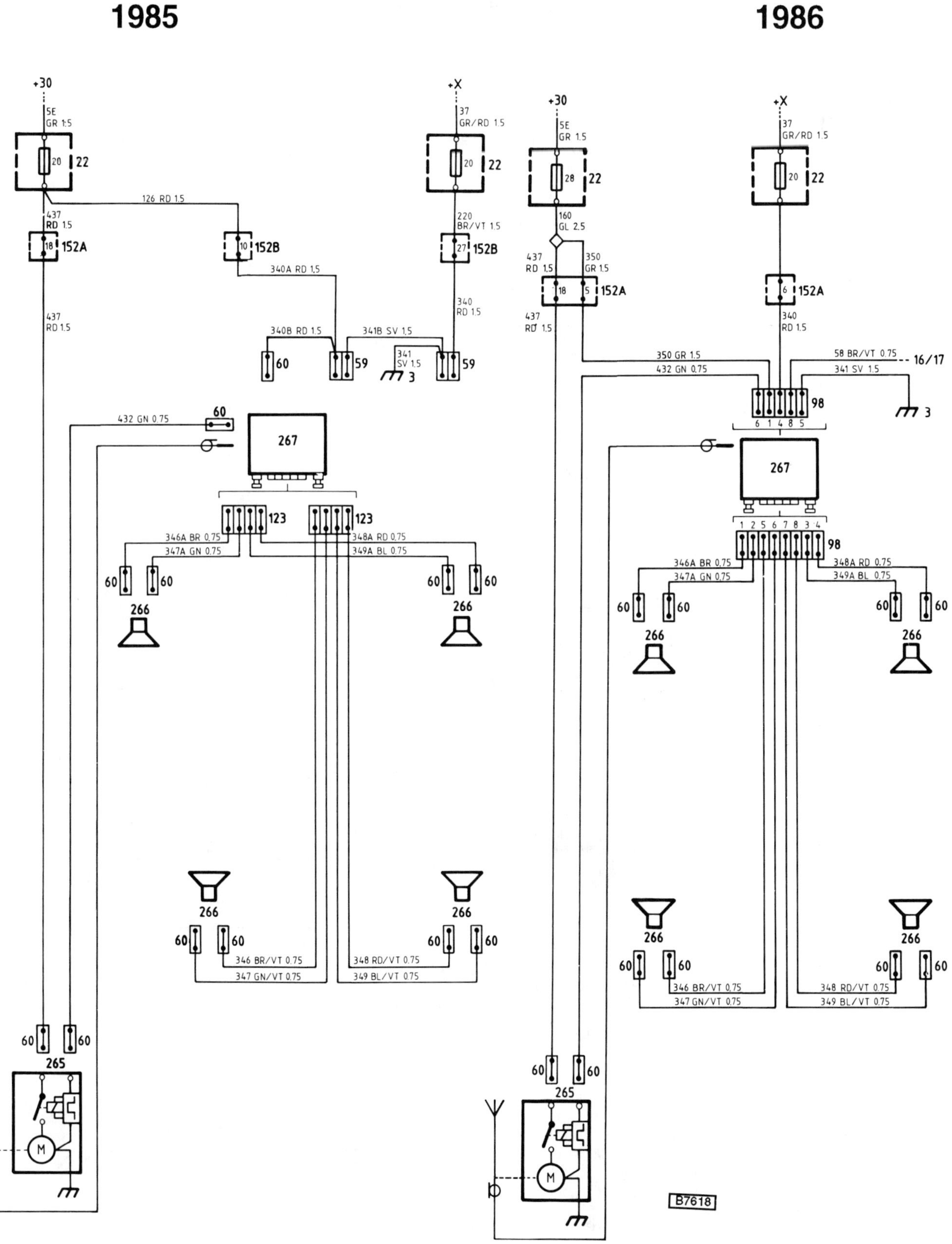
1985
1986
+30
+X
5E GR 1.5
37 GR/RD 1.5
22
152A
152B
126 RD 1.5
437 RD 1.5
340A RD 1.5
220 BR/VT 1.5
340 RD 1.5
340B RD 1.5
341B SV 1.5
341 SV 1.5
59
60
3
432 GN 0.75
267
123
346A BR 0.75
347A GN 0.75
348A RD 0.75
349A BL 0.75
266
346 BR/VT 0.75
347 GN/VT 0.75
348 RD/VT 0.75
349 BL/VT 0.75
265
M
160 GL 2.5
350 GR 1.5
58 BR/VT 0.75
16/17
98
B7618

Radio

1987-1990

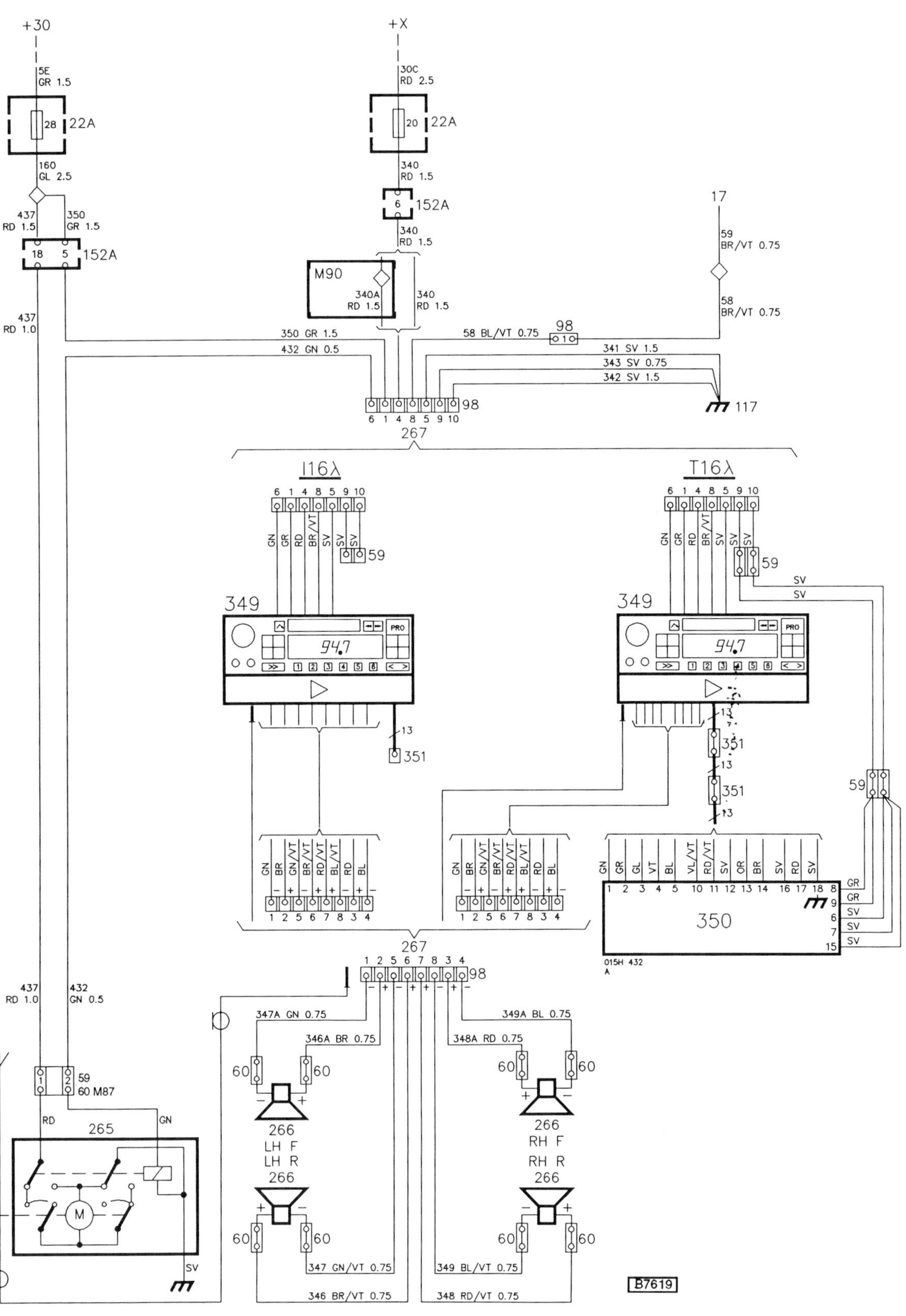

Radio
1991

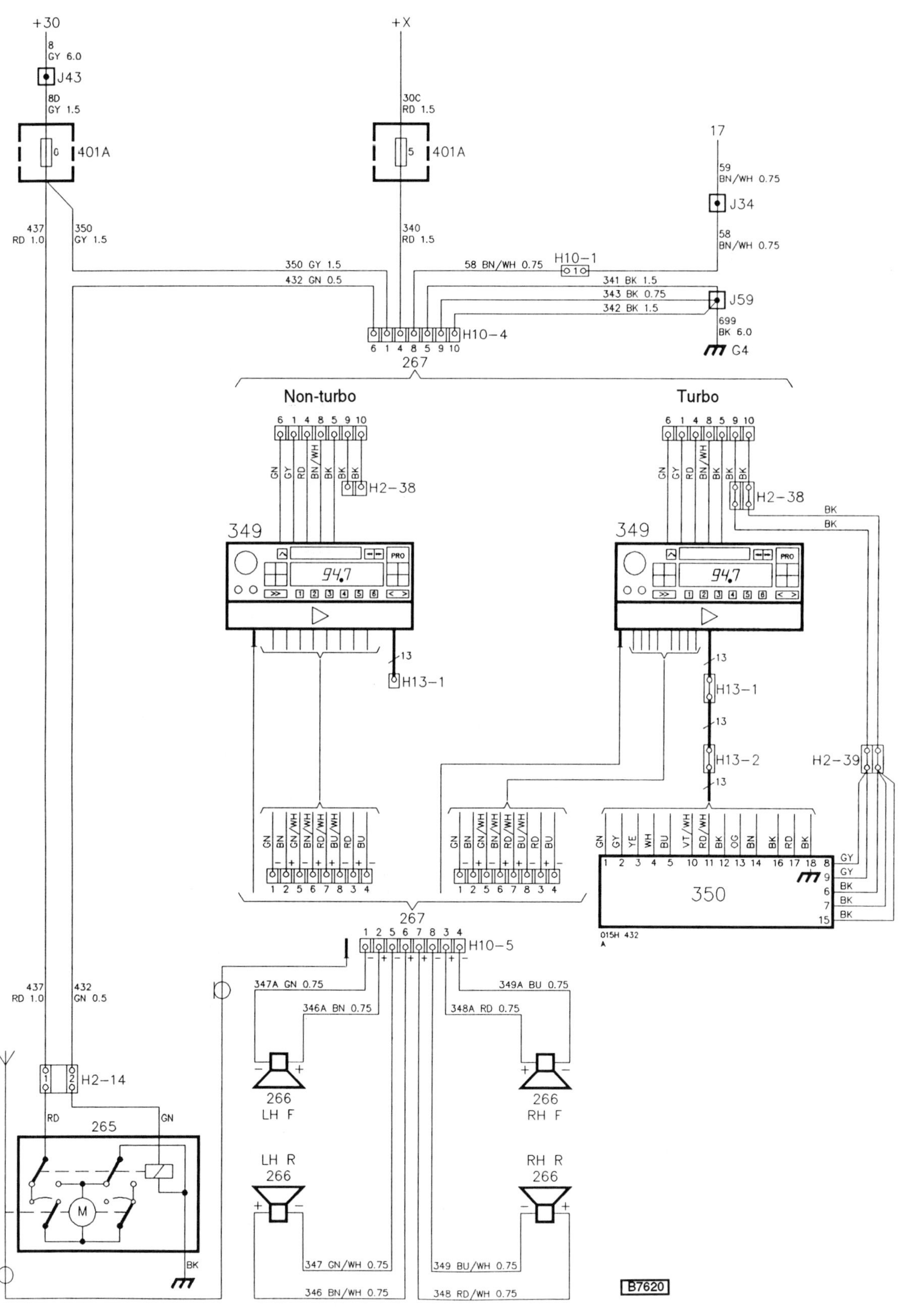

+30
+X
J43
401A
17
J34
J59
G4
H10-1
H10-4
267
Non-turbo
Turbo
349
H2-38
H13-1
H13-2
H2-39
350
H10-5
266
LH F
RH F
LH R
RH R
265
H2-14
B7620

Radio

1992 and later

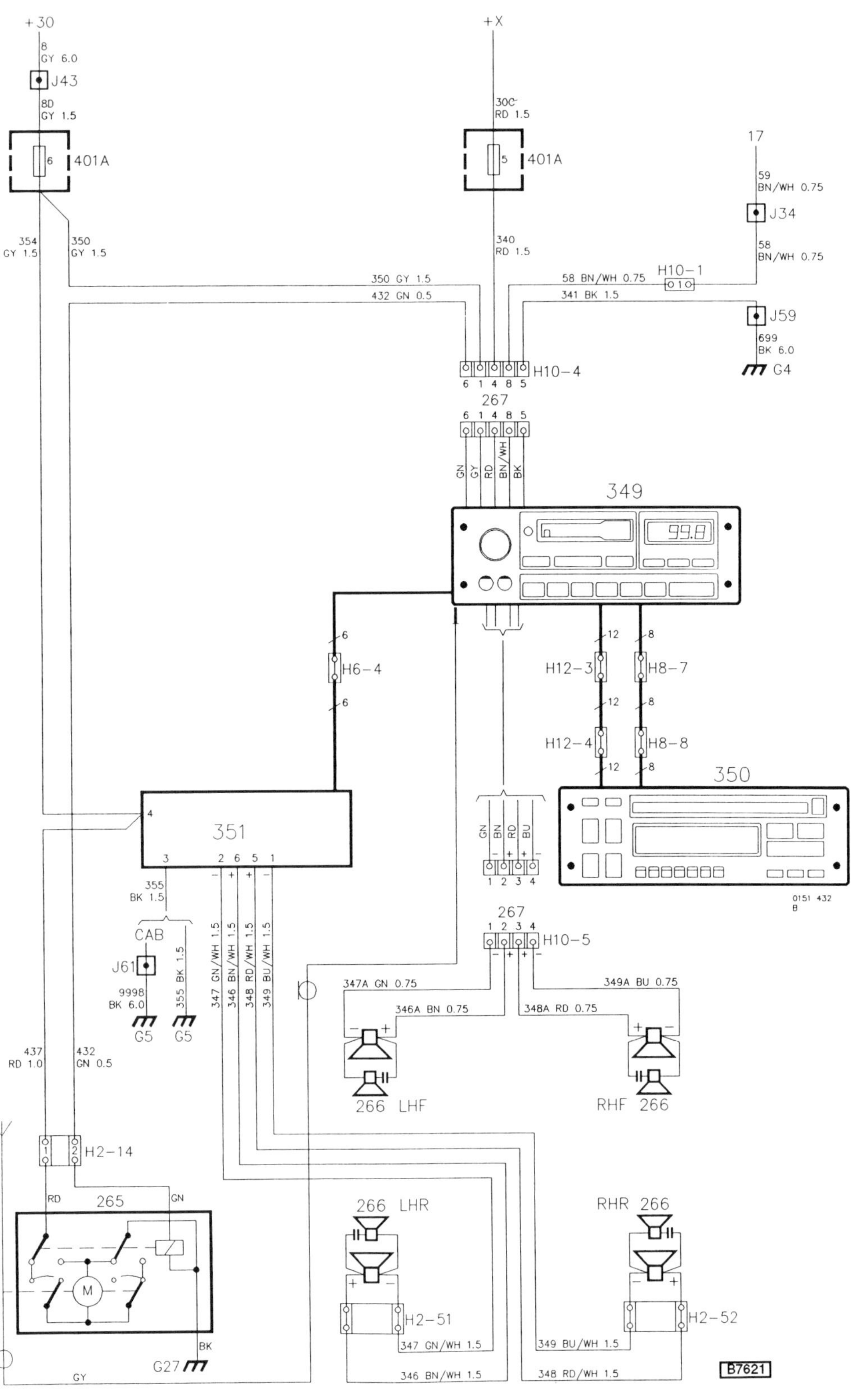

Seat Belt and Ignition Key Warning

Operation

The seat belt and ignition key warning system warns the driver to fasten his seat belt. The system also warns the driver whenever the key is left in the ignition and the door is open.

For information on removing and repairing the ignition lock and ignition switch see **432 Manual Transmission Controls**.

Fault Tracing

1. Check the fuses.
2. Check that the door switch wire has continuity to ground when the door is opened, and has no continuity to ground when the door is shut.
3. Check for voltage at terminals 3, 15, and L of the seat belt warning relay (82) with the key in the run position.

Component Locations

20 ignition switch in center console
22 main fuse/relay panel
54 door switches on the door jamb
69 passenger seat belt switch under seat cover
70 seat belt switch, driver side between driver and passenger seat
72 seat belt warning light at center of instrument panel
82 seat belt warning relay under the rear seat

Connector Locations

1985-1990

58 12-pin connector to left of steering column
60 1-pin connector under center console
98 10-pin connector to left of steering column
152A 29-pin bulkhead connector behind main fuse/relay panel
152B 29-pin bulkhead connector behind main fuse/relay panel

1991 and later

H3-18 3-pin connector under passenger seat
H8-1 8-pin connector under passenger seat
H8-2 8-pin connector under driver seat
H12-1 12-pin connector behind instrument panel, left of steering column
H29-2 29-pin bulkhead connector behind main fuse/relay panel (1991-1991 1/2)
H33-2 33-pin bulkhead connector behind main fuse/relay panel (1991 1/2 and later)

Ground Locations

1985-1990

117 ground point under handbrake

1991 and later

G4 ground point between ignition switch and handbrake

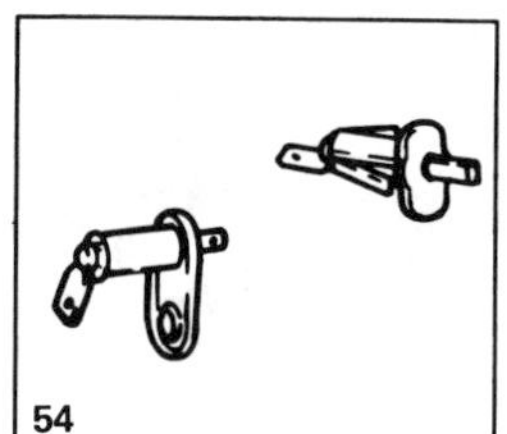
54

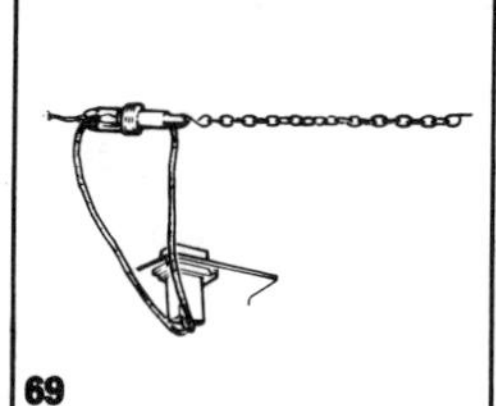
69

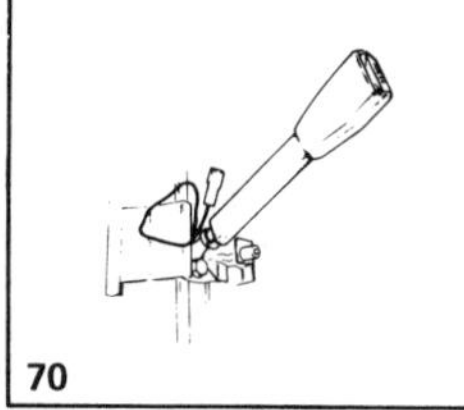
70

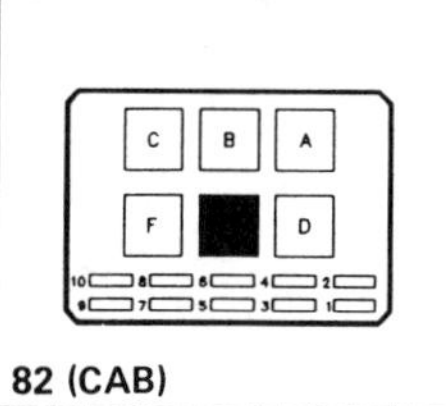

82 (CAB)

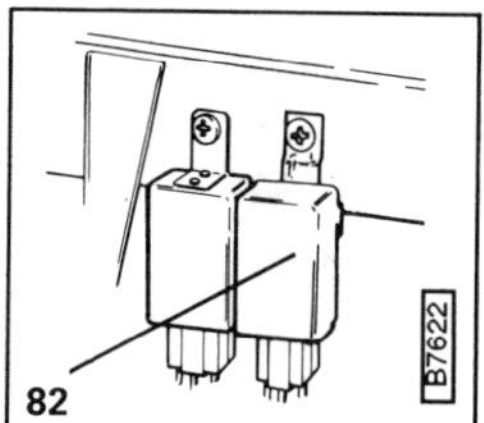

82

Seat Belt and Ignition Key Warning

1985-1986

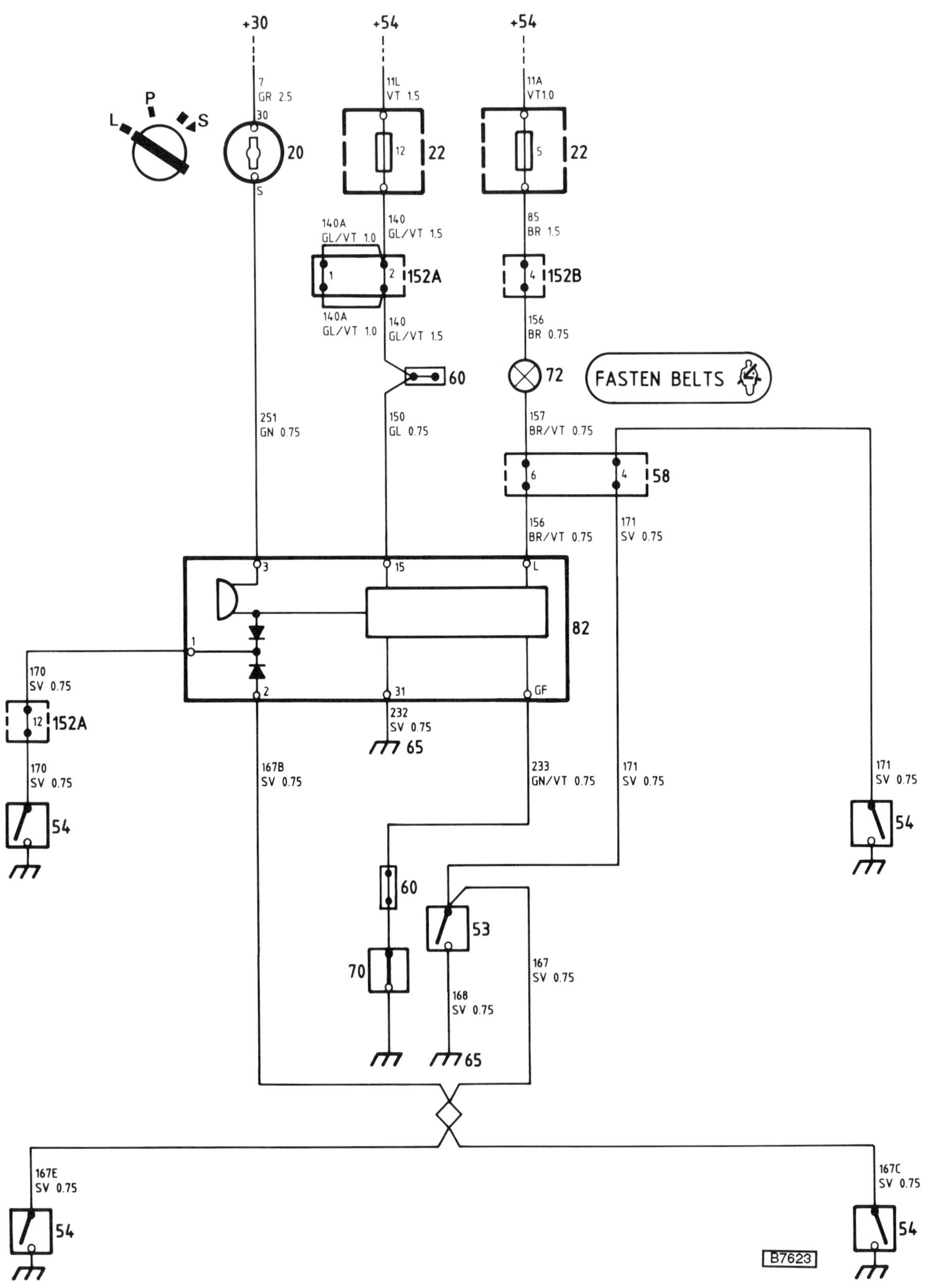

Seat Belt and Ignition Key Warning

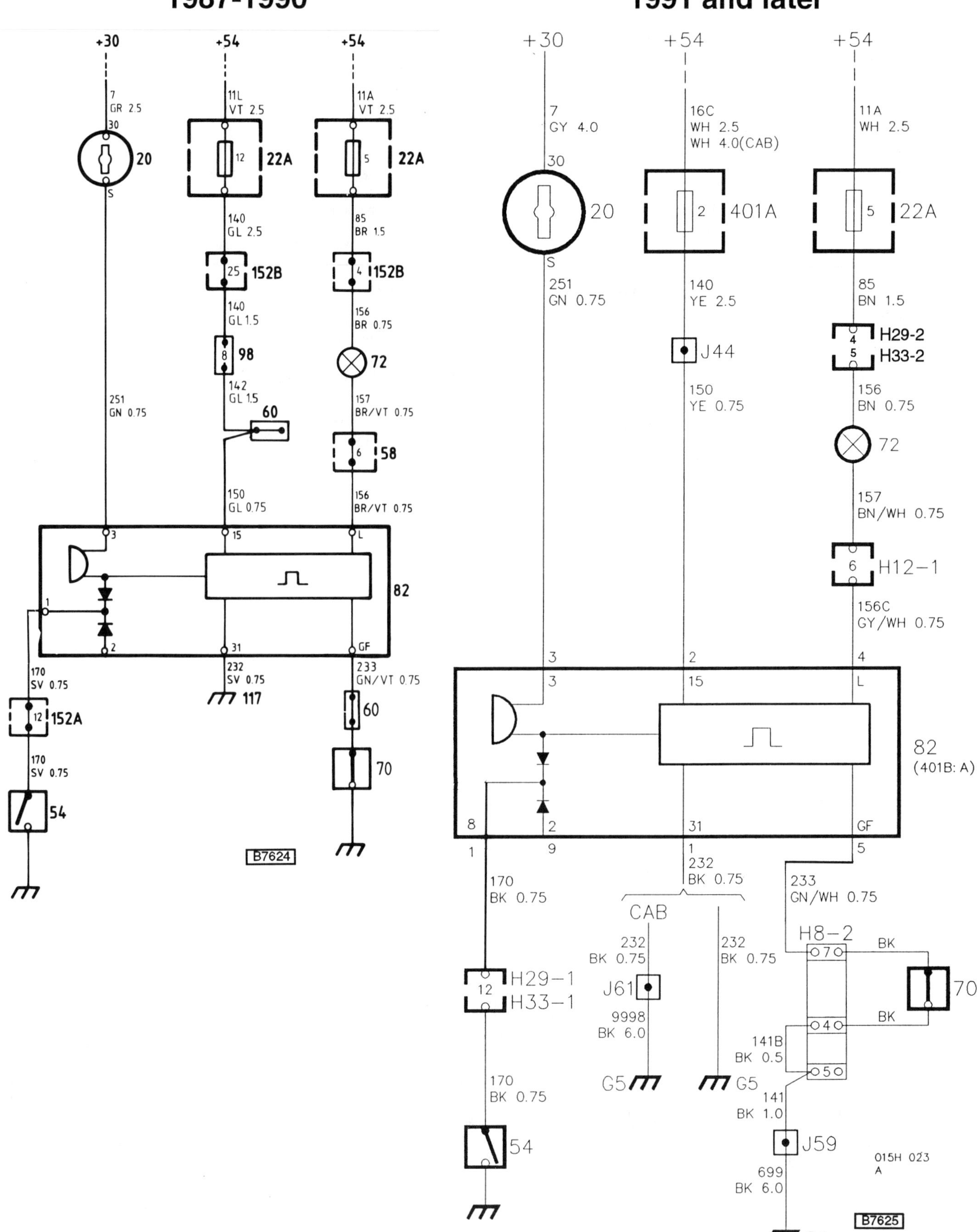

Shift-up Indicator

Operation

The shift-up indicator is installed on cars with manual transmission only. The light in the instrument cluster lights up indicating to the driver when to shift up. The light will stay off if the car is in fifth gear, if the engine temperature is below 95°F (35°C), or if the throttle is in the rest position. A time delay function of 1.7 seconds prevents the light from flashing and causing irritation. This time delay function is incorporated in the shift-up indicator relay (270). 1989 and later models have shift-up incorporated into the LH control unit.

NOTE
For shift-up wiring diagrams on 1989 and later models, see **Combined Instruments** elsewhere in this section.

Fault Tracing

1. Check the fuses with the key in the run position.
2. Check for voltage at the shift-up relay (270) terminal G and terminal 15. The car should be in first gear and the engine temperature cold (less than 95°F).
3. Check the shift-up lamp (47K) in the instrument cluster.

Component Locations

22A main fuse/relay panel
47K shift-up indicator lamp
146 ignition amplifier in front of left wheel housing
147 ignition pulse amplifier in main fuse/relay panel, position D
158 ground (–) distribution in main fuse/relay panel
176 EZK control unit at inner left fender
203 throttle angle transmitter on throttle housing
261 throttle contacts for shift-up indicator at throttle housing
262 temperature switch for shift-up indicator between center intake ports of intake manifold
263 vacuum switch for shift-up indicator at left wheel housing
264 5 gear switch for shift-up indicator at front side cover of gearbox
270 shift-up indicator relay in main fuse/relay panel

Connector Locations

59 2-pin connector behind the instrument panel
152B 29-pin bulkhead connector at main fuse/relay panel

Ground Locations

3 ground point behind instrument panel
201 ground point for fuel injection at engine lifting lug, 2 points

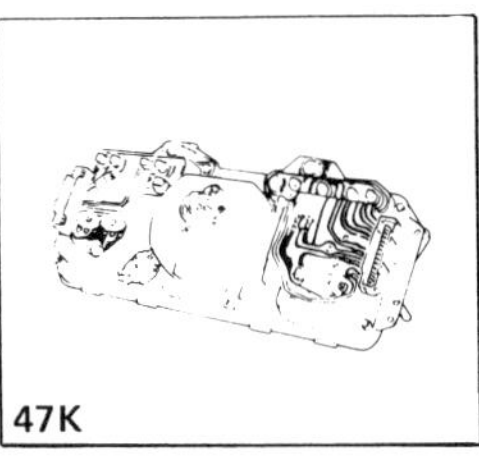
47K

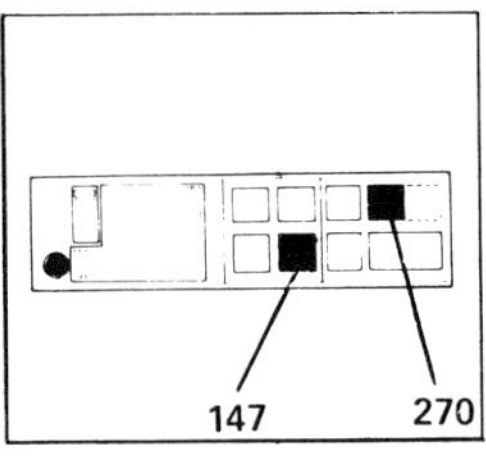

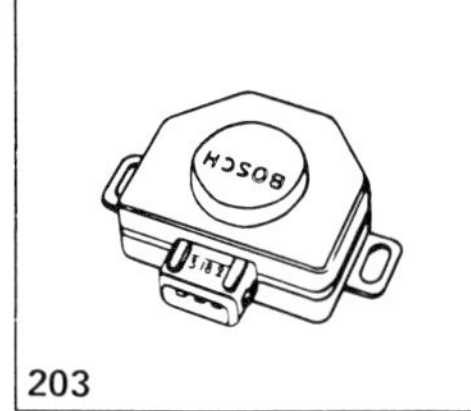

203

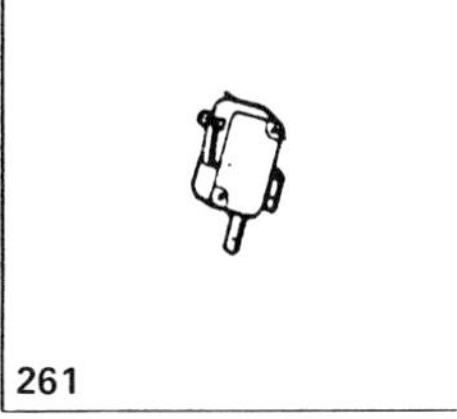
261

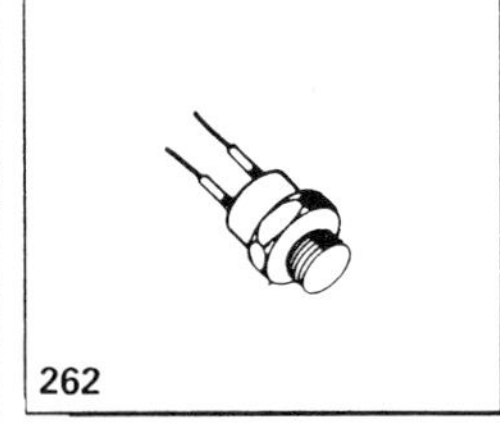
262

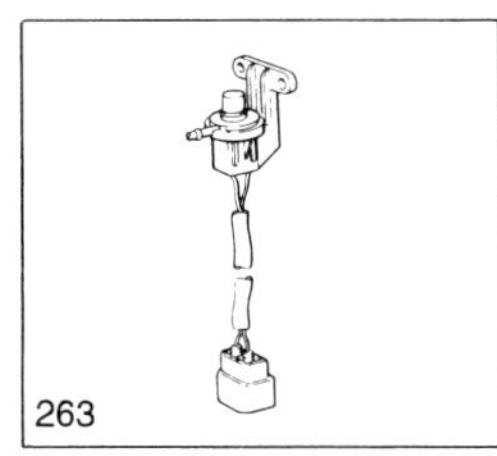
263

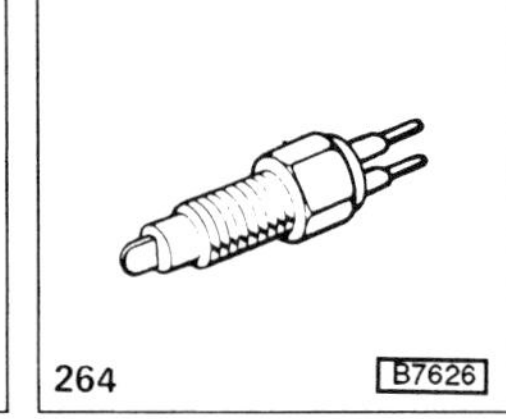
264

B7626

Shift-up Indicator
1985-1988

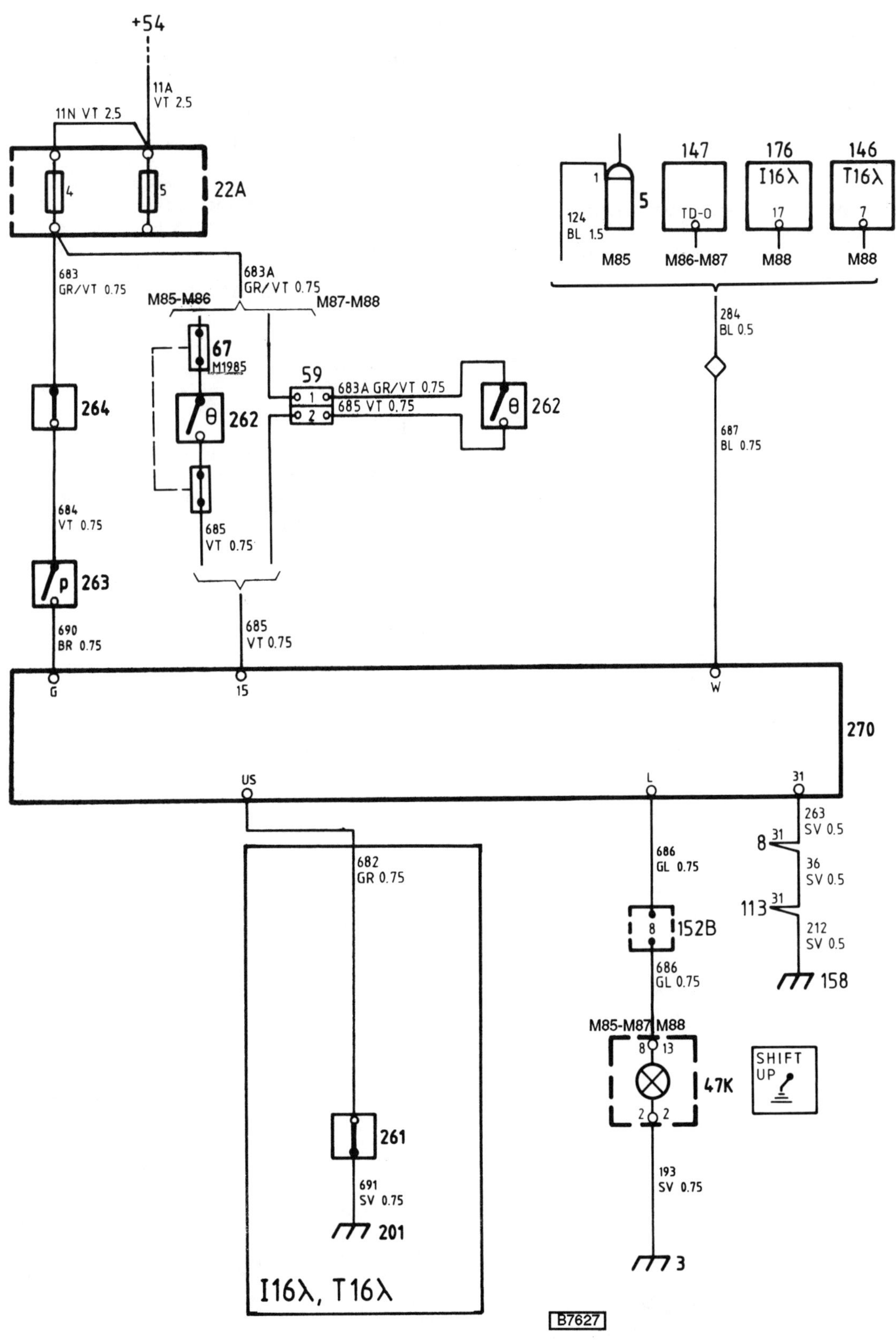

Starting System

Operation

For information on removing and repairing the starter see **331 Starter**. For more information on replacing and adjusting the neutral safety switch on automatics, see **444 Automatic Transmission Controls**.

WARNING
Batteries generate explosive gasses. Keep sparks and open flame away. Do not smoke.

CAUTION
- Do not disconnect the battery when the engine is running. The alternator could be destroyed.
- Always disconnect the negative (–) battery cable first when servicing the starter. Reconnect the negative (–) battery cable last.

Fault Tracing

1. Check for battery voltage at terminal 30 of the starter.
2. Check for battery voltage at terminal 50 of the starter when the key is in the start (crank) position. If no voltage is present, check the ignition switch and ignition relay.
3. Check for continuity between the engine block and battery negative (–) terminal.
4. On 1992 convertible models, check the start interlock relay 423 for the burglar alarm, located under the rear seat.

Component Locations

- 1 battery
- 4 starter motor under intake manifold
- 20 ignition switch at center console
- 75 distribution block at right wheel housing
- 77 neutral safety switch (automatics only) at gear selector lever
- 289 burglar alarm control unit (1992 and later Convertible) under rear seat
- 423 burglar alarm start interlock relay (1992 and later Convertible) under rear seat

Connector Locations

1985-1990

- 60 2-pin connector at main fuse/relay panel
- 152A 29-pin bulkhead connector behind main fuse/relay panel

1991 and later

- H1-18 1-pin connector under center console
- H2-53 2-pin connector under rear seat
- H29-1 29-pin bulkhead connector behind main fuse/relay panel (1991-1991 1/2)
- H33-1 33-pin bulkhead connector behind main fuse/relay panel (1991 1/2 and later)

Ground Locations

1985-1990

- 7 ground point at radiator cross member
- 211 ground point at gearbox

1991 and later

- G1 ground point at radiator cross member
- G25 ground point at gearbox

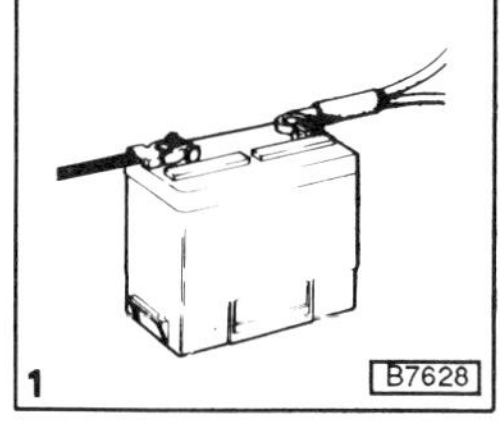

1

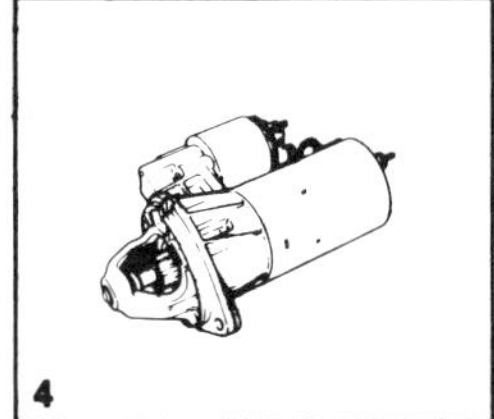
4

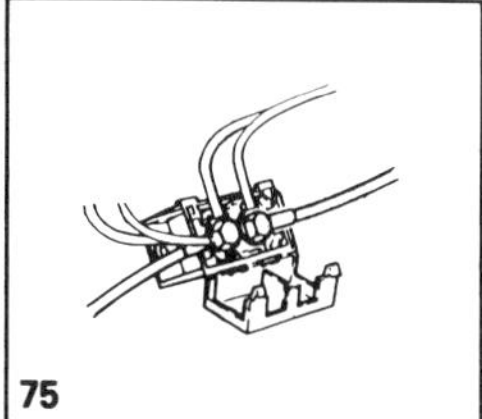
75

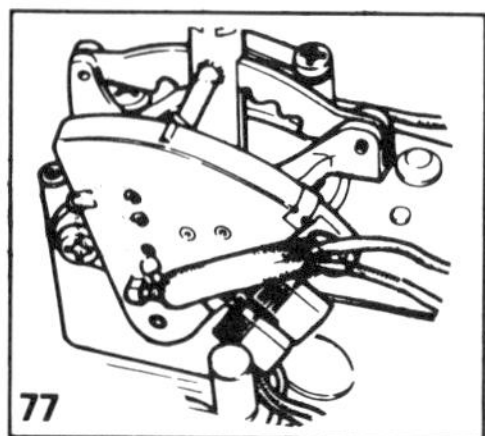
77

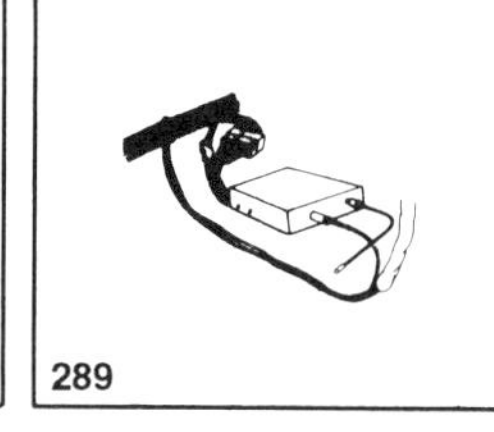
289

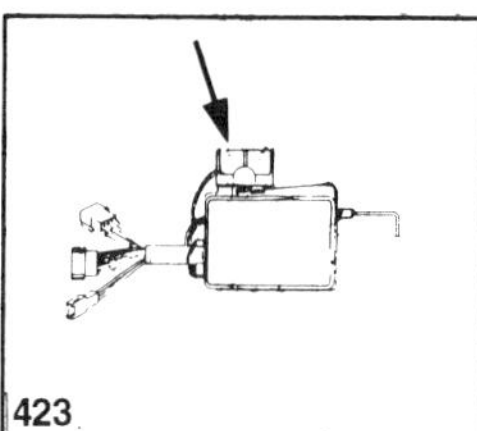
423

Starting System
1985-1990

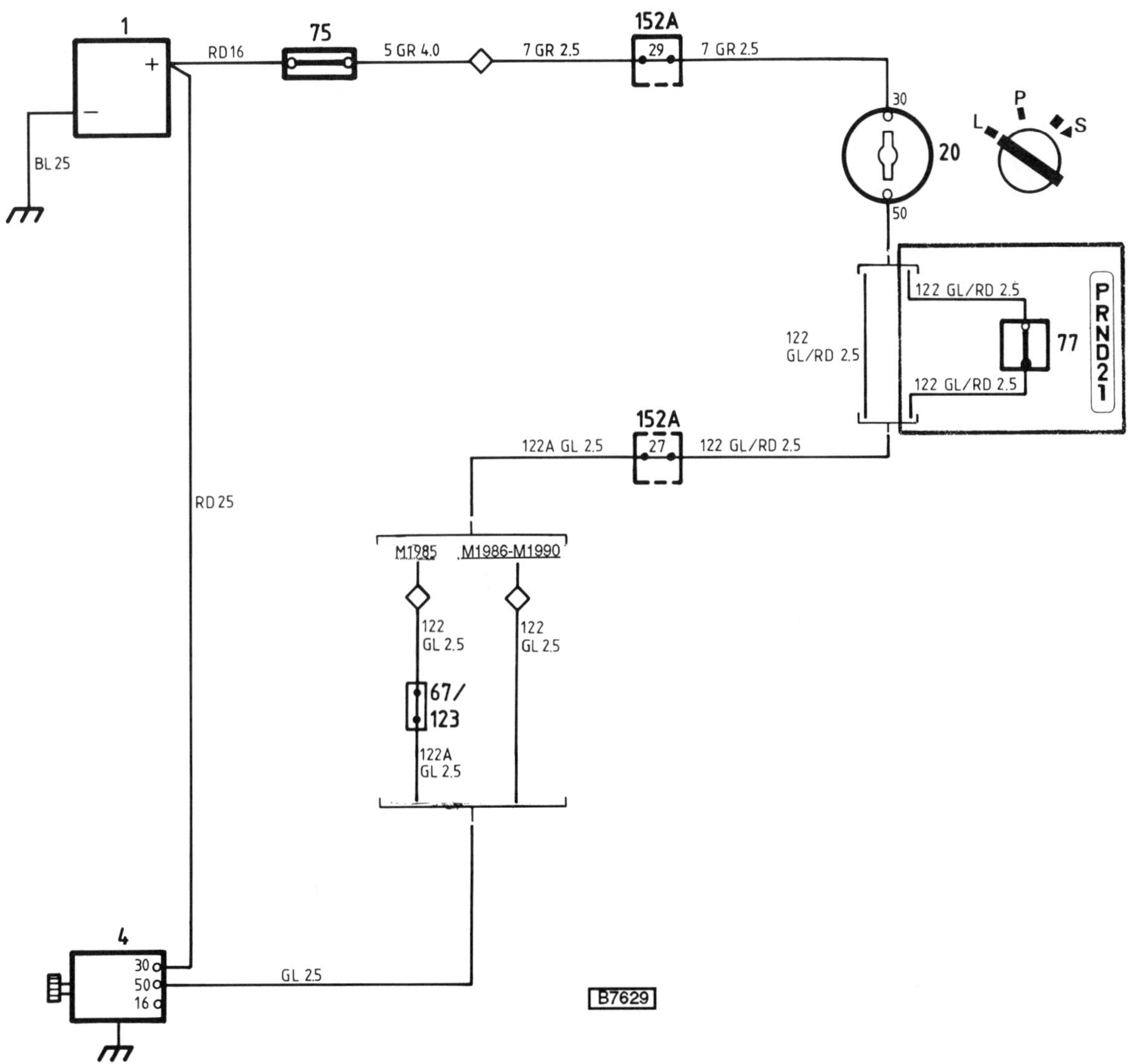

Starting System

1991 and later

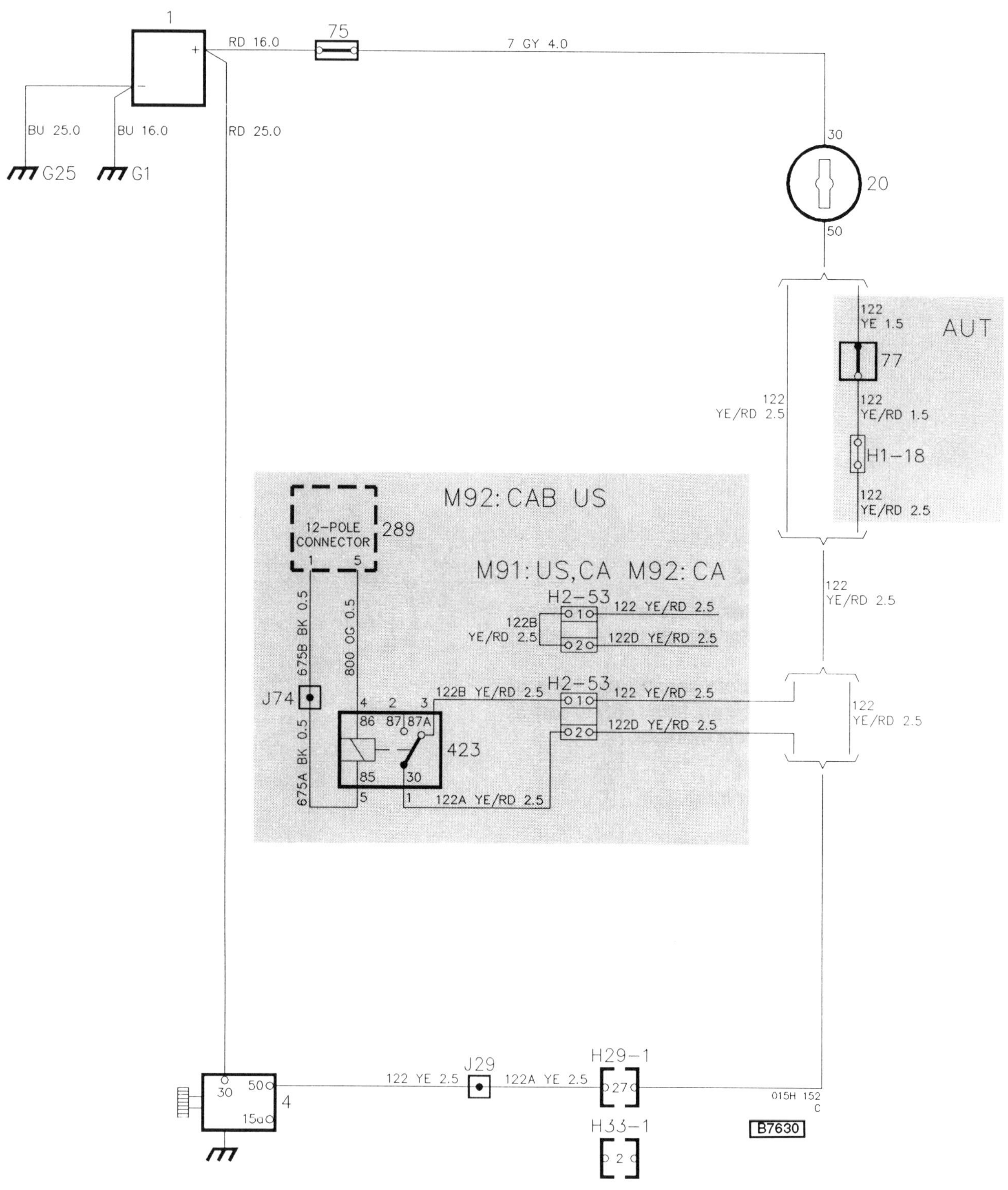

Supplemental Restraint System (SRS)—Airbag

Operation

The supplemental restraint system (SRS) consists of two front sensors, a control unit, a safety sensor, and the airbag with gas generator. If a fault should occur in the system, the SRS lamp in the instrument cluster will flash when the ignition switch is turned to the run position. Fault codes in the system's memory can be read by an authorized Saab dealer using special diagnostic equipment.

WARNING

- The airbag is an explosive device. Do not attempt to remove the steering wheel or service the wiring in the steering column assembly without first disarming the SRS system. You could accidentally ignite the airbag, causing serious personal injury. See an authorized Saab dealer for any repairs to the SRS system or to disarm the system.

- The components and wiring used in the system should not be altered or repaired as they are unique in design and construction. Additionally, do not connect ground wires from other systems to the mounting screws for the front sensors or the electronic unit since this may cause disturbances in the system, rendering it inoperative.

Fault Tracing

The following fault tracing should be used as a guide only. Comprehensive fault tracing should be carried out by an authorized Saab dealer who has the necessary diagnostic equipment and training.

1. Check the fuses.

Component Locations

1 battery at right front of engine compartment
20 ignition switch
21 ignition switch relay in main fuse/relay panel
22A main fuse/relay panel at left wheel housing
47E charging lamp in instrument cluster
47K shift up indicator lamp
47T SRS airbag warning lamp (see SRS warnings)
75 distribution block at right wheel housing
158 ground (–) distribution in main fuse/relay panel
331 SRS airbag control unit behind instrument panel, left grille. See SRS warning
332A SRS airbag left sensor at left wheel housing in engine compartment. See SRS warning.
332B SRS airbag right sensor at right wheel housing in engine compartment. See SRS warning.
333 SRS airbag in steering wheel. See SRS warning.
336 slip ring contact in steering wheel

Connector Locations

1990

98 10-pin connector behind instrument panel to left of steering column
98 10-pin connector next to SRS airbag electronic unit
123 4-pin connector at the SRS airbag electronic unit
123 4-pin connector at the left SRS airbag sensor
123 4-pin connector at the right SRS airbag sensor
152A 29-pin bulkhead connector at main fuse/relay panel
152B 29-pin bulkhead connector at main fuse/relay panel
330 SRS airbag 10-pin connector in center console under rubber bellows. See SRS warning
335 SRS airbag 2-pin orange connector below steering column. Pins are short circuited when connector is separated. See SRS warnings

1991 and later

H3-16 3-pin connector at the SRS airbag left front sensor
H3-17 3-pin connector at the SRS airbag right front sensor
H4-10 4-pin connector at the SRS airbag control unit
H4-10 4-pin connector at the SRS airbag at the control unit
H4-11 4-pin connector at the SRS airbag at the control unit
H10-1 10-pin connector behind instrument panel, left of steering column
H10-2 10-pin connector at the SRS airbag control unit, left speaker grille. See warning.
H12-1 12-pin connector behind instrument panel, left of steering column
H29-1 29-pin bulkhead connector behind main fuse/relay panel (1991-1991 1/2)
H29-2 29-pin bulkhead connector behind main fuse/relay panel (1991-1991 1/2)
H33-1 33-pin bulkhead connector behind main fuse/relay panel (1991 1/2 –on)
H33-2 33-pin bulkhead connector behind main fuse/relay panel (1991 1/2 –on)

Ground Locations

7 ground point at radiator cross member
211 ground point at gearbox
334 SRS airbag ground point for electronic unit adjacent to electronic unit. See SRS warning.
400 SRS airbag redundant ground point behind instrument panel, left side. See SRS warning.

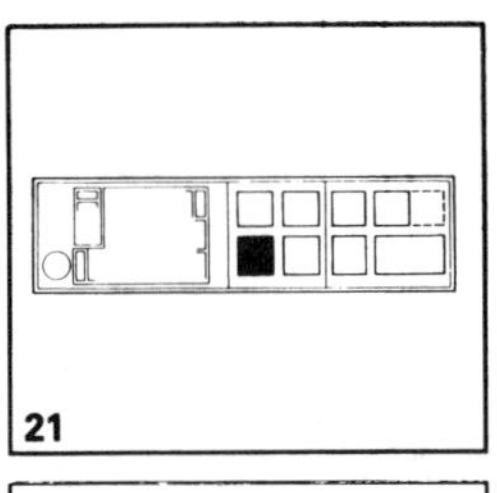
21

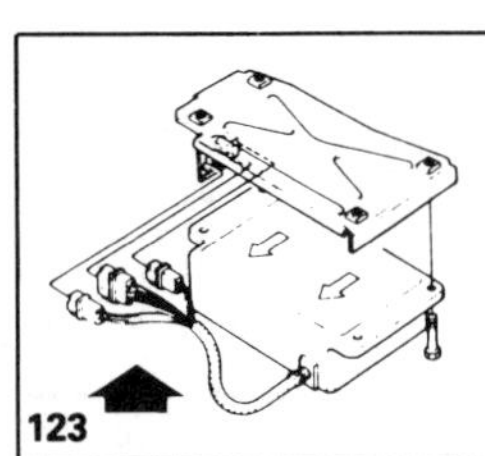
123

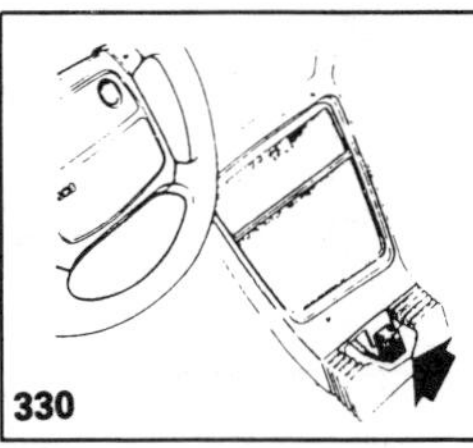
330

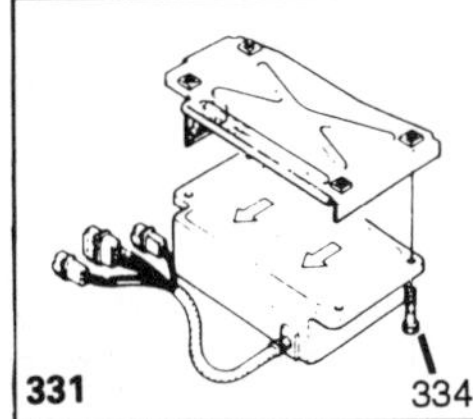

331

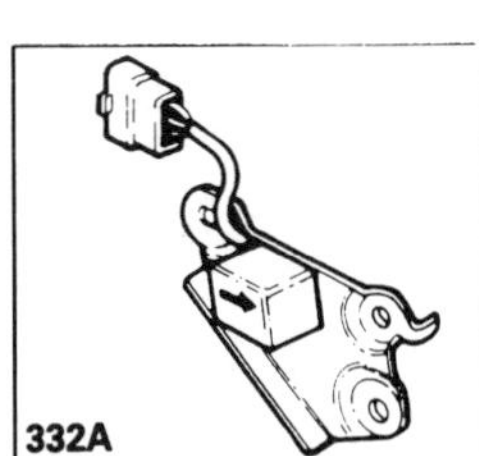
332A

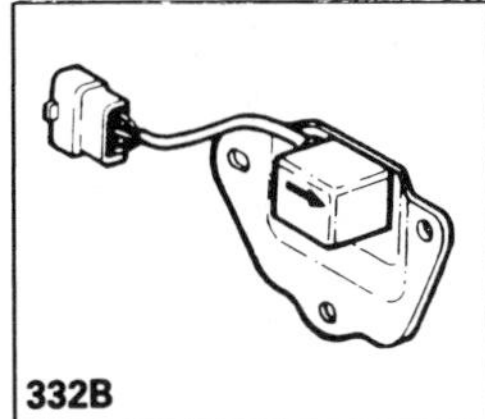
332B

333

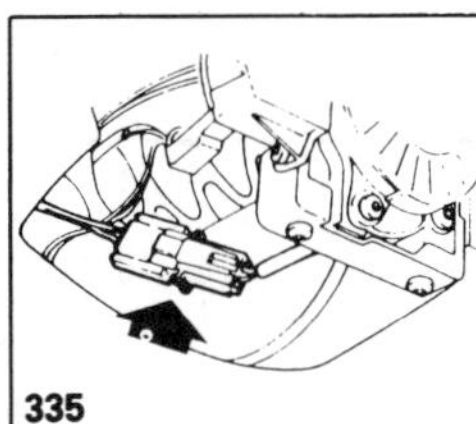
335

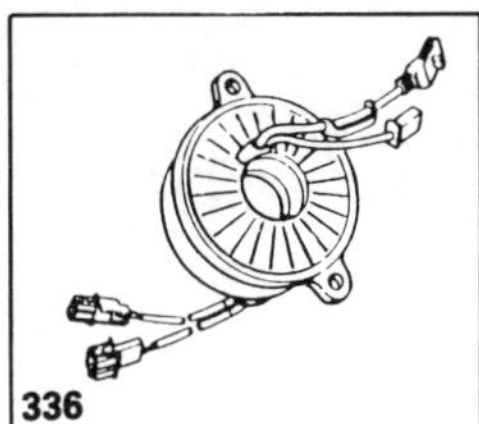
336

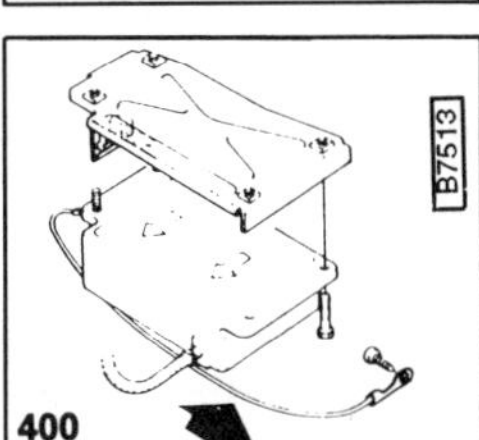

400

Supplemental Restraint System (SRS)—Airbag

1990

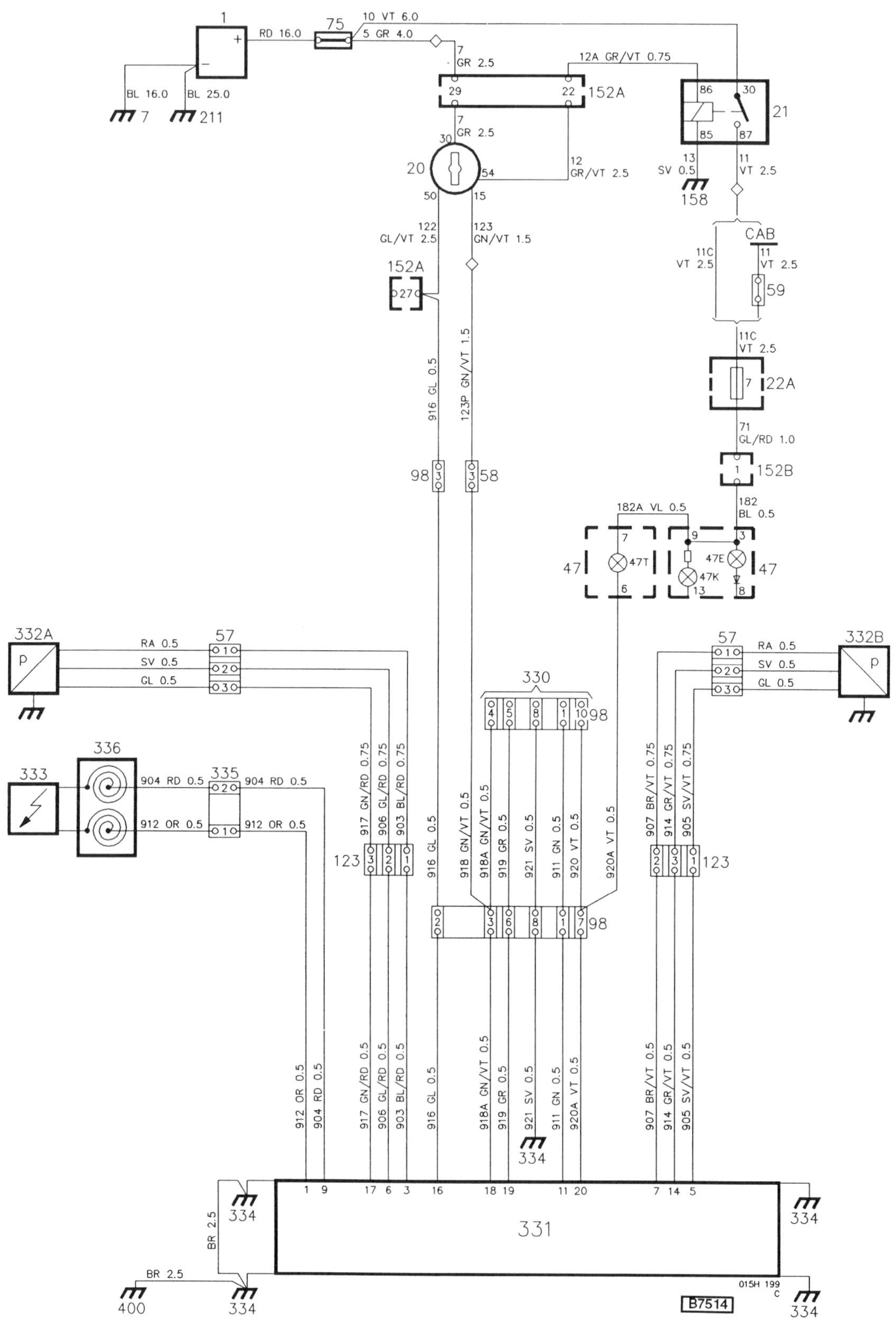

Supplemental Restraint System (SRS)—Airbag

1991 and later

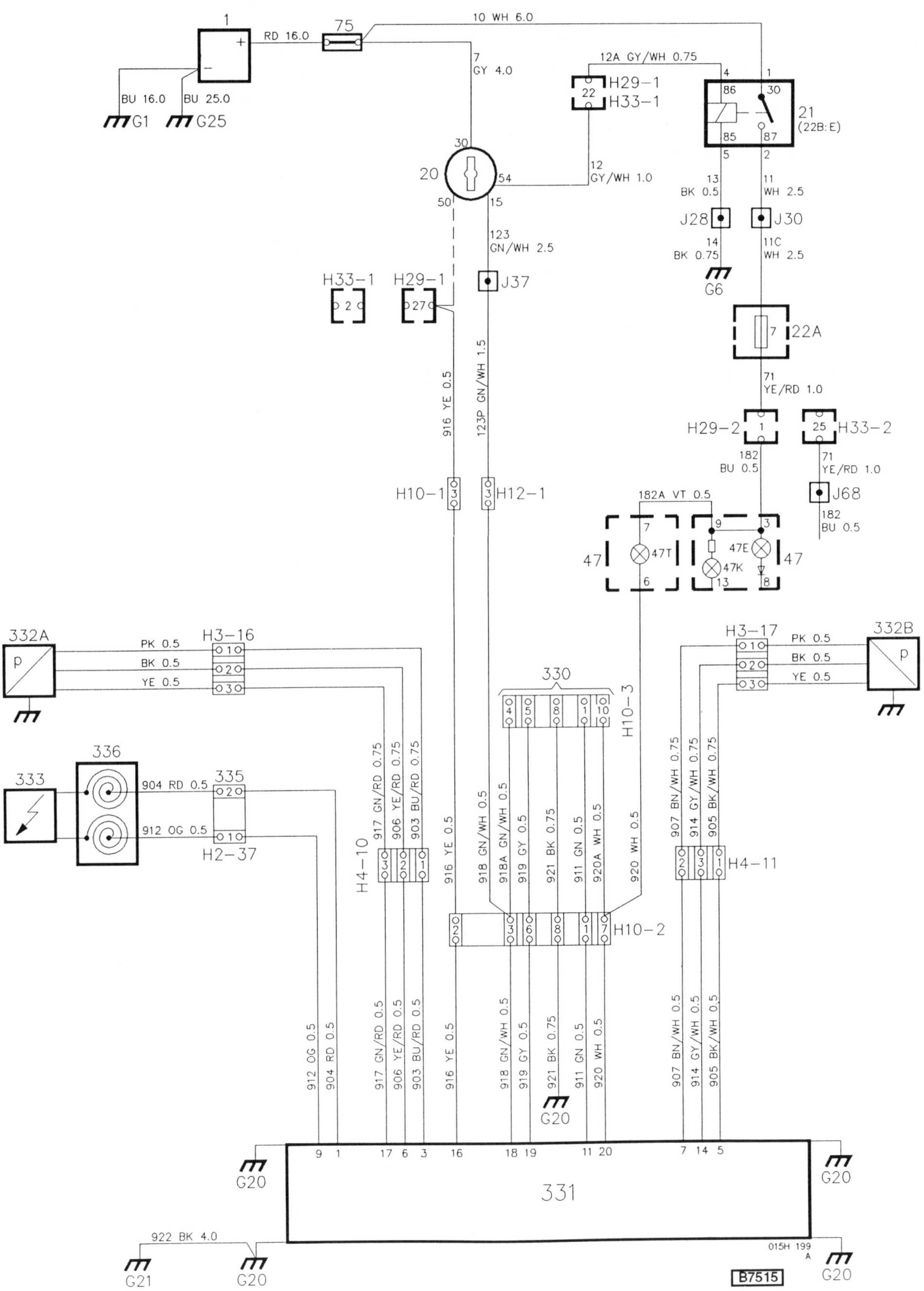

Ventilation Fan

Operation

The ventilation fan, located behind the instrument panel on the right side, is controlled by the fan and air distribution switches. Normally there are three fan speeds. If the air distribution switch (149) is switched to position 1, the fan switch (35) is overridden and the fan runs at high. The resistor pack provides various resistor values for different fan speeds. The resistor pack (74) is thermally protected internally and will blow the fuse if overheated.

For information on the related A/C systems, see the **Air Conditioner (A/C)** wiring diagram elsewhere in this section.

For information on repairing the heating and air conditioning system, see **854 Heating and Air Conditioning.**

Fault Tracing

1. Check the fuse. If the fuse blows repeatedly, check the resistor pack (74).

Component Locations

22A main fuse/relay panel at left wheel housing
35 ventilation fan switch in instrument panel
36 ventilation fan motor under right speaker grille
74 resistor pack for ventilation fan under left speaker grille
149 main switch for ventilation fan integrated in air distribution switch
150 air distribution switch in instrument panel

Connector Locations

1985-1990

152B 29-pin bulkhead connector at main fuse/relay panel

1991 and later

H29-2 29-pin bulkhead connector behind main fuse/relay panel (1991-1991 1/2)
H33-2 33-pin bulkhead connector behind main fuse/relay panel (1991 1/2 and later)

Ground Locations

1985-1990

3 ground point behind instrument panel

1991 and later

G8 ground point behind instrument panel

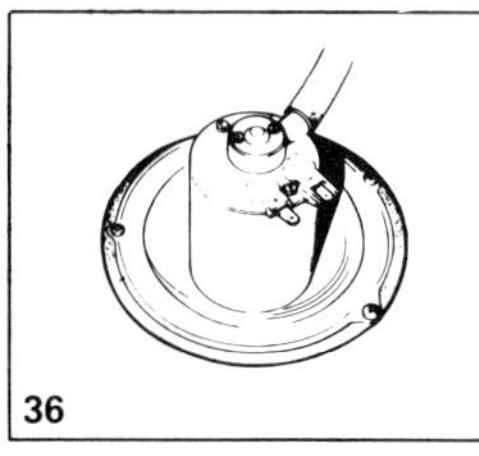

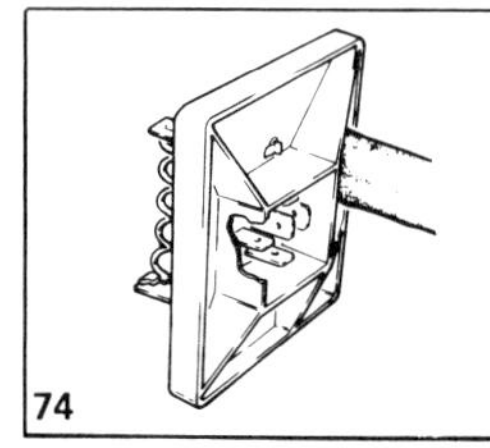

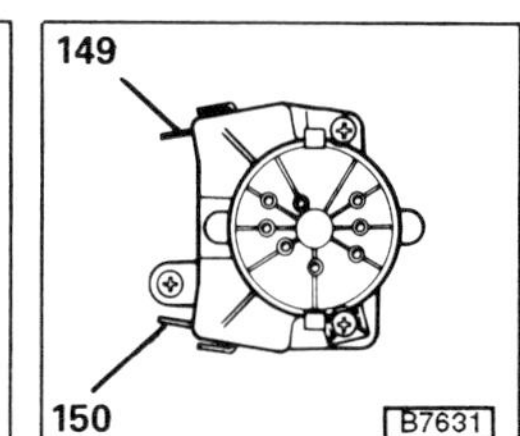

Ventilation Fan

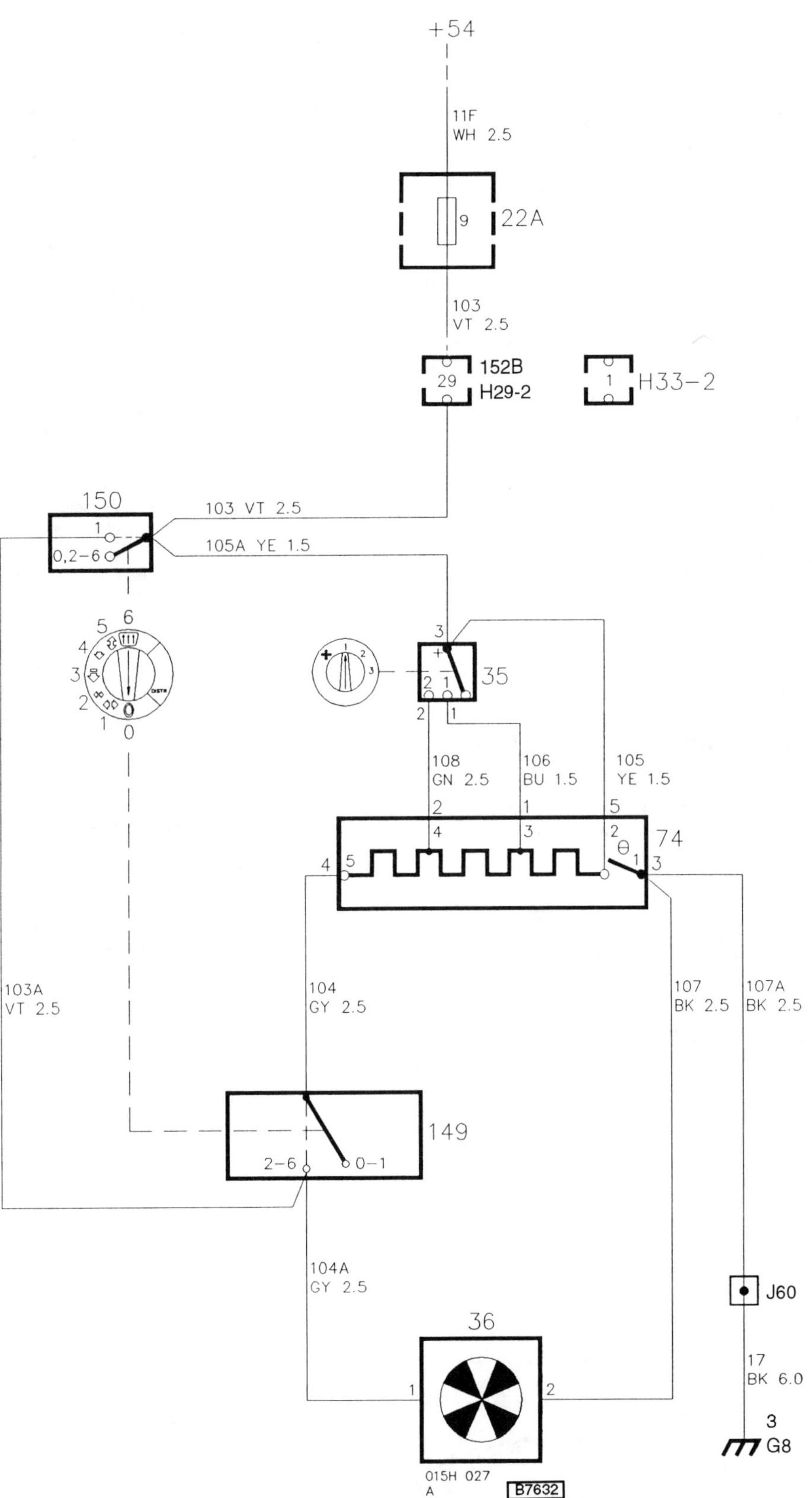

Wipers and Washers

Operation

The windshield wipers have three speeds controlled by the wiper stalk switch (61). The intermittent speed is controlled by the intermittent windshield wiper relay (83). The windshield wiper motor (62) has a park switch that interrupts voltage to correctly park the wiper blades at the base of the windshield after the stalk switch has been shut off.

The headlight wipers are controlled by the wiper stalk switch (61). When the wiper stalk switch is pulled toward the driver, the windshield washer pump (63) is energized and the wipers will run (via the intermittent relay 83) for 5 cycles. The headlight wiper motor (66), has a park switch that interrupts voltage to correctly park the wiper blades at the base of the headlight after the stalk switch has been released.

See **363 Wipers and Washers** for information on removing and installing the wiper motor mechanism, the headlight wipers, and the washer pump.

Fault Tracing

1. Check the fuses. Check for approximate battery voltage with the key in the run position using the table below.

Table a. Wiper and Washer Electrical Tests

Position	Switch terminal (pin)	Windshield wiper motor terminal (pin)	Intermittent relay terminal (pin)
0 off	53A (1)	53A (2)	15 (2)
I INT	53A (1) INT (5)	53A (2)	15 (2), I (8)
II slow	53A (1), 53 (2)	53A (2) 53 (5)	15 (2)
III fast	53A (1) 53B (4)	53A (2) 53B (4)	15 (2)
A* wash	53A (1) 54 (7), 31B (3), 53 (2)	53 (5)	T (5), 15 (2), 53M (1)

* check for voltage at the windshield washer pump (63), and headlight wiper motors

Component Locations

22A main fuse/relay panel
61 wiper stalk switch on steering column
62 windshield wiper motor at engine compartment firewall
63 windshield washer motor below fluid bottle in engine compartment
66 headlight wiper motor behind headlight assembly
83 intermittent windshield wiper relay to left of steering column, behind instrument panel
158 ground (–) distribution in main fuse/relay panel

Connector Locations

1985-1990

59 2-pin connector at the washer bottle
152B 29-pin bulkhead connector at main fuse/relay panel
152C 29-pin bulkhead connector at main fuse/relay panel

1991 and later

H3-1 3-pin connector at front of engine compartment, right wiper motor
H3-2 3-pin connector at front of engine compartment, left wiper motor
H29-2 29-pin bulkhead connector behind main fuse/relay panel (1991-1991 1/2)
H29-3 29-pin bulkhead connector behind main fuse/relay panel (1991-1991 1/2)
H33-2 33-pin bulkhead connector behind main fuse/relay panel (1991 1/2 and later)
H33-3 33-pin bulkhead connector behind main fuse/relay panel (1991 1/2 and later)

Ground Locations

1985-1990

3 ground point behind instrument panel
7 ground point at radiator cross member

1991 and later

G1 ground point at radiator cross member
G6 ground distribution in main fuse/relay panel
G8 ground point behind instrument panel

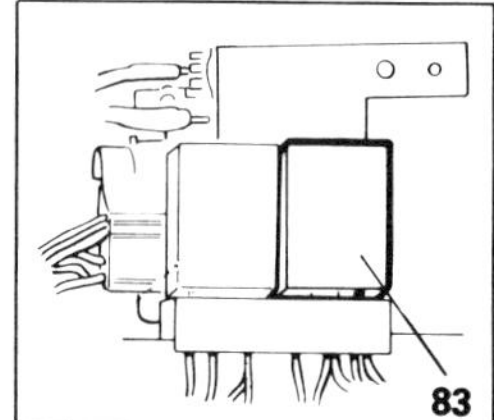

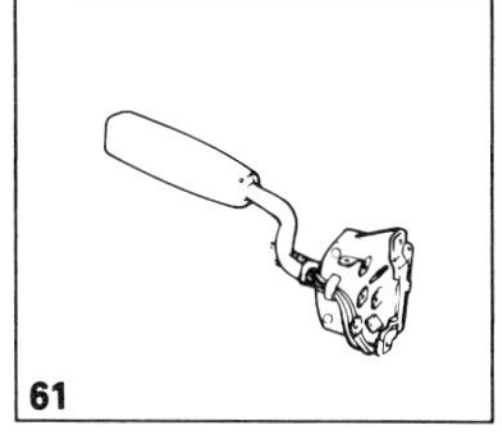

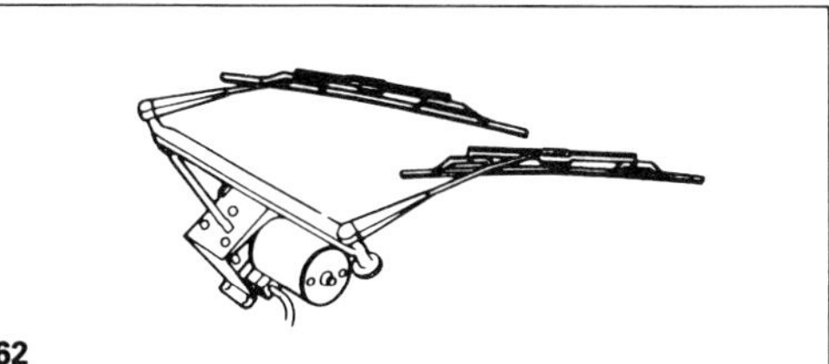

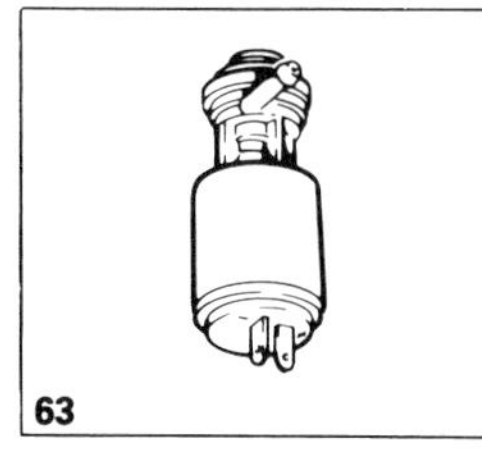

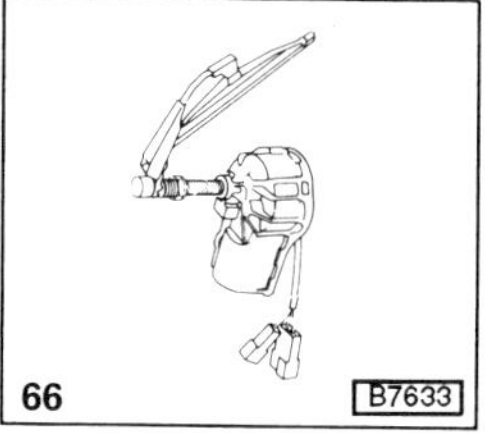

Wipers and Washers

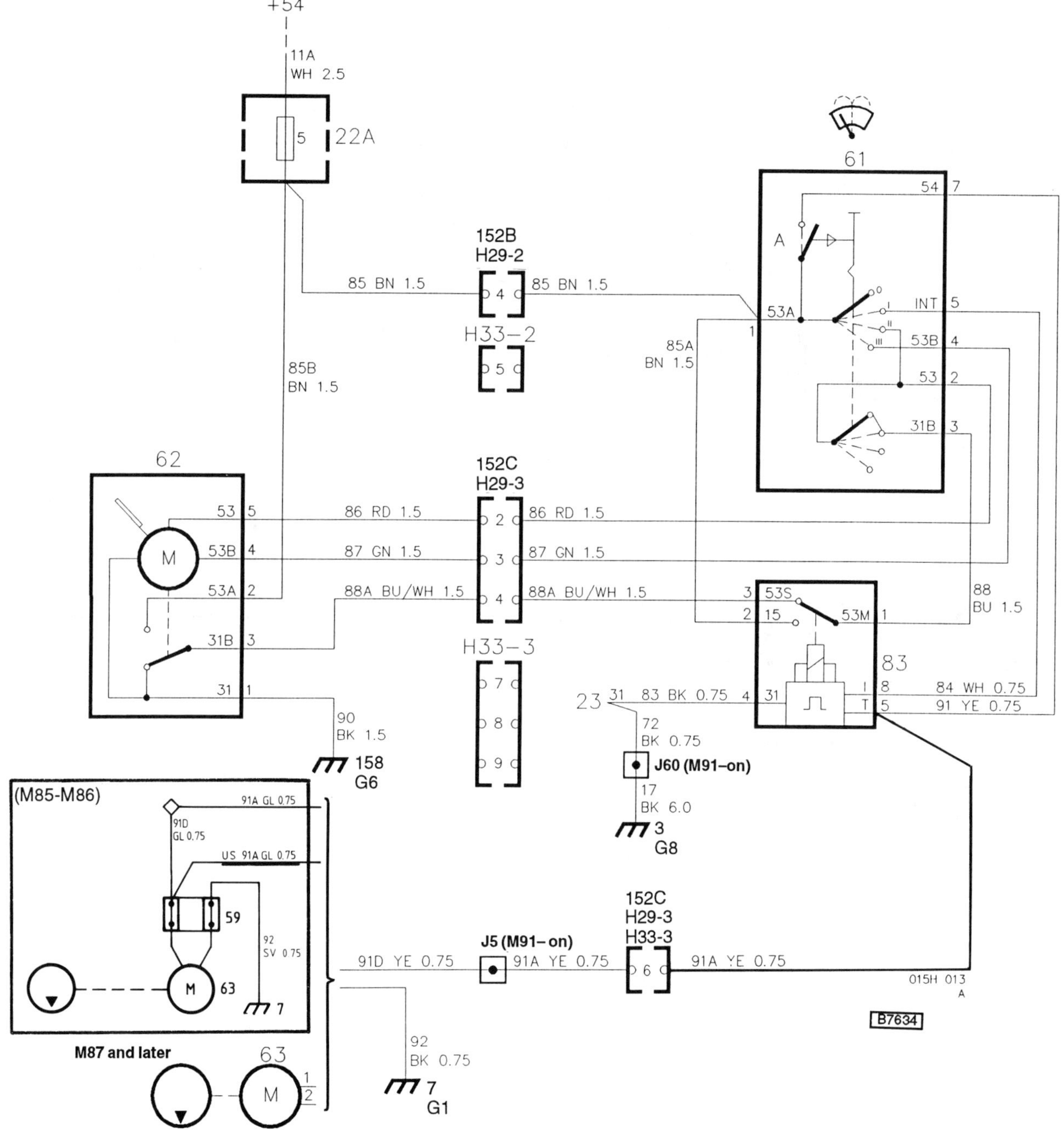

Headlight Wipers

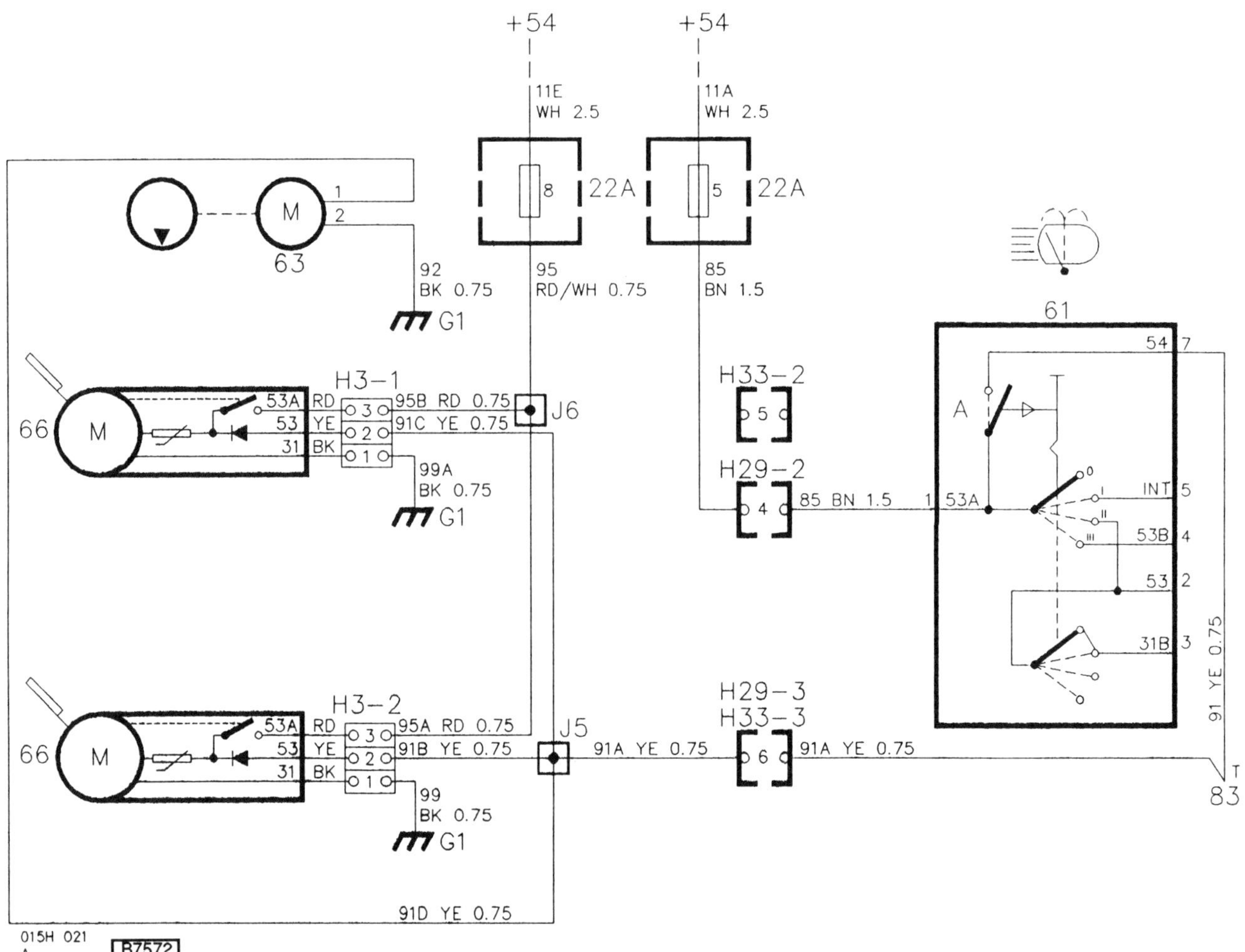

Component List—Numerical
(page 1 of 4)

1 battery—right front of engine compartment
2 alternator—back of engine compartment
3 ground point—behind instrument panel
4 starter motor—under intake manifold
5 ignition coil—on top of radiator
6 ignition distributor—end of cylinder head
7 ground point—radiator cross member
8 headlight relay—main fuse/relay panel
9 ground point—luggage compartment
10 lighting switch
11 high beam headlight
12 low beam headlight
13 parking lights
14 rear lights
15 license plate lights
16 rheostat for instrument cluster
17 rheostat for instrument panel lighting
18 instrument lighting
19 glove compartment light
20 ignition switch
21 ignition switch relay—main fuse/relay panel
21A ignition switch relay—in fuse/relay panel (401) under rear seat
22/22A main fuse/relay panel—left wheel housing
23 flasher relay—behind instrument panel, left side
24 direction indicator stalk switch
25 hazard warning switch
26 coolant fan time delay relay—front left wheel housing
27 left-hand direction indicator lamps
28 right hand direction indicator lamps
29 brake light switch—brake pedal cluster
30 brake lamps
31 backup light switch—gear selector housing
32 backup lights
33 rear fog lights
35 ventilation fan switch—instrument panel
36 ventilation fan motor—under right speaker grille
37 radiator cooling fan motor—behind radiator
38 recirculation valve—behind instrument panel, near right side A pillar
39 coolant fan temperature switch—upper left corner of radiator
40 horn—engine compartment
41 horn switch—in steering wheel
42 brake fluid level switch—brake fluid reservoir
43 handbrake switch—under handbrake
44 oil pressure switch—left side of engine, above oil filter
45 coolant temperature transmitter—front of cylinder head
46 fuel level transmitter—in fuel tank, accessible in luggage compartment
47 instrument cluster
47A fuel level gauge
47B fuel warning light
47C coolant temperature gauge
47D oil pressure warning light
47E charging lamp in instrument cluster
47F brake warning light
47G full—beam warning light
47H left-hand direction indicator warning lamp
47I right-hand direction indicator warning lamp
47J rear window heater warning lamp
47K shift-up indicator lamp
47M handbrake warning lamp
47N rear fog light warning lamp
47P CHECK ENGINE light
47Q ABS warning lamp
47S passive seat belt warning lamp
47T SRS airbag warning lamp (see warnings)
47U cruise control warning lamp
48 cigarette lighter
49 clock
50 roof lamp/switch—to left of driver
51 front roof lamp—center rear view mirror
52 ignition switch light—next to ignition switch, center console
53 interior light switch—center console
54 door switches—on door jamb
55 luggage compartment light—storage area
56 luggage compartment light switch—storage area
57 3-pin connector
58 12-pin connector
59 2-pin connector
60 1-pin connector
61 wiper stalk switch—steering column
62 windshield wiper motor—engine compartment firewall
63 windshield washer motor—below fluid bottle in engine compartment
64 heated seat pad with thermostat—in seat cushion and backrest
65 ground point—at handbrake
66 headlight wiper motor—behind headlight assembly
67 6-pin connector
68 horn relay—main fuse/relay panel
69 passenger seat belt switch—under seat cover
70 seat belt switch, driver side—between driver and passenger seat
71 seat belt switch, passenger side—between driver and passenger seat
72 seat belt warning light—center of instrument panel
73 TSI (test service instrument) socket—in main fuse/relay panel
74 resistor pack for ventilation fan—under left speaker grille
75 distribution block—right wheel housing
76 switch for raising idle speed (automatic transmission)—center console
77 neutral safety switch (automatics only)—gear selector lever
82 seat belt warning relay—under rear seat
83 intermittent windshield wiper relay—behind instrument panel, left side
85 fog lamps
88 switch for fog lamps
89 left fender direction indicator
90 right fender direction indicator
91 gear indicator light—at gear selector lever (automatics)
93 ground point—left wheel housing
94 starting injector—throttle housing
98 10-pin connector
101 supply fuel pump—in fuel tank
102 fuel pump relay—at LH control unit 200, forward of r.f. door
103 main fuel pump—in fuel tank
107 relay for extra lamps
109 third brake lamp (high mount brake light)
110 tachometer
113 time delay relay for heated rear window—under rear seat
115 rear window heater element
116 rear heated window switch
117 ground point—at handbrake
118 cornering lights—in front clusters
119 side backup lights in front light clusters
121 passenger seat switch for heated seats—under passenger seat
122 8-pin connector
123 4-pin connector
124 left power mirror switch—instrument panel
125 right power mirror switch—instrument panel
126 left power mirror motor—in left mirror
127 right power mirror motor—in right mirror
128 speed control relay—behind instrument panel, left side
131 control unit for cruise control—behind instrument panel, left side
132 speed transmitter—at rear of instrument cluster
133 clutch switch for cruise control—at clutch pedal
134 brake switch for cruise control—at brake pedal
136 lambda exhaust sensor—in exhaust manifold
141 selector for cruise control—direction indicator stalk
143 recirculation switch
144 boost pressure switch (turbo)
145 EZK test connector—next to main fuse/relay panel
146 ignition control unit (non-EZK ignition)
ignition amplifier (EZK ignition)—in front of left wheel housing

Component List—Numerical

(page 2 of 4)

147 ignition pulse amplifier—main fuse/relay panel, position D
148 ashtray lighting
149 over-ride switch for ventilation fan—integrated in air distribution switch
150 air distribution switch—instrument panel
151 interior lighting time delay relay—under rear seat
152A 29-pin bulkhead connector—main fuse/relay panel (white)
152B 29-pin bulkhead connector—main fuse/relay panel (red)
152C 29-pin bulkhead connector—main fuse/relay panel (black)
153 cigarette lighter lamp
154 heater control lighting
155 relay for A/C cooling fan—main fuse/relay panel
156 A/C compressor relay—main fuse/relay panel
157 sparkplug
158 negative (ground) distribution in main fuse/relay panel
159 +15 distribution in main fuse/relay panel
160 glovebox light switch—side of glovebox
161 rear fog light switch
162 switch for driver power window—center console
163 switch for passenger power window—center console
164 power window motor—left front door
165 power window motor—right front door
166 A/C pressure switch for cooling fan—on receiver/dryer unit
167 A/C throttle switch—throttle housing
168 A/C coolant temperature switch—radiator hose near distributor
169 A/C switch—instrument panel
170 A/C compressor—top of engine near firewall
171 A/C anti freeze-up thermostat—behind instrument panel, right side
172 A/C cooling fan—behind radiator
173 A/C compressor diode—engine wiring harness, rear of valve cover
174 relay for daytime driving lights
175 central locking control unit—behind instrument panel right side
176 EZK control unit—inner left fender
177 APC control unit–under back seat (1985), ahead of left wheel housing (1986 and later)
178 knock sensor—engine block, below intake manifold
179 APC boost pressure solenoid valve—above radiator fan on radiator
180 boost pressure sensor behind instrument panel to left of steering column
181 power sunroof or convertible switch
182 power sunroof motor—luggage compartment at spare tire compartment
183 key switch for driver's central door locking—driver door
184 central door lock motor—passenger door
185 central door lock motor—right rear door
186 central door lock motor—left rear door
187 cruise control vacuum pump—engine compartment left wheel housing
188 central door lock motor—tailgate lock
189 lockout switch for rear power windows
190 switch for left rear power window—center console
190a switch for left rear power window—left rear door
191 switch for right rear power window—center console
191a switch for right rear power window—right rear door
193 power window motor—left rear door
194 power window motor—right rear door
200 LH fuel injection control unit—forward of right front door, behind trim
201 LH ground point for fuel injection—engine lifting lug, 2 points
202 LH engine temperature transmitter—intake manifold flange, between cylinders 2 and 3
203 LH throttle angle transmitter—on throttle housing
204 LH test connector—engine compartment, behind right wheel housing
205 LH air mass meter—in throttle intake hose
206 fuel injectors—intake manifold
207 heated rear view mirrors—front doors
208D passive seat belt door switch—driver door
208P passive seat belt door switch—passenger door
211 ground point—gearbox
215 headlight dip switch
225 reading lights, convertible—back seat
229 LH fuel injection main relay—at LH control unit 200, behind A pillar trim at passenger door
233 cruise control vacuum switch—engine compartment left wheel housing
234 side marker lights in front light clusters
252 driver heated seat rheostat—instrument panel
254 driver seat temperature thermostat—in driver seat
257 ground point—alternator bracket
261 throttle contacts for shift-up indicator—throttle housing
262 temperature switch for shift-up indicator—between center intake ports of intake manifold
263 vacuum switch for shift-up indicator—left wheel housing
264 5 gear switch for shift-up indicator—front side cover of gearbox
265 electric radio antenna—left rear body panel
266 radio speakers—(4) two in front, two in rear
267 radio connector—instrument panel
270 shift-up indicator relay—main fuse/relay panel
271 lambda preheater (integral with lambda sensor)
272 AIC valve (LH idle speed motor)—front left side of cylinder head
273 motor for convertible hydraulic pump—under rear seat, right side
274 fuse for burglar alarm under rear seat
275 burglar alarm siren—engine compartment near right headlamp
276 burglar alarm hood switch—under hood at front of wheel housing
277 relay for raising convertible top (1987-1988)—under rear seat on bulkhead
277 relay for raising convertible top (1989 and later)—under rear seat in fuse/relay panel 401
278 relay for lowering convertible top (1987-1988)—under rear seat on bulkhead
278 relay for lowering convertible top (1989 and later)—under rear seat in fuse/relay panel 401
279 mercury switch for convertible heated rear window—left side top mounting
283 diodes for convertible top (1987-1988)—under rear seat in wiring harness
285 fuse for lambda sensor—engine compartment, next to fresh air intake
287 power window relay for automatic control—under rear seat
288 burglar alarm switch—center console
289 burglar alarm control unit—under rear seat
290A fuse for convertible top—engine compartment, next to distribution block 75
290B fuse for convertible top—engine compartment, next to distribution block 75
291 ABS control unit (1989)—engine compartment, left wheel housing
291 ABS control unit (1990 and later)—under rear seat, right side
292 ABS system relay (1989)—ABS distribution box, engine compartment, left wheel housing
292 ABS system relay (1990 and later)—ABS distribution box, behind right wheel housing
293 ABS pump relay (1989)—ABS distribution box, left wheel housing
293 ABS pump relay (1990 and later)—ABS distribution box, behind right wheel housing
294 ABS pressure switch—on 302 ABS electrical distribution box (1990 and later)—engine compartment, behind right wheel housing
295 ABS master valve—on hydraulic unit, engine compartment
296 ABS valve block—forward of left wheel housing
297 ABS hydraulic pump motor—engine compartment at hydraulic unit
298A ABS wheel sensor—left front wheel
298B ABS wheel sensor—right front wheel
298C ABS wheel sensor—left rear wheel
298D ABS wheel sensor—right rear wheel
299 ABS brake fluid level sensor—brake fluid reservoir
300 ABS ground point—at front of hydraulic unit, engine compartment
302 ABS electrical distribution box (1989)—engine compartment, forward of left wheel housing
302 ABS electrical distribution box (1990 and later)—engine compartment, behind right wheel housing

Component List—Numerical
(page 3 of 4)

302A ABS fuse holder (1989)—engine compartment, forward of left wheel housing
302A ABS fuse holder (1990 and later)—engine compartment, behind right wheel housing
303B ABS diode (1989)—engine compartment, forward of left wheel housing
303B ABS diode (1990 and later)—engine compartment, behind right wheel housing
304 burglar alarm motion detector—under rear seat
305 burglar alarm LED—left speaker grille
306 logic box for passive seat belts—under rear seat, left side
307D passive seat belt belt reel—driver seat
307P passive seat belt belt reel—passenger seat
308D passive seat belt motor with limit switches—driver seat
308P passive seat belt motor with limit switches—passenger seat
309 passive seat belt g sensor—under rear seat, left side
310D passive seat belt fuse for driver seat—under rear seat
310P passive seat belt fuse for passenger seat—under rear seat
311D passive seat belt motor relay for driver seat—under rear seat
311P passive seat belt motor relay for passenger seat—under rear seat
312D passive seat belt motor relay for driver seat—under rear seat
312P passive seat belt motor relay for passenger seat—under rear seat
313 burglar alarm relay—under rear seat
314 burglar alarm seat switch—driver seat
315 burglar alarm seat switch—passenger seat
316 burglar alarm diode—under rear seat in wiring harness
320 ignition coil with integrated amplifier—inner right fender, near battery
321 charcoal canister valve (ELCD)—engine compartment ahead of left wheel housing
322 LH coding connector—at LH control unit 200, forward of r.f. door
323 fuel pump—in fuel tank
330 SRS airbag 10-pin connector—center console under rubber bellows. See SRS warning.
331 SRS airbag control unit—behind instrument panel, left grille. See SRS warning.
332A SRS airbag left sensor—left wheel housing in engine compartment. See SRS warning.
332B SRS airbag right sensor—right wheel housing in engine compartment. See SRS warning.
333 SRS airbag—in steering wheel. See SRS warning.
334 SRS airbag ground point for electronic unit—adjacent to electronic unit. See SRS warning.
335 SRS airbag 2-pin orange connector—pins are short circuited when connector is separated. See SRS warning.
336 SRS airbag slip ring contact—in steering wheel. See SRS warning.
345 EZK crankshaft sensor—behind crankshaft pulley
347 LH diagnostic test connector—under rear seat, right side
349 radio contact box with amplifier—instrument panel
350 contact box for CD player or equalizer—center console top compartment
351 audio amplifier—under rear seat below ABS control unit (291)
352 slip ring switch—in steering wheel
386 switch assembly for power windows and sunroof—center console
389 LH NTC resistor—under intake manifold
390 LH EGR modulating valve—ahead of left wheel housing
396 radiator fan relay—main fuse/relay panel
397 ABS diagnostic test socket—near hydraulic unit in engine compartment, wiring harness
400 SRS airbag redundant ground point—behind instrument panel, left side. See SRS warning.
401 auxiliary fuse/relay panel—under rear seat
412 burglar alarm service mode switch—under passenger seat
413 burglar alarm glass breakage detector—under passenger seat
423 burglar alarm start interlock relay (convertible)—under rear seat
424 burglar alarm hazard warning light relay (convertible)—under rear seat at control unit
425 door lock switch—center console
426 switch for rear seat—under rear seat

G1 ground point—radiator cross member
G3 ground point—luggage compartment
G4 ground point—between ignition switch and handbrake
G5 ground point—under rear seat
G6 ground distribution—main fuse/relay panel
G7 ground point—engine lifting lug
G8 ground point—behind instrument panel
G9 ground point—luggage compartment
G12 ground point—left wheel housing
G16 ground point—front of ABS hydraulic unit
G19 ground point—hatchback
G20 ground point—SRS airbag ground at electronic unit. See SRS warning.
G21 ground point—SRS airbag redundant ground. See SRS warning.
G25 ground point—gearbox
G26 ground point—right C pillar on sedans
G27 ground point—electric antenna
G32 ground point—alternator bracket
H1-1 1-pin connector—engine compartment, upper left door hinge
H1-2 1-pin connector—next to bulkhead connectors, left side behind instrument panel
H1-3 1-pin connector—engine compartment, upper right door hinge
H1-5 1-pin connector—behind instrument panel to left of steering column
H1-6 1-pin connector—right B pillar, behind trim
H1-7 1-pin connector—left B pillar, behind trim
H1-8 1-pin connector—behind instrument panel to left of steering column
H1-9 1-pin connector—near lambda sensor, right wheel housing
H1-10 1-pin connector—near A/C compressor in engine compartment
H1-12 1-pin connector—engine compartment, right side near air intake
H1-14 1-pin connector—in left front door
H1-15 1-pin connector—in right front door
H1-16 1-pin connector—under center console next to shift selector (automatic)
H1-17 1-pin connector—under center console
H1-18 1-pin connector—under center console
H1-19 1-pin connector—near LH control unit, behind right A pillar trim
H1-21 1-pin connector—for LED, under left speaker grille
H1-22 1-pin connector—for LED, under left speaker grille
H1-27 1-pin connector—engine compartment, next to distribution block 75
H1-28 1-pin connector—under rear seat
H2-1 2-pin connector—at radiator fan motor
H2-2 2-pin connector—next to A/C cooling fan (172)
H2-3 2-pin connector—behind instrument cluster
H2-4 2-pin connector—engine compartment near right door hinge
H2-5 2-pin connector—engine compartment near top left door hinge
H2-6 2-pin connector—behind instrument cluster, left of steering column
H2-7 2-pin connector—instrument panel at light switch
H2-8 2-pin connector—engine compartment near right door hinge
H2-10 2-pin connector—behind cigarette lighter
H2-11 2-pin connector—engine compartment, near top right door hinge
H2-12 2-pin connector—under rear seat, left side
H2-13 2-pin connector—at fuel pump in storage area
H2-14 2-pin connector—left rear wheel housing in luggage compartment
H2-17 2-pin connector—hatchback, left side or sedan, under parcel shelf
H2-18 2-pin connector—hatchback, left side
H2-19 2-pin connector—trunk lid
H2-20 2-pin connector—luggage compartment, left wheel housing
H2-21 2-pin connector—luggage compartment, left wheel housing
H2-22 2-pin connector—engine compartment near ABS hydraulic unit
H2-23 2-pin connector—engine compartment right side partition
H2-24 2-pin connector—under rear seat, left side
H2-25 2-pin connector—under rear seat, right side
H2-27 2-pin connector—main fuse/relay panel
H2-30 2-pin connector—left rear door
H2-31 2-pin connector—right rear door
H2-32 2-pin connector—luggage compartment near central lock motor
H2-33 2-pin connector—near lambda sensor in engine compartment
H2-34 2-pin connector—left wheel housing
H2-35 2-pin connector—above roof lining at rear view mirror

Component List—Numerical
(page 4 of 4)

H2-40 2-pin connector—for burglar alarm siren, behind headlamp
H2-41 2-pin connector—under passenger seat, right side
H2-42 2-pin connector—trunk lid
H2-43 2-pin connector—left hinge, convertible
H2-46 2-pin connector—left reading lamp, convertible
H2-47 2-pin connector—right reading lamp, convertible
H2-48 2-pin connector—at convertible top motor
H2-51 2-pin connector—left rear speaker
H2-52 2-pin connector—right rear speaker
H2-53 2-pin connector—under rear seat
H3-1 3-pin connector—front of engine compartment, right wiper motor
H3-2 3-pin connector—front of engine compartment, left wiper motor
H3-3 3-pin connector—left of starter motor
H3-4 3-pin connector—main fuse/relay panel
H3-5 3-pin connector—engine compartment, left of air intake
H3-7 3-pin connector—engine compartment near left door hinge
H3-10 3-pin connector—right B pillar, behind trim
H3-11 3-pin connector—left B pillar, behind trim
H3-13 3-pin connector—luggage compartment, left air outlet
H3-14 3-pin connector—near LH control unit, behind right A pillar trim
H3-15 3-pin connector—in driver door
H3-16 3-pin connector—SRS airbag left front sensor
H3-17 3-pin connector—SRS airbag right front sensor
H3-18 3-pin connector—under passenger seat
H4-1 4-pin connector—left wheel housing
H4-1 4-pin connector—instrument panel right side behind trim
H4-2 4-pin connector—engine compartment, near top left door hinge
H4-3 4-pin connector—engine compartment, near top right door hinge
H4-4 4-pin connector—right B pillar behind trim
H4-5 4-pin connector—left B pillar behind trim
H4-6 4-pin connector—instrument panel left side
H4-7 4-pin connector—at LH control unit, forward of right front door
H4-8 4-pin connector—in left front door
H4-9 4-pin connector—in right front door
H4-10 4-pin connector—SRS airbag at control unit
H4-11 4-pin connector—SRS airbag at control unit
H4-12 4-pin connector—trunk lid, left air outlet
H4-15 4-pin connector—under rear seat, next to fuse/relay panel 401
H4-16 4-pin connector—behind instrument panel to left of steering column
H6-1 6-pin connector—engine compartment right wheel housing
H6-2 6-pin connector—engine compartment right wheel housing
H6-4 6-pin connector—behind instrument panel
H8-1 8-pin connector—under passenger seat
H8-2 8-pin connector—under driver seat
H8-3 8-pin connector—under rear seat
H8-7 8-pin connector—behind instrument panel
H8-8 8-pin connector—behind instrument panel
H10-1 10-pin connector—behind instrument panel, left of steering column
H10-2 10-pin connector—at SRS airbag control unit, left speaker grille
H10-5 10-pin connector—behind instrument panel
H10-6 10-pin connector—at auxiliary fuse/relay panel under rear seat
H10-8 10-pin connector—under rear seat at burglar alarm control unit
H12-1 12-pin connector—behind instrument panel, left of steering column
H12-3 12-pin connector—behind instrument panel
H12-4 12-pin connector—behind instrument panel
H29-1 29-pin bulkhead connector—behind main fuse/relay panel
H29-2 29-pin bulkhead connector—behind main fuse/relay panel
H29-3 29-pin bulkhead connector—behind main fuse/relay panel
H33-1 33-pin bulkhead connector—behind main fuse/relay panel
H33-2 33-pin bulkhead connector—behind main fuse/relay panel
H33-3 33-pin bulkhead connector—behind main fuse/relay panel

Component List—Alphabetical

(page 1 of 4)

Component	No.
5th gear switch for shift-up indicator—front side cover of gearbox	264
+15 distribution terminal—main fuse/relay panel, engine compartment	159
ABS brake fluid level sensor—brake fluid reservoir	299
ABS control unit (1989)—engine compartment, left wheel housing	291
ABS control unit (1990 and later)—under rear seat, right side	291
ABS diagnostic test socket—near hydraulic unit in engine compartment, wiring harness	397
ABS diode (1989)—engine compartment, forward of left wheel housing	303B
ABS diode (1990 and later)—engine compartment, behind right wheel housing	303B
ABS electrical distribution box (1989)—engine compartment, forward of left wheel housing	302
ABS electrical distribution box (1990 and later)—engine compartment, behind right wheel housing	302
ABS fuse holder (1989)—engine compartment, forward of left wheel housing	302A
ABS fuse holder (1990 and later)—engine compartment, behind right wheel housing	302A
ABS ground point—at front of hydraulic unit, engine compartment	300
ABS hydraulic pump motor—engine compartment at hydraulic unit	297
ABS master valve—on hydraulic unit, engine compartment	295
ABS pressure switch—on ABS hydraulic unit	294
ABS pump relay (1989)—ABS distribution box, left wheel housing	293
ABS pump relay (1990 and later)—ABS distribution box, behind right wheel housing	293
ABS system relay (1989)—ABS distribution box, engine compartment, left wheel housing	292
ABS system relay (1990 and later)—ABS distribution box, behind right wheel housing	292
ABS valve block—forward of left wheel housing	296
ABS warning lamp	47Q
ABS wheel sensor—front wheel, left	298A
ABS wheel sensor—front wheel, right	298B
ABS wheel sensor—rear wheel, left	298C
ABS wheel sensor—rear wheel, right	298D
A/C anti freeze-up thermostat—instrument panel, right side	171
A/C compressor—top of engine near firewall	170
A/C compressor diode—engine wiring harness, rear of valve cover	173
A/C compressor relay—main fuse/relay panel, engine compartment	156
A/C coolant temperature switch—radiator hose near distributor	168
A/C cooling fan—behind radiator	172
A/C pressure switch for cooling fan—on receiver/dryer unit	166
A/C switch—instrument panel	169
A/C throttle switch—throttle housing	167
AIC valve (LH idle speed motor)—front left side of cylinder head	272
air distribution switch—instrument panel	150
alternator—back of engine compartment	2
APC boost pressure solenoid valve—above radiator fan on radiator	179
APC control unit—under back seat (1985), ahead of left wheel housing (1986 and later)	177
ashtray lighting	148
audio amplifier—under rear seat below ABS control unit (291)	351
auxiliary fuse/relay panel—under rear seat	401
backup light switch—gear selector housing	31
battery—right front of engine compartment	1
battery—right front of engine compartment	1
boost pressure sensor—behind instrument panel to left of steering column	180
boost pressure switch (turbo)	144
brake fluid level switch—brake fluid reservoir	42
brake lamps	30
brake light switch—brake pedal cluster	29
brake switch for cruise control—at brake pedal	134
brake warning light	47F
burglar alarm control unit—under rear seat	289
burglar alarm diode—under rear seat in wiring harness	316
burglar alarm glass breakage detector—under passenger seat	413
burglar alarm hazard warning light relay (convertible)—under rear seat at control unit	424
burglar alarm hood switch—under hood at front of wheel housing	276
burglar alarm LED—left speaker grille	305
burglar alarm motion detector—under rear seat	304
burglar alarm relay—under rear seat	313
burglar alarm seat switch—driver seat	314
burglar alarm seat switch—passenger seat	315
burglar alarm service mode switch—under passenger seat	412
burglar alarm siren—engine compartment near right headlamp	275
burglar alarm start interlock relay (convertible)—under rear seat	423
burglar alarm switch—center console rear seat at control unit	288
central door lock motor—left rear door	186
central door lock motor—passenger door	184
central door lock motor—right rear door	185
central door lock motor—tailgate lock	188
central locking control unit—behind instrument panel right side	175
charcoal canister valve(ELCD)—engine compartment ahead of left wheel housing	321
charging lamp—in instrument cluster	47E
CHECK ENGINE light	47P
cigarette lighter	48
cigarette lighter lamp	153
clock	49
clutch switch for cruise control—at clutch pedal	133
coding connector—at LH control unit 200, behind A pillar trim	322
combined instruments	47
connector, 1-pin	60
connector, 2-pin	59
connector, 3-pin	57
connector, 4-pin	123
connector, 6-pin	67
connector, 8-pin for burglar alarm—under rear seat	122
connector, 10-pin	98
connector, 12-pin	58
connector, 29-pin—main fuse/relay panel	152A
connector, 29-pin—main fuse/relay panel	152B
connector, 29-pin—main fuse/relay panel	152C
connector, 1-pin—engine compartment, upper left door hinge	H1-1
connector, 1-pin—next to bulkhead connectors, left side behind instrument panel	H1-2
connector, 1-pin—engine compartment, upper right door hinge	H1-3
connector, 1-pin—behind instrument panel to left of steering column	H1-5
connector, 1-pin—right B pillar, behind trim	H1-6
connector, 1-pin—left B pillar, behind trim	H1-7
connector, 1-pin—behind instrument panel to left of steering column	H1-8
connector, 1-pin—near lambda sensor, right wheel housing	H1-9
connector, 1-pin—near A/C compressor in engine compartment	H1-10
connector, 1-pin—engine compartment, right side near air intake	H1-12
connector, 1-pin—in left front door	H1-14
connector, 1-pin—in right front door	H1-15
connector, 1-pin—under center console next to shift selector (automatic)	H1-16
connector, 1-pin—under center console	H1-17
connector, 1-pin—under center console	H1-18
connector, 1-pin—near LH control unit, behind right A pillar trim	H1-19
connector, 1-pin—for LED, under left speaker grille	H1-21
connector, 1-pin—for LED, under left speaker grille	H1-22
connector, 1-pin—engine compartment, next to distribution block 75	H1-27
connector, 1-pin—under rear seat	H1-28
connector, 2-pin—at radiator fan motor	H2-1
connector, 2-pin—next to A/C cooling fan (172)	H2-2
connector, 2-pin—behind instrument cluster	H2-3
connector, 2-pin—engine compartment near right door hinge	H2-4
connector, 2-pin—engine compartment near top left door hinge	H2-5
connector, 2-pin—behind instrument cluster, left of steering column	H2-6
connector, 2-pin—instrument panel at light switch	H2-7

Component List—Alphabetical

(page 2 of 4)

Component	Location
connector, 2-pin—engine compartment near right door hinge	H2-8
connector, 2-pin—behind cigarette lighter	H2-10
connector, 2-pin—engine compartment, near top right door hinge	H2-11
connector, 2-pin—under rear seat, left side	H2-12
connector, 2-pin—at fuel pump in storage area	H2-13
connector, 2-pin—left rear wheel housing in luggage compartment	H2-14
connector, 2-pin—hatchback, left side or sedan, under parcel shelf	H2-17
connector, 2-pin—hatchback, left side	H2-18
connector, 2-pin—trunk lid	H2-19
connector, 2-pin—luggage compartment, left wheel housing	H2-20
connector, 2-pin—luggage compartment, left wheel housing	H2-21
connector, 2-pin—engine compartment near ABS hydraulic unit	H2-22
connector, 2-pin—engine compartment right side partition	H2-23
connector, 2-pin—under rear seat, left side	H2-24
connector, 2-pin—under rear seat, right side	H2-25
connector, 2-pin—main fuse/relay panel	H2-27
connector, 2-pin—left rear door	H2-30
connector, 2-pin—right rear door	H2-31
connector, 2-pin—luggage compartment near central lock motor	H2-32
connector, 2-pin—near lambda sensor in engine compartment	H2-33
connector, 2-pin—left wheel housing	H2-34
connector, 2-pin—above roof lining at rear view mirror	H2-35
connector, 2-pin—for burglar alarm siren, behind headlamp	H2-40
connector, 2-pin—under passenger seat, right side	H2-41
connector, 2-pin—trunk lid	H2-42
connector, 2-pin—left hinge, convertible	H2-43
connector, 2-pin—left reading lamp, convertible	H2-46
connector, 2-pin—right reading lamp, convertible	H2-47
connector, 2-pin—at convertible top motor	H2-48
connector, 2-pin—left rear speaker	H2-51
connector, 2-pin—right rear speaker	H2-52
connector, 2-pin—under rear seat	H2-53
connector, 3-pin—front of engine compartment, right wiper motor	H3-1
connector, 3-pin—front of engine compartment, left wiper motor	H3-2
connector, 3-pin—left of starter motor	H3-3
connector, 3-pin—main fuse/relay panel	H3-4
connector, 3-pin—engine compartment, left of air intake	H3-5
connector, 3-pin—engine compartment near left door hinge	H3-7
connector, 3-pin—right B pillar, behind trim	H3-10
connector, 3-pin—left B pillar, behind trim	H3-11
connector, 3-pin—luggage compartment, left air outlet	H3-13
connector, 3-pin—near LH control unit, behind right A pillar trim	H3-14
connector, 3-pin—in driver door	H3-15
connector, 3-pin—under passenger seat	H3-18
connector, 4-pin—left wheel housing	H4-1
connector, 4-pin—instrument panel right side behind trim	H4-1
connector, 4-pin—engine compartment, near top left door hinge	H4-2
connector, 4-pin—engine compartment, near top right door hinge	H4-3
connector, 4-pin—right B pillar behind trim	H4-4
connector, 4-pin—left B pillar behind trim	H4-5
connector, 4-pin—instrument panel left side	H4-6
connector, 4-pin—at LH control unit, forward of right front door	H4-7
connector, 4-pin—in left front door	H4-8
connector, 4-pin—in right front door	H4-9
connector, 4-pin—trunk lid, left air outlet	H4-12
connector, 4-pin—under rear seat, next to fuse/relay panel 401	H4-15
connector, 4-pin—behind instrument panel to left of steering column	H4-16
connector, 6-pin—engine compartment right wheel housing	H6-1
connector, 6-pin—engine compartment right wheel housing	H6-2
connector, 6-pin—behind instrument panel	H6-4
connector, 8-pin—under passenger seat	H8-1
connector, 8-pin—under driver seat	H8-2
connector, 8-pin—under rear seat	H8-3
connector, 8-pin—behind instrument panel	H8-7
connector, 8-pin—behind instrument panel	H8-8
connector, 10-pin—behind instrument panel, left of steering column	H10-1
connector, 10-pin—at SRS airbag control unit, left speaker grille	H10-2
connector, 10-pin—behind instrument panel	H10-5
connector, 10-pin—at auxiliary fuse/relay panel under rear seat	H10-6
connector, 10-pin—under rear seat at burglar alarm control unit	H10-8
connector, 12-pin—behind instrument panel, left of steering column	H12-1
connector, 12-pin—behind instrument panel	H12-3
connector, 12-pin—behind instrument panel	H12-4
connector, 29-pin—at bulkhead, behind main fuse/relay panel	H29-1
connector, 29-pin—at bulkhead, behind main fuse/relay panel	H29-2
connector, 29-pin—at bulkhead, behind main fuse/relay panel	H29-3
connector, 33-pin—at bulkhead, behind main fuse/relay panel	H33-1
connector, 33-pin—at bulkhead, behind main fuse/relay panel	H33-2
connector, 33-pin—at bulkhead, behind main fuse/relay panel	H33-3
contact box for CD player or equalizer—center console, top compartment	350
control unit for cruise control—behind instrument panel, left side	131
coolant fan temperature switch—upper left corner of radiator	39
coolant fan time delay relay—front left wheel housing	26
coolant temperature gauge	47C
coolant temperature transmitter—front of cylinder head	45
crankshaft sensor—behind crankshaft pulley	345
cruise control vacuum pump—engine compartment left wheel housing	187
cruise control vacuum switch—engine compartment left wheel housing	233
cruise control warning lamp—instrument cluster	47U
diodes for convertible top (1987-1988)—under rear seat in wiring harness	283
direction indicator lamps, left-hand	27
direction indicator lamps, right-hand	28
direction indicator stalk switch	24
direction indicator warning lamp, left-hand	47H
direction indicator warning lamp, right-hand	47I
distribution block—right wheel housing	75
door lock switch—center console	425
door switches—on door jamb	54
driver heated seat rheostat—instrument panel	252
driver seat temperature thermostat—in driver seat	254
EGR modulating valve—ahead of left wheel housing	390
electric radio antenna—left rear body panel	265
EZK control unit—engine compartment, left bulkhead	176
EZK knock sensor—engine block, below intake manifold	178
EZK test connector—next to main fuse/relay panel	145
fender direction indicator, left	89
fender direction indicator, right	90
flasher relay—behind instrument panel, left side	23
fog lamps	85
front roof lamp—center rear view mirror	51
fuel injectors—intake manifold	206
fuel level gauge	47A
fuel level transmitter—in fuel tank, accessible in luggage compartment	46
fuel pump—in fuel tank	323
fuel pump relay—at LH control unit 200, forward of r.f. door behind A pillar trim	102
fuel warning light	47B
full beam warning light	47G
fuse for burglar alarm under rear seat	274
fuse for convertible top—engine compartment, next to distribution block 75	290A
fuse for convertible top—engine compartment, next to distribution block 75	290B
fuse for lambda sensor—engine compartment, next to fresh air intake	285
gear indicator light—at gear selector lever (automatics)	91
glovebox light	19
glovebox light switch—side of glovebox	160
ground distribution—main fuse/relay panel	G6
ground point—alternator bracket	257
ground point—alternator bracket	G32
ground point—behind instrument panel	3
ground point—behind instrument panel	G8

Component List—Alphabetical

(page 3 of 4)

Component	No.
ground point—between ignition switch and handbrake	G4
ground point—C pillar, right on sedans	G26
ground point—electric antenna	G27
ground point—engine lifting lug	G7
ground point—front of ABS hydraulic unit	G16
ground point for fuel injection—engine lifting lug, 2 points	201
ground point—gearbox	211
ground point—gearbox	G25
ground point—at handbrake	117
ground point—at handbrake	65
ground point—hatchback	G19
ground point—radiator cross member	7
ground point—radiator cross member	G1
ground point—luggage compartment	G3
ground point—luggage compartment	9
ground point—luggage compartment	G9
ground point—under rear seat	G5
ground point—wheel housing, left	93
ground point—wheel housing, left	G12
handbrake switch—under handbrake	43
handbrake warning lamp	47M
hazard warning switch	25
headlight dip switch	215
headlight switch	10
headlight wiper motor—behind headlight assembly	66
heated rear view mirrors—front doors	207
heated seat pad with thermostat—in seat cushion and backrest	64
heater control lighting in instrument cluster	154
high beam headlight	11
horn—engine compartment	40
horn relay—main fuse/relay panel	68
horn switch—in steering wheel	41
ignition amplifier—in front of left wheel housing	146
ignition coil—on top of radiator	5
ignition coil with integrated amplifier—inner right fender, near battery	
ignition control unit—in front of left wheel housing	320
ignition distributor—end of cylinder head	6
ignition pulse amplifier—main fuse/relay panel, position D	147
ignition switch	20
ignition switch light—next to ignition switch, center console	52
ignition switch relay—main fuse/relay panel	21
ignition switch relay—in fuse/relay panel (401) under rear seat	21A
instrument cluster	47
instrument lighting	18
interior light switch—center console	53
interior lighting time delay relay—under rear seat	151
intermittent windshield wiper relay—behind instrument panel, left side	83
key switch for driver's central door locking—driver door	183
knock sensor—engine block, below intake manifold	178
lambda exhaust sensor—in exhaust manifold	136
lambda preheater (integral with lambda sensor)	271
LH air mass meter—in throttle intake hose	205
LH coding connector—at LH control unit 200, forward of r.f. door	322
LH diagnostic test connector (sedan, hatchback)—under rear seat, right side	347
LH diagnostic test connector (convertible)—under center console bellows	347
LH diagnostic test connector—under rear seat, right side	347
LH engine temperature transmitter—intake manifold flange, between cylinders 2 and 3	202
LH fuel injection control unit—forward of right front door, behind trim	200
LH fuel injection main relay—at LH control unit 200, behind A pillar trim, passenger door	229
LH NTC resistor—under intake manifold	389
LH test connector—engine compartment, behind right wheel housing	204
license plate lights	15
lighting relay—main fuse relay panel	8
lockout switch for rear power windows	189
logic box for passive seat belt s—under rear seat, left side	306
low beam headlight	12
luggage compartment light—storage area	55
luggage compartment light switch—storage area	56
main fuel pump—in fuel tank	103
main fuse/relay panel—in engine compartment	22A
mercury switch for convertible heated rear window—left side top mounting	279
motor for convertible hydraulic pump—under rear seat, right side	273
negative (ground) distribution in main fuse/relay panel	158
neutral safety switch (automatics only)—gear selector lever	77
oil pressure switch—left side of engine, above oil filter	44
oil pressure warning light	47D
over-ride switch for ventilation fan—integrated in air distribution switch (150)	149
parking lights	13
passenger seat switch for heated seats—under passenger seat	121
passenger seat belt switch—under seat cover	69
passive seat belt belt reel—driver seat	307D
passive seat belt belt reel—passenger seat	307P
passive seat belt door switch—driver door	208D
passive seat belt door switch—passenger door	208P
passive seat belt fuse for driver seat—under rear seat	310D
passive seat belt fuse for passenger seat—under rear seat	310P
passive seat belt g sensor—under rear seat, left side	309
passive seat belt motor relay for driver seat—under rear seat	311D
passive seat belt motor relay for passenger seat—under rear seat	311P
passive seat belt motor relay for driver seat—under rear seat	312D
passive seat belt motor relay for passenger seat—under rear seat	312P
passive seat belt motor with limit switches—driver seat	308D
passive seat belt motor with limit switches—passenger seat	308P
passive seat belt warning lamp	47S
power mirror motor, left—in left mirror	126
power mirror motor, right—in right mirror	127
power mirror switch, left—instrument panel	124
power mirror switch, right—instrument panel	125
power sunroof or convertible switch	181
power window motor—left front door	164
power window motor—left rear door	193
power window motor—right front door	165
power window motor—right rear door	194
power window relay for automatic control—under rear seat	287
radiator cooling fan motor—behind radiator	37
radiator fan relay—main fuse/relay panel	396
radio connector—instrument panel	267
radio contact box with amplifier—instrument panel	349
radio speakers—(4) two in front, two in rear	266
reading lights, convertible—back seat	225
rear lights	14
rear fog lights	33
rear fog light switch	161
rear fog light warning lamp	47N
rear window heater element	115
rear window heater warning lamp	47J
recirculation switch—instrument cluster	143
recirculation valve—behind instrument panel, near right side A pillar	38
relay for A/C cooling fan—main fuse/relay panel	155
relay for daytime driving lights	174
relay for extra foglamps	107
rear heated window switch	116
relay for raising convertible top (1987-1988)—under rear seat on bulkhead	277
relay for raising convertible top (1989 and later)—under rear seat in fuse/relay panel 401	277
relay for lowering convertible top (1987-1988)—under rear seat on bulkhead	278

Component List—Alphabetical
(page 4 of 4)

relay for lowering convertible top (1989 and later)—under rear seat in fuse/relay panel 401 278
resistor pack for ventilation fan—under left speaker grille 74
rheostat for instrument cluster 16
rheostat for instrument panel lighting 17
roof lamp/switch—to left of driver 50
seat belt switch, driver side—between driver and passenger seat 70
seat belt warning light—center of instrument panel 72
seat belt warning relay—under rear seat 82
selector for cruise control—direction indicator stalk 141
shift-up indicator lamp 47K
shift-up indicator relay—main fuse/relay panel 270
side backup lights in front light clusters 119
side marker lights in front light clusters 234
slip ring switch—in steering wheel 352
sparkplug—center of valve cover 157
speed control relay—behind instrument panel, left side 128
speed transmitter—at rear of instrument cluster 132
SRS airbag 2-pin orange connector—pins are short circuited when connector is separated. See SRS warning. 335
SRS airbag 10-pin connector—center console under rubber bellows. See SRS warning. 330
SRS airbag—in steering wheel. See SRS warning. 333
SRS airbag control unit—behind instrument panel, left grille. See SRS warning. 331
SRS airbag ground point for electronic unit—adjacent to electronic unit. See SRS warning. 334
SRS airbag left sensor—left wheel housing in engine compartment. See SRS warning. 332A
SRS airbag redundant ground point—behind instrument panel, left side. See SRS warning. 400
SRS airbag right sensor—right wheel housing in engine compartment. See SRS warning. 332B
SRS airbag slip ring contact—in steering wheel. See SRS warning. 336
SRS airbag warning lamp. See SRS warning. 47T
starter motor—under intake manifold 4
starting injector—throttle housing 94
supply fuel pump—in fuel tank 101
switch assembly for power windows and sunroof—center console 386
switch for driver power window—center console 162
switch for fog lamps 88
switch for left rear power window—center console 190
switch for left rear power window—left rear door 190a
switch for passenger power window—center console 163
switch for raising idle speed (automatic transmission)—center console 76
switch for rear seat—under rear seat 426
switch for right rear power window—center console 191
switch for right rear power window—right rear door 191a
tachometer 110
temperature switch for shift-up indicator—between center intake ports of intake manifold 262
third brake lamp (high mount brake light) 109
throttle angle transmitter—on throttle housing 203
throttle contacts for shift-up indicator—throttle housing 261
time delay relay for heated rear window—under rear seat 113
TSI (test service instrument) socket—in main fuse/relay panel 73
vacuum switch for shift-up indicator—left wheel housing 263
ventilation fan switch—instrument panel 35
ventilation fan motor—under right speaker grille 36
voltage distribution block—engine compartment right bulkhead 75
windshield washer motor—below fluid bottle in engine compartment 63
windshield wiper motor—engine compartment firewall 62
wiper stalk switch—steering column 61

400 Transmission—General

TABLES

GENERAL

The repair groups found within the **4 TRANSMISSION** section contain manual and automatic transmission service and repair information. Some of the information contained in these repair groups is intended to be used as a guide for the professional or experienced automotive technician. In addition, some of the operations require special equipment. Transmission and final drive rebuilding are specialized repairs requiring many special Saab tools. Therefore, these operations are not within the scope of this manual and have not been included.

Procedures for changing the manual transmission lubricant, automatic transmission fluid, or final drive fluid (automatics only) are covered in **1 LUBRICATION AND MAINTENANCE**. Removal of the transmission is covered in **2 ENGINE**.

Transmission Assembly

The Saab transmission is a unique design in that it is bolted directly to the bottom of the engine. The top section of the transmission housing serves as the engine oil sump and the engine oil is completely sealed off from the manual transmission lubricant.

Power is transferred from the engine down to the transmission via a chain at the front of the engine/transmission assembly. Power then flows through the gearset to the final drive and out to the drive axles to drive the front wheels.

MANUAL TRANSMISSION

The 5-speed transmission is shown in Fig. 1. The transmission case contains the primary chain, the mainshaft, and the layshaft. At the end of the transmission is the integral final drive housing containing the differential, and the ring and pinion gears. The transmission and final drive housing has one common bath of lubricating oil.

The clutch, pressure plate, and release bearing can all be serviced without removing the engine or transmission. In addition, the clutch slave cylinder and engine flywheel can be serviced in the car as well. See **2 ENGINE** for information on removing the flywheel.

WARNING
The clutch disc contains asbestos fibers. Asbestos materials can cause asbestosis. Always wear an OSHA approved respirator and protective clothing when handling components containing asbestos. Do not use compressed air. Do not grind, heat, weld, or sand on or near any asbestos materials. Only approved cleaning equipment should be used to service the clutch disc or areas containing asbestos dust or asbestos fibers.

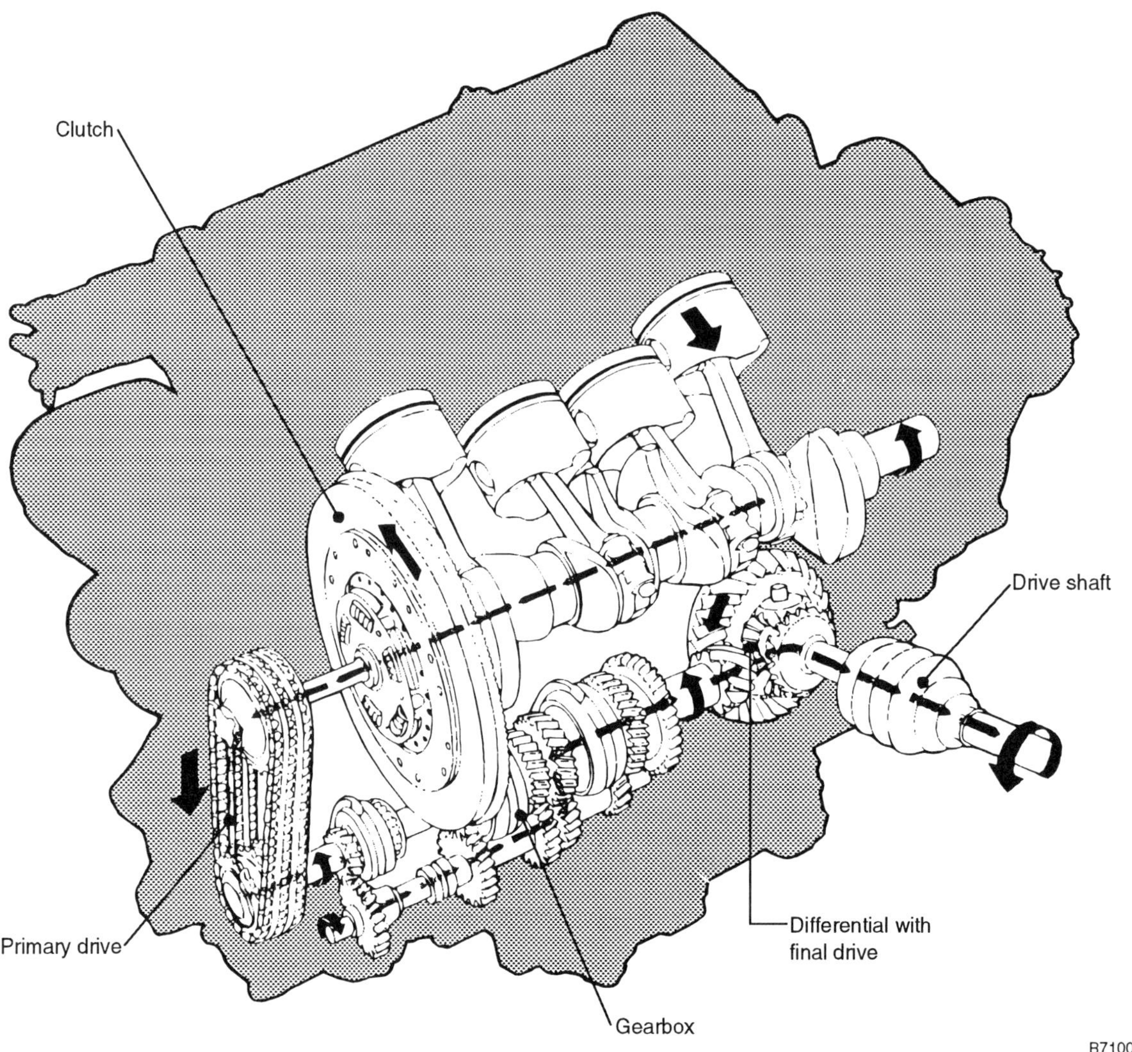

Fig. 1. Manual transmission with integral final drive.

Fig. 2. shows the internal components of the transmission. A description of several of the main components is given. Remember that power flows from the engine to the transmission via the clutch and primary chain. From the chain, power flows down into the gearbox, and to the final drive where the drive axles attach.

Clutch, Pressure Plate, Release Bearing

The clutch disc, pressure plate, and release bearing are located at the front of the car behind a plastic cover. They are removed and installed together. The clutch disc transmits power to the primary chain via a splined input shaft. See **411 Clutch**.

Clutch Master and Slave Cylinders

The clutch is hydraulically actuated. The master cylinder supplies pressure to the slave cylinder. The brake fluid reservoir supplies the clutch master cylinder with hydraulic fluid. The slave cylinder moves the release bearing, which presses on the fingers of the pressure plate allowing the clutch disc to rotate independent of engine speed. See Fig. 3. See **412 Clutch Control**.

AUTOMATIC TRANSMISSION

The automatic transmission is shown in Fig. 4. At one end of the transmission is the integral final drive housing. Inside the final drive housing are the differential and the ring and pinion gears. The final drive housing, containing oil for lubricating the final drive gears, is completely sealed off from the transmission case. The transmission case contains automatic transmission fluid (ATF) for the ATF pump, the hydraulic controls, and the planetary gear system. See Fig. 5. ATF does not circulate unless the engine is running, so the transmission parts are only partially lubricated when the engine is turned off.

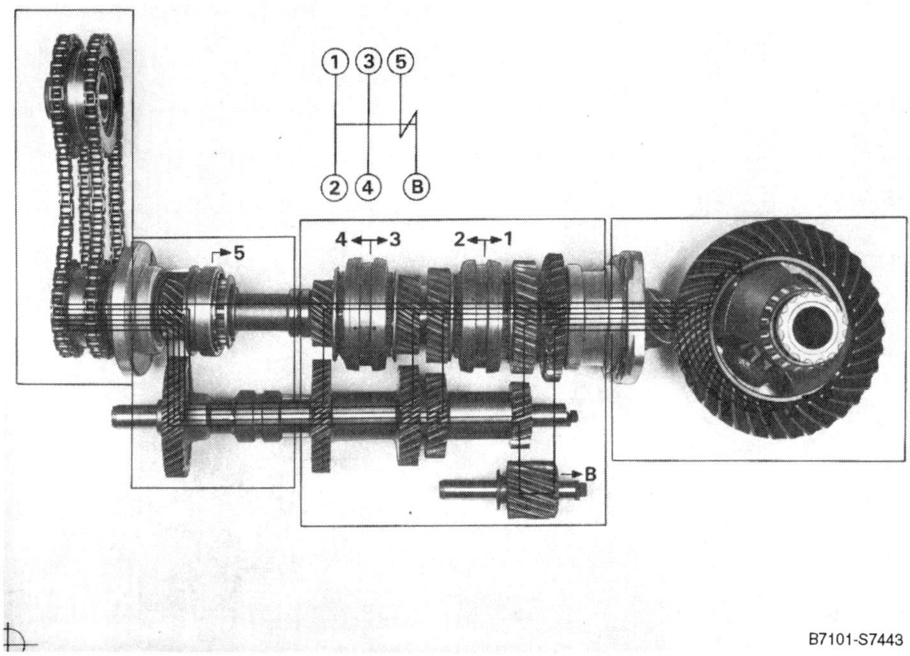

Fig. 2. Schematic view of manual transmission with primary chain (left) and final drive (right).

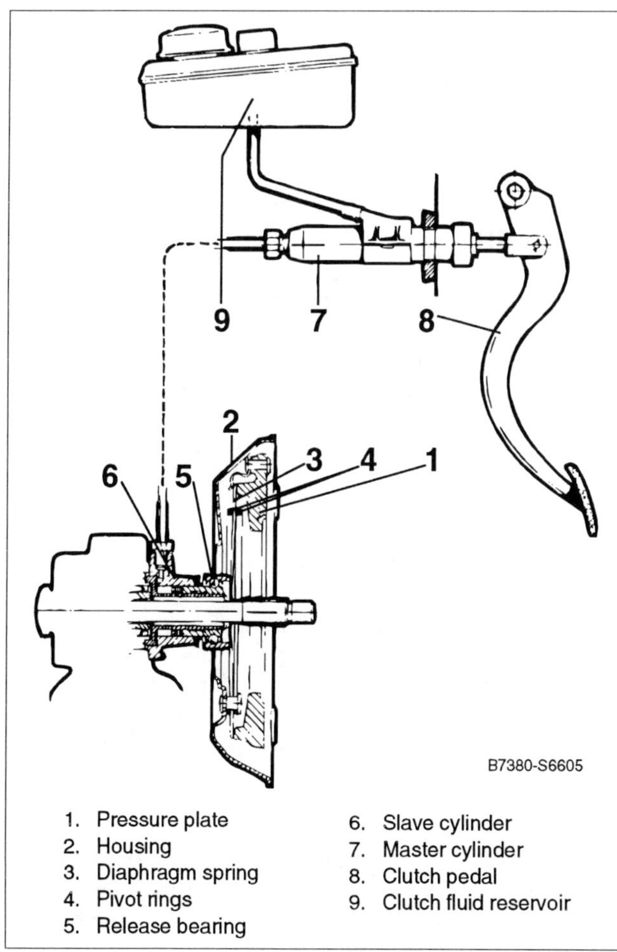

1. Pressure plate
2. Housing
3. Diaphragm spring
4. Pivot rings
5. Release bearing
6. Slave cylinder
7. Master cylinder
8. Clutch pedal
9. Clutch fluid reservoir

Fig. 3. Clutch components.

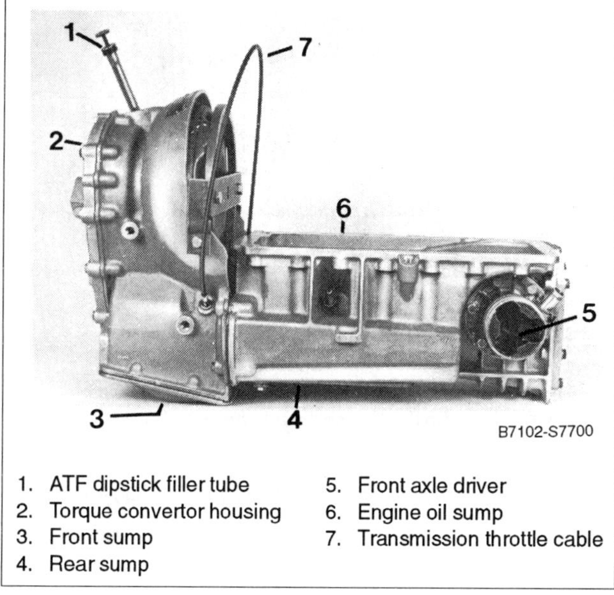

1. ATF dipstick filler tube
2. Torque convertor housing
3. Front sump
4. Rear sump
5. Front axle driver
6. Engine oil sump
7. Transmission throttle cable

Fig. 4. Automatic transmission with integral final drive.

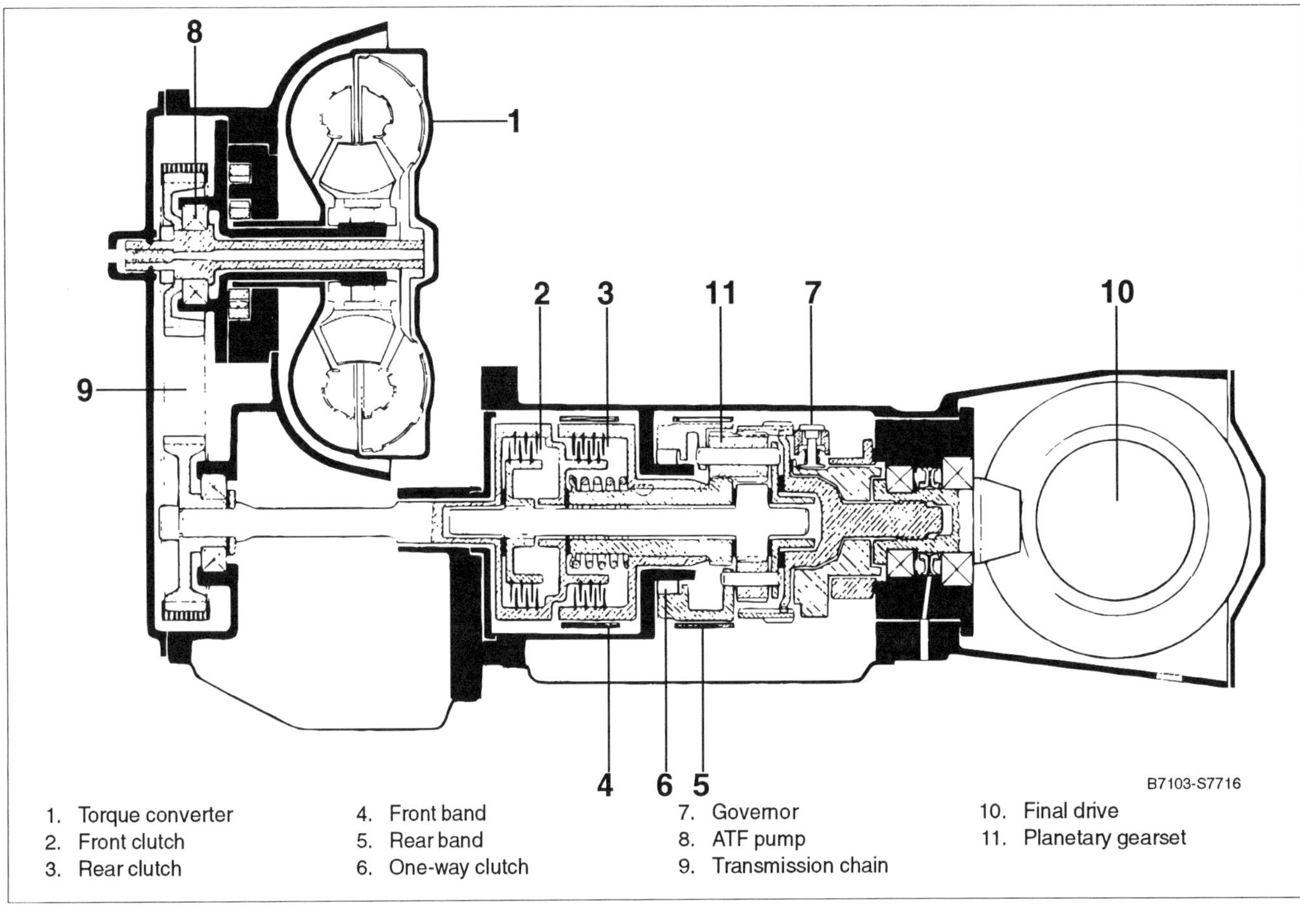

Fig. 5. Cutaway view of automatic transmission.

CAUTION

- The following rules must be observed if a car with automatic transmission has to be towed:
- The selector lever must be in position **N**.
- The ATF level must be topped up an additional 2.0 l (2.1 qt.). After towing, drain the fluid so the transmission has the correct level.
- The car must not be towed a distance greater than 40 to 50 km. (25 to 30 miles).
- The towing speed must not exceed 25 mph (40 km/h)

Torque Converter

The torque converter is a doughnut-shaped assembly located between the engine and the transmission. The torque converter is a fluid coupling. The torque converter transmits engine output to the transmission, and also multiplies engine torque at low vehicle speeds. The engine and transmission must be removed and separated to service the torque converter and drive plate.

ATF Pump

The automatic transmission fluid (ATF) circulates through the transmission under pressure. The ATF pump that creates this pressure is located at the top front of the transmission. The splined pump driveshaft is connected directly to the torque converter housing, so ATF circulates whenever the engine is running. ATF is drawn from the ATF sump through a strainer into the pump.

Planetary Gear System

A torque converter alone cannot supply the torque multiplication needed for all driving conditions. The torque converter therefore drives through a planetary gear system which can operate at different drive ratios. The planetary gear system consists of two sun gears, two sets of pinions, a pinion carrier and a ring gear.

The two hydraulically-operated multiple-disc clutches control the routing of power to the planetary gearsets. The front clutch connects the converter to the forward sun gear. In reverse, the rear clutch connects the converter to the reverse sun gear.

Hydraulic System and ATF Cooler

The ATF pump supplies the system with fluid. A governor provides automatic control of the upshift and downshift points by routing fluid to the valve body shift valves. The shift valves provide hydraulic control of transmission functions by opening and closing ports. The transmission throttle cable controls a shift valve for downshifting during hard acceleration.

All models have an external ATF cooler that is one of two types: an engine coolant heat exchanger, or an air heat exchanger. See Fig. 6. Additionally, some models have an inline thermostat. For more information see **472 Automatic Transmission Seals and Gaskets**.

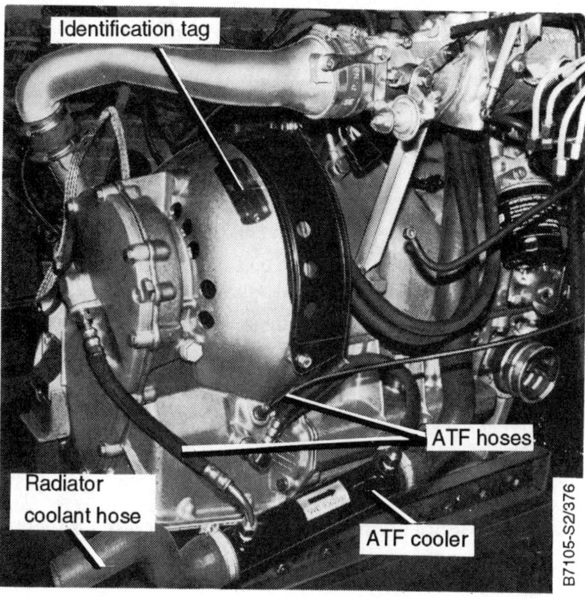

Fig. 6. Automatic with ATF cooler. Cooler shown is engine coolant type.

DIFFERENTIAL AND FINAL DRIVE

The final drive, including differential, is at the rear of the transmission case. On manual transmissions the final drive is lubricated by the transmission lubricant. On automatics the final drive has its own lubricant, separate from the ATF.

IDENTIFICATION CODES AND SPECIFICATIONS

Due to different power characteristics and performance requirements, there are minor variations of the basic transmission. On manual transmissions, the different versions are identified by code letters found stamped in the front case. See Fig. 7. On automatics, an identification tag is located on the torque converter housing. See Fig. 6 above. **Table a** gives specifications for the manual transmission. **Table b** gives specifications for the automatic transmission. For more information on checking or changing the fluids, see **1 LUBRICATION AND MAINTENANCE**.

Fig. 7. Identification stamp (arrow) on manual transmission.

Table a. Manual Transmission and Clutch Specifications

Clutch type	Fichtel & Sachs
Clutch diameter*	
non-turbo	204 mm (8 in.)
turbo	216 mm (8.5 in.)
Transmission oil capacity	3.0 l (3.5 qt.)
Transmission oil type	Engine oil SAE 10 W 30 or SAE 10 W 40
Clutch/brake master cylinder fluid	DOT 4 brake fluid

* approximately

Table b. Automatic Transmission Specifications

Type	Borg Warner 37
ATF volume	8.0 l (8.5 U.S. qts.)
ATF grade	Ford spec M2C-33F/G
Final drive fluid volume	1.25 l (1.3 U.S. qts.)
Final drive fluid type	SAE 10W 30

MANUAL TRANSMISSION TROUBLESHOOTING

This troubleshooting section applies to problems affecting the manual transmission.

The source of most problems is apparent from the symptoms. For example, difficulty in engaging a gear or imprecise shifting may be caused by air trapped in the clutch hydraulic system or it may be a more serious internal transmission problem. Other symptoms, such as clutch slippage, vibration or shuddering when releasing the clutch may be solved by repairing or replacing the clutch components only.

Noises may be the result of a failure in the gear train, or of the final drive. What appears to be a transmission oil leak may be engine oil leaking from a faulty rear crankshaft oil seal, especially if the leak is near the bottom of the transmission housing. See **2 ENGINE** for information on crankshaft oil seals.

NOTE

To pinpoint the location of leaks, have the undercarriage and transmission degreased. Remember that air turbulence from driving can cause fluids to appear to be leaking from other locations.

Transmission problems fall into two categories: those that can be fixed by external service, and those that require disassembly of the transmission. Problems that at first appear to be caused by internal faults, such as gear shifting difficulty or noisy operation, may be corrected by external adjustments such as gearshift lever adjustment, or bleeding the clutch hydraulic system.

Begin with a thorough visual inspection, both in the engine compartment and from beneath. Check all parts of the gearshift mechanism for wear that might cause misalignment and shifting difficulty. Look for wet spots that may indicate oil leaks. High or low oil level, or the wrong type of oil may be the cause of hard shifting or noise. Accurate pinpointing of leaks may require that the suspected area be cleaned and reinspected.

Correct leaks and oil level before acting on suspected internal problems. The gearshift mechanism is covered in **432 Manual Transmission Controls**. Checking and correcting oil level is covered in **1 LUBRICATION AND MAINTENANCE**.

Observation of the symptoms is the key to isolating and identifying transmission problems. A road test is an important step. Determining whether the problem is present in all gears, only during acceleration, when the clutch is engaged, or in some other special condition may help isolate the source of the problem.

Table c lists manual transmission and clutch symptoms, their probable causes, and recommended corrective actions. The numbers in bold type in the corrective action column refer to the repair group in this section where the suggested repairs are described.

Table c. Manual Transmission Troubleshooting

Symptom	Corrective action
1. Difficult or noisy shifting	**a.** Insufficient oil. Correct oil level. See **1 LUBRICATION AND MAINTENANCE**
	b. Adjust incorrect idle speed. See **2 ENGINE**
	c. Bleed or repair clutch hydraulic system. See **412**

continued

Table c. Manual Transmission Troubleshooting

Symptom	Corrective action
1. Difficult or noisy shifting (cont'd)	**d.** Lubricate or replace binding clutch disc on input shaft. See **411**
	e. Repair worn gearshift linkage. See **432**
	f. Replace seized input shaft bearing in flywheel. See **2 ENGINE**
	g. Replace worn or damaged internal gear train components.
2. Transmission fails to engage a gear or jumps out of gear	**a.** Repair worn gearshift linkage or loose shift console. See **432**
	b. Repair worn or damaged internal gear train components.
3. Poor acceleration or slipping	**a.** Replace worn or burnt clutch friction surfaces. See **411**
4. Clutch not fully engaging	**a.** Inspect clutch disc for binding on input shaft. See **411**
	b. Replace release bearing, flywheel bearing for input shaft, clutch disc, or pressure plate. See **411**
	c. Replace oil soaked clutch disc and faulty oil seals. See **411**
	d. Check for faulty engine/transmission mounting. See **2 ENGINE**

AUTOMATIC TRANSMISSION TROUBLESHOOTING

This troubleshooting section applies to problems affecting the automatic transmission.

External adjustments to the transmission are covered in this manual, but some of the troubleshooting information in this section describes problems which can only be remedied by disassembly and internal repair. Internal transmission repairs require specialized knowledge and equipment and are, therefore, beyond the scope of this manual. The publisher recommends that such repairs be left to an authorized Saab dealer or other qualified automatic transmission repair shop.

NOTE

- To pinpoint the location of leaks, have the undercarriage and transmission degreased. Remember that air turbulence from driving can cause fluids to appear to be leaking from other locations.

- If the car has been in a collision, it is possible that the magnet located in the ATF sump has been dislodged to block the oil pickup tube, or that the oil pickup tube has been knocked loose. Remove the oil pan and check for the proper location of the magnet and tube. See **1 LUBRICATION AND MAINTENANCE**.

Basic Principles

In order for automatic transmission troubleshooting to provide meaningful results, the engine must be in good mechanical condition and properly tuned. See **1 LUBRICATION AND MAINTENANCE** for engine tuning.

Inspect the transmission for external damage, loose or missing fasteners, and for any obvious leaks. Many automatic transmission problems can be traced to an incorrect ATF level, incorrect ATF type, contaminated ATF, or to misadjusted transmission controls. Also check the final drive fluid level and type. See **1 LUBRICATION AND MAINTENANCE** for information on checking and changing the ATF and final drive fluid.

Check to see if the ATF is dirty or has a burned odor. A burned odor indicates overheated fluid. This may be accompanied by burned clutches, as well as friction material which may be clogging the valve body passages.

Minor automatic transmission problems can often be corrected merely by performing the following tasks. In any event, do these things before beginning any internal tear down or repair.

Preliminary service

- drain and refill the ATF
- drain and refill the final drive fluid
- clean or replace the ATF filter screen
- check the operation of the shift lever and cable
- check the operation of the transmission throttle cable

Table d is given as a guide for experienced transmission repair specialists. Special tools and techniques are required to repair major faults. The engine–transmission assembly must be removed from the car to disassemble the transmission.

Table d. Automatic Transmission Troubleshooting

Symptom	Corrective Action
1. No drive (car will not move)	a. Check ATF level. See **1 LUBRICATION AND MAINTENANCE** b. Check shift cable adjustment. See **444** c. Check for clogged fluid screen. See **1 LUBRICATION AND MAINTENANCE**
2. Does not shift properly	a. Check transmission throttle cable. See **444** b. Check for binding governor. See **444** c. Check pipes between governor and valve body. See **444**
3. Slips when shifting	a. Check throttle cable. See **444**
4. Starts in wrong gear	a. Check governor for binding. See **444**
5. Incorrect upshift speed	a. Check throttle cable adjustment. See **444** b. Check fluid pressure at idle. See **444** c. Check for binding governor. See **444**
6. Parking pawl does not hold	a. Check shift cable adjustment. See **444**
7. Noise	a. Check ATF level. See **1 LUBRICATION AND MAINTENANCE** b. Check final drive fluid level. See **1 LUBRICATION AND MAINTENANCE** c. Check shift cable adjustment. See **444** d. Check for broken engine drive plate. See **2 ENGINE**
8. Fluid leaks	a. Check all sealing surfaces. See **472** b. Check ATF pump seal. See **472** c. Check pinion bearing seal.

continued

Table d. Automatic Transmission Troubleshooting

Stall Speed Test

This test is used to check for faults in the torque converter and planetary gear system when there is no other apparent cause for poor performance and acceleration. The test results are meaningless if the engine is not running properly. A precise tachometer must be used for the rpm measurements, as dashboard instruments are not sufficiently accurate.

CAUTION

The stall speed test should be as short as possible and should never extend beyond 10 seconds maximum. Prolonging the test may overheat the transmission and damage the seals or internal components.

To perform stall speed test

1. Drive the car to normal operating temperature. On turbo engines, connect a pressure boost gauge and unplug the APC solenoid.

NOTE

For more information on the APC solenoid and its location, see **2 ENGINE**.

---

2. Connect a tachometer according to the instrument manufacturer's instructions, so that it can be read from the driver's seat, then start the engine.

3. Set the parking brake and depress the foot brake firmly to hold the vehicle stationary.

4. Place the selector lever in **D**.

WARNING
Be certain that no one is in front of or behind the car during the test.

---

5. While holding the car stationary with the brakes, floor the accelerator for no more than 10 seconds. Note the tachometer readings. The rpm should increase, and then hold steady. Maximum rpm achieved under these conditions is the stall speed.

Stall speed specifications depend on the transmission code numbers found on the torque converter housing. Shown below is a general range for stall speeds and can be used as a guide. See an authorized Saab dealer for exact stall speed specifications.

General stall speed specifications
- 2250 to 2700 rpm
- charging pressure* (turbo models only) . . . . 0.40 bar

*APC solenoid valve unplugged

A stall speed that is 300 hundred rpm below the specified range is probably due to reduced engine performance. A stall speed that is 800 rpm or more below the specified range indicates a faulty torque converter.

If the stall speed is substantially higher than normal, there is slippage in the forward clutch or lack of fluid to the torque converter. All of these faults require that the transmission be removed and disassembled for repair.

Pressure Test

A main pressure test will reveal internal leaks, sticking control valves, or other troubles in the hydraulic controls. Engine idle speed must be correctly adjusted.

Tool required
- ATF pressure gauge . . . . . . .Saab tool no. 87 91 592 or equivalent

To perform pressure test

1. Connect the pressure gauge to the main pressure tap on the transmission, as shown in Fig. 8.

2. Make sure the engine and transmission are at normal operating temperature, let the engine idle.

3. Set the parking brake.

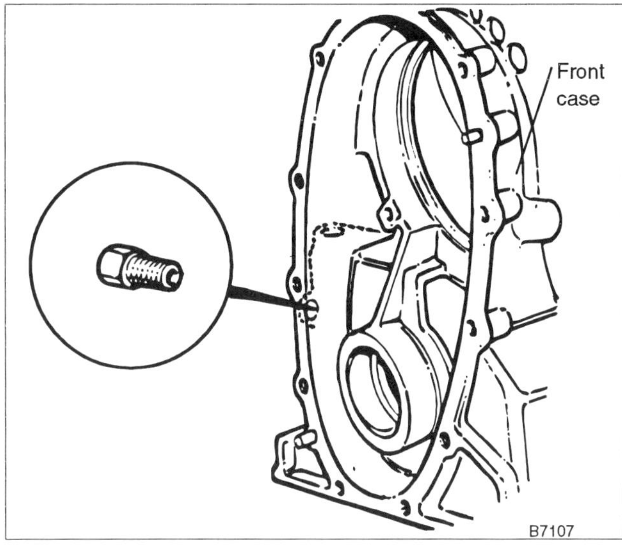

Fig. 8. Main pressure tap on transmission case, located on exhaust side of engine.

4. Depress the foot brake firmly to hold the vehicle stationary.

5. With the gear selector in **D**, check the main pressure. Correct test values are given below.

Automatic transmission line pressure
- 4.2 to 4.9 bar (61 to 71 psi) at idle, gear selector in D

6. Put the gear selector in **P** and shut off the engine. Disconnect the pressure gauge hose and reinstall the plug for the pressure tap. Torque the plug. Top up the ATF if necessary.

Pressure tap tightening torque
- 5 to 7 Nm (44 to 62 in-lb)

Any pressure that is higher or lower than specified usually indicates a malfunctioning valve body and valves, probably due to contamination. The valve body can be removed, cleaned, and reinstalled with the transmission in place by removing the ATF pan and filter screen. See **1 LUBRICATION AND MAINTENANCE**. However, the valve body contains many precision parts which must be reassembled in their exact locations. Because of the complexity of the valve body assembly, we recommend that these repairs be left to an authorized Saab dealer or other qualified repair shop.

Low pressure may also indicate a worn ATF pump or internal ATF pump leaks past seals, gaskets, and metal mating surfaces. These repairs require that the transmission be removed and disassembled.

411 Clutch

GENERAL

The clutch, pressure plate, and release bearing can all be serviced without removing the engine or transmission. In addition, the clutch slave cylinder and engine flywheel can be serviced after removing the clutch and pressure plate. See **2 ENGINE** for information on removing the flywheel.

The clutch, pressure plate, slave cylinder, and release bearing are located behind a plastic cover at the front of the engine. A splined input shaft transmits engine power from the clutch disc to the primary chainwheel. The clutch is non-adjustable and is actuated by the hydraulic slave cylinder. Brake fluid from the brake fluid reservoir supplies the clutch master cylinder.

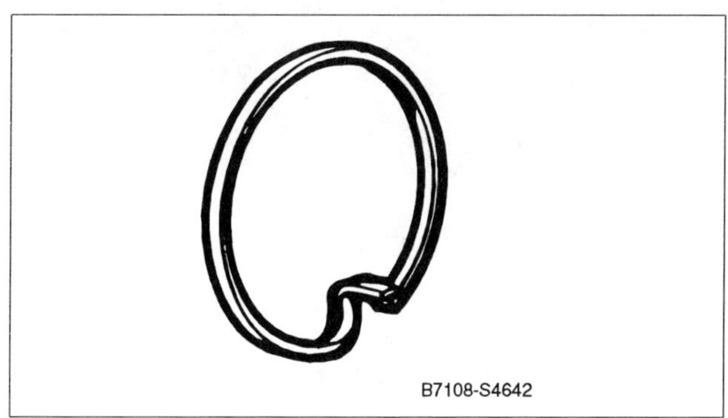

Fig. 1. Spacer ring (Saab tool no. 87 91 618) to disengage pressure plate.

CLUTCH, PRESSURE PLATE, RELEASE BEARING AND SLAVE CYLINDER

The clutch, pressure plate, release bearing and slave cylinder are removed and installed as a unit. This is because there is little clearance in the flywheel housing.

To remove clutch, pressure plate, release bearing and slave cylinder

Tools required

- spacer ring . . . . Saab tool no. 87 91 618 and /or 83 90 023
- lever arm (optional). . . . . . . Saab tool no. 83 94 033

NOTE

Two different clutch assemblies were installed on the cars covered by this manual. Most early cars (approximately 1988 and earlier models) were equipped with a smaller clutch that required a different spacer ring (Saab tool no. 83 90 023) for its removal. All newer cars and all clutch replacement parts use a larger spacer ring (Saab tool no. 87 91 618). Therefore, early cars still equipped with the original smaller clutch will need both special tools to replace the clutch. See an authorized Saab dealer for more information.

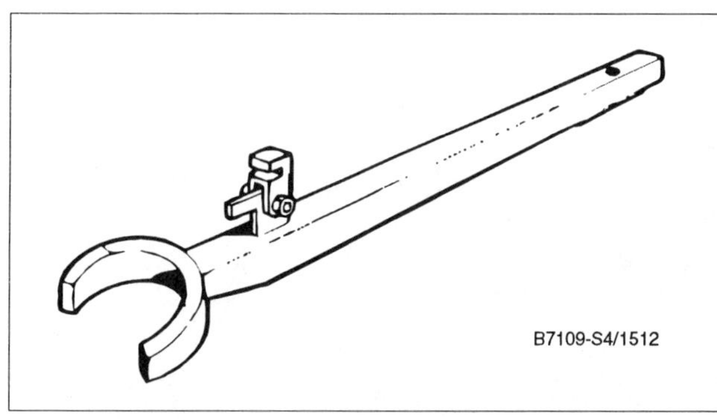

Fig. 2. Lever arm (Saab tool no. 83 94 033) to hold pressure plate fingers if clutch hydraulic system is not working.

1. Disconnect the negative (–) battery cable. Remove the hood. Remove the air intake rubber bellows. On turbo models, remove the turbo pipes above the clutch cover.

2. Remove the left radiator fan as described in **261 Radiator and Cooling System.**

3. Remove the plastic clutch cover. See Fig. 3.

411

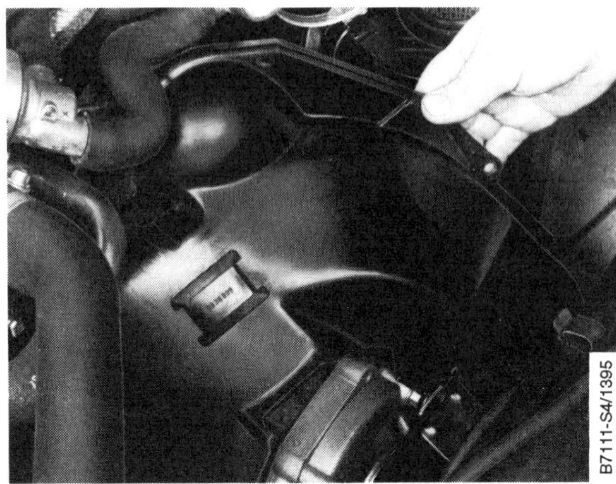

Fig. 3. Plastic cover being removed.

4. Have a helper depress and hold the clutch pedal. Insert the special spacer ring under the fingers of the pressure plate. See Fig. 4. Release the pedal.

NOTE

If the Saab tool no. 87 91 618 or tool no. 83 90 023 is not available, a length of sparkplug wire can be used under the fingers of the pressure plate.

Fig. 4. Spacer being inserted between fingers and housing of pressure plate.

NOTE

- Inserting the spacer creates the necessary clearance to remove the pressure plate, clutch, release bearing, and slave cylinder from the flywheel housing.

- If a helper is not available, wedge a long stick against the clutch pedal and the seat.

- If the clutch hydraulic system doesn't work, the special Saab tool no. 83 94 033 will be required to compress the pressure plate fingers in order to install the spacer ring.

---

5. Remove the spring clip and cover as shown in Fig. 5. Unscrew the plastic propeller from the input shaft.

CAUTION

The plastic propeller circulates oil to the bearing. Failure to reinstall the propeller after completing repairs may cause bearing seizure.

Fig. 5. Spring clip and cover to be removed to withdraw input shaft.

6. Thread an 8 mm bolt with flat washer into the front of the clutch input shaft. Using a pry bar, slide the clutch input shaft out by levering against the flat washer. See Fig. 6.

CAUTION

Be careful not to hit the radiator or fan with the pry bar or input shaft.

Fig. 6. Clutch input shaft being pried out using special tool (Saab tool no. 83 94 033).

NOTE
The shaft does not need to be fully removed.

7. Remove the three internal hex-head screws for the slave cylinder. See Fig. 7.

Fig. 7. Slave cylinder screws being removed.

NOTE
- The three internal hex-head screws can be difficult to loosen. Clean the head of the screw so the wrench will grip tightly.
- Do not disconnect the hydraulic line to the slave cylinder.

8. Remove the bolts holding the pressure plate assembly to the flywheel. Remove as a unit, the pressure plate, clutch disc, release bearing, and slave cylinder.

CAUTION
Do not step on the clutch pedal while the slave cylinder is removed.

9. Inspect the flywheel and pressure plate assembly for burn marks or scoring. Inspect the input shaft bearing in the flywheel and replace if necessary. See **2 ENGINE** for more information.

Note which side of the clutch disc faces the flywheel as a guide to reassembly. Carefully inspect the clutch input shaft seal located at the transmission case surface. If leaking, replace the seal using an appropriate seal driver. Apply grease to the seal lip before installing the shaft.

NOTE
Inspect for oil leakage at the rear of the transmission chain housing, directly below the clutch release bearing. If oil is present on the housing, it may be leaking past the chain tensioner bolts. Because oil will quickly ruin a new clutch disc, it is recommended that the oil leak be corrected by removing the tensioner bolts and reinstalling them using a thread sealer. Accessing the bolts requires supporting the engine/transmission assembly and removing the front engine mount and the front transmission chain cover. Be sure to use a new gasket at the front chain cover.

To install clutch, pressure plate, release bearing and slave cylinder

1. Working at the bench, use a press and cylinder of the correct diameter to depress the pressure plate fingers uniformly so the spacer ring can be installed.

NOTE
The diameter of the cylinder used to compress the pressure plate fingers should be equivalent to the diameter of the release bearing contact area.

2. Lubricate the input shaft splines with molybdenum disulfide grease. Assemble the pressure plate, clutch, release bearing, and slave cylinder in the proper order.

3. Install the pressure plate, clutch disc, release bearing, and slave cylinder into the flywheel housing. See Fig. 8.

Fig. 8. Pressure plate, clutch disc, and release bearing with slave cylinder being installed into flywheel housing. Also shown is spacer ring (arrow).

4. Hand tighten two of the pressure plate bolts to hold the assembly in place. Slide the input shaft into engagement with the clutch splines, then tap the shaft into the case with a plastic hammer until it bottoms out. See Fig. 9.

Fig. 9. Input shaft being tapped into case. Snap ring will lock shaft in the case.

5. Install the three slave cylinder screws using thread sealing compound.

Tightening torque

- slave cylinder mounting screws . . . . . 6 to 14 Nm (53 to 124 in-lb)

---

6. Install the plastic propeller, input shaft cover and spring clip.

7. Install and tighten the remaining pressure plate bolts.

8. Remove the spacer ring from the pressure plate while a helper depresses the clutch pedal. If the pedal is spongy the system needs to be bled, see **412 Clutch Control**.

CAUTION

Only press the pedal enough to remove the spacer. Otherwise the slave cylinder seal may be damaged.

---

9. Push the plastic sleeve toward the flywheel while someone holds the clutch pedal down. See Fig. 10. Finally, check the clutch pedal to make sure it doesn't bind.

NOTE

The plastic shield will automatically position itself when the clutch pedal is released.

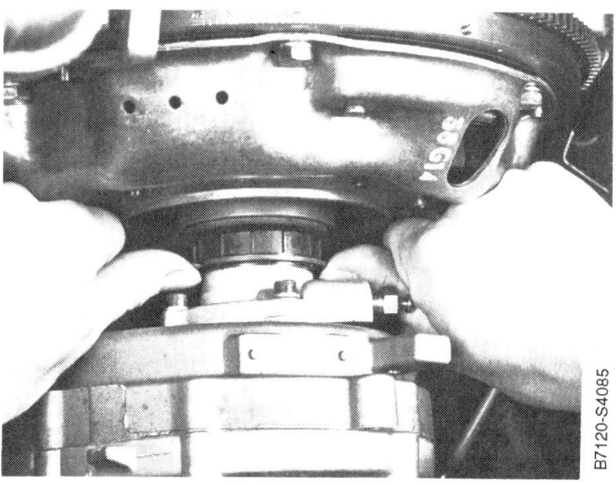

Fig. 10. Plastic sleeve being pushed toward flywheel while clutch pedal is held down.

10. Reinstall the plastic cover, the hood, the air intake rubber bellows, and the turbo pipes (where applicable).

412 Clutch Control

GENERAL

The clutch master cylinder and slave cylinder can be serviced without removing the engine or transmission. However, the clutch slave cylinder can only be removed together with the pressure plate assembly, clutch disc, and release bearing. See **411 Clutch** for information on removing these components.

The clutch is non-adjustable. Typical problems with the clutch hydraulic system are fluid leaks, and air trapped in the system that creates a spongy feel to the clutch pedal. Fluid leaks are usually apparent around the component. Internal leakage past a seal can occur which results in a loss of pressure when the pedal is pushed.

To replace clutch master cylinder

1. Working in the engine compartment, pinch off the fluid supply hose from the brake fluid reservoir to the clutch master cylinder. See Fig. 1.

Fig. 1. Fluid reservoir **B** for clutch master cylinder and master cylinder **A**. Arrow shows fluid supply hose.

2. Remove the hydraulic pipe from the master cylinder. See Fig. 2. Remove the clip that holds the pipe to the body.

CAUTION
Brake fluid can damage paint and bodywork. Immediately rinse any spills with water.

NOTE
On cars equipped with ABS, it may be necessary to remove the alternator belt tensioner and move the alternator to one side to reach the master cylinder.

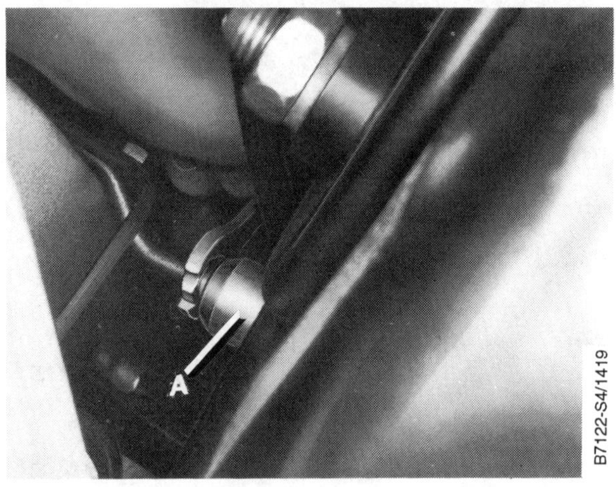

Fig. 2. Clutch master cylinder hydraulic pipe being removed. Master cylinder is located at **A**.

3. Inside the car, remove the left hand footwell air duct. See Fig. 3. Remove the clevis pin and the master cylinder self-locking mounting nuts. See Fig. 4.

WARNING
Always replace self-locking nuts with new ones.

4. Installation is the reverse of removal. Bleed the system as described below. Replenish the fluid in the brake master cylinder reservoir as necessary.

NOTE
Do not allow the reservoir to empty, otherwise the entire system will need to be bled after the reservoir is refilled.

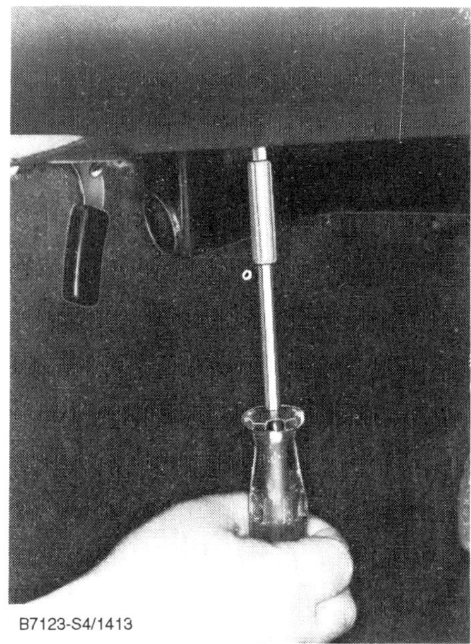

Fig. 3. Left hand footwell air duct being removed.

Fig. 4. Clevis pin (arrow) and clutch master cylinder self-locking nuts **A** to be removed. Master cylinder is removed from engine compartment.

To bleed clutch master and slave cylinders

Tool required

- cooling system pressure tester with cap or equivalent

Bleeding the clutch master cylinder requires that the brake fluid reservoir be pressurized using special equipment. Saab recommends using a coolant system pressure tester and an adaptor that screws onto the brake fluid reservoir. A brake system pressure bleeding kit can also be used for this procedure. These tools and kits are available from automotive tool manufacturers and supply stores.

1. Place a 6 mm. (1/4 in.) inside diameter hose on the slave cylinder bleeder nipple. See Fig. 5. Put the other end of the hose in a container.

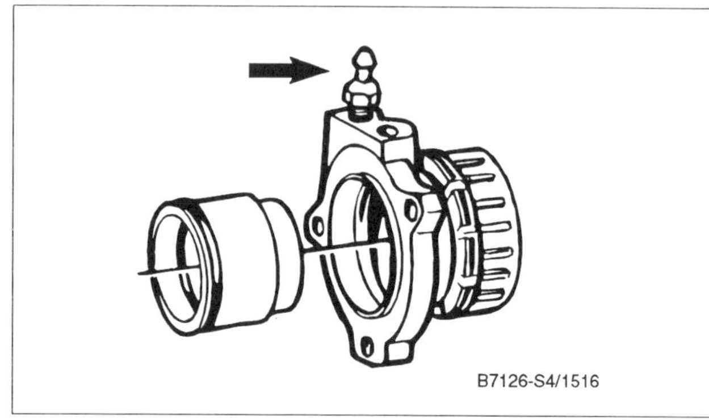

Fig. 5. Slave cylinder bleeder nipple (arrow).

2. Fill the master cylinder reservoir with brake fluid. Place the cooling system pressure tester on the master cylinder.

3. Open the bleeder nipple 1/2 of a turn.

4. Slowly pump up the tester only once or twice until fluid flows out of hose. Allow the fluid to flow until it is free of bubbles.

CAUTION

Too much pressure applied to the system will damage the seals.

---

5. Shut off the bleeder nipple, recheck the fluid level and check the clutch pedal operation.

NOTE

Do not allow the reservoir to empty, otherwise the entire system will need to be bled after the reservoir is refilled.

---

432 Manual Transmission Control

MANUAL TRANSMISSION CONTROL

This section covers repair and adjustment of the gear lever and gear selector rod. Also covered is replacement of the ignition lock cylinder and switch. Many of the fasteners used in the console area are Torx® T25 fasteners. Plan to have this size wrench on hand before performing any work. Also, before doing any adjustments, check the all engine mounts to be sure they are tight and not broken.

To remove gear lever housing

Tool required

- gear lever housing nut wrench .... Saab tool no. 87 90 370

1. Disconnect the negative (–) battery cable and remove the driver's seat. Pull up the handbrake, engage reverse and remove the key.
2. Remove the gear shift bellows, and the two front console screws. See Fig. 1.

Fig. 1. Console front screws (arrows) being removed.

3. Remove the screws under the rear ashtray. See Fig. 2. Disconnect the wires to the interior light switch and remove the console.

NOTE

After removing all console screws, insert the key and disengage reverse gear to help in removing the console.

Fig. 2. Console rear screws (arrows) being removed.

4. Using the special Saab wrench, remove the gear lever housing nuts. See Fig. 3. Label and remove the wires to the ignition switch and reverse switch.

NOTE

- If replacing just the ignition switch, remove the cover plate screws shown in Fig. 4 then remove the two ignition switch screws shown in Fig. 5.
- An impact driver will help remove stuck screws.

432

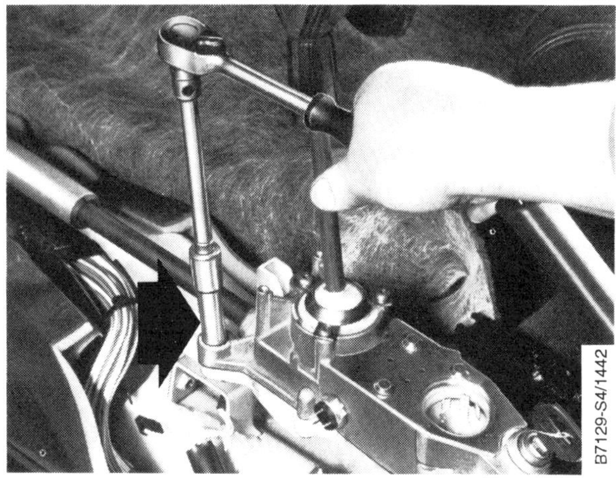

Fig. 3. Gear lever housing nuts being removed with special wrench, Saab tool no. 87 90 370.

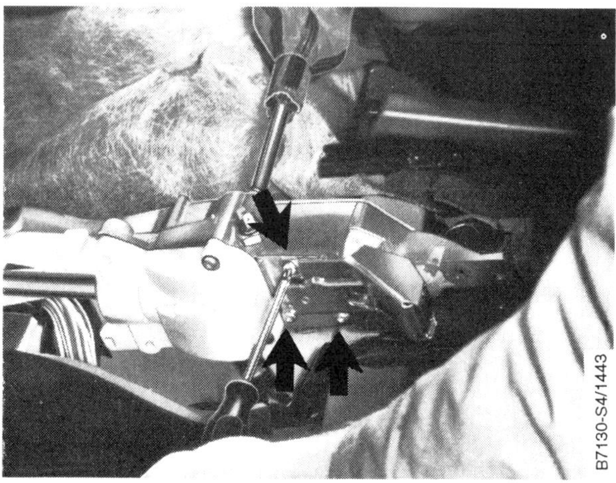

Fig. 4. Cover plate screws (arrows) being removed to replace ignition switch.

Fig. 5. Ignition switch being removed.

NOTE

- Engage the slot in the ignition switch with the tab in the gear lever housing when reinstalling the switch.
- For ignition switch replacement, no further disassembly is required. Adjust the gear shift control as described below.

---

5. Raise and rotate the gear lever housing on its side. Remove the screws securing the plastic bottom cover, remove the housing. See Fig. 6.

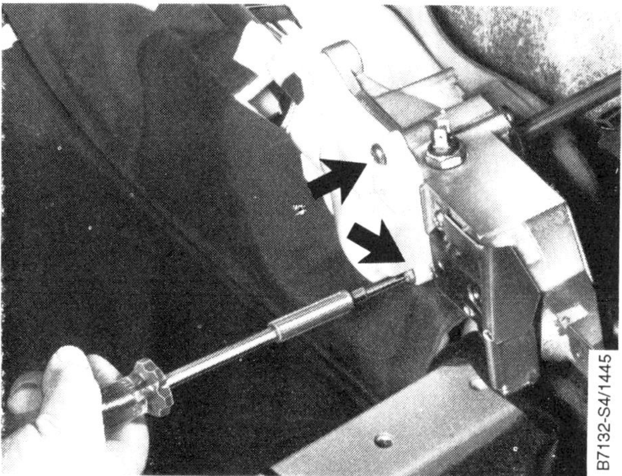

Fig. 6. Plastic bottom cover screws (arrows) being removed.

To remove ignition lock barrel

1. Remove the gear lever housing as described above.
2. Mount the housing in a vise and turn the key to the position shown in Fig. 7.

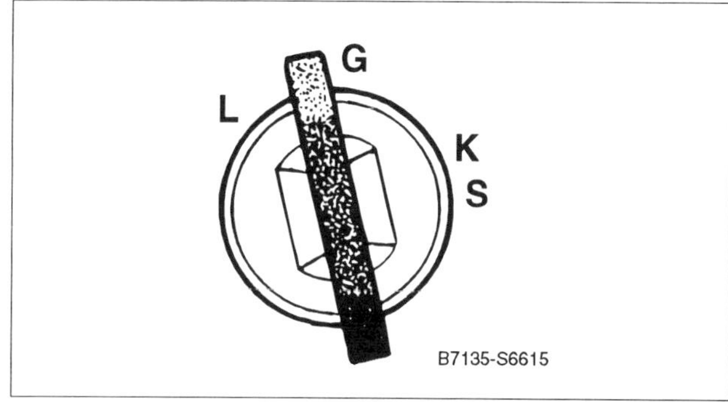

Fig. 7. Position of ignition key to remove lock barrel. View is from above key.

3. Using a stiff wire tool inserted in the hole in the housing, push in the spring loaded pin in the housing while pulling the lock barrel out with the key. See Fig. 8.

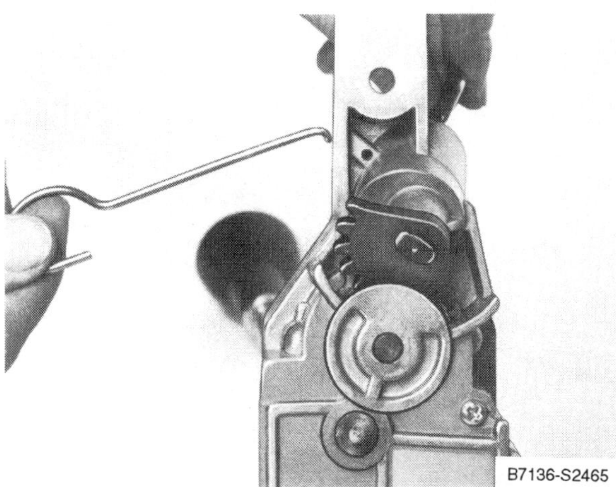

Fig. 8. Ignition lock barrel pin being pushed in. Pull on the key while pushing the pin.

NOTE

If the ignition key is missing, drill a hole in the side of the housing and drive in the pin as shown in Fig. 9.

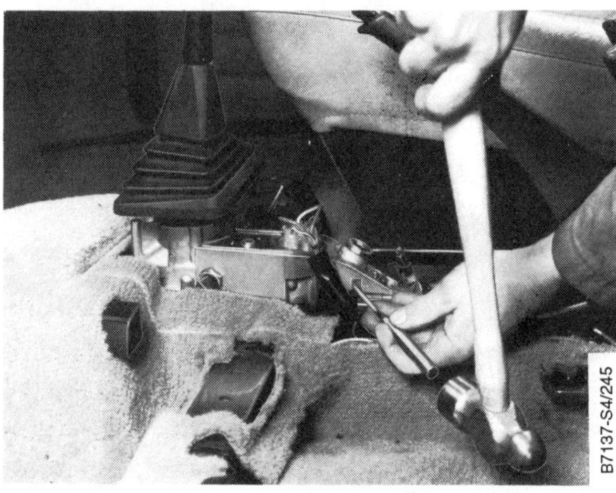

Fig. 9. Ignition lock barrel being removed when key is missing. Drill hole where the punch is located.

To install ignition lock barrel

1. Turn key in the new lock barrel to the position shown in Fig. 7 above.

2. Check that the tooth segment driver pins in the gear lever housing are in the correct position to accept the lock barrel.

3. Push in the spring loaded pin on the lock barrel and insert the barrel in the gear lever housing until it clicks.

To remove gear selector rod

1. Remove the gear lever housing as described above.

2. Loosen the clamp on the selector rod where the rod comes through the firewall. See Fig. 10.

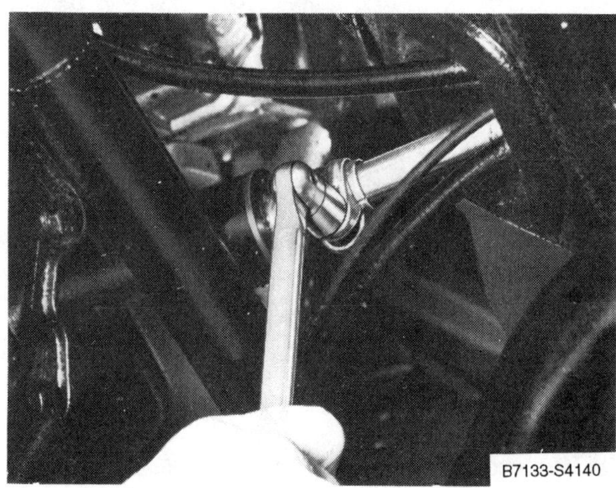

Fig. 10. Selector rod clamp being loosened.

3. Remove the rod from inside the passenger compartment.

4. After installing the rod, adjust the gear shift control as described below. Torque the clamp bolt.

Shift rod clamp bolt

• tightening torque . . . . . . .30 to 35 Nm (22 to 25 ft-lb)

NOTE

Inspect and replace any worn rubber bushings. Worn bushings may cause hard shifting or jumping out of gear.

To disassemble gear shift lever

1. Remove the gear lever housing as described above.

2. Remove the three screws and remove the gear shift lever. See Fig. 11.

3. Measure and record the length of the latch stud as shown in Fig. 12.

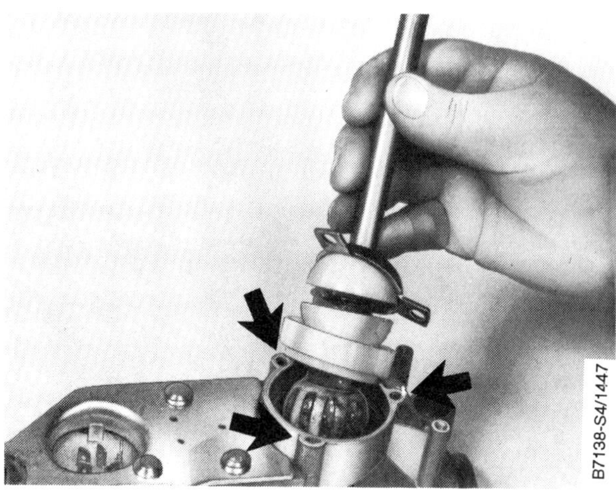

Fig. 11. Gear shift lever being removed after removing screws located at arrows.

CAUTION
The latch stud prevents the shift lever from accidentally going into reverse when attempting to shift into 5th gear. The length of the latch stud must not be altered or the lockout feature may not work.

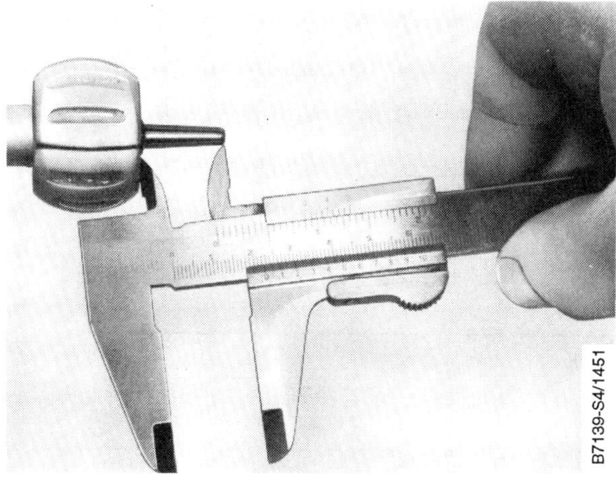

Fig. 12. Gear shift lever latch stud being measured. The length is adjustable.

Gear shift lever latch stud
- projecting length
  22±0.5 mm (55/64 in.)

4. Remove the wire clip, sleeve, spring, and bearings. See Fig. 13.

5. Unscrew the latch stud from the rod. See Fig. 14. Remove the rubber bellows and shift knob.

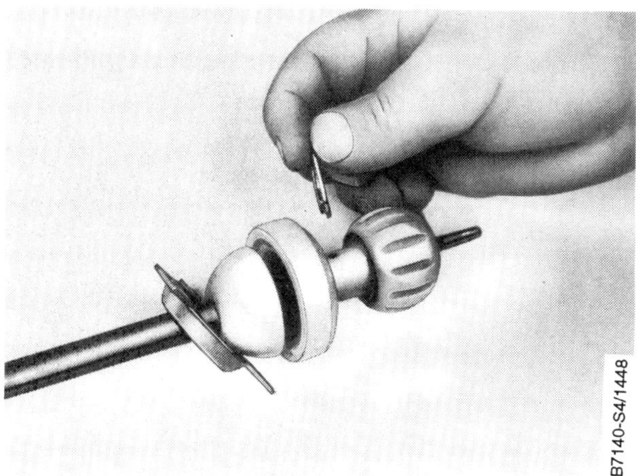

Fig. 13. Gear shift lever being disassembled.

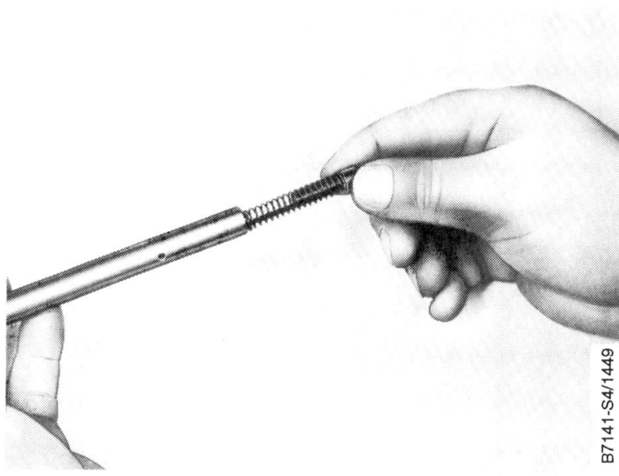

Fig. 14. Gear shift lever latch stud being unscrewed.

6. Inspect and replace any worn components. Adjust the latch stud projecting length to the value given above. See Fig. 12.

7. Reassemble the lever and housing. Grease all sliding components with soft EPI grease. See Fig. 15 for an exploded view of the assembly.

To adjust gear shift control (up to mid 1986)

1. Remove just the console as described earlier. Engage reverse gear, and release the clamp on the shift rod. See Fig. 10 above.

2. Lock the gear shift lever in position by inserting a 6 mm (1/4 in.) pilot tool in the hole as shown in Fig. 16.

NOTE
A drill bit or drift works well as a pilot tool.

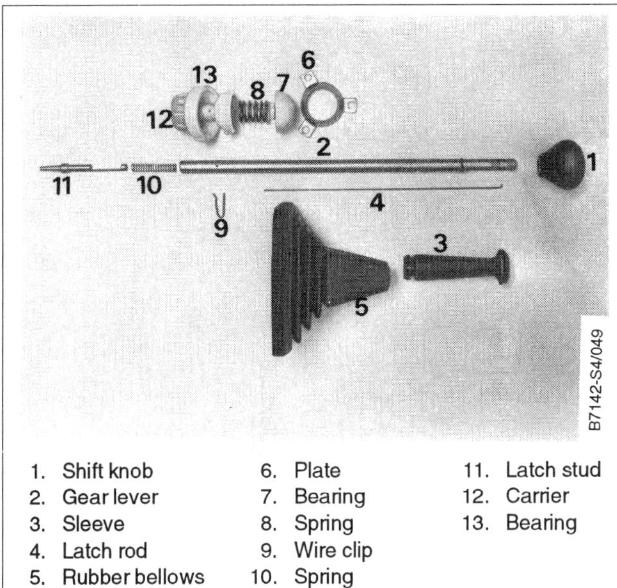

Fig. 15. Gear shift lever assembly exploded view.

Fig. 16. Gear shift lever being locked into reverse prior to tightening shift rod clamp. Turbo model shown with console bellows (arrow) removed. Other models are similar.

3. Tighten the clamp on the shift rod to the torque given below. Remove the pilot tool and reinstall the console.

Shift rod clamp bolt

• tightening torque . . . . 30 to 35 Nm (22 to 25 ft-lb)

To adjust gear shift control (from mid 1986)

Tool required

• shift rod alignment tool . . . . Saab tool no. 87 91 576

---

1. Remove only the console as described earlier under removing the gear selector housing. Engage third gear and insert the special tool in the differential cover as shown in Fig. 17.

Fig. 17. Shift rod alignment tool (arrow) installed in back of differential cover. Shift lever must be in third gear.

2. Loosen the shift rod clamp bolt. See Fig. 10 above.

3. Lock the gear shift lever in third gear by inserting a 6 mm (1/4 in.) pilot tool in the hole as shown in Fig. 18.

Fig. 18. Gear shift lever being locked in 3rd gear prior to tightening shift rod clamp.

NOTE
A drill bit or drift works well as a pilot tool.

4. Tighten the shift rod clamp. Remove the special tool from the differential cover and remove the pilot tool. Reinstall the console.

Tightening torque
- Shift rod clamp bolt. . . . . 30 to 35 Nm (22 to 25 ft-lb)

To adjust centering of gear shift lever in neutral gate (up to mid 1986 only)

The gear shift lever is in its proper neutral position if it can be shifted straight forward into third gear without having to "fish" around for the gear. No adjustment can be done on models from mid 1986 on.

1. To adjust models up to mid 1986, pull the carpeting away from the front of the shift lever, then engage third gear.

2. Loosen the two retainer screws. Move the bracket so the rollers drop into the plastic block grooves. See Fig. 19.

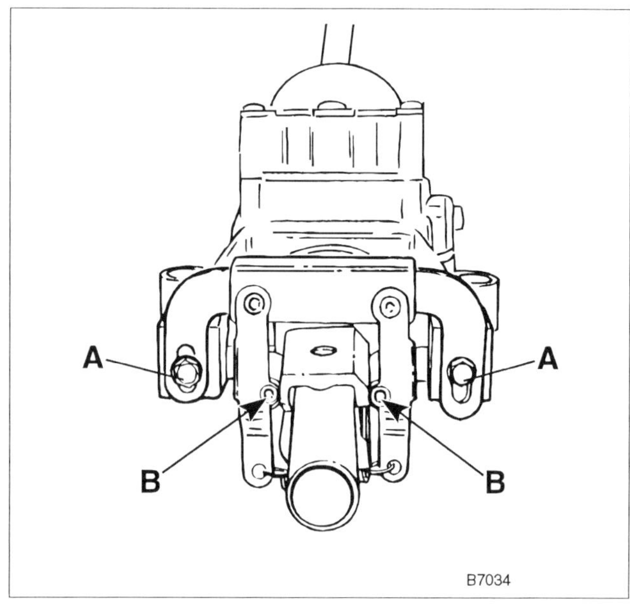

Fig. 19. Gear shift centering mechanism retainer screws **A** and rollers **B**. Adjustment is done with gearshift in 3rd gear.

3. Tighten the retaining screws and recheck the adjustment as described above. Reinstall the console pieces.

444 Automatic Transmission Controls

TRANSMISSION CONTROLS

To check shift lever and linkage

1. Move the selector lever to the **N** position. Press the pawl button and move the lever slightly back and forth.
2. Release the pawl button and check that the lever is positioned exactly at position **N**. If not, then adjust the gear selector cable as described below.

CAUTION
Correct adjustment of the gear selector cable is vital to the functioning and life of the transmission.

Fig. 1. Shift indicator plate being moved to reveal cover screw (arrow) below. Screw on opposite side (not shown) must also be removed.

To remove gear selector cable

Tool required
- gear selector housing wrench — Saab tool no. 87 90 370

1. Disconnect the negative (–) battery cable. Move the front seats to their fully rear position. Apply the handbrake.
2. Move the gear selector to **P** and remove the ignition key.
3. Remove the indicator plate and slide it toward the shift knob. See Fig. 1.
4. Remove the cover screws and slide the plastic console up enough to disconnect the wires to the interior light switch. Remove the console. See Fig. 2.
5. Working at the transmission, remove the cable retaining bolt. See Fig. 3.
6. Slide back the spring loaded cable sleeve and unhook it from the transmission shift rod. See Fig. 4.
7. Remove the gear selector housing nuts using special Saab wrench no. 87 90 370. Rotate the housing onto its side then remove the circlip and pin from the end of the cable.

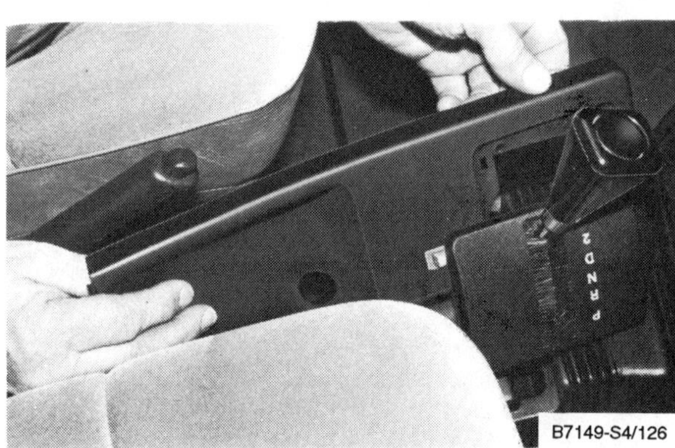

Fig. 2. Gear selector housing console being removed.

Fig. 3. Transmission cable retaining bolt (arrow).

444

Fig. 4. Transmission cable being unhooked from transmission shift rod. Shift lever must be in **P**.

8. Remove the setscrew that secures the cable to the lever. See Fig. 5. Loosen the cable jacket nuts and remove the cable.

NOTE
The cable jacket nuts hold the cable to the bottom of the shift lever housing.

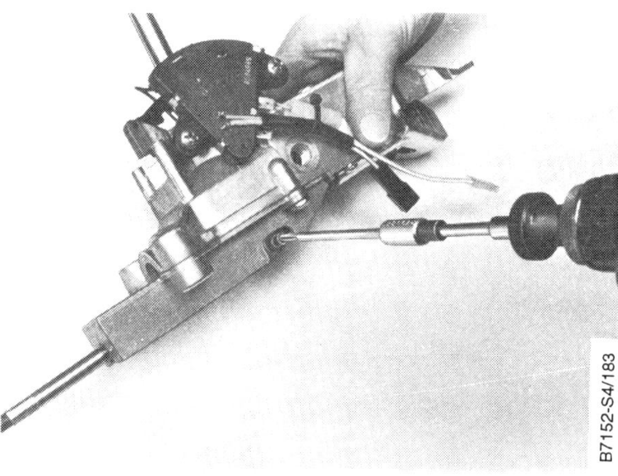

Fig. 5. Transmission cable setscrew being removed using internal-hex head wrench. Housing removed from car for clarity.

9. Remove the carpeting, heater duct, and the old cable.

To install and adjust gear selector cable

NOTE
Proper transmission operation and service life depends on the correct adjustment of the selector cable.

---

1. Install the new cable and check for a proper seal where the cable passes through the firewall.

2. Hook the cable to the transmission shift rod in the transmission, then insert the cable into the transmission case and install the retaining bolt to the case.

3. In the car, install the end of the cable into the selector lever hole and secure with the pin and circlip. Tighten the cable jacket nuts.

4. Withdraw the wire in the cable as far as possible, corresponding to position **P** as if the cable were attached to the shift lever. Move the cable in two notches corresponding to position **N**.

5. Move the gear selector to position **N** without disturbing the cable position. Install and tighten the cable setscrew. See Fig. 5 above.

Tightening torque
• Cable setscrew. . . . . 2.5 Nm (23 in-lb)

---

6. Install the gear selector housing nuts using the special Saab wrench no. 87 90 370.

CAUTION
The gear selector housing must be securely fastened to the floor console.

---

7. Perform a final check by moving the selector lever to position **D**. Release the pawl button and move the lever to position **2**. Increasing resistance should be felt in both directions. Slight movement should be felt before the lever is locked by the selector lever housing detent. If not, then the cable is not adjusted correctly.

The remaining is the reverse of removal. Be sure to check the operation of the neutral safety switch, interior lighting switch and the parking pawl.

To remove and install transmission throttle cable

The transmission throttle cable enters the transmission below the torque converter on the driver's side. It moves a cam in the transmission valve body. After replacment, the cable must be adjusted and the ATF must be topped up.

1. Disconnect the cable from the throttle lever and from its attachment to the retaining plate on the throttle housing.

2. Drain the ATF from the transmission and remove the forward sump cover. See **472 Automatic Transmission Seals and Gaskets**. Remove the ATF strainer.

CAUTION

- Do not dislodge any of the pipes in the valve body. The transmission will have to be removed from the car to reinstall these pipes.

- Do not allow any dirt to enter the transmission, or damage may result.

3. Detach the throttle cable from the cam on the control valve at the valve body. See Fig. 6. Unscrew the cable from the transmission housing. See Fig. 7.

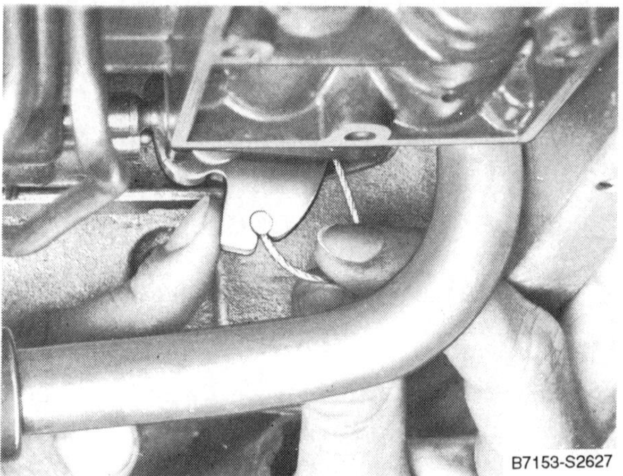

Fig. 6. Transmission throttle cable being unhooked from cam at valve body.

Fig. 7. Transmission throttle cable being unscrewed from transmission housing.

4. Connect a new cable to the transmission housing. Hook the cable end onto the cam at the control valve at the valve body.Make sure that the cable wire is seated in the cam guide.

5. Working at the other end of the cable, straighten the cable and pull the wire until slight tension of the cam is felt. Using pliers, clamp the stop clip next to the threaded cable sheath. See Fig. 8.

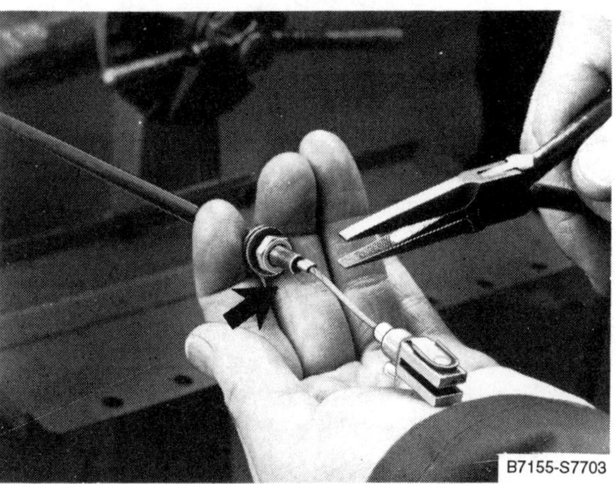

Fig. 8. Stop clip (arrow) being clamped on a new cable. The cable must be straight and slightly tensioned against cam in valve body.

6. Connect the cable to the throttle housing. Floor the accelerator pedal and adjust the nuts until the highest point of the cam on the control valve is aligned as shown in Fig. 9. This is the kickdown position.

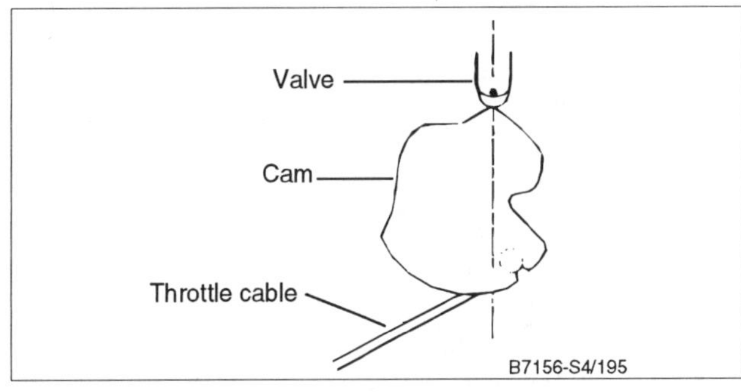

Fig. 9. Cam in valve body in kickdown position for initial throttle cable adjustment at throttle housing.

The remaining is the reverse of removal. Use a new ATF strainer if clogged or damaged. Install a new sump gasket and refill the transmission with new ATF. Check and correct any binding in the accelerator pedal linkage. Finally, do the precision adjustment described below.

To adjust transmission throttle cable

Precise adjustment of the cable should be done after installation of a new cable or if the kickdown function is inoperative. A helper is needed to complete the adjustment procedure.

Tool required

- ATF pressure gauge — Saab tool no. 87 91 592 or equivalent

1. Remove the pressure tap on the transmission and install the pressure gauge. See **400 Transmission–General** for information on performing a pressure test.

2. Block the wheels and apply the handbrake. Start the engine and check for correct idle speed with the gear selector in position **P**.

3. Disconnect the transmission throttle cable from the throttle lever.

4. Firmly apply the footbrake. Engage **D** with the selector lever. Pull and release the cable wire several times. Record the gauge pressure with the wire released.

NOTE

If pressure does not return to the same value, the control valve in the valve body may be sticking and needs to be cleaned.

---

5. Reconnect the cable to the throttle lever. Line pressure should increase by 0.1 bar (1.5 psi). If pressure does not increase by 0.1 bar (1.5 psi), adjust the cable at the throttle lever while watching the pressure gauge. The correct pressure values are given below.

Line pressure

- 4.2 to 4.9 bar (61 to 71 psi)

To remove governor

The governor controls when the transmission shifts. Most problems with the governor occur from dirty ATF. See **400 Transmission–General** for more information on troubleshooting the governor.

The governor can be removed without disassembling the transmission. Extreme cleanliness must be observed when installing the sump cover. Refill the transmission with ATF as described in **1 LUBRICATION AND MAINTENANCE**.

1. Apply the handbrake and block the wheels. Set the selector lever to **N**. Drain the automatic transmission fluid.

NOTE

Do not drain the final drive fluid.

---

2. Remove the support member under the sump.

3. Clean the bottom part of the transmission around the rear sump pan. Remove the sump bolts.

4. Remove the pan by rotating it 1/8 of a turn to gain clearance around the cross member. See Fig. 10.

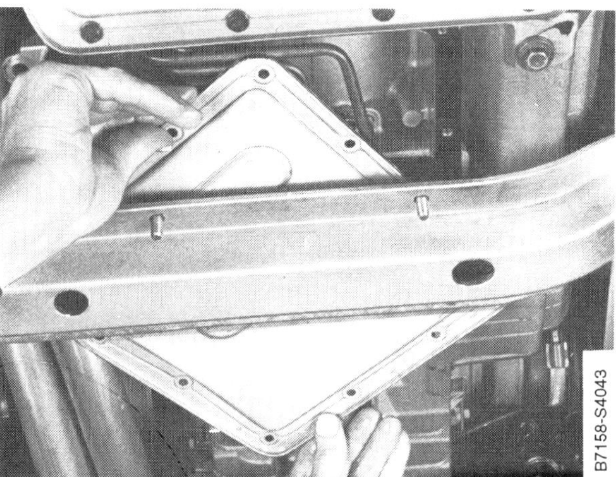

Fig. 10. ATF sump pan being removed from car.

5. Remove the two screws and remove the governor. See Fig. 11.

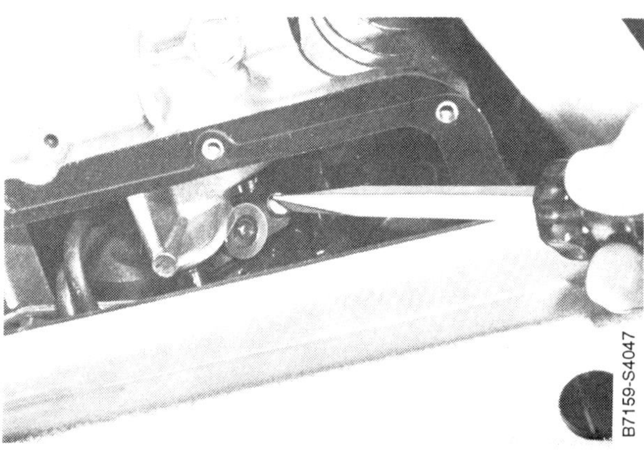

Fig. 11. Governor being removed from transmission.

NOTE

To gain access to the governor screws, rotate one of the wheels while holding the other stationary. This will change the position of the governor.

Installation is the reverse of removal. Be sure the cover plate for the governor faces toward the pinion bearing housing. Reinstall the ATF sump pan with a new gasket. See **472 Automatic Transmission Seals and Gaskets**. Fill the transmission with new fluid, and check for leaks.

Tightening torques

- ATF sump pan bolts . . . . 8 to 12 Nm (71 to 106 in-lb)
- ATF sump pan drain plug . . 5 to 8 Nm (44 to 71 in-lb)

---

472 Automatic Transmission Seals and Gaskets

GENERAL

This repair group covers replacement of the automatic transmission pan (sump) gasket and replacement of the automatic transmission fluid cooler only. Other automatic transmission gaskets and seals require disassembly of the transmission, which is not covered in this manual.

Automatic Transmission Pan Gasket

The gaskets used on sump pans are easily replaced in the car by removing the bolts around the pan. See Fig. 1. Refill the sump with new ATF, then start the car and select **P** for 15 seconds, select **D** for 15 seconds and select **R** for 15 seconds to circulate the ATF. Reselect **P** and check the fluid level at idle. Shut off the engine and check for leaks.

WARNING
Always firmly apply the handbrake before starting the engine.

Fig. 1. ATF front cover sump bolts being removed. Rear sump cover can be seen in background. The ATF drain plug is located at **A**.

Tightening torques
- ATF sump pan bolts . . . 8 to 12 Nm (71 to 106 in-lb)
- ATF sump pan drain plug. . . . . 5 to 8 Nm (44 to 71 in-lb)

Automatic Transmission Specifications
- Grade of ATF—Ford Specification M2C-33F (alternate: Ford Specification G)
- ATF capacity 8.5 quarts (8.0 liters)

CAUTION
- Use only Ford spec M2C-33F/G ATF. Do not use other types of fluid.
- Do not allow any dirt to enter the transmission or damage may result.

Other areas where leakage can occur are at the torque converter-to-ATF pump seal and at the front cover gasket. The pump seal is integral with the ATF pump housing. Replacing this seal requires that the front cover, primary chain and sprocket, and the ATF pump be removed from the transmission housing.

The pinion bearing housing seals can leak allowing ATF and final drive fluid to mix. The only remedy is to disassemble the transmission and replace the seals. Special tools and techniques are required for the above procedures and are best left to an authorized Saab dealer.

Automatic Transmission Fluid Cooler

The cooler should be replaced if it is visibly leaking. The cooler can also leak internally, causing the engine coolant to mix with the ATF. When this happens, the ATF usually has a milky appearance.

To replace ATF cooler

1. Drain the engine coolant as described in **261 Radiator and Cooling System.**

2. Disconnect the coolant hose clamps and the ATF hoses. Then remove the cooler. See Fig. 2. Some models are equipped with an ATF thermostat in-line with the ATF cooler.

Fig. 2. ATF cooler. Arrows show coolant hose clamps and ATF hoses to be removed.

ATF cooler connection nut
- 13 to 16 Nm (10 to 12 ft-lb)

Installation is the reverse of removal. Always replace O-rings and gaskets. Be sure to top up the ATF.

CAUTION
- Always replace the ATF and flush out all ATF hoses if coolant contamination has occurred.
- If a reconditioned transmission is being installed, flush out the ATF cooler and hoses with clean ATF.

---

500 Brakes—General

TABLES

GENERAL

All cars covered by this manual are equipped with disc brakes at all four wheels. See Fig. 1. The brake system is hydraulically actuated by the master cylinder and has power assist. The brakes are self-adjusting. The parking brake system is mechanical using cables connected to the calipers. Some later models are equipped with an anti-lock braking system (ABS).

Models without ABS use a vacuum booster for power assist. Models with ABS provide power assist through the ABS unit.

The brake disc, also known as the rotor, is mounted to each wheel hub. Two brake pads, one on either side of the disc are located within the caliper. The caliper piston applies force to the brake pads. When the brakes are applied, the friction-surfaced brake pads slow the car. See Fig. 2. A combination of flexible and rigid brake lines connect the calipers to the hydraulic system and master cylinder.

The brake pedal directly actuates the master cylinder. The master cylinder creates pressure in two hydraulic circuits. The two hydraulic circuits form the dual-diagonal braking system where diagonally opposite wheels are braked by one circuit. The system assures a level of braking control if one circuit should fail.

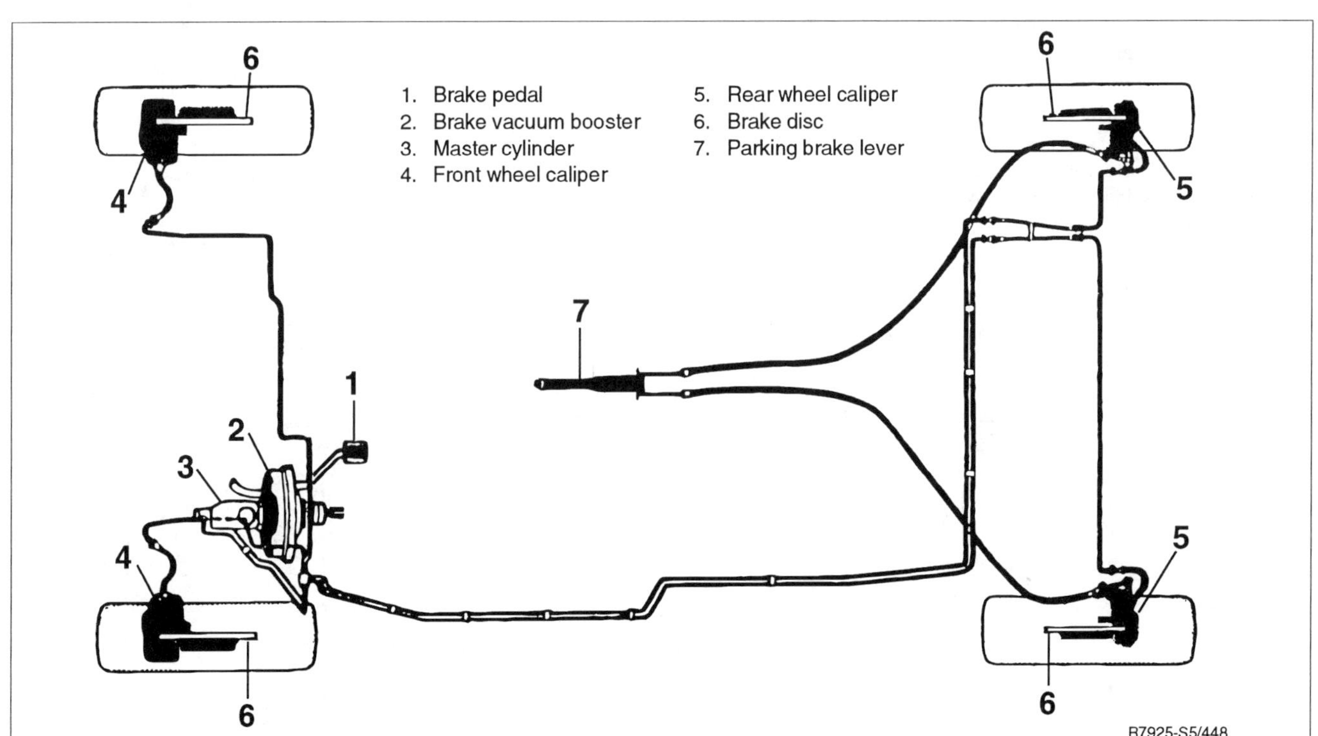

Fig. 1. Four wheel disc brake system

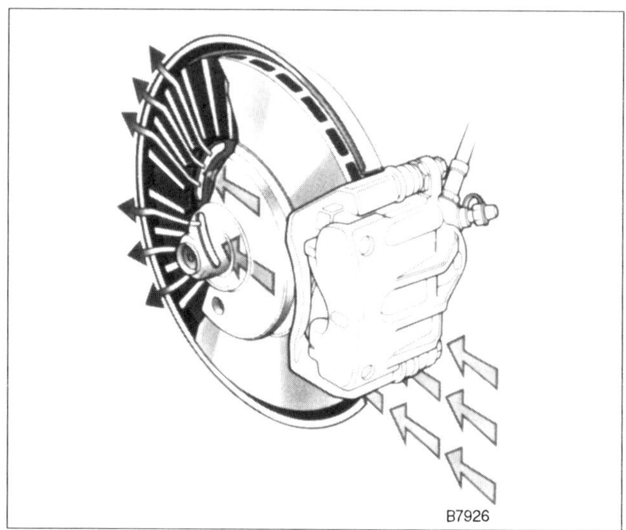

Fig. 2. Brake disc and caliper. Airflow over the brakes (arrows) helps cool the caliper and disc.

ANTI-LOCK BRAKING SYSTEM (ABS)

The ABS system, used on some late models, was developed to ensure optimum braking ability under widely varying road and weather conditions. See Fig. 3. The system monitors and automatically controls braking at the front wheels individually and the rear wheels as a pair—preventing the wheels from locking during emergency braking situations. Steering control is maintained during braking and the shortest possible stopping distance is achieved. The ABS system only operates during emergency stops or hard braking. During most normal braking situations, the system is not in operation.

The ABS system can be simplified into four basic components that operate in a closed loop. See Fig. 4. The wheel speed sensors at all four wheels measure wheel speed. The control unit constantly compares these signals to determine when one wheel is not rotating at the same speed as the others—indicating a potential lock-up condition. Using this information, the control unit regulates the opening and closing of the solenoid valves to adjust the fluid (hydraulic) pressure to the calipers.

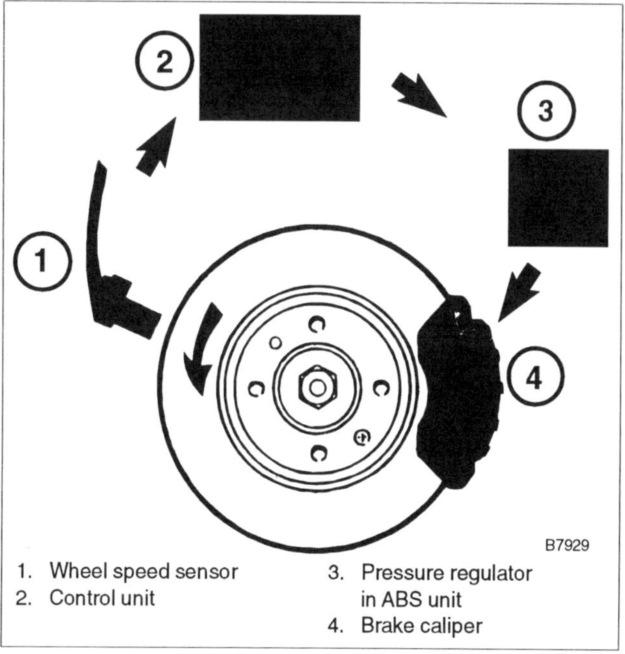

Fig. 4. Basic representation ABS system closed-loop operation.

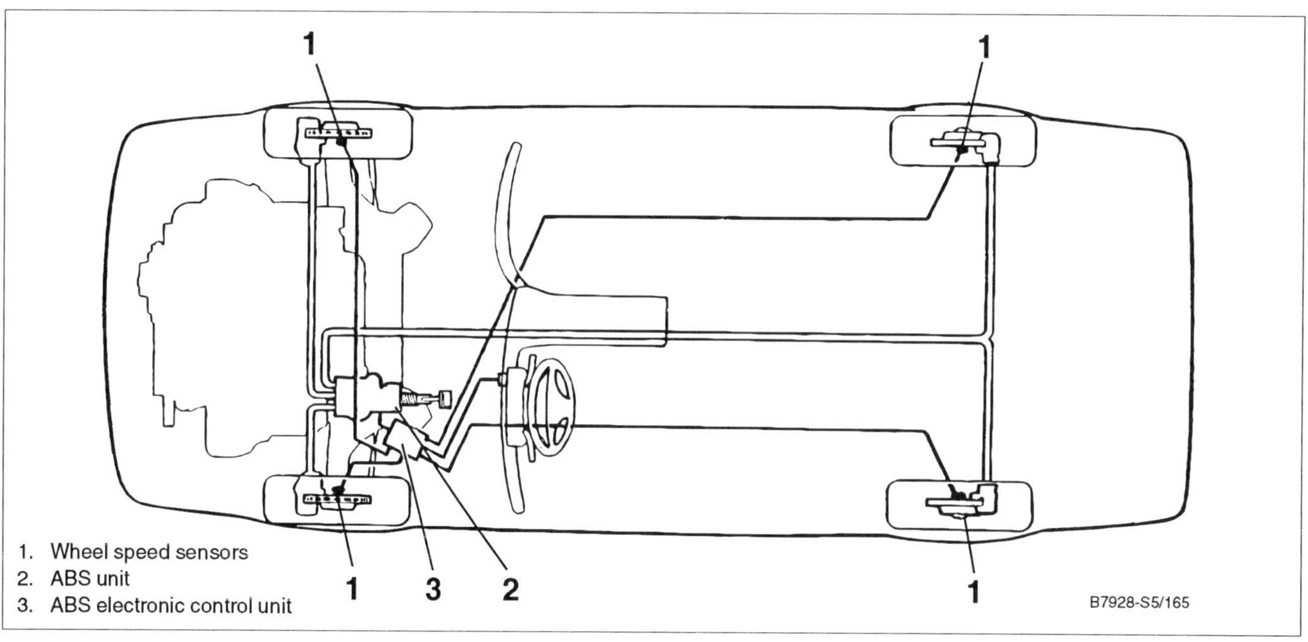

Fig. 3. Schematic of ABS system.

The ABS unit is shown in Fig. 5. The pump pressurizes the accumulator to provide power assist normally provided by the vacuum booster. The accumulator holds enough pressure in the system to provide power assist for approximately twenty stops if the pump should fail. The ABS system is able to monitor itself and if there is a sensor or control system failure it will revert to the non-ABS mode.

NOTE
For information on replacing the ABS unit, see **521 Brake Master Cylinder**. For ABS wiring and ABS wheel speed sensor testing, see **371 Wiring Diagrams, Fuses and Relays**

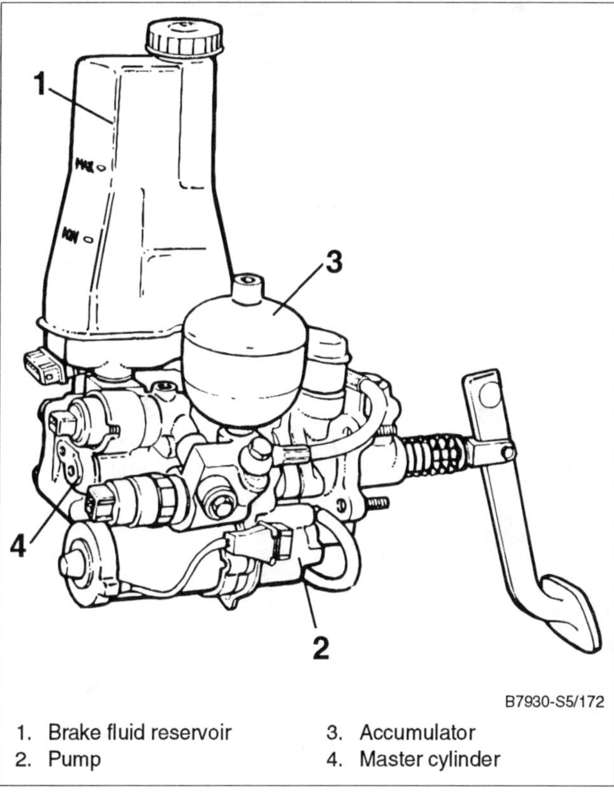

1. Brake fluid reservoir
2. Pump
3. Accumulator
4. Master cylinder

Fig. 5. ABS unit.

The ANTI-LOCK and the BRAKE FLUID warning lamps in the instrument cluster monitor the system. The ANTI-LOCK warning lamp will light up if a problem or fault occurs in the ABS system. The BRAKE FLUID warning lamp will light up if the brake fluid level in the reservoir falls too low. See an authorized Saab dealer if either warning lamps come on.

WARNING
If the ANTI-LOCK and the BRAKE FLUID warning lamp should come on, the car must not be driven. Brake failure may occur. Have the problem corrected promptly by an authorized Saab dealer.

WARNING
On cars with ABS, dangerously high pressure may be retained in the system, even though the car is not running or has not been driven recently. Before loosening any components, depressurize the system by disconnecting the battery negative cable and pressing the brake pedal 25 to 30 times, or until there is a noticeable increase in pedal effort. Never attempt to open the pressure accumulator.

NOTE
The control unit has the capability to detect and store fault codes, although retrieving these faults codes requires special test equipment. See an authorized Saab dealer for additional information on ABS fault codes.

To replace ABS wheel speed sensor

Replacement of wheel speed sensors is similar for either the front or the rear. The sensor is a sealed unit and cannot be repaired. Be sure to have a new fiber washer on hand when removing or replacing the sensor. The washer is used to precisely set the air gap between the sensor and the toothed wheel.

1. Working in the engine compartment, disconnect the negative battery cable and the wheel speed sensor connectors. See Fig. 6.

NOTE
The wheel speed sensor connectors for the rear wheels are located under the rear seat.

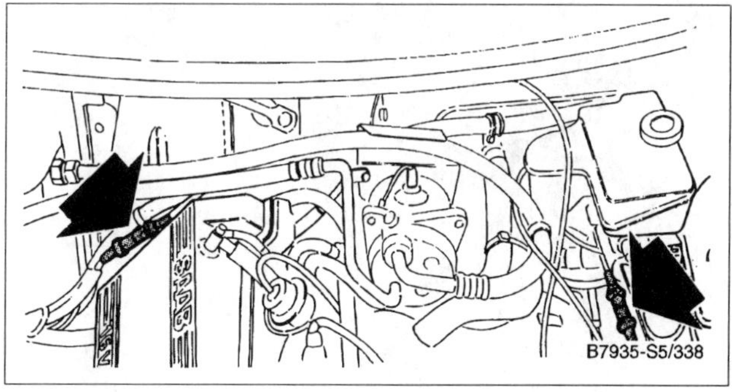

Fig. 6. Location of front wheel speed sensor connectors (arrows).

2. Raise the car and support it with jackstands. Remove the road wheels.

WARNING
Make sure the car is well supported with jackstands. Never use just a jack to support a car.

3. Remove the sensor harness from the steering member. Carefully pull the sensor lead through the rubber grommet in the wheel arch. See Fig. 7.

NOTE

The rubber grommets for the rear wheel speed sensors are located in the floor pan and can be found by tracing the harness from the wheel.

Fig. 7. Front ABS wheel speed sensor harness guide **A** and rubber grommet **B**.

4. Remove the wheel speed sensor. See Fig. 8 and Fig. 9.

Fig. 8. Front wheel speed sensor retaining screw being removed.

5. Remove the plastic sleeve from the sensor housing. See Fig. 10.

Fig. 9. Rear wheel speed sensor retaining screw being removed.

NOTE

When removing rear wheel speed sensors, remove the parking brake cable guide from the suspension spring link then remove the wheel speed sensor harness from the clips. See Fig. 11.

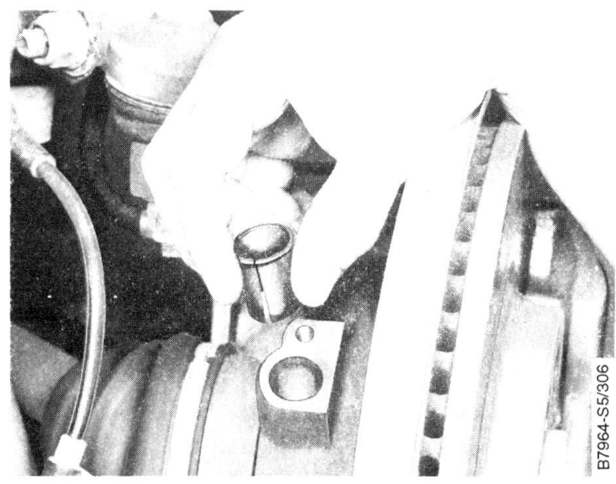

Fig. 10. Plastic sleeve being removed from sensor housing.

6. Clean out the sensor housing in the steering member or axle. Spin the wheel hub slowly and clean out any debris in the toothed wheel.

7. Working at the bench, clamp the sensor adjusting sleeve in a vice and remove the setscrew. See Fig. 12. Remove the sensor from the adjusting sleeve.

CAUTION

Clamp only the sensor sleeve. Do not clamp the metal part of the sensor, as this will damage it.

Fig. 11. Parking brake cable guide (**A**) and wire harness clip (**B**) holding wheel speed sensor harness to rear suspension spring link.

Fig. 12. Setscrew being removed from wheel speed sensor sleeve.

8. Clean any debris from the end of the wheel speed sensor and sensor sleeve using a wire brush. Lightly lubricate the sensor body.

9. Glue a new fiber spacer to the tip of the wheel speed sensor. Install the new sensor in the sensor sleeve.

CAUTION

The fiber spacer has a thickness of 0.65 mm to provide the sensor with the proper clearance to the toothed wheel. Do not spin the toothed wheel until the sensor has been completely installed. If the fiber washer is damaged, the sensor may be incorrectly installed.

Specification

- ABS wheel speed sensor air gap . . . . 0.65 mm (0.026 in.)

---

10. Install the wheel speed sensor and tighten the retaining screw. See Fig. 8 or 9 above.

11. Gently press the sensor body against the sensor wheel then tighten the setscrew.

The remainder of installation is the reverse of removal. Check that the ABS warning light comes on for several seconds when starting the engine. It should then go out.

BRAKES TROUBLESHOOTING

This troubleshooting section applies mainly to the mechanical and hydraulic components regardless of whether or not the car is equipped with ABS. It is important to realize that ABS only operates when one or more wheels are about to lock during emergency or otherwise hard braking. It is very unlikely that ABS components are the cause of more conventional brake noise or grabbing symptoms.

NOTE

This troubleshooting section does not specifically include troubleshooting for ABS. If an ABS system fault exists, see an authorized Saab dealer who has the necessary training and diagnostic equipment to properly service the system.

The most common brake problems and repairs involve the brake calipers, pads, and brake discs since these components are exposed to heat, water, chemicals, and corrosion.

Table a. Brake Troubleshooting

Symptom	Probable cause	Corrective action
1. Brake squeak or squeal	**a.** Normal condition **b.** Brake pads installed incorrectly **c.** Calipers or brake pads binding, brake caliper guide pins or caliper dirty or corroded **d.** Brake pad lining worn **e.** Brake pad linings heat-glazed or oil-soaked	**a.** See **516 Brake Discs** **b.** Check installation. **517 Brake Pads** **c.** Clean calipers and/or guide pins. **523 Brake Calipers**, **517 Brake Pads** **d.** Install new pads. **517 Brake Pads** **e.** Replace brake pads. Clean discs. Replace leaking calipers as required. **517 Brake Pads**, **516 Brake Discs**, **523 Brake Calipers**
2. No brakes, pedal goes to floor	**a.** Brake fluid level too low **b.** Master cylinder faulty **c.** Failed line or hose, loose union, or other major fluid leak	**a.** Check fluid level. Check for leaks. Fill and bleed system. **520 Brake Fluid and Brake Bleeding** **b.** Replace master cylinder. **521 Brake Master Cylinder** **c.** Check for leaks. Fill and bleed system. **522 Brake Lines**
3. Low pedal, (brakes properly bled, no signs of leakage)	**a.** Master cylinder faulty	**a.** Replace master cylinder. **521 Brake Master Cylinder**
4. Pedal feels spongy or brakes work only after pedal is pumped	**a.** Insufficient brake fluid **b.** Air in brake fluid **c.** Master cylinder faulty **d.** Leaking line and hose unions	**a.** Check fluid level. Check for leaks. Fill and bleed system. See **520 Brake Fluid and Brake Bleeding** **b.** Bleed system. **520 Brake Fluid and Brake Bleeding** **c.** Replace master cylinder. **521 Brake Master Cylinder** **d.** Check for leaks. Fill and bleed system. **522 Brake Lines**
5. High pedal effort required (braking performance poor)	**a.** Brake pads wet **b.** Brake pads heat-glazed or oil-soaked **c.** Vacuum booster or vacuum connections faulty (non-ABS cars only) **d.** Faulty master cylinder	**a.** Use light pedal pressure to dry brakes while driving. **b.** Replace brake pads. Clean discs. Replace leaking calipers as required. **517 Brake Pads**, **516 Brake Discs**, **523 Brake Calipers** **c.** Inspect vacuum lines and check valve. Test booster and replace as required. **541 Brake Vacuum Booster** **d.** Replace master cylinder. **521 Brake Master Cylinder**
6. Brakes pulsate, chatter, or grab	**a.** Warped brake discs **b.** Brake pads worn **c.** Brake pads heat-glazed or oil-soaked	**a.** Recondition or replace discs. **516 Brake Discs** **b.** Recondition brakes. **517 Brake Pads** **c.** Replace brake pads. Clean discs. Replace leaking calipers as required. **517 Brake Pads**, **516 Brake Discs**, **523 Brake Calipers**
7. Uneven braking, car pulls to one side	**a.** Incorrect tire pressures **b.** Brake pads heat-glazed or oil-soaked **c.** Brake caliper or brake pads binding **d.** Brake fluid contaminated **e.** Worn tires or suspension components	**a.** Check and correct tire pressures. See **1 LUBRICATION AND MAINTENANCE** **b.** Replace brake pads. Clean discs. Replace leaking calipers as required. **517 Brake Pads**, **516 Brake Discs**, **523 Brake Calipers** **c.** Clean and recondition brakes. Check parking brake adjustment. **517 Brake Pads**, **516 Brake Discs**, **523 Brake Calipers**, **551 Parking Brake** **d.** Drain, flush, refill, and bleed brake system. **520 Brake Fluid and Brake Bleeding** **e.** See **6 STEERING AND WHEEL ALIGNMENT**, **7 SUSPENSION**
8. Brakes drag, bind, or overheat	**a.** Parking brake dragging **b.** Brake caliper or brake pad binding **c.** Master cylinder faulty	**a.** Adjust parking brake. Replace caliper or caliper return spring. **551 Parking Brake** **b.** Clean and recondition brakes. **517 Brake Pads**, **516 Brake Discs**, **523 Brake Calipers** **c.** Replace master cylinder. **521 Brake Master Cylinder**
9. Brakes make loud clunk when backing up	**a.** Caliper yoke worn **b.** Caliper guide pins worn or pre-set bend in pin no longer exists	**a.** Replace caliper assembly. **523 Brake Calipers** **b.** Replace guide pins. **523 Brake Calipers**

516 Brake Discs

TABLES

GENERAL

Fig. 1 is an exploded view of the front disc brake. Two types of front discs—ventilated and solid—are used on cars covered by this manual, depending on models and model year. See **Table a.** The rear discs are solid on all models. The brake disc is bolted to the wheel hub and can be removed once the caliper is removed.

Table a. Front Brake Disc Applications

Model year and Model	Disc type
1985 through 1987 900	Solid
1985 and 1986 900s	Solid
1985 Turbo	Solid
1987 900s	Ventilated
1986 through 1987 Turbo, including convertible	Ventilated
1988 and later, All	Ventilated

Discs and brake pads are subject to the greatest wear and are the components most often requiring service. While it possible to restore the brakes by replacing only the brake pads, the discs should be resurfaced or replaced at the same time to achieve full braking performance and to maximize pad life.

INSPECTING AND REPLACING BRAKE DISCS

Inspecting the brake discs should be done during regular service or when the brakes are reconditioned. The discs should be checked for cracks, scoring, glazing and warpage.

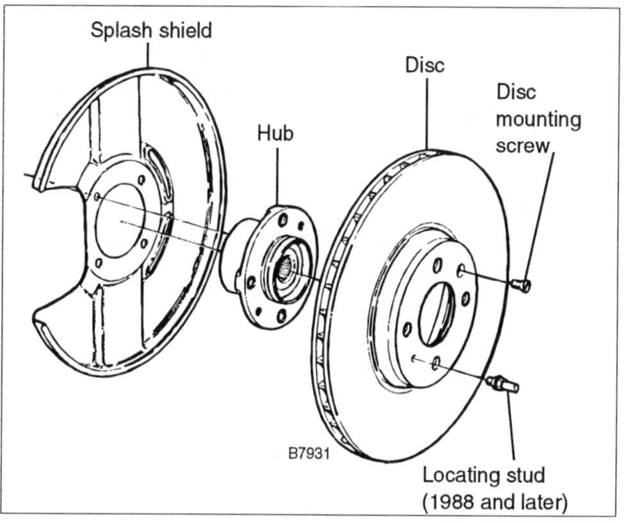

Fig. 1. Front disc assembly (ventilated front disc shown).

Brake discs must be replaced when they cannot be resurfaced without exceeding the specified minimum thickness given below.

Brake discs that are glazed or lightly scored may be resurfaced. Cracked discs should always be replaced. Discs should be replaced or resurfaced in pairs only. If the disc is being resurfaced, both faces should be resurfaced by equal amounts. See **Table b** and **Table c** for disc specifications.

Table b. Rear Disc Specifications

thickness (new)	9.0 mm (0.354 in.)
thickness (wear limit)	7.0 mm (0.276 in.)
brake surface lateral runout (maximum)	0.1 mm (0.004 in.)

Table c. Front Disc Specifications

	Solid disc	Ventilated disc (1986-1987)	Ventilated disc (1988 and later)
thickness (new)	12.7 mm (0.50 in.)	20 mm (0.784 in.)	23.5 mm (0.93 in.)
thickness (wear limit)	11.2 mm (0.441 in.)	18 mm (0.709 in.)	21.5 mm (0.85 in.)
brake surface lateral runout (maximum)	0.1 mm (0.004 in.)	0.1 mm (0.004 in.)	0.08 mm (0.003 in.)

NOTE

If the brake pads are soaked with oil, grease, or brake fluid, the cause of the contamination must be found and corrected before new brake pads or discs are installed.

To remove brake disc

New replacement brake discs should be cleaned with a grease-free solvent, such as brake cleaner, before installing the caliper and brake pads. The procedure below applies to front and rear brake discs.

1. Raise the car and support it with jackstands. Remove the wheel.

WARNING

Make sure the car is well supported with jackstands. Never use just a jack to support a car.

---

2. Remove the brake pads as described in **517 Brake Pads**.

WARNING

Friction materials in the brake pads may contain asbestos fibers. Avoid breathing any asbestos fibers or dust. Always use a respirator. Do not create dust by grinding or sanding, or by cleaning the pads or disc with compressed air.

---

3. Without removing the flexible brake hose, remove the caliper as described in **523 Brake Calipers**. Suspend the caliper from the body using stiff wire. See Fig. 2.

CAUTION

Do not allow the removed caliper to hang by the flexible brake hose.

NOTE

If the brake hose remains connected, it will not be necessary to bleed the brakes.

---

4. Remove the disc mounting screws or road wheel locating stud (where applicable). See Fig. 3.

Fig. 2. Caliper removed from disc and suspended using stiff wire.

Fig. 3. Arrows show locating stud and disc mounting screw.

NOTE

- On 1985 through 1987 models, the disc is mounted with two screws. On 1988 and later cars, the disc is mounted with a screw and a locating stud.

- Use a penetrating oil in advance to help loosen corroded screws. Keep penetrating oil away from rubber parts.

---

5. Remove the brake disc from the wheel hub. See Fig. 4.

NOTE

If the disc is frozen to the hub, tap it loose with a soft faced mallet.

Fig. 4. Disc being removed from hub.

Installation is the reverse of removal. Use a new caliper mounting bolt locking plate when installing the caliper. Reinstall the brake pads and gently pump the brake pedal several times to seat the pads on the disc. Install the wheels and tighten the wheel lugs. Test the footbrake and parking brake functions.

Tightening torques

- front brake caliper to steering member (1985 to 1987) . . . . . . 110 to 130 Nm (81 to 96 ft-lb)
- front brake pad carrier to steering member (1988 models and later) . . . . . 70 to 110 Nm (52 to 81 ft-lb)
- rear brake caliper to axle (1985 to 1987) . . . . 70 to 90 Nm (52 to 66 ft-lb)
- rear brake pad carrier to axle (1988 models and later) . . . . 40 to 54 Nm (30 to 49 ft-lb)
- road wheel locating stud to wheel hub . . . . 25 to 30 Nm (18 to 22 ft-lb)
- wheel to wheel hub
  - lug nuts . . . . 90 to 110 Nm (66 to 88 ft-lb)
  - lug bolts . . . . 105 to 125 Nm (77 to 92 ft-lb)
- all other fasteners
  - M5 bolt . . . . 5 Nm (44 in-lb)
  - M6 bolt . . . . 10 Nm (89 in-lb)
  - M8 bolt . . . . 20 Nm (15 ft-lb)
  - M10 bolt . . . . 40 Nm (30 ft-lb)

517 Brake Pads

GENERAL

Since the disc brake assemblies and the parking brake are self-adjusting it is not possible to judge the condition of the brake pads from brake pedal travel or from the parking brake lever. Pads should be inspected during regular service or when any abnormal brake noise is noticed. The brake discs should also be inspected during pad replacement as described in **516 Brake Discs**.

INSPECTING BRAKE PADS

Inspection of the brake pads can be done after removing the road wheel. The pads are made up of friction material and are designed to wear away. Pad thickness is measured by how much friction material is left. See Fig. 1.

Fig. 1. Disc brake pads as viewed through opening in caliper (road wheel removed). Minimum brake pad thickness shown by dimension **A**.

WARNING

- Do not reuse any self-locking nuts or bolts. These fasteners are designed to be used only once and should be replaced anytime they are loosened or removed.

- Friction materials in the brake pads may contain asbestos fibers. Avoid breathing any asbestos fibers or dust. Always use a respirator. Do not create dust by grinding or sanding, or by cleaning the pads or disc with compressed air.

NOTE

The front brake pads will usually wear out before the rear pads owing to the fact that the front brakes do most of the stopping.

Always replace brake pads in complete sets. If the old pads are to be reinstalled, make sure they are refitted in their original locations. Inspect other parts such as springs, shims, hoses, and cables and replace as necessary.

Brake Pad Lining

Model	Minimum thickness (dimension A)
1985 to 1987 models	1.0 mm (0.04 in.)
1988 and later models	4.0 mm (0.16 in.)

REPLACING BRAKE PADS

The brake pads can be easily replaced without disconnecting the flexible brake hose or the handbrake cable. This eliminates the need to bleed the brake system. In some cases, special tools may be required to replace the pads. Read the procedures completely before starting the job.

CAUTION
Different brake pads are used on different models. In addition, some models require different inner and outer front brake pads. Check with an authorized Saab dealer for the latest in parts information.

To replace front brake pads (1985-1987 models)

Fig. 2 shows the front brake assembly used on 1985 through 1987 models. Owing to the self-adjusting caliper assemblies, the caliper piston ratchets out as the brake pads are used up. In order to fit the thicker new pads to the caliper, the piston needs to be screwed back into the caliper housing and this requires a special tool. See Fig. 3.

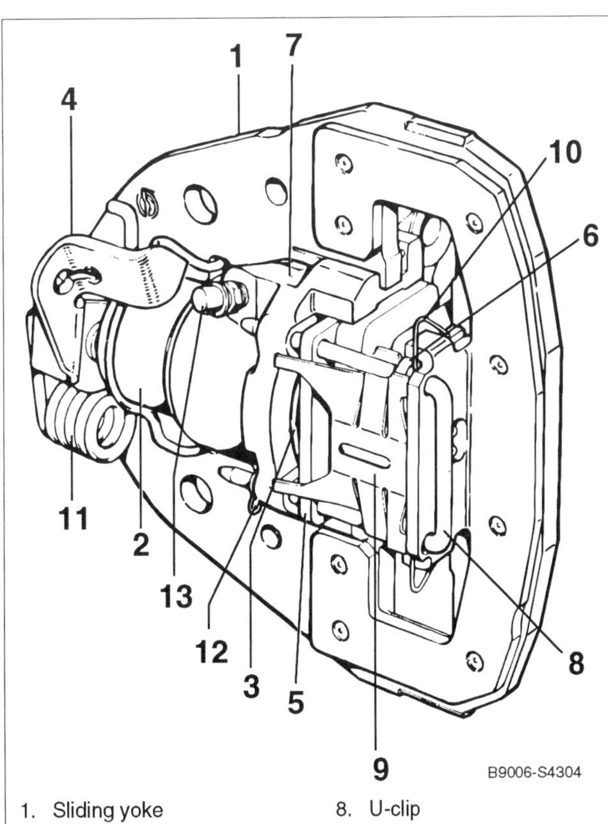

1. Sliding yoke
2. Indirect piston
3. Direct piston
4. Parking brake lever
5. Inner brake pad
6. Outer brake pad
7. Piston housing
8. U-clip
9. Damper (anti-rattle clip)
10. Anti-rattle spring
11. Parking brake lever return spring
12. U-clip retaining pin
13. Bleeder

Fig. 2. Front brake assembly used on 1985 through 1987 models.

1. Raise the car and support it with jackstands. Remove the front wheels.

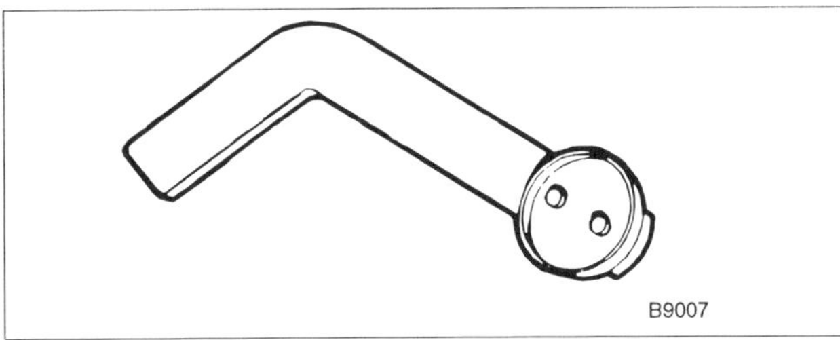

Fig. 3. Special brake piston wrench (Saab tool no. 89 96 043) needed for pad replacement.

WARNING
Make sure the car is well supported with jackstands. Never use just a jack to support a car.

2. Release the parking brake. Remove any rust and debris from the brake disc.

3. Working at the caliper, push the parking brake lever towards the sliding yoke and unhook the parking brake cable from the lever.

CAUTION
The parking brake lever must operate correctly. If the lever sticks, the pads will not fully release from the brake disc. This can lead to premature brake pad wear or even brake system failure due to the constant heat.

NOTE
Check the operation of the parking brake lever by pushing it fully towards the yoke and then releasing it. The return spring should cause the lever to snap back and contact the yoke. If the parking brake lever does not fully release, the lever is sticking in the caliper or the lever return spring is damaged. If the lever cannot be made to move freely, the caliper must be replaced as described under **523 Brake Calipers.**

4. Reconnect the parking brake cable to the lever. Check that the parking brake cables are correctly adjusted by checking for a small gap between the parking brake lever and yoke. Measure the gap as shown in Fig. 4. If the clearance is incorrect, adjust the parking brake cables as described in **551 Parking Brake**.

5. Remove the small retaining pin at the bottom of the U-clip, then pull the U-clip from the caliper. If necessary, gently pry the U-clip out evenly using a large screwdriver.

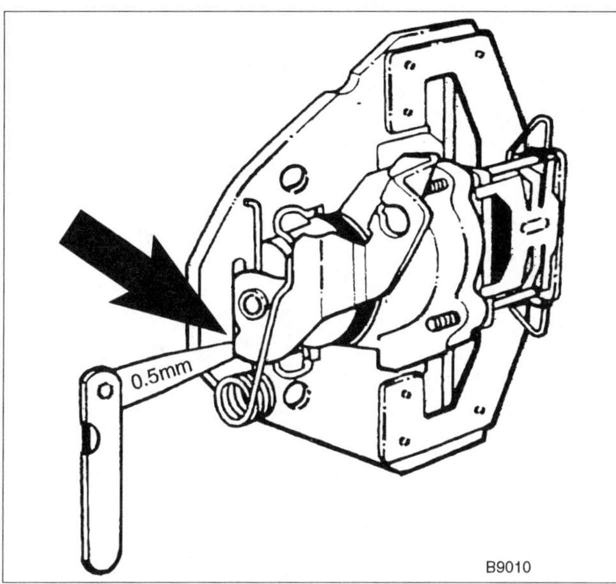

Fig. 4. Parking brake lever gap being measured. Cable must be connected to lever when making measurement.

Parking brake adjustment	
parking brake lever to caliper clearance	0.5±0.1 mm (0.019±0.003 in.)

NOTE

Observe the position of the damper (anti-rattle clip) behind the U-clip. During installation, the damper should be reinstalled in the same position.

6. Remove the inner and outer pads from the caliper. The pads can be removed from the caliper by grabbing the pad using large pliers. As an alternative, a special brake pad puller is available to help remove the pads. See Fig. 5.

Fig. 5. Brake pads being removed from caliper. Special brake pad puller (Saab tool no. 89 95 771) shown.

CAUTION

Do not step on the brake pedal or apply the parking brake with the brake pads removed. The piston will be forced out of the caliper making it impossible to reinstall the pads without removing the caliper.

7. Clean the caliper assembly using brake cleaner and a small wire brush. Be careful not to damage rubber seals with the wire brush. Check that the yoke slides freely in its groove in the caliper.

8. Lubricate the sliding surfaces between the caliper and yoke using Gleitmo 540 lubricant, which is available from an authorized Saab dealer. See Fig. 6.

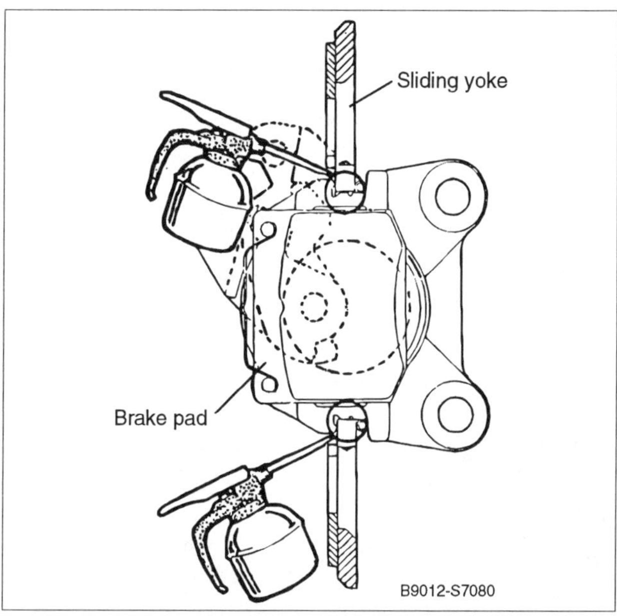

Fig. 6. Sliding surfaces of yoke to be lubricated using special grease (Gleitmo 540).

9. Using the special brake piston wrench, engage the pins of the wrench in the piston face and rotate the piston clockwise. See Fig. 7. Remove the wrench and push the piston into the caliper. If necessary, gently pry the piston in using a screwdriver. Repeat the process until the pads can be fitted.

CAUTION

Do not thread the piston in beyond the face of the caliper. See Fig. 8. The piston seal and dust cover can be damaged. If the piston is threaded all the way in and there still is not enough clearance to install the pads, install the wrench to the piston and carefully slide the yoke away from the caliper. Continue to thread the piston in until the pads can be fitted.

NOTE

The piston can only be rotated a small amount at one time with the wrench. After rotating the piston about 1/4 turn, remove the wrench and push the piston in.

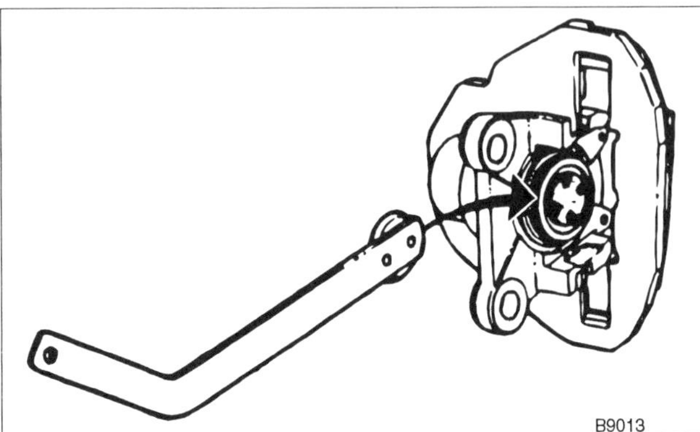

Fig. 7. Special wrench (Saab part no. 89 96 043) used to screw caliper piston in. Rotate piston clockwise only.

NOTE

Pushing the caliper piston in may cause brake fluid to overflow the master cylinder reservoir. To prevent this, use a clean syringe or some equivalent to remove some fluid from the reservoir.

Fig. 8. Piston shown flush to face of caliper (arrow). Piston must not be threaded beyond this point. If necessary, carefully slide yoke away from caliper to rotate piston in further.

10. Install the new brake pads, damper and U-clip. Install a new retaining pin in the U-clip.

NOTE

Saab recommends that the U-clips and dampers (anti-rattle clips) be replaced whenever replacing brake pads. The U-clips are pre-bent to help prevent brake noise (clunking noise when backing up). During normal use, the bends in the U-clips tend to straighten out and the damper spring tension tends to weaken.

---

11. Pull up the handbrake lever in the passenger compartment 7 notches (clicks). Start the engine and gently pump the brake pedal several times. Release the lever and then raise it 9 to 10 notches. The parking brake should now be fully applied.

NOTE

Pulling up the hand brake lever 7 notches blocks the self adjusting mechanism of the caliper and prevents over adjustment. If the caliper is over adjusted, the brake pads will drag.

---

12. Install the road wheels and lower the car. Check the brake fluid level and top up as necessary.

WARNING

New brake pads require some break-in. Allow for slightly longer stopping distances for the first 100 to 150 miles of city driving, and avoid hard stops.

Tightening torque

- wheel to wheel hub (lug nuts) . . . . 90 to 110 Nm (66 to 88 ft-lb)

To replace rear brake pads (1985-1987 models)

Fig. 9 shows the rear brake assembly on 1985 through 1987 models.

1. Raise the car and support it with jackstands. Remove the rear wheels.

WARNING

Make sure the car is well supported with jackstands. Never use just a jack to support a car.

---

2. Using a 2.5 mm drift, tap out the brake pad retaining pins. See Fig. 10.

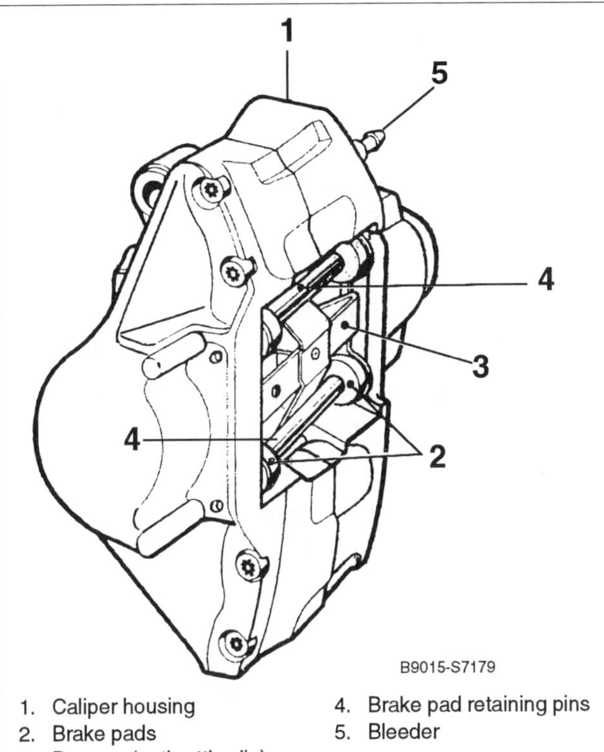

1. Caliper housing
2. Brake pads
3. Damper (anti-rattle clip)
4. Brake pad retaining pins
5. Bleeder

Fig. 9. Rear brake assembly used on 1985 through 1987 models.

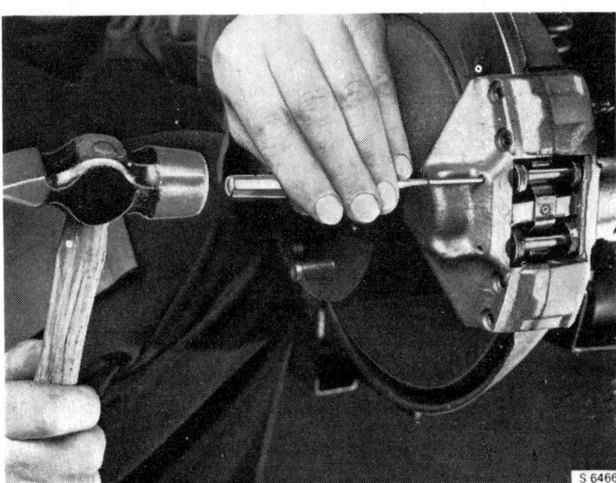

Fig. 10. Brake pad retaining pins being tapped out of caliper.

NOTE

Observe the position of the damper (anti-rattle clip) behind the retaining pins. During installation, the damper should be reinstalled in the same position.

---

3. Remove the inner and outer pads together with pad shims.

NOTE

- The brake pad shims are located on the rear of the pads. Label the shims during removal, as they are different between the left and right wheels.
- The pads can be removed from the caliper by grabbing them with a large pliers. As an alternative, a special brake pad puller is available to help remove the pads. See Fig. 11.

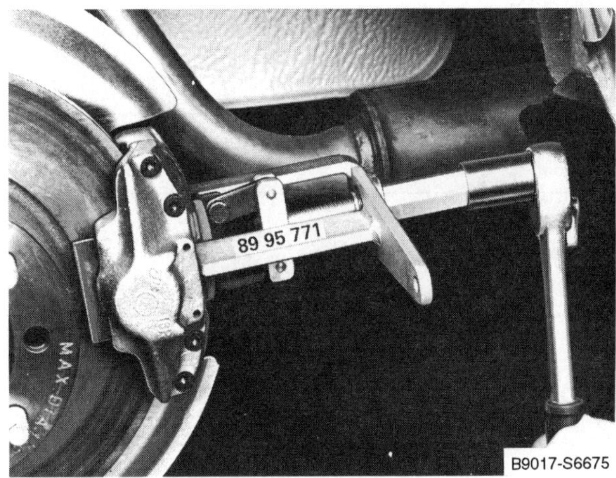

Fig. 11. Brake pads being removed from caliper. Special brake pad puller (Saab tool no. 89 95 771) shown.

CAUTION

Do not step on the brake pedal with the brake pads removed. The piston will be forced out of the caliper.

---

4. Clean and inspect the caliper assembly, the pad retaining pins, and the shims using brake cleaner and a small wire brush. Replace any worn components. Be careful not to damage rubber seals with the wire brush. Inspect the piston rubber dust cover and replace if necessary.
5. Using a screwdriver, gently push the piston back into the caliper. Install the new brake pads with the shims.

CAUTION

Push the piston in just far enough to install the new brake pads. Pushing the piston in too far may damage the piston seals.

NOTE

Pushing the caliper piston in may cause brake fluid to overflow the master cylinder reservoir. To prevent this, use a clean syringe or some equivalent to first remove some fluid from the reservoir.

---

6. Install the damper (anti-rattle clip) and the pad retaining pins. Tap the retaining pins in using a drift until they are fully seated.

7. Install the road wheels and lower the car. Gently pump the brake pedal several times to seat the pads. Check the brake fluid level and top up as necessary.

WARNING
New brake pads require some break-in. Allow for slightly longer stopping distances for the first 100 to 150 miles of city driving, and avoid hard stops.

Tightening torque
- wheel to wheel hub (lug nuts) . . . . 90 to 110 Nm (66 to 88 ft-lb)

To replace front brake pads (1988 and later models)

Fig. 12 shows the front brake assembly used on 1988 and later models.

1. Raise the car and support it with jackstands. Remove the front wheels.

WARNING
Make sure the car is well supported with jackstands. Never use just a jack to support a car.

---

2. Working through the opening in the caliper, press the brake piston back into the caliper housing using large pliers. See Fig. 13.

3. While holding the lower guide pin stationary, remove the brake caliper mounting bolt from the end of the guide pin. See Fig. 14.

4. Swing the caliper up out of the way and remove the brake pads. See Fig. 15.

CAUTION
Do not step on the brake pedal with the brake pads removed. The piston will be forced out of the caliper damaging the seals.

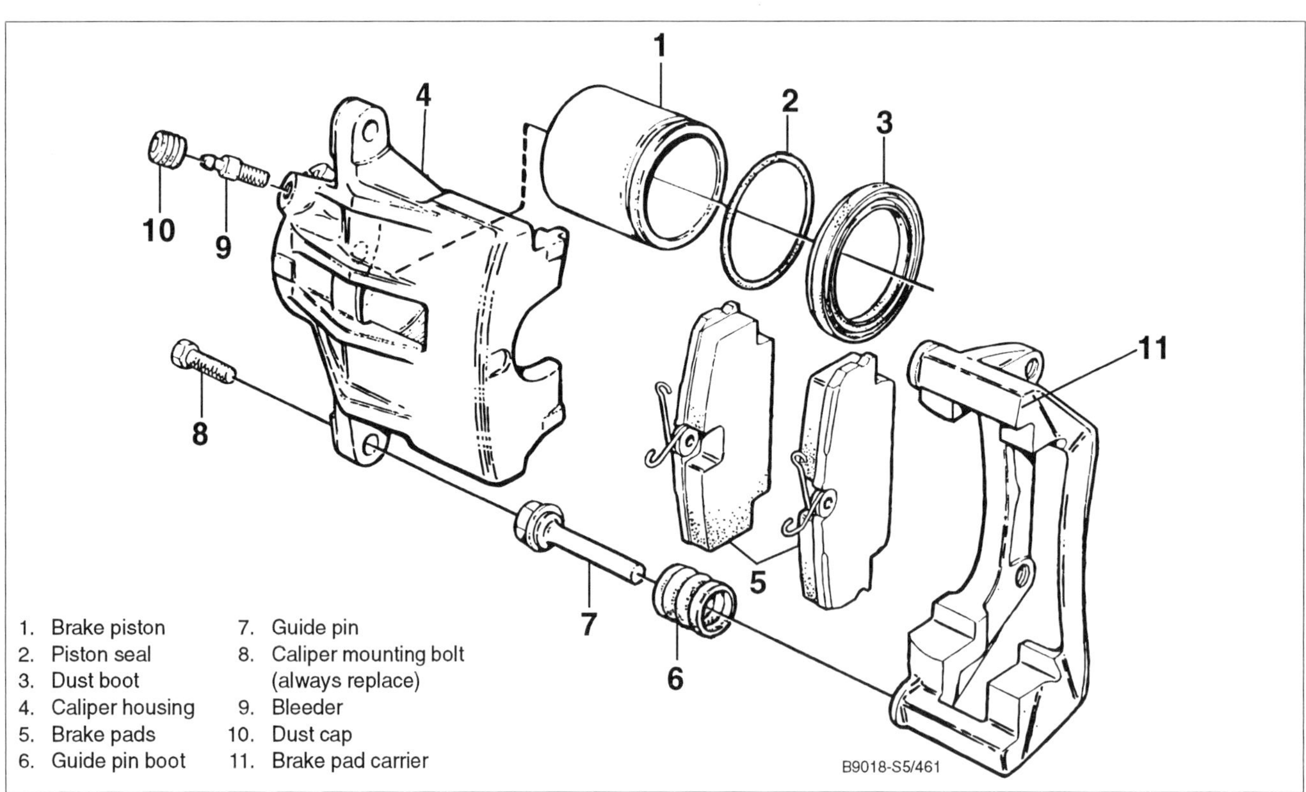

Fig. 12. Exploded view of front brake assembly (1988 and later models).

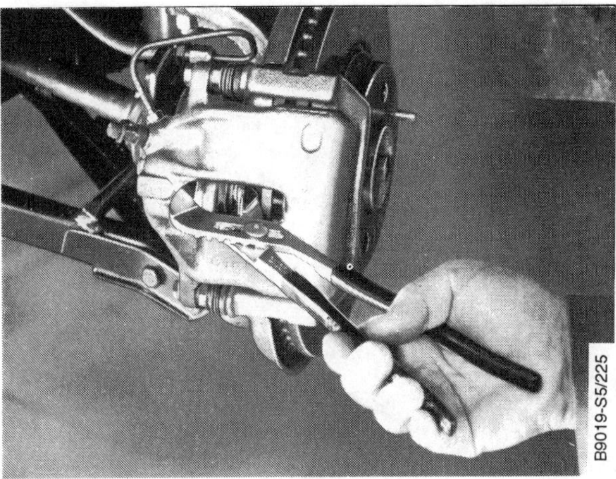

Fig. 13. Piston being pressed into caliper housing.

Fig. 14. Caliper mounting bolt being removed from lower guide pin. Open-end wrench (arrow) being used to hold guide pin stationary.

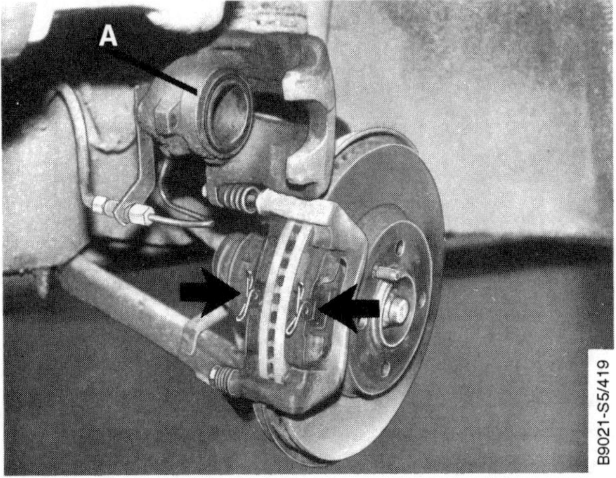

Fig. 15. Caliper (**A**) pivoted up to remove brake pads. Arrows show brake pads.

NOTE

To prevent the piston from creeping out of the caliper, place a strong rubber band around the piston and caliper to hold the piston in.

---

5. Clean and inspect the caliper assembly, the guide pin, and the pad carrier using brake cleaner and a small wire brush. Replace any worn parts. Be careful not to damage rubber seals with the wire brush. Inspect the rubber dust covers for the piston and the guide pins. Replace if necessary. Lightly lubricate the guide pins.

6. Using large pliers and a protective cloth covering the piston, press the piston back into the caliper just enough to install the new pads.

7. Install the new pads into the pad carrier and pivot the caliper down into position. If necessary, push the lower guide pin in as the caliper is lowered into position.

8. Install a new caliper mounting bolt in the lower guide pin and tighten it while holding the guide pin stationary.

WARNING

Do not reuse the caliper self-locking mounting bolts. These are designed to be used only once and should be always be replaced.

Tightening torque

- caliper mounting bolt to guide pin . . . . 30 to 35 Nm (22 to 26 ft-lb)

---

9. Install the road wheels and lower the car. Gently pump the brake pedal several times to seat the pads. Check the brake fluid level and top up as necessary.

Tightening torque

- wheel lug bolts . . . . . . 105 to 125 Nm (77 to 92 ft-lb)

WARNING

New brake pads require some break-in. Allow for slightly longer stopping distances for the first 100 to 150 miles of city driving, and avoid hard stops.

To replace rear brake pads (1988 and later models)

Fig. 16 shows the rear brake assembly used on 1988 and later models.

1. Raise the car and support it with jackstands. Remove the rear wheels.

WARNING
Make sure the car is well supported with jackstands. Never use just a jack to support a car.

---

2. Disconnect the parking brake cable from the lever at the caliper. See Fig. 17.

3. Remove the plug covering the piston adjusting screw. See Fig. 18.

4. Loosen the piston adjusting screw using a 4 mm internal-hex head wrench until the piston moves against its stop. See Fig. 19.

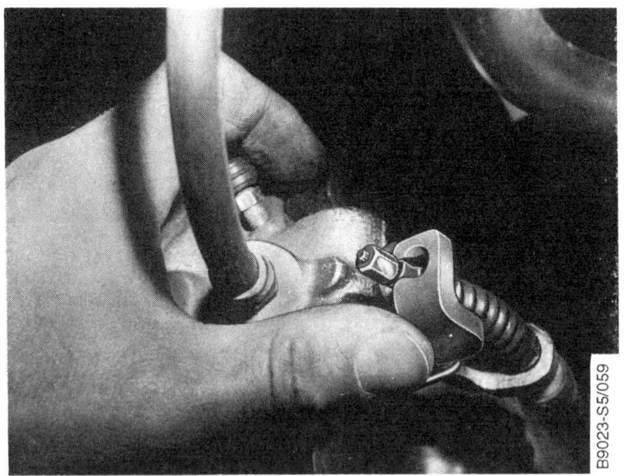

Fig. 17. Parking brake cable being disconnected from caliper.

5. Remove the dust caps from the guide pins then unscrew the upper and lower guide pins using a 7 mm internal-hex head wrench. See Fig. 20.

6. Remove the pad retaining clip. See Fig. 21.

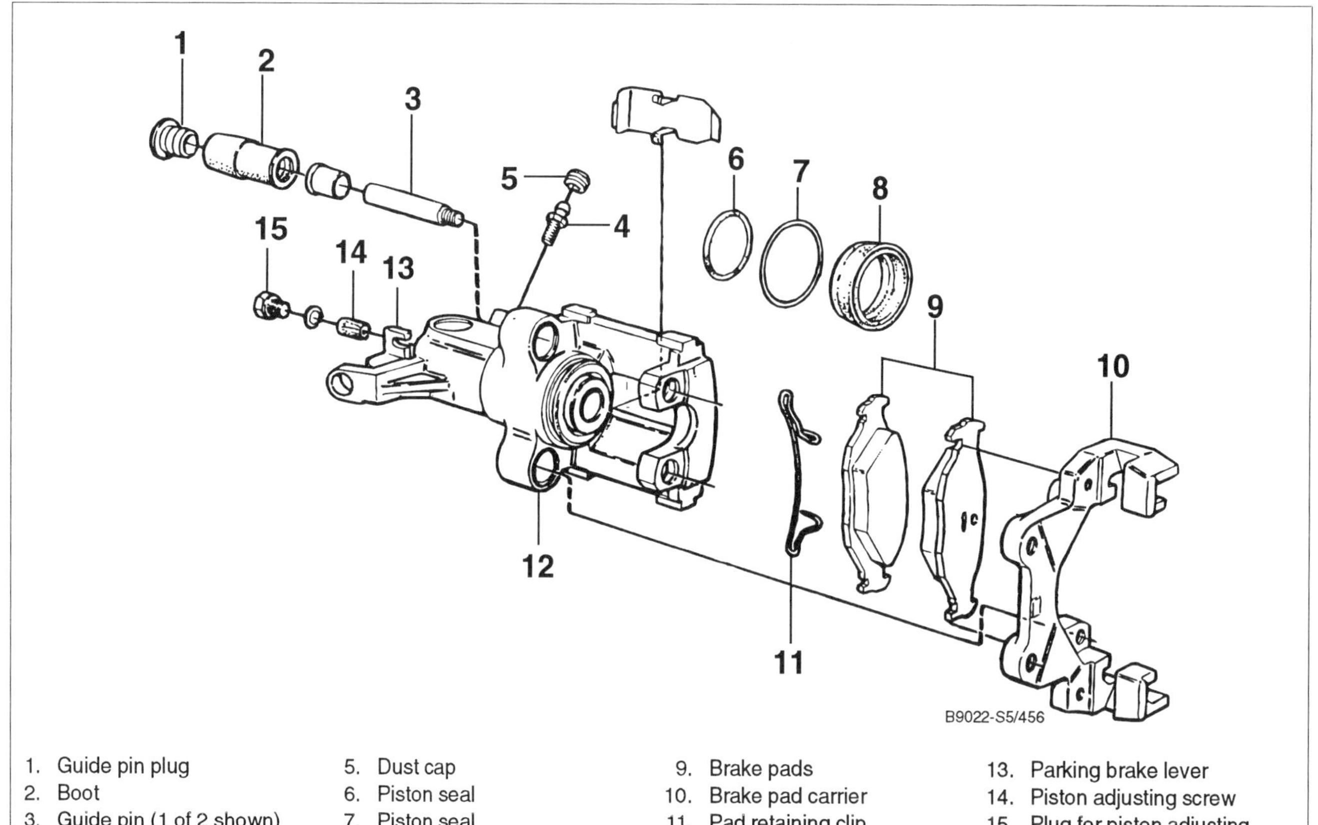

1. Guide pin plug
2. Boot
3. Guide pin (1 of 2 shown)
4. Bleeder
5. Dust cap
6. Piston seal
7. Piston seal
8. Dust boot
9. Brake pads
10. Brake pad carrier
11. Pad retaining clip
12. Brake caliper
13. Parking brake lever
14. Piston adjusting screw
15. Plug for piston adjusting screw

Fig. 16. Exploded view of rear brake assembly used on 1988 and later models.

Fig. 18. Piston adjusting screw plug being removed using wrench (arrow).

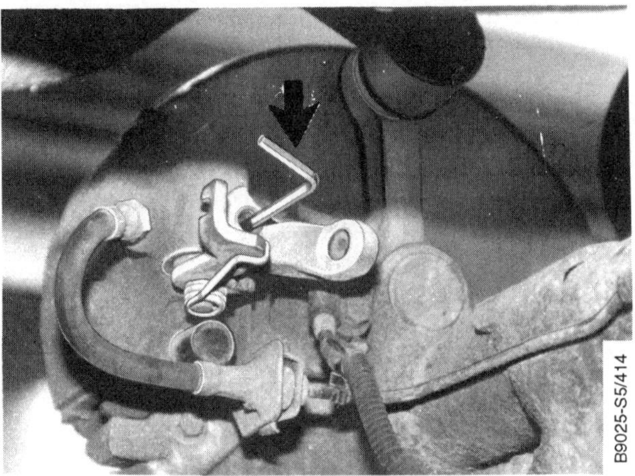

Fig. 19. Internal-hex head wrench (arrow) to loosen piston adjusting screw.

Fig. 20. Lower guide pin being removed from caliper. Upper guide pin shown at arrow.

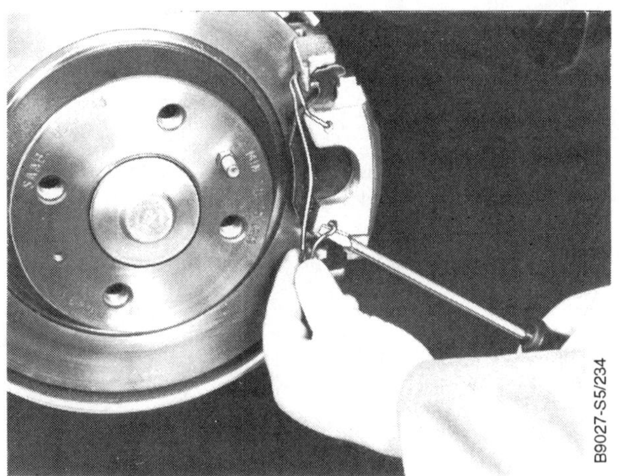

Fig. 21. Pad retaining clip being removed.

7. Remove the caliper from the pad carrier. Remove the brake pads from the carrier. See Fig. 22.

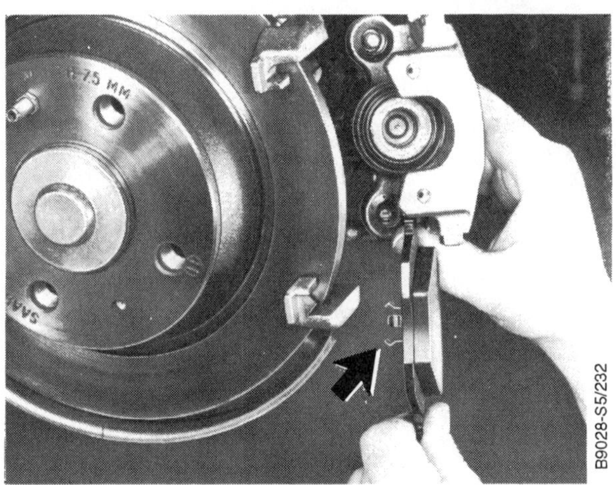

Fig. 22. Caliper being removed from pad carrier. Brake pad with spring clip (arrow) is on piston side of caliper.

CAUTION

Do not step on the brake pedal with the brake pads removed. The piston will be forced out of the caliper.

NOTE

To prevent the piston from creeping out of the caliper, place a strong rubber band around the piston and caliper to hold the piston in.

---

8. Clean and inspect the caliper assembly, the guide pins, and the pad carrier using brake cleaner and a small wire brush. Replace any worn parts. Inspect the rubber dust covers for the piston and the guide pins. Replace if necessary.

CAUTION
Be careful not to damage rubber seals with the wire brush.

9. Using large pliers and a protective cloth over the piston, press the piston back into the caliper.

10. Install the new pads in the pad carrier then install the caliper.

11. Install and tighten the guide pins then install the guide pin dust caps.

NOTE
No lubrication is specified for the rear guide pins.

Tightening torque
- rear caliper to pad carrier (guide pins) . . . . 25 to 30 Nm (18 to 22 ft-lb)

12. Install the pad retaining clip as shown above in Fig. 21.

13. Turn the piston adjusting screw all the way. See Fig. 19 above. Then back the screw out 1/4 to 1/2 turn. Check that the brake disc rotates freely.

14. Install the plug for the adjusting screw then reconnect the parking brake cable.

15. Check the adjustment of the parking brake cable as described in **551 Parking Brake**. Adjust the cable if necessary.

16. Install the road wheels and lower the car. Gently pump the brake pedal several times to seat the pads. Check the brake fluid level and top up as necessary.

WARNING
New brake pads require some break-in. Allow for slightly longer stopping distances for the first 100 to 150 miles of city driving, and avoid hard stops.

Tightening torque
- wheel to wheel hub (lug bolts) . . . . 105 to 125 Nm (77 to 92 ft-lb)

520 Brake Fluid and Brake Bleeding

GENERAL

Brake fluid has the job of transmitting the force applied at the pedal to the brake pads. In order for the fluid to properly transmit the force, it must be free of air and moisture. Because of the moisture-absorbing properties of brake fluid, it is essential that the fluid be replaced on a regular basis to prevent corrosion of brake parts and brake system failure. See **110 Maintenance Program** for the specified intervals for changing brake fluid.

BLEEDING AND CHANGING BRAKE FLUID

Bleeding is the process used to purge air bubbles or flush contaminated fluid from the system. Bleeding brakes periodically is good preventative maintenance, but it is also essential any time the system has been opened, such as when disconnecting a brake line. A spongy feeling brake pedal is a sign that brakes may need to be bled.

Bleeding the brake system can be done using pressure bleeding equipment, vacuum bleeding equipment, or by conventional means using two people.

WARNING

- Brake fluid is poisonous. Wear safety glasses when working with brake fluid. Wear rubber gloves to prevent brake fluid from entering the bloodstream through cuts of scratches. Do not siphon brake fluid with your mouth.

- Brake fluid is considered a hazardous waste. Catch brake fluid in a suitable container. Dispose of brake fluid in a manner that is mindful of the environment and meets ordinances governing disposal of wastes.

- On cars equipped with ABS, the ABS system is self-pressurizing and maintains very high hydraulic pressure, as much as 210 bar (3045 psi). Before working on any part of the ABS system, switch off the ignition and disconnect the cable from the battery negative (-) terminal.

NOTE

It is good practice to flush the clutch hydraulic system whenever the brake fluid is being changed. See **412 Clutch Control** to bleed the clutch hydraulic system.

Bleeding the Brake System

The procedure below is for bleeding the brakes using a manual method and requires a helper. When using other methods—such as vacuum or pressure bleeding equipment, follow the instructions given by the equipment's manufacturer.

CAUTION

Use only DOT 4 brake fluid. Do not use silicone based (DOT 5) brake fluid.

To bleed brake system (cars without ABS)

Bleeding the brakes or replacing the brake fluid must be done in a particular order as shown in **Table a.**

CAUTION

Brake fluid absorbs moisture from the air. Add only unused fluid to the system and only from well-sealed or previously unopened containers. Do not use fluid expelled from the system, even if it is fresh fluid.

Table a. Order for Bleeding Brakes (Cars without ABS)

1985-1987 models	1988-1989 models
1. Right front wheel	1. Left rear wheel
2. Left rear wheel	2. Right front wheel
3. Left front wheel	3. Right rear wheel
4. Right rear wheel	4. Left front wheel

1. Check the level of the brake fluid in the master cylinder reservoir. If only bleeding the brakes, top up the reservoir using fresh brake fluid from a sealed container.

520

- Brake fluid — DOT 4

NOTE

- When replacing the brake fluid, remove as much of the old fluid from the reservoir as possible, then fill the reservoir with new brake fluid. Plan to have approximately 1.2 liters of new fluid on hand to flush the system.
- Brake fluid is very harmful, especially to paint and rubber parts. Spilled brake fluid should be cleaned up immediately.

2. Starting at the first caliper listed in **Table a**, place a hex wrench over the caliper bleeder. Then connect a length of clear tubing to the bleeder. Place the other end of the tube in a container. See Fig. 1.

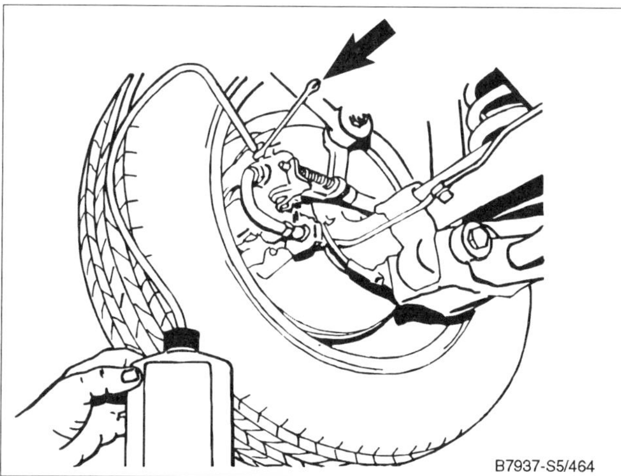

Fig. 1. Tube and container to bleed brake caliper. Arrow shows wrench on bleeder.

NOTE

The bleeder is a small hex-head fitting with a hollow center and usually has a rubber dust boot over it. See Fig. 2.

3. Have a helper pump the brake pedal slowly three times and hold it down.

4. Open (unscrew) the bleeder about 1/2 turn. As the pedal goes to the floor and the fluid stops flowing, close the bleeder. Release the pedal and repeat step 3 until the pedal feels hard or all of the air has been expelled from the system.

NOTE

When replacing the brake fluid, remove at least 1 pint (500 cc) of brake fluid from each caliper to completely expel the old fluid.

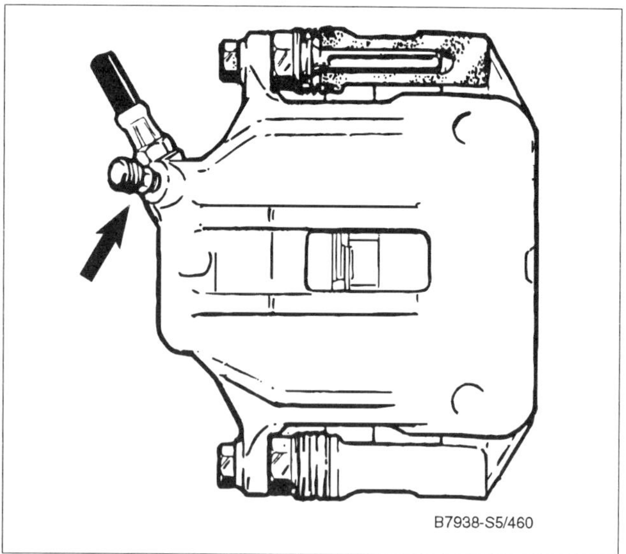

Fig. 2. Front caliper bleeder (arrow).

5. Repeat the above from procedure (step 1 through step 4) bleeding the next caliper in the order given above in **Table a.**

To bleed brake system (cars with ABS)

On cars with ABS the front brakes must be bled first. The front brakes can be bled using pressure bleeding equipment or they can be bled manually. The rear brakes are bled using the ABS pump as described below.

1. Bleed the front brakes using the technique described above. Bleed the right front caliper then the left front caliper.

NOTE

- When replacing the brake fluid, remove as much of the old fluid from the reservoir as possible, then fill the reservoir with new brake fluid.
- When replacing the brake fluid, remove at least 1 pint (500 cc) of brake fluid from each caliper to completely expel the old fluid.

2. Bleed the rear calipers by connecting a length of clear tubing to the bleeder and placing the other end in a container. See Fig. 3.

3. Have a helper turn the ignition key to run (engine off) then press the brake pedal. The ABS pump will come on.

4. Working at the caliper, loosen (unscrew) the bleeder about 1/2 turn and let the fluid flow until it is free of bubbles. Close the bleeder.

Fig. 3. Rear caliper being bled on model with ABS.

5. Check the level of the fluid in the reservoir. If necessary, repeat steps 2 through 4 at the other rear caliper.

CAUTION
- Do not allow the ABS pump to run more than 2 minutes or it may overheat. After running 2 minutes, allow the pump to cool for 10 minutes.
- Do not allow the ABS pump to run without fluid. Damage to the pump may result.

Top up the brake fluid in the reservoir as necessary and replace any dust caps.

521 Brake Master Cylinder

MASTER CYLINDER AND FLUID RESERVOIR

The master cylinder, on cars without ABS, has two chambers that create pressure in two hydraulic circuits. One chamber controls the right front and left rear brakes. The second chamber controls the left front and right rear brakes. This design—known as dual diagonal braking—assures a high level of braking control if one circuit fails. Fig. 1 shows an exploded view of the master cylinder used on cars without ABS.

The master cylinder has an integral brake fluid reservoir. The fluid reservoir has chambers for the brake master cylinder and for the clutch master cylinder (where applicable). The reservoir cap has a float switch that signals the driver when the fluid level is low.

CAUTION
Whenever the brake system is open, plug all openings to prevent dirt from entering the system. Even a minute particle of dirt can cause problems.

On cars with ABS, the master cylinder has three brake circuits: Individual circuits for each front wheel and one circuit for the rear wheels. The master cylinder is integrated with other ABS components to form the ABS unit. See Fig. 2.

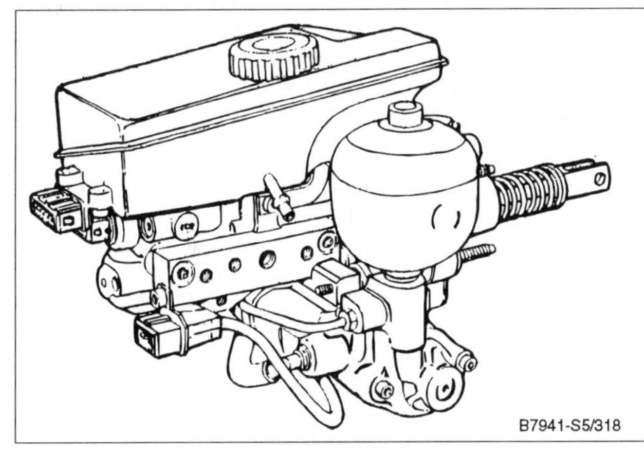

Fig. 2. ABS braking unit with integral master cylinder.

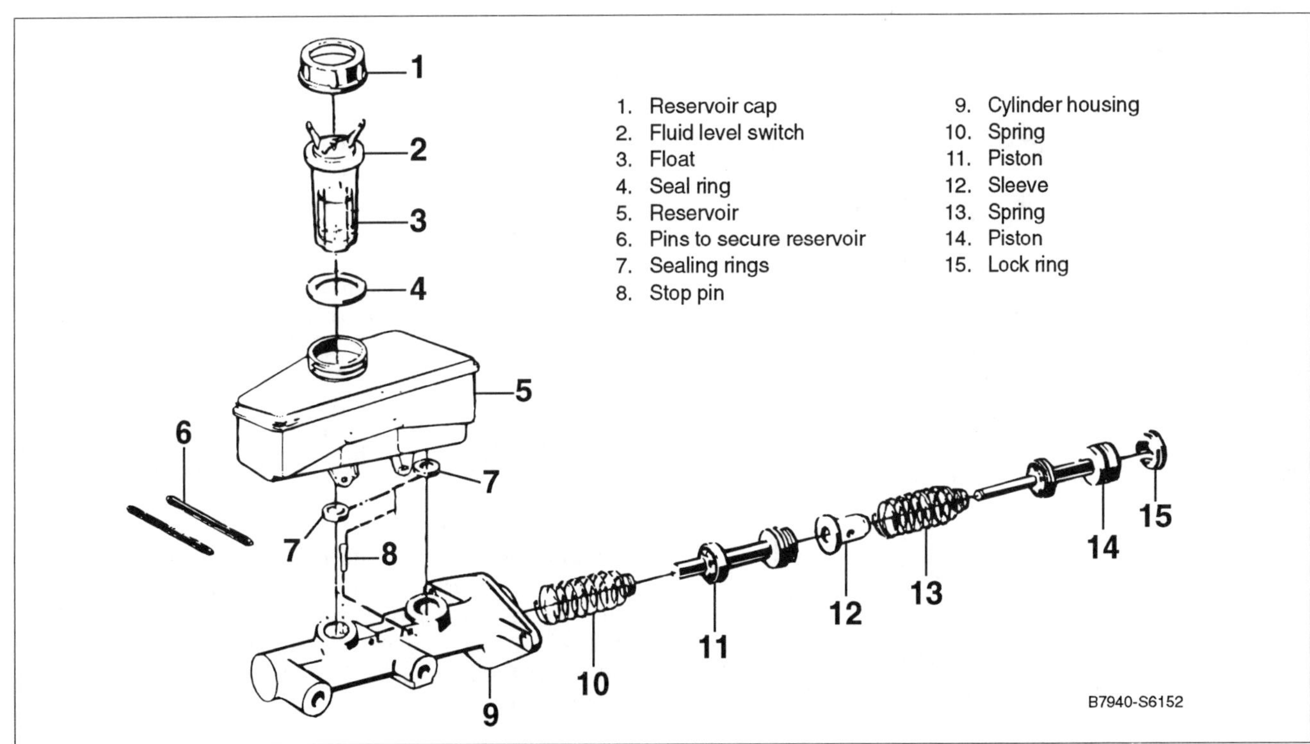

1. Reservoir cap
2. Fluid level switch
3. Float
4. Seal ring
5. Reservoir
6. Pins to secure reservoir
7. Sealing rings
8. Stop pin
9. Cylinder housing
10. Spring
11. Piston
12. Sleeve
13. Spring
14. Piston
15. Lock ring

Fig. 1. Exploded view of brake master cylinder.

The master cylinder displaces brake fluid when the brake pedal is depressed. The displaced fluid moves a piston in each caliper, which in turn presses the brake pads against the rotor. The master cylinder must displace fluid without losing pressure or leaking. When it cannot do this, it must be replaced. If there is any leakage from around the master cylinder the master cylinder is probably faulty and should be replaced. For troubleshooting information see **500 Brakes—General**.

NOTE

- Unexplained fluid loss from the reservoir could be due to brake fluid leaking from the master cylinder into the vacuum booster. The fluid is drawn into the engine through the vacuum booster hose. Look for seepage at the master cylinder to vacuum booster flange. Replace both the master cylinder and the vacuum booster as the diaphragm in the booster may be damaged.

- Check the master cylinder by holding the pedal down hard with the car stopped and the engine running. The pedal should feel solid and stay solid. If the pedal slowly falls to the floor, either the master cylinder is leaking internally, or fluid is escaping from the system. If no leaks can be found, the master cylinder is faulty and should be replaced.

To remove master cylinder

1. Disconnect the electrical wires from the fluid reservoir cap.

2. Remove the vacuum hose with check valve from the vacuum booster. See Fig. 3.

Fig. 3. Vacuum hose and check valve (arrow) removed from vacuum booster.

3. Using a syringe, remove as much brake fluid from the reservoir as possible.

4. On cars with manual transmission, pinch off the fluid supply hose to the clutch master cylinder. See Fig. 4. Remove the supply hose and plug the fittings.

Fig. 4. Special clamping pliers (arrow) used to pinch off supply line to clutch master cylinder.

WARNING

- Brake fluid is poisonous. Wear eye and hand protection when working with brake fluid.

- Brake fluid is considered a hazardous waste. Recycle or dispose of brake fluid in a manner that is mindful of the environment and meets ordinances governing disposal of wastes.

CAUTION

Brake fluid is very harmful, especially to paint and rubber parts. Spilled brake fluid should be cleaned up immediately.

5. Using a brake line (flare) wrench, loosen the brake line fittings and remove the two brake lines from the master cylinder. See Fig. 5.

NOTE

To make access to the brake lines easier, remove the mounting bolt holding the coolant expansion tank and move the tank out of the way. It is not necessary to drain the coolant.

6. Remove the two nuts holding the master cylinder to the vacuum booster. Remove the master cylinder.

Installation is the reverse of removal. Inspect the seal between the master cylinder and the vacuum booster and replace if necessary. A faulty seal can be the source of a vacuum leak, causing a reduction in braking performance and/or an erratic idle speed. Bleed the brakes as described in **520 Brake Fluid and Brake Bleeding** using DOT 4 brake fluid from a sealed container.

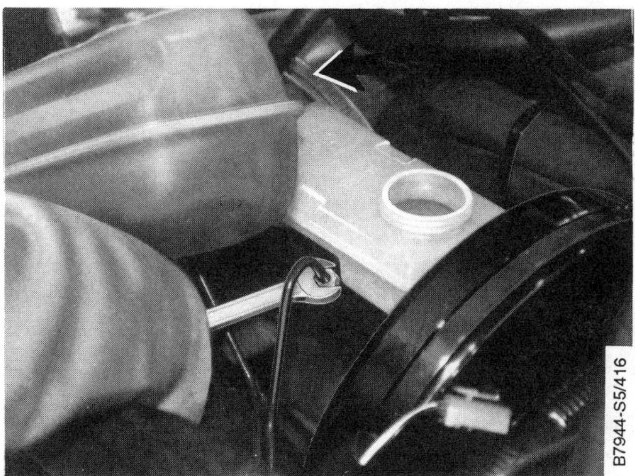

Fig. 5. Brake line being removed. Coolant tank (arrow) has been moved out of way.

CAUTION
Always start the brake line fittings by hand to prevent stripping the threads.

NOTE
It is good practice to flush the clutch hydraulic system whenever the brake fluid is being changed or the master cylinder is being replaced. See **412 Clutch Control** for details on bleeding the clutch hydraulic system.

To remove ABS unit

The ABS unit is removed from the car as a complete assembly. Certain replacement parts for the ABS unit are available from an authorized Saab dealer. See your dealer for the latest parts information.

WARNING
• Dangerously high pressure may be retained in the ABS system, even though the car is not running or has not been driven recently. Never attempt to open or disassemble the pressure accumulator, which contains a nitrogen gas charge and is under high pressure.

• If the ANTI-LOCK and the BRAKE FLUID warning lamps should come on, the car must not be driven. Brake failure may occur. Have the problem corrected promptly by an authorized Saab dealer.

---

1. Depressurize the ABS system before loosening any components by disconnecting the battery negative cable and pressing the brake pedal 25 to 30 times, or until there is a noticeable increase in pedal effort.

2. Remove the lower dashboard pad and footwell heating duct as described in **851 Interior Trim and Upholstery**.

3. Working at the brake pedal assembly, remove the padded insulating material. Then remove the defroster hose from the heater box.

4. Remove the brake pedal pushrod pin locking clip and the pushrod pin from the ABS unit. See Fig. 6.

CAUTION
Inspect the pushrod locking clip and clevis pin and replace them with new ones if they are in anyway damaged or deformed.

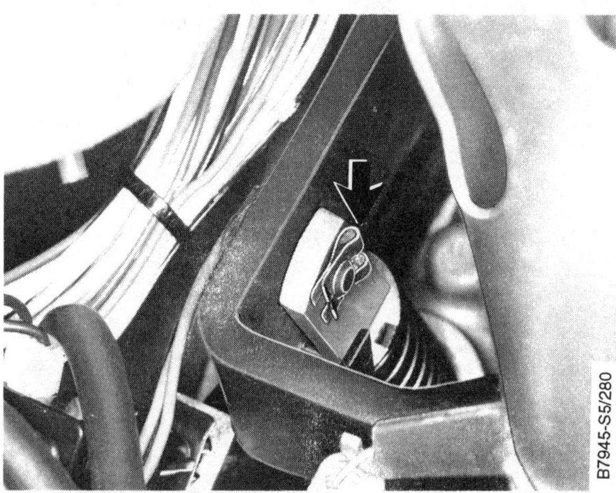

Fig. 6. Brake pedal pushrod locking clip (arrow). Note the orientation of the pin and locking clip.

5. Working at the front of the engine compartment, remove the air intake duct. See Fig. 7.

Fig. 7. Air intake duct being removed.

6. Remove the coolant expansion tank to body mounting bolt and move the tank aside. See Fig. 8. Do not disconnect any cooling hoses or remove the cap from the tank.

Fig. 8. Coolant expansion tank being moved out of way.

7. Disconnect all electrical connectors from the ABS unit. Remove the ground lead. See Fig. 9.

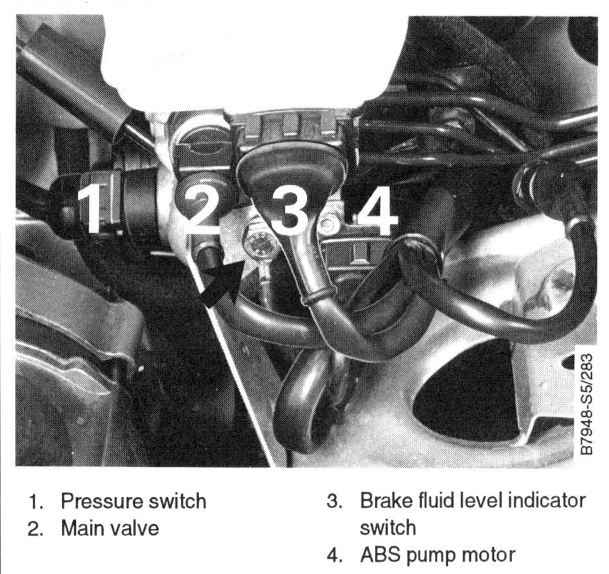

1. Pressure switch
2. Main valve
3. Brake fluid level indicator switch
4. ABS pump motor

Fig. 9. ABS unit electrical connectors. Arrow shows ground lead.

8. Remove the ABS unit mounting bracket. See Fig. 10.

9. Using a syringe, siphon off the brake fluid from the reservoir.

Fig. 10. ABS unit mounting bracket being removed.

WARNING

- Brake fluid is poisonous. Wear eye and hand protection when working with brake fluid.
- Brake fluid is considered a hazardous waste. Recycle or dispose of brake fluid in a manner that is mindful of the environment and meets ordinances governing disposal of wastes.

CAUTION

Brake fluid is very harmful, especially to paint and rubber parts. Spilled brake fluid should be cleaned up immediately.

10. On cars with manual transmission pinch off the supply hose to the clutch master cylinder. Remove the hose from the reservoir. See Fig. 11.

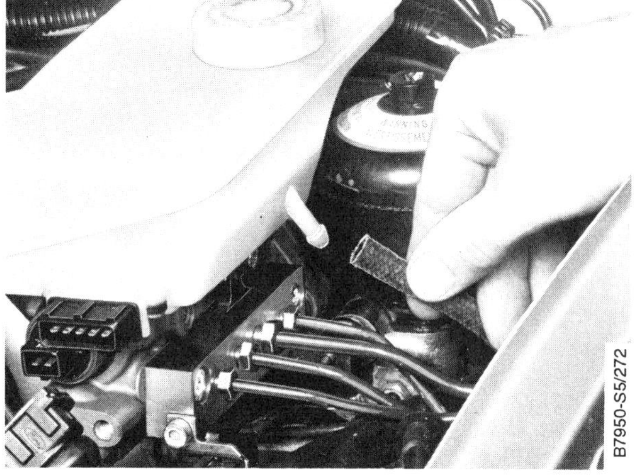

Fig. 11. Supply hose to clutch master cylinder being removed. Brake lines can be seen below hose fitting.

11. Label and remove the brake lines from the ABS unit using a brake line (flare) wrench.

NOTE

Plug or cover the brake lines and the openings in the ABS unit to prevent dirt from entering system.

12. Working in the passenger compartment above the pedals, remove the four nuts that hold the ABS unit to the bulkhead. See Fig. 12.

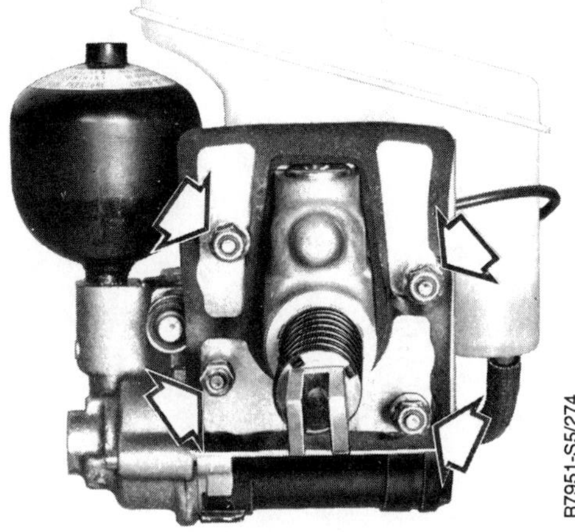

Fig. 12. ABS unit mounting nuts (arrows). Nuts are accessible in passenger compartment above pedal assembly.

To install ABS unit

1. Carefully install the ABS unit in the opening in the bulkhead. Position the ABS unit pushrod so it correctly aligns with the brake pedal.

CAUTION

Use care when installing the ABS unit through the bulkhead. The brake light switch and cruise control switches on the pedal assembly can be easily damaged.

2. Working in the passenger compartment, install the pedal pushrod pin and locking clip through the ABS unit pushrod. See Fig. 6 above.

3. Install and tighten the four new nuts that hold the ABS unit to the bulkhead. See Fig. 12 above.

WARNING

Always use new self-locking nuts to mount the ABS unit to the bulkhead.

Tightening torque

- ABS unit to bulkhead . . . . 26±4 Nm (19±3 ft-lb)

4. Connect the brake lines to the ABS unit. See Fig. 11 above.

CAUTION

Always start the brake line fittings by hand to prevent stripping the threads.

The remainder of installation is the reverse of removal. Fill the reservoir with DOT 4 brake fluid from a sealed container. Switch on the ignition and check that the ABS pump comes on. Bleed the system, including the clutch, as described in **520 Brake Fluid and Brake Bleeding** and **412 Clutch Control**.

Check that there are no leaks and that the warning lights go out after the car is started. Finally, test drive the car to check all brake functions. Recheck the brake fluid level.

522 Brake Lines

BRAKE LINES AND HOSES

The brake lines carry brake fluid and transmit hydraulic pressure to the calipers at each wheel. They are rigid up to their connecting points with the flexible hoses near the wheels. The flexible hoses are used to accommodate suspension and steering movement. Normally, no maintenance is required other than inspecting the lines and hoses for leaks or deterioration. Fig. 1 shows the typical brake line and hose routing.

Brake lines are available from Saab pre-formed to fit without any bending or modification. See an authorized Saab dealer for the latest parts information.

WARNING
- On cars equipped with ABS, dangerously high pressure may be retained in the ABS system even though the car is not running or has not been driven recently. Before loosening any brake line fitting, depressurize the system by disconnecting the battery negative cable and pressing the brake pedal 25 to 30 times, or until there is a noticeable increase in pedal effort.
- Brake fluid is poisonous. Wear hand and eye protection.

WARNING
Brake fluid is considered a hazardous waste. Catch brake fluid in a suitable container and label it. Recycle or dispose of brake fluid in a manner that is mindful of the environment and meets ordinances governing disposal of wastes.

To replace brake lines or brake hoses

1. Clean the connections of the brake line at both ends.
2. Remove any brake line clamps or tie-downs. Loosen the fittings using a brake line (flare) wrench.

NOTE
Brake lines to the rear brakes travel under the carpeting in the passenger compartment on the driver side. See **8 BODY** for information on removing the seats, sill plates, and carpeting.

3. Remove the brake line or hose.

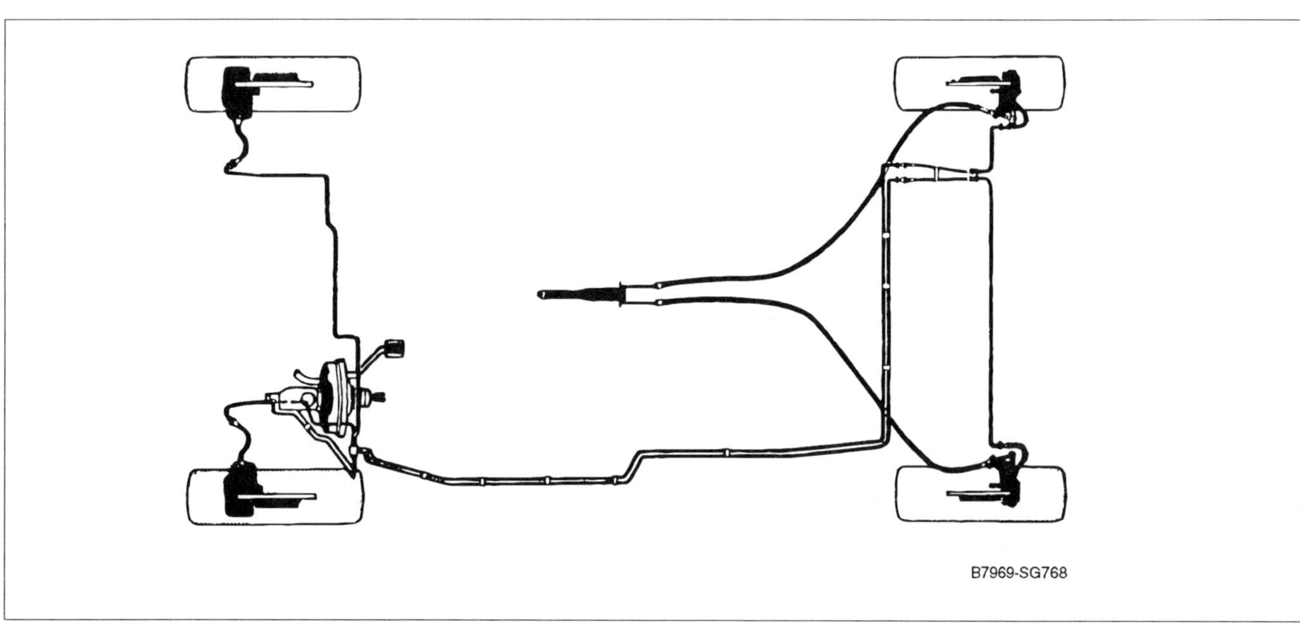

Fig. 1. Brake lines and hoses. Also shown is parking brake with cables.

522

CAUTION

- Brake fluid is harmful to paint and rubber parts. Spilled brake fluid should be cleaned up immediately.
- Plug the openings in the hydraulic system to prevent dirt from entering the system. Even a minute particle of dirt can cause problems.

4. Clean the inside of the new brake line or hose with compressed air.
5. Place the line or hose in position and hand tighten the fittings. When connecting lines to hoses, counter hold the fittings using two wrenches during tightening.

CAUTION

- Always start the brake line fittings by hand to prevent stripping the threads.
- When fitting flexible hoses, be sure the hose is not twisted and is properly positioned. Check that the hose does not contact any suspension or steering parts.

NOTE

When replacing front flexible brake hoses, jack the car up and support it so the road wheels are freely suspended and pointing straight ahead. This will ensure that there is the proper amount of slack in the hose when the car is jacked up.

6. Tighten the brake fittings using a brake line wrench, and, if necessary, reinstall any clamps or tie-downs.

CAUTION

Never attempt to bend or twist brake lines after the fittings have been tightened. If any lines are at all kinked they must be replaced.

The rest of installation is the reverse of removal. Fill the reservoir with DOT 4 brake fluid from a sealed container. Bleed the system as described in **520 Brake Fluid and Brake Bleeding**. Check that there are no leaks. Finally test drive the car to check all brake functions. Recheck the brake fluid level.

523 Brake Calipers

GENERAL

Two basic brake caliper configurations are used on cars covered by this manual. On 1985 through 1987 cars, the front calipers contain the parking brake assembly. On all 1988 and later cars, the rear calipers contain the parking brake assembly. On all cars, the front calipers are bolted to the steering swivel member while the rear calipers are bolted to the axle.

Brake fluid seeping or leaking from around the caliper piston is the result of a failed or damaged piston seal. The seal can be replaced. However, corrosion, scoring, or pitting on the piston will quickly destroy a new seal. It is recommended that the caliper be replaced to remedy a leaking piston seal and to prevent future problems.

WARNING

- Friction materials in the brake pads may contain asbestos fibers. Avoid breathing any asbestos fibers or dust. Do not create dust by grinding or sanding, or by cleaning the pads or disc with compressed air. Always use a respirator.

- Brake fluid is poisonous. Always wear hand and eye protection.

NOTE

- Saab recommends that the brake pad U-clips and dampers (anti-rattle clips) be replaced whenever replacing brake pads or calipers on 1985 through 1987 cars. The U-clips are prebent to help prevent brake noise (clunking noise when backing up). During normal use, the bends in the clip tend to straighten out and the damper spring tension weakens.

- If the parking brake lever does not fully release, the lever is sticking in the caliper or the lever return spring is damaged. This can lead to brake system failure and premature brake pad wear. If the lever cannot be made to move freely, the caliper must be replaced as described below.

NOTE

Always plug or cover the brake line or hose fittings whenever the system has been opened to prevent dirt from getting into the system. Even a minute particle of dirt can cause problems.

REPLACING BRAKE CALIPERS (1985-1987 MODELS)

To remove front calipers on 1985 through 1987 models

1. Raise the car and support it with jackstands. Remove the front wheels.

WARNING

Make sure the car is well supported on the jackstands. Never use just a jack to support a car.

---

2. Release the parking brake. Remove any rust and debris from the brake disc and caliper. Clean the hose fittings.

3. Working at the caliper, push the parking brake lever towards the sliding yoke and unhook the parking brake cable from the lever. Remove the small circlip then pull the cable from the sliding yoke.

4. Remove the brake pads as described in **517 Brake Pads.**

5. Pinch off the flexible hose using special brake hose clamping pliers. Unscrew the rigid brake line fitting at the brake hose. See Fig. 1.

CAUTION

If the special hose clamping pliers are not available, remove the brake fluid from the fluid reservoir using a syringe. Do not clamp the hose using any other type of pliers. Internal damage to the hose may result.

NOTE

Plug the hose fittings to prevent dirt from entering the system.

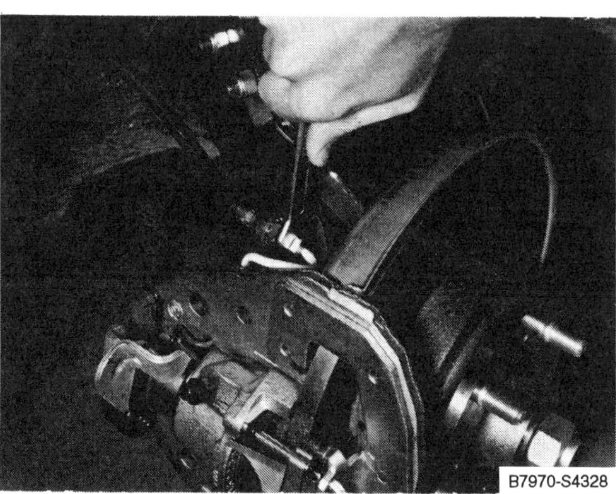

Fig. 1. Brake line fitting being unscrewed.

6. Working from the rear of the caliper, bend the locking plate tabs away from the caliper mounting bolt heads. Remove the two mounting bolts. See Fig. 2.

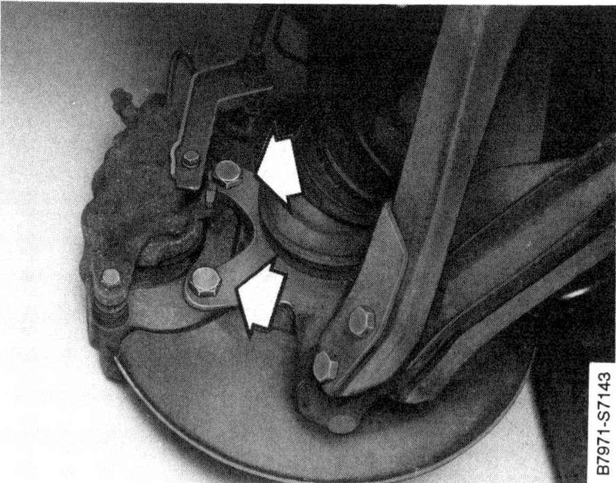

Fig. 2. Front caliper mounting bolts (arrows). Caliper shown is slightly different than those covered here.

Installation is the reverse of removal. Tighten the caliper mounting bolts. Then, using a new locking plate, lock the bolts in position by bending the tabs over the bolt heads. Do not twist or bend the flexible brake hose when connecting the brake line. Install the brake pads and reconnect the parking brake cable as described in **517 Brake Pads**. Bleed the system as described in **520 Brake Fluid and Brake Bleeding**. Adjust the parking brake cables as described in **551 Parking Brake.** Install the wheels and tighten the wheel lug nuts or bolts. Test all brake functions for correct operation.

NOTE

The front calipers have a sliding yoke that requires cleaning and lubrication as part of caliper replacement. Lubricate the sliding surfaces between the caliper and yoke using Gleitmo 540 lubricant, which is available from an authorized Saab dealer.

Tightening torques
- front caliper to steering member .... 110 to 130 Nm (81 to 96 ft-lb)
- wheel lug nuts .... 90 to 110 Nm (66 to 81 ft-lb)

To remove rear calipers on 1985 through 1987 models

Fig. 3. shows an exploded view of rear caliper used on 1985 to 1987 cars.

1. Raise the car and support it with jackstands. Remove the rear wheels.

WARNING

Make sure the car is well supported on the jackstands. Never use just a jack to support a car.

CAUTION

Do not place a jack under the rear axle to raise up the car. The axle may be damaged.

2. Remove any rust and debris from the brake disc and caliper. Clean the hose fittings.
3. Remove the brake pads as described in **517 Brake Pads.**
4. Remove the rigid brake line fitting at the brake caliper.

NOTE

Plug the hose fittings to prevent dirt from entering the system.

5. Bend the locking plate tabs away from the caliper mounting bolt heads. Remove the two mounting bolts holding the caliper to the axle.

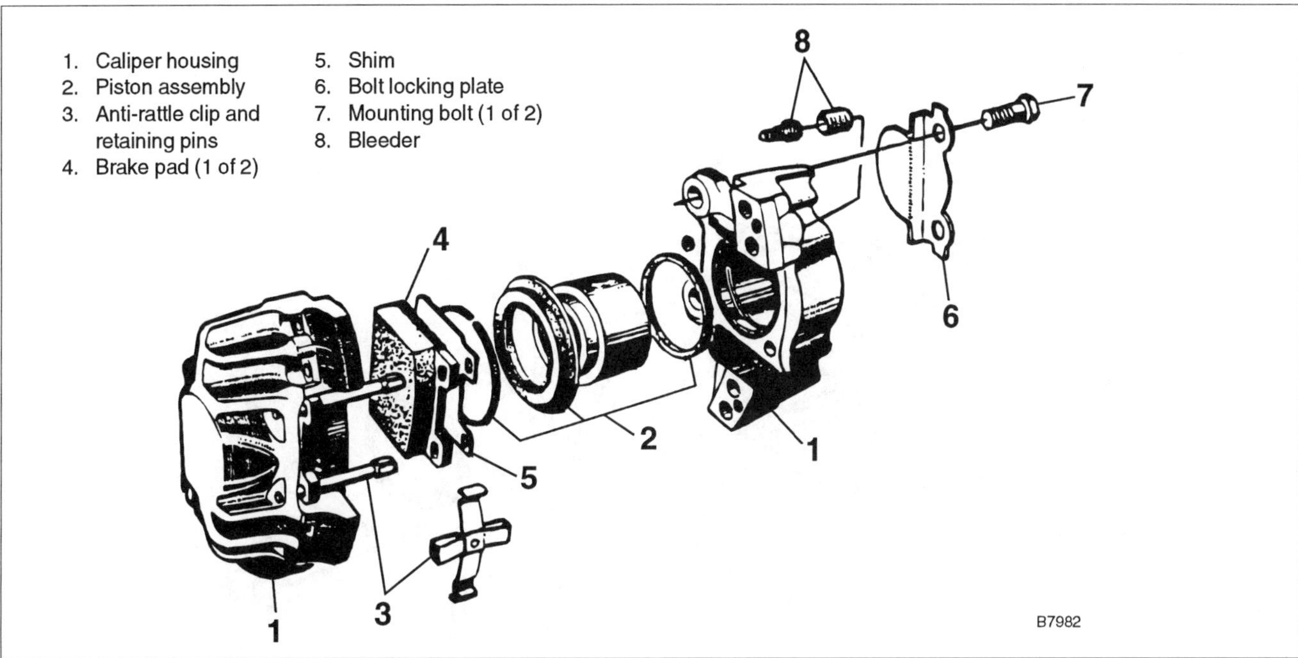

Fig. 3. Exploded view of rear calipers on 1985 to 1987 models.

Installation is the reverse of removal. Tighten the caliper mounting bolts. Then, using a new locking plate, lock the bolts in position by bending the tabs down over the bolt heads. Install the brake pads as described in **517 Brake Pads**. Tighten the brake hose and bleed the system as described in **520 Brake Fluid and Brake Bleeding**. Install the wheels and tighten the wheel lug nuts. Test all brake functions for correct operation.

Tightening torques

- rear caliper to axle. . . . . .70 to 90 Nm (52 to 66 ft-lb)
- wheel lug nuts . . . . .90 to 110 Nm (66 to 81 ft-lb)

REPLACING BRAKE CALIPERS (1988 AND LATER MODELS)

To remove front calipers on 1988 and later models

Fig. 4 is an exploded view of the front caliper used on 1988 and later models.

1. Raise the car and support it with jackstands. Remove the front wheels.

WARNING

Make sure the car is well supported on the jackstands. Never use just a jack to support a car.

---

2. Remove any rust and debris from the brake disc and caliper. Clean the hose fittings.

3. Using special brake hose clamping pliers, pinch off the flexible brake hose. Remove the brake line fitting to the caliper using a brake line (flare) wrench. See Fig. 5.

WARNING

If the special hose clamping pliers are not available, remove the brake fluid from the fluid reservoir using a syringe. Do not clamp the hose using any other type of pliers. Internal damage to the hose may result.

---

4. Remove the bracket that holds the brake hose to the caliper. See Fig. 6.

NOTE

Note how the bracket dimples fit into the caliper.

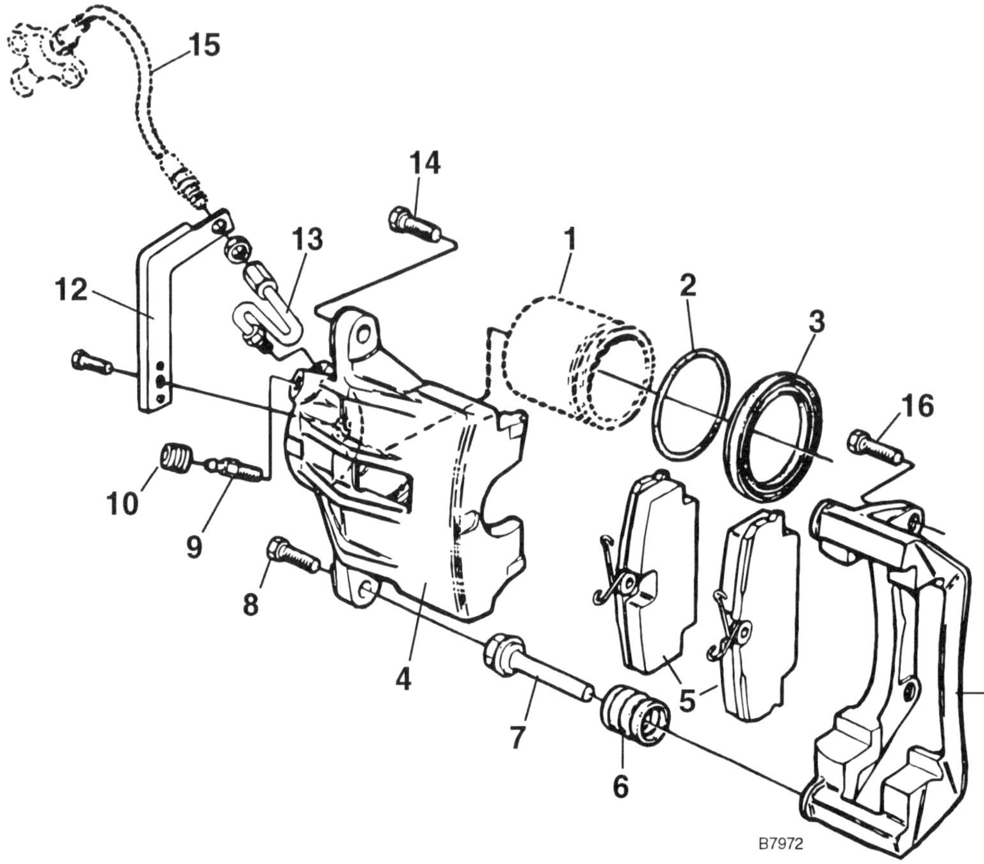

B7972

1. Brake piston
2. Piston seal
3. Dust boot
4. Caliper housing
5. Brake pads
6. Guide pin boot
7. Guide pin (1 of 2 shown)
8. Caliper mounting bolt (always replace)
9. Bleeder
10. Dust cap
11. Pad carrier
12. Brake hose bracket
13. Brake line
14. Caliper mounting bolt (always replace)
15. Brake hose
16. Brake pad carrier mounting bolt

Fig. 4. Exploded view of front caliper assembly used on 1988 and later models.

Fig. 5. Brake line fitting being removed.

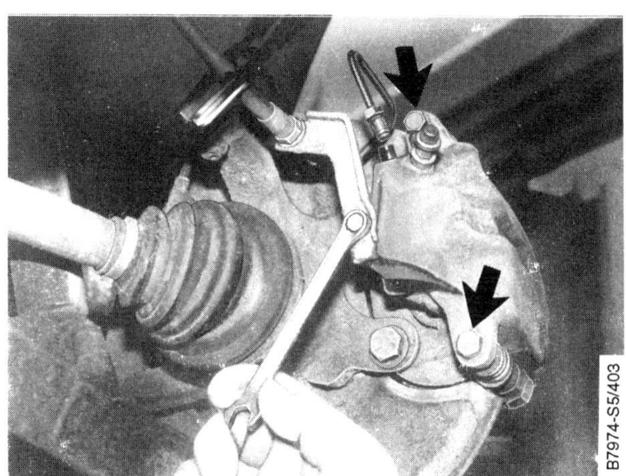

Fig. 6. Brake hose bracket being removed. Arrows show upper and lower caliper mounting bolts.

5. While holding the guide pins stationary, remove the upper and lower caliper mounting bolts. See Fig. 7. Remove the caliper.

Fig. 7. Hold guide pins stationary using open-end wrench (**A**) when loosening caliper mounting bolts (**B**).

6. Remove the brake pad carrier by removing the two bolts holding it to the steering member.

Installation is the reverse of removal. Do not twist or bend the flexible brake hose when connecting the brake line. Inspect the rubber boots for the guide pins and replace as necessary. Use new self-locking bolts when installing the caliper to the pad carrier. Install the brake pads as described in **517 Brake Pads**. Bleed the system as described in **520 Brake Fluid and Brake Bleeding**. Install the wheels and tighten the wheel lug bolts. Test all brake functions for correct operation.

CAUTION
Always replace the front caliper mounting bolts with new ones. These bolts are designed to be used only once and may fail when used a second time.

Tightening torques
- caliper mounting bolt to guide pin . . . . 30 to 35 Nm (22 to 26 ft-lb)
- front pad carrier to steering member (1988 and later models) . . . . . 70 to 110 Nm (52 to 81 ft-lb)
- wheel lug bolts . . . . . . 105 to 125 Nm (77 to 92 ft-lb)

To remove rear calipers on 1988 and later models

Fig. 8. shows the rear caliper used on 1988 and later models.

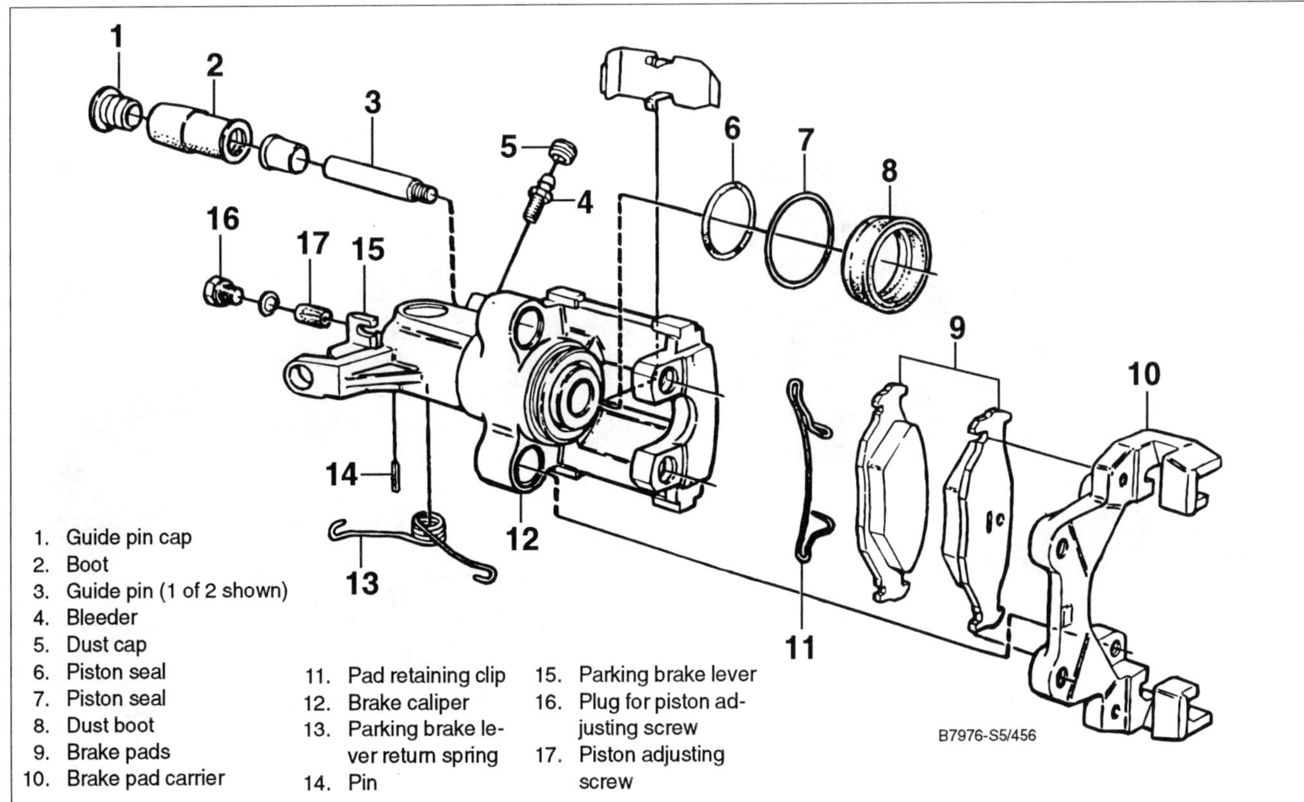

Fig. 8. Exploded view of rear caliper assembly used on 1988 and later models.

1. Raise the car and support it with jackstands. Remove the rear wheel.

WARNING

Make sure the car is well supported on the jackstands. Never use just a jack to support the car.

---

2. Unhook the parking brake cable from the caliper lever. See Fig. 9. Pull the cable out of the caliper housing.

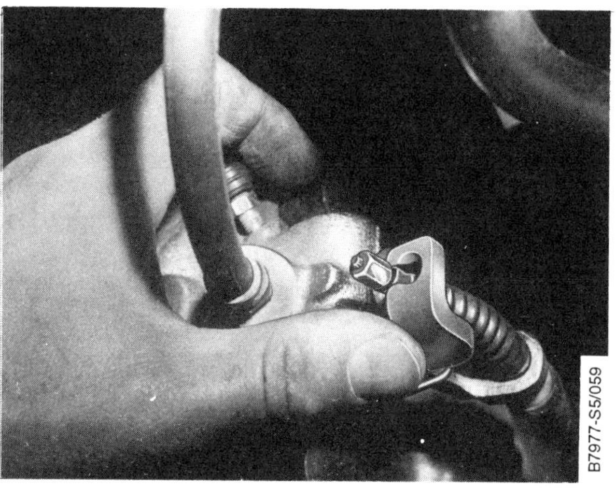

Fig. 9. Parking brake cable being unhooked from caliper.

3. Remove the pad retaining clip. See Fig. 10.

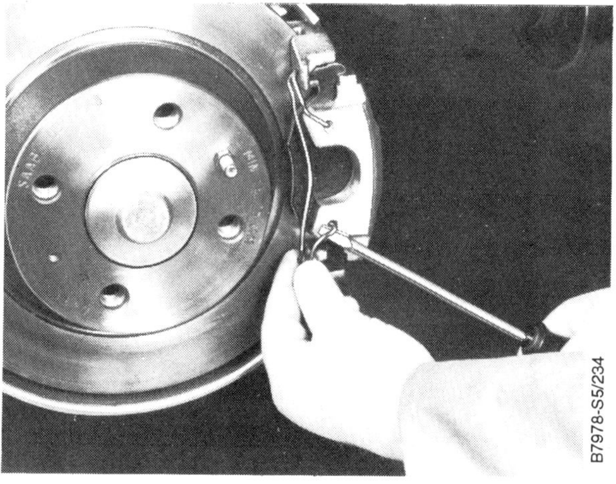

Fig. 10. Pad retaining clip being removed.

4. Remove any rust and debris from the brake disc and caliper. Clean the hose fittings.

5. Remove the threaded screw plug covering the piston adjusting screw. Then unscrew the piston adjusting screw using a 4 mm internal-hex head wrench. See Fig. 11.

NOTE

The piston caliper adjusting screw positions the piston to the pads. The screw needs to be backed out of the caliper so that the piston can be pushed away from the pads. More information on the piston adjusting screw is given in **517 Brake Pads**.

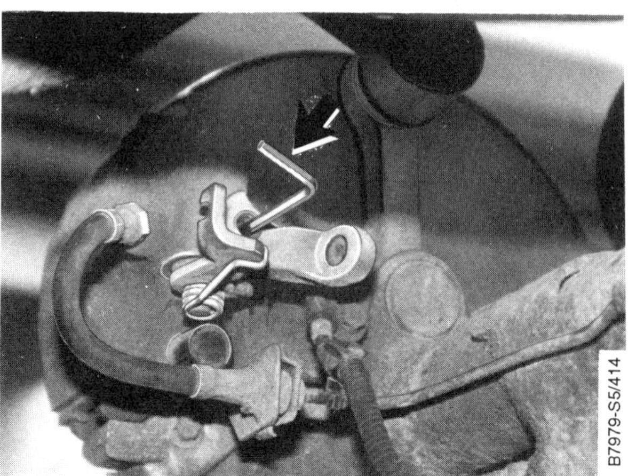

Fig. 11. Internal-hex head wrench (arrow) used to loosen caliper piston adjusting screw.

6. Using special brake hose clamping pliers, pinch off the flexible brake hose. Loosen slightly, but do not remove, the brake hose. See Fig. 12.

WARNING

If the special hose clamping pliers are not available, remove the brake fluid from the fluid reservoir using a syringe. Do not clamp the hose using any other type of pliers. Internal damage to the hose may result.

Fig. 12. Brake hose being loosened at rear caliper.

7. Remove the guide pin dust caps and then remove the two guide pins using a 7 mm internal-hex head wrench. See Fig. 13.

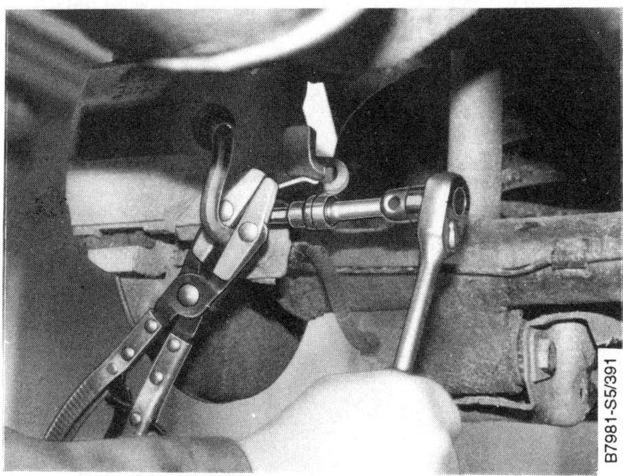

Fig. 13. Lower caliper guide pin being removed. Remove upper guide pin also.

8. Lift the caliper housing off the pad carrier and remove the brake pads.

9. While holding the flexible brake hose stationary, unscrew the caliper. Plug the hose and caliper openings to keep out dirt.

10. Remove the two bolts holding the pad carrier to the axle then remove the two bolts holding the dust shield. See Fig. 14.

Installation is the reverse of removal. Reinstall the brake pads and adjust the piston as described in **517 Brake Pads.** Tighten the hose and bleed the system as described in **520 Brake Fluid and Brake Bleeding.** Reconnect the parking brake cable and check the cable adjustment as described in **551 Parking Brake.** Install the wheels and tighten the wheel lug bolts. Test all brake functions for correct operation.

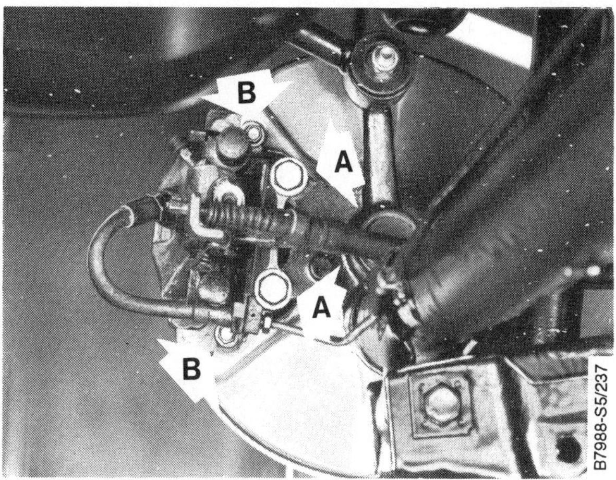

Fig. 14. Pad carrier bolts (**A**) and dust shield bolts (**B**).

Tightening torques

- rear caliper to pad carrier (pins). . . . . 25 to 30 Nm (18 to 22 ft-lb)
- brake pad carrier to rear axle (1988 and later models). . . . . . 40 to 54 Nm (30 to 40 ft-lb)
- wheel lug bolts. . . . . . 105 to 125 Nm (77 to 92 ft-lb)
- all other fasteners
  - M5 bolt . . . . 5 Nm (44 in-lb)
  - M6 bolt . . . . 10 Nm (89 in-lb)
  - M8 bolt . . . . 20 Nm (15 ft-lb)
  - M10 bolt . . . . 40 Nm (30 ft-lb)

524 Brake Pedal Mechanism

GENERAL

The brake pedal mechanism consists of the brake pedal and connecting linkage that transmits the mechanical force from the driver's foot to the master cylinder. The mechanism is located next to the steering column in the passenger compartment. See Fig. 1.

WARNING
On cars equipped with an SRS airbag system, do not attempt to service the wiring in the steering wheel, steering column assembly, or airbag control unit without first disarming the SRS system. The airbag may ignite causing injury. See an authorized Saab dealer for any repairs necessary to the SRS wiring or components.

To remove brake pedal

1. Remove the lower dashboard pad and footwell heating duct as described in **851 Interior Trim and Upholstery**.

2. Working at the brake pedal assembly, remove the padded insulating material then remove the defroster hose from the heater box.

3. Unhook the brake pedal return spring. See Fig. 2.

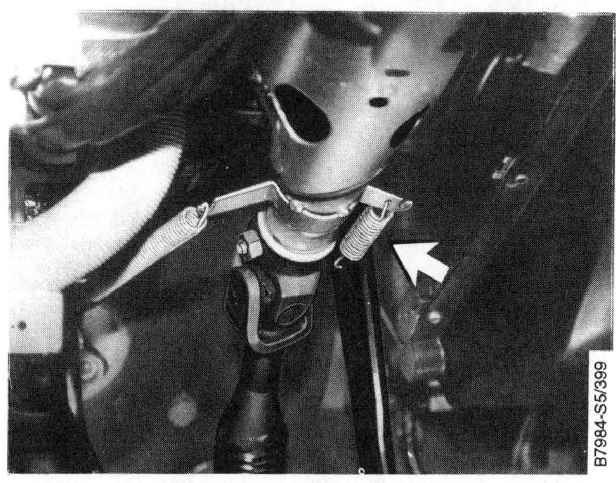

Fig. 2. Brake pedal return spring (arrow).

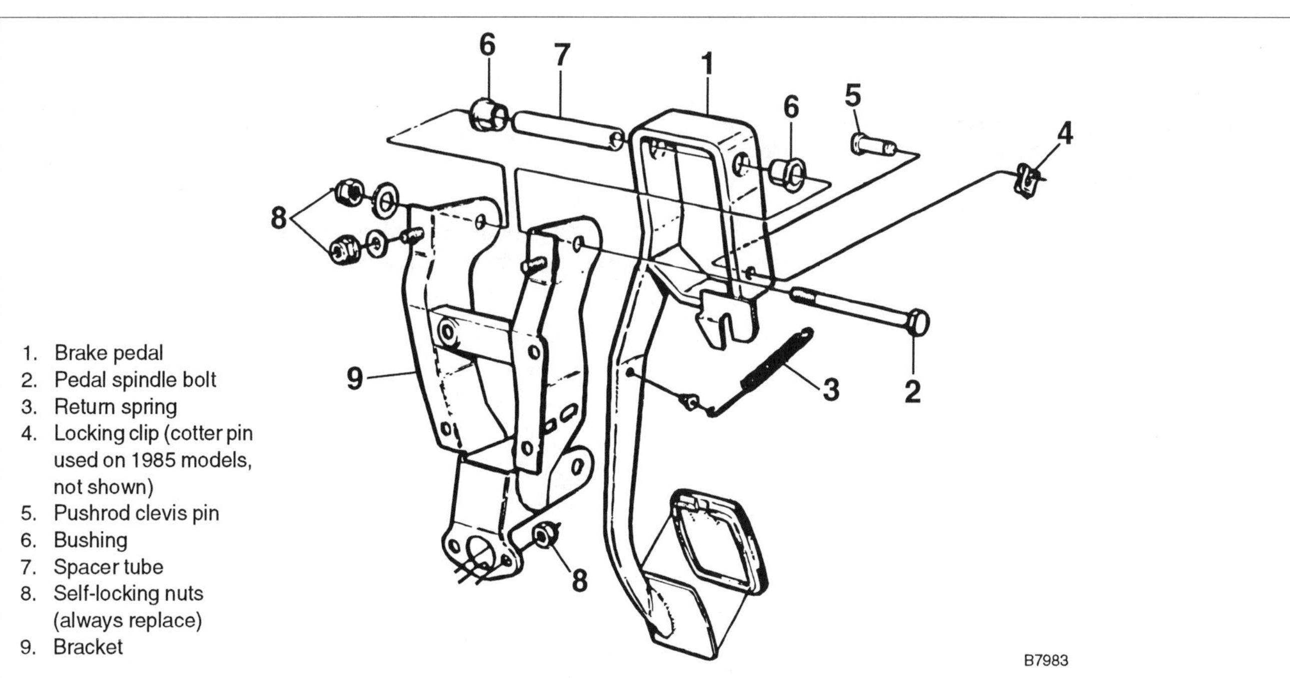

Fig. 1. Exploded view of brake pedal assembly.

4. Remove the locking clip (or cotter pin) and the pushrod pin for the master cylinder pushrod. See Fig. 3.

Fig. 3. Locking clip (arrow) for pushrod pin on master cylinder. 1985 models use a cotter pin instead of a locking clip.

NOTE
Note the orientation of the pushrod pin and locking clip (or cotter pin).

---

5. Remove the mounting plate for the brake light switch.

6. Remove the self-locking nut for the pedal spindle bolt. Remove the bolt.

WARNING
Always replace the self-locking nut with a new one. Self-locking nuts are designed to be used only once and may loosen and fall off when used a second time.

---

7. Remove the brake pedal. It may be necessary to rotate the pedal as it is being removed. Be sure to save the bushings and spacer tube. See Fig. 4.

NOTE
Inspect the bushings and spacer tube for any signs of wear and replace as necessary.

Fig. 4. Brake pedal being removed.

Installation is the reverse of removal. Always replace self-locking nuts with new ones. On 1985 models, use a new cotter pin. Adjust the brake light switch as described in **364 Electric Controls and Switches**.

CAUTION
Inspect the pushrod locking clip and replace it with a new one if it is in anyway damaged or deformed.

Test all braking functions and check that the brake lights are working. Where applicable, test cruise control functions.

541 Brake Vacuum Booster

General

The vacuum booster is used to assist braking by reducing the effort required of the driver to operate the master cylinder. Engine manifold vacuum, ported to the booster, acts on a diaphragm to boost the driver's own force on the master cylinder. See Fig. 1. The vacuum booster is a sealed unit and cannot be repaired.

NOTE
A vacuum booster is not used on cars with ABS. Instead, the brake assist is handled through the ABS unit. See **500 Brakes—General** for more information on the ABS system.

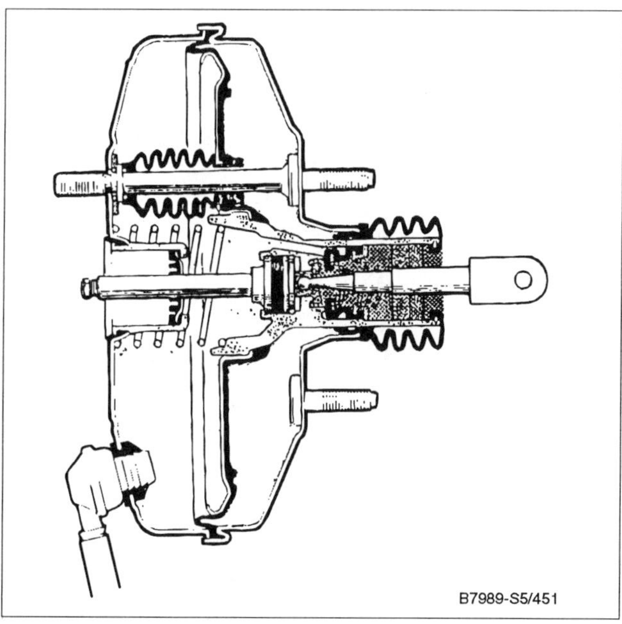

Fig. 1. Vacuum booster unit.

A quick-check of the vacuum booster can be made by pumping the brake pedal approximately 10 times with the engine off. Then while holding the pedal down, start the engine. the pedal should fall slightly. If not, the booster may be faulty.

NOTE
For a more accurate check of the vacuum booster and check valve, create a vacuum in the booster using a hand-held vacuum pump. Apply vacuum at the vacuum hose from the intake manifold. The system should not leak. See Fig. 2.

Fig. 2. Vacuum booster unit and check valve (**A**). Apply vacuum at hose (arrow) to test unit.

Replacing Vacuum Booster

The vacuum booster should be replaced if braking pedal effort is too high from a fault with the vacuum booster. If the booster is unable to hold vacuum after the engine is stopped, the vacuum check valve and seal may be defective or there may be a leak in the seal between the vacuum booster and the master cylinder.

Replacing the vacuum booster involves disconnecting the pushrod linkage at the brake pedal and removing the brake master cylinder first.

To remove vacuum booster unit

1. Disconnect the battery negative (–) cable.

2. Remove the lower dashboard pad and footwell heating duct as described in **851 Interior Trim and Upholstery**.

WARNING
On cars equipped with an SRS airbag system, do not attempt to service the wiring in the steering wheel, steering column assembly, or airbag control unit without first disarming the SRS system. The airbag may ignite causing injury. See an authorized Saab dealer for any repairs necessary to the SRS wiring or components.

3. Working at the brake pedal assembly, remove the padded insulating material then remove the defroster hose from the heater box.

4. Remove the locking clip and the pushrod pin for the vacuum booster pushrod. See Fig. 3.

NOTE

- 1985 models use a split (cotter) pin rather than a locking clip.
- Inspect the pushrod pin for wear and replace if necessary.

Fig. 3. Locking clip (arrow) for pushrod pin on master cylinder.

NOTE

Note the orientation of the pushrod pin and locking clip so they can be reinstalled correctly.

5. Working in the engine compartment, disconnect the vacuum supply hose from the brake booster. See Fig. 2 above.

6. Remove the master cylinder as described in **521 Brake Master Cylinder**.

7. Working in the passenger compartment, remove the four nuts holding the vacuum booster to the bulkhead. Remove the vacuum booster from the engine compartment.

Installation is the reverse of removal. Inspect the seal between the vacuum booster and the master cylinder and replace as necessary. Replace any self-locking nuts with new ones. Bleed the master cylinder as described in **521 Brake Master Cylinder**. Test all braking functions.

551 Parking Brake

GENERAL

The parking brake system, working through cables, moves a lever at the calipers to force the brake pads against the brake disc. On 1985 through 1987 models, the parking brake mechanism operates through the front calipers. On 1988 and later models, the parking brake mechanism operates through the rear calipers. The parking brake system is self-adjusting, so that as the pads wear the play between the pads and the brake disc is taken up automatically and the clearance is kept constant. The system should be periodically checked for proper operation.

PARKING BRAKE ASSEMBLY

The parking brake mechanically actuates the brake calipers and is independent of the hydraulic brake system. The ratcheting parking brake lever operates two separate, replaceable cables that connect to the calipers. If the parking brake mechanism at the caliper is damaged or seized, the caliper must be replaced.

NOTE

For additional information on checking the parking brake lever on the caliper, see **517 Brake Pads**. Information on replacing the calipers can be found in **523 Brake Calipers**.

To remove parking brake cables (1985-1987 models)

Fig. 1 shows the front parking brake system.

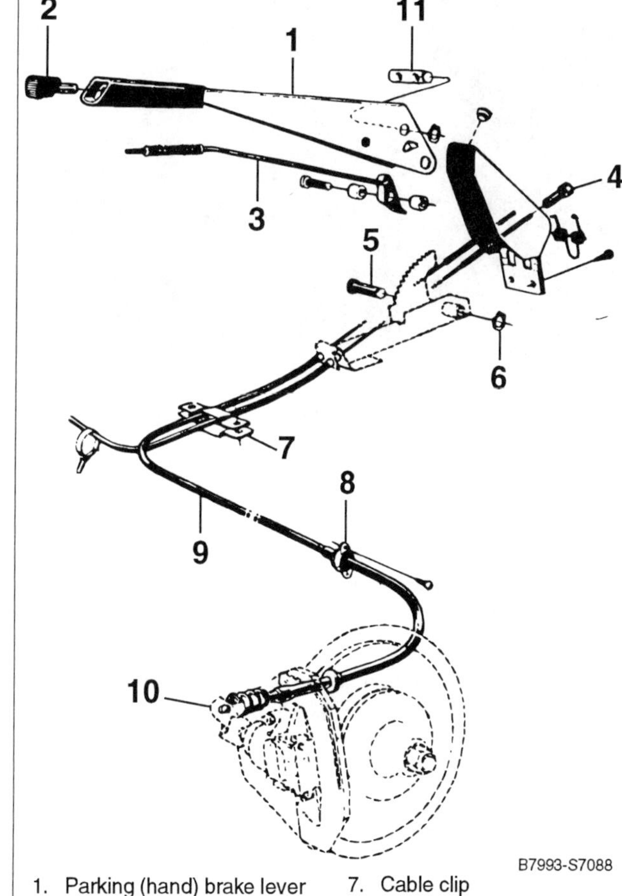

1. Parking (hand) brake lever
2. Release button
3. Release link
4. Cable adjusting nut (1 of 2)
5. Pin
6. Circlip
7. Cable clip
8. Wheel housing grommet
9. Cable
10. Caliper lever
11. Pivot pin

Fig. 1. Parking brake system used on 1985 through 1987 models.

1. Raise the car and support it with jackstands.

WARNING

Make sure the car is well supported on the jackstands. Never use just a jack to support a car.

---

2. Release the parking brake.

3. Remove the driver's seat and sill plates, then pull back the front carpeting to expose the heating duct. See **851 Interior Trim and Upholstery**.

4. Remove the center console beneath the handbrake lever as described in **432 Manual Transmission Controls**. Where applicable, remove the center storage console as described in **853 Dashboard and Consoles**.

5. Remove the center heating duct.

6. Remove the adjusting nuts from the cable ends at the parking brake lever. See Fig. 2.

Fig. 2. Parking brake cable adjusting nuts (arrow). Center console removed.

NOTE
Individual cables are available as replacement parts.

---

7. Remove the cable hold-down clip that anchors the cables to the floor. See Fig. 1 above.

NOTE
The cables cross over each other just ahead of the cable clip.

---

8. Working at the wheel housing, remove the rubber grommet that holds the cable to the body. Unhook the cable end from the caliper lever. Remove the small circlip the holds the cable to the caliper and slide the cable out of the caliper. See Fig. 3.

9. Working below the engine compartment, cut any cable ties from the parking brake cable. Then pull the cables through the bulkhead grommet and out of the passenger compartment. Pull the other end of the cable through the opening in the wheel housing.

Fig. 3. Parking brake cable (arrow) being disconnected at caliper lever.

NOTE
Note how the cable runs through the engine compartment so the new cable can be installed in the same location.

To install parking brake cables (1985-1987 models)

1. Working below the engine, inspect the rubber grommet in the bulkhead and replace it if necessary.

2. Install the cables through the bulkhead grommet into the passenger compartment.

NOTE
It may help to spray the rubber grommet and cable jacket with silicone spray as an aid to installation.

---

3. Working in the passenger compartment, install the cable ends into the pivot pin in the handbrake lever and thread the adjusting nuts on to the cable. See Fig. 2 above.

NOTE
Check that the cables cross over each other just inside the passenger compartment.

---

4. Install the cable hold-down clip over the cables.

5. Working under the car, feed the other end of the cable through the opening in the wheel housing and connect the cable end to the caliper lever. See Fig. 3 above.

The rest of the installation is the reverse of removal. Replace any cable ties as necessary. Apply the parking brake lever several times to stretch the cables then adjust the cables as described below. Check that the parking brake warning lamp operates correctly.

NOTE
Adjust the parking brake as described below before reinstalling the center console. The adjusting nuts cannot be reached as easily after the console has been fitted.

To adjust parking brake (1985-1987 models)

1. With the parking brake fully released, back off the adjusting nuts at the hand brake lever until no tension is on the actuating lever at the caliper. Then insert a 0.5 mm feeler gauge between the caliper lever and yoke as shown in Fig. 4.

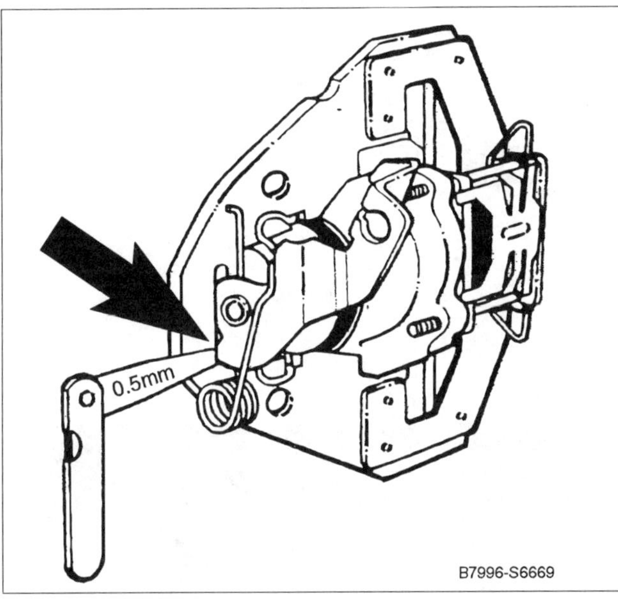

Fig. 4. Parking brake lever gap being measured at caliper. Cable must be connected to lever.

parking brake lever	
to yoke clearance	0.5±0.1 mm (0.019±0.003 in.)

2. Then working at the hand brake lever, adjust the parking brake cable adjusting nut(s) in the passenger compartment just until the feeler gauge falls out of the caliper. Recheck the gap with the feeler gauge.

NOTE
While a helper pulls up and then releases the handbrake lever in the passenger compartment, check that the caliper lever fully releases. If not, the lever is sticking in the caliper or the lever return spring is damaged. If the lever cannot be made to move freely, the caliper should be replaced. See **523 Brake Calipers.**

Check that the parking brake is fully applied when the hand brake lever is pulled up 9 to 10 notches (clicks). Check that the parking brake warning lamp works correctly.

To remove parking brake cables (1988 and later models)

Fig. 5 is an exploded view of the parking brake system used on 1988 and later models.

1. Remove the center console beneath the hand brake lever as described in **432 Manual Transmission Controls**. Release the parking brake after removing the center console.

2. Remove the rear seat cushion and rear sill plates as described in **851 Interior Trim and Upholstery**. Pull back the rear carpeting.

3. On 1991 and later models, remove the sound absorbing padding and the metal cover over the handbrake cables. See Fig. 6.

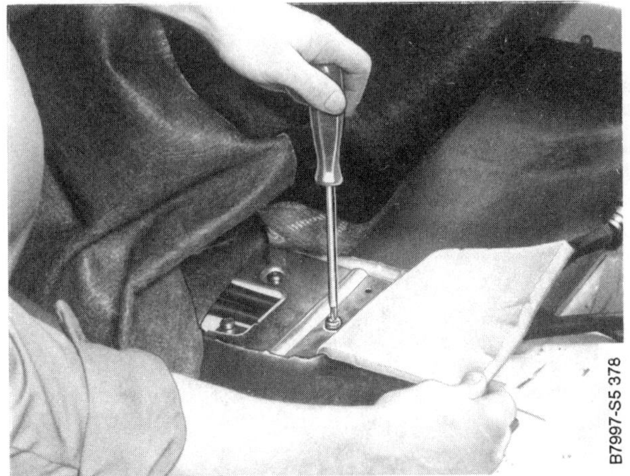

Fig. 6. Handbrake cable metal cover mounting screws being removed on 1991 and later models. Cover is mounted with 3 screws.

4. Remove the adjusting nut from the end of the cable. See Fig. 7.

5. Remove the cable locking plate and slide the cable out of the parking brake console. See Fig. 8.

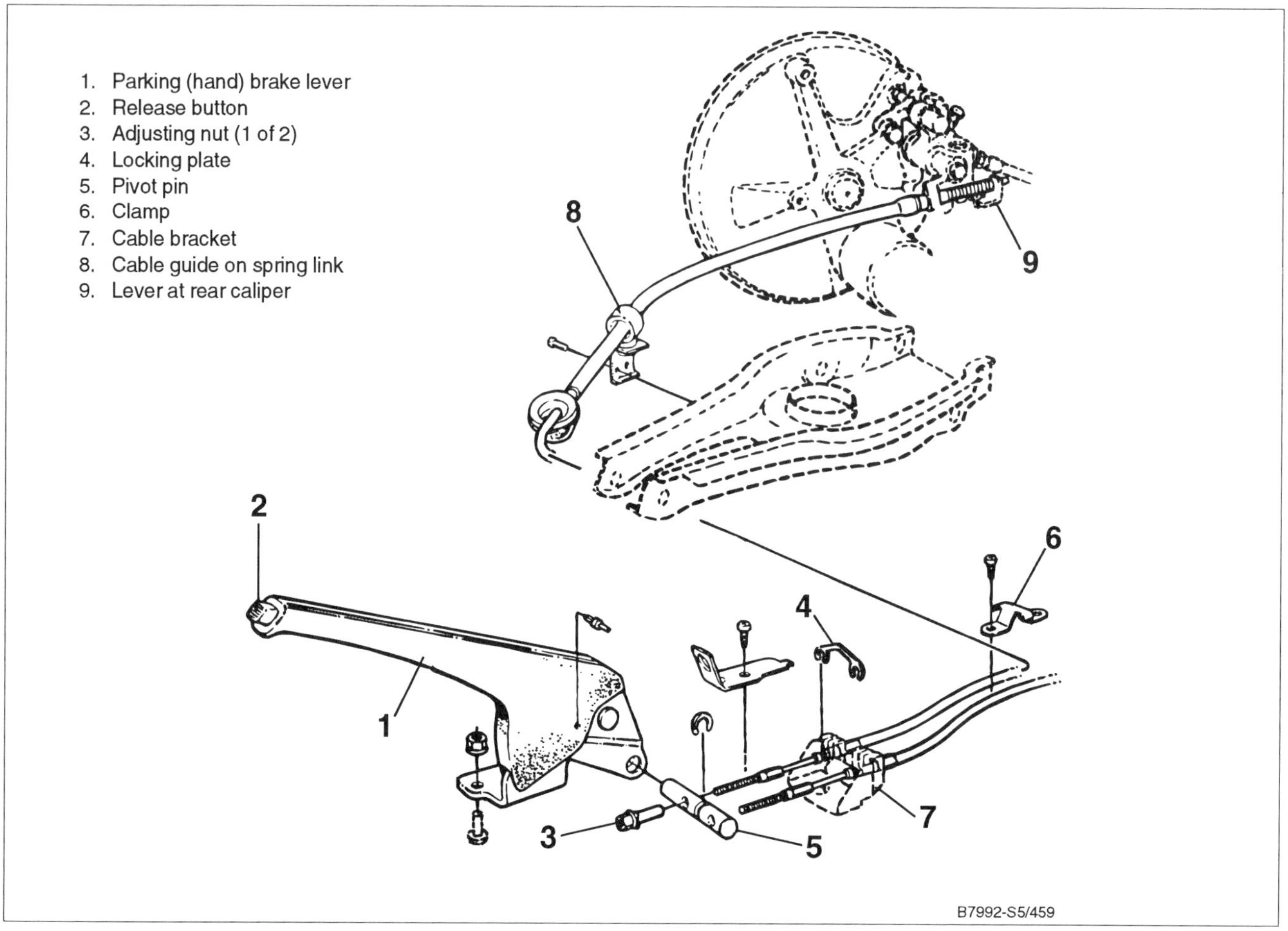

1. Parking (hand) brake lever
2. Release button
3. Adjusting nut (1 of 2)
4. Locking plate
5. Pivot pin
6. Clamp
7. Cable bracket
8. Cable guide on spring link
9. Lever at rear caliper
B7992-S5/459

Fig. 5. Parking brake mechanism on 1988 and later models.

A
B
B7998-S5/205

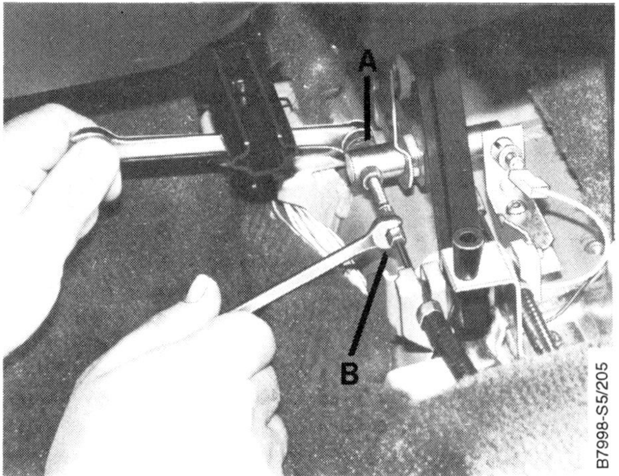

Fig. 7. Cable adjusting nut (**A**) being removed while cable (**B**) is held stationary.

B7999-S5/204

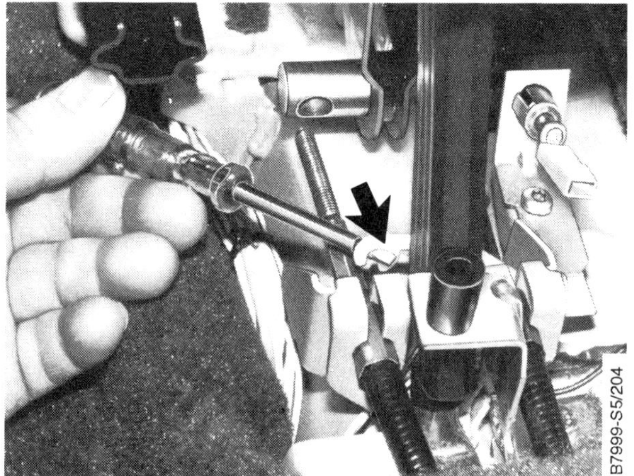

Fig. 8. Cable locking plate (arrow) being removed.

6. Remove the cable hold-down clamp under the carpeting in the center of the floor. See Fig. 9.

NOTE
On models with ABS, cut the tie wraps holding the wheel speed sensor to the parking brake cable.

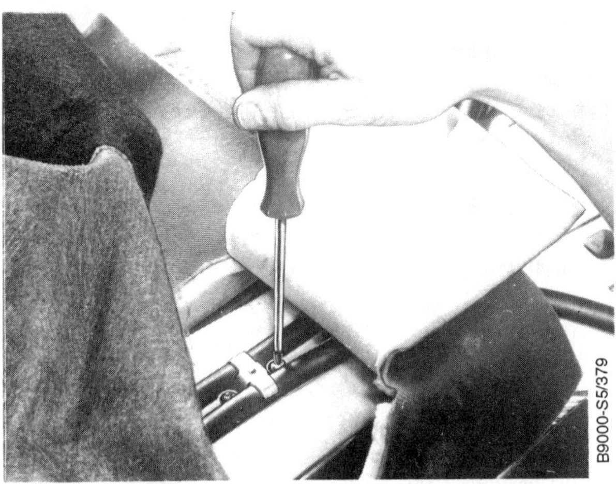

Fig. 9. Cable hold-down clamp being removed. Clamp is on center of floor.

7. Raise the rear of the car and support it with jackstands. Remove the rear wheels.

WARNING
Make sure the car is well supported on the jackstands. Never use just a jack to support a car.

---

8. Remove the cable guide from the rear suspension spring link. See Fig. 10.

Fig. 10. Cable guide on rear suspension link.

9. Remove the cable end from the brake caliper lever. See Fig. 11.

Fig. 11. Cable end being removed from caliper lever.

10. Working inside the passenger compartment, remove the cables. See Fig. 12.

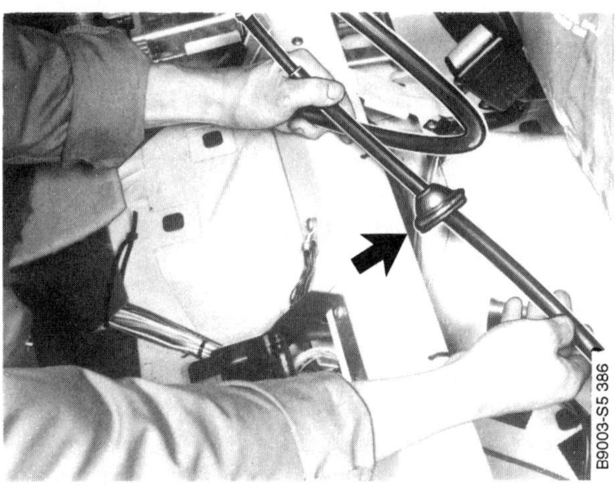

Fig. 12. Cables being removed. Rubber grommet (arrow) seals body opening.

To install parking brake cables (1988 and later models)

1. On 1991 and later cars, unscrew the adjusting sleeve locknut until the cable bottoms out in the adjusting sleeve. See Fig. 13. Then screw the locknut clockwise until it contacts the sleeve, plus an additional three turns. This will preset the cable length.

2. Insert the new cable through the hole under the rear seat and into the parking brake console. Install the cable adjusting nut(s) hand tight and then install the locking plate. See Fig. 8 above.

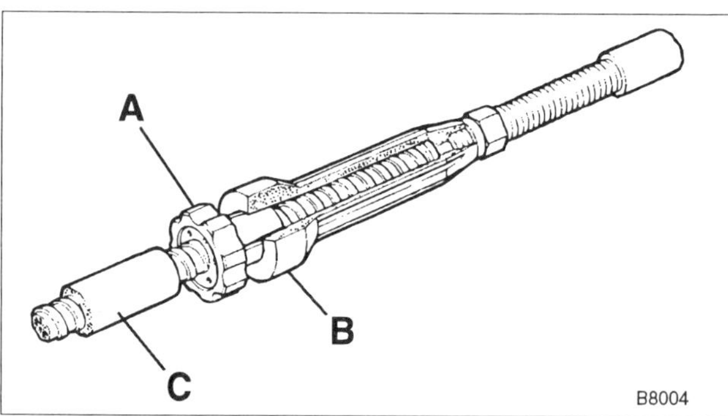

Fig. 13. Cable locknut (**A**) and adjusting sleeve (**B**). Loosen locknut then bottom out cable (**C**) in sleeve.

3. Install the cable hold-down clamp as shown in Fig. 9 above.
4. On 1991 and later cars, install the metal cover and sound absorbing padding.
5. Feed the cable through the body opening towards the caliper. Install the rubber grommet to the body.

NOTE
On cars with ABS, install a new wire tie to hold the wheel speed sensor harness to the parking brake cable.

---

6. Slide the cable guide onto the cable then install it to the rear suspension spring link. See Fig. 10 above.
7. Connect the cable end to the rear caliper lever.

Apply and release the parking brake lever several times to stretch the new cables then adjust the parking brake as described below. The rest of the installation is the reverse of removal. Leave the center console off until the parking brake has been adjusted. Check for correct operation of the parking brake warning light.

To adjust parking brake (1988-1990 models)

Two versions of parking brake cables are used on the cars covered by this manual, depending on model year. Adjusting procedures vary depending on cable installed.

On 1988 through 1990, the cables are adjusted at the parking brake console. On 1991 and later models the cables are adjusted at the adjusting sleeves under the rear seat cushion.

NOTE
On 1988 and later convertible models and on all 1991 and later models, the right hand cable is slightly longer than the left hand cable.

---

1. Remove the center console as described in **432 Manual Transmission Controls**. Release the parking brake after removing the center console.
2. Working at the caliper, remove the plug covering the piston adjusting screw then loosen the adjusting screw using a 4 mm internal-hex head wrench until the piston moves out against its stop.

NOTE
More information on locating the piston adjusting screw can be found in **517 Brake Pads**.

---

3. Turn the piston adjusting screw all the way in then back the screw out 1/4 to 1/2 turn. Check that the brake disc rotates freely.
4. Install the plug for the adjusting screw then reconnect the parking brake cable.
5. Insert a feeler gauge between the parking brake caliper lever and its stop. See Fig. 14. Adjust the cable through the adjusting nut(s) at the console (see Fig. 7 given earlier) until the feeler gauge falls out.

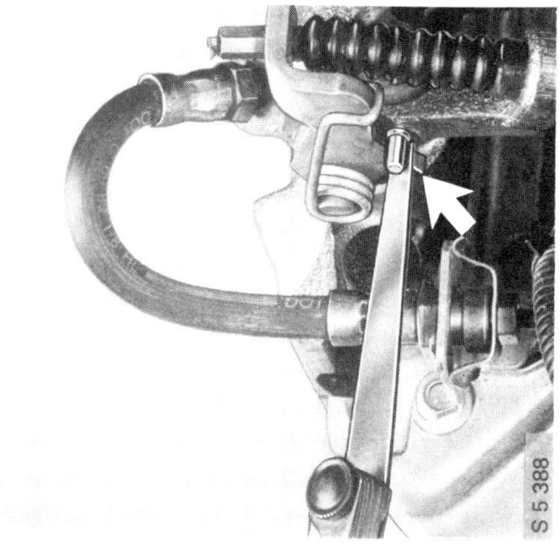

Fig. 14. Parking brake lever gap being measured with feeler gauge (arrow). Cable must be connected to lever.

parking brake lever to caliper clearance	1.0±0.5 mm (0.04±0.02 in.)

The rest of installation is the reverse of removal.

To adjust parking brake (1991 and later models)

1. Remove the rear seat cushion as described in **851 Interior Trim and Upholstery**. Release the parking brake before making adjustments to the parking brake.

2. Working at the caliper, remove the plug covering the piston adjusting screw, then loosen the adjusting screw using a 4 mm internal-hex head wrench until the piston moves out against its stop.

NOTE

More information on locating the piston adjusting screw can be found in **517 Brake Pads**.

---

3. Turn the piston adjusting screw all the way in, then back the screw out 1/4 to 1/2 turn. Check that the brake disc rotates freely.

4. Install the plug for the adjusting screw then reconnect the parking brake cable.

5. Working at the caliper, insert a feeler gauge (between the parking brake caliper lever and its stop. See Fig. 14 above.

parking brake lever to caliper clearance	0.5 to 2.0 mm (0.02 to 0.08 in.)

6. Locate the cable adjusting sleeve under the rear seat, then carefully pry the sleeve away from the sleeve's locknut to remove the slack in the cable. See Fig. 15. Then screw in the locknut (approximately 3 turns) until the feeler gauge falls out.

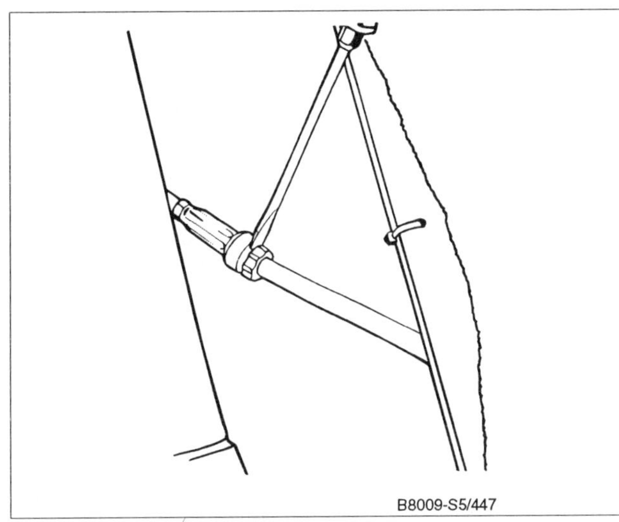

Fig. 15. Locknut being pried away from adjusting sleeve to remove slack in cable.

NOTE

- Apply and release the parking brake several times and check the adjustment again. Make sure the lever moves freely.

- While a helper pulls up and then releases the handbrake lever in the passenger compartment, check that the caliper lever fully releases. If not, the lever is sticking in the caliper or the lever return spring is damaged. If the lever cannot be made to move freely, the caliper should be replaced. See **523 Brake Calipers.**

---

600 Steering and Wheel Alignment—General

GENERAL

Steering

All of the cars covered by this manual have power steering. The steering rack is located at the rear of the engine compartment. The belt-driven power steering pump is mounted on a bracket at the back of the engine, on the passenger side. Fig. 1 shows the power steering system.

> **NOTE**
> For drive axle repair information, see **774 Wheel Bearings and Drive Axles.**

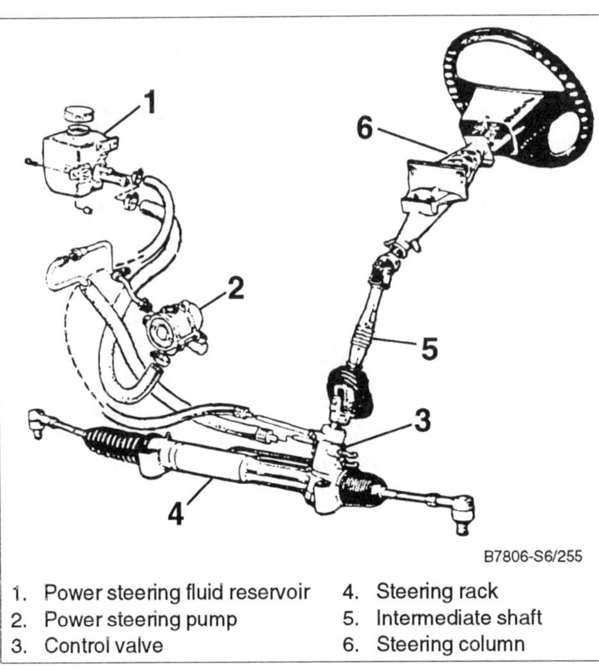

Fig. 1. Power-assisted steering system.

The steering column connects to the steering rack via an intermediate shaft an a universal joint. The column is collapsible in the event of a serious accident. Some models are equipped with an SRS airbag system. The airbag itself is located in the steering wheel pad. Tie rods with replaceable ends connect the steering rack to the steering swivel member.

> **WARNING**
> On cars equipped with an SRS airbag system, do not attempt to service the wiring in the steering wheel, steering column assembly, or airbag control unit without first disarming the SRS system. The airbag may ignite causing injury. See an authorized Saab dealer for any repairs necessary to the SRS wiring or components.

Wheel Alignment

Wheel alignment is the precise adjustment of the steering and suspension components to ensure that all wheels are orientated correctly, compared to the other wheels, the chassis and the direction of travel. Small changes can have a big effect on the how the car drives. Proper alignment provides the best compromise between responsiveness, stability, and tire wear.

Wheel alignment is adjustable only on the front wheels. Toe-in, Caster, and Camber are the three wheel alignment adjustments that are made using special front-end alignment equipment.

Toe-in is the difference between dimension A and dimension B shown in Fig. 2. If the wheels are exactly parallel, with the two dimensions equal, the toe-in will be zero. For proper steering and road control, the toe-in value must always be positive. In other words, dimension B must be greater than dimension A. This small amount of toe-in helps to offset the forces that tend to spread the tires outward as the car is travelling forward at speed.

Camber refers to the angle formed between the wheel and the vertical. See Fig. 3. If the wheel tilts outwards, the camber angle is said to be positive; if it tilts inwards, the angle is said to be negative. Proper wheel geometry on the Saab 900 requires positive camber. The camber angle influences cornering and directional stability.

600

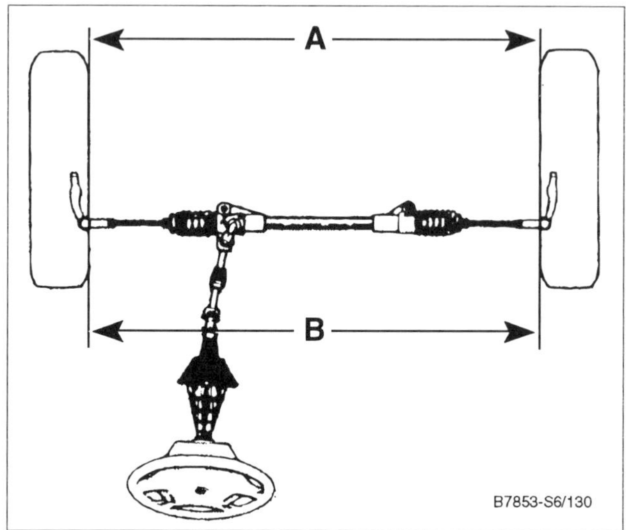

Fig. 2. Toe-in is the difference between dimension **A** and dimension **B**.

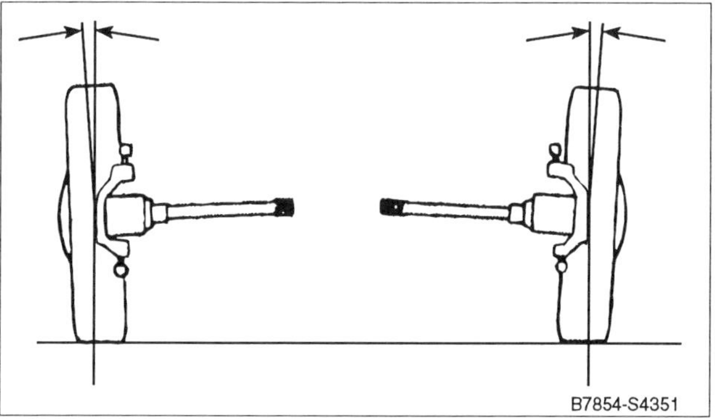

Fig. 3. Camber as viewed from front or rear.

Caster is the angle at which the swivel member (king pin) deviates from the vertical when viewed from the side. See Fig. 4. When the swivel member axis is inclined backwards, the caster is said top be positive; when the axis is inclined forward, the caster is said to be negative. The 900 is designed with positive caster. Positive camber helps to provide self-centering steering and directional stability.

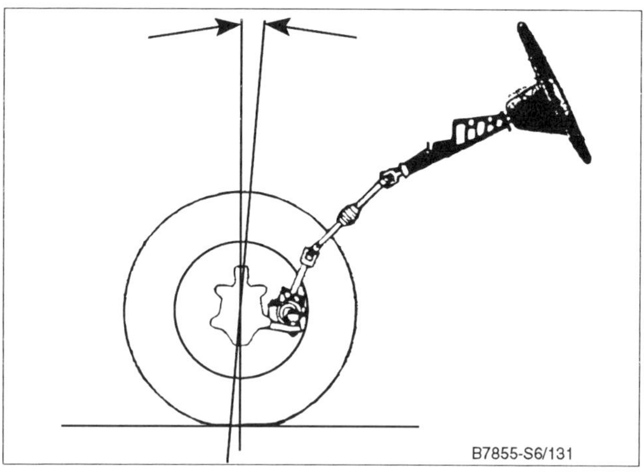

Fig. 4. Caster as viewed from the side.

TROUBLESHOOTING

This troubleshooting section applies to problems affecting steering and wheel alignment. Such problems are usually caused by faults in the steering system, but a problem such as consistently pulling to one side may also be caused by faulty brakes or a damaged drive-axle joint.

The steering system must precisely position the wheels so that the car is stable and controllable. Instability or imprecise road feel may be caused by worn or damaged steering components or incorrectly aligned wheels.

Tire wear is good indicator of steering and wheel alignment problems. Tire wear and incorrect inflation pressures can dramatically affect handling. Subtle irregularities in wheel alignment angles also affect stability. Mixing different types or sizes of tires, particularly on the same end of the car, can affect alignment and may unbalance a car's handling.

Steering and wheel alignment problems can usually be isolated and at least partially diagnosed by careful observation of the symptoms and inspection of the components that are the most likely cause. **Table a** lists symptoms of steering and wheel alignment problems and their probable causes, and suggests corrective actions.

Table a. Steering and Wheel Alignment Troubleshooting

Symptom	Probable cause	Corrective action
1. Pull to one side, wandering	**a.** Incorrect tire pressure **b.** Defective/unevenly worn tire **c.** Incorrect wheel alignment **d.** Faulty brakes (pulls only under braking)	**a.** Check and correct tire pressures **b.** Inspect tires and replace as needed **c.** Check and adjust wheel alignment. **601 Wheel Alignment** **d.** See **5 BRAKES**
2. Little or no power assist when car/engine is cold	**a.** Worn control valve and seals	**a.** Replace steering rack. **644 Power Steering**
3. Steering heavy, noisy, poor return-to-center	**a.** Incorrect tire pressure **b.** Low power steering fluid **c.** Loose, worn or broken power steering pump V-belt **d.** Worn front suspension parts, such as rubber bushings. **e.** Worn or damaged steering column universal joint **f.** Faulty power steering pump **g.** Air in power steering fluid	**a.** Check and correct tire pressures **b.** Check power steering fluid and add as required. See **1 LUBRICATION AND MAINTENANCE** **c.** Inspect V-belt. Tighten or replace as necessary. See **1 LUBRICATION AND MAINTENANCE** **d.** Inspect and replace any worn parts found. See **7 SUSPENSION** **e.** Replace universal joint. **641 Steering Column** **f.** Test and, if necessary, replace pump. **644 Power Steering** **g.** Repair air leak and, if necessary, add fluid. **644 Power Steering**
4. Front-end vibration or shimmy	**a.** Unbalanced wheels/tires or front wheels out of alignment **b.** Loose wheel lug bolts **c.** Bent wheel rim (radial or lateral runout) **d.** Tire(s) out-of-round (radial runout) **e.** Severely worn shock absorbers **f.** Worn control arm bushings	**a.** Balance tires. Align front wheels. Check tires for uneven wear patterns **b.** Tighten lug bolts to proper torque **c.** Inspect wheels and replace as necessary **d.** Measure tire radial runout and remount or replace as necessary **e.** Replace worn shocks and shock bushings. See **7 SUSPENSION** **f.** Replace bushings. **632 Control Arms**
5. Knocking, thumping or clicking noises from front end	**a.** Worn shock absorber bushings **b.** Worn front suspension bushings **c.** Loose suspension mounting bolts **d.** Worn CV joints or wheel bearings	**a.** Check and, if necessary, replace bushings. **731 Front Suspension** **b.** Check and, if necessary, replace bushings. **731 Front Suspension** **c.** Retorque all front suspension fasteners. **731 Front Suspension** **d.** Replace worn CV joints or wheel bearings. **774 Wheel Bearings and Drive Axles**
6. Steering loose, imprecise	**a.** Incorrect tire pressure **b.** Worn steering rack bushings **c.** Worn tie rod end(s) **d.** Faulty front wheel bearings **e.** Worn or damaged steering column universal joint **f.** Worn or damaged steering rack	**a.** Check and correct tire pressures **b.** Replace bushings. **644 Power Steering** **c.** Replace tie rod end(s) and align wheels. **643 Tie Rod Ends, 601 Wheel Alignment** **d.** Replace wheel bearing. **774 Wheel Bearings and Drive Axles** **e.** Replace universal joint. **641 Steering Column** **f.** Replace steering rack. **644 Power Steering**

601 Wheel Alignment

TABLES

WHEEL ALIGNMENT SPECIFICATIONS

The specifications and procedures given in this repair group are designed to be used in conjunction with special wheel alignment equipment. Only the alignment of the front wheels is adjustable, although rear wheel alignment can be checked. Checking wheel alignment is normally necessary whenever new tires are installed, if the tires are wearing abnormally, or if the car wanders to one side or handles irregularly.

Checking tire balance is recommended when doing a front wheel alignment.

There are two chassis used on the cars covered by this manual; a standard chassis and a sport chassis. To identify the type of chassis, measure the distance between the top of the wheel rim and the seam line between the fender and the hood. See Fig. 1.

Fig. 1. Chassis ride height measurement (dimension **B**).

Chassis Ride Height (dimension **B**)
- standard chassis. . . . . 243 mm (9.56 in.)
- sport chassis
  - with 15 in. wheel . . . . 230 mm (9.06 in.)
  - with 16 in. wheel . . . . 217 mm (8.54 in.)

WARNING
On cars equipped with an SRS airbag system, do not attempt to remove the steering wheel without first disarming the SRS system. The airbag may ignite causing injury. See an authorized Saab dealer for any repairs necessary to the SRS system.

When checking front wheel alignment, the car should be on a level surface with a full tank of gas. There should be no passengers or additional weight in the car. **Table a** lists wheel alignment specifications for cars covered by this manual. Always make sure that tire pressures are correct and that no suspension or steering components are worn.

Table a. Wheel Alignment Specifications

Measurement	Model	
	except sport chassis	sport chassis
Front		
Caster	2°±0.5	2°±0.25
Camber	0.5°±0.5	0.25°±0.25
Toe-in	2±1 mm (0.08±0.04 in.)	1.5±0.5 mm (0.06±0.02 in)
Swivel pin inclination	11.5°±1	11.5°±1
Steering angle—outer wheel	20°	20°
Steering angle—inner wheel	20.75°±0.50	20.75°±0.50
Rear		
Toe-in	4±1 mm (0.16±0.04 in.)	4±1 mm (0.16±0.04 in.)
Camber	–0.5°±0.25	–0.5°±0.25

CAUTION
The front wheel toe-in specifications listed in **Table a** are only applicable when making measurements directly from the rim, such as when using a toe bar. If optical alignment equipment is used, the specifications need to be corrected based on type of equipment being used. Most modern alignment equipment is based on a universal 28.64 in. circle.

NOTE

Swivel pin inclination, also known as king pin inclination, is not adjustable. If the swivel pin inclination is incorrect, the swivel member must be replaced as described under **774 Wheel Bearings and Drive Axles**.

Front Wheel Toe-in

Toe-in is adjusted by varying the length of the threaded tie rod in the tie rod end. Screwing the rod into the tie rod end will decrease toe-in and screwing the rod out will increase toe-in.

To adjust toe-in

1. Working from below, loosen the tie rod lock nut. See Fig. 2.

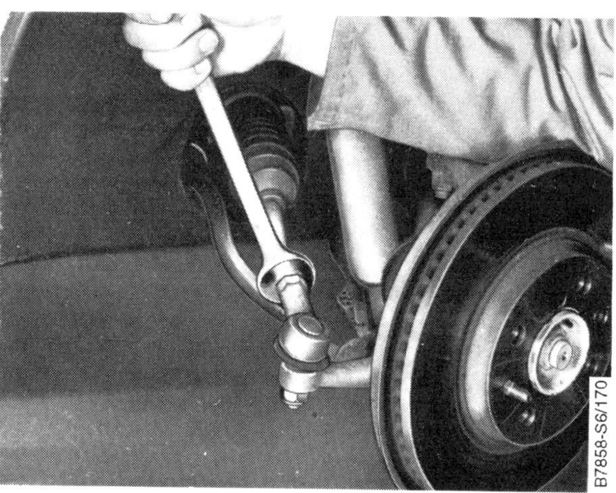

Fig. 2. Tie rod locknut being loosened. (Wheel shown removed for clarity.)

2. Using a locking pliers, turn the tie rod in or out to obtain the correct setting.

CAUTION

When the toe-in setting is correct, tighten the tie rod lock nut.- The length of the tie rod from the locknut to the stepped part of the rod must never exceed 125 mm (4.92 in). See Fig. 2. Also, the difference in length between the two rods must not exceed 2 mm (0.08 in.). For example, if the right rod measured 124 mm, the left rod must measure between 122 mm and 125 mm. See Fig. 3.

Tightening torque

- steering tie rod to tie rod end (locknut) . . . . 60 to 80 Nm (44 to 59 ft-lb)

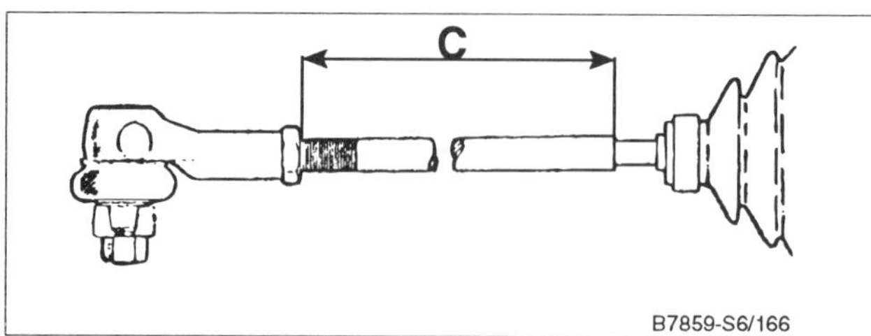

Fig. 3. Maximum permissible length (**C**) of tie rod must not exceed 125 mm (4.92 in.).

Front Wheel Camber and Caster

Camber and caster are adjusted by varying the number of shims under the upper control arm bearing brackets. See Fig. 4. The shims are available from an authorized Saab dealer in thicknesses of 0.5 mm, 1.0 mm and 2.0 mm.

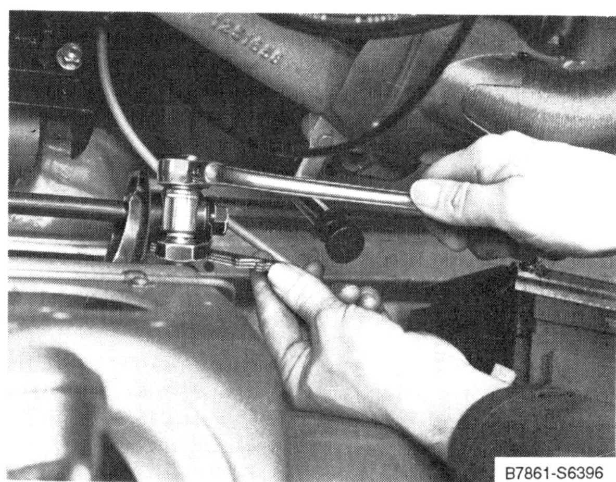

Fig. 4. Camber/caster shims being removed from upper control arm bearing bracket.

Camber is adjusted by changing the number of shims equally under both the front and rear brackets. Removing an equal number of shims from beneath both brackets will increase positive camber. Adding shims will reduce positive camber.

Caster is adjusted by changing the number of shims from either the left or the right bearing brackets. Moving shims from the front bearing bracket to the rear bearing bracket will increase the caster. Moving shims from the rear bracket to the front bracket will reduce caster. Once the final adjustments have been made, torque the bracket bolts.

Tightening torque

- upper control arm bearing bracket to body . . . . 40 to 55 Nm (30 to 40 ft-lb)

---

631 Ball Joints

CHECKING AND REPLACING BALL JOINTS

The ball joints locate the steering swivel member to the upper and lower control arms. See Fig. 1. The ball joints are permanently lubricated and do not require any service. If found to be worn, they must be replaced. See **632 Control Arms** for illustrations of ball joint mountings to the control arms.

> **WARNING**
> Do not reuse self-locking nuts. These parts are designed to be used only once and must always be replaced once loosened or removed.

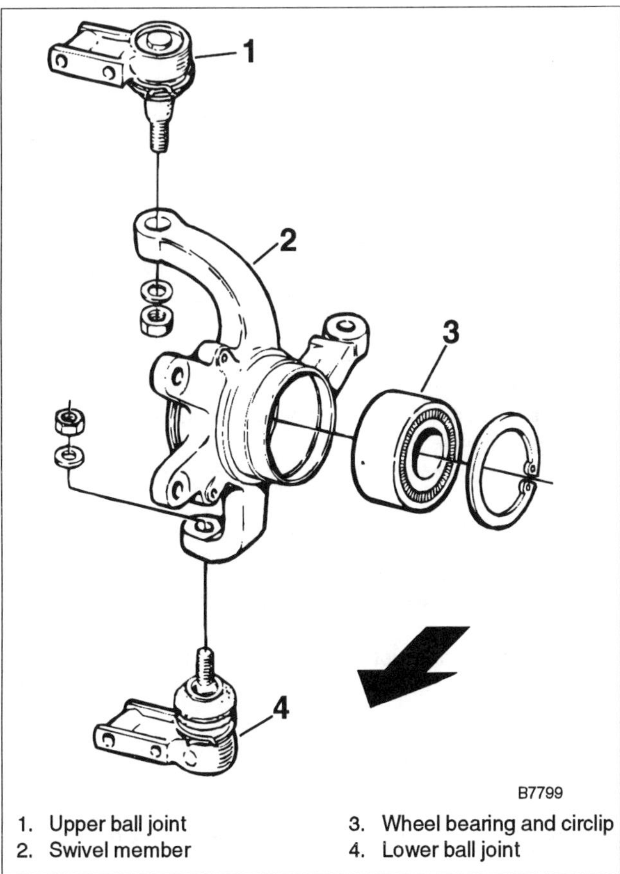

1. Upper ball joint
2. Swivel member
3. Wheel bearing and circlip
4. Lower ball joint

Fig. 1. Exploded view of steering swivel member.

To check ball joint play

To accurately check ball joints for wear, the coil spring tension on the control arm must be relieved. A special tool, as shown below, is available for this purpose.

1. With the car on the ground, insert spacer tool (Saab part no. 83 93 209) between the upper control arm and the body. See Fig. 2.

Fig. 2. Spacer tool (arrow) inserted between upper control arm and body. The spacer tool relieves suspension loading on the ball joints.

2. Loosen the wheel lug bolts or nuts, then raise the front of the car and support it securely on jack stands designed for the purpose. Remove the wheel.

3. Carefully inspect the ball joint rubber boots. If any boot is torn or cracked, the complete ball joint should be replaced.

4. Using water pump pliers, check the axial (up-down) play of the upper and lower ball joints. See Fig. 3. If the play is excessive, the ball joint must be replaced.

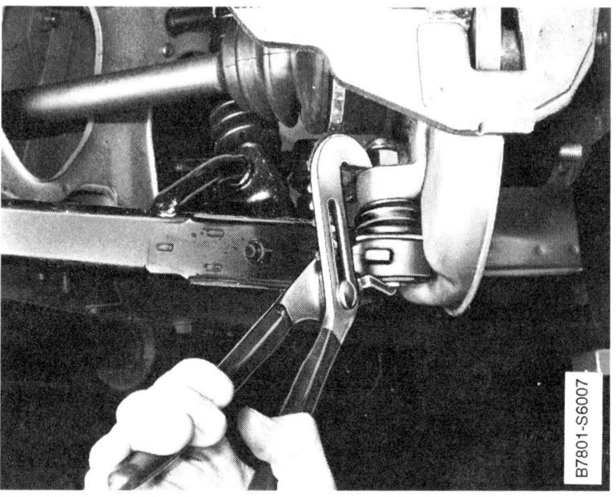

Fig. 3. Lower ball joint being checked for axial (up-down) play using water pump pliers.

Ball joint wear limit
- maximum axial play . . . . 2 mm (0.078 in.)

---

5. Using a pry bar, check the radial (side-to-side) play of the upper and lower ball joint. Gently pry the joint back and forth to check for play. See Fig. 4. If the play is excessive, the ball joint must be replaced.

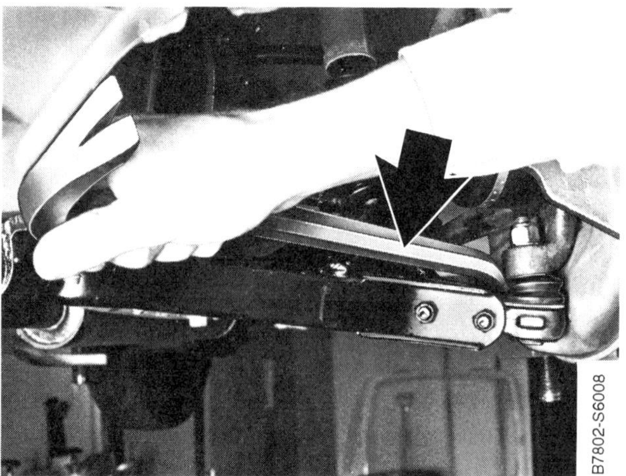

Fig. 4. Lower ball joint radial (side-to-side) play being checked using pry-bar (arrow).

Ball joint wear limit
- maximum radial play . . . . 1 mm (0.040 in.)

CAUTION
Use care not to damage the ball joint rubber boot with the pry bar.

If the ball joints are in good shape, loosely install the wheel. Lower the car and tighten the wheel bolts or nuts. Remove the spacer tool from the opening in the body.

Tightening torque
- road wheel to wheel hub
  lug nuts . . . . 90 to 110 Nm (66 to 81 ft-lb)
  lug bolts. . . . . 105 to 125 Nm (77 to 92 ft-lb)

To replace ball joint

The procedure below applies to both upper and lower ball joints.

WARNING
Do not reuse self-locking nuts. These parts are designed to be used only once and must always be replaced once loosened or removed.

---

1. With the car on the ground, insert spacer tool (Saab no. 83 93 209) between upper control arm and body. See Fig. 2 above.

2. Loosen the wheel lug bolts or nuts, then raise the front of the car and support it securely on jack stands designed for the purpose. Remove the wheel.

WARNING
Always check that the car is stable on the jack stands before starting any work.

---

3. Using a jack under the control arm, raise the lower control arm slightly. Remove the lower shock absorber mounting nut and pull the shock off its mount. See Fig. 5.

4. Lower the jack just until the drive axle is just contacting the body opening. Lock the jack in position for support.

5. Remove the self-locking nut holding the ball joint to the steering member.

6. Separate the ball joint using a press tool. See Fig. 6.

Fig. 5. Shock absorber being removed from control arm mounting.

CAUTION

Do not use a ball joint separator fork to remove the ball joint from the steering member. The steering member may be damaged as a result.

Fig. 6. Upper ball joint being pressed out of steering swivel member. Special press tool (Saab tool no. 89 95 409) shown.

7. Remove the two through-bolts holding the ball joint to the control arm. See Fig. 7. Remove the ball joint by sliding it out of the control arm.

Fig. 7. Ball joint-to-control arm mounting bolts shown at arrows. Upper ball joint shown, lower ball joint is similar.

CAUTION

If the upper ball joint is being removed, do not remove the bolt for the spring saddle as the spring is under compression.

Installation is the reverse of removal. Replace the ball joint bolts and all self-locking nuts. Torque the bolts and nuts to the values given below. Be sure to remove the spacer tool when the job is complete.

Tightening torques

- balljoint to steering swivel member
  (self-locking nut) ...... 35 to 50 Nm (26 to 37 ft-lb)
- balljoint to control arm bolts
  (self-locking nuts)...... 40 to 55 Nm (30 to 40 ft-lb)
- road wheel to wheel hub
  lug nuts............ 90 to 110 Nm (66 to 81 ft-lb)
  lug bolts .... 105 to 125 Nm (77 to 92 ft-lb)

---

632 Control Arms

GENERAL

The independent front suspension for each front wheel consists of two control arms, each of which is pivot-mounted to the unibody by bearing brackets fitted with rubber bushings. The steering swivel member is mounted to the control arms via ball joints. See Fig. 1.

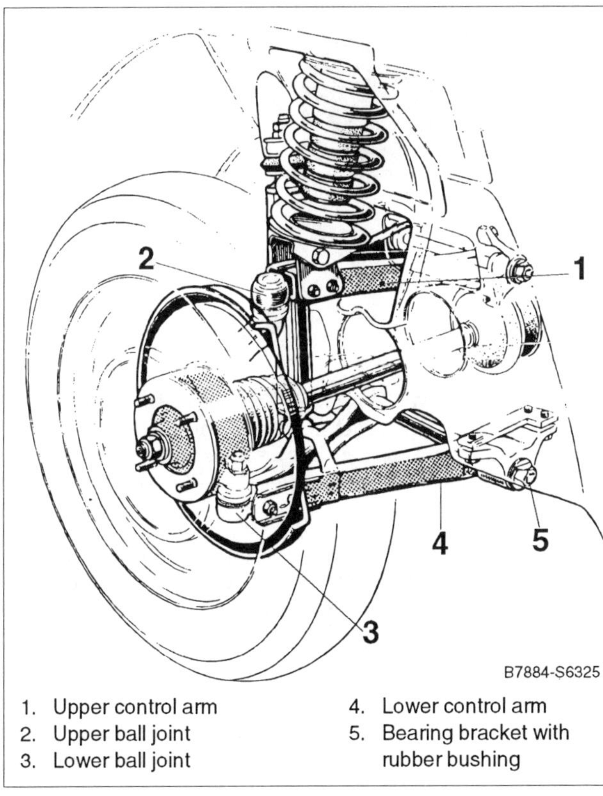

Fig. 1. Cut-away view of control arms and front suspension.

CONTROL ARMS AND CONTROL ARM BUSHINGS

The control arms are not normally replaced unless damaged. The control arm bushings, on the other hand, are prone to wear under normal use and high mileage. Inspecting the control arms includes checking for distortion or damage due to collisions or road hazards. The bushings should be inspected for wear or deterioration. Fig. 2 shows an exploded view of the lower control arm and it bushings. The upper control arm is similar.

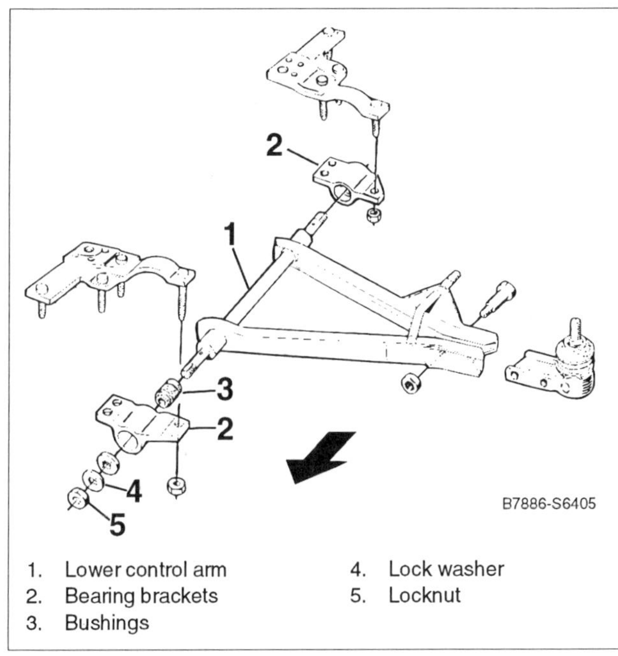

Fig. 2. Exploded view of lower control arm.

WARNING

If the controls arms have been subjected to violent stresses as a result of a collision or a road hazard, they must be carefully inspected for bending or distortion. Be sure to also inspect the bearing brackets and their mountings to the body.

NOTE

Ball joint inspection is covered in **631 Ball Joints.** Steering tie rod end inspection is covered in **643 Tie Rod Ends.**

Worn control arm bushings are often noticed through knocking or clunking sounds when traveling over rough road surfaces. Before inspecting for damaged parts or worn bushings, first check the tightness of all fasteners using a torque wrench. See Fig. 3.

632

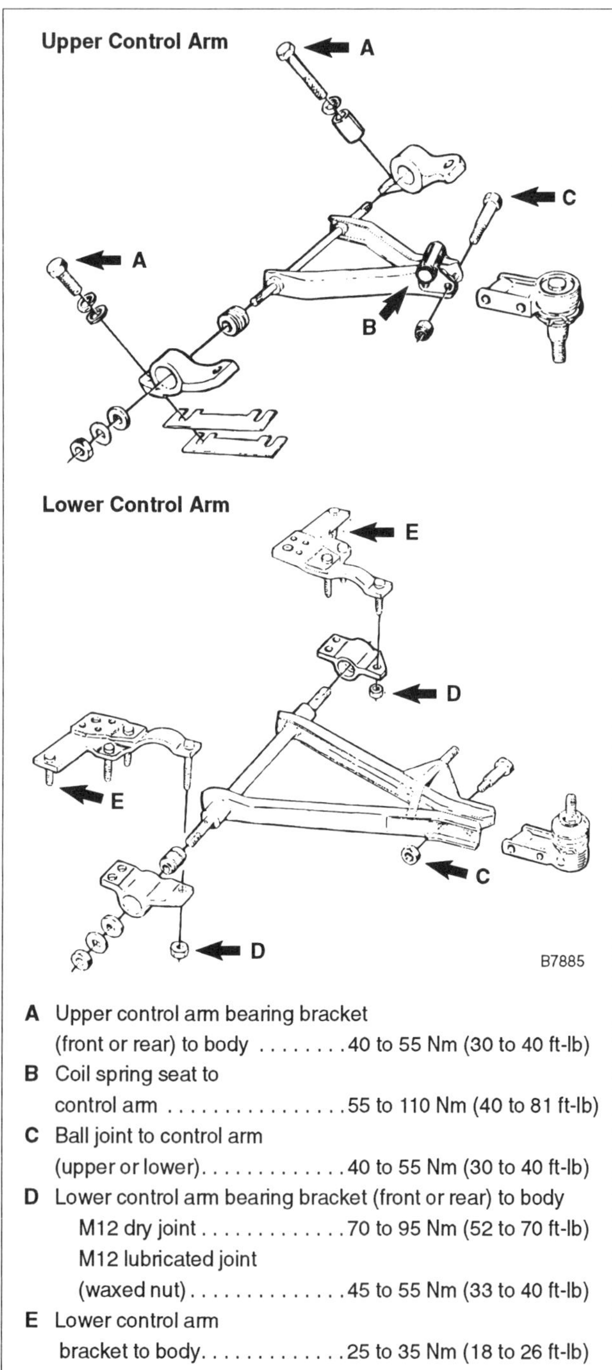

A Upper control arm bearing bracket (front or rear) to body . . . . 40 to 55 Nm (30 to 40 ft-lb)
B Coil spring seat to control arm . . . . 55 to 110 Nm (40 to 81 ft-lb)
C Ball joint to control arm (upper or lower). . . . . 40 to 55 Nm (30 to 40 ft-lb)
D Lower control arm bearing bracket (front or rear) to body
M12 dry joint . . . . 70 to 95 Nm (52 to 70 ft-lb)
M12 lubricated joint (waxed nut) . . . . 45 to 55 Nm (33 to 40 ft-lb)
E Lower control arm bracket to body. . . . . 25 to 35 Nm (18 to 26 ft-lb)

Fig. 3. Exploded view of upper and lower control arm fasteners.

To replace control arm bushings

1. Remove the control arm as described below. Remove the bearing brackets from the control arm.

2. Press the old bushing out of the bracket. Thoroughly clean the bearing brackets. Apply soapy water to the new bushing and press it into the bracket. See Fig. 4.

CAUTION
Oil or grease must not be allowed to come into contact with the bushings. Use only soapy water.

Fig. 4. Special press tool used to install control arm bushing.

NOTE
Saab tool no. 78 41 349 is used to replace lower control arm bushings (as shown above) and Saab tool no. 78 41 331 is used to replace the upper control arm bushings.

---

3. Install the bearing brackets to the control arm and position them as shown in Fig. 5. Tighten the locknut while holding the brackets in position. Recheck the angle of the bracket. Bend over the lock washer to lock the nut in place.

Bearing bracket to control arm (locknut and lock washer)

- upper control arm bracket to control arm . . . . 55 to 70 Nm (40 to 52 ft-lb)
- lower control arm bracket to control arm . . . . 75 to 90 Nm (55 to 66 ft-lb)

---

4. Install the control arm as described below.

Removing and Installing Control Arms

Removing and installing the driver's side upper control arm will require removal of the engine. With the engine installed, there is not enough clearance to pull the control arm from the

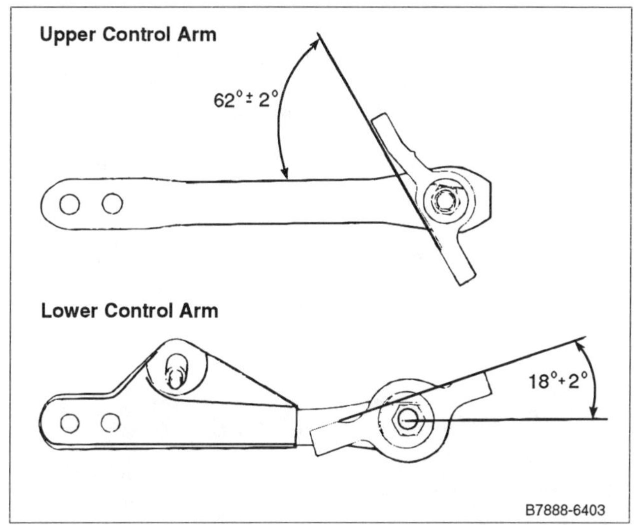

Fig. 5. Control arm bearing bracket installation angles.

body. Removing the passenger's side upper control arm requires that the engine be suspended with a hoist so that an engine mount can be removed. Special tools are required to remove the upper control arms. Read the procedures completely before starting any work.

WARNING

- Special spring compressing tools (Saab tool no. 88 18 791 or equivalent) are required to remove and install the upper control arms. Do not attempt to remove the upper control arms without the proper tools, as serious injury could result.

- Do not reuse self-locking nuts or locking washers. These parts are designed to be used only once and must be replaced once removed.

To remove upper control arm

1. If removing the driver's side control arm, remove the engine as described in **201 Engine Removal and Installation.**

2. Loosen the wheel lug bolts or nuts, then raise the front of the car and support it securely on jack stands designed for the purpose. Remove the front wheel.

WARNING

Always check that the car is stable on the jack stands before starting any work.

---

3. Using a jack under the control arm, raise the lower control arm slightly. Remove the lower shock absorber mounting nut and pull the shock off its mount. See Fig. 6. Remove the jack.

Fig. 6. Shock absorber being removed from control arm mounting.

4. Compress the suspension coil spring using a spring compressor (Saab no. 88 18 791 and 88 18 809 or equivalent). Remove the spring from the car. See Fig. 7.

WARNING

Work carefully as the spring is compressed. Check to make sure that the spring compressor is always securely seated on the spring.

Fig. 7. Compressed coil spring being removed from car.

5. Remove the spring seat and upper ball joint mounting bolts. See Fig 8. Remove the spring seat and ball joint from the control arm.

Fig. 8. Upper ball joint bolts (**1**) and spring seat bolt (**2**).

6. If removing the passenger's side control arm, use a suitable hoist to support the engine. Then remove the right side engine mount. See Fig. 9. Remove the engine mounting bracket from the engine block and engine support bracket.

CAUTION
Be careful not to damage the inner drive axle rubber boot when removing the engine mount bracket.

Fig. 9. Right side engine mount being removed. Mount is bolted in place from above and below. (Hydraulic engine mount shown, rubber engine mount is similar.)

7. Remove the four bolts holding the control arm to the body. Note the number of shims under each bearing bracket. See Fig. 10. Remove the control arm from the car.

CAUTION
The shims should be re-installed in their exact positions. The shims are used to align the front wheels. If the shims are incorrectly installed, a front wheel alignment will be necessary. See **601 Wheel Alignment.**

NOTE
The control arms are not symmetrical. If removing more than one control arm, mark their locations during removal.

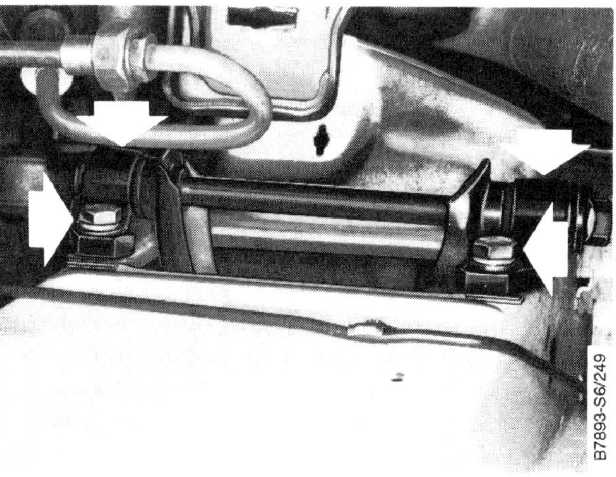

Fig. 10. Upper control arm mounting bolts (arrows) as viewed from above.

Installation is the reverse of removal. If the bearing brackets were removed from the control arms, be sure to reinstall them as shown above in Fig. 5. Be sure to replace all self-locking nuts and locking washers. Torque all control arm fasteners to the values given in above in Fig. 2. Tighten the engine mounts to their final torques with the car on the ground and engine hoist removed. Check and adjust wheel alignment if necessary. See **601 Wheel Alignment.**

To remove lower control arm

1. Loosen the wheel lug bolts, then raise the front of the car and support it securely on jack stands designed for the purpose. Remove the front wheel.

2. Raise the lower control arm slightly using a jack at the outside of the control arm. Remove the shock absorber from its lower mount and remove the ball joint from the control arm. See Fig. 11. Remove the jack.

NOTE
Where applicable, move the anti-roll bar out of the way.

Fig. 11. Lower ball joint mounting bolts (**1**) and shock absorber mounting nut (**2**). Anti-roll bar mount shown at **A**.

3. Remove the six control arm bracket-to-body mounting nuts. See Fig. 12. Remove the control arm from the car.

Installation is the reverse of removal. If the bearing brackets were removed from the control arms, be sure to reinstall them as shown above in Fig. 5. Replace all self-locking nuts and torque all fasteners to the values given in Fig. 2. Check and adjust wheel alignment if necessary. See **601 Wheel Alignment.**

Fig. 12. Lower control arm mounting nuts (arrows).

641 Steering Column

GENERAL

The steering column assembly consists of three sections, connected by universal joints. See Fig. 1. The top perforated cage-like section is deformable and the steering wheel shaft is telescopic. The intermediate shaft is made of a flexible sheet steel, which will allow the steering column to collapse when subjected to high loads.

On 1990 and later models, an SRS airbag system is used, with the airbag itself located in the steering wheel pad.

WARNING
- The SRS (Supplemental Restraint System) uses an explosive device to inflate the airbag. Do not attempt to service the wiring in the steering wheel, steering column assembly, or airbag unit. The airbag may ignite causing serious injury. See an authorized Saab dealer for any repairs necessary to the SRS wiring or components, including removal of the steering wheel and steering column.

- Do not reuse self-locking nuts. These parts are designed to be used only once and must be replaced whenever loosened or removed.

CAUTION
- When spinning the steering wheel via the front road wheels (front wheels off the ground), move the wheels slowly from lock to lock to avoid damaging the collapsible steering column.

- Do not push or pull on the steering wheel (for example when trying to roll the car). Doing so can strain the steering column, causing it to collapse.

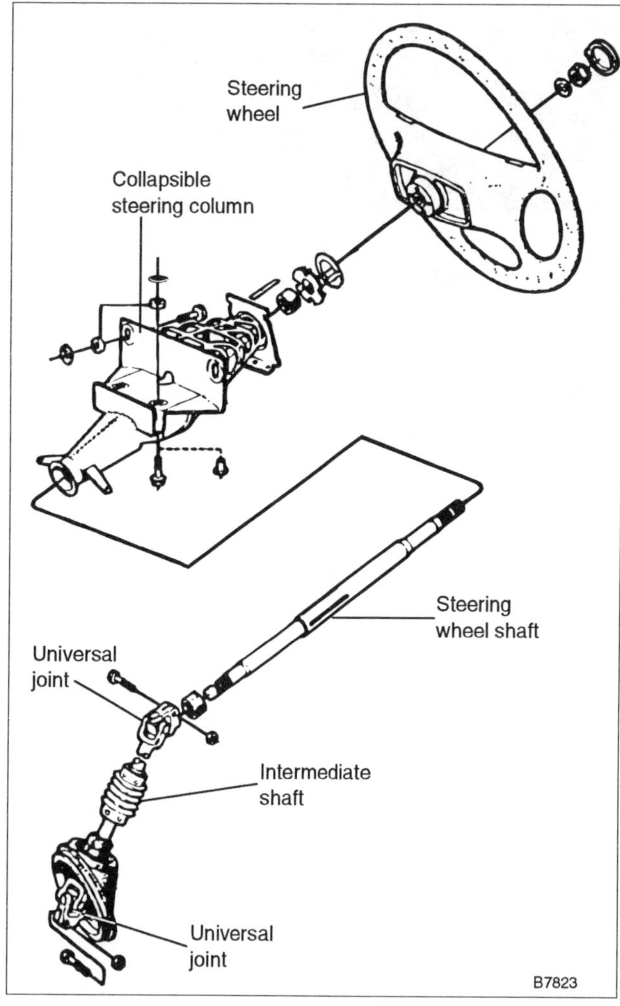

Fig. 1. Exploded view of steering column assembly.

To remove steering wheel

The procedure below does not cover removing the steering wheel on SRS (airbag) equipped cars. Cars with SRS can be identified by the three letter markings on the steering wheel pad.

WARNING
Removing the steering wheel on cars equipped with SRS airbag requires that the airbag unit be disarmed, removed, and stored in a safe place. Due to the inherent danger involved in this operation, it should be left to an authorized Saab dealer.

---

1. Position the steering wheel so that the road wheels are straight ahead.

2. On three-spoke steering wheels, carefully pry off the steering wheel pad and disconnect the electrical connectors for the horn. See Fig. 2.

3. On four-spoke steering wheels, pry out the badge in the center of the wheel.

4. Place matching marks on the steering wheel and the steering wheel shaft. Remove the center steering wheel nut and washer. See Fig. 3.

Fig. 2. Steering wheel pad being removed on cars with three-spoke wheels.

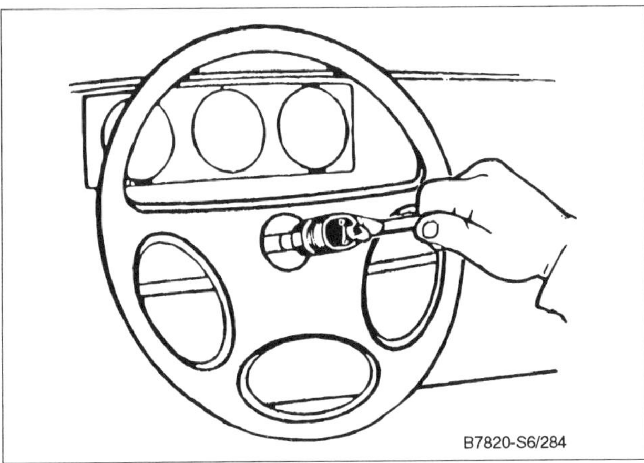

Fig. 3. Steering wheel mounting nut being removed.

5. Pull the steering wheel straight off the steering wheel shaft. If the wheel does not pull off easily, use a suitable puller to assist in removal. See Fig. 4.

CAUTION
Do not hammer on the steering wheel or steering wheel shaft in an attempt to loosen the steering wheel. This may damage the collapsible steering column.

Installation is the reverse of removal. Always replace the self-locking nut.

Tightening torque
- steering wheel to steering column (self-locking nut). . . . . 25-28 Nm (18 to 21 ft-lb)

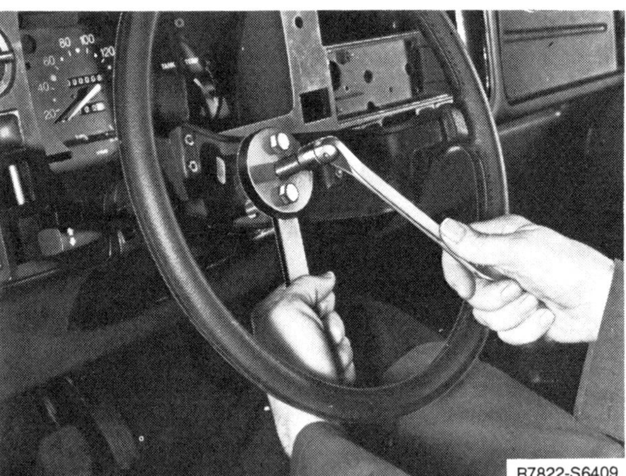

Fig. 4. Puller (Saab tool no. 89 96 258) being used to remove steering wheel. The two side bolts on the puller thread into the steering wheel itself and the center bolt is threaded down onto the steering wheel shaft.

To remove steering column assembly

The procedure below does not cover removing the steering column assembly on SRS (airbag) equipped cars. Cars with SRS can be identified by the three letter markings on the steering wheel pad.

WARNING
Removing the steering column assembly on cars equipped with SRS airbag requires that the airbag unit be disarmed, removed, and stored in a safe place. Due to the inherent danger involved in this operation, it should be left to an authorized Saab dealer.

---

1. Working from the engine compartment, remove the clamping bolt that holds the steering column universal joint to the steering rack. See Fig. 5. Push the steering column protective boot off the firewall bulkhead and into the passenger compartment.

2. Remove the steering wheel as described above.

3. Remove the center storage console and the lower instrument padding as described in **853 Dashboard and Consoles**.

4. Remove the steering column lower trim piece.

5. Remove the directional indicator and wiper/washer stalk switches from the steering column. Label the electrical connectors before unplugging them.

6. Unplug the connectors for the horn and cruise control (where applicable). Cut any cable ties holding the wiring harness to the steering column.

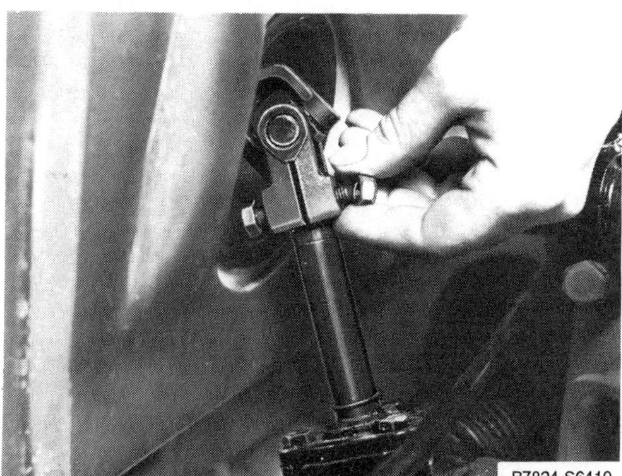

Fig. 5. Steering column universal joint clamping bolt being removed.

7. If applicable, remove the anti-chafing pad from the right side of the steering column.

NOTE

If an anti-chafing material is used, note its position before removing it.

---

8. Remove the four steering column-to-console bolts and spacers. See Fig. 6.

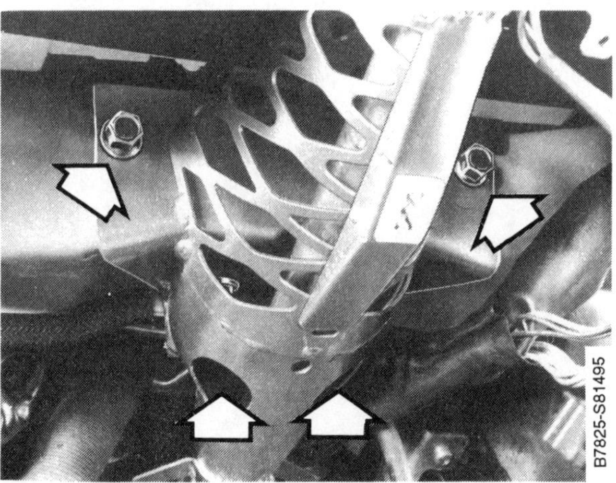

Fig. 6. Steering column mounting bolts (arrows).

9. Lower the column slightly and pull the entire assembly out of the car. See Fig. 7.

WARNING

Use care when handling the removed steering column assembly. Do not alter the position of the telescopic steering wheel shaft or the collapsible function of the column assembly may be impaired.

Fig. 7. Steering column assembly being removed from car.

Installation is the reverse of removal. Make sure that the steering column universal joint is fully seated on the steering rack pinion shaft so that the clamping bolt properly engages the groove in the shaft. See Fig. 8.

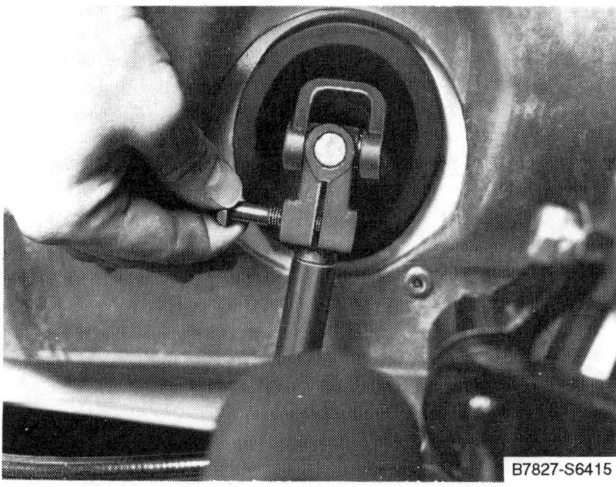

Fig. 8. Steering column-to-steering rack pinion shaft clamping bolt being installed. Bolt must engage groove in shaft.

Apply Loctite to the four steering column-to-body mounting bolts during installation. Replace all self-locking nuts. Check the universal joints for free movement. Universal joints that are seized or do not swivel freely should be replaced. Tighten all bolts to their recommended torques.

Tightening torques

- steering column to steering rack (clamping bolt, self-locking nut) .... 20 to 27 Nm (15 to 20 ft-lb)
- steering column to body (bolts, install with Loctite).......... 20 to 27 Nm (15 to 20 ft-lb)
- steering wheel to steering column (self-locking nut) .... 25-28 Nm (18 to 21 ft-lb)

---

643 Tie Rod Ends

GENERAL

The tie rod ends connect the steering rack tie rods to the steering swivel member. They thread onto the end of the tie rod and are securely fastened to the swivel member with a self-locking nut. No maintenance or lubrication is needed for the life of the joint. See Fig. 1.

CAUTION
Do not reuse self-locking nuts. These parts are designed to be used only once and must be replaced if loosened or removed.

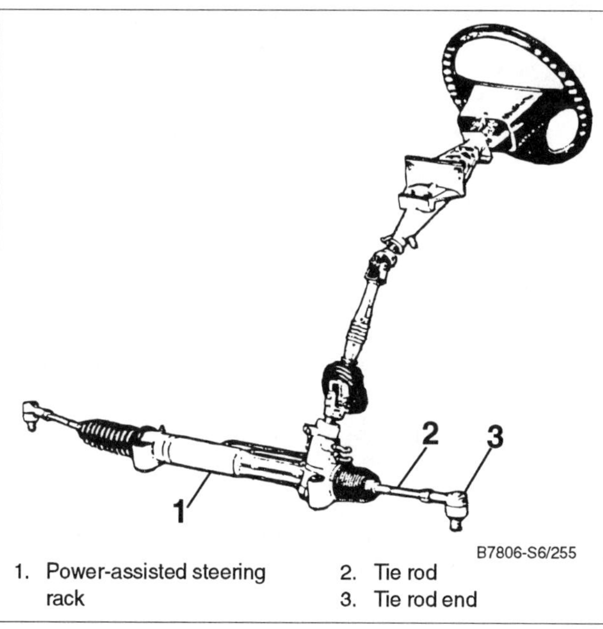

Fig. 1. Steering system.

Tie rod ends should be checked for wear at regular intervals. The rubber boots around the joints should also be inspected for tears, cracks or general deterioration. Replace the tie rod end if any faults are found.

Tie rod ends are best checked for wear with the front wheels off the ground. Grasp both sides of the tire and gently rock the wheel back and forth. If any noticeable play is present, the tie rod end is probably worn and should be replaced.

CAUTION
A new style tie rod end was introduced during the 1989 model year on the 900 models. This new tie rod end can be identified by a slot cut in the end of the threaded stud. See Fig. 2. The two tie rod ends must never be interchanged between the early cars and later cars, as steering geometry will be affected.

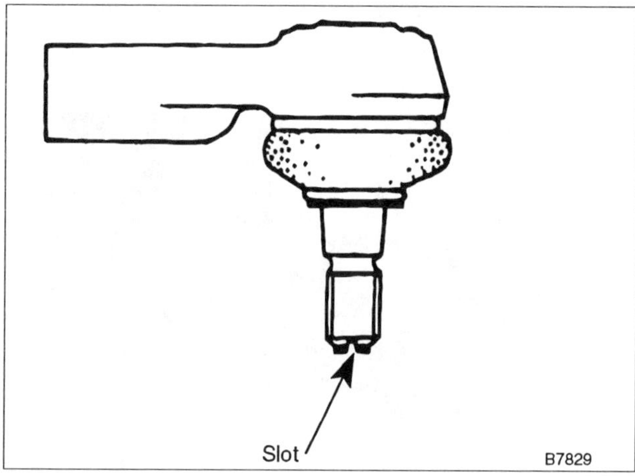

Fig. 2. New style tie rod end used on early 1989 and later models. This new tie rod end can be identified by slot cut into threaded end of stud.

To remove tie rod end

Removing the tie rod end will alter the alignment (toe-in) of the front wheels. It is highly recommended that the front wheels be aligned after replacing a tie rod end.

1. Loosen the wheel lug nuts or bolts, then raise the front of the car and support it securely on jack stands designed for the purpose. Remove the wheel.

WARNING
Always check that the car is stable on the jack stands before starting any work.

2. Loosen the locknut that secures the tie rod end to the tie rod. Remove the self-locking nut securing the tie rod end to the steering swivel member. See Fig. 3.

3. Using a press tool, remove the joint from the steering swivel member. See Fig. 4.

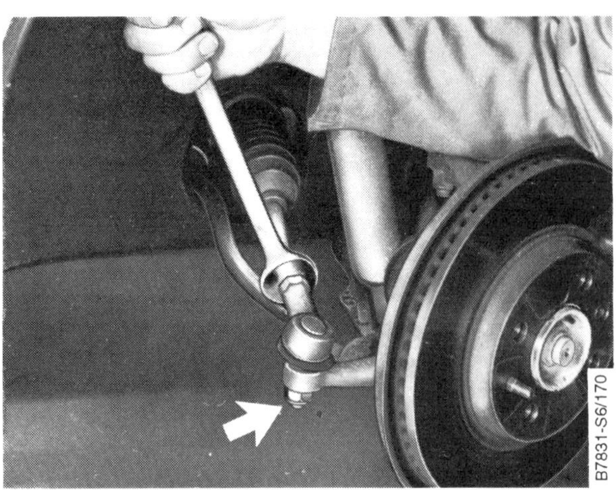

Fig. 3. Tie rod end locknut being loosened. Tie rod end self-locking nut shown at arrow.

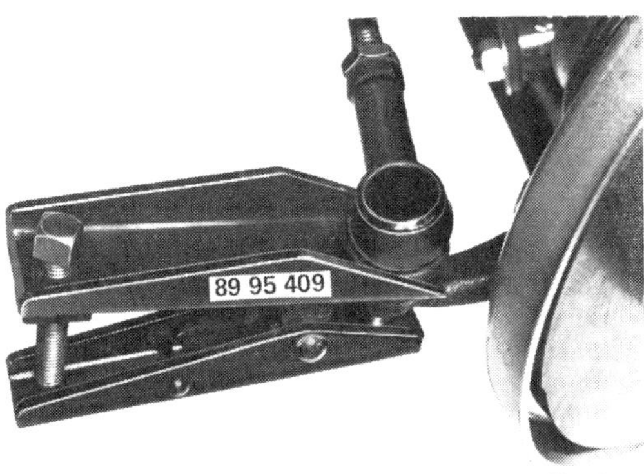

Fig. 4. Tie rod end being removed from steering swivel member using press. Saab tool no. 89 95 409 shown.

WARNING

A tie rod end removal fork should not be used to remove the tie rod end. Do not hammer on the tie rod end in an attempt to remove it from the steering member. Doing this may damage the steering rack, the collapsible steering column, or the steering swivel member.

---

4. Mark the position of the tie rod end to the tie rod. Thread the tie rod end off the tie rod, counting the number of turns it takes to get it off.

NOTE

If the position of the tie rod end on the tie rod is carefully marked, the new tie rod end can be positioned where the old tie rod was prior to removal so the car can be safely driven.

---

5. Install the new tie rod end to the tie rod, threading it on the same number of turns counted above in step 4. Insert the tie rod end into the steering member and install and tighten a new self-locking nut.

Tightening torque

- tie rod end to steering member (self-locking nut). . . . . . . 50 to 60 Nm (37 to 44 ft-lb)

WARNING

The length of the tie rod from the locknut to the stepped part of the rod must never exceed 125 mm (4.92 in). See Fig. 2. Also, the difference in length between the two tie rods must not exceed 2 mm (0.08 in.). For example, if the right rod measured 124 mm, the left rod must measure between 122 mm and 125 mm. See Fig. 5.

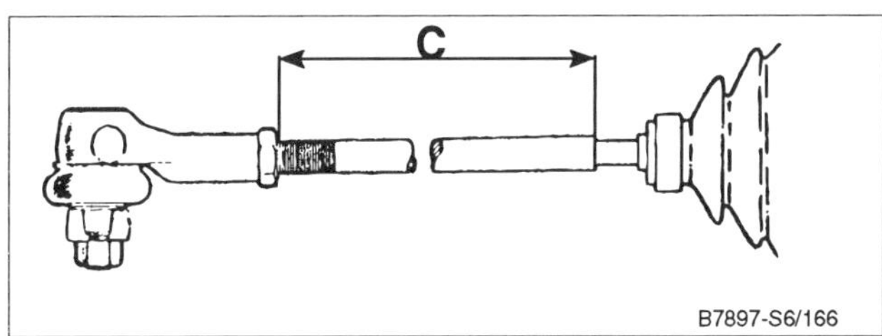

Fig. 5. Maximum permissible length (**C**) of tie rod must not exceed 125 mm (4.92 in.).

6. Adjust the toe-in using special wheel alignment equipment. Tighten the tie rod lock nut.

Tightening torque

- steering tie rod to tie rod end (locking nut). . . . 60 to 80 Nm (44 to 59 ft-lb)

---

644 Power Steering

POWER STEERING SYSTEM

The power-assisted steering rack is mounted at the lower rear of the engine compartment. A belt driven hydraulic pump supplies fluid under pressure to the control valve in the steering rack to help reduce steering effort. See Fig. 1.

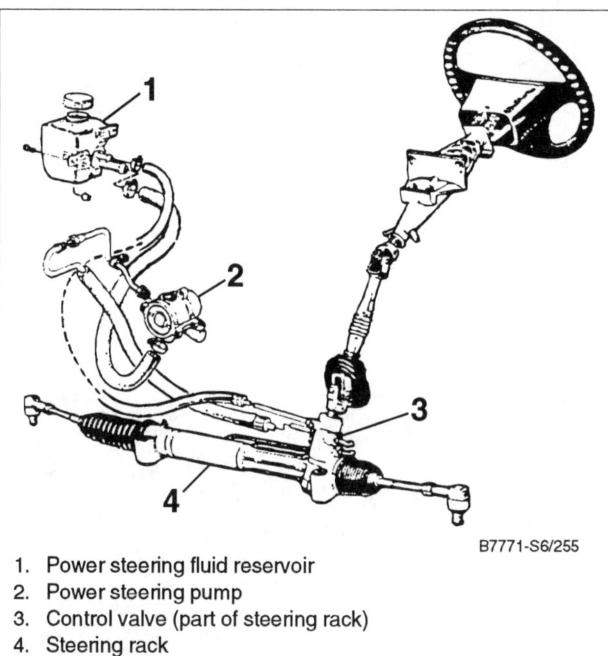

1. Power steering fluid reservoir
2. Power steering pump
3. Control valve (part of steering rack)
4. Steering rack

Fig. 1. Power steering system.

There is no routine maintenance for the power steering system other than checking the fluid level, see **1 LUBRICATION AND MAINTENANCE.** Checking the steering tie rod ends is described in **643 Tie Rod Ends.**

CAUTION

- Do not reuse self-locking nuts. These parts are designed to be used only once and must always be replaced whenever loosened or removed.
- Do not hold the steering wheel at full lock for extended periods with the engine running. This may overheat the pump and damage it.

To remove power steering rack

WARNING

Removing or replacing the steering rack will affect front wheel alignment. Always have the front end aligned after doing any work to the steering rack or related steering components. See **601 Wheel Alignment** for more information on aligning the wheels.

---

1. Loosen the wheel lug bolts, then raise the front of the car and support it securely on jack stands designed for the purpose. Remove the wheels.

WARNING

Always check that the car is stable on the jack stands before starting any work.

---

2. Drain the power steering fluid by removing the return hose from the fluid reservoir. See Fig. 2. Place the disconnected hose in a quart-sized container. Plug the open hose fitting at the reservoir.

NOTE

If necessary, connect an extension hose to the return hose.

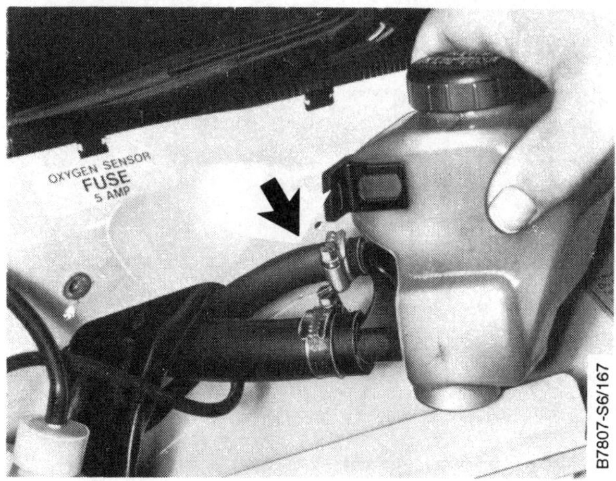

Fig. 2. Power steering pump return hose (arrow) at fluid reservoir.

3. Start the engine and allow the fluid to pump out of the system and into the container. Rotate the steering wheel slowly from lock to lock. Shut off the engine as soon as the system is empty. Reconnect the return hose to the reservoir.

4. Working at the wheels, loosen the tie rod end locknut at both tie rods. See Fig. 3.

Fig. 3. Tie rod end locknut being loosened.

5. Using a vernier caliper, measure and record the tie rod length from the tie rod end to the stepped part tie rod. See Fig. 4.

NOTE

It may be necessary to push the bellows back slightly to access the stepped part of the tie rod.

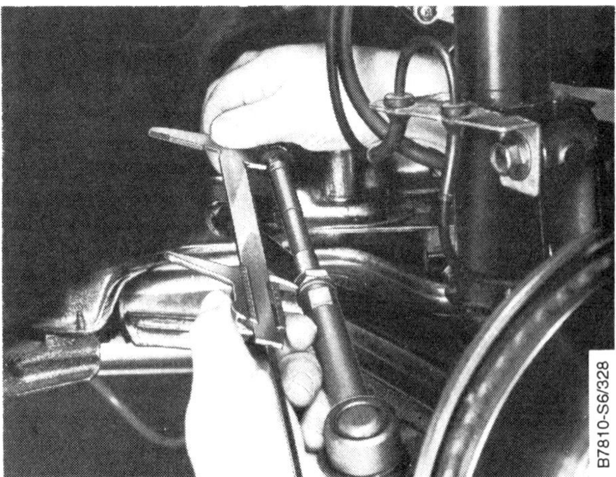

Fig. 4. Tie rod length being measured using vernier caliper. Car shown is Saab 9000.

6. Unscrew the tie rods from the tie rod ends. Hold the inner rubber bellows stationary while unscrewing the rods. See Fig. 5.

Fig. 5. Tie rod being unscrewed from tie rod end.

7. Thoroughly clean the area around the two hydraulic pipe fittings on the steering rack. See Fig. 6. Disconnect the pipes from the rack and plug the pipe openings. Remove the clamps holding the pipes to the rack.

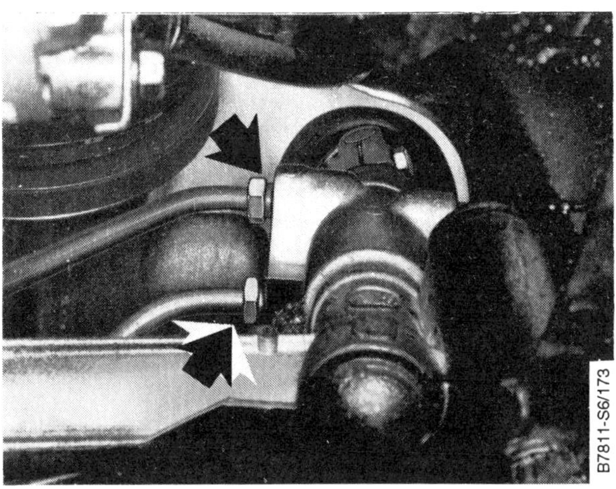

Fig. 6. Hydraulic pipe fittings on steering rack (arrows).

8. Working from the rear of the engine compartment, remove the clamping bolt holding the steering column universal joint to the steering rack. See Fig. 7.

9. Remove the bolts holding the steering rack to the body. See Fig. 8.

10. Separate the steering rack from the steering column universal joint.

11. Rotate the steering rack until its pinion shaft is pointing downward. See Fig. 9.

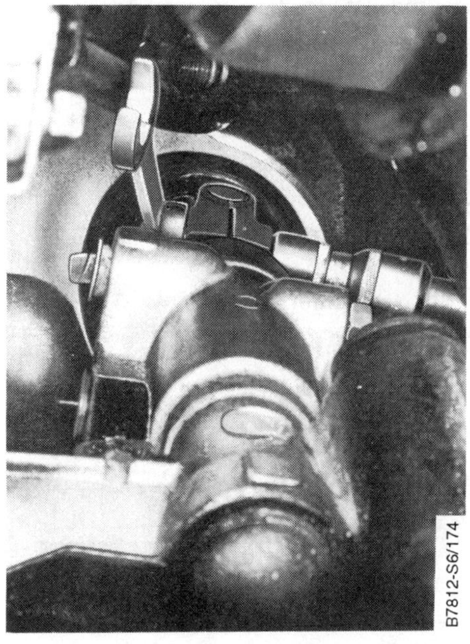

Fig. 7. Steering column clamping bolt being removed.

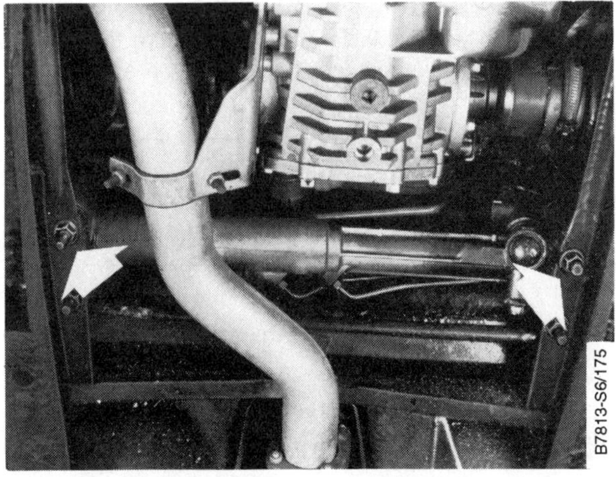

Fig. 8. Steering rack mounting bolts (arrows).

12. Slide the steering rack toward the passenger side of the car.

13. Turn the steering rack pinion shaft until the right-hand (passenger's) side tie rod is fully extended. Lift the left-hand (driver's) side tie rod over the subframe. See Fig. 10.

CAUTION
Turn the shaft using pliers. Place a rag over the pinion shaft to protect the splines.

---

14. Slide the entire rack toward the driver's side of the car and remove the rack assembly.

Fig. 9. Steering rack pinion shaft positioned correctly for removal of rack.

Fig. 10. Left-hand (driver's) side tie rod shown lowered from car body.

To install power steering rack

Inspect the rubber bellows and the rubber mounting bushings. Replace any worn or damaged parts.

1. Turn the pinion shaft until the driver's side tie rod is fully extended. Place the rack up and into the body with the pinion shaft pointing down. See Fig. 11.

2. Turn the pinion shaft until the passenger's side tie rod is fully extended. Lift the left-hand (driver's) side tie rod up and over the subframe member. Center the steering rack.

NOTE
When the steering rack is centered, the slot in the pinion shaft for the clamping bolt should be toward the rear of the car (shaft pointing downward).

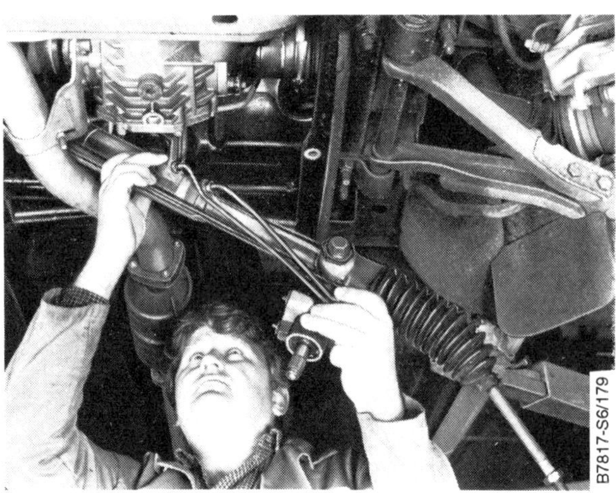

Fig. 11. Steering rack being installed into body.

3. Rotate the entire rack up and connect the pinion shaft to the steering column universal joint. Loosely install the clamping bolt and new a self-locking nut.

CAUTION
Make sure the pinion shaft fully engages the universal joint. The clamping bolt must go through the slot in the pinion shaft.

---

4. Install and tighten the steering rack mounting bolts and the steering column clamping bolt.

Tightening torques
- power steering rack to body . . . . 60 to 80 Nm (44 to 59 ft-lb)
- universal joint to pinion shaft (clamping bolt and self-locking nut) . . . . 25 to 34 Nm (18 to 25 ft-lb)

---

5. Install and tighten the hydraulic pipes to the control valve. Replace the O-rings at the pipe connections where necessary.

Tightening torque
- power steering hose fittings . . . . 20 to 34 Nm (15 to 25 ft-lb)

---

6. Install new clamps to hold the pipes to the steering rack housing.

CAUTION
Use care not to pinch or damage the pressure-equalizing tube between the rubber bellows.

---

7. Thread the tie rods into the tie rod ends. Adjust the tie rod to the dimensions recorded above in Fig. 4. Tighten the locknuts.

Tightening torque
- tie rod end to tie rod . . . 60 to 80 Nm (44 to 59 ft-lb)

---

8. Fill the reservoir with power steering fluid. With the engine off, slowly turn the steering wheel three or four times from lock to lock.

CAUTION
Do not use ATF in the power steering system. Use only GM (General Motors) Specification Power Steering Fluid.

Power steering fluid
- GM power steering fluid (GM 9985010), Texaco TL4634 or equivalent . . . . 75 cl (0.8 qt)

---

9. Install the wheels, lower the car and start the engine. Turn the wheels from lock to lock two more times.

Tightening torques
- wheel lug bolts . . . . . . 105 to 125 Nm (78 to 92 ft-lb)
- wheel lug nuts . . . . 90 to 110 Nm (66 to 81 ft-lb)

---

10. Check the front wheel alignment and adjust if necessary.

To remove power steering pump and lines

1. Drain the power steering fluid by removing the return hose from the fluid reservoir. See Fig. 2 above. Place the disconnected hose in a quart-sized container. If necessary, connect an extension hose to the return hose. Plug the open hose fitting at the reservoir.

2. Start the engine and allow the fluid to pump out of the system and into the container. Rotate the steering wheel slowly from lock to lock. Shut off the engine as soon as the system is empty. Reconnect the return hose to the reservoir.

3. Working in the engine compartment, cut the cable ties holding the main engine harness to the rear of the cylinder head. Rest the harness on top of the valve cover.

4. Slacken the pump bracket nut and bolt. Fully loosen the bracket adjusting screw. See Fig. 12. Remove the pump V-belt.

Fig. 12. Pump bracket nut (**1**), bracket bolt (**2**), adjusting screw (**3**), and outlet pipe (**4**).

5. Disconnect the fluid outlet pipe at the union shown in the above figure.

6. Working from below the car, remove the bracket's lower mounting bolt. Disconnect the inlet hose. See Fig. 13.

NOTE

Note the order of the rubber bushings, spacers, and washers for the lower mounting bolt.

---

7. Working from the engine compartment, remove the pump bracket top nut and bolt. Swivel the pump toward the wheel arch and remove it from the car. See Fig. 14.

Installation is the reverse of removal. Tighten the hose fittings to the specified torque. Adjust the belt tension as described in **1 LUBRICATION AND MAINTENANCE**. Fill and bleed the system as described above under the steering rack installation procedure.

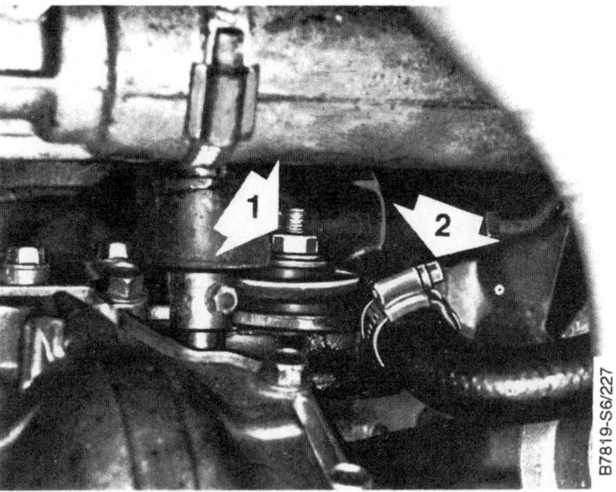

Fig. 13. Pump bracket lower mounting bolt (**1**) and inlet hose (**2**) as viewed from below car.

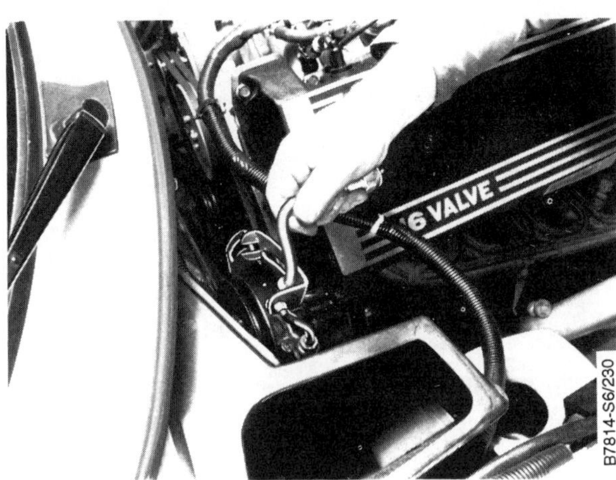

Fig. 14. Power steering pump being removed.

Tightening torque

- power steering pump hose fittings . . . . 20 to 34 Nm (15 to 25 ft-lb)

---

700 Suspension—General

FRONT SUSPENSION

The Saab 900 is equipped with an independent front suspension. See Fig. 1. The upper and lower control arms are pivot-mounted to the body. A double-acting shock absorber and coil spring controls suspension travel, which is limited by a rubber buffer. The steering swivel member is mounted to the control arms through ball joints.

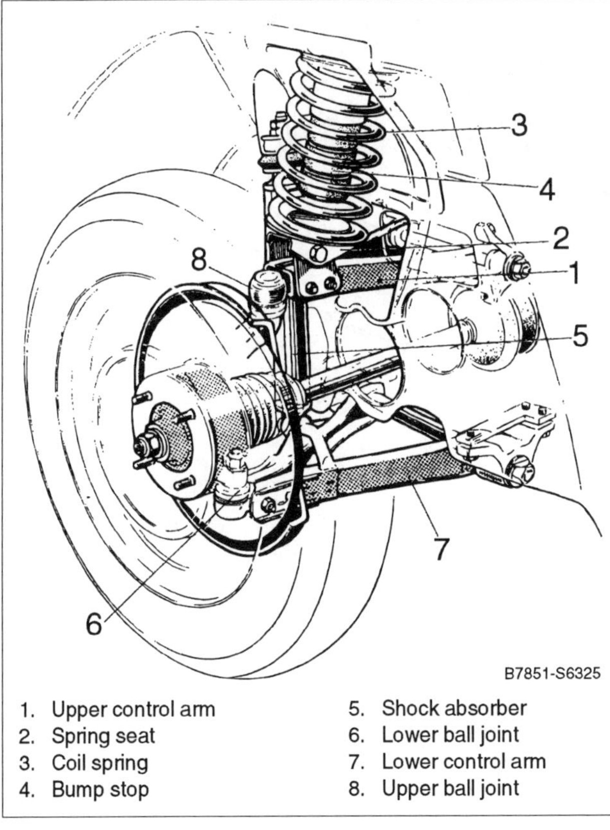

1. Upper control arm
2. Spring seat
3. Coil spring
4. Bump stop
5. Shock absorber
6. Lower ball joint
7. Lower control arm
8. Upper ball joint

Fig. 1. Front suspension.

The front wheel bearing is pressed into the steering member and the wheel bearing hub is in turn pressed into the wheel bearing. See Fig. 2.

The splined drive axle with integral constant velocity (CV) joint passes through the wheel bearing and is firmly bolted to the splined wheel bearing hub. The brake caliper is bolted to the steering swivel member and the brake disc is mounted to the wheel bearing hub. The steering rack is connected to the steering swivel member through the tie rod ends.

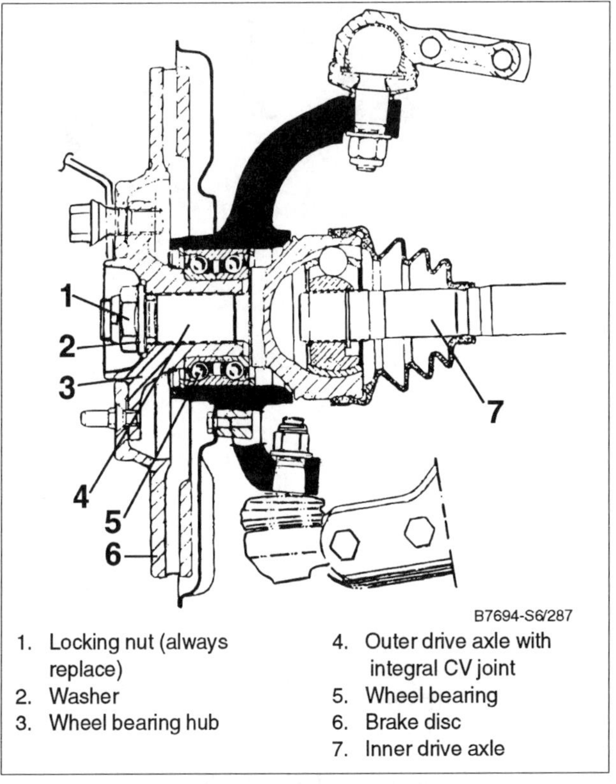

1. Locking nut (always replace)
2. Washer
3. Wheel bearing hub
4. Outer drive axle with integral CV joint
5. Wheel bearing
6. Brake disc
7. Inner drive axle

Fig. 2. Steering swivel member.

REAR SUSPENSION

The rear axle is a lightweight tube located by five links designed to keep the rear wheels parallel and stable. See Fig. 3. The panhard rod absorbs the lateral cornering forces. The spring links and torque arms prevent the axle from rotating during braking and accelerating. On some models, a rear stabilizer bar further controls body sway or roll during cornering. Upward and downward movement of the axle is limited by the double acting shock absorbers and suspension coil springs.

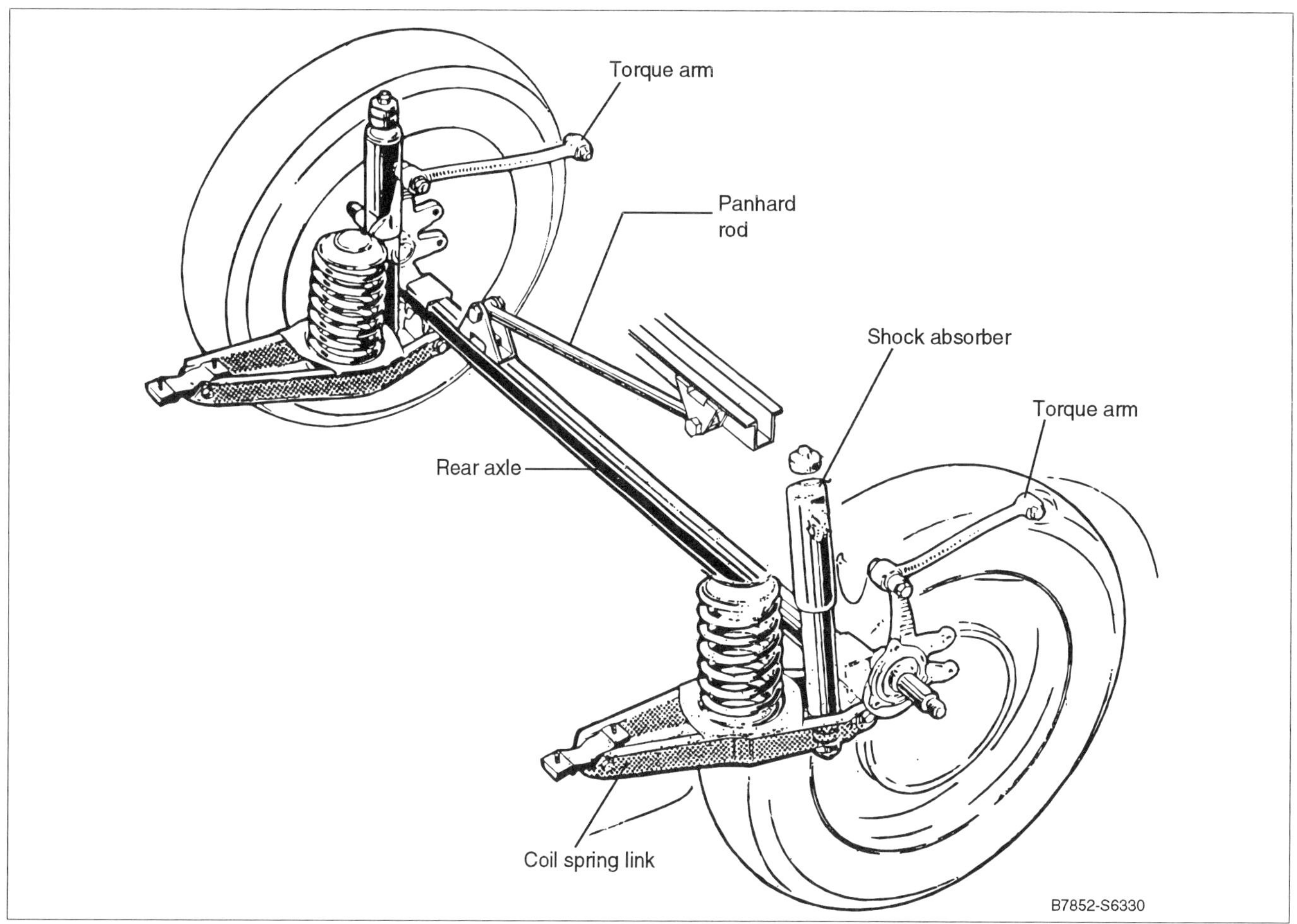

Fig. 3. Rear suspension.

SUSPENSION TROUBLESHOOTING

Stable handling and ride comfort depends on the integrity of the suspension components that gradually become worn with time and mileage. In addition to worn suspension parts, troubleshooting must consider the condition of the wheels, tires, and their alignment. General suspension and wheel alignment troubleshooting information can be found in **600 Steering and Wheel Alignment—General**.

731 Front Suspension

General

This section covers replacement of the front shock absorbers, coil springs, and anti-roll bar only. For information on replacing the ball joints and the control arms, see **631 Ball Joints** and **632 Control Arms.**

Shock Absorbers

The function of a shock absorber, or damper, is to moderate the action of the coil spring. The shock slows the spring's bounce and allows it to return to its normal position more quickly. See Fig. 1.

Shocks require no routine maintenance and cannot be serviced. The shock absorbers are easily replaced using ordinary hand tools and should always be replaced in pairs.

Fig. 1. Front shock absorber and pivoted suspension springs.

The best evidence of worn shock absorbers is their road handling behavior in normal driving. Worn shocks will allow skittishness over bumps and a less controlled, often wallowing, feel after bumps or in corners. Very worn shocks may reach the limits of their travel by knocking when going over bumps.

The most common—though not entirely accurate—test of shock absorber function involves vigorously bouncing each corner of the car and then releasing and observing how quickly the bouncing stops. More than one bounce usually suggests the shocks are not properly dampening and should be replaced. As a final check, look for oil leaks on the outside of the shock. If any signs of oil are present, the shocks should be replaced.

If a rattling or clunking noise is noticeable while traveling over rough road surfaces, check the lower shock absorber bushings. These bushing are available separately from an authorized Saab dealer. In addition, replacement shock absorbers come with new upper and lower bushing sets. See Fig. 2.

WARNING
Gas shock absorbers are under high pressure (400 to 600 psi) and can cause severe injury if handled improperly. Do not heat, weld, cut or deform the shock absorber in any way. Gas shock absorbers should be disposed of properly. See an authorized Saab dealer for information on gas shock disposal.

NOTE
The Saab 900 shock absorbers are of a unique design incorporating a special stop. Always replace them with Saab original equipment shock absorbers or damage to the suspension may result.

To remove front shock absorbers

1. Working in the engine compartment, remove the shock absorber upper mounting nuts. Loosen the top locknut first while holding the lower nut stationary. See Fig. 3.

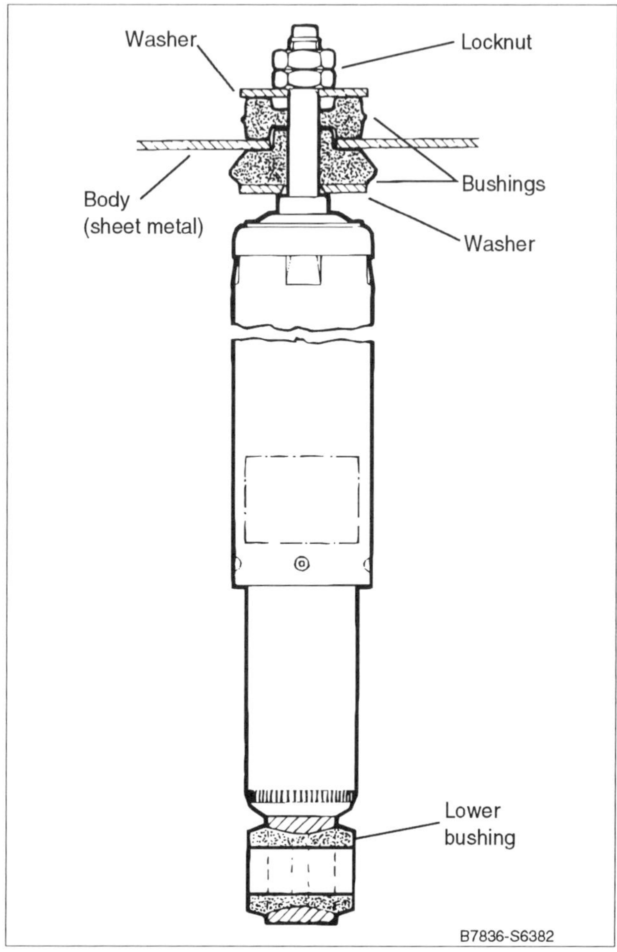

Fig. 2. Front shock absorber.

NOTE

- If the shock shaft turns while trying to loosen the nuts, cut the plastic protective tube off the shock from below and then use a locking pliers to hold the shaft stationary.
- When removing the driver's side shock, the mounting nuts can be more easily accessed if the coolant expansion tank is moved out of the way. Do not remove the hoses or cap. Remove only the fasteners holding the tank to the body.

2. Loosen the wheel lug bolts, then raise the front of the car and support it securely on jack stands designed for the purpose. Remove the front wheel.

WARNING

Always check that the car is stable on the jack stands before starting any work.

3. Remove the shock absorber lower mounting nut and washer. Remove the shock absorber. See Fig. 4. If necessary, pry the shock off its control arm mount.

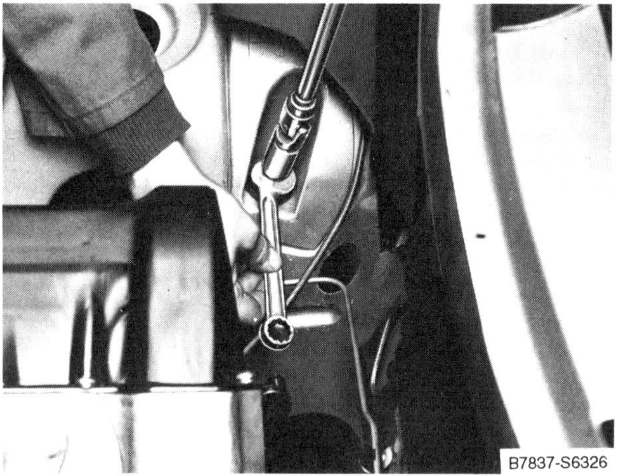

Fig. 3. Shock absorber upper mounting nut being removed. Open-end wrench is used to prevent lower nut from spinning when loosening top nut.

Fig. 4. Shock absorber being removed from lower control arm mount.

To install front shock absorbers

1. Lubricate the lower mount bushings with petroleum jelly. Install the shock absorber to the lower mount. Tighten the nut to the value given below.

Tighting torque

- front shock absorber to lower control arm . . . . 90 to 100 Nm (66 to 74 ft-lb)

2. Install the washer and bushing (lower) onto the top of the shock. See Fig. 5.

3. Using a jack, raise the control arm slightly while guiding the shock into its opening in the body. See Fig. 6. Working in the engine compartment, install the bushing (upper), the washer and nuts. Tighten the nuts.

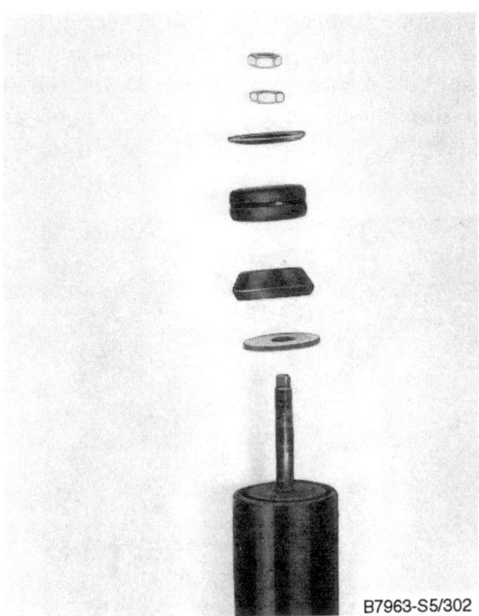

Fig. 5. Shock absorber mounting bushings, washers and nuts. Note the orientation of the upper dished washer (concave faces up) and the taper on the lower bushing.

NOTE
Tighten the shock upper mounting nuts just until the upper bushing is expanded to the outer edges of the washer.

Fig. 6. Raise lower control arm slightly using jack.

4. Lower the jack from under the control arm. Install and tighten the wheel bolts or nuts. Lower the car. Install the coolant reservoir if necessary.

Tightening torques
- wheel lug bolts ..... 105 to 125 Nm (78 to 92 ft-lb)
- wheel lug nuts ...... 90 to 110 Nm (66 to 81 ft-lb)

SUSPENSION COIL SPRINGS

Fig. 7 shows the suspension coil spring. The coil springs do not require any service or maintenance and are not normally replaced unless damaged or fatigued. Coil springs should always be replaced in sets. Removing the coil springs requires special tools. Read the procedures through before starting the job.

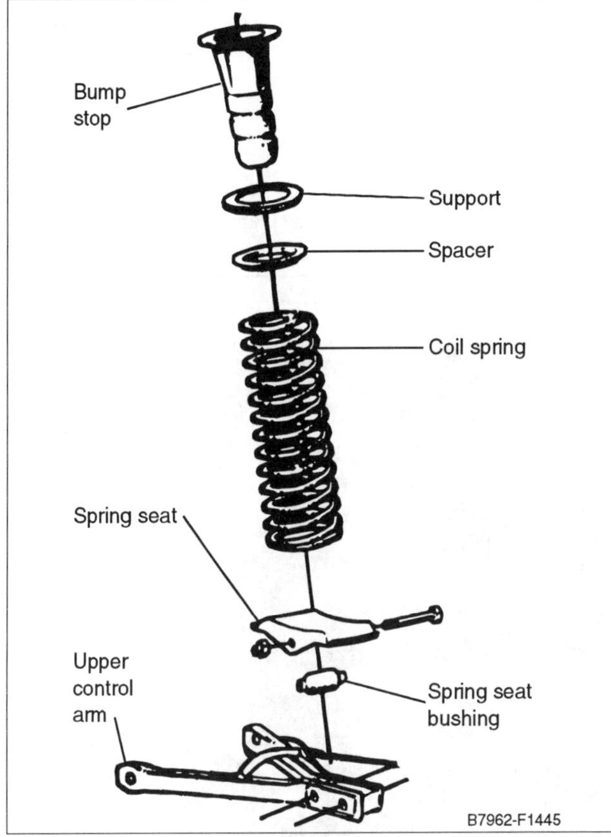

Fig. 7. Exploded view of front suspension coil spring and related components.

WARNING
Do not attempt to service the coil springs without a spring compressor designed specifically for this purpose. Attempting this job without the proper tools can result in serious injury.

To remove coil springs

1. Loosen the wheel lug bolts, then raise the front of the car and support it securely on jack stands designed for the purpose. Remove the front wheel.

WARNING
Always check that the car is stable on the jack stands before starting any work.

---

2. Remove the shock absorber lower mounting nut and washer and remove the shock from its control arm mount. If necessary, pry the shock from the mount.

3. Install the coil spring compressor to the spring. Slowly compress the spring and remove it from car. See Fig. 8.

WARNING
Work carefully as the spring is compressed. Check to make sure that the spring compressor is always securely seated on the spring.

NOTE
Mark the coil spring as an aid to installation. Used coil springs should always be installed in their original position and orientation.

Fig. 8. Compressed coil spring being removed from car. Spring compressor shown is Saab tool no. 88 18 791 and tool no. 88 18 809.

Installation of the spring is the reverse of removal. Inspect all rubber parts for wear or deterioration and replace any faulty parts found. Check the spring free length as described below. Inspect the protective coating on the spring. The springs are treated with an anti-corrosion agent, which should be touched up with paint or an equivalent sealer.

When installing the spring, position it so that the spring end is fitted against the stop on the spring seat. See Fig. 9. Be sure to install the spring's support and spacer on the top of the spring. Install the shock absorber lower mount as described above. Install the road wheel and lower the car.

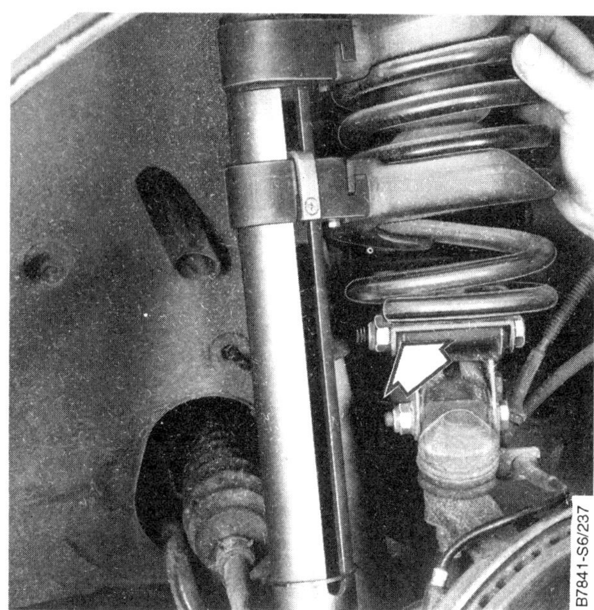

Fig. 9. Spring end (arrow) correctly positioned against spring stop on spring seat.

Tightening torques
- front shock absorber to lower control arm . . . . 90 to 100 Nm (66 to 74 ft-lb)
- wheel lug bolts . . . . . . 105 to 125 Nm (78 to 92 ft-lb)
- wheel lug nuts . . . . 90 to 110 Nm (66 to 81 ft-lb)

Checking Coil Springs

A function of the coil spring is to control the ride height of the car. Therefore, a damaged or fatigued coil spring will usually result in a noticeable difference in ride height. **Table a** lists spring specifications. The spring must be removed from the car to measure its free length.

Various springs are installed depending on model and model year. The springs are color-coded with a paint dot. In addition, the left and right springs on some models may be different. In all cases, the new spring should match the old spring being replaced.

> **NOTE**
> For chassis ride height specifications see **601 Wheel Alignment.**

Table a. Front Coil Spring Specifications

Spring color codes	Spring free length
Standard chassis	
green, light green, black, or white	373 mm (14.7 in.)
yellow or red	380 mm (15.0 in.)
pink or brown	388 mm (15.3 in.)
blue or light blue	372 mm (14.6 in.)
Sport chassis	
silver or bronze	301 mm (11.8 in.)

To remove front coil spring seat and bushing

The front coil spring seat and bushing can be replaced after the coil spring has been removed.

1. Remove the coil spring as described above. Remove the bolt for the spring seat and remove the spring seat.

2. Press out the spring seat bushing using a suitable press (Saab tool no. 89 96 274 or equivalent). See Fig. 10.

Fig. 10. Spring seat bushing being pressed out.

3. Lubricate the new bushing with petroleum jelly and install it using a press (Saab part no. 89 96 274 or equivalent). See Fig. 11.

4. Install the spring seat with the spring stop facing out. See Fig. 12. Loosely tighten the spring seat bolt using a new self-locking nut.

Fig. 11. Spring seat bushing being pressed in.

> **WARNING**
> Do not reuse self-locking nuts. These parts are designed to be used only once and must be replaced whenever loosened or removed.

Fig. 12. Spring stop (arrow) on spring seat faces out.

Install the coil spring as described above. Make sure the end of the coil spring is against the stop on the spring seat as shown earlier in Fig. 9. When the weight of the car is on the wheels, tighten the spring seat mounting bolt.

> **Tightening torque**
> - coil spring seat to control arm . . . . 55 to 110 Nm (40 to 81 ft-lb)

ANTI-ROLL BAR

The front anti-roll bar is rigidly mounted to the body and to the lower control arms to control body sway or roll during cornering. The anti-roll bar bushings should be periodically inspected for deterioration, wear, or oil contamination. Special tools are needed to remove the anti-roll bar. Read the procedure through before starting the job.

To remove front anti-roll bar

1. With the car on the ground, insert a special spacer tool (Saab part no. 83 93 209) between the upper control arm and the body on each side of the car. See Fig. 13.

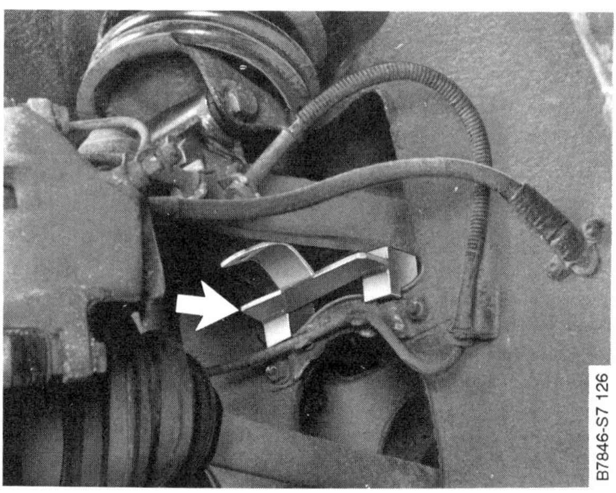

Fig. 13. Spacer tool (arrow) inserted between upper control arm and body. Insert one tool on each side of the car (2 tools needed). The spacer tool relieves suspension loading on the anti-roll bar.

2. Loosen the wheel lug bolts, then raise the front of the car and support it securely on jack stands designed for the purpose. Remove the front wheels.

WARNING
Always check that the car is stable on the jack stands before continuing any work.

3. Working at the lower control arms, remove the anti-roll bar mounting bolts. See Fig. 14. Remove the rubber end pieces.

4. Working from below the car, remove the two U-clamps and split rubber bushings holding the roll bar to the floor pan. See Fig. 15.

NOTE
Save the shims when the U-clamps are removed.

Fig. 14. Anti-roll bar to control arm mounting bolts (arrows).

Fig. 15. Anti-roll bar U-clamp mounting bolt being removed. Arrow shows additional nut to be removed.

5. Unbolt the steering rack and move it forward slightly. See Fig. 16.

CAUTION
Do not reuse self-locking fasteners. These parts are designed to be used only once and must be replaced whenever loosened or removed.

6. Turn the bar until the ends are facing up and slide the bar from the body. See Fig. 17.

Installation is the reverse of removal. Lubricate all rubber bushings with Molycote 1-4382 or equivalent. Loosely install the roll bar. Insert the U-clamp split rubber bushings with the split toward the front of the car. See Fig. 18. Loosely install the U-clamps, shims and nuts. Center the roll bar in the outer bushings and tighten the nuts. Tighten the U-clamp nuts and finally install and tighten the steering rack mounting bolts.

Fig. 16. Steering rack mounting bolts (arrows).

Fig. 17. Anti-roll bar being removed.

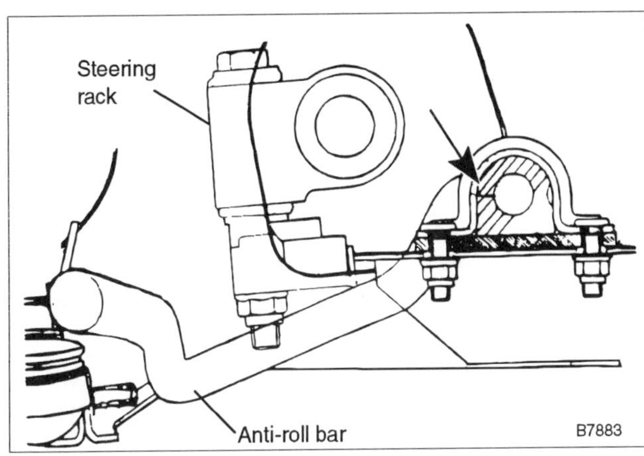

Fig. 18. Correctly installed anti-roll bar bushing with split (arrow) facing forward.

Tightening torques

- anti-roll bar bracket to lower control arm. . . . . 40 to 55 Nm (30 to 40 ft-lb)
- power steering rack to body . . . . 60 to 80 Nm (44 to 59 ft-lb)
- all other fasteners
  - M5 bolt . . . . 5 Nm (44 in-lb)
  - M6 bolt . . . . 10 Nm (89 in-lb)
  - M8 bolt . . . . 20 Nm (15 ft-lb)
  - M10 bolt . . . . 40 Nm (30 ft-lb)

732 Rear Suspension

SHOCK ABSORBERS

The function of a shock absorber, or damper, is to moderate the action of the coil spring. See Fig. 1. The shock slows the spring's bounce and allows it to return to its normal position more quickly. For a quick check to assess the general condition of the rear shocks, see **731 Front Suspension.**

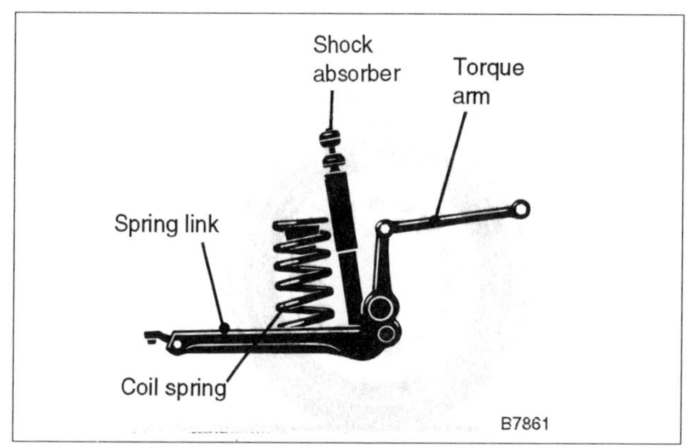

Fig. 1. Rear shock absorber and related suspension components.

WARNING

Gas shock absorbers are under high pressure (400 to 600 psi) and can cause severe injury if handled improperly. Do not heat, weld, cut or deform the shock absorber in any way. Gas shock absorbers should be disposed of properly. See an authorized Saab dealer for information on gas shock disposal.

NOTE

The Saab 900 shock absorbers are of a unique design incorporating a special stop. Always replace them with Saab original equipment shock absorbers or damage to the suspension may result.

To remove rear shock absorbers

Fig. 2 shows the shock absorber and it related mounting hardware. The rubber bushings should always be replaced as part of shock replacement.

1. Loosen the rear wheel lug bolts or nuts, then raise the rear of the car and support it securely on jack stands designed for the purpose. Remove the rear wheels.

WARNING

Always check that the car is stable on the jack stands before starting any work.

---

2. Using a jack, raise the spring link slightly to relieve the suspension load on the shock. Remove the shock's lower mounting nut and bolt. See Fig. 3.

3. Slowly lower the jack slightly, but do not remove it.

4. Working in the wheel well, remove the upper shock absorber mounting nuts, washers, and rubber bushings. See Fig. 4. Remove the shock absorber from the body.

To install rear shock absorbers

1. Install the washer and lower bushing to the top of the shock. Use Fig. 2 as a guide to bushing and washer orientation.Guide the shock into the opening in the body. Install the upper bushing, washer and lock nuts. Tighten the nuts just until the upper bushing is expanded to the outer edges of the washer.

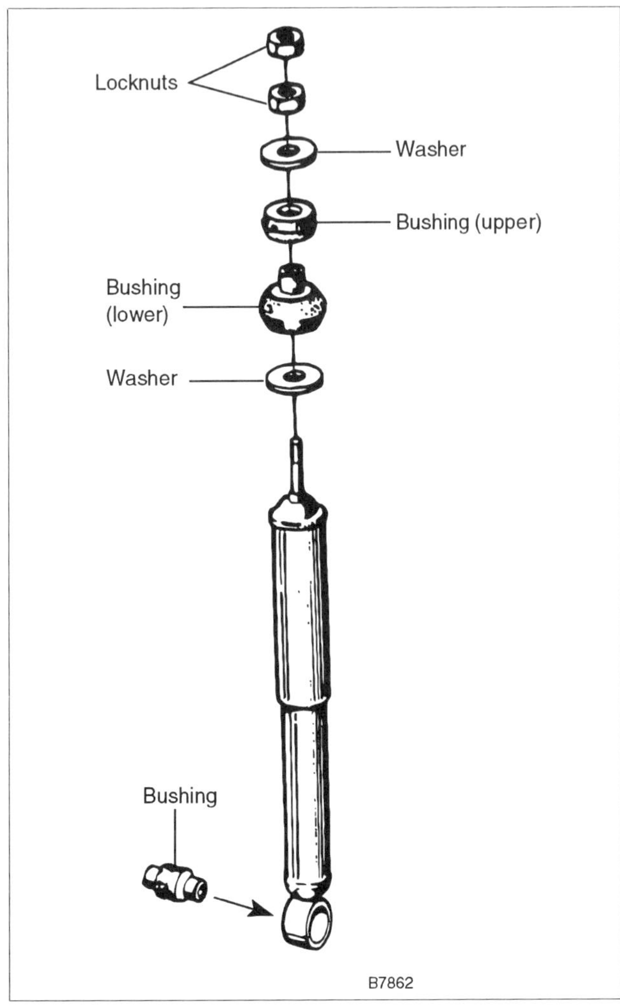

Fig. 2. Rear shock and mounting hardware.

Fig. 3. Shock absorber lower mounting bolt being removed.

Fig. 4. Shock absorber upper mounting nuts being removed.

2. Raise the spring link slightly until the lower mounting hole in the link is aligned with the shock mounting hole. Install and tighten the bolt using a new self-locking nut. Remove the jack.

WARNING
Do not reuse self-locking nuts. These parts are designed to be used only once and should be replaced once loosened or removed.

---

3. Install the wheel and lower the car.

Tightening torques
- wheel lug bolts . . . . . . 105 to 125 Nm (78 to 92 ft-lb)
- wheel lug nuts . . . . 90 to 110 Nm (66 to 81 ft-lb)

COIL SPRINGS

Fig. 5 shows the suspension coil spring. The springs do not require any service or maintenance and are not normally replaced unless damaged or fatigued. Coil springs should always be replaced in sets.

To remove coil spring

1. Loosen the rear wheel lug bolts or nuts, then raise the rear of the car and support it securely on jack stands designed for the purpose. Remove the rear wheels.

WARNING
Always check that the car is stable on the jack stands before starting any work.

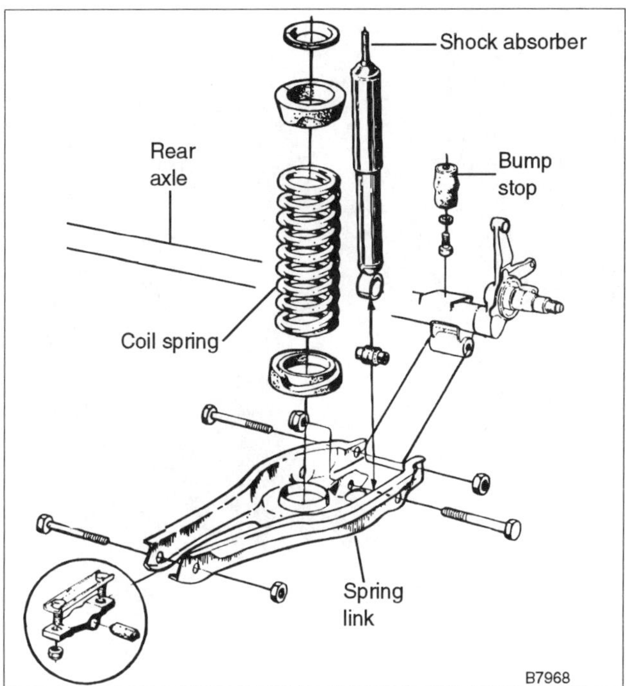

Fig. 5. Exploded view of coil spring and related suspension components.

2. On 1988 and later models, remove the handbrake cable hold down clamp from the spring link. See Fig. 6

Fig. 6. Handbrake cable hold down being removed from spring link.

3. On cars with ABS, remove the wheel speed sensor from the rear axle housing. See Fig. 7. Release the sensor harness from the clips on the spring link.

4. Using a jack, slightly raise the spring link. Then remove the shock absorber lower mounting bolt. See Fig. 3 shown earlier.

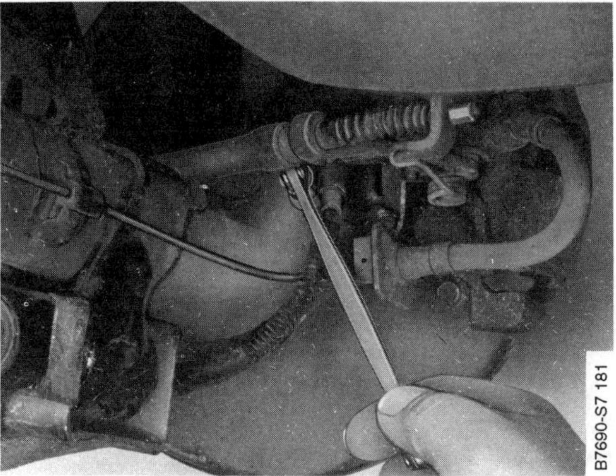

Fig. 7. ABS wheel speed sensor mounting bolt being removed from rear axle housing.

NOTE
The jack should be positioned under the rear of the spring link.

5. Remove the bolt and nut from the spring link rear mounting. See Fig. 8.

WARNING
Do not remove the front spring link mounting bolts while the spring is installed. Serious personal injury could result.

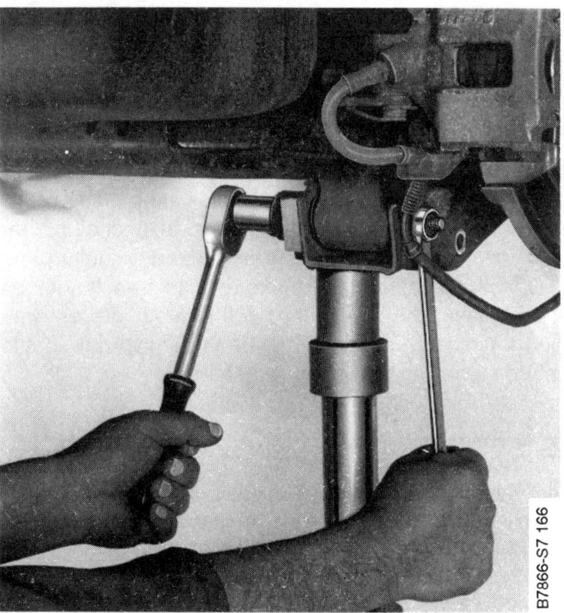

Fig. 8. Spring link rear mounting bolt being removed.

6. On cars equipped with a rear an anti-roll bar, jack up the spring link on the opposite side of the car and remove the mounting bolt from the rear of the other spring link.

7. Loosen, but do not remove, the anti-roll bar front mounting bolts and swivel the anti-roll bar down and out of the way. See Fig. 9.

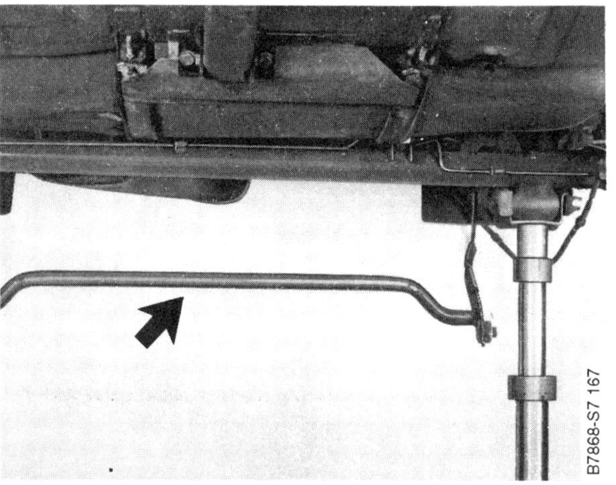

Fig. 9. Anti-roll bar (arrow) shown lowered from spring link.

8. Support the rear axle from below using a set of jack stands. Slowly lower the spring link by means of the jack. Remove the coil spring. If necessary, repeat the procedure for the other spring. See Fig. 10.

CAUTION

The rear axle must be supported to avoid damaging the flexible brake lines.

Installation is the reverse of removal. Be sure to replace all self-locking nuts. Where applicable, install the parking brake bracket and the ABS wheel speed sensor. Inspect all rubber parts for wear or deterioration and replace any faulty parts found. Check the spring by measuring its free length as described below. The coil springs are treated with an anti-corrosion agent. If the coating has been damaged it should be touched up before the spring is installed.

WARNING

Do not reuse self-locking nuts. These parts are designed to be used only once and should be replaced whenever loosened or removed.

NOTE

If the bolt mounting hole in the spring link does not align with the bolt mounting hole in the rear axle, use a large water pump pliers and a screwdriver to align the holes. See Fig. 11.

Fig. 10. Coil spring being removed from car after lowering spring link.

Fig. 11. Rear axle being aligned with spring link using large water-pump pliers and screwdriver.

Tightening torques

- wheel lug bolts . . . . . . 105 to 125 Nm (78 to 92 ft-lb)
- wheel lug nuts . . . . 90 to 110 Nm (66 to 81 ft-lb)
- all other fasteners
  - M5 bolt . . . . 5 Nm (44 in-lb)
  - M6 bolt . . . . 10 Nm (89 in-lb)
  - M8 bolt . . . . 20 Nm (15 ft-lb)
  - M10 bolt . . . . 40 Nm (30 ft-lb)

Checking Suspension Coil Springs

A function of the coil spring is to control the ride height of the car. Therefore, a damaged or fatigued coil spring will usually result in a noticeable difference in ride height. **Table a** lists spring specifications. The spring must be removed from the car to measure their free length.

NOTE

For chassis ride height specifications see **601 Wheel Alignment.**

Various springs are installed depending on model and model year. The springs are color-coded with a paint dot. In addition, the left and right springs on some models may be different. In all cases, the new spring should match the old spring being replaced.

Table a. Rear Coil Spring Specifications

Spring color codes	Spring free length
Standard chassis	
black or white (left spring)	311 mm (12.24 in.)
green or light green (right spring)	308 mm (12.12 in.)
Sport chassis	
silver or bronze	293 mm (11.5 in.)

To remove rear coil spring link

1. Remove the coil spring as described above.

2. On cars equipped with an anti-roll bar, remove the spring link front mounting nuts on both sides of the car. Then remove the anti-roll bar from the spring links. See Fig. 12.

NOTE

If the spring link front mounting bolt was installed with the bolt head on the anti-roll bar side of the link, the bolt will have to be removed to remove the anti-roll bar.

---

3. Remove the two bolts that hold the spring link front mount to the body. See Fig. 13. Remove the spring link from the car.

Installation is the reverse of removal. Inspect the front and rear spring link rubber bushings and replace any parts that are worn or deteriorated. Be sure to install the spring link front mounting through-bolt so that the bolt head is towards the outside of the car.

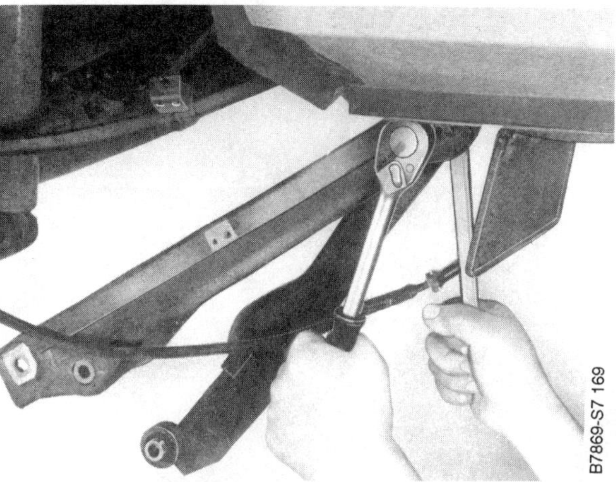

Fig. 12. Spring link front mounting nut being removed.

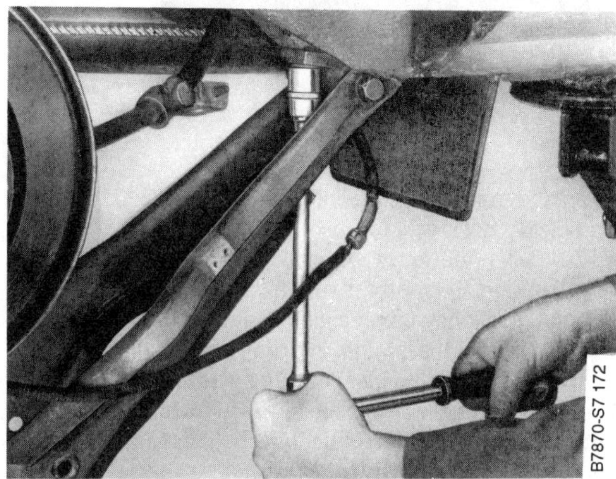

Fig. 13. Spring link front mount bolt being removed.

Tightening torques

- spring link front mount to body . . . . 70 to 90 Nm (52 to 66 ft-lb)
- all other fasteners
  - M5 bolt . . . . 5 Nm (44 in-lb)
  - M6 bolt . . . . 10 Nm (89 in-lb)
  - M8 bolt . . . . 20 Nm (15 ft-lb)
  - M10 bolt . . . . 40 Nm (30 ft-lb)

Replacing Spring Link Bushings

Replacing the spring link bushings requires special press tools.

To replace the spring link front bushing, the spring will need to be removed from the car as described above. With the link removed, Use a press and an appropriate press sleeve to remove and install the bushing. See Fig. 14. Lubricate the bushing with petroleum jelly prior to installation.

Fig. 14. Front spring link bushing being pressed out of front mount.

To replace the rear spring link bushing, the coil spring and spring link do not need to be removed, but the rear of the spring link will need to be lowered to access the bushing in the axle housing. Support the rear axle, then raise the rear of the spring link slightly using a jack. Remove the shock lower mounting bolt and the spring link rear mounting bolt. Lower the spring link (using the jack) until the bushing can be easily worked on. Then using the special press tools shown in Fig. 15, remove and install the bushing. Lubricate the bushing with petroleum jelly prior to installation.

Fig. 15. Spring link rear mount bushing (in rear axle) being pressed out using special press tools (Saab tool no. 89 96 274 shown). Same tool is used to install bushing.

ANTI-ROLL BAR

Some models are equipped with an anti-roll bar to reduce body roll while cornering. The anti-roll bar is rigidly mounted to both spring links.

To remove rear anti-roll bar

1. Loosen the rear wheel lug bolts or nuts, then raise the rear of the car and support it securely on jack stands designed for the purpose. Remove the rear wheels.

WARNING
Always check that the car is stable on the jack stands before continuing any work.

---

2. Raise the rear of the spring links slightly using a jack. Then remove the spring link rear mounting bolts on both sides of the car. See Fig. 16.

NOTE
After the anti-roll bar has been removed, reinstall the nuts for the rear mounting bolts.

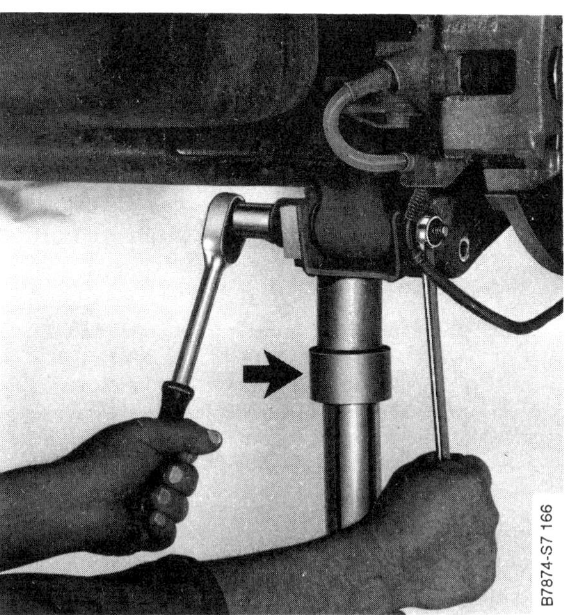

Fig. 16. Spring link rear mounting bolt being removed. Jack (arrow) shown under spring link.

3. Remove the nuts from the spring link front mounting bolts. Do not remove the bolts.

CAUTION

If the spring link front mounting bolt was installed with the bolt head on the anti-roll bar side of the link, the spring link will have to be removed as described above. Do not remove the front spring link mounting bolt without first removing the suspension coil spring.

4. Remove the anti-roll bar by prying it off the front mounting bolt. See Fig. 17.

Fig. 17. Anti-roll bar being removed front mounting bolt.

Installation is the reverse of removal. Leave the spring link front mounting nuts loosely installed until the rear bolts have been installed and tightened.

REAR AXLE

Read the entire procedure before beginning any work. Extra jacks are required to support the axle during removal.

CAUTION

Do not place a jack under the rear axle to jack up the car. The axle may be damaged.

To remove rear axle

1. Loosen the rear wheel lug bolts or nuts, then raise the rear of the car and support it securely on jack stands designed for the purpose. Remove the rear wheels.

WARNING

Always check that the car is stable on the jack stands before starting any work.

2. Unbolt the panhard rod from the rear axle. See Fig. 18. Tie the rod up out of the way.

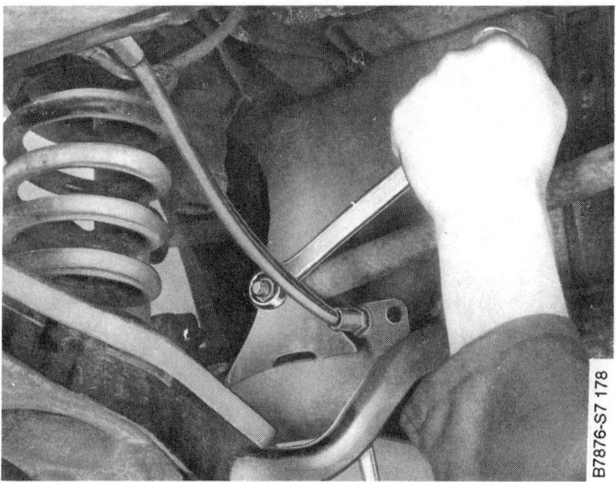

Fig. 18. Panhard rod mounting bolt being removed from rear axle.

3. Pinch off the brake line with a special hose clamp plier. As an alternative, drain the brake system as described in **520 Brake Fluid and Brake Bleeding.** Then separate the flexible brake hoses from the brake line unions on the rear axle. See Fig. 19.

WARNING

The flexible brake hoses must only be pinched off using special hose clamping pliers. Do not use any other type of clamping device or locking pliers, as the hose may become damaged and internally weakened.

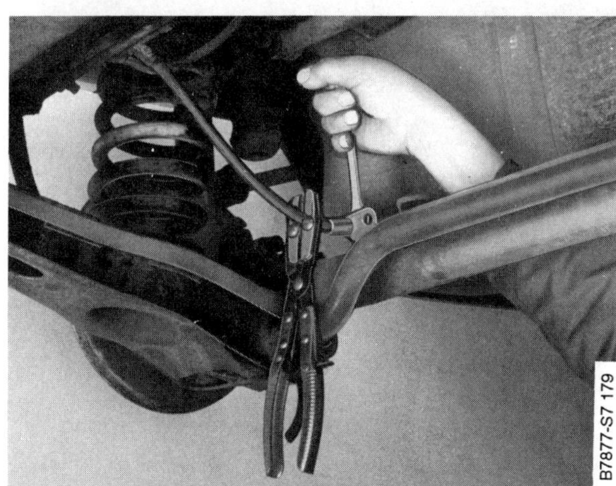

Fig. 19. Brake hoses being disconnected from brake line fitting on rear axle. Special brake hose clamping pliers shown on hose.

4. On cars with ABS, remove the wheel speed sensors from each side of the rear axle housing. See Fig. 20. Release the sensor harness from the clips on the spring link.

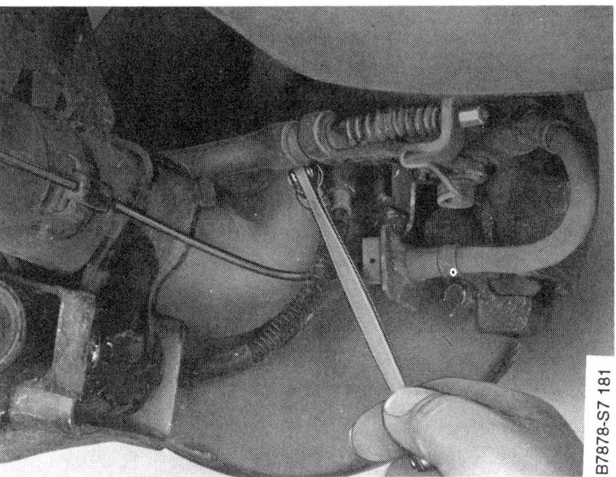

Fig. 20. ABS wheel speed sensor mounting bolt being removed from rear axle housing.

5. On 1988 and later models, disconnect the handbrake cables from the brake caliper levers. See Fig. 21. Remove the handbrake cable hold-down bracket from the axle (see Fig. 6 shown earlier).

Fig. 21. Handbrake cable (**A**) disconnected from brake lever (**B**).

6. Place a jack beneath the rear of each spring link. Slightly raise the spring links and remove the rear mounting bolts. See Fig. 16 shown earlier.

7. Place a jack under the center of the axle. Then unbolt the torque arms from both sides of the axle.

8. Lower the spring links slightly. Raise the axle up just enough to remove it from the spring link mountings and remove the axle from the car.

Installation is the reverse of removal. Replace all self-locking fasteners. Bleed the brakes as described in **520 Brake Fluid and Brake Bleeding**. Check all braking functions including the handbrake.

CAUTION

When installing the panhard rod to the axle, be certain that the bolt head is toward the fuel tank. Damage to the fuel tank may result if the bolt is installed incorrectly. Tighten the wheels to the torque values given below.

Tightening torques

- wheel lug bolts . . . . . . 105 to 125 Nm (78 to 92 ft-lb)
- wheel lug nuts . . . . 90 to 110 Nm (66 to 81 ft-lb)
- all other fasteners
  - M5 bolt . . . . .5 Nm (44 in-lb)
  - M6 bolt . . . . .10 Nm (89 in-lb)
  - M8 bolt . . . . 20 Nm (15 ft-lb)
  - M10 bolt . . . . 40 Nm (30 ft-lb)

TORQUE ARM AND PANHARD ROD

The torque arm and panhard rod are shown in Fig. 22. The rubber bushings in the torque arms and the panhard rod can wear out, often causing a groaning or squeaking sound. The bushings are pressed into place and require special press tools to remove and install them.

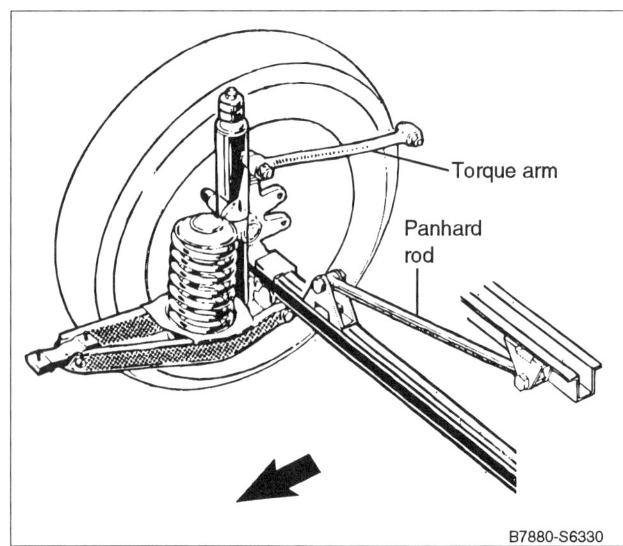

Fig. 22. View of passenger side rear suspension. Arrow points toward front of car.

To remove torque arm

1. Loosen the rear wheel lug bolts or nuts, then raise the rear of the car and support it securely on jack stands designed for the purpose. Remove the rear wheels.

WARNING
Always check that the car is stable on the jack stands before starting any work.

---

2. Remove the front and rear torque arm mounting bolts. See Fig. 23. Remove the torque arm.

Fig. 23. Torque arm front mounting bolt being removed.

3. Press out the torque arm front bushing using a 24 mm sleeve or equivalent. See Fig. 24. Press out the rear bushing using a slightly smaller sleeve.

4. Lubricate the new bushings with petroleum jelly and press them into the torque arm.

5. Install the torque arm in its mountings and loosely hand tighten the nuts.

6. Put the wheels back on the car, tighten the wheel lug bolts or nuts. Lower the car to the ground and tighten the torque arm mounting bolts.

NOTE
The torque arm mounting bolts are torqued after the suspension is loaded by the car's weight to prevent bushing distortion.

Fig. 24. Torque arm bushing being pressed out.

Tightening torques
- wheel lug bolts...... 105 to 125 Nm (78 to 92 ft-lb)
- wheel lug nuts .... 90 to 110 Nm (66 to 81 ft-lb)
- torque arm mounting bolts
  lubricated bushings.... 21 to 35 Nm (16 to 26 ft-lb)
  dry bushings......... 40 to 70 Nm (30 to 52 ft-lb)

To remove panhard rod

1. Raise the car.

NOTE
The rear wheels do not have to be removed.

---

2. Remove the bolts for the panhard rod mountings. Note the orientation of the panhard rod.

3. Press out the rubber bushings using a suitable size sleeve. Lubricate the new bushings with petroleum jelly and press them into the rod.

4. Install the panhard rod in its mountings and loosely hand tighten the nuts.

CAUTION
Install the panhard rod-to-axle mounting bolt so that the bolt head is toward the fuel tank. Damage to the fuel tank may result if the bolt is installed incorrectly.

---

5. Lower the car to the ground. Tighten the panhard rod mounting bolts to the value given below.

NOTE

The panhard rod mounting bolts are torqued after the suspension is loaded by the car's weight to prevent bushing distortion.

Tightening torque

- panhard rod mounting bolts . . . . 40 to 70 Nm (30 to 52 ft-lb)

To replace rubber bump stop

1. Loosen the rear wheel lug bolts or nuts, then raise the rear of the car and support it securely on jack stands designed for the purpose. Remove the rear wheels.

WARNING

Always check that the car is stable on the jack stands before continuing any work.

2. Remove the screw in the middle of the bump stop using an internal 6mm hex-head socket. See Fig. 25. Remove the bump stop and spacer.

Fig. 25. Suspension bump stop being removed.

Installation is the reverse of removal. Torque the wheel lug bolts or nuts.

Tightening torques

- wheel lug bolts . . . . . . 105 to 125 Nm (78 to 92 ft-lb)
- wheel lug nuts . . . . 90 to 110 Nm (66 to 81 ft-lb)

774 Wheel Bearings and Drive Axles

DRIVE AXLES AND FRONT WHEEL BEARINGS

The drive axle assembly is shown in Fig. 1. Each end of the axle is fitted with a swivel joint. The outer Constant Velocity (CV) joint is splined to the wheel bearing hub to drive the front wheel and the inner universal joint fits into the driver on the side of the transmission. Both joints are lubricated with a special grease and are protected from road dirt and other hazards by rubber boots. The only maintenance required of the drive axles and its joints is to periodically inspect the protective boots for damage. For information on troubleshooting a front end problem see **600 Steering and Wheel Alignment—General**.

The front wheel bearing is pressed into the steering swivel member and retained by large circlips. The wheel hub is in turn pressed into the bearing and retained by a large locking nut on the end of the outer CV joint. See Fig. 2.

CAUTION
Do not install the road wheel and lower the car to the ground while the drive axle is removed, as the wheel hub is not supported. The weight of the car can damage the wheel bearing.

To remove and install steering swivel member

1. Disconnect the battery negative (–) cable. Block the rear wheels and put the car in neutral.

2. Remove the center wheel cover from the wheel. Using a punch, tap the staked part of the drive axle nut up and away from the groove in the axle.

CAUTION
Make sure the staked part of the nut does not interfere with the threads on the CV joint. If the threads are damaged, the CV joint will have to be replaced.

3. With the car on the ground, loosen, but do not remove the center drive axle nut.

WARNING
Loosen the center drive axle nut only while the car is on the ground. The leverage required to do this could topple the car from a lift or jackstand.

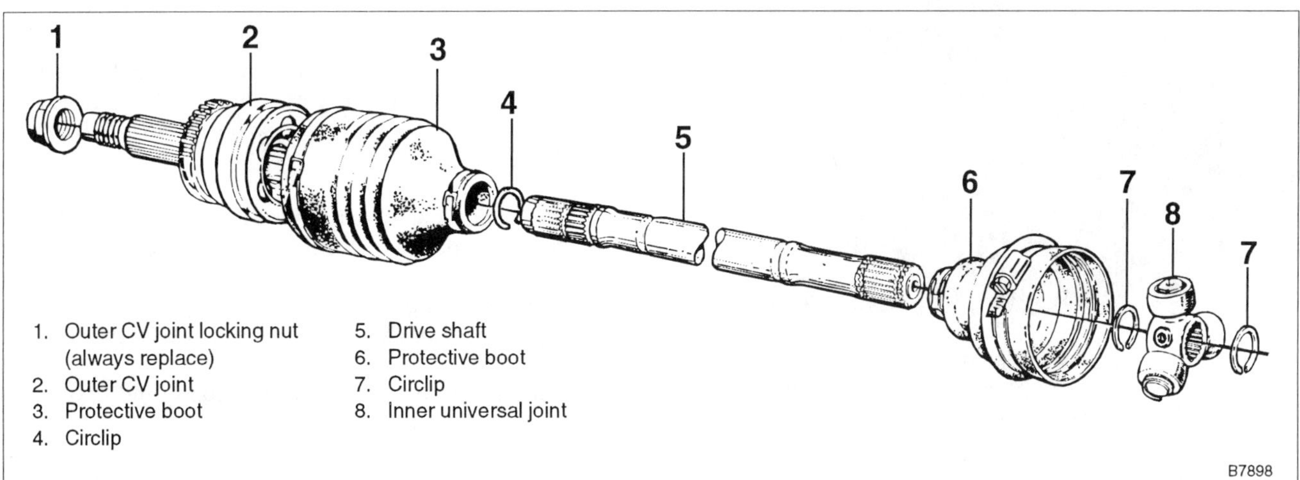

Fig. 1. Exploded view of front drive axle.

774

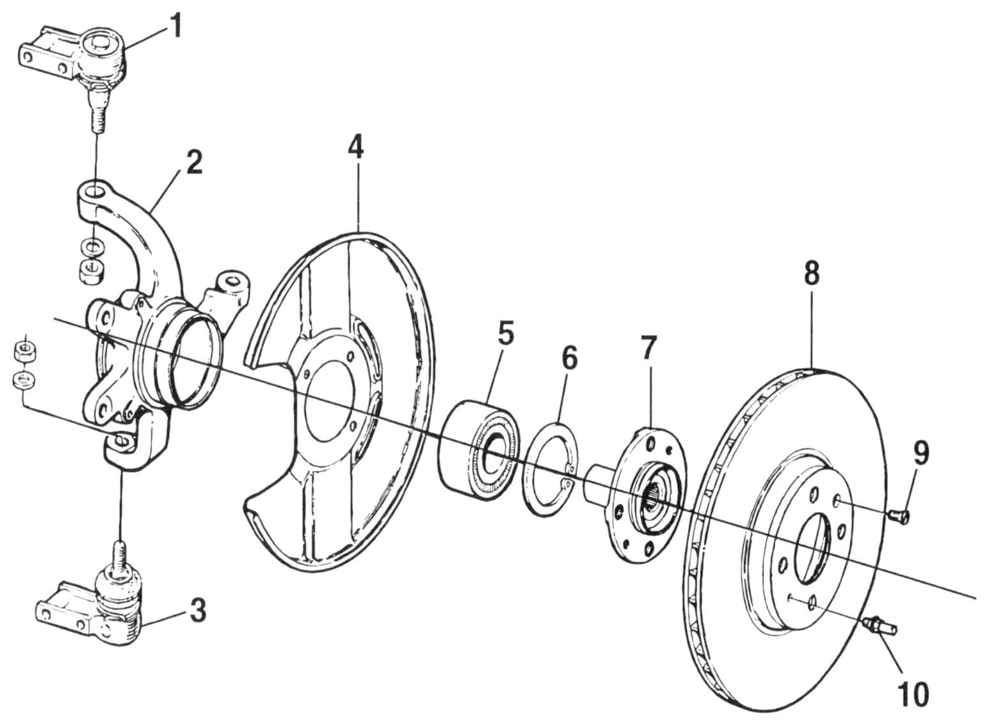

B7899

1. Upper ball joint
2. Steering swivel member
3. Lower ball joint
4. Brake dust shield
5. Wheel bearing
6. Circlip (inner circlip not shown)
7. Wheel hub
8. Brake disc
9. Brake disc mounting screw
10. Road wheel locating stud (1988 and later models)

Fig. 2. Exploded view of front wheel bearing and steering swivel member.

4. Insert the special spacer tool (Saab part no. 83 93 209) between the upper control arm and the body. See Fig. 3.

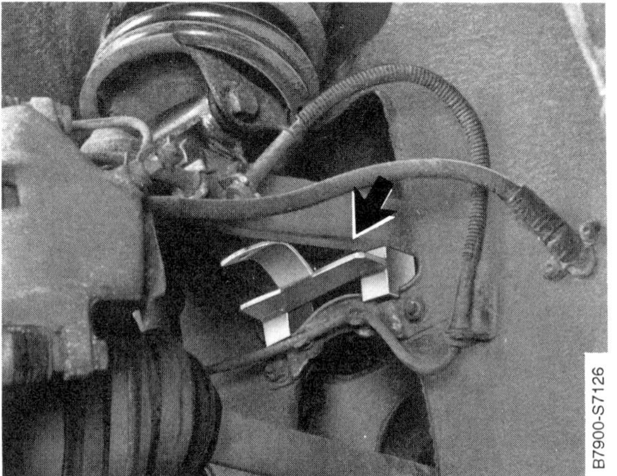

Fig. 3. Spacer tool (arrow) inserted between upper control arm and body. The spacer tool relieves upper control arm suspension loading on the steering member.

5. Raise the car and support it with jackstands. Remove the front wheel, the center drive axle nut and washer (where applicable).

WARNING
Always check that the car is stable on the jackstands before starting any work.

---

6. Remove the brake caliper as described in **523 Brake Calipers**. Suspend the caliper from the body using stiff wire. Remove the brake disc as described in **516 Brake Discs.**

7. Where applicable, remove the ABS wheel speed sensor from steering member. See **500 Brakes—General**.

8. Remove the steering rack tie rod end from the steering swivel member as described in **643 Tie Rod Ends.**

9. Remove the bolts securing the upper and lower ball joints to the control arms. See Fig. 4.

NOTE
If necessary, drive the bolts out of the control arms using a punch.

Fig. 4. Lower ball joint mounting bolt being removed. Upper ball joint mounting bolts shown at arrows.

NOTE
Some later cars are equipped with an anti-roll bar that mounts to the lower ball joint bolts.

10. Using stiff wire, support the drive axle by wiring it to the upper control arm. Then pull the steering swivel member from the drive axle and control arms. See Fig. 5.

CAUTION
Do not let the drive axle fall when removing the steering swivel member. The drive axle boots may be damaged.

NOTE
If necessary, use a soft-faced hammer to tap the drive axle out of the steering swivel member. See Fig. 6.

11. Apply grease (Molycote G or equivalent) to the splines of the drive axle. Then install the steering member to the drive axle. See Fig. 7.

12. Install the upper and lower ball joints in the control arms. Reinstall the bolts using new self-locking nuts.

Fig. 5. Steering swivel member being removed from drive axle.

Fig. 6. Drive axle being tapped out of steering swivel member.

WARNING
Do not reuse self-locking nuts. These parts are designed to be used only once and must be replaced whenever loosened or removed.

Tightening torque
• ball joint to
control arm (bolts) ..... 40 to 54 Nm (30 to 40 ft-lb)

13. Install the tie rod end, the brake caliper, and the brake disc. Where applicable, install the ABS wheel speed sensor.

14. Install the washer (where applicable) and a new center drive axle nut. Reinstall the wheel and lower the car to the ground. Tighten the drive axle nut and then stake it to the groove in the CV joint. See Fig. 8.

Fig. 7. Steering swivel member being installed on drive axle.

> **WARNING**
> Tighten the center drive axle nut only while the car is on the ground. The leverage required to do this could topple the car from a lift or jackstand.

Tightening torques
- wheel hub to drive axle (locking nut) . . . . .290-310 Nm (214- 229 ft-lb)
- wheel lug nuts . . . . 90-110 Nm (66-88 ft-lb)
- wheel lug bolts . . . . .105-125 Nm (77- 92 ft-lb)

Fig. 8. Center drive axle nut being staked. Always use a new nut.

15. Remove the spacer tool. Pump the brake pedal several times to seat the brake pads.

To remove drive axle

> **CAUTION**
> Do not install the road wheel and lower the car to the ground while the drive axle is removed, as the wheel hub is not supported. The weight of the car can damage the wheel bearing.

> **NOTE**
> A new drive axle assembly was introduced on 1987 models. This drive axle is 6 mm longer than the earlier version and is not interchangeable between models. Always check with an authorized Saab dealer for the latest parts and service information.

1. Remove the steering swivel member as described above.

2. Loosen the boot clamp from the inner universal joint. See Fig. 9. Pull the drive axle out of the inner driver. Wrap or cover the driver.

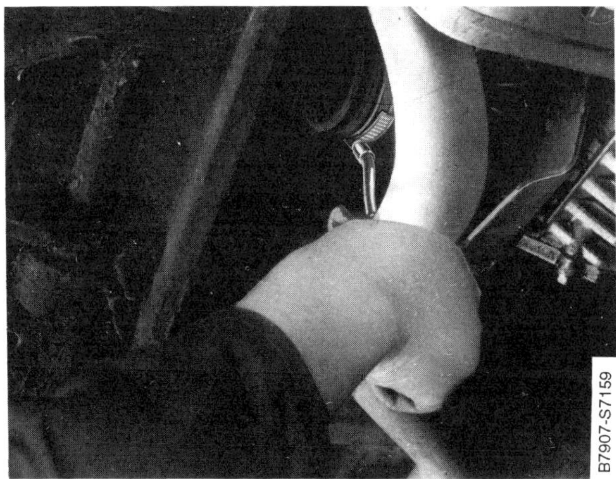

Fig. 9. Inner drive axle boot clamp being loosened.

> **CAUTION**
> Handle the drive axle and axle joints with care. Wrap or cover the joints to protect them from dirt and to prevent the bearing rollers and needle bearings from falling out of the joints.

Installation is the reverse of removal. Replace any damaged drive axle boots. Place the drive axle in the transmission driver and install the steering member as described earlier. Install the drive axle washer (where applicable) and a new center drive axle nut. Reinstall the wheel and lower the car to the ground. Tighten the drive axle nut and then stake it to the groove in the CV joint. See Fig. 8. Install and tighten the inner boot clamp.

WARNING
Do not reuse locking nuts. These parts are designed to be used only once and must be replaced whenever loosened or removed..

Tightening torques
- wheel hub to drive axle (locking nut) . . . . 290-310 Nm (214- 229 ft-lb)
- wheel lug nuts . . . . 90-110 Nm (66-88 ft-lb)
- wheel lug bolts. . . . . 105-125 Nm (77- 92 ft-lb

To replace outer CV joint and joint boot

When replacing the CV joint, be sure to have on hand the special CV joint grease, a new boot, new clamps, and a new drive axle nut.

CAUTION
The outer CV joint should be lubricated with a special CV joint grease specifically designed for the purpose. Do not use any other type of lubricant. See an authorized Saab dealer for the correct grease.

1. Remove the drive axle from the car as described earlier.
2. Remove the old clamps from the boot and then cut the boot off the joint.
3. Expand the drive axle circlip shown in Fig. 10 and pull the CV joint off the shaft.
4. Thoroughly clean and degrease the joint and the drive axle. Allow the parts to dry.

CAUTION
When the grease is removed from the CV joint, the balls can fall out if the joint is positioned the right way.

5. Install the new boot clamps and the boot to the shaft. Slide the boot down the shaft.

NOTE
The old boot clamps should not be reused.

6. Repack the CV joint with the special grease. Work the grease into the joint.

Fig. 10. Circlip pliers being used to expand CV joint circlip. Insert pliers in circlip opening. As an alternative, use a flat blade screwdriver to spread the circlip open.

Outer CV joint lubricant
- Esso nebula EP2 grease or equivalent . . . . 80 grams (approx. 3 oz.)

7. While expanding the circlip, slide the greased CV joint onto the shaft until it locks into place. Check that the CV joint is locked on the shaft by trying to pull it off.
8. Slide the boot and clamps into position. Release any trapped air in the boot by peeling up a corner of the boot and giving it a light squeeze.
9. Crimp the clamps using the appropriate crimping pliers (Knipex 1099 or equivalent). See Fig. 11.
10. Install the drive axle using a new locking nut as as described earlier. Be sure to stake the nut to the axle as shown in Fig. 8.

To replace inner universal joint and joint boot

Fig. 12 shows the inner universal joint and the transmission driver. When replacing the universal joint, be sure to have on hand the special grease, a new boot, and new clamps.

CAUTION
The universal joint should be lubricated with a special grease specifically designed for the inner joint. Do not use any other type of lubricant. See an authorized Saab dealer for the correct grease. The grease used to lubricate the inner joint is different than the grease used in the outer joint.

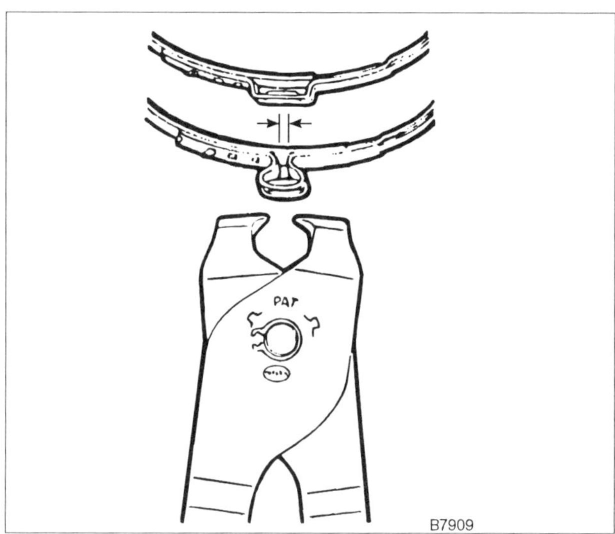

Fig. 11. CV boot clamp and crimping pliers.

NOTE

A new drive axle assembly was introduced on 1987 models. This drive axle is 6 mm longer than the earlier version and is not interchangeable between models. Always check with an authorized Saab dealer for the latest parts and service information..

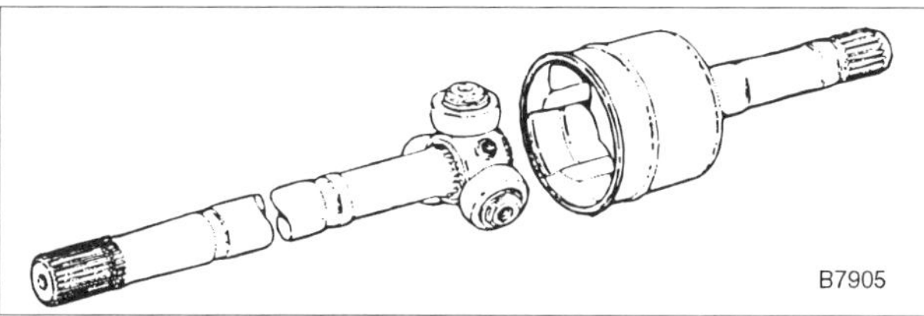

Fig. 12. Inner universal joint and transmission driver.

1. Remove the drive axle as described earlier. Mount the drive axle in a vise with the inner joint facing up.

2. Remove the circlip from the end of the drive axle. See Fig. 13. Pull the joint off the shaft while holding the roller bearings to the joint.

NOTE

Use care when removing the joint from the shaft. The rollers and small needle bearings can fall off the joint.

---

3. Remove the boot clamp and slide the boot off the shaft.

4. Thoroughly clean and degrease the joint, the drive axle, and the driver on the side of the transmission. Allow the parts to dry. If necessary, wipe the parts dry with a clean cloth. Where applicable, inspect the inner circlip and replace if damaged.

Fig. 13. Circlip being removed from inner drive axle joint.

5. Install the new boot and the new clamp on the shaft. Crimp the clamp using the appropriate crimping pliers (Knipex 1099 or equivalent). See Fig. 11 shown above.

6. Install the joint on the drive axle and install the circlip.

7. Pack the universal joint and the transmission driver with the appropriate amount of the specified grease.

Inner Universal Joint Grease

- Mobil GS57C or equivalent
- universal joint . . . . 60 g (approx. 2 oz.)
- transmission driver . . . . 115 g (approx. 4 oz.)

---

8. Install the drive axle as described earlier.

CAUTION

Do not let any dirt fall into the inner universal joint during installation of the drive axle. Temporarily wrap or cover the inner joint and boot during installation.

To replace front wheel bearing

Special tools, including a service press, are required to replace the front wheel bearings.

CAUTION

Do not install the road wheel and lower the car to the ground while the drive axle is removed, as the wheel hub is not supported. The weight of the car can damage the wheel bearing.

NOTE

Some cars (up through mid-1990 models) may experience a clunking or snapping noise at the wheel when backing up at low speeds with the steering at full lock (such as when parking). This noise is most likely caused by the wheel bearing sliding back and forth in the steering member. This problem can be corrected by installing a new bearing and the appropriate shims. See an authorized Saab dealer for more information on this repair.

1. Remove the steering swivel member from the car as described earlier in this section.

2. Using the special wheel bearing press fixture tools (Saab tool nos. 89 96 449 and 89 96 456), press the hub out of the steering member. See Fig. 14.

NOTE

Pressing the hub out of the bearing destroys the bearings. In most cases, the bearing inner race will remain on the hub.

Fig. 15. Bearing inner race being pulled off hub.

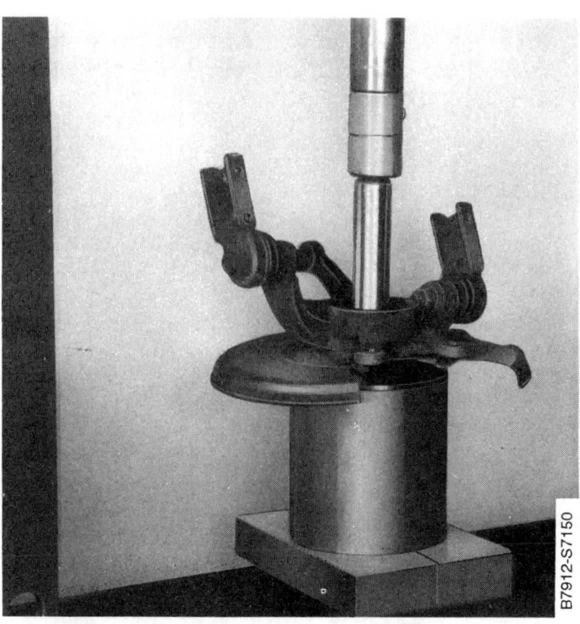

Fig. 14. Wheel hub being pressed out of wheel bearing.

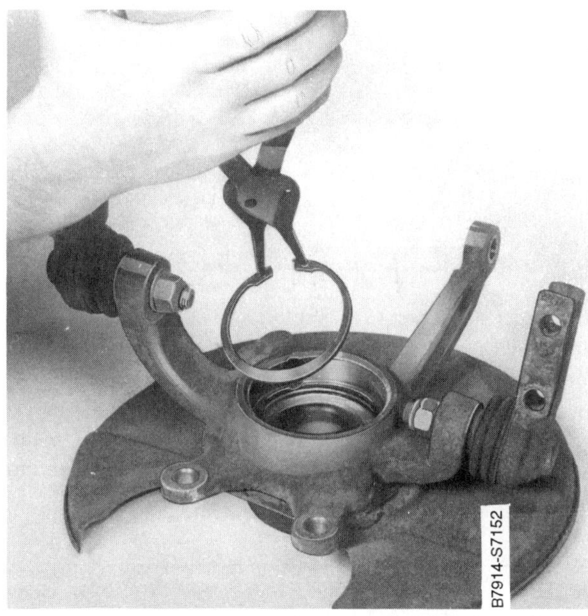

Fig. 16. Circlip being removed from rear of wheel bearing. Circlip on other side of wheel bearing must also be removed.

3. If necessary, pull the inner bearing race off the hub using a two-jaw puller. See Fig. 15.

4. Remove the circlips from the steering swivel member. See Fig. 16.

5. Using the special wheel bearing press fixture tools (Saab tool nos. 89 96 449, 89 96 456, and 83 90 114), press the wheel bearing out of the steering swivel member. See Fig. 17.

6. Clean the steering member housing. Install the inner circlip in the steering member. See Fig. 18. Lubricate the inside of the steering member with Molycote G grease or an equivalent.

NOTE

Inspect the circlip carefully. If it is deformed or will not expand into the groove, replace it with a new one.

Fig. 17. Wheel bearing being pressed out of steering member.

Fig. 18. Inner circlip being installed to circlip groove in steering member.

7. Using the special press tools (Saab part nos. 83 90 114 and 89 96 464), press the new bearing into the steering member until it is firmly seated on the circlip. See Fig. 19.

NOTE
Be sure to position Saab tool no. 89 96 464 so that the larger diameter collar is facing up.

---

8. Install the outer circlip.

NOTE
- Inspect the circlip carefully. If it is deformed or will not expand into the groove, replace it with a new one.
- Before pressing the hub into the steering member, inspect the wheel studs (where applicable) and replace any that are worn. Wheel studs are pressed out of the hub after the hub is removed from the steering member.

Fig. 19. Front wheel bearing being pressed into steering swivel member. Numbers shown are Saab tool numbers.

9. Press the wheel hub into the bearing in the steering member using special tools (Saab tool nos. 83 90 114 and 89 96 464). See Fig. 20.

Fig. 20. Wheel Hub (arrow) being pressed into steering member.

Install the steering swivel member as described above.

WARNING
Do not reuse self-locking nuts. These parts are designed to be used only once and must be replaced whenever loosened or removed.

Replacing Front Wheel Studs

Saab recommends that the wheel hub be pressed out of the steering member to replace the wheel studs. It may by possible in some cases to tap the stud out of the hub after removing the brake disc. See **516 Brake Discs** for information on removing the brake disc. A special press tool (Saab tool no. 89 95 920) can be used to press the studs out of the hub.

REAR WHEEL BEARINGS AND WHEEL HUBS

The rear wheel bearing and hub are replaced as an assembly. Neither the bearing or the hub are available as separate replacement parts. The bearing is permanently sealed and does not require any maintenance. There are two types of rear hubs and bearings used on cars covered by this manual. See Fig. 21.

The rear wheel bearing is integral with the wheel hub. The wheel bearing hub assembly is fitted to the stub axle on the rear axle and retained by a large locking nut.

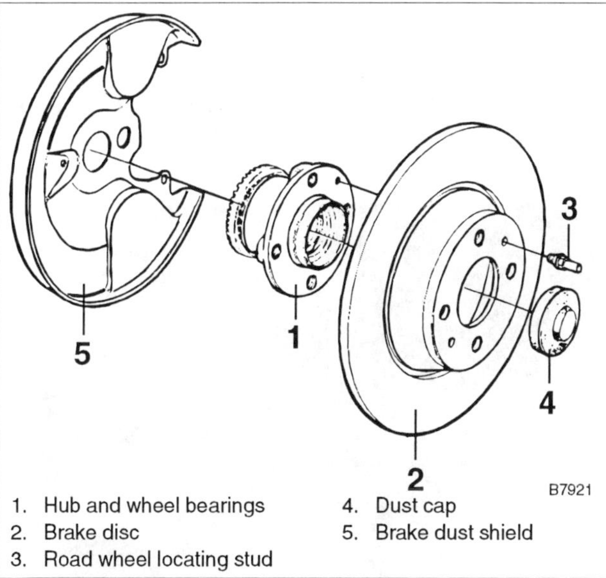

1. Hub and wheel bearings
2. Brake disc
3. Road wheel locating stud
4. Dust cap
5. Brake dust shield

Fig. 21. Exploded view of rear hub and brake disc (center axle nut not shown).

To replace rear wheel bearing

1. Working at the rear wheel, remove the hub dust cap.

2. Using a punch, pry up the staked material on the center axle nut. With the car on the ground, loosen, but do not remove the center axle nut.

WARNING

Loosen and tighten the center axle nut only while the car is on the ground. The leverage required to do this could topple the car from a lift or jackstand.

CAUTION

Make sure the staked part of the center axle nut does not interfere with the spindle threads. If the threads are stripped, the entire axle has to be replaced.

---

3. Raise the car and support it with jackstands. Remove the rear wheel, the center axle nut and washer (where applicable).

WARNING

Make sure the car is well supported with jackstands. Never use just a jack to support a car.

---

4. Remove the brake caliper as described in **523 Brake Calipers**. Suspend the caliper with stiff wire.

5. Remove the brake disc as described in **516 Brake Discs**. Where applicable, remove the ABS wheel speed sensor and handbrake cable.

6. Remove the hub.

NOTE

On 1985-1987 models press off the hub using special tool (Saab tool no. 89 96 084). See Fig. 22.

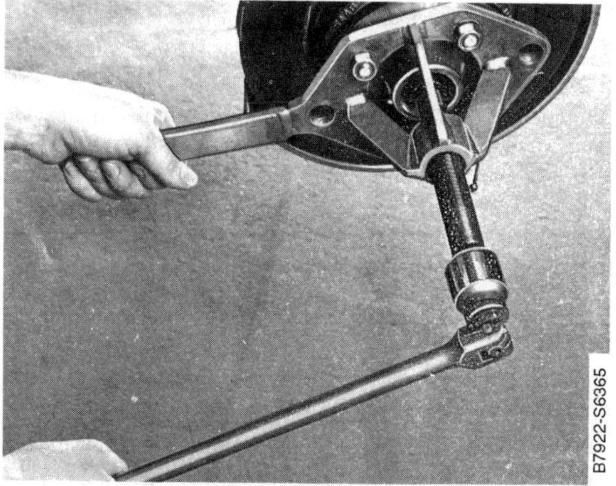

Fig. 22. Rear hub being pressed off axle on 1985 to 1987 models.

Installation is the reverse of removal. Clean the stub axle and remove any burrs or pits with an emery cloth. Lubricate the stub axle with thin oil.

NOTE
- The hub and bearings are replaced as an assembly.
- Install the hub and bearings using thumb pressure against the bearing race to prevent the race from sliding. See Fig. 23.

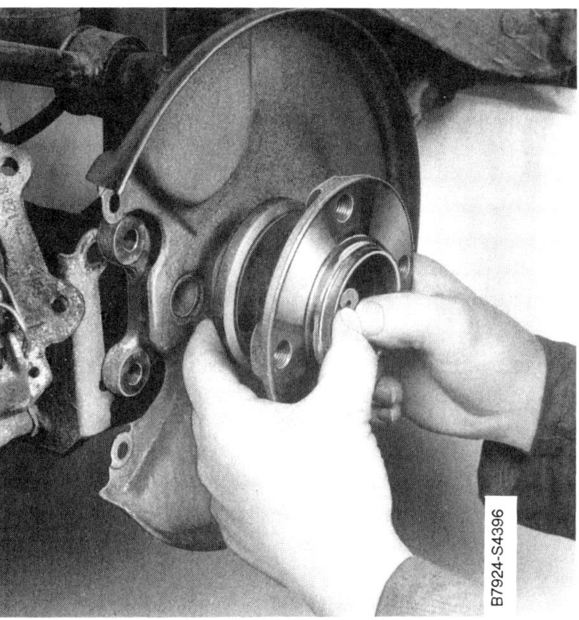

Fig. 23. Rear hub and bearing being installed.

Replace the center axle nut with a new one and torque it to the value given below with the car on the ground. Stake the nut as shown earlier.

NOTE
Early models have a replaceable seal and bearings. On later models, the bearings and seal are integral with the hub and are not available separately. See your Saab dealer for exact parts applications.

Tightening torques
- center axle nut to rear axle . . . . 300±10 Nm (220±9 ft-lb)
- wheel lug nuts . . . . 90 to 110 Nm (66 to 81 ft-lb)
- wheel lug bolts . . . . . . 105 to 125 Nm (77 to 92 ft-lb)

To replace rear wheel studs

NOTE
It may be possible in some cases to tap the wheel studs (where applicable) out of the hub using a brass or plastic hammer. If it is not possible to tap out the studs, a special press is available from Saab. The pressing procedure is given below. The new studs should be fully seated in the hub by putting the wheel on and torquing the wheel lug nuts to the correct value given elsewhere in this section.

1. Raise the car and support it with jackstands. Remove the rear wheel.

WARNING
Make sure the car is well supported with jackstands. Never use just a jack to support a car.

2. Remove the brake caliper as described in **523 Brake Calipers**. Suspend the caliper with stiff wire.
3. Remove the brake disc as described in **516 Brake Discs.**
4. Press out the wheel stud using the special tool (Saab tool no.89 95 920) and a sleeve located behind the hub. See Fig. 24.

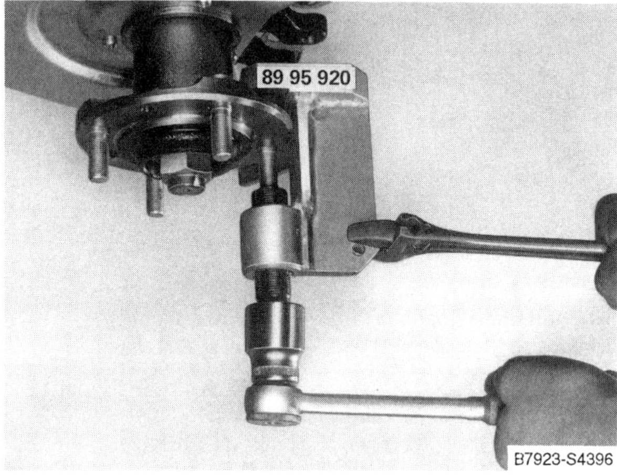

Fig. 24. Rear wheel stud being pressed out of hub. Number shown is Saab tool number.

5. Press in the new stud using the same tool. Position the sleeve on the outside of the hub.
6. Install the wheel and tighten the lug nuts.

800 Body–General

Body

Fig. 1 shows the overall body dimensions for the three 900 body styles. The hood, the grille, the doors, and the trunk lid are all removable. These bolt-on components are easily replaced even if you have little or no knowledge of auto body repair. The front fenders, however, are welded to the main body structure. Because very few screws and bolts are used in assembling the body, fewer rattles are likely to develop. The ride is quieted further by the application of sound-dampening material to the floor plates and the body panels.

The Saab 900 body is of welded, unitized construction, meaning it does not have a separate frame. This design forms a very rigid passenger compartment, with large crumple zones in the front and rear for energy absorption in the event of a collision. See Fig. 2.

During manufacture, the various body panels, subassemblies, and a number of smaller pressed-steel panels and plates are joined by electric welding. Although all body panels are available as replacement parts, many of these replacement panels must be butt-welded to the body after the damaged panels have been cut away.

For corrosion protection, all steel is treated with a multi-layer finish. The body seams are then sealed using a PVC compound. The body is undercoated and all interior cavities are flooded with a rust preventative sealant. The front fenders are open to allow trapped moisture to evaporate. See Fig. 3.

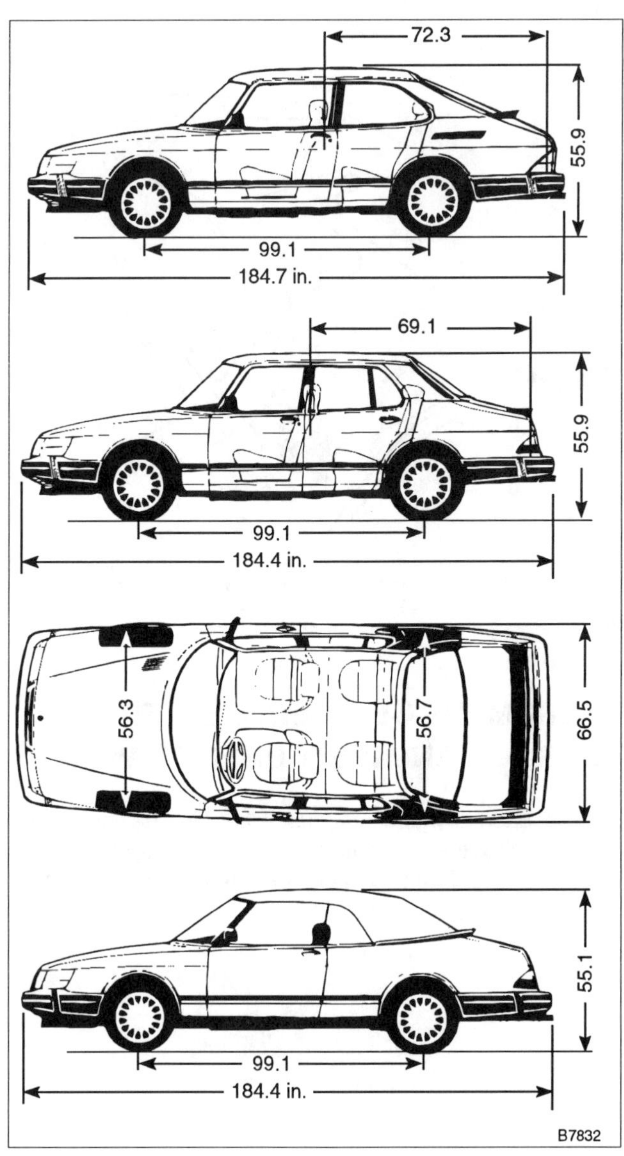

Fig. 1. Body dimensions. Dimensions on some sport models may vary slightly

Seats, Seat Belts, and Interior

The front seats are mounted to the floor. Rear seats are bolted to the body and are easily removed for access to the rear seat belt mountings. The seat belts are typical three-point belts that cross the hips and the shoulder. Some later models use a motorized passive restraint seat belt system. Most interior trim is easily removed using ordinary hand tools.

Fig. 2. Unitized Saab 900 body shell.

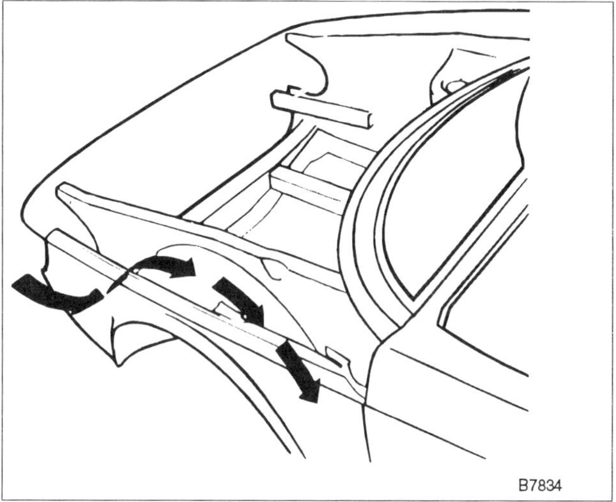

Fig. 3. Front fenders are ventilated (arrows) for corrosion protection.

INSTRUMENT CLUSTER, CENTER CONSOLE, AND INSTRUMENT PANEL

The padded instrument panel houses the instrument cluster and the ventilation and heating system. It is fastened to the body and can be removed using ordinary hand tools. The instrument cluster is removable as a unit without removing the instrument panel. All electrical repairs to the instrument cluster are covered in **3 ELECTRICAL SYSTEM**.

Some of the cars covered by this manual may be equipped with a Supplemental Restraint System (SRS) that automatically deploys an airbag. See Fig. 4.

WARNING

The SRS airbag unit uses an explosive device to electrically ignite a powerful gas. Use extreme care when working on the body, the steering wheel or steering column on cars equipped with SRS. Working involving the SRS, the steering wheel or the steering column should only be performed by an authorized Saab dealer.

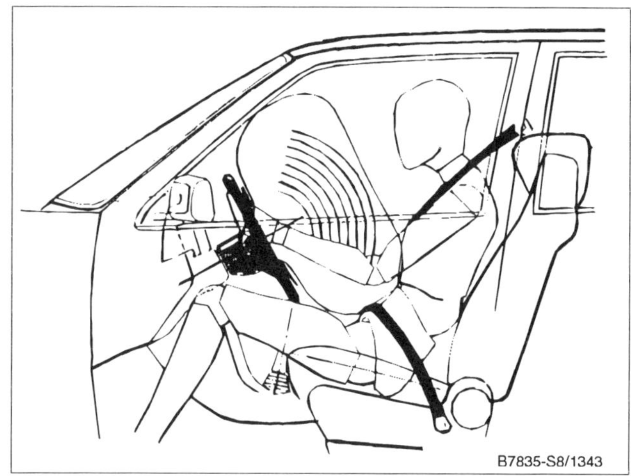

Fig. 4. Schematic of SRS (airbag) system.

812 Convertible Top

GENERAL

The convertible top consists of a top cover, a frame assembly, and an inner headliner. See Fig. 1. The top has a heated rear window element. A mercury switch prevents the heated rear window from coming on if the top is in the down position. See **371 Wiring Diagrams, Fuses and Relays** for the heated rear window circuit.

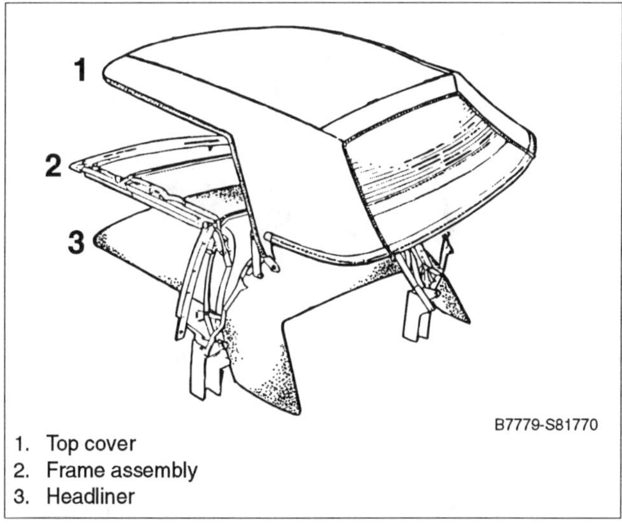

1. Top cover
2. Frame assembly
3. Headliner

Fig. 1. Convertible top.

The top is operated by an electrically-controlled hydraulic system. The system consists of an electric motor/pump assembly, two actuating pistons, a bypass valve, and connecting hoses. See Fig. 2. The motor/pump assembly is located under the rear seat and is thermally-protected (the motor shuts off after approximately 20 seconds of operation). A bypass valve enables the top to be operated manually in the event of an electrical failure. This valve is behind a trim flap at the back of the luggage compartment.

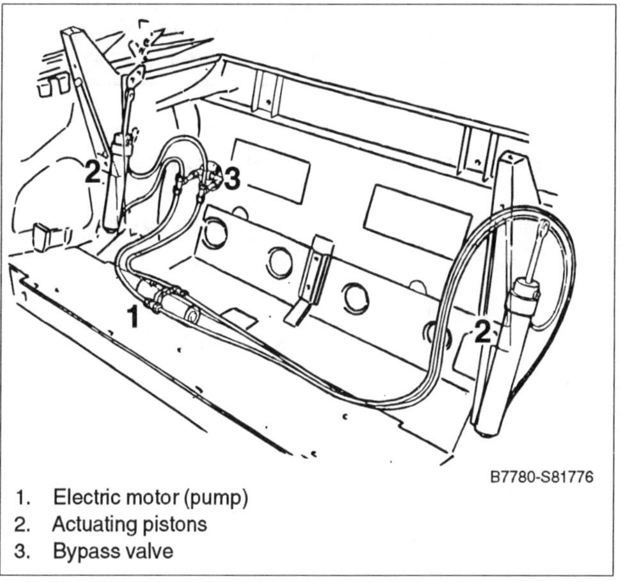

1. Electric motor (pump)
2. Actuating pistons
3. Bypass valve

Fig. 2. Hydraulic system beneath rear seat.

TOP ASSEMBLY

The top does not require any maintenance other than normal cleaning. Operate the top periodically to check that it functions correctly.

Replacement of the top requires special techniques and equipment and is beyond the scope of this manual. Information on removing and adjusting the side windows can be found in **830 Doors, Windows, and Lids**.

Adjustments

This section covers adjustments that can be made to the top. Keep in mind that doing one adjustment can affect the alignment of the top in other areas. There are five adjustments that can be made.

Water and wind leaks are usually the result of a defective seal between the weatherstripping and the top. Water leaks into the passenger compartment are most easily found using two people. One person can aim a garden hose at the car while the other person checks for the leak inside the car. Wind noise is not as easy to find. One technique is to tape over a suspected area and then test drive the car to check if the noise still exists.

The weatherstrips and seals are installed at the factory using adhesive and screws. Generally, seals are glued into place using 3M® Super Weatherstrip Adhesive. The seals are non-adjustable once installed. All fasteners should be checked and tightened before beginning any adjustment.

NOTE
A service campaign to adjust the convertible top was initiated by Saab for 1986-1987 models and some 1988 models. See an authorized Saab dealer for more information on this campaign.

To check and adjust park position

The park position allows the top to be latched easily while at the same time pulling the top taught.

1. Raise the top until it stops. The leading edge of the top should be above the windshield by the amount shown in Fig. 3.

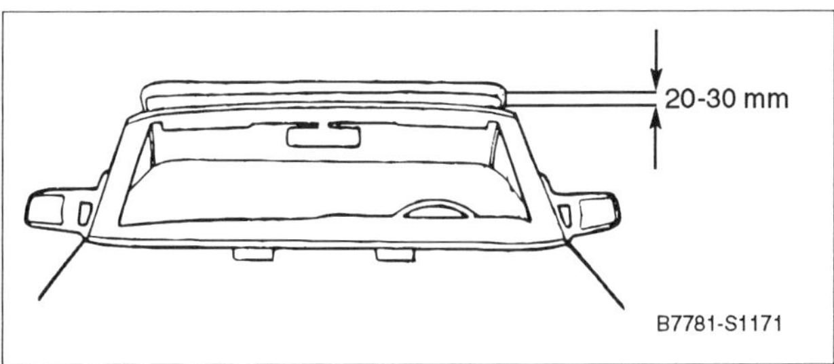

Fig. 3. Correct park position of top.

2. If the gap is incorrect, adjust the cam links on each side of the top until the gap is as specified. See Fig. 4.

NOTE
The adjustment is made using an internal hex-head key. Be sure to tighten the locknut after adjustment.

To check and adjust latched position

When the top is latched closed, there should be no side-to-side or up-down play. The guide pins, which control side-to-side movement, do not usually require adjustment. The latching hooks, which control up and down play, can be easily adjusted. See Fig. 5.

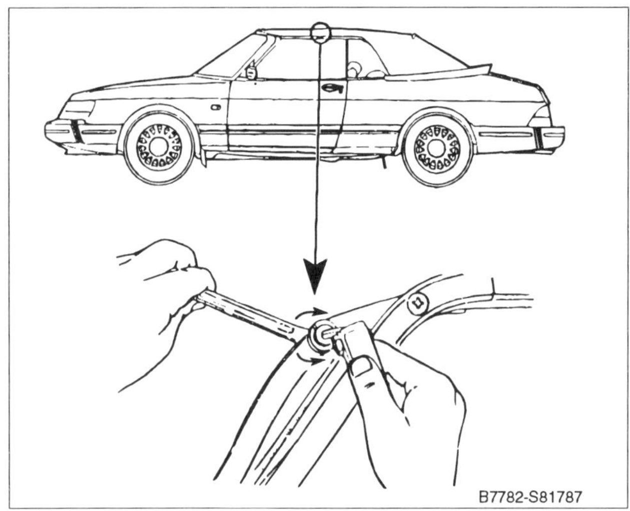

Fig. 4. Park position adjusting cam being adjusted. Cams are located above windows.

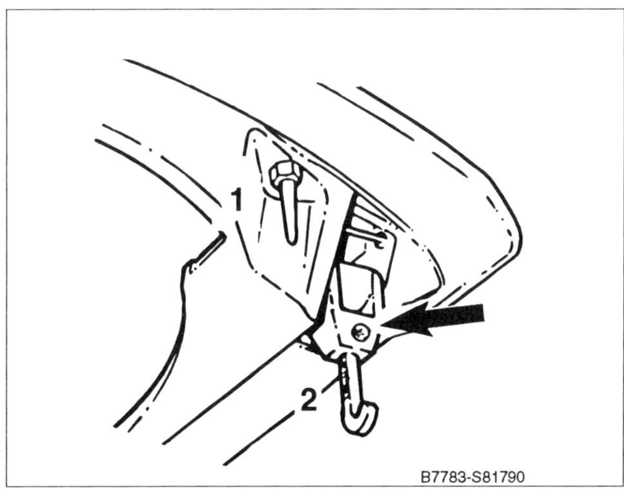

Fig. 5. Guide pin **1** and latching hook **2**. Arrow shows location of Torx adjusting screw.

1. With the top latched in position, push down on each corner of the top. If any play is found, the latching hooks should be adjusted.

2. Adjust the height of the latching hook by loosening the Torx screw and rotating the hook.

NOTE
One turn of the hook changes the height by 1 mm (0.04 in.).

To check and adjust side rail position

The side rail position controls the seal between the front windows and the top.

1. Check that the side rail is parallel with the windows. Check that no air gap exists. If any faults are found, the side rail should be adjusted.

2. Adjust the side rail by loosening the hinge screw between the front and middle rail sections. Adjust the rails sections until they are in parallel with the window and then tighten the screw. See Fig. 6.

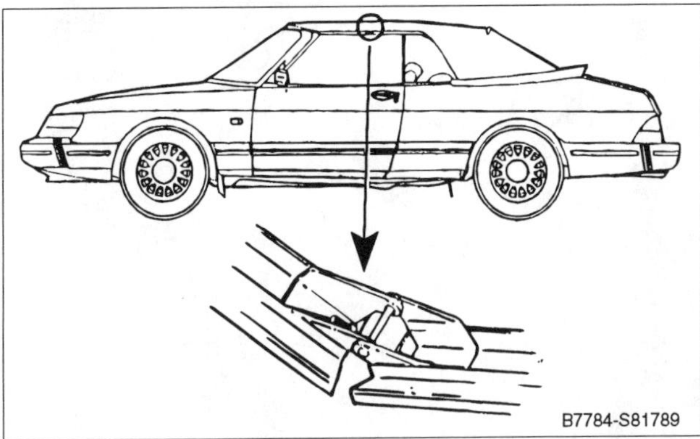

Fig. 6. Front section side rail hinge.

To check and adjust fully open position

Checking and adjusting the fully open and stowed position of the top requires a special gauge that can be made from wood or cardboard.

1. To check the open position of the top, open the top to its fully stowed position. Using the special gauge, check the top position as shown in Fig. 7.

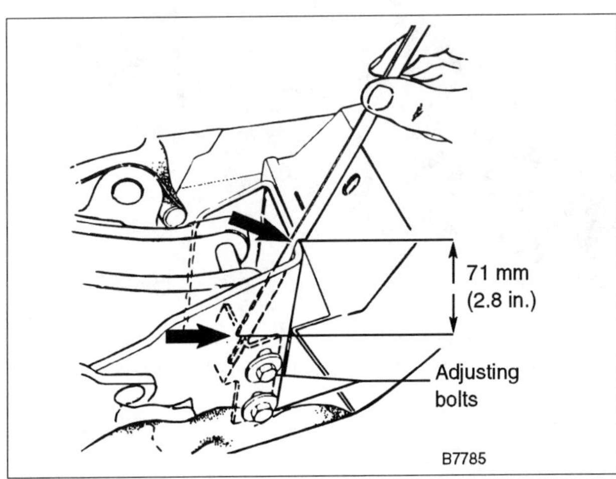

Fig. 7. Stop bracket position being checked (arrows) using special gauge. If position is incorrect loosen adjusting bolts.

2. If the position is incorrect, loosen, but do not remove, the adjusting bolts and adjust the stop bracket. Tighten the bolts.

HYDRAULIC SYSTEM

If the top does not operate, begin by checking the motor fuses. There are two fuses used in the circuit. See **371 Wiring Diagrams, Fuses and Relays** for locations. Check the fluid level in the pump reservoir. See Fig. 8. If the level is low, check for any visible leaks. Use only the special Saab hydraulic fluid when adding fluid to the system.

CAUTION
Use only the approved hydraulic fluid when adding or replacing fluid. Engine oil or ATF should not be used in the system.

Pump hydraulic fluid
- Aeroshell Fluid 4/Shell Code 60 421 (Saab part no. 30 18 694)

Fig. 8. Hydraulic pump fluid level. Fluid level should be at **A** with top down and at **B** with top up. Fill plug is shown at **C.**

To replace an individual component, the entire hydraulic system should be removed from the car as described below. This allows for proper bleeding of the system and also prevents any spilled hydraulic fluid from contacting and damaging painted surfaces.

WARNING
Do not allow the top to be operated when your hands are near the top mechanisms. The pistons have sufficient force to cause injury.

CAUTION
Leaking hydraulic fluid can damage paint and upholstery. Correct any leaks as soon as possible.

To remove hydraulic system

1. Remove the rear seat as described in **851 Interior Trim and Upholstery**.

2. Remove the interior trim panels below the rear side windows as described in **830 Doors, Windows, and Lids**.

3. Working in the luggage compartment, open the bypass valve to release the pressure in the system. See Fig. 9.

Fig. 9. Hydraulic system bypass valve in luggage compartment. Lift up carpet flap to access.

4. Release the handbrake to allow for slack in the hand-brake cables near the pump.

5. Working in the passenger compartment, release the hydraulic hoses from the body clips.

6. Remove the split pin and clevis pin from the pistons on both sides of the car. Note the position of the washers and spacers. See Fig. 10.

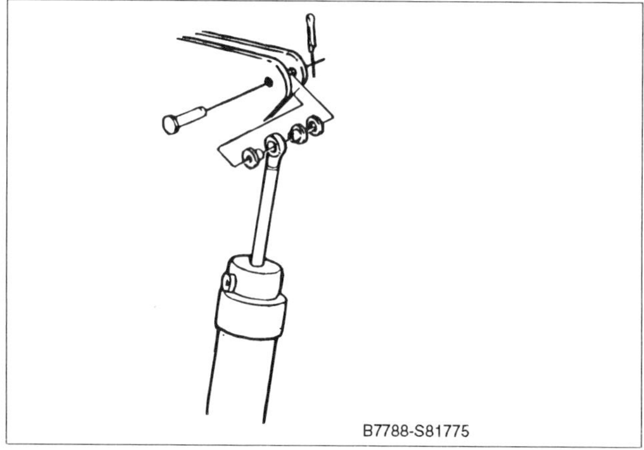

Fig. 10. Split pin, clevis pin and washers for piston.

7. Close the bypass valve. Switch on the ignition and fully retract the pistons by placing the top switch in the down position. Switch off the ignition.

8. Remove the bolts holding the piston to the side body panel. See Fig. 11.

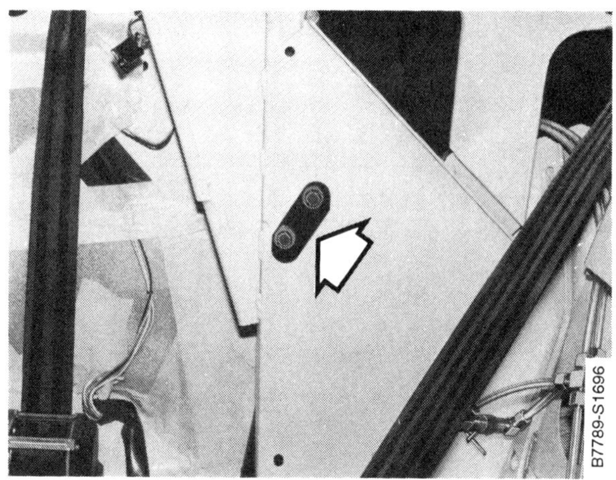

Fig. 11. Piston mounting bolts (arrow).

9. On 1987 and 1988 models, remove the pump from its mountings and disconnect the harness connectors from the relays on the bulkhead. Remove and label the pump wires from the relay connectors. See Fig. 12.

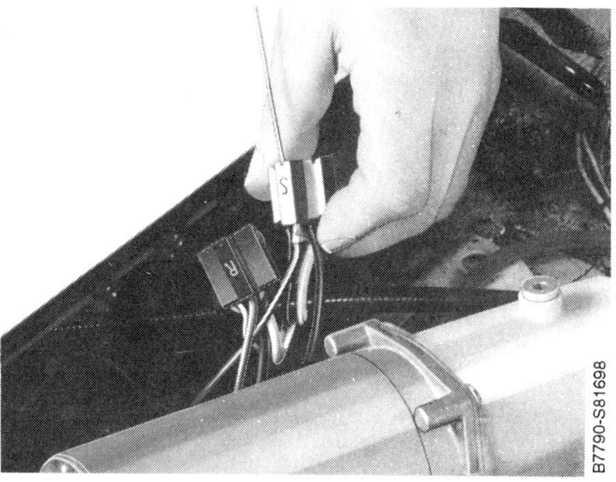

Fig. 12. Pump wiring being removed from relay connector on 1987 and 1988 moldels. Label wires before removal.

10. On 1989 and later models, disconnect the pump harness connector.

11. Remove the moisture barrier from each body panel cavity.

12. Remove the pistons by lifting them up while feeding the bottom of the piston through the cutout in the body

13. Label each piston and bracket before removing the entire hydraulic system from the car. Carefully slide the right-hand piston out from under the fuel lines and the parking brake cable during removal. See Fig. 13

NOTE

If the piston brackets are to be removed, label their positions before removal. The left and right brackets are different.

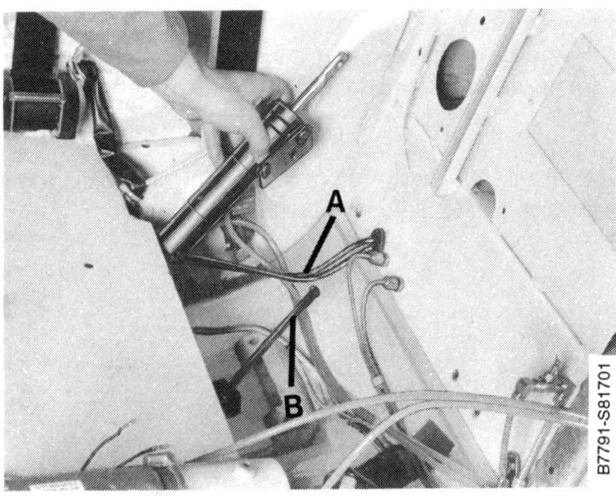

Fig. 13. Right-hand piston must pass under fuel lines **A** and handbrake cable **B** to remove.

If necessary, the individual components can be replaced once the system is removed. If any component is replaced or the system has been opened, the system must be bled as described below before installing the system.

Tightening torque

- Hydraulic hose fittings . . . . 5.1 to 6.2 Nm (45 to 54 in-lb)

To install hydraulic system

1. Make sure the pistons are fully retracted. If necessary run the pump as described below.

2. Slide the right-hand piston and hoses under the fuel lines and handbrake cable.

3. Install the pump under the handbrake cable. Plug in the pump electrical connectors. If applicable, reconnect the harness connectors to the relays. Fit the pump to its mount.

4. Install the pistons in the body cavities. Make sure the hose connections on the pistons are toward the rear of the car.

5. Reinstall the moisture barrier in each body cavity.

6. Mount the bypass valve and hoses in their clips.

7. Operate the pump to fully extend the pistons. With the top unlatched, install the washers, spacers, clevis pin and split pin in the piston. See Fig. 10.

The remaining of installation is the reverse of removal.

To bleed hydraulic system

The hydraulic system is bled with the complete system removed from the car. This will prevent any damage to painted surfaces.

1. With all lines connected, place the pump on a workbench. Place the pistons in a tray on the floor. The pistons should be at a lower level than the pump.

2. Fill the reservoir with hydraulic fluid up to the top level mark. See Fig. 14. Leave the fill plug off.

Pump hydraulic fluid

- Aeroshell Fluid 4/Shell Code 60 421 (Saab part no. 30 18 694)

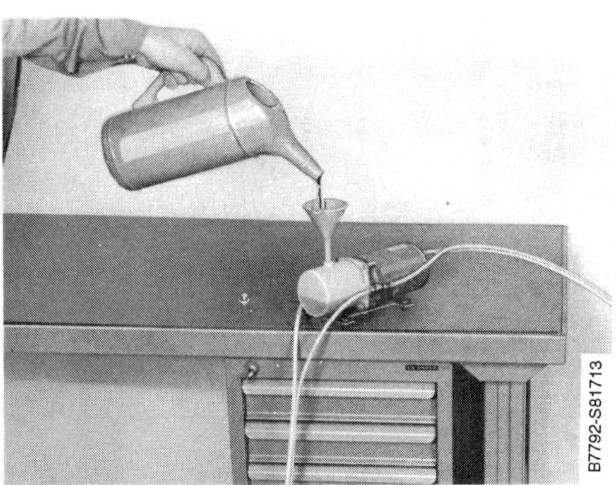

Fig. 14. Hydraulic pump being filled with hydraulic oil.

3. Loosen one hose fitting at one of the pistons. Allow fluid to run out until no air bubbles are present. Tighten the hose and repeat the procedure at the remaining three fittings. See Fig. 15.

4. Connect a battery to the pump. Run the system to fully retract or fully extend the pistons.

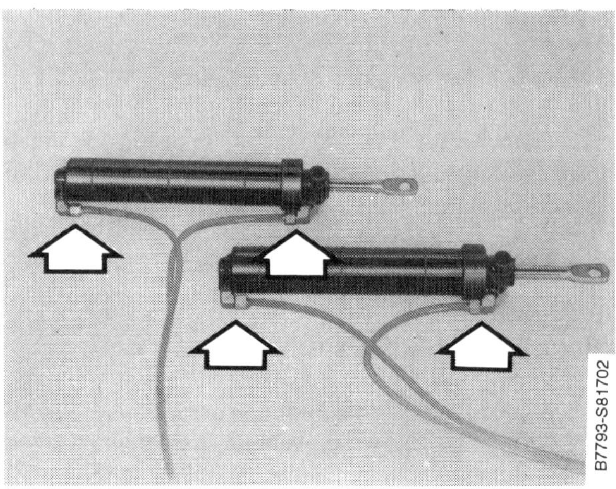

Fig. 15. Hydraulic hose fittings (arrows) at pistons used to bleed lines.

NOTE
- The electrical connection should have fuse protection. Use the same rating fuse as used in the circuit.
- Replenish the hydraulic fluid as the level drops during bleeding.

---

5. Repeat step 3 above. Run the pump and pistons in the opposite direction.
6. Repeat step 5 until the system is free of air.
7. Top up the fluid, tighten all hose connections, reinstall the fill plug and check for leaks.

Tightening torque
- Hydraulic hose fittings. . . . . 5.1 to 6.2 Nm (45 to 54 in-lb)

NOTE
The hydraulic system can be tested using a pressure gauge and fitting. The pressure gauge can be installed in place of the rear T-fitting. Be sure to bleed the system after pressure testing the pump.

Hydraulic pump
- minimum working pressure . . . . 25 bar (363 psi)

SPOILER ASSEMBLY

The spoiler assembly is held to the body using adhesive tape and nuts. There are two side pieces and one trunk lid piece.

To remove spoiler

1. Remove the rear seat as described in **851 Interior Trim and Upholstery**.
2. Remove the interior trim panels below the rear side windows as described in **830 Doors, Windows, and Lids**.
3. With the top down, remove the front nut holding the side spoiler to the body. See Fig. 16.

Fig. 16. Spoiler mounting nut (arrow) in body cavity.

4. Open the top approximately half-way and remove the center nut. See Fig. 17.

NOTE
Cars from VIN L701110 and later do not have a center nut.

WARNING
Do not allow anyone to operate the top when your hands are near the mechanism. The pistons have sufficient force to cause injury.

---

5. Working in the luggage compartment, remove the rear nut through the cutout in the carpeting. See Fig. 18.

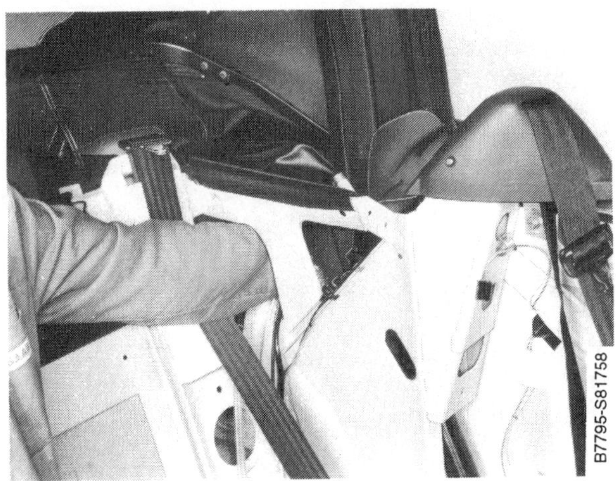

Fig. 17. Side spoiler center nut being removed through body side cavity.

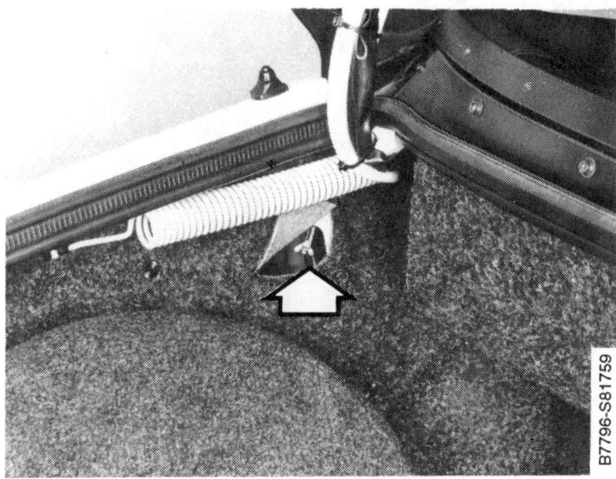

Fig. 18. Side spoiler rear nut (arrow) behind carpet cutout.

6. Unplug the hi-mount brake light connector. Remove the rubber plugs, retaining bolts and nuts for the rear mount spoiler. See Fig. 19.

7. Heat the spoiler with a heat gun to release the adhesive tape. See Fig. 20. Remove the spoiler.

CAUTION

• Use care when applying heat. Too much heat will damage the paint and spoiler.

• Pull the spoiler off gently to prevent damage to the paint.

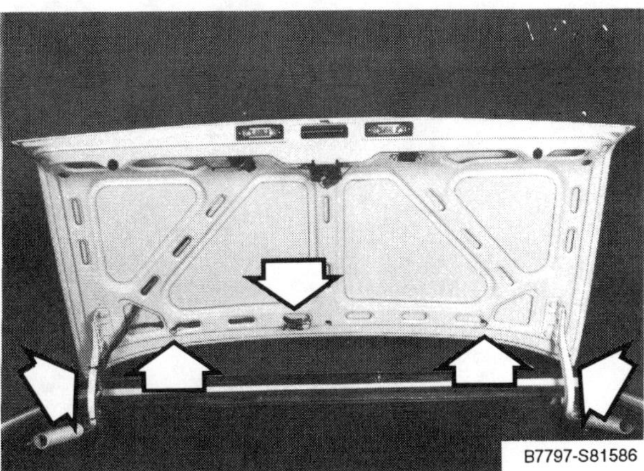

Fig. 19. Arrows show rear mount spoiler nuts and bolts to be removed from trunk lid.

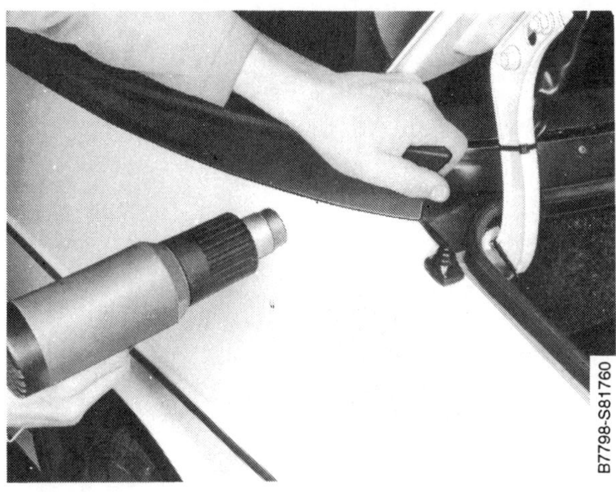

Fig. 20. Heat being applied to spoiler to loosen adhesive.

NOTE

The side spoiler has a cable at the rear mounting hole. This cable should be saved if the spoiler is being replaced.

---

8. Remove all old adhesive from the paint and spoiler.

Installation is the reverse of removal. New double-sided adhesive tape should be installed to the spoiler. If installing a new spoiler, install the cable for the side spoiler rear mount and a rubber washer on each stud. Apply a water sealant such as Sikaflex 255 around the hole for the hi-mount brake light wire harness.

820 Hood and Fenders

GENERAL

Fig. 1 shows an exploded view of the hood and related components. The hood is bolted to hinges at the radiator crossmember. The rear of the hood has locating pins and guides. The hood release mechanism is also mounted to the radiator crossmember. When the hood is closed, the locking pin engages the release mechanism. A safety catch prevents the hood from opening fully after the release mechanism has been disengaged.

WARNING

- Welding and grinding coated steel can produce a poisonous gas containing zinc-oxide. This type of work should always be carried out by experienced body technicians having the proper respiratory equipment and work area.

- 1990 and later models are equipped with an airbag or SRS system. The airbag is an explosive device. Do not do electric (arc) welding to cars equipped with SRS (airbag) without first disarming and removing the airbag unit. You could accidentally ignite the airbag, causing serious personal injury. See an authorized Saab dealer to disarm the system.

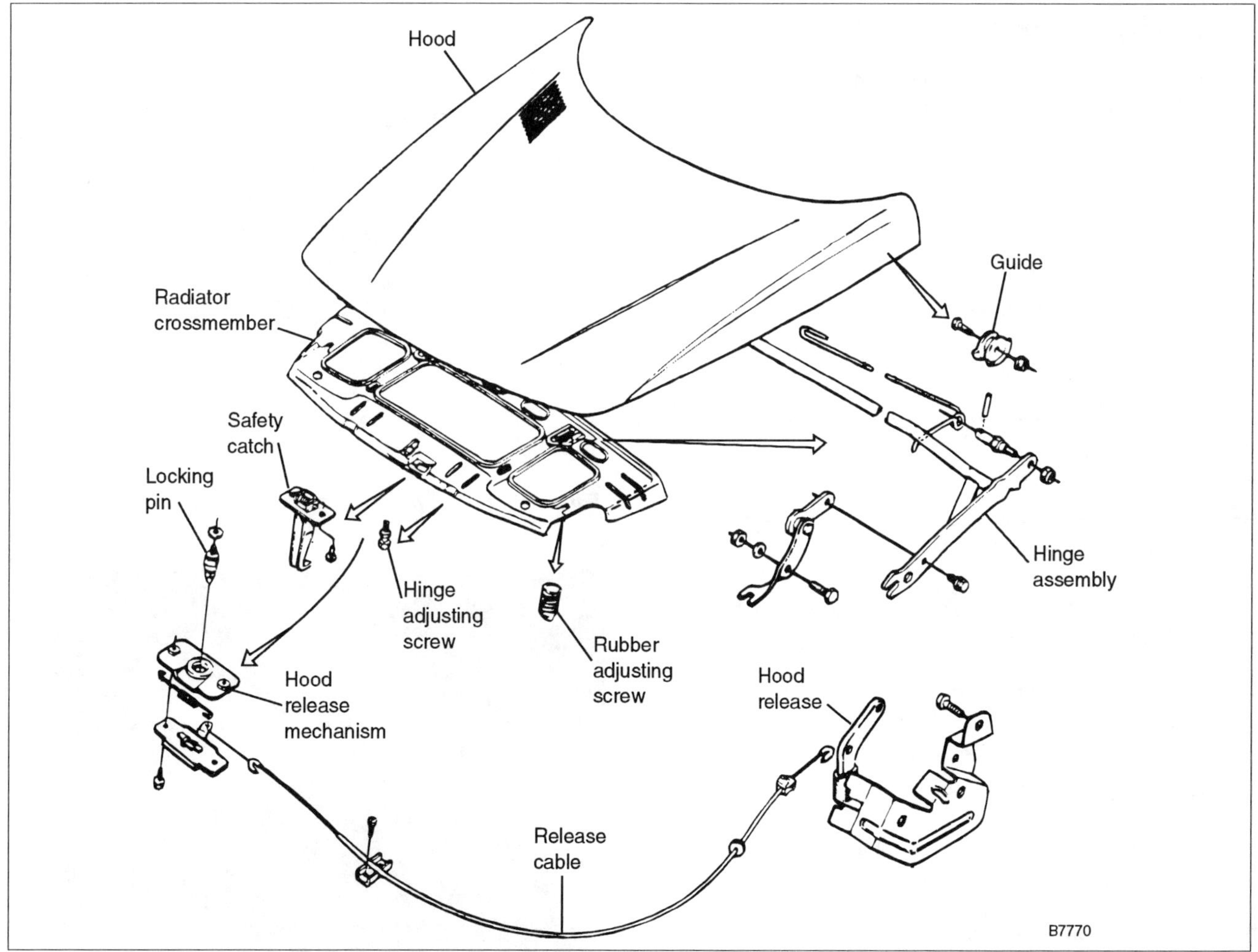

Fig. 1. Exploded view of hood assembly.

820

The front fenders are welded to the body to form part of the unit-body construction. See Fig. 2. Special tools and welding equipment are needed to replace a fender. Therefore, fender replacement is not covered in this manual.

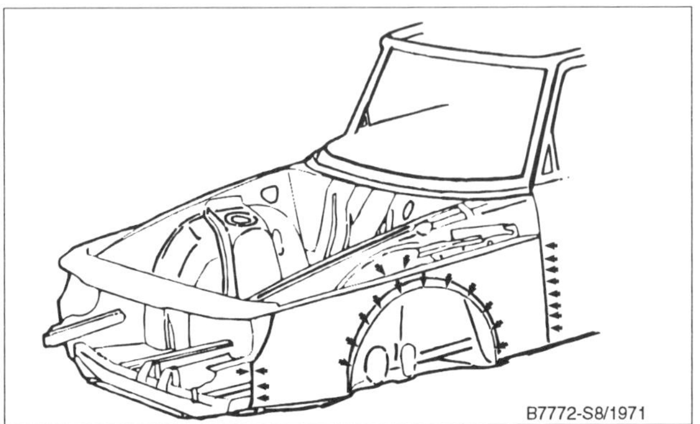

Fig. 2. Front fender welds (arrows).

To open hood if release cable is broken

If the hood cannot be opened using the hood release, a wire tool can be made to release the hood locking pin through the front grille. The tool dimensions are shown in Fig. 3.

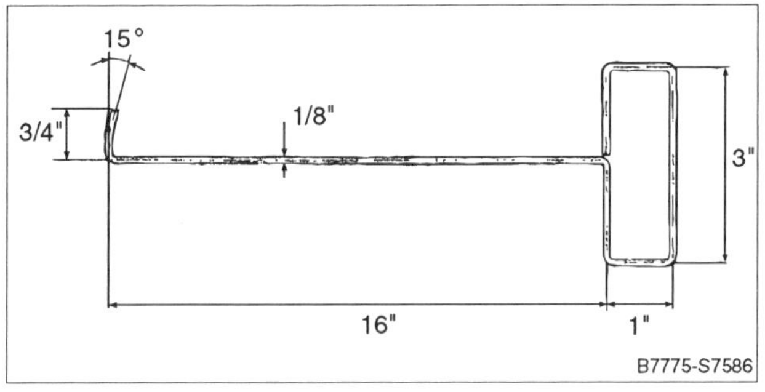

Fig. 3. Hood release tool can be made using 1/8 in. diameter wire. All dimensions are approximate.

1. Insert the tool through the grille and hook the rear of the lock mechanism. See Fig. 4.

2. Pull the latch toward the driver's side of the car until the hood releases.

To remove hood

1. Open the hood and then disconnect the hose for the windshield washer nozzles. See Fig. 5.

2. While supporting the hood with the aid of a helper, remove the mounting bolts for the hinge links. See Fig. 6.

3. Carefully lift the hood off the car.

Fig. 4. Hood lock being released using special tool. Grille shown removed for clarity.

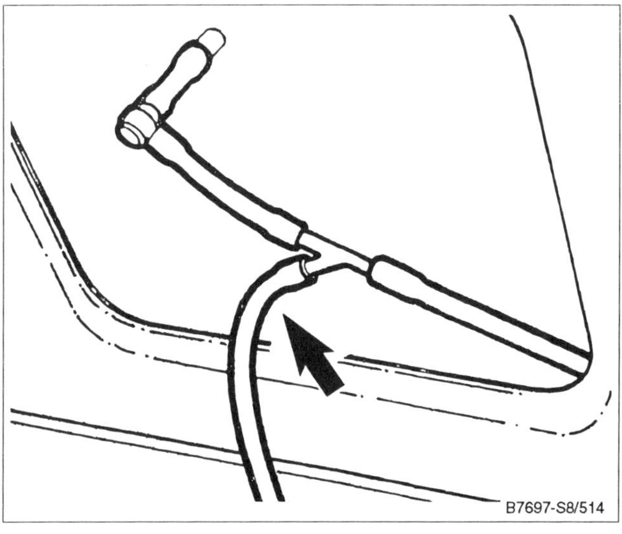

Fig. 5. Windshield washer nozzle hose (arrow).

Fig. 6. Hood hinge link mounting bolt being removed (arrow).

Installation is the reverse of removal. If installing a new hood, adjust its fit as described below.

Hood Alignment and Adjustment

The hood can be adjusted up-down, left-right, and fore-aft. The front up-down adjustment may require special shims on 1985 through 1989 models.

To adjust the up-down position at the front of the hood, loosen the locking pin. See Fig. 7. On 1985 through 1989 models, add or subtract shims under the pin until the adjustment is correct. On 1990 and later models, the shims are not required owing to the return spring. When the lock pin adjustment is correct, turn the two rubber adjusting screws (shown in Fig. 1) so that there is no play when pressing down on the top of the hood.

NOTE
A maximum shim thickness of 5 mm (3/16 in.) can be added between the pin and the hood.

Fig. 7. Locking pin on 1985 through 1989 models. Adjustment shims are between pin and hood (arrow).

To adjust the up-down position and the left-right position at the rear of the hood, the guides and guide pin plates can be repositioned. The guide is mounted to the hood (see Fig. 1) and the guide pin plate is mounted to the body with the internal-hex head screws. Loosen the guide plate mounting screws and then adjust the position of the guides. When the guide position is correct, tighten the guide pin plate screws.

If the front of the hood is not centered from left to right, the release mechanism mounting bolts can be loosened to reposition the mechanism. See Fig. 8.

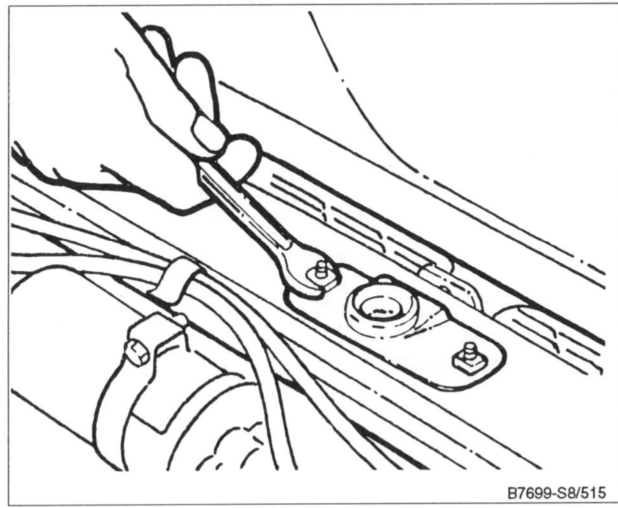

Fig. 8. Hood release mechanism mounting bolt being loosened.

Adjusting the fore/aft position of the hood can be done by changing the position of the hinge adjusting bolts at the radiator member. See Fig. 9. Making this adjustment requires removal of the front grille.

Fig. 9. Hood fore/aft adjusting screw at front radiator crossmember.

830 Doors, Windows, and Lids

DOORS AND WINDOWS

This section covers the removal and installation of the doors, the interior door panels, the window regulators, and the window glass.

Doors

The doors can be easily removed once the interior trim panels have been removed and the electrical connectors disconnected. Models with Torx head hinge bolts require a special Torx socket. After installing, adjust the door so that it correctly aligns with the body allowing it to open and close properly.

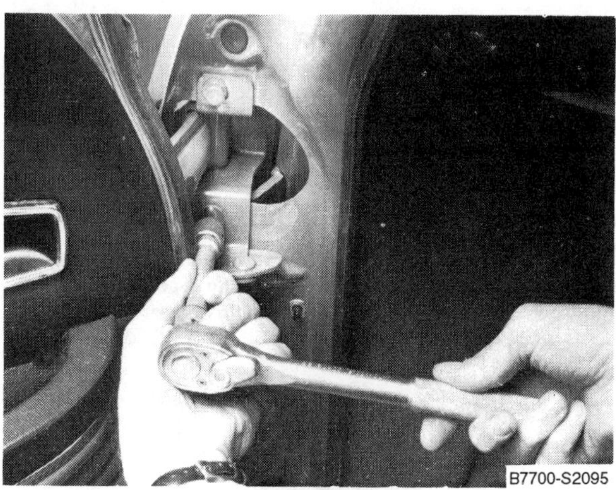

Fig. 1. Front door hinge-to-body bolts being removed.

To remove and install doors

1. Disconnect the negative (–) battery cable.

2. Remove the interior door panel and moisture barrier as described later under **To remove interior door panel.** Where applicable, disconnect the connectors for the power windows, power mirrors, and central locking. Pull the wiring harness from the door.

3. Have a helper hold the door, then remove the six hinge bolts for the upper and lower hinges and remove the door. See Fig. 1.

NOTE

• Before loosening the bolts, scribe a mark showing the position of the hinge on the body so the door can be realigned in its original position.

• If a helper is not available, support the door with a floor jack and protective padding.

• On rear doors, the trim covering the B-pillar must be removed to reach the nuts. See Fig. 2.

Fig. 2. Rear door hinge-to-body nuts being removed. Trim (arrow) has been removed from the B-pillar to reveal nuts.

Installation is the reverse of removal. After installing the door, adjust it as described below. When installing a new replacement door, the door parts from the old door will have to be transferred to the new door.

To adjust doors

Correct adjustment or alignment of the door allows for proper opening and closing. Adjustment also prevents wind noise. If the hinge bolts inside the door or the striker plate have not been disturbed, there is no need to adjust them.

NOTE

Some models have a locating screw in the hinge plate which must be removed before adjusting the door. See Fig. 3. This screw can be discarded after adjusting the door.

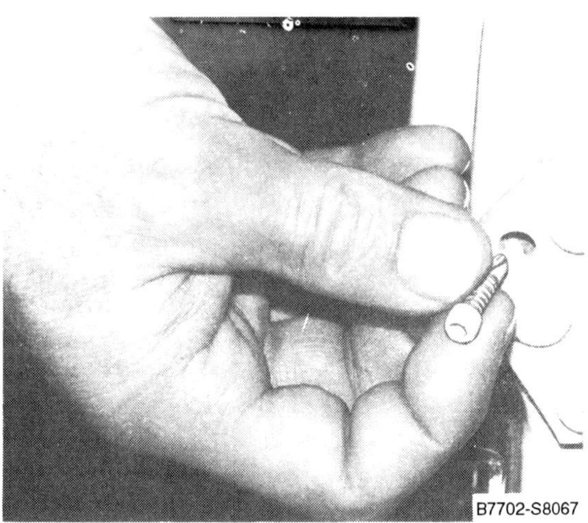

Fig. 3. Locating screw being removed before adjusting door.

1. Lubricate the hinges and latch mechanism with engine oil.

2. To adjust the flush fit of the front doors to the body, loosen the hinge-to-body bolts as shown in Fig. 1 above. The door can then be moved on the slotted holes in the hinge. Tighten the bolts, close the door and check the adjustment. Readjust as necessary.

3. To adjust the up-down or fore-aft position of the front doors, loosen the hinge-to-door bolts. See Fig. 4. This adjustment can only be done after the interior trim panel has been removed.

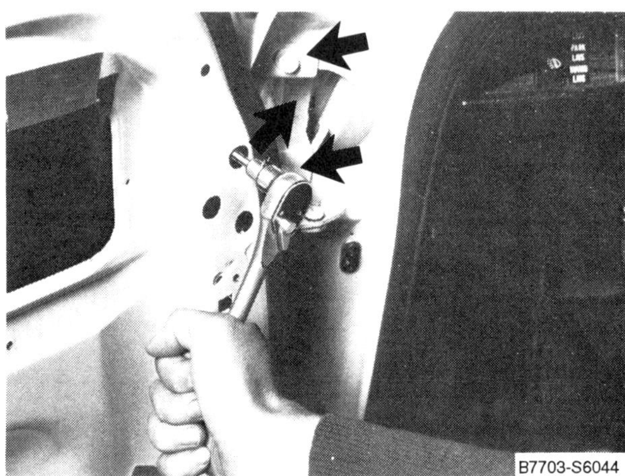

Fig. 4. Hinge-to-door bolt being loosened to adjust up-down or for-aft position of front door. The bolts for adjusting the flush fit of the door can also be seen (arrows).

4. Rear door flush fit and up-down position can be adjusted after loosening the hinge-to-door bolts. See Fig. 5.

Fig. 5. Rear hinge-to-door bolt being loosened to adjust flush fit and up-down position of door.

5. Adjust the striker plate so the door is not forced up or down when closing. Also check that the door opens and closes smoothly. Loosen the screws as shown in Fig. 6 to adjust the striker plate.

Fig. 6. Striker plate being adjusted. An impact driver can be used to loosen screws.

NOTE
Additional adjustment of the rear doors can be done by loosening the hinge-to-body nuts. See Fig. 2 shown above.

To remove interior door panel

Although the procedures given below apply to the front doors, they can also be used as a guide for removing the interior trim for the rear doors.

1. Unscrew the locking knob. Where applicable, carefully pry off the disc from the window crank and remove the crank screw and crank. See Fig. 7.

NOTE
Before removing the window crank, make a note of its position with the window closed.

---

2. On sedan models, pry out the trim cover for the inner door handle. Remove the screws that hold the armrest to the door. Then carefully pry off the panel by working around the perimeter of the door. The panel is held in place by retaining clips. Lift the panel up slightly to remove it.

3. On hatchback and convertible models, remove the door pull retaining screw and remove the door pull. Slide the trim insert panel up and off its mounting clips. Remove the screws holding the panel to the door. See Fig. 8.

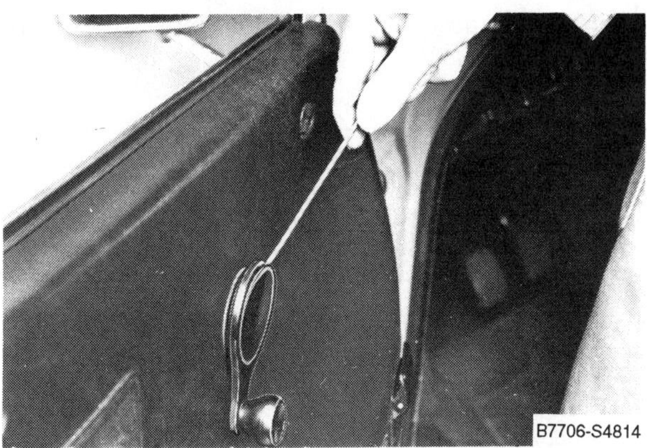

Fig. 7. Window crank trim cover being pried off.

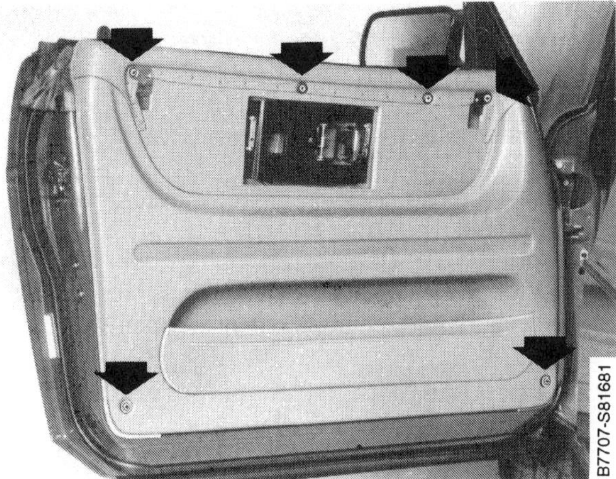

Fig. 8. Door panel retaining screws (arrows) on hatchback and convertible models. Door pull and upper trim insert panel removed.

4. Carefully remove the moisture barrier from the door.

Installation is the reverse of removal. Always test the window, mirror, and locking functions before reinstalling the panel. Replace any damaged retaining clips. If the moisture barrier is handled carefully and kept clean, it can be reused. Apply thread locking compound to the window crank handle screw.

NOTE
Always replace the moisture barrier if it becomes damaged.

Windows

This section covers removal and installation of the door windows, window regulators, and power window motors. The door windows are controlled by window regulators that move the glass in fixed channels. To replace the power window motor, the regulator assembly must first be removed from the door.

WARNING
Always disconnect the electric window motor when working on it. The motor is powerful enough to cause injury if it should come on by accident.

NOTE
Replacement of the windshield, the rear windows, and fixed side windows is not covered here. These windows are held in place with weather-tight seals. Special equipment and techniques are required to replace these windows.

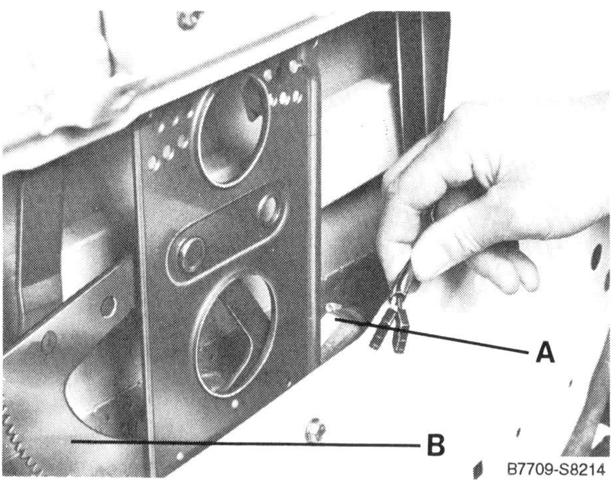

Fig. 10. Connector for power window motor disconnected. Also shown is motor **(A)** and gear sector **(B)**.

To remove and install front power window regulator

1. Disconnect the negative (–) battery cable.
2. Remove the interior door trim and moisture barrier as described earlier.
3. Pry off the inner window weatherstrip spring clips and remove the inner weatherstrip from the door. See Fig. 9.

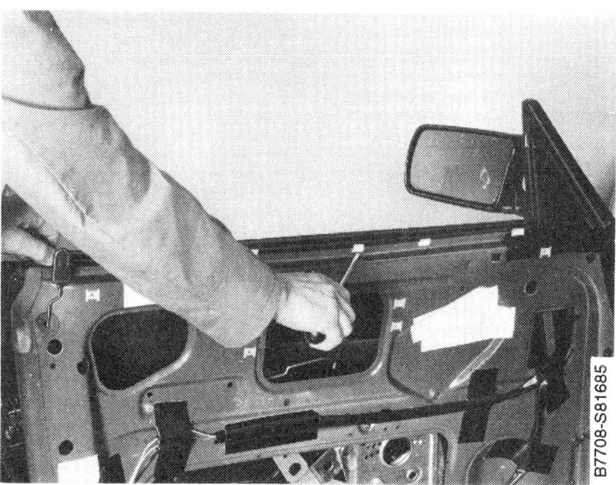

Fig. 9. Spring clip for inner weatherstrip being removed.

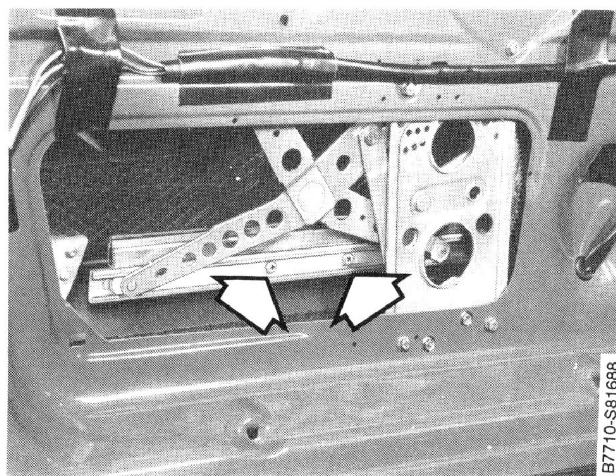

Fig. 11. Regulator-to-window glass support mounting screws (arrows). Support glass after removing screws.

4. Locate the window motor electrical connector inside the door and disconnect it. See Fig. 10.
5. While supporting the window glass, remove the screws holding the glass to the regulator. See Fig. 11.
6. Remove the window glass by rotating it to the vertical position and sliding it up out of the door.
7. Remove the four bolts holding the regulator assembly to the door and remove the assembly through the opening in the door. See Fig. 12.

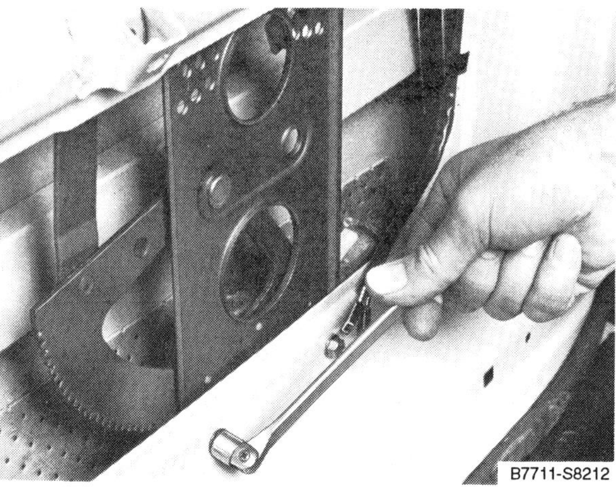

Fig. 12. Regulator-to-door mounting bolt being removed. Two bolts (not shown) at top must be removed also.

8. Remove the three bolts holding the motor to the regulator. See Fig. 13.

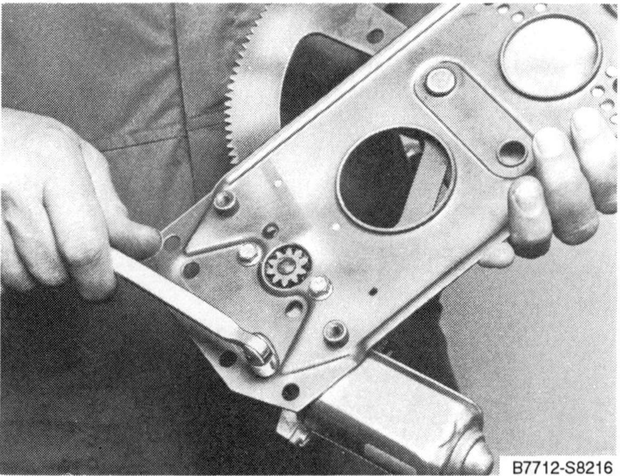

Fig. 13. Power motor mounting bolt being removed.

NOTE

The plastic moisture barrier on the old motor must be reinstalled on the new motor to keep out moisture.

Installation is the reverse of removal. Test the new motor before installing it in the door. A thin film of white grease can be applied to moving parts.

NOTE

The power motor can be tested by disconnecting the connectors at the motor and testing for voltage when the window switch is pushed in either direction (ignition key on). If power is present at the connector, the motor is faulty. If voltage is not present, the problem lies in the switch or other part of the circuit. Troubleshoot the power window circuit using the appropriate diagram in **371 Wiring Diagrams, Fuses and Relays**.

To remove and install rear power window regulator (except convertible)

1. Disconnect the negative (–) battery cable. Remove the window switch from the interior trim.

2. Remove the interior door trim and moisture barrier as described earlier. Disconnect the electrical connector for the power window located inside the door.

3. While supporting the window glass, remove the screws that hold the glass to the regulator arm. See Fig. 11 shown above. Then push the window up until it is fully closed.

CAUTION

Once the window-to-regulator screws are removed, the window should be supported. With the window fully closed, tape the glass to the door frame to prevent it from falling.

NOTE

Removal of the rear door window requires that the fixed side pane be removed so that the rear window channel can be moved out of the way. The window channel is held in place with two screws that can be accessed after removing the rubber concealing plugs in the door.

---

4. Remove the five screws that hold the regulator assembly to the door. See Fig. 14. Remove the assembly through the opening in the door.

NOTE

Slide the regulator arm forward to help in removing the assembly from the door.

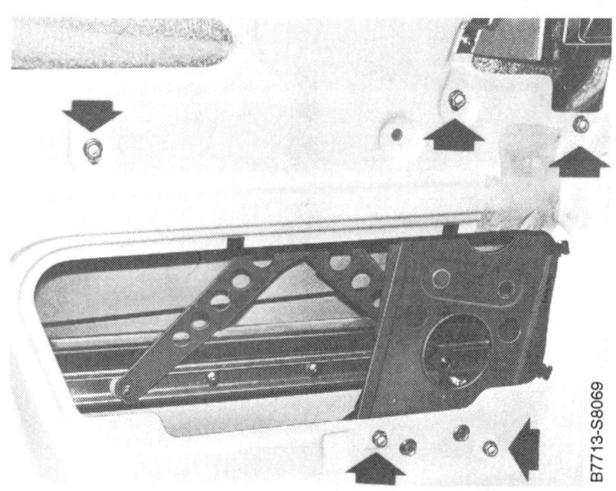

Fig. 14. Rear door regulator mounting screws (arrows).

5. Remove the screws that hold the motor to the regulator.

NOTE

Always reinstall the old protective cover to the window motor.

Installation is the reverse of removal. Test the new motor before installing it in the door. A thin film of white grease can be applied to moving parts.

To remove and install rear power window regulator (convertible)

The regulator assembly on convertibles is located in the body cavity. The regulator is removed as a complete assembly together with the window glass.

1. Disconnect the negative (–) battery cable.

2. Remove the rear seat cushion, backrest, and interior trim panel as described in **851 Interior Trim and Upholstery**.

3. Remove the seatbelt cover screws and slide the cover down. See Fig. 15.

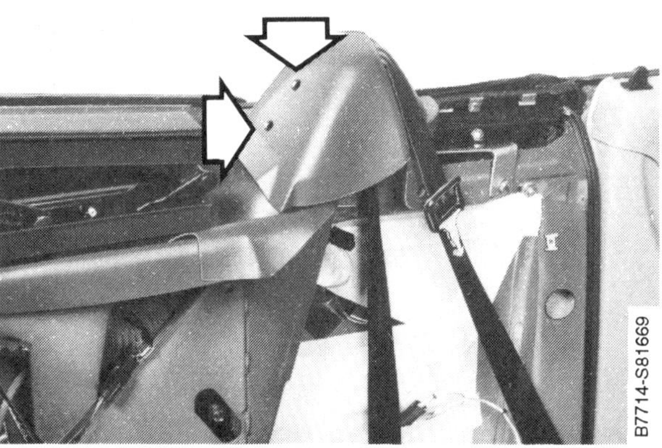

Fig. 15. Screws for seatbelt cover (arrows) to be removed. Slide cover down seatbelt.

4. Loosen the seatbelt guide bolt and pivot the belt guide in. Remove the two window bracket bolts. See Fig. 16.

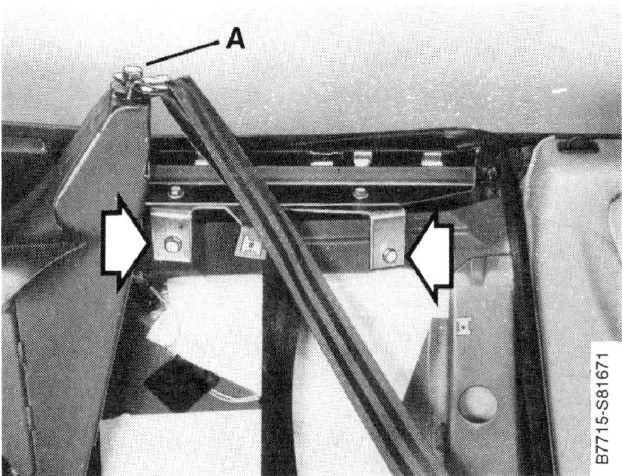

Fig. 16. Loosen seatbelt guide bolt **A**. Remove two window bracket bolts (arrows).

5. Carefully pry off the outer window seal.

NOTE
The front of the seal is glued to the body.

---

6. Raise the window up until it contacts the window stop. Remove the four nuts holding the regulator assembly to the body.

7. Using a hex key, screw the regulator studs in. See Fig. 17.

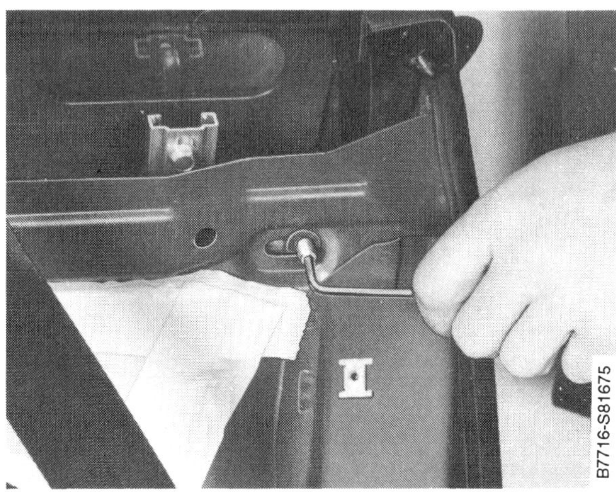

Fig. 17. Regulator mounting stud being turned in to gain clearance with body panel.

8. Pull the window glass and regulator assembly out of the body.

NOTE
The glass can be removed from the regulator by removing the three regulator-to-glass mounting bolts.

Installation is the reverse of removal. Tighten the seatbelt guide bolt to the value given below. Reinstall the outer window seal using contact adhesive around the seal and the molding.

Tightening torque
- seatbelt guide bolt to body (convertible models) . . . 24 to 40 Nm (18 to 30 lb-ft)

To remove and install front manual window regulator

1. Remove the interior door trim and moisture barrier as described above.

2. While supporting the window glass, remove the screws that hold the glass to the regulator arm. See Fig. 11 above.

NOTE

The window glass can be removed from the door after removing the inner weatherstrip from the door. See Fig. 9 above. With the weatherstrip removed, rotate the glass to a vertical position and slide it up and out of the door.

3. Remove the four bolts holding the regulator to the door and remove the regulator. See Fig. 18.

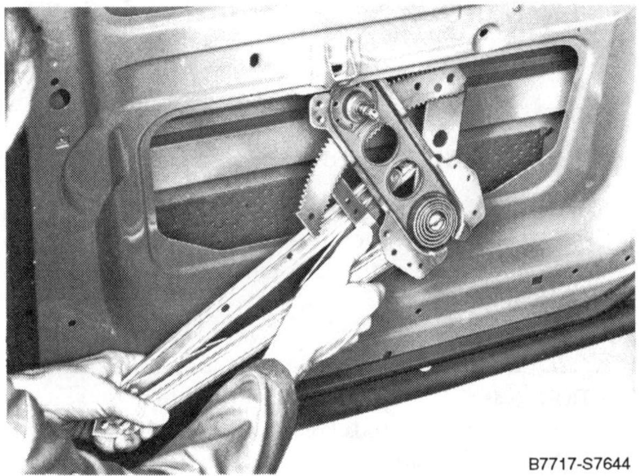

Fig. 18. Regulator being removed from front door.

Installation is the reverse of removal. A thin film of white grease can be applied to moving parts. Test the window regulator before installing the interior door trim.

To remove and install rear manual window regulator

1. Remove the door handle, interior door trim and moisture barrier as described above.

2. Support the window glass while removing the screws that hold the glass to the regulator arm. Slide the window up until it is in its fully closed position.

3. Remove the bolts holding the regulator to the door and remove the regulator. See Fig. 19.

Installation is the reverse of removal. A thin film of white grease can be applied to moving parts. Test the window regulator before installing the interior door trim.

NOTE

Removal of the rear door window requires that the fixed side pane be removed so that the rear window channel can be moved out of the way. The window channel is held in place with two screws that can be accessed after removing the rubber concealing plugs in the door.

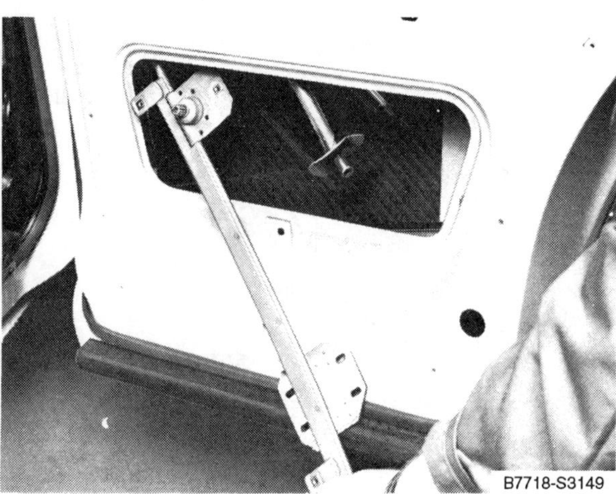

Fig. 19. Rear door manual regulator being removed.

LOCKS, HANDLES, AND LATCH MECHANISMS

This section covers replacement of the lock cylinders, the door handles, and the latch mechanisms. Also covered here is replacement of the central locking motors.

For information on repairing the ignition lock cylinder see **432 Manual Transmission Controls**. For information on wiring for the central locking system see **371 Wiring Diagrams, Fuses and Relays.**

NOTE

- Always test all of the latch and locking functions including the child safety feature after completing any repairs.
- When working on the locking system always keep a spare key outside the car in case the system locks accidentally.

To replace door handle

1. Remove the interior door trim and moisture barrier as described earlier. Working inside the door, remove the front door handle mounting screw.

2. Working at the outside door edge, loosen the rear screw for the door handle bracket about four turns. See Fig. 20.

NOTE

On 4-door models, the rear screw for the rear door is hidden behind the weather strip.

3. Rotate the handle to the position shown in Fig. 21 and remove the handle from the door.

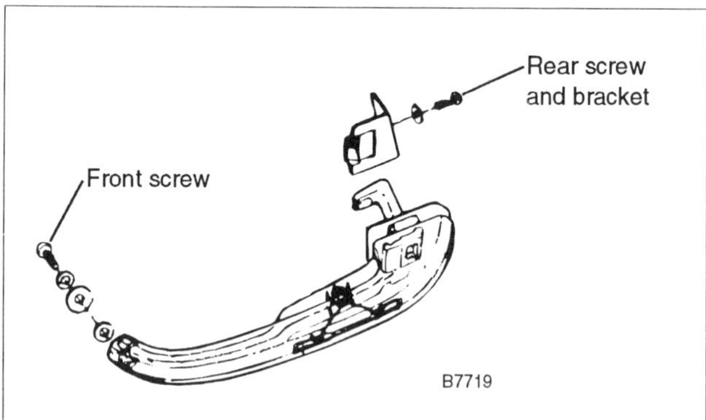

Fig. 20. Door handle assembly.

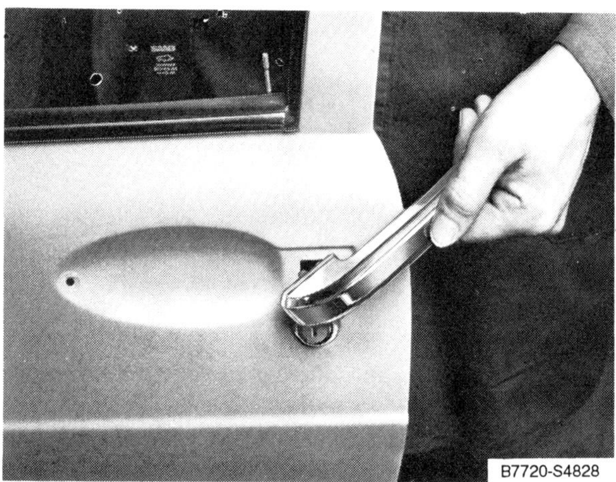

Fig. 21. Rotate door handle as shown to remove.

CAUTION
Do not force the handle when removing it from the door. The latch mechanism inside the door could be damaged.

Installation is the reverse of removal.

To replace door lock mechanism

Fig. 22 shows the front and rear door lock mechanisms.

1. Close the window. Remove the locking knob, interior door trim and moisture barrier as described above.

2. Manually rotate the latch mechanism on the door jamb to the latched (closed) position and remove the three retaining screws on the door edge.

NOTE
If the screws are frozen they can be removed with an impact driver.

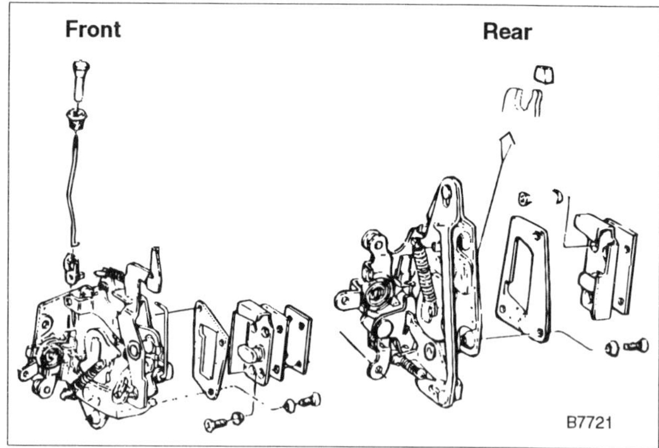

Fig. 22. Front (left) and rear (right) door lock mechanisms.

3. Working inside the door, remove the link rods from the inside door handle, the lock cylinder, and the central lock motor.

CAUTION
• When removing the link rods from plastic parts do not stress the plastic as it will break.

• Do not bend or distort the link rods. The latch mechanism will not work properly when the bent links are reinstalled.

NOTE
The central lock motor can be removed to gain more working space inside the door. Remove the locking motor as described below.

---

4. Loosen, but do not remove, the screws for the outer door handle as described above.

NOTE
Loosening the outer door handle screws will allow some clearance for the latch mechanism to be removed. The outer door handle can be completely removed if necessary.

---

5. Carefully work the latch mechanism free and remove it from the door.

Installation is the reverse of removal. Apply a thin film of chassis grease (Saab special chassis grease —ESSO Nebula EP2 or equivalent) to the latch mechanism. Test all the latch functions before installing the interior trim panel.

To replace trunk lid lock mechanism

1. Remove the central lock motor as described later under the appropriate heading.

CAUTION
When removing the link rods from plastic parts do not stress the plastic as it will break.

2. Remove the trunk lid lock cylinder as described below.

3. Remove the two bolts for the latch mechanism, then carefully remove the latch from its mount.

Installation is the reverse of removal.

To replace hatchback lock mechanism

1. Remove the interior trim panel from the lid.

2. Working from inside the lid, disconnect the link rod from the control arm on the lock cylinder. Remove the two screws that hold the latch mechanism to the lid and remove the latch mechanism. See Fig. 23.

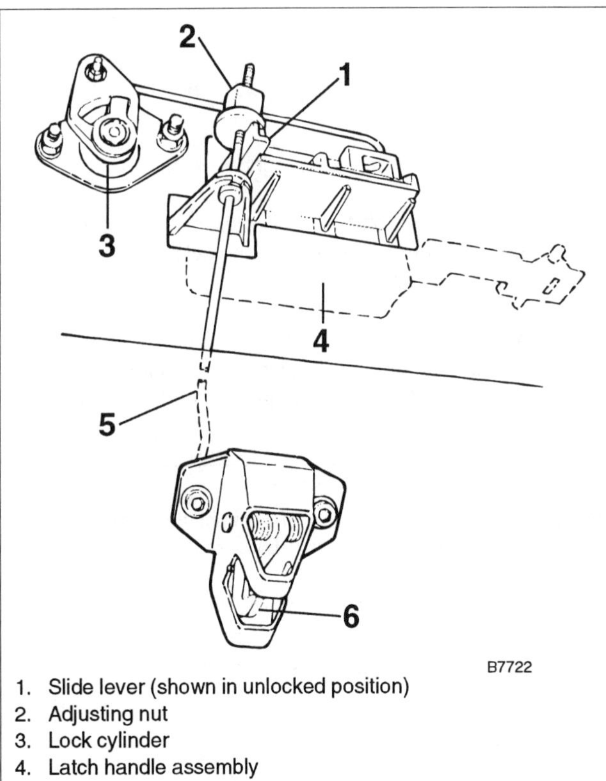

1. Slide lever (shown in unlocked position)
2. Adjusting nut
3. Lock cylinder
4. Latch handle assembly
5. Link rod
6. Latch mechanism

Fig. 23. Latch mechanism used on hatchback models.

3. Working inside the lid remove the five nuts holding the latch handle assembly to the lid. Disconnect the license plate light connectors. Remove the handle assembly.

Installation is the reverse of removal. Clean, then lubricate all sliding surfaces with a thin film of grease. The adjusting nut can be adjusted so the handle has a little slack before it releases the hatchback lid.

To replace door lock cylinder

Replacing the door lock cylinder requires removing the interior trim panel from the door. Fig. 24 shows an exploded view of the lock including the U-shaped spring clip that holds the lock to the door.

NOTE
Lock cylinders matching your key code can be specially ordered from Saab. The key code is also stamped on the lock cylinder barrel.

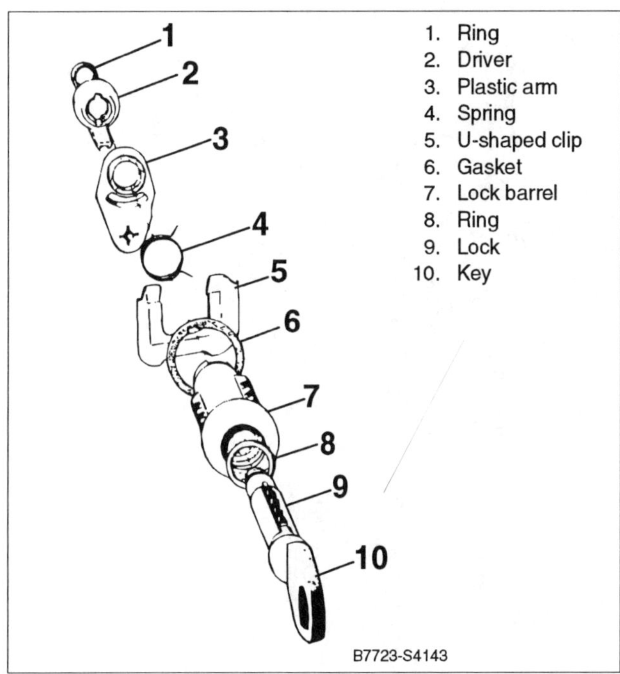

1. Ring
2. Driver
3. Plastic arm
4. Spring
5. U-shaped clip
6. Gasket
7. Lock barrel
8. Ring
9. Lock
10. Key

Fig. 24. Door lock cylinder.

1. Put the window in the closed (up) position. Remove the interior door panel trim as described earlier.

2. Unhook the link rod from the lock cylinder plastic arm.

3. Carefully pull down the U-shaped clip using pliers. Note the cutouts in the lock cylinder body for the clip.

NOTE

It is always a good idea to replace the U-shaped clip with a new one when replacing the lock. The old clip may become distorted and will not hold the lock cylinder properly.

Installation is the reverse of removal. Lubricate the lock cylinder with lock lubricant after installation.

To replace trunk lid or hatchback lid lock cylinder

Fig. 25 shows the exploded view of the trunk lid lock cylinder. The hatchback lid lock cylinder is shown in Fig 26.

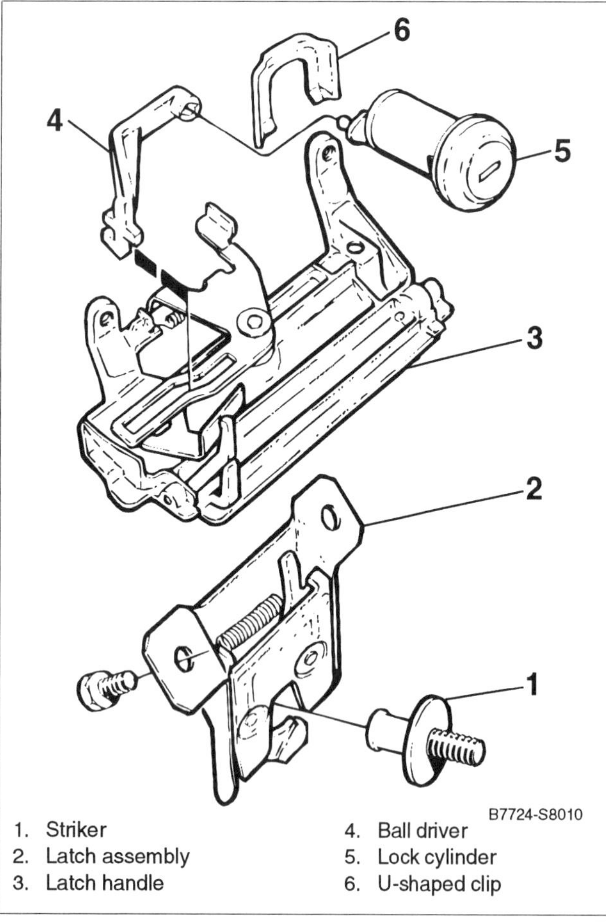

Fig. 25. Exploded view of lock cylinder and latch handle on sedan trunk lid.

NOTE

Lock cylinders matching your key code can be specially ordered from Saab. The key code is also stamped on the lock cylinder barrel.

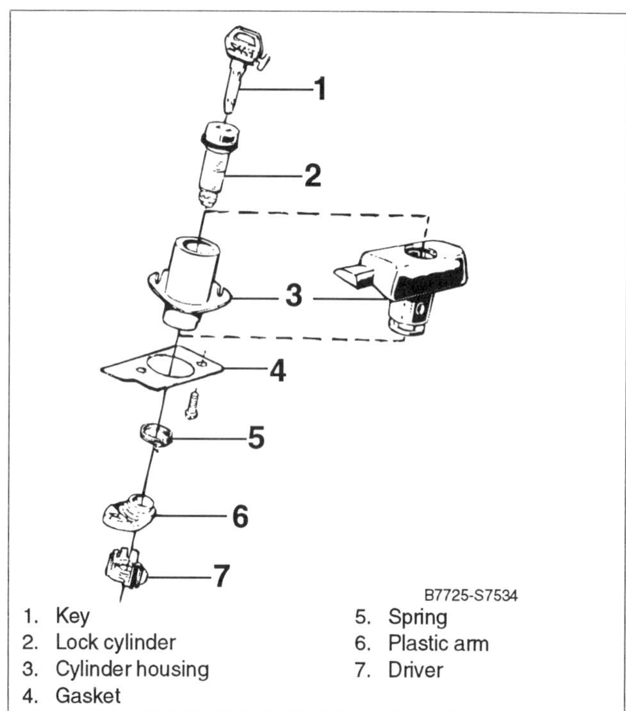

Fig. 26. Exploded view of lock cylinder for hatchback lid.

1. Remove interior trim as described earlier.
2. On sedans, pull off the U-shaped clip and disconnect the ball driver from the back of the cylinder. Pull the lock center from the trunk lid.
3. On hatchbacks, remove the link rod from the plastic arm. Remove the two lock cylinder mounting screws and then pull the lock cylinder assembly from the lid.

NOTE

On models with central locking, disconnect the locking motor then remove the motor retaining bolts and move the motor slightly.

Installation is the reverse of removal.

To remove central locking motors

For more information on electrical tests of the central locking system, see **371 Wiring Diagrams, Fuses and Relays**.

1. Where applicable, make sure the door windows are closed. Remove the interior trim panel as described earlier.
2. Locate the door/lid lock motor and unhook the link rod from the motor.

3. Disconnect the electrical connector for the lock motor. Remove the two screws holding the motor to the door or lid.

NOTE
Front door and hatchback lock motors are mounted on brackets.

Installation is the reverse of removal. Test the central lock motor before reinstalling the interior trim panels.

CAUTION
The lock motors should not be tested using a battery or power supply. Damage to the motor may result. Test the motors only through the central locking control unit.

HATCHBACK AND TRUNK LID

The hatchback or trunk lid can easily be removed. After installation, the fit of the lid should be carefully adjusted.

WARNING
The hatchback lid is very heavy and should not be removed unless two people, or more, are available to help.

To remove and install hatchback lid

1. Disconnect the negative (–) battery cable. Remove the ground strap near the hinge. Disconnect the electrical connectors to the heating element, central locking motor, and any lighting.

2. Mark the position of the hinges using a scribe. Loosen, but do not remove, the hinge screws.

3. With a helper supporting the rear of the lid, remove the gas assist struts on each side.

WARNING
- The hatchback lid has no support once the gas assist struts are removed. The lid could fall causing injury.
- Do not attempt to disassemble the gas assist struts. They are under very high pressure and could explode.

4. Remove the hinge screws that were loosened earlier, then carefully lift the lid from the body.

NOTE
After removing the lid, place small blocks of wood under the lid hinges to help position the hinge during installation. See Fig. 27.

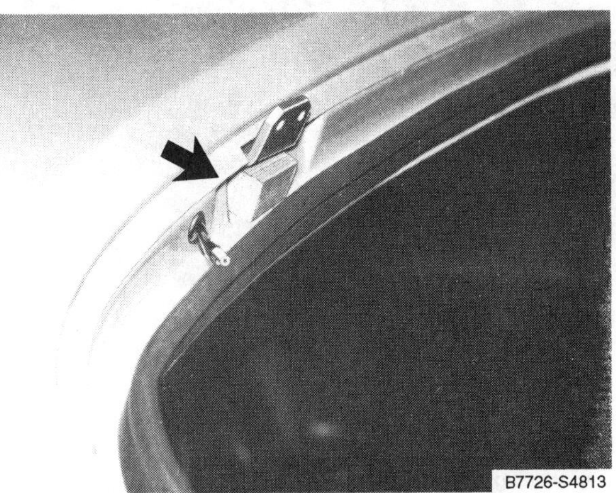

Fig. 27. Small blocks of wood (arrow) used to hold lid hinges in up position for lid installation. Be sure to remove the blocks before shutting the lid.

Installation is the reverse of removal. The lid can be adjusted for proper alignment by loosening the screws at the hinges or striker plate. Always test the heated rear window and central locking functions.

CAUTION
Do not close the hatchback lid if the gas assist struts are not attached to the lid. The struts and the body could be damaged.

To remove and install trunk lid

1. Disconnect the negative (–) battery cable. Disconnect the electrical connectors next to the left hinge and cut any wire ties holding the harness to the lid.

2. Mark the position of the hinges on the lid. Remove the two nuts holding the trunk lid to the hinge mounting. See Fig. 28.

3. Installation is the reverse of removal. Adjustment to the lid is made by loosening the nuts shown in Fig. 28.

After completing the adjustment, secure the wiring harness to the lid and test all electrical functions.

Fig. 28. Trunk lid hinge mounting nuts (**A**) to be removed. The mounting nuts (**B**) at the hinge holes do not need to be removed.

NOTE

The opening effort of the assist springs can be adjusted by repositioning the spring end into one of the three openings in the body. See Fig. 29.

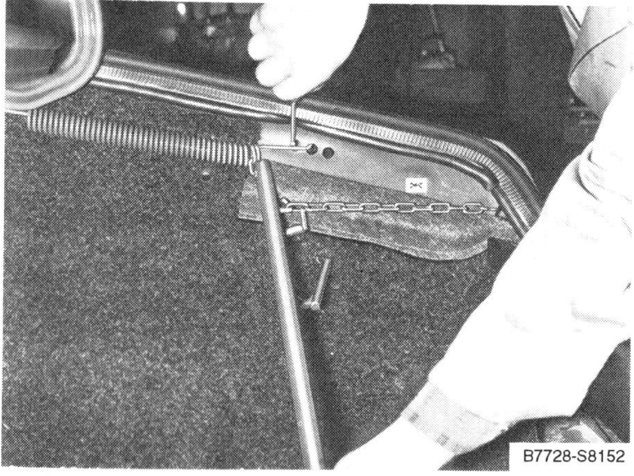

Fig. 29. Trunk lid assist being adjusted by positioning spring in second cutout. The tool shown is used to stretch the

SUNROOF

Two types of sunroofs, electric and manual, are installed in cars covered by this manual. This section covers removal, installation, and adjustment of the sunroof. For troubleshooting information of the power sunroof see **371 Wiring Diagrams, Fuses and Relays**.

The electric sunroof is driven by a motor and cable assembly. The motor is located in the luggage compartment, near the spare tire. The drive cables run along each C-pillar up to the sunroof.

NOTE

To replace the drive cables, the interior headliner and the entire sunroof assembly must first be removed. On sedans, the headliner can only be removed after the rear window has been removed. Because of the nature of this procedure, it is not covered in this manual.

Water drainage hoses are located at the corners of the sunroof assembly. The front hoses run down through the corner A-pillars. The rear hoses run down through the rear pillars. These hoses must not be clogged or water may leak into the passenger compartment.

To remove sunroof

1. Slide the sunroof back and remove the four screws at the front edge of the roof panel. See Fig. 30.

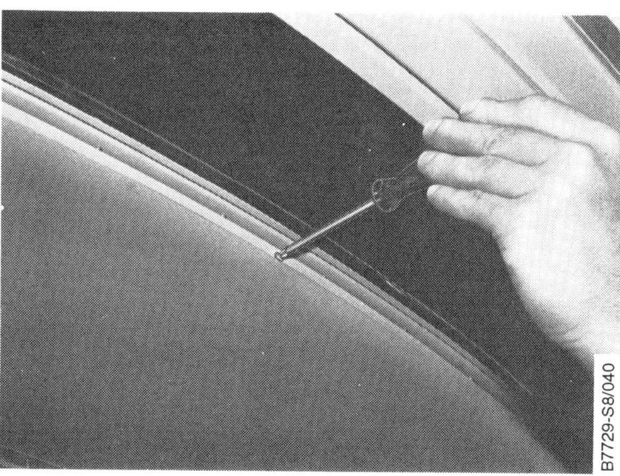

Fig. 30. Screws being removed at sunroof front edge.

2. Close the sunroof panel until a gap of 3/4 in (19 mm) remains. Then remove the top panel by raising it up at the front and pulling it forward and out.

3. Working at the front corners, remove the guide clip nuts and the clips. See Fig. 31.

4. Working at the rear corners, pry back the locking tabs for the rear guide nuts. Remove the guide nuts and pull the rear guides off of the sunroof panel frame. See Fig. 32. Where applicable, set aside the springs, mountings, bushings and sleeves.

5. Push the panel forward as far as it will go. Loosen, but do not remove the screws at the rear guide clips. See Fig. 33. Slide the clips outward as far as possible.

6. Remove the panel frame by raising the front edge while pulling it forward.

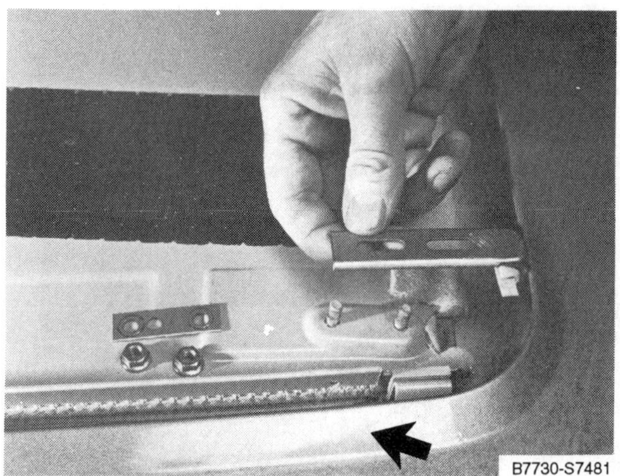

Fig. 31. Front guide clip being removed. Windbreak shown at arrow.

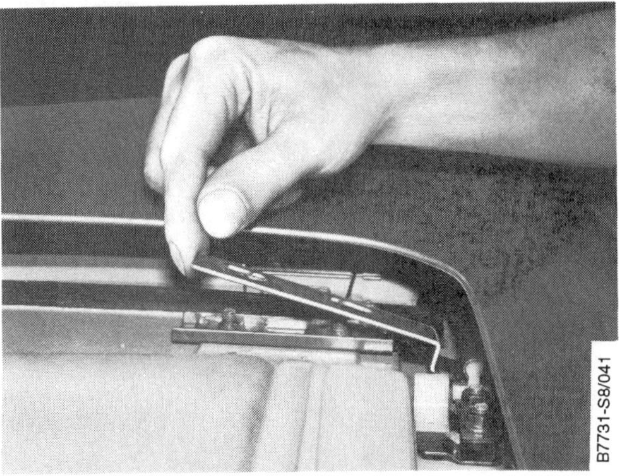

Fig. 32. Rear guide being removed. Model with power sunroof shown.

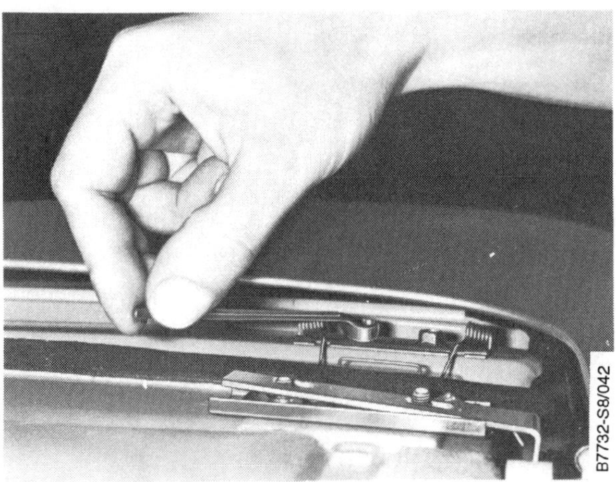

Fig. 33. Rear guide clip being loosened. Early model shown uses nuts instead of screws.

To install sunroof

Before installing the sunroof assembly, lubricate all sliding surfaces with a coat of petroleum jelly (Vaseline).

1. Install and position the panel frame against the front stops, center the frame in the sunroof opening and tighten the front guide clip nuts to obtain the clearance shown below. See Fig. 34.

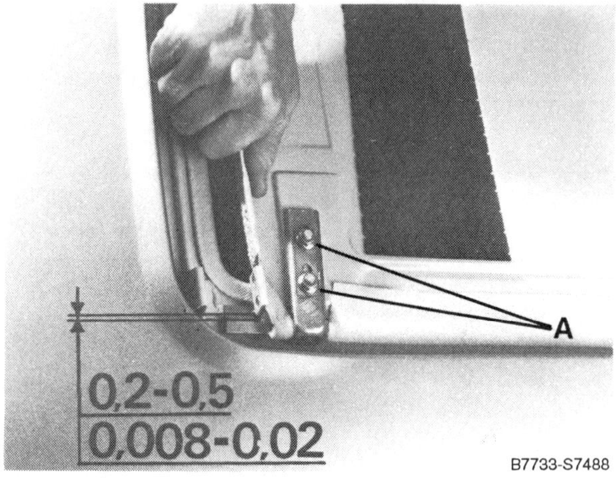

Fig. 34. Sunroof panel clearance being adjusted. Tighten nuts (**A**) when clearance is correct.

2. With the panel against the front stops, install the rear guide clips and loosely install the clip screws if they were removed earlier.

3. Have a helper gently press up on the rear edge of the panel from inside the car and then slide the guide clips into position.

NOTE

Pressing up on the rear of the panel frame will bend it slightly allowing the rear guide clips to be pushed back to their original positions.

---

4. Tighten the rear guide clip and the rear guide fasteners.

5. Position the sunroof frame as far forward as possible.

6. Install the sunroof panel into the sunroof panel frame, inserting the back first. Make sure the tab on the panel engages the spring clips on the frame. Push down and back on the panel until it locks into place.

7. Carefully slide the sunroof back while checking that the sunroof clears the panel. Install the four screws at the front edge.

CAUTION
If the sunroof top contacts the panel the paint may be scratched. Move the panel slowly to check that it clears the body sufficiently.

8. Close the sunroof top and check for a uniform gap around the opening.

9. Check that the rear of the sunroof top is flush with the roof when closed. If necessary, adjust the sunroof top height by first removing it as described above. Adjust the guide shoe screw as shown in Fig. 35. Reinstall the sunroof top and recheck the height.

CAUTION
Be careful not to scratch the paint when adjusting the screw.

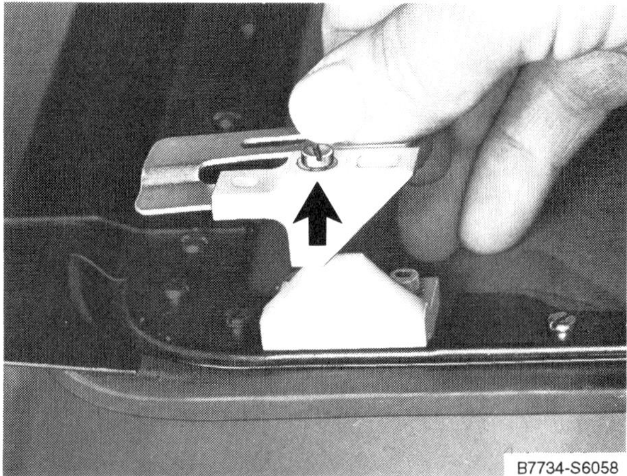

Fig. 35. Guide shoe adjusting screw (arrow) to adjust sunroof top flush with roof.

851 Interior Trim and Upholstery

SEATS AND SEATBELTS

The front seats are bolted to the floor pan via rails. The rails provide fore-aft seat adjustment. All models have heating elements in the front seats. Some models have a power seat adjustment. For information on testing the heating element see **371 Wiring Diagrams, Fuses and Relays.**

The seat belts are a combination lap-shoulder belt except for the center belt for the rear seat. The belts should be inspected periodically for webbing defects such as cuts or pulled threads. They should also be tested for proper retracting.

WARNING

- For maximum protection from injury, seat belts should be replaced as a set (including all hardware) if they are subjected to occupant loading in a collision.
- Seat belts should not be modified or repaired. The seat belt anchorage points should not be changed or modified.
- Do not install seat belts or seat belt hardware purchased from an auto-recycler or salvage yard. These parts may have been subjected to occupant loading from a collision. Only Saab original replacement equipment mounting bolts and hardware should be used. Check with an authorized Saab dealer for the latest parts information.
- Seat belt assemblies must remain together as a matched set. Improper latching of the seat belt may occur if the components have been mixed from other sets or other cars.
- Do not bleach or dye seat belt webbing. Webbing that is severely faded or redyed will not meet the strength requirements and must be replaced.

To remove front seats

1. Slide the seat to the rear. Remove the two front socket head screws holding the seat to the adjusting mechanism.
2. Disconnect the electrical connectors for the seat heater and power function (where applicable).
3. To remove the passenger's seat, slide the seat forward. Remove the nuts holding the rails to the height adjusting mechanism. Remove the seat.
4. To remove the driver's seat, release the front catch by sliding the seat back to the limit of its travel. Tilt the seat back and then lift it upward and forward, removing it from the car. See Fig. 1.

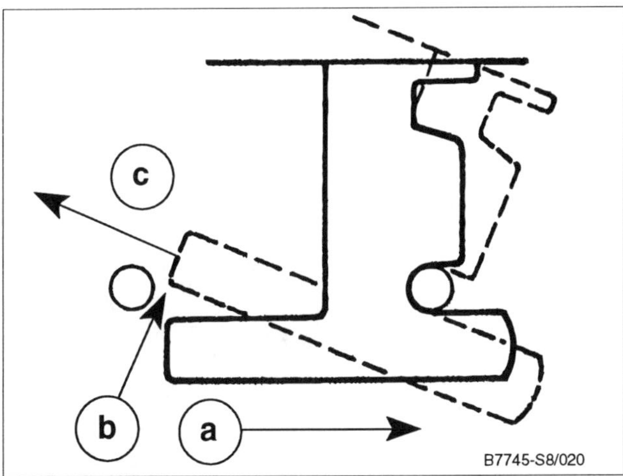

Fig. 1. To remove driver's seat, slide seat to rear (**a**), tilt seat back (**b**), and lift seat out of car (**c**).

The seat heating elements and thermostat are located under the seat covering. The bottom cover is held on with upholstery clips. The backrest cover can be removed after removing the headrest and unzipping the cover at the bottom.

To remove rear seat

1. To remove the rear seat bottom, remove the bolts along the front edge of the seat bottom or remove the seat hinge bolts. See Fig. 2. Pull the seat out of the car.

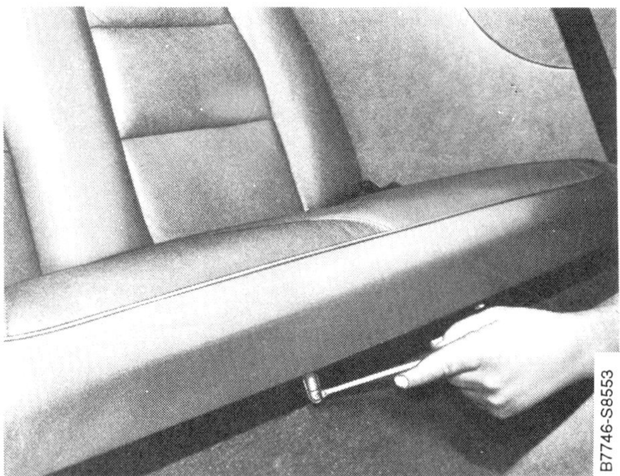

Fig. 2. Rear seat bottom cushion being removed on convertible model.

2. To remove the rear seat backrest, pivot the lower seat cushion up and into the cargo position. Release the rear seat back cushion and pivot it forward slightly. Then unbolt the hinges from the body. See Fig. 3.

NOTE

On convertible models, two anchor bolts located at the top of the backrest must also be removed. These bolts can be found behind each headrest, beneath the small cutouts in the upholstery. Two bolts at the bottom must be removed as well.

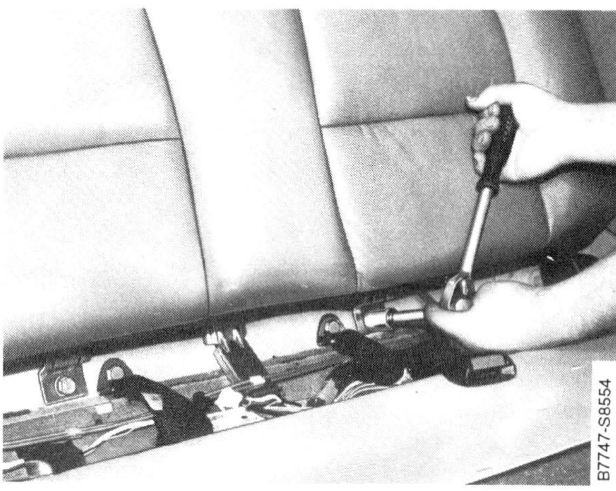

Fig. 3. Rear seat backrest being removed.

Removing Seat Belts

Removal of some of the seat belt assemblies may require removal of interior trim panels as described later in this section. When reinstalling the seat belt, always check that the seat belt retracts correctly and that the belt guides do not bind the belt. Always replace any damaged or worn components.

Tightening torque

- seat belt guide bolt to body (convertible models). . . . 24 to 40 Nm (18 to 30 lb-ft)
- all other seat belt mounting bolts . . . . 45±10 Nm (33±7 ft-lb)

NOTE

Servicing the passive (motorized) seat belts requires special equipment and techniques and is therefore beyond the scope of this manual. See an authorized Saab dealer for repairs to the passive seat belt system. For passive seat belt wiring diagrams, see **371 Wiring Diagrams, Fuses and Relays.**

NOTE

For information on removing the interior trim on convertible models, see **830 Doors, Windows, and Lids**.

CARPETS

The interior carpet is a nylon fiber on fabric. It is secured using press studs and tape fasteners.

To remove carpets

1. Remove both front seats as described earlier.

2. Remove the center console as described in **432 Manual Transmission Controls**. Remove the storage console (where applicable) as described in **853 Dashboard and Consoles**.

3. Remove the metal door sill plates. Carefully pull up the carpet and remove it from the car.

Installation is the reverse of removal. Check and correct any water leakage into the floor area before reinstalling the carpet.

Interior Body Trim

To remove headliner

On hatchback models the headliner can be removed through the hatch opening. On two-door sedans the headliner can be very carefully removed through the right door opening. On four-door sedans, the rear window must be removed to remove the headliner.

1. Disconnect the battery negative (–) cable. On hatchbacks, remove the rear parcel shelf and put the rear seat down.

2. Remove the mirror, sunvisors, assist handles, coat hooks, and dome light. On models equipped with a sunroof, remove the edging around the sunroof opening.

CAUTION
Extra care should be taken not to stress the molded headliner particularly around the mirror and sun visors, as it will crack.

3. Remove the trim around the B-pillar seat belt. On hatchback models, remove the brackets for the rear parcel shelf. See Fig. 4. Pry off the plastic covers for the hatchback hinges. See Fig. 5.

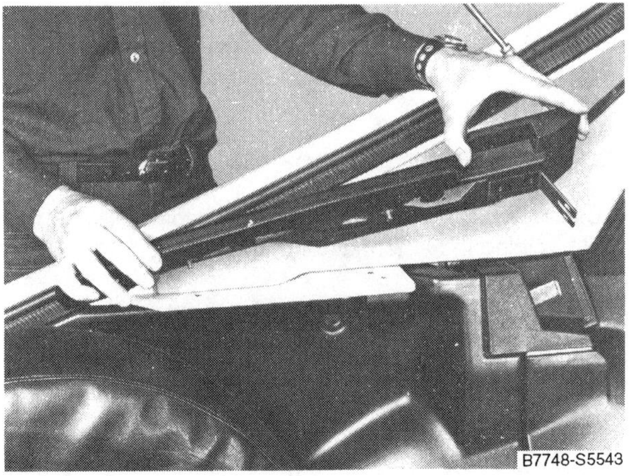

Fig. 4. Rear parcel shelf brackets being removed.

4. Remove the trim pieces from the rear corner pillars. See Fig. 6.

NOTE
The rear corner trim pieces are held on with clips. Carefully pry the piece away from the body.

5. Pull the headliner back slightly to free it from the windshield pillar trim and remove the headliner.

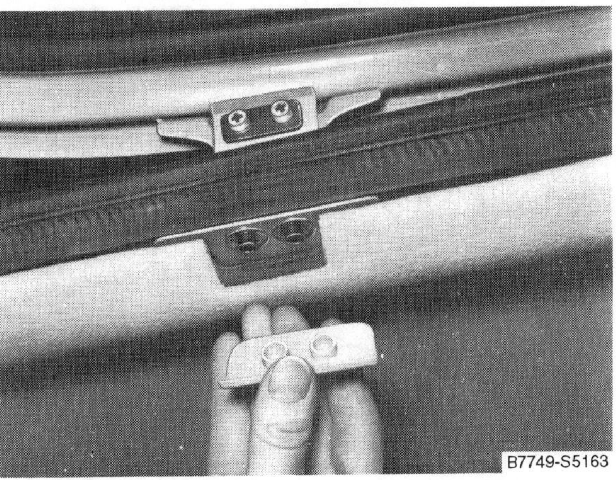

Fig. 5. Plastic trim cover for hatchback hinge.

Fig. 6. Rear trim piece being removed.

Installation is the reverse of removal.

To remove lower instrument pad

1. Remove the center storage console as described in **853 Dashboard and Consoles**.

2. Remove the ashtray and the ashtray holder screws. Remove the bolt in the ashtray opening.

3. Working in the engine compartment, remove the instrument pad nuts, one near the left door hinge and the other near the right door hinge. See Fig. 7. Remove the lower instrument pad.

NOTE
Do not mistake the small nut that holds the lower instrument pad with the larger two bolts that hold the entire instrument panel assembly. The two larger bolts should not be removed.

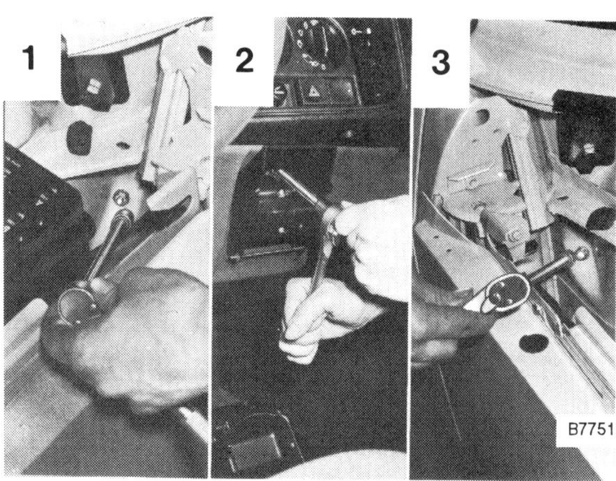

Fig. 7. Mounting points for lower instrument pad to body (**1** and **3**). Center dash pad mounting bolt shown at **(2).**

To remove interior side trim

1. Remove the back seat cushions as described earlier.

NOTE
On sedan models, the lower seat cushion does not require removal, as the cushion can be tilted forward to reach the lower trim screws.

---

2. Remove the screws holding the trim to the body. See Fig. 8. On some models, a special plastic fastener is used in place of the screws. To remove these fasteners turn them 90° counter-clockwise to unfasten.

Fig. 8. Remove screws (arrows). Convertible model shown.

NOTE
On convertibles, the speaker and reading light connectors must be disconnected.

To remove luggage compartment side trim (hatchback models)

1. Remove the rear floor panel and floor plate.

2. Remove the side carpet sections.

NOTE
Some models use a molded plastic trim piece in place of the carpet section. This piece is held in with special plastic fasteners which are removed by turning them 90°.

ANTENNA

To test electric antenna

1. Remove the luggage compartment side trim as described above.

2. Check that the ground wire to the chassis is tight.

3. Test for battery voltage at the red wire (motor supply).

4. Test for battery voltage at the green wire (up/down signal) when the radio is first turned on.

If voltage is as specified, the antenna is faulty. If voltage is not as specified, check the wiring and relay using the appropriate wiring diagram. listed in **371 Wiring Diagrams, Fuses and Relays.**

To replace electric antenna mast

1. Disconnect the battery negative (–) cable. Remove the nut holding the antenna to the body.

2. Working inside the car, pull back the luggage compartment side carpeting. Remove the screws holding the antenna assembly to the body. Disconnect the wires.

3. Remove the screws holding the antenna tube to antenna housing. See Fig. 9. Remove the tube after making a note of its position.

4. Connect the motor leads to a battery. Black wire to ground (–). Red and green wires to positive (+). Wait until the motor has stopped with the antenna in the extended position.

NOTE
The motor will stop after several seconds. The gear rack/mast assembly can now be pulled out of the motor.

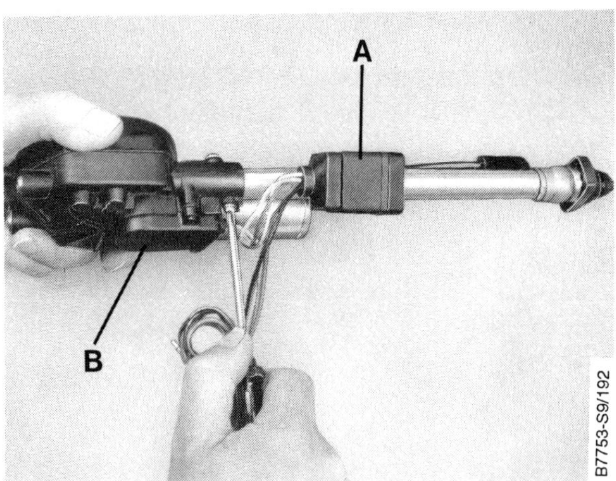

Fig. 9. Antenna tube screws being removed. Also shown is the relay **(A)** and the park position switch cover **(B)**.

5. Insert the new mast/gear rack into the motor with the teeth facing the motor. See Fig. 10.

NOTE
The new gear rack should be greased with a multipurpose grease.

---

6. Connect the electrical leads as described above. Gently engage the rack teeth into the motor.

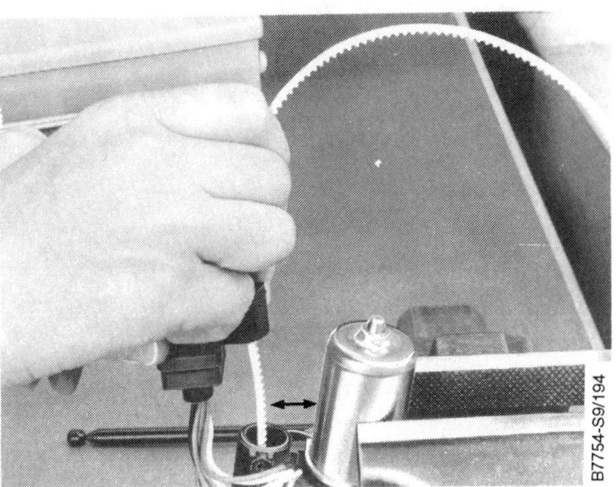

Fig. 10. Antenna gear rack correctly installed with teeth facing motor (arrow).

NOTE
To help engage the rack, momentarily touch the motor red lead to the battery several times.

---

7. When the gear rack is all the way in, disconnect the leads.

8. Replace the antenna tube in its correct position. Reinstall the antenna in the car.

853 Dashboard and Consoles

DASHBOARD

The one-piece padded dashboard panel is removed after the instrument panel, radio and steering wheel have been removed. Removal of the steering wheel is given in **641 Steering Column.** Removal of the instrument panel that holds the dashboard switches is covered in **364 Electric Controls and Switches.**

WARNING

1990 and later models are equipped with an airbag or SRS system. The airbag is an explosive device. Do not attempt to remove the steering wheel or service the wiring in the steering column assembly. You could accidentally ignite the airbag, causing serious personal injury. See an authorized Saab dealer for any repairs to the SRS system or to disarm the system prior to removing the steering wheel.

NOTE

Removal of the center console between the front seats is covered in **432 Manual Transmission Controls.**

To remove padded dashboard

1. Remove the battery negative (–) cable.

2. Remove the instrument panel as described in **364 Electric Controls and Switches.**

3. Remove the left and right front speaker grilles.

NOTE

Use an offset screwdriver to remove the speaker grille mounting screws.

---

4. Working through the speaker grille openings, remove the left and right upper dashboard mounting screws. See Fig. 1

5. Working below the glove box, remove the two screws shown in Fig. 2.

6. Working under the left-hand side of the dash, remove the corner mounting screw shown in Fig. 3.

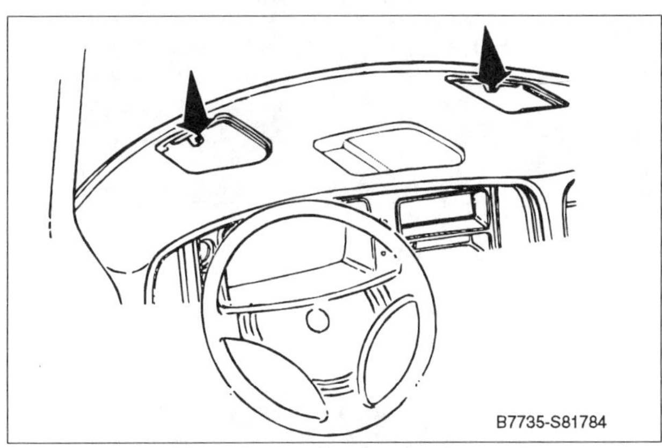

Fig. 1. Dashboard upper mounting screws (arrows).

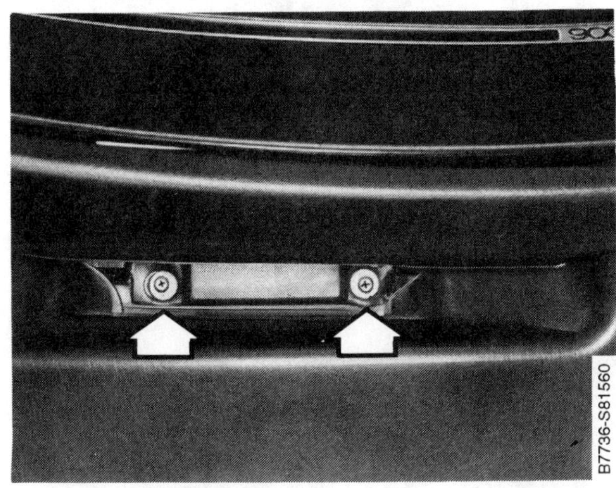

Fig. 2. Lower dashboard mounting screws below glovebox (arrows).

7. Remove the dashboard as shown in Fig. 4.

Installation is the reverse of removal. Check that the defroster hoses are attached to the speaker grilles. Check all instrument panel functions.

To remove storage console

1. Remove the rubber boot in front of the shift lever by squeezing it in pulling it out. See Fig. 5.

2. Remove the ashtray. Remove the screws holding the ashtray bracket to the console. See Fig. 6.

853

Fig. 3. Mounting screw on under left-hand side of dash (arrow).

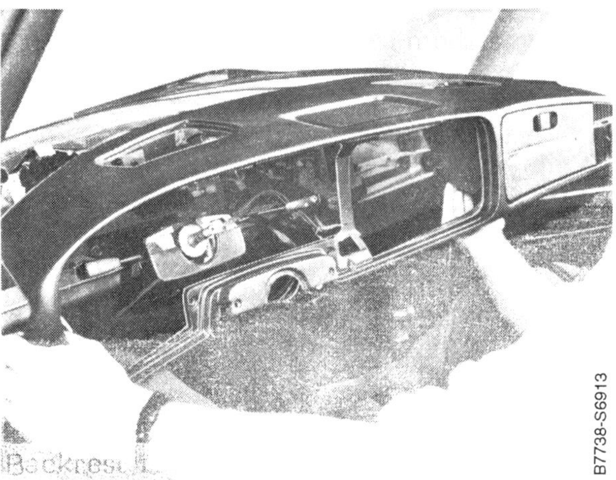

Fig. 4. Padded dashboard being removed.

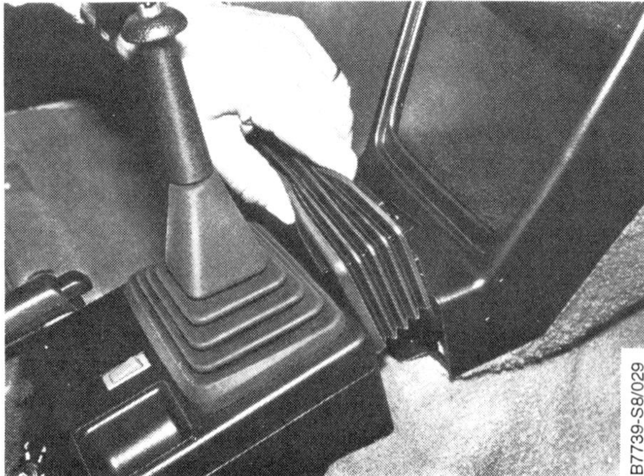

Fig. 5. Rubber boot being removed.

3. Working through the ashtray opening, remove the bolt holding the console to the dashboard.

Fig. 6. Ashtray bracket being removed. Console bolt (not shown) is removed through opening (arrow).

4. Disconnect the ashtray illumination wires and remove the bulb holder.

5. Where applicable, remove the gauges or the radio equipment in the center of the console. Disconnect and label the wiring.

6. Remove the six screws holding the console to the car body and dash. Remove the console.

INSTRUMENT CLUSTER

The instrument cluster can be easily removed once the instrument panel is removed as described in **364 Electric Controls and Switches**. To replace bulbs in the cluster, remove the left speaker grille and reach into the opening. See Fig. 7. The bulbs can be removed and tested by checking for continuity at the socket terminals.

Fig. 7. Instrument cluster bulbs (arrows) as viewed through left speaker opening

Instrument cluster bulb rating

- instrument illum ination . . . . 3 watt
- charge warning lamp. 2 watt
- other warning/indicator lamps . . . . 1.2 watt

To remove instrument cluster

1. Remove the battery negative (–) cable. Remove the steering wheel as described in **641 Steering Column**.

WARNING

1990 and later models are equipped with an airbag or SRS system. The airbag is an explosive device. Do not attempt to remove the steering wheel or service the wiring in the steering column assembly. You could accidentally ignite the airbag, causing serious personal injury. See an authorized Saab dealer for any repairs to the SRS system or to disarm the system prior to removing the steering wheel.

2. Remove the instrument panel as described in **364 Electric Controls and Switches**.

3. Remove the left speaker grille.

4. Working through the speaker grille, disconnect the electrical connectors at the back of the cluster. Disconnect the speedometer cable by bending the spring out of the way and pulling the cable from the instrument. See Fig. 8.

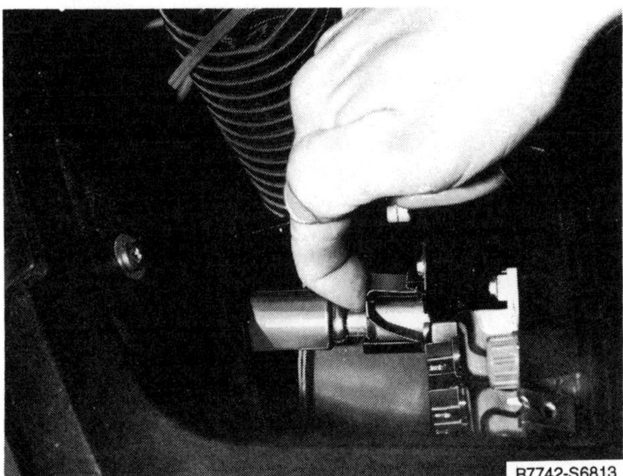

Fig. 8. Speedometer cable retaining clip being pried up to removed cable from speedometer.

NOTE

If the speedometer cable is being replaced, free the cable from the grommet in the bulkhead then pull the cable into the engine compartment. Remove the other end of the cable from the transmission.

5. Remove the screws holding the cluster to the dash. See Fig. 9. Remove the cluster.

Fig. 9. Instrument cluster retaining screw being removed.

NOTE

- Replacement instruments are available from an authorized Saab dealer. Fig. 10 shows the individual instruments removed from the cluster housing.

- Laws in some areas require that you fill out an odometer verification sticker when replacing a speedometer.

Fig. 10. Instruments.

854 Heating and Air Conditioning

TABLES

GENERAL

This section of the manual covers repairs and troubleshooting for the heating and air conditioning (A/C) systems. This includes repair information for the heater core, the heater valve, the ventilation blower, the dash-mounted controls, and the A/C components.

CAUTION
The A/C system is a sealed system and should only be serviced by an authorized Saab dealer or other qualified repair shop. Special tools and equipment are necessary to service the A/C system.

NOTE
- Repairs to the cooling system, including heater hose replacement, are covered in **261 Radiator and Cooling System**.
- Additional electrical troubleshooting is covered in **371 Wiring Diagrams, Fuses and Relays.**

Fig. 1 shows the heating and air conditioning system's air distribution system. Fresh air enters the car through the vent in the hood and passes through the A/C evaporator and through the heater core. Air exits through the rear slots near the luggage area. Air flow through the system is directed through vacuum-actuated dampers.

Temperature, air flow, and ventilation fan speeds are controlled by separate instrument panel knobs. The air distribution knob also contains electric contacts for the ventilation blower.

Heating is controlled by regulating coolant flow through the heater core via the heater valve. The temperature regulating knob is directly connected to the heater valve, using a control rod.

All of the cars covered by this manual are equipped with factory-installed A/C. The major components of the A/C system are shown in Fig. 2.

The A/C system is protected by a pressure switch, a fuse for the compressor, an anti-frost switch and an A/C coolant temperature switch. See **261 Radiator and Cooling System** for information on the A/C coolant temperature switch. These components switch off the compressor to prevent damage to the A/C system.

WARNING
- Adding refrigerant or servicing the A/C system without the proper tools, equipment, or knowledge may cause severe personal injury as well as damage to the A/C components.
- Wear eye protection when inspecting the system. R-12 at normal atmospheric pressures can evaporate and freeze anything it contacts.
- At normal operating temperature the heating system is pressurized with hot engine coolant. Allow the system to cool as long as possible before opening—a minimum of an hour—then release the coolant expansion cap very slowly to allow safe release of pressure.
- Releasing cooling system pressure lowers the coolant's boiling point, and the coolant may boil suddenly. Use heavy gloves and wear eye and face protection to guard against scalding.

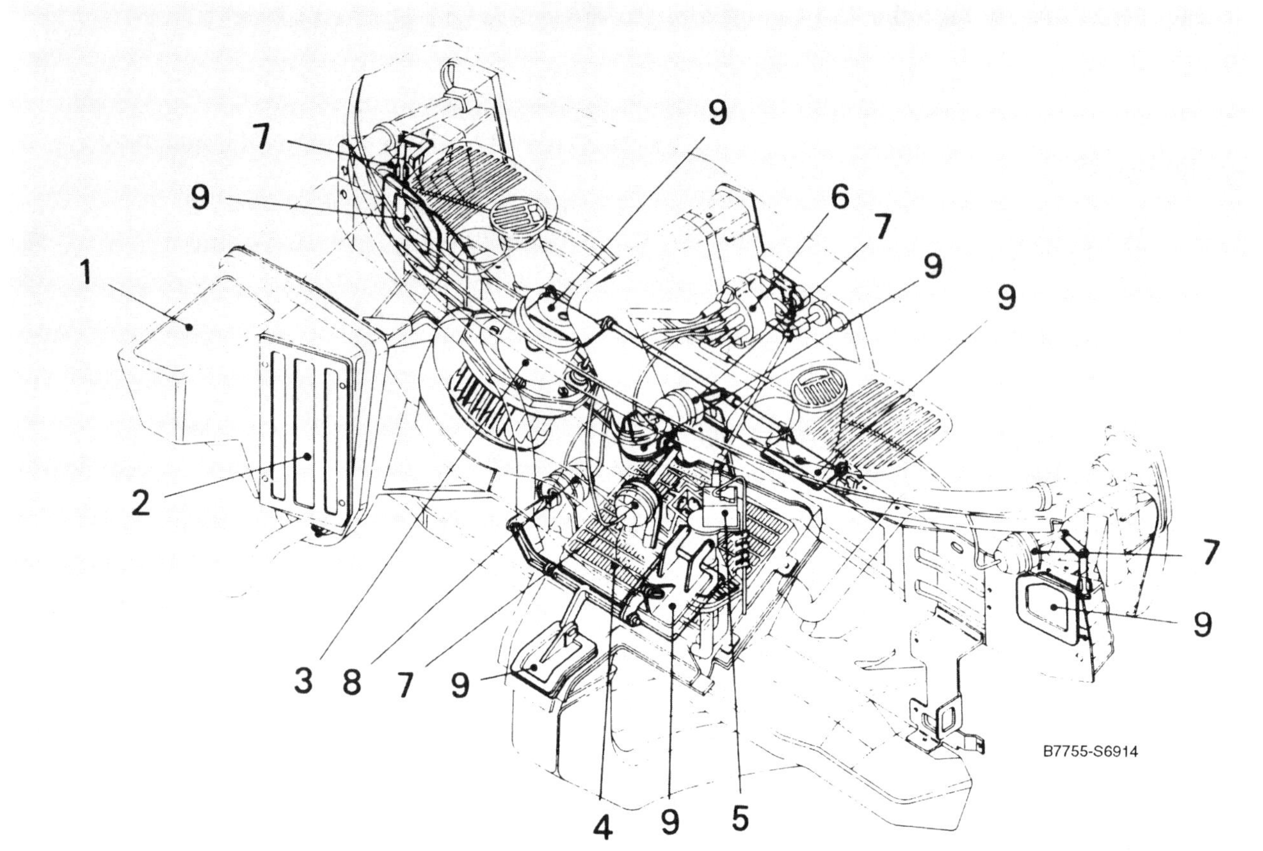

1. Air intake
2. Evaporator
3. Blower motor
4. Heater core
5. Heater valve
6. Air distribution switch
7. Vacuum servo (single stage)
8. Vacuum servo (dual stage)
9. Vacuum controlled flaps

Fig. 1. Cut-away view of air distribution system.

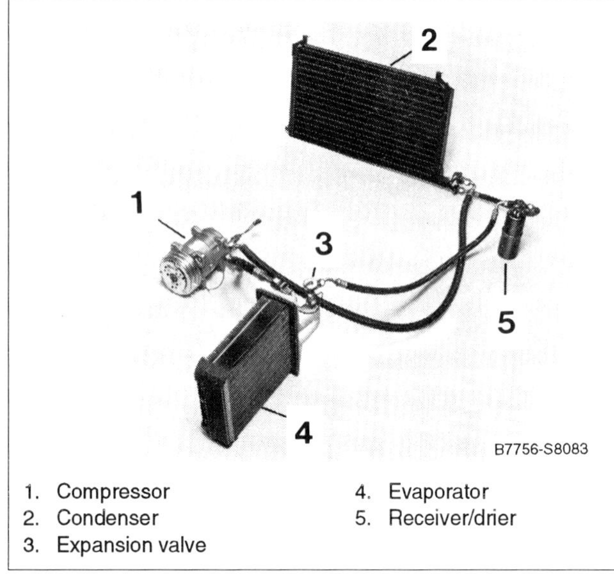

1. Compressor
2. Condenser
3. Expansion valve
4. Evaporator
5. Receiver/drier

Fig. 2. A/C components.

> **CAUTION**
> Avoid adding cold water to the coolant while the engine is hot or overheated. If it is absolutely necessary to add coolant to a hot system, do so only with the engine running and coolant pump turning.

TROUBLESHOOTING

Table a shows common heating and air conditioning problems. Each system has its own causes and corrective actions.

Insufficient heater output may be caused by a faulty heater valve, an air flap not opening, or a cooling system fault. Coolant leaking visibly into the passenger compartment is a sign of a faulty heater core. A sweet, anti-freeze odor in the car's interior, or a constantly fogged windshield may also indicate a faulty core. Inspect the carpet and the area near the footwell vents for any moisture or coolant. Water appearing on the carpets or near the footwells could be a clogged A/C evaporator condensation drain hose.

Table a. Heating and Air Conditioning System Troubleshooting

Symptom	Probable cause	Corrective action
1. Heater output inadequate (temperature gauge reading normal)	a. Heater hose restricted b. Heater core or heater valve clogged or faulty c. Heater controls broken	a. Replace hose. See **261 Radiator and Cooling System** b. Clean or replace heater valve. Have heater core cleaned c. Inspect and replace any faulty controls
2. Heat always present at side vents, temperature regulation erratic—cannot be regulated to cooler settings	a. Heater valve not fully closed due to disconnected or damaged control rod b. Internal seals in heater valve faulty	a. Check control rod operation b. Replace heater valve
3. A/C cooling output inadequate	a. System charge (refrigerant) low b. Anti-frost switch faulty c. Expansion valve faulty	a. Check system charge at sight glass. Have system recharged if necessary. Check for leaks b. Test switch and replace if necessary c. Test system pressure and replace expansion valve if necessary

HEATER AND CONTROLS

Heater Core and Heater Valve

Coolant flow through the heater core is controlled by the heater valve. The heater valve is connected directly to the temperature knob. See Fig. 3. There are no adjustments that can be made to the valve or control rod.

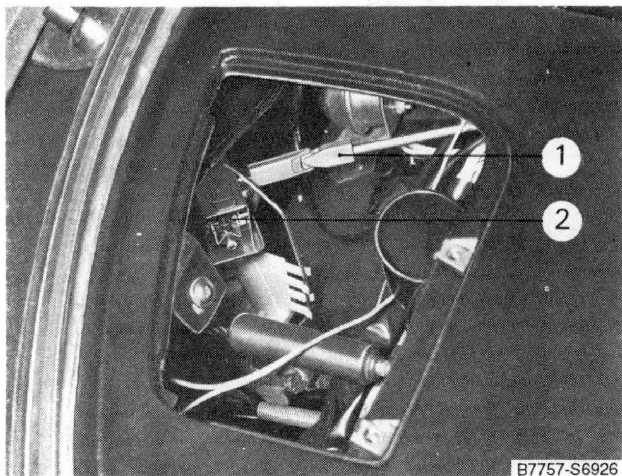

Fig. 3. Heater valve (**2**) and control rod (**1**) as viewed through left-front speaker grille opening.

To replace heater valve and heater core

1. Disconnect the negative (–) cable from the battery.

2. Drain the coolant as described in **261 Radiator and Cooling System**.

3. Working in the engine compartment, label and remove the heater hoses at the heater valve fittings. Plug the ends of the fittings on the valve.

4. Remove the lower steering column cover, the storage console (where applicable), and lower dashboard pad as described in **851 Interior Trim and Upholstery**.

WARNING

1990 and later models are equipped with an airbag or SRS system. The airbag is an explosive device. Do not attempt to remove the steering wheel or service the wiring in the steering column assembly. You could accidentally ignite the airbag, causing serious personal injury. See an authorized Saab dealer for any repairs to the SRS system or to disarm the system prior to removing the steering wheel.

---

5. Remove the left speaker grille, then slide the heater control rod forward to disengage it from the knob. Slide rod backwards to remove it from the heater valve. See Fig. 3 above.

6. If removing just the heater valve use a long 4-mm hex-head driver to remove the screws securing the heater valve to the heater core. See Fig. 4.

NOTE

A ball type (swivel) hex-head driver will help make removal and installation of the heater valve screws easier.

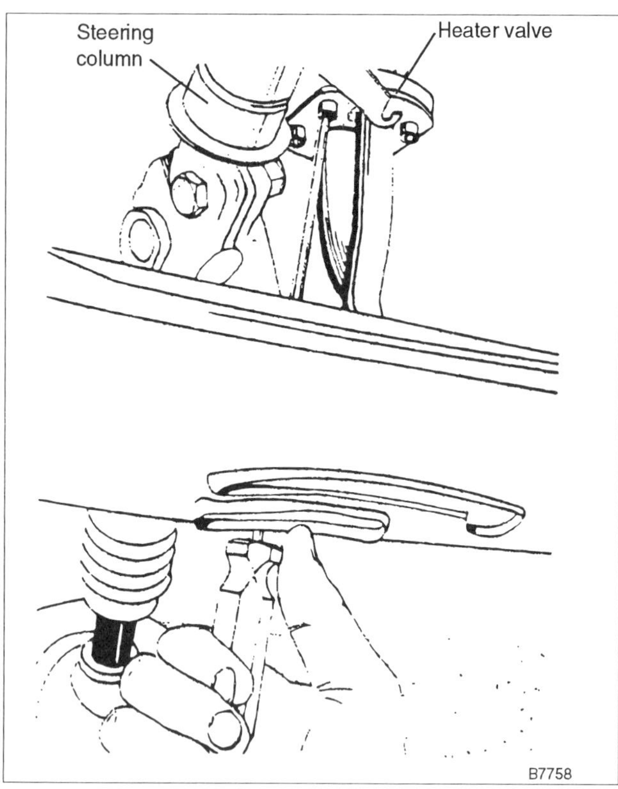

Fig. 4. Heater valve being removed from heater core.

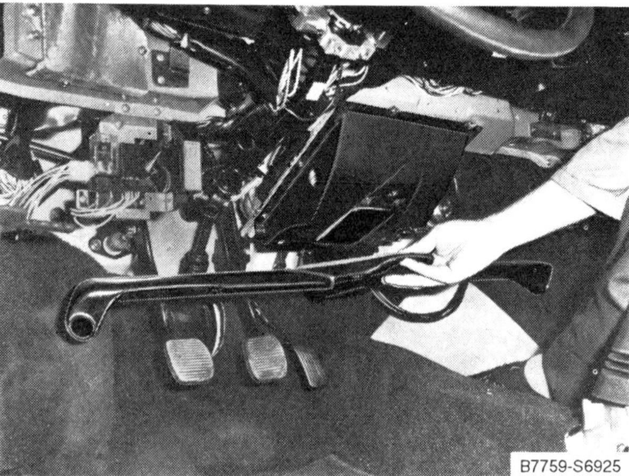

Fig. 5. Ventilation air diffuser being removed.

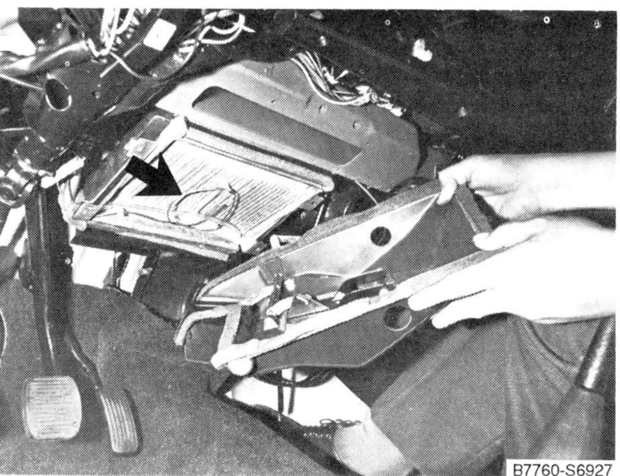

Fig. 6. Lower heater box section being removed. Also visible is the heater valve capillary tube (arrow).

WARNING

- Replacement heater valves may interfere with throttle pedal operation and require a new throttle pedal arm. See an authorized Saab dealer for correct parts information.

- On cars with cruise control, be sure to refit the actuator chain guard to the heater valve to prevent interference with the chain.

---

7. Remove the ventilation air diffuser in the footwell. See Fig. 5.

8. Remove the screws securing the lower section of the heater box and remove the lower section. See Fig. 6.

9. Unhook the brake pedal return spring from the pedal and depress the pedal slightly. Lower the heater core and heater valve assembly out of the car.

10. Where applicable, remove the heater valve capillary tube from the heater core. Separate the heater valve from the heater core. See Fig. 7.

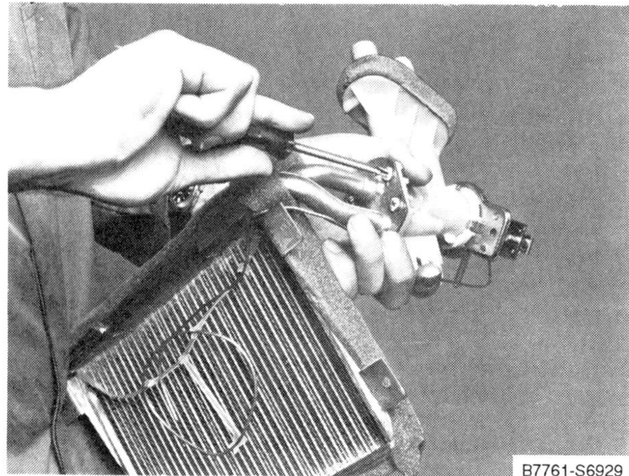

Fig. 7. Heater valve being removed from heater core.

CAUTION

Handle the capillary tube carefully. Do not crease or bend the tube.

Installation is the reverse of removal. Always replace the heater core-to-heater valve O-rings. The heater valve should be in the off position (flat surface up) before connecting the control rod. Reconnect the heater hoses to the valve. Check the operation of all foot pedals before installing the lower dash pad. Refill and bleed the cooling system as described in **261 Radiator and Cooling System** and check the operation of the heater functions.

NOTE

Reinstall the heater hoses to the heater valve so that the top hose leads to the water pump and the lower hose comes from the intake manifold.

Ventilation Blower and Blower Switch

The blower assembly is mounted in the passenger compartment footwell and runs except when the air distribution switch is in the 0 (six o'clock) position. A blower resistor pack, located below the left speaker grille, controls the speed of the blower motor. There are three resistors for three speeds of the motor. If the resistor pack overheats, an internal switch closes and blows the fuse on the main fuse/relay panel.

To quickly test the blower motor, remove the right speaker grille and probe the connector with a test lamp. If there is no voltage reaching the motor with the ignition on and the blower switch on high, check the fuse on the main fuse/relay panel and check the wiring. See **371 Wiring Diagrams, Fuses and Relays.** If voltage is present, the motor is probably faulty.

NOTE

- A blower motor that runs only when the air distribution switch is in position 1 (7 o'clock position) usually indicates a fault with the blower motor resistors or blower switch.

- To replace the blower switch, remove the switch panel as described in **364 Electric Controls and Switches**, then remove the clip holding the switch and the wire connector.

To remove and install ventilation blower

1. Disconnect the negative (–) cable from the battery.

2. Remove the dashboard instrument panel as described in **364 Electric Controls and Switches.**

3. Remove the padded dashboard as described in **853 Dashboard and Consoles.**

4. Disconnect the blower wiring from the blower.

5. Remove right defroster housing mounting screws.

6. Remove the three blower mounting screws and remove the blower. See Fig. 8.

Fig. 8. Blower motor being removed.

Installation is the reverse of removal.

NOTE

A sound insulation kit is available from Saab to reduce blower motor noise. See an authorized Saab dealer for the correct application and part number.

Air Distribution Control Switch, Vacuum Servos and Air Flaps

Vacuum operated flaps direct air flow to the various air outlets. The panel-mounted air distribution switch routes vacuum to the correct vacuum servo to open and close the air flaps. See Fig. 9. The vacuum for the system is supplied via a vacuum storage tank. The switch also functions to close microswitches for the ventilation blower motor and the recirculation valve.

NOTE

To replace the air distribution switch, the instrument panel must be removed. See **364 Electric Controls and Switches.**

There are six vacuum servos that open and close air flaps. The recirculation switch on the instrument panel controls an electric solenoid that routes vacuum to the recirculation door servo. See Fig. 10.

To test vacuum servos and air flaps

Many vacuum related faults are the result of pinched or disconnected hoses. Always inspect the hoses carefully when experiencing problems with the servos.

1. With the engine running, check for vacuum at the vacuum tank on the passenger side wheel liner.

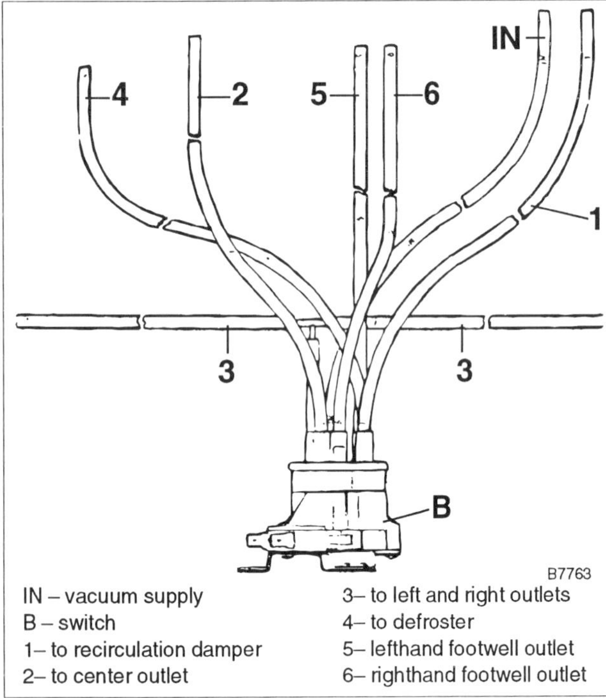

IN – vacuum supply
B – switch
1– to recirculation damper
2– to center outlet
3– to left and right outlets
4– to defroster
5– lefthand footwell outlet
6– righthand footwell outlet

Fig. 9. Air distribution switch showing vacuum hose routing.

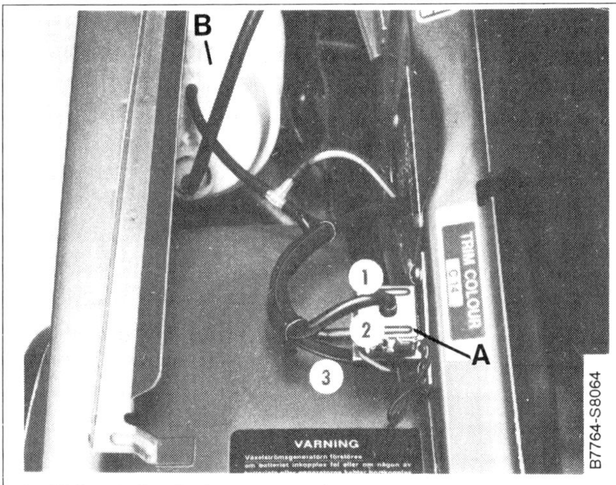

1. Yellow to heater box vacuum box.
2. Blue to recirculation servo
3. White to T connection vacuum tank

Fig. 10. Air recirculation solenoid (**A**) on wheel housing next to vacuum tank (**B**) on 1985 through 1987 models. Recirculation solenoid on 1988 and later models is in passenger compartment, behind right footwell kickpanel.

2. Check the operation of the system servos and the air distribution switch using the information found in **Table b.**

NOTE

The servos should be visible when making the tests outlined in the table below. Remove the two speaker grilles to gain access to the outer vent and defroster servos. The lower instrument panel should be removed as described in **853 Dashboard and Consoles** to check the lower servos and flaps. The switch panel must be removed to test the air distribution switch.

Table b. Vacuum Servo Fault Tracing

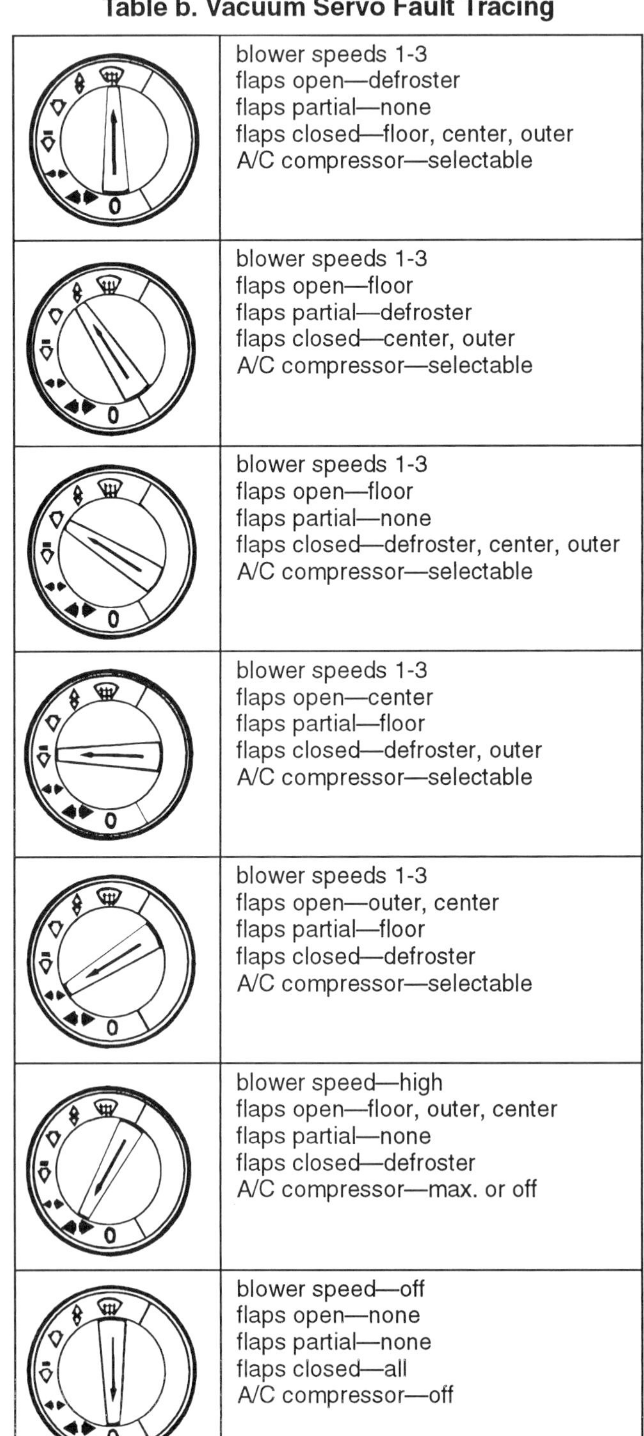

	blower speeds 1-3 flaps open—defroster flaps partial—none flaps closed—floor, center, outer A/C compressor—selectable
	blower speeds 1-3 flaps open—floor flaps partial—defroster flaps closed—center, outer A/C compressor—selectable
	blower speeds 1-3 flaps open—floor flaps partial—none flaps closed—defroster, center, outer A/C compressor—selectable
	blower speeds 1-3 flaps open—center flaps partial—floor flaps closed—defroster, outer A/C compressor—selectable
	blower speeds 1-3 flaps open—outer, center flaps partial—floor flaps closed—defroster A/C compressor—selectable
	blower speed—high flaps open—floor, outer, center flaps partial—none flaps closed—defroster A/C compressor—max. or off
B7765	blower speed—off flaps open—none flaps partial—none flaps closed—all A/C compressor—off

Vacuum Servo Location

- outer vent — below speaker grilles
- defroster vents — behind center of dash
- center vent — above heater box
- footwell — passenger side of heater box
- fresh air intake — in engine compartment at A/C evaporator housing

3. If any faults are found, use a hand vacuum pump to check the operation of the servos. If the servo operates correctly, check the hose from the switch. If no faults are found, the switch is faulty and should be replaced.

NOTE

The vacuum tank, the switch and the lines can also be checked for leaks using the hand pump.

AIR CONDITIONING

It is recommended that all service to the A/C system be left to an authorized Saab dealer or other qualified repair shop. For information on the A/C selector switch as well as other electrical components, see **371 Wiring Diagrams, Fuses and Relays.**

Dismounting of the A/C compressor and the condenser, without disconnecting the hoses, is covered as part of the engine removal procedure in **201 Engine Removal and Installation**. If any of the hoses or components are disconnected and the system is opened, special equipment will be needed to remove moisture from the system before it is closed back up.

WARNING

Air conditioning (A/C) service and repair requires special equipment and knowledge. Incorrect procedures may not only damage the system, but may also be hazardous. Pressures in excess of 300 psi are created in the system when it is operating. The refrigerant R-12 is poisonous. In its vapor form it can accumulate in areas with poor ventilation and cause suffocation. Also, in vapor or liquid form R-12 can immediately freeze anything it contacts, including eyes and skin.

System Description

Fig. 11 is a schematic view of a typical Saab A/C system. In an A/C system, the heat from the passenger compartment is absorbed by the refrigerant (R12) in the evaporator, causing ther refrigerant to boil (evaporate). This heat is then released into the atmosphere when the R-12 is cooled and condensed into a liquid at the condenser. Moisture is removed at the evaporator in the same way that water drops form on a cold glass. The moisture drips onto the water tray in the evaporator housing and is routed away via a drain hose. This is the reason a water puddle is often be seen under the car when the A/C is operating.

The compressor forces the R-12 through the system and at the same time pressurizes it, raising the R-12's boiling point to make it more easily condensed. The compressor is engaged by an electro-magnetic clutch that is actuated when the A/C is turned on.

The condenser, which looks like a small radiator, is located in front of the engine radiator. The receiver/drier, located behind the battery, removes small amounts of moisture and dirt from the system. The evaporator and expansion valve are located in the engine compartment on the passenger side at the firewall.

WARNING

Wear eye protection when inspecting the system. R-12 at normal atmospheric pressures can evaporate and freeze anything it contacts.

NOTE

- Run the air conditioning system for a few minutes, every few weeks, to keep the seals lubricated.
- Check that the condensation drain hose from the evaporator housing is clear. This can be accomplished by blowing it out with a low pressure compressed air nozzle.

Checking Refrigerant Charge

Inspect the refrigerant charge by starting the engine and turning the air conditioner on to MAX A/C. With the compressor running (clutch cycled on) view the sight glass on the top of the receiver/drier (located near the battery). There should be few or no bubbles visible in the glass. See Fig. 12.

Discharging, Evacuating and Recharging the A/C System

Discharging the system is necessary any time a defective component is replaced. To prevent component damage, a totally discharged system must be evacuated (sometimes called pulling a vacuum) using special equipment before recharging. This removes any moisture from the lines and components, which can damage the system. For system discharging, evacuating and recharging, see an authorized Saab dealer or other shop qualified to do A/C repair work.

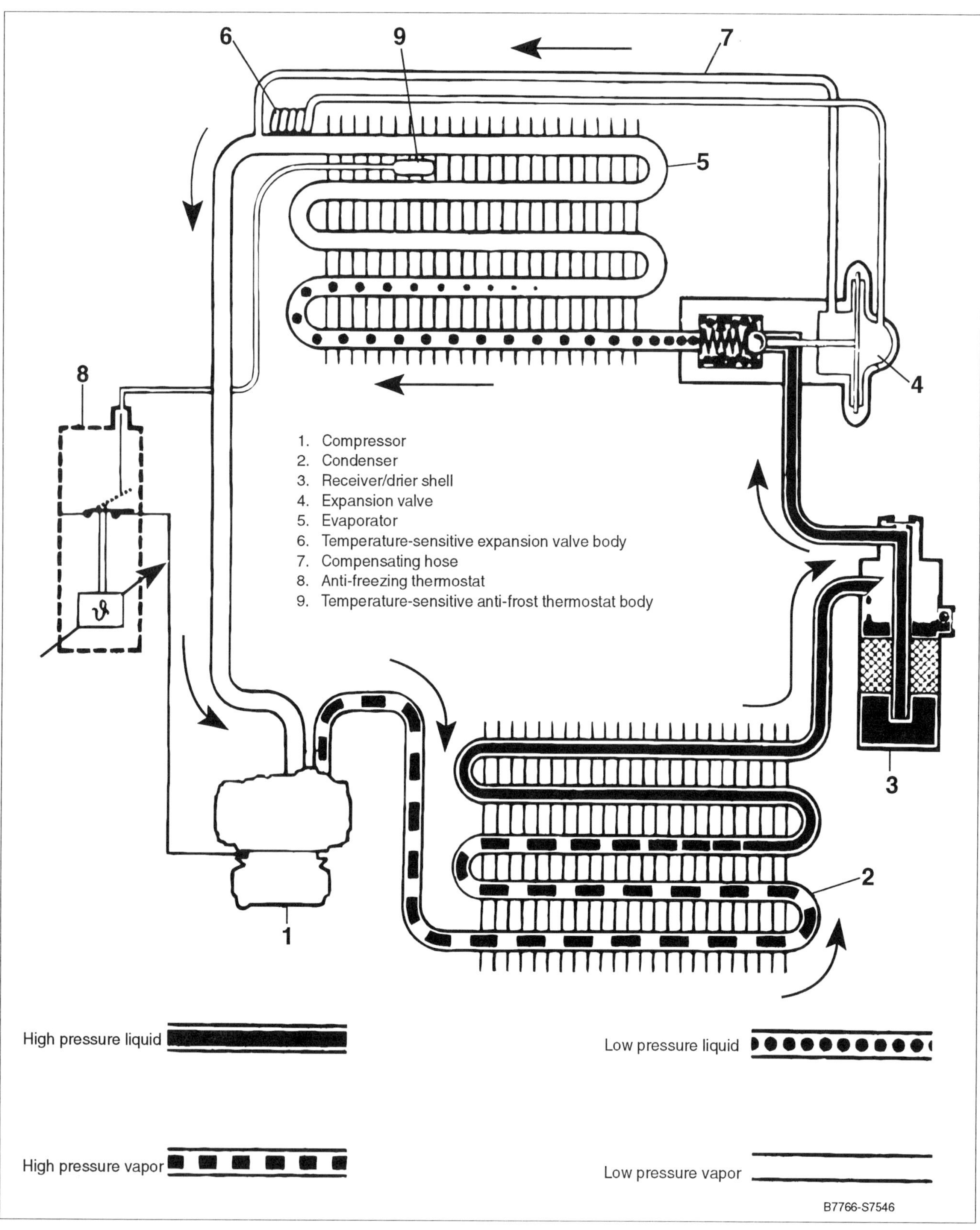
6
9
7
5
8
4
1. Compressor
2. Condenser
3. Receiver/drier shell
4. Expansion valve
5. Evaporator
6. Temperature-sensitive expansion valve body
7. Compensating hose
8. Anti-freezing thermostat
9. Temperature-sensitive anti-frost thermostat body
3
2
1
High pressure liquid
Low pressure liquid
High pressure vapor
Low pressure vapor
B7766-S7546

Fig. 11. Schematic view of A/C system.

Clear sight glass - system correctly charged or overcaharged

Occasional bubbles - system not fully charged

Heavy stream of bubbles -serious shortage of refrigerant

Oil streaks on glass - no refrigerant in system

Dark or clouded sight glass - contaminants present
B7767

Fig. 12. Air conditioning sight glass indicators.

WARNING
Discharging the system or adding refrigerant without the proper tools, equipment, or knowledge may cause severe personal injury as well as damage to the A/C components.

A/C Component Replacement

The information given below is intended to be used by those experienced in A/C service. When replacing components, always use new O-rings and gaskets. Lubricate the fittings and O-rings with refrigerant oil during installation. **Table c** lists the appropriate amount of refrigerant oil that should be added to the system when replacing individual components. Fig. 13 shows tightening torques for the various hoses and components.

WARNING
The system must be discharged before replacing any A/C components or hoses. Always evacuate the system before recharging it.

CAUTION
The oil filler plug on the A/C compressor is not an oil level plug. Do not check the compressor oil level through this plug.

NOTE
If the A/C system has been opened up to the atmosphere for more than five minutes the receiver/drier must be replaced.

Table c. A/C System Refrigerant Specifications

Refrigerant capacity (R12)	1.0 kg. (2.2 lb)
Refrigerant oil capacity (compressor replacement)	1.75 dl (4.9 oz.)
Refrigerant oil capacity per component (due to sudden leakage)	
Evaporator	0.5 dl (1.4 oz.)
Receiver/drier	0.2 dl (0.57 oz.)
Condenser	0.2 dl (0.57 oz.)
Hose	0.2 dl (0.57 oz.)
Oil fill plug torque	8–12 Nm (6–9 ft-lb)

Air Conditioning Electrical Tests

Covered under this heading are tests for the A/C compressor clutch, pressure and temperature safety switches, and the A/C selector switch.

NOTE
Additional wiring information can be found in **371 Wiring Diagrams, Fuses and Relays**.

To test A/C compressor

1. Turn the ignition on and turn the temperature regulating knob to its full cold position. Turn the A/C switch on and listen for the compressor clutch to click on. If no click is heard, the compressor clutch may not be receiving voltage or the clutch itself may be faulty.

2. Check for voltage between the single-wire connector leading out of the compressor and ground. If voltage is present, the compressor clutch is faulty and should be replaced.

3. If voltage is not present, check for a faulty compressor fuse in the main fuse/relay panel. Check the A/C coolant temperature switch, the low pressure switch, and the anti-frost switch as described below. Check for damaged wiring or a faulty (open) suppression diode using an ohmmeter.

NOTE
The A/C diode is in the wiring harness at the rear of the camshaft cover. See **371 Wiring Diagrams, Fuses and Relays** for A/C wiring diagrams.

4. If no faults are found up to this point, test the anti-frost valve as described below.

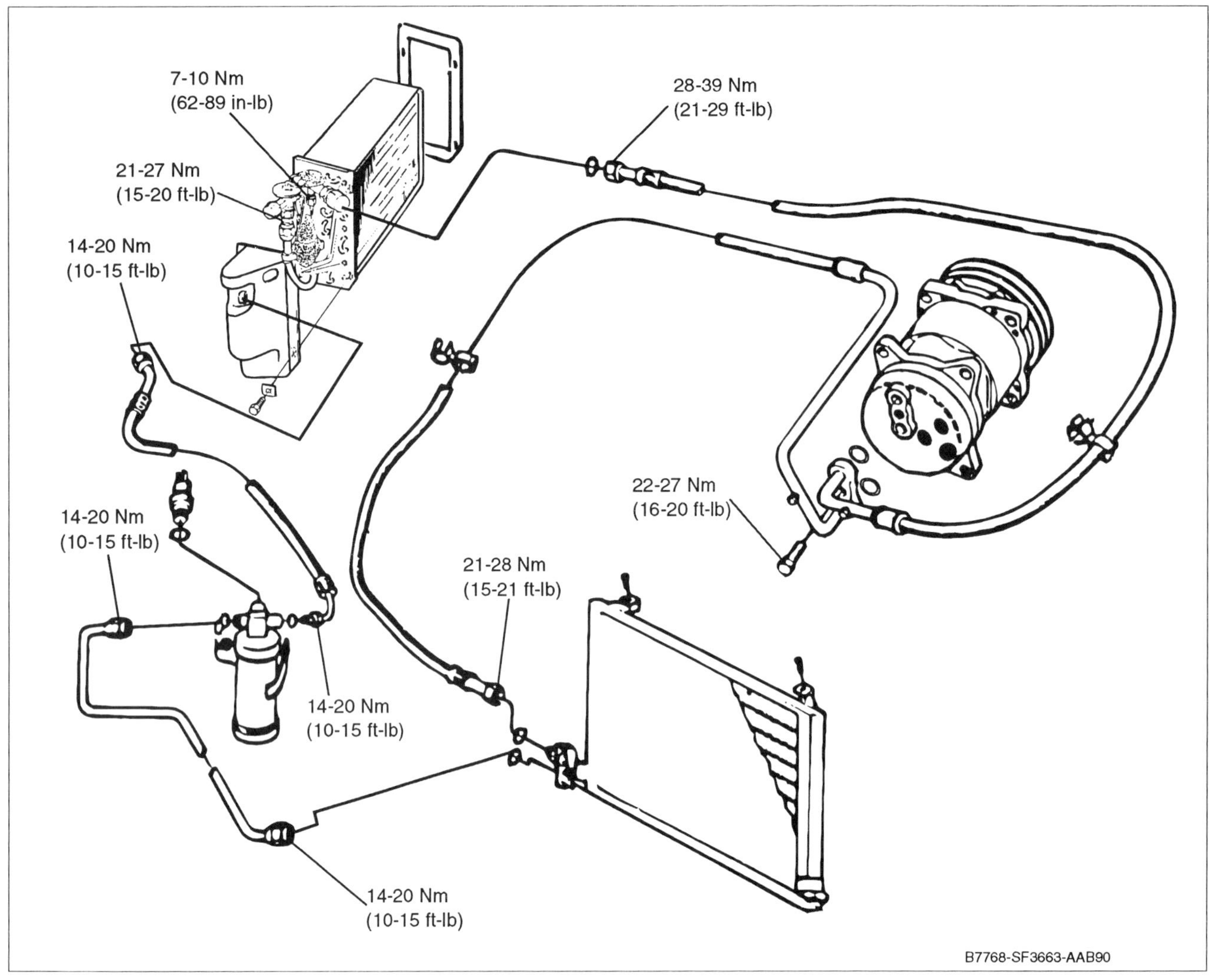

Fig. 13. A/C hose and component tightening torques.

To test A/C safety switches

A low pressure switch in the receiver/drier interrupts power to the compressor clutch if the pressure is too low. An anti-frost switch automatically disengages the compressor clutch when the temperature at the evaporator drops below a certain level. An A/C coolant temperature switch on the hose to the thermostat interrupts the compressor if the coolant temperature is excessive.

NOTE

The radiator cooling fan should run when the A/C is switched on (key on). When the compressor clutch cycles (engine running), the additional cooling fan should also run.

A/C Safety Switches

- Low pressure switch
  opening pressure .... 2.9 bar (42 psi)
- Coolant temperature switch
  opening temperature............. 115°C (239°F)
- Anti-frost switch
  switch closed....... 4.0 to 6.2 °C (39.2 to 43.1 °F)
  switch open..........0.4 to 2.6 °C (33 to 36.6 °F)

1. Disconnect the connector from the low pressure switch and connect and ohmmeter across the switch terminals. With the engine running and the A/C on, there should continuity. If not, either the refrigerant charge is low or the switch is faulty.

WARNING

- Do not loosen or remove the low pressure switch. Refrigerant will be expelled. The system must be discharged before this switch is removed.

- Operate the A/C only long enough to make the tests.

2. Check the anti-frost switch by disconnecting the switch connector and connecting and ohmmeter across the switch terminals. There should continuity with the switch at room temperature. If not the switch is faulty and should be replaced. See Fig. 14.

NOTE

- When installing a new anti-frost switch, be sure the capillary tube is in its original position.

- Check that the capillary tube does not interfere with the recirculation door.

3. Check the A/C coolant temperature switch by disconnecting the switch connector and connecting and ohmmeter across the switch terminals. There should be continuity across the terminals at all temperatures up to 239°F (115°C). If the switch is open, it is faulty and should be replaced.

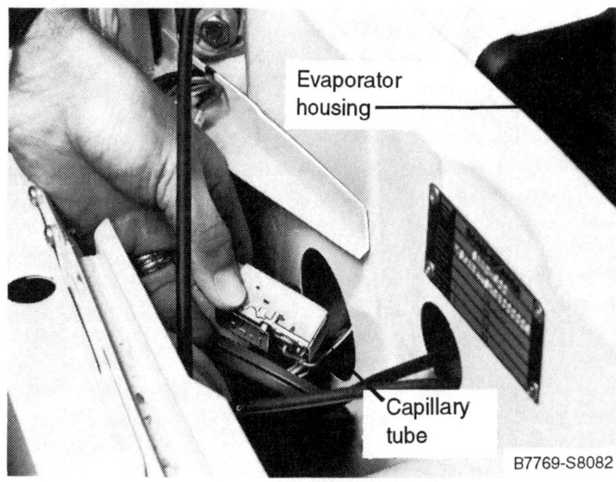

Fig. 14. Anti-frost switch being removed from evaporator housing.

NOTE

To replace the A/C coolant temperature switch, drain the coolant as described in **261 Radiator and Cooling System**.

860 Bumpers

REMOVING AND INSTALLING BUMPERS

Two types of bumpers are used on cars covered by this manual, depending on model year. See Fig. 1 and Fig. 2.

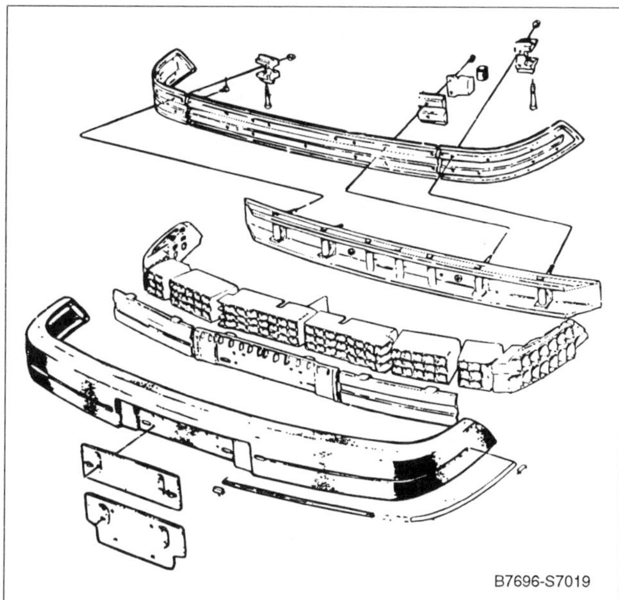

Fig. 1. Exploded view of front bumper used on 1985 and 1986 models. Rear bumper is similar.

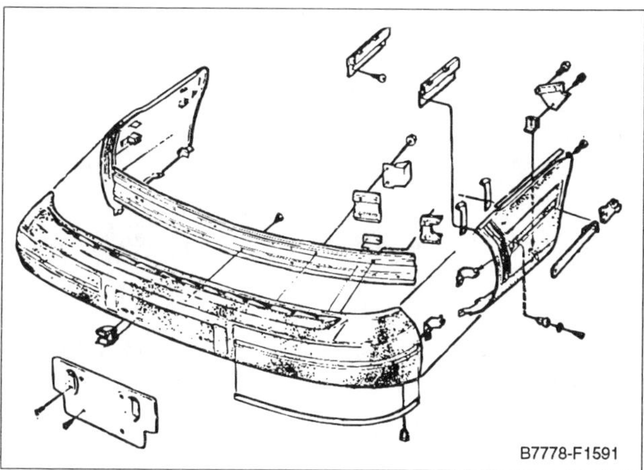

Fig. 2. Exploded view of front bumper used on 1987 and later models. Rear bumper is similar.

To remove bumpers

1. To remove the front bumper, remove the two internal-hex head screws holding the bumper to the bumper brackets. See Fig. 3. Remove the bumper.

NOTE

On cars with headlight wipers, remove the wipers before removing the front bumper as described in **363 Wipers and Washers.**

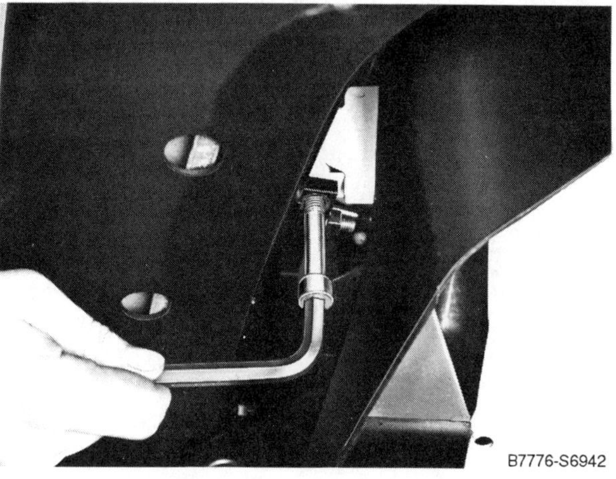

Fig. 3. Front bumper internal-hex head screw as viewed from below. Early style bumper shown.

2. To remove the rear bumper, remove the four nuts holding the bumper to the bumper mounting brackets. See Fig. 4.

860

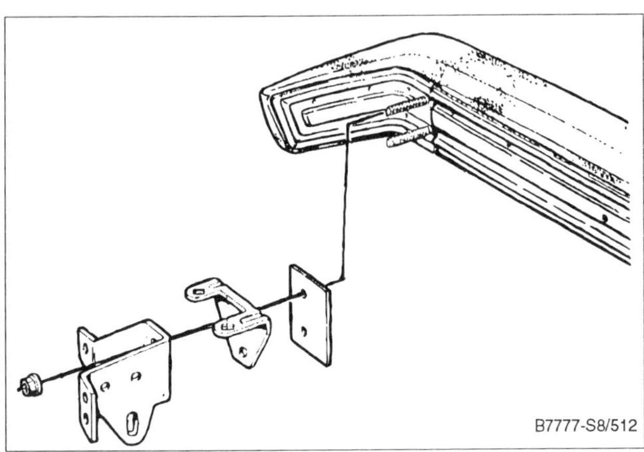

Fig. 4. Rear bumper mounting bracket (right-hand side). Early style bumper shown.

Installation is the reverse of removal. Individual bumper replacement parts are available from an authorized Saab dealer.

INDEX

Subjects are indexed by repair group number, followed by the page number(s) within the repair group where the subject can be found. For example **210**-4 refers to repair group **210 Engine Disassembly and Assembly**, page 4.

> ***WARNING —***
> *• Automotive service and repair is serious business. You must be alert, use common sense, and exercise good judgement to prevent personal injury and complete the work safely.*
>
> *• Before beginning any work on your vehicle, thoroughly read the safety notice, disclaimer, and all the Cautions and Warnings listed near the front of this manual.*
>
> *• Always read the complete procedure before you begin the work. Pay special attention to any Cautions and Warnings that accompany that procedure, or other information on a specific topic.*

A

B

INDEX

Subjects are indexed by repair group number, followed by the page number(s) within the repair group where the subject can be found. For example **210**-4 refers to repair group **210 Engine Disassembly and Assembly**, page 4.

> ***WARNING —***
> *• Automotive service and repair is serious business. You must be alert, use common sense, and exercise good judgement to prevent personal injury and complete the work safely.*
> *• Before beginning any work on your vehicle, thoroughly read the safety notice, disclaimer, and all the Cautions and Warnings listed near the front of this manual.*
> *• Always read the complete procedure before you begin the work. Pay special attention to any Cautions and Warnings that accompany that procedure, or other information on a specific topic.*

INDEX

Subjects are indexed by repair group number, followed by the page number(s) within the repair group where the subject can be found. For example **210**-4 refers to repair group **210 Engine Disassembly and Assembly**, page 4.

> ***WARNING —***
> *• Automotive service and repair is serious business. You must be alert, use common sense, and exercise good judgement to prevent personal injury and complete the work safely.*
> *• Before beginning any work on your vehicle, thoroughly read the safety notice, disclaimer, and all the Cautions and Warnings listed near the front of this manual.*
> *• Always read the complete procedure before you begin the work. Pay special attention to any Cautions and Warnings that accompany that procedure, or other information on a specific topic.*

V

W

RICHARD GROSS

PSYCHOLOGY

THE SCIENCE OF MIND AND BEHAVIOUR

SEVENTH EDITION

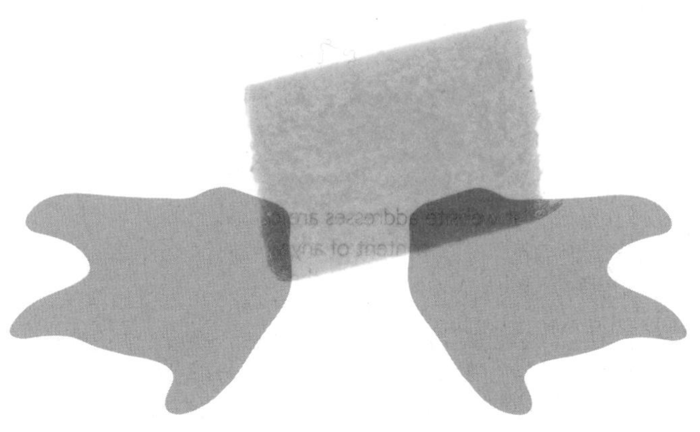

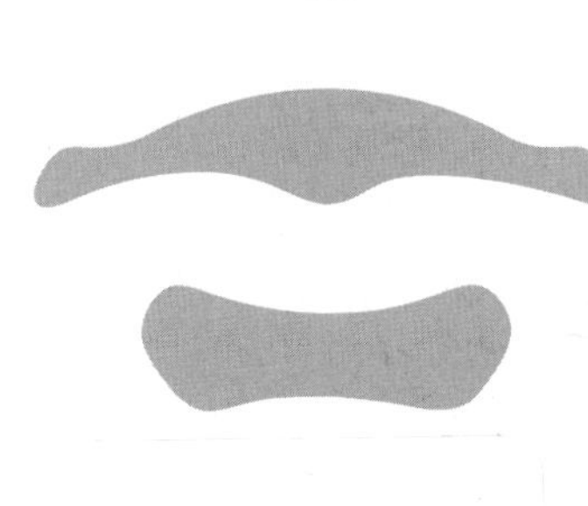

HODDER EDUCATION
AN HACHETTE UK COMPANY

Dedication

To my beautiful daughters, T.N. and J.G., in the hope that, given time, love will prevail.

Although every effort has been made to ensure that website addresses are correct at time of going to press, Hodder Education cannot be held responsible for the content of any website mentioned in this book. It is sometimes possible to find a relocated web page by typing in the address of the home page for a website in the URL window of your browser.

Hachette UK's policy is to use papers that are natural, renewable and recyclable products and made from wood grown in sustainable forests. The logging and manufacturing processes are expected to conform to the environmental regulations of the country of origin.

Orders: please contact Bookpoint Ltd, 130 Milton Park, Abingdon, Oxon OX14 4SB. Telephone: (44) 01235 827720. Fax: (44) 01235 400454. Lines are open from 9.00–5.00, Monday to Saturday, with a 24-hour message answering service. You can also order through our website www.hoddereducation.com

First published in 2015

by Hodder Education

An Hachette UK Company

Carmelite House, 50 Victoria Embankment, London EC4Y 0DZ

Impression number 5 4 3 2

Year 2019 2018 2017 2016

Illustrations by Peter Lubach, and Kate Nardoni/Cactus Design

Typeset in 9/11 Bembo Std/55 Roman by Integra Software Services Pvt. Ltd, Pondicherry, India.

Printed in India

A catalogue record for this title is available from the British Library

ISBN: 978 1471 829734

CONTENTS

PART 4: SOCIAL PSYCHOLOGY

PART 5: DEVELOPMENTAL PSYCHOLOGY

PART 6: INDIVIDUAL DIFFERENCES

PART 7: ISSUES AND DEBATES

GUIDED TOUR

Helps you to analyse, evaluate and assess the validity of this scientific information — a crucial component of A level and undergraduate study.

Critical Discussion 50.2

Are shared environments really that unimportant?

Scarr (1992) acknowledges the influence of the environment on behaviour but claims that, in reality, the environment is very similar for many individuals. According to the 'average [. . .]

Psychology is a research-driven field. These updates let you see how scientific explanations change in light of new information, showing you 'how science works'.

Research Update 42.1

Freud and neuroscience

As we noted in Chapter 2, support for certain aspects of Freud's theories has been provided by the relatively new sub-discipline of *neuropsychoanalysis* (NP), one of the many spin-offs [. . .]

Understanding the cultural context of scientific findings helps you to explain and evaluate a variety of methods and results from different psychological studies.

Cross-Cultural Study 35.1

Trobriand Island boys and their fathers (Malinowski, 1929)

- Among the Trobriand Islanders of Papua New Guinea, boys were traditionally disciplined by their maternal uncle (their mother's brother), rather than by their own [. . .]

With some key questions in mind (if not always answers!) you will more easily understand the major studies and theories.

Ask Yourself

- Do you agree with Skinner's claim that thoughts and other 'covert behaviours' don't explain our behaviour (because they cannot determine what we do)?

It can be hard to link theories to real life. Case studies give you concrete examples of people's stories, and how they confirm or challenge psychological research.

Case Study 4.1

The case of the phantom hand

Tom Sorenson lost a hand in a car accident, after which his arm was amputated just above the elbow. When his face was touched in various places, he experienced [. . .]

This feature explains the methods, results and implications of some of the more iconic or innovative work in Psychology.

Key Study 4.1

When the left brain literally doesn't know what the left hand is doing (Sperry, 1968)

- Participants sit in front of a screen, their hands free to handle objects that are behind the screen but which are obscured from sight.

There is a lot to take in for your exams and essays. This feature will help you revise, build up your knowledge of the key points and how they fit together.

Chapter Summary

- **Biopsychology** is the branch of neuroscience that studies the biological bases of behaviour. Biopsychologists are only interested in biology for what it can tell them about behaviour and mental processes.

Helps you evaluate a particular theory or piece of research by understanding its connections with others.

Links with Other Topics/Chapters

Chapter 28 ⟶ Babies' sociability has its adult counterpart in the *need for affiliation*, the basis of *interpersonal attraction*

Some of the top psychology researchers in the world talk in a more personal way about why they asked the questions they did. The methods they used, and the stories behind their research, will help you explain and evaluate the impact of their own and others' work in this continually developing science.

MEET THE RESEARCHER

Viv Burr

Constructions of the family in popular culture: the case of *Buffy the Vampire Slayer*

PREFACE

By the time this 7th edition of *Psychology: The Science of Mind and Behaviour* is published, it will be 28 years since the first edition appeared (and 30 years since the contract for that first edition was signed!). Needless to say, much has changed within Psychology in that time, and yet some of the basic questions that researchers have been exploring – and philosophers before them – are still being asked.

Despite the advent of e-books and the evolution of electronic media in general, the task of the textbook author has remained essentially the same. Something that you, as a student having to write essays, seminar papers, and dissertations, and I, as a textbook author, have in common, is the challenge of deciding what is best to include and exclude within what are always finite resources – time, money, words, and so on. Users of this book are (mainly) students new to Psychology, who need to know something of its past in order to appreciate where it is now – and where it might be going in the future. In order to make room for discussion of recent developments, I have continued what was started in the 6th edition, namely, to reduce the amount of detail when describing the older (but never redundant) material. Also, I've sometimes sign-posted the reader to alternative sources of material, rather than providing a cursory summary of a particular study or theory.

One of the features new to the 6th edition, and which has been retained in the 7th, is the 'Meet the Researcher' feature. While these haven't been updated, in all cases their original contributions remain as relevant and informative as they were when they first appeared. As well as providing additional material to what's covered in the main body of the textbook, what their contributions show is that there's always a 'story' behind a theory or chosen research project. Research doesn't appear out of nowhere and what particular Psychologists investigate isn't a random event. So, every time you read about a particular study, psychological concept or construct, or full-blown theory, remember that behind it are one or more human beings, each with their 'story' of how they came to be researching that topic rather than some other area of Psychology.

For the first time in this book, I've chosen to refer to the discipline of Psychology (and sub-disciplines) with an upper case 'P'. This applies also 'Psychologists'. When used as an adjective ('psychological'), or when referring to what Psychologists actually study (various aspects of human and non-human psychology), a lower case 'p' is used. This isn't just a matter of stylistic preference; distinguishing between 'Psychology' as a scientific discipline and 'human psychology' as what Psychologists investigate highlights the unique nature of Psychology: it's where people study themselves *as* people, using the same human abilities that they (often) are investigating. Even more importantly, what Psychologists tell us about ourselves may actually change us, i.e. our psychology.

Part of the appeal of previous editions was that they catered for the needs of students on a wide range of courses, without being written specifically or exclusively for any one group. I hope – and trust – that the same can be said of this 7th edition. As before, please let me know what you think of my efforts (via the publisher) – it's not just students who need feedback!

Richard Gross

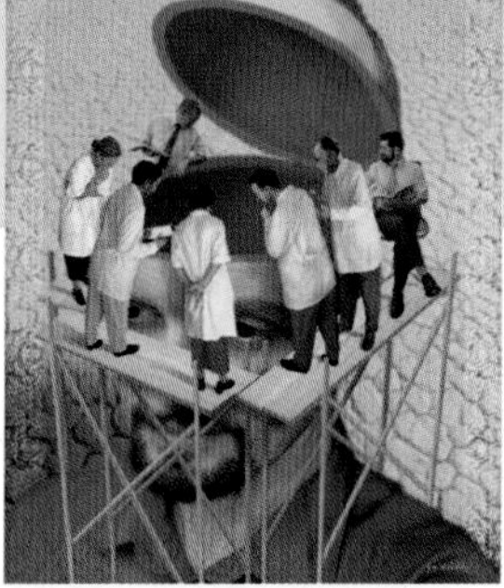

CHAPTER 1

WHAT IS THIS THING CALLED PSYCHOLOGY?

A brief history

Classifying the work of Psychologists

INTRODUCTION and OVERVIEW

Ask Yourself

- If you're completely new to Psychology, what do you expect it to consist of?
- If you've studied it before, how would you define it and what's the range of topics/subjects it covers?
- How does it differ from other disciplines, such as physiology, sociology and anthropology?

The opening chapter in any textbook is intended to 'set the scene' for what follows, and this normally involves defining the subject or discipline. In the case of Psychology, this isn't as straightforward as you might expect. Definitions of Psychology have changed frequently during its relatively short history as a separate field of study; this reflects different, and sometimes conflicting, theoretical views regarding the nature of human beings and the most appropriate methods for investigating them (see Chapter 2).

These theoretical differences partly reflect the complexity of the subject-matter. Perhaps more importantly, there's a very real sense in which we are all 'Psychologists' in our everyday lives: Psychologists as scientists/researchers use fundamental cognitive processes in order to investigate those same processes (such as perception and memory); hence, **P**sychologists (with an upper-case 'P') study human **p**sychology (with a lower-case 'p'), making the relationship between the discipline and the subject matter unique. However, there are important differences between the Psychologist-as-investigator and the person-as-'Psychologist'.

Also, the boundaries between Psychology and other subject disciplines aren't clearly drawn, and what this chapter aims to do is make them sufficiently clear to enable you, the reader, who may be 'visiting' Psychology for the first time, to find your way around this book – and the subject – relatively easily.

In Greek mythology, Psyche was represented by a butterfly. She became the wife of Eros, the god of love (renamed Cupid by the Romans).
And logos means "knowledge", "study": like all "ologies"!

Figure 1.1

A BRIEF HISTORY

The word 'psychology' is derived from the Greek *psyche* (mind, soul or spirit) and *logos* (knowledge, discourse or study). Literally, then, Psychology is the 'study of the mind'. The emergence of Psychology as a separate discipline is generally dated from 1879, when Wilhelm Wundt opened the first psychological laboratory at the University of Leipzig in Germany. Wundt and his co-workers were attempting to investigate 'the mind' through *introspection* (observing and analysing the structure of their own conscious mental processes). Introspection's aim was to analyse conscious thought into its basic elements and perception into its constituent sensations, much as chemists analyse compounds into elements. This attempt to identify the structure of conscious thought is called *structuralism*.

Wundt and his co-workers measured and recorded the results of their introspections under controlled conditions, using the same physical surroundings, the same 'stimulus' (such as a clicking metronome), the same verbal instructions to each participant, and so on. This emphasis on measurement and control marked the separation of the 'new Psychology' from its parent discipline of philosophy.

Philosophers had discussed 'the mind' for thousands of years. For the first time, scientists (Wundt was a physiologist) applied some of scientific investigation's basic methods to the study of mental processes. This was reflected in James's (1890) definition of Psychology as:

> *the Science of Mental Life, both of its phenomena and of their conditions ... The Phenomena are such things as we call feelings, desires, cognition, reasoning, decisions and the like.*

However, by the early twentieth century, the validity and usefulness of introspection were being seriously questioned, particularly by John B. Watson, an American Psychologist. Watson believed that the results of introspection could never be proved or disproved: if two people produce different introspective accounts, how can we ever decide whose is correct? Objectively, of course, we cannot: introspection is subjective, and only the individual can observe his/her own mental processes.

Consequently, Watson (1913) proposed that Psychologists should confine themselves to studying *behaviour*, since only this is measurable and observable by more than one person. Watson's *behaviourism* largely replaced introspectionism, advocating that people should be regarded as complex animals and studied using the same scientific methods as those used in chemistry and physics. For Watson, the only way Psychology could make any claim to being scientific was to emulate the natural sciences and adopt its own objective methods. Watson (1919) defined Psychology as:

> *that division of Natural Science which takes human behaviour – the doings and sayings, both learned and unlearned – as its subject matter.*

The study of inaccessible, private, mental processes was to have no place in a truly scientific Psychology.

Especially in the USA, behaviourism (in one form or another) remained the dominant force for the next 40 years or so. The emphasis on the role of learning (in the form of conditioning) was to make that topic one of the central areas of psychological research as a whole (see Chapters 2 and 11).

In the late 1950s, many British and American Psychologists began looking to the work of computer scientists to try to understand more complex behaviours which, they felt, had been either neglected altogether or greatly oversimplified by learning theory (conditioning). These complex behaviours were what Wundt, James and other early scientific Psychologists had called 'mind' or *mental processes*. They were now called *cognition* or *cognitive processes*, and refer to all the ways in which we come to know the world around us, how we attain, retain and regain information, through the processes of perception, attention, memory, problem-solving, decision-making, language and thinking in general.

Cognitive Psychologists see people as *information-processors*, and Cognitive Psychology has been heavily influenced by computer science, with human cognitive processes being compared to the operation of computer programs (the *computer analogy*). Cognitive Psychology now forms part of cognitive science, which emerged in the late 1970s (see Figure 1.2). The events which together constitute the 'cognitive revolution' are described in Box 3.3 (page 40).

Although cognitive processes can only be *inferred* from what a person does (they cannot be observed literally or directly), they're now accepted as being valid subject matter for Psychology, provided they can be made 'public' (as in memory tests or problem-solving tasks). Consequently, what people say and do are perfectly acceptable sources of information *about* their cognitive processes; however, the processes themselves remain inaccessible to the observer, who can study them only indirectly.

Box 1.1 Psychoanalytic Theory and Gestalt Psychology

- In 1900, Sigmund Freud, a neurologist living in Vienna, first published his *psychoanalytic* theory of personality in which the unconscious mind played a crucial role. In parallel with this theory, he developed a form of psychotherapy called *psychoanalysis*. Freud's theory (which forms the basis of the *psychodynamic* approach) represented a challenge and a major alternative to behaviourism (see Chapter 2, pages 18–21).
- A reaction against both structuralism and behaviourism came from the Gestalt school, which emerged in the 1920s in Austria and Germany. Gestalt Psychologists were mainly interested in perception, and believed that perceptions couldn't be broken down in the way that Wundt proposed (see Chapter 3) and behaviourists advocated for behaviour (see Chapters 3 and 11). They identified several 'laws' or *principles of perceptual organisation* (such as 'the whole is greater than the sum of its parts'), which have made a lasting contribution to our understanding of the perceptual process (see Chapter 15 for a detailed discussion).

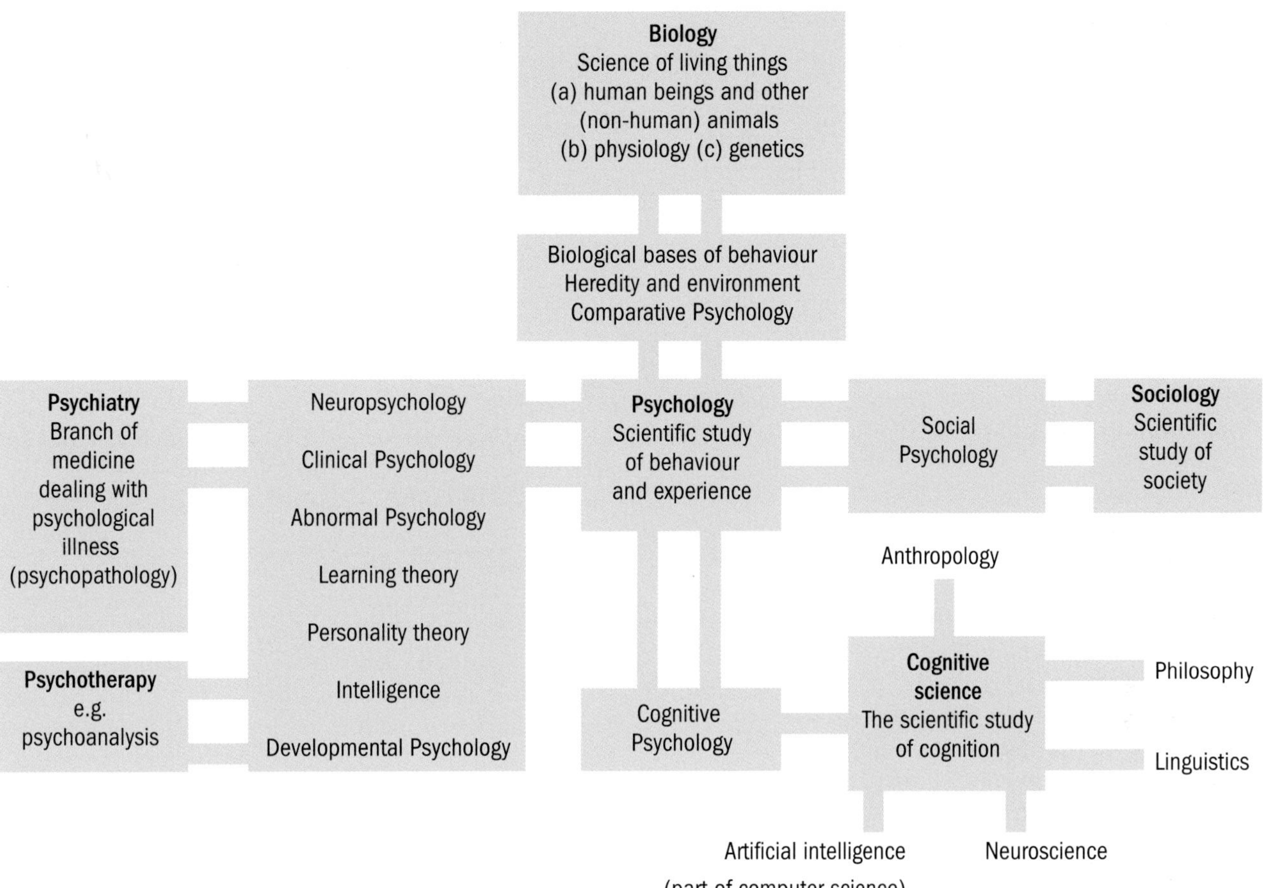

Figure 1.2 The relationship between Psychology and other scientific disciplines

The influence of both behaviourism and Cognitive Psychology is reflected in Clark and Miller's (1970) definition of Psychology as:

> *the scientific study of behaviour. Its subject matter includes behavioural processes that are observable, such as gestures, speech and physiological changes, and processes that can only be inferred, such as thoughts and dreams.*

According to the British Psychological Society (BPS; www.bps.org.uk), Psychology is:

> *the scientific study of people, the mind and behaviour. It is both a thriving academic discipline and a vital professional practice.*

CLASSIFYING THE WORK OF PSYCHOLOGISTS

Despite Behaviourist and Cognitive Psychology's influence during the last 90 years or so, much more goes on within Psychology than has been outlined so far. There are other theoretical approaches or orientations, other aspects of human (and non-human) activity that constitute the special focus of study, and different kinds of work that different Psychologists do.

The BPS's distinction between the academic and professional (i.e. applied) branches of Psychology is reflected in Figure 1.4. *Academic Psychologists* carry out research and are attached to a university or research establishment, where they also teach undergraduates and supervise postgraduate research. Research is both *pure* (done for its own sake and intended, primarily, to increase our knowledge and understanding) and *applied* (aimed at solving a particular problem). Applied research is usually funded by a government institution such as the Home Office, National Health Service (NHS) or the Department for Education and Employment (DfEE), or by some commercial or industrial institution. The range of topics that may be investigated is as wide as Psychology itself, but they can be classified as focusing either on the processes or mechanisms underlying various aspects of behaviour, or more directly on people (Legge, 1975).

The process approach

This is divided into three main areas: Physiological, Cognitive and Comparative Psychology.

Physiological (or Bio-)Psychology (Chapters 4–12)

Physiological (or Bio-)Psychologists are interested in the physical basis of behaviour, how the functions of the nervous system (in particular the brain) and the endocrine (hormonal) system are related to and influence behaviour and mental processes. For example, are there parts of the brain specifically concerned with particular behaviours and abilities (localisation of brain function)? What role do hormones play in the experience of emotion and how are these linked to brain processes? What is the relationship between brain activity and different states of consciousness (including sleep)?

A fundamentally important biological process with important implications for Psychology is *genetic transmission*. The *heredity and environment* (or *nature–nurture*) issue draws on what geneticists have discovered about the characteristics that can be passed from parents to offspring, how this takes place, and how genetic factors interact with environmental ones (see Chapters 41, 44 and 50). Other research areas include motivation and stress (an important topic within *Health Psychology*: see Chapter 12), and sensory processes, which are closely connected with perception (see Chapter 15).

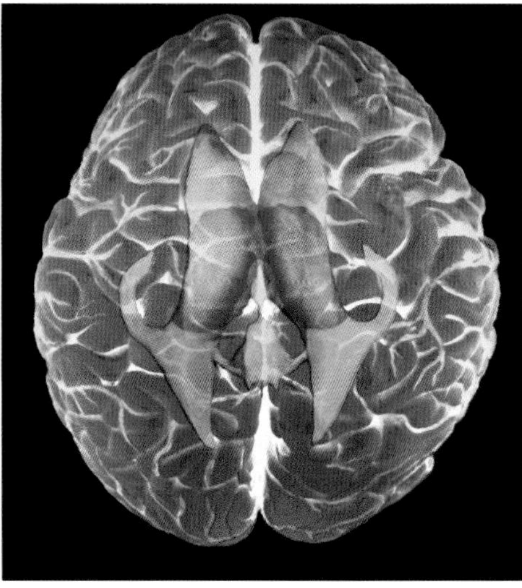

Figure 1.3 A brain-scan image of the underside of the human brain

Cognitive Psychology (Chapters 13–21)

As we saw earlier, cognitive processes include *attention, memory, perception, language, thinking, problem-solving, decision-making, reasoning* and *concept-formation* ('higher-order' mental activities). Although these are often studied for their own sake, they may also have important practical implications, such as understanding the memory processes involved in *eyewitness testimony* (see Chapter 21). Social Psychology (classified here as belonging to the person approach) is heavily cognitive in flavour: many Social Psychologists study the mental processes we use when trying to explain people's behaviour, for example (social cognition). Also, Piaget's theory (again, belonging to the person approach) is concerned with cognitive development.

Comparative Psychology

Comparative Psychology is the study of the behaviour of non-human animals, aimed at identifying similarities and differences between species. It also involves studying non-human animal behaviour to gain a better understanding of human behaviour. The basis of Comparative Psychology is evolutionary theory. Research areas include classical and operant conditioning (see Chapter 11), animal communication, language and memory (see Gross, 2012a), and evolutionary explanations of human behaviour (see, for example, Chapter 2, pages 30–34). Teaching language to non-humans is discussed in relation to language development (Chapter 19).

The person approach

Social Psychology (Chapters 22–31)

Some Psychologists would claim that 'all Psychology is Social Psychology', because all behaviour takes place within a social context and, even when we're alone, our behaviour continues to be influenced by others. However, other people usually have a more immediate and direct influence upon us when we're actually in their presence (as in *conformity* and *obedience*: see Chapters 26 and 27).

Social Psychology is also concerned with *social* (or *interpersonal*) *perception* (forming impressions of others), *interpersonal relationships*, *prejudice* and *discrimination*, and *pro- and antisocial behaviour* (especially *aggression*). Chapter 31 looks at the Social Psychology of sport.

Developmental Psychology (Chapters 32–40)

Developmental Psychologists study the biological, cognitive, social and emotional changes that occur in people over time. One significant change during the past 30 years or so is the recognition that development isn't confined to childhood and adolescence, but is a lifelong process (the *lifespan approach*): development continues beyond childhood and adolescence into adulthood and old age.

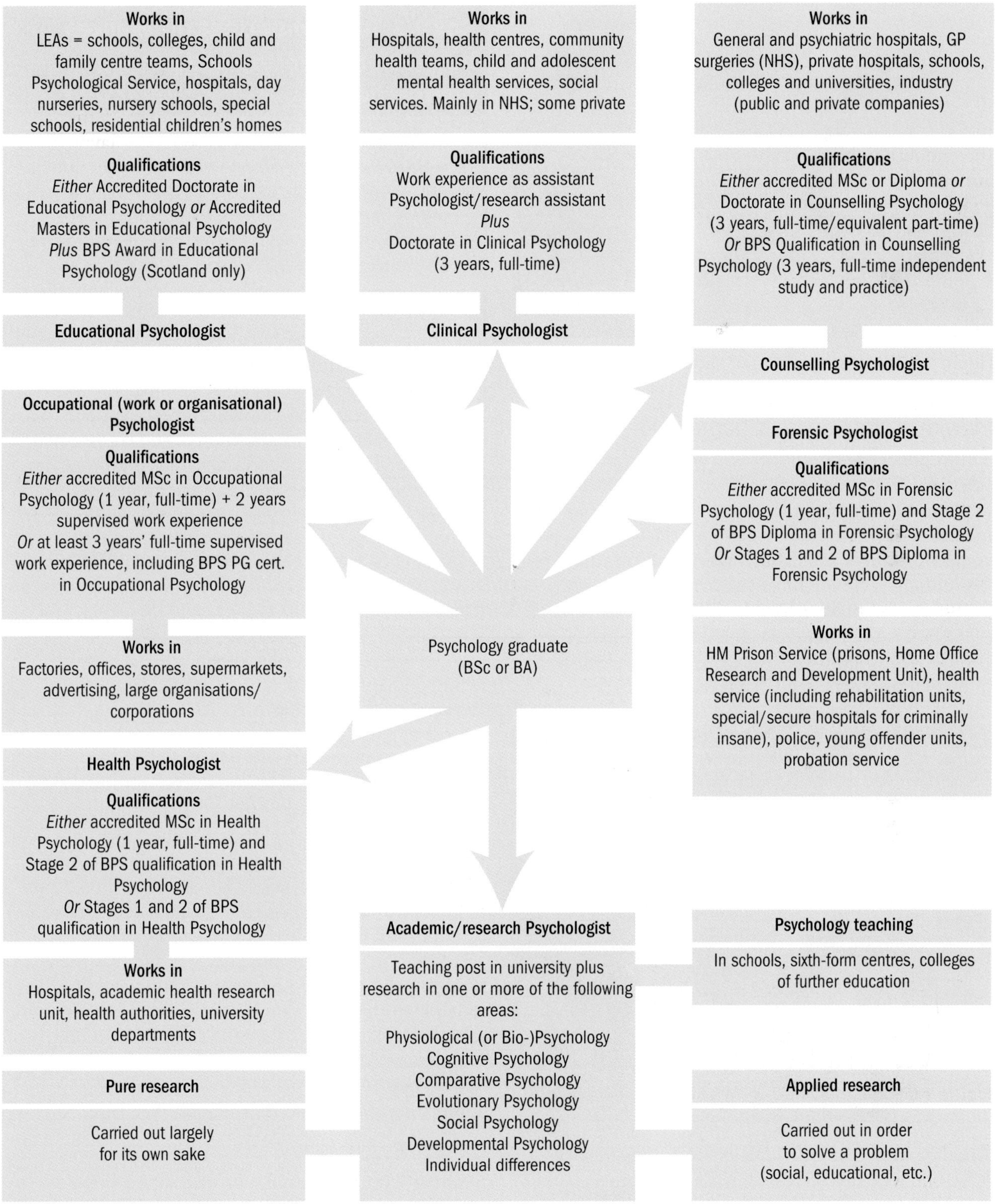

Works in
LEAs = schools, colleges, child and family centre teams, Schools Psychological Service, hospitals, day nurseries, nursery schools, special schools, residential children's homes

Qualifications
Either Accredited Doctorate in Educational Psychology *or* Accredited Masters in Educational Psychology *Plus* BPS Award in Educational Psychology (Scotland only)

Educational Psychologist

Works in
Hospitals, health centres, community health teams, child and adolescent mental health services, social services. Mainly in NHS; some private

Qualifications
Work experience as assistant Psychologist/research assistant
Plus
Doctorate in Clinical Psychology (3 years, full-time)

Clinical Psychologist

Works in
General and psychiatric hospitals, GP surgeries (NHS), private hospitals, schools, colleges and universities, industry (public and private companies)

Qualifications
Either accredited MSc or Diploma *or* Doctorate in Counselling Psychology (3 years, full-time/equivalent part-time)
Or BPS Qualification in Counselling Psychology (3 years, full-time independent study and practice)

Counselling Psychologist

Occupational (work or organisational) Psychologist

Qualifications
Either accredited MSc in Occupational Psychology (1 year, full-time) + 2 years supervised work experience
Or at least 3 years' full-time supervised work experience, including BPS PG cert. in Occupational Psychology

Works in
Factories, offices, stores, supermarkets, advertising, large organisations/corporations

Psychology graduate (BSc or BA)

Forensic Psychologist

Qualifications
Either accredited MSc in Forensic Psychology (1 year, full-time) and Stage 2 of BPS Diploma in Forensic Psychology
Or Stages 1 and 2 of BPS Diploma in Forensic Psychology

Works in
HM Prison Service (prisons, Home Office Research and Development Unit), health service (including rehabilitation units, special/secure hospitals for criminally insane), police, young offender units, probation service

Health Psychologist

Qualifications
Either accredited MSc in Health Psychology (1 year, full-time) and Stage 2 of BPS qualification in Health Psychology
Or Stages 1 and 2 of BPS qualification in Health Psychology

Works in
Hospitals, academic health research unit, health authorities, university departments

Academic/research Psychologist

Teaching post in university plus research in one or more of the following areas:

Physiological (or Bio-)Psychology
Cognitive Psychology
Comparative Psychology
Evolutionary Psychology
Social Psychology
Developmental Psychology
Individual differences

Psychology teaching

In schools, sixth-form centres, colleges of further education

Pure research

Carried out largely for its own sake

Applied research

Carried out in order to solve a problem (social, educational, etc.)

Figure 1.4 Some of the main areas of academic and applied Psychology open to Psychology graduates

Developmental Psychology isn't an isolated or independent field, and advances in it depend on progress within Psychology as a whole, such as behaviour genetics, (Neuro)Physiological Psychology, learning, perception and motivation. Equally, Piaget's theory of cognitive development is considered to have made a major contribution to Psychology as a whole (see Chapter 34). While the focus is on normal development, Chapter 40 is concerned with exceptional/atypical development.

Figure 1.5 Three generations of the same family

Individual differences (Chapters 41–46)

This is concerned with the ways in which people can differ from one another, including personality, intelligence and psychological abnormality. Major mental disorders include schizophrenia, depression, anxiety disorders and eating disorders. Abnormal Psychology is closely linked to Clinical Psychology, one of the major applied areas of Psychology (see below). Each major theoretical approach has contributed to both the explanation and the treatment of mental disorders (see Chapters 2 and 45).

Figure 1.6 Some individual differences are very obvious

Another source of individual differences is *criminal behaviour*, which is discussed in Chapter 46.

Areas of Applied Psychology

Discussion of the person/process approaches has been largely concerned with the academic branch of Psychology. Since the various areas of Applied Psychology are all concerned with people, they can be thought of as the applied aspects of the person approach.

Box 1.2 Some important differences between the process and person approaches

- The **process approach** is typically confined to the laboratory (where experiments are the method of choice). It makes far greater experimental use of non-human animals and assumes that psychological processes (particularly learning) are essentially the same in all species, and that any differences between species are only *quantitative* (differences of degree).
- The **person approach** makes much greater use of field studies (such as observing behaviour in its natural environment) and of non-experimental methods (e.g. correlational studies). Typically, human participants are studied, and it's assumed that there are *qualitative* differences (differences in kind) between humans and non-humans.

According to Hartley and Branthwaite (1997), most applied Psychologists work in four main areas: *Clinical*, *Educational* and *Occupational Psychology*, and government service (such as *Forensic* or *Criminological* Psychologists). In addition, Coolican *et al.* (2007) identify *Counselling*, *Sport and Exercise*, *Health* and *Environmental* Psychologists.

Each of these eight areas is represented by a division within the BPS. Other divisions are (a) Teachers and Researchers; and (b) Neuropsychology. *Neuropsychologists* investigate the relationship between the brain and cognitive or physiological processes; like Clinical Psychologists, they may also help to assess and rehabilitate brain-injured people and those with neurological disorders (such as strokes, dementia, tumours and degenerative brain diseases).

Hartley and Branthwaite (1997) argue that the work Psychologists do in these different areas has much in common: it's the subject matter of their jobs that differs, rather than the skills they employ. Consequently, they consider an Applied Psychologist to be a person who can deploy specialised skills appropriately in different situations. (See Box 1.3.)

Clinical Psychology

Clinical Psychology represents the largest single division within the BPS (Coolican *et al.*, 2007) and the USA (Atkinson *et al.*, 1990). They usually work as part of a team with, for example, social workers, medical practitioners and other health professionals. In the UK, most work in the NHS, but some work in private practice. (See Box 1.4.)

Psychotherapy is usually carried out by psychiatrists (medically qualified doctors specialising

Box 1.3 Seven major skills (or roles) used by Applied Psychologists

- **Psychologist as counsellor**: helping people to talk openly, express their feelings, explore problems more deeply, and see these problems from different perspectives. Problems may include school phobia, marriage crises and traumatic experiences and the counsellor can adopt a more or less directive approach (see Chapter 2, pp. 21–23, and Chapter 45).
- **Psychologist as colleague**: working as a member of a team and bringing a particular perspective to a task, namely drawing attention to the human issues, such as the point of view of the individual end-user (be it a product or a service of some kind).
- **Psychologist as expert**: drawing upon specialised knowledge, ideas, theories and practical knowledge to advise on issues ranging from incentive schemes in industry to appearing as an 'expert witness' in a court case.
- **Psychologist as toolmaker**: using and developing appropriate measures and techniques to help in the analysis and assessment of problems, including questionnaire and interview schedules, computer-based ability and aptitude tests, and other psychometric tests (see Chapters 41 and 42).
- **Psychologist as detached investigator**: many Applied Psychologists carry out evaluation studies to assess the evidence for and against a particular viewpoint. This reflects the view of Psychology as an objective science, which should use controlled experimentation whenever possible. The validity of this view is a recurrent theme (see, in particular, Chapter 3).
- **Psychologist as theoretician**: theories try to explain observed phenomena, suggesting possible underlying mechanisms or processes. They can suggest where to look for causes and how to design specific studies that will produce evidence for or against a particular point of view.
- **Psychologist as agent for change**: helping people, institutions and organisations, based on the belief that their work will change people and society for the better. However, some changes are much more controversial than others, such as the use of psychometric tests to determine educational and occupational opportunities, and the use of behaviour therapy and modification techniques to change abnormal behaviour (see Chapters 41, 45, 47 and 48).

(Based on Hartley and Branthwaite, 2000)

Box 1.4 The major functions of the Clinical Psychologist

- Assessing people with learning difficulties (LDs), administering psychological tests to brain-damaged patients, devising rehabilitation programmes for long-term psychiatric patients and assessing the elderly for their fitness to live independently.
- Planning and carrying out programmes of therapy, usually behaviour therapy/modification (both derived from learning theory principles) or psychotherapy (group or individual) in preference to, or in addition to, behavioural techniques (see Chapter 45).
- Carrying out research into abnormal psychology, including the effectiveness of different treatment methods ('outcome' studies); patients are usually adults, many of whom will be elderly, in psychiatric hospitals, psychiatric wards in general hospitals and psychiatric clinics.
- Involvement in community care, as psychiatric care in general moves out of the large psychiatric hospitals.
- Teaching other groups of professionals, such as nurses, psychiatrists and social workers.

Figure 1.7 A Clinical Psychologist working in a day-centre for the elderly

in psychological medicine) or psychotherapists (who've undergone special training, including their own psychotherapy). In all its various forms, psychotherapy is derived from Freud's psychoanalysis (see Chapters 2 and 45), and is distinguished from both behavioural treatments and physical (somatic) treatments (those based on the medical model: see Chapters 43 and 45).

Counselling Psychology

Counselling Psychologists work within the NHS (in general and psychiatric hospitals and GP surgeries), in private hospitals and in private practice, in schools, colleges and universities, within the prison service, in industry and in public and private corporate institutions. They may work directly with individuals, couples, families and groups, or act as consultants (see Chapter 45).

Forensic Psychology

Forensic Psychology is the application of psychological principles and methods to the criminal justice system. It is rooted in empirical research and draws on Cognitive, Developmental, Social and Clinical Psychology. One main focus is the study of criminal behaviour and its management, but in recent years research interests have expanded to include other areas, most notably those with a high media profile (such as stalking: see Chapter 46). Like Clinical Psychologists, a crucial part of their work involves research and evaluation of what constitutes successful treatment.

The largest single employer of Forensic Psychologists in the UK is HM Prison Service (which includes the Home Office Research and Development Unit as well as prisons). Forensic (formerly 'Criminological') Psychologists also work in the health service (including rehabilitation units and special/secure hospitals for the criminally insane, such as Broadmoor and Rampton), the police service, young offender units and the probation service. Some work in university departments or in private consultancy.

Box 1.5 Some recent areas of research interest among Forensic Psychologists

- Jury selection
- The presentation of evidence
- Eyewitness testimony (see Chapter 21)
- Improving the recall of child witnesses
- False memory syndrome and recovered memory (see Chapter 21)
- Offender profiling (see Chapter 46)
- Crime prevention (see Chapter 46)
- Devising treatment programmes (such as anger management, see Chapter 46)
- Assessing the risk of releasing prisoners (see Chapter 46)

(From Coolican *et al*., 1996)

Educational Psychology

Before 2006, people wanting to train as Educational Psychologists were required to have a teaching qualification and experience. Now, all that's required is a three-year postgraduate training in Educational Psychology (see Figure 1.4) (Frederickson and Miller, 2008).

Educational Psychologists' clients are mostly aged up to 18 years, but most fall into the 5–16 age group. They regularly liaise with other professionals from the departments of education, health and social services. A growing number work as independent or private consultants (British Psychological Society, 2004).

Box 1.6 Some of the responsibilities of the Educational Psychologist

- Administering psychometric tests, particularly intelligence (or IQ) tests, as part of the assessment of LDs (see Chapters 40 and 41).
- Planning and supervising remedial teaching; research into teaching methods, the curriculum (subjects taught), interviewing and counselling methods and techniques.
- Planning educational programmes for those with mental and physical impairments (including the visually impaired and autistic), and other groups of children and adolescents who aren't attending ordinary schools (special educational needs; see Chapter 40).
- Advising parents and teachers on how to deal with children and adolescents with physical impairments, behaviour problems or LDs.
- Teacher training.

In the USA, *Educational Psychology* is concerned with theory, methodology and applications to a broad range of teaching, training and learning issues. *School Psychology* refers to the delivery of psychological services to children, adolescents and families in schools and other applied settings (Frederickson and Miller, 2008).

Occupational (Work or Organisational) Psychology

Occupational Psychologists are involved in the selection and training of individuals for jobs and vocational guidance, including administration of aptitude tests and tests of interest. (This overlaps with the work of those trained in personnel management.)

Figure 1.8 An Educational Psychologist working in a special needs school

Box 1.7 Other responsibilities of the Occupational Psychologist

- Helping people who, for reasons of illness, accident or redundancy, need to choose and retrain for a new career (*industrial rehabilitation*).
- Designing training schemes, as part of 'fitting the person to the job'; teaching machines and simulators (such as an aeroplane cockpit) often feature prominently in these schemes.
- 'Fitting the job to the person' (human engineering/Engineering Psychology or *ergonomics*) – findings from Experimental Psychology are applied to the design of equipment and machinery in order to make the best use of human resources and to minimise accidents and fatigue; examples include telephone dialling codes (memory and attention) and the design of decimal coinage (tactile and visual discrimination).
- Advising on working conditions in order to maximise productivity (another facet of ergonomics – the study of people's efficiency in their working environments); occupational groups involved include computer/VDU operators, production-line workers and air-traffic controllers.
- Helping the flow of communication between departments in government institutions, or 'industrial relations' in commerce and industry (Organisational Psychology); the emphasis is on the *social*, rather than the physical or practical, aspects of the working environment.
- Helping to sell products and services through advertising and promotions; many Psychologists are employed in the advertising industry, where they draw on what Experimental Psychologists have discovered about human motivation, attitudes and cognition (see Chapter 24).

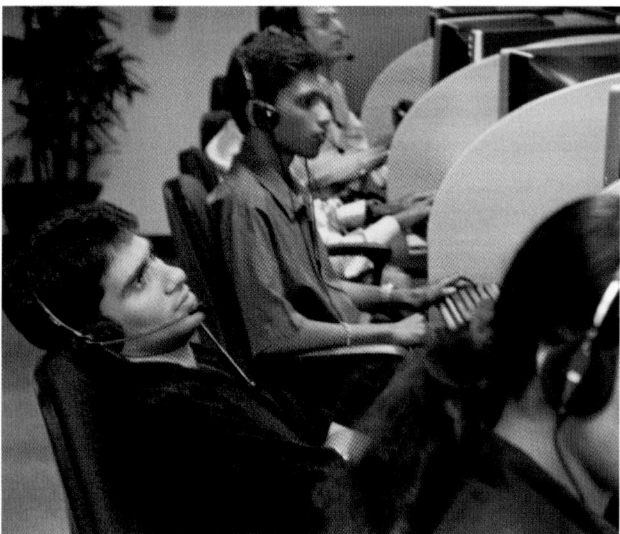

Figure 1.9 An Indian call centre

Health Psychology

Health Psychology, which involves the use of psychological principles to promote changes in people's attitudes and behaviour about health and illness, is one of the newer fields of Applied Psychology.

Health Psychologists work in a variety of settings, such as hospitals, academic health research units, health authorities and university departments. They may deal with problems identified by health care agencies, including NHS Trusts and health authorities, health professionals (such as GPs, nurses and rehabilitation therapists) and employers outside the health care system. (See Box 1.8.)

Box 1.8 The breadth of Health Psychology

- The use of psychological theories and interventions to prevent damaging behaviours (such as smoking, drug abuse and poor diet), and to change health-related behaviour in community and workplace settings.
- Promoting and protecting health by encouraging behaviours such as exercise, healthy diet, teeth brushing, health checks/self-examination.
- Investigating the processes that can explain, predict and change health and illness behaviours (health-related cognitions).
- The nature and effects of communication between health care practitioners and patients, including interventions to improve communication, facilitate adherence (such as taking medication), prepare for stressful medical procedures, and so on.
- Looking at the psychological impact of acute and chronic illness on individuals, carers and families.

Chartered Psychologists

The BPS is the representative body for Psychology and Psychologists in the UK and the only professional body for British Psychologists incorporated by Royal Charter. It has national responsibility for the development, promotion and application of Psychology for the public good, and promotes the efficiency and usefulness of its members by maintaining a high standard of professional education and knowledge.

Since 1987, the BPS has been authorised under its Charter to keep a Register of *Chartered Psychologists*. Entry to the Register is restricted to members of the Society who've applied for registration and who have the necessary qualifications or experience to have reached a standard sufficient for professional practice in Psychology without supervision (Gale, 1990).

Figure 1.10 Logo of the British Psychological Society

All the applied areas described above (Clinical, Counselling, Forensic, Educational, Occupational and Health), plus Sport and Exercise Psychology, lead to chartered status. This is also true of Teaching and Research, which requires either (a) a PhD in psychology or (b) for teachers, at least three years' full-time experience as a teacher of Psychology including the BPS's Diploma in the Applied Psychology of Teaching. As yet, psychotherapy doesn't grant chartered status (British Psychological Society, 2004).

Ask Yourself

- What, if anything, has come as a surprise to you regarding what goes on in the name of 'Psychology'?

The language of Psychology

- As in all sciences, there's a special set of technical terms (jargon) to get used to, and this is generally accepted as an unavoidable feature of studying the subject. But over and above this jargon, Psychologists use words that are familiar to us from everyday speech in a technical way, and it's in these instances that 'doing Psychology' can become a little confusing.
- Some examples of this are 'behaviour' and 'personality'. For a parent to tell a child to 'behave yourself' is meaningless to a Psychologist's ears: behaving is something we're all doing all the time (even when we're asleep). Similarly, to say that someone 'has no personality' is meaningless because, as personality refers to what makes a person unique and different from others, you cannot help but have one!
- Other terms that denote large portions of the research of Experimental Psychology, such as memory, learning and intelligence, are *hypothetical constructs* – that is, they don't refer to anything that can be directly observed but only inferred from observable behaviour (see above, page 2). They're necessary for explaining the behaviour being observed, but there's a danger of thinking of them as 'things' or 'entities' (*reification*), rather than as a way of trying to make sense of behaviour.
- Another way in which Psychologists try to make sense of something is by comparing it with something else using an analogy. Often something complex is compared with something more simple. Since the 1950s and the development of computer science, the *computer analogy* has become very popular as a way of trying to understand how the mind works. As we saw earlier, the language of computer science has permeated the cognitive view of human beings as information processors (see Chapter 2, pp. 23–26).
- A *model* is a kind of metaphor, involving a single, fundamental idea or image; this makes it less complex than a *theory* (although sometimes the terms are used interchangeably). A theory is a complex set of interrelated statements that attempt to explain certain observed phenomena. But in practice, when we refer to a particular theory (for example, Freud's or Piaget's), we often include description as well. Thomas (1985) defines a theory as 'an explanation of how the facts fit together', and he likens a theory to a lens through which to view the subject matter, filtering out certain facts and giving a particular pattern to those it lets in. A *hypothesis* is a testable statement about the relationship between two or more variables, usually derived from a model or theory (see Chapter 3).

Psychology and common sense

Ask Yourself

- What do you understand by the term 'common sense'?
- In what ways are we all Psychologists?
- How might a 'common-sense' understanding of human behaviour and experience differ from that of professional Psychologists?

We all consider we know something about people and why they behave as they do, and so there's a sense in which we're all Psychologists (see Chapters 22 and 23, and Gross, 2014). This is a theme explored at length by Joynson in *Psychology and Common Sense* (1974). He begins by stating that human beings aren't like the objects of natural science – we understand ourselves and can already predict and control our behaviour to a remarkable extent. This creates for the Psychologist a paradoxical task: what kind of understanding can you seek of a creature that already understands itself?

"Ok, let's try reverse psychology. Andrew... don't eat all your dinner up!"

Figure 1.11

For Joynson, the fundamental question is: If the Psychologist did not exist, would it be necessary to invent him? Conversely, for Skinner (1971), 'it is science or nothing' and Broadbent (1961) also rejects the validity of our everyday understanding of ourselves and others (Joynson calls this 'the behaviourists' prejudice'). Yet we cannot help but try to make sense of our own and other people's behaviour (by virtue of our cognitive abilities and the nature of social interaction) and, to this extent, we're all Psychologists. Heather (1976) points to ordinary language as embodying our 'natural' understanding of human behaviour: as long as human beings have lived they've been Psychologists, and language gives us an 'elaborate and highly refined conceptual tool, developed over thousands of years of talking to each other'.

Formal versus informal Psychology

Legge (1975) and others resolve this dilemma by distinguishing between *formal* and *informal* Psychology (or professional versus amateur, scientific versus non-scientific).

Our common sense, intuitive or 'natural' understanding is unsystematic and doesn't constitute a body of knowledge. This makes it very difficult to 'check' an individual's 'theory' about human nature, as does the fact that each individual has to learn from his/her own experience. So, part of the aim of formal Psychology is to provide such a systematic body of knowledge, which represents the unobservable basis of our 'gut reactions'.

Yet it could be argued that informal Psychology *does* provide a 'body of knowledge' in the form of proverbs or sayings or folk wisdom, handed down from generation to generation (for example, 'Birds of a feather flock together', 'Too many cooks spoil the broth' and 'Don't cross your bridges before you come to them'). While these may contain at least a grain of truth, for each one there's another proverb that states the opposite ('Opposites attract', 'Many hands make light work' and 'Time and tide wait for no man' or 'Nothing ventured, nothing gained') (Rolls, 2007).

However, formal Psychology may help us reconcile these contradictory statements. For example, there's evidence to support both proverbs in the first pair (see Chapter 28). Formal Psychology tries to identify the conditions under which each statement applies; they appear contradictory if we assume that only one or the other can be true! In this way, scientific Psychology throws light on our everyday, informal understanding, rather than negating or invalidating it.

Legge (1975) believes that most psychological research should indeed be aimed at demonstrating 'what we know already', but that it should also aim to go one step further. Only the methods of science, he believes, can provide us with the public, communicable body of knowledge that we're seeking. According to Allport (1947), the aim of science is 'Understanding, prediction and control above the levels achieved by unaided common sense', and this is meant to apply to Psychology as much as to the natural sciences (see Chapters 3 and 42).

CONCLUSIONS

Psychology is a diverse discipline. Psychologists investigate a huge range of behaviours and mental or cognitive processes. There is a growing number of applied areas, in which theory and research findings are brought to bear in trying to improve people's lives in a variety of ways. During the course of its life as a separate discipline, definitions of Psychology have changed quite fundamentally, reflecting the influence of different theoretical approaches. Rather than having to choose between our common-sense understanding of people and the 'scientific' version, Psychology as a scientific discipline can be seen as complementing and illuminating our 'everyday' psychological knowledge.

Chapter Summary

- Early Psychologists, such as Wundt, attempted to study the mind through **introspection** under controlled conditions, aiming to analyse conscious thought into its basic elements (**structuralism**).
- Watson rejected introspectionism's **subjectivity** and replaced it with **behaviourism**. Only by regarding people as complex animals, using the methods of natural science and studying observable behaviour, could Psychology become a true science.
- **Gestalt Psychologists** criticised both structuralism and behaviourism, advocating that 'the whole is greater than the sum of its parts'. Freud's **psychoanalytic theory** was another major alternative to behaviourism.
- Following the **cognitive revolution**, people came to be seen as **information-processors**, based on the **computer analogy**. Cognitive processes, such as perception and memory, became an acceptable part of Psychology's subject matter.
- **Academic** Psychologists are mainly concerned with conducting research (**pure** or **applied**), which may focus on underlying processes/mechanisms or on the person.
- The **process approach** consists of Physiological, Cognitive and Comparative Psychology, while the **person approach** covers Developmental and Social Psychology and individual differences.
- While the process approach is largely confined to **laboratory experiments** using **non-humans**, the person approach makes greater use of **field studies** and **non-experimental methods** involving **humans**. The two approaches see species differences as **quantitative** or **qualitative** respectively.
- Most **Applied Psychologists** work in **Clinical**, **Counselling**, **Forensic**, **Educational** or **Occupational** Psychology. Newer fields include **Health** and **Sport and Exercise** Psychology.
- There's a sense in which we're all Psychologists, creating a dilemma for Psychologists: are they necessary? One solution is to distinguish between **informal/common-sense** and **formal/ scientific Psychology**. The latter aims to go beyond common-sense understanding and to provide a public, communicable body of knowledge.

Recommended Reading

Benson, N.C. & Grove, G. (1998) *Psychology for Beginners*. Cambridge: Icon Books.

Equally relevant to Chapter 2.

Butler, G. & McManus, F. (1998) *Psychology: A Very Short Introduction*. Oxford: Oxford University Press.

Danziger, K. (1990) *Constructing the Subject: Historical Origins of Psychological Research*. Cambridge: Cambridge University Press.

Fancher, R.E. (1996) *Pioneers of Psychology* (3rd edn). New York: Norton.

Equally relevant (if not more so) to Chapters 2 and 3.

McGhee, P. (2000) *Thinking Psychologically*. Basingstoke: Palgrave.

Just as relevant to Chapters 2 and 3.

Useful Websites

www.bps.org.uk The official website of the British Psychological Society/BPS. www.apa.org/ (The official site of the American Psychological Association/APA)

http://changingminds.org/ (Provides huge number of links to all research areas. Especially relevant here are: (i) 'The ABC of Psychology – a glossary of 1200 terms; (ii) 'Psych Site' – links to all things psychological; and (iii) Psybox – a Psychology dictionary.)

http://psychology.about.com/od/profilesofmajorthinkers/p/watson.htm (Lots of useful links to other major figures.)

CHAPTER 2

THEORETICAL APPROACHES TO PSYCHOLOGY

- The Biopsychological approach
- The Behaviourist approach
- The Psychodynamic approach
- The Humanistic approach
- The Cognitive approach
- The Social Constructionist approach
- The Evolutionary approach

INTRODUCTION and OVERVIEW

As noted in Chapter 1, different Psychologists make different assumptions about what particular aspects of a person should be the focus of study; this helps to determine an underlying model/image of what people are like. In turn, this determines a view of psychological normality, the nature of development, preferred methods of study, the major cause(s) of abnormality, and the preferred methods and goals of treatment.

A theoretical approach is a perspective that isn't as clearly outlined as theory and that:

> *provides a general orientation to a view of humankind. It says, in effect, we see people as operating according to these basic principles and we therefore see explanations of human behaviour as needing to be set within these limits and with these or those principles understood. (Coolican et al., 1996)*

As we shall see, most of the major approaches include two or more distinguishable theories, but within an approach they share certain basic principles and assumptions that give them a distinct 'flavour' or identity. The focus here is on the Biopsychological, Behaviourist, Psychodynamic, Humanistic, Cognitive, Social Constructionist and Evolutionary approaches.

THE BIOPSYCHOLOGICAL APPROACH

Theoretical and practical contributions

As noted in Chapter 1, Biopsychology forms part of the process approach (Legge, 1975) and a crucially important biological process with important implications for Psychology is *genetic transmission* (see Box 2.1). For example, *behaviour geneticists* attempt

Box 2.1 Basic principles and assumptions

Toates (2001) identifies four strands of the application of biology to understanding behaviour:

1. How things work in the 'here and now', i.e. the immediate *determinants* of behaviour. In some cases, a biological perspective can provide clear insights into what determines people to act in a particular way. For example, when someone treads on a thorn (a cause) and cries out in pain soon afterwards (an effect), we know the pathways of information in the body that mediate between such causes and effects. What this example shows is that behaviour is an integral part of our biological make-up.
2. We inherit *genes* from our parents and these genes play a role in determining the structure of our body; through this structure, and perhaps most obviously through that of our *nervous system* (NS), genes play a role in behaviour.
3. A combination of genes and environment affects the growth and maturation of our body, with the main focus being the NS and behaviour. Development of the *individual* is called *ontogenesis*.
4. The assumption that humans have evolved from simpler forms, rooted in Darwin's (1859) theory of *evolution*, relates to both the physical structure of our body and our behaviour: we can gain insight into behaviour by considering how it has been shaped by evolution. Development of *species* is called *phylogenesis*.

(See Figure 4.1, p. 52.)

to quantify how much of the variability of any given trait (e.g. intelligence, aggressiveness or schizophrenia) can be attributed to:

(a) genetic differences between people (*heritability*);

(b) *shared environments* (i.e. between-family variation, such as socio-economic status (SES)); and

(c) *non-shared environments* (within-family variations, such as how parents treat different children differently) (Pike and Plomin, 1999).

The two major methods used by behaviour geneticists to determine how much each of these factors contributes to individual differences are twin studies and adoption studies. These methods are able to *disentangle* the effects of genetic and environmental factors, which otherwise become *confounded* (or confused). For example, knowing that the children of a parent (or both parents) with schizophrenia are significantly more likely to become schizophrenic themselves compared with their cousins or unrelated children, could be explained in terms of *either* genetic *or* environmental factors. However, as the genetic similarity between people increases, so does the similarity of their environments: parents and offspring usually live in the same households, whereas unrelated people don't.

One way of overcoming this problem is to compare the rates of schizophrenia among monozygotic (identical) twins reared together (MZsRT) with those for monozygotic twins reared apart (MZsRA). Studies of MZs reared apart represent one kind of *adoption study*.

Biopsychology is the study of the biological bases, or the physiological correlates, of behaviour and is a branch of *neuroscience* (or the brain sciences), the study of the NS (see Critical discussion 2.1 below). 'Biopsychologists aren't interested in biology for its own sake, but for what it can tell them about behaviour and mental (cognitive) processes' (Pinel, 1993).

The influence of the Biopsychological approach can be seen very clearly in the: (i) *biomedical model* of illness and disease (see Chapter 12); (ii) the concept of addiction, which is based on the *addiction-as-disease model* (see Chapter 8).

Critical Discussion 2.1

Neuroscience: Scientific breakthrough or neurotrash?

- The claims, over recent years, to have identified the areas of the brain that underlie a wide range of human behaviours and cognitive processes, using brain imaging (in particular, functional magnetic resonance imaging (fMRI)), have produced some extreme reactions within the scientific community. The resulting multi-coloured images (see Figure 1.3) have become iconic symbols of science in general, and neuroscience in particular.
- What makes fMRI so persuasive is that it claims to show brain activity in *real time*: the areas that 'light up' while the participant is engaged in some particular task (such as reading some text or reacting to pictures of faces) are taken to be the neural *correlates* of the behaviours/cognitions involved in the task. But is this interpretation valid?
- According to Satel and Lilienfeld (2013), brain scan images aren't what they seem: they're not photographs of the brain in action in real time. Scientists cannot just look 'in' the brain and see what it does. Those 'beautiful colour-dappled images' are in fact representations of particular brain areas that are working the hardest – as measured by increased oxygen consumption. The powerful computer located within the scanning machine transforms changes in oxygen levels into the now familiar images.

... Despite well-informed inferences, the greatest challenge of imaging is that it is very difficult for scientists to look at a fiery spot on the brain scan and conclude with accuracy what is going on in the mind of the person. (Satel and Lilienfeld, 2013)

- fMRI doesn't directly measure synaptic and neuronal activity (see Chapter 4), which occurs over the course of milliseconds; by contrast, changes in oxygen consumption occur over the course of seconds.
- So, claims to have found the religious centre (the area that's most active when the participant is asked to think of God) or the love centre cannot be taken literally. Indeed, neuroscientists themselves sometimes refer disparagingly to such studies as 'blobology'; others (usually non-neuroscientists) are less restrained and talk about 'neuromania', 'neurohubris', 'heurohype' and 'neuro-bollocks' (if you're British!).
- More seriously, criminal defence lawyers (especially in the USA) are increasingly drawing on neuroscientific findings to argue that their client's brain 'made' them commit murder or some other violent act ('*neurodeterminism*'). Clearly, such arguments are central to the whole notion of criminal (and moral) responsibility and, more broadly, free will (see Chapters 21 and 49). This is symptomatic of a wider tendency to grant a kind of inherent superiority to brain-based explanations

over all other ways of accounting for human behaviour; Satel and Lileinfeld (2013) call this *neurocentrism*, a form of *reductionism* (again, see Chapter 49, and text below).

- According to Vul *et al.* (2009), the findings from many recent studies are virtually meaningless: 54 per cent of the studies in their literature search had used a seriously biased method of analysis, a problem that probably also undermines the findings of fMRI studies in other areas of Psychology. These studies had identified small areas of brain activity (voxels, 3-D pixels about the size of a pea comprising about one million neurons: Koch, 2012b) that varied according to the experimental condition of interest (e.g. being rejected or not), and had then focused on just those voxels that showed a correlation, above a given threshold, with the psychological measure (e.g. feeling rejected).
- Ideally, they should have used *two* sets of scans: one set to identify which voxel clusters are highly activated during the experiment and a second set to confirm that the first wasn't the result of random fluctuations (similar to static/white noise on an untuned television). But many researchers made the mistake of using just one data set for both the initial and final analysis: this allows the random noise to inflate an apparent link to a behavioural response or trait.
- Finally, they'd arrived at their published brain–behaviour correlations by taking the average correlation from among just this select group of voxels – or, in some cases, just one 'peak voxel'. According to Vul *et al.* (2009), this procedure makes it almost impossible not to find a significant brain–behaviour correlation. (Social neuroscience is discussed in Meet the Researcher, Chapter 22.)
- According to Chen (2013), these faulty methods of data collection seem to be used less often now. However, he cites a 2012 study which showed that an fMRI experiment could be analysed in nearly 7000 ways, with results varying hugely depending on which method of analysis was chosen. With so much flexibility, neuroimagers can unintentionally (or indeed deliberately) analyse their data in a way that produces the most favourable results.
- However, the reverse problem has also been identified: based on a survey of 730 studies examining the risk factors and treatment for neurological disorders (such as chronic pain, see Chapter 12; and Alzheimer's disease, see Chapter 39), the average 'statistical power' was about 20 per cent; in other words, four out of five studies might have missed the actual biological effect or mechanism they were looking for (and so reported 'false negatives'). The most common reason for these 'failures' was that the sample size was too small (Chen, 2013).
- In the context of education, Bennett (2013) dismisses the creative right brain/logical left brain distinction (see Chapter 4) as a 'neuromyth'. Satel and Lilienfeld (2013) apply the criticisms described above to the neuroscientific study of addiction (see Chapter 8), advertising ('neuromarketing', see Chapter 24), and lie detection.
- However, Robson (2013) warns that the danger of such 'neuroscepticism' is that we may throw the baby out with the bathwater. Brain imaging is, after all, an infant technology which is developing very quickly; there are now new, more finely tuned scans that are less error-prone (such as portable scanners that allow us to take a peek at brain activity in more natural settings).

An evaluation of the Biopsychological approach

- The Biopsychological approach is *reductionist*: it attempts to explain human – and non-human – psychological processes and behaviour in terms of the operation of physical/physiological structures (such as interactions between neurons/nerve cells and hormones). In turn, these processes are explained in terms of smaller constituent processes, such as synaptic transmission between neurons. Ultimately, reductionism claims that all Psychology can be explained in terms of biology, which in turn can be understood in terms of chemistry and physics. Some Psychologists believe that this loses sight of the whole person and fails to reflect experience and everyday interaction with other people. (See Critical discussion 2.1 and Chapter 49.)
- Reductionism has been effective in scientific research. For example, the greatest insight into the cause and possible cure of Parkinson's disease (PD) has been obtained from reducing it to the biological level: we know that Parkinson's disease is caused by the malfunction and death of certain neurons in a particular part of the brain (Toates, 2001). However, while there may be a fairly straightforward causal link between this neuron malfunction and the movement disorder that characterises PD, things are rather more complex

when it comes to explaining the associated mood disorder. This, in turn, raises the more general *philosophical* issue regarding the relationship between the brain and the mind (or consciousness) (the 'mind–body' or 'brain–mind' problem; see Gross, 2014).

- The Biopsychological approach tends to remove the person from his/her social context, focusing almost exclusively on physical processes within the body. This is both another form of reductionism and a form of *determinism*. However, outside the laboratory there's a limit to how far biological manipulation can take place in order to reveal a simple cause–effect behavioural chain (a major assumption of determinism): biological factors need to be interpreted within a context of rather subtle psychological principles (Toates, 2001).
- The Human Genome Project (HGP) was a 13-year research project, aimed at identifying all human genes (the *genome*), that is, determining the sequences of chemical base pairs that make up human DNA (see Chapter 50). This was duly completed in 2003, the achievement described as a 'landmark event' in the biomedical sciences (Carter, 2004). Several writers discuss the possibility that unethical scientists may abuse this knowledge in the form of genetic manipulation/engineering and selective breeding (*eugenics*, see Chapters 41 and 47).

Ask Yourself

- Dip into some of these chapters, just to familiarise yourself with the range of topic areas to which the Biopsychological approach has been applied (and to help you find your way round the book).

THE BEHAVIOURIST APPROACH

Basic principles and assumptions

As we saw in Chapter 1, Watson (1913) revolutionised Psychology by rejecting the introspectionist approach and advocating the study of observable behaviour. Only by modelling itself on the natural sciences could Psychology legitimately call itself a science. Watson was seeking to transform the very subject matter of Psychology (from 'mind' to 'behaviour') and this is often called *methodological behaviourism*. According to Skinner (1987):

> *'Methodological' behaviourists often accept the existence of feelings and states of mind, but do not deal with them because they are not public and hence statements about them are not subject to confirmation by more than one person.*

In this sense, what was revolutionary when Watson (1913) first delivered his 'behaviourist manifesto' (see Box 3.2, p. 40) has become almost taken for granted, 'orthodox' Psychology. It could be argued that all psychologists are methodological behaviourists (Blackman, 1980). Belief in the importance of empirical methods, especially the experiment, as a way of collecting data about humans (and non-humans), which can be quantified and statistically analysed, is a major feature of *mainstream Psychology* (see Chapter 3). By contrast, as Skinner (1987) asserts:

> *'Radical' behaviourists ... recognise the role of private events (accessible in varying degrees to self-observation and physiological research), but contend that so-called mental activities are metaphors or explanatory fictions and that behaviour attributed to them can be more effectively explained in other ways.*

For Skinner, these more effective explanations of behaviour come in the form of the principles of reinforcement derived from his experimental work with rats and pigeons. What's 'radical' about Skinner's *radical behaviourism* is the claim that feelings, sensations and other private events cannot be used to explain behaviour, but are to *be explained in* an analysis of behaviour. Methodological behaviourism proposes to ignore such inner states (they're inaccessible). But for Skinner they're irrelevant: they can be translated into the language of reinforcement theory (Garrett, 1996).

Given this important distinction between methodological and radical behaviourism, we need to consider some principles and assumptions that apply to Behaviourism in general.

Figure 2.1 B.F. Skinner (1904–1990)

Box 2.2 Basic principles and assumptions made by the Behaviourist approach

- Behaviourists emphasise the role of environmental factors in influencing behaviour, to the near exclusion of innate or inherited factors (see Chapter 50). This amounts essentially to a focus on learning. The key form of learning is conditioning, either *classical* (Pavlovian or respondent), which formed the basis of Watson's behaviourism, or *operant* (instrumental), which is at the centre of Skinner's radical behaviourism. Classical and operant conditioning are often referred to (collectively) as learning theory, as opposed to 'theories of learning', which usually implies non-behaviourist theories (see Chapter 11).
- Behaviourism is often referred to as 'S–R' Psychology ('S' standing for 'stimulus' and 'R' for 'response'). Both classical and operant conditioning explain observable behaviour (responses) in terms of environmental events (stimuli), but they define the stimulus and response relationship in fundamentally different ways. Only in classical conditioning is the stimulus seen as triggering a response in a predictable, automatic way, and this is what's conveyed by 'S–R' Psychology. It is, therefore, a mistake to describe operant conditioning as an 'S–R' approach (see Chapter 11).
- Both types of conditioning are forms of *associative learning*, whereby associations or connections are formed between stimuli and responses that didn't exist before learning takes place.
- For Watson, introspectionism invoked too many vague concepts that are difficult, if not impossible, to define and measure. According to the *law of parsimony* (or 'Occam's razor'), the fewer assumptions a theory makes, the better (more 'economical' explanations are superior).
- Behaviourists stress the use of *operational definitions* (defining concepts in terms of observable, measurable, events).
- The aim of a science of behaviour is to *predict* and *control* behaviour.

Theoretical contributions

Behaviourism made a massive contribution to Psychology, at least up to the 1950s, and explanations of behaviour in conditioning terms recur throughout this book. For example, apart from a whole chapter on learning and conditioning (Chapter 11), imagery as a form of organisation in memory and as a memory aid is based on the principle of association, and the interference theory of forgetting is largely couched in stimulus–response terms (Chapter 17). Language, moral and gender development (Chapters 19, 35 and 36) have all been explained in terms of conditioning, and some influential theories of the formation and maintenance of relationships focus on the concept of reinforcement (Chapter 28). The behaviourist approach also offers one of the major models of abnormal behaviour (Chapter 45). Finally, Skinner's notorious views on free will are discussed in detail in Chapter 49.

Theorists and researchers critical of the original, 'orthodox' theories have modified and built on them, making a huge contribution in the process. Noteworthy examples are Tolman's (1948) *cognitive behaviourism* (see Chapter 11) and Bandura's *social learning theory* (see Chapters 29, 35 and 36).

Ask Yourself

- Repeat the exercise suggested for the biopsychological approach (see p. 16).

Practical contributions

Methodological behaviourism, with its emphasis on experimentation, operational definitions, and the measurement of observable events (see Box 2.1), has been a major influence on the practice of scientific Psychology in general (what Skinner (1974) called the 'science of behaviour'). This is quite unrelated to any views about the nature and role of mental events. Other, more 'tangible' contributions include:

- *Behaviour therapy* and *behaviour modification* (based on classical and operant conditioning, respectively) as major approaches to the treatment of abnormal behaviour (see Chapter 45) and one of the main tools in the Clinical Psychologist's 'kit bag' (see Box 1.4, p. 7)
- *Behavioural pharmacology* involves the use of schedules of reinforcement (see Chapter 11) to assess the behavioural effects of new drugs that modify brain activity; most importantly, the research has illustrated how many behavioural effects of drugs are determined as much by the current behaviour and reinforcement contingencies as by the effects of the drug on the brain (Leslie, 2002, see Chapter 8)
- *Biofeedback* as a non-medical treatment for stress-related symptoms, derived from attempts to change rats' autonomic physiological functions through the use of operant techniques (see Chapter 12)
- *Teaching machines* and *programmed learning*, which now commonly take the form of *computer-assisted learning* (CAL).

An evaluation of behaviourism

In addition to the criticisms – both general and specific – that occur in the particular chapters where behaviourist explanations are presented, two evaluative points will be made here:

1. The 'Skinner box' is an 'auto-environmental chamber', in which rats' and pigeons' environments can be totally controlled by the experimenter (see Chapter 11). This is central to Skinner's analysis of behaviour. A rat pressing a lever was intended to be equivalent to a cat operating an escape latch in Thorndike's puzzle box (1898), so counting the number of lever presses (the response rate) became the standard measure of operant learning. Despite Skinner's claim that he doesn't have a theory, 'the response' in operant conditioning has largely considered only the *frequency* of behaviour, ignoring intensity, duration and quality. As Glassman (1995) observes:

   While the focus on frequency was a practical consideration, it eventually became part of the overall conceptual framework as well – a case of research methods directing theory.

   But in everyday life, frequency isn't always the most meaningful aspect of behaviour. For example, should we judge an author's worth by how many books s/he publishes, rather than their content?

Ask Yourself

- Do you agree with Skinner's claim that thoughts and other 'covert behaviours' don't explain our behaviour (because they cannot determine what we do)?

2. Skinner's claim that human behaviour can be predicted and controlled in the same way as the behaviour of non-humans is usually accepted only by other behaviour analysts. Possessing language allows us to communicate with each other and to think about 'things' that have never been observed (and may not even exist), including rules, laws and principles (Garrett, 1996). While these can only be expressed in or thought about in words, much of our behaviour is governed by them. According to Garrett, when this happens:

   ... behaviour is now shaped by what goes on inside their [people's] heads ... and not simply by what goes on in the external environment.

So, what people think is among the important variables determining what they do and say, the very opposite of what Skinner's radical behaviourism claims.

However, behaviour analysts recognise the limitations of their approach. For example, Leslie (2002) admits that operant conditioning cannot provide a complete account of psychology from a behavioural perspective, even in principle. Similarly, O'Donohue and Ferguson (2001) acknowledge that the science of behaviour cannot account for creativity, as in music, literature and science.

Figure 2.2 Behaviourists have difficulty explaining creativity or any kind of novel behaviour

THE PSYCHODYNAMIC APPROACH

The term 'psychodynamic' denotes the active forces within the personality that motivate behaviour, and the inner causes of behaviour (in particular, the unconscious conflict between the different structures that compose the whole personality). While Freud's *psychoanalytic theory* was the original psychodynamic theory, the psychodynamic theories of Jung (1964), Adler (1927) and Erikson (1950) aren't psychoanalytic. Because of their enormous influence, Freud's ideas will be the focus of this section.

Basic principles and assumptions

Freud's concepts are closely interwoven, making it difficult to know where a description of them should begin (Jacobs, 1992). Fortunately, Freud himself stressed the acceptance of certain key theories as essential to the practice of *psychoanalysis*, the form of psychotherapy he pioneered and from which most others are derived.

Figure 2.3 Sigmund Freud (1856–1939)

Box 2.3 The major principles and assumptions of Psychoanalytic theory

- Much of our behaviour is determined by unconscious thoughts, wishes, memories, and so on. What we're consciously aware of at any one time represents the tip of an iceberg: most of our thoughts and ideas are either not accessible at that moment (*pre-conscious*) or are totally inaccessible (*unconscious*). These unconscious thoughts and ideas can become conscious through the use of special techniques, such as *free association*, *dream interpretation* and *transference*, the cornerstones of psychoanalysis (see Chapter 45).
- Much of what's unconscious has been made so through repression, whereby threatening or unpleasant experiences are 'forgotten' (see Chapter 21, pp. 355–57). They become inaccessible, locked away from our conscious awareness. This is a major form of *ego defence* (see Chapter 42). Freud singled out repression as a special cornerstone 'on which the whole structure of psychoanalysis rests. It is the most essential part of it' (Freud, 1914). Repression is closely related to *resistance*, interpretation of which is another key technique used in psychoanalysis (see Chapter 45).
- According to the *theory of infantile sexuality*, the sexual instinct or drive is active from birth and develops through a series of five *psychosexual stages*. The most important of these is the *phallic stage* (spanning the ages 3–5/6), during which all children experience the Oedipus complex (see Chapter 35). In fact, Freud used the German word 'Trieb', which translates as 'drive', rather than 'Instinkt', which was meant to imply that experience played a crucial role in determining the 'fate' of sexual (and aggressive) energy (see Box 50.2, p. 872).
- Related to infantile sexuality is the general impact of early experience on later personality (see Chapter 32). According to Freud (1949):

It seems that the neuroses are only acquired during early childhood (up to the age of 6), even though their symptoms may not make their appearance until much later ... the child is psychologically father of the man and ... the events of its first years are of paramount importance for its whole subsequent life.

Theoretical contributions

As with behaviourist accounts of conditioning, many of Freud's ideas and concepts have become part of mainstream Psychology's vocabulary. You don't have to be 'Freudian' to use concepts such as 'repression', 'unconscious', and so on, and many of the vast number of studies of different aspects of the theory have been conducted by critics hoping to discredit it (such as Eysenck, 1985; Eysenck and Wilson, 1973).

Also like behaviourist theories, Freud's can be found throughout Psychology. His contribution is extremely rich and diverse, offering theories of motivation (see Chapter 9), dreams and the relationship between sleep and dreams (Chapter 7), forgetting (Chapter 21), attachment and the effects of early experience (Chapter 32), moral and gender development (Chapters 35 and 36), aggression (Chapter 29) and abnormality (Chapter 45). Psychoanalytic theory has also influenced Gould's (1978, 1980) theory of the evolution of adult consciousness (Chapter 38) and Adorno *et al.*'s (1950) authoritarian personality account of prejudice (Chapter 25).

Finally, and as noted earlier, Freud's theories have stimulated the development of alternative theories, often resulting from the rejection of some of his fundamental principles and assumptions, but reflecting his influence enough for them to be described as psychodynamic. Some major examples include:

- *Ego psychology* (e.g. Freud's daughter, Anna Freud, 1936)
- *Psychosocial theory* (Erikson, 1950, 1968)
- *Analytical psychology* (Jung, 1964)
- *Individual psychology* (Adler, 1927)
- *Object relations school* (Fairbairn, 1952; Klein, 1932; Mahler, 1975; Winnicott, 1965).

Anna Freud (1895–1982)

Erik Erikson (1902–1994)

Carl Gustav Jung (1875–1961)

Alfred Adler (1870–1937)

Figure 2.4 Major alternative psychodynamic theorists

Ask Yourself

- Repeat the exercise suggested for the Biopsychological approach (see p. 16).

Practical contributions

The current psychotherapy scene is highly diverse, with only a minority using Freudian techniques (see Chapter 45), but, as Fancher (1996) points out:

> *Most modern therapists use techniques that were developed either by Freud and his followers or by dissidents in explicit reaction against his theories. Freud remains a dominating figure, for or against whom virtually all therapists feel compelled to take a stand.*

Both Rogers, the major humanistic therapist (see below) and Wolpe, who developed systematic desensitisation (a major form of behaviour therapy, see Chapter 45), were originally trained in Freudian techniques. Perls, the founder of Gestalt therapy, Ellis, the founder of rational emotive therapy (RET) (see Chapter 45) and Berne, who devised transactional analysis (TA), were also trained psychoanalysts.

Even Freud's fiercest critics concede his influence, not just within world psychiatry but in philosophy, literary criticism, history, theology, sociology, and art and literature. Freudian terminology is commonly used in conversations between therapists well beyond Freudian circles, and his influence is brought daily to therapy sessions as part of the cultural background and experience of nearly every client (Jacobs, 1992).

Many mental health practitioners (including psychotherapists, counsellors and social workers), although not formally trained as psychoanalysts, have incorporated elements of Freudian thought and technique into their approaches to helping their clients (Nye, 2000).

An evaluation of the psychodynamic approach

- A criticism repeatedly made of Freudian (and other psychodynamic) theories is that they're unscientific because they're *unfalsifiable* (incapable of being disproved). For example, if the Freudian prediction that 'dependent' men will prefer big-breasted women is confirmed, then the theory is supported. However, if such men actually prefer small-breasted women (Scodel, 1957), Freudians can use the concept of *reaction formation* (an ego-defence mechanism, see Table 42.4, p. 728) to argue that an unconscious fixation with large breasts may manifest itself as a conscious preference for the opposite, a clear case of 'heads, I win, tails you lose' (Eysenck, 1985; Popper, 1959).
- However, it's a mistake to see reaction formation as typical of Freudian theory as a whole. According to Kline (1984, 1989), for example, the theory comprises a collection of hypotheses, some of which are more central to the theory than others, and some of which have more supporting evidence than others. Also, different parts of the theory have been tested using different methods (see Chapter 42).
- According to Zeldow (1995), the history of science reveals that those theories that are the richest in explanatory power have proved the most difficult to test empirically. For example, Newton's Second Law couldn't be demonstrated in a reliable, quantitative way for 100 years, and Einstein's general theory of relativity is still untestable. But even if it were true that psychoanalytic theory were untestable (as claimed by Eysenck, Popper and others):

> *... the same thing could (and should) be said about any psychological hypotheses involving complex phenomena and worthy of being tested ... psychoanalytic theories have inspired more empirical research in the social and behavioural sciences than any other group of theories ...* (Zeldow, 1995)

- Support for certain aspects of Freud's theories has been provided by the relatively new sub-discipline of *neuropsychoanalysis*, one of the many spin-offs of neuroscientific research (see Critical Discussion 2.1 and Chapter 42). According to Bargh (2014), contemporary Cognitive Psychologists have recast the Freudian worldview, adopting a more pragmatic view of what defines our unconscious self. For example, Nobel laureate Daniel Kahneman (2011) has described the modern distinction between *automatic* and *controlled* thought processes (corresponding to unconscious and conscious, respectively); these are discussed in relation to decision-making in Chapter 20.
- Automatic thought processes represent one facet of the 'cognitive unconscious'. This can manifest itself in several ways, including *stereotyping* (see Chapter 22), the cognitive component of prejudice (see Chapter 25). A way of tapping the unconscious emotional/affective component of prejudice is through the Implicit Association Test (IAT) (Greenwald *et al.*, 1998).
- Bargh (2014) also describes unconscious (or 'non-conscious') dimensions to emotion (see Chapter 10), observational learning (a major feature of social learning theory, see above), advertising

(see Chapter 24), the treatment of alcoholism (see Chapter 8) and antisocial and prosocial behaviour (see Chapters 29 and 30).

- Freud's theory provides methods and concepts that enable us to interpret and 'unpack' underlying meanings (it has great *hermeneutic strength*). Popper's and Eysenck's criticism above helps to underline the fact that these meanings (both conscious and unconscious) cannot be measured in any precise way. Freud offers a way of understanding that, while less easily tested, may capture the nature of human experience and action more appropriately (Stevens, 1995; see Chapter 3). According to Fancher (1996):

> *Although always controversial, Freud struck a responsive chord with his basic image of human beings as creatures in conflict, beset by irreconcilable and often unconscious demands from within as well as without. His ideas about repression, the importance of early experience and sexuality, and the inaccessibility of much of human nature to ordinary conscious introspection have become part of the standard western intellectual currency.*

- Reason (2000) believes it's time to re-acknowledge Freud's greatness as a Psychologist. Like James, he had a rare gift for describing and analysing the phenomenology of mental life. According to Kline (1998):

> *... after 100 years, Freudian theory cannot be uncritically accepted just as it cannot be totally rejected. However ... Freudian theory contains some profound observations and understanding of human behaviour. These must be incorporated into any adequate human psychology, not only its theory but also its methods ...*

THE HUMANISTIC APPROACH

Basic principles and assumptions

As we noted earlier, Rogers, a leading Humanistic Psychologist (and therapist), was trained as a psychoanalyst. Although the term 'humanistic psychology' was coined by Cohen (1958), a British Psychologist, this approach emerged mainly in the USA during the 1950s. Maslow (1968), in particular, gave wide currency to the term 'humanistic', calling it a 'third force' (the other two being Behaviourism and Freudianism). However, Maslow didn't reject these approaches but hoped to unify them, thus integrating both subjective and objective, the private and public aspects of the person, and providing a complete, holistic Psychology.

Box 2.4 Some basic principles and assumptions of the Humanistic approach

- Both the Psychoanalytic and Behaviourist approaches are *deterministic*. People are driven by forces beyond their control, either unconscious forces from within (Freud) or reinforcements from outside (Skinner). Humanistic Psychologists believe in free will and people's ability to choose how they act (see Chapter 49).
- A truly scientific Psychology must treat its subject matter as fully human, which means acknowledging individuals as interpreters of themselves and their world. Behaviour, therefore, must be understood in terms of the individual's *subjective experience*, from the perspective of the actor (a *phenomenological approach*, which explains why this is sometimes called the 'humanistic-phenomenological' approach). This contrasts with the *positivist approach* of the natural sciences, which tries to study people from the position of a detached observer. Only the individual can explain the meaning of a particular behaviour and is the 'expert' – not the investigator or therapist.
- Maslow argued that Freud supplied the 'sick half' of Psychology, through his belief in the inevitability of conflict, neurosis, innate self-destructiveness, and so on, while he (and Rogers) stressed the 'healthy half'. Maslow saw *self-actualisation* at the peak of a *hierarchy of needs* (see below and Chapter 9), while Rogers talked about the *actualising tendency*, an intrinsic property of life, reflecting the desire to grow, develop and enhance our capacities. A *fully functioning person* is the ideal of growth. Personality development naturally moves towards healthy growth (unless it's blocked by external factors), and should be considered the norm (see Chapter 42).
- Maslow's contacts with Wertheimer and other Gestalt Psychologists (see Box 1.1 and Chapter 15) led him to stress the importance of understanding the whole person, rather than separate 'bits' of behaviour.

(Based on Glassman, 1995)

Theoretical contributions

Maslow's hierarchy of needs (see Chapter 9, pp. 144–5) distinguishes between motives shared by both humans and non-humans and those that are uniquely human, and can be seen as an extension of the psychodynamic approach. Freud's id would represent physiological needs (at the hierarchy's base), Horney (a major critic of the male bias in Freud's theory, see Chapter 35) focused on the need for safety and love (corresponding to the next two levels), and Adler (see above) stressed esteem needs (at the fourth level). Maslow added self-actualisation to the peak of the hierarchy (Glassman, 1995).

Figure 2.5 Abraham H. Maslow (1908–1970)

According to Rogers (1951), while awareness of being alive is the most basic of human experiences, we each fundamentally live in a world of our own creation and have a unique perception of the world (the *phenomenal field*). It's our *perception* of external reality that shapes our lives (not external reality itself). Within our phenomenal field, the most significant element is our sense of self, 'an organised consistent gestalt, constantly in the process of forming and reforming' (Rogers, 1959, see Chapter 42). This view contrasts with those of many other self-theorists, who see it as a central, unchanging core of personality (see Chapter 33).

Ask Yourself

- Repeat the exercise as for the Biopsychological, Behaviourist and Psychodynamic approaches.

Practical contributions

By far the most significant practical influence of any Humanistic Psychologist is Rogers' form of psychotherapy: originally (in the 1950s) called '*client-centred therapy*' (CCT), since the mid-1970s it has been known as '*person-centred therapy*' (PCT) (see Chapter 45). According to Rogers (1959):

> *... psychotherapy is the releasing of an already existing capacity in a potentially competent individual.*

The change in name was meant to reflect more strongly that the person, in his/her full complexity, is the centre of focus. Also, Rogers wanted to convey that his assumptions were meant to apply broadly to almost all aspects of human behaviour – not just to therapeutic settings. According to Nye (2000):

> *A wide range of individuals – psychotherapists, counsellors, social workers, clergy and others – have been influenced by Rogers' assumptions that, if one can be a careful and accurate listener, while showing acceptance and honesty, one can be of help to troubled persons.*

Less well known is the prolific research that Rogers undertook during the 1940s, 1950s and 1960s into this form of therapy. According to Thorne (1992):

> *This body of research constituted the most intensive investigation of psychotherapy attempted anywhere in the world up to that time ... The major achievement of these studies was to establish beyond all question that psychotherapy could and should be subjected to the rigours of scientific enquiry.*

Rogers helped develop research designs (such as Q-sorts) which enable objective measurement of the self-concept, ideal self and their relationship over the course of therapy, as well as methodologies (such as rating scales and the use of external 'consultants') for exploring the importance of therapist qualities. These innovations continue to influence therapeutic practice, and many therapists are now concerned that their work should be subjected to research scrutiny. Research findings are now more likely than ever before to affect training procedures and clinical practice across many different therapeutic orientations (Thorne, 1992, see Chapter 45).

By emphasising the therapist's personal qualities, Rogers opened up psychotherapy to Psychologists and contributed to the development of therapy provided by non-medically qualified therapists (*lay therapy*). This is especially significant in the USA, where (until recently) psychoanalysts had to be psychiatrists (i.e. medically qualified). Rogers originally used the term 'counselling' as a strategy for silencing psychiatrists who objected to Psychologists practising 'psychotherapy'. In the UK, the outcome of Rogers' campaign has been the evolution of a counselling profession whose practitioners are drawn from a wide variety of disciplines. Counselling skills are used in a variety of settings throughout education, the health professions, social work, industry and commerce, the armed services, and international organisations (Thorne, 1992).

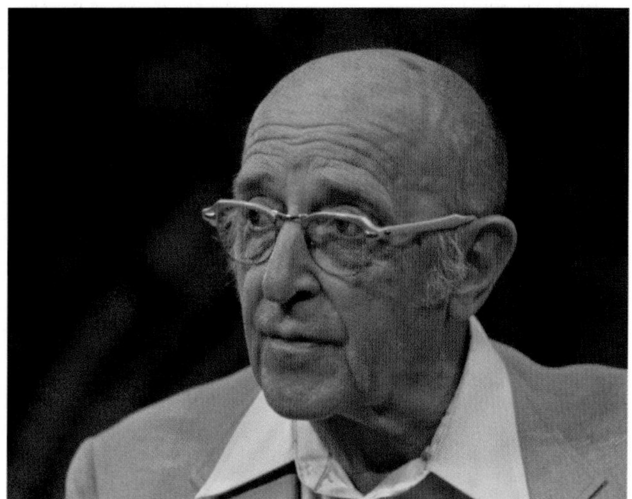

Figure 2.6 Carl Rogers (1902–1987)

An evaluation of the humanistic approach

- According to Wilson *et al.* (1996), the Humanistic approach isn't an elaborate or comprehensive theory of personality, but should be seen as a set of uniquely personal theories of living created by humane people optimistic about human potential. It has wide appeal to those who seek an alternative to the more mechanistic, deterministic theories.
- However, like Freud's theory, many of its concepts are difficult to test empirically (such as self-actualisation), and it cannot account for the origins of personality. Since it describes but doesn't explain personality, it's subject to the *nominal fallacy* (Carlson and Buskist, 1997).
- Nevertheless, for all its shortcomings, the Humanistic approach represents a counterbalance to the Psychodynamic (especially Freud) and Behaviourist approaches, and has helped to bring the 'person' back into Psychology. Crucially, it recognises that people help determine their own behaviour and aren't simply slaves to environmental contingencies or to their past. The self, personal responsibility and agency, choice, and free will are now legitimate issues for psychological investigation.

THE COGNITIVE APPROACH

Basic principles and assumptions

Despite its undoubted influence within Psychology as a whole (see below and Chapter 3), it's more difficult to define the boundaries of Cognitive Psychology compared with the other major approaches. Its identity isn't as clearly established, and it cannot be considered to be a specific, integrated set of assumptions and concepts. It has several contemporary forms, with many theories, research programmes and forms of psychotherapy having a 'cognitive tilt' (Nye, 2000).

Also, there's no specific figure who can be identified as being central to its development in the same way as Watson, Freud and Rogers can with their respective approaches. As Wade and Tavris (1990) say:

> *Cognitive psychology does not yet have a unifying theory, and unlike other 'brands' of psychology ... it lacks an acknowledged spokesperson.*

Figure 2.7 The mind as an information-processing device

Theoretical contributions

We noted earlier that two major modifications to 'orthodox' learning theory are Tolman's *cognitive behaviourism* and *social learning theory* (associated primarily with Bandura). Both these theories stress the central role of cognitive processes in the learning process. The influence of the information-processing approach is obvious in relation to attention, pattern recognition and memory (see Box 2.6), but it has permeated many other areas of Psychology. As noted in Chapter 1, *social cognition* is now a commonly used term to refer to many aspects of the perception of people (see Chapter 22), attribution (see Chapter 23), attitudes and attitude change (including prejudice, see Chapters 24 and 25), and other areas of Social Psychology.

The information-processing approach also represents an increasingly influential view of cognitive development (see Chapter 34) and of the nature of intelligence (see Chapter 41). Cognitive behaviour therapy (CBT) also represents a major approach to the treatment of mental disorders (see Chapter 45 and 'Practical contributions' below).

Box 2.5 Some basic principles and assumptions of the Cognitive approach

- According to Parkin (2000), psychologists in general, and Cognitive Psychologists in particular, face a problem not faced by other scientists:

The human brain is not like other organs of the body in that looking at its structure does not reveal anything about how it functions. We can see that the wall of the small intestine acts as an absorptive surface, the heart as a pump, and the kidney as a filter. The brain, however, is a large mass of cells and fibres which, no matter how clearly we look at it, gives no indication of how we think, speak and remember ...

For these reasons, Cognitive Psychologists are forced to seek *analogies* and *metaphors* when trying to describe a construct within the brain – that is, how the brain works is compared with the operation of something we already understand. As we saw in Chapter 1, by far the most dominant is that internal mental abilities are *information processing systems* (drawing on ideas from telecommunications and computer science: the *computer analogy*). Included within this overall analogy are several central ideas or concepts, such as coding, channel capacity, and serial/parallel processing (see Chapter 20).

- Every telecommunication system uses some form of *coding*. For example, a telephone receives and translates our voice into an electromagnetic code, which is then decoded back into our voice at the other end. Cognitive Psychologists realised that the concept of coding was central to understanding the representations used by the brain. When we see a picture, for example, we extract information from it that forms a code, which is, therefore, a symbol of the original stimulus (see Chapters 5 and 15).
- *Channel capacity* is the idea that any transmission system has a finite limit to the amount of information it can hold. Nowadays, with the advent of optic fibres, channel capacity can be huge – but it's still limited. This is also true of human beings: most of our mental activities are capacity-constrained, such as our attentional processes (see Chapter 13). But compared with physical communication devices, human coding is more flexible, and can take account of the form of the input in order to reduce the amount and nature of information that's actually formed into a code (as demonstrated in span of apprehension experiments and chunking (see Chapter 17). Unlike humans, physical systems reduce all information to fundamental units ('bits'), which in turn allows the absolute capacity of the system to be defined (which is impossible for human information processing).

(Based on Parkin, 2000)

According to the website of the Centre for Evolutionary Psychology (www.psych.ucsb.edu/research/cep/primer.html):

> *the human brain consists of a large collection of functionally specialised computational devices that evolved to solve the adaptive problems regularly encountered by our hunter-gatherer ancestors.*

Evolution by natural selection has endowed all human beings with a set of psychological adaptations, or 'mental organs'. These include psychological mechanisms (or 'functionally specialised computational devices') for *language* (see Chapter 19), *face recognition* (see Chapter 14), and *spatial perception* (see Chapters 14–16). (Others include tool use, mate attraction and retention, and parental care; see Chapters 28 and 32). (See discussion of Evolutionary Psychology below.)

Ask Yourself

- Repeat the exercise as for the Biopsychological, Behaviourist, Psychodynamic and Humanistic approaches.

Practical contributions

In relation to counselling and psychotherapy, Ellis's *rational emotive behaviour therapy* (REBT, previously just called rational emotive therapy or RET) deserves special attention (Nye, 2000). According to Rorer (1998), 'the cognitive revolution in psychotherapy began with the publication of (Ellis's 1962 book) *Reason and Emotion in Psychotherapy*'. REBT is the predecessor of the current cognitive and cognitive-behaviour therapies (see Chapter 45), and continues to evolve and gain in popularity. His emphasis on the primacy of cognition in psychopathology is at the forefront of practice and research in Clinical Psychology (Nye, 2000).

REBT attempts directly and actively to get clients to dispute their irrational and unscientific beliefs, and replace them with rational beliefs, which are less likely to be associated with extremely negative emotional states or maladaptive behaviours. The key concept underlying REBT (and other cognitive approaches) is that people are disturbed not by events themselves but by their *perception* of them. (This is similar to Rogers' phenomenal field, see above.)

Although Ellis (1987) believes that people have a biological tendency to think irrationally, REBT is an optimistic approach. It emphasises that:

... people have enormous power to think about their thinking, to use rationality and the scientific method, and to radically control and change their emotional destiny – providing they really work at doing so. (Ellis, 1987)

Figure 2.8 Albert Ellis (1913–2007)

Another practical contribution is helping children who experience difficulties in learning to read, based on research into *working memory* (see Chapter 17).

An evaluation of the cognitive approach

Ask Yourself

- Try to identify some of the similarities between computers and humans as information processors.
- Can you think of some limitations of the computer analogy? (See Box 2.6 and Chapter 20, pp. 342.) One issue you may wish to focus on is the role of emotion in human information-processing.

- The parallels between human beings and computers are compelling (Parkin, 2000). According to Lachman *et al.* (1979):

Computers take a symbolic input, recode it, make decisions about the recoded input, make new expressions from it, store some or all of the input, and give back a symbolic input. By analogy that is what most cognitive psychology is about. It is about how people take in information ... recode and remember it, how they make decisions, how they transform their internal knowledge states, and how they translate these states into behavioural outputs.

Box 2.6 Some other similarities between computers and humans as information processors

- Computers operate in terms of *information streams*, which flow between different components of the system. This is conceptually similar to how we assume symbolic information flows through human information channels (for example, see Atkinson and Shiffrin's multi-store model (MSM) of memory, Chapter 17, p. 287).
- All computers have a *central processing unit*, which carries out the manipulation of information. At the simplest level, a central processor might take a sequence of numbers and combine them according to a particular rule in order to compute an average. Many Cognitive Psychologists saw this as comparable to how people would perform the same operation.
- Computers have *databases* and *information stores*, which are permanent representations of knowledge the computer has acquired. In many ways, this is comparable to our permanent (long-term) memory.
- Information sometimes needs to be held for a period of time while some other operation is performed. This is the job of the *information buffer*, which is a feature of computers and information-processing models of human attention (see Chapter 13) and memory (again, see the section on the MSM in Chapter 17).

(Based on Parkin, 2000)

- Information-processing accounts invariably address some specific aspect of mental processing, rather than being all-embracing accounts of cognition. A good example (in addition to those given in Box 2.6) is Bruce and Young's (1986) model of *face recognition* (see Chapter 14, pp. 238–9). A model is more than a mere analogy (see Chapter 1): the proposed information-processing system is specified in sufficient detail to enable clear predictions to be made about how humans would behave in certain situations.
- Cognitive Psychologists implicitly adopted, at least initially, a strong *nomothetic* view of human mental processes – that is, they assumed that any information-processing model would apply equally to everyone (see Chapter 42). But the influence of *individual differences* soon became apparent. The general rule is that the more complex the cognitive process, the more likely there are to be individual differences (Parkin, 2000).
- Until the mid-1980s, mainstream Cognitive Psychologists took little interest in the study

of how brain damage affects subsequent cognitive and behavioural functioning. *Cognitive Neuropsychologists* now study people with acquired cognitive deficits in order to learn about the nature and organisation of cognitive functioning in normal people (the *cognitive architecture* of mental processes; see Chapter 4).

THE SOCIAL CONSTRUCTIONIST APPROACH

Basic principles and assumptions

Social constructionism (SC) has played a central role in the various challenges that have been made to mainstream, academic Psychology during the last 30 years or so (see Chapter 3). The emergence of SC is usually dated from Gergen's (1973) paper 'Social psychology as history'. In this, he argued that all knowledge, including psychological knowledge, is historically and culturally specific, and that we therefore must extend our enquiries beyond the individual into social, political and economic realms for a proper understanding of the evolution of present-day Psychology and social life. Since the only constant feature of social life is that it's continually changing, Psychology in general – and Social Psychology in particular – becomes a form of historical undertaking: all we can ever do is try to understand and account for how the world appears to be at the present time.

Gergen's paper was written at the time of 'the crisis in Social Psychology'. Starting in the late 1960s and early 1970s, some Social Psychologists were becoming increasingly concerned that the 'voice' of ordinary people was being omitted from social psychological research. By concentrating on *decontextualised* laboratory behaviour, it was ignoring the real-world contexts that give human action its meaning. Several books were published, each proposing an alternative to positivist science and focusing on the accounts of ordinary people (e.g. Harré and Secord, 1972). These concerns are clearly seen today in SC.

Ask Yourself

- Try to formulate some arguments for and against the view that people are basically the same, regardless of culture and historical period (the *universalist assumption*).

While there's no single definition of SC that would be accepted by all those who might be included under its umbrella, we could categorise as social constructionist any approach that is based on one or more of the following key attitudes (as proposed by Gergen, 1985). Burr (2003) suggests we might think of these as 'things you would absolutely have to believe in order to be a social constructionist'.

- *A critical stance towards taken-for-granted knowledge*: our observations of the world don't reveal in any simple way the true nature of the world, and conventional knowledge isn't based on objective, unbiased 'sampling' of the world (see Table 3.1, p. 43). The categories with which we understand the world don't necessarily correspond to natural or 'real' categories/distinctions. Belief in such natural categories is called *essentialism*, so Social Constructionists are *anti-essentialism*.
- *Historical and cultural specificity*: how we commonly understand the world, and the categories and concepts we use, are historically and culturally *relative*. Not only are they specific to particular cultures and historical periods, they're seen as products of that culture and history, and this must include the knowledge generated by the social sciences. The theories and explanations of Psychology thus become time- and culture-bound, and cannot be taken as once-and-for-all descriptions of human nature (the 'true' nature of people and social life, Burr, 2003).
- *Knowledge is sustained by social processes*: our current accepted way of understanding the world ('truth') doesn't reflect the world as it really is (*objective reality*), but is constructed by people through their everyday interactions. Social interaction of all kinds, and particularly language, is of central importance for Social Constructionists: it's other people, both past and present, who are the sources of knowledge.

> *We are born into a world where the conceptual frameworks and categories used by the people of our culture already exist ... Concepts and categories are acquired by each person as they develop the use of language and are thus reproduced every day by everyone who shares a culture and language. This means that the way a person thinks, the very categories and concepts that provide a framework of meaning for them, are provided by the language that they use. Language therefore is a necessary pre-condition for thought as we know it ... (Burr, 2003)*

If knowledge is culturally created, then we shouldn't assume that our ways of understanding are necessarily any better (closer to 'the truth') than other ways. Yet this is precisely what mainstream (Social) Psychology has done. According to Much (1995), a new *(trans) cultural* Psychology has emerged in North America (e.g. Bruner, 1990; Cole, 1990; Shweder, 1990) as an attempt to overcome the bias of ethnocentrism that has too often limited the scope of understanding in the social sciences (see Chapter 47).

By giving a central role to *social interactions* and seeing these as actively producing taken-for-granted knowledge of the world, it follows that language itself is more than simply a way of expressing our thoughts and feelings (as typically assumed by mainstream Psychology). When people talk to each other, they (help to) construct the world, such that language use is a form of action (it has a '*performative*' role; see Chapter 18).

- *Knowledge and social action go together*: these 'negotiated' understandings could take a wide variety of forms, so that there are many possible 'social constructions' of the world. But each different construction also brings with it, or invites, a different kind of action: how we account for a particular behaviour (what caused it) will dictate how we react to and treat the person whose behaviour it is (see Chapter 23).

Mainstream Psychology looks for explanations of social phenomena inside the person – for example, by hypothesising the existence of attitudes, motives, cognitions, and so on (*individualism*, see Box 47.1, p. 825). This can also be seen as *reductionist* (see Chapter 49). Social Constructionists reject this view: explanations are to be found neither inside the individual psyche, nor in social structures or institutions (as advocated by sociologists), but in the interactive processes that take place routinely between people. For Burr (2003):

> *Knowledge is therefore seen not as something that a person has or doesn't have, but as something that people do together ...*

Theoretical contributions and an evaluation of Social Constructionism

Social Constructionism and social representation theory

- According to *social representation theory* (SRT), people come to understand their social world by way of images and social representations (SRs) shared by members of a social group. These representations act like a map which makes a baffling or novel terrain familiar and passable, thereby providing evaluations of good and bad areas. Attitudes are secondary phenomena, underpinned by SRs. SRT tries to provide a historical account of people's understanding of the world (Potter, 1996).
- During the 1950s, the French Psychologist, Moscovici, conducted one of the classic pieces of research on SRs. He was interested in how the ideas/concepts of psychoanalytic theory could be absorbed within a culture (post-Second World War France), based on women's magazines, church publications and interviews. He concluded that psychoanalytic theory had trickled down from the analytic couch and learned journals into both 'high' culture and popular common sense: people 'think' with psychoanalytic concepts, without it seeming as if they are doing anything theoretical at all. But rather than the general population of Paris being conversant with/conversing with psychoanalytic theory in all its complexities, they were working with a simplified image of it, with some concepts having a wide currency (such as repression) and others not (such as libido) (Potter, 1996).

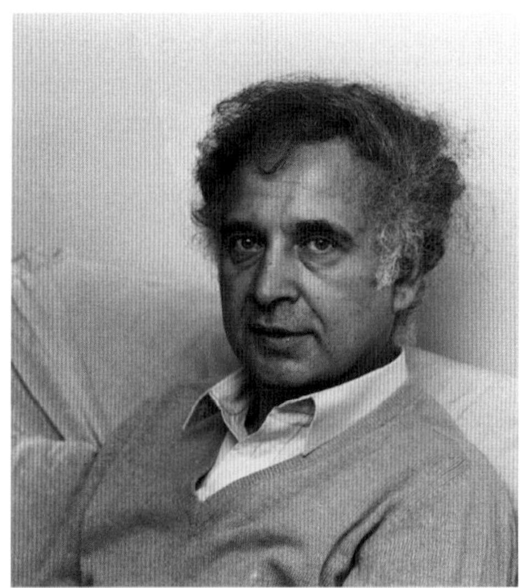

Figure 2.9 Serge Moscovici (born 1925)

- SRT is a *constructionist* theory: instead of portraying people as simply perceiving (or misperceiving) their social worlds, it regards these worlds as constructed, and an SR is a device for doing this construction. It allows someone to make sense of something potentially unfamiliar and to evaluate it. For Moscovici, all thought and understanding are based on the working of SRs, each of which consists of a mixture of concepts, ideas and images; these are both in people's minds and circulating in society.

Figure 2.10 The power of the media to circulate social representations by capturing the 'national mood'

MEET THE RESEARCHER

Viv Burr

Constructions of the family in popular culture: the case of *Buffy the Vampire Slayer*

Contrary to how it appears in many psychology books, I believe that the research psychologists (and other scientists) undertake often arises from a strong personal interest rather than a disinterested concern to build on previous research findings. This is exactly how I began my recent research and writing on the TV show *Buffy the Vampire Slayer* (*BtVS*). To me, *BtVS* seemed to offer the opportunity to become drawn into an alternative world which nevertheless addressed real-life issues. As a psychologist, my own and others' interest in the programme was itself intriguing; much of what is interesting about people lies not in abnormal or unusual behaviour but in the experiences that make up our mundane lives. Today, popular culture, especially television, is very much a part of this experience, and so I became interested in *BtVS* for my research.

Questioning 'common sense' discourses

For many years, my theoretical framework and epistemological perspective has been informed by Social Constructionism and Critical Psychology. These argue that the phenomena of our social world are constructed through the language and images used by people in daily life (sometimes referred to as 'discourses'), and that certain constructions or discourses become predominant; they become our 'common sense'. But our common sense ways of thinking about the world sometimes need to be questioned. We should be 'critical' of them because they can support practices that are oppressive. For example, a few decades ago, it was commonplace for gay people to be constructed as 'sick' or 'evil', and these constructions supported social practices limiting their freedom and opportunities. So my approach to *BtVS* was intuitively a constructionist one: I was interested in the constructions of people and social phenomena it offered.

US reactions to the portrayal of non-normative lifestyles in *BtVS*

Of course, psychologists have been interested in television for a long time and there is a large body of research on 'media effects'. This literature focuses upon measuring the effects of watching certain kinds of television, often violence. But the constructionist perspective is doubtful about identifying 'causes' and 'effects' when trying to understand human behaviour; rather, it focuses on the social constructions that people build and share, and on how people engage with these constructions to understand their own lives.

My approach to this research in fact bore more similarity to recent trends in the fields of cultural studies and media studies. Here, audiences are seen not as passive recipients of 'messages' or 'influences' present in popular culture but as actively engaged in making sense of media texts, reflecting upon their content and making their own 'reading' of the text. This was significant because *BtVS* had been heavily criticised, particularly in the USA, for its violent content and for its positive portrayal of non-normative sexuality. But my constructionist and critical perspective led me to view these criticisms as driven less by worries that viewers may unthinkingly imitate dangerous behaviour and more by the fact that viewers may conclude that non-normative lifestyles can be a defensible personal choice.

The focus for the research was influenced by a chance meeting with a colleague, also a fan of *BtVS*, who worked in the School of Education (part of the University of Huddersfield), and we decided to work on a joint publication. After some discussion, we agreed that 'constructions of the family' would be an appropriate focus. It is often the conventional, nuclear family that is portrayed on television, despite the fact that there is an increasing diversity of living arrangements in modern western societies. Families and households today include single parents, step-families and unrelated people co-habiting. Among other things, these changes indicate that people today do not stay in unsatisfactory relationships as they often did a few decades ago. Rather than performing family roles through obligation, people are giving their own personal needs for happiness and fulfilment higher priority, and are continually re-negotiating their relationship commitments; there is an increasing tendency in contemporary society to feel that relationships within the family should be based on mutual care, respect and equality, rather than obligation and obedience. But it is not surprising that what people may think of as the 'normal' family is a construction that we regularly see portrayed positively in television shows; people who have rejected traditional relationship and family forms may be happier for doing so, but non-normative family forms can also be seen as problematic because of the difficulties they then create for the state in terms of housing shortages, childcare needs, care of the elderly and so on.

How common is it to see non-normative families represented in popular culture?

It seemed to us that *BtVS* offered constructions of family life that were not limited to the conventional nuclear family (and that were indeed critical of it) and so were more likely to reflect the experiences of many young people today. In addition, we felt that its representation of non-normative family forms offered its audience the opportunity to reflect upon the advantages and disadvantages of different family arrangements, and we saw this as potentially beneficial rather than problematic. So we set about analysing and documenting the various portrayals of families as they occur throughout the series (at the time this research was carried out, *BtVS* was in its sixth, penultimate, season on terrestrial TV in the UK).

Identifying family forms in *BtVS*

Through our analysis, we identified representations of three different family forms: the 'feudal' family structure of vampires; the conventional 'nuclear' family; and the alternative 'chosen' family of friends. However, these were not necessarily portrayed as wholly good or bad. The vampire 'families' were constructed as unhealthy; they offered their members a strong sense of belonging, but appeared feudal in their emphasis upon obedience, servitude and punishment for pursuing individual desires. By contrast, the values of the conventional nuclear family were often endorsed: care, strong emotional bonds and tolerance of individual differences. However, *BtVS* also portrays the conventional family as often failing to live up to its ideal: parents leave or are emotionally distant or violent; potential step-parents can fail to relate to their acquired offspring; parents may fail to understand their children's problems or try to exert too much control over their choices.

The alternative presented in *BtVS* is the 'chosen' family, the friendship group. *BtVS* explores how a family can function without traditional compulsions and expectations, where belonging is based on choice and free will. Together, Buffy and her friends care for the child of this 'family' – Buffy's sister, Dawn. Belonging to this family is based on voluntary choice and commitment. But this too is shown to bring dangers as people leave unexpectedly when their own needs become pressing; the family provides love and care, but inconsistently and unpredictably. However, the benefits for Dawn are also shown: she is involved in decision-making; she is exposed to multiple perspectives on matters; and there is (usually) someone there who can help her. The viewer is given the opportunity of weighing up the advantages of this more 'democratic' family style against its potential dangers.

Conclusions

Popular culture may be a very ordinary aspect of our daily lives, but I see it as a rich source of 'constructions' of the social world that deserve psychologists' attention. My research on *BtVS* also includes constructions of sexuality, and I am currently looking at how individuals engage with this 'text' by analysing interviews with a sample of viewers.

Dr Viv Burr is a Reader in Psychology at the University of Huddersfield, UK. She has published over 35 peer-reviewed articles and is author of *Social Constructionism*, 2nd edn. Routledge, London, 2003.

- SRT wasn't published in English until the early 1980s. Since then research has snowballed, especially in Europe, Australia and South America (though it's been largely ignored by mainstream North American Social Psychologists in the experimental cognitive tradition). Potter (1996) suggests that one reason for this may be that the latter's pursuit of general laws and processes is directly challenged by SRT's emphasis on the specific content of a culture's or group's SR as the main object of analysis.

THE EVOLUTIONARY APPROACH

Basic principles and assumptions

Sociobiology, 'the systematic study of the biological basis of all social behaviour' (Wilson, 1975), grew out of the work of evolutionary biologists in the 1960s. Wilson set out to explain all non-human and human social behaviour in terms of evolution and other biological principles. It concentrated on the evolutionary origins of behaviour and tended to imply rigid genetic control (Archer, 1996). Since then, many of these principles have been used to study topics covered by the social sciences – including Psychology.

Evolutionary Psychology (EP) (Buss, 1995) is a development of sociobiology (and is often referred to as 'neo- or modern Darwinism'). Unlike sociobiologists, Evolutionary Psychologists try to explain human behaviour in terms of the underlying computations that occur within the mind. This was an important addition: as well as studying phenomena which sociobiologists studied (such as mate choice and parent–offspring conflict), EP now embraced phenomena which formed part of Cognitive Psychology (such as memory, reasoning, and perception). This put EP squarely in the centre ground of Psychology (Workman and Reader, 2008).

Theoretical contributions

As indicated in Box 2.7, explanations from EP (and sociobiology) can be found throughout Psychology. For example, *fear* is commonly regarded as an adaptive response to threatening stimuli and events, while

Box 2.7 Some basic principles and assumptions of Evolutionary Psychology (EP)

- According to Workman and Reader (2008), the fundamental assumption of EP is that the human mind is the product of evolution just like any other bodily organ, and that we can gain a better understanding of the mind by examining evolutionary pressures that shaped it. This occurred in the Environment of Evolutionary Adaptedness/Adaptation (EEA), thought to be the African savannah (Rose, 2000) during the Pleistocene period between 10,000 and one million years ago (Tooby and Cosmides, 1997).
- While acknowledging their debt to sociobiology, Evolutionary Psychologists contend that it often ignored the role of the mind in mediating links between genes and behaviour. According to Barkow *et al.* (1992), the mind consists of a collection of specialised, independent mechanisms or *modules*, designed by natural selection to solve problems that faced our hunter-gatherer ancestors, such as acquiring a mate, raising children and dealing with rivals. The solutions often involve such emotions as lust, fear, affection, jealousy and anger. Together, these modules and the related emotions constitute *human nature*.
- Traditionally, Psychology has tried to identify *proximate mechanisms*, that is, causes that relate to the individual's goals, knowledge, disposition or life history. By contrast, EP asks *ultimate questions*: for example, instead of Psychology's 'Why are some people more prejudiced than others?' (see Chapter 25), EP asks 'Why is prejudice present in human beings at all?' i.e. what evolutionary advantage did prejudice provide to human beings (Workman and Reader, 2008).
- EP rejects the Standard Social Science Model (SSSM), which makes several broad assumptions about human beings (Workman and Reader, 2008):
  (a) Humans are born as blank slates: knowledge, personality traits and cultural values are acquired from the cultural environment. There's no such thing as 'human nature'.
  (b) Human behaviour is infinitely malleable: there are no biological constraints as to how people develop.
  (c) Culture is an autonomous force and exists independently of people.
  (d) Human behaviour is determined by a process of learning, socialisation or indoctrination.
  (e) Learning processes are general: they can be applied to a variety of phenomena.
- EP is, in general, about *universal* features of the mind. In so far as individual differences exist, the default assumption is that they're expressions of the same universal human nature as it encounters different environments. *Gender* is the crucial exception to this rule. Natural selection has constructed the mental modules of men and women in very different ways as a result of their divergent reproductive roles (*sexual dimorphism*) (see Chapter 36).

anxiety is an 'aberration' (see Chapter 44). Similarly, while the body's stress response evolved to help us cope with life-threatening situations (emergencies), most 'modern-day' stressors aren't like this. Consequently, our bodies react in an inappropriate and potentially life-threatening way to 'chronic' stress (see Chapter 12).

Because men can never be sure that a child is theirs, their jealousy tends to be triggered by fears of a mate's sexual infidelity. Women, on the other hand, become more upset at the thought of losing a mate's emotional commitment – and thus his resources. In turn, women make greater 'parental investment' in their children than men do (Buss, 1994; see Chapter 32).

Perhaps the best-known, and also one of the most controversial, claims of sociobiology is Dawkins' (1976) 'selfish-gene' theory (see Chapter 30).

Ask Yourself

- Repeat the exercise as for the other approaches.
- Look at the arguments you formulated for and against the universalist assumption (in relation to Social Constructionism). Are any of these relevant in evaluating EP?

An evaluation of EP

Some common misconceptions of EP

Workman and Reader (2008) identify four major misrepresentations of EP:

1. Everything is an adaptation.
2. EP is deterministic (see Chapter 50).
3. EP is reductionist (see Chapter 49).
4. EP is politically incorrect (see Chapter 47).

Ask Yourself

- Is culture unique to human beings?
- You may first want to define (human) culture, before consulting Chapter 47.

Four fallacies of EP

Buller (2009, 2013) identifies four fallacies of what he calls 'Pop EP', best represented by Buss, Pinker, Symons, Tooby and Cosmides (see above).

1. *Analysis of Pleistocene adaptive problems provides clues to the mind's design.* As we've seen, EP is based on the belief that the human mind is adapted to cope with life as a Pleistocene hunter-gatherer (H-G) (which we were for about two million years before the ancient Chinese, Indian, Egyptian, and Sumerian civilisations; Abdulla, 1996). Forms of behaviour and social organisation that evolved adaptively over many generations in human H-G society may or may not be adaptive in modern industrialised society, but they have become, to a degree, fixed by humanity's evolutionary experience in the Palaelothic EEA (Rose, 2000). The story of our human H-G ancestors is, inevitably, partly a work of fiction (Turney, 1999) or 'just so' accounts (Rose, 2000). Evolutionary Psychologists imagine how the abilities that human beings possess now may have evolved, then propose this constructed past as the cause of these current abilities: this is *circular* reasoning. As Buller (2009, 2013) puts it:

> *To know how a solution to an adaptive problem evolved ... it is necessary to know something about the pre-existing trait that was recruited and modified to solve the problem. Without knowledge of our ancestors' psychological traits – which we don't have – we can't know how selection tinkered with them to create the minds we now possess.*

Figure 2.11 Can we use 'images' like these of our hunter-gatherer ancestors to explain how our current human abilities evolved?

2. *We know, or can discover, why distinctively human traits evolved. The comparative method* attempts to address the problem of adaptation quite directly. Like other species, humans need to find and consume food, find a mate, reproduce, and so on. It's likely, therefore, that similarities exist between humans and our closest relatives, the apes, regarding how they solve these particular problems. Testing whether particular behaviours are adaptive is easier to do for non-humans: we can assume that they're living under similar conditions to those of their ancestors (Workman and Reader, 2008).
While Pinker is probably correct in claiming that language is an adaptation (see above), discovering why it evolved, what it is an adaptation for,

MEET THE RESEARCHER

Lance Workman

Evolutionary psychology: lateralisation, mate choice and the social brain

My particular brand of psychology treats humans as a species of animal where both physical and psychological traits are regarded as the products of evolution. I began my career researching how the left and right sides of a bird's brain respond differentially to visual stimuli and how this changes with age in an adaptive (evolved) manner. Working first with Richard Andrew at the University of Sussex and then with Lesley Rogers at the University of New England, we uncovered evidence that, in the domestic chick, the right hemisphere is very much involved in processing visuospatial information to allow for topographical learning about the environment, while the left hemisphere is adapted to undertake food discrimination tasks (Workman and Andrew, 1989). It has also been shown by Andrew and his co-workers that the right hemisphere is important in controlling emotional type responses such as fear of novelty (Rogers and Andrew, 2002). This broad distribution of abilities between the two hemispheres of the forebrain – known as lateralisation of function – seemed to me to show remarkable parallels with human lateralisation. We know that in humans the right hemisphere is particularly good at processing visuospatial information (e.g. when reading a map) and emotional responses; the left is good at discrimination tasks and language. If there is this broad similarity between chicks and humans in the pattern of lateralisation then it seemed feasible that it is evolutionarily very ancient and might predate the evolution of birds and mammals. In fact, other researchers working on lateralisation in a wide range of vertebrate species from frogs to apes have subsequently shown that this broad pattern of lateralisation is quite widespread – hence adding support to the notion that it is an evolutionarily ancient adaptation (Rogers and Andrew, 2002; and below).

Lateralisation in humans

In recent years, I have shifted my attention to lateralisation in humans with regard to both language and emotional processing in order to determine whether this fits in with findings from other species. Looking at

These chicks are about to put lateralisation of right and left brain functions into practice

the ability to recognise emotional faces, my colleagues and I uncovered evidence that this ability is related to development of the right hemisphere that mirrors the time course for the development of language in the left hemisphere (Workman *et al.*, 2006). It appears that these developments during early childhood are adaptive as children grow and begin to engage with others outside their families. As this occurs, they need to understand both the linguistic and emotional signals others give off. Clearly for our early hominid (ape-like) ancestors, being able to communicate and pick up on emotional states is likely to have had positive repercussions for survival.

Adaptation

My work on lateralisation is informed by knowledge of evolution, but also illustrates difficulties faced by evolutionary psychologists. Both the strengths and weaknesses of our field are related to the Darwinian concept of 'adaptation'. Evolutionary psychologists seek to determine how various states of mind and behavioural responses might have come about due to their ability to aid survival and reproduction during our evolutionary past. Behaviours that evolved to aid survival and reproduction are often said to be 'adaptive'. Critics of evolutionary psychology see the concept of adaptations when applied to human behaviour as problematic, caricaturing them as a series of post hoc 'just-so' stories (like Rudyard Kipling's tales of how, for example, the elephant got its trunk – it was stretched by a crocodile's jaws). The problem is that, although we can formulate reasonable hypotheses about how and why various human traits evolved, we cannot go back in a time machine and observe their evolution (Workman and Reader, 2008). This makes testing evolutionary hypotheses difficult, but not impossible. One way is to observe human behaviours across different cultures. Common responses or preferences across these cultures might suggest they have come about through evolution via a common ancestor rather than as the products of culture itself. David Buss has used this cross-cultural approach to study sex differences in mate choice behaviour, uncovering evidence from 37 different cultures that males rate attractiveness more highly than females, and females rate status and wealth more highly than males (Buss, 1989). He also discovered that, across these cultures, males prefer younger females and females prefer older males. These findings suggest that, since females have a relatively short period of fertility (typically ages 13–50), then ancestral males who found indicators of youth and fertility attractive in females would have left more surviving offspring than those who did not. Hence this evolved tendency is still with us today. Likewise, Buss argues that since males have an extended period of fertility (age 13 potentially to end of life!) and because it is often older men that have accumulated wealth and status, the tendency to favour such males would have helped our female ancestors to produce and support more surviving offspring. Therefore Buss has accumulated evidence that this sex difference in mate preferences is an adaptation in our species.

Evidence from 37 different cultures has shown that males prefer younger females and females prefer older males

Social brain hypothesis

Comparing across cultures can help us understand which responses are likely to be adaptive and it has been relatively successful when studying mate choice. But this does have limitations when attempting to test some other evolutionary-based theories. Another evolutionary theory, Robin Dunbar's 'social brain hypothesis', uses the comparative method (i.e. comparing between species). The social brain hypothesis suggests that we evolved a particularly large forebrain in order to use language to solve the complexities of living in such large social groups (Dunbar, 1993). Dunbar suggests that when our hominid ancestors came down from the trees and began to live on the open savannah, they formed larger groups in order to fight off the big cats they encountered there. This increase in group size – from approximately 20–150 – led to a huge increase in time spent grooming and getting around the group. Dunbar suggests that our ancestors solved this by evolving language (and a large brain to support this) allowing us vocally to 'groom' more than one individual at a time. The social brain theory is supported by the fact that there is a strong positive correlation between the group size of a particular species of primate and its forebrain size. This method of comparing across species is important. Because we are dealing with an entity that does not vary between cultures (forebrain size), we have to make use of this comparative method to test the social brain hypothesis. In fact, today it is known that the relationship between brain size and social group size extends beyond the primates and is also true for birds (Emery and Clayton, 2004). This is powerful evidence of what drove us to evolve such a large brain because we observe the same pattern of a positive correlation between brain size and social group size in a wide range of species. This suggests a general evolutionary explanation for increases in brain size for social species. Of course, how this fits in with my own less high-profile work on lateralisation of the brain and how my work might relate to human mate choice preferences is still to be determined. But I am pleased to see that evolutionary psychologists have returned to testing birds to help us understand the evolution of human brain and behaviour – which is, after all, where I came in!

Dr Lance Workman is Head of Psychology at the School of Social Sciences at Bath Spa University and Head of the Biopsychology Research Unit (BPU). He has published a large number of articles on biological psychology and on animal behaviour. The second edition of his book *Evolutionary Psychology* (Workman and Reader) was published by Cambridge University Press in 2008.

requires identifying the adaptive functions that language served among early language users. To use the comparative method to answer such questions, we need to compare human language in species with which we share a common ancestor. This is tricky! Our closest living relatives, chimpanzees and bonobos, don't spontaneously use language (although, arguably, they can be taught it; see Chapter 19), So, we cannot identify the environmental conditions that may have influenced the appearance of language as an adaptive trait. The species in the genus *Homo* are, of course, all extinct, and dead hominims tell us (almost) nothing about their evolutionary histories (Buller, 2009, 2013).

3. *Our modern skulls house a Stone Age mind.* Evolutionary psychologists claim that the timescale of human history has been too short for evolutionary selection pressures to have produced significant change. Buller (2009, 2013) believes that the claim is mistaken at both ends of the scale:
   (a) some human psychological mechanisms emerged in a more ancient evolutionary past. For example, Panskepp (in Buller) claims that the emotional systems that he calls Care, Panic and Play date back to early primate evolutionary history, while Fear, Rage, Seeking and Lust have even earlier, pre-mammalian origins;
   (b) the idea that we're stuck with a Pleistocene-adapted psychology greatly underestimates the rate at which natural and sexual selection can drive evolutionary change. Selection can radically alter the life-history of a population in as few as 18 generations (for humans, roughly 450 years). Environmental changes since the Pleistocene – both natural (such as climate change; McKie, 2002) and human-made (such as the agricultural and industrial revolutions) – have unquestionably altered the selection pressures on human psychology. If, as EP maintains, human psychological characteristics are the product of an interaction between genes and the environment, then even with negligible genetic evolution since the Pleistocene, such environmental changes would have produced traits that are likely to differ in important ways from those of our Pleistocene ancestors.
4. *The psychological data provide clear support for EP.* Some of these data will be discussed at various points in the chapters that follow. One example will be given here, which produces a criticism usually reserved for Freud's theories (see above). According to Daly and Wilson (1988a, 1988b), children under the age of two were at least 60 times more likely to be killed by a step-parent – and almost always a stepfather – than by a natural parent. This is exactly what evolutionary theory would predict, since step-parents and step-children are genetically unrelated, while a child inherits half its genes from each biological parent. However, most stepfathers don't kill or abuse, and a minority of biological fathers do; these findings are difficult to square with any explanation based on shared/non-shared genes. More seriously, in discussing women who kill their newborn babies, Pinker (1997b) claimed that when such an act takes place in conditions of poverty, it could be regarded as an *adaptationist* response. The psychological module that normally induces protectiveness in mothers of newborns is switched off by the challenge of an impoverished environment. This means that both killing and protecting are explained by evolutionary selection. As Hilary Rose (2000) says, this explains everything and, therefore, nothing.

Figure 2.12 Steven Pinker (born 1954)

CONCLUSIONS

The focus of this discussion of various theoretical approaches within Psychology has been on how each conceptualises human beings. Freud's 'tension-reducing person', Skinner's 'environmentally controlled person' and Rogers' 'growth-motivated person' really are quite different from each other (Nye, 2000). The person-as-organism, person-as-information-processor, and the person-as-shaped-by-our-evolutionary-past are different again – both from each other and from the first three approaches. SC's image of the person is rather less concrete and more elusive: what people are like and what they do is relative to their culture, historical period, and so on.

However, we've also noted some important similarities between different approaches, such as the deterministic nature of Freud's and Skinner's theories, and the influence of the Biopsychological and information-processing approach on EP. As we shall see throughout this book, each approach has something of value to contribute to our understanding of ourselves – even if it is only to reject the particular explanation it offers. The diversity of approaches reflects the complexity of the subject matter, so, usually, there's room for a diversity of explanations.

Chapter Summary

- Different theoretical **approaches/perspectives** are based on different models/images of the nature of human beings.
- Central to the **Biopsychological approach** (a branch of **neuroscience**) is the role of **genes** in determining behaviour via the **nervous system**.
- **Behaviour geneticists** attempt to quantify how much of the **variability** of any given trait can be attributed to **heritability**, **shared environments**, or **non-shared environments**.
- They do this through the use of studies of **separated MZs** and **adoption studies**; these both allow researchers to separate the effects of genetic and environmental factors.
- The influence of the Biopsychological approach is clearly seen in the **addiction-as-disease model**.
- Untenable claims based on neuroscientific research using **fMRI scans** have been accused of being **neurocentric**. This mirrors the **reductionist** nature of the Biopsychological approach as a whole.
- **Methodological behaviourism** focuses on what can be quantified and observed by different researchers. Skinner's **radical behaviourism** regards mental processes as both **inaccessible** and **irrelevant** for explaining behaviour.
- The **Behaviourist approach** stresses the role of environmental influences (**learning**), especially **classical** and **operant conditioning**. Psychology's aim is to **predict** and **control** behaviour.
- Tolman's **cognitive behaviourism** and **social learning theory** represent modifications of 'orthodox' learning (conditioning) theory.
- Methodological behaviourism has influenced the practice of scientific Psychology in general. Other practical contributions include **behaviour therapy** and **modification**, **behavioural neuroscience** and **pharmacology**, and **biofeedback**.
- The **Psychodynamic approach** is based on Freud's **psychoanalytic theory**. Central aspects are the **unconscious** (especially **repression**), **infantile sexuality** and the impact of **early experience**.
- Freud's ideas have become part of **mainstream Psychology**, contributing to our understanding of motivation, sleep and dreams, forgetting, attachment, aggression and abnormality.
- Major modifications/alternatives to Freudian theory include **ego psychology**, **Erikson's psychosocial theory**, Adler's **individual psychology**, Jung's **analytical psychology**, and the **object relations school**.
- All forms of **psychotherapy** stem directly or indirectly from **psychoanalysis**. Many trained psychoanalysts have been responsible for developing radically different therapeutic approaches, including Rogers, Perls and Wolpe.
- Maslow called the **humanistic approach** the 'third force' in psychology. It believes in **free will**, adopts a **phenomenological perspective**, and stresses the **positive aspects** of human personality.
- Rogers was a prolific researcher into the effectiveness of his **client/person-centred therapy**, opened up psychotherapy to psychologists and other non-medically qualified practitioners, and created a **counselling profession** that operates within a wide diversity of settings.
- The **cognitive approach** lacks both a central figure and a unifying theory. It uses **analogies** and **metaphors** when trying to describe what's going on inside the brain, in particular the **computer analogy** and the view of people as **information processors**.
- Other important features of the cognitive approach include the concepts of **coding**, **channel capacity** and **serial/parallel processing**.
- A major application of the cognitive approach has been **cognitive behaviour therapy**, as in Ellis's **rational emotive behaviour therapy** (REBT).
- While the computer analogy is a useful way of understanding cognitive processes, there are also some important differences between how computers and people process information.
- One of the goals of **social constructionism** is to correct the tendency of mainstream psychology to **decontextualise** behaviour. Related to this is the **universalist assumption**, which is challenged by **(trans)cultural** (as distinct from **cross-cultural**) **psychology**.
- **Social representation theory** is a social constructionist theory, and many **feminist psychologists** adopt a social constructionist approach in challenging mainstream psychology.
- **Evolutionary psychology** grew out of sociobiology. Unlike the latter, EP puts the mind in centre stage, identifying several independent **mental mechanisms** or **modules**. These form the core of **human nature**.
- A major assumption of EP is that these mental modules have become fixed by our hunter-gatherer ancestors' experience in the **Palaeolithic Environment of Evolutionary Adaptation** (EEA). But knowledge of the EEA is largely speculative, and there's good reason to believe that human traits have changed since that time.

Links with Other Topics/Chapters

Chapter 3 → The description of classical and operant conditioning as forms of associative learning reflects the philosophical roots of behaviourism, namely the *empiricist* philosophy of John Locke. This was a major influence on the development of science in general, as well as on Behaviourism in particular

Chapters 3 and 48 → Defining the aims of a science of behaviour as prediction and control raises both *conceptual* questions (about the *nature of science*, in particular the role of theory) and *ethical* questions (for example, about *power* and the role of *Psychologists as agents of change*)

Chapters 45 and 48 → The ethics of some forms of *behaviour modification* (such as the *token economy*) and certain aspects of *applied behaviour analysis* (especially the use of punishment with vulnerable individuals) have been seriously questioned

Chapter 7 → Many Psychologists would agree that there are degrees or levels of *consciousness*, but most wouldn't share Freud's distinction between the conscious, pre-conscious and unconscious mind

Chapter 47 → The distinction between cultural Psychology and cross-cultural Psychology corresponds to the *emic–etic distinction*

Chapter 18 → Social Constructionism is consistent with Whorf's *linguistic relativity hypothesis* and the more general theory of *linguistic determinism* (language determines thought)

Chapter 24 → *Discursive Psychology* (a social constructionist approach) finds nothing odd about the common finding that *attitudes are often poor predictors of behaviour*

Chapter 22 → Social representations are an important part of *social cognition* and *social perception*

Recommended Reading

Burr, V. (2003) *Social Constructionism* (2nd edn). London: Routledge.

Cohen, D. (2004) *Psychologists on Psychology*. London: Hodder & Stoughton.

Glassman, W.E. (2006) *Approaches to Psychology* (4th edn). Maidenhead: Open University Press.

Harré, R. (2006) *Key Thinkers in Psychology*. London: Sage.

Nye, D. (2000) *Three Psychologies: Perspectives from Freud, Skinner and Rogers* (6th edn). Belmont, CA: Wadsworth/Thomson Learning.

Rose, H. & Rose, S. (eds) (2000) *Alas, Poor Darwin: Arguments Against Evolutionary Psychology*. London: Jonathan Cape.

Workman, L. & Reader, W. (2008) *Evolutionary Psychology: An Introduction* (2nd edn). Cambridge: Cambridge University Press.

Useful Websites

www.freud.org.uk

www.psychoanalysis.org.uk

http://psychology.about.com/od/profilesofmajorthinkers/p/watson.htm

www.en.wikipedia.org/wiki/Cognitive_revolution

www.en.wikipedia.org/wiki/Social_constructionism

www.psych.ucsb.edu/research/cep/ (Centre for Evolutionary Psychology)

www.emory.edu/LIVING_LINKS/ (Centre for the Advanced Study of Ape and Human Evolution)

novaonline.nvcc.edu/eli/spd110td/interper/self/linksselftheoryidentityhumanistic.html

(For further weblinks, see Chapter 42.)

CHAPTER 3

PSYCHOLOGY AS A SCIENCE

Some philosophical roots of science and Psychology

What do we mean by 'science'?

The scientific study of human behaviour

INTRODUCTION and OVERVIEW

As we saw in Chapter 1, Psychology is commonly defined as the scientific study of behaviour and cognitive processes (or mind or experience). In effect, this book as a whole looks at how different Psychologists have put this definition into practice, through their use of various investigative methods to study a wide variety of behaviours and cognitive processes.

This chapter turns the spotlight once more on the definition of Psychology given above. It does this by examining the nature of science (including the major features of scientific method), and by tracing some of the major developments in Psychology's history as a scientific discipline. This enables us to address the question of how appropriate it is to use scientific method to study human behaviour and cognitive processes, and to assess the validity of this widely accepted definition.

SOME PHILOSOPHICAL ROOTS OF SCIENCE AND PSYCHOLOGY

The seventeenth-century French philosopher Descartes was the first person to distinguish formally between mind and matter (*philosophical dualism*; see Chapter 49), which had an enormous impact on the development of both Psychology as a science and science in general. Dualism allowed scientists to treat matter as inert and completely distinct from human beings, which meant that the world could be described objectively, without reference to the human observer. *Objectivity* became the ideal of science, and was extended to the study of human behaviour and social institutions in the mid-1800s by Comte, who called it *positivism*.

Descartes also promoted *mechanism*, the view that the material world comprises objects which are assembled like a huge machine and operated by mechanical laws. He extended this view to living organisms, including, eventually, humans. Because the mind (unlike the physical world) is non-material, Descartes believed that it can be investigated only through *introspection* (observing one's own thoughts and feelings, see Chapter 1). He was also one of the first advocates of *reductionism* (see Chapter 49).

Figure 3.1 René Descartes (1596–1650)

Empiricism refers to the ideas of the seventeenth- and eighteenth-century British philosophers, Locke, Hume and Berkeley. They believed that the only source of true knowledge about the world is *sensory experience* (what reaches us through our senses or can be inferred about the relationship between such sensory facts). Empiricism is usually contrasted with *nativism* (or *rationalism*), according to which knowledge of the world is largely innate or inborn.

The word '*empirical*' ('through the senses') is often used to mean 'scientific', implying that what scientists do, and what distinguishes them from non-scientists, is carry out experiments and observations as ways of collecting data or 'facts' about the world (hence, 'empirical methods' for 'scientific methods'). Empiricism proved to be one of the central influences on the development of physics and chemistry.

Empiricism and Psychology

Prior to the 1870s, there were no laboratories devoted specifically to psychological research, and the early scientific Psychologists had trained mainly as physiologists, doctors, philosophers, or some combination of these. The two professors who set up the first two Psychology laboratories and who deserve much of the credit for the development of academic Psychology were Wundt (1832–1920) in Germany, and James (1842–1910) in the USA (Fancher, 1979).

Wundt's contribution

A physiologist by training, Wundt is generally regarded as the 'founder' of the new science of Experimental Psychology ('a new domain of science': Wundt, 1874). Having worked as Helmholtz's assistant (see Chapter 15), Wundt eventually became professor of 'scientific philosophy' at Leipzig University in 1875, illustrating the lack of distinct boundaries between the various disciplines that combined to bring about Psychology's development (Fancher, 1979).

Figure 3.2 Wilhelm Wundt (1832–1920)

In 1879, Wundt converted his 'laboratory' at Leipzig into a 'private institute' of Experimental Psychology. For the first time, a place had been set aside for the explicit purpose of conducting psychological research, and hence 1879 is widely accepted as the 'birth date' of Psychology as a discipline in its own right. From its modest beginnings, the institute began to attract people from all over the world, who returned to their own countries to establish laboratories modelled on Wundt's.

Ask Yourself

- Consider the difficulties that might be involved in relying on introspection to formulate an account of the nature of conscious experience (i.e. an account that applies to *people in general*).
- In what ways is structuralism *reductionist*? (See Chapter 49.)
- Which major theory of perception rejects this structuralist approach, and what are its principal features? (See Chapter 15.)

Box 3.1 Wundt's study of the conscious mind: introspectionism and structuralism

- Wundt believed that conscious mental states could be scientifically studied through the systematic manipulation of *antecedent variables* (those that occur before some other event), and analysed by carefully controlled techniques of *introspection*.
- Introspection was a rigorous and highly disciplined technique for analysing conscious experience into its most basic elements (sensations and feelings). Participants were always advanced Psychology students, who'd been carefully trained to introspect properly.
- Sensations are the raw sensory content of consciousness, devoid of all 'meaning' or interpretation, and all conscious thoughts, ideas and perceptions were assumed to be combinations of sensations. Based on his experiment in which he listened to a metronome beating at varying rates, Wundt concluded that feelings could be analysed in terms of pleasantness–unpleasantness, tension–relaxation and activity–passivity.
- Wundt believed that introspection made it possible to cut through the learned categories and concepts that define our everyday experience of the world, and so expose the 'building blocks' of experience.
- Because of introspection's central role, Wundt's early brand of Psychology was called *introspectionism*, and his attempt to analyse consciousness into its elementary sensations and feelings is known as *structuralism*.

(Based on Fancher, 1979)

James's contribution

James taught anatomy and physiology at Harvard University in 1872, and by 1875 was calling his course 'The Relations Between Physiology and Psychology'. In the same year, he established a small laboratory, used mainly for teaching purposes. In 1878, he dropped anatomy and physiology, and for several years taught 'pure Psychology'.

His view of Psychology is summarised in *The Principles of Psychology* (1890), which includes discussion of instinct, brain function, habit, the stream of consciousness, the self (see Chapter 33), attention (Chapter 13), memory (Chapter 17), perception (Chapters 15 and 16), free will (Chapter 49), and emotion (Chapter 10).

The Principles of Psychology provided the famous definition of Psychology as 'the science of mental life' (see Chapter 1). But ironically, James was very critical both of his book and of what Psychology could offer as a science. He became increasingly interested in philosophy, although in 1894 he became the first

Figure 3.3 William James (1842–1910)

American to call favourable attention to the recent work of the then little known Viennese neurologist, Sigmund Freud (Fancher, 1979).

James proposed a point of view (rather than a theory) that directly inspired *functionalism*, which emphasises the purpose and utility of behaviour (Fancher, 1979). Functionalism, in turn, helped to stimulate interest in *individual differences*, since they determine how well or poorly individuals adapt to their environments. These attitudes made Americans especially receptive to Darwin's (1859) ideas about individual variation, evolution by natural selection, and the 'survival of the fittest' (see Chapters 2, 28 and 30).

Figure 3.4 Charles Darwin (1809–1882)

Watson's behaviourist revolution

Watson took over the Psychology Department at Johns Hopkins University in 1909, and immediately began cutting Psychology's ties with philosophy and strengthening those with biology. At that time, Wundt's and James's studies of consciousness were still the 'real' Psychology, but Watson was doing research on non-human animals and became increasingly critical of the use of introspection.

Figure 3.5 John Broadus Watson (1878–1958)

In particular, Watson argued that introspective reports were unreliable and difficult to verify. It's impossible to check the accuracy of such reports, because they're based on purely *private experience*, which is inaccessible to the investigator. As a result, Watson redefined Psychology in his famous 'behaviourist manifesto' of 1913.

Ask Yourself

- **Try to formulate arguments for and against Watson's claim that there's only a quantitative difference between the behaviour of humans and non-humans.**

In his 1915 presidential address to the American Psychological Association, Watson talked about his recent 'discovery' of Pavlov's work on conditioned reflexes in dogs. He proposed that the conditioned reflex could become the foundation for a full-scale human Psychology.

The extreme environmentalism of Locke's empiricism (see above) lent itself well to the behaviourist emphasis on learning (through the process of Pavlovian or classical conditioning). While Locke had described the mind at birth as a *tabula rasa* ('blank slate') on which experience writes, Watson, in rejecting the mind as suitable for a scientific Psychology, simply swapped mind for behaviour: it's now behaviour that's shaped by the environment.

According to Miller (1962), empiricism provided Psychology with both (a) a *methodology* (stressing the role of observation and measurement) and (b) a *theory*, including *analysis into elements* (such as stimulus–response units) and *associationism* (which explains how simple elements can be combined to form more complex ones).

Box 3.2 Watson's (1913) 'Behaviourist Manifesto'

Watson's article 'Psychology as the behaviourist views it' is often referred to as the 'behaviourist manifesto', a charter for a truly scientific Psychology. It was Behaviourism that was to represent a rigorous empiricist approach within Psychology for the first time. According to Watson:

> *Psychology as the behaviourist views it is a purely objective natural science. Its theoretical goal is the prediction and control of behaviour. Introspection forms no essential part of its methods, nor is the scientific value of its data dependent upon the readiness with which they lend themselves to interpretation in terms of consciousness. The behaviourist ... recognises no dividing line between man and brute. The behaviour of a man ... forms only a part of the behaviourist's total scheme of investigation.*

Three features of this 'manifesto' deserve special mention:

1. Psychology must be purely *objective*, excluding all subjective data or interpretations in terms of conscious experience. This redefines Psychology as the *'science of behaviour'* (rather than the 'science of mental life').
2. The goals of Psychology should be to *predict* and *control* behaviour (as opposed to describing and explaining conscious mental states), a goal later endorsed by Skinner's *radical behaviourism* (see Chapter 2).
3. There's no fundamental (*qualitative*) distinction between human and non-human behaviour. If, as Darwin had shown, humans evolved from more simple species, then it follows that human behaviour is just a more complex form of the behaviour of other species (the difference is merely *quantitative* – one of degree). Consequently, rats, cats, dogs and pigeons became the major source of psychological data. Since 'psychological' now meant 'behaviour' rather than 'consciousness', non-humans that were convenient to study, and whose environments could be easily controlled, could replace people as experimental subjects.

(Based on Fancher, 1979; Watson, 1913)

Behaviourism also embodied positivism, in particular the emphasis on the need for scientific rigour and objectivity. Humans were now conceptualised and studied as 'natural phenomena', with subjective experience, consciousness, and other characteristics (traditionally regarded as distinctive human qualities) no longer having a place in the behaviourist world.

The cognitive revolution

Academic Psychology in the USA and the UK was dominated by behaviourism for the next 40 years. However, criticism and dissatisfaction with it culminated in a number of 'events', all taking place in 1956, which, collectively, are referred to as the 'cognitive revolution'.

Box 3.3 The 1956 'Cognitive Revolution'

- At a meeting at the Massachusetts Institute of Technology (MIT), Chomsky introduced his theory of language (see Chapter 19), Miller presented a paper on the 'magical number seven' in short-term memory (see Chapter 17), and Newell and Simon presented a paper on the logical theory machine (or logic theorist), with a further paper by Newell *et al.* (1958), which Newell and Simon (1972) extended into the general problem-solver (GPS; see Chapter 20).
- The first systematic attempt to investigate concept formation (in adults) from a cognitive psychological perspective was reported (Bruner *et al.*, 1956).
- At Dartmouth College, New Hampshire (the 'Dartmouth Conference'), ten academics met to discuss the possibility of producing computer programs that could 'behave' or 'think' intelligently. These academics included McCarthy (generally attributed with having coined the term 'artificial intelligence'), Minsky, Simon, Newell, Chomsky and Miller (see Chapter 20).

(Based on Eysenck and Keane, 1995)

Figure 3.6 George A. Miller (1920–2012)

This new way of thinking about and investigating people was called the *information-processing approach*. At its centre is the *computer analogy*, the view that human cognition can be understood by comparing it with the functioning of a digital computer. It was now acceptable to study the mind again, although its conceptualisation was very different from that of Wundt, James and the other pioneers.

Science, scientism and mainstream Psychology

Despite this major change in Psychology after 1956, certain central assumptions and practices within the discipline have remained essentially the same, and these are referred to as *mainstream Psychology*. Harré (1989) refers to the mainstream as the 'old paradigm', which he believes continues to be haunted by certain 'unexamined presuppositions'. One of these is *scientism*, defined by Van Langenhove (1995) as:

> *... the borrowing of methods and a characteristic vocabulary from the natural sciences in order to discover causal mechanisms that explain psychological phenomena.*

Scientism maintains that all aspects of human behaviour can and should be studied using the methods of natural science, which claims to be the sole means of establishing 'objective truth'. This can be achieved by studying phenomena removed from any particular context (*'context-stripping'* exposes them in their 'pure' form), and in a *value-free* way (there's no bias on the investigator's part). The most reliable way of doing this is through the laboratory experiment, the method providing the greatest degree of control over relevant variables (see Box 3.6, p. 48). As noted earlier, these beliefs and assumptions add up to the traditional view of science known as positivism.

Ask Yourself

- Try to find examples of experimental studies of human behaviour that fit the definition of 'context-stripping' given above. Probably the 'best' examples will come from Social Psychology, which in itself should suggest criticisms of this approach to studying behaviour. (See also Chapter 47.)

Although much research has moved beyond the confines of the laboratory experiment, the same positivist logic is still central to how psychological enquiry is conceived and conducted. Method and measurement still have a privileged status:

> *Whether concerned with mind or behaviour (and whether conducted inside or outside the laboratory), research tends to be constructed in terms of the separation (or reduction) of entities into independent and dependent variables and the measurement of hypothesised relationships between them. (Smith et al., 1995)*

Despite the fact that since the mid-1970s the natural sciences model has become the subject of vigorous attacks, Psychology is still to a large extent dominated by it. The most prominent effect of this is the dominance of experiments (Van Langenhove, 1995). This has far-reaching effects on the way Psychology pictures people as more or less passive and mechanical information-processing devices, whose behaviour can be split up into variables. It also affects the way Psychology deals with people. In experiments, people aren't treated as single individuals, but as interchangeable 'subjects'. There's no room for individualised observations (see Gross, 2014).

WHAT DO WE MEAN BY SCIENCE?

The major features of science

Most Psychologists and philosophers of science would probably agree that for a discipline to be called a science, it must possess certain characteristics. These are summarised in Box 3.4 and Figure 3.7.

Box 3.4 The major features of science

- **A definable subject matter**. This changed from conscious human thought to human and non-human behaviour, then to cognitive processes, within Psychology's first 80 years as a separate discipline.
- **Theory construction**. This represents an attempt to explain observed phenomena, such as Watson's attempt to account for (almost all) human and non-human behaviour in terms of classical conditioning, and Skinner's subsequent attempt to do the same with operant conditioning (see Chapters 2 and 11).
- **Hypothesis testing**. This involves making specific predictions about behaviour under certain conditions (for example, predicting that by combining the sight of a rat with the sound of a hammer crashing down on a steel bar just behind his head, a small child will learn to fear the rat, as in the case of Little Albert: see Key Study 11.1).
- **Empirical methods**. These are used to collect *data* (*evidence*) relevant to the hypothesis being tested.

What is 'scientific method'?

The account given in Box 3.4 and Figure 3.7 of what constitutes a science is non-controversial. However, it fails to tell us how the scientific process takes place, the sequence of 'events' involved (such as where the theory comes from in the first place, and how it's related to observation of the subject matter), or the exact relationship between theory construction, hypothesis testing, and data collection.

Collectively, these 'events' and relationships are referred to as (the) scientific method. Table 3.1 summarises some common beliefs about both science and scientific method, together with some alternative views.

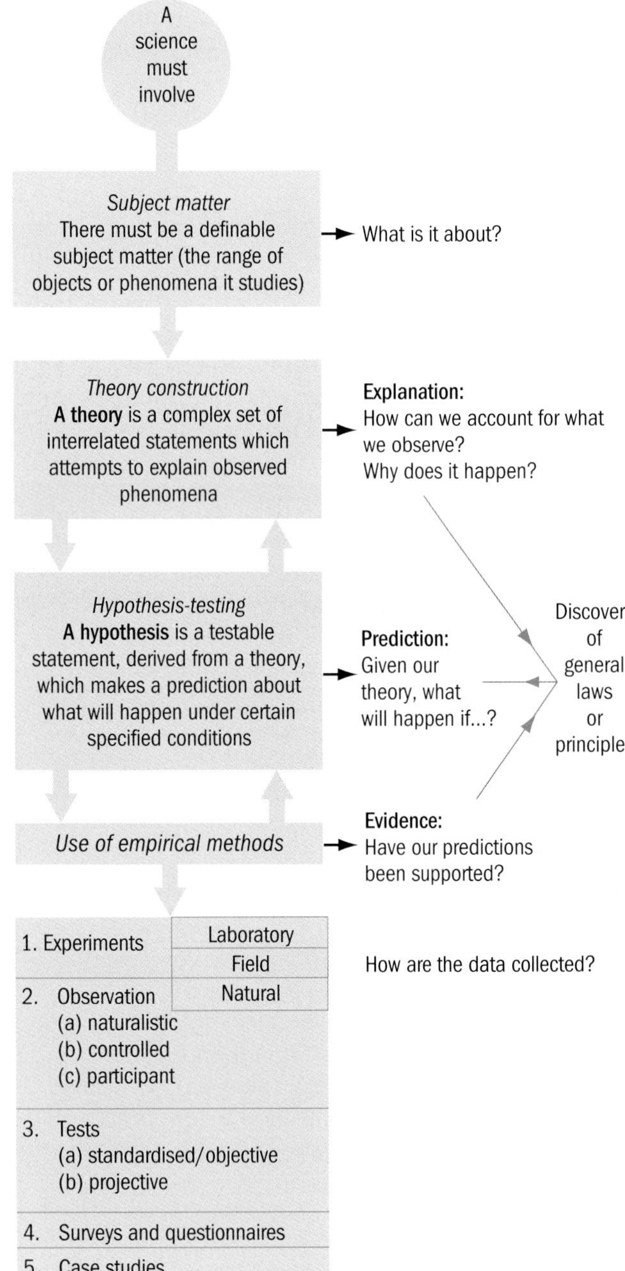

Figure 3.7 A summary of the major features of a science

As a result of the first two beliefs identified in Table 3.1, Popper (1972) has revised the stages of the scientific process as proposed by the classical view (the *inductive method*). This, together with Popper's revised version, is shown in Table 3.2.

Can Psychology be a science if Psychologists cannot agree what Psychology is?

As we noted earlier, definitions of Psychology have changed during its lifetime, largely reflecting the influence and contributions of its major theoretical approaches or orientations. In this chapter (and Chapter 2), we've seen that each approach rests upon a different image of what people are like. This, in turn, determines what's considered worthy of investigation, as well as the methods of study that can and should be used to investigate it. Consequently, different approaches can be seen as self-contained disciplines, as well as different facets of the same discipline (Kline, 1988; Kuhn, 1962, 2012).

Ask Yourself

- What is the underlying image of the person associated with each of the major theoretical approaches within Psychology?
- Which of these do you consider captures your own experience, and your experience of others, most accurately, and why? (You might find it helpful to refer to both Chapters 2 and 45.)

Does Psychology have a paradigm?

Kuhn (a philosopher of science) argues that a field of study can only legitimately be considered a science if a majority of its workers subscribe to a common, global perspective or *paradigm*. This means that Psychology is *preparadigmatic*: it lacks a paradigm, without which it's still in a state (or stage) of *prescience*. Whether Psychology has, or has ever had, a paradigm, is hotly debated. As Table 3.3 shows, some Psychologists agree with Kuhn's view of Psychology as prescientific; others believe it has already undergone at least two revolutions, and is in a stage of *normal science*, with Cognitive Psychology the current paradigm. A third view, which represents a blend of the first two, is that Psychology currently, and simultaneously, has a number of paradigms.

For example, Smith *et al.* (1998) identify psychoanalysis, behaviourism, sociobiology, and the information-processing, and cognitive–developmental approaches as paradigms, with the last being the most important as far as child development is concerned (see Chapters 34 and 35). For Davison *et al.* (2004) the current paradigms in psychopathology and therapy are the biological, psychoanalytic, humanistic and existential, learning (behaviourist) and cognitive (see Chapter 45).

Table 3.1 Some common beliefs and alternative views about 'science' and 'scientific method'

Common beliefs	Alternative views
● Scientific discovery begins with simple, unbiased, unprejudiced observation: the scientist simply 'samples' the world without any preconceptions, expectations or predetermined theories.	● There's no such thing as unprejudiced observation: Observation is always selective, interpretative, prestructured, and directed: we must have at least some idea of what we're looking for, otherwise we cannot know when we've found it. Goldberg (2000) cites a philosophy professor who asserted that what we call 'data' (that which is given) should more accurately be called 'capta' (that which is taken).
■ From the resulting sensory evidence ('data'/sense-data), generalised statements of fact will take shape: we gradually build up a picture of what the world is like based on a number of separate 'samples'.	■ 'Data' don't constitute 'facts': evidence usually implies measurements, numbers, and recordings, which need to be interpreted in the light of a theory. Facts don't exist objectively and cannot be discovered through 'pure observation'. 'Fact' = Data + Theory (Deese, 1972).
▲ The essential feature of scientific activity is the use of empirical methods, through which the sensory evidence is gathered: what distinguishes science from non-science is performing experiments, etc.	▲ Despite the central role of data collection, data alone don't make a science. Theory is just as crucial, because without it data have no meaning (see point above).
▼ The truth about the world (the objective nature of things, what the world is 'really like') can be established through properly controlled experiments and other ways of collecting 'facts': science can tell us about reality as it is independently of the scientist or the activity of observing it.	▼ Scientific theory and research reflect the biases, prejudices, values and assumptions of the individual scientist, as well as of the scientific community s/he belongs to. Science isn't value-free (see Chapter 47).
♦ Science involves the steady accumulation of knowledge: each generation of scientists adds to the discoveries of previous generations.	♦ Science involves an endless succession of long, peaceful periods ('normal science') and 'scientific revolutions' (Kuhn, 1962: see Table 3.3, p. 44).
	✻ Science has a warm, human, exciting, argumentative, creative 'face' (Collins, 1994).

(Based on Medawar, 1963; Popper, 1972)

Table 3.2 Comparison between the classical, inductive view of science and Popper's revised version

Inductive method	Popper's version
Observation and method	Problem (usually a refutation of an existing theory or prediction)
Inductive generalisation	Proposed solution or new theory
Hypothesis	Deduction of testable statements (hypotheses) from the new theory. This relates to the hypothetico-deductive method, which is usually contrasted with/opposed to the *inductive method*. In practice, both approaches are involved in the scientific process and are complementary
Attempted verification of hypothesis	Tests or attempts to *refute* by methods including observation and experiment
Proof or disproof	Establishing a preference between competing theories
Knowledge	

(Based on Popper, 1972)

Table 3.3 Stages in the development of a science (▲) and their application to psychology (■)

▲	*Prescience*: No paradigm has evolved, and there are several schools of thought or theoretical orientations.
■	Like Kuhn, Joynson (1980) and Boden (1980) argue that Psychology is preparadigmatic. Kline (1988) sees its various approaches as involving different paradigms.
▲	*Normal science*: A paradigm has emerged, dictating the kind of research that's carried out and providing a framework for interpreting results. The details of the theory are filled in, and workers explore its limits. Disagreements can usually be resolved within the limits allowed by the paradigm.
■	According to Valentine (1982), *behaviourism* comes as close as anything could to a paradigm. It provides: (a) a clear *definition of the subject matter* (behaviour as opposed to 'the mind'); (b) *fundamental assumptions*, in the form of the central role of learning (especially conditioning), and the analysis of behaviour into stimulus–response units, which allow prediction and control; (c) a *methodology*, with the controlled experiment at its core.
▲	*Revolution*: A point is reached in most established sciences where the conflicting evidence becomes so overwhelming that the old paradigm has to be abandoned and is replaced by a new one (*paradigm shift*). For example, Newtonian physics was replaced by Einstein's theory of relativity. When this paradigm shift occurs, there's a return to *normal science*.
■	Palermo (1971) and LeFrancois (1983) argue that Psychology has already undergone several paradigm shifts. The first paradigm was *structuralism*, represented by Wundt's introspectionism. This was replaced by Watson's *behaviourism*. Finally, *Cognitive Psychology* largely replaced behaviourism, based on the computer analogy and the concept of information processing. Glassman (1995) disagrees, claiming that there's never been a complete reorganisation of the discipline, as has happened in physics.

Lambie (1991) believes it's a mistake to equate 'paradigm' with 'approach'. As noted in Table 3.2, while theory is an essential part of a paradigm, there's much more involved than this. For example, different theories can co-exist within the same overall approach, such as classical and operant conditioning within 'learning theory' (the behaviourist approach), and Freud's and Erikson's theories within the psychodynamic approach.

One of the 'ingredients' that makes a paradigm different from an approach is its social psychological dimension. Paradigms refer to assumptions and beliefs held in common by most, if not all, the members of a given scientific community. This issue is discussed further in the following section.

THE SCIENTIFIC STUDY OF HUMAN BEHAVIOUR

The social nature of science: the problem of objectivity

'Doing science' is part of human behaviour. When Psychologists study what people do, they're engaging in some of the very same behaviours they're trying to understand (such as thinking, perceiving, problem-solving and explaining). This is what's meant by the statement that Psychologists are part of their own subject matter, which makes it even more difficult for them to be objective than other scientists.

According to Richards (1996b):

> *Whereas in orthodox sciences there is always some external object of enquiry – rocks, electrons, DNA, chemicals – existing essentially unchanging in the non-human world (even if never finally knowable 'as it really is' beyond human conceptions), this is not so for psychology. 'Doing psychology' is the human activity of studying human activity; it is human psychology examining itself – and what it produces by way of new theories, ideas and beliefs about itself is also part of our psychology!*

Knowable 'as it really is' refers to objectivity, and Richards is claiming that it may be impossible for any scientist to achieve complete objectivity. One reason for this relates to the social nature of scientific activity. As Rose (1997) says:

> *How biologists – or any scientists – perceive the world is not the result of simply holding a true reflecting mirror up to nature: it is shaped by the history of our subject, by dominant social expectations and by the patterns of research funding.*

Does this mean that 'the truth' only exists 'by agreement'? Does science not tell us about what things are 'really' like, but only what scientists happen to believe is the truth at any particular time?

Ask Yourself

- Given the sometimes very intense feelings aroused in individual scientists during the course of their work, in what ways do you think science can be described as a social activity? (It might be useful to think about why you do practical work/labs – other than because you have to!)

According to Richardson (1991), whatever the logical aspects of scientific method may be (deriving hypotheses from theories, the importance of refutability, and so on), science is a very *social* business. Research must be qualified and quantified to enable others to replicate it, and in this way the procedures, instruments and measures become standardised, so that scientists anywhere in the world can check the truth of reported observations and findings. This implies the need for universally agreed conventions for reporting these observations and findings (Richardson, 1991).

Kuhn's concept of a paradigm also stresses the role of agreement or consensus among scientists working within a particular discipline. Accordingly, 'truth' has more to do with the popularity and widespread acceptance of a particular framework within the scientific community than with its 'truth value'. The fact that revolutions do occur (paradigm shifts; see Table 3.3) demonstrates that 'the truth' can and does change.

Figure 3.8 Science is essentially a social process

For example, the change from classical Newtonian mechanics to quantum mechanics (Einsteinian physics) reflected the changing popularity of these two accounts. For Planck (in Kuhn, 1970), who helped to shape the 'Einsteinian revolution':

> *A new scientific theory does not triumph by convincing its opponents and making them see the light, but rather because its opponents eventually die, and a new generation grows up that is familiar with it.*

The popularity or acceptability of a theory, however, must be at least partly determined by how well it explains and predicts the phenomena in question. In other words, both social and 'purely' scientific or rational criteria are relevant.

However, even if there are widely accepted ways of 'doing science', 'good science' doesn't necessarily mean 'good Psychology'. Is it valid to study human behaviour and experience as part of the natural world, or is a different kind of approach needed altogether? After all, it isn't just Psychologists who observe, experiment and theorise (Heather, 1976).

Kuhn's emphasis on the importance of communities of scientists clustered round a shared paradigm triggered the growth of a new academic discipline – the sociology of science – in which researchers began to examine scientific disciplines much as anthropologists studied exotic tribes, and in which science was regarded as just another subculture (Naughton, 2012).

Indeed, the Psychology of Science (which dates from about 2003) is concerned with 'empirically investigating the full range of psychological processes behind scientific behaviour, interest, talent and creativity' (Feist, 2013). According to Feist:

> *... to fully appreciate and understand scientific thought and behaviour – from the infant trying to figure out her world to the historically great scientific discoveries – we must apply the best theoretical and empirical tools available to psychologists. Psychology is extraordinarily well suited to unpack the mechanisms behind scientific thought and behaviour.*

The Psychology experiment as a social situation

To regard empirical research in general, and the experiment in particular, as objective involves two related assumptions:

1. Researchers only influence the participants' behaviour (the outcome of the experiment) to the extent that they decide what hypothesis to test, how the variables are to be operationalised, what design to use, and so on.

2. The only factors influencing the participants' performance are the objectively defined variables manipulated by the experimenter.

> **Ask Yourself**
>
> - Try to formulate some arguments against these two assumptions.
> - What do the experimenter and participant bring with them to the experimental situation that isn't directly related to the experiment, and how may this (and other factors) influence what goes on in the experimental situation? (See Chapter 47.)

Experimenters are people too: the problem of experimenter bias

According to Rosenthal (1966), what the experimenter is *like* is correlated with what s/he *does*, as well as influencing the participant's perception of, and response to, the experimenter. This is related to *experimenter bias*. (See Box 3.5.)

> **Ask Yourself**
>
> - How could you explain the findings from the studies described in Box 3.5?
> - How could experimenter expectations actually bring about the different performances of the two groups of rats and children?

Participants are Psychologists too: demand characteristics

Instead of seeing the person being studied as a passive responder to whom things are done ('subject'), Orne (1962) stresses what the person does, implying a far more active role. Participants' performance in an experiment could be thought of as a form of problem-solving behaviour. At some level, they see the task as working out the true purpose of the experiment and responding in a way which will support (or not support, in the case of the unhelpful participant) the hypothesis being tested.

In this context, the cues that convey the experimental hypothesis to participants represent important influences on their behaviour, and the sum total of those cues are called the *demand characteristics* of the experimental situation. These cues include:

> *... the rumours or campus scuttlebutt [gossip] about the research, the information conveyed during the original situation, the person of the experimenter, and the setting of the laboratory, as well as all explicit and implicit communications during the experiment proper. (Orne, 1962)*

> **Box 3.5 Some examples of experimenter bias**
>
> - According to Valentine (1992), experimenter bias has been demonstrated in a variety of experiments, including reaction time, psychophysics, animal learning, verbal conditioning, personality assessment, person perception, learning and ability, as well as in everyday life situations.
> - What these experiments consistently show is that if one group of experimenters has one hypothesis about what it expects to find and another group has the opposite hypothesis, both groups will obtain results that support their respective hypotheses. The results aren't due to the mishandling of data by biased experimenters, but the experimenter's bias somehow creates a changed environment, in which participants actually behave differently.
> - When experimenters were informed that rats learning mazes had been specially bred for this ability ('maze-bright'), they obtained better learning from their rats than did experimenters who believed their rats were 'maze-dull' (Rosenthal and Fode, 1963; Rosenthal and Lawson, 1964). In fact, both groups of rats were drawn from the same population and were randomly allocated to the 'bright' or 'dull' condition. The crucial point is that the 'bright' rats did actually learn faster. The experimenters' expectations in some way concretely changed the situation.
> - In a natural classroom situation, children whose teachers were told they'd show academic 'promise' during the next academic year showed significantly greater gains in measured intelligence (IQ) than children for whom such predictions weren't made (although this latter group also made substantial improvements). In fact, the children were *randomly* allocated to the two conditions. But the teachers' expectations actually produced the predicted improvements in the 'academic promise' group – that is, there was a *self-fulfilling prophecy* (Rosenthal and Jacobson, 1968).
>
> (Based on Valentine, 1992; Weisstein, 1993)

This tendency to identify the demand characteristics is related to the tendency to play the role of a 'good' (or 'bad') experimental participant.

Key Study 3.1

The lengths some people will go to please the experimenter (Orne, 1962)

- Orne points out that if people are asked to do five push-ups as a favour, they'll ask 'Why?', but if the request comes from an experimenter, they'll ask 'Where?'
- Similarly, he reports an experiment in which people were asked to add sheets of random numbers, then tear them up into at least 32 pieces. Five and a half hours later, they were still doing it, and the experimenter had to tell them to stop!
- This demonstrates very clearly the strong tendency of people to want to please the experimenter, and not to 'upset the experiment'. It's mainly in this sense that Orne sees the experiment as a social situation, in which the people involved play different but complementary roles. In order for this interaction to proceed fairly smoothly, each must have some idea of what the other expects of him or her.

The expectations referred to in Key Study 3.1 are part of the culturally shared understandings of what science in general, and Psychology in particular, involves and without which the experiment couldn't 'happen' (Moghaddam *et al.*, 1993). So, not only is the experiment a social situation, but science itself is a *culture-related phenomenon*. This represents another respect in which science cannot claim complete objectivity.

The problem of representativeness

Traditional, mainstream experimental Psychology adopts a *nomothetic* ('law-like') approach. This involves generalisation from limited samples of participants to 'people in general', as part of the attempt to establish general 'laws' or principles of behaviour (see Figure 3.9 and Chapter 42).

Ask Yourself

- Figure 3.8 captures a fairly typical scene as far as participant characteristics in mainstream psychological research are concerned.
- In this photograph of one of Asch's famous conformity experiments (see Chapter 26), what are the most apparent characteristics of the experimental participants, and how are they similar to/different from those of Asch (who's pictured furthest right)?

Figure 3.9

Despite the fact that Asch's experiments were carried out in the early 1950s, very little has changed as far as participant samples are concerned. In American Psychology, at least, the typical participant is a Psychology undergraduate, who's obliged to take part in a certain number of studies as a course requirement, and who receives 'course credits' for so doing (Foot and Sanford, 2004; Krupat and Garonzik, 1994).

Mainstream British and American Psychology has implicitly equated 'human being' with 'member of western culture'. Despite the fact that the vast majority of research participants are members of western societies, the resulting findings and theories have been applied to 'human beings', as if culture made no difference (they are 'culture-bound and culture-blind' (Sinha, 1997)). This *Anglocentric* or *Eurocentric* bias (a form of *ethnocentrism*) is matched by the *androcentric* or *masculinist bias* (a form of *sexism*), according to which the behaviours and experiences of men are taken as the standard against which women are judged (see Chapter 47).

In both cases, while the bias remains implicit and goes unrecognised (and is reinforced by Psychology's claim to be objective and value-free), research findings are taken as providing us with an objective, scientifically valid, account of what 'women/people in general are like'. Once we realise that scientists, like all human beings, have prejudices, biases and values, their research and theories begin to look less objective, reliable and valid than they did before.

The problem of artificiality

Criticisms of traditional empirical methods (especially the laboratory experiment) have focused on their *artificiality*, including the often unusual and bizarre tasks that people are asked to perform in the name of science (see Key Study 3.1). Yet we cannot be sure that the way people behave in the laboratory is an accurate indication of how they're likely to behave outside it (Heather, 1976).

What makes the laboratory experiment such an unnatural and artificial situation is the fact that it's almost totally structured by one 'participant' – the experimenter. This relates to *power differences* between experimenters and their 'subjects', which is as much an ethical as a practical issue (see Chapter 48).

Traditionally, participants have been referred to as 'subjects', implying something less than a person, a

Box 3.6 Some difficulties with the notion of experimental control

- While it's relatively easy to control the more obvious situational variables, this is more difficult with *participant variables* (such as age, gender and culture), either for practical reasons (such as the availability of these groups), or because it isn't always obvious exactly what the relevant variables are. Ultimately, it's down to the experimenter's judgement and intuition: what s/he believes is important (and possible) to control (Deese, 1972).
- If judgement and intuition are involved, then control and objectivity are matters of degree, whether in Psychology or physics (see Table 3.1).
- It's the *variability/heterogeneity* of human beings that makes them so much more difficult to study than, say, chemicals. Chemists don't usually have to worry about how two samples of a particular chemical might be different from each other, but Psychologists need to allow for *individual differences* between participants.
- We cannot just assume that the IV (or 'stimulus' or 'input') is identical for every participant, definable in some objective way, independent of the participant, and exerting a standard effect on everyone. The attempt to define IVs (and DVs) in this way can be regarded as a form of *reductionism* (see Chapter 49).
- Complete control would mean that the IV alone was responsible for the DV, so that experimenter bias and the effect of demand characteristics were irrelevant. But even if complete control were possible (in other words, if we could guarantee the *internal validity* of the experiment), a fundamental dilemma would remain. The greater the degree of control over the experimental situation, the more different it becomes from real-life situations (the more artificial it gets and the lower its *external validity*).

dehumanised and depersonalised 'object'. According to Heather (1976), it's a small step from reducing the person to a mere thing or object (or experimental 'subject'), to seeing people as machines or machine-like ('mechanism' = 'machine-ism' = mechanistic view of people). This way of thinking about people is reflected in the popular definition of Psychology as the study of 'what makes people tick' (see Chapter 1).

The problem of internal versus external validity

If the experimental setting (and task) is seen as similar or relevant enough to everyday situations to allow us to generalise the results, we say that the study has high *external* or *ecological validity*. But what about *internal validity*? Modelling itself on natural science, Psychology attempts to overcome the problem of the complexity of human behaviour by using experimental control. This involves isolating an independent variable (IV) and ensuring that extraneous variables (variables other than the IV likely to affect the dependent variable) don't affect the outcome. But this begs the crucial question 'How do we know when all the relevant extraneous variables have been controlled?'

As Box 3.6 indicates, in order to discover the relationships between variables (necessary for understanding human behaviour in natural, real-life situations), Psychologists must 'bring' the behaviour into a specially created environment (the laboratory), where the relevant variables can be controlled in a way that's impossible in naturally-occurring settings. However, in doing so, Psychologists have constructed an artificial environment and the resulting behaviour is similarly artificial. It's no longer the behaviour they were trying to understand!

CONCLUSIONS

Psychology as a separate field of study grew out of several other disciplines, both scientific (such as physiology) and non-scientific (in particular philosophy). For much of its life as an independent discipline, and through what some call revolutions and paradigm shifts, it has taken the natural sciences as its model (scientism). This chapter has highlighted some of the major implications of adopting methods of investigating the natural world and applying them to the study of human behaviour and experience. In doing this, the chapter has also examined what are fast becoming outdated and inaccurate views about the nature of science. Ultimately, whatever a particular science may claim to have discovered about the phenomena it studies, scientific activity remains just one more aspect of human behaviour.

Chapter Summary

- **Philosophical dualism** enabled scientists to describe the world **objectively**, which became the ideal of science. Its extension by Comte to the study of human behaviour and social institutions is called **positivism**.
- Descartes extended **mechanism** to the human body, but the mind remained accessible only through **introspection**.
- **Empiricism** emphasises the importance of sensory experience, as opposed to **nativism**'s claim that knowledge is innate. 'Empirical' implies that the essence of science is collecting data/facts through experiments and observations.
- Wundt is generally regarded as the founder of the new science of Experimental Psychology. He used introspection to study conscious experience, analysing it into its basic elements (**structuralism**).
- James is the other pioneer of scientific Psychology. As well as helping to make Freud's ideas popular in the USA, he influenced **functionalism** which, in turn, stimulated interest in **individual differences**.
- Watson argued that for Psychology to be objective, it must study **behaviour** rather than mental life, its goals should be **prediction** and **control**, and there are only **quantitative differences** between human and animal behaviour.
- Dissatisfaction with behaviourism culminated in the 1956 '**cognitive revolution**'. At the centre of this new **information-processing approach** lay the **computer analogy**.
- **Scientism** maintains that all aspects of human behaviour can and should be studied using the methods of natural science. It involves '**context-stripping**' and the value-free, objective use of **laboratory experiments** in particular.
- A **science** must possess a **definable subject matter**, involve **theory construction and hypothesis testing**, and use **empirical methods** for **data collection**. However, these characteristics fail to describe the **scientific process/scientific method**.
- While the classical view of science is built around the **inductive method**, Popper's revised view stresses the **hypothetico-deductive** method. The two methods are complementary.
- Different theoretical approaches can be seen as self-contained disciplines, making Psychology **pre-paradigmatic** and so still in a stage of **prescience**.
- Only when a discipline possesses a paradigm has it reached the stage of **normal science**, after which **paradigm shifts** result in **revolution** (and a return to normal science).
- Science is a very **social** activity. Consensus among the scientific community is paramount, as shown by the fact that revolutions involve redefining 'the truth'.
- Environmental changes are somehow produced by experimenters' expectations (**experimenter bias**), and **demand characteristics** influence participants' behaviours by helping to convey the experimental hypothesis. The experiment is a **social situation** and science itself is **culture-related**.
- The **artificiality** of laboratory experiments is largely due to their being totally structured by experimenters. Also, the higher an experiment's **internal validity**, the lower its **external validity** becomes.

Links with Other Topics/Chapters

Chapter 50 → Empiricism and nativism lie at the heart of the *nature–nurture debate* (or the *heredity and environment issue*). Sometimes, this concerns the *causes of universal abilities or behaviours*, such as:

Chapter 16 → Perception

Chapter 19 → Language

Chapter 29 → Aggression

Chapter 32 → Attachment

Chapter 36 → Development of gender

Chapters 41 and 44 → Most controversially, the debate focuses on individual differences, in particular intelligence and mental disorders (such as schizophrenia and depression)

Chapter 47 → Feminist Psychologists are highly critical of the scientific method in general and context-stripping (and the related individualism) in particular. They also argue that sexism and androcentrism (together with ethnocentrism) demonstrate how Psychology is far from being objective and value-free

Chapter 48 → The treatment of people as 'subjects' in Psychology experiments has both methodological and ethical implications

Chapter 42 → Treating 'subjects' as interchangeable (group data are all-important) represents a nomothetic approach to studying people

Chapter 49 → Rose (1997) calls experimental control *reductionism as methodology*

Recommended Reading

Deese, J. (1972) *Psychology as Science and Art*. New York: Harcourt Brace Jovanovich.

Koestler, A. (1970) *The Act of Creation*. London: Pan Books.

Richards, G. (2002) *Putting Psychology in Its Place: A Critical Historical Overview* (2nd edn). Hove: Routledge. Also relevant to Chapters 1 and 2.

Rosnow, R.L. & Rosenthal, R. (1997) *People Studying People: Artifacts and Ethics in Behavioural Research*. New York: W.H. Freeman & Co.

Useful Websites

methods.fullerton.edu/noframesindex.html (Methods in Behavioural Research)

www.socialpsychology.org/expts.htm (Social Psychology Network: 202 web-based experiments, surveys, and other studies)

www.eeng.dcu.ie/~tkpw/ (Karl Popper website)

www.qualitativeresearch.uga.edu/QualPage/ (Resources for Qualitative Research)

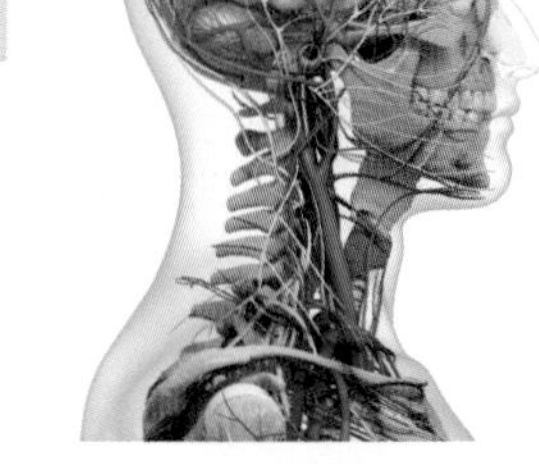

CHAPTER 4

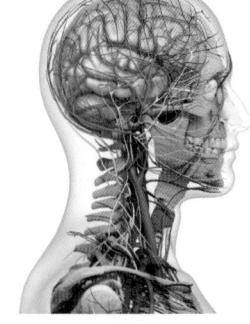

THE NERVOUS SYSTEM

An overview of the human nervous system (NS): structure and function

The central nervous system (CNS)

The major structures and functions of the brain

The spinal cord

The localisation and lateralisation of brain function

The autonomic nervous system (ANS)

The endocrine system

INTRODUCTION and OVERVIEW

As we noted in Chapter 1, Biopsychology is the study of the biological bases, or the physiological correlates, of behaviour and is a branch of neuroscience (or the 'brain sciences'), the study of the nervous system. Biopsychology is also sometimes referred to as 'Psychobiology', 'Behavioural neuroscience' and 'Physiological Psychology'. According to Pinel:

> *... biopsychology's unique contribution to neuroscientific research is a knowledge of behaviour and of the methods of behavioural research ... the ultimate purpose of the nervous system is to produce and control behaviour.*

In other words, Biopsychologists aren't interested in biology for its own sake, but for what it can tell them about behaviour and mental processes. In general terms:

- the kind of behaviour an animal is capable of depends very much on the kind of body it possesses; for example, humans can flap their arms as much as they like but they'll never fly (unaided) – arms are simply not designed for flying, while wings are; however, we're very skilled at manipulating objects (especially small ones), because that's how our hands and fingers have developed during the course of evolution;
- the possession of a specialised body is of very little use unless the nervous system is able to control it; of course, evolution of the one usually mirrors evolution of the other;
- the kind of nervous system also determines the extent and nature of the learning of which a species is capable. As you move along the *phylogenetic* (evolutionary) scale, from simple, one-celled amoebae, through insects, birds and mammals, to primates (including *Homo sapiens*), the nervous system gradually becomes more complex. At the same time, behaviour becomes increasingly the product of learning and environmental influence, rather than instinct and other innate, genetically determined factors.

AN OVERVIEW OF THE HUMAN NERVOUS SYSTEM (NS): STRUCTURE AND FUNCTION

As Figure 4.1 shows, the NS involves a number of sub-divisions. Before looking at these in detail, we need to look at some of the general characteristics of the NS.

Neurons

The NS as a whole comprises approximately 100 billion (100,000,000,000) neurons, the basic structural units, or building blocks, of the NS. About 80 per cent of all neurons are found in the brain, particularly in the *cerebral cortex*, the topmost outer layer. Information is passed from neuron to neuron in the form of electrochemical impulses, which constitute the 'language' of the NS. There are three main kinds of neuron:

1. *sensory* (or *afferent*), which carry information from the sense organs to the central nervous system (CNS)

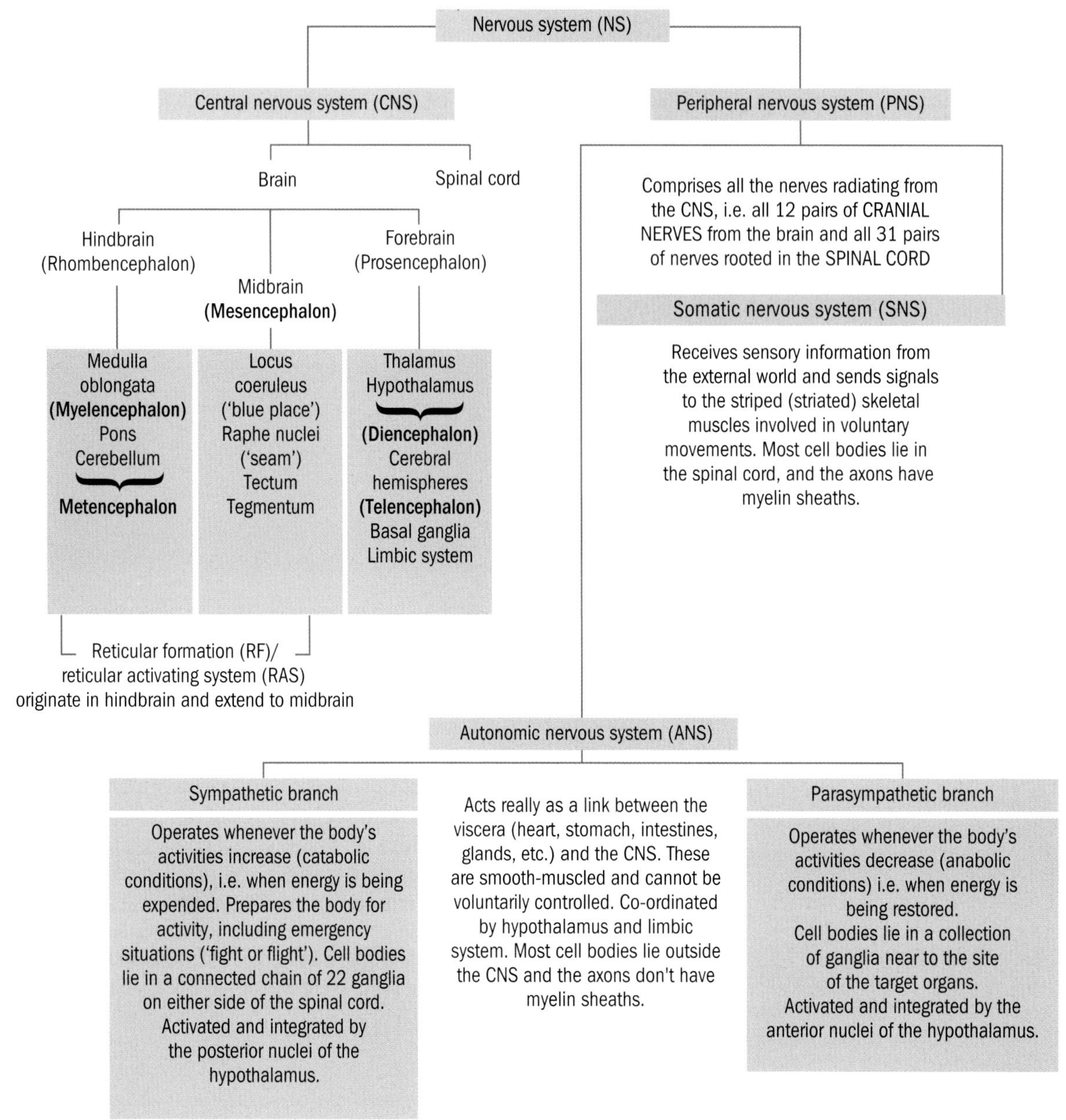

Figure 4.1 Major subdivisions of the human nervous system (including the main subdivisions of the brain)

2. *motor* (or *efferent*), which carry information from the CNS to the muscles and glands
3. *interneurons* (or *connector*), which connect neurons to other neurons and integrate the activities of sensory and motor neurons; interneurons are the most numerous and constitute about 97 per cent of the total number of neurons in the CNS.

Although no two neurons are identical, most share the same basic structure, and they work in essentially the same way. Figure 4.2 shows a typical motor neuron.

The *cell body* (or *soma*) houses the *nucleus* (which contains the genetic code), the *cytoplasm* (which feeds the nucleus) and the other structures common to all living cells. The *dendrites* branch out from the cell body, and it's through the dendrites that the neuron makes electrochemical contact with other neurons, by receiving incoming signals from neighbouring neurons. The *axon* is a thin cylinder of protoplasm, which projects away from the cell body and carries the signals received by the dendrites to other neurons. The myelin sheath is a white, fatty substance, which insulates the axon and speeds up the rate of conduction of signals down the axon and towards the *terminal buttons* (or *synaptic knobs*). The myelin sheath isn't continuous but is interrupted by the *nodes of Ranvier*.

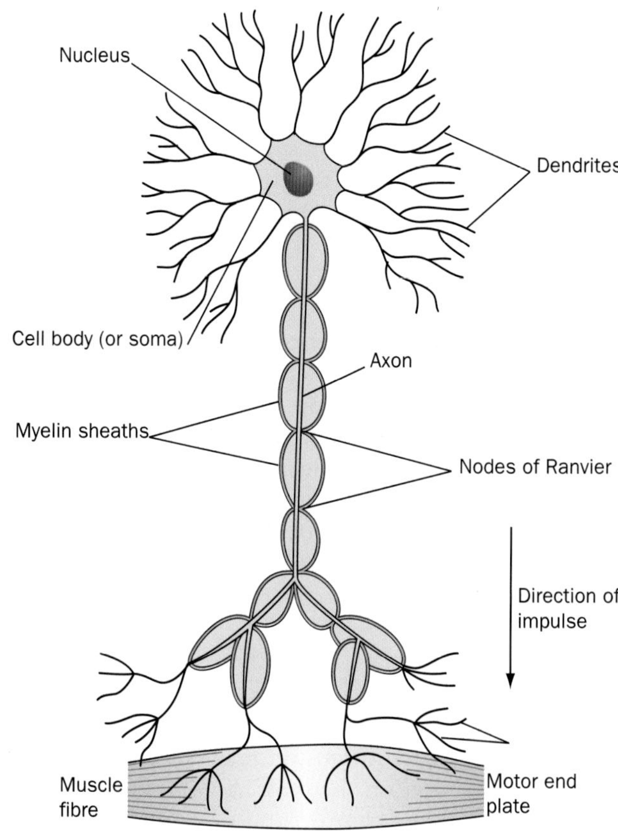

Figure 4.2 A typical motor neuron

A *nerve* is a bundle of elongated axons belonging to hundreds or thousands of neurons. Twelve pairs of cranial nerves leave the brain through holes in the skull, and 31 pairs of spinal nerves leave the spinal cord through the vertebrae. Together, they constitute the nerves of the *peripheral nervous system* (PNS, see Figure 4.1).

Communication between neurons

As Figure 4.3 shows, the terminal buttons house a number of tiny sacs, or *synaptic vesicles*, which contain between 10 and 100,000 molecules of a chemical messenger called a *neurotransmitter*. When an *electrochemical impulse* has passed down the axon, it arrives at a terminal button and stimulates the vesicles to discharge their contents into the minute gap between the end of the terminal button (the *presynaptic membrane*) and the dendrite of the receiving neuron (the *postsynaptic membrane*) called the *synaptic cleft* (or *gap*).

The neurotransmitter molecules cross the synaptic gap and combine with special receptor sites in the postsynaptic membrane of the dendrite of the receiving neuron. So, the term 'synapse' refers to the junction between neurons (although there's no actual physical contact between them), at which signals are passed from a sending to a receiving neuron through the release of neurotransmitters.

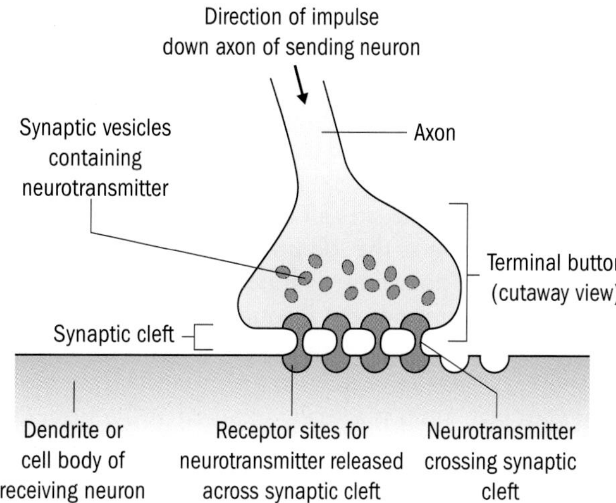

Figure 4.3 The synapse

The complexity of the resulting network is staggering. With the 100 billion neurons each having 1000 synapses, the result is 100 trillion interconnections. If you started to count them at one per second, you'd still be counting 30 million years from now! (O'Shea, 2013).

Although this synaptic transmission is the most common form of communication between neurons (Iversen, 1979), 20 per cent of the brain is completely devoid of neurons. Instead of forming a solid mass, the neurons are interspersed with a convoluted network of fluid-filled spaces or cavities. According to Mitchell (1999), there's a growing body of opinion that neurons can communicate with large regions of the brain by releasing chemicals into these watery spaces. This is called *volume transmission*, which is seen as complementary to synaptic transmission.

Electrochemical impulses

The electrochemical signal that passes down the axon is called an *action potential*. Before the action potential occurs, an inactive neuron contains positively charged potassium (K+) ions (electrically charged potassium atoms) and large, negatively charged protein molecules. Outside the neuron, in the surrounding fluid, there are concentrations of positively charged sodium ions (Na+) and negatively charged chloride ions (Cl−). The large, negatively charged, protein ions are trapped inside the neuron, while the positively charged sodium ions are kept out by the action of the *sodium-potassium pumps* in the cell membrane, which allow potassium (and chloride) ions to move in and out fairly freely.

The overall effect of this uneven distribution of ions is that the inside of the cell is electrically negative relative to the outside (by about 70 millivolts). The neuron is said to be *impermeable* to the positively charged sodium ions (its *resting state* or *resting potential*).

When an action potential occurs, the inside of the neuron momentarily changes from negative to positive (+40 millivolts), the sodium channels are opened (for one millisecond) and sodium ions flood into the neuron (it's now permeable to sodium ions). This sets off a chain reaction, whereby the sodium channels open at adjacent membrane sites all the way down the axon. But almost as soon as the sodium channels are opened, they close again: potassium channels are opened instead, allowing potassium ions out through the membrane and restoring the negative resting potential.

Because the myelin sheath isn't continuous, but is segmented (the axon is actually exposed at the nodes of Ranvier; see Figure 4.2), the action potential jumps from one node to another down the axon. This is called *saltatory conduction*, which is actually faster than if the sheaths were continuous.

Different types of synapse

Some synapses are *excitatory* (they 'instruct' the receiving neuron to 'fire' – that is, to conduct an action potential), while others are *inhibitory* (they 'instruct' the receiving neuron not to 'fire'). Because each neuron may have between 1000 and 10,000 synapses, some of which will be excitatory and some inhibitory, the 'decision' to fire or not will depend on the combined effect of all its receiving synapses. If enough excitatory synapses are active, their combined effect may add up to exceed the threshold for firing of the receiving neuron (this is called *summation*).

Inhibitory synapses are important because they help control the spread of excitation through the highly interconnected NS, keeping activity channelled in appropriate networks or 'circuits'. Epileptic seizures (fits), for example, may be caused by excitation of many different brain circuits at the same time and, if it weren't for inhibition, we might all be having seizures much of the time.

Different types of neurotransmitter

What makes a synapse either excitatory or inhibitory is the particular neurotransmitter(s) contained within the vesicles of the synaptic button. A region on the surface of the receptor site is precisely tailored to match the shape of the transmitter molecule (in a lock-and-key fashion). The effect of the transmitter is brought to an end either by *deactivation* (where it's destroyed by special enzymes) or by *reuptake* (where it's pumped back into the presynaptic axon, either for destruction or recycling).

According to Iversen (1979), there are at least 30 different neurotransmitters in the brain, each with its specific excitatory or inhibitory effect on certain neurons. Neurotransmitters aren't randomly distributed throughout the brain, but are localised in specific groups of neurons and pathways. Some of the major transmitters and their effects are shown in Table 4.1.

As a general rule, a single neuron will store and release the same neurotransmitter in all its axon

Table 4.1 Major transmitters and their effects

Neurotransmitter	Effect on receiving neuron	Related behaviour
Acetylcholine (ACh)	Generally *excitatory*, but can be *inhibitory*, depending on the type of receptor molecule involved	Voluntary movement of muscles, behavioural inhibition, drinking, memory. In Alzheimer's disease, there's a degeneration of ACh-producing neurons
Noradrenaline (norepinephrine)*	*Inhibitory* (in CNS); *excitatory* (in ANS)	Wakefulness and arousal (behavioural and emotional), eating, depression and mania (see Chapters 44 and 45)
Dopamine*	*Inhibitory* and *excitatory*	Voluntary movement, emotional arousal. Parkinson's disease involves degeneration of dopamine-releasing neurons. Schizophrenia is associated with excess dopamine (see Chapter 44)
Serotonin*	*Inhibitory* and *excitatory*	Sleep (see Chapter 7), temperature regulation
GABA (gamma aminobutyric acid)	*Inhibitory* (the most common inhibitor in CNS)	Motor behaviour. Huntington's disease may result from degeneration of GABA cells in the corpus striatum
Glycine	*Inhibitory* (found in spinal cord)	Spinal reflexes and other motor behaviour
Neuromodulators (neuropeptides, e.g. enkephalins and endorphins)	*Inhibitory* and *excitatory*	Sensory transmission, especially pain (see Chapter 12)

*Monoamine (MAO) transmitters

Box 4.1 Opioids: the brain's natural painkillers?

- The enkephalins and endorphins are also known as *opioids*, because functionally they resemble the opium drugs morphine, heroin and opium itself (see Chapter 8). Morphine is commonly used for the relief of severe, intractable pain, and the discovery of 'opiate receptors' in the neurons strongly suggested that the brain creates its own powerful painkiller.
- Enkephalins and endorphins seemed to fit the bill, and they may work by interfering with the release of transmitters from the presynaptic membrane of neurons that transmit information about pain.
- It's thought that they're released during acupuncture and hypnosis, producing a reduction in perceived pain, although pain information probably still reaches the brain (as it's not the pain receptors that are directly influenced; see Chapter 12).
- It's also believed that *placebos* ('dummy drugs') work by influencing the release of endorphins in response to the belief that an active drug was given (Hamilton and Timmons, 1995; see Chapters 12 and 45).

Research Update 4.1

Glial cells: the other half of the brain; and spindle cells: the cells that make us human

- *Glial cells* (or *glia*) are mostly smaller than neurons and nine to ten times more numerous. They come in different forms, the most important being *astrocytes* (star-shaped glial cells) and *oligodendrocytes*.
- It used to be thought that they merely 'fill in the space' between neurons, and serve just a maintenance role (bringing nutrients from the blood vessels to neurons, maintaining a healthy balance of ions in the brain, and warding off pathogens that evaded the immune system.
- Glia also play an important role in regulating synapse development and functioning; they promote neuronal survival and protection after injury, support learning and memory, and regulate mood. They're also implicated in a range of diseases/disorders (including epilepsy, major depression, multiple sclerosis, and Alzheimer's disease (AD)). *Radial glia* could be important for ensuring healthy brain energy metabolism and preventing neurodegeneration (especially relevant to understanding AD).
- Imaging studies have shown that neurons and glial cells engage in a two-way dialogue, beginning in the embryo and continuing through to old age. Astrocytes modify the connections between neurons (through regulating signals across the synapse); this is one way in which the brain revises its responses to stimuli as it accumulates experience (in other words, how it learns and remembers).They influence the formation of synapses, and oligodendrocytes provide the insulating myelin sheath around the axon of the neuron.
- The proportion of glial cells to neurons increases considerably as animals move up the evolutionary ladder. Extensive connectivity among astrocytes might contribute to greater learning capacity. It could be that what distinguishes geniuses (such as Einstein) from 'mere mortals' is a higher concentration of glial cells, or a more potent type of glia.
- *Microglia* are 'master multitaskers': (i) they respond to injuries by getting rid of debris and allowing healing to begin; (ii) during rest times, they control the growth of new neurons, new connections and neuronal pruning (the latter especially important in adolescence, but also in the adult brain, see Chapter 37). Once the new synapse is formed, they may monitor and tweak the pre- and post-synaptic receptors. They may also facilitate learning, by helping the formation of memories; they seem to be highly active in the hippocampus (see text below and Chapter 17). All these functions relate to the brain's *plasticity*. The loss of these functions is implicated in AD (see Chapter 36) and autism (see Chapter 40).
- *Spindle cells* are a recently evolved type of brain cell unique to higher primates (including chimpanzees and gorillas). These strikingly large cells, with unusually long spindle-shaped bodies, are found only in the front (anterior) part of the cingulated cortex (the ACC; see below). While normal brains have very few (100,000 at most), patients with Alzheimer's disease have about 75 per cent fewer.
- Spindle cells are believed to help regulate a brain system that controls intuitive behaviour during social interactions. Our emotional response to others, especially those we love ('social emotions') are precisely those which people with autism fail to display or understand. During the development of autistic brains, the spindle cells might fail to migrate to their normal positions. The spindle cells of patients with schizophrenia also appear to be abnormal (see Chapter 44).

(Source: based on Constandi, 2013; Fields, 2004; Moyer, 2013a, 2013b; Phillips, 2004a)

terminals. So, *cholinergic*, *noradrenergic*, *dopaminergic* and *serotonergic* neurons use ACh, noradrenaline, dopamine and serotonin, respectively.

Neurotransmitters have a fairly direct influence on receiving neurons. But *neuromodulators* 'tune' or 'prime' neurons, enabling them to respond in a particular way to later stimulation by a neurotransmitter. Neuromodulators include certain *neuropeptides* (see Table 4.1), notably the *enkephalins* ('in the head') and the *endorphins* ('morphine within').

Other neuropeptides are found as hormones, including:

- *vasopressin*, which is thought to play a role in memory (see Chapter 17)
- *corticosteroids* ('stress hormones') and *adrenocorticotrophic hormone* (ACTH), which are involved in stress reactions (see Chapter 12) and emotional arousal (see Chapter 10)
- *androgens* (male sex hormones), which regulate sex drive in both sexes (see Table 4.3, p. 70 and Box 36.1, p. 611).

THE CENTRAL NERVOUS SYSTEM (CNS)

Methods of studying the brain

Clinical/anatomical methods

One of the earliest methods used to study the CNS was the study of patients who'd suffered brain damage following an accident, stroke or tumour. A famous and early example is Paul Broca's discovery of a specialised area of the brain for speech. In 1869, Broca, a French physician, reviewed evidence from a number of cases of brain damage. He concluded that injury to a certain part of the left cerebral hemisphere (the left half of the brain) caused the patient's speech to become slow and laboured, but that the ability to understand speech was almost completely unaffected. What's now called *Broca's area* seems to control the ability to produce speech, and damage to it causes *motor* (or *expressive*) *aphasia*. In 1874, Carl Wernicke reported that injury to a different part of the left hemisphere caused *receptive aphasia*, the inability to understand speech (one's own or someone else's).

These clinical studies of the brain have normally been conducted in parallel with anatomical studies, usually during the course of postmortem examinations. Studying structure and function in a complementary way is essential for an adequate understanding of such a complex organ as the brain. *Split-brain patients* have undergone surgery for epilepsy when all other treatments have failed. The surgery (*commissurotomy*) involves cutting the tissue which connects the two halves of the brain (the corpus callosum). Roger Sperry and his colleagues in the 1960s and 1970s made full use of the unique opportunity to study these 'split brains' (see pp. 66–67).

Invasive methods

Parts of the brain may be surgically removed (*ablation*) or an area of the brain may be damaged (rather than removed: the *lesion method*). An early user of the first method was Karl Lashley, working with rats in the 1920s, and it has been used extensively to study the role of the brain in eating (see Chapter 9).

Psychologists are usually interested in destroying areas or structures located deep within the brain. To do this, a *stereotaxic apparatus* is used, which allows the researcher to operate on brain structures that are hidden from view. While the subjects are exclusively non-human animals, *stereotaxic surgery* is also used with humans, including psychiatric patients (see Chapter 45).

Ask Yourself

- Is it ethically acceptable to use invasive methods with non-human animals?
- How could you justify their use?

(See Chapter 48, pp. 846–850.)

Instead of surgically removing or damaging the brain, it can be *stimulated*. This can be done either (a) *chemically* (using micropipettes to drop drugs known to either increase or decrease the activity of particular neurotransmitters on to specific areas of the brain) or, more commonly, (b) *electrically*, using microelectrodes, whereby precise locations can be stimulated. Again, it's usually non-human animals that are involved (see Figure 4.4 and Chapter 9), but sometimes patients already undergoing surgery for a brain tumour or some other abnormality (such as epilepsy) are studied. Here, the neurosurgeon takes advantage of the fact that the patient is conscious, alert and able to report memories, sensations, and so on, produced by the stimulation. Wilder Penfield pioneered this kind of research in the 1950s (and through it discovered the 'Penfield homunculus'; see Figures 4.5 and 4.10).

Microelectrodes are also used to record the electrical activity in individual neurons when the subject (usually a cat or monkey) is presented with various kinds of stimuli. This method was used by Hubel and Wiesel in the 1960s to study visual feature detectors (see Chapters 5 and 14).

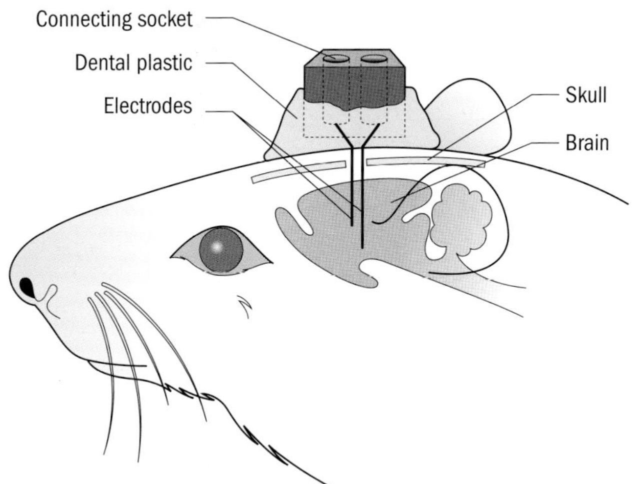

Figure 4.4 Electrical stimulation of the brain

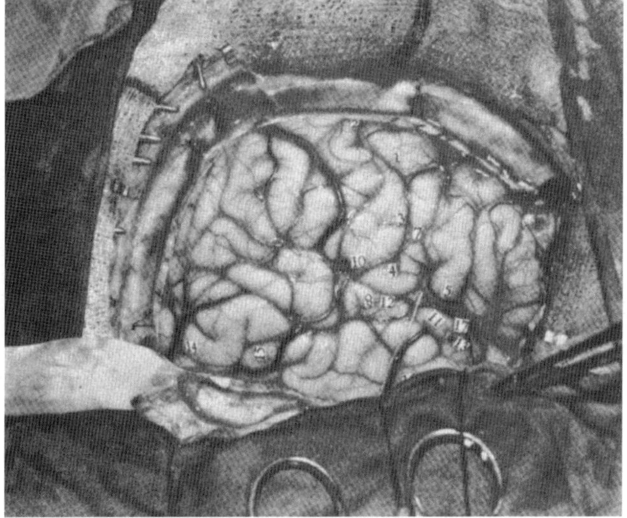

Figure 4.5 Photograph taken during surgery carried out by Penfield. The numbers refer to the parts of the cortex stimulated (from Penfield. W. (1947) Some observations on the cortex of man. *Proceedings of the Royal Society, 134* (876), 349.)

Non-invasive methods

The electroencephalogram (EEG)

The electrical activity of the brain can also be recorded from the outside, by fitting electrodes (passive sensors) to the scalp. The activity can be traced on paper, and typical brainwave patterns associated with various states of arousal have been found. The EEG records action potentials for large groups of neurons and has been used extensively in the study of states of consciousness, including sleep. Related to this is the *electromyogram* (EMG), which records the electrical activity of muscles, and the *electrooculogram* (EOG), which records eye movements, both of which are, like the EEG, used in sleep research (see Chapter 7).

Average evoked potentials (AEPs)

A brief change in the EEG may be produced by the presentation of a single stimulus, but the effect may well be lost (or obscured) in the overall pattern of waves. However, if the stimulus is presented repeatedly and the results averaged by a computer, other waves cancel out and the evoked response can be detected. This technique has shown that an identical visual stimulus yields different AEPs according to the meaning the participant attaches to it.

EEG imaging and the geodesic net

While the EEG involves a small number of electrodes, EEG imaging records the brain's electrical activity using 32 electrodes. This is fed to a computer, which translates it into coloured moving images on a monitor. While originally developed for investigating convulsive seizures, it has been adapted for studying brain development in babies in the form of a *geodesic net*. This consists of 64 or 132 electrodes, whose combined output produces a map of the active regions across the baby's head. The computer then calculates the likely brain areas that generated the voltages observed on the scalp. The geodesic net is unlikely to rival the spatial accuracy of adult scanning methods (see below), but its resolution over time is far superior, allowing the study of brain events 'at the speed of thought' (Johnson, 2000). One area of research that has made use of the geodesic net is infants' perception of faces (see Chapter 16).

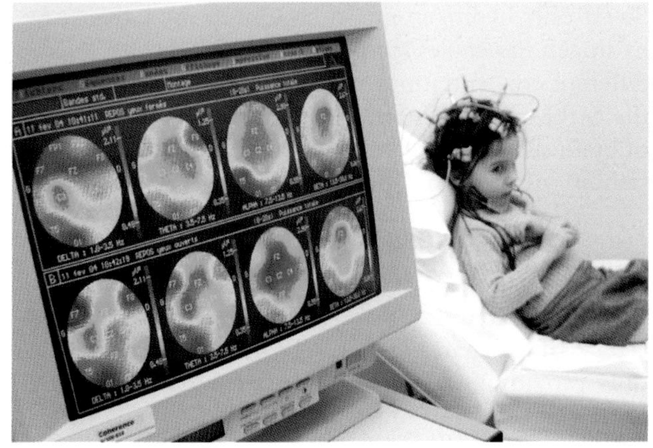

Figure 4.6 A geodesic sensor net being used to study brain activity

Radioactive labelling

This takes advantage of the brain's flexible use of blood-borne oxygen. A radioactive isotope is added to the blood, causing low levels of radioactivity, which increase as greater blood flow occurs in more active areas of the brain. A scanner next to the head feeds radiation readings to a computer, which produces a coloured map of the most and least active brain regions: different regions change colour as the person attempts a variety of tasks or is presented with a variety of stimuli.

Computerised axial tomography (CAT)

A moving X-ray beam takes pictures from different positions around the head, and these are converted by the computer into 'brain slices' (apparent cross-sections of the brain). CAT scanning is used primarily for the detection and diagnosis of brain injury and disease.

Positron emission tomography (PET)

This uses the same computer-calculation approach as CAT, but uses radiation for the information from which the brain slices are computed. A radioactive tracer is added to a substance used by the body (such as oxygen or glucose). As the marked substance is metabolised, PET shows the pattern of how it's being used. For example, more or less use of glucose could indicate a tumour, and changes are revealed when the eyes are opened or closed. PET diagnoses brain abnormalities more efficiently than CAT.

Magnetic resonance imaging (MRI)

This is like a CAT scan, but instead of using radiation, it passes an extremely strong magnetic field through the head and measures its effects on the rotation of atomic nuclei of some element in the body. Again, a computerised cross-sectional image is produced. So far only hydrogen nuclei have been used. Because hydrogen molecules are present in substantially different concentrations in different brain structures, the MRI can use the information to prepare pictures of brain slices which are much clearer (higher resolution) than CAT pictures.

Functional MRI (fMRI)

The MRI can identify the smallest tumour, or the slightest reduction in blood flow in a vein or artery. But it shares with CAT the limitation of only providing still images of brain slices. This tells us very little about brain function. To remedy this, fMRI monitors blood flow in the brain over time as people perform different kinds of task, so it's used as much to study the normal as the damaged/diseased brain.

SPECT and SQUID

More recent imaging techniques include single-photon/positron emission computerised tomography (SPECT, which, like PET, tracks blood flow through the brain), and superconducting quantum imaging/interference device (SQUID, which detects tiny changes in magnetic fields). Their main advantage is that they can focus on tiny areas of the brain. SPECT has revealed that there is significant loss of functioning in the front part of the brain in patients with Korsakoff's syndrome, caused by prolonged and heavy use of alcohol (see Chapter 8).

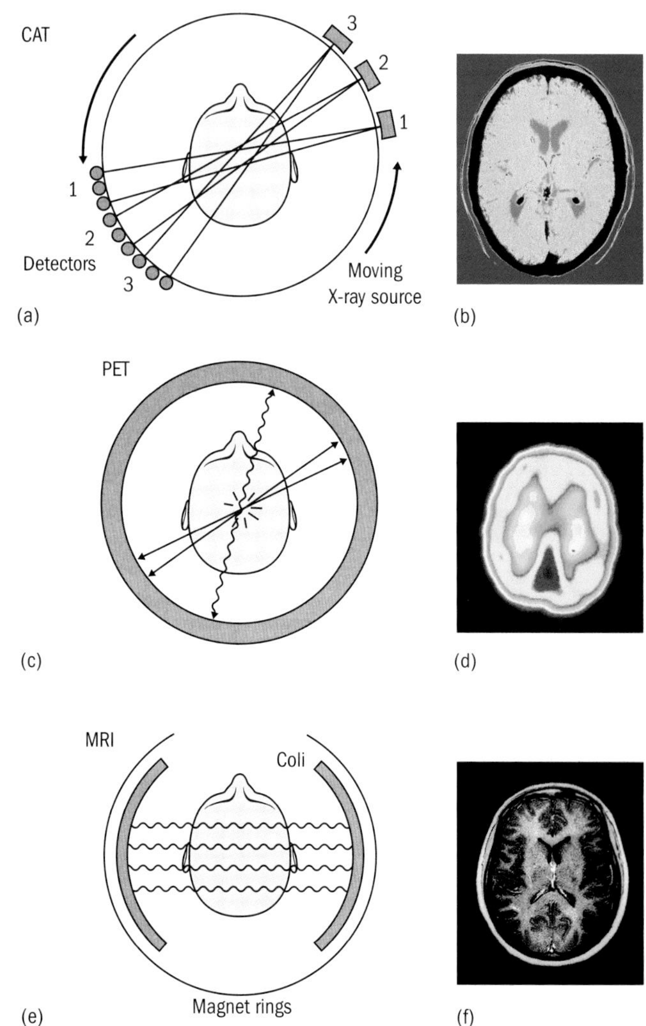

Figure 4.7 Non-invasive techniques (a), (c) and (e) used to study detailed sections of the living human brain (b), (d) and (f)

3-D Brain mapping

Most recently, researchers have created a revolutionary high-resolution 3-D brain atlas that allows the user to zoom in and navigate around the human brain almost at the level of single cells. Called the BigBrain map, this could help increase the accuracy of implantation of deep-brain stimulation (see Chapter 45). Ultimately, it's hoped that it will help with the larger mission of the European Union's Human Brain Project, which aims at constructing a working computational model of the entire human brain (Jarrett, 2013a). An American equivalent, the Brain Activity Map (BAM), aims to build a comprehensive map of the brain's activity. This is intended to do for the brain what the Human Genome Project did for genetics (see Chapter 2) (Jarrett, 2013b).

Ask Yourself

- What would you say are the main advantages of using scanning/imaging techniques compared with other methods?

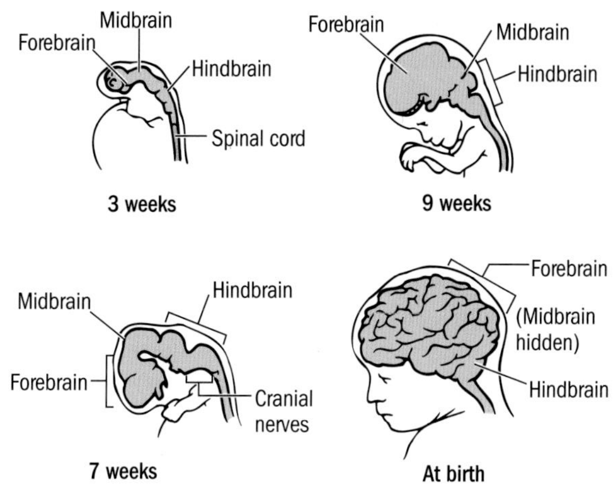

Figure 4.8 The human brain at four stages of development

THE MAJOR STRUCTURES AND FUNCTIONS OF THE BRAIN

As Figure 4.8 shows, during the first few weeks of foetal life, the neural tube changes its shape to produce five bulbous enlargements. These are generally accepted as the basic divisions of the brain, namely the *myelencephalon* (the medulla oblongata), the *metencephalon* (the pons and cerebellum), the *mesencephalon* (the tectum and tegmentum), the *diencephalon* (thalamus and hypothalamus) and the *telencephalon* (the cerebral hemispheres or cerebrum, basal ganglia and limbic system). 'Encephalon' means 'within the head'.

As shown in Figure 4.1, the myelencephalon and metencephalon together make up the *hindbrain*, the mesencephalon constitutes the *midbrain*, and the diencephalon and telencephalon make up the *forebrain*.

The forebrain

The cerebral hemispheres (or cerebrum)

Many of our uniquely human abilities arise in the forebrain, which expanded rapidly during the evolution of our mammalian ancestors (O'Shea, 2013). The cerebral hemispheres are the two largest structures at the top of the brain, which enfold (and, therefore, conceal from view) most other brain structures. If you removed an intact brain, its appearance would be dominated by the massive hemispheres, with just the cerebellum showing at the back (see Figure 4.9).

The top layer of the cerebrum (about 1 cm at its deepest) is the *cerebral cortex* (usually just called 'cortex', which means 'bark'). The cortex is pinkish-grey in colour (hence 'grey matter'), but below it the cerebrum consists of much thicker white matter, composed of myelinated axons (the cortex consists of cell bodies).

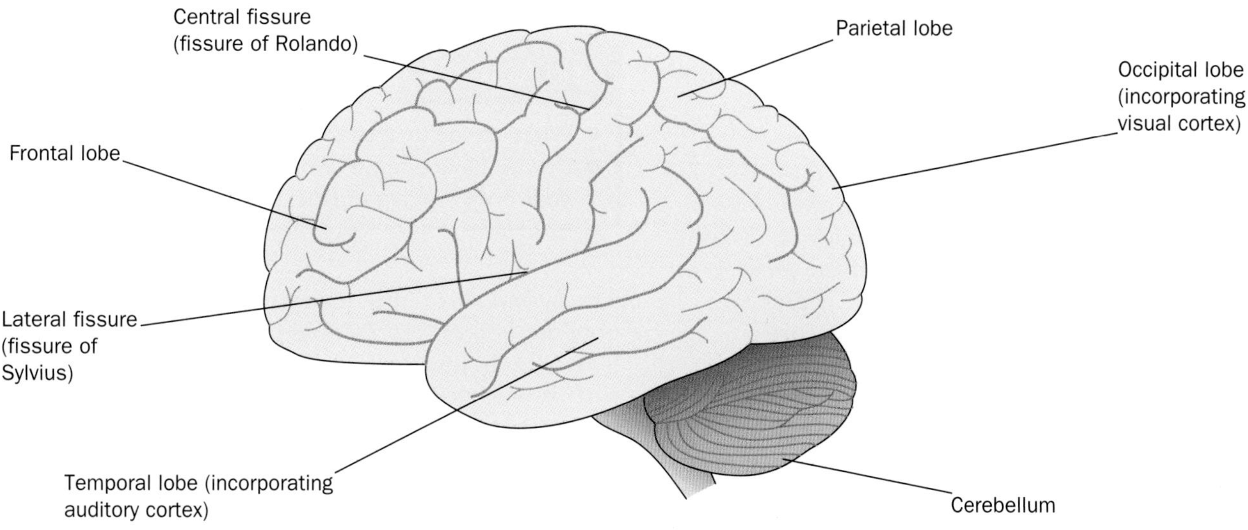

Figure 4.9 Lateral (side-on) view of the human brain (left cerebral hemisphere)

Research Update 4.2

What shape is your brain in?

- As can be seen in Figure 4.8, during foetal development the outside of the brain gradually becomes more folded/wrinkled (or *convoluted*); this is necessary if its 2.5-ft^2 surface area is going to fit inside the relatively small skull.
- New research indicates that a network of nerve fibres physically pulls the pliable cortex into shape during development and holds it in place throughout life. Disturbances to this network during development or later (through a stroke or injury) can have far-reaching consequences for brain shape and neural communication.
- As the axons grow more and more taught, stretching like rubber bands, folds begin to appear in the cortex. But these mechanical forces are also affecting its *layered structure*: the cortex comprises horizontal tiers of cells, stacked like a multilayered cake. Most areas have six layers, and individual layers in those areas vary in thickness and composition. Folding changes the relative thickness of the layers.
- The brains of patients with schizophrenia show reduced cortical folding overall (and, hence, a different shape) compared with those of non-schizophrenics (see Chapter 44).
- Similarly, people with autism have abnormal cortical convolutions; specifically, some of their sulci (the fissure of Sylvius is a sulcus, see Figure 4.9) appear to be deeper and slightly out of place compared with those of normal people. This has led to the recent suggestion that autism arises from the miswiring of the brain (see Research Update 4.1). The finding that communication between brain areas close to each other increases, while it decreases between more distant areas, may explain the difficulties in ignoring irrelevant stimuli and shifting attention appropriately that many people with autism experience.

(Based on Hilgetag and Barbas, 2009)

There's a large crevice running along the cerebrum from front to back (the *longitudinal fissure/sulcus*), which divides the two hemispheres. But they're connected further down by a dense mass of commissurial ('joining') fibres called the *corpus callosum* (or 'hard body').

There are two other natural dividing lines in each hemisphere: the *lateral fissure* (or *fissure of Sylvius*) and the *central fissure* (or *fissure of Rolando*). The lateral fissure separates the temporal lobe from the frontal lobe (anteriorly: towards the front) and from the parietal lobe (posteriorly: from the back), while the central fissure separates the frontal and parietal lobes. The occipital lobe is situated behind the parietal lobe and is at the back of the head. This division of the cortex into four lobes – named after the bones beneath which they lie – is a feature of both hemispheres, which are mirror images of each other.

The *primary visual cortex* is found in the occipital lobe, the *primary auditory cortex* in the temporal lobe, the *primary somatosensory* (or *body-sense*) *cortex* in the parietal lobe, and the *primary motor cortex* in the frontal lobe (see Chapter 5). The somatosensory cortex and motor cortex are perhaps the most well-defined areas, both showing *contralateral control*: areas in the right hemisphere receive information from, and are concerned with the activities of, the left side of the body, and vice versa. The crossing over (*corticospinal decussation*) takes place in the medulla (part of the brainstem). These areas represent the body in an upside-down fashion, so information from the feet, for example, is received by neurons at the top of the area.

Furthermore, the amount of cortex devoted to different parts of the body is related to the sensitivity and importance of that part of the body – not to its size. For example, fingers have much more cortex devoted to them than the trunk in the motor cortex, and the lips have a very large representation in the somatosensory cortex (see Figure 4.10). Broca's area is found in the frontal lobe and Wernicke's area borders the temporal and parietal lobes, but only in the left hemisphere. (See pp. 65–68.)

The cortex and body image

Ask Yourself

- What do you understand by the term 'body image'?
- Do you have a sense of being 'in' your body, or is your body just a part or extension of 'you'?

The *homunculus* ('little man') in Figure 4.10 depicts how the body is represented by the brain. We each have a 'body image', which forms a fundamental part of our overall sense of ourselves as a stable, embodied 'self' (see Chapter 33). Usually, we just 'know' what our arms and legs are doing without having to look: they do what we 'ask' them to. The 'body map' represented by the homunculus may appear to be 'hard-wired' into our brain. But

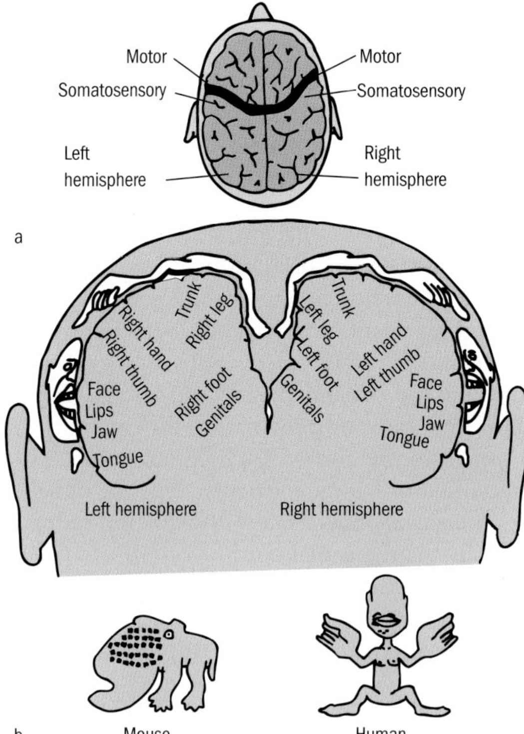

Figure 4.10 Animunculi and homunculi showing how much cortical tissue is devoted to each body area. The mouse explores with its nose and each whisker has its own cortical area. We can use our hands for sensing, although we normally rely more on vision. The large face of the homunculus reflects the large cortical areas necessary for the control of speech. This is sometimes called the Penfield homunculus, after Wilder Penfield who discovered it

our body image can become distorted, and when it does, the disability it causes can be every bit as devastating as injuring the equivalent part of the body. If a stroke or accident damages the brain region housing the body map, patients may lose the use of a perfectly healthy limb – even though the brain areas that directly control movement remain intact (Phillips, 2000). Conversely, amputees can continue to experience their missing arm or leg as if it were still attached: this is the *phantom limb phenomenon*.

As Ramachandran and Blakeslee (1998) point out, the Penfield 'map' doesn't represent precisely the body's basic organisation. For example, the face isn't near the neck, where it 'should be', but is below the hand. The genitals, instead of being between the thighs, are located below the foot (they cite the case of a female leg amputee, who had strange sensations in her phantom foot after sex!). This lack of a perfect match can help explain at least some cases of phantom limbs (see Case Study 4.1 and Figure 4.11).

Case Study 4.1

The case of the phantom hand

Tom Sorenson lost a hand in a car accident, after which his arm was amputated just above the elbow. When his face was touched in various places, he experienced sensations in his phantom thumb, index finger, little finger and so on. The whole surface of his hand was mapped out beautifully on his cheek. As Figure 4.11 shows, Tom also had a second 'map' of the missing hand, tucked into his left upper arm a few inches above the amputation line. Stroking the skin surface on this second map also produced precisely localised sensations on individual fingers.

How can we explain this apparently bizarre phenomenon? Ramachandran and Blakeslee (1998) believe the secret lies in the peculiar mapping of body parts in the brain. On the Penfield map, the hand area in the brain is flanked below by the face area and above by the upper arm/shoulder area. Sensory fibres originating from Tom's face (which normally activate only the face area in the cortex) invaded space left vacant by the amputated hand. The same happened with fibres originating in the upper arm/shoulder. The brain generated the feeling of the hand from the signals coming from another part of the body.

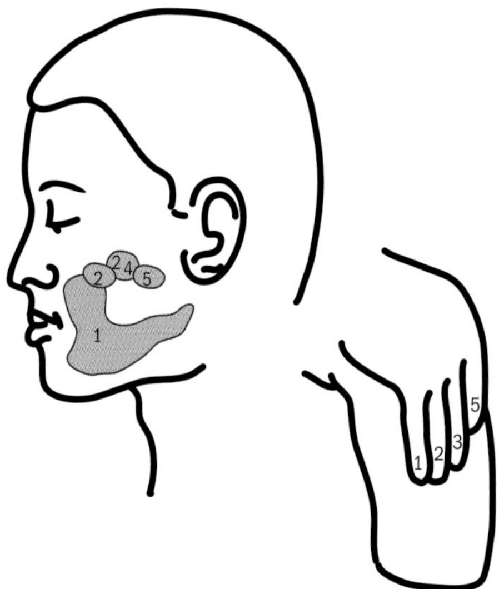

Figure 4.11 Points on the body surface that produced referred sensations in the phantom hand (from Ramachandran and Blakeslee, 1998, reproduced with permission from HarperCollins Publishers Ltd)

According to Frith (2007), most phantom limbs occur because a limb has been amputated; in such cases, there's no brain damage involved. But phantom limbs can also occur after brain damage, as described in Case Study 4.2.

Case Study 4.2

The woman with three arms (Hari *et al.*, 1998, in Frith, 2007)

E.P. is a Finnish woman who went into hospital with a severe headache and paralysis on the left side of her body. The cause was found to be a burst blood vessel at the front of her brain, and she underwent surgery to repair it. However, E.P. was left with permanent damage in a small region at the front of her brain concerned with the control of movements. Several years later, while fully recovered, she frequently experiences an extra 'ghost' arm on the left side of her body. This phantom arm appears in the same position that her real left arm was in a minute or two before. When the phantom is present, it feels to her as if she has three arms. The phantom left arm disappears if she looks at her real left arm. The perception of an extra arm is so strong that she sometimes worries that she'll bump into people when shopping – it feels as if she's carting a large bag in each of her three hands.

Aplasic phantoms are phantoms of limbs that are missing since birth. This raises the possibility that the body schema is innate (inborn) or acquired in the womb. According to Brugger and Funk (2007):

> *... there's extensive limb use during foetal life, and the possibility that a representation of a physically absent limb may be formed* in utero *by use of the contralateral limb cannot be dismissed.*

According to Ramachandran and Blakeslee (1998), just as an amputee might experience a phantom limb, so our entire body image is a phantom – something the brain constructs for convenience. As Ramachandran and Rogers-Ramachandran (2010) put it, our sense of inhabiting our body is just as tenuous an internal construct as any of our other perceptions – and just as vulnerable to illusion and distortion.

Association areas in the cortex

The primary motor and sensory areas account for only about 25 per cent of the cortex's surface area, leaving about 75 per cent without an obvious sensory or motor function. This *association cortex* is where the 'higher mental functions' (thinking, reasoning, planning and deciding etc.) probably 'occur'. However, much less is known about where these functions are localised, compared with certain aspects of memory, perception and language.

What is clear is that the cortex isn't necessary for biological survival (which is controlled by various *subcortical structures*). Some species (birds, for example) don't have one to begin with, and in those that do, surgical removal doesn't prevent the animal from displaying a wide range of behaviour (although it becomes much more automatic and stereotyped). The human brain has a greater proportion of association cortex than any other species.

The thalamus ('deep chamber')

There are actually two thalami, situated deep in the forebrain (between the brainstem and the cerebral hemispheres). Each is an egg-shaped mass of grey matter and represents a crucial link between the cerebrum and the sense organs. All sensory signals pass through the thalamus, which serves as a *relay station* or major integrator of information flowing in from the sense organs to the cortex. Each contains nuclei that are specialised to handle particular types of signal:

- the *ventrobasal complex* takes information fed in from the body via the spinal cord
- the *lateral geniculate* ('bent') body (LGB) processes visual information (see Chapter 5)
- the *medial geniculate body* (MGB) processes auditory information.

The thalamus also receives information from the cortex, mainly dealing with complex limb movements, which are directed to the cerebellum. Another part of the thalamus plays a part in sleep and waking (see Chapter 7).

Ask Yourself

- What role does the thalamus play in theories of emotion? (See Chapter 10)

The hypothalamus ('under the thalamus')

For its size (about equal to the tip of your index finger), the hypothalamus is a remarkable and extremely important part of the brain. It plays a major part in *homoeostasis* (control of the body's internal environment) and *motivation*, including eating and drinking (see Chapter 9), sexual behaviour, emotional arousal and stress (see Chapter 12). Seven areas can be identified, each with its own special function: *posterior* (sex drive); *anterior* (water balance); *supraoptic* (also water balance); *presupraoptic* (heat control); *ventromedial* (hunger); *dorsomedial* (aggression); and *dorsal* (pleasure).

The hypothalamus works basically in two ways:

1. by sending electrochemical signals to the entire ANS (see Figure 4.1), so that it represents a major link between the CNS and the ANS
2. by influencing the *pituitary gland*, to which it's connected by a network of blood vessels and neurons.

The pituitary gland is situated in the brain, just below and to one side of the hypothalamus. However, it's actually part of the *endocrine* (hormonal) system (see pp. 68–70).

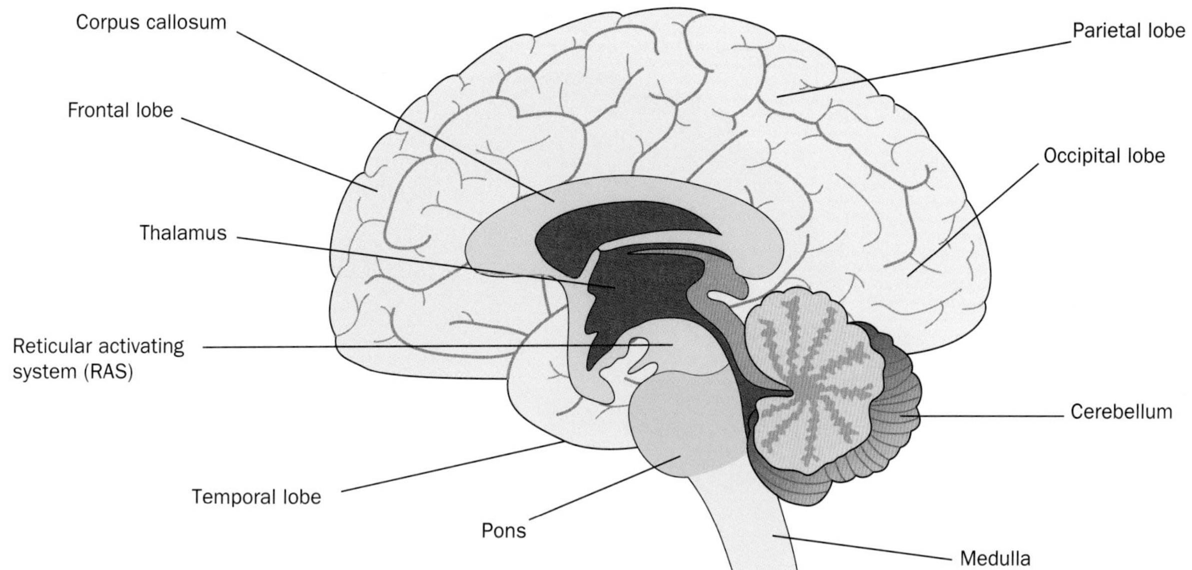

Figure 4.12 Front-to-back cross-section of the right cerebral hemisphere

Basal ganglia ('nerve knots')

These are embedded in the mass of white matter of each cerebral hemisphere. They are themselves small areas of grey matter, comprising a number of smaller structures:

- the *corpus striatum* ('striped body'), composed of the *lentiform nucleus* and caudate nucleus
- the *amygdala* ('almond')
- the *substantia nigra* (which is also part of the *tegmentum*, usually classified as part of the midbrain).

These structures are closely linked to the thalamus. They seem to play a part in muscle tone and posture by integrating and co-ordinating the main voluntary muscle movements, which are the concern of the great descending motor pathway (the *pyramidal system*). Information from the cortex is relayed to the brainstem and cerebellum.

The limbic system ('bordering')

This isn't a separate structure, but comprises a number of highly interrelated structures which, when seen from the side, seem to nest inside each other, encircling the brainstem in a 'wishbone' (see Figure 4.13). The major structures are: (i) the *thalami bodies*; (ii) *hypothalamus*; (iii) *mamillary bodies*; (iv) *septum pellucidum*; (v) *cingulate gyrus*; (vi) *hippocampus*; (vii) *amygdala*; (viii) *fornix*; and (ix) *olfactory bulbs*.

The human limbic system is very similar to that of primitive mammals, and so is often called 'the old mammalian brain'. It's also sometimes called the 'nose brain', because much of its development seems to have been related to the olfactory sense (and, of course, the olfactory bulb, which is concerned with the sense of smell, is one of its components). It's closely involved with behaviours that satisfy certain motivational and emotional needs, including feeding, fighting, escape and mating.

The midbrain

This is really an extension of the brainstem connecting the forebrain to the spinal cord. The main structure is the *reticular activating system* (RAS) or *reticular formation* (RF). This ascends from the spinal cord to the forebrain carrying mainly sensory information (the ARAS), and descends from the forebrain to the spinal cord carrying mainly motor information. Since it begins in the spinal cord and passes through the brainstem, it's often classified as part of the hindbrain in addition to the midbrain.

Box 4.2 Major functions of the ARAS

- The ARAS is vitally important in maintaining our general level of arousal or alertness (it's often called the '*consciousness switch*') and plays an important part in the sleep–wake cycle (see Chapter 7).
- It also plays a part in selective attention. Although it responds unselectively to all kinds of stimulation, it helps to screen extraneous sensory information by, for example, controlling *habituation* to constant sources of stimulation, and making us alert and responsive mainly to *changes* in stimulation (see Chapter 7).
- Sleeping parents who keep 'one ear open' for the baby who might start to cry are relying on their ARAS to let only very important sensory signals through. So, it acts as a kind of sentry for the cortex. Damage can induce a coma-like state of sleep.

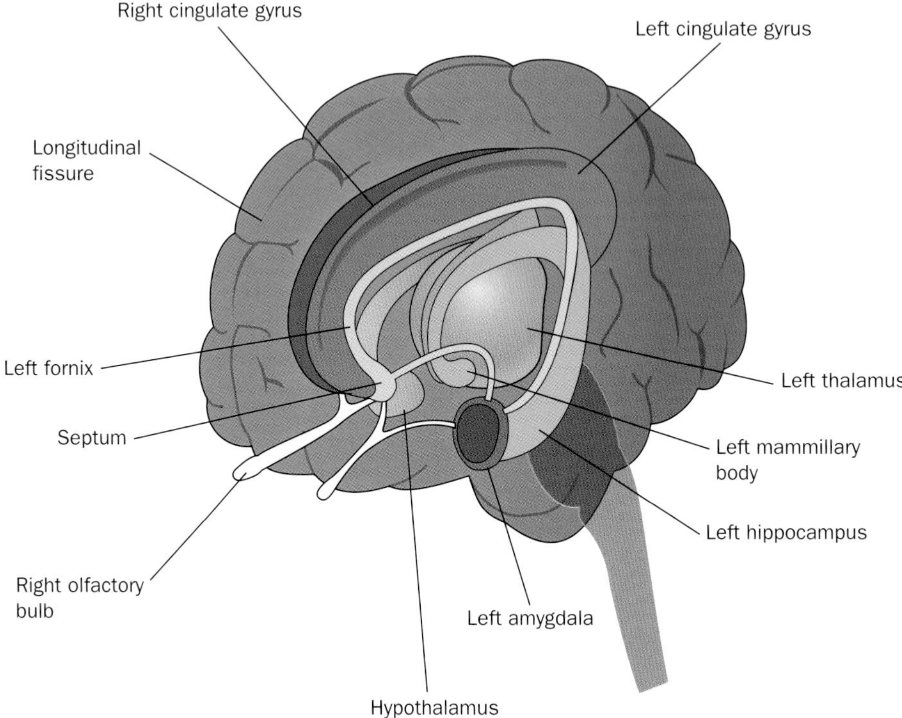

Figure 4.13 The major structures of the limbic system: the thalami bodies, the hypothalamus, the mammillary bodies, the hippocampus, the amygdala, the septum, the fornix and the cingulate gyrus. Also illustrated are the olfactory bulbs, which are connected to several limbic structures

The midbrain also contains important centres for visual and auditory reflexes, including the *orienting reflex*, a general response to a novel stimulus. Other structures include the *locus coeruleus* (see Chapter 7), the *raphne nuclei*, the *tectum* and the *tegmentum*.

The hindbrain

Cerebellum ('little brain')

Like the cerebrum, the cerebellum (which accounts for about 11 per cent of the brain's entire weight) consists of two halves or hemispheres, and is even more convoluted than the cortex. It plays a vital role in the coordination of voluntary (skeletal) muscle activity, balance and fine movements (such as reaching for things). Motor commands that originate in higher brain centres are processed here before transmission to the muscles. Damage to the cerebellum can cause hand tremors, drunken movements and loss of balance.

Once learned, complex movements like those involved in picking up a glass, walking and talking seem to be 'programmed' into the cerebellum. This allows us do them 'automatically' without having to think consciously about what we're doing (it acts as an 'automatic pilot' inside the brain).

The pons ('bridge')

This is a bulge of white matter that connects the two halves of the cerebellum. It's an important connection between the midbrain and the medulla, and is vital in integrating the movements of the two sides of the body. Four of the twelve cranial nerves (which originate in the brain) have their nuclei ('relay stations') here, including the large *trigeminal nerve*. It's the middle portion of the brainstem.

The medulla oblongata ('rather long marrow')

This is a fibrous section of the lower brainstem (about 2 cm long), and is really a thick extension of the spinal cord. In evolutionary terms, it's the oldest part of the brain and is the site of the crossing over of the major nerve tracts coming up from the spinal cord and coming down from the brain. It contains vital reflex centres, which control breathing, cardiac function, swallowing, vomiting, coughing, chewing, salivation and facial movements. The midbrain, pons and medulla together make up the *brainstem*.

THE SPINAL CORD

The spinal cord (about the thickness of a little finger) passes from the brainstem down the whole length of the back and is encased in the vertebrae of the spine; it represents the main communication 'cable' between the brain (CNS) and the peripheral nervous system (PNS), providing the pathway between body and brain.

Each of the 31 pairs of spinal nerves innervates a different and fairly specific part of the body and are 'mixed nerves': they contain both *motor neurons* (carrying information from the NS to the muscles) and *sensory neurons* (carrying information from the sensory receptors to the NS) for most of their length. But at the junction with the cord itself, the nerves divide into two roots – the *dorsal root* (towards the back of the body), which contains sensory neurons, and the *ventral root* (towards the front of the body), which contains motor neurons.

The basic functional unit of the NS is the *spinal reflex arc*, such as the knee-jerk reflex. This involves just two kinds of neuron: a sensory neuron conveys information about stimulation of the patella tendon (knee cap) to the spinal cord, and this information crosses a single synapse within the grey 'butterfly' (which runs inside the centre of the cord). This causes a motor neuron to stimulate the appropriate muscle groups in the leg, which causes the leg to shoot up in the air.

However, most spinal reflexes are more complex than this. For example, withdrawing your hand from a hot plate will involve an *interneuron* (as well as a sensory and motor neuron) and two synapses. Commonly, the experience of pain follows one to two seconds after you have withdrawn your hand – this is how long it takes for sensory information to reach the cortex.

THE LOCALISATION AND LATERALISATION OF BRAIN FUNCTION

Ask Yourself

- What do you understand by these two terms?
- How are they different?

When describing the cortex earlier, we saw that different functions, such as vision, hearing, movement and sensation, are *located* in different lobes (occipital, temporal, parietal and frontal, respectively). Remember also that all four lobes are found in both cerebral hemispheres, so, in this respect, the hemispheres can be regarded as mirror images of each other. We also noted that there are distinct areas dealing with speech production and comprehension (Broca's area and Wernicke's area, respectively), again illustrating *functional localisation*. However, these are found only in the left hemisphere, illustrating *functional lateralisation* (or *hemispheric asymmetry*).

Lateralisation, language and handedness

Much of the research into lateralisation has focused on language. From studies of stroke victims in particular, it's generally agreed that for the majority of right-handed people, their left hemisphere is dominant for speech (and language ability in general). People paralysed down their *right* side must have suffered damage to the *left* hemisphere and, if they've also suffered *aphasia*, then we can infer that language is normally controlled by the *left* hemisphere.

But this needs to be qualified, since it applies mainly to *higher-order* cognitive processes relating to language. For example, split-brain studies (see below) have shown that basic language processes (such as vocabulary) are present in *both* hemispheres. However, only the left has the specialised neural processes needed to carry out the complex linguistic functions of everyday life (Gazzaniga, 2000). In the vast majority of intact brains, only the left hemisphere retains the ability to speak, enabling verbal report of conscious experience (Colvin and Gazzaniga, 2007).

Some people seem to have much more lateralised brains than others, while some have language more or less equally represented on both sides (*bilateral representation;* Beaumont, 1988). The left hemisphere seems to be dominant for language for 95 per cent of right-handed patients, while only 5 per cent had their right hemisphere dominant. But with left-handers, things are much less clear-cut: 75 per cent had their left hemisphere dominant, none had the right dominant, but 25 per cent showed bilateral representation (based on a review by Satz (1979) of all studies between 1935 and 1975; cited in Beaumont, 1988). But what happens if a person only has a right hemisphere? (See Case Study 4.3.)

Case Study 4.3

The boy with just a right hemisphere (Danelli *et al.*, 2013)

A 14-year-old adolescent, E.B., underwent a left hemispherectomy (near-total removal of the hemisphere) at the age of 2.5 years (due to vascular abnormalities). After initial aphasia, his language skills recovered within two years, except for some word-finding problems.

Over the years, neuropsychological assessments showed that E.B.'s language was near-to-normal in almost all areas. In addition, his accuracy and speed in both reading and writing were mostly within the normal range.

His fMRI patterns for several linguistic and metalinguistic tasks were similar to those observed in the left hemisphere of control participants, although some differences were reminiscent of children with dyslexia. Despite these deficits, the overall pattern of findings suggests that his language network conforms to a left-like linguistic neural blueprint.

Split-brain patients

Remember that split-brain patients have undergone surgery (normally in the treatment of epilepsy) to cut their *corpus callosum* (CC), which joins the two hemispheres and allows them to exchange information. While the surgery may relieve the epilepsy, it has a major side-effect: the two hemispheres become functionally separate (they act as two separate, independent brains). Sperry (based on a number of studies in the 1960s and 1970s, for which he was awarded the Nobel Prize for Medicine in 1981) and Ornstein (1975) believe that split-brain studies reveal the 'true' nature of the two hemispheres, and that each embodies a different kind of consciousness (see below and Chapter 7). A typical split-brain experiment is described in Key Study 4.1.

Figure 4.14 Apparatus for studying lateralisation of visual, tactile, lingual and associated functions in the surgically separated hemispheres (from Sperry, 1968)

Key Study 4.1

When the left brain literally doesn't know what the left hand is doing (Sperry, 1968)

- Participants sit in front of a screen, their hands free to handle objects that are behind the screen but which are obscured from sight. While fixating on a spot in the middle of the screen, a word (for example, 'key') is flashed on to the left side of the screen for a tenth of a second (this ensures that the word is only 'seen' by the right hemisphere).
- If asked to select the key from a pile of objects with the left hand (still controlled by the right hemisphere), this can be done quite easily. However, the participant is unable to say what word appeared on the screen (because the left hemisphere doesn't receive the information from the right as it normally would), and literally doesn't know why s/he chose the key.
- This time, a word (for example, 'heart') is flashed on the screen, with 'he' to the left and 'art' to the right of the fixation point. If asked to name the word, participants will say 'art', because this is the portion of the word projected to the left hemisphere. However, when asked to point with the left hand to one of two cards on which 'he' and 'art' are written, the left hand will point to 'he', because this is the portion projected to the right hemisphere.

Ask Yourself

- What do the findings in Key Study 4.1 suggest regarding the right hemisphere's linguistic abilities?

These examples show that the right hemisphere doesn't completely lack language ability – otherwise participants couldn't successfully point or select. However, it clearly lacks the left hemisphere's ability to name and articulate what has been experienced. In the second example, both hemispheres are handicapped if information isn't conveyed from one to the other – the whole word ('heart') isn't perceived by either! (But see Case Study 4.3.)

A similar, but perhaps more dramatic, example involved sets of photographs of different faces. Each photo was cut down the middle and halves of two different faces were pasted together. They were then presented in such a way that the left side of the photo would only be visible to the right hemisphere and vice versa.

Ask Yourself

- If a picture of an elderly man were presented to the left hemisphere and a young boy to the right, and participants were asked to describe what they'd seen (the left hemisphere responding), what would they have said?
- If asked to point with their left hand to the complete photo of the person they'd seen (the right hemisphere responding), which picture would they have pointed to?

In the first case, they said 'an elderly man', and in the second case, they pointed to the young boy. It seems that two completely separate visual worlds can exist within the same head!

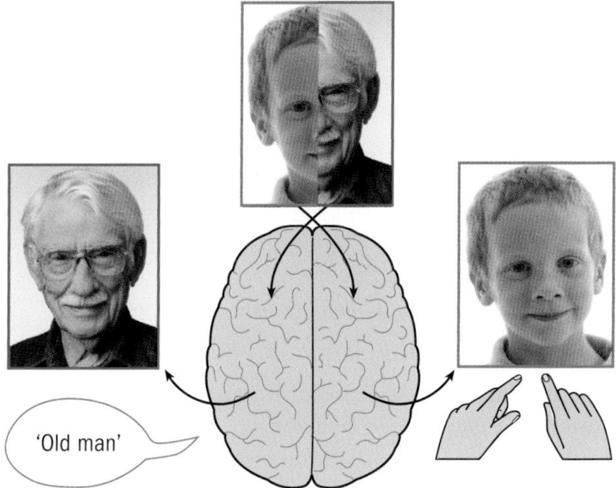

Figure 4.15 Responses given by the left and right hemispheres to a chimeric

CC and brain plasticity

Wolf (2013) describes the case of Sarah Mellnik, who was born without a CC (agenesis of the CC). Such individuals often have cognitive deficits, ranging from autistic-like symptoms to mild learning difficulties, as in the case of autistic-savant, Kim Peek (see Chapter 40). However, there's also considerable evidence that many affected individuals have normal intelligence (assuming no other brain abnormalities); the activity of their two hemispheres often look very similar to that of normal brains. Wolf *et al.* (2011) found that the two hemispheres are able to relay complex information between themselves, a finding consistent with the belief that other pathways are formed during critical periods in brain development.

> *... The ability of a brain during childhood to find different wiring patterns reveals its extraordinary malleability and plasticity. (Wolf, 2013)*

One brain or two? One mind or two?

These and many more equally dramatic experiments led Sperry, Ornstein and others to conclude that each of the separated hemispheres constitutes a separate mind, a separate sphere of consciousness (Sperry, 1964). Levy-Agresti and Sperry (1968) concluded that the:

> *... mute, minor hemisphere is specialised for Gestalt perception, being primarily a synthesist in dealing with information input. The speaking, major hemisphere, in contrast, seems to operate in a more logical, analytic, computer-like fashion ...*

Ask Yourself

- Should we generalise about hemispheric differences from studies of split-brain patients?

Cohen (1975) argues that long-standing presurgical pathology might have caused an abnormal reorganisation of the brains of these split-brain patients, so that generalising to normal people might not be valid. Several attempts have been made to move beyond the simplistic left hemisphere/right hemisphere, verbal/non-verbal distinction, both in normal participants and in split-brain patients. In a review of research, Annett (1991) says that 'it is evident that each hemisphere has some role in the functions assigned to the other'. For example, the right hemisphere has a considerable understanding of language and it's been suggested that it might be responsible for semantic errors made by deep dyslexics (see Chapter 40). Similarly, the left hemisphere is almost certainly responsible for the production of imagery, 'which is likely to be required in much spatial thinking'.

Box 4.3 The major differences between the left and right hemispheres

Ornstein (1986) summarises the differences as follows:

- The *left* is specialised for *analytic* and *logical thinking* (breaking things down into their component parts), especially in verbal and mathematical functions, processes information *sequentially* (one item at a time), and its mode of operation is primarily *linear* (straight line).
- The right is specialised for *synthetic thinking* (bringing different things together to form a whole), particularly in the area of spatial tasks, artistic activities, crafts, body image and face recognition, processes information more *diffusely* (several items at once), and its mode of operation is much *less linear* (more *holistic*).

According to Gazzaniga (1985), the brain is organised in a modular fashion – that is, organised into relatively independent functioning units, which work in parallel. Many of the modules operate at a non-conscious level, in parallel to our conscious thought, with the left hemisphere interpreting the processing of these modules.

Sternberg (1990) believes that Gazzaniga's view isn't widely accepted by neuropsychologists; but many would also reject the degree of separation between the hemispheres suggested by Sperry and his co-workers. An alternative view is one of *integration*: the two hemispheres should be seen as playing different parts in an integrated performance (Broadbent, 1985, cited in Sternberg, 1990). Most everyday tasks involve a mixture of 'left' and 'right' skills. For example, in listening to speech, we analyse both the words and the intonation pattern, and when reading we analyse visual shapes and draw on our linguistic knowledge. Far from doing their own thing, the two hemispheres work very much together (Cohen, 1975).

McCrone (1999) concludes that researchers have come to see the distinction between the two hemispheres as a subtle one of *processing style*, with every mental faculty shared across the brain, and each side contributing in a complementary, not exclusive, fashion. Evidence from imaging studies suggests that the left hemisphere 'prefers' (or pays more attention to) detail (such as grammar and specific word production), while the right prefers the overall meaning of what's being said (as conveyed by intonation and emphasis). This is consistent with the finding that people with right-hemisphere stroke damage become much more literal in their interpretation of language. However, a 'smart' brain is one that responds in both ways.

Rowson and McGilchrist (2013) argue that in the West we've become dominated by the left hemisphere's way of looking at the world. Unfortunately, the dominant doesn't understand things, jumps to conclusions, is narcissistic and uses everything – education, art, morality, the natural world – for its own ends. In contrast, the side-lined right hemisphere takes a more holistic, reasoned approach, understands context, and is more interconnected with the body; overall, it's more in touch with reality. The authors base these distinctions on brain-imaging studies and split-brain patients conducted over more than 20 years. They argue that this shift to predominantly left hemisphere thinking is responsible for the recent financial crash, the increase in depression, and environmental problems.

THE AUTONOMIC NERVOUS SYSTEM (ANS)

As shown in Figure 4.1, the ANS is the part of the PNS that controls the body's internal organs and glands over which we have little (or no) voluntary control. It comprises two branches:

1. the *sympathetic*, which takes over whenever the body needs to use its energy (as in emergencies: the 'fight or flight' syndrome)
2. the *parasympathetic*, which is dominant when the body is at 'rest' and energy is being built up.

Although the two branches work in essentially opposite ways, they're both equally necessary for the maintenance of the delicately balanced internal state of *homoeostasis* (see Chapter 9). Sometimes, a sequence of sympathetic and parasympathetic activity is required. For example, in sexual arousal in men, erection is primarily parasympathetic, while ejaculation is primarily sympathetic.

The ANS produces its effects in two ways:

1. by direct neural stimulation of body organs
2. by stimulating the release of hormones from the endocrine glands (see below).

In both cases, the hypothalamus is the orchestrator. The ANS is discussed further in Chapter 10, in relation to emotion, and in Chapter 12, in relation to stress.

THE ENDOCRINE SYSTEM

Endocrine glands secrete *hormones* (chemical messengers) which, unlike neurotransmitters, are released directly into the bloodstream and are carried throughout the body. While an electrochemical impulse can convey a message in a matter of milliseconds, it may take several seconds for a hormone to be stimulated, released and reach its destination. Consequently, where an immediate behavioural reaction is required (for example, a reflex action), the NS plays a major role. Hormones are better suited to communicating steady, relatively unchanging messages over prolonged periods of time (for example, the body changes associated with puberty, see Chapter 37).

Box 4.4 The pituitary gland

- This is the major endocrine gland, which is physically (but not functionally) part of the brain (situated just below the hypothalamus).
- It's often called the 'master gland', because it produces the largest number of different hormones, and also because it controls the secretion of several other endocrine glands.
- The pituitary comprises two independently functioning parts: the *posterior* pituitary transmits hormones that are thought to be manufactured in the hypothalamus, while the *anterior* is stimulated by the hypothalamus to produce its own hormones.
- The major hormones of the posterior and anterior lobes of the pituitary are shown, along with their effects, in Table 4.3.

Table 4.2 Major sympathetic and parasympathetic reactions

	Organ or function affected	Sympathetic reaction	Parasympathetic reaction
1	Heart rate	Increase	Decrease
2	Blood pressure	Increase	Decrease
3	Secretion of saliva	Suppressed (mouth feels dry)	Stimulated
4	Pupils	Dilate (to aid vision)	Contract
5	Limbs (and trunk)	Dilation of blood vessels of the voluntary muscles (to help us run faster, for example)	Contraction of these blood vessels
6	Peristalsis (contraction of stomach and intestines)	Slows down (you don't feel hungry in an emergency)	Speeds up
7	Galvanic skin response (GSR) (measure of the electrical resistance of the skin)	Decreases (due to increased sweating associated with increased anxiety)	Increases
8	Bladder muscles	Relaxed (there may be temporary loss of bladder control)	Contracted
9	Adrenal glands	Stimulated to secrete more adrenaline and noradrenaline	Reduced secretion
10	Breathing rate	Increased (through dilation of bronchi)	Decreased
11	Liver	Glucose (stored as glycogen) is released into the blood to increase energy	Sugar is stored
12	Emotion	Experience of strong emotion	Less extreme emotions

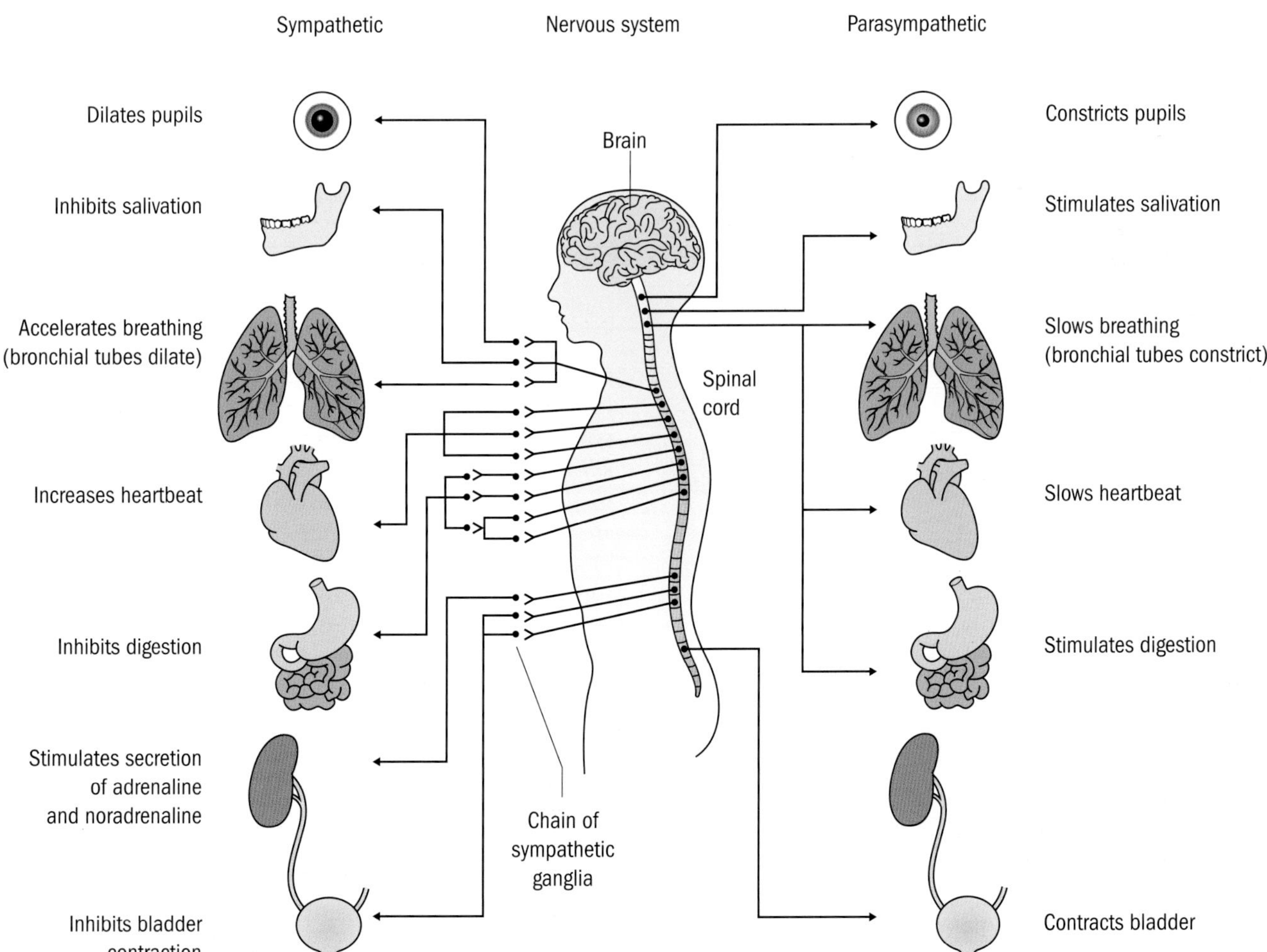

Figure 4.16 Some of the major organs affected by the two branches of the ANS (from Hassett and White, 1989)

Table 4.3 Major pituitary hormones and their effects

Hormone	Endocrine gland or organ stimulated	Effects
Growth hormone (somatotrophin)	Body tissues	Increases growth of bones and muscles, particularly in childhood and adolescence. Too little produces pituitary dwarfism and too much gigantism
Gonadotrophic hormones 1. Luteinising hormone (LH)	Gonads (testes, male; ovaries, female)	Development of sex (germ) cells: Ova (female), Sperm (male) Production of sex hormones: Oestrogen and progesterone (female), Testosterone (male)
2. Follicle-stimulating hormone (FSH)	Ovaries	Production of follicles in ovary during ovulation
Thyrotrophic hormone (TTH)	Thyroid gland	Secretion of thyroxin which controls metabolic rate – too little causes lethargy and depression, too much causes hyperactivity and anxiety
Lactogenic hormone (Prolactin)	Breasts	Milk production during pregnancy
Adrenocorticotrophic hormone (ACTH)	Adrenal glands 1. Adrenal medulla 2. Adrenal cortex	Secretion of adrenaline and noradrenaline Secretion of adrenocorticoid hormones (or corticosteroids), e.g. cortisol and hydrocortisone (important in coping with stress) (see Chapter 12)
Oxytocin	Uterus (womb)	Causes contractions during labour and milk release during breast feeding
Vasopressin (also a neurotransmitter)	Blood vessels	Causes contraction of the muscle in the walls of the blood vessels and so raises blood pressure
Antidiuretic hormone (ADH)	Kidneys	Regulates the amount of water passed in the urine

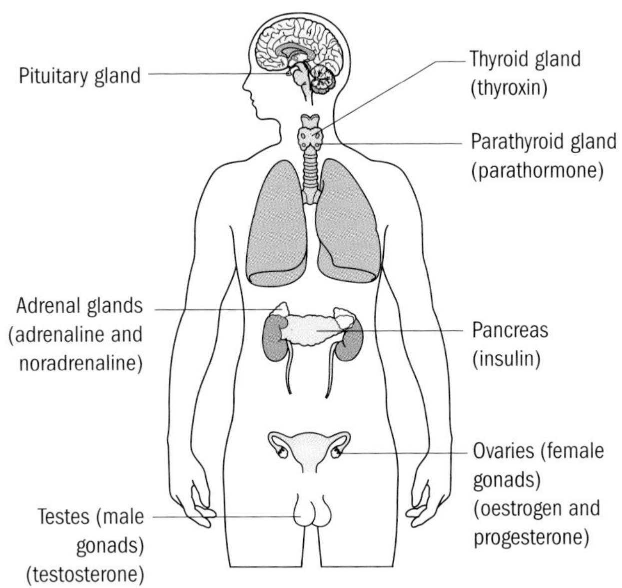

Figure 4.17 Some major glands of the endocrine system and the hormones they produce

Other important endocrine glands are the *adrenals* (situated just above the kidneys), each of which comprises the *adrenal medulla* (inner core) and the *adrenal cortex* (outer layer). As Table 4.3 shows, the medulla secretes adrenaline and noradrenaline, which are the transmitter substances for the sympathetic branch of the ANS.

Other endocrine glands include:

- Thymus – situated in the chest; functions unknown, but thought to involve production of antibodies (see Chapter 12)
- Pancreas – secretes insulin (anti-diabetic hormone), given in the treatment of diabetes. Controls the body's ability to absorb glucose and fats
- Pineal body/gland – situated near corpus callosum, functions unknown but may play a role in sleep–waking cycle (see Chapter 7)

Chapter Summary

- **Biopsychology** is the branch of neuroscience that studies the biological bases of behaviour. Biopsychologists are only interested in biology for what it can tell them about behaviour and mental processes.
- The **nervous system** (NS) comprises 10–12 billion **neurons**, 80 per cent of which are found in the brain, mainly in the cerebral cortex. There are nine to ten times as many **glial cells** (including **astrocytes, radial glia**, and **microglia**). Other, recently discovered brain cells are **spindle cells.**
- Neurons are either **sensory/afferent, motor/efferent** or **interneurons/connector**. They vary enormously in length, but share a basic structure.
- A **nerve** is a bundle of elongated axons. Twelve pairs of **cranial nerves** leave the brain through holes in the skull, while 31 pairs of **spinal nerves** leave the spinal cord through the vertebrae. Together, they constitute the nerves of the **peripheral nervous system** (PNS).
- When an **electrochemical signal/action potential** occurs, the inside of the neuron momentarily changes from negative to positive. The **resting potential** is almost immediately restored.
- **Synapses** are either **excitatory** or **inhibitory**, depending on the particular **neurotransmitter** contained within the **synaptic button**. Whether or not a particular neuron will fire depends on **summation.**
- Once the transmitter molecules have crossed into the **postsynaptic membrane,** their effect is ended either by **deactivation** or **reuptake.**
- **Neuromodulators** 'prime' receiving neurons for later stimulation by a neurotransmitter. Neuromodulators include **neuropeptides,** in particular the **enkephalins** and **endorphins/ opioids**.
- **Clinical/anatomical methods** of studying the brain involve patients who've suffered accidental brain damage or disease, and **split-brain** patients.
- **Invasive methods** involve **ablation**, **stimulating** the brain (either **electrically** or **chemically**), and **microelectrode recording**.
- **Non-invasive methods** include the **electroencephalogram** (EEG), **electromyogram** (EMG), **electrooculogram** (EOG) and **average evoked potentials** (AEPs).
- Computers are also used in a number of **scanning/ imaging devices**. These include **computerised axial tomography** (CAT), **positron emission tomography** (PET), **functional magnetic resonance imaging** (fMRI) and **3-D brain mapping**.
- The **cerebral hemispheres/cerebrum** enfold and conceal most other brain structures. The top layer is the highly convoluted cortex.
- Each hemisphere is naturally divided into the **occipital lobe** (which houses the **visual cortex**), the **temporal lobe (auditory cortex)**, the **parietal lobe (somatosensory/body-sense cortex)**, and the **frontal lobe (motor cortex)**.
- The whole body is represented on the surface of the cortex as a 'body map' (**homunculus**).
- The **association cortex** is where higher mental processes 'occur'.
- The cortex isn't necessary for biological survival, which is controlled by various **subcortical** structures.
- The cerebral hemispheres are part of the **forebrain,** together with the **thalamus, hypothalamus, basal ganglia** and the **limbic system**.
- The **midbrain** is an extension of the brainstem and connects the forebrain to the spinal cord. The **reticular activating system** (RAS) begins in the spinal cord and passes through the brainstem.
- The **hindbrain** consists of the **medulla oblongata,** the **pons** and the **cerebellum.**
- The **spinal cord** is encased in the vertebrae and is the main communication cable between the CNS and the PNS. Messages enter and leave via 31 pairs of spinal nerves.
- There's considerable evidence for both **functional localisation** and **functional lateralisation**. The left hemisphere is dominant for language in most right-handed people, but some people seem to have much more lateralised brains than others, while others display **bilateral representation**.
- The **phantom limb phenomenon** suggests that the adult brain is also very malleable.
- The findings from **split-brain studies** have led to the view that each hemisphere constitutes a separate mind or sphere of consciousness. An alternative interpretation is that the brain is organised in the form of **modules,** which work in parallel and often non-consciously. A third view is that the two hemispheres differ in their **processing styles,** yet represent a highly integrated system.
- The **autonomic nervous system** (ANS) comprises the **sympathetic** and **parasympathetic branches**. It works either by direct neural stimulation of body organs, or by stimulating the release of hormones from the endocrine system.
- The **pituitary gland** produces the largest number of different hormones and controls the secretion of several other endocrine glands, such as the adrenal glands.

Links with Other Topics/Chapters

Chapter 8 ⟶ Both neuropharmacology and psychopharmacology are relevant to understanding *substance addictive behaviour*

Chapter 44 ⟶ Several neurotransmitters are thought to be involved in major mental disorders, such as *schizophrenia* and *depression*

Chapter 45 ⟶ Some of the most important evidence for their role in causing these disorders comes from what's known about how drugs used to treat them affect these neurotransmitters

Some neuropeptides occur as hormones, including those that are involved in:

Chapter 10 ⟶ *emotional arousal*

Chapter 12 ⟶ *stress reactions*

Chapter 36 ⟶ *sex drive*

Chapter 16 ⟶ *perceptual development*

Chapter 7 ⟶ *Non-invasive methods* (in particular, the EEG, EMG and EOG) have been used extensively in relation to *sleep*

Chapter 33 ⟶ Body image is one important component of the *self-concept*

Chapter 44 ⟶ Distorted body image is a feature of *body dysmorphia* and *eating disorders* (in particular, *anorexia nervosa* and *bulimia nervosa*)

One of the ways the ANS produces its effects is by stimulating the release of hormones from the endocrine glands. The ANS is relevant to understanding:

Chapter 10 ⟶ *emotion*

Chapter 12 ⟶ *stress*

Chapter 48 ⟶ Much of the *ethical controversy* surrounding the use of non-human animals in experiments focuses on the invasive methods used to study the brain

These methods have been used in relation to:

Chapter 5 ⟶ *sensory processes*

Chapter 9 ⟶ *eating*

Chapter 12 ⟶ *stress*

Chapter 14 ⟶ *pattern recognition*

Chapter 49 ⟶ The study of split-brain patients raises fundamental issues regarding the *relationship between the brain and mind/consciousness*

Chapter 2 ⟶ Bennett (2013) dismisses the creative right brain/logical left brain distinction as a 'neuromyth'.

Recommended Reading

Gross, R. (2012b) *Key Studies in Psychology* (6th edn). London: Hodder Education, Chapter 15.

Pinel, J.P.L. (2002) *Biopsychology* (5th edn). Boston: Allyn & Bacon.

Ramachandran, V.S. (2011) *The Tell-Tale Brain: Unlocking the Mystery of Human Nature*. London: Windmill Books.

Ramachandran, V.S. & Blakeslee, S. (1998) *Phantoms in the Brain*. London: Fourth Estate. Also relevant to Chapter 49.

Toates, F. (2001) *Biological Psychology: An Integrative Approach*. Harlow: Pearson Education Ltd.

Useful Websites

www.psy.cmu.edu/~rakison/plasticity%20and%20the%20brain.pdf (Kolb *et al*. (2003) Brain Plasticity & Behaviour. Canadian Centre for Behavioural Neuroscience.)

www.cogneuro.ox.ac.uk (McDonnel Network for Cognitive Neuroscience, University of Oxford)

www.fmrib.ox.ac.uk/ (University of Oxford FMRIB centre: Department of Clinical Neurology)

psy.ucsd.edu/chip/ramabio.html (V.S. Ramachandran website; also relevant to textbook Chapter 15)

https://bigbrain.loris.ca (Big Brain project: 3-D model of human brain)

http://humanconnectome.org (Human Connectome Project, launched in the USA 2010)

http://humanbrainproject.eu (Human Brain Project, launched by the European Union 2013)

CHAPTER 5

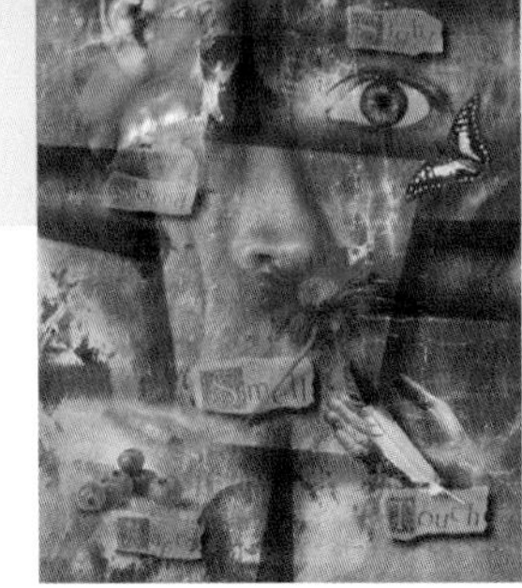

SENSORY PROCESSES

INTRODUCTION and OVERVIEW

When we move our eyes or our heads, the objects we see around us remain stable. Similarly, when we follow a moving object, we attribute the movement to the object and not to ourselves. When we walk towards someone in the street, we don't experience them as gradually growing 'before our eyes', and we recognise objects seen from various angles.

These examples of how we experience the world may seem mundane and obvious, until we realise what's actually taking place physically. If we compare what we experience (a world of objects that remain stable and constant) with what our sense organs receive in the form of physical stimulation (a world in a continuous state of flux), it's almost as if there were two entirely different worlds involved. The one we are aware of is a world of objects and people (*perception*), and the one we're not aware of is a world of sense data (*sensation*).

While perception cannot occur without sensation (the physical stimulation of the sense organs), the sense data constitute only the 'raw material' from which our awareness of objects is constructed. Although we feel we're in direct and immediate contact with the world as it really is, in fact our awareness of things is the end-product of a long and complex process. According to Durie (2005), perception is the 'added value' that the organised brain gives to raw sensory data; it goes way beyond the 'palette of sensations' and involves memory, past experience and higher-level processing. The process begins with physical energy stimulating the sense organs (light in the case of vision, sound waves in the case of hearing), and ends with the brain interpreting the information received from the sense organs.

This chapter concentrates on sensation, the physical processes necessary for the psychological process of perception (see Chapters 15 and 16).

THE SENSES: PROVIDING THE RAW MATERIAL OF PERCEPTION

According to Ornstein (1975), we don't perceive objective reality but, rather, our *construction* of reality. Our sense organs gather information, which the brain modifies and sorts, and this 'heavily filtered input' is compared with memories, expectancies, and so on, until, finally, our consciousness is constructed as a 'best guess' about reality.

In a similar vein, James (1902) maintained that 'the mind, in short, works on the data it receives much as the sculptor works on his block of stone'. However, different artists use different materials, and, similarly, different sensory systems provide different kinds of sense data for the perceiver-sculptor to 'model'. Each of our various sensory systems is designed to respond only to a particular kind of stimulation.

The nature of light

Light is one form of *electromagnetic radiation*, which includes radio waves, microwaves, infrared and ultraviolet light, as well as the visible spectrum. Although the entire spectrum ranges from less than 1 billionth of a metre to more than 100 metres, the human eye, by design, responds only to the tiny portion between 380 and 780 billionths of a metre (nanometres) which we call light (Bruce and Green, 1990).

CLASSIFYING SENSORY SYSTEMS

The senses have been classified in several ways. It was originally Aristotle who identified the 'famous five' senses: vision, hearing, taste, smell and touch. Since then, researchers have added many more to the list, including senses for balance, pain, time, temperature, limb positioning, and the ability to register hunger and thirst. In addition, brain-imaging studies have

Box 5.1 Sensation and evolution

A related and equally important point (often overlooked) is that our sensory systems also function as *data reduction systems* (Ornstein, 1975). If something cannot be sensed (because our senses aren't responsive or sensitive to it), it doesn't exist for us. While we normally regard our senses as the 'windows' to the world, a major job they perform is to discard 'irrelevant' information and to register only what's likely to be of practical value (clearly, something that has occurred as a result of evolutionary forces). We'd be overwhelmed if we responded to the world as it is: different forms of energy are so diverse they're still being discovered. Each species has developed particular sensitivity to certain of these different forms of energy, which have aided their survival. According to Bruce and Green (1990):

> *Sensitivity to diffusing chemicals and to mechanical energy gives an animal considerable perceptual abilities but leaves it unable to obtain information rapidly about either its inanimate world or about silent animals at a distance from itself ... The form of energy that can provide these kinds of information is light, and consequently most animals have some ability to perceive their surroundings through vision ...*

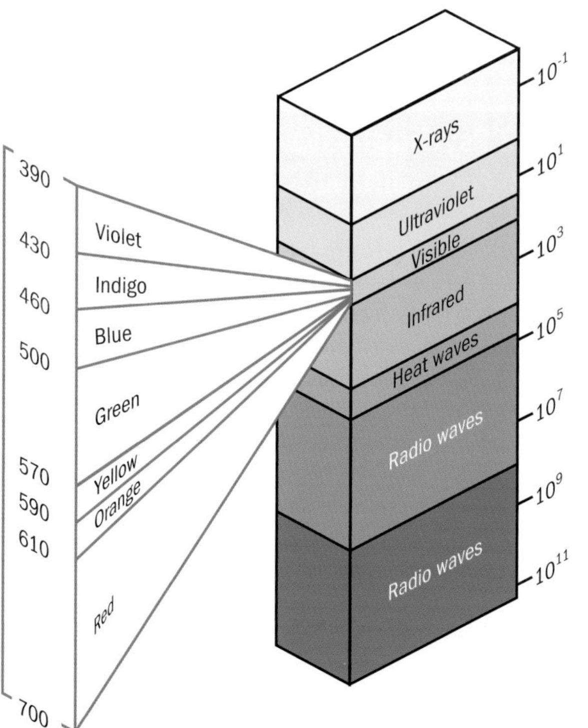

Figure 5.1 The spectrum of electromagnetic radiation. Wavelengths are given in nanometres (1 nm = 10^{-9} m). The visible part of the spectrum is shown on the left, with the colours of different wavelengths of light (redrawn from Bruce and Green, 1990)

identified neural pathways for processing numbers and letters, colours, shapes and faces (Bleicher, 2012).

Sherrington (1906) identified three kinds of receptor:

1. *exteroceptors*, which tell us about the external environment
2. *interoceptors*, which tell us about the internal environment (e.g. pain, hunger and thirst, body temperature, emotion)
3. *proprioceptors*, which deal with the position of our body in space and its movement through space.

Exteroception includes the five 'traditional' senses of sight (*vision*), hearing (*audition*), smell (*olfaction*), taste (*gustation*) and touch (*cutaneous* or *skin senses*). Interoception includes the internal receptors for oxygen, carbon dioxide, blood glucose, and so on. Proprioception is usually subdivided into: (i) the *kinaesthetic sense*, which monitors movements of the limbs, joints and muscles; and (ii) the *vestibular sense*, which responds to gravity and the movements of the head.

Gibson (1966) rejected proprioception as a distinct sensory system (and saw taste and smell as representing the same system), and Legge (1975) includes proprioception under the general heading of interoception.

CHARACTERISTICS OF SENSORY SYSTEMS

However we classify them, all sensory systems (or modalities) share certain characteristics.

- They each respond to particular *forms of energy or information*.
- They each have a *sense organ* (or *accessory structure*), which is the first 'point of entry' for the information that will be processed by the system (the sense organ 'catches' the information).
- They each have *sense receptors* (or *transducers*), specialised cells that are sensitive to particular kinds of energy, and which then convert it into electrical nerve impulses, the only form in which this physical energy can be dealt with by the brain (see Chapter 4).
- They each involve a *specialised part of the brain* that interprets the messages received from the sense receptors and (usually) results in perception of an object, a person, a word, a taste, etc.
- A certain minimum stimulation of the sense receptors is necessary before any sensory experience will occur (the *absolute threshold*). In practice, instead of finding a single intensity value below which people never detect the stimulus and above which they always detect it, a range of values is found and the absolute threshold is taken to be the value at which the stimulus is detected 50 per cent of the time.

These characteristics for the six major sense modalities are described in Table 5.1.

Table 5.1 Sense organs, sense receptors and brain areas for the six major sense modalities

Sense modality	Sense organ (accessory structure)	Sense receptor (transducer)	Brain area
Vision (sight)	Eye (in particular, the lens)	Rods and cones (in the retina)	Occipital lobe (striate cortex, extrastriate/ prestriate cortex) (via optic nerve)
Audition (hearing)	Outer ear (pinna), middle ear (eardrum and ossicles), inner ear (cochlea)	Specialised hair cells in organ of Corti (in cochlea)	Temporal lobe (via auditory nerve)
Gustation (taste)	Tongue (in particular the taste buds and papillae, the ridges around the side of the tongue)	Specialised receptors in taste buds, which connect with sensory neurons	Temporal lobe (via gustatory nerve)
Olfaction (smell)	Nose (in particular the olfactory mucosa of nasal cavity)	Transducers in the olfactory mucosa	Temporal lobe and limbic system (via olfactory bulb and olfactory tracts)
Skin/cutaneous senses (touch)	Skin	There are about 5 million sensors, of at least seven types, including: Meissner's corpuscles (touch); Krause end bulbs (cold)	Parietal lobe (somatosensory cortex) and cerebellum
Proprioception (kinaesthetic and vestibular senses)	Inner ear (semicircular canals, vestibular sacs)	Vestibular sensors (otoliths or 'earstones'), tiny crystals attached to hair cells in vestibular sacs which are sensitive to gravity	Cerebellum (via vestibular nerve)

Sensory thresholds

Not only does the absolute threshold vary from individual to individual, but it varies for the same individual at different times, depending on physical state, motivation, physical conditions of presentation, and so on.

The *difference threshold* is the minimum amount of stimulation necessary to discriminate between two stimuli (also known as the *just noticeable difference* (*jnd*)). Weber's law states that the *jnd* is a constant value, but this, of course, will differ from one sense modality to another. For example, 1/133 is the value needed to tell apart the pitch of two different tones, and 1/5 for discriminating between saline solutions.

The Weber–Fechner law holds only approximately through the middle ranges of stimulus intensities. An alternative approach is *signal detection theory*, which rejects the notion of thresholds altogether. Each sensory channel always carries *noise* (any activity that interferes with the detection of a signal): the stronger the stimulus, the higher the signal-to-noise ratio and the easier it is to detect the stimulus. The detection of a stimulus, therefore, then becomes a statistical matter (a question of *probabilities*).

Box 5.2 Psychophysics and the Weber–Fechner law

- Fechner (1860) reformulated Weber's law: the Weber–Fechner law (as it's come to be known) states that large increases in the intensity of a stimulus produce smaller, proportional increases in the perceived intensity.
- Fechner's was one of the first attempts to express a psychological phenomenon mathematically, and was an important contribution to *psychophysics*. This studies the relationship between physical stimuli and how they're subjectively experienced.
- Psychophysics is of enormous historical importance in the development of Psychology as a science (see Chapter 3 and Gross, 2014).

THE VISUAL SYSTEM

The fundamental job of a single-chambered eye (such as the human eye) is to map the spatial pattern in the optic array onto the retina by forming an image. The optic array is the pattern of light reaching a point in space from all directions (Gibson, 1966; see

Chapter 15). All light rays striking the eye from one point in space are brought to a focus at one point on the retina (Bruce and Green, 1990). *Visual acuity* is a way of describing the efficiency with which the eye does this. Pinel (1993) defines acuity as 'the ability to see the details of objects'. Acuity is limited by several processes, in particular:

- the efficiency with which the optical apparatus of the eye maps the spatial pattern of the optic array on to the retina
- the efficiency with which the receptor cells convert that pattern into a pattern of electrical activity
- the extent to which information available in the pattern of receptor cells activity is detected by the neural apparatus of the retina and the brain.

We'll now look at each of these aspects of acuity in turn.

The sense organ: the eye

Ask Yourself

- Why do you think vision is considered to be the most important of the human sense modalities?

Ornstein (1975) describes the eye as 'the most important avenue of personal consciousness', and it's estimated that 80 per cent of the information we receive about the external world reaches us through vision (Dodwell, 1995). Research interest has focused largely on vision, both as a sensory system and a perceptual system. The sense organ of vision is the eye (see Figure 5.2).

Box 5.3 The pupil and the ANS

- The *pupil* (the hole in the iris) regulates the amount of light entering the eye via the *iris* (the coloured part of the eye), which has tiny sets of muscles that dilate and contract the pupil. (Pupil size is also regulated by the *ciliary muscles*.)
- In bright light, the pupil contracts to shut out some of the light rays; when light is dim or we're looking at distant objects, the pupils dilate to let more light in. *Sensitivity* rather than acuity is what's crucial.
- Ultimately, pupil size is controlled by the *autonomic nervous system* (ANS), and so is outside conscious control. The *parasympathetic branch* of the ANS controls change in pupil size as a function of change in illumination. The *sympathetic branch* dilates the pupils under conditions of strong emotional arousal, as in an 'emergency' situation when we need to see 'better' (see Chapters 9, 10 and 12).

The *cornea* is a transparent membrane, which protects the lens and through which light enters the eye. The *lens*, situated just behind the iris, is enclosed in a capsule held firmly in place by the *suspensory ligaments*; it focuses light on the retina as an *inverted* (upside-down) *image*, and its shape is regulated by the ciliary muscles. As with certain reptiles, birds and other mammals, the lens of the human eye thickens and increases its curvature (and the ciliary muscles contract) when focusing on nearby objects. When viewing more distant objects, it becomes flatter (and the ciliary muscles are fully relaxed). This process is called *accommodation*.

Between the cornea and the lens is the anterior chamber filled with *aqueous humour*, a clear, watery fluid; behind the lens is the larger posterior chamber filled with *vitreous humour*, a jelly-like substance. Both fluids give the eyeball its shape and help to keep it firm.

The *sclerotic coat* is the thickest layer of the eyeball and forms the outer, white part of the eye. It consists of a strong, fibrous membrane, except in the front where it bulges to form the cornea. The *choroid coat* is a dark layer containing black-coloured matter, which darkens the chamber of the eye and prevents reflection of light inside the eye. In front, it becomes the iris, which is seen through the transparent cornea.

Eye movements

Primates' eyes make the largest, most rapid and most precisely controlled eye movements of all animals, except the chameleon.

Box 5.4 Different types of eye movement

1. Our eyes constantly dart about, fixating for a fraction of a second, then moving on. These jerky, sudden, intermittent jumps of eye position are called *saccades*, each lasting between 20 and 200 microseconds; they occur when we try to fixate an object when looking directly at it (*foveal vision*). Even when we think we're looking steadily at something, or when we read or look at a picture, our eyes make several saccades each second to scan it.
2. Once an object has been fixated, smooth and continuous *pursuit movements* keep it in foveal vision as the object or the observer moves.
3. If the distance of the object from the observer changes, smooth and continuous *convergence movements* keep it fixated by the foveas of both eyes.

(Source: based on Bruce and Green, 1990)

Is the eye a camera?

Ask Yourself

- In what ways can the eye be thought of as a camera?
- What are some of the major similarities and differences?

In a camera, light striking each light-sensitive grain in the film comes from a narrow segment of the optic array, and this is also true of the retinal image (Bruce and Green, 1990). Both also have a lens that projects the image on to the film or the retina. So the camera is a useful analogy for understanding the optics of the eye.

However, Bruce and Green point out a number of important differences:

- If judged by the same standards as a camera, even the most sophisticated eye forms an image of an extremely poor quality. Optical aberrations produce blur, aberrations of the lens and cornea cause distortions in the image, and the curvature of the retina means that images of straight lines are curved and metrical relations in the image don't correspond to those in the world.
- A camera that moved as much as the eye would produce blurred pictures.
- The retinal image has a yellowish cast, particularly in the macular region, and contains shadows of the blood vessels that lie in front of the receptor cells in the retina.
- While the purpose of a camera is to produce a static picture for people to look at, the purpose of the eye and brain is to extract the information from the changing optic array needed to guide a person's actions or to specify important objects or events. The optic nerve doesn't transmit a stream of pictures to the brain (as a television camera does to a television), but instead transmits information about the pattern of light reaching the eyes. The brain then has to interpret that information.

The *retina* is the innermost layer of the eyeball, formed by the expansion of the optic nerve, which enters at the back and a little to the nasal side of the eye.

Box 5.5 The three layers of the retina

1. *Rods and cones*, photosensitive cells that convert light energy into electrical nerve impulses (and form the rear layer of the retina).
2. *Bipolar cells*, connected to the rods, cones and ganglion cells.
3. *Ganglion cells*, whose fibres (axons) form the beginning of the optic nerve leading to the brain.

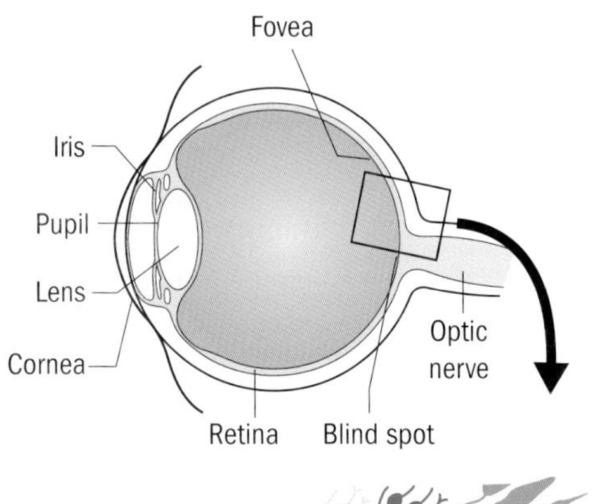

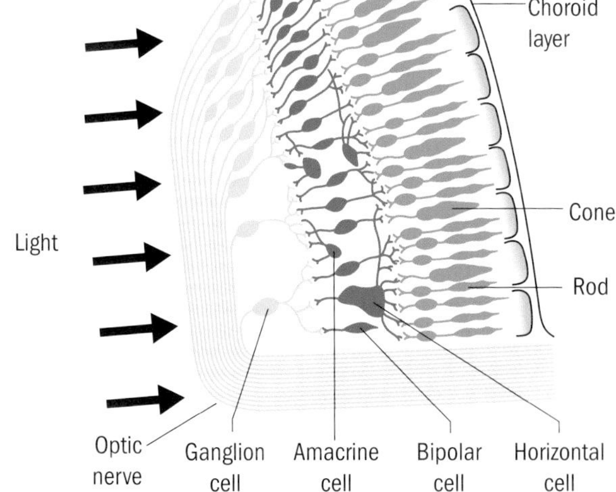

Figure 5.2 A diagrammatic section through the eye and a section through the retina at the edge of the blind spot (from Atkinson *et al*., 1983)

The receptors: rods and cones

Gregory (1966) estimated that only about 10 per cent of the light entering the eye actually reaches the transducers (rods and cones), the rest being absorbed by the accessory structures (the rest of the eye).

Box 5.6 The distribution of rods and cones

- The rods are 1000 times more sensitive than the cones – that is, they're far more likely to respond to low levels of illumination.
- They're also far more numerous: in each retina there are 120 million rods and 7 million cones.
- Their distribution around the retina also differs. Cones are much more numerous towards the centre of the retina. The *fovea*, a pit-like depression, is part of a cone-rich area (the *macula lutea*), where there's a concentration of about 50,000 cones. By contrast, the rods are distributed fairly evenly around the periphery (but aren't found in the fovea).

What do rods and cones do?

The rods are specialised for vision in dim light (including night-time vision) and contain a photosensitive chemical (*rhodopsin*), which changes structure in response to low levels of illumination. They help us see black, white and intermediate greys (*achromatic colour*), and this is referred to as *scotopic vision*. The cones are specialised for bright-light vision (including daylight) and contain *iodopsin*. They help us see chromatic colour (red, green, blue, and so on) and provide *photopic vision* (from 'photon', the smallest particle of light that travels in a straight line).

This chemical difference between the rods and cones explains the phenomenon of *dark adaptation*. If you go into a dark cinema from bright sunlight, you'll experience near blindness for a few seconds. This is because the rods need a little time to take over from the cones, which were responding outside. The rhodopsin in the rods is being regenerated (resynthesised), having been 'bleached' by the bright sunlight. It takes 30 minutes for the rods to reach their maximum level of responding.

Rods, cones and adaptation

According to Bruce and Green (1990), the difference between the sensitivity of rods and cones explains the correlation between the rod:cone ratio in an animal's retina and its ecology. *Diurnal animals* (which are active by day and sleep at night) have a higher proportion of cones than *nocturnals* (which are active by night and sleep by day, see Chapter 7). Pure-cone retinas are rare (mostly confined to lizards and snakes), as are pure-rod retinas (confined to bats and deep-sea fish, which never leave their dark habitats).

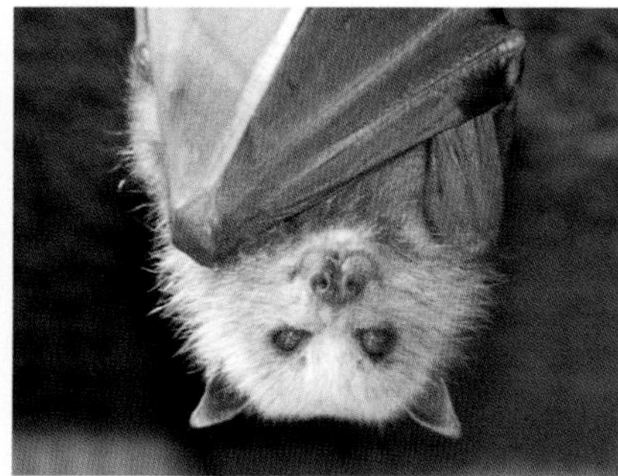

Figure 5.3 Dogs are diurnal and have relatively more cones than nocturnal animals, such as bats

Rods, cones and ganglion cells

The 127 million rods and cones are 'reduced' to 1 million *ganglion* cells, which make up the optic nerve. This means that information reaching the brain has already been 'refined' to some extent compared with the relatively 'raw' information received from other sensory nerves. However, the degree of reduction (or *summation*) differs considerably for different areas of the retina. In the periphery, up to 1200 rods may combine to form a single ganglion cell, and so connect to a single axon in the optic nerve. This provides only very general visual information. At the fovea, only 10–12 cones may be summed for each ganglion cell, providing much more detailed information.

Two other kinds of cell, horizontal and amacrine, interconnect with groups of the other cells. This further increases the degree of information processing that takes place in the retina itself. Horizontal cells connect receptors and bipolar cells, while amacrine cells connect bipolar and ganglion cells (see Figure 5.2).

Box 5.7 What's the best way of looking at an object?

- When focusing on objects in bright light, the most sharply defined image is obtained by looking directly at them, thereby projecting the light on to the fovea (which, remember, is packed with cones).
- In night light, however, the sharpest image is actually produced by looking slightly to one side of the object (for example, a star in the sky), thereby stimulating the rods (which are found in the periphery of the retina).
- The dense packing of cones helps explain *acuity*: the more densely packed the receptors, the finer the details of a pattern of light intensity that can be transformed into differences in electrical activity. The difference between a human's acuity and, say, a falcon's is the result of a difference in receptor packing: receptors are three times more densely packed in the falcon (Bruce and Green, 1990).

Ganglion cells and receptive fields

Each ganglion cell has a *receptive field*, a (usually) roughly circular region of the retina, in which stimulation affects the ganglion cell's firing rate. There are (at least) three kinds of ganglion cell, each with a different kind of receptive field:

1. *on-centre cells* are more neurally active when light falls in the centre of the receptive field, but less active when it falls on the edge
2. *off-centre cells* work in the opposite way
3. *transient cells* have larger receptive fields and seem to respond to movements, especially sudden ones.

The combined activity of on-centre and off-centre cells provides a clear definition of contours ('edges'), where there's a sudden change in brightness. These contours are essential in defining the shape of objects to be perceived (Beaumont, 1988). Further analysis of contours takes place in the striate cortex by simple, complex and hypercomplex cells (see below).

Box 5.8 Is the retina back-to-front?

- As Beaumont (1988) points out, the retina appears to be built back-to-front: the receptors don't point to the source of the light but towards the supporting cells at the back of the eye. Before it arrives at the receptors, light must pass through the layers of retinal cells and blood vessels inside the eye (see Figure 5.2). In view of this, it's surprising that such high-quality vision can still be achieved.
- When you look up at the sky, especially a cloudless blue sky, you see small transparent bubbles floating in front of you: these are red blood cells.

Visual pathways: from eye to brain

As Figure 5.4 shows, the pathways from the half of each retina closest to the nose cross at the *optic chiasma* (or *chasm*) and travel to the *opposite hemisphere* (*crossed pathways*). The pathways from the half of each retina furthest from the nose (*uncrossed pathways*) travel to the hemisphere on the same side as the eye. So, when you fixate on a point straight ahead (such that the eyes converge), the image of an object to the *right* of fixation falls on the left half of each retina, and information about it passes along the crossed pathway from the right eye to the left hemisphere and along the uncrossed pathway from the left eye to the left hemisphere. No information is passed directly to the right hemisphere.

All these relationships are reversed for an object to the *left* of the fixation point, so that information is passed directly only to the right hemisphere. It follows that any damage to the visual area of just one hemisphere will produce blind areas in both eyes; however, the crossed pathway ensures that complete blindness in either eye won't occur.

Before reaching the cortex, the optic nerve travels through the *lateral geniculate nucleus* (LGN), which is part of the thalamus (see Chapter 4). Optic nerve fibres terminate at synapses with LGN cells arranged in layers (laminae), each lamina containing a *retino-optic map* of half the visual field.

LGN cells have concentric receptive fields similar to those of retinal ganglion cells, and the axons of LGN cells project to the *occipital lobe*. In monkeys, all LGN cells project to area 17, which is the *visual* or *striate* cortex (called the *geniculostriate path*).

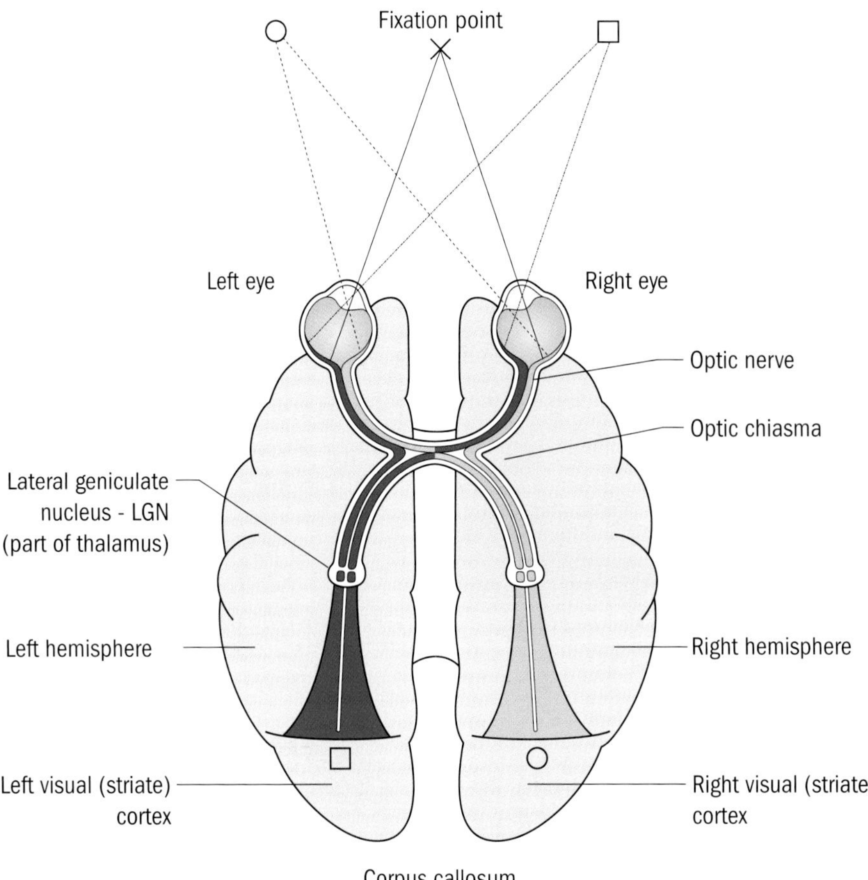

Figure 5.4 The visual system

Blindsight

In humans, the geniculostriate path must be intact for conscious experience of vision to be possible. People with damage to their visual cortex will report complete blindness in part or all of the visual field. Even so, they'll show some ability to locate or even identify objects that they cannot consciously see; Weiskrantz (1986) called this *blindsight*.

This was based originally on intensive study of D.B., who had an operation meant to reduce the number of severe migraines he suffered. Despite being left with an area of subjective blindness, he could detect whether or not a visual stimulus had been presented to the blind area and also identify its location. However, he seemed to possess only a rudimentary ability to discriminate shapes (see Case Study 5.1).

This suggests that, while most visual functions rely on the 'primary' *geniculostriate path*, the 'secondary' *retinotectal path* (some ganglion cells are projected to the paired *superior colliculi* structures in the midbrain) carries enough information to guide some actions in an unconscious way. In the intact brain, these two paths function interdependently: the *corticotectal path* provides the superior colliculi with input from the cortex.

Explaining blindsight

In birds and fish, the superior colliculus (SC) is the main structure receiving input from the eyes; in mammals, it's overshadowed by the visual cortex but remains involved in controlling eye movements and other visual functions. Blindsight would exploit information travelling from the retina to the SC without first going through the primary visual cortex. In the human brain, the SC acts as an interface between sensory processing (sight) and motor processing (leading to the patient's action), thereby contributing to visually-guided behaviour in a way that's apparently separate from the pathways involving the cortex and entirely outside conscious visual experience. Blindsight of emotions also involves the SC and the amygdala. (See Case Study 5.2.)

Ungerleider and Mishkin (1982) distinguished between two essential and complementary aspects of visual perception:

- the *ventral system*, passing from primary visual cortex (V1) to the inferior temporal lobe, which is concerned with *object identification* (the 'what' system)
- the *dorsal system*, passing from V1 to the posterior parietal lobe, which is concerned with *object localisation* (the 'where' system).

While plenty of supporting evidence for the ventral/dorsal system distinction was found (in the monkey brain) during the 1980s and 1990s, researchers began to suggest that 'what versus *how*' might describe the functional distinction more accurately. This, together with other evidence from monkey experiments, strongly suggested that:

(a) D.F.'s perceptual problems could have arisen from severe damage to the ventral stream, which supplies suitably abstract representations of the visual world and which provides our immediate visual experience – as well as our visual memories

(b) her spared *visuomotor* skills could perhaps be attributed to a functionally intact dorsal stream, which acts entirely in real time, guiding the

Case Study 5.1

T.N., D.B. and G.Y. (De Gelder, 2010)

- T.N., blind as a result of two strokes suffered in 2003, proceeds down a long corridor strewn with boxes, chairs and other objects. He has no idea the objects are there and yet he avoids them all. This is probably the most dramatic demonstration of blindsight ever reported.
- Personalised psychophysical tests to assess his conscious vision hadn't found any visual functioning, including detection of big targets; his ability to negotiate the corridor was reminiscent of sleepwalking. He insisted that he'd simply walked along the hallway: not only was he unaware of seeing anything but was also oblivious to how he'd manoeuvered around the unseen objects; he was at a loss to explain or even describe his actions.
- G.Y. had lost all his primary visual cortex on the left side in childhood, causing blindness on the right side of his visual field. He could reliably guess facial expressions on faces he didn't consciously perceive, but he seemed truly blind to various non-emotional facial attributes (such as personal identity and gender).
- In 2009, both G.Y. and D.B. were shown still images of faces and whole bodies expressing happiness and fear, using *emotional contagion* (a tendency to match one's own facial expressions to those of others) as measured by *facial electromyography* (as in sleep research; see Chapter 7). All the stimuli triggered emotional reactions, regardless of whether the image was on the patient's sighted or blind side. In fact, surprisingly, the unseen images produced a *faster* response than those seen consciously. The unseen fearful images produced the strongest pupil dilation (a measure of physiological arousal); apparently, the more consciously aware we are of an emotional signal, the slower and weaker our reaction.

programming and unfolding of our actions at the instant we make them; this enables the smooth and effective movements that allowed our primate ancestors to survive in a hostile and unpredictable world.

Using fMRI, Goodale and Milner found support for their hypothesis. Essentially, this is a distinction between *vision for perception* and *vision for action* (Goodale and Milner, 2006). This is now referred to as the *dual-stream model of visual processing*.

Case Study 5.2

D.F. (Goodale and Milner, 2004)

- D.F. suffered carbon monoxide poisoning, which damages part of the visual system concerned with shape recognition. She has a vague impression of light, shade and colour, but cannot recognise anything because she cannot see what shape it is. She seems to be able to walk around and pick things up far better than would be expected given that she's almost blind. Several experiments, over a period of years, have confirmed that there's a big discrepancy between what she could *see* and what she could *do*.
- In one experiment, you hold up a rod and ask D.F. about its orientation. She's unable to say whether it's horizontal or vertical or at an angle. It's as if she cannot see the rod and is just guessing. Then you ask her to reach out and grasp the rod. She does this normally: she rotates her hand so that her fingers have the same orientation as the rod, she grasps it smoothly whatever its angle.
- This shows that D.F.'s brain 'knows' about the angle of the rod and can use this information to control the movements of her hand. Her brain knows something about the physical world, while her conscious mind doesn't (Frith, 2007).
- Again, despite being unable to report (verbally or manually) the width of a rectangular block, she would still tailor her finger–thumb grip size perfectly in advance of picking it up. In other words, she could guide her movements using visual cues of which she seemed to be completely unaware (Milner *et al*., 1991; Goodale *et al*., 1991).

However, Himmelbach *et al*. (2102), after comparing D.F.'s performance with that of 20 female, age-matched healthy controls, concluded that she was severely impaired in her reaching and grasping; this seems to undermine Milner and Goodale's dual-stream interpretation.

Hubel and Wiesel's studies of cortical cells

The first recordings from single cells in the striate cortex of cats and monkeys were made by Hubel and Wiesel (1959, 1962, 1968). They identified three kinds of cortical cell. (See Box 5.9.)

Box 5.9 Simple, complex and hypercomplex cells

- *Simple cells* respond only to particular features of a stimulus (such as straight lines, edges and slits) in particular orientations and in particular locations in the animal's visual field. For example, a bar presented vertically may cause a cell to 'fire', but if the bar is moved to one side or out of vertical, the cell will not respond.
- *Complex cells* also respond to lines of particular orientation, but location is no longer important. For example, a vertical line detector will respond wherever it is in the visual field. It seems that complex cells receive inputs from larger numbers of simple cells sharing the same orientation sensitivity.
- *Hypercomplex cells* are 'fed' by large numbers of complex cells and are similar to complex cells, except that they take length into account too (that is, they are most responsive to a bar or edge not extending beyond their receptive field).

Some researchers have questioned the existence of hypercomplex cells as a distinct class of cell (Bruce and Green, 1990). However, Hubel and Wiesel's research demonstrates that the visual cortex isn't a homogeneous mass of tissue, with randomly scattered cells of different kinds. Rather, it shows an astonishingly precise and regular arrangement of different cell types, which Hubel and Wiesel (1962) called the *functional architecture* of the visual cortex.

The six main layers of the striate cortex can be recognised under the microscope. The cortical area devoted to the central part of the visual field is proportionately larger than that devoted to the periphery. Hubel and Wiesel (1977) suggest that the cortex is divided into roughly square blocks of tissue (about 1 mm^2), extending from the surface down to the white matter (*hypercolumns*).

The extrastriate (prestriate) cortex

Single-cell recordings have revealed many regions of the *extrastriate* (or *prestriate*) cortex, to the front of the striate, which can be considered 'visual areas'. However, it's proved more difficult to map these, compared with the striate cortex.

Maunsell and Newsome (1987) reviewed studies involving macaque monkeys. They concluded that there are 19 visual areas, covering large areas of the occipital, temporal and parietal lobes. The deep folding of the cortex means that some areas, lying within folds (*sulci*), aren't visible from the exterior.

Each area sends output to several others and most, if not all, connections are matched by reciprocal connections running in the opposite direction. Van Essen (1985) lists 92 pathways linking the visual areas. Most can be classified as either *ascending* (leading away from V1) or *descending* (leading towards V1). When the pathways are classified in this way, a consistently hierarchical pattern emerges, with areas placed at different levels.

The hierarchical processing of colour and number

According to Ramachandran and Hubbard (2003), neural signals from the retina initially travel to area 17 in the occipital lobe. The image is processed further within local clusters or blobs into such simple attributes as colour, motion, form and depth. The information about these separate features is then sent forward and distributed to several far-flung regions in the temporal and parietal lobes.

In the case of colour, information is sent to V4 in the *fusiform gyrus* of the temporal lobe. It's then passed to areas lying further up in the hierarchy of colour centres, including a region near a patch of cortex called TPO (standing for the junction of the temporal, parietal and occipital lobes). These areas may be concerned with more sophisticated aspects of colour processing, such as *colour constancy* (see below).

Numerical computation also occurs in stages. An early step also occurs in the fusiform gyrus, where the actual shapes of numbers are represented. A later stage occurs in the *angular gyrus*, a part of the TPO concerned with numerical concepts such as ordinality (sequence) and cardinality (quantity).

The way in which colour and number are processed could help explain the fascinating phenomenon of *synaesthesia*.

Synaesthesia

Ask Yourself

- Does it make sense to say that we can taste shapes, see sounds, or hear colours?
- Have you ever associated particular numbers with particular colours?
- Could the way that different kinds of visual information (colour, motion, form and depth) are processed help explain these phenomena (see text above)?

Not only have neuroscientists identified many more senses than was traditionally believed (see above), but they're discovering the *interconnections* between them. The brain links and synchronises sensory information from diverse sources in ways that we cannot consciously observe. Not only are the senses highly interconnected, but the brain is also very good at substituting one sensory input for another, even using the ears to construct remarkably sight-like pictures of the world (Bleicher, 2012).

Case Study 5.3

Daniel Kish and echolocation

- Daniel Kish is the most scientifically studied person who 'sees' with sound. He lost both eyes to cancer as a one-year-old.
- As a toddler, he worked out that if he made sharp, quick clicks with his tongue and listened to their echoes, he could get around his neighbourhood quite efficiently.
- This human *echolocation* produces scenes that have form, texture, depth and continuity – but they are colourless and restricted to about the size of a tennis ball. Nevertheless, he's able to go dancing, hikes in the dark and rides his bike in city traffic.
- He often uses the vocabulary of vision to describe his echolocation and brain scans revealed why. Thaler *et al.* (2011) used fMRI to scan Kish's brain, along with that of another blind echolocator and two control participants, while they listened to recordings of clicks and their echoes. They also heard clicks without echoes.
- The visual cortex (specifically, the *calcarine sulcus/fissure* in the occipital lobe) was found to be active only in the echolocators and only when they heard the echoes – not other background noises. The auditory cortex seemed to play no special role in converting echoes into images. The activity was greater in Kish, who was an 'early' echolocator compared with the other blind participant.
- Thaler *et al.* conclude that processing of click-echoes recruits brain regions that are typically devoted to *vision* (rather than audition).

A small number of otherwise 'normal' people experience the ordinary world in extraordinary ways, and

> *... seem to inhabit a mysterious no-man's land between fantasy and reality. For them, the senses – touch, hearing, vision and smell – get mixed up instead of remaining separate. (Ramachandran and Hubbard, 2003)*

Examples include associating letters of the alphabet, or musical notes played on the piano, with colours, and numbers and shapes with tastes. *Synaesthesia* is commonly defined as a joining of the senses, where sensations in one modality (e.g. hearing) produce sensations in another (e.g. colour vision). But this is an oversimplification, because synaesthetic experiences are often driven by *symbolic* rather than sensory representations (as the examples above involving letters and numbers demonstrate) (Ward, 2003).

How does synaesthesia happen?

According to Ramachandran and Hubbard (2003), recent research has begun to uncover brain processes that could account for this phenomenon. One possibility is *cross-wiring*. As we noted earlier, both colours and numbers are initially processed in the fusiform gyrus, and subsequently near the angular gyrus. Number–colour synaesthesia might be caused by (a) cross-wiring between V4 and the number–appearance area (both located within the fusiform gyrus), or (b) between higher-colour areas and the number–concept area (both located within the TPO). The hearing centre in the temporal lobes is also close to the higher brain area that receives colour signals from V4. This could explain sound–colour synaesthesia.

Ask Yourself

- Look at the figures below.
- Which of these is a 'bouba' and which a 'kiki'?

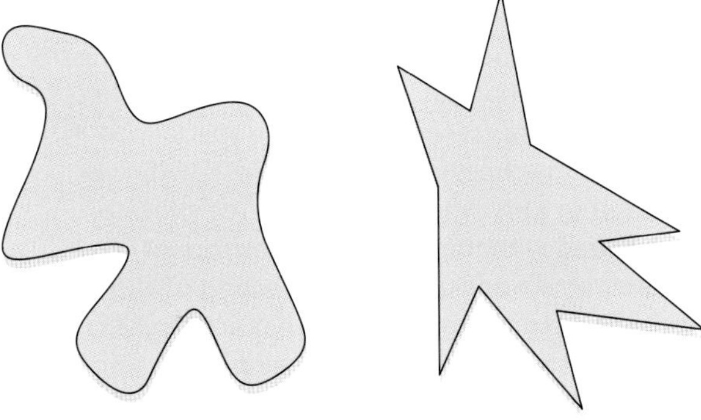

Figure 5.5

Are we all 'closet synaesthetes'?

According to Ramachandran and Hubbard, 98 per cent of people pick the inkblot (left) as 'bouba'. Why? Perhaps the gentle curves of the amoeba-like figure *metaphorically* mimic the gentle undulations of the sound 'bouba' as represented in the brain's hearing centres, as well as the gradual inflections of the lips as they produce the curved 'bouba' sound. The sharp inflection of the tongue on the palate when saying 'kiki' mimics the sudden changes in the jagged visual shape. People with damage to their angular gyrus fail to make the bouba/kiki distinction. Ramachandran and Hubbard suggest that the angular gyrus (which is disproportionately large in humans compared with apes and monkeys) evolved originally for cross-modal associations – but then was taken over for other, more abstract functions, such as metaphor. Significantly, synaesthetes are seven times more common among creative people, many of whom share the skill of using metaphor (in some form or another). It's as if their brains are set to make links between seemingly unrelated conceptual domains.

COLOUR VISION AND COLOUR BLINDNESS

Light can be described *physically* by its *energy spectrum* (intensities at different wavelengths) or *phenomenologically* by three dimensions:

1. *brightness* (perceived intensity)
2. *hue* (perceived colour)
3. *saturation* (the purity of hue: how much colour or how much white).

Although both hue and saturation are aspects of 'colour', hue is what theories of colour vision and discussion of colour vision defects are concerned with.

Rushton and Campbell (1954, cited by Rushton, 1987) were the first to measure the visual pigments in the living human eye, applying the familiar observation that a cat's eye will reflect back light shone into it. Instead of the cat's shining *tapetum lucidium*, we have a very black surface behind the retina – the choroid coat – which reflects very faint light. Rushton and Campbell identified rhodopsin, plus red and green pigments. However, insufficient blue light is reflected to measure the blue cone pigment (Rushton, 1987).

Later, Marks *et al.* (1964, cited by Rushton, 1987) used fresh retinas from monkeys and human eyes removed during surgery to measure visual pigments in single cones. They found the blue-green and red-sensitive cones, thus supporting the Young–Helmholtz trichromatic theory (see below). Rushton and Campbell's findings were also confirmed using living colour-blind participants, who possessed only one of the two pigments they measured.

Theories of colour vision

The Young–Helmholtz trichromatic theory

The *trichromatic theory* (Young, 1801) claims that colour is mediated by three different kinds of cone, each responding to light from a different part of the visible spectrum. Blue-sensitive, green-sensitive and red-sensitive cones are maximally responsive to short, medium and long wavelengths, respectively. While the sum of the three wavelengths (B + G + R) determines brightness, their ratio or pattern (B:G:R) determines colour. This is essentially what's believed today (Rushton, 1987).

This explains the painter's experience that mixing a few paints will produce a whole range of colours. It also implies that every colour (including white) should excite B, G and R cones in a characteristic set of ratios, so that a mixture of red and green and blue lights, adjusted to produce this same set of ratios, should appear white or whatever the initial colour was. This was systematically tested by Maxwell (1854), who found that every colour can be matched by a suitable mixture of blue, green and red 'primaries' (the *trichromacy of colour*). This was later confirmed by Helmholtz (Rushton, 1987). Hence, this is often called the *Young–Helmholtz trichromatic theory*.

The opponent process theory

While the Young–Helmholtz theory can explain the effects of mixing colours of different wavelengths, it has difficulty explaining colour blindness (see Box 5.10) and the phenomenon of *negative after-images*. Both of these can be explained more easily by the major alternative to the trichromatic theory, namely the *opponent process (tetrachromatic) theory* (Hering, 1878). This claims that colour analysis depends on the action of two types of detector, each having two modes of response. One signals red or green, the other signals yellow or blue. A third type of detector, black–white, contributes to the perception of brightness and saturation.

Evidence for the opponent process theory

- If you stare at a coloured surface (for example, red) and then look at a plain surface, you'll perceive an after-image that is coloured in the 'opposite direction' (i.e. green). This is called a *complementary* (or *negative*) *after-image*.
- The retina encodes in terms of three constituent components (a blue-green-red 'component' system: stage one of colour vision). But output through the bipolar and ganglion cells and on to the LGN (stage two) becomes recoded in terms of opponent processes (DeValois and Jacobs, 1984). There seem to be four kinds of LGN cell: (i) those that increase activity to red light but decrease with green (R+ G−); (ii) those that increase activity to green light but decrease with red (G+ R−); and similarly (iii) for blue and yellow (B+Y−) and (iv) yellow and blue (Y+ B−). Still other LGN cells simply respond to black and white (Beaumont, 1988).

Box 5.10 Colour blindness

- People with defective colour vision (usually called '*colour blind*') usually fail to distinguish between red and green. This is the most common form of defect, caused by a recessive sex-linked gene that affects more males (about 8 per cent) than females (about 0.4 per cent).
- Sufferers have *dichromatic vision* (normal vision is *trichromatic*): they possess only red- or green-sensitive cone pigments, but they can match every colour of the rainbow exactly with a suitable mix of only two coloured lights (for example, red and blue). Most people need the green primary as well if every colour is to be matched.
- Next most common is *true* colour blindness, which involves an absence of any cones at all (*monochromatic vision*).
- Least common of all is yellow-blue blindness. These findings are clearly consistent with the opponent colour theory.
- While men are more susceptible to colour blindness (of any kind), women are potentially *tetrachromatic* ('super-sighted'), able to distinguish, for example, between two apparently identical shades of green (Hollingham, 2004).

Must we choose between the two theories?

The generally held view is that a complete theory of colour vision must draw on elements from both theories. Indeed, Helmholtz himself showed that the two theories aren't incompatible, as a simple transformation could change the three receptor outputs to two different signals, plus one additive signal (Troscianko, 1987). According to Harris (1998), the theories are compatible, and neurophysiological evidence exists for both.

Colour constancy

Any chromatic light hitting the retina is composed of different amounts of the three primary colours (for example, turquoise might be 70 per cent blue, 30 per cent green). So, blue-sensitive cones would 'fire' quite quickly, and green-sensitive ones quite slowly (and red-sensitive wouldn't fire at all). However, perceived colour isn't solely determined by the wavelength composition of the light reflected from the object (the *spectral reflectance* of the object).

According to McCann (1987), our visual system is built to tell us about the permanent colours of objects, as opposed to the spectral composition of the light falling on a local area of the retina.

Box 5.11 Factors influencing the perception of colour

- The relative proportions of different wavelengths in the light falling on the object (the *spectral composition* of the illumination)
- Prior stimulation of the retina (as shown by complementary or negative after-images)
- The nature of the surroundings, such as the simultaneous contrast created by adjacent areas of different colour or brightness; for example, a grey square will look brighter set against a black background than against a white background). (See Figure 5.6.)

Figure 5.6 Our familiarity with, and knowledge of, an object's colour, which is part of the psychological phenomenon of *colour constancy*

CONCLUSIONS

The crucial role of the brain

Saccades (see Box 5.4) occur about three times per second and last up to 200 milliseconds. With each fixation, your visual system takes in high-resolution detail which it somehow weaves together to create an illusion of completeness; this is remarkable, given that we're effectively blind during saccades themselves. Similarly, every five seconds or so, we blink. But we're not usually aware of the resulting 'blackouts', because the brain edits then out (Lawton, 2011).

Given that we perform approximately 150,000 saccades every day, our visual system is 'offline' for a total of about four hours per waking day even without blinking. Yet, we don't notice anything amiss! So, how does the brain fill in the gaps? One popular hypothesis is that, in order to formulate a hypothesis about what is happening now, the brain must somehow predict the future. Information striking the fovea cannot be relayed instantaneously to conscious perception: first it has to travel down the optic nerve and be processed by the brain. This takes several hundred milliseconds, by which time the world has moved on. So, the brain predicts what the world will look like about 200 m/sec into the future – and that is what we see (Lawton, 2011).

However, things are even more complicated than this. According to Freeman *et al.* (2013), the 'same' event in the outside world seems to be perceived by different parts of the brain as happening at different times. So, rather than one unified 'now', there are many clocks in the brain, all measuring their individual 'nows' relative to their average. This claim is based on the case of P.H., the first confirmed case of someone who hears people speak *before* registering their lips have moved.

Because light and sound travel at different speeds, when someone speaks, visual and auditory inputs arrive at our eyes and ears at *different* times. Despite the signals then being processed in different brain areas, we perceive the events as happening simultaneously.

P.H., a 67-year-old man, was found to have two lesions in areas that may play a part in hearing, timing and movement. Freeman *et al.* gave him a *temporal order judgement test*: he was shown clips of people talking and was asked whether the voice came before or after the lip movements. He said it came before; for him to perceive them as simultaneous, the voice had to be played about 200 m/sec *later* than the lip movements. A second test was presented, based on the *McGurk illusion*: listening to one syllable while watching someone mouth a different one results in the perception of a third syllable. It was expected that the illusion would work with P.H. when the voice was *delayed*. However, the *opposite* result was found: presenting the voice 200 m/sec earlier than the lip movements triggered the illusion. This suggests that his brain was processing the sight before the sound.

In P.H.'s case, one or more of the brain clocks has been significantly slowed – possibly as a result of the lesions. Freeman *et al.* (2013) are looking for a way to slow down his hearing so that it matches what he sees.

Chapter Summary

- **Sensation** is necessary for **perception**, since sense data represent the 'raw material' from which conscious awareness of the world is constructed.
- Each **sensory system** or **modality** is sensitive to a particular form of physical energy, but each also acts as a **data reduction system**.
- **Light** is one form of **electromagnetic radiation**. The human eye responds to only a tiny fraction of the visible **electromagnetic spectrum**.
- **Exteroceptors** include the five traditional senses of sight, hearing, smell, taste and touch; **interoceptors** include receptors for the internal environment; **proprioceptors** are usually subdivided into the **kinaesthetic** and **vestibular senses**.
- Every sense modality comprises a **sense organ/ accessory structure, sense receptors/transducers**, a **specialised brain area** that processes the sensory messages, and an **absolute threshold**.
- The **Weber–Fechner law** is an attempt to predict **difference threshold/jnd** and is an important part of **psychophysics**, which studies the relationship between physical stimuli and subjective experience.
- **Signal detection theory** rejects the notion of thresholds, and instead uses the concept of **signal-to-noise ratio**.
- The fundamental job of the human eye is to focus an image of the **optic array** on to the retina with maximum **acuity**. About 80 per cent of our information about the world comes through vision.
- The **pupil** regulates the amount of light entering the eye by contracting or dilating. Pupil size is controlled by the ciliary muscles and by the ANS.
- The **lens** focuses light on the retina as an **inverted image**, and its shape is regulated through **accommodation**.
- The retinal image is continuously moving, and other kinds of movement include **saccades, pursuit movements** and **convergence**.
- Unlike a camera, what's sent to the brain isn't a picture, but information about the pattern of light reaching the eyes. This information must then be interpreted.
- The **retina** contains 120 million **rods** and 7 million **cones** (the **photosensitive cells**). It also comprises **bipolar** and **ganglion** cells.
- The rods help us see **achromatic colour** (**scotopic vision**) and the **cones** help us see **chromatic colour** (**photopic vision**).
- When focusing on objects in bright light, the sharpest image is obtained by projecting the image on to the **fovea**, which is densely packed with cones.
- The rods and cones are 'reduced' to 1 million ganglion cells (**summation**) but this varies according to which part of the retina is involved. There are (at least) three kinds of ganglion cell, each with a different kind of receptive field.
- The pathways from the half of each retina closest to the nose cross at the **optic chiasma/chasm**, through the LGN, then on to the **visual/striate cortex** in the occipital lobe. This is called the **geniculostriate path**.
- Cases of **blindsight** suggest that the **retinotectal path** carries enough information to allow some 'unconscious' vision. Normally, these two paths work together.
- **Simple**, **complex** and **hypercomplex** cells in the striate cortex of cats and monkeys respond to particular stimulus features. These cells are arranged in **hypercolumns**.
- Research with monkeys has shown that large areas of the occipital, temporal and parietal lobes are involved in vision.
- **Synaesthesia** may result from the cross-wiring between parts of the brain that normally process different types of information separately. The highly interconnected nature of sensory systems is demonstrated in cases of human **echolocation**.
- The **Young–Helmholtz trichromatic theory of colour vision** stresses the ratio or pattern of the three wavelengths of light, while the **opponent process/tetrachromatic theory** is based on the two modes of response of two types of detector.
- Some of the evidence supporting the opponent process theory comes from the study of **colour-blind people**. Both theories are seen as valid and complementary.

Links with Other Topics/Chapters

Chapters 15 and 16 → Sensation provides the 'raw material' for *perception*

Chapter 4 → Sensory information is fed to the CNS via the SNS (part of the PNS). Sensory information is processed in various parts of the brain, and 'vision' denotes the sense organ, sense receptor and specialised area of the brain *working as a system*

Chapters 1 and 3 → *Psychophysics* was a significant development in Psychology's emergence as a discipline in its own right

Recommended Reading

Gregory, R.L. & Colman, A.M. (eds) (1995) *Sensation and Perception*. London: Longman.

Ramachandran, V.S. & Hubbard, E.M. (2003) Hearing colours, tasting shapes. *Scientific American*, *288*(5), 42–9.

Ward, J. (2003) Synaesthesia. *The Psychologist*, *16*(4), 196–9.

Useful Websites

www.senseofsmell.org/ (The Fragrance Foundation)

http://people.hws.edu/uwolfe/psych100/

www.multimediaplace.com/asa (American Synaesthesia Association)

http://asj.gr.jp/2006/data/kashi/index.html

www.faculty.ucr.edu/~rosenblu/lab-index.html (The 'McGurk effect')

http://blogs.scientificamerican.com/observations/2010/04/22/blindsight-seeing-without-knowing-it (An account of Weiskrantz's experiments, including video footage.)

CHAPTER 6

PARAPSYCHOLOGY

- The historical roots of Parapsychology (PP)
- Parapsychology (PP) and Anomalistic Psychology (AP): Defining the field
- Experimental investigation of paranormal phenomena
- Some recurring issues in parapsychological research

INTRODUCTION and OVERVIEW

Most Psychologists believe that the sensory systems or modalities described in Chapter 5 are the only means by which we can acquire information about our environment (both physical objects and other people). However, there are some phenomena that seem to involve meaningful exchanges of information between organisms and their environment, and yet at the same time appear somehow to exceed the capacities of the sensory and motor systems as they are currently understood (Rao and Palmer, 1987). For these reasons, such phenomena are considered to be *anomalous*; they include what's commonly referred to as *paranormal* phenomena (or '*psi*', short for 'psychic ability'), the subject matter of *Parapsychology*.

Such phenomena include 'extra-sensory perception' (ESP). The term unambiguously implies that there are ways of acquiring information about the world that don't depend on vision, hearing and so on. Similarly, psychokinesis (PK) refers to the influence of physical events by purely mental means. So, 'anomalous' or 'paranormal' is used for phenomena apparently lying outside the range of normal scientific explanations and investigations. However, most Anomalistic and Parapsychologists consider themselves to be scientists applying the usual rules of scientific enquiry to admittedly unusual phenomena. Indeed, the term 'Parapsychology' was first introduced in the 1930s to refer to the scientific investigation of paranormal phenomena (Evans, 1987a).

THE HISTORICAL ROOTS OF PARAPSYCHOLOGY (PP)

According to Evans (1987a), the history of PP can be conveniently divided into three overlapping phases or periods: *spiritualistic research/spiritualism*, *psychical research*, and *modern PP*.

Spiritualistic research/spiritualism

Most Victorian scientists brought up as orthodox Christians were expected to believe in the reality of an immortal, non-physical soul. So a substantial number of them became involved in the minority religion of *spiritualism*: if souls or spirits survived the death of the physical body, they must exist somewhere in the universe and should, in principle, be contactable (for example, through mediums). Some of the outstanding brains of the time, including physicists, biologists and anthropologists, solemnly tried to induce spirit forms to materialise in their laboratories. The Society for Psychical Research was founded in London in 1882 and, soon after, the *Journal of the Society for Psychical Research*.

Other, more critical or sceptical colleagues conducted their own experiments. Medium after medium was exposed as fraudulent, and the pioneers were shown to be gullible, incompetent, or both. By 1900, scientific interest was moving away from seances and towards 'more plausible' aspects of the paranormal.

Psychical research

This was the era of the 'ghost hunter'. Scientists and affluent amateurs turned to phenomena such as manifestations in haunted houses, poltergeist activity, demonic possession, apparitions and premonitions. There was also a growing number of casual studies of telepathy and precognitive dreams.

Modern PP

According to Blackmore (1995), credit for the founding of PP (in the 1930s) was almost entirely due to J.B. Rhine and Louisa Rhine (although Louisa is often not mentioned, as in Evans' 1987a, account).

They were biologists who wanted to find evidence against a purely materialist view of human nature. Despite sharing the same objectives, they wanted to dissociate themselves from spiritualism and bring their new science firmly into the laboratory. They renamed their research 'Parapsychology', established a department of PP at Duke University in the USA, began to develop new experimental methods, and defined their terms operationally.

PARAPSYCHOLOGY (PP) AND ANOMALISTIC PSYCHOLOGY (AP): DEFINING THE FIELD

Ask Yourself

- What do you understand parapsychological/ paranormal phenomena to be?
- Do you believe they exist as real phenomena (regardless of how you might explain them)?

According to Henry (2005), *Parapsychology* is the study of *psychic phenomena*, that is:

> *... the exchange of information or some other interaction between an organism and its environment, without the mediation of the senses ...*

Similarly, Irwin and Watt (2007) define PP as:

> *... the scientific study of experiences which, if they are as they seem to be, are in principle outside the realm of human capabilities as presently conceived by conventional scientists ...*

For these reasons, such phenomena are considered to be *anomalous* (or *exceptional*).

J.B. Rhine introduced the term 'extra-sensory perception' (ESP) in 1934. This was a general term used to cover three types of communication that supposedly occur without the use of the senses, namely *telepathy*, *clairvoyance* and *precognition*. These, and other commonly researched phenomena in PP, are defined in Box 6.1.

Box 6.1 The four types of psi

- **Telepathy**: '... the transmission of information from one mind to another, without the use of language, body movements, or any of the known senses ...' (Evans, 1987b). It was previously called 'thought transference'.
- **Clairvoyance**: '... the acquisition by a mind or brain of information which is not available to it by the known senses, and, most important, which is not known at the time to any other mind or brain ...' (Evans, 1987b).
- **Precognition**: '... the apparent ability to access information about future events before they happen ...' (Morris, 1989).

These are all forms of *extrasensory perception* (ESP). In all cases, the direction of influence is from environment to person.

- **Psychokinesis (PK)** (movement by the psyche): '... the supposed power of the mind to manipulate matter at a distance without any known physical means ...' (Evans, 1987b).

A distinction is made between (a) *macro-PK*, where solid objects are affected and the result can be seen by the naked eye (such as spoon-bending, apports ('gifts' that 'materialise' from non-physical to physical reality) or moving an object purely via intention); and (b) *micro-PK*, where ultra-sensitive instruments (such as strain gauges and random number generators (RNGs), see below) are apparently affected by intention and the significance of the results is assessed statistically.

Macro-PK is still highly controversial; it's an area where experimenters have to take particular care to guard against fraud (Wiseman, 2001, see below)

Naturally-occurring PK (*recurrent spontaneous PK* (RSPK)) is associated with phenomena such as poltergeists. Direct mental interaction with a living system (DMILS) refers to PK on a live organism where physiology, such as electrodermal (skin conductance) activity, or blood pressure, is altered purely by intention. Another example is distant and non-contact healing (Henry, 2005).

For PK, the direction of influence is from person to environment (the reverse of ESP).

Apparitional phenomena

Apparitions are experienced as external to the self, the classic example being a ghost. Sometimes the apparition appears to be fairly solid, at other times less obviously person-like. In previous centuries, reports of demon visitations were quite common. In the latter half of the twentieth century, reflecting technological developments, similar experiences have often been interpreted as visits by aliens. (This has parallels in the kind of 'thought-insertion' symptoms commonly reported by patients with schizophrenia; see Chapter 44). In non-western cultures, experiences of spirits of some kind are often accepted as part of life, but in the West such reports are rare (though there are some well-known cases of visions of the Virgin Mary) (Henry, 2005).

Anomalous or exceptional experience

In contrast to apparitions, *anomalous experiences* (such as *out-of body experiences* (OBEs), *near-death experiences* (NDEs), *past-life experiences* (PLEs) and *coincidence experiences* (CEs)) are felt as happening to the individual him/herself. There are other anomalous experiences (such as UFOs) and (other) *exceptional experiences* (such as altered states of consciousness and mystical experiences) that are traditionally studied by researchers other than Parapsychologists. This is seen as a reason for categorising anomalous and exceptional experiences together.

For example, White (1993) offers a classification of exceptional experiences which brings together phenomena traditionally studied by Parapsychologists and others interested in anomalous and exceptional experiences. These are:

- mystical experiences (including peak experiences, stigmata, transformational experience)
- psychic experiences, including apports, synchronicity, telepathy, PK, and OBEs
- encounter-type experiences (including apparitions, angels, UFO encounters, sense of presence)
- death-related experiences, such as NDEs and PLEs
- exceptional normal experiences (such as *déjà vu* and hypnogogia).

Hypnosis, hallucinations and lucid dreams used to be considered part of PP, until Psychologists made progress in understanding them. As Boring (1966) said, a scientific success is a failure for psychical research; in other words, PP is concerned with those phenomena that 'mainstream' or 'regular' Psychology cannot explain with its currently available models and theories (see above).

Paranormal beliefs

While the definitions of PP so far have focused on the study of paranormal experiences and abilities, in some ways a more fundamental feature of PP is the study of paranormal *beliefs*. Irwin (2009) provides a 'working definition' of paranormal belief as:

> *... a proposition that has not been empirically attested to the satisfaction of the scientific establishment but is generated within the non-scientific community and extensively endorsed by people who might normally be expected by their society to be capable of rational thought and reality testing ...*

For these people, the belief (like all their other beliefs) is phenomenologically a part of their sense of reality and truth rather than 'a proposition they endorse'. Such beliefs aren't idiosyncratic but reasonably common within the individual's sociocultural group. In some societies, ESP is regarded as a human skill that falls entirely within the natural order, yet in western societies it's generally thought of as paranormal. Indeed, Northcote (2007) argues that the term 'paranormal' is fundamentally a western ontological category.

However, even though the definition of PP may itself be culturally relative, cultural differences are still consistent with the view that it has a claim to being part of the world of science. Not only are paranormal beliefs culturally relative, they're also *temporally* relative – a proposition that's deemed paranormal at one time might not be so regarded at another time, either because it becomes empirically substantiated to the satisfaction of mainstream science or it's no longer extensively endorsed within the community. (See below.)

Box 6.2 Paranormal beliefs

As many Parapsychologists demonstrate (e.g. Irwin, 2009; Irwin and Watt, 2007), 'paranormal belief' encompasses different varieties of beliefs, including

(a) beliefs in psychic abilities (or *psi*)
(b) beliefs in all-powerful deities and the power of prayer
(c) beliefs in the survival of the soul after death and the ability to communicate with the deceased
(d) superstitious beliefs
(e) beliefs that organisms can be healed, or harmed, through the direct action of mental intention
(f) beliefs that the earth is visited by intelligent alien life forms.

It's not only Parapsychologists who have explored these beliefs: anthropologists, sociologists and Psychologists have also approached them from their own particular perspectives. Because Parapsychologists don't rule out the possibility that psi is real, part of their research looks at the relationship between belief in psi and actual performance on controlled laboratory tests of psychic ability (see below). In contrast, anthropologists and sociologists are interested in the social and cultural function that such beliefs serve – regardless of their reality. Psychologists are perhaps the most sceptical about the reality of psi, and some of their criticism of parapsychological research is based on the assumption that such beliefs are basically misguided and maladaptive. Other, more open-minded Psychologists explore how such beliefs have arisen and what psychological function they may serve (Watt and Wiseman, 2009).

MEET THE RESEARCHER

Susan Blackmore

Why I had to change my mind

It was 1970, the tail end of the hippy era, when I arrived in Oxford as an enthusiastic young fresher. I was thrilled by the intellectual atmosphere, and threw myself into late nights, early lectures, New Age theories, crazy clothes and mind-opening cannabis.

I joined the Oxford University Society for Psychical Research and blundered into occultism, mediumship and the paranormal – ideas that clashed tantalisingly with everything I was learning for my degree in physiology and psychology. Then late one evening something very strange happened. I was sitting around with friends, smoking, listening to music and enjoying the vivid imagery of rushing down a dark tunnel of leaves towards a bright light, when my friend spoke and I couldn't reply.

'Where are you, Sue?' he asked, and suddenly I seemed to be on the ceiling looking down.

'Astral projection!' I thought and I (or some imagined flying 'I') set off across Oxford, over the country and way beyond. For more than two hours I explored strange scenes, entered mystical states beyond space and time, and ultimately lost myself.

Drawing of a tunnel that Susan made in 1970 after her out-of-body experience

It was an extraordinary and life-changing experience. Everything seemed brighter and more real than ordinary life; something seemed to tell me that this mattered more than anything else. I could not understand; yet I longed to.

Perhaps understandably I jumped to obvious but wrong conclusions – that my spirit had left my body and that this must prove phenomena that most scientists reject, like telepathy, clairvoyance and life after death. I decided, with youthful overconfidence, that I was going to become a parapsychologist and prove all those 'closed-minded' scientists wrong.

Research into ESP and memory

My tutors said I'd never have a future in research if I did parapsychology, but I did not care. Somehow I got a PhD place to test what I thought was my brilliant and original 'memory theory of ESP' (extra-sensory perception), and funded myself by part-time teaching. I believed that all minds were connected through a psychic field and that memory was a special case of telepathy. So I set to work on a long series of experiments comparing ESP and memory.

The results were a shock. Whether I looked for telepathy or precognition or clairvoyance, I got only chance results. I trained fellow students in imagery; chance results. I tested twins in pairs; chance results. I worked in playgroups with very young children; chance results. I trained as a Tarot reader; chance results.

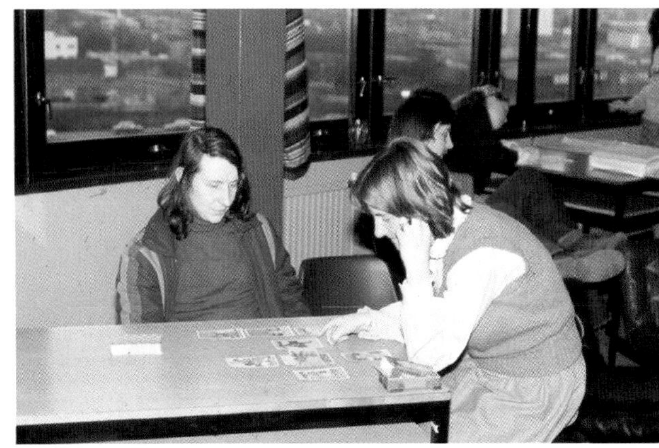

Susan doing a tarot reading for a student in her experiment (c.31976)

Occasionally, I got a significant result. Oh the excitement! Then, as a scientist must, I repeated the experiment, checked for errors, redid the statistics, varied the conditions, and every time either I found the error or got chance results again. Sometimes my enthusiasm waned and I began to doubt. But there was always another beckoning claim, always another 'X' to try. By the end of my PhD I had run out of 'X's.

Turning point

At some point, something snapped. Instead of struggling to fit my chance results into yet another doomed theory of the paranormal, I faced up to the awful possibility that I might have been wrong from the start – that perhaps there were no paranormal phenomena at all. I had to change my mind.

At first this was terribly hard because my whole persona was based on my beliefs – from my New Age clothes to training as a witch, visiting Spiritualist churches, using the Tarot, I-Ching and crystal balls, and hunting ghosts. My friends couldn't understand how I could join the 'sceptics'. But deep down I was a scientist and always had been. These results were telling me something very loud and clear. I was wrong! I had to reassess the way I saw the world and that is what I did.

Being a 'rent-a-sceptic'

On the one hand, I became what I called 'rent-a-sceptic', appearing on TV programmes to counter psychic claims with rational explanations (a task that brought much hate mail as well as enjoyment). On the other I began research trying to understand why people have near-death and out-of-body experiences (OBEs), if nothing actually leaves the body.

BBC 2 Horizon programme on 'Close Encounters', broadcast 28 November 1994

There is no question that they do. In surveys, between 10 and 20 per cent of people claim to have had an OBE, and the experiences are similar across ages and cultures. But why? The answer is not that we all have a spirit or soul, but that our brains are similar. In certain states induced by drugs, shock, deep relaxation or special techniques, random excitation of neurons causes odd consequences. Activation in visual cortex produces tunnels and spirals, activation in the temporal lobe arouses memories as though one's whole life is flashing past and – most interestingly – a certain spot near the right temporo-parietal junction produces body image distortions and OBEs. So the experiences are real enough but do not prove life after death or the existence of souls.

I also wondered why so many people believe in paranormal phenomena if they do not exist. I did experiments showing that people who are worst at judging the likelihood of chance events are more likely to be believers, along with husband, Tom Troscianko. I studied lucid dreams (in which you know you are dreaming) and sleep paralysis (in which you wake up paralysed, hearing strange noises and convinced there is someone else in the room). This was especially helpful when I came to investigate alien abductions because many turn out to be unrecognised sleep paralysis. Once again people try truthfully to report what happened to them, but their explanations are wrong – just as I had done they jump to obvious but false conclusions.

Return to academia

After many years of working on my own, with little money and no job, I became a senior lecturer, and then reader, at the University of the West of England in Bristol. So my tutors were finally proved wrong – though it took a long time. I got tired of being the hated sceptic, battling against people's hopes of worlds beyond and paranormal phenomena, and having mediums, psychics and believers tell me that I didn't have an open mind. 'Do you know what it means to have an open mind?' I wanted to shout sometimes. 'It means being able to change your mind when the evidence shows you are wrong.' That is what science is all about. That is how we learn the truth about human nature rather than clinging to what we want to be true – like telepathy and life after death.

Perhaps I will always get involved in controversial topics. I became fascinated by the concept of memes – the cultural analogue of genes. I took up Zen meditation in my twenties and eventually wrote a book about Zen questioning. I got involved in debates about free will, drugs and the harmful effects of religion. Eventually I realised that the common thread in all of this, beginning with that original experience, is the mystery of consciousness. As we learn more and more about the brain it seems ever more peculiar that a vast number of neurons all connected together in complex patterns can bring about an experience of a world with me in it. How can this be? I don't think I will ever get bored of exploring the mystery of consciousness.

Professor Susan Blackmore is a psychologist and writer researching consciousness, memes, and anomalous experiences, and a Visiting Professor at the University of Plymouth. She blogs for the *Guardian* and *Psychology Today*, and often appears on radio and television. Her book *The Meme Machine* (1999) has been translated into 13 languages.

Paranormal beliefs are very widely held. Around the world, surveys consistently show that about 50 per cent of people hold one or more, and, of these, about 50 per cent believe that they've themselves had a genuinely paranormal experience. According to Watt and Wiseman (2009):

> *... Regardless of whether these beliefs and experiences are 'correct', they are clearly an important part of what it means to be human. Paranormal beliefs occur in every culture around the world. Therefore academics have a responsibility to attempt to understand what causes these beliefs, and the consequences to individuals and to society of holding them ...*

Why do we believe in the paranormal?

According to Wiseman (2012):

> *... Belief in the paranormal is not the provenance of a select group of individuals who are fundamentally different form the rest of us. We are all wired for weird.*

One of the most popular explanations of people's belief in ghosts involves a neural mechanism called the *agency-detection device* (Barrett, 2004). The parts of the brain responsible for detecting the reasons/motives behind people's actions can cause most of us to see human-like behaviour in even the most meaningless stimuli. A classic demonstration of this is Heider and Simmel's (1944) study of animated triangles (one small, one large) and a circle, around which participants instantly created elaborate stories to explain the movement of the shapes. This demonstrates the very strong tendency to *attribute* motives and intentions (usually to people, but here to geometric shapes) (see Chapter 23).

If Barrett is right, seeing ghosts might be the price we pay for having remarkable brains that can effortlessly figure out why other people behave as they do (Wiseman, 2012). By the same token, our normally highly reliable *face-recognition system* can become hyperactive, leading us to see eyes and mouths everywhere (see Chapter 14).

Other Psychologists believe that individuals differ in the extent to which they rely on the two hemispheres, thus making them more experiential (right) or rational (left) in their preferred way of thinking about themselves and the world.

Ask Yourself

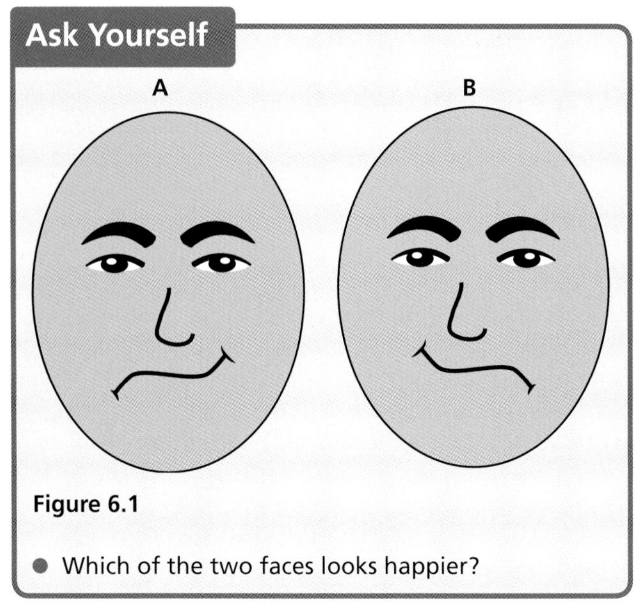

Figure 6.1

- Which of the two faces looks happier?

In drawing A, the person is smiling on the *right* side of the face; in B, it's on the *left*. Since it's our *opposite* hemisphere that perceives the face, if we judge B to be happier, then it's our *right* hemisphere that's making the judgement. People who claim to have had paranormal experiences do tend to opt for B; they also demonstrate a preference for their right hemisphere in other tests. According to Brugger and Graves (1997), such individuals would be especially likely to make associations between unconnected events, see faces in ambiguous shapes, and sense patterns where there are none; in turn, this makes them prone to experiencing seemingly impossible phenomena (such as ghostly faces in photographs and prophetic dreams).

EXPERIMENTAL INVESTIGATION OF PARANORMAL PHENOMENA

ESP and Zener cards

The Rhines were convinced that the supposedly paranormal powers of the mind were essentially psychological phenomena, and so should be investigated with the tools of traditional psychological research. Throughout the 1930s, they conducted a lengthy series of *telepathy* experiments, in which a *receiver* had to guess the identity of a target being looked at by an *agent*. To make the task as easy as possible, a set of simple symbols was developed and made into Zener cards (named after their designer) or 'ESP cards'. They come as a pack of 25 cards, consisting of five circles, five squares, five crosses, five stars and five wavy lines.

Figure 6.2 Zener card symbols

The rationale for these studies was that they allowed the experimenter to compare the results achieved with what would be expected by chance. So, in a pack of 25 cards comprising five of each of five distinct symbols, we'd expect, on average, five to be *guessed* correctly (i.e. by chance alone). If receivers repeatedly scored above chance over long series of trials, this would suggest that they were 'receiving' some information about the cards. This would, in turn, imply that, if the experiments had been sufficiently tightly controlled as to exclude all normal or known sensory cues, then the information must be coming via ESP (Evans, 1987a). In *clairvoyance* experiments, the cards were randomised out of sight of anyone, and in *precognition* experiments, the card order was decided only *after* the receiver had made his/her guesses.

The order was determined initially by shuffling, and later by the use of random number tables. It's extremely important for targets in ESP experiments to be properly randomised, so that results cannot be affected by any kind of systematic biases: shuffling isn't adequate (Blackmore, 1995).

What were the Rhines' findings?

The technique seemed to be successful, and the Rhines reported results that were way beyond what could be expected by chance (Blackmore, 1995). They claimed that they'd established the existence of ESP. However, these claims produced considerable opposition from the psychological establishment.

For example, were the Rhines' receivers physically completely isolated from the experimenter, so that information couldn't be passed unwittingly (for example, by unconsciously whispering or other non-deliberate cues)? Were checks on the data records precise enough to ensure minor errors weren't made (unconsciously or deliberately) to bias the results in a pro-ESP direction?

The Rhines tightened up their procedures on both counts by (a) separating receiver and experimenter in different buildings, and (b) arranging independent verification and analysis of the results. As a consequence, the above-chance results became more rare, although they remained sufficiently common to constitute apparently indisputable evidence for ESP. However, then came another, more fundamental criticism. When Psychologists not committed to a belief in ESP tried to replicate the Rhines' findings in their own laboratories, they simply failed to produce any positive results.

In response to this potentially fatal blow, the Parapsychologists argued that a significant factor in ESP might be the *experimenter's attitude* to the phenomenon under investigation: sceptical or dismissive experimenters ('goats') might have a 'negative effect' on the results (the Rhines, and other believers, being 'sheep'). This argument seems to imply that only believers are fit to investigate ESP, which is contrary to the spirit of scientific research (Evans, 1987a; see Chapter 3).

Ask Yourself

- Are you a sheep or a goat?

Free-response ESP

One drawback of the early Rhine research was that guessing long series of cards is extremely boring. By contrast, reports of psychic dreams, premonitions and other cases of spontaneous psi abounded. The challenge was to capture these under laboratory conditions (Blackmore, 1995). *Free-response ESP* represents the most important attempts to meet this challenge and now forms the dominant paradigm in ESP research (Irwin and Watt, 2007). By far the most successful free-response method has been the *Ganzfeld* ('ganz' = 'whole'; 'feld' = 'field'), first used for psi research by Honorton in 1974. He argued that why ESP occurs in dreams, meditation and reverie is that they're all states of reduced sensory input and increased internal attention. He tried to find a way of producing such a 'psi-conducive' state without the expense of a dream laboratory (see Chapter 7 and Box 6.3).

The 'Ganzfeld debate'

Honorton (1985) analysed 28 studies using the Ganzfeld procedure (totalling 835 sessions, conducted in 10 different laboratories). He reported a 38 per cent correct

Box 6.3 The Ganzfeld

- Halved ping-pong balls are taped over the receiver's eyes and red light is shone into them, so all that can be seen is a pinkish glow. Soothing sea sounds or hissing 'white noise' (like a radio that's not properly tuned in) are played through headphones while the participant lies on a comfortable couch or reclining chair. While this doesn't constitute total sensory deprivation (see Chapter 9), the Ganzfeld deprives receivers of patterned input and encourages internal imagery. They typically report a pleasant sensation of being immersed in a 'sea of light'.
- The *sender* (an experimenter acting as an agent) is situated in a separate, acoustically isolated room. A visual stimulus (a picture, slide or brief video sequence) is randomly selected from a large pool of similar stimuli to serve as the *target*. While the sender concentrates on the target (for about 15 minutes), the receiver tries to describe it by providing a continuous verbal report of his/her ongoing imagery and free associations.
- The sender stays in the room for another 10 minutes. From a separate room, the *experimenter* can both hear (via a microphone) and see (via a one-way mirror) the receiver, and is blind to the target (doesn't know what the target is).
- At the end of the experimental session, the receiver is presented with four stimuli (one of which is the target), and is asked to rate the degree to which each one matches the imagery and associations experienced during the session. A 'direct hit' is recorded if the receiver assigns the highest rating to the target.
- The sender is then called in and reveals the target. A typical experiment involves about 30 sessions.

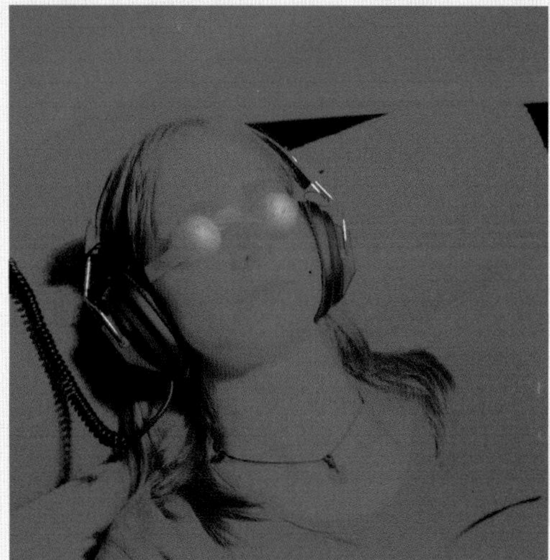

Figure 6.3 A receiver in the Ganzfeld

selection of the target, which compares with a 25 per cent success rate by chance alone (i.e. by guessing). Statistically, this is highly significant: the chances of obtaining a 38 per cent success rate by chance alone is less than one in a billion (Honorton, 1985).

However, a critical review by Hyman (in the *Journal of Parapsychology*, 1985) pointed out discrepancies in the scoring systems used, and procedural flaws (such as the failure to use proper randomisation for selecting the targets). Hyman also claimed to have found correlations between the quality ratings for studies and outcome, with the sloppier studies giving the 'better' results. However, in the same journal, Honorton claimed to have found no such evidence. Rosenthal provided a commentary on the debate, generally regarded as favouring Honorton's interpretation (Blackmore, 1995).

Hyman and Honorton issued a joint 'communiqué' (Hyman and Honorton, 1986), in which they agreed that the studies as a whole fell short of ideal, but that something beyond selective reporting, or inflated significance levels, seemed to be producing the non-chance outcomes. They also agreed that the significant outcomes had been produced by several different researchers. Further replication would decide which of their interpretations was correct.

This debate, which Morris (1989) describes as 'an outstanding example of productive interaction between critic and researcher', brought Parapsychologists and sceptics together to try to agree what would constitute an acceptable experiment. As a consequence, Honorton designed a *fully automated* Ganzfeld experiment, leaving little scope for human error or deliberate fraud. Several experiments produced significant results, which were published in the *Psychological Bulletin* in 1994 (one of the world's most prestigious Psychology journals).

SOME RECURRING ISSUES IN PARAPSYCHOLOGICAL RESEARCH

We've seen above just how divided opinion is between those who believe in the reality of ESP ('sheep') and those who don't ('goats'). Also, accusations of fraud – the deliberate invention or modification of procedures or results – have been a

Box 6.4 Meta-analysis: a better way of analysing Ganzfeld results?

Meta-analysis (MA) refers to the use of statistical methods to synthesise and describe experiments and their outcomes. MA focuses on studies not just in terms of their statistical significance levels (the traditional approach), but also allows diverse studies to be compared on a single measure, called an *averaged effect size*. When MA is used to assess the effectiveness of treatments for mental disorder, effect size refers to 'an index of the magnitude of the effects of a treatment ... averaged across all studies ...' (Lilienfeld,1995; see Chapter 7).

By 1997, over 2500 Ganzfeld sessions had been conducted around the world with an average success rate of 33 per cent. This appeared to provide impressive evidence for a psi effect. However, a MA of 30 subsequent Ganzfeld studies (Milton and Wiseman, 1999) found an effect near chance; Milton (1999) found a significant but lower effect size. Henry (2005) cites Bem *et al.*'s (2001) reanalysis of 40 subsequent studies, including Milton and Wiseman's 30; this suggested that those studies that followed the classic Ganzfeld procedure closely (such as using similar visual targets) did come very close to replicating the original effect size, whereas those trying something different (such as using musical targets) didn't (Henry, 2005). These mixed results suggest that the next step in the search for strong evidence of psi will involve more systematic research to identify what, if any, variables affect performance in Ganzfeld ESP studies – if ESP is, indeed, a genuine phenomenon (Milton, 2005).

feature of the history of parapsychological research in general. Arguably, this makes the study of psi unique as an area of psychological enquiry. At least as far as goats are concerned, Parapsychologists are guilty unless proven innocent. In other words, if psi doesn't exist (as goats maintain), then any claims by sheep that it does must be based on fraudulent (or, at best, unreliable and/or invalid) data. So, rather than simply trying to produce evidence that supports the existence of psi, Parapsychologists are constantly having to show that they're *not cheating*! But how can you prove a negative?

Critical Discussion 6.1

Parapsychology and science

According to Roberts and Groome (2001):

> *... In practice there is considerable overlap between what is regarded as 'paranormal' and what is considered to be merely 'unusual' ...*

Because scientific knowledge changes so rapidly, and because most Parapsychologists consider themselves to be scientists applying the accepted rules of scientific enquiry to difficult-to-explain phenomena, the field of PP is ever shrinking.

For example, hypnosis, hallucinations and lucid dreams used to be considered part of PP – until Psychologists made progress in understanding them. This, in turn, suggests that 'paranormal' implies phenomena that *apparently* lie outside the range of normal scientific explanations and investigations. As Boring (1966) said, a scientific success is a failure for psychical research; in other words, PP is concerned with phenomena that mainstream Psychology cannot explain with its currently available models and theories.

Irwin and Watt (2007) describe Parapsychology's relationship with science as paradoxical: despite the fact that parapsychological phenomena appear to be contrary to conventional scientific wisdom, they're investigated using the methods of science:

> *... A feature of modern parapsychology is that investigation of its phenomena is staged in the controlled environment of the psychological laboratory whenever possible. Scientific methodology is emphasised also in field studies of the sort that predominated in the days when such interests were known as* psychical research, *the study of phenomena apparently mediated directly by the mind or 'soul'. (Irwin and Watt, 2007; emphasis in original)*

Paranormal experiences are defined in terms of *appearances* – how they *seem* to be. This means that a fundamental task of researchers is to investigate the actual bases of these experiences, determining the extent to which they can be explained within the framework of accepted principles of mainstream science. Researchers should also show how that framework can be extended in order to accommodate relevant empirical findings (Irwin and Watt, 2007). (For further discussion, see Gross, 2014.)

The history of PP also seems to highlight a number of methodological issues that, while they recur throughout all areas of psychological research, assume a more exaggerated or extreme form in relation to psi. These include:

- the question of the *'conclusive' experiment*
- the *replication problem*
- *publication bias* (or the *file-drawer problem*)
- the *inadequacy of controls*
- *experimenter effects*.

The question of the 'conclusive' experiment

According to Abelson (1978), then editor of *Science*, 'extraordinary claims require extraordinary evidence' (quoted in Rao and Palmer, 1987). This implies that the strength of evidence needed to establish a new phenomenon is directly proportional to how incompatible the phenomenon is with our current beliefs about the world. If we reject the possibility of this new phenomenon (its *subjective probability* is zero), then no amount of empirical evidence will be sufficient to establish the claim. However, as Rao and Palmer point out:

> *... In serious scientific discourse ... few would be expected to take a zero-probability stance because such a stance could be seen to be sheer dogmatism, and the very antithesis of the basic assumption of science's open-endedness.*

Abelson's 'extraordinary evidence' sometimes means, in practice, demands for a 'foolproof' experiment that would control for all conceivable kinds of error, including experimenter fraud. This assumes that at any given time, one can identify all possible sources of error and how to control for them.

Ask Yourself

- Is this assumption valid? (See Box 3.6, p. 48.)

According to Rao and Palmer (1987):

> *... The concept of a 'conclusive' experiment, totally free of any possible error or fraud and immune to all skeptical doubt, is a practical impossibility for empirical phenomena. In reality, evidence in science is a matter of degree ... a 'conclusive' experiment [should] be defined more modestly as one in which it is highly improbable that the result is artifactual ...*

In other words, there are no *absolutes* in science (no certainty, no once-and-for-all 'proof'), only *probabilities* (see Chapter 3); in this latter sense, Rao and Palmer believe that a case *can* be made for 'conclusive' experiments in PP.

Box 6.5 Schmidt's (1969) random event generator (REG)

- Schmidt, a physicist at the Boeing Scientific Research Laboratories in the USA, designed a test for the possibility of ESP.
- A specially-built machine seemed to rule out all artefacts arising from recording errors, sensory cues or receiver cheating. The machine randomly selected targets with equal probability, and recorded both target selections and receivers' responses. The receiver's task was to guess which of four lamps would light and press the corresponding button if aiming for high scores (or avoid pressing if aiming for low scores).
- Random lighting of the lamps was achieved by a sophisticated electronic random event generator (REG), which was tested extensively in control trials and found not to deviate significantly from chance.

The REG experiments:

- represent one of the major experimental paradigms in contemporary PP
- are regarded by most Parapsychologists as providing good evidence for psi
- have been subjected to detailed scrutiny by critics.

Despite this, and almost inevitably, they have been criticised. For example, Hansel (1980) claimed that Schmidt's highly significant results haven't been replicated by other researchers (see below), and these criticisms are routinely taken as valid by most sceptics (such as Alcock, 1981).

The replication problem

Rao and Palmer (1987) argue that science is concerned with establishing general laws, not unique events (this relates to the *idiographic–nomothetic* debate; see Chapter 42). The ability to repeat an experiment would seem to be a reasonable thing to demand of a field aiming to achieve scientific respectability (*New Scientist*, 2004; see Chapter 3).

However, many sceptics argue that only 'replication on demand' (i.e. absolute replication) can produce conclusive proof of psi. According to Rao and Palmer, an experiment isn't either replicable or not replicable, but rather it's on a continuum:

> *... In this sense of statistical replication, an experiment or an effect may be considered replicated if a series of replication attempts provides statistically significant evidence for the original effect when analysed as a series. (Rao and Palmer, 1987)*

In other words, on balance, does the accumulated evidence, based on a large number of replication attempts, point towards the existence of psi, or not? But while this is fine in principle, in practice it's proved impossible to reach any kind of consensus.

Meta-analysis (MA) provides a precise estimate of how unlikely it is that the results of the entire group of studies being examined arose by chance alone (*cumulative probability*) (see Box 6.4). In order to make this calculation, the probability associated with each study's outcome is calculated and the probabilities are combined to reflect the overall outcome. In most PP meta-analyses, the results have been significantly above chance. In large groups of studies, the results go well beyond mere statistical significance and have astronomical odds against having arisen by chance (a 'fluke') (Milton, 2005).

However, between 1995 and 1999, 30 Ganzfeld experiments were conducted. Four different meta-analytic studies of these experiments were also performed: two concluded that the findings were significant, while the other two concluded that they weren't! The biggest discrepancy between them was the inclusion (or not) of a hugely successful study by Dalton (1997) carried out at Edinburgh University. It was omitted from two of the MAs on the grounds that it was an 'outlier': because its results were so much better than any others, it should be discounted (an accepted practice in MA). But another accepted practice is that MAs must use *all* available data. So, the other two included Dalton's study (*New Scientist*, 2004). So much for scientific objectivity!

Also, many Parapsychologists argue that any failure to replicate should be taken as a positive result: it confirms what they knew all along, namely that paranormal phenomena are inherently elusive. You cannot expect to pin them down in the laboratory (New Scientist, 2004).

Publication bias (or the 'file-drawer' problem)

A recurring issue within science in general, and PP in particular, is the concern that only successful studies tend to be published (i.e. those that produce significant results), while those that find no effect or an effect in the opposite direction from the one predicted are more often left in researchers' file drawers (and so *don't* get published). This is the so-called *file-drawer problem*. This would mean that those that are published (the database of known studies) may not accurately reflect the true state of affairs: there will be a strong bias in favour of psi.

With the usual cut-off point for statistical significance being set at 0.05, on average, one in 20 studies will be apparently successful by chance alone. This makes it necessary to know how many studies have been conducted in total (Milton, 2005).

But how is it possible to establish how many studies may have been 'binned'?

Box 6.6 Solving the file-drawer problem

- Parapsychologists are more sensitive to the possible impact of unreported negative results than most other scientists. In the USA, the Parapsychological Association (PA) has advocated publishing all methodologically sound experiments, regardless of the outcome. Since 1976, this policy has been reflected in publications of all affiliated journals (such as the *Journal of Parapsychology*) and in papers accepted for presentation at annual PA conventions.
- There are relatively few Parapsychologists, and most are aware of ongoing work in the various laboratories around the world. When conducting a MA, they actively seek out unpublished negative studies at conventions and through personal networks.
- MA allows the calculation of the number of studies with an average zero effect that would have to be in the research 'file drawer' to bring the observed overall result in a MA down to the point at which it became statistically non-significant. In most MAs to date, the file-drawer estimates are so large that selective publication *doesn't* appear to be a reasonable counter-explanation for the observed results.

(Source: based on Atkinson *et al.*, 1990; Milton, 2005; Rao and Palmer, 1987)

Case Study 6.1

A classic case of publication bias

- In 2011, Parapsychologist Daryl Bem published a series of nine experiments, involving over 1000 participants, that seemed to support the existence of precognition ('feel the future'). The results appeared in the prestigious *Journal of Personality & Social Psychology*, with Bem inviting other researchers to conduct replications. Accepting the invitation, Ritchie, Wiseman and French each ran his own independent study and Bem actually provided each researcher with the software he'd used in the original study. All three studies obtained null results.
- However, when they submitted their results for publication (in 2012), several journals, including the *Journal of Personality & Social Psychology*, refused to review them on the grounds that they didn't publish attempted replications. This isn't just a problem for PP but for mainstream Psychology in general. To verify that an effect is genuine, it's vital that other researchers attempt replications in their own laboratories. By refusing to publish attempted replications, journals make it virtually impossible to assess a finding and so can leave both Psychologists and the public with the mistaken impression that an effect is much more robust than it actually is (Wiseman, 2012).
- Finally, their results were published by *PLoS ONE*, an open-access journal. They received widespread coverage around the world, raising doubts about the validity of Bem's original findings and leading to much-needed discussion of the place of replication in science and the strengths and weaknesses of the current system of peer review. (Bem was one of two reviewers for the *British Journal of Psychology*; not surprisingly, he didn't recommend it for publication) (French, 2012).

The inadequacy of controls

While it's true that replicating an effect implies nothing directly about its cause, it's also a basic premise of experimental science that replication reduces the probability of some causal explanations, particularly those related to the honesty or competence of individual experimenters (Rao and Palmer, 1987). As Alcock (1981) says:

> *It is not enough for a researcher to report his observations with respect to a phenomenon; he could be mistaken, or even dishonest. But if other people, using his methodology, can independently produce the same results, it is much more likely that error and dishonesty are not responsible for them.*

If psi experiment results were due to poor methodological controls rather than to genuine phenomena, we might expect each study's quality to be negatively related to its effect size; in other words, the better controlled the study, the smaller its outcome. However, in almost all PP MAs, *no* statistically significant relationships have been demonstrated between overall quality and effect size (Milton, 1995).

Experimenter effects

As we saw in Chapter 3, whenever human participants are involved, they will try to make sense of the experimental situation – they look for the *demand characteristics* in the experimental situation (Orne, 1962). Equally important are *experimenter effects*, that is, methodological problems arising from the influence of the experimenter on the data.

The experimental system in parapsychological research is a particularly 'open' one. Not only are demand characteristics and experimenter effects potential problems, but the parapsychological experimenter effect (PEE) represents an additional source of bias: it denotes the partial dependence of the obtained data on the parapsychological abilities of the experimenter (Kennedy and Taddonio, 1976; Schmeidler, 1997; White, 1976). The PEE assumes the existence of psi, but it raises the question of whether it's possible for a researcher to investigate the nature of ESP (Irwin and Watt, 2007).

The usual 'blind' methods used to prevent or limit the experimenter's unintentional influence on the participants' behaviour do not apply here. If ESP really exists, can the participant read the experimenter's mind? Can the experimenter use PK to directly influence delicate physical instruments? If this is possible, the experimental environment is even more open than was previously thought.

One of the most consistent findings in parapsychological research is that some experimenters, using well-controlled methods, repeatedly produce significant results, while others, using exactly the same methods, consistently produce non-significant results. Experimenters can affect the outcome of experiments unwittingly (see Chapter 3). These experimenter effects have long been explicitly recognised and discussed in PP. (See Box 6.7.)

How should we interpret these findings?

The PEE is one of Parapsychology's longest-standing controversies. This is largely due to the 'heads I win, tails you lose' interpretation that many

Box 6.7 Psi-permissive, psi-inhibitory and psi-conducive experimenters

- Some experimenters seem capable of creating a climate in which participants' psi abilities are allowed to express themselves (*psi-permissive experimenters*), while others have the opposite effect and produce consistently negative results (*psi-inhibitory results*). These differences seem to be related to:
  (i) the pleasantness/unpleasantness of the experimental setting for the participant – a relaxed participant is more likely to display psi abilities (Crandall, 1985)
  (ii) the experimenter's expectations – participants are more likely to display psi abilities if the experimenter expects positive results (Taddonio, 1976).
- According to Schmiedler (1997), some experimenters have produced particularly high levels of positive results with participants who fail to repeat their performance later. This could be explained in terms of a highly motivated experimenter, who has strong psi abilities him/herself. S/he may somehow transfer these abilities to participants during the course of the experiments (but not beyond). These are referred to as *psi-conducive experimenters*. This transfer can distort the experimental findings.

Parapsychologists (sheep) place on the findings described in Box 6.7. In other words, the fact that positive results are obtained by researchers with psi abilities – but not by those without – 'proves' that psi exists. Rather than being a confounding variable as sceptics would claim, believers argue that experimenter effects in the context of parapsychological research actually *demonstrate* the phenomena under investigation.

The PEE itself is now the object of intense research. New explanations for it are also emerging. For example, some Parapsychologists claim that it arises not through experimenters' influence over mind or matter, but because they use their extra-sensory powers to pick the right moments to sample a fluctuating process and catch any 'fluky', but natural, departures from randomness (McCrone, 2004). (See Research Update 6.1.)

CONCLUSIONS: THE CONTROVERSY GOES ON

Holt *et al.* (2012) assess the scientific status of PP in terms of a number of criteria that have been proposed for defining a field of study as a science (e.g. Popper's (1959) concept of *falsifiability*; see Chapter 3) or as a pseudoscience (e.g. Mousseau, 2003) (see Gross, 2014). Holt *et al.* conclude that:

Box 6.8 Evolution, individual differences and the paranormal

Sheep, compared with goats, are more likely to display *transliminality* – the tendency for information to pass between our subconscious and conscious mind (Thalbourne, in Wilson, 2006). Several studies have shown that the better you are at tuning into your subconscious, the more likely you are to be a sheep. But sheep are also better at perceiving meaningful patterns in apparently random 'noise'. The classic example of this trait, known as *pareidolia*, is when people claim to see images of the Virgin Mary, say, on the wall of a building or a tortilla. Pareidolia can also be auditory, as shown by the current craze for detecting electronic voice phenomena (EVP), supposed messages from the dead buried in the random noise of audio recordings.
Seeing patterns that aren't there (a type 1 error) is, from an evolutionary perspective, the price we pay for protection from type 2 errors (failing to spot the tiger hiding in the grass). At least if you always see tigers and always run away, you're not dead! (Wilson, 2006).

> *In general, parapsychology appears to meet the implicit criteria of science, to a greater or lesser extent, rather better than it meets the criteria of pseudoscience.*

Perhaps the real significance of psi and of PP as areas of research is that they force us to question some of our basic beliefs and assumptions about the world and ourselves. Both scientists and non-scientists are capable of prejudice and closed-mindedness, and PP can be seen as a case study in 'doing science', which isn't the unbiased, objective activity many scientists take it to be (see Chapters 3 and 47).

Matthews (2004) believes that parapsychological studies are often better designed, and their results more impressive, than clinical drug trials:

> *... by all the normal rules for assessing scientific evidence, the case for ESP has been made. And yet most scientists still refuse to believe the findings, maintaining that ESP simply does not exist ...*

Matthews concludes that science alone cannot give us what we seek – an objective view of reality. As he says:

> *More than any other scientific discipline, parapsychology pushes the scientific process to its limits and reveals where its faults lie. In particular, it has highlighted that, contrary to the insistence of many scientists, data alone can never settle this or any other issue.*

Research Update 6.1

Investigating the parapsychological experimenter effect

- Ongoing research into the PEE is being conducted jointly by Wiseman (University of Hertfordshire, UK) and Schlitz (Institute of Noetic Sciences, California, USA). This is a classic sceptic (Wiseman) versus believer (Schlitz) experiment.
- The experiment is an example of *Direct Mental Interaction with Living Systems* (DMILS) – that is, attempts to use mental connection to influence distant biological systems. This can take the form of *remote staring* (as in the Wiseman–Schlitz research), and affecting the growth rates of seedlings and yeast cultures.
- Participants sit in an isolated room, wired up to electrodes that measure arousal levels through slight changes in sweating of the hands (galvanic skin response (GSR).
- In another room, the experimenter can see the participant on CCTV.
- The experimenter has either to stare at the participant or look away, according to a random 16-minute schedule divided into 30-second blocks.
- The hypothesis being tested is that if participants know they're being stared at, they should show detectable shifts in arousal while they're under surveillance.
- Schlitz and others have been claiming small but statistically significant results for more than a decade. In the mid-1990s, Wiseman (a professional magician before he trained as a Psychologist) tried the same experiment and found no effect. The collaboration between them began in 1996; they published two joint articles in 1997 and 1999. They've swapped laboratories and shared participant pools. According to Wiseman, Schlitz's results are on 'the very knife-edge of significance'.
- These first two collaborations obtained evidence of 'experimenter effects', that is, experiments conducted by:
- Schlitz (the sheep) obtained significant results, but those conducted by Wiseman (the goat) didn't. So, does the experimenter effect come from somewhere other than the experimenter's psychic powers?
- In the most recent study from Edinburgh University (Schlitz *et al.*, 2006), the 'meet and greet' part of the experiment was split from the experimental phase. On some trials, the experimenter carried out both; on others, these jobs were shared with another experimenter. Interactions between experimenters and participants were videotaped and independently rated for factors such as warmth. They failed to replicate the findings of the earlier studies. This could be because (a) some aspect of the study disrupted the production of a genuine psychic effect; (b) the results of the earlier experiments were actually a fluke and there's really *no* remote detection of staring effect.

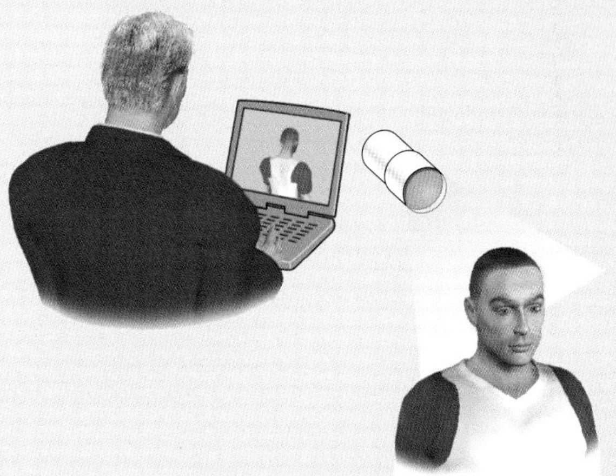

Figure 6.4 The Wiseman–Schlitz experiment tests whether participants can tell if they're being watched via a CCTV link

(Source: based on McCrone, 2004; Schlitz *et al.*, 2006)

Chapter Summary

- **Parapsychology** (**PP**) is the scientific study of **paranormal phenomena** (or '**psi**'), which appear to exceed the sensory means by which we normally acquire information about the environment. For this reason, they're considered **anomalous** (exceptional or unusual).
- **Anomalistic psychology** (**AP**) is the scientific study of all exceptional experiences (including psi, apparitions/ghosts, UFO encounters, near death experiences (NDEs), out-of-body experiences (OBEs), and mystical experiences).
- Many Psychologists have denied the possibility of the existence of such experiences, and the history of PP is littered with accusations of fraud.
- Modern PP was founded in the 1930s by the Rhines, and grew out of **spiritualistic research/ spiritualism** and **psychical research** dating back to the 1880s.
- **Extra-sensory perception** (**ESP**) consists of **telepathy**, **clairvoyance** and **precognition**. The direction of influence is from environment to person. The other major type of psi is **psychokinesis (PK)** (**macro** or **micro**) in which the influence is from person to environment.
- Paranormal **beliefs** are widely held around the world, and are both **culturally** and **temporally relative**; they are investigated by anthropologists and sociologists as well as Psychologists.
- An important distinction is made between parapsychological **experiences** and **processes**, the former defined in terms of **appearances**.
- Early ESP research used **Zener cards**, which allowed the experimenter to compare the results with what would be expected by chance. In **telepathy** experiments, a **receiver** had to guess the identity of a **target** symbol being looked at by an **agent/sender**. In **clairvoyance** experiments, the cards were randomised out of sight of everyone, and in **precognition** experiments, card order was determined only after the receiver had made his/her guesses.
- **Free-response methods** include **remote-viewing** and the **Ganzfeld**. The so-called **Ganzfeld debate** between Honorton and Hyman, resulting in their joint statement identifying areas of agreement between them, brought Parapsychologists and sceptics together in an effort to define an acceptable experiment. This resulted in a **fully automated Ganzfeld**, but the dispute between 'sheep' and 'goats' continues.
- In addition to Parapsychologists continually having to prove they're not cheating, several **methodological issues**, while not unique to PP, assume a more extreme form in relation to psi. These include the **'conclusive' experiment**, the **replication problem**, **publication bias** (or the **file-drawer problem**), the **inadequacy of controls** and **experimenter effects**.
- Schmidt's **random event generator (REG)** is regarded by many Parapsychologists as constituting a 'conclusive' experiment, but critics disagree. The safest conclusion is that there's no such thing as a fraud-proof experiment.
- Parapsychologists are more sensitive to the file-drawer problem than most other scientists, and they've taken a number of steps to get round it. These include the use of **meta-analysis (MA)** to calculate the number of studies with negative results needed to cancel out a series of positive results.
- One of the most robust findings in parapsychological research concerns the consistency with which different experimenters produce positive or negative results. These experimenter differences have been classified as **psi-permissive**, **psi-inhibitory** and **psi-conducive**. Important individual differences between participants relevant to psi abilities have also been identified.

Links with Other Topics/Chapters

Chapter 3 → Parapsychology raises fundamental questions regarding the *nature of science* – in particular, its *objectivity*; this is related

Chapter 47 → to the *biases and prejudices of scientists themselves*

Chapters 4 and 49 → The reality of psi has fundamental implications for theories of the *mind–brain relationship*, especially those *reductionist* theories which claim that any psychological account of 'the mind' can be replaced by a neurophysiological one. It also has implications

Chapter 49 again → for the *free will and determinism* debate

Chapter 42 → There's evidence that people with particular *personality characteristics* (such as extroverts: Honorton *et al*., 1990) may be more likely to display psi abilities

Recommended Reading

Blackmore, S. (1995) Parapsychology. In A.M. Colman (ed.) *Controversies in Psychology*. London: Longman.

Blanke, O. & Thut, G. (2007) Inducing out-of-body experiences. In S. Della Sala (ed.) *Tall Tales About the Mind & Brain: Separating Fact from Fiction*. New York: Oxford University Press.

Gross, R. (2012b) *Key Studies in Psychology* (6th edn). London: Hodder Education. Chapter 16.

Henry, J. (ed.) (2005) *Parapsychology: Research on Exceptional Experiences*. London: Routledge.

Holt, N.J., Simmonds-Moore, C., Luke, D., French, C.C. (2012) *Anomalistic Psychology*. Basingstoke: Palgrave Macmillan.

Irwin, H.J. (2009) *The Psychology of Paranormal Belief: A Researcher's Handbook*. Hatfield: University of Hertfordshire Press.

Irwin, H.J. & Watt, C.A. (2007) *An Introduction to Parapsychology* (5th edn). Jefferson, NC: McFarland & Co. Inc.

Useful Websites

www.iands.org (International Association of Near-Death Studies)

www.northampton.ac.uk (The Centre for the Study of Anomalous Psychological Processes/CSAPP)

www.parapsych.org (Parapsychological Association)

www.goldsmiths.ac.uk/apru (Anomalistic Psychology Research Unit, Goldsmiths College, University of London)

www.koestler-parapsychology.psy.ed.ac.uk (Koestler Parapsychology Unit, Edinburgh University)

www.spr.ac.uk (Society for Psychical Research)

www.aspr.com (American Society for Psychical Research)

www.ehe.org (Exceptional Human Experience Network)

www.rhine.org (Rhine Research Center)

CHAPTER 7

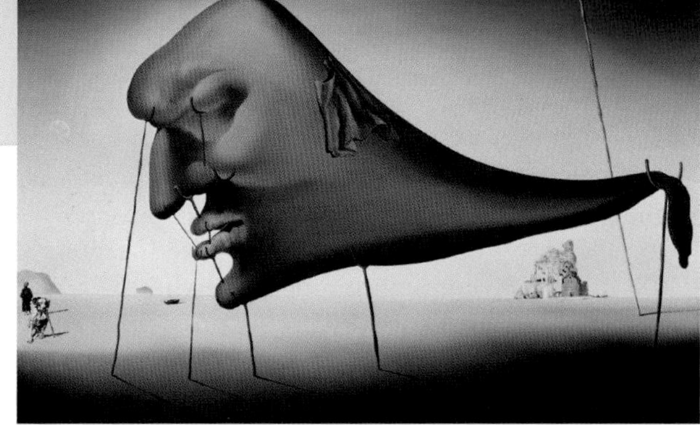

STATES OF CONSCIOUSNESS AND BODILY RHYTHMS

What is 'consciousness'?

Consciousness, arousal and alertness

Consciousness and attention

Consciousness and the brain

The functions of consciousness: what is it for?

Consciousness and the electroencephalogram (EEG)

Sleep

Dreaming

INTRODUCTION and OVERVIEW

For the first 30 or so years of its life as a separate discipline, pioneered by figures such as James and Wundt, Psychology took *conscious human experience* as its subject matter. As we saw in Chapter 1, *introspection* – the observation of one's own mind – was the primary method used to study it. This interest in consciousness shouldn't come as a surprise, given how fundamental it is to everything we do (Rubin and McNeill, 1983).

Yet it's the very *subjectivity* of our experience that led Watson to reject introspectionism in favour of a truly scientific (i.e. *objective*) approach to the study of Psychology, namely behaviourism. Writing from the perspective of a modern neuroscientist, Greenfield (1998) states that:

> *Any scientific explanation of consciousness must be objective and embrace physical properties of the brain: but at the same time it must, nonetheless, somehow take account of the subjective. This is why consciousness has been such an anathema to scientists, because the whole essence of science is objectivity. And yet we are going to deal with a phenomenon that is subjective …*

However, as part of the 'cognitive revolution' in the 1950s (which removed behaviourism from its dominant position within Psychology), 'the mind' once more became an acceptable focus of psychological research. Reflecting the current interest in consciousness among neuroscientists, philosophers and Psychologists, one of the questions we'll be asking is: How might the brain generate consciousness?

Since the 1950s, there's been a considerable amount of research into *sleep* as a state of consciousness, much of which involves trying to find correlations between objective measures of physiological activity and subjective experience, in particular *dreaming*. Sleep is increasingly being discussed in relation to bodily rhythms; disruption of these through our modern lifestyle is increasingly being seen as a risk to health. According to Hobson (1995), the rhythm of rest and activity, 'the primordia of sleeping and waking', represents one of the most universal and basic features of life. So, the study of sleep is of interest to biologists as well as to Psychologists.

WHAT IS 'CONSCIOUSNESS'?

Are only human beings 'conscious'?

Ask Yourself

- In what sense could non-human animals be described as conscious?

If being conscious means having sensations of pain, cold, hunger, fear, and so on, then most species can be said to be conscious (although '*sentient*' might be a better term than 'conscious'; see Chapter 48).

If by conscious we mean having *self-consciousness*, then humans may be unique (with the possible exception of some higher primates; see Chapters 19 and 33). According to Singer (1998), *self-awareness* (normally used synonymously with 'self-consciousness') is the experience of one's own individuality, the ability to experience oneself as an autonomous individual with subjective feelings. It's considered to be 'the result of social interactions, and hence of cultural evolution'. This suggests that it's a rather human thing to have.

Singer also claims that when we say we're conscious, we usually mean that we perceive and remember in a way that makes it possible to report on the perceived and remembered content, or to make it the object of intentional deliberations. Given the crucial role of language in these processes, and given that language is regarded by many as unique to humans (but see Chapter 19), the rest of this chapter will focus on consciousness as a characteristic of human beings.

Ask Yourself

- Can you think of some other ways in which we use the term '(un)conscious/consciousness' in everyday conversation?

Freud's theory of consciousness

Freud saw consciousness as a whole comprising three levels:

1. the *conscious* – what we're fully aware of at any one time
2. the *preconscious* – what we could become aware of quite easily if we switched our attention to it
3. the *unconscious* – what we've pushed out of our conscious minds, through *repression*, making it *inaccessible*, although it continues to exert an influence on our thoughts, feelings and behaviour (see Chapters 2 and 42).

Most Psychologists would agree that thoughts, feelings, memories, and so on, differ in their degree of accessibility. But most wouldn't accept Freud's formulation of the unconscious (based on repression). Indeed, other psychodynamic theorists, in particular Jung, disagreed fundamentally with Freud's view of the unconscious (see Chapter 42).

Rubin and McNeil (1983) define consciousness as 'our subjective awareness of our actions and of the world around us'. So, consciousness points both *inwards*, towards our thoughts, feelings, actions, and so on, and *outwards*, towards external, environmental events (including other people). This mirrors the 'mental' orientation of Wundt and James, and Cognitive Psychologists since the mid-1950s, and Watson's (and Skinner's) Behaviourist orientation, respectively.

CONSCIOUSNESS, AROUSAL AND ALERTNESS

Objective physiological measures, such as the *electroencephalogram* (EEG), *electromyogram* (EMG), *electrooculogram* (EOG) (see below), breathing and heart rates, and other correlates of consciousness, are often described as measures of level of *arousal or alertness*. Both subjectively and with regards overt behaviour, there's an obvious difference between being sleepy and being wide awake in terms of degree of arousal or alertness. Less obvious are the smaller changes that occur during normal wakefulness and that are of two kinds – tonic and phasic. These are mediated by different brain systems (Lloyd *et al.*, 1984).

Tonic alertness

Changes in tonic alertness reflect *intrinsic* (and usually quite slow) changes of the basic level of arousal throughout a 24-hour period (or even across a lifetime). They are closely related to various *biological rhythms*, in particular the *circadian rhythm* (see below). It was originally thought that the reticular formation (RF)/reticular activating system (RAS) was solely responsible for arousing and maintaining consciousness (in Chapter 4, the RAS was described as a 'consciousness switch'). For instance, if the brainstem is severed *below* the RAS, the animal will be paralysed but will remain fully alert when awake and will show normal sleep–wake EEG patterns. However, if it's sectioned *above* the RAS, it will fall into a state of continuous slow-wave sleep (see below).

During both wakefulness and sleep, there are periodic, fairly predictable changes in the degree of alertness: the daytime changes are governed by a *diurnal rhythm* and the sleep (night-time) changes by an *ultradian rhythm*.

Phasic alertness

Changes in *phasic alertness* involve short-term, temporary variations in arousal, over a period of seconds, initiated by novel and important environmental events. An important component of these changes is the *orienting response* to arousing stimuli. It involves a *decrease* in heart rate and breathing rate, pupil dilation, tensing of the muscles and characteristic changes in the EEG, which becomes *desynchronised*.

CONSCIOUSNESS AND ATTENTION

Although consciousness is difficult to describe because it's fundamental to everything we do (Rubin and McNeil, 1983), one way of trying to 'pin it down' is to study what we're paying attention to – what is in the

Box 7.1 Phasic alertness and evolution

- If stimuli are continuously presented, the orienting response is replaced by *habituation*: the person or animal stops responding to them.
- Habituation is, in fact, a form of *adaptation*. It's more important from a survival point of view to respond to novel stimuli rather than constant ones, and since most stimuli are relatively constant, we need to be able to attend selectively to those that are different and/or unexpected.
- It's the *changing* aspects of the environment that demand, and usually receive, our attention.

forefront of our consciousness. According to Allport (1980a), 'attention is the experimental psychologist's code name for consciousness'.

Focal and peripheral attention

Focal attention/awareness (what Beyerstein, 2007, calls 'executive consciousness') is what we're currently paying deliberate attention to and what's in the centre of our awareness (this corresponds to Freud's 'conscious'). All those other aspects of our environment (as well as our own thoughts and feelings), which are on the fringes of our awareness, but which could easily become the object of our focal attention, are within our *peripheral attention/awareness* (corresponding to Freud's 'preconscious').

We seem to be capable of doing many things quite unconsciously or automatically (without having to think about what we're doing). A good illustration of this is perception. It's difficult to imagine what it would be like if we were aware of how we perceive.

Conversely, something we normally do quite automatically, such as walking down stairs, might well be disrupted if we try to bring it into focal awareness (for example, thinking about each step as we take it – don't try this at home!). In general, being able to do things automatically makes sense in terms of freeing us to attend to those environmental events that are unfamiliar or threatening in some way. As Beyerstein (2007) puts it:

> *... one of the jobs of executive consciousness is to make as much of our behaviour as possible unconscious, i.e. to practise new skills while we must still pay careful attention to them, in an attempt to make as many behaviours as we can automatic ...*

In this way, the limited processing capacity of focal awareness can be freed up for attending to those things that do require our moment-to-moment

Box 7.2 Perception as an automatic process: doing what comes naturally

Ask Yourself

- If you haven't seen the picture below before, what do you see?
- If you have seen it before, try to explain how you saw what you saw when you first looked at it?

Figure 7.1 Boring's old/young 'woman'

- To select consciously one version of the ambiguous/reversible 'old/young woman' figure, we must either know that there's a young and an old woman 'in' the picture, or we must have already perceived both versions. (In which case, how did the original perception come about?)
- You may have had difficulty yourself perceiving the old woman if your immediate perception was of the young woman, even though you consciously 'searched' for, and tried to see, the alternative version.
- This illustrates the very important difference between *conception* and *perception*: most of the time, perception is something that we 'just do'. (See Chapter 15.)

monitoring and deliberation (Beyerstein, 2007). Learning to drive a car is a classic example (see Chapter 13).

Nisbett and Wilson (1977) go so far as to claim that *all* psychological activities (including social behaviour) are governed by processes of which we're unaware. If people are asked about what they think governed their behaviour after participating in a Social Psychology experiment, the answers they give don't usually correspond very well with the explanations Psychologists offer for the same behaviour (and which they believe are the *real reasons*).

Nisbett and Wilson argue that our belief that we can account for our own behaviour ('common sense' or *intuitive explanations*) is illusory, because what *really* guides our behaviour isn't available to consciousness. We don't have direct or 'privileged' access to our cognitive processes themselves, only to the products/outputs of those processes. Joynson (1974), Heather (1976) and other Psychologists present an opposing view, arguing that people are Psychologists, and that common-sense explanations may be as valid as theoretical, scientific ones (see Chapter 1 and Gross, 2014). Nisbett and Wilson are describing the *cognitive unconscious*, a dramatic demonstration of which is *blindsight* (see Chapter 5). (Also see Chapter 2 for a discussion of *neuropsychoanalysis*.)

Ask Yourself

- Do you lean towards Nisbett and Wilson on this issue, or Joynson and Heather?
- How might you try to choose between them?
- Is there a convergence between Nisbett and Wilson's ideas and Freud's, regarding the reasons 'ordinary' people give for their own behaviour and the explanations provided by Psychologists? (See Chapter 42.)

CONSCIOUSNESS AND THE BRAIN

Are there specific areas for consciousness?

Consistent with Nisbett and Wilson's claims regarding the cognitive unconscious is the finding that the neocortex can be active without necessarily giving rise to a conscious experience (Koch, 2012a). According to van Gaal (e.g. Wokke *et al.*, 2011), different brain regions must exchange information before consciousness can 'happen'. Similarly, Boly *et al.* (2011) demonstrated that feedback between the frontal cortex and the lower-level sensory areas is crucial to producing conscious experience. Diagnosis of patients in a vegetative state (VS) or minimally conscious state (MCS) is extremely difficult; the misdiagnosis rate can be as high as 40 per cent (Monti and Owen, 2010) (see below).

Similarly, Greenfield (1998) claims that a recurring problem in neuroscience in general is the difficulty of 'location of function'. Vision, memory and other brain/mind functions seem almost certainly to not be related in a modular way to single respective brain regions. Many different regions play parallel roles, analysing the outside world in various ways and reintegrating it into a connected whole. This is also likely to be true of consciousness.

However, we now know that some regions of the cortex have a privileged relationship to consciousness and that they don't all contribute equally to generating a conscious experience (Koch, 2012b). Two such regions are the *anterior cingulate cortex* (ACC) and the *fronto-insular* (FI) cortex, in both of which are found giant brain cells, called *von Economo neurons* (VENs). Both areas are heavily involved in many of the more advanced aspects of our inner lives, such as reacting to socially relevant cues (e.g. facial expressions and strong emotions); they also play a key role in the 'salience network', which keeps a subconscious tally of what's going on around us and directs our attention to the most pressing events, as well as detecting changes in bodily sensations (Williams, 2012). The ACC and FI are also both active when we recognise our reflection in the mirror, suggesting that they underlie our sense of self – a key component of consciousness (see Chapter 33).

Dementia, autism and consciousness

In *fronto-temporal dementia*, patients (sometimes in their 30s) lose large numbers of VENs in the ACC and FI early in the disease, when the main symptom is a complete loss of social awareness, empathy and self-control.

Postmortems of the brains of people with autism also support the idea that VENs are central to our emotional reactions and empathy. Some are found to have *too many* VENs; this may make emotional systems fire too intensely, causing the individual to feel overwhelmed (as many say they do) (Williams, 2012). (See Chapter 40.)

Consciousness in other species

VENs have now been identified in chimpanzees and gorillas, elephants, and some whales and dolphins. As Williams (2012) observes, many of these species live in large social groups and show signs of empathy and even grief (elephants); many also display mirror self-recognition (see Chapter 33). Yet VENs are also found in mantees, hippos, giraffes, and macaques, none of which is especially 'social' or has demonstrated mirror self-recognition.

Consciousness and brain damage

Monti and Owen (2010) describe the case of Martha, a brain-injured patient whose eyes are now open. In medical terms, the return of alternating cycles of sleep and wakefulness mark her progression from *coma* (comatose state) to a *vegetative state* (VS) (Jennet and Plum, 1972). However, although her eyes are open and she gives the impression of 'seeing', in fact she doesn't. Visual information may well reach several centres of her brain dedicated to processing visual information, and her brain may even respond differently to different categories of objects. But this doesn't mean she's aware of what it is she's looking at.

Consciousness can be conceptualised as comprising two key components (Laureys, 2005): (a) *level* (i.e. wakefulness) and (b) *content* (i.e. awareness). Table 7.1 shows how these two components are typically present or absent in different normal and abnormal states/conditions.

Table 7.1 The appearance of level (wakefulness) and content (awareness) of consciousness as displayed in different normal and abnormal states/conditions (based on Monti and Owen, 2010)

	Consciousness	
Normal/abnormal states/conditions	Level (wakefulness)	Content (awareness)
Healthy (awake) individual	✓	✓
Comatose patient	X	X
Under general anaesthetic	Very low	Very low
From deep sedation/sleep → wakefulness	✓	✓
Vegetative state (VS)	✓ (apparent)	X
REM ('dream') sleep and (other) oneiric (dream-related) experiences	X	✓

Unlike the healthy (awake) individual and comatose patient, in whom wakefulness and awareness vary together, in the VS they seem to *dissociate*: VS patients appear to be awake but they aren't aware. The reverse dissociation occurs naturally during REM sleep, and especially during *oneiric* experiences, where a subjective feeling of awareness is often present despite the individual not being awake. (See Gross, 2012a.)

Detecting consciousness via functional neuroimaging

In the past ten years, an increasing number of research studies have highlighted the possibility that functional neuroimaging technology (such as PET and fMRI) can be used to look directly into the brain for indicators of consciousness. Monti and Owen (2010) cite two such studies which highlighted the fact that, despite severe brain injury, it's possible to retain relatively high-level brain activity. The crucial question is: can brain activity be used as a substitute for voluntary motor behaviour in revealing the presence of consciousness? This can be answered by viewing voluntary brain activity as a form of non-muscle-dependent behaviour which, like voluntary motor behaviour, implies the presence of awareness (Owen and Coleman, 2008). A striking application of this idea is described in Box 7.3.

Box 7.3 Playing tennis, walking and consciousness

- A patient who failed to display any voluntary behaviour when tested at the bedside (and so was diagnosed VS), could voluntarily modulate brain activity by producing different kinds of mental imagery (Owen *et al.*, 2006). When tested with fMRI, the patient was asked to imagine playing tennis and, at a different time, to imagine walking around the rooms of her home. Importantly, while the patient was instructed to sustain the imagery for 30-second periods, the only sensory stimulation was a one-second-long aural cue instructing her to focus on one or other of the imagery tasks.
- Strikingly, despite being unable to produce any type of wilful motor behaviour to demonstrate that she was conscious, the patient was able to produce wilful 'brain behaviour' by up-and-down modulation of her brain activity; this confirmed that she was engaging in the two imagery tasks.
- When control participants (healthy individuals) were tested, it was found that unless they understood the task instructions and had decided to comply with them, no brain activity was observed (Owen *et al.*, 2007). This totally discounts the possibility that the patient's brain activity may have reflected an automatic response.
- Monti *et al.* (2009) presented a listener with a series of emotionally neutral words, and alternately instructed them to either listen passively, or to count how many times a given target word was repeated. The types of words used, their number and repetition were all controlled. When a patient with severe brain injury was tested, the counting task revealed activation of the fronto-parietal regions typically associated with detecting targets and *working memory* (see Chapter 17). Unless the patient had understood the instructions, decided to co-operate, and retailed a level of cognitive processing sufficient to perform the task, how could the same stimuli have led to systematically different activations?

Such non-invasive neuroimaging techniques are now beginning to allow us to redefine the meaning of 'appearance' and 'acts' to include non-muscle-dependent 'brain acts'. Indeed, functional neuroimaging can be used to allow aware, but non-responsive, patients to convey their state of consciousness without relying on muscle-dependent behaviour.

Building on their earlier work, Naci and Owen (2013) have developed a strategy to enable people in a VS to answer questions with yes/no answers. This is described in Key Study 7.1

Key Study 7.1

Every word counts (Naci and Owen, 2013)

- The aim of the study was to test whether selective auditory attention can be used to detect conscious awareness and communicate with behaviourally non-responsive patients.
- The participants were three patients with severe brain injury – two MCS (minimally conscious state) and one VS (for 12 years).
- After asking questions, such as about their name, and whether they were in a hospital, the researchers repeated the word 'yes' several times, interspersing the word 'yes' with distracting, random numbers. They did the same for 'no'.
- The patients had been told beforehand to indicate their answer by paying close attention to how many times their desired answer was repeated.
- fMRI was used to indicate when they were concentrating. The task was so demanding that they could easily ignore their non-preferred answer.
- All three showed the ability to follow the instructions; one of the MCS patient and the VS patient were also able to guide their attention to repeatedly communicate correct answers to several yes/no questions.

THE FUNCTIONS OF CONSCIOUSNESS: WHAT IS IT FOR?

Like perception, many cases of problem-solving seem to involve processes that are 'out of consciousness'. For example, solutions often seem to 'pop into our head' and we don't know how we reached them. If what's important is the solution (as opposed to the process involved in reaching it), then consciousness may be seen as incidental to information processing (consistent with Nisbett and Wilson's view). But while perception and other basic cognitive and behavioural processes may not *require* consciousness, they're at least usually *accompanied* by consciousness. Assuming that most other species lack our kind of consciousness, then we can infer that it evolved in human beings for some purpose.

Ask Yourself

- From an evolutionary perspective, what advantages do you think (self-) consciousness might have conferred on human beings?
- What does it allow you to do in relation to other people?

The complexity of our nervous system, which makes our consciousness possible, provided our ancestors with the flexibility of behaviour that helped them survive. However, it's less obvious whether consciousness was itself adaptive or simply a side-effect or byproduct of a complex nervous system. Some Psychologists and biologists believe that consciousness is a powerful agent for controlling behaviour, which has evolved *in its own right*. Accordingly, non-conscious problem-solving systems are seen as the servants of consciousness (Ruch, 1984).

Box 7.4 Evolution of the 'inner eye'

- Humphrey (1986, 1993) argues that if consciousness (what he calls the 'inner eye') is the answer to anything at all, it must be to a biological challenge that human beings have had to meet, namely the human need to understand, respond to and manipulate the behaviour of other human beings:

  ... The first use of human consciousness was – and is – to enable each human being to understand what it feels like to be human and so to make sense of himself and other people from the inside. (Humphrey, 1993)
- This inner eye allowed our ancestors to raise social life to a new level, so that consciousness is essential for human social activity. We are natural psychologists in a way that species lacking consciousness cannot be (see Gross, 2014).

CONSCIOUSNESS AND THE ELECTROENCEPHALOGRAM (EEG)

Electroencephalography (literally, 'electric-in-head writing') detects the output of minute electrical 'ripples', caused by changes in the electrical charges in different parts of the brain (usually the synchronised activity of large groups of neurons). Although there are characteristic patterns common to all individuals of a particular age or developmental stage, individuals' brain activity is as unique and distinctive as their fingerprints. Brain activity is traced on paper by pens which appear as rows of oscillating waves.

The waves vary in *frequency*, measured as the number of oscillations per second – the more oscillations, the higher the frequency. One complete oscillation is a cycle, and the frequency is expressed as cycles per second (cps) or hertz (Hz).

Box 7.5 The four major types of brain wave (measured in frequency)

- **Delta (1–2 Hz)**: found mainly in infants, sleeping adults or adults with brain tumours
- **Theta (3–7 Hz)**: found mainly in children aged 2–5 years, and in psychopaths (see Chapter 46); may be induced by frustration
- **Alpha (8–12 Hz)**: found mainly in adults who are awake, relaxed and whose eyes are closed; most reliably recorded from the back of the scalp
- **Beta (13 Hz and over)**: found mainly in adults who are awake and alert, whose eyes are open, and who may be concentrating on some task or other; most reliably recorded from the middle of the scalp, and related to activity in the somatosensory and motor cortex.

(See Table 7.2, p. 115)

Computerised electroencephalography has recently been used to detect evoked potentials. Often the average of a number of responses to similar kinds of stimuli is used – the *average evoked potential* (AEP) – in order to amplify the signal-to-noise ratio. AEPs are used to study newborns, some children with learning problems, patients in a coma, stroke victims, tumour patients and patients with multiple sclerosis. However, for certain brain conditions, brain scanning has largely replaced the EEG (Diagram Group (1982); see Chapter 4).

SLEEP

Sleep and the circadian rhythm

Ask Yourself

- Blakemore (1988) asks what would happen if we removed all the external cues to the nature of time (*zeitgebers*), both natural (day and night) and manufactured (clocks, mealtimes).
- Would our bodies still have their own rhythmic existence?

According to Blakemore (1988):

> *For all the advances of modern society, we cannot afford to ignore the rhythms of the animal brain within us, any more than we can neglect our need to breathe or eat. Without the biological clocks in our brains, our lives would be chaotic, our actions disorganised. The brain has internalised the rhythms of Nature, but can tick on for months without sight of the sun ...*

Most animals display a *circadian rhythm* (from the Latin '*circa dies*' = 'about one day'). This is a rhythmical alternation (*periodicity*) of various physiological and behavioural functions, synchronised to the 24-hour cycle of light and dark. So, during a 24-hour period, there's a cycle of several physiological functions (heart rate, metabolic rate, breathing rate, body temperature, hormonal secretion, urine excretion, immune function, alertness, and so on), which all tend to reach maximum values during the late afternoon and early evening, and minimum values in the early hours of the morning.

Box 7.6 Aschoff: the founder of chronobiology

- Aschoff's experiments conducted in a disused Munich bunker in the 1960s were the first to reveal the body's independent sleep–wake cycle in its naked state.
- For several weeks, his participants lived in isolation, collecting their own urine and monitoring their body temperatures. Dim lights were entirely under their control, but no time clues or information from the outside world was allowed.
- Despite no exposure to sunrise, participants still tended to sleep for 8 hours. However, their awake time stretched slightly beyond 16 hours; this revealed an internal clock that ran 20 minutes slower than the 24-hour day. Their days settled into a pattern of about 24.3 hours, so that with each passing day, they went to sleep later and later until they were entirely out of sync with the rhythms of normal life.
- Aschoff's participants spent at most 28 days in the bunker.

(Based on Gamble, 2013)

The internal or biological clock

Rats, like humans, have an inherent rhythm of about 25 hours, which dictates their cycle of sleep and waking if they're put in the dark. This internal clock is as reliable and regular as most manufactured ones – the rhythm deviates by no more than a few minutes

Case Study 7.1

Siffre and the 25-hour day

- In 1972, Michel Siffre, a young French geologist, spent eight weeks underground with no clues as to the time of day.
- He had adequate food, water, books and exercise equipment, and his only contact with the outside world was via a telephone that was permanently staffed. He was linked up to a computer and video camera, by which scientists on the surface could monitor his physiological functions and state of mind.
- He organised his life into a fairly normal pattern of alternating periods of activity and sleep, and his 'day' was broken up by a normal meal pattern.
- However, his *subjective* time had passed at half the speed of clock time. He'd made a transition to a 48-hour day (36 hours activity, 12 hours sleep). He later confirmed this when spending six months in Texan caves.

(Source: Blakemore, 1988)

over several months. So how is the internal (biological) clock reset each day to the cycle of the real world, and where is the 'clock' to be found?

It's thought to be a tiny cluster of neurons, the *suprachiasmatic nucleus* (SCN), situated in the medial hypothalamus. For example, damage to the SCN in rats produces complete disappearance of the circadian rhythm: the sleep–wake cycle, eating and drinking, hormone secretion, and so on, become completely random during the course of the 24-hour period. Most of what's known about the SCN is based on experiments with non-human animals using ablation (see Chapter 4), and we cannot make direct electrophysiological recordings from the human brain. But anatomical studies show that humans have an SCN (Empson, 1993) whose function is to synchronise all the bodily functions that are governed by the circadian rhythm.

The SCN is situated directly above the optic chiasma (the junction of the two optic nerves en route to the brain; see Chapter 5). A tuft of thin nerve fibres branches off from the main nerve and penetrates the hypothalamus above, forming synaptic connections with cells in the SCN. This anatomically insignificant pathway is the link between the outside world and the brain's own clock (Blakemore, 1988). So the retina projects directly onto the SCN, which ensures that the sleep–wake cycle is tuned to the rhythm of night and day. If this connection with the retina is severed, the cycle goes 'haywire'.

The effects of disrupting the biological clock

So, in human adults at least, it appears that the circadian rhythm doesn't depend primarily on external cues, although it's surprisingly easy to outsmart our body clock by external means, such as alarm clocks.

Ask Yourself

- What is an average night's sleep for you?
- Is that as much as you really need?
- If not, what ill-effects are you experiencing?

Figure 7.2 Whatever happened to lunchbreaks? Our work-hungry society demands that we eat at our work-stations – part of our '24/7' lifestyle

Is too little sleep harmful?

There's plenty of evidence (scientific and anecdotal) connecting lack of sleep with both accidents and mental disorder. Dement (2000) believes that most of us carry a heavy 'sleep debt', a deficit of sleep built up over days, weeks and months. Sleep debt is dangerous, and potentially lethal. The RAC warned that sleepy drivers were responsible for 20,000 crashes in 2005 (Revill, 2006), including those who actually fall asleep at the wheel. In addition, pilots may be too sleepy to land planes safely, and surgeons may botch surgical procedures because they're exhausted. Both the Exxon Valdez and the Challenger space shuttle disasters were attributed to human error caused by extreme sleep deprivation.

The physiology of sleep

When darkness falls, the eyes indirectly inform the *pineal gland* (the 'third eye'). This is a tiny structure at the top of the brainstem, which keeps track of the body's natural cycles and registers external factors such as light and darkness. The pineal gland secretes *melatonin* in response to darkness, making us drowsy. Melatonin ('nature's sleeping draught'; Downing,

Figure 7.3 The 1986 Challenger space shuttle exploding on live TV, killing all seven astronauts on board

1988) is a hormone that affects brain cells, which produce serotonin, concentrated in the raphe nuclei (situated near the pons), and these secrete a substance that acts on the RAS to induce light sleep. Jouvet (1967) found that lesions of the *raphe nuclei* in cats produced severe insomnia, and naturally occurring lesions in humans seem to have a very similar effect.

Another important sleep centre is the *locus coeruleus* (LC), a tiny structure on each side of the brainstem, whose cells are rich in noradrenaline, thought to be involved in inducing active (or rapid eye movement (REM)) sleep (see below). The LC may well serve many of the functions previously attributed to the RAS. Studies with rats suggest that the LC regulates the animal's level of *vigilance* to environmental stimuli (Empson, 1993).

There's also evidence that a substance called *factor S* accumulates gradually in the brains of animals while they're awake. If this is removed from the fluid surrounding the brain and transferred into another animal, sleep will be induced. It's likely that factor S contributes to our feelings of sleepiness (Diagram Group, 1982).

Varieties of sleep and the ultradian rhythm

In the typical sleep laboratory, a volunteer settles down for the night with not only EEG wires attached, but also wires from an *electrooculogram* (EOG) ('oculo' meaning eye) and an *electromyogram* (EMG) ('myo' meaning muscle) (see Figure 7.6). Collectively, these are called *polysomnography* (PSG) (Nishida *et al.*, 2009).

A typical night's sleep comprises between four and five *ultradian cycles* (lasting approximately 90 minutes), and each cycle consists of a number of stages (see Table 7.2). The cycle then goes into reverse, so we re-enter stage 3 and then stage 2, but instead of re-entering stage 1, a different kind of sleep (*active sleep*) appears. Pulse and respiration rates increase, as does blood pressure, and all three processes become less regular. EEGs begin to resemble those of the waking state, showing that

Critical Discussion 7.1

Insomnia and mental disorder

Young (2009) cites a 1987 American study of 1053 male medical students who'd been followed for an average of 34 years after graduation. During that time, 101 of them had developed clinical depression, 13 of whom had committed suicide. Those who'd reported suffering from insomnia were twice as likely to become depressed as those with no sleep problems. One conclusion drawn from these data was that insomnia can predispose people to depression. Consistent with this conclusion, Young cites evidence that treating depressed patients' sleep problems (with a drug such as benzodiazepine; see Chapters 44 and 45) can produce a dramatic improvement in their mood disorder. For some patients, insomnia seems to cause depression. *Sleep apnea* may cause or aggravate psychiatric symptoms and the oxygen deprivation may harm cells or disrupt normal brain functioning (Levine, 2012).

Impaired sleep can also induce the manic episodes involved in *bipolar disorder* (see Chapter 44), as well as failure of a sleep-dependent component of *procedural learning* (such as mastering a piece of machinery) associated with schizophrenia (Stickgold, 2004, cited in Young, 2009).

During REM sleep (see text below), the *visceral* component of our memories (the experience of anger, fear, etc.) is stripped away from the more *cognitive* component. This happens because the neurotransmitters associated with stress, fear, and the fight-or-flight response, serotonin and noradrenaline, are shut down. So, although dreams can be emotional, they gradually take the 'emotional edge' off our memories (Young, 2009, see text below).

Another aspect of the sleeping disorders problem is that many people will be taking hypnotics (sleeping pills) and anti-depressants prescribed to help with the problem, but which produce problems of their own (see Chapters 8 and 45). Conversely, many more people are taking recently marketed drugs designed to help people *stay awake*. For example, *modafinil* is a stimulant (launched in 1999) which doesn't appear to have the side-effects of other stimulants such as caffeine and amphetamines, including the jitters, euphoria and eventual crash (Lawton, 2006).

the brain is active, supported by increases in oxygen consumption, blood flow and neural firing in many brain structures. But it's even more difficult to wake us from this kind of sleep than the deep stage 4 sleep, which is why it's called *paradoxical sleep* (Aserinsky and Kleitman, 1953).

Another characteristic of active sleep is the rapid eye movements (the eyeballs moving back and forth, up and down, together) under the closed lids (hence *rapid eye movement* (REM) *sleep*). Finally, while the brain may be very active, the body isn't. REM sleep is characterised by muscular paralysis (especially the muscles of the arms and legs), so that all the tossing and turning and other typical movements associated with sleep in fact only occur during stages 1–4 (*non-rapid eye movement* (NREM) *sleep*). The distinction between REM and NREM sleep was originally made by Dement and Kleitman (1957).

Another feature of REM sleep is the appearance of *pontine-geniculo-occipital* (PGO) *spikes/waves*, which are generated in the pons and travel through the lateral geniculate nucleus (LGN). These were discovered by Jouvet working with cats in the 1960s. PGO spikes typically occur in bursts, often preceding individual eye movements. According to the *activation-synthesis model* of dreaming (see below), PGO activity is the prime source of dreaming experience (Empson, 1993).

After 15 minutes or so in REM sleep, we re-enter NREM sleep (stages 2–4), and so another ultradian cycle begins. However, with each 90-minute cycle, the duration of REM sleep *increases* and that of NREM sleep *decreases*. The first cycle normally provides the deepest sleep and the shortest REM period. As the night goes on, we spend relatively more time in REM and less in NREM sleep. In later cycles, it's quite common to go from REM to stage 2, and then straight back into REM sleep (bypassing stages 3 and 4). Natural waking usually occurs during a period of REM sleep (see Figure 7.5).

According to Empson (1993):

> *While most all-night recording experiments are over brief periods (of up to a week), some very extended studies have been done and there is no evidence that the patterns of sleep we observe over short periods (after the first night) are in any way peculiar to the unfamiliarity of the laboratory environment.*

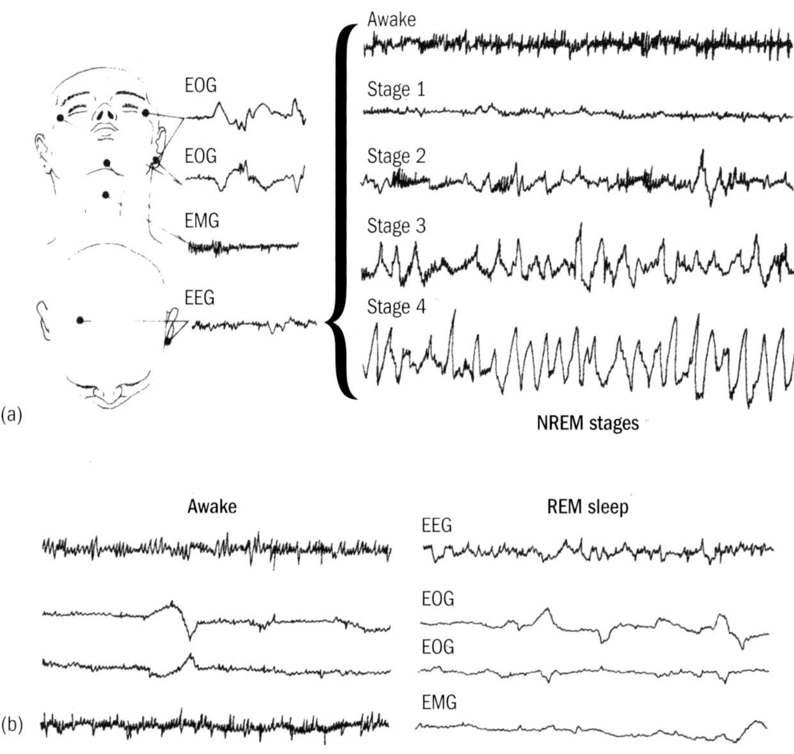

Figure 7.4 Comparison of physiological measures for different types of sleep. (a) The non-rapid eye movement (NREM) stages are represented in typical order of appearance; in reality each one gradually blends into the next. (b) Rapid eye movement (REM) sleep is in some ways similar to waking but in others quite different; the EEG is more similar to waking than to that of any NREM stage and REMs are present, but the body muscles are deeply inhibited

Table 7.2 A typical night's sleep: The four stages of non-rapid eye movement (NREM) sleep

After we shut our eyes and prepare to sleep, *alpha waves* begin to punctuate the high frequency *beta waves* of active wakefulness. The transition from being awake to entering stage 1 sleep is called the *hypnagogic period*, and is sometimes included in stage 1.
Stage 1: When we first fall asleep, the EEG is irregular and lacks the pattern of alpha waves which characterises the relaxed waking state. At first there's a reduction in frequency of alpha waves, which are then replaced by low voltage, slow *theta waves*, accompanied by slow rolling eye movements. Heart rate begins to slow down, the muscles relax, but we can still be woken up easily.
Stage 2: This is a deeper state of sleep, but we can still be woken fairly easily. The EEG shows bursts of activity called *sleep spindles* (1- to 2-second waxing and waning bursts of 12–14 Hz waves). There are also occasional sharp rises and falls in amplitude of the whole EEG (*K complexes*), which last up to two seconds.
Stage 3: Sleep becomes deeper, the spindles disappear and are replaced by long, slow *delta waves* for up to 50 per cent of the EEG record. We're now quite unresponsive to external stimuli, and so it's difficult to wake us up. Heart rate, blood pressure and body temperature all continue to drop.
Stage 4: We now enter *delta sleep* (deep or 'quiet sleep': 50 per cent and more of the record consists of delta waves) and will spend up to 30 minutes in stage 4. About an hour has elapsed since stage 1 began. As in stage 3, it's difficult to wake us, unless something happens that's of great personal significance (such as our baby crying). But this is when *sleepwalking* is most likely to occur, especially in children/adolescents. Other parasomnias (unwanted behaviours during sleep) can occur at any one/more sleep stages (including NREM and REM) (Idzikowski, 2013).
Stages 2–4 collectively are called *slow-wave sleep* (SWS). As we pass from stages 1 to 4, the frequency of the waves decreases, and the amplitude/voltage increases. Also, muscle tone steadily declines.

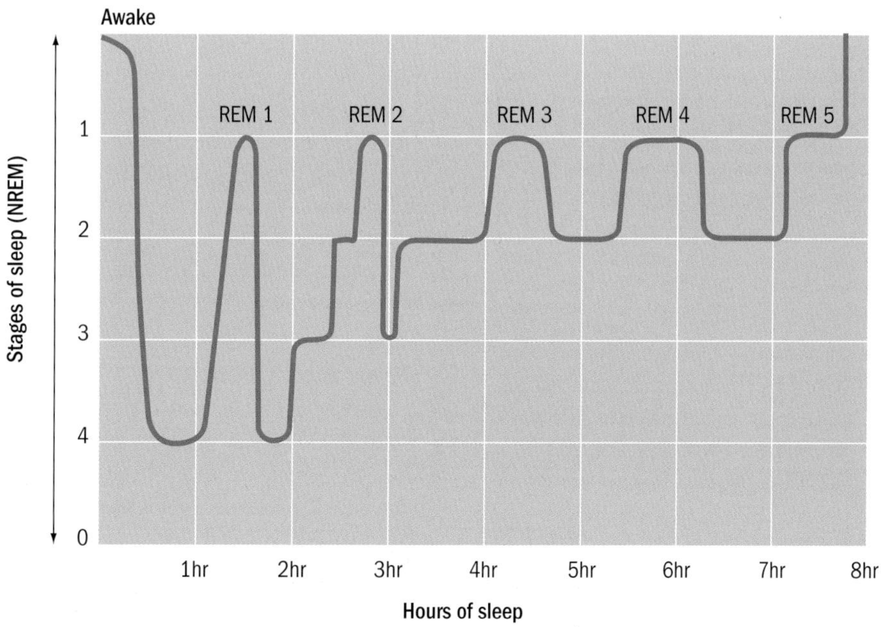

Figure 7.5 A typical night's sleep (note the disappearance of stages 3 and 4 and the relative increase in the length of REM periods)

Ask Yourself

- Construct a summary table of differences between REM and NREM sleep.

Functions of sleep

Problem-solving

Research has shown that REM sleep aids problem-solving (PS). For example, Wamsley and Stickgold (2010) asked participants to navigate a virtual maze. After some practice, they had either a waking break, REM sleep, or a non-REM sleep period. Only REM was found to sharpen their performance. When participants were woken or interrupted and asked what they were thinking/dreaming, the theme was often the maze – but only when this thinking occurred in REM sleep did they perform better the next time they tackled the maze. Because REM sleep is associated with dreaming, these studies imply that dreaming might have something to do with creative PS (Barrett, 2011).

Kekule's famous dream of the structure of benzene (in the form a snake made of atoms taking its tail into its mouth) illustrates the two distinctive features of PS in dreams: (i) the brain areas that usually restrict our thinking to the logical and the familiar are more *disinhibited* during REM sleep; (ii) the high activity in the visual areas of the sleeping brain allows it to visualise solutions more readily than when awake. Dreamed solutions tend to have unusual visual characteristics (Barrett, 2011).

Sleep and learning

While it has been demonstrated that sleep can strengthen previously acquired memories (see below), whether humans can acquire entirely new information hadn't been demonstrated until a study by Arzi *et al.* (2012) (See Key Study 7.2.)

Sleep and memory

The prevailing view amongst researchers claims that recently formed memories are 'replayed' during sleep and become consolidated in the process: synaptic connections that have been strengthened while the individual is awake are further reinforced while sleeping (Castro, 2012). This process is known as '*synaptic potentiation*'.

This view arose from studies over the past 20 years, first in rats, then in humans, which showed that patterns of neural activity during sleep resemble those recorded while the 'subject' is awake. For example, when a rat learns to navigate a maze, certain neurons in the hippocampus fire in specific sequences; during subsequent sleep, rats 'replay' these sequences more often than predicted by chance (Tononi and Cirelli, 2013).

Key Study 7.2

Learning to sniff in your sleep (Arzi *et al.*, 2012)

- While asleep, dozens of participants were exposed to pleasant (deodorant or shampoo) or unpleasant (rotten fish or carrion) odours. The pleasant smells triggered deeper sniffs compared with the unpleasant.
- Using partial-reinforcement trace conditioning (see Chapter 11), the odours were paired with distinct auditory tones.
- Later in the night, the tones were presented alone and the still-sleeping participants sniffed more deeply to tones previously paired with a pleasant smell.
- This acquired behaviour pattern persisted throughout the night and into the morning when the participants were awake – but this latter finding applied only to NREM sleep.
- Participants had no memory of what had happened while asleep.

However, Tononi and Cirelli's (2013) *synaptic homeostasis hypothesis* (SHY) turns this accepted view on its head, by claiming that sleep performs the vital function of synaptic *weakening*. The neural circuits underlying new memories can only be strengthened so many times before reaching their maximum strength: sleep serves as a reset button, loosening neural connections throughout the brain, restoring it to a flexible state (plasticity) in which (new) learning can take place (Castro, 2012).

For the brain to be able to integrate new and old memories, it needs respite from all the stimulation that comes from the external environment: this is precisely what sleep offers.

What evidence do Tononi and Cirelli offer for their SHY? (See Box 7.7.)

Sleep and dreaming

Rapid eye movements and dreams

Since Aserinsky and Kleitman's (1957) distinction between REM and NREM sleep, REM sleep has come to be equated with dreaming ('dream sleep' or the 'D-state'). This was based on studies using the basic methodology in which sleeping volunteers are deliberately woken from one or other kind of sleep. REMs seem to be a very reliable indicator that someone is dreaming (especially in combination with the fairly high-frequency and low-amplitude brain waves).

Box 7.7 Evidence for SHY (Tononi and Cirelli, 2013)

- Strong synapses consume more energy than weak ones and the brain doesn't have unlimited energy stores. The brain accounts almost 20 per cent of the body's total energy budget, with two-thirds of that devoted to supporting synaptic activity.
- Building and strengthening synapses is a major source of cellular stress.
- Synaptic weakening during sleep would restore brain circuitry to a baseline level of strength, thereby avoiding excessive energy consumption and cellular stress.
- In principle, SHY can account for the essential, universal purpose of sleep: the risk we take by becoming disengaged from the external environment for hours at a time is the price we pay for this 'neural recalibration'. Clearly, this applies differently to different species (as discussed in the text below on the evolutionary theory).
- More generally, sleep is the price we pay for the brain's plasticity – its ability to modify its wiring in response to experience. Again the human brain is uniquely plastic (see Gross, 2012a), which implies that SHY is especially relevant to explaining human sleep.
- Based on computer simulations and experiments with both humans and non-humans, Tononi and Cirelli conclude that (i) the large, steep slow waves early in the night indicate that synapses have been strengthened by prior wakefulness, whereas (ii) the small, shallow slow waves early in the morning indicate that synapses have become weaker during sleep (*down selection*) (see Table 7.2). SWS seems to pull the brain back to some kind of equilibrium that being awake has disturbed.
- While it's been accepted for a long time that SWS is necessary and restorative, Tononi and Cirelli report that people deprived of SWS tend to compensate for it with longer and more intense bouts subsequently.

The correlation between dreams and REM sleep is real enough – but it isn't perfect. (Vivid) dreaming is reported from 70–95 per cent of REM awakenings, but only 5–10 per cent of NREM awakenings (Blackmore, 2003) Mentation (mental activity) of some sort is reported in about 50 per cent of NREM awakenings. The figures vary according to the criteria used (Empson, 2001). So, being in REM sleep doesn't guarantee dreaming, and, conversely, dreaming can and does occur in NREM sleep.

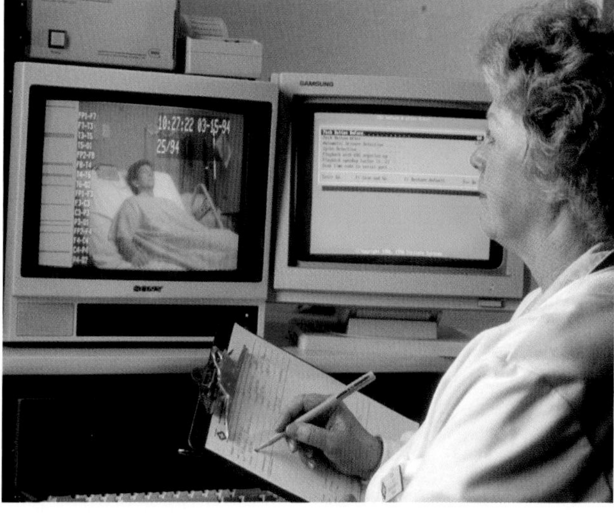

Figure 7.6 A modern sleep laboratory

Solms and Turnbull (2007) cite a 1997 study of six patients who, despite damage to the REM-generating regions of the *pons*, still considered they were still dreaming. Over 40 other patients with damage to two specific parts of the *forebrain* (nowhere near the critical REM-generating structures) *did* experience a cessation of dreaming – even though their REM state was preserved.

Human foetuses spend about 15 hours per day in REM sleep – but they couldn't be 'dreaming' (since experience of the world is the 'raw material' of dreams; see below). The combination of all this evidence, together with what we know about REM sleep in other species (and from what we believe about their dreams and state of consciousness) leads to only one conclusion: that the 'REM sleep = dreaming' equation is seriously mistaken.

There are also *methodological* problems involved in equating REM sleep with dreaming, as discussed in Box 7.8.

However, evidence from studies of sleep deprivation seems to support the view of REM sleep as a dream-state sleep quite independently of the sleeper's report of having dreamed (or not).

The effects of sleep deprivation

As far as rats are concerned, long-term sleep deprivation is definitely not good for their health: it causes impaired thermoregulation, metabolic dysfunction and eventually death (Hobson, 1995). For example, Rechtschaffen *et al.* (1989a, 1989b) selectively deprived rats of either REM or both REM and NREM sleep. After a week of total deprivation, they showed progressive weight loss despite increased food intake. This became more pronounced after two weeks, and after four weeks they died. (According to Siegel (in Young, 2008), it was *stress* that killed them, rather than sleep deprivation.)

Box 7.8 The methodology of dream recall

- Beaumont (1988) argues that being woken from NREM sleep may lead to the dream being forgotten before the participant is sufficiently awake to report it (since this is a deeper kind of sleep in which the brain is much less active).
- By contrast, being woken from REM sleep may allow the ongoing dream to be remembered and then reported (here the brain is much more active).
- Clearly, if this is so, then we've stumbled upon a major confounding variable that challenges the very basis of much of the sleep/dream research.
- Foulkes (1962, cited in Solms and Turnbull, 2007) observed that you're most likely to have dreams in NREM sleep just after you've 'dropped off' (that is, during the *sleep-onset* phase/descending stages 1 and 2). If woken during this first few minutes, participants report dreams about 70 per cent of the time. Most people don't remember these dreams when they wake up in the morning, which means they cannot be misremembered REM dreams as some theorists have claimed.

In the case of human beings, studies have been remarkably consistent in failing to show any marked changes in heart and breathing rates, blood pressure, skin conduction, body temperature, EMG or EEG, even when deprivation continues for up to 200 hours (Pinel, 1993). But as we saw above, this is very different from the chronic sleep deprivation that is symptomatic of our modern (western) lifestyle.

Webb and Bonnet (1979) limited participants to two hours' sleep on one particular night; they suffered no ill-effects the following day, but that night they fell asleep more quickly and slept longer than usual. Longer periods of sleep deprivation may result in some unpleasant psychological effects, but people are remarkably able to do without sleep. Webb and Bonnet gradually reduced the length of sleep in a group of volunteers from eight to four hours per night over a two-month period, with no detectable effect.

Theories of sleep

According to Blakemore (1988):

> *... Even human beings, the most spectacularly successful species, spend one-third of their lives more or less paralysed and senseless. If sleep is so risky, it must bestow a huge benefit on animals that indulge in it, or it would have been eliminated by the powerful forces of natural selection. Animals that did not need sleep would surely have evolved and prevailed over their sleepy competitors ... sleep must surely be valuable ...*

Box 7.9 The REM rebound

- When sleep is abruptly reduced (as, for example, in the case of hospital doctors, who may be on duty for 50 hours at a stretch), the effects are rather more serious. These effects include irritability, intellectual inefficiency, and an intense fatigue and need for sleep.
- These effects mirror those produced by depriving participants of approximately two hours of REM sleep (but otherwise allowing them to sleep normally). The following night, there's an increase in REM sleep (to compensate for the previous night's loss). This is called the *REM rebound*.
- When volunteers are able to get by on greatly (but gradually) reduced amounts of sleep, it's apparently because they pack their two hours of REM tightly into their sleeping time (thus reducing the amount of NREM sleep in between their dreams). When sleep is abruptly reduced, there's no time to adopt this alternative dreaming-sleep pattern.
- Dement (1960) woke participants from their REM sleep on five successive nights (while those in a control group were only woken during NREM sleep periods). When they were allowed to sleep uninterruptedly, they did 60 per cent more dreaming until they'd made up their lost REM time. For as many as five nights following their REM deprivation, they spent more time in REM sleep than usual, and on some nights they doubled their REM time.

Empson (1993) maintains that even though physiologists have made great strides in understanding sleep mechanisms, this hasn't greatly helped in understanding what sleep is *for*. While sleep has the features of a *primary drive* (such as hunger and sex), what makes it unique as a primary biological drive is that the need for sleep is reflected in *decreased levels of arousal*, and its satisfaction is associated with further decreases. Sleep, therefore, represents a serious exception to the view that organisms seek a single optimal level of (non-specific) arousal (Lloyd *et al.*, 1984; see Chapter 9).

The restoration theory

Oswald (1966) maintained that both REM and NREM sleep serve a restorative, replenishing function. NREM restores bodily processes that have deteriorated during the day, while REM sleep is a time for replenishing and renewing brain processes, through the stimulation of protein synthesis.

Box 7.10 REM sleep and the developing brain

- Restoration theory helps explain the large proportion of babies' sleeping time spent in REM sleep.
- During much of their first year, babies are sleeping for about 18 hours per 24, and by about 12 months they have two periods of sleep every 24 hours (one during the day and one at night). Not until about 5 years has an 'adult' pattern become established, probably as a result of both environmental and maturational factors.
- Within these changing patterns, the relative proportions of REM and NREM sleep change quite dramatically. Whereas newborns spend half their 18 hours in REM sleep, adults usually spend only one-quarter of their eight hours in REM sleep.
- The developing brain needs a great deal of protein synthesis for cell manufacture and growth, and REM sleep helps to achieve this.

An evaluation of restoration theory

- Patients who survive drug overdoses and withdrawal, and other brain 'insults', such as intensive electroconvulsive therapy (see Chapter 45), experience prolonged increases in REM sleep. These increases are consistent with the estimated time for the half-life of proteins in the brain: in a six-week period, about half the brain's total protein is replaced, and this is the approximate length of the increased REM period.
- Nocturnal secretion of growth hormone (which produces bodily protein synthesis) depends on uninterrupted stage 4 sleep. In adults, a chronic lack of normal stage 4 is found in fibrositis sufferers, whose EEG during sleep is characterised by 'alpha-delta' patterns, a mixture of sleeping and waking EEG (typically experienced as fitful, 'unrestorative sleep'). The disturbance of stage 4 in healthy volunteers produces the symptoms of fibrositis.
- According to Empson (1993), all this evidence is consistent with a general *anabolic function* for sleep: REM sleep underlies brain growth, repair and memory functions, and slow-wave (stage 4) sleep promotes bodily growth and repair. However, cell repair goes on 24 hours a day (even though it reaches a peak at night).
- A more serious objection is that REM sleep is an active state (at least as far as the brain is concerned), and probably burns up a substantial amount of energy. Indeed, blood flow to the brain *increases* during REM sleep, and this would actually *prevent* high levels of protein synthesis. In view of this kind of evidence, Oswald (1974) maintained that *both* types of sleep are involved in the process of restoring *bodily tissue*.
- However, Oswald may have been a little premature. According to Siegel (2003), although most brain cells are at least as active during REM sleep as in waking, there's a specific group of cells that goes against this trend. These are the cells that produce the *monoamine neurotransmitters* (noradrenaline, serotonin and histamine). These key neurotransmitters inhibit body movement and reduce awareness of the environment, and the cells that produce them stop discharging completely during REM sleep. This interruption may allow the receptor systems to 'rest' and regain full sensitivity, which may be crucial during waking for mood regulation. The monoamines also play a part in rewiring the brain to respond to new experiences. So, turning them off during REM may help prevent changes in brain connections that might otherwise be 'accidentally' created as a consequence of the activation of other neurons during REM sleep. The REM rebound might result from the need to rest monoamine systems and other 'off' systems (Siegel, 2003).
- One of these 'off' systems might be the brainstem (see Chapter 4). In land mammals, brainstem activity drops sharply during NREM sleep and bounces back to normal waking levels during REM sleep. So, REM sleep might simply allow individuals to wake in a more alert state: we usually wake naturally from a period of REM sleep and both humans and non-humans are usually groggier when woken from NREM sleep. Alternatively, REM sleep might have evolved to spare the brainstem from long periods of inactivity during NREM sleep. Either way, there'd be no need for REM sleep without NREM sleep (Siegel, cited in Young, 2008).

Evolutionary theory

Different species characteristically sleep for different periods. Those at risk from predators, which cannot find a safe place to sleep, or which spend large parts of each day searching for and consuming food and water (such as herd animals), sleep very little (for example, zebras sleep for only two to three hours per day). Predators that sleep in safe places, and can satisfy their food and water needs fairly quickly, sleep for much of the day. Lions, for example, often sleep more or less continuously for two to three days after gorging themselves on a kill.

According to Meddis (1975), sleep keeps the animal immobilised for long periods, making it less conspicuous to would-be predators and, therefore, safer. The safer the animal from predators, the longer it's likely to sleep. Meddis also argues that the long sleep periods of babies have evolved to prevent exhaustion in their mothers and, in this sense, sleep is still functional – at least for mothers of babies and small children! As to the need for immobilisation, this no longer seems viable as an explanation of sleep in humans, and so may be regarded as a remnant of our evolutionary past.

This view is echoed by Siegel (cited in Young, 2008). Instead of performing some vital biological function (such as eating or mating), the fundamental purpose of sleep is simply to conserve energy and keep an individual out of danger. This is the most effective way of passing on your genes (so, *indirectly* perhaps, sleep *is* performing some vital biological function).

An evaluation of evolutionary theory

- According to the theory, a preyed-upon species may sleep for shorter periods (because of the constant need to stay on guard against predators) as well as longer periods (because this makes it safer from predators). In other words, whatever sleep pattern a species has, it can be explained in 'evolutionary' terms – an example of *non-falsifiability* (see Chapter 3).
- Empson (1993) characterises Meddis's theory as a 'waste of time' theory. He believes that the fact that all animals sleep contradicts the theory, as does the finding that sleep deprivation can be fatal (Kleitman, 1927; Rechtschaffen *et al.*, 1989a, 1989b: but see Siegel's interpretation above).
- A weaker version of the 'waste of time' theory was proposed by Horne (1988), who distinguishes between *core sleep* (which is necessary) and *optional sleep* (which isn't). Evidence from sleep deprivation experiments (both partial and total) shows that accumulated sleep 'debts' are made up to some extent on recovery nights, but never entirely. This suggests that only the first three hours of sleep are truly necessary (core sleep), and the rest is optional (having no physiological function).
- But most of us eat more than we absolutely need to, yet no biologist would say that because a proportion of feeding was optional that feeding was only partly functional (Empson, 1993). Empson concludes by saying:

> *... sleep appears to be ubiquitous and necessary; it is a complex function of the brain involving far-reaching changes in body physiology as well as brain physiology. It is difficult to believe that it does not have an important function and the restorative theories provide a coherent account of what this might be.*

Hobson's levels

Although not a discrete theory, Hobson (1995) proposes that the function of sleep can be analysed at different levels.

- At the *behavioural level*, sleep suppresses activity at a time (night-time/darkness) when the chances of finding food or a mate are relatively low. Also, such activities have a high energy cost in warm-blooded animals when the temperature is low. This makes sleep behaviourally very efficient. In addition, the enforced nature of sleep and its relation to resting activity serves to unite animals in a family or pair-bonded situation, which may encourage sexual behaviour and promote the care and development of the young. Incredibly, ethologists have failed to recognise and systematically study sleep as a form of behaviour (see Chapter 2).
- At the *developmental level*, a function of REM sleep for developing organisms could be the guaranteed activation of neural circuits underlying crucial, survival behaviours. From an evolutionary point of view, there would be great advantages gained from ensuring the organised activation of the complex systems of the brain before the organism has developed the ability to test them in the real world. In both the developing and the adult animal, REM sleep could constitute a form of behavioural rehearsal.
- At the *metabolic level*, the recurring cycles of NREM/REM sleep are accompanied by major changes in all the body's physiological systems. NREM sleep involves decreased blood pressure, heart and breathing rates, as well as the release of growth and sex hormones from the pituitary (consistent with the restoration theory), while REM sleep involves increased blood pressure, heart and breathing rates, as well as penile erection and clitoral engorgement.

DREAMING

Ask Yourself

- How do dreams differ from waking consciousness?

According to Empson (1993), a starting point in trying to understand the nature of dreams must be to establish clearly how dreaming differs from waking consciousness. Empson identifies four such differences:

1. Dreams *happen to us* as opposed to being a product of our conscious control. *Lucid dreaming*, in which the dreamer 'knows' s/he is dreaming and decides how the dream plot should develop, is very rare.
2. The logic of waking consciousness is suspended (see Freud's theory, Chapter 42).
3. Dreams reported in the laboratory tend to be mundane and lack the *bizarre quality* of 'normal' dreams, probably because only the strangest experiences are remembered when we wake normally after a night's sleep.

4. Dreams have a *single-mindedness*: the imagery of the dream totally dominates the dreamer's consciousness. But when we're awake, we normally reflect on the stream of consciousness as it goes on, and can be aware of one thing but simultaneously imagine something else.

Theories of dreaming

REM sleep has been called 'dream sleep' or the 'D-state' and some have gone as far as to call it the 'third state of existence', because in many ways it's as different from NREM sleep (the 'S-state') as it is from waking. This leads us to ask why we need to dream.

Ask Yourself

- Do dreams have a function of their own, or are they just an accompaniment to certain sleep states?
- Why do we dream?

Reorganisation of mental structures

According to Ornstein (1986), REM sleep and dreaming may be involved in the reorganisation of our *schemas* (mental structures), so as to accommodate new information. People placed in a 'disturbing and perplexing' atmosphere for four hours just prior to sleep (asked to perform difficult tasks with no explanation) spend longer in REM sleep than normal. REM time also increases after people have had to learn complex tasks. This may explain why REM sleep decreases with age (see Box 7.10).

Activation-synthesis model (Hobson and McCarley, 1977; McCarley, 1983)

The *activation* aspect of the model claims that dreaming (i.e. REM sleep) is 'switched on' (activated) by acetylcholine (cholinergic mechanisms) in the *pontine brainstem* (top of the spinal column, at the base of the brain); this switches *off* NREM sleep. This activation is what *causes* dreaming and is 'motivationally neutral'. The *synthesis* aspect argues that the forebrain frantically attempts to piece together (synthesise) the meaningless, apparently random images, thoughts and feelings that are randomly thrown up by the brainstem. These PGO waves (see above) are indistinguishable from signals that would normally have been relayed from the eyes/ears.

So, dreams are a conscious interpretation (synthesis) of all this activity; the forebrain's contribution to the process is *secondary* to a brainstem-driven process, making 'the best of a bad job'. Hence, dreams are *epiphenomena* (byproducts) produced by the REM state and are *inherently* meaningless (Solms and Turnbull, 2007).

While the motor cortex is highly active (generating activity that would normally produce bodily movement), these commands don't reach the muscles of the limbs but are 'switched off' at a 'relay station' at the top of the spinal column: we're effectively paralysed (*output blockade*). There's also inhibition of incoming signals produced by the sensory systems, causing perceptions of the 'real' world to be selectively attenuated (*input blockade*).

It's the unusual intensity and rapidity of brain stimulation which account for the highly changeable and sometimes bizarre content of dreams. According to Hobson (1995):

> *... the now autoactivated and autostimulated brain processes these signals and interprets them in terms of information stored in memory ...*

Evaluation of the activation-synthesis model

- Hobson and McCarley's model rests heavily on the *assumption* that dreaming and REM sleep are *synonymous*. However, we've seen above that this equation is unjustified (Solms and Turnbull, 2007): while they may be *correlated*, they *aren't* the same thing.
- Crick and Mitchison (1983) proposed a modified version of the model, which they called *reverse learning*. The basic idea is that we dream *in order to forget*. The cortex (unlike other parts of the brain) is composed of richly interconnected neuronal networks. The problem with such a network system is that it malfunctions when there's overload of incoming information. To deal with such overload, the brain needs a mechanism to 'debug' or 'clean up' the network, and REM sleep is that mechanism. In this way, we awake with a cleaned-up network, and the brain is ready for new input. According to Crick and Mitchison, trying to remember our dreams may not be a good idea: they are the very patterns of thought the system is trying to tune out.

Ask Yourself

- Is *reverse learning* consistent with SHY (Tononi and Cirelli, 2013, see Box 7.7)?
- For others, especially psychodynamic psychologists, it's essential that we *do* remember our dreams, so that we can try to understand their meaning. For example, both Freud and Jung saw *symbolism* as being of central importance in dreams, which put the dreamer in touch with parts of the self usually inaccessible during waking life (see Chapter 42). Hall (1966) saw dreams as 'a personal document, a letter to oneself' and, like Jung, advocated the study of *dream series*, rather than single, isolated dreams. Far from being meaningless or motivationally neutral, dreams are a major source of self-understanding.

CONCLUSIONS: INTEGRATING NEUROBIOLOGICAL, EVOLUTIONARY AND PSYCHOLOLGICAL ACCOUNTS OF DREAMING

Winson (1997) argues that neural and psychological theories of dreams *aren't* mutually exclusive. While Crick and Mitchison argue that we need to forget our dreams, Winson claims that:

> *... dreams may reflect a memory-processing mechanism inherited from lower species, in which information important for survival is reprocessed during REM sleep. This information may constitute the core of the unconscious.*

To maintain sleep, locomotion had to be suppressed by inhibiting motor neurons. But suppressing *eye movements* wasn't necessary, because these don't disturb sleep. With the evolution of REM sleep, each species could process the information most needed for its survival (such as the location of food, and means of predation or escape). In REM sleep, this information may be re-accessed and integrated with past experience to provide an ongoing strategy for behaviour. Similarly, *threat simulation theory* (Revonso, 2000) claims that dreaming evolved to simulate the very real threats to individuals' physical survival (and hence to reproductive success) during human evolution. Ways of dealing with these threats could be 'practised' in dreams.

According to Humphrey (1986, 1993), dreams are also about practising all sorts of physical, intellectual and social skills ('dreaming as play'). It may be true that dreams are just an evolutionary 'epiphenomenon', without any adaptive function (Flanagan, 2000), and it may also be true that many people function perfectly well without remembering their dreams (Hobson, 2002). Nevertheless, we can still use dreaming in our waking lives:

> *... studying our own dreams can be valuable in all sorts of ways. They can reveal our inner motivations and hopes, help us face our fears, encourage growing awareness, and even be a source of creativity and insight ... (Blackmore, 2003)*

Chapter Summary

- Since the cognitive revolution dislodged behaviourism from its dominant position in Psychology, cognitive processes and consciousness have once more become important areas of Psychological research.
- Freud distinguished three **levels of consciousness**: **conscious, preconscious** and **unconscious**. Most psychologists do not accept Freud's view of the unconscious as based on repression, but they would accept that there is a **continuum of consciousness**.
- **Arousal/alertness** can be defined objectively in terms of various physiological measures, such as EEGs, EOGs, EMGs, breathing and heart rates. These are **correlates** of consciousness.
- Changes in **tonic alertness** are closely linked to various biological rhythms, especially the **circadian rhythm**. The RF/RAS plays an important role in arousing/maintaining consciousness. Alertness changes in fairly predictable ways both during wakefulness (controlled by a **diurnal rhythm**) and sleep (**ultradian rhythm**).
- Changes in **phasic alertness** involve changes in the **orienting response** to arousing stimuli. This is complemented by **habituation**, a form of adaptation. Human and non-human nervous systems have evolved such that they are especially responsive to **change**.
- Consciousness can be experimentally pinned down by studying **attention** (**focal** or **peripheral**). Perception seems to take place largely unconsciously, and many behaviours are carried out quite automatically, allowing us to attend consciously to the unfamiliar or threatening aspects of our environment.
- Nisbett and Wilson claim that all psychological activities are governed by processes unavailable to consciousness. However, Humphrey maintains that the 'inner eye' of consciousness evolved to allow our ancestors to relate to others based on understanding others' experience of being human.
- While many different brain regions are involved in consciousness, some regions of the cortex are particularly important, including the **anterior cingulate cortex** (ACC) and the **fronto-insular** (FI) **cortex**. Both regions contain **von Economo neurons** (VENs).
- VENs are implicated in dementia and autism and have been found in several non-human species, both social and non-social.
- Consciousness can be conceptualised in terms of **level** (wakefulness) and **content** (awareness). In **vegetative state** (VS) patients, there's a **dissociation** between these two levels.

- **Functional neuroimaging** is used to detect consciousness in brain-damaged patients with no motor function.
- Most animals display a **circadian rhythm** synchronised to the 24-hour cycle of light and dark, involving a rhythmical alternation of various physiological and behavioural functions.
- The **internal/biological clock** is thought to be the **suprachiasmatic nucleus** (SCN), part of the hypothalamus. The retina projects directly onto the SCN, ensuring that the sleep–wake cycle is tuned to the rhythm of night and day.
- When darkness falls, the **pineal gland** begins to secrete **melatonin**, making us drowsy. It affects brain cells that produce serotonin concentrated in the **raphe nuclei**; these secrete a substance that acts on the RAS to induce light sleep. The **locus coeruleus** (LC) is rich in noradrenaline, which induces REM sleep.
- Sleep is measured in the laboratory using **polysomnography** (PSG): an **electrocephalogram** (EEG), **electrooculogram** (EOG) and **electromyogram** (EMG).
- A typical night's sleep comprises four to five **ultradian cycles**, each consisting of several stages. Stages 2–4 are collectively called **slow-wave sleep** (SWS) or 'deep' sleep; stages 1–4 are collectively called **non-rapid eye movement** (NREM) sleep.
- **Rapid eye movement** (REM) or **active sleep** replaces stage 1 at the beginning of the next cycle. Physiological processes increase and EEGs begin to resemble those of the waking state, yet it's more difficult to wake someone than from stage 4 sleep (making it **paradoxical**). With each ultradian cycle, the duration of REM sleep increases.
- Depriving people of REM sleep produces the **REM rebound**, suggesting that dreaming associated with REM sleep is perhaps the most important function of sleep.
- Sleep has also been shown to facilitate **problem-solving, learning** and **memory**.
- According to the **synaptic homeostasis hypothesis** (SHY), sleep acts as a reset button, restoring the brain's plasticity so that new learning can take place.
- According to Oswald's **restoration theory**, REM and NREM sleep help replenish bodily and brain processes respectively. However, the fact that cell repair goes on 24 hours a day, and that the brain is highly active during REM sleep, led Oswald to claim that both REM and NREM sleep are involved in restoration of bodily tissue.
- Meddis's **evolutionary theory** claims that sleep keeps the animal immobilised and so safer from predators, so longer sleep is associated with greater safety. But danger from predators is also associated with shorter sleep, because of the need to stay alert, and longer sleep is also characteristic of certain predators such as lions. This makes the theory **unfalsifiable**.
- According to Hobson and McCarley's **activation-synthesis model**, forebrain **activation** by signals from the **pontine brainstem** during REM sleep is consciously interpreted (**synthesis**) in the form of a dream.
- While the activation-synthesis model sees dreams as **meaningless, psychodynamic** theorists, such as Freud, Jung and Hall, stress their **significance** for the dreamer.
- According to Crick and Mitchison's **reverse learning theory**, dreams are a way of 'cleaning up' the cortex's neural networks and preparing them for new input. So, we need to forget our dreams. Psychodynamic theories, however, stress the need to remember them.
- Different theories of dreaming aren't mutually exclusive. REM sleep may have evolved to help animals' biological survival, but they continue to serve a vital function for individuals, helping them to survive psychologically.

Links with Other Topics/Chapters

Chapters 1, 3 and 48 → The distinction between conscious(ness) and self-conscious(ness)/self-awareness is crucial for understanding the *difference between humans and non-humans*

Chapter 33 → Self-awareness is a key feature of the *self-concept* and there's debate as to whether humans are the only primates who possess it

Chapter 19 → This debate is also relevant when assessing attempts to *teach language to chimpanzees and other non-human primates*

Chapter 13 → Definitions of consciousness are relevant to *attention and performance*

Chapters 2 and 42 → Freud's *psychoanalytic theory*

Chapter 4 → Ways of measuring consciousness (in terms of arousal and alertness, sleep and dreams) involve methods used to study the *nervous system* in general

Chapter 2 → Explanations of the functions of consciousness (including theories of sleep and dreams) often take an *evolutionary perspective*

Chapter 12 → The *disruption of circadian rhythms* is a source of *stress*

Recommended Reading

Blackmore, S. (2003) *Consciousness: An Introduction*. London: Hodder & Stoughton. Also relevant to Chapters 8 and 20.

Blackmore, S. (2005) *Consciousness: A Very Short Introduction*. Oxford: Oxford University Press.

Damasio, A. (1999) *The Feeling of What Happens: Body, Emption and the Making of Consciousness*. London: Vintage. Also relevant to Chapters 10 and 33.

Empson, J. (2001) *Sleep and Dreaming* (3rd rev edn). Basingstoke: Palgrave Macmillan.

Gross, R. (2012b) *Key Studies in Psychology* (6th edn). London: Hodder Education. Also for Chapters 14 and 15.

Humphrey, N. (1986, 1993) *The Inner Eye*. London: Vintage.

Humphrey, N. (1992) *A History of the Mind*. London: Vintage.

Velmans, M., Schneider, S. (eds) (2007) *The Blackwell Companion of Consciousness*. Oxford: Blackwell Publishing.

Useful Websites

www.lboro.ac.uk/departments/ssehs/research/behavioural-medicine/clinical-sleep-research-centre/unit/keyinterests (University of Loughborough Sleep Research Centre)

faculty.washington.edu/chudler/sleep.html (What is sleep, why do we do it?)

www.sleepnet.com (Take a sleep test)

www.sleeping.org.uk (British Sleep Society)

www.aasmnet.org (American Academy of Sleep Medicine)

www.asdreams.org (International Association for the Study of Dreams)

www.dreamresearch.net (Quantitative Study of Dreams, A. Schneider & G.W. Domhoff, 2009)

http://assc.caltech.edu/index.htm

www.ai.mit.edu/projects/humanoid-robotics-group

www.consciousentities.com/?p=64

www.consciousness.arizona.edu/ (Center for Consciousness Studies)

www.fil.ion.ucl.ac.uk

CHAPTER 8

ADDICTIVE BEHAVIOUR

INTRODUCTION and OVERVIEW

For thousands of years, people have taken substances to alter their perception of reality, and societies have restricted the substances their members are allowed to take. These substances, which we usually call drugs, are *psychoactive*, denoting a chemical substance that alters conscious awareness through its effect on the brain. Most drugs fit this definition. Some – for example, aspirin – are *indirectly* psychoactive: their primary purpose is to remove pain, but being headache-free lifts our mood. Others, however, are designed to change mood and behaviour. These are collectively referred to as *psychotherapeutic* drugs, such as those used in the treatment of anxiety, depression and schizophrenia (see Chapter 45).

This chapter is mainly concerned with psychoactive drugs used to produce a temporarily altered state of consciousness for the purpose of *pleasure*. These include *recreational drugs*, which have no legal restrictions (such as alcohol, nicotine and caffeine), and *drugs of abuse*, which are illegal. However, just as recreational drugs can be abused (such as alcohol), so illegal drugs are taken recreationally (such as ecstasy). 'Substance abuse', therefore, doesn't imply particular types of drug, but refers to the extent to which the drug is used, and the effects – emotional, behavioural and medical – on the abuser.

According to Veitia and McGahee (1995):

> *Cigarette smoking and alcohol abuse permeate our culture and are widespread enough to be considered ordinary addictions ... The degree to which these drugs permeate our culture and the extent to which they are accepted by our society distinguish them from other addictive but illegal substances such as heroin and cocaine.*

While 'addiction' is usually equated with drugs of abuse and these 'ordinary addictions', the concept is being used to refer to an ever-increasing range of activities (hence 'addictive behaviours') which don't involve chemical substances at all (such as sex, the internet, gambling, and even anorexia nervosa as mentioned below).

THE DIVERSITY OF 'ADDICTION': IS THERE MORE TO ADDICTION THAN DRUGS?

Ask Yourself

- What do terms such as 'workaholic', 'shopaholic' and 'chocoholic' tell you about the nature of addictive behaviour?
- Can you define addiction in a way that can cover such non-drug behaviours?
- What might they all have in common?

The concept of addiction has been heavily criticised, leading some to reject it in favour of terms such as 'abuse' and 'dependence' (see below). However, some researchers argue that the concept should be *broadened*, in order to cover certain recent forms of 'addictive' behaviour that don't involve chemical substances at all. According to Shaffer *et al.* (1989):

> *Addictive behaviours typically serve the addict in the short run at the price of longer-term destructiveness. Physical dependence is not a requisite for addiction ... addictive behaviours organise the addict's life. All of life's other activities fit in the gaps that the addictive behaviour permits.*

The addiction can be to a substance or an experience: shopping, gambling, or eating (or abstaining from eating; see Chapter 44). Drawing on current definitions of substance dependence, pathological gambling, and eating disorders, Walters (1999) suggests that addiction may be defined as 'the persistent and repetitious enactment of a behaviour pattern', which includes:

- *progression* (increase in severity)
- *preoccupation* with the activity
- *perceived loss of control*
- *persistence* despite negative long-term consequences.

Similarly, Griffiths (e.g. 2005) maintains that addiction isn't confined to drugs. Several other behaviours, including gambling, watching television, playing amusement machines, overeating, sex, exercise, playing computer games, and using the internet are all potentially addictive. Social pathologies are beginning to surface in cyberspace in the form of *technological addictions*, which are:

> ... non-chemical (behavioural) addictions that involve human–machine interaction. They can be either passive (e.g. television) or active (e.g. computer games). The interaction usually contains inducing and reinforcing features (e.g. sound effects, colour effects ...) that may promote addictive tendencies. (Griffiths, 1995)

Griffiths (1996, 2005) argues that these behaviours display the same *core components* of addiction (complementing Walters' 'four Ps' above), namely:

- *salience*
- *mood modification*
- *tolerance*
- *withdrawal symptoms*
- *conflict*
- *relapse.*

(See Meet the Researcher, pp. 130–1.)

How useful/valid is the concept of addiction?

Alcoholism and drug addiction as 'paradigm cases': addiction-as-disease

Until recently, the study and treatment of drug problems were organised around the concept of *addiction*: people with drug problems have problems because they're addicted to the drug (Hammersley, 1999). Addicts are compelled by a physiological need to continue taking the drug, experience horrible physical and psychological symptoms when trying to stop, and will continue taking it despite these symptoms because of their addictive need. Their addiction will also change them psychologically for the worse, they will commit crimes to pay for the drug, neglect their social roles and responsibilities, and even harm the people around them. In addition, some drugs are considered inherently much more addictive than others (see below), and substance users can be divided into addicts and non-addicts. As Bennett (2006) says:

> Ask someone to describe an addict and they will usually give a stereotypical description of someone addicted to 'hard' drugs such as heroin or cocaine ...

This stereotype is based on the *addiction-as-disease* (AAD) model. In other words, alcoholism and drug addiction are 'paradigm cases', and the AAD model is the 'paradigmatic account of addiction in general'. Even though the AAD was developed as a way of trying to explain alcoholism and (illegal) drug addiction, it has been criticised from several perspectives (see below). Given that we've considered several other addictions that are non-chemical/behavioural, the question arises as to how valid an addiction-as-disease model can be in trying to account for these. For example, gambling would appear to be 'purely' behavioural (so that the AAD doesn't seem appropriate), while smoking has both chemical and behavioural components (as do alcoholism and drug addiction), so that the AAD would appear to be more appropriate.

Criticisms of the concept of addiction

It's an oversimplification. Most professionals who deal with people with any kind of problem – medical, criminal, educational, social – will have seen many clients who aren't exactly addicts, but whose drug use seems to have contributed to, or worsened, their other problems (Hammersley, 1999). According to Sussman and Ames (2008):

> ... [with drug abuse] defined as a disease, the capacity for self-management and assuming responsibility for one's behaviour may be undermined ...

Four further problems with the AAD model are discussed in Critical Discussion 8.1. below.

According to Hammersley (1999), 'addiction' now usually refers to a field of study, covering substance use, abuse and dependence, rather than to a theory of why people become dependent.

Substance use and abuse

According to Hammersley (1999), the concept of abuse is something of a compromise, because it's debatable whether any use of a substance can be entirely risk-free. For example,

Critical Discussion 8.1

Limitations of the addiction-as-disease model

Sussman and Ames (2001, 2008) identify four major problems with this model.

1. *There's no independent means of verifying the existence of the disease.* In the case of addictive behaviour (and behaviour disorders in general), it's difficult to separate *factors* (e.g. a poison or a virus) from *symptoms* (e.g. high temperature).
   If the problem were merely one of behaviour, then no longer taking the drug would stop the problem. But relapse rates never fall to zero and are 65 per cent in the first year following treatment, halving each year after that. This is true regardless of the substance involved. High relapse rates imply underlying factors, but there are no independent measures of assessing the underlying factors. However, recent research evidence has thrown light on the 'addicted brain', and this might provide the independent assessment of underlying factors required by the disease model (see Research Update 8.1).
2. *Variation in disordered behavioural symptoms.* Behavioural symptoms may be defined as more or less disordered depending on the social context. For example, someone who gets drunk and obnoxious once a month may be seen as an alcoholic in a church-going community – but not in a college dorm. Also, drug abuse can be seen as falling somewhere on a *continuum*, rather than a binary (yes/no) state, which is often used to define a disease ('you're either an addict or you're not') (see Chapter 43). However, heart disease, for example, also falls along a continuum, which is why it can be 'missed' or misdiagnosed (even though there are objective tests that can detect it).
3. *Variation in behavioural symptoms may not reflect the same underlying processes.* For example, there are various patterns of drug abuse, from a single-episode catastrophe to periodic problem use, to heavy or uncontrolled use. It's unclear whether these variations all reflect the same underlying cause.
4. *The aetiological factors for drug abuse as a behavioural disorder aren't known.* We don't know what makes people abuse drugs. The AAD model regards various addictive behaviours (e.g. compulsive gambling, drug abuse, overeating) as being *qualitatively* different: the possibility that there might be some common underlying cause isn't considered. Indeed, drug abuse is associated with various problem behaviours, including crime, violence, sensation-seeking and poor diet, which may precede the abuse as a disease.

(See risk factors in text below, pp. 139–40.)

Figure 8.1 George Best (1946–2005), gifted footballer and famous alcoholic

> *... The health risks of tobacco smoking now seem so substantial that all smoking is probably abuse – there is no negligible-risk use of tobacco ...*

However, he believes that most other drugs can be used in ways that make risks negligible.

Abuse and dependence

The American Psychiatric Association's Diagnostic and Statistical Manual of Mental Disorders (DSM-IV-TR, 2000), distinguished between substance abuse and dependence. DSM-5 (2013) removed this distinction, reflecting what many practising clinicians believed was an arbitrary distinction (Grohol, 2013). 'Substance use disorders' (now listed under 'Substance-related disorders and behavioural disorders'; see Chapter 43) are now rated as 'mild', 'moderate' or 'severe' depending on how many criteria are met (2–3, 4–5, 6 or more, respectively).

Also, the traditional distinction between physiological and psychological dependence is removed; 'craving' is an added criterion. Despite its removal, the distinction is still useful. *Physiological dependence* is related to *withdrawal and/or tolerance* (which relates to the traditional concept of addiction), while *psychological dependence* isn't. However, being deprived of something that's highly pleasurable can induce anxiety. Since the symptoms of anxiety (rapid pulse, profuse sweating, shaking, and so on) overlap with withdrawal symptoms, people may mistakenly believe that they're physiologically dependent. Psychological dependence is, though, part of the overall *dependence syndrome* (see Figure 8.4).

Research Update 8.1

The 'addicted brain' (based on Nestler and Malenka 2004; Solis, 2013)

- Neurobiologists have long known that drugs have their effect because they ultimately boost the activity of the brain's reward system: a complex circuit of neurons which evolved to make us feel 'flush' after eating or sex. At least initially, stimulating this system makes us feel good, which encourages us to repeat whatever induced the pleasure.
- But new research indicates that chronic drug use can induce changes in the structure and function of the system's neurons that last for weeks, months or years after the fix.
- A key part of the circuit is the pathway extending from dopamine-producing neurons of the *ventral tegmental area* (VTA) (in the midbrain) to dopamine-sensitive neurons in the *nucleus accumbens* (NA), situated deep beneath the frontal cortex. These changes contribute significantly to the tolerance, dependence and craving that fuel repeated use and that lead to relapses even after long periods of abstinence.
- The VTA, rich in dopamine neurons, sends projections through the medial forebrain bundle to a set of *limbic brain regions*, including the NA and *amygdala*, and to the *prefrontal cortex* (PFC). Together, these, and related structures, are known as the 'common reward pathway': their stimulation is experienced as pleasurable and reinforcing (see Chapter 9).
- There are also pathways linking the NA and VTA with other brain regions that can help make addicts highly sensitive to reminders of past highs (such as drug paraphernalia and places where they've scored), vulnerable to relapse when stressed and unable to control the urge to seek drugs.
- The VTA–NA pathway acts as a 'rheostat of reward': it 'tells' other brain centres how rewarding an activity is. The more rewarding, the more likely the organism is to remember it well and repeat it.
- fMRI and PET scans (see Chapter 4) show that the NA in cocaine addicts' brains 'lights up' when offered a snort, shown a video of someone using cocaine or even a photograph of white lines on a mirror.

The amygdala and some areas of the cortex also respond. While being scanned, they rate their feelings of rush and craving on a scale of 0–3. Such studies show that (a) the VTA and sublenticular extended amygdala are important to the cocaine-induced rush, and (b) the amygdala and NA influence both the rush and the craving for more of the drug, which becomes stronger as the euphoria wears off (as shown in Figure 8.3).

Figure 8.2 This image is enough to excite a cocaine addict's brain

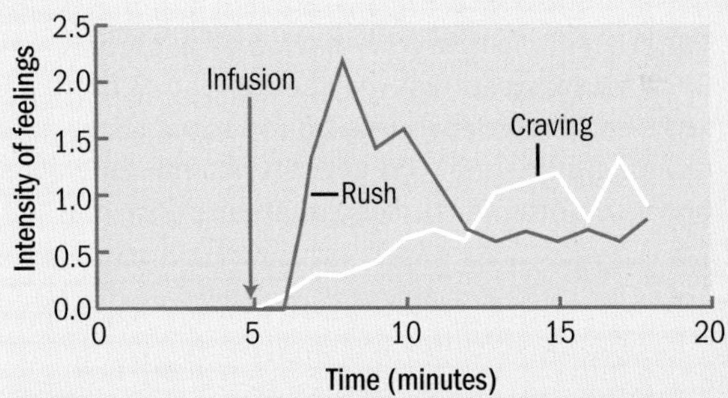

Figure 8.3 From Nestler and Malenka (2004) (reprinted with permission from Hans C. Breiter, Massachusetts General Hospital)

The same regions react in compulsive gamblers shown images of slot machines.

Addiction affects much of the molecular machinery present at synapses. The connections between the decision-making PFC and the habit-learning NA are damaged, which makes changing a routine extremely difficult for addicts. The synapses become rigid, unable to respond to new information such as 'I want to stop using drugs'. Glutamate is central to the normal, flexible functioning of these synapses (see Chapter 4) and drug use destroys this flexibility by altering glutamate-related machinery. Protein pumps in nearby glial cells fail to maintain normal levels of glutamate in the extracellular space.

Teenagers are at particular risk, because their PFC is slow to mature; this isn't just the seat of inhibitory (self-) control, but also of working memory (see Chapter 17) (Hopson, 2013).

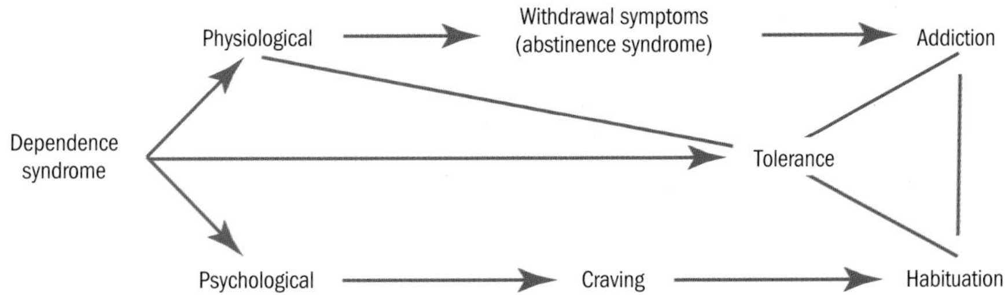

Figure 8.4 Summary of major components of dependence syndrome

Imipramine, used to treat depression (see Chapter 45), illustrates the difference between the two types of dependence. When it's stopped after prolonged use, there may be nausea, muscle pain, anxiety and difficulty in sleeping, but there's never a compulsion to resume taking it (Lowe, 1995):

> *Habituation is the repeated use of a drug because the user finds that use increases pleasurable feelings or reduces feelings of anxiety, fear, or stress. Habituation becomes problematic when the person becomes so consumed by the need for the drug-altered state of consciousness that all his or her energies are directed to compulsive drug-seeking behaviour ... (Lowe, 1995)*

Physiologically addictive drugs, such as heroin and alcohol, typically also cause habituation. Most widely used recreational drugs, including cannabis, cocaine, LSD, PCP (see Table 8.1), and methylenedioxymethamphetamine (MDMA, otherwise known as 'ecstasy'), *don't* cause physiological dependence – but people do become habituated.

CLASSIFYING DRUGS

Psychoactive drugs have been classified in several different ways. For example, Hamilton and Timmons (1995) identify three broad groups:

1. *stimulants* temporarily excite neural activity, arouse bodily functions, enhance positive feelings and heighten alertness; in high doses, they cause overt seizures
2. *depressants* (or *sedatives*) depress neural activity, slow down bodily functions, induce calmness and produce sleep; in high doses, they cause unconsciousness
3. *hallucinogens* produce distortion of normal perception and thought processes; in high doses, they can cause episodes of psychotic behaviour (see Chapters 43 and 44).

A fourth category is *opiates*. These also depress activity in the CNS, but have an *analgesic* property – that is, they reduce sensitivity to pain without loss of consciousness. The Royal College of Psychiatrists (1987) identified *minor tranquillisers* as a separate category, but in Table 8.1 they've been included under the general category of depressants. Cannabis doesn't fall easily into any of these other categories.

Another way of classifying drugs is in terms of their *description*. As Table 8.2 shows, in this approach the same drug can appear in more than one category.

Ask Yourself

- How do the three drug classifications (Cooper, 1995; Hamilton and Timmons, 1995; and Sussman and Ames, 2008) interrelate/overlap?

THE EFFECTS OF DRUGS

According to Greenfield (in Ahuja, 2000):

> *As a person, you are the configuration of your brain cells ... Drugs are specifically designed to alter that configuration. So when you blow your mind on drugs, you really are blowing your mind. They may not kill you, but they may dramatically alter the person you are ...*

Children and teenagers, whose relatively malleable brains are still being moulded, are particularly vulnerable. Teenagers, for various social and cultural reasons, are especially likely to take drugs, including those that pose the greatest threat to physical and mental health (see Chapter 37).

Depressants

Alcohol

Despite the difficulties in assessing the relationship between level of intake and harmful effects, certain 'safe levels' are widely accepted (Gelder *et al.*, 1999). These are expressed in terms of *units* of alcohol, which is equal to eight grams of ethanol (the equivalent of half a pint of beer, a small glass of wine, a glass of sherry or a standard (pub) measure of spirits).

MEET THE RESEARCHER

Mark Griffiths

Addictions

When most people think of the word 'addiction' they probably think of 'chemical' addictions, like alcoholism or a heroin addiction. However, there is now a growing movement that views a number of behaviours as potentially addictive including behaviours that do not involve the ingestion of a psychoactive substance like alcohol or nicotine. These include behaviours as diverse as gambling, overeating, sex, exercise, videogame playing, love, internet use and work (Griffiths, 2005). In fact, you can almost become addicted to anything. Such diversity has led to new all-encompassing definitions of what constitutes an addictive behaviour, such as:

> *A repetitive habit pattern that increases the risk of disease and/or associated personal and social problems. Addictive behaviours are often experienced subjectively as 'loss of control' – the behaviour contrives to occur despite volitional attempts to abstain or moderate use. These habit patterns are typically characterised by immediate gratification (short-term reward), often coupled with delayed deleterious effects (long-term costs). Attempts to change an addictive behaviour (via treatment or self-initiation) are typically marked with high relapse rates (Marlatt* et al.*, 1988: 224).*

The key idea here that is common to previous ideas about chemical addictions is the idea of 'loss of control'. The person with the addiction is not able to regulate their behaviour as they would like and their behaviour becomes extreme.

All kinds of addictive behaviour have elements in common and these are reminiscent of the clinical criteria for diagnosing substance dependence. However, some individuals engage in behaviours that have addictive elements without it necessarily being a full-blown addiction. If someone has no negative withdrawal effects after stopping their excessive cocaine use or gambling, are they really addicted? If the cocaine use or gambling does not conflict with anything else in that person's life, can it be said to be an addiction? In very simple terms, the difference between an excessive enthusiasm and an addiction is that enthusiasms add to life, whereas addictions take away from it.

For many years I have been using what I call the 'components model' of addictive behaviour. It is my belief that all addictive behaviours comprise a number of core components. These are briefly outlined below.

Salience

Salience refers to how important the behaviour becomes to the individual. Addictive behaviours become the most important activity for a person, so that even when they are not doing it they are thinking about it. It should also be noted that some addictive behaviours, such as smoking (nicotine) and drinking (alcohol), are activities that can be engaged in concurrently with other activities and therefore do not tend to dominate an addict's thoughts or lead to total preoccupation. For instance, a smoker can carry around their cigarettes and still engage in other day-to-day activities. However, if that person were in a situation in which they were unable to smoke for a long period (such as a 24-hour plane flight), smoking would be the single most important thing in their life and would totally dominate their thoughts and behaviour. This is what could be termed 'reverse salience' with the addictive activity becoming the most important thing in that person's life when they are prevented from engaging in the behaviour.

Mood modification

Mood modification is the experience people report when they carry out their addictive behaviour. People with addictive behaviour patterns commonly report a 'rush', or a 'buzz' or a 'high' when they are taking their drugs or when they are gambling, for example. What is interesting is that a person's drug or activity of choice can have the capacity to achieve different mood-modifying effects at different times. For instance, a nicotine addict may use cigarettes first thing in the morning to get the arousing 'nicotine rush' they need to get going for the day. By the end of the day they may not be using nicotine for its stimulant qualities, but may in fact be using nicotine as a way of de-stressing and relaxing. It appears that addicts can use their addiction to bring about mood changes and this is as true for gamblers as it is for drug addicts.

Tolerance

Tolerance refers to the increasing amount of activity that is required to achieve the same effect. The classic example of tolerance is a heroin addict's need to increase the size of their 'fix' to get the type of feeling (e.g. an intense 'rush') they once got from much smaller doses. In gambling, tolerance may involve the gambler gradually having to increase the size of the bet to experience a mood-modifying effect that was initially obtained by a much smaller bet. It may also involve spending longer and longer periods gambling.

Withdrawal symptoms

Withdrawal symptoms are the unpleasant feelings and physical effects that occur when the addictive behaviour is suddenly discontinued or reduced. This can include 'the shakes', moodiness and irritability. These symptoms are commonly believed to be a response to the removal of a chemical to which the person has developed a tolerance. However, these effects can also be experienced by gamblers, so the effects might be due to withdrawal from the behaviour as well as the substance.

Conflict

People with addictive behaviours develop conflicts with the people around them, often causing great social misery. They also develop conflicts within themselves. Continual choosing of short-term pleasure and relief leads to disregard of adverse consequences and long-term damage, which in turn increases the apparent need for the addictive activity as a coping strategy.

Relapse

This refers to the tendency for repeated reversions to earlier patterns of the particular activity to recur and for even the most extreme patterns typical of the height of the addiction to be quickly restored after many years of abstinence or control. The classic example of relapse behaviour is in smokers who often give up for a period of time only to return to full-time smoking after a few cigarettes. However, such relapses are common in all addictions, including behavioural addictions such as gambling.

Importance of research

Research shows that singular approaches to explaining addictions have major shortcomings in providing a comprehensive explanation for addictive behaviour. Furthermore, psychological explanations are insufficient to explain the full complexity of addiction and that a unified theory of addiction will be complex and biopsychosocial. Whether ongoing behaviour is explained in terms of biological, behavioural or cognitive theories, it still remains unclear why one person engages more heavily in one behaviour than another. In other words, while it seems likely that increased involvement with a particular behaviour is likely to contribute to loss of control over behaviour, development of irrational beliefs and greater psychological dependence, it is important to determine what makes some people more susceptible to these factors than others. It is here that research into biological and personality factors becomes important.

Dr Mark Griffiths is Professor of Gambling Studies at Nottingham Trent University. He has been researching behavioural addictions since 1987 and has published over 235 peer review papers, three books and over 60 book chapters. His latest book is *Problem Gaming in Europe: Challenges, Prevention, and Interventions* (2009, New York: Springer).

Table 8.1 Some examples of the major categories of psychoactive drugs

Major category	Examples	Slang name(s)
Depressants (sedatives)	alcohol	
	barbiturates	'downers', 'barbs', various other names derived from names or colour of pill/capsule (e.g. 'blueys')
	tranquillisers	'tranx'
	solvents	
Stimulants	caffeine	
	nicotine	
	amphetamines	'uppers', 'speed', 'sulphate', 'sulph', 'whizz'
	MDMA	'ecstasy', 'E', and many names derived from shape/colour of drugs
	cocaine	'coke', 'snow', 'crack', 'freebase', 'base', 'wash', 'rock'
Opiates	morphine	
	heroin	'junk', 'skag', 'H', 'smack'
	codeine	
	methadone	'amps' (injectable), 'linctus' (oral)
Hallucinogens	lysergic acid diethylamide (LSD)	'acid'
	mescaline	
	psilocybin	'magic mushrooms', 'mushies'
	phencyclidine (PCP)	'angel dust'
Cannabis	cannabis sativa	'pot', 'dope', 'blow', 'draw', 'smoke'
	herbal cannabis	'grass', 'marijuana', 'ganja'
	cannabis resin	'weed', 'the herb', 'skunk'
	cannabis oil	'hash', 'hashish'

(Based on Cooper, 1995)

For *men*, up to 21 units per week, and for women, up to 14 units is considered safe, provided the whole amount isn't taken all at once and that there are occasional drink-free days. Anything over 50 and 35 units, respectively, is considered 'dangerous'. The British legal driving blood alcohol limit is 80 mg per 100 ml (equivalent to two or three drinks).

The effects of alcohol on memory

Ask Yourself

- Either from your own experience, or from observing others, how would you describe the effects of alcohol on memory?

Alcohol interferes with normal sleep patterns. Although it causes sedation, alcohol also suppresses REM sleep by as much as 20 per cent (see Chapter 7). There also appears to be a link between alcohol-induced sleepiness and memory loss. People who get drunk and then forget what happened have memory impairments similar to those suffered by people with sleep disorders, such as daytime sleepiness (Motluk, 1999).

In both cases, the person cannot recall how they got home, or what happened while at work or at the pub. It's the *transfer* of information into long-term memory that seems to be disrupted. The GABA signals that induce the sleepiness can interfere with both the early and late stages of memory formation (*stimulus registration* and *consolidation*, respectively). Chemicals that mimic GABA can do this, and there are many GABA receptors in the hippocampus. Another memory disorder associated with chronic alcohol consumption is *Korsakoff's syndrome* (see Chapters 17 and 50).

Table 8.2 Drug use terms and descriptions (based on Sussman and Ames, 2008)

Terms	General description	Example(s)
Drug	A substance that can be taken into the body that alters one or more bodily processes	Alcohol, nicotine, cocaine, marijuana, etc.
Street drug	Any drug that's misused: may have dangerous consequences and is considered improper to use either intrinsically or within the social conditions in which it's used	Alcohol (in underage drinking), heroin, methamphetamine, crack cocaine, marijuana
Hard drug	A drug that's generally considered to be more dangerous, with a higher risk of dependence, than soft drugs	Heroin, methamphetamine, crack cocaine
Soft drug	A drug whose use supposedly doesn't result in as severe a degree of dependence as hard drugs, and is often considered less dangerous by society – although the negative consequences may be just as/more severe (e.g. tobacco use → lung cancer)	Marijuana, alcohol, nicotine
Illicit drug	An illegal drug (not legally prescribed)	Marijuana, cocaine, heroin, LSD
Designer drug	A synthetic drug very similar chemically to an existing drug, exerting similar pharmacological effects	Ecstasy
Club drug	A drug used primarily in clubs, bars, and trance parties (such as raves), usually by adolescents or young adults	Ecstasy, Rohypnol ('roofies'), GHB, ketamine ('special K'), LSD, mephedrone ('m-cat'/'meow')

Stimulants

Amphetamines

These were first synthesised in the 1920s. Their general effect is to increase energy and enhance self-confidence. For this reason, they were used extensively by the military in the Second World War to reduce fatigue and give soldiers going into battle more confidence. Amphetamines also suppress appetite and are hence the main ingredient of 'slimming pills', such as Methedrine, Dexedrine and Benzedrine.

Amphetamines are swallowed in pill form, inhaled through the nose in powder form or injected in liquid form. Small amounts cause increased wakefulness, alertness and arousal. Users experience a sense of energy and confidence, and feel that any problem can be solved and any task accomplished. Once the drug wears off, users experience a 'crash' or 'hangover', characterised by extreme fatigue and depression, irritability, disorientation and agitated motor activity. They counteract this by taking the drug again. Large amounts can cause restlessness, hallucinations and paranoid delusions (or amphetamine psychosis), which is virtually indistinguishable from paranoid schizophrenia (see Chapter 44). Long-term use has also been linked with severe depression, suicidal tendencies, disrupted thinking and brain damage.

Tolerance and *psychological dependence* develop quickly. The amphetamine 'hangover' is indicative of *withdrawal*, suggesting that there's also *physiological dependence*.

Cocaine

Cocaine hydrochloride is a powerful CNS stimulant extracted from the leaves of the coca shrub, native to the Andes mountains in South America. The Peruvian Indians originally discovered that chewing the leaves could increase stamina and relieve fatigue and hunger. While they still chew the leaves, elsewhere in the world cocaine is inhaled in powder form, injected into the veins in liquid form or smoked. When smoked, the drug reaches the brain in 5–10 seconds, much faster than the other methods. It can also be swallowed, rubbed on the gums or blown into the throat.

In general, the effects of cocaine are similar to those of amphetamines, but they tend to last only 15–30 minutes (compared with several hours). Typically, the user experiences a state of euphoria, deadening of pain, increased self-confidence, energy and attention. There's also a 'crash' when the drug wears off.

Even in small amounts, the stimulating effects can cause cardiac arrest and death. Young people who use cocaine (and amphetamines) may be increasing their risk of having a stroke (brain haemorrhage) (Laurance, 2000; Taylor, 2002). This is overshadowing the traditional risk factors for stroke, such as high blood pressure; this is much more common in older people, as are strokes, but it's becoming increasingly common for people under 30 to suffer strokes after taking drugs.

Cocaine (and amphetamines) produces a surge in blood pressure. Repeated inhalation constricts the blood vessels in the nose and the nasal septum may become perforated, necessitating cosmetic surgery.

Formication refers to the sensation that 'insects' ('coke bugs') are crawling beneath the skin. Although this is merely random neural activity, users sometimes try to remove the imaginary insects by cutting deep into their skin. Cocaine definitely produces *psychological dependence*, but there's much more doubt regarding physiological dependence, tolerance and withdrawal. Unlike heroin-dependent people, most cocaine users will get over their drug problem without professional help (Hammersley, 1999).

Box 8.1 Crack

- Crack is a form of cocaine that first appeared in the 1980s.
- It's made using cocaine hydrochloride, ammonia or baking soda and water. When heated, the ammonia or baking soda produces a 'cracking' sound. The result is a crystal, which has had the hydrochloride base removed (hence the term '*free basing*' to describe its production).
- Its effects are more rapid and intense than cocaine's, but the 'crash' is also more intense.

Opiates

These are derived from the unripe seed pods of the opium poppy ('plant of joy'). One constituent of opium is morphine, from which *codeine* and *heroin* can be extracted.

Figure 8.5 Extreme dehydration and hyperthermia, plus MDMA, can be a lethal cocktail

Morphine and heroin

In general, the opiates *depress* neural functioning and suppress physical sensations and responses to stimulation. In Europe, *morphine* was first used as an *analgesic* during the Franco-Prussian War (1870–71). However, it quickly became apparent that it produced physiological dependence (the 'soldier's disease'). The German Bayer Company developed *heroin* (the 'hero' that would cure the 'soldier's disease') in order to prevent this dependence, but, unfortunately, it also causes physiological dependence and has many unpleasant side effects.

Heroin can be smoked, inhaled or injected intravenously. Puffing the heated white powder ('chasing the dragon') is now the preferred method because syringes are seen as dirty and dangerous (Khan, 2003). The immediate effects (the 'rush') are described as an overwhelming sensation of pleasure, similar to sexual orgasm but affecting the whole body. Such effects are so pleasurable that they override any thoughts of food or sex. Heroin rapidly decomposes into morphine, producing feelings of euphoria, well-being, relaxation and drowsiness.

Long-term users become more aggressive and socially isolated, as well as less physically active. Opiates in general may damage the body's immune system, leading to increased susceptibility to infection. The impurity of the heroin used, users' lack of adequate diet and the risks from contaminated needles, all increase health risks. Overdoses are common.

Figure 8.6 Anna Nicole Smith, who died in 2007 (aged 39) apparently as the result of an overdose of prescription drugs

Heroin produces both *physiological and psychological dependence*. *Tolerance* develops quickly. *Withdrawal symptoms* initially involve flu-like symptoms, progressing to tremors, stomach cramps, and alternating chills and sweats. Rapid pulse, high blood pressure, insomnia and diarrhoea also occur. The skin often breaks out into goosebumps, where the skin resembles that of a plucked turkey (hence the term '*cold turkey*' to describe attempts to abstain). The legs jerk uncontrollably (hence '*kicking the habit*'). These symptoms last about a week, reaching a peak after about 48 hours.

Box 8.2 Heroin and endorphins

- As we saw in Chapter 4, the brain produces its own opiates (*opioid peptides* or *endorphins*).
- When we engage in important survival behaviours, endorphins are released into the fluid that bathes neurons. Endorphin molecules stimulate opiate receptors on some neurons, producing an intensely pleasurable effect just like that reported by heroin users.
- Regular use of opiates overloads endorphin sites in the brain, and the brain stops producing its own endorphins (Snyder, 1977). When the user abstains, neither the naturally occurring endorphins nor the opiates are available. Consequently, the internal mechanism for regulating pain is severely disrupted, producing some of the withdrawal symptoms described earlier.

Hallucinogens

These produce the most profound effects on consciousness. This is why they're sometimes called *psychedelics* ('mind expanding'). *Mescaline* comes from the peyote cactus, while *psilocybin* is obtained from the mushroom *psilocybe mexicana*. LSD and PCP are both chemically synthesised.

LSD

First produced in the 1940s, LSD was used during the 1960s for a variety of medical purposes, including pain relief for the terminally ill. But it became widely known during that period – and widely used – as a recreational drug. This use of LSD was largely inspired by Timothy Leary, a Harvard University Psychologist, who coined the slogan 'Tune out' of traditional society, 'Turn on' to mind-altering drugs, and 'Tune in' to one's inner nature. LSD, peace and love were central to the 1960s hippy movement ('flower power').

Figure 8.7 Timothy Leary (1920–1996)

LSD is usually impregnated on blotting paper and swallowed. Unlike other drugs, its effects may not appear until an hour or so after being taken. These include:

- distorted sensory experiences, such as the intensification of sights and sounds, and changing form and colour; this can be pleasurable or terrifying (a 'bad trip'), depending on mood and expectations
- the dramatic slowing down of subjective time
- *synaesthesia* – for example, music may be experienced visually (see Chapter 5)
- *depersonalisation* – a state in which the body is perceived as being separate from the self; users report being able to see themselves from afar, similar to out-of-body experiences (see Chapter 6)
- *flashbacks* – some long-term users experience distorted perceptions or hallucinations days or weeks after the drug was taken; these might be psychological or physiological in origin.

There's *no* evidence of physiological dependence or withdrawal, but *tolerance* can develop quickly. Whether LSD produces psychological dependence is disputed.

Cannabis

This is second only to alcohol in popularity. The *cannabis sativa* plant's psychoactive ingredient is *delta-9-tetrahydrocannabinil* (THC). THC is found in the branches and leaves of the male and female plants (*marijuana*), but is highly concentrated in the resin of the female plant. *Hashish* is derived from the sticky resin and is more potent than marijuana (see Table 8.1).

Cannabis is usually smoked with tobacco or eaten. When smoked, THC reaches the brain within seven seconds. Small amounts produce a mild, pleasurable 'high', involving relaxation, a loss of social inhibition, intoxication and a humorous mood. Speech becomes slurred and coordination is impaired. Increased heart rate, reduced concentration, enhanced appetite and impaired short-term memory are also quite common effects. Some users report fear, anxiety and confusion.

Cannabis is commonly taken along with MDMA (and other drugs). Regular cannabis users often display worse memory scores than non-drug users; *combined* MDMA/cannabis users display even worse memory profiles. Cannabis is broadly similar to alcohol in the extent of damage it can cause, although the profile of deficits is very different (Parrott, 2008).

Large amounts produce hallucinogenic reactions, but these aren't full blown as with LSD. THC remains in the body for up to a month, and both male sex hormones and the female menstrual cycle can be disrupted. If used during pregnancy, the foetus may fail to grow properly, and cannabis is more dangerous to the throat and lungs than cigarettes. While tolerance is usually a sign of physiological dependence, with cannabis *reverse tolerance* has been reported: regular use leads to a *lowering* of the amount needed to produce the initial effects. This could be due to a build-up of THC, which takes a long time to be metabolised. *Withdrawal effects* (restlessness, irritability and insomnia) have been reported, but they seem to be associated only with continuous use of very large amounts. *Psychological dependence* almost certainly occurs in at least some people.

Heavy use can contribute to respiratory/cardiovascular problems, as well as short-term memory impairments. Indeed, recent evidence has shown that sudden deaths from cardiac arrhythmia (abnormal heart rhythms) can be caused by cannabis intoxication in individuals with no history of cardiac problems (Hartung *et al.*, 2014). However, most people suffer no ill-effects from a single or occasional use of the drug. On the positive side, it can reduce dangerously high internal eye pressure (glaucoma) that can lead to vision loss; it can also provide pain relief and reduce nausea/vomiting from chemotherapy, and limit severe weight loss in AIDS and other diseases (Arkowitz and Lilienfeld, 2012a).

Ask Yourself

- Sixteen US states have now legalised cannabis for medical use and many more are considering doing so (Arkowitz and Lilienfeld, 2012a).
- Do you agree with the government's decision to *reclassify* cannabis back to a Class B drug in 2009? (It was 'downgraded' to a Class C drug (alongside tranquillisers and steroids) in 2004.)
- Do you think it should be legalised (decriminalised)?
- Why/why not?

EXPLAINING SUBSTANCE ABUSE AND DEPENDENCE

According to Lowe (1995):

> *... It is now generally agreed that addictive behaviours are multiply determined phenomena, and should be considered as biopsychosocial entities.*

Most researchers believe that social, personal, family and lifestyle factors are important, as well as the action of the drug itself. However, it's not yet understood fully how these work and interact. According to Hammersley (1999), theories of dependence have two dimensions. These are concerned with the extent to which dependence is:

1. supposedly caused by *biological*, as opposed to *social*, factors
2. the result of *abnormal/pathological* processes, as opposed to the extreme end of normal processes.

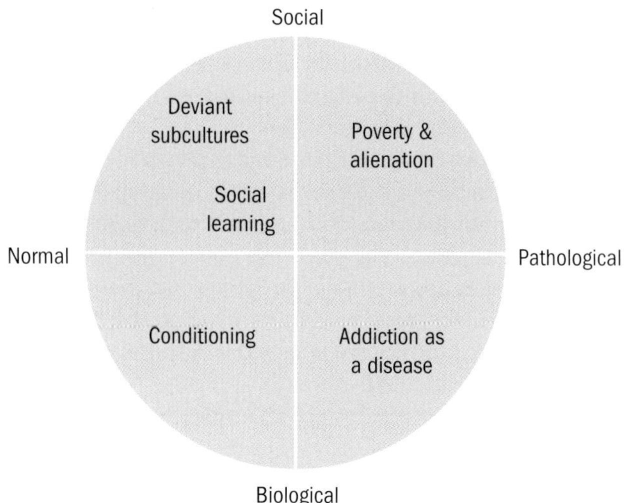

Figure 8.8 Five main theories of addiction (from Hammersley, 1999)

Critical Discussion 8.2

Cannabis and psychosis

- New, stronger strains of cannabis, such as *skunk*, are showing the darker side of a drug once considered to be relatively harmless. Concerns about its links with psychosis, and its ability to act as a 'gateway drug' into addiction, have prompted a sea change in popular opinion about cannabis (Doward and Templeton, 2008). Skunk accounts for 80 per cent of the cannabis used in the UK.
- According to Arkowitz and Lilienfeld (2012a), many studies have found that most people who used other illicit drugs had, in fact, used marijuana first. Although results such as these are consistent with the *gateway hypothesis*, they don't prove that using marijuana *causes* the other drug use. Those who are drawn to marijuana may simply be predisposed to drug use in general, regardless of their exposure to pot. Also, individuals often smoke cigarettes or drink alcohol *before* they try pot. Should we also be asking whether nicotine and alcohol are gateway drugs?
- Greenfield (in Ahuja, 2000) considers cannabis to be pretty potent. It takes 0.3 mg to induce the same kind of effects as 7000 mg of alcohol, primarily feelings of well-being and relaxation. This potency suggests that specific cannabis receptors exist in the brain.
- Laurance (2004a) cites several studies showing a link between cannabis and psychosis. A four-year Dutch study followed 2437 people aged 14–24 years, finding that of those who smoked cannabis regularly and had a pre-existing risk of psychosis, 50 per cent developed psychotic symptoms over this period. This was twice the rate among those who didn't use and more than three times higher than those who were neither users nor vulnerable.
- According to Murray (2002), people with schizophrenia don't take more alcohol, heroin or ecstasy than the rest of us – but they're twice as likely to smoke cannabis regularly. While this doesn't demonstrate that cannabis *causes* schizophrenia, it's consistent with other evidence that shows it *exacerbates* schizophrenia (unlike heroin or morphine). However, other evidence exists which demonstrates a causal link (Arkowitz and Lilienfeld, 2012a).
- However, there hasn't been a corresponding increase in the incidence of psychosis since cannabis use became common in the 1960s and 1970s (Iversen, cited in Laurance, 2007); indeed, incidence of schizophrenia has *fallen* between 1996 and 2005 (Doward and Templeton, 2008). Also, cannabis use among 16–24-year-olds has *fallen* by about 20 per cent since 2004 (when cannabis was 'downgraded' to a Class C): if classification itself made a difference, we'd expect cannabis use to have *increased* (Blakemore, 2008).

The disease model of alcohol dependence

Rush, widely regarded as the father of American psychiatry, is commonly credited with being the first major figure to conceptualise alcoholism as a 'disease', in the early 1800s. At about the same time, the British doctor, Trotter, likened alcoholism to a mental disorder. Both men saw it as a product of a distinct biological defect or dysfunction, much like cancer, diabetes or TB (Lilienfeld, 1995).

In 1935, a doctor and former alcoholic, Smith, and Wilson (a stockbroker) founded Alcoholics Anonymous (AA) in the USA. AA assumes that certain individuals possess a physiological susceptibility to alcohol analogous to an allergy: a single drink is sufficient to trigger an unquenchable desire for more, resulting in an inevitable loss of control.

Perhaps the most influential champion of the disease model was Jellinek, a physiologist. Based on questionnaire data with AA members, Jellinek (1946, 1952, 1960) proposed that alcoholism was a biological illness with a highly characteristic and predictable course. It comprises four major stages:

1. *pre-alcoholic phase* – alcohol provides a means of reducing tension and increasing self-confidence (*alpha* alcoholics)
2. *prodromal phase* – the alcoholic begins to drink secretly and heavily, and to experience blackouts (*beta* alcoholics)
3. *crucial phase* – the alcoholic begins to lose control, engage in 'benders' and to experience severe withdrawal symptoms (*delta*, *epsilon* and *gamma* alcoholics)
4. *chronic phase* – the alcoholic drinks almost constantly and neglects almost all social and occupational responsibilities (*gamma* alcoholics).

Evaluating the disease model

(We considered some limitations of the AAD model in Critical Discussion 8.1).

According to Lilienfeld (1995), the course of alcoholism appears to be far more variable than this, and many drinkers don't fit into any of Jellinek's categories. Nevertheless, his research was instrumental in persuading many scientists that alcoholism is best regarded as a physiological illness with a distinctive natural history.

This was the single most influential theory for much of the twentieth century. It's still the dominant view underlying psychiatric and other medically oriented treatment programmes, but is much less influential among psychologically based programmes since the 1980s.

Peele (1989) lists six major assumptions made by the disease model.

1. alcoholics drink too much, not because they intend to, but because they can't control their drinking
2. alcoholics inherit their alcoholism, and so are born as alcoholics
3. alcoholism as a disease can strike any individual, from any sociocultural background (it's an 'equal-opportunity destroyer')
4. alcoholism always gets worse without treatment; alcoholics can never cut back or quit on their own
5. treatment based on the AA principles is the only effective treatment
6. those who reject the AA principles, or observers who reject any of the above, are in denial.

Peele argues that there's no evidence to support any of these assumptions. Regarding the second assumption, Lilienfeld (1995) observes that it implies that all individuals drink heavily for the same – or at least very similar – reasons. However, Cloninger (1987) proposed that *Group 1 alcoholics* are at risk of 'Type 1' alcoholism:

- they drink primarily to reduce tension, are predominantly female, are prone to anxiety and depression, and tend to have relatively late onset of problem drinking.

By contrast, *Group 2 alcoholics* are at risk of 'Type 2' alcoholism:

- they drink primarily to relieve boredom, give free rein to their tendency towards risk-taking and sensation-seeking, are predominantly male, prone to antisocial and criminal behaviour, and tend to have relatively early onset of drinking behaviour.

Although the evidence for Cloninger's model is tentative and indirect, it challenges the disease model in a quite fundamental way. If he's correct, alcoholism may represent the culmination of two very different (and, in fact, essentially opposite), pathways (Lilienfeld, 1995).

Alcohol dependence syndrome (ADS) (Edwards, 1986) is a later version of the disease model. It grew out of dissatisfaction with 'alcoholism' and with the traditional conception of alcoholism as disease. The term 'syndrome' adds flexibility, suggesting a group of concurrent behaviours that accompany alcohol dependence. They needn't always be observed in the same individual, nor are they observable to the same degree in everyone. According to Lowe (1995):

> *Simple disease models have now been largely replaced by a more complex set of working hypotheses based, not on irreversible physiological processes, but on learning and conditioning, motivation and self-regulation, expectations and attributions.*

It's important to make some observations about the risk factors described in Box 8.3.

Box 8.3 Risk factors for addictive behaviour

Griffiths (2013) identifies four major risk factors for addictive behaviour:

1. **Stress**: There's a well-established link between long-term stress from childhood abuse (physical, emotional and/or sexual) and later development of both chemical and behavioural addictions. Clearly, not everyone who suffers such abuse goes on to develop an addiction, but it makes it much more likely.
2. **Peer influence**: Some researchers claim that peer influence is the single most important risk factor during adolescence (see Table 8.3). If asked, teenage addicts often blame peers for both initiation and maintenance of their addictive habit (a case of *normative social influence*; see Chapter 26).
3. **Age**: Related to (2) above is the finding that young people are at greater risk of developing addictive behaviour: decision-making and judgement skills are still developing. However, addiction can occur at any age. The adolescent is particularly susceptible to lifetime addiction partly because adolescence is a time for risk-taking (see Chapter 37). A consistent research finding is that the earlier someone first engages in a potentially addictive behaviour, the more likely it is to become a problem.
4. **Personality**: In terms of the five-factor model of personality (see Chapter 42), alcohol-abuse disorders are positively correlated with neuroticism (N) and negatively correlated with agreeableness (A) and conscientiousness (C). Some studies have found an association between substance-use disorders and high scores on N and openness (O), and lower scores on extroversion (E), A and C compared with those suffering from other mental disorders. Andreassen *et al.* (2013) have also found relationships between these dimensions and (i) facebook addiction; (ii) video game addiction; (iii) internet addiction; (iv) mobile phone addiction; (v) exercise addiction; (vi) compulsive buying; and (vii) study addiction.

Other studies (e.g. Ersche *et al.*, 2010) have shown that impulsivity and sensation-seeking (an interest in searching out new experiences, even if they're risky or potentially dangerous) are risk factors for drug addiction.

- There's little evidence for an 'addictive personality' as such (Griffiths, 2013).
- Risk factors aren't *deterministic*: they don't automatically and inevitably lead to addiction, but increase the probability of this happening (Smith, 2013).
- Smith (2013) cites evidence that some people are able to take (potentially) addictive substances recreationally without developing dependence (even heroin). These individuals (including many returning American soldiers from Vietnam and Afghanistan, where heroin was highly accessible and the need for self-medication great) seem to have *protective factors* against developing compulsive drug-taking tendencies.

The influence of sociocultural factors on drug use

Sussman and Ames (2008) discuss (a) the effects people in one's immediate support systems might have on whether an individual initiates drug use; and (b) macro-level physical and environmental influences on the development of substance use. These are summarised in Tables 8.3 and 8.4, respectively, below.

APPROACHES TO THE TREATMENT OF DRUG DEPENDENCE

A wide range of treatments and therapies is used in an attempt to change people's addictive behaviours (including both chemical and non-chemical dependence), reflecting some of the major theoretical approaches discussed in Chapter 2.

Addictive behaviour is just another psychological disorder, which may be treated using *psychological* and/or *biological* methods (see Chapter 45). Some examples of each type are given below:

1. *Aversion therapy*, *covert sensitisation* and *imagined sensitisation* (all based on classical conditioning) for treating alcohol abuse.
2. *Contingency management*, *behavioural self-control training* (including one or more of: *stimulus control*, *modification of the topography of drinking*, *reinforcing abstinence*) (all based on operant conditioning) for alcohol abuse.
3. Cognitive interventions, including *relapse prevention training* for cocaine abusers, *cognitive behavioural therapy* (CBT) with both alcohol and cocaine abusers, pathological gamblers, *relaxation* and *positive self-talk* with smokers.

Table 8.3 Social interaction and social group influences on drug use (adapted from Sussman and Ames, 2008)

Family unit and parenting	Family interactions may serve as protective or risk factors for subsequent drug use (e.g. conflict-ridden *vs* warm interactions)
	Parenting styles affect problem behaviours
	Quality and quantity of family time a child experiences and parental monitoring of child's activities can predict future drug use
Peer social influence	Friends and peer affiliation can inhibit or promote drug use behaviours: friend/peer group drug use considered to be one of strongest predictors of drug use among teens (see Chapter 26)
Social/cognitive theory	Drug use can develop through vicarious learning (modelling/observational learning), and/or reinforcement of drug-related behaviour
	Role models act as teachers of time and place, quantity, and methods of drug use
	Cognitive processes primarily regulate behaviour (see Chapters 29, 35 and 36)
Social support	The assistance people in social networks provide each other with, through family, friends, acquaintances, or community agencies. Includes companionship, instrumental support, conformity and informational support (see Chapters 25, 26 and 28)
Social networks	Social networks influence an individual's choices about those with whom s/he has contact and interacts, which can determine behaviour, either through constraint or promotion of action
	Individuals occupying central positions within a network tend to be more influential in disseminating information and regulating behavioural norms (see Chapters 26 and 27)
Deviant subcultures	Differential socialisation may lead to group norms that serve to rationalise problem behaviour or deviant subcultures (see Chapter 35)
Group identification	The tendency for people to identify with a consensually recognised and labelled group; this may promote or inhibit drug use
	Groups indicate successful/unsuccessful ways of participating in a particular culture (see Chapter 25)

Table 8.4 Wider social and physical environmental influences on drug use (adapted from Sussman and Ames, 2008)

Neighbourhood disorganisation	A lack of centralised authority or rapid changes of authority can produce a lack of behavioural monitoring. Individuals living in more chaotic areas may be more heavily exposed to social disobedience. Abandoned buildings and enclosed public spaces may result in greater incidence of exposure to drugs and criminal activities
Socioeconomics	Adverse socioeconomic conditions may prevent the promotion or availability of prosocial activities and increase exposure drug-related criminal activity
	A decrease in protective factors (familial or social support) may influence some to self-medicate under disadvantaged circumstances. Individuals of high socioeconomic status (SES) may be able to afford large quantities of drugs, leading to addiction
Environmental availability	Ease of distribution, access and acquisition of drugs within the individual's environment
Cultural influences	Life habits/rituals, normative structures/expectations, and beliefs about drug use/its effects
Gender differences	Gender-role expectations within one's environment and differential stigma associated with drug use
Ethnicity	Ethnicity may interact with demographics such as gender, age and type of drug in predicting drug use. Ethnic pride may play a role as protective factor in many ethnic groups
Acculturation	Exposure to changes in cultural rituals, drug use norms, or beliefs about drugs: the degree to which individuals adopt a 'host' culture to which they're recently exposed may inhibit or promote drug use, depending on their 'home' culture and the new one
Media and worldwide access to information	Advertisements promoting certain drug-related behaviours (e.g. movies glamorise cigarette smoking and alcohol use)
	Mass media can disseminate large amounts of information quickly and to various sources (e.g. the internet shows how to manufacture and obtain particular drugs)

4. *Antidepressant drugs* (such as *selective serotonin reuptake inhibitors* (SSRIs)) with pathological gamblers.
5. *Anxiolytic* (anti-anxiety) *drugs* (such as *diazepam/* Valium) as part of *detoxification* with alcohol abusers and *disulfiram* (Antabuse) to maintain abstinence.
6. *Nicotine gum, patches* or *inhalers*.
7. *Brain stimulation* (including *deep brain stimulation, cortical stimulation* and *transcranial magnetic stimulation* (TMS)) for drug abuse.
8. *Heroin substitutes*, such as *methadone*. This is a synthetic *opiate* (or *opioid*) created to treat physiological dependence on heroin and other opiates. Methadone acts more slowly than heroin, and doesn't produce the heroin 'rush'. While heroin users may be less likely to take heroin if they're on methadone, they're likely to become at least psychologically dependent on it. By the early 1980s, long-term prescribing of methadone (*methadone maintenance*) began to be questioned, both in terms of effectiveness and the message it conveyed to users.
9. *Modafinil, topiramate* and *vigabatrin*, all drug therapies designed specifically either to satisfy a cocaine addict's cravings or dampen the reward responses in the brain (see Research Update 8.1) (Sergo, 2008).

Chapter Summary

- Drugs are **psychoactive** substances. They may be used **therapeutically** or for **pleasure**, the latter being subdivided into **recreational** and **drugs of abuse**.
- Which drugs are legal or illegal changes over time within the same society and between societies. Cigarette smoking and alcohol abuse are so widespread that they may be considered 'ordinary addictions'.
- The concept of **addiction** has been criticised for being oversimplified and for reflecting the **disease model**.
- Some researchers argue that the concept of addiction should be **broadened**, so as to cover forms of addictive behaviour which don't involve chemical substances at all. Addictive behaviours may display the same components, regardless of the particular substance or activity involved.
- **Dependence** can be either **psychological** or **physiological**, the latter indicated either by **tolerance** or **withdrawal**. Both types of dependence are part of the **dependence syndrome**.
- Physiologically addictive drugs, such as alcohol and heroin, typically also cause **habituation**. Most widely used recreational drugs, including cannabis, cocaine and ecstasy, produce habituation without causing physiological dependence.
- Major **categories** of drugs include **depressants (sedatives)**, **stimulants**, **opiates**, **hallucinogens (psychedelics)** and **cannabis**.
- **Alcohol** is a **depressant** and can produce several life-threatening physical diseases, as well as causing **foetal alcohol syndrome**. It also impairs memory function, an extreme form being **Korsakoff's syndrome**.
- **Stimulants** include **amphetamines**, which produce both physiological and psychological dependence, **cocaine**, which definitely causes only psychological dependence, and **MDMA** (or ecstasy).
- Ecstasy is associated with raves and clubbing, making it difficult to infer the drug's effect on various mental and physical reactions.
- **Morphine** and **heroin** are **opiates**. Heroin produces both psychological and physiological dependence, and withdrawal symptoms are severe and extremely unpleasant. It's thought that regular use of opiates causes the brain to stop producing its own **endorphins**.
- **LSD** is a **hallucinogen**, which may produce psychological dependence, but not physiological dependence.
- **Cannabis** doesn't fit neatly into the other categories. It comes in different forms and can be taken in a variety of ways. There's some evidence of **reverse tolerance**, and psychological dependence is likely for some people.
- **Theories of dependence** differ according to whether they see the causes as **biological** or **social**, and whether dependence is seen as pathological or the extreme end of normal processes.
- The single most influential theory of alcohol dependence is the **disease model**. It assumes that everyone is dependent for the same reasons and supporting evidence is very limited. **Alcohol dependence syndrome** (ADS) is a more flexible version of the disease model.
- **Risk factors** include stress, peer influence, age (younger people), and certain personality factors. But there's no 'addictive personality' as such, and risk factors aren't deterministic.
- The influence of **sociocultural factors** (such as family, peer group, physical environment and the broader cultural context) need to be taken into account **in addition** to the physiological effects of the abused substance.
- As with interventions for psychological abnormality as a whole, several different **biological** and **psychological** treatments and therapies have been used with both chemical and non-chemical abuse and dependence.

Links with Other Topics/Chapters

Chapter 43 ⟶ Substance abuse disorders are included in DSM-5's classification of *mental disorders*

Chapter 44 ⟶ Several (non-chemical) addictions share many of the characteristics of drug addiction, including *eating disorders*

Chapter 7 ⟶ Alcohol also suppresses *REM sleep*

Chapter 37 ⟶ Increased alcohol consumption among younger people has been related to the trend toward 'perpetual adolescence': *puberty* starts earlier

Chapter 12 ⟶ The disease model of addiction is one example of the more general *biomedical model* of disease. *Health Psychology* represents a major challenge to the biomedical model, favouring the *biopsychosocial model* of health and illness

Chapter 44 ⟶ Several drugs (such as amphetamines and hallucinogens) can induce *psychotic reactions*

Chapter 17 ⟶ *Korsakoff's syndrome* is an extreme memory disorder associated with chronic alcohol consumption

Chapter 38 ⟶ and men and women are postponing both *marriage* and having *children*

Chapter 4 ⟶ The effects of long-term heroin use can be understood in terms of the brain's own *opiates* (*endorphins*)

Chapter 46 ⟶ Cloninger's group 2 alcoholics have a crime-prone personality

Recommended Reading

Baker, A. (ed.) (2000) *Serious Shopping: Essays in Psychotherapy and Consumerism*. London: Free Association Books. Chapter 2 (by Baker). Chapter 6 (by Corbett) examines shopping addiction in relation to women's body image (and so is relevant to eating disorders; see Chapter 44).

Griffiths, M. (1999) internet addiction: Fact or Fiction? *The Psychologist*, 12(5), 246–50.

Powell, J. (2000) Drug and alcohol dependence. In L. Champion, M. Power (eds) *Adult Psychological Problems: An Introduction* (2nd edn). Hove: Psychology Press.

Sussman, S., Ames, S.L. (2008) *Drug Abuse: Concepts, Prevention and Cessation*. New York: Cambridge University Press.

Useful websites

www.cannabis.net (Cannabinoids, cannabis, marijuana, and hemp)

www.samhsa.gov (The Substance Abuse and Mental Health Services Administration within the US Department of Health and Human Services.)

www.sciencemag.org/cgi/content/abstract/sci;251/5001/1580 (Access to several science articles on the psychology and neurophysiology of cocaine addiction)

CHAPTER 9

MOTIVATION

INTRODUCTION and OVERVIEW

Trying to define motivation is a little like trying to define Psychology itself. Taking as a starting point the lay person's view of Psychology as the study of 'what makes people tick', motivation is concerned with why people act and think the way they do. 'Why' questions – and related 'how' questions – usually imply *causes* and *underlying mechanisms* or *processes*.

Each of the major theoretical approaches discussed in Chapter 2 (*Biopsychological, Behaviourist, Cognitive, Psychodynamic, Humanistic, Social Constructionist* and *Evolutionary*), tries to identify the key processes and mechanisms. At the heart of each approach lies an image of human beings that, in essence, is a theory of the causes of human behaviour.

Motivated behaviour is *goal-directed*, purposeful behaviour. It's difficult to think of any behaviour, human or non-human, that isn't motivated in this sense. However, just how the underlying motives are conceptualised and investigated depends very much on the persuasion of the Psychologist. For example:

- For a *Biopsychologist*, what's crucial are bodily events and processes taking place in the CNS, the ANS and the endocrine system, or interactions between these different systems (see Chapter 4).
- A *Psychodynamic* Psychologist will try to discover internal, unconscious drives and motives (see Chapter 42).
- A *Behaviourist* will look for environmental *schedules of reinforcement*, which can explain the behaviour of rats and pigeons as effectively as that of human beings (see Chapter 11).
- A *Humanistic* Psychologist, such as Maslow, will try to understand a person's behaviour in terms of a *hierarchy of needs/motives*, with *self-actualisation* at the top of the hierarchy.

While Maslow's hierarchy of needs is useful as a general framework for examining other approaches, this chapter has a very 'biological' flavour. *Homeostatic drive theories* try to explain hunger and thirst, but even in the case of such basic biological motives as these, cognitive and other individual factors, as well as social and cultural factors, play a crucial role. *Non-homeostatic needs* and *drives*, include electrical self-stimulation of the brain (ES-SB), competence and cognitive motives, and some important social motives.

WHAT IS MOTIVATION?

According to Rubin and McNeil (1983), motives are a special kind of cause that 'energise, direct and sustain a person's behaviour (including hunger, thirst, sex and curiosity)'. Similarly:

> *Motivation refers, in a general sense, to processes involved in the initiation, direction, and energisation of individual behaviour ... (Geen, 1995)*

The word 'motive' comes from the Latin for 'move' (*movere*), and this is captured in Miller's (1962) definition:

> *The study of motivation is the study of all those pushes and prods – biological, social and psychological – that defeat our laziness and move us, either eagerly or reluctantly, to action.*

Several attempts have been made to classify different kinds of motives. For example, Rubin and McNeil (1983) identify (i) survival or physiological motives, and (ii) competence or cognitive motives. Social motives represent a third category. Clearly, humans share survival motives with all other animals, as well as certain competence motives (see below). But other motives are peculiarly and uniquely human, notably self-actualisation, which lies at the peak of Maslow's (1954) 'hierarchy of needs'.

Maslow's hierarchy of needs

Although Maslow's theory is commonly discussed in relation to personality (see Chapter 42), its focus on needs makes it equally relevant to motivation. (The book in which he first proposed his hierarchy was called *Motivation and Personality*.) According to Maslow, we're subject to two quite different sets of motivational states or forces:

1. those that ensure survival by satisfying basic physical and psychological needs (physiological, safety, love and belongingness, and esteem), and
2. those that promote the person's self-actualisation – that is, realising one's full potential, 'becoming everything that one is capable of becoming' (Maslow, 1970), especially in the intellectual and creative domains.

As Maslow states:

> *We share the need for food with all living things, the need for love with (perhaps) the higher apes, [and] the need for Self-Actualisation with [no other species].*

Behaviours that relate to survival or deficiency needs (*deficiency* or *D-motives*) are engaged in because they satisfy those needs (a means to an end). But those that relate to self-actualisation are engaged in for their own sake, because they're intrinsically satisfying (*growth*, *being* or *B-motives*). The latter include the fulfilment of ambitions, the acquisition of admired skills, the steady increase of understanding about people, the universe or oneself, the development of creativeness in a particular field or, most important, simply the ambition to be a good human being. It's simply inaccurate to speak in such instances of tension reduction, which implies the overcoming of an annoying state, for these states aren't annoying (Maslow, 1968). (Another term for tension reduction is drive reduction, which is discussed below.) Maslow's argument is that to reduce the full range of human motives to drives, which must be satisfied or removed, is simply mistaken.

The hierarchical nature of Maslow's theory is intended to highlight the following points.

- Needs lower down in the hierarchy must be satisfied before we can attend to needs higher up. For example, if you're reading this while your stomach is trying

Self-actualisation
'Realising one's full potential' 'becoming everything one is capable of becoming'.
Aesthetic needs
Beauty – in art and nature – symmetry, balance, order, form.
Cognitive needs
Knowledge and understanding, curiosity, exploration, need for meaning and predictability.
Esteem needs
The esteem and respect of others, and self-esteem and self-respect. A sense of competence.
Love and belongingness
Receiving and giving love, affection, trust and acceptance. Affiliating, being part of a group (family, friends, work).
Safety needs
Protection from potentially dangerous objects or situations, (e.g. the elements, physical illness). The threat is both physical and psychological (e.g. 'fear of the unknown'). Importance of routine and familiarity.
Physiological needs
Food, drink, oxygen, temperature regulation, elimination, rest, activity, sex.

Figure 9.1 Maslow's hierarchy of needs (based on Maslow, 1954)

to tell you it's lunchtime, you probably won't absorb much about Maslow. Similarly if you're tired or in pain. Yet you can probably think of exceptions, such as the starving artist who finds inspiration despite hunger, or the mountain climber who risks his/her life for the sake of adventure (what Maslow would call a 'peak' experience – if you'll forgive the pun!).

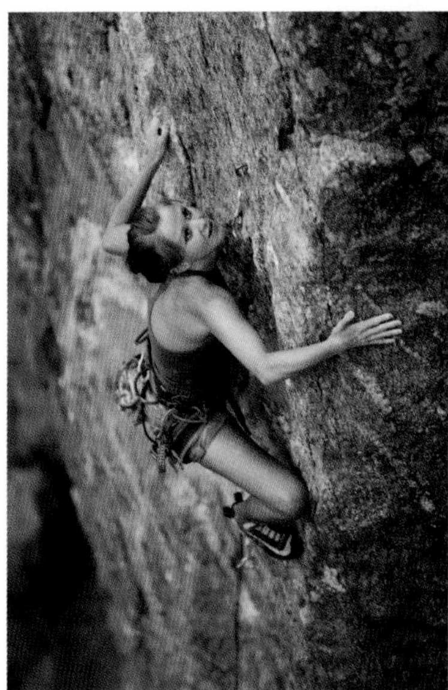

Figure 9.2 Because it's there

- Higher-level needs are a later evolutionary development: in the development of the human species (*phylogenesis*), self-actualisation is a fairly recent need. This applies equally to the development of individuals (*ontogenesis*): babies are much more concerned with their bellies than with their brains. But it's always a case of one need *predominating* at any one time, *not* excluding all other needs.
- The higher up the hierarchy we go, the more the need becomes linked to life experience, and the less 'biological' it is. Individuals will achieve self-actualisation in different ways, through different activities and by different routes. This is related to experience, not biology:

  > *A musician must make music, an artist must paint, a poet must write, if he is to be ultimately at peace with himself. What a man can be, he must be. (Maslow, 1968)*

  This captures nicely the *idiographic* nature of Maslow's theory – that is, the view that every individual is unique (see Chapter 42).
- The higher up the hierarchy we go, the more difficult it becomes to achieve the need. Many human goals are remote and long-term, and can only be achieved in a series of steps. This pursuit of aims/goals that lie very much in the future is unique to human beings, although individuals differ in their ability to set and realise such goals.

Ask Yourself

- Do you consider Maslow's hierarchy to be a useful way of thinking about human motivation? Do you think he's omitted any important motives?
- To what extent might the hierarchy reflect the culture and the historical time in which Maslow lived and wrote?

THE EARLY STUDY OF MOTIVATION

As with many other aspects of Psychology, the study of motivation has its roots in philosophy (see Chapters 1 and 3). *Rationalists* saw human beings as free to choose between different courses of action. This makes the concept of motivation almost unnecessary: it's our *reason* that determines our behaviour. This idea of freedom and responsibility is a basic premise of both Humanistic and Cognitive approaches (see Chapter 49).

The seventeenth-century British philosopher Hobbes proposed the theory of *hedonism*. This maintains that all behaviour is determined by the seeking of pleasure and the avoidance of pain. These are the 'real' motives (whatever we may believe) and this idea is central to Freud's psychoanalytic theory, captured in the concept of the *pleasure principle*. Similarly, the basic principles of *positive* and *negative reinforcement* correspond to the seeking of pleasure and avoidance of pain, respectively, and these are central to Skinner's operant conditioning.

Box 9.1 Motives as instincts

- The concept of instinct played a major role in early psychological approaches to motivation. Many Psychologists, inspired by Darwin's (1859) theory of evolution (see Chapter 2), which argued that humans and animals differ only *quantitatively*, identified human instincts that would explain human behaviour.
- For example, McDougall (1908) originally proposed 12 and, by 1924, over 800 separate instincts. But to explain behaviour by labelling it is to explain nothing (e.g. 'We behave aggressively because of our aggressive instinct' is a circular statement). This, combined with the sheer proliferation of instincts, seriously undermined the whole approach.
- However, the concept of instinct – with certain important modifications – remains a central feature of the *ethological approach* to behaviour, in particular, non-human animal behaviour (see Chapter 2 and Gross *et al.*, 2000).

During the 1920s, the concept of instinct was largely replaced by the concept of *drive*. The term was first used by Woodworth (1918), who compared human behaviour with the operation of a machine: the mechanism of a machine is relatively passive and drive is the power applied to make it 'go'. The concept of drive has taken two major forms: *homeostatic drive theory* (Cannon, 1929), which is a physiological theory, and *drive reduction theory* (Hull, 1943), which is primarily a theory of learning.

HOMEOSTATIC DRIVE THEORY

The term *homeostasis* is derived from the Greek *homos* (meaning 'same') and *stasis* (meaning 'stoppage'). It was coined by Cannon (1929) to refer to the process by which an organism maintains a fairly constant internal (bodily) environment – that is, how body temperature, blood sugar level, salt concentration in the blood, and so on, are kept in a state of relative balance or equilibrium.

When a state of imbalance arises (for example, through a substantial rise in body temperature), something must happen to correct the imbalance and restore equilibrium (sweating). In this case, the animal doesn't have to 'do' anything, because sweating is completely automatic and purely physiological. However, if the imbalance is caused by the body's need for food or drink (*tissue need*), the hungry or thirsty animal has to do something to obtain food or water. This is where the concept of a *homeostatic drive* becomes important. Tissue need leads to internal imbalance, which leads to homeostatic drive, which leads to appropriate behaviour, which leads to restoration of internal balance, which leads to drive reduction.

The internal environment requires a regular supply of raw materials from the external world (Green, 1980). While oxygen intake, for example, is involuntary and continuous, eating and drinking are *voluntary* and *discontinuous* (or spaced). We talk about a hunger and thirst drive, but we don't talk about an 'oxygen drive'. Because of the voluntary nature of eating and drinking, hunger and thirst are the homeostatic drives that Biopsychologists have been most interested in. We shall focus here on hunger.

Hunger and eating

Does hunger cause eating?

Ask Yourself

- What makes you eat?
- Why do you get hungry?

If there's a common-sense theory of eating, it's that we eat because – and when – we're hungry. What could be simpler? If asked why we get hungry, most people would probably say that 'our bodies get hungry' – that is, certain events take place in our bodies when we haven't eaten for a certain period of time, and these act as the 'signal' to eat. We experience that signal as hunger.

This fits very neatly with the hunger drive outlined above. If we place the experience of hunger in between 'internal imbalance' and 'homeostatic drive', we get a nice blend of the common-sense and drive-reduction theories, with hunger towards the end of a chain of causation that results in eating.

But is hunger either a necessary or sufficient condition for eating to occur? Can eating occur in the absence of hunger, and is it possible that we might not eat despite being hungry? We've all been tempted by the look or the smell of food when not feeling hungry, and we're not usually still hungry by the time the dessert trolley comes along. In other words, we often eat simply because we like it. This suggests that *hunger isn't necessary* for eating. Conversely, people who go on diets or hunger strike aren't eating (or are eating less than they might otherwise do) despite being very hungry, suggesting that *hunger isn't sufficient*.

So, there seems to be no biological inevitability about the hunger–eating relationship. However, as Blundell and Hill (1995) point out, under many circumstances there's a close relationship between the pattern of food intake and the rhythmic fluctuation of hunger. For example, many experimental studies confirm the strong link between the intensity of experienced hunger sensations and the amount of food eaten. This fairly consistent finding has been interpreted as showing that there's a causal connection between hunger and the size of a following meal. But in reality, certain physiological mechanisms are probably producing *both* the sensations of hunger and the eating behaviour.

Blundell and Hill propose an *appetite control system*, in which hunger, eating and physiological mechanisms are coupled together, but the coupling isn't perfect. There will be circumstances where uncoupling can occur, as in the hunger strike example, or in cases of eating disorders (such as obesity and anorexia nervosa; see below and Chapter 44). So, what might some of these physiological mechanisms be? Assuming that, normally, these are 'coupled' (or correlated) with hunger, what happens when the 'body gets hungry'?

What prompts us to eat?

Carlson (1992) points out that the physiological signals that cause eating to begin aren't necessarily the ones that cause it to end. There's considerable delay between the act of eating (the *correctional mechanism*) and a change in the state of the body. So, while we may start eating because the level of nutrients has fallen below a certain point, we certainly don't stop because that level has been restored to normal. In fact, we usually stop eating long before this, since digestion takes several hours to complete. Therefore, the signals for hunger and for *satiety* (the state of no longer being hungry) are sure to be different. Probably the earliest formal theory of hunger was proposed by Cannon.

Key Study 9.1

'Swallow a balloon if you're hungry' (Cannon and Washburn, 1912)

- Cannon originally believed that the hunger drive is caused by stomach contractions ('hunger pangs') and that food reduces the drive by stopping the contractions.
- Washburn swallowed an empty balloon tied to the end of a thin tube. Then Cannon pumped some air into the balloon and connected the end of the tube to a water-filled glass U-tube, so that Washburn's stomach contractions would cause an increase in the level of water at the other end of the U-tube. He reported a 'pang' of hunger each time a large stomach contraction was recorded.
- These results were soon confirmed by a case study (cited in Carlson, 1992) of a patient with a tube implanted through his stomach wall, just above the navel. He'd accidentally swallowed some acid, which caused the walls of his oesophagus (the muscular tube that carries food from the throat to the stomach) to fuse shut. The tube allowed him to feed himself and provided a means of observing his stomach activities.
- When there was food in his stomach, small rhythmic contractions (subsequently named *peristaltic contractions/peristalsis*) mixed the food and moved it along the digestive tract. When it was empty, the contractions were large and associated with the patient's reports of hunger.

An evaluation of Cannon's 'hunger pangs' theory

Sometimes patients have their stomachs removed (because of disease) and the oesophagus is 'hooked up' directly to the duodenum or small intestine (the upper portion of the intestine through which most of the glucose and amino acids are absorbed into the bloodstream; see below). They continue to report feeling hungry and satiated. Even though their stomachs are bypassed, they maintain normal body weight by eating more frequent, smaller meals (Pinel, 1993).

Similarly, cutting the *vagus nerve* connections between the gastrointestinal tract (GIT) (mainly the stomach and intestine) and the brain has little effect on food intake – either in experimental animals or human patients.

These findings suggest that Cannon exaggerated the importance of stomach contractions in causing hunger. But this doesn't mean that the stomach and the GIT play no part in hunger and satiety. If the vagus nerve is cut, signals arising from the gut can still be communicated to the brain via the circulatory system. These signals convey information about the components of the food that's been absorbed. Some of the nutrients whose depletion acts as a signal to start eating are fats (*lipids*), carbohydrates (including glucose), vitamins/mineral salts and proteins/amino acids. Fats and carbohydrates are burnt up in cellular reactions and provide the energy to fuel *metabolic* processes (essential for the body's normal functioning).

Also, the presence of food in the stomach (*stomach loading*) is important in the regulation of feeding: if the exit from the stomach to the duodenum is blocked off, rats will still eat normal-sized meals. It seems that information about the stretching of the stomach wall caused by the presence of food is passed to the brain (via the vagus nerve), allowing the brain's feeding centres to control meal size.

Glucostatic and lipostatic theories

When we engage in vigorous physical activity, our muscles are fuelled by fats and carbohydrates, which are stored as energy reserves. The cells that store our fat reserves are called adipocytes, and they clump together as *adipose tissue* (or simply 'fat'). Carbohydrates are stored as glycogen. Two major accounts of why we start eating are the *glucostatic* and *lipostatic* theories.

- According to *glucostatic theory* (GT), the primary stimulus for hunger is a decrease in the level of blood glucose below a certain set point. Glucose is the body's (especially the brain's) primary fuel. The *glucostat* was assumed to be a neuron (probably in the hypothalamus), which detects the level of blood glucose in much the same way as a thermostat measures temperature.
- According to Green (1994), *lipostatic theory* (LT) focuses on the *end product* of glucose metabolism, namely the storage of fats (lipids) in *adipocytes*. Body fat is normally maintained at a relatively constant level. Similarly, fluctuations in the amount of stored fats largely determine variations in body weight. According to Nisbett's (1972) version of LT, we all have a body weight set point around which our weight fluctuates within quite narrow limits; this is determined by the level of fats in the adipocytes.

Ask Yourself

- What are your two or three favourite foods (or meals)?
- What exactly is it about them that you like so much?
- How much, if at all, do you consider social factors play a part in your eating behaviour?

Other factors that influence eating

According to Pinel (1993):

> *The modern era of feeding research has been characterised by an increasing awareness of the major role played by learning in determining when we eat, what we eat, how much we eat, and even how the food that we eat is digested and metabolised. The concept of the feeding system has changed from that of an immutable system that maintains glucose and fat levels at pre-determined set points, to that of a flexible system that operates within certain general guidelines but is 'fine-tuned' by experience ...*

Eating for pleasure

Both humans and other animals are *drawn* to eat (rather than *driven* to eat) by food's *incentive properties* – that is, its anticipated pleasure-producing effects (or *palatability*). According to *incentive theories*, both internal and external factors influence eating in the same way, namely by changing the incentive value of available foods. Signals from the taste receptors seem to produce an immediate decline in the incentive value of *similar tasting food*, and signals associated with increased energy supply from a meal produce a general decrease in the incentive properties of *all foods*.

Support for this view comes from the discovery of neurons in the lateral hypothalamus (LH) that respond to the incentive properties of food, rather than food itself (Rolls and Rolls, 1982). When monkeys were repeatedly allowed to eat one palatable foodstuff, the response of LH neurons to it declined (a form of habituation?), although not to other palatable foods. Neurons that responded to the sight of food would begin to respond to a neutral stimulus that reliably predicted the presentation of food. These findings explain very neatly the common experience of our 'mouths watering' (salivating) at the mere mention of our favourite food – or even a picture of it. (See Key Study 9.2.)

Knowing what to eat: evolutionary influences

If learning is involved in the way humans and other animals respond to foods that are already palatable, could learning be involved in what is found palatable in the first place?

Key Study 9.2

Learning to salivate (Pavlov, 1927)

- The smell of food and the dinner bell are *food-predicting cues* (or *classically conditioned stimuli*).
- They trigger digestive and metabolic events, such as salivation, insulin secretion and gastric secretions (*classically conditioned responses*). These digestive/metabolic events are also called *cephalic phase responses*.
- Pavlov (1927) was the first to demonstrate that a cephalic phase response can be conditioned: the sight or smell of milk produced abundant salivation in puppies raised on a milk diet, but not in those raised on a solid diet.
- Feeling hungry at those times of the day when we usually eat (whether or not we're experiencing an energy deficit) is another example of a classically conditioned response (see Chapter 11).

- We have innate preferences for tastes that are associated in nature with vital nutrients. For example, sweetness detectors on the tongue are probably there because they helped our ancestors identify food that's safe to eat. Even when we're not particularly hungry, we tend to find a sweet taste pleasant, and eating something sweet tends to increase our appetite (Carlson, 1992).
- Both humans and other animals also have the ability to learn the relationship between taste and the post-ingestion consequences of eating certain food. In *taste aversion studies*, rats learn to avoid novel tastes that are followed by illness (Garcia *et al.*, 1966; see Chapter 11). Rats are also able to learn to prefer tastes that are followed by the infusion of nutrients and flavours that they smell on the breath of other rats.
- Rats and human beings have in common a metabolism that requires them to eat a variety of different foods: no single food provides all essential nutrients. We generally find a meal that consists of moderate amounts of several different foods more interesting than a huge plate of only one food, however palatable that food might be. If we have access to only one particular food, we soon become tired of it (*sensory-specific satiety*) (S-SS). This encourages the consumption of a varied diet and is related to explaining gluttony/obesity in humans (see Box 9.2).
- *Cultural evolution* helps the selection of balanced diets. For example, Mexicans increased the calcium in their diet by mixing small amounts of mineral lime into their tortillas. But in the industrialised societies of Europe and North America, we seem

Box 9.2 Sensory-specific satiety (S-SS) (based on Simring, 2013)

- S-SS has nothing to do with metabolic satiety (the feeling of 'fullness' that signals the body has consumed enough energy).
- According to research in the 1990s, S-SS is processed in the orbitofrontal cortex, involved in sensory integration, reward processing and decision-making. Neurons in that region respond strongly when we first taste food, then gradually weaken with successive bites; if another food in tasted, neuronal activity jumps back up to the high initial levels. This can continue even after we feel full – provided the next bite has a radically different sensory profile.
- In the first long-term study of S-SS, Tey *et al.* (2012) found that sticking to the same food meal after meal tends to *increase* its palatability, i.e. we'll go on eating more of it than we would have if we'd enjoyed more variety. Also, people reach S-SS much faster when they eat foods with complex, intense or unfamiliar flavours, as opposed to mild or bland flavours.

Figure 9.3

Ask Yourself

- Which would you rather eat?

to prefer diets that are fundamentally detrimental to our health (see Chapter 12). Manufacturers tend to sell foods that are highly palatable and energy-dense, but that often have little nutritional value. This encourages us to overeat and, as a result, to increase fat deposits and body weight. Blundell and Hill (1995) maintain that in evolutionary terms, overeating makes good sense:

> *... For human beings it can be supposed that during most of the tens of thousands of years of human evolution, the biggest problem facing human-kind was the scarcity of food ... the existence of an abundance of food, highly palatable and easily available, is a very recent development in evolutionary terms. Accordingly, it is unlikely that evolutionary pressure has ever led to the development of mechanisms to prevent overconsumption ...*

What stops us eating?

According to Blundell and Hill (1995), *satiety* (feeling 'full up' or satisfied) is, by definition, not instantaneous but something that occurs over a considerable period of time. It's useful, therefore, to distinguish different phases of satiety associated with different mechanisms that, together, comprise the *satiety cascade*. Most important for understanding the suppression and subsequent control of hunger are:

- *post-ingestive effects*, which include gastric distension, the rate of gastric emptying, the release of hormones (such as cholecystokinin (CCK)) and the stimulation of certain receptors along the GIT
- *post-absorptive effects*, which refer to mechanisms arising from the action of glucose, fats, amino acids (and other metabolites) after absorption across the intestine into the bloodstream.

The brain's control of eating

It's been known since the early 1800s that tumours of the hypothalamus can cause *hyperphagia* (excessive overeating) and obesity in humans (Pinel, 1993). But not until the advent of *stereotaxic surgery* in the late 1930s (see Chapter 4) were experimenters able to assess the effects of damage to particular areas of the hypothalamus on the eating behaviour of experimental animals.

The VMH syndrome

Paradoxically, VMH-lesioned rats aren't 'hell bent' on eating – they won't eat anything and everything.

Key Study 9.3

Hyperphagia in rats (Hetherington and Ranson, 1942)

- Hetherington and Ranson found that large, bilateral lesions in the lower, central portion of the hypothalamus (the *ventromedial nucleus* (VMN)) cause *hyperphagia*: the rat will carry on eating until it becomes grotesquely fat, doubling or even trebling its normal body weight.
- Although several structures were damaged by such lesions, it was generally assumed that the *ventromedial hypothalamus* (VMH) was the crucial structure.
- The resulting hyperphagia was taken to indicate that the normal function of the VMH is to *inhibit* feeding when the animal is 'full'. Hence, the VMH became known as the *satiety centre*. It's been found in rats, cats, dogs, chickens and monkeys (Teitelbaum, 1967).

Figure 9.4 A hyperphagic rat

The taste of food seems to be especially important in hyperphagic rats. Most animals will eat even bad-tasting food ('you'll eat anything if you're hungry enough'), but hyperphagic rats are very fussy, and will refuse their regular food if quinine is added – even if this means that they become underweight (Teitelbaum, 1955).

What about people?

One possible explanation for the 'finicky' eating of VMH-lesioned rats is that they become less sensitive to *internal* cues of satiation (such as blood glucose level and body fat content) and more responsive to *external* cues (such as taste). Schachter (1971) claims that this may also apply to overweight people. Schachter *et al.* (1968) found that normal-weight people responded to the internal cue of stomach distension ('feeling bloated') by refusing any more food. But obese people tended to go on eating. The latter seemed to be responding to the *availability of food*. However, they're less willing to make an effort to find food compared with normal-weight people, who'll search for food – but only if they're genuinely hungry (Schachter, 1971).

- Overweight people also tend to report that they feel hungry at prescribed eating times, even if they've eaten a short while before. Normal-weight people tend to eat only when they feel hungry, and this is relatively independent of clock time. However, this increased sensitivity to external cues isn't necessarily what causes some people to become obese – it could just as easily be an *effect* of obesity.
- Although people with hypothalamic tumours tend towards obesity, there's no evidence that the hypothalamus doesn't function properly in overweight people generally.

Differences in basal metabolic rate largely determine our body weight, and are probably hereditary. There's very little evidence to suggest that lack of impulse control, poor ability to delay gratification or eating too quickly contribute to overweight (Carlson, 1992). Up until quite recently, the role of complex psychological variables has been studied much more extensively in relation to *anorexia nervosa* and *bulimia nervosa* (see Chapter 44).

Explaining obesity: food addiction?

Every decision we make about eating is influenced by mental and physiological forces that are often outside of our awareness and control. The way a particular food looks, tastes and feels in our mouth can trick our brain into eating well past what we need from an energy point-of-view: packaged, processed, high sugar and fat foods are especially effective in tricking us in this way (Simring, 2013).

Being surrounded by a large variety of delicious food plays a key role in triggering the brain's reward response. Johnson and Kenny (2010) found that rats that could eat whenever they wanted from a buffet of highly palatable foods ate more and more over time, became obese, and showed a disruption of their brain's reward system, compared with rats fed normally. The obese rats had fewer dopamine D2 receptors (which signal pleasure) in the striatum: their sensitivity to food was reduced, meaning they need to consume more to get the same 'high'. (This is equivalent to *tolerance* in the dependence syndrome; see Chapter 8.) Similar decreases in D2 receptors are seen in overweight people, as well as rats and people addicted to heroin and cocaine.

This kind of binge eating can trigger more binging. Oswald *et al.* (2011) found that rats specially bred for binge eating would endure painful electric shock to obtain a desired food – a hallmark of addiction. If humans are like rats, then dieters who break a strict diet with a binge may be putting themselves at risk for addiction. Frequent consumption of highly palatable food, high in sugar and fat, may trip a kind of overeating trigger in the *nucleus acumbens* (NA); this kind of diet appears to make the NA hypersensitive to GABA (see Chapter 4). Also, injecting endorphins into the NA induced the same hypersensitivity as the palatable diet (Simring, 2013).

Appetite-controlling hormones affect certain pathways of neurons – feeding circuits – in the hypothalamus; they also affect systems in the brain that control feelings of reward (i.e. food will taste really good if you haven't eaten for several hours and you'll spend a great deal of time, effort and money to get it!) (Kenny, 2013).

During periods of hunger, hormones increase the reactivity of food-related reward circuits, especially in the striatum, which contains high concentrations of endorphins. As you eat, your stomach and gut release appetite-suppressing hormones (such as leptin and insulin) that decrease pleasure signals triggered by the striatum and other parts of the reward system; this makes food seem less attractive. However, this normal 'balance' between hunger and eating is disturbed by high fat/sugar foods (which are also often visually very appealing); they activate our reward circuits more powerfully than leptin's ability to shut them down (Kenny, 2013).

Therein lies the rub. We have evolved an efficient brain system to help maintain a healthy and consistent body-weight by signalling when it is time to eat and when it is time to stop. But highly appetising foods can often override these signals and drive weight gain (Kenny, 2013).

However, food addiction is different from obesity: many food addicts have normal weight and some obese people aren't food addicts (see Table 9.1). Also, not all the criteria for drug addiction apply when applied to food (see Chapter 8): we need food to survive in a way that we don't need recreational drugs. Nevertheless, the food addiction concept is gaining empirical support.

Table 9.1 Similarities and differences between obesity and addiction (based on Kenny, 2013)

	Obesity	Addiction
Similarities	1. Same patterns of neural activity in brain areas associated with *rewarding experiences* (e.g. fewer dopamine D2 receptors (D2R) in striatum); these respond to dopamine	→
	2. People born with reduced D2R levels are at greater genetic risk of obesity	→
	3. Reduced sensitivity to food (*tolerance*)	→
	4. High sugar/fat diets prompt cycles of *craving/withdrawal*	Recovering drug/alcohol addicts tend to gain weight
	5. Gastric bypass surgery often → *relapse* to overeating and weight gain. These patients are also at risk for other addictions	→
	6. Environmental cues/temptations = major cause of craving/relapse	→
Differences	1. Although highly-processed, quickly-digested carbohydrates could be the ingredient that triggers food cravings, no one ingredient seems to provoke addiction-like behaviours. (It's the combination of fats, sugars, and calorie content that → 'hedonic impact')	1. Nicotine in cigarettes and methanol in alcohol are well-established 'hooks'/triggers
	2. Not included in DSM-5 (American Psychiatric Association, 2013) as an eating disorder	2. Substance use disorder in DSM-5 combines substance abuse and dependence from DSM-IV; gambling disorder also included as a behavioural addiction

HULL'S DRIVE-REDUCTION THEORY

As we noted earlier, Hull's motivational theory must be considered in the context of his theory of learning. Drive-reduction theory was intended to explain the fundamental principle of *reinforcement*, both *positive* (the reduction of a drive by the presentation of a stimulus) and *negative* (the reduction of a drive by the removal or avoidance of a stimulus).

Hull was interested in the *primary* (physiological), *homeostatic* needs and drives of hunger, thirst, air, avoiding injury, maintaining an optimum temperature, defecation and urination, rest, sleep, activity and propagation (reproduction). He believed that all behaviour (human and animal) originates in the satisfaction of these drives.

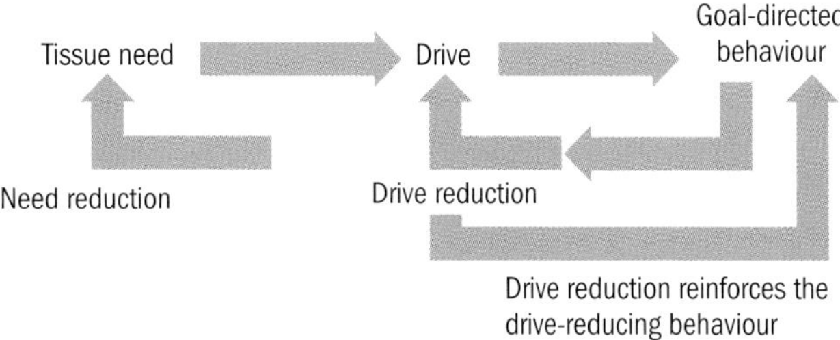

Figure 9.5 Summary of drive-reduction theory

Needs versus drives

While the terms 'need' and 'drive' are often used interchangeably, they're fundamentally different:

- *needs* are *physiological* and can be defined objectively (for example, in terms of hours without food or blood sugar level)
- *drives* are *psychological* (*behavioural*), and are *hypothetical constructs* – that is, abstract concepts that refer to processes/events believed to be taking place inside the person/animal, but that cannot be directly observed or measured.

However, Hull *operationalised* drives as hours of deprivation. He proposed a number of equations, which were meant to be testable in laboratory experiments (Walker, 1984). Perhaps the most important of these was:

$$sEr = D \times V \times K \times sHr$$

where *sEr* stands for the intensity or likelihood of any learned behaviour which can be calculated if four other factors are known, namely:

- *D* – the drive or motivation, measured by some indicator of physical need, such as hours of deprivation
- *V* – the intensity of the signal for the behaviour
- *K* – the degree of incentive, measured by the size of the reward or some other measure of its desirability
- *sHr* – habit strength, measured as the amount of practice given, usually in terms of the number of reinforcements.

Evaluation of drive-reduction theory

Ask Yourself

- Try to formulate some arguments against drive-reduction theory.

- Hull's basic premise is that animals (and, by implication, people) always and only learn through primary drive reduction. But the relationship between primary drives and needs is very unclear, as we saw earlier when discussing the eating behaviour of obese people.
- At its simplest, needs can arise without specific drives, as in learning what and how much to eat (see above). For example, we need vitamin C, but we wouldn't normally talk of a 'vitamin C drive' (in the way that we talk about a general hunger drive).
- Conversely, drives can occur in the absence of any obvious physiological need. An important example of a non-homeostatic drive in rats is *electrical (self-) stimulation of the brain* (ES-SB) or *intracranial self-stimulation* (ICSS) (Toates, 2001) (see Key Study 9.4).

Brain stimulation is such a powerful reinforcer that a male rat with an electrode in its *lateral hypothalamus* (LH) will self-stimulate in preference to eating if hungry, drinking when thirsty or having access to a sexually receptive female. This effect has been found in rats, cats, monkeys and pigeons (and humans, occasionally). The main reward site for ES-SB is the *median forebrain bundle* (MFB), a fibre tract that runs from the brainstem up to the forebrain through the LH (Beaumont, 1988; Carlson, 1992). The effect seems to depend on the presence of dopamine and noradrenaline. These reward centres are generally thought of as the neural substrate of 'pleasure', so that any behaviour defined as pleasurable involves their activation (see Chapter 8). ES-SB is seen as a 'short-cut' to pleasure, eliminating the need for natural drives and reinforcers.

- Tolman's *cognitive behaviourism* challenged Skinner's theory of operant conditioning, because it showed that learning could take place in the absence of reinforcement (*latent learning*; see Chapter 11). By implication, Tolman showed that learning could take place in the absence of drive reduction.
- Hull's theory emphasised primary (homeostatic) drives to the exclusion of *secondary* (*non-homeostatic*) drives. Primary drives are based on primary (innate) needs, but much human (and, to a lesser extent, non-human) behaviour can be understood only in terms of secondary (acquired) drives. Several Behaviourist Psychologists – notably Miller (1948), Mowrer (1950), and Dollard and Miller (1950) – modified Hull's theory to include acquired drives (in particular, anxiety), which led to a great deal of research on avoidance learning in the 1950s (see Chapters 11, 32, 44 and 45).

Key Study 9.4

What a rat wouldn't do for a shock (Olds and Milner, 1954)

- Olds and Milner implanted an electrode near a rat's septum (part of the limbic system), so that every time it pressed a lever, it would receive an electric shock.
- Rats made between 3000 and 7500 lever-pressing responses in a 12-hour period.
- Olds (1956) reported that one rat stimulated itself more than 2000 times per hour for 24 consecutive hours.
- Olds (1958) reported that rats, which normally press a lever 25 times per hour for food reward, will press 100 times per minute for a reward of ES-SB.

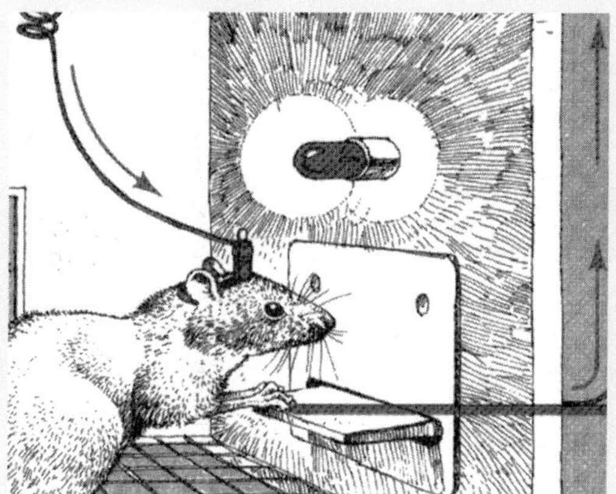

Figure 9.6 Olds (1956) implanted electrodes in the hypothalami of rats. The rats could trigger an electrical stimulus by depressing a lever. Clearly, the region where the electrode was implanted constitutes some kind of pleasure centre (adapted from J. Olds ©1956 Pleasure centres in the brain. *Scientific American*, Inc. All rights reserved)

- In Maslow's terms, drive-reduction theory deals only with survival needs, completely ignoring the self-actualisation (or 'growth') needs, which make human motivation distinctively different from that of non-humans.

NON-HOMEOSTATIC NEEDS AND DRIVES

Just as ES-SB cannot be accommodated by drive reduction when considering only non-human motivation, so non-humans seem to have other non-homeostatic drives that they share, to some degree, with humans. The rest of this chapter will be devoted to these important, and pervasive, non-homeostatic needs and drives.

Ask Yourself

- When we – and non-humans – aren't eating, drinking and doing all the other things we have to do to survive, what do we do?
- Why do we do it?
- Are all our activities ultimately aimed at survival, or are even non-humans capable of doing things 'just for the sheer hell of it'?

Competence motives: motives without specific primary needs

According to White (1959), the 'master reinforcer' that keeps most of us motivated over long periods of time is the need to confirm our *sense of personal competence*: our capacity to deal effectively with the environment. It's *intrinsically* rewarding and satisfying to feel that we're capable human beings, to be able to understand, predict, and control our world (aims which also happen to be the major aims of science; see Chapter 3).

Unlike hunger, which comes and goes, competence seems to be a continuous, ongoing motive. We can't satisfy it and then do without it until it next appears, because it's not rooted in any specific physiological need. This is why it isn't very helpful to think of the competence motive as a drive that pushes us into seeking its reduction. Competence motives often involve the *search for stimulation*.

Seeking stimulation

If rats are allowed to become thoroughly familiar with a maze, and then the maze is changed in some way, they'll spend more time exploring the altered maze. This occurs even in the absence of any obvious extrinsic reward, such as food. They're displaying a *curiosity drive* (Butler, 1954). Butler (1954) and Harlow *et al.* (1950) gave monkeys mechanical puzzles to solve, such as undoing a chain, lifting a hook and opening a clasp. The monkeys did these puzzles over and over again, for hours at a time, with no other reward: they were displaying their *manipulative drive* (Harlow *et al.*, 1950). (See Figure 9.7.)

Play and motivation

Much of the behaviour normally described as play can be thought of in terms of the drives for curiosity, exploration and manipulation. The purpose of play from the child's point of view is simple enjoyment. It doesn't consciously play in order to find out how things work, or to exercise its imagination, but simply because it's fun and intrinsically satisfying. Any learning that does result is quite incidental.

Figure 9.7 Research by Butler and Harlow has shown that animals are motivated to explore and manipulate their environments, quite unrelated to biological drives such as hunger and thirst. Monkeys will learn and work in order to open a door which allows them to view an electric train. They will also work diligently to open locks which lead to no tangible reward

Piaget (1951) distinguishes between play, which is performed for its own sake, and '*intellectual activity*' or *learning*, which has an external aim or purpose. This distinction is meant to apply to all three major types of play he describes: *mastery*, *symbolic/make-believe* and *play with rules*. (Piaget's theory is discussed in detail in Chapter 34.) Nor is play confined to humans. The young of many species engage in activities that seem to have little to do with homeostatic or survival needs. However, the higher up the evolutionary scale the species, the more apparent and purposeful the play becomes, and the more the nature of play changes as the young animal develops (Fontana, 1981). (See Figure 9.8.)

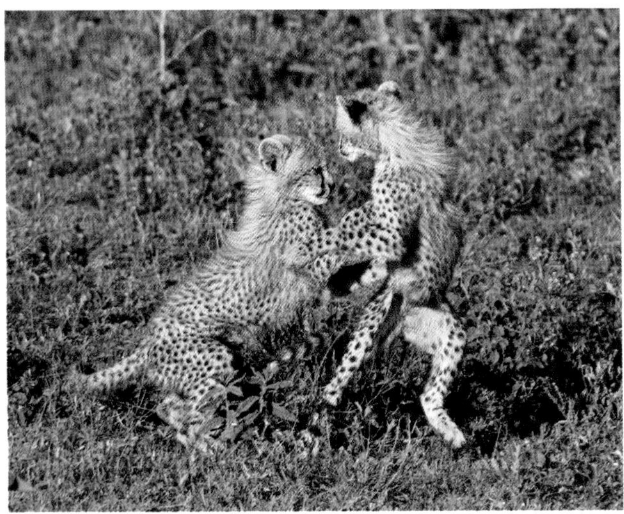

Figure 9.8 Play – both pleasurable and purposeful

Box 9.3 Play isn't just for children

Although researchers usually stress the benefits of play for the developing brain, they've found that play is also important for adults. Without play, adults may end up getting burned out from the stresses of everyday life (see Chapter 12) (Bekoff, cited in Wenner, 2009). Adults who don't play may become unhappy and exhausted without knowing why. So, how can adults get more play into their lives. Brown (cited in Wenner, 2009) suggests three ways:

1. *Body play*: participate in some form of active movement that has no time pressures or expected outcome (if you're working out in order to lose weight, that's not play!).
2. *Object play*: Use your hands to create something you enjoy (again, there shouldn't be a specific goal).
3. *Social play*: Join other people in seemingly purposeless social activities.

Ask Yourself

- What did you enjoy doing as a child?
- How could you 'translate' this into a more appropriate form for your age and circumstances?

Brown's suggestions all share the implication that for an activity to count as play, it must be *intrinsically/inherently* enjoyable, interesting, etc. – that is, entered into *for its own sake* (see Piaget's definition of play in text above).

Motivation and adaptation

Piaget saw play as essentially an *adaptive activity*. Throughout development, play helps to consolidate recently acquired abilities, as well as aiding the development of additional cognitive and social skills. In the same way, the competence motives of curiosity, exploration and manipulation undoubtedly have adaptive significance for an individual and, ultimately, for the species.

Optimal level (or arousal) theories

According to Berlyne (1960), investigation and exploration are based on an inbuilt tendency to seek a certain 'optimum' level of stimulation or activity. Exploring the unfamiliar increases arousal, but if it's too different from what we're used to, arousal will be too high (we'll feel anxious and tense). If it's not different enough, arousal is too low (we'll soon become bored).

Optimum level theories are supported by *sensory deprivation experiments*. In classic experiments carried out by Hebb and his colleagues at McGill University in the 1950s (Bexton *et al.*, 1954; Heron, 1957), participants were almost completely cut off from their normal sensory stimulation, by wearing blindfolds, earmuffs, cardboard tubes on their arms and legs, and so on. They soon began to experience extreme psychological discomfort, reported hallucinations, and couldn't tolerate their confinement for usually more than three days.

Cohen and Taylor (1972) studied the psychological effects of long-term imprisonment, and found that sensory deprivation and monotony are experiences that prisoners share with explorers, space travellers and round-the-world sailors. Conversely, excessive stimulation ('*sensory overload*') is also debilitating, and may be responsible for some kinds of psychological disorders in our highly urbanised society (see the discussion of stress in Chapter 12).

The need for control

Another major kind of competence motive is the need to be in control of our own destiny, and not at the mercy of external forces (Rubin and McNeil, 1983). This is closely linked to the need to be free from the controls and restrictions of others, and not be dictated to. According to Brehm (1966), when our freedom is threatened, we tend to react by reasserting our freedom (*psychological reactance*; see Chapter 49).

When people initially expect to have control over the outcomes of their actions, the first experience of not doing so is likely to produce reactance, but further bad experiences are likely to result in *learned helplessness* (Seligman, 1975). Rotter's (1966) concept of *locus of control* refers to individual differences in people's beliefs about what controls events in their everyday lives (see Chapter 12).

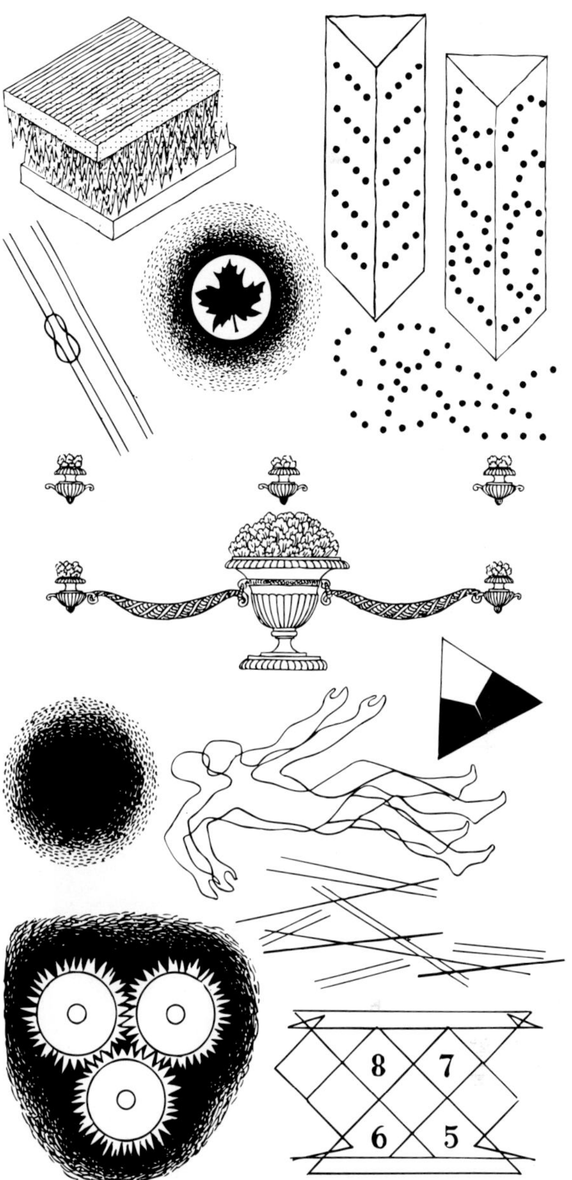

Figure 9.9 Hallucinations of sensory-deprived participants

Cognitive motives

Consistency and achievement

One of the most researched cognitive motives is the need for *cognitive consistency*, which is discussed in Chapter 24 in relation to attitudes and attitude change. Another that has generated an enormous amount of research and theorising is *achievement motivation/need for achievement* (nAch). This was one of the 20 human motives identified by Murray in 1938. He drew a sharp distinction between *psychogenic* (or psychological) needs, which are learned, and *viscerogenic* (or physiological) needs, which are innate.

Murray agreed with Freud that people express their true motives more clearly in free association than in direct self-reports (or questionnaire-type personality tests; see Chapter 42). Based on this belief, Murray

(Morgan and Murray, 1935) devised the *Thematic Apperception Test* (TAT).

Individuals are presented with a subset (typically 5 to 12) of 31 cards displaying pictures of ambiguous situations, mostly involving people (such as a distraught woman clutching an open door, and the two women depicted in Figure 9.10). (Other versions include the Children's Apperception Test, featuring animals in ambiguous situations, and the Blacky Test, featuring the adventures of a black dog) (Lilienfeld *et al.*, 2005).

Figure 9.10 Sample TAT picture

The participant is told that the TAT is a test of imagination and asked to make up a story that describes:

- what is happening and who the people are
- what has led up to the situation
- what the characters are thinking and feeling
- what will happen later.

The pictures are sufficiently ambiguous to allow a wide range of interpretations: how a person interprets them reveals their own unconscious motives. Hence, the TAT is a major *projective test* used in motivation and personality research (see Chapter 42).

Social motives

According to Geen (1995), *social motivation* refers to the activation of processes involved in the initiation, direction and energisation of individual behaviour 'by situations in which other people are in close contact with the individual'. It's usually assumed that these situations don't provide specific cues for individual behaviour (they're 'weak'). He contrasts them with 'strong' situations, such as those in which there's direct social influence (as in obedience experiments; see Chapter 27). Geen gives three main examples:

1. *social facilitation* – the enhancing effect on behaviour of the mere presence of others (see Chapter 31)
2. *social presentation* – behaving in ways that attempt to present a desirable impression to others (see Chapter 22)
3. *social loafing* – the tendency for individual effort to diminish in group task situations, partly as a result of diffusion of responsibility (again, see Chapter 31).

Each of these may be thought of as a manifestation of the more general influence of *social anxiety*, a state created when a person who wishes to make a certain impression on others doubts that this impression can actually be made. But why should the fear of making a bad impression be such a powerful motive for individual behaviour?

One answer can be found at quite a low level of Maslow's hierarchy, namely love and belongingness. This includes the *need for affiliation*, the company of other people (especially family, friends and work colleagues), and the need to be accepted by, and included within, society. Certain kinds of conformity can be understood in terms of this basic need (a survival need in Maslow's terms, see Chapter 26). But does this need itself stem from some other, even more fundamental need?

According to Greenberg *et al.*'s (1992) *terror management theory*, human culture, which society represents, provides a buffer against facing one's own vulnerability and mortality. Society provides a 'cultural drama' that gives meaning to life and without which the individual would experience a dread of being alive. We are, therefore, motivated to play an approved role in that drama: by meeting cultural standards, the individual achieves the approval and acceptance of others, and avoids rejection and isolation. This can be seen in relation to safety needs, the second level of Maslow's hierarchy, and includes 'fear of the unknown'. The ultimate example of this is the fear of death (see Chapter 39, and Gross, 2012a). Affiliation and our attraction to particular others are discussed in Chapter 28 on interpersonal relationships.

Fiske (2004) argues that we're motivated to get along with other people, because it's *adaptive* to do so. She identifies five core social motives: belonging (see above), which, in turn, underlies *understanding*, *controlling*, *self-enhancing* and *trusting*.

Chapter Summary

- The study of motivation is the study of the **causes of behaviour**. While there's general agreement that motivated behaviour is purposeful, goal-directed behaviour, different theoretical approaches see the underlying causes in very different ways.
- 'Motive' comes from the Latin for 'move' and denotes that which energises and gives direction to people's behaviour.
- Motives have been classified in various ways, but the most comprehensive classification is Maslow's **hierarchy of needs**, which distinguishes survival, deficiency or **D-motives**, and growth, being or **B-motives**.
- **Hedonism** can be seen as a central theme in both Freud's **psychoanalytic theory** and Skinner's **operant conditioning**.
- Influenced by Darwin's **theory of evolution**, many early Psychologists tried to explain human behaviour in terms of large numbers of **instincts**. This approach was replaced by Woodworth's concept of **drive**.
- Two major forms of drive theory are Cannon's **homeostatic drive theory** and Hull's **drive-reduction theory**.
- **Hunger** and **thirst** are the homeostatic drives that have been most researched by Biopsychologists. The earliest formal theory of hunger was Cannon's theory of **stomach contractions**.
- According to the **glucostatic theory**, the primary stimulus for hunger is a decrease in the level of blood glucose below a certain **set point**. The **glucostat** (probably a neuron in the hypothalamus) detects the level of blood glucose in the way a thermostat measures temperature.
- The other major set-point theory is the **lipostatic theory**, which focuses on the storage of **lipids** (fats) in the **adipose tissue**.
- Eating, in both humans and other animals, is partly determined by food's **palatability**. Food-predicting cues elicit **cephalic phase responses**, such as salivation, through **classical conditioning**.
- **Sensory-specific satiety** (S-SS) encourages the consumption of a varied diet. Although humans are capable of learning which diets best meet their biological needs, people in industrialised societies seem to prefer diets that are fundamentally harmful to health.
- Lesions in the VMN of the rat's hypothalamus cause **hyperphagia**, and the VMH became known as the **'satiety centre'**. However, the **VMH syndrome** also involves increased sensitivity to external cues of satiation. This also seems to be true of obese humans.
- Lesions to the LH cause **aphagia**, which suggests it's a feeding centre. However, the effects of LH lesions are much more diffuse than originally thought.
- The ability of leptin and insulin to make food seem less attractive is reduced by high fat/sugar foods, which are both visually appealing and taste delicious.
- While there are many similarities between **obesity** and **food addiction**, many food addicts have normal weight and some obese people aren't food addicts.
- Hull's **drive-reduction theory** was intended to explain the principle of **reinforcement**. However, needs can arise without specific drives and drives can occur in the absence of any obvious tissue need, as in **ES-SB**. Brain stimulation is a very powerful reinforcer, which can override the primary drives of hunger, thirst and sex.
- **Latent learning** shows that learning can take place in the absence of reinforcement. Much behaviour can only be understood in terms of secondary (**non-homeostatic**) drives, such as anxiety and its avoidance.
- Humans and non-humans share certain non-homeostatic needs and drives, such as **curiosity**, **manipulation** and **play**. These are linked to the **search for stimulation** and the **need for competence**, important for **adaptation** to our environment.
- **Optimal level theories** can help explain why both **sensory deprivation** and **sensory overload** can be stressful and disturbing.
- **Cognitive consistency** and **need for achievement** (**nAch**) are two very important **cognitive motives**.
- Many kinds of social behaviour can be seen as a manifestation of **social anxiety**, which in turn may reflect the more fundamental need for safety and protection from our fear of death.
- **Core social motives** include **belonging**, **understanding**, **controlling**, **self-enhancing** and **trusting**.

Links with Other Topics/Chapters

Chapters 2 and 4 → Each *major theoretical approach* tries to identify key processes and mechanisms ('causes') underlying human behaviour

Chapter 42 → Maslow's hierarchy of needs is commonly discussed in relation to *personality*. It represents an *idiographic* theory, seeing every individual as unique

Chapter 48 → Many of the experiments designed to understand the mechanisms involved in eating and drinking involve surgical procedures performed on rats (including damaging parts of their brain). This raises fundamental questions about the *ethics of animal experimentation*

Chapter 44 → The study of *obesity* can help identify some of the psychological variables involved in eating, but these have been explored much more extensively in relation to other eating disorders, in particular *anorexia nervosa* and *bulimia nervosa*

Chapter 11 → Hull's drive-reduction theory was meant to explain the principle of *reinforcement*, and a major challenge to it (and to Skinner's *operant conditioning*) came from Tolman's *cognitive behaviourism*

Several Behaviourist Psychologists modified Hull's theory by including acquired drives, especially anxiety, which is relevant to understanding:

Chapter 11 → *learning*

Chapter 44 → *phobias* (and other mental disorders)

Chapter 45 → *behavioural treatments* for those disorders

Chapter 34 → *Play* represents an important competence (non-homeostatic) motive, which Piaget saw as essentially an *adaptive* activity

Chapter 49 → *Psychological reactance* is a response to threats to our *freedom* and the need to feel in control

Chapter 24 → A major cognitive motive is *cognitive consistency*, which is central to certain theories of *attitude change*

Social motives underlie many of the major areas of social psychological research. These include:

Chapter 22 → *social presentation/self-enhancing*

Chapter 23 → *understanding*

Chapters 26 and 27 → *belonging*

Chapter 29 → *control*

Chapter 30 → *trust*

Chapter 31 → *social facilitation and social loafing*

Recommended Reading

Cohen, J. (1970) *Homo Psychologicus*. London: George Allen & Unwin Ltd.

Evans, P. (1975) *Motivation*. London: Methuen.

Most of Freud's books could be thought of as dealing with (unconscious) motivation. (See Chapter 42.)

Frankl, V.E. (2004) *Man's Search for Meaning* (originally published, in German, in 1946). London: Rider.

Maslow, A. (1970) *Motivation and Personality* (2nd edn). New York: Harper & Row. Also relevant to Chapter 42.

Weiner, B. (1992) *Human Motivation: Metaphors, Theories and Research*. Newbury Park, CA: Sage. Also relevant to Chapters 10, 23, 29 and 30.

Useful Websites

http://psychclassics.yorku.ca/Maslow/motivation.htm (Maslow's (1943) 'A Theory of Human Motivation' article, in which he describes his hierarchy of needs)

www.csun.edu/~vcpsy00h/students/explore.htm (Curiosity Exploration: Susan Edelman (1997))

http://tip.psychology.org/motivate.html (Motivation; provides many links, including to Edelman, 1997)

CHAPTER 10

EMOTION

What is emotion?

Theories of emotion

INTRODUCTION and OVERVIEW

Mr Spock in *Star Trek* often points out to Captain Kirk how much energy human beings waste through reacting emotionally to things, when a more logical and rational approach would be more productive. But would we be human at all if we didn't react in this way? This isn't to advocate losing control of our feelings or being unable to consider things in a calm and detached way, but it's the richness of our emotions, and our capacity to have feelings as well as to think things through and to reason, which makes us unique as a species. Emotions set the tone of our experience and give life its vitality. They are internal factors that can energise, direct and sustain behaviour (Rubin and McNeill, 1983).

At the same time, we often respond emotionally to events and situations that we believe make demands on us that we cannot meet – either because we don't have the necessary abilities or resources, or because they force us to make very difficult choices and decisions. We describe these negative kinds of events/situations as *stressful*, and our emotional responses to them as the experience of stress (see Chapter 12).

One of the key issues running through research into the nature of emotional experience is to what extent it's a *physiological* phenomenon. Related to this is the question of whether different *subjective* emotions (feeling angry, afraid, and so on) are also *physiologically* distinct. More recent theories have emphasised the role of *cognitive* factors in our experience of emotion, and are collectively referred to as *cognitive appraisal theories*.

WHAT IS EMOTION?

Ask Yourself

- What gives emotions their 'flavour'?
- Do different emotions share certain basic dimensions?

Definitions of emotion

Table 10.1 shows how some of the leading emotion researchers define the concept; note the strong evolutionary flavour of the second and fourth of these definitions.

Table 10.1 Some definitions of emotion

Arnold and Gasson (1954)	An emotion or an affect can be considered as the felt tendency towards an object judged suitable or away from an object judged unsuitable, reinforced by specific bodily changes
Tooby and Cosmides (1990)	... each emotional state manifests design features 'designed' to solve particular families of adaptive problems, whereby psychological mechanisms assume unique configuration
Lazarus (1991)	Emotions are organised psychophysiological reactions to news about ongoing relationships with the environment
Ekman (1992)	Emotions are viewed as having evolved through their adaptive value in dealing with fundamental life-tasks. Each emotion has unique features: signal, physiology, and antecedent events. Each emotion also has characteristics in common with other emotions: rapid onset, short duration, unbidden occurrence, automatic appraisal, and coherence among responses
Oatley *et al.* (2006)	*... multi-component responses to challenges or opportunities that are important to the individual's goals, particularly social ones* (emphasis in the original)

Ekman *et al.* (1972) and Ekman and Friesen (1975) identified *six primary emotions*: surprise, fear, disgust, anger, happiness and sadness (based on photographs of posed facial expressions, see Figure 10.1). Based on their early studies in Brazil, Japan, Borneo, New Guinea, and the USA, these are taken to be *universal*.

This suggests very strongly that they're innate, and is supported by studies of congenitally blind people: they express these emotions in the same way as sighted people, despite never having seen an emotional expression (Matsumoto and Willingham, 2009).

Happiness

Disgust

Surprise

Sadness

Anger

Fear

Figure 10.1 Six universal facial expressions

However, there's evidence that facial expressions may *not* be universal.

Key Study 10.1

Facial expressions aren't universal (Jack *et al.*, 2012)

- Jack *et al.* used a graphics package to generate 4800 expressions by randomly combining facial muscle positions.
- These were presented to 15 European and 15 Chinese participants.
- Their task was to categorise the faces in terms of the basic emotions identified by Ekman (see text above).
- The Europeans (who were shown European-looking faces) could do this quite easily, with high levels of agreement between them. But the Chinese participants produced much more overlapping categorisations and disagreed much more.
- When the Chinese participants were free to choose their own labels, the findings confirmed the view that culture does have an influence.
- While certain facial expressions may have a biological origin, humans have had culture for 80,000 years; this is plenty of time for the expressions to be reshaped by cultural evolution, allowing regional variations to arise.

'Basic' or 'primary' emotions

For Ekman (1994), 'basic' is meant to emphasise the role that evolution has played in shaping both the unique and the common features that emotions display, as well as their current function. Emotions evolved for their adaptive value in dealing with fundamental life tasks: they helped species to survive (see Table 10.1). Three major characteristics of emotions follow from this adaptive function.

1. There will be certain common elements in the contexts in which emotions are found to occur, despite individual and cultural differences in social learning
2. They're likely to be observable in other primates (while it's possible that there are certain emotions that are unique to humans, there's no convincing evidence that this is so). (One possible exception to this is *crying* (Walter, 2006/7).)
3. They can be aroused so quickly that they start to happen before we're even aware of them:

> *Quick onset is central to the adaptive value of emotions, mobilising us quickly to respond to important events ... (Ekman, 1994)*

So, emotions can occur with very rapid onset, through automatic appraisal (see below), with little awareness, and with involuntary changes in expression and physiology. Indeed, we often experience emotions as happening *to* us, rather than chosen by us.

As discussed below, evidence exists for distinctive patterns of autonomic nervous system (ANS) activity for various emotions. Ekman believes that these patterns are likely to have evolved because they support patterns of motor behaviour that were adaptive for each of these emotions, preparing the organism for quite different actions. For example, fighting might well have been the adaptive action in anger (which is consistent with the finding that blood flow increases to the hands when we're angry). There may also be unique patterns of CNS activity for each emotion, which aren't found in other mental activity.

Similarly, Averill (1994) defines basic emotions as those 'that fulfil vital biological functions' (vital to the survival of the species). Like Ekman, he believes that basic emotions should be universal, be seen (at least in rudimentary form) in non-human primates, and be heritable. However, the original biological purpose of happy smiles, angry scowls or sad frowns have so far eluded researchers. Yet they remain very powerful ways of communicating inner states to other human beings – even if they didn't evolve for this signalling purpose (Humphries, 2012). At the same time, *pride* and *shame* have more recently been added to the list of basic emotions: their original (physiological) function may have been to prepare for confrontation (by increases in testosterone and lung capacity) and to reduce/hide bodily targets from potential attack, respectively (Humphries, 2012).

Figure 10.2 What emotion is this woman experiencing?

Most basic of all are emotions that are *psychologically* basic: when people are asked to recount emotional episodes that evoked their 'true feelings', they typically describe incidents that reinforce or transform or enhance their sense of self (Morgan and Averill, 1992).

Components of emotion

For each distinct emotion, there are three components:

1. the *subjective experience* of happiness, sadness, anger, and so on
2. *physiological changes*, involving the autonomic nervous system (ANS) and the endocrine system, over which we have little, if any, conscious control; however, we may become aware of some of their effects (such as 'butterflies in the stomach', gooseflesh and sweating: see Chapter 4)
3. *associated behaviour* such as smiling, crying, frowning, running away and being 'frozen to the spot'.

The second and third components are sometimes categorised together as 'bodily reactions', with the former being called *visceral* and the latter *skeletal*. This distinction relates to the ANS and central nervous system (CNS), respectively. However, while running away is largely under voluntary (CNS) control, crying or sweating definitely aren't – yet in all three cases we infer another person's emotional state from this observable behaviour.

Different *theories* of emotion are distinguished by:

- how they see the relationship between the three components
- the relative emphasis given to each component
- how they see the relationship between the components and our cognitive *appraisal* or *interpretation* of the emotion-producing stimulus or situation.

Critical Discussion 10.1

The social construction of emotions

- According to *social constructionism* (SC) (see Chapter 2), emotions are the products of culture. Human cultures influence the emotions by influencing their members' beliefs, values and social environments.
- Emotions may be understood as enmeshed within an entire system of beliefs and values, so they cannot exist independently of the culture.
- For example, *accida* is an emotion that existed in western cultures in medieval times but seems to have become extinct by about 1400. It involved a mixture of boredom with one's religious duties, attempting to put off carrying them out, sadness about one's religious failings, and a sense of loss of one's former religious enthusiasm. It disappeared during the Renaissance when values changed (Parrott, 2004).
- Today, someone facing the same religious 'crisis' is likely to feel guilt, an emotion related to a culture based on individual responsibility (rather than spiritual duty) (Harré and Finlay-Jones, 1986).
- According to Markus and Kitayama (1991), 'ego-focused' emotions (such as anger, frustration and pride) will be experienced more by people in *individualist* cultures with more independent selves. 'Other-focused' emotions (such as shame, belongingness and sympathy) will be more common in *collectivist* cultures with more interdependent selves (see Chapter 47).
- According to Barrett (2011), rather than being biologically based, emotions/emotional expressions are *culturally learned symbols*; like spoken language, there are both common elements and cultural differences. When we observe emotions in others, the categories we use are culturally constructed, learned and context-dependent. We rarely see faces in isolation from posture, voice, other faces and the wider context. Also, viewing the *same* expression labelled alternately with 'anger', 'surprise' and 'fear' changes how people perceive it (Barrett *et al.*, 2011).
- What's considered basic also varies between cultures and within the same culture over time. For example, in the Middle Ages, *hope* was classified as a basic emotion, while today it's regarded as secondary (if it's considered an emotion at all) by most emotion theorists (Averill, 1994).

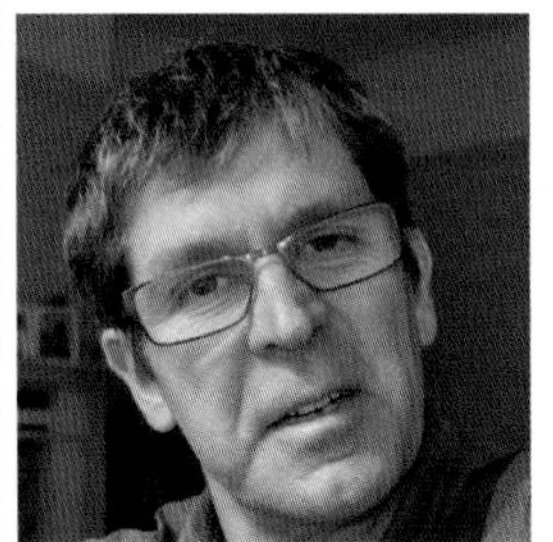

MEET THE RESEARCHER

Brian Parkinson

Emotions in and outside the laboratory

One of the things that first got me interested in emotions was Schachter and Singer's famous experiment (Schachter and Singer, 1962; see p. 168). I liked the idea that you could tinker with the ingredients of emotions in order to work out how they were put together, and I was impressed by the elaborate manipulations and deceptions practised on unwitting participants. Despite their counter-intuitive basis, I found the study's main predictions strangely plausible. The proposal that participants who did not know that their feelings of physiological arousal (e.g. increased heart rate, dry mouth) were caused by an adrenaline injection should interpret these symptoms as anger when exposed to an angry person but as euphoria when exposed to someone else expressing euphoria did not seem in any way outlandish or incredible to me. Perhaps this was because, at that age, I sometimes struggled to make sense of my own emotional states. I say 'at that age', but even after studying emotions for so long, I guess I still do.

Implications of Schachter and Singer's findings

As it happens, Schachter and Singer's findings were not as clear cut as claimed at the time and although the other person's response clearly had some impact, the adrenaline injection had less consistent effects on emotion. Despite its inconclusive findings, the experiment has two implications that I continue to think are quintessential. The first is that emotions are not entirely defined by the bodily changes that often accompany them. We do not recognise an instance of anger or euphoria simply by turning attention inwards and checking off internal symptoms. The second implication is that emotions and our interpretations of them are closely associated with what other people say and do.

Emotions and interpersonal life

Too often, psychologists neglect this social aspect and think of emotions as purely private and personal reactions. By contrast, my colleagues and I have tried to examine how emotions relate to interpersonal life, how they affect other people and how other people's reactions can change the way our emotions unfold and develop over time.

To illustrate, here is an everyday anger experience described by a participant in one of my studies: 'I was in a bad mood anyway and loads of people were in my room watching telly and I was trying to concentrate and one of my flatmates would not stop talking really, really loudly.' What made the participant angry was not a simple stimulus or event but a series of developing obstacles – the fact that other people were in the way whatever the participant attempted to do. Indeed, we sometimes get cross when other people fail to understand what we are trying to tell them. For example, think how it feels when another driver cuts in front of you without even noticing they got in your way.

Obstacles to research

Investigating real-life emotions like this can be challenging because researchers cannot easily track people and assess their reactions wherever they go and whatever they do (and even if they could, the fact that researchers were observing you would likely change the way you responded to potentially emotional events). Often the best available evidence comes instead from people's reports of what is happening, collected as soon as possible after the event.

Recent studies

For example, one of our recent studies (Parkinson and Simons, 2009) asked people to carry around palm-top computers so they could report on their own and other people's emotions at key moments. Our particular focus fell on how anxiety can affect decision-making, and we found, as expected, that when someone else is worried about the potential consequences of a course of action, that tends to make us more worried too. Being worried, in turn, can make us see a decision option as more risky and change our ultimate decision.

Although people's descriptions of their own and others' emotional experiences can be revealing (especially when we can get someone's second opinion to corroborate them), emotions often involve expressions and experiences that are not explicitly registered or interpreted. Indeed, we are often influenced by someone else's emotions not because the person tells us what they are feeling but because their physical orientation to what is happening affects us more directly. For instance, we instinctively respond to a wide-eyed stare directed at something behind us by turning to look in the same direction. In order to investigate this kind of non-verbal process thoroughly, it is useful to video-record people's bodily and facial movements over time.

Laboratory research

Most of the research currently conducted in our laboratory (see figure below) involves assessing, over time, the effects of one person's facial expressions on another's. For example, in a series of recent studies, participants played a *Who Wants to be a Millionaire?*-style quiz in which they received advice about the correct answer from another participant (in a separate cubicle, see right) before giving their own final response. We were particularly interested in how the other person's facial expressions of uncertainty, worry or confidence might affect the contestant while answering the question. Surprisingly, seeing the other person's face across a video link led to lower rather than higher scores in the quiz. It seemed that participants were unable to make use of the information conveyed by facial expression when there was no direct contact with the quiz partner. In face-to-face conversations, we see the other person's expression and they see ours, so our responses are mutually attuned to what each of us is doing or communicating (e.g. making eye contact or smiling at each other). Perhaps, then, facial expressions need to be interpersonally co-ordinated in order to be informative. Perhaps, like physiological arousal, they need to be put into a social context before making clear emotional sense.

Set-up for quiz game experiments. This participant can see the face of the 'helper' participant in a separate cubicle while both participants read the question on the other monitor

Control room in emotion communication laboratory showing equipment for video mixing, monitoring and recording

To test this idea, we compared the effects of one- and two-way video links using the same quiz procedure. As we predicted, scores were higher when both quiz partners could see each other than when the contestant could see the other person but the other person could not see the contestant.

Having documented some of the ways in which we are affected by other people's emotions and emotional expressions, our research group is now turning its attention to the purposes served by expressing emotion to someone else. This research is part of a wider project on Emotion Regulation of Others and Self (EROS, see www.erosresearch.org) sponsored by the Economic and Social Research Council (ESRC). In particular, our current studies look at the ways people use emotional expressions to influence others. For example, if a friend is worried about something, we may empathise by expressing worry ourselves or we may attempt to alleviate their concern by expressing excitement about the opportunities associated with the impending event. Of course, when a friend tries to influence our own emotion at the same time as we try to influence theirs, the interpersonal process becomes even more complex and interesting. By examining moment-by-moment changes in recorded facial expressions, and participants' perceptions of what their own and the other person's facial expressions mean, we hope to clarify how emotional meanings are constructed not from registration of internal symptoms, but by mutual co-ordination of communication and action.

Dr Brian Parkinson is a Lecturer in Experimental Psychology at Oxford University. He has been studying emotion since conducting an undergraduate project into the effects of false autonomic feedback at Manchester University. Publications include the books *Ideas and Realities of Emotion* (1995) and *Emotion in Social Relations* (2005) (with Agneta Fischer and Tony Manstead).

Consistent with this is Parrott's (2004) definition of an emotion as:

> *... a reaction to personally significant events, where 'reaction' is taken to include biological, cognitive and behavioural reactions, as well as subjective feelings of pleasure or displeasure ...*

THEORIES OF EMOTION

Darwin's evolutionary theory

The publication of *The Expression of Emotions in Man and Animals* (1872) represents the first formal attempt, by any scientist, to study emotion. Based largely on anecdotal evidence, Darwin argued that particular emotional responses (such as facial expressions) tend to accompany the same emotional states in humans of all races and cultures, even those who are born blind. (This claim is supported by Ekman and Friesen's research, see above.) Like other human behaviours, the expression of human emotion is the product of evolution.

Ask Yourself

- What would you say is the 'common-sense' theory of emotion?
- Is it 'obvious' how emotional reactions are triggered (that is, what makes us have emotional experiences)?
- How does the experience of emotion relate to bodily/behavioural changes?
- Draw a diagram to summarise a typical 'emotional reaction' sequence of events.

The James–Lange theory

If there's a common-sense theory of emotion, it is that something happens that produces in us a subjective emotional experience and, as a result of this, certain bodily and/or behavioural changes occur. James (originally in 1878 and then in 1890) and Lange (1885, at first quite independently of James) turned this common-sense view on its head. They argued that our emotional experience is the *result*, not the cause, of perceived bodily changes.

To give an example used by James, the common-sense view says that we meet a bear, are frightened and run. The James–Lange theory maintains that we're frightened *because* we run! Similarly, 'We feel sorry because we cry, angry because we strike, afraid because we tremble ...'. According to James (1890):

> *... the bodily changes follow directly the perception of the exciting fact, and ... our feeling of the same changes as they occur is the emotion.*

Ask Yourself

- Do you agree with James?
- Does the emotional experience always precede the associated behaviour (as common sense would have it), or can the behaviour come first (as the James–Lange theory claims)?

The crucial factor in the James–Lange theory is feedback from the bodily changes (see Figure 10.3). We label our subjective state by inferring how we feel based on perception of our own bodily changes ('I'm trembling, so I must be afraid', see Chapter 18).

You may be able to think of situations in which you've reacted in a fairly automatic way (for example, you've slipped coming down the stairs), and only after you've grabbed the banisters do you become aware of feeling frightened (and a little shaken). It's almost as if the sudden change in your behaviour has caused the fear, quite apart from why you grabbed the banisters in the first place.

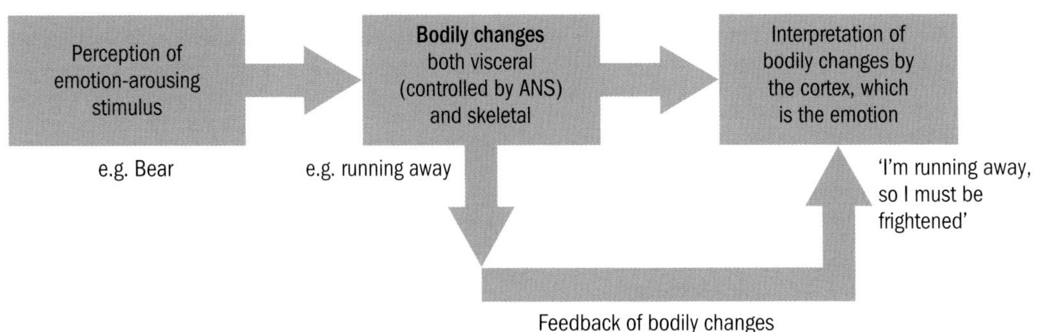

Figure 10.3 The James–Lange theory of emotion

Evaluation of the James–Lange theory

The theory implies that by deliberately altering our behaviour, we can control our emotional experiences. Try smiling – do you feel any happier? A crucial test (which James admitted would be very difficult to perform) would be to examine the emotional experience of someone who's completely anaesthetised, but not intellectually or motor impaired.

In the examples that James himself gives of inferring emotion from bodily changes (such as running away from a bear), he clearly attaches much more importance to *skeletal* as opposed to *visceral* changes. Parrott (2004) calls this the 'peripheral' approach. In this respect, the James–Lange theory probably differs from other theories, which usually mean 'visceral' when they say 'physiological'. Given this emphasis on skeletal changes, there are two important studies that support the James–Lange theory.

The Valins and Laird studies suggest that overt behaviour may cause subjective feelings without there being any obvious physiological arousal taking place: visceral changes may not be necessary. But neither Valins nor Laird attempted to measure any accompanying visceral changes. What if smiling triggers certain physiological changes? Might these be the *real* cause of our feeling happy, rather than the change in our facial muscles? And, if so, isn't this quite damaging to the James–Lange theory, which places so much emphasis on behavioural (skeletal) changes?

Levenson *et al.* (1990) asked participants to move particular facial muscles (to simulate the emotional expression of fear, anger, surprise, disgust, sadness and happiness). They also monitored several physiological responses controlled by the ANS while this was going on. They found that the simulated expressions did alter ANS activity. For example, anger increased heart rate and skin temperature, fear increased heart rate but decreased skin temperature, while happiness decreased heart rate without affecting skin temperature.

There's also recent evidence that peripheral feedback from facial muscles and skin (using the facial feedback hypothesis) influences neural activity in the amygdala (see Key Study 10.3).

Key Study 10.2

Listen to your heart and smile if you want to be happy (Valins, 1966; Laird, 1974)

- Valins provided male participants with feedback of their heart rate while watching slides of semi-nude *Playboy* pin-ups. The heart rate was in fact pre-recorded and programmed to increase in response to presentation of half the slides: participants believed the feedback was an indication of their true response (*the false feedback paradigm*). The slides associated with the apparent heart rate increase were judged to be more attractive than those associated with unchanged heart rate.
- Laird tested the *facial feedback hypothesis* by falsely informing 32 students that they were participating in an experiment to measure activity in facial muscles. Bogus electrodes were attached to their faces (as if to measure physiological response), and they were instructed to raise their eyebrows, contract the muscles in their forehead, and make other facial expressions. They didn't realise the emotional significance of what they were being asked to do. While this was going on, cartoon slides were projected onto a screen. Regardless of their content, participants rated the slides they'd seen while 'smiling' as funnier. They also described themselves as happier when 'smiling', angrier when 'frowning', and so on.

Key Study 10.3

Botox can affect your amygdala

- Hennenlotter *et al.* (2008) studied a group of women who'd received Botox (botulinum toxin) injections to their face (for cosmetic reasons), making them unable to flex the frown muscles (*corrugators supercilii*).
- 38 women had their brains scanned while they imitated pictures of sad or angry facial expressions. Crucially, half of them were tested *before* receiving the injections, while the other half were tested two weeks *afterwards* (when the effects of Botox are greatest).
- As expected, imitating an angry or sad facial expression increased activity on both sides of the amygdala in both groups. But for angry expressions, activity in the left amygdala was *lower* in the women who'd already had the injections compared with those who hadn't. This suggests that pulling an angry face affects the amygdala via *both* the neural command to flex the facial muscles *and* the movement of the facial muscles and skin.

In the James–Lange theory, skeletal bodily changes occur *spontaneously*, not consciously and deliberately. This makes it difficult to draw any firm conclusions from experiments like those of Valins and Laird. However, both studies strongly suggest that physiological arousal isn't *sufficient* to account for emotional experience. The fact that participants in the Valins study were prepared to infer emotion on the basis of (false) information about their reactions to stimuli suggests it may not even be necessary, and that cognitive factors may be sufficient (Parkinson, 1987).

According to Parrott (2004), for the body to 'know' how to respond appropriately, more than just 'perception of the exciting fact' must be involved. The event (e.g. the bear) must be interpreted or evaluated (or *appraised*) as a threat. The James–Lange theory fails to account for why the bear is seen as frightening in the first place! (We shall return to this issue below.)

Cannon's critique of the James–Lange theory

According to Cannon (1929), there are four major faults with the James–Lange theory:

1. It assumes that for each subjectively distinct emotion there's a corresponding set of physiological changes enabling us to label the emotion we're experiencing.
2. Even if this assumption were true, physiological arousal would still not be sufficient.
3. Physiological arousal may not even be necessary.
4. The speed with which we often experience emotions seems to exceed the speed of response of the viscera, so how could the physiological changes be the source of sudden emotion?

Cannon argued that, 'the same visceral changes occur in very different emotional states and in non-emotional states'. In other words, the James–Lange theory was built on the (false) assumption that *different* emotional stimuli induce *different* patterns of ANS activity, and that perception of these different patterns results in different emotional experiences.

According to the *Cannon–Bard theory* (see below), the ANS responds in the *same* way to *all* emotional stimuli, namely, the *fight-or-flight syndrome* (see Chapter 4). This means that there must be more to our emotional experience than simply physiological arousal, otherwise we wouldn't be able to tell one emotional state from another.

Evidence for physiological specificity

According to LeDoux (1994), this represents 'one of the most pesky problems in emotion research'. He points out that the emphasis of research has been on ANS activity, and this emphasis is partly due to Cannon's criticism of the James–Lange theory.

Key Study 10.4

Be afraid: the Ax man's coming (Ax, 1953)

- In a famous (but ethically highly dubious) experiment, Ax measured various aspects of *electrodermal* (skin conductance), *electromyographic* (muscle action potential), *cardiovascular* and *respiratory* activity in participants who were deliberately frightened and made angry.
- They were told they were participating in a study of *hypertension* (high blood pressure), and were asked to lie quietly on a couch while physiological measures were being taken. As electrodes were being attached, it was casually mentioned that the regular technician was sick, and a man who'd recently been fired for incompetence and arrogance was filling in for him. After baseline measures had been recorded, either the anger condition occurred, followed by the fear condition, or vice versa.
- In the *fear condition*, a continuous mild shock was administered to one finger (without any warning or explanation). The intensity gradually increased, until the participant complained. Then sparks were made to jump.
- In the *anger condition*, the technician (an actor) entered the room and spent five minutes checking the wiring. During this time, he jostled the participant, criticised the attending nurse and blamed the participant for causing a fault in the equipment.
- Of 14 different measures taken, Ax found that seven were significantly different between the two conditions. For example, fear was associated with increased heart rate, skin conduction level, muscle action potential frequency, and breathing rate (reflecting the effects of adrenaline). Anger was accompanied by increased diastolic blood pressure, frequency of spontaneous skin conduction responses and action potential size (reflecting the greater influence of noradrenaline).

Ax's findings have been replicated by others (e.g. Frankenhaeuser, 1975). Schachter (1957) confirmed Ax's original findings that fear is influenced largely by adrenaline. But he also found that anger produces a mixed adrenaline–noradrenaline response, and pain produces a noradrenaline-like pattern. Schachter and Singer (1962) concluded that:

> *Whether or not there are physiological distinctions among the various emotional states must be considered an open question. Any differences which do exist are at best rather subtle and the variety of emotion, mood and feeling states do not appear to be matched by an equal variety of visceral patterns.*

This conclusion is consistent with Schachter's (1964) cognitive labelling theory (see below).

Less extreme and controversial methods than Ax's include:

- the *directed facial action method*, in which participants are instructed to make the facial expressions characteristic of various emotions while ANS activity is recorded
- the *relived emotion method*, in which participants are asked to think about previous emotional experiences while these measures are being made.

Based on a series of experiments using both kinds of method, Levenson (1994) maintains that it's a 'myth' that every emotion is autonomically different. It seems far more likely that reliable differences will only be found between emotions for which there are different associated typical *behaviours*, and even among this smaller set, it's quite unlikely that they won't share some features.

Ask Yourself

- Given James' emphasis on skeletal, as opposed to visceral, changes, could it be argued that Cannon's first criticism is not strictly relevant?
- Since we're almost completely unaware of visceral changes, could James have claimed that 'visceral feedback' is the emotion?

Even if there were identifiable patterns of physiological response associated with different subjective emotions, Cannon argued that such physiological changes themselves don't necessarily produce emotional states (physiological arousal *isn't sufficient*). This was demonstrated by Marañon (1924), who injected 210 people with adrenaline: 71% said they experienced only physical symptoms, with no emotional overtones at all; most of the rest reported 'as if' emotions. The few who experienced genuine emotion had to imagine – or remember – a highly emotional event.

However, a study by Hohmann (1966) suggests that, although physiological changes aren't sufficient for the experience of 'full-blooded' emotions, they may still be *necessary*.

Key Study 10.5

Real emotions need an intact ANS (Hohmann, 1966)

- Hohmann studied 25 adult males with spinal cord injuries, who suffered corresponding ANS damage.
- They reported significant changes in the nature and intensity of certain emotional experiences, especially anger, fear and sexual feelings. Generally, the higher the lesion in the spinal cord, the greater the disruption of visceral responses, and the greater the disturbance of normal emotional experiences.
- Like Marañon's participants, they reported 'as if' emotions – a 'mental kind of anger', for example.

A replication of Hohmann's study (Bermond *et al.*, 1991) involved interviews with 37 people who'd suffered spinal injuries during the previous one to nine years. They were asked separately about (a) the intensities of physiological disturbances and (b) the subjective intensities of emotional experiences. Neither in the whole group, nor in the 14 people with injuries in the neck region (producing the greatest sensory loss), was there any reduction in rated emotional intensity.

Ask Yourself

- What implications do the studies of Marañon, Hohmann, and Bermond *et al.* have for the James–Lange theory?
- What's their relevance to Schachter's cognitive labelling theory? (See below.)

The Cannon–Bard theory

Dana (1921) studied a patient with a spinal cord lesion: despite having no sympathetic functioning and extremely limited muscular movement, the patient showed a range of emotions, including grief, joy, displeasure and affection. Similarly, Chwalisz *et al.* (1988) found that people with spinal cord injuries (who have no sensation in much of their body) experience emotion as intensely as before the injury, as intensely as 'normal' people, and as intensely as people with spinal cord injuries that don't block bodily sensations. These findings seem to support Cannon's view.

So what's different about Cannon's theory (known as the Cannon–Bard theory)? As Figure 10.4 shows,

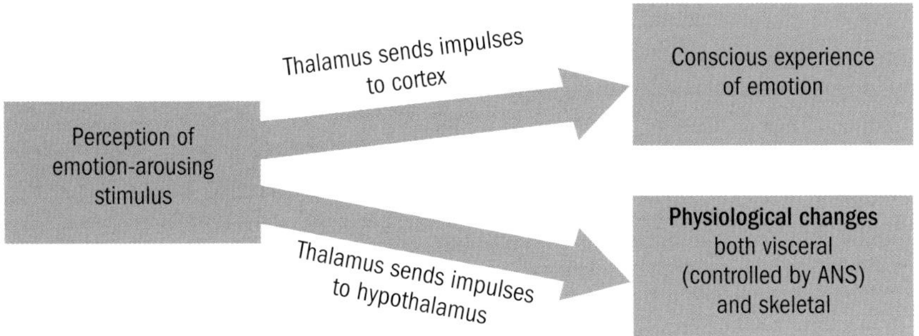
Thalamus sends impulses to cortex
Conscious experience of emotion
Perception of emotion-arousing stimulus
Physiological changes both visceral (controlled by ANS) and skeletal
Thalamus sends impulses to hypothalamus

Figure 10.4 The Cannon–Bard theory of emotion

the subjective emotion is quite independent of the physiological changes involved. The emotion-producing stimulus is processed by the thalamus. This sends impulses to the cortex, where the emotion is consciously experienced, and to the hypothalamus, which sets in motion certain autonomic physiological changes.

An evaluation of the Cannon–Bard theory

Cannon also argued that, because we often feel emotions quite rapidly, yet the viscera are quite slow to react, how could the physiological changes be the source of such sudden emotion (as required by the James–Lange theory)? However, although the viscera aren't sensitive to certain kinds of stimulation (such as burning and cutting), they provide much better feedback than Cannon suspected. Many visceral changes can occur sufficiently quickly that they *could* be the causes of feelings of emotion (Carlson, 1992).

Pinel (1993) advocates a position falling between the extreme views represented by the Cannon–Bard and James–Lange theories. On the one hand, the Cannon–Bard view that the ANS responds in the same way to all emotional stimuli is clearly incorrect (see above). On the other hand, there's insufficient evidence to make a strong case for the James–Lange view that each emotion is characterised by a different pattern of ANS activity.

Schachter's cognitive labelling theory

According to Schachter (1964), Cannon was wrong in thinking that bodily changes and the experience of emotion are independent, and the James–Lange theory was mistaken in claiming that physiological changes cause the feeling of emotion. While sharing the James–Lange belief that physiological changes *precede* the experience of emotion, Schachter argues that we have to *decide* which particular emotion we're feeling. The label we attach to our arousal depends on what we attribute that arousal to.

Schachter is saying that physiological arousal (factor 1) is *necessary* for the experience of emotion, but the nature of arousal is immaterial – what's important is how we *interpret* that arousal (factor 2). Hence, the theory is also known as the *two-factor theory of emotion*. The classic experiment that demonstrates this cognitive theory of emotion is Schachter and Singer's (1962) 'adrenaline experiment' (see Key Study 10.6).

Key Study 10.6

Schachter and Singer's (1962) adrenaline experiment

Participants were given what they were told was a vitamin injection, in order to see its effect on vision. In fact, it was adrenaline, and they were tested under one of four conditions.

1. *Group A* participants were given *accurate information* about the side-effects of the injection (palpitations, tightness in the throat, tremors and sweating).
2. *Group B* participants were given *false information* about the side-effects (itching and headache).
3. *Group C* participants were given *no information* about the side-effects (true or false).
4. *Group D* (control group) participants were given a *saline injection* (and otherwise treated like group C).

Before being given a 'vision test', each participant (one at a time) sat in a waiting room with another 'participant' (a stooge of the experimenters). For half the participants in each condition, the stooge acted either in a happy, frivolous way (making paper aeroplanes, laughing out loud and playing with a hula-hoop: *euphoria condition*), or very angrily (eventually tearing up the questionnaire which he and every participant was asked to complete: *anger condition*). (In fact, the group B condition was run only with a euphoric stooge.)

Participants' emotional experience was assessed in two ways: (1) observers' ratings of the degree to which they joined in with the stooge's behaviour; and (2) self-report scales.

As predicted:

- Groups A and D were much less likely to join in with the stooge or to report feeling euphoric or angry
- Groups B and C were much more likely to assume the stooge's behaviour and emotional state.

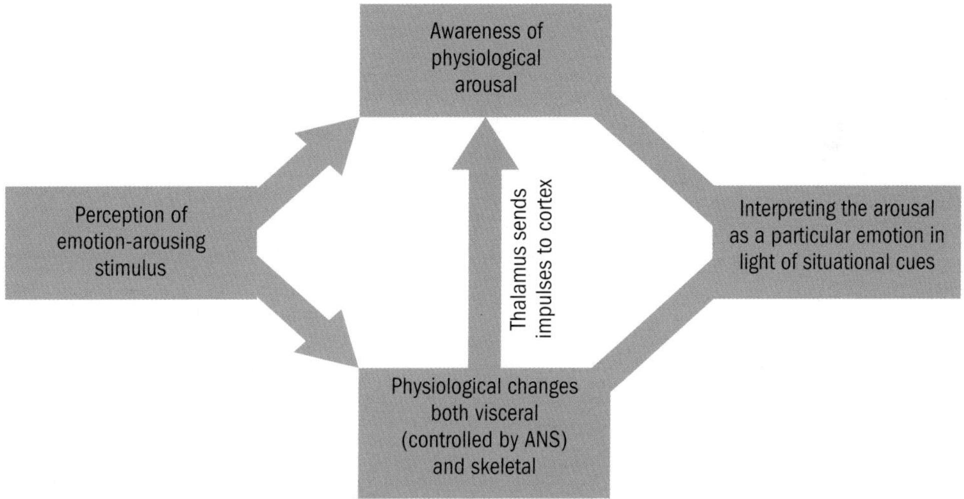
Awareness of physiological arousal
Perception of emotion-arousing stimulus
Thalamus sends impulses to cortex
Interpreting the arousal as a particular emotion in light of situational cues
Physiological changes both visceral (controlled by ANS) and skeletal

Figure 10.5 Schachter's cognitive labelling theory (or two-factor theory)

Ask Yourself

- Can you account for these findings in terms of Schachter's cognitive labelling/two-factor theory?

Schachter and Singer were testing three interrelated hypotheses regarding the *interaction* between physiological and cognitive factors in the experience of emotion.

1. If we experience a state of physiological arousal for which we have no immediate explanation, we'll 'label' this state and describe it in terms of the cognitions available. So, precisely the same state of arousal could receive different labels (e.g. 'euphoria'/'anger' – groups B and C). (Physiological arousal and cognitive labelling are necessary.)
2. If we experience a state of physiological arousal for which we have a completely appropriate explanation (e.g. 'I've just been given an injection of adrenaline'), we'll 'label' this state accordingly (group A).
3. Given the same circumstances, we'll react emotionally or describe our feelings as emotions only to the extent that we experience a state of physiological arousal (all three groups). (Physiological arousal is necessary.)

An evaluation of cognitive labelling theory

- Schachter and Wheeler (1962) confirmed these results by injecting participants either with adrenaline or chlorpromazine (which inhibits arousal); controls were injected with a placebo. While watching a slapstick comedy, the adrenaline participants laughed more, and the chlorpromazine participants less, than the controls.
- Dutton and Aron's (1974) study (see Key Study 10.7) confirms Schachter's claim that the autonomic arousal that accompanies all emotions is similar, and that it's our *interpretation* of that arousal that matters – even though this sometimes results in our *misidentifying* our emotions. Dutton and Aron's suspension bridge participants seemed to be *mislabelling* their fear as sexual attraction to the interviewer.

Ask Yourself

- What do you think the outcome might have been if the interviewer had been male?

- The focus of Schachter's model is an atypical state of affairs, where the participant is unsure about the cause of arousal (groups B and C). Schachter (1964) himself admitted that we usually *are* aware of a precipitating situation prior to the onset of arousal (which usually takes 1–2 seconds to reach consciousness). So, it's normally perfectly obvious to us what aspects of the situation have provoked the emotion. However, even here the meaning of the emotion-inducing circumstances requires *some* cognitive analysis before the emotion can be labelled.
- Schachter claims that the *quantitative* aspect of emotion can arise without cognitive mediation ('Am I in a state of emotional arousal?': as in Valins' study). But the *qualitative* aspect requires prior cognition ('What emotion is it I am experiencing?': as in Laird's study). Mandler (1984) has called Schachter's theory the *'jukebox' theory* – arousal is like the coin that gets the machine going, and cognition is the button pushed to select the emotional tune.

Key Study 10.7

Falling in love on a suspension bridge (Dutton and Aron, 1974)

- The participants were unsuspecting males, aged 18–35, visiting the Capilano Canyon in British Columbia, Canada.
- An attractive female interviewer approached the men and asked them questions as part of a survey on the effects of scenery on creativity. One of the things they were asked to do was to invent a short story about an ambiguous picture of a woman (a picture from the Thematic Apperception Test (TAT); see Chapter 9). This was later scored for sexual content, taken to reflect the men's sexual attraction towards the interviewer.
- Some men were interviewed on an extremely unstable suspension bridge, 5 feet wide, 450 feet long, composed of wooden boards attached to wire cables, running from one side of the canyon to the other. This bridge, 230 feet above the canyon, tended to sway, tilt and wobble, giving the impression that one could fall over the side at any moment; it had only very low handrails of wire cable for support (*high arousal condition*).
- Other men were interviewed on a solid wooden bridge upstream, a mere 10 feet above a shallow rivulet, with high handrails and without any swaying or tilting (*low arousal condition*).
- As predicted, the stories of the men in the high arousal condition contained significantly more sexual imagery. The interviewer also invited the men to call her if they wanted more information about the research. Again in line with predictions, four times as many men from the high arousal condition called her compared with the low arousal condition.
- To show that arousal was the independent variable, Dutton and Aron also arranged for another group of men to be interviewed 10 or more minutes after crossing the suspension bridge. By this time, the symptoms of their physical arousal should have been declining. These non-aroused men didn't show the signs of sexual arousal shown by those in the high arousal condition.

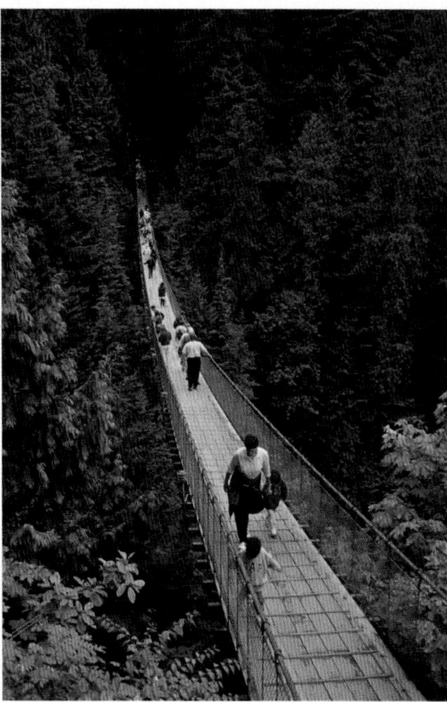

Figure 10.6 The Capilano River bridge

- According to Parkinson (1987), the view that affect (emotion) is *post-cognitive* is now probably the most popular view among emotion theorists. But even accepting the important role of cognitive factors, are environmental cues really as easily accepted as the basis for inferences about our own feelings as Schachter claims (Fiske and Taylor, 1991)?
- Using the original Schachter and Singer paradigm, several studies (Marshall and Zimbardo, 1979; Maslach, 1979; Plutchik and Ax, 1967) have concluded that when we try to explain a state of arousal, we don't merely use others' behaviour as a guide to what we're feeling. We call on many other sources of information as well, particularly previous occasions on which we felt this arousal state to explain why it's occurring now. While other people's behaviour might suggest – or even dictate (through conformity) – how we should *behave* in that situation, it doesn't tell us how we're *feeling*. At the very least, others' behaviour must in some way be appropriate (Weiner, 1992).
- These later studies also found that people who don't have a ready-made explanation for their adrenaline-produced arousal are more likely to attach a *negative* emotional label to it (such as unease or nervousness, similar to 'free-floating anxiety').

- Many theorists now believe that Schachter overstated how easy it is to influence emotional interpretations. Because our attributions about, and appraisals of, emotional situations usually determine our autonomic as well as emotional reactions in the first place (e.g. Lazarus, 1991), we often know *in advance* what we're going to feel (Parkinson, 2008).

The role of attribution

According to Schachter, group A participants in the adrenaline experiment could attribute their arousal to the injection (they had a ready-made explanation and so didn't need an emotional explanation). But for those in groups B and C, no such ready-made explanation was available, and so the stooge's behaviour was used as a cue for explaining their own state of arousal (as either euphoria or anger).

Taking one of James' original examples (running away from a bear), the original cause of the bodily reactions (the bear) is irrelevant. This is because our emotional experience is based on feedback from our bodily reactions (running away). But for Schachter, it's what we attribute our arousal to that determines the label we give to it. In the adrenaline experiment, the initially unexplained arousal is attributed to the (rather extreme) behaviour of the confederate, and so is labelled euphoria or anger accordingly.

Similarly, the men in Dutton and Aron's experiment who were tested on the swaying suspension bridge, were unaware of the 'real' cause of their arousal. They attributed it instead to the female interviewer. We know that arousal was the independent variable, and it's highly likely that if the attractive interviewer hadn't approached them, they'd have labelled their arousal 'fear', because it would have been attributed to a frightening stimulus (the bridge).

What all these examples show is that the cognitive labelling theory is essentially based on *attributional principles* (see Chapter 23). This represents a major form of influence that Schachter's theory has had on cognitive theories of emotion in general.

The misattribution effect

What the adrenaline and the suspension bridge experiments show is that people can make mistakes in how they attribute their arousal. This mislabelling of our feelings, and drawing mistaken conclusions about the causes of those feelings, is called the *misattribution effect* (Ross and Nisbett, 1991).

As part of their suspension bridge experiment, and in a later experiment, Dutton and Aron (1974, 1989) invited male students to participate in a learning experiment. After meeting an attractive female partner, half the students were frightened with the news that they'd be suffering some 'quite painful' electric shocks. Before the experiment was due to begin, they were given a short questionnaire 'to get some information on your present feelings and reactions, since these often influence people on the learning task'. Asked how much they would like to date and kiss their partner, the aroused (frightened) men expressed more intense attraction than the non-frightened men.

By definition, the female partner was sexually attractive, and so it was far easier for the men to transfer their arousal to her, and to mislabel it as sexual arousal. In this way, she represented a *salient* or *credible* source of arousal (Olson and Ross, 1988). (She also represented a clear, unambiguous source of arousal.) Similarly, if female participants are shown slides of attractive male nudes, it may be easy to alter their preferences among the pictures based on false heart rate feedback, whereas this would be very difficult to achieve if the male nudes were replaced by slides of naked hippos! (This is a deliberately modified version of an example given by Taylor *et al.*, 1994.)

Figure 10.7

Cognitive appraisal or affective primacy?

When evaluating the James–Lange theory earlier, we noted that it fails to take into account our *appraisal* of the emotional 'stimulus'. Appraisal is the thinking that leads to emotion (Parrott, 2004), and appraisal theory is a development of Schachter's cognitive labelling theory. The importance of appraisal is demonstrated in Key Study 10.8.

Key Study 10.8

Subincision in the Arunta (Speisman *et al.*, 1964)

- Participants saw a film (*Subincision in the Arunta*), which shows aboriginal boys undergoing circumcision as part of a puberty rite. The boys are seen having their penises cut with a jagged flint knife. This usually causes high levels of stress in viewers of the film (and probably in the boys too!). The soundtrack was manipulated, so that:
  (i) The pain, jaggedness of the knife, and so on, were emphasised (*trauma*).
  (ii) The boys' anticipation of entering manhood was emphasised (*denial*).
  (iii) The emotional elements were ignored and the traditions of the aboriginal people were emphasised (*intellectualisation*).
  (iv) There was no commentary (*silent control*).
- As predicted, arousal (measured by GSR and heart rate) was highest in the trauma condition, next highest in the control condition and lowest in the other two. What we tell ourselves about external situations (*cognitive appraisal*) influences our level of arousal.

According to Lazarus (1982), some degree of cognitive processing is an essential prerequisite for an affective reaction to a stimulus to occur, and is an integral feature of all emotional states. For Lazarus,

> *... emotion results from evaluative perception of a relationship (actual, imagined or anticipated) between a person (or animal) and the environment.*

He proposes that cognitive appraisal invariably *precedes* any affective reaction, although it doesn't have to involve any conscious processing. Zajonc (1984) argues that there's generally little direct evidence of either the existence or nature of such preconscious cognitive processing (although the study of *subliminal perception* suggests otherwise; see Chapter 15). Zajonc (1980a) argues that cognition and affect operate as *independent* systems, and an emotional response may precede cognitive processes under certain circumstances. For example, we may meet someone very briefly and form a positive or negative impression, despite not being able to remember any detailed information about them later (Eysenck and Keane, 1990).

Ask Yourself

- Try to formulate some arguments against Zajonc's claim that cognition and affect are separate, independent systems.

Parrott (2004) asks how it's possible to call certain emotions 'irrational' if emotions don't intrinsically entail beliefs. Also, most emotions are 'about' something – and this is cognitive. The most important problem for Zajonc is that how we think about a situation obviously influences how we feel (for example, why we think someone behaved as they did determines whether we feel angry or sympathetic; see Chapter 23).

Zajonc seems to overestimate the amount of cognitive processing that Lazarus and other cognitive appraisal theorists are claiming. For example, Lazarus simply argues that some minimal cognitive analysis at some level always precedes emotional experience. But this can be quite automatic, and so 'cognitive appraisal' is quite consistent with the sense of 'immediacy' that so much emotional experience has (and which Frijda (1994) sees as a characteristic of emotion).

CONCLUSIONS

Manstead (2005) points out that some of the leading emotion researchers, including Schachter, Lazarus, Ekman and Scherer are social and personality Psychologists. This makes it all the more surprising that appraisal theorists fail to pay sufficient attention to the *social context*: the tendency has been to study emotional phenomena at the level of the socially isolated individual.

Chapter Summary

- Ekman and Friesen identify six **primary, universal** emotions, which are probably innate.
- An **evolutionary approach** to understanding primary or basic emotions includes considering their current **function**. But 'basic' emotions differ between cultures and over time within the same culture. They may be psychologically or culturally basic – not biologically.
- According to **social constructionism** (SC), emotions are **culturally** and **historically relative**. They exist within a system of beliefs and values, which differs between cultures and changes over time.
- For each distinct emotion there are the **subjective experience, physiological changes, associated behaviour** and **cognitive appraisal** of the emotion-producing stimulus/situation.
- Darwin saw emotional behaviour, like other behaviour as having **evolved** because they benefited those animals that used them effectively.
- The **James–Lange theory** turns the common-sense theory of emotion on its head, claiming that our emotional experience is the result of perceived bodily changes – in particular, skeletal changes.
- Studies by Valins (using the **false feedback paradigm**) and Laird (testing the **facial feedback hypothesis**) and Hennenlotter *et al*. support the James–Lange theory, although they fail to take into account any **visceral** changes that may be taking place. They both suggest that physiological arousal isn't sufficient to account for emotional experience.
- Cannon criticised the James–Lange theory for assuming that different emotional states are associated with different patterns of ANS activity. The **Cannon–Bard theory** claims that the ANS responds in the same way to all emotional stimuli.
- Using the **directed facial action** and the **relived emotion methods**, Levenson found physiological differences between anger, disgust, fear and sadness. Both the James–Lange and Cannon–Bard theories take too extreme a view regarding **physiological specificity**, and the truth lies somewhere in between.
- Marañon's and Hohmann's studies support Cannon's claim that physiological arousal isn't sufficient for emotional experience, although they indicate that it is necessary. However, Dana's study of a patient with a spinal cord lesion suggests that it might not even be necessary.
- According to Schachter's **cognitive labelling theory,** the experience of emotion depends both on **physiological changes** and the **interpretation of those changes**. Cannon, therefore, was mistaken in claiming that emotional experience and bodily changes are independent.
- Schachter and Singer's 'adrenaline experiment' demonstrates that while physiological arousal is necessary, the nature of the arousal is irrelevant. What's crucial is the **cognitive label** we give that arousal.
- Dutton and Aron's 'suspension bridge' experiment supports Schachter's theory, but also shows that how we label our arousal can be mistaken (the **misattribution effect**).
- Failure to replicate the adrenaline experiment suggests that emotional experience is much less malleable than Schachter claims, and that unexplained arousal is likely to be interpreted *negatively*.
- Lazarus's **cognitive appraisal theory** claims that some minimal cognitive analysis always precedes emotional experience, although this can be unconscious and automatic. Zajonc's **affective primacy theory** claims that emotional responses can occur without any cognition being involved.
- The basic disagreement between Lazarus and Zajonc seems to be about the **level** of processing involved, rather than whether or not any cognitive processing takes place.
- The cognitive appraisal approach is based on an underlying view of people as socially isolated and so has largely ignored the importance of the **social context**.

Links with Other Topics/Chapters

Chapter 2 ⟶ The study of emotion has always been influenced by an *evolutionary approach*

Chapter 23 ⟶ Schachter's cognitive labelling theory has had a major impact on cognitive theories of emotion in general. One major form of this influence relates to the role of *attribution*, including the *misattribution effect*

Chapter 11 ⟶ Abramson and Martin (1981) grafted attributional principles onto Seligman's (1975) theory of *learned helplessness*

Chapter 44 ⟶ in an attempt to explain *major depressive disorder/clinical depression*

Chapter 30 ⟶ The way we account for other people's behaviour (and the resulting emotions we experience) can influence *helping behaviour/ bystander intervention*

Chapter 12 ⟶ The experience of certain kinds of negative emotions is what we commonly mean by *stress*, and Lazarus's appraisal theory is often discussed in this context

Recommended Reading

Cox, T. (1978) *Stress*. London: Macmillan Education Ltd. Also useful for Chapter 12.

Ekman, P. & Davidson, R.J. (eds) (1994) *The Nature of Emotion: Fundamental Questions*. New York: Oxford University Press.

Gross, R. (2008) *Key Studies in Psychology* (5th edn). London: Hodder Education. Chapter 18.

Lazarus, R.S. (1991) *Emotion and Adaptation*. Oxford: Oxford University Press.

Lazarus R.S. (1999) *Stress and Emotion: A New Synthesis*. London: Free Association Books. Probably more relevant to Chapter 12.

LeDoux, J. (1998) *The Emotional Brain: The Mysterious Underpinnings of Emotional Life*. New York: Simon & Schuster.

Oatley, K., Keltner, D., Jenkins, J.M. (2006) *Understanding Emotions* (2nd edn). Oxford: Blackwell Publishing Ltd. Some chapters are relevant to Chapters 44 and 45.

Useful Websites

www.loc.gov./loc/brain/emotion/Damasio.html ('The Science of Emotion': Damasio; part of the Project on the Decade of the Brain, 1990–2000)

www.cns.nyu.edu/home/ledoux (The LeDoux laboratory)

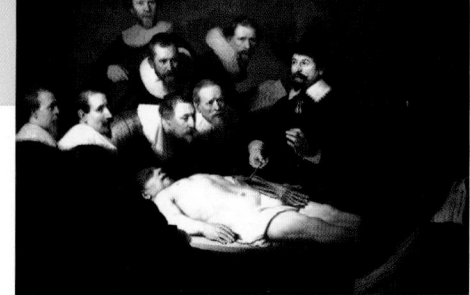

CHAPTER 11

LEARNING AND CONDITIONING

What is learning?

Behaviourist approaches

Cognitive approaches

INTRODUCTION and OVERVIEW

We've seen in earlier chapters how American Psychology in particular was dominated by *behaviourism* for much of the first half of the twentieth century. Given the central role of learning in philosophical behaviourism, it's not surprising that the topic of learning itself should be central within Psychology as a whole.

The concept of learning is a good example of the discrepancy between the everyday, common-sense use of a term and its technical, scientific use (see Chapter 1). In everyday conversation, the emphasis is usually on *what* is learned (the *end product*), such as learning to drive a car, use the internet or speak French. But when Psychologists use the term, their focus is on *how* the learning takes place (the *learning process*).

When the focus is on the end product, we generally infer that the learning is *deliberate.* For example, we pay for driving lessons that will help us, eventually, to acquire a driving licence. But, for Psychologists, learning can take place without a 'teacher'. We can learn, for example, by merely *observing* others, who may not even know they're being observed. Learning can also happen without other people being involved at all, as when we observe recurring environmental events ('thunder always follows lightning').

Partly because the concept of learning as used by Psychologists is very broad, they disagree as to exactly what's involved in the learning process. Watson, the founder of behaviourism, was the first Psychologist to apply Pavlov's concept of the *conditioned reflex/response* to human behaviour. A more active view of learning was taken by Thorndike, whose work formed the basis of Skinner's *operant conditioning*. Skinner's contribution, above all others, made behaviourism such a force within Psychology as a whole (see Chapter 2).

WHAT IS LEARNING?

Learning is a *hypothetical construct*: it cannot be directly observed, but only inferred from observable behaviour. Learning normally implies a fairly *permanent* change in a person's behavioural performance. However, permanent changes in behaviour can also result from things that have nothing to do with learning, such as the effects of brain damage on behaviour, or the changes associated with puberty and other maturational processes. So, if a change in behaviour is to be counted as learning, the change must be linked to some kind of *past experience* (regardless of whether there was any attempt to bring about that change).

For these reasons, Psychologists usually define learning as 'a relatively permanent change in behaviour due to past experience' (Coon, 1983) or 'the process by which relatively permanent changes occur in behavioural potential as a result of experience' (Anderson, 1995a).

Learning versus performance

Anderson's definition has one major advantage over Coon's, namely that it implies a distinction between learning (*behavioural potential*) and performance (*actual behaviour*).

Ask Yourself

- What things have you learned to do/learned about that you're not actually doing/thinking about right now?

If you can swim, you're almost certainly not doing so as you read this chapter – but you could readily do so if faced with a pool full of water! So what you *could do* (potential behaviour based on learning) and what you're *actually doing* (current performance) are two different things. Ultimately, of course, the only proof of learning is a particular kind of performance (such as exams). Performance can fluctuate due to fatigue, drugs and emotional factors, and so is much more variable than learning, which is more permanent. (Exams come to mind again – many students have left an exam knowing what they could not demonstrate during the exam itself.)

Learning and other abilities

Howe (1980) defines learning as 'a biological device that functions to protect the human individual and to extend his capacities'. In this context, learning is neither independent of, nor entirely separate from, several other abilities, in particular memory and perception. Indeed, learning and memory may be regarded as two sides of the same coin (see Chapter 17).

According to Howe, learning is also *cumulative*: what we learn at any time is influenced by our previous learning. Also, most instances of learning take the form of *adaptive changes*, as reflected in Anderson's (1995a) definition as 'the mechanism by which organisms can adapt to a changing and nonpredictable environment'.

Some basic questions about learning

While it's generally agreed by Psychologists that learning is relatively permanent and due to past experience, there's much less agreement about exactly what changes when learning takes place, and what kinds of past experience are involved. Put another way, how do the changes occur and what mechanisms are involved? One important issue that divides Psychologists is the extent to which they focus on the *overt, behavioural changes* as opposed to the *covert, cognitive changes*.

BEHAVIOURIST APPROACHES

Skinner (1938) made the crucial distinction between *respondents* (or *respondent behaviour*), which are triggered automatically by particular environmental stimuli, and *operants* (or *operant behaviour*), which are essentially voluntary. A related distinction is that between *classical* or *respondent (Pavlovian) conditioning* and *operant* or *instrumental (Skinnerian)* conditioning.

Classical conditioning: why do dogs drool over bells?

Ivan Pavlov was a physiologist interested in the process of digestion in dogs. He was awarded the Nobel Prize in 1904 (the year Skinner was born). He developed a surgical technique for collecting a dog's salivary secretions: a tube was attached to the outside of its cheek, so the drops of saliva could easily be measured.

Pavlov (1927) noticed that the dogs would often start salivating *before* they were given any food: when they looked at the food or saw the feeding bucket, or even when they heard the footsteps of the laboratory assistant coming to feed them. These observations led to the study of what's now called classical (or Pavlovian) conditioning: a stimulus (such as a bell), which wouldn't normally produce a particular response (such as salivation), eventually comes to do so by being paired with another stimulus (such as food) which does normally produce the response.

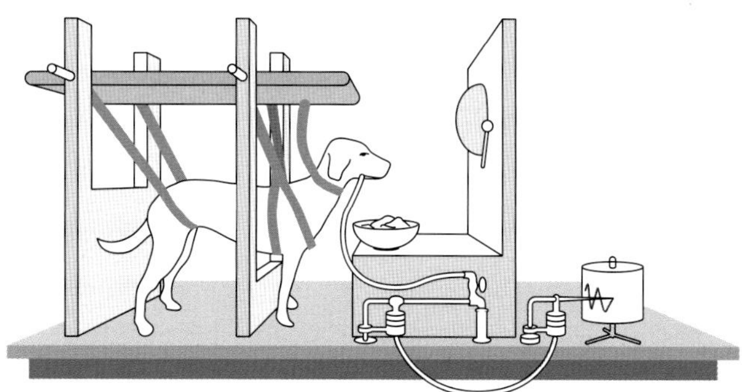

Figure 11.2 The apparatus used by Pavlov in his experiments on conditioned reflexes

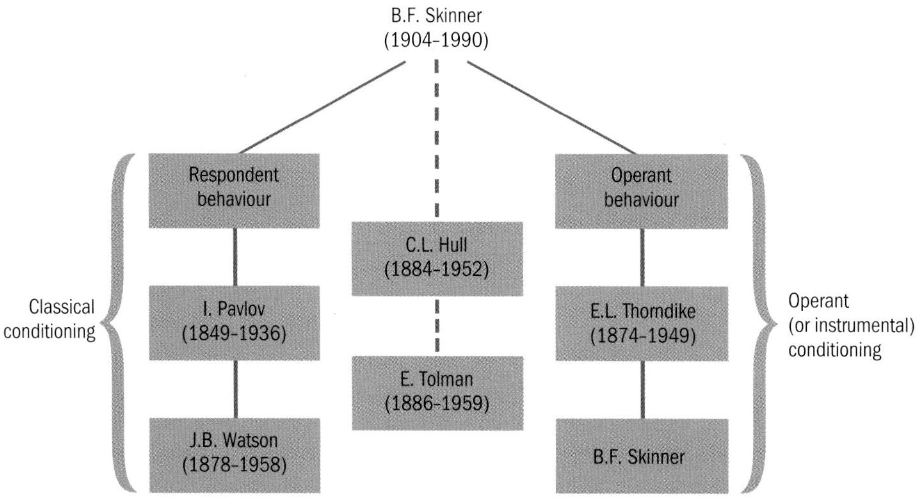

Figure 11.1 Major figures in the behaviourist (learning theory) tradition

- *Before* conditioning, the taste of food will naturally and automatically make the dog salivate, but the sound of a bell won't. So, the food is referred to as an *unconditioned stimulus* (UCS), and the salivation is an *unconditioned response* (UCR): an automatic, reflex, biologically built-in response. The dog doesn't have to learn to salivate in response to food, because it does so naturally.
- *During* conditioning, the bell is paired with the food. Because the bell doesn't naturally produce salivation, it's called a *conditioned stimulus* (CS): it only produces salivation *on the condition* that it's paired with the UCS. It's also *neutral* with regard to salivation prior to conditioning.
- If the bell and food are paired often enough, the dog starts to salivate as soon as it hears the bell and *before* the food is presented. When this occurs, conditioning has taken place. The salivation is now referred to as a *conditioned response* (CR), because it's produced by a conditioned stimulus (CS) – the bell.

This basic procedure can be used with a variety of conditioned stimuli, such as buzzers, metronomes, lights, geometric figures, and so on. The exact relationship between the CS and the UCS can also be varied to give different kinds of conditioning. What I've described above is *delayed/forward conditioning* (see Table 11.1).

Ask Yourself

- In the basic procedure described above, the CS is presented about a half-second before the UCS.
- What do you think might happen if the CS is presented *after* the UCS?

Table 11.1 Four types of classical conditioning based on different CS–UCS relationships

1. Delayed or forward	The CS is presented *before* the UCS, and remains 'on' while the UCS is presented and until the UCR appears. Conditioning has occurred when the CR appears before the UCS is presented. A half-second interval produces the strongest learning. As the interval increases, learning becomes poorer. This type of conditioning is typically used in the laboratory, especially with non-humans.
2. Backward	The CS is presented *after* the UCS. Generally this produces very little, if any, learning in laboratory animals. However, much advertising uses backward conditioning (e.g. the idyllic tropical scene is set, and then the coconut bar is introduced).
3. Simultaneous	The CS and UCS are presented *together*. Conditioning has occurred when the CS on its own produces the CR. This type of conditioning often occurs in real-life situations (e.g. the sound of the dentist's drill accompanies the contact of the drill with your tooth).
4. Trace	The CS is *presented and removed* before the UCS is presented, so that only a 'memory trace' of the CS remains to be conditioned. The CR is usually weaker than in delayed or simultaneous conditioning.

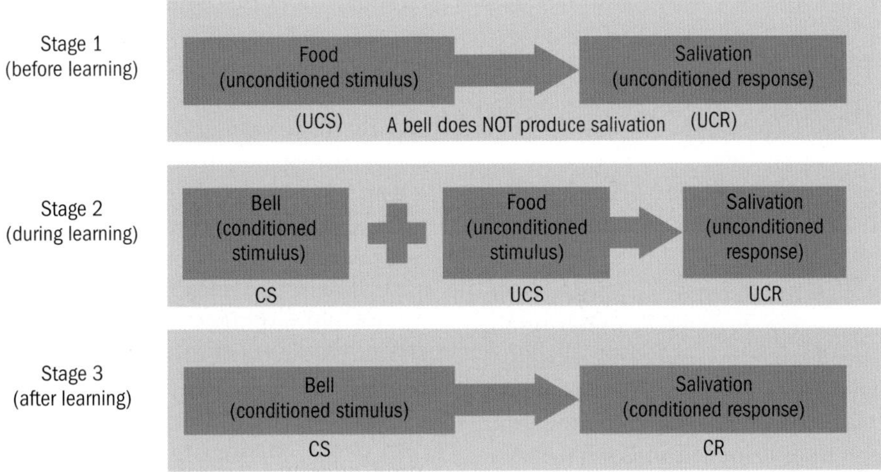

Figure 11.3 The basic procedure involved in classical conditioning

Higher-order conditioning

Pavlov demonstrated that a strong CS could be used instead of food, to produce salivation in response to a new stimulus that had never been paired with food. For example, a buzzer (previously paired with food) is paired with a black square. After ten pairings (using delayed conditioning), the dog will salivate a small but significant amount at the sight of the black square before the buzzer is sounded. Remember, the black square has never been associated with food directly, but only indirectly, through association with the buzzer. The CS is functioning as a UCS.

The buzzer and food combination is referred to as *first-order conditioning*, and the black square and buzzer pairing as *second-order conditioning*. Pavlov found with dogs that learning couldn't go beyond third- or fourth-order conditioning. Even so, conditioning is beginning to look a rather more complex process.

Generalisation and discrimination

In *generalisation*, the CR transfers spontaneously to stimuli similar to, but different from, the original CS. For example, if a dog is trained using a bell of a particular pitch and is then presented with a bell a little higher or lower in pitch, it will still salivate, although only one bell (the original CS) was actually paired with food. However, if the dog is presented with bells that are increasingly different from the original, the CR will gradually weaken and eventually stop altogether – the dog is showing *discrimination*.

CS1 (The bell used in the original conditioning procedure) → CR (salivation)

Bells CS2, CS3 and CS4 are of increasingly lower pitch but still produce salivation through **GENERALISATION**	CS2 → CR CS3 → CR CS4 → CR	Salivation is gradually becoming weaker as the pitch becomes lower compared with CS1
Bells CS5, CS6 and CS7 fail to produce salivation because they're sufficiently different from CS1 The dog is showing **DISCRIMINATION**	CS5 ↛ CR CS6 ↛ CR CS7 ↛ CR	No salivation occurs

Figure 11.4 An example of discrimination occurring spontaneously as a result of generalisation stopping

Pavlov also trained dogs to discriminate in the original conditioning procedure. For example, if a high-pitched bell is paired with food but a low-pitched bell isn't, the dog will start salivating in response to the former, but not the latter (*discrimination training*). An interesting phenomenon related to discrimination is what Pavlov called *experimental neurosis* (see Box 11.1).

Box 11.1 Experimental neurosis: how to drive a dog mad

- Pavlov (1927) trained dogs to salivate to a circle but not to an ellipse, and then gradually changed the shape of the ellipse until it became almost circular.
- As this happened, the dogs started behaving in 'neurotic' ways – whining, trembling, urinating and defecating, refusing to eat, and so on.
- It was as if they didn't know how to respond: was the stimulus a circle (in which case, through generalisation, they 'ought' to salivate) or was it an ellipse (in which case, through discrimination, they 'ought not to' salivate)?

Extinction and spontaneous recovery

If dogs have been conditioned to salivate to a bell, and the bell is repeatedly presented *without* food, the CR of salivation gradually becomes weaker and eventually stops altogether (*extinction*). However, if a dog that's undergone extinction is removed from the experimental situation, and then put back a couple of hours or so later, it will start salivating again. Although no further pairing of the bell and food has occurred, the CR of salivation reappears in response to the bell (*spontaneous recovery*). This shows that extinction doesn't involve an 'erasing' of the original learning, but rather a learning to *inhibit* or *suppress* the CR when the CS is continually presented without a UCS.

Classical conditioning and human behaviour

There have been many laboratory demonstrations involving human participants. It's relatively easy to classically condition and extinguish CRs, such as the eye-blink and galvanic skin response (GSR). But what relevance does this have for understanding human learning and memory, let alone thinking, reasoning or problem-solving (see Chapter 20)?

In normal adults, the conditioning process can apparently be overridden by instructions: simply *telling* participants that the UCS won't occur causes *instant* loss of the CR, which would otherwise extinguish only slowly (Davey, 1983). Most participants in a conditioning experiment are aware of the experimenter's *contingencies* (the relationship between stimuli and responses), and in the absence of such awareness often fail to show evidence of conditioning (Brewer, 1974).

There are also important differences between very young children, or those with severe learning difficulties, and older children and adults, regarding their behaviour in a variety of operant conditioning and discrimination learning experiments. These seem largely attributable to language development (Dugdale and Lowe, 1990; see Chapter 19).

All this suggests that people have rather more efficient, language- or rule-based forms of learning at their disposal than the laborious formation of associations between a CS and UCS. Even *behaviour therapy*, one of the apparently more successful applications of conditioning principles to human behaviour, has given way to *cognitive-behavioural therapy* (Mackintosh, 1995; see Chapter 45).

Classical conditioning and phobias

Watson was the first Psychologist to apply the principles of classical conditioning to human behaviour. He did this in what's considered to be one of the most ethically dubious Psychology experiments ever conducted. See Key Study 11.1.

Ask Yourself

- Why do you think Watson and Rayner's experiment is considered to be so ethically unsound?

It's unclear whether Watson and Rayner intended to remove Albert's phobia; what's certain is that his mother removed him before this could happen.

They might have attempted to remove it through the method of *direct unconditioning*, as used by Jones (1924). See Key Study 11.2. This is an early example of what Wolpe (1958) called *systematic desensitisation* (see Chapter 45).

Key Study 11.2

The case of Little Peter (Jones, 1924)

- Peter was a 2-year-old living in a charitable institution. Jones was mainly interested in those children who cried and trembled when shown an animal (such as a frog, rat or rabbit). Peter showed an extreme fear of rats, rabbits, feathers, cotton wool, fur coats, frogs and fish, although in other respects he was regarded as well-adjusted. It wasn't known how these phobias had arisen.
- Jones, supervised by Watson, put a rabbit in a wire cage in front of Peter while he ate his lunch. After 40 such sessions, Peter ate his lunch with one hand and stroked the rabbit (now on his lap) with the other.
- In a series of 17 steps, the rabbit (still in the cage) had been brought a little closer each day, then let free in the room, eventually sitting on Peter's lunch tray.

Key Study 11.1

The case of Little Albert (Watson and Rayner, 1920)

- Albert was described as 'healthy from birth' and 'on the whole stolid and unemotional'. When he was about 9 months old, his reactions to various stimuli were tested – a white rat, a rabbit, a dog, a monkey, masks with and without hair, cotton wool, burning newspapers and a hammer striking a four-foot steel bar just behind his head. Only the last of these frightened him, so this was designated the UCS (and fear the UCR). The other stimuli were neutral, because they *didn't* produce fear.
- When Albert was just over 11 months old, the rat and the UCS were presented together: as Albert reached out to stroke the animal, Watson crept up behind the baby and brought the hammer crashing down on the steel bar.
- This occurred seven times in total over the next seven weeks. By this time, the rat (the CS) *on its own* frightened Albert, and the fear was now a CR. Watson and Rayner had succeeded in deliberately producing in a baby a phobia of rats.
- The CR transferred spontaneously to the rabbit, the dog, a sealskin fur coat, cotton wool, Watson's hair and a Santa Claus mask. But it didn't generalise to Albert's building blocks, or to the hair of two observers (so Albert was showing *discrimination*).
- Five days after conditioning, the CR produced by the rat persisted. After ten days it was 'much less marked', but was still evident a month later.

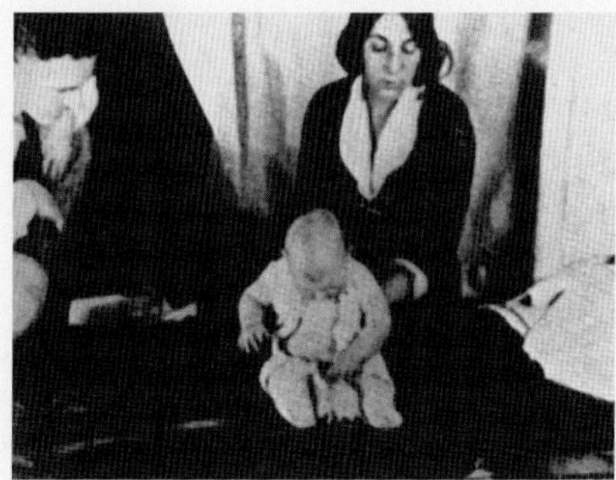

Figure 11.5 A very rare photograph of John Watson and Rosalie Rayner during the conditioning of Little Albert

Behaviour therapists, such as Eysenck, regard the Little Albert experiment as demonstrating how *all* phobias are acquired in everyday life.

Ask Yourself

- How could the basic classical conditioning procedure help to explain someone's fear of the dentist?

A fear of the dentist could be learnt in the following way:

- drill hitting a nerve (UCS) → pain/fear (UCR)
- sound of drill (CS) + drill hitting nerve (UCS) → pain/fear (UCR)
- sound of the drill (CS) → fear (CR).

If you're looking at the dentist who's peering into your mouth, you may become afraid of upside-down faces; if s/he's wearing a mask, you may acquire a fear of masks too. Also, through generalisation, you can come to fear all drill-like noises or white coats worn by medical personnel or lab technicians.

Human phobias may be perpetuated through *avoiding* the object of our fears. In other words, we don't give the fear a chance to undergo extinction (see Chapters 44 and 45). This occurs in conjunction with *operant conditioning*, whereby the avoidance behaviour becomes strengthened through negative reinforcement.

Operant conditioning: why do rats press levers?

When Skinner drew the distinction between respondent and operant behaviour, he wasn't rejecting the discoveries of Pavlov and Watson. Rather, he was arguing that most animal and human behaviour isn't triggered or elicited by specific stimuli. He was interested in how animals *operate on their environment*, and how this operant behaviour is *instrumental* in bringing about certain consequences, which then determine the probability of that behaviour being repeated. Skinner saw the learner as much more *active* than did Pavlov or Watson.

Just as Watson's ideas were based on the earlier work of Pavlov, so Skinner's study of operant conditioning grew out of the earlier work of another American, Edward Thorndike.

Thorndike's law of effect

Thorndike (1898) built puzzle-boxes for use with cats, whose task was to operate a latch that would automatically cause the door to spring open, freeing them. Each time they managed to escape from the puzzle-box, there was a piece of fish, visible from inside the puzzle-box, waiting for them. The cats were deprived of food for a considerable time before the experiments began, and so were highly motivated. After eating the fish, the cats were put straight back in, and the whole process was repeated.

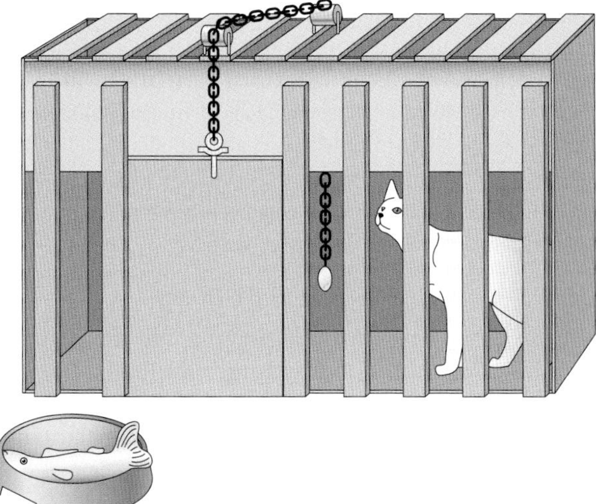

Figure 11.6 Thorndike's puzzle-box

At first the cats struggled to get out, behaving in a purely random way, and it was only by chance that the first escape was made. But each time they were returned to the puzzle-box, it took them less time to operate the latch and escape. For instance, with one of the boxes, the average time for the first escape was 5 minutes, but after 10–20 trials this was reduced to about 5 seconds.

Thorndike accounted for this by claiming that the learning was essentially *random* or *trial and error*. There was no sudden flash of insight into how the releasing mechanism worked, but rather a gradual reduction in the number of errors made and hence escape time (see Chapter 20). What was being learned was a connection between the stimulus (the manipulative components of the box) and the response (the behaviour that allowed the cat to escape). Further, the stimulus–response connection is 'stamped in when pleasure results from the act, and stamped out when it doesn't' (*law of effect*). This is crucially important as a way of distinguishing classical and operant conditioning, which Skinner did 40 years later.

Skinner's 'analysis of behaviour'

Skinner used a form of puzzle-box known as a *Skinner box*. This was designed for a rat or pigeon to do things in, rather than escape from. The box has a lever (in the case of rats) or illuminated discs (in the case of pigeons), under which is a food tray. The experimenter decides exactly what the relationship shall be between pressing the lever and the delivery of a food pellet, providing total *control* of the animal's environment. But it's the animal that has to do the work.

Figure 11.7 Rat in a Skinner box (or 'operant chamber')

Skinner used the term *strengthen* in place of Thorndike's 'stamping in', and *weaken* in place of 'stamping out'. He regarded Thorndike's terms as too mentalistic, and his own as more objective and descriptive.

Box 11.2 Skinner's analysis of behaviour (or the ABC of operant conditioning)

The analysis of behaviour requires an accurate but neutral representation of the relationship (or contingencies) between:

- **A**ntecedents (the stimulus conditions, such as the lever, the click of the food dispenser, a light that may go on when the lever is pressed)
- **B**ehaviours (or operants, such as pressing the lever)
- **C**onsequences (what happens as a result of the operant behaviour – reinforcement or punishment).

This is the ABC of operant conditioning.

According to Skinner's version of the law of effect, 'behaviour is shaped and maintained by its consequences'. The consequences of operants can be *positive reinforcement*, *negative reinforcement* or *punishment*.

While both positive and negative reinforcement *strengthen* behaviour (making it more probable), each works in a different way. *Positive reinforcement* involves presenting something pleasurable (such as food), while *negative reinforcement* involves the removal or avoidance of some 'aversive' (literally 'painful') state of affairs (such as electric shock). Punishment *weakens* behaviour (making it less probable), through the presentation of an aversive stimulus.

Primary and secondary reinforcers

Primary reinforcers (such as food, water, sex) are *natural* reinforcers (reinforcing in themselves). *Secondary reinforcers* acquire their reinforcing properties through association with primary reinforcers – that is, we have to *learn* (through classical conditioning) to find them reinforcing. Examples of human secondary (or *conditioned*) reinforcers are money, cheques and tokens (see Chapter 45).

In a Skinner box, if a click accompanies the presentation of each pellet of food, the rat will eventually come to find the click on its own reinforcing. The click can then be used as a reinforcer for getting the rat to learn some new response. (Clickers are used in dog training, at first in conjunction with a primary reinforcer, such as a food 'treat', then on their own.) Secondary reinforcers are important, because they 'bridge the gap' between the response and the primary reinforcer, which may not be presented immediately.

Schedules of reinforcement

Another important aspect of Skinner's work is concerned with the effects on behaviour of how frequently and how regularly (or predictably) reinforcements are presented. Ferster and Skinner (1957) identified five major *schedules*, each of which is associated with a characteristic pattern of responding. This part of Skinner's research is largely counterintuitive (Walker, 1984).

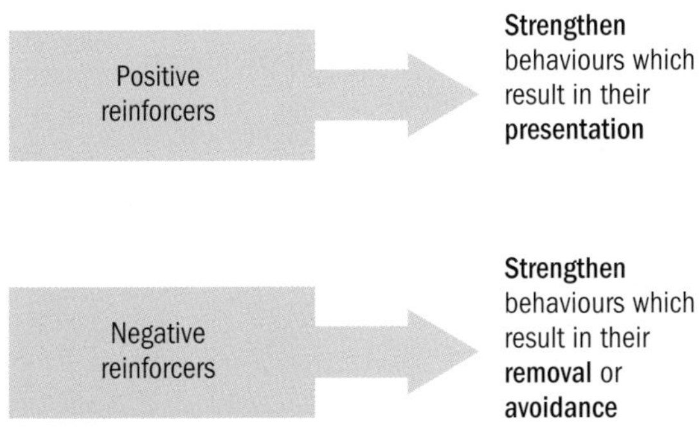
Positive reinforcers
Strengthen behaviours which result in their **presentation**
Negative reinforcers
Strengthen behaviours which result in their **removal** or **avoidance**

Punishers
Weaken behaviours which result in their **presentation**

Figure 11.8 The consequences of behaviour and their effects

Rats and pigeons (and probably most mammals and birds) typically 'work harder' (press the lever/peck the disc at a faster rate) for scant reward: when reinforcements are relatively infrequent and irregular or unpredictable, they'll go on working long after the reinforcement has actually been withdrawn. So, each schedule can be analysed in terms of (a) *pattern and rate of response*; and (b) *resistance to extinction* (see Table 11.2).

The rate of response can be represented by plotting responses cumulatively as steps along a vertical axis, against the time when they're made along the horizontal axis. Skinner called this a '*cumulative record*' (see Figure 11.9).

A *continuous schedule* is normally used only when some new response is being learned. Once it's being emitted regularly and reliably, it can be maintained by using one of the four *partial* or *intermittent schedules*. But this change must be gradual. If the animal is switched from a continuous schedule to, say, a VR 50, it will soon stop responding. Skinner (1938) originally used an interval schedule because a reinforcer is guaranteed, sooner or later, so long as one response is made during the interval.

Table 11.2 Common reinforcement schedules, and associated patterns of response and resistance to extinction

Reinforcement schedule	Example	Pattern and rate of response	Resistance to extinction	Example of human behaviour
Continuous reinforcement (CRF)	Every single response is reinforced	Response rate is low but steady	Very low – the quickest way to bring about extinction	1. Receiving a high grade for every assignment 2. Receiving a tip for every customer served
Fixed interval (FI)	A reinforcement is given every 30 seconds (FI 30), provided the response occurs at least once during that time	Response rate speeds up as the next reinforcement becomes available; a pause after each reinforcement. Overall response rate fairly low	Fairly low – extinction occurs quite quickly	1. Being paid regularly (every week or month) 2. Giving yourself a 15-minute break for every hour's studying done
Variable interval (VI)	A reinforcement is given on average every 30 seconds (VI 30), but the interval varies from trial to trial. So, the interval on any one occasion is unpredictable	Response rate is very stable over long periods of time. Still some tendency to increase response rate as time elapses since the last reinforcement	Very high – extinction occurs very slowly and gradually	Many self-employed people receive payment irregularly (depending on when the customer pays for the product or the service)
Fixed ratio (FR)	A reinforcement is given for a fixed number of responses, however long this may take, e.g. one reinforcement every ten responses (FR 10)	There's a pronounced pause after each reinforcement, and then a very high rate of responding leading up to the next reinforcement	As in FI	1. Piece work (the more work done, the more money earned) 2. Commission (extra money for so many goods made or sales completed)
Variable ratio (VR)	A reinforcement is given on average every ten responses (VR 10), but the number varies from trial to trial. So, the number of responses required on any one occasion is unpredictable	Very high response rate – and very steady	Very high – the most resistant of all the schedules	Gambling

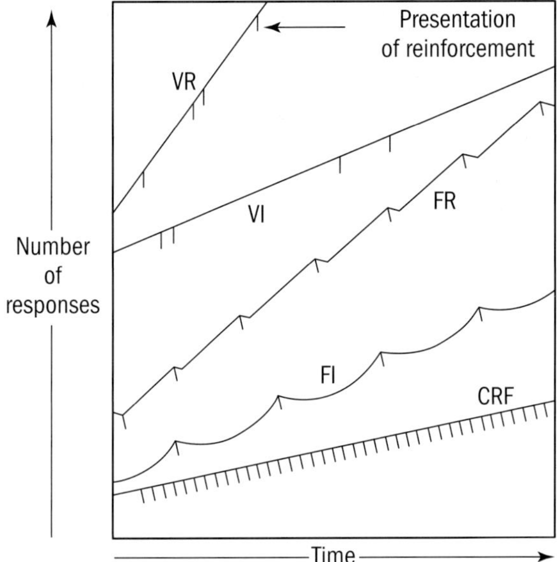

Figure 11.9 Typical cumulative records for a response (such as lever pressing) reinforced using five schedules of reinforcement

Shaping: the reinforcement of successive approximations

Reinforcement can be used to build up relatively complex behaviour (not part of the animal's natural repertoire) by reinforcing closer and closer approximations to the desired behaviour (*shaping*). First, the behaviour must be broken down into a number of small steps, each of which is reinforced in sequence. Gradually, what the animal can do is much more like what the experimenter is trying to teach it. This is what animal trainers have been doing for hundreds of years, and is the method of reinforcement Skinner used to teach pigeons to play ping-pong or turn a full (anticlockwise) circle. Most human skills are learned in this step-by-step manner.

Shaping also provides an important foundation for *behaviour modification*. This is used to teach children and adults with learning difficulties to use the toilet, feed and dress themselves, and other social skills. It's also been used to develop speech in autistic children and adults with schizophrenia (see Chapter 45).

Negative reinforcement: escape and avoidance learning

Escape and avoidance learning are the two major ways in which negative reinforcement has been studied in the laboratory. *Escape learning* is relatively simple. For example, rats can learn to press a lever to turn off electric shock. *Avoidance learning* is more complex and more relevant to certain aspects of human behaviour. (See Box 11.3.)

Box 11.3 Avoidance learning through negative reinforcement

- Most laboratory studies use a *shuttle box*, a box divided into two compartments, sometimes with a barrier or door between them. Electric shocks can be delivered through the floor of either compartment independently of the other. Neither side is permanently safe, but only one is electrified at a time.
- The animal's task is to find which is the safe side on any one occasion. A *warning signal* (a light or buzzer) is given whenever the electrified side is to be changed, so the animal can always avoid being shocked if it switches sides when it hears (or sees) the signal.

According to the *two factor theory* (Mowrer, 1960) or the *two process theory* (Gray, 1975):

- The animal first learns to be afraid (the warning signal elicits an anticipatory emotional response of fear/anxiety through *classical conditioning*).
- It then learns a response to reduce the fear (jumping the barrier is *negatively reinforced* through avoiding the shock before it's switched on).

Punishment

Skinner maintained that, with both humans and non-humans, positive (and, to a lesser extent, negative) reinforcement is a much more potent influence on behaviour than punishment. This is largely because punishment can only make certain responses less likely: you cannot teach anything new by punishment alone.

However, Campbell and Church (1969) argue that punishments are, if anything, a *stronger* influence on behaviour than the incentive effects of reinforcements (at least as far as laboratory animals are concerned). But punishment produces unpleasant side-effects, such as stress, anxiety, withdrawal and aggression.

Estes (1970) concluded that punishment merely *suppresses* lever pressing in the short term, but doesn't weaken it. Other experiments have shown that the strength and duration of the suppression effect depend on the intensity of the punishment and the degree of deprivation. However, the response is still suppressed rather than unlearned.

When alternative ways of obtaining reinforcers are available, punishment has a more powerful suppressive effect on the punished behaviour (Howe, 1980). For example, Azrin and Holz (1966) combined punishment and reinforcement, so that response A was punished while response B (incompatible with A) was positively reinforced. Skinner advocates this with human beings.

The antecedents of behaviour: stimulus control

In operant conditioning, the stimulus indicates the likely consequence of emitting a particular response: the operant behaviour is more likely to occur in the presence of some stimuli than others. If a rat has been reinforced for pressing the lever, it's more likely to go on emitting that response as the lever becomes associated both with reinforcement and the action of pressing (probably through classical conditioning). Technically, lever pressing has now come under the *stimulus control* of the lever. But there's still no inevitability about pressing it, only an *increased probability*. (This is why the term 'S–R Psychology' is sometimes used only to refer to classical conditioning.)

Similarly, drivers' behaviour is brought under the stimulus control of traffic signals, road signs, other vehicles, pedestrians, and so on. Much of our everyday behaviour can be seen in this way. Sitting on chairs, answering the telephone, turning on the television, and so on, are all operants that are more likely to occur in the presence of those stimuli because of the past consequences of doing so.

A special case of stimulus control is a *discriminative stimulus*. If a rat in the Skinner box is reinforced for lever pressing only when a light is on, the light soon becomes a discriminative stimulus (the rat presses only when the light is on).

Ask Yourself

- What are the major similarities and differences between classical and operant conditioning?

Does conditioning work in the same way for all species?

The fact that many experiments involving a variety of species can all be described as classical conditioning doesn't in itself mean that there's only one mechanism involved, or only one explanation that applies, equally, to all species and all cases (Walker, 1984). Although *conditionability* seems to be an almost universal property of nervous systems (including those of sea snails, flatworms and fruit flies), many Psychologists have argued that there can be no general laws of learning (Seligman, 1970).

If such laws do exist, one of them is likely to be the *law of contiguity*: events (or stimuli) that occur close together in time and space are likely to become associated with each other. Most of the examples of conditioning we've considered so far would appear to 'obey' the law of contiguity. The *taste aversion* experiments described in Key Study 11.3 represent important exceptions.

Box 11.4 Major similarities and differences between classical and operant conditioning

Similarities

- They're both types of *associative learning*.
- *Generalisation*, *discrimination*, *extinction* and *spontaneous recovery* occur in both.

Differences

- In *classical*, the UCR or CR is *elicited* (triggered automatically) by the UCS or CS (it's essentially a reflex, involuntary response). In *operant*, behaviour is *emitted* by the organism and is essentially voluntary.
- In *classical*, the stimulus is guaranteed to produce the response, while the likelihood of a particular operant response being emitted is a function of the past consequences of such behaviour (it's more or less probable, but never certain).
- In *classical*, the UCS works in basically the same way regardless of whether it's pleasurable (such as food) or aversive (such as electric shock). In *operant*, responses that result in pleasurable outcomes are likely to be repeated, while those that result in aversive outcomes aren't.
- In *classical*, completely new S–R connections are formed, while *operant* involves the strengthening or weakening of response tendencies already present in the animal's behavioural repertoire.
- In *classical*, the reinforcer (UCS) is presented regardless of what the animal does, and is presented *before* the response. In *operant*, the reinforcer is only presented if the animal emits some specified, pre-selected behaviour, and is presented *after* the behaviour.
- In *classical*, the strength of conditioning is typically measured in terms of *response magnitude* (e.g. how many drops of saliva) and/or *latency* (how quickly a response is produced by a stimulus). In *operant*, strength is measured mainly as *response rate* (see Table 11.2).

Key study 11.3

Learning to feel as sick as a rat (Garcia and Koelling, 1966; Garcia *et al.*, 1966)

- Rats were given a novel-tasting solution, such as saccharine-flavoured water (the CS), prior to a drug, apomorphine (the UCS), which has a delayed action, inducing severe intestinal illness (the UCR).
- In two separate experiments, the precise time lapse between tasting the solution and onset of the drug-induced nausea was either (a) 5, 6, 7, 8, 9, 10, 11, 12, 15, 16, 17, 18, 19, 20, 21 and 22 minutes, or (b) 30, 45, 75, 120 and 180 minutes.
- In (a), the rats received just four treatments (one every third day). In all cases, there was a conditioned aversive response to the solution: intestinal illness became a CR (a response to the solution alone). In some replications, just a single treatment has been required.

While rats can also be conditioned to novel smells, auditory, visual and tactile stimuli aren't so readily associated with internal illness. As for pigeons, it's impossible to deter them from water and, for other species, taste aversions are very difficult to establish, even if the animal is made very ill. In almost all species, aversions are learned more easily to new flavours than to familiar ones (saccharine solution is a novel taste for the rat).

Biological constraints on conditioning

It seems, then, that there are definite biological limitations on the ability of animals to develop a conditioned aversion. Similarly, rats typically learn very quickly to avoid shock in a shuttle box and to press a lever for food. However, they don't learn very readily to press a lever to avoid shock. Pigeons can be trained quickly to fly from one perch to another in order to avoid shock, but it's almost impossible to train them to peck a disc to avoid shock.

Findings like these have led Bolles (1980) and others to conclude that we cannot regard the basic principles of learning as applying equally to all species in all situations. We must take into account the evolutionary history of the species, as well as the individual organism's learning history. According to the concept of *preparedness* (Seligman, 1970), animals are biologically prepared to learn actions that are closely related to the survival of their species (such as learned water or food aversions), and these *prepared* behaviours are learned with very little training. Equally, *contraprepared* behaviours are contrary to an animal's natural tendencies, and so are learned with great difficulty, if at all. Seligman believes that most of the behaviour studied in the laboratory falls somewhere in between these two extremes.

As far as human behaviour is concerned, much of the relevant data relates to how easily certain conditioned fear responses can be induced in the laboratory or how common certain naturally occurring phobias are compared with others. For example, Ohman *et al.* (1975a, 1975b) paired slides of snakes and spiders with a strong electric shock, and quickly established conditioned emotional responses to these slides – but not to slides of flowers, houses or berries.

Seligman (1972) observed that human phobias tend to fall into certain narrow categories, mostly animals or dangerous places. Most common of all were the fear of snakes, spiders, the dark, high places and closed-in places, and often there's no previous evidence for the fear actually having been conditioned (see Chapters 43 and 45). Also, classically conditioned responses extinguish faster in humans than animals. This is because the CRs are modulated by more complex human memories (Weiskrantz, 1982).

COGNITIVE APPROACHES

The role of cognition in conditioning

According to Mackintosh (1978), conditioning cannot be reduced to the strengthening of S–R associations by the automatic action of a process called reinforcement. It's more appropriate to think of it as a matter of detecting and learning about *relations between events*. Animals typically discover what signals or causes events that are important to them, such as food, water, danger or safety. Salivation or lever pressing are simply a convenient index of what the subject has learned, namely that certain relationships exist in its environment.

Classical conditioning

Pavlov himself described the CS as a 'signal' for the UCS, the relationship between CS and the UCS as one of 'stimulus substitution', and the CR as an 'anticipatory' response (or 'psychic secretions'), suggesting that his dogs were *expecting* the food to follow the bell. Consistent with this interpretation, Rescorla (1968) presented two groups of animals with the same number of CS–UCS pairings, but the second group also received additional presentations of the UCS on its own without the CS. The first group showed much stronger conditioning than the second, indicating that the most important factor (at least in classical conditioning) is how *predictably* the UCS follows the CS, *not* how often the CS and UCS are paired.

Blocking also supports a more cognitive interpretation (Kamin, 1969). For example, if an animal is shown a light, quickly followed by an electric shock, the light soon comes to elicit fear as a CR. If a noise is then added (noise + light + shock), then the noise should also soon become a CS, because it, too, is being paired with shock. However, this isn't what happens. If the noise is later presented alone, it fails to produce a CR. It seems that the noise has somehow been 'blocked' from becoming a CS because of the previous conditioning to the light. In cognitive terms, since the light already predicts shock, the noise is *irrelevant*. It provides no additional information – the animal already 'knows' that shock will follow the light.

Operant conditioning

Key Study 11.4

Learned helplessness (Seligman, 1974, 1975)

- Dogs were strapped into a harness and given a series of shocks from which they couldn't escape. They were later required to jump a barrier in a shuttle box within 10 seconds of a warning signal, or suffer 50 seconds of painful shock.
- Control dogs (which hadn't been subjected to the inescapable shocks) learned the avoidance response very quickly.
- But about two-thirds of the experimental dogs seemed unable to do so. They seemed passively resigned to suffering the shock, and even if they did successfully avoid the shock on one trial, they were unlikely to do so the next. Some dogs had to be pushed over the barrier 200 times or more before this learned helplessness wore off.

According to Seligman, the dogs learned that no behaviour on their part had any effect on the occurrence (or non-occurrence) of a particular event (the shock). This has been demonstrated using human participants by Miller and Norman (1979), and Maier and Seligman (1976) have tried to explain depression in humans in terms of learned helplessness (see Chapters 12 and 44).

Skinner's claim that reinforcements and punishments *automatically* strengthen and weaken behaviour has been challenged by Bandura (1977a). For Bandura:

> *Reinforcements serve principally as an informative and motivational operation rather than as a mechanical response strengthener.*

Reinforcement provides the learner with *information* about the likely consequences of certain behaviour under certain conditions – that is, it improves our prediction of whether a given action will lead to pleasant (reinforcement) or unpleasant (punishment) outcomes in the *future*. It also *motivates* us, by causing us to *anticipate* future outcomes. Our present behaviours are largely governed by the outcomes we *expect* them to have, and we're more likely to learn behaviour if we value its consequences.

This cognitive reinterpretation of reinforcement forms part of Bandura's *social learning theory* (SLT), which is discussed in more detail in relation to aggression (Chapter 29), moral and gender development (Chapters 35 and 36), and personality (Chapter 42). While not denying the role of both classical and operant conditioning, SLT focuses on *observational learning* (or *modelling*), in which cognitive factors are crucial. This is reflected in Bandura's renaming (1986, 1989) of SLT as *social cognitive theory*.

Tolman's cognitive behaviourism

Although he was working within the Behaviourist tradition in the 1920s, 1930s and 1940s, Tolman would today be regarded as a Cognitive Psychologist. He explained the learning of rats in terms of inferred cognitive processes, in particular *cognitive* or *mental maps*.

Ask Yourself

- How might you explain Tolman and Honzik's findings?
- Could the distinction between learning and performance help?

Clearly, group 3 rats had been learning their way through the maze during the first 10 days, but that learning was *latent* (hidden or 'behaviourally silent'). In other words, it didn't show up in their actual behaviour until they received the incentive of the reinforcement on day 11. Tolman and Honzik concluded that reinforcement may be important in relation to *performance* of learned behaviour, but that it *isn't* necessary for the learning itself.

Tolman's (1948) *place learning* (or *sign learning*) *theory* maintains that rats learn expectations as to which part of the maze will be followed by which other part of the maze. Tolman called these expectations *cognitive maps*, a primitive kind of perceptual map of the maze, an understanding of its spatial relationships (much like the mental map you have of familiar streets leading to home or college).

Key Study 11.5

Latent learning – who needs reinforcement? (Tolman and Honzik, 1930)

- *Group 1* rats were reinforced every time they found their way through a maze to the food box.
- *Group 2* rats were never reinforced.
- *Group 3* rats received no reinforcement for the first 10 days of the experiment, but did so from day 11.
- Not surprisingly, group 1 learned the maze quickly and made fewer and fewer mistakes, while group 2 never reduced the time it took to find the food, and moved around aimlessly much of the time.
- Group 3 made no apparent progress during the first 10 days. But they then showed a sudden decrease in the time it took to reach the goal box on day 11, when they received their first reinforcement. They caught up almost immediately with Group 1.

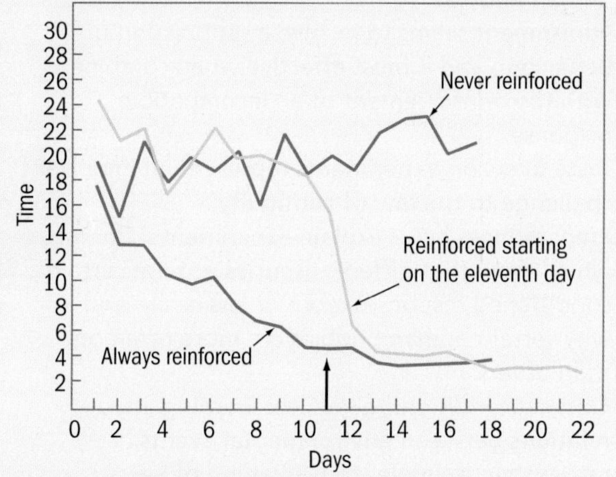

Figure 11.10 The results of Tolman and Honzik's study of latent learning in rats

Although a cognitive map can only be inferred from actual behaviour, it's difficult to know how else to explain the findings that rats will take short-cuts to the food box if the old path is blocked. Similarly, if the maze were rotated, they could find the usual food location from several different starting points (Tolman *et al.*, 1946). Restle (1957) flooded a maze immediately after a group of rats had learnt to run it, and they were able to swim to the goal box with no more errors than when they'd walked. This clearly supports Tolman's interpretation.

Insight learning

Insight learning represents a view of learning as 'purely cognitive'. It stems from the Gestalt school of Psychology, which is diametrically opposed to the S–R approach. The Gestalt Psychologists are best known for their work on perception (see Chapter 15), and their view of learning is directly linked to their view of perception.

Insight learning can be defined as a *perceptual restructuring* of the elements that constitute a problem situation: a previously missing 'ingredient' is supplied, and all the parts are seen in relation to each other, forming a meaningful whole. Some of the most famous studies of insight learning were conducted by Köhler, one of the founders of Gestalt Psychology, with chimps. These, and other Gestalt studies of problem-solving, are discussed in Chapter 20.

Learning sets

According to Harlow (1949), S–R learning and insight learning are essentially two different phases of the same, continuous process. S–R learning predominates in the early stages, and insight develops out of prior S–R connections. Harlow suggests that the concept of a *learning set* (or 'learning to learn') represents an intervening process between S–R and insight learning. The greater the number of sets, the better equipped the learner is to adapt to a changing environment; a very large number of different sets 'may supply the raw material for human thinking'.

A learning set involves learning a general skill applicable to a whole new class of problems, a simple rule or code, based on a *conceptual* (not a perceptual) relationship. In experiments with monkeys, Harlow demonstrated that insightful learning is itself (at least partially) *learned* and grows out of more random, trial-and-error learning.

CONCLUSIONS: TRANSFER OF LEARNING

A learning set represents a special case of a more general phenomenon known as *transfer of learning* (or *training*). Essentially, transfer refers to the influence of earlier learning on later learning, which is an inherent feature of the learning process in general (Howe, 1980). Some kinds of transfer take the form of simple stimulus generalisation, while in more complex learning situations transfer may depend on the acquisition of rules or principles that apply to a variety of different circumstances. Learning sets can be viewed as intermediate between simple generalisation, and the more complex transfer phenomena involved in hierarchically organised skills (Howe, 1980).

Koestler (1970) believes that the debate between the S–R and cognitive theorists derives to a large extent from a refusal to take seriously the notion of *ripeness*. By this, he means a person's or animal's readiness to make a discovery or solve a problem, based on relevant knowledge, skills and past experience. Rats and cats have generally been presented with tasks for which they are biologically ill-fitted, and so the resulting learning was bound to appear gradual, piecemeal and at first quite random. But Köhler set chimps problems for which they were (almost) ripe, which gave the impression that all learning is based on insight.

Chapter Summary

- **Learning** has played a major part in the development of Psychology as a scientific discipline and is central to the **Behaviourist approach**.
- Psychologists are interested in learning **as a process**. Theories of learning differ as to the nature of the process involved, especially the role played by **cognitive factors**.
- It's generally agreed that learning involves a **relatively permanent change** in behaviour due to **past experience**. The distinction between **learning** and **performance** refers to **potential** and **actual** behaviour, respectively.
- The distinction between **respondent** and **operant behaviour** corresponds to **classical** (**respondent** or **Pavlovian**) and **operant** (**instrumental** or **Skinnerian**) **conditioning**, respectively.
- In **classical conditioning**, the pairing of a conditioned and an unconditioned stimulus results in the former eliciting a response that formerly was produced only by the latter.
- **Delayed/forward**, **backward**, **simultaneous** and **trace** conditioning differ according to the relationships between the conditioned and the unconditioned stimuli.
- **Generalisation**, **discrimination**, **extinction** and **spontaneous recovery** represent conditioning phenomena, which make it more complex and versatile. Spontaneous recovery demonstrates that extinction involves a learning to **inhibit/suppress** the conditioned response.
- Watson applied classical conditioning to human behaviour for the first time by inducing fear of a rat in Little Albert. Jones removed animal phobias from Little Peter using an early form of **systematic desensitisation**.
- Compared with classical, **operant conditioning** sees learning as a much more **active process**. Skinner was interested in how animals **operate on their environment**, and how their activity is **instrumental** in producing certain consequences.
- Skinner's work was based on Thorndike's **law of effect**. He designed a form of puzzle-box (a **Skinner box**), and called the consequences of behaviour **positive reinforcement**, **negative reinforcement** and **punishment**.
- **Reinforcement** (both positive and negative) **strengthens** behaviour, while **punishment weakens** it.
- **Primary reinforcers** are naturally reinforcing, while **secondary/conditioned reinforcers** come to be reinforcing through association with primary reinforcers.
- Different **schedules of reinforcement** can be analysed in terms of **pattern/rate of response** and **resistance to extinction**. **Variable** schedules involve high, steady rates of response and high resistance to extinction, compared with **fixed** and **continuous** schedules.
- **Shaping** involves the reinforcement of **successive approximations** to the desired behaviour.
- **Escape** and **avoidance learning** are two forms of **negative reinforcement**.
- According to the **two-factor theory**, both classical and operant conditioning are involved in avoidance learning, which can account for the persistence of human **phobias**.
- **Punishment** seems to involve a suppression of behaviour, and is most effective when combined with the reinforcement of an **incompatible** response.
- **Taste aversion experiments** represent an important challenge to the **law of contiguity**.
- **Preparedness** helps explain experimental findings which show that different species acquire certain conditioned responses more or less easily, and why certain human phobias are more common than others.
- Classical conditioning involves learning about **relations between environmental events**, rather than a simple strengthening of S–R associations. Seligman's concept of **learned helplessness** illustrates the complexity of operant conditioning and has been used to explain human depression.
- Tolman's studies of **latent learning** show that learning can take place in the absence of reinforcement. Rats learn a **cognitive map** of a maze, not the individual movements of walking or running that take them to the food box.
- **Gestalt** Psychologists saw **insight learning** as involving the **perceptual restructuring** of the elements that constitute a problem situation.
- Harlow's concept of a **learning set** shows that insight and trial and error aren't necessarily opposed forms of learning. A learning set represents a special case of the more general **transfer of learning**.

Links with Other Topics/Chapters

Chapter 2 ⟶ Learning, in the form of conditioning, lies at the heart of *behaviourism*, one of the major *theoretical approaches* within Psychology

Chapter 1 ⟶ The distinction between *philosophical* and *methodological behaviourism* is important both in the *history* of Psychology

Chapter 3 ⟶ and the debate over the *scientific status of Psychology*

Chapter 17 ⟶ Learning and *memory* are closely interrelated processes

Chapter 44 ⟶ The Little Albert experiment is taken by many behaviour therapists (such as Eysenck) as demonstrating how *all phobias* are acquired in everyday life

Chapter 45 ⟶ The 'direct unconditioning' used in the Little Peter experiment is an early example of *systematic desensitisation*, a major form of *behaviour therapy*, used in the treatment of phobias

Chapter 45 ⟶ Shaping provides the basis of *behaviour modification*, used with a range of patients, including *autistic children* and *adult schizophrenics*

Chapter 44 ⟶ Seligman and others have drawn on the concept of *learned helplessness* to explain *human depression*

Social learning theory has been applied to the study of:

Chapter 29 ⟶ *aggression*

Chapter 35 ⟶ *moral development*

Chapter 36 ⟶ *gender development*

Gestalt Psychology is best known for:

Chapter 15 ⟶ its *principles* of *perceptual organisation*

Chapter 20 ⟶ research into *problem-solving*

Recommended Reading

Anderson, J.R. (1995) *Learning and Memory: An Integrated Approach.* New York: John Wiley & Sons. Equally relevant to Chapter 17.

Catania, A.C. (1992) *Learning* (3rd edn). Englewood Cliffs, NJ: Prentice-Hall. Also useful for Chapters 17, 19, 35 and 36.

Gross, R. (2008) *Key Studies in Psychology* (5th edn). London: Hodder Education. Chapter 23.

Leslie, J.C. (2002) *Essential Behaviour Analysis.* London: Arnold. Also relevant to Chapters 19, 44 and 45.

O'Donohue, W. & Ferguson, K.E. (2001) *The Psychology of B.F. Skinner.* London: Methuen.

Walker, S. (1984) *Learning Theory and Behaviour Modification.* London: Methuen. Also relevant to Chapter 45.

Useful Websites

www.brembs.net/classical/classical.html (Basic Concepts in Classical Conditioning)

www.wagntrain.com/OC/ (An Animal Trainer's Introduction to Operant and Classical Conditioning)

www.tinyurl.com/py3ptx5 (YouTube explanatory video)

www.tinyurl.com/088hv2u (Account of Pavlov's work in *British Medical Journal*)

www.tinyurl.com/y8d2py4 (Pavlov's own account of classical conditioning at PsychClassics site)

www.tinyurl.com/nehqx9v (Simple conditioning of a simulated dog)

CHAPTER 12

HEALTH PSYCHOLOGY

INTRODUCTION and OVERVIEW

According to Ogden (2004), Health Psychology (HP) represents one of several challenges that were made during the 20th century to the *biomedical model* (Engel, 1977, 1980). This maintains that:

- Individuals aren't responsible for their illnesses, which arise from biological changes beyond their control, such as chemical imbalances, bacteria, viruses or genetic predisposition; people who are ill are victims.
- Treatment should consist of vaccination, surgery, chemotherapy or radiotherapy, all of which aim to change the physical state of the body.
- Responsibility for treatment rests with the medical profession.
- Health and illness are qualitatively different – you're either healthy or ill, and there's no continuum between them.
- Mind and body function independently of each other; the abstract mind relates to feelings and thoughts, and is incapable of influencing physical matter.
- Illness may have psychological consequences, but not psychological causes.

In opposition to these ideas, HP maintains that human beings should be seen as complex systems. Illness is often caused by a combination of biological (e.g. viruses), psychological (e.g. behaviours and beliefs), and social (e.g. employment) factors. These assumptions reflect the *biopsychosocial model* of health and illness (Engel, 1977, 1980).

The biopsychosocial model reflects fundamental changes in the nature of illness, causes of death and overall life expectancy during the twentieth century. Since the Industrial Revolution in the mid-1800s, average female life expectancy has increased in western societies from about 45 years to currently more than 80 (men live on average four to five years fewer; Westendorp and Kirkwood, 2007). This is due mainly to the virtual elimination of infectious diseases – such as pneumonia, flu, tuberculosis (TB), diphtheria, scarlet fever, measles, typhoid and polio – as causes of death. Although HIV and AIDS increased the percentage of infection-related deaths during the 1980s and early 1990s, today's major killers are cardiovascular diseases (heart disease and strokes) and cancers, the former accounting for about 40 per cent of deaths in industrialised countries (Stroebe, 2000).

By conceptualising disease in purely biological terms, the biomedical model has little to offer the prevention of chronic diseases through efforts to change people's health beliefs, attitudes and behaviour.

WHAT IS HEALTH PSYCHOLOGY?

A brief history

HP formally began with the founding of the Division of Health Psychology within the American Psychological Association in 1978. The journal *Health Psychology* followed in 1982. In 1986, a Special Health Psychology Group was established within the British Psychological Society, which became a Division in 1997. There's also a European Health Psychology Society.

It became evident in the 1970s that national health spending in western countries was getting out of control. Consequently, many countries began to explore disease *prevention*. The most powerful preventative strategy may be *health promotion*, and HP has made significant contributions in this area since the mid-1970s (Maes and van Elderen, 1998).

Definitions

According to Turpin and Slade (1998), HP in the UK is an *extension* of Clinical Psychology, focusing specifically on people with physical health problems and their associated psychological needs. As Abraham *et al.* (2008) say, the two sub-disciplines overlap, because some of the psychological processes that affect physical health are also important for mental health (such as stress and anxiety responses). According to Abraham *et al.* (2008):

> *Health psychologists seek to understand the processes which link individual perceptions, beliefs and behaviours to biological processes, which, in turn, result in physical health problems. ... Health psychologists also study social processes including the effect of wider social structure (such as socio-economic status) and face-to-face interactions with others ... because these social processes shape perceptions, beliefs and behaviour. ... In addition, health psychologists explore individual processes that shape health outcomes and health behaviours ... and social processes which influence the effectiveness of health care delivery ...*

In the above, Abraham *et al.* are describing the *biopsychosocial model*.

Figure 12.1 Health Psychology and related disciplines (From French, D. *et al.* (2010) *Health Psychology* (2nd edn). BPS Blackwell, Oxford.)

Health and illness

Ask Yourself

- What do you understand by the terms 'health' and 'illness'?
- Are you healthy if you're not ill, or is health a more positive state than that?

Revisiting the biomedical model

According to the biomedical model, disease is a deviation from a measurable biological norm. This view, which still dominates medical thinking and practice, is based on several invalid assumptions. Most importantly, the *specificity assumption* maintains that understanding of an illness is greater if it can be defined at a more specific biochemical level. This *reductionist* view (see Chapter 49) originated when infectious diseases were still the major causes of death (Maes and van Elderen, 1998; see above).

Revisiting the biopsychosocial model

In contrast with the biomedical model's reductionist view, the biopsychosocial model adopts a *holistic* approach – that is, the person *as a whole* needs to be taken into account. Both 'micro-level' (small-scale causes, such as chemical imbalances) and 'macro-level' (large-scale causes, such as the extent of available social support) processes interact to determine someone's health status (see Figure 12.1).

According to Halligan (2007), crucial to the biopsychosocial perspective is:

> *... the belief that illness is not just the result of discrete pathological processes but can be meaningfully explained in terms of psychological and sociocultural factors. In particular, beliefs held by patients about their health and illness are central to the way they present, respond to treatment and evaluate their capacity for work.*

According to Ogden (2004), for most people in the West being healthy is the norm and beliefs about being ill exist in the context of beliefs about being healthy (for example, illness means not being healthy or feeling different from normal). Healthiness is most people's natural state and represents the backdrop to their beliefs about being ill.

Acculturation

Cross-cultural Psychologists believe that there's a complex pattern of continuity and change in how people who've developed in one cultural context behave when they move to and live in a new cultural context. This process of adaptation to the new ('host') culture is called *acculturation*. With increasing acculturation (the longer immigrants live in the host country), health status 'migrates' to the national norm (Berry, 1998).

For example, coronary heart disease (CHD) among Polish immigrants to Canada increased (their rates were initially lower), while for immigrants from Australia and New Zealand the reverse was true. Data for immigrants from 26 out of 29 countries shifted their rates towards those of the Canadian-born population. Similar patterns have been found for stomach and intestinal cancer among immigrants to the USA (Berry, 1998).

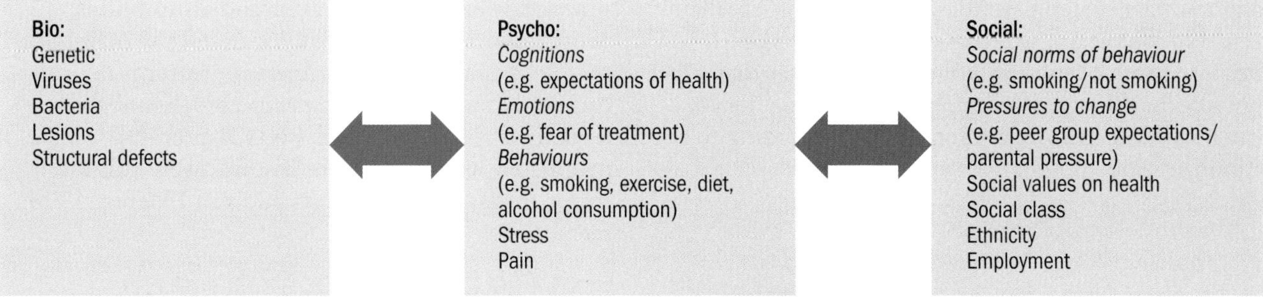

Figure 12.2 The biopsychosocial model of health and illness (adapted from Ogden, 2004)

Box 12.1 Health and disease as cultural concepts

- Many studies have shown that the very concepts of health and disease are defined differently across cultures. While 'disease' may be rooted in pathological biological processes (common to all), 'illness' is now widely recognised as a culturally influenced subjective experience of suffering and discomfort (Berry, 1998).
- Recognising certain conditions as either healthy or as a disease is also linked to culture. For example, trance is seen as an important curing (health-seeking) mechanism in some cultures, but may be classified as a sign of psychiatric disorder in others.
- Similarly, how a condition is expressed is also linked to cultural norms, as in the tendency to express psychological problems *somatically* (in the form of bodily symptoms) in some cultures (e.g. Chinese) more than in others (see Chapter 43).
- Disease and disability are highly variable. Cultural factors (such as diet, substance abuse and social relationships within the family) contribute to the prevalence of diseases including heart disease, cancer and schizophrenia (Berry, 1998).

Figure 12.3 Was ET's near-fatal illness due to acculturation – or did he simply want to go home?

Ask Yourself

- How could you explain such findings?
- What is it about living in a different cultural situation that can increase or decrease your chances of developing life-threatening diseases?

One possibility is exposure to widely shared risk factors in the physical environment (e.g. climate, pollution, pathogens), over which there's little choice. Alternatively, it could be due to choosing to pursue *assimilation* (or possible integration) as the way to acculturate. This may expose immigrants to *cultural* risk factors, such as diet, lifestyle and substance abuse. This 'behavioural shift' interpretation would be supported if health status both improved *and* declined relative to national norms.

However, the main evidence points to a *decline*, supporting the 'acculturative stress' (or even 'psychopathology') interpretation – that is, the very process of acculturation may involve risk factors that can reduce health status. This explanation is supported by evidence that stress can lower resistance to diseases such as hypertension and diabetes (Berry, 1998).

MODELS OF HEALTH BEHAVIOUR

Understanding why people do or don't practise behaviours to protect their health can be assisted by the study of *models/theories of health behaviour*, such as:

- the Theory of Reasoned Action (TRA)
- the Theory of Planned Behaviour (TPB), and
- the Health Belief Model (HBM).

According to Ogden (2004), these various models/ theories are often referred to, collectively, as *social cognition models*, because they regard cognitions as being shared by individuals within the same society. But Ogden prefers to distinguish between:

- *social cognition models* (such as TRA and TPB), which aim to account for social behaviour in general and are much broader than health models, and

- *cognition models* (such as HBM), which are specifically *health models*.

A fundamentally important question for HP is why people adopt – or don't adopt – particular health-related behaviours. Models of health behaviour try to answer this question, and those discussed below belong to the family of *expectancy-value models* (Stroebe, 2000). These assume that decisions between different courses of action are based on two types of cognition:

- *subjective probabilities* that a given action will produce a set of expected outcomes
- *evaluation* of action outcomes.

Individuals will choose from among various alternative courses of action the one most likely to produce positive consequences and avoid negative ones. Different models differ in terms of the types of belief and attitude that should be used in predicting a particular class of behaviour. They are *rational reasoning models*, which assume that individuals consciously deliberate about the likely consequences of the behavioural alternatives available to them before engaging in action.

Ask Yourself

- Do you agree with this view of people as rationally/consciously choosing health behaviours?
- How would you explain your own behaviours in relation to diet, smoking, alcohol, exercise, and so on?

The health belief model (HBM)

This was originally developed by Social Psychologists working in the US Public Health Service (Becker, 1974; Janz and Becker, 1984). They wanted to understand why people failed to make use of disease prevention and screening tests for early detection of diseases not associated with clear-cut symptoms (at least in the early stages). It was later also applied to patients' responses to symptoms, and compliance with/adherence to prescribed medication among acutely and chronically ill patients. More recently, it's been used to predict a wide range of health-related behaviours (Ogden, 2000).

The HBM assumes that the likelihood that people will engage in a particular health behaviour is a function of:

- the extent to which they believe they're *susceptible* to the associated disease
- their perception of the *severity of the consequences* of getting the disease.

Together, these determine the *perceived threat* of the disease. Given the threat, people then consider whether or not the action will bring benefits that outweigh the costs associated with the action. In addition, *cues to action* (such as advice from others, a health problem or mass-media campaigns) increase the likelihood that the action will be adopted. Other important concepts include *general health motivation* (the individual's readiness to be concerned about health matters) and *perceived control* (for example, 'I'm confident I can give up smoking' (Becker and Rosenstock, 1987)).

Evaluation of the HBM

- The HBM allows for demographic variables (such as age and gender) and psychological characteristics (such as ways of coping with stress and locus of control, see below) that might affect health beliefs (Forshaw, 2002). For example, young women are likely to engage in dieting behaviour. So:

> *... the HBM covers most, if not all, of the factors which, on the face of it, should be relevant in determining if a person engages in a particular behaviour ...*

- There's considerable evidence supporting the HBM's predictions in relation to a wide range of behaviours. Dietary compliance, safe sex, having vaccinations, having regular dental checks, participation in regular exercise programmes, are all related to people's perception of their susceptibility to the related health problem, their belief that the problem is severe, and their perception that the benefits of preventative action outweigh the costs (e.g. Becker, 1974; Becker and Rosenstock, 1984; Becker *et al.*, 1977).
- According to Dunn (2007), these examples include behaviours which occur once or over a short period of time (such as immunisation and attending screenings), as well as those that are longer term (such as dieting, exercise, and the use of condoms). The most important predictor of the likelihood of health behaviour seems to be perceived barriers, followed by susceptibility, benefits and severity. Relatively little research has been conducted on the effects of cues to action or health motivation (Dunn, 2007).
- There's also conflicting evidence. For example, Janz and Becker (1984) found that healthy behavioural intentions are related to low perceived seriousness (not high, as the model predicts). Also, several studies have suggested an association between low susceptibility (not high) and healthy behaviour (Ogden, 2004).

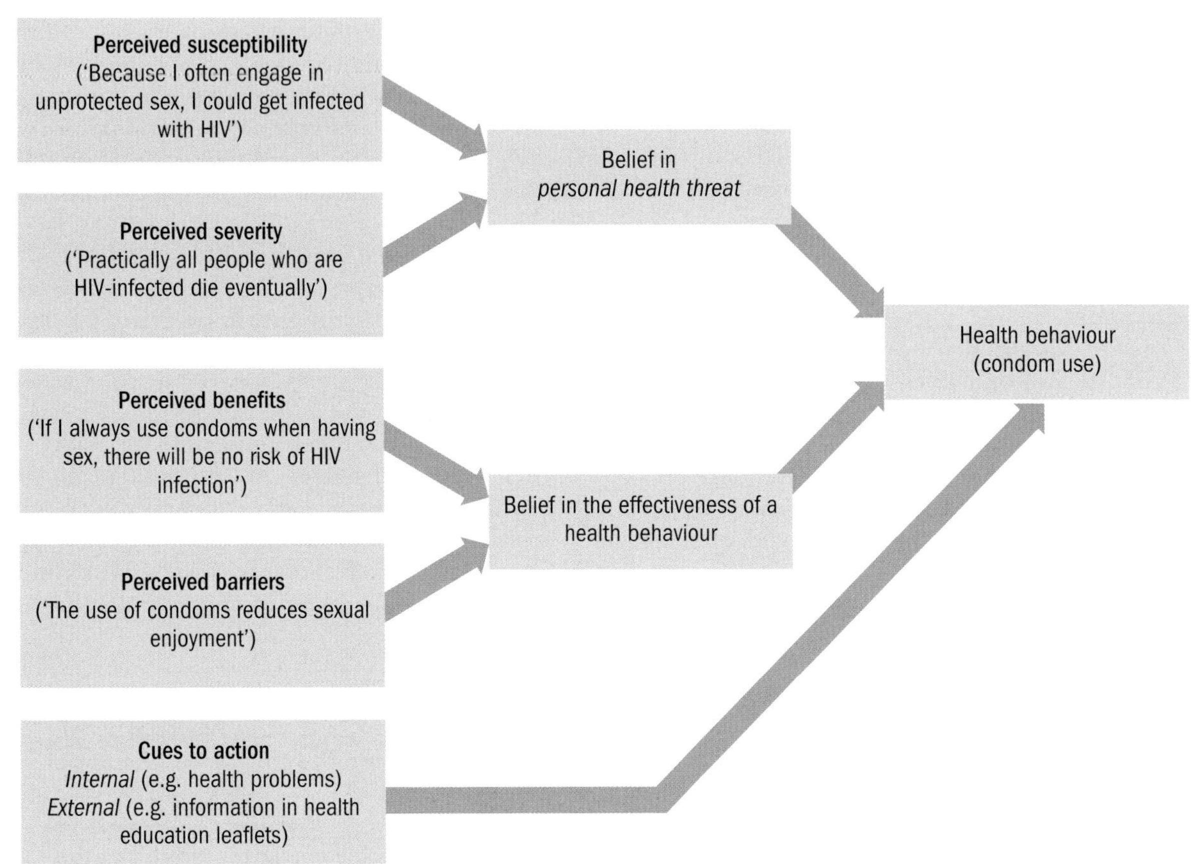

Figure 12.4 Main components of the health belief model (adapted from Stroebe, 2000, reproduced with kind permission of the Open University Press/McGraw-Hill publishing company)

- There's been a lack of standardised measures used to assess the model's various components, such as perceived susceptibility (Penny, 1996). A factor that may explain the persistence of unhealthy behaviours is people's inaccurate perceptions of risk and susceptibility. While fear might dissuade someone from experimenting with drugs in the first place, once addictive behaviours have become habitual, they'll be carried out with little conscious deliberation. In addition, people under the influence of alcohol or other drugs may have impaired judgement and may be unable to think logically (Dunn, 2007). (See Chapter 8.)

Box 12.2 Are we unrealistic optimists?

- Weinstein (1983, 1984) asked participants to examine a list of health problems and to state 'Compared with other people of your age and sex, are your chances of getting [the problem] greater than, about the same, or less than theirs?' Most believed they were less likely, displaying what Weinstein called *unrealistic optimism:* not everyone can be less likely to experience a particular problem! Weinstein identified four cognitive factors contributing to unrealistic optimism:
  - (i) lack of personal experience with the problem
  - (ii) belief that the problem is preventable by individual action
  - (iii) belief that if the problem hasn't yet appeared, it won't appear in the future
  - (iv) belief that the problem is uncommon.
- This suggests that perception of one's own risk isn't a rational process. People show *selective focus,* ignoring their own risk-taking behaviour (for example, the times they've not used a condom) and concentrating primarily on their risk-reducing behaviour (the times they have used one).
- This is compounded by the tendency to ignore others' risk-reducing, and emphasise their risk-taking, behaviour. These tendencies produce unrealistic optimism.

Unlike TRA and TPB (see below), there's no explicit reference to behavioural *intention* in HBM. Instead, central beliefs and perceptions act directly on the likelihood of behaviour. But it's been shown that adding intention to HBM increases its level of predictability, so it's now typically added when testing the model. However, this blurs the distinction between HBM and other models. The trend is towards developing generic models of health behaviour that incorporate the best 'bits' of other models (Harris and Middleton, 1995).

The theory of reasoned action (TRA)

This is a more general theory than the HBM and was central to the debate within Social Psychology regarding the relationship between attitudes and behaviour (see Chapter 24). TRA (Ajzen and Fishbein, 1970; Fishbein, 1967; Fishbein and Ajzen, 1975) assumes that behaviour is a function of the *intention* to perform that behaviour. A behavioural intention is determined by:

- a person's *attitude* to the behaviour, which is determined by (a) beliefs about the outcome of the behaviour, and (b) evaluation of the expected outcome
- *subjective norms*: a person's beliefs about the desirability of carrying out a certain health behaviour in the social group, society and culture s/he belongs to. (See Figure 12.5.)

Evaluation of the TRA

- The TRA has successfully predicted a wide range of behaviours, including blood donation, smoking marijuana, dental hygiene and family planning.
- However, attitudes and behaviour are only weakly related: people don't always do what they say they intend to (see Chapter 24).
- The model doesn't consider people's past behaviour, despite evidence that this is a good predictor of future behaviour. Nor does it account for people's irrational decisions (Penny, 1996). Similarly, Maes and van Elderen (1998) argue that:

> *... The assumption that behaviour is a function of intentions ... limits the applicability or heuristic value of the model to volitional behaviour, that is, to behaviours that are perceived to be under personal control ...*

The theory of planned behaviour (TPB)

This represents a modification of the TRA, in particular the addition of Bandura's (1977a, 1986) concept of self-efficacy – our belief that we can act effectively and exercise some control over events that influence our lives (see Chapter 35). According to Ajzen (1991), control beliefs are important determinants of perceived behavioural control (PBC), that is, feeling confident that our current skills and resources will enable us to achieve the desired behaviour and overcome any external barriers. This is crucial for understanding motivation: if, for example, you think you're unable to quit smoking, you probably won't try. PCB can have a direct effect on behaviour, bypassing behavioural intentions. (See Figure 12.6.)

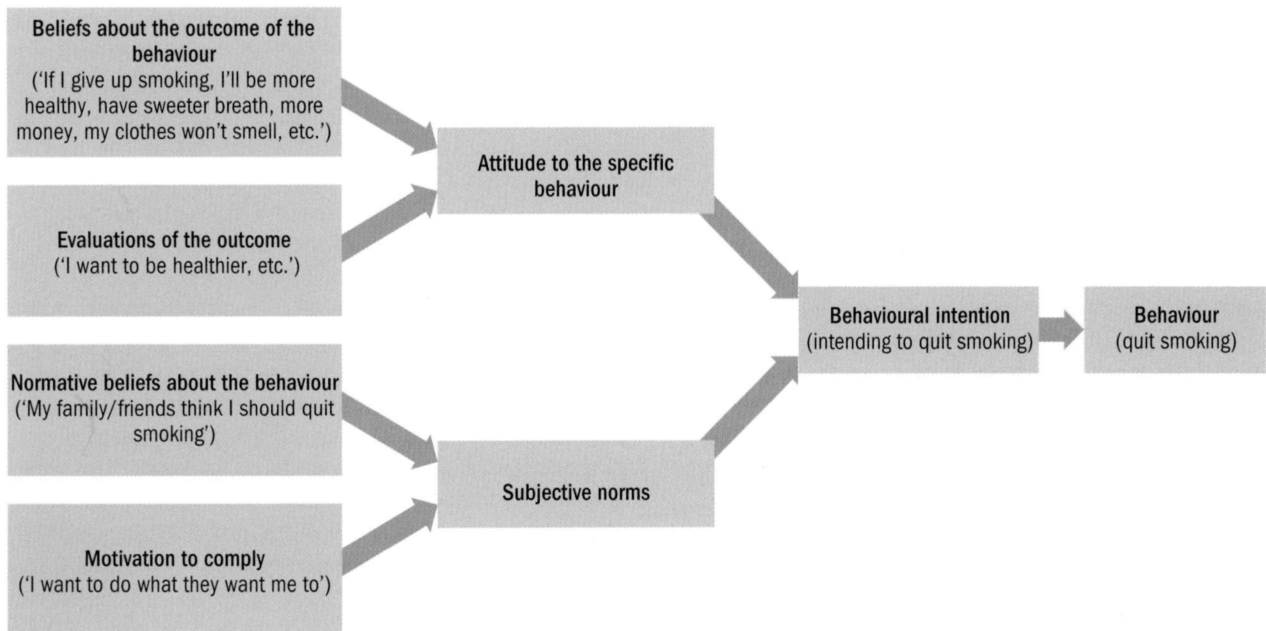

Figure 12.5 Main components of the theory of reasoned action (adapted from Penny, 1996; Maes and van Elderen, 1998)

found this really interesting and it supported other work I had done looking at success stories across a number of different behaviours. My dieting work showed that trying to control what you eat can lead to loss of control. But the surgery work indicated that taking control away from the individual made them feel more in control. I called this 'the paradox of control' and it resonated with so many other areas of successful behaviour change interventions such as seat belt laws, smoking bans and the removal of fizzy drink machines from schools. Relying on will power and self-control can have a rebound effect, but imposing control can be liberating.

Covert and overt control

These findings also parallel my work on parental control. Parents often control what their children eat saying things like 'eat your vegetables and you can have pudding'. But much research shows that in doing so children are taught that the unhealthy foods are preferable to the ones they are allowed. Therefore when given free choice children will eat more of the foods that have been forbidden. But does this mean that children should be allowed to eat whatever they want? Such an approach would be manageable in a world of healthy foods, but given the constant supply of sweets and junk food this didn't feel like a satisfactory conclusion. Surely there must be some form of parental control that worked? To date the literature seemed to have focused on 'overt' forms of control as they could be detected by the child (e.g. eat less chocolate, eat more vegetables, be good and you can have cake). But there seemed to be another more 'covert' form of control that couldn't be detected by the child such as not bringing unhealthy food into the house or avoiding fast food restaurants. I developed a measure of covert and overt forms of control and explored their relationship with children's diets. To date, these studies indicate that covert control may be a better way of controlling children's diets than overt control and that controlling what children eat in ways that are less obvious might reduce the likelihood of a rebound effect later on (e.g. Ogden *et al*., 2006b).

'Overt' control: eat your greens and you can have some cake for pudding

'Covert' control would involve a parent removing all these foods from their house

Conclusions

I have worked in a number of different health-related fields. But my work seems to have been dominated by issues of control, and central to this is the paradox of control. Conscious control in all its forms, whether it be will-power, denial, self-management or even empowerment may work in the short term, but for many in the longer term it results in a rebound effect and the very behaviour the person is trying to avoid. In contrast, imposed control in the form of changes in the environment (whether it be the home, school or society) or even surgery can take control away from the individual but leave them feeling liberated and more in control in the longer term.

Professor Jane Ogden graduated from the University of Sussex and then completed her PhD on eating behaviour at London University. She is currently Professor in Health Psychology at the University of Surrey. Jane is currently interested in sustained changes in behaviour and obesity surgery.

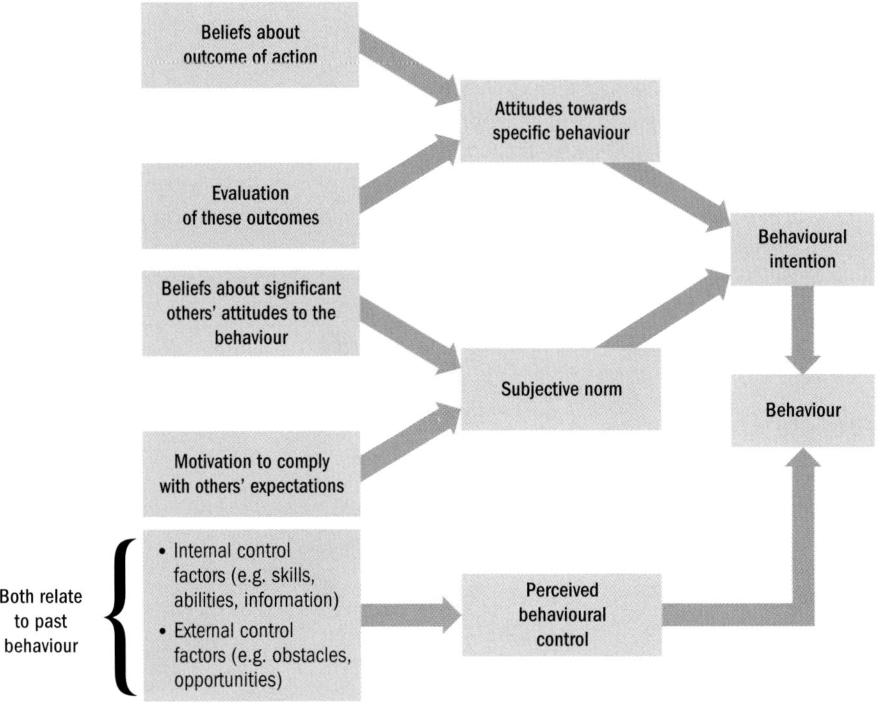

Figure 12.6 Main components of the theory of planned behaviour (adapted from Ogden, 2004)

Evaluation of the TPB

- According to Walker *et al.* (2004), TPB is currently the most popular and widely used social cognition model in HP, and it's been used to assess a variety of health-related behaviours. For example, Brubaker and Wickersham (1990) examined its different components in relation to testicular self-examination: attitude, subjective norm and behavioural control (measured as self-efficacy) all correlated with the behavioural intention. Schifter and Ajzen (1985) found that weight loss was predicted by the model's components, especially PBC.
- TPB has been particularly successful in predicting behaviours such as smoking, alcohol consumption, and exercise, with PCB and self-efficacy proving to be the key components (Dunn, 2007). However, the TPB (and the HBM) relates only to the motivational or intention-formation stage, and so doesn't address what can be called the action stage (the translation of intention into behaviour) (Dunn, 2007). Even when intention is strong, people don't always follow through with the intended behaviour. Where intention has been deliberately manipulated, the impact on behaviour is still modest (Webb and Sheeran (2006), cited in Dunn (2007)).

Overall evaluation of models of health behaviour

- A limitation shared by all the models is their failure to consistently predict behavioural intentions. Most serious of all is the *intention-behaviour gap*, see Box 12.3.
- The models are all very general, covering all kinds of health-related behaviour; it may simply be invalid to apply the same model to a whole range of behaviours and illnesses. It may be necessary to model specific behaviour, such as in the threat of AIDS (as in Catania *et al.*'s (1990) risk-reduction model).
- To date, most models have been designed and tested in a western cultural context and are, therefore, likely to be biased: they're culturally relative and we cannot just assume that they apply universally (Forshaw, 2002; Uskul, 2010). For example, Sisson Joshi's (1995) study of causal beliefs about insulin-dependent diabetes in England and India found that far more Indian diabetics believed that eating too much sweet food caused their diabetes (38 per cent compared with 6 per cent of the English sample).
- According to Uskul (2010), the incorporation of sociocultural factors into existing health models can contribute to a comprehensive understanding of

the moderating factors that determine how illness cognitions are shaped or when behaviour is likely to change:

It is time to collate the vast amount of knowledge accumulated in the hitherto disconnected subfields of cultural and health psychology and to explore the degree to which theories and models developed in the West can be used to understand health and illness-related psychological experiences elsewhere. (Uskul, 2010)

Box 12.3 The 'intention-behaviour' gap

- The *intention-behaviour gap* refers to the fact that intentions are far from perfect predictors of behaviour. A limitation shared by all the models is their inability to predict actual behaviour.
- One of the most promising research developments is *implementation intentions* (IIs) (e.g. Gollwitzer, 1993, 1999). Asking someone to make an II requires them to make a specific plan as to what, when and where they'll carry out the behaviour. The reasoning behind this is that when they find themselves in that situation, they'll be cued to perform the behaviour.
- For example, Kellar and Abraham (2005) found that Psychology undergraduates who'd been asked to plan vegetables for their lunch and evening meals, ate significantly more of those foods in the week following the plan-making compared with students who hadn't made specific plans.
- Similar effects have been found for a range of other health behaviours, including exercise, breast self-examination, and consumption of vitamins (Sheeran *et al.*, 2005).
- IIs appear to be particularly effective in overcoming common problems in enacting intentions, namely, forgetting. Provided effective cues are identified in the II (ones that will be commonly encountered and are sufficiently distinctive), forgetting is much less likely (Abraham *et al.*, 2008).

- The TPB has the advantage over the HBM (as does the TRA) of including a degree of irrationality (in the form of evaluations), and it attempts to address the problem of social and environmental factors (normative beliefs). The extra 'ingredient' of PBC provides a role for past behaviour. For example, if you've tried several times in the past to quit smoking, you're less likely to believe you can do so successfully in the future and, therefore, you're less likely to intend to try (Ogden, 2000; Penny, 1996).

PATIENT ADHERENCE: DOING WHAT YOU'RE TOLD

'*Adherence*' is now preferred to 'compliance' (e.g. Haynes *et al.*, 1979), because it implies a *collaborative* relationship between health care professionals (HCPs) and their patients, in which they work together to plan and implement treatments (Damrosch, 1995; Myers and Abraham, 2005) (see Chapter 27). The need for such co-operation has been highlighted more recently by the suggestion that HCPs and patients should reach *'concordance'* – a mutual understanding and agreement about treatment and its implementation (Myers and Abraham, 2005).

Operationalising adherence/non-adherence

There are numerous ways in which patients' behaviour can deviate from recommendations, with varying implications for clinical outcomes (Horne and Clatworthy, 2010), For example, a patient could:

- Take all the required medication but not at the correct time.
- Miss occasional doses.
- Take 'drug holidays' (i.e. miss three or more days' doses).
- Take lower/fewer doses than prescribed.
- Never take the medication.
- Take larger/more frequent doses than prescribed.

While there's no universally accepted way of measuring adherence/non-adherence, the method that's adopted can impact the resulting adherence *rates* (see below). Table 12.1 describes some common methods used for measuring medication adherence.

None of these methods represents a 'gold standard' and all have disadvantages. For example, indirect, behavioural measures may provide objective measures but are subject to the *Hawthorne effect*: people may change their behaviour because they know they're being monitored (see Chapter 3). In this way, they may in themselves act as adherence interventions, rather than giving an accurate estimation of adherence

Table 12.1 Methods of measuring medication adherence

Direct	
Observation	Directly observing patients taking their medication. Widely used in treatment of tuberculosis (TB) but more as an intervention than as means of measuring adherence
Biological assays	Usually blood or urine samples are taken and analysed to detect levels of the drug/drug metabolites
Indirect	
Pill count	Patients are asked to bring all their medication containers to their appointment. The remaining tablets are counted and the percentage of prescribed doses taken is calculated
Self-report	Patients are asked to describe their adherence either in an interview or through completion of a questionnaire or diary
Repeat prescription/ pharmacy refill records	Records of when the patients collect/fill prescriptions are monitored. Actual collect/fill date is compared with the date medication would have been needed if all doses had been taken as prescribed
Electronic monitor	Caps of medication bottles contain a computer chip which records each time the container is opened. Caps are scanned and the data downloaded onto a computer

levels. Conversely, while self-report measures are often criticised for being subjective and prone to response bias (such as overestimating adherence), they're the only means of finding out why the person was non-adherent (e.g., was it intentional or unintentional?) (Horne and Clatworthy, 2010).

Focusing specifically on medication adherence and using an objective outcome measure, a review of 21 studies found that the odds of dying among those with high adherence was almost half those of low adherers (Simpson, 2006). A different kind of impact of non-adherence is the financial burden it places on health care providers. NICE (2009) estimated that hospital admissions resulting from medication non-adherence costs the NHS up to £196 million annually. In addition, up to £4 billion per year is wasted on prescribed medication that's not taken as directed.

Ask Yourself

- Have you ever been non-adherent? For example, have you ever failed to complete a course of antibiotics?
- Why weren't you adherent?
- Why do you think it's important to understand non-adherence?

The extent of non-adherence

According to Myers and Abraham (2005), approximately 50 per cent of patients don't take prescribed medications as recommended; across the whole range of recommendations made by HCPs, 15–93 per cent of patients don't adhere.

In addition, 10–25 per cent of hospital admissions can be attributed to non-adherence. These include patients who've received an organ transplant: their non-adherence can lead to rejection of the organ and/or death of the patient (Abraham *et al.*, 2008; Damrosch, 1995; Myers and Abraham, 2005).

Why are patients non-adherent?

Patients tend to overestimate their degree of adherence, because they wish to convey a *socially desirable impression*. Practitioners also tend to overestimate their patients' adherence.

Myers and Abraham (2005) identify two major reasons for patient non-adherence:

1. Some patients intend to take recommended actions but forget or find it difficult to do so.
2. Others may disagree with the doctor's diagnosis or the medication regimen.

Patients often have key questions regarding their condition and the prescribed treatment unanswered (or inadequately answered) (such as 'Do I really need this treatment?', 'What side-effects will it have?'), leaving them to reach their own conclusions and formulate a different plan from that recommended by the HCP (Abraham *et al.*, 2008).

Characteristics of health care practitioners

Doctors' sensitivity to patients' non-verbal expression of feelings (such as tone of voice) is a good predictor of adherence. This, along with his/her concern, respect and competence, contribute to patient *satisfaction*; this, in turn, is significantly correlated with adherence (Ley, 1988).

How practitioners communicate their beliefs to patients also influences adherence. Misselbrook and Armstrong (2000) asked patients whether they'd accept treatment to prevent a stroke, and presented the effectiveness of this treatment in four different ways. Although the actual risk was the same in all four cases:

1. 92 per cent said they'd accept the treatment if it reduced their chances of a stroke by 45 per cent (*relative risk*)
2. 75 per cent if it reduced the risk from 1/400 to 1/700 (*absolute risk*)
3. 71 per cent if a doctor had to treat 35 patients for 25 years to prevent one stroke (*number needed to treat*)
4. 44 per cent if treatment had a 3 per cent chance of doing them good and a 97 per cent chance of doing no good/not being needed (*personal probability of benefit*).

According to Ogden (2004), these results indicate that:

> *... not only do health professionals hold their own subjective views, but ... these views may be communicated to the patient in a way that may then influence the patient's choice of treatment.*

How can adherence be made easier?

Oral information is poorly recalled; repeating advice/instructions can improve recall, as can writing it down for the patient. (But, of course, the language used must be appropriate.) Telling someone what you're about to tell them (*explicit categorisation*) makes it more likely they'll remember, because this assists *encoding* (see Chapter 17). Also, *more specific* advice (such as 'Stop smoking' or 'Make an appointment for two weeks' time') is easier to remember than *general* suggestions (such as 'Cut down the amount you smoke' or 'Come in again soon') (Myers and Abraham, 2005).

Cue-dose training refers to individualising recommendations to improve medication recall at specific times of the day (e.g. when brushing one's teeth or at mealtimes). Patients might (also) be advised to leave medication in a prominent place associated with a routine event (e.g. beside the bed or in the fridge). Related to these examples are *implementation intentions* (Gollwitzer, 1993: Box 12.3).

Box 12.4 What makes patients adhere?

According to Damrosch (1995), there's theoretical agreement regarding the importance of the factors that make patients more likely to adhere:

1. They perceive the high severity of the disorder (*serious consequences*). For example, Brewer *et al.* (2002) found that belief in the serious consequences of very high cholesterol was positively related to medication and cholesterol control.
2. They believe the probability of getting the disorder is also high (*personal susceptibility*).
3. They have confidence in their ability to perform the behaviour prescribed to reduce the threat (*self-efficacy*).
4. They're also confident that the prescribed regimen will overcome the threat (*response efficacy*).
5. They have the intention to perform the behaviour (*behavioural intention*).

Damrosch refers to these five points as the *double high/double efficacy/behavioural intention* model.

PAIN

What is it?

Ask Yourself

- Can you describe the experience of pain?
- Are there different kinds of pain?
- If so, how do they differ?
- Is pain a purely physical, bodily phenomenon?

According to the International Association for the Study of Pain (IASP, 1986), pain is:

> *... an unpleasant sensory and emotional experience associated with actual or potential tissue damage, or described in terms of such damage ...*

This definition indicates that pain is a subjective, personal experience involving both sensory (e.g. shooting, burning, aching) and emotional (e.g. frightening, annoying, sickening) qualities. Fear/anxiety can increase the perception of pain, and depression often accompanies chronic pain and is positively associated with the pain intensity ratings of chronic pain patients (Bradley, 1995).

While pain is a physiological *protective mechanism* for the body (Collins, 1994), this doesn't explain the pain *experience*, which includes both the pain sensation, and certain autonomic responses and 'associated feeling states' (Zborowski, 1952). For example, understanding the physiology of pain cannot explain the acceptance of intense pain in torture, or the strong emotional reactions of certain individuals to the slight sting of a hypodermic needle. 'Pure' pain is never detected as an isolated sensation. It's always accompanied by emotion and meaning, so that each pain is unique to the individual.

Figure 12.7 Chinese torture. The prisoner kneels on a steel chain while tied to a cross, forced to remain in that position for days

The IASP definition recognises that an individual needn't suffer actual tissue damage at a specific body site in order to perceive pain at that site, as in the 'phantom limb' phenomenon (see Chapter 4). In describing treatment of phantom limb pain, Ramachandran and Blakeslee (1998) maintain that:

> *... pain is an* opinion *on the organism's state of health rather than a mere reflexive response to an injury. There is no direct hotline from pain receptors to 'pain centres' in the brain. On the contrary, there is so much interaction between different brain centres, like those concerned with vision and touch, that even the mere visual appearance of an opening fist can actually feed all the way back into the patient's motor and touch pathways, allowing him to feel the fist opening, thereby killing an illusory pain in a nonexistent hand.*

Ultimately, the *subjective* nature of pain makes it difficult to find a satisfactory scientific definition.

Pain without injury

Phantom limb pain is one of several examples of how it's possible to experience pain in the absence of any physical damage/injury. Others include *neuralgia* (nerve pain) and *caucalgia* (a burning pain that often follows a severe wound, such as stabbing), both of which develop *after* the wound/injury has healed. This represents the converse of phantom limb pain.

Injury without pain

People with *congenital analgesia* are incapable of feeling pain (a potentially life-threatening disorder), while those with *episodic analgesia* only experience pain minutes or even hours after the injury has occurred. This can sometimes be *life-saving*, as when soldiers suffer horrific injuries, but suffer little/no pain while waiting for medical attention (e.g. Beecher, 1956).

Cultural aspects of pain

According to Rollman (1998), to say that pain is universal doesn't imply that it can be understood in only physiological or biochemical terms. The human pain experience comprises sensory, emotional and cognitive components. In both its expression and management, biological, psychological and social factors interact in complex ways. The influence of culture on the expression of pain almost certainly begins at birth and extends throughout a person's lifetime. Members of different cultures may assume differing attitudes towards different types of pain.

African Americans (and others of African or Asian descent) display a greater sensitivity to painful stimuli compared with white Caucasian people, at least under laboratory conditions (Jarrett, 2011; Wickelgren, 2009).

Palmer *et al.* (2007) found that reports of all-over body pain were four times higher on average among a sample of South Asian participants living in the UK compared with white Europeans. Crucially, such reports were *negatively* correlated with participants' degree of assimilation into British culture: the lesser the degree of assimilation, the greater the reported all-over body pain. Perhaps those who identify with their ethnic group are more susceptible to these cultural influences, which, in turn, are likely to be mediated via neurobiological factors and processes (Jarrett, 2011).

Cognitive aspects of pain

Trusting the doctor's ability to ease your suffering (whether this takes the form of a cure or merely the relief of pain and suffering) represents part of the *cognitive appraisal* aspect of pain – that is, the belief that the illness/symptoms are controllable. If we attribute our symptoms to something that's controllable, this should make us feel more optimistic (see Chapter 10). The *meaning* of our illness may be a crucial factor in how we react to it, which in turn may affect the illness itself.

For the soldiers studied by Beecher (see above), their injuries represented the end of their war and they could look forward to resuming their lives away from the dangers of the battleground. Compared with just 32 per cent of wounded soldiers who requested pain relief medication, Beecher found that 83 per cent of civilians with similar (or less severe) wounds following surgery requested pain relief:

surgery represented for them the beginning of a long and challenging disruption to their lives.

If patients are allowed to perform necessary painful procedures on themselves (such as debridement of dead skin in severe burn cases), they tend to perceive the pain as *less* intense compared with the same procedure performed by a nurse (Melzack and Wall, 1991). This suggests that *control* is influencing the patient's level of anxiety, which, in turn, affects subjective pain.

Expectations and the modulatory pathway

Since the 1970s, researchers have been uncovering, piece by piece, a circuit in the brain and spinal cord that functions as a kind of volume control for pain, adjusting the amount a person perceives depending on the circumstances (Fields, 2009). For example, patients with severe chronic pain obtain significant, though temporary, relief from electrical stimulation of a site in the midbrain called the *periqueductal grey* (PG). The pain-control circuit extends from the frontal cortex through underlying structures (including the PG) to the spinal cord, where pain-sensitive nerve fibres connect to neurons that transmit pain signals from the rest of the body. Neurons in this pathway synthesise *endorphins* (see Chapter 4).

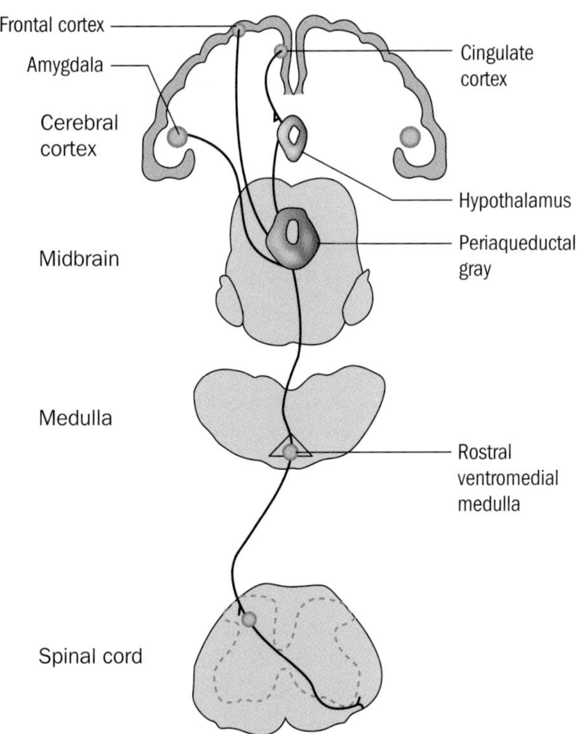

Figure 12.8 Pain modulatory pathway

Neuroscientific research is finding that cognitive influences on pain (including the expectation of pain relief from a *placebo*; see Chapter 45) operate through this modulatory pathway (Fields, 2009). Positive expectations of healing from painful injuries (such as traffic-accident-related whiplash) can produce faster recovery (Ozegovic *et al.*, 2009). Relief can also come from the mere anticipation of a natural incentive (such as food or sex). Conversely, predicting pain amplifies activity on the pain transmission pathway, leading to greater subjective pain.

STRESS

What is it?

Ask Yourself

- What do you understand by the term 'stress'?
- Is the term used in different ways to refer to different things or processes?
- What makes you feel stressed, and how does it feel?

According to Bartlett (1998):

> *... the notion that stress is bad for you and can make you ill has become a modern cultural truism. However, there is also a significant body of research evidence which lends support to this idea ... The study of stress must ... be central to ... health psychology which concerns, at its most basic level, the role of psychosocial processes in health and disease.*

Definitions of stress fall into three categories (Bartlett, 1998; Goetsch and Fuller 1995):

1. stress as a *stimulus*
2. stress as a *response*
3. stress as *interaction* between an organism and its environment.

This classification corresponds very closely to the three models of stress identified by Cox (1978), as described below.

1. The *engineering model* sees external stresses giving rise to a stress reaction, or strain, in the individual. The stress is located in the stimulus characteristics of the environment: stress is *what happens to a person* (not what happens within a person).

Up to a point, stress is inevitable and can be tolerated, and moderate levels may even be beneficial (*eustress*: Selye, 1956). Complete absence of stress (as measured, say, by anxiety or physiological arousal) could be positively detrimental (for example, you're so relaxed that you fail to notice the car speeding towards you as you're crossing the road). Stress helps to keep us alert, providing some of the energy required to maintain an interest in our environment, to explore it and adapt to it (see Chapter 9).

However, when we're 'stretched beyond our limits of elasticity', it becomes positively harmful.

2. The *physiological model* is primarily concerned with *what happens within the person* as a result of stress (the 'response' aspects of the engineering model), in particular the physiological changes.

The impetus for this view of stress was Selye's (1956) definition that 'Stress is the non-specific response of the body to any demand made upon it'. While a medical student, Selye noticed a general syndrome associated with 'being ill', regardless of the particular illness, characterised by: (i) a loss of appetite; (ii) an associated loss of weight and strength; (iii) loss of ambition; and (iv) a typical facial expression associated with illness.

Further examination of extreme cases revealed major physiological changes, (confirmed by Cox, 1978). This non-specific response to illness reflected a distinct phenomenon, which Selye called the *General Adaptation Syndrome* (GAS, see below).

3. The *transactional model* represents a kind of blend of the first two models and owes much to the work of Lazarus (1966) and Lazarus and Folkman (1984), for whom stress is

> *... a particular relationship between the person and the environment that is appraised by the person as taxing or exceeding his or her resources and endangering his or her well-being (Lazarus and Folkman, 1984)*

Because it's the person's *perception* of this mismatch between demand and ability that causes stress, the model allows for important *individual differences* in what produces stress and how much stress is experienced. There are also wide differences in how people attempt to *cope* with stress, psychologically and behaviourally.

The *engineering model* is mainly concerned with the question 'What causes stress?', and the *physiological model* with the question 'What are the effects of stress?' The transactional model is concerned with *both* these questions, plus 'How do we cope with stress?'

What causes stress?

Lazarus and Folkman's definition above implies that *stressors* cannot be defined *objectively* (independently of people's perceptions). So, in this section we're really identifying *potential* stressors, the kinds of event or experience that most people are likely to find exceed their capacity to handle the demands that are involved.

Disruption of circadian rhythms

As we saw in Chapter 7, the word 'circadian' (meaning 'about one day') describes a particular periodicity or rhythm of a number of physiological and behavioural functions that can be seen in almost all living creatures. Many studies have shown that these rhythms persist if we suddenly reverse our activity pattern and sleep during the day and are active during the night. This indicates that these rhythms are internally controlled (*endogenous*).

However, our circadian rhythms are kept on their once-every-24-hours schedule by regular daily environmental (*exogenous*) cues called *zeitgebers* (from the German meaning 'time givers'). The most important zeitgeber is the daily cycle of light and dark. If we persist with our reversal of sleep and activity, the body's circadian rhythms will (after a period of acclimatisation) reverse and become synchronised to the new set of exogenous cues.

Individual differences and the effects of shift work

Ask Yourself

- Look back at Chapter 7.
- What is it about the disruption of circadian rhythms that could account for the effects of shift work and jet lag?

Hawkins and Armstrong-Esther (1978) found significant differences between nurses on a seven-night period of night duty, with some appearing relatively undisturbed and others never really adjusting at all. A survey of 279 nurses found that a growing number are finding that night duty is detrimental not only to their own health, but also to the safety of their patients. Chronic fatigue was the most common complaint, plus difficulty in sleeping during the day. Also frequently mentioned were gastrointestinal problems (nausea/vomiting, constipation, indigestion, appetite disturbances and abdominal pain). Psychological problems included depression, mood swings, inability to concentrate, irritability and episodes of confusion (Humm, 2000).

But not all physiological functions reverse at the same time: body temperature usually reverses inside a week for most people, while the rhythms of adrenocortical hormone take much longer. During the changeover period, the body is in a state of *internal desynchronisation* (Aschoff, 1979). This is very stressful: in shift work, the zeitgebers stay the same, but workers are forced to adjust their natural sleep–wake cycles in order to meet the demands of changing work schedules (Pinel, 1993).

The effects of jet lag

Other occupational groups affected by disruption to their circadian rhythms are airline pilots and cabin crew, who experience jet lag because they cross time zones during the course of a flight.

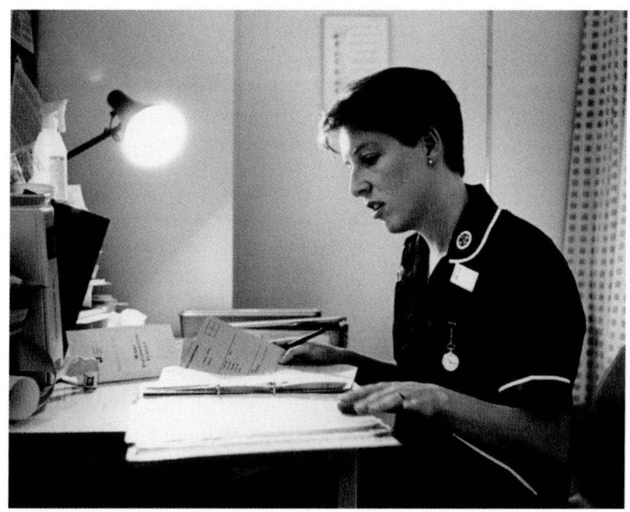

Figure 12.9 Night shift involves an enforced adjustment of sleep-wake cycles

When going west ('chasing the sun'), the day is temporarily lengthened. Because the natural circadian rhythm cycle is 25 hours (see Chapter 7), an increase in day length is much easier to deal with than a decrease. Secretion of *melatonin* reaches a peak during the night, helping to make us sleepy. After a long flight, the cyclical release of melatonin stays locked into the day/night pattern of the home country for some days. This could account for the fatigue felt during the day and the insomnia at night. If jet-lagged volunteers are given melatonin during the evening, far fewer report feeling jet-lagged than controls who receive only a placebo (Blakemore, 1988).

Cabin crew flying across time zones had significantly raised salivary *cortisol* (one of the *glucocorticoid stress hormones*, see Figure 12.10, p. 208) compared with when the same cabin crew flew short distances, and with ground crew. In a response-time test, the jet-lagged crew performed more poorly when there was a 25-second delay between presentation of the target symbol and having to recognise the symbol (but not when the delay was only 1–5 seconds) (Cho *et al.*, 2000). De Quervain *et al.* (2000) found poorer recognition memory among non-flight crew participants given *cortisone* (another glucocorticoid). Raised glucocorticoid levels may cause impairments in memory retrieval in such stressful situations as exams, job interviews, combat and courtroom testimony (see Chapter 17).

Life changes: the SRRS

Holmes and Rahe (1967) examined 5000 patient records, and made a list of 43 life events, of varying seriousness, which seemed to cluster in the months preceding the onset of their illness. Out of this grew the *Social Readjustment Rating Scale* (SRRS) (see Table 12.2).

The amount of life stress a person has experienced in a given period of time, say one year, is measured by the total number of life change units (LCUs). These units result from the addition of the values (shown in the right column) associated with events that the person has experienced during the target time period. The mean values (item weightings) were obtained empirically by telling 100 judges that 'marriage' had been assigned an arbitrary value of 500 and asking them to assign a number to each of the other events in terms of 'the intensity and length of time necessary to accommodate … regardless of the desirability of the

Table 12.2 Selected items from the Social Readjustment Rating Scale

Rank	Life event	Mean value
1	Death of spouse	100
2	Divorce	73
3	Marital separation	65
4	Jail term	63
5	Death of close family member	63
6	Personal injury or illness	53
7	Marriage	50
8	Fired at work	47
9	Marital reconciliation	45
10	Retirement	45
11	Change in health of family member	44
12	Pregnancy	40
13	Sex difficulties	39
16	Change in financial state	38
17	Death of close friend	37
18	Change to different line of work	36
22	Change in responsibilities at work	29
23	Son or daughter leaving home	29
28	Change in living conditions	25
30	Trouble with boss	23
31	Change in work hours or conditions	20
32	Change in residence	20
38	Change in sleeping habits	16
41	Vacation	13
42	Christmas	12
43	Minor violations of the law	11

event relative to marriage'. The average of the numbers assigned each event was divided by ten and the resulting values became the weighting of each life event.

Holmes and Masuda (1974) described an LCU score of over 150 in a single year as a life crisis, 150–199 is a mild crisis, 200–299 a moderate crisis, and over 300 a major crisis. They also reported that life crises were linked to deterioration in health (including sudden cardiac death, heart attacks (non-fatal), TB, diabetes, leukaemia, accidents and even athletics injuries). Further studies in the 1970s by Rahe and colleagues suggested that high LCU scores were related to heart disease (Abraham et al., 2008).

Evaluation of studies using the SRRS

- Many studies may have found statistically significant *correlations* between LCUs and subsequent illness; this means that, instead of life events causing illness, some life events (e.g. being fired from work, sexual difficulties, change in sleeping habits) are themselves early manifestations of an already developing illness (Brown, 1986; Davison *et al.*, 2004; Penny, 1996).
- Many of these studies are also *retrospective*. People are asked to recall both the illnesses and the stressful life events that occurred during the specified period, which is likely to produce distorted, unreliable data (see Chapter 17). For example, what people say about a past illness may be different from what the illness was actually like (Davison *et al.*, 2004). For this reason, only *prospective* studies (which assess life events prior to diagnosis or onset of the illness) are today given any credibility (Abraham *et al.*, 2008).
- While isolated studies (such as Chen *et al.*'s 1995 study claiming a link between life events and breast cancer) grab the public's attention through the media, literature reviews and meta-analyses tend to conclude that there's little evidence of such a link (Abraham *et al.*, 2008).

Evaluation of the SRRS

- The SRRS assumes that any change, by definition, is stressful – that is, certain events are *inherently* stressful. But the *undesirable* aspects of events are at least as important as the fact that they change people's lives (Davison and Neale, 1994). A quick glance at Table 12.2 suggests that life changes have a largely *negative* feel about them (especially those in the top ten, which receive the highest LCU scores). So, the scale may be confusing 'change' and 'negativity'.
- Some of the items are *ambiguous* (e.g. those that refer to 'changes in …' could be positive or negative changes). Others (e.g. 6 and 12) refer to states of health, so the total LCU score is already contaminated with an individual's current health status (Penny, 1996).
- The list of life events is *incomplete*. For example, there's no death of a child, no reference to the problems of old age, and no mention of natural or 'man-made' disasters (Lazarus, 1999).
- It fails to take individual circumstances into account. For example, the impact of the death of a spouse will be affected by the partner's age at the time, the nature of their relationship, and the cause of death (Forshaw, 2002).
- The SRRS was developed almost 50 years ago. This makes some of the original LCU scores associated with particular life events potentially out of date.
- Life changes may only be stressful if they're *unexpected* and, in this sense, *uncontrollable*: it may not be change as such that's stressful, but change we cannot prevent or reverse. Studies have shown that when people are asked to classify the undesirable life events on the SRRS as either 'controllable' or 'uncontrollable', only the latter are significantly correlated with subsequent onset of illness (Brown, 1986). According to Parkes (1993), the *psychosocial transitions* that are most dangerous to health are those that are sudden and allow little time for preparation (e.g. the sudden death of a relative from a heart attack, in an accident or as a result of crime; see Chapter 39).
- According to Dohrenwend (2006), *test-retest reliability* declines dramatically over periods of several weeks (untrustworthy memory again?).
- Despite all these limitations of life events research, it's an approach that seems to be here to stay, with the number of studies increasing every decade (Dohrenwend, 2006).

The hassles and uplifts of everyday life

By definition, most of the 43 changes included in the SRRS aren't everyday occurrences. Kanner *et al.* (1981) designed a *hassles scale* (comprising 117 items), and an uplifts scale (135 items). Kanner *et al.* define hassles as:

> *… the irritating, frustrating, distressing demands that to some degree characterise everyday transactions with the environment. They include annoying practical problems, such as losing things or traffic jams, and fortuitous occurrences such as inclement weather, as well as arguments, disappointments, and financial and family concerns.*

Daily uplifts are:

> *… positive experiences such as the joy derived from manifestations of love, relief at hearing good news, the pleasure of a good night's rest, and so on.*

In a study of 100 men and women aged 45–64 over a 12-month period, Kanner *et al.* confirmed the prediction that hassles were positively related to undesirable psychological symptoms. But the effect of uplifts was unclear, and research interest waned (Bartlett, 1998). They also found that hassles were a more powerful predictor of symptoms than life events (as measured by SRRS). 'Divorce', for example, may exert stress by any number of component hassles, such as cooking for oneself, handling money matters and having to tell people about it. So, daily hassles may intervene between major life events and health. It's the *cumulative impact* of these day-to-day problems that may prove detrimental to health.

Evaluation of the hassles and uplifts scales

- According to Lazarus (1999), life events (as measured by the SSRS) are *distal* (remote) causes of stress. We need to know the psychological *meaning* a person attaches to an environmental event, the personal significance of what's happening (the *proximal* cause). This is what makes Kanner *et al.*'s scales a more valid approach.
- A number of more recent studies have shown that daily hassles can have a substantial cumulative effect on health and well-being (e.g. Zautra, 2003; Almeida, 2005). While life-events researchers look at *long-term* effects (such as the likelihood of contracting cancer and other serious diseases), those who study the effects of daily hassles focus on much more *proximal* changes in stress-related physiological markers, or the occurrence of minor ailments (such as colds).
- This focus has helped them to shed more light on exactly *how* stress impacts on disease. Abraham *et al.* (2008) cite several studies which, taken together, indicate that daily hassles can influence health and illness processes by disrupting habitual health behaviours, increasing the release of stress hormones, as well as exacerbating already existing symptoms and disrupting self-care behaviours in people with chronic conditions. They also indicate the potential benefits of *stress-management programmes*.

What are the effects of stress?

The general adaptation syndrome (GAS)

According to Selye (1956), GAS represents the body's defence against stress. The body responds in the same way to any stressor, whether it's environmental or arises from within the body itself. Selye initially observed that injecting extracts of ovarian tissue into rats produced enlargement of the adrenal glands, shrinkage of the thymus gland, and bleeding ulcers. When he used extracts of other organs (pituitary, kidney, spleen), as well as substances not derived from bodily tissue, the same responses were produced. He eventually found that this same 'triad' of 'non-specific' responses could be produced by such different stimuli as insulin, excessive cold or heat, X-rays, sleep and water deprivation, and electric shock. Selye (1956) defined stress as:

> *... the individual's psychophysiological response, mediated largely by the autonomic nervous system and the endocrine system, to any demands made on the individual ...*

GAS comprises three stages: the *alarm reaction*, *resistance* and *exhaustion*.

Alarm reaction

When a stimulus is perceived as a stressor, there's a brief, initial *shock phase*. Resistance to the stressor is lowered. But this is quickly followed by the *countershock phase*. The sympathetic branch of the ANS is activated, which, in turn, stimulates the *adrenal medulla* to secrete increased levels of adrenaline and noradrenaline (*catecholamines*).

These are associated with sympathetic changes, collectively referred to as the *fight or flight response* (FOFR) (see Chapter 4). The catecholamines mimic sympathetic arousal ('*sympathomimetics*'), and noradrenaline is the transmitter at the synapses of the sympathetic branch of the ANS. Consequently, noradrenaline from the adrenals prolongs the action of noradrenaline released at synapses in the ANS. This prolongs sympathetic arousal after the stressor's removal. This is referred to as the *ANS–adrenal–medulla system* (or *sympathetic adrenal medullary* (SAM) *response system*).

Resistance

If the stressor isn't removed, there's a *decrease* in sympathetic activity, but an *increase* in output from the other part of the adrenal gland, the *adrenal cortex*. This is controlled by the amount of *adrenocorticotrophic hormone* (ACTH) in the blood. ACTH is released from the anterior pituitary on instructions from the hypothalamus. The adrenal cortex is essential for the maintenance of life and its removal results in death.

The effect of ACTH is to stimulate the adrenal cortex to release *corticosteroids* (or *adrenocorticoid hormones*), one group of which is the *glucocorticoid hormones* (chiefly, corticosterone, cortisol and hydrocortisone). These control and conserve the amount of glucose in the blood (*glucogenesis*), which functions to resist stress of all kinds. The glucocorticoids convert protein into glucose, make fats available for energy, increase blood flow and generally stimulate behavioural responsiveness. In this way, the *anterior pituitary–adrenal cortex system* (or *hypothalamic–pituitary–adrenal* (HPA) axis response system) contributes to the FOFR.

Exhaustion

Once ACTH and corticosteroids are circulating in the bloodstream, they tend to inhibit the further release of ACTH from the pituitary. If the stressor is removed during the resistance stage, blood sugar levels will gradually return to normal. But when the stress situation continues, the pituitary–adrenal excitation will continue. The body's resources are now becoming depleted, the adrenals can no longer function properly, blood glucose levels drop and, in extreme cases, *hypoglycaemia* could result in death.

It's at this stage that *psychophysiological disorders* develop, including high blood pressure (hypertension), heart disease (coronary artery disease (CAD)), coronary heart disease (CHD), asthma and peptic (stomach) ulcers. Selye called these the *diseases of adaptation*.

Evaluation of GAS

Lazarus (1999) cites a study of patients dying from injury or disease. Postmortem examination showed that those who remained unconscious

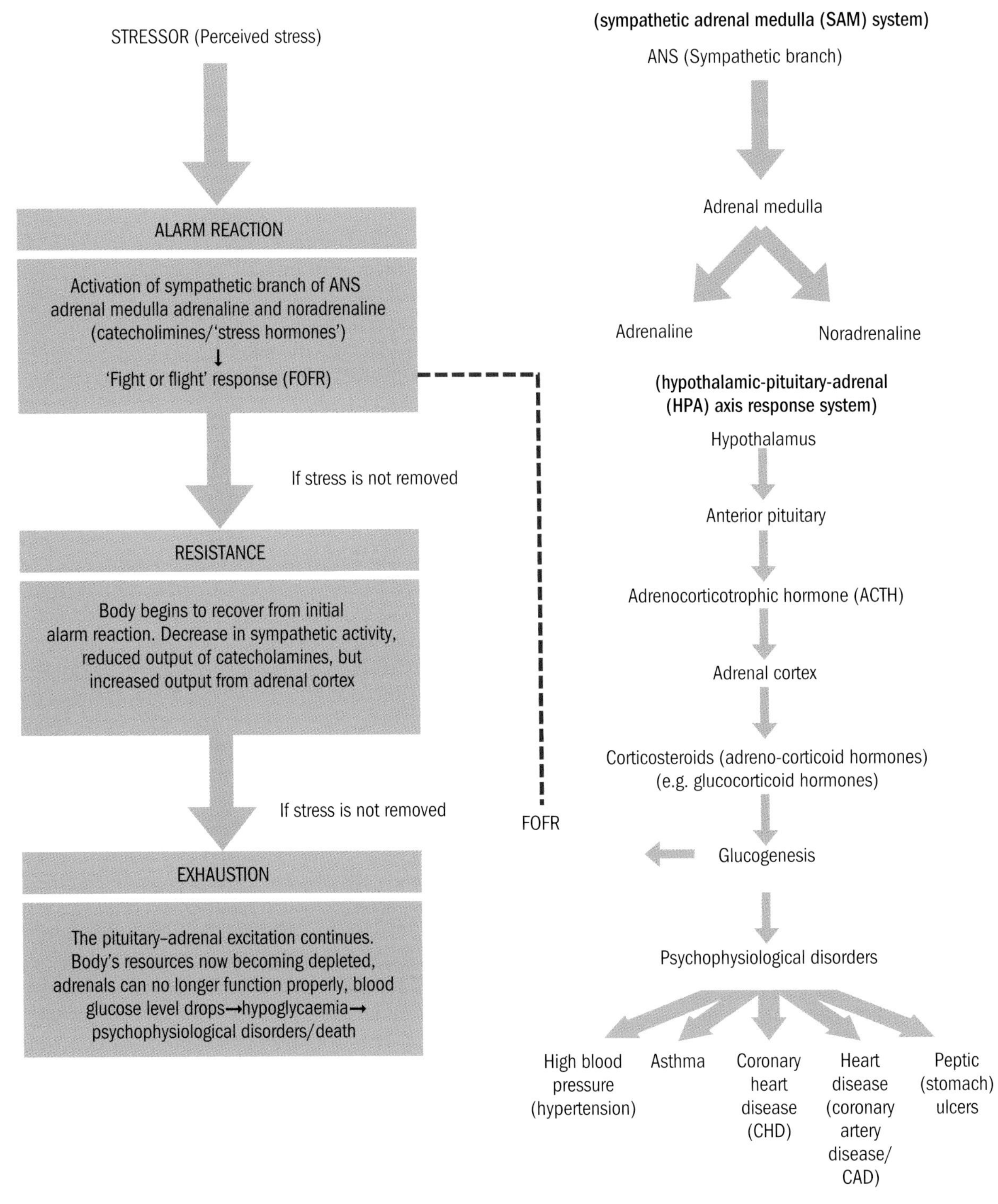

Figure 12.10 Summary diagram of the three stages of the general adaptation syndrome (GAS) (Selye, 1956) and their relationship to the physiological changes associated with (i) the SAM and (ii) HPA response systems

had normal levels of corticosteroids, while the opposite was true for those who were conscious (presumably aware they were dying). Lazarus infers from this that:

> *... some psychological awareness – akin to a conscious perception or appraisal – of the psychological significance of what is happening may be necessary to produce the adrenal cortical changes of the GAS.*

While Selye helped us understand how stressors affect the body, in order to understand what makes a psychological event stressful, we must put the person into the equation. In effect, says Lazarus:

> *... it takes both the stressful stimulus conditions and a vulnerable person to generate a stress reaction ...*

How does stress make us ill?

Box 12.5 Evolutionarily basic and modern stressors, acute and chronic stress, and the PFC

- The sympathetic branch of the ANS responds as a unit, causing a state of generalised, undifferentiated arousal. This was probably of crucial importance in our evolutionary past, when our ancestors were frequently confronted by life-threatening dangers. This is precisely what the FOFR is for. While an increase in heart rate may be necessary to supply more blood to the muscles when facing a hungry-looking bear, it may be quite irrelevant to most of the stressors we face in modern life, which involve a far higher psychological element.
- Most stressors *don't* pose a physical threat, but our nervous and endocrine systems have evolved in such a way that we typically react to stressors *as if* they did. Most everyday stressors are either frequent daily hassles or long-term, chronic stressors. What may have been adaptive responses for our ancestors have become maladaptive today.
- In addition, the unique human ability to *time travel* (i.e. to reflect on the past and contemplate the future) has a very significant disadvantage: we're able to think about stressors *in their absence* (in space or time) and this is sufficient to produce the same potentially harmful physiological effects as our ancestors experienced in life-threatening situations. Chronic stress responses are probably a rather recent human 'invention' (Thayer and Brosschot, 2010).
- The cognitive representation of stressors, before or after their occurrence, is called *perseverative cognition* (PC) (Brosschot *et al.*, 2006; Watkins, 2008). A key area of the brain involved in PC is the pre-frontal cortex (PFC), which serves as a control centre that mediates our highest cognitive abilities (including concentration, planning, decision-making, insight, judgement and the ability to retrieve memories). The PFC is the most recent part of the brain to have evolved and can be extremely sensitive to even temporary everyday anxieties and worries (Arnsten *et al.*, 2012).
- Recent research demonstrates that acute, uncontrollable stress triggers a series of chemical events that weaken the influence of the PFC, while strengthening the dominance of the brain's older parts, in particular the amygdala; this is involved in the control of emotional behaviour (see Chapter 4).

Figure 12.11 A modern stressor

> *As the older parts take over, we may find ourselves either consumed by paralysing anxiety or else subject to impulses that we usually manage to keep in check: indulgence in excesses of food, drink, drugs ... Quite simply, we lose it.* (Arnsten et al., 2012)

- In the case of heart rate and blood pressure (BP), chronic stress will involve repeated episodes of increases in heart rate and BP which, in turn, produce increases in plaque formation within the cardiovascular system.
- Stress also produces an increase in blood cholesterol levels, through the action of adrenaline and noradrenaline on the release of free fatty acids. This produces a clumping together of cholesterol particles, leading to clots in the blood and in the artery walls, and occlusion of the arteries (*atherosclerosis*). In turn, raised heart rate is related to a more rapid build-up of cholesterol on artery walls. High BP results in small lesions on the artery walls, and cholesterol tends to get trapped in these lesions (Holmes, 1994).

Stress and the immune system

The *immune system* is a collection of billions of cells that travel through the bloodstream and move in and out of tissues and organs, defending the body against invasion by foreign agents (such as bacteria, viruses and cancerous cells). These cells are produced mainly in the spleen, lymph nodes, thymus and bone marrow. The study of the effect of psychological factors on the immune system is called *psychoneuroimmunology* (PNI).

While the immune system is so vital, Sternberg and Gold (1997) warn that:

> *... its responses are so powerful that they require constant regulation to ensure that they are neither excessive nor indiscriminate and yet remain effective. When the immune system escapes regulation, autoimmune and inflammatory diseases or immune deficiency syndromes result.*

As we've seen, the GAS involves the release of cortisol (one of the major glucocorticoids) into the bloodstream. But the immune system, too, is capable of triggering this stream of biological events: it has a direct line to the hypothalamus. When our immune system is activated to fight an illness or infection, it sends a signal to the hypothalamus to produce its stress hormones (including cortisol). The flow of hormones, in turn, *shuts off* the immune response. This ingenious negative feedback loop allows a short burst of immune activity, but prevents the immune system from getting carried away. In this way, a little stress is 'good for you'. But *chronic* stress produces such a constant flow of cortisol, that the immune system is dampened too much. This helps explain how stress makes us ill (Sternberg, 2000).

Moderators and mediators of stress

Moderator variables are antecedent conditions (such as personality, ethnic background and gender) that interact with exposure to stress to affect health outcome. *Mediator variables* intervene in the link between stress exposure and health outcome (for example, *appraisal*: Folkman and Lazarus, 1988). If they *reduce* the impact of a stressful event, they're called 'protective' or 'buffering' variables (they soften or cushion the impact; Bartlett, 1998).

Personality

Type A behaviour pattern (TAPB)

The TABP (originally called 'Type A personality') comprises a set of overt behavioural responses that are elicited from susceptible individuals by challenging and stressful environments (Friedman and Rosenman, 1974; Matthews, 1982). The pattern is characterised by *competitive drive*, *impatience*, sense of *time urgency*, *hostility* and *anger*. Rosenman *et al*.'s (1975) Western Collaborative Group Study found that men with TABP were twice as likely to experience CHD after controlling for traditional risk factors (such as cholesterol and cigarette smoking).

Subsequent reviews showed that, while TABP was reliably related to CHD, the average strength of the correlation had decreased during the subsequent decade, especially in those who already had CHD (Booth-Kewley and Freidman, 1987; Penny, 1996). The risks are only *relative:* the vast majority of Type As *don't* develop CHD and many Type Bs *do* (Davison and Neale, 1994).

The focus shifted to specific Type A components, namely *hostility* and *anger,* which are most predictive of CHD, including atherosclerosis and CHD deaths (Miller *et al*., 1996). However, an almost exclusive concern with hostility/anger may have been premature: hyper-reactivity is an initial response to uncontrollable stressful events, especially in Type A individuals who display increased efforts to assert and maintain control in the face of its possible loss (Glass, 1977; Glass and Contrada, 2012).

Box 12.6 Allostatic load and immune system

- The account above of how the immune system can be shut down in the face of chronic stress is consistent with the concept of *allostatic load.*
- *Allostasis* is contrasted with *homeostasis* (see Chapter 4): physiological parameters must be maintained *outside* the normal range to match chronic demands (physical or psychological), essentially altering the normal homeostatic 'set point' for all physiological systems.
- While homeostatic changes (such as ANS response to acute threat) may be adaptive, maintaining an allostatic state in the long term causes physiological wear and tear, leading to pathology (LeMoal, 2007).
- The *allostatic load model* (Sterling and Eyer, 1988) aims to explain why biological changes designed to *protect* the organism can also be *harmful.* Consistent with the model, stress mediators can be both protective (allostatic) and harmful (allostatic load). Adrenal glands promote allostasis together with other catecholamines by helping to move immune cells ('trafficking') to organs and tissues where they're needed to fight infection. But chronic overactivity of these same mediators can produce *immunosuppressive effects* (McEwan and Seeman, 1999).

According to Glass and Contrada's (2012) *hyper-/hypo-reactivity model*, this initial response to uncontrollable stressors (hyper-reactivity) is displayed both by TABP individuals and those with bipolar disorder (BPD) (see Chapter 44). However, subsequent difficulty in coping will produce depression-like affect and behaviour, including helplessness and reduced motivation (hypo-reactivity); again, this applies to both those who display TABP and individuals with BPD. The autonomic, neuroendocrine and associated physiological changes that accompany these mood fluctuations over an extended period of time, may promote atherosclerosis and CHD (Glass and Contrada, 2012).

Type C

According to Temoshok (1987), Type C personalities are *cancer-prone*. The Type C personality has difficulty expressing emotion and tends to suppress or inhibit emotions, particularly negative ones such as anger. Such individuals also display 'pathological niceness', conflict avoidance, high social desirability, over-compliance and over-patience. While there's no clear-cut evidence that these personality characteristics can actually *cause* cancer, it does seem likely that they influence the progression of cancer and, hence, the survival time of cancer patients (Weinman, 1995).

Greer and Morris (1975) found that women diagnosed with breast cancer showed significantly more emotional suppression than those with benign breast disease (especially among those under 50). This had been a characteristic for most of their lives. Cooper and Faragher (1993) reported that experiencing a major stressful event is a significant predictor of breast cancer. This was especially so in women who didn't express anger, but used denial as a form of coping.

Key Study 12.1

Beating breast cancer (Greer *et al.*, 1979)

- Greer *et al.* studied women who'd had a mastectomy after being diagnosed with breast cancer.
- Those who reacted either by *denying* what had happened ('I'm being treated for a lump, but it's not serious'), or by showing *'fighting spirit'* ('This is not going to beat me'), were significantly more likely to be free of cancer five years later than women who stoically accepted it ('I feel an illness is God's will ...') or were described as 'giving up' ('Well, there's no hope with cancer, is there?').
- A follow-up at 15 years (Greer *et al.*, 1990) confirmed the improved prognosis.

Interestingly, a Danish study has claimed that high levels of daily stress *reduce* the chances of women developing breast cancer in the first place by 40 per cent. The study involved 6500 women, followed over an 18-year period. It seems that sustained high stress levels (as in career women) may reduce levels of *oestrogen* (the female hormone), which is known to affect the development of breast cancer (Laurance, 2005).

In men, the combination of the tendency to internalise or deny their emotions, and putting work/career before their marriage and family (often to the detriment of the latter) is associated with an increased risk of developing prostate cancer (Hill, 2007b).

Hardiness

Other personality variables can be protective. For example, Kobasa and her colleagues (Kosaba, 1979; Kobasa *et al.*, 1982) describe *hardiness,* which comprises the three Cs:

- *commitment* – a tendency to involve oneself in whatever one is doing, and to approach life with a sense of curiosity and meaningfulness
- *control* – this is related to Rotter's (1966) *locus of control* (i.e. individual differences in people's beliefs regarding what controls events in their everyday lives)
- *challenge* – a tendency to believe that change, as opposed to stability, is normal in life, and to anticipate change as an incentive to personal growth and development rather than a threat to security.

According to Funk (1992), hardiness seems to moderate the stress–illness relationship by reducing cognitive appraisals of threat, and reducing the use of regressive coping.

Cultural/ethnic background

In evaluating the TABP research, Penny (1996) observes that competitiveness and striving for achievement are common goals in capitalist societies, but probably not in more traditional, communal ones. Similarly, the SRRS has been criticised for not taking account of cultural and ethnic differences in the kinds of potential stressors that people are exposed to.

For many years, it's been noted that both the physical and mental health of African-Americans is worse than that of whites, especially in terms of the spread of AIDS and hypertension. While this is partly due to the direct negative effects of poverty, such as poor diet, low levels of education and poor medical care, there are many psychological and social stressors involved as well. Although these are extremely difficult to measure, especially across cultures:

> *... there is little dispute that blacks in North America and Europe face a unique kind of stress – racial discrimination. (Cooper* et al.*, 1999)*

Critical Discussion 12.1

Resilience: Bouncing back from trauma

The conventional/traditional view holds that psychological resilience in the face of life's more extreme stresses is a fairly rare event. However, Bonanno's (2009) research into bereavement, and responses to sexual abuse, the 9/11 attacks and the SARS epidemic in Hong Kong, suggest that resilience (from the Latin *re* for 'back' and *salire* for 'to leap') is, in fact, relatively commonplace.

Most bereaved people/victims soon begin to recover and ultimately emerge largely emotionally intact: most of us demonstrate astonishing natural resilience to the worst that life throws our way (Stix, 2011).

The study of resilience is uncovering a series of underlying mechanisms – biochemical, genetic and behavioural – which act together to restore our emotional equilibrium. The initial response to life-threatening events is often FOFR, which relates to the hyper-reactivity component of Glass and Contrada's (2012) *hyper /hypo-reactivity model* (see text above). However, as we've also already seen, chronic stress results in the production of stress hormones, in particular cortisol, which can actually damage brain cells in the hippocampus and amygdala.

Stress hormones, aided by certain protective biochemicals, seem to switch off more readily in resilient people. These chemicals include dehydroepiandrosterone (DHEA), which reduces the effect of cortisol, and neuropeptide Y, which appears to reduce anxiety by counteracting the effects of corticotrophin-releasing hormone (released by the hypothalamus).

Consistent with the resilience research, considerable research within positive psychology has found evidence for *post-traumatic growth* (Tedeschi and Calhoun, 1996); this denotes how trauma can serve as a catalyst for positive psychological change (in relationships, self-concept and outlook on life as a whole). (See Gross, 2014.)

Resilience can be enhanced through *cognitive reappraisal* (as in CBT, for example) and *mindfulness meditation* (see text below) (Southwick and Charney, 2013).

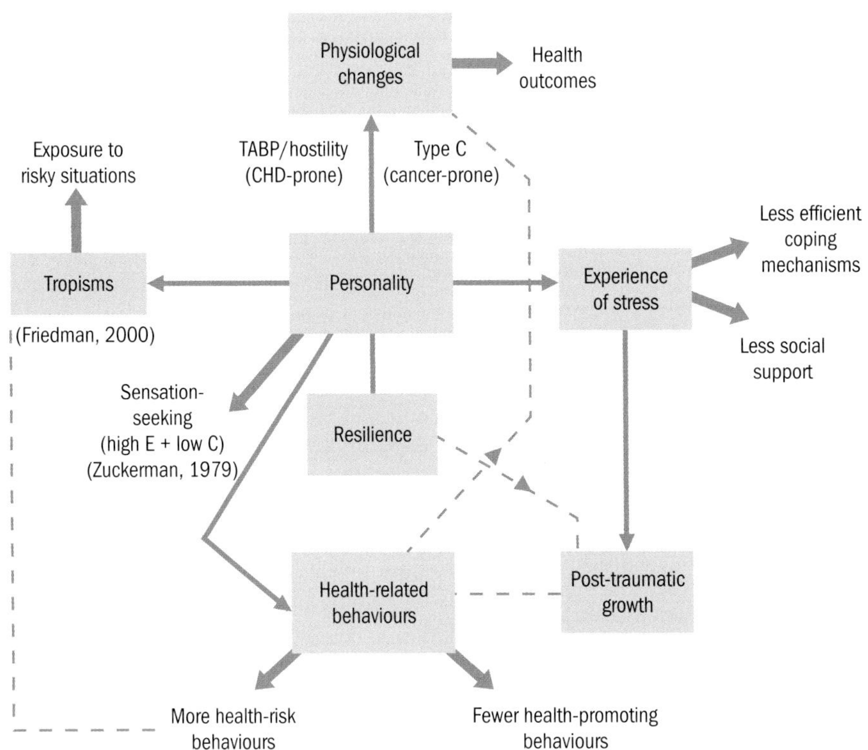

Figure 12.12 Potential harmful and positive effects of personality on health outcomes

Ask Yourself

- Can you think of ways in which racial discrimination increases the stress levels of its victims? (See Chapter 25)
- Can you think of ways in which sexism might adversely affect women's health?
- Do women have access to protective factors that men don't?

How do we cope with stress?

What do we mean by coping?

Lazarus and Folkman (1984) define coping as:

> *... constantly changing cognitive and behavioural efforts to manage external and/or internal demands that are appraised as taxing or exceeding the resources of the person.*

This mirrors their definition of stress (see above, p. 204).

Different kinds of coping

Primary appraisal of an event as in some way harmful or threatening is really only the beginning of the coping process.

Cohen and Lazarus (1979) have classified all the coping strategies that a person might use into five general categories:

1. *direct action response* – the individual tries directly to change or manipulate his/her relationship to the stressful situation, such as escaping from/removing it
2. *information seeking* – the individual tries to understand the situation better, and to predict future events that are related to the stressor
3. *inhibition of action* – doing nothing; this may be the best course of action if the situation is seen as short-term
4. *intrapsychic or palliative coping* – the individual reappraises the situation (for example, through the use of psychological defence mechanisms) or changes the 'internal environment' (through drugs, alcohol, relaxation or meditation)
5. *turning to others* for help and emotional support.

These five categories of coping overlap with the distinction between problem-focused and emotion-focused coping (see Box 12.7).

Box 12.7 Problem-focused and emotion-focused coping (Lazarus and Folkman, 1984)

- *Problem-focused coping* (PFC) involves taking direct action in order to solve the problem, or seeking information that's relevant to a solution.
- *Emotion-focused coping* (EMC) involves trying to reduce the negative emotions that are part of the experience of stress.

Ask Yourself

- Which of the above coping responses best describes your typical response to stressful situations?
- How about your best friend or partner?
- Does the way you cope depend on the nature of the stressor?

Evaluation of different coping methods

Many researchers simply assume that EFC is a less adaptive way of dealing with stress (de Ridder, 2000). But Lazarus and Folkman argue that effective coping depends on the situation, and sometimes using both kinds might offer the 'best solution'. For example, a situation that's controllable calls for more problem-focused efforts because the individual is in a position to do something about it. In contrast, situations that don't allow for control require management of the emotions they trigger (Folkman, 1984). Effectiveness must also take account of how long the stressor lasts.

Several studies report that women engage more often in EFC than men, but the majority of female coping is PFC: the observation that women are emotion-oriented copers is a *relative* one (de Ridder, 2000). Stanton *et al.* (1994) have questioned the very concept of EFC. They found that women more often worked through their emotions than men and that this greater effort to understand and express their emotions was *more adaptive for them*. Similarly, Stroebe (1998) has suggested that widowers may be more vulnerable to physical illness and depression than widows, because widowers find it easier to avoid confrontation with feelings and to deal with the problems created by their wife's death rather than dealing with their grief. Widows can access their emotions and express them more easily.

Stress management

Much of what we've said about coping with stress refers to what people do in a largely *spontaneous* (and often unconscious) way. In this *informal* sense, we all 'manage our stress' more or less effectively, through the various *coping strategies/mechanisms* described above.

But, more *formally*, *stress management* (SM) refers to a range of psychological techniques used in a quite deliberate way, in a professional setting, to help people reduce their stress. These techniques may be used singly or in combination.

- In the case of *biofeedback* (see Chapter 2), the focus is on treating the symptoms of stress rather than the stressor itself.
- The same is true for a number of procedures used to bring about a state of relaxation, in particular *progressive muscle relaxation* (see Chapter 45), *meditation* (including *mindfulness*) and *hypnosis*.
- Mindfulness is a type of dispassionate focus on the present: it helps to ward off stress and anxiety that arise from 'time travel' into the remembered past and the imagined future (*rumination*). A large body of data shows that *mindfulness* training helps to reduce stress-related diseases in adults (Wickelgren, 2012).
- *Cognitive restructuring* refers to a number of specific methods aimed at trying to change the way individuals think about their life situation and self, in order to change their emotional responses and behaviour. This approach is based largely on the work of Beck (the *treatment of automatic thoughts*) and Ellis (*rational emotive therapy*), two major forms of *cognitive behavioural therapy* (CBT) (see Chapter 45). This approach provides information to reduce uncertainty and to enhance people's sense of control.

Chapter Summary

- While traditional medicine is based on the **biomedical model** of disease, **Health Psychology** (HP), rests on the **biopsychosocial model.**
- HP focuses on normal behaviour and psychological processes in relation to health and illness, although some see it as an extension of Clinical Psychology.
- **Cultural factors** contribute to the prevalence of certain diseases between cultures, and **acculturation** may expose immigrants to risk factors within the host culture.
- **Expectancy-value models** try to account for people's adoption/failure to adopt particular health behaviours. They are **rational reasoning** models.
- In the **health belief model (HBM)**, belief in susceptibility to, and perception of severity of the consequences, of the disease, together determine the **perceived threat.**
- A factor that may explain the persistence of unhealthy behaviours is people's tendency towards **unrealistic optimism**. This suggests that perception of one's own risk isn't a rational process.
- The **theory of reasoned action (TRA)** assumes that behaviour is a function of **behavioural intention,** jointly determined by a person's attitude and subjective norms.
- The **theory of planned behaviour (TPB)** is a modification of the TRA. The extra ingredient is **perceived behavioural control (PBC)** based on Bandura's concept of **self-efficacy.**
- All the models are poor predictors of actual behaviour (the **intention–behaviour gap**). One response to this criticism is the concept of **implementation intentions.**
- Research indicates that patient **non-adherence** is very common. It applies to both chronic and acute conditions, and to organ transplant patients.
- **Adherence** is affected by **practitioner variables,** including how doctors communicate their beliefs to patients.
- Although **pain** is basically physiological, the **pain experience** has **emotional, cognitive** and **cultural components. Phantom limb** pain illustrates that people can feel pain in the absence of physical injury, and **congenital analgesia** illustrates the converse.
- **Stress** can be conceptualised as a **stimulus** (corresponding to the **engineering model**), a **response** (corresponding to the **physiological model**) or as an **interaction** between organism and environment (corresponding to the **transactional model**).
- The **causes** of stress include **disruption of circadian rhythms,** as in shift work and jet lag.
- **Major life changes** have been studied using the **Social Readjustment Rating Scale (SRRS)**. An alternative to the SRRS is the **hassles scale.**
- Selye's **General Adaptation Syndrome (GAS)** represents the body's defence against stress. It comprises the **alarm reaction, resistance** and **exhaustion.**
- The alarm reaction involves the **fight or flight response (FOFR)**, in which the **sympathetic adrenal medulla (SAM) system** is activated. In resistance, the **hypothalamic-pituitary-adrenal (HPA) system** is activated.
- While the FOFR may have been adaptive in our **evolutionary past**, it's inappropriate as a response to most 'modern' stressors. Stress can cause illness through maintaining a dangerously high level of physiological arousal.
- **Psychoneuroimmunology** studies the relationship between stress and health by assessing its effects on the **immune system.**
- Consistent with the **allostatic load model,** stress **mediators** can be both protective (**allostatic**) and harmful (**allostatic load**).
- FOFR is related to the **hyper-reactivity** component of the **hyper-/hypo-reactivity model.**

- **Moderators** of stress include **personality** and **ethnic background.**
- Consistent with the study of **resilience** is evidence for **post-traumatic growth**.
- Considerable research has investigated the link between **Type A Behaviour Pattern (TABP)** and CHD, and between **Type C personalities** and cancer. Unlike these, **hardiness** is a **protective factor** against the harmful effects of stress.
- **Coping** with stress involves **primary** and **secondary appraisals, problem-focused** and **emotion-focused coping** (**PFC** and **EFC**), and **coping mechanisms**. These represent **informal** ways of dealing with stress.
- **Stress management** (**SM**) refers to **formal, deliberate** attempts to reduce stress, including **biofeedback, progressive muscle relaxation, mindfulness** and **cognitive restructuring**.

Links with Other Topics/Chapters

Chapters 8 and 43 ⟶ The biomedical model of illness is closely related to the *disease model of addiction* and the *medical model of mental disorder*

Chapter 47 ⟶ *Culture* determines what is commonly understood by 'health' and 'illness', as well as helping to determine the prevalence of certain diseases. Pain may also be understood as a cultural phenomenon

Chapter 47 ⟶ Models of health behaviour are culturally relative, and western culture seems to value and encourage the competitive component of TAPB

Chapter 25 ⟶ *Racial discrimination* is a unique form of stress that can account for the greater susceptibility of African-Americans to certain health problems

Chapter 24 ⟶ The TRA has been central to the debate within Social Psychology regarding the *relationship between attitudes and behaviour*

Chapter 35 ⟶ The TPB is a modification of the TRA, reflecting the influence of Bandura's concept of *self-efficacy*

Chapter 24 ⟶ Perceptions of invulnerability demonstrate how people rationalise behaviour that conflicts with aspects of their self-concept, as explained by Festinger's *cognitive dissonance theory*

Chapter 27 ⟶ Patient 'compliance' implies the doctor's role as an authority figure, with the less powerful patient in a submissive (obedient) role

Chapter 11 ⟶ Biofeedback is used in the treatment of pain and stress-related disorders, and is derived from work with rats, which demonstrated how autonomic responses could be modified using *operant conditioning* techniques

Chapters 44 and 45 ⟶ Both pain and stress are also treated through cognitive behavioural techniques, including Beck's *treatment of automatic thoughts* and Ellis's *rational emotive therapy*

Chapter 7 ⟶ The *disruption of circadian rhythms* is a major cause of stress

Chapter 44 ⟶ People working in the emergency services are especially susceptible to *post-traumatic stress disorder* (PTSD)

Chapter 4 ⟶ Stressors adversely affect health through their impact on the *autonomic nervous system* (ANS) and *endocrine system*

Chapter 10 ⟶ For something to be perceived as a stressor, it first has to be appraised as potentially threatening. Appraisal also applies to *theories of emotion*

Chapter 42 ⟶ Coping mechanisms are often contrasted with Freud's account of *ego defence mechanisms*

Recommended Reading

Abraham, C., Conner, M., Jones, F., O'Connor, D. (2008) *Health Psychology.* London: Hodder Education.

Bartlett, D. (1998) *Stress: Perspectives and Processes.* Buckingham: Open University Press.

Forshaw, M. (2002) *Essential Health Psychology.* London: Arnold.

French, D., Vedhara, K., Kaptein, A.A., Weinman, J. (eds) (2010) *Health Psychology* (2nd edn). Oxford: BPS Blackwell.

Ogden, J. (2004) *Health Psychology: A Textbook* (3rd edn). Maidenhead: Open University Press/McGraw-Hill Education.

Stroebe, W. (2000) *Social Psychology and Health.* Buckingham: Open University Press.

Useful Websites

http://health-psych.org/ (The American Psychological Association's Division 38 Health Psychology)

www.bps.org.uk/networks-and-communities/member-microsite/division-health-psychology (The British Psychological Society's Division of Health Psychology)

www.stressfree.com (Stress Free Network)

www.psychosomatic.org (American Psychosomatic Society)

www.isbm.info (International Society for Behavioural Medicine)

CHAPTER 13

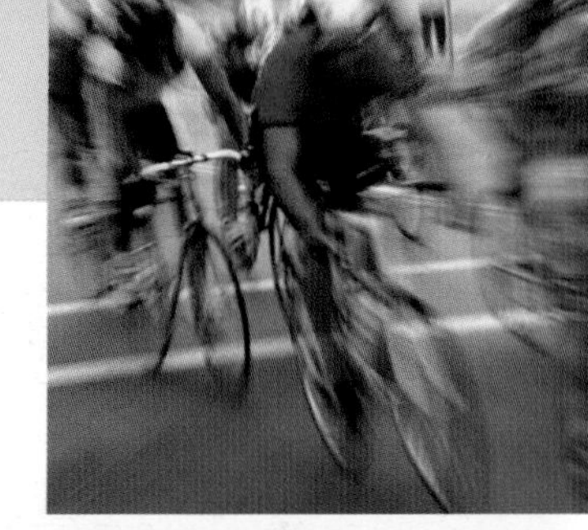

ATTENTION

INTRODUCTION and OVERVIEW

According to Titchener (1903), a student of Wundt:

> *The doctrine of attention is the nerve of the whole psychological system.*

However, the Gestalt Psychologists believed the concept of attention was unnecessary (a stimulus array's properties are sufficient to predict the perceptual response to it; see Chapter 15). The Behaviourists argued that since 'attention' was unobservable, it wasn't worthy of experimental study (see Chapters 2 and 3).

Interest in the study of attention re-emerged following the publication of Broadbent's (1958) *Perception and Communication*, which also had a great impact on the development of Cognitive Psychology overall. Broadbent argued that the world is composed of many more sensations than can be handled by the perceptual and cognitive capabilities of the human observer. To cope with the flood of available information, humans must selectively attend to only some information, and somehow 'tune out' the rest. Attention, therefore, is the result of a *limited-capacity information-processing* system. Solso (1995) calls this a 'pipeline' theory. To understand our ability to attend selectively to things, researchers study *focused* (or *selective*) *attention*.

Central to the information-processing approach is the *computer analogy*. This is arguably most evident in explanations of memory (see Chapter 17) and attention. Concepts such as buffer store and limited-capacity processor are drawn from information technology and built into the models of attention discussed in this chapter.

Almost all the early models of attention assumed *serial processing*, a step-by-step process in which each operation is carried out in turn. The first of these was Broadbent's (1958) *filter model*, followed by Treisman's (1964) *attenuation model*, and the *pertinence model* (Deutsch and Deutsch, 1963; Norman, 1969). These are all 'single-channel models' of selective attention. But early attempts to explain *divided attention*, such as Kahneman's (1973) *central capacity theory*, also assumed serial processing. In *parallel processing,* two or more operations are carried out at the same time. This is the view taken in Allport's (1980b) *multi-channel theory* of divided attention (doing more than one thing at a time).

A fairly recent way of thinking about and investigating divided attention is in the form of *multitasking*, which is related to the more general phenomenon of *attention switching*. An even more general area of research interest concerns how we're able to attend (i.e. concentrate/keep focused) to *anything at all.*

WHAT IS ATTENTION?

Ask Yourself

- What do you understand by the term 'attention'? (See Chapters 7 and 9.)

One famous definition of attention is that of William James (1890), according to whom:

> *It is the taking possession by the mind, in clear and vivid form, of one out of what seem several simultaneously possible objects or trains of thought. Focalisation, concentration of consciousness are of its essence. It implies withdrawal from some things in order to deal effectively with others.*

Although we cannot necessarily equate attention with consciousness (see below), James' definition underlines the *selective* nature of attention. This is echoed in Solso's (1995) definition: 'the concentration of mental effort on sensory or mental events'. However, this is only one of two major ways in which attention has been defined and investigated. A crucial distinction is made between:

1. the mechanisms by which certain information is registered and other information is rejected, whether or not the latter enters conscious awareness (*selective* or *focused attention*)
2. some upper limit to the amount of processing that can be performed on incoming information at any one time (*capacity* or *divided attention*).

The term 'attention' has also been used to refer to *arousal level*, *vigilance* and the ability to *stay alert* and *concentrate* (see Chapters 7 and 9).

Figure 13.1 How many things can you do at once?

METHODS OF STUDYING ATTENTION

Selective attention

People are presented with two or more simultaneous 'messages', and are instructed to process and respond to only one of them. The most popular way of doing this is to use *shadowing*, in which one message is fed into the left ear and a different message into the right ear (through headphones). Participants have to repeat one of these messages aloud as they hear it.

The shadowing technique is really a particular form of *dichotic listening* (Broadbent, 1954). This is the simultaneous reception of two different stimulus inputs, one to each ear. Shadowing was first used by Cherry (1953), who wanted to study the *cocktail party phenomenon*, in which we manage to select one or two voices to listen to from the hubbub of conversations taking place at the same time in the same room. The participant is asked to select, which can tell us something about the selection process and what happens to unattended stimuli. Most studies have looked at *auditory* attention.

Divided attention

In the *dual-task technique*, people are asked to attend and respond to both (or all) the messages. Whereas shadowing focuses attention on a particular message, the dual-task method deliberately *divides* people's attention. This provides useful information about a person's processing limitations, and also about attention mechanisms and their capacity.

SELECTIVE (OR FOCUSED) AUDITORY ATTENTION

Cherry's dichotic listening and shadowing research

In his initial experiments, Cherry's participants wore headphones through which pairs of spoken prose 'messages' were presented to both ears simultaneously (*binaural listening*). Cherry found that various physical differences affected a person's ability to select one of the messages to attend to, in particular voice intensity, the speaker's location and the speaker's gender. He also found that when these differences were controlled for in the two messages (so that each message was, say, spoken in an equally intense female voice), their meaning was extremely difficult to separate. In later experiments, he used dichotic listening and shadowing. While participants were able to shadow the specified message, they remembered little of the non-shadowed message.

Box 13.1 Other research findings using shadowing

- Little of the non-shadowed message was remembered, even when the same word was presented 35 times to the non-shadowed ear (Moray, 1959).
- Participants didn't notice if the message was spoken in a foreign language or changed from English to a different language.
- While speech played backwards was reported as having 'something queer about it', most participants believed it to be normal speech.
- A pure tone of 400 cycles per second was nearly always noticed, as was a change of voice from male to female or female to male (Cherry and Taylor, 1954).

Ask Yourself

- What conclusions can you draw from these findings?

These data suggested that while the *physical properties* of the message in the non-shadowed ear were 'heard', *semantic content* (its *meaning*) was completely lost.

Researchers quickly moved on from Cherry's original question about how we can attend to one conversation, and began to ask why so little seemed to be remembered about the other conversations (Hampson and Morris, 1996).

Broadbent's split-span studies

Broadbent (1954) reported the results of a series of studies using the *split-span procedure*. In this, three digits (such as 8, 2 and 1) are presented via headphones to one ear at the rate of one every half a second. Simultaneously, three different digits (such as 7, 3 and 4) are presented to the other ear. The task is to listen to the two sets of numbers and then write down as much as can be remembered.

The digits can be recalled either:

1. according to the ear of presentation (*ear-by-ear recall*: the numbers above could be recalled as either 8, 2, 1, 7, 3, 4 or 7, 3, 4, 8, 2, 1), or
2. according to their chronological order of presentation (*pair-by-pair recall*); since the digits have been presented in pairs, this would involve recalling the first pair (8, 7 or 7, 8), followed by the second pair (2, 3 or 3, 2) and finally the third pair (1, 4 or 4, 1).

When people are simply given a list of six digits at a rate of one every half a second, serial recall is typically 95 per cent accurate. However, Broadbent found that the split-span procedure produced accurate recall only 65 per cent of the time. Moreover, pair-by-pair recall was considerably poorer than ear-by-ear recall. If given a choice, people preferred ear-by-ear recall.

SINGLE-CHANNEL THEORIES OF FOCUSED AUDITORY ATTENTION

Single-channel theories propose that somewhere in information processing there's a 'bottleneck' or filter that allows some information to be passed on for further analysis, while the rest is either discarded or processed to only a limited degree. The three theories that have been proposed differ mainly over whether the filtering takes place early or late in information processing. This means that they differ in terms of the nature and extent of processing of the non-attended material.

Broadbent's early selection filter theory

Broadbent's (1958) theory was the first systematic attempt to explain both Cherry's findings and those of split-span experiments. Broadbent assumes that our ability to process information is *capacity-limited*. Information from the senses passes 'in parallel' to a short-term store. This is a temporary 'buffer system' which holds information until it can be processed further and, effectively, extends the duration of a stimulus (see Chapter 17). The various types of information (such as two or more voices) are preserved in their original form, and then passed to a *selective filter*. This operates on the basis of the information's physical characteristics, selecting one source for further analysis and rejecting all others.

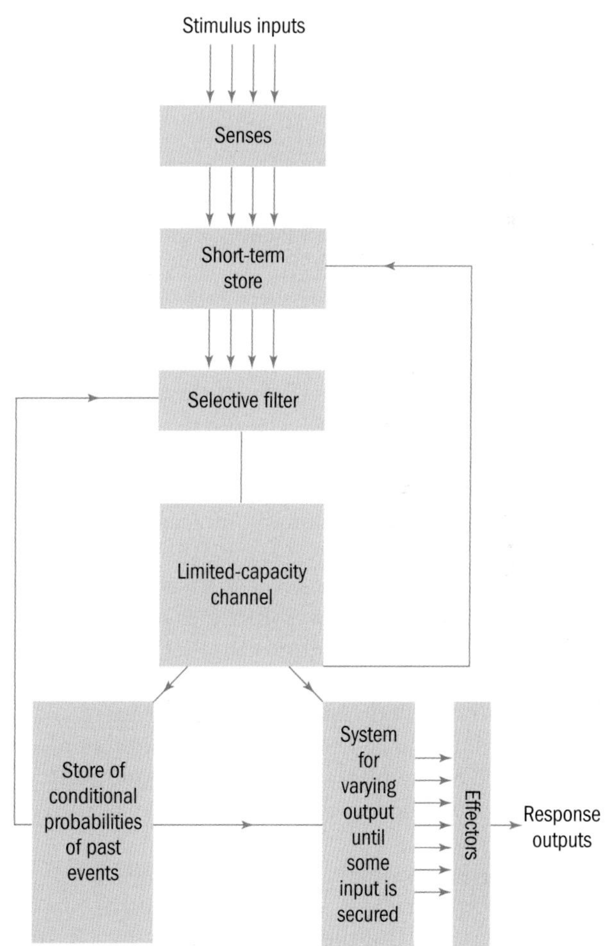

Figure 13.2 Broadbent's theory of the flow of information between stimulus and response

Information allowed through the filter reaches a limited-capacity channel (the filter is necessary precisely because the channel is capacity-limited). This corresponds to the 'span of consciousness' (James, 1890) or what we experience as happening *now*. The information allowed through the filter is analysed in that it's recognised, possibly rehearsed, and then transferred to the motor effectors (muscles), producing an appropriate response.

Broadbent considered the short-term store to be capable of holding information for a period of time before it decayed. So, two simultaneous stimuli can be processed provided the processor can get back to the store before the information in it has disappeared. Consequently, attending to one thing doesn't necessarily mean that everything else is lost. However, Broadbent maintained that processing two different pieces of information from two channels would always take longer, and be less efficient, than processing the same information from one channel: switching attention between channels takes a substantial period of time.

Tests of Broadbent's theory

Ask Yourself

- How can Broadbent's theory explain (a) Cherry's findings concerning the fate of the non-shadowed message, and (b) the data from the split-span experiments?

According to the filter theory, (a) the non-shadowed message isn't allowed to pass through the filter, and (b) the input to the relevant ear is the physical property which is the basis for selecting the information.

However, the theory assumes that because the non-shadowed message is filtered out according to its physical characteristics, its meaning shouldn't be subject to any sort of higher-level analysis. But when we're at a party, our attention sometimes switches from the person we're chatting with to another part of the room (if, for example, we hear our name spoken). This was demonstrated experimentally by Moray (1959), who found that when the participant's name was presented to the non-attended (non-shadowed) ear, attention switched to that ear about one-third of the time.

According to Broadbent, participants should have reported 'ob-two-tive', or 'six-jec-nine'. This, of course, is nonsense. But the filter model maintains that it's the physical nature of the auditory signal (which ear receives which input), and not meaning which determines what's attended to and, hence, what's recalled.

What participants *actually* reported was 'objective' or 'Dear Aunt Jane', etc. In other words, they acted 'intelligently'. The ears don't always function as different information channels, and switching between channels is fairly easy to do.

Key Study 13.1

Why use one ear when two will do? (Gray and Wedderburn, 1960)

- Gray and Wedderburn presented, to each ear alternately, the syllables composing a word, plus random digits. Thus, when one ear 'heard' a syllable, the other 'heard' a digit. For example, in one experiment, participants heard:
  Left ear: OB 2 TIVE
  Right ear: 6 JEC 9
- In other experiments, phrases were used in place of words, such as 'Dear Aunt Jane', 'Mice eat cheese' and 'What the hell'.

Figure 13.3

Ask Yourself

- What would Broadbent have predicted about participants' responses when asked to repeat what they'd heard in one ear (or channel)?

An evaluation of Broadbent's theory

The importance of meaning

- Broadbent's pioneering research highlights the role of audition (hearing) as the 'sentinel of the senses'. Ears (unlike eyes) are never pointing in the wrong direction and are never closed; they're alert to changes in the auditory environment even when the conscious mind is diverted or switched off (as demonstrated by our ability to wake when the alarm clock goes off – sometimes!) (Beaman, 2006).
- Treisman (1960) found that if meaningful material presented to the attended ear was switched in mid-sentence to the non-attended ear, participants would occasionally change the focus of their attention to the non-attended ear, and shadow that material before changing back to the attended ear.
- Treisman (1964) discovered that if a French translation of the shadowed material was presented as non-shadowed material, some bilingual participants realised that the shadowed and non-shadowed material had the same meaning.

- Corteen and Wood (1972) conditioned participants to produce a galvanic skin response (GSR) whenever they heard a particular target word. A small electric shock was delivered immediately after the target word was heard. The target word produced a GSR when presented to the non-attended ear, as did synonyms. However, GSRs didn't occur every time the conditioned words were presented.
- Mackay (1973) presented the word 'bank' in a sentence, and participants subsequently had to recognise the sentence they'd heard. Recognition was influenced by whether the word 'river' or 'money' had been presented to the non-attended ear.

What these studies, and that of Gray and Wedderburn (see Key Study 13.1), suggest is that the *meaning* of the input to the non-attended ear is processed at least some of the time. Further, Underwood (1974) found that participants trained at shadowing can detect two-thirds of the material presented to the non-attended ear. This throws doubt on Broadbent's claim that the non-shadowed message is always rejected at an early stage of processing. Also, when material used is sufficiently different (such as one being auditory and the other visual), memory for the non-shadowed message is good. This indicates that it must have been processed at a higher level than proposed by Broadbent (Allport *et al.*, 1972).

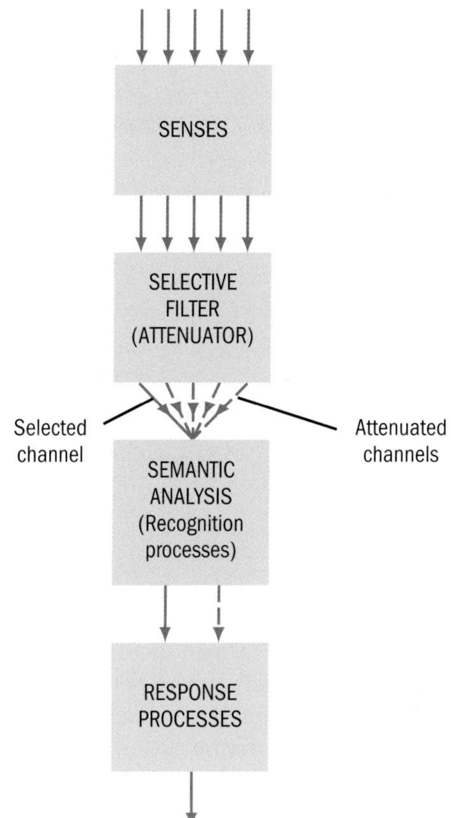

Figure 13.4 Treisman's attenuation model

Treisman's attenuation (or stimulus-analysis system) model

According to Treisman (1960, 1964), competing information is analysed for things other than its physical properties, including sounds, syllable patterns, grammatical structure and the information's meaning (Hampson and Morris, 1996). Treisman suggested that the non-shadowed message isn't filtered out early on, but that the selective filter *attenuates* it: a message that isn't selected on the basis of its physical properties wouldn't be rejected completely, but its 'volume' would be 'turned down'.

Both non-attenuated and attenuated information undergoes these further analyses. This may result in an attenuated message being attended to, depending on its features.

Treisman suggested that biologically relevant and emotionally important stimuli may be 'pre-sets' to which attention is switched, irrespective of the attenuated message's content. This accounts for our ability to switch attention to a different conversation when our name is mentioned.

Since it's the features of a stimulus that determine whether or not it's attended to, the concept of *probabilistic filtering* is perhaps a better way of appreciating Treisman's theory than that of attenuation (Massaro, 1989).

The Deutsch–Norman late-selection filter model

Deutsch and Deutsch (1963) and Norman (1968, 1976) completely rejected Broadbent's claim that information is filtered out early on. According to the Deutsch–Norman model, filtering or selection occurs only *after* all inputs have been analysed at a high level, for example after each word has been recognised by the memory system and analysed for meaning.

The filter is placed nearer the *response* end of the processing system; hence, it's a 'late' selection filter. Because processing will have already been undertaken on the information that's been presented, some information will have been established as *pertinent* (most relevant) and have activated particular memory representations. This is why it's sometimes called the *pertinence model*. When one memory

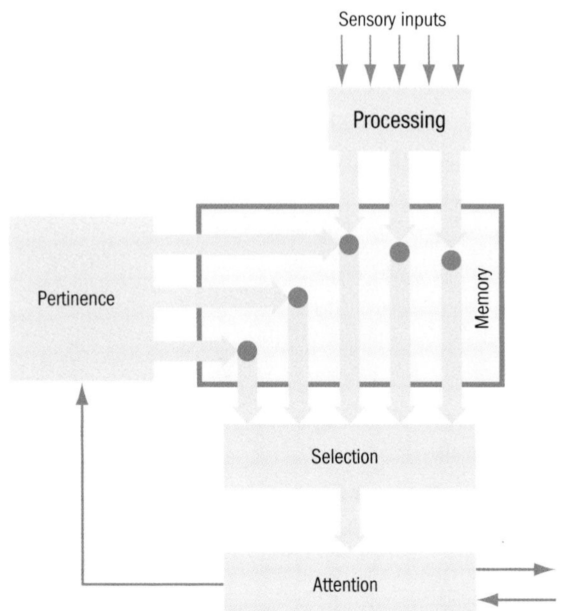

Figure 13.5 The Deutsch–Norman theory of focused attention. All sensory inputs receive perceptual processing and are recognised in the sense that they excite their representations (the circles) in memory. The information selected is that which has the greatest pertinence (Norman, 1968)

representation is selected for further processing, attention becomes selective. The model implies that we perceive everything we encounter, but are consciously aware of only some of it (Hampson and Morris, 1996).

Tests of the Treisman and the Deutsch–Norman models

Both the Treisman and the Deutsch–Norman models can account for the processing of non-shadowed material (whereas Broadbent's theory cannot). If the Deutsch–Norman model is correct, then participants should be able to identify as many target words in the non-shadowed message as in the shadowed message, since both are allegedly completely analysed for meaning. Treisman and Geffen (1967), however, found that target words were much better detected in the shadowed message (87 per cent) than the non-shadowed message (8 per cent). This is consistent with Treisman's view that the non-shadowed message is attenuated.

However, Treisman and Geffen's findings assume that the shadowed and non-shadowed messages are equally important. Deutsch and Deutsch (1967) argued that this assumption isn't valid, because participants had to indicate when they heard a target word by tapping. In other words, they had to shadow and tap in one message, but only tap in the other. This made the target words in the shadowed message more important than those in the non-shadowed message. Treisman and Riley (1969) overcame this problem by requiring participants to stop shadowing and to tap as soon as they detected a target word in either ear. Under such conditions, performance was still better for the shadowed message (76 per cent) than for the non-shadowed message (33 per cent).

This finding is consistent with Treisman's model, but inconsistent with the Deutsch–Norman claim that performance shouldn't differ. However, the detection rate for the non-attended ear in Treisman and Riley's study (33 per cent) was much higher than that in the Treisman and Geffen study (8 per cent). This provides some support for the Deutsch–Norman model.

The Deutsch–Norman model predicts that participants asked immediately afterwards should be able to repeat back the words presented to the non-shadowed ear. However, the non-shadowed message gets into short-term memory for only a brief period and is then forgotten very quickly. Norman (1969) found that participants could remember the last couple of words presented to the non-attended ear if tested immediately, but not after a short continuation of the shadowing task. This finding was replicated by Glucksberg and Cowan (1970).

Ask Yourself

- Can you think of examples where you've remembered something later that you weren't aware of hearing at the time (such as something somebody said)?
- Which of the theories of attention discussed above best accounts for these occurrences?

An evaluation of single-channel models

- Despite some support for the Deutsch–Norman model, Wilding (1982) believes that less is known about non-attended messages than it claims. However, more is known than can be explained by either Broadbent's or Treisman's models.
- The major criticism of single-channel theories is their lack of flexibility, and several more 'flexible' theories have been advanced. According to Johnston and Heinz (1979), attentional selectivity can occur at several different stages of processing, depending on the demands made by the experimental task. To minimise demands on capacity, selection is made as early as possible.

- Johnston and Heinz (1979) and Johnston and Wilson (1980) presented findings consistent with their view that processing is more flexible than predicted by single-channel theories. For example, Johnston and Wilson showed that participants processed words presented to both ears, but only when they didn't know to which ear particular target words would be presented. These data suggest that non-target words are processed only to the extent necessary to perform a task.
- Many researchers question whether any single, general purpose, limited-capacity central processor can, in principle, account for the complexities of selective attention (Allport, 1980b; Neisser, 1976; Norman and Bobrow, 1975). Much of the relevant evidence comes from dual-task studies, which are more directly concerned with processing capacity, i.e. divided attention (see below).

FOCUSED VISUAL ATTENTION

According to Driver (1996):

> *The cluttered scenes of everyday life present more objects than we can respond towards simultaneously, and often more than we can perceive fully at any one time. Accordingly, mechanisms of attention are required to select objects of interest for further processing. In the case of vision, one such mechanism is provided by eye movements, which allow us to fixate particular regions so that they benefit from the greater acuity of the fovea.*

The fovea (see Figure 5.2) provides maximum acuity for visual stimuli. So, when we fixate on an object, maximum visual processing is carried out on the object whose image is projected on to the fovea. The resources given to the other parts of the visual field are 'attenuated' (Anderson, 1995b).

Posner *et al.* (1978, 1980) found that when people are told to fixate on one part of the visual field, it's still possible to attend to stimuli seven or so degrees either side of the fixation point. Also, attention can be shifted more quickly when a stimulus is presented in an 'expected' rather than an 'unexpected' location. Thus, visual attention isn't confined to the part of the visual field which is processed by the fovea, but can be shifted without corresponding changes in eye movements. Indeed, such shifts in attention frequently *precede* the corresponding eye movement (Anderson, 1995b). Posner (1980) calls this *covert attention*.

Posner likened covert attention to an *internal mental spotlight* that 'illuminates' any stimulus in the attended region, so that it's perceived in greater detail. It essentially duplicates the functions of eye movements *internally*, by allowing a particular region of space to be perceptually enhanced (Driver, 1996).

The fate of unattended visual stimuli

For Johnston and Dark (1986), stimuli beyond the focus of visual attention are subject to no, or virtually no, semantic processing. Any such processing is limited to mainly simple physical features. However, Driver (1996) disagrees. For example, when a picture is shown as the unattended stimulus on one trial, it slows the processing of an attended word with an identical or similar meaning on the next trial (*negative priming*). This slowing suggests that the meaning of the unattended stimulus must have been subject to some sort of processing (Tipper and Driver, 1988).

Attention and the visual search procedure

In the *visual search procedure*, participants are presented with an array of visual material in which a target item is embedded on some trials but absent on others, and the 'distractor' items can be varied so that they're similar to the target letter, or different from it. The participant's task is to decide if the target is present or absent.

```
X P T L A B N T

A R H N J I F R

E W R N P A Z X

A H Y 5 Y T E S

A N H C E S T I

G D T K D Y U I
```

Figure 13.6 A visual search array. The task is to find the number five among the letters

Neisser (1967) argued that when people perform a visual search task, they process many items simultaneously, without being fully 'aware' of the exact nature of the distractor items. Visual information processing might occur *pre-attentively*, depending on the nature of the stimuli (such as whether they have angular or curved features when the task is to detect a particular letter).

However, Treisman argues that attention must be focused on a stimulus before its features can be synthesised into a pattern. In one of Treisman and Gelade's (1980) experiments, participants were required to detect the presence of the letter T among an array of Is and Ys. Because the horizontal bar at the top of a T distinguishes it from an I and a Y, this could

Box 13.2 Real-world visual search: the low prevalence effect and inattentional blindness

- Unlike the visual search experiments described above, real-world visual search often involves 'whole objects' rather than individual letters.
- For example, professional searchers, such as the crews who look for survivors in storm wreckage, are looking for something they're unlikely to find – something that in the overwhelming majority of cases will not be present (the *low prevalence effect*); it can greatly reduce accuracy (Hout and Goldinger, 2013).
- Hout and Goldinger cite a 2010 Norwegian study which suggested that the rate of misses for radiologists who pore over mammogram films looking for breast tumours is 20–30 per cent – a lot higher, we'd presume, than your personal failure rate for, say, finding your keys!
- Miss rates were even greater in a study by Drew *et al.* (2013), in which 24 experienced radiologists were asked to scan lung X-rays to look for tumours. Unbeknown to the radiologists, a small picture of a gorilla had been inserted into one of the slides. A full 83 per cent of the doctors failed to notice the gorilla image because they were looking for something else (*inattentional blindness*).

be done fairly easily just by looking for the horizontal bar. Participants took around 800 milliseconds to detect the T, and the detection time wasn't affected by the size of the array (that is, the number of Is and Ys).

In another experiment, the T was embedded in an array of Is and Zs. Here, looking for a horizontal bar on its own doesn't aid detection, since the letter Z also has a horizontal bar on top of it. To detect a T, participants needed to look for the conjunction of a horizontal and vertical line. This took around 1200 milliseconds. Moreover, detection time was longer when the size of the array was increased. On the basis of these (and other) findings, Treisman (1988) proposed her *feature-integration theory*.

Attention switching

Many researchers are interested in the brain regions involved in attention (e.g. Muller and Maxwell, 1994; Halligan, 1995; Driver, 1996). People who've suffered a right-hemisphere stroke involving the parietal lobe may completely ignore stimuli occurring on the left side (see Chapter 4). For example, they may fail to eat food from the left side of their plate, and be unaware of their body on that side. The fascinating thing about this *unilateral visual neglect* (VN) is that these effects occur even though the pathways from the receptors to the central nervous system for the neglected information remain intact.

According to Ramachandran and Rogers-Ramachandran (2009), VN is, fundamentally, a disorder of attention. It's also a 'floridly exaggerated' version of the kind of neglect we all engage in to avoid sensory overload. Curiously, it is *only* seen with damage to the *right* hemisphere; this is believed to have more attentional resources and plays a major role in spatial vision, so that it can survey the entire visual scene. So, when the *left* hemisphere is damaged, the right can compensate.

Figure 13.7 Drawing of a parrot by a person with left-side neglect

Apart from the more 'obvious' signs of neglect (such as a man only shaving the right side of his face, or a woman applying make-up only to the right side of hers), when a patient is asked to draw a clock, s/he will begin by drawing the whole circle (This is an overlearned 'ballistic' response that doesn't require focused attention). But then the numbers 1–12 are packed into the right side of the circle (or only 1–6 are inserted). Also, even if, say, a plate of food is placed entirely into the patient's right visual field, only the food on the right half of the plate will be eaten. In all these examples, the patient is largely unaware of the neglect (Ramachandran and Rogers-Ramachandran, 2009).

According to Posner and Petersen (1990), the parietal lobe is responsible for disengaging attention from its present focus, and patients with damage to the *pulvinar nucleus* (part of the thalami) have difficulty in shifting attention to a new target (Rafal and Posner, 1987).

Interestingly, among 4- to 10-year-old children, those who took less time to switch attention in a specially devised computer game were more likely to show awareness of traffic as they approached a busy road (Dunbar *et al.*, 1999).

How does it happen?

Voluntary and involuntary attention

Sometimes, our attention is 'grabbed' beyond our control (*involuntary attentional capture* (IAC)). For example, when we respond to an extremely loud noise or bright light (or an extremely attractive or unusual-looking person), we do so *involuntarily*. An experimental example involves presentation of a display containing three squares: when one of the squares briefly flashes (the cue) attention rapidly orients to the flash (within 1/10 of a second). This is an *automatic process*: we cannot stop our attention from moving to the flash even if we try (Tipper, 2005). This contrasts with our (usual) ability to consciously and deliberately focus on some particular aspect of the environment (*voluntary attentional vigilance* (VAV)).

A famous demonstration of IAC is the *Stroop effect*.

How do we manage to focus on anything?

According to Beaman (2006), the existence of these two different types of attentional effects (IAC and VAV) highlight the central difficulty of *selection*.

According to one view, the act of concentration induces the brain to become blinkered to irrelevant distractions, so that it won't process them at all; the opposite view claims that we perceive everything, but the brain prioritises what's important. Lavie (1997) found evidence showing that both views are mistaken: concentrating in itself cannot screen out distractions (as in IAC) and there's an upper limit to what our eyes can take in at any one time.

The results from Forster and Lavie's experiment (see Research Update 13.1) suggest that a visually more demanding task 'loads' the brain's attention: we become increasingly blind to distractions and our performance improves (reaction times get faster and error rate drops). In other words, the *harder you have to concentrate, the less likely you are to be distracted*. This can be thought of as a way of tricking the brain into paying attention by tapping into the way it focuses attention. Loading the brain to make it blind to distractions has been replicated many times and the concept has been widely accepted (Fisher, 2007).

Change blindness

Ask Yourself

- How quickly can you spot the difference between the two pictures in Figure 13.8?

Research Update 13.1

Measuring distractability

- Forster and Lavie (2007) have devised a test which, for the first time, makes it possible to obtain an objective measure of an individual's ability to concentrate in the face of a visual distraction.
- It takes the form of a simple computer game, in which participants are asked to concentrate on letters flashing up in a particular area on the screen, and to press one key if they see an N and another key if they see an X. Outside this area, other letters pop up as distractions. It measures how much these distractions increase the time taken to press the correct key and the number of mistakes people make. At the end of the test, participants are given an 'index of distractability', a measure of their powers of concentration.
- Forster and Lavie have found that while distractions slowed everyone's reaction time, some people slowed by almost twice as much as others. Some people didn't even notice they'd made any mistakes.
- Interestingly, during visually more intensive tasks (when the area of the screen to focus on is more cluttered with letters), most people are able to *ignore* the distractions: individual differences found on the easier tasks actually disappear.

Figure 13.8

In the lower picture, one of the engines is missing! Despite this being right in the middle of the picture, occupying a large space, it's commonly missed. According to Frith (2007), you quickly perceive the gist of the scene: *a military transport plane on a runway*. But you don't actually have all the details in your mind and you might need to have your attention deliberately drawn to it.

In a *change blindness* demonstration in the laboratory, a blank grey screen is displayed between each scene: as the screen goes from being multicoloured to grey – and back again – there's a big visual change *everywhere*, in every region of the screen. The brain receives no signal to indicate where the important change is happening.

DIVIDED ATTENTION

Ask Yourself

- What are you doing now, apart from reading this sentence?
- What other examples can you give of being able to do more than one thing at a time?
- How can you explain this ability?

Some demonstrations of dual-task performance

Allport *et al.* (1972) showed that skilled pianists were able to read music successfully while shadowing speech. Later, Shaffer (1975) reported the case of an

Box 13.3 Attention and evolution

- The basic finding of hundreds of *task-switching* studies is that humans are much slower and make more errors on *switch trials* (e.g. responding to digits based on whether they're odd/even, than according to whether they're lower/higher than 6) than on *repeat trials* (odd/even followed by odd/even, or lower/higher than 6 followed by lower/higher than 6). The *performance cost* caused by switching is calculated by subtracting the average time needed to do the tasks on the switch trials from the average on repeat trials.
- But surprisingly, compared with people, monkeys don't show switch costs under the same conditions (Stoet and Snyder, 2003). If (as most Psychologists do) switch costs are interpreted as reflecting the limited capacity of our mental flexibility, then we'd expect monkeys to have *larger* switch costs. After ruling out the role of the extensive training monkeys need to perform switch tasks, Stoet explains this monkey superiority in terms of the *evolutionary advantage of switch costs*.
- During the course of evolution, humans acquired the capacity to concentrate on a single task for a long time; this appears to be uniquely human. In order to achieve this, humans must be capable of resisting all external distractions. The human brain might be optimised to concentrate on tasks and possess special mechanisms that prevent distraction and jumping too quickly to another task; switch costs might reflect this resistance. If human social groups shared responsibility for food production and protection against predators, individuals could focus on producing high-quality artefacts (tools, weapons, etc.) (Stoet and Snyder, 2007).
- Conversely, IAC (see text above) evolved to protect us in hostile environments. For example, if the sudden movement out the corner of my eye is a snake about to strike, it's critical that I give this my full attention and take appropriate action (Tipper, 2005).

expert typist who could type accurately from sight while shadowing speech. But perhaps the most striking example of dual-task performance comes from Spelke *et al.* (1976), who had two students spend five hours a week training at performing two tasks simultaneously.

Initially, the students were required to read short stories while writing down dictated words. At first they found this difficult, and both their comprehension and writing suffered. But after six weeks of training, they could read as quickly, and comprehend as much of what they read, when reading with dictation as when reading without it. Interestingly, though, they could remember very little of what they'd written down, even though thousands of words had been dictated to them over the course of the experiment.

At this point, the task was altered and the students had to write down the category a word belonged to (requiring more processing of the words), while simultaneously reading the short stories. Although the task was again difficult initially, they eventually performed it without any reduction in their comprehension of the stories.

Theories of divided attention

As we noted earlier, models of selective attention assume the existence of a limited-capacity filter capable of dealing with one information channel at a time. As Hampson and Morris (1996) have observed, these theories:

> *... imply a series of stages of processing, starting with superficial, physical analysis, and working 'upwards' towards the 'higher' cognitive analyses for meaning.*

In Hampson and Morris's view, these processes are better thought of as an integrated mechanism, with the high and low levels interacting and combining in the recognition of stimuli. Accordingly, it's better to look at the system's overall processing.

Limited-capacity theories

Kahneman's theory

According to Kahneman (1973), humans have a limited amount of processing capacity, and whether or not tasks can be performed successfully depends on how much demand they make on the limited-capacity processor. Some tasks require little processing capacity, leaving plenty available for performing another task simultaneously. Others require much more, leaving little 'spare'.

The process of determining how much capacity is available ('effort') is related to the allocation of that capacity. How much capacity a task requires depends on things like its difficulty and a person's experience of it. How capacity is allocated depends on *enduring dispositions*, *momentary intentions* and the *evaluation of the attentional demands* (see Figure 13.6). The *central processor* is responsible for the allocation policy, and constantly evaluates the level of demand. When demand is too high, the central processor must decide how available attention should be allocated.

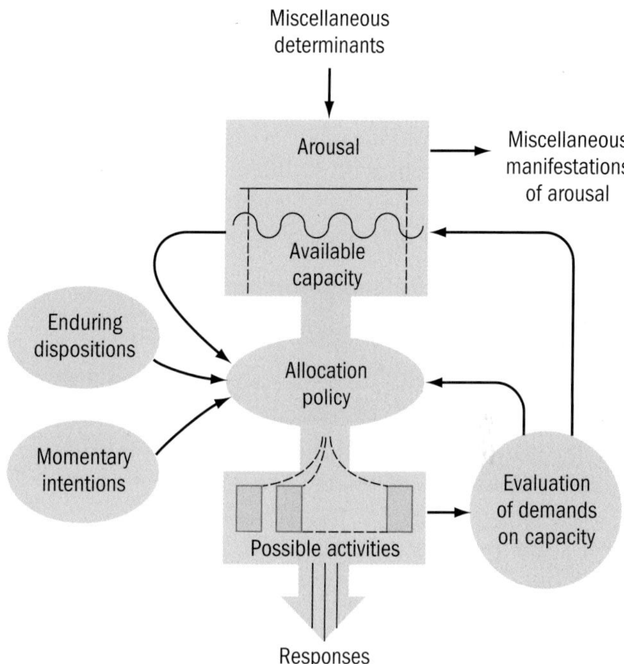

Figure 13.9 Kahneman's theory of attention. Enduring dispositions are the rules for allocating capacity which are outside voluntary control. These include allocating capacity to novel stimuli and hearing one's own name used in a different conversation. Momentary intentions are voluntary shifts in attention such as listening to a message in a dichotic listening task. Evaluation of demands on capacity include rules for overload on the system, such as deciding to complete one task rather than failing to complete two

Kahneman sees arousal as playing an important part in determining how much capacity is available. Generally, more attentional resources are available when we're aroused and alert than when we're tired and lethargic. Attention can be divided between tasks provided the total available capacity isn't exceeded. This explains the findings of the dichotic listening tasks discussed earlier: shadowing requires almost all of the capacity available, leaving the non-shadowed message insufficient capacity. Kahneman's theory also predicts that as skill at carrying out a task increases, so less capacity is needed for it and more becomes available for other tasks. Thus, when people are trained at shadowing, they become able to shadow and to attend to the non-shadowed message (Underwood, 1974).

Evaluation of Kahneman's theory

- Kahneman's theory portrays attention as a much more flexible and dynamic system than do the models of focused attention. However, it doesn't address the issue of how decisions to channel attention are made. The difficulty in defining the general limits of capacity has led some researchers to suggest that the concept of a limited capacity should be abandoned (Hampson and Morris, 1996).
- A second limited-capacity theory is Norman and Bobrow's (1975) *central capacity interference theory* (CCIT). Its central feature is the distinction between *resource-limited* and *data-limited* processes.
- Broadly consistent with Kahneman's theory is the concept of 'cognitive band width' (Mullainathan and Shafir, 2014), as described in Box 13.4.

Box 13.4 Cognitive 'bandwidth': cognitive capacity and executive control (Mullainathan and Shafir, 2014)

According to Mullainathan and Shafir, 'bandwidth' refers to two broad, related components of mental function:

- *cognitive capacity:* the psychological mechanisms that underlie our ability to solve problems, retain information, engage in logical reasoning, etc. A specific example is *fluid intelligence*, the ability to think and reason abstractly and solve novel problems (see Chapter 41).
- *executive control:* the mechanism that underlies our ability to manage our cognitive activities, including *attention,* planning, and initiating and inhibiting actions.

These are both affected by *scarcity*: this can mean, literally, limited resources (such as poverty), more abstract lack (such as time), more temporary states (such as sleep deprivation), loneliness, inadequate diet and exercise, or any other unmet need that preoccupies us and captures our attention, thus impeding our ability to focus on other things. A fixation on scarcity taxes our cognitive capacity and executive control, which in turn diminishes (fluid) intelligence and impulse control, among other things.

Multi-channel theories

Supporters of limited-capacity models defend their approach by pointing out that the attentional system breaks down as more and more is demanded of it. Also, if data from divided-attention studies are considered carefully it's not true that two tasks can be performed together with no disruption at all (Broadbent, 1982). Nevertheless, several researchers have rejected the concept of a general-purpose, limited-capacity processor completely. For Allport (1980b, 1989, 1993), the concept of attention is often used synonymously with 'consciousness', with no specification of how it operates. This has done little to increase our understanding of the very problems it's meant to explain.

Modules and multiple resources

According to Allport, it's difficult to see how the neurology of the brain could produce a system of processing capacity that was completely open to any of the tasks that might be presented to it (Hampson and Morris, 1996). It's much more profitable to view the data in terms of tasks competing for the *same* specialised processing mechanisms or *modules*, each of which has a limited capacity but none of which is uniquely 'central'.

When two tasks are highly similar, they compete for the same modules, and this leads to performance impairments. However, because dissimilar tasks use different modules, both can be performed simultaneously. Certainly, the findings of dual-task studies (e.g. Allport *et al.*, 1972) are consistent with the idea of different processing mechanisms handling the requirements of different tasks.

However, this approach is also *non-falsifiable*, since any pattern of data can be explained by proposing the existence of a particular pattern of modules (Navon, 1984). If multiple resources do operate in parallel, they must do so in a highly integrated way, since our behaviour is typically coherent (Eysenck and Keane, 1995).

Attempts at synthesising capacity and module accounts

According to Eysenck (1982, 1984, 1997a) and Baddeley (1986), a much better way of accommodating the data from divided-attention studies is to see capacity and module accounts as being *complementary* rather than competitive. *Synthesis models* propose the existence of a modality-free central capacity processor, which is involved in the coordination and control of behaviour, and specific processing systems. In Baddeley's (1986) *working memory* (WM) *model*, for example, there are two independently operating and specific systems, an *articulatory/phonological loop* and a *visuo-spatial scratch pad*. These systems can explain why overt repetition of an overlearned sequence of digits doesn't interfere with verbal reasoning, since the former uses an articulatory loop and the latter a central processor (see Chapter 17).

Reference to the WM model indicates that memory and attention are intimately related, even though they're traditionally been studied by separate groups of researchers (Tipper, 2005). Tipper's own research shows that certain attention processes (such as inhibition and excitation), rather than being transient states that dissipate rapidly, may, under some circumstances, leave a trace in memory. When retrieval cues are strong enough, such attentional states might be reactivated and help with our current processing (as when we're looking for objects/people that are important to us).

Ask Yourself

- Thinking of a skill you possess (such as driving a car or playing a musical instrument), how did demands on your attention and concentration change during the course of acquiring it?
- Can you now do things at the same time as performing this skill that you couldn't have done while learning it?

Figure 13.10 At first, learning to drive a car, like other psychomotor skills, requires focused attention. The experienced driver, however, displays automaticity

Automatic versus controlled processing

As we've seen, both laboratory evidence and everyday experience indicate that we can learn to perform two tasks simultaneously and highly efficiently. For some researchers, this is because many processes become *automatic*, that is, they make no attentional demands, if they're used/practised often enough. Two important theoretical contributions are those of Schneider and Shiffrin (1977) and Norman and Shallice (1986).

Schneider and Shiffrin's automaticity model

Schneider and Shiffrin (Schneider and Shiffrin, 1977; Shiffrin and Schneider, 1977) distinguish between controlled and automatic attentional processing as follows:

- *controlled processing* makes heavy demands on attentional resources, is slow, capacity-limited, and involves consciously directing attention towards a task
- *automatic processing* makes no demands on attentional resources, is fast, unaffected by capacity limitations, unavoidable and difficult to modify (it always occurs in the presence of an appropriate stimulus), and isn't subject to conscious awareness.

The results of several studies (e.g. Schneider and Fisk, 1982) are consistent with Schneider and Shiffrin's view. If people are given practice at a task, they can perform it quickly and accurately, but their performance is resistant to change. An example of apparent automaticity in real life occurs when we learn to drive a car. At first, focused attention is required for each component of driving, and any distraction can disrupt performance. Once we've learned to drive, and as we become more experienced, our ability to attend simultaneously to other things increases.

Logan (1988) suggests that automaticity develops through practice, because automatic responses involve an almost effortless retrieval of an appropriate and well-learned response from memory. This doesn't involve conscious memory, because no thought processes intervene between the presentation of a stimulus and the production of an appropriate response. In Logan's view, then, automaticity occurs when stored information about the sequence of responses necessary to perform a task can be accessed and retrieved rapidly.

An evaluation of Schneider and Shiffrin's model

Despite its intuitive appeal, it's unclear whether automaticity results from a speeding up of the processes involved in a task, or a change in the nature of the processes themselves. Also, the view that automatic processing makes no demands on attention has been challenged by findings indicating that allegedly automatic tasks *do* influence the performance of simultaneously performed tasks (e.g. Hampson, 1989). Additional problems occur with the Stroop effect (see www.tinyurl.com/3gtk4).

Norman and Shallice's SAS model

To overcome what Eysenck (1993) calls the 'unavoidability criterion', Norman and Shallice (1986) proposed that processing involves two separate control systems: *contention scheduling* and the *supervisory attentional system* (SAS). Some behaviours involve fully automatic processing, which occurs with little conscious awareness of the processes involved, and is controlled by *schemas* (organised plans for behaviour; see Chapter 21).

However, such processes are capable of disrupting behaviour, and so contention scheduling occurs as a way of resolving conflicts among schemas. This produces *partially automatic processing*, which generally involves more conscious awareness than fully automatic processing, but doesn't require deliberate direction or conscious control. *Deliberate control* involves the SAS and occurs in decision-making and trouble-shooting, allowing flexible responding to occur in novel situations. Baddeley (1997) claims that the SAS is like the operation of free will, while contention scheduling leaves no place for free will (see Chapter 49).

An evaluation of Norman and Shallice's model

According to Eysenck and Keane (1995), Norman and Shallice's model is superior to Schneider and Shiffrin's because it provides a more natural explanation for the fact that some processes are fully automatic, whereas others are only partially automatic.

Their SAS model isn't worked out in the same degree of detail, nor empirically tested as extensively as Schneider and Shiffrin's automaticity model. But it provides a very useful basis for conceptualising the central executive of the WM model (Baddeley, 1997; see Chapter 17).

Action slips

Ask Yourself

- Have you ever done something you didn't intend to do or, conversely, failed to do something you did intend to do?
- How might you explain these 'lapses' in terms of attentional processes?

Action slips have been defined as the performance of unintended actions, or actions which deviate from the actor's intentions, and have been extensively researched by Reason (1979, 1992). Reason originally asked 36 participants to keep a diary record of the action slips

Critical Discussion 13.1

Multitasking: can *anyone* really do several things at once?

According to Marois (cited in Motluk, 2007), there are three 'sticking points 'in our ability to multitask:

1. Simply identifying what we're looking at can take a few tenths of a second, during which time we're unable to see and recognise a second item (the *attentional blink*). Experiments have shown that if you're looking out for a particular event and a second event occurs unexpectedly within this few tenths-of-a second 'window', it may register in your visual cortex but you'll be unable to act on it.
2. It's estimated that we can keep track of about four items at a time (fewer if they're complex). This capacity shortage can help explain *change blindness* (see text above).
3. Choosing which stimulus to respond to also takes some tenths of a second (*response selection bottleneck*).

- Apparently simultaneous awareness and processing of information actually takes place in '3-second windows': in these 3-second increments, the brain takes in all the data about the environment *as a block* and subsequent events are then processed in the next window. Switching tasks also takes time (see text above).
- Strayer and Watson (2012) believe that effective multitasking is a myth, as is the idea that members of the 'mutitasking generation', who grew up with video games, smart phones and e-readers, can somehow concentrate on several things at once.
- Strayer and Watson have been researching how we balance driving and talking on our mobiles. Performance deteriorates drastically when we attempt to focus on more than one task at a time: even simple behaviours such as walking and chewing gum can be impaired with sufficient cognitive load.
- Mobile phone drivers' reactions are slower, they have difficulty staying in their lane and maintaining appropriate following distance, and are more likely to go over red lights and miss other important details in the driving environment. The crash risk for those talking on a mobile or texting often exceeds the level observed with drivers at the legal limit of alcohol. Lapses in attention essentially render the driver partially blind to significant details directly in their gaze ('*attention blindness*'; see text above).
- Using EEGs, Strayer and Watson compared the brain signals associated with the detection of the brake lights on the vehicle in front (in a simulator). A particularly interesting component of these brain waves, the P300, is sensitive to how much attention a person is paying to a particular stimulus. The amplitude of P300 increases as more attention is allocated to a task. When drivers talk on their mobile, the P300 amplitude reduced by 50 per cent. Both hand-held and hands-free equipment causes equivalent interference, which shows that this is a form of *cognitive* distraction – as opposed to, say, a visual distraction that draws the driver's eye from the rod or manual distraction. These findings support the current campaign in the UK to ban hands-free.
- But what about the 2.5 per cent of the 700 participants that Strayer and Watson have identified as 'supertaskers', whose performance doesn't deteriorate when completing two simultaneous tasks? They showed *less* brain activity at the more difficult levels of the multitasking test: for most people, a tougher challenge recruits more brain resources, but supertaskers showed little/no such changes. The most striking differences were in three frontal cortex areas: the *frontopolar PFC*, *dorsolateral PFC*, and the *anterior cingulate cortex*.

they made over a four-week period; they recorded 433 action slips between them. Reason was able to place 94 per cent of these into one of five categories.

Box 13.5 Reason's five categories of action slips

Storage failures (40 per cent): repeating an action that's already been completed (e.g. pouring a second kettle of boiling water into a teapot of freshly made tea without any recognition of having made the tea already).
Test failures (20 per cent): forgetting the goal of a particular sequence of actions and switching to a different goal (e.g. intending to turn on the radio, but walking past it and picking up the telephone instead). These occur, presumably, because a planned sequence of actions isn't monitored sufficiently at some crucial point in the sequence.
Sub-routine failures (18 per cent): either omitting or re-ordering the stages in a sequence of behaviour (e.g. making a pot of tea, but failing to put any tea bags in).
Discrimination failures (11 per cent): failing to discriminate between two objects involved in different actions (e.g. mistaking toothpaste for shaving cream).
Programme assembly failures (5 per cent): incorrectly combining actions (e.g. unwrapping a sweet, putting the paper in your mouth and throwing the sweet in the waste-bin).
(Source: based on Reason, 1992; Eysenck, 1997b)

Reason and Mycielska (1982) believe that a thorough understanding of the nature of action slips is necessary to avoid potential disaster occurring in the real world. Eysenck (1995) maintains that action slips would be eliminated if we were to use *closed-loop control* for all behaviours, but this would be a waste of valuable attentional resources! The frequency of action slips reported by Reason's (1979) participants (an average of about one per day) suggests that people alternate between closed-loop and *open-loop control* as the circumstances dictate. For Eysenck (1995):

> *The very occasional action slip is a price which is generally worth paying in order to free the attentional system from the task of constant monitoring of our habitual actions.*

As Reason (1984) puts it, 'Absent-minded errors demonstrate misapplied competence rather than incompetence'.

CONCLUSIONS

'Attention' is really an umbrella term for a number of processes and abilities. These include the ability to focus attention on a single aspect of the environment or activity (voluntary attentional vigilance) at one extreme, and automatic, uncontrollable responses to unusual or unexpected events (involuntary attentional capture) at the other. Both may have evolved to aid the survival of the human species.

While the selective nature of attention seems almost inevitable, given the sheer quantity of sensory data reaching the sense organs, it's also an advantage being able to divide one's attention between two different tasks, although how this is achieved hasn't yet been satisfactorily explained. Whether or not we can truly multitask is a matter of ongoing debate.

The idea that many processes become automatic and make no demands on attention has some support, and helps explain why we sometimes perform behaviours we didn't intend. Action slips involve behaviours that are highly practised, and are the price we pay for not having to continuously monitor our actions.

Chapter Summary

- According to Broadbent, who was trying to account for Cherry's **cocktail party phenomenon**, humans must **selectively attend** to some information and 'tune out' the rest.
- Using **binaural listening**, Cherry identified several physical differences affecting selective attention to one of two messages. Using **dichotic listening**, in which participants had to **shadow** one of the messages, participants remembered little, if anything, of the non-shadowed message, whose meaning was completely lost.
- Three **single-channel models** share the belief in a 'bottleneck' or **filter** which allows some information to be passed on for further processing, either discarding the rest or processing it only to a limited degree. They differ mainly in terms of how early or late the filtering takes place.
- Broadbent's **early selection filter theory** accounts for Cherry's findings and his own **split-span** data. But people's ability to switch attention to the non-attended ear when their name is spoken, together with other research findings relating to the processing of **meaning**, are inconsistent with Broadbent's account.
- According to Treisman's **attenuation model**, competing information is analysed for its physical properties, and for sounds, syllable patterns, grammatical structures and meaning. The selective filter 'turns down' the non-shadowed message.
- The Deutsch–Norman **late-selection filter theory/ pertinence model** sees selection as occurring only after all inputs have been analysed at a high level. The filter is nearer the **response end** of the processing system.
- Mechanisms involved in **focused visual attention** include eye movements that allow us to fixate specific regions of the visual field. But visual attention isn't confined to the part of the visual field processed by the fovea, as demonstrated by **covert attention**. This is like an **internal mental spotlight**.
- A way of trying to explain **attention switching** by reference to the distinction between **voluntary attentional vigilance (VAV) and involuntary attentional capture (IAC)**.
- Both VAV and IAC seem to have given our human ancestors an **evolutionary advantage**.
- Forster and Lavie's research shows that visually more demanding tasks '**load**' the brain, tricking it into paying attention.
- Demonstrations of **change blindness** show how difficult it is to focus on specific aspects of the environment.
- Researchers interested in **divided attention** typically measure **dual-task performance**.
- Apparent **multitasking** is limited by the **attention blink** and **response selection bottleneck.** Car accidents involving mobile phone users illustrate the potential hazards of divided attention.
- According to Kahneman, humans have only a **limited processing capacity**. Different tasks require different amounts of processing capacity, leaving more or less available for performing other tasks. The **central processor** controls the allocation policy and constantly evaluates demand level.
- Norman and Bobrow's **central capacity interference theory** (CCIT) distinguishes between **resource-limited** and **data-limited performance**.
- Several researchers argue that the most useful way of interpreting the data is in terms of tasks competing for the same **modules**, each of which has a limited capacity but none of which is uniquely 'central'.
- **Synthesis models** propose the existence of a modality-free central capacity processor, plus specific independent processing systems, such as Baddeley's **working memory** (WM) **model**.
- Schneider and Shiffrin distinguish between **controlled** and **automatic processing**. The **'Stroop effect'** shows that well-learned, automatic skills (such as reading) can interfere with other tasks (such as naming the colour of a written word).
- **Contention scheduling** is used to resolve conflicts among **schemas**, which control **fully automatic processing** and produces **partially automatic processing**. The **supervisory attentional system** (SAS) is involved in deliberate control, which allows flexible responses in novel situations.
- The most common types of **action slips** are **storage failures**. Other categories include **test, sub-routine, discrimination** and **programme assembly failures**.
- Action slips reflect an over-reliance on **open-loop control** when **closed-loop control** (focused attention) is needed.

Links with Other Topics/Chapters

Chapters 7 and 9 ⟶ The concept of attention has been defined in more *biological/ physiological* ways, as referring to *arousal level*, *vigilance* and *alertness* (consciousness)

Chapters 1, 2, 3 and 20 ⟶ It also features prominently in the cognitive revolution, in which *information processing* and the *computer analogy* are central

Chapter 17 ⟶ The dependent variable (DV) in many experimental studies of both selective and divided attention is operationalised in terms of *recall* and other forms of *remembering*

Chapter 17 ⟶ Baddeley and Hitch's *working memory* (WM) model (of *short-term memory*) is essentially a synthesis model of divided attention. Norman and Shallice's SAS provides a useful basis for conceptualising the *central executive*

Chapter 21 ⟶ Sellen and Norman's (1992) schema theory of action slips stems from Bartlett's research into *reconstructive memory* and the more general *schema theory* of everyday memory

Chapter 5 ⟶ Explanations of focused visual attention go beyond what's known about the sensitivity of the *fovea*

Chapter 4 ⟶ A person who suffers damage to the right *parietal lobe* will suffer left-sided unilateral visual neglect

Chapter 49 ⟶ Controlled processing and deliberate control (which involves the supervisory attentional system/ SAS) can be seen in terms of *free will*, while automatic processing and contention scheduling leave no room for free will

Chapter 41 ⟶ Fluid intelligence (a form of 'cognitive capacity') is measured by Raven's Progressive Matrices test

Recommended Reading

Braisby, N., Gellatly, A. (eds) (2005) *Cognitive Psychology.* Oxford: Oxford University Press in association with the Open University. Chapter 2.

Eysenck, M.W., Keane, M.T. (2000) *Cognitive Psychology: A Student's Handbook* (4th edn). Hove: Psychology Press. Chapter 5.

Groome, D., Dewart, H., Esgate, A., Gurney, K., Kemp, R., Towell, N. (1999) *An Introduction to Cognitive Psychology: Processes and Disorders.* Hove: Psychology Press. Chapter 2. Also relevant to Chapter 15.

Solso, R.L. (1995) *Cognitive Psychology* (4th edn). Boston: Allyn & Bacon. Also relevant to Chapter 15.

Useful Websites

www.diku.dk/hjemmesider/ansatte/panic/eyegaze/node15.html (Visual Selective Attention)

www.cse.psu.edu/~rcollins/CSE597E/papers/treismanFeatIntegration.pdf (Treisman's feature integration theory)

http://psych.princeton.edu/psychology/research/treisman/index.php (Treisman's research at Princeton.)

www.bioscience.org/2000/v5/d/alain/alain.pdf (Alain, C. & Arnott, S.R. (2000) Selectively Attending to Auditory Objects. *Frontiers in Bioscience, 5,* d202-12)

Change blindness demonstrations

www.theinvisiblegorilla.com/videos.html (Simons and Chabris' famous gorilla experiment (1999) plus several others.)

CHAPTER 14

PATTERN RECOGNITION

Theories of pattern recognition (PR)

Face recognition

INTRODUCTION and OVERVIEW

Pattern recognition is the process by which we assign meaning to visual input by identifying the objects in the visual field (Eysenck, 1993). Although our ability to recognise, identify and categorise objects seems effortless, it actually comprises several remarkably complex achievements. While we're usually aware only of structured, coherent objects:

> *Our visual systems have to 'decide' which edges, surfaces, corners and so on go together to form units or wholes. (Roth, 1995)*

As Roth says, what theories of pattern recognition must do is explain the complexity of a process which 'is so ingrained in our experience that we rarely even notice that we do it' (Houston *et al.*, 1991). A way of illustrating this challenge is to consider the ease with which we're able to recognise the letter 'T', whether it's printed on paper, handwritten or spoken.

TTTTTTTT7TTTTTTTTTTTTTTTTT

Figure 14.1

A major contribution to our understanding of this process comes in the form of the Gestalt laws of perception, which are discussed in Chapter 15. Pattern (or object) recognition can be regarded as the central problem of perception and, indeed, the terms are almost synonymous. To this extent, all the theories of perception discussed in Chapter 15 can be thought of as trying to account for pattern recognition (PR).

However, the theories discussed here are usually referred to as theories of PR (rather than perceptual theories). Face recognition is a special case of PR.

THEORIES OF PATTERN RECOGNITION (PR)

Template-matching hypothesis

According to the *template-matching hypothesis* (TMH), incoming sensory information is matched against miniature copies (or *templates*), stored in long-term memory, of previously presented patterns or objects. Template matching is used by computerised cash registers, which identify a product and its cost by matching a bar code with some stored representation of that code. Every product has a unique bar code.

Figure 14.2 The bar codes on the goods we buy identify them. When the bar code is read by a computerised cash register (scanned), the computer supplies the price, which is then entered on the cash register tape. The code is read by template-matching on the basis of the positions, widths and spacing of the lines

An evaluation of TMH

Given the complexity of the environment, we'd need an incredibly large number of templates, each corresponding to a specific visual input. Even if we were able to use a wheelbarrow to carry around the cerebrum needed for this, the time needed to search for a specific template would be inordinately long, and we'd never recognise unfamiliar patterns (Solso, 1995).

Ask Yourself

- How would you describe (a) a cup, (b) a torch, (c) a penguin?
- What kinds of basic components could they be broken down into?

Biederman's geon theory

Biederman's (1987) *geon theory* of PR ('geon' stands for 'geometrical icon'), or *recognition-by-components model*, is intended to overcome TMH's limitations. Biederman's starting point is the everyday observation that if we're asked to describe an object, familiar or unfamiliar, we tend to use the same basic strategy. We almost certainly divide it into parts or components (*parsing/segmentation*), comprising various three-dimensional-shape concepts (*volumetric concepts* or *geons*), such as 'block', 'cylinder', 'funnel' and 'wedge'.

The regions of the object used to divide it up are probably the regions of greatest *concavity* (where one part makes a sharp angle with another part). According to geon theory, a very large range of different objects can be described by combining geons in various ways. Geons (simple geometric 'primitives') can be combined to produce more complex ones.

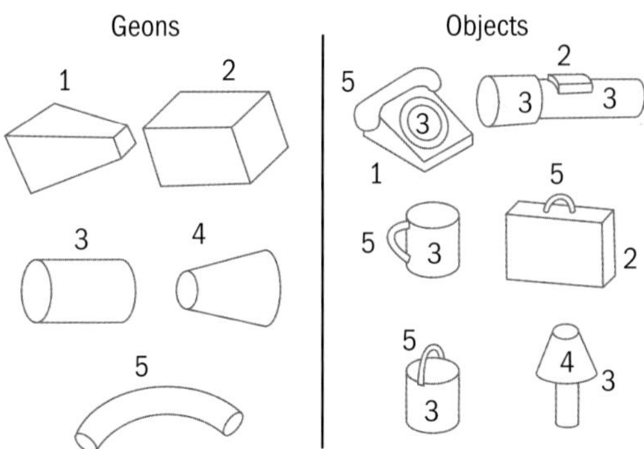

Figure 14.3 Biederman's geons (left) and some of the objects they can combine to make (right)

Component- or geon-based information extracted from the visual object is matched in parallel against stored representations of 36 geons that make up the basic set. The identification of any visual object is determined by whichever stored representation provides the best fit. But for a complete object to be recognised, there must also be a store of *complete* object descriptions, in which both the characteristic geon set and *relationships* among it are specified (Roth, 1995).

Tests of geon theory

According to Roth (1995), Biederman's theory was designed to:

- provide an intuitively plausible account of how we recognise objects in terms of their obvious components
- explain the fact that this recognition is both rapid and accurate, despite variations in angle of viewing and the 'degraded' information available (such as poor lighting, one object obscuring another, and so on).

One general prediction is that since an appropriate arrangement of geons provides a very powerful cue for object recognition, this recognition will occur even when an object's full complement of geons is absent.

A more stringent test is participants' ability to identify degraded versions of objects, in which the normal contours are *disrupted*. In a second experiment (using the same basic procedure as the first), Biederman presented stimulus objects like those shown in Figure 14.4.

These stimuli were presented for 100, 200 or 750 m/sec, with 25, 45 or 65 per cent of their contours removed. Once again, results supported the theory.

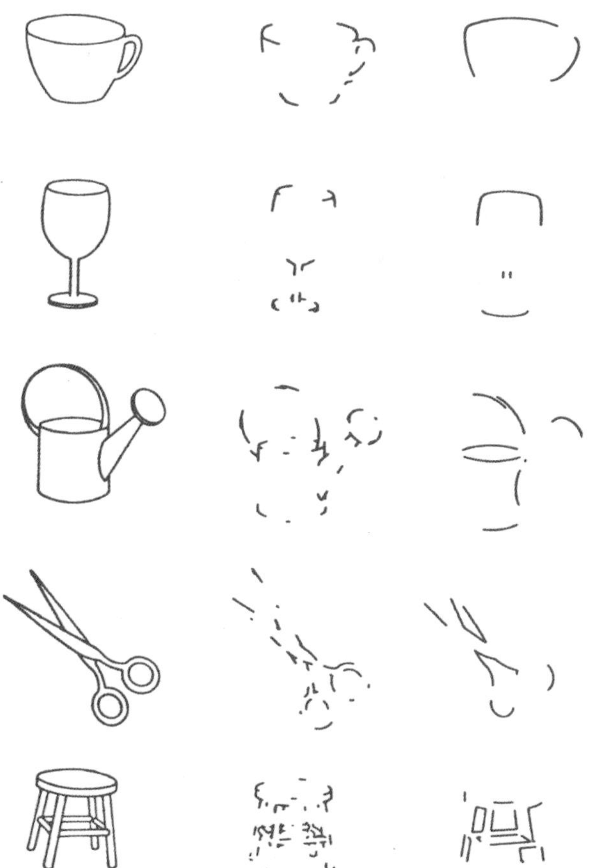

Figure 14.4 The middle column shows degraded but 'recognisable' versions; the right-hand column shows 'non-recognisable' versions

Key Study 14.1

Geons can be so degrading (Biederman, 1987)

- Biederman produced line drawings of 36 common objects, differing in complexity (the number of basic geon components needed to draw them ranged from two to nine).
- For each drawing, there were 'partial' versions (one or more geons were missing), and each stimulus was presented for 100 m/sec via a tachistoscope. Participants had to name the object aloud as quickly as possible.
- Error rates for 'partial' objects were extremely low, with 90 per cent accuracy even for complex objects with two-thirds of their components missing.
- So, even the simplest line drawings can be readily and correctly identified, provided the relevant geons are present. These findings are consistent with geon theory.
- Also, response times were almost as fast for partial as for complete objects, although complex complete objects were identified slightly more quickly than simple ones. This, too, is consistent with the theory: if an object's geons are simultaneously matched with stored geon descriptions, then the greater the number of such geons available, the faster the critical level needed for a 'match' will be reached.

An evaluation of geon theory

Roth (1995) believes that geons are intuitively appealing, and that they also offer a relatively flexible and comprehensive system for describing objects. Geons include a range of different shapes that can be applied not only to artefacts such as chairs, tables and houses, but also to mammals and other animals.

Although the theory makes clear predictions that can be experimentally tested, identification of the 36 geons and structural relationships is based more on 'hunch' than empirical evidence. There have been no tests to determine whether it's *these* geons that are used in object recognition, rather than other components.

Feature-detection theories

Feature-detection theories (FDTs) represent the most influential approach to PR, maintaining that every stimulus can be thought of as a configuration of elementary features. The letters of the alphabet, for example, are composed of combinations of 12 basic features (such as vertical lines, horizontal lines and closed curves) (Gibson *et al.*, 1968).

In *visual scanning* (or search) *tasks*, participants search lists of letters as quickly as possible to find a randomly placed target letter (see Chapter 13). Since finding a target letter entails detecting its elementary features, the task should be more difficult when the target and non-target letters have more features in common. This is exactly what researchers (e.g. Rabbitt, 1967) have found. Additional support comes from studies of eye movements and fixation. Presumably, the more a feature in a pattern is looked at, the more information is being extracted from it. The perception of features within complex patterns depends on higher cognitive processes (such as attention and purpose; see Chapter 13), as well as the nature of the physical stimuli being looked at.

It's also well established that the visual systems of some vertebrates contain both *peripheral* (retinal) and *central* (cortical) cells that respond only to particular features of visual stimuli. In their pioneering research, Hubel and Wiesel (1968) identified three kinds of cortical cell ('simple', 'complex' and 'hypercomplex', referring to the types of stimuli the cells respond to, see Box 5.9, p. 82).

More recently, it's been claimed that there are *face-specific cells* in the monkey's infero–temporal cortex (Ono *et al.*, 1993). In humans, Perrett (cited in Messer, 1995) has identified cells that respond to specific aspects of a face or to a set of features. There may also be cells that respond to many different views of a face, 'summing' inputs from a variety of sources. Going even further, there may be individual cells that respond exclusively to particular individuals (*gnostic neurons* or *'grandmother cells'*).

An evaluation of FDTs

Whether such cells constitute the feature detectors proposed by FDTs is unclear. These neurological detectors may be a necessary pre-condition for higher-level (or cognitive) pattern task analysis. However, FDTs typically assume a *serial* form of processing, with feature extraction being followed by feature combination, which itself is then followed by PR (Eysenck, 1993). For example, Hubel and Wiesel saw the sequence of simple, complex and hypercomplex cells representing a serial flow of information, whereby only particular information is processed at any one time before being passed on to the next level upwards, and so on.

The alternative and widely held view is that considerable *parallel* processing takes place in the visual cortex, and that the relationship between different kinds of cortical cell is more complex than originally believed. An early example of a non-serial processing computer program is Selfridge's (1959) Pandemonium model.

FACE RECOGNITION

Just as we can identify different categories of dogs or chairs, so we can identify 'baby's face', 'man's face' or, say, 'Japanese face'. We also have some ability to identify individual dogs or chairs, but in the case of human faces this ability to identify individuals is of paramount importance (Bruce, 1995). Recognising faces is probably one of the most demanding tasks that we set our visual systems. Unlike most other cases of object identification, the task is to identify one specific instance of the class of objects known as faces (Groome *et al.*, 1999).

Strictly, face recognition (using the face to identify an individual) is part of the broader process of *face perception*. According to Eysenck and Keane (1995), more is known about the processes involved in face recognition than about those involved in most other forms of PR.

Are faces more than the sum of their parts?

Ask Yourself

- Choose a familiar face (friend, lecturer, film star) and describe it.
- What makes this face unique – that is, what enables you to recognise it as that specific face?
- What do all faces have in common?

Based on theories of basic-level PR (such as Biederman's geon theory), faces could be described as a set of parts (the features) and their spatial arrangement. When we're asked to describe a face, or speculate about how individual faces are represented in memory, we're likely to think in terms of separate features. This tendency is undoubtedly created partly by our language, which has discrete terms for the different functional parts of the face. But the visual system may not describe faces in this way. According to Bruce and Young (1998):

> *... there is a good deal of evidence that face patterns are treated more as wholes or as interrelationships between different features, than simply as a list of their features ...*

In other words, it seems more valid to describe faces in a more *configural* way (Bruce, 1995) (see Box 14.1).

Box 14.1 The meanings of 'configural'

According to Bruce (1995), although Psychologists tend to agree that a face is greater than the sum of its parts, studies of face perception haven't always made explicit which sense of 'configural' is being investigated. She identifies three meanings.

1. The *spatial relationships* between features are as important as the features themselves.
2. Facial features *interact* with one another (for example, perception of mouth shape is affected by the shape of the nose).
3. Faces are processed *holistically* (they aren't analysed into separable features at all).

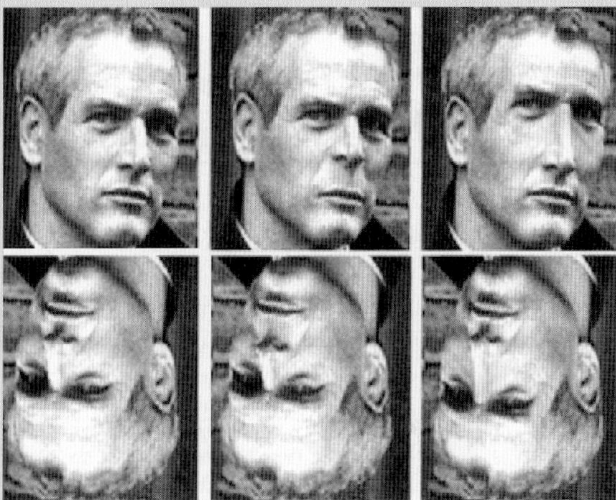

Figure 14.5 You should find it easy to detect which image shows the real Paul Newman, though the distortions are much easier to see in the upright than in the inverted images (from Bruce and Young, 1998)

However, early research into face recognition implicitly assumed that a part-based description might be appropriate, comprising a list of features each with different specific values. Many Psychologists during the 1970s used *artificially constructed faces*, such as Bradshaw and Wallace's (1971) use of *Identikit*. This refers to a set of varying line-drawn features used by the police to construct a criminal/suspect's face, based on a witness's description (see Chapter 21).

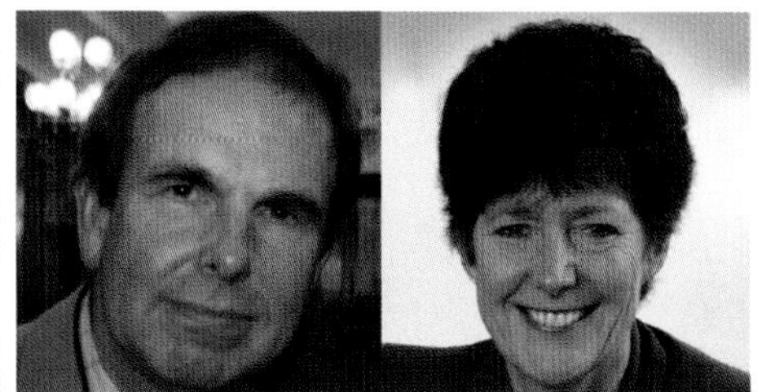

MEET THE RESEARCHERS

Andy Young and Vicki Bruce

Face perception

Faces loom large in our social world. We use them to infer people's feelings, help us understand their speech, tell their age and sex, and recognise whether we have met them before. Arguably, the face offers the richest source of social meanings of any visual stimulus, yet when we began working on face perception, research on visual perception and cognition was dominated by the study of much simpler and often relatively meaningless patterns.

Perception: analysis as a whole or in parts?

To understand face perception, we need to know how different things we do with faces (e.g. interpreting expressions, estimating age, recognising familiar people) relate to each other. One possibility is that, because faces are both common and socially important, everything to do with them is analysed together. If this view were correct, we would expect that brain injuries affecting the critical region responsible for these analyses would compromise all aspects of face perception more or less similarly. This does not seem to be the case; many examples in the research literature show that brain injury can affect some aspects of face perception more than others, e.g. people with prosopagnosia have profound difficulties recognising the identities of faces but are better able to interpret facial expressions.

A contrasting position is that different aspects of face perception are carried out relatively independently. This was the view we put forward (Bruce and Young, 1986), and it continues to sit more comfortably with known facts about the effects of brain injury. We suggested an organisational framework for understanding face perception and recognition that schematised what was known at that time, and offered suggestions and a few guiding principles for future research. We wrote this initially to stimulate discussion at a meeting in 1985 attended by a number of researchers interested in the perception and recognition of faces, substantially influenced by seminal work started in the 1970s by a group at Aberdeen University, where Hadyn Ellis and others were among the first to investigate face recognition with a sustained programme of research. Their experiments provided compelling insights into important practical questions, such as eyewitness identification.

Shortcomings of the Bruce and Young model

We are both proud and a bit perplexed that the 'Bruce and Young model' is still so widely discussed. Proud that it seems to have stood the test of time (so far), but perplexed because it had obvious shortcomings that needed to be fixed with something better. In part, standing the test of time reflects the fact that the framework was very much a group effort via that important 1985 meeting. Nevertheless, there were a number of unresolved issues in 1986, and new directions have emerged since. Here, we briefly discuss two unresolved issues and some questions of contemporary research interest that go beyond our thinking in 1986.

The first is: why are different aspects of face perception allocated to different specialist regions in the way we proposed? We had little to say about this in 1986, but an appealing suggestion offered by Jim Haxby and his colleagues (Haxby *et al.*, 2000) is that it may reflect a more general division between interpreting those things about the face that change from moment to moment (such as expressions) for which patterns of movement are important, and those that are relatively invariant (age, sex, identity) and likely to be based primarily on the perception of static form.

Haxby *et al.*'s model

Haxby *et al.*'s (2000) model is shown in the figure opposite. It proposes separable pathways for the visual analysis of changeable aspects of faces such as expression (inferior occipital gyri and superior temporal sulcus) and relatively non-changeable aspects such as identity (inferior occipital gyri and lateral fusiform gyrus). The pathways in this core system are themselves interconnected and link to an extended system comprising further specialist brain regions.

The fact that Haxby *et al.*'s (2000) model is explicitly framed in terms of the contributions of different brain regions brings us to our second unresolved issue: how does Bruce and Young's explicitly 'functional' model relate to underlying neuroanatomy? We deliberately avoided this question in 1986, because we were sceptical about a lot of the information concerning sites of brain injuries collected in an era when brain imaging techniques were very limited. It was also widely held in the 1980s that psychological (functional) and neuroanatomical levels of description were of different logical status, and need not map precisely to each

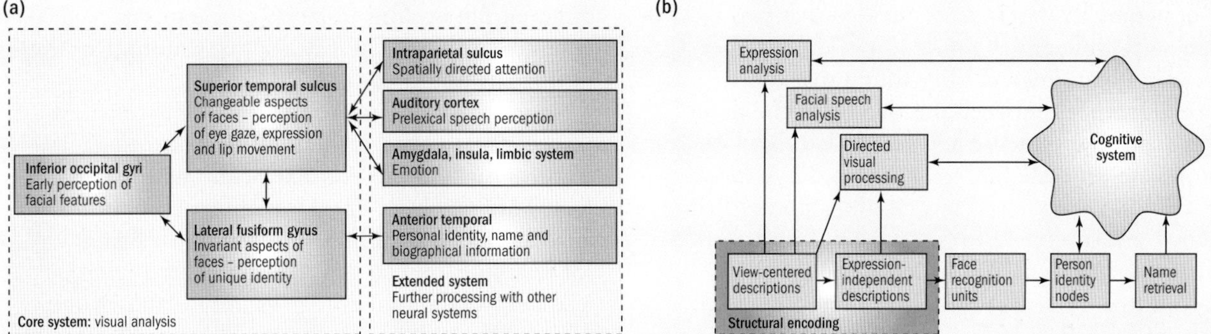

Model of face perception proposed by Haxby *et al.* (2000), and a redrawn version of Bruce and Young (1986). (Figure adapted from Box 1 in Calder and Young, 2005.)

other. A commonly used analogy was that the hardware (cf. neuroanatomy) of a computer did not account for what its software (cf. psychology) might do. The point is still seen in critiques of what psychology can learn from brain imaging (e.g. Coltheart, 2006).

However, the figure redraws Bruce and Young's functional model rotated through 90 degrees (from Calder and Young, 2005) to highlight the overall similarities to Haxby *et al.*'s (2000) more neuroanatomical account. Something particularly appealing about Haxby *et al.*'s position is that it not only explains a potential organising principle underlying part of the 'division of labour' in face perception, but also it links this to a more general system of visual pathways for perceiving motion and static form in the cerebral cortex, making the neuroanatomy and psychology fit neatly alongside each other. We think one of the strongest points of Bruce and Young (1986) was that it sought to use ideas that were consistent across as wide a range of evidence as possible. This approach, technically called 'converging operations', helps to reduce the risk that a particular conclusion is incorrect because of a problem with a specific research technique. We therefore see the emerging convergence with neuroanatomy as additional grounds for thinking the overall framework remains valid.

Some of the most exciting recent developments in the psychology of face perception sit very comfortably with the Haxby *et al.* approach, e.g. Bruce and Young were silent about gaze perception, yet Haxby *et al.* clearly indicated gaze as one of the 'changeable' features handled within the superior temporal sulcus. The perception of gaze and other aspects of social attention and perception is currently a hot topic in social cognitive neuroscience (see Frith, Chapter 22). Another example is the perception of dynamic information from faces, where the Haxby model provides a very good way of thinking about intriguing findings such as the benefits for face identification of seeing faces displaying their characteristic motions (e.g. Lander and Bruce, 2000).

Some problems, however, endure. Research in the 1970s and 1980s was provoked in part by problems of eyewitness memory for faces. Today, issues arise from related applied questions about the verification of identities from CCTV camera images and/or identity cards. Many of us like to think we are good at recognising faces, but this reflects our recognition of people we know quite well. Several studies have shown that comparing the identities of unfamiliar faces shown in different image formats is actually surprisingly error-prone (e.g. Kemp *et al.*, 1997; Bruce *et al.*, 1999). This highlights a critical theoretical question: how unfamiliar faces become familiar, or, in Bruce and Young's (1986) terms, how 'face recognition units' are created. There is still plenty more to be done!

If you'd been at the scene of the crime, how many details do you think you'd be able to give the police about this man's face?

Professor Andy Young is Professor of Neuropsychology at the University of York and **Professor Vicki Bruce** is Professor of Psychology at Newcastle University. They grew up in nearby streets in Tyneside and travelled to school on the same train, yet never met until they both started working on face recognition. Each has over 35 years' experience in research on face perception, motivated by both theoretical and applied questions, and including work with people with brain injuries and neurodevelopmental or psychiatric disorders.

Bradshaw and Wallace presented pairs of faces to see how quickly participants decided that two faces in a pair were different as a function of the number of features that differed. They found that the more differences between the two faces, the faster participants responded. They concluded that facial features are processed *independently* and *in sequence*. Sergent (1984) reviewed several other studies that reached similar conclusions.

However, Sergent also noted that faces that differed in several features also differed more in terms of overall configuration than those differing only in a few. If features really are processed independently, the number of feature differences shouldn't affect how quickly a 'difference' judgement is made (the judgement can be made as soon as any one feature difference is spotted). Accordingly, Sergent constructed eight slightly different faces from the same 'kit' of face features, but each had one of two different *chins*, *eye colours* and *internal space* (arrangements of internal features). 'Different' pairs (one, two or three feature differences) were intermixed with pairs of identical faces, and participants were asked to decide whether the 'different' pairs were the same or different.

Sergent confirmed Bradshaw and Wallace's finding that the more features that differed, the faster a 'difference' decision was made. However, when only a *single* feature differed, 'difference' decisions were *faster* when this involved *chins* (and this was true for all participants). When something *in addition* to chins differed, the decisions were even faster. This latter finding suggests that there's *interactive processing* of different dimensions of facial appearance: a *configuration* emerges from a set of features that's more than the sum of its parts (see Box 14.1).

Another way of assessing holistic processing is the *whole-part effect*: it's harder to recognise facial features outside the context of the whole face (e.g. Wang *et al.*, 2012). Also, object recognition appears not to depend on holistic processing; for example, objects are less affected by *inversion* (see below) than faces (e.g. Valentine and Bruce, 1986). This adds to the evidence for *domain-specific processing mechanisms* (i.e. face recognition involves specific mechanisms; see Critical Discussion 14.1) (Davis *et al.*, 2013).

Are upright and inverted faces processed differently?

Ask Yourself

- Before reading on, look at the photographs of Margaret Thatcher (in Box 14.2).
- Describe what you see.

An interesting additional finding from Sergent's study was that when she repeated the experiment using inverted face images, the results supported the view that the face is processed as a set of *independent* features. Several other studies have confirmed this finding.

Box 14.2 Evidence relating to differential processing of upright and inverted faces

- Tanaka and Farah (1993) found that facial features learned in the context of an upright normal face were more likely to be identified correctly in the context of that face (as opposed to being tested in isolation). However, this advantage wasn't found for inverted faces. They concluded that the representation of whole faces is based on a *holistic* description, while inverted faces (as well as houses and scrambled faces, see Chapter 16) are represented as a set of *independent components*.
- According to Yin (1969), while upright faces are recognised more accurately than physical objects, the reverse is true for inverted faces. Somehow, the different features in inverted faces cannot be integrated to give a coherent impression. This finding was replicated by Leder and Carbon (2006).
- Young *et al.* (1987) took pictures of well-known faces and sliced them horizontally to form separate upper and lower face halves. They then paired the upper half with a 'wrong' lower half. Participants were asked to name the top halves of faces presented either in isolation or when paired with the 'wrong' lower halves. The top halves were much harder to name when combined with the wrong lower halves than when shown alone, or when the two correct halves were misaligned. Young *et al.*'s explanation was that combining the two halves produced a 'new' configuration (see the 'Gazzaker' images, Figure 14.7). Significantly, when composite faces were inverted, participants named them *more* accurately than when they were presented upright.
- In Thompson's (1980) Thatcher illusion, the eyes and mouth are cut out and inverted within the face.

When viewed upright, this produces a grotesque appearance, but when inverted, it looks quite similar to the 'normal' version.

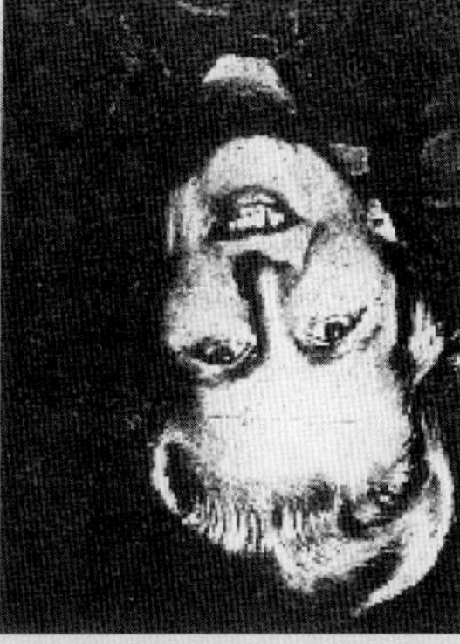

Figure 14.6 Thompson's (1980) Thatcher illusion

According to Bartlett and Searcy (1993), the most likely explanation of the Thatcher illusion is the *configural processing hypothesis.* The relationship between the features is more difficult to perceive when the face is inverted (so the features are processed independently), and the strangeness of the grotesque face cannot be seen (since it arises from the relationship between the features).

- Leder and Bruce (1998) doctored pictures of faces to alter just their features or the *spatial relation* between the features. Both types of change made the faces equally more distinctive and easier for participants to recognise compared with the original face. But when the faces were inverted, those with unusual feature *relations* proved far *less* distinctive or familiar than those with doctored features. Leder and Bruce concluded that face perception involves processing *both* the individual features *and* their configuration – but inverting a face disrupts the latter.
- This was confirmed when participants were asked to identify faces either by unique combinations of features (such as eye and hair colour) or by distinctive relations between features; inverting the faces made the latter much harder to identify (Leder and Bruce, 2000). But unexpectedly, when the faces with odd configurations were inverted, participants found these harder to identify than faces with *both* distinctive attributes (unique features *and* relations). This lends further support to the configuration explanation.

Figure 14.7 Who can you see?

Leder and Carbon (2006) suggest that configural processing might be *face-specific.* Is this necessarily the case? A study by Diamond and Carey (1986) of dog breeders and judges suggests that expertise may be the crucial variable. These dog experts were just as affected by the inversion of dog pictures as non-experts were by the inversion of human faces. So, configural processing might enable experts to make fine discriminations within a particular category, in which all the members share the same overall structure. When it comes to human face recognition, we all appear to be experts.

Disorders of face processing

While we might all be experts at face recognition, there are rare but dramatic cases of people who are unable to recognise familiar faces, including those of their spouses, other relatives and friends. The most common such disorder is *prosopagnosia* ('face blindness').

Prosopagnosia

Bate (2014) distinguishes between two forms of the disorder:

1. *Acquired prosopagnosia* (AP) is a rare form of the disorder that occurs after brain damage; these people had normal face recognition skills prior to their injury. Typically, the occipital and temporal lobes are affected, including the *fusiform gyrus* (FG). While damage to the FG produces difficulties in face *perception*, damage to other areas of the temporal lobe is associated with difficulties in *remembering* (i.e. recognising) faces. These correspond to *apperceptive prosopagnosia* and *associative prosopagnosia*, respectively.

2. More commonly, *developmental prosopagnosia* (DP) appears from an early age and is actually more common than autistic spectrum disorder (ASD).

The core deficit involved in prosopagnosia seems to be the inability to use configural processing; this is associated with some defect in the right PFC (Renzi *et al.*, 2013). Research that tracks eye movements shows that people with prosopagnosia tend to focus on the hair and ears (as do babies; see Chapter 16), rather than the internal features, Interestingly, both of these abnormalities are found in both AP and DP (Bate, 2014).

However, other research suggests that, rather than being a distinct disorder, DP may simply represent one extreme end of a 'normal' face-processing continuum; at the other extreme sits *super-recognisers*, who are about as good at face recognition as people with DP are bad (e.g. Russell *et al.*, 2009). Evidence from *eye-witness testimony* research shows the considerable variation between members of the general population in face-processing skills (Bate, 2014; see Chapter 21).

It's also interesting that people with prosopagnosia, unlike most people, don't find inverted face processing any more difficult than upright faces; this suggests that they're unable to process faces holistically and rely on feature-based processing (Davis *et al.*, 2013).

Case Study 14.1

W.J. (McNeil and Warrington, 1993)

- W.J. was a 51-year-old man who suffered a series of strokes, causing lesions in his left occipital, frontal and temporal lobes (see Chapter 4).
- When shown a set of three photographs (one famous and two unfamiliar faces), he couldn't select the famous one. However, if he was asked 'Which one is ...?', his performance improved significantly (*covert recognition*).
- Following the onset of his prosopagnosia, he acquired a flock of sheep which he photographed. He knew them by number and could recognise at least 8 of the 16 pictures. This represents remarkable evidence of an ability to learn to recognise individual sheep, while still being profoundly prosopagnosic for human faces (Groome *et al.*, 1999).

The case of W.J. (Case Study 14.1) demonstrates that prosopagnosia appears to be a face-specific deficit. Several other case studies have shown that patients can still identify personal possessions (including non-human animals), and can recognise faces if tested indirectly. Covert recognition suggests that prosopagnosia *isn't* a memory deficiency (Groome *et al.*, 1999).

Some of these patients can derive particular kinds of meaning from faces (including emotional expression), despite being unable to recognise them. Conversely, some patients with a form of dementia find it difficult to recognise emotional expressions, while still being able to classify famous faces according to occupation (which requires knowledge of personal identity) (Kurucz and Feldmar, 1979). The task of recognising individual identity from a face, therefore, seems to be quite separate from that of recognising an emotional expression.

The impairment is often so severe that it cannot only impair recognition of faces of friends and family, but also one's own face. This can have a devastating effect on the individual's life, leading to anxiety or the tendency to withdraw from social situations (Bate, 2013).

Capgras' delusion/syndrome

Once thought to be extremely rare, *Capgras' syndrome* has been increasingly recognised and reported in recent years. Some studies suggest that it may be present in up to 4 per cent of psychotic patients (see Chapter 44), and up to a third of Alzheimer's patients may display the syndrome at some point during their illness (see Chapter 39) (Enoch and Ball, 2001). It's one of the most extensively studied forms of *delusional misidentification*.

It involves the belief that one or more close relatives have been replaced by near-identical imposters. Cases have been found in many cultures and show a consistent pattern. Patients can be otherwise rational and lucid, and able to appreciate that they're making an extraordinary claim (Bruce and Young, 1998).

Case Study 14.2

Arthur (Ramachandran, 1998)

Arthur had been in a near-fatal car accident and lay in a coma for three weeks. When he finally awoke, he seemed restored to his former self, except for this one incredible delusion about his parents – they were imposters. Nothing could convince him otherwise. Ramachandran asked him, 'Arthur, who brought you to the hospital?'

'That guy in the waiting room,' Arthur replied. 'He's the old gentleman who's been taking care of me.'

'You mean your father?'

'No, no, doctor. That guy isn't my father. He just looks like him. But I don't think he means any harm.'

'Arthur, why do you think he's an imposter? What gives you that impression?'

'... Maybe my real father employed him to take care of me, paid him some money so that he could pay my bills.'

Arthur's parents revealed that he didn't treat them as imposters when they spoke to him on the phone, but only in face-to-face encounters. This implied that Arthur wasn't amnesic regarding his parents, and that he wasn't simply 'crazy'.

Critical Discussion 14.1

Is there a specialised area in the brain for face recognition?

- According to Young and Bruce (1998):

Because faces are of such fundamental social importance to a creature that lives in a complex society, extensive areas of the brain are involved in their perception.

- The brain seems to 'farm out' different aspects of the task to different specialised areas. For example, some regions are more closely involved in determining an individual's identity from their facial appearance, and others in interpretation of facial expressions of emotion (Young *et al*., 1993).
- According to Ellis and Young (1990), when we look at the faces of people we know, we recognise who they are and parts of our brains set up preparatory emotional responses for the types of interaction that are likely to follow (the *orienting response*). Recognising *who* it is, and the orienting response, involve *separate* neurological pathways. If the pathway responsible for the orienting response is damaged, and the orienting response is impaired, faces that can still be recognised (and so look familiar) can somehow seem strange (because they don't elicit the usual reactions).
- The *temporal lobes* contain regions that specialise in face and object recognition (the '*what pathway*'). Normally, these face recognition areas relay information to the *limbic system* (specifically, the *amygdala*), which then helps to generate emotional responses to particular faces. For example, our GSR increases when we see someone familiar (or just see their photograph), but we'd expect this not to happen in the case of Capgras patients. This was confirmed in the case of Arthur (see Case Study 14.2). The discrepancy between recognition and the emotional response (there is none) produces a highly disturbing sense of strangeness. The delusional belief might simply be a *rationalisation* of that disturbing experience (Bruce and Young, 1998; Young and Bruce, 1998).
- Patients with prosopagnosia have particular problems matching faces when the faces only differ by their features' spatial relations (consistent with the configuration explanation; see Box 14.2 above) (Bublitz, 2008). *f*MRI studies involving people *without* prosopagnosia have revealed the *fusiform gyrus* (or fusiform face area (FFA)) as one area that responds selectively to faces (Bublitz, 2008; Williams, 2006). Significantly, sufferers often show *no* deficit in their FFA response, However, they sometimes fail to show *adaptation* (reduced activity in the FFA when the same face is presented twice in succession). While there's some other conflicting evidence, few researchers believe that the FFA tells the whole story (Williams, 2006).
- The FFA is larger in adults than in children, who don't achieve adult-like proficiency at recognising faces until about 14 years. So, although innate neural mechanisms may exist, experience of looking at the human face also very likely plays a role in maturation of the brain's face areas (Bublitz, 2008).
- According to Konorski's (1967, cited in Gaschler, 2006) theory of 'gnostic neurons' (from the Greek *gnosis*, meaning 'recognition'), the activity of one or just a few neurons can represent the abstract concept of a specific thing or person (such as our grandmother; hence 'grandmother cells'). Using implanted electrodes (see Chapter 4) with epilepsy patients in the 1990s, Quiroga and colleagues found a Bill Clinton cell was located deep within one female patient's amygdala. This cell responded to three different pictures of Clinton, but showed no response to pictures of any other US President. In other patients, cells responsive only to the Beatles, the Simpsons, and Jennifer Aniston (all in the medial temporal lobe) were found, and a 'Halle Berry' neuron was found in one patient's hippocampus (sensitive to merely seeing her name). Despite these findings, Quiroga *et al.* (2008) argue that true grandmother (i.e. single) cells cannot account for face recognition.
- Renzi *et al.* (2013) used transcranial magnetic stimulation (TMS) to help identify specific brain areas for face recognition. Interfering with the *left PFC*, they affected *featural processing*, i.e. the ability to identify the individual components of the face (facial features), while interfering with the *right PFC* impaired the ability to distinguish the relationship between features, such as the distance between nose and eyes (*configural processing*). This is the first time that a causal relationship has been shown between these areas and different aspects of face recognition.

Figure 14.8 Is there a Halle Berry neuron?

CONCLUSIONS

Face recognition represents a particular kind of pattern recognition (PR). The importance of face recognition clearly lies in the fact that it's essential for our normal social interaction in general, and our ability to maintain relationships with particular individuals. One of the 'debates' within this area of research concerns those who believe that face recognition represents a distinct mental module (controlled by specific brain areas) on the one hand, and those who argue that our constant encounter with other people from birth onwards helps us to acquire the skill of face recognition. The former view is one that would be favoured by Evolutionary Psychologists, although this shouldn't be equated with a nativist argument. Indeed, the finding that it's not until they're about 14 that children acquire face recognition ability on a par with adults, suggests that, however specialised the human brain may be, experience is crucial for the normal development of such specialised abilities.

Chapter Summary

- **Pattern recognition (PR)** is the process of assigning meaning to visual input by identifying the objects in the visual field. Like perception, with which it's almost synonymous, PR is a deceptively simple process.
- According to the **template matching hypothesis (TMH)**, incoming sensory information is matched against miniature copies (or **templates**) of patterns/objects stored in long-term memory. However, TMH fails to account for our ability to recognise unfamiliar patterns.
- Biederman's **geon theory** (or **recognition-by-components model**) tries to overcome TMH's limitations. Descriptions of objects usually divide them into **volumetric concepts** or **geons**, and the regions used to divide them up are probably those of greatest **concavity**.
- Geon theory has been supported by experiments using 'partial' objects. A more stringent test involves the use of 'degraded' objects. While geons are intuitively appealing, there's little empirical support for the specific geons Biederman identifies.
- **Feature-detection theories (FDTs)** are the most influential approach to PR. Every stimulus can be regarded as a configuration of elementary features. **Visual scanning tasks** and studies of **eye movements/fixations** support FDTs.
- Hubel and Wiesel identified three kinds of **cortical cell**, which may or may not be the feature detectors proposed by FDTs. There may be **face-specific cells** in the monkey cortex, and there also appear to be cells in the human cortex that respond to specific aspects of faces.
- While FDTs typically assume a **serial form of processing**, it's widely believed that the visual cortex involves considerable **parallel processing**.
- **Face recognition** involves the identification of individual faces. It's part of **face perception**, which includes inferring emotional states and other information from the face. Probably more is understood about face recognition than about any other aspect of PR.
- Although faces could be described in terms of basic components, it seems more valid to describe them in a more **configural** way. However, this can refer to different things, including the **interaction between features** and the **holistic processing** of the whole face.
- Early research often used **artificially constructed** faces, such as **Identikit** faces, and indicated that facial features are processed independently and in sequence. However, some features (such as chins) seemed to influence facial judgements more than others, and there was evidence of **interactive processing**.
- According to the **configural processing hypothesis**, the relationship between the features is more difficult to perceive when the face is **inverted** (they're processed **independently**). In a normal upright face, the configuration of the features is crucial.
- Patients with **prosopagnosia** ('face-blindness') are unable to recognise familiar faces, despite an otherwise normal capacity for recognising individual objects or animals.
- Studies involving patients with prosopagnosia and other face-perception disorders, and normal adults, suggest that recognising individual identity is quite separate from recognising emotional expression.
- In **Capgras' delusion**, the normal integration of face recognition and orienting response appears to be impaired. This is thought to mirror the breakdown of the normal link between the **temporal lobe** (which contains the **'what pathway'**) and the **limbic system** (especially the **amygdala**).
- Another brain area involved is the **fusiform gyrus (fusiform face area (FFA))**. This responds normally in people with prosopagnosia, except for a lack of **adaptation** in some cases.
- According to Konorski's **gnostic neurons theory**, activity of one or just a few 'grandmother' neurons is sufficient for representing the abstract concept of a person. Not all researchers believe this is possible.

Links with Other Topics/Chapters

Chapter 15 ⟶ PR is almost synonymous with perception, and *theories of perception* can be thought of as trying to account for PR

Chapter 5 ⟶ The three kinds of *cortical cell* that respond to different features of *visual stimuli* (identified by Hubel and Wiesel) may be the feature detectors proposed by feature-detection theories

Chapter 20 ⟶ The serial processing proposed by FDTs contrasts with the parallel processing thought to take place in the visual cortex. This distinction is also relevant to the debate about *artificial intelligence* (AI)

Chapter 15 ⟶ A major limitation of FDTs in general is their failure to take account of the role of *context*, and *perceiver characteristics* (such as *expectations*)

Chapter 21 ⟶ Early research into face recognition assumed that faces could be analysed into individual features, as in Bradshaw and Wallace's *Identikit*, used by the police to construct a suspect's face based on witnesses' descriptions

Chapters 5 and 13 ⟶ People who suffer strokes in the right parietal lobe display left-sided neglect (*unilateral neglect*), which involves a deficit in *eye movements* (which normally ensure that we scan the whole picture)

Chapters 39 and 44 ⟶ Capgras' syndrome is found in about 4 per cent of psychotics and up to a third of Alzheimer's patients

Chapter 4 ⟶ In Capgras' syndrome there seems to be a breakdown in communication between areas in the *temporal lobe* (concerned with object/face recognition) and the *amygdala* (part of the *limbic system*), which helps generate emotional responses

Chapter 17 ⟶ Relevant to evaluating Bruce and Young's functional model of face recognition is the *tip-of-the-tongue* (TOT) phenomenon

Chapter 2 ⟶ The claim that the human brain is specialised for face recognition is consistent with the claims of *Evolutionary Psychology*

Chapter 50 ⟶ The development of face recognition demonstrates the *interaction between nature and nurture*

Chapter 16 ⟶ *Face perception* has been studied extensively in *newborns* and data exist to support both innate and learned aspects

Chapter 40 ⟶ There's a suggested link between prosopagnosia and autistic spectrum disorder

Recommended Reading

Bruce, V. (1995) Perceiving and recognising faces. In I. Roth & V. Bruce (eds) *Perception and Representations: Current Issues* (2nd edn). Buckingham: Open University Press.

Bruce, V., Young, A. (1998) *The Eye of the Beholder: The Science of Face Perception.* Oxford: Oxford University Press.

Roth, I. (1995) Object recognition (in the book by Roth and Bruce above). Also relevant to Chapter 15.

(Also see Recommended Reading for Chapter 13.)

Useful Websites

www.psychologicalscience.org/index.php/news/releases/why-do-some-people-never-forget-a-face.html (Some very useful links on face perception)

www.utdallas.edu/~otoole/face_try.html (Human Face Perception and Recognition, University of Texas at Dallas)

CHAPTER 15

PERCEPTION: PROCESSES AND THEORIES

Gestalt Psychology and perceptual organisation

Depth perception

Perceptual constancy

Illusions

Theories of visual perception

INTRODUCTION and OVERVIEW

Perception is the *organisation* and *interpretation* of incoming sensory information to form inner representations of the external world.

This chapter begins by looking at some basic visual perceptual phenomena, namely, form and depth perception, perceptual constancy and visual illusions. Many of the principles that govern human visual perception were first identified by the German 'school' of Gestalt Psychology. As Dodwell (1995) has observed:

> *To perceive seems effortless. To understand perception is nevertheless a great challenge.*

One response to this challenge claims that our perception of the world is the end result of a process which also involves making *inferences* about what things are like. Similarly, most of what we see is a confabulation of our brain: it 'makes stuff up based on the sparse data it gets from our eyes' (Macknik and Martinez-Conde, 2014). In this sense, we don't perceive 'reality' at all but only how our brain *interprets* it.

Those who subscribe to this 'end result' view, such as Bruner (1957), Neisser (1967) and Gregory (1972, 1980), are called *top-down* (or *conceptually driven*) perceptual processing theorists. Making inferences about what things are like means that we perceive them *indirectly*, drawing on our knowledge and expectations of the world. Others argue that our perception of the world is essentially determined by the information presented to the sensory receptors, so that things are perceived quite *directly*. The most influential of these *bottom-up* (or *data-driven*) perceptual processing theorists is Gibson (1966, 1979). Others still, notably Marr (1982), display elements of both approaches.

According to Frith (2007):

> *... By hiding from us all the unconscious inferences that it makes, our brain creates the illusion that we have direct contact with objects in the physical world ...*

GESTALT PSYCHOLOGY and PERCEPTUAL ORGANISATION

Von Ehrenfels (1890) claimed that many groups of stimuli acquire a pattern quality that is greater than the sum of their parts. A square, for example, is more than a simple assembly of lines – it has 'squareness'. Ehrenfels called this 'emergent property' *Gestalt qualität* (or form quality). In the early 1900s, Gestalt Psychologists (notably Wertheimer, Koffka and Köhler) attempted to discover the principles through which sensory information is interpreted. They argued that as well as creating a coherent perceptual experience that's more than the sum of its parts, the brain does this in regular and predictable ways. They believed that these organisational principles are largely innate (see Chapter 16).

Form perception

In order to structure incoming sensory information, we must perceive objects as being separate from other stimuli and as having meaningful form.

Figure and ground

Ask Yourself

- What do you see in Figure 15.1?
- Although it's visually quite simple, can you suggest how it might illustrate a basic principle of how we see things?

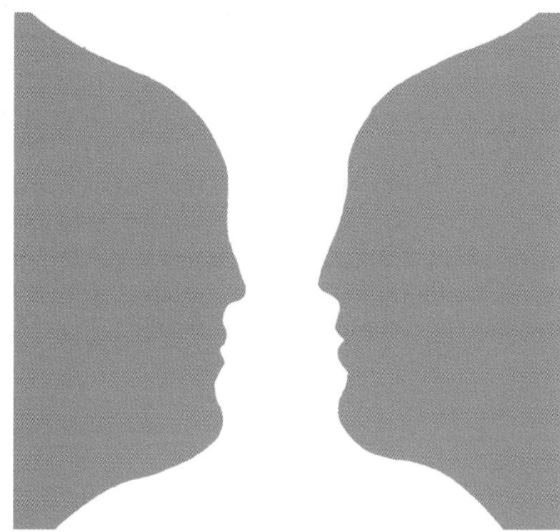

Figure 15.1

The first perceptual task when confronted with an object (or *figure*) is to recognise it (see Chapter 14). To do this, we must perceive the figure as being distinct from its surroundings (or *ground*). A figure's familiarity can help determine whether it's perceived as figure or ground, but unfamiliar and even meaningless 'blobs' are also seen as figures. One of the strongest determinants of figure and ground is *surroundedness*. Areas enclosed by a contour are generally seen as figures, whereas the surrounding area is generally seen as ground. Size, orientation and symmetry also play a role in figure–ground separation.

Sometimes, though, there may not be enough information in a pattern to allow us to distinguish easily between figure and ground. A good example of this is shown in Figure 15.2, which illustrates the principle underlying *camouflage*.

Figure 15.2 The Dalmatian dog (the figure) is difficult to distinguish from the ground because it has few visible contours of its own

In *figure–ground reversal*, a figure may have clear contours, but is capable of being perceived in two very different ways: it's unclear which part of it is the figure and which the ground. A famous example is Figure 15.1, usually called Rubin's vase (Rubin, 1915). Here, the figure–ground relationship continually reverses, so that it's perceived as either a white vase with a dark background, or two dark profiles on a white background. However, the stimulus is always organised into a figure seen against a ground, and the reversal indicates that the same stimulus can trigger more than one perception.

Ask Yourself

- Can you think of some 'everyday' examples of figure–ground (reversible or not)?
- Can you think of some non-visual examples?

A map is another example. We normally see the land as figure and the sea as (back)ground, because we're more familiar with the shape of Africa, say, than with the shape of the Atlantic ocean. An auditory example is the *cocktail party phenomenon* (see Chapter 13). Here's another: try repeating 'over-run' out loud and you'll find the two words alternating as figure and ground.

Grouping

Once we've discriminated figure from ground, the figure can be organised into a meaningful form. Gestalt Psychologists believed that objects are perceived as *gestalten* ('organised wholes', 'configurations' or 'patterns') rather than combinations of isolated sensations. They identified several 'laws' of perceptual organisation or grouping, which illustrate their view that the perceived whole of an object is more than the sum of its parts.

These laws can be summarised under one heading, the law of *prägnanz* ('precision'), according to which:

> *Psychological organisation will always be as good as the prevailing conditions allow. In this definition, 'good' is undefined. (Koffka, 1935)*

'Good' can be defined as possessing a high degree of internal redundancy, that is, the structure of an unseen part is highly predictable from the visible parts (Attneave, 1954). Similarly, according to Hochberg's (1978) *minimum principle*, if there's more than one way of organising a given visual stimulus, we're most likely to perceive the one requiring the least amount of information to perceive it.

In practice, the 'best' way of perceiving is to see things as symmetrical, uniform and stable, and this is achieved by following the laws of prägnanz. (See Box 15.1.)

Box 15.1 Gestalt laws of perception

Proximity: Elements appearing close together in space or time tend to be perceived together, so that different spacings of dots produce four vertical lines or four horizontal lines:

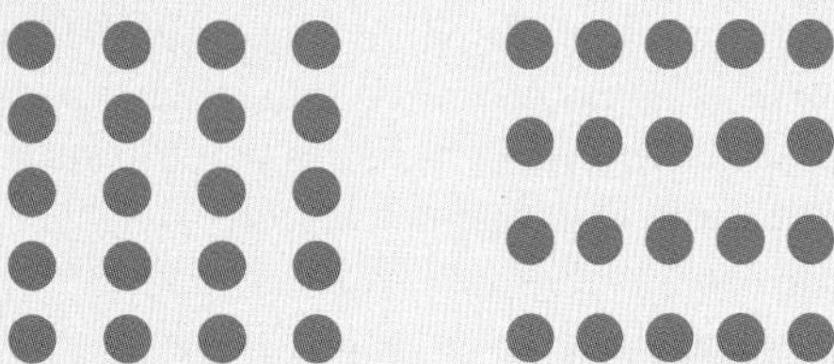

Figure 15.3a

An auditory example would be the perception of a series of musical notes as a melody, because they occur soon after one another in time.

Similarity: Similar figures tend to be grouped together. So, the triangles and circles below are seen as columns of similar shapes rather than rows of dissimilar shapes.

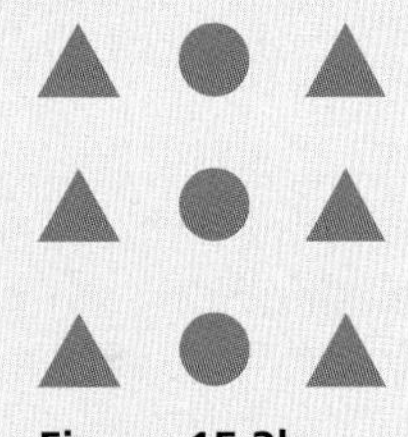

Figure 15.3b

Hearing all the separate voices in a choir as an entity illustrates the principle of similarity.

Continuity: We tend to perceive smooth, continuous patterns rather than discontinuous ones. The pattern below could be seen as a series of alternating semi-circles, but tends to be perceived as a wavy line and a straight line.

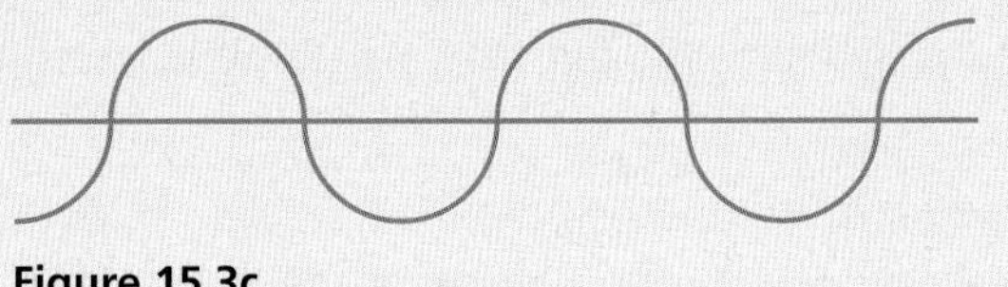

Figure 15.3c

Music and speech are perceived as continuous, rather than a series of separate sounds.

Closure: Closed figures are perceived more easily than open/incomplete ones. So, we often supply missing information to close a figure and separate it from its background. By filling in the gaps, the illustrations below are seen as a triangle and a seashell.

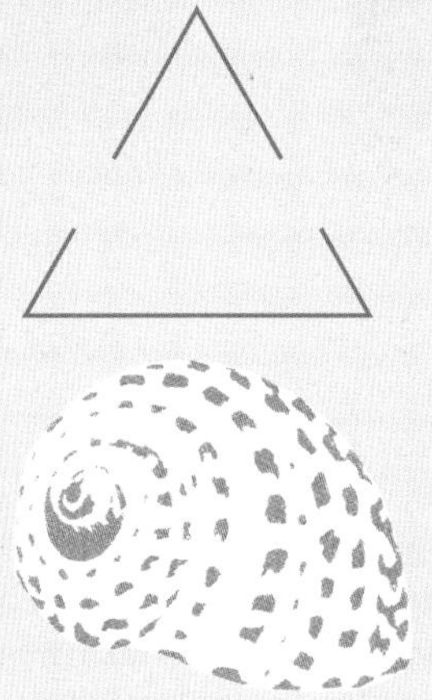

Figure 15.3d

Part–whole relationship: As well as illustrating continuity and proximity, the three figures below illustrate the principle that 'the whole is greater than the sum of its parts'.

Despite the similarity of the parts (each pattern is composed of twelve crosses), the gestalten are different.

Figure 15.3e

The same melody can be recognised when hummed, whistled or played with different instruments and in different keys.

An evaluation of the Gestalt contribution

A major philosophical influence on Gestalt Psychology was *phenomenology*, which refers to our individual *experience* of the world. Koffka, for example, believed that the most important question for perceptual Psychologists was 'Why do things look as they do?', and for Köhler:

> *There seems to be a single starting point for psychology, exactly as for all the other sciences: the world as we find it, naïvely and uncritically.*

The most comprehensive account of perceptual grouping is still that provided by the Gestaltist Psychologists (Roth, 1986), and in Gordon's (1989) view, Gestalt Psychology's discoveries 'are now part of our permanent knowledge of perception'.

However, many contemporary researchers (e.g. Greene, 1990) have argued that, as originally expressed, the various Gestalt 'laws' are at best only *descriptive* and at worst extremely imprecise and difficult to measure. While there's plenty of experimental support, the Gestalt laws are difficult to apply to the perception of solid (three-dimensional/3-D) objects (as opposed to two-dimensional/2-D drawings). Our eyes evolved to see 3-D objects, and when 3-D arrays have been studied, Gestalt laws haven't been consistently upheld (Eysenck, 1993). The world around us comprises 'whole' scenes, in which single objects are but 'parts' (Humphreys and Riddoch, 1987). Because many of the Gestalt displays involve single objects, they have very low *ecological validity,* that is, they're not representative of 'the objects and events which organisms must deal with in order to survive' (Gordon, 1989).

DEPTH PERCEPTION

From the 2-D images that fall on our retinas, we manage to organise 3-D perceptions. This ability is called *depth perception,* and it allows us to estimate an object's distance from us. Some of the cues used to transform 2-D retinal images into 3-D perceptions involve both eyes and rely on their working together. These are called *binocular cues. Monocular cues* are available to each eye separately.

Ask Yourself

- How do we judge the distance of objects from us?
- Is it always done unconsciously, or do we sometimes try to 'work it out' consciously?

Non-pictorial (primary) cues

Most preyed-upon non-humans (such as rabbits) have their eyes on the sides of the head, allowing them to see danger approaching over a wide area. Most predators (such as lions) have their eyes set close together on the front of the head, equipping them with binocular vision, which helps in hunting prey. Like non-human predators, humans have predatory vision, which influences the way we perceive the world. Four important non-pictorial cues are *retinal disparity, stereopsis, accommodation* and *convergence.* These are all binocular, except accommodation.

- Because our eyes are nearly three inches apart, each retina receives a slightly different image of the world. The amount of *retinal disparity* (the difference between the two images) detected by the brain provides an important cue to distance.

Ask Yourself

- Hold your finger directly in front of your nose.
- Look first with your right eye closed and then with the left. The difference between the two retinal images is large.
- When the finger's held at arms' length, retinal disparity is much smaller.

- Ordinarily, we don't see double images, because the brain combines the two images in a process called *stereopsis* (literally, 'solid vision': Harris, 1998). This allows us to experience one 3-D sensation, rather than two different images.
- In *accommodation,* which is a muscular cue, the lens of the eye changes shape when we focus on an object, thickening for nearby objects and flattening for distant objects (see Chapter 5).
- *Convergence,* another muscular cue to distance, is the process by which the eyes point more and more inward as an object gets closer. By noting the angle of convergence, the brain provides us with depth information over distances from about 6 to 20 feet (Hochberg, 1971).

Pictorial (secondary) cues

Except with relatively near objects, each eye receives a very similar retinal image when looking ahead. At greater distances, we depend on *pictorial cues.* These refer to features of the visual field itself (rather than to the eyes), and are all also monocular (see Table 15.1).

Figure 15.4 Linear perspective

PERCEPTUAL CONSTANCY

Having perceived an object as a coherent form and located it in space, we must next recognise the object without being 'fooled' by changes in its size, shape, location, brightness or colour. The ability to perceive an object as unchanging, despite changes in the sensory information that reaches our eyes, is called *perceptual constancy.*

Table 15.1 Some pictorial depth cues

Depth cue	Description
Relative size	In an array of different-sized objects, smaller ones are usually seen as more distant (especially if they're known to have a constant size)
Relative brightness	Brighter objects normally appear to be nearer
Superimposition (or overlap)	An object which blocks the view of another is seen as being nearer
Linear perspective	Parallel lines (e.g. railway tracks) appear to converge as they recede into the distance
Aerial perspective	Objects at a great distance appear to have a different colour (e.g. the hazy, bluish, tint of distant mountains)
Height in the horizontal plane	When looking across a flat expanse (e.g. the sea), objects that are more distant seem higher (closer to the horizon) than nearer objects, which seem lower (closer to the ground)
Light and shadow	3-D objects produce variations in light and shade (for example, we normally assume that light comes from above)
Texture gradient	Textured surfaces (e.g. sand) look rougher close up than from a distance. A stretch of beach looks more smooth and uniform
Motion parallax	This is the major *dynamic* depth cue (pictorial/non-pictorial). Objects nearer to us seem to move faster than more distant objects (e.g. telegraph poles seen from a (moving) train window flash by when close to the track)

Size constancy

The image on the retina of an average-height person would be the same size for a dwarf seen from close up or a giant viewed from a distance (Ramachandran and Rogers-Ramachandran, 2004). *Size constancy* occurs because the perceptual system takes into account an object's distance from the perceiver. So, perceived size is equal to retinal image size taking distance into account.

The perception of an *after-image* demonstrates how distance can be varied without changing the retinal image's size.

Ask Yourself

- Stare at a bright light for a few seconds, and then look away.
- You'll experience an after-image. This has a fixed size, shape and position on the retina.
- Now quickly look at a nearby object, and then an object further away.
- The after-image seems to shrink and swell, appearing to be largest when you look at a more distant object.

Real objects cast smaller images the further away they are, and to maintain perceptual constancy the brain 'scales up' the image (*constancy scaling*). The same constancy scaling is applied to an after-image, producing changes in its apparent size.

Shape constancy

We often view objects from angles at which their 'true' shapes aren't reflected in the retinal image they project. For example, rectangular doors often project trapezoid shapes and round cups often project elliptical-shaped images. Just as with size constancy, the perceptual system maintains constancy in terms of shape.

Figure 15.5 No matter what angle a door is viewed from, it remains a door

However, shape and size constancy don't always work. When we look down at people from the top of a very tall building, they do look more like ants to us, even though we know they're people. Sometimes, people lose their conscious recognition of shape altogether (see Case Study 5.2, p. 82).

Location constancy

Moving our heads around produces a constantly changing pattern of retinal images. However, we don't perceive the world as spinning around. This is because kinaesthetic feedback from the muscles and balance organs in the ear are integrated with the changing retinal stimulation in the brain to inhibit perception of movement (see Chapter 5). To keep the world from moving crazily every time we move our eyes, the brain subtracts the eye-movement commands from the resulting changes on the retina. This helps to keep objects in a constant location.

Brightness constancy

We see objects as having a more or less constant brightness, even though the amount of light they reflect changes according to the level of illumination. For example, white paper reflects 90 per cent of light falling on it, whereas black paper reflects only 10 per cent. But in bright sunlight, black paper still looks black, even though it may reflect 100 times more light than does white paper indoors. Perceived brightness depends on how much light an object reflects relative to its surroundings (*relative luminance*).

Ask Yourself

- View sunlit black paper through a narrow tube, so that nothing else is visible.
- It will appear greyish, because in bright sunlight it reflects a fair amount of light.
- Now view it without the tube.
- It appears black again, because it reflects much less light than the colourful objects around it.

Colour constancy

Familiar objects retain their colour (or, more correctly, their *hue*) under a variety of lighting conditions (including night light), provided there's sufficient contrast and shadow. However, when we don't already know an object's colour, colour constancy is less effective. If you've bought new clothes under fluorescent light without viewing them in ordinary lighting conditions, you'll probably agree.

ILLUSIONS

Although perception is usually reliable, our perceptions sometimes misrepresent the world. When our perception of an object doesn't match its true physical characteristics, we've experienced an illusion. Some illusions are due to the physical distortion of stimuli, whereas others are due to our misperception of stimuli (Coren and Girgus, 1978). An example of a physical illusion is the bent appearance of a stick when placed in water. Gregory (1983) identifies four types of perceptual illusion:

1. *distortions* (or *geometric illusions*)
2. *ambiguous* (or *reversible*) *figures*
3. *paradoxical figures* (or *impossible objects*)
4. *fictions*.

Distortions

Figure 15.6 shows several examples of distortions.

Ambiguous figures

In addition to Rubin's vase, another well-known reversible figure is shown in Figure 15.7a: the cube undergoes a *depth reversal*, such that it can be perceived with the crosses being drawn either on the back side of the cube or on the top side looking down. Although our perceptual system interprets this 2-D line drawing as a 3-D object, it seems unsure as to which of the two orientations should be perceived. Hence, the cube spontaneously reverses in depth orientation if looked at for about 30 seconds. Two more, less well-known, examples are Mori's 'Man/Donkey' and 'Memento Mori' (Figure 15.7b and c); this time, you have to *invert* the pictures (or stand on your head!)

Paradoxical figures

While paradoxical figures look ordinary enough at first, on closer inspection we realise they cannot exist in reality (hence 'paradoxical'). Figure 15.8a–d illustrates four such paradoxical figures.

According to Hochberg (1970), it takes us a few seconds to realise that a figure is impossible. This is because we need time to examine it fully or scan it and organise its parts into a meaningful whole. When we look at a figure, our eyes move from place to place at the rate of about three changes per second (Yarbus, 1967). So, when we look at an impossible figure, it takes time for us to scan it and perceive its form, and only after this scanning can we appreciate its impossible nature. (However, 3-D models have been built creating the same illusion as 2-D drawings.)

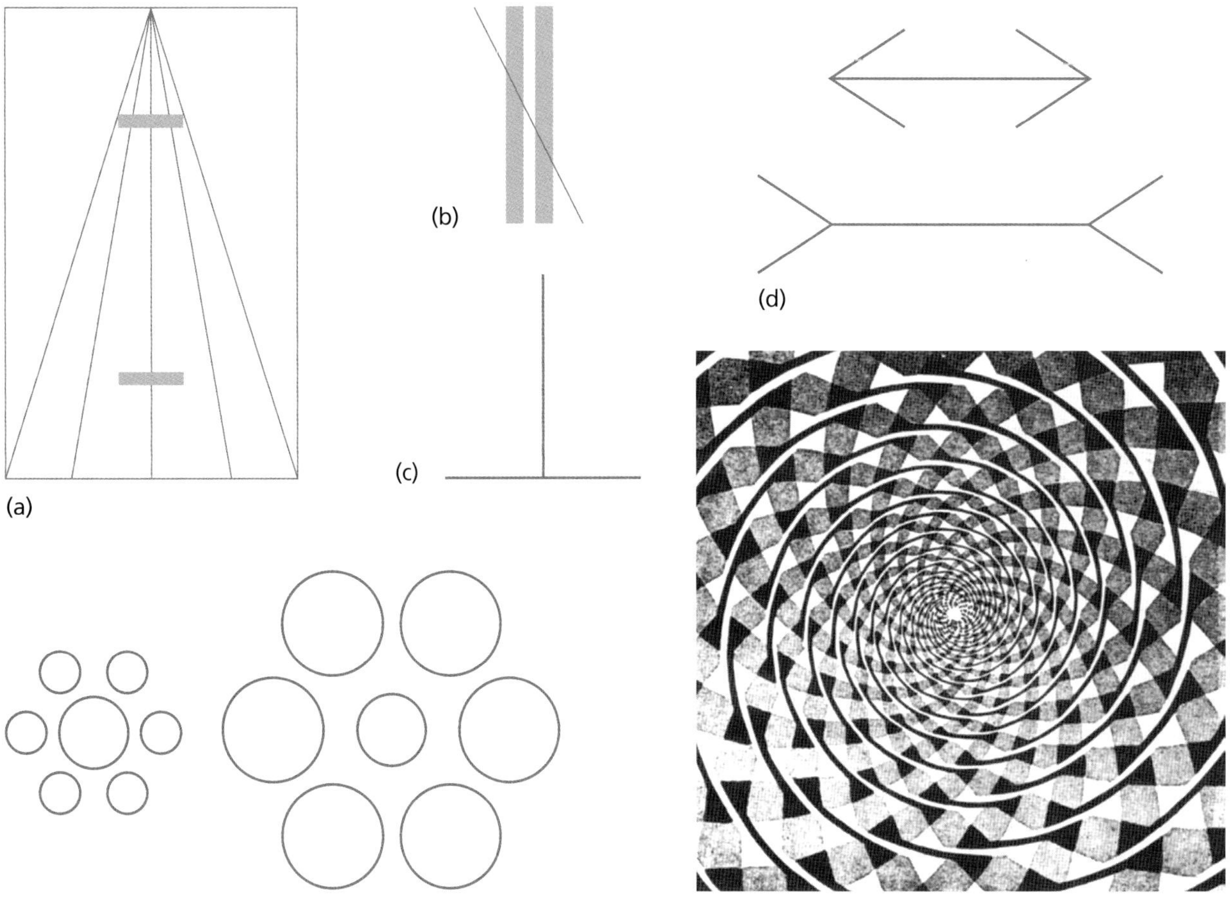

(b)

(d)

(a)

(c)

(e)

(f)

Figure 15.6 Distortions (or geometric illusions). (a) In the **Ponzo illusion**, the horizontal bar at the top is seen as being longer than the horizontal line at the bottom, even though they're both the same length. (b) The **Poggendorf illusion** suggests that the segments of the diagonal line are offset, even though they're not. (c) In the **horizontal-vertical illusion**, the vertical line appears longer than the horizontal line – even though they're of equal length. (d) In the **Müller–Lyer illusion,** the line with the outgoing fins appears to be longer than the line with the ingoing fins, but in fact they're the same length. (e) In **Titchener's circles**, the central circle in the left-hand group is seen as being larger than the central circle of the right-hand group, but they're both the same size. Finally, (f) in the **twisted card illusion**, the twisted cards appear to be a spiral pattern, but the circles are, in fact, concentric

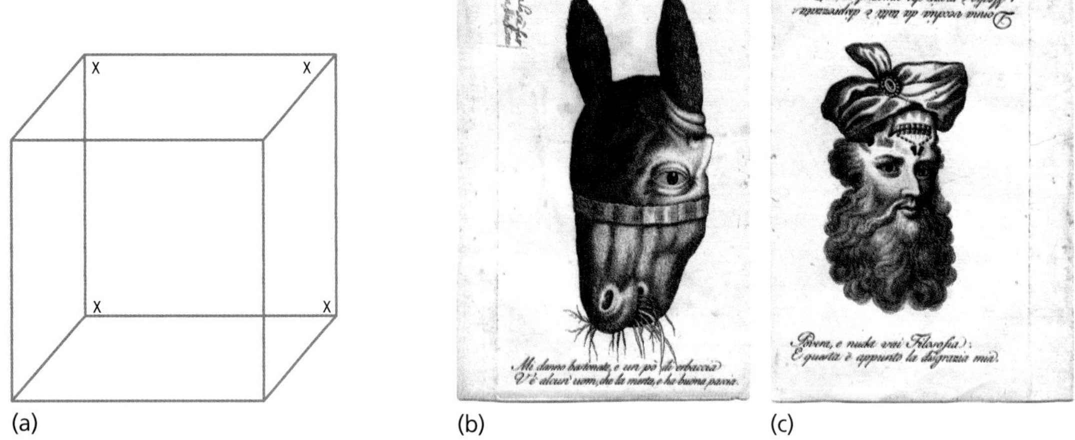

Figure 15.7 Three ambiguous/reversible figures: (a) the Necker cube; and (b) and (c) Giuseppe's engravings: 'Man/Donkey' and 'Memento Mori' (turn the page upside-down)

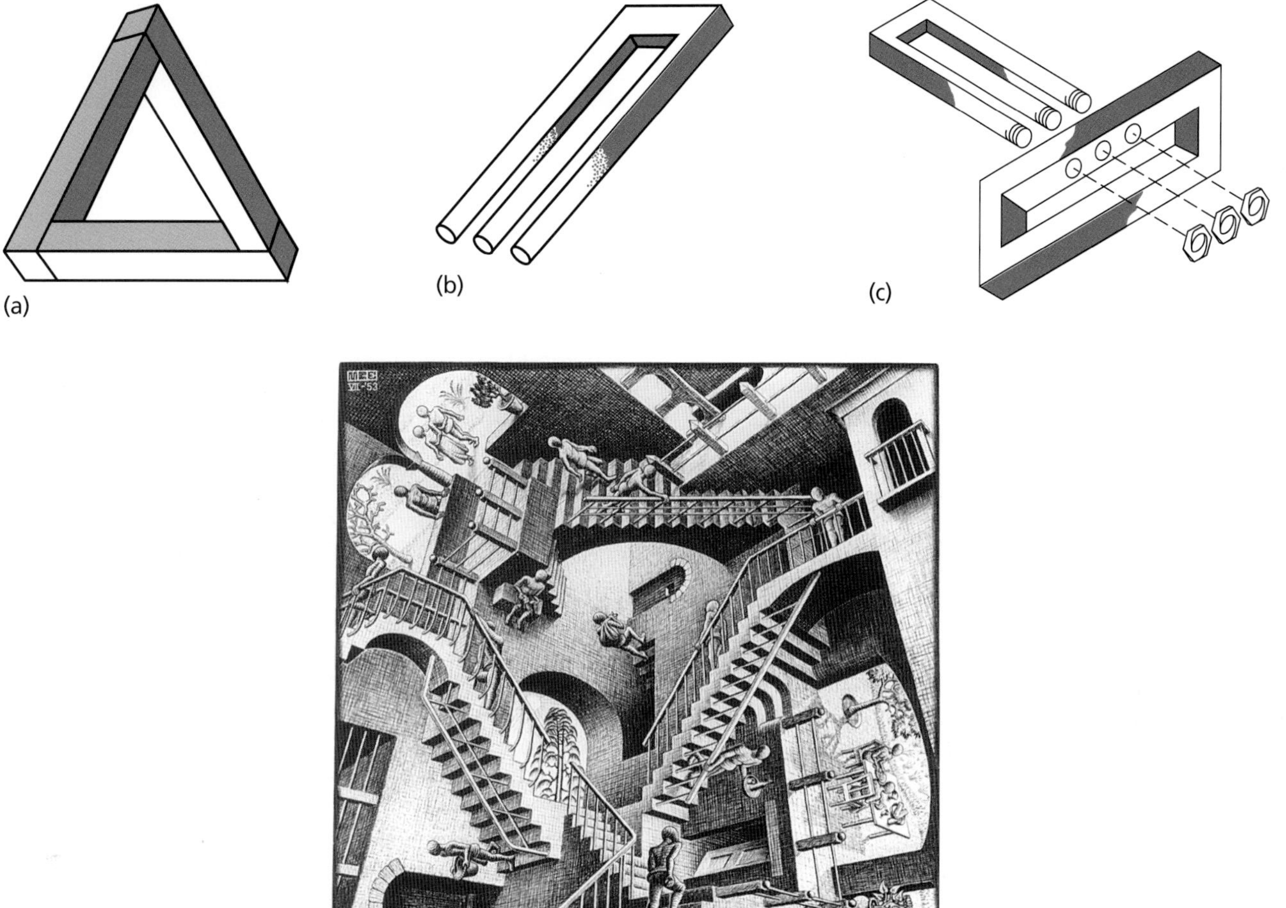

Figure 15.8 Four paradoxical objects: (a) Penrose impossible triangle and (b) variously known as 'Trident' and 'The Devil's Pitchfork'. In (c), Trident has been combined with another impossible object. (d) M.C. Escher's *Relativity*. Although working in two dimensions, Escher has used perceptual cues in such a way as to encourage the viewer to perceive a three-dimensional figure

Fictions

Fictions help explain how we perceive that objects possess specific shapes. The idea that shape is determined by the physical contours of an object (which cause edge-detector cells in the visual system to fire; see Chapter 5) has been challenged by the existence of *subjective contours*. These are the boundaries of a shape perceived in the absence of physical contours (Kanizsa, 1976).

In Figure 15.9a, there's no white triangular contour physically present. But we perceive the shape of a white triangle, which appears to be opaque and lighter than the background. There are some contours that are physically present (the overlap of the triangle and the disc), which might cause enough edge-detector cells to fire. However, this explanation cannot account for the fact that in Figure 15.9b, the partial and straight physical contours give rise to a curved triangle. Nor can it explain the subjective contour in Figure 15.9c, which is marked by lines in a totally different orientation (Krebs and Blackman, 1988).

Ask Yourself

- Can you think of any 'real-life' illusions – that is, illusions that haven't been deliberately created by Psychologists (or artists) to study perception?

Illusions of movement

We're surrounded by illusions in our everyday life. The use of perspective cues by artists leads us to infer depth and distance, that is, we add something

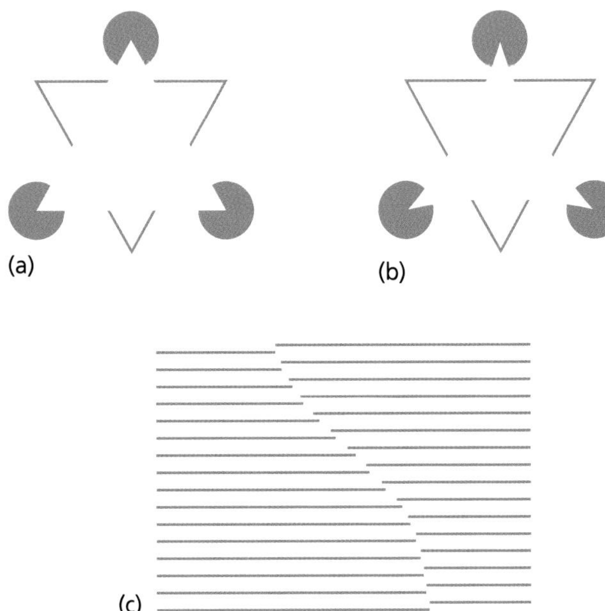

Figure 15.9 Three fictions. In (a), the 'white triangle' is banded by a subjective contour, rather than a continuous physical one. In (b), the subjective contours are curved. In (c), lines of different orientation produce a subjective contour

to a picture which isn't physically present, just as we do to the images projected on our television screens. Television pictures also use the illusion of movement. Just as it's possible for changes in patterns of retinal stimulation not to be accompanied by the perception of movement, so it's possible to perceive movement without a successive pattern of retinal stimulation (Ramachandran and Anstis, 1986). This is called *apparent movement*. (See Box 15.2.)

Illusions of shading

According to Ramachandran and Rogers-Ramachandran (2004), the visual image is inherently ambiguous. Perception is partly a matter of using certain assumptions about the world in order to resolve such ambiguities, and illusions can help uncover the brain's hidden rules and assumptions.

Ask Yourself

- How would you describe the group of disks on the left in Figure 15.10?
- How would you describe those on the right?
- Can you try to explain the different perceptions?

In Figure 15.10, the disks on the left are usually seen as eggs, while those on the right are seen as cavities. The eggs are light on the top, and the cavities are light on the bottom. According to Ramachandran and Rogers-Ramachandran, this reveals an assumption made by the visual system, namely that it expects light to shine from *above*.

Box 15.2 Some examples of apparent movement

The autokinetic effect: If you look at a stationary spot of light in an otherwise completely dark room, the light will appear to move. According to Gregory (1973), this illusion is produced by small and uncontrollable eye movements. Another explanation suggests that it's caused by the absence of a stimulating background to provide a frame of reference for measuring movement. This is supported by the fact that the autokinetic effect disappears if other lights are introduced.

Stroboscopic motion: The illusion of movement is created by the rapid succession of slightly different stationary images. If these are presented sufficiently quickly (around 16–22 frames per second), an illusory impression of continuous movement is produced. This is the mechanism by which moving pictures operate. With fewer than 16 frames per second, the moving picture looks jumpy and unnatural. Smooth slow motion is achieved by filming at a rate of 100 or more frames per second, and then playing back at about 20 frames per second.

The phi phenomenon: This is a simpler form of stroboscopic motion, in which a number of separate lights are turned on and off in quick succession. This gives the impression of a single light moving from one position to another. Both stroboscopic motion and the phi phenomenon can be explained by the *law of continuity* (see Box 15.1).

Induced movement: This occurs when we perceive an object to be moving, although in reality it's stationary and the surroundings are moving. Movie stars, for example, are often filmed in a stationary car with a projection of a moving background behind them. Similarly, when the moon is seen through a thin cover of moving clouds, we sometimes perceive it to be moving very quickly.

Motion after-effects: People who work on inspection belts in factories experience movement after-effects when the belt suddenly stops but is then perceived as moving backwards. Similarly, if you stare at a waterfall and then switch your gaze to the ground surrounding it, the ground appears to be moving in the opposite direction.

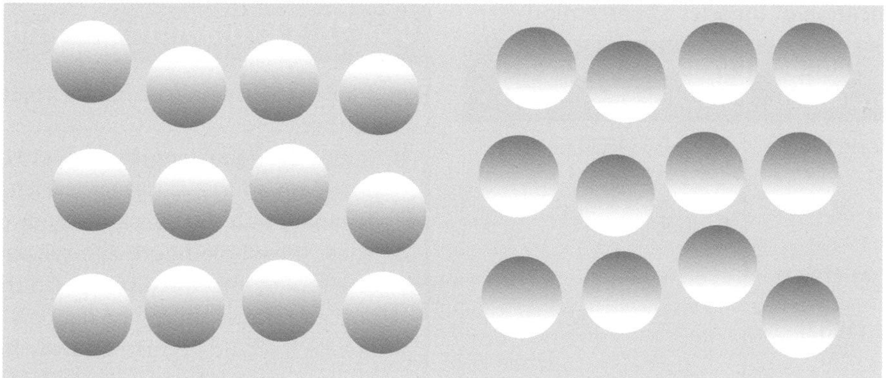

Figure 15.10 From Ramachandran and Rogers-Ramachandran (2004). Reproduced with permission of Scientific American.

Ask Yourself

- Turn the page upside down.
- In Figure 15.10, all the eggs and cavities instantly switch places.
- Ask a friend to hold the page right side up for you. Then bend down and look between your legs at the page (which is now behind you).
- Again, the switch occurs, 'as if the sun is stuck to your head and shining upward from the floor' (Ramachandran and Rogers-Ramachandran, 2004).

Our brain is always abstracting and interpreting the world around us. Even when we know the true nature of an illusion, this insight often does not change our experience. As far as the brain is concerned, if an event is an illusion, it might as well be real (Hood, 2012).

THEORIES OF VISUAL PERCEPTION

Classifying theories

As we noted in the *Introduction and overview,* one way in which theories of perception differ is in terms of whether they regard perception as a *direct* (*bottom-up/data-driven*), or an *indirect* (*top-down/conceptually driven*) process. Bruce and Green (1990) call these 'ecological' and 'traditional', respectively. The term 'ecological' was used by Gibson, the major bottom-up theorist, to imply that visual information from the whole physical environment is available for analysis by retinal receptor cells.

Another issue which divides theories relates to the *nature–nurture debate* (see Chapter 50). *Empiricists* regard perception as primarily the result of learning and experience, while *nativists* believe it's essentially an innate ability, requiring little, if any, learning. All the top-down theorists are also empiricists, and the major nativists are the Gestalt Psychologists. Gibson was influenced by the Gestalt school, but he's generally regarded as an empiricist. Finally, Marr's theory has both top-down and bottom-up components, and he too was influenced by some of the Gestalt laws.

Critical Discussion 15.1

Are illusions real?

- Several studies since the early 1980s have shown that the brain interprets various visual illusions as if they are real.
- For example, Ramachandran (1985) reported that a common trick used by animators to create the perception of an object's movement also applies to illusory contour images. When these illusory shapes are transposed between two locations on subsequent frames, they appear to have migrated. A 2006 neuroimaging study showed that the apparent movement of these shapes activates motion-sensitive regions of the visual cortex. The brain treats these geometric ghosts as if they were real moving objects (Hood, 2012).
- Laeng and Sulutvedt (2013) used pupil dilation to reveal the most dramatic example to date of the real effects of illusions. They used an infrared sensor to measure the pupil sizes of observers as they looked at a brightness illusion, in which one design seems very much brighter than another, even though they're in fact equally bright (the same amount of *physical luminance*). Participants' pupils constricted more in response to the subjectively brighter design: a *subjective* experience of brightness, rather than an *objective* measure, governs the response (traditionally thought of as involuntary, see Chapter 5).
- Examples like this demonstrate that we have no *direct* contact with reality.

Gregory's constructivist theory

According to Gregory (1966):

> *Perception is not determined simply by stimulus patterns. Rather, it is a dynamic searching for the best interpretation of the available data … [which] involves going beyond the immediately given evidence of the senses.*

Table 15.2 A classification of theories of perception

	Direct (bottom-up/ecological)	Indirect (top-down/traditional)
Empiricist	Gibson (1966, 1979)	Gregory (1966, 1972, 1980)
		Bruner (1957)
	Neisser (1967)	
	Marr (1982)	
Nativist	Gestalt	

To avoid sensory overload, we need to *select* from all the sensory stimulation which surrounds us. Also, we often need to *supplement* sensory information, because the total information we need might not be directly available to the senses. This is what Gregory means by 'going beyond the immediately given evidence of the senses', and it's why his theory is known as *constructivist*. For Gregory, we make inferences about the information the senses receive (based on Helmholtz's nineteenth-century view of perception as consisting of *unconscious inferences*).

Gregory's theory and perceptual constancies

Perceptual constancies tell us that visual information from the retinal image is sketchy and incomplete, and that the visual system has to 'go beyond' the retinal image in order to test hypotheses which fill in the 'gaps' (Greene, 1990). To make sense of the various sensory inputs to the retina *(low-level information)*, the visual system must draw on all kinds of evidence, including distance cues, information from other senses, and expectations based on past experience (*high-level knowledge*). For all these reasons, Gregory argues that perception must be an indirect process involving a construction based on physical sources of energy.

Gregory's theory and illusions

Gregory argues that when we experience a visual illusion, what we perceive may not be physically present in the stimulus (and hence not present in the retinal image). Essentially, an illusion can be explained in terms of a perceptual hypothesis which isn't confirmed by the data: our attempt to interpret the stimulus figure turns out to be inappropriate. In other words, an illusion occurs when we attempt unsuccessfully to construe the stimulus in keeping with how we normally construe the world.

All illusions illustrate how the perceptual system normally operates by forming a 'best guess', which is then tested against sensory inputs. For Gregory (1966), illusions show that perception is an active process of using information to suggest and test hypotheses. What we perceive aren't the data, but an *interpretation* of them: a perceived object is a *hypothesis*, suggested and tested by sensory data. This makes the basis of knowledge 'indirect and inherently doubtful' (Gregory, 1996).

When we view a 3-D scene with many distance cues, the perceptual system can quickly select the hypothesis that best interprets the sensory data. However, reversible figures supply few distance cues to guide the system. For example, the spontaneous reversal of the Necker cube (see Figure 15.7a) occurs because the perceptual system continually tests two equally plausible hypotheses about the nature of the object represented.

One striking illusion is the *rotating hollow mask* (Gregory, 1970) (see Figure 15.11). There's sufficient information for us to see the mask as hollow, but it's impossible not to see it as a normal face. The perceptual system dismisses the hypothesis that the mask is an inside-out face, because it's so improbable. The hypothesis we select is strongly influenced by our past experiences of faces (Gregory, 1970).

Box 15.3 Explaining the Ponzo Illusion

In the Ponzo illusion (see Figure 15.6a), our system can either:

- accept the equal lengths of the two central bars as drawn on a flat 2-D surface (which would involve assuming that the bars are equidistant from us), or
- 'read' the whole figure as a railway track converging into the distance (so that the two horizontal bars represent sleepers, the top one of which would be further away from us but appears longer, since it 'must' be longer in order to produce the same length image on the retina).

The second interpretation is clearly inappropriate, since the figure is drawn on a flat piece of paper with no actual distance differences. As a result, we experience an illusion.

Ask Yourself

- Knowing what you do about Gregory's theory, how do you think he might try to explain the Müller–Lyer illusion (see Figure 15.6d)? You may find Box 15.3 helpful.

Misapplied size constancy theory

According to Gregory, the Müller–Lyer illusion can be explained as follows.

- The arrow with the *ingoing fins* provides linear *perspective cues*, suggesting that it could be the *outside corner* of a building. Hence, the fins are seen as walls receding away from us, making the shaft look closer to us.

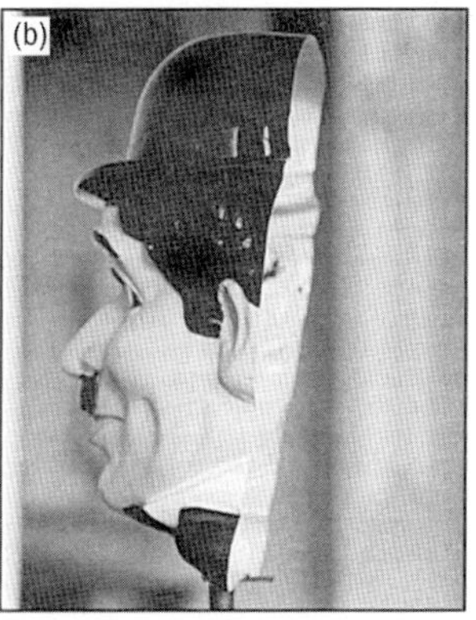

Figure 15.11 The rotating hollow mask. (a) shows the normal face which is rotated to (d), which is a hollow face. However, (d) appears like a normal face rotating in the opposite direction

- In the arrow with the *outgoing fins*, the cues suggest that it could be the *inside corner* of a room, and the outgoing fins as walls coming towards us. This would make the shaft appear 'distant'.

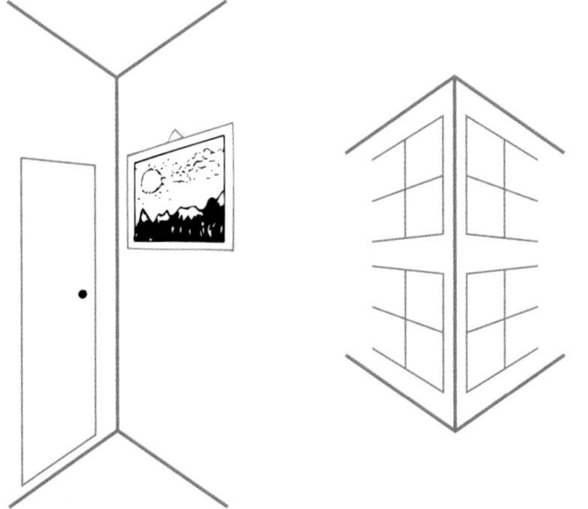

Figure 15.12 A representation of the Müller–Lyer illusion as suggested by Gregory's misapplied size constancy theory

- The retinal images produced by the arrows are actually equal and, according to size constancy, if equally sized images are produced by two lines, one of which is further away from us than the other, then the line which is furthest from us must be longer! Because this interpretation is taking place unconsciously and quickly, we perceive the illusion immediately.

However, if the perspective cues are removed, the illusion remains, suggesting that the misapplied size constancy theory is itself misapplied (see Figure 15.13). Alternatively, the apparent distance of the arrow could be caused by the apparent size of the arrows rather than, as Gregory claims, the other way around (Robinson, 1972).

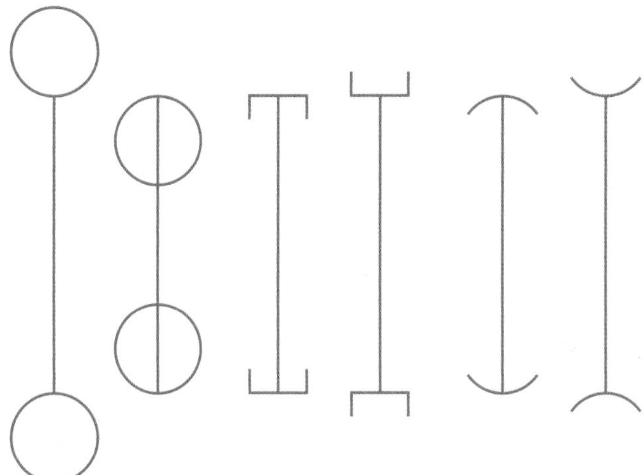

Figure 15.13 The Müller–Lyer illusion with the depth cues removed (after Delboeuf, 1892)

In the Müller–Lyer illusion, we *know* the arrows are the same length, yet we still experience the illusion. Our knowledge should enable us to modify our hypotheses in an adaptive way. While some illusions can be explained in terms of the same unconscious processes occurring (an example being size constancy), not all illusions are amenable to explanation in the way Gregory proposes (Robinson, 1972).

Gregory's theory and perceptual set

Perceptual set is directly relevant to Gregory's view that perception is an active process involving selection, inference and interpretation. Allport (1955) describes perceptual set as:

> *... a perceptual bias or predisposition or readiness to perceive particular features of a stimulus.*

It refers to the tendency to perceive or notice some aspects of available sense data and ignore others. According to Vernon (1955), set acts as:

- a *selector* – the perceiver has certain expectations which help focus attention on particular aspects of the incoming sensory information, and
- an *interpreter* – the perceiver knows how to deal with the selected data, how to classify, understand and name them, and what inferences to draw from them.

Several factors can influence or induce set, most of them being *perceiver* (or *organismic*) variables. An example of this is *wishful seeing*, as described in Box 15.4.

Box 15.4 Wishful seeing: seeing what we want to see

- A common method used for testing *wishful seeing* is to create in participants a desire (e.g. to avoid embarrassment) in order to test how this affects their interpretation of an ambiguous stimulus (see Figure 15.7) (Balcetis and Dunning, 2010).
- Wishful seeing is a robust phenomenon that occurs outside conscious control and despite pressures to change one's perceptual experience. Wishes, hopes and desires affect what people see quickly and without their awareness (Balcetis, 2014).
- One function of wishful seeing may be to help us achieve our goals. If we're tuned and ready to see the good things in our surroundings, we might be better prepared to pursue them (Bruner, 1957). This might explain why thirsty people see a glass of water as bigger (Veltkamp *et al.*, 2008) and a bottle of water as closer (Balcetis and Dunning, 2010).
- Similarly, coins appear larger to poor people (Bruner and Goodman, 1947) and the powerless (Dubois *et al.*, 2010). Money also appears closer to financially strapped college students (Balcetis and Dunning, 2010).
- Research also suggests that people most motivated to make it to a finish line or to make it to the top of a mountain actually see the environment as *less extreme* (Cole *et al.*, 2013).

Other factors influencing/inducing set relate to the nature of the stimulus or the conditions under which it's perceived (*stimulus* or *situational* variables). Both types influence perception *indirectly*, through *directly* influencing set which, as such, is a perceiver variable or characteristic.

An evaluation of Gregory's theory

- Gregory's theory raises many important questions which have yet to be answered satisfactorily (Gordon, 1989). For example, if perception is essentially constructive, then we need to know how it gets started and why there's such common experience among different people, all of whom have had to construct their own idiosyncratic perceptual worlds. Given that perception is typically accurate (and our hypotheses are usually correct), it seems unlikely that our retinal images are really as ambiguous and lacking in detail as Gregory suggests.

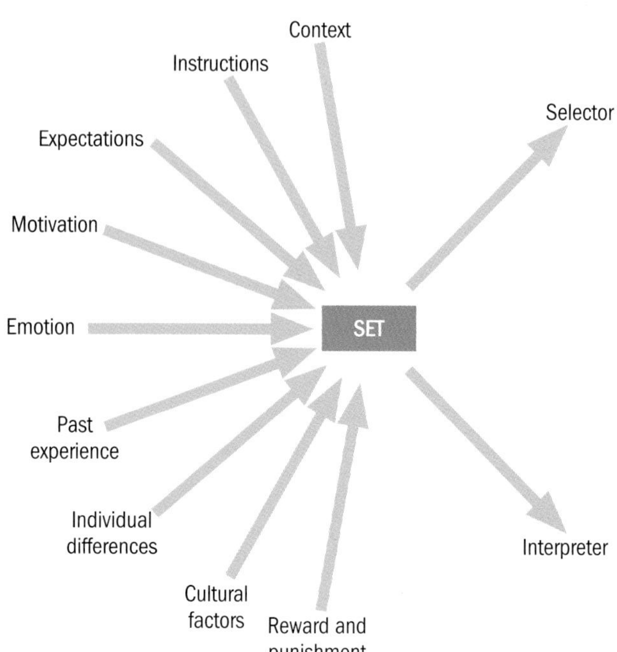

Figure 15.14 The indirect influence of perceiver and stimulus variables on perception through their direct influence on set

- Gregory has been much more successful in explaining at least some types of illusion than in explaining perception as a whole (Eysenck and Keane, 1995). His theory may be most relevant when stimuli are ambiguous or incomplete, presented very briefly, or their processing interrupted (Groome *et al.*, 1999). In Gordon's (1989) view, constructivist theories have underestimated the richness of sensory evidence in the real world. For Gordon:

> *It is possible that we perceive constructively only at certain times and in certain situations. Whenever we move under our own power on the surface of the natural world and in good light, the necessary perceptions of size, texture, distance, continuity, motion and so on, may all occur directly and reflexively.*

Gibson's theory of direct perception

Constructivists use the retinal image as their starting point for explaining perception. According to Gibson (1966), this approach mistakenly describes the input for a perceiver in the same terms as that for a single photoreceptor, namely a stream of photons. For Gibson, it's better to begin by considering the input as a pattern of light extended over time and space (an *optic array* containing all the visual information from the environment striking the eye of a stationary perceiver).

The optic array provides unambiguous, invariant information about the layout and relevant properties of objects in space. This information takes three main forms: *optic flow patterns*, *texture gradient* and *affordances*. Perception essentially involves 'picking up' the rich information provided by the optic array in a direct way, which involves little or no (unconscious) information processing, computations or internal representations (Harris, 1998).

Optic flow patterns

During the Second World War, Gibson prepared training films describing the problems pilots experience when taking off and landing. He called the information available to pilots *optic flow patterns* (OFPs). As shown in Figure 15.15, the point to which a pilot moves appears motionless, with the rest of the visual environment apparently moving away from that point. Thus, all around the point there's an apparent radial expansion of textures flowing around the pilot's head.

Figure 15.15 The optic flow patterns as a pilot approaches the landing strip (from Gibson, 1950)

The lack of apparent movement of the point towards which the pilot moves is an *invariant*, unchanging feature of the optic array. Such OFPs provide unambiguous information about direction, speed and altitude. OFPs in general refer to changes in the optic array as the perceiver moves about.

Texture gradients

Textures expand as we approach them and contract as they pass beyond our heads. This happens whenever we move toward something, so that over and above the behaviour of each texture element, there's a 'higher-order' pattern or structure available as a source of information about the environment (and so the flow of the texture is invariant). Texture gradients (or *gradients of texture density*) are important depth cues perceived directly without the need for any inferences. The depth cues described in Table 15.1 are all examples of directly perceived, invariant, higher-order features of the optic array. For Gibson, then, the third dimension (depth) is available to the senses as directly as the other two dimensions, automatically processed by the sense receptors, and automatically producing the perceptual experience of depth.

Affordances

Affordances are directly perceivable, potential uses of objects, such as surfaces that are stand-on-able or sit-on-able, objects that are graspable or throwable, or that afford eating (are 'edible'). In other words, affordances are the *meanings* that an environment has for an animal, and the relationship between perceiver and environment is vitally important.

An evaluation of Gibson's theory

- Gibson was concerned with the problem of how we obtain constant perception in everyday life, based on continually changing sensations. According to Marr (1982), this indicates that he correctly regarded the problem of perception as that of recovering from sensory information 'valid properties of the external world'.
- However, as Marr points out, Gibson failed to recognise two equally critical things:

> *First, the detection of physical invariants, like image surfaces, is exactly and precisely an information-processing problem ... Second, he vastly underrated the sheer difficulty of such detection.*

- An interesting study by Lee and Lishman (1975) tends to support Gibson's belief in the importance of movement in perception, and the artificiality of separating sensory and motor aspects of behaviour (see Key Study 15.1).
- Gibson's concept of affordances is part of his attempt to show that all the information needed to make sense of the visual environment is directly available in the visual input (a purely 'bottom-up' approach to perception). Bruce and Green (1990) argue that this concept is most powerful and useful in the context of visually guided behaviour, as in insects. Here, it makes sense to speak of an organism detecting information available in the light needed to organise its activities, and the idea of it needing a conceptual representation of its environment seems redundant.
- However, humans act in a *cultural* as well as physical environment. It's inconceivable that we don't need any knowledge of writing or the postal system in order to detect that a pen affords writing or a postbox affords posting a letter, and that these are directly perceived invariants. People see objects and events as what they are in terms of a culturally given conceptual representation of the world, and Gibson's theory says much more about '*seeing*' than about '*seeing as*'.

Key Study 15.1

If the room sways, there may be an experiment going on (Lee and Lishman, 1975)

- Lee and Lishman used a specially built swaying room (suspended above the floor), designed to bring texture flow under experimental control. As the room sways (so changing the texture flow), adults typically make slight unconscious adjustments, and children tend to fall over. Normally, the brain is very skilled at establishing correlations between changes in the optic flow, signals to the muscles, and staying upright.
- Arguably, the most important reason for having a visual system is to be able to anticipate when contact with an approaching object is going to be made. Lee and Lishman believe that estimating 'time to contact' is crucial for actions such as avoidance of objects and grasping them, and thus represents extremely important ecological information. This can be expressed as a formula:

$$\text{Time to contact} = \frac{\text{size of retinal image}}{\text{rate of expansion of retinal image}}$$

- This is a property shared by all objects, and so is another invariant, demonstrating the unambiguous nature of the retinal image.
- Measures of optic flow have also provided some understanding of how skilled long-jumpers control their approaches to the take-off position (Gordon, 1989).

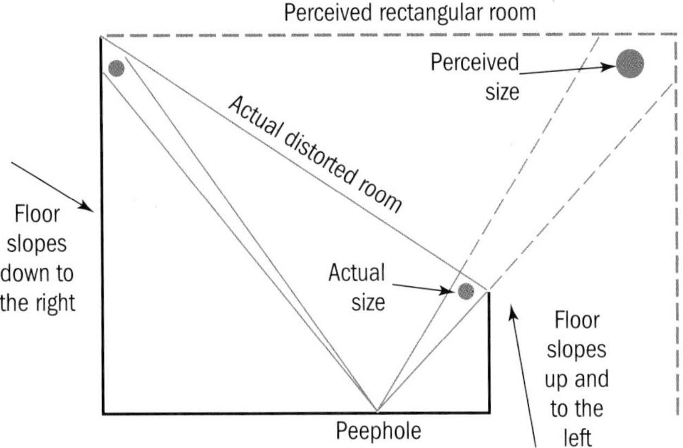

Figure 15.16 The Ames room and a schematic representation of its 'secret'. The room is constructed in such a way that, when viewed with one eye through a peephole, a person at one end may appear very small and the person at the other end very tall. When they cross the room, they appear to change size. The room itself appears perfectly normal and regular to an observer

'Seeing' and 'seeing as'

According to Fodor and Pylyshyn (1981):

> *What you see when you see a thing depends upon what the thing you see is. But what you see the thing as depends upon what you know about what you are seeing.*

This view of perception as 'seeing as' is the fundamental principle of *transactionalism*. Transactionalists (such as Ames, cited in Ittelson, 1952) argue that because sensory input is always ambiguous, the interpretation selected is the one most likely to be true given what's been perceived in the past.

In the Ames distorted room (see Figure 15.16), the perceiver has to choose between two different beliefs about the world built up through past experience. The first is that rooms are rectangular, consist of right angles, and so on. The second is that people are usually of 'average' height. Most observers choose the first, and so judge the people to be an odd size. However, a woman who saw her husband in the room and judged the room to be odd, shows that particularly salient past experiences can override more generalised beliefs about the world.

The Ames room is another example of a visual illusion, and the inability of Gibson's theory to explain mistaken perception is perhaps its greatest single weakness. Gibson argues that most 'mistaken perceptions' occur in situations very different from those which prevail in the natural environment. However, to suggest that illusions are nothing but laboratory tricks designed to baffle ordinary people isn't true: at least some produce effects similar to those found in normal perception. A striking example is the 'hollow mask' illusion (Bruce and Green, 1990; see Figure 15.11).

A possible synthesis of Gregory's and Gibson's theories

Despite the important differences between Gibson's and Gregory's theories, they also agree on certain points.

Similarities

- Visual perception is mediated by light reflected from surfaces and objects.
- Some kind of physiological system is needed to perceive.
- Perception is an active process. (In Gibson's, 1966, view, 'a perceiving organism is more like a map-reader than a camera').
- Perceptual experience can be influenced by learning.

Differences

- Gregory believes that meaningless sensory cues must be supplemented by memory, habit, experience and so on, in order to construct a meaningful world. Gibson argues that the environment (initially the optic array) provides us with all the information we need for living in the world. Perceptual learning consists not in 'gluing' together sensory 'atoms', but in coming to differentiate and discriminate between the features of the environment as presented in the optic array.
- To the extent that Gibson acknowledges the role of learning (albeit a different kind of learning from Gregory), he may be considered an empiricist (see above), together with his emphasis on what's provided by the physical world. In other respects, though, Gibson can be considered a nativist. As we noted earlier, he was very much influenced by the Gestalt Psychologists, stressing the organised quality of perception. However, while for Gibson this organised quality is part of the physical structure of the light impinging on the observer's eye, for Gestaltists it's a function of how the brain is organised.

Eysenck and Keane (1995) argue that the relative importance of bottom-up and top-down processes is affected by several factors. When viewing conditions are good, bottom-up processing may be crucial. However, with brief and/or ambiguous stimuli, top-down processing becomes increasingly important. Gibson seems to have been more concerned with optimal viewing conditions, while Gregory and other constructivists have tended to concentrate on sub-optimal conditions (Eysenck, 1993). In most circumstances, both bottom-up *and* top-down processes are probably needed, as claimed by Neisser (1976).

Box 15.5 Neisser's (1976) analysis-by-synthesis model

- Neisser assumes the existence of a perceptual cycle involving schemata, perceptual exploration and stimulus environment.
- Schemata contain collections of knowledge based on past experience (see Chapter 21), and these direct perceptual exploration towards relevant environmental stimulation. Such exploration often involves moving around the environment, leading the perceiver actively to sample the available stimulus information. If this fails to match the information in the relevant schema, then the hypothesis is modified accordingly.
- An initial analysis of the sensory cues/features (a bottom-up process) might suggest the hypothesis that the object being viewed is, say, a chair. This initiates a search for the expected features (such as four legs and a back), which is based on our schema of a chair (and this synthesis is a top-down process).
- But if the environmental features disconfirm the original hypothesis (the 'chair' has only three legs and no back), then a new hypothesis must be generated and tested (it might be a stool), and the appropriate schema activated.
- Neisser argues that perception never occurs in a vacuum: our sampling of sensory features of the environment is always guided by our knowledge and past experience. Perception is an interactive process, involving both bottom-up feature analysis and top-down expectations.

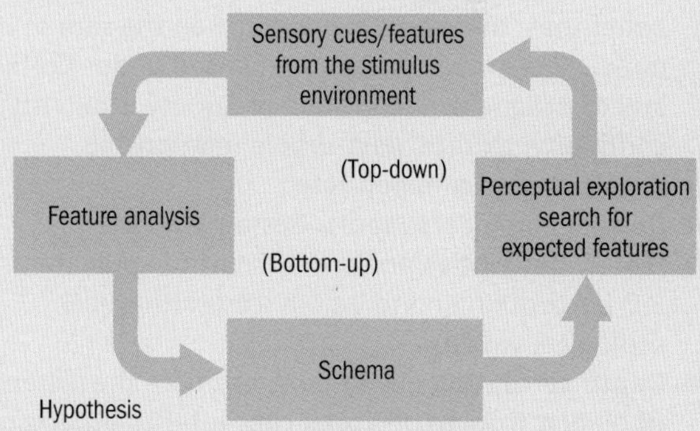

Figure 15.17 Neisser's analysis-by-synthesis model of perception

Marr's computational theory of vision

According to Marr (1982), the central 'problem' of perception is identifying the precise mechanisms and computations by which useful information about a scene is extracted from that scene ('useful information' being what will guide the thoughts or actions of the total system of which the visual system is part). Marr's theory begins by asking 'What is the visual system for?', because only by answering this can we understand how it works.

For Marr, there are three levels at which *any* process must be understood:

- The *computational theory level* is a theoretical analysis of the tasks performed by a system (in this case, the visual system), and the methods needed to perform them.
- The *algorithmic level* is concerned with identifying the actual operations by which perceptual tasks (processes and representations) are achieved.

- The *hardware or implementation level* is concerned with the mechanisms underlying the system's operation. In the case of a biological visual system, these are neuronal or nervous system structures.

Marr argues that vision's main 'job' is to derive a representation of the *shape* of objects from information contained in the retinal image. This happens via four successive *stages* or *modules*:

1. The image (or grey-level description)
2. The primal sketch (raw and full)
3. 2½-D sketch
4. 3-D model representation.

Each stage/module takes as its input the information it receives from the previous stage/module, converting it into a more complex description/representation. By taking the image as the starting point, Marr's approach is strictly bottom-up (Roth, 1995). However, there are also top-down aspects.

CONCLUSIONS

Form and depth perception, perceptual constancy and visual illusions are all concerned with *perceptual organisation*, and many of the principles governing perceptual organisation are commonly referred to as Gestalt laws.

While Gregory's constructivist ('top-down') and Gibson's direct ('bottom-up') approaches may appear to contradict each other, it's possible to see them as complementary. According to Harris (1998):

> *Perception is not just a single task but ... contributes in many different ways to everyday life ... Some of these ... are obviously more difficult than others and it seems likely that some can be accomplished directly, as Gibson maintained, whilst others may require sophisticated internal knowledge and are thus better described by the indirect approach.*

Chapter Summary

- **Sensation** involves physical stimulation of the sense organs, while **perception** is the organisation and interpretation of incoming sensory information.
- **Gestalt Psychologists** identified innately determined principles through which sensory information is interpreted and organised. The most basic of these is **form perception**, which organises incoming sensory information into **figure and ground.**
- Laws for grouping stimuli together all rest on the belief that 'the whole is greater than the sum of its parts'. These laws can be summarised under Koffka's **law of prägnanz** and include **proximity, similarity, continuity, closure, part–whole relationship, simplicity** and **common fate.**
- Despite empirical support, Gestalt laws are merely **descriptive** and are difficult to apply to 3-D perception and to whole scenes (they lack **ecological validity**).
- **Depth perception** allows us to estimate the distance of objects from us. **Pictorial cues** refer to aspects of the visual field, and are **monocular. Non-pictorial cues** include **convergence** and **retinal disparity,** which are **binocular.**
- **Perceptual constancy** refers to the ability to recognise an object as unchanging despite changes in its **size, shape, location, brightness** and **colour.**
- Four main kinds of **visual illusion** are **distortions/ geometric illusions, ambiguous/reversible figures, paradoxical figures** and **fictions.** Others include those involving **apparent movement** and **shading.**
- According to **top-down (conceptually driven) theorists**, perception is the end result of an **indirect** process that involves making inferences about the world, based on knowledge and expectations.
- **Bottom-up (data-driven) theorists** argue that perception is a **direct** process, determined by the information presented to the sensory receptors.
- According to Gregory's **constructivist theory,** we often supplement perception with **unconscious inferences.** His **misapplied size constancy theory** claims that we interpret the ingoing and outgoing fins of the arrows in the Müller–Lyer illusion as providing perspective cues to distance.
- **Perceptual set** acts as a **selector** and **interpreter,** and can be induced by **perceiver/organismic** and **stimulus/situational** variables. Perceiver variables include expectations, which often interact with context.
- According to Gibson, the **optic array** provides information about the layout and properties of objects in space requiring little or no (unconscious) information processing, computations or internal representations. **Optic flow patterns (OFPs), texture gradients** and **affordances** are all **invariant**, unchanging and 'higher-order' features of the optic array.
- Gibson overlooked the role of **culturally determined knowledge** in perception. He also failed to distinguish between **seeing** and **seeing as,** the latter forming the basic principle of **transactionalism.**
- Both Gibson and Gregory agree that perception is an **active** process, influenced by **learning** (making

them **empiricists**), although they propose different kinds of learning. Gibson is also a **nativist** in certain respects and was influenced by the Gestalt Psychologists.

- Bottom-up processing (Gibson) may be crucial under **optimal viewing conditions**, but under **sub-optimal conditions**, top-down processing (Gregory) becomes increasingly important.
- According to Neisser's **analysis-by-synthesis model,** perception is an **interactive** process, involving both bottom-up feature analysis and top-down expectations (appearing at different stages of a perceptual cycle).
- Marr's **computational theory** states that vision's main function is to derive a representation of **object shape** from information in the retinal image. This is achieved via a series of four increasingly complex **stages/modules**: the **image/grey-level description**, the **primal sketch**, the **2½-D sketch,** and the **3-D model representation/object recognition**.

Links with Other Topics/Chapters

Chapter 5 ⟶ Although perception and *sensation* are different, there are some important areas of overlap, as in non-*pictorial depth cues*, *colour* and *brightness constancy*, and the importance of *eye movements*

Chapter 14 ⟶ All the major theories of perception, and in particular the Gestalt principles of perceptual organisation, can be seen as concerned with *pattern recognition*

Chapter 50 ⟶ Most theories of perception can be classified as *empiricist*, the main exception being the Gestalt theory, which is *nativist*

Chapter 20 ⟶ The Gestalt Psychologists contributed to early research into *problem-solving*

Chapters 22, 23 and 24 ⟶ Gestalt principles have also had a considerable impact on many aspects of *Social Psychology*, in particular *social perception* (the perception of people), *attribution theory* and *theories of attitude change*

Chapter 26 ⟶ Sherif used the autokinetic effect in his famous *conformity* experiment

Recommended Reading

Gregory, R.L. (1966) *Eye and Brain*. London: Weidenfeld and Nicolson.

Gregory, R.L. (1970) *The Intelligent Eye*. London: Weidenfeld and Nicolson.

Also Chapters 2 and 3 in Eysenck and Keane (2000), and Chapter 3 in Solso (1995) (see Chapter 13).

Useful Websites

http://cvr.yorku.ca (Centre for Vision Research)

http://persci.mit.edu/ (Perceptual science group @ MIT)

http://webspace.ship.edu/cgboer/gestalt.html (Biographies of Gestalt theorists and their ideas)

http://dogfeathers.com/java/necker.html (Mark Newbold's Animated Necker Cube)

http://plato.stanford.edu/entries/relativism/supplement1.html (Stanford Encyclopaedia of Philosophy: Relativism and the constructive aspects of perception)

www.britannica.com/EBchecked/topic/232098/Gestalt-psychology (Very useful links to other aspects of perception)

www.tinyurl.com/qho4cmf (Illusion demonstrations)

CHAPTER 16

THE DEVELOPMENT OF PERCEPTUAL ABILITIES

Overview of the research

Studies of human cataract patients

Non-human animal experiments

Perceptual adaptation/readjustment studies

Studying neonate and infant visual perception

Cross-cultural studies

INTRODUCTION and OVERVIEW

Chapters 5 and 15 showed that visual perception is a complex set of interconnected and overlapping abilities, including perception of depth, shape and movement. Whether these are present at birth or develop through experience has been one of Psychology's most enduring debates. This chapter examines the evidence concerning the development of visual perception.

In Chapter 15, we distinguished between *nativists* and *empiricists*. While these terms originally denoted philosophical schools of thought (see Chapters 1 and 3), they're still used in the context of psychological debates regarding the origins of human abilities, such as language (see Chapter 19) and perception. Nativists are 'naturists', who believe that we're born with certain capacities to perceive the world in particular ways. These abilities may take time to appear, but they do so through the genetically determined process of *maturation*, with little or no learning being involved (see Chapter 50). Empiricists, by contrast, are 'nurturists', maintaining that all our knowledge and abilities are acquired through experience; that is, they're *learned*. For Locke (1690), the mind at birth is a blank slate (or *tabula rasa*) on which experience 'writes'. Locke's belief was supported by James (1890), according to whom:

> *The baby, assailed by eyes, ears, nose, skin and entrails at once, feels it all as one great booming, buzzing confusion.*

Most present-day Psychologists wouldn't take such extreme views. They'd probably consider themselves to be *interactionists*, believing that while we may be born with certain capacities, environmental influences are crucial for determining how – and even whether – these capacities actually develop. Although particular abilities may be more affected by genetic or environmental influences, *all* abilities are the product of an interaction between both sets of factors.

In a different sense, empiricists are also interactionists. Segall (1994) says that every perception is the result of an interaction between a stimulus and a perceiver, shaped by prior experience. This is essentially a 'top-down' view consistent with Gregory's theory (see Chapter 15). However, it also helps to underline an important, but rarely acknowledged, similarity between those who favour the nativist or empiricist approaches: the perceiver isn't a passive responder to external stimuli, but in some way contributes to, and influences, the perceptual experience.

OVERVIEW of the RESEARCH

Ask Yourself

- What do you consider might be the main advantage and disadvantage of studying (a) newborn babies and (b) non-human animals in trying to understand the development of perceptual abilities?

An evaluation of the research methods

- Investigating the perceptual abilities of newborn babies (or *neonates*) represents the most *direct* way of investigating the nature–nurture issue.

In general, the earlier a particular ability appears, the more likely it is to be under the influence of genetic factors. But the fact that it develops some time after birth doesn't necessarily mean it's been learnt: it could take time to mature. However, there are other special difficulties involved in studying speechless participants.

- *Non-human animal experiments* often involve depriving animals of normal sensory and perceptual stimulation, and recording the long-term effects on their sensory and perceptual abilities. Others study how animals' brains control perceptual abilities. From a research point of view, the main advantage of studying animals is that we can manipulate their environments in ways that aren't permissible with humans. *Deprivation studies* can tell us how much and what kinds of early experience are necessary for normal perceptual development in those species being studied. But we must be very cautious about generalising these findings to humans. We must also be aware of the ethical objections to such research (see Chapter 48).
- Studies of *human cataract patients* represent the human counterpart to non-human deprivation experiments. These patients have been deprived of normal visual experience through a physical defect, rather than through experimental manipulation/interference, and constitute a kind of 'natural experimental group'. Their vision is restored through surgical removal of the cataract, and the abilities that are evident immediately after removal of the bandages are normally taken to be unlearned. However, generalising from 'unusual' adults can be misleading.
- In studies of *perceptual adaptation/readjustment*, human volunteers wear special goggles which distort the visual world in various ways. If they can adapt to such a distorted-looking world, then human 'perceptual habits' cannot be as fixed or rigid as they would be if they were under genetic control. However, the adaptation involved may be motor, rather than perceptual, that is, learning to move about successfully in a very different-looking environment. If this is the case, then we cannot be sure that our perceptual 'habits' are habits at all (learned in the first place), but only that we're good at changing our body movements to 'match' what we see.
- *Cross-cultural studies* attempt to test whether or not the way that people in western culture perceive things is universal, that is, perceived in the same way by people who live in cultures very different from our own. The most common method of testing is to present members of different cultural groups with the same stimulus material, usually visual illusions. Cross-cultural studies prevent us from generalising from a comparatively small sample of the earth's population (Price-Williams, 1966; see Chapter 47). Consistent differences between different cultural groups are usually attributed to environmental factors of some kind. Such studies, therefore, enable us to discover the extent to which perceiving is structured by the nervous system (and so common to all human beings), and to what extent by experience. But Psychologists cannot agree as to the key features of such cultural experience.

What general conclusions can we draw?

As we noted in the *Introduction and overview*, most psychologists are interactionists. However, some attempts have been made to test directly the merits of the nativist and empiricist positions, particularly in relation to neonates and infants. Most of the evidence supporting the nativist view derives from infant studies.

Although the bulk of the evidence supports the interactionist position, there are grounds for concluding that relatively simple perceptual abilities are controlled more by genes and less susceptible to environmental influence; the reverse is true for more complex abilities. The most clear-cut demonstration of this comes from human cataract patients.

Ask Yourself

- Looking back at Chapters 5 and 15, identify some examples of what you think may count as simple and complex visual abilities.
- What determined your choice; in other words, what makes them simple or complex?

STUDIES of HUMAN CATARACT PATIENTS

Most of the evidence comes from the work of von Senden (1932), a German doctor, who reported on 65 cases of people who had undergone cataract-removal surgery between 1700 and 1928. A cataract is a film over the lens of the eye, which prevents normal (patterned) light from entering the eye. Cataracts can be present at birth or develop any time afterwards, and their removal 'restores' vision.

Hebb (1949) re-analysed von Senden's data in terms of:

- *figural unity*, the ability to detect the presence of a figure or stimulus, and
- *figural identity*, being able to name or in some other way identify the object, to 'say' what it is.

Initially, cataract patients are bewildered by an array of visual stimuli (rather like the 'booming, buzzing confusion' of newborn babies). However, they can distinguish *figure from ground* (see Chapter 15), *fixate* and *scan* objects, and follow moving objects with their eyes. But they cannot identify by sight alone those objects already familiar through touch (including faces), or distinguish between various geometrical shapes without counting the corners or tracing the outline with their fingers. They also fail to show *perceptual constancy*. However, this is contradicted by Bower's research with neonates, which suggests that size and shape constancy are innate.

So, the more simple ability of figural unity is available very soon after cataract removal and doesn't seem to depend on prior visual experience. But the more complex figural identity seems to require learning. Hebb believes that this is how these two aspects of perception normally develop. Further evidence comes from the case of S.B. (see Case Study 16.1).

Evaluation of cataract patient studies

- Adult patients aren't the same as babies. While infants' sensory systems are all relatively immature, adults have other well-developed sensory modalities which tend to compensate for the lack of vision (especially touch and hearing). These other channels may actually hinder visual learning, because the patient may have to 'unlearn' previous experience. For example, S.B.'s continued preference for touch over vision may reflect a tendency to stick with what's familiar, rather than experiment with the unknown. This may be a safer conclusion to draw than Hebb's, which is that figural identity is (normally) learned.
- Traditionally, cataract patients haven't been adequately prepared for their 'new world of vision'. The resulting confusion and general emotional distress following the operation may make it difficult to be sure just what they can and cannot see. When blind, S.B. would cross the street by himself, but he was too scared to do it once he could see the traffic. In fact, he died three years after his operation, at least partially from depression (which was also common amongst von Senden's cases).
- Some physical deterioration of the visual system may have occurred during the years of blindness. This could account for the absence of figural identity, rather than lack of visual stimulation and learning (as Hebb maintains).

Case Study 16.1

S.B. (Gregory and Wallace, 1963)

- S.B. was 52 when he received his sight after a corneal graft operation.
- His judgement of size and distance was good, provided he was familiar with the objects in question.
- Unlike most of the cases studied by Hebb, he could recognise objects visually if he was already familiar with them through touch (he displayed good *cross-modal transfer*). However, he seemed to have great difficulty in identifying objects visually if he wasn't already familiar with them in this way. A year after his operation, he still couldn't draw the front of a bus although the rest of the drawing was very well executed (see Figure 16.1).
- As the months passed, it became clear that S.B. was in some ways like a newborn baby when it came to recognising objects and events by sight alone. For instance, he found it impossible to judge distances by sight alone. He knew what windows were, but, of course, he'd never been able to look out from a top-floor window, and he thought 'he would be able to touch the ground below the window with his feet if he lowered himself by his hands'. The window in question was the one in his hospital room – 40 feet above the ground!
- He never learnt to interpret facial expressions, although he could infer a person's mood from the sound of their voice. He preferred to sit in the dark all evening, instead of putting on the light.

Figure 16.1 This was drawn after S.B. had had some experience of sighted travel. Basically, it shows the parts he knew by touch but clearly he had also, by this time, noticed the bright advertisement for Typhoo Tea on the side of the bus

Key Study 16.1

Project Prakash: What newly-sighted children can tell us (Sinha, 2013)

- Project Prakash is a combination of cataract-removal among some of India's huge numbers of congenitally blind children and young adults, and a scientific investigation of how the brain learns to make sense of visual information.
- Typically, the newly-sighted display profound impairments. For example, (i) they cannot organise the many regions of different colours and brightness into larger assemblies; (ii) many features of ordinary objects are perceived as entirely separate objects (not component parts of the same larger structure).
- It's as if the visual scene is a collage of many unrelated areas of colour and luminance (like an abstract painting). This perceptual *overfragmentation* makes it difficult to detect whole objects.
- While there was no evidence of Gestalt principles of organisation (see text below), interesting changes occur over time.
- Consistent with Gregory and Wallace's findings, S.K. had a hard time delineating whole objects; his new visual world was a bewildering collection of colours and brightnesses, with little to glue them together into coherent entities. He didn't appear particularly thrilled with his new vision.
- However, images that were hopelessly confusing for S.K. when static became interpretable when their constituent parts *moved.* Eighteen months later, he expressed his happiness about his improved vision. S.K.'s experience was replicated in that of other, much younger, participants.
- Replicating Hebb's findings, but contrary to Gregory and Wallace's, participants tended to display poor *inter-(cross) modal transfer:* the inability to recognise visually what they could identify just through touch.
- However, within just a few weeks, this ability appeared. Other higher-order visual functions that can be acquired include the ability to differentiate objects in an image, detecting faces, and mentally reasoning about the spatial arrangements of objects they observe.
- At the same time, some key lower-level visual abilities, such as *acuity, spatial contrast* and *optical stability*, are compromised by extended deprivation; these deficits appear to be permanent.

... taken together, these studies suggest that many years of congenital blindness do not preclude the development of sophisticated visual ability at a relatively advanced age ... neural plasticity – the ability of the visual system, for one, to adapt to new experiences – exists even late in childhood or in young adults ... (Sinha, 2013)

- Sinha's findings seem to be broadly consistent with Hebb's: the lower-order abilities that fail to develop are normally innate, while the higher-order functions can develop given the right amount and kind of visual experience.

- The reliability of the case histories themselves is open to doubt. There's great variability in the ages of the patients, when they underwent surgery, and when their cataracts first appeared, and hence in the amount of their previous visual experience.

NON-HUMAN ANIMAL EXPERIMENTS

An early experiment by Riesen (1947), in which one group of chimps was raised in darkness until they were 16 months old, served only to show that a certain amount of light is physically necessary to maintain the visual system and allow it to mature normally (Weiskrantz, 1956).

Later, Riesen (1965) reared three chimps from birth to seven months of age, under three different conditions:

- Debi spent the whole time in darkness.
- Kova spent 1½ hours per day exposed to *diffuse* (or unpatterned) light by wearing translucent goggles; the rest of the time was spent in darkness.
- Lad was raised in normal lighting conditions.

Ask Yourself

- What do you think the outcome of this experiment was?
- For example, which chimp suffered retinal damage, and what effects might exposure to unpatterned light have had?

As expected, only Debi suffered retinal damage. Lad was no different, perceptually, from any other normally reared chimp. It was Kova who was of special interest, because she was only exposed to unpatterned light (patches of different colours and brightnesses – not distinguishable shapes or patterns), but without suffering any retinal damage. Her perceptual development was noticeably retarded.

These, and similar experiments with monkeys, chimps and kittens, suggest that:

- light is necessary for normal physical development of the visual system (at least in chimps, some monkeys and kittens)

- patterned light is also necessary for the normal development of more complex visual abilities (in those species), such as following a moving object, differentiating between geometrical shapes, perceiving depth and distinguishing a moving from a stationary object.

Other animal experiments have also shown the impact of early experience on perceptual abilities.

Key Study 16.2

Kitten carousel experiment (Held and Hein, 1963)

- Held and Hein used a kitten carousel to study kittens' ability to guide their movements using vision (see Figure 16.2).
- For their first eight weeks, kittens were kept in darkness. They then spent three hours each day in the carousel, the rest of the time being spent in darkness. The 'active' kitten could move itself around (its legs were free), and its movements were transmitted to the 'passive' kitten via a series of pulleys. Every time the active kitten moved, the passive kitten moved the same distance, at the same speed. Since the visual environment was constant, both kittens had exactly the same visual experience.

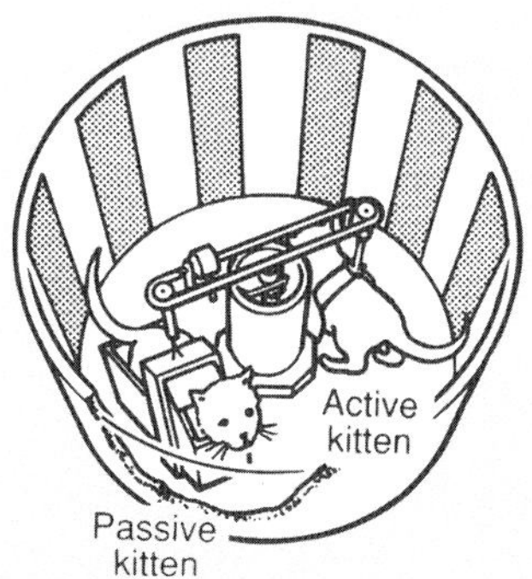

Figure 16.2 The kitten carousel (from Held, 1965)

- When paw–eye co-ordination was tested several weeks later, the passive kittens were markedly inferior. For example, they showed no evidence of depth perception when placed on the deep side of the visual cliff apparatus (see text below and Figure 16.8).
- However, they soon learned the normal avoidance responses on the deep side of the cliff when allowed to run around in a lighted environment. This suggests that what they'd failed to learn were the correct *motor responses* associated with depth perception (*sensorimotor coordination*), rather that depth perception as such (see the section on perceptual readjustment studies below).

Blakemore and Cooper (1970) raised kittens from birth in darkness, except for a five-hour period each day when they were placed in a large, round chamber. This had either vertical or horizontal stripes painted on the inside, and a glass floor which reflected the pattern of stripes. The kittens wore special collars which prevented them from seeing their own bodies, and the stripes were the only visual stimuli they encountered.

At five months old, the kittens were tested for line recognition by being presented with a moving pointer held either vertically or horizontally. Those reared in the 'vertical world' would reach out only to a vertical pointer, while those raised in the 'horizontal world' reached only for a horizontal pointer. Depending on their early visual experience, the kittens acted as if they were blind in the presence of the other kind of visual stimulus.

This 'behavioural blindness' mirrored 'physiological blindness'. By placing microelectrodes into individual cells in the visual cortex, Blakemore and Cooper found that the 'vertical' kittens didn't possess cells that were responsive to bars of light moved horizontally, and the reverse was true for the 'horizontal' kittens. The only receptive fields to have developed were those which reflected the kittens' early visual experience (see Chapter 5). The findings suggest very strongly that certain kinds of perceptual ability are learned in some species.

Evaluation of non-human animal experiments

- A general problem with non-human animal studies (as with studies of human infants) is that we can only *infer* their perceptual experiences through observing their behaviour or their physiological responses. We cannot be certain that animals deprived in particular ways don't perceive particular stimuli, only that they don't *behave* as if they do.

Ask Yourself

- Do you consider the experiments by Riesen, Held and Hein, and Blakemore and Cooper to be ethically acceptable?
- What kinds of scientific justification could be made in their defence?

PERCEPTUAL ADAPTATION/ READJUSTMENT STUDIES

If it can be shown that people are capable of perceiving the world in a different way from normal, and adjusting to this altered perception, then perception is probably learned. Neither salamanders (Sperry, 1943) nor chickens (Hess, 1956) show any evidence of being able to adapt to distorted perceptions, suggesting that genetic factors largely control their perceptual abilities.

One of the earliest recorded human studies was that of Stratton. (See Key Study 16.3.)

Key Study 16.3

Turning the world upside down (Stratton, 1896)

- Stratton fitted himself with a telescope on one eye which 'turned the world upside down'. The other eye was kept covered. He wore the telescope for a total of 87 hours over an eight-day period, wearing blindfolds at night and at other times when not wearing the inverting lens. As far as possible, Stratton went about his normal routine.
- For the first three days, he was aware that part of his environment – the part not in his immediate field of vision but on the periphery – was in a different orientation.
- But by day four, he was beginning to imagine unseen parts as also being inverted, and by day five he had to make a conscious effort to remember that he actually had the telescope on. He could walk round the house without bumping into furniture, and when he moved his surroundings looked 'normal'. However, when he concentrated hard and remained still, things still appeared upside down.
- By day eight, everything seemed 'harmonious'; he began to 'feel' inverted, but this was quite normal and natural to him.

When Stratton removed the telescope, he immediately recognised the visual orientation as the one that existed before the experiment began. He found it surprisingly bewildering, although definitely not upside-down. This absence of an inverted after-image/after-effect means that Stratton hadn't actually learnt to see the world in an upside-down fashion. If he had, removal of the telescope would have caused the now normal (right-way-up) world to look upside-down again! Instead, it suggests that the adaptation took the form of learning the appropriate *motor responses* in an upside-down-looking world. But Stratton did experience an after-effect which caused things before him to 'swing and sweep' as he moved his eyes, showing that *location constancy* had been disrupted.

In another experiment, Stratton made goggles which visually displaced his body, so that he always appeared horizontally in front of himself (see Figure 16.3). Wherever he walked, he 'followed' his own body image, which was suspended at right angles to his actual body. When he lay down, his body would appear above him, vertically, again at right angles. After three days, he was able to go out for a walk on his own – and lived to tell the tale!

Figure 16.3 One of Stratton's experiments in which goggles displaced the wearer's body image at right angles

Gilling and Brightwell (1982) replicated Stratton's inverted goggles experiment (see Case Study 16.2).

This account supports the view of vision as an active process, enabling us to deal with the world. When Susannah removed the goggles, she was annoyed that nothing seemed any different! She reverted to normal vision within a few minutes, very relieved that the experiment was over. Like Stratton, she learnt to match her vision with signals reported by the rest of her body. According to Gilling and Brightwell (1982):

> *She was not just seeing, but sampling the world as a whole with her senses, and organising them so that they told stories which could be sensibly related to each other. She saw with her whole body, the whole apparatus of her senses, as it were, and not just with her eyes ...*

Snyder and Pronko (1952) made goggles which inverted and reversed the visual world. Their results showed that motor adaptations are extremely resistant to forgetting.

Ask Yourself

- What conclusions can you draw from adaptation studies?

Case Study 16.2

Susannah Fienues (Gilling and Brightwell, 1982)

Susannah Fienues, a young art student, wore inverted goggles for a period of seven days. After first putting them on she reported:

The cars are going upside down. They're going the wrong way. It's all going completely the wrong way to what you'd expect. It's really strange.

After one hour, she reported:

In fact, looking at people in cars was quite normal, I didn't think they were upside down, and I just got adjusted to it, I think. But the difficult thing is just walking and being very disorientated, because how you feel is completely different to what you're doing ... As for things being upside down, it just doesn't feel like that at all because I know very well that I'm sitting here and so I think my brain still knows that, so it's all right.

Like Stratton, she at first had great difficulty in pouring milk from a jug into a glass. By the fourth day, she could walk without difficulty, from the bedroom to the sitting room. And she could now pour the milk! She felt 'just fine ... I don't notice that things are upside down at all.' She could write her name normally, but only if she closed her eyes. With her eyes open, she could write it so that it appeared normal to her but inverted to anyone else!

By day seven, her early problems seemed to have vanished – she could ride her bike, walk, run, climb stairs, turn corners, and make coffee. Only using a knife and fork still presented problems:

Evaluation of adaptation studies

- When volunteers adapt to a distorted perceptual world, they're not, for the most part, actually learning to see 'normally', but are developing the appropriate *motor behaviour* which helps them to get around and function efficiently in their environment. What's learnt is not a new way of perceiving the world, but a new set of body movements.
- The visual system, at least in adults, is extremely flexible, and can adjust to distorted conditions. This strongly suggests that learning plays an important role in perceptual development, since a totally or largely innate system wouldn't allow such adaptation to occur.
- The volunteers are adults, who've already undergone a great deal of learning and in whom maturation has already taken place. This makes it difficult to generalise from these studies to how babies develop under normal circumstances.

STUDYING NEONATE and INFANT VISUAL PERCEPTION

Before looking at the perceptual world of the human neonate, we need to be familiar with some of the methods that have been used in this area (see Box 16.1).

The perceptual abilities of babies

According to Schaffer (2004), any deficiencies that exist in the newborn's visual system are soon made up as a result of visual experience ('Looking ... is improved by looking'). But babies aren't merely passive recipients of stimulation:

> *... from a very early age on they can be observed actively to explore their environment with their eyes, looking for interesting sights and in this way supplying their own stimulation ...*
> *(Schaffer, 2004)*

Pattern (or form) perception

Using the preferential looking technique, Fantz (1961) presented one- to 15-week-olds with pairs of stimuli (see Figure 16.4). The stimuli were presented at weekly intervals, and Fantz measured how long the babies spent looking at each. There was a distinct preference for more complex stimuli; that is, stimuli which contain more information and in which there's more 'going on'. According to Fantz:

> *The relative attractiveness of the two members of a pair depended on the presence of a pattern difference. There were strong preferences between stripes and bull's-eyes and between checkerboard and square. Neither the cross and circle nor the two triangles aroused a significant differential interest. The differential response to pattern was shown at all ages tested, indicating that it was not the result of a learning process.*

This preference for complexity is apparently a function of age. The babies tested at weekly intervals could discriminate between stimuli with progressively narrower stripes. Later, Fantz showed that two- to four-month-olds prefer patterns to colour or brightness, as shown in Figure 16.4.

Box 16.1 Some methods used to study neonate and infant perception

Spontaneous visual preference technique (or **preferential looking**): Two stimuli are presented simultaneously to the neonate. If more time is spent looking at one, we can infer that (a) the baby can discriminate between the stimuli; and (b) the baby prefers the one it looks at longer.

Sucking rate: A dummy (or pacifier) is used and the sucking rate in response to different stimuli is measured. First, a baseline sucking rate is established, and then a stimulus introduced; this may produce an increase or decrease in sucking rate but, eventually, *habituation* will occur: the baby will stop responding. If the stimulus is changed and another increase or decrease in sucking rate occurs, we can infer that the baby has responded to the change as a novel stimulus, and hence can tell the difference between the two stimuli.

Habituation: Used as a method in its own right, if an external stimulus and a baby's representation of it match, then the baby presumably recognises the stimulus and will eventually ignore it. Mismatches will maintain the baby's attention, so that a novel (and discriminable) stimulus presented after habituation to a familiar stimulus re-excites attention (the baby starts responding again).

Conditioned head rotation: The infant is operantly conditioned to turn its head in response to a stimulus. The stimulus can then be presented in a different orientation, and the presence or absence of the conditioned response recorded. It's been used to test for *shape constancy* and in *auditory perception* (Bornstein, 1988).

Physiological measures: If a physiological change (such as heart rate or breathing rate) occurs when a new stimulus is presented, we can infer that the infant can discriminate between the old and new stimuli.

Measures of electrical activity in the brain: By using electrodes attached to the scalp, researchers can look for visually evoked potentials (VEPs) occurring in response to particular stimuli. If different stimuli produce different VEPs, the infant can presumably distinguish between those stimuli. A recent piece of equipment used for doing this is the 'geodesic hair-net' (see Chapter 4).

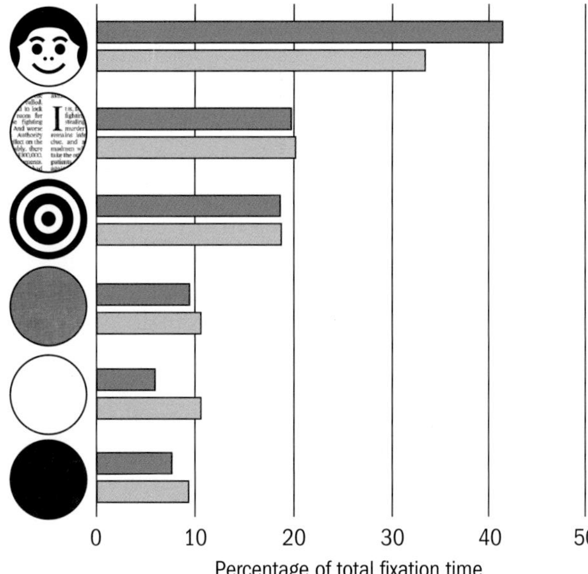

Figure 16.4 Preference for complex stimuli over simple stimuli. The dark bars show the percentage of fixation time for two- to three-month-olds. The light bars show the percentage of fixation time for four-month-olds (Fantz, 1961). Reproduced with permission of Scientific American.

The preference for increasing complexity suggests that the baby's capacity for differentiation steadily improves. Possibly this is because its ability to *scan* becomes more efficient and thorough. Support for this comes from studies showing that very young infants confine their scanning to one corner of a triangle, suggesting a preference for areas of greatest contrast (Salapatek, 1975). Only later does the baby begin to explore all around the stimulus and inside it, and attend to the whole pattern and not just specific parts. Before two months of age, neonates probably discriminate between shapes on the basis of *lower-order variables*, such as orientation and contrast (Slater and Morison, 1985). But after two months, 'true form perception' begins (Slater, 1989), and babies respond to *higher-order variables* (such as configurational invariance and form categories).

The perception of human faces

Ask Yourself

- Can you think of any reasons why it would be a 'good idea' for babies to have an inborn knowledge of/preference for faces?
- What is it about faces that babies are likely to find particularly attractive?

Eye movements already occur in the womb and in the dark, so they aren't just a reaction to being stimulated. Rather, they're a sign that babies are born prepared to explore their visual world and this is by no means a random process. Babies will scan their surroundings actively searching for those features of their visual world that matter to them. This is best illustrated by their interest in the human face (Schaffer, 2004).

The human face is three-dimensional, contains high-contrast information (especially the eyes, mouth and hairline), constantly moves (the eyes, mouth and head), is a source of auditory information (the voice), and regulates its behaviour according to the baby's own activities. Thus, the human face combines complexity, pattern and movement (it's a *supernormal stimulus*: Rheingold, 1961), all of which babies appear innately to prefer. As Schaffer (2004) says:

> *... It is as though nature has ensured that babies are preadapted to attend to that aspect of their environment that is most important to their survival and welfare, namely, other people ...*

A crucial question is whether preference for faces occurs because of this combination of factors, or whether there's an innate perceptual knowledge of a face *as a face*.

Fantz (1961) presented babies aged between four days and six months with all possible pairs of the three stimuli shown in Figure 16.5. The stimuli were coloured black, presented against a pink background, and of the approximate shape and size of an adult's head.

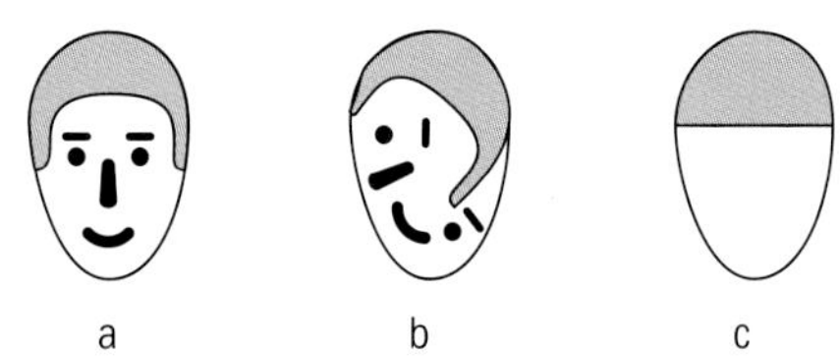

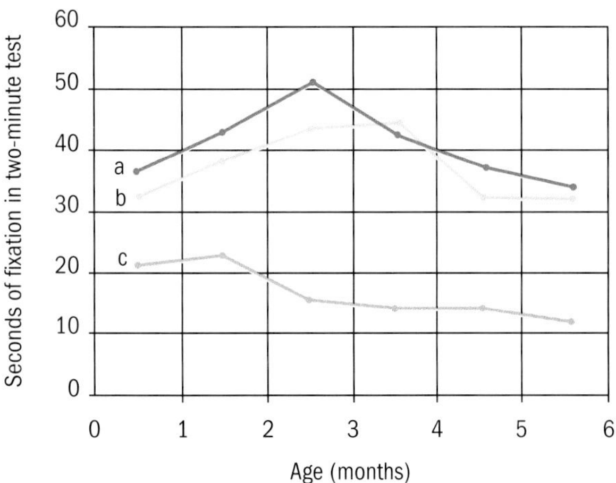

Figure 16.5 Looking times for each of the stimuli used in Fantz's study of the perception of faces (from Fantz, 1961). Reproduced with permission of Scientific American.

Irrespective of age, the babies preferred to look at the schematic representation of a face (a) more than the 'scrambled' face (b). The control stimulus (c) was largely ignored. Even though the difference between (a) and (b) was small, Fantz concluded that 'there is an unlearned, primitive meaning in the form perception of infants', and that babies have an innate preference for 'facedness'.

But according to Bremner (2003), (a) contained more information around the edge of the stimulus. This is important, because, as we noted earlier, young infants tend to scan around the periphery of complex stimuli. This alone could explain their preference for (a). Hershenson *et al.* (1965) argued that both (a) and (b) were more complex than (c), and this might account for Fantz's findings, rather than a preference for looking at human faces. So they presented neonates with all possible pairs of three equally complex stimuli:

- a real female face
- a distorted picture, which retained the outline of head and hair but altered the position of the other features
- a scrambled face (stimulus (b) in Fantz's experiment).

They found no preference for any of the three stimuli, and concluded that a preference for real faces isn't innate, and doesn't appear until about four months of age.

Perception of real faces

Since Hershenson *et al.*'s study, several studies have found that young babies can discriminate between their mother's face and that of a female stranger (e.g. Carpenter, 1974; Maurer and Salapatek, 1976). Even newborns with only a few hours' contact with their mother show this preference (Bushnell, 2001; Field *et al.*, 1984).

But a possible confounding variable is the infant's ability to recognise the mother through *smell*. Bushnell *et al.* (1989) controlled for this by using a strong-smelling perfume to act as an olfactory mask, and they still found the same preference for the mother among babies as young as 12–36 hours. It thus appears clear that newborns are capable of discriminating between the faces of their mother and a female stranger (Bremner, 2011).

Meltzoff and Moore (1977) found that two- to three-week-old babies, and even newborns (1983) can imitate facial expressions, including sticking out their tongues, opening their mouths and protruding their lips. To achieve this, infants must be able to perceive the *internal* parts of the face making the gestures, and be able to *match* this to the equivalent parts of their own face (Bremner, 2011).

Key Study 16.4

Early evidence of face preference (Johnson *et al.*, 1991)

- Lying on their backs, neonates (with an average age of 43 minutes) saw one of four patterned boards moved in an arc in front of their faces. Their eyes followed the most face-like pattern longer than the un-face-like patterns.
- Even the most face-like board was only a schematic representation, with only moderate realism. But it still contains intensity changes, which approximate (or even exaggerate) those of real faces, and for an innate mechanism, that's all that's needed (Bruce and Young, 1998).

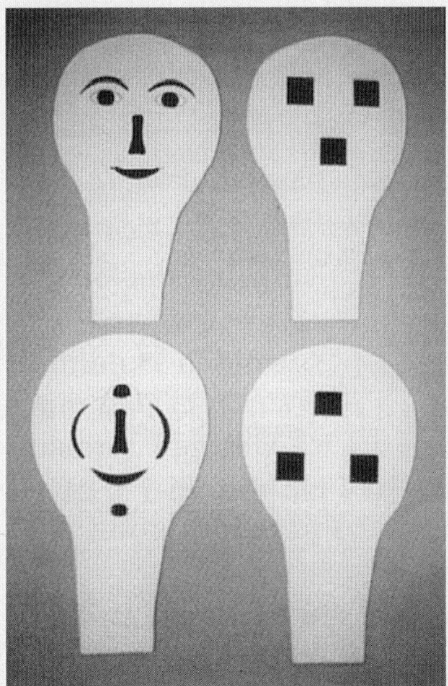

Figure 16.6 Four face-like boards

Figure 16.7 Baby imitating facial expressions

This perception of the internal features could also explain the very early recognition of the mother's face. Bremner (2003) claims that it's distinctly possible that even newborns can discriminate on the basis of *configurational differences* (see Chapter 14). But this seems to conflict with the finding that young babies only scan the outside of a stimulus (see above) – and they would have to be exceptionally fast learners!

According to Slater (1994), the evidence indicates that:

> *Some knowledge about faces is present at birth, suggesting that babies come into the world with some innate, genetically determined knowledge about faces.*

Box 16.2 Babies' preference for beauty as an evolutionary adaptation

- Using the preferential looking technique, Slater (2004, in Connor, 2004) has found that newborns show a distinct preference for female faces judged to be more attractive by adults. Slater believes that this preference is linked to the evolutionary need for babies to be able to identify human faces as soon as they're born.
- What's inborn could be a visual template or *prototype* of the human face based on a statistical average of facial features. If you average loads of faces, then the resulting prototype (typical face) is actually extremely attractive (see Chapter 28).
- Slater believes that evolution has built into the developing visual system an innate representation of the face, which, to all intents and purposes, corresponds to a very attractive-looking face. Newborns prefer to look at the attractive face because it most closely resembles the prototype.
- But this *doesn't* affect their overriding interest in the face of their own mother.

However, preference for specifically *female* faces isn't present at birth, and when it develops it only appears for *same-race* faces (Quinn *et al.*, 2008). It could be that the innate, very general system for face recognition, tuned to a very general prototype and permitting discrimination of faces in other species and races, is gradually replaced, through experience with a specific race, by a more specific face system tuned to the race the baby encounters (Slater *et al.*, 2010). (Something very similar happens in relation to speech perception: Bremner, 2011; see Chapter 19).

Depth perception

Perhaps the most famous way of investigating infants' depth perception is Gibson and Walk's (1960) *visual cliff apparatus* (see Figure 16.8). This consists of a central platform, on the shallow side of which is a sheet of plexiglass. Immediately below this is a black-and-white checkerboard pattern. On the deep side is another sheet of plexiglass, this time with the checkerboard pattern placed on the floor, at a distance of about four feet. This gives the appearance of a 'drop' or 'cliff'. The baby is placed on the central platform, and its mother calls and beckons to it, first from one side and then the other.

Gibson and Walk found that most babies aged between 6 and 14 months wouldn't crawl on to the 'deep' side when beckoned by their mothers. This was interpreted as indicating that neonates have the innate ability to perceive depth. Those babies who did venture onto the deep side did so 'accidentally', either by backing on to it or resting on it. It's likely that their poor motor control was responsible for this, rather than their inability to perceive depth.

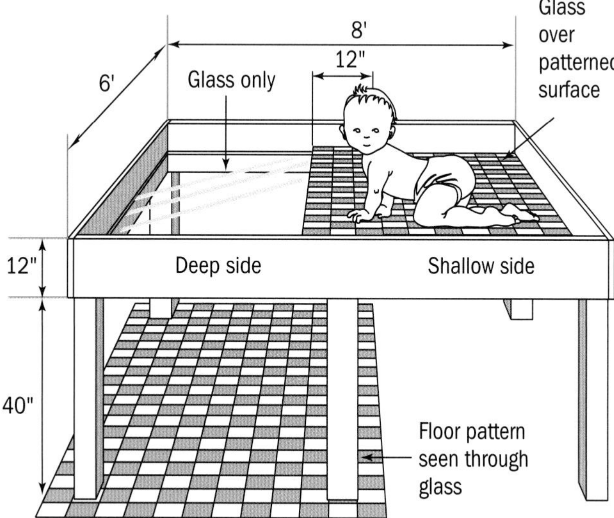

Figure 16.8 The visual cliff (from Dworetzky, 1981)

Ask Yourself

- Can you think of an alternative interpretation of Gibson and Walk's findings?

The visual cliff apparatus required the use of babies who could crawl, the youngest being six months old. By that age, the babies might have *learned* to perceive depth. Gibson and Walk subsequently tested a number of members of *precocial species* (capable of moving about independently at or shortly after birth), namely chicks, goat kids, lambs, and rats with their sensitive whiskers removed. None would venture on to the deep side. If forcibly placed on the deep side, they invariably 'froze'.

This was confirmed by Dahl *et al.* (2013). (See Key Studies 16.5 and 16.6.)

Key Study 16.5

Using heart rate to measure depth perception (Campos *et al.*, 1970)

- In an ingenious way of assessing babies younger than six months, Campos *et al.* used heart rate as an index of depth perception. Babies of various ages had their heart rates monitored while they were on the visual cliff.
- When placed on the 'deep' side, older babies (nine months) showed an *increased* heart rate (presumably indicating fear), while the youngest (two months) showed a *decreased* heart rate. They were less likely to cry, more attentive to what was underneath them, and clearly not frightened by what they saw. No such changes were observed when the infants were placed on the 'shallow' side.
- It seems that even two-month-old babies can perceive depth, and that avoidance behaviour is probably learnt (perhaps after having a few experiences of falling).

Perceptual organisation: constancies and Gestalt principles

Size constancy

Despite a newborn's vision being much poorer than an adult's, its visual world is highly organised (Slater, 1994). According to *empiricists*, constancy is learned, and so neonates are likely to be 'tricked' by the appearance of things (for example, if something *looks* smaller – projects a smaller retinal image – then it *is* smaller). *Nativists*, however, would argue that neonates are innately able to judge the size of an object regardless of retinal image.

Bower recorded the number of times each stimulus produced the conditioned response (CR), and used this as a measure of how similar the neonate considered the stimulus to be to the original. The original stimulus produced a total of 98 CRs, while

Key Study 16.6

Go-carting babies know vertigo (Dahl *et al.*, 2013)

- Dahl *et al.* put babies who couldn't yet crawl into go-carts that they could control with joysticks.
- After three weeks of training, the babies were lowered towards a 1.3 metre drop-off. Their heart rate increased by 5 beats per minute, suggesting they were anxious; the heart rates of non-driving babies remained the same.
- Babies were also tested in a 'moving room': moving walls and ceiling created the sensation of being projected forwards. The go-carting babies recoiled backwards when the walls moved, while the other babies moved far less.
- This suggests that the act of propelling yourself around in spaces teaches your brain to become aware of information in the peripheral visual field and use it to correct balance.
- The babies that reacted most to the moving room also showed the greatest increase in heart rate when lowered over the drop-off.
- In a separate experiment, babies who could already crawl were tested in both the moving room and the visual cliff. Those who reacted most dramatically to the former were most likely to avoid crossing the 'deep' side.

Key Study 16.7

'Peek-a-boo' and size constancy, too (Bower, 1966)

To assess nativist and empiricist claims, Bower initially conditioned two-month-olds to turn their heads whenever they saw a 30-centimetre cube at a distance of one metre (an adult popping up in front of the baby whenever it performed the desired behaviour served as a powerful reinforcer). Once the response was conditioned, the cube was replaced by one of three different cubes:

(a) A 30-centimetre cube at a distance of three metres (producing a retinal image *one-third of the size* of the original)

(b) A 90-centimetre cube at a distance of one metre (producing a retinal image *three times* the size of the original)

(c) A 90-centimetre cube at a distance of three metres (producing exactly the *same-sized* retinal image as the original).

(See Figure 16.9.)

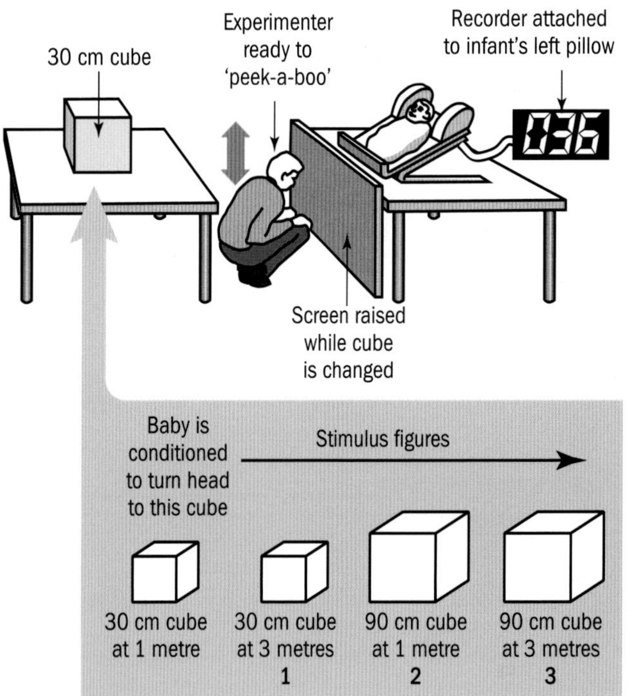

Figure 16.9 The experimental set-up in Bower's study of size constancy

(a) produced 58, (b) 54 and (c) 22. This indicates that the baby was responding to the *actual size* of the cube, irrespective of its distance. This suggests the presence of size constancy, and supports the nativist view that this constancy is inbuilt. Empiricists would have expected (c) to produce the most CRs.

Bower's findings have been replicated with two-day-old babies by Slater *et al.* (1990). Although these findings demonstrate that size constancy is an organising feature of perception present at birth, learning still plays some part (Slater, 1994). For example, in the Slater *et al.* study, the procedure depends on infants learning the characteristics of the cubes in the early 'familiarisation trials'.

Shape constancy

Neonates have the ability to extract the constant real shape of an object independently of (transformation in) its spatial orientation (Slater, 1989). For example, Bower (1966) found that if a two-month-old was conditioned to turn its head to look at a rectangle, it would continue to make the conditioned response when the rectangle was turned slightly to produce a trapezoid retinal image.

After reviewing studies of both size and shape constancy, Bornstein (1988) concluded that 'babies, still only in the first year of life can perceive form *qua* form': they demonstrate the ability to perceive the shape (and size) of objects despite changes in the angle (or distance) from which they're viewed. Bremner (2003) believes that shape constancy is an *innate* ability.

Gestalt principles

Bower has also looked at how neonate perception is organised in terms of certain Gestalt principles (see Chapter 15). Bower wanted to discover if *closure* (or *occlusion*) is an inborn characteristic.

Key Study 16.8

Closure (Bower, 1977)

Two-month-olds were conditioned to respond to a black wire triangle with a black iron bar across it (Figure 16.10, top). Then various stimuli (Figure 16.10, bottom) were presented.

Ask Yourself

- If nativists are correct, and closure is an inborn ability, to which of A, B, C or D should the CR generalise?

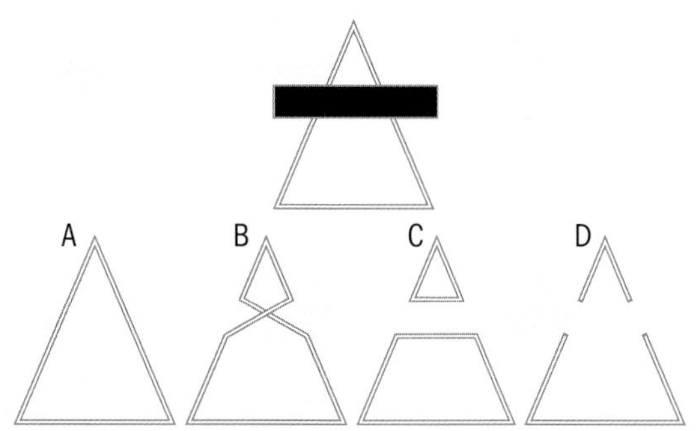

Figure 16.10 The stimulus figures used in Bower's study of closure

- Bower found that the CR was generalised to the complete triangle (A), suggesting that the babies perceived an unbroken triangle to lie behind the black iron bar.
- Given that they were unlikely to have encountered many triangles, Bower concluded that closure is almost certainly an inborn feature of neonate perceptual ability.

Bruce and Young (1998) sum up like this:

> *These studies of infants allow us to glimpse the intricate interplay between the innate organisation of the brain and its astonishing capacity for perceptual-learning ... the infant's brain is highly plastic – ready to be moulded by the experiences it encounters. But it also contains crafty mechanisms (such as attention-capturing properties for face-like stimuli) which keep the odds high that these experiences will be optimal for what the baby will need to learn.*

CROSS-CULTURAL STUDIES

Ask Yourself

- We noted earlier that if we find consistent perceptual differences between different cultural groups, then we're likely to attribute them to environmental factors.
- In what ways do cultures differ that could suggest what these environmental factors might be?

Studies using visual illusions

There's a long history of cross-cultural research into perceptual development using visual illusions.

The carpentered world hypothesis

According to Segall *et al.*'s (1963) carpentered world hypothesis (CWH), people in western cultures:

> *... live in a culture in which straight lines abound and in which perhaps 90 per cent of the acute and obtuse angles formed on [the] retina by the straight lines of [the] visual field are realistically interpretable as right angles extended in space.*

Segall *et al.*, therefore, believe that we tend to interpret illusions, which are 2-D drawings, in terms of our past experiences. In the 'carpentered world' of western societies, we add a third dimension (depth), which isn't actually present in the drawing, and this leads to the illusion experience (cf. Gregory's account of visual illusions in Chapter 15).

Jahoda (1966) compared the Lobi and Dagomba tribes of Ghana, who live in open parkland in round huts, with the Ashanti, who live in dense forest in roughly rectangular huts. The prediction that the Lobi and Dagomba would be significantly more susceptible to the horizontal–vertical illusion, while the Ashanti would be significantly more susceptible to the Müller–Lyer, wasn't supported. Similarly, Gregor and McPherson (1965) found no significant differences between two groups of Australian aborigines on the two illusions, despite one group living in a relatively urbanised, carpentered environment and the other living primitively out of doors. However, both groups were significantly less

Box 16.3 Some early research into cross-cultural differences using visual illusions

- Rivers (1901) compared English adults and children with adult and child Murray Islanders (a group of islands between New Guinea and Australia) using the Müller–Lyer and the horizontal–vertical illusions. The Murray Islanders were less susceptible to the Müller–Lyer illusion than their English counterparts, but more susceptible to the horizontal–vertical illusion.
- Allport and Pettigrew (1957) used the *rotating trapezoid illusion*. This is a trapezoid with horizontal and vertical bars attached to it to give the impression of a window.

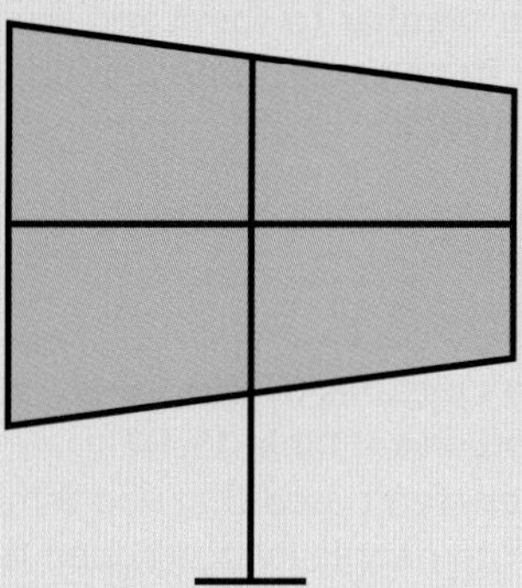

Figure 16.11 The trapezoid window

- When attached to a motor and revolved in a circle, most western observers report seeing a rectangle oscillating backwards and forwards, rather than a trapezoid rotating through 360° (which it actually is). Allport and Pettigrew reasoned that for people unfamiliar with windows (at least as people from western cultures know them), the illusion wouldn't be perceived. When the trapezoid was viewed with both eyes and from a short distance, Zulus (who live in a rather 'circular environment') were less likely than either urban Zulus or Europeans to perceive an oscillating rectangle, and more likely to perceive a rotating trapezoid.
- Segall *et al.* (1963) used the Müller–Lyer illusion with members of African and Filipino cultures. Compared with white South Africans and Americans, the Africans and Filipinos were much less susceptible to the illusion. But on the horizontal–vertical illusion, members of two African cultures (the Batoro and the Bayankole) were most susceptible. People of these cultures live in high, open country where vertical objects are important focal points used to estimate distances. For example, when a tree or pole falls away from you, it seems to grow shorter (foreshortening), but when it falls to the left or right across your field of vision its length doesn't appear to change (Price and Crapo, 1999). The Bete, who live in a dense jungle environment, were least likely of all groups tested to see the illusion. The white South Africans and Americans fell between the extremes of the three African cultures.
- Stewart (1973) used the Ames distorted room (see Figure 15.16) with rural and urban Tongan children. The rural children were less likely to see the illusion than those living in urban environments and European children. This was also true for other illusions, including the Müller–Lyer.

prone to the Müller–Lyer than Europeans and more prone to the horizontal–vertical.

Despite some inconsistent evidence regarding illusion susceptibility and its interpretation, Segall *et al.* (1999) conclude their review by stating:

> *... people perceive in ways that are shaped by the inferences they have learned to make in order to function most effectively in the particular ecological settings in which they live ... we learn to perceive in the ways that we need to perceive. In that sense, environment and culture shape our perceptual habits.*

Studies of other perceptual phenomena

In various African cultures, children and adults find it difficult to perceive depth in both pictorial material and under certain conditions in the real world, too.

Case Study 16.3

Confusing your buffalo with your insects (Turnbull, 1961)

- The BaMbuti pygmies live in the dense rainforests of the Congo, a closed-in world without open spaces. When a BaMbuti archer was taken to a vast plain and shown a herd of buffalo grazing in the distance, he claimed he'd never seen such insects before. When informed that the 'insects' were buffalo, the archer was offended.
- They then rode in a jeep towards the buffalo. The sight of the buffalo in the distance was so far removed from the archer's experience that he was convinced Turnbull was using magic to deceive him. The archer lacked experience with distance cues, preventing him from relating distance to size (Price and Crapo, 1999).

'Reading' pictures

Hudson (1960) showed people from various African cultures a series of pictures depicting hunting scenes (see Figure 16.12). Participants were first asked to name all the objects in the scene, and then they were asked about the relationship between them, such as 'Which is closer to the man?' If the 'correct' interpretation was made, and depth cues were taken into account, respondents were classified as having 3-D vision. If such cues were ignored, they were classified as having 2-D vision. Hudson reported that both children and adults found it difficult to perceive depth in the pictorial material.

Figure 16.12 Hudson (1960) found that when shown the top picture and asked which animal the hunter is trying to spear, members of some cultures reply 'the elephant'. This shows that some cultures don't use cues to depth (such as overlap and known size of objects). The second picture shows the hunter, elephant and antelope in true size ratios when all are the same distance from the observer

Deregowski (1972) refers to a description given of an African woman slowly discovering that a picture she was looking at portrayed a human head in profile:

> *She discovered in turn the nose, the mouth, the eye, but where was the other eye? I tried turning my profile to explain why she could see only one eye, but she hopped round to my other side to point out that I possessed a second eye which the other lacked.*

The woman treated the picture as an object, rather than a 2-D representation of an object, that is, she didn't 'infer' depth in the picture. What she believed to be an 'object' turned out to have only two dimensions, and this is what the woman found bewildering. But when familiar pictorial stimulus material is used, recognition tends to be better (Serpell, 1976). Thus, some (but not all) of the Me'en of Ethiopia found it much easier to recognise material when it was presented in the form of pictures painted on cloth (which is both familiar to them and free of distracting cues such as a border) than line drawings on paper (Deregowski, 1972).

Ask Yourself

- In Hudson's pictures (Figure 16.12), which depth cues are used (see Table 15.1)?
- Which cues aren't used that you think could be important to people living in open terrain?

Are Hudson's pictures biased?

Hudson's pictures use *relative size* and *overlap/superimposition*, but *texture gradient*, *binocular disparity* and *motion parallax* are all missing. When the pictures were redrawn to show texture gradients (by, for example, adding grass to open terrain), more Zambian children gave 3-D answers than in Hudson's original study (Kingsley *et al.*, cited in Serpell, 1976). Research summarised by Berry *et al.* (1992) indicates that the absence of certain depth cues in pictorial material makes the perception of depth difficult for non-western peoples (see Gross, 2008).

CONCLUSIONS: NATURE, NURTURE or an INTERACTION?

According to Bee (2000), as researchers have become increasingly ingenious in devising ways of testing infants' perceptual skills, they've found more and more skills already present in neonates and very young infants. There's growing evidence to support Kagan's (1971) claim that:

> *Nature has apparently equipped the newborn with an initial bias in the processing of experience. He does not ... have to learn what he should examine.*

Slater (1994) is a little more cautious. Auditory perception and learning about the auditory world (not dealt with in this chapter) are well advanced even in very young babies, and a nativist view is closest to the truth. But in the case of vision, the truth lies somewhere in-between a nativist and empiricist view. Evidence suggests that the newborn infant:

> *... comes into the world with a remarkable range of visual abilities ... Some rudimentary knowledge and understanding of important stimuli such as objects and faces is present at birth, and experience builds on this genetically or evolutionarily provided range of abilities. (Slater, 1994)*

Some of the strongest evidence in support of the role of nurture comes from cross-cultural studies, deprivation studies using non-humans, and studies of human cataract patients. However, nature and nurture are never entirely separable. For example, the neonate's ability to discriminate between the mother's face and that of a similar-looking female must be the result of experience, but the capacity to make the distinction must be built in. As Bee (2000) says, whenever there's a dispute between nativists and empiricists, *both* sides are correct. Both nature and nurture are involved.

Chapter Summary

- **Nativists** argue that we're born able to perceive the world in particular ways, with little or no learning necessary. **Empiricists** believe that our perceptual abilities develop through learning and experience. Most Psychologists reject these extreme viewpoints in favour of an **interactionist** position.
- Studying **neonates** represents the most **direct** source of evidence, but we can only **infer** what their perceptual experience is.
- **Non-human animal experiments** usually involve **deprivation** of normal sensory experience, raising serious **ethical questions**. There's also the problem of generalising the results of such studies to humans.
- Studies of **human cataract patients** represent the human counterpart to non-human animal experiments. Problems in interpretation of the research findings include possible physical deterioration of the visual system and dubious reliability of the case histories.
- Studies of **perceptual adaptation/readjustment** demonstrate the **flexibility** of human perception, but caution is needed in deciding whether perceptual or motor adaptation is involved.
- **Cross-cultural studies** help to identify the influences on perceptual development, in particular the role of learning and experience. But Psychologists disagree as to the key features of **cultural learning**.
- When analysing data from cataract patients, Hebb distinguished between **figural unity**, which he believed is largely innate, and **figural identity** which is largely learnt.
- Deprivation experiments suggest that light is necessary for normal physical development of the visual system, and that **patterned light** is necessary for the normal development of more complex abilities in chimps, cats and monkeys.
- Perceptual adaptation/readjustment studies illustrate the enormous adaptability of the human visual system, but this seems to involve learning appropriate **motor behaviour.**
- Methods used to study neonate perception include **spontaneous visual preference/preferential looking, sucking rate, habituation, conditioned head rotation, physiological measures** and measures of **electrical brain activity**.
- Babies show a preference for **complexity**, which is a function of age. This is probably related to improvement in the ability to scan the whole pattern, rather than just areas of greatest contrast.
- Evidence that babies quickly learn to prefer their mothers' faces (and voices) is contributing to the view that the human face has **species-specific significance** from birth onwards.
- **Depth perception** has been studied using the **visual cliff apparatus**. Heart rate measures support Gibson and Walk's original claim (based on crawling) that depth perception is probably innate.
- Bower believes that babies have an inborn understanding **size** and **shape constancy** and the **Gestalt principle of closure**.
- Cross-cultural studies involve giving members of different cultural groups the same test materials, usually visual illusions, including the Müller–Lyer, horizontal–vertical, and the rotating trapezoid.
- Segall *et al.* proposed the **carpentered world hypothesis (CWH)** to explain why different cultural groups are more/less susceptible to different illusions. This stresses the role of the physical environment on perception.
- Evidence that contradicts the carpentered world hypothesis has led to the proposal that exposure to western **cultural variables** may be more important, such as 2-D drawings and photographs.
- Perceptual development after birth involves a complex **interaction** between **genetic/maturational** and **environmental/experiential** influences.

Links with Other Topics/Chapters

Chapters 1, 3 and 50 → The continuing debate within Psychology about the relative influence of *nature and nurture* partly reflects its *philosophical roots*

Chapter 15 → Vision consists of a large number of abilities, some more simple, others more complex and it's likely that the relative contributions of genetic and environmental factors vary between different abilities

Chapter 48 → The experimental study of non-human animals, especially those involving deprivation or any kind of pain or suffering, raise fundamental *ethical issues*

Chapter 15 → Cross-cultural studies have made considerable use of visual illusions

Chapter 47 → *Cross-cultural Psychology* helps to question the *universality* of the theories and research findings reported using western-only populations. But it's still mainly western Psychologists that conduct this cross-cultural research, using methods and instruments designed in the West

Chapters 2 and 32 → An inborn attraction to human faces makes the baby interested in its caregivers, which, in turn, encourages them to provide the care the baby needs. The very rapid learning to recognise the mother could be seen as *evolutionarily determined attachment behaviour*

Chapter 28 → The newborn's inborn preference for attractive faces based on 'averageness' is mirrored in research involving adults

Recommended Reading

Cross-cultural studies

Berry, J., Poortinga, Y.H., Segall, M.H. & Dasen, P.R. (eds) (1992) *Cross-Cultural Psychology: Research and Applications.* New York: Cambridge University Press. Especially Chapter 6. Also relevant to Chapter 47.

Gross, R. (2008) *Key Studies in Psychology* (5th edition). London: Hodder Education. Chapter 4.

Segall, M.H., Dasen, P.R., Berry, J.W. & Poortinga, Y.H. (1999) *Human Behaviour in Global Perspective: An Introduction to Cross-Cultural Psychology* (2nd edition). Boston: Allyn & Bacon. Especially Chapter 4.

Perceptual abilities of infants

Bower, T.G.R. (1989) The perceptual world of the newborn child. In A. Slater & G. Bremner (eds) *Infant Development.* London: Lawrence Erlbaum.

Bremner, G. (2003) Perceptual Knowledge and Action. In A. Slater & G. Bremner (eds) *An Introduction to Developmental Psychology.* Oxford: Blackwell Publishing.

Muir, D.W., Humphrey, D.E. & Humphrey, G.K. (1999) Pattern and Space Perception in Young Infants. In A. Slater & D. Muir (eds) *The Blackwell Reader in Developmental Psychology.* Oxford: Blackwell.

Slater, A. & Bremner, G. (2011) *An Introduction to Developmental Psychology* (2nd edition). BPS Blackwell. Chapter 5.

Useful Website

www.richardgregory.org/papers/recovery_blind/2-the-case.htm (Gregory, R.L. and Wallace, J.G. (1963) The Case of S.B. *Experimental Psychology Society Monographs*, No.2.)

CHAPTER 17

MEMORY AND FORGETTING

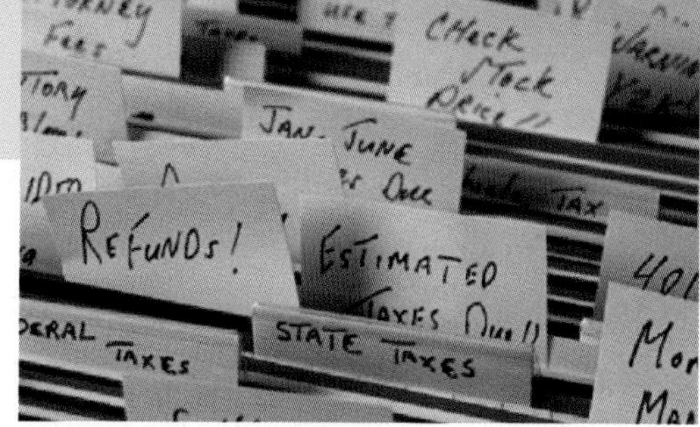

- The meanings of 'memory'
- Storage
- Retrieval
- The multi-store model (MSM)
- Alternatives to the MSM
- Theories of forgetting

INTRODUCTION and OVERVIEW

As we noted in Chapter 11, learning and memory represent two sides of the same coin: learning depends on memory for its 'permanence', and memory would have no 'content' without learning. Hence, we could define memory as the retention of learning and experience. As Blakemore (1988) says:

> *In the broadest sense, learning is the acquisition of knowledge and memory is the storage of an internal representation of that knowledge ...*

Blakemore expresses the fundamental importance of memory like this:

> *... Without the capacity to remember and to learn, it is difficult to imagine what life would be like, whether it could be called living at all. Without memory, we would be servants of the moment, with nothing but our innate reflexes to help us deal with the world. There could be no language, no art, no science, no culture. Civilisation itself is the distillation of human memory ...*

Both learning and memory featured prominently in the early years of Psychology as a science (see Chapters 1, 3 and 11). William James was arguably the first to make a formal distinction between *primary* and *secondary memory*, which correspond to *short-term* and *long-term memory* respectively. This distinction is central to Atkinson and Shiffrin's (1968, 1971) very influential *multi-store model* (MSM).

As with other cognitive processes, memory remained a largely unacceptable area for psychological research until the cognitive revolution of the mid-1950s, reflecting the dominance of behaviourism up until this time. However, some Behaviourists, especially in the USA, studied 'verbal behaviour' using paired–associate learning. This *associationist approach* was (and remains) most apparent in *interference theory*, an attempt to explain forgetting. Other theories of forgetting include *trace decay*, *displacement*, *cue-dependent forgetting* and *repression*.

Several major accounts of memory have emerged from criticisms of the limitations of the MSM. These include Craik and Lockhart's *levels-of-processing* approach, Baddeley and Hitch's *working-memory model*, and attempts to identify different types of long-term memory (e.g. Tulving, 1972). Psychologists are increasingly interested in *everyday memory*, rather than studying it merely as a laboratory phenomenon.

THE MEANINGS of 'MEMORY'

Memory, like learning, is a *hypothetical construct* denoting three distinguishable but interrelated processes:

- *registration* (or *encoding*) – the *transformation* of sensory input (such as a sound or visual image) into a form which allows it to be entered into (or registered in) memory. With a computer, for example, information can only be encoded if it's presented in a format the computer recognises
- *storage* – the operation of *holding* or *retaining* information in memory. Computers store information by means of changes in the system's electrical circuitry; with people, the changes occurring in the brain allow information to be stored, though exactly what these changes involve is unclear
- *retrieval* – the process by which stored information is *extracted* from memory.

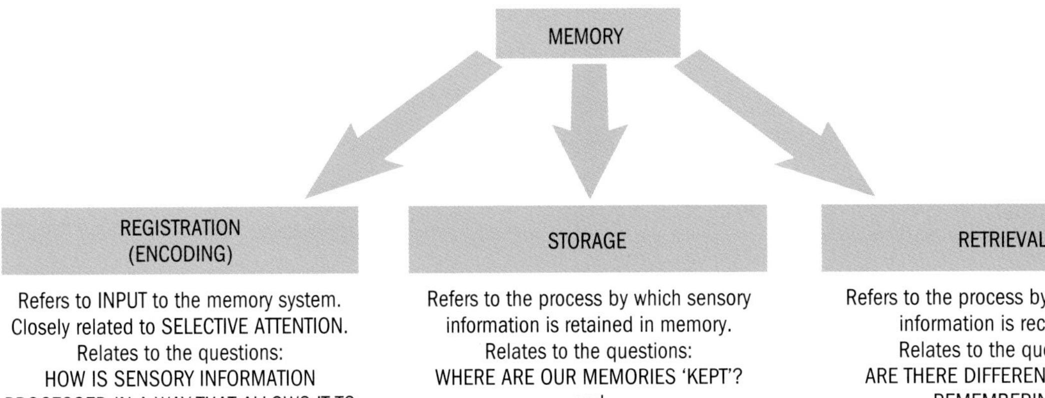

Figure 17.1 The three processes of memory

Registration can be thought of as a necessary condition for storage to take place, but not everything which registers on the senses is stored. Similarly, storage is a necessary, but not sufficient, condition for retrieval: we cannot recover information which hasn't been stored, but the fact that we know it is no guarantee that we'll remember it on any particular occasion. This is the crucial distinction between *availability* (whether or not the information has been stored) and *accessibility* (whether or not it can be retrieved), which is especially relevant to theories of forgetting.

STORAGE

Ask Yourself

- Can saying 'I can't remember' mean different things?
- Do you consider yourself to have a 'good/poor' memory? What criteria do you apply in making that assessment?

In practice, storage is studied through testing people's ability to retrieve. This is equivalent to the distinction between learning and performance: learning corresponds to storage, while performance corresponds to retrieval (see Chapter 11). But there are several kinds of retrieval (see below). So, if we're tested by *recall* it may look as though we haven't learnt something, but a test of *recognition* may show that we have. For these reasons, it's useful to distinguish between *memory as storage* and *memory as retrieval*. When people complain about having a 'poor memory', they might mean storage or retrieval (but they simply say 'I can't remember').

Ebbinghaus (1885), the pioneer of memory research, would have accepted James' distinction between primary and secondary memory. Many Psychologists since James have also made the distinction, including Hebb (1949), Broadbent (1958), and Waugh and Norman (1965). In Atkinson and Shiffrin's (1968, 1971) multi-store model, they're called short-term memory (STM) and long-term memory (LTM) respectively. Strictly, STM and LTM refer to experimental procedures for investigating short-term and long-term *storage* respectively.

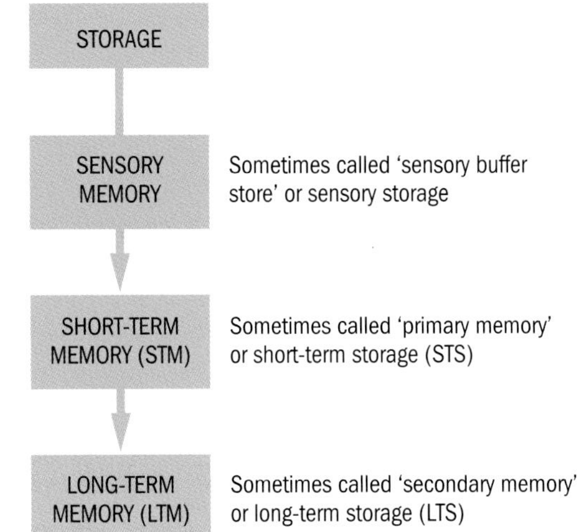

Figure 17.2 The three forms of storage

Sensory memory

Sensory memory gives us an accurate account of the environment as experienced by the sensory system. We retain a 'literal copy' of the stimulus long enough for us to decide whether it's worthy of further processing. Any information we don't attend to or process further is forgotten. It's probably more useful to think of sensory memory as an aspect of perception and as a necessary requirement for storage proper (that is, STM).

There's a definite resemblance between sensory memory (or storage) and Broadbent's sensory 'buffer' store (Eysenck and Keane, 1990: see Chapter 13); Broadbent's *filter model of selective attention* was, in many ways, the main precursor of the multi-store approach to memory (see below).

Short-term memory (STM)

Probably less than one-hundredth of all the sensory information that impinges on the human senses every second reaches consciousness; of this, only about 5 per cent is stored permanently (Lloyd *et al.*, 1984). Clearly, if we possessed only sensory memory, our capacity for retaining information about the world would be extremely limited. However, according to models of memory such as Atkinson and Shiffrin's MSM (1968, 1971), some information from sensory memory is successfully passed on to STM.

STM (and LTM) can be analysed in terms of:

- *capacity* – *how much* information can be stored
- *duration* – *how long* the information can be held in storage
- *coding* – *how* sensory input is represented by the memory system.

Capacity

Ebbinghaus (1885) and Wundt (in the 1860s) were two of the first Psychologists to maintain that STM is limited to six or seven bits of information. But the most famous account is given by Miller (1956) in his article 'The magical number seven, plus or minus two'. Miller showed how *chunking* can be used to expand the limited capacity of STM by using already established memory stores to categorise or encode new information.

If we think of STM's capacity as seven 'slots', with each slot being able to accommodate one bit or unit of information, then seven individual letters would each fill a slot and there'd be no 'room' left for any additional letters. But if the letters are chunked into a word, then the word would constitute one unit of information, leaving six free slots. In the example below, the 25 bits of information can be chunked into (or reduced to) six words, which could quite easily be reduced further to one 'bit' (or chunk) based on prior familiarity with the words:

S	A	V	A	O
R	E	E	E	G
U	R	S	Y	A
O	O	D	N	S
F	C	N	E	R

To be able to chunk, you have to know the 'rule' or the 'code', which in this case is: starting with F (bottom left-hand corner) read upwards until you get to S and then drop down to C and read upwards until you get to A, then go to N and read upwards and so on. This should give you 'four score and seven years ago'.

Chunking is involved whenever we reduce a larger amount of information to a smaller amount. This (a) increases the capacity of STM, and (b) represents a form of encoding information, by imposing a *meaning* on otherwise meaningless material. For example:

- arranging letters into words, words into phrases, phrases into sentences
- converting 1066 (four bits of information) into a date (one chunk), so a string of 28 numbers could be reduced to seven dates
- using a rule to organise information: the series 149162536496481100121 (21 bits) is generated by the rule by which 1[squared] = 1, 2[squared] = 4, 3[squared] = 9, and so on. The rule represents a single chunk, and that's all that has to be remembered.

These examples demonstrate how chunking allows us to bypass the seven-bit 'bottleneck'. Although the amount of information contained in any one chunk may be unlimited (e.g. the rule above can generate an infinitely long set of digits), the number of chunks which can be held in STM is still limited to seven plus or minus two.

Duration

A way of studying 'pure' STM was devised by Brown (1958) and Peterson and Peterson (1959), and is called the *Brown–Peterson technique*. By repeating something that has to be remembered (*maintenance rehearsal*), information can be held in STM almost indefinitely.

Coding

Conrad (1964) presented participants visually with a list of six consonants (such as BKSJLR), each of which was seen for about three-quarters of a second. They were then instructed to write down the consonants. Mistakes tended to be related to a letter's *sound*. For example, there were 62 instances of B being mistaken for P, 83 instances of V being mistaken for P, but only two instances of S being mistaken for P. These *acoustic confusion errors* suggested to Conrad that STM must code information according to its sound. Even when information is presented visually, it must somehow be transformed into its acoustic code (see also Baddeley's, 1966, study below).

Critical Discussion 17.1

Is there a magical number after all?

Ask Yourself

- How many capital cities can you name?
- Note any pattern of remembering that occurs.

Broadbent (1975) questioned just how fundamental the number seven actually is. Although people typically remember up to about seven items, perhaps more meaningful was the number of items people could remember *flawlessly* (because, presumably, those items are recalled without relying on a mental strategy that can fail). Memory was nearly flawless for sets of only *three* items: adding a fourth or fifth item resulted in a set that could usually be recalled correctly, and adding more made things more difficult. Broadbent pointed out that when we try to recall items from a category in *LTM*, we tend to do so in bursts of three items.

According to Cowan (2001), across many types of experiment, there exists something like a semi-magical number *four* (plus or minus two, varying across individuals and situations). This applies only to procedures in which the items are well known and in which it's impossible to form larger chunks. Based on a review of recent research, Cowan *et al.* (2007) conclude by saying that the limit of three or four chunks serves as a useful guideline for theory and research.

Key Study 17.1

The Brown–Peterson technique (Peterson and Peterson, 1959)

- In the *Brown–Peterson technique,* participants hear various *trigrams* (such as XPJ). Only one trigram is presented on each trial. Immediately afterwards, they're instructed to recall what they heard or to count backwards, in threes, out loud, from some specified number for 3, 6, 9, 12, 15 or 18 seconds (the *retention interval*). The function of this *distractor task* is to prevent rehearsal. At the end of the time period, participants try to recall the trigram.
- Peterson and Peterson found that the average percentage of correctly recalled trigrams was high with short delays, but decreased as the delay interval increased. Nearly 70 per cent was forgotten after only a nine-second delay, and 90 per cent after 18 seconds.
- In the absence of rehearsal, then, STM's duration is very short, even with very small amounts of information. If a more difficult distractor task is used, it can be made even shorter.

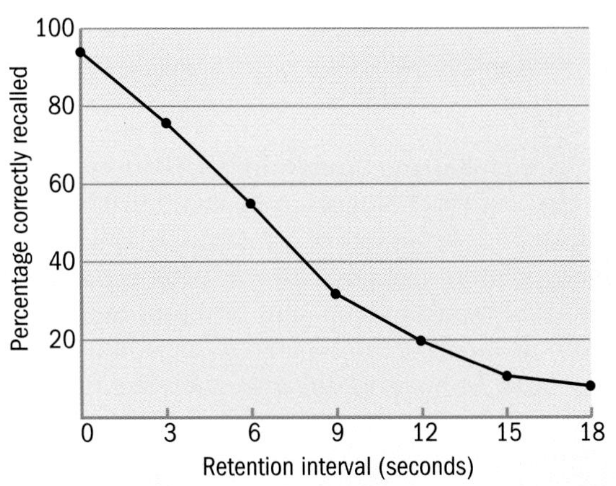

Figure 17.3 The data reported by Peterson and Peterson in their experiment on the duration of STM

Other forms of coding in STM

Shulman (1970) showed participants lists of ten words. Recognition of the words was then tested using a visually presented 'probe word', which was either:

- a *homonym* of one of the words on the list (such as 'bawl' for 'ball')
- a *synonym* (such as 'talk' for 'speak'), or
- *identical* to it.

Ask Yourself

- Shulman found that homonym and synonym probes produced similar error rates.
- What does this tell us about the types of coding used in STM?

If an error was made on a synonym probe, some matching for meaning must have taken place (i.e. *semantic coding*).

Visual images (such as abstract pictures, which would be difficult to store using an acoustic code) can also be maintained in STM, if only briefly.

Long-term memory (LTM)

Capacity and duration

It's generally accepted that LTM has *unlimited* capacity. It can be thought of as a vast storehouse of all the information, skills, abilities and so on, which aren't being currently used, but which are potentially retrievable. According to Bower (1975), some of the kinds of information contained in LTM include:

- a spatial model of the world around us
- knowledge of the physical world, physical laws and properties of objects
- beliefs about people, ourselves, social norms, values and goals
- motor skills, problem-solving skills, and plans for achieving various things
- perceptual skills in understanding language, interpreting music, and so on.

Many of these are included in what Tulving (1972) calls *semantic memory* (see below).

Information can be held for between a few minutes and several years (and may in fact span the individual's entire lifetime).

Coding

With verbal material, coding in LTM appears to be mainly semantic. For example, Baddeley (1966) presented participants with words which were either:

- *acoustically similar* (e.g. 'caught', 'short', 'taut', 'nought')
- *semantically similar* (e.g. 'huge', 'great', 'big', 'wide')
- *acoustically dissimilar* (e.g. 'foul', 'old' and 'deep'), or
- *semantically dissimilar* (e.g. 'pen', 'day', 'ring').

When recall from STM was tested, acoustically similar words were recalled less well than acoustically dissimilar words. This supports the claim that acoustic coding occurs in STM. There was a small difference between the number of semantically similar and semantically dissimilar words recalled (64 and 71 per cent respectively). This suggests that while some semantic coding occurs in STM, it's not dominant.

When an equivalent study was conducted on LTM, fewer semantically similar words were recalled, while acoustically similar words had no effect. This suggests that LTM's dominant code is semantic. Similarly, Baddeley found that immediate recall of the order of short lists of unrelated words was seriously impeded if the words were acoustically similar, but not if they were semantically similar. After a delay, however, exactly the opposite effect occurred.

Does LTM use only semantic coding?

Findings such as Baddeley's don't imply that LTM uses only a semantic code (Baddeley, 1976). Our ability to picture a place we visited on holiday indicates that at least some information is stored or coded visually. Also, some types of information in LTM (such as songs) are coded acoustically. Smells and tastes are also stored in LTM, suggesting that it's a very flexible system, as well as being large and long-lasting.

Figure 17.4 Long-term memory of this scene requires the use of a visual code

Table 17.1 Summary of main differences between STM and LTM

	Capacity	Duration	Coding
STM	Seven bits of (unrelated) information. Can be increased through *chunking*	15–30 seconds (unaided). Can be increased by (maintenance) rehearsal	Mainly acoustic. Some semantic. Visual is also possible
LTM	Unlimited	From a few seconds to several years (perhaps permanently)	Semantic, visual, acoustic, and also olfactory (smells) and gustatory (tastes). Very flexible

RETRIEVAL

There are many different ways of recovering or locating information which has been stored; that is, 'remembering' can take many different forms. Likewise, there are also different ways of measuring memory in the laboratory.

How is memory measured?

The systematic scientific investigation of memory began with Ebbinghaus (1885) (see Key Study 17.2).

Other techniques for measuring memory include the following:

- *Recognition:* This involves deciding whether or not a particular piece of information has been encountered before (as in multiple-choice tests, where the correct answer is presented along with incorrect ones). The sensitivity of recognition as a form of retrieval is demonstrated by Standing (1973) (see Key Study 17.3).
- *Recall:* This involves participants actively searching their memory stores in order to retrieve particular information (as in timed essays). Retrieval cues are missing or very sparse. The material can be recalled either in the order in which it was presented (*serial recall*) or in any order at all (*free recall*).
- *Memory-span procedure:* This is a version of serial recall, in which a person is given a list of unrelated digits or letters, and then required to repeat them back immediately in the order in which they were heard. The number of items on the list is successively increased until an error is

Key Study 17.3

Recognising how to ask people to remember (Standing, 1973)

- Participants were shown series of slides of either pictures or words (20 or so per series), each slide for five seconds, and each series at three-minute intervals. Two days later they were shown further series of slides using a double projector. Thus they saw two pictures side by side, one taken from the original series, the other being new. They had to indicate which looked more familiar.
- Amazingly, as Standing went on increasing the number of images up to 10,000, the error rate continued to stay very low, and didn't seem to increase at all with the number of items to be remembered. Standing concluded that, for all practical purposes, there's no upper limit to memory capacity.
- Contrary to the evidence that there are limits to what's transferred from STM to LTM (see text below), it seems that some accessible trace of each item must have been left – enough to enable a new item to be compared with the trace and classified as familiar or unfamiliar. According to Rose (2003):

... On this basis, it could be argued that nothing is forgotten, provided we know how to ask if it is remembered ...

Key Study 17.2

Pure memory (Ebbinghaus, 1885)

- To study memory in its 'purest' form, Ebbinghaus invented three-letter nonsense syllables (a consonant followed by a vowel followed by another consonant, such as XUT and JEQ).
- Ebbinghaus spent several years using only himself as the subject of his research. He read lists of nonsense syllables out loud, and when he felt he'd recited a list sufficiently to retain it, he tested himself. If he could recite a list correctly *twice* in succession, he considered it to be learnt. After recording the time taken to learn a list, he then began another one.
- After specific periods of time, he'd return to a particular list and try to memorise it again. He calculated the number of attempts (or trials) it took him to relearn the list, as a percentage of the number of trials it had originally taken to learn it (a *savings score*).
- He found that memory declines sharply at first, but then levels off. For example, in one set of experiments involving a series of eight different lists of 13 nonsense syllables, he found savings scores of:
  - 58 per cent, 20 minutes after training
  - 44 per cent, 60 minutes after training
  - 34 per cent, 24 hours after training
  - 21 per cent, 31 days after training.

... Thus, most of the memory loss occurred within the first minutes after training; once the memory had survived this hurdle it seemed much more stable ... (Rose, 2003)

This finding has subsequently been replicated many times.

made. The maximum number of items that can consistently be recalled correctly is a measure of *immediate memory span*.

- *Paired-associate recall:* Participants are required to learn a list of paired items (such as 'chair' and 'elephant'). When one of the words (e.g. 'chair') is re-presented, the participant must recall the paired word ('elephant').

THE MULTI-STORE MODEL (MSM)

Atkinson and Shiffrin's (1968, 1971) *multi-store model* (MSM) (sometimes called the *dual-memory model* because of the emphasis on STM and LTM) was an attempt to explain how information flows from one storage system to another. The model sees sensory memory, STM and LTM as *permanent structural components* of the memory system (built-in features of the human information-processing system). In addition to these structural components, the memory system comprises more *transient control processes*, of which *rehearsal* is key. Rehearsal serves two main functions:

1. to act as a *buffer* between sensory memory and LTM by maintaining incoming information within STM
2. to *transfer* information to LTM.

Information from sensory memory is scanned and matched with information in LTM, and if a match (i.e. *pattern recognition*) occurs, then it might be fed into STM along with a verbal label from LTM. (See Figure 17.5.)

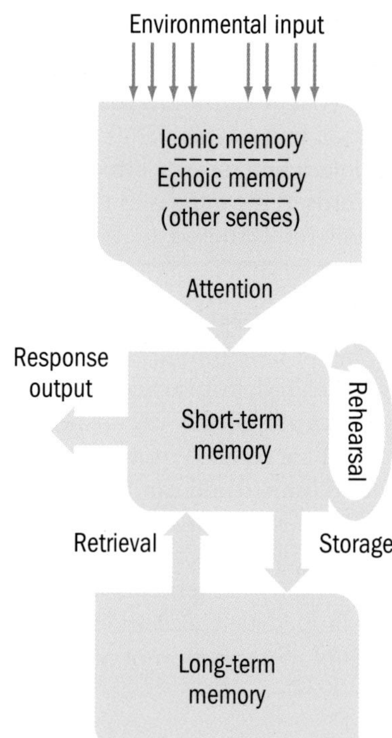

Figure 17.5 The multi-store/dual-memory model of memory proposed by Atkinson and Shiffrin

Evidence for the MSM

Three kinds of evidence are relevant here:

1. experimental studies of STM and LTM (sometimes referred to as *two-component tasks*)
2. studies of *coding*
3. studies *of brain-damaged patients.*

Experimental studies of STM and LTM

The serial position effect

Murdock (1962) presented participants with a list of words at a rate of about one per second; they were required to free-recall as many of these as they could. The probability of recalling any word depended on its position in the list (its *serial position*: hence the graph shown in Figure 17.6 is a *serial position curve*).

Participants typically recalled those items from the end of the list first, and got more of these correct than earlier items (the *recency effect*). Items from the beginning of the list were recalled quite well relative to those in the middle (the *primacy effect*), but not as well as those at the end. Poorest recall is for items in the middle. The serial position effect holds regardless of the length of the list (Murdock, 1962).

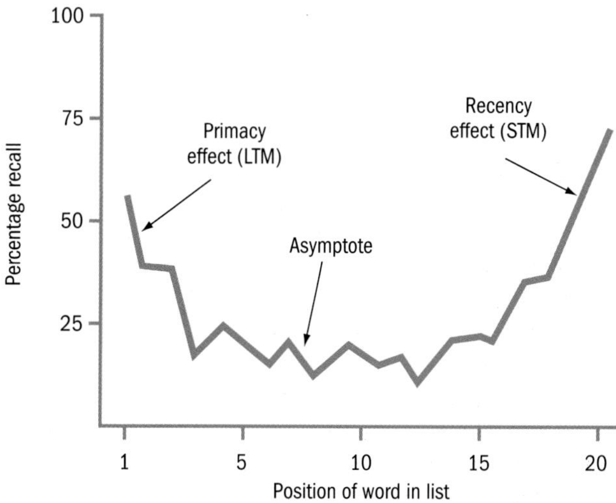

Figure 17.6 A typical serial position curve (Reprinted from *Journal of Verbal Learning and Verbal Behaviour, 5*, Glanzer and Cunitz, 1966, Two storage mechanisms in free recall, 928–935, © 1966, with permission from Elsevier)

Ask Yourself

- Using what you already know about STM, LTM and rehearsal, try to explain:
  (a) the primacy and recency effects
  (b) why words in the middle of the list are the least well remembered.

The primacy effect occurs because the items at the beginning of the list have (presumably) been rehearsed and transferred to LTM, from where they're recalled. The recency effect presumably occurs because items currently in STM are recalled from there. Because STM's capacity is limited and can hold items for only a brief period of time, words in the middle are either lost from the system completely, or are otherwise unavailable for recall. The last items are remembered only if recalled first and tested immediately, as demonstrated by Glanzer and Cunitz (1966) in a variation of Murdock's study (see Key Study 17.4).

Key Study 17.4

Removing the recency effect (Glanzer and Cunitz, 1966)

- Glanzer and Cunitz presented two groups of participants with the same list of words. One group recalled the material *immediately* after presentation, while the other group recalled *after 30 seconds*. They had to count backwards in threes (the Brown–Peterson technique), which prevented rehearsal and caused the recency effect to disappear.
- The primacy effect was largely unaffected.

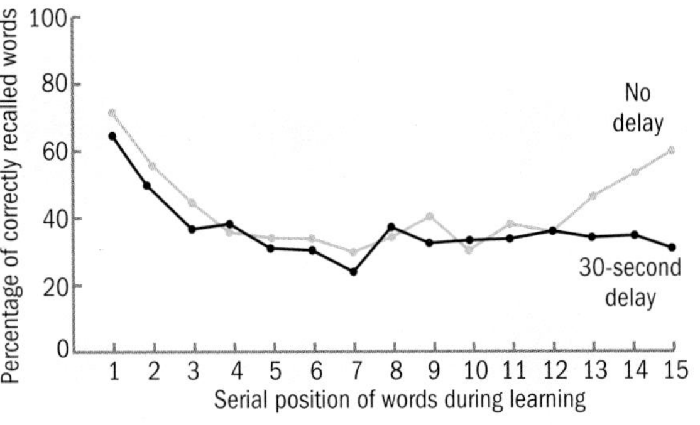

Figure 17.7 Data from Glanzer and Cunitz's study showing serial position curves after no delay and after a delay of 30 seconds

Ask Yourself

- Try to account for Glanzer and Cunitz's findings.

It's likely that the earlier words had been transferred to LTM (from where they were recalled), while the most recent words were 'vulnerable' to the counting task (Eysenck, 1993).

Brown–Peterson technique and rehearsal

When discussing the characteristics of STM earlier, we noted the rapid loss of information from memory when rehearsal is prevented using the Brown–Peterson technique. This is usually taken as evidence for the existence of a STM with rapid forgetting. But the concept of rehearsal itself has been criticised as both unnecessary and too general.

Key Study 17.5

Maintenance versus elaborative rehearsal (Craik and Watkins, 1973)

- Craik and Watkins asked participants to remember only certain 'critical' words (those beginning with a particular letter) from lists presented either rapidly or slowly. The position of the critical words relative to the others determined the amount of time a particular word spent in STM, and the number of potential rehearsals it could receive.
- Long-term remembering was unrelated to either how long a word had spent in STM, or the number of explicit or implicit rehearsals it received.
- Based on this and later findings, Craik and Watkins distinguished between:
  (a) *maintenance rehearsal*, where material is rehearsed in the form in which it was presented ('rote'), and
  (b) *elaborative rehearsal* (or *elaboration of encoding*), which elaborates the material in some way (such as by giving it a meaning, or linking it with pre-existing knowledge stored in LTM).

It seems that what's important is the *kind* of rehearsal or processing, rather than how much. This has been investigated in particular by Craik and Lockhart (1972), in the form of the levels-of-processing approach (see below).

Studies of coding

Table 17.1 indicates that the major form of coding used in STM is acoustic, while LTM is much more flexible and varied in how it encodes information. It also suggests that semantic coding is used primarily by LTM. This is usually taken to support the MSM. However, not everyone accepts this view.

Chunking, STM and LTM

According to Miller (1956), chunking represents a *linguistic recoding* which seems to be the 'very lifeblood of the thought process'. But this cannot occur until certain information in LTM is activated, and a match made between the incoming items and their representation in LTM.

Miller and Selfridge (1950) gave participants 'sentences' of varying lengths, which resembled (or approximated to) true English to different degrees, and asked them to recall the words in their correct order. The closer a 'sentence' approximated normal English, the better it was recalled. This suggests that knowledge of semantic and grammatical structure (presumably stored in LTM) is used to aid recall from STM.

Clearly, an acoustic code isn't the only one used in STM. According to Wickelgren (1973), the kind of coding might reflect the processing which has occurred in a given context, rather than being a property of the memory store itself.

The study of brain-damaged patients

Anterograde amnesia and the amnesic syndrome

If STM and LTM really are distinct, then there should be certain kinds of brain damage which impair one without affecting the other. One such form of brain damage is *anterograde amnesia*. (See Case Study 17.1.)

Based on a steady decline in H.M.'s ability to define, spell, and pronounce words familiar to him before his surgery, MacKay (2014. MacKay and Johnson, 2013) reasoned that the hippocampal region must be involved not just in making new memories, but preserving old ones. The hippocampus can craft new memories to replace those that have been degraded or fragmented with time. In H.M.'s case, this hippocampal maintenance system was defunct: he had no way of rejuvenating depleted memories through practice or relearning (Mackay, 2014).

An equally dramatic, but in many ways more tragic case is that of Clive Wearing (see Case Study 17.2).

Ask Yourself

- In what ways do the cases of H.M. and Clive Wearing support the MSM?
- In what ways do they challenge it?

Atkinson and Shiffrin regard the kind of memory deficits displayed by H.M. and Clive Wearing as 'perhaps the single most convincing demonstration of a dichotomy in the memory system'. According to Parkin (1987), the *amnesic syndrome* (AS) isn't a general deterioration of memory function, but a *selective impairment* in which some functions (such as learning novel information) are severely impaired, while others (including memory span and language) remain intact.

If amnesics do have an intact STM, they should show a similar recency effect (based on STM) but a poorer primacy effect (based on LTM) compared with normal controls. This is exactly what's found (e.g. Baddeley and Warrington, 1970). However, this difference in STM and LTM functioning could mean that:

Case Study 17.1

H.M. (Milner *et al.*, 1968)

- H.M. (Henry Molaison) is probably the single most studied amnesic patient in the history of Neuropsychology (Rose, 2003). He'd been suffering epileptic fits of devastating frequency since the age of 16. In 1953 (aged 27), he underwent surgery aimed at alleviating his epilepsy. The anterior two-thirds of his hippocampus, most of his amygdala, plus part of the temporal lobe (on both sides of his brain) were removed (see Chapter 4).
- While this was fairly successful in curing his epilepsy, at the time the role of these brain structures in memory was unknown, and he was left with severe *anterograde amnesia*: he had near normal memory for anything learned before the surgery, but severe memory deficits for events that occurred afterwards.
- He showed preserved STM (e.g. immediate memory span) and episodic memory, could retain verbal information for about 15 seconds without rehearsal, and for much longer with rehearsal. But he couldn't transfer information into LTM or, if he could, was unable to retrieve it. He seemed entirely incapable of remembering any new fact or event.
- He was able to learn and remember perceptual and motor skills, but had to be reminded each day just what skills he possessed.
- He forgot all the news almost as soon as he'd read about it, had no idea what time of day it was unless he'd just looked at the clock, couldn't remember that his father had died or that his family had moved house. He reread the same magazine without realising he'd already read it.
- People he met after the operation remained, in effect, total strangers to him. Brenda Milner knew him for 25 years, yet she was a stranger to him each time they met. He died in 2008.

Case Study 17.2

Clive Wearing (based on Baddeley, 1990; Blakemore, 1988; Wearing, 2005)

- Clive Wearing was the chorus master of the London Sinfonietta and a world expert on Renaissance music, as well as a BBC radio producer. In March 1985, he suffered a rare brain infection caused by the cold sore virus (*Herpes simplex*). The virus attacked and destroyed his hippocampus, along with parts of his cortex.
- Like H.M., he lives in a snapshot of time, constantly believing that he's just awoken from years of unconsciousness. For example, when his wife, Deborah, enters his hospital room for the third time in a single morning, he embraces her as if they'd been parted for years, saying, 'I'm conscious for the first time' and 'it's the first time I've seen anybody at all'.
- At first, his confusion was total and very frightening to him. Once he held a chocolate in the palm of one hand, covered it with the other for a few seconds until its image disappeared from his memory. When he uncovered it, he thought he'd performed a magic trick, conjuring it up from nowhere. He repeated it again and again, with total astonishment and growing fear each time.
- Like H.M., he can still speak and walk, as well as read music, play the organ and conduct. In fact, his musical ability is remarkably well preserved. Also like H.M, he can learn new skills (e.g. mirror-reading), which he performed just as well three months later. Yet for Clive, it's new every time.
- But unlike H.M., his capacity for remembering his earlier life is extremely patchy. For example, when shown pictures of Cambridge (where he'd spent four years as an undergraduate and had often visited subsequently) he only recognised King's College Chapel – the most distinctive Cambridge building – but not his own college. He couldn't remember who wrote *Romeo and Juliet*, and he thought the Queen and the Duke of Edinburgh were singers he'd known from a Catholic church.
- According to Deborah, 'without consciousness he's in many senses dead'. In his own words, his life is 'Hell on earth – it's like being dead – all the bloody time'.

- the problem for amnesics is one of *transfer* from STM to LTM, which is perfectly consistent with the MSM, or, alternatively
- amnesics have difficulties in retrieval from LTM (Warrington and Weiskrantz, 1968, 1970).

Another major implication of cases such as those of H.M. and Clive Wearing is that the MSM's *unitary* LTM is a gross oversimplification (see the next section).

Retrograde amnesia

In *retrograde amnesia,* a patient fails to remember what happened *before* the surgery or accident that caused the amnesia. It can be caused by head injuries, electroconvulsive therapy (ECT: see Chapter 45), carbon monoxide poisoning, and extreme stress (see Chapter 12). As in anterograde amnesia, there's typically little or no disruption of STM, and the period of time for which the person has no memories may be minutes, days or even years. When retrograde amnesia is caused by brain damage, it's usually accompanied by anterograde amnesia. Similarly, patients with Korsakoff's syndrome (caused by severe, chronic alcoholism involving damage to the hippocampus) usually experience both kinds of amnesia.

Retrograde amnesia seems to involve a disruption of *consolidation* whereby, once new information has entered LTM, time is needed for it to become firmly established physically in the brain (see the discussion of forgetting below).

ALTERNATIVES to the MSM

Multiple forms of LTM

Episodic and semantic memory

Despite their brain damage, H.M. and Clive Wearing retained many skills, both general and specific (such as talking, reading, walking, playing the organ). They were also capable of acquiring (and retaining) new skills – although they didn't know that they had them! This suggests very strongly that there are different kinds of LTM. But as far as the MSM is concerned, there's only 'LTM'.

Our 'general' knowledge about, say, computers (part of semantic memory or 'SM') is built up from past experiences with particular computers (part of episodic memory or 'EM'), through abstraction and generalisation. This suggests that, instead of regarding EM and SM as two quite distinct systems within the brain (which is what Tulving originally intended), it might be more valid to see SM as made up from multiple EMs (Baddeley, 1995). (See Box 17.1.)

Flashbulb memories

Flashbulb memories (FMs) are a special kind of EM, in which we can give vivid and detailed recollections of where we were and what we were doing when we first heard about some major public national or international event (Brown and Kulik, 1977).

Box 17.1 Episodic and semantic memory (Tulving, 1972)

Episodic memory (EM): an 'autobiographical' memory responsible for storing a record of our past experiences – the events, people, objects and so on which we've personally encountered. EMs usually have a *spatio-temporal context*: e.g. 'Where did you go on your holiday last year?' and 'What did you have for breakfast this morning?'). They have a *subjective* (self-focused) reality, but most could, in principle, be verified by others.
Semantic memory (SM): our store of general, factual knowledge about the world, including concepts, rules and language, 'a mental thesaurus, organised knowledge a person possesses about words and other verbal symbols, their meanings and referents' (Tulving, 1972). SM can be used without reference to where and when that knowledge was originally acquired. But SM can also store information about ourselves (such as how many brothers and sisters we have, or how much we like Psychology).

Ask Yourself

- Where were you and what were you doing when you heard of the death of Michael Jackson?

Figure 17.8 Michael Jackson

Box 17.2 FMs: how accurate are they?

- Research from the last 25 years shows that 'FM' is a misnomer. Memories formed under strong emotions are often considerably distorted: they seem so vivid that we have a misplaced confidence in their accuracy (Chen, 2012).
- The first detailed evidence of the inaccurate nature of FMs emerged from surveys conducted following the space shuttle *Challenger* disaster in 1986.
- More recently, Hirst *et al.* (2009) surveyed more than 3000 people in New York, Washington and five other US cities one week after the terrorist attacks, in subsequent years (and again in 2011). Compared with their initial reports, participants were only 63 per cent correct on the when-where-how types of details about learning of the attack one year later; after that, the decline slowed. Yet they were 'absolutely confident' that their memory was correct.
- Surprisingly, people were least accurate when describing their emotional state on 9/11 (42 per cent accuracy one year later). Initial shock may give way to sadness or frustration over time; we tend to reconstruct our emotional past in a way that's consistent with how we're *currently* emotionally reacting. (See discussion of Bartlett's account of *reconstructive memory* in Chapter 21.)
- However, accuracy for the key details, such as the number of hijacked planes and crash sites, was better. This can be explained (at least in part) by the repeated and ongoing media coverage. As Hirst *et al.* observe, our memory isn't independent of the larger social context we live in.
- Similarly, Neisser (1982) argues that the durability of FMs stems from their frequent rehearsal and retelling after the event. (See Critical Discussion 17.2 below.)

According to Brown and Kulik (1982), a neural mechanism is triggered by events that are emotionally arousing, unexpected or extremely important, with the result that the whole scene becomes 'printed' on the memory. But how accurate are they?

Procedural versus declarative memory

Procedural memory (PM) refers to information from LTM which cannot be inspected consciously (Anderson, 1985; Tulving, 1985). For example, riding a bike is a complex skill which is even more difficult to describe. In the same way, native speakers of a language cannot usually describe the complex grammatical rules by which they speak correctly (perhaps because they weren't learnt consciously in the first place: see Chapter 19). By contrast, EM and SM are both amenable to being inspected consciously, and the content of both can be described to another person.

Cohen and Squire (1980) distinguish between PM and *declarative memory* (DM), which corresponds to Ryle's (1949) distinction between *knowing how* and *knowing that* respectively (see Figure 17.9). Anderson (1983) argues that when we initially learn something, it's learned and encoded declaratively, but with practice it becomes compiled into a procedural form of knowledge. (This is similar to the distinction between controlled/automatic processing discussed in Chapter 13.)

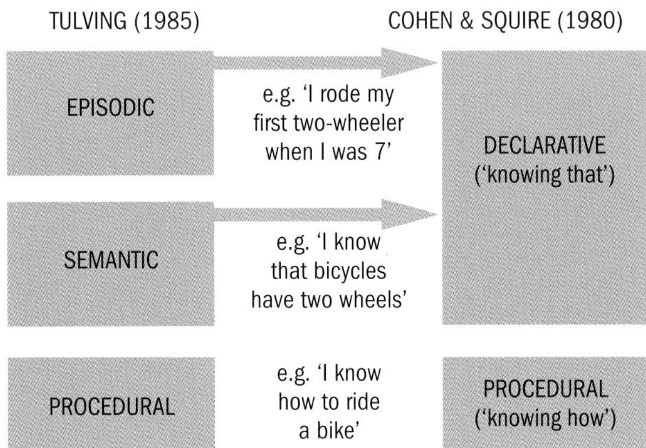

Figure 17.9 Distinctions between different kinds of LTM

PM involves more automatic processes, and allows patients to demonstrate learning without the need for conscious recollection of the learning process. But DM involves conscious recollection of the past. Damage to a number of cortical and subcortical areas (including the temporal lobes, hippocampus and mamillary bodies) seriously impairs DM in amnesic patients. PM doesn't appear to be impaired by damage to these areas (Baddeley, 1995).

The working-memory (WM) model: rethinking STM

In their MSM, Atkinson and Shiffrin saw STM as a system for temporarily holding and manipulating information. However, Baddeley and Hitch (1974) criticised the model's concept of a *unitary* STM. While accepting that STM rehearses incoming information for transfer to LTM, they argued that it was much more complex and versatile than a mere 'stopping-off station' for information. Instead of a single, simple STM, Baddeley and Hitch proposed a more complex, *multi-component* WM. This comprises a *central executive*, which is in overall charge, plus *sub-* or *slave systems*, whose activities are controlled by the central executive. These are the *articulatory* (or *phonological*) *loop* and the *visuospatial scratch* (or *sketch*) *pad*. Later, Baddeley (2000) added a fourth component, the *episodic buffer*.

The central executive

This is thought to be involved in many higher mental processes, such as decision-making, problem-solving and making plans (see Chapter 20). More specifically, it may co-ordinate performance on two separate tasks, and attend selectively to one input while inhibiting others (Baddeley, 1996). Although capacity-limited, it's very flexible and can process information in any sense modality (it's *modality-free*). It resembles a pure attentional system (Baddeley, 1981: see Chapter 13).

The articulatory (or phonological) loop

This is probably the most extensively studied component of the model. It was intended to explain the extensive evidence for acoustic coding in STM (Baddeley, 1997). It can be thought of as a *verbal rehearsal loop* used when, for example, we try to remember a telephone number for a few seconds by saying it silently to ourselves. It's also used to hold words we're preparing to speak aloud. It uses an *articulatory/phonological code*, in which information is represented as it would be spoken (the *inner voice*).

Its name derives from the finding that its capacity isn't limited by the number of items it can hold, but by the length of time taken to recite them (Baddeley *et al.*, 1975). Lists of words that took longer to pronounce weren't recalled as well as lists of the same number of words that could be pronounced more quickly. Similarly, the faster you recite something into a microphone, the more words you can record on a short loop of recording tape (Groome *et al.*, 1999).

The visuospatial scratch (or sketch) pad

This can also rehearse information, but deals with visual and/or spatial information as, for example, when we drive along a familiar road, approach a bend, and think about the road's spatial layout beyond the bend (Eysenck, 1986). It uses a visual code, representing information in the form of its visual features such as size, shape, and colour (the *inner eye*).

The scratch pad appears to contain separate visual and spatial components. The *more active spatial component* is involved in movement perception and control of physical actions, while the *more passive visual component* is involved in visual pattern recognition (Logie, 1995).

The episodic buffer

One weakness of the original version of the WM model is that least was known about the most important component, namely the central executive (Hampson and Morris, 1996). It could apparently carry out an enormous variety of processing activities in different conditions, making it difficult to describe its precise function. It was like a *homunculus* ('little man': see Chapter 4) who sits there in the theory and can be conveniently called upon whenever the theorist is unsure how to explain something. But if any result can be explained, how do you test and develop the theory? (Baddeley, 2008).

Baddeley's answer is that you try to chip away gradually at the tasks the homunculus is required to perform. In this context, the original assumption that the central executive was a purely attentional system and couldn't itself store information was questioned: how did the phonological loop and visuospatial sketchpad work together if they don't have a common code or language? And how could the whole system interface with LTM?

The *episodic buffer* (EB) was proposed as the answer to these questions. As shown in Figure 17.10, it sits between the slave systems, LTM, and the central executive. It's a limited-capacity (about four episodes or chunks) system that provides temporary storage of information held in a *multimodal code*, which is capable of combining information from the slave systems, and from LTM, into a unitary episodic representation (Baddeley, 2000). So, the EB acts as a buffer between these other parts of WM: when you try to form a mental image of a person's face or voice, all these conscious experiments are assumed to be represented within the EB. At first, it was thought of as being accessible through conscious awareness (it's the stage at which conscious mental action occurs); but it's now seen as an essentially *passive* store:

> *... a television screen rather than a stage, in which the hard work goes on elsewhere, but which depends on the buffer for its display. (Baddeley, 2008)*

An evaluation of the WM model

- It's generally accepted that (a) STM is better seen as a number of relatively independent processing mechanisms than as the MSM's single unitary store, and (b) attentional processes and STM are part of the same system (they're probably used together much of the time in everyday life). Indeed, Baddeley (e.g. 2007) identified the central executive with the *supervisory attentional system* (SAS) proposed by Norman and Shallice (1980: see Chapter 13).
- The idea that any one slave system (such as the phonological loop) may be involved in the performance of apparently very different tasks (such as memory span, mental arithmetic, verbal reasoning, and reading) is a valuable insight.
- An important *theoretical* development is to ask: why has the phonological loop evolved?

Box 17.3 Evolution and the phonological loop

- As Baddeley (2008) wittily points out, the phonological loop presumably didn't evolve because nature was preparing us for telephone numbers!
- He tested a patient who, following a stroke, had developed a pure deficit in her phonological STM. After being given a telephone number of more than two digits, she'd immediately forget it. Although her language skills were normal, she had great difficulty in learning new words (such as Russian words). This led Baddeley to suggest that the loop might have evolved for *language learning*.
- Further evidence to support this hypothesis came from the study of 8-year-old children with *specific language impairment*. They had normal general intelligence, but the language development of 6-year-olds. When given non-words (such as *prindle*, *skiticult* and *contramponist*) to repeat back, they performed like 4-year-olds; as the non-word length increased, so did their failure rate. Baddeley also found a correlation between level of vocabulary development in young normal children and their capacity to repeat back non-words; this is what would be expected if the loop had evolved for new world learning.

- These theoretical developments, in turn, have *practical applications* (Gathercole, 2008; Gathercole and Baddeley, 1990; Gathercole *et al.*, 2006).

The levels of processing (LOP) model

Rehearsal and the MSM

As we noted above, the MSM sees rehearsal as a key control process which helps to transfer information from STM to LTM. There's also only one type of rehearsal as far as the model is concerned, what

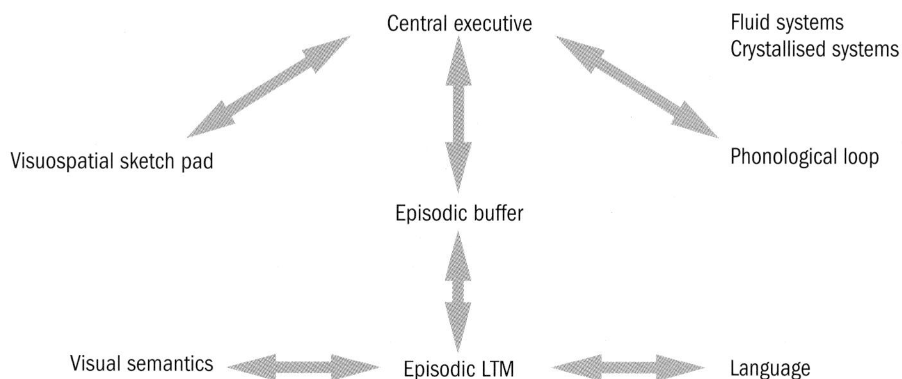

Figure 17.10 The working memory model, showing the central executive and its subsystems

Critical Discussion 17.2

Intermind: How Google is changing our memory (Wegner and Ward, 2013)

- According to Wegner and Ward, the internet is not just replacing other people as sources of memory and someone to share information with, but also our own cognitive faculties, undermining the impulse to ensure that some important, just-learned facts get inscribed into our biological memory banks. They call this the *Google effect.*
- Sparrow *et al.* (2011) asked participants to copy 40 memorable factoids (e.g. 'An ostrich's eye is bigger than its brain') into a computer. Half were told their work would be saved on the computer; the other half were told that it would be deleted. In addition, half of each group was asked to remember the information, regardless of whether it was being saved.
- Those participants who believed the computer had saved their work were much *worse* at remembering; this tendency persisted when they were explicitly asked to keep the information in mind.
- Wegner and Ward describe another study which looked at how quickly we turn to the internet when trying to answer a question. Participants completed two Stroop (see Chapter 13) tests, one after trying to answer easy trivia questions, the other after trying to answer difficult ones (e.g. 'Do all countries have at least two colours in their flags?'). The words in the Stroop tests related *either* to the internet (e.g. 'Google' in red letters or 'Yahoo' in blue) *or* to general brand names (e.g. 'Nike' in yellow).
- There was a particularly striking effect in relation to the difficult questions: participants were significantly slower in answering the colour of internet-related words than general brand-related words.
- This suggests that the internet comes to mind quickly when we don't know the answer to a question: our first impulse is to think of our all-knowing 'friend' that can provide the information we need.
- Research has shown that participants who have just found answers on a website experience the illusion that their *own* mental capacities had produced this information – not Google. Using Google gives people the sense that the internet has become part of their own cognitive tool set.

... The immediacy with which a search result pops onto the screen of a smartphone may start to blur the boundaries between our personal memories and the vast digital troves distributed across the internet ...

... The advent of the 'information age' seems to have created a generation of people who feel they know more than ever before – when their reliance on the internet means that they may know ever less about the world around them. (Wegner and Ward, 2013)

Craik and Watkins (1973) call *maintenance* (as opposed to *elaborative*) rehearsal (see Key Study 17.5). This means that what matters is *how much* rehearsal occurs. But maintenance rehearsal may not even be necessary for storage. Jenkins (1974) found that participants could remember material even though they weren't expecting to be tested – and so were unlikely to have rehearsed the material. This is called *incidental learning*.

According to Craik and Lockhart (1972), it's the *kind* of rehearsal or processing that's important. Craik and Lockhart also considered that the MSM's view of the relationship between structural components and control processes was, essentially, the wrong way round.

Ask Yourself

- How does the MSM see the relationship between structural components and control processes?

According to the MSM, the *structural components* (sensory memory, STM and LTM) are fixed, while *control processes* (such as rehearsal) are less permanent. Craik and Lockhart's *levels-of-processing* (LOP) model begins with the proposed control processes. The structural components (the memory system) are what results from the operation of these processes. In other words, memory is a *by-product of perceptual analysis*. This is controlled by the central processor, which can analyse a stimulus (such as a word) on various levels:

- at a *superficial* (or *shallow*) level, the surface features of a stimulus (such as whether the word is in upper or lower case) are processed
- at an *intermediate* (*phonemic* or *phonetic*) level, the word is analysed for its sound
- at a *deep* (or *semantic*) level, the word's meaning is analysed.

The level at which a stimulus is processed depends on both its nature and the processing time available. The more deeply information is processed, the more likely it is to be retained.

(See Gross, 2008, for further discussion of the LOP model.)

THEORIES of FORGETTING

To understand why we forget, we must recall the distinction between *availability* (whether or not material has been stored) and *accessibility* (being able to retrieve what's been stored). In terms of the MSM, since information must be transferred from STM to LTM for permanent storage:

- availability mainly concerns STM and the transfer of information from STM into LTM
- accessibility has to do mainly with LTM.

Forgetting can occur at the encoding, storage or retrieval stages.

One way of looking at forgetting is to ask what prevents information staying in STM long enough to be transferred to LTM (some answers are provided by *decay* and *displacement theories*). Some answers to the question about what prevents us from locating the information that's already in LTM are offered by *interference theory, cue-dependent forgetting* and *motivated forgetting* (or *repression*: this is discussed in Chapter 21).

Decay theory

Decay (or *trace decay*) *theory* tries to explain why forgetting increases with time. Clearly, memories must be stored somewhere, the most obvious place being the brain. Presumably, some sort of structural change (the *engram*) occurs when learning takes place. According to decay theory, metabolic processes occur over time which cause the engram to degrade/break down, unless it's maintained by repetition and rehearsal. This results in the memory contained within it becoming unavailable.

Hebb (1949) argued that while learning is taking place, the engram which will eventually be formed is very delicate and liable to disruption (the *active trace*). With learning, it grows stronger until a permanent engram is formed (the *structural trace*) through neurochemical and neuroanatomical changes.

Decay in STM and LTM

The active trace corresponds roughly to STM, and, according to decay theory, forgetting from STM is due to disruption of the active trace. Although Hebb didn't apply the idea of decay to LTM, other researchers have argued that it can explain LTM forgetting if it's assumed that decay occurs through disuse (hence, *decay-through-disuse theory*). So, if certain knowledge or skills aren't used or practised for long periods of time, the corresponding engram will eventually decay away (Loftus and Loftus, 1980).

Ask Yourself

- **Try to think of skills/knowledge that, contrary to decay-through-disuse theory, aren't lost even after long periods of not being used/practised.**

Is forgetting just a matter of time?

Peterson and Peterson's (1959) experiment (see Key Study 17.1) has been taken as evidence for the role of decay in STM forgetting. If decay did occur, then we'd expect poorer recall of information with the passage of time, which is exactly what the Petersons reported.

The difficulty with the Petersons' study in particular, and decay theory in general, is that other possible effects need to be excluded before we opt for a decay-based account. The ideal way to study the role of decay in forgetting would be to have people receive information and then do nothing, physical or mental, for a period of time. If recall was poorer with the passage of time, it would be reasonable to suggest that decay had occurred. Such an experiment is, of course, impossible. However, Jenkins and Dallenbach (1924) were the first to attempt an approximation to it.

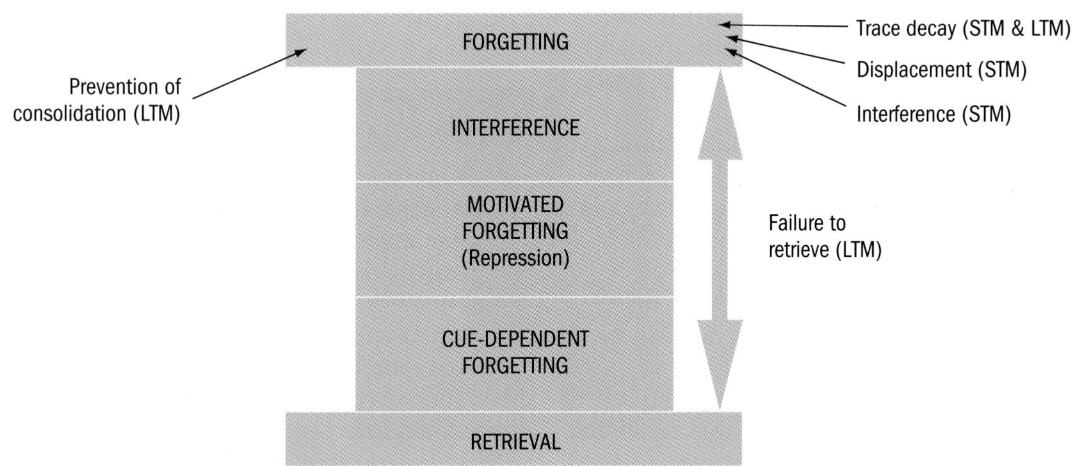

Figure 17.11 Different theories of forgetting, including retrieval failure

Key Study 17.6

If you want to remember, sleep on it (Jenkins and Dallenbach, 1924)

- Participants learnt a list of ten nonsense syllables. Some then went to sleep immediately (approximating the ideal 'do nothing' state), while the others continued with their normal activities. After intervals of one, two, four or eight hours, all participants were tested for their recall of the syllables.
- While there was a fairly steady increase in forgetting as the retention interval increased for the 'waking' participants, this wasn't true for the sleeping participants (see Figure 17.12).
- If decay is a natural result of the passage of time alone, then we should have expected equal forgetting in *both* groups. The results suggest that it's what happens *in between* learning and recall that determines forgetting, not time as such. This led Jenkins and Dallenbach to conclude that:

Forgetting is not so much a matter of decay of old impressions and associations as it is a matter of interference, inhibition or obliteration of the old by the new.

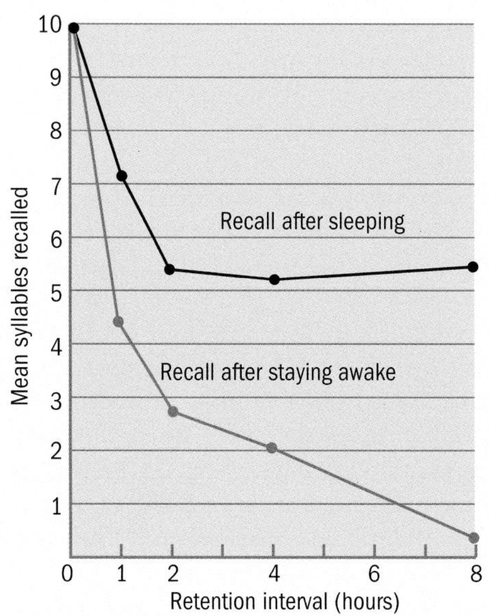

Figure 17.12 Mean number of syllables recalled by participants in Jenkins and Dallenbach's experiment

Although some data exist suggesting that neurological breakdown occurs with age and disease (such as Alzheimer's disease), there's no evidence that the major cause of forgetting from LTM is neurological decay (Solso, 1995).

Displacement theory

In a limited-capacity STM system, forgetting might occur through *displacement*. When the system is 'full', the oldest material in it would be displaced ('pushed out') by incoming new material. This possibility was explored by Waugh and Norman (1965) using the *serial probe task*. Participants were presented with 16 digits at the rate of either one or four per second. One of the digits (the 'probe') was then repeated, and participants had to say which digit followed the probe. Presumably:

- if the probe was one of the digits at the beginning of the list, the probability of recalling the digit that followed would be small, because later digits would have displaced earlier ones from the system
- if the probe was presented towards the end of the list, the probability of recalling the digit that followed would be high, since the last digits to be presented would still be available in STM.

When the number of digits following the probe was small, recall was good, but when it was large, recall was poor. This is consistent with the idea that the earlier digits are replaced by later ones.

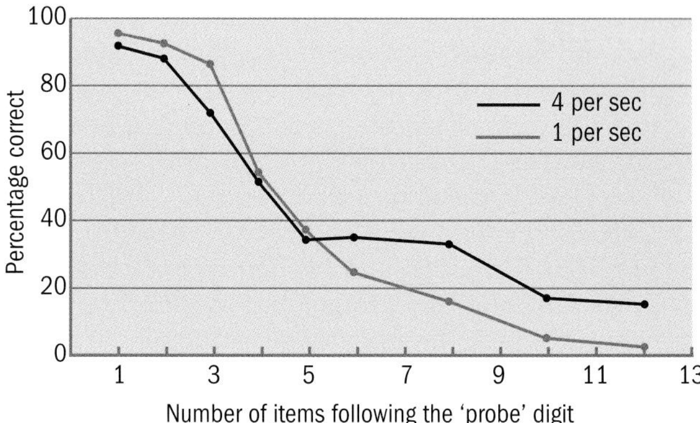

Figure 17.13 Data from Waugh and Norman's serial probe experiment

Ask Yourself

- Waugh and Norman also found that recall was generally better with the faster (four per second) presentation rate. How does this support decay theory?

Since less time had elapsed between presentation of the digits and the probe in the four-per-second condition, there would have been less opportunity for those digits to have decayed away. This makes it unclear whether displacement is a process distinct from decay.

Retrieval-failure theory and cue-dependent forgetting

According to *retrieval-failure theory*, memories cannot be recalled because the correct retrieval cues aren't being used. The role of retrieval cues is demonstrated by the *tip-of-the-tongue phenomenon* (TOT), in which we know that we know something but cannot retrieve it at that particular moment in time (Brown and McNeill, 1966).

Key Study 17.7

It's on the tip of my tongue (Brown and McNeill, 1966)

- Brown and McNeill gave participants dictionary definitions of unfamiliar words, and asked them to provide the words themselves. Most participants either knew the word or knew that they didn't know it.
- Some, however, were sure they knew the word but couldn't recall it (it was on the tip of their tongue). About half could give the word's first letter and the number of syllables, and often offered words which sounded like the word or had a similar meaning. This suggests that the required words were in memory, but the absence of a correct retrieval cue prevented them from being recalled.
- Examples of definitions used by Brown and McNeill:
  1. A small boat used in the harbours and rivers of Japan and China, rowed with a scull from the stern, and often having a sail
  2. Favouritism, especially governmental patronage extended to relatives
  3. The common cavity into which the various ducts of the body open in certain fish, reptiles, birds and mammals.

Answers: sampan; nepotism; cloaca

Tulving (1974) used the term *cue-dependent forgetting* to refer jointly to *context-dependent* and *state-dependent forgetting*. (See Table 17.2.)

Table 17.2 Cue-dependent forgetting

Context-dependent forgetting	State-dependent forgetting
Occurs in absence of relevant environmental or contextual variables. These represent *external* cues.	Occurs in absence of relevant psychological or physiological variables. These represent *internal* cues.
Abernathy (1940): One group had to learn and then recall material in the same room, while a second group learned and recalled in different rooms. The first group's recall was superior.	Clark *et al.* (1987): Victims' inabilities to recall details of a violent crime may be due at least partly to the fact that recall occurs in a less emotionally aroused state. (See Chapter 21.)
Godden and Baddeley (1975): Divers learned lists of words either on land or 15 feet under water. Recall was then tested in the same or a different context. Those who learned and recalled in different contexts showed a 30% deficit compared with those who learned and recalled in the same context.	McCormick and Mayer (1991): The important link may be between mood and the sort of material being remembered. So we're more likely to remember happy events when we're feeling happy rather than sad.

Interestingly, when Godden and Baddeley (1980) repeated their 'underwater' experiment using *recognition* as the measure of remembering, they found no effect of context. They concluded that context-dependent forgetting applies only to *recall*. According to Baddeley (1995), large effects of context on memory are found only when the contexts in which encoding and retrieval occur are *very* different. Although less marked changes can produce some effects, studies (other than Abernathy's) looking at the effects of context on examination performance have tended to show few effects. This may be because when we're learning, our surroundings aren't a particularly salient feature of the situation, unlike our internal state (such as our emotional state).

Interference theory

According to *interference theory*, forgetting is influenced more by what we do before or after learning than by the mere passage of time (see Key Study 17.6).

- In *retroactive interference/inhibition* (RI), *later* learning interferes with the recall of *earlier* learning. For example, if you originally learned to drive in a manual car, then learned to drive an automatic, when returning to a manual, you might try to drive it as though it were an automatic.
- In *proactive interference/inhibition* (PI), *earlier* learning interferes with the recall of *later* learning. For example, say you learned to drive on a car in which the indicator lights are turned on by

using the stalk on the left of the steering wheel, and the windscreen wipers by the stalk on the right. After passing your driving test, you buy a car in which this arrangement is reversed. When you're about to turn left or right, you activate the windscreen wipers!

Interference theory has been extensively studied in the laboratory using *paired-associate lists*. The usual procedure for studying interference effects is shown in Figure 17.14.

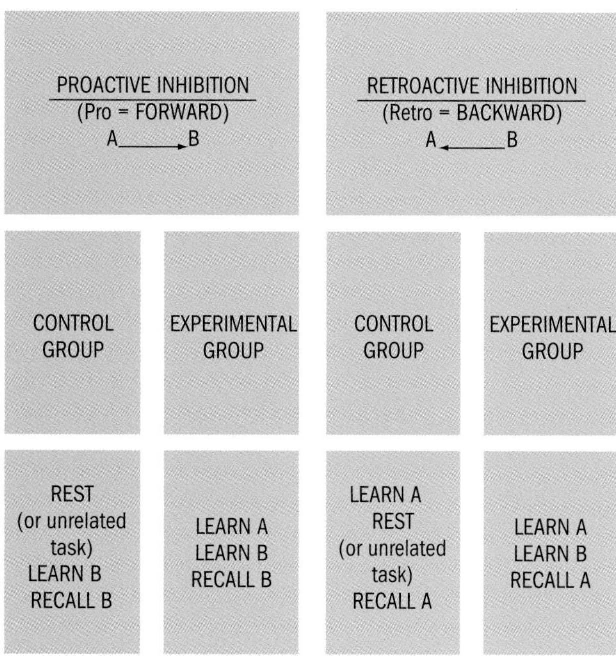

Figure 17.14 Experimental procedure for investigating retroactive and proactive interference

Usually, the first member of each pair in list A is the same as in list B, but the second member of each pair is different in the two lists.

- In RI, the learning of the second list interferes with recall of the first list (the interference works *backwards* in time).
- In PI, the learning of the first list interferes with recall of the second list (the interference works *forwards* in time).

Limitations of laboratory studies of interference theory

The strongest support for interference theory comes from laboratory studies. However, the following points should be borne in mind:

- Learning in such studies doesn't occur in the same way as it does in the real world, where learning of potentially interfering material is spaced out over time. In the laboratory, learning is artificially compressed in time, which maximises the likelihood that interference will occur (Baddeley, 1990). Such studies therefore lack ecological validity.
- Laboratory studies tend to use nonsense syllables as the stimulus material. When meaningful material is used, interference is more difficult to demonstrate (Solso, 1995).
- When people have to learn, say, the response 'bell' to the stimulus 'woj', the word 'bell' isn't actually learned in the laboratory, since it's already part of SM. What's being learned (a specific response to a specific stimulus in a specific laboratory situation) is stored in EM. SM is much more stable and structured than EM, and so is much more resistant to interference effects. No amount of new information will cause someone to forget the things they know that are stored in their SM (Solso, 1995).
- However, in support of interference theory, it's generally agreed that if students have to study more than one subject in the same time-frame, these should be as *dissimilar* as possible.

Ask Yourself

- Think of examples of subjects that (a) should definitely *not* be studied together in the same time-frame, and (b) *could* be studied together without much risk of interference.

According to Schacter (2002), efficient forgetting is a crucial part of having a fully functioning memory. When we forget something useful, the pruning system is working just a little too well. In his book *The Seven Sins of Memory* (2001), Schacter describes several ways that we forget, including:

- *Transience* is a strategy whereby we discard information that's out of date (such as old telephone numbers or what we had for lunch last week).
- *Absent-mindedness* might involve failing to properly encode information about where we put our keys because our attention is tied up elsewhere (see Chapter 13).
- *Blocking* refers to the brain holding back on one memory in favour of a competing memory, so that we don't get muddled (this prevents interference).

Each of these strategies has an adaptive purpose, preventing us from storing mundane, confusing or out-of-date memories. (See Critical Discussion 17.3 and Case Study 17.3.) Explaining HSAM is more difficult than describing it; it's possible that it relies not just on how information is encoded but also on how it's retrieved (Marshall, 2008).

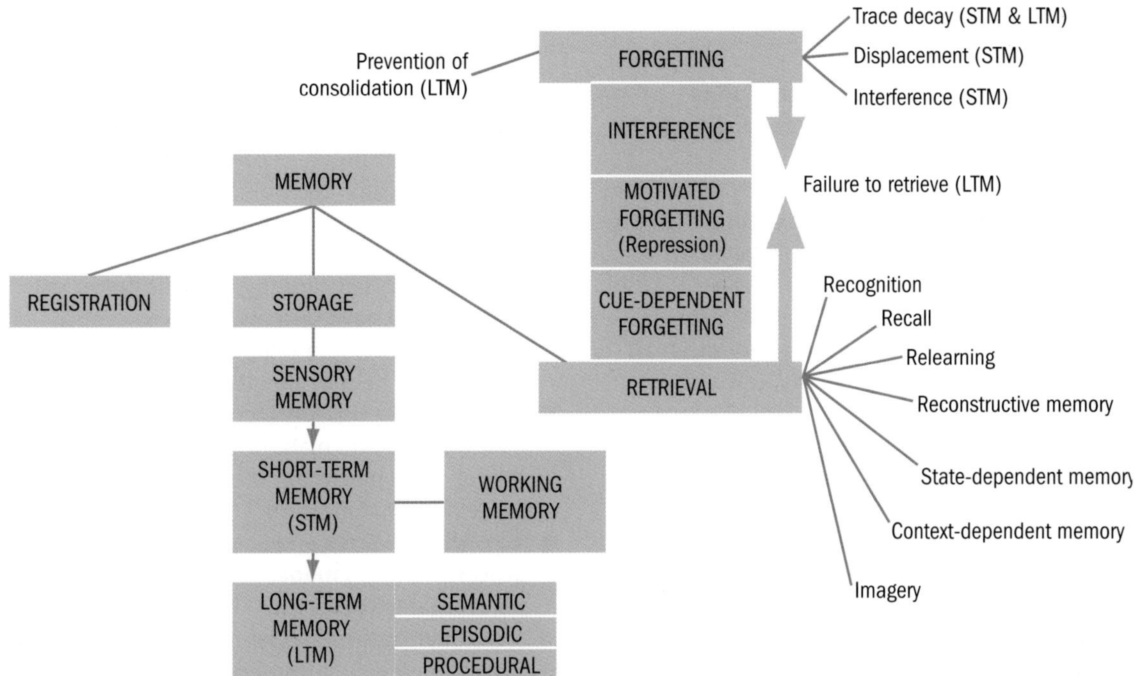

Figure 17.15 A summary of the three components of memory and theories of forgetting

Critical Discussion 17.3 and Case Study 17.3

Why we need to forget: The Case of A.J. (Parker *et al.*, 2006)

- A 42-year-old woman from California, A.J., (real name, Jill Price) remembers every day of her life since her teens in extraordinary detail. Mention any date since 1980, and she's immediately transported back in time, picturing where she was, what she was doing, and what made the news that day. She can also identify the day of the week for any date since 1980 and give the correct date for apparently insignificant events.
- She's locked in a cycle of remembering that she describes as 'running a movie that never stops'. She describes her constant recall as 'non-stop, uncontrollable and totally exhausting' and as a 'burden' of which she's both warden and victim.
- Parker *et al*. coined the term 'hyperthymestic syndrome' (from the Greek 'thymesis' = 'remembering'). It's also referred to as highly superior autobiographical memory (HSAM) (McGaugh and Le Port, 2014).
- MRI and PET scans of the brains of other people with HSAM have identified two memory-related regions, the uncinate fascicle (a nerve tract linking the temporal and frontal cortex) and the parahippocampal gyrus.
- Independent evidence shows that injury to the uncinate fascicle impairs autobiographical memory (McGaugh and Le Port, 2014). HSAM is quite different from the memory of 'S', made famous by Luria (1968) in *The Mind of a Mnemonist* (see Rolls, 2010).

CONCLUSIONS

According to Rose (2003):

> *... Memory defines who we are and shapes the way we act more closely than any other single aspect of our personhood ...*

Whatever happens to us (including losing a limb), we're still, in an important sense, recognisably ourselves provided our memories are intact. However:

> *... Lose your memory and you, as you, cease to exist ... (Rose, 2003)*

> *A bit of healthy editing and shading is far better in helping us understand who we are, where we have come from, and where we might be heading in the future. The primary role of autobiographical memory is helping us understand our place in the world, past, present and future. (Morrison, 2013)*

Chapter Summary

- **Memory** can be defined as the **retention of learning** or **experience**. Learning and memory are **interdependent** processes.
- Ebbinghaus began the systematic study of memory, using **nonsense syllables**. He showed that memory declined very rapidly at first, then levelled off.
- Memory is now studied largely from an **information-processing approach**, which focuses on **registration/encoding**, **storage**, and **retrieval**. Storage corresponds to **availability**, retrieval to **accessibility**.
- Techniques for measuring memory include **recognition**, **recall** (**serial** or **free**), **paired associates recall,** and the **memory-span procedure**.
- James' distinction between **primary** and **secondary** memory corresponds to that between **short-term memory (STM)** and **long-term memory (LTM)**.
- **Sensory memory** is probably best thought of as an aspect of **perception** and as a prerequisite for storage proper (i.e. STM).
- The limited capacity of STM can be increased by **chunking**, which draws on LTM to encode new information in a meaningful way. **Rehearsal** is a way of holding information in STM almost indefinitely, and the primary code used by STM is **acoustic**. But semantic and visual codings are also used.
- LTM probably has an **unlimited capacity,** and information is stored in a **relatively permanent** way. Coding is mainly **semantic**, but information may also be coded visually, acoustically and in other ways.
- Atkinson and Shiffrin's **multi-store model** (**MSM**) sees sensory memory, STM and LTM as **permanent structural components** of the memory system. Rehearsal is a **control process**, which acts as a **buffer** between sensory memory and LTM, and helps the **transfer** of information to LTM.
- The **primacy effect** reflects recall from LTM, while the **recency effect** reflects recall from STM. Together they comprise the **serial position effect.**
- Studies of **brain-damaged, amnesic patients** appear to support the STM–LTM distinction. While STM continues to function fairly normally, certain aspects of LTM functioning are impaired.
- LTM isn't unitary, but comprises **semantic (SM)**, **episodic (EM)**, and **procedural memory (PM)**. **Autobiographical memory** (**AM**) and **flashbulb memories** are two kinds of EM. An overlapping distinction is that between PM and **declarative memory/learning**.
- Baddeley and Hitch's **working-memory (WM) model** rejected the MSM's view of STM as unitary. Instead, STM is seen as comprising a **central executive**, which controls the activities of the **phonological loop (inner voice)**, and **visuospatial scratch pad (inner eye)**.
- A passive, limited capacity **episodic buffer** sits between the slave systems, LTM and central executive, providing temporary storage of information held in a **multimodal code.**
- Craik and Watkins' distinction between **maintenance** and **elaborative rehearsal** implies that it's not the amount but the **kind** of rehearsal or processing that matters.
- According to Craik and Lockhart's **levels-of-processing (LOP) model,** memory is a **by-product of perceptual analysis**, such that STM and LTM are the consequences of the operation of control processes.
- The more deeply information is processed, the more likely it is to be retained. **Semantic** processing represents the **deepest** level.
- **Decay/trace decay theory** attempts to explain why forgetting increases over time. STM forgetting is due to **disruption** of the **active trace**, and **decay through disuse** explains LTM forgetting.
- **Displacement theory** is supported by data from Waugh and Norman's **serial probe task**. However, displacement may not be distinct from decay.
- According to **retrieval-failure theory**, memories cannot be recalled because the correct **retrieval cues** are missing. This is demonstrated by the **tip-of-the-tongue (TOT) phenomenon**.
- **Cue-dependent forgetting** comprises **context-dependent** and **state-dependent** forgetting, which refer to **external** and **internal cues** respectively.
- According to **interference theory**, forgetting is influenced more by what we do before/after learning than by the mere passage of time. **Retroactive interference/inhibition** (**RI**) works **backwards** in time, while **proactive interference/inhibition (PI)** works **forwards** in time.
- Laboratory studies of interference lack **ecological validity**, and interference is more difficult to demonstrate when material other than nonsense syllables is used.
- The need to forget redundant information is a fundamental aspect of a fully functioning memory; this is lacking in people with **hyperthymestic syndrome** (or **highly superior autobiographical memory** (HSAM).

Links with Other Topics/Chapters

Chapter 13 ⟶ Broadbent's filter model of selective attention was, in many ways, the precursor to Atkinson and Shiffrin's MSM, and sensory memory is very similar to Broadbent's concept of a sensory 'buffer' store

Chapter 3 ⟶ The case study method, in practice at least, often involves unusual or abnormal behaviour. While this can shed light on 'normal' behaviour, critics argue that we cannot generalise from such cases, making it unscientific

Chapter 42 ⟶ Traditional science adopts a *nomothetic* ('law-like') approach, while the case study is central to the *idiographic* ('uniqueness') approach

Chapter 39 ⟶ Rose (2003) argues that cases like those of H.M. and Clive Wearing involve brain damage that is clinically unique, making it impossible to generalise as can be done from patients with Korsakoff's syndrome or Alzheimer's disease

Chapter 13 ⟶ The distinction between PM and declarative memory is similar to that between controlled and automatic processing

Chapter 20 ⟶ Chess masters' phenomenal STM only for non-random board positions demonstrates an important difference between how people and computers 'think' and solve problems

Chapter 40 ⟶ A.J. and other people with hyperthymestic syndrome display obsessive qualities similar to those of autistic individuals (such as an unusual interest in dates)

Chapters 7 and 44 ⟶ The need to forget is considered important for people suffering from post-traumatic stress disorder (PTSD) and is the central concept in Crick and Mitchison's reverse learning theory of dreaming

Recommended Reading

Baddeley, A. (1997) *Human Memory: Theory and Practice* (revised edition). Hove: Psychology Press.

Baddeley, A. (1999) *Essentials of Human Memory.* Hove: Psychology Press.

Draaisma, D. (2004) *Why Life Speeds Up As You Get Older.* Cambridge: Cambridge University Press. Also relevant to Chapters 6, 21, and 40.

Gross, R. (2008) *Key Studies in Psychology* (5th edition). London: Hodder Education. Chapter 5.

Parkin, A.J. (1987) *Memory and Amnesia: An Introduction.* Oxford: Blackwell.

Rose, S. (2003) *The Making of Memory: From Molecules to Mind* (revised edition). London: Vintage. Also useful for Chapter 49.

Useful Websites

http://memory.uva.nl/index_en (Memory Psychology for a general audience: University of Amsterdam)
www.exploratorium.edu/memory/index.html (Memory exploratorium)
www.york.ac.uk/res/wml (Centre for Working Memory and Learning: University of York)
www.livescience.com/38280-what-is-deja-vu.html (Some very useful links to other aspects of memory)
www.tinyurl.com/qf97j66 (Short-term memory demonstrations, including serial position curve)
www.tinyurl.com/nh6r2xd (Demonstration of chunking and cueing effects)

CHAPTER 18

LANGUAGE AND THOUGHT

Language and thought are the same

Thought is dependent on, or caused by, language

Language is dependent on, and reflects, thought

Thought and language as initially separate activities

INTRODUCTION and OVERVIEW

The relationship between language and thought is one of the most fascinating and complex issues within Psychology and has been debated by philosophers for more than 2000 years. Our thinking often takes the form of imagery, and our thoughts and feelings are often expressed (unconsciously) through gestures and facial expressions. Artists 'think' non-linguistically. Knowing what we want to say, but being unable to 'put it into words', is one of several examples of thought taking place without language (Weiskrantz, 1988).

However, the exact *relationship* between language and thought has been the subject of much debate. Views fall into four main categories.

1. *Thought is dependent on, or caused by, language.* This view is taken by people working in a variety of disciplines, including Psychology, sociology, linguistics, and anthropology. Sapir (a linguist and anthropologist) and Whorf (a linguist) were both interested in comparing languages, which they saw as a major feature of a culture. Language is shared by all members of a culture, or subcultures within it, and this makes it a determining influence on how individuals think. Bernstein (a sociologist) focused on subcultural (social class) differences in language *codes*, which he saw as a major influence on intelligence and educational attainment. *Social constructionists* (e.g. Gergen) regard language as providing a basis for all our thought, a system of categories for dividing up experience and giving it meaning (see Chapter 2).
2. *Language is dependent on, and reflects, thought.* Probably the most extreme version of this view is Piaget's, according to whom language reflects the individual's level of cognitive development (see Chapter 34).
3. *Thought and language are initially quite separate activities*, which then come together and interact at a later point in development (about age two). This view is associated with the Russian Psychologist, Vygotsky (again, see Chapter 34).
4. *Language and thought are one and the same.* This rather extreme view is associated mainly with Watson, the founder of Behaviourism (see Chapters 1 and 2).

The focus of this chapter is the various versions of the first of these viewpoints.

LANGUAGE and THOUGHT are the SAME

Watson's 'peripheralist' approach

The earliest psychological theory of the relationship between language and thought was proposed by Watson (1913). In his view, thought processes are really no more than the sensations produced by tiny movements of the speech organs too small to produce audible sounds. Essentially, then, thought is talking to oneself very quietly. Part of Watson's rejection of 'mind' was his denial of mentalistic concepts such as 'thought' (see Chapter 3), and hence his reduction of it to 'silent speech' (see Chapter 49).

Watson's theory is called *peripheralism*, because it sees 'thinking' occurring peripherally in the larynx, rather than centrally in the brain. Movements of the larynx do occur when 'thought' is taking place. But this indicates only that such movements may *accompany* thinking, not that the movements *are* thoughts or that they're necessary for thinking to occur.

Ask Yourself

- Can you think of any ways in which you might test Watson's theory?

Smith *et al.* (1947) attempted to test Watson's theory by giving himself an injection of curare, a drug that causes total paralysis of the skeletal muscles without affecting consciousness. The muscles of the speech organs and the respiratory system are paralysed, and so Smith had to be kept breathing artificially. When the drug's effects had worn off, he was able to report on his thoughts and perceptions during the paralysis.

Additionally, Furth (1966) has shown that people born deaf and mute, and who don't learn sign language, can also think in much the same way as hearing and speaking people. For Watson, deaf and mute individuals should be incapable of thought, because of the absence of movement in the speech organs.

THOUGHT is DEPENDENT ON, or CAUSED BY, LANGUAGE

Bruner (1983) has argued that language is essential if thought and knowledge aren't to be limited to what can be learned through our actions (the *enactive mode of representation*) or images (the *iconic mode*). If the *symbolic mode* (going beyond the immediate context) is to develop, then language is crucial (see Chapter 34).

Social constructionists (e.g. Gergen, 1973) have argued that our ways of understanding the world derive from other people (past and present), rather than from objective reality. We're born into a world where the conceptual frameworks and categories used by people in our culture already exist. Indeed, these frameworks and categories are an essential part of our culture, since they provide meaning, a way of structuring experience of both ourselves and the world of other people. Language is of fundamental importance in this process. This view has much in common with the 'strong' version of the *linguistic relativity hypothesis,* the most extensively researched of the theories arguing that thought is dependent on, or caused by, language.

Ask Yourself

- What would you say are some of the fundamental categories that exist in contemporary Britain, taken-for-granted ways of thinking and perceiving, which we may/may not share with other western cultures?

The linguistic relativity hypothesis (LRH)

According to the philosopher Wittgenstein (1921), 'The limits of my language mean the limits of my world'. By this he meant that people can only think about and understand the world through language and that if a particular language doesn't possess certain ideas or concepts, these couldn't exist for its native speakers.

The view that language determines how we think about objects and events, or even *what* we think (our ideas, thoughts and perceptions), can be traced to the writings of Sapir (1929) and Whorf (1956), a student of Sapir. Their perspective is often called the *Sapir–Whorf linguistic relativity hypothesis* (LRH), and is sometimes referred to as the *Whorfian hypothesis* in acknowledgement of the greater contribution made by Whorf. For Whorf (1956):

> *We dissect nature along the lines laid down by our native languages. The categories and types that we isolate from the world of phenomena we do not find there because they stare every observer in the face; on the contrary, the world is presented in a kaleidoscopic flux of impressions that has to be organised by our minds – and this means largely by the linguistic systems in our minds. We cut nature up, organise it into concepts and ascribe significance as we do, largely because we are parties to an agreement to organise it this way – an agreement that holds throughout our speech community and is codified in patterns of our language.*

According to Whorf's *linguistic determinism*, language determines our concepts, and we can think only through the use of concepts. So acquiring a language involves acquiring a 'world view' (or *Weltanschauung*). People who speak different languages have different world views (hence linguistic 'relativity').

Ask Yourself

- In a general sense, do you agree with the claims of linguistic determinism? Is language really that 'powerful'? Have another read of this chapter's *Introduction and overview*.
- If people who speak different (native) languages really do have different world views, what would that imply for communication between them?

What was Whorf's evidence?

Whorf compared standard average European (SAE) languages, such as English, French, and Italian (Indo-European), with Native American languages, particularly Hopi. While in English we have a single word for snow, the Inuit Eskimos have approximately 20 (including one for fluffy snow, one for drifting snow, another for packed snow, and so on). The Hopi Indians have only one word for 'insect', 'aeroplane', and 'pilot' and the Zuni Indians don't distinguish, verbally, between yellow and orange.

Figure 18.1 According to Whorf, the fact that Inuit Eskimos have 20 different words for snow means that they literally perceive more varieties of snow than native English speakers who have only one or two words

Whorf also saw a language's grammar as determining an individual's thought and perception. In the Hopi language, for example, no distinction is made between past, present, and future which, compared with English, makes it a 'timeless language'. In European languages, 'time' is treated as an objective entity, with a clear demarcation between past, present, and future. Although the Hopi language recognises duration, Hopis talk about time only as it appears subjectively to the observer. For example, rather than saying 'I stayed for ten days', Hopis say 'I stayed until the tenth day' or 'I left on the tenth day'.

In English, nouns denote objects and events, and verbs denote actions. But in the Hopi language, 'lightning', 'wave', 'flame', 'meteor', 'puff of smoke' and 'pulsation' are all verbs, since events of necessarily brief duration must be verbs. As a result, a Hopi would say 'it lightninged', 'it smoked' and 'it flamed'.

Ask Yourself

- Does the finding that Inuit Eskimos have 20 words for snow (if true) necessarily mean that native speakers of Inuit actually perceive more varieties of snow than speakers of English?
- Did Whorf show that the Hopi Indians cannot discriminate between past, present and future in essentially the same way as SAE speakers?

Greene (1975) asks us to imagine a Hopi linguist applying a Whorfian analysis to English. Would s/he think that we have 'primitive' beliefs that ships are really female or that mountains have feet, or that 'driving a car', 'driving off in golf' and 'driving a hard bargain' all involve the same activity? Of course not.

Figure 18.2 Do mountains really have feet?

Testing the LRH

Miller and McNeill (1969) distinguish between three different versions of the LRH, all consistent with it but varying in the strength of claim they make:

- the *strong version* claims that language determines thought
- the *weak version* claims that language affects perception
- the *weakest version* claims that language influences memory – information that's more easily

described in a particular language will be better remembered than information that's more difficult to describe.

The questions and criticisms that we considered above relate mainly to the strong version, but almost all the research has focused on the weak and weakest versions. One of the few attempts to test the strong version was a study by Carroll and Casagrande (1958).

Key Study 18.1

How Navaho children shape up on cognitive development (Carroll and Casagrande, 1958)

- Carroll and Casagrande compared Navaho Indian children who spoke either only Navaho (*Navaho–Navaho*) or English and Navaho (*English–Navaho*) with American children of European descent who spoke only English, on the development of *form or shape recognition*.
- The Navaho language stresses the importance of form, such that 'handling' verbs involve different words depending on what's being handled. For example, long and flexible objects (such as string) have one word form, whereas long and rigid objects (such as sticks) have another. American children of European descent develop object recognition in the order: size, colour, and form or shape.
- If, as the strong version of the LRH claims, language influences cognitive development, then the developmental sequence of the Navaho children should differ from the English-only American children, and their form or shape recognition abilities should be superior. This is what Carroll and Casagrande found, thus supporting the strong version of the LRH.
- However, they also found that the English–Navaho group showed form recognition *later* than the English-only American children, which *doesn't* support the LRH strong version. Carroll and Casagrande attributed the superior performance of the English-only children to the fact that they'd had a great deal of experience of shape classification at nursery school. This made them an atypical sample.

Perception and memory of colour

Attempts at testing the 'weak' and 'weakest' versions of the LRH have typically involved the *perception and memory of colour*. The Jalé (New Guinea) only have terms for black and white, while the Dani (New Guinea) use 'mola' for bright, warm hues, and 'mili' for dark, cold hues. The Shona people (Zimbabwe) have three colour words, and members of the Ibibio culture (Nigeria) have terms for black, white, red, and green.

Ask Yourself

- Would the Jalé or the Ibibio find tests of colour perception and memory more difficult, according to the weak and weakest versions of the LRH?

According to the weaker versions of the LRH, tests of colour perception and memory should be more difficult for the Jalé than the Ibibio. Since the Ibibio word for green encompasses the English green, blue, and yellow, the Ibibio should find colour perception and memory tasks more difficult than English speakers. Taking a previous example, since the Zuni language doesn't distinguish between yellow and orange, Zuni speakers should be unable to discriminate them (they should be 'blind' for these two colours).

Brown and Lenneberg (1954) found that Zuni Indians did make more mistakes than English speakers in recognising these colours. But Lenneberg and Roberts (1956) found that the number of errors made by *bilingual* Zuni–English speakers in distinguishing orange and yellow fell *midway* between that of monolingual Zuni and monolingual English speakers. This suggests that the two languages don't determine two different sets of conflicting perceptions, but rather two sets of *labels* for essentially the same colour perceptions. Language serves to draw attention to differences in the environment and acts as a label to help store these differences in memory.

Sometimes the label we apply to what we see may *distort* our recall of what was seen, since the label determines how we code our experiences into memory storage (see Chapter 17). This was demonstrated in an experiment by Carmichael *et al.* (1932).

So, while there's very little direct evidence to support the strong form of the LRH, there's rather more support for the weaker versions. Language merely predisposes people to think or perceive in certain ways or about certain things (Brown, 1958). However, Brown and Lenneberg's (1954) results (and those of other researchers using a similar methodology) have been challenged in a way that throws doubt even on the weaker versions

Perceiving focal colours

Berlin and Kay (1969) used a chart with an array of 320 small coloured chips, comprising virtually all the hues that the human eye can discriminate. They asked native speakers of 20 languages (other than English) (a) to trace the boundaries of each of their native language's basic colour terms, and (b) to point to the chip which was the best example of each basic colour term. A basic or *focal colour* was defined by a list of linguistic criteria, including:

- A term should consist of only a single unit of meaning (e.g. 'red' as opposed to 'dark red'), and

- It should name only colours and not objects (e.g. 'purple' as opposed to 'wine').

As expected from anthropological research, there was considerable variation in the placement of boundaries. But the choice of best examples was surprisingly similar. The largest clusters were for black and white and red, for which all the 20 languages have colour terms, then 19 for green, 18 yellow, 16 blue, 15 brown and purple, 14 grey, and 11 pink and orange. Berlin and Kay concluded that 'colour categorisation is not random and the foci of basic colour terms are similar in all languages'.

So, while cultures may differ in the number of basic colour terms they use, all cultures draw their focal terms from only 11 colours: black, white, red, green, yellow, blue, brown, purple, pink, orange and grey. Moreover, the colour terms emerge in a particular sequence in the history of languages (as shown in Figure 18.3).

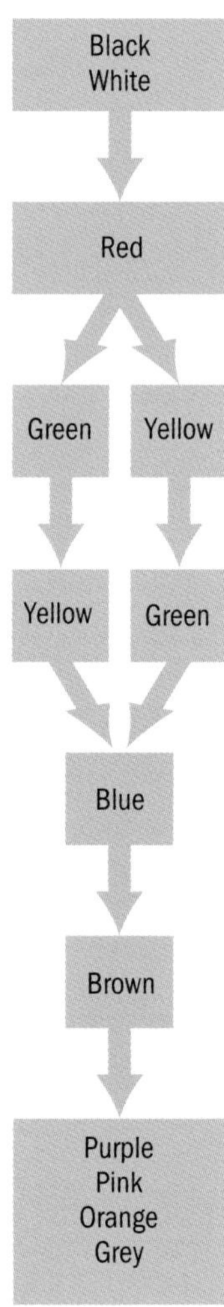

Figure 18.3 The sequence in which focal colours emerge (Berlin and Kay, 1969)

For cultures with only two colours, these will always be black and white, whereas in cultures with three colours, these will always be black, white and red (Newstead, 1995). As Newstead has observed:

> *... It had been assumed that verbal labels were chosen more or less arbitrarily, and that those chosen influenced the way in which colour was perceived. Berlin and Kay's findings suggest that there are certain focal colours which will always be labelled if colour terms are used at all. This suggests an alternative explanation for Brown and Lenneberg's findings: that the colours which participants in their study had found easier to learn were the focal colours and these were easy to remember not because they had verbal labels but because they were the most basic colours.*

A study which supports Berlin and Kay's findings (Heider and Oliver, 1972) is described in Key Study 18.2.

Key Study 18.2

Colour naming among the Dani (Heider and Oliver, 1972)

- As we noted earlier, the Dani (a Stone-Age agricultural people of Indonesian New Guinea) have only two words for colours, whereas native English speakers have words for 11 basic colours. Heider and Oliver gave both Dani and English-speaking participants a coloured chip which they were allowed to look at for five seconds. After a 30-second delay, participants were asked to pick out a chip of the same colour among a set of 40 different-coloured chips.
- On the *weakest* version of the LRH, the Dani's colour vocabulary should have influenced their memory for colours, and on the *weak* version they should have had difficulty discriminating similar colours of a slightly different hue that they'd labelled with the same name. Both the Dani-speaking and English-speaking participants made many mistakes. But there were no significant differences between them in their rate of confusion of similar colours, despite the differences in their colour vocabularies.
- In other research, Heider showed that both Dani and English speakers were better at recognising focal colours than non-focal colours, and that the Dani found it much easier to learn labels for focal than non-focal colours.

Heider (1972) concluded that:

> *Far from being a domain well suited to the study of the effects of language on thought, the colour-space would seem a prime example of the influence of underlying perceptual–cognitive factors on the formation and reference of linguistic categories.*

By this, Heider (sometimes referred to as Rosch – her married name) means that her data are better explained in terms of *physiological factors* underlying colour vision, rather than linguistic factors. Thus, people are sensitive to focal colours because the human visual system processes reality in a certain way (Lakoff, 1987). Indeed, evidence suggests that focal colours can be discriminated before any verbal labels for them have been learned. Bornstein (1988), for example, has argued that preverbal infants categorise the visible spectrum in a similar way to adults, namely, on the basis of the relatively discrete hues of blue, green, yellow and red.

However, Kay (in Ross, 2004) denies that there's any evidence to support a physiological explanation. In addition, a study of another New Guinea people, the Berinmo, casts doubt on Heider's interpretation, and seems to support the weakest and weak versions of the LRH.

Critical Discussion 18.1

The Berinmo and colour naming universals

- According to Kay and Regier (2007), the 'lingusitic relativity' versus 'linguistic universals' debate regarding colour has revolved around two related, but separate questions, which are often confounded:
  1. Do the languages of the world lexically carve up the colour space largely arbitrarily?
  2. Where colour-naming differences among languages occur, do they correlate with corresponding differences in memory, learning and discrimination of colours?
- While supporters of the LRH (such as Whorf) want the answers to both questions to be 'Yes', supporters of the universalist position (such as Heider/Rosch) want a 'No'. Kay and Regier (2007) argue that currently available evidence points strongly towards 'No' and 'Yes' to questions 1 and 2 respectively. While there are non-trivial (non-arbitrary) universal tendencies across languages in colour naming, at the same time colour-naming differences do occur and are correlated with colour memory, learning and discrimination
- Studies of the Berinmo people, who live a simple hunter-gatherer lifestyle in remote forests, illustrate the need to separate the two questions. The Berinmo language has five colour names: one for green, blue and purple, another for yellow, orange and brown, a third for all dark colours, a fourth for white and all light colours; and a fifth for all shades of red and pink.

Using a procedure similar to Heider and Oliver's (1972), Robertson *et al.* (2000; 2005) found that the Berinmo could remember only those colours which matched their colour names, and that they were unable to discriminate between colours which their language didn't discriminate (for example, green and blue). This is inconsistent with Rosch's well-known finding of better memory for focal colours (see text above and Key Study 18.2). Although all the focal colours were 'represented' by the Berinmos' five colour names, the fact that green, blue and purple were lumped together, as were yellow, orange and brown, and also red and pink, seems inconsistent with the claim that colour terms emerge in a particular order in the history of languages (see Figure 18.3).

As Kay and Regier (2007) point out:

> *... These focal colours have been understood to be the cognitive underpinning for cross-language naming universals; to challenge their existence or effectiveness is implicitly to challenge one of the bases for universals of colour naming ...*

After reanalysing Robertson *et al.*'s data, Kay and Regier (2007) found that, while linguistic category boundaries do affect colour discrimination and memory in Berinmo speakers (and in other languages), the placement of those boundaries is constrained by universal forces (i.e. they're not arbitrary). Current evidence supports *both* the existence of universal constraints on colour naming *and* the influence of colour-naming differences on colour memory and discrimination.

	5R	10R	5YR	10YR	5Y	10Y	5GY	10GY	5G	10G	5BG	10BG	5B	10B	5PB	10PB	5P	10P	5RP	10RP
9	3	2	5	Wap	2				1	1			Wap	1	5	12	6	3		2
8				9	6	2	3										1			
7			2	5	4	4	1	1		2										
6		Mehi		2	1			2	3		1									
5	6	2			Wor	1		6	7	4	Nol	2	2						Mehi	3
4	19								5			3								11
3	2			Kel							1		1		1					1
2		1	1	3	4	6	12				2	1	4	3	4	4	Kel	2		

Berinmo

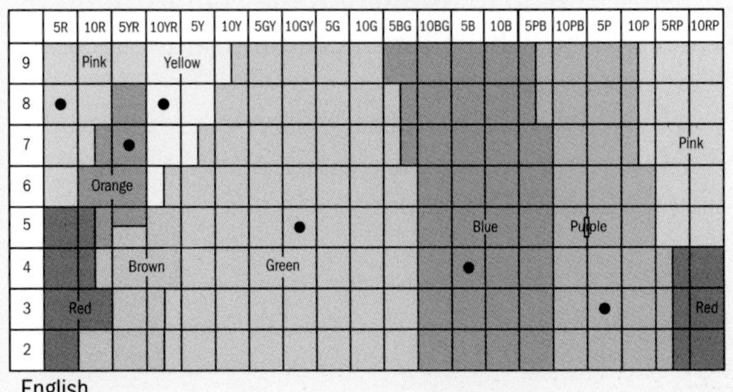

Figure 18.4 Colour categories in Berinmo and English.

Evaluation of the LRH

- Berry *et al.* (1992) and Jackendoff (1993) have argued that Whorf's evidence was anecdotal rather than empirical, and that he exaggerated the differences between Hopi and other languages. Moreover, far from having 'over 20' words for 'snow', the Inuit Eskimos have relatively few such words (Newstead, 1995), and no more than do English speakers (Pinker, 1997a). According to Pagel (1995), Whorf simply got his facts wrong.
- There's an important difference between a language's grammar and our perceptual experience. The fact that Hopi can be translated into English (and vice versa) implies a universally shared knowledge of the world that's independent of the particular language in which it's expressed (Pagel, 1995).
- A crucial question that Whorf seems to have overlooked is *why* Eskimos have so many names for snow (if, indeed, they do) and SAE languages so few. One answer is that the more significant an experience or some feature of our environment is for us, the greater the number of ways of expressing it in the language. In other words, while Whorf argued that language structures the Eskimo's world, it could equally well be argued that the Eskimo's language develops as a result of his/her different perception of the world (Baddeley, 1999). According to Solso (1995):

> *The development of specific language codes ... is dependent on cultural needs; the learning of these codes by members of a language group also involves the learning of significant values of the culture, some of which must be related to survival ...*

- Solso's view is supported by the fact that English-speaking skiers learn to discriminate between varied snow conditions and invent a vocabulary to describe these differences. Such terms include 'sticky snow', 'powder', 'corn' and 'boilerplate' (or ice: Crooks and Stein, 1991). Similarly, the Hanunoo people of the Philippines have modified their language in response to environmental conditions. For example, women have developed a more complex vocabulary for shades of blue to distinguish the colours of dyed textiles that have been introduced into their society (Price and Crapo, 1999).
- It's now widely accepted that Whorf overestimated the importance of language differences. As Berry *et al.* (1992) have observed:

> *Language as an instrument for thinking has many cross-culturally variant properties. As humans, we may not all be sharing the same thoughts, but our respective languages do not seem to predestine us to different kinds of thinking.*

- What language may do, though, is to affect the ease of information processing. Newstead (1995), for example, describes research conducted by Hunt and Agnoli (1991) which supports this view. The English word 'seven' has two syllables, whereas the equivalent French word ('sept') has only one. The English word 'eleven' has three syllables, whereas the French word 'onze' has one. Hunt and Agnoli argue that when a name is shorter, information is processed more quickly, and so French speakers would have an advantage over English speakers when performing mental arithmetic involving these numbers, at least in processing terms.
- According to Price and Crapo (1999), the study of semantic domains (such as colour naming) helps us to discover what's important in the daily lives of different cultural groups, as well as the changing cultural history of a society. Similarly, Kay (in Ross, 2004) argues that the degree to which the world is *man-made* seems to explain the variation in the number of colour words. Hunter-gatherers need fewer, because colour data rarely provide much crucially distinguishing information about a natural scene or object. But industrialised societies get a bigger 'information pay-off' for colour words.
- Kay (in Ross, 2004) claims that his research into focal colours has been interpreted by some as undermining the LRH as a whole. But Berlin and he were concerned with one restricted domain, namely colour. Even if it's accepted that the colour perception research doesn't support the LRH, there's no reason to rule it out in relation to other domains.

Key Study 18.3

'There's a fly to the north of your nose'

- Ross (2004) cites a study of speakers of Guugu Yimithirr (a language of Australia). Like several world languages, this lacks subjective terms equivalent to 'left' and 'right', and instead uses absolute directions akin to 'north' and 'south'. In such a language, you might say 'There's a fly to the north of your nose.'
- If Guugu speakers are presented with an arrow pointing to their left, they'll later draw it pointing to the left only if they're still facing in the direction in which they saw the arrow originally. But if they turn round, they'll draw it pointing to the right – that is, in the same absolute direction as the original arrow.
- This illustrates quite strikingly how linguistic categories can mould thought and behaviour (Ross, 2004).

The LRH, social class and race

Black English

A version of English spoken by segments of the African-American community is called 'Black English'. For example, when asked to repeat the sentence 'I asked him if he did it, and he said he didn't do it', one five-year-old girl repeated the sentence like this: 'I asks him if he did it, and he says he didn't did it, but I knows he did' (Labov, 1973). Bernstein (1961) argued that Black English is a restricted code, and that this makes the thinking of Black English speakers less logical than that of their white *elaborated-code* counterparts.

One major difference between Black and standard English relates to the use of verbs (Rebok, 1987). In particular, Black English speakers often omit the present tense copula (the verb 'to be'). So, 'he be gone' indicates standard English 'he's been gone for a long time' and 'he gone' signifies that 'he's just gone'. Black English is often termed *sub-standard* and regarded as illogical rather than *non-standard* (Bereiter and Engelman, 1966). According to Labov (1970), Black English is just one dialect of English, and speakers of both dialects are expressing the same ideas equally well.

Black English and prejudice

While the grammatical rules of Black English differ from those of standard English, Black English possesses consistent rules which allow the expression of thoughts as complex as those permitted by standard English (Labov, 1973). Several other languages, such as Russian and Arabic, also omit the present-tense verb 'to be', and yet we don't call them 'illogical'. This suggests that black dialects are considered sub-standard as a matter of convention or prejudice, and not because they're poorer vehicles for expressing meaning and logical thinking. However, because the structure of Black English does differ in important ways from standard English, and since intelligence tests are written in standard English, Black English speakers are at a linguistic disadvantage (as, indeed, are white working-class children: see Chapters 41 and 47).

Language in context

Labov also showed that the social situation can be a powerful determinant of verbal behaviour. A young boy called Leon was shown a toy by a white interviewer and asked to tell him everything he could about it. Leon said very little and was silent for much of the time, even when a black interviewer took over. However, when Leon sat on the floor and shared a packet of crisps with his best friend and with the same black interviewer introducing topics in a local black dialect, Leon became a lively conversationalist. Had he been assessed with the white or black interviewers on their own, Leon might have been labelled 'non-verbal' or 'linguistically retarded'.

Black children may actually be *bilingual*. In the classroom, and when talking to anyone in authority, they must adopt standard English with which they're unfamiliar. This results in short sentences, simple grammar and strange intonation. But out of school, their natural language is easy, fluent, creative and often gifted. So, while Black English is certainly non-standard, it's another language with its own grammar which is certainly *not* sub-standard.

LANGUAGE is DEPENDENT on, and REFLECTS, THOUGHT

According to Piaget (1950), children begin life with some understanding of the world and try to find linguistic ways of expressing their knowledge. As language develops, it 'maps' onto previously acquired cognitive structures, so language is dependent upon thought (Piaget and Inhelder, 1969). For example, a child should begin talking about objects that aren't present in its immediate surroundings only after *object permanence* has developed. Similarly, children who could conserve liquid quantity understood the meaning of phrases and words such as 'as much as', 'bigger' and 'more'. However, children who couldn't conserve didn't improve their performance of the correct use of these words after receiving linguistic training (Sinclair-de-Zwart, 1969). (See Chapter 34.)

In Piaget's view, children can be taught words, but they won't understand them until they've mastered certain intellectual skills during the process of cognitive growth. So, language can exist without thought, but only in the sense that a parrot can 'speak'. Thought, then, is a necessary forerunner to language if language is to be used properly.

Contrary to Piaget's view that thought structures language, Luria and Yudovich (1971) suggest that language plays a central role in cognitive development (see Case Study 18.1).

Support for Piaget, however, comes from two recent sources.

The second source of support comes from a recent account of the Pirahas, a small and remote tribe in the Brazilian interior who speak one of the least understood languages in the world. The Piraha have just two numerical words ('hoi' with an accent' and 'hoi' without, signifying 'one' and 'two', respectively); they use a 'one-to-many' counting system, in which quantities above two are simply referred to as 'many'.

After testing members of the tribe, Gordon (2004) concluded that their impoverished counting system

Case Study 18.1

The Russian twins (Luria and Yudovich, 1971)

- Luria and Yudovich studied 5-year-old twin boys whose home environment was unstimulating. They played almost exclusively together and had only a very primitive level of speech.
- The boys received little adult encouragement to speak, and made little progress towards the symbolic use of words.
- Essentially, their speech was *synpraxic*, a primitive form in which words cannot be detached from the action or object they denote.
- The twins hardly ever used speech to describe objects or events or to help them plan their actions. They couldn't understand other people's speech and their own constituted a kind of *signalling* rather than symbolic system.
- Although they never played with other children, and played with each other in a primitive and repetitive way, they were otherwise normal.
- After being separated, one twin was given special remedial treatment for his language deficiency, but the other wasn't. The former made rapid progress and, ten months later, was ahead of his brother. However, *both* made progress, and their synpraxic speech died away.
- For Luria and Yudovich:

The whole structure of the mental life of both twins was simultaneously and sharply changed. Once they acquired an objective language system, [they] were able to formulate the aims of their activity verbally, and after only three months we observed the beginnings of meaningful play.

Box 18.1 The evolutionary roots of thought

- Pinker (2007), linguist and Evolutionary Psychologist, argues that language lays bare the basic categories used by the human mind.
- By studying how verbs work, for instance, we can see how our minds categorise actions. Actions that work because of gravity are classified differently from those that use other kinds of force (which is why you can 'pour wine into the glass' but not 'fill wine into the glass': Papineau, 2007).
- Applying this method across a wide range of linguistic constructions, Pinker pieces together the basic concepts we use to structure the world.
- Although many such concepts are very 'modern', reflecting historical and cultural change, modern thought is still built on the patterns laid down in our evolutionary past. All humans share a universal 'language of thought' comprising basic concepts of space, time, force and other essentially *practical* concerns.
- While not all spoken languages express these categories using identical grammatical constructions, all societies have some way of marking these fundamental environmental features. Three million years as hunter-gatherers have left their imprint on human thought-language merely reflects it.

truly limits their ability to enumerate exact quantities when set sizes exceed two or three items. This, of course, is consistent with the LRH. However, despite its lack of number words, counting, colour words and other features that characterise English (and many other Indo-European languages), Everett (2009) believes that the Pirihas can put into words (probably) any thought they can entertain, which means that that human creativity lies in human thought, not in human language.

THOUGHT and LANGUAGE as INITIALLY SEPARATE ACTIVITIES

For Vygotsky (1981), language is by far the most important psychological tool the human species possesses, capable of transforming how we think about the world and altering 'the entire flow and structure of mental functions'. So, while for Piaget thought is prior to language, Vygotsky sees language as prior to thought (developing the ability to use words makes representational thought possible) (Schaffer, 2004).

According to Vygotsky (1962), language and thought begin as separate and independent activities. Early on, thinking occurs without language (consisting primarily of images) and language occurs without thought (as when babies cry or make other sounds to express feelings, or attract attention). But at about age 2, prelinguistic thought and pre-intellectual language meet and join to initiate a new kind of behaviour, in which thought becomes verbal and speech rational (Vygotsky, 1962)

Vygotsky believed that between ages 2 and 7, language performs two functions:

1. An *internal* function, which enables internal thought to be monitored and directed
2. An *external* function, which enables the results of thinking to be communicated to others.

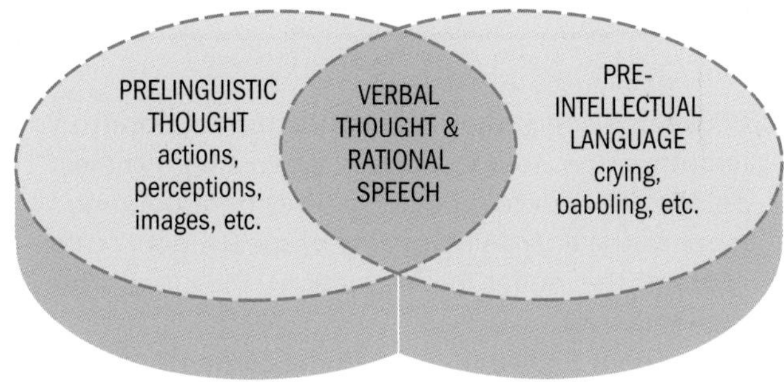

Figure 18.5 A diagrammatic representation of Vygotsky's views on the relationship between language and thought

However, children cannot yet distinguish between the two functions and, as a result, their speech is *egocentric*: they talk out loud about their plans and actions, and can neither think privately nor communicate publicly to others. Instead, they're caught somewhere between the two, and cannot distinguish between 'speech for self' (what Piaget calls *autistic speech*) and 'speech for others' (*socialised speech*).

Around the age of 7 (when children typically enter Piaget's concrete operational stage of cognitive development: see Chapter 34), overt language begins to be restricted to communication, while the thought function of language becomes internalised as *internal speech* (*verbal thought*). For Piaget, egocentric speech is a kind of 'running commentary' on the child's behaviour. At about age 7, it simply fades away and is replaced by socialised (or communicative) speech.

But for Vygotsky (1962), the function of egocentric speech was similar to that of inner speech. It doesn't merely accompany the child's activity but:

> *... Serves mental orientation, conscious understanding; it helps in overcoming difficulties; it is speech for oneself, intimately and usefully connected with the child's thinking. In the end it becomes inner speech ...*

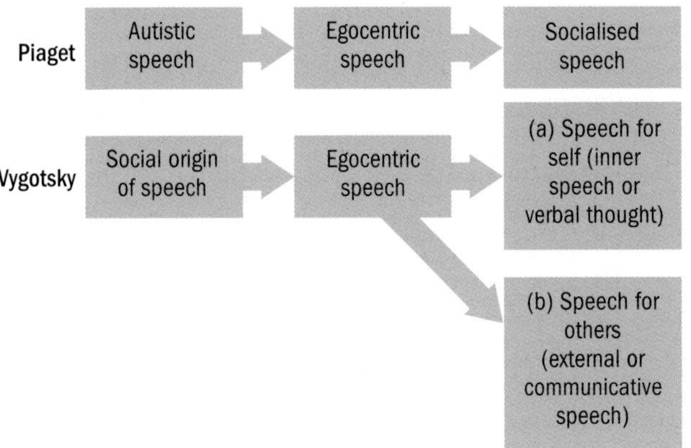

Figure 18.6 The difference between Piaget and Vygotsky with respect to egocentric speech

An evaluation of Vygotsky's position

- A considerable body of research into inner speech has largely supported Vygotsky's account, demonstrating how closely language and thought become intertwined during development (Schaffer, 2004).
- Egocentric speech commonly accompanies problem-solving, even in young children. But with age, it becomes less and less audible, and eventually becomes silent. For example, Bivens and Berk (1990) observed 6- to 7-year-olds as they worked on maths problems. This was repeated one to two years later. The overall incidence of egocentric speech was extremely high and remained high over the three years of observation. But *task-relevant speech* increased greatly, and the nature of the speech changed – there were more inaudible mutterings and lip movements. These changes were paralleled by the children's greater ability to inhibit extraneous movements and restlessness, and to pay closer attention to the task. This is consistent with Vygotsky's belief that inner speech is used increasingly to aid the child's *self-regulation/self-control* (Schaffer, 2004). (See Box 18.2.)
- Both inner speech and egocentric speech differ from speech for others in that they don't have to satisfy grammatical conventions. Thus, both are abbreviated, incomplete and concerned more with the essential meaning rather than how it's expressed. For Vygotsky, inner speech is a 'dynamic, shifting and unstable thing which "flutters" between word and thought' (see Figure 18.6).
- If inner speech is derived from external speech, we'd expect both to activate the same neural networks. Indeed, fMRI studies have linked inner speech to the *left inferior frontal gyrus*, including Broca's area (Fernyhough, 2013). Again, if inner speech is just external speech without articulation, it should be associated with the same qualities of tone, timbre and accent as our ordinary overt speech. Fernyhough cites research that seems to support this hypothesis. Inner speech can also serve motivational functions (as in athletes 'psyching' themselves up) and is an important component of *metacognition* (see Chapters 34 and 41).

CONCLUSIONS

While there are many examples indicating that thought can occur without language, the exact relationship between thought and language remains unclear. However, since language represents such a central feature of culture, both shaping it and being shaped by it, any theory which fails to take account of cultural factors is likely to be inadequate.

Box 18.2 Language and self-regulation

According to Luria (1961), a colleague and supporter of Vygotsky, there are three stages in children's ability to use language for directing their behaviour.

1. Up to about 3, another person's verbal instructions can trigger an action, but not inhibit it. For example, given a rubber bulb to squeeze, children will correctly squeeze in response to 'Squeeze', but 'Stop' will simply make them squeeze again.
2. Between 4 and 5, they respond to instructions in an impulsive way: told to squeeze when a light comes on, they'll squeeze repeatedly. They're responding more to the energising quality of speech than to its content (the louder the instructions, the more often they squeeze).
3. After about 5, they respond to the contents of speech and become capable of using it to inhibit or activate their behaviour.

Cultural transmission allows the best thoughts of one generation to be passed onto the next, and language (spoken and written) plays a major role in that process. Regardless of one's particular culture, it is widely agreed that the use of symbols allows us to disengage our thought from perception. This 'decoupling' is a striking feature of human thought and may be facilitated (and perhaps even require) the use of symbols, especially language (Bayne, 2013).

> *Language ... is a tool that allows us to augment our powers of thought. By putting thoughts into language we are able to take a step back and subject them to critical evaluation ... (Bayne, 2013)*

Chapter Summary

- According to Watson's **peripheralism**, thought is no more than sensations produced by tiny movements of the larynx, too small to produce audible sounds.
- Contrary to Watson's view, thinking can occur despite complete paralysis, and people born deaf and mute are also capable of thinking.
- Bruner argues that language is essential for thought and knowledge to progress beyond the **enactive** and **iconic modes of representation** to the **symbolic mode**.
- **Social constructionists** claim that conceptual frameworks and categories provide meaning within a culture, a way of structuring our experience of ourselves and the world.
- According to the **Sapir–Whorf linguistic relativity hypothesis (LRH)**, language determines how we think about objects and events, and even what we think. This is related to **linguistic determinism**.
- The '**weak**' and '**weakest**' versions of the LRH have typically been tested through perception and memory of **colour**. The fewer colour words there are in a language, the more difficult native speakers should find tests of colour perception and memory.
- Early studies seemed to support these two versions. But while cultures may differ in the number of basic colour terms they use, all cultures draw their colour terms from only 11 **focal colours**, which emerge in a particular sequence in the history of languages.
- Whorf's evidence was **anecdotal** rather than empirical, and he exaggerated the differences between Hopi and other languages. Also, he mistakenly equated language's grammar with perceptual experience. Translation between languages implies a universally shared knowledge of the world independent of any particular language.
- Differences between standard and **Black English** have resulted in the latter being called **sub-standard**, rather than **non-standard**. According to Labov, this is an expression of prejudice.
- Black children may be **bilingual**, using the accepted register fluently at home and with their peers, but adopting unfamiliar standard English in the classroom.
- According to Piaget, language 'maps' on to previously acquired **cognitive structures**, so that **language is dependent on thought**. Words can be understood only if certain intellectual skills (such as **object permanence** and **conservation**) have already been mastered.
  - Pinker agrees with Piaget, arguing from the perspective of **Evolutionary Psychology**. 'Modern' thought still reflects its roots in our hunter-gatherer past.
  - Additional support for Piaget comes from study of the Piraha people, who can express any thought despite the differences between their own and other world languages.

- For Vygotsky, language and thought are **initially separate and independent** activities. At around age 2, **pre-linguistic thought** and **pre-intellectual language** begin to interact to form **verbal thought** and **rational speech**.
- Between the ages of 2 and 7, language performs both **internal** and **external** functions. The child's failure to distinguish between them results in **egocentric speech**. For Vygotsky, this indicates the separation of the two functions.
- According to both Vygotsky and Luria, language plays a vital role in **self-regulation/self-control.**

Links with Other Topics/Chapters

Chapters 2, 3 and 49 →	Watson's peripheralism demonstrates both his Behaviourist *rejection of mentalistic terms* (Chapters 2 and 3) and the *reductionist* approach of behaviourism (Chapter 49)
Chapters 2, 3 and 47 →	*Social constructionism* (SC) is a theoretical orientation that lies behind a number of recent alternative approaches to the study of human beings as social animals, including *Critical Psychology*, *Discourse analysis* and *Feminist Psychology*
Chapters 15 and 17 →	The weak version of the LRH claims that language affects *perception*, while the weakest version claims that language (Chapter 15) influences *memory*
Chapter 25 →	Regarding Black English as sub-standard (rather than non-standard) is an expression of *prejudice*
Chapters 41 and 47 →	Since standard *intelligence (IQ) tests* are written in standard English, Black English speakers are at a linguistic disadvantage, as are white working-class children
Chapter 34 →	Bruner's, Piaget's and Vygotsky's accounts of the relationship between language and thought are part of their more general theories of *cognitive development*

Recommended Reading

Carroll, J.B. (1956) *Language, Thought and Reality: Selected Writings of Benjamin Lee* Whorf. Cambridge, MA: MIT Press.

Everett, D.L. (2009) *Don't Sleep, There are Snakes: Life and Language in the Amazonian jungle*. London: Profile Books.

Rosch, E. (1977) Human categorisation. In N. Warren (ed.) *Studies in Cross-Cultural Psychology*, Volume 1. New York: Academic Press.

Vygotsky, L.S. (1962) *Thought and Language* (translated by E. Haufmann & G. Vakar). Cambridge, MA: MIT Press.

Useful Websites

http://anthro.palomar.edu/language/language_5.htm (Language and Thought Processes)

http://ojs.academypublisher.com/index.php/tpls/article/viewFile/tpls0203642646/4439 (Article by Hussein, 2012: The Sapir-Whorf Hypothesis Today)

http://plato.stanford.edu/entries/relativism/supplement2.html (Stanford Encyclopaedia of Philosophy: The Linguistic Relativity Hypothesis)

CHAPTER 19

LANGUAGE ACQUISITION

INTRODUCTION and OVERVIEW

Since our brains seem specially designed to enable us to use speech (see Chapter 4), it's hardly surprising that language is so crucial to most human activities. Many Psychologists and philosophers have claimed that language is what makes us unique as a species; *Evolutionary Psychologists* in particular stress the benefits afforded by language to our hunter-gatherer ancestors (see Chapter 2 and Gross, 2012a).

Until quite recently, the study of language was largely the domain of *linguistics*, which is concerned primarily with the structure of language (its *grammar*). According to Durkin (1995), while Developmental Psychologists have always been interested in language, during the mid-twentieth century it became marginalised as an area of psychological research. As we noted in Chapter 18, Piaget saw language as merely reflecting cognitive structures – a lens through which to inspect the child's thought.

However, there's been a revival of interest in language since the 1960s, inspired largely by Chomsky's (1959) theory of an innate *language acquisition device* (LAD). The 'marriage' between Psychology and linguistics (Chomsky is a linguist) is called *psycholinguistics*, which studies the perception, understanding and production of language, together with their development.

According to *learning theory,* associated with Skinner and Bandura, language development can be attributed primarily to environmental input and learning. But Chomsky's *nativist* approach argues that, although the environment may supply the content of language, grammar is an inherent, biologically determined capacity of human beings. Hence, the process of language development is essentially one of *acquisition* (as distinct from learning). Attempts to teach language to non-humans have major implications for Chomsky's claim that language is a uniquely human ability.

WHAT is LANGUAGE?

According to Brown (1965), language is a set of arbitrary symbols:

> *... which, taken together, make it possible for a creature with limited powers of discrimination and a limited memory to transmit and understand an infinite variety of messages and to do this in spite of noise and distraction.*

This 'infinite variety of messages' is called *productivity*, which Kuczaj and Hill (2003) describe as the most important characteristic of human language.

While other species are able to communicate with each other, they can do so only in limited ways, and it's perhaps the 'infinite variety of messages' part of Brown's definition that sets humans apart from non-humans. For example, wild chimpanzees use over 30 different vocalisations to convey a large number of meanings, and repeat sounds in order to intensify their meaning. However, they don't string these sounds together to make new 'words' (Calvin, 1994). The claim that chimpanzees are capable of using language is based largely, and until recently, on deliberate training (see below). Human language is mastered spontaneously and quite easily within the first five years of life.

What makes productivity possible is that humans acquire a *rule system*. This rule system is called (*mental*) *grammar*. However, for Psycholinguists, grammar is much more than the parts of speech we learn about in school. It's concerned with the description of language, the rules that determine how a language 'works', and what governs patterns of speech (Jackendoff, 1993).

THE MAJOR COMPONENTS of GRAMMAR

Grammar consists of *phonology*, *semantics* and *syntax* (see Figure 19.2).

Phonology

Phonologists are concerned with a language's sound system – what counts as a sound and what constitutes an acceptable sequence of sounds. Basic speech sounds are called *phones* (or *phonetic segments*), and are represented by enclosing symbols inside square brackets. For example, [p] is the initial phone in the word 'pin'. Some languages have as few as 15 distinguishable sounds, and others as many as 85. The English language has 46 phones (Solso, 1995).

The phones that matter are those that affect the *meaning* of what's being said. For example, the difference between [p] and [d] matters because it can lead to two words with different meanings (such as 'pin' and 'din'). Because [p] and [d] cannot be interchanged without altering a word's meaning, they belong to different functional classes of phones called *phonemes* (*phonological segments*). Languages differ in their number of phonemes. Phonological rules constrain the permitted sequence of phonemes, which correspond roughly to the vowels and consonants of a language's alphabet. However, languages (including English) can have more phonemes than letters in the alphabet. This is because some letters, such as 'o', can be pronounced differently (as in 'hop' and 'hope').

Semantics

Semantics is the study of the *meaning* of language, and can be analysed at the level of morphemes and phrases/sentences. *Morphemes* are a language's basic units of meaning and consist mainly of words. Other morphemes are prefixes (such as 'pre' and 're') and suffixes (word-endings, such as 's' to make a plural). Most morphemes are 'free' (they have meaning when they stand alone, as most words have). But single words have only a limited meaning, and are usually combined into longer strings of phrases and sentences.

Syntax

Syntax refers to the rules for combining words into phrases and sentences. One example of a *syntactic rule* is *word order*. This is crucial for understanding language development. Clearly, the sentences 'The dog bit the postman' and 'The postman bit the dog' have very different meanings!

Another example of a syntactic rule occurs in the sentence 'The dog chased the ...' In English, only a noun can complete this sentence. Some sentences may be syntactically correct but lack meaning. For example, 'The player scored a goal' and 'The goal post scored a banana' are both syntactically correct, but one has much more meaning than the other. While sentences have sounds and meanings, syntax refers to the structures which relate the two.

Figure 19.1 'Then you should say what you mean', the March Hare went on. 'I do,' Alice hastily replied; 'at least – at least I mean what I say – that's the same thing, you know.' 'Not the same thing a bit!' said the Hatter. 'Why, you might just as well say that 'I see what I eat' is the same thing as 'I eat what I see'!'

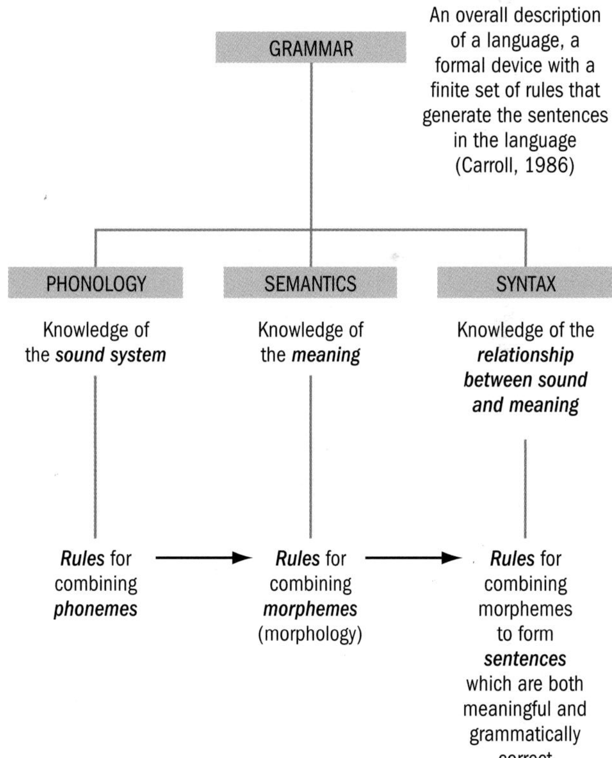

Figure 19.2 The major components of grammar

STAGES in LANGUAGE DEVELOPMENT

It's generally agreed that language development follows a universal timetable – that is, regardless of their language or culture, all children pass through the same sequence of stages at approximately the same ages (although their *rate* of development may vary). While this belief implies the role of *maturation*, children can come to speak a language only if they're exposed to it.

It's also generally agreed that there are three major stages in language development: the *prelinguistic stage* (0–12 months), the *one-word stage* (12–18 months), and the *stage of two-word sentences*. This third stage is divided into two sub-stages: *stage 1 grammar* (18–30 months) and *stage 2 grammar* (30 months and beyond).

The prelinguistic stage (0–12 months)

In their first year, babies are essentially *prelinguistic*. They make various sounds with their vocal organs (including crying) long before they can talk. Crying tends to dominate in the first month, with parents gradually learning to discriminate between the various cries (Gustafson and Harris, 1990). By one month, babies are able to distinguish between phonemes (such as 'ba' and 'pa') and other sounds, even though these may be physically and acoustically almost identical (Aslin *et al.*, 1983). This perceptual ability (*categorical speech perception*) is probably innate.

The development of babbling

This is the major development in the first year of life, and usually begins between 6 and 9 months. Phonemes are produced and take the form of combinations of consonants and vowels (such as 'ma' and 'da'). These may be repeated to produce *reduplicated monosyllables* (such as 'mama' and 'dada'). Although these are very different from the earlier cooing sounds, they have no meaning.

Babies spend more time making noises, especially when alone in their cots (*spontaneous babbling*), and they seem to enjoy exercising their voices for the sake of it. This has *intonational patterns*, just like speech, with rising inflections and speech-like rhythms; by one year, syllables are often produced over and over again (as in 'dadadada'), a phenomenon called *echolalia*. Babbling occurs at around the same age in all babies regardless of culture.

Babies initially produce only a few phonemes, but by 2 months they produce every phoneme in all the world's languages (*phonemic expansion*) (Kuhl *et al.*, 1992). At around 9–10 months, *phonemic contraction* begins: phoneme production is now restricted to those used in the baby's native language. At this stage, babies of different 'native tongues' can already be distinguished by the sounds they produce. Additionally, deaf babies usually stop babbling at around this time, presumably because of the lack of feedback from their own voices.

Box 19.1 There's more to babbling than meets the ear

Petitto *et al.* (2001) studied three babies with normal hearing, who, because their parents were deaf, had no systematic exposure to speech. However, they were 'cooed over' in sign language, and the babies began to 'babble' with their hands ('silent babbling') just as children born to hearing parents babble out loud. Deaf parents sign to their babies using a rhythmic sets of hand movements quite different from those they would use if signing to other adults. This is a silent form of 'motherese' (see text below).

Comparing these children with three born to hearing parents, Petitto *et al.* found that the former moved their hands in a rhythmical way that contrasted with the latter's random arm waving; these movements are 'linguistic' and the babies are babbling with their hands.

Holowka and Pettito (2002) believe that babbling is linked to the language processing centres in the baby's brain. When babies babble, they open the *right* side of the mouth more widely than the left, reflecting activity in the *left* hemisphere (see Chapter 4); this also applies to adult speech, but we're usually unaware of this asymmetry. Holowka and Pettito made videotapes of ten Canadian babies (five from French-speaking, five from English-speaking families), aged 5–12 months. Two people (who didn't know what the researchers were looking for) scored the tapes for babbling and non-babbling sounds, and smiles. All the babies showed right-mouth asymmetry when babbling, equal mouth opening for non-babbling, and left-mouth asymmetry for smiling.

One-word stage (12–18 months)

Ask Yourself

- How do words differ from a baby's babbling?
- When people ask parents 'Is your baby talking yet?', what do they mean?

Typically, a child produces its first word at around one year, although there's considerable variability in this (Rice, 1989). Babies don't, of course, suddenly switch from babbling to the production of words, and non-words (*jargon*) continue to be produced for up to another six months. Their first words (or *articulate sounds*) are often invented, quite unlike 'adult words', phonologically the easiest (most similar to their babbling). This also explains why the words for mother and father are so similar across a wide range of different languages (Siegler, 1998).

Scollon (1976) defined a word as 'a systematic matching of form and meaning'. On this definition, 'da' is a word if it's consistently used to refer to a doll, since the same sound is being used to label the same thing or kind of thing, and there's a clear intention to communicate.

However, an infant's earliest words are usually *context-bound*, produced in only very limited and specific situations or contexts in which particular actions or events occur (Barrett, 1989). For example, one infant, at least initially, only produced the word 'duck' while hitting a toy duck off the edge of a bath. The word was never used in any other context. Barrett argues that an infant's first words often don't serve a communicative purpose as such. Rather, they function as '*performatives*': some words may be more like the performance of a ritualised action than the expression of a lexical meaning to another person. However, words seem to have either:

- An *expressive function* – they communicate internal states (such as pleasure and surprise) to others, or
- A *directive function* – the behaviour of others is directed (by, for example, requesting or obtaining and directing attention).

The one-word stage is also characterised by the use of *holophrases* (see Box 19.2).

Box 19.2 Holophrases: making a sentence out of a word

- In *holophrastic speech*, a single word (such as 'milk') is used to convey a much more complex message (such as 'I want some more milk' or 'I have spilt my milk').
- Because holophrases are accompanied by gestures and tone of voice to add full meaning to an individual word, they may be seen as precursors of later, more complex sentences (Greenfield and Smith, 1976). They represent 'two-word meanings' (word plus gesture) before two words are actually used together in speech (Bates *et al.*, 1987). But they depend on the recipient of the holophrase making the 'correct' interpretation.

The kinds of things that first words refer to are the things that matter to a 1-year-old: parents, siblings, pets, toys, clothes and food. Things that move are also more likely to be named (e.g. a bus rather than the road) (Schaffer, 2004). However, Tardif *et al.* (2008) found certain differences between 8–16-month-old Chinese-speaking and English-speaking children.

Children understand more words than they can produce. For example, a child who uses 'bow-wow' to refer to all small animals will nonetheless pick a picture of a dog, rather than any other animal, when asked to select a 'bow-wow' (Gruendel, 1977). The child's *receptive vocabulary* (the words it can understand) is therefore much bigger than its *expressive vocabulary* (the words it uses in speech).

Even before age 2, children begin acquiring words at the rate of about 20 per day (Miller, 1978). While some of these are context-bound, they gradually become more *decontextualised*. Other words are used from the start in a decontextualised way (Barrett, 1989). As the one-word stage progresses, the child becomes able to ask and answer questions, and provide comments on people and objects in the immediate environment. These abilities enable the child to participate in very simple conversations with other people.

Stage of two-word sentences

Like the one-word stage, the two-word stage is universal (although individual differences become more marked). Also, like the transition from babbling to the one-word stage, the transition to the two-word stage is gradual (Slobin, 1979). As well as continued vocabulary development, the understanding of grammar grows. Brown (1973) divides this stage into *stage 1* and *stage 2 grammars*.

Stage 1 grammar (18–30 months)

Here, the child's speech is essentially *telegraphic* (Brown, 1973): only those words which convey the most information (*contentives*) are used. Purely grammatical terms (*functors*), such as the verb 'to be', plurals and possessives, are omitted. For example, children will say, 'There cow,' to convey the underlying message, 'There is a cow'. It seems that irrespective of culture, children express basic facts about their environment (Brown, 1973).

Telegraphic speech has a rigid word order, which seems to preserve a sentence's meaning. For example, if asked, 'Does Shayla want some milk?', the child might reply 'Shayla milk' (or, later on, 'Shayla want milk'). Adult speech, by contrast, doesn't rely exclusively on word order to preserve meaning.

Children's imitations of adult sentences are also simple and retain the original sentence's word order. For example, 'Ellie is playing with the dog' is imitated as 'Play dog' (*imitation by reduction*: Brown, 1965). Complementary to this is *imitation with expansion*, in which the adult imitates the child's utterances by inserting the 'missing' functors.

The rigid order of the child's utterances makes it easier to interpret their meaning, but gestures and context still provide important clues (as with the one-word stage).

Ask Yourself

- How would you adapt your speech when talking to a young child compared with how you talk to adults?

Box 19.3 Motherese

Babies are exposed to an undifferentiated series of speech sounds (*speech stream*: Jusczyk, 1997), but they need to separate this into individual sounds and sound combinations in order to learn the relevant sounds of their language (phonemes and morphemes). For example, the way an adult might ask a 7-year-old a question could be represented as, 'Wheredidyougowithgrandpa?' (the words are joined when they're being spoken). But long before the child learns to read (where the words are spaced), how does it learn to hear 'Where did you go with grandpa?' (Slobin, 1979)?
Part of the answer is *motherese* (or *infant-directed speech*). Compared with talking to one another, adults talking to children tend to use much shorter sentences and simpler syntax, raise the pitch of their voice for emphasis, use their voice more rhythmically, and repeat or paraphrase much of what the child says. This helps to achieve a mutual understanding with children who haven't yet mastered the full complexity of language. Sensitivity to the child's vocabulary and its intellectual and social knowledge is an example of a *pragmatic rule* for ensuring a degree of shared understanding (Greene, 1990). It also supports a social-interaction approach to language acquisition (see text below).

According to Cromer's (1974) *cognition hypothesis*, word order in two-word utterances seems to reflect the child's *prelinguistic knowledge*. Children form schemata to understand the world and then talk about it; a good example is *object permanence* (see Chapter 34). If a child didn't already understand the relationships between objects, people and events in the real world, its first words would be like random unconnected lists.

Stage 2 grammar (from about 30 months)

This lasts until around age 4 or 5, and while it may be different for different languages, the rule-governed nature of language development is universal. The child's vocabulary grows rapidly, and sentences become longer and more complex. *Mean length of utterance* (MLU) is the number of words in a sentence divided by the total number of sentences produced.

The increase in MLU shown in Figure 19.3 is due largely to the inclusion of the functors that are omitted from the telegraphic speech of stage 1 grammar. For example, 'Daddy hat,' may become, 'Daddy wear hat,' and finally, 'Daddy is wearing a hat'. Sentences also become longer because conjunctions (such as 'and' and 'so') are used to form *compound* sentences. Stage 2 grammar, then, really begins with the first use of purely grammatical words. While most children up to 20 months still use one- or two-word sentences, by 24 months the longest sentences include four to five words. By 30 months, this has risen to between eight and ten. This is strongly linked to vocabulary development (Fenson *et al.*, 1994).

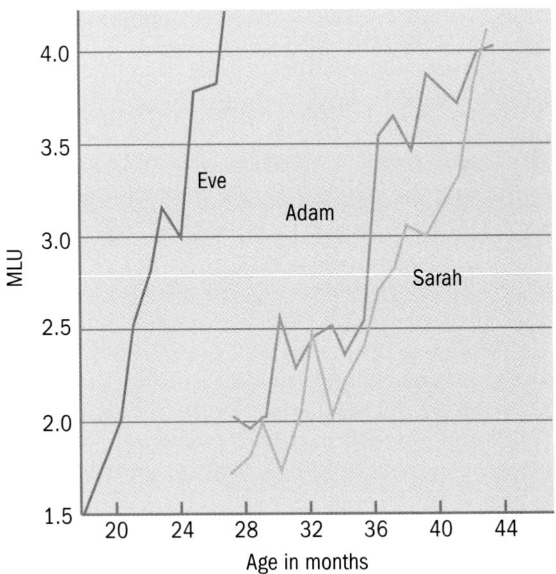

Figure 19.3 Mean length of utterance (MLU) plotted against age in months for three children (based on Brown, 1973)

Brown (1973) found a distinct regularity among English-speaking children in terms of the order in the addition of grammatical complexities. Similarly, de Villiers and de Villiers (1979) found that, irrespective of culture, children acquire functional words in the same general order but at different rates. Each function word corresponds to a syntactic rule. Several studies show that when children begin to apply these rules (such as the rule for forming plurals), they're not just imitating other people.

Key Study 19.1

Wugs rule OK (Berko, 1958)

- Berko showed children a picture of a fictitious creature called a wug and told them 'This is a wug'.

This is a wug

Figure 19.4a

- They were then shown a second picture in which there were two of the creatures and told 'Now there is another one. There are two of them'.

Now there is another one.
There are two of them.
There are two ______

Figure 19.4b

- The children were asked to complete the sentence 'There are two ...'
- Three- and four-year-olds answered 'wugs' despite never having seen a 'wug' before. Although the children couldn't have been imitating anybody else's speech, and hadn't been told about the rule for forming plurals, they were able to apply this rule. Significantly, they weren't consciously aware of having acquired the rule for forming a plural, and couldn't say what the rule was.

Ask Yourself

- Can you think of any other examples of grammatical rules that children of this age display (including their speech errors)?

The rule-governed nature of language is also shown in children's grammatical *mistakes*. For example, while the rule 'add an 's' to a word to form a plural' usually works, there are exceptions to it (such as 'sheep' rather than 'sheeps' and 'geese' rather than 'gooses'). Similarly, the rule 'add 'ed' to form the past tense' usually works, but not in the case of 'cost' and 'go'. The observation that children use words like 'costed' and 'goed', without ever having heard others use them, suggests that they're applying a rule rather than just imitating. But the rule is being *overgeneralised* or the language *over-regularised*. It also shows that children are actively and quite spontaneously involved in rule learning, and that they're trying to make sense of the whole business of how to talk (Schaffer, 2004).

By age 4 or 5, basic grammatical rules have been acquired, but a typical 5-year-old will have difficulty understanding passive sentences. There are also many irregular words still to be learned, and this aspect of grammatical development will take several more years.

By age 13, most English-speaking children have a vocabulary of 20,000 words, and by age 20, this will have risen to 50,000 or more (Aitchison, 1996). This vocabulary is acquired at an average rate of ten words per day (Pinker, 1994).

THEORIES of LANGUAGE DEVELOPMENT

Learning theory: operant conditioning

Ask Yourself

- Given what you know about operant conditioning (see Chapter 11), how do you think Skinner might have tried to explain language development?

According to Skinner (1985):

> *Verbal behaviour evidently came into existence when, through a critical step in the evolution of the human species, the vocal musculature became susceptible to operant conditioning.*

Skinner (1957) first applied operant conditioning principles to explain language development when he argued that:

> *A child acquires verbal behaviour when relatively unplanned vocalisations, selectively reinforced, assume forms which produce appropriate consequences in a given verbal community.*

While Skinner accepted that prelinguistic vocalisations, such as cooing and babbling, were probably inborn, he argued that adults *shape* the baby's sounds into words by reinforcing those which approximate the form of real words. Through *selective reinforcement*, words are shaped into sentences with correct grammar being reinforced and incorrect grammar ignored.

One form of positive reinforcement is the child getting what it asks for (*mands*). For example, 'May I have some water?' produces a drink that reinforces that form of words. Reinforcement may also be given by parents becoming excited and poking, touching, patting and feeding children when they vocalise. The mother's delight on hearing her child's first real word is exciting for the child, and so acquiring language becomes reinforcing in itself.

Skinner also believed that *imitation* (emitting *echoic responses*) plays an important role. When children imitate verbal labels (*tacts*), they receive immediate reinforcement in the form of parental approval to the extent that the imitations resemble correct words. As children continue to learn new words and phrases through imitation, so their language becomes progressively more like that of adults (Moerk and Moerk, 1979).

An evaluation of Skinner's theory

Ask Yourself

- How easily can operant conditioning explain the stages of language development described above?

- Brodbeck and Irwin (1946) found that, compared with institutionalised children who received less attention, children whose parents reinforced their early attempts at meaningful sounds tended to vocalise more. Parents often reinforce children when they imitate adult language, and, using behaviour modification, Lovaas (1987) has shown that selective reinforcement can be used successfully to teach language to emotionally disturbed or developmentally delayed children (see Chapter 45). However, Skinner's views have been challenged by a number of researchers.
- While imitation must be involved in the learning of accent and vocabulary, its role in complex aspects of language (syntax and semantics) is less obvious. As we saw earlier, when children do imitate adult sentences, they tend to convert them to their own currently operating grammar. So, between 18 and 30 months, the child's imitations are as telegraphic as its own spontaneous speech. However, a child is more likely to imitate a correct grammatical form after an adult has *recast* the child's own sentences than when the adult uses the same grammatical form spontaneously in normal conversation (Farrar, 1992; Nelson, 1977). Recasting, though, is relatively rare (or sometimes non-existent) in normal toddler–parent conversations, yet children still acquire a complex grammar (Bee, 2000). Since at least some adult language is ungrammatical, imitation alone cannot explain how children ever learn 'correct language'. Even if we don't always use correct grammar ourselves, we still know the difference between good and bad grammar.
- In response to these criticisms, Bandura (1977a) has broadened the concept of imitation. *Deferred imitations* are those word sequences and language structures stored in a child's memory for long periods before being used (often in the same situation in which they were first heard). *Expanded imitations* are repetitions of sentences or phrases not present in the original form (Snow, 1983). Children's language production sometimes exceeds their competence in that they imitate forms of language they don't understand. By storing examples of adult language in memory, children have a sort of 'delayed replay' facility that enables them to produce language forms after they've been acquired.
- Operant conditioning cannot explain the *productivity* (or creativity) of language. As Chomsky (1968) states:

> *The normal use of language is innovative, in the sense that much of what we say in the course of normal language use is entirely new [and] not a repetition of anything that we have heard before.*

- Operant conditioning cannot account for children's ability to understand sentence as opposed to word meaning. A sentence's meaning is not simply the sum of the meanings of the individual words. The structure of language is comparable to the structure of perception as described by the Gestalt psychologists (Neisser, 1967: see Chapter 15).

Chomsky's LAD and the biological approach

Although language cannot develop without some form of environmental input, Chomsky (1957, 1965, 1968), Lenneberg (1967) and McNeill (1970) believe that environmental factors could never explain language development adequately. Chomsky proposed the existence of an innate *language acquisition device* (LAD), whereby children are born already programmed to formulate and understand all types of sentences even though they've never heard them before.

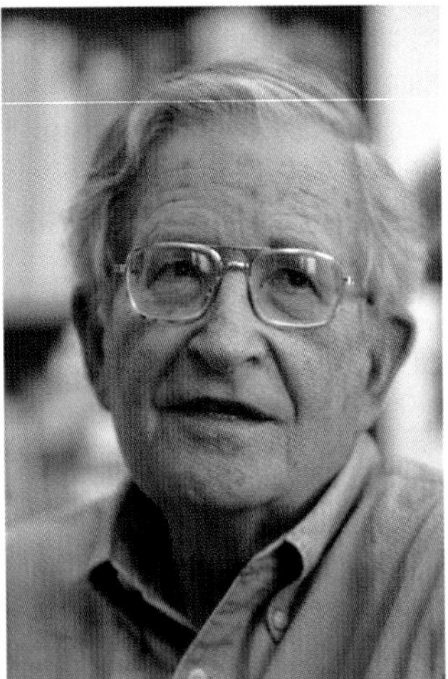

Figure 19.5 Noam Chomsky (born 1928)

Chomsky (1957) argued that language is much more complex and much less predictable than Skinner believed. Central to his theory of *transformational grammar* (TG) are *phrase-structure rules*, which specify what are acceptable/unacceptable utterances in a speaker's native language. When applied systematically, these rules generate sentences in English (or any other language).

While phrase-structure rules specify some important aspects of language, they don't specify them all (Chomsky, 1957).

Rule (1) An S (sentence) consists of (or can be broken down into) NP (noun phrase) and VP (verb phrase)

Rule (2) NP ——→ Article + (Adjective) + Noun

(The brackets denote 'optional')

Rule (3) VP ——→ Verb + NP

Rule (4) Article ——→ a(n), the

Rule (5) Adjective ——→ big, small, red, etc.

Rule (6) Noun ——→ boy, girl, stone, etc.

Rule (7) Verb ——→ hit, threw, helped, etc.

} These are *lexical rewrite rules.* The commas imply that only *one* word should be selected from the list.

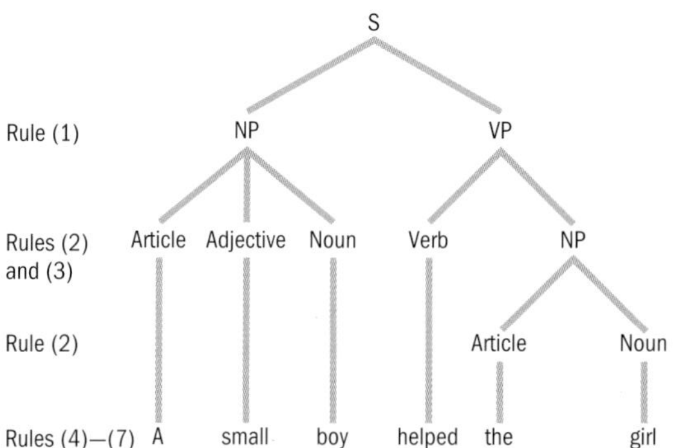

Figure 19.6 Some of Chomsky's phrase-structure rules and an example of a sentence produced by using them

Box 19.4 Deep and surface structure and TG

- A sentence's *surface structure* refers to the actual words or phrases used in the sentence (its *syntactical structure*), while its *deep structure* more or less corresponds to the *meaning*.
- Chomsky argues that when we hear a spoken sentence, we don't 'process' or retain its surface structure, but transform it into its deep structure.
- Transformational grammar (TG) is knowing how to transform a sentence's meaning into the words that make it up (and vice versa). This knowledge is an innate LAD, and is what enables us to produce an infinite number of meaningful sentences.
- A single surface structure may have more than one deep structure, as in the sentence 'The missionary was ready to eat'. This could be interpreted either as, 'The missionary is ready to consume a meal' or, 'The missionary has been prepared for consumption by others'.
- Conversely, different surface structures can have the same deep structure (as in the sentences 'A small boy helped the girl' and 'The girl was helped by a small boy').

Ask Yourself

- Try a Chomsky-type analysis on the following:
  - (a) Cleaning ladies can be delightful.
  - (b) Shaving men can be dangerous.

For Chomsky, children are equipped with the ability to learn the rules for transforming deep structure into various surface structures. They do this by looking for certain kinds of linguistic features common to all languages, such as the use of consonants and vowels, syllables, modifiers and so on. Collectively, these linguistic features (*linguistic universals*) provide the deep structure. They must be universal, because all children can learn any language to which they're exposed. Chomsky argues that only some kind of LAD can account for children's learning and knowledge of grammatical rules in view of the often ungrammatical and incomplete samples of speech they hear (see above).

Chomsky didn't suggest that we go through the procedures of phrase structure and TG each time we prepare to speak a sentence (Hampson and Morris, 1996). A language's grammar is an *idealised description* of the *linguistic competence* of its native speakers. Any model of how this competence is applied in actual performance must acknowledge certain psychologically relevant factors, such as memory, attention, the workings of the nervous system, and so on (Lyons, 1970).

An evaluation of Chomsky's theory

- Aitchison (1983) agrees with Chomsky's claim that children are 'wired' with the knowledge that language is rule-governed, and that they make a succession of hypotheses about the rules underlying speech. However, she disputes the claim that the LAD also consists of TG (what she calls 'Content Cuthbert'). Aitchison prefers a *process approach*, in which children are seen as having inbuilt puzzle-solving equipment that enables them to process linguistic data along with other sorts of data ('Process Peggy').
- By contrast, Chomsky (1979) argues that innate language ability exists *independently* of other innate abilities, because the mind is constructed of 'mental organs' which are:

> *... Just as specialised and differentiated as those of the body ... and ... language is a system easy to isolate among the various mental faculties.*

- According to Chapman (2000), belief in some kind of LAD has persisted despite evidence that language structure is acquired piecemeal, occurs over a period of many years, and that there are wide variations in how quickly children acquire language. Also, language input to young children is well-formed, responsive to the child's communicative attempts, well-adapted to the child's current focus of attention and understanding. This suggests that language development needs to be understood within the context of the child's social interactions, rather than by focusing almost exclusively on what the child possesses in the form of a LAD.

- The data relating to parents' influence on children's syntactic development support Chomsky's claim that parents' role isn't significant (Hill and Kuczaj, 2011; Kuczaj and Hill, 2003). However, 'they do in fact learn the language that they have heard their parents speak'. Parents do a much better job of providing children with good examples of grammatical sentences than Chomsky gives them credit for.
- But Chomsky insists that, however grammatically correct parents' speech might be, and however much they might adapt their speech to children's needs and abilities (see Box 19.3), it still consists only of *surface structure*. The only source of *deep structure*, he says, is an innate LAD. But Kuczaj and Hill (2003) draw a distinction between a *predisposition* to learn language (which is relatively uncontroversial and widely accepted) and *innate knowledge* of language (Chomsky's much more controversial claim that is accepted by very few).

Critical Discussion 19.1

Chomsky, evolution and the search for language genes

- Chomsky believes that newborns' ability to make *phonetic discriminations* represents the first linguistic universals the baby discovers. As we've seen above, meaning can be expressed through gesture, implying that sound isn't an inherent feature of language. However, sound is the 'default medium' – so what makes it so special?
- According to Workman and Reader (2008), (a) using sound enables *multitasking* (you can talk and do something else at the same time); (b) you don't have to look at the person you're talking to, allowing you to attend visually to other, potentially important things; and (c) you can communicate in the dark (important in our ancestral environment of equatorial Africa).
- Despite Chomsky's claim that language constitutes a distinct 'mental organ', he denies that it has been shaped by natural selection. Rather, he proposed that the language organ evolved for some other purpose and was 'co-opted' for its current purpose. More recently, Chomsky and his colleagues (Hauser *et al.*, 2002) extended this idea by distinguishing between 'the faculty of language in the broad sense' (FLB) and in the narrow sense (FLN). FLB refers to what we commonly call language (verbal communication) and includes all the cognitive operations that support it (such as auditory perception and planning), while FLN denotes only those features of language that are specific to language itself.
- Chomsky proposes that a fundamental language-specific feature which distinguishes human from animal communication is *recursion*, the process by which relative clauses are embedded within sentences to produce an infinite set of possibilities. Is there any known human language that *lacks* recursion? According to Everett (2008), Piraha (see Chapter 18), instead of saying, 'The man, who was tall, came into the house', they say, 'The man came into the house. He was tall'. This one known exception to the 'recursion rule' means that there's *no* universal grammar. Everett believes that the Piraha lack of recursion derives from 'the immediacy of experience principle': Pirahas have little interest in what they cannot directly verify, so they communicate through a sequence of simple declarative assertions, removing the need for embedded clauses.
- According to Jakendoff and Pinker (2005), even if it were true that *all* the underlying cognitive operations involved in language were co-opted (as Chomsky originally claimed), this still wouldn't mean that language didn't evolve: natural selection usually works by modifying what's already present, rather than creating new structures. Whether co-opted or not, it's now widely accepted that language involves a complex design of interacting parts that surely couldn't have evolved by accident (Workman and Reader, 2008). But if language is 'in the genes', do we have any idea what these might be?
- Research into *specific language impairment* (SLI) may have provided some vital clues. Gopnik and her colleagues (e.g. Gopnik, 1994; Crago and Gopnik, 1994) studied a British family (the 'KEs'), comprising close-knit cousins and siblings; 16 out of 30 members displayed a particularly severe form of SLI. Some have speech which is almost incomprehensible to outsiders, and many struggle when given the 'wug' test (see Key Study 19.1). Those with SLI seem to have inherited a mutated form of a single, dominant gene, located on chromosome 7, known as FOXP2 (Lai *et al.*, 2001). While not unique to humans, the specific version of FOXP2 present in humans is subtly different from those found in other species. However, this is *not* a 'grammar gene'; it acts as a *regulator gene*, controlling the activity of other genes. In the womb, it appears to switch on genes responsible for the development of normal brain circuitry underlying language. However, it's also been suggested that FOXP2 might be associated with the motor control of our jaw and tongue rather than language abilities, as such (Vargha-Khadern, in McKie, 2001).

Some alternatives to learning theory and biological approaches

Ask Yourself

- What aspects of the interaction between a baby and its caregiver might be important for the baby's future language development? Think of this from the perspective of both partners.

The language and social-interaction approach

One alternative explanation to Chomsky's of the rule-bound nature of children's speech is that it arises from the child's *prelinguistic knowledge* (as in Cromer's *cognition hypothesis*). During the 1970s, Psychologists began to look at language development in the first 12–18 months of life because the basic skills acquired then contribute substantially to the syntactic skills characteristic of adult language.

A purely syntactic analysis of language cannot explain how children 'discover' their language; that is, how they learn that there's such a thing as language which can be used for communicating, categorising, problem-solving and so on. Smith *et al.*'s (1998) *language and social-interaction approach* sees language as being used to communicate needs and intentions, and as an enjoyable means of entering into a community.

Several studies have indicated how babies initially master a social world on to which they later 'map' language. Snow (1977), for example, notes that adults tend to attach meaning to a baby's sounds and utterances. As a result, burps, grunts, giggles and so on are interpreted as expressions of intent and feeling, as are non-verbal communications (such as smiling and eye contact). Snow sees this as a kind of primitive conversation (or *proto-conversation*). This has a rather one-sided quality, in that it requires a 'generous' adult attributing some kind of intended meaning to the baby's sounds and non-verbal behaviours. From this perspective, the infant is an inadequate conversational partner. (But see Box 19.5.)

Figure 19.7 Peek-a-boo: the fun of turn-taking

Language acquisition support system (LASS): the active adult

According to Bruner (1983), formats comprise the *language acquisition support system* (LASS). He's concerned with the pragmatics and functions of language (what language is *for*). In Bruner's view:

> *Entry into language is entry into discourse that requires both members of a dialogue pair to interpret a communication and its intent. Learning a language ... consists of learning not only the grammar of a particular language, but also learning how to realise one's intentions by the appropriate use of that grammar.*

Box 19.5 Visual co-orientation, formats and turn-taking: two-way interaction

- *Visual co-orientation* (or *joint attention*) and *formats* (Collis and Schaffer, 1975) are far more *two-way* than proto-conversations.
- *Visual co-orientation* involves two individuals coming to focus on some common object. This puts an infant's environmental explorations into a social context, so that an infant–object situation is converted into an infant–object–mother situation (Schaffer, 1989). This entails *joint attention*, which provides opportunities for learning how to do things. So, as parents and children develop their mutual patterns of interaction and share attention to objects, some activities recur (such as joint picture-book reading).
- Bruner (1975, 1978) uses *'formats'* to refer to rule-bound activity routines, in which the infant has many opportunities to relate language to familiar play (as when the mother inserts name labels into a game or activity), initially in indicating formats and later in requesting them. These ritualised exchanges stress the need for *turn-taking* (which occurs in games such as peek-a-boo), and so help the baby to discover the social function of communication. As a result, the infant can learn about the structures and demands of social interaction, and prepare and rehearse the skills that will eventually become essential to successful interchanges such as conversation.
- As Schaffer (2004) says:

> *... The acquisition of language is very much a social interactive process and ... any attempt to understand it in terms of the activities of the learner alone is doomed to failure ...*

The emphasis on intent requires a far more active role on the adult's part in helping a child's language acquisition than just being a 'model', or providing the input for the child's LAD. According to Moerk (1989), 'the LAD was a lady', that is, the lady who does most of the talking to the child (namely its mother). Mothers simplify linguistic input and break it down into helpful, illustrative segments for the child to practise and build on (see Box 19.3). This view sees language development as a very sophisticated extension of the processes of meaningful interaction that the caregiver and child have constructed over several months (Durkin, 1995).

The active child

Another way of looking at the 'partnership' is to see the infant as being the more 'active' partner. The view of language as a *cause–effect analytic device* has been summarised by Gauker (1990), for whom:

> *The fundamental function of words is to bring about changes in the speaker's environment ... Linguistic understanding consists of a grasp of these causal relations.*

Gauker sees language as comprising a set of symbols whose use results in a change of behaviour in the listener. The use of words as communicative tools is shown in the emergence of *communicative intentionality*.

During the prelinguistic stage, children have no awareness that they can gain a desired effect indirectly by changing somebody else's behaviour. So, they may cry and reach for something, but not direct the cry towards the caregiver or look back at the caregiver. The cry merely expresses frustration and isn't a communicative signal designed to affect the other's behaviour. This describes *first-order causality*.

The emergence of communicative intentionality involves *second-order causality*, the awareness that it's possible to bring about a desired goal by using another person as a tool. Pointing gestures and glances now rapidly increase as a means of asking others to look at or act upon an object. According to Savage-Rumbaugh (1990), the child is beginning to understand in a general sense:

> *... that it is possible to 'cause' others to engage in desired actions through the mechanism of communication about those actions.*

TEACHING LANGUAGE to NON-HUMAN ANIMALS

As we've seen, Chomsky believes that language is unique to human beings. Similarly, Lenneberg (1967) claims that it represents a *species-specific* behaviour, common to all humans and found only in humans. But if non-humans can be taught to use language, then they must have the capacity for language. The obvious subjects for such language training are our closest evolutionary relatives, chimpanzees and gorillas (the non-human primates).

Criteria for language

We need to define language in a way that will enable us to evaluate the results of studies where humans have tried to teach it to speechless non-humans. Hockett (1960) proposed 13 'design features' of language and based on these, Aitchison (1983) proposed that ten criteria should be sufficient (not all of these are included in Hockett's list). These are shown in Table 19.1.

Table 19.1 Ten criteria for language (Aitchison, 1983, based on Hockett, 1960)

1 Use of the vocal–auditory channel	**6** Turn-taking (conversation is a two-way process)
2 Arbitrariness (use of neutral symbols – words – to denote objects, actions, etc.)	**7** Duality (organisation into basic sounds plus combinations/sequences of sounds
3 Semanticity (use of symbols to mean or refer to objects, actions, etc.)	**8 Displacement** (reference to things not present in time or space)
4 Cultural transmission (handing down the language from generation to generation)	**9 Structure dependence** (the patterned nature of language/use of 'structured chunks' (e.g. word order)
5 Spontaneous usage (freely initiating speech)	**10 Creativity** (what Brown calls **productivity**: the ability to produce/understand an infinite number of novel utterances

N.B. Items in bold are criteria unique to humans

It's in terms of these four highlighted criteria that attempts to teach language to non-human primates have been evaluated.

Early studies

Early attempts to teach chimpanzees to speak (Kellogg and Kellogg, 1933; Hayes and Hayes, 1951) were almost totally unsuccessful: the vocal apparatus of a chimp is unsuited to making English speech sounds.

However, this doesn't rule out the possibility that chimps may still be capable of learning language in some non-spoken form. This is precisely what several

Psychologists have tried to demonstrate since the 1960s in what have come to be called *production-based training*.

Ask Yourself

- Why do we need to know if non-human primates are capable of language?
- Has this research any potential practical implications for the subjects?
- Does it have implications for how we see ourselves as a species?

Evaluating production-based studies

One way of evaluating the studies summarised in Table 19.2 is to ask whether the languages of children and chimps are qualitatively different.

As far as *semanticity* is concerned, is the correct use of signs to refer to things a sufficient criterion? Savage-Rumbaugh *et al.* (1980) seriously doubt whether any of the apes (including their own, Lana) used the individual elements of their vocabularies as words. Terrace (1987) argues that the deceptively simple ability to use a symbol as a name required a cognitive advance in the evolution of human intelligence at least as significant as the advances that led to grammatical competence.

The function of much of a child's initial vocabulary is to inform another person (usually an adult) that it has noticed something (MacNamara, 1982). A child often refers to the object spontaneously, showing obvious delight from the sheer act of naming. This hasn't been observed in apes. MacNamara believes that no amount of training could produce an ape with such an ability: the act of referring isn't learnt but is a 'primitive of cognitive psychology' (and is a necessary precursor of naming). Instead, a chimp usually tries to 'acquire' an object (approach it, explore it, eat it), and shows no sign of trying to communicate the fact that it has noticed an object as an end in itself (Terrace, 1987).

Several critics have claimed that the linguistic abilities of chimps amount to a wholly 'instrumental use' of symbols. Referring to Savage-Rumbaugh's work with Kanzi (see below), Seidenberg and Petitto (1987) claim that Kanzi 'may not know what the symbols mean' but only 'how to produce behaviours that others can interpret'. However, Gauker (1990) proposes that this may be essentially what *human* understanding of words involves.

Helping chimps be more like children

Since the 1980s, Savage-Rumbaugh, at the Yerkes Primate Centre and Georgia State University, has been working with chimps in a way which is much more like how children acquire language (and in certain respects more like that of the pioneers in this field, the Kelloggs and the Hayeses). Instead of putting the chimps through rote learning of symbols, gradually building up a vocabulary a symbol at a time, Savage-Rumbaugh aimed to use a large vocabulary of symbols from the start, using them as language is used around human children.

Table 19.2 The major studies which have attempted to teach language to non-human primates

Study	Subject	Method of language training
Gardner & Gardner (1969)	Washoe (female chimp)	American sign language (ASL or Ameslan). Based on a series of gestures, each corresponding to a word. Many gestures visually represent aspects of the word's meaning.
Premack (1971)	Sarah (female chimp)	Small plastic symbols of various shapes and colours, each symbol standing for a word; they could be arranged on a special magnetised board. e.g. a mauve △ = 'apple'; a pale blue ✧ = 'insert'; a red □ = 'banana'.
Rumbaugh *et al.* (1977)/Savage-Rumbaugh *et al.* (1980)	Lana (female chimp)	Special typewriter controlled by a computer. Machine had 50 keys each displaying a geometric pattern representing a word in a specially devised language ('Yerkish'). When Lana typed, the pattern appeared on the screen in front of her. 'Lana' 'Eat'
Patterson (1978, 1980)	Koko (female gorilla)	American sign language
Terrace (1979)	Nim Chimpsky (male chimp)	American sign language

Operant conditioning is used in all these studies when signs, etc. are correctly used.

This represents a move away from an emphasis on grammatical structure (at least in the beginning) and towards *comprehension*.

This new approach was applied on a limited scale with Austin and Sherman, two common chimps. But it really got going with some pygmy chimps (*bonobos*), which are slightly smaller than common chimps, and more vocal and communicative through facial expressions and gestures. In 1981, work began with Matata, who six months earlier had kidnapped a newborn infant, Kanzi, and kept him as her own. Instead of ASL, Savage-Rumbaugh used an extensive 'lexigram', a matrix of 256 geometrical shapes on a board (see Figure 19.8). Instructors touch the symbols, which represent verbs and nouns, to create simple requests or commands. At the same time, the sentence is spoken, with the aim of testing comprehension of spoken English. When the chimpanzee presses a symbol, a synthesised voice from the computer 'speaks' the word.

Although clearly intelligent in many ways, Matata was a poor learner and used only about six symbols. However, despite no attempt to teach Kanzi anything, he picked up the symbols Matata knew, as naturally as human children do. From that point onwards, an even greater effort was made to place language learning in a naturalistic context. Kanzi acquired a sister, Mulika, when he was 2-and-a-half years old and they grew up together.

According to Savage-Rumbaugh (1990), production-based language training can be said to disrupt the 'normal course' of language acquisition in the ape. Kanzi was the first to demonstrate that *observational exposure* is sufficient for the acquisition of lexical and vocal symbols. Three other chimps (two pygmy and one common) have also learned symbols without training (so Kanzi's ability is unique neither to him nor to his species). According to Savage-Rumbaugh (1990), chimps learn where one word ends and the next begins, that is, what the units are, through the learning of routines which emerge out of daily life that has been constructed for the chimpanzees.

Figure 19.8 Panbanisha and Panzee, a common chimp raised with Panbanisha, using the lexigram keyboard

Ask Yourself

- Is it ethically acceptable to use chimps and other apes for this kind of research?
- Is it right that they're treated as if they were human when they're not? (See Chapter 48.)

Case Study 19.1

Kanzi

By age 10 (1991), Kanzi had a vocabulary of some 200 words. But it's not so much the size of his vocabulary that's impressive, rather what the words apparently mean to him.

He was given spoken requests to do things, in sentence form, by someone out of his sight. Savage-Rumbaugh's assistants in the same room with Kanzi wore earphones, so they couldn't hear the instructions and thereby cue Kanzi, even unconsciously. None of the sentences was practised and each one was different. 'Can you put the raisins in the bowl?' and, 'Can you give the cereal to Karen?' posed no problems for Kanzi. Nor did, 'Can you go to the colony room and get the telephone?' (there were four or five objects in the colony room, which weren't normally there).

More testing still was the instruction 'Go to the colony room and get the orange' when there was an orange in front of Kanzi. This caused him confusion about 90 per cent of the time. But if asked to 'Get the orange that's in the colony room', he did so without hesitation, suggesting that the syntactically more complex phrase is producing better comprehension than the simple one (Savage-Rumbaugh, in Lewin, 1991).

Kanzi showed this level of comprehension when he was 9 years old, but not when he was younger than 6. He also showed understanding of the syntactic rule that in two-word utterances, action precedes object and, significantly, he went from a random ordering initially to a clear, consistent preference.

When almost 20, Kanzi's grammatical comprehension was officially assessed as exceeding that of a 2 and a half-year-old child, and he understood about 2000 words. His 15-year-old sister, Panbanisha, had a vocabulary of at least 3000 words, and Nyota, Panbanisha's son, was learning faster than his mother and uncle. It seems that the researchers' expectations were higher for those who came after Kanzi (Cohen, 2000).

CONCLUSIONS: IS LANGUAGE UNIQUELY HUMAN?

According to Aitchison (1983), the apparent ease with which children acquire language, compared with apes, supports the suggestion that they're innately programmed to do so. Similarly, although these chimps have grasped some of the rudiments of human language, what they've learned and the speed at which they learn it are *qualitatively different* from those of human beings (Carroll, 1986).

Aitchison and Carroll seem to be talking for a majority of Psychologists. However, the criticisms of ape studies and the conclusions that have been drawn from them are based on production-based studies. Savage-Rumbaugh believes there's only a *quantitative difference* (one of degree) between ape and human language. Responding to criticisms by Terrace that Kanzi still uses his symbols only in order to get things done, to ask for things, rather than to share his perception of the world, Savage-Rumbaugh observes that so do young children. In fact, the predominant symbol use of normal children is 'requesting'.

Kanzi's capacity for comprehension far outstrips his capacity for producing language using the lexigram. This makes him extremely frustrated, at which times he often becomes very vocal, making high-pitched squeaks. Is he trying to speak? If Kanzi were to talk, maybe the first thing he'd say is that he's fed up with Terrace claiming that apes don't have language (Lewin, 1991).

Chapter Summary

- Language involves the acquisition of a rule system (**grammar/mental grammar**), which consists of **phonology**, **semantics**, and **syntax**.
- During the **prelinguistic stage**, babies make various non-speech sounds including crying and cooing. But **babbling** involves the production of **phonemes**. **Phonemic expansion** is replaced at around 9–10 months by **phonemic contraction**.
- The child's **first words** are often invented and **context-bound**, denoting specific actions, events or objects. They serve less of a communicative function and more of a **performative function**.
- The full meaning of **holophrases** is provided by accompanying gestures and tones of voice. They can be thought of as precursors of later, more complex sentences.
- Language in **stage 1 grammar** is **telegraphic**, consisting of **contentives** but no **functors**, and involving a **rigid word order**. The child's **imitation by reduction** is complemented by the adult's **imitation with expansion**.
- Word order seems to reflect the child's **prelinguistic knowledge**, as claimed by Cromer's **cognition hypothesis**. Similarly, Piaget believes that language development reflects the child's stage of cognitive development.
- In **stage 2 grammar**, sentences become longer and more complex, as measured by the **mean length of utterance** (MLU). MLU increase is due largely to the inclusion of functors missing from stage 1 telegraphic speech.
- Each functor corresponds to a **syntactic rule**. The rule-governed nature of language is also illustrated in children's grammatical mistakes, which often involve the **overgeneralised/over-regularised** application of a rule.
- According to Skinner, verbal behaviour is acquired through **operant conditioning.** Cooing and babbling are **shaped** by adults into words, and **selective reinforcement** shapes words into grammatically correct sentences.
- Operant conditioning cannot explain the **culturally universal** and **invariant sequence** in the stages of language development. It also fails to explain the **creativity** of language.
- According to Chomsky, children are innately equipped with a **language acquisition device (LAD)**, which consists essentially of **transformational grammar (TG)**. TG enables us to transform **surface** into **deep structure** and vice versa.
- LAD is used to look for **linguistic universals,** which collectively provide the deep structure. Children can learn any language they're exposed to with equal ease.
- According to **integrative theorists,** children are active learners of language whose learning of grammar is based on important already acquired concepts. The language and **social-interaction approach** emphasises children's prelinguistic knowledge.
- Early attempts to teach chimps to speak failed because their vocal apparatus is unsuited to making speech sounds. **Production-based training** studies have found that, compared with children, chimps show little spontaneous naming of objects, and they seem to use symbols in a purely instrumental way.
- Since the 1980s, Savage-Rumbaugh has been using a **comprehension-based** approach, with Kanzi and other bonobos. This structures the environment in a way that allows the chimp to acquire language through **observational learning**, much like a child, by exposing it to language in the course of daily life routines.
- Data from comprehension-based studies suggest that there's only a **quantitative difference** between ape and human language. Rejection of the claim that chimps are capable of language has arisen from the earlier, production-based studies.

Links with Other Topics/Chapters

Chapters 18 and 34 → Cromer's cognition hypothesis sees word order in two-word utterances as dependent on the child's prelinguistic knowledge, in particular Piaget's concept of *object permanence*. This is consistent with Piaget's view of the *relationship between language and thought*

Chapter 34 → The use of animate tools (other people) in communicative intentionality (second-order causality) parallels the use of inanimate tools (physical objects). This is an important feature of *sensorimotor intelligence*, the first stage in Piaget's *theory of cognitive development*

Chapter 48 → Attempts to teach language to bonobos and other chimps raise fundamental philosophical, scientific and *ethical* issues

Chapters 2, 11 and 49; 35 and 36 → Skinner's theory of language development is based on the same principles of *operant conditioning* that are applied to all other (voluntary) behaviours. But he also sees (Chapters 2, 11 and 49) *imitation* as playing an important role, which is more a feature of *social learning theory*

Chapter 45 → Some support for Skinner comes from the use of *behaviour modification* to teach language to emotionally disturbed/developmentally delayed children

Chapters 16 and 50 → Language (like perception) is one of the major arenas (Chapter 16) for the *nature–nurture debate* and Chomsky's LAD represents one of the major *nativist* theories within Psychology as a whole – past or present

Recommended Reading

Barrett, M. (1989) Early Language Development. In Slater, A. & Bremner, G. (eds) *Infant Development.* Hillsdale, NJ: Erlbaum.

Chomsky, N. (author), Belletti, A. & Luigi, R. (eds) (2002) *On Nature and Language.* Cambridge: Cambridge University Press.

Gross, R. (2012) *Key Studies in Psychology* (6th edition). London: Hodder Education. Chapter 3.

Jackendoff, R. (1993) *Patterns in the Mind: Language and Human Nature.* Hemel Hempstead: Harvester Wheatsheaf.

Hill, H.M. & Kuczaj, S.A. (2011) The Development of Language. In Slater, A. & Bremner, G. (eds) *An Introduction to Developmental Psychology.* Oxford: Blackwell Publishing Ltd. (2nd edition).

Pinker, S. (2004) *The Language Instinct.* New York: Morrow.

Savage-Rumbaugh, S. & Lewin, R. (1994) *The Ape at the Brink of the Human Mind.* New York: John Wiley.

Schaffer, H.R. (2004) *Introducing Child Psychology.* Oxford: Blackwell Publishing Ltd. Chapter 9. Also relevant to Chapter 37.

Useful Websites

www.literacytrust.org.uk/talktoyourbaby/theories.html (Website of the Literacy Trust)

www.kidsdevelopment.co.uk LanguageDevelopmentStagesYoungChildren.html (Kids' Development: Links to accounts of cognitive and social development, etc.)

www.youtube.com/watch?v=rnLWSC5p1XE (Video of Talk by Chomsky (2008) and several related videos)

www.davidmswitzer.com/apelang.html ('Language in Apes: How much Do They Know and How Much Should We Teach Them' by D. Switzer (1995, 1999))

www.ted.com/talks/susan_savage_rumbaugh_on_apes_that_write.html (Video of talk by Sue Savage-Rumbaugh, filmed 2004; posted 2007. Also several related videos)

www.ted.com/talks/susan_savage_rumbaugh_on_apes_that_write?language=en (Talk by Sue Savage-Rumbaugh plus film footage.)

CHAPTER 20

PROBLEM-SOLVING, DECISION-MAKING AND ARTIFICIAL INTELLIGENCE

- The nature of problems
- Explaining problem-solving (PS)
- Decision-making
- Artificial intelligence (AI)

INTRODUCTION and OVERVIEW

The basic cognitive processes we've considered in the previous chapters are all aspects of 'thought'. However, there's more to thinking than perception, attention and language. Two closely related aspects of thinking of interest to Cognitive Psychologists are *problem-solving* (PS) and *decision-making* (DM). DM is a special case of PS, in which we already know the possible solutions (or options). A problem can be defined as arising whenever a path to a desired goal is blocked.

In another sense:

> *... all thinking involves problem-solving, no matter how simple, immediate and effortless it may appear ... (Boden, 1987a)*

A good example of what Boden means is *perception*. As we noted in Chapter 15, the effortless and (usually) accurate nature of perception suggests that there's no problem-solving involved (no 'vision problem'). But that's not how Psychologists – and other researchers – see it.

Much of the work of computer simulation and *artificial intelligence* (AI) has been concerned with PS. If we can create computer programs that will solve 'human' problems, we might understand better how we solve them. This research is based on the argument that both computers and human problem-solvers are *information-processing machines* (Greene, 1987).

Significantly, some early research into human PS was going on during the 1920s and 1930s in Germany and elsewhere in Europe, where the impact of American behaviourism was minimal. It wasn't until the mid-1950s that behaviourism's domination of American Psychology gave way to Cognitive Psychology. The new information-processing approach to PS was quite different from early PS research, being largely inspired by computer scientists, including those working within AI.

THE NATURE of PROBLEMS

Classifying problems

Garnham (1988) distinguishes between two broad classes of problem, *adversary* and *non-adversary*.

Adversary problems

Adversary problems involve two or more people pitting their wits against each other, as in chess. Garnham says that game-playing is a special kind of PS, in which the problem is to find a winning strategy or the best current move. The focus of AI research here has been on two-player games, in which each player always has complete information about the state of play, and in which there's no element of chance. Apart from chess, games used include noughts and crosses (tic-tac-toe) and draughts (checkers).

Non-adversary problems

Most problems fall into the *non-adversary* category, in which another person is only involved as the problem setter. Some of the most commonly used include the following:

- The **eight-puzzle**: a 3 × 3 matrix containing the numbers one to eight, with one vacant square, must be moved until the numbers are in order.

5	4	8
7	2	6
3		1

Figure 20.1 The eight-puzzle

- The **missionaries and cannibals** (or '**hobbits and orcs**') **problem**: the three missionaries and three cannibals must be transported across the river in a single boat, which can hold only two people but needs at least one to get it across the river. The cannibals must never outnumber the missionaries on either bank (or they'll be eaten).

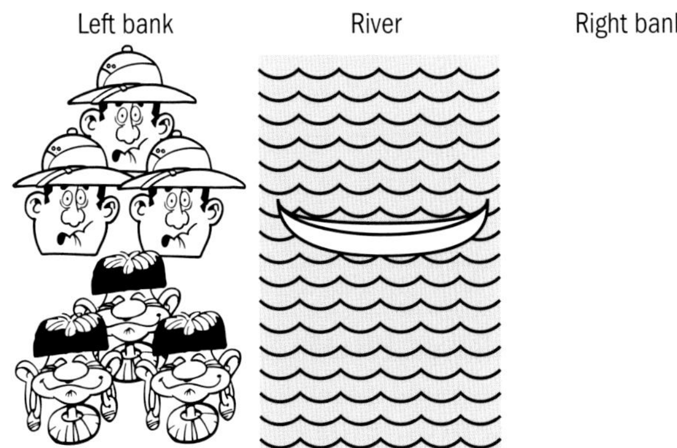

Figure 20.2 The missionaries and cannibals problem

- The **Tower of Hanoi problem**: there are three vertical pegs with four (or more) discs of increasing size stacked on one peg. The problem is to transfer the discs to the second peg, moving only one at a time and never placing a larger disc on top of a smaller one.

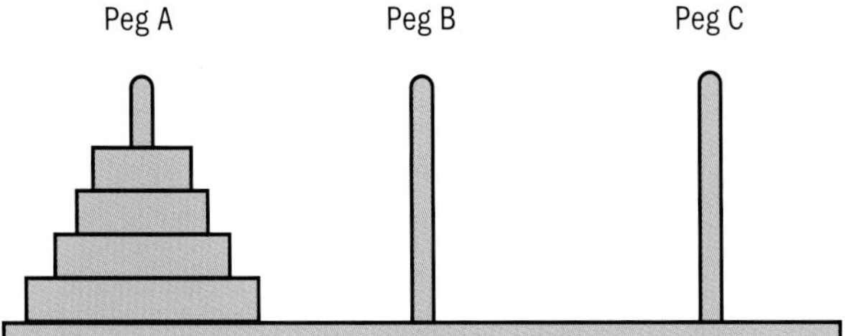

Figure 20.3 The Tower of Hanoi problem

- **Cryptarithmetic** (Bartlett, 1958): given that D = 5 and each letter stands for a digit (0–9), find the digits which make the sum correct.

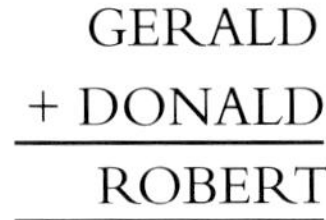

> **Ask Yourself**
>
> - Have a go at solving these puzzles, trying to monitor the strategies you adopt as you do so.

EXPLAINING PROBLEM-SOLVING (PS)

The Gestalt approach

According to Behaviourists, PS is essentially a matter of *trial-and-error* and *accidental success* (Thorndike, 1911: see Chapter 11). As acquired habits are learned, so PS (essentially a chain of stimulus–response associations) improves. While trial-and-error can be effective in solving some problems, Gestalt Psychologists saw PS as involving the *perceptual restructuring* of the problem, resulting in *insight*.

Functional fixedness

Functional fixedness (or '*fixity*') is a type of *mental set* (see below), in which we fail to see that an object may have functions (or uses) other than its normal ones. Duncker (1926, 1945) gave participants a candle and a box of drawing pins, and instructed them to attach the candle to a wall over a table so that it would stay upright and not drip on to the table underneath. Most tried to tack the candle directly to the wall, or glue it by melting it. Few thought of using the inside of the tack-box as a candle-holder and tacking that to the wall. Participants were 'fixated' on the box's normal function, and they needed to reconceptualise it (use *lateral thinking*: de Bono, 1967). Their past experience was leading them away from the solution. When people are shown an empty box and the drawing pins are scattered on a table, the box is much more likely to be used as a candle-holder (Glucksberg and Weisberg, 1966).

In Scheerer's (1963) nine-dot problem (see Figure 20.4), the task is to draw four continuous straight lines, connecting all the dots, without lifting the pencil from the paper. Most people fail, because they assume that the lines must stay within the square formed by the dots – they 'fixate' on the shape of the dots. (The solution can be found on p. 344.)

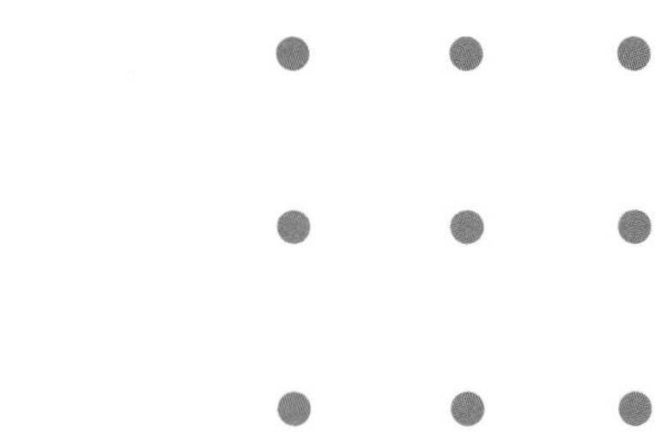

Figure 20.4 Scheerer's nine-dot problem

Table 20.1 The water container problems used by Luchins and Luchins (1959)

	Containers with capacity in fluid ounces			Obtain exactly these amounts of water
Problem no.	**Container A**	**Container B**	**Container C**	
1	21	127	3	100
2	14	163	25	99
3	18	43	10	5
4	9	42	6	21
5	20	59	4	31
6	23	49	3	20
7	10	36	7	3

Mental set

In *mental* (or *problem-solving*) *set* we tend to continue using a previously successful strategy to solve new problems, even when more efficient strategies exist. Luchins (1942) and Luchins and Luchins (1959) asked people to imagine they had three different containers, each of a different size. The task was to use the containers to obtain a specific volume of liquid. Once this problem had been solved, the task was repeated, but participants had to imagine a different set of three containers. (See Table 20.1.)

Problems 1–5 can be solved using the formula B–2C–A (that is, fill container B, pour its contents into container C twice, and then pour what remains in container B into container A to leave the desired amount in container B). While problem 6 can also be solved using this formula, there's a more direct solution, namely A–C. Problem 7 cannot be solved using the formula B–2C–A, but can be solved using the formula A–C.

Once people discovered a solution to the first problem, they continued to use it even when (in the case of problem 6) it was less efficient, or (in the case of problem 7) it didn't apply. In Gestalt terms, mental set produces *reproductive thinking* (what Luchins and Luchins called the *Einstellung* effect), when in fact a problem calls for *productive thinking* (Maier, 1931; Scheerer, 1963).

Recent research that tracks the eye movements of highly skilled chess players has found that they're *literally* blind to certain areas of the chess board that would have provided clues to better (faster) check-mate positions (Bilalic and McLeod, 2014). They tend to stick with a well-known sequence of moves that has proved successful in the past. In fact, the *Einstellung* effect was powerful enough to temporarily lower expert chess masters to the level of much weaker players (Bilalic and McLeod, 2014).

In *productive thinking*, problems are solved by the principle of *reorganisation*, or solving a problem by perceiving new relationships among its elements. Consider, for example, trying to arrange six matchsticks into four equilateral triangles with each side equal to one stick. If you try to arrange the matchsticks by pushing them around on a table, the problem cannot be solved. But through reorganisation, and realisation that the matchsticks don't have to be arranged in two dimensions, the problem can be solved (as shown on p. 344). The principle of reorganisation is similar to what Köhler (1925) called *insight* in his studies of PS in chimpanzees. (See Key Study 20.1.)

An evaluation of the Gestalt approach

- Gestalt Psychologists made a significant contribution to our understanding of the processes involved in solving certain types of problem, but they didn't develop a theory that applies to all aspects of PS.
- The concepts of 'insight' and 'restructuring' are attractive, because they're easily understood (especially when accompanied by perceptual demonstrations). But they're extremely vague and ill-defined as theoretical constructs: it's very unclear under what conditions they occur and exactly what insight involves (Eysenck and Keane, 1995).
- However, in many ways, the spirit of Gestalt research, with its emphasis on the goal-directed and non-associationist nature of thinking, provides a basis for the information-processing approach. It also left a large body of experimental problems and

Key Study 20.1

Sultan and the banana (Köhler, 1925)

Köhler suspended, out of reach, a bunch of bananas from the ceiling of the cage of a chimpanzee called Sultan. In the cage were several items that could be used to reach the bananas (such as sticks of different lengths), although none on its own was sufficient. Eventually, Sultan solved the problem by placing empty boxes beneath the bananas and climbing on the boxes.

Later, Köhler allowed Sultan to see a box being placed in the corridor leading to his cage. Sultan was then taken to his cage where, again, bananas were suspended from the ceiling. Sultan's first strategy was to remove a long bolt from the open cage's door. Quite suddenly, though, he stopped, ran down the corridor, and returned with the box which was again used to retrieve the bananas.

For Köhler, Sultan's behaviour was a result of sudden *perceptual reorganisation* or *insight*, which was different from trial-and-error learning. Other experiments showed that Sultan's perceptual reorganisation was maintained as a plan of action. So, when the bananas were placed outside the cage, Sultan still built several boxes. Experience can sometimes be an obstacle to PS!

Figure 20.5

evidence for which any later theory had to be able to account; 'the legacy of the school was, therefore, substantial' (Eysenck and Keane, 1995).

The information-processing approach

Information-processing approaches analyse cognitive processes in terms of a series of separate stages. In the case of PS, the stages are: representing the problem, generating possible solutions, and evaluating those solutions.

Algorithms

An *algorithm* is a systematic exploration of every possible solution until the correct one is found. For example, to solve the anagram YABB, we could list all the possible combinations of letters, checking each time to see whether the result is a real word. So, we might generate BBAY (non-word), BYAB (non-word) and so on, until we eventually arrive at BABY. Algorithms guarantee a solution to a problem, and are effective when the number of possible solutions is small (as in the above example). But when there's a very large number of possible solutions, algorithms are time-consuming (unless we're fortunate enough to find the solution early).

Heuristics

Heuristics are 'rules of thumb':

> *... guidelines for selecting actions that are most likely to lead a solver towards a goal, but may not always do so. (Greene, 1987)*

So, while not guaranteeing a solution to a problem, heuristics can result in solutions being reached more quickly (Newell *et al.*, 1958). These 'fuzzy' procedures are based on intuition, past experience, and any other relevant information. With solving anagrams, for example, a heuristic approach would involve looking for letter combinations that are/are not permitted in the English language. BB isn't a permitted combination of letters at the beginning of a word, and so this would immediately exclude BBAY as a solution to the example above. Heuristic devices applied to longer anagrams might not be successful, and we might miss a solution based on a lack of intuition, past experience, and other relevant factors. Heuristic devices include *means–end analysis* (MEA) (Newell and Simon, 1972).

Well-defined and ill-defined problems

Garnham (1988) believes that in everyday problems, and those requiring a high degree of creative thinking, one or more of: (i) the initial state; (ii) the goal state; or (iii) the operators are typically *ill-defined* (not made explicit). This makes it difficult to write AI programs designed to solve such problems. But in the missionaries and cannibals problem, Tower of Hanoi and other puzzle problems, all three are clearly specified (they're *well-defined* problems) and AI programs are relatively successful in solving them. According to Greene (1987), there are two major differences between puzzle problems and real-life problems:

1. Puzzle problems are unfamiliar problems about which the solver has little knowledge, whereas many everyday problems require considerable amounts of knowledge. The knowledge which is relevant in puzzle problems is called *general-purpose* (or *domain-independent heuristic*) knowledge. For example, MEA can be applied in a wide range of different situations (domains). By contrast, everyday problems require substantial *domain-specific knowledge*; this is also required in adversary problems, such as chess (see below).
2. The knowledge required to solve puzzles is present in the statement of the problem, whereas much of the difficulty with everyday problems is finding the relevant information needed to solve them.

Solving adversary problems: the case of chess

According to Ginsberg (1998):

> *The world watched with considerable amazement in May 1997 as IBM's chess computer, Deep Blue, beat Garry Kasparov, the world champion, in a six-game match. With a machine's victory in this most cerebral of games, it seemed that a line had been crossed, that our measurements of ourselves might need tailoring.*

However, the contest was very close (two wins, one defeat and three ties), and Kasparov clearly wasn't on top form. Although Deep Blue and other recent chess-playing programs generally play well, Ginsberg observes that:

> *As an element of artificial intelligence, game-playing software highlights the key differences between the brute-force calculation of machines and the often intuitive, pattern-matching abilities of humans.*

The number of possible sequences of moves in a game of chess is frighteningly large (there are an estimated 10^{20} possible games of chess, compared with a mere 10^{12} microseconds per century: Garnham, 1988). Human players will consider tens (or perhaps hundreds) of positions when selecting a move, which represents a tiny fraction of the potential moves, and only rarely can they think through to a win, lose or stalemate situation. Chess-playing computer programs used to be like human players. They selected a small number of moves to follow up, then used the *minimax procedure* (minimising the maximum loss that can be inflicted by the opponent) to analyse these in detail. Programs run on small computers still operate in this way.

But top programmers have access to the most powerful machines available, and they often revert to a more algorithmic method; for example, examining every possible position that can be reached in the next five moves by each player (which involves comparing hundreds of thousands of positions). While modern computers can perform many millions of operations per second (through 'brute-force' methods), this provides few insights for cognitive scientists, since it bears no relationship to the way that people solve difficult problems (Garnham, 1991).

Box 20.1 Key differences between human and computer chess masters

- Considering the far superior computational capacity of computers, it might seem unlikely that humans could ever win. But although people look at a mere handful of successive positions, they tend to look at the right handful. They identify the best positions to consider through *pattern matching (*or PR: see Chapter 14). Chess experts compare a given board position with the vast number of such positions they've seen during their career, using lessons learned from analysing those other positions to identify good moves in the current game. For Deep Blue, however, there are no pre-existing lists of positions it can use to evaluate the current game. As Boden (1987b) puts it:

  > *Master chess players develop global perceptual schemata in terms of which they can see threats and oppositions on the board much as a lesser mortal can see complex emotional response in a cartoon face ...*

- Pattern matching is a *parallel process,* while the computer's capacity for searching through vast numbers of possibilities is a *serial process*. Since the brain is a massively parallel structure, it's far superior to computers at recognising patterns.

According to Boden (1987b):

> *Like problem-solving in other ... domains ... chess playing needs more than quick thinking and a retentive memory: it requires an appreciation of the overall structure of the problem, so that intelligent action can be economically planned ...*

de Groot (1965, 1966) compared the performance of five grand masters and five expert players on choosing a move from a particular board position. He asked participants to think aloud, and then determined the number and type of different moves they'd considered. Grand masters didn't consider more alternative moves or search any deeper than experts, and yet they took slightly less time to make a move. Independent raters judged the final moves of the masters to be superior to those of the experts.

de Groot's initial explanation for these differences was in terms of knowledge of different board positions stored in LTM. When participants were given a five-second presentation of board positions from actual games and asked to reconstruct them from memory, the masters were correct 91 per cent of the time compared with 41 per cent for the experts. Clearly, the masters could recognise and encode the various configurations of pieces using prior knowledge. When pieces were randomly arranged on the board, both groups did equally badly.

Figure 20.6 Chess experts are only better at remembering the position of chess pieces when they're positioned as they might be during a game. If the pieces are placed randomly, the experts are no better than non-experts at memorising their positions (de Groot, 1966)

This specific memory ability must be the result of training, because grandmasters do no better than others in general tests of memory, Similar results have been demonstrated in bridge players, computer programmers and musicians. This memory ability is a standard criterion for the existence of *expertise* (Ross, 2006).

Experts and domain-specific knowledge

According to Sternberg (1990):

> *... intelligent systems rely to a great extent on stored problem patterns when they face a familiar task. Instead of creating solutions from scratch for every problem situation, they make use of previously stored information in such a way that it facilitates their coping with the current problem.*

As we've seen above, experts aren't faster thinkers, with better memories than non-experts (Hampson and Morris, 1996): the key difference seems to be the reduced strain put on *working memory* (see Chapter 17). Since PS strategies depend on knowledge which is already available, 'the more you know, the less you have to think' (Greene, 1987).

According to Greene (1987), what's missing from AI accounts of human PS are the different experiences people bring to different tasks.. Expertise is more far-reaching than simple knowledge of the rules which apply to a particular problem (otherwise we'd all be chess masters!).

DECISION-MAKING

As we noted in the *Introduction and overview, decision-making* (DM) is a special case of PS, in which we already know the possible solutions (or choices). Some decisions we have to make are relatively trivial. Others are more important, such as deciding which university to attend, or whether or not to have children. In DM, then, we're faced with various alternative choices from which one must be selected and the others rejected.

Ask Yourself

- Think of a situation in which you had to choose between various options (e.g. which college or university to go to, or which subjects to study).
- How did you make your decision?

Compensatory and non-compensatory models of DM

Compensatory models

If we were completely logical in our DM, we'd evaluate how all the desirable potential outcomes of a particular decision might compensate for all the undesirable ones. According to the *additive compensatory model*, we start the DM process by listing common features of various alternatives and assigning arbitrary weights that reflect their value to us. The weights are then added up to arrive at a separate score for each alternative. Provided the criteria have been properly weighted and each criterion has been correctly rated, the alternative with the highest score is the most rational choice given the available information.

Another compensatory model is the *utility–probability model*. This proposes that important decisions are made by weighting the desirability of each potential outcome according to its *utility* (the value placed on potential positive or negative outcomes) and *probability* (the likelihood that the choice will actually produce the potential outcome).

Non-compensatory models

Evidence suggests that we actually use various, and less precise, *non-compensatory models*. In these, we may not consider every feature of each alternative and features don't compensate for each other. There are at least four such models.

Box 20.2 Some non-compensatory DM models

Elimination by aspects: When faced with complex decisions, we eliminate various options if they don't meet particular criteria, irrespective of their quality on other criteria (Tversky, 1972). This assumes that we begin with a maximum criterion and use it to test the various options. If, after applying this criterion, more than one alternative remains, the second most important criterion is used. The procedure continues until just one option remains; this is the chosen option.

Maximax strategy: After comparing the various options according to their best features, we then select the one with the strongest best feature.

Minimax strategy: After considering the weakest feature of each option, we select the option whose weakest feature is most highly rated.

Conjunctive strategy: This involves setting a 'minimum' acceptable value on each option. The next step is to discard any option which doesn't meet, or exceed, this value as the criteria are considered from most to least important. The chosen option is the one that meets or exceeds the minimum acceptable value on each criterion.

Heuristics in DM

Clearly, important decisions should be approached rationally and systematically. But it's not always easy to make rational decisions, even in important matters, because of the absence of information about the various alternatives. Moreover, with all the decisions we have to make daily, there isn't time to engage in the rational processes described above. We also have only a limited capacity for reasoning according to formal logic and probability theory (Evans and Over, 1996). As a result, we often rely on *heuristics*. Two of these are the *availability heuristic* (or *bias*) and the *representativeness heuristic* (or *bias*: Tversky and Kahneman, 1973).

Availability heuristic (or bias)

Sometimes, decisions must be made on the basis of whatever information is most readily available in LTM. The availability heuristic is based on the assumption that an event's probability is directly related to the frequency with which it has occurred in the past and that more frequent events are usually easier to remember than less frequent events.

Ask Yourself

- Does the letter K appear more often as the first letter of a word or as the third letter?

Most people say the former. In fact, 'K' is three times more likely to appear as the third letter, but because words beginning with 'K' come to mind more easily, we assume they're more commonplace (Hastie and Park, 1986).

Figure 20.7 The availability heuristic plays a role in our tendency to overestimate the chances of being the victim of a violent crime or a plane crash (Tyler and Cook, 1984). This is because the extensive media coverage of these statistically very rare events brings vivid examples of them to mind very readily

Representativeness heuristic (or bias)

Ask Yourself

Steve is very shy and withdrawn, invariably helpful, but with little interest in people, or in the world of reality. A meek and tidy soul, he has a need for order and structure, and a passion for detail.

- Try to guess Steve's occupation: is he a musician, pilot, physician, salesperson or librarian?
- Why did you choose the one you did?

Tversky and Kahneman (1973) found that most of their participants chose librarian, presumably because his personality characteristics matched certain *stereotypes* of librarians (see Chapter 22). Whenever we judge the likelihood of something by intuitively comparing it with our preconceived ideas of a few characteristics we believe represent a category, we're using the *representativeness heuristic*. It can also explain the *gambler's fallacy* (see Box 20.3) and the *base rate fallacy*.

Box 20.3 The gambler's fallacy

Ask Yourself

- Consider the following possible outcomes of tossing a coin six times:

  HHHHHH, TTTTTT and HTTHTH.

- Which of these is the *least*, and which the *most*, likely?

Most people believe the *first* outcome is the *least* likely of the three and the *third* the *most* likely. In fact, the probability of the three sequences is *identical*.

Our assumption that coin tossing produces a random sequence of heads and tails leads us to decide that the third is the most likely (it *looks* the most random). Indeed, if people observe five consecutive heads, and are then asked to estimate the probability of the next toss being a head, they tend to say that a tail is the more likely outcome – even though the probability of either heads or tails is actually 0.5! This tendency is called the *gambler's fallacy*.

In the *base rate fallacy*, we ignore important information about base rates (the relative frequency of different objects/events in the world). For example, Tversky and Kahneman (1973) asked participants to decide whether a student who could be described as 'neat and tidy', 'dull and mechanical' and 'a poor writer' was a computer-science student or a humanities student. Over 95 per cent decided the student studied computing. Even after they were told that over 80 per cent of students at their school were studying humanities, their estimates remained virtually unchanged. So, even when we know the relative frequency of two things, we tend to ignore this information and base a decision on how well something matches our stereotype; that is, how *representative* it is.

However, if prior odds are the *only* relevant information (base rates without the description of the student), then participants will estimate correctly. People may also be more inclined to take account of base rate information when it seems to be *causally* relevant (Tversky and Kahneman, 1980).

Gambling and risk-taking

Many laboratory studies have used gambling as a model of risk-taking behaviour, despite the fact that it isn't typical of the risks we take in everyday life (Jones, 1998). However, the heuristics discussed above (which are based largely on laboratory studies) can help explain an increasingly common case of real-life gambling, namely, playing the UK National Lottery. Although the odds against winning the jackpot are 14 million to one (far greater than any other form of average gambling return), 90 per cent of the population are estimated to have bought at least one ticket, and 65 per cent claim to play regularly (Hill and Williamson, 1998). Given these odds, it's likely that the ordinary 'social gambler' doesn't think about the actual probability of winning, but relies on heuristic strategies for handling the available information (Griffiths, 1997b).

The fact that there are so many heuristics and biases, and that several can be applied to any one particular situation, gives them little predictive value (Griffiths, 1997b; Wagenaar, 1988). However, the availability bias, illusory correlations, and illusion of control can help explain the persistence of gambling (Griffiths, 1997b; Hill and Williamson, 1998). Uncovering the false beliefs underlying people's mistakes when becoming involved in a risk situation can help to reduce the irrational thinking of a potential gambler (Griffiths, 1990; Walker, 1992).

Ask Yourself

- Try to relate these heuristics and biases to explanations of *risky health behaviours* (see Chapter 12) and *addictive behaviours* (see Chapter 8).

Table 20.2 Heuristic strategies and biases that might be used by lottery players

Heuristic	Application to lottery participation
Availability bias	Wide publicity concerning winners, and pleasant memories of an occasional small prize, make winning more salient than losing
Randomness bias: not expecting a random sequence to have any apparent biases and regularities (Teigen, 1994)	Despite the mechanical and random nature of the draw, many people seem to be trying to predict which numbers will be drawn (Haigh, 1995). So, there's difficulty in choosing six random numbers from 49
Representativeness bias: equating a 'random' sample with a 'representative' sample (Tversky and Kahneman, 1971)	A tendency to choose numbers that appear 'random' (irregular, no pattern), and avoid those which appear less random (adjacent numbers and repeating digits)
Gambler's fallacy: the belief that subsequent events will cancel out previous events to produce a representative sequence (Holtgraves and Skeel, 1992), and that the probability of winning will increase with the length of an ongoing run of losses (Wagenaar, 1988; see also Box 20.3)	Choosing numbers which have been least drawn (they are therefore 'due'), and overestimating the chances of winning
Illusory correlations: the use of superstitious behaviour when it's believed variables correlate when they don't (Wagenaar, 1988; see also Chapter 22)	Choosing 'lucky numbers' – birthdays, house numbers, etc. – which causes players to discard statistical probabilities
Flexible attribution: tendency to attribute success to personal skill and failures to some external influence (Wagenaar, 1988; see Chapter 23)	Preference for choosing own numbers rather than buying 'lucky dips', so that any win is due to player's own skill (game of luck), whereas losses are due to features of the game (game of chance)
Illusion of control: an expectancy of success which is greater than the objective probability warrants (Langer, 1975)	Being able to choose own numbers induces skill orientations, which cause players to feel inappropriately confident
Sunk cost bias: continuing an endeavour once an investment has been made (Arkes and Blumer, 1985)	Continuing to buy lottery tickets while experiencing losses. The more money that's spent, the more likely people are to continue 'investing', and to inflate their estimations of winning

(Based on Griffiths, 1997b; Hill and Williamson, 1998)

Critical Discussion 20.1

Thinking, Fast and Slow (Kahneman, 2013)

This is the title of a recent book by Kahneman, in which he distinguishes between two kinds of systems in the mind:

- *System 1*: this is based on instinct and intuition and is where the representativeness and other heuristics belong (see text above). It works in a reflex way, using a limited amount of information to reach a conclusion quickly and in a shallow way. The 'solution' seems obvious, but you cannot explain how you reached it. It can triumph in situations where slowness = death.
- *System 2:* this thinks deeply, logically and slowly, taking everything into account (the 'professor'). It can triumph where avoiding error is paramount. It's what we use to solve problems that require attention and reasoning and it's where the compensatory/non-compensatory models (see text above) belong.

However, this account involves something of a false dichotomy, for underlying System 1's heuristics is a considerable amount of mental effort. Also, Systems 2's highest achievements sometimes depend on System 1's insights into the way things work (Strevens, 2013). While System 2 generally produces better outcomes, attention, concentration and reasoning are finite resources: most everyday mental tasks are left to System 1, leaving us vulnerable to errors. Our minds are biased and flawed, but in a systematic way; human behaviour is irrational, but predictably so (Lawton, 2013).

ARTIFICIAL INTELLIGENCE (AI)

Throughout the chapter so far, we've talked about computers as problem-solvers and have looked at some of the important differences between them and human problem-solvers. Also, we've discussed mainly puzzle problems. But what about the kind of 'problem' referred to in the *Introduction and overview,* such as vision and language understanding, which humans are 'designed' for? Can computers be programmed to mimic these basic human abilities and, if so, what can we learn about the way we use them?

Defining AI

According to Garnham (1988), AI is 'the science of thinking machines' and, again:

> *... an approach to understanding behaviour based on the assumption that intelligence can best be analysed by trying to reproduce it. In practice, reproduction means simulation by computer. AI is, therefore, part of computer science ...*

Garnham observes that most contemporary AI research is influenced more or less by consideration of how people behave. Very few researchers simply try to build clever machines disregarding the principles underlying its behaviour, and many still have the explicit goal of writing a program which works in the way people do (such as Marr's computational theory of vision: see Chapter 15). So, Cognitive Psychologists and workers in AI share an interest in the scientific understanding of cognitive abilities.

Abilities such as vision, language, PS and DM are all part of 'intelligence' in the broadest sense of that term, and intelligence has always been a central concern of Psychologists (see Chapters 34 and 41). As we saw in Chapter 1, since the late 1970s, Cognitive Psychology and AI have both become component disciplines of *cognitive science.* By the late 1970s, Cognitive Psychologists had more in common with AI researchers than with other psychologists and AI researchers had more in common with Cognitive Psychologists than with other computer scientists (Garnham, 1988).

Boden (1987b) defines AI as '... the science of making machines do the sorts of things that are done by human minds ...' The 'machines' in question are, typically, digital computers. But she's at pains to make clear that AI isn't the study of computers but the study of intelligence in thought and action. Computers are its tools, because its theories are expressed as computer programs which are tested by being run on a machine.

What is a computer?

The initial concept of the 'computer', and the first attempts to build the modern digital computer, were made by the Cambridge mathematician, Charles Babbage (1792–1871).

Box 20.4 Turing machines

Turing (1936) described an abstract computing device (a *Turing machine*), which performs its calculations with the help of a tape divided into squares, each with a symbol printed on it. Its basic operations comprise reading and writing symbols on the tape and shifting the tape to the left or right. It uses a finite vocabulary of symbols, but the tape is indefinitely long.

A *universal* Turing machine can mimic the operation of any other Turing machine. To do this, it must be given a description of how that machine works, which can be written onto its tape in standard Turing machine format.

Every general-purpose digital computer is an approximation to the universal Turing machine (since no real machine has an indefinitely large memory). When it runs a program, it behaves as if it were a machine for performing just the task the program performs.

Figure 20.8 Alan Turing (1912–1954)

A digital computer's memory consists of chips (silicon wafers with transistors engraved on them), which store data in the form of a *binary code* – that is, each unit can exist in one of two states (on/off, represented by the symbols 0/1) (Rose, 2003). These two states can symbolise an indefinitely large number of things (as can the 26 letters of the alphabet), because they can be grouped together in indefinitely numerous ways. As described by Turing, they are machines that change according to the problem to be solved (based on the particular instructions contained within the program). 'Digital' refers to the finger, and the fingers can be used as a kind of abacus, a simple form of computing machine. Computers are, in essence, *autonomous abaci* – working without continuous human intervention (Gregory, 1981).

Although originally designed as calculating machines ('compute' means to 'calculate'), computers aren't mere 'number crunchers' or supercalculating arithmetic machines. Digital computers are, in fact, *general-purpose symbol manipulating machines*. It's up to the programmer to decide what interpretations can sensibly (consistently) be made of the symbols of machine and programming languages, which, in themselves, are meaningless (Boden, 1987a).

Strong and weak AI, and the computational theory of mind

Ask Yourself

- Do you believe that computers literally think/behave intelligently (that is, are *reproducing/duplicating* the equivalent human thinking/behaviour) or are they merely *simulating* (mimicking) human thought/intelligence?

This distinction corresponds to the one made by Searle (1980) between strong and weak AI, respectively:

> *According to weak AI, the main value of the computer in the study of the mind is that it gives us a very powerful tool, e.g. it enables us to formulate and test hypotheses in a more rigorous and precise fashion than before. But according to strong AI the computer is not merely a tool; rather, the appropriately programmed computer really is a mind in the sense that computers given the right program can be literally said to understand and have other cognitive states ...*

Searle is very critical of strong AI, a view advocated by computer scientists such as Minsky (1975), who defines AI as '... the science of making machines do things that would require intelligence if done by men'. The implication of such a definition is that machines must be intelligent if they can do what humans can do (although this rather begs the question as to what it means to display intelligence). Underlying strong AI is the *computational theory of mind* (CTM), one supporter of whom is Boden (1987a):

> *Intelligence may be defined as the ability creatively to manipulate symbols, or process information, given the requirements of the task in hand. If the task is mathematical, then numerical information may need to be processed. But if the task is non-numerical (or 'semantic') in nature ... then the information that is coded and processed must be semantic information, irrespective of the superficial form of the symbols used in the information code ...*

Symbols have no inherent similarity to what they symbolise and represent something in a purely formal way. Hence, computer programs comprise *formal systems*, 'a set of basic elements or pieces and a set of rules for forming and transforming the elements or pieces' (Flanagan, 1984). In computer languages, symbols stand for whatever objects, relations or processes we wish. The computer manipulates the symbols, not their meaning. Programs consist of rules for manipulating symbols and don't refer to anything in the world.

However, CTM defines all intelligent systems as symbol manipulators which, of course, include human minds. If symbols are meaningless to a computer, it follows that they're also meaningless to a human mind. But in that case, what's the 'meaning' which, according to Boden, the human programmer attaches to the meaningless symbols? Searle's attack on strong AI and CTM takes the form of a *Gedanken* experiment ('thought experiment') called the Chinese room.

The Chinese room and the Turing test

Searle believes the Chinese room demonstrates quite conclusively that there's more to intelligence and understanding than mere manipulation of symbols. In particular, he's trying to show that the *Turing test* (or *imitation game*) (see Box 20.6) isn't the ultimate test of machine intelligence that supporters of strong AI have traditionally claimed it is.

Box 20.5 The Chinese room (Searle, 1980)

- Suppose that I am locked in a room and am given a large batch of Chinese writing. Suppose that I know no Chinese, either written or spoken …
- After this first batch of Chinese writing, I am given a second batch together with a set of rules for correlating the second batch with the first batch. The rules are in English and I understand them as well as any other English native speaker. They enable me to correlate one set of formal symbols with another set of formal symbols and all that 'formal' means here is that I can identify the symbols entirely by their shapes.
- I am then given a third batch of Chinese symbols together with some instructions, again in English, which enable me to correlate elements of this third batch with the first two batches and these rules instruct me how to give back certain Chinese symbols with certain sorts of shapes in response to certain sorts of shapes provided by the third batch.
- Unknown to me, the people giving me all these symbols call the first batch a 'script', the second batch a 'story', the third batch 'questions', the symbols I give back in response to the third batch, 'answers to the questions' and the set of English rules 'the program' …
- After a while I get so good at following the instructions for manipulating the Chinese symbols and the programmers get so good at writing the program that, from the point of view of somebody outside the room, my answers are indistinguishable from those of native Chinese speakers … However … I am manipulating uninterpreted formal symbols and in this respect I am simply behaving like a computer, i.e. performing computational operations on formally specified elements … I am simply a realisation of the computer program.

Box 20.6 The Turing test (Turing, 1950)

Turing suggested that a suitable test for success in AI would be an 'imitation game', in which a human judge would hold a three-way conversation with a computer and another human and try to tell them apart. The judge would be free to turn the conversation to any topic and the successful machine would be able to chat about it as convincingly as the human. This would require the machine participant to understand language and conversational conventions and to have a general ability to reason.

If the judge couldn't tell the difference after some reasonable amount of time, the machine would pass the test: it would seem human to a human.

> *I believe that in about 50 years time it will be possible to program computers … to make them play the imitation game so well that, on average, the interrogator will not have more than a 70 per cent chance of making the right identification after five minutes of questioning. When this occurs, there is no contradiction in the idea of thinking machines. (Turing, 1950)*

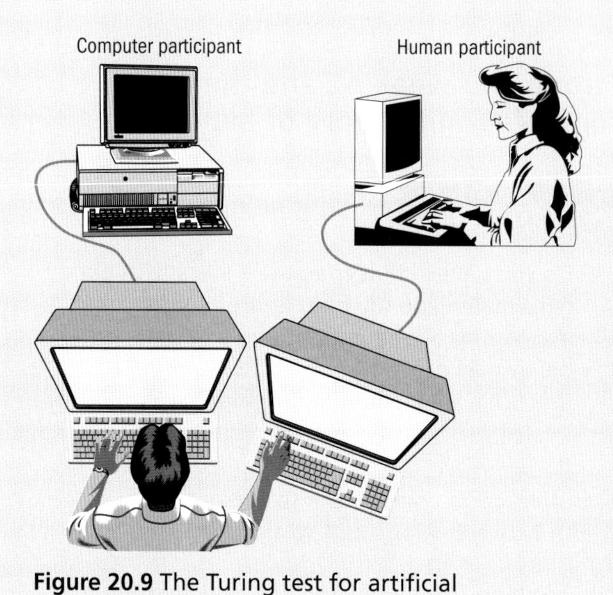

Figure 20.9 The Turing test for artificial intelligence

Both the Chinese room and the Turing test have been criticised. Gregory (1987b) argues that, because it's such a highly restricted and artificial environment:

> *The Chinese room parable does not show that computer-based robots cannot be as intelligent as we are – because we wouldn't be intelligent from this school either.*

Boden (1993) contends that a functioning program is comparable to Searle-in-the-Chinese-room's understanding of *English* (not Chinese). A word in a language one understands is a mini-program, which causes certain processes to be run in one's mind. Clearly, this doesn't happen with the Chinese words, because Searle-in-the-Chinese-room doesn't understand Chinese.

According to Block (in Raley, 2006), the Turing test tests only whether or not a computer *behaves* (verbally and cognitively) in a way that's identical to a human being. Imagine we could program a computer with all possible conversations of a certain finite length. When the interrogator asks a question (Q), the computer looks up the conversation in which Q occurred, then types out the answer that followed (A). When the interrogator asks the next question, P, the computer now looks up the string Q,A,P and types out the answer that followed in this conversation (B). Block believes that such a computer would have the intelligence of a toaster – but it would pass the Turing test.

Supporters of strong AI might reply that the problem Block raises for computers also applies to human beings: all the evidence we *ever* have for whether a human being can think is the behaviour the thought produces. Consequently, we can never really know if our interlocutor (conversation partner) is having a 'real' conversation (Raley, 2006). In turn, Searle would respond by appealing to the Chinese room demonstration that a computer can pass the Turing test without ever understanding the meaning of a single word it uses. The whole AI debate is, surely, based on the belief (shared by both 'camps') that human beings *do* understand the words they use.

The real aims of AI

According to Ford and Hayes (1998), the central defect of the Turing test is that it is *species-centred*: it assumes that human thought is the ultimate, highest form of thinking against which all others must be judged. Most contemporary AI researchers explicitly *reject* the goal of the Turing test. Instead, Ford and Hayes maintain that:

> *The scientific aim of AI research is to understand intelligence as computation, and its engineering aim is to build machines that surpass or extend human mental abilities in some useful way. Trying to imitate a human conversation (however 'intellectual' it may be) contributes little to either ambition.*

Ford and Hayes draw an analogy between AI and artificial flight. They argue that the traditional view of (strong) AI's goal – to create a machine that can successfully imitate human thought – is mistaken. The Turing test should be relegated to the history of science, in the same way that the aim of imitating a bird was eventually abandoned by the pioneers of flight. The development of aircraft succeeded only when people stopped trying to imitate birds:

> *In some ways, aircraft may never match the elegant precision of birds. But in other ways, they outperform them dramatically. Aircraft do not land in trees, scoop fish from the ocean or use the natural breeze to hover motionless above the countryside. But no bird can fly at 45,000 feet or faster than sound.*

Rather than limiting the scope of AI to the study of how to mimic (or reproduce) human behaviour, Ford and Hayes argue that the proper aim of AI is to create a computational science of intelligence itself, whether human, animal or machine. This brings us back to the CTM.

Do we need brains to be brainy?

For supporters of strong AI, our bodies – including our brains – are in no way necessary to our intelligence. In Boden's terms: 'You don't need brains to be brainy' (in Rose, 2003). What she means by this is that you can model mind processes using the latest and most powerful computer systems without paying attention to the underlying biology. Putting it another way, what matters is the program (*software*): the brain (*hardware*) is incidental. Strong AI claims that any physical system capable of carrying out the necessary computational processes can be described as intelligent, even if it's 'made of old beer cans' (in Searle's words). But many, as noted below, have argued that our brains are necessary.

- Flanagan (1984) finds it highly unlikely that our evolutionary history, genes, biochemistry, anatomy and neurophysiology have nothing essential to do with our defining features (even though it remains logically possible).
- Searle (1987) believes that mental states and processes are real biological phenomena in the world, as real as digestion, photosynthesis, lactation and so on (they are 'caused by processes going on in the brain').
- Penrose (1987) agrees that there's more to understanding than just carrying out some appropriate program and that the actual physical construction of the brain is also important. He argues that a computer designed to follow the logical operations of every detail of the workings of the human brain would itself not achieve 'understanding', even though the person whose brain is being considered would claim to understand.
- The earlier generations of computers were essentially *serial processors*. They could perform – although admittedly incredibly quickly – only

one operation at a time in sequence (in a *linear* fashion). AI researchers became convinced that real (biological) brains don't work like this at all, but instead carry out many operations in *parallel* and in a *distributed* manner: many parts of a network of cells are involved in any single function, and no single cell is uniquely involved in any. These considerations caused an explosion of interest in new computer designs based on *parallel distributed processing* (PDP) principles, promising new generations of machines.

- The central principle of this new brain-modelling approach is *connectionism*, based on the idea that the brain is composed of neural networks with multiple connections between them (see Chapter 4). If the aim of AI is to construct models which offer insights into human cognition, then it was necessary to look much more closely at the microstructure of the brain itself, to see if insights into the power of this natural information-processing engine might help develop a more realistic modelling system. Most PDP researchers were interested in how individual components (neurons) might operate collectively to produce the brain's information-processing capacity.
- According to Rose (2003), strong AI's separation of the mind from the brain is a form of mind–body dualism (see Chapter 49). But equally:

> *... the insistence on treating the brain as a sort of black box whose internal biological mechanisms and processes are irrelevant and all that matters is to match input to output, is reminiscent of the behaviourist programme in psychology ...*

CONCLUSIONS: CAN COMPUTERS EVER be LIKE BRAINS?

According to Rose (2003), the very concept of AI implies that intelligence is simply a property of the machine itself. However, the neuronal system of brains, unlike computers, is radically indeterminate:

> *... brains and the organisms they inhabit, above all human brains and human beings, are not closed systems, like the molecules of a gas inside a sealed jar. Instead they are open systems, formed by their own past history and continually in interaction with the natural and social worlds outside, both changing them and being changed in their turn ...*

This is consistent with the view that for a computer to understand the meaning of the symbols it manipulates, it would have to be equipped with a *sensory apparatus* (such as a camera); this would enable it to *see* the objects represented by the symbols (Harnad, in Raley, 2006). Harnad proposes a 'Robotic Turing Test': to merit the label 'thinking', a machine would have to pass the test *and* be connected to the outside world. To build machines that can think, we first need to build their bodies (Hughes, 2011).

Brains are capable of modifying their structural, chemical and physical output in response to environmental events (they're highly *plastic*). They're also extraordinarily resilient in the face of injury, with undamaged parts taking over the function of damaged areas (they're highly *redundant*).

Rose argues that brains process and remember information based on its meaning, which isn't equivalent to information in a computer sense. An essential difference between human and computer memory is that:

> *... each time we remember, we in some sense do work on and transform our memories, they are not simply being called up from store and, once consulted, replaced unmodified. Our memories are re-created each time we remember ... (Rose, 2003)*

(See Chapters 17 and 21.)

At least for the foreseeable future, it seems that brains will continue to outperform computers when doing the kinds of things that they were naturally designed to do.

One of these might be consciousness (see Chapters 4 and 7). Currently, we simply don't know what makes the brain conscious and so we cannot design a conscious machine. But since the brain is a physical entity and is conscious, it must have some design features (presumably physical) which make it conscious (McGinn, 1987). This doesn't mean that a machine *couldn't* be conscious, only that it would have to be the same kind of machine the brain is. Agreeing with Searle, Teichman (1988) states that, while we know that the computer hardware doesn't produce (initiate) the program, it's highly probable that the brain *does* help to produce mental states (see Chapter 49).

Chapter Summary

- The **Behaviourist** view of **PS** as **trial-and-error** and **accidental success** was challenged by the **Gestalt** Psychologists, who looked at how we impose **structure** on a problem.
- **Functional fixedness** is a type of **mental PS set**, in which we fail to see that an object may have functions/uses other than its normal ones. One example of this is the Einstellung **effect**.
- **Algorithms** and **heuristics** are two ways of generating possible solutions to a problem. Algorithms guarantee a solution, but can be time-consuming. Heuristics don't guarantee a solution, but can help produce solutions more quickly, as in **means–end analysis (MEA)**.
- Chess experts are only better at remembering board positions that could appear in an actual game, as opposed to random positions. Chess masters develop **global perceptual schemata** which allow them to see possible threats.
- **Expertise** reduces the strain on **working memory (WM)** by enabling the expert to draw on already available, **domain-specific knowledge** stored in long-term memory (LTM).
- **Expert systems (ESs)** apply knowledge in specific areas (such as medical diagnosis), enabling a computer to function as effectively as a human expert. But human experts cannot always say explicitly how they solve particular problems or make particular decisions.
- **DM** is a special case of PS, in which we already know the possible solutions or choices. According to **compensatory models**, we evaluate how all desirable potential outcomes might compensate for undesirable ones.
- **Non-compensatory models** are less precise but more commonly used approaches, in which not all features of each alternative are considered, and features don't compensate for each other.
- Because of the absence of information and time, rational decisions cannot always be made. So, we often resort to the **availability** and **representativeness heuristics**.
- **Gambling** is a form of **risk-taking** behaviour. Playing the National Lottery can be explained in terms of several heuristic strategies and biases, including the representativeness bias (which can explain the **gambler's fallacy**) and availability bias, **randomness bias, illusory correlation, flexible attribution, illusion of control** and **sunk cost bias.**
- Every general-purpose digital computer is an approximation to a **universal Turing machine**. Although originally designed as powerful calculators, computers are **general-purpose, symbol-manipulating machines**.
- According to **weak AI**, computers merely **simulate/mimic** thought or intelligence, while according to **strong AI**, they literally reproduce/duplicate thinking and intelligence.
- Underlying strong AI is the **computational theory of mind (CTM)**, according to which intelligence is the ability to manipulate symbols. This is as true of a human mind as it is of a computer.
- Searle's **Chinese room thought experiment** is meant to show that the **Turing test** isn't the ultimate test of machine intelligence. But both have been criticised, and human intelligence shouldn't be regarded as the only or truest form of intelligence.
- According to CTM, the possession of a brain/the structure and mode of operation of the human brain are irrelevant. But many biologists, Psychologists and others believe that there must be certain **design features** of the brain that have evolved to make it conscious.
- While digital computers process information in a **serial** fashion, brains operate in a **parallel** and also in a **distributed** manner. These considerations led to the development of **parallel distributed processing (PDP)**.
- Brains and human beings are **open systems**, constantly interacting with the natural and social world. Brains can perform certain tasks that are currently beyond the capability of any computer.

Links with Other Topics/Chapters

Chapter 15 ⟶ The Gestalt approach to PS is directly related to Gestalt *principles of perceptual organisation*

Chapter 12 ⟶ The way that doctors frame the risks involved have been shown to influence *patients' adherence with medical advice and treatment*

Chapters 11 and 49 ⟶ The Behaviourist emphasis on *trial-and-error learning* of *stimulus-response associations* is a *reductionist* account, while the Gestalt emphasis on the relationship between all the elements is a *holistic* approach

Chapter 17 → Chess experts have phenomenal *short-term memory* for board positions – provided they're arranged non-randomly (according to the rules of chess). Knowledge of chess is stored in *long-term memory*

Chapter 22 → The illusory correlation can help explain the formation of *negative stereotypes of racial and other minority groups*

Chapter 21 → Rose's (2003) claim that human memories (unlike a computer's) are re-created each time we remember is closely related to Bartlett's *theory of reconstructive memory*, which has had a major influence on research into *eyewitness testimony* (EWT)

Chapter 49 → According to Rose (2003), the PDP approach is *reductionist*. It takes the neuron as the unit of functioning and tries to simulate some of the brain's known properties using a new generation of supercomputers that perform parallel processing. By contrast, the CTM approach (which attempts to model minds rather than brains) is *holistic*

Chapter 23 → Flexible attribution combines elements of the *actor-observer effect* (AOE) and the *self-serving bias* (SSB)

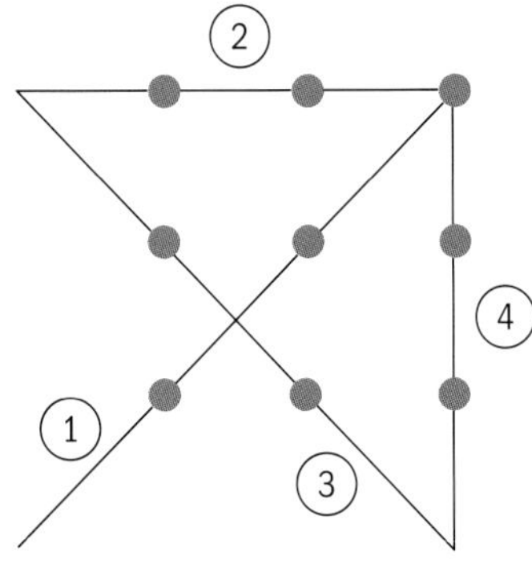

Figure 20.10a Solution to the nine-dot problem

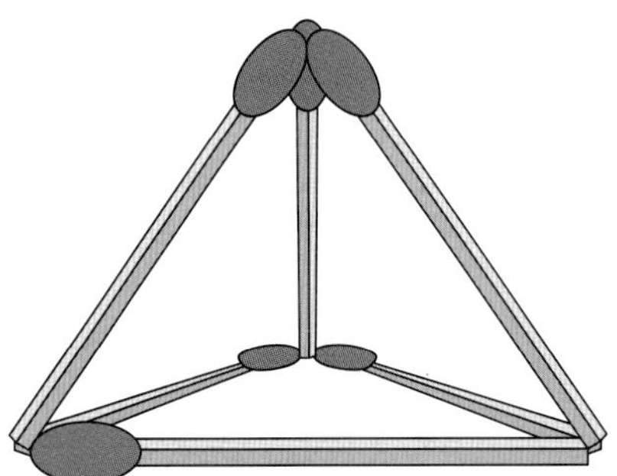

Figure 20.10b Solution to the matchsticks problem

Recommended Reading

Bilalic, M. & McLeod, P. (2014) Why Good Thoughts Block Better Ones. *Scientific American, l 310* (3), 58–63.

Broadbent, D. (ed.) (1993) *The Simulation of Human Intelligence.* Oxford: Blackwell.

Gross, R. (1994) *Key Studies in Psychology* (2nd edition). London: Hodder & Stoughton. Chapter 3.

Rose, S. (2003) *The Making of Memory: From Molecules to Mind* (revised edition). London: Vintage. Chapter 4.

Useful Websites

www.csl.sony.fr (Sony Computer Science Laboratory, Paris)

http://arti.vub.ac.be/ (Artificial Intelligence Laboratory)

www.sjdm.org (Society for Judgement and Decision Making)

http://en.wikipedia.org/wiki/Daniel_Kahneman/ (Daniel Kahneman's webpage)

CHAPTER 21

COGNITION AND THE LAW

- Schema theory and everyday memory
- Reconstructive memory
- Eyewitness testimony (EWT)
- Repression and the false-memory debate

INTRODUCTION and OVERVIEW

This chapter is concerned mainly with *memory* and *forgetting*. But unlike Chapter 17, we'll be focusing on these crucially important cognitive processes from an *applied* perspective. Specifically, how has psychological research into memory and forgetting helped us understand and deal with certain situations that arise within our legal system, in particular, the issue of *eye-witness testimony* (EWT) and the controversy surrounding the *recovery of repressed memories* (sometimes referred to as the *false-memory debate*).

In 1973, the Devlin Committee was set up to look at over 2000 legal cases in England and Wales that had involved identification parades (or line-ups). In 45 per cent of cases, suspects were picked out, and of those people prosecuted after being picked out, 82 per cent were subsequently convicted. Of the 347 cases in which prosecution occurred when EWT was the only evidence against the defendant, 74 per cent were convicted (Devlin, 1976). This indicates the overwhelming weight given to EWT (Baddeley, 1999).

Nevertheless, the *reconstructive* nature of memory has led some researchers to question the accuracy of EWT (e.g. Wells, 1993). The view of memory as reconstructive stems from the work of Bartlett (1932), and central to his theory is the concept of a *schema*. Bartlett has had an enormous impact on Loftus's research into EWT.

Since the early 1990s, considerable publicity has been given to court cases in the USA, where parents are being sued for damages by their teenage or adult children, who accuse them of child sexual abuse (CSA). This has been remembered during the course of psychotherapy. It's assumed that these *recovered memories* had been repressed since the alleged CSA happened, and that the safety and support provided by the therapist allow them to become conscious many years later.

However, accused parents and retractors (those who accused their parents, then later withdrew the accusations) have also sued therapists and hospitals for implanting false memories in the children's minds. The False Memory Syndrome Foundation was set up in the USA in 1992 and, in 1993, the British False Memory Society was founded. *Repression* is a theory of forgetting originally proposed by Freud, regarded by many as at least partly responsible for the phenomenon of *false-memory syndrome*.

SCHEMA THEORY and EVERYDAY MEMORY

It became increasingly obvious during the 1970s that semantic memory (SM) must contain structures considerably larger than the simple concepts involved in Collins and Quillian's (1969) *hierarchical network model* and Collins and Loftus's (1975) *spreading-activation model*. This 'larger unit' is the *schema*, a concept first used by Bartlett (1932) as part of his theory of reconstructive memory (see below).

At the core of schema theory is the belief that what we remember is influenced by what we already know, and that our use of past experience to deal with new experience is a fundamental feature of the way the human mind works. Our knowledge is stored in memory as a set of schemas, simplified, generalised mental representations of everything we understand by a given type of object or event based on our past experience. Schemas operate in a 'top-down' way to help us interpret the 'bottom-up' flood of information reaching our senses from the outside world.

Two major modern schema theories are those of Rumelhart (1975), and Schank (1975) and Schank and Abelson (1977). There's a good deal of overlap between them, and the broad characteristics they share are summarised by Rumelhart and Norman (1983, 1985), as follows:

- A schema is a *packet of information* comprising a *fixed/compulsory value* plus a *variable/optional value.* For example, a schema for buying something in a shop would have relatively fixed slots for the exchange of money and goods, while the variable values would be the amount of money and the nature of the goods. In particular cases, a slot may be left unspecified and can often be filled with a 'default' value (a best guess given the available information).
- *Schemas can be related together to form systems.* They aren't mutually exclusive packets of information, but can overlap. For example, a schema for a picnic may be part of a larger system of schemas including 'meals', 'outings' and 'parties'.
- *Schemas represent knowledge at all levels of abstraction.* They can relate to abstract ideologies, abstract concepts (e.g. justice) or concrete objects (e.g. the appearance of a face).
- *Schemas embody knowledge and experience of the world,* rather than abstract rules.
- *Schemas are active recognition devices.* This is very similar to Bartlett's 'effort after meaning', whereby we try to make sense of ambiguous and unfamiliar information in terms of our existing knowledge and understanding (see below).

According to Schank (1975) and Schank and Abelson (1977), schemas or *scripts* represent commonly experienced social events, such as catching a bus and going to a restaurant. These allow us to fill in much of the detail not specified in any text that we might read. For example:

> *We had a tandoori chicken at the Taj Mahal last night. The service was slow and we almost missed the start of the play ...*

can only be interpreted by bringing in a great deal of additional information (Baddeley, 1990). Scripts are essential ways of summarising common cultural assumptions, which not only help us to understand text and discourse but also predict future events and behave appropriately in given social situations. Scripts contain the sequences of actions we go through when taking part in familiar events, including the sorts of objects and actors we're likely to encounter.

Ask Yourself

- Try writing a script for going to a restaurant, i.e. what sequence of events typically occurs when you go out for a meal, and who's involved at different times?

Figure 21.1 (posed by models)

RECONSTRUCTIVE MEMORY

The Bartlett 'approach'

As we saw in Chapter 17, Ebbinghaus was the first to study memory systematically, using nonsense syllables. Although this 'tradition' is still popular with today's memory researchers, Bartlett (1932) argued that:

- Ebbinghaus's use of nonsense syllables excluded 'all that is most central to human memory'.
- The study of 'repetition habits' had very little to do with memory in everyday life.
- Research should examine people's active search for meaning, rather than their passive responses to meaningless stimuli presented by an experimenter.

Although meaningful material is more complex than meaningless material, Bartlett argued that it, too, could be studied experimentally. As we saw earlier, Bartlett's concept of a schema is central to theories which attempt to explain the structure and organisation of knowledge in SM (a major part of LTM). Because of the large amount of work on the *organisational* aspects of memory (see Chapter 17), and because of the growing recognition of the need to study *meaningful material* (as opposed to lists of unrelated words, numbers and so on), there has been a 'rediscovery' of Bartlett's work.

Serial reproduction and 'The War of the Ghosts'

One method used by Bartlett was *serial reproduction,* in which one person reproduces some material, a second person has to reproduce the first reproduction, a third has to reproduce the second reproduction and so on, until six or seven reproductions have been made. The method is meant to duplicate, to some extent, the process by which gossip or rumours are spread, or legends passed from generation to generation (and may be more familiar as 'Chinese whispers'). One of the most famous pieces of material Bartlett used was '*The War of the Ghosts*', a North American folk tale (see Box 21.1).

Box 21.1 'The War of the Ghosts'

One night two young men from Egulac went down to the river to hunt seals and while they were there it became foggy and calm. Then they heard war-cries and they thought: 'Maybe this is a war party'. They escaped to the shore and hid behind a log. Now canoes came up and they heard the noise of paddles and saw one canoe coming up to them. There were five men in the canoe and they said: 'What do you think? We wish to take you along. We are going up the river to make war on the people'. One of the young men said 'I have no arrows'. 'Arrows are in the canoe', they said. 'I will not go along. I might be killed. My relatives do not know where I have gone. But you', he said, turning to the other, 'may go with them'. So one of the young men went but the other returned home. And the warriors went on up the river to a town on the other side of Kalama. The people came down to the water and they began to fight and many were killed. But, presently, the young man heard one of the warriors say: 'Quick, let us go home; that Indian has been hit'. Now he thought: 'Oh, they are ghosts'. He did not feel sick but they said he had been shot. So the canoes went back to Egulac and the young man went ashore to his house and made a fire. And he told everybody and said: 'Behold, I accompanied the ghosts and we went to fight. Many of our fellows were killed and many of those who attacked us were killed. They said I was hit and I did not feel sick'. He told it all and then he became quiet. When the sun rose he fell down. Something black came out of his mouth. His face became contorted. The people jumped up and cried. He was dead.

When used with English participants, who were unfamiliar with its style and content, the story changed in certain characteristic ways as it was retold.

- The story became noticeably *shorter.* Bartlett found that after six or seven reproductions, it shrank from 330 to 180 words.
- Despite becoming shorter and details being omitted, the story became *more coherent.* No matter how distorted it became, it remained a story: the participants were interpreting the story as a whole, both listening to it and retelling it.
- It also became *more conventional*, retaining only those details which could be easily assimilated to the participants' shared past experiences and cultural backgrounds.
- It became *more clichéd* – any peculiar or individual interpretations tended to be dropped.

Replications of Bartlett's findings

Using the '*The War of the Ghosts'* and the serial reproduction method, Hunter (1964) found similar changes to those originally reported by Bartlett. But the use of this folk tale has been criticised because it's written in an unusual style, making it difficult for western participants to find connections between different parts of the story.

Another method used by Bartlett, *repeated reproduction*, involves the same participants recalling the story on different occasions. This produced similar results to those obtained with serial reproduction. Wynn and Logie (1998) used this alternative method, but they used a real-life event, namely first-year undergraduates' recollections of details of their first week at university. They were asked to recall this information in November, January, March and May (the students being unaware that this would happen).

Contrary to Bartlett's findings, Wynn and Logie found that the accuracy of the descriptions was maintained across the different intervals and regardless of the number of repeated recalls. This suggests that memories for distinctive events can be relatively resistant to change over time, even when repeatedly reproduced.

Schemas and reconstructive memory

Bartlett concluded from his findings that *interpretation* plays a major role in the remembering of stories and past events. Learning and remembering are both active processes involving 'effort after meaning'; that is, trying to make the past more logical, coherent and generally 'sensible'. This involves making *inferences* or *deductions* about what could or should have happened. We reconstruct the past by trying to fit it into our existing understanding of the world (i.e. schemas). Unlike a computer's memory, where the output exactly matches the input, human memory is an 'imaginative reconstruction' of experience.

Schemas (or schemata):

- provide us with ready-made expectations, which help to interpret the flow of information reaching the senses
- help to make the world more predictable
- allow us to 'fill in the gaps' when our memories are incomplete
- can produce significant distortions in memory processes, because they have a powerful effect on the way in which memories for events are encoded; this happens when new information conflicts with existing schemas.

For example, Allport and Postman (1947) showed white participants a picture of two men evidently engaged in an argument (see Figure 21.2).

Cross-Cultural Study 21.1

Remembering as a cultural activity

- An important implication of Bartlett's work is that memory is a *social phenomenon* that cannot be studied as a 'pure' process. Because he emphasised the influence of previous knowledge and background experience, Bartlett found that remembering is integrally related to the social and cultural contexts in which it's practised. When members of western and non-western cultures are compared on tasks devised in Psychology laboratories, such as free-recalling lists of unrelated words, the former do better; this seems to reflect the meaninglessness of such tasks for the latter (see Chapter 17).
- According to Mistry and Rogoff (1994), 'remembering' is an activity with goals whose function is determined by the social and cultural contexts in which it takes place. This helps to explain the phenomenal memory for lines of descent and history of Itamul elders in New Guinea, needed to resolve disputes over claims to property by conflicting clans. Bartlett himself described the prodigious ability of Swazi herdsmen to recall individual characteristics of their cattle. But since Swazi culture revolves around the possession and care of cattle, this ability isn't so surprising.
- What these examples show is that remembering is a means of achieving a culturally important goal, rather than the goal itself (Mistry and Rogoff, 1994).

Figure 21.2 The stimulus material used by Allport and Postman (1947). The two men are engaged in an argument. The better-dressed man is black and the white man has a cut-throat razor in his hand

After looking briefly at the picture, participants were asked to describe the scene to someone who hadn't seen it. This person was then required to describe the scene to another person, and so on. As this happened, details changed. The most significant change was that the cut-throat razor was reported as being held by the black man.

Ask Yourself

- What method was involved in Allport and Postman's experiment?
- What can you infer about the schema that the participants were using, which helps account for the distortion that took place?
- If the participants had been black, would you expect a similar distortion to have taken place?
- Are these results consistent with Bartlett's theory of reconstructive memory? Explain your answer.

Allport and Postman used serial reproduction. Presumably, the white participants used a schema which included the belief that black men are prone to violence. Black participants would be expected to have a rather different schema of black men, making them less likely to distort the details in the picture. Allport and Postman's findings are consistent with Bartlett's theory of reconstructive memory.

EYEWITNESS TESTIMONY (EWT)

Loftus's research

Bartlett's view of memory as reconstructive was adopted by Loftus, who has investigated it mainly in relation to *eyewitness testimony* (EWT). Loftus argues that the evidence given by witnesses in court cases is highly unreliable, and this is explained largely by the kind of *misleading questions* that witnesses are asked. Lawyers are skilled in asking such questions deliberately, as are the police when interrogating suspects and witnesses to a crime or accident.

Loftus has tried to answer the following questions:

- Is EWT influenced by people's tendency to reconstruct their memories of events to fit their schemas?
- Can subtle differences in the wording of a question cause witnesses to remember events differently?
- Can witnesses be misled into 'remembering' things that didn't actually occur?

EWT, episodic memory (EM) and SM

According to Fiske and Taylor (1991), it's easy to see how a witness could confuse the mention of something in a question with its actual presence at the scene of the crime, if that something is commonly found in such situations. For example, a 'leading' question might refer to things that weren't actually present at the scene of the crime (stored in EM), but which might well have been (based on our schemas and stereotyped beliefs about the world stored in SM).

Similarly, a witness who examines a preliminary identification parade may later remember having seen one of the suspects before, but fail to distinguish between the identification parade and the scene of the crime – the innocent suspect may be misidentified as the criminal because s/he is familiar. This can be taken one stage further back. Several studies have shown that when witnesses view a line-up after having looked at mug shots, they're more likely to identify one of those depicted (regardless of whether that person actually committed the crime) than people who aren't shown the mug shot (Memon and Wright, 1999).

These (and the case of the Australian Psychologist below) are examples of *source confusion* (or *misattribution*) – you recognise someone, but you're mistaken about where you know them from. This can have very serious consequences for the person who is misidentified!

The legal status of eyewitness identification

The Devlin Committee Report (1976) (see *Introduction and overview*) recommended that the trial judge be required to instruct the jury that it isn't safe to convict on a single eyewitness's testimony alone, except in exceptional circumstances (such as where the witness is a close friend or relative of the accused, or where there's substantial corroborative evidence).

This recommendation is underlined by a famous case of misidentification involving an Australian Psychologist. The Psychologist in question had appeared in a TV discussion on EWT, and was later picked out in an identity parade by a very distraught woman who claimed that he'd raped her. The rape had in fact occurred while the victim was watching the Psychologist on TV. She correctly recognised his face but not the circumstances!

In fact, Lord Devlin's recommendation was rejected by the judiciary and the Home Office. Instead, juries would be warned of the dangers of honest mistakes by eyewitnesses – a policy still in force today (Davies, 2008). Many of the key factors relating to the nature of the incident that influence an eyewitness's ability to remember it were identified in the 'Turnbull ruling' (1977) and can be recalled using the mnemonic '*ADVOKATE* (Kebbell and Wagstaff, 1999)':

Amount of time suspect was under observation
Distance of the witness from the suspect or event
Visibility (night, day, lighting?)
Obstructions to the witness's view
Knows the suspect or seen before (when and where?)
Any special reason for remembering the suspect?
Time lapse: how long has elapsed since witness saw the suspect?
Error or significant discrepancy between the witness's initial and the suspect's actual appearance.

How useful are these guidelines?

These guidelines seem to have been based on judicial intuition, rather than any systematic review of existing research evidence. Davies (2008) believes that the 'common sense' feel of the list is its weakness. For example, lighting and distance often interact: is a witness more likely to accurately identify a suspect seen under a street light at 25 metres than one seen in a darkened room at 3 metres? *ADVOKATE* cannot answer such questions and only psychological research can help. For example, Davies cites Wagenaar's 'the rule of fifteen', which states that the suspect should be no more than 15 metres away from the witness and lighting should be no less than 15 lux (about the amount of light in a dimly-lit room).

The powerful effect of EWT and EW credibility

Recent convictions for murder and other serious crimes have highlighted the value of DNA profiling and CCTV for securing vital evidence. In the USA, the Innocence Project has used DNA techniques to establish the innocence of people previously convicted on the strength of other evidence (including EWT): many prisoners serving lengthy sentences for rape and murder have been exonerated. Of the first 70 wrongful convictions highlighted by the project, 61 were based on mistaken EW identifications – sometimes by more than one witness. Nevertheless, evidence in the majority of crimes comes in the form of EWT in court (Davies, 2008).

Using a fictitious case, Loftus (1974) asked students to judge the guilt or innocence of a man accused of robbing a grocer's and murdering the owner and his 5-year-old granddaughter. On the evidence presented, only nine of the 50 students considered the man to be guilty. Other students were presented with the same case, but were also told that one of the shop assistants had testified that the accused was the man who had committed the crimes. Thirty-six of these 50 students judged him to be guilty.

A third group of 50 students was presented with the original evidence and the assistant's EWT. However, they were also told that the defence lawyer had discredited the assistant: he was short-sighted, hadn't been wearing his glasses when the crime occurred, and so couldn't possibly have seen the accused's face from where he was standing at the time.

Ask Yourself

- How many students in the third group do you think judged the accused to be guilty?
- Explain your answer and say what this tells us about the importance of EWT.

In fact, 34 out of 50 thought he was guilty! So, a mistaken witness does seem to be 'better' than no witness.

Apart from the impact of EWT itself, what other factors influence EW credibility in the eyes of jurors (see Box 21.2)?

Factors influencing EWT

Factors relating to the incident

ADVOKATE refers mainly to factors relating to the event/crime. Others include *emotional arousal* and *violence/the presence of weapon*.

The weapons-focus effect

Overall, the evidence suggests that memory for violent events is stronger than for a neutral event (Baddeley, 1999). A crime is typically classified as emotionally arousing if emotional stimuli are present at the crime scene (such as a gun). *Weapons-focus effect* (WFE) research has found that memory for certain details (e.g. the perpetrator's face) is impaired, while memory for other details (e.g. a weapon) is enhanced (Hammond and Thole, 2008; Memon and Thomson, 2007). So,

> *... fear may put a crucial feature of a situation into sharp focus, but may reduce the reliability of the witness's account of peripheral features. (Baddeley, 1999)*

Factors relating to the witness

Race: The race of both the witness and the suspect can influence accuracy of identification. Errors are more likely to occur when the suspect and witness are racially *different* (Brigham and Malpass, 1985; Meissner and Brigham, 2001). So, we're much better at recognising members of our own racial groups than members of other racial groups. Memon and Thomson (2007) cite a survey which found that 90 per cent of experts believe that the so-called *cross-race identification effect* (or *own-race bias*) is robust enough to present in court, and mock juror research suggests that the layperson is insensitive to the effect.

Box 21.2 Factors influencing EW credibility?

Confidence: There's ample evidence to suggest that how confident an EW seems is one of the most important factors determining whether or not jurors will believe an EW – regardless of accuracy (Clifasefi *et al.*, 2007). For example, confident witnesses are more likely to be seen as credible (i.e. accurate) compared with anxious witnesses, even though actual accuracy may not differ (Nolan and Markham, 1998). Lindsay *et al.* (1998) found that under the right conditions (e.g. good view of the perpetrator for a lengthy period of time), confidence and accuracy can be positively correlated. However, just because we're confident about something doesn't necessarily mean we're right (Clifasefi *et al.*, 2007).

There are many ways in which an EW can become more confident about his/her initial testimony. For example, Wells *et al.* (2003) have shown that when a witness identifies a suspect in a line-up and then receives feedback (such as, 'Good, you identified the suspect,') the EW becomes more confident that s/he was right – even when the suspect isn't in the line-up.

Detail: Another common misconception about memory is the belief that the amount of detail is related to accuracy. Studies have shown that that the degree of detail contained in an EW statement is an important influence on jurors' decision-making processes (Clifasefi *et al.*, 2007). For example, Bell and Loftus (1989) found that when EWs provide greater detail, they're judged not only as more credible, but also to have a better memory for the perpetrator's face and to have paid more attention to them.

Consistency: EWs who are consistent in their testimony (say, between their initial statement to the police and under cross-examination in court) are more credible. However, the fact that s/he may inaccurately describe one aspect of an incident doesn't mean that s/he's also inaccurate about other details (Clifasefi *et al.*, 2007). In other words, *perceived* consistency and *objective* accuracy aren't strongly correlated.

Emotional intensity: A common belief is that if a person displays a strong emotional response to a particular memory, this is reliable evidence that the event actually happened. However, McNally (2003) found that the belief that one has been traumatised (e.g. abducted by aliens) is sufficient to evoke intense emotional/physiological reactions similar to those displayed by war veterans. Therefore, real and false memories cannot be distinguished by the intensity of emotional reactions (Clifasefi *et al.*, 2007). (See text below.)

Age: The typical finding from laboratory studies of unfamiliar face recognition (recognition of faces seen just once before) is that older adults (60–80 years) are more likely to choose an incorrect face from a line-up of photographs compared with, say, 18–32-year-olds (Memon and Thomson, 2007). This can be explained in terms of reduced perceptual abilities and visual acuity, together with increased difficulty in storing and retrieving information.

At the other extreme, children usually make less effective witnesses than adults; their memories are less efficient and they're less articulate (Hammond and Thole, 2008). According to Sutherland *et al.* (2007), given that researchers have dedicated 20 years or so to investigating how to interview children, how to obtain accurate testimony and how to facilitate their giving of evidence in court, we might expect Psychologists to have 'cracked' it. But they haven't.

Clothing: Witnesses pay more attention to a suspect's clothing than to more stable characteristics, such as height and facial features. It seems that criminals are aware of this, since they change what they wear prior to appearing in a line-up (Brigham and Malpass, 1985).

Social influence: One source of social influence (see Chapter 26) is contact and exchange of information among witnesses. For example, Memon and Wright (1999) describe a study in which participants were asked in pairs whether they'd seen several cars in a previous phase of the study. When responding second, people were influenced by the first person's answers. If the first person said s/he did see the car previously, the second person was more likely to say the same, irrespective of whether the car really was previously seen.

Post-event influences

Misleading questions and suggestibility: It seems that both adults and children are subject to reconstructive errors in recall, particularly when presented with misleading information. In other words, a witness can be highly suggestible. Different types of misleading question include:

1. *Leading questions*, as illustrated by Loftus and Palmer's (1974) experiment (see Key Study 21.1)
2. Questions which introduce *after-the-event information*, as illustrated by Loftus (1975; see Key Study 21.2).

What do leading questions actually do?

Loftus and Palmer wanted to know if memory for events actually changes as a result of misleading questions, or whether the existing memory is merely *supplemented*. Memory-as-reconstruction implies that memory itself is transformed at the point of retrieval, so that what was originally encoded changes when it's recalled.

Key Study 21.1

The effect of leading questions (Loftus and Palmer, 1974)

- Loftus and Palmer tested the effect of changing single words in certain critical questions on the judgement of speed. Participants were shown a 30-second videotape of two cars colliding, and were then asked several questions about the collision.
- One group was asked, 'About how fast were the cars going when they hit?' For others, the word 'hit' was replaced by 'smashed', 'collided', 'bumped' or 'contacted'. These words have very different connotations regarding the speed and force of impact, and this was reflected in the judgements given.
- Those who heard the word 'hit' produced an average speed estimate of 34.0 mph. For 'smashed', 'collided', 'bumped' and 'contacted', the average estimates were 40.8, 39.3, 38.1 and 31.8 mph respectively (see Figure 21.3).

Figure 21.3 Assessments of speeds of crashing vehicles can be influenced by the verb used to describe the impact. While (a) represents 'two cars hitting', (b) represents 'two cars smashing'. Which word is used in a question can influence people's estimates of how fast the cars were travelling at the time of impact

To test this, Loftus and Palmer's (1974) study included a follow-up experiment. A week after the original experiment, those participants who'd heard the word 'smashed' or 'hit' were asked further questions, one of which was whether they remembered seeing any broken glass (even though there was none in the film). If 'smashed' really had influenced participants' memory of the accident as being more serious than it was, then they might also 'remember' details they didn't actually see, but which are consistent with an accident occurring at high speed (such as broken glass).

Of the 50 'smashed' participants, 16 (32 per cent) reported seeing broken glass. Only seven (14 per cent) of the 50 'hit' participants did so. These results appear to support the memory-as-reconstruction explanation.

Similarly, Loftus and Zanni (1975) showed participants a short film of a car accident, after which they answered questions about what they'd witnessed. Some were asked if they'd seen *a* broken headlight, while others were asked if they'd seen *the broken* headlight; the latter were far more likely to say 'yes' than those asked about *a* headlight.

Key Study 21.2

The effect of 'after-the-event' information (Loftus, 1975)

- Participants watched a short film of a car travelling through the countryside. They were all asked the same ten questions about the film, except for one critical question.
  (a) Group A was asked 'How fast was the white sports car going when it passed the 'Stop' sign while travelling along the country road?' (There was a 'Stop' sign in the film.)
  (b) Group B was asked 'How fast was the white sports car going when it passed the barn while travelling along the country road?' (There was no barn.)
- 'The' barn implies that there actually was a barn in the film, which is what makes it misleading.
- A week later, all the participants were asked ten new questions about the film. The final question was 'Did you see a barn?' Of group A participants, only 2.7 per cent said 'yes', while 17.3 per cent of group B participants said 'yes'.

Memory-as-reconstruction sees questions that provide misleading new information about an event (as with leading questions) becoming integrated with how the event is already represented in memory.

Suggestibility and source misattribution

As the Loftus studies show, witnesses may come to believe that they actually remember seeing items in an event that in fact have been (falsely) suggested to them. Currently, the most popular explanation for suggestibility effects is *source misattribution*. Witnesses are confusing information obtained outside the context of the witnessed event (*post-event information*) with the witnessed event itself (Memon and Wright, 1999). Memories of details from various sources can be combined with memories of that event (*memory blending*). (For a review of 'Earwitness testimony', see Dunn, 2013.)

An evaluation of Loftus's research

- While the evidence described above suggests that eyewitnesses are unreliable, are they really as unreliable as Loftus believes?
- Bekerian and Bowers (1983) have argued that Loftus questions her witnesses in a rather unstructured way. If questions followed the order of events in strict sequence, then witnesses weren't influenced by the biasing effect of subsequent questions. Despite some failures to replicate these findings (e.g. McCloskey and Zaragoza, 1985), an important practical consequence of Bekerian and Bower's research is the cognitive interview (see Box 21.3).
- Contrary to the memory-as-reconstruction interpretation, Baddeley (1995) believes that 'the Loftus effect is not due to destruction of the memory trace but is due to interfering with its retrieval' (see Chapter 17).
- Stephenson (1988) points out that the bulk of the work on EWT has been carried out in laboratories, and has concentrated on eyewitness identification of people seen under fairly non-threatening conditions, or even people seen on films. In sharp contrast was a study of eyewitness accounts of a shooting which occurred outside a gun shop in full view of several witnesses (in Vancouver, Canada) (Yuille and Cutshall (1986): see Case study 21.1).
- Loftus herself acknowledges that when misleading information is 'blatantly incorrect', it has no effects on a witness's memory. For example, Loftus (1979) showed participants colour slides of a man stealing a red purse from a woman's bag. 98 per cent correctly identified the purse's colour and, when they read a description of the event which referred to a 'brown purse', all but 2 per cent continued to remember it as red. This suggests that our memory for obviously important information accurately perceived at the time isn't easily distorted, as shown by Yuille and Cutshall's (1986) study.

Case Study 21.1

Eyewitness memory of a crime (Yuille and Cutshall, 1986)

- Twenty-one of the witnesses were interviewed by the police shortly after the event, and 13 of them agreed to take part in a research interview four to five months later. In both sets of interviews (police and research), verbatim accounts of the incident were obtained and follow-up questions were asked in order to clarify points of detail. Also, Yuille and Cutshall asked two misleading questions based on Loftus's 'a broken headlight'/'the broken headlight' technique.
- The sheer volume of accurate detail produced in both sets of interviews is truly impressive. The researchers obtained much more detail than did the police, because they were concerned with memory for details which had no immediate forensic value. Witnesses who were central to the event gave more details than did peripheral witnesses, but there was no overall difference in accuracy between the two groups.
- Significantly, the wording of the misleading questions had no effect and those who were most deeply distressed by the incident were the most accurate of the witnesses.

- According to Cohen (1993), people are more likely to be misled if:
  (a) the false information they're given concerns insignificant details that aren't central to the main event
  (b) the false information is given after a delay (when the memory of the event has had time to fade)
  (c) they have no reason to distrust it.

The cognitive interview

An increasing number of police forces are using the *cognitive interview* (CI). Traditionally, police officers and lawyers have used the standard interview procedure, which involves a period of free recall about the event, followed by specific questions about details that emerge from the free recall. The CI draws on Tulving's research concerning the relationship between encoding and retrieval cues (see Chapter 17); the four principles ('mnemonics') described in Box 21.3 are designed to enhance both the quantity and quality of the information produced.

The first two 'stages' are based on the concept of *encoding specificity*, that is, trying to provide maximum overlap between the context in which the crime was committed and the context in which the recall attempt is made. The second two try to capitalise on the idea that material can be retrieved using a number of different routes that may produce information about rather different aspects of the original event (Baddeley, 1999).

Box 21.3 The cognitive interview (Geiselman *et al.*, 1985)

Reinstating the context: The interviewer and interviewee try to recreate the context in which the incident occurred (the surroundings, such as the temperature, smells, sounds, the witness's feelings) before any attempt is made to recall the events themselves.
Reporting the event: The interviewee is asked to report absolutely *everything*, regardless of how unimportant/irrelevant it may seem.
Recalling the event in several orders: This includes reporting the event in *reverse* order.
Reporting the event from multiple perspectives: The interviewee is asked to recall the event from, say, the perspective of the cashier in the case of a bank robbery.

The initial test of the CI (Geiselman *et al.*, 1985) used a police training film of a violent crime. Participants were interviewed 48 hours later, using either the new CI, or the standard Los Angeles police interview, or hypnosis prior to being asked to recall the incident using the standard procedure. Although the three methods didn't differ in the amount of false information they produced, the standard interview produced the least overall amount of information (an average of 29.4 items); the CI produced *the most* (41.2 items).

A second experiment introduced misleading information during the interview: 'Was the guy with the green backpack nervous?' (It wasn't green.) Those tested with the CI were the *least likely* to be misled by false information.

Fisher and Geiselman (1988) have continued to develop the CI, using hints obtained from watching 'good' and 'poor' interviewers. These include the greater use of open-ended questions and attempts to fit the order of questioning to the witness's order of experience. This has increased accurate reporting from 40 to 60 per cent. Bekerian and Dennett (1993) reviewed 27 experiments comparing the effects of the CI with more standard techniques. The CI proved superior in all cases: on average, about 30 per cent more information is accurately reported, with false information being slightly less common.

Harrower (1998) maintains that the CI procedure may be particularly beneficial for those interviewing child witnesses, especially those who may have been the victims of physical or sexual abuse. However, the interviewer must be trained in assessing the linguistic and cognitive competence of each child interviewee, and adapt the interview accordingly.

Some remaining problems with the CI

Despite its obvious superiority over standard interview techniques, which have led to its use by police forces and law enforcement agencies all over the worlds, there are still problems associated with the approach (Hammond *et al.*, 2006):

- If used inaccurately, or by untrained interviewers, the CI can produce a notable number of errors and inaccurate information. (But is this a limitation of the technique itself?)
- Police officers often encounter difficulties using the CI, sometimes failing to follow the correct procedures. (Again, is this the 'fault' of the CI?)
- Using a CI can be time-consuming, both in terms of interviewer training and the interview itself. It requires rapport-building (to help the witness relax), as well as free and cued recall. Establishing a supportive working relationship with the interviewee can be challenging – especially when the interviewee is the suspect. The CI assumes a willing respondent, keen to remember as much as possible; with an unwilling suspect, the interview has to take a very different form (Canter, 2010).

However, overall the CI has proven a valuable means of enhancing EWT and continues to be endorsed by police forces, academics and forensic practitioners alike (Hammond and Thole, 2008).

Ask Yourself

- Without looking back at the photograph on p. 346 of two men involved in a violent incident, try to answer the following questions.
  1. What are the two men doing?
  2. In which hand is one of the men holding a knife?
  3. Are both men clean-shaven?
  4. Is there anyone else in the picture?
  5. How would you describe the man who isn't holding the knife?
- Now look back at the photograph and check your answers.

Recognising faces

While the face isn't the only route to person identification, it's probably the most reliable (Bruce and Young, 1998). Laboratory experiments have shown that people are remarkably accurate at remembering briefly viewed, previously unfamiliar faces, typically scoring over 90 per cent correct when asked to decide which of a large set of faces were previously presented. But this may seem to be at odds with our sometimes embarrassing failure to recognise or identify faces in everyday life (e.g. Young *et al.*'s 1985 diary study).

Figure 21.4 Bill Clinton and Al Gore? Same face, different hair

Helping people to remember faces

Two major techniques used to probe witnesses' memory for faces are *reconstruction* and *identification*.

Reconstruction

Reconstruction involves producing, from the witness's description, an image of the criminal for circulation to other police forces or for the general public. This may involve the use of *forensic artists,* who use pencils or crayons to sketch the face by hand. More typically, the witness, with or without a trained operator, tries to construct a target face using a 'kit' of isolated facial features. Performance using Photofit (and other similar 'kits', such as PRO-fit: Frowd *et al.*, 2008) is generally very poor (e.g. Ellis *et al.*, 1978). One problem is that kits assume that a face can be deconstructed into its component parts. But facial identity may be more holistic than this, and relationships between features are at least as important as the features themselves (see Chapter 14). Photofit offers only limited opportunities for the manipulation of such factors. There's a small number of 'cardinal' features, which people use regularly and reliably to describe and categorise faces (such as face shape, hair and age), but these are difficult to manipulate directly using Photofit (Bruce and Young, 1998).

The rapid development of powerful computer graphics at relatively low cost has made it possible to develop more interactive systems. E-fit, for example, although still based around a basic 'kit' of photographic face parts, provides much greater opportunity for the blending and elaboration of these parts. This results in much more realistic images (Bruce and Young, 1998). Currently, as a witness gives a description of, say, the eyes, the computer chooses the best set of eyes for you. The witness doesn't see the face until it's completed. However, a modified 'jigsaw' E-fit, being pioneered by the UK Face Processing Research Group, allows the witness to watch the face being built up. But because it's important that the features are always seen as part of a face, a cartoon outline and features are used to replace those elements that haven't yet been described (Greenhaigh, 2000).

Figure 21.5 An E-fit face

It's possible to reduce the perceptual impact of the external features of an unfamiliar face by using a Gaussian filter, a 'blurring technique' which allows the inner face to appear more prominent while maintaining a complete face context (important for holistic face-processing). Preliminary research suggests that this technique significantly improves the quality of internal features recognition (Frowd *et al.*, 2008).

Even with a good view of the criminal's face and the use of CI techniques, many witnesses are unable to provide a satisfactory description. Building on witnesses' confidence that they could recognise the person if they saw them again, several researchers are designing composite systems based more on recognition than recall. One example is EvoFIT (Frowd *et al.*, 2004). This presents sets of whole faces, 18 per screen. Witnesses select faces that look something like the criminal's and EvoFIT 'breeds' them together to produce another set. While the initial faces have random characteristics, repeating the selection and breeding procedure a few times normally allows a good likeness to 'evolve' (Frowd *et al.*, 2008).

Identification

Identification involves looking through photographs in an album of 'mug shots', or looking at a live 'line-up'/identity parade of potential offenders. Witnesses can be unconsciously nudged into selecting the person the police believe is the offender; they may also feel pressurised into selecting *someone* (Canter, 2010).

REPRESSION and the FALSE-MEMORY DEBATE

Motivated-forgetting theory (repression)

According to Freud (1901), forgetting is *motivated*, rather than the result of a failure to learn or other processes. Memories which are likely to induce guilt, embarrassment, shame or anxiety are actively, but unconsciously, pushed out of consciousness as a form of ego defence (see Chapter 42):

> *The essence of repression lies simply in turning something away, and keeping it at a distance, from the conscious ... (Freud, 1915)*

Unconscious or repressed memories are exceedingly difficult to retrieve (they're *inaccessible*) but remain *available* ('in storage': see Chapter 17). They continue to exert a great influence over us, even though we have no awareness of them.

Evidence for repression

Clinical evidence

It's widely accepted that repression plays a crucial role in different types of *psychogenic* (or *functional*) *amnesia*, such as *fugue* and *multiple personality* (or *dissociative identity*) *disorder* (see Gross, 2008). These disorders involve a loss of memory associated with a traumatic experience (as opposed to brain injury or surgery). A relatively common form of psychogenic amnesia is *event-specific amnesia*: loss of memory for a fairly specific period of time. For instance, some violent criminals claim they cannot remember carrying out their crimes (see Chapter 46). Even when we have ruled out both malingering and the effects of intoxication at the time the crime was committed, there's still a substantial number of criminals whose memories of their crimes seem to have been repressed (Parkin, 1993). This is especially likely when murder victims are close relatives or lovers of the murderer killed in a crime of passion (Taylor and Kopelman, 1984).

Contrary to what we might expect, in a study of children who'd seen a parent killed, none showed evidence of repression; on the contrary, the experience tended to be recalled all too frequently (Baddeley, 1999). This, and the observation that psychogenic amnesia can disappear as suddenly as it appeared, are difficult for motivated-forgetting theory to explain.

Parkin (1993) also cites evidence that repressive mechanisms may play a beneficial role in enabling people with *post-traumatic stress disorder* (PTSD) to adjust (see Chapter 44). For example, survivors of the Holocaust judged to be better adjusted were significantly less able to recall their dreams when woken from REM sleep (see Chapter 7) than less well-adjusted survivors (Kaminer and Lavie, 1991).

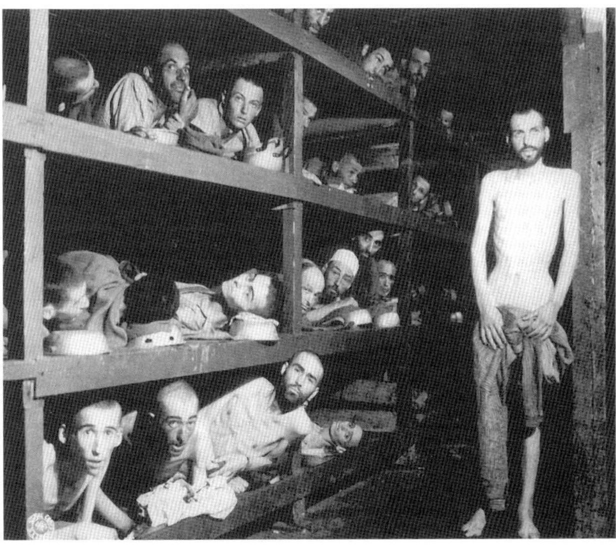

Figure 21.6 For those who endured them, are these horrors best forgotten?

However, 'repression' doesn't necessarily imply a strictly Freudian interpretation. When the concept is considered more broadly than Freud intended, that is, in the general sense that our memory systems can in some way block particular forms of memory, it deserves to be taken seriously (Parkin, 2000). This is also the view taken by the British Psychological Survey (BPS) on 'Recovered Memories' (BPS, 1995: see below). Similarly, although traumatic experiences can undoubtedly produce memory disturbances, there's greater doubt as to whether Freud's explanation is the best one (Anderson, 1995a).

Experimental evidence

Key Study 21.3

Testing Freud's repression hypothesis (Levinger and Clark, 1961)

- Levinger and Clark looked at the retention of associations to negatively charged words (such as 'quarrel', 'angry', 'fear') compared with those for neutral words (such as 'window', 'cow', 'tree').
- When participants were asked to give immediate free associations to the words (to say exactly what came into their minds), it took them longer to respond to the emotional words. These words also produced higher galvanic skin responses (GSR: a measure of emotional arousal).
- Immediately after the word association tests had been completed, participants were given the cue words again and asked to try to recall their associations. They had particular trouble remembering the associations to the emotionally charged words.
- This is exactly what Freud's repression hypothesis predicted, and for some years the study stood as the best experimental demonstration of repression (Parkin, 1993).

However, other studies show that, while highly arousing words tend to be poorly recalled when tested immediately, the effect *reverses* after a delay (Eysenck and Wilson, 1973). If the words are being repressed, this shouldn't happen (they should stay repressed), suggesting that *arousal* was the crucial factor.

Ask Yourself

- If you were to repeat the Levinger and Clark experiment, what change would you introduce in order to test the 'arousal hypothesis'?

Parkin *et al.* (1982) replicated the original study, but added a *delayed recall* condition: participants were asked to recall their associations seven days after the original test. The results supported Eysenck and Wilson's interpretation – higher arousal levels inhibit immediate recall but increase longer-term recall. Bradley and Baddeley (1990) used an immediate and a 28-day delayed condition and found clear support for the arousal hypothesis. But later research hasn't always supported the arousal interpretation, and the question of emotional inhibition remains open (Parkin, 1993). (Further evidence relating to repression can be found in Chapters 2 and 42.)

Recovered memories and the false-memory debate

As noted in the *Introduction and overview*, from the perspective of adults who accuse their parents of CSA and their therapists, the discovery of repressed memories are *recovered memories* (RMs). However, from the perspective of the accused parents, these are *false memories* (FMs), implanted by therapists into the minds of their emotionally vulnerable patients/clients. These unethical, unscrupulous therapists are, in turn, accused by parents of practising *recovered-memory therapy*, which induces *false-memory syndrome* (FMS).

This brief account of the FM debate raises several, interrelated issues, spanning the psychology of memory and forgetting, the nature of psychotherapy (in particular, Freudian psychoanalysis), and the ethics of psychotherapy in general. When children sue their parents over alleged CSA, the family is inevitably torn apart and individual lives can be ruined. But the false memory debate has also caused division amongst Psychologists, as well as between Psychologists and psychiatrists. Key questions that need to be asked are:

1. Do RMs exist?

2. Do FMs exist? If so, how might they be created?

Do recovered memories exist?

The answer to this question depends very largely on how the concept of repression is understood. If these memories have been repressed and are now retrieved from the unconscious during the course of therapy, then there must first be sound evidence for the existence of repression. When discussing repression above, we saw that the strongest evidence is clinical, but that this is far from conclusive. We also need to take a closer look at Freud's view of memory. (See Box 21.4.)

Box 21.4 Freud and Screen Memories

According to Mollon (2000), it's sometimes asserted that Freud believed that the events of a person's life are all recorded accurately somewhere in the mind, like video recordings. They're supposedly preserved in their original form, available but made inaccessible by repression.
However, in a paper on *Screen Memories* (1899), Freud argued that memories, especially of events of long ago, may be constructed like dreams. A 'screen memory' is one that's apparently emotionally insignificant, but is actually a substitute for a more troubling memory with which it's become associated. However, the distinction between screen memories and other memories from childhood is unclear:

> *... Our childhood memories show us our earliest years not as they were but as they appeared at the later periods when the memories were aroused. In these periods of arousal, the childhood memories did not, as people are accustomed to say, emerge; they were found at that time. And a number of motives, with no concern for historical accuracy, had a part in forming them, as well as in the selection of the memories themselves. (Freud, 1899)*

Thus, Freud argued that memories of childhood may not be what they seem. The subjective sense of remembering doesn't mean that the memory is literally true. Memories are like dreams or works of fiction, constructed out of psychodynamic conflict, serving wish-fulfilment and self-deception (see Chapter 45). True memories of childhood may simply be unobtainable. Our apparent memories may be fabrications created later (Mollon, 2000).

If Freud is right, then RMs can no longer be memories of actual CSA, but *phantasies* of abuse. This reflects Freud's rejection of the *seduction theory* in favour of the Oedipal theory (see Chapter 35). Essentially, these correspond to actual abuse and phantasised abuse, respectively, as causes of adult neurosis. But, rightly or wrongly:

> *... that adult emotional disorders originate from repression of memories of experiences in early childhood which can be 'uncovered' by psychoanalysis ... [is] ... part and parcel of Freud's heritage. ... [It is an] essential element ... in the recovered memory therapist's armoury. (Esterson, 2000: personal communication)*

Freud appears to be in a no-win situation. Esterson claims that Freud's theory of repression and his therapeutic methods are the basic tools of RM therapists, which makes Freud the arch-enemy of accused parents. However, if memories are essentially *constructed*, rather than 'discovered' or 'recovered' ('unearthed' to use an archaeological analogy which Freud himself used), it becomes easier to understand how FMS occurs: vulnerable patients can easily be 'persuaded' that a constructed memory (a phantasy that CSA took place) is, in fact, an objectively true, historically verifiable event (the CSA actually happened).

MEET THE RESEARCHER

Elizabeth F. Loftus

Illusions of memory

Memory is a funny thing, especially when it goes awry. A good example came to light in early 2008, when Hillary Clinton was running for the Presidency of the USA. While campaigning, she recalled a harrowing trip she had taken to Bosnia some 12 years earlier, 'I remember landing under sniper fire ... There was supposed to be some kind of a greeting ceremony at the airport, but instead we just ran with our heads down to get into the vehicles to get to our base.' Her memory ran into trouble when the media began showing photographs of her actual arrival in Bosnia that day. These photos depicted a peaceful landing; she walked from the helicopter with her daughter as they were greeted peacefully by schoolchildren. After thorough fact-checking – and interviews with celebrities who had joined the trip to entertain the troops – proved her memory was wrong, one commentator gave Hillary's memory 'four Pinocchios'. The memory was wrong in at least four ways. There was no 'corkscrew' landing, nor was there any sniper fire. There was no cancelled airport reception, only that greeting from the schoolchildren. And she was not the first wife of a US President to go into a war zone (Alter, 2008).

The research that I and many other psychological scientists have done has taught us about the malleability of human memory. Thousands of experiments conducted over the last century reveal this truth: despite the value of human memory for allowing us to manage our lives effectively, it is not very hard to get people to remember things that never happened. What Hillary's tale tells us is that vivid and detailed memory distortions can even happen to highly intelligent, highly educated, almost-presidents of the USA.

Studying memory distortion

In initial studies, conducted in the 1970s, I showed what can happen when a person sees a crime or accident and is later questioned about the incident in a biased way. Since then, hundreds of studies have documented the ways in which exposure to misinformation can supplement, contaminate or distort our memories. We pick up misinformation not only from biased and leading questions, but also from other people who (consciously or inadvertently) give us an erroneous version of a past event (Loftus, 2005). Inaccuracy in memory caused by erroneous information provided after an event is known in psychology as the *misinformation effect*.

Rich false memories

To explore whether highly suggestive therapy procedures (e.g. guided imagery, dream interpretation, hypnosis and exposure to false information) could lead to rich false memories, researchers developed procedures that were inspired by some of the problematic therapies. Using suggestion, my colleagues and I initially got people to believe that when they were children they had been lost in a shopping mall for an extended time. The *lost-in-the-mall technique* used information obtained from their parents to help create scenarios that described some true events and also the false event about getting lost. The scenarios were then fed to participants as if they were entirely true. In that initial work, about one-quarter of participants fell sway to the misinformation and claimed to have been lost in the suggested fashion.

Later research using this technique showed that people would also accept suggestions that they experienced events that were more bizarre and upsetting. In one study, about one-third of participants were persuaded that as children they had nearly drowned and had to be rescued by a lifeguard. In another, researchers succeeded in convincing half of participants that something as horrible as being a victim of a vicious animal attack had occurred in their childhood (Loftus, 2003).

False memory?

Subsequent work showed that comparatively subtle suggestions can also lead people to develop false beliefs and memories. One such technique, common in some psychotherapy offices, is *guided imagination*, in which a therapist says something like, 'You don't remember your abuse, but you have all the symptoms. Why don't you just close your eyes and try to imagine who might have done it?' This technique persists despite good evidence that imagining an event that didn't happen (like breaking a window with your hand) can lead people to think that it did happen. Researchers call this phenomenon *imagination inflation*.

Using suggestive procedures, researchers have been able to get people to remember all sorts of things that did not happen, including the implausible or even impossible. In several studies, participants were led to believe they had met Bugs Bunny at a Disney resort after exposure to a single fake advertisement. Participants look at the advert and evaluate it on a variety of characteristics. Later, many participants will claim they met Bugs at Disney even though this could not have happened because Bugs Bunny is a Warner Brothers character.

False memories matter

My own research on memory distortion has recently taken a new twist. After years of planting false memories into the minds of experimental participants, my collaborators and I became interested in the *consequences* of planting memories. Our earliest effort to explore this issue involved planting a false memory about being sick as a child after eating either hard-boiled eggs or dill pickles. After planting this belief, participants were less inclined to want to eat the foods at an outdoor party. The same thing happened when we planted a false memory about being sick on a fattening food – strawberry ice cream (Bernstein *et al.*, 2005). We and others have shown that such planted memories can influence eating behaviour and continued their influence for quite some time (Scoboria *et al.*, 2008; Geraerts *et al.*, 2008). Moreover, false positive memories about a healthy food (asparagus) also had repercussions. Participants who fell for the suggestions said they liked asparagus better than controls, that they wanted to eat it more, that they would pay more for asparagus and that they found photographs of asparagus more appealing (Laney *et al.*, 2008). Taken together, these findings take us beyond the mere demonstrations that memory is malleable and can be supplemented or altered by new information. They show that memory distortions can have repercussions for people – affecting behaviours that occur long after the pseudomemories have taken hold. Of course, along with this power to contaminate memory and control behaviour come some ethical considerations. When should we use this kind of mind technology and should we ever ban its use?

False memories and society

Communicating what we have learned to the broader public will go a long way towards minimising the damage that false memories can cause. If there is one lesson to be learned from our findings, it is this: just because a memory is expressed with confidence, just because it contains detail, just because it is expressed with emotion, does not mean it really happened. We cannot yet reliably discriminate true memories from false ones; we still need independent corroboration. Advances in neuroimaging and other techniques may one day aid in this endeavour. But in the meantime, we as a society would do well to continually keep in mind that memory – like liberty – is fragile.

Professor Elizabeth Loftus is Professor of Psychology and adjunct Professor of Law at the University of Washington. She received her PhD in Psychology from Stanford University in 1970. Her research has focused on human memory, eyewitness testimony and courtroom procedure. Her book *Eyewitness Testimony* won a National Media Award from the American Psychological Foundation.

In defence of Freud, Ofshe (in Jaroff, 1993) contends that RM therapists have invented a mental mechanism ('robust' repression) that supposedly causes a child's awareness of sexual abuse to be driven entirely from consciousness. There's no limit to the number of traumatic events that can be repressed, or to the length of time over which the series of events can occur.

According to Loftus (in Jaroff, 1993), the idea of repression as a trauma filter or blocker which pops up at any sign of trouble to shield us from harm only to fail years later and redeliver us a complete enough picture to shock us once more goes against the very concept of memory. She believes repression is the mind's choice to avoid thinking about a disagreeable experience, and it can only hold out for so long before thoughts creep back in.

Many practising psychotherapists would agree with Loftus. A report published in the *British Journal of Psychiatry* (Brandon *et al.*, 1998) distinguishes between (a) CSA that's reported in childhood or kept secret although unforgotten, and (b) RMs of CSA, previously completely forgotten, that emerge in adulthood during therapy, usually in women in their thirties or forties. For some patients, RMs can escalate into FMS, in which a person's identity comes to centre around the:

> *... memory of a traumatic experience which is objectively false but in which the person strongly believes ... The individual avoids confrontation with any evidence that might challenge the memory ...*

Brandon *et al.* summarise the findings of studies that have compared these two kinds of CSA:

- 90 per cent of RM patients are women, while in documented abuse cases the sex ratio is close to 50:50
- While only 3 per cent of RM accusations are made against stepfathers, they are much more likely to be involved in documented childhood cases
- While documented abuse usually involves older children or adolescents, RM cases recall abuse before the age of four, or even in infancy.

Ask Yourself

- What conclusions can you draw from these reported differences about the validity of RMs?
- Do you find it plausible that we can recall events that happened to us as infants?
- What's your earliest childhood memory?

How might FMs be created?

In 'Meet the Researcher' (pp. 358–359), Loftus (who has been voted the most influential female Psychologist of all time: Sutton, 2013) describes her more recent research into what she calls 'Rich FMs'. One of these (Laney *et al.*, 2008) investigated the long-term consequences of FMs concerning asparagus (see Gross, 2012b). More recently still, she explored the impact of receiving a false suggestion about becoming ill after drinking rum or vodka before the age of 16 (Clifasefi *et al.*, 2013). Results indicated that participants who received this suggestion reported increased confidence that this had, indeed, happened; they also showed a strong tendency to report reduced liking of this alcohol. While further research clearly needs to explore the behavioural effects of such false suggestions and its implications for alcohol interventions, the researchers acknowledge the ethical issues raised by this type of research (see Chapter 48).

CONCLUSIONS

McNally and Geraerts (2009) propose that some memories of CSA are indeed recovered spontaneously, *not* because they've been repressed, but because either (a) the experience hasn't been recalled since it occurred, or (b) prior recollections have been forgotten. The abuse probably wasn't perceived as traumatic at the time (consistent with many real-life accounts and helping to explain why it may take so long to be recalled), although reappraising the experience as an adult is often traumatic. They conclude by saying that a genuine recovered CSA memory doesn't require repression, trauma or even complete forgetting.

The fact that FMs can be created doesn't mean that all RMs are false (Loftus, 1997). The BPS has published a draft set of new guidelines for Psychologists working with clients in contexts in which issues related to RMs may arise. The preamble states that:

> *... There can be no doubt for psychologists of the existence of ... (CSA) as a serious social and individual problem with long-lasting effects. In addition, there can be little doubt that at least some recovered memories of CSA are recollections of historical events. However, there is a genuine cause for concern that some interventions may foster in clients false beliefs concerning CSA or can lead them to develop illusory memories.*
> *(Frankland and Cohen, 1999)*

Based on their review of the research, Clifasefi *et al.* (2013) challenge the notion that memory is permanent: when we remember experiences, we often incorporate new information or interpret things in line with what we believe to be true now. People can be confident, emotional, detailed and consistent in their EWT and their memories can still be mistaken.

... False memories can be created precisely because they are not entirely false. They are made up of some false things combined together to make a false event. They are not spun out of whole cloth so much as woven from the idiosyncrasies of our lives. (Clifasefi et al., 2013)

Chapter Summary

- **Schema theory** sees schemas as the 'units' of SM, rather than simple concepts. Our knowledge is stored in memory as simplified mental representations of objects and events, which we use to interpret new experiences. One influential form of schema theory is the notion of **scripts**.
- Bartlett introduced the concept of **schema** to help explain how we remember **meaningful material,** such as stories. Memory isn't a 'pure' process that can be studied outside the **social/cultural contexts in** which it takes place.
- Bartlett used **serial reproduction** to study **reconstructive memory,** which uses schemas (schemata) to interpret new information. While schemas help to make the world more **predictable,** they can also **distort** our memories.
- Loftus has applied Bartlett's view of memory as reconstructive to the study of **eyewitness testimony (EWT)**. The Devlin Committee recommended that convictions shouldn't be based on a single EWT alone (except in exceptional circumstances).
- **Source confusion/misattribution** can account for why suspects may be mistakenly selected from line-ups/identification parades. EWT appears to be a persuasive source of evidence, even if the witness is discredited by the defence lawyer.
- Factors influencing EWT include those relating to the **incident** (as reflected in ADVOKATE, plus the **weapons-focus effect/WFE**), and the **witness** (such as **race, age, clothing** and **social influence**).
- **Post-event influences** include **misleading questions**, which can take the form of either **leading questions** or those which introduce **after-the-fact information**. Both types can induce **reconstructive errors**.
- Loftus believes that leading questions actually **change** the memory for events, rather than merely **supplementing** the existing memory. The 'Loftus effect' may relate only to the **retrieval** of the original memory.
- Blatantly incorrect information has no effect on EWT. People are more likely to be misled if the false information is insignificant, presented after a delay, and believable.
- An alternative to the standard witness interview is the **cognitive interview (CI)**, which involves **reinstating the context**, **reporting the event** and **recalling the event in several orders** and from **several perspectives**.
- Witnesses can be helped to remember **faces** through the use of 'kits' such as **Photofit, E-fit**, and **EvoFIT**. These are aids to memory **reconstruction**, while line-ups are designed to help witness **identification**.
- According to Freud's **motivated-forgetting theory**, unacceptable memories are made inaccessible through **repression**.
- While cases of **psychogenic amnesia** are consistent with Freud's theory, a strictly Freudian interpretation may not be necessary and experimental support for the repression hypothesis is inconclusive.
- There is currently great controversy over **recovered memories (RMs)** of CSA and **false-memory syndrome.** RM therapists are accused of implanting **false memories (FMs)** of CSA into patients, while patients accuse their parents of the abuse.

Links with Other Topics/Chapters

Chapter 4 → The term 'schema' was borrowed from the neurologist Henry Head, who used it to represent a person's concept of the location of limbs and body: see Penfield's *homunculus*

Chapter 20 → Schank and Abelson (1977) built their scripts into a *computer program* (SAM), which they claim is capable of answering questions about restaurants and understanding stories about restaurants

Chapter 22 → *Stereotypes* are a type of schema that help to explain Allport and Postman's findings, as well as other evidence relating to *selective remembering*

Chapter 17 → The cognitive interview draws on Tulving's research into the relationship between *encoding* and *retrieval cues*

Chapter 14 → Photofit, E-fit and EvoFIT are based on the assumption that faces can be deconstructed into their *component parts*. But facial identity is much more *holistic* than this – it's the *relationship between the features* that's crucial

Chapter 46 → Some of the *clinical* support for Freud's theory of repression comes from the *event-specific amnesia of violent criminals* for their crimes

Chapters 45 and 48 → The FM debate raises fundamental questions regarding the very nature of our memories of childhood, as well as the *nature of psychotherapy*. It also highlights some of the *ethical issues* (Chapter 45) relating to psychotherapy, including therapist *power* and the patient *vulnerability*

Recommended Reading

Gross, R. (2012b) *Key Studies in Psychology* (6th edition). London: Hodder Education. Chapter 2.

Loftus, E.F. (1997) Creating false memories. *Scientific American, 277*(3), 50–5.

Mollon, P. (2000) *Freud and False Memory Syndrome.* Cambridge: Icon Books.

Useful Websites

www.bartlett.psychol.cam.ac.uk (The F.C. Bartlett Archive)

http://faculty.washington.edu/eloftus (Elizabeth Loftus website)

www.EvoFIT.co.uk (The EvoFIT website)

www.bfms.org.uk (British False Memory Society/BFMS)

www.jimhopper.com/memory (Recovered Memories of Sexual Abuse: Scientific Research and Scholarly Resources)

www.fmsfonline.org (False Memory Syndrome Foundation)

http://blogs.brown.edu/recoveredmemory/ (The Recovered Memory Project)

CHAPTER 22

SOCIAL PERCEPTION

INTRODUCTION and OVERVIEW

Social (or person) perception refers to the perception of people (as opposed to physical objects: see Figure 22.1). The focus of this chapter is on *interpersonal perception* or *ordinary personology*, the process by which:

> *Ordinary people come to know about each others' temporary states (such as emotions, intentions, and desires) and enduring dispositions (such as beliefs, traits, and abilities) from their actions … (Gilbert, 1998)*

This is included in what Fiske and Taylor (1991) call *social cognition* ('the process by which people think about and make sense of other people, themselves and social situations'). According to Fiske (2004), social cognition builds on attribution theory, which is discussed in Chapter 23.

The *impression-formation* research represents some of the earliest research conducted in Social Psychology, and it flourished during the 1950s, 1960s and 1970s. It was carried out largely from the perspective of the *perceiver* and looked at *central versus peripheral traits*, the *primacy–recency effect*, *implicit personality theory* and *stereotyping*. But we'll also discuss it from the *actor's* point of view (that is, the person being perceived), by considering (a) how being stereotyped can affect behaviour and self-concept; and (b) some of the ways in which we try to influence others' impressions of us (*impression management/self-presentation*).

Since the 1980s, these traditional perspectives of person perception have largely been replaced by that of social cognition. This differs from the earlier research more in terms of the overall approach than the phenomena being investigated. The study of impression formation was concerned with the content of our thoughts about others. But social cognition reflects the *information-processing approach;* this is concerned less with the content and more with the, often unconscious, automatic processes that underlie our (usually) conscious impressions of others.

PERCEIVING OBJECTS and PERCEIVING PEOPLE

According to Fiske (2004), when we form impressions of other people it seems to happen immediately ('automatically'). But in fact we:

> *… search the social horizon unaware that [we] are using mental binoculars and that things are much farther away than they appear. All our experience … is actually mediated or filtered through a psychological lens, our perceiving apparatus. Although we experience the world as if we take in a literal, unfiltered copy, each person passes reality through a different lens…*

We're aware only of the *end product* of this process, which is our experience of the person. Part of Heider's (1958) *common-sense psychology* (equivalent to ordinary personology) is this direct experience of the world, which he contrasts with the *scientific* analysis of how people perceive it (see Chapter 23). As Figure 22.1 shows, both social (or person) and object perception involve selection, organisation and inference (see Chapter 15). As applied to perceiving people, this might mean:

- focusing on people's physical appearance or on just one particular aspect of their behaviour (*selection*)
- trying to form a complete, coherent impression of a person (*organisation*)
- attributing characteristics to someone for which there's no direct or immediate evidence, as in stereotyping (*inference*).

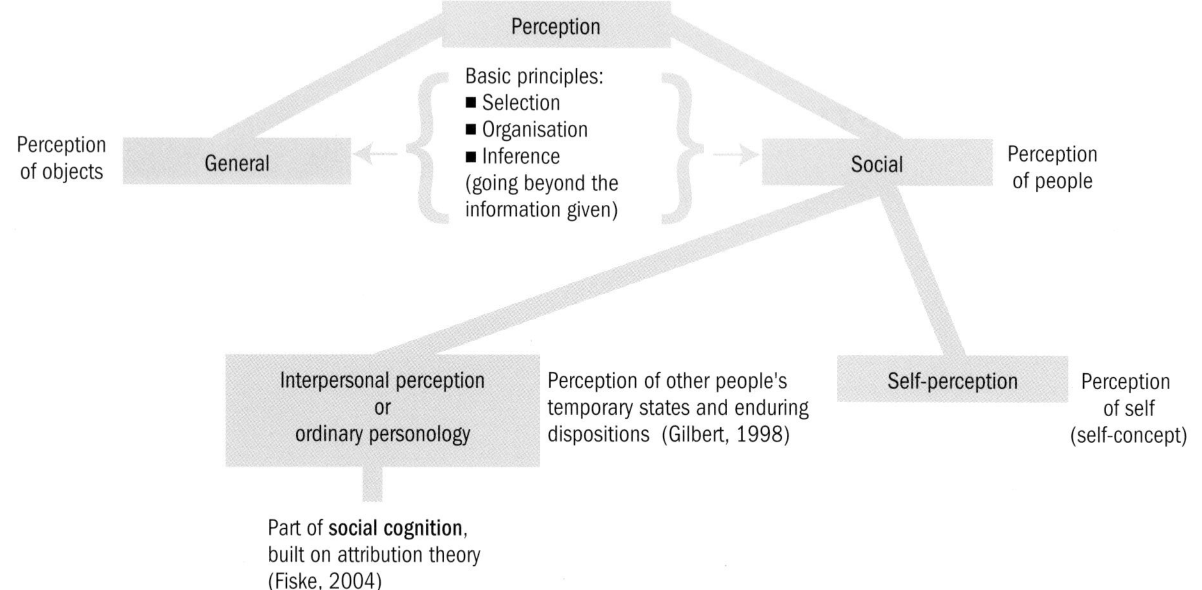

Figure 22.1 Relationship between general and social perception

> **Ask Yourself**
>
> - In what ways does perceiving people differ from perceiving objects?

- People *behave* (but objects don't). It's often behaviour which provides the data for making inferences about what people are like.
- People are *causal agents* – that is, they intend to act on their environment (Fiske and Taylor, 1991).
- People *interact* with other people (but they don't interact with objects or objects with each other). One person's behaviour can influence another's: behaviour is *mutually influential*.
- People *anticipate* being observed, and this is related to *self-presentation* (Fiske and Taylor, 1991).
- People are generally more *changeable* than objects, and it's harder to verify the accuracy of observations about people (what they're 'really' like) (Fiske and Taylor, 1991: see Chapter 42).
- People *perceive* and *experience* (but objects cannot). One person's perception can influence the other's (especially his/her non-verbal behaviour), so that each person's perception of the other is at least partly a product of the other's perception of him/her. As Fiske and Taylor (1991) put it, social perception is *mutual perception*.

Phenomenological Psychologists regard *experience* as the major source of 'data' (as opposed to behaviour) in social interaction (see Chapter 2). For example, Laing (1967) argued that the task of *social phenomenology* is to relate 'my experience of your behaviour to your experience of my behaviour'. In other words, it studies the relationship between experience and experience. In his book *Knots* (1970), Laing dramatically (and often humorously) demonstrates the kinds of tangles that human relationships can get into. He does this in the form of short prose poems and diagrammatic poems. Here are two of the shorter and more straightforward examples.

1. Jack frightens Jill that he will leave her because he is frightened she will leave him.
2. Jack: 'You are a pain in the neck.
   To stop you giving me a pain in the neck
   I protect my neck by tightening my neck muscles,
   Which gives me the pain in the neck you are.'
   Jill: 'My head aches through trying to stop you giving me a headache.'

For Laing, 'knots' like these illustrate how 'my experience of another is a function of the other's experience of me' and vice versa.

ARE WE ALL PSYCHOLOGISTS?

> **Ask Yourself**
>
> - In what ways can we all be considered psychologists?

As we noted earlier, everyone tries to 'figure people out', explain, predict and, very often, control others' behaviour, as part of their everyday living in a social world. These also happen to be the three traditionally accepted aims of science, including Psychology (see Chapter 3). Gahagan (1984) defines interpersonal perception as 'the study of how the layperson uses theory and data in understanding people'. She breaks this definition down further into three main components:

1. The study of how people perceive others as *physical objects* and form impressions of their physical appearance, actions and the social categories to which they can be assigned. Often the first thing we notice about other people is some aspect of their appearance (such as their clothes or hair: see Chapter 21), and to this extent we're treating them as no more than 'things'. This is usually the first step involved in stereotyping, since we usually categorise people on the basis of physical appearance.
2. The study of how people perceive others as *psychological entities*. We form impressions of what kind of person they are, or we infer what their feelings, motives, personality traits and so on might be (having already categorised them).
3. The study of *the lay person as a psychologist*. According to Nisbett and Ross (1980):

> *We are all psychologists. In attempting to understand other people and ourselves, we are informal scientists who construct our own intuitive theories of human behaviour. In doing so, we face the same basic tasks as the formal scientist ...*

'Intuitive theories' is another way of referring to 'implicit personality theories' (see below, p. 372).

THE PERSON AS THINKER

People are thinking organisms (as opposed to emotional organisms or mindless automatons) who 'reside' between stimulus and response (a S–O–R model as opposed to an S–R model: see Chapters 2 and 11). Social cognition represents a fairly recent way of looking at the thinking involved in our social interactions.

According to Fiske and Taylor (1991), there are four guises that the cognitive tradition has assumed. They see the thinker, respectively, as follows:

1. *Consistency seeker*. This refers to the principle of *cognitive consistency*, around which a number of theories of attitude change were built in the 1950s, the most influential being Festinger's cognitive dissonance theory (see Chapter 24). All the theories claim that we're highly motivated to *reduce* cognitive inconsistency.
2. *Naïve scientist*. Attribution theories are central to the view that, by trying to infer unobservable causes from observable behaviour, we all operate as amateur scientists (see above). This view was first proposed by Heider, the 'father of attribution theory', in 1958, but most attribution theories were formulated between the mid-1960s and early 1970s. They attempted to account for how people *ought* to attribute causes to behaviour under 'ideal' conditions (they're *normative*). They also took the 'naïve scientist' model too far, by seeing ordinary people as completely logical and systematic in their thinking (see Chapter 23).
3. *Cognitive miser*. Partly as a reaction against normative attribution theories, Nisbett and Ross (1980), Taylor (1981) and others introduced the term 'cognitive miser' to convey the idea that people are limited in their capacity to process information. We take shortcuts whenever we can, adopting strategies that simplify complex problems. This might lead us to draw biased and hence inaccurate conclusions (relative to what the normative theories predict), but seeing people as fallible thinkers represents a much more *descriptively accurate* account of how people actually think about behaviour. This is reflected in studies of error and bias in the attribution process, but also, more generally, in *heuristics* (Tversky and Kahneman, 1974) or 'rules of thumb' (see Chapter 20). Some examples are given in Table 22.1.
4. *Motivated tactician*. This refers to a development of the cognitive miser view, 'putting back' the motivational and emotional variables that were removed from the original cognitive consistency model. The motivated tactician is a:

> *... fully engaged thinker who has multiple cognitive strategies available and chooses among them based on goals, motives, and needs ... (Fiske and Taylor, 1991)*

This corresponds to what Leyens and Codol (1988) call the 'cognitive–affective human being'.

Evaluation of social cognition: what's happened to the 'social'?

- Critics of social cognition (e.g. Moscovici, 1982; Zajonc, 1989) have argued that it may have taken Social Psychology too far towards Cognitive Psychology, so that there may not be any 'social' in social cognition. Many of the cognitive processes and structures that have been proposed seem to be unaffected by social context: they seem to be taking place within an apparently isolated person who (just happens to be) thinking about social objects. But this isn't what's meant by 'social cognition'. Instead, we should be focusing on the link between people and the social object. This is truly social, because it's concerned with how cognition is socially constructed, shared and maintained by different members of a given social group, or

Table 22.1 Some examples of heuristics used in uncertain or ambiguous situations

Availability: We judge the frequency/probability of an event according to the number of instances of it that can readily be brought to mind (remembered), and so which are cognitively available. For example, being able to think of several friends who are studying Psychology in other colleges/universities leads you to believe that Psychology is nationally one of the most popular subjects (which, in fact, it is!).
Representativeness: We decide whether a particular person/event is an example of a particular category. For example, if X has long hair, is wearing a skirt, has a high-pitched voice and is called Jo, then there's a good chance X is female – but not necessarily! It's a safe bet, because there's a match between the person in front of you and your stereotyped belief (or prototype) of what females are like.
Simulation: Judging what's likely to be/have been the outcome of some event, according to how easily different outcomes can be brought to mind. For example, we're often much more angry and upset by 'near misses' than when we 'missed it by a mile' – we can imagine 'If only I'd …', or 'If only that man in front of me …' much more easily in the former than in the latter.
Anchoring: When we have no information about a particular event, we may draw on information about a similar event as a reference point or 'anchor'. For example, if asked to estimate how many hours per week a fellow Psychology student studies, in the absence of any specific knowledge you may base your answer on how many (or few!) hours you yourself put in.

even a whole society. To study 'social' cognition by studying what's going on inside the head of individuals is *reductionist* (see Chapter 49).

- *Stereotypes* illustrate the shared nature of cognition, but perhaps the best example of how cultural knowledge may be constructed and transmitted is Moscovici's (1961, 1981) *theory of social representations* (see Chapter 2).

Social representations (SRs)

According to Moscovici (1981), social representations are:

> *… A set of concepts, statements and explanations originating in daily life in the course of inter-individual communications. They are the equivalent, in our society, of the myths and belief systems in traditional societies; they might even be said to be the contemporary version of common sense …*

Characteristics of SRs

- Moscovici (1961) showed that people have simplified (and often mistaken) ideas about Freud's psychoanalytic theory. Many people have heard of Freud, just as they've heard of Einstein or Stephen Hawking, but most will have only the vaguest knowledge of their respective ideas and theories. This illustrates the *personification* of new and complex ideas, that is, linking them with a person.

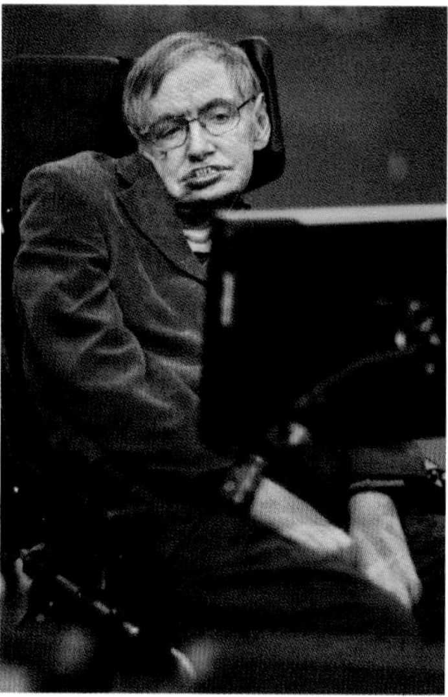

Figure 22.2 Stephen Hawking (born 1942). You don't have to be a cosmologist, physicist or mathematician to have heard of him, or even to have read one of his books

- Complex ideas are also often converted into the form of visual images, as in a cartoon where the darker side of a person's nature is portrayed as a devil and his/her conscience as an angel. This kind of *figuration* is sometimes used to convey Freud's concepts of the id and superego respectively (with the person him/herself being the ego) (see Figure 22.3)
- Both personification and figuration are examples of *objectification*, that is, the need to make the abstract concrete (Moscovici and Hewstone, 1983). For example, thinking of God as 'a father' gives some sort of reality to a supernatural concept. We also need to anchor new and unfamiliar ideas into some pre-existing system (see Table 22.1).

An example of anchoring is given in Jodelet's (1980) study of the re-housing of ex-psychiatric hospital patients in a French village. They were immediately labelled 'bredins' (a local term for vagrants or 'half-wits'). Despite the term's almost total inaccuracy, it served to reduce something totally unknown and alien to something familiar.

Figure 22.3 A representation of Freud's concept of the id, ego and superego, using figuration

The functions of SRs

- They facilitate communication between individuals and groups by establishing a shared 'social reality'. They also guide social action: individuals will interpret their own and others' behaviour in the light of this shared knowledge.
- Through socialisation, shared SRs are impressed on the child, infiltrating to the 'core of the personality', and imposing limits to perceptions and attitudes (Moscovici and Hewstone, 1983).
- In a way, the study of SRs is the study of the transformation from knowledge to common sense (Moscovici and Hewstone, 1983) or 'popular consciousness', and the theory of SRs 'explains how the strange and the unfamiliar become, in time, the familiar' (Farr and Moscovici, 1984). It's the study of how SRs evolve and are communicated between groups and individuals that makes this true social cognition.

Ask Yourself

- Can you think of any other examples of SRs?
- Where do you think they come from?

SRs provide an evolving framework for making sense of the world, deriving from the mass media, scientific and religious movements, and intergroup relations (Moscovici, 1984). They also have important consequences for how we deal with one another, and how society responds to particular individuals and groups. For example, whether abnormal behaviour is conceptualised in moral, biological, religious, or social terms will determine how social policy-makers, the government, as well as the general public, will respond to it (see Chapter 43). When the Yorkshire Ripper was convicted for multiple rapes and murders, he was held to be criminally responsible (despite his schizophrenia). As Hogg and Abrams (2000) point out:

> *Such distinctions are dependent more on society's current social representations of good and evil, sanity and insanity, than they are on objectively measurable criteria.*

Whenever people engage in conversation or debate controversial issues, such as 'what to do with paedophiles', whether homosexuals should be allowed to become foster/adoptive parents, whether cannabis should be legalised or whether we should pay higher taxes to fund public services like the NHS, SRs become apparent.

SRs, prejudice and discrimination

According to Horton (1999), underlying much racist talk or discourse is a hidden core, which consists of:

> *... a social representation of human nature, including the belief in a hereditary factor in natural character. Biological, psychological and religious images and ideas make up this inner core. Racialism corresponds to a social representation which gives replies to questions such as 'What is man?', 'What are his origins?' and 'Why are people different?'*

Billig's (1978) participant observational study of the National Front (now the British National Party/BNP) revealed that beneath black stereotypes and active hostility towards blacks laid a complex set of ideas. These included the need for racial cleansing and belief in a Zionist conspiracy. By offering scapegoats instead of a rational analysis of the situation, the Nazis gave hope to the German people by attributing the crisis to a cause that was relatively easily controllable by elimination – the Jews.

For Horton, SR theory, by providing a lay theory of causality:

> *... Offers a social psychological explanation of 'prejudice' that takes into full account the phenomena of active hostility towards, and persecution and elimination of, outgroups, which experimental social psychology has not been able to offer.*

Figure 22.4 Residents campaigning against the planned move of a convicted paedophile into their neighbourhood on his release from prison. The belief that they cannot help but reoffend is part of the social representation of paedophiles

Box 22.1 The social representation of AIDS

- According to Joffe (1996), the early representation of AIDS in the West, by both the scientific and lay communities, was in terms of *outgroups*, namely, homosexuals and/or Africans. This anchoring acts as a form of identity-protection, and has operated throughout the ages.
- Joffe gives the example of syphilis as it swept through Europe in the fifteenth century. It became associated with foreigners and outgroups: the English called it the 'French pox', and for the Japanese it was the 'Chinese disease'. This applied also to typhus, leprosy, polio and cholera (the pandemic diseases).
- 'Blaming the foreigner' is necessary in order to punish the perceived cause of the crime and prevent its return. This scapegoating is vital for maintenance of the social order, and the greater the potential threat, the greater the need to exterminate the 'demons' (Poliakov, 1980, in Horton, 1999).

FORMING GLOBAL IMPRESSIONS of PEOPLE

Central versus peripheral traits

Certain information we have about a person (certain traits we believe they possess) may be more important in determining our overall impression of that person than other information. This was demonstrated in Asch's (1946) classic study, which led him to distinguish between *central* and *peripheral* traits. (See Box 22.2.)

Box 22.2 Central and peripheral traits (Asch, 1946)

- *Central traits* have a disproportionate influence on the overall impression we form of someone based on those traits (such as 'warm–cold'). They're implicitly *evaluative*, so that including 'warm' produced an overall *positive* impression, while 'cold' produced an overall *negative* impression (despite the other traits in the list being the same).
- *Peripheral traits* (such as 'polite-blunt') have little impact on the impression we form of another person.

Kelley (1950) found that the description of the target person as 'warm' or 'cold' influenced participants' behaviour towards a *real* (as opposed to hypothetical) person.

What makes central traits central?

For Asch, a set of traits produces a coherent impression or configuration (a *gestalt*: see Chapter 15), in which the meaning of one trait has been influenced by the others. The *principle of coherence* makes all the traits fit together into a well-integrated portrait (Fiske, 2004). Central traits exert a major organising influence, and can generate inferences about additional traits not given in the set, while peripheral traits have little or no influence. However:

- The *meaning* of various traits may nevertheless be altered by the context in which they appear, as Asch originally suggested. For example, if someone is described as 'proud', this is rated as closer to 'confident' when it appears in the context of positive traits, but as closer to 'conceited' when presented in the context of negative traits (Zebrowitz, 1990)
- According to Anderson's (1974) *averaging/algebraic model*, people extract the evaluative element from each component of the impression (that is, each trait's inherent likeability). They then average the separate evaluations into an overall evaluation – this is an explicitly piecemeal, elemental account, which sees traits as completely independent of each other and having no influence on each other (Fiske, 2004)
- Bruner and Tagiuri (1954) argued that both general impressions and inferences about additional traits are due to people's implicit personality theories (IPTs: see below).

The primacy–recency effect

> **Ask Yourself**
>
> - Do you believe that first impressions are more influential than later impressions? If so, why?
> - Does it make a difference if the person is a potential sexual partner (i.e. does the element of potential sexual attraction affect the impact of initial impressions)?

The other major explanation of global perception concentrates on the *order* in which we learn things about a person:

- The *primacy effect* refers to the greater impact of what we learn *first* about someone ('first impressions count').
- The *recency effect* refers to the greater impact of what we learn *later* on.

Initial support for a primacy effect came in another study by Asch (1946). He used two lists of adjectives describing a hypothetical person, one in the order: intelligent, industrious, impulsive, critical, stubborn and envious, and the other in the reverse order. Participants given the first list formed a favourable overall impression, while those given the second list formed an unfavourable overall impression. Luchins (1957) found further evidence of a primacy effect.

Both the Luchins and Asch studies involved hypothetical people. In a study by Jones *et al.* (1968), participants watched a student (a stooge of the experimenters) trying to solve a series of difficult multiple-choice problems. They were then asked to assess his intelligence. The student always solved 15 out of 30 correctly, but one group saw him get most of the right answers towards the beginning, while another group saw him get most of the right answers towards the end.

> **Ask Yourself**
>
> - Which group do you think assessed him as more intelligent?
> - According to common sense, which group would judge him to be more intelligent?

The common-sense prediction would be that when the student got most right towards the end, he'd be judged as more intelligent: he'd seem to be learning as he went along. When he got most right towards the beginning, his early successes could be attributed to guesswork or 'beginner's luck'. Jones *et al.* in fact made the common-sense prediction that there'd be a recency effect. But what they found was a primacy effect. Significantly, when asked to recall how many problems the student had solved correctly, those who'd seen the 15 bunched at the beginning said 20.6 (on average), while those who'd seen them bunched at the end said 12.5 (on average). These memory distortions (over- and underestimations) also reflected the impact of the primacy effect.

Explaining the primacy effect

- Anderson (1974) maintained that people pay more attention to information presented when they're first trying to form an impression about someone. Having formed some initial impression, they pay less attention to any subsequent information.
- Asch's explanation was that the first bit of information affects the meaning of later information, which is made consistent with the former. For example, if you initially find out that someone is courageous and frank, and you later learn that he's also undecided, you may take that to mean 'open-minded' rather than 'wishy-washy' (Zebrowitz, 1990).
- However, a *negative* first impression appears to be more resistant to change than a positive one. One explanation is that negative information carries more weight, because it's likely to reflect socially undesirable traits or behaviour and, therefore, the observer can be more confident in attributing the trait or behaviour to the person's 'real' nature. (This is relevant to Jones and Davis's attribution theory: see Chapter 23.) It may be more adaptive for us to be aware of negative traits than positive ones, since the former are potentially harmful or dangerous.

> **Ask Yourself**
>
> - Can you think of any experiences like this that you have had?

INFERRING WHAT PEOPLE are LIKE

The halo effect

Asch's original finding that the inclusion of 'warm' produces a more positive impression compared with the same list including 'cold' demonstrates the *halo effect*. If we're told a person is warm, then we tend to attribute them with other favourable characteristics (a *positive* halo). The reverse is true if we're told the person is 'cold' – we attribute them with a *negative* halo. The halo effect seems to illustrate very well two basic principles of perception (see Figure 22.1):

- We like to see people in as *consistent* (or organised) a way as possible. It's easier to regard someone as having either all good or all bad qualities than a mixture of good and bad. Two quite extreme examples of this are when lovers regard each other as perfect and faultless ('love is blind': see Chapter 28) and the '*mirror-image phenomenon*', where enemies see each other as all bad (see Chapter 25)

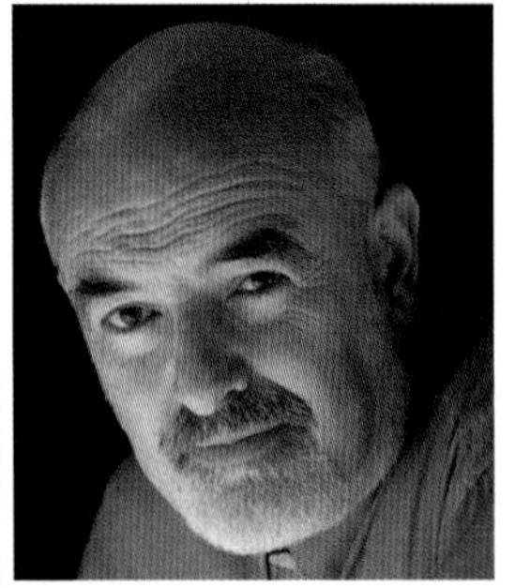

MEET THE RESEARCHER

Chris Frith

Social neuroscience

At the beginning of my career as a psychologist, I knew very little about the brain and even less about social psychology. During my clinical training, I became fascinated by patients with a diagnosis of schizophrenia and I tried to think what might cause their strange symptoms. This fascination eventually led to my interest in the brain and in social aspects of behaviour.

In the late 1970s, my medical colleagues and I demonstrated a specific brain difference in schizophrenia (enlarged ventricles) and also a specific role for dopamine in controlling the development of symptoms. The exciting implication of these results is that it must be possible to understand the strange subjective experiences, the hallucinations and delusions associated with schizophrenia in terms of abnormal brain function. This brought home to me the more general idea that, when we study psychology, whether we concentrate on behaviour or subjective experience, we are also studying how the brain works. (See Chapter 44.)

Autism and ToM tasks

In parallel with my work on schizophrenia, my wife Uta Frith was working on autism. In 1985, she and her colleagues demonstrated that autism was associated with a specific problem in solving *theory of mind* tasks. To solve such tasks you have to recognise that peoples' behaviour is determined by their beliefs, rather than the reality of the situation. If Maxi believes his chocolate is in the cupboard, then that is where he will look for it even though his belief is false. He doesn't know that his mother has moved his chocolate onto the fridge. This ability to *read* the minds of others and to use this knowledge about their intentions and beliefs to predict what people are going to do next seems to be a uniquely human ability and thus a very important component of social cognition. (See Chapter 40.)

Hearing voices

I realised that some of the symptoms of schizophrenia might also reflect *theory of mind* problems, though of a different kind from those associated with autism. For example, patients with delusions of persecution make entirely wrong inferences about the intentions of other people. Indeed, most of the symptoms of schizophrenia have a strong social component: hearing voices, believing that other people are controlling their actions, believing that other people are communicating with them through some kind of telepathy. I developed an account of the various symptoms associated with schizophrenia in terms of deviant cognitive processes and speculated how these might relate to the brain (Frith, 1992).

Studies using brain scanning techniques

At this point, my progress might have stopped, but for an entirely unexpected technological development. By using positron emission tomography (PET) and subsequently functional magnetic resonance imaging (fMRI), it became possible to see activity in the brain when healthy volunteers performed various psychological tasks. I was lucky enough to be at the right time and place to be part of the group who first applied these techniques in the UK.

One of the first experiments we did was to scan people while they were performing a *theory of mind* task. Our observations that autism and schizophrenia were associated with *theory of mind* problems while other intellectual faculties remained intact suggested that there might be a circumscribed brain region or network involved with performance of theory of mind tasks. Our 1995 PET study suggested that this was indeed the case. Performance of *theory of mind* tasks in comparison to similar tasks that did not involve thinking about people's mental states, activated a small number of regions including medial prefrontal cortex and the temporo-parietal junction.

Other research

Our study of *theory of mind* was just one in a torrent of studies that has appeared during the last decade about the role of the brain in social behaviour. A major theme to emerge was driven by the discovery of mirror neurons by the Italian neuroscientist Giacomo Rizzolatti and his colleagues. They found neurons that fire when a monkey performs a particular motor act, such as picking up a peanut, but also fire when the monkey observed the experimenter performing the same action. This result demonstrates that there is a neural basis for the long-established idea in psychology that actions are represented in a form that applies to actions we perform, as well as to actions we imagine performing or see someone else performing. To generate this common code, the brain has to solve the correspondence problem: linking the visual signals we receive when watching someone act with the motor signals we generate when performing the same action. Delineating the precise form of this computational mechanism is currently one of the hot topics in social neuroscience.

Subsequent studies have shown that there are many mirror systems in the human brain. We do not just mirror the actions that others perform, but also their emotions and experiences. Furthermore, these effects are largely automatic and unconscious.

Two recent experiments nicely illustrate this point. Sarah-Jayne Blakemore and colleagues scanned volunteers and touched them on the face or neck. As expected, this stimulation activated areas of the brain concerned with the sense of touch (primary and secondary somatosensory cortex). The exciting new result was that precisely these same areas were activated when the volunteers saw someone else being touched on the face or neck. But this activity does not break through into consciousness. The vast majority of people do not consciously feel touch when they see someone else being touched. However, there are a small number of people who do report that, when they see someone else being touched, they feel the touch on their own body. But most of us share the experience without even knowing it.

In the other experiment, Roman Liepelt and colleagues used a standard choice reaction time paradigm. Volunteers had to lift their first or second finger in response to the cue '1' or '2' appearing on the screen in front of them. The novel feature of this experiment was that these cues appeared superimposed on a picture of a hand (see figure). In one condition all the fingers in this photo of a hand were free. In another condition the first and second fingers in the photo were held down by metal clamps. The striking result was that the reaction time of the volunteers was slowed down simply by seeing a hand in which the fingers were clamped, even though their own fingers were completely free. This result shows that our actions are automatically effected by the situations of the other people we are with.

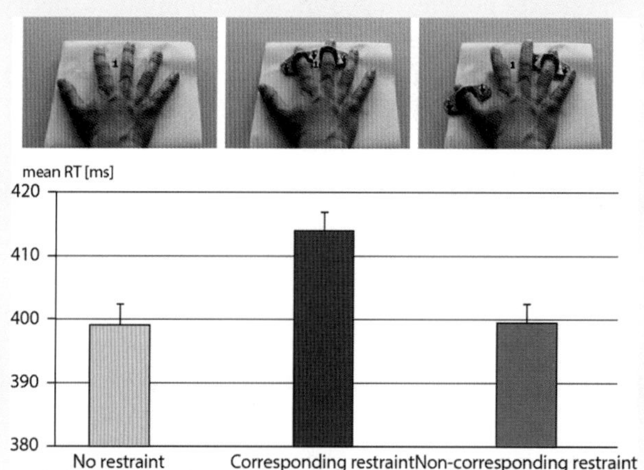

Liepelt and colleagues experiment in which volunteers raise one of two fingers in response to a cue

These are just two of the many recent experiments that show we are much more embedded in the social world than we realise. These automatic and unconscious processes make us more socially orientated and less selfish, but are probably quite independent of the processes that allow us to perform *theory of mind* tasks. Exploring the precise relationship between mirroring and *theory of mind* is another currently hot topic in social cognitive neuroscience.

We know that human beings are social creatures through and through. So it is slightly surprising that neuropsychologists have only recently started to explore the neural bases of our social behaviour and interactions. Are there certain brain regions that are specialised for social interactions? I would go further and suggest that the main function of the human brain is to allow us to engage in fruitful social interactions.

Professor Chris Frith FRS FBA is Emeritus Professor of Neuropsychology at the Wellcome Trust Centre for Neuroimaging at University College London. After several years researching schizophrenia, his interests turned to brain imaging and social neuroscience. He is author of *Schizophrenia: A Very Short Introduction* (with Eve Johnstone) and *Making up the Mind: How the Brain Creates Our Mental World*.

- The halo effect is a very general form of *implicit personality theory* (IPT). These theories enable us to infer what people are like when we have only very limited information about them.

Implicit personality theories (IPTs)

As we saw earlier, we all have 'implicit' theories about what makes people 'tick'. One kind of implicit theory is to do with how personality is structured and what traits tend to go together or cluster. Zebrowitz (1990) refers to these as 'person type' IPTs.

The importance of names

Our names are part of the central core of our self-image (see Chapter 33) and they can sometimes form the basis for others' expectations (e.g.. Harari and McDavid, 1973). Christenfeld and Larsen (2008) identify a number of ways in which our names could influence us. For example, if our family name comes near the beginning of the alphabet we're likely to enjoy certain advantages compared with those whose names come towards the end. Rare names and rare spellings, and those that are stereotypically black rather than white, tend to be judged as less favourable by others. Although it's very difficult to disentangle the effects of nature and nurture:

> *... it seems that ... names do shape, in some ways, the fate of their bearers. Perhaps the thousands of baby-naming books should add a new section reporting not only on the past of a name, but also on the future ... (Christenfeld and Larsen, 2008)*

Key Study 22.1

Names and psychiatric diagnosis (Birmingham, in Adler, 2000)

- Birmingham, a forensic psychiatrist at Southampton University, asked 464 British psychiatrists to provide a diagnosis based on a one-page description of a 24-year-old who'd assaulted a train conductor.
- When they were asked to assess 'Matthew', over 75 per cent gave him a sympathetic hearing, proposing that he was suffering from schizophrenia and in need of medical help.
- But when renamed 'Wayne', psychiatrists gave him a more sinister character: he was twice as likely as Matthew to be diagnosed as a malingerer, a drug abuser, or suffering from a personality disorder (see Chapter 43).

The importance of physical appearance

Another kind of IPT involves inferring what somebody is like psychologically from certain aspects of their physical appearance. Allport (1954) gave examples of widely held, but totally unfounded, beliefs that fat people are jolly, high foreheads are a sign of superior intelligence, eyes too close together are a sign of untrustworthiness, and redheads have fiery tempers.

A number of studies have demonstrated the 'attractiveness stereotype'; that is, the tendency to infer that physically attractive people also have more attractive personalities (see Chapter 28).

Stereotypes and stereotyping

Stereotypes can be thought of as a special kind of IPT that relate to an entire social group. The term was introduced into social science by Lippman (1922), who defined stereotypes as 'pictures in our heads'. Table 22.2 gives some other definitions.

Table 22.2 Some definitions of stereotypes and stereotyping

'... the general inclination to place a person in categories according to some easily and quickly identifiable characteristic such as age, sex, ethnic membership, nationality or occupation, and then to attribute to him qualities believed to be typical to members of that category ...' (Tagiuri, 1969)
'... a shared conception of the character of a group ...' (Brown, 1986)
'... the process of ascribing characteristics to people on the basis of their group memberships ...' (Oakes *et al.*, 1994)
'... widely shared assumptions about the personalities, attitudes and behaviour of people based on group membership, for example ethnicity, nationality, sex, race and class ...' (Hogg and Vaughan, 1995)
'... applying to an individual one's cognitive expectancies and associations about the group. As such, stereotypes represent one specific kind of schema ...' (Fiske, 2004)

The process of stereotyping involves the following reasoning:

- We assign someone to a particular group (for example, on the basis of their physical appearance)
- We bring into play the belief that all members of the group share certain characteristics (the *stereotype*), and
- We infer that this particular individual must possess these characteristics.

The basic method of studying ethnic stereotypes is that used by Katz and Braly (1933) in one of the earliest studies of its kind (see Key Study 22.2).

> **Key Study 22.2**
>
> **Studying stereotypes at Princeton (Katz and Braly, 1933)**
>
> - One hundred undergraduates at Princeton University, USA, were presented with a list of ethnic groups (Americans, Jews, Negroes, Turks, Germans, Chinese, Irish, English, Italians and Japanese) and 84 words describing personality. For each ethnic group, they were asked to list the five or six traits that were 'typical' of that group.
> - The aim was to find out whether traditional social stereotypes (as typically portrayed in newspapers and magazines) were actually held by Princeton students. In fact, they showed considerable agreement, especially about negative traits.
> - Rather disturbingly, most of the students had had no personal contact with any members of most of the ethnic groups they had to rate. Presumably, they'd absorbed the images of those groups prevalent in the media.

Gilbert (1951) studied another sample of Princeton students, and this time found less uniformity of agreement (especially about unfavourable traits) than in the 1933 study. Many expressed great irritation at being asked to make generalisations at all. In 1967, Karlins *et al.* repeated the study (but reported their findings in 1969). Many students again objected to doing the task, but there was greater agreement compared with the 1951 study. There seemed to be a re-emergence of social stereotyping, but towards more favourable stereotypical images.

> **Ask Yourself**
>
> - Do you think that stereotypes/stereotyping are inherently bad/wrong?
> - Give reasons for your answer.

The traditional view of stereotypes: are they inherently bad?

For most of the time that Psychologists have been studying stereotypes and stereotyping, they've condemned them for being both false and illogical, and dangerous, and people who use them have been seen as prejudiced and even pathological (see Chapter 25).

Lippman (1922), for example, described stereotypes as selective, self-fulfilling and ethnocentric, constituting a 'very partial and inadequate way of representing the world'. The research started by Katz and Braly (1933) was intended to trace the link between stereotypes and prejudice: stereotypes are public fictions arising from prejudicial influences 'with scarcely any factual basis'. So, should they be dismissed as completely unacceptable?

According to Allport (1954), most stereotypes do contain a 'kernel of truth', and Lippman had recognised the categorisation processes involved in stereotyping as an important aspect of general cognitive functioning. Allport built on these ideas, arguing that 'The human mind must think with the aid of categories ...' However, he also believed that prejudiced people tend to make extremely simple *dichotomous* (either/or) judgements compared with tolerant, non-prejudiced people.

Asch (1952) also rejected the view of stereotyping as 'faulty processing'. In a great many situations, the behaviour of individuals (for example, members of audiences, committees, families, football teams, armies) is determined by their group membership. So, representing people in terms of these group memberships (stereotyping) could be seen as an important way of representing social reality. In keeping with his belief in Gestalt principles, Asch argued that groups have distinct psychological properties which cannot be reduced to the characteristics of the individual members (see Chapter 15).

Sherif (1967) also argued that stereotypes aren't in themselves deficient, but serve to reflect the reality of intergroup relations. Instead of asking if they are objectively true or accurate, we need to understand stereotypes in this *intergroup* context. To this extent, they are highly flexible, since changes in the relationship with other groups will result in changes to the stereotyped images of those groups (see Chapter 25). But according to Operario and Fiske (2004), it's precisely this broader context of stereotypes, reflected in social hierarchy and history that defines their truly insidious nature.

The changing face of stereotypes: are they 'normal' after all?

Almost all the researchers whose views of stereotyping we've discussed so far are American. According to Taylor and Porter (1994), there are compelling reasons why American Psychologists should condemn stereotyping and wish to rid society of this evil. One of these is the political ideology, according to which everyone who lives in America is first and foremost 'American' regardless of the country they might have come from or their ethnic/cultural origins. This is the 'melting pot' idea, whereby differences are 'boiled away', leaving just one culture.

By contrast, European Social Psychologists, notably Tajfel, had been brought up in contexts where it was normal to categorise people into groups, where they expected society to be culturally diverse, and where people were proud of their cultural identities. From this personal experience, Tajfel and others mounted a challenge to the American view of stereotyping. Tajfel (1969), for example, reconceptualised stereotyping as the product of quite normal cognitive processes common to all (non-prejudiced) individuals. Specifically, it's a special case of *categorisation*, which involves an exaggeration of similarities within groups and of differences between groups (the *accentuation principle*). According to Oakes *et al.* (1994), Tajfel's contribution is widely seen as having been revolutionary. One effect of his ideas was to move researchers away from studying the *content* of stereotypes and towards the study of the *process of stereotyping* in its own right.

Figure 22.5 Millwall and West Ham United fans displaying stereotypical behaviour, 2009

Stereotyping as a normal cognitive process

According to Brislin (1993):

> Stereotypes should not be viewed as a sign of abnormality. Rather, they reflect people's need to organise, remember and retrieve information that might be useful to them as they attempt to achieve their goals and to meet life's demands ...

Stereotypes are 'categories about people' (Allport, 1954; Brislin, 1981), and categories in general, and stereotypes in particular, are shortcuts to thinking. From a purely cognitive point of view, there's nothing unique about stereotypes. They're universal and inevitable, 'an intrinsic, essential and primitive aspect of cognition' (Brown, 1986).

Lippmann (1922) himself argued that stereotypes serve a crucially important practical function:

> ... The real environment is altogether too big, too complex and too fleeting for direct acquaintance. We are not equipped to deal with so much subtlety, so much variety, so many permutations and combinations, and although we have to act in that environment, we have to reconstruct it on a simpler model before we can manage it.

Ask Yourself

- How does this view of stereotyping relate to the view of the person as thinker (Fiske and Taylor, 1991: see above, p. 365)?

According to the *cognitive miser* perspective, stereotypes are resource-saving devices. They simplify the processing of information about other people. As Fiske (2004) says:

> ... Under the busy conditions of ordinary interaction, people can save cognitive resources by using stereotype-consistent information ...

This is a good example of the *selective* nature of person perception.

The accuracy of stereotypes

Definitions claim that stereotypes are *exceptionless generalisations* (see Table 22.2). But, clearly, the degree of generalisation involved is too great to make a stereotype factually true: no group is completely homogeneous, and individual differences are the norm. Yet in Katz and Braly's study, the instruction to list the traits typical of each ethnic/national group was taken to mean 'true of all members of each group' (Brown, 1986). However, the early studies never actually found out what participants understood by 'typical'. McCauley and Stitt (1978) attempted to rectify this, concluding that typical seems to mean *characteristic*, that is, true of a higher percentage of the groups in question that of *people in general*.

Stereotypes, then, seem to be schemas about what particular groups are like relative to 'people in general'. They *aren't* exceptionless generalisations. Perhaps this is how we should understand Allport's claim that stereotypes do contain a 'kernel of truth'.

Consistent with this conclusion, Operario and Fiske (2004) claim that stereotypes are more *ambivalent* than is commonly recognised: they comprise both positive and negative attributes about social groups (as illustrated by the stereotypes of 'Negroes' in the Katz and Braly (1933) study: superstitious/lazy/happy-go-lucky/ignorant/musical). Minority groups tend to be viewed as either (a) highly competent but not nice, or (b) extremely incompetent but nice, and stereotype content reflects this pattern. (See Box 22.3 below.)

Ask Yourself

- Based on Operario and Fiske's distinction, which of the following groups would you classify as 'nice but incompetent' or 'not nice but competent': Jews, the mentally retarded, feminists, the blind, black professionals, housewives, business women, the elderly, Asians, the physically disabled?

According to Operario and Fiske, you're likely to have answered as follows:

- 'nice but incompetent': the mentally retarded, housewives, the elderly, the physically disabled, the blind
- 'not nice but competent': feminists, business women, black professionals, Asians, Jews.

The beliefs associated with these two clusters reflect the particular group's relationship with the dominant majority (white, male, middle class, able-bodied). The first cluster presents no threat to the majority, while the second cluster poses a significant threat. However, research participants have become much more reluctant to engage in stereotyping over the past 80 years (Fiske, 2004), and stereotypes do change. For example, the most negatively rated groups in Katz and Braly's (1933) study (Negroes, Turks, Chinese) are now neutral or even slightly more positive than the most positively rated (Americans), who are rated less positively than they were (Leslie *et al.*, 2003).

Stereotypes, ingroups and outgroups

Instead of seeing comments such as 'They're all the same' as simply bigoted and discriminatory, research has shown that such statements may stem from the *outgroup homogeneity effect* (Quattrone, 1986). People tend to perceive members of an outgroup as highly similar to each other (stereotype), whereas they tend to see all kinds of individual differences among members of their own groups (the *ingroup differentiation hypothesis*: Linville *et al.*, 1989). These are consequences of the act of categorisation, and could be seen as an extension of Tajfel's accentuation principle (see above).

This differential perception of ingroup and outgroup members isn't necessarily indicative of outgroup prejudice, but is the natural outcome of social interaction patterns. We tend to interact with members of our own groups and therefore perceive differences within them. We may have limited interaction with other social groups, and this encourages a simplified social representation of these groups. In this context, it's both necessary and useful to see all outgroup members as similar. Ironically, study of the processes involved in stereotyping has suggested that it's the content that should – and can – be modified: the process itself may be 'hard-wired' as an element of human cognition, so that there's nothing we can do about it (Taylor and Porter, 1994).

Box 22.3 Stereotyping and social categorisation theory (SCT) (Turner *et al.*, 1987)

- When a crowd of demonstrators is confronted by massed ranks of riot police, it would be profoundly dysfunctional for the demonstrators to consider what the police are like as individuals.
- What matters in this context is what the police have in common and how, as police, they're likely to act. Categorical perception here is neither less accurate than individual perception, nor a distortion of reality: it's a reflection of a social categorical reality (Reicher *et al.*, 2012).
- Similarly, the *content* of our stereotypic views is a reflection of social reality. According to SCT, stereotypes are *contextually* valid perceptions: they accurately represent what makes the groups that are salient in a given situation distinctive from each other. So,
  (i) the accuracy pertains to *groups* and their inter-relations, *not* to individuals within groups;
  (ii) the accuracy of stereotypes is always limited to a specific intergroup context and cannot be asserted in general terms;
  (iii) accuracy is related the description of *differences*, not to their evaluation. In other words, SCT draws a clear and clear distinction between stereotypes and prejudice.
- In a nutshell, stereotypes are about *groups* in relation to each other; they reflect *social reality* and *social practices,* as distinct from individual cognition.

Stereotypes, expectations and memory

Buckhout (1974) gave participants a series of drawings in which some stereotypical pattern was violated. One drawing (based on Allport and Postman's (1947) experiment: see Chapter 21) showed a casually dressed white man threatening a well-dressed black man on a subway train, with the white man holding a razor (see Figure 22.6). After seeing the picture briefly, approximately half the (white) participants 'remembered' seeing a black man holding a razor.

Similarly, Rothbart *et al.* (1979) found that people often recall better those facts that support their stereotypes (*selective remembering*), and Howard and Rothbart (1980) found that people have better recall of facts which are critical of the minority group than facts which are favourable (*negative memory bias*).

Duncan (1976) showed white participants a video of a discussion between two males, and told them it was a 'live' interaction over CCTV. At one point, the discussion became heated, and one actor gave the other a shove – the screen then went blank. Participants were asked to classify the shove as 'playing around', 'dramatising', 'aggressive behaviour' or 'violent behaviour'. Different participants saw different versions of the video, which differed only in the race of the two actors – two whites, two blacks, a white who shoved a black, or a black who shoved a white.

Figure 22.6 One of the drawings used by Buckhout (1974) Reproduced with permission of Scientific American.

Ask Yourself

- How do you think participants classified the shove under different conditions?
- How could you explain the results?
- What relevance do all the above studies have for eyewitness testimony (EWT) (see Chapter 21)?

Duncan found that many more participants classified the black man's shove as violent behaviour, especially if he shoved a white man.

Stereotypes, expectations and behaviour

Our expectations of people's personalities or capabilities may influence the way we actually treat them, which in turn may influence their behaviour in such a way that confirms our expectation (the *self-fulfilling prophecy*). This illustrates how stereotypes can (unwittingly) influence our behaviour towards others, and not just our perception and memory of them.

Box 22.4 Stereotyping and the brain

- Adler (2000) cites research using EEG recordings to see what happens in people's brains when stereotypes are activated. Sentences in which gender stereotypes are violated (such as, 'The surgeon prepared herself for the operation') provoke the same surge of electrical activity as sentences that don't make grammatical sense (such as, 'The cat won't eating'). The tell-tale signal is a strong positive brainwave (the P600), which is often associated with surprise (see Chapter 7).
- The brains of men and women showed this reaction, even if they consciously found the sentence completely acceptable. Their brains seemed to be 'saying' one thing and their overt responses something quite different.
- Other researchers have used MRI scans to measure the differing reactions in the amygdala of white participants to black and white faces. The amygdala is thought to act like a spotlight, focusing attention on frightening or other emotionally charged events (see Chapter 4). There's greater amygdala activity in response to black faces or race-related words and images.

Stereotypes also affect our expectations of ourselves, which, in turn, can influence our behaviour. This may take place under naturalistic conditions and over a substantial period of time, as when members of minority groups internalise the negative stereotypes of them prevalent in the majority culture (see Chapter 25). But it can also happen under more artificial, experimental conditions in the short term.

According to Pendry (2008), Bargh *et al.*'s (1996) experiment (and two others reported in the same article) stimulated a great deal of subsequent research and remains a classic as an initial demonstration of 'automatic social behaviour'. For example, Dijksterhuis *et al.* (1998) asked participants to unscramble sentences containing words associated with negative stereotypes of the elderly. Half were asked to make judgements about Princess Julianna (the then 89-year-old Dutch Queen Mother). All the participants were then shown to the lifts, situated at the end of the corridor, and the time taken to reach them was recorded. Those who'd been primed with Princess Julianna walked significantly *faster*.

Key Study 22.3

How stereotypes can slow you down (Bargh *et al.*, 1996)

- Under the guise of a language proficiency experiment, 30 male and female college students were asked to unscramble sentences scattered with either negative age-related words (such as 'grey'/'bingo'/wrinkle') or neutral, non-age-specific words. This represented the *priming phase*, making attributes of the elderly (the 'elderly stereotype') more accessible in participants' minds. Words relating to slowness (a common part of the stereotype of the elderly) were *excluded* from the elderly priming condition.
- Students who had sorted sentences containing negative words walked down the corridor at the end of the experiment significantly more slowly, and remembered less about the experiment, than students who had sorted neutral words.

Ask Yourself

- Try to explain the findings described by Bargh *et al.* (1996) and Dijksterhuis *et al.* (1998).

The studies illustrate that when general stereotypes are activated, we may automatically adopt some of those characteristics ourselves. But when images of specific extreme individuals (exemplars) are activated, we automatically make a contrast between ourselves and the exemplar: this makes us react in the *opposite* way to how we think that person would react (Hogg and Abrams, 2000).

So, it's not stereotypes themselves which are dangerous or objectionable, but how they affect behaviour. While the experiments described above show that anyone can be affected by negative stereotypes, under normal circumstances it's the elderly who are affected by negative stereotypes of the elderly (see Chapter 39). The same applies, of course, to ethnic minority groups and race stereotypes, and to women and gender stereotypes (see Chapters 25 and 36). According to Operario and Fiske (2004):

> *... Stereotypes are both (a) basic human tendencies inherent within our mental architecture; and (b) potentially damaging belief systems, depending on the power of the situation ...*

Stereotype threat

One way in which negative stereotypes can be damaging is *stereotype threat* (ST) (Steele and Aronson, 1995). They impose an intellectual burden on many minorities and on others who think that the people around them perceive them as inferior in some way; these individuals worry that they'll fail in a way that affirms the derogatory stereotype (such as female students in advanced maths classes earning lower grades than the males) (e.g. Steele, 1997).

Hundreds of studies have confirmed that ST undermines performance, producing the very failure they dread (a *self-fulfilling prophecy*). Some people become trapped in a vicious cycle in which poor performance produces more worry, which, in turn, impedes performance even more. However, although the threat is real, some researchers question how well some of the laboratory studies reflect anxiety in real-world settings (Yong, 2013).

According to Schmader (2010), one way in which ST can produce its harmful effects is through depletion of *working memory*: people tend to overthink actions that would otherwise be automatic and become more sensitive to cues that might indicate discrimination. It can also manifest as weakened self-control and day-dreaming.

By thwarting ST, researchers have shown that the stereotypes themselves are unfounded. Performance gaps between black and white students or between male and female scientists don't indicate differences in ability; rather, they reflect prejudices that we can change (see Chapter 25) (Yong, 2013).

INFLUENCUNG HOW OTHERS SEE US

Impression management

It's difficult to think of a social situation in which we're not trying (consciously or otherwise) to manipulate how others perceive us. This fundamental aspect of social interaction is referred to as *impression management* (or *self-presentation*) (Baumeister, 1982; Leary and Kowalski, 1990), which Turner (1991) defines as 'the process of presenting a public image of the self to others'. Sometimes we may be trying to influence particular people on a particular occasion, such as in a job interview, or we may be trying to maintain an image of ourselves (as a caring or competent person, for example).

According to Leary and Kowalski (1990), impression management can increase our subjective wellbeing by meeting three primary motivations:

1. Maximising the reward of social relationships (*belonging*: its major function)
2. Enhancing self-esteem (*self-enhancement*)
3. Establishing desired identities (*self-understanding*).

It's widely agreed that we usually try to influence others in a positive way – that is, we want them to have a favourable impression of us (Schlenker, 1980; Turner, 1991).

Critical Discussion 22.1

Is stereotyping an automatic process?

According to Devine (1989), (a) familiarity with racial stereotypes is culturally shared, even by those who don't endorse them; and (b) stereotype activation is an automatic process (i.e. it's unconscious, not requiring intention, attention or effort: Pendry, 2012). Devine found that participants' prior level of racial prejudice made little difference to their susceptibility to 'black primes' (terms presented too quickly to be consciously recognised, such as 'blacks', 'niggers', 'poor' and 'lazy') when subsequently asked to form an impression of a person who engaged in ambiguously hostile behaviour.

Several studies during the 1990s supported Devine's second hypothesis. In addition, as we saw in the text above, stereotypes, once activated, can affect not just expectations and memory, but also behaviour. However, the case for the automatic activation of stereotypes is far from proven. Several factors have been identified as influencing this process.

1. For example, Macrae *et al.* (1997) challenged the view that mere exposure to a member of a stereotyped group is sufficient to activate the associated stereotypes. The crucial variable is the extent to which we're interested in the *social meaning* of the stimuli we encounter (what they are and what they're called: *semantic processing*). This study highlights the *goal-dependent* nature of stereotype activation.
2. According to Moskowitz *et al.* (1999), 'chronic egalitarians' may possess an effortless, pre-conscious form of cognitive control that prevents stereotype activation.

So, evidence exists which suggests that stereotype activation *isn't* the inevitable, automatic process which Devine originally took it to be (Pendry, 2012). But what happens if such activation occurs (beyond our control) – is there anything we can do about it?

In books such as *The Presentation of Self in Everyday Life (*1971), Goffman, the Canadian sociologist, offers a 'dramaturgical' analysis of social interaction. To create a successful impression requires the right setting, props (e.g. the way you're dressed), skills, and a shared understanding of what counts as 'backstage'. For example, the person who takes *self-disclosure* too far (see below), may be regarded as bringing on to stage what should be kept 'backstage', and so creates an unfavourable impression.

How is impression management carried out?

Impression management requires us to 'take the role of the other' (see Cooley and Mead's theories of self: Chapter 33). We must be able, psychologically, to step into someone else's shoes to see how we look from their viewpoint, and to adjust our behaviour accordingly. Fiske and Taylor (1991) and Fiske (2004) identify several components of impression management, ways of adjusting our behaviour to take into account other people's viewpoints (see Table 22.3).

Are some positive impressions more positive than others?

Ask Yourself

- Can you think of any exceptions to the rule that we always try to create favourable impressions in others?
- Do we sometimes go about creating negative impressions in a defensive, self-protective way?

It isn't surprising that we're usually – and predominantly – motivated to be evaluated positively by others. After all, being regarded favourably by others is a prerequisite for many positive life outcomes (such as respect, friendship, romantic relationships and job success) (Leary, 2004). Sometimes, however, people believe that their interests will be best served by projecting an unfavourable impression, leading to a negative evaluation.

For example, you might protect yourself from anticipated failure by engaging in behaviours that will produce insurmountable obstacles to success. So, when the inevitable failure happens, you've a ready-made excuse (*behavioural self-handicapping*). Alternatively, you may blame, in advance, things about yourself that could explain the failure (apart from your lack of competence). For example, lecturers at exam time get quite used to students telling them how badly they're going to do because of lack of sleep, always getting anxious about exams, and so on (*self-reported handicaps*).

One way of thinking about self-handicapping is to see it as an attempt to influence the kind of *attribution* other people make about our behaviour. This also applies to making excuses for/confessing our socially undesirable behaviour (Weiner, 1992: see Chapter 23).

Self-monitoring

Individuals differ in the extent to which they can and do exercise intentional control over their self-presentation. Although Social Psychology as a whole isn't concerned with individual differences, *self-monitoring* is profoundly social psychological. It refers to how much people attend to the social situation as guides for their behaviour, as

Table 22.3 Major components involved in impression management (based on Fiske and Taylor, 1991; Fiske, 2004)

In **behaviour matching**, we try to match the target person's behaviour. For example, if the other person is self-disclosing, we'll tend to do so to a comparable degree.
When we **conform to situational norms**, we use our knowledge of what's appropriate behaviour in a particular situation to adopt that behaviour ourselves. For every social setting, there's a pattern of social interaction which conveys the best identity for that setting (the 'situated identity'). *High self-monitors* (see text below) are more likely to make a favourable impression.
Appreciating or flattering others (**ingratiation**) can sometimes produce a favourable response from the target person, especially if it's done sincerely. But if seen for what it is, flattery (or laughing at their jokes, etc.) can backfire on the flatterer, who'll be seen as deliberately trying to achieve his/her own ends (a hypocrite or sycophant: an 'arse-licker' in popular terminology).
If we show **consistency** among our beliefs, or between our beliefs and behaviour, we're more likely to impress other people favourably. Inconsistency is usually seen as a sign of weakness.
Our **verbal and non-verbal behaviours** should match, which they usually do if we're sincere. But if we're flattering, or in some other way being dishonest, the non-verbal channel will often 'leak', giving away our true feelings. When people perceive an inconsistency between what someone says and what they're trying to convey with their body, the latter is usually taken as revealing the 'true' message (Argyle *et al.*, 1972; Mehrabian, 1972).
Self-promotion is an attempt to be seen as competent, but this can conflict with the wish to be liked. Also, there's the danger of being seen as conceited and, at worst, a fraud.
Intimidation is meant to convey the impression of being dangerous ('don't mess with me'). But empty threats can produce a loss of credibility (as with parents and children).
In **exemplification**, the person wants to be seen as worthy, moral and saintly. The downside is being seen as sanctimonious, 'holier than thou' (a 'pain').
Supplication (pleading/begging) is the strategy of last resort. The aim is to be seen as helpless ('strategic incompetence'), but the downside is being perceived as lazy, calculating and manipulative.

opposed to their own internal states (Snyder, 1974; 1987). *High self-monitors* are particularly talented in this way compared with low self-monitors (Snyder, 1995).

High self-monitors are concerned with behaving in a socially appropriate manner, and so are more likely to monitor the situation (rather than themselves), looking for subtle cues as to 'how to behave'. They're more skilled in using facial expressions and their voices to convey particular emotions, and can interpret others' non-verbal communication more accurately compared with low self-monitors (Ickes and Barnes, 1977; Snyder, 1979). But carried to an extreme, their perceptiveness and social sensitivity can make them look like self-interested opportunists who change themselves and their opinions to suit the situation (Snyder, 1987). Their behaviour shows greater *cross-situational inconsistency* – they behave differently in different situations.

Low self-monitors remain 'themselves' regardless of the situation, rarely adapting to the norms of the social setting. They monitor their behaviour in relation to their own enduring needs and values. Carried to an extreme, they can be seen as insensitive, inflexible and uncompromising (Snyder, 1987). They show greater *cross-situational consistency*.

According to Fiske (2004):

> *Both levels of self-monitoring can be useful in the social world. Groups need people who are sensitive to norms and flexible about adjusting to them, and groups also need people who stand up for enduring principles, so a mix of high and low self-monitors is arguably good for group survival.*

Self-disclosure

How accurately others perceive us is determined partly by how much we reveal to them about ourselves (*self-disclosure*). Wiemann and Giles (1988) define it as:

> *... the voluntary making available of information about one's self that would not ordinarily be accessible to the other at that moment.*

According to Jourard (1971), we disclose ourselves through what we say and do (as well as what we omit to say and do). This means that we have greater control over some aspects of self-disclosure than others since, generally, we have greater control over verbal than non-verbal behaviour. However, Jourard believes that the decision to self-disclose (or to become 'transparent') is one taken freely, and the aim in disclosing ourselves is to 'be known, to be perceived by the other as the one I know myself to be'.

Jourard believes that we can learn a great deal about ourselves through mutual self-disclosure, and our intimacy with others can be enhanced. It's a way of both achieving and maintaining a healthy personality, but only if the self-disclosure meets the criterion of *authenticity* (or honesty).

Ask Yourself

- Think of your various relationships. What determines the nature and extent of what you disclose to other people?

Factors influencing disclosure

- *Reciprocity:* The more personal the information we disclose to someone, the more personal the information they're likely to disclose to us. This relates to the *norm of reciprocity* (Gouldner, 1960), according to which our social behaviours 'demand' an equivalent response from our partners. We might sometimes feel the other person is giving too much away (or doing so too quickly), but we're still likely to reveal more about ourselves than we otherwise would.
- *Norms:* The situation we're in often determines how much (or what kind of) disclosure is appropriate. For instance, it's acceptable for someone we meet at a party to tell us about their job, but not to reveal details about medical problems or political beliefs.
- *Trust:* Generally, the more we trust someone, the more prepared we are to self-disclose to them.
- *Quality of relationships:* Altman and Taylor's (1973) *social penetration theory* maintains that the more intimate we are with somebody, the greater the range of topics we disclose to them and the more deeply we discuss any particular topic. Equally, a high degree of mutual self-disclosure can enhance the intimacy of the relationship, and is an excellent predictor of whether couples stay together over a four-year period (see Chapter 28).
- *Gender:* Women generally disclose more than men, and Jourard (1971) argues that men's limited self-disclosure prevents healthy self-expression and adds stress to their lives.

CONCLUSIONS

It would be quite appropriate to begin a textbook on Psychology with a chapter on social perception. Since most of us are, by definition, neither Psychologists nor any other kind of scientist in a literal sense, the person-as-psychologist is a metaphor. However, it combines two essential truths about human beings:

1. Science (including Psychology) is conducted by people and, as far as we know, is uniquely human.
2. Observing, explaining, predicting and trying to control others' behaviour are activities shared by professional Psychologists and all other human beings.

Chapter Summary

- **Interpersonal perception** refers to how we all attempt to explain, predict and, to some degree, control the behaviour of other people. In these ways, we can all be thought of as psychologists.
- Although Social Psychology in general, and interpersonal perception in particular, has always been concerned with the content of people's thoughts about others, **social cognition** emphasises the **information-processing approach**.
- Both object and person perception involve **selection, organisation** and **inference**. But only people behave, interact with each other, perceive and experience.
- **Social phenomenologists** regard **experience**, rather than behaviour, as the major source of 'data' in social interaction.
- Four views of people as thinking organisms have been identified, seeing us as **consistency seekers, naïve scientists, cognitive misers** and **motivated tacticians**.
- As cognitive misers, we use **heuristics** as shortcuts to thinking, including **availability, representativeness, simulation** and **anchoring**.
- **Social representations** (**SRs**) refer to 'common sense', simplified, widely shared understanding of complex theories and ideas, and involve **personification** and **figuration**.
- **Central traits** exert a major organising influence on our overall impression of a person, while **peripheral traits** have little or no influence. An alternative, but not contradictory explanation, is that overall impressions and inferences about additional traits reflect our **implicit personality theories** (**IPTs**).
- While most of the evidence supports a **primacy effect** with regard to strangers, a **recency effect** may be more powerful with regard to people we know well.
- The **halo effect** is one kind of IPT, which enables us to infer what people are like when we have only limited information about them. IPTs may be based on people's names and their physical attractiveness.
- **Stereotypes** represent a special kind of IPT and they characterise entire **groups.** Traditionally, American researchers studied stereotypes in relation to prejudice and regarded them as false, illogical **overgeneralisations.**
- European Psychologists saw the **categorisation** of people as normal and expected. From a cognitive point of view, stereotyping is a **normal mental shortcut**.
- The act of categorising people produces the **accentuation principle**, the **outgroup homogeneity effect** and the **ingroup differentiation hypothesis**. The **illusory correlation** can help explain the formation of negative stereotypes of minority groups.
- **Stereotyping** affects **attention**, **perception** and **memory**, as well as people's **behaviour** towards members of outgroups, and the behaviour of outgroup members themselves, through the **stereotype threat** (ST).
- We try actively to influence the impression that others form of us through **impression management/ self-presentation**. Strategies used to create favourable impressions include **behaviour matching, appreciating/flattering others**, showing **consistency** among our beliefs and **matching our verbal and non-verbal behaviours**.
- **High self-monitors** try to match their behaviour to the situation, while **low self-monitors** are more likely to 'be themselves'.
- Important factors that influence **self-disclosure** include **reciprocity, norms, trust, quality of relationship** and **gender**.

Links with Other Topics/Chapters

Chapter 15 ⟶ Perception of people has much in common with *object perception*

Chapter 23 ⟶ Social cognition is built on *attribution theories*, which originated with Heider's (1958) account of the *naïve scientist*

Chapters 24 and 26 ⟶ Consistency is a concept central to many theories of attitude change (Chapter 24) and minority influence

Chapter 25 ⟶ Social representations (SRs) are the basis of much racist talk/discourse

Chapter 2 ⟶ SR theory is also a major *social constructionist approach*

Chapter 15 ⟶ Asch's research into impression formation was heavily influenced by the *Gestalt principles of perceptual organisation*

Chapters 24 and 25 ⟶ Stereotypes represent the *cognitive component of attitudes* (Chapter 24) and *prejudice* may be thought of as an *extreme attitude*

Chapter 17 ⟶ Stereotypes can help explain *selective remembering* and the *negative memory bias*

Chapter 28 ⟶ Impression management/self-presentation is relevant to *interpersonal attraction*: instead of simply sitting back and letting others be impressed (or not), we can take an active role in making ourselves likeable to others (Duck, 1988)

Chapters 24, 26, 29 and 30 ⟶ According to Turner (1991), several studies suggest that concerns with self-presentation may underlie a whole range of phenomena, including: *cognitive dissonance*, *conformity*, *aggression and deindividuation*, *bystander intervention*

Recommended Reading

Oakes, P.J., Haslam, S.A. & Turner, J.C . (1994) *Stereotyping and Social Reality.* Oxford: Blackwell.

Operario, D. & Fiske, S.T. (2004) Stereotypes: Content, Structure, Processes and Context. In M.B. Brewer & M. Hewstone (eds) *Social Cognition.* Oxford: Blackwell Publishing.

Potter, J. (1996) Attitudes, social representations, and discursive psychology. In M. Wetherell (ed.) *Identities, Groups and Social Issues.* London: Sage/ The Open University. Also relevant to Chapter 24.

Zebrowitz, L.A. (1990) *Social Perception.* Milton Keynes: Open University Press. Also relevant to Chapter 23.

Useful Websites

www.colorado.edu/conflict/peace (International Online Training Program on Intractable Conflict)

www.indiana.edu/~soccog/arcpaps.html (Social Cognition Paper Archive and Information Centre.)

CHAPTER 23

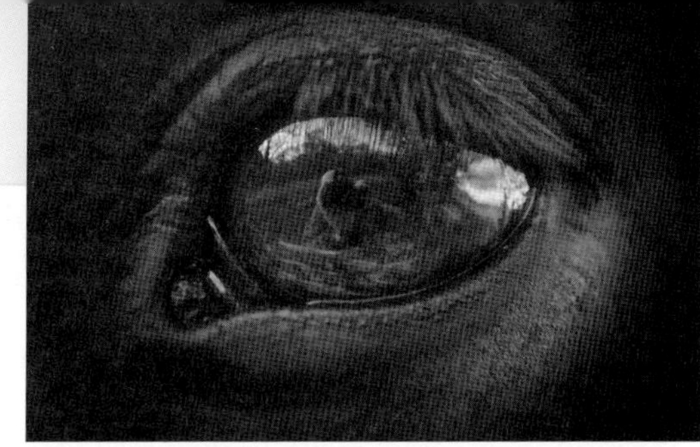

ATTRIBUTION

Attribution and the naïve scientist

Jones and Davis's correspondent inference theory (CIT)

Kelley's covariation and configuration models

Weiner's attributional theory of emotion and motivation

Error and bias in the attribution process

INTRODUCTION and OVERVIEW

As we noted at the beginning of Chapter 22, attribution is an important aspect of social perception, theories of which flourished during the 1950s to the 1970s. Most of our impressions of others are based on their overt behaviour and the setting in which it occurs. How we judge the causes of someone's behaviour (the 'actor') will have a major influence on the impression we form of them. Was their behaviour something to do with them 'as a person', such as their motives, intentions or personality (an *internal* cause)? Or was it something to do with the situation, including some other person or some physical feature of the environment (an *external* cause)?

Unless we can make this sort of judgement, we cannot really use the person's behaviour as a basis for forming an impression of them. Although we might mistakenly attribute the cause to the person instead of the situation, an attribution still has to be made.

Attribution theory deals with the general principles governing how we select and use information to arrive at causal explanations for behaviour. *Theories of attribution* draw on the principles of attribution theory, and predict how people will respond in particular situations (or life domains: Fiske and Taylor, 1991).

Rather than being a single body of ideas and research, attribution theory is a collection of diverse theoretical and empirical contributions sharing several common concerns (or mini-theories: Antaki, 1984). Six different traditions form the 'backbone' of attribution theory (Fiske and Taylor, 1991). These are: Heider's (1958) *'common-sense'* psychology, Jones and Davis's (1965) *correspondent inference theory*, Kelley's (1967, 1972, 1983) *covariation* and *configuration models*, Schachter's (1964) *cognitive labelling theory* (of emotion: see Chapter 10), Bem's (1967, 1972) *self-perception theory* (of attitude change: see Chapter 24), and Weiner's (1986) *attributional theory of motivation*.

The models and theories of Heider, Jones and Davis, and Kelley see people as logical and systematic in their explanations of behaviour. In practice, however, people tend to make attributions quickly, based often on very little information, and show clear tendencies to offer certain types of explanation for particular behaviours (Hewstone and Fincham, 1996). As Fiske (2004) says:

> *... Using an intuitive and relatively automatic process, people do not think about making attributions; they just do it. People are experts at understanding other people – at least we all think we are – but we do not actually understand how we do it until we reflect on it. And attribution theory is one way of systematically reflecting on it.*

ATTRIBUTION and the NAÏVE SCIENTIST

The process by which we make judgements about internal/external causes is called the *attribution process,* which was first investigated by Heider (1958). In a famous study, Heider and Simmel (1944) demonstrated the strength of the human tendency to explain people's behaviour in terms of intentions. Participants were shown animated cartoons of three geometrical shapes, which they described in terms of human characteristics (such as intentions).

We noted in Chapter 22 that there's a sense in which we're all psychologists. Perhaps this is most apparent in the case of attribution theory, which promises to:

> *... Uncover the way in which we, as ordinary men and women, act as scientists in tracking down the causes of behaviour; it promises to treat ordinary people, in fact, as if they were psychologists ... (Antaki, 1984)*

Heider's 'common-sense' psychology

Heider (1958) argued that the starting point for studying how we understand the social world is the 'ordinary' person. He asked 'How do people usually think about and infer meaning from what goes on around them?' and 'How do they make sense of their own and other people's behaviours?' These questions relate to what he called 'common-sense' psychology. In Heider's view, the 'ordinary' person is a naïve scientist who links observable behaviour to unobservable causes; these causes (rather than the behaviour itself) provide the meaning of what people do.

What interested Heider was the fact that members of a culture share certain basic assumptions about behaviour. These assumptions belong to the belief system that forms part of the culture as a whole, and distinguishes one culture from another. As Bennett (1993) has observed:

> *It is important that we do subscribe to a common psychology, since doing this provides an orienting context in which we can understand, and be understood by, others. Imagine a world in which your version of everyday psychology was fundamentally at odds with that of your friends – without a shared 'code' for making sense of behaviour, social life would hardly be possible.*

Ask Yourself

- Can you see any parallels between Heider's common-sense psychology and Moscovici's social representations? (See Chapter 22.)

As we noted in the *Introduction and overview*, we explain people's behaviour in terms of *dispositional* (or personal/internal) factors, such as ability or effort, and *situational* (or environmental/external factors); we tend to attribute its cause to one or other of these two general sources. This represents one of these culturally shared beliefs about behaviour that forms part of common-sense psychology.

Although Heider didn't formulate his own theory of attribution, he inspired other Psychologists to pursue his original ideas. As well as his insight relating to personal and situational factors as causes of behaviour, three other ideas have been particularly influential (Ross and Fletcher, 1985):

1. When we observe others, we tend to search for enduring, unchanging, and dispositional characteristics
2. We distinguish between intentional and unintentional behaviours
3. We tend to attribute behaviours to events (causes) that are present when the outcome is present, and absent when the outcome is absent.

JONES and DAVIS'S CORRESPONDENT INFERENCE THEORY (CIT)

Correspondent inferences and intentionality

Very much influenced by Heider, Jones and Davis (1965) argued that the goal of the attribution process is to be able to make *correspondent inferences*. We need to be able to infer that both the behaviour and the intention that produced it correspond to some underlying, stable feature of the person (a *disposition*). An inference is 'correspondent' when the disposition attributed to an actor 'corresponds' to the behaviour from which the disposition is inferred. For instance, if someone gives up his seat on the bus to allow a pregnant woman to sit down, we'd probably infer that he's 'kind and unselfish'. This is a correspondent inference, because both the behaviour and the disposition can be labelled in a similar way ('kind and unselfish'). But if we attribute the behaviour to compliance with someone else's demands ('he' is a husband whose wife has told him to give up his seat), then we wouldn't be making a correspondent inference.

According to Jones and Davis, a precondition for a correspondent inference is the attribution of *intentionality*, and they specify two criteria or conditions for this. We have to be confident that the actor:

- is capable of having produced the observed effects, and
- knew the effects the behaviour would produce.

The analysis of uncommon effects

Having made these preliminary decisions, how do we then proceed to infer that the intended behaviour is related to some underlying disposition? One answer is the *analysis* of *uncommon effects*. When more than one course of action is open to a person, a way of understanding why s/he chose one course rather than another is to compare the consequences of the chosen option with the consequences of those that weren't. In other words, what's *distinctive* (or *uncommon*) about the effects of the choice that's made?

For example, you've a strong preference for one particular university, even though there are several that are similar with regard to size, reputation, type of course and so on. The fact that all the others require you to be in residence during your first year suggests that you've a strong preference for being independent and self-sufficient.

Generally, the fewer differences between the chosen and the unchosen alternatives, the more confidently we can infer dispositions. Also, the more negative elements involved in the chosen alternative, the more confident still we can be of the importance of the distinctive consequence. (If living out of residence means a lot of extra travelling, or is more expensive, then the desire to be self-sufficient assumes even greater significance.)

Other factors affecting dispositional attributions

Because the analysis of uncommon effects can lead to ambiguous conclusions, other cues must also be used.

- *Choice* is self-explanatory: is the actor's behaviour influenced by situational factors or a result of free will?
- *Social desirability* relates to the norms associated with different situations. Because most of us conform most of the time, the need to explain other people's behaviour doesn't often arise. We base our impressions of others more on behaviour which is in some way unusual, novel, bizarre or antisocial, than on behaviour that's expected or conventional.

Ask Yourself

- Do you agree with this account of social desirability?
- Give your reasons.
- Can you think of an example from your own experience, or something in the media, that is consistent with Jones and Davis's account?

'Deviant' behaviour seems to provide more information about what the person is like, largely because when we behave unconventionally we're more likely to be ostracised, shunned or disapproved of (which, presumably, people don't want).

For example, at a funeral, people are expected to dress soberly, look sad and talk respectfully of the deceased. So, when we observe such behaviour, we can easily attribute it to the situation ('that's how one acts at funerals'). But if somebody arrives in brightly coloured clothes, making jokes and talking disrespectfully of the deceased, s/he is 'breaking the rules'. His/her behaviour needs explaining, and we're likely to attribute it to personal/dispositional characteristics. This was demonstrated in an experiment by Jones *et al.* (1961) (see Key Study 23.1).

Social desirability can also be explained in terms of the *positivity bias* (see Box 23.1).

Key Study 23.1

If you want to be an astronaut, be a loner (Jones *et al.*, 1961)

- Participants heard a tape-recording of a job interview, where the applicant was, supposedly, applying to be an astronaut or a submariner.
- Prior to hearing the tape, participants were informed of the ideal qualities for the job: astronauts should be inner-directed and able to exist without social interaction, while submariners should be other-directed and gregarious. The participants believed the candidates also understood these ideal qualities.
- The tape presented the candidate as either displaying these qualities or behaving in the opposite way, and participants had to give their impressions of the candidate.
- When the candidate behaved in the *opposite* way, participants more confidently rated him as actually being like that, compared with those who heard a 'conforming' candidate.

- *Roles* refer to another kind of conformity. When people in well-defined roles behave as they're expected to, this tells us relatively little about their underlying dispositions (they're 'just doing their job'). But when they display out-of-role behaviour, we can use their actions to infer 'what they're really like'. This is similar to the effects of social desirability, except that the norms are associated with particular social positions within an overall social context, rather than with the context or situation itself.

Pope damns paedophile priests

Figure 23.1 An extreme case of out-of-role behaviour

- *Prior expectations* are based on past experiences with the same actor. The better we know someone, the better placed we are to decide whether his/her behaviour on a particular occasion is 'typical'.

Box 23.1 The positivity bias, vigilance and the 'Pollyanna principle'

We usually see people as 'good', trustworthy, and so on (the *positivity bias*) (Fiske, 2004). Similarly, according to the 'Pollyanna principle' (Matlin and Stang, 1978), people seek the pleasant and avoid the unpleasant, communicate good news more often than bad, judge pleasant events as more likely than unpleasant events, recall pleasant life experiences more accurately than unpleasant experiences, rate themselves better than the average and as more happy than not, and evaluate each other positively. Also, desirable traits are perceived as more common than undesirable traits (Rothbart and Park, 1986). North Americans, at least, view their future as unequivocally positive (Ross and Newby-Clark, 1998), and positive words even outnumber negative words in most languages (Zajonc, 1998).

> *... The positivity assumption, then, is widespread in people's expectations about life experiences, but people expect positive outcomes from other people even more than from events in general ... positivity implies approach rather than avoidance, so it encourages interaction with other people and the environment ...* (Fiske, 2004)

Positivity is offset by *vigilance*: unexpected bad behaviour grabs people's attention. Why is this? According to Fiske: (a) if negative events are perceived as rare, they should provide more information about the individual – they set the person apart from the norm; (b) negative events might also be more *diagnostic* – that is, allow more confident categorisation of the person as a particular kind or other, regardless of the norm.

If it's 'atypical', we're more likely to dismiss it, or play down its significance, or explain it in terms of situational factors.

An evaluation of Jones and Davis's CIT

- While there are data consistent with Jones and Davis's theory, several weaknesses have been identified.
- Eiser (1983) has argued that intentions aren't a precondition for correspondent inferences. When someone is called 'clumsy', that dispositional attribution doesn't imply that the behaviour was intentional. In Eiser's view, behaviours which are unintended or accidental are beyond the scope of Jones and Davis's theory.
- It isn't just undesirable or unexpected behaviour that's informative. 'Conforming' behaviour can also be informative, as when behaviour confirms a stereotype (Hewstone and Fincham, 1996: see Chapter 22).
- Although CIT continues to attract interest, most of the studies supporting it didn't measure causal attributions (Gilbert, 1995). Indeed, the model focuses on the covariation (*correlation*) of actions and their *consequences* as the key to attribution (Fiske, 2004). Inferring a disposition isn't the same as inferring a cause, and each appears to reflect different underlying processes (Hewstone and Fincham, 1996).
- Both of Kelley's models discussed next are concerned with the processes that determine whether an internal or external attribution is made for a behaviour's cause. Focusing on the covariation of actions and their potential causes is complementary to CIT (Fiske, 2004).

KELLEY'S COVARIATION and CONFIGURATION MODELS

Ask Yourself

- One of your fellow students (let's call her Sally) is late for Psychology class one morning. How might you explain her late arrival?
- What kinds of information would you need in order to make a causal attribution?

The covariation model

Kelley's *covariation model* (1967) tries to explain how we make causal attributions where we have some knowledge of how the actor usually behaves in a variety of situations, and how others usually behave in those situations. The principle of covariation states that:

> *An effect is attributed to one of its possible causes with which, over time, it covaries.*

In other words, if two events repeatedly occur together, we're more likely to infer that they're causally related than if they very rarely occur together. If the behaviour to be explained is thought of as an effect, the cause can be one of three kinds, and the extent to which the behaviour covaries with each of these three kinds of possible cause is what we base our attribution on. To illustrate the three kinds of causal information, let's take the hypothetical example of Sally.

- *Consensus* refers to the extent to which other people behave in the same way. In this example, are other students late for Psychology? If all (or most) other

students are late, then consensus is *high* (she's in good company), but if only Sally is late, consensus is *low*.
- *Distinctiveness* refers to the extent to which Sally behaves in a similar way towards other, similar, 'stimuli' or 'entities'. Is she late for other subjects? If she is, then distinctiveness is *low* (there's nothing special about Psychology), but if she's late only for Psychology, then distinctiveness is *high*.
- *Consistency* refers to how stable Sally's behaviour is over time. If she's regularly late for Psychology, consistency is *high*, but if she's not (this is a 'one-off'), then consistency is *low*.

Kelley believes that a combination of *low consensus* (Sally is the only one late), *low distinctiveness* (she's late for all her subjects) and *high consistency* (she's regularly late) will lead us to make a *person* (*internal* or *dispositional*) *attribution*. In other words, the cause of Sally's behaviour is something to do with Sally, such as being a poor timekeeper. Any other combination would normally result in an *external* or *situational attribution*. For example, if Sally is generally punctual (low consistency), or if most students are late for Psychology (high consensus), then the cause of Sally's lateness might be 'extenuating circumstances' in the first case or the subject and/or the lecturer in the second.

Table 23.1 Causal attributions based on three different combinations of causal information (based on Kelley, 1967)

Consensus	Distinctiveness	Consistency	Causal Attribution
Low	Low	High	Person (actor/ internal)
Low	High	Low	Circumstances (external)
High	High	High	Stimulus/ target (external)

Evaluation of Kelley's covariation model

Ask Yourself

- Can you relate consensus, distinctiveness and consistency information to components of Jones and Davis's CIT?

- According to Gilbert (1998), the similarities between Kelley's covariation model and CIT are often overlooked: (a) *consensus* is similar to Jones and Davis's social *desirability* (if consensus is high, then the behaviour is socially desirable); (b) *distinctiveness* is similar to Jones and Davis's concern with *uncommon/unique effects* (the more distinctive the choice, the more it has to do with the unique effects of the choice); (c) *consistency* reflects an enduring *disposition* (as opposed to temporary circumstances).
- While a number of empirical studies have found support for Kelley (see Key Study 23.2), not all three types of causal information are used to the same extent. Distinctiveness influences entity attributions the most, and consistency influences circumstances attribution the most. Also, contrary to predictions, consensus doesn't influence person attributions the most.

Key Study 23.2

A funny thing happened on the way to the laboratory (McArthur, 1972)

- McArthur presented participants with one-sentence descriptions of various behaviours relating to emotions, accomplishments, opinions and actions (for example, 'John laughs at the comedian', 'Sue is afraid of the dog', 'George translates the sentence incorrectly').
- Each description was accompanied by high or low consensus information ('Almost everyone ...' or 'Hardly anyone ...'), high or low distinctiveness information (this person does/ does not respond the same way to 'almost every other ... comedian ... dog, etc.'), and high or low consistency information ('In the past ... has almost always ...' or 'almost never').
- The task was to attribute each behaviour to (a) characteristics of the actor, (b) the stimulus (target), (c) circumstances or (d) some combination of these.
- Predictions based on Kelley's model were strongly supported.

- Major (1980) found that participants show a marked preference for consistency over the other two, with consensus being the least preferred. Similarly, Nisbett and Borgida (1975) found surprisingly weak effects of consensus information when they asked university students to explain the behaviour of a participant in a Psychology experiment. This participant, like most others involved, had agreed to tolerate a high level of electric shock. But the students who were told that 16 of the 34 participants had tolerated the highest possible shock level, were no more likely to make situational attributions than those who'd been given no consensus information at all. According to Nisbett and Borgida, people's judgements are less responsive to the dull and abstract base rates that constitute consensus information than to the more vivid information regarding the behaviour of one, concrete target person.

- However, consensus information can have more of an impact if it's made more salient (for example, if it's contrary to what we might expect most people to do: Wells and Harvey, 1977). This proposal is consistent with Hilton and Slugoski's (1986) *abnormal conditions focus model*; this can help explain why the three types of causal information aren't used to the same extent (see Box 23.2).

Box 23.2 The abnormal conditions focus model (Hilton and Slugoski, 1986)

Kelley's three types of information are useful to the extent that the behaviour requiring explanation contrasts with the information given. So, with *low consensus* information, the *person* is abnormal, whereas with *low consistency* information the *circumstances* are abnormal. With *high distinctiveness* information, the *stimulus/target* is abnormal.

Another way of looking at 'abnormality' is, in Table 23.1, to read down the columns. Two 'values' are the same and different from the third. For example, high consensus (the 'odd one out') corresponds to the stimulus/target, low distinctiveness corresponds to the person/actor and low consistency corresponds to the circumstances.

Although 'abnormal' here refers to the causal information, rather than the causal attribution, the end result seems to be the same.

The model proposes that we attribute as a cause the necessary condition that's abnormal when compared with the background of the target event (Slugoski and Hilton, 2000).

- Just because people make attributions as if they're using covariation 'rules', doesn't necessarily mean they are (Hewstone and Fincham, 1996). Kelley seems to have overestimated people's ability to assess covariation. He originally compared the social perceiver to a naïve scientist (as did Heider), trying to draw inferences in much the same way as the formal scientist draws conclusions from data. More significantly, it's a *normative* model which states how, ideally, people should come to draw inferences about others' behaviour. However, the actual procedures that people use aren't as logical, rational and systematic as the model suggests. (This criticism also applies to Jones and Davis's CIT: see the section on error and bias, below.)

The configuration model

Kelley recognised that in many situations (most notably when we don't know the actor), we might not have access to any or all of the covariation model's three types of information. Indeed, often the only information we have is a single occurrence of the behaviour of a particular individual. Yet we still feel able to explain the behaviour. The *configuration model* was Kelley's attempt to account for attributions about such single occurrence behaviours.

Causal schemata

When we make 'single event attributions' we do so using *causal schemata* (Kelley, 1972, 1983). These are general ideas (or ready-made beliefs, preconceptions, and even theories: Hewstone and Fincham, 1996) about 'how certain kinds of causes interact to produce a specific kind of effect' (Kelley, 1972). According to Fiske and Taylor (1991), causal schemata provide the social perceiver with a 'causal shorthand' for making complex inferences quickly and easily. They come into play when causal information is otherwise ambiguous and incomplete.

The two major kinds of causal schemata are *multiple necessary schemata* and *multiple sufficient schemata*.

Box 23.3 Multiple necessary and multiple sufficient schemata

Multiple necessary causes: Experience tells us that to win a marathon, for example, you must not only be fit and highly motivated, but you must have trained hard for several months beforehand, you must wear the right kind of running shoes and so on.

Even if all these conditions are met, there's no guarantee of success, but the absence of any one of them is likely to produce failure. So, in this sense, success is more informative than failure. Thus, there are many causes needed to produce certain behaviours – typically, those which are unusual or extreme.

Multiple sufficient causes: With some behaviours, any number of causes are sufficient to explain their occurrence. For example, a sportsman/woman who advertises shampoo may do so because s/he genuinely believes it's a good product or because s/he's being paid a large sum of money to advertise it – either of these is a sufficient cause.

Ask Yourself

- In this last example, do you think one of the proposed causes is more likely to be the real cause than the other (believing in the product or receiving a large fee)?
- If so, which one?
- What do you base this attribution on?

Since it's reasonable to assume that it's the fee which accounts for the sportsperson's appearance in the commercial, we're likely to reject the other cause ('belief' in the product) according to the *discounting principle* (Kelley, 1983). According to this:

> *Given that different causes can produce the same effect, the role of a given cause is discounted if other plausible causes are present.*

Multiple sufficient schemata are also associated with the *augmenting principle* (Kelley, 1983). This states that:

> *The role of a given cause is augmented or increased if the effect occurs in the presence of an inhibitory factor.*

So, we're more likely to make an internal attribution (to effort and ability) when a student passes an exam after (say) suffering the death of a relative, than would be the case for a student who'd passed without having suffered such a loss.

WEINER'S ATTRIBUTIONAL THEORY of EMOTION and MOTIVATION

As the name suggests, Weiner's (1986) theory is really an application of basic attributional principles to human emotion and motivation (see Chapters 9 and 10). According to Weiner, the attributions we make about our own and others' successes and failures produce specific kinds of emotional response, but these attributions are more complex than described by Heider, Jones and Davis or Kelley.

For Weiner, there are three dimensions of causality. These are:

1. The *locus dimension*: causes can be internal/external (person/situation)
2. The *stability dimension*: causes can be stable/transient (permanent/temporary)
3. The *controllability dimension*: causes can be controllable or uncontrollable.

For example, we may blame failure in an exam on a really difficult paper (external, stable, uncontrollable), which is likely to make us feel *angry*. Or we may blame the really bad headache we awoke with on the morning of the exam (internal, unstable, uncontrollable), which may make us feel both *angry* and *disappointed*. But a third possibility is that we blame our failure on our basic lack of ability (internal, stable, uncontrollable), which is likely to make us feel quite *depressed*.

What's important here is that not all internal or external causes are of the same kind. For Weiner, causes are *multidimensional*.

ERROR and BIAS in the ATTRIBUTION PROCESS

As we've already seen, people are far less logical and systematic (less 'scientific') than required by Kelley's covariation model. Also, both this and Jones and Davis's CIT are *normative* models: an *idealised* view of how people would think if provided with all the available information, with unlimited time and displaying no bias (Fiske, 2004).

Research into sources of error and bias seems to provide a much more accurate account of how people *actually* make causal attributions. Zebrowitz (1990) defines sources of bias as:

> *... The tendency to favour one cause over another when explaining some effect. Such favouritism may result in causal attributions that deviate from predictions derived from rational attributional principles, like covariation ...*

Even though almost all behaviour is the product of *both* the person and the situation, our causal explanations tend to emphasise one or the other. According to Jones and Nisbett (1971), we all want to see ourselves as competent interpreters of human behaviour, and so we naïvely assume that simple explanations are better than complex ones. To try to analyse the interactions between personal and situational factors would take time and energy, and we seldom have all the relevant information at our disposal.

One kind of bias is the uneven use of different kinds of causal information as identified by Kelley's covariation model. As we saw earlier, they're not used to an equal extent; people use consistency the most, distinctiveness moderately and consensus the least (Kruglanski, 1977).

The fundamental attribution error (FAE)

The *fundamental attribution error* (FAE) refers to the general tendency to overestimate the importance of personal/dispositional factors relative to situational/environmental factors as causes of behaviour (Ross, 1977). This will tend to make others' behaviour seem more predictable which, in turn, enhances our sense of control over the environment.

Ask Yourself

- Can you relate the FAE to any of the Gestalt laws of perception (see Chapter 15)?

Heider (1958) believed that behaviour represents the 'figure' against the 'ground', comprising context, roles, situational pressures and so on. In other words, behaviour is conspicuous and situational factors are less easily perceived. For Zebrowitz (1990):

> *... The fundamental attribution error is best viewed as a bias towards attributing an actor's behaviour to dispositional causes rather than as an attribution error. This bias may be limited to adults in western societies and it may be most pronounced when they are constrained to attribute behaviour to a single cause ...*

(See Critical Discussion 23.1.)

The term 'FAE' implies the view that it's a pervasive, inescapable process. However, subsequent research suggests that it's more context-dependent that such a description implies (Parkinson, 2008). Studies such as those of Krull (1993) indicates that automatic dispositional attributions only occur if the experimental task is to understand the actor, rather than the situation the actor is in (Parkinson, 2008). For these reasons, the FAE is often referred to as the *correspondence bias* (Gilbert and Malone, 1995)

The FAE and the just world hypothesis (JWH)

Related to the FAE, but not usually cited as an example of an attribution error, is the *just world hypothesis* (JWH) (Lerner, 1965, 1980). According to this, 'I am a just person living in a just world, a world where people get what they deserve'. When 'bad' things happen to people, we believe it's because they're in some way 'bad' people, so that they have at least partly 'brought it on themselves'. This can help explain the phenomenon of 'blaming the victim'. In rape cases, for example, the woman is often accused of having 'led the man on' or giving him the sexual 'green light' before changing her mind.

Myers (1994) gives the example of a German civilian who, on being shown round the Bergen–Belsen concentration camp after the British liberation, commented 'What terrible criminals these prisoners must have been to receive such treatment'. What this person seems to have been saying is that s/he found it totally unbelievable that such horrors (as had obviously been perpetrated in that camp) could have happened to innocent people – if they happened to them, why couldn't they happen to me? Believing in a just world gives us a sense of being in control: so long as we're 'good', only 'good' things will happen to us.

The actor–observer effect (AOE)

Related to the FAE is the tendency for actors and observers to make different attributions about the same event. This is called the *actor–observer effect* (AOE) (Jones and Nisbett, 1971; Nisbett *et al.*, 1973).

- Actors usually see their own behaviour as primarily a response to the situation, and therefore as quite variable from situation to situation (the cause is external).
- The observer typically attributes the same behaviour to the actor's intentions and dispositions, and therefore as quite consistent across situations (the cause is internal). The observer's attribution to internal causes is, of course, the FAE.

Nisbett *et al.* (1973) found that students: (a) assumed that actors would behave in the future in ways similar to those they'd just witnessed; (b) described their best friend's choices of girlfriend and college major in terms referring to dispositional qualities of their best friend (while more often describing their own similar choices in terms of properties of the girlfriend or major); and (c) attributed more personality traits to other people than to themselves.

One explanation for the AOE is that what's *perceptually salient* or vivid for the actor is different from what's perceptually salient or vivid for the observer (this is the figure–ground explanation which we noted when discussing the FAE). An important study by Storms (1973) supports this perceptual salience explanation of the AOE.

The general implication of the Storms study is that we can correct for inattention to situational factors by manipulating attention (Parkinson, 2012).

The self-serving bias (SSB)

Several studies have found that the AOE is most pronounced when judging *negative* behaviours, and may be absent or even reversed for positive ones.

Ask Yourself

- **Try to account for this finding.**

Naturally, no one wants to admit to being incompetent, so we're more likely to 'blame' our failures on something external to ourselves. This is the *self-protecting bias,* which protects our self-esteem. However, we're quite happy to take the credit for our successes. This is the *self-enhancing bias*, which enhances our self-esteem. Together, they constitute the *self-serving bias* (SSB) (Miller and Ross, 1975).

There's some evidence that positively valued outcomes (e.g. altruism) are more often attributed to people, and negatively valued outcomes (e.g. being late) to situational factors, regardless of who committed them. However, when either the self or someone closely associated with the self has committed the action, credit for positive events and denial of responsibility for negative ones are even stronger.

Key Study 23.3

Videotape and the attribution process (Storms, 1973)

- Two actor participants at a time engaged in a brief, unstructured conversation, while two observers looked on. Later, a questionnaire was used to measure the actors' attributions of their own behaviour in the conversation, and the observers' attributions of the behaviour of one of the two actors to whom they'd been assigned.
- Visual orientation was manipulated by the use of videotapes of the conversation so that:
  (a) the *no video* (control) group simply completed the questionnaire
  (b) the *same orientation* group simply saw a video of what they saw during the original conversation (before completing the questionnaire)
  (c) the *new orientation* group saw a video which reversed the original orientation: actors saw themselves and observers saw the other actor (again, before completing the questionnaire).
- As predicted, in the first two groups the usual AOE was found. But, also as predicted, the AOE was reversed in the third group: actors made more dispositional attributions than did observers.

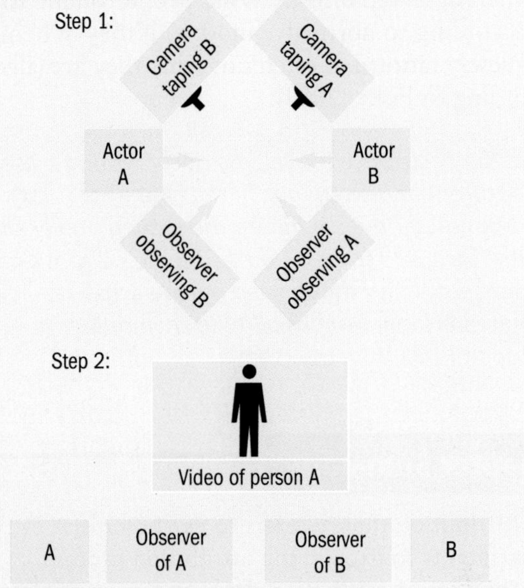

Figure 23.2 Diagram depicting the arrangement in the Storms (1973) experiment

Critical Discussion 23.1

Cultural differences in attributional errors and biases

Although the FAE has been assumed to be universal, more recent research suggests it may actually be specific to *individualist* (predominantly western) cultures (Fiske *et al.*, 1998: see Chapter 47). In *collectivist* (mainly non-western) cultures, people are more likely to attribute someone's behaviour to situational factors as opposed to personality characteristics. They don't expect people to be consistent on their behaviour: different behaviours may be required when the situation calls for it (Nagayama Hall and Barongan, 2002). Roles or duties describe a person better than individual traits, which calls into question the universality of the FAE in its usual form (Abrahamson, 2014).

English-language newspapers reporting murders emphasise dispositional causes (such as a deeply disturbed, driven personality, very bad temper/'short fuse'), while Chinese-language papers reporting the same crime emphasise situational causes (relationships, rivalry and isolation, the social availability of guns, achievement pressure and the immediate context, such as having recently been sacked) (Morris and Peng, 1994).

While all cultures encourage a search for invariant dispositions, some locate them more in individual actors, others in collective actors (Morris *et al.*, 2001).

The SSB isn't found among Asians, who are more likely to attribute their successes to external factors (such as luck) and their failures to internal factors (such as lack of effort) (Kitayama and Markus, 1995). This, in turn, reflects a bias towards self-effacement, which is more likely to maintain one's self-esteem in a collectivist culture (where the achievements of the individual are minimised). This strategy for maintaining self-esteem is also often used by women in individualist cultures:

> *... Whose belief system can also be characterised as collectivist in nature, in that they value relationships, put other people's needs before their own, and define themselves in terms of their connectedness to others ... (Nagayama Hall and Barongan, 2002)*

CONCLUSIONS

All these errors and biases fall under the heading of *descriptive models*. They emphasise what people actually do when observed directly. What people 'ought' to do (according to normative models) if they're being completely rational, is often not what they actually do. According to Fiske (2004):

> ... The descriptive models, by documenting biases, capture that discrepancy. In the case of ordinary personology, people ignore the hidden power of situations and focus on other people's dispositions more than they should, and people attribute more personal responsibility to themselves for good events than they should.

According to Edwards and Potter (1993), attributions are formulated to meet *conversational goals* (such as persuading, undermining, blaming and accusing). The different ways that defence and prosecution lawyers try to explain the behaviour of accused and victims in trials is a classic demonstration of such conversational goals. But Edwards and Potter believe that *any* attribution is aimed at meeting some such goal. As Parkinson (2012) says:

> ... *attributions do not function as attempts to explain a separately existing social reality, but* instead to construct *a version of reality suited to the current conversational business. Attributions are not descriptive representations but rhetorical moves in an ongoing dialogue.* (emphasis in original)

Chapter Summary

- **Attribution theory** refers to Psychologists' attempts to explain the **attribution process**. **Theories of attribution** draw on the principles of attribution theory to predict how people will respond in particular life domains.
- Heider's 'common-sense' psychology sees people as **naïve scientists**, inferring unobservable causes (or meaning) from observable behaviour. In western culture, behaviour is explained in terms of both **personal (dispositional/internal)** and **situational (environmental/external)** factors.
- Jones and Davis were concerned with explaining why we make **correspondent inferences** about people's dispositions. One way of looking for dispositions that could have caused behaviour is through the **analysis of uncommon effects**.
- The likelihood of making dispositional attributions is influenced by **free choice**, **social desirability**, **roles** and **prior expectations**.
- Kelley's **covariation model** is concerned with the processes by which we make internal and external attributions for the causes of behaviour. The principle of **covariation** says that we're more likely to infer that two events are causally related if they repeatedly co-occur.
- Attributions about some effect/behaviour depend on the extent of its covariation with causal information regarding **consensus**, **consistency** and **distinctiveness**.
- Kelley's **configuration model** tries to account for 'single event attributions' in terms of **multiple necessary** and **multiple sufficient causal schemata**. The latter are associated with the **augmenting principle**, and we choose between two or more possible causes by using the **discounting principle**.
- Weiner's attribution theory identifies three dimensions of causality: **locus**, **stability** and controllability. It applies basic attributional principles to emotion and motivation.
- People are actually less rational and scientific than Jones and Davis's, and Kelley's **normative models** require. A more accurate account of the attribution process involves looking at **systematic biases** in the attribution of cause.
- The **fundamental attribution error (FAE)** (also known as the **correspondence bias**) is the tendency to exaggerate the importance of internal/dispositional factors relative to external/situational factors.
- In the **actor–observer effect (AOE)**, actors see their behaviours as responses to situational factors, whereas observers explain the same behaviours in dispositional terms.
- The AOE is most pronounced when one explains one's own negative behaviour (**self-protecting bias**). Personal successes tend to be explained in dispositional ways (**self-enhancing bias**). Together, they comprise the **self-serving bias (SSB)**.
- There are important **cultural differences** with regard to the FAE and SSB in particular. These are related to **individualist** and **collectivist** cultures.

Links with Other Topics/Chapters

Chapters 10 and 24 → Two of the traditions that form the backbone of attribution theory are Schachter's *cognitive labelling theory of emotion* (Chapter 10) and Bem's *self-perception theory of attitude change*

Chapters 9, 22, 30 and 36 → The multidimensional nature of causes, combined with the emotional responses associated with different attributions (Weiner) have important implications for: *impression management/self-presentation*, *self-esteem* (especially in relation to gender differences in nAch) and *helping behaviour*

Chapter 35 → The claim that women's collectivist belief system is a means of maintaining their self-esteem is directly relevant to *Gilligan's account of female morality*

Chapters 25 and 30 → In combination with the FAE, the JWH can help to explain (certain aspects of) *prejudice* and *helping behaviour*

Chapter 44 → An interesting exception to the SSB is the case of *clinically depressed people* (Abramson *et al.*, 1978)

Chapter 12 → Women are more likely than men to cope with *stress* by blaming themselves for their plight

Chapter 28 → The SSB might be useful in the short run, but not adaptive in the long term. For example, blaming one's partners is correlated with *marital dissatisfaction*; the data suggest that blame actually causes the unhappiness

Recommended Reading

Fiske, S.T. & Taylor, S.E. (1991) *Social Cognition* (2nd edition) New York: McGraw-Hill. Chapters 2 and 3 are especially relevant.

Gross, R. (2008) *Key Studies in Psychology* (5th edition). London: Hodder Education. Chapter 14.

Weiner, B. (1992) *Human Motivation: Metaphors, Theories and Research.* Newbury Park, CA: Sage. Chapters 6 and 7.

Useful Websites

http://tip.psychology.org/weiner.html (Attribution Theory – B. Weiner)

http://changingminds.org/explanations/theories/attribution_theory.htm (Changing Minds org: Attribution Theory)

www.newworldencyclopedia.org/entry/Fritz_Heider (New World Encyclopedia: Fritz Heider)

CHAPTER 24

ATTITUDES AND ATTITUDE CHANGE

- What are attitudes?
- What are attitudes for?
- The measurement of attitudes
- The relationship between attitudes and behaviour
- Social influence and behaviour change
- Theories of attitude change

INTRODUCTION and OVERVIEW

According to Gordon Allport (1935):

> *The concept of attitudes is probably the most distinctive and indispensable concept in contemporary American social psychology …*

More than 50 years later, Hogg and Vaughan (1995) claim that:

> *Attitudes continue to fascinate research workers and remain a key, if controversial, part of social psychology.*

However, the study of attitudes has undergone many important changes during that time, with different questions becoming the focus of theory and research.

According to Stainton Rogers *et al.* (1995), Psychologists have tried to answer four fundamental questions over the last 70 years:

1. Where do attitudes come from? How are they moulded and formed in the first place?
2. How can attitudes be measured?
3. How and why do attitudes change? What forces are involved and what intrapsychic mechanisms operate when people shift in their opinions about particular 'attitude objects'?
4. How do attitudes relate to behaviour? What is it that links the way people think and feel about an attitude object, and what they do about it?

In this chapter, the emphasis is on some of the answers that have been offered to questions 3 and 4. This discussion is also relevant to prejudice, considered as an extreme attitude (see Chapter 25).

During the 1940s and 1950s, the focus of research was on attitude change, in particular *persuasive communication*. Much of the impetus for this came from the use of propaganda during the Second World War, as well as a more general concern over the growing influence of the mass media, especially in the USA. The power of advertising was also beginning to interest Psychologists and other social scientists. This period also saw the birth of a number of theories of attitude change, the most influential of these being Festinger's *cognitive dissonance theory*.

The 1960s and 1970s was a period of decline and pessimism in attitude research, at least partly due to the apparent failure to find any reliable relationship between measured attitudes and behaviour (Hogg and Vaughan, 1995). However, the 1980s saw a revival of interest, stimulated largely by the cognitive approach, so attitudes represent another important aspect of *social cognition* (see Chapter 22).

WHAT ARE ATTITUDES?

Allport (1935) regarded the study of attitudes as the meeting ground for the study of social groups, culture and the individual. Similarly, Festinger (1950) emphasised the integral *interdependence* of individual and group: 'an attitude is correct, valid and proper to the extent that it is anchored in a group of people with similar beliefs, opinions and attitudes'. But, with a few notable exceptions, attitude research has focused on *internal* processes, ignoring the influence of groups on attitude formation and change (Cooper *et al.,* 2004). Even Allport's definition in Table 24.1 reflects this bias. Warren and Jahoda's definition is probably the most 'social'.

Attitudes can vary in two important ways: (a) *valence* (or direction) and (b) *strength* (Haddock and Maio, 2012).

Table 24.1 Some definitions of attitudes

An attitude is a mental and neural state of readiness, organised through experience, exerting a directive or dynamic influence upon the individual's response to all objects and situations with which it is related. (Allport, 1935)
A learned orientation, or disposition, toward an object or situation, which provides a tendency to respond favourably or unfavourably to the object or situation … (Rokeach, 1968)
… Attitudes have social reference in their origins and development and in their objects, while at the same time they have psychological reference in that they inhere in the individual and are intimately enmeshed in his behaviour and his psychological make-up. (Warren and Jahoda, 1973)
The term attitude should be used to refer to a general, enduring positive or negative feeling about some person, object, or issue. (Petty and Cacioppo, 1981)
An attitude is an evaluative disposition toward some object. It's an evaluation of something or someone along a continuum of like-to-dislike or favourable-to-unfavourable … (Zimbardo and Leippe, 1991)
An overall evaluation of an object that is based on cognitive, affective and behavioural information. (Maio and Haddock, 2012).
Inherent in definitions of attitudes is the idea that reporting an attitude involves the expression of an *evaluative judgement* about a stimulus object (a particular issue, object or person), i.e. liking/disliking, approving/disapproving, favouring/disfavouring. (Haddock and Maio, 2012) (emphasis in original)

According to Rosenberg and Hovland (1960), attitudes are 'predispositions to respond to some class of stimuli with certain classes of response'. These classes of response are:

- *Affective*: what a person feels about the attitude object, how favourably or unfavourably it's evaluated
- *Cognitive*: what a person believes the attitude object is like, objectively
- *Behavioural* (sometimes called the '*conative*'): how a person actually responds, or intends to respond, to the attitude object.

This *three-component model*, which is much more a model of *attitude structure* than a simple definition (Stahlberg and Frey, 1988), is shown in Figure 24.1. It sees an attitude as an intervening/mediating variable between observable stimuli and responses, illustrating the influence that behaviourism was still having, even in Social Psychology, at the start of the 1960s. A major problem with this multi-component model is the assumption that the three components are highly correlated.

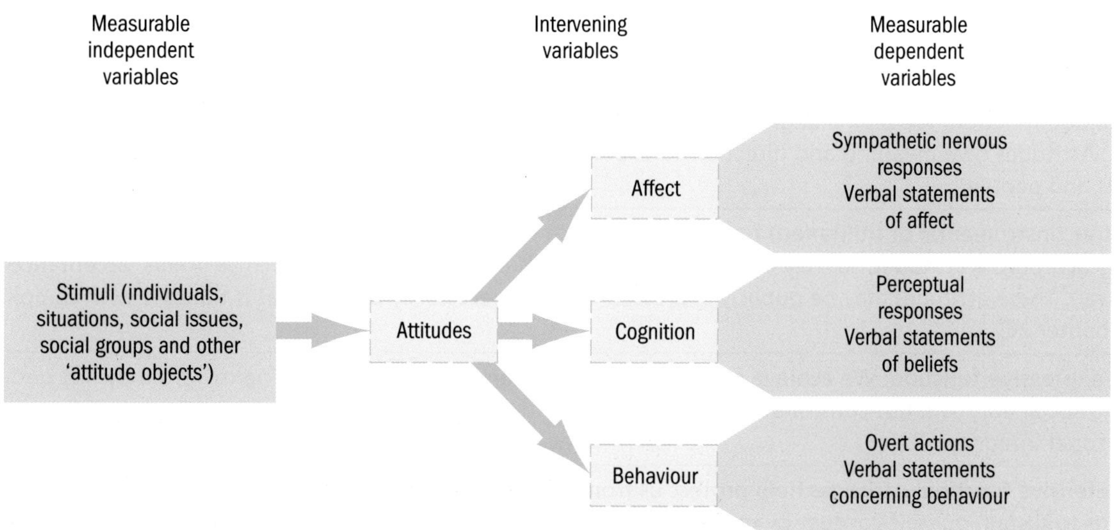

Figure 24.1 Three-component view of attitudes (Rosenberg and Hovland, 1960). From Stahlberg, D. and Frey, D. (1988) 'Attitudes 1: Structure, measurement and functions'. In Hewstone, M. *et al.* (eds) *Introduction to Social Psychology*. Oxford, Blackwell

Attitudes, beliefs and values

An attitude can be thought of as a blend or integration of beliefs and values. Beliefs represent the knowledge or information we have about the world (although these may be inaccurate or incomplete) and, in themselves, are non-evaluative. According to Fishbein and Ajzen (1975), 'a belief links an object to some attribute' (e.g. 'America' and 'capitalist state'). To convert a belief into an attitude, a 'value' ingredient is needed. Values refer to an individual's sense of what is desirable, good, valuable, worthwhile, and so on. While most adults will have many thousands of beliefs, they have only hundreds of attitudes and a few dozen values.

Ask Yourself

- Try to identify some of your most cherished values (there should be a relatively small number of these). Then try to identify some related attitudes, which are less abstract than values.

WHAT ARE ATTITUDES FOR?

According to Hogg and Vaughan (1995):

> *... Attitudes are basic and pervasive in human life ... Without the concept of attitude, we would have difficulty construing and reacting to events, trying to make decisions, and making sense of our relationships with people in everyday life ...*

In other words, attitudes provide us with ready-made reactions to, and interpretations of events, just as other aspects of our cognitive 'equipment' do, such as schemas (see Chapter 21) and stereotypes (see Chapters 22 and 25). Attitudes save us energy, since we don't have to work out how we feel about objects or events each time we come into contact with them.

However, not all attitudes serve the same function. Katz (1960), influenced by Freud's psychoanalytic theory, believes that attitudes serve both conscious and unconscious motives. He identified four major functions of attitudes (see Table 24.2).

Katz's functional approach implies that some attitudes will be more resistant to efforts to change them than others, in particular those that serve an ego-defensive function. This is especially important when trying to account for prejudice and attempts to reduce it (see Chapter 25).

THE MEASUREMENT of ATTITUDES

Attitudes cannot be measured directly; because they're *hypothetical constructs*, they have to be *inferred* from the individual's responses to questions about the attitude object (Fazio and Olson, 2003). Most attitude scales rely on verbal reports, and usually take the form of standardised statements which clearly refer to the attitude being measured. Such scales make two further assumptions: (i) the same statement has the *same meaning* for all respondents; and, more fundamentally, (ii) subjective attitudes, when expressed verbally, can be *quantified* (represented by a numerical score).

Haddock and Maio (2012) distinguish between *explicit* and *indirect* attitude measures:

- *Explicit* measures require respondents' conscious attention to the attitude being measured and *directly* ask people to think about and report their attitude. Most attitude measures fall into this category and examples include the Likert scale and the semantic differential.

Table 24.2 Four major functions of attitudes (based on Katz, 1960)

Knowledge function: We seek a degree of predictability, consistency and stability in our perception of the world. Attitudes give meaning and direction to experience, providing frames of reference for judging events, objects and people.
Adjustive (instrumental or utilitarian) function: We obtain favourable responses from others by displaying socially acceptable attitudes, so they become associated with important rewards (such as others' acceptance and approval). These attitudes may be publicly expressed, but not necessarily believed, as is the case with compliance (see Chapter 26).
Value-expressive function: We achieve self-expression through cherished values. The reward may not be gaining social approval but confirmation of the more positive aspects of our self-concept, especially our sense of personal integrity.
Ego-defensive function: Attitudes help protect us from admitting personal deficiencies. For example, prejudice helps us to sustain our self-concept by maintaining a sense of superiority over others. Ego defence often means avoiding and denying self-knowledge. This function comes closest to being unconscious in a Freudian sense (see Chapters 2 and 42).

- *Implicit* measures don't require such conscious attention, assessing attitudes without *directly* asking respondents for a verbal report. Examples include sociometry, evaluative priming and the implicit association test (IAT).

Explicit (direct) methods

Likert scale (1932)

This comprises a number of statements, for each of which participants indicate whether they strongly agree/agree/undecided/disagree/strongly disagree. If possible, statements are selected so that for half 'agree' represents a positive attitude and for the other half a negative attitude. This controls for *acquiescence response set*, the tendency to agree or disagree with items consistently, or to tick the 'undecided' point on the scale.

LIKERT SCALE

'I believe that under no circumstances can animal experiments be justified'

5	4	3	2	1
Strongly agree	Agree	Undecided	Disagree	Strongly disagree

Figure 24.2 An illustration of a Likert scale

The Likert scale is one of the most popular standard attitude scales, partly because it's more statistically reliable, and easier to construct, than the Thurstone scale. It makes no assumptions about *equal intervals*.

Semantic differential (Osgood *et al.*, 1957)

This assumes a hypothetical semantic space, in which the meaning or connotation of any word or concept can be represented somewhere on a seven-point scale. Unlike other scales, this allows different attitudes to be measured on the same scale. The attitude object is denoted by a single word (e.g. 'father'), and the scale comprises seven bipolar scales of adjectives (a value of seven usually being given to the positive end).

good _ _ _ _ _ _ bad (illustrates the *evaluative factor*)
strong _ _ _ _ _ weak (illustrates the *potency factor*)
active _ _ _ _ _ passive (illustrates the *activity factor*)

Implicit (indirect) methods

A problem with attitude scales (explicit self-report methods) is that participants may be reluctant to reveal their true feelings. This can produce *social desirability* effects, in which participants give answers they think are expected or 'proper'. Incorporating a *lie scale* can help detect this tendency (see Chapter 42). Reassurance that their answers will remain anonymous, and stressing the importance of giving honest answers, can also help reduce the social desirability effect.

Sociometry (Moreno, 1953)

This represents a method for assessing interpersonal attitudes in 'natural' groups (at school, college, work); that is, it assesses who likes whom. Each group member is asked to name another who'd be his/her preferred partner for a specific activity or as a friend. The product of these choices is a *sociogram*, which charts the friendship patterns, revealing the popular and unpopular members, the 'isolates', and so on.

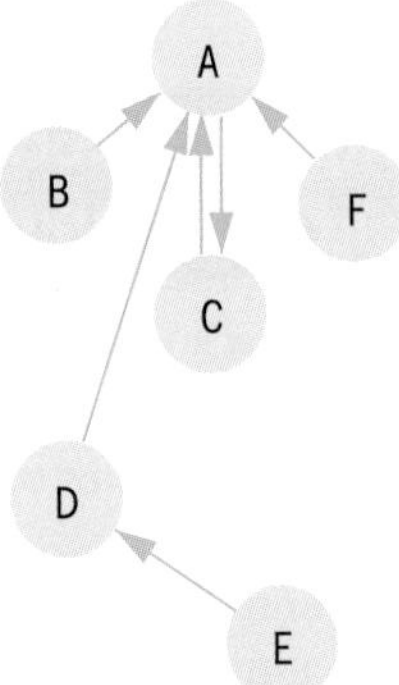

Figure 24.3 A sociogram

Each circle in Figure 24.3 represents a group member, and the arrows indicate direction of preference.

Ask Yourself

- Who's the most popular member of the group?
- Who's most isolated?

Evaluative priming

According to Fazio (1995), an attitude is an association in memory between an attitude object and a summary evaluation; these associations vary in strength, which determines the accessibility of the attitude. Accessibility could be defined in terms of how quickly an individual responds to an evaluative word after having been briefly presented with the attitude object (Fazio *et al.*, 1995). In a typical experiment, participants are seated in front of a computer screen; the name of an attitude object (e.g. 'abortion') is replaced by an evaluative object (e.g. 'immoral') and the participant's task is to indicate the *valence* of the adjective (its positivity or negativity) as quickly as possible. In the example, if someone feel very strongly that abortion is wrong, they should respond faster to negative than to positive adjectives.

This approach has been used in studies of numerous attitude objects, including those that might raise social desirability issues if used on explicit measures (Haddock and Maio, 2012). For example, Fazio *et al.* (1995) instructed white participants that their task was to indicate the meaning of positive and negative adjectives. But prior to the presentation of each individual adjective, a photograph of a black or white person was briefly shown. Compared to response times to white faces, presentation of a black face produced faster responses to negative adjectives and slower responses to positive adjectives. Black participants didn't show these response patterns. In addition, white participants who showed this pattern most strongly were more likely to display more negative behaviour towards a black experimenter. Fazio *et al.* interpreted these response differences as reflecting a negative attitude towards blacks.

Box 24.1 The Implicit Association Test (IAT) (Greenwald *et al.*, 1998)

- Participants respond on a computer keyboard (a) with their *right* hand to words that name *pleasant* things and, say, names of flowers; and (b) with their *left* hand to words that name *unpleasant* things, and say, insect names.
- Then, the task is changed: participants now have to give the first response to *pleasant* words + insect names, and the second response to *unpleasant* words + flower names.
- While the first task is generally very easy, the second becomes hugely difficult.
- In a second experiment, participants were consistently faster when presented with 'White'/'pleasant' and 'Black'/'unpleasant' than they were when presented with ''White'/'unpleasant' and 'Black'/'pleasant'. This suggests that the former set of concepts is more strongly associated than the second set.
- This demonstrates underlying, implicit, unconscious prejudice (see Chapter 25).

The IAT and other implicit measures have become increasingly popular among attitude researchers because they assess attitudes without the necessity of asking participants for a direct verbal report; this reduces the influence of giving socially desirable report (Fazio and Olson, 2003). However, the (sometimes) low correlation between implicit and explicit measures implies that they're assessing *different* constructs. Haddock and Maio (2012) believe that they've allowed Social Psychologists to generate novel and important questions regarding the underlying causes of behaviour. They're especially useful in relation to socially sensitive attitudes, in particular, prejudice.

THE RELATIONSHIP between ATTITUDES and BEHAVIOUR

Once we've established people's attitudes, can we then accurately predict how they'll behave? As we noted earlier, Rosenberg and Hovland's (1960) three-components model implies that the behavioural component will be highly correlated with the cognitive and affective components.

Ask Yourself

- Do people's expressed attitudes (cognitive and affective components) necessarily coincide with their overt actions (behavioural component)?
- Do we always act in accordance with our attitudes?

An early study showing the inconsistency between attitudes and behaviour is that of LaPiere (1934).

Key Study 24.1

Some of my best friends are Chinese ... (LaPiere, 1934)

- Beginning in 1930 and for the next two years, LaPiere travelled around the USA with a Chinese couple (a young student and his wife), expecting to encounter anti-Oriental attitudes which would make it difficult for them to find accommodation.
- But in the course of 10,000 miles of travel, they were discriminated against only once and there appeared to be no prejudice. They were given accommodation in 66 hotels, auto-camps and 'Tourist Homes' and refused at only one. They were also served in 184 restaurants and cafés and treated with '... more than ordinary consideration ...' in 72 of them.
- However, when each of the 251 establishments visited was sent a letter six months later asking: 'Will you accept members of the Chinese race as guests in your establishment?', 91 per cent of the 128 which responded gave an emphatic 'No'. One establishment gave an unqualified 'Yes' and the rest said 'Undecided: depends upon circumstances'.

Ask yourself

- Try to account for LaPiere's findings.

Influences on behaviour

It's generally agreed that attitudes form only one determinant of behaviour. They represent *predispositions* to behave in particular ways, but how we actually act in a particular situation will depend on the immediate consequences of our behaviour, how we think others will evaluate our actions and habitual ways of behaving in those kinds of situations. In addition, there may be specific *situational factors* influencing behaviour. For example, in the LaPiere study, the high quality of his Chinese friends' clothes and luggage and their politeness, together with the presence of LaPiere himself, may have made it more difficult to show overt prejudice. Thus, sometimes we experience a conflict of attitudes and behaviour may represent a compromise between them.

Compatibility between attitudes and behaviour

The same attitude may be expressed in a variety of ways. For example, having a positive attitude towards the Labour Party doesn't necessarily mean that you actually become a member, or that you attend public meetings. But if you don't vote Labour in a general or local election, people may question your attitude. In other words, an attitude should predict behaviour to some extent, even if this is extremely limited and specific.

Indeed, Ajzen and Fishbein (1977) argue that attitudes can predict behaviour, provided that both are assessed at the same level of generality: there needs to be a high degree of *compatibility* (or *correspondence*) between them. Specifically, measures of attitude and behaviour need to correspond in four key areas: (a) *action* - the behaviour being performed (e.g. voting Labour); (b) the *target* of the behaviour (e.g. a particular political candidate); (c) *context* – the environment in which the behaviour's performed (e.g. private ballot or public show of hands); (d) *time* (e.g. is the election this week or in two years' away). Measures of attitude and behaviour are compatible to the extent that these four elements are assessed at *identical levels of generality or specificity* (Ajzen, 1988).

Ajzen and Fishbein (1977) argue that much of the earlier research (LaPiere's study included) suffered from either trying to predict specific behaviours from general attitudes, or vice versa, and this accounts for the generally low correlations. A study by Davidson and Jaccard (1979) tried to overcome this limitation. (See Key Study 24.2.)

The reliability and consistency of behaviour

Many of the classic studies which failed to find an attitude–behaviour relationship assessed just single instances of behaviour (Stroebe, 2000). As we noted earlier, behaviour depends on many factors in addition to the attitude. This makes a single instance of behaviour an unreliable indicator of an attitude (Jonas *et al.*, 1995). Only by sampling many instances of the behaviour will the influence of specific factors 'cancel out'. This *aggregation principle* (Fishbein and Ajzen, 1974) has been demonstrated in a number of studies.

Key Study 24.2

Attitudes can predict behaviour if you ask the right questions (Davidson and Jaccard, 1979)

- Davidson and Jaccard analysed correlations between married women's attitudes towards birth control and their actual use of oral contraceptives during the two years following the study.
- When 'attitude towards birth control' was used as the attitude measure, the correlation was 0.08. Clearly, the correspondence here was very low. But when 'attitudes towards oral contraceptives' were measured, the correlation rose to 0.32, and when 'attitudes towards using oral contraceptives' were measured, the correlation rose still further to 0.53.
- Finally, when 'attitudes towards using oral contraceptives during the next two years' was used, it rose still further, to 0.57. Clearly, in the last three cases, correspondence was much higher.

According to Hogg and Vaughan (1995), what emerged in the 1980s and 1990s is a view that attitudes and overt behaviour aren't related in a simple one-to-one fashion. In order to predict someone's behaviour, it must be possible to account for the interaction between attitudes, beliefs and behavioural intentions, as well as how all of these connect with the later action. One attempt to formalise these links is the *theory of reasoned action* (TRA) (e.g. Ajzen and Fishbein, 1970). This is discussed in relation to health behaviour in Chapter 12.

Figure 24.4 A demonstration of attitude–behaviour consistency that amazed the world; a pro-democracy Chinese student stands up for his convictions and defies tanks sent in against fellow rebels in Tiananmen Square, Beijing, China. Some 2000 demonstrators died in the subsequent massacre and the student was tried and shot a few days later

The strength of attitudes

Most modern theories agree that attitudes are represented in memory, and that an attitude's *accessibility* can exert a strong influence on behaviour (Fazio, 1986). By definition, strong attitudes exert more influence over behaviour, because they can be *automatically activated*. According to the MODE model ('motivation and opportunity as determinants': Fazio, 1986, 1990), spontaneous/automatic attitude–behaviour links occur when people hold highly accessible attitudes towards certain targets. These spontaneously guide behaviour, partly because they influence people's selective attention and perceptions of a particular target or situation.

One factor that seems to be important is *direct experience*. For example, Fazio and Zanna (1978) found that measures of students' attitudes towards Psychology experiments were better predictors of their future participation if they'd already taken part in several experiments than if they'd only read about them.

MODE acknowledges that, in some situations, people engage in *deliberate, effortful thinking* about their attitudes when deciding how to act (forming behavioural *intentions*). For example, a student deciding which university to go to will probably scrutinise his/her attitudes before making a choice. But research conducted under MODE focuses on *automatic processing* (Cooper *et al.*, 2004). The *theory of planned behaviour* (TPB: Ajzen, 1991), which built on the TRA, was designed to explain the relationship between attitudes and behaviour when deliberate, effortful processing is required. According to the TPB, it's *behavioural intentions*, rather than attitudes, that directly influence behaviour (again, see Chapter 12).

SOCIAL INFLUENCE and BEHAVIOUR CHANGE

Persuasive communication

According to Laswell (1948), in order to understand and predict the effectiveness of one person's attempt to change the attitude of another, we need to know 'Who says what in which channel to whom and with what effect'. Similarly, Hovland and Janis (1959) say that we need to study:

- the *source* of the persuasive communication, that is, the communicator (Laswell's 'who')
- the *message* itself (Laswell's 'what')
- the *recipient* of the message or the audience (Laswell's 'whom'), and
- the *situation* or *context*.

The basic paradigm in laboratory attitude-change research involves three steps or stages:

1. Measure people's attitude towards the attitude object (*pre-test*)
2. Expose them to a persuasive communication (manipulate a source, message or situational variable, or isolate a recipient-variable as the independent variable: see Figure 24.6)
3. Measure their attitudes again (*post-test*).

Critical Discussion 24.1

So attitudes don't predict behaviour: what's the problem?

The so-called *attitude–behaviour problem*, that is, the failure to find a reliable relationship between attitudes and behaviour, threatened to undermine the entire study of attitudes. As we saw in the *Introduction and overview*, attitude research was a cornerstone of Social Psychology in general, and social cognition in particular, for much of their history (Stainton Rogers *et al.*, 1995). But from the perspective of *Discursive Psychology* (DP) there's no reason to expect such a correlation: inconsistency between attitudes and behaviour is what we'd expect to find.

Traditional, mainstream, attitude research is based on the fallacy of *individualism*, according to which attitudes 'belong' to individuals (see Chapter 3). This implies something fairly constant and which is expressed and reflected in behaviour. From a discursive perspective, attitudes are versions of the world that are *constructed* by people in the course of their interactions with others.

DP is concerned with *action*, as distinct from cognition. In saying or writing things, people are performing actions, whose nature can be revealed through a detailed study of the discourse (e.g. recordings of everyday conversations, newspaper articles, TV programmes). Social Psychologists have underestimated the centrality of conflict in social life; an analysis of *rhetoric* highlights the point that people's versions of events, and their own mental life, are part of ongoing arguments, debates and dialogues (Billig, 1987, 1992, in Potter, 1996).

Compared with traditional attitude research, DP tries to shift the focus away from single, isolated, individuals towards interactions between individuals and groups, a more *relational* or *distributed* focus (Potter, 1996).

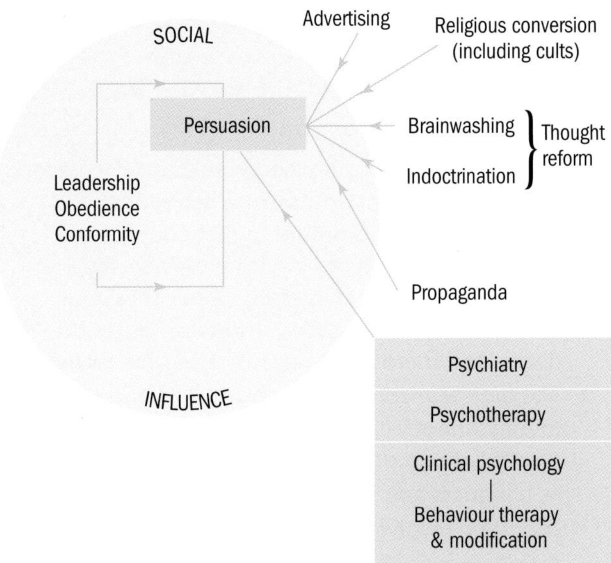

Figure 24.5 Different kinds of attempt to change people's attitudes and behaviour. These range from professional help for emotional and behavioural problems, through inevitable features of social interaction/social influence, to deliberate attempts to manipulate and control others for the benefit of the manipulator

If there's a difference between pre- and post-test measures, then the persuasive communication is judged to have 'worked'.

The early research into persuasive communication was conducted for the US War Department's Information and Education Department. This largely pragmatic approach is known as the *Yale approach*, with Hovland being one of the leading figures involved. It told us a great deal regarding when attitude change is most likely to occur and how, in practical terms, it can be produced. But it told us less about *why* people change their attitudes in response to persuasive messages.

Theories of systematic processing

According to theories of *systematic processing*, what's important is that the recipient processes the message content in a detailed way. This approach began with Hovland *et al.*'s (1953) proposal that the impact of persuasive messages can be understood in terms of a sequence of processes:

Attention to message → Comprehension of the content → Acceptance of its conclusions

If any of these fail to occur, persuasion is unlikely to be achieved.

McGuire (1969) proposed a longer chain of processes. We should ask if the recipient (i) *attended* to the message; (ii) *comprehended* it; (iii) *yielded* to it (*accepted* it); (iv) *retained* it; and (v) *acted* as a result. As with Hovland *et al.*'s theory, the failure of any one of these steps will cause the sequence to be broken.

Since the recipient must go through each of these steps if the message is to persuade, and since it's unlikely that any given step will be at its maximum effectiveness, McGuire's framework helps explain why it's often difficult to induce behaviour change through information campaigns (Stroebe, 2012a).

Typically, the impact of a 'persuasive' message in an experimental study is assessed immediately after its presentation; this effectively corresponds to just steps (i)–(iii). Also, (i) and (ii) are usually combined into a single step of *reception* of the message; thus, McGuire's model can be reduced to a two-step process, according to which the probability of a message producing attitude change is the joint of function of reception

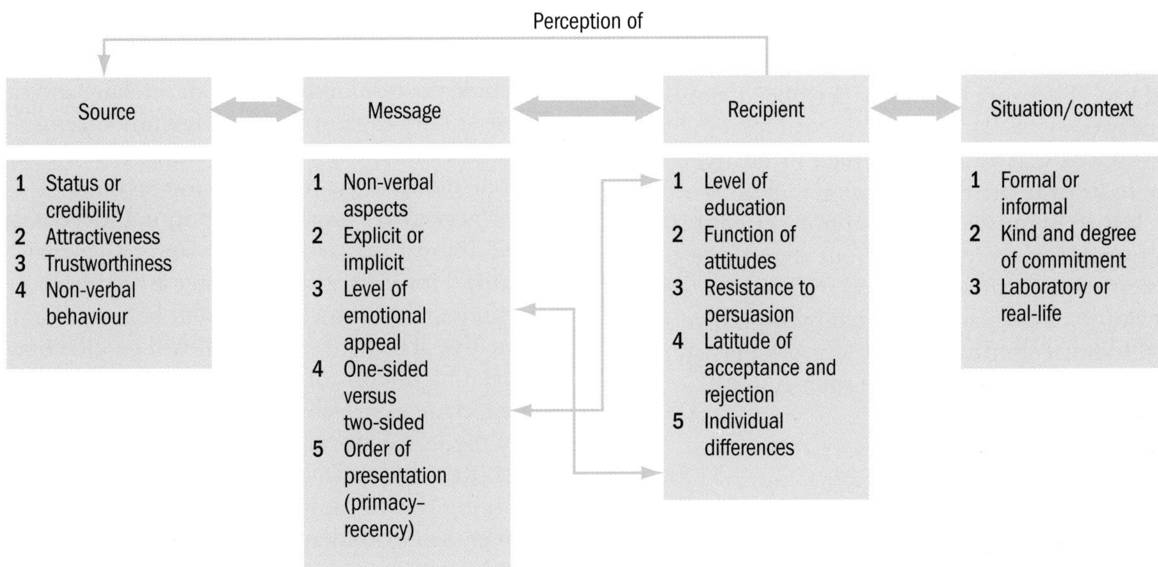

Figure 24.6 The four major factors involved in persuasive communication (arrows between boxes indicate examples of interaction between variables)

and yielding. There's little experimental support for this two-step model, which also lacks a theoretical account of the relationship between yielding and attitude change (Stroebe, 2012a).

The *cognitive response model* (Greenwald, 1968; Petty *et al.*, 1981) attempts to fill this theoretical 'hole'.

Dual-process models

Dual-process models of persuasion integrate both theories of systematic processing and processes that aren't based on systematic analysis of message arguments (such as classical conditioning – see Chapter 11 – the mere exposure effect – see Chapter 28 -, and heuristic processing – see Chapter 20 and below).

According to Stroebe (2012a), two major, overlapping dual-process models are (a) the *heuristic-systematic model* (HSM) (Chaiken, 1987; Chaiken *et al.*, 1989; Chen and Chaiken, 1999; see below); and (b) the *elaboration-likelihood model* (ELM) (Petty and Cacioppo, 1986; Petty and Wegener, 1999).

Heuristics are rules of thumb or mental shortcuts, which we use in processing social or any other kind of information (see Chapters 20 and 22). When a situation is personally involving (for example, it involves attitudes which are salient for the individual concerned), careful, cognitive analysis of the input occurs. The degree of attitude change depends largely on the quality of the arguments presented.

However, when personal involvement is low, individuals rely on various heuristics to determine whether to change their attitudes. Much of the Yale approach, in fact, deals with the content of these heuristics. For example, experts are more believable than non-experts (Eagly and Chaiken, 1993) and so we're more easily persuaded by the former, as we are by likeable sources (compared with non-likeable). Other examples of heuristics include being more persuaded by a greater number of arguments backed up by statistics than a smaller number and 'if other people think something is right (or wrong), then I should too'. These are essentially peripheral, non-content issues.

It's assumed that attitudes formed or changed on the basis of heuristic processing will be less stable, less resistant to counter-arguments and less predictive of subsequent behaviour than those based on systematic processing. Several studies have shown that attitude change accompanied by high levels of issue-relevant cognitive activity is more persistent than that accompanied by little such activity (Stroebe, 2000).

Fear and persuasion

A famous early attempt to induce attitude change through the manipulation of fear was made by Janis and Feshbach (1953) (see Key Study 24.3).

Key Study 24.3

Fear of the dentist as a means to healthier teeth (Janis and Feshbach, 1953)

- The message was concerned with dental hygiene, and degree of fear arousal was manipulated by the number and nature of consequences of improper care of teeth (which were also shown in colour slides). Each message also contained factual information about the causes of tooth decay, and some advice about caring for teeth.
- The *high fear condition* involved 71 references to unpleasant effects (including toothache, painful treatment and possible secondary diseases, such as blindness and cancer). The *moderate fear condition* involved 49 references and the *low fear condition* just 18. The *control group* heard a talk about the eye.
- Before the experiment, participants' attitudes to dental health, and their dental habits, were assessed as part of a general health survey. The same questionnaire was given again immediately following the fear-inducing message, and one week later.
- The results show that the stronger the appeal to fear, the greater their anxiety (an index of attitude change). But as far as actual changes in dental *behaviour* were concerned, the high fear condition proved to be the *least* effective. Eight per cent of the high fear group had adopted the recommendations (changes in tooth brushing and visiting the dentist in the weeks immediately following the experiment), compared with 22 per cent and 37 per cent in the moderate and low fear conditions respectively.

Similar results were reported by Janis and Terwillinger (1962), who presented a mild and strong fear message concerning the relationship between smoking and cancer.

These studies suggest that, in McGuire's terms, you can frighten people into attending to a message, comprehending it, yielding to it and retaining it, but not necessarily into acting upon it. Indeed, fear may be so great that action is *inhibited* rather than facilitated. However, if the audience is told how to avoid undesirable consequences and believes that the preventative action is realistic and will be effective, then even high levels of fear in the message can produce changes in behaviour. The more specific and precise the instructions, the greater the behaviour change (the *high availability factor*). It's critical when using fear to motivate behaviour change to also encourage self-confidence that the person can do something effective to reduce the threat (Dunn, 2007).

Ask Yourself

- Can you relate the high availability factor to one of the principles we identified when discussing the measurement of attitude–behaviour correlations?

Figure 24.7 Part of an anti-smoking commercial based on the appeal to fear

According to Stroebe (2000), mass media campaigns designed to change some specific health behaviour should use arguments aimed mainly at changing beliefs relating to that specific behaviour – rather than focusing on more general health concerns. This is another example of the compatibility principle. For example, to persuade people to lower their dietary cholesterol, it wouldn't be very effective merely to point out that coronary heart disease (CHD) is the major killer and/or that high levels of saturated fat are bad for one's heart. To influence diet, it would have to be argued that very specific dietary changes (such as less animal fat and red meat) would have a positive impact on blood cholesterol levels, which, in turn, should reduce the risk of developing CHD.

In situations of minimal or extreme fear, the message may fail to produce any attitude change, let alone any change in behaviour. According to McGuire (1968), there's an inverted U-shaped curve in the relationship between fear and attitude change (see Figure 24.8).

In segment 1 of the curve, the participant isn't particularly interested in (aroused by) the message: it's hardly attended to and may not even register. In segment 2, attention and arousal increase as fear increases, but the fear remains within manageable proportions. In segment 3, attention will decrease again, but this time because defences are being used to deal with extreme fear: the message may be denied ('it couldn't happen to me') or repressed (see Chapter 12). This inverted U curve is no more than a theoretical account of the relationship between fear and attitude change.

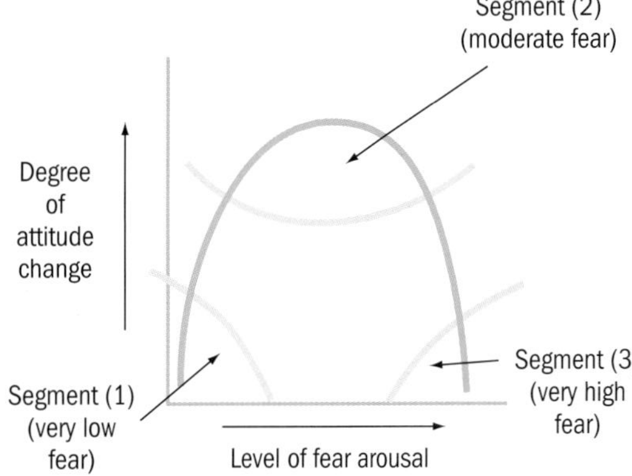

Figure 24.8 Inverted U curve showing relationship between attitude change and fear arousal (based on McGuire, 1968)

Despite evidence of defensive processing, Stroebe (2000) maintains that:

> *... The overwhelming majority of studies on fear appeals has found that higher levels of threat resulted in greater persuasion than did lower levels. However, the effectiveness of high-fear messages appeared to be somewhat reduced for respondents who feel highly vulnerable to the threat ...*

The importance of feeling vulnerable

In order to arouse fear, it isn't enough that a health risk has (objective) serious consequences: the individual must also feel personally at risk (i.e. vulnerable). There's some evidence that unless individuals feel vulnerable to a threat, they're unlikely to form the intention to act on the recommendations in the message (Kuppens *et al.*, 1996). Fear appeals are also most likely to be effective for individuals who are unfamiliar with a given health risk. For example, when the dangers involved in unprotected anal intercourse among homosexuals became known in the early 1980s, the information appeared to produce an enormous reduction in such practices. But over time, the impact of that knowledge declined and the rate of unprotected anal intercourse began to rise again. Similarly, knowledge of/acknowledgement of the dangers of smoking no longer distinguish between smokers and non-smokers (if it ever did). So, there's no guarantee that individuals will be made to feel vulnerable through simple fear appeals based on information regarding the possible consequences of their risky behaviour (Stroebe, 2000: see Chapter 12).

Feeling vulnerable relates to what McGuire calls the initial level of concern. Clearly, someone who has a high level of initial concern will be more easily pushed into segment 3 of the curve than someone with a low level. The former may be overwhelmed by a high-fear message (in which case defences are used against it), while the latter may not become interested and aroused enough for the message to have an impact.

Propaganda and war

'Propaganda' refers to a deliberate attempt to manipulate, often by concealed or underhand means, the minds of other people for ulterior ends (Brown, 1963). This change can be dated from the official use of propaganda as a weapon in the total warfare of modern times, beginning with the First World War. But this was itself an effect of changes in the nature of communication within technically advanced societies. Pratkanis and Aronson (2001) define propaganda as:

> *... mass suggestion or influence, through the manipulation of symbols and the psychology of the individual. Propaganda is the communication of a point of view with the ulterior goal of having the recipient of the appeal come to 'voluntarily' accept this position as if it were his or her own.*

According to Brown (1963):

> *There is nothing like a war for breaking down class and other barriers and creating feelings of friendship and co-operation within a country because all its previously inwardly directed aggression and resentment comes to be directed against an external enemy, and it is only in the last stages of a losing effort or after a war has been won that disunity begins to show itself once more ...*

Ask Yourself

- How does Brown's quote relate to Tajfel's social identity theory (SIT) as one explanation of prejudice and discrimination, and to Allport's advocacy of equal status contact and the pursuit of common goals as one means of reducing them? (See Chapter 25.)

Advertising

An interesting link between Psychology and advertising comes in the form of J.B. Watson, the founder of behaviourism (see Chapter 3). Following dismissal from his academic position at Johns Hopkins University, during which he devised health promotion films on venereal disease for the American military (propaganda?), Watson joined the J. Walter Thompson advertising agency, becoming one of the first and most successful applied Psychologists (Banyard and Hayes, 1994).

Box 24.2 Some specific techniques used in propaganda

The use of stereotypes: The Nazi portrayal of Jews (as shown below) is a good illustration of how a generalised belief about an entire group of people is exaggerated in the form of a caricatured portrayal of that group – the negative characteristics are taken to an extreme form (see Chapter 22).
The substitution of names: Favourable or unfavourable names, with an emotional connotation, are substituted for neutral ones, for example, 'Red' (replaces 'Communist' or 'Russian'), 'Union bosses' (for the presidents of trade unions), 'Huns'/'Krauts' ('Germans') and 'Yids' ('Jews'). Conversely, 'free enterprise' sounds better than 'capitalism'.
Selection: From a mass of complex facts, selection is made for propaganda purposes. *Censorship* is one way of achieving this and thus is a form of propaganda.
Repetition: If a statement or slogan is repeated often enough, it will eventually come to be accepted by the audience, such as Hitler's 'Ein Volk, ein Reich, ein Fuhrer' ('One people, one empire, one leader'). During the First World War, there were demands for 'A War to End War' and to 'Make the World Safe for Democracy'.
Assertion: Instead of argument, bald assertions are used to support the propagandist's case, as in the presentation of only one side of the picture, the deliberate limitation of free thought and questioning.
Pinpointing the enemy: It's useful to present a message not only *for* something but also *against* some real or imagined enemy who's supposedly frustrating the audience's will. This is demonstrated by the Nazi campaign against the Jews (the scapegoats for Germany's humiliation and economic hardships following the First World War, which pervaded every aspect of life in Germany in the 1930s (see Chapter 25). An example of this is the beer-mat with the inscription 'Whoever buys from a Jew is a traitor to his people'. (The caricatured face also illustrates the use of stereotypes.)

Figure 24.9 Caricature on beer-mat (based on Brown, 1963).

Scott (1909, in Brown, 1963) wrote the first textbook published in Britain on advertising. In it, he identified a number of principles, the most fundamental being *association*. Not until the late 1930s did advertisers discover Freud – but little came of it until the late 1940s and early 1950s (Brown, 1963).

Ask Yourself

- Taking some advertisements you're familiar with, try to identify the way that (a) association (as demonstrated by classical conditioning: see Chapter 11), and (b) aspects of Freud's psychoanalytic theory (see Chapter 42) are used. Are these 'techniques' more likely to influence:
  - Developing a need (i.e. convincing people they want or need the product)
  - Noticing the product
  - Purchasing the product
  - Behaviour after the purchase (encouraging repeat purchases)?

(Based on Banyard, 1996)

Subliminal advertising

This is by far the most controversial aspect of advertising. It originated with Jim Vicary, an American market researcher, who arranged with the owner of a New Jersey cinema to install a second special projector which, during a film, flashed on the screen phrases such as 'Hungry? Eat Popcorn' and 'Drink Coca-Cola'. These were either flashed so quickly, or printed so faintly, that they couldn't be consciously perceived (*'subliminal perception'* means recognition without awareness), even after a warning that they were about to appear.

Vicary claimed that sales of popcorn rose by almost 50 per cent and soft drinks by about 18 per cent, although he believed it unlikely that a subliminal stimulus could produce any response at all, unless prospective customers already intended buying the product. Subsequent research seems to have supported Vicary's belief (Bargh, 2014). Nevertheless, and despite the current belief that it was all just a publicity hoax (Pratkanis and Aronson, 2001), subliminal advertising was banned in the USA, UK and Australia.

Subliminal messages made a comeback in the mid-1970s. In *The Exorcist* (1974), for example, a death mask was flashed on to the screen subliminally and, more recently, in order to reduce theft, several department stores in the USA began mixing barely audible and rapidly repeated whispers (such as 'I am honest. I will not steal') with their piped music. Many stores reported dramatic decreases in shoplifting. Also, audio cassette tapes are readily available which supposedly cure stress with soothing sub-audible messages covered by mood music or the ambient sounds of nature (Zimbardo and Leippe, 1991).

In 1990, the heavy metal band Judas Priest went on trial, accused of triggering a suicide attempt by two young fans through, allegedly, *backmasking/backward masking*), in which spoken words ('Do it') were recorded backwards onto an album track. The case was dismissed on the grounds that there was no scientific evidence that backmasking worked (Stroebe, 2012b).

According to Stroebe (2012a), while no one likes to feel manipulated, the fact is that our surroundings colour our choices all the time – without us consciously realising it. His research indicates that subliminal messages hold sway over our behaviour in the same way as these environmental influences do. However, to have any genuine effect, subliminal slogans would have to be short, delivered near the time of a decision and relate to a person's immediate intentions or habits. In practice, subliminal messaging is far less powerful than first thought; it might even be out to good use, as when millisecond exposures of 'relax' can definitely reduce blood pressure and heart rate (albeit short-lived).

THEORIES of ATTITUDE CHANGE

The most influential theories of attitude change have concentrated on the principle of *cognitive consistency*. Human beings are seen as internally active information-processors, who sort through and modify a large number of cognitive elements in order to achieve some kind of cognitive coherence. This need for cognitive consistency means that theories such as Heider's *balance theory* (1958), Osgood and Tannenbaum's *congruity theory* (1955), and Festinger's *cognitive dissonance theory* (1957) aren't just theories of attitude change, but are also theories of human motivation (see Chapter 9).

Cognitive dissonance theory (CDT)

According to *cognitive dissonance theory* (CDT), whenever we simultaneously hold two cognitions which are psychologically inconsistent, we experience *dissonance*. This is a negative drive state, a state of 'psychological discomfort or tension', which motivates us to reduce it by achieving consonance. Attitude change is a major way of reducing dissonance. Cognitions are 'the things a person knows about himself, about his behaviour and about his surroundings' (Festinger, 1957), and any two cognitions can be consonant (A implies B), dissonant (A implies not-B) or irrelevant to each other.

For example, the cognition 'I smoke' is psychologically inconsistent with the cognition 'smoking causes cancer' (assuming that we don't wish to get cancer).

Ask Yourself

- How might someone who smokes try to reduce dissonance?

Perhaps the most efficient (and certainly the healthiest!) way to reduce dissonance is to stop smoking, but many people will work on the other cognition; for example, they might:

- Belittle the evidence about smoking and cancer (e.g. 'The human data are only correlational')
- Associate with other smokers (e.g. 'If so-and-so smokes, then it can't be very dangerous')
- Smoke low-tar cigarettes
- Convince themselves that smoking is an important and highly pleasurable activity.

These examples illustrate how CDT regards human beings not as rational but *rationalising* creatures: attempting to appear rational, both to others and to themselves.

Dissonance following a decision

If we have to choose between two equally attractive objects or activities, then one way of reducing the resulting dissonance is to emphasise the undesirable features of the one we've rejected. This adds to the number of consonant cognitions and reduces the number of dissonant ones.

This was demonstrated in a study by Brehm (1956). Female participants had to rate the desirability of several household appliances on an eight-point scale. They then had to choose between two of the items (their reward for participating). For one group the items were ½ to 1½ point apart on the scale (*high dissonance condition*), while for a second group they were a full three points apart (*low dissonance condition*). When they were asked to re-evaluate the items they'd chosen and rejected, the first group showed increased liking for the chosen item and decreased liking for the rejected one.

CDT also predicts that there'll be *selective exposure* to consonant information: seeking consistent information which isn't present at the time. However, *selective perception* also includes *selective attention* (looking at consistent information which is present) and *selective interpretation* (perceiving ambiguous information as being consistent with our other cognitions). According to Fiske and Taylor (1991), the evidence overall is stronger for selective attention and interpretation than for selective exposure.

Dissonance resulting from effort

When a voluntarily chosen experience turns out badly, the fact that we chose it motivates us to try to think that it actually turned out well. The greater the sacrifice or hardship associated with the choice, the greater the dissonance and, therefore, the greater the pressure towards attitude change (the *suffering-leads-to-liking effect*) (see Key Study 24.4).

Engaging in counter-attitudinal behaviour

This aspect of CDT is of most relevance to our earlier discussion of the relationship between attitudes and behaviour (see Key Study 24.5).

Ask Yourself

- How would CDT explain these findings? (You first need to ask yourself who experienced the greater dissonance.)

The large, 20-dollar incentive gave those participants ample justification for their counter-attitudinal behaviour, and so they experienced very little dissonance. But the 1-dollar group experienced considerable dissonance: they could hardly justify their counter-attitudinal behaviour in terms of the negligible reward (hence, the change of attitude to reduce the dissonance). As Stroebe (2012b) puts it, being paid 20 dollars to lie is a good reason to *discount* one's behaviour as a source of information regarding one's attitude.

Festinger and Carlsmith's findings have been replicated by several studies, in which children are given either a mild or a severe threat not to play with an attractive toy (Aronson and Carlsmith, 1963; Freedman, 1965). If children obey a mild threat, they'll experience greater dissonance, because it's more difficult for them to justify their behaviour than for children given a severe threat. So, the mild threat condition produces greater reduction in liking of the toy.

Key Study 24.4

Preferring things that turn out for the worst (Aronson and Mills, 1959)

- Female college students volunteered for a discussion on the psychology of sex, with the understanding that the research was concerned with the dynamics of group discussion. Each student was interviewed individually and asked if she could participate without embarrassment; all but one said yes.
- Students assigned to the *control condition* were simply accepted. But for acceptance to the *severe embarrassment condition*, they had to take an 'embarrassment test' (reading out loud to a male experimenter a list of obscene words and some explicit sexual passages from modern novels – remember the year was 1959!). For acceptance to the *mild embarrassment condition*, they had to read aloud words like 'prostitute' and 'virgin'.
- The participants then all heard a tape-recording of an actual, extremely dull, discussion (by a group which they believed they'd later join) about sex in lower animals. Finally, they had to rate the discussion, and the group members, in terms of how interesting and intelligent they found them.
- As predicted, the *severe embarrassment group* gave the most *positive ratings* – because they'd experienced the greatest dissonance!

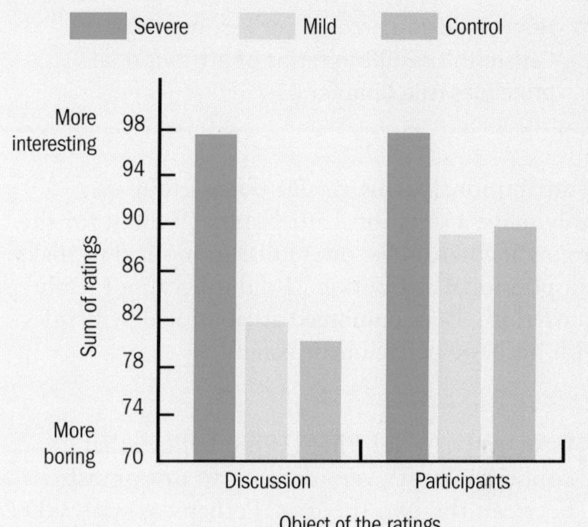

Figure 24.10 Female students' ratings of how interesting a group discussion was in relation to degrees of embarrassment which they suffered in order to get accepted for the discussion (based on Aronson and Mills, 1959)

Key Study 24.5

The '1 dollar/20 dollar' experiment (Festinger and Carlsmith, 1959)

- College students were brought, one at a time, into a small room to work for 30 minutes on two extremely dull and repetitive tasks (stacking spools and turning pegs). Later, they were offered either 1 dollar or 20 dollars to enter a waiting room and to try to convince the next 'participant' (in fact, a female stooge) that the tasks were interesting and enjoyable.
- Common sense would predict that the 20-dollar students would be more likely to change their attitudes in favour of the tasks (they had more reason to do so) and this is also what *reinforcement/incentive theory* (Janis *et al.*, 1965) would predict (the greater the reward/incentive, the greater the attitude change).
- However, as predicted by CDT, it was in fact the 1-dollar group that showed the greater attitude change (the *less-leads-to-more effect*).

However, dissonance occurs only when the behaviour is *volitional* (voluntary); that is, when we feel we've acted of our own free will. If we believe we had no choice, there's no dissonance, and hence no attitude change. A study by Freedman (1963) shows that dissonance theory and reinforcement theory aren't mutually exclusive; instead, they seem to apply to voluntary and involuntary behaviour respectively.

Self-perception theory (SPT)

According to Bem's *self-perception theory* (SPT) (1965, 1967), the concept of dissonance is both unnecessary and unhelpful. Any self-report of an attitude is an *inference* from observation of one's own behaviour, and the situation in which it occurs. This is because we don't have 'privileged access' to our own thoughts and feelings, but find out about them in the same way as we learn about other people's. (Bem was a Behaviourist.)

If the situation contains cues (such as the offer of a large 20-dollar incentive) which imply that we might have behaved that way regardless of how we personally felt (we lie about the task being interesting even though it was boring), then we don't infer that the behaviour reflected our true attitudes. But in the absence of obvious situational pressures (1-dollar condition), we assume that our attitudes are what our behaviour suggests they are.

> **Ask Yourself**
>
> - How could you account for Festinger and Carlsmith's results in terms of attributional principles (see Chapter 23)?

In attributional terms, the 20-dollar group can easily make a situational attribution ('I did it for the money'), whereas the one-dollar group had to make a dispositional attribution ('I did it because I really enjoyed it'). Bem combined attributional principles with his basic behaviourist beliefs.

An evaluation of CDT and SPT

- Eiser and van der Pligt (1988) believe that, conceptually, it's very difficult to distinguish between the two theories. Perhaps, as with CDT and incentive theories, both processes operate but to different extents under different circumstances. Fazio *et al.* (1977), for example, argue that dissonance may apply when people behave in a way which is contrary to their initial attitude (*counter-attitudinal behaviour*), while self-perception may apply better where their behaviour and initial attitude are broadly consistent (*attitude-congruent behaviour*). According to Fiske (2004), Bem's theory best accounts for those circumstances where we don't know our own mind or attitudes ahead of time.
- Zanna and Cooper's (1974) experiment provides support for both CDT and SPT (see Key Study 24.6).

> **Key Study 24.6**
>
> **Is there a dissonance-reduction pill? (Zanna and Cooper, 1974)**
>
> - Participants were asked to write a counter-attitudinal essay under instructions that implied either high or low freedom of choice. Consistent with previous findings, the prediction that high-choice participants change their opinions more than low-choice participants was confirmed.
> - The novel feature of the experiment was that participants were also given a placebo pill: they were either told it would make them feel tense or relaxed, or they were told nothing about it at all.

> **Ask Yourself**
>
> - The dissonance theory prediction was upheld when participants were given no information about the pill, and upheld even more strongly when they were told it would relax them. But when they were told it would make them feel tense, no difference between the high- and low-choice conditions was found. How can you explain these findings?

- If participants believe the pill will either relax them or have no effect, and they also believe they're acting of their own free will, they change their opinions, presumably because they experience an internal state of dissonance. But if told the pill will make them tense, they will (mis) attribute their tension to the pill, and so little attitude change will occur (as is also true of low-freedom-of-choice participants). This attributional explanation is consistent with SPT, and so the Zanna and Cooper experiment offers support for both Festinger and Bem.
- Fiske (2004) believes that one of the most provocative lines of research to have emerged from SPT is the overjustification effect. If one has a situational justification for one's behaviour (such as an external reward), then one doesn't need to make a dispositional attribution for it. For example, if a child enjoys reading and receives a gold star for each book completed, s/he may infer that the reading is motivated by the reward. If the rewards are discontinued, the reading may too (the opposite effect to what was intended).
- Conflict or inconsistency often arise between two attitudes, rather than between an attitude and behaviour. Both situations can be explained by CDT but, because SPT is based on attribution principles, it requires some overt behaviour from which we then make an inference about our attitudes.
- According to some impression management theorists (e.g. Schlenker, 1982; Tedeschi and Rosenfield, 1981: see Chapter 22), many dissonance experiments might not reflect genuine cases of 'private' attitude change (a drive to be consistent). Rather, they reflect the need to appear consistent, and hence to avoid social anxiety and embarrassment, or to project positive views of one's own identity. So, the 1-dollar group's attitude change is genuine, but is motivated by social (rather than cognitive) factors.
- Despite these and other challenges and reconceptualisations, Hogg and Vaughan (1995) maintain that:

... Cognitive dissonance theory remains one of the most widely accepted explanations of attitude change and many other social behaviours. It has generated over one thousand research studies and will probably continue to be an integral part of social psychological theory for many years ...

CONCLUSIONS: ARE THEORIES of ATTITUDE CHANGE CULTURALLY BIASED?

Although lying to another 'participant' (as in the 1 dollar/20 dollar experiment) may contravene the norms of many cultures, other commonly used dissonance paradigms may not induce the same level of dissonance in all cultures (Cooper *et al.*, 2004).

For example, Heine and Lehman (1997) used the 'free choice' method used by Brehm (1956: see above). Japanese and Canadian participants were asked to rate a selection of western rock and pop CDs, then asked to choose between two that they'd rated similarly. The Canadians showed the usual dissonance effect, but the Japanese didn't. Heine and Lehman concluded that Japanese people may not be as concerned about the inconsistency that arises when they 'lose' the positive aspect of the unchosen option and 'accept' the negative aspects of the chosen option.

The tendency to change one's attitude or behaviour in order to be more consistent (and so reduce dissonance) reflects a need to view behaviour as driven by internal factors. But members of *collectivist cultures* don't demonstrate these tendencies. They're willing to sacrifice consistency to maintain a sense of harmony with others (Nagayama Hall and Barongan, 2002). It may even be considered selfish to act according to one's own desires, or to express one's attitudes, if they make others feel uncomfortable (Fiske *et al.*, 1998).

The evidence for the over-justification effect is strong in the USA, but it rests on that culture's bias towards individual autonomy and perceived choice (Fiske, 2004). In more *interdependent* (i.e. collectivist) cultures, children's intrinsic motivation increases when choices are made for them by trusted authorities and peers (Iyengar and Lepper, 1999).

Chapter Summary

- The **three-component model** sees attitudes as comprising **affective, cognitive** and **behavioural** components. Attitudes have much in common with beliefs and values.
- Katz identifies the **knowledge, adjustive, value-expressive** and **ego-defensive functions** of attitudes.
- **Explicit (direct)** methods of **attitude measurement** (such as the Likert scale and semantic differential) rely on verbal reports of people's opinions about the attitude object. **Implicit (indirect)** methods include sociometry, evaluative priming and the Implicit Association Test.
- Problems associated with self-report scales include **acquiescent response set** and the effects of **social desirability**.
- Early research into the **relationship between attitudes and behaviour** showed that attitudes are very poor predictors of behaviour. But attitudes represent only one of several determinants of behaviour, including situational factors.
- Attitudes can predict behaviour, provided there's a close correspondence between the way the two variables are defined and measured (the **principle of compatibility**). Also, measures of a representative sample of behaviours relevant to the attitude must be made (the **aggregation principle**).
- According to **Discursive Psychologists**, attitudes are **constructed** in the course of social interaction, rather than possessed by isolated individuals.
- **Persuasive communication** has traditionally been studied in terms of the influence of four interacting factors: the **source** of the persuasive message, the **message** itself, the **recipient** of the message, and the **situation/context**.
- Early models of **systematic processing** see the impact of persuasive messages as dependent on a sequence of processes, including **attending** to the message, **comprehending** it, **accepting** its conclusions, **retaining** it and **acting** as a result.
- The more recent **cognitive response model** focuses on **why** people change their attitudes, not merely when and how it's likely to happen.
- **Dual-process models** include the **heuristic-systematic model** of persuasion, which explains why we're more likely to be persuaded when the situation isn't personally involving or if the arguments are convincing. Overlapping with this is the **elaboration-likelihood model (ELM)**.
- People can be frightened into attending to, comprehending, accepting and retaining a message, but the **high availability factor** is necessary for any behaviour change to take place.
- People also need to feel personally **vulnerable** if fear appeals are to have any impact. There appears to be an **inverted U curve** in the relationship between fear and attitude change.
- **Propaganda** tries deliberately to limit people's choices, either through **censorship** or through use

of **caricature, stereotypes, emotive names** and **repetitive slogans**.

- **Subliminal messages** can influence judgements when superimposed on consciously attended-to material, producing general reactions (such as increasing the desire to eat popcorn). However, their influence on behaviour is much less certain.
- The major **theories of attitude change** share the basic principle of **cognitive consistency**. The most influential of these is Festinger's **cognitive dissonance theory** (**CDT**).
- Dissonance is most likely to occur after making a **very difficult choice/decision**, when putting ourselves through **hardship or making a sacrifice** only to find it was for nothing, or when engaging voluntarily in **counter-attitudinal behaviour**.
- Bem's **self-perception theory** (**SPT**) explains the results of dissonance experiments in terms of **attributional principles**. CDT may apply under conditions of 'true' counter-attitudinal behaviour, while SPT applies to **attitude-congruent behaviour**.
- **Impression management theory** stresses the **social** rather than the **cognitive** motivation underlying attitude change.
- Like most western Psychology, theories of attitude change are **culturally biased**.

Links with Other Topics/Chapters

Chapter 17 ⟶ Strong attitudes influence behaviour partly through their automatic activation from within *memory*

Chapter 28 ⟶ Personal (direct) experience also helps activate attitudes automatically, which can be explained by the *mere exposure effect* (Zajonc, 1968)

Chapters 20, 22 and 23 ⟶ Heuristic models of attitude change have their counterparts in: *problem-solving, interpersonal perception, social cognition/attribution*

Chapter 12 ⟶ The *theory of reasoned action* (TRA) and *theory of planned behaviour* (TPB) are attempts to explain the attitude–behaviour relationship in the context of Health Psychology

Chapter 25 ⟶ The *stereotyping* used in propaganda is the cognitive component of *prejudice*

Chapter 49 ⟶ The over-justification effect is sometimes referred to as the *paradox of reward*, which is relevant to the debate on *free will*

Recommended Reading

Ajzen, I. (1988) *Attitudes, Personality and Behaviour.* Milton Keynes: Open University Press.

Cooper, J., Kelly, K.A. & Weaver, K. (2004) Attitudes, Norms, and Social Groups. In M.B. Brewer & M. Hewstone (eds) *Social Cognition.* Oxford: Blackwell Publishing.

Gross, R. (2008) *Key Studies in Psychology* (5th edition). London: Hodder Education. Chapter 9.

Haddock, G. & Maio, G.R. (2012) Attitudes. In M. Hewstone, W. Stroebe & K. Jonas (eds) *An Introduction to Social Psychology* (5th edition). Oxford: BPS/Blackwell.

Stroebe, W. (2012b) Strategies of Attitude and Behaviour Change. In M. Hewstone, W. Stroebe & K. Jonas (eds) *An Introduction to Social Psychology* (5th edition). Oxford: BPS/Blackwell.

Zimbardo, P.G. & Leippe, M.R. (1991) *The Psychology of Attitude Change and Social Influence.* New York: McGraw-Hill.

Useful Websites

www.calvin.edu/academic/cas/gpa/ (Nazi and East German Propaganda Guide Page)

https://implicit.harvard.edu/implicit/research/ (Project Implicit. You have the opportunity to take one or more Implicit Association Tests/IATS, which measure your unconscious attitudes towards a range of attitude objects)

CHAPTER 25

PREJUDICE AND DISCRIMINATION

Prejudice as an attitude

Theories of prejudice and discrimination

Reducing prejudice and discrimination

> *... Fifty years after the [Nazi] extermination and concentration camps were liberated, genocide continues unabated, neither punished nor prevented. In what used to be ... [Yugoslavia], torture, murder, rape and starvation are everyday occurrences ... (Hirsch, 1995)*

INTRODUCTION and OVERVIEW

While genocide – the systematic destruction of an entire cultural, ethnic or racial group – is the most extreme form of discrimination, the prejudice that underlies it is essentially the same as that which underlies less extreme behaviours.

Prejudice is an *attitude* that can be expressed in many ways, or which may not be overtly or openly expressed at all. Like other attitudes, prejudice can be regarded as a *disposition* to behave in a prejudiced way (to practise *discrimination*), so the relationship between prejudice and discrimination is an example of the wider debate concerning the attitude–behaviour relationship. As we saw in Chapter 24, LaPiere's early study of this relationship was concerned with anti-Oriental prejudice and discrimination in the USA in the 1930s.

Theories of prejudice and discrimination try to explain their origins: how do people come to be prejudiced and to act in discriminatory ways? Answers to these questions potentially answer the further question: how can they be reduced or even prevented altogether? This, of course, has much greater practical significance for people's lives, as the quote from Hirsch conveys.

PREJUDICE as an ATTITUDE

As an *extreme* attitude, prejudice comprises the three components common to all attitudes:

- The *cognitive* component is the *stereotype* (see Chapter 22)
- The *affective* component is a *strong feeling of hostility*
- The *behavioural* component can take different forms.

Allport (1954) proposed five stages of this component:

1. *Antilocution* – hostile talk, verbal denigration and insult, racial jokes
2. *Avoidance* – keeping a distance but without actively inflicting harm
3. *Discrimination* – exclusion from housing, civil rights, employment
4. *Physical attack* – violence against the person and property
5. *Extermination* – indiscriminate violence against an entire group (including genocide).

As we noted in the *Introduction and overview*, 'discrimination' is often used to denote the behavioural component, while 'prejudice' denotes the cognitive and affective components. But just as the cognitive and affective components may not necessarily be manifested behaviourally (as in LaPiere's study), so discrimination doesn't necessarily imply the presence of cognitive and affective components. People may discriminate if the prevailing social norms dictate that they do so, and if their wish to become or remain a member of the discriminating group is stronger than their wish to be fair and egalitarian (see below).

According to Fiske (2004), the *affective* component is crucial. This is illustrated by the findings that (a) individual differences in emotional prejudice correlate with discrimination better than do stereotypes (Dovidio *et al.*, 1996) and (b) affective reactions to gay men predict discrimination far better than do stereotypes (Talaska *et al.*, 2003). Although the relationship between prejudice and discrimination is moderate, it's comparable to the general attitude–behaviour relationship (Fiske, 2004: see Chapter 24).

Definitions of prejudice

Although most definitions of prejudice stress the hostile, negative kind, prejudice can also be positive (just as stereotypes can be positive such as, 'women are caring' or neutral, such as, 'men are tall'). However, the research which tries to identify how prejudice arises, and how it might be reduced, focuses on *hostile* prejudice.

Table 25.1 Some definitions of prejudice and discrimination

... An antipathy based on faulty and inflexible generalisation directed towards a group as a whole or towards an individual because he is a member of that group. It may be felt or expressed. (Allport, 1954)
Prejudice is an attitude (usually negative) toward the members of some group, based solely on their membership in that group ... (Baron and Byrne, 1991)
Prejudice is a learned attitude towards a target object that typically involves negative affect, dislike or fear, a set of negative beliefs that support the attitude and a behavioural intention to avoid, or to control or dominate, those in the target group ... Stereotypes are prejudiced beliefs ... when prejudice is acted out, when it becomes overt in various forms of behaviour, then discrimination is in practice ... (Zimbardo and Leippe, 1991)

The definitions in Table 25.1 locate prejudice squarely *within the individual*. However, Vivian and Brown (1995) prefer to see prejudice as a special case of *intergroup conflict*. Although conceptually distinct, prejudice and intergroup conflict often coexist. For Vivian and Brown, intergroup conflict occurs when:

> *... People think or behave antagonistically towards another group or its members in terms of their group membership and seem motivated by concerns relating to those groups ...*

They also distinguish intergroup conflict and *interpersonal* conflict, a distinction we shall return to when discussing attempts to reduce prejudice.

Defining prejudice in terms of intergroup conflict 'lifts' it to the social plane. Consistent with this is Fernando's (1991) distinction between 'racial prejudice' and 'racism': the former denotes an attitude possessed by an individual, while the latter refers to a political and economic *ideology*, which is a characteristic of society. Similarly, Littlewood and Lipsedge (1989) argue that:

> *Racist attitudes may be manifest as a highly articulated set of beliefs in the individual, but they are also found in less conscious presuppositions, located in society as a whole ...*

Strictly, then, it is societies (or institutions, such as the police or the armed forces) that are racist, and individuals who are racially prejudiced.

Ask Yourself

- Apart from racism, what other '-isms' are there that meet these criteria for being social, rather than individual, phenomena?

Until quite recently, most of the theory and research into prejudice and discrimination were concerned with racism, '... the quite specific belief that cultural differences between ethnic groups are of biological origin and that groups should be ranked in worth' (Littlewood and Lipsedge, 1989). However, gender (as in *sexism*: see Chapters 36 and 47), sexual orientation or preference (as in *heterosexism*: see Chapters 43 and 47) and age (as in *ageism*: see Chapter 39) can all be targets for hostility and discrimination.

Figure 25.1 Sexual orientation is a target for hostility and discrimination in a heterosexist society

Institutionalised prejudice and discrimination

A great deal of prejudice and discrimination is unconscious, reflected in basic, stereotyped assumptions that we make about others. These assumptions influence our behaviour towards them, which may not be necessarily overtly hostile or 'anti'. It's this pervasive form of prejudice and discrimination that's perhaps the most difficult to break down, because we're unaware of it, and because it reflects institutionalised heterosexism, racism and so on.

Both Cochrane (1983) and Littlewood and Lipsedge (1989) show how ethnic minorities in England are more often hospitalised for mental illness than the white majority This is interpreted as reflecting an implicit, unwitting, prejudice against minority groups which pervades the National Health Service as an institution. This definition of 'institutionalised racism' as 'unwitting' was included in the Government Report (1999) on the behaviour of the police in their investigation of the murder of the black London teenager, Stephen Lawrence (in Horton, 1999).

Figure 25.2 Stephen Lawrence

THEORIES of PREJUDICE and DISCRIMINATION

Attempts to explain prejudice and discrimination fall into three broad categories:

1. Those that see prejudice as stemming from *personality variables* and other aspects of the psychological make-up of individuals
2. Those that emphasise the role of *environmental factors* (sometimes called the *conflict approach*)
3. Those that focus on the effects of the mere fact of *group membership*.

Each approach may be important to a complete understanding of the causes of intergroup conflict and prejudice, and to their reduction (Vivian and Brown, 1995).

Prejudice and personality

The authoritarian personality

Adorno *et al.* (1950) proposed the concept of the *authoritarian personality* (in a book of the same name); someone who's prejudiced by virtue of specific personality traits which predispose them to be hostile towards ethnic, racial and other minority or outgroups.

Adorno *et al.* began by studying antisemitism in Nazi Germany in the 1940s and drew on Freud's theories to help understand the relationship between 'collective ideologies' (such as fascism) and individual personality (Brown, 1985). After their emigration to the USA, studies began with over 2000 college students and other native-born, white, non-Jewish, middle-class Americans (including school teachers, nurses, prison inmates and psychiatric patients). These involved interviews concerning their political views and childhood experiences and the use of *projective tests* (in particular, the thematic apperception test/TAT: see Chapter 9) designed to reveal unconscious attitudes towards minority groups.

Figure 25.3 A banner reading 'Germans, don't buy from Jews' in front of a synagogue in Berlin, *c.*1937

A number of scales were developed in the course of their research (see Table 25.2).

The term 'ethnocentrism' was first defined by Sumner (1906) as:

> *A view of things in which one's own group is the centre of everything, and all others are scaled and rated with reference to it ... each group ... boasts itself superior ... and looks with contempt on outsiders. Each group thinks its own folkways the only right one.*

According to Brown (1965), Adorno *et al.* never referred to the *Potentiality for fascism* (F) *scale* as the authoritarianism scale. But since it's supposed to identify the kind of personality the book is talking about, it's reasonable to suppose that the scale could also be correctly called the authoritarianism scale (as it has been in many subsequent research reports). It was intended to measure implicit authoritarian and antidemocratic trends in personality, making someone with such a personality susceptible to explicit fascist propaganda. The 38 items were subclassified under nine general headings (six of which are included in Table 25.2).

Table 25.3 shows the correlations between the different scales.

Ask Yourself

- What conclusions can you draw from the correlations in Table 25.3?

Table 25.3 Correlations between scores on the different scales used by Adorno *et al.* (1950)

AS	E	PEC	F
AS	0.80	0.43	0.53
E		0.57	0.65
PEC			0.57
F (final version)	0.75		

The pattern of intercorrelations suggests that:

- scores on the AS, E and F scales all correlate with each other much more strongly than any of them does with the PEC score, and, following from this
- people who are antisemitic are also likely to be hostile towards 'Negroes', 'Japs' and any other minority group or 'foreigner' (all *outgroups*) – the authoritarian personality is prejudiced in a very *generalised* way.

Table 25.2 Sample items from the various scales used by Adorno *et al.* (1950)

Antisemitism (AS) scale	The trouble with letting Jews into a nice neighbourhood is that they gradually give it a typically Jewish atmosphere.
Ethnocentrism (E) scale	Negroes have their rights, but it's best to keep them in their own districts and schools and to prevent too much contact with white people.
Political and economic conservatism (PEC) scale	In general, full economic security is harmful; most men wouldn't work if they didn't need the money for eating and living.
Potentiality for fascism (F) scale	
1. Conventionalism	Obedience and respect for authority are the most important virtues children should learn.
2. Authoritarian submission	Young people sometimes get rebellious ideas, but as they grow up they ought to get over them and settle down.
3. Authoritarian aggression	Sex crimes, such as rape and attacks on children, deserve more than mere imprisonment; such criminals ought to be publicly whipped or worse.
4. Power and toughness	People can be divided into two distinct classes: the weak and the strong.
5. Projectivity	Nowadays, when so many different kinds of people move around and mix together so much, a person has to protect himself especially carefully against catching an infection or disease from them.
6. Sex	Homosexuals are hardly better than criminals and ought to be severely punished.

What's the authoritarian personality like?

Typically, authoritarian personalities are hostile to people of inferior status, servile to those of higher status and contemptuous of weakness. They're also rigid and inflexible, intolerant of ambiguity and uncertainty, unwilling to introspect feelings and upholders of conventional values and ways of life (such as religion). This belief in convention and intolerance of ambiguity combine to make minorities 'them' and the authoritarian's membership group 'us'; 'they' are, by definition, 'bad' and 'we' are, by definition, 'good'.

How does the authoritarian personality become prejudiced?

Based on the interview and TAT data, Adorno *et al.* claimed that authoritarians have often experienced a harsh, punitive, disciplinarian upbringing, with little affection. While they consciously have very high opinions of their parents, they often reveal considerable latent (unconscious) hostility towards them, stemming from the extreme frustration they experienced as children.

Drawing on Freudian theory, Adorno *et al.* proposed that such unconscious hostility may be *displaced* onto minority groups, which become the targets for the authoritarian's hostility. Authoritarians also project onto these groups their own unacceptable, antisocial impulses (especially sexual and aggressive), so that they feel threatened by members of these groups. They have very little self-understanding (insight), and their prejudice serves a vital *ego-defensive function*: it protects them from the unacceptable parts of themselves (see Table 24.2, p. 396).

Evaluation of the authoritarian personality theory

- While some evidence is broadly consistent with the theory, there are a number of serious methodological and other problems which make it untenable.
- The items on the AS, E and F scales (all Likert-type questions: see Chapter 24) were worded in such a way that agreement with them always implies antisemitism, ethnocentrism and potential fascism, respectively. Adorno *et al.* recognised the possibility that *acquiescent response set* might be a problem (see Chapter 24).
- The interview and TAT data were intended partly to validate the F scale. But the clinical interviews were flawed, since the interviewer knew the interviewee's F score. This represents a serious source of *experimenter bias* (see Chapter 3).

Figure 25.4 The attack by Japan on Pearl Harbor in 1941 brought the USA into the Second World War

The open and closed mind

Another criticism of the authoritarian personality theory is that it assumed that authoritarianism is a characteristic of the *political right*, implying that there's no equivalent authoritarianism on the left. According to Rokeach (1960), 'ideological dogmatism' refers to a relatively rigid outlook on life and intolerance of those with opposing beliefs. High scores on the *dogmatism scale* reveal: (i) closedness of mind; (ii) lack of flexibility; and (iii) authoritarianism, regardless of particular social and political ideology.

Dogmatism is a way of *thinking*, rather than a set of beliefs (Brown, 1965). The dogmatic individual tends to accentuate differences between 'us and them' and displays *self-aggrandisement* (e.g. 'If I had to choose between happiness and greatness, I'd choose greatness'). S/he also has a *paranoid* outlook on life ('I often feel people are looking at me critically') and is *uncompromising* in his/her beliefs and intolerant of others. These characteristics serve as defences against a sense of personal inadequacy.

Rokeach (1960) gave the F scale and the dogmatism scale to five English groups of different political persuasions, including a group of 13 communist students. While the communists scored low on the F scale, they had the highest dogmatism scores. This supported Rokeach's claim that the F scale measures only right-wing authoritarianism.

MEET THE RESEARCHER

Celia Kitzinger

Researching sexuality and gender

Nicky calls a dentist's receptionist and asks if she can register her 'partner' (who is in acute pain and unable to make the call personally) for emergency dental treatment. The receptionist asks, 'What was his name?' Nicky replies, 'Sandra Ferry'. ('Sandra' is a pseudonym – but the first name she uses is a common English name for females.) After checking she has heard the name correctly, the puzzled receptionist asks, 'Is it for him *or for you?' (Land and Kitzinger, 2005)*

The most exciting development in research on gender and sexuality in recent years has been a shift from asking people questions about gender and sexuality to observing them *doing* gender and sexuality in ordinary interactions. In my early research (Kitzinger, 1987), I interviewed lesbians and gave them questionnaires asking about their attitudes, beliefs and behaviour. In my current research I do not ask people any questions at all. Instead I work with recordings of naturally occurring interactions (like Nicky's phone conversation with the receptionist) and analyse them using a method called 'conversation analysis' (Wilkinson and Kitzinger, 2008) to reveal what these interactions show us about the ways in which people 'do gender' and 'do sexuality' in the course of their everyday lives.

Studies into same-sex relationships

Research on gender and sexuality has always been concerned to document and challenge prejudice and discrimination. The first ever sex survey was in 1903 by the Scientific Humanitarian Committee, the world's first organisation dedicated to advancing the civil rights of homosexuals. Its motto was 'Justice through Science' (Adam, 1987). In the aftermath of the trial of Oscar Wilde, the famous playwright arrested and imprisoned for 'the love that dare not speak its name', the British Society for the Study of Sex Psychology (founded in 1914) published research showing that homosexuality was biological in origin, and not a sinful choice for which people should be punished. Over the last century psychologists have challenged the psychiatric classification of homosexuality as a mental illness, demonstrated the range and variety of homosexualities, documented the existence of long-term stable same-sex relationships, established gay people's parenting skills, and explored the intersecting oppressions experienced by (for example) ageing lesbians and gay men, those with learning disabilities and those who are members of faith communities (e.g. Catholics, Muslims). I recommend the textbook by Clarke *et al.* (2010) for an excellent overview of psychological research on lesbian, gay bisexual, transgender and intersex (LGBTI) issues. Psychology has always addressed the social concerns and prejudices of the period; with changing social attitudes, psychological research questions change too.

Assumptions about normative heterosexuality

Compared with 40 years ago, when I first came out as lesbian (I describe my personal experience in Peel and Clarke, 2005), the world is a much kinder and fairer place for LGBTI people. Nonetheless, interactions with heterosexuals can sometimes be problematic, and in my recent research I have wanted to capture and analyse these. The conversation between Nicky and the dentist's receptionist is a real-life (recorded) example. It shows that the word 'partner' still conjures up, at least for some people, an *opposite-sex* partner. The receptionist first uses the masculine pronoun in asking for the partner's name ('What was his name?') and then tries to solve the problem of why she has been given a feminine name by checking out which member of the (presumed different-sex) couple is in need of treatment ('Is it for *him* or for you?'). The expectation that a female speaker's 'partner' will be male is so strong that, even given the contradictory evidence of the partner's name, this receptionist overlooks the obvious explanation: Nicky is in a lesbian relationship. The difficulty for Nicky is then how to respond to the question 'Is it for *him* or for you?' – and how to manage the effect of her response on the receptionist – at a time when her overriding preoccupation is to get help for her suffering partner. (What would you say, and what kind of reaction might you expect?) You can see the whole of Nicky's conversation – and others like it – in Land and Kitzinger (2005).

Our recordings of 150 everyday interactions show how taken-for-granted assumptions about normative heterosexuality underwrite ordinary activities, such as making a dentist appointment, buying car insurance or making arrangements with a plumber to fix a leaking pipe. By analysing conversations like these we can begin to understand both how the heterosexual presumption is displayed in talk, and the hassles it creates for people who are not heterosexual. In other research I have shown how, in conversations between heterosexuals, the heteronormative presumption functions to smooth the interaction and facilitate the business of the talk (Kitzinger 2005a, 2005b). This is a concrete example of heterosexual privilege in action.

This new interactionally based approach to research is sometimes described as a 'bottom up' approach – that is, it is based on the idea that society is created in part by the daily mundane interactions we all of us have with other people. By contrast, 'top down' approaches focus on the ways in which society is constructed for us by institutions such as the law, social policy, education. Given the continuing oppression of LGBTI people worldwide, I believe that psychology needs *both* 'bottom up' and 'top down' approaches.

Human rights

In many countries, LGBTI people are executed, imprisoned, tortured, raped and forced to undergo 'treatment' in state institutions because of their sexual or gender identities (see the Amnesty International LGBT website). In the UK, psychologists have documented bullying of lesbian and gay youth (Rivers, 2001), discrimination in healthcare provision for lesbians and gay men (Warwick and Aggleton, 2002), and widespread reluctance among heterosexual students to act in support of lesbian and gay rights (Ellis, 2002).

One human right denied to same-sex couples in all but a handful of countries (do you know which?) is the right to marry. In Britain, the government refuses to accept same-sex marriage. Instead, since 2005, there has been a separate institution for same-sex couples only ('civil partnership'), reserving marriage for different-sex couples only. Psychologists have pointed out that this adds to the life stresses of same-sex couples and their children (American Psychological Association, 2004) and that it is 'not valid or defensible on psychological or other grounds' (Hegarty *et al.*, 2006). My own same-sex marriage, legally made in Canada, is not acknowledged as a marriage in Britain. (Britain does of course accept the Canadian marriages of British *different-sex* couples.) The ban on same-sex marriage is a form of oppression that cannot be fixed by 'bottom up' research aimed at improving interpersonal interactions (Wilkinson and Kitzinger, 2005, 2006; Kitzinger and Wilkinson 2006).

Celebrity couple Sir Elton John and David Furnish leave as a married couple following their civil partnership ceremony at the Guildhall, Windsor on December 21, 2005 in Windsor, Berkshire

However, what unites different approaches in psychological research on gender and sexuality is their commitment to justice and equality for LGBTI people.

Professor Celia Kitzinger is Professor of Gender, Sexuality and Conversation Analysis at the University of York. Her first book was *The Social Construction of Lesbianism* (1987) and since then she has published a further eight books and around 150 articles and chapters. For information about her campaign for equal marriage rights for same sex couples, see www.equalmarriagerights.org.

[Since this piece was written marriage between same-sex couples has been legalised in the UK (in 2014). It is now legal in 17 other countries, as well as in 25 US States.]

Social dominance theory (SDT)

The central focus of SDT is on *social dominance orientation* (SDO); this measures how much an individual accepts general cultural ideologies concerning equality or inequality within society (Pratto, 1999; Sidanius and Pratto, 1999). In the face of widespread status and power differences between social groups in society, some individuals accept or even favour a clear stratification of dominant and subordinate groups as being just and consistent with a natural order:

- Individuals with a *high* SDO have a strong desire to promote intergroup hierarchies and for their ingroups to dominate their outgroups; they also reject politics aimed at establishing equality.
- Individuals with a *low* SDO believe that inequality is unjust and support views and political policies designed to reduce social inequalities.

At the heart of SDO are various *legitimising myths*, defined as 'consensually held values, attitudes, beliefs, stereotypes or cultural ideologies that provide moral and intellectual justification for group-based oppression and inequality' (Kessler and Mummendey, 2008). They serve to justify the oppression of some groups by others (and the related status differences); ultimately, SDT provides an *evolutionary-psychological* explanation for the organisation of human societies as group-based hierarchies (Kessler and Mummendey, 2008) (see Critical Discussion 25.1).

Evaluation of social dominance theory

- Kessler and Mummendey (2008) cite several studies which have shown that SDO (measured by the SDO scale: Pratto *et al.*, 1994; Sidanius and Pratto, 1999) is related to non-egalitarian political and social attitudes (including sexism, racism and nationalism). However, there's less evidence that people with high SDO display specific intergroup bias in order to achieve or maintain ingroup domination.

Scapegoating: the frustration–aggression hypothesis

According to Dollard *et al.*'s (1939) *frustration–aggression hypothesis*, frustration always gives rise to aggression, and aggression is always caused by frustration (see Chapter 29). The source of frustration (whatever prevents us from achieving our goals) might often be seen as a fairly powerful threat (such as parents or employers) or may be difficult to identify. Drawing on Freudian theory, Dollard *et al.* claim that when we need to vent our frustration but are unable to do this directly, we do so *indirectly* by displacing it on to a substitute target (we find a *scapegoat*).

Ask Yourself

- Can you see any parallels between the frustration–aggression hypothesis and certain parts of Adorno *et al.*'s theory?

The choice of scapegoat isn't usually random. In England during the 1930s and 1940s, it was predominantly the Jews, who were replaced by West Indians during the 1950s and 1960s and, during the 1970s, 1980s and 1990s, by Asians from Pakistan. In the southern USA, lynchings of black people from 1880 to 1930 were related to the price of cotton: as the price dropped, so the number of lynchings increased (Hovland and Sears, 1940). While this is consistent with the concept of displaced aggression, the fact that white people chose black people as scapegoats rather than some other minority group suggests that there are usually socially approved (legitimised) targets for frustration-induced aggression.

Limitations of the personality approach

- Several researchers (e.g. Billig, 1976; Brown, 1988; Hogg and Abrams, 1988) have argued that any account of prejudice and discrimination in terms of individuals (*intrapersonal behaviour*) is *reductionist* (see Chapter 49). In other words, the social nature of prejudice and discrimination requires a social explanation (in terms of *intergroup behaviour*).
- Adorno *et al.* imply that racism is the product of the abnormal personality of a small minority of human beings, rather than a social and political ideology. This distinction is of great practical, as well as theoretical, importance because what's considered to be the cause of prejudice has very real implications for its reduction. Indeed, Adorno *et al.* recognised that society provides the content of attitudes and prejudice and defines the outgroups.
- According to Brown (1988), if prejudice is to be explained in terms of individual differences, how can it then be manifested in a whole population or, at least, a vast majority of that population? In pre-war Nazi Germany, for example (and in many other places since), consistent racist attitudes and behaviour were shown by hundreds of thousands of people, who must have differed on most other psychological characteristics.
- Similarly, how can Adorno *et al.*'s theory account for the sudden rise and fall of prejudice in particular societies at specific historical periods? Antisemitism in Nazi Germany grew during a decade or so, which is much too short a time for a whole

generation of German families to have adopted new forms of childrearing practices giving rise to authoritarian and prejudiced children (Brown, 1988). Even more dramatic was the anti-Japanese prejudice among Americans following the attack on Pearl Harbor. Brown believes that such examples strongly suggest that:

> *... The attitudes held by members of different groups towards each other have more to do with the objective relations between the groups – relations of political conflict or alliance, economic interdependence and so on – than with the familial relation in which they grew up!*

The role of environmental factors

The impact of social norms: prejudice as conformity

Individual bigotry is only part of the explanation of racial discrimination. For example, even though overt discrimination has, traditionally, been greater in the southern USA, white southerners haven't scored higher than white people from the north on measures of authoritarianism (Pettigrew, 1959). So, clearly, conformity to social norms can prove more powerful as a determinant of behaviour than personality factors.

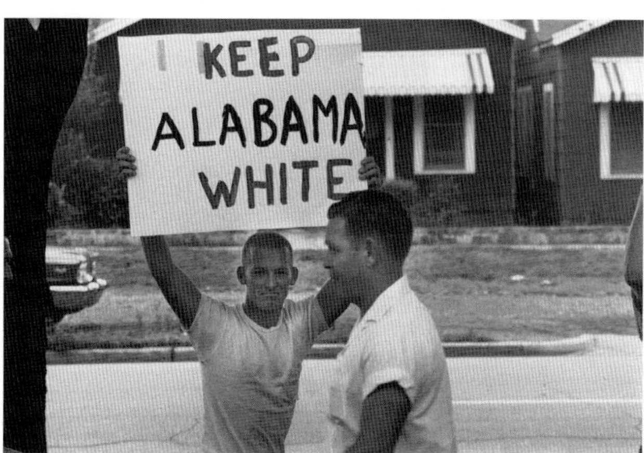

Figure 25.5 Racial discrimination in the southern USA during the 1950s was as much a way of life as apartheid in South Africa

Minard (1952) found that black and white coalminers in West Virginia followed a pattern of almost complete integration below ground, but almost complete segregation above! This makes sense only when viewed in terms of conformity to the norms which operated in those different situations.

Ask Yourself

- What do you think the two sets of norms may have been?

Pettigrew (1971) also found that Americans in the south are no more antisemitic or hostile towards other minority groups than those from the north: prejudice *isn't* the generalised attitude which Adorno *et al.* claimed. According to Reich and Adcock (1976), the need to conform and not be seen as different may cause milder prejudices. But active discrimination against, and ill treatment of, minorities reflects a prejudice which already exists, and which is maintained and legitimised by conformity.

Relative deprivation theory

According to the frustration–aggression hypothesis, people experience frustration when they feel deprived of something they believe they're entitled to. The discrepancy between our actual attainments (such as standard of living) and expectations (the standard of living we feel we deserve) is our *relative deprivation* (Davis, 1959). When attainments suddenly fall short of rising expectations, relative deprivation is particularly acute, resulting in collective unrest. This is expressed as a J-curve (Davies, 1969).

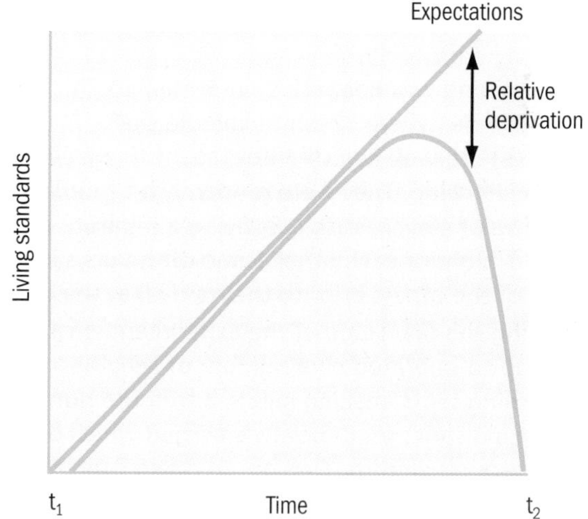

Figure 25.6 The J-curve hypothesis of relative deprivation (based on Davies, 1969)

A good example of such acute relative deprivation is the 1992 Los Angeles riots. The immediate cause was the acquittal, by an all-white jury, of four LA police officers accused of beating a black motorist, Rodney King. Against a background of rising unemployment and continuing disadvantage, the acquittal was seen by black people as symbolic of their low esteem in the eyes of the white majority (Hogg and Vaughan, 1995). The great sense of injustice at the acquittal seemed to demonstrate in acute form the injustice which is an inherent feature of discrimination – and of relative deprivation.

Figure 25.7 The 1992 Los Angeles riots were triggered by an all-white jury's acquittal of four Los Angeles police officers accused of beating a black motorist, Rodney King

The LA riots illustrate *fraternalistic relative deprivation*, based on a comparison either with dissimilar others or with other groups (Runciman, 1966). This is contrasted with *egoistic relative deprivation*, which is based on comparison with other similar individuals. Vanneman and Pettigrew (1972) found that white people who expressed the most anti-black attitudes were those who felt most strongly that white people, as a group, were badly off relative to black people. Objectively, they were actually better off, showing the subjective nature of relative deprivation. It has also been found that the most militant black people seem to be those of higher socio-economic and educational status. They probably have higher expectations, both for themselves and for their group, and consequently experience relative deprivation more acutely (Vivian and Brown, 1995).

Realistic group conflict theory (RGCT)

According to Sherif's (1966) *realistic group conflict theory* (RGCT), intergroup conflict arises as a result of a conflict of interests. When two groups want to achieve the same goal but cannot both have it, hostility is produced between them. Indeed, Sherif claims that conflict of interest (or competition) is a *sufficient* condition for the occurrence of hostility or conflict. He bases this claim on the Robber's Cave experiment, which Brown (1986) describes as the most successful field experiment ever conducted on intergroup conflict.

Key Study 25.1

The Robber's Cave experiment (Sherif *et al.*, 1961)

- The setting was Robber's Cave State Park in Oklahoma, where 22 white, middle-class, Protestant, well-adjusted boys spent two weeks at a summer camp. They were randomly assigned to two groups of eleven, each occupying a separate cabin, out of sight of each other. None of the boys knew any of the others prior to their arrival at the camp.
- During the *first stage* of the experiment, each group co-operated on a number of activities (pitching tents, making meals, a treasure hunt) and soon a distinct set of norms emerged which defined the group's identity. One group called itself 'the Rattlers', and the other 'the Eagles'. Towards the end of the first week, they were allowed to become aware of the other's existence and an 'us and them' language quickly developed.
- The *second stage* began with the announcement that there was to be a grand tournament between the two groups, comprising ten sporting events, plus points awarded for the state of their cabins and so on. A splendid trophy, medals and four-bladed knives for each of the group members would be awarded to the winning group.
- Before the tournament began, the Rattlers' flag was burned and the camp counsellors (the experimenters) had to break up a fight between the two groups. With some 'help' from the counsellors, the Eagles won and later the Rattlers stole their medals and knives. There was a strong ingroup preference. Rattlers stereotyped all Rattlers as brave, tough and friendly, and (almost) all Eagles as sneaky, stinkers and smart alecks. The reverse was true for the Eagles.

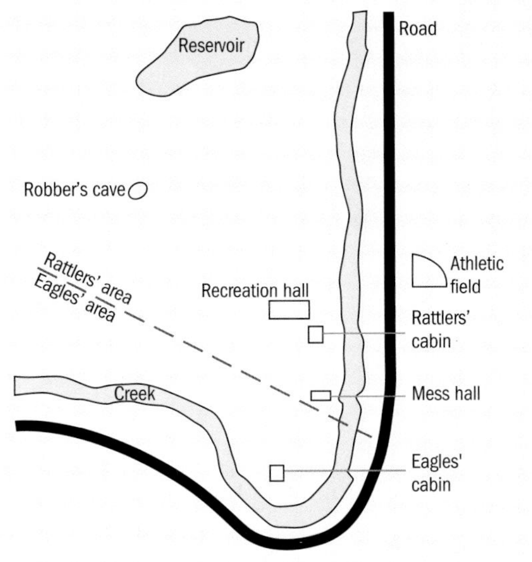

Figure 25.8 A map of Robber's Cave State Park

An evaluation of RGCT

- According to Fiske (2004), RGCT is the most obvious explanation for prejudice and discrimination. However, it has received only limited and inconsistent support, and the perceived, symbolic threat posed by outgroups matters more than any real or tangible threat. For this reason, the 'realistic' may as well be dropped from its name, and the theory renamed 'perceived group conflict theory'.
- Perceived conflict does predict negative attitudes towards outgroups (Brown *et al.*, 2001; Hennessy and West, 1999), and conflict only matters when people identify with their ingroups. More importantly, ingroup identification by itself can account for intergroup hostility, even in the absence of competition (Brewer and Brown, 1998). Intangible outcomes (such as group recognition, status, prestige) produce conflict far more often than do tangible resources. Even when the conflict appears to involve resources, often the real pay-off is pride in one's own identification with a group capable of winning them. As Fiske (2004) says:

> *... Group conflict is an inherently social competition that goes beyond concrete self-interest. One result of the struggle for positive identity is bias against the outgroup ...*

- This is related to social identity theory (see below, pp. 422–24).
- Tyerman and Spencer (1983) challenged Sherif *et al.*'s conclusions that competition is a sufficient condition for intergroup conflict. They observed English boy scouts at their annual camp. The boys knew each other well before the start of camp, and much of what they did there was similar to what the Rattlers and Eagles did at Robber's Cave (see Key Study 25.1). They were divided into four 'patrols', competing in situations familiar to them from previous camps, but the friendship ties which existed prior to arrival at camp were maintained across the patrol groups. Competition remained friendly, and there was no increase of ingroup solidarity. The four groups continued to see themselves as part of the whole group, something that was deliberately encouraged by the leader.
- Tyerman and Spencer concluded that Sherif *et al.*'s results reflect the transitory nature of their experimental group. The fact that the English boys knew each other beforehand, had established friendships, were familiar with camp life and had a leader who encouraged cooperation, were all important *contextual/situational influences* on the boys' behaviour.
- It seems, then, that 'competition' may not be a sufficient condition for intergroup conflict and hostility after all. If we accept this conclusion, the question arises whether it's even necessary; in other words, can hostility arise in the *absence* of conflicting interests?

The influence of group membership

Minimal groups

According to Tajfel *et al.* (1971), the *mere perception* of another group's existence can produce discrimination. When people are arbitrarily and randomly divided into two groups, knowledge of the other group's existence is a sufficient condition for the development of pro-ingroup and anti-outgroup attitudes. These artificial groups are known as *minimal groups*.

Before any discrimination can occur, people must be categorised as members of an ingroup or an outgroup (making categorisation a necessary condition). More significantly, the very act of categorisation produces conflict and discrimination (making it also a sufficient condition). These conclusions are based on the creation of artificial groups among 14–15-year-old Bristol schoolboys. The criteria used to create the groups were arbitrary and superficial and differed from experiment to experiment. They included:

- Chronic 'overestimations' or 'underestimations' on a task involving estimating the number of dots appearing on slide projections
- Preference for paintings by Klee or Kandinsky
- The toss of a coin.

In the Tajfel *et al.* experiments, the actual group assignments were always made randomly, whatever the boys believed to be the basis for the categorisation (see Box 25.1).

An evaluation of minimal group experiments

- The minimal group experiment must stand as one of the most influential and provocative in the study of intergroup processes (Oakes, 2004).
- Billig and Tajfel (1973) and Locksley *et al.* (1980) went even further than Tajfel *et al.*, by actually telling the participants they were being randomly assigned, tossing the coin in front of them, and giving them obviously meaningless names (such as As and Bs, or Kappas and Phis). Even under these conditions, the groups still showed a strong ingroup preference.
- According to Brown (1988), intergroup discrimination in this minimal group situation has proved to be a remarkably robust phenomenon. In more than two dozen independent studies in several different countries, using a wide range of experimental participants of both sexes (from young children to adults), essentially the same result has been found: the mere act of allocating people into arbitrary social categories is sufficient

Box 25.1 The minimal group paradigm (Tajfel *et al.*, 1971)

- Once these arbitrary groups had been formed, each boy worked alone in a cubicle on a task that required various matrices to be studied (see Figure 25.9).
- He had to decide how to allocate points to a member of his own group (but not himself) and a member of the other group. The boys were also told that the points could be converted to money after the study.
- The only information each boy had about another boy was whether he was a member of the same group or the other group; otherwise he was anonymous, unknown, unseen and identified only by a code number.
- The top line in the figure represents the points that can be allocated to the boy's own group and the bottom line the points to the other group. For example, if 18 points are allocated to the boy's own group, then five are allocated to the other group. If 12 are allocated to the boy's own group, 11 are allocated to the other group, and so on.

MATRIX 4

18	17	16	15	14	13	12	11	10	9	8	7	6	5
5	6	7	8	9	10	11	12	13	14	15	16	17	18

Figure 25.9 One of the matrices used by Tajfel *et al.* (1971)

to elicit biased judgements and discriminatory behaviours. However, Wetherell (1982) maintains that intergroup conflict *isn't* inevitable. She studied white and Polynesian children in New Zealand, and found the latter to be much more generous towards the outgroup, reflecting cultural norms which emphasised co-operation.

- The minimal group paradigm has been criticised on several methodological and theoretical grounds, especially its artificiality and meaninglessness (e.g. Schiffman and Wicklund, 1992; Gross, 2008). Tajfel (1972), however, argues that it's precisely the need to find meaning in an 'otherwise empty situation' (especially for the self) that leads participants to act in terms of the minimal categories ('Klee' or 'Kandinsky', etc.). In fact, you can turn the meaninglessness argument on its head and argue that:

> *... The power of minimal categorisations to produce group-based behaviour reflects the customary significance and usefulness of categorical perception which participants import to the laboratory – when a context is defined in social categorical terms participants expect the categories to mean something ... (Oakes, 2004)*

Social identity theory (SIT)

Tajfel (1978) and Tajfel and Turner (1986) explain the minimal group effect in terms of *social identity theory* (SIT). According to SIT, an individual strives to achieve or maintain a positive self-image. This has two components: *personal identity* (the personal characteristics and attributes which make each person unique), and *social identity* (a sense of who we are, derived from the groups we belong to).

In fact, each of us has several social identities, corresponding to the different groups we identify with (ingroups). In each case, the more positive the image of the ingroup, the more positive our own social identity, and hence our self-image. By emphasising the desirability of the ingroup(s) and focusing on those distinctions which enable our own group to come out on top, we help to create for ourselves a satisfactory social identity. This can be seen as lying at the heart of prejudice.

Some individuals may be more prone to prejudice because they have an intense need for acceptance by others. Their personal and social identities may be much more interconnected than for those with a lesser need for social acceptance. Prejudice can be seen as an adjustive mechanism which bolsters the self-concept of individuals who have feelings of personal inadequacy – but with potentially undesirable social implications.

Evaluation of SIT

- While there's considerable empirical support for the theory, much of this comes from minimal group experiments. Not only have they been criticised (see above), but SIT was originally proposed to explain the findings from those experiments. So, there's a circularity involved, making it necessary to test SIT's predictions in other ways.

- SIT has been criticised on the grounds that it presents racism (and other forms of prejudice) as 'natural', helping to justify it. Stemming from Allport's (1954) claims that stereotypes are 'categories about people' and that 'the human mind must think with the aid of categories' (see Chapter 22), Tajfel (1969; Tajfel *et al.*, 1971) saw the process of categorisation as a basic characteristic of human thought. SIT implies that intergroup hostility is natural and built into our thought processes as a consequence of categorisation. If this is correct, then racism (conceived as a form of intergroup hostility or ingroup favouritism) may also be construed as natural.
- Of course, Tajfel never intended SIT to be seen as a justification of racism. Indeed, he was a life-long opponent of racism, having lost his family and community in the Holocaust. Taken out of context and elevated to the status of a universal human characteristic, SIT is easily *misrepresented* as an explanation and justification of racism (Milner, 1991, in Howitt and Owusu-Bempah, 1994).
- Although there's abundant evidence of intergroup discrimination, this appears to stem from raising the evaluation of the ingroup, rather than denigrating the outgroup (Vivian and Brown, 1995). Indeed, SIT suggests that prejudice consists largely of liking 'us' more than disliking 'them': favouring the ingroup is the core phenomenon, *not* outgroup hostility (Brewer, 1999; Hewstone *et al.*, 2002). However, one form that ingroup favouritism can take is 'modern racism'. (See Box 25.2.)
- Wetherell (1996) believes that racism is only inevitable given a particular social context, where 'racial' categories become significant and acquire meaning as group divisions. These categories aren't natural, but become powerful as a result of social history.

Box 25.2 Modern racism and subtle prejudice

According to Fiske (2004), most estimates put 70–80 per cent of white people as relatively high on *modern/subtle* forms of racism. These are 'cool' and indirect, automatic, unconscious, unintentional, ambiguous and ambivalent. This is in sharp contrast with the crude and blatant racist abuse associated with Allport's 'antilocution' (see text above). This is sometimes referred to as *symbolic racism*; Henry and Sears' (2002) *The Symbolic Racism 2000 Scale* attempts to assess this 'new' form of racism through items such as the following:

1. It's really a matter of some people not trying hard enough; if black people would only try harder they could be just as well off as white people (1–4: strongly agree to strongly disagree).
2. Irish, Italian, Jewish and many other minorities overcame prejudice and worked their way up. Black people should do the same (1–4: strongly agree to strongly disagree).

Hostility is no longer attached to race as such but to newly emerging racial issues such as *affirmative action* (positive discrimination) and welfare programs (Kessler and Mummendey, 2008).

Subtle prejudice isn't a uniquely American, white-on-black phenomenon. (Pettigrew, 1998; Pettigrew and Meertens, 1995). In Europe, there's French/North Africans, British/South Asians, Germans/Turks.

Aversive racists advocate fairness and justice for all social/racial groups and believe strongly that they're non-racist. But this non-prejudiced self-image is combined with the tendency to discriminate against minority groups in situations where the normative structure is weak and the guidelines of appropriate behaviour are vague (Kessler and Mummendey, 2008) – or whenever they believe it's 'safe' to be racist. A classic example in the UK involved Ron Atkinson, an eminent ex-football manager and TV football pundit, who was heard to make 'old-fashioned' racist remarks about a black player when he thought his microphone was switched off. In his defence, he claimed, 'What I said was racist – but I'm not a racist. I am an idiot' (in Eboda, 2004). He was sacked from his job.

Figure 25.10 The late Jade Goody famously referred to her *Big Brother* housemate, Shilpa Shetty, as 'Shilpa Poppadom'. Jade denied that this – and other offensive remarks – were racist (as did Shetty herself)

- According to SIT, whether or not differentiation results in negative treatment of the outgroup depends on what's valued within the group's belief system. Indeed, SIT challenges the notion that people in groups are inherently inclined to act oppressively towards others, and thereby challenges the view that there are fundamental biases in collective thinking (Reicher *et al.*, 2012). However, recent evidence suggests that the mere act of categorising ourselves as belonging to an ingroup (and so, by definition, defining others as belonging to an outgroup) is sufficient for us to see less humanity in the faces of the latter (see Key Study 25.2).

Key Study 25.2

Do outgroup members have minds? (Hackel *et al.*, 2014)

- Participants were shown people images from a computer-generated series in which the face of a Barbie doll morphs incrementally into a human face.
- If the face was designated as one of their own group (a fellow-student at their university), participants perceived it as looking human *sooner* than if they believed it was the face of someone from a different university, i.e. the threshold for perceiving an ingroup member was *lower* (i.e. less stringent). ('Being human' was defined as having a mind, so the more human the image *looked,* the sooner it was *attributed* with a mind.)
- So, outgroup members required more humanness than in-groupers to be perceived as having minds.
- Significantly, scans of their brains showed corresponding increases in activity in the 'theory of mind' (ToM) network (see Chapter 40.) Hackel *et al.* regard ToM as the essence of human cognition and they conclude by saying that our social identity powerfully affects how we evaluate others, including how much humanness we accord them. These evaluations happen rapidly, perhaps even within the first half-second of seeing someone.

Critical Discussion 25.1

Prejudice, the brain and evolution: Is prejudice natural and adaptive?

According to Buchanan (2007), many researchers argue that prejudice is part of human nature; only by facing up to our authentic nature can we gain real insight into the forces that drive group conflict, and learn how we might manage and defuse such urges.

Phelps, a *social neuroscientist*, has used *f*MRI (see Chapter 4) to examine changes in blood flow within the brains of people shown race-relevant stimuli under different conditions. This research has shown a link between social categorisation and the amygdala. For example, Phelps *et al.* (2000) found that white participants' greater amygdala activation in response to black versus white faces was significantly correlated with their implicit racial prejudice (see Chapter 24) only when the faces were of *unknown* black people – but not when the faces were of famous and popular individuals.

According to Stroebe *et al.* (2008), these (and other similar) findings implicate the role of social learning and personal experience. The involvement of biological processes doesn't imply something fundamental and unchangeable; in fact, social neuroscience stresses that *social* factors can *influence* biological processes (Phelps and Thomas, 2003).

Consistent with this view of the role of social learning is the belief that our hunter-gatherer ancestors wouldn't normally have come into contact with people of a different skin colour to themselves. However, many researchers now believe that we have evolved a tendency to divide the world along ethnic lines. According to Boyd (in Buchanan, 2007), our ancestors would have needed skills for perceiving the important groups individuals belonged to. Being attuned to ethnic differences would have allowed individuals to identify others who shared the same social norms. It would have been advantageous to attend to cultural differences (such as clothing, scarification, manner of greeting) that marked one group out from another.

While this might help explain ingroup favouritism, what about hostility towards outgroups? If we reject ingroup members who violate social norms, this response is easily transferred to members of other ethnic groups. Unconsciously, we may see people from other ethnic groups not simply as different, but as cheats, morally corrupt, bad people (as we do deviants within our ingroup) (Gil-White, in Buchanan, 2007).

If ethnocentrism is an evolved adaptation to facilitate smooth social interactions, it's a rather crude one. But it may serve the same cognitive purpose as stereotyping, namely to save effort and enable us to make swift judgements – and responses (see Chapter 22). Ending on a positive note, Buchanan (2007) claims that:

If the seeds of racism are in our nature, so too are the seeds of tolerance ... By better understanding what sorts of situations ... are conducive to both, we may be able to promote our better nature.

REDUCING PREJUDICE and DISCRIMINATION

The contact hypothesis

Probably the first formal proposal of a set of social–psychological principles for reducing prejudice was Allport's (1954) *contact hypothesis* (as it's come to be called), according to which:

> *Prejudice (unless deeply rooted in the character structure of the individual) may be reduced by equal status contact between majority and minority groups in the pursuit of common goals. The effect is greatly enhanced if this contact is sanctioned by institutional supports (i.e. by law, custom or local atmosphere) and provided it is of a sort that leads to the perception of common interests and common humanity between members of the two groups.*

Most programmes aimed at promoting harmonious relations between groups that were previously in conflict have operated according to Allport's 'principles', in particular *equal status contact* and the *pursuit of common (superordinate) goals.*

Equal status contact

When people are segregated, they're likely to experience *autistic hostility*, that is, ignorance of others, which results in a failure to understand the reasons for their actions. Lack of contact means there's no 'reality testing' against which to check our own interpretations of others' behaviour, and this in turn is likely to reinforce negative stereotypes. By the same token, ignorance of what 'makes them tick' will probably make 'them' seem more dissimilar from ourselves than they really are. Bringing people into contact with each other should make them seem more familiar and, at least, offers the possibility that this negative cycle can be interrupted and even reversed.

Related to autistic hostility is the *mirror-image phenomenon* (Bronfenbrenner, 1960), whereby enemies come to see themselves as being in the right (with 'God on our side') and the other side as in the wrong. Both sides tend to attribute to each other the same negative characteristics (the 'assumed dissimilarity of beliefs'). Increased contact provides the opportunity to disconfirm our stereotypes. The outgroup loses its strangeness, and group members are more likely to be seen as unique individuals, rather than an 'undifferentiated mass' (see Figure 25.11). This represents a reduction in the *illusion of outgroup homogeneity* (see Chapter 22).

How effective is equal status contact?

It's generally agreed that increased contact alone won't reduce prejudice. Despite evidence that we prefer people who are familiar (see Chapter 28), if this contact is between people who are consistently of

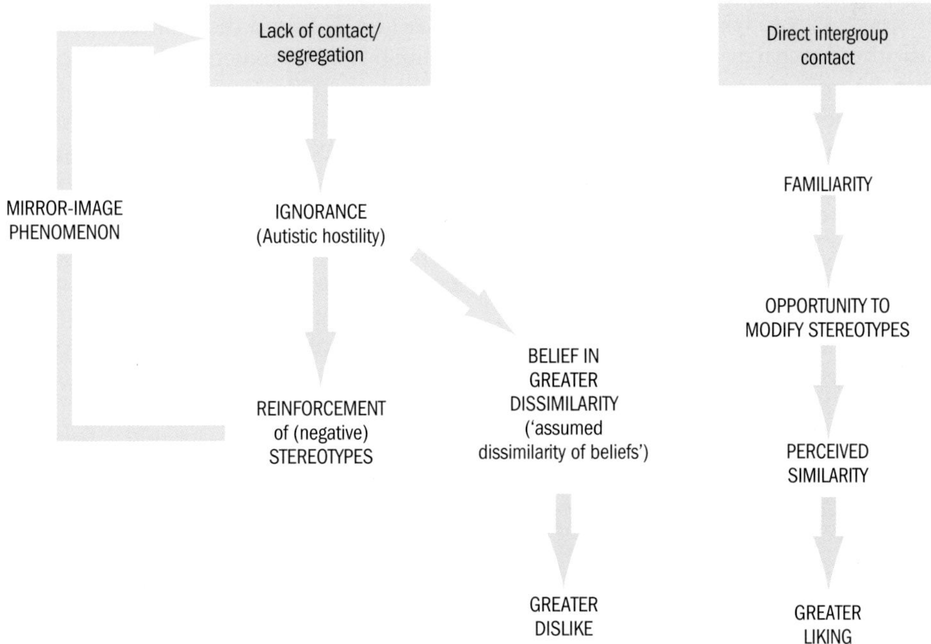

Figure 25.11 Summary of how the negative cycle of lack of contact/segregation between racial/ethnic groups and reinforcement of negative stereotypes can be broken by direct contact (as advocated by Allport's contact hypothesis)

unequal status, then 'familiarity may breed contempt'. Aronson (1980) points out that many white people (in the USA) have always had a great deal of contact with black people – as dishwashers, toilet attendants, domestic servants and so on. Such contacts may simply reinforce the stereotypes held by white people of black people as being inferior. Similarly, Amir (1994) argues that we need to ask 'Under what conditions does intergroup contact have an impact, for whom and regarding what outcomes?'

One early study of equal status contact (Deutsch and Collins, 1951) compared two kinds of housing project, one of which was thoroughly integrated (black people and white people were assigned houses regardless of race) and the other segregated. Both casual and neighbourly contact was greater in the integrated housing, with a corresponding decrease in prejudice among white people towards black people.

As noted earlier, in Minard's study of miners in West Virginia, black and white miners were (equal status) colleagues underground, but the norms operating above ground clearly didn't permit equality of status. Similarly, Stouffer *et al.* (1949) and Amir (1969) found that interracial attitudes improved markedly when black people and white people served together as soldiers in battle and on ships, but relationships weren't so good at base camp.

Stephan (1978) reviewed a number of studies of desegregation of American schools and concluded that white prejudice towards black people wasn't reduced, while black prejudice towards white people seemed to have increased. Several studies have found that, at first, interaction and friendship are totally governed by group attitudes and then slowly start to take account of personal qualities. But racial attitudes change very little. Aronson (2000) believes that the main reason for this failure was that very few of the studies reviewed by Stephan involved a school situation where all three of Allport's requisites – equal status contact, pursuit of common goals, and sanction by authority – were in place at the same time.

Pursuit of common (superordinate) goals

In a co-operative situation, the attainment of one person's goal enhances the chances of attainment of the goals of other group members; this is the reverse of a competitive situation (Brown, 1986). (See Key Study 25.3.)

One influential attempt to realise both mutual co-operation and equal status contact is Aronson *et al.*'s (1978) *jigsaw method*.

Do common goals always work?

The imposition of superordinate goals may sometimes even *increase* antagonism towards the outgroup – if the co-operation fails to achieve its aims. Groups need distinctive and complementary roles to play, so that each group's contributions are clearly defined. When this doesn't happen, liking for the other group may actually *decrease*, perhaps because group members are concerned with the integrity of the ingroup (Brown, 1988).

> **Key Study 25.3**
>
> **Robber's Cave revisited (Sherif *et al.*, 1961)**
>
> - In a *third stage* of their field experiment (see Key Study 25.1), Sherif *et al.* created seven *equal status contact* situations (including filling out questionnaires, watching movies, and having meals). None of these, nor all in combination, helped reduce friction between the Rattlers and Eagles.
> - But it was also arranged that the camp's drinking water supply was cut off, and the only way to restore it was by a *co-operative effort*. In order to afford to hire a movie, both groups had to chip in, and on a trip to Cedar Lake, the truck got stuck and they all had to pull on a rope together to get it free.
> - In the final few days, the group divisions disappeared and the boys actually suggested travelling home together in one bus. Sixty-five per cent of their friendship choices were now made from the other group and their stereotypes became much more favourable.

Maintaining group boundaries (*mutual differentiation*: Fiske, 2004) is essential for promoting generalisation from the particular outgroup members to the whole outgroup (Hewstone, 2003). For example, Harwood *et al.* (2003) found that contact with grandparents was a much better predictor of more positive attitudes towards the elderly in general, when young people reported being aware of age groups during contact.

But isn't there the danger that emphasising group/category boundaries during contact will reinforce perceptions of group differences and increase *intergroup anxiety* (Islam and Hewstone, 1993: see below)? It certainly shouldn't be done in the initial stages of contact, especially when intergroup relationships are very negative. According to Hewstone (2003), the best approach is:

> *... To promote contact that is simultaneously both 'interpersonal' (e.g. involving personal exchange within a close relationship) and 'intergroup' (i.e. both members are still aware that they belong to different groups) ...*

An evaluation of the contact hypothesis (CH)

- The reduction in prejudice among children who participate in the racially mixed jigsaw classroom doesn't generalise to those ethnic groups as a whole.

This is a crucial criticism of the CH (Hewstone and Brown, 1986). But there's now much greater optimism that positive effects can generalise in several ways: across situations, from specific outgroup members to the whole outgroup, from the immediate outgroup to other outgroups (the *secondary transfer effect*: Pettigrew, 2009) and across different types of responses (Gaertner and Dovidio, 2000; Hewstone, 1996; New, 2013; Pettigrew, 1997). For example, Tausch *et al.* (2010) found that contact across the sectarian divide in Northern Ireland (i.e. between Catholics and Protestants) promoted not only more positive attitudes towards the religious outgroup, but also towards racial minorities.

- But contact can also 'work' via more subtle processes than generalisation (Hewstone, 2003). For example, it can help reduce the 'almost automatic fear' caused by interacting with members of outgroups ('intergroup awe': Stephan and Stephan, 1985). Contact has been shown to play a crucial mediating role in reducing anxiety between Hindus and Muslims in Bangladesh and between Catholics and Protestants in Northern Ireland (Hewstone, 2003).
- In a meta-analysis ('study of studies'; see Chapter 6) of over 500 studies, Pettigrew and Tropp (2000, 2006) found that the greater the contact between groups, the lower the prejudice expressed. Only about 6 per cent showed the *reverse* effect. Pettigrew and Tropp conclude that Allport's original contact conditions aren't *necessary* for positive contact effects to occur, but they are *facilitating* conditions likely to make contact more effective.
- Based on their meta-analysis, Pettigrew and Tropp (2000, 2006) proposed a reformulation of the CH; instead of conditions necessary for positive contact, they identified negative conditions that must be *avoided* to prevent positive contact effects being erased. Contact opportunities should (i) occur often enough; (ii) not induce threat or anxiety; and (iii) encourage the development of cross-group friendships. This reformulation provides a much more optimistic view than the original CH: preconditions for positive effects can now be met more easily (Kessler and Mummendey, 2008).

CONCLUSIONS: WHAT to do with STEREOTYPES?

According to Brislin (1993):

> *In many cultures, stereotypes of certain groups are so negative, so pervasive, and have existed for so many generations that they can be considered part of the culture into which children are socialised …*

As we saw in Chapter 22, stereotypes represent a way of simplifying the extraordinarily complex social world we inhabit by placing people into categories; this alone would explain why they're so resistant to change. But they also influence selective attention and selective remembering, processes that are to a large extent outside conscious control. However, these automatic stereotyped reactions (like one I'm still 'guilty' of, namely inferring that 'doctor' denotes 'he') can be seen simply as habits that can be broken. Prejudice reduction is a *process* (rather than an all-or-none event), which involves learning to inhibit these automatic reactions and deciding that prejudice is an inappropriate way of relating to others (Devine and Zuwerink, 1994). But trying to suppress your stereotypes may actually *strengthen* their automaticity. Hogg and Abrams (2000) argue that:

> *The knack would seem to be to get people to have insight into their stereotypes – to understand them and see through them rather than merely to suppress them …*

Relying on stereotypes to form impressions of strangers (*category-driven processing*) represents the cognitively easiest, least strenuous, route, while relying on their unique characteristics (*attribute-driven processing*) represents the most strenuous route (Fiske and Neuberg, 1990). While people are very skilled at preserving their stereotypes ('You're OK, it's the others'), the more often they come into contact with members of a particular group who don't fit the stereotype, the more likely it is to lose its credibility.

Similarly, Crisp and Meleady (2012) identify two cognitive systems we have for thinking about social groups:

- *System 1* is fast and automatic and is demonstrated by stereotyping; we classify people by social category in a matter of milliseconds.
- *System 2* allows us to override crude ingroup/outgroup categorisation, making it possible to form new alliances. This can be activated when our attention is drawn to an outsider having multiple group memberships, especially if these co-occur relatively rarely (e.g. a German Muslim). This reduces prejudice by highlighting the person's individuality. Similarly, prejudice can be reduced if attention is drawn to the individual's membership of one of our own groups (e.g. a German Muslim of the same age).

Policy-makers need to recognise the kind of social contexts that switch-on System 2. (See Kahneman's research, Chapter 20.) Any attempt at 're-drawing' the boundaries between 'us' and 'them' ('we') should help to activate System 2. (This relates to the *recategorisation/common group identity model:* Gaertner *et al.*, 1989). Van Bavel and Cunningham (2012) demonstrated this by assigning participants to small groups that were randomly defined – except that each included both black people and white people. Not only did participants rate members of their own group more positively than outsiders regardless of skin colour, but they were also more likely to remember group members' faces despite having seen them for just a few seconds. This is surprising, given that people are usually worse at remembering the faces of other racial/ethnic groups (*own-race bias*: see Chapter 21).

Finally, propaganda, education and the raising of consciousness can all contribute to the reduction and prevention of prejudice. (See Key Study 25.4.)

In a follow-up study of the students when they were 18, Elliott found that they reported themselves as being more tolerant of differences between groups and actively opposed to prejudice.

Elliott's experiment (in Aronson and Osherow, 1980) demonstrates the potential impact of experiencing prejudice and discrimination first-hand. Prejudice is mindless. If we teach people, especially children, to be mindful of others, to think of them as complex, whole individuals, stereotypic reactions could be reduced (Hogg and Vaughan, 1995).

Key Study 25.4

The blue eyes–brown eyes experiment (Elliott, in Aronson and Osherow, 1980)

- Aronson and Osherow reported an experiment with nine-year-olds conducted by their teacher, Jane Elliott. She told her class one day that brown-eyed people are more intelligent and 'better' people than those with blue eyes. Brown-eyed students, though in the minority, would be the 'ruling class' over the inferior blue-eyed children and be given extra privileges. The blue-eyed students were to be 'kept in their place' by being last in line, seated at the back of the class and given less break-time. They also had to wear special collars as a sign of their low status.
- Within a short time, the blue-eyed children began to do more poorly in their schoolwork, became depressed and angry and described themselves more negatively. The brown-eyed group grew mean, oppressing the others and making derogatory comments about them.
- The next day, Elliott announced that she'd made a mistake and that it was really blue-eyed people who are superior. The pattern of prejudice and discrimination quickly switched from the blue-eyed as victims to the brown-eyed.
- At the end of the experiment, Elliott debriefed the children. She told them its purpose was to provide them with an opportunity to experience the evils of prejudice and discrimination in a protected environment.

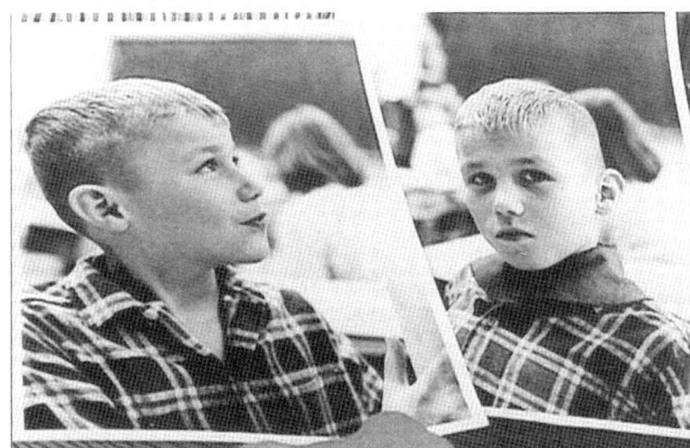

Figure 25.12 Stills from the film of Elliot's classroom experiment, in which wearing collars as an overt sign of low status was part of the discrimination sanctioned by the teacher

Chapter Summary

- As an extreme attitude, **prejudice** comprises **cognitive (stereotype)**, **affective (hostility)** and **behavioural** components. **Discrimination** usually refers to any kind of prejudiced behaviour.
- Most definitions of prejudice identify it as the characteristic of an individual, but it's often associated with **intergroup conflict**. Racism, sexism, heterosexism and ageism can all be regarded as **ideologies**, which are characteristics of society, not individuals.
- The most influential 'individual' theory of prejudice is the **authoritarian personality.** Adorno *et al.* concluded that the authoritarian personality is prejudiced in a **generalised** way.
- This reflects a personality structure that divides the world rigidly into 'us' and 'them', and a punitive, unloving upbringing, from which considerable **repressed hostility** towards the parents is **displaced** and **projected** onto minority groups.
- Methodological problems with these data include **acquiescent response set** and **experimenter bias.** A major theoretical problem is how a theory of individual differences can account for the uniformity of prejudice as found in Nazi Germany.
- Rokeach's theory of **ideological dogmatism** identifies authoritarianism as an extreme way of thinking (the 'closed mind'), rather than a particular political persuasion.
- According to Dollard *et al.*'s **frustration–aggression hypothesis**, frustration-induced aggression is often displaced onto minority groups, which act as **scapegoats**.
- The central focus of social dominance theory (SDT) is on **social dominance orientation (SDO)**. This measures an individual's acceptance of general cultural ideologies relating to equality/inequality. Central to SDO are **legitimising myths**.
- **Relative deprivation theory** claims that we experience frustration when attainments fall short of expectations. **Fraternalistic relative deprivation** will produce intergroup hostility, particularly if there's a sudden shortfall of attainments.
- According to Sherif's **realistic group conflict theory (RGCT), competition** between groups for scarce resources is a **sufficient** condition for inter-group hostility. This was demonstrated in the Robber's Cave field experiment.
- **Minimal group experiments** demonstrate that intergroup conflict can occur without competition, and that the **mere categorisation** of oneself as belonging to one group rather than another is **sufficient** for intergroup discrimination.
- The minimal group effect is explained in terms of Tajfel's **social identity theory (SIT)**, according to which we try to increase self-esteem by accentuating the desirability of our ingroup(s). Prejudice can be seen as part of the attempt to boost self-image.
- The involvement of **biological** processes in prejudice (as revealed by brain-scanning) is consistent with both **social learning** and **evolutionary** accounts.
- An important framework for attempts to reduce prejudice is Allport's **contact hypothesis (CH)**, which stresses the need for **equal status contact** and the **pursuit of common (superordinate) goals** between members of different ethnic groups.
- Group segregation can produce **autistic hostility** and the related **mirror-image phenomenon**, with the likely reinforcement of negative stereotypes. Unequal status contact can also reinforce stereotypes.
- In **equal status situations**, there needs to be a balance between **mutual group differentiation** (which maintains **intergroup contact)** and **interpersonal contact**.
- There's considerable support for the CH, which doesn't just apply to relationships between ethnic/racial groups but to a wide range of social groups. The key mechanism involved seems to be creating **affective ties**, including the reduction of **intergroup awe**.
- Stereotypes (**category-driven processing**) are very resistant to change because they often form part of the culture. They can be activated automatically/unconsciously but may be broken if people are encouraged to focus on the unique characteristics of individuals (**attribute-driven processing**).

Links with Other Topics/Chapters

Chapters 43 and 47 → Social institutions other than the police that may be guilty of institutional racism include *psychiatry* and *Psychology* itself (the '-isms' including *sexism*, *heterosexism*, and *ethnocentrism*

Chapter 22 → *Stereotypes* represent the cognitive component of prejudice

Chapter 29 → The frustration–aggression hypothesis is, of course, relevant to understanding *human aggression*

Chapter 49 → Explanations of prejudice and discrimination in terms of individual personality (intrapersonal behaviour), rather than interpersonal/intergroup, are *reductionist*

Chapter 23 → The *ultimate attribution error* (UAE) (Pettigrew, 1979) refers to the belief that the negative behaviours of an outgroup member are caused by immutable, genetic characteristics of the group as a whole (the 'bedrock assumption of racist doctrine')

Recommended Reading

Allport, G.W. (1954) *The Nature of Prejudice.* Reading, MA: Addison-Wesley.

Brown, R. (1995) *Prejudice: Its Social Psychology.* Oxford: Blackwell.

Gross, R. (2008) *Key Studies in Psychology* (5th edition). London: Hodder Education. Chapter 12

Howitt, D. & Owusu-Bempah, J. (1994) *The Racism of Psychology: Time for Change.* Hemel Hempstead: Harvester Wheatsheaf. Also relevant to Chapters 47 and 48.

Oakes, P. (2004) The Root of All Evil in Intergroup Relations? Unearthing the Categorisation Process. In M.B. Brewer & M. Hewstone (eds) *Social Cognition.* Oxford: Blackwell.

Plaudi, M.A. (1992) *The Psychology of Women.* Dubuque, Iowa: W.C.B. Brown and Benchmark. Also relevant to Chapter 47.

Useful Websites

www.socialinclusion.org.uk/home/index.php (National Social Inclusion Programme)

www.tolerance.org (Teaching Tolerance: Project of the Southern Poverty Law Center)

www.understandingprejudice.org/links/antisem.htm (Understanding Prejudice: Antisemitism)

www.socialpsychology.org/social.htm#prejudice (Social Psychology Network) (Also relevant to Chapters 22, 24, and 26.)

www.iupui.edu/~anthkb/ethnocen.htm (Ethnocentrism: Barger (2008))

www.bbc.co.uk/programmes/b01j5mym (Radio discussion featuring Miles Hewstone)

CHAPTER 26

CONFORMITY AND GROUP INFLUENCE

INTRODUCTION and OVERVIEW

It's impossible to live among other people and not be influenced by them in some way. According to Allport (1968), Social Psychology as a discipline can be defined as:

> *... An attempt to understand and explain how the thoughts, feelings and behaviours of individuals are influenced by the actual, imagined, or implied presence of others.*

Sometimes, other people's attempts to change our thoughts or behaviour are very obvious, as when, for example, a traffic warden tells us not to park our car in a particular place. If we do as we're told and move the car, we're demonstrating *obedience,* which implies that one person (in this example, the traffic warden, an authority figure) has more social power than others (motorists). Obedience is discussed in Chapter 27.

In common with obedience, other forms of *active* social influence involve deliberate attempts by one person to change another's thoughts or behaviour.

Ask Yourself

- Try to identify some other examples of *active social influence* (see previous chapters in the 'Social' part of this book and the 'Links with other topics/chapters' section at the end of this chapter).

However, on other occasions, social influence is less direct and deliberate and may not involve any explicit requests or demands at all. For example, sometimes the mere presence of other people can influence our behaviour. This can take the form of *inhibiting* our behaviour, as in bystander intervention (see Chapter 30) or social loafing, or *enhancing* it, as in social facilitation (see Chapter 31).

Another form of indirect or passive social influence occurs when your choice of clothes or taste in music is affected by what your friends wear or listen to. This is *conformity*. Your peers (equals) exert pressure on you to behave (and think) in particular ways, a case of the majority influencing the individual (*majority influence*). But majorities can also be influenced by minorities (*minority influence*). Related to conformity are other group processes, such as the *risky shift phenomenon* and *group polarisation*.

According to Turner (1991):

> *The key idea in understanding what researchers mean by social influence is the concept of a social norm. Influence relates to the processes whereby people agree or disagree about appropriate behaviour, form, maintain or change social norms, and the social conditions that give rise to, and the effects of, such norms ...*

Turner defines a social norm as:

> *... A rule, value or standard shared by the members of a social group that prescribes appropriate, expected or desirable attitudes and conduct in matters relevant to the group ...*

MAJORITY INFLUENCE

What is conformity?

Conformity has been defined in a number of ways. For Crutchfield (1955), it is 'yielding to group pressure'. Mann (1969) agrees with Crutchfield, but argues that it may take different forms and be based on motives other than group pressure. Zimbardo and Leippe (1991) define conformity as:

> *... A change in belief or behaviour in response to real or imagined group pressure when there is no direct request to comply with the group nor any reason to justify the behaviour change.*

Ask Yourself

- What do these definitions have in common?

Group pressure is the common denominator in definitions of conformity, although none of them specifies particular groups with particular beliefs or practices. Pressure is exerted by those groups that are important to the individual at a given time; these may consist of 'significant others', such as family or peers (*membership groups*), or groups whose values a person admires or aspires to, but to which s/he doesn't actually belong (*reference groups*).

Conformity, then, doesn't imply adhering to any particular set of attitudes or values. Instead, it involves yielding to the real or imagined pressures of any group, whether it has majority *or* minority status (van Avermaet, 1996) (see below).

Experimental studies of conformity

A study by Jenness (1932) is sometimes cited as the very first experimental study of conformity, although it's usually discussed in the context of social facilitation (see Chapter 31). Jenness asked individual students to estimate the number of beans in a bottle and then had them discuss it to arrive at a group estimate. When they were asked individually to make a second estimate, there was a distinct shift towards the group's estimate. Sherif (1935) used a similar procedure in one of the classic conformity experiments. (See Key Study 26.1.)

Key Study 26.1

If the light appears to move, it must be the Sherif (Sherif, 1935)

- Sherif used a visual illusion called the *autokinetic effect*: a stationary spot of light seen in an otherwise dark room appears to move (see Chapter 15). He told participants he was going to move the light and their task was to say how far they thought the light moved.
- Participants were first tested individually, being asked to estimate the extent of movement several times. The estimates fluctuated to begin with, but then 'settled down' and became quite consistent (despite wide individual differences).
- They then heard the estimates of two other participants (the group condition). Under these conditions, the estimates of different participants *converged* (they became more *similar*). Thus, a *group norm* developed, which represented the average of the individual estimates.
- Just as different individuals produced different estimates, so did different groups. This happened both under the conditions already described, and also when participants were tested in small groups right from the start.

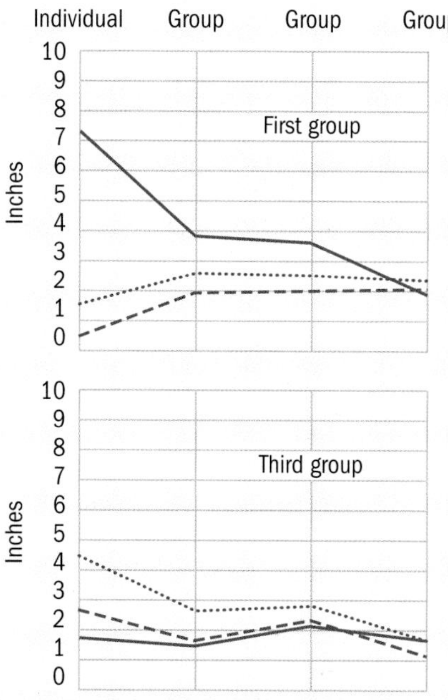

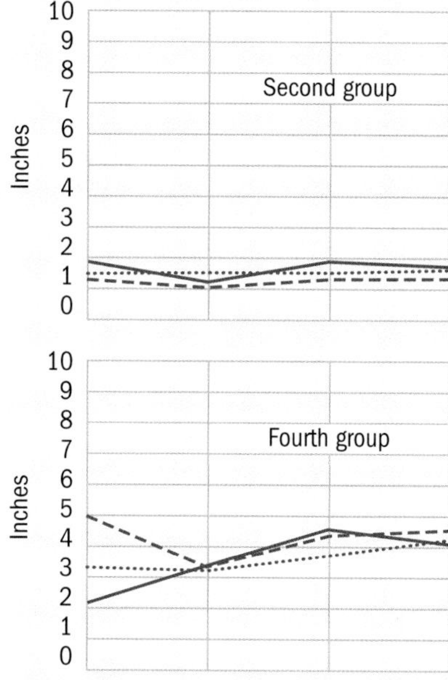

Figure 26.1 Median judgements of the apparent movement of a stationary point of light given by participants in Sherif's (1935) experiment. The figure shows the estimates given by four groups.

According to Sherif, participants used others' estimates as a frame of reference in what was an ambiguous situation. Note that:

- Participants weren't in any way instructed to agree with the others in the group (unlike the Jenness study).
- When participants were tested again individually, their estimates closely resembled the group norm (rather than their original, individual, estimates).

An evaluation of Sherif's experiment

- According to Brown (1996), Sherif's study is one of the classics of Social Psychology. But it seems to raise questions rather than provide answers.
  - In what sense can Sherif's participants be described as a group?
  - Can we speak of group norms without any direct interaction taking place or participants seeing themselves as engaged in some kind of joint activity?
- In post-experimental interviews, participants all denied being influenced by others' judgements. They also claimed that they struggled to arrive at the 'correct' answers on their own. In other words, they didn't consider themselves part of a group (although there's always doubt about taking participants' reports about the motivation for their behaviour at face value).
- While Sherif believed he'd demonstrated conformity, others, notably Asch, disagreed. According to Asch, the fact that the task used by Sherif was *ambiguous* (there was no right or wrong answer) made it difficult to draw any definite conclusions about conformity. Conformity should be measured in terms of the individual's tendency to agree with other group members who unanimously give the *wrong answer* on a task where the solution is obvious or unambiguous. This is a much stricter test of conformity than where there's no correct or incorrect answer to begin with.
- Asch devised a simple perceptual task that involved participants deciding which of three comparison lines of different lengths matched a standard line. In a pilot study, Asch tested 36 participants individually on 20 slightly different versions of the task shown in Figure 26.2. They made a total of only three mistakes in the 720 trials (an error rate of 0.42 per cent).

Ask Yourself

- What was the purpose of the pilot study?
- What conclusions do you think Asch drew from its results?

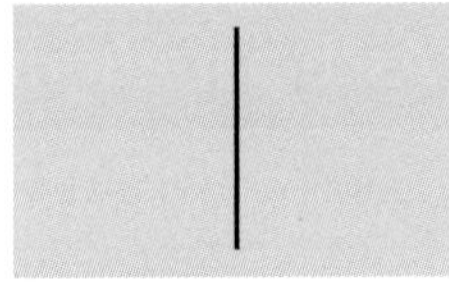

Standard line

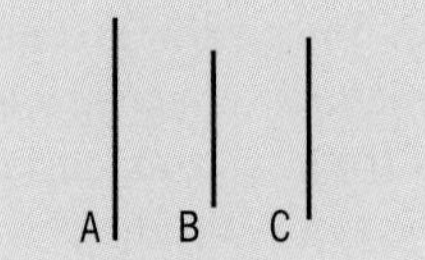

Comparison lines

Figure 26.2 Stimulus cards used in Asch's conformity experiments (1951, 1952, 1956)

The purpose of the pilot study (which involved participants who weren't to take part in the actual experiment) was to establish that the task really was simple and the answers obvious and unambiguous. Asch concluded that they were. Because his procedure for studying conformity can be adapted to investigate the effects of different variables on conformity, it's known as the *Asch paradigm* (see Box 26.1).

The important measure in the Asch paradigm is whether the naïve participant conforms and gives the same wrong answer as the unanimous stooges on the critical trials or remains independent and gives the obviously correct answer. Asch found a mean conformity rate of 32 per cent; that is, participants agreed with the incorrect majority answer on about one-third of the critical trials.

As shown in Table 26.1, there were also wide *individual differences*:

- No one conformed on all the critical trials and 13 of the 50 participants (26 per cent) never conformed
- One person conformed on 11 of the 12 critical trials and about 75 per cent conformed at least once.

Given that the task was simple and unambiguous, such findings indicate a high level of conformity. As van Avermaet (1996) has remarked:

> *The results reveal the tremendous impact of an 'obviously' incorrect but unanimous majority on the judgements of a lone individual.*

How did the naïve participants explain their behaviour?

When interviewed at length following the experiment, participants gave a number of specific reasons for conforming.

- Some wanted to act in accordance with the experimenter's wishes and convey a favourable impression of themselves by not 'upsetting the

Box 26.1 The Asch paradigm

Some of the participants who'd taken part in the pilot study were asked to act as 'stooges' (or 'confederates: accomplices of the experimenter). The stooges were told they'd be doing the task again, but this time in a group that would contain one person (a naïve participant) who was completely unaware that they were stooges.

On certain *critical* trials, all the stooges were required to say out loud the same *wrong* answer. In Asch's original experiment, the stooges (usually seven to nine of them) and the naïve participant were seated either in a straight line or round a table. The situation was rigged so that the naïve participant was always the last or last but one to say the answer out loud.

On the first two trials (*neutral* trials), all the stooges gave the correct answers. But the next trial was a critical trial. This happened a further 11 times (making 12 critical trials in total) with four additional neutral trials (making six in total) between the critical trials.

Figure 26.3 A minority of one faces a unanimous majority (Courtesy William Vandivert and *Scientific American,* November 1955)

Table 26.1 The findings from Asch's original experiment

No. of conforming responses made	No. of people making those responses
0	13
1	4
2	5
3	6
4	3
5	4
6	1
7	2
8	5
9	3
10	3
11	1
12	0

experiment' (which they believed they would have done by disagreeing with the majority); they thought some obscure 'mistake' had been made.

- A few, who had no reason to believe that there was anything wrong with their eyesight, genuinely doubted the validity of their own judgements by wondering if they were suffering from eye-strain, or if their chairs had been moved so that they couldn't see the cards properly.
- Some denied being aware of having given incorrect answers – they'd unwittingly used the confederates as 'marker posts' (Smith, 1995).
- Others said they wanted to be like everyone else, didn't want to 'appear different', 'be made to look a fool', a 'social outcast' or 'inferior'. So, for these participants there was a discrepancy between the answer they gave in the group and what they privately believed: they knew the 'wrong' answer was wrong, but went along with it nonetheless. Contrast this with Sherif's participants, for whom there was no conflict between the group's estimate and their own, individual estimates.
- According to Reicher *et al.* (2012), recent analyses have shown that these explanations of their own responses show that participants weren't blindly and passively conforming. Rather, they were faced with a strange and alarming situation of which they had to try to make sense.

Factors affecting conformity

So far, we've described the original, basic experiment. Asch (1952, 1955) subsequently manipulated different variables in order to identify the crucial influences on conformity.

Size of the majority and unanimity

With one naïve participant and just one stooge, conformity was very low (about 3 per cent), ('it's my word against yours'). Where there were two stooges and one participant, conformity increased to 14 per cent and, with three stooges, it reached the 32 per cent that Asch originally reported. But beyond three, conformity didn't continue to rise. This suggests that it's the *unanimity* of the majority which is important (the stooges all agree with each other), rather than the actual size of the majority (the number of stooges).

This was demonstrated when one of the stooges (a *dissenter*) agreed with the naïve participant. With one 'supporter', conformity dropped from 32 to 5.5 per cent. Significantly, a dissenter who disagrees with *both* the naïve participant and the majority has almost as much effect on reducing conformity as one who agrees with the naïve participant. In both cases, the majority is no longer unanimous. Thus, just breaking the unanimity of the majority is sufficient to reduce conformity (Allen and Levine, 1971). According to Asch (1951):

> *... A unanimous majority of three is, under the given conditions, far more effective than a majority of eight containing one dissenter ...*

However, this reduction in conformity only seems to apply to unambiguous stimulus situations (like Asch's perceptual task), and not where opinions are being asked for (Allen and Levine, 1968).

Also, Gerard *et al.* (1968) and Latané and Wolf (1981) claim that adding more stooges will increase conformity, although the *rate of increase* falls with each extra majority member. Contrary to both Asch and these later studies, Mann (1969) claims that as group size increases, so conformity goes on increasing (a *linear relationship*). However, this will only occur if the majority members are perceived as independent judges, and not as sheep following each other or as members of a group who've jointly reached a judgement.

Fear of ridicule

In the original experiment, it seems that participants were justified in fearing they'd be ridiculed by the rest of the group if they gave the answer they believed to be correct. When a group of 16 naïve participants and a single stooge were tested, the stooge's wrong answers on the critical trials were greeted with sarcasm, exclamations of disbelief and mocking laughter!

Task difficulty

When Asch made the comparison lines more similar in length (making the task more difficult), participants were more likely to yield to the incorrect majority answer – especially when they felt confident there was a right answer. When tasks are more ambiguous, in the sense that they involve expressing opinions or stating preferences, conformity actually *decreases*.

Giving answers in private

Critics of Asch's experiment have pointed out that participants may conform because they're reluctant or too embarrassed to expose their private views in face-to-face situations (as many of them indicated in post-experimental interviews). If so, the level of conformity should decrease if they're allowed to write their answers down, or where they remain anonymous in some other way.

For example, Deutsch and Gerard (1955) used partitions which shielded participants from each other, with responses showing up on a light panel in front of them – the naïve participant had to press one of three buttons. Under these conditions, conformity was lower than in Asch's face-to-face situation. Indeed, when Asch himself allowed the naïve participant to answer in writing (while the stooges still gave their answers publicly), conformity dropped to 12.5 per cent.

Crutchfield (1954) also used a non-face-to-face procedure. He criticised Asch's experiments for being time-consuming and uneconomical since only one participant could be tested at a time. So, he changed the experimental situation so that several (usually five) naïve participants could be tested at the same time. Altogether, he tested over 600.

Replications of Asch's research

Key Study 26.2

Who needs confederates? (Mori and Arai, 2010)

- Mori and Arai adapted the MORI technique (Manipulation of Overlapping Rivalrous Images by polarising filters – used previously in eyewitness research): by wearing glasses similar to those used for watching 3-D movies, participants can view the same display and yet see three *different* things.
- Over 100 Japanese participants (male and female) were tested in groups of four; three wore identical glasses, with the fourth wearing a different pair. As in Asch's study, participants stated their answers publicly, with the minority participant always going third.
- For women only, the results closely matched Asch's. But the males were *not* at all influenced by the majority.
- Not only were these participants from a different culture and generation from Asch's, but they knew each other. Mori and Arai argue that conformity among acquaintances is more important as a psychological research topic than among strangers. Conformity usually takes place within families, friendship or colleague groups, and the Asch experiment lacks ecological validity.

Were Asch's findings a reflection of the times? Asch began his research expecting to show that people weren't as suggestible as was commonly believed at the time – and as suggested by Sherif's experiments. He believed that Americans could act independently, even when faced with a majority that saw the world differently from themselves.

Larsen (1974) found significantly lower conformity rates than Asch had found among groups of American students and suggested that this was because of a changed climate of opinion in America in the 1970s towards independence and criticism and away from conformity. However, in a later study, Larsen *et al.* (1979) found results very similar to those of Asch. Perhaps the pendulum had begun to swing back again. Why might this have happened?

The early 1950s was the McCarthyism era in the USA. This is named after the US Senator Joseph McCarthy, who claimed to have unearthed an anti-American Communist plot. This resulted in a witch-hunt of alleged Communist sympathisers, which included academics and Hollywood stars. Under these social and political conditions, high conformity is to be expected (Spencer and Perrin, 1998). By the early 1970s, there was a more liberal climate, but this may have changed again by the late 1970s.

In Britain, Perrin and Spencer (1981) found very low rates of conformity among university students during a period of self-expression and tolerance. As Spencer and Perrin (1998) say, 'The Asch findings are clearly an indicator of the prevailing culture'.

Ask Yourself

- Perrin and Spencer (1981) tested young offenders on probation, with probation officers as stooges.
- How do you think conformity rates with these participants compared with those of Asch?
- Explain your answer.

We might expect the general social and political climate in Britain in the early 1980s to have had a different impact on university students than on young offenders. Additionally, the stooges were adult authority figures, which means that the group wasn't composed of peers (or equals). Not surprisingly, conformity rates were much higher than for the undergraduates and were similar to those reported by Asch.

It's also possible that experimenters exert an influence. As Brown (1985) has noted, experimenters may also have changed over time. Perhaps their expectations of the amount of conformity that will occur in an experiment are unwittingly conveyed to the participants, who respond accordingly (see Chapter 3).

Cross-cultural studies of conformity

As shown in Table 26.2, the vast majority of conformity studies using the Asch paradigm have been carried out in Britain and the USA. However, using meta-analysis (see Chapter 6), Bond and Smith (1996) were able to compare the British and American studies with the small number carried out in other parts of the world. After all relevant factors have been taken into account, the studies can be compared in terms of an *averaged effect size*, in this case, the conformity rate.

Table 26.2 Asch conformity studies by national culture (based on Bond and Smith, 1996; from Smith and Bond, 1998)

Nation	Number of studies	Averaged effect size
Asch's own US studies	18	1.16
Other US studies	79	0.90
Canada	1	1.37
UK	10	0.81
Belgium	4	0.91
France	2	0.56
Netherlands	1	0.74
Germany	1	0.92
Portugal	1	0.58
Japan	5	1.42
Brazil	3	1.60
Fiji	2	2.48
Hong Kong	1	1.93
Arab samples (Kuwait, Lebanon)	2	1.31
Africa (Zimbabwe, Republic of the Congo [Zaire], Ghana)	3	1.84

Ask Yourself

- Are there any patterns in the conformity rates (averaged effect size) in Table 26.2?
- For example, are those countries with the highest and lowest conformity geographically and/or culturally related?

According to Smith and Bond (1998), the countries represented in Table 26.2 can be described as *individualist* (such as the USA, the UK and other western European countries) or *collectivist* (such as Japan, Fiji and the African countries). In individualist cultures, one's identity is defined by personal choices and achievements, while in collectivist cultures it's defined in terms of the collective group one belongs to (such as the family or religious group). As might be expected, the tendency is for more conformity in collectivist cultures (but see Key Study 26.2).

An evaluation of the Asch paradigm

- According to Fiske (2004), Asch's research could be seen as focusing on a 'stripped-down' form of social influence, without any real interaction – 'Asch's groups weren't very groupy'. This mirrors Brown's criticism of Sherif's experiments (see above).
- Asch took an individualist view of groups, rather than a more social interactionist view – that is, he focused on participants as individuals within a group as distinct from a group process as such. None of his groups actually interacted, and he concentrated on individual naïve participants' *independence* rather than group members' *interdependence* (Leyens and Corneille, 1999).

Why do people conform?

Different types of social influence

One very influential and widely accepted account of group influence is Deutsch and Gerard's (1955) distinction between *informational social influence* (ISI) and *normative social influence* (NSI).

Informational social influence (ISI)

Underlying ISI is the need to be right, to have an accurate perception of reality. So when we're uncertain or face an ambiguous situation, we look to others to help us perceive the stimulus situation accurately (or define the situation: see Chapter 30). This involves a *social comparison* with other group members in order to reduce the uncertainty.

As we saw earlier, Sherif's experiment involves an inherently ambiguous situation: there's no actual movement of the light, and so there cannot be any right or wrong answers. Under these conditions, participants were only too willing to validate their own estimates by comparing them with those of others. The results were consistent with Sherif's *social reality hypothesis*, which states that:

> *The less one can rely on one's own direct perception and behavioural contact with the physical world, the more susceptible one should be to influence from others … (Turner, 1991)*

According to Festinger's (1954) *social comparison theory*, people have a basic need to evaluate their ideas and attitudes and, in turn, to confirm that they're correct. This can provide a reassuring sense of control over one's world, and a satisfying sense of competence. In novel or ambiguous situations, social reality is defined by what others think and do. Festinger saw this as necessary if the group is to reach its goals (*group locomotion*). Significantly, Sherif's participants were relatively unaware of being influenced by the other judges. As Turner (1991) observes:

> *They appear to be largely unconsciously adjusting their judgement in the light of others' reports to arrive at a stable, agreed picture of a shared but initially unstructured world.*

Normative social influence (NSI)

Underlying NSI is the need to be accepted by other people, and to make a favourable impression on them. We conform in order to gain social approval and avoid rejection – we agree with others because of their power to reward, punish, accept, or reject us.

In Asch's experiment, most participants weren't unsure about the correct answer. Rather, they were faced with a conflict between two sources of information, which in unambiguous situations normally coincide, namely their own judgement and that of others. If they chose their own judgement, they risked rejection and ridicule by the majority. Recall, though, that some participants were unaware of any conflict or of having given an incorrect response.

Internalisation and compliance

Related to ISI and NSI are two kinds of conformity:

1. *Internalisation* occurs when a private belief or opinion becomes consistent with a public belief or opinion. In other words, we say what we believe

and believe what we say. Mann (1969) calls this *true conformity* and it can be thought of as a *conversion* to other people's points of view, especially in ambiguous situations.

2. *Compliance* occurs when the answers given publicly aren't those that are privately believed (we say what we don't believe and what we believe we don't say). Compliance represents a compromise in situations where people face a conflict between what they privately believe and what others publicly say they believe.

Ask Yourself

- Which kind of conformity was most common in Sherif's and Asch's experiments?
- How are internalisation and compliance related to NSI and ISI?

In Sherif's experiment, participants internalised others' judgements and made them their own. Faced with an ambiguous situation, participants were guided by what others believed to reduce their uncertainty. So, internalisation is related to ISI.

By contrast, most of Asch's participants knew that the majority answers on the critical trials were wrong, but often agreed with them publicly. They were complying with the majority to avoid ridicule or rejection. So, compliance is related to NSI. (See Figure 26.4.)

Do we have to choose between ISI and NSI?

The ISI/NSI distinction has proved very influential. But like all distinctions, it faces the problem of being a *false dichotomy:* are they really separate, opposite forms of influence? A study by Insko *et al.* (1983) suggests that they can operate together (see Key Study 26.3).

Remember that when Asch made the three comparison lines much more similar – and hence the task more difficult – conformity increased. Clearly, ISI was involved here. If we believe there's a correct answer and are uncertain what it is, it seems quite logical to expect that we'd be more influenced by a unanimous majority. This is why having a supporter, or the presence of a dissenter, has the effect of reducing conformity. By breaking the group consensus, the participant is shown both that disagreement is possible and that the group is fallible. As Turner (1991) puts it:

> *... the more consensual the group and the more isolated the individual (i.e. the less others agree with the deviant), the greater the power of the group to define reality, induce self-doubt in the deviant as to both her competence and social position, and threaten her with ridicule and rejection for being different.*

In other words, both ISI and NSI can operate in conjunction with each other, and shouldn't be seen as opposed processes of influence.

Key study 26.3

The compatibility of ISI and NSI (Insko *et al.*, 1983)

- Insko *et al.* had participants, in groups of six, judge whether a colour shown on a slide was more similar to another colour shown to the left or to one shown to the right.
- On critical trials, four stooges who answered before the naïve participant, and another who answered last, gave answers which deviated from those given by most participants in a control condition who were tested alone.
- There were two independent variables:
  1. Participants answered either publicly or privately
  2. The experimenter said that he either was or wasn't able to determine which response was more correct (in the 'determined' condition, he referred to an apparatus through which he could accurately measure which response was more correct; in the 'undetermined' condition, he said this was impossible).
- Two hypotheses were tested:
  1. There will be greater conformity in the public than the private condition due to NSI
  2. There will be greater conformity in the determined than the undetermined condition due to ISI.
- Both hypotheses were confirmed. Also, the determined condition produced greater conformity in both private and public conditions, and all four conditions produced greater conformity than the control condition. Hence, even with 'objective stimuli', ISI can add to the effect of NSI (van Avermaet, 1996).

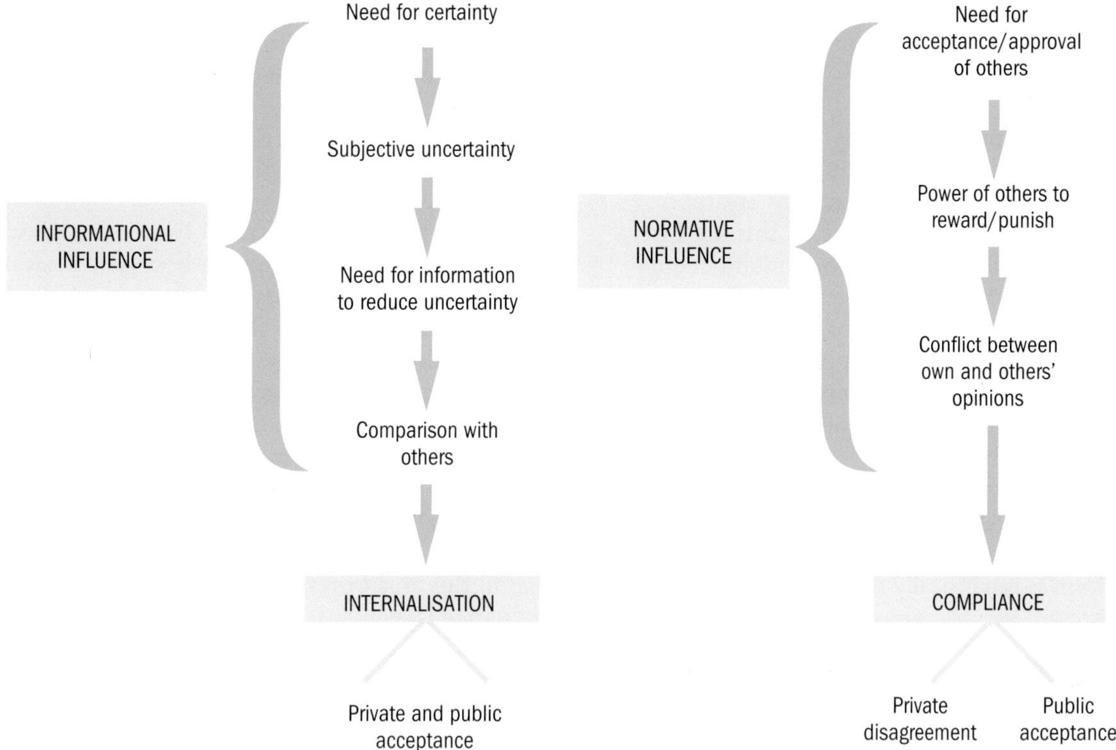

Figure 26.4 The relationship between different kinds of influence and different kinds of conformity

Conformity and group belongingness

The distinction between NSI and ISI has been called the *dual process dependency model* (DPDM) of social influence (e.g. Turner, 1991). But this model underestimates the role of group 'belongingness'. One important feature of conformity is that we're influenced by a group because, psychologically, we feel we belong to it; this is why a group's norms are relevant standards for our own attitudes and behaviour. The DPDM emphasises the *interpersonal* aspects of conformity experiments, which could just as easily occur between individuals as group members.

The *self-categorisation approach* suggests that in Sherif's (1935) experiment, for example, participants assumed that the autokinetic effect was real, and expected to agree with each other. In support of this, it's been shown that when participants discover that the autokinetic effect is an illusion, mutual influence and convergence cease – the need to agree at all is removed (Sperling, 1946). If, however, we believe that there is a correct answer, and we're uncertain what it is, then only those whom we categorise as belonging to 'our' group will influence our judgements. As Brown (1988) has remarked:

Key Study 26.4

Knowing what to think by knowing who you are (Abrams *et al.*, 1990)

- Abrams *et al.* replicated Sherif's experiment with Psychology students, but manipulated categorisation: stooges were introduced as students at a nearby university, but were either fellow Psychology students or students of ancient history.
- Convergence only occurred when others were categorised as being equivalent to self, that is, a member of the ingroup (fellow Psychology students). So self-categorisation may set limits on ISI.
- It should also set limits on NSI since individuals will presumably have a stronger desire to receive rewards, approval and acceptance from those categorised in the same way as themselves than from those categorised differently.
- Using the Asch paradigm but again manipulating categorisation, Abrams *et al.* found that conformity exceeded the usual level of 32 per cent in the ingroup condition, but was greatly below this level in the outgroup condition.

There is more to conformity than simply 'defining social reality': it all depends on who is doing the defining.

Social influence occurs, then, when we see ourselves as belonging to a group and possessing the same characteristics and reactions as other group members. Turner (1991) calls this kind of self-categorisation, in which group membership is relevant, *referent social influence* (RSI). What's important isn't the validation of physical reality or the avoidance of social disapproval, but the upholding of a group norm: people are the source of information about the appropriate ingroup norm. (See Key Study 26.4.)

According to Fiske (2004), a social categorisation approach sees the NSI/SIS distinction as (another) false dichotomy (see Key Study 26.3), since 'information is intrinsically social'.

Ask Yourself

- What do you understand Fiske to mean when she says that 'Information is intrinsically social'? (A look back at Chapter 3 should offer you some clues.)

MINORITY INFLUENCE

Majority or minority influence in Asch-type experiments?

Typically, the findings from experiments using the Asch paradigm have been interpreted as showing the impact of a (powerful) majority on the (vulnerable) individual (who's usually in a minority of one). While the stooges are, numerically, the majority, Asch himself was interested in the social and personal conditions that induce individuals to resist group pressure. (In 1950s' USA, this group pressure took the form of McCarthyism: see above.)

Spencer and Perrin (1998) ask if reports of Asch's experiments have overstated the power of the majority to force minority individuals to agree with obviously mistaken judgements. Indeed, Moscovici and Faucheux (1972) argued that it's more useful to think of the naïve participant as the majority (s/he embodies the 'conventional', self-evident 'truth') and the stooges as the minority (they reflect an unorthodox, unconventional, eccentric and even outrageous viewpoint). This corresponds to the distinction between the ingroup and the outgroup, respectively: Moscovici wanted to demonstrate the conditions under which people actually conform to the outgroup. In Asch's experiments, this minority/outgroup influenced the majority 32 per cent of the time, and it's those participants remaining independent who are actually the conformists!

Is the majority always right?

Looked at from Moscovici and Faucheux's perspective, Asch-type experiments suggest how new ideas may come to be accepted (they explain *innovation*), rather than providing evidence about maintenance of the *status quo*. If groups always followed a majority decision rule ('the majority is always or probably right, so best go along with it'), or if social influence were about the inevitable conforming to the group, where would innovation come from? (Spencer and Perrin, 1998: see Box 26.2.)

According to Moscovici (1976), there's a *conformity bias* in this area of research, such that all social influence is seen as serving the need to adapt to the *status quo* for the sake of uniformity and stability (the 'tyranny of the majority': Martin and Hewstone, 2001; Wood, 2000). However, change is sometimes needed to adapt to changing circumstances, and this is very difficult to explain given the conformity bias. Without active minorities, social and scientific innovations would simply never happen (van Avermaet, 1996).

How do minorities exert an influence?

Moscovici (1976) reanalysed the data from one of Asch's (1955) experiments, in which he varied the proportion of neutral to critical trials. In the original experiment this proportion was 1:2 (see Box 26.1). When the proportion was 1:6, the conformity rate was 50 per cent, but when it was 4:1 it dropped to 26.2 per cent.

Ask Yourself

- Try to account for these findings.
- Why should conformity rate *increase* as the ratio of neutral to critical trials *decreases*, but *decrease* when it *increases*?

Moscovici interpreted these findings in terms of *consistency*. When there were more critical than neutral trials (the ratio *decreases*), the stooges (who embody the minority viewpoint) appear more consistent as a group, and this produces a higher conformity rate. They're more often agreeing with each other about something unconventional or novel, which makes it more likely they'll change the views of the majority (as represented by the naïve participant).

Key Study 26.5

Blue/green colour slide experiment (Moscovici *et al.*, 1969)

- Moscovici *et al.* used groups of six participants, of whom four were naïve and two were stooges. The stooges played the role of the minority. Before the experiment began, participants' colour vision was tested. They all passed. This meant that the naïve participants couldn't explain the stooges' wrong answers by claiming they were colour blind.
- All the participants gave their answers out loud. The stooges sat either in the first and second position, or first and fourth.
- On 36 separate trials, slides that were clearly blue (based on a *control* condition comprised of six naïve participants) – but which differed in brightness – were presented on a screen.
- In the *consistent* condition, the stooges called it green every time. This yielded a 'green' response rate of over 8 per cent among the naïve participants. In the *inconsistent* condition, the stooges answered 'green' 24 times and 'blue' 12 times. This time, the green responses were made 1.25 per cent of the time. This was a significant difference. 32 per cent of naïve participants gave at least one green response.
- There were really two types of group: one where nobody was influenced by the minority and one where several were influenced. Where the stooges sat made no difference.

Moscovici *et al.*'s experiment clearly showed that a consistent minority can affect the judgements made by the majority. Although the minority doesn't have a numerical advantage, their consistent behavioural style makes them influential. In conformity experiments, the influence of the (numerical) majority is evident from the start; but minority influence only begins to show after a while.

However, consistency doesn't necessarily have to involve repeating the same response. Nemeth *et al.* (1974) replicated the Moscovici *et al.* experiment, but added two conditions: the stooges said 'green' on half the trials and 'green-blue' on the other half. In the *random* condition, the green and green-blue responses were randomly distributed across the trials (there was no consistency in their responses). In the *correlated* condition, whether they said green or green-blue depended on the brightness of the slide (so, there was still a pattern to their responses).

Compared to a no-influence *control* condition, the random condition had no effect. But in the correlated condition, almost 21 per cent of the responses were wrong (minority) answers. Where stooges consistently repeated the green response, there was no minority influence. In other words, there's more to minority influence than just consistency: it also matters how the majority interprets the minority's answers, which must relate to the stimulus in some predictable way. In Nemeth *et al.*'s study, it was the brightness of the slide that counted.

Minority influence is achieved not so much by a particular style of behaviour in the group, but more by a combination of attributes and behaviour (Smith, 1995). Moscovici (1980) proposes that while majorities impose their views through directly requiring compliance (which often requires 'surveillance'), minorities use more *indirect* means to achieve a more lasting conversion.

As Gardikiotis (2013) points out, minority members sometimes need to negotiate their ideas with the majority. Flexible negotiation entails a moderate style and includes making compromises, while rigid negotiation entails a more extreme style; the former is usually more effective. An inflexible minority can be more easily discounted, especially when the minority's psychological characteristics are significant: they could be seen as responsible for the inflexibility.

Box 26.2 The importance of consistency and other factors in minority influence

According to Hogg and Vaughan (1998), consistency has five main effects:

1. It disrupts the majority norm, producing uncertainty and doubt
2. It draws attention to itself as an entity
3. It conveys the existence of an alternative, coherent point of view
4. It demonstrates certainty and an unshakeable commitment to a particular point of view
5. It shows that the only solution to the current conflict is the minority viewpoint.

Minorities are more efficient if they:

- are seen to have made significant personal/material sacrifices (*investment*)
- are perceived as acting out of principle rather than ulterior motives (*autonomy*)
- display a balance between being 'dogmatic' (rigid) and 'inconsistent' (*flexible*)
- are seen as being similar to the majority in terms of age, gender and social category, particularly if they're categorised as part of the ingroup.

Ask Yourself

- Can you relate the importance of consistency to Kelley's covariation model of attribution? (See Chapter 23.)

When minority group members *consistently* adopt a unique (non-majority, unconventional) response (that is, there's *low consensus*), this is likely to lead majority members to make an *internal/dispositional attribution* (they sincerely believe in what they say).

Figure 26.5 Scene from *Twelve Angry Men*, starring Henry Fonda as the only dissenter in an (all-male) jury. He succeeds in overturning an 11-to-1 majority favouring a guilty verdict (see www.filmsite.org/twelve.html)

According to Wood *et al.* (1994), minority influence most often occurs *privately* – that is, on measures that protect the converted majority individuals from appearing publicly to abandon their majority position. For the same reason, influence is often *indirect,* emerging on issues merely *related* to the controversial issues or *delayed* beyond the immediate context (Crano, 2000):

> *... Thus, majorities can be converted by minorities, but majority individuals do not admit it to others, and perhaps not to themselves, thereby avoiding public identification with the unpopular minority position ... (Fiske, 2004)*

Are minority and majority influence different processes?

According to Moscovici's (1976, 1980) *conversion theory*, minority and majority influence are *qualitatively different* processes. While being faced with a counter-attitudinal majority (one that holds a different/opposing opinion) leads to *compliance* based on *comparison* (see above), a counter-attitudinal *minority* leads to *conversion* based on a *validation* process. (This is equivalent to *internalisation*.) Validation involves focusing on the content of the message in order to understand exactly what's being said, with attitude change occurring mainly unconsciously, indirectly and gradually.

According to Moscovici, we actually tend to think longer and harder about a minority argument precisely because it's unusual: minority opinions demand more – and more elaborate – cognitive processing. However, according to Mackie's (1987) *objective-consensus approach*, it's a counter-attitudinal *majority* that requires greater cognitive processing: it breaks consensus expectations (we expect that most people will agree with us) and this motivates us to analyse the argument in order to understand the discrepancy.

Martin and Hewstone's (2008) *source-context-elaboration model* proposes that both majority and minority can lead to more (or less) thinking, depending on the cognitive demands of the influence situation. The question is to what extent the situation in which the attempt to influence us allows or encourages elaboration of the source's message. However, most such situations don't involve either very high or low processing demands; this will tend to favour the systematic processing of only the *minority* arguments.

Research has exposed the *power dimension* of group dynamics. According to Gardikiotis (2013):

> *... We can think of majority and minority not only in terms of 'us' and 'them' but also in terms of the 'many' and the 'few', the 'normative' versus the 'anti-normative' and so on. Therefore, minority influence exemplifies how psychological research can be simultaneously scientifically rigorous and socially relevant.*

OTHER GROUP PROCESSES

Risky shift

Based on the traditional interpretation of conformity studies as being concerned with majority influence and with how the *status quo* is maintained, the common-sense prediction is that groups, relative to individuals, will be more cautious and conservative. Convergence towards a group mean in Sherif's experiment is a clear demonstration of this prediction. However, Stoner (1961) found the *opposite* to be true. He presented participants with 12 decision dilemmas faced by hypothetical people, and their task was to advise the person about how much risk to take. Initially this was done individually, then in groups of about five.

To everyone's amazement, the group decisions were usually *riskier* than the individuals'. In other words, the group advised the hypothetical person to take a greater risk than the average of the individuals' advice (*the risky shift phenomenon*).

Stoner sparked a wave of research into group decision-making, which initially found considerable support for risky shift, involving people of varying ages, occupations and from 12 different countries. However, it was eventually found that risky shift wasn't universal after all. It was possible to present decision dilemmas on which people became *more cautious* after discussion (Myers, 1994). So, is there a general principle that will predict how risky or cautious people's advice will be?

Group polarisation

One of the most robust findings in Social Psychology is that when group members with similar initial attitudes engage in group discussion to achieve agreement about difficult decisions, the discussion *strengthens* the average individual inclinations (Cooper *et al.*, 2004). For this reason, risky shift came to be seen as part of a much wider phenomenon called *group polarisation* (GP) (Moscovici and Zavalloni, 1969). This is the tendency for groups to make decisions that are more extreme than the mean of individuals' initial positions, in the direction already favoured by that mean (Myers and Lamm, 1975; Wetherell, 1987). So, groups are likely to adopt more *extreme* views than individual members, but this can be in either a riskier or a more cautious direction. Why does it occur?

- According to Brown (1986), the mere *exchange of information* about which members made which decisions can produce GP. In group discussion, group members may point out relevant information that others have missed, exposing individuals to supportive arguments they might not previously have thought of. This relates to ISI.
- Group members wish to define their identity more positively and distinctively, in contrast to members of other groups whom they might expect to adopt more average positions (Turner, 1991). This is supported by studies in which groups are told of the presumed decisions of other groups relevant to them (Smith, 1995). This is related to NSI.
- Several studies suggest that *social categorisation processes* also play a significant role in GP. It seems to occur through three steps: (i) categorisation of self as a member of a group (the ingroup); (ii) identification of the prototypical characteristics, behaviours and norms of the ingroup that differentiate it from other (out)groups; and (iii) stereotyping the self as a member of the ingroup (Cooper *et al.*, 2004). According to Hewstone and Martin (2012), juries clearly show GP, as well as majority and minority influence.

Groupthink

Groupthink (Janis, 1971, 1982) is an example of how group decisions may become very extreme. Groupthink is defined as a mode of thinking in which the desire to reach unanimous agreement overrides the motivation to adopt proper, rational, decision-making procedures. Using archive material (people's retrospective accounts and content analysis), Janis analysed how the decisions were taken that led to certain major political/military fiascos, such as Pearl Harbor (1941), the Bay of Pigs invasion of Cuba (1961) which led to the Cuban Missile Crisis (1962), and the Vietnam War.

It's been suggested that groupthink is merely a specific instance of risky shift, in which a group that already tends towards making risky decisions polarises, through discussion, to an even riskier one (Myers and Lamm, 1975). According to Levine and Moreland (1998), it's an extreme form of problems associated with the failure to exchange information (or, at least, different views) among group members. Janis believes that groupthink stems from an excessively cohesive, close-knit group, the suppression of dissent in the interests of group harmony and a directive leader who signals what decisions s/he favours. According to Hewstone and Martin (2012):

> *... In essence, groupthink constitutes an extreme form of normative influence, where the norm to reach and maintain consensus and harmony within the group completely eliminates any informational influence that could show how disastrous the group's intended decision is likely to be.*

CONCLUSIONS: CONFORMITY – GOOD or BAD?

Ask Yourself

- **Is conformity always and necessarily desirable, and is failure to conform always and necessarily undesirable?**

Sometimes, dissent is just an expression of disagreement, a refusal to 'go along with the crowd' (Maslach *et al.*, 1985). On other occasions, it's more creative or constructive, as when someone suggests a better solution to a problem. A refusal to 'go along with the crowd' may be an attempt to remain independent as a *matter of principle* (what Willis, 1963, calls *anticonformity*), and may betray a basic fear of a loss of personal identity.

According to Zimbardo and Leippe (1991), in most circumstances conformity serves a valuable social purpose in that it:

> *... Lubricates the machinery of social interaction [and] enables us to structure our social behaviour and predict the reactions of others.*

For most people, though, the word 'conformity' has a negative connotation. As a result, it's implicitly assumed that independence is 'good' and conformity is 'bad', a value judgement made explicit by Asch (1952). However, conformity can be highly functional, helping us to satisfy social and non-social needs, as well as being necessary (at least to a degree) for social life to proceed at all.

Since each of us has a limited (and often biased) store of information on which to make decisions, other people can often provide valuable additional information and expertise. Conforming to others under these circumstances may be a rational judgement. However, while conformity can help preserve harmony:

> *There are obvious dangers to conformity. Failure to speak our minds against dangerous trends or attitudes (for example, racism) can easily be interpreted as support ... (Krebs and Blackman, 1988)*

The term conformity is often used to convey undesirable behaviour. However, in the context of his famous obedience studies, Milgram showed that the presence of two defiant peers significantly reduced the obedience rate among naïve participants, and he wrote an article (1965) called 'Liberating effects of group pressure' (see Chapter 27).

Also, whether conformity is considered good or bad is a matter of *culture*. In *individualist* cultures, people are often distressed by the possibility that others can influence their behaviour against their will: they prefer to believe they're in control of their destiny. So 'conformity', 'compliance', 'obedience' and other similar terms have negative connotations. But in *collectivist* cultures, adjusting one's behaviour to fit the requests and expectations of others is highly valued, and sometimes even a moral imperative (Fiske *et al.*, 1998); conformity is seen as necessary for social functioning, rather than a sign of weakness (Nagayama Hall and Barongan, 2002).

Chapter Summary

- **Social influence** can be **active** and **deliberate** (as in persuasive communication and obedience) or **passive** and **non-deliberate** (as in social facilitation and conformity). A common feature of all social influence is the concept of a **social norm**.
- Definitions of **conformity** commonly refer to **group pressure**, whether the group is a **membership** or a **reference** group.
- In Sherif's experiment using the **autokinetic effect**, individual estimates **converged** to form a group norm. Asch criticised Sherif's use of an ambiguous task, and in his own experiments used a comparison of lines task for which there was a correct answer.
- Asch found that the **unanimity of the majority** is crucial, not its size. The presence of a **supporter** or **dissenter** reduces conformity, because the majority is no longer unanimous.
- Conformity is increased when the task is made more difficult (more ambiguous), and reduced when participants give their answer anonymously.
- Replications of Asch's experiment have produced higher or lower rates of conformity according to when and where they were conducted. Both **socio-historical** and **cultural factors** seem to play a part.
- Asch's findings are usually interpreted as demonstrating **majority influence.** But Moscovici believes that the stooge majority should be thought of as embodying unconventional, minority beliefs, and that conformity experiments show how new ideas come to be accepted (**innovation**).
- One way in which **minority influence** works is by displaying **consistency**, together with **investment**, **autonomy**, and a balance between **rigidity** and **flexibility**.
- Two major motives for conformity are the need to be right (**informational social influence/ISI**) and the need to be accepted by others (**normative social influence/NSI**).
- ISI is related to Sherif's **social reality hypothesis** and Festinger's **social comparison theory** and is demonstrated through **internalisation/true conformity**. NSI is linked to **compliance**.
- ISI and NSI aren't opposed forms of influence, but the **dual process dependency model** (DPDM) tends to emphasise the **interpersonal** aspects of conformity experiments. In contrast, **referent social influence/RFI** stresses the importance of **group membership** and **self-categorisation**.
- According to Moscovici, minority and majority influence are **qualitatively different** processes.
- Evidence for the **risky shift phenomenon** is mixed. It has come to be seen as part of **group polarisation/GP**, in which group decisions tend to become more extreme than the mean of individuals' initial positions.
- One demonstration of GP is **groupthink**, which stems from excessively cohesive groups with a directive leader.
- While **independence** is often seen as preferable to conformity, conformity also serves an important social function. Milgram has shown how it can have liberating effects in an obedience situation.

Links with Other Topics/Chapters

Chapters 22, 24 and 27 ⟶ Other examples of active social influence apart from *obedience include impression management persuasive communication, propaganda* and *advertising*

Chapter 31 ⟶ *Social loafing* and social *facilitation* are both forms of indirect/passive social influence relevant to the *Social Psychology of sport*

Chapter 47 ⟶ The finding that conformity is generally higher in *collectivist cultures* demonstrates the importance of cross-cultural research in general, and the need to counteract *ethnocentrism* and *Eurocentrism* in particular

Chapter 25 ⟶ Self-categorisation and intergroup relationships are crucial for understanding *prejudice and discrimination*

Recommended Reading

Asch, S.E. (1952) *Social Psychology*. Englewood Cliffs, NJ: Prentice-Hall.

Hewstone, M. & Martin, R. (2012) Social Influence. In M. Hewstone, W. Stroebe & K. Jonas (eds) *An Introduction to Social Psychology* (5th edition). Oxford: BPS/Blackwell.

Milgram, S. (1992) *The Individual in a Social World: Essays and Experiments* (2nd edition). New York: McGraw-Hill. Also relevant to Chapter 27.

Turner, J.C. (1991) *Social Influence*. Milton Keynes: Open University Press.

Useful Websites

http://facultystaff.richmond.edu/~dforsyth/gd/ (University of Richmond, Virginia: Group Dynamics Resource Page)

http://en.wikipedia.org/wiki/Asch_conformity_experiments (Asch conformity experiments)

www.bbc.co.uk/radio4/science/mindchangers1.shtml (BBC Radio 4: Mind Changers, Programme 1: Solomon Asch – Conformity)

CHAPTER 27

OBEDIENCE

Compliance: requesting, selling and convincing

How does obedience differ from conformity?

Experimental studies of obedience

The power of social situations

INTRODUCTION and OVERVIEW

As we saw at the beginning of Chapter 26, obedience is an active or deliberate form of social influence, which involves someone in authority requiring us to behave in a particular way in a particular situation. If we obey, we are said to be *complying* with the authority figure's request or instruction. We also discussed compliance as a major kind of *conformity*, namely one in which overt behaviour doesn't reflect private beliefs.

Compliance also occurs whenever we do what someone else 'asks' us to do, that is, whenever people make direct requests, such as when a friend asks us for a 'favour' or a salesperson 'invites' us to try a product or service. Many researchers believe that attempts to gain compliance through direct requests is the most common form of social influence (Hogg and Vaughan, 1995).

Cialdini (2004) identifies six basic tendencies of human behaviour that come into play in generating a positive response when one person tries to influence another's attitudes or actions. These are: *reciprocity* (*reciprocation*), *liking*, *consistency*, *social validation*, *authority* and *scarcity*. Most of these are best understood as 'tactics' used by a salesperson trying to sell a product (Cialdini, 1988). Consistency was discussed in Chapter 26 in relation to minority influence, and authority relates directly to obedience.

Like the demands of an authority figure, these tactics (some more subtle than others) are active and deliberate attempts to make us behave in particular ways. Unlike both obedience and conformity, there's no obvious 'penalty' to pay for not complying. And as we find in some obedience and conformity situations, the salesperson may be perceived as an expert with access to information (and goods/services) that we need. So, it's clear that these various forms of social influence share many characteristics.

COMPLIANCE: REQUESTING, SELLING and CONVINCING

- *The norm of reciprocity:* Giving a free estimate for a job, or a 'free pen' in charity donation envelopes, may put the potential customer/donor under a sense of obligation. This is based on the social norm that 'we should treat others the way they treat us' (and on the further principle that 'there's no such thing as a free lunch'). Survey researchers have found that attaching a small incentive (financial or otherwise) increases return rate by almost 20 per cent, while a payment dependent on completing the questionnaire doesn't have the same effect. It's the *unsolicited* gift that does the trick (Tourangeau, 2004). This can apply to other relationships too, as in the belief that 'one good turn deserves another'.
- *Liking:* people prefer to say 'yes' to people they like. This can be manipulated through physical attractiveness, agreeing with others and in other ways showing them how we're similar to them, paying them compliments (even flattering them), and co-operating with them ('I'm on your side'). This is sometimes referred to as *ingratiation* (see Chapter 22).
- *Social validation*: requesters can stimulate compliance by demonstrating (or implying) that others 'just like you' have already complied (for example, telling us how many people have already subscribed to X or signed in support of Y). But this can backfire, as in:

> *... The understandable but potentially misguided tendency of health educators to call attention to a problem by depicting it as regrettably frequent. Information campaigns stress that alcohol and drug abuse are intolerably high, that adolescent suicide rates are alarming and that polluters are spoiling the environment ... (Cialdini, 2004)*

- Although the claims are both true and well intentioned, this may produce a boomerang effect.
- *Scarcity*: This relates to people's tendency to value rare/scarce resources. They'll try to obtain items that are going out of stock ('while stocks last') or that are almost out of reach ('once-in-a-lifetime opportunity'). The resources can take the form of information (as in newspaper 'scoops' or exclusives). On the same principle, 'secret' affairs can be more exciting, and 'absence makes the heart grow fonder' (Cialdini, 2004: see Chapter 28).
- The *'foot in the door' tactic* (FITD) (Freedman and Fraser, 1966): Getting someone to agree to a small request makes them more likely to comply with a larger request at some later point, than if the larger request had been made initially. This can be explained partly in terms of people's need to appear consistent – to both themselves and others (see Chapter 24). To be effective, the FITD usually requires a delay between the initial small request and the later, larger one. If they come too close together, people feel exploited and often refuse. Similarly, people refuse to comply when the same person makes both requests (Fiske, 2004). For people to maintain their relationships, they must abide by the norm of reciprocity (Cialdini and Trost, 1998: see above).
- According to Hogg and Vaughan (1995), the FITD represents one of three multiple-request tactics, whereby an initial request functions as a set-up for a second (real) request. The other two are:
  (a) The *'door-in-the-face' tactic* (DIF), in which a large, unreasonable request is followed up with a second, much more reasonable request, which is more difficult to refuse. Compliance takes the form of a 'concession', and trades on the requester appearing to 'back off' and the target person feeling guilty and perhaps needing to reciprocate by agreeing to the more moderate request (Fiske, 2004); however it works, it works (O'Keefe and Hale, 2001)
  (b) The *'low-ball'* (LB) tactic – for example, having induced a customer to commit him/herself to a purchase, the salesperson then reveals certain hidden costs that weren't previously mentioned (the term comes from US baseball; in the UK, we might talk of 'moving the goal posts').

Ask Yourself

- Can you identify any of these tactics in your own experience with salespeople?
- Have you possibly employed one or more of them yourself?

HOW DOES OBEDIENCE DIFFER from CONFORMITY?

Ask Yourself

- Based on what you know about conformity (see Chapter 26), try to identify some of the basic *similarities* and *differences* between conformity and obedience.

According to Milgram (1992), both conformity and obedience involve the 'abdication of individual judgement in the face of some external social pressure'. However, there are three major *differences* between them.

1. In conformity, there's no explicit requirement to act in a certain way, whereas in obedience we're being ordered or instructed to do something.
2. In conformity, those who influence us are our peers (equals) and people's behaviour becomes more alike (*homogenisation of behaviour*). In obedience, there's a difference in status from the outset, with the authority figure influencing another person who has inferior power or status: there's no mutual influence.
3. Conformity has to do with the psychological 'need' for acceptance by others, and entails going along with one's peers in a group situation. Obedience has to do with the social power and status of an authority figure in a hierarchical situation. Although we typically deny that we conform (because it seems to detract from our sense of *individuality*), in the case of obedience we usually *deny responsibility* for our behaviour ('He made me do it,' or 'I was only doing what I was told').

In addition, Brown (1986) says that conformity behaviour is affected by *example* (from peers or equals), while obedience is affected by *direction* (from somebody in higher authority).

EXPERIMENTAL STUDIES of OBEDIENCE

In the experiments of Sherif, Asch and others (see Chapter 26), participants showed conformity by giving a verbal response of some kind or pressing buttons representing answers on various tasks. In the most famous and controversial of all obedience experiments, Milgram's participants were required to 'kill' another human being.

Milgram's research

Figure 27.1 Stanley Milgram (1933–1984)

Milgram was attempting to test 'the "Germans are different" hypothesis'. This has been used by historians to explain the systematic destruction of millions of Jews, Poles and others by the Nazis during the 1930s and 1940s. It maintains that:

- Hitler couldn't have put his evil plans into operation without the co-operation of thousands of others, and
- the Germans have a basic character defect, namely a readiness to obey authority without question regardless of the acts demanded by the authority figure; it's this readiness to obey that provided Hitler with the co-operation he needed.

It's really the second part of the hypothesis that Milgram was trying to test. After piloting his research in the USA, he planned to continue it in Germany. But his results showed this was unnecessary.

The participants

The participants in the original (1963) experiment were 20–50-year-old men, from all walks of life. They answered advertisements that came by post or appeared in local newspapers, which asked for volunteers for a study of learning to be conducted at Yale University. It would take about one hour and there would be a payment of $4.50.

Public Announcement

WE WILL PAY YOU $4.00 FOR ONE HOUR OF YOUR TIME

Persons Needed for a Study of Memory

***We will pay five hundred New Haven men to help us complete a scientific study of memory and learning. The study is being done at Yale University.**

***Each person who participates will be paid $4.00 (plus 50c carfare) for approximately 1 hour's time. We need you for only one hour: there are no further obligations. You may choose the time you would like to come (evenings, weekdays, or weekends).**

***No special training, education, or experience is needed. We want:**

Factory workers	Businessmen	Construction workers
City employees	Clerks	Salespeople
Laborers	Professional people	White-collar workers
Barbers	Telephone workers	Others

All persons must be between the ages of 20 and 50. High school and college students cannot be used.

***If you meet these qualifications, fill out the coupon below and mail it now to Professor Stanley Milgram, Department of Psychology, Yale University, New Haven. You will be notified later of the specific time and place of the study. We reserve the right to decline any application.**

***You will be paid $4.00 (plus 50c carfare) as soon as you arrive at the laboratory.**

TO:
PROF. STANLEY MILGRAM, DEPARTMENT OF PSYCHOLOGY, YALE UNIVERSITY, NEW HAVEN, CONN. I want to take part in this study of memory and learning. I am between the ages of 20 and 50. I will be paid $4.00 (plus 50c carfare) if I participate.

NAME (Please Print)....................................

ADDRESS ....

TELEPHONE NO. .... Best time to call you ....

AGE........OCCUPATION.................... SEX......

CAN YOU COME:

WEEKDAYS .... EVENINGS ......WEEKENDS.........

Figure 27.2 Announcement placed in a local newspaper to recruit participants (from Milgram, 1974)

The basic procedure

The original (1963) experiment involved what Milgram called the *remote-victim condition*; this was the first of a series of 18 different experiments, all variations on the same basic theme. In this particular experiment, Mr Wallace was scripted to pound loudly on the wall at 300 volts and, after 315 volts, to stop pounding and give no further answers. In the second experiment (*voice feedback*), teachers heard a tape-recorded series of verbal responses, which they believed were the spontaneous reactions of Mr Wallace to the increasing shock levels.

- At 75, 90 and 105 volts, he made a little grunt.
- At 120 volts, he shouted to the experimenter that the shocks were becoming painful.
- At 135 volts, he made pained groans.
- At 150 volts, he cried out, 'Experimenter, get me out of here! I won't be in the experiment anymore!

Box 27.1 The basic procedure used in Milgram's obedience experiment

- When participants arrived at Yale University Psychology department, they were met by a young man in a grey laboratory coat, who introduced himself as Jack Williams, the experimenter. Also present was a Mr Wallace, introduced as another participant, in his late 50s, an accountant, a little overweight and generally a very mild and harmless-looking man. In fact, Mr Wallace was a stooge, and everything that happened after this was preplanned, staged and scripted: everything, that is, except the degree to which the real participant obeyed the experimenter's instructions.
- The participant and Mr Wallace were told that the experiment was concerned with the effects of punishment on learning. One of them was to be the teacher and the other the learner. Their roles were determined by each drawing a piece of paper from a hat: both, in fact, had 'teacher' written on them. Mr Wallace drew first and called out 'learner', so, of course, the real participant was always the teacher.
- They all went into an adjoining room, where Mr Wallace was strapped into a chair with his arms attached to electrodes, which would deliver a shock from the shock generator situated in an adjacent room.
- The teacher and experimenter then moved next door, where the generator was situated. The teacher was given a 45-volt shock to convince him/her that it was real, for s/he was to operate the generator during the experiment. However, that was the only real shock that either the teacher or the learner was to receive throughout the entire experiment.
- The generator had a number of switches, each clearly marked with voltage levels and verbal descriptions, starting at 15 volts and going up to 450 in intervals of 15:

15–60	Slight shock
75–120	Moderate shock
135–180	Strong shock
195–240	Very strong shock
255–300	Intense shock
315–360	Intense to extreme shock
375–420	Danger: severe shock
435–450	XXX

- The teacher had to read out a series of word pairs, and then the first of one pair (the stimulus word) followed by five words, of which one was the original paired response. The learner had to choose the correct response to the stimulus word by pressing one of four switches, which turned on a light on a panel in the generator room. Each time s/he made a mistake, the teacher had to deliver a shock and each successive mistake was punished by a shock 15 volts higher than the one before.

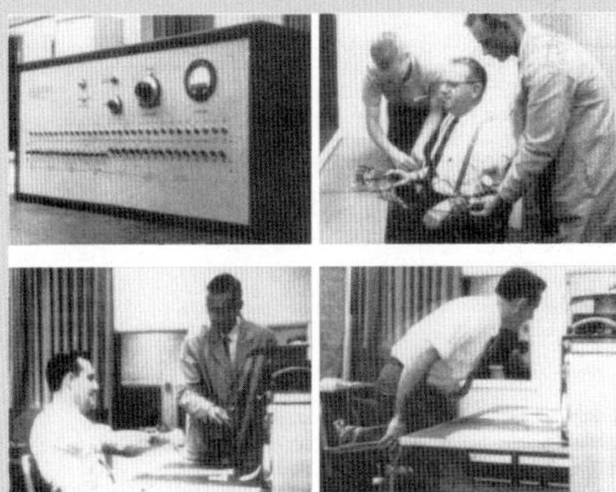

Figure 27.3 1 Shock generator used in the experiments. Fifteen of the 30 switches have already been depressed. 2 Learner is strapped into chair and electrodes are attached to his wrist. Electrode paste is applied by the experimenter. 3 Subject receives sample shock from the generator. 4 Subject breaks off experiment. (Copyright 1965 by Stanley Milgram from the film *Obedience*, distributed by the Pennsylvania State University, Audio Visual Services.) (From Milgram, 1974)

I refuse to go on!' This continued with rising intensity until at 180 volts, he shouted, 'I can't stand the pain!'
- At 270 volts, he let out an agonised scream. (He continued to insist on being released.)
- At 300 volts, he shouted desperately that he would no longer provide answers.
- At 315 volts, he let out a violent scream, reaffirming vehemently that he was no longer participating.
- After 330 volts, ominous silence!

The teacher was instructed to treat no response as if it were an incorrect response, so the shocks could continue beyond 300 volts. In addition, the experimenter had a script prepared for whenever the teacher refused to continue or showed any resistance or reluctance to do so:
- 'Please continue' or 'Please go on'
- 'The experiment requires that you continue'
- 'It's absolutely essential that you continue'
- 'You have no other choice, you must go on.'

There were also 'special prods' to reassure the participant that s/he wasn't doing the learner any permanent harm: 'Although the shocks may be painful there is no permanent tissue damage, so please go on.'

Ask Yourself

- If you'd been one of Milgram's teacher-participants, how far up the voltage scale would you have continued to punish 'wrong answers'?

The results

Milgram asked 14 Psychology students to predict what would happen for 100 participants in this situation. They thought that a few would break off early on, most would stop somewhere in the middle and a few would continue right up to 450 volts. He also asked 40 psychiatrists, who predicted that, on average, less than one per cent would administer the highest voltage.

In the first (remote-victim) experiment, every teacher shocked up to at least 300 volts, and 65 per cent went all the way up to 450 volts. In the voice-feedback condition, 62.5 per cent of participants went on giving shocks up to 450 volts.

Many displayed great anguish, attacked the experimenter verbally, twitched nervously or broke out into nervous laughter. Many were observed to:

> *... sweat, stutter, tremble, groan, bite their lips and dig their nails into their flesh. Full-blown, uncontrollable seizures were observed for three subjects. (Milgram, 1974)*

Indeed, one experiment had to be stopped because the participant had a violently convulsive seizure.

To determine why the obedience levels were so high, Milgram conducted several variations using the voice-feedback condition as his baseline measure. In all, a further 16 variations were performed. (See Key Study 27.1.)

Ask Yourself

- For each of the variations described in Key Study 27.1, estimate the rates of total obedience (the percentage of participants going all the way up to 450 volts).
- Try to explain why it might have been higher or lower than the 62.5 per cent in the voice-feedback condition.

- In variation 10, the obedience rate was 47.5 per cent. This still-very-high figure suggests that the institutional context played some part, but wasn't a crucial factor.
- In variation 3, the obedience rate dropped to 40 per cent, and in variation 4 it dropped further to 30 per cent. While it became much more uncomfortable for participants to see – as well as hear – the effects of their obedience, the figures are still very high.
- In variation 7, obedience dropped to 20.5 per cent. Indeed, participants often pretended to deliver a shock or delivered one lower than they were asked to. This suggests that they were trying to compromise between their conscience and the experimenter's instructions. In his absence, it was easier to follow their conscience.

Key Study 27.1

Some variations on Milgram's basic procedure

Institutional context (variation 10): In interviews following the first experiment, many participants said they continued delivering shocks because the research was being conducted at Yale University, a highly prestigious institution. So, Milgram transferred the experiment to a run-down office in downtown Bridgeport.

Proximity and touch proximity (variations 3 and 4): In the original procedure, the teacher and learner were in adjacent rooms and couldn't see one another. But in variation 3, they were in the same room (about 1.5 ft/46 cm apart), and in variation 4 the teacher was required to force the learner's hand down on to the shock plate.

Remote authority (variation 7): The experimenter left the room (having first given the essential instructions) and gave subsequent instructions by telephone.

Two peers rebel (variation 17): The teacher was paired with two other (stooge) teachers. The stooge teachers read out the list of word-pairs, and informed the learner whether the response was correct. The naïve participant delivered the shocks. At 150 volts, the first stooge refused to continue and moved to another part of the room. At 210 volts, the second stooge did the same. The experimenter ordered the real teacher to continue.

A peer administers the shocks (variation 18): The teacher was paired with another (stooge) teacher and had only to read out the word-pairs (the shock being delivered by the stooge).

- In variation 17, there was only 10 per cent obedience. Most stopped obeying when the first or second stooge refused to continue. According to Milgram (1965):

> *The effects of peer rebellion are most impressive in undercutting the experimenter's authority.*

- In other words, seeing other participants (our peers) disobey shows that it's *possible* to disobey, as well as *how* to disobey. Indeed, some participants said they didn't realise they could. This is a demonstration of the effects of *conformity*.
- In variation 18, obedience rose to 92.5 per cent. This shows that it's easier for participants to shift responsibility from themselves to the person who actually 'throws the switch'.

Why do people obey?

According to Milgram (1974):

> *The most fundamental lesson of our study is that ordinary people simply doing their jobs, and without any particular hostility on their part, can become agents in a terrible destructive process.*

Unless there's reason to believe that people who go all the way up to 450 volts are especially sadistic and cruel, or are unusually obedient (which 'the "Germans are different" hypothesis' claimed about a whole nation), explanations of obedience must look 'outside' the individual participant. In this way, the emphasis is shifted away from personal characteristics to the characteristics of the social situation: most people facing that situation would probably act in a similar (obedient) way. What might some of these situational factors be?

Diffusion of responsibility

Many participants raised the issue of responsibility for any harm to the learner. Although the experimenter didn't always discuss this, when he did say 'I'm responsible for what goes on here', participants showed visible relief. Indeed, when participants are told they're responsible for what happens, obedience is sharply reduced (Hamilton, 1978).

Milgram saw this *diffusion of responsibility* as crucial to understanding the atrocities committed by the Nazis, and Eichmann's defence that he was 'just carrying out orders'. It can also explain the behaviour of William Calley, a US soldier who was court-martialled for the 1968 massacre by troops under his command of several hundred Vietnamese civilians at My Lai. This is related to the *agentic state* (see below).

Figure 27.4 Eichmann at his trial in Jerusalem, 1960. He had been in charge of the transportation of Jews and others to extermination camps, and was eventually arrested in South America

The perception of legitimate authority

As mentioned earlier, many participants showed signs of distress and conflict; so diffusion of responsibility cannot tell the whole story. The conflict seems to be between two opposing sets of demands – the external authority of the experimenter who says, 'Shock', and the internal authority of the conscience which says, 'Don't shock'. The point at which conscience triumphs is, of course, where the participant (finally) stops obeying the experimenter, who, in a sense, ceases to be a legitimate authority in the eyes of the participant. 35 per cent in the original experiment reached that point somewhere before 450 volts, and for many, the crucial 'prod' was when the experimenter said, 'You have no other choice, you must go on'. They were able to exercise the choice which, of course, they had from the start.

The most common mental adjustment in the obedient participant is to see him/herself as an agent of external authority (the *agentic state*). This represents the opposite of an *autonomous state*, and is what makes it possible for us to function in a hierarchical social system. For a group to function as a whole, individuals must give up responsibility and defer to others of higher status in the social hierarchy. Legitimate authority thus replaces a person's own self-regulation (Turner, 1991). In Milgram's (1974) words:

> The essence of obedience consists in the fact that a person comes to view himself as the instrument for carrying out another person's wishes, and he, therefore, no longer regards himself as responsible for his actions. Once this critical shift of viewpoint has occurred in the person, all the essential features of obedience follow.

According to Hirsch (1995), many of the greatest crimes against humanity are committed in the name of obedience. He maintains that *genocide* (a term first used in 1944) tends to occur under conditions created by three social processes:

1. *Authorisation* relates to the 'agentic state' – that is, obeying orders because of where they come from
2. *Routinisation* refers to massacre becoming a matter of routine, or a mechanical and highly programmed operation
3. *Dehumanisation* involves the victims being reduced to something less than human, allowing the perpetrators to suspend their usual moral prohibition on killing.

Ask Yourself

- What was it about Jack Williams, the experimenter, that conveyed to participants that he was 'in charge' in the experimental situation?

Authority figures often possess highly visible symbols of their power or status that make it difficult to refuse their commands. In Milgram's experiments, the experimenter always wore a grey laboratory coat to indicate his position as an authority figure.

Another major study that demonstrates the impact of uniforms and other symbols of authority is Zimbardo *et al.*'s (1973) 'prison simulation experiment' (see below).

'Entrapment'

According to Gilbert (1981), Milgram's participants may have been 'sucked in' by the series of graduated demands. These began with the 'harmless' advertisement for volunteers for a study of learning and memory and ended with the instruction to deliver what appeared to be potentially lethal electric shocks to another person. Having begun the experiment, participants may have found it difficult to remove themselves from it (*entrapment*). (This is similar to the FITD tactic: see above.)

Figure 27.5 One of the many statues of Lenin brought crashing down in Eastern Europe after the collapse of Communism in 1989

Socialisation

Despite our expressed ideal of independence, obedience is something we're socialised into from a very early age by significant others (including our parents and teachers). Obedience may be an ingrained habit that's difficult to resist (Brown, 1986).

An evaluation of Milgram's research

- In evaluating Milgram's experiments, ethical issues are usually more prominent than scientific ones. These are discussed in detail in Chapter 48. However, Milgram asks whether the ethical criticisms are based as much on the nature of the (unexpected) results as on the procedure itself. Aronson (1988) asks if we'd question the ethics if none of the participants had gone beyond the 150-volt level, which is the point at which most people were expected to stop (according to Milgram's students and the 40 psychiatrists he consulted). Aronson manipulated the results experimentally, and found that the higher the percentage going right up to 450 volts, the more harmful the effects of the experiment are judged to be.

Methodological issues

- One criticism is that Milgram's sample was unrepresentative of the American population. However, a total of 636 participants were tested (in the 18 separate experiments combined), representing a cross-section of the population of New Haven, thought to be a fairly typical small, American town. Milgram admits that those who went on obeying up to 450 volts were more likely to see the learner as responsible for what happened to him and not themselves! They seemed to have a stronger authoritarian character and a less advanced level of moral development. But as Rosenthal and

Rosnow (1966) and others have found, people who volunteer for experiments are, on the whole, considerably *less* authoritarian than those who don't.

- Only 40 women were included in Milgram's sample (Experiment 8). But they showed a 65 per cent obedience rate, just like their male counterparts.
- According to Orne and Holland (1968), Milgram's experiments lack *experimental realism*, that is, participants might not have believed the experimental set-up they found themselves in, and knew the learner wasn't really being given electric shocks. However, a study by Sheridan and King (1972) seems to exclude this possibility.

Key Study 27.2

Obedience training for puppies (Sheridan and King, 1972)

- A college professor told 13 male and 13 female students that their task was to train a puppy to learn a discrimination task by punishing it with increasingly severe and real electric shocks whenever it made an error (up to 450 volts).
- Although the puppy actually received only a small shock, the participants could see it and hear its squealing and jumping around the electrified grid. After a time, an odourless anaesthetic was released into the puppy's cage, causing it to fall asleep.
- Although participants were very upset and complained about the procedure (and some even cried), they were reminded that the puppy's failure to respond was a punishable error, and that they should continue to give shocks.
- A total of 75 per cent of participants delivered the maximum shock possible (54 per cent of the males, 100 per cent of the females). A similar result was found in an unpublished study involving adolescent high school girls (Zimbardo, 2007).

- As well as contradicting Orne and Holland's criticism regarding lack of experimental realism, Sheridan and King's findings support the important role of the perception of legitimate authority.
- Orne and Holland also criticised Milgram's experiments for their lack of *mundane realism* (*external* or *ecological validity*), that is, the results don't extend beyond the particular laboratory setting in which they were collected. They base this claim on the further claim that cues in the experimental setting influenced the participants' perceptions of what was required of them. Obedience, then, might simply have been a response to the *demand characteristics* of the highly unusual experimental setting (see Chapter 3). However, naturalistic studies of obedience dispute this.

Key Study 27.3

A naturalistic study of nurses (Hofling *et al.*, 1966)

- Twenty-two nurses working in various American hospitals received telephone calls from a stooge 'Dr Smith of the psychiatric department', instructing them to give Mr Jones (Dr Smith's patient) 20 mg of a drug called Astrofen. Dr Smith said that he was in a desperate hurry and would sign the drug authorisation form when he came to see the patient in ten minutes' time.
- The label on the box containing the Astrofen (actually a harmless sugar pill) clearly stated that the maximum daily dose was 10 mg. So, if the nurse obeyed Dr Smith's instructions she'd be exceeding the maximum daily dose. Also, she'd be breaking the rules requiring written authorisation before any drug is given, and that a nurse be absolutely sure that 'Dr Smith' is a genuine doctor.

Ask Yourself

- What do you think you'd have done if you'd been one of the nurses?

- Presented with this scenario for discussion, 21 out of 22 graduate nurses who hadn't participated in the actual experiment said they wouldn't have given the drug without written authorisation, especially as it exceeded the maximum daily dose.
- A real doctor was posted nearby, unseen by the nurse, and observed what the nurse did following the telephone call. Out of the 22 nurses, 21 complied without hesitation, and 11 later said they hadn't noticed the dosage discrepancy!

According to Milgram (1974), while there are, of course, differences between laboratory studies of obedience and the obedience observed in Nazi Germany:

> *Differences in scale, numbers and political context may turn out to be relatively unimportant as long as certain essential features are retained …*

The 'essential features' that Milgram refers to is the agentic state (see above).

According to Reicher and Haslam (2011a), the main problem with this account is that the studies themselves provide no real evidence of such an agentic state; it doesn't tally with how participants actually behaved and it certainly cannot explain differences between different experimental conditions. Agreeing, Burger (2011) claims that few serious researchers talk about an agentic state these days; instead, they attribute participants' behaviour to situational variables embedded in the experimental setting, in particular: (i) the use of small increments (or 'entrapment'); (ii) diffused or missing responsibility; (iii) placing participants in a novel situation; and (iv) limited time for participants to act. ((i) and (ii) have been discussed in the text above.). There's empirical support for all four factors and this is discussed in detail in Gross (2012b).

- A further methodological criticism concerns the *cross-cultural replicability* of Milgram's findings:

Table 27.1 Cross-cultural replications of Milgram's obedience experiment (adapted from Smith and Bond, 1998)

Study	Country	Participants	Percentage Obedient
Ancona and Pareyson (1968)	Italy	Students	85
Kilham and Mann (1974)	Australia	Male students	40
		Female students	16
Burley and McGuiness (1977)	UK	Male students	50
Shanab and Yahya (1978)	Jordan	Students	62
Miranda *et al.* (1981)	Spain	Students	over 90
Schurz (1985)	Austria	General population	80
Meeus and Raajimakers (1986)	The Netherlands	General population	92

Unfortunately, it's very difficult to compare these studies because of methodological discrepancies between them (Smith and Bond, 1998). For example, different types of stooges were used (e.g. a 'long-haired student' in Kilham and Mann's study), some of whom may have been perceived as more vulnerable – or more deserving of shocks – than others. In the Meeus and Raajimakers study, the task involved participants having to harass and criticise someone who was completing an important job application.

While Milgram found no gender differences, the Australian female students were asked to shock another female (but the learner was always male in Milgram's experiments). Also, with the exception of Jordan (Shanab and Yahya, 1978), all the countries studied have been western industrialised nations, so we should be cautious when concluding that a universal aspect of social behaviour has been identified. But Smith and Bond (1998) observe that:

> *In none of the countries studied is obedience to authority the kind of blind process that some interpreters of Milgram's work have implied. Levels of obedience can and do vary greatly, depending on the social contexts that define the meaning of the orders given.*

- As we noted earlier, the legacy of Milgram's research is as much to do with the *ethics* of social psychological research as the science. Ironically, as a direct result of the ethical 'fall-out' from Milgram's experiments (e.g. Baumrind, 1964; Kaufmann, 1967), ethical codes and guidelines have been constructed that would make these experiments in their original form totally unacceptable today (Elms, 1995; Reicher and Haslam, 2011b). (See Chapter 48.)
- However, creative ways have been found to get round the ethical concerns. One of these involves the use of *virtual reality* (e.g. Slater *et al.*, 2006); another involves Burger's (2006) replication of the original studies only up to a specific shock level (150 volts) (Burger, 2009). Burger's study is entitled 'Replicating Milgram: Would people still obey today?' His results suggest that average Americans react to this laboratory situation today much the way they did in the 1960s. Although changes in social attitudes can affect behaviour, Burger's findings indicate that the same situational identified above still operate today.

What do Milgram's studies tell us about ourselves?

Perhaps one of the reasons Milgram's research has been so heavily criticised is that it paints an unacceptable picture of human beings. Thus, it's far easier for us to believe that a war criminal like Eichmann was an inhuman monster than that 'ordinary people' can be destructively obedient (what Arendt, 1965, called the *banality of evil*).

But is it possible that Eichmann was more the inhuman monster, and that evil is less banal, than commentators like Arendt, and Psychologists like Milgram, would have us believe? Arendt (1965) herself described Eichmann as taking great pride in the way he transported millions to their deaths 'with great zeal and meticulous care'. He didn't receive detailed instructions from 'on high' regarding the 'final solution'; he had to elaborate these himself (Haslam and Reicher, 2007).

THE POWER of SOCIAL SITUATIONS

Milgram's whole research programme placed great emphasis on the power of the situation (a fundamental premise of Social Psychology in general). While personality isn't irrelevant to understanding obedience, the power of situations is such that most people are capable of destructive obedience (Miller, 1986). But this fact doesn't exonerate the perpetrators of evil: while evil deeds may have been *instigated* by situational factors, individuals can and do make choices (see Chapter 49).

Social roles provide models of power and powerlessness, as in parent–child, teacher–student, and employer–employee relationships. Rather than asking what makes some people more obedient than others, or how we'd have reacted if we'd been one of Milgram's participants, we could instead ask how we would behave if put into a position of authority ourselves. How easily could we assume the role and use the power that goes with it?

Zimbardo's research

Almost as famous – and controversial – as Milgram's obedience studies is the prison simulation experiment or Stanford prison experiment (SPE) (Haney *et al.*, 1973; Zimbardo *et al.*, 1973). The SPE demonstrates aspects of conformity, obedience, and, most significantly, the *power of social situations* on people's behaviour.

After an initial 'rebellion' had been crushed, the prisoners began to react passively as the guards stepped up their aggression each day (by, for example, having a head count in the middle of the night simply to disrupt the prisoners' sleep). This made the prisoners feel helpless and no longer in control of their lives.

Social power became the major dimension on which everyone and everything was defined. Every guard at some time or another behaved in an abusive, authoritarian way. Many seemed to positively enjoy the newfound power and the almost total control over the prisoners which went with the uniform. For example:

Key Study 27.4

The prison simulation experiment (Zimbardo *et al.*, 1973)

- Zimbardo *et al.* recruited male participants through newspaper advertisements asking for student volunteers for a two-week study of prison life. From 75 volunteers, 24 were selected. They were judged to be emotionally stable, physically healthy, and 'normal to average' (based on personality tests). They also had no history of psychiatric problems and had never been in trouble with the police.
- Participants were told they'd be randomly assigned to the role of either 'prisoner' or 'prison guard'. At the beginning of the experiment, then, there were no differences between those selected to be prisoners and guards. They constituted a relatively homogeneous group of white, middle-class college students from all over the USA.
- The basement of Stanford University Psychology department was converted into a 'mock prison'. Zimbardo *et al.* wished to create a prison-like environment which was as psychologically real as possible. The aim was to study how prison life impacts upon both prisoners and guards.
- The experiment began one Sunday morning, when those allocated to the prisoner role were unexpectedly arrested by the local police. They were charged with a felony, read their rights, searched, handcuffed and taken to the police station to be 'booked'. After being fingerprinted, each prisoner was taken blindfolded to the basement prison.
- Upon arrival, the prisoners were stripped naked, skin-searched, deloused and issued with uniforms and bedding. Each prisoner wore a loose-fitting smock with his identification number on the front and back, plus a chain bolted around one ankle. He also wore a nylon stocking to cover his hair (rather than having his head shaved). They were referred to by number only and accommodated in 6 × 9 feet 'cells', three to a cell.
- The guards wore military-style khaki uniforms, silver reflector sunglasses (making eye contact with them impossible) and carried clubs, whistles, handcuffs and keys to the cells and main gate. They were on duty 24 hours a day, each working eight-hour shifts with complete control over the prisoners, who were kept in their cells around the clock, except for meals, toilet privileges, head counts and work.

(a)
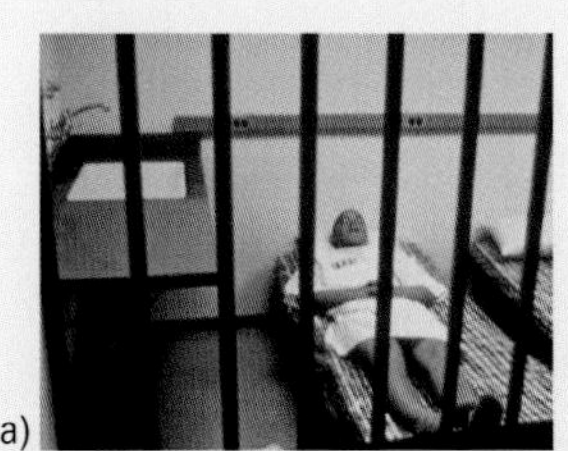

(b)

Figure 27.6 (a) A prisoner in one of the three-bedded cells; (b) A prison guard asserting his authority over a prisoner

MEET THE RESEARCHER

Alex Haslam

Social identity and the positive psychology of groups

It is no accident that most of the classic studies in Psychology are studies of Social Psychology, and that their impact has been felt not just in psychology but in the world at large. As a student, I was drawn in both by the details of these studies and by the much larger messages they conveyed about human nature. They were beautifully crafted, clever and exciting. But they were also shocking. One reason for this is that, at heart, the classic studies tend to present a very depressing picture of human nature. Humans, they suggest, are victims of their psychology, slaves to processes that not only pervert their own behaviour but also have tragic consequences for society.

Of all the studies that convey this bleak picture, the Stanford Prison Experiment (SPE) (Haney *et al.*, 1973) is probably the most alarming. As a student I was startled to learn about the well-adjusted students who were assigned roles as prisoners and guards in a specially constructed prison, and then began a rapid 'descent into hell' in which the groups conformed quickly and willingly to their roles as brutalisers and brutalised.

Is conformity 'natural'?

Although I read that this conformity to role was 'natural', I became increasingly troubled by this conclusion and the model of human nature the classic studies promote. This was due largely to the influence of several brilliant scholars who shaped my development as a Psychologist. First, my PhD supervisor, John Turner, alerted me to the fact that the tendency to focus on processes of conformity, obedience and repression while simultaneously ignoring a range of countervailing processes constitutes a clear example of what Serge Moscovici (1976) termed *conformity bias*. By suggesting that social problems are the product of irresistible psychological forces, this encourages us to think that those problems are inevitable and insurmountable. Yet for all the pessimism that conformity bias engenders, a striking feature of the social world is that people do not always go along with others. Sometimes they say 'no'. And when they do, this can lead to powerful forms of *social change.*

Resistance to peer-group pressure

The seeds of such change can be seen in all the classic studies. Thus while 65 per cent of the participants in Milgram's (1963) 'standard' obedience paradigm showed total obedience to the experimenter, 35 per cent did not. Likewise, although Asch's (1955) studies of line judgement are usually understood as demonstrations of peer-group pressure, in fact the dominant response was to resist such pressure (on critical trials, 67 per cent of participants' responses were correct). And although approximately one-third of Zimbardo's guards responded enthusiastically to their role, the remaining two-thirds did not. Moreover, at some point in all these research programmes there was evidence of systematic and substantial resistance. For example, in one variant of Milgram's studies, disobedience rose to 90 per cent when participants were exposed to a confederate who refused to follow the experimenters' instructions.

Resistance and liberation politics

The simple fact, then, is that people do not appear to yield mindlessly to the wishes of others. As an illustration of this point (this time from a real prison), it is instructive to read Nelson Mandela's account of the prisoners who were incarcerated on Robben Island under the Apartheid regime in South Africa. The prison's brutal conditions were designed to crush both the prisoners' spirit and that of the broader movement they supported. Yet, ultimately, the prison became a crucible for liberation politics that played a major part overthrowing Apartheid (Mandela, 1995). If people tend only to 'go along' with the social systems in which they find themselves, what are we to make of this?

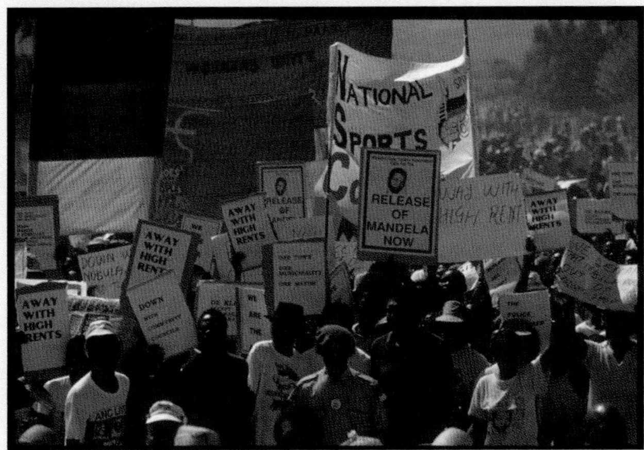

Groups: a force for good as well as evil

Social identity theory

In trying to answer such questions, I was influenced enormously by ideas that John Turner developed with Henri Tajfel at the University of Bristol in the 1970s. In particular, their social identity theory (SIT) argues that people are prepared to challenge the thinking and actions of dominant groups if they see the treatment of their own group as illegitimate and changeable, and if they come to define themselves and other group members in terms of a shared *social identity* – as 'us'. Under these circumstances, SIT suggests, individuals are likely to work together with other members of their group to try to challenge the system. This, for example, is what happened when participants united with the dissenting confederate to disobey the experimenter in the variant of Milgram's obedience studies described above.

The BBC Prison Study

Over the last 30 years, these ideas have been supported by a massive amount of laboratory-based research. As a result, SIT is one of the most influential theories in Social Psychology today. Nevertheless, it was apparent both to me and another close colleague, Steve Reicher (University of St Andrews), that these ideas had not been tested in a way or that would allow comparison with the classic studies of yesteryear. It was this realisation that led us to work together to design and conduct the BBC Prison Study (BPS) in late 2001. In this, we wanted to revisit Zimbardo's prison paradigm in order to establish (a) whether oppression would be a product of blind conformity to role or else of active processes of social identification, and (b) whether, as well as being a basis for tyranny, social identification might also be a basis for *resistance*.

Conclusions

To cut a long story short, as well as supporting some of SIT's core ideas, the study also challenged the received wisdom derived from the SPE (Haslam and Reicher, 2007; Reicher and Haslam, 2006). In particular, the guards did not take on their roles uncritically and the prisoners did not succumb passively to the guards' authority. Indeed, the upshot of this was that on day 6 of the study, the prisoners mounted a revolt that brought the guards' regime to a dramatic end. After this, the study descended towards a tyranny akin to that witnessed in the SPE. Importantly, though, it was clear that this did not result from participants' blind conformity to role but from a conviction that their actions were appropriate and necessary.

In this way, the BPS breaks from the tradition of a long line of classic studies in Social Psychology that suggest human beings' instinctive conformity takes them down an inevitable path towards conflict, abuse and tyranny. This is not inconsistent with us living in a world where these phenomena are all too prevalent. Where they occur, though, our analysis suggests that these things do not result from zombie-like compliance, but rather from individuals' active identification and engagement with the groups of which they are part.

Moreover, as much as these processes can lead us into the darkness, they can also take us into the light. Groups do not rob us of choice, they *give* us choices – not least because they are the principal means by which we can bring about social change (for better or for worse). By neglecting this fact, we see that Social Psychology has itself been imprisoned (Turner, 2006). It is time to escape.

You can learn more about the BBC Prison Study by visiting the website: www.bbcprisonstudy.org.

Professor Alex Haslam is Professor of Social and Organisational Psychology at the University of Exeter and a former Commonwealth Scholar at Macquarie University (Sydney) and Jones Scholar at Emory University (Atlanta). He is currently on the editorial board of eight journals (including EJSP, PSPB, BJM, JPSP and *Scientific American Mind*).

- Guard A said: 'I was surprised at myself – I made them call each other names and clean the toilets out with their bare hands. I practically considered the prisoners cattle and I kept thinking I have to watch out for them in case they try something.'
- Guard B (preparing for the visitors' first night): 'I made sure I was one of the guards on the yard, because this was my first chance for the type of manipulative power that I really like – being a very noticed figure with complete control over what is said or not.'
- Guard C: 'Acting authoritatively can be fun. Power can be a great pleasure.'
- After less than 36 hours, one prisoner had to be released because of uncontrolled crying, fits of rage, disorganised thinking and severe depression. Three others developed the same symptoms and had to be released on successive days. Another prisoner developed a rash over his whole body, which was triggered when his 'parole' request was rejected. Prisoners became demoralised and apathetic and even began to refer to themselves and others by their numbers. The whole experiment, planned to run for two weeks, was abandoned after six days because of the pathological reactions of the prisoners.

An evaluation of the prison simulation experiment

- An outside observer, who had a long history of imprisonment, believed that the mock prison, and both the guards' and prisoners' behaviours, were strikingly similar to real prison life. This supports Zimbardo *et al.*'s major conclusion that what make prisons such evil places are prisons themselves – not prisoners or guards. As Zimbardo (1973) says:

> *Not that anyone ever doubted the horrors of prison, but rather it had been assumed that it was the predispositions of the guards ('sadistic') and prisoners ('sociopathic') that made prisons such evil places. Our study holds constant and positive the dispositional alternative and reveals the power of social, institutional forces to make good men engage in evil deeds.*

Ask Yourself

- What does Zimbardo mean by 'Our study holds constant and positive the dispositional alternative'?

- Volunteers were selected for their emotional stability and 'normality', and then randomly allocated to the prisoner/guard roles. Therefore, their different behaviours and reactions couldn't be attributed to their personal characteristics (or dispositions). Rather, the differences could only be explained in terms of the different roles they played in the context of the mock prison. However, not all the guards acted brutally (Haslam and Reicher, 2007).
- But according to Banuazizi and Mohavedi (1975), the behaviour of both guards and prisoners may have arisen from the stereotyped expectations of their respective roles. The participants were 'merely' role-playing (based on their prior expectations about how guards and prisoners 'ought' to behave). However, one reply to this criticism is to ask at what point 'mere' role-playing becomes a 'real' experience. As Zimbardo (1971, quoted in Aronson, 1992) says:

> *It was no longer apparent to us or most of the subjects where they ended and their roles began. The majority had indeed become 'prisoners' or 'guards', no longer able to clearly differentiate between role-playing and self.*

- This strongly suggests that their experiences were very real, and that even if they were 'merely' role-playing at the beginning, they were soon taking their roles very seriously, indeed! This was 'aided and abetted' by the environmental conditions. A brutalising atmosphere, like the 'mock' prison, produces brutality. Had the roles been reversed, those who suffered as the prisoners may just as easily have inflicted suffering on those who were randomly chosen as guards. However, during 'orientation', Zimbardo (acting as 'superintendent') gave them a sense of how he wanted them to behave, namely, to create in the prison a sense of 'powerlessness' (Haslam and Reicher, 2007).
- The study has provoked almost as much controversy regarding its ethics as did Milgram's experiments (see Chapter 48).
- Replications and extensions include the BBC's prison study *The Experiment*. (See Meet the Researcher pp. 456–7 and Gross, 2012b.)

CONCLUSIONS: RESISTING OBEDIENCE and the LIMITS of SITUATIONAL POWER

In 1992, an East German judge sentenced a former East German border guard for having shot a man trying (three years earlier) to escape to the West. The judge's comments echo the spirit of the Nuremberg Accords which followed the Nazi war crimes trials:

> *Not everything that is legal is right ... At the end of the twentieth century, no one has the right to turn off his conscience when it comes to killing people on the orders of authorities ... (cited in Berkowitz, 1993)*

As we've seen, it's difficult to disobey authority. But we're most likely to rebel when we feel that social pressure is so strong that our freedom is under threat (what Brehm, 1966, called *psychological reactance:* see Chapter 49). Milgram himself felt that obedience would be reduced by:

- *educating* people about the dangers of blind obedience
- *encouraging* them to question authority
- *exposing* them to the actions of disobedient models.

According to Zimbardo (2007), the design of the SPE revealed that initially the guards were 'good apples', some of whom turned sour over time by powerful situational forces. But by his own detailed evidence, a small number of guards were a little sour even before the roles were allocated – and despite the best efforts to recruit only good ones. In other words, the power of social situations isn't limitless; ultimately, it's individuals, not 'the System', that's responsible for individuals' behaviour.

Zimbardo himself, as well as several independent investigators, have drawn parallels between the SPE and Abu Ghraib prison in Iraq. The abusive, dehumanising treatment by a few 'bad apples' (US soldiers) of Iraqi prisoners mirrors the treatment by some guards of the prisoner participants. In both cases, the psychological dynamics made such behaviour possible and permissible; but also in both cases, it was displayed only by a small minority.

Chapter Summary

- **Compliance** is an element common to different kinds of social influence, including conformity, obedience and our responses to other people's direct requests.
- Attempts to change people's opinions and behaviour used by salespeople and others include **reciprocity, liking (ingratiation), scarcity, social validation, foot-in-the-door (FITD), door-in-the-face (DIF)** and **low-ball (LB)** tactics.
- While both conformity and obedience involve the **abdication of personal responsibility,** obedience involves orders from someone in **higher authority**, with influence being in one direction only.
- Milgram's series of 18 obedience experiments involve a basic procedure (**remote victim/voice feedback**) and variations on this, involving the manipulation of critical variables.
- Increasing the proximity to the victim, reducing the proximity of the experimenter and having the social support of 'rebel' fellow teachers all reduced obedience, while having someone else actually deliver the shock increased it.
- Two related variables that are crucial for understanding obedience are **acceptance/denial of responsibility** and the **agentic state**. The wearing of uniform and other such symbols of authority are also important.
- Milgram's experiments have caused great ethical controversy, but have also been criticised on scientific grounds. The results have been replicated **cross-culturally**, although identical procedures haven't always been used, making it difficult to draw comparisons. But blind obedience hasn't been found anywhere and social context influences obedience levels.
- The **mundane realism** of the procedure is supported by Hofling *et al.*'s naturalistic experiment involving nurses, and Milgram believes that obedience is essentially the same process regardless of the particular context.
- Many of the greatest crimes against humanity are committed in the name of obedience. Genocide tends to occur under conditions of **authorisation, routinisation** and **dehumanisation**.
- Zimbardo's **Stanford prison experiment (SPE)**, like Milgram's obedience studies, demonstrates the **power of social situations** to make people act in uncharacteristic ways. A brutalising atmosphere, like a prison, can induce brutality in people who aren't usually brutal.
- Participants were selected for their emotional stability and general 'normality', and then randomly allocated to the roles of prisoner or prison guard. Therefore, their pathological reactions couldn't be attributed to their personal characteristics.
- While they may have been merely **role-playing** at the beginning of the experiment, they soon 'became' prisoners or guards.

Links with Other Topics/Chapters

Chapter 28 ⟶ Liking as a tactic used to influence people's attitudes or behaviour is related to *interpersonal attraction* (one aspect of *interpersonal relationships*)

Chapter 22 ⟶ Liking/ingratiation is a major component of *impression management*, and the norm of reciprocity is a factor influencing *self-disclosure*

Chapter 49 ⟶ Feeling exploited by attempts to change our opinions/behaviour through the FITD may reflect *psychological reactance*

Chapter 30 ⟶ Diffusion of responsibility is a factor involved in *helping behaviour/ bystander intervention*

Chapter 26 ⟶ Milgram's 'Two peers rebel' experiment demonstrates how obedience and *conformity* can operate together

Chapter 48 ⟶ Both Milgram's and Zimbardo's research highlights the *double obligation dilemma*

Chapters 23 and 47 ⟶ The SPE found support for the influence of social situations, rather than individual personality (the *dispositional hypothesis*), in explaining the behaviour of people in prisons

Recommended Reading

Gross, R. (2012b) *Key Studies in Psychology* (6th edition). London: Hodder Education. Chapters 11 and 12.

Hirsch, H. (1995) *Genocide and the Politics of Memory: Studying Death to Preserve Life.* Chapel Hill, NC: University of North Carolina Press. Chapters 9–11 are especially relevant here (also relevant to Chapter 25).

Milgram, S. (1974) *Obedience to Authority.* New York: Harper & Row.

Zimbardo, P. (2007) *The Lucifer Effect – Understanding How Good People Turn Evil.* London: Ebury.

Useful Websites

www.tinyurl.com/m2foazl (Includes some stills/video clips of Milgram's original studies)

www.tinyurl.com/lttd7uf (Video of Burger's partial replication)

www.prisonexp.org (The Stanford prison study website)

www.bbcprisonstudy.org (Haslam and Reicher's 2001 BBC series *The Experiment*, including many video clips)

www.muskingum.edu/~psych/psycweb/history/milgram.htm (The Stanley Milgram website)

www.LuciferEffect.com (The official website of *The Lucifer Effect*)

www.sonoma.edu/users/g/goodman/zimbardo.htm (Holocaust Studies Center, Sonoma State University, 1999 Holocaust Lectures: 'Transforming People into Perpetrators of Evil' – P. Zimbardo)

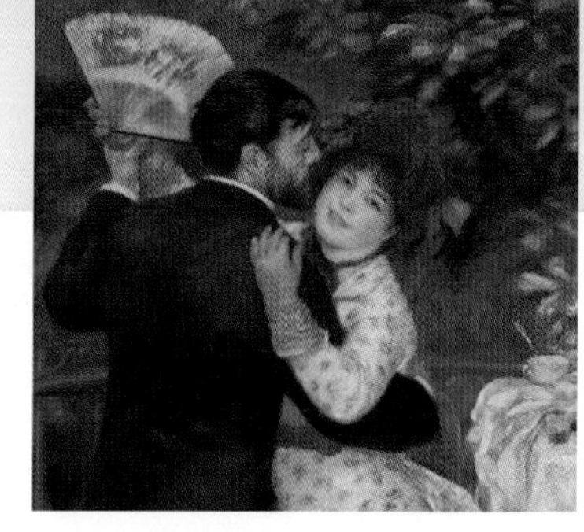

CHAPTER 28

INTERPERSONAL RELATIONSHIPS

INTRODUCTION and OVERVIEW

According to popular belief, it's love that makes the world go round. But according to Rubin and NcNeil (1983), liking perhaps more than loving is what keeps it spinning. How are liking and loving related? Are there different kinds of love, and can this help us understand how romantic relationships develop over time and why some break down? How do we get into relationships in the first place?

The importance of relationships, both sexual and non-sexual, is 'obvious'. According to Duck (1999):

> *… We need merely to reflect for a moment on the sources of our greatest pleasure and pain to appreciate that nothing else arouses the extremes of emotion that are experienced in the course of personal relationships with other human beings …*

Relationships make life meaningful, whether they're good or bad. When asked 'What's necessary for your happiness?' most people say, before anything else, satisfying close relationships with friends, family and romantic partners (Berscheid, 1985).

Most relationship research has focused on 'voluntary' relationships. When describing relationships breaking up (or down), we often use language that implies a degree of choice ('Why don't you get out of that relationship?' or 'I wish I'd never got involved in the first place.'). One way of trying to understand the *dissolution* of relationships is to see it as the process of relationship *formation* in reverse.

Traditionally, Social Psychologists have been interested in *interpersonal attraction*, which relates to the question 'How do relationships start?' But during the last 20 years or so, the emphasis has shifted to relationships *as a process* (Duck, 1999), reflected in two further questions: 'What makes people stay in relationships (maintenance and progression)?' and 'Why and how do relationships go wrong (breakdown or dissolution)?'

AFFILIATION: THE NEED for OTHER PEOPLE

Affiliation is the basic human need for the company of other human beings. The need to belong and to be accepted by others is one of Maslow's basic survival needs (see Chapter 9) and is also a major motive underlying conformity (see Chapter 26). We also saw in Chapter 26 that conformity can be explained in terms of the need to evaluate our beliefs and opinions by comparing them with other people's, especially in ambiguous or unstructured situations. This is the central idea in Festinger's (1954) *social comparison theory*.

According to Duck (1988), we're more 'affiliative' and inclined to seek others' company under certain conditions than others, for example, when we're anxious, when we've just left a close relationship (the 'rebound' situation) and when we've moved to a new neighbourhood. *Anxiety* is one of the most powerful factors.

Ask Yourself

- What do these results (Key Study 28.1) tell you about the students' motives for affiliation?

Key Study 28.1

'Anxiety loves anxious company' (Schachter, 1959)

- Female Psychology students were led to believe they'd be receiving electric shocks. One group was told the shocks would be painful (*high anxiety condition*), while another group was told they wouldn't be at all painful (*low anxiety condition*).
- They were then told that there'd be a delay while the equipment was set up and they were given the option of waiting either alone or with another participant (this was the dependent variable and no actual shock was given).
- As predicted, the high anxiety group showed a greater preference for company (20 out of 32) than the low anxiety group (10 out of 30).
- In a separate, related experiment, all the participants were told the shocks would be painful, but for half the choice was between waiting alone and waiting with another participant in the same experiment, and for the other half it was between waiting alone and waiting with another student who was waiting to see her teacher.
- For the first group, there was a strong preference for waiting with another high anxiety participant, while the second group preferred to wait alone.

Schachter's results strongly suggest that *social comparison* was the motive for affiliation (rather than distraction) – if we have something to worry about, we prefer to be with other worriers. As Schachter (1959) says, 'Misery doesn't love just any kind of company, it loves only miserable company'.

Kulik and Mahler (1989) reached the same conclusions when studying patients about to undergo coronary-bypass surgery. Most preferred to share a room with someone who'd already undergone coronary surgery, rather than another patient waiting for the same operation. The main motive for this preference seemed to be the need for information about the stress-inducing situation. Not only were those assigned a post-operative roommate less anxious, they were more mobile post-operatively and had faster post-operative recoveries (Kulik *et al.*, 2003).

LOVE and INTIMACY

Ask Yourself

- What is a relationship and what makes a relationship a close one?
- What different kinds of relationship are there?
- Are there different types of love?

Relationships: definitions and varieties

According to Berscheid and Ammazzalorso (2004), the concept of a relationship:

> *... refers to two people whose behaviour is* interdependent *in that a change in behaviour in one is likely to produce a change in behaviour of the other ...* (emphasis in original)

A 'close' relationship denotes an interaction pattern which takes place over a long period of time; the partners' influence on each other is strong and frequent and many different types of behaviour are affected (Kelley *et al.*, 1983).

In common with other close relationships, romantic relationships involve interdependence, strong feelings, committed intent and overlapping self-concept. But unique to romantic relationships are passion and exclusive commitment (Fiske, 2004).

Voluntary/involuntary relationships

According to Moghaddam *et al.* (1993), interpersonal relationships in western cultures tend to be *individualistic*, *voluntary* and *temporary*; those in non-western cultures are more *collectivist*, *involuntary* and *permanent*. As they say:

> *The cultural values and environmental conditions in North America have led North American social psychologists to be primarily concerned with first-time acquaintances, friendships and intimate relationships, primarily because these appear to be the relationships most relevant to the North American urban cultural experience.*

In other words, western Psychologists tend to equate 'relationships' with 'western relationships' (a form of *ethnocentrism*: see Chapter 47).

The examples given in the quote from Moghaddam *et al.* are all voluntary; but western Psychologists have studied a wide range of such relationships during the past 20 years or so, some of which may seem more voluntary than others. Duck (1999) gives the following examples: relationships of blended families, cross-sex non-romantic friendships, romantic or friendly relationships in the workplace, relationships between cooperative neighbours, relationships between prisoners and guards, sibling relationships, children relating to other children and adults' relationships with their parents.

Marriage is found in all known cultures (Fletcher, 2002) and is usually taken to be a voluntary relationship. But there are several reasons for asking if it really is.

- There are wide and important cultural variations in marital arrangements. From a western perspective, the 'natural' form of marriage is *monogamy* (marriage to one spouse at any one time). This belief is enshrined in the law (bigamy is a criminal offence) and reflects basic Judeo–Christian doctrine. But monogamy is only one of the forms that marriage can take. (See Box 28.1.)
- According to Duck (1999), the choice to marry is voluntary, presumably. But once the marriage is a few years old, it's much less voluntary than it was, since getting out of it is accompanied by a great deal of 'social and legal baggage':

> *... Thus when we talk about 'voluntary relationships', we need to recognise not only that the exercise of apparently free choice is always tempered by the social realities and constraints that surround us, but also that, once exercised, some choices are then disabled, and cannot be easily or straightforwardly remade. To that extent, therefore, their consequences become non-voluntary ...*
> *(Duck, 1999)*

Arranged marriages

Ask Yourself

- Do you consider that arranged marriages are necessarily wrong or undesirable?
- Do you come from a cultural background in which they are the norm?
- Is there a sense in which all marriages are 'arranged'?

Box 28.1 Culture and marriage

- *Polygamy* refers to having two or more spouses at once.
- It can take the form of *polygyny* (one man having two or more wives) or (less commonly) *polyandry* (one women with two or more husbands).
- Another arrangement is *mandatory marriage to specific relatives*, as when a son marries the daughter of his father's brother (his first cousin: Triandis, 1994).
- A total of 84 per cent of known cultures allow polygyny, but only 5–10 per cent of men in such cultures actually have more than one wife (Fletcher, 2002).
- Probably less than 0.5 per cent of human societies have practised polyandry as a common or preferred form of marriage (Price and Crapo, 1999). However, throughout Tibet and the neighbouring Himalayan areas in India, Nepal and Bhutan, it's been common for generations. Usually, a woman marries two or more brothers (*fraternal polyandry*); this helps to keep family numbers down in order to cope with scarce resources.
- *Polyamory* ('group marriage') refers to open but committed relationships with more than one (same and/or opposite sex) lover or partner (or spouse) simultaneously. While polyamorists ('ethical sluts') are released from the burdens of traditional marriage vows, they seem to keep their long-term relationships intact (Newitz, 2006). They're found mainly in California but increasingly in the UK (Frith, 2005).

Figure 28.1 Polygyny in Nevada, USA is alive and well!

According to Kerckhoff and Davis's (1962) *filter model* (see below), our choice of potential (realistic) marriage partners is limited by demographic variables (age, education, ethnic and religious background, and so on). To this extent, most relationships are 'arranged'. As Duck (1999) says:

> *Many of us would perhaps not recognise – or accept – that marriages are actually 'arranged' by religion, social position, wealth, class, opportunity and other things over which we have little control, even within our own culture …*

Conversely, parentally arranged marriages in some cultures are gladly entered into and are considered perfectly normal, natural relationships that are anticipated with pleasure (Duck, 1999).

Gupta and Singh (1982) found that couples in Jaipur, India, who married for love reported *diminished* feelings of love if they'd been married for more than five years. By contrast, those who'd undertaken arranged marriages reported *more* love if they weren't newlyweds. These findings reveal that passionate love 'cools' over time, and that there's scope for love to flourish within an arranged marriage.

In cultures where arranged marriages occur, courtship is accepted to a certain degree, but love is left to be defined and discovered after marriage (Bellur, 1995). This, of course, is the reverse of the 'Hollywood' picture, where love is supposed to precede marriage and be what marriage is all about. But even in traditional cultures that practise arranged marriages, brides (and grooms) are typically given some choice in the matter (Fletcher, 2002). For example, in Sri Lanka, men and women who like one another (or fall in love) usually let their parents know their choices in advance through indirect channels (de Munck, 1998). Families often use similar criteria that the individuals themselves might use if they had a free choice (including matching on attractiveness: see below). The classic example is the Jewish custom of having a *matchmaker* (Rockman, 1994).

Arranged marriages are far more common in *collectivist* cultures, where the whole extended family 'marries' the other extended family ('social networks motivate marriages': Fiske, 2004). For example, almost 25 per cent of marriages in Japan are arranged (Iwao, 1993). This contrasts with *individualist* cultures, in which the individuals marry one another (Triandis, 1994). Here, it's presumed that marriage is motivated by romantic love between two mutually attracted individuals, who freely choose to commit (Fiske, 2004).

In general, *divorce rates* among those who marry according to parents' wishes are much *lower* than among those who marry for love. This is an argument in favour of arranged marriages. Indeed, it's difficult to argue for the superiority of western (especially American) marital arrangements given the 50 per cent divorce rate and an average marriage that lasts for just seven years (Fiske, 2004). As Triandis (1994) argues:

> *Marriage, when seen as a fifty-year relationship, is more likely to be a good one if people enter it after careful, rational analysis, which is more likely to be provided by older adults than by sexually aroused young people …*

Traditional forms of matchmaking are, however, on the wane in most cultures, reflecting the growing western influence, and divorce rates among 'arranged couples' are rising. Personal freedom is gaining in importance, and traditional structures that define set roles for family members are becoming less valid. Among the more liberal-minded Asians living in the West, arranged marriages operate more like a dating facility ('arranged meetings' rather than 'arranged marriages').

Gay and lesbian relationships

Ask Yourself...

- Do you believe that the differences between gays and lesbians and heterosexuals are greater than the similarities?
- What are the major differences and similarities?
- What is your belief based on?

The focus on the long-term relationships of heterosexuals has now been supplemented with discussion of gay and lesbian relationships (Duck, 1999); this includes studies of their stability and dissolution (Kurdeck, 1991, 1992).

Compared with same-sex friendships and cross-sex non-romantic friendships, gay and lesbian partners experience extra social burdens in terms of the influence of other people's reactions (Huston and Schwartz, 1995). Weston (1991) argues that 'blood-family' is often replaced for homosexuals by 'families of choice'. Gays and lesbians often aren't 'out' to blood-family, or may be estranged from their blood-families specifically because of their homosexuality; as a result, the blood-family can function very differently for gays and lesbians compared with heterosexuals. Not only are they less likely to tell their parents and siblings of 'new' relationships; they're less likely to talk about intimate relationships that have already developed (Huston and Schwartz, 1995).

According to Kitzinger and Coyle (1995), psychological research into homosexuality since the mid-1970s has moved away from a 'pathology model' towards one comprising three overlapping themes:

1. Rejection of the concept of homosexuality as a central organising principle of the personality in favour of recognising the diversity and variety of homosexuals as individuals
2. An assertion that homosexuality is as natural, normal and healthy as heterosexuality
3. Denial of the idea that homosexuals pose any threat to children, the nuclear family or the future of society as we know it.

According to Bee (1994), homosexual partnerships are far more like heterosexual ones than they are different. In terms of sexual behaviour, apart from their sexual preferences, gays and lesbians don't look massively different from their heterosexual counterparts (Fletcher, 2002).

Gender differences

Researchers have repeatedly found that many of the same gender differences between heterosexual men and women occur when comparing gays and lesbians. For example, straight men and gays have higher sex drives than straight women and lesbians, and females (straight or lesbian) are more relationship-focused than males (straight or gay). In other words:

> *... Many central patterns of sexual attitudes and behaviour are more closely linked to gender than to sexual orientation. If one wants to understand gays and lesbians, a good place to start is by looking at heterosexual men and women respectively ... (Fletcher, 2002)*

One danger of emphasising the sameness of hetero- and homosexual couples is the failure to explore the *marginalisation* of the latter in the wider society (Clarke *et al.*, 2005). Similarly, Kitzinger and Coyle (1995) argue that certain factors are omitted or distorted when homosexual relationships are assessed in terms derived from heterosexual relationships.

The very fact of them being of the same sex/gender may explain the greater instability of gay/lesbian relationships (LeVay, 2006). They may experience a kind of 'anti-homophily': they find it difficult to develop the reciprocal dependency that is central to a stable, loving relationship because they have 'nothing to trade'. In addition, they may have difficulty seeing their partner as sufficiently 'other' or 'exotic' for romantic passion to persist.

Figure 28.2 Does this couple conform to the stereotype of how gay men are supposed to look?

'Electronic' friendships

Ask Yourself

- Have you had an online relationship?
- What do you think the potential benefits and dangers of such a relationship might be?

Probably one of the most unexpected uses of the internet is the development of *online relationships* (or *cyber affairs*: Griffiths, 2000). In the UK, one newspaper reported that there have been over 1000 weddings resulting from internet meetings.

Indeed, Cacioppo (2013) reports that more than a third of the 19,131 adult Americans who married between 2005 and 2012 met their spouse online. An online meeting was also associated with a lower rate of marital break-up than other venues (5.96 versus 7.67 per cent) plus a higher rate of marital satisfaction. Factors that might explain these findings include access to more potential partners online and the fact that communicating electronically has, in other studies, been found to produce greater self-disclosure (see Chapter 22). Griffiths (2000) claims that 'electronic communication is the easiest, most disinhibiting and most accessible way to meet potential new partners'.

Different types of love

Berscheid and Walster (1978) distinguish between: (a) *companionate love* ('true love' or 'conjugal love'), 'the affection we feel for those with whom our lives are deeply entwined', including very close friends and marriage partners; and (b) *passionate love* (romantic love, obsessive love, infatuation, 'love sick' or 'being in love'). Romantic love is 'A state of intense absorption in another … A state of intense physiological arousal.' These are qualitatively different, but companionate love is only a more extreme form of liking ('the affection we feel for casual acquaintances') and corresponds to Rubin's 'love'.

Similarly, Sternberg (1988b) has proposed a 'triangular' model of love, in which three basic components (intimacy, passion and decision/commitment) can be combined to produce *consummate love.* When only two are combined, the resulting love is *romantic, companionate* or *fatuous*. (See Figure 28.3.)

The power of love

Is romantic love unique to western culture?

American researchers have focused mainly on romantic relationships as the basis for marriage (Fiske, 2004). According to the popular ('Hollywood') view individuals learn that in order to be happy and fulfilled, they must be in love and live for love (Moghaddam, 2002). However, as we've seen, in cultures where arranged marriages occur, the relationship between love and marriage is the other way around, and marriage is seen as the basis on which to explore a loving relationship (Bellur, 1995). As Bellur notes, the cultural background in which people have learned about love is important in shaping their concept of it.

Ask Yourself

- If someone had all the other qualities you desired in a marriage partner, would you marry this person if you weren't in love?

When Kephart (1967) asked Americans this question, well over twice as many men replied 'no' as did women. When Simpson *et al.* (1986) repeated the study, more than 80 per cent of both men and women said 'no'.

Ask Yourself

- How might you account for the difference between Kephart's and Simpson *et al.*'s findings?

This can be explained at least partly by the fact that, 20 years later, financial independence has

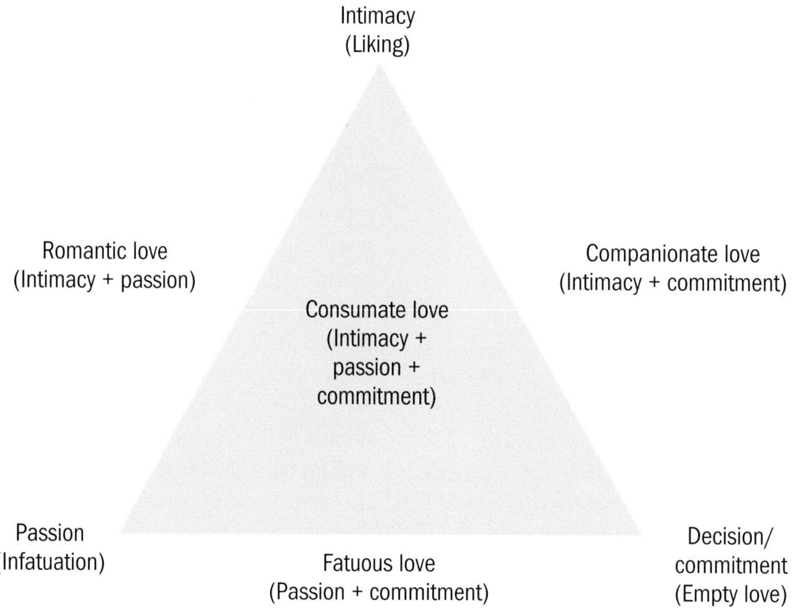

Figure 28.3 Robert Sternberg's (1988b) model of different kinds of love as combinations of three basic components of love (from Myers, D.G. (1994), *Exploring Social Psychology*. New York, McGraw-Hill)

allowed women to choose marriage partners for reasons other than material necessity. But this doesn't explain why romantic love has become so central for both American men and women (Moghaddam, 1998).

Figure 28.4 Nicole Kidman and Ewan McGregor in *Moulin Rouge* (2001)

As non-western societies become westernised, there's a greater tendency for young people to say 'no' to the question asked by Kephart and Simpson *et al.* Even in collectivist cultures (such as India and Pakistan), about 50 per cent of young people said 'no', and the indications are that this percentage is rising (Moghaddam, 2002).

However, cultural differences still exist. For example, Levine *et al.* (1995) studied young people in Australia, Brazil, England, Hong Kong, India, Japan, Mexico, Pakistan, the Philippines, Thailand and the USA. Participants from India, Thailand and Pakistan gave the highest proportion of 'yes' replies, while those from England and the USA gave the lowest. These are collectivist and individualist cultures, respectively.

According to Nakielska and Goodwin (2013), researchers claim that it's not the *feeling* of love that differs between cultures, but rather the social and cultural *meaning* and *value* assigned to the feeling. One of the dimensions that differentiates attitudes to romantic love and relationships is *individualism-collectivism* (see above and Chapter 47).

An evolutionary theory of love: love as attachment

An *evolutionary* account of love focuses on the functions that love evolved to meet. Compared with other primates, humans are dependent on their parents for an exceptionally long period of time. As length of childhood (and related brain size) increased steadily over the last million years or so of *Homo* evolution, so there were strong selection pressures toward the development of (relatively) *monogamous pair-bonding*. In other words:

> *Love is ... an evolutionary device to persuade couples to stay together for long enough to give their children a good shot at making it to adulthood ... (Fletcher, 2002)*

In our hunter-gatherer ancestral environment, two parents were better than one. Attachment bonds between procreative partners would have greatly enhanced the survival of their offspring (Zeifman and Hazan, 2000).

Bowlby (1969) identified three basic behavioural systems that bond male–female pairs together: attachment, caregiving and sex. Shaver *et al.* (1996) have proposed a theory of adult romantic love in terms of these three systems. So, when we say 'I love you', we can mean any or all of the following.

- *Love as attachment:* 'I am emotionally dependent on you for happiness, safety and security; I feel anxious and lonely when you're gone, relieved and stronger when you're near. I want to be comforted, supported emotionally, and taken care of by you ...'
- *Love as caregiving*: 'I get great pleasure from supporting, caring for and taking care of you; from facilitating your progress, health, growth and happiness ...'
- *Love as sexual attraction*: 'I am sexually attracted to you and can't get you out of my mind. You excite me, "turn me on", make me feel alive ... I want to see you, devour you, touch you, merge with you, lose myself in you, "get off on you" ...'

Zeifman and Hazan (2000) believe that there are four stages of adult attachment that mirror Bowlby's (1969) four phases of infant attachment to the mother(-figure). These are summarised in Table 28.1.

STAGE THEORIES of RELATIONSHIPS

Ask Yourself

- Do you think there are any 'natural' stages that all intimate (romantic and non-romantic) relationships go through? (Assuming the 'romantic' ones last a reasonable amount of time – one-night-stands don't count!)

Table 28.1 The four stages of adult attachment in relation to Bowlby's four phases of infant attachment development

Bowlby's phases of infant attachment	Pre-attachment (0–3/4 months)	Attachment-in-the-making (3/4–6/7 months)	Clear-cut attachment (6/7–12/18 months)	Goal-directed partnership (12–18 months onwards)
Four stages of adult attachment	Attraction and flirting	Falling in love	Loving	Life as usual

Based on Zeifman and Hazan (2000)

Our own experience tells us that intimate relationships change and develop over time. Indeed, those which stagnate ('we're not going anywhere'), especially sexual/romantic relationships, may well be doomed to failure (Duck, 1988).

The filter model (Kerckhoff and Davis, 1962)

Kerckhoff and Davis compared 'short-term couples' (together for less than 18 months) with 'long-term couples' (18 months or more) over a seven-month period. According to their *filter model*:

- *Similarity of sociological* (or *demographic*) variables determines the likelihood of individuals meeting in the first place. To some extent, our choice of friends and partners is made for us; social circumstances reduce the '*field of availables'* (Kerckhoff, 1974) – that is, the range of people that are *realistically* (as opposed to *theoretically*) available for us to meet. There's considerable *preselection* of the types of people we come into contact with, namely those from our own ethnic, racial, religious, social class and educational groups; these are the types of people we tend to find most attractive initially, since similarity makes communication easier and we've something immediately in common with them. At this point, attraction has little to do with other people's individual characteristics (this is the first 'filter')
- The second filter involves individuals' *psychological characteristics*, specifically *agreement on basic values*. This was found to be the best predictor of the relationship becoming more stable and permanent; those who'd been together for less than 18 months tended to have a stronger relationship when the partners' values coincided
- For the long-term couples, *complementarity of emotional needs* was the best predictor of a longer-term commitment (the third filter). Complementary behaviours take account of each other's needs, helping to make a perfect whole and the relationship feel less superficial (Duck, 1999).

An evaluation of the filter model

- According to Winch (1958), happy marriages are often based on each partner's ability to fulfil the other's needs. For example, a domineering person could more easily satisfy a partner who needs to be dominated than one who's equally domineering. Despite some experimental support for this hypothesis regarding *interpersonal styles* (Dryer and Horowitz, 1997) the evidence is sparse, and we're more likely to marry others whose needs and personalities are *similar* to ours (the *matching phenomenon*: e.g. Berscheid and Walster, 1978). In other words, 'birds of a feather flock together' (rather than 'opposites attract').
- Berscheid and Reis (1998) argue that the overwhelming evidence favours the similarity-attraction principle. In direct contradiction of the opposites-attract hypothesis, Felmlee (1998) examined 'fatal attractions' to a partner with qualities that differed from the partner and from the average. Descriptions of these terminated relationships indicated that even when these dissimilar, unique or extreme qualities might have been intriguing or appealing to begin with, it was the self-same qualities that eventually produced disenchantment.
- Instead of complementary needs, what about complementarity of *resources* (Brehm, 1992)? Men seem to give a universally higher priority to 'good looks' in their female partners than do women in their male partners. The reverse is true when it comes to 'good financial prospect' and 'good earning capacity'.

From his study of 37 cultures, Buss (1989) concluded that these sex differences '... appear to be deeply rooted in the evolutionary history of our species ...' (see below, pp. 474–6).

Figure 28.5 Richard and Judy – complementarity personified!

Stimulus–value–role theory (Murstein, 1976, 1986, 1987)

According to Murstein's *stimulus-value-role* (SVR) theory, intimate relationships proceed from:

- a *stimulus stage,* in which attraction is based on external attributes (such as physical appearance), through
- a *value stage*, in which similarity of values and beliefs becomes much more important, and finally to
- *a role stage*, which involves a commitment based on successful performance of relationship roles, such as husband and wife.

Although all three factors have some influence throughout a relationship, each one assumes greatest significance during one particular stage. (See Figure 28.6.)

An evaluation of stage theories

- Brehm (1992) points out that many studies have provided only weak evidence for a fixed sequence of stages in intimate relationships. 'Stages' are probably best regarded as 'phases' that take place at different times for different couples. However, the claim that relationships change and develop isn't in dispute, and it's useful to think of this as involving a beginning, a middle and an end, corresponding to the three questions that were posed at the beginning of the chapter (see *Introduction and overview*). For example, how each partner understands the role of husband and wife, and how well each performs their role, are relatively late influences in a given courtship. The matching of partners' role concepts will be irrelevant to the success of the early stages of the courtship (Duck, 1999).

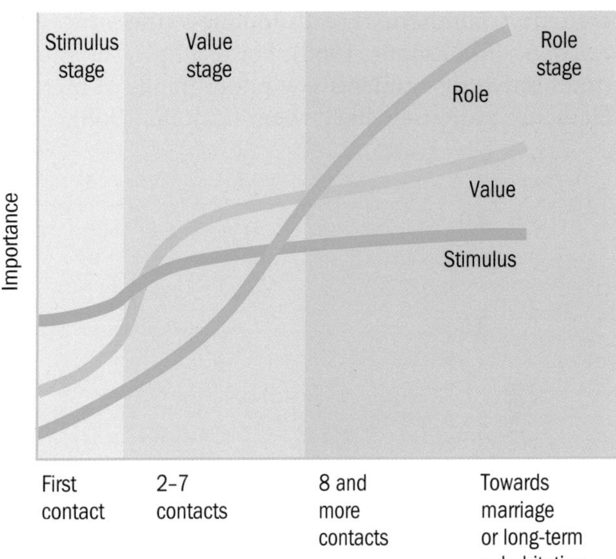

Figure 28.6 States of courtship in SVR theory (Murstein, 1987, based on Brehm, 1992)

INTERPERSONAL ATTRACTION: HOW RELATIONSHIPS GET STARTED

A general theoretical framework for explaining initial attraction is *reward theory* (Clore and Byrne, 1974; Lott and Lott, 1974). The more rewards someone provides for us, the more we should be attracted to that individual. A number of factors have been found to influence initial attraction through their reward value, including *proximity*, *exposure* and *familiarity*, *similarity* and *physical attractiveness*.

Proximity

Proximity (physical closeness or *propinquity*) represents a minimum requirement for attraction: the further apart two people live, the lower the probability they'll ever meet, let alone become friends or marry. Festinger *et al.* (1950) studied friendship patterns in a university campus housing complex for married students. People were more friendly with those who lived next door, next most friendly with those living two doors away, and least friendly with those who lived at the end of the corridor. On any one floor, people who lived near stairways had more friends than those living at the end of a corridor.

However, physical proximity has become less important with the creation and expansion of internet dating sites, chat rooms and email. It's much easier now to become friends, even lovers, with individuals at great geographical distance (Buunk and Dijkstra, 2008: see above).

Exposure and familiarity

Proximity increases the opportunity for interaction (*exposure*), which, in turn, increases *familiarity*. There's considerable evidence that, far from breeding contempt, familiarity breeds fondness (the *mere exposure effect*: Zajonc, 1968). For example, the more times university students saw photographs of men's faces, the more they liked them (Zajonc, 1968).

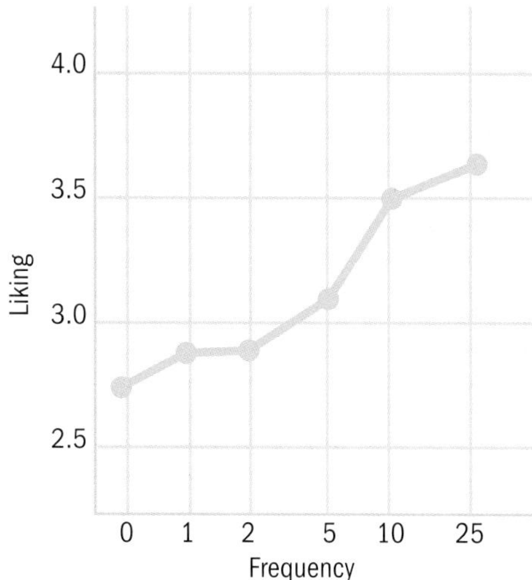

Figure 28.7 The relationship between frequency of exposure and liking. Participants were shown photographs of different faces and the number of times each face was shown was varied. The more they saw a particular face, the more they said they liked the person shown (based on Zajonc, 1968)

According to Argyle (1983), the more two people interact, the more *polarised* their attitudes towards each other become – usually in the direction of greater liking. This, in turn, increases the likelihood of further interaction, but only if the interaction is on an equal footing.

People form friendships with those they encounter frequently (as the mere exposure effect would predict). Asian-Americans date Euro-Americans when they're in close proximity (Fujino, 1997), high-school students form friendships within their own academic subjects (Kubitschek and Hallinan, 1998), and older, relocated adults make friends among their nearest neighbours (Dugan and Kivett, 1998).

Similarity

Ask Yourself

- Do you consider your friends to be similar to you? If so, in what ways?
- Does this also apply to sexual partners?

This was discussed above in relation to Kerckhoff and Davis's *filter model*.

Newcomb (1943) studied students at an American college with a liberal tradition among teaching staff and senior students. Many students coming from conservative backgrounds adopted liberal attitudes in order to gain the liking and acceptance of their classmates. Griffitt and Veitch (1974) paid 13 males to spend ten days in a fall-out shelter. Those with similar attitudes and opinions liked each other most by the end of the study, particularly if they agreed on highly salient issues.

Ask Yourself

- What is it about similarity that makes it an influence on attraction?
- Why should we prefer people who (we believe) are like us?

According to Fiske (2004), if someone resembles prior experience or the self, then at least we have the illusion of knowing 'what makes them tick'. In this respect, familiarity and similarity influence attraction in comparable ways. We mostly seek out others who make us feel good about ourselves:

> *... People who resemble us or agree with us also reassure us. People who validate us and like us presumably won't do us any harm ...*
> *(Fiske, 2004)*

According to the *similarity-attraction principle,* if familiarity underlies attraction, and if the most familiar people are those who are like us, then people like us are attractive. This stems in part from *consistency theories* of attitude change (see Chapter 24); the most relevant here is Heider's (1958) *balance theory*. We prefer and infer affective, cognitive and behavioural consistency – in ourselves and others: we like to agree with our friends and to befriend those who agree with us. This describes *interpersonal balance*, 'a harmonious state, one in which the entities comprising the situation and the feelings about them fit together without stress' (Heider, 1958). (See 'Meet the Researcher', pp. 472–3.)

Physical attractiveness

While it often takes time to find out about other people's attitudes and values, their physical attractiveness is immediately apparent. Physical attractiveness has been studied as an influence on attraction in its own right, as well as one aspect of similarity.

The attractiveness stereotype

As we saw in Chapter 22, we tend to perceive attractive-looking people as also having more attractive personalities (the *attractiveness stereotype*). Dion *et al.* (1972) found that photographs of attractive people, compared with unattractive people, were consistently credited with more desirable qualities – sexually warm and responsive, kind, strong, outgoing, nurturant, sensitive, interesting, poised, sociable, exciting dates, better character, happily married, socially and professionally successful and enjoying more fulfilling lives. So, 'what is beautiful is socially good' (Fiske, 2004).

The power of the physical attractiveness stereotype is demonstrated in a classic study by Snyder *et al.* (1977).

Key Study 28.2

The self-fulfilling nature of the attractiveness stereotype (Snyder *et al.*, 1977)

- Male undergraduates received photographs of women before a getting-acquainted telephone conversation. The photographs, independently rated as either quite attractive or quite unattractive, didn't depict their actual partners, who were unaware of the experimental manipulation.
- Before the telephone conversation, the men rated the supposedly attractive partner as more sociable, poised, humorous and adept.
- During the conversation, independent judges rated these men as more sociable, sexually warm, outgoing, interesting, independent, bold, humorous and adept.
- In response, their (actual) partners, who'd been randomly allocated to the 'attractive' or 'unattractive' conditions, behaved in similar ways.
- So, the men's expectations about their partners, based on the photographs, influenced the women's behaviour in line with those expectations (a *self-fulfilling prophecy*).

However, Dermer and Thiel (1975) found that extremely attractive women were judged (by female participants) to be egotistic, vain, materialistic, snobbish and less likely to be successfully married. Similarly, attractive people are judged as more snobbish, less modest and less faithful (Singh, 2004). This suggests that it's not always to our advantage to be seen as highly attractive, and one situation where this may apply is where a criminal's good looks played a part in the crime.

Dion and Dion (1995) observe that stereotyping based on facial attractiveness appears at least as early as six years old. They also suggest that this might be linked to the *just world hypothesis,* such that there's a positive bias towards 'winners', equivalent to 'blaming the victim' (see Chapter 23). However, the attractiveness stereotype applies predominantly to *female* faces (Smolak, 2012).

Is the attractiveness stereotype culturally relative?

Like most attractiveness research, studies of the attractiveness stereotype are largely American, the prime example of an individualist culture. Although a physical attractiveness stereotype can be found in some collectivist cultures (such as Korea and Taiwan), the content differs. For example, in Korea attractive people aren't seen as more powerful but as showing more concern for others and more integrity. In other words, 'the beautiful receive the benefits of social status, embodying that culture's ideal values' (Fiske, 2004).

Different cultures have different criteria concerning physical beauty. For example, chipped teeth, body scars, artificially elongated heads and bound feet have all been regarded as beautiful, and in western culture, definitions of beauty change over time, as in the 'ideal' figure for women (see Chapter 44.)

Figure 28.8 Joan Van Ark, former Dallas actress, is known for having had plastic surgery.

Figure 28.9 Ideas about what constitutes female beauty have changed over the centuries

MEET THE RESEARCHER

Steve Duck

Interpersonal relationships

Relationships run right through everyday life, and for this reason everyone is interested in how relationships work and how to make them work better. Paradoxically, study of relationships is difficult because taken-for-granted assumptions make it hard to stand back and think about how they work.

Research difficulties

One difficulty in relationship research is the direction of causality (what causes what). Friends may tend to be similar to one another in personality, but that is merely correlational data and, scientifically, does not demonstrate whether friends become more similar during acquaintance or they become friends in the first place because of similarity in personalities.

The 'bogus stranger paradigm'

Donn Byrne (1971) revised an ingenious strategy – originally used by Smith (1957) – to test the hypothesis that similarity in attitudes caused people to be more attracted to one another, rather than the other way about (attraction causes similarity). The technique had a participant fill out a questionnaire and then a few minutes later read another questionnaire allegedly filled out by a stranger in a different room, whom the participant would eventually meet. In fact this 'other participant' did not exist (i.e. was bogus) and the experimenter had, in the time that it took to apparently collect the other questionnaire from the stranger, created a questionnaire filled out to a precise percentage of similarity to the one filled out by the original participant (for example, 10 per cent similar, 20 per cent similar, 50 per cent similar). This controlling of the degree of similarity manipulates the independent variable accurately and makes it possible to observe the degree to which the similarity affects liking, because right after reading the stranger's questionnaire the participant was asked to say how much they liked the stranger. By this method, which became known as the 'bogus stranger paradigm', Byrne was able to state the effect of the degrees of similarity on the degrees of liking. He was therefore, for the first time from a scientific perspective, able to say which came first – the similarity or the liking. Similarity exactly predicted the degree of liking. Although many people were critical of the style of experiment as unrealistic and unrepresentative of real-life experience, it was a notable step in determining the importance of similarity in subsequent friendship.

Meantime, other early research was concerned with 'self-disclosure', a term created by Sidney Jourard (1971) to refer to the extent to which someone reveals inner thoughts/personal secrets. Jourard, a Clinical Psychologist, believed that a healthy person would show high self-disclosure. Relationship researchers in turn assumed that self-disclosure was a significant process in relationship development, with greater disclosure leading to greater

intimacy. It was also demonstrated that there are norms about self-disclosure: the more self-disclosure one person gives to another, the more it is expected in return. More recent research suggests a subtle twist – that women are expected to self-disclose more than men.

Relating research to real life

Two questions arising from these studies are: the extent to which self-disclosure outside of lab experiments is relevant to development of relationships; and whether experimental studies accurately reflect the *processes* that happen in everyday common experience. Along with other kinds of variables that have been investigated experimentally, I find it hard to believe that these methods tell us anything about real life, which is a blooming buzzing confusion of conversation. From this conversation people are, of course, able to deduce the degrees of similarity that exist between them, but it is a process that takes work and effort – and nobody ever gives us their attitude scales to read, so we cannot even be sure that we have guessed right about someone else's personality.

It is important to recognise that everyday-life relationships are conducted through words and symbols. The self-disclosure that people do with one another displays subtle landscapes of their mental structure, and any particular direct reference to attitudes and beliefs can help us to understand more clearly how they function and think. In a series of studies, Duck *et al.* (1991) measured individual reports on the amount and style of talk as people engaged in everyday-life communication, using a measure that became known as the Iowa Communication Record. Among other things, they were able to establish that more conflict happens on a Wednesday, and that the *quality of communication* is able to distinguish friends from distant acquaintances and strangers.

Technology and interpersonal relationships

I have recently taken a more adventurous approach to the whole of social life (Duck and McMahan, 2010) and have interpreted all of everyday experience in terms of relationships that exist between the parties involved. For example, this approach recognises the importance of 'new technology' as in fact *relational* technology. It also explains such phenomena as the decisions taken in groups in terms of the relationships that exist between the members of the group. Even the uses and influence of mass media can be explained by the relationships that exist between individuals in the society: mass communication has its effects mediated by everyday communication between people who know one another.

New approaches to relationships

Finally, I've gone further in Duck (2010) and proposed an entirely new approach to relationships as based on knowledge and shared understanding rather than emotion. I point out that personality can be reinterpreted as a person's understanding of the world based on the reactions of others from an early point in life. Physical sex affects each person's knowledge of the way in which the world is to be understood (and the relationships that may be had between people). Also, the knowledge shared between members of the society is what is responsible for the significance of exchange of gifts, love tokens, tie-signs and many other aspects of relationships previously explained by Psychologists in terms of similarity of attitudes. By transforming Byrne's approach towards attitudes into one that deals with *knowledge* and *shared understanding*, this new look at relationships undermines many comfortable myths that most of us have previously been happy to live with.

Professor Steve Duck was the Founder and first Editor of the *Journal of Social and Personal Relationships* and has written or edited 50 books on relationships. He was recently appointed a Collegiate Administrative Fellow in the College of Liberal Arts and Sciences, University of Iowa.

The evolutionary approach: Sex differences and sexual selection – what do males and females find attractive?

Evidence suggests that humans are a *mutually* sexually-selected species, that is, both males and females have evolved preferences for certain behavioural and/or anatomical features in the opposite sex. According to Ridley (1993):

> *People are attracted to people of high reproductive and genetic potential – the healthy, the fit and the powerful …*

So, how exactly do we choose our mates?

While the stage theories of Kerkhoff and Davis and Murstein put physical (sexual) attractiveness into a social and also a temporal (time-related) context, Evolutionary Psychologists try to explain mate choice in terms of 'built-in' preferences that have developed through the course of human evolution.

Ask Yourself

- Think of someone you find extremely facially attractive; try to specify what it is about their face that you like.

The importance of facial symmetry

Although any two individuals can vary widely in what they consider facially attractive, these differences actually vary around an underlying norm, which is surprisingly consistent across cultures (Berry, 2000; Langlois and Roggman, 1990). Langlois *et al.* (1987) found that when babies under one year are shown faces that adults consider attractive or unattractive, they spend longer looking at the former (implying that they prefer them: see Chapter 16). Clearly, they're too young to have learned cultural standards of beauty.

Langlois and Roggman (1990) took photographs of faces with standard pose, expression and lighting, and then scanned them into a computer. Each image was then divided into a very large number of tiny squares (or *pixels*), and the brightness of corresponding pixels in different same-sex faces were *averaged* to produce *computer-composite images* (see Figure 28.10). When people were asked to judge the attractiveness of these composite faces (made from four, eight, 16, or 32 faces), they rated them as increasingly attractive the more faces that went into each image. This applied to both male and female faces.

The greater the number of faces making up a composite image, the more the peculiarities of particular faces become ironed out – that is, the more *symmetrical* they become. Most faces are (to varying degrees) asymmetrical around the vertical midline, and even those that are highly asymmetrical can be made more attractive. Hence, as Bruce and Young (1998) observe, moving a facial image closer to the average increases its perceived attractiveness.

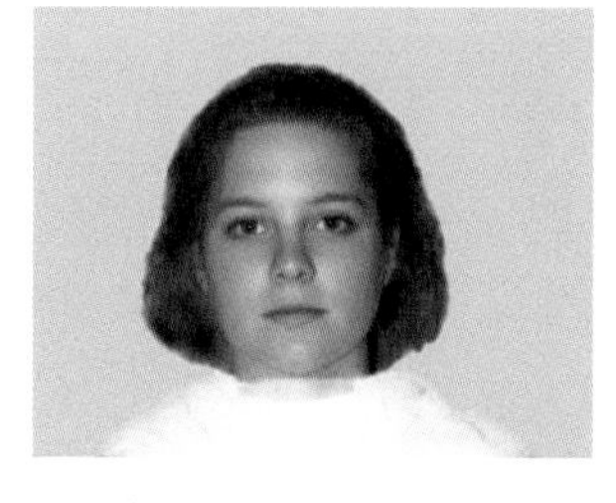

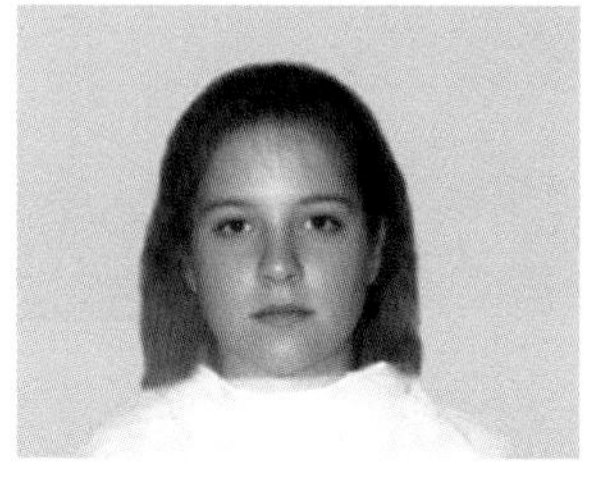

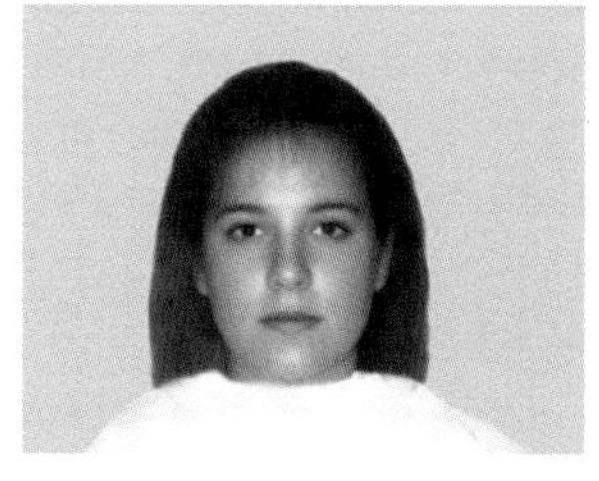
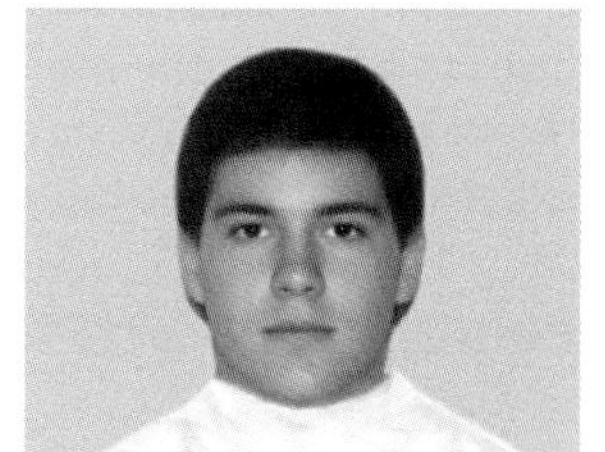
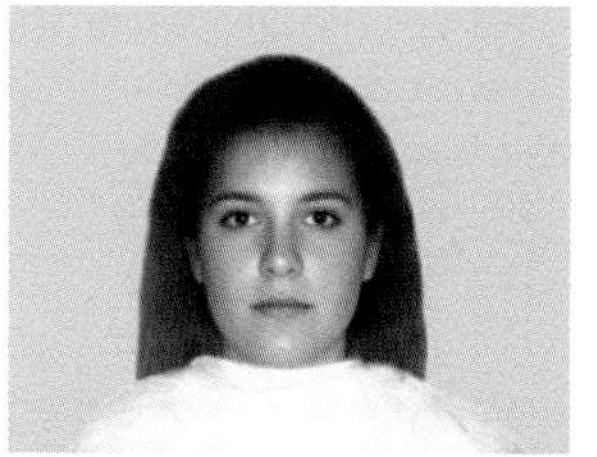

Figure 28.10 Computer-composite faces. The columns show composite sets created from female faces (left) or from male faces (right). From top to bottom, rows show composites created by averaging across 4, 8, 16 and 32 faces (from Bruce and Young, 1998)

Studies have shown men prefer photographs of women with symmetrical faces – and vice versa (Cartwright, 2000). It seems likely that symmetry (which shows a tendency to be inherited) equates with *reproductive fitness* (the capacity to reproduce one's genetic material).

Is attractiveness really no more than averageness?

This seems unlikely. For example, if we describe someone as 'average looking', we usually mean that s/he is neither 'good-looking' nor 'ugly', and movie stars and sex symbols *aren't* obviously average (otherwise most of us would be sex symbols!).

According to Perret *et al.* (1994), the average derived from highly attractive faces is consistently preferred to the average of the entire set of photographs they were taken from. This wouldn't happen if 'attractive' equalled 'average'. When the difference between the average shape of attractive faces and the average shape of the entire set was increased, perceived attractiveness of the former also increased. But the effect of this was to make the resulting faces *more different* from the average. Perret *et al.* found exactly the same pattern of results for European and Japanese faces, regardless of whether they were judged by European or Japanese people.

Body symmetry and waist-to-hip ratio (WHR)

Facial symmetry is also the best predictor of *body symmetry*. Research indicates that women with symmetrical male partners have the most orgasms, and women with symmetrical breasts are more fertile than more asymmetrically-breasted women (Cartwright, 2000). Males and females with near-perfect body symmetry report two to three times as many sexual partners as those with the most asymmetrical bodies. But it may not be symmetry itself that is directly attractive: other characteristics that are correlated with body symmetry, such as being more dominant, or having higher self-esteem, might be crucial.

Another physical characteristic shown to be a universally major determinant of attractiveness concerns *body shape*. In a series of studies conducted in the early 1990s, Singh (e.g. 1993) identified *waist-to-hip ratio* (WHR) as reliably conveying information about female mate value. WHR refers to fat distribution (regulated by sex hormones) that sculpts typical male-female body shape differences: after puberty, females have greater amounts of body fat deposited in the lower part of the body, such that their WHR is greater than men's, giving them their 'curves' or hour-glass figure.

Singh (1993) used archival data from the previous 50 years to examine the WHR of beauty contest winners and *Playboy* centrefolds. He found that a small waist set against full hips was a consistent feature of female attractiveness, while bust-line, overall body weight and physique varied over the years. He concluded that a larger WHR was associated with better health status and greater reproductive capacity (i.e. fertility). The optimum WHR is 0.7, which happens to correspond closely to the measurements of supermodels like Anna Nicole Smith (0.69), Kate Moss (0.66) and Cindy Crawford (0.69) (Swami and Furnham, 2006). (For males the ideal is more like 0.85–0.9.)

This fits in perfectly with Darwinian theories of human mate selection, which claim that both men and women select partners who enable them to enhance reproductive success, thus ensuring the survival of their genes into the next generation.

Although *Playboy* centrefolds have shown a 20 per cent decline in plumpness over the years (see Chapter 44), they've shown a consistent WHR of 0.7.

Figure 28.11 As well as her facial beauty, 1960s model Twiggy's WHR was (surprisingly) an attractive 0.733

However, cross-cultural replications haven't generally supported the claim that there's a universal preference for a low WHR (such as 0.7). Singh himself argued that the WHR acts as an initial 'filter' (screening out those who are unhealthy or have low reproductive capacity), after which the face and/or *body weight* (which may vary between cultures) are used in final mate selection (Swami and Furnham, 2006).

Is physical attractiveness more important to men?

A very general example of *sexual dimorphism* (the different characteristics of females and males of the same species) is that men use physical attractiveness as an indicator of reproductive fitness to a much greater extent than women do. This was demonstrated in a much-cited study by Buss (1989) of 37 cultures (including Nigeria, South Africa, Japan Estonia, Zambia, Columbia, Poland, Germany, Spain, France, China, Palestinian Arabs, Italy and the Netherlands) involving over 10,000 people. Men seem to give a universally higher priority to 'good looks' in their female partners, while the situation is reversed when it comes to 'good financial prospect' and 'good earning capacity'. According to Buss, these sex differences 'appear to be deeply rooted in the evolutionary history of our species'. Why should they have evolved?

Men value female partners in terms of *fecundity*, that is, the ability to produce and care for children.

Men often have to rely on a woman's physical appearance in order to estimate her age and health, with younger, healthier women being perceived as more attractive ('fitter'). The preference for the large eyes and lips, etc. (see above) is also related to the need to estimate a woman's age and hence her reproductive fitness.

Women's reproductive success is less dependent on finding fertile males, for whom age is a much less reliable indicator of fertility. Also, male fertility cannot be assessed as accurately from their physical appearance as can females' (Buss, 1995). Consequently, women's mate selection depends on their need for a provider to take care of them during pregnancy and nursing: men seen as powerful and controlling resources that contribute to the mother and child's welfare will be seen as especially attractive. However, although physical attractiveness may be less important to females, they tend to be much choosier in selecting a mate since they have greater *investment* in their offspring (Buss and Malamuth, 1996).

Critical Discussion 28.1

The tricky case of homosexuality

How can Evolutionary Psychology (in particular, *sexual selection theory*) account for same-sex romantic relationship? They seem to have existed in most cultures throughout recorded history regardless of prevailing attitudes towards homosexuality and bisexuality. Both evolutionary accounts of mating and research into adult romantic relationships in terms of attachment theory (including Bowlby's evolutionary theory of attachment: see text above and Chapter 32) have been heavily biased towards heterosexual relationships.

For Bowlby, the sexual behavioural system of homosexuals isn't serving its functional goal of reproduction. But at the same time he never denied that legitimate, psychologically healthy same-sex romantic attachments exist. Similarly, Ainsworth (1985) maintained that same-sex romantic attachments are likely to function in the same way as opposite-sex attachments: the main difference between them is that only the latter are socially acceptable.

Evolutionary theorists have assumed that there's a *genetic* component to homosexuality and bisexuality; further, 'gay genes' offer a direct reproductive advantage (such as homosexuals possessing traits such as charm, empathy and intelligence that are attractive to females: McKnight, 1997). Alternatively, one version of the *kin-selective altruism hypothesis* claims that males with gay genes instinctively feel at a reproductive disadvantage and decide to divert their energies into supporting the reproductive fitness of close relatives (e.g. Wilson, 1975).

However, the great variability in sexual behaviour among lesbian, gay and bisexual (LGB) individuals, as well as recent developments in artificial insemination and family structures, mean that significant numbers of LGB people do have children (Patterson, 1995; Roughgarden, 2004). Thus, same-sex romantic relationships may also increase individuals' ability to provide for their children, as appears to be the case for opposite-sex couples (Weiss, 1982: see Chapter 32). According to Roughgarden (2004), homosexuality is much too common for it to be considered a genetic aberration.

Arguably, the most viable explanation of same-sex relationships derives from the model proposed by Shaver *et al.* (1996) (see text above, p. 467), which distinguishes between the evolved social-behavioural systems of *attachment, caregiving* and *sexuality.* Although romantic adult attachments typically integrate all three systems, they in fact have distinct origins, functions and underpinnings. Research into the brain substrates of both human and non-human sexuality and pair-bonding has confirmed this view (e.g. Bartels and Zeki, 2000, in Diamond, 2006).

This view of romantic love and sexual desire as fundamentally distinct has profound implications for our understanding of the nature and development of same-sex relationships. Specifically, if love and desire are based in independent systems, then one's *sexual orientation* needn't correspond with experiences of *romantic attachment* to same-sex or opposite-sex partners.

> *This, of course, runs directly counter to the implicit presumption among both scientists and laypeople that heterosexual individuals fall in love only with other-sex partners and lesbian and gay individuals fall in love only with same-sex partners. (Diamond, 2006)*

Diamond (2006) reports on a study of 79 women (aged 18–23), most describing themselves as either lesbian or bisexual. One important finding was that the experience of being attracted to 'the person and not the gender' is appreciably distinct from that of needing an emotional bond with another person in order to be physically attracted to them. Unsurprisingly, non-gendered attraction was strongly associated with bisexuality.

Ask Yourself

- How might these arguments be used to explain the growing number of *asexual* individuals? According to Westphal (2004), the number of asexual people is close to the number of homosexual people.

The matching hypothesis

According to *social exchange theory* (e.g. Thibaut and Kelley, 1959: see below), people are more likely to become romantically involved if they're fairly closely matched in their ability to reward one another. Ideally, we'd all have the 'perfect partner' because, the theory says, we're all selfish. But since this is impossible, we try to find a compromise solution. The best general bargain that can be struck is a *value-match,* a subjective belief that our partner is the most rewarding we could realistically hope to find.

Several studies have tested the matching hypothesis (MH) (Walster *et al.*, 1966; Dion and Berscheid, 1974; Berscheid *et al.,* 1971; Silverman, 1971; Murstein, 1972; Berscheid and Walster, 1974). These studies generally show that people rated as being of high, low or average attractiveness tend to choose partners of a corresponding level of attractiveness. Indeed, the matching phenomenon of physical attraction between marriage partners is stable within and across generations (Price and Vandenberg, 1979).

The findings from the various MH studies imply that the kind of partner we'd be satisfied with is one we feel won't reject us, rather than one we positively desire. Brown (1986), however, maintains that we learn to adjust our expectations of rewards in line with what we believe we have to offer others.

An evaluation of attraction research

According to Duck (1999), the 'magnetic metaphor' of attraction implies that people are unwittingly, and almost against their will, pulled towards one another's inherent, pre-existing characteristics. This caricatures real relationships as the 'unthinking domain of reactive magnetism'.

More recent research has considered the *dynamics* of relationships (how they develop and unfold over time), and how relationships are actually conducted in real life. One feature of 'real' relationships is their inherent tensions, such as the need to balance our desire for disclosure and openness, connectedness and interdependence on the one hand, and the desire for autonomy and independence, privacy and the right to retain secrets on the other. Not surprisingly, this shift has involved fewer controlled laboratory studies, and more exploration of life as it's lived 'out there' (Duck, 1999). This now includes such diverse research areas as homosexual and electronic relationships (see above).

WHAT KEEPS PEOPLE TOGETHER?

Ask Yourself

- What do all the important relationships in your life have in common?

You may say something to the effect that they provide you with security, happiness, contentment, fun and so on, and (if you're honest) that they can also be complex, demanding and, at times, even painful. If all relationships involve both positive and negative, desirable and undesirable aspects, what determines our continued involvement in them?

Social exchange theory (SET)

Social exchange theory (SET) provides a general framework for analysing all kinds of relationship, both intimate and non-intimate, and is really an extension of reward theory (see above).

According to Homans (1974), we view our feelings for others in terms of *profits* (the amount of reward obtained from a relationship minus the cost). The greater the reward and lower the cost, the greater the profit and hence the attraction. Blau (1964) argues that interactions are 'expensive': they take time, energy and commitment, and may involve unpleasant emotions and experiences. Because of this, what we get out of a relationship must be more than what we put in.

Similarly, Berscheid and Walster (1978) argue that in any social interaction there's an exchange of rewards (such as affection, information and status), and that the degree of attraction or liking will reflect how people evaluate the rewards they receive relative to those they give.

Ask Yourself

- Is it appropriate to think of relationships in this economic, capitalistic, way?
- Are relationships really like that?

An evaluation of SET

- SET sees people as fundamentally selfish and human relationships as based primarily on self-interest. But this is a *metaphor* for human relationships, and it shouldn't be taken too literally. However, although we like to believe that the joy of giving is as important as the desire to receive, we have to admit that our attitudes toward other people are determined to a large extent by our assessments of the rewards they hold for us (Rubin, 1973).
- Equally, though, Rubin believes that SET doesn't provide an adequate, complete account:

Human beings are sometimes altruistic in the fullest sense of the word. They make sacrifices for the sake of others without any consideration of the rewards they will obtain from them in return ...

- Altruism is most often and most clearly seen in close interpersonal relationships (see Chapter 30).
- Some Psychologists make the distinction between 'true' love and friendship, which are altruistic, and less admirable forms which are based on considerations of exchange (Brown, 1986). Fromm (1962) defines true love as giving, as opposed to the false love of the 'marketing character' which depends upon expecting to have the favours returned. Support for this distinction comes from studies by Clark and Mills (1979, 1993),who identified two kinds of intimate relationship:
  (a) The *communal couple*, in which each partner gives out of concern for the other
  (b) The *exchange couple,* in which each keeps mental records of who's 'ahead' and who's 'behind'.
- SET implies that all relationships are of the exchange variety. Exchange might describe some kinds of relationship, such as impersonal friendships and relationships between business associates, but in communal relationships, people don't track outcomes (who did what for whom: Clark, 1984). Instead, they track each other's needs, and one partner may need more than the other, at different times, or even throughout the relationship (Clark *et al.,* 1986). Fiske (2004) suggests that thinking of family relationships as communal explains why parents don't normally 'charge' their children for their upbringing. According to Clark and Grote (1998), communal relationships operate by different norms from exchange relationships.
- One of those norms is *reciprocity*, which involves the repayment of specific benefits ('you scratch my back and I'll scratch yours': see Chapter 27). Perhaps contrary to what most people would expect, reciprocity is particularly strong in most casual relationships, but weaker in more intimate communal relationships (Clark and Mills, 1993). Indeed, 'exchange' implies that people reciprocate benefit for benefit, resulting in an equivalence of outcomes (Fiske, 2004). The communal couple's responsiveness to each other's needs represents a broader type of reciprocity. In some form, reciprocity appears to be a fundamental aspect of human social exchanges (Dovidio and Penner, 2004), evident in all known cultures (Moghaddam *et al.*, 1993).
- Clearly, SET is a greatly oversimplified account of human relationships and cannot accommodate their rich diversity and complexity. At best, it may describe a certain type of superficial and probably short-term relationship.

RELATIONSHIP BREAKDOWN and DISSOLUTION

Ask Yourself

- Think of your most unsuccessful relationship(s).
- Why did it/they go wrong?
- Was it to do with you as individuals, or 'circumstances', or a mixture of the two?

Why do relationships go wrong?

According to Duck (2001), there's an almost infinite number of reasons why relationships break up. But they can be put into three broad categories:

1. *Pre-existing doom*: incompatibility and failure are almost predestined (for example, 'Schoolgirl, 17, marries her 50-year-old teacher, who's already a grandfather')
2. *Mechanical failure*: two suitable people of goodwill and good nature nevertheless find they cannot live together (the most common cause)
3. *Sudden death*: the discovery of a betrayal or infidelity can lead to the immediate termination of a romantic relationship (see below).

Duck believes that the 'official' reasons given to others (including the partner) to justify the break-up are far more interesting psychologically than the real reasons. The psychology of break-up involves a whole layer of individual psychological processes, group processes, cultural rules and self-presentation. But this applies mainly to romantic relationships, rather than friendships. When you fall out with a friend, there's usually no formal or public 'announcement': friendships aren't *exclusive* in the way that most sexual relationships are (it's 'normal' to have several friends at once, but not several partners!). As Duck says:

... Truly committed romantic relationships necessarily involve the foregoing of other romantic relationships and commitment to only one partner ('forsaking all others', as it says in the marriage ceremony) ...

Marital unhappiness and divorce

Duck (1988, 1992) has identified several factors that make it more likely that a marriage will be unhappy and/or end in divorce. Marriages that involve the following tend to be more unstable:

- Partners who are *younger than average*. This can be understood by reference to Erikson's concept of *intimacy* (see Chapter 38). Such marriages often involve early parenthood; the young couple has little time to adjust to the new responsibilities of marriage before financial and housing problems are added with the arrival of a baby (Kellmer Pringle, 1986).

- Couples from lower socio-economic groups and educational levels. These are also the couples that tend to have their children very early in marriage.
- Partners from different demographic backgrounds (race, religion and so on) (see Kerckhoff and Davis's filter model).
- People who've experienced parental divorce as children, or who've had a greater number of sexual partners than average before marriage.

While these factors are important, only a proportion of marriages involving such couples actually end in divorce. Conversely, many divorces will involve couples who don't fit any of these descriptions. So what other factors may be involved?

According to Brehm (1992), there are two broad types of cause: *structural* (gender, duration of the relationship, the presence of children and role strain created by competing demands of work and family) and *conflict resolution*.

Gender differences

In general, women report more problems, and there's some evidence that the degree of female dissatisfaction is a better predictor than male unhappiness of whether the relationship will end (perhaps because women are more sensitive to relationship problems than men). Alternatively, men and women may come into relationships with different hopes and expectations, with men's generally being fulfilled to a greater extent than women's.

Consistent with this possibility is evidence of gender differences in the specific type of problems that are reported. For example, divorcing men and women are equally likely to cite communication problems as a cause of their splitting up. But women stress basic unhappiness and incompatibility more than men do.

Past research has indicated that, while men are more likely to be jealous of sexual indiscretions, for women it's emotional infidelity that matters. These findings have been explained in terms of evolutionary theory (see above), but Levy and Kelly (2010) offer an explanation in terms of attachment theory. Both men and women with a dismissing (or avoidant) insecure attachment were the most likely to report being jealous of sexual infidelity; men are more likely to have such an attachment style. (See Chapter 32.)

Men also seem particularly upset by 'sexual withholding' by a female partner, while women are distressed by a male partner's sexual aggression. This is consistent with the finding that men tend to fall in love more easily than women (Baumeister and Bratslavsky, 1999), which is contrary to the popular myth about women demanding commitment and men fighting shy of it. Men also seem to respond more quickly to any intimacy changes (positive and negative), at both earlier and later stages of a relationship (Fiske, 2004).

BOX 28.2 The dark side of love: when intimacy becomes violent (Finkel and Duffy, 2013)

- Tina Turner endured what Johnson (2008) calls *intimate terrorism* at the hands of husband and musical partner, Ike.
- Less widely recognised – but actually more common – is *situational couple violence* (SCV), which is mutual and emerges from relationship conflict that gets out of hand. For example, the late Amy Winehouse and Blake Fielder-Civil reportedly shared an intense love; their passion intermittently boiled over into mutual violence.
- Could SCV be akin to a mistake (like having unprotected sex), i.e. an impulse we wish we'd suppressed? Do people in intimate relationships often experience aggressive urges towards their partner, which are usually kept in check?
- Finkel and Duffy (2013) found that while half the undergraduate students they questioned had been tempted to act violently, only 21 per cent had succumbed.
- Other research with married couples mirrored these findings (25 and 9 per cent, respectively). These figures applied equally to men and women.
- Finkel *et al.* (2013) asked 120 married couples (married, on average, 11 years) to write about the most significant marital conflict they'd experienced in the previous four months. They repeated this exercise twice within one year. They also reported on their overall satisfaction with their marriage. Although marital quality declined during the first year, it only declined during the second year for those who hadn't been given an extra task: describing the conflict from the perspective of a neutral third party. This exercise seemed to reduce their anger and distress (it was repeated every four months).

Duration of relationships and the passage of time

The longer partners have known each other before marriage, the more likely they are to be satisfied in the marriage, and the less likely they are to divorce. However, couples who've cohabited before marriage report fewer barriers to ending the marriage, and the longer a relationship lasts, the more people blame their partners for negative events.

According to Pineo's (1961) *linear model* (see Figure 28.12) there's an inevitable fading of the romantic 'high' of courtship before marriage. Also, people marry because they've achieved a 'good fit' with their partner, so any changes that occur in either partner will reduce their compatibility. For example, if one partner becomes more self-confident (ironically, through the support gained from the relationship), there may be increased conflict between two 'equals' competing for superiority.

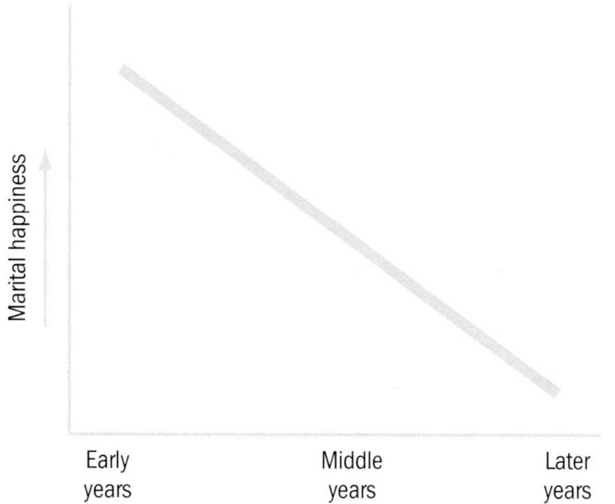

Figure 28.12 A linear life-cycle (based on Brehm, 1992)

Burr's (1970) *curvilinear model* (see Figure 28.13) proposes that marital happiness is greatest in the earliest years. Marital satisfaction declines as children are born and grow up, then increases again as they mature and leave home.

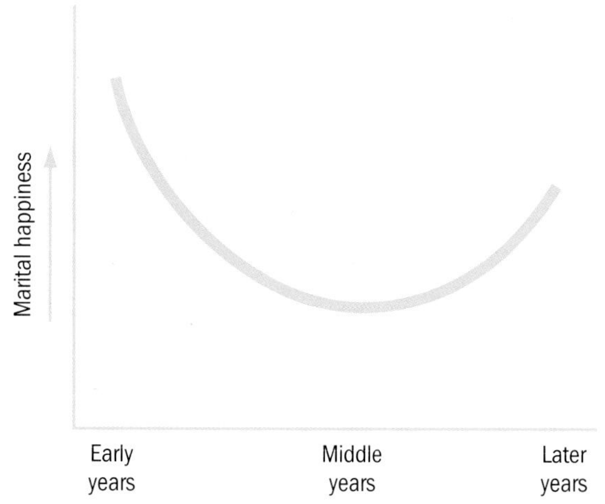

Figure 28.13 A curvilinear life cycle (based on Brehm, 1992)

While it's generally agreed that there's a decline in satisfaction during the early years, whether there's an actual increase or just a levelling off after that remains a matter of debate. Gilford and Bengtson (1979) argue that it's an oversimplification to talk about 'marital satisfaction'. Instead, we should look at two life cycles: the pattern of positive rewards, and the pattern of negative costs. The early years are associated with very high rewards and very high costs, while in the middle years there's a decline in both. In the later years, costs continue to decline, but there's an increase in rewards.

Conflict resolution

According to Duck (1988), some kind and degree of conflict is inevitable in all relationships. But the process of resolving conflicts can often be positive, promoting relationship growth (Wood and Duck, 1995). The important question, therefore, isn't whether there's conflict, but *how* it's handled. However, recurring conflicts may indicate an inability to resolve the underlying source; the partners may come to doubt each other as reasonable persons, leading to a 'digging in of the heels', a disaffection with each other and, ultimately, a 'strong falling out' (Berry and Willingham, 1997).

Some degree of overt conflict ('getting it out in the open') can improve a relationship. According to Bradbury and Fincham (1990), happy and unhappy couples resolve conflict in typically different ways, which can be understood as different *attributional patterns* (see Chapter 23). Happy couples use a *relationship-enhancing pattern*, while unhappy couples use a *distress-maintaining* (or *conflict-promoting*) *pattern* see Figure 28.14).

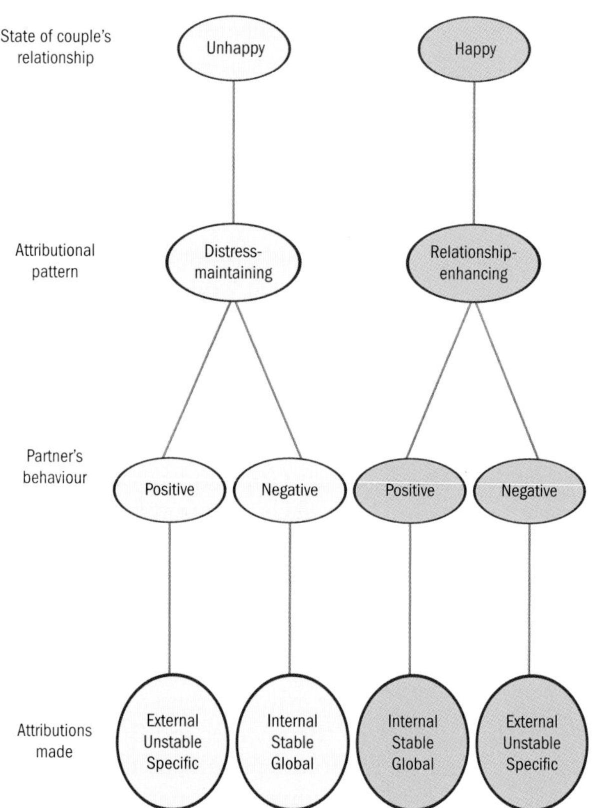

Figure 28.14 Attributions made by happy and unhappy couples

According to Fincham (2004), the evidence for an association between attribution and marital satisfaction is overwhelming, making it possibly the most robust, replicable phenomenon in the study of marriage. There's also increasing evidence that the causal link between attributions and marital satisfaction is *bidirectional* (they influence each other) (Fincham, 2004). However, couples' changing attributions over time predict their marital satisfaction more than satisfaction predicts attributions (Karney and Bradbury, 2000).

Rule-breaking and deception

Ask Yourself

- What's the worst thing that a friend or partner could do as far as your relationship is concerned?
- Is there anything that, in principle, you wouldn't tolerate?

Argyle and Henderson (1984) and Argyle *et al.* (1985) identified a number of rules thought to apply to all or most relationships, such as 'Should respect the other's privacy', 'Should not discuss what is said in confidence', 'Should be emotionally supportive'. There are additional rules for particular types of relationship. Relationships fall into clusters (such as (i) spouse, siblings, close friends; (ii) doctor, teacher, boss), with similar rules applying within a cluster.

Trust probably represents the most important rule that shouldn't be broken. Although what counts as deception will depend on the nature of the relationship, if you cannot trust your friend or partner, the relationship is almost certainly doomed.

Relationship dissolution as a process

Duck's model

Duck's (1982) model comprises four phases, each of which is initiated when a *threshold* is broken (see Table 28.2). The ending of a romantic relationship indicates that the two people are now legitimately available as partners for other relationships. This requires them to create a story for the end of the relationship that leaves them in a favourable light as potential partners. Romantic relationships are, therefore, typically ended publicly in a way that announces the ex-partner's freedom from the expectations of exclusive commitment.

'Dressing the grave' involves 'erecting a tablet' that provides a credible, socially acceptable account of the life and death of the relationship. While helping to save face, it also serves to keep alive some memories and to 'justify' the original commitment to the ex-partner. As Duck (1988) puts it:

Table 28.2 A sketch of the main phases of dissolving personal relationships (based on Duck, 1982, from Duck, 1988)

Breakdown–dissatisfaction with relationship

Threshold: 'I can't stand this anymore' 

INTRAPSYCHIC PHASE

- Personal focus on partner's behaviour
- Assess adequacy of partner's role performance
- Depict and evaluate negative aspects of being in the relationship
- Consider costs of withdrawal
- Assess positive aspects of alternative relationships
- Face 'express/repress dilemma'

Threshold: 'I'd be justified in withdrawing' 

DYADIC PHASE

- Face 'confrontation/avoidance dilemma'
- Confront partner
- Negotiate in 'our relationship talks'
- Attempt repair and reconciliation?
- Assess joint costs of withdrawal or reduced intimacy

Threshold: 'I mean it' 

SOCIAL PHASE

- Negotiate post-dissolution state with partner
- Initiate gossip/discussion in social network
- Create publicly negotiable face-saving/blame-placing stories and accounts
- Consider and face up to implied social network effect, if any
- Call in intervention team

Threshold: 'It's now inevitable' 

GRAVE-DRESSING PHASE

- 'Getting over' activity
- Retrospective; reformative post-mortem attribution
- Public distribution of own version of break-up story

> … Such stories are an integral and important part of the psychology of ending relationships … By helping the person to get over the break-up they are immensely significant in preparing the person for future relationships as well as helping them out of old ones.

Duck (2001) identifies a number of classic formats for a break-up story (such as 'X suddenly changed and I had to get out';'X betrayed me';'We grew apart'). The crucial ingredients of such stories are those that show the speaker:

- is open to relationships but doesn't enter them thoughtlessly
- is aware of others' deficiencies but isn't overly critical
- is willing to work to improve a relationship or take decisive action when partners turn nasty or break the rules of relating
- is rational and sensible, and brings closure to relationships only after trauma, hard work or on reasonable grounds after real effort to make things work.

Rollie and Duck's (2005) modification of the 1982 model emphasises the complexity and uncertainty of the dissolution process, including the psychological need to prepare oneself for the next step rather than to be preoccupied with what's going on now (Duck, 2005).

CONCLUSIONS: WHAT HAPPENS AFTER DIVORCE?

One growing area of research interest is 'postmarital' and 'remarital' relationships and family reorganisation after divorce. The increasing incidence of divorce is making *blended families* the norm. Indeed, there's a shift in ideology, from viewing divorce as pathology to viewing it as an institution (Duck, 1999). This enables researchers to attend to a much wider range of issues, such as 'getting over' and prevention, and as much to the processes of entering new relationships as to those to do with leaving the old ones (Masheter, 1997).

According to Berscheid and Ammazzalorso (2004):

> … It is one of the saddest facts of the human condition that even the closest and happiest of relationships end – if not by some circumstance of fate that causes separation, then by the death of one of the partners …

The loss, through death, of a loved one is often accompanied by the experience of the strongest negative emotions of which human beings are capable. (See Chapter 39.)

Chapter Summary

- The **need for affiliation** represents a precondition for attraction, and can be related to the need for **social comparison**. Both are enhanced under conditions of increased anxiety.
- Interpersonal relationships in **western cultures** tend to be **individualistic, voluntary** and **temporary**, whereas those in **non-western cultures** tend to be more **collectivist, involuntary** and **permanent**.
- Western Psychologists tend to equate 'relationships' with 'western relationships'. This is a form of ethnocentrism, specifically, **Anglo**- or **Eurocentrism**.
- **Marriage** is found in all cultures. But there are important cultural variations in marital arrangements, including **monogamy, polygamy (polygyny, polyandry, polyamory)**, and **mandatory marriage to specific relatives**.
- **Arranged marriages** are far more common in collectivist cultures, but even here, brides and grooms are typically given some choice about who they marry. Traditionally, **divorce rates** have been much lower among 'arranged couples' but these are now increasing.
- The focus on long-term **heterosexual** relationships has now been supplemented with discussion of **gay** and **lesbian** relationships.
- Up to the mid-1970s, psychological research into homosexuality adopted a 'pathology model', which has been replaced by one that emphasises the underlying similarity between homosexuals and heterosexuals. This approach, however, omits or distorts certain key differences, such as those relating to **cohabitation, sexual exclusivity** and **sex roles**.
- One of the most unexpected uses of the internet is in the development of online relationships (**cyber affairs** or **electronic friendships**).
- Berscheid and Walster distinguish between **companionate** ('true' or 'conjugal') and **passionate** (romantic or obsessive) **love**. These are **qualitatively** different, but companionate love is only a more extreme form of **liking**.

- Sternberg's **triangular theory** of love comprises three basic components (**intimacy, passion** and **decision/commitment**), which can be combined to form different kinds of love.
- These models reflect the popular western ('Hollywood') view of the relationship between love and marriage, which isn't universal. However, the notion of people falling in love is found in one form or another in most human societies, even where marriages are traditionally arranged.
- Bowlby's **evolutionary** account of love focuses on love as **attachment**. This is one of three meanings of 'I love you', the others being love as **caregiving** and love as **sexual attraction**. This can help account for homosexuality, which cannot easily be explained in terms of **reproductive fitness.**
- In support of Kerckhoff and Davis's **filter model** (and other **stage** theories), it's generally agreed that relationships change and develop; although there's little evidence for the **complementarity** of **psychological needs**, there's more support for complementarity of **resources**.
- A general theoretical framework for explaining **initial attraction** is that the presence of others must be **rewarding**. This can help explain the impact of **proximity**, **exposure** and **familiarity**, **similarity** and **physical attractiveness**.
- **Proximity** provides increased opportunity for interaction, which increases familiarity through the **mere exposure effect.**
- **Similarity** of attitudes and values is a powerful influence on attraction, but this usually only emerges as the relationship develops. However, physical attractiveness is immediately apparent.
- There are important cultural differences in what counts as **physical beauty**, but there's a universal tendency for men to regard physical attractiveness as more important than women.
- Humans appear to be a **mutually** sexually selected species; **mate choice** is determined by 'built-in' preferences that have developed through the course of human evolution.
- The **symmetry** of the face around the vertical midline (its '**averageness**') appears to be an important determinant of attractiveness and is quite consistent across cultures. Symmetry equates with **fitness.**
- Symmetry is also important for bodily attractiveness (for both sexes), as is **waist-to-hip ratio** (**WHR**) (for females).
- The **matching hypothesis** (**MH**) is derived from **social exchange theory** (**SET**), which is a major explanation of all kinds of relationships, both intimate and non-intimate. Its different versions see people as fundamentally selfish, concerned only with getting as much out of a relationship as possible. But humans are capable of altruism as well as selfishness.
- Marriages are more **unstable** if the couple are teenagers, from lower socio-economic groups and different demographic backgrounds, whose parents were divorced, who've been sexually active prior to marriage and who experience early parenthood.
- **Conflict** is an inherent part of all relationships; what's crucial is how constructively it's resolved. Happy couples tend to deal with conflict in a **relationship-enhancing way**, while unhappy couples use a **distress-maintaining pattern** of conflict resolution.
- **Rule-breaking** is a major cause of relationship breakdown, especially **deception.**
- Relationship breakdown is a **process**. Research is increasingly concerned with the aftermath of relationship break-down, especially divorce, and not just the breakdown itself.

Links with Other Topics/Chapters

Chapter 22 ⟶ Interpersonal attraction, including the attractiveness *stereotype*, is really one aspect of *interpersonal* (or *social*) *perception*

Chapter 26 ⟶ Affiliation can be understood in relation to *conformity*, especially the need to belong. We also *compare ourselves with others* when we're unsure what to do or think

Chapter 47 ⟶ Ethnocentricism is a form of *bias* involved when western Psychologists equate 'relationships' with 'western relationships'

Chapter 43 ⟶ Homosexuality is discussed in relation to definitions and classification of *psychological abnormality*

Chapter 10 → Seeing love as a label we attach to our state of physiological arousal is consistent with the *cognitive labelling theory of emotion*

Chapters 2 and 32 → An evolutionary theory of love (love as *attachment*) is one aspect of *Evolutionary Psychology*

Chapter 24 → The similarity-attraction principle is related to *consistency theories of attitude change* (including Heider's *balance theory*)

Chapter 44 → Ideas about what makes people (especially women) physically attractive are relevant to discussion of *eating disorders*

Chapter 14 → Analysing the factors that account for facial attractiveness is related to *facial perception* (including *face recognition*)

Chapter 39 → The tendency to equate beauty with youthfulness is the flip-side of *prejudice* against old age (*ageism*)

Chapter 30 → The SET view of people as fundamentally selfish is relevant to discussion of *altruism*

Chapter 38 → Erikson's concept of *intimacy* is part of his *psychosocial theory of development*

Recommended Reading

Brehm, S.S. (1992) *Intimate Relationships* (2nd edition). New York: McGraw-Hill.

Duck, S. (1999) *Relating to Others* (2nd edition). Buckingham: Open University Press.

Fletcher, G. (2002) *The New Science of Intimate Relationships*. Oxford: Blackwell Publishing. Also relevant to Chapter 29.

Ickes, W. & Duck, S. (eds) (2000) *The Social Psychology of Personal Relationships.* Chichester: John Wiley & Sons Ltd.

Karremans, J.C. & Finkenauer, C. (2012) Affiliation, Attraction and Close Relationships. In M. Hewstone, W. Stroebe & K. Jonas (eds) *Introduction to Social Psychology* (5th edition). Oxford: BPS/Blackwell.

Kitzinger, C. & Coyle, A. (1995) Lesbian and gay couples: Speaking of difference. *The Psychologist, 8*(2), 64–9. Also relevant to Chapter 47.

Useful Websites

www.gov.uk/government/organisations/government-equalities-office (Women and Equality Unit, Lesbian and Gay Issues)

www.beautyanalysis.com/index2_mba.htm (Marquardt Beauty Analysis: as exploration of every aspect of facial beauty)

www.socialpsychology.org/social.htm#divorce (also relevant to textbook Chapter 38.) (Both these websites are part of the Social Psychology Network)

www.iarr.org (International Association for Relationship Research)

http://myweb.uiowa.edu/blastd (Steve Duck's homepage)

CHAPTER 29

AGGRESSION AND ANTISOCIAL BEHAVIOUR

INTRODUCTION and OVERVIEW

Philosophers and Psychologists have been interested in human aggression for a long time. According to Hobbes (1651), people are naturally competitive and hostile, interested only in their own power and gaining advantage over others. Hobbes argued that to prevent conflict and mutual destruction, people need government.

This pessimistic view of human nature was shared by Freud and Lorenz, albeit for different theoretical reasons. Like McDougall, Freud and Lorenz saw aggression as an *instinct* (see Chapter 9). In Freud's *psychoanalytic theory*, aggression is inherently self-destructive, but in practice is directed outwards mainly at other people, demonstrated all too clearly in the carnage of war. According to Lorenz's *ethological theory*, human beings have lost the means of controlling their aggression that other species possess, and in addition have invented weapons that allow aggression to take place from a distance. *Evolutionary Psychologists* regard male aggression – and violence – as *adaptive*, even when children and women are the victims.

Other explanations have combined elements of instinct theories with those of learning theory, such as Dollard *et al.*'s *frustration–aggression hypothesis*, and Berkowitz's *aggressive-cue theory*. Bandura's study of *observational learning's* role in aggression stimulated research into the effects of violence in television and computer games and, currently, *cyberbullying*. Perhaps the 'purest' social psychological account of aggression is the theory of *deindividuation*.

Baron and Richardson (1994) define antisocial behaviours as those 'which show a lack of feeling and concern for the welfare of others'. While aggression represents just one such lack of feeling and concern, it's the one that Psychologists have focused on.

DEFINING AGGRESSION

Ask Yourself

- What do you understand by 'aggression'?
- Are there different kinds of aggression?
- Is aggression the same as violence?

We all seem to recognise aggression when we witness it, but defining it often proves much more difficult. When used as a noun, aggression usually conveys some behaviour which is intended to harm another (or at least which has that effect). Yet even this definition is too broad: self-defence and unprovoked attack may both involve similar 'acts' and degrees of aggression, but only the latter would normally be considered 'antisocial' (and the law also recognises this distinction). When used as an adjective, 'aggressive' can convey that an action is carried out with energy and persistence (Lloyd *et al.*, 1984), something which may be regarded as socially desirable.

The importance of intention

Moyer (1976) and Berkowitz (1993) see aggression as always involving behaviour, either physical or symbolic, performed with the intention of harming someone. Similarly, Fiske (2004) defines aggression as entailing 'any *behaviour* whose *proximate intention* is to harm another person'. Aggressive thoughts, without the behaviour, aren't aggressive. Bushman and Anderson (2001a) distinguish between two types of intention: *proximate* (the closest and most immediate) and *primary* (ultimate). Aggressors operate with *multiple motives*. For example, perpetrators of school shootings may have the primary intent of revenge, suicide or fame. Terrorist attacks may have various primary intentions, such as revenge, escalating tensions, genocide, political control, moral influence, personal salvation or publicity. Domestic abuse can be motivated by control, self-enhancement, and relief from tension. According to Fiske (2004):

> ... Because people's motives are complex, focusing on the most immediate, closest, or proximate goal seems more fruitful than trying to decide the primary one.

Moyer and Berkowitz reserve the word *violence* to describe an extreme form of aggression involving a deliberate attempt to inflict serious physical injury on another person.

Other important distinctions include:

- *Hostile aggression*, aimed solely at hurting another (gratuitous aggression or 'aggression for aggression's sake'); this would exclude self-defence; it's also angry, impulsive and automatic; and
- *Instrumental aggression*, a means to an end (and so would include self-defence: Buss, 1961; Feshbach, 1964); it's controlled and premeditated.

Ask Yourself

- Can you think of any exceptions to this distinction between hostile and instrumental aggression?

Hostile aggression can sometimes be controlled, as when an angry person plots revenge over time. This is similar to *appetitive aggression*, which arises from the thrill of the hunt: even the act of planning an attack can arouse intense excitement (Weierstall *et al.*, 2013). Conversely, instrumental aggression can sometimes be impulsive, as when a child hits another child to get its toy back. Fiske (2004) believes that examples like these make the distinction less useful.

THEORIES of AGGRESSION

Lorenz's ethological approach

Ethologists consider aggression to be instinctive in all species and important in the evolutionary development of the species. It allows individuals to adapt to their environments, survive in them, and successfully reproduce (see Chapter 2 and below). When space or food is scarce, many species limit their reproduction and survive by marking off living space which they defend against 'trespassers' (*territoriality*). Aggressiveness is clearly important in competing successfully for limited resources, in defending territory, and for basic survival.

According to Lorenz (1966), it's legitimate to make direct comparisons between different species, although his theory of human aggression is based on the study of non-primates, and mainly non-mammals (mainly fish and insects). He defines aggression as:

> ... The fighting instinct in beast and man which is directed against members of the same species ...

Evolutionary explanations

Ask Yourself

- Is it possible to agree with the rape adaptation hypothesis but not see it as justifying rape? (See Critical Discussion 29.1.)

Freud's psychoanalytic approach

Freud's theory is normally regarded as an *instinct theory* (see Chapter 9). It wasn't until late in his life that Freud recognised aggression as an instinct distinct from sexuality (libido), a response to the horrific carnage of the First World War. In *Beyond the Pleasure Principle* (1920) and *The Ego and the Id* (1923), he distinguished between the *life instinct* (or *Eros*), including sexuality, and the *death instinct* (*Thanatos*).

Thanatos represents an inborn destructiveness, directed primarily against the self. The aim (as with all instincts in Freud's view) is to reduce tension or excitation to a minimum and, ultimately, to eliminate it completely. This was the idyllic state we enjoyed in the womb, where our needs were met as soon as they arose, and, for a while, at our mother's breast. But after this, the only way of achieving such a *Nirvana* is through death.

Self-directed aggression, however, conflicts with the life instinct, especially the self-preservative component. But because the impulse to self-destruction is so strong, we must destroy some other thing or person if we're not to destroy ourselves; this conflict results in our aggression being *displaced* onto others. More positively, aggression can be *sublimated* into sport, physical occupations and domination and mastery of nature and the world in general. Like Freud, Lorenz also argued that we need to acknowledge our aggressiveness and to control it

Critical Discussion 29.1

Sexual dimorphism and rape

Evolutionary Psychologists see the mind as comprising a number of specialised mechanisms or modules, designed by natural selection to solve problems that faced our hunter–gatherer ancestors, such as acquiring mates, raising children and dealing with rivals. The solutions often involve emotions such as lust, fear, affection, jealousy and anger. (See Chapter 2.)

Although the focus is on *universal* features of the mind, individual differences are seen as the expression of the same universal human nature as it encounters different environments. The crucial exception to this rule is *gender*: natural selection has constructed the mental modules of men and women very differently as a result of their divergent reproductive roles.

Buss (1994) claims that there's a distinct gender gap in 'mate choice', and Thornhill and Wilmsen-Thornhill (1992) argue that human sexual psychology is *dimorphic*. The sexes differ in their feelings about whether, when and how often it's in their interests to mate. Because women are more selective about their mates and more interested in evaluating them and delaying intercourse, men, to get sexual access, must often break through female resistance. According to Thornhill and Wilmsen-Thornhill's *'rape adaptation hypothesis'*, during human evolutionary history there was enough directional selection on males in favour of traits that solved the problem of forcing sex on a reluctant partner to produce a psychological tendency specifically towards rape.

In other words, not only does this hypothesis recast an oppressive form of behaviour in a much more positive light (it's 'adaptive'), but it also represents it as a natural characteristic of men ('they can't help it'). Not surprisingly, it's been condemned as not simply trying to *explain* men's sexual coercion, but *justifying* it (Edley and Wetherell, 1995).

However, in their book on rape, co-authors Thornhill and Palmer (2000) disagree as to whether rape is a direct adaptation (Thornhill) or a side-effect of the male sex drive (Palmer) (Workman and Reader, 2008). Thornhill and Palmer were accused of political incorrectness and caused a storm by suggesting that women should consider that their behaviour and clothing might contribute to their being raped in certain circumstances. While many feminists were outraged, some actually agreed (e.g. McElroy, in Workman and Reader).

through sport (e.g. the Olympics), expeditions, explorations, and so on, especially if international cooperation is involved (Lorenz called these 'displacement' activities). Freud shared Lorenz's view that aggressive energy builds up until eventually it has to be discharged in some way (see Key Study 29.1).

Figure 29.1 Opening ceremony to the 2012 London Olympic Games

An evaluation of Freud's theory

- Despite supportive evidence such as Megargee's (see Key Study 29.1), Freud's ideas on aggression made little impact either on the public imagination or on other Psychologists (including other psychoanalysts) until Dollard *et al.* (1939) proposed their *frustration–aggression hypothesis* (see below).
- Fromm's *The Anatomy of Human Destructiveness* (1977) was influenced by Freud's ideas, as was Storr's *Human Aggression* (1968). Storr (like Fromm, a psychoanalyst) dedicated his book to Lorenz, and in the introduction he says:

> *... the extremes of 'brutal' behaviour are confined to man; and there is no parallel in nature to our savage treatment of each other ... we are the cruellest and most ruthless species that has ever walked the earth;... we know in our hearts that each one of us harbours within himself those same savage impulses which lead to murder, to torture and to war.*

Key Study 29.1

The overcontrolled violent criminal (Megargee, 1966)

- Megargee reported that brutally aggressive crimes are often committed by *overcontrolled* individuals. They repress their anger and, over a period of time, the pressure to be aggressive builds up. Often it's an objectively trivial incident which provokes the destructive outburst. The aggressor then returns to his previously passive state, once again seeming incapable of violence.
- In Phoenix, an 11-year-old boy who stabbed his brother 34 times with a steak knife was described by all who knew him as being extremely polite and softly spoken, with no history of violent behaviour. In New York, an 18-year-old youth who confessed he'd assaulted and strangled a 7-year-old girl in a church, and later tried to burn her body in the furnace, was described in the press as an unemotional person who planned to be a minister. A 21-year-old man from Colorado accused of the rape and murder of two little girls had never been a discipline problem.
- In these cases, the homicide wasn't just one more aggressive offence in a person who'd always displayed inadequate controls. Rather, it was a completely uncharacteristic act in a person who'd always displayed extraordinarily high levels of control. According to Megargee and Mendelsohn (1962):

> ... The extremely assaultive person is often a fairly mild-mannered, long-suffering individual who buries his resentment under rigid but brittle controls. Under certain circumstances he may lash out and release all his aggression in one, often disastrous, act. Afterwards he reverts to his usual overcontrolled defences. Thus he may be more of a menace than the verbally aggressive 'chip-on-the-shoulder' type who releases his aggression in small doses.

The frustration–aggression hypothesis (FAH)

Dollard *et al.*'s (1939) *frustration–aggression hypothesis* (FAH) was intended partly to 'translate' some of Freud's psychoanalytic concepts into learning theory terms. It claims that:

> *... aggression is always a consequence of frustration and, contrariwise ... the existence of frustration always leads to some form of aggression ...*

While agreeing with Freud that aggression is an innate response, Dollard *et al.* argued that it would be triggered only by frustrating situations and events. Some support for this view comes from the *displacement* of aggression, as demonstrated in the *scapegoating* account of racial discrimination (see Chapter 25).

Indeed, evidence for this form of *indirect* aggression is stronger than for direct aggression (Fiske, 2004). A meta-analysis of laboratory studies found a sizeable effect of provocation on aggression towards innocent third parties when retaliation against the provoking person isn't possible (Marcus-Newhall *et al.*, 2000). Displaced aggression often focuses on a weaker, safer target than the frustrating agent. Related research into *bullying* and *partner abuse* shows that aggression towards others is an attempt to exert control over someone in a weaker position (Fiske, 2004).

Ask Yourself

- Can you think of any exceptions to the claims made by the frustration–aggression hypothesis?
- Do we necessarily become aggressive when we're frustrated?

Some criticisms of the original FAH

Despite the evidence for displaced aggression, it soon became apparent that the FAH, in its original form, was an overstatement.

- Miller (1941) argued that frustration is an *instigator* of aggression, but situational factors (such as *learned inhibition* and *fear of retaliation*) may prevent actual aggressive behaviour from occurring. So, although frustration may make aggression more likely, it's far from being a sufficient cause of aggression.
- Bandura (1973) argued that frustration might be a source of *arousal*, but frustration-induced arousal (like other types of arousal) could have a variety of outcomes, of which aggression is only one. Whether it actually occurs is more the result of learned patterns of behaviour triggered by environmental cues.
- Frustration may also produce different responses in different people in different situations. For example, experiments seem to suggest that

frustration is most likely to produce aggression if (a) the person is close to achieving his/her goal, or (b) the frustrating event seems arbitrary (Miell, 1990). Berkowitz (1993) says that if a frustration is either arbitrary or illegitimate, it's seen as unfair.

Key Study 29.2

Don't frustrate me without a good reason (Kulik and Brown, 1979)

- Kulik and Brown found that frustration was more likely to produce aggression if it wasn't anticipated, and if participants believed that the person responsible for frustrating them did so deliberately and without good reason. This shows the importance of *cognitive* factors as cues for aggressive behaviour.
- Participants were told they could earn money by telephoning people and persuading them to make a pledge to charity. One group expected that about two-thirds of those contacted would agree to make a pledge, while a second group expected a very low response rate. All the people telephoned were stooges, none of whom agreed to pledge.
- The first group of participants showed more aggression by slamming down the phone, speaking more aggressively, and so on. Also, those given reasonable excuses (such as 'I can't afford it') showed less aggression than those given less reasonable excuses (such as 'Charities are a waste of time and a rip-off').

The attributional perspective

Ask Yourself

- How would you expect an attributional account of aggression to predict the conditions under which frustration is converted into aggression?

One of the important cognitive factors identified by Kulik and Brown (1979) is the *attribution of intention*. According to Berkowitz (1993), we aren't usually bothered by a failure to reach our goals unless we believe that the frustrater intentionally or improperly tried to interfere with our efforts. In other words, the attribution must involve a cause that's seen as *internal*, *controllable*, and *improper* (in violation of generally accepted rules of conduct). This is consistent with Weiner's (1986) theory (see Chapter 23), and with the definition of aggression as the (perceived) intention to harm another person (see above). If there are *mitigating circumstances*, the cause may now be seen as external and uncontrollable (although still improper).

Chronically aggressive children appear to have a particular type of *attributional style*. They display a strong hostile attributional bias (HAB) towards seeing others as acting against them with hostile intent, especially in ambiguous situations (Nasby *et al.*, 1979). Such biased attributions often lead to *retaliatory aggression* (Taylor *et al.*, 1994). Individuals who are sensitive to provocations from others more readily interpret others' behaviours as being more provoking – producing a vicious circle of aggression (Lawrence, 2011). In this way, traits can influence how the context is perceived in the first place: if the trait results in more hostile attributions, the likelihood of aggressive behaviour in response increases (Lawrence, 2013).

Aggressive children make attributions rapidly and based on only some of the relevant information relating to perceived threat (Dodge and Tomlin, 1987). This suggests a state of chronic arousal and vigilance that other people experience only sporadically. The phenomenon of *excitation transfer* describes how arousal from an irrelevant prior source persists and then spills over into the next (unrelated) setting to which it's then misattributed (Zillman, 1988: see below). HAB also highlights the *social construction* of aggression (Mummendey, 1996: see below).

Larger frustrations may facilitate aggression because they're more likely to trigger a (perhaps biased) search for an explanation favouring a dispositional attribution about the frustrater. The presence of *aggressive cues* is also more likely to trigger hostile attributions (Fiske, 2004).

Aggressive-cue theory (ACT)

According to Berkowitz (1966), frustration produces *anger* rather than aggression. According to *aggressive-cue* (or *cue–arousal*) *theory* (ACT), for anger/psychological pain to be converted into actual aggression, certain cues are needed. These are environmental stimuli associated either with aggressive behaviour, or with the frustrating object or person.

Aggressive or violent behaviour is, at least partly, a reaction to specific features of the surrounding situation which 'pull out' responses that heighten the strength of the behaviour. This happens either when the environmental cues are associated in the aggressor's mind with aggression, and/or when they somehow remind the aggressor of decidedly unpleasant experiences.

Box 29.1 Berkowitz's paradigm for investigating cue-related aggression

- When participants arrive, they're told they'll be paired with another person (a stooge) in a study concerned with the physiological reactions to stress. To do this, they'll be asked to offer a written solution to a problem. Stress will be introduced by their solution being evaluated by their partner, who will deliver between one and ten electric shocks to them (according to his/her evaluation of the solution).
- After completing their solutions, half the participants receive a single shock, while the rest receive seven (all fairly mild), the lower number of shocks indicating a very favourable evaluation.
- Following this first stage, participants take their turn in evaluating the stooge's solution, either after seeing a violent film (*Champion*, depicting a brutal prize fight and starring Kirk Douglas), or a non-violent film (showing highlights of an exciting track race), or in the presence of objects that are/aren't associated with violence. Aggression is measured as the number of shocks the participant delivers.

Experimental tests of ACT

Berkowitz and Green (1966) introduced the stooge to the real participant as either Bob Anderson or Kirk Anderson. As expected, the largest number of shocks was delivered by participants who were angry (had received seven shocks from the confederate), had witnessed the violent film, and believed the confederate's name was Kirk (his name was linked to the witnessed aggression through Kirk Douglas).

In a parallel experiment, the stooge was introduced either as Bob Kelly, Bob Dunne or Bob Riley: Dunne was the name of the victorious character in *Champion*, and Kelly (played by Kirk Douglas) was the loser. As predicted, the stooge received more shocks from participants who'd seen the violent film, but most importantly, he received most shocks when he was called Kelly.

Ask Yourself

- Try to account for these findings.

In both cases (the stooge called 'Kirk' or 'Kelly' receiving the most shocks), participants encountered someone who reminded them of the victim in the witnessed aggression. He was associated with an instance of successful (i.e. rewarded) aggression, which made it more likely that anger would be converted into aggression (Berkowitz, 1993).

Berkowitz and LePage's (1967) participants were taken to a 'control room' and shown the shock apparatus. For some, there was a shotgun and a revolver on a table next to the shock apparatus, while for others there were badminton rackets and some shuttlecocks. For each participant, these objects were pushed aside by the experimenter, who said that 'they must have been left there by another experimenter'. There was a third group for whom there were no 'planted' objects. As predicted, angry participants delivered more shocks to the stooge if a shotgun and revolver were nearby (objects associated with violence) than when badminton rackets were present. This is known as the *weapons effect* (see Figure 29.2).

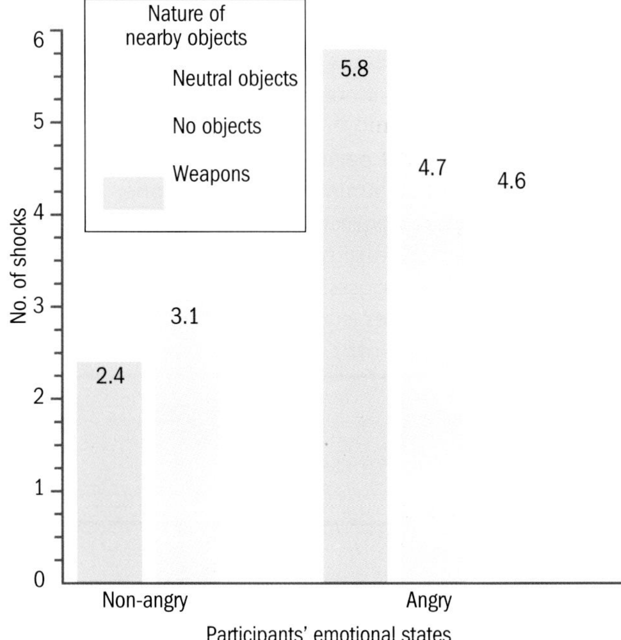

Figure 29.2 Mean number of shocks given as a function of presence of weapons (adapted from Berkowitz and LePage, 1967). (Copyright 1967 by the American Psychological Association. Adapted by permission)

An evaluation of ACT

- These and several other similar studies seem to suggest that people's actions towards others are sometimes influenced in a relatively thoughtless, automatic way by particular details of the immediate situation. The mere physical presence of weapons, even when not used in the performance of aggressive actions, may still increase the occurrence of such behaviour. As Berkowitz (1968) put it:

> *Guns not only permit violence, they can stimulate it as well. The finger pulls the trigger, but the trigger may also be pulling the finger ...*

- Overall support for the weapons effect is impressive (Krahé, 2008). From their meta-analysis of 57 studies, Carlson *et al.* (1990) concluded that aggression-related cues within experimental settings increase aggressive behaviour.
- Exposure to a weapon produces *automatic priming* (Anderson *et al.,* 1998). For example, people can identify aggression-related words faster after seeing a weapon name or picture; this suggests that weapons make aggressive thoughts more accessible. Violent media can do the same: after seeing a violent video, people list more aggressive associations to both ambiguous and non-aggressive words, as well as identifying aggressive words faster (Bushman, 1998).
- Consistent with both ACT and the weapons effect is the correlation between the availability of firearms and firearms homicide rates, both in the USA and across 16 European countries. Not only do guns make aggression more lethal when they are involved (hardly surprising), but: '... guns also provoke aggression in their own right, simply by being there ...' (Fiske, 2004)
- Berkowitz (1995) points to a number of successful replications, including studies carried out in Belgium, Canada, Croatia, Italy and Sweden. In the Swedish study (Frodi, 1975), the weapons effect was shown by high-school boys even when they hadn't been 'angered' (i.e. shocked). According to Baron (1977):

> *It is clear that Berkowitz's more general proposal that aggression is 'pulled' or elicited from without by external stimuli rather than merely 'pushed' from within has attained widespread acceptance ...*

The social learning theory approach and media violence

According to *social learning theory* (SLT), aggressive behaviours are learned through reinforcement and the imitation of aggressive 'models' (Bandura, 1965, 1973, 1994: see Chapters 35 and 42).

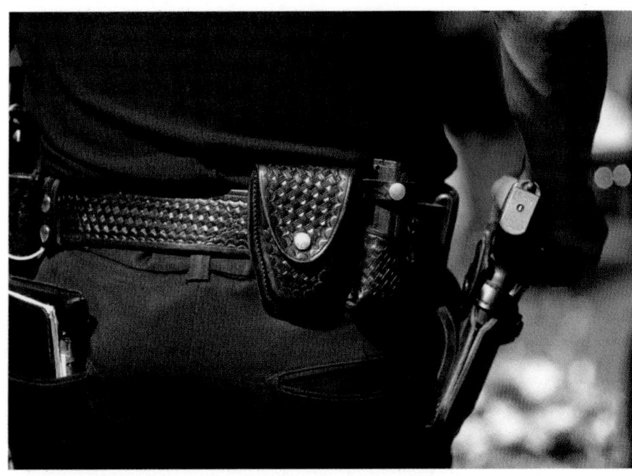

Figure 29.3 Gun culture creates gun crime

Imitation is the reproduction of learning through observation (*observational learning*), and involves observing other people who serve as models for behaviour. Bandura *et al.* (1961, 1963) demonstrated how a child's aggressive tendencies can be strengthened through *vicarious reinforcement* (seeing others being rewarded for behaving aggressively).

Box 29.2 Bandura *et al.*'s procedure for investigating the effects of observed aggression

- Three-, 4- and 5-year-old children were exposed to an adult model behaving aggressively towards an inflated plastic 'Bobo' doll. Later, the children were allowed to play with the doll themselves. The number of acts of *imitative aggression* was the main dependent variable.
- Bandura made the important distinction between *learning* and *performance*: learning of aggressive responses (*acquisition*) doesn't necessarily mean that they'll be displayed in the child's behaviour (*performance*). In other words, a failure to imitate doesn't imply the absence of learning.
- For example, Bandura (1965) showed that when children who'd seen the model being punished for his behaviour were themselves offered rewards for behaving aggressively, they showed they'd learned the model's behaviours just as well as those who'd seen the behaviours being positively reinforced (see Chapter 35).

SLT and the effects of the media

According to Baron (1977), the Bobo doll experiments constitute 'phase one' of scientific research into the effects of media violence: almost all involved filmed (*symbolic*) models. The basic finding was that young children can acquire new aggressive responses not previously in their behavioural repertoire, merely through exposure to a filmed or televised model. If children could learn new ways of harming others through such experience, then mass-media portrayals of violence might be contributing, in some degree, to increased levels of violence in society (Baron, 1977).

However, Bandura himself (1965) warned against such an interpretation in the light of his distinction between learning and performance. Nevertheless, the mere *possibility* of such effects was sufficient to focus considerable public attention on his research. There were also several methodological problems with the Bobo doll research, which made it very difficult to generalise from it to 'real world' media influence. This helped to promote 'phase two' of the study of the effects of media violence, with Berkowitz being one of the leading figures.

How do viewers perceive violence?

According to Gunter and McAleer (1997), viewers can be highly discriminating when it comes to portrayals of violence and don't invariably read into TV content the same meanings researchers do. Thus, merely knowing how often certain pre-defined incidents occur in programmes doesn't tell us how significant these features are for viewers. Viewers' perceptions of how violent TV content is, then, may not agree with objective counts of violence in programmes. According to Gunter (2000), the potential for emotional upset is increased:

- by violent portrayals in realistic settings – real-life incidents in news and documentary programmes are generally rated as being more violent than those in fictional settings
- when the violence is depicted as justified or rewarded
- when viewers strongly identify with the characters
- when the victim's pain and suffering are shown graphically.

Very young children are frightened by monsters they can see on the screen (such as *The Incredible Hulk*), while older children (9–12-year-olds) are scared by hidden evils in disguise or that lurk unseen off-camera (as in *Poltergeist*, where much of the 'horror' is covert and depends on a more sophisticated reading of story events: Gunter, 2000).

Programmes which are extremely violent according to 'objective' counts of violent acts can be seen by children as 'containing hardly any violence', and this is especially true of cartoons. Subjective assessment of violence should, therefore, be incorporated into assessments of the amount of violence shown on TV (Gunter and McAleer, 1997).

Figure 29.4 Tom and Jerry – and friend. Evidence suggests that children see such cartoons as less violent than more realistic portrayals

Methods used to study TV violence

Correlational studies

Typically, these involve asking people which programmes they like best and which they watch most often; these data are then correlated with measures of aggression given by parents, teachers, peers, self-reports and so on. Despite some inconsistency, the overall finding is that amount of viewing is related to self-reports of aggressive behaviour. Of course, it's possible that those who watch violent TV are different in some way from those who don't, and the impossibility of inferring cause and effect from correlational studies weakens this methodology.

Laboratory studies

These are designed to enable the causal link between watching violent TV and behaving aggressively to be established (if it exists). For example, Liebert and Baron (1972) randomly assigned children to two groups: Group 1 watched *The Untouchables*, a violent TV programme; Group 2 watched an equally engaging and arousing, but non-violent, sports competition. Afterwards, the children were allowed to play; those in Group 1 behaved more aggressively.

The problem with laboratory studies is that most use small and unrepresentative samples which are exposed to the independent variable under highly contrived and unnatural viewing conditions. The measures of TV viewing and aggression tend to be so far removed from normal everyday behaviour that it's doubtful whether such studies have any relevance to the real world (Gunter and McAleer, 1997).

Field experiments

These have much more *ecological validity*, and involve children or teenagers being assigned to view violent or non-violent programmes for periods of a few days or weeks. Measures of aggressive behaviour, fantasy, attitude, and so on are taken before, during and after the periods of controlled viewing. To ensure control over actual viewing, children in group or institutional settings are studied, mostly from nursery schools, residential schools, or institutions for adolescent boys (e.g. Parke *et al.*, 1977). In general, the results show that children who watch violent TV are more aggressive than those who don't.

Key Study 29.3

Creating aggression – a cottage industry? (Parke *et al.*, 1977)

- Parke *et al.* studied Belgian and American male juvenile delinquents living in small-group cottages in low-security institutions.
- Their normal rates of aggressive behaviour were assessed (using several measures of physical and verbal aggression).
- Then the boys in one cottage were exposed to five commercial films involving violence over a period of one week, while boys in another cottage saw five non-violent films during the same period.
- The former showed significant increases in aggressive behaviour for some of the categories, but increases in other measures of aggression were confined to boys who were naturally high in aggression (and who saw the violent film).

Ask Yourself

- What do you consider to be the major disadvantage of field experiments compared with laboratory experiments?
- What particular limitations did the Parke *et al.* study have?

In field experiments, the setting cannot be controlled as well as in laboratory experiments. Consequently, we cannot be certain that the only difference between the children is the watching of either violent or non-violent TV, especially when participants aren't assigned randomly to conditions. In Parke *et al.*'s study, for example, 'cottages' (or pre-existing groups), rather than individuals, were assigned to the viewing conditions. Also, their participants (juvenile delinquent males) aren't representative of children or adolescents in general.

Natural experiments

Here, the researcher doesn't manipulate an independent variable, but takes advantage of fortuitous and naturally occurring events. Williams (1986) studied a community in Canada ('Notel'), where TV had only recently been introduced. This community was compared with one in which there was a single TV channel, and another with several channels. Verbal and physical aggression in both male and female 6–11-year-olds increased over a two-year period following the introduction of TV to 'Notel'. No such increase occurred in the communities that already had TV. Another example is described in Key Study 29.4.

Key Study 29.4

A natural experiment on the island of St. Helena (Charlton and Hannan, 2005)

- Television (CNN) was introduced to the South Atlantic island of St. Helena in 1995. Further services were added later, including movie, documentary, sports and children's channels.
- This provided the opportunity for a quasi-experimental investigation of TV's impact on 59 pre-schoolers (monitored until they were 13) and all 800 children of first- and middle-school age.
- Prior to 1995, data were collected on children's leisure-time activities and school-related behaviour; these key dependent measures were then assessed annually. Also, after 1995, data were collected re: TV viewing habits and other TV-related matters.
- Self-report data from children were supplemented by data from older students and teachers.
- The study as a whole comprised nine component studies. The overall conclusions were as follows:
  1. *Displacement effects:* Most children became enthusiastic – though not excessive – viewers. Viewing time appeared to be most displaced from activities such as 'unorganised play', 'sleeping', 'eating' and 'walking', along with 'watching video'.
  2. *Content effects:* Findings challenge simplistic notions that viewing TV encourages antisocial behaviour. Discussions with older children suggested that family and community factors were more persuasive in shaping behaviour than mere exposure to TV.
  3. *Future research:* Potentially adverse outcomes of TV viewing can be limited by equitable social controls operating within family and community structures.

Longitudinal panel studies

Like experiments, but unlike correlational studies, longitudinal panel studies can say something about cause and effect, and normally use representative samples. In this case, their aim is to discover relationships that may exist or develop over time between TV viewing and behaviour. These studies look at TV's *cumulative* influence and whether or not attitudes and behaviour are linked with watching it.

How does television exert its effects?

Huesmann *et al.* (2003) have identified a number of psychological processes which underlie either the short-term or long-term effects of exposure to television and other media (such as movies and video games). These are shown in Table 29.1.

Table 29.1 Psychological processes underlying the short-term and long-term effects of media exposure (based on Huesmann *et al.*, 2003)

Underlying process	
Short-term effects	1. Priming of already existing cognitions or scripts for behaviour.
	2. Immediate mimicking (imitation) of observed behaviours.
	3. Changes in emotional arousal and the misattribution of that arousal (*excitation transfer*).
Long-term effects	1. Observational learning of behavioural scripts, world schemas and normative beliefs.
	2. Activation and desensitisation of emotional processes.
	3. Didactic learning processes.

These processes and effects don't apply specifically, or exclusively, to aggression/violence, and some have already been discussed above. For a detailed discussion, see Dubow *et al.* (2007). A few additional points are worth making:

- An example of *priming* is the *weapons effect* (e.g. Berkowitz and LePage, 1967).
- Huesmann *et al* distinguish between *short-term mimicking* (imitation) and *long-term observational learning*. The former requires only one exposure to an observed behaviour (as when a newborn imitates an adult's facial expression; Meltzoff and Moore, 2000: see Chapter 16), whereas the latter usually requires repeated exposures over a period of time, with the scripts, schemas and beliefs becoming increasingly complex. For example, extensive observation of violence biases children's world schemas toward attributing hostility to others' actions, which in turn increases the likelihood that they'll behave aggressively themselves. This is related to *disinhibition*, the reduction of inhibitions about behaving aggressively oneself, or coming to believe that aggression is a permitted or legitimate way of solving problems or attaining goals. This relates to Berkowitz's ACT (see above).

SL theorists acknowledge the role of cognitive factors as *mediating* between stimulus and response (Bandura, 1994). How TV violence is *perceived* and *interpreted*, and the issue of realism, are clearly important intervening variables for both children and adults (see Chapter 35).

- *Desensitisation* is the reduction in emotional response (habituation: see Chapter 9) to TV violence (and an increased acceptance of violence in real life) as a result of repeatedly viewing it. Increasingly violent programmes may be required to produce an emotional response (Gadow and Sprafkin, 1989). Violent scenes become less physiologically arousing over time, and brief exposure to media violence can reduce physiological reactions to real-world violence (Dubow *et al.*, 2007).
- While observational learning and desensitisation can happen outside the child's awareness, *didactic learning* involves persuasive messages that require conscious, 'effortful' processing, as when counter-stereotypical content is presented (see Chapter 22); cognitive changes in middle childhood make children more active processors of media content, applying the schemas they've acquired and becoming more interested in its abstract, conceptual meanings (Huston and Wright, 1997: see Chapter 36).

Moderators of media effects

In order to be able to properly evaluate data regarding the impact of exposure to media violence on aggressive behaviour, we must first consider the moderating role of individual differences and cultural and contextual factors. By acknowledging the importance of such factors, we're recognising that media violence (and other media content) has only an *indirect* effect on the viewer's behaviour; the role of cognitive factors discussed above illustrates this point.

Dubow *et al.* (2007) present what they call an organisational framework for understanding media effects on cognitions, behaviour and emotions (including the processes discussed above). This is summarised in Figure 29.5 (and see Key Study 29.4).

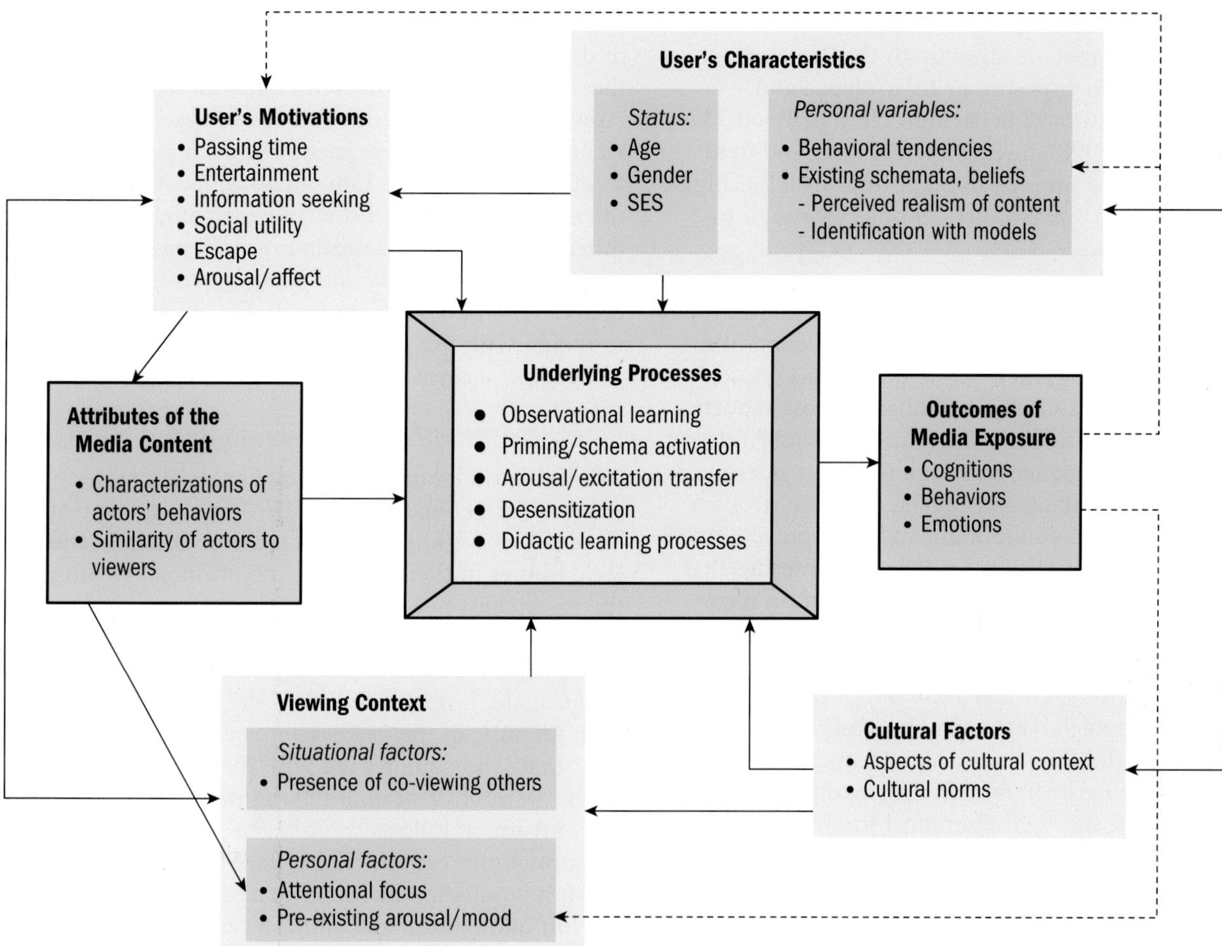

Figure 29.5 Organisational framework for understanding media effects on cognitions, behaviours, and emotions. (From Dubow *et al.*, 2007)

What's the evidence for the harmful effects of media violence?

American (e.g. Eron and Huesmann, 1985; Lefkowitz *et al.*, 1972; Phillips, 1986) and British research (e.g. Bailey, 1993; Sims and Gray, 1993) shows that such a link exists. Sims and Gray, for example, reviewed an extensive body of literature linking heavy exposure to media violence and subsequent aggressive behaviour. Similarly, Bailey's study of 40 adolescent murderers and 200 young sex offenders showed repeated viewing of violent and pornographic videos to be 'a significant causal factor'. This was particularly important in adolescents who carried out abusive acts while babysitting, where videos provided 'a potential source of immediate arousal for the subsequent act', including imitating violent images.

However, some studies have failed to find such a link. Milavsky *et al.* (1982) found only small associations between exposure to violent programmes and verbal and physical aggression amongst 3,200 elementary school children and adolescents. Variables such as family background, social environment, and school performance were actually much better predictors of aggressiveness, if not of actual crime (Ford, 1998).

Based on Huesmann and Eron's (1986) cross-national survey in six countries (Holland, Australia, USA, Israel, Poland and Finland), Comstock and Paik (1991) concluded that viewing TV violence at an early age is a predictor of later aggression. However, Cumberbatch (1997) cites several studies which cast doubt on claims regarding the connections between media violence and children's aggression.

According to Taylor *et al.* (1994):

> *... Media violence is not a sufficient condition to produce aggressive behaviour, nor is it a necessary one. Aggressive behaviour is multiply determined and media violence in and of itself is unlikely to provoke such behaviour ... However ... media violence can be a contributing factor to some aggressive acts in some individuals ....*

Others, however, disagree.

Paik and Comstock (1994) conducted the most comprehensive meta-analysis up to that time of the link between exposure to TV violence and aggressive or antisocial behaviour. They analysed 217 studies (1957–1990), including laboratory and field experiments and surveys, and reported small but highly significant effect sizes for pre-schoolers through to college students.

Bushman and Anderson (2001b) and Anderson and Bushman (2002) conducted a MA of 280 studies (up to the year 2000) of the effects of violent content in TV, movies, video games, comic books, and music. They found effect sizes very similar to those reported by Paik and Comstock (1994). Bushman and Anderson argue that the evidence for a link is almost as strong as that between smoking and cancer, and even stronger than that between condom use and HIV prevention.

Researchers seem to have reached a consensus that media violence increases the likelihood of aggressive and violent behaviour in both immediate and long-term contexts (Anderson *et al.*, 2003). This conclusion is derived from the combination of (a) laboratory experiments which have unambiguously demonstrated a causal link; (b) cross-sectional field studies in which correlations have been found in many different real-world settings; and (c) longitudinal studies which have found that children who are exposed to more violence grow up to be more aggressive independently of other variables known to be associated with aggression (e.g. low IQ, low socio-economic status, poor parenting: see Chapter 46) (Dubow *et al.*, 2007).

According to Fiske (2004):

> *Research unequivocally demonstrates that media violence facilitates aggression … review after review supports the conclusion … The link of violent media to aggression is one of the most reliable findings in social psychology …*

Deindividuation

Ask Yourself

- Do you think people are more likely to behave in antisocial ways in a group or crowd than when they're alone?
- If so, why?

The concept of *deindividuation* has been used to try to explain why people in groups may behave in an uncharacteristically aggressive way (and in other antisocial ways), compared with their individual behaviour. When an individual's identity is lost in a mass of people, and when the markers of personality are reduced, the individual is said to be *deindividuated* (Gergen and Gergen, 1981).

Festinger *et al.* (1952) first introduced the concept of deindividuation, based on Le Bon's (1895) study of the aggressive behaviour sometimes associated with crowds. They defined deindividuation as a state of affairs in a group where members don't pay attention to other individuals as individuals and, correspondingly, the members don't feel they're being singled out by others. Belonging to a group not only provides people with a sense of identity and *belongingness* (see Maslow's hierarchy of needs – Chapter 9), but allows individuals to merge with the group, to forego individuality, and to become *anonymous*.

Empirical studies of deindividuation

While most relevant studies have been laboratory experiments, Diener *et al.*'s (1976) field experiment involved over 700 Halloween trick-or-treaters visiting local houses in their Halloween costumes. Friends of the researchers put out bowls of sweets or coins, each bowl being labelled 'TAKE ONE'. Some children arrived alone, others in groups. In the *non-anonymous condition*, the homeowner asked the child to reveal their identity; in the *anonymous condition*, s/he made it clear that s/he couldn't tell who they were.

The amount of stealing (taking more than one sweet or coin) was as follows:

- Anonymous groups: 57 per cent
- Anonymous and alone: 21 per cent
- Non-anonymous and alone: 8 per cent
- Non-anonymous groups: 21 per cent.

Clearly, not being identifiable and being in a group of other anonymous children *combined* to produce the highest rate of antisocial behaviour.

Zimbardo (2007) describes an unpublished experimental study, also involving children and Halloween costumes. Zimbardo describes the data as 'striking testimony to the power of anonymity'. Aggression among the young schoolchildren increased significantly as soon as they put the costumes on.

An evaluation of deindividuation research

- This basic paradigm has been repeated with comparable results in many laboratory and field studies, involving a wide range of participants (Zimbardo, 2007). Deindividuation of the guards (through their military-style uniforms and silver reflecting sunglasses) was also a feature of the SPE (see Chapter 27).
- The hoods and lab coats worn by Zimbardo's (1969) participants resembled that worn by the Ku Klux Klan (see Figure 29.6) and may have acted as a *demand characteristic* (see Chapter 3): the participants believed they should behave in a more extreme way (Johnson and Downing, 1979). In support of this, Johnson and Downing found that when participants wore surgical masks and gowns, they delivered

Key Study 29.5

Anonymity can be bad for your health (Zimbardo, 1969)

- Female students had to deliver electric shocks to another student in a study of 'creativity under stress'. Each participant was given a 75 volt shock to convince her that it hurt (no other actual shocks were administered).
- Half wore bulky lab coats and hoods that hid their faces, were spoken to in groups of four, and were never referred to by name. The other half wore their normal clothes, were given large name tabs to wear, were introduced to each other by name, and could see each other dimly while giving the shock.
- The student who received the shock was seen through a one-way mirror and pretended to be in extreme discomfort – writhing, twisting, grimacing and finally tearing her hand away from the strap.
- The key dependent variable was the *duration* of shock administered. The hooded, deindividuated participants gave twice as much shock as the individuated group and also increased shock time over the 20 trials. If they were told that the student receiving the shock was honest, sincere and warm, she didn't receive any less shock than those believed to be conceited or critical.
- By contrast, the individuated participants did adjust the shock they delivered according to the victim's character.

Figure 29.6 Deindividuated participants in Zimbardo's (1969) experiment

significantly less electric shock than those participants whose names and identities were emphasised. This suggests that the participants' clothing and related behavioural expectations, rather than deindividuation, may have influenced their behaviour.

- Similarly, in another of Zimbardo's (1969) studies, the participants were Belgian soldiers. When these soldiers wore hoods, they didn't behave more aggressively but became self-conscious, suspicious and anxious. Their apparently individuated counterparts, who wore army-issue uniform, retained their 'normal' level of deindividuation resulting from their status as uniformed soldiers.
- One of the functions of uniforms in the 'real world' is to reduce individuality and hence, at least indirectly, to increase deindividuation (Brown, 1985). Indeed, dispossessing people of their 'civilian' clothes is a major technique of depersonalising them in 'total institutions' such as prisons and psychiatric hospitals (Goffman, 1968, 1971). As Brown (1985) observes, the victims of aggression are often dehumanised by having their heads shaved and being dressed in ill-fitting clothes, making them appear less human. This, in turn, makes it easier for people to humiliate and abuse them.
- The deindividuation produced by wearing military or police uniform increases the likelihood of the wearer's brutality. By the same token, the anonymity of massed ranks of police or soldiers may make them appear less human, making them a more obvious target for a rioting crowd's violence.

The social constructionist approach

Mummendey (1996) has proposed that whether or not a behaviour is considered aggressive depends on a judgement made by either an observer or the performer: the appraisal of a behaviour as aggressive involves going beyond a description to an *evaluation* of it. For Mummendey:

> *When asking about the causes of aggression, more is of interest than simply the conditions for the occurrence of that behaviour. Of even greater importance are the conditions for judging the individual behaviour as 'aggressive'.*

A case in point is soccer hooliganism.

Ask Yourself

- How might the theories of aggression discussed above explain soccer hooliganism?
- How easily can they account for the fact that most people at soccer matches *don't* behave in this way?

MEET THE RESEARCHER

Barbara Krahé

Does playing violent video games make adolescents more aggressive?

There is evidence from experimental studies that watching a violent film or playing a violent video game increases users' aggressive thoughts, feelings and behaviours. In addition, surveys asking people to report on their use of violent media and their readiness to engage in aggressive behaviour also support a link between media violence and aggression (Anderson and Bushman, 2002). Other authors have denied that there is conclusive evidence that violent media make users more aggressive (e.g. Ferguson, 2007). We conducted two studies with secondary school students in Germany to further address this controversy. Both studies focused on the use of violent video games as a particularly popular type of violent media among young people.

Study 1

The first study (Krahé and Möller, 2004) looked at the link between playing violent video games and two types of aggression-related thoughts: (1) the belief that using physical aggression is acceptable; and (2) the tendency to attribute hostile intentions to other people (called 'hostile attributional style').

A sample of 115 girls and 116 boys (average age, 13.6 years) indicated how often they played each game of a list of 25 popular video games and listed five favourite games they would recommend to a friend. For each game, journalists from computer magazines rated the level of violence. Students also stated to what extent they would find it acceptable to show different aggressive responses (e.g. 'To threaten to beat another person up who has made one angry is: (a) totally OK; (b) somewhat OK; (c) not really OK; (d) not at all OK'). To measure participants' hostile attributional style, they were asked to imagine being in a situation where someone caused some form of harm to them and they had to indicate whether they thought the person had done it on purpose. One of the scenarios read:

> *Imagine it is break time at school. You and your friends are hanging out in the school yard, standing together in a group and chatting. A group from another class is standing next to you. You are thirsty and so you open a can of coke. You are about to take the first sip when someone gives you a push from behind. The coke is spilt all over your new white shirt and you are wet and sticky all over.*

Participants were asked to rate how certain they were that the other person had spilt the coke on purpose, using a scale ranging from 'not at all' (1) to 'very much' (5).

The main findings showed that boys played violent games more frequently than girls and recommended more violent games to their friends. For both boys and girls, the more often participants played violent games and the more violent the games they recommended to a friend, the more they found it acceptable to act aggressively. In turn, the more they found physical aggression acceptable, the more they tended to attribute hostile intentions to the person in the story.

Correlational studies such as this can show that there is a link between the amount of violent video game usage and aggression. However, they cannot tell us if the more frequent use of violent video games is a *cause* of aggression because both aggression and use of violent games were measured at the same time. Therefore, we conducted a second study where reports about use of violent video games were related to participants' aggression 30 months later.

Study 2

This longitudinal study (Möller and Krahé, 2009) was conducted with 153 girls and 142 boys who were contacted twice over 30 months. Average age at the first measurement was 13.4 years. On both occasions, participants reported how frequently they used violent video games and rated their own tendency to behave aggressively by responding to items such as, 'If somebody hits me, I hit back' – response scale ranging from 'not at all like me' (1) to 'completely like me' (5). The belief that physical aggression is acceptable and hostile attributional style were also measured twice, using similar measures as in Study 1. The figure below shows the links between usage of violent video games and aggressive behaviour over 30 months.

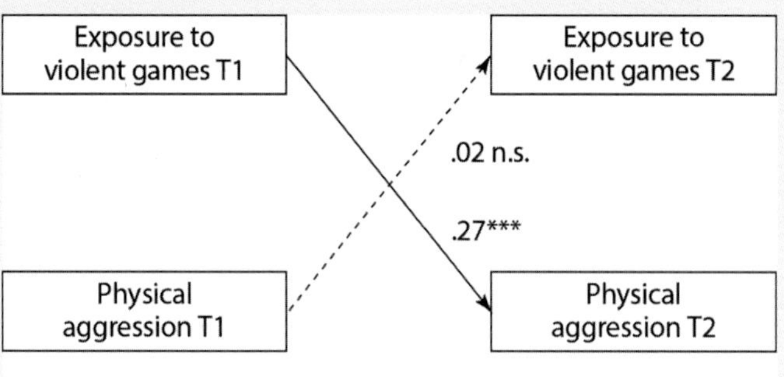

Links between playing of violent video games and physical aggression over a three-month period (based on Möller and Krahé, 2009: 84)

The more violent video game usage participants reported at the first occasion (T1), the more aggressive they were 30 months later (T2) by their own description. The correlation of 0.27 is small, but significant, indicating that about 7 per cent of differences in aggression between participants at T2 can be explained through knowing their different use of violent video games at T1. By contrast, aggressive behaviour at T1 was unrelated to reported use of violent video games at T2 30 months later. These findings suggest that using violent video games has an effect over time on aggressive behaviour and that the reverse hypothesis – namely that more aggressive individuals are more likely to select violent video games – received no support by these data. Confirming the findings from Study 1, the more violent video game use participants reported at T1, the more they thought 30 months later that using physical aggression was acceptable. In turn, the more they believed that aggression was acceptable, the more they attributed hostile intentions to others and the more aggressive they rated themselves to be at T2. The findings are presented below.

In combination, these studies show a link between the frequency of using violent video games and aggressive thoughts and behaviour. However, it must be stressed that the link was established at the group level. Those who played a lot of violent games tended to be more aggressive on average, but this does not mean that every single user was more aggressive. In addition, although statistically significant – i.e. unlikely to be due to chance – the obtained links are relatively small. This means that in explaining why some people are more aggressive than others, differences in the use of violent video games provides only a small part of the answer. So the message of this research is two-fold: spending a lot of time playing violent video games may make adolescents more aggressive over time, but using violent video games is only one of many risk factors for aggressive behaviour.

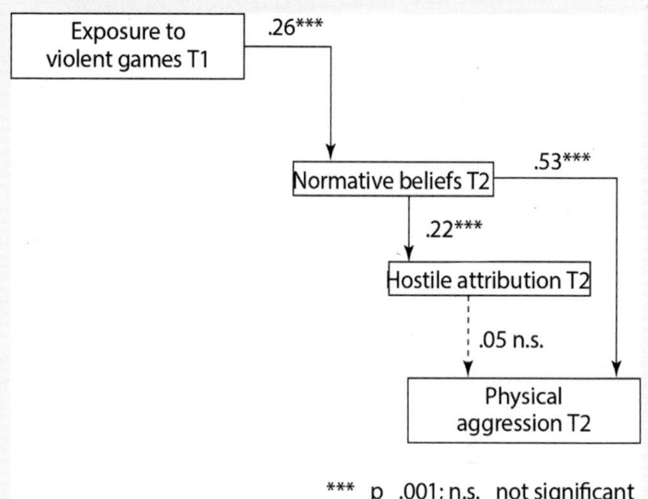

Predication of physical aggression from use of violent video games (based on Möller and Krahé, 2009: 84)

Professor Barbara Krahé is Professor of Psychology at the University of Potsdam, Germany. She is author of *The Social Psychology of Aggression* (2001; 2nd edn, 2013).

Critical Discussion 29.2

The online disinhibition effect and cyberbullying

- *The online disinhibition effect* (ODE) is a lowering of behavioural inhibitions in the online environment. Many of the behaviours witnessed in cyberspace, including cyberbullying and self-disclosure (see Chapter 22) and giving help and advice (see Chapter 30) may be attributed to the ODE (e.g. Joinson, 1998).
- Cyberbullying refers to a variety of destructive behaviours on the internet, mobile phones or other electronic devices. These behaviours include *flaming* (mutual denigration), *harassment* (recurrent insults), *denigration* (spreading rumours), *outing* and *trickery* (blaming), *exclusion, impersonation* (taking on a different identity), *happy slapping* (publishing embarrassing/ compromising pictures or movies) and *cyberstalking* and *cyberthreatening* (Kowlaski *et al.,* 2008).
- *Flaming* is an example of what Suler (2004) calls *toxic disinhibition.*
- A relevant finding in the context of the media and aggression is that the degree to which adolescents engage in cyberbullying depends on the degree to which they used media in general (Müller, 2013, cited in Ittel *et al.*, 2014). This suggests that different factors determine whether (or not) adolescents engage in cyberbullying or in-person bullying (Ittel *et al.,* 2014).
- Joinson (2003, 2007) and Suler (2004) have proposed a number of satiation-specific factors that appear to account for the ODE, including *anonymity, invisibility, asynchronicity* and *textuality.*
- Lapidot-Lefler and Barak (2012) found that *lack of eye contact* has a significant effect on the ODE, including self-reported flaming incidents and threats. They also operationalised anonymity as *unidentifiability* (and coined the new term 'online sense of unidentifiability'); this includes lack of eye contact (as well as non-disclosure of personal details and invisibilty).

CONCLUSIONS

Taking the example of soccer hooliganism, violence and aggression need to be explained at several different levels. Most of the theories we've discussed are *individualistic.* Stemming from Le Bon's original study of rioting crowds, even deindividuation theory stresses how crowds release the primitive, uncivilised/ unsocialised tendencies within the psyche of every *individual.*

What's needed is an analysis which integrates many levels of explanation. While the largely symbolic and ritualistic nature of much football supporter behaviour can be explained in terms of the 'rules' identified by Marsh *et al* (1978):

> *... Individual or group frustrations coupled with the highly emotional atmosphere of a match may occasionally tip the balance towards real aggression. In the mix, there may also be individuals who are simply aggressive, and who find the ferment of a match an ideal context in which to indulge in overt aggression ... (Hogg and Abrams, 2000)*

Chapter Summary

- Lorenz's **ethological** account seriously underestimated the role of **cultural evolution**.
- The highly controversial **rape adaptation hypothesis** isn't accepted by all Evolutionary Psychologists. While some see it as an evolved **adaptation** to the problem of securing a reluctant mate, others see it as a **side-effect** of the male sex drive.
- According to Freud, our self-destructive death instinct is 'diverted' into outwardly directed aggression. Both Freud and Lorenz believed that aggression builds up spontaneously and needs regular release. Some support for this view comes from studies of **overcontrolled violent criminals**.
- Dollard *et al.*'s **frustration–aggression hypothesis (FAH)** represented an attempt to integrate some of Freud's ideas with those of learning theory. Several modifications were made to the original theory, concerning the conditions under which frustration is likely to produce aggression.
- According to Berkowitz's **aggressive-cue theory (ACT)**, environmental stimuli which have an aggressive **meaning** are necessary for anger to be converted into aggressive behaviour. One demonstration of this is the **weapons effect.**
- Zillman's **excitation-transfer theory (ETT)** sees the arousal–aggression relationship as a **sequence.**

However, the existence of 'neutral' arousal has been questioned. The cognitive approach sees anger and aggression as **parallel** processes.

- Bandura's Bobo doll experiments were carried out in the context of his **social learning theory (SLT)**, which gives central place to **observational learning/ modelling**. They represent the first phase of scientific research into the effects of media violence.
- Perception of the level of **TV violence** is subjective and may not correspond with objective counts of violent incidents. Real-life incidents in news and documentaries are generally rated as more violent than those in fictional settings or cartoons.
- Several different **methodologies** have been used to study the effects of media violence, including **correlational studies, laboratory, field** and **natural experiments** and **longitudinal panel studies**.
- Processes underlying the effects of media violence include **priming, mimicking (imitation)**, **arousal** and **excitation transfer** (short-term), **observational learning, activation** and **desentization of emotional processes** and **didactic learning processes** (long-term).
- Allowing for the role of **moderating variables** (such as age, gender, motivation, attributes of the media content, and viewing context), the consensus seems to be that exposure to media violence makes aggressive behaviour significantly more likely.
- **Deindividuation** explains aggression in terms of the reduction of inhibition against antisocial behaviour when individuals are part of a group. In this setting, there's a **loss of individuality** and an **increase in anonymity**.
- Anonymity has been operationalised by wearing hoods and masks, which make it more likely that individuals will give more punitive electric shocks to an innocent person.
- **Cyberbullying** involves many of the components of deindividuation.
- **Social constructionists** see behaviour as being aggressive or non-aggressive if that's how it's **evaluated**.

Links with Other Topics/Chapters

Chapter 46 ⟶ The case of terrorism in general, and the *suicide bomber* in particular, illustrate the controlled, premeditated nature of hostile aggression. This is one aspect of *Criminological Psychology*

Chapters 44 and 46 ⟶ Storr (1968) identifies four forms of psychopathology attributable to the inadequate resolution of the aggressive drive, namely *depression*, *schizoid behaviour*, *paranoia* and *psychopathy*

Chapters 42 and 44 ⟶ Frustration can produce a variety of responses (of which aggression is one), including *regression, depression* and *lethargy* (Seligman, 1975)

Chapter 22 ⟶ Apologising or confessing can have a similar effect to the presence of mitigating circumstances in changing the attributions made about a frustrater (Weiner, 1992), and represent important aspects of *impression management*

Chapter 10 ⟶ Excitation transfer as a way of explaining the misattribution of emotional arousal is consistent with Schachter's *cognitive labelling theory*

Chapter 8 ⟶ Desensitisation in response to TV violence is the equivalent of developing *tolerance to drugs* with repeated use

Chapters 25 and 46 ⟶ Taylor *et al.* (1994) argue that TV and movies contribute only a small incentive effect to *crime* and violence over and above the contribution of social factors such as *racial prejudice, unemployment*, and the widespread availability of *drugs* and *guns*

Recommended Reading

Archer, J. (ed.) (1994) *Male Violence*. London: Routledge. Also relevant to Chapters 2, 36 and 50.

Berkowitz, L. (1993) *Aggression: Its Causes, Consequences and Control*. New York: McGraw-Hill.

Gross, R. (2008) *Key Studies in Psychology* (5th edn). London: Hodder Education. Chapter 24

Siann, G. (1985) *Accounting for Aggression: Perspectives on Aggression and Violence*. London: Allen and Unwin.

Useful Websites

www.socialpsychology.org/social.htm#violence (Social Psychology Network)

www.suicidology.org (American Association of Suicidology)

www.bullying.co.uk (Bullying UK)

www.israsociety.com (International Society for Research on Aggression)

www.melissainstitute.org (Melissa Institute for Violence Prevention)

www.angermanage.co.uk (British Association of Anger Management)

CHAPTER 30

ALTRUISM AND PROSOCIAL BEHAVIOUR

Defining prosocial behaviour

Helping and bystander intervention

Television and prosocial behaviour

INTRODUCTION and OVERVIEW

What do human kidney donors and rabbits that drum their feet on the ground have in common? At first sight, very little. But on closer inspection, they both seem to be doing things that benefit others (another person or other rabbits, respectively). In the case of the kidney donor, this is self-evident. In the case of the rabbit, drumming its feet serves as a warning to other rabbits of some threat or danger.

These are both examples of *helping behaviour,* a major form of *prosocial behaviour*. They're also often cited as cases of *altruism*, that is, help performed for the benefit of others with no expectation of personal gain. But are people – let alone rabbits – capable of acting in a purely unselfish way? Is our helping always motivated by the prospect of some benefit for ourselves – however subtle? According to Batson (2000):

> *We want to know whether anyone ever, in any degree, transcends the bounds of self-interest and helps out of genuine concern for the welfare of another. We want to know whether altruism – motivation with the ultimate goal of increasing another's welfare – exists.*

According to the theory of *universal egoism*, people are fundamentally selfish and altruism is impossible (Dovidio, 1995). This has been, and still is, the dominant ethos in social science, including Psychology. Similarly, sociobiologists consider acts of *apparent* altruism to be acts of selfishness in disguise.

Philosophers have debated for centuries whether people are by nature selfless or selfish. McDougall (1908) proposed that 'sympathetic instincts' are responsible for altruistic acts (see Chapter 10).

Only about 20 psychological studies of helping were published before 1962, but the murder of Kitty Genovese in 1964 opened up the floodgates of research into *bystander intervention* and altruism (Schroeder *et al.*, 1995). Latané and Darley were the pioneers of this research.

DEFINING PROSOCIAL BEHAVIOUR

According to Schroeder *et al.* (1995), *prosocial behaviour* includes behaviour intended to benefit others, such as helping, comforting, sharing, cooperating, reassuring, defending, donating to charity and showing concern. It follows that acts that *unintentionally* help others don't count, while those that are intended to help but actually *fail* to help *do* count.

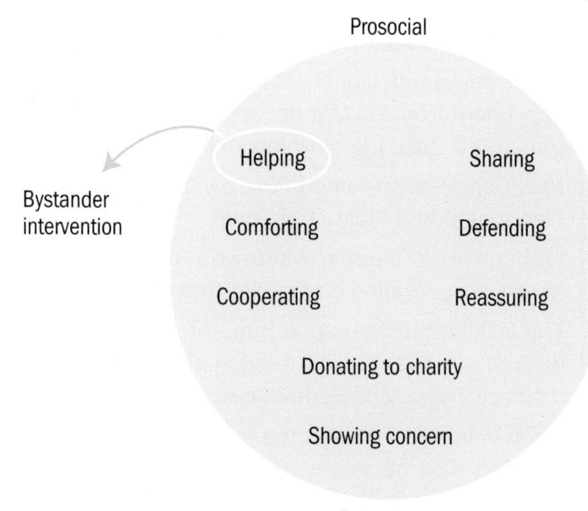

Figure 30.1 The varieties of prosocial behaviour, including helping and bystander intervention

Fiske (2004) observes that what actually benefits another person is socially defined, changing with time and place. Depending on the context, prosocial acts might include circumcision, foot-binding, piercing, scarring, tooth-pulling and ruthless criticism.

The altruism concept underlies the sub-set of prosocial behaviours that are motivated mainly out of a consideration of *another's* needs rather than one's own (Piliavin and Charng, 1990). As a motive, altruism involves self-sacrificial costs and the absence of any 'obvious' external rewards (Batson, 1998).

HELPING and BYSTANDER INTERVENTION

Ask Yourself

- What do you think you'd have done if you'd been one of Kitty's neighbours? (See Case Study 30.1.)

Since 1964, doubt has been cast on many of the details as reported above. For example, Manning *et al.* (2007)

Case Study 30.1

Kitty Genovese (adapted from the *New York Times*, March 1964)

37 Who Saw Murder Didn't Call the Police

Apathy at Stabbing of Queens Woman Shocks Inspector

By Martin Gansberg

For more than half an hour, 38 respectable, law-abiding citizens in Queens watched a killer stalk and stab a woman in three separate attacks ...

Twice the sound of their voices and the sudden glow of their bedroom lights interrupted him and frightened him off. Each time he returned, sought her out and stabbed her again. Not one person telephoned the police during the assault; one witness called after the woman was dead.

'He Stabbed Me!'

... She screamed. Lights went on in the ten-storey apartment house ... Windows slid open and voices punctured the early morning stillness.

Miss Genovese screamed: 'Oh, my God, he stabbed me! Please help me! Please help me!'

From one of the upper windows in the apartment house, a man called down: 'Let that girl alone!'

The assailant looked up at him, shrugged and walked ... toward a white sedan parked a short distance away. Miss Genovese struggled to her feet.

Lights went out. The killer returned to Miss Genovese, now trying to make her way around the side of the building ... to her apartment. The assailant grabbed her again.

'I'm dying!' she shrieked.

'I'm dying!'

A City Bus Passed

Windows were opened again, and lights went on in many apartments. The assailant got into his car and drove away. Miss Genovese staggered to her feet. It was 3.35 a.m.

The assailant returned. By then, Miss Genovese had crawled to the back of the building ... he saw her slumped on the floor at the foot of the stairs. He stabbed her a third time – fatally.

It was 3.50 by the time the police received their first call, from a man who was a neighbour of Miss Genovese ...The man explained that he had called the police after much deliberation ... 'I didn't want to get involved,' he sheepishly told the police.

Suspect is Arrested

Today witnesses from the neighbourhood ... find it difficult to explain why they didn't call the police.

The police said most persons had told them they had been afraid to call, but had given meaningless answers when asked what they had feared.

'We can understand the reticence of people to become involved in an area of violence,' Lieutenant Jacobs said, 'but where they are in their homes, near phones, why should they be afraid to call the police?'

... A housewife ... said, 'We thought it was a lovers' quarrel.' A husband and wife both said, 'Frankly, we were afraid.' ... A distraught woman ... said, 'I didn't want my husband to get involved.'

One couple ... said they heard the first screams ... 'We went to the window to see what was happening,' he said, 'but the light from our bedroom made it difficult to see the street.' The wife, still apprehensive, added: 'I put out the light and we were able to see better.'

Asked why they hadn't called the police, she shrugged and replied, 'I don't know.'

questioned whether individual witnesses standing at their windows can be meaningfully described as an unresponsive group. Nevertheless, what is beyond doubt is that the Kitty Genovese murder, together with findings from their laboratory studies, led Latané and Darley to introduce the concept of the *unresponsive bystander* (or *bystander apathy*) to denote people's typically uncaring attitude towards others in need of their help.

While the American media thought it remarkable that out of 38 witnesses not a single one did anything to help, Latané and Darley believed that it was precisely *because* there were so many that Kitty Genovese wasn't helped. So, how does the presence of others determine whether any particular individual will intervene in an emergency, and what other influences are involved?

The decision model of bystander intervention

According to Latané and Darley's (1970) *decision model*, before someone helps another, that person must:

- notice that something is wrong
- define it as a situation requiring help
- decide whether to take personal responsibility
- decide what kind of help to give
- implement the decision to intervene.

This represents a logical sequence of steps: a negative response at any one step means that the bystander won't intervene, and the victim won't receive help (at least not from that bystander: see Figure 30.2).

Noticing that something is wrong

Studies conducted in several different countries (including the USA, UK, Saudi Arabia and Sudan) have found that people living in urban areas tend to be less helpful than those in rural settings (Hedge and Yousif, 1992; Yousif and Korte, 1995).

Ask Yourself

- Why do you think there should be this urban/rural divide?
- Does it surprise you?

Milgram (1970) believes it may represent a way in which urban dwellers cope with *stimulus overload*: they restrict their attention mainly to personally relevant events. Strangers and their situations of need may, therefore, go unnoticed.

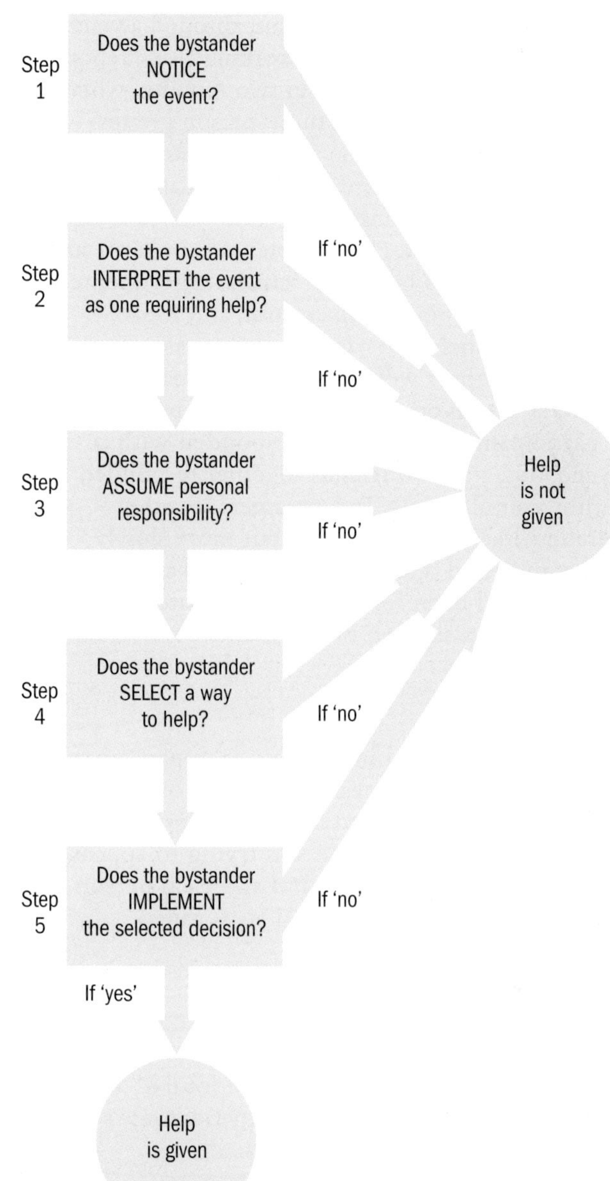

Figure 30.2 Latané and Darley's five-step decision model of bystander intervention and non-intervention (based on Schroeder *et al.*, 1995)

Regardless of location, people are also more likely to be attentive to others when they're in a good mood (which, in turn, makes them more likely to help) (Dovidio and Penner, 2004).

Defining the situation as an emergency

In one of the first bystander experiments (Latané and Darley, 1968), participants were shown into a room in order to complete some questionnaires. In one condition they were alone, while in another there were two others present. After a time, steam (resembling smoke) began to pour through a vent in the wall. 75 per cent of those working alone reported the smoke, half of them within two minutes, while 62 per cent of those in the three-person groups carried on working for the full six minutes (by which time it was difficult to see the questionnaires and the experiment was terminated).

Latané and Rodin (1969) obtained similar results when participants heard the female experimenter in an adjoining room fall, cry out, and moan. They were much faster to react when alone than when others were present. In a variation of Latané and Rodin's experiment, 70 per cent of participants on their own responded within 65 seconds, and two friends together responded within a similar time. Two strangers together were less likely to react at all (but more slowly if they did), and if someone was paired with a stooge who'd been instructed not to intervene at all, that person showed the least and slowest reaction of all.

Pluralistic ignorance

In post-experimental interviews, each participant reported feeling very hesitant about showing anxiety, so they looked to others for signs of anxiety. But since everyone was trying to appear calm, these signs weren't found and each person defined the situation as 'safe'. This is called *pluralistic ignorance*.

Ask Yourself

- Can pluralistic ignorance account for the inaction of the witnesses to Kitty Genovese's murder?

There seems little doubt that the witnesses realised at the time what was going on. Although one woman claimed she thought it was a 'lovers' quarrel', most claimed they were afraid to intervene (they didn't deny that help was needed), and Kitty's second lot of screams (if not the first) must have made the nature of the situation quite unambiguous.

Genuine ambiguity may sometimes account for lack of intervention, as in situations of domestic violence. According to Shotland and Straw (1976), we'd be much more likely to help a victim if we believed s/he didn't know the attacker than if we believed a relationship existed between the two. Male participants were shown a staged fight between a man and a woman. In one condition the woman screamed, 'I don't even know you', while in another, she screamed 'I don't even know why I married you!' Three times as many men intervened in the first condition as in the second condition.

Accepting personal responsibility or diffusing responsibility

Ask Yourself

- Try to account for Darley and Latané's findings in Key Study 30.1.
- Can pluralistic ignorance explain them?

While pluralistic ignorance may make it less likely that we'll define a situation as an emergency in the first place, this cannot apply in Darley and Latané's study. The best explanation is *diffusion of responsibility*, that is, the denial of personal responsibility and the belief that someone else will probably do what's necessary. The more bystanders that are present (or believed to be present), the lower the probability that any one of them will accept responsibility. This is more likely to happen when the victim is remote (can only be 'heard' from some other room in the building).

Kitty Genovese could be both heard and seen (by those who made the effort to look out of their windows), and the second lot of screams must have made it obvious that no one had gone for help!

Piliavin *et al.* (1981) use the term *dissolution of responsibility* to describe what happens when the behaviour of other witnesses cannot be observed and the participant 'rationalises' that someone else must have already intervened (as in the 'seizure' experiment). *Diffusion* occurs when all the witnesses accept responsibility. Regardless of which term is used, it's consistently found that the presence of others *inhibits* an individual from intervening.

However, there are limits to diffusion of responsibility. Piliavin *et al.* (1969) found that help was offered on crowded subways in New York as frequently as on relatively empty ones (see Key Study 30.3). As Brown (1985) suggests, perhaps it's more difficult not to help in a face-to-face situation and in an enclosed space.

Choosing a way to help: the role of competence

Related to diffusion of responsibility, and something which may interact with it, is a bystander's *competence* to intervene and offer appropriate help. In the presence of others, one or more of whom you believe is better

Key Study 30.1

The stresses of urban living (Darley and Latané, 1968)

- College students were recruited to discuss the problems of living in a high-pressure urban environment.
- Instead of face-to-face discussion, they communicated via an intercom system ('so as to avoid any embarrassment'). Each participant would talk for two minutes, then each would comment on what the others had said. The other 'participants' were, in fact, tape recordings.
- Early in the discussion, the victim (a stooge) casually mentioned that he had epilepsy and that the anxiety and stress of urban living made him prone to seizures. Later, he became increasingly loud and incoherent, choking, gasping and crying out before lapsing into silence.
- Darley and Latané were interested in the percentage of participants who responded within five minutes (by coming out of the small room to look for the victim).
- Of those who believed they were the only other participant, 85 per cent intervened. Of those who believed there were two others (three altogether), 62 per cent intervened, and of those who believed there were five others (six altogether), only 31 per cent intervened. The most responsive group was also the fastest to respond. These findings were confirmed by Latané *et al.* (1981).

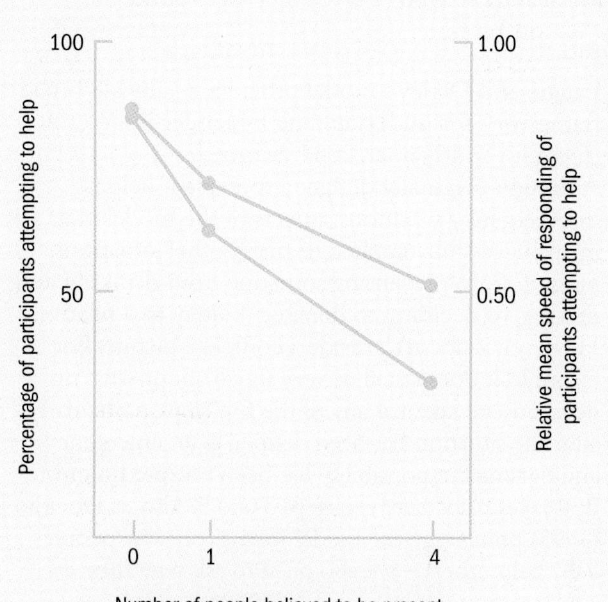

Figure 30.3 Percentage of participants attempting to help (by leaving their room to look for the 'victim' within five minutes) as a function of the number of others believed to be present, and the relative mean speed of responding of participants attempting to help (adapted from Darley and Latané, 1968)

equipped to offer help, diffusion of responsibility will be increased. However, if you believe you're best equipped to help, the presence of others will have relatively little effect on your behaviour. For example, if a swimmer is in trouble, we'll usually let the lifeguard go to the rescue, and even if we were the only other person at the pool, we'd be extremely unlikely to dive in if we couldn't swim ourselves! But if we're an excellent swimmer and trained in life-saving skills, we'd be much more likely to help even if others were present (Baron and Byrne, 1991).

According to Schroeder *et al.* (1995), we shouldn't take the inhibiting effects of other people as necessarily indicating bystander apathy, as Latané and Darley did. People may be truly concerned about the victim's welfare, but sincerely believe that someone else is more likely – or better qualified in some way – to help. For example, Bickman (1971) replicated the 'seizure' experiment, but manipulated the participants' belief about proximity to the victim. Those who believed the other person was as close to the victim as they were (in the same building) and equally capable of helping, were less likely to help

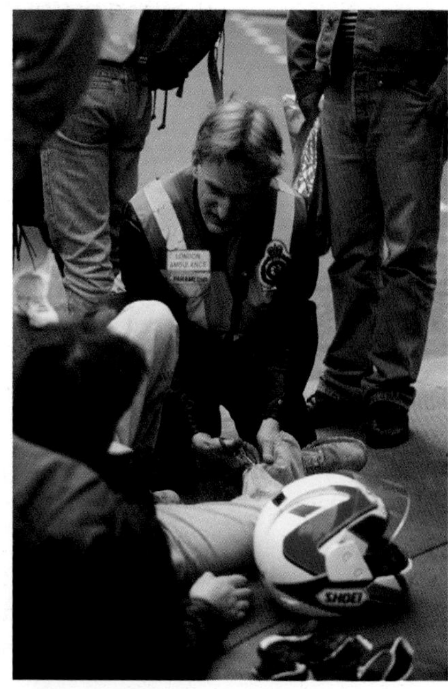

Figure 30.4 We're happy to diffuse responsibility when more competent bystanders are present

than those who believed they were alone (diffusion of responsibility). But when they believed the other person was in another building and so unable to help, they helped as much as those who believed they were alone.

Evaluation of the decision model

- Latané and Darley's model provides a valuable broad framework for understanding bystander intervention (Dovidio and Penner, 2004; Schroeder *et al.,* 1995).
- Although originally designed to explain helping in emergency situations, aspects of the model have been successfully applied to many other situations, ranging from preventing someone from drinking and driving, to deciding to donate a kidney to a relative.
- However, it doesn't provide a complete picture. For example, it doesn't tell us very much about why 'no' decisions are taken at any of the five steps, particularly after the situation has been defined as an emergency and personal responsibility has been accepted: a great deal takes place between steps 3 and 5. Also, as Dovidio (1995) points out, the model focuses on why people *don't* help others – we also need to ask why they *do*.

The arousal–cost–reward (ACR) model

The *arousal–cost–reward* (ACR) *model* (Piliavin *et al.*, 1969, 1981; Dovidio *et al.*, 1991) is a major alternative to the decision model, and represents a kind of 'fine-tuning' of some of the processes involved. It identifies a number of critical situational and bystander variables, which can help predict how likely it is that intervention will take place under any particular set of circumstances.

The ACR model was first introduced by Piliavin *et al.* (1969) as a 'heuristic device' in attempting to account for the results of the New York subway experiment (see Key Study 30.3). It was subsequently revised and expanded to cover both emergency and non-emergency helping (Piliavin *et al.*, 1981).

The model identifies two conceptually distinct but functionally interdependent influences on helping:

1. *Arousal* in response to the need or distress of others is an emotional response. This is the basic *motivational* construct. When arousal is attributed to the victim's distress, it's experienced as unpleasant, and the bystander is motivated to reduce it.
2. The *cost–reward* component involves cognitive processes by which bystanders assess and weigh up the anticipated costs and rewards associated with both helping and not helping.

According to Dovidio *et al.* (1991):

> *People are aroused by the distress of others and exhibit emotionally empathic reactions to the problems and crises of others ... also ... the severity and clarity of another person's emergency and the relationship to the victim systematically influence arousal ...*

While arousal and helping are often only correlated, the ACR model sees arousal as *causing* the helping. There's considerable empirical support for this claim (Dovidio *et al.,* 1991). The model proposes that bystanders will choose the response that most rapidly and completely reduces the arousal, incurring as few costs as possible. So, the emotional component provides the motivation to do something, while the cognitive component determines what the *most efficient* or *effective response* will be.

Ask Yourself

- Try to remember a situation in which you helped someone who was clearly upset or distressed.
- How did you reach the decision to help?
- What were your motives for helping – at the time and in retrospect?

The cost–reward analysis

Research has concentrated on this part of the ACR model and, specifically, on the relative costs of helping and not helping. (But see the section on arousal below.)

- The *costs of helping* include lost time, effort, possible physical danger, embarrassment, disruption of ongoing activities, and psychological aversion (as in the case of a victim who's bleeding or drunk).
- The *rewards of helping* include fame, gratitude from the victim and relatives, the intrinsic pleasure and self-satisfaction derived from the act of helping, the avoidance of guilt (for not helping) and even money.
- The *costs of not helping* include guilt, blame from others and cognitive and/or emotional discomfort associated with knowing that another person is suffering.

What's high cost for one person may be low cost for another (and vice versa). Cost may also differ for the same person from one situation to another.

Table 30.1 is based largely on the ACR model as it had been proposed prior to 1981. Piliavin *et al.* (1981) and Dovidio *et al.* (1991) elaborated the model by considering the influence of a new range of variables, such as bystander personality and mood, the clarity of the emergency, victim characteristics, the relationship between the victim and potential helpers, and attributions made by potential helpers of the victim's deservingness. Many of these variables interact and contribute to (a) how aroused the bystander is and (b) the perceived costs and rewards for direct intervention.

Different kinds of costs

Two kinds of costs associated with not helping are *personal costs* (e.g. self-blame, public disapproval) and *empathy costs* (e.g. knowing that the victim continues to

Table 30.1 Costs of helping/not helping in emergencies/non-emergencies, and the likelihood/type of intervention, as predicted by the arousal–cost–reward model (based on Piliavin *et al.*, 1969)

Costs of helping/not helping and likely outcome	Examples
Costs of helping are low	You're unlikely to be injured yourself; the victim is only shocked
Costs of not helping are high	You'd feel guilty; other people would blame you
Likelihood of intervention **very high – and direct**	
Costs of helping are high	You don't like the sight of blood; you're unsure what to do
Costs of not helping are high	It's an emergency – the victim could die
Likelihood of intervention **fairly high – but indirect**	Call for ambulance/police, or ask another bystander to assist
Or **redefine the situation** (see text)	Ignore the victim and/or leave the scene
Costs of helping are high	'This drunk could turn violent or throw up over me'
Costs of not helping are low	'Who'd blame me for not helping?'
Likelihood of intervention **very low**	Bystander may well turn away, change seats, walk away, etc
Costs of helping are low	'It wouldn't hurt to help this blind man across the road'
Costs of not helping are low	'He seems capable of looking after himself; there's very little traffic on the road'
Likelihood of intervention **fairly high**	Bystanders will vary, according to individual differences and how they perceive the norms operating in the particular situation

suffer). According to Dovidio *et al.* (1991), in general, costs for not helping affect intervention primarily when the costs for helping are low.

Although *indirect helping* becomes more likely as the costs for helping increase (as in serious emergencies), it's relatively infrequent. This may be because it's difficult for bystanders to pull themselves away from such involving situations in order to seek other people to assist (Schroeder *et al.*, 1995). The most common (and positively effective) way of resolving the *high-cost-for-helping/high-cost-for-not-helping dilemma* (see section 2 of Table 30.1) is *cognitive reinterpretation*. This can take one of three forms:

1. Redefining the situation as one not requiring help
2. Diffusing responsibility
3. Denigrating (blaming) the victim.

Each of these has the effect of reducing the perceived costs of not helping. Schroeder *et al.* (1995) stress that cognitive reinterpretation doesn't mean that bystanders are uncaring (or 'apathetic'). On the contrary, it's the fact that they care that creates the dilemma in the first place.

The cost of time

The importance of loss of time as a motive for not helping was shown in a content analysis of answers given in response to five written traffic accident scenarios (Bierhoff *et al.*, 1987, in Bierhoff and Klein, 1988). We're often in a hurry in many real-life situations, and waiting can be very frustrating; this is why the willingness to sacrifice time for a person in need can be seen as generous ('time is money'). The most frequently mentioned motives for helping were enhancement of self-esteem and moral obligation.

The experiment by Darley and Batson (1973) (see Key Study 30.2) shows that seemingly trivial variables can exert a profound effect on altruistic responses (Bierhoff and Klein, 1988). By contrast, Bierhoff (1983) asked students to volunteer for a Psychology experiment; if they participated without payment, the money would be sent to children in need. They could choose up to 12 half-hour sessions and, on average, students volunteered for 3.71 sessions. These findings indicate that the general level of helpfulness is higher than some pessimists might have assumed.

Different types of helping

Certain kinds of *casual helping* (McGuire, 1994) or *low-cost altruism* (Brown, 1986) seem to be fairly common, such as giving a stranger directions or telling them the time. Latané and Darley (1970) had Psychology students approach a total of 1,500 passers-by in New York to ask them such routine, low-cost favours.

Key Study 30.2

If you need help, avoid a late Samaritan (Darley and Batson, 1973)

- The participants were students at a theological seminary, who were instructed to present a talk in a nearby building. Half the students were to give a talk on the Good Samaritan, while for the other half it was about jobs most enjoyed by seminary students. Each student was then told:
  - (a) He was ahead of schedule and had plenty of time (to get to the other building), or
  - (b) He was right on schedule, or
  - (c) He was late.
- On the way to give their talk, all the students passed a man (a stooge) slumped in a doorway, coughing and groaning.
- Although the topic given for the talk had little effect on helping, time pressures did: the percentages offering help were 63, 45 and ten for conditions a, b and c, respectively.
- Ironically, on several occasions the 'late' students who were on their way to talk about the Good Samaritan literally stepped over the victim!

Depending on the nature of the favour, between 34 and 85 per cent of New Yorkers proved to be 'low-cost altruists'. However, most people refused to tell the student their names.

Generally, as the type of intervention that's required changes from casual helping through 'substantial personal helping' (such as helping someone move house) and 'emotional helping' (such as listening to a friend's personal problems) to 'emergency helping' (which is what's involved in most of the studies discussed so far), the costs of intervention increase. But so do the costs of not helping.

Helping different kinds of victim

Ask Yourself

- Would you be more likely to go to the aid of a stranger who collapses apparently due to the effects of alcohol or for some other (medical) reason?
- If the victim were bleeding, would you be more or less likely to offer help?

Key Study 30.3

Good Samaritanism – an underground phenomenon? (Piliavin *et al.*, 1969)

- Student experimenters pretended to collapse in subway train compartments – they fell to the floor and waited to see if they'd be helped.
- Sometimes they were carrying a cane (the *lame condition*); sometimes they were wearing a jacket which smelled very strongly of alcohol and carried a bottle in a brown paper bag (the *drunk condition*).
- As predicted, help was offered much less often in the 'drunk' than in the 'lame' condition (20 per cent compared with 90 per cent, within 70 seconds).

In a second study, the person who 'collapsed' bit off a capsule of bloodlike dye, which trickled down his chin. The helping rate dropped from 90 to 60 per cent. People were much more likely to get someone else to help, especially someone they thought would be more competent in an emergency (Piliavin and Piliavin, 1972).

Similarly, Piliavin *et al.* (1975) found that when the victim had an ugly facial birthmark, the rate of helping dropped to 61 per cent. Other studies have reported that a smartly dressed and well-groomed stranded motorist is far more likely to receive help from passing motorists than one who's casually dressed or looks untidy.

The importance of difference

The greater the victim's distress, injury or disfigurement, or the more we disapprove of them or blame their plight on their undesirable behaviour, the more likely we are to perceive them as being different from ourselves. This, in turn, makes it less likely that we'll offer them help. The psychological costs of helping someone perceived as being different from ourselves seem to be greater than the same help offered to someone perceived as being similar.

On this basis, we'd expect help to be offered less often to someone of a different racial group from the bystander. But the evidence isn't so clear-cut. For example, in the New York subway experiment, there was no evidence of greater same-race helping when the victim was apparently ill. However, when he appeared drunk, blacks were much more likely to help a black drunk and whites a white drunk.

Ask Yourself

- How might you account for this finding in terms of different types of racism? (See Chapter 25.)

Many whites who may truly believe they're not prejudiced still harbour unconscious negative feelings. As a result of possessing both conscious, non-prejudiced convictions and unconscious, prejudiced feelings, *symbolic* (or *aversive*) racists discriminate in certain situations but not others. Where the social norms for appropriate behaviour are clear and unambiguous (for example, people who are ill should be helped), aversive racists won't discriminate. If they did behave in a discriminatory way, their self-concept (as non-racists) would be threatened, incurring significant costs. However, when social norms are weak or ambiguous, or where aversive racists can justify a negative response based on some factor other than race/ethnic group ('drunks can turn nasty, so leave them alone'), then discrimination will occur.

Figure 30.5 Foreign beggars on the streets of London. Are they less likely to be given money because they are foreigners – or more likely because they have children?

Key Study 30.4

Diffusion of responsibility as a 'cover' for racism (Gaertner and Dovidio, 1977)

- Gaertner and Dovidio used the cubicle and intercom procedure, as in the Darley and Latané (1968) 'seizure' experiment (see Key Study 30.1).
- White bystanders, who believed they were the only witness to an emergency and when appropriate behaviour was clearly defined, didn't discriminate against a black victim. In fact, they were slightly more likely to help a black than a white victim (94 per cent compared with 81 per cent).
- But when they believed there were other bystanders, they helped a black victim about half as often as a white victim (38 and 75 per cent respectively).
- The opportunity to diffuse responsibility offered a non-race-related excuse to treat blacks differently, thereby allowing them to avoid recognising racial bias as a factor (Schroeder *et al.,* 1995).

Individual differences and helping

As Table 30.1 shows, individual differences will have their main impact when the costs for helping and not helping are both low, and when the situation is ambiguous and 'psychologically weak' or less 'evocative'. But the more emergency-like the situation (and, hence, the more compelling and evocative it is), the less relevant person variables will be. According to Dovidio and Penner (2004), although personality is now recognised as an important factor in helping, personality traits typically play a less substantial role in helping than do situational factors (see Meet the Researcher, pp. 514–15.).

Gender differences and helping

Although both men and women experience physiological arousal in response to others' distress, women are more likely to interpret this arousal as a positive *empathic response* to others' needs (Eisenberg and Lennon, 1983). This would predict greater helping by women. However, Eagly and Crowley (1986) reviewed 172 studies and found that men turn out to be significantly *more* helpful than women. How can we reconcile these two things?

According to Eagly (1987), the female gender role involves caring for others, providing friends with personal favours, emotional support, counselling about personal problems, and so on (*communal helping*). By contrast, the male gender role requires heroism and chivalry: men are more likely to help another when there's an audience present to witness the helping act, and/or where there's an element of risk involved in helping (*agentic helping*). Most studies of bystander intervention (at least those involving emergencies) seem to require agentic helping.

Gender roles also affect perception of the costs and rewards associated with various types of helping. For example, Otten *et al.* (1988) found that in response to friends' requests for psychological support, women (compared with men) said they'd feel worse for not visiting the friend (higher cost for not helping) and perceived the visit to be less of an imposition on their time (lower cost for helping). Similarly, men (compared with women) are more likely to see the cost of failing to act heroically as greater, and the cost of intervening (such as personal harm) as lower (Eagly and Crowley, 1986).

Evaluation of the arousal–cost–reward model

- As noted in the *Introduction and overview*, the crucial question as regards altruism is *why* we help other people.

Ask Yourself

- Is helping ever motivated by a genuine wish to benefit someone else, or are we always motivated by self-interest?

Universal egoism

Underlying the ACR model (like exchange theory on which it's partly based) is an *economic* view of human behaviour: people are motivated to maximise rewards and minimise costs (Dovidio *et al.*, 1991). Faced with a potential helping situation, we weigh the probable costs and rewards of alternative courses of action, then arrive at a decision that produces the best outcome – *for ourselves*. This is one form of *universal egoism*: everything we do, no matter how noble and beneficial to others, is really directed towards the ultimate goal of self-benefit.

Another form of universal egoism relates to the arousal component of the ACR model. According to the *negative state relief* (NSR) model (Cialdini *et al.*, 1982, 1987), harming another person or witnessing another being harmed can induce negative feelings (such as guilt and sadness). This motivates the harmer/observer to reduce these feelings. Through socialisation and experience, we learn that the good feelings derived from helping can reduce these negative feelings, making us feel better. In other words, people are motivated primarily to feel good, and the motivation for helping others is essentially egoistic.

Empathy–altruism

Those who advocate the *empathy–altruism hypothesis* (EAH) (for example, Batson, 1991) don't deny that much of what we do (including what we do for others) is egoistic. But under certain circumstances, we're capable of a qualitatively different form of motivation, whose ultimate goal is to *benefit others*.

Empathic emotions include sympathy, compassion and tenderness, and are associated with *empathic concern*. These empathic emotions can and should be distinguished from the more self-oriented emotions of discomfort, anxiety and upset, which are associated with personal distress. (This corresponds to the distinction between personal and empathic costs for not helping: see above.) While personal distress produces an egoistic desire to reduce one's own distress, empathic concern produces an altruistic desire to reduce the other's distress. These are qualitatively different responses.

According to Darley (1991):

> *In the United States and perhaps in all advanced capitalistic societies, it is generally accepted that the true and basic motive for human action is self-interest. It is the primary motivation, and is the one from which other motives derive. Thus it is the only 'real' motivation …*

Testing the EAH

If helping benefits the person in need and the helper (as it often does), how are we to know the ultimate goal? If ultimate goals are reached by the same behaviour, how are we ever to know which goal or goals are ultimate? According to Batson (2000), this puzzle has led many scientists to give up on the question of the existence of altruism – it cannot be answered empirically. But Batson disagrees.

Over the past 20 years, Batson and others have conducted a series of laboratory experiments in which people are given an unexpected opportunity to help someone in need. Some are induced to feel empathy, others not. In addition, circumstances have been systematically varied in order to disentangle the altruistic ultimate goal (benefiting others) and one or more possible egoistic ultimate goals (benefiting self).

One way of teasing these goals apart is to vary the situation, so that sometimes the arousal can be reduced in a less costly way than by helping. If the ultimate goal is to reduce one's own arousal, then aroused individuals should help less when they believe they'll no longer be exposed to the person in need of help. But if the ultimate goal is to reduce the other's distress, this variation should have no effect. Several experiments using this logic have supported the EAH (Batson, 2000).

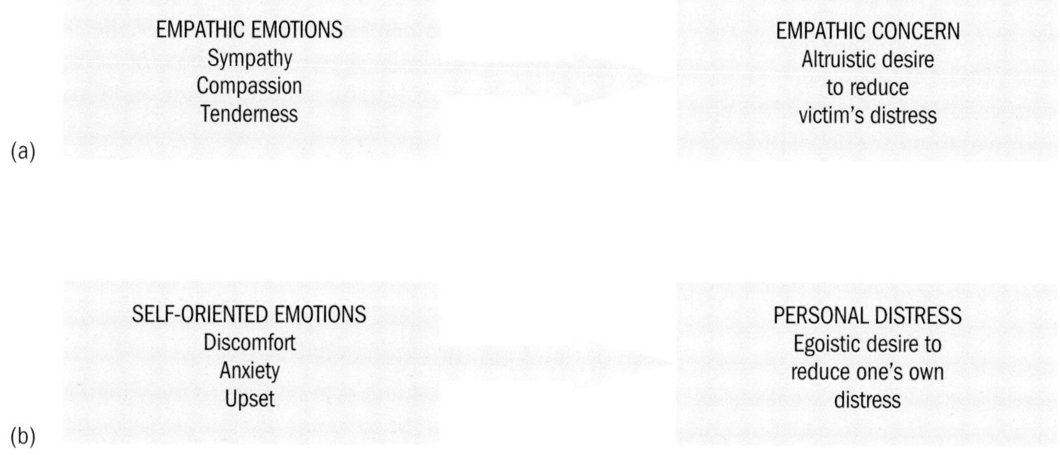

Figure 30.6 Summary of (a) the empathy–altruism hypothesis and (b) the universal egoism account of helping behaviour

These and other experiments have led to what Piliavin and Charng (1990) call a 'paradigm shift' away from universal egoism, indicating that the dominant view of human motivation – and indeed of human nature – is wrong. As Batson (2000) says:

> *... It is not true that everything we do is directed towards the ultimate goal of benefiting ourselves. It seems that we are capable of being altruistic as well as egoistic.*

But according to the *empathy-specific reward* (ESR) interpretation, people only help because they expect a reward from the victim, or from others who witnessed the act, or from themselves ('empathic joy'). Batson *et al.* (1991), however, found that participants who reported high levels of empathic concern (and were, presumably, altruistically motivated) showed high levels of helping *regardless* of whether they'd had the opportunity to experience empathic joy. In reviewing this and other egoistic challenges to the EAH, Dovidio and Penner (2004) conclude that:

> *... the preponderance of evidence from the 20 or so years of experimentation on this question strongly suggests that truly altruistic motivation may exist and all helping is not necessarily egoistically motivated.*

The evolutionary approach: Universal egoism and the paradox of altruism

If, according to universal egoists, all human acts of apparent altruism are really driven by self-interest, we might not be surprised to find a similar interpretation of the equivalent behaviours in non-human animals. There are many examples of apparently altruistic behaviour in non-humans. This is referred to as the *paradox of altruism*.

Box 30.1 The paradox of altruism

If survival is necessary for *reproductive fitness,* then Darwin's original theory of evolution by natural selection faced a major difficulty: behaviour that's commonly observed in many non-human species (including blackbirds, rabbits and lions), as well as human, serves to enhance the fitness of *another* animal (the recipient or 'beneficiary') at the cost of the performer's own fitness. For example, when a rabbit bangs on the ground as a warning to others of a potential predator, it increases the chances of the others escaping but draws attention to itself and so puts itself at greater risk. Natural selection would predict that, in a competitive world, the altruist would quickly lose the evolutionary 'race' – and this trait wouldn't survive (altruists would have very low reproductive fitness). So, how can altruism be explained in evolutionary terms?

The contribution of sociobiology

Two major *sociobiological* explanations share the view of altruism as only *apparent*, such that there *is* an inherent gain for the altruist:

(a) According to *kin selection theory* (Hamilton, 1964), traits which directed an individual's altruism towards its relatives – but not to non-relatives – would evolve. By increasing the reproductive fitness of relatives, the altruist is *indirectly* enhancing its own fitness: relatives, by definition, share some of the altruist's genes which will be reproduced via the surviving relatives. This is called *inclusive fitness*. These relatives are likely to be genetically predisposed to be altruistic. Also, the closer the genetic tie, the greater the altruistic sacrifices.

(b) Where the altruist and the beneficiary *aren't* related, the altruist is later 'repaid' by help from the unrelated recipient: short-term reduction in individual fitness is followed by a gain in fitness for both individuals. This is called *reciprocal altruism theory* ('you scratch my back, and I'll scratch yours') (Trivers, 1971).

What makes sociobiological explanations different from a 'classical' Darwinian one is the former's emphasis on the *set of genes* in contrast with the latter's 'individual animal' as the basic unit of evolution. In other words, it's not as important for individuals to survive as it is for their genes to do so. According to *selfish gene theory* (e.g. Dawkins, 1976, 1989), what appears as an altruistic act at the individual level turns out to be a *selfish* act at the gene level. Any behaviour of an organism is specifically 'designed' to maximise the survival of its genes; from the 'gene's point of view', the body is a sort of survival machine created to enhance the gene's chances of continued replication.

According to Holmes (2009), however, this focus on genes may not tell the whole story. A small but growing number of evolutionary biologists argue that it ignores crucial evolutionary processes at higher levels – among groups, species and even whole ecosystems. For example, genes rarely act alone but operate as part of networks of interacting genes; on this basis, it's the network that's selected, *not* the individual gene. Even Dawkins agrees that the idea of 'species selection' has some credibility.

Biological and psychological altruism

The sociobiological explanation of altruism fails to make the fundamental distinction between *biological* (or *evolutionary*) and *psychological* (or *vernacular*) altruism (Sober, 1992). Biological altruism is the kind displayed by birds, bees, ants, rabbits and so on. We wouldn't normally attribute the rabbit which warns its fellow rabbits with altruistic motives or intentions: it's simply part of its biologically determined repertoire. Psychological altruism is displayed by higher mammals, in particular, primates and, especially, human beings.

MEET THE RESEARCHER

Hans-Werner Bierhoff

Prosocial behaviour as a function of the person and the situation

For decades, Social Psychologists have expressed serious doubts about the existence of individual differences in prosocial behaviour (e.g. Darley and Latané, 1970). Only recently, the notion of a prosocial personality reappears in the field of Social Psychology as a viable concept. The new evidence stems from three different methodological approaches:

- questionnaire studies, which include personality measures and altruism scales
- studies in which emergencies are simulated in order to explore the relationship between intervention/non-intervention and personality
- studies of authentic emergencies in which the personality characteristics of persons who intervened in real emergencies are examined.

In this presentation we focus on the third approach, which is the most promising. Rescuers of Jews in Nazi Germany are a group of people who have clearly demonstrated their willingness to act prosocially. Results by Oliner and Oliner (1988) indicate that these rescuers were similar to matched non-rescuers in many characteristics. For example, the opportunity to help was quite comparable for rescuers and non-rescuers. However, rescuers were different from their comparison group in that they showed more benevolence towards Jews, placed more emphasis on adhering to ethical principles, and attached more importance to personal responsibility and proactive behaviour. In correspondence with this description, rescuers scored higher on social responsibility and internal locus of control. Bandura (2002: 112) commented on this evidence: 'In the case of proactive moral courage, the individual triumphs as a moral agent over compelling situational forces.'

Research into the motivations of first-aiders

Whereas Oliner and Oliner obtained their results in a retrospective study, which presupposes that current personalities of participants are related with their action or inaction decades ago, our goal was to shorten this timespan substantially (Bierhoff *et al.* 1991). Although we were convinced that Oliner and Oliner had inferred an important determinant of prosocial behaviour – namely, the person who is engaged in moral agency – we hoped to obtain more direct and more valid evidence on the issue. For example, a large time delay between the helping episode and personality measurement does not take into account processes of personality development, which might have taken place in the time interval. Therefore, an improved design provides for the immediate measurement of the personality profile of first-aiders, who intervened on behalf of accident victims.

Results

Compared with a matched control group of non-helpers, first-aiders scored higher on internal locus of control, just-world belief, social responsibility and emotional empathy (see Figure below).

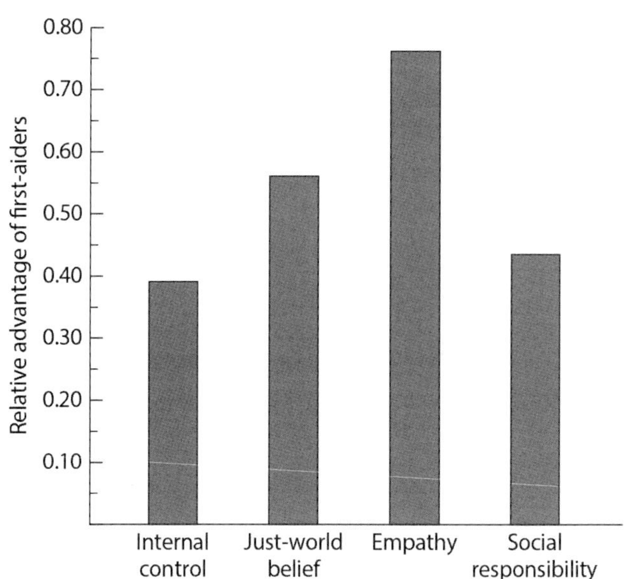

Relative advantage of first-aiders over non-helpers (from Bierhoff *et al.* 1991). All scales were assessed on six-point scales. Higher scores indicate more positive responses of the first-aiders relative to non-helpers.

The just-world belief focuses on individual differences in the belief that everyone gets what they deserve. The results attest to the fact that belief in a just world is a positive determinant of helping when the perceived effectiveness of helping is high. Whereas helpers surpassed non-helpers on all scales illustrated in the Figure, the opposite pattern of results occurred for hostile and selfish intentions, which were more pronounced in non-helpers.

The importance of the prosocial personality was acknowledged centuries ago under a different name. Both Plato and Thomas Aquinas described moral virtues that are compatible with the facets of the prosocial personality (Jeffries, 1998). The main virtues are temperance, fortitude, justice, charity and prudence. The empirical results confirm the relevance of these virtues for prosocial behaviour. For example, justice is linked to the just-world belief, which is based on justice considerations.

In attempting to identify the prosocial personality profile, researchers have used three distinct approaches. The other two approaches mentioned earlier also support the notion of a prosocial personality, which is likewise confirmed by longitudinal research on the stability of prosocial dispositions from childhood to adulthood (Eisenberg *et al.* 1999). (See Chapter 35.)

Therefore, research has unequivocally proven that the prosocial personality contributes significantly to prosocial action. Individual differences are important. At the same time, much evidence indicates that the situation exerts control over whether a person acts prosocially or not. An example is the diffusion of responsibility effect. A person is more willing to help when they are alone as a potential helper than in a situation in which several potential helpers are present (Latané and Nida, 1981).

Individual differences and contextual variables both influence prosocial behaviour. Combining these two research traditions, the question arises whether the prosocial personality is dependent on situational circumstances. More specifically, does the profile of the prosocial personality differ from situation to situation?

Voluntary and involuntary conditions

An important situational distinction focuses on voluntariness of action. One might juxtapose a voluntary condition with an obligatory condition. Whereas people in the voluntary condition can decide freely whether or not to help, in the obligatory condition social pressure is exerted that suggests not to leave the situation. This distinction was introduced by Batson (1991), who created a voluntary setting by giving participants the permission to leave the situation if they wished (easy-escape condition) and an obligatory setting by demanding that the participants not leave until the end of the experiment (difficult-escape condition). Whereas in the voluntary condition altruistically motivated helping was elicited, in the obligatory condition egoistically motivated helping was predominant. Results of a large number of experiments confirm the co-existence of these two motivational systems, which is the essence of the empathy-altruism hypothesis.

Social responsibility

Moral fulfilment of expectations and adherence to social prescriptions are two components of social responsibility, which are represented by subscales (Bierhoff, 2002). Whereas moral fulfilment of expectations refers to moral agency, adherence to social prescriptions is based on the internalisation of prosocial societal norms. Is the prosocial behaviour in voluntary situations influenced by fulfilment of the justified expectations of others and in obligatory situations by adherence to social rules of conduct?

Recent research

Bierhoff and Rohmann (2004) conducted an experiment in which easy- and difficult-escape conditions were compared, which were carefully constructed in accordance with Batson's experimental procedures. Participants had the opportunity to help a person in need who appeared to be suffering. The actual level of prosocial behaviour was scaled from 1 (no help) to 3 (high level of help). In addition, participants filled out the social responsibility questionnaire, which included the two subscales.

The results of the experiment indicate that – as expected – two distinct profiles of the prosocial personality emerged that were linked to easiness of escape. Whereas moral fulfilment of expectations was primarily related to prosocial behaviour in the voluntary condition of easy escape, adherence to social prescriptions was primarily associated with prosocial behaviour in the obligatory condition of difficult escape.

These results that illustrate the Prosocial Person × Situation interaction support the assumption that two prosocial personality profiles are operative depending on the social situation. Additional data indicate that the one which is relevant in voluntary situations corresponds to the personality profile of first-aiders in the study by Bierhoff *et al.* (1991), whereas the second one has been less researched until now and deserves further scrutiny.

Professor Hans-Werner Bierhoff is Professor of Social Psychology at the Ruhr-University Bochum. He is the author of *Prosocial Behaviour* and has written many scholarly books, chapters and articles on topics in Social Psychology. His main research interests are prosocial behaviour, proactive behaviour, fairness in social relationships and narcissism.

Are humans capable of biological altruism?

According to Brown (1986), the closeness of kinship is construed very differently from one society to another, so there's no simple correspondence between perceived and actual (genetic) kinship. If altruistic behaviour directly reflected actual kinship, rather than learned conceptions of kinship, it would be impossible for adoptive parents to give their adopted children the quality of care they do.

As a species, much of our behaviour is altruistic, and as Brown says:

> *Human altruism goes beyond the confines of Darwinism because human evolution is not only biological in nature but also cultural, and, indeed, in recent times primarily cultural.*

However, biological altruism may be triggered under very specific conditions, such as a highly arousing emergency situation. People often display a rapid, almost unthinking, reflexive type of helping (*impulsive helping*) in extreme situations such as natural – and other kinds of – disasters.

Figure 30.7 Biological altruism in the 2004 tsunami disaster

TELEVISION and PROSOCIAL BEHAVIOUR

If television can have harmful effects as a result of watching antisocial behaviour (see Chapter 29) then, presumably, it can have beneficial effects by promoting prosocial behaviour. According to Gunter and McAleer (1997):

> *...Television programmes contain many examples of good behaviour, of people acting kindly and with generosity. It is equally logical to assume that these portrayals provide models for children to copy.*

Box 30.2 Evidence for the prosocial effects of TV

- **Laboratory studies with specially produced instructional film or video materials:** Specially prepared materials have been shown to influence courage, the delay of gratification, adherence to rules, charitable behaviour, friendliness and affectionate behaviour.
- **Laboratory studies with educational broadcasts specially produced for social skills teaching purposes:** TV productions designed to enhance the social maturity and responsibility of young viewers include *Sesame Street* and *Mister Roger's Neighbourhood.* Children who watch these programmes are able to identify and remember the cooperative and helping behaviours emphasised in certain segments.
- **Laboratory studies with episodes from popular TV series:** Specially manufactured TV programmes or film clips influence children's prosocial tendencies, at least when the prosocial behaviour portrayed is very similar to that requested of the child. But there's only limited evidence that ordinary broadcast material can enhance a wide range of helping behaviours.
- **Field studies relating amount of viewing of prosocial TV content to strength of prosocial behaviour tendencies:** Children who watch little TV, but watch a lot of programmes with high levels of prosocial content, are more likely than others to behave prosocially. But the correlations between viewing habits and prosocial behaviour are lower than those between viewing habits and antisocial behaviour. In part, this may be because prosocial behaviours are verbally mediated and often subtle, whereas antisocial behaviours are blatant and physical. Children learn better from simple, direct and active presentation, and so aggressive behaviours may be more readily learned. Also, the characters who display prosocial behaviour (typically female and non-white) and antisocial behaviour (typically male and white) may confound the relative influence of prosocial and antisocial behaviours with the types of character that portray them.

(From Gunter and McAleer, 1997; Gunter, 1998)

Television violence and catharsis

Ask Yourself

- How might Freud's and Lorenz's theories of aggression explain the benefits of watching TV violence (see Chapter 29)?

One positive effect of TV might be that witnessing others behaving aggressively helps viewers to get their aggressive feelings 'out of their systems' and hence be less likely to behave aggressively. The claim that TV can act as a form of *vicarious catharsis* is based partly on Freud's and Lorenz's theories of aggression.

However, the evidence doesn't support the view that TV is cathartic for everybody. If a discharge of hostile feelings occurs at all, it's probably restricted to people of a particular personality type or those who score high on cognitive measures of fantasy, daydreaming and imagination (Singer, 1989). Only for some people does TV violence have positive effects and provide a means of reducing aggressive feelings (Gunter and McAleer, 1990).

Can computer games enhance prosocial behaviour?

Computer games:

- give children access to 'state of the art' technology, a sense of confidence and equip them with computer-related skills for the future (Surrey, 1982)
- may also promote *social interaction*; Mitchell (1983, in Griffiths, 1993) found that families generally viewed computer games as promoting interaction in a beneficial way through cooperation and competition
- may be *cathartic* in that they allow players to release their stress and aggression in a non-destructive way, and relax them (Kestenbaum and Weinstein, 1985). Other benefits include enhancing cognitive skills, a sense of mastery, control and accomplishment, and a reduction in other youth problems due to 'addictive interest'(!) in video games (Anderson and Ford, 1986).

Griffiths (1997a) points out that many of the assertions made above were subjectively formulated, and not based on empirical research findings.

CONCLUSIONS

In March 1984, the Catherine (Kitty) Genovese Memorial Conference on Bad Samaritanism was held. Experts shared what they had learned in the 20 years since her murder. *The New York Times* again reported on the conference:

> *It's held the imagination because looking at those 38 people, we were really looking at ourselves. We might not have done anything either. That's the ugly side of human nature. [O'Connor, law professor]*

At the conference, Psychology professor, Stanley Milgram, noted that the most evident thing about the case was that it struck to the very heart of the nature of human fear. If we need help, will those around provide it? Will they ignore us? Will they look on? Or, worse, will they aid our destruction?

According to Dovidio and Penner (2004):

> *... helping is a complex multidimensional behaviour. Whether it is spontaneous and short-term or planned and sustained, helping is an evolutionarily important behaviour that is shaped by fundamental cognitive and affective processes, involves self- and other-directed motives, and has consequences that are central to one's self-image and social relationships ...*

Chapter Summary

- **Helping** as a form of **prosocial behaviour** has been studied largely in the form of **bystander intervention.** The murder of Kitty Genovese, together with early laboratory experiments, led Latané and Darley to introduce the concept of the **unresponsive bystander/ bystander apathy.**
- According to Latané and Darley's **decision model,** a bystander will pass through a logical series of steps before actually offering any help. A negative decision at any step leads to **non-intervention.**
- The more potential helpers there are (believed to be) present, the more likely it is that **diffusion** (or **'dissolution') of responsibility** will take place.
- How **competent** we feel to offer appropriate help will influence diffusion of responsibility. This suggests that diffusion of responsibility *doesn't* imply apathy about what happens to the victim.
- The decision model emphasises only why people don't help, rather than why they do. The **arousal–cost–reward (ACR) model** is an extension of the decision model, identifying a number of critical **situational** and **bystander variables,** which help predict the likelihood of helping under particular circumstances.
- **Arousal** constitutes the **motivational** part of the model, while **cost–reward** involves the **cognitive** weighing-up of anticipated costs and rewards for both helping and not helping.
- The most common solutions to the **high-cost-for-helping/high-cost-for-not-helping dilemma** are **re-defining the situation, diffusing responsibility** and **blaming the victim.** These are all forms of **cognitive reinterpretation.**
- The costs of helping and not helping differ according to the **type of help required, victim characteristics** (including perceived similarity to the bystander) and **bystander gender.**

- Helping can be called **altruism** only if the motive is to benefit the victim (**empathic concern**). According to the **empathy–altruism hypothesis** (**EAH**), human beings are capable of altruistic acts, but according to **universal egoism**, helping is always motivated by **personal distress**.
- According to the **negative state relief (NSR) model,** people are motivated to help others in need by their own egoistic need to reduce/remove their state of negative arousal caused originally by the victim's plight.
- While non-humans are incapable of **psychological altruism**, humans are capable of **biological altruism** (**impulsive helping**), triggered by highly arousing emergency situations, especially where friends or relatives are involved.
- **Field studies** indicate that the amount of **prosocial TV content** viewed is related to the strength of **prosocial behaviour**. But this relationship is weaker than that between viewing habits and antisocial behaviour. This may be because antisocial behaviours are learnt more easily than verbal and subtle prosocial behaviours.
- The **benefits of computer games** could include providing an opportunity for releasing stress and aggression in a non-destructive way.

Links with Other Topics/Chapters

Chapter 28 ⟶ The cost–reward component of the ACR model corresponds to the *exchange theory explanation of intimate relationships*

Chapter 23 ⟶ Denigrating the victim (as a form of cognitive reinterpretation when dealing with the high-cost-for-helping/high-cost-for-not-helping dilemma) is another application of the *'just world' hypothesis*

Chapter 24 ⟶ The three forms of cognitive reinterpretation could also be seen as *rationalisations* that reduce the bystander's *cognitive dissonance*

Chapter 35 ⟶ Graziano and Eisenberg (1997) identify individual differences in empathy as one kind of evidence supporting the claim that personality traits can account for variance in prosocial behaviour. This complements Eisenberg's research into the development of *prosocial moral reasoning*

Chapters 35 and 45 ⟶ *Self-efficacy* (as a personality characteristic that can make some people more likely to act prosocially than others) is also relevant to (a) Bandura's (1986, 1989) *social cognition theory* of *moral development* and (b) Bandura's (1977a) account of why *psychotherapy* works

Chapter 35 ⟶ Typical differences between male and female helping are related to Gilligan's (1982) research into differences in their *morality/moral reasoning*

Chapters 10 and 23 ⟶ The ACR model maintains that only arousal attributed to the victim's plight will motivate helping. This is especially relevant to Weiner's *attributional theory of motivation* and to Schachter's *cognitive labelling theory of emotion*

Chapters 28 and 32 ⟶ The finding that impulsive helping is more likely in the case of close friends or loved ones can be (partly) explained in terms of *familiarity* and *attachments*

Recommended Reading

Dovidio, J.F. and Penner, L.A. (2004) Helping and Altruism. In M.B. Brewer and M. Hewstone (eds) *Emotion and Motivation.* Oxford: Blackwell Publishing.

Gross, R. (2012) *Key Studies in Psychology* (6th edition). London: Hodder Education. Chapter 13.

Schroeder, D.A., Penner, L.A., Dovidio, J.E. and Piliavin, J.A. (1995) *The Psychology of Helping and Altruism: Problems and Puzzles.* New York: McGraw-Hill.

Useful Websites

www.socialpsychology.org/social.htm#prosocial (Social Psychology Network)

http://heroicimagination.org/public-resources/social-influence-forces/bystander-effect-and-diffusion (Lots of video clips of staged emergencies and the Kitty Genovese murder. Also Zimbardo and links to several aspects of Social Psychology)

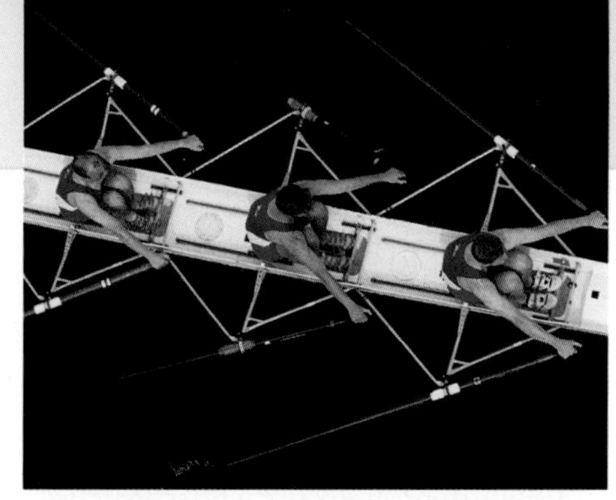

CHAPTER 31

THE SOCIAL PSYCHOLOGY OF SPORT

What is Sport Psychology?

Social facilitation

Influences on group performance

INTRODUCTION and OVERVIEW

As we saw in Chapter 30, sociobiologists believe that an individual animal should be seen as a set of genes, and that these *selfish genes* (Dawkins, 1976) aim to secure their own survival. This view of evolution implies that there's no such thing as society: sociobiologists have ridiculed the idea that groups of organisms might gain a survival advantage over other groups because they shared some beneficial trait.

However, as we also saw, biologists are starting to understand that evolution takes place on a variety of levels (Dicks, 2000; Holmes, 2009). Natural selection may favour certain genes, but it can also favour particular societies. Provided a group of individuals can co-operate without any cheats trying to sneak an unfair advantage, then it may evolve as a single unit. Indeed, Darwin's solution to the paradox of altruism was to suggest that natural selection operates among groups of organisms. As Dicks (2000) puts it:

> *A group of people who are kind and helpful to each other may not do so well individually, but as a team they may do better than other groups of people, and so the tendency to work as a team spreads through the population.*

While not all sport is team sport, of course, applications of Social Psychology to sport tend to focus on group processes (see Chapter 26), such as *social facilitation*, factors affecting group performance (such as *social loafing*), and *group cohesion*.

WHAT IS SPORT PSYCHOLOGY?

Walley and Westbury (1996) define Sport Psychology as the:

> *... scientific study of human behaviour and experience in sport (where ... 'sport' is used to cover various levels of recreational activities, competitive sports, and health-oriented exercise programmes) ...*

A brief history

Triplett's (1898) study of social facilitation (see below) is often cited as the first Social Psychology experiment, but on closer inspection it had stronger links with psychophysiology and Sport Psychology (Hogg and Vaughan, 1998). Indeed, Sport Psychology is generally seen as having started with Triplett's study (Hardy, 1989) (see Key Study 31.1). But it first became recognised as an academic discipline in the UK in the late 1960s, going from strength to strength since the early 1980s, with the Psychology content of sports science degrees gradually increasing.

However, it wasn't until 1992 that the British Psychological Society (BPS) acknowledged Sport Psychology by forming an interest group. A fully fledged Sport and Exercise Psychology section was established in 1993, and in 2004 a division of Sport and Exercise Psychology was established within the BPS; this gave Sport and Exercise Psychologists the opportunity to apply for a chartered status (see Chapter 1).

During most of the 1990s, Sport and Exercise Psychology were discussed together (under the title 'Sport Psychology', as reflected in Walley and Westbury's definition above). But since then, the two sub-disciplines have diverged into two distinct areas of study (Coolican *et al.*, 2007).

How do Exercise and Sport Psychology differ?

According to Coolican *et al.* (2007), *exercise* refers to structured and relatively formal physical activity, usually carried out in gyms, health clubs or sport/leisure centres. Exercise Psychology is related to health (Chapter 12) and Clinical (Chapters 43-45) Psychology. For example, theoretical understanding of health-related behaviour has helped Exercise Psychologists understand why some people adopt and maintain a physically active lifestyle, while others don't.

Exercise Psychology also examines the positive impact activity and exercise can have on psychological well-being.

Sport Psychology has links with Organisational/Occupational Psychology, as well as with counselling psychology (see Chapter 1). Theoretical understanding from these areas of applied Psychology help the Sport Psychologist to address performance-related issues, such as poor team dynamics, low confidence, and performance anxiety. Its aims are to help athletes and teams fulfil their potential as performers, and to manage the related stresses (Coolican *et al.*, 2007).

Not surprisingly, another major link is with *Social Psychology*; because of the latter's concern with groups and group processes, theoretical understanding of these can be applied to sports teams and their performance. So, the focus of this chapter will be on the *social psychological* aspects of *sport* (as distinct from exercise).

The scope of Sport Psychology (SP)

According to Walley and Westbury (1996):

> *The image that many people have of a sport psychologist is someone who comes in to 'psych up' players before a game, the purpose being to make them more competitive or even aggressive ...*

They believe this image is very misleading (see Box 31.1).

The role of stress in athletic performance grew out of the early interest in social facilitation (see below). According to Hardy (1989):

> *Competitive athletes ... may represent an invaluable microcosm within which we may test and refine our understanding of human adaptation. The athlete must learn to cope with a wide range of stressors – performance standards, the experience of failure, ageing and so on. In evaluating our theories and developing new treatment techniques, the athlete may, therefore, be an able and willing ally ...*

Another area of research within SP is identification of personality factors underlying elite performance and attraction to different sports (very popular in the late 1960s and early 1970s: see Chapter 42).

Zuckerman's (1979) *sensation-seeking scale* has been successful in predicting leisure preferences and participation. The high-sensation seeker displays a need for varied, novel sensations, and appears willing to take physical and social risks to gain these experiences (Furnham and Heaven, 1999). As predicted by Zuckerman's scale, white-water canoeists and kayak paddlers showed higher than average scores (especially on the thrill and adventure-seeking subscales; Campbell *et al.*, 1993). Also, athletes scored higher than non-athletes, contact sports athletes scored higher than non-contact sports athletes, and male athletes scored higher than female athletes (Schroth, 1995). (See Box 31.2.)

Box 31.1 Different areas of work involving Sport Psychologists

Clinical Sport Psychology: Trained Clinical Psychologists (see Chapter 1) deal with performers' emotional and behavioural problems. Several Olympic-standard US and British performers have been successfully treated for a range of problems, including acute anxiety, eating disorders, depression, and obsessive–compulsive behaviour (see Chapter 44).

Research Sport Psychology: This is a largely applied area of research, concerned with real-life problems confronting coaches and players. Researchers also try to ensure that their findings are made available not just to the academic community, but also to coaches, athletes, and teachers. Some of the issues addressed are how stress affects performance, what factors affect performers' decision to drop out of sport, and how complex skills are learned and controlled.

Education Sport Psychology: This aims to teach participants in sport mental skills that will enhance both their performance in, and enjoyment of, sport. Sport Psychologists may be consulted on:

- how to manage performance-related stress and anxiety
- how to increase and maintain self-confidence
- how to use mental rehearsal to facilitate learning of skills
- team-building
- coach education.

Teaching and consultancy: Until the late 1990s, most Sport Psychologists in the UK were based in universities, combining research and consultancy roles with teaching undergraduate and postgraduate students. Then many sports received additional funding for world-class performance through the National Lottery. National and Regional Institutes of Sport were established around the UK, providing support services for athletes. Most of these institutes employ Sport Psychology support staff to work with elite and developing athletes (following the US and Australian pattern).

(Based on Coolican *et al.*, 2007; Walley and Westbury, 1996)

Box 31.2 T types and the adrenaline rush

- Type T (for 'thrill') personalities thrive on taking risks (Farley, in Schueller, 2000).
- The most visible members of the type T group today are the *extreme athletes*, such as the hang-gliders, bungee jumpers, and those who jump off tall buildings. For example, Kristen Ulmer considers herself to be a full-time 'adrenaline sports' athlete. As well as being voted the craziest skier in North America, she rock climbs, paraglides, and dabbles in ice climbing and mountain biking.
- But Farley believes that you can get an adrenaline rush without jumping off a building or hang-gliding. It can come from sex or gambling (see Chapter 8), and those who push the frontiers of the mind rather than the body are also thrill seekers. Adrenaline surges have been recorded during chess tournaments, and Farley cites Einstein as a mental T type. Type Ts need to push their abilities – physical or intellectual – to the limits.
- What makes a type T may be at least partly due to 'thrill-seeking' genes, which affect dopamine receptors in the brain (see Chapter 4).

Figure 31.1

- Farley believes that human progress demands risk-taking. There's a very simple motive underlying creativity, risk-taking, exploring, and adventure; namely, thrill.

(Based on Schueller, 2000b)

SOCIAL FACILITATION

Triplett's research

As we noted earlier, Triplett (1898) carried out what is widely considered to be the first Social Psychology experiment. But it seems to be at least as relevant to SP.

Cycling had increased enormously in popularity in the last decade of the nineteenth century, both as a pastime and a sport. Triplett's interest was stimulated by the common observation that racing cyclists go faster when racing or being paced than when riding alone (Stroebe *et al.*, 2012).

Ask Yourself

- Why do you think this effect might occur?

Triplett identified various possible explanations for this superior performance. His preferred explanation was a *dynamogenic theory*, which proposed that racing another person aroused a 'competitive instinct', which released 'nervous energy' (similar to arousal). The sight of movement in another rider suggested a higher speed and inspired greater effort. The energy of a movement was proportional to the idea of that movement. (It was believed at the time that to perform an action or movement, there first had to be an 'idea' of that action/movement; the idea 'suggested' the action/movement to be performed) (Hogg and Vaughan, 1998).

Figure 31.2 Competition can increase speed regardless of the kind of bicycle being ridden

Key Study 31.1

Is this a wind-up or a Social Psychology experiment? (Triplett, 1898)

- In his most famous experiment, 40 boys and girls aged 8 to 17 years were tested under two conditions: working alone and working in pairs, each child competing against the other member of the pair.
- The apparatus consisted of two fishing reels, which turned silk bands around a drum (a 'competition machine'). Each reel was connected by a loop of cord to a pulley two metres away, and a small flag was attached to each cord. To complete one trial, a flag sewn to the silk band had to travel four times around the wheel.
- Some of the children were slower when competing against another child, most were faster, and others little affected.
- The faster children showed the effects of both 'the arousal of their competitive instincts and the idea of a faster movement'. The slower ones were overstimulated or 'going to pieces'.

In expanding on the dynamogenic theory, Triplett emphasised the *ideo-motor responses*, that is, the effects of one child's bodily movements acting as a cue for another child. These are essentially *non-social*. According to Hogg and Vaughan (1998), Triplett himself cannot be considered a Social Psychologist. So, while Triplett's experiment is often cited as a (very early) study of social facilitation, it's not strictly a social psychological study at all. According to Stroebe *et al.* (2012), it's Floyd Allport who should be considered the first true Social Psychologist.

Allport's research

According to Floyd Allport (1924), Triplett's narrow view of the role of competition could be broadened to include a more general principle: an improvement in performance can be produced by the mere presence of *conspecifics* (members of the same species). This is a form of influence he called *social facilitation*.

Allport instructed his participants not to try to compete against one another (and also prevented any collaboration) while engaging on a variety of tasks. These included crossing out all the vowels in a newspaper article, multiplication, and finding logical flaws in arguments. He found they performed better when they could see others working than when they worked alone, and he called this form of social facilitation the *co-action effect*.

Social facilitation also occurs when someone performs a task in front of an audience, that is, other people who aren't doing what s/he is doing. This is the *audience effect*. Other studies have shown that social facilitation can occur by simply telling participants that others are performing the same task elsewhere (Dashiell, 1935).

For the sportsperson, the fact that the presence of others may improve or impair performance is of considerable interest. Although most of the research has taken place in non-sports settings, it still has a direct bearing on sports situations (Woods, 1998).

Ask Yourself

- In your own experience, do you 'perform' better when there are other people around?
- Does it matter that they're engaged in the same task as you?
- Might an 'audience' inhibit you?
- How is all of this affected by the particular task you're engaged in?

Explaining social facilitation

Zajonc's drive theory

The considerable research interest in social facilitation (much of it involving a range of species and a range of behaviours, from eating to copulation) died down at the end of the 1930s. But it was revived by Zajonc's (1965) *drive theory*, according to which social facilitation depends on the nature of the task, in particular, how simple and well learned it is. According to Zajonc:

> *... an audience impairs the acquisition of new responses and facilitates the emission of well-learned responses.*

In other words, things a person already knows how to do (such as cancelling numbers and letters, and simple multiplication) are done *better* when others are present, but things which are complex or which participants are required to learn are done *less well* when others are present. These findings have been confirmed by others. But why should this happen?

Because people are relatively unpredictable, there's a clear advantage to the species for their presence to induce in us a state of alertness or readiness. So, an instinctive response to the presence of others (in whatever capacity) is an increase in drive level (or *level of arousal*). This, in turn, energises (causes us to perform) our *dominant responses*, that is, our best learned or habitual responses in that situation. On subjectively simple tasks (those considered to be simple by the performer), those dominant responses are likely to be correct. Hence, the presence of others will facilitate performance on simple tasks (*task enhancement*).

However, when the task is complex, the effect of increased arousal is to make it more likely that incorrect or irrelevant responses will be performed and, hence, more errors are made (*task impairment*). The arousal produced by the presence of others, together with that produced by the task itself, produces a level beyond the optimum for ideal performance.

An evaluation of Zajonc's drive theory

Some critics have argued that even on well-learned tasks, a skilled athlete may perform poorly in front of others. This can be better explained by the inverted U theory (based on the Yerkes–Dodson law (see Figures 31.3 and 24.8, p. 403).

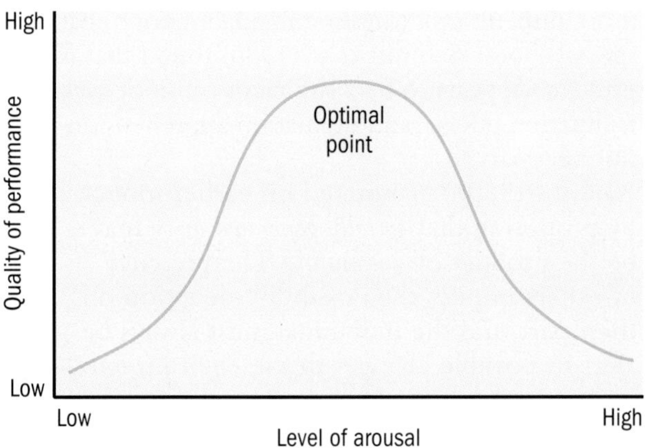

Figure 31.3 Graph showing the inverted U relationship between arousal and performance

Oxendine (1970) found an inverted U relationship in several sports, but the amount of arousal necessary for optimal performance depended on the nature of the skill involved. More complex skills (putting in golf) need a lower level of arousal, because arousal interferes with fine muscle movement and coordination, and cognitive activities such as concentration. But high arousal is useful in less complex skills that require strength, endurance, and speed (like tackling in football).

Many skills involve both strength and complexity, which are difficult to separate out (Jones and Hardy, 1990). For example, preparing to putt requires low muscle activity in the forearms, but high cognitive activity, while performing a maximum bench press in the gym requires high muscle activity in the forearms and lower cognitive activity.

Open and closed skills

According to Woods (1998), arousal can be more detrimental to performance of open than closed skills.

- *Open skills* are performed in an unpredictable environment, so they make more cognitive demands on the performer. The environment is constantly changing and players don't know what will happen; they have to make rapid decisions about what to do and when to do it.

Ask Yourself

- Give an example of an open skill.

An example is that of a basketball player who has to be able to control the ball while noting the movement of team-mates and opposing players, as well as making tactical decisions. Dribbling a basketball is best learned by practising under a variety of conditions, so that it can be performed effectively whatever the circumstances.

- *Closed skills* are performed in a constant, predictable environment, so the performer knows in advance what to do and when to do it. Learning involves refining the skill until it's as perfect as possible, and then repeating it until it can be performed automatically (it becomes habitual).

Ask Yourself

- Give an example of a closed skill.

A gymnast starting a routine is performing a closed skill, which is self-paced. But closed skills may also occur in an 'open' situation. For example, a netball player taking a penalty shot is performing a closed skill, but she must take account of environmental factors, such as the position of other players and likely rebounds. So, the penalty shot cannot be purely habitual and has some characteristics of an open skill (Woods, 1998).

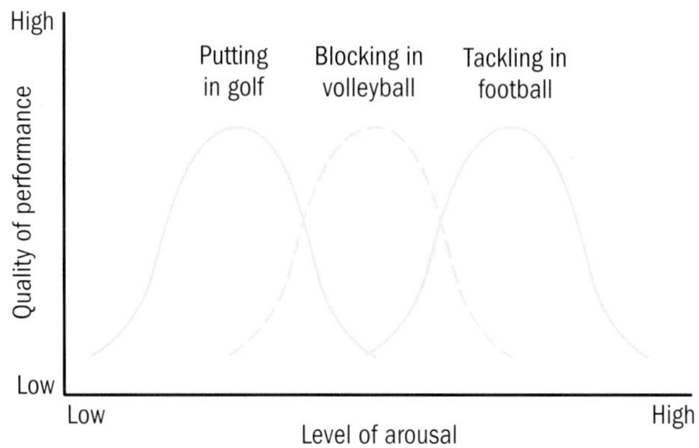

Figure 31.4 Graph showing the relationship between level of arousal and level of performance in three skills

Level of expertise

To perform well, someone just learning a sport should experience only very low levels of arousal; the experienced performer will need much higher levels in order to achieve optimum performance. Because the learner's skills aren't yet automatic, s/he uses cognitive abilities to direct, monitor, and control them. Any additional arousal may interfere with concentration, reducing the ability to control the skill successfully. (See Chapter 13.)

Personality

Performers with low impulsivity (low extroversion/E and low neuroticism/N: see Chapter 42) tend to be more highly aroused during the early part of the day. By contrast, those high on impulsivity are more highly aroused later in the day. This has implications for performance. For example, athletes rated high on impulsivity will need to use more relaxation and stress-reduction strategies when running in an evening compared with a morning race (Woods, 1998).

Cottrell's evaluation apprehension model (EAM)

Cottrell *et al.* (1968) found no social facilitation effect on three well-learned tasks when the two-person audience was inattentive (blindfolded) or merely present (only incidentally present, while supposedly waiting to participate in a different experiment). However, a non-blindfolded audience that carefully attended to the participant's performance and had expressed an interest in watching, did produce a social facilitation (audience) effect.

According to EAM, it's *not* the presence of other people that increases arousal (as Zajonc's drive theory claims), but *apprehension* about being evaluated by them. We quickly learn that the social rewards and punishments (such as approval and disapproval) are dependent on others' evaluations of us, so the presence of others triggers an acquired arousal drive based on evaluation apprehension.

An evaluation of Cottrell's model

- If we're confident about our ability, then the awareness of being watched makes us perform well; but if we're not confident, then we're constantly worrying about how others are evaluating us.
- Cottrell *et al.* also showed that the more expert the audience, the more the performance was impaired (the greater the evaluation apprehension).

Ask Yourself

- Have you had personal experience of this (not necessarily in an athletic context)? (Consult the answers you gave to the Ask Yourself box on page 522.)

- Markus (1978) found support for Cottrell on an easy task (dressing in one's own clothes, having first undressed), but support for drive theory on a more difficult task (dressing in a laboratory coat and special shoes). Schmitt *et al.* (1986) found that mere presence appears to be a sufficient cause of social facilitation effects, and evaluation apprehension is not necessary.
- Zajonc (1980b) elaborated his earlier model by proposing that *socially generated drive* may be the product of *uncertainty*. The presence of others implies the possibility of action on their part, and the individual must always be alert to possible changes in the environment caused by others' behaviour. Uncertainty may be caused by the inability to anticipate how they'll act (Geen, 1995).

Baron's distraction–conflict theory (DCT)

The amount of information we can attend to at the same time is limited (see Chapter 13). Little attention is needed to perform an easy task, but more is needed for a complex one. According to Baron's (1986) DCT, while distraction alone can impair task performance, attentional conflict can also induce a drive that facilitates dominant responses. Together, these processes improve performance of easy tasks, but impair performance of difficult ones. The presence of other people makes demands on our attention, which can either impair or enhance performance, depending on the nature of the task.

Attention overload causes people to narrow their attention and focus on a small number of central cues. Complex tasks require attention to a large number of cues, so attention narrowing is likely to impair performance. On simple tasks (which involve few central cues), attention narrowing eliminates distraction and is likely to improve performance. This corresponds to Manstead and Semin's (1980) distinction between *controlled* and *automatic task performance*.

An evaluation of distraction–conflict theory

- Sanders *et al.* (1978) had participants perform easy and difficult tasks, either alone or co-acting with someone performing either the same or a different task. The reasoning is that someone performing a *different* task wouldn't be a relevant source of social comparison, and so distraction should be minimal, while another person performing the *same* task would be highly distracting. As predicted, participants in the same-task (*distraction*) condition made more mistakes on the difficult task and did better on the simple task, compared with the other conditions.
- Research shows that *any* form of stimulation (such as noise, movement, flashing lights) – not only the presence of other people – can produce the same facilitation or distraction effects (Hogg and Vaughan, 1998). An implication of this theory is that one way of preventing 'overload' is to cut out awareness of others and focus on the task in hand (Woods, 1998).

An evaluation of explanations of social facilitation

- There are many different accounts of what might originally have seemed a rather basic, straightforward social phenomenon. Some have fared better than others, and many questions remain unanswered.
- In a meta-analysis of social facilitation experiments involving over 24,000 participants, Bond and Titus (1983) concluded that the mere presence of other people accounted for no more than 0.3–3.0 per cent of the variation in individual performance.
- It's now widely accepted that we need to adopt a multifaceted approach to explain why the presence of others on individual task performance moves from harmless to harmful as the perceived complexity of the task increases (Hewstone and Martin, 2008).

Social facilitation in a sports setting

Most of the research described above has involved passive, and unbiased, audiences. But in a sports context, the 'audience' is usually far from unbiased. Rather, it's composed of active, often passionate, supporters. While research involving 'real' audiences is rare, one relevant area of research has looked at 'home advantage'.

Figure 31.5 Patriotic British tennis fans at Wimbledon

Box 31.3 Home advantage (based on Woolfson, 2012)

- Home advantage has a massive impact on national, continental, and international competitions. Bookies determine their odds with the venue firmly in mind, and a team's stadium is often referred to as its 'fortress'.
- Statistics consistently show better performance at home than away in almost all team sports, including basketball, hockey, baseball, cricket, rugby, and football. At the modern Olympics, the host country wins three times as many medals as its average, with 14 of the 17 hosts achieving their highest-ever haul on home turf (Clarke, 2000). At London 2012, Team GB won 65 medals, of which 29 were gold – 18 more than Beijing in 2008 (and the best since London in 1908).
- British athletes often cited the overwhelming support of the home crowd as a major factor in their success. However, the crowd can sometimes be distracting, especially during a critical event.
- Analyses of both Summer and Winter Olympics throughout the twentieth century reveal that home advantage occurs mainly in events that are subjectively assessed by judges.
- Neave and Wolfson (2003) found a significant surge in testosterone among footballers before home matches compared to away games and baseline measures. Similar increases have been found in lower animals defending their territory, along with impressive improvements in their ability to triumph against larger and more powerful rivals.

Ask Yourself

- If you support a football or rugby team, for example, check their results for last season. Did they perform better at home or away? (The chances are that unless they either won the championship or got relegated – in which case they probably performed consistently well or badly home and away – they did better at home.)

INFLUENCES ON GROUP PERFORMANCE

Social inhibition

The Ringelmann effect

Can the presence of others have an *inhibiting* effect on performance, as well as a facilitating effect? Several years after Triplett's experiments, Ringelmann, a French professor of engineering, reported a series of studies in which the presence of others seemed to produce a loss in motivation. (The studies had actually been conducted prior to Triplett's research, so strictly speaking these are the very first experiments in Social Psychology [Geen, 1995; Smith, 1995].) Ringelmann found that the more members there were in a tug-of-war team, the less hard each member pulled; that is, as the size of the group increased, so the amount of force exerted per person decreased (the *Ringelmann effect*). Ringelmann explained this largely in terms of a loss of physical coordination, but he conceded that loss of motivation could also be involved.

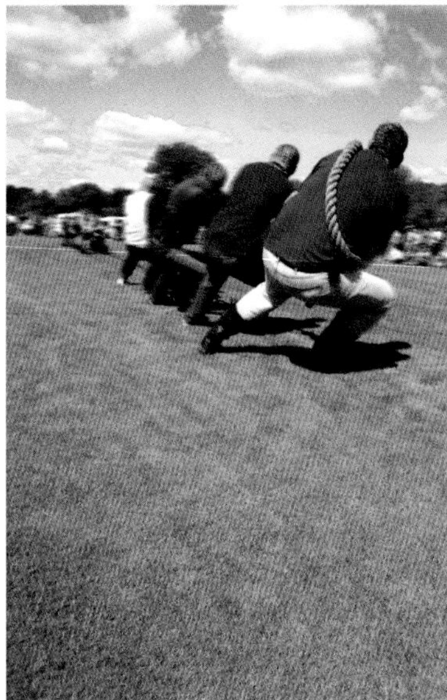

Figure 31.6 How hard he pulls depends on how many others are pulling

Social loafing

Latané *et al.* (1979) revived the Ringelmann effect under the term *social loafing*. Early demonstrations involved simple physical acts, such as shouting and hand-clapping, individually or in groups, with the general result that the intensity of output per person declined as additional members were added. For example, when participants were asked to cheer and clap as loudly as possible, the amount of noise produced per person (compared with individual performance) dropped by 29 per cent in a pair, 49 per cent in a four-person group, and 60 per cent in a six-person group.

Social loafing can be defined as the tendency for individuals to work less hard (to loaf) on a task when they believe that others are also working on the task, and that one's own effort will be pooled with that of the other group members, compared with either working alone or *co-actively* (where others are doing the same task but independently of each other). According to Geen (1995), the data are consistent with one of the major claims of *social impact theory* (Latané and Nida, 1980): when a person is a member of a group subjected to social forces, the impact of those forces on each person in the group is diminished in inverse proportion to the number of people in the group – the larger the group, the smaller the impact.

Later studies have shown the effect to be very reliable and general, occurring in both physical and cognitive tasks, in laboratory and naturalistic settings, in both genders, and in several cultures. However, a review by Karau and Williams (1995) concluded that gender and culture appear to moderate people's tendency to loaf. Although men and women in different cultures are susceptible to loafing, the effect is smaller for women than men, and for people living in Eastern cultures. Both women and people living in Eastern cultures tend to be more group or collectively oriented in their thinking and behaviour (see Chapters 35 and 47).

Explanations of social loafing

Geen (1995) identifies four main explanations:

- '*Free-riding*' (Kerr, 1983) occurs when each member of a group perceives that there's a high probability that some other group members will solve the problem at hand, and that the benefits from this person's performance will go to all members. Each individual concludes that his/her contribution is dispensable, and so puts little effort into the group task.
- Related to this is the *equalisation of perceived output* (or the *sucker effect*): if people expect their fellow group members to become free-riders ('goof off'), they may respond by loafing in an effort to bring equality to an inequitable situation ('Why should I make more effort than the others?' or 'I'm no

sucker'). This is sometimes called the *output equity hypothesis* (McIlveen, 1995). Men seem to dislike the sucker role more than women.

- *Evaluation apprehension*, as we saw earlier when discussing social facilitation, refers to anxiety about how others will judge us. If, as has been claimed, the tasks commonly used in social loafing studies are boring and meaningless, people will try to avoid doing them. If the efforts of group members are pooled, individuals can remain anonymous ('hide in the crowd', which is very similar to free-riding). It follows that making each person's contribution identifiable should eliminate social loafing. This was demonstrated by Williams *et al.* (1981), who simply informed participants that their shouting responses would be identifiable to the experimenter. Participants are especially likely to become apprehensive about being evaluated by the experimenter when they believe their performance is being compared with that of their co-actors performing the same task (effectively, they're in competition). The higher the level of evaluation apprehension, the lower the level of social loafing (Harkins and Jackson, 1985).
- *Matching to standard* assumes that apprehension over the possibility of being evaluated by the experimenter causes the participant to match a standard for performance set by the experimenter (and that this matching is avoided under conditions that allow social loafing). According to Szymanski and Harkins (1987), the explicit statement of a standard relevant to the activity is sufficient to reduce social loafing.

Implications of social loafing for sports coaches

Ask Yourself

- Based on the social loafing research discussed above, what advice would you give sports coaches?

According to Woods (1998), social loafing is essentially the result of a decrease in motivation. While 'There's no "I" in "team"' is a well-worn sporting cliché, she believes that research on social loafing shows that coaches ignore the 'I' at their peril.

> *Group goals are achieved by individuals, so it is important to identify individual behaviours which help group performance and try to encourage those behaviours. Monitoring and feedback on performance (to both individuals and the group) are better than feedback only on group performance ... (Woods, 1998)*

Group cohesion

Ask Yourself

- How would you define a 'team'?
- Is it more than just the sum of the individual members (as with any group)?
- Apart from their skill levels, how do teams differ from each other?

According to Hogg and Vaughan (1998), *group cohesion* (or *cohesiveness*) is one of the most basic properties of a group, and is otherwise known as solidarity, *esprit de corps*, team spirit, or morale. A cohesive group or team is:

> *... the way it 'hangs together' as a tightly knit, self-contained entity characterised by uniformity of conduct and mutual support among members ...*

Cohesion can vary between groups, contexts, and across time. Groups with extremely low levels of cohesion hardly appear to be groups at all, and so the term may capture the very essence of being a group: the psychological process that transforms a collection of individuals into a group.

Festinger (1950) defined cohesiveness as a field of forces acting on the individual deriving from the attraction of the group and its members, and the degree to which the group satisfies individual goals. Cohesiveness is responsible for the continuity of group membership and adherence to group norms/standards.

Figure 31.7 Tottenham Hotspur's triumphant Carling Cup winning team, 2008

According to Hogg (1992), most research defines cohesiveness in terms of attraction to the group and interpersonal attraction. Factors that increase interpersonal attraction (such as similarity, cooperation, interpersonal acceptance, and shared threat: see Chapter 28) generally increase cohesiveness. This, in turn, causes, or is associated with, conformity to group norms, accentuated similarity, improved in-group communication, and increased liking.

Personal versus social attraction

Hogg (1992, 1993) proposed a distinction between *personal attraction* (true interpersonal attraction based on close relationships) and *social attraction* (inter-individual liking based on common group membership). As Hogg and Vaughan (1998) say, personal attraction is nothing to do with groups, while social attraction is the 'liking' component of group membership.

Ask Yourself

- How might social attraction be understood in terms of social-identity theory (SIT: see Chapter 25)?
- In what other ways might SIT be relevant to understanding group cohesiveness?

Attraction is one of a large number of effects produced by *self-categorisation*, as specified in *social-identity theory* (SIT). One advantage of this distinction between personal and social attraction is that group cohesiveness isn't reduced to interpersonal attraction, and it also applies equally to small interactive groups and to large-scale social categories (such as 'ethnic group' and 'nation').

Hogg and Hardie (1991) gave questionnaires to a football team in Australia. Perceptions of team *prototypicality* (the typical/ideal defining features of team members) and norms were significantly related to measures of group-based social attraction, but not to measures of interpersonal attraction. This differential effect was strongest among members who themselves identified most strongly with the team. Similar findings were obtained with netball teams (Hogg and Hains, 1996).

Task versus social cohesion

Athletes often report that team cohesion is a source of satisfaction in their lives. Yet there is conflicting evidence as to whether the most cohesive teams are always the most successful. This is related to whether teams have been analysed in terms of:

- *task cohesion* – the degree to which group members work together and are committed to achieve common goals, such as winning a match, or
- *social cohesion* – the degree to which group members like each other and get on well, trust, and support each other.

These two aspects/dimensions are independent of each other. You might be very committed to achieving your team's goals, but not be particularly attached to the other team members. A team in which members get on well and are very committed to achieving common goals is at the *performing stage* of group development (Tuckman, 1965). This team may be successful. But equally, a team in which there are major disputes (and which is at the *storming stage* [Tuckman, 1965]) could do well if there's a high degree of commitment to the common goal (Woods, 1998).

Factors associated with group cohesion

In *interactive* sports, such as football, the cohesive team (where members rely on each other to perform successfully) tends to be more successful. But in *co-active* sports, such as swimming (in which individual performance doesn't depend on others' performance), degree of cohesion seems to have little effect.

Ask Yourself

- Analyse other sports in terms of the interactive/co-active distinction. Do some sports combine elements of both?
- Can a similar distinction be made with respect to opponents?

Box 31.4 Other factors associated with group cohesion

Stability: Greater stability in group membership allows time for relationships between members to develop.
Group size: The smaller the group, the greater the cohesion. This may be because there's more opportunity for members to interact, and less chance that faulty group processes will occur.
Similarity: The more similar the members (in terms of status and characteristics, such as age and skill level), the greater the cohesion.
Success: The more successful the team, the greater the cohesion.
External threats: These may increase group cohesion by forcing members to ignore internal divisions and conflicts.
(Based on Woods, 1998)

Ask Yourself

- Can you relate external threats to *common/superordinate goals*, as discussed in Chapter 25?

Factors affecting group performance

A good team is more than a group of skilled players. Members need to work together effectively in order to be successful. According to Steiner (1972), this can be expressed as:

Actual productivity = Potential productivity – Losses due to faulty group processes

In other words, to improve team performance, coaches need to increase the skills and performance of individuals (potential productivity), while reducing faulty group processes. The latter include coping with *excess arousal* and dealing with *social loafing* (both discussed above), *competitiveness*, and *poor co-ordination*.

CONCLUSIONS: COMPETITION, CO-OPERATION AND CO-ORDINATION FACTORS

Although competitiveness is an essential part of sporting activity, co-operation is also essential, especially in team sports. In a review of the research, Johnson and Johnson (1985) concluded that co-operation produced higher standards in many more situations than competitiveness (including individual situations). But most of these studies weren't conducted in sports settings, in which competitiveness can produce exceptional effort, as well as damaging consequences.

Co-ordination factors refer to the degree to which each player's skills are meshed together as tightly as possible, and are a central feature of interactive sports (such as football, rugby, and volleyball). Training time should include practice in passing, timing, and the pattern of players' movements. For example, co-ordination between the three players involved in taking a penalty corner in hockey is crucial. Co-active sports (such as swimming and golf), where individual performance doesn't depend on others, suffer much less from co-ordination factors (Woods, 1998).

Chapter Summary

- **Sport Psychology** is part of the BPS Division of Sport and Exercise Psychology. While Exercise Psychology is concerned with recreational activities and exercise, SP is defined as the scientific study of human behaviour and experience in competitive sport.
- Major roles/areas of Sport Psychologists' work include **clinical, research, education, teaching** and **consultancy**. Many of the issues they address draw on areas of research in mainstream and Applied Psychology, such as treatment of mental disorders, stress management, skill learning, and the role of personality factors.
- Zuckerman's **sensation-seeking scale** has successfully predicted attraction to sporting activities that involve high levels of risk and thrill.
- **Extreme athletes** have been described as **T types,** who may have fewer dopamine receptors in their brains. But adrenaline surges have also been recorded during more mental activities, such as chess.
- Triplett proposed a number of **non-social explanations** for why racing cyclists go faster when racing or being paced, compared with riding alone.
- Allport coined the term **social facilitation** to refer to improved performance caused by the mere presence of **conspecifics.** Two forms of social facilitation are the **co-action** and **audience effects**.
- Several explanations of social facilitation have been proposed, including Zajonc's **drive theory**, Cottrell's **evaluation apprehension model (EAM)**, and Baron's **distraction–conflict theory (DCT)**.
- There's evidence for an **inverted U relationship** between performance and arousal. This depends on the **nature of the skill** involved (such as **open/closed)**, level of **expertise** and **personality**.
- The **'Ringelmann effect'** describes one way in which the presence of others can **inhibit** performance. This idea was later revived and renamed **social loafing.**
- Major explanations of social loafing include **'free-riding'**, the **equalisation of perceived output/sucker effect, evaluation apprehension**, and **matching to standard**.
- **Group cohesion/cohesiveness** is a basic property of a group. Most research defines cohesiveness in terms of attraction, but fails to distinguish between **personal** and **social attraction**. Only social attraction is relevant to group membership as such.
- Factors affecting group cohesion include the **type of sport (interactive** or **co-active)**, **stability**, **group size**, **similarity**, and **external threats**.
- Factors affecting **group performance** include **arousal, social loafing, competitiveness, co-operation**, and **co-ordination**.

Links with Other Topics/Chapters

Chapter 12 ⟶ Exercise is widely accepted as a means of *stress reduction*, and also has several other benefits for both *physical and mental health*

Chapters 8 and 46 ⟶ One study of T types has found that people with certain *addictive and impulsive personality traits* have fewer dopamine receptors to record sensations of pleasure and satisfaction. This drives them to overindulge in *substances or activities* that stimulate their existing receptors

Chapter 9 ⟶ Zajonc's explanation of social facilitation is based on *Hull's learning theory*

Chapters 7 and 24 ⟶ The Yerkes–Dodson law (1908) is concerned with the general *relationship between arousal and performance* and has been applied to the relationship between *fear arousal and attitude change*

Chapter 44 ⟶ Evaluation apprehension is a form of *social anxiety*

Chapter 30 ⟶ The free-riding explanation of social loafing is similar to the *diffusion of responsibility* explanation of *bystander intervention*

Chapter 47 ⟶ In group-oriented (*collectivist*) cultures, such as China and Japan, making the tasks more realistic and relevant to everyday life not only eliminates social loafing but reverses it. The presence of others enhances performance on the same tasks which, in more *individualist,* Western cultures produce social loafing (Smith and Bond, 1993)

Chapters 22, 25 and 26 ⟶ Other effects produced by self-categorisation, as specified by SIT, include *stereotyping intergroup differentiation, ethnocentrism* and *in-group solidarity* and *conformity*

Recommended Reading

Coolican, H. (ed.) (2007) *Applied Psychology* (2nd edition). London: Hodder Arnold. Chapter 9.

Cox, R.H. (1994) *Sports Psychology: Concepts and Applications* (3rd edition). Dubuque, Iowa: WC Brown & Benchmark.

Kremer, J. & Scully, D. (1994) *Psychology in Sport.* East Sussex: Taylor & Francis.

Woods, B. (2001) *Psychology in Practice: Sport.* London: Hodder & Stoughton.

Useful Websites

www.issponline.org (International Society of Sport Psychology)

www.bps.org.uk/spex (The BPS Division of Sport and Exercise Psychology)

http://courses.essex.ac.uk/bs/sportpsy/specific_sports.htm (Sports Psychology by sport: resources on sport psychology in general and specifically for tennis, golf, cycling, volleyball and swimming)

CHAPTER 32

EARLY EXPERIENCE AND SOCIAL DEVELOPMENT

- The development and variety of attachments
- Theories of the attachment process
- Individual and cultural variations in attachment
- Deprivation and privation
- Continuity between early and later attachment patterns

INTRODUCTION and OVERVIEW

The study of attachments and their loss or disruption represents an important way of trying to understand how early experience can affect later development. Although it was a central tenet of Freud's psychoanalytic theory that experience during the first five years of life largely determines the kind of adults we become, it's really only since the 1950s that Developmental Psychologists have systematically studied the nature and importance of the child's tie to its mother.

This began with the English psychiatrist John Bowlby. He was commissioned by the World Health Organization (WHO) to investigate the effects on children's development of being raised in institutions. The central concept discussed in his report (*Maternal Care and Mental Health*: Bowlby, 1951) was *maternal deprivation*, which has become almost synonymous with the harmful effects of not growing up within a family.

However, Bowlby has been criticised for exaggerating the importance of the mother–child relationship. There's much more to attachment than attachment to the mother: fathers are attachment figures in their own right, as are siblings. Children's social development involves the expansion of the network of relationships to include teachers, neighbours, and classmates, some of whom will become their friends.

There's now a considerable body of research into attachments beyond infancy and childhood, especially between adult sexual partners, and many Psychologists have questioned the deterministic nature of the early years.

According to Schaffer (2004), whether the nature of our earliest relationships exerts as profound an influence on all subsequent close relationships as Freud suggested remains a contentious issue. But there's no question that relationship formation remains a lifelong issue, and that:

> *... relationships provide the context in which all of a child's psychological functions develop ... What is also certain is that differences among children in the nature of their relationships with others can have profound implications for the particular developmental path that each child embarks upon ... (Schaffer, 2004)*

THE DEVELOPMENT AND VARIETY OF ATTACHMENTS

What is attachment?

According to Kagan *et al.* (1978), an attachment is:

> *... an intense emotional relationship that is specific to two people, that endures over time, and in which prolonged separation from the partner is accompanied by stress and sorrow.*

While this definition applies to attachment formation at any point in the life cycle, our first attachment acts as a *prototype* (or model) for all later relationships. Similarly, although the definition applies to any attachment, the crucial first attachment is usually taken to be with the mother.

Phases in the development of attachments

The attachment process can be divided into several phases (Schaffer, 1996a).

1. The *pre-attachment phase* lasts until about 3 months of age. From about 6 weeks, babies develop an attraction to other human beings in preference to physical aspects of the environment. This is shown through behaviours such as nestling, gurgling, and smiling (the *social smile*) which are directed to just about anyone.
2. At about 3 months, infants begin to discriminate between familiar and unfamiliar people, smiling much more at the former (the social smile has now disappeared). However, they allow strangers to handle and look after them without becoming noticeably distressed, provided they're cared for adequately. This *indiscriminate attachment phase* lasts until around 7 months.
3. From about 7 or 8 months, infants begin to develop specific attachments. This is demonstrated through actively trying to stay close to certain people (particularly the mother) and becoming distressed when separated from them (*separation anxiety*). This *discriminate attachment phase* occurs when an infant can consistently tell the difference between its mother and other people, and has developed *object permanence* (the awareness that things – in this case, the mother – continue to exist even when they cannot be seen; see Chapter 34).

   Also at this time, infants avoid closeness with unfamiliar people and some, though not all, display the *fear-of-strangers response*. This includes crying and/or trying to move away, which are usually triggered only when a stranger tries to make direct contact with the baby (rather than when the stranger is just 'there').
4. In the *multiple attachment phase* (from about 9 months onwards), strong additional ties are formed with other major caregivers (such as the father, grandparents, and siblings) and with non-caregivers (such as other children). Although the fear-of-strangers response typically weakens, the strongest attachment continues to be with the mother.

THEORIES OF THE ATTACHMENT PROCESS

'Cupboard love' theories

According to *psychoanalytic* accounts, the infant becomes attached to its caregiver (usually the mother) because of his/her ability to satisfy its instinctual needs. For Freud (1926):

> *The reason why the infant in arms wants to perceive the presence of its mother is only because it already knows that she satisfies all its needs without delay.*

Freud believed that healthy attachments are formed when feeding practices satisfy the infant's needs for food, security, and oral sexual gratification (see Chapter 42). Unhealthy attachments occur when infants are *deprived* of food and oral pleasure, or are *overindulged*. Thus, psychoanalytic accounts stress the importance of feeding, especially breastfeeding, and of the maternal figure.

Figure 32.1 Is this really all there is to attachment formation?

Ask Yourself

- What do you think the behaviourist account of attachment might be? (See Chapter 11.)

The *behaviourist* view of attachment also sees infants as becoming attached to those who satisfy their physiological needs. Infants associate their caregivers (who act as *conditioned or secondary reinforcers*) with gratification/satisfaction (food being an *unconditioned or primary reinforcer*), and they learn to approach them to have their needs met. This eventually generalises into a feeling of security whenever the caregiver is present.

An evaluation of 'cupboard love' theories

Both behaviourist and psychoanalytic accounts of attachment as 'cupboard love' were challenged by Harlow's studies involving rhesus monkeys

Key Study 32.1

A cuddle's worth more than food to a rhesus monkey (Harlow, 1959; Harlow and Zimmerman, 1959)

- To determine whether food or the close comfort of a blanket were more important, Harlow placed infant rhesus monkeys in cages with two 'surrogate (substitute) mothers'.
- In one experiment, one of the surrogate mothers was made from wire and had a baby bottle attached to 'her'. The other was made from soft and cuddly terry cloth, but didn't have a bottle attached.
- The infants spent most of their time clinging to the cloth mother, even though 'she' provided no nourishment. Harlow concluded from this that monkeys have an unlearned need for *contact comfort*, which is as basic as the need for food.

Ask Yourself

- If the cloth mother had been fitted with a bottle, but the wire mother hadn't, would the baby's preference for the cloth mother still have indicated an unlearned need for contact comfort?

- By fitting only the wire mother with a bottle, Harlow was trying to separate the two variables (the need for food and the need for something soft and cuddly), so as to assess their relative importance. If the cloth mother had been fitted with a bottle, it would have been impossible to interpret the infants' clinging behaviour: was it due to the food or to her being soft and cuddly?

Figure 32.2 Rhesus monkey displaying contact comfort

(e.g. Harlow, 1959; Harlow and Zimmerman, 1959). In the course of studying learning, Harlow separated new-born monkeys from their mothers and raised them in individual cages. Each cage contained a 'baby blanket', to which the monkey became intensely attached, showing great distress when it was removed for any reason.

The cloth surrogate also served as a 'secure base' from which the infant could explore its environment.

The rhesus monkeys reared exclusively with their cloth 'mothers' failed to develop normally: they became extremely aggressive adults, rarely interacted with other monkeys, made inappropriate sexual responses, and were difficult (if not impossible) to breed. Harlow's research indicates that rhesus monkeys develop normally only if they interact with other rhesus monkeys during the first six months of life.

Research on attachment in humans also casts doubt on 'cupboard love' theories.

Key Study 32.2

Feeding isn't everything for Scottish infants (Schaffer and Emerson, 1964)

- Sixty infants were followed up at four-weekly intervals throughout their first year, and then again at 18 months.
- Mothers reported on their infants' behaviour in seven everyday situations involving separations, such as being left alone in a room, with a babysitter, and put to bed at night. For each situation, information was obtained regarding whether the infant protested or not, how much and how regularly it protested, and whose departure elicited it.
- Infants were clearly attached to people who didn't perform caretaking activities (notably the father). Also, in 39 per cent of cases, the person who usually fed, bathed, and changed the infant (typically the mother) wasn't the infant's primary attachment figure.

Schaffer and Emerson concluded that the two features of a person's behaviour which best predicted whether s/he would become an attachment figure for the infant are:

- *responsiveness* to the infant's behaviour
- the *total amount of stimulation* s/he provided (such as talking, touching, and playing).

For Schaffer (1971), 'cupboard love' theories of attachment put things the wrong way round. Instead of infants being passive recipients of nutrition (they 'live to eat'), he prefers to see them as *active seekers of stimulation* (they 'eat to live').

The ethological approach

The term 'attachment' was actually introduced to Psychology by *ethologists*. Lorenz (1935) showed that some non-humans form strong bonds with the first moving objects they encounter (usually, but not always, the mother). In *precocial species* (in which the new-born is able to move around and possesses well-developed sense organs), the mobile young animal needs to learn rapidly to recognise its caregivers and to stay close to them. Lorenz called this *imprinting*. Since imprinting occurs simply through perceiving the caregiver without any feeding taking place, it too makes a 'cupboard love' account of attachment seem less valid, at least in goslings.

Imprinting is an example of a *fixed-action pattern* (FAP), which occurs in the presence of a *species-specific releasing stimulus* (or *sign stimulus*). According to Lorenz, imprinting occurs only during a brief *critical period* of life (a restricted time period during which certain events must take place if normal development is to occur; Bornstein, 1989); once it has occurred, it's *irreversible*. However, studies have shown that the critical period can be extended by changing the environment in certain ways. This has led some researchers (e.g. Sluckin, 1965) to propose instead the existence of a *sensitive period*: learning is *most likely* to happen at this time, and will occur most easily, but it may still occur at *other times*. Also, imprinting is reversible (at least in the laboratory).

Ask Yourself

- How relevant are Harlow's and Lorenz's findings with rhesus monkeys and goslings, respectively, to understanding human attachments?

Bowlby's evolutionary theory

Bowlby was greatly influenced by ethological theory, especially by Lorenz's concept of imprinting, and his theory represents the most comprehensive account of human attachment formation. Bowlby (1969, 1973) argued that because new-born human infants are entirely helpless, they're *genetically programmed* to behave towards their mothers in ways that ensure their survival.

Figure 32.3 John Bowlby (1907–1990)

The mother also inherits a genetic blueprint that programmes her to respond to the baby. There's a critical period during which the *synchrony of action* between mother and infant produces an attachment. In Bowlby's (1951) view, mothering is useless for all children if delayed until after 2 and a half to 3 years, and for most children if delayed until after 12 months.

Strictly speaking, it's only the child who's *attached* to the mother, while she is *bonded* to her baby. The child's attachment to its mother helps to regulate how far away from her the child will move, and the amount of fear it will show towards strangers. Generally, attachment behaviours are more evident when the child is distressed, unwell, afraid, or in unfamiliar surroundings.

Bowlby believed that infants display a strong innate tendency to become attached to one particular adult female (not necessarily the natural mother), a tendency he called *monotropy*. This attachment to the mother figure is *qualitatively different* (different in kind) from any later attachments. For Bowlby (1951):

> *Mother love in infancy is as important for mental health as are vitamins and proteins for physical health.*

Box 32.1 Species-specific behaviours used by infants to shape and control their caregivers' behaviour

Sucking: While sucking is important for nourishment, not all sucking is nutritive. *Non-nutritive sucking* seems to be an innate tendency that inhibits a newborn's distress. In Western societies, babies are often given 'dummies' (or 'pacifiers') to calm them when they're upset.
Cuddling: Human infants adjust their postures to mould themselves to the contours of the parent's body. The reflexive response that encourages front-to-front contact with the mother plays an important part in reinforcing the caregiver's behaviour.
Looking: When parents don't respond to an infant's eye contact, the infant usually shows signs of distress; an infant's looking behaviour, therefore, acts as an invitation to its mother to respond. If she fails to do so, the infant becomes upset and avoids further visual contact. By contrast, mutual gazing is rewarding for an infant.
Smiling: This seems to be an innate behaviour, since babies can produce smiles shortly after birth. Although the first 'social smile' doesn't usually occur before 6 weeks (see text above), adults view the smiling infant as a 'real person', which they find very rewarding.
Crying: Young infants usually cry only when hungry, cold, or in pain, and crying is most effectively ended by picking up and cuddling them.

Ask Yourself

- Do you agree with Bowlby that the infant's relationship with its mother is unique, or are men just as capable as women of providing adequate parenting and becoming attachment figures for their young children?

An evaluation of Bowlby's theory

- Infants and young children display a whole range of attachment behaviours towards a variety of attachment figures other than their mothers. In other words, the mother isn't special in the way the infant shows its attachment to her (Rutter, 1981).
- Although Bowlby didn't deny that children form multiple attachments, he saw attachment to the mother as being unique: it's the first to develop and is the strongest of all. However, Schaffer and Emerson (see Key Study 32.2) showed that multiple attachments seem to be the rule rather than the exception:
  - at about 7 months, 29 per cent of infants had already formed several attachments simultaneously (10 per cent had formed five or more)
  - at 10 months, 59 per cent had developed more than one attachment
  - by 18 months, 87 per cent had done so (one-third had formed five or more).
- Although there was usually one particularly strong attachment, most infants showed multiple attachments of varying intensity:
  - only half of the 18-month-old children were most strongly attached to their mothers
  - almost one-third were most strongly attached to their fathers
  - about 17 per cent were equally attached to both parents.
- Given the critical influence of attachment theory in our understanding of the influences of early relationship experiences on later relationships, and given the fact that attachment theory is an evolutionary theory, it's useful to point out some of the limitations and re-interpretations of attachment theory in the light of Evolutionary Psychology.
- Bowlby's (1969) original formulation of his theory maintained that attachment behaviour had evolved in order to promote the *survival of the species*. But, as Belsky (1999) observes, attachment behaviour wouldn't have evolved if it had only functioned to protect the individual child and thereby to promote survival, because survival as such clearly *isn't* the goal of natural selection: unless survival enhanced the *reproductive fitness* of ancestral human infants, there wouldn't have been sufficient evolutionary pressure for attachment behaviour to evolve. So, human attachment evolved because the protection and survival it promoted increased the chances of successful reproduction of those individuals who tended to maintain proximity and/or seek contact with their caregivers.
- Bowlby later recognised his mistake and acknowledged that evolution works at the levels of the *gene* and the *individual* – not the species

(reproductive fitness, not just survival) (Belsky, 1999). (But see Chapter 30.)

- Other criticisms apply more to Ainsworth *et al.*'s (1971, 1978) extensions of Bowlby's theory.

What about fathers?

For Bowlby, the father is only of *indirect* value to the infant – as an emotional and economic support for the mother. Evolutionary Psychologists (see Chapter 2) see mothers as having a greater parental investment in their offspring, and hence are better prepared for child rearing and attachment (Kenrick, 1994). However, Bowlby's views on fathers as attachment figures are disputed by findings such as those of Schaffer and Emerson.

Figure 32.4 Does the baby really mind that the person who feeds it isn't female?

INDIVIDUAL AND CULTURAL VARIATIONS IN ATTACHMENT

A pioneering study of individual differences in children's attachment to their mothers was conducted by Ainsworth (1967) in Uganda. Ainsworth replicated her Ugandan study in Baltimore, USA (Ainsworth *et al.,* 1971, 1978), which Van Ijzendoorn and Schuengel (1999) describe as the most important study in the history of attachment research. Like the earlier study, both interviews and naturalistic observation were used, but the latter now played a much greater role.

Also like the Uganda study, the Baltimore study was *longitudinal*: 26 mother–infant pairs were visited at home every three to four weeks, each visit lasting three to four hours, for the first year of the baby's life. In order to make sense of the enormous amount of data collected for each pair (72 hours' worth), there needed to be an *external criterion* measure (some standard against which to compare the observations). The criterion chosen was the *Strange Situation Test* (*SST*; see Figure 32.6, and Table 32.1).

Figure 32.5 Mary Ainsworth (1913–1999)

Figure 32.6 One of the eight episodes in the 'Strange Situation' Test

The SST had been devised earlier by Ainsworth and Wittig (1969), who wanted to study how the baby's tendencies towards attachment and exploration interact under conditions of low and high *stress*. They believed that the balance between these two systems could be observed more easily in an unfamiliar environment. In the Baltimore study, the SST was modified to enable the infant and maternal behaviour patterns to be classified.

Group data confirmed that babies explored the playroom and toys more vigorously in the mothers' presence than after the stranger entered or while the mother was absent. However, Ainsworth was particularly fascinated by the unexpected variety of infants' reactions to the mothers' return (*reunion behaviours*: see Table 32.2). This provides a clearer picture of the state of attachment than even the response to separation itself (Marrone, 1998).

Table 32.1 The eight episodes of the 'Strange Situation' Test

Episode	Person present	Duration	Brief description
1	Mother, baby, observer	30 seconds	Observer introduces mother and baby to experimental room, then leaves
2	Mother, baby	3 minutes	Mother is non-participant while baby explores; if necessary, play is stimulated after two minutes
3	Stranger, mother, baby	3 minutes	Stranger enters. First minute: stranger silent. Second minute: stranger converses with mother. Third minute: stranger approaches baby. After three minutes, mother leaves unobtrusively
4	Stranger, baby	3 minutes or less*	First separation episode. Stranger's behaviour is geared to the baby's
5	Mother, baby	3 minutes or more**	First reunion episode. Stranger leaves. Mother greets and/or comforts baby, then tries to settle baby again in play. Mother then leaves, saying 'bye-bye'
6	Baby	3 minutes or less*	Second separation episode
7	Stranger, baby	3 minutes or less*	Continuation of second separation. Stranger enters and gears her behaviour to baby's
8	Mother, baby	3 minutes	Second reunion episode. Mother enters, greets baby, then picks up baby. Meanwhile, stranger leaves unobtrusively

* Episode is ended early if baby is unduly distressed.

** Episode is prolonged if more time is required for baby to become reinvolved in play.

(Based on Ainsworth *et al.*, 1978; Krebs and Blackman, 1988)

Table 32.2 Behaviour associated with three types of attachment in 1-year-old infants using the 'Strange Situation' Test

Category	Name	Sample (%)
Type A	**Anxious–avoidant**	**15**
Typical behaviour: Baby largely ignores mother, because of indifference towards her. Play is little affected by whether she's present or absent. No or few signs of distress when mother leaves, and actively ignores or avoids her on her return. Distress is caused by being alone, rather than being left by the mother. Can be comforted as easily by the stranger as by the mother. In fact, *both adults are treated in a very similar way.*		
Type B	**Securely attached**	**70**
Typical behaviour: Baby plays happily while the mother is present, whether the stranger is present or not. Mother is largely 'ignored', because she can be trusted to be there if needed. Clearly distressed when the mother leaves, and play is considerably reduced. Seeks immediate contact with mother on her return, quickly calms down in her arms, and resumes play. The distress is caused by the mother's absence, not by being alone. Although the stranger can provide some comfort, *she and the mother are treated very differently.*		
Type C	**Anxious–resistant**	**15**
Typical behaviour: Baby is fussy and wary while the mother is present. Cries a lot more than types A and B, and has difficulty using mother as a safe base. Very distressed when she leaves, seeks contact with her on her return, but simultaneously shows anger and resists contact (may approach her and reach out to be picked up, then struggles to get down again). This demonstrates the baby's *ambivalence* towards her. Doesn't return to play readily. *Actively resists stranger's efforts to make contact.*		

The *dynamics* of the attachment relationship can be seen in terms of a balance between (a) exploratory behaviour directed towards the environment, and (b) attachment behaviour directed towards the caregiver. Looked at in this light, securely attached babies have got the balance right (Meins, 2003). But in both patterns of insecure attachment, the balance is tipped to one or other extreme: the *anxious–avoidant* baby shows high levels of *environment-directed* behaviour to the detriment of attachment behaviour, while the *anxious–resistant* baby is preoccupied with the *caregiver* to the detriment of exploration and play.

Evaluation of the Strange Situation Test

- The SST is widely accepted as the 'gold standard' measure of security in early life. But one of the drawbacks of its remarkable success is that it's tended to focus attention on security/insecurity to the exclusion of other aspects of attachment (Rutter *et al.*, 2009). (See Critical Discussion 32.1 below.)
- According to Goldberg (2000) the SST:

  > *... represents a unique combination of experimental and clinical methods, as the procedure itself is well standardised but allows controlled opportunities for natural interactions ...*

  The observer focuses on the infant, with the mother's caregiving behaviour regarded primarily as the context for the infant's behaviour. The advantage of this is that while the mother may try to please the experimenter and show herself to be a 'good mother', infant behaviour is free of such biases and is more transparent.
- When the family's living conditions don't change, the children's attachment patterns also remain fairly constant, both in the short term (6 months; Waters, 1978) and the long term (up to 5 years; Main *et al.*, 1985). This is commonly interpreted as reflecting a fixed characteristic of the child, such as temperament.
- But Vaughn *et al.* (1980) showed that attachment type may change depending on variations in the family's circumstances. Children of single parents living in poverty were studied at 12 and 18 months. Significantly, 38 per cent were classified differently on the two occasions, reflecting changes in the families' circumstances, particularly changes in accommodation and the mothers' degree of stress. This suggests that attachment types aren't necessarily permanent characteristics. In general, the longer the gap between assessments, the more likely it is that children will be found to have changed classification status (Schaffer, 2004).
- Patterns of attachment to mothers and fathers are *independent*, so the same child might be securely attached to its mother, but insecurely attached to its father (Main and Weston, 1981). This shows that attachment patterns derived from the SST reflect qualities of distinct relationships, rather than characteristics of the child. If temperament, for example, were the main cause of attachment classification, the same child should develop the same kind of attachment pattern to both parents (van Ijzendoorn and De Wolff, 1997).
- According to Main (1991; Main and Hesse, 1990), many babies don't fit neatly into Ainsworth *et al.*'s three attachment types. She identifies a fourth type, namely *insecure–disorganised* (type D). This describes a baby whose behaviour appears to lack observable goals, intentions or exploration. There are contradictory behaviours (either sequential or simultaneous), misdirected, incomplete and interrupted movements, stereotyped behaviour, freezing/stilling and apparent fear of the parent (Rutter *et al.*, 2009). Type D has been linked to infant maltreatment or hostile caregiving, maternal history of loss through separation, divorce or death (Lyons-Ruth *et al.*, 1991), maternal depression (Radke-Yarrow *et al.*, 1995), and being raised in institutions (Rutter *et al.*, 2009; see below).

Ask Yourself

- How could the SST be criticised on ethical grounds?

- As we noted above, the SST is designed to see how young children react to stress, with the stranger becoming more intrusive over the course of the eight episodes. According to Marrone (1998), although the SST has been criticised for being stressful, it's modelled on common, everyday experiences: mothers do leave their children for brief periods of time in different settings, and often with strangers, such as baby-sitters. However, deliberately exposing children to stress as part of a psychological study is very different from what happens in the course of normal, everyday life (see Chapter 48).

Cross-cultural similarities and differences

Cross-cultural studies have revealed important differences, both within and between cultures. Van Ijzendoorn and Kroonenberg (1988) carried out a major review of 32 worldwide studies involving eight countries and over 2000 infants, and reached three main conclusions.

1. There are marked differences within cultures in the distribution of types A, B and C. For example, in one of two Japanese studies, there was a complete absence of type A but a high proportion of type C, while the other study was much more consistent with Ainsworth *et al.*'s findings.

Critical Discussion 32.1

Attachment styles and evolution

It's widely believed that the *environment of evolutionary adaptedness* (EEA) was neither as uniform nor as benign as Bowlby seems to have imagined (Chisholm, 1996, in Belsky, 1999; see Chapter 2). It's very likely that in some ecological niches food was abundant and maternal care was sensitively responsive (as it appears to be in certain present-day hunter–gatherer societies); but it's more than likely that in others (or at least at certain times) resources were scarce or of poor quality, making care mostly insensitive. Assuming that there were many different EEAs and that attachment behaviour probably evolved within these different contexts, it becomes very difficult to believe that one single pattern of attachment (namely, secure) was or is 'species-typical' or normative. As Belsky (1999) says:

> *...Under the diverse conditions in which hominids evolved, it seems more reasonable to presume that no pattern of attachment was primary and others secondary, but rather that what evolved was a repertoire of attachment behaviours that could be flexibly organised into different patterns contingent on ecological and caregiving conditions...*

By the same token, there's no reason to believe that sensitive maternal responsiveness is any more species-typical, normative or characteristic of ancestral humans (i.e. 'natural') than insensitivity (Belsky, 1999).

We cannot simply claim that insecure attachments are '*mal*adaptations' because they compromise the capacity for dealing with later developmental issues, especially those surrounding intimate social relationships and parenting (Sroufe, 1988). It makes just as much sense to regard them as *evolved* responses to contextual demands (i.e. mothering practices) that *enable* the individual to reproduce 'successfully' (or at least once did so in some EEAs). The variability in types of human attachment pattern prepares the young of the species to adapt to parents' pattern of investment in their offspring; infants increase their chances of survival if they can adapt to the particular caregiving conditions they encounter (Miller, 2002). If parents are heavily invested, and so are sensitive and responsive, then environmental risks to the children decrease, and they can explore more freely from their safe base. But if parents are unwilling/unable to invest heavily, then resistant or avoidant attachment styles may be *more* adaptive.

From an evolutionary perspective, insecure attachments are just as 'natural' as secure attachments are (Belsky, 1999).

2. The overall worldwide pattern, and that for the USA, was similar to the Ainsworth *et al.* 'standard' pattern. But within the USA, there was considerable variation between samples.
3. There seems to be a pattern of cross-cultural differences: while type B is the most common, type A is relatively more common in Western European countries, and type C is relatively more common in Israel and Japan.

Japanese children are rarely separated from their mothers, so that the departure of the mother is the most upsetting episode in the SST. Japanese mothers commonly sleep with their infants, and are in constant bodily contact with them during the day, carrying them around in slings. This suggests that the SST is an inappropriate and inaccurate measure of attachment security within Japanese culture, since the procedure is too far removed from the infant's everyday experiences of caregiving (Meins, 2003). For children raised on Israeli kibbutzim (small, close-knit groups), the entrance of a stranger was the main source of distress. Valid interpretations of the SST in cross-cultural settings require intimate knowledge of child-rearing customs and goals (Goldberg, 2000).

Figure 32.7 Constant bodily contact with the mother would make the Strange Situation Test an extremely stressful – and inappropriate – way of trying to assess this baby's attachment to her

DEPRIVATION AND PRIVATION

Bowlby's maternal-deprivation hypothesis

As noted earlier, Bowlby argued for the existence of a critical period in attachment formation. This, along with his theory of monotropy, led him to claim that the mother–infant attachment couldn't be broken in the first few years of life without serious and permanent damage to social, emotional, and intellectual development. For Bowlby (1951):

> *An infant and young child should experience a warm, intimate and continuous relationship with his mother (or permanent mother figure) in which both find satisfaction and enjoyment.*

Bowlby's *maternal-deprivation hypothesis* (MDH) was based largely on studies conducted in the 1930s and 1940s of children brought up in residential nurseries and other large institutions (such as orphanages), notably Goldfarb (1943), Spitz (1945, 1946) and Spitz and Wolf (1946).

Bowlby, Goldfarb, Spitz and Wolf explained the harmful effects of growing up in an institution in terms of what Bowlby called maternal deprivation. In doing so, they failed to:

- recognise that the understimulating nature of the institutional environment, as well as (or instead of) the absence of maternal care, could be responsible for the effects they observed
- disentangle the different types of deprivation and the different kinds of retardation produced (Rutter, 1981)
- distinguish between the effects of deprivation and privation. Strictly, *deprivation* ('de-privation') refers to the *loss*, through separation, of the maternal attachment figure (which assumes that an attachment has already developed); *privation* refers to the *absence* of an attachment figure (there's been no opportunity to form an attachment in the first place: Rutter, 1981).

Poor, unstimulating environments are generally associated with learning difficulties and retarded language development (which is crucial for overall intellectual development). Hence, a crucial variable in intellectual development is the amount of intellectual stimulation a child receives, not the amount of mothering.

The early studies of children raised in institutions are most accurately thought of as demonstrating the effects of *privation*. However, Bowlby's own theory and research were mainly concerned with *deprivation*. By only using the one term ('deprivation'), he confused two very different types of early experience, which have very different types of effect (both short- and long-term).

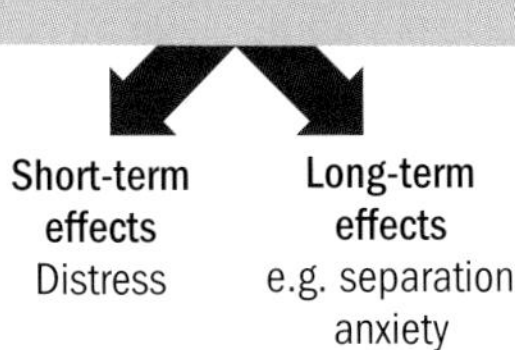
Deprivation (loss/separation)
e.g. child/mother going into hospital, mother going out to work, death of mother (which may occur through suicide or murder witnessed by the child), parental separation/divorce, natural disasters. These are all examples of acute stress (Schaffer, 1996a).
Short-term effects
Distress
Long-term effects
e.g. separation anxiety

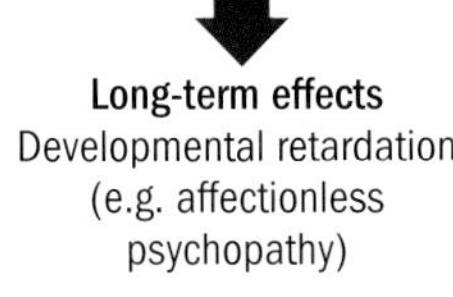
Privation (lack/absence)
e.g. being raised in an orphanage/other institution or suffering chronic adversity (Schaffer, 1996a), as in the case of the Czech twins (Koluchova, 1972, 1991) and the Romanian orphans (Chisolm et al., 1995).
Long-term effects
Developmental retardation
(e.g. affectionless psychopathy)

Figure 32.8 Examples of the difference between deprivation and privation, including their effects

Deprivation (separation or loss)

Short-term deprivation and its effects

One example of short-term deprivation (days or weeks, rather than months or years) is that of a child going into a nursery while its mother goes into hospital. Another is that of the child itself going into hospital. Bowlby showed that when young children go into hospital, they display distress, which typically involves three components or stages (see Box 32.2).

One *long-term effect* of short-term separation is *separation anxiety*.

Long-term deprivation and its effects

Long-term deprivation includes the permanent separation resulting from *parental death*, and the increasingly common separation caused by *divorce*. Perhaps the most common effect of long-term deprivation is what Bowlby called *separation anxiety* (the fear that separation will occur again in the future). This may manifest itself in:

- *increased aggressive behaviour* and greater demands towards the mother
- *clinging behaviour* – the child is unable to let the mother out of its sight.
- *detachment* – the child becomes apparently self-sufficient, because it cannot afford to be let down again
- some *vacillation* between clinging and detachment
- *psychosomatic* (*psychophysiological*) reactions.

Long-term effects of divorce

With few exceptions, the consensus is that adolescents and young adults from divorced families are more likely to be insecurely attached than those from intact families, with most evidence

Box 32.2 The components or stages of distress

Protest: The initial, immediate reaction takes the form of crying, screaming, kicking, and generally struggling to escape, or clinging to the mother to prevent her from leaving. This is an outward and direct expression of the child's anger, fear, bitterness, and bewilderment.
Despair: The struggling and protest eventually give way to calmer behaviour. The child may appear apathetic, but internally still feels all the anger and fear previously displayed, keeping these feelings 'locked up' and wanting nothing to do with other people. The child may no longer anticipate the mother's return, and barely reacts to others' offers of comfort, preferring to comfort itself by rocking, thumb-sucking, and so on.
Detachment: If the separation continues, the child begins to respond to people again, but tends to treat everyone alike and rather superficially. If reunited with the mother at this stage, the child may well have to 'relearn' its relationship with her and may even 'reject' her (as she 'rejected' her child).

Figure 32.9 John (17 months) experienced extreme distress while spending nine days in a residential nursery when his mother was in hospital having a second baby. According to Bowlby, he was grieving for the absent mother. Robertson and Robertson (1967–73) (who made a series of films called *Young Children in Brief Separation*) found that the extreme distress was caused by a combination of factors: loss of the mother, strange environment and routines, multiple caretakers and lack of a mother substitute

pointing towards a greater likelihood of becoming more anxiously attached (fearful or preoccupied; see below) as adults (Feeney and Monin, 2008). They're likely to hold less positive attitudes towards marriage and relationships, to show less trust, to have problems with dependency and control, to be less optimistic, and to believe that disagreement is destructive.

Box 32.3 The effects of divorce on children's attachment security

- According to Feeney and Monin (2008):

  ...To the extent that divorce reduces a child's confidence in who and where his or her attachment figures are; in his or her perceived acceptability in the eyes of attachment figures; and in the availability, accessibility, and sensitive responsiveness of attachment figures... divorce is likely to affect the child's attachment security...

- The mere fact that parents are living apart may undermine a child's feelings of security: parental accessibility becomes more tenuous. Bowlby (1980) noted that some children who've experienced loss or separation from one parent may fear the loss or separation from the other parent. Divorce often contributes to depression, anxiety or substance abuse in one or both parents and the consequent reduction in security and love may be more damaging for children than the original conflict (Arkowitz and Lilienfeld, 2013).
- Yet despite the stresses involved, most children are resilient enough to adapt to their parents' divorce eventually (Hetherington and Stanley-Hagan, 1999). Several factors have been identified as moderating the effects of divorce on young children's attachment security (Feeney and Monin, 2008). Most importantly: (i) quality of parenting; (ii) father visitation patterns (which influence mother–infant attachment)/continuity of contact with the non-custodial parent; and (iii) maternal education and family income.
- According to Arkowitz and Lilienfeld (2013), researchers have found that only a relatively small percentage of children experience serious problems in the wake of divorce. While most children are affected in the short term (e.g. anxiety, anger, shock and disbelief), they recover rapidly; by the end of the second year, all but a minority are problem-free.
- While parental conflict is generally regarded as the single most harmful factor, relief from conflict after separation/divorce can sometimes be a welcome change. Also, if conflict is muted or kept 'secret' from the children, the divorce may come as a shock.

Nevertheless, the evidence suggests that most children of divorce become well-adjusted adults (Amato, 2000; Hetherington and Kelly, 2002).

The effects of day care

This is regarded by some as another form of long-term deprivation. According to Scarr (1998), day care includes all varieties of non-maternal care of children who reside with their parent(s) or close relatives, and so excludes foster care and institutional (residential) care.

A deep-seated and widely held assumption is that child care provided by anyone other than the child's mother is *non-normative* (it's not how most children are cared for). This partly reflects the continuing influence of Bowlby's theory of attachment. However, shared child care is actually a *normative* experience for contemporary American (and British) children, the vast majority of whose mothers are employed. For example, just over 52 per cent of women in the UK with children under five worked in 2003 (Hinsliff, 2004). According to Scarr (1998), non-maternal shared care is normative, both historically and culturally (and so is universal).

Despite these changing patterns of female employment, the belief that women are born and reared to be, first and foremost, mothers (the *motherhood mystique/mandate*) remains an influence on our attitudes about working mothers (Kremer, 1998).

Figure 32.10 Non-maternal shared care is both historically and culturally normative

Ask Yourself

- What would Bowlby's theory predict about the effects of working mothers on the development of their child's attachment?

According to Bowlby, a child whose mother goes out to work experiences maternal deprivation. If this happens during the child's first year (before an attachment has formed), an attachment may not develop at all (strictly, this is privation). If it happens after an attachment has developed, the child will be distressed, may experience separation anxiety, and so on (see above).

Belsky and Rovine (1988) claimed that infants were more likely to develop insecure attachments (especially anxious–avoidant; 43 per cent) if they'd been receiving day care for at least four months before their first birthday and for more than 20 hours per week. Clarke-Stewart (1989) reported insecure attachment rates of 36 per cent. (These figures compared with 26 and 29 per cent for groups with no or limited early child care experience). Lamb *et al.* (1992) found comparable rates of elevated insecurity/avoidance for infants receiving as little as five hours of day care per week.

However, Clarke-Stewart (1989) argues that the use of the SST is an inappropriate technique for children in day care. As we saw earlier, the SST is based on the assumption that repeated separations from the mother put children under stress, and so highlight their attempts at security seeking. But children in day care are used to such separations and so may not experience stress. When they respond to the mother's return in the SST with (what looks like) indifference, they may be showing *independence* and *self-reliance*, not the 'avoidance' or 'resistance' that are used to classify children as insecurely attached. According to Schaffer (1996a):

> *It is possible that the Strange Situation procedure is not psychologically equivalent for children of working and of non-working mothers. If that is so, it becomes even more important to ensure that any conclusions are based on a variety of assessment techniques.*

Ask Yourself

- If day care were harmful to young children's attachments, what kind of distribution of secure and insecure attachments would you expect among those whose mothers work compared with those who don't (e.g. what percentage of type A and type C attachments)?

- The observed distribution of insecure infants of working mothers in the USA (22 per cent type A; 14 per cent type C) is virtually identical to the overall distribution for studies around the world (21 per cent and 14 per cent, respectively, based on almost 2000 children of mainly non-working mothers; Van Ijzendoorn and Kroonenberg, 1988).
- In theory, an attachment is a *relationship*, not a global personality trait. If the children of working mothers are more insecure with them, this doesn't necessarily mean that they're emotionally insecure

in general. We need to assess their emotional health in a range of situations, with a variety of attachment figures. Several studies have shown that children who were in day care as infants do as well as those who weren't, using measures of security, anxiety, self-confidence, and emotional adjustment (Clarke-Stewart, 1989).

- Howes and Spieker (2008) reviewed three studies concerned specifically with the effects of child care experience during the development of primary attachments in infancy on the security of the infant–mother attachment. One conclusion from these studies (consistent with Ahnert *et al.*'s (2006) meta-analysis) is that children's attachments to caregivers in child care are less secure when group size and child-caregiver ratios are large. While it may be quite difficult to provide really good-quality care (at least for very young children) in group settings where caregiving is shared and not individualised (Rutter, 2008), Howes and Spieker claim that:

  > *... It may be that children under these adverse circumstances develop strategies with all of their caregivers that are adapted to increase the probability of protection and survival under threatening conditions, which after all is the evolutionary purpose of attachment.*

  (See Critical Discussion 32.1 above.)
- Although not looking at attachment security/insecurity specifically or exclusively, two recent studies suggest very strongly that working mothers do not put their children at risk. These are:
  - the US National Institute of Child Health and Human Development Study of Early Child Care (NICHD-SECC; National Institute of Child Health and Human Development 2010). This longitudinal study followed more than 1000 children up to age 7 from ten geographic areas, tracking their development and family characteristics. Taking everything into account, the net effect was *neutral*; however, part-time work (i.e. up to 30 hours per week) provided more desirable outcomes than full-time employment.
  - Lucas-Thompson *et al.*'s (2010) meta-analysis (see Chapter 6) of 69 studies concluded that overall, maternal employment wasn't significantly associated with later decreases in achievement or increases in behaviour problems. The results highlighted the importance of *social context* for identifying under which conditions, and for which subgroups (e.g. two/single-parent families, low/high-risk families) early maternal employment is associated with positive or negative child outcomes.

Privation

Given the importance of the child's first relationship as a prototype of relationships in general, failure to develop an attachment of any kind is likely to affect adversely all subsequent relationships.

Harlow's research (see above) showed that monkeys brought up with only surrogate mothers were very disturbed in their later sexual behaviour. For example, females had to be artificially inseminated because they wouldn't mate naturally. The unmothered females also became very inadequate mothers, rejecting their infants whenever they tried to cling to their bellies and, literally, walking all over them.

Affectionless psychopathy

According to Bowlby, maternal deprivation in early childhood causes *affectionless psychopathy*: the inability to care and have deep feelings for other people and the consequent lack of meaningful interpersonal relationships, together with the inability to experience guilt.

Key Study 32.3

Growing up with tuberculosis (Bowlby *et al.*, 1956)

- Bowlby *et al.* studied 60 children aged 7–13 years who'd spent between five months and two years in a tuberculosis (TB) sanatorium (which provided no substitute mothering) at various ages up to four. About half had been separated from their parents before they were 2 years old.
- When compared with a group of non-separated 'control' children from the same school classes, the overall picture was that the two groups were more similar than different.
- The separated children were more prone to 'daydreaming', showed less initiative, were more over-excited, rougher in play, concentrated less well, and were less competitive. But they weren't more likely to show affectionless psychopathy, regardless of when their separation had occurred (before or after 2).

Bowlby *et al.* admitted that 'part of the emotional disturbance can be attributed to factors other than separation', such as the common occurrence of illness and death in the sanatorium children's families. So, there was very little evidence for the link between affectionless psychopathy and separation (or bond disruption). However, Bowlby may have provided evidence for an association with privation instead (a failure to form bonds in early life). According to Rutter (1981), privation is likely to lead to:

- an initial phase of clinging, dependent behaviour
- attention-seeking, and uninhibited, indiscriminate friendliness
- a personality characterised by lack of guilt, an inability to keep rules, and an inability to form lasting relationships.

Are the effects of privation reversible?

There are (at least) three kinds of study that demonstrate that it's possible to undo the effects of early privation.

1. *Case studies* of children who've endured *extreme early privation*, often in near complete isolation. Examples include the Czech twins studied by Koluchova (1972, 1991; see Case Study 32.1) and the concentration camp survivors (Freud and Dann, 1951; see Case Study 32.2).
2. Studies of *late adoption*: children raised in institutions are adopted after Bowlby's critical period for attachment development (12 months for most children, up to 2 and a half/3 years for the rest). Studies include those of Tizard and her colleagues (e.g. Hodges and Tizard, 1989; see Key Study 32.4), Chisolm *et al.* (1995), Rutter and the ERA Study Team, 2004; Rutter *et al.* (2007) (see Key Study 32.4), and the Bucharest Early Intervention Project (BEIP) (Almas *et al.*, 2012; Nelson *et al.*, 2007) (see Key Study 32. 5).
3. Studies of *developmental pathways*.

Studies of extreme privation

This represents the toughest test of the hypothesis that early experience, important at the time, will have long-term effects only if similar experiences occur subsequently (Clarke and Clarke, 2000). What happens to children who suffer extreme early privation but are then 'rescued' and enjoy much improved conditions?

Clearly, the twins' experience of prolonged privation didn't predestine them to a permanent condition of severe handicap (Clarke and Clarke, 2000).

The fate of the Holocaust survivors seems to highlight the fundamental importance of having somebody (not necessarily a mother figure) with whom to form an emotional bond. According to Tizard (1986), Freud and Dann's study provides evidence of the *protective function* of attachments in development, even when they are not directed to the mother, or indeed to an adult. In other words, it is *attachment formation* as such that's important for the development of social and emotional relationships in later childhood and adulthood, rather than who the particular attachment figure is.

Studies of late adoption

Tizard (1977) and Hodges and Tizard (1989) studied children who, on leaving care between the ages of two and seven, were either adopted or returned to their own families. The institutions they grew up in provided good physical care and appeared to provide adequate intellectual stimulation. However, staff turnover was high, and they operated a policy against allowing strong

Case Study 32.1

The case of PM and JM (Koluchova, 1972, 1991)

- Identical twin boys, born in 1960 in the former Czechoslovakia, lost their mother shortly after birth. They were cared for by a social agency for a year, then fostered by a maternal aunt for a further six months. They then went to live with their father who'd remarried, but his new wife proved to be excessively cruel to the twins, banishing them to the cellar for the next five and a half years. They were also harshly beaten.
- When discovered in 1967, they were very short in stature, had rickets, no spontaneous speech (communicating largely by gestures), and were terrified of many aspects of their new environment.
- Having been removed from their parents, they first underwent a programme of physical rehabilitation and entered a school for children with severe learning difficulties. They were subsequently adopted by two exceptionally dedicated women.
- Academically, they caught up with their peers and achieved emotional and intellectual normality. At follow-up in 1974 (at age 14), they showed no signs of psychological abnormality or unusual behaviour. They'd gone on to technical school, training as typewriter mechanics, but later went on to further education, specialising in electronics.
- They both had very good relationships with their adoptive mothers, their adopted sisters, and the women's relatives. Both were drafted for national service, and later married and had children. At the age of 29, they were said to be entirely stable, with no abnormalities, and enjoying warm relationships. One had become a computer technician and the other a technical training instructor (Koluchova, 1991).

Case Study 32.2

Childhood survivors of the Holocaust (Freud and Dann, 1951)

- Anna Freud and Sophie Dann studied six German-Jewish orphans rescued from a concentration camp at the end of the Second World War. They'd all been orphaned when a few months old, after which they were kept together as a group in a deportation camp. They were cared for by camp inmates, who were successively deported to Auschwitz.
- During their time in the camp, they'd been subjected to many terrifying experiences, including witnessing camp hangings. On release, at age 3, all were severely malnourished, normal speech had hardly developed, and they'd developed the same kind of intense attachment to each other that children normally have for their parents – but there was none of the jealousy and rivalry usually found among siblings. They refused to be separated even for a moment, and were extremely considerate and generous to each other. But they showed cold indifference or fearful hostility towards adults. After the camp was liberated, they were flown to Bulldog's Bank in England.
- They obviously cared greatly – and only – for each other. But gradually they began to form attachments to specific adult caretakers, and they showed a spurt in social and language development. In a one-year follow-up, it was clear that they were hypersensitive, aggressive, and difficult to handle. But, as Freud and Dann observe:

... they were neither deficient, delinquent nor psychotic. They ... had mastered some of their anxieties, and developed social attitudes. That they were able to acquire a new language in the midst of their upheavals, bears witness to a basically unharmed contact with their environment.

- Within the next two years, all but one of the children had been adopted. All six were traced and interviewed by Moskovitz during 1979 and 1980 (Moskovitz, 1983, 1985). While it had previously been thought that they'd been irreparably damaged:

What now became apparent ... was the wide range of adaptation when there was theoretically no reason to see anything positive ... Many made adaptations that are not only impressive but inspiring ... (Clarke and Clarke, 2000)

attachments to develop between the staff and children. Consequently, the children had little opportunity to form close, continuous relationships with adults. Indeed, by age 2, they'd been looked after for at least a week by an average of 24 different caregivers (50 by age 4). The children's attachment behaviour was very unusual and, in general, the first opportunity to form long-term attachments came when they left the institutions and were placed in families.

By age 8, the majority of the adopted children had formed close attachments to their adoptive parents (who very much wanted a child), despite the lack of early attachments (Tizard and Hodges, 1978). But only some of those children returned to their own families had formed close attachments: the biological parents often had mixed feelings about having the child back, with other children competing for their attention (as well as material hardship). As reported by their parents, the ex-institutional children as a whole didn't display more problems than a comparison group that had never been in care. But their teachers described them as displaying attention-seeking behaviour, restlessness, disobedience, and poor peer relationships.

Developmental pathways

Quinton and Rutter (1988) wanted to find out whether children deprived of parental care become depriving parents themselves. They observed one group of women, brought up in care, interacting with their own children, and compared them with a second group of non-institutionalised mothers. The women brought up in care were, as a whole, less sensitive, supportive, and warm towards their children. This difference could be explained in terms of both:

- various subsequent experiences the women had as a result of their early upbringings (such as teenage pregnancy, marrying unsupportive spouses, and marital breakdown)
- their actual deprived childhoods.

However, there was also considerable variability within the group brought up in care, with some women displaying good parenting skills. This could be explained in terms of *developmental pathways* (or *trajectories*; Schaffer, 2004). For example, some of the women had more positive school experiences than others. This made them three times more likely as adolescents or young adults to make proper career and marriage partner choices (Rutter, 1989). Such positive experience represents an escape route from the early hardships associated with being brought up in care (see Figure 32.11).

Similar adverse childhood experiences can have multiple outcomes (Schaffer, 1996b, 2004). *Starting off* at a disadvantage doesn't necessarily mean having to *finish up* at a disadvantage: early disadvantage doesn't inevitably set off a chain reaction of more and more

Key Study 32.4

Late adoption of Romanian orphans (Rutter, 2006; Rutter and the ERA study team, 1998, 2004; Rutter *et al.*, 2007)

- Rutter and the English and Romanian Adoptees (ERA) study team (1998) reported their findings from a study of 111 Romanian children raised in poor to appalling 'hospitals' or 'orphanages' and adopted before the age of 2 by English families (educationally and occupationally above general population norms).
- The Romanian children were compared with 52 control group children (within-UK adoptees, who hadn't suffered early privation). The Romanian children, as a whole, were more severely deprived – physically and psychologically – than almost any other sizeable group of children previously studied; they showed major developmental retardation.
- By age 4, the Romanian adoptees showed 'spectacular' *developmental catch-up* (especially cognitive), particularly marked in those adopted before 6 months. However, two follow-up studies suggest that there's a continuing strong effect of their early privation.
- In the first follow-up, they were studied up to the age of 6 (Rutter and the ERA study team, 2004). Many children displayed *disinhibited attachment* (DA), which in many ways resembles the attachment behaviour of Hodges and Tizard's ex-institution sample: a lack of close confiding relationships; rather indiscriminate friendliness; a relative lack of differentiation in response to different adults; a tendency to go off with strangers; and a lack of checking back with a parent in anxiety-provoking situations. DA is one form of *reactive attachment disorder* (RAD).
- This pattern persisted from ages four to six, and Rutter (2006) argued that it might reflect some form of biological programming, that is, an effect on brain structure and functioning which occurs as a form of adaptation to an abnormal environment during a sensitive period of development. On this basis, we'd expect this pattern of behaviour to continue into middle childhood/early adolescence.
- Indeed, parents' reports of a persistence of DA from age 6 to 11 were confirmed by Rutter *et al.* (2007) – but it did become less frequent.

Key Study 32.5

The Bucharest Early Intervention Project (BEIP) (Almas *et al.*, 2012; Nelson *et al.*, 2007)

- Like the study described in Key Study 32.4, the BEIP examined the effects on a child's brain and behaviour of living in Romanian state institutions and whether foster care could improve the effects of being raised in such impoverished conditions.
- A total of 136 children free of neurological, genetic, and other birth defects were selected for the study; all had been abandoned to institutions in the first weeks/months of life and their average age in 2000 was 22 months. Half the children were randomly assigned to a foster care intervention (all foster parents were licenced and received special training), while the other half remained in one of six institutions. A third group of children who'd been raised by their biological families in Bucharest was recruited.
- Beginning in 2000, the BEIP was the first ever *randomised controlled study* (RCS), providing a level of experimental precision that hadn't been previously available (Nelson *et al.*, 2013). This meant that any developmental or behavioural differences between the two groups could be attributed to where they were reared.
- At 30, 40 and 52 months, the average IQ of the institutionalised group was in the low-middle 70s, about 10 points lower than that of the fostered group (and 100 for the family control group).
- Consistent with the findings of the ERA study team, there was a *sensitive period* when a child was able to achieve a maximum gain in IQ: a child fostered before age 2 had a significantly higher IQ than a later-adopted child. According to Nelson *et al.* (2013):

> ...the Romanian children living in institutions provide the best evidence to date that the initial two years of life constitute a sensitive period in which a child must receive intimate emotional and physical contact or else find personal development stymied.

- When assessed at 42 months, fostered children displayed dramatic improvements in making emotional attachments: almost half were securely attached to another person (compared with 18 per cent of the institutionalised children). Again, those who were fostered before 24 months were more likely to form secure attachments compared with those fostered later.

- While foster care reduced the incidence of anxiety and depression by about half, it didn't affect behavioural diagnoses (ADHD and conduct disorder). However, there was no evidence of a sensitive period for mental health.
- Children raised in institutions showed a less mature pattern of brain activity, while those who were fostered before 24 months were indistinguishable from the family-reared children. While fostering children at any age had no effect on increasing the amount of *grey* matter, it did increase *white* matter volume.
- The evidence as a whole suggests that the earlier children are cared for by stable, emotionally invested adults, the better their chances of a more normal developmental trajectory. The children are being followed up into adolescence (Nelson *et al.*, 2013).

disadvantage. Periodically, individuals reach turning points where choices must be made, and the path that's taken can either reinforce or help to minimise the consequences of previous experience (Schaffer, 2004).

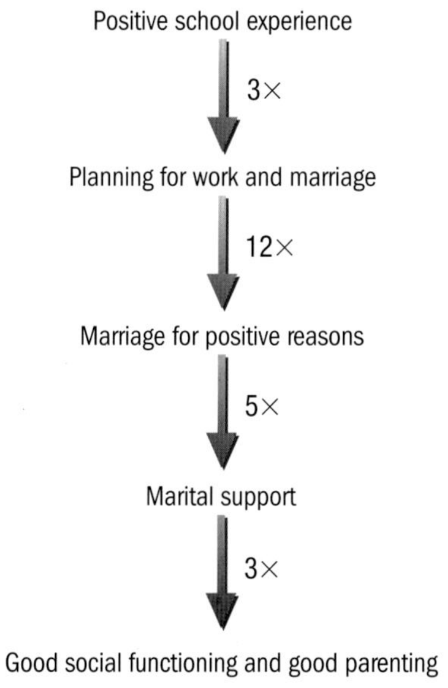

Positive school experience

↓ 3×

Planning for work and marriage

↓ 12×

Marriage for positive reasons

↓ 5×

Marital support

↓ 3×

Good social functioning and good parenting

Figure 32.11 A simplified adaptive chain of circumstances in institution-raised women (based on Quinton and Rutter, 1988; Rutter, 1989)

CONTINUITY BETWEEN EARLY AND LATER ATTACHMENT PATTERNS

The effects of early attachments on later adult relationships

Although until recently attachment was studied almost exclusively within parent–child relationships, Bowlby (1977) maintained that 'attachment behaviour is held to characterise human beings from the cradle to the grave'. According to Hazan and Shaver (1987), attachment theory, as developed by Bowlby and Ainsworth in particular, offers a valuable perspective on adult romantic love, helping to explain both positive emotions (caring, intimacy, and trust) and negative emotions (fear of intimacy, jealousy, and emotional 'ups and downs').

Hazan and Shaver were the first to apply Ainsworth *et al.*'s three basic attachment styles to adult–adult sexual/romantic relationships, asking how adults' attachment patterns (in their adult relationships) are related to their childhood attachments to their parents.

Key Study 32.6

Romantic love conceptualised as an attachment process (Hazan and Shaver, 1987)

- Ainsworth *et al.*'s three attachment styles were 'translated' in a way that would make them suitable for the study of adult attachments. As part of a 'love quiz' in a local newspaper, respondents were asked to indicate which of three descriptions best applied to their feelings about romantic relationships.
- They were also asked to complete a simple adjective checklist describing their childhood relationships with their parents (their recollections of the kind of parenting they received). This was then correlated with their chosen attachment style.
- Fifty-six per cent of respondents were classified as securely attached, 24 per cent as anxious–avoidant, and 20 per cent as anxious–ambivalent.

Ask Yourself

- Compare Hazan and Shaver's findings with those of Ainsworth *et al.*
- Overall, do they match?

Hazan and Shaver's findings closely mirror Ainsworth *et al.*'s findings with 12- to 18-month-old infants. Although these results provided encouraging support for an attachment perspective on romantic love,

Hazan and Shaver warned against drawing any firm conclusions about the continuity between early childhood and adult experience. It would be excessively pessimistic, at least from the point of view of the insecurely attached person, if continuity were the rule, rather than the exception. The correlations suggest that as we go further into adulthood, continuity with our childhood experiences decreases. The average person participates in several important friendships and love relationships, which provide opportunities for revising our *mental models* (or what Bowlby, 1973, called *internal working models* [IWMs]) of self and others (see below).

Intergenerational continuity

Another way of looking at the continuity between early and later attachment patterns is to ask how *parents'* attachment styles are related to their *children's* attachment styles: do people parent their children as they themselves were parented? This is the issue of *intergenerational continuity* (or *intergenerational transfer* of attachment patterns; Meins, 2003).

A commonly used measure of how parents are/were attached to their own parents is the *Adult Attachment Interview* (AAI). Apart from the SST, the AAI is probably the most widely used and best-developed measure of attachment (Goldberg, 2000). It's based on the assumption that what's crucial for predicting parenting behaviour isn't so much the objective facts about our early attachments, but rather how we construe these facts, that is, the nature of our IWMs. (See Box 32.4)

So, the AAI may predict how the mother's child will be attached to her as determined by the SST (Heard and Lake, 1997; Main, 1995). However, it's possible that these findings are affected by the mother's selective recall: how she remembers her childhood might be influenced by her current experiences with her own child.

Ask Yourself

- How could you try to control this potential confounding variable?

Fonagy *et al.* (1991) tried to rule out this possibility by giving the AAI to 96 women *before* the birth of their children (i.e. during pregnancy), then classifying the children (using the SST) when they were 12 and 18 months old. As Table 32.3 shows, Main *et al.*'s (1985) results were largely replicated (with the exception

Box 32.4 The Adult Attachment Interview (Main *et al.*, 1985)

The Adult Attachment Interview (AAI) is a structured interview, comprising 15 questions designed to tap an individual's experience of attachment relationships in childhood, and how s/he considers those experiences to have influenced later development and present functioning. More specifically, for each parent, the person is asked to choose five adjectives which best describe that relationship during childhood. The person then has to illustrate each of these choices by drawing on childhood memories.

Later, the person is asked how they reacted when upset, to which parent they felt closest and why, whether they ever felt rejected or threatened, why parents may have acted as they did, how these relationships may have changed, and how these earlier experiences (including major loss up to the present time) may have affected their adult functioning and personality.

Each interview (which lasts about 90 minutes) is classified as a whole, giving an overall 'state of mind' regarding attachment. Four attachment styles are possible:

Secure/autonomous (F): These individuals discuss childhood experiences openly, coherently and consistently, acknowledging both positive and negative events and emotions. This is the most common style among parents of *securely attached* infants.

Dismissing (D): These individuals seem cut off from the emotional nature of their childhood, denying especially their negative experiences and dismissing their significance. They appear cooperative, but contradictions make them seem dishonest. This is the most common style among parents of *anxious–avoidant* infants.

Preoccupied/entangled (E): Such people are overinvolved with what they recollect, appearing so overwhelmed that they become incoherent, confused, even angry. They're still actively trying to please their parents. This is the most common style among parents of *anxious–resistant* infants.

Unresolved/disorganised (U): This style describes mainly those who've experienced a trauma (which may include physical or sexual abuse), or the early death of an attachment figure, and who haven't come to terms with it or worked through the grieving process (see Chapter 39). This is the most common style among parents of *disorganised* infants.

(Based on Goldberg, 2000; Heard and Lake, 1997; Main *et al.*, 1985; Schaffer, 1996a)

of the preoccupied mothers). The correlation was especially strong for the autonomous mother–secure child pairing.

Table 32.3 Mother's prenatal AAI classification and children's Strange Situation Test classification (based on Fonagy *et al.*, 1991)

	Classification of the mother		
Classification of the children	**Dismissing**	**Autonomous**	**Preoccupied**
Anxious-avoidant	15	8	7
Secure	5	45	5
Anxious-resistant	2	6	3

These results have been replicated in later studies by Fonagy and his colleagues, for both infant–mother attachment (Fonagy *et al.*, 1994; Steele *et al.*, 1995) and father–infant attachment (Steele *et al.*, 1996). Overall, mothers' perceptions of their own childhood attachments predicted their children's attachments to them 75 per cent of the time. While acknowledging the need to explain the 25 per cent 'failure' rate (Clarke and Clarke, 2000), how can we explain this evidence for intergenerational continuity?

Inner working models

According to Bowlby (1973), expectations about the availability and responsiveness of attachment figures are built into our IWMs of attachment. These reflect memories and beliefs stemming from our early experiences of caregiving, which are carried forward into new relationships, both during childhood and beyond. They play an active role in guiding perceptions and behaviour.

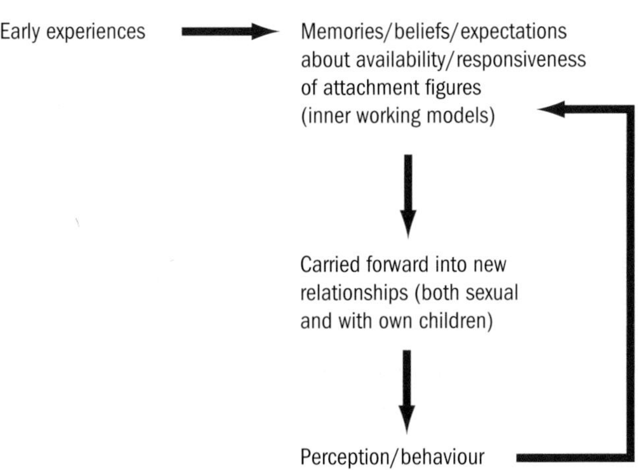

Figure 32.12 How inner working models link early caregiving experiences and later relationships

Bowlby (1973) argued that, at least under normal circumstances, our IWMs are resistant to change:

> *Because ... children tend unwittingly to identify with parents and therefore to adopt, when they become parents, the same patterns of behaviour towards children that they have themselves experienced during their own childhood, patterns of interaction are transmitted, more or less faithfully, from one generation to another.*

However, IWMs usually can be updated or modified as new interactions develop. While for young children such change must be based on actual physical events, such direct interaction isn't necessary in older children and adults. Main *et al.* (1985), for example, found that some adults, who reported being insecure in their relationships with their own parents, managed to produce children who were securely attached, at both 12 months and 6 years. They'd mentally worked through their unpleasant experiences with their parents, and their IWMs were now more typical of secure types (Hazan and Shaver, 1987).

Van Ijzendoorn and Bakjermans-Kranenburg (1996) reviewed 33 studies involving the AAI. Similar proportions of mothers, fathers, and older adolescents fell into the four attachment categories, but people from lower socio-economic groups were slightly more likely to be classified as dismissing. The largest difference is for people having treatment for mental disorder, who are very unlikely to score as autonomous. Some mothers who've had very negative early experiences seemed to have come to terms with them, explaining them in rational terms (such as marital stress, overwork). They were more likely to have secure infants, perhaps because they'd successfully updated their own IWMs. In fact, Bowlby (1988) recognised that attachment behaviour and IWMs cannot be regarded as fixed in infancy and unchanging throughout life.

CONCLUSIONS

Together with studies of adopted children (see above), Golombok's research (Golombok *et al.*, 1995, 1999, 2001) into the effects of 'reduced' or 'minimal' parenting shows that:

> *... a 'blood-bond' is not necessary for the development of sound parent–child relationships: this can be found even when the role of parenthood is fragmented between a biological and psychological parent ... (Schaffer, 2004)*

While evolutionary theory would predict a more troublesome or weaker parent–child relationship in the absence of a genetic bond, attachment theory wouldn't (Rutter, 2008). To date, the evidence seems to support attachment theory. (See Meet the Researcher pp. 550–1.)

MEET THE RESEARCHER

Susan Golombok

Children in new family forms

The birth in 1978 of Louise Brown, the first 'test-tube' (IVF) baby, has had a fundamental impact on the way in which mothers and fathers may be related to their children. With IVF, when the mother's egg and father's sperm are used, both parents are genetically related to their child. When a donated egg is used (egg donation), the father is genetically related to the child but not the mother, and when donated sperm are used (donor insemination), the mother is genetically related to the child but not the father. When both egg and sperm are donated (embryo donation), neither parent is genetically related to the child, a situation that is like adoption except that the parents experience the pregnancy and the child's birth. With surrogacy, one woman hosts a pregnancy for another woman. There are two forms of surrogacy: non-genetic surrogacy, which uses the egg of the mother who will raise the child; and genetic surrogacy where, in addition to hosting the pregnancy, the surrogate mother provides the egg. It is now possible for a child to have five parents: an egg donor, a sperm donor, a surrogate mother who hosts the pregnancy, and the two social parents whom the child knows as Mum and Dad.

A further change to the family that occurred in the 1970s was an increase in the number and visibility of lesbian mother families. The majority of lesbian families at that time were formed by women who had their children while married or cohabiting with a male partner and then moved into a lesbian household. Today, many women have children after coming out as lesbian, either singly or as a couple, often by means of donor insemination. There has also been an increase in the number of gay men who are bringing up children. Although it has always been the case that married gay men have had children, it is only in recent years that children have been raised in gay father families. Not only are children of previously married gay men more likely to live with their father following divorce but also more gay men are adopting children, some are having children with lesbian women, and gay men in the USA are becoming fathers through surrogacy.

How do these ways of creating families affect the psychological development of children, or influence the relationships between children and their parents? A team from the Centre for Family Research at the University of Cambridge has been studying new family forms in order to provide answers to these questions.

Israeli gay couple Omer Gher (L) and Yonatan pose with their 1-month old son Evyatar, who was conceived through an Indian surrogate mother, at a hospital in Mumbai on November 17, 2008. The Israeli gay couple became parents to a child conceived through a Mumbai-based fertility clinic

The European Study of Assisted Reproduction Families

In the first psychological study of assisted reproduction families, we assessed almost 500 children in the Netherlands, Italy, Spain and the UK at ages 6 (Golombok *et al.*, 1995, 1996), 12 (Golombok *et al.*, 2001, 2002a, 2002b) and 18 years (Golombok *et al.*, 2009). Children born following IVF or donor insemination were compared with adopted and naturally conceived children. Contrary to the concerns that had been raised about assisted reproduction families, the parents had very positive relationships with their children and the children themselves were functioning well. The most striking finding was that very few donor insemination parents had told their child about the nature of their conception, so the children were unaware that the man they thought of as their father was not their genetic parent.

The Millennium Study of Assisted Reproduction Families

Our next study began 15 years later. By this time, children were being born through egg donation and surrogacy, and we wanted to examine the impact on family relationships and child development of procedures involving the lack of a genetic and/or gestational relationship between a parent and the child. The findings regarding the quality of parent–child relationships and children's psychological well-being were very similar to those of the earlier European study (Golombok *et al.*, 2004a, 2004b, 2005, 2006). By age 7, only a minority of egg donation and donor insemination parents had told their child about their donor conception. The children in this study were born before the change in UK law that removed donor anonymity. From 2023 onwards, identifying information about the donor will be available to donor-conceived individuals at age 18, and it is likely that more parents will be open with their children about their genetic origins.

Donor sibling families

We have been able to learn about the consequences of donor identification from the USA where it is possible for donor offspring to search for their donor relations through a website, the Donor Sibling Register (DSR). Since its launch, more than 24,000 people have registered with the website and more than 6500 matches have been made. At the Centre for Family Research, we have been collaborating with the DSR in a survey of almost 800 donor insemination parents and almost 200 offspring about their experiences of searching for donor relations (Freeman *et al.*, 2009; Jadva *et al.*, 2009). One key finding is that the older the donor offspring are when told about their donor conception, the more likely they are to feel upset, angry, shocked and confused. Those told as young children are much more accepting. Another fascinating, and unexpected, finding is that donor offspring are particularly interested in meeting their donor siblings, i.e. their genetic half-siblings who are growing up in other families. On average, children are finding around five donor siblings, many are finding more than ten, and the maximum number reported in the survey was 55! Most donor siblings maintain contact with each other and, for the large majority, finding their donor siblings has proved to be a positive experience. Thus the website has created a new phenomenon whereby family relationships based on genetic connections between children are being formed across multiple family units.

Same-sex parents

Studies of children in lesbian mother families have tended to focus on two aspects of development: psychological adjustment and gender-role behaviour. Comparisons between children in lesbian families and their counterparts from heterosexual families have found no differences in psychological well-being or in the gender-role behaviour of boys or girls (Tasker and Golombok, 1995; Golombok and Tasker, 1996). These findings have been replicated in studies of children raised in lesbian families from birth (Golombok *et al.*, 1997; MacCallum and Golombok, 2004) and in investigations of general population samples (Golombok *et al.*, 2003). The only clear difference identified between family types is that co-mothers in lesbian families are more involved with the children than are fathers in heterosexual homes.

The circumstances of children in gay father families are more unusual than those of children raised by lesbian mothers. Not only are they being raised by same-sex parents but also it is rare for fathers, whether heterosexual or gay, to be the primary parent. Research on the development of children in gay father families is just beginning.

Conclusion

The assumptions and speculations about the potentially negative influences for children's psychological development of assisted reproduction or same-sex parenting appear to be unfounded. Whether created by IVF, donor insemination, egg donation or surrogacy, and whether headed by same-sex or opposite-sex parents, what seems to matter most for children's psychological well-being is not the structure of their family but the quality of family life.

Professor Susan Golombok is Professor of Family Research and Director of the Centre for Family Research at the University of Cambridge. Her research focuses on the impact on children's psychological development, and on parent–child relationships, of new family forms. She is author of *Parenting: What really counts?*

Schaffer (1998) believes that psychological development is far more flexible than was previously thought. Our personalities aren't fixed once and for all by events in the early years. Given the right circumstances, the effects of even quite severe and prolonged deprivation can be reversed. As Clarke and Clarke (2000) conclude:

> *... there is no suggestion that what happens in the early years is unimportant. For most children, however, the effects of such experiences represent no more than a first step in an ongoing life path ... There is little indication that any one point of development is more critical than another; all are important ...*

Chapter Summary

- The attachment process can be divided into **pre-attachment, indiscriminate, discriminate,** and **multiple attachment phases.**
- The development of specific attachments is shown through separation anxiety. Some babies also display the **fear-of-strangers response**.
- According to **'cupboard love' theories**, attachments are learned through satisfaction of the baby's need for food. However, Schaffer and Emerson found that not only were infants attached to people who didn't perform caretaking activities, but those who did weren't always their primary attachment figures.
- According to Bowlby's **evolutionary theory**, new-born humans are **genetically programmed** to behave towards their mothers in ways that ensure their survival. There's a **critical period** for attachment development, and attachment to the mother figure is based on **monotropy**.
- The **Strange Situation Test (SST)** is used to classify the baby's basic attachment to the mother into three main types: **anxious–avoidant (type A), securely attached (type B)** and **anxious–resistant (type C)**. The crucial feature determining the quality of attachment is the mother's **sensitivity**.
- Patterns of attachment to mothers and fathers are **independent**. Attachment type may change depending on variations in the family's circumstances, and there are also **cultural variations** in the distribution of attachment types.
- Given that the **environment of evolutionary adaptation (EEA)** was more variable than Bowlby originally claimed, it's unlikely that any one pattern of attachment was/is 'species-specific' or normative ('natural').
- Bowlby's **maternal-deprivation hypothesis (MDH)** was used to explain the harmful effects of growing up in institutions. But this fails to recognise the understimulating nature of the institutional environment, and to disentangle the different kinds of retardation produced by different types of **privation**.
- According to Bowlby's theory, **short-term deprivation** produces **distress**. **Privation** produces long-term **developmental retardation** (such as **affectionless psychopathy**).
- Parental death and divorce are examples of **long-term deprivation**, and are associated with long-term effects, particularly **separation anxiety**.
- Since children in **day care** experience regular separations, the SST may be an inappropriate method for assessing their attachments.
- Case studies of children who've endured **extreme privation**, studies of **late adoption**, and the study of **developmental pathways**, all indicate that the effects of early privation are **reversible**.
- Attachment is a **lifelong phenomenon**, and patterns established in childhood parent–child relationships tend to structure the quality of later bonds in their adult relationships.
- This hypothesis was tested in Hazan and Shaver's ground-breaking study of adult romantic relationships. They found a similar distribution of attachment styles as was found for young children, as well as a correlation between adult attachment style and **type of parenting** received as a child.
- Hazan and Shaver also found evidence that adults with different attachment styles display different characteristic **mental models** of themselves and their closest relationships. This is related to Bowlby's **inner working models (IWMs)**.
- The **Adult Attachment Interview (AAI)** is a structured interview designed to tap an individual's experience of attachment relationships in childhood and how s/he considers those experiences to have influenced later development and present functioning.
- According to the AAI, four attachment styles are possible: **secure/autonomous (F), dismissing (D), preoccupied/entangled (E)** corresponding to the three identified by Ainsworth *et al.*, and **unresolved/disorganised (U)**.
- Many studies have used the AAI in the context of intergenerational **continuity** or **intergenerational transfer of attachment patterns**.

Links with Other Topics/Chapters

Chapter 28 → Babies' sociability has its adult counterpart in the *need for affiliation*, the basis of *interpersonal attraction*

Chapter 16 → The pre-attachment phase of attachment development is supported by all the research that demonstrates babies' *preference for human faces* (*facedness*) over aspects of the physical world. Also, the baby's ability to *imitate facial expressions* may facilitate its relationship with attachment figures (Miller, 2002)

Chapter 16 → *Object permanence* (necessary for specific attachments to develop) is part of the *object concept*

Chapter 34 → and an important part of the *sensorimotor stage* of Piaget's *theory of cognitive development*

Chapter 36 → Discussion of fathers as (principal) parents raises some of the same issues as are raised by discussion of *gay and lesbian couples as parents*

Chapter 12 → Separation anxiety in the form of psychosomatic (*psychophysiological*) reactions refers to physical symptoms associated with/caused by *stress, anxiety* or other *psychological factors*

Chapter 37 → The effects of divorce on children include *adolescent behaviours* (such as earlier age of having sex, teenage pregnancies and leaving home)

Chapter 38 → earlier age of *cohabitation and marriage*, and more distant relationships with parents in *adulthood*

Chapter 44 → greater frequency of depression

Chapter 46 → higher incidence of *antisocial and delinquent behaviour* during childhood and adolescence

Chapter 38 → The effects on children of day care is part of a wider debate about the *roles of men and women* and their respective responsibilities for/contributions to child care

Chapter 22 → An assumption made by many Psychologists (and a feature of *social representations* of the effects of early experience)

Chapter 2 → is that children are highly malleable and their early experiences determine the course of their personality once and for all. Both *Freud and Watson* argued that early experience has unique significance

Chapter 28 → Hazan and Shaver's study can help to explain why some *romantic relationships* last and others don't – in terms of *incompatibility* between partners' attachment styles

Recommended Reading

Cassidy, J. & Shaver, P.R. (eds) (2008) *Handbook of Attachment: Theory, Research and Clinical Applications* (2nd edn). New York: The Guilford Press.

Clarke, Ann & Clarke, Alan (2000) *Early Experience and the Life Path.* London: Jessica Kingsley Publishers.

Goldberg, S. (2000) *Attachment in Development.* London: Arnold.

Gross, R. (2008) *Key Studies in Psychology* (5th edn). London: Hodder Education. Chapters 15 and 27.

Holmes, J. (1993) *John Bowlby and Attachment Theory.* London: Routledge.

Useful Websites

www.youtube.com/watch?v=VAAmSqv2GV8 (Video of talk by Bowlby on attachment and loss; lots of related videos)

www.thebowlbycentre.org.uk/aboutCAPP home.htm (The Bowlby Centre (2007–9))

www.psychology.sunysb.edu/attachment (Attachment Theory and Research – at Stony Brook)

www.personalityresearch.org/attachment.html (Attachment Theory)

www.fnf.org.uk (Families Need Fathers)

www.fathers-4-justice.org (Fathers4Justice official website)

CHAPTER 33

DEVELOPMENT OF THE SELF-CONCEPT

INTRODUCTION and OVERVIEW

According to Hampson (1995), the human capacity for self-awareness permits us to try to see ourselves as others see us. When Personality Psychologists study personality via self-reports, such as questionnaires (see Chapter 42), they're assessing people's perceptions of themselves. Social Psychologists also study people's self-perceptions through their study of the self-concept.

The self-concept (or simply 'self') is clearly a *hypothetical construct*: it's a 'theory' each one of us develops about who we are and how we fit into society. It's repeatedly revised during childhood in the light of both cognitive development and social experience. On the one hand, as children get older they become more competent at self-awareness and more realistic; on the other hand, other people's perceptions and responses will come to play a more central role in shaping the nature of that awareness (Schaffer, 2004).

Adolescence is a crucial period for the development of the self-concept. A major account of how the self-concept changes in adolescence is Erikson's *psychosocial theory* (see Chapter 37). But the formation of the self is never complete. At no time does the self function as a closed system – it's always affected by others' evaluations of us (Schaffer, 2004). This is consistent with the view of the self as 'social to the core' (Fiske, 2004). Even when tracing how self-perception changes in the individual, we'll see that this is an *inherently social process*, as reflected in the early theories of James, Cooley and Mead. More recent extensions of these see the self as *constructed in language* (e.g. Harré).

CONSCIOUSNESS AND SELF-CONSCIOUSNESS

Ask Yourself

- What do you think is the difference between consciousness and self-consciousness?

When you look in the mirror at your face, or think about something you've done, you're both the person who's looking/thinking (*subject*) and that which is looked at/thought about (*object*). 'I' refers to ourselves as subject and 'me' to ourselves as object, and this represents a rather special relationship we have with ourselves, namely *self-consciousness/self-awareness*.

While other species possess consciousness (they're *sentient* creatures), only humans possess self-consciousness (see Chapter 48). We often use the term 'self-conscious' to describe our response to situations where we're made to feel object-like or exposed in some way (for example, we leave home in the morning to discover our sweater's on back-to-front). But this is a secondary meaning; the *primary* meaning refers to this unique relationship in which the same person, the same self, is both subject and object.

What is the self?

'Self' and 'self-concept' are used interchangeably to refer to an individual's overall self-awareness. According to Murphy (1947), 'the self is the individual as known to the individual', and Burns (1980) defines it as 'the set of attitudes a person holds towards himself'.

According to Leary (2004), the self is a *cognitive structure* that permits self-reflection and organises information about oneself. It also has motivational features, in particular:

- *self-consistency* (to maintain, if not verify, one's existing view of oneself)
- *self-evaluation* (self-assessment – to see oneself accurately)
- *self-enhancement* (to maintain a positive image of oneself).

One's existing view of oneself is one's *self-image,* and our evaluation of ourselves determines our *self-esteem*. Self-enhancement can be both private and public.

- *Private self-enhancement* also relates to *self-esteem*. According to Greenwald (1980), the self-esteem motive acts like a totalitarian political regime that suppresses information and rewrites history to preserve a particular desired image of the government. In the same way, the 'totalitarian ego' distorts facts about the self and rewrites one's memory of personal history in order to maintain one's own positive evaluation.
- *Public self-enhancement* relates to *self-presentation* (or *impression management*), our deliberate attempts to influence others' impressions of us (see Chapter 22).

Private versus public self

Murphy's and Burns' definitions of the self are really definitions of the private self. According to Leary (2004):

> *... at the most fundamental level, the self is the cognitive apparatus that permits self-reflexive thought – the cognitive structures and associated processes that permit people to take themselves as an object of their own thought and to think consciously about themselves ...*

This describes the 'subject'/'object' relationship we discussed above (self-consciousness/awareness) and corresponds to the 'I'/'me' distinction. Leary claims that, strictly, there is *only* a private self. So, what does the public self refer to? It's been used to refer to three distinct entities:

1. the image we convey to others (including reputation and roles)
2. our beliefs about our public image (how we think others perceive us)
3. the impressions others actually form about us.

Whichever of these we mean, the term refers to a very different concept from the private, psychological self, which allows us to think about and control these public impressions. This so-called public self resides either within the individual's own private sense of self or in others' minds, respectively; in either case, it is not a 'self' in the true sense of the term (Leary, 2004).

However, both Goffman's (1971) *dramaturgical approach*, and the *social constructionist approach* reject the view of the self as a private feature of individuals, seeing it as *wholly social/public* (see below).

Components of the self-concept

The self-concept is a general term that normally refers to three major components: *self-image, self-esteem,* and *ideal self.*

Self-image

Ask Yourself

- Give 20 different answers to the question 'Who am I?'

Self-image refers to the way we describe ourselves, what we think we're like. One way of investigating self-image is to ask people the question 'Who am I?' 20 times (Kuhn and McPartland, 1954). This typically produces two main categories of answer.

1. *Social roles* are usually objective aspects of the self-image (e.g. son, daughter, brother, sister, student). They are 'facts' that can be verified by others.
2. *Personality traits* are more a matter of opinion and judgement, and what we think we're like may be different from how others see us. But how others behave towards us has an important influence on our self-perception (see below).

As well as social roles and personality traits, people's answers often refer to their physical characteristics (such as tall, short, fat, thin, blue-eyed, brown-haired). These are part of our *body image/bodily self,* the 'bodily me' which also includes bodily sensations (which are mainly temporary/transitory experiences). A more permanent feature of our body image relates to what we count as part of our body (and hence belonging to us), and what we don't.

Allport (1955) gives two rather dramatic examples of how intimate our bodily sense is, and just where we draw the boundaries between 'me' and 'not me'.

> **Ask Yourself**
> - Imagine swallowing your saliva – or actually do it. Now imagine spitting it into a cup and drinking it.
> - Imagine sucking blood from a cut on your finger (something we do quite automatically). Now imagine sucking the blood from a plaster on your finger!

Clearly, once we've spat out our saliva, we've disowned it – it no longer belongs to us.

Similarly, once the blood has soaked into the plaster it has ceased to be part of ourselves.

Box 33.1 The psychological impact of visible difference (Based on Harcourt and Rumsey, 2008)

- According to the charity Changing Faces, there are over 2,300,000 people in the UK with a significant disfigurement of the face caused by accidents, surgery (such as for cancer), strokes (such as facial paralysis), skin conditions (such as psoriasis or acne), or some congenital or birth conditions (such as birthmarks, cleft lips/palates).
- The term 'disfigurement' is widely understood by the general public and is enshrined in the 1995 Disability and Discrimination Act (DDA). Changing Faces uses the word primarily as a noun ('a person *has* a disfigurement, not '*is* disfigured') but some people prefer to talk about 'visible differences' or 'unusual appearance'. Changing Faces also encourages spelling out the cause of the disfigurement.
- A detailed understanding of the psychosocial impact of disfigurement is complicated by the need to take account of the many different types of difference, causes, and body sites affected, how visible it is to other people, the individual's age, and a whole variety of factors affecting self-perceptions and adjustment. Despite this, there's remarkable consensus concerning the 'headline' difficulties reported by people with a visible difference, namely (i) the experience of negative emotions (e.g. self-consciousness, anxiety and depression); (ii) detrimental effects on self-evaluations (negative self-perceptions and self-esteem: see text below); (iii) difficult encounters with others (e.g. intrusive questioning and staring); and (iv) behavioural consequences (e.g. social avoidance).

Figure 33.1 Simon Weston, survivor – and casualty – of the Falklands War in 1982

Whenever our body changes in some way, so our body image changes. In extreme cases (such as losing a limb, being scarred, or having cosmetic surgery), we'd expect a correspondingly dramatic change in body image (see Box 33.1, and Gross and Kinnison, 2014).

Self-esteem

While the self-image is essentially *descriptive*, self-esteem (or *self-regard*) is essentially *evaluative*. It refers to how much we like and approve of ourselves, how worthy a person we think we are. Coopersmith (1967) defined it as 'a personal judgement of worthiness, that is expressed in the attitudes the individual holds towards himself'.

How much we like or value ourselves can be an overall judgement, or it can relate to specific areas of our lives. For example, we can have a generally high opinion of ourselves and yet not like certain of our characteristics or attributes (such as our curly hair when we want it straight). Conversely, it may be very difficult to have high overall esteem if we're very badly disfigured, or are desperately shy.

Our self-esteem can be regarded as how we evaluate our self-image, that is, how much we like the kind of person we think we are. Clearly, certain characteristics or abilities have a greater value in society generally, and so are likely to influence our self-esteem accordingly (for example, being physically attractive as opposed to unattractive; see Chapter 28). The value attached to particular

Critical Discussion 33.1

Behavioural economics: ownership and personal identity

It seems that, at all stages of life, 'we are what we own'. James (1890) was one of the first to appreciate that the things we own serve an important function as markers for self-identity.

According to Hood (2012), *behavioural economics* (BE) attempts to unravel the cognitive processes that lead humans to make decisions about ownership and transactions. One robust finding is that the concept of ownership develops very early, especially for those objects that children use for comfort and grow attached to.

Over the course of our lives, we increasingly use objects to express our self-identity. Simply choosing an object endows it with more value in our minds than an identical object we didn't select. This partiality appears to be rooted in brain mechanisms that evaluate potential losses and gains in terms of their emotional significance.

> *... At least in western cultures, humans treat objects as extensions of themselves, explaining why some of us seem to overreact to the loss of, or damage to, our personal possessions. (Hood, 2012)*

Most western parents will probably observe their child become inseparably attached to a particular soft toy or cuddly blanket; however, such *transitional objects* are much less common in Japan, where infants sleep with their mothers into middle childhood (Hobara, 2003).

Prisons – and other 'total institutions' (see Chapter 27) – show their understanding of the importance of ownership by deliberately removing them from inmates; this eradicates the sense of self. Some of the most harrowing images from the Nazi concentration camps are the piles of personal possessions taken from inmates (including dentures, hair, shoes, suitcases – and dolls); these are now regarded as sacred.

Figure 33.2 Personal possessions taken from inmates at Auschwitz

Box 33.2 The pros and cons of high self-esteem

- According to Baumeister *et al.* (2003), people with high self-esteem perform only slightly better academically than those with low self-esteem.
- Similarly, self-esteem is only weakly related to children's popularity in school and tenuously tied to the quality of a person's relationships in general. It also has little effect on how likely someone is to be violent or engage in risky behaviours (such as smoking and drug use).
- However, high self-esteem does seem to make people more persistent. Those high self-esteem participants also reported feeling happier and less depressed (Baumeister *et al.*, 2003).
- One serious drawback of high self-esteem is that it makes it more difficult to see our own shortcomings. Considerable research evidence consistently finds that high self-esteem individuals tend to have an unrealistically positive self-image. They believe they're more attractive, successful, likable, clever, and moral than others do. When they receive negative feedback, these individuals become defensive, blaming everything and everyone but themselves (Crocker and Carnevale, 2013).

characteristics will also depend on culture, gender, age, and social background (see Critical Discussion 33.2, p. 560).

Ideal self

Self-esteem is also partly determined by how much the self-image differs from the ideal self. If our self-image is the kind of person we think we *are*, then our ideal self (*ego-ideal* or *idealised self-image*) is the kind of person we'd *like* to be. This can vary in extent and degree. We may want to be different in certain aspects, or we may want to be a totally different person. (We may even wish we were someone else!) Generally, the greater the gap between our self-image and our ideal self, the lower our self-esteem (see Rogers' self theory: Chapter 42).

Figure 33.3 Jocelyne Wildenstein (the 'Cat Woman') has had several plastic surgery procedures to make herself look like a cat

Self-schemata

We not only represent and store information about other people, we also do so about ourselves – but in a more complex and varied way. This information about the self constitutes the self-concept.
We tend to have very clear conceptions of ourselves (*self-schemata*) on some dimensions (such as those that are very important to us), but not others.
For example, if you think of yourself as athletic, as definitely not unathletic, and being athletic is important to you, then you are self-schematic on that dimension (it is part of your self-concept; Hogg and Vaughan, 1995).

Ask Yourself

- What are you self-schematic on?

Most people have a complex self-concept with a relatively large number of self-schemata, including an array of possible selves, future-oriented schemata of what we'd like to become (ideal self) (Markus and Nurius, 1986). Visions of future possible selves may influence how we make important life decisions, such as career choice.

The idea of *multiple selves* raises the question of whether there's any one self that's more real or authentic than the others.

Ask Yourself

- Do you feel most real (most 'yourself') when you're with a particular person (your best friend, perhaps?).

Personality theorists tend to assume that the person has a single, unitary self. This is implied by the fact that typical instructions at the top of a personality questionnaire don't specify which self the respondent should describe (Hampson, 1995). By contrast, Social Psychologists recognise the possibility that the self refers to a complex set of perceptions, composed of a number of schemata relating both to what we're like and how we *could* be.

THEORIES OF SELF

James' theory: self-as-subject/self-as-object

It was James (1890) who first made the distinction between *self-as-subject* or *knower* ('I') and *self-as-object* or *known* ('me'). The 'I' represents the principal form of the self, lying at the centre of our state (or 'stream') of consciousness. But we have as many selves as we have social relationships: the self is *multifaceted*. This is consistent with the widely shared view that we modify our behaviour to some extent depending on whom we're with: different others bring out different aspects of our personality (Hampson, 1995).

Goffman's dramaturgical theory

James' view of multiple selves is also consistent with Goffman's (1971) account of *self-presentation*, which he defined as the creation and maintenance of a *public self*. By analogy with the theatre, each participant in a social interaction is engaged in a performance designed as much for its effect on the audience as it is for honest and open expression of the self. Indeed, according to this *dramaturgical approach*, personality is equated with the various roles the person plays in life.

So, for Goffman (1971), the only true self is a public one. In discussing the link between self and self-presentation, he says:

> *A correctly staged and performed scene leads the audience to impute a self to a performed character, but this impression – this self – is a product of a scene that comes off and is not a cause of it. The self shouldn't be regarded as an internal, organic thing, but rather as the dramatic effect of a person's public presentation.*

James' idea of multiple selves goes much further than this, by suggesting that different personalities are constructed in the context of every relationship one has (Hampson, 1995).

Ask Yourself

- Do you agree with James or Goffman, or do you believe there is just one 'self', that remains constant regardless of whom we're interacting with or the context of the interaction?

Cooley's theory: the looking-glass self

According to Cooley's (1902) *theory of the looking-glass self,* the self is reflected in the reactions of other people, who are the 'looking-glass' for oneself. That is, in order to understand what we're like, we need to see how others see us, and this is how children gradually build up impressions of what they're like. We receive reflections of judgements and evaluations of our behaviour and appearance, which produce some form of self-feeling (such as pride or shame).

Consistent with the notion of multiple selves, Cooley claims that the looking-glass isn't a 'mere mechanical reflection', because it will differ depending on whose view we take. The individual and society are opposite sides of the same coin (Denzin, 1995).

Mead's symbolic interactionism

Symbolic interactionism is mainly associated with Mead (1934), who was influenced by the earlier theories of James and Cooley. Human beings act towards things in terms of their *meanings*: we exist in a *symbolic* as well as a physical environment and the importance of a social interaction is derived from the meaning it holds for us. The 'interaction' refers specifically to the fact that people communicate with each other, which provides the opportunity for meanings to be learned. Because we share a common language and have the ability for symbolic thought, we can (at least in principle) look at the world from the point of view of other perceivers – that is, *take the role of the other*. According to Mead, this is essentially the process by which the self develops.

Mead turned James and Cooley on their heads. The self isn't mentalistic (something privately going on inside the individual) but, like mind, is a cognitive process lodged in the *ongoing social world*. However, like Cooley, he saw self and society as two terms in a reciprocal process of interaction (Denzin, 1995). Knowledge of self and others develops simultaneously, both being dependent on social interaction.

Possessing a self converts us into a special kind of actor, transforming our relation to the world: we're an object to ourselves and can interact with ourselves, which is a great influence upon our transactions with the world in general, and with other people in particular. Self-interaction is a *reflexive process* (Mead's way of making the 'I'/'me' distinction): the experiencing 'I' cannot be an object, it cannot itself be experienced, since it's the very act of experiencing. What we experience and interact with is our 'me'.

As important as language is in (self-)interaction, the key process by which we develop a concept of self is *role-taking*. By placing ourselves in the position of others, we can look back on ourselves. The idea of self can develop only if the individual can 'get outside himself (experientially) in such a way as to become an object to himself' (Mead, 1934); that is, to see ourselves from the standpoint of others. (See Box 33.3.)

Social constructionist approaches

Influenced by Mead, many sociologists and Social Psychologists see the role of language as fundamental to the construction and maintenance of the self. What we say about ourselves often depends on who's listening. In selecting what to say and not to say, we're actively constructing a self in relation to another person. The self is not a static, internal entity but a constantly changing *process* (Petkova, 1995).

According to Harré (1985, 1989), our understanding and experiences of ourselves as human beings, our subjective experiences of selfhood, are laid down by the beliefs about being a person that are implicit in our language. The structure of our language implies certain assumptions/beliefs about human nature, which we live out in our daily interactions with others. For example, the words 'I' and 'me' mislead us into believing that each of us is represented by a coherent, unified self that operates mechanisms and processes (the subject matter of Psychology) which are responsible for our actions. But 'self', 'ego', 'mind' and so on don't refer to anything that exists objectively in the world: they're *hypothetical constructs* which perform the very important function of helping us to organise and structure our world (Burr, 1995).

According to Harré (1995; 1999), what 'I' actually does is specify a *location* for the acts performed by a speaker. It draws attention to the body of one particular speaker who occupies a unique location, both physically and socially. It also commits that individual to the consequences of his/her utterance. We use words such as 'I' in conversation to perform actions in a *moral universe*:

Box 33.3 Mead's Developmental Theory of the Self

- Initially, the child thinks about his conduct as 'good or bad only as he reacts to his own acts in the remembered words of his parents'. 'Me' at this stage is a combination of the child's memory of his own actions and the kind of reaction they received.
- In the next stage, the child's pretend play, in particular 'playing at mummies and daddies' or 'doctors or nurses', helps the child understand and incorporate adult attitudes and behaviour. Here, the child isn't merely imitating but also 'calls out in himself the same response as he calls out in the other'. For example, he's being the child *and* the parent and, as the parent, is responding to himself as the child.
- Play is distinguished from games, which involve rules: 'The child must not only take the role of the other, as he does in the play, but he must assume the various roles of all the participants in the game, and govern his action accordingly...'. Games are a later development than play.
- In this way, the child acquires a variety of social viewpoints or 'perspectives' (mother, father, nurse, doctor), which are then used to accompany, direct and evaluate his own behaviour. This is how the *socialised* part of the self (Mead's 'me') expands and develops.
- At first, these viewpoints or perspectives are based upon specific adults. But in time, the child comes to react to himself and his behaviour from the viewpoint of a 'typical mother', a 'typical nurse' or 'people in general' (the *generalised other*). This marks the final, qualitative change in the 'me'. 'It is this generalised other in his experience which provides him with a self.'
- Our 'me' is an image of self seen from the perspective of a judgemental, non-participant observer. By its very nature, 'me' is social, because it grows out of this role-playing, whereby the child is being the other person.

(Based on Mead, 1934)

> *... 'I' ... is a form of life, a moral community that has been presupposed by the uses of the first person, not a kind of hidden inner cognitive engine ... (Harré, 1989)*

Similarly, Potter and Wetherell (1987) argue that the very experience of being a person, the kind of mental life one can have, are dependent on the particular ways of accounting for/talking about ourselves available in our culture. These 'stories' or accounts, whose meaning is shared by members of a culture, are called *discourses*. Since these differ from culture to culture, it follows that members of different cultures will experience being human ('selves') in different ways (see Chapter 24 and Critical Discussion 33.2.).

Critical Discussion 33.2

The self-concept as a cultural phenomenon

In Maori culture, the person is invested with a particular kind of power (*mana*), given by the gods in accordance with the person's family status and birth circumstances. This is what enables the person to be effective, whether in battle or everyday dealings with others. But this power isn't a stable resource, and can be increased or decreased by the person's day-to-day conduct. For example, it could be reduced by forgetting a ritual observance, or committing some misdemeanour.

People's social standing, and successes and failures, are seen as dependent on external forces, not internal states (such as personality or level of motivation). In fact, mana is only one of these external forces which inhabit the individual. People living in such a culture would necessarily experience themselves quite differently from what people in western culture are used to. Instead of representing themselves as the centre and origin of their actions, which is crucial to the western concept of the self:

> *The individual Maori does not own experiences such as the emotions of fear, anger, love, grief; rather they are visitations governed by the unseen world of powers and forces ... (Potter and Wetherell, 1987)*

According to Moscovici (1985), 'the individual' is the greatest invention of modern times. Only recently has the idea of the autonomous, self-regulating, free-standing individual become dominant, and this has fundamental implications for the debate about free will and determinism (see Chapter 49). Smith and Bond (1998) distinguish between *independent* and *interdependent* selves: the former is what's stressed in western, *individualist* cultures, and the latter by non-western, *collectivist* cultures (see Chapter 47).

FACTORS INFLUENCING THE DEVELOPMENT OF THE SELF-CONCEPT

Much of the research into factors that influence the self-concept can be understood in relation to the symbolic interactionist position. But the importance of these factors extends beyond childhood – our self-concept is constantly being revised. The most significant 'change' is probably the time when it's first being formed.

Argyle (1983) identifies four major influences:

1. the reaction of others
2. comparison with others
3. social roles
4. identification (see Chapters 35 and 36).

The reaction of others

We've already seen in the theories of Cooley and Mead how central the reactions of others are in the formulation of our self-concept. Any attempt to explain how we come to be what we are, and how we change, involves us in the question of what kind of evidence we use. Kelly (1955), like Cooley and Mead, believes that we derive our pictures of ourselves through what we learn of other people's pictures of us (see Chapter 42). So, the central evidence is the reaction of others to us, both what they say of us and the implications of their behaviour towards us. We filter others' views of us through our views of them. We build up continuous and changing pictures of ourselves out of our interaction with others.

Guthrie (1938) tells the famous story of a dull and unattractive female student. Some of her classmates decided to play a trick on her by pretending she was the most desirable girl in the college, and drawing lots to decide who would take her out first, second, and so on. By the fifth or sixth date, she was no longer regarded as dull and unattractive.

Ask Yourself

- Try to explain this change in the student.

By being treated as attractive she had, in a sense, *become* attractive (perhaps by wearing different clothes and smiling more), and her self-image had clearly changed. For the boys who dated her later, it was no longer a chore! 'Before the year was over, she had developed an easy manner and a confident assumption that she was popular' (Guthrie, 1938).

Preschool children are extremely concerned with how adults view them, and few things are more relevant than the reactions to them of *significant others* (parents, older siblings, and other people whose opinions the child values). Strictly speaking, it's the

Figure 33.4 Teachers – major new significant others for younger children

child's *perception* of others' reactions that makes such an important contribution to how the child comes to perceive itself. After all, the child has no frame of reference for evaluating parental reactions: parents are all-powerful figures, and what they say is 'fact'. If a child is consistently told how beautiful or intelligent she is, she'll come to believe it (it will become part of her self-image) through *introjection* (a process very similar to identification, whereby we come to incorporate into our own personality the perceptions, attitudes and reactions to ourselves of our parents; Argyle, 1983). It's through others' reactions that the child learns its *conditions of worth*, that is, which behaviours will produce *positive regard* and which will not (Rogers, 1959; see Chapter 42).

When the child starts school, the number and variety of significant others increase to include teachers and peers. At the same time, the child's self-image is becoming more differentiated, and significant others then become important in relation to different parts of the self-image. For example, the teacher is important as far as the child's academic ability is concerned, parents as far as how loveable the child is, and so on.

How others' reactions influence self-esteem

Coopersmith's (1967) study of 9- and 10-year-old white, middle-class boys, found that the optimum conditions for the development of high self-esteem involve a combination of (i) firm enforcement of limits on the child's behaviour; and (ii) a good deal of acceptance of the child's autonomy and freedom within those limits. Firm management helps the child to develop firm inner controls: a predictable and structured social environment helps the child to deal effectively with the environment, and, hence, to feel 'in control' of the world (rather than controlled by it).

Coopersmith followed these boys through into adulthood, and found that the high self-esteem boys consistently outperformed the low self-esteem boys, both educationally and occupationally

Box 33.4 The schizophrenic self

- In contrast with the parents of high-esteem boys in Coopersmith's study is the study of interaction between parents and their schizophrenic children.
- These parents tend to deny *communicative support* to the child, and often fail to respond to the child's statements and demands for recognition of its opinions. When the parents do communicate with the child, it's often in the form of an interruption or an intrusion, rather than a response to the child. In fact, they respond selectively to those of the child's utterances that they themselves have initiated, rather than those initiated by the child.
- Laing (1970) suggests that these kinds of communication patterns within the family make the development of *ego boundaries* in the child very difficult – that is, there's a confusion between *self* and *not-self* (me and not me). This impaired autonomy of the self and appreciation of external reality are often found to be fundamental characteristics of schizophrenic adolescents and adults (see Chapter 44).

Comparison with others

Ask Yourself

- Can you think of any examples of where comparison with others (either made by others or yourself) has affected your self-image/self-esteem (either favourably or unfavourably)?

According to Bannister and Agnew (1976), the personal construct of 'self' is intrinsically *bipolar* – that is, having a concept of self implies a concept of not-self. (This is similar to Cooley and Mead's view that self and society are really two sides of a coin.) So, one way in which we come to form pictures of what we're like is to see how we compare with others. Indeed, certain components of self-image are meaningful only through comparison with others. For example, 'tall' and 'fat' aren't absolute characteristics (like, say, 'blue-eyed'): we're tall or fat only in relation to others who are shorter or thinner than us. This is true of many other characteristics, including intelligence (see Chapter 41).

Parents and other adults often react to children by comparing them with other children (such as siblings). A child of above-average intelligence who's grown up in the shadow of a brilliant brother or sister may be less successful academically than an average or even below-average child who's not had to face these unfavourable comparisons.

Ask Yourself

- Do you think it's possible for the converse to be true – in other words, can one's view of self affect how we compare ourselves with others?

According to Tesser (2004), recent research has demonstrated exactly this effect. For example, the poorer our performance in, say, athletics, the more charitable we are in evaluating others' athletic performance. If I do poorly, then others who do poorly are 'OK'; if I do well, then people who do poorly are rated down. Under some conditions, when we're outperformed by others, we don't downgrade our view of self but, instead, upgrade their performance (Alicke *et al.*, 1997). It's less threatening to be outperformed by a 'genius' than someone of normal/average ability (we're 'out of their league').

Social roles

As we noted earlier, social roles are what people commonly regard as part of 'who they are'. Kuhn (1960) asked 7-year-old children and undergraduate students to give 20 different answers to the question, 'Who am I?' The 7-year-old children gave an average of five answers relating to roles, while the undergraduates gave an average of ten. As we get older, we incorporate more and more roles into our self-image, reflecting the increasing number and variety of roles we actually take on. The preschooler is a son or daughter, perhaps a brother or sister, has other familial roles, and may also be a friend to another child. But the number and range of roles are limited compared with those of the older child or adult.

DEVELOPMENTAL CHANGES IN THE SELF-CONCEPT

How do we get to know ourselves?

Achieving identity, in the sense of acquiring a set of beliefs about the self (a *self-schema*), is one of the central developmental tasks of a social being (Lewis, 1990). It progresses through several levels of complexity, and continues to develop through the lifespan (see Chapters 38 and 39).

During the first few months, the baby gradually distinguishes itself from its environment and from other people, and develops a sense of *continuity through time* (the *existential self*). But at this stage, the infant's self-knowledge is comparable to that of other species (such as monkeys). What makes human self-knowledge distinctive is becoming aware that we have it – we're conscious of our existence and uniqueness (Buss, 1992).

According to Maccoby (1980), babies are able to distinguish between themselves and others on two counts:

1. their own fingers hurt when bitten (but they don't have any such sensations when they're biting their rattle or their mother's fingers)
2. probably quite early in life, they begin to associate feelings from their own body movements with the sight of their own limbs and the sounds of their own cries. These sense impressions are bound together into a cluster that defines the *bodily self*, so this is probably the first aspect of the self-concept to develop.

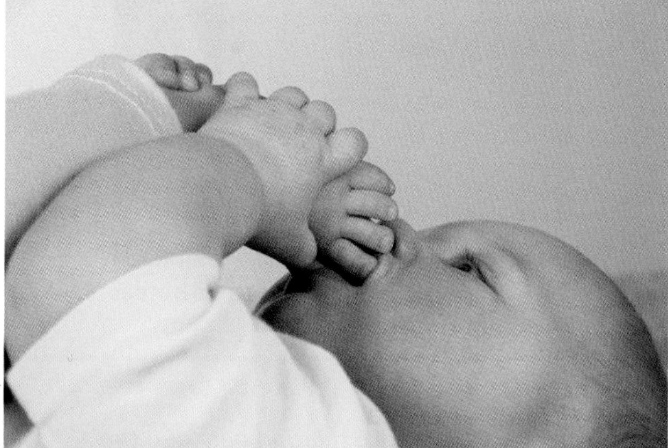

Figure 33.5 A baby acquiring its bodily self

Other aspects of the self-concept develop by degrees, but there seem to be fairly clearly defined stages of development. Young children may know their own names, and understand the limits of their own bodies, and yet be unable to think about themselves as coherent entities. So, self-awareness/self-consciousness develops very gradually.

According to Piaget, an awareness of self comes through the gradual process of *adaptation to the environment* (see Chapter 34). As the child explores objects and accommodates to them (thus developing new *sensorimotor schemas*), it simultaneously discovers aspects of its self. For example, trying to put a large block into its mouth and finding that it won't fit is a lesson in selfhood, as well as a lesson about the world of objects.

Self-recognition

One way in which the development of bodily self has been studied is through *self-recognition*, and this involves more than just a simple discrimination of bodily features. To determine that the person in a photograph or a film or reflected in a mirror is oneself, certain knowledge seems to be necessary:

- at least a rudimentary knowledge of oneself as continuous through time (necessary for recognising ourselves in photographs or movies) and space (necessary for recognising ourselves in mirrors), and
- knowledge of particular features (what we look like).

Although other kinds of self-recognition are possible (e.g. one's voice or feelings), only visual self-recognition has been studied extensively, both in humans and non-humans.

Many non-human animals (including fish, birds, chickens and elephants) react to their mirror images as if they were other animals, although there are exceptions (such as magpies; Prior *et al.*, 2008). Most research has focused on the higher primates – chimpanzees and other great apes (see Key Study 33.1).

A number of researchers (e.g. Lewis and Brooks-Gunn, 1979) have used modified forms of Gallup's technique with 6- to 24-month-old children. The mother applies a dot of rouge to the child's nose (while pretending to wipe its face), and the child is observed to see how often it touches its nose. It is then placed in front of a mirror, and again the number of times it touches its nose is recorded. While touching the dot was never seen before 15 months, between 15 and 18 months, 5–25 per cent of infants touched it, and 75 per cent of the 18- to 24-month-old infants did.

In order to use the mirror image to touch the dot on its nose, the baby must also have built up a schema of how its face should look in the mirror before (otherwise, it wouldn't notice the discrepancy created by the dot). This doesn't develop before about 18 months. This is also about the time when, according to Piaget, *object permanence* is completed, so object permanence would seem to be a necessary condition for the development of self-recognition (see Chapter 34).

Interpreting Gallup's findings

It's generally agreed that passing the mirror test is strong evidence that a chimp has a self-concept, and that only chimps, orang-utans and humans consistently pass it. However, Gallup (1998) infers much more than this. He claims that:

> *... species that pass the mirror test are also able to sympathise, empathise and attribute intent and emotions in others – abilities that some might consider the exclusive domain of humans.*

He believes that self-awareness or self-consciousness is the expression of some underlying process that allows organisms to use their experience as a means of modelling the experience of others. The best support for this *mindreading hypothesis* (MRH) comes

Key Study 33.1

Mirror, mirror ... (Gallup, 1977)

- Gallup, working with preadolescent, wild-born chimps, placed a full-length mirror on the wall of each animal's cage. At first, they reacted as if other chimps had appeared – they threatened, vocalised, or made conciliatory gestures. But this quickly faded out, and by the end of three days had almost disappeared. They then used their images to explore themselves. For example, they'd pick up food and place it on their faces, which couldn't be seen without the mirrors (see Figure 33.6).
- After ten days' exposure, each chimp was anaesthetised and a bright red spot was painted on the uppermost part of one eyebrow ridge, and a second spot on the top of the opposite ear, using an odourless, non-irritating dye.
- When the chimp had recovered from the anaesthetic, it was returned to its cage, from which the mirror had been removed, and it was observed to see how often it touched the marked parts of its body. The mirror was then replaced, and each chimp began to explore the marked spots around 25 times more often than it had done before.
- The procedure was repeated with chimps that had never seen themselves in the mirror, and they reacted to the mirror image as if it were another chimp (they didn't touch the spots). So, the first group had apparently learned to recognise themselves.
- Lower primates (monkeys, gibbons, and baboons) are unable to learn to recognise their mirror images.

Figure 33.6 Chimpanzees learn to use mirrors to explore parts of their bodies they cannot usually see

from mirror studies involving human infants and young children (see above). Gallup's research also points to the *right prefrontal cortex* as the brain area that mediates self-awareness and mental states (such as deception and gratitude) – and this is the brain region that grows most rapidly between 18 and 34 months (see Chapter 4).

As additional support for his MRH, Gallup cites studies by Povinelli and his colleagues involving chimps. These studies are often taken to show that chimps have a 'theory of mind' (see Chapter 40). Ironically, Povinelli (1998) himself disagrees with Gallup's MRH. While agreeing that passing the mirror test indicates that chimps possess a self-concept, he disagrees that this means that they also possess the deep psychological understanding of behaviour that seems so characteristic of humans. (See Key Study 33.2.)

Based on these findings, Povinelli believes that self-recognition in chimps – and human toddlers – is based on recognition of the self's *behaviour,* not the self's psychological states. When chimps and orang-utans see themselves in a mirror, Povinelli (1998) believes they:

> *... form an equivalence relation between the actions they see in the mirror and their own behaviour. Every time they move, the mirror image moves with them. They conclude that everything that is true for the mirror image is also true for their own bodies, and vice versa. Thus, these apes can pass the mirror test by correlating coloured marks on the mirror images with marks on their own bodies. But the ape does not conclude, 'That's me!'. Rather the animal concludes, 'That's the same as me!'*

In short, chimps possess explicit mental representations of the positions and movements of their own bodies, which Povinelli calls the *kinaesthetic self-concept* (see Chapter 5).

Gallup's MRH relates to what Dunbar (2004) calls *second order intentionality* (the capacity to reflect on the contents of someone else's mind). His research suggests that humans are limited to fifth order intentionality ('I suppose [1] that you believe [2] that I want [3] you to think [4] that I intend [5] ...'). Chimps (and perhaps other great apes) may be capable of second order, and

Key Study 33.2

Stickers, lies and videotape (Povinelli, 1998)

- In a series of experiments, children were videotaped while they played an unusual game. The experimenter placed a large, brightly coloured sticker secretly on top of the child's head. Three minutes later, they were shown either (i) a live video image of themselves, or (ii) a recording made several minutes earlier, which clearly depicted the experimenter placing the sticker on the child's head.
- Two- and 3-year-old children responded very differently, depending on which video they saw. With the live image (equivalent to seeing themselves in a mirror), most reached up and removed the stickers from their heads. But with the recording, only about one-third did so. However, this wasn't because they failed to notice the stickers (when the experimenter drew their attention to them and asked 'What is that?' most gave the correct answer).
- They also 'recognised' themselves in the recording – they all confidently responded with 'Me' and stated their name when asked 'Who is that?' But this reaction didn't seem to go beyond a recognition of facial and bodily features. When asked 'Where is that sticker?' they often referred to the 'other' child (e.g. 'It's on her/his head'), as if they were trying to say 'Yes, that looks like me, but that's not me – she's not doing what I'm doing right now'. One 3-year-old said 'It's Jennifer' (her name), then hurriedly added 'but why is she wearing my shirt?'
- By about four, a significant majority of the children began to pass the delayed self-recognition test. Most 4- and 5-year-old children confidently reached up to remove the stickers after watching the delayed video images of themselves. They no longer referred to 'him/her' or their proper names.

monkeys stop at first order (along with most mammals and birds). Dunbar believes that these capacities are a linear function of the relative size of the frontal lobe: a large neocortex in general, and frontal lobes in particular, is a 'primate speciality'. However, mind reading isn't a specialised primate or even human capacity: there's only a *quantitative difference* between species in the number of orders of intentionality they can travel. (See Box 33.5.)

Self-definition

Piaget, Mead, and many others have pointed to the importance of language in consolidating the early development of self-awareness, by providing labels which permit distinctions between self and not-self ('I', 'you', 'me', 'it'). The toddler can then use these labels to communicate notions of selfhood to others. One important kind of label is the child's *name*. Names aren't usually chosen arbitrarily – either the parents particularly like the name, or they want to name the child after a relative or famous person; nor are they neutral labels in terms of how people respond to them and what they associate with them.

Indeed, they can be used as the basis for *stereotyping* (see Chapter 22). Jahoda (1954) described the naming practices of the Ashanti tribe of West Africa. Children born on different days of the week are given names accordingly, because of the belief that they have different personalities. Police records showed that among juvenile delinquents, there was a very low percentage of boys born on Monday (believed to have quiet and calm personalities), but a very high rate of Wednesday-born boys (thought to be naturally aggressive).

Box 33.5 Self-awareness and the brain

- In their study of 'ecstatic epileptic seizures', Picard and Craig (2009) identified the *insula* as a possible neurological origin of the disorder.
- The insula (or *insular cortex*) is buried inside the fissure dividing the frontal and parietal lobes from the temporal lobe within each hemisphere.
- Its main function seems to be to integrate *interoceptive* signals from inside the body (such as heartbeat) with *exteroceptive* signals (such as touch sensations) (see Chapter 5).
- There's also evidence that the processing of these signals gets progressively more sophisticated looking from the back of the insula to the front. The portion closest to the back of the head deals with objective properties (such as body temperature) and the front (anterior) portion with subjective feelings of body states and emotions, both good and bad. The anterior insula, therefore, determines how we feel about our body and ourselves, helping to create a conscious feeling of 'being' (the *sentient self*) (Ananthaswamy, 2014).
- *Depersonalisation* and *derealisation* disorders (in which the body and self seem to become detached, and the familiar becomes unfamiliar, respectively) are associated with a dysfunctional or underactive insula. People with these disorders describe the world as being drained of sensory and perceptual reality (Ananthaswamy, 2014).

Ask Yourself

- How might the boys' names have contributed to these statistics?

These findings can be explained in terms of the *self-fulfilling prophecy*. It's reasonable to believe that these Ashanti boys were treated in a way consistent with the name given to them, and that, as a result, they 'became' what their name indicated they were 'really' like. In English-speaking countries, days of the week (e.g. Tuesday) and months of the year (April, May and June) are used as names, and they have associations which may influence others' reactions (for example, 'Monday's child is fair of face, Tuesday's child is full of grace …').

The psychological self

Maccoby (1980) asks what children mean when they refer to themselves as 'I' or 'me'. Are they referring to anything more than a physical entity enclosed by an envelope of skin?

Key Study 33.3

There's more to children than meets the eye (Flavell *et al.*, 1978)

- Flavell *et al*. (1978) investigated development of the psychological self in 2 and a half to 5-year-olds.
- In one study, a doll was placed on the table in front of the child, and it was explained that dolls are like people in some ways – they have arms, legs, hands, and so on (which were pointed to). Then the child was asked how dolls are different from people, whether they know their names and think about things, and so on. Most children said a doll doesn't know its name and cannot think about things, but people can.
- They were then asked, 'Where is the part of you that knows your name and thinks about things?' and 'Where do you do your thinking and knowing?', and 14 out of 22 children gave fairly clear localisation for the thinking self, namely 'in their heads', while others found it very difficult. The experimenter then looked directly into the child's eyes and asked, 'Can I see you thinking in there?' Most children thought not.

These answers suggest that by 3 and a half to 4 years, a child has a rudimentary concept of a private, thinking self that's not visible even to someone looking directly into its eyes. The child can distinguish this from the bodily self, which it knows is visible to others. In other words, by about age 4, children begin to develop a *theory of mind*, the awareness that they – and other people – have mental processes (e.g. Leekam, 1993; Shatz, 1994; Wellman, 1990). However, one group failing to develop a theory of mind is autistic children (see Chapter 40).

The categorical self

Age and *gender* are both parts of the central core of the self-image. They represent two of the categories regarding the self which are also used to perceive and interpret the behaviour of others. Interestingly, recent research has found that by 9 months, babies can differentiate faces of their own race more easily than those of other races (Vogel *et al.*, 2012).

Age is probably the first social category to be acquired by the child (and is so even before a concept of number develops). Lewis and Brooks-Gunn (1979) found that 6- to 12-month-olds can distinguish between photographs, slides, and papier-mâché heads of adults and babies. By 12 months, they prefer interacting with unfamiliar babies to unfamiliar adults. Also, as soon as they've acquired labels like 'mummy' and 'daddy' and 'baby', they almost never make age-related mistakes.

Before age 7, children tend to define the self in physical terms – hair colour, height, favourite activities, and possessions. Inner, psychological experiences and characteristics aren't described as being distinct from overt behaviour and external, physical characteristics. During middle childhood through to adolescence, self-descriptions now include many more references to internal, psychological characteristics, such as competencies, knowledge, emotions, values and personality traits (Damon and Hart, 1988). However, Damon and Hart also report important *cultural* differences in how the self-concept develops (see Critical Discussion 33.2).

School highlights others' expectations about how the self should develop and provides a social context in which new goals are set and comparisons with others (peers) are prompted. This makes evaluation of the self all the more important (Durkin, 1995). This comparison becomes more important still during adolescence (see Chapter 37).

Chapter Summary

- An important distinction is that between **consciousness** and **self-consciousness/awareness**. Self-awareness allows us to see ourselves as others see us.
- Our **self-concept** refers to our perception of our personality, and comprises the **self-image** (which includes **body image/bodily self**), **self-esteem**, and **ideal self**. It can also be defined in terms of a complex set of **self-schemata**, which themselves include an array of **possible** selves.
- A major theoretical approach to the self is **symbolic interactionism**, associated mainly with Mead, who was influenced by James's **'I'/'me' distinction** and by Cooley's **theory of the looking-glass self.**
- Mead denied that the self is mentalistic, seeing it as a **process of social interaction**. It develops through **role-taking**, in particular, taking the perspective of the **'generalised other'** in the context of the child's play.
- Based on Mead, many sociologists and Social Psychologists see **language** as fundamental to how the self is **constructed**, providing stories or accounts of what being a person is like ('**discourses**').
- Discourses differ between **cultures**. The view of people as independent, self-contained individuals is a relatively recent invention of western, **individualist** cultures.
- Two major influences on the development of the self-concept are the **reaction of others** and **comparison with others**. Much of the relevant research is consistent with the theories of James, Cooley and Mead.
- The self-concept develops in fairly regular, predictable ways. During the first few months, the **existential self** emerges, but the **bodily self** is probably the first aspect of the self-concept to develop.
- The bodily self has been studied through (mainly visual) **self-recognition in mirrors**. Self-recognition appears at about 18 months in children, and is also found in chimps.
- While it's generally agreed that passing the mirror test implies a self-concept, this may be no more than a **kinaesthetic self-concept**, which doesn't involve an understanding of psychological states.
- **Self-definition** is related to the use of language, including the use of labels, such as names. By 3 and a half to 4, children seem to have a basic understanding of a **psychological self** (or **'theory of mind'**).
- **Age** and **gender** are two basic features of the **categorical self**, which changes from being described in **physical** to more **psychological** terms during middle childhood through to adolescence.

Links with Other Topics/Chapters

Chapter 7 ⟶ '*Consciousness*' has several meanings and should be distinguished from 'self-consciousness'/'self-awareness'

Chapters 23 and 24 ⟶ One account of how we get to know ourselves is Bem's *self-perception theory*

Chapter 10 ⟶ Another, specifically concerned with our emotional experience, is Schachter's *cognitive labelling theory*

Chapter 48 ⟶ The fact that non-humans are sentient raises fundamental *ethical issues* about using them in psychological (and medical) research. The possibility that certain non-human primates may also possess self-consciousness makes their use all the more controversial

Chapter 37 ⟶ The bodily changes involved in *puberty* affect the *adolescent's body image*, which, in turn, affects the self-concept as a whole

Chapter 36 ⟶ *Biological sex* is another fundamental aspect of body image, and our *gender/gender identity* is another part of the central core of our self-image

Chapter 39 ⟶ *Ageing* involves an inevitable decline in the body's ability to function, as well as characteristic changes in physical appearance

Chapter 29 ⟶ High but fragile and inflated self-esteem can help explain many cases of *aggression and violence*

Chapter 24 → The *self-consistency motive* implies that self-esteem is threatened by inconsistency (Tesser, 2004). Festinger's *cognitive dissonance theory* has come to be interpreted in terms of threat to self-esteem

Chapter 2 → Harré's analysis of the concept of self is made from the perspective of *discursive psychology*, which is a *social constructionist approach*

Chapter 25 → The Adorno *et al.* (1950) *authoritarian personality theory* claims that *prejudice and discrimination* are functional – they can help conceal our own inadequacies

Chapter 47 → The importance of *possessions* – and the *kind* of possessions that matter – is likely to differ between different kinds of culture

Chapters 40 and 44 → Abnormal functioning of the insula may help explain *anorexia nervosa, autistic spectrum disorder*, and other mental disorders (Arnold, 2012)

Recommended Reading

Burr, V. (2002) *The Person in Psychology.* East Sussex: Taylor & Francis. Also relevant to Chapter 2.

Gallup, G. (1998) Can animals empathise? Yes. *Scientific American Presents, 9*(4), 66, 68–71

Povinelli, D.J. (1998) ...Maybe not. *Scientific American Presents, 9*(4), 67, 72–5.

Leary, M.R. (2004) The Self We Know and the Self We Show: Self-esteem, Self-presentation, and the Maintenance of Interpersonal Relationships. In M.B. Brewer & M. Hewstone (eds) *Emotion and Motivation.* Oxford: Blackwell Publishing. Also relevant to Chapter 22.

Tesser, A. (2004) Self-esteem. In M.B. Brewer & M. Hewstone (eds) *Emotion and Motivation.* Oxford: Blackwell Publishing.

Useful Websites

www.self-esteem-nase.org (National Association for Self-Esteem)

http://novaonline.nvcc.edu/eli/spd110td/interper/self/self.html (Self-Concept)

CHAPTER 34

COGNITIVE DEVELOPMENT

Piaget's theory: the child as scientist

Vygotsky's theory: the child as apprentice

Bruner's theory

The Information-processing approach

INTRODUCTION and OVERVIEW

According to Meadows (1993, 1995), cognitive development is concerned with the study of 'the child as thinker'. However, different theoretical accounts of how the child's thinking develops rest on very different images of what the child is like:

- Piaget sees the child as an organism *adapting to its environment*, as well as *a scientist constructing its own understanding of the world*
- Vygotsky, in contrast to Piaget (and the information-processing approach), sees the child as *a participant in an interactive process*, by which socially – and culturally – determined knowledge and understanding gradually become *individualised*
- Bruner, like Vygotsky, emphasises the *social aspects* of the child's cognitive development
- information-processing theorists see children, like adults, as *symbol manipulators*.

Some years ago, Piaget's theory was regarded as the major framework or paradigm within Child Development. Despite remaining a vital source of influence and inspiration, both in psychology and education, today there are hardly any 'orthodox' Piagetians left (Dasen, 1994). Many fundamental aspects of Piaget's theory have been challenged, and fewer and fewer Developmental Psychologists now subscribe to his or other 'hard' stage theories (Durkin, 1995). Nonetheless, Piaget's is still the most comprehensive account of how children come to understand the world (Schaffer, 2004). Arguably, however, it was a little too 'cold' – that is, concerned with purely intellectual functions that supposedly can be studied separately from socio-emotional functions. Vygotsky tried to redress the balance (Schaffer, 2004).

PIAGET'S THEORY: THE CHILD AS SCIENTIST

Rather than trying to explain individual differences (why some children are more intelligent than others: see Chapter 41), Piaget was interested in how intelligence itself changes as children grow. He called this *genetic epistemology*.

According to Piaget, cognitive development occurs through the interaction of innate capacities with environmental events, and progresses through a series of *hierarchical, qualitatively different, stages*.

- All children pass through the stages in the same sequence without skipping any or (except in the case of brain damage) regressing to earlier ones (they're *invariant*).
- The stages are also the same for everyone irrespective of culture (they're *universal*).
- Underlying the changes are certain *functional invariants*, fundamental aspects of the developmental process which remain the same and work in the same way through the various stages. The most important of these are *assimilation, accommodation*, and *equilibration*.
- The principal cognitive structure that changes is the *schema* (plural *schemas* or *schemata*).

Schemas (or schemata)

A *schema* (or *scheme*) is the basic building block or unit of intelligent behaviour. Piaget saw schemas as mental structures which organise past experiences and provide a way of understanding future experiences. For Bee (2000), they're not so much categories as the *action of categorising* in some particular way. Life begins with simple schemas, which are largely confined to inbuilt reflexes (such as sucking and grasping). These operate independently of other reflexes, and are activated only when certain objects are present. As we grow, so our schemas become increasingly complex.

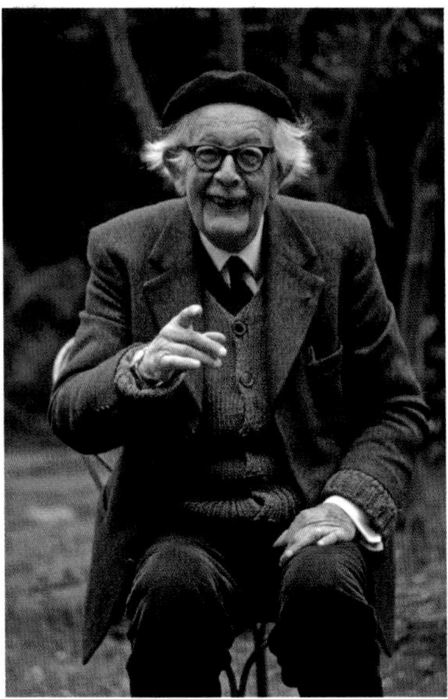

Figure 34.1 Jean Piaget (1896–1980)

Assimilation, accommodation and equilibration

Assimilation is the process by which we incorporate new information into existing schemas. For example, babies will reflexively suck a nipple and other objects, such as a finger. To learn to suck from a bottle or drink from a cup, the initial sucking reflex must be modified through *accommodation*.

When a child can deal with most, if not all, new experiences by assimilating them, it's in a state of *equilibrium* (brought about through *equilibration*, the process of seeking 'mental balance'). But if existing schemas are inadequate to cope with new situations, cognitive *disequilibrium* occurs. To restore equilibrium, the existing schema must be 'stretched' in order to take in (or 'accommodate') new information. The necessary and complementary processes of assimilation and accommodation constitute the fundamental process of *adaptation* (see Figure 34.2).

Stages of cognitive development

Each of Piaget's four stages represents a stage in the development of intelligence (hence *sensorimotor intelligence, pre-operational intelligence*, and so on), and is a way of summarising the various schemas a child has at a particular time. The ages shown in Table 34.1 are approximate: children move through the stages at different rates due to differences in both the environment and their biological maturation. Children also pass through transitional periods, in which their thinking is a mixture of two stages.

Table 34.1 Piaget's four stages of cognitive development

Stage	Approximate age
Sensorimotor	0–2 years
Pre-operational	2–7 years
Concrete operational	7–11 years
Formal operational	11 years onwards

The sensorimotor stage

This lasts for approximately the first two years of life. Infants learn about the world primarily through their senses ('sensori-'), and by doing ('motor'). Based on observations of his own children, Piaget (1952) divided the sensorimotor stage into six substages.

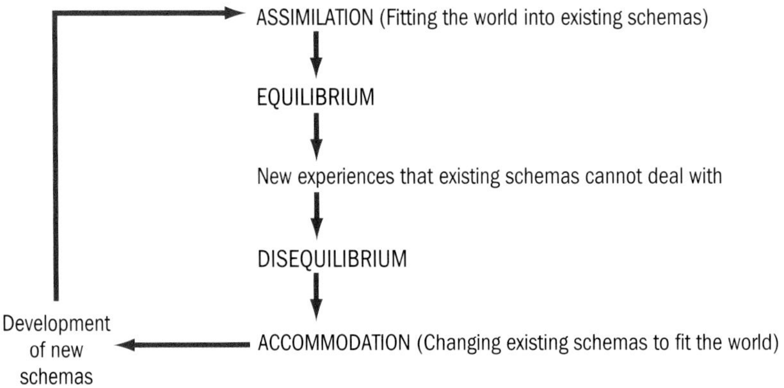

Figure 34.2 Relationship between assimilation, equilibrium, disequilibrium and accommodation in the development of schemas

Object permanence

Frequent interaction with objects ultimately leads to the development of *object permanence*. But this will take 18 months to become fully developed.

In the fourth substage (*the coordination of secondary circular reactions*: 10–12 months), the baby will search for a hidden object ('out of sight' is no longer 'out of mind') but will persist in looking for it where it was *last* hidden, even when it's hidden somewhere else (see Figure 34.3).

1. Baby sees ball placed under cloth on his left (A)
A
2. He retrieves it and the sequence is repeated
A

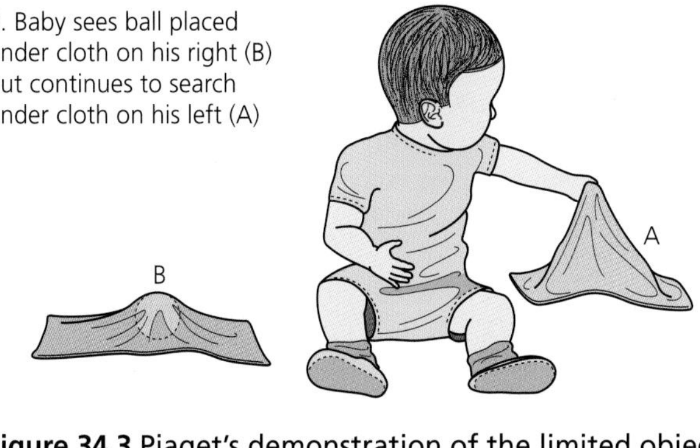
3. Baby sees ball placed under cloth on his right (B) but continues to search under cloth on his left (A)
B
A

Figure 34.3 Piaget's demonstration of the limited object permanence of babies between 8 and 12 months. They can retrieve a hidden object only from its original hiding place, not where it was last hidden. Not until about 12 months will they search under the cushion where they last saw the object hidden; they can do this even when three or four cushions are used. (Others have suggested that this ability appears as early as 9 months.) (From Barnes-Gutteridge, 1974)

While after 12 months infants will look for an object where they last saw it hidden (*tertiary circular reactions*: 12–18 months), object permanence isn't yet fully developed. Suppose an infant sees an object placed in a matchbox, which is then put under a pillow. When the infant's not looking, the object is removed from the matchbox and left under the pillow. If the matchbox is given to the infant, it will open it expecting to find the object. On not finding it, the infant won't look under the pillow. This is because it cannot take into account the possibility that something it hasn't actually seen might have happened (*failure to infer invisible displacements*). Once the infant can infer invisible displacements (after 18 months), the development of object permanence is complete (*invention of new means through mental combinations*: 18–24 months).

Box 34.1 The general symbolic function

- Other cognitive structures that have developed by the end of the sensorimotor stage include *self-recognition* (see Chapter 33), and *symbolic thought* (such as *language*).
- *Deferred imitation* is the ability to imitate or reproduce something that's been perceived but is no longer present (Meltzoff and Moore, 1983).
- *Representational* (or *make-believe*) *play* involves using one object as though it were another. Like deferred imitation, this ability depends on the infant's growing ability to form mental images of things and people in their absence (to *remember*).

The pre-operational stage

The main difference between this and the sensorimotor stage is the continued development and use of internal images (or '*interiorised*' schemas), symbols and language, especially important for the child's developing sense of self-awareness (see Chapter 33). However, the child tends to be influenced by how things *look*, rather than by logical principles or operations (hence the term 'pre-operational').

Piaget subdivided the stage into the *pre-conceptual* (ages 2–4) and the *intuitive* substages (ages 4–7). The absolute nature of the pre-conceptual child's thinking makes relative terms such as 'bigger' or 'stronger' difficult to understand (things tend to be 'biggest' or just 'big'). The intuitive child can use relative terms, but its ability to think logically is still limited.

Syncretic thought, transductive reasoning, and animism

Syncretic thought is the tendency to link together any neighbouring objects or events on the basis of what individual instances have in common. For example, if a 3-year-old is given a box of wooden shapes of different colours and asked to pick out four that are alike, the child might pick the shapes shown in Figure 34.4. Here, the characteristic the child focuses on changes with each second shape that's chosen: a blue square is followed by a blue circle, which is followed by a purple circle, which is followed by a purple triangle. There's no one characteristic that all four have in common. A 5-year-old would be able to select four of the same shape, or four of the same colour, and say what they have in common.

Box 34.2 Examples of children's animism during the pre-operational stage (from Piaget, 1973)

- Cli (3 years, 9 months) speaking of a motor in a garage: 'The motor's gone to bye-byes. It doesn't go out because of the rain ...'
- Nel (2 years, 9 months) seeing a hollow chestnut tree: 'Didn't it cry when the hole was made?' To a stone: 'Don't touch my garden! ... My garden would cry.' Nel, after throwing a stone onto a sloping bank, watching the stone rolling down said: 'Look at the stone. It's afraid of the grass.'
  Nel scratched herself against a wall. Looking at her hand: 'Who made that mark? – It hurts where the wall hit me.'
- Dar (1 year, 8 months/2 years, 5 months) bringing his toy motor to the window: 'Motor see the snow.' Dar stood up in bed, crying and calling out: 'The mummies (the ladies) all on the ground, hurt!' Dar was watching the grey clouds. He was told that it was going to rain. 'Oh, look at the wind! Naughty wind, smack wind.' ... On a morning in winter when the sun shone into the room: 'Oh, good! The sun's come to make the radiator warm.'

Transductive reasoning involves drawing an inference about the relationship between two things based on a single shared attribute. If both cats and dogs have four legs, then cats must be dogs. This sort of reasoning can lead to *animism*, the belief that inanimate objects are alive.

Ask Yourself

- Can you think of any examples of adults displaying animistic thinking?
- Do you ever think this way yourself?

Centration

Centration involves focusing on only a single perceptual quality at a time. A pre-conceptual child asked to divide apples into 'big and red' ones and 'small and green' ones will either put all the red (or green) apples together irrespective of their size, or all the big (or small) apples together irrespective of their colour. Until the child can *decentre*, it will be unable to classify things logically or systematically. Centration is also associated with the *inability* to conserve (see below).

Ask Yourself

- How is centration illustrated by syncretic thought (see above)?

Egocentrism

According to Piaget, pre-operational children are *egocentric*, that is, they see the world from their own standpoint and cannot appreciate that other people might see things differently (they cannot put themselves 'in other people's shoes'). Consider the following example (Phillips, 1969) of a conversation between an experimenter and a 4-year-old boy:

Experimenter:	'Do you have a brother?'
Child:	'Yes.'
Experimenter:	'What's his name?'
Child:	'Jim.'
Experimenter:	'Does Jim have a brother?'
Child:	'No'

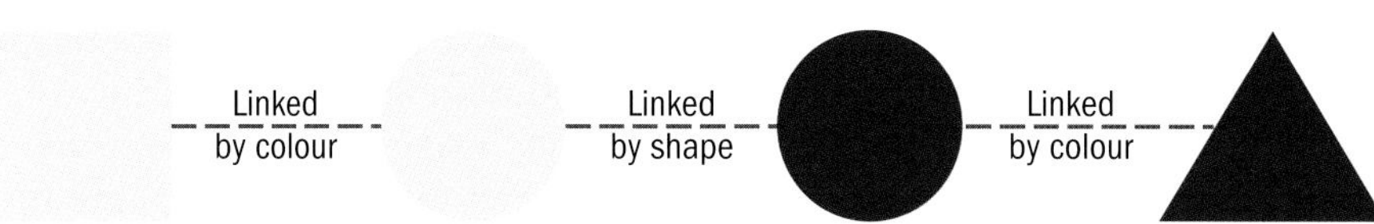

Figure 34.4 Simple example of syncretic thought

Key Study 34.1

The 'Swiss mountain scene' test of egocentrism (Piaget and Inhelder, 1956)

- The three papier-mâché model mountains shown in Figure 34.5 are of different colours. One has snow on the top, one a house, and one a cross.
- The child walks round and explores the model, and then sits on one side while a doll is placed at some different location. The child is shown ten pictures of different views of the model and asked to choose the one that represents how the doll sees it.
- Four-year-olds were completely unaware of perspectives other than their own, and always chose a picture which matched their view of the model. Six-year-olds showed some awareness, but often chose the wrong picture. Only 7- and 8-year-olds consistently chose the picture that represented the doll's view.
- According to Piaget, children below the age of 7 are bound by the *egocentric illusion*. They fail to understand that what they see is *relative to their own position*, and instead take it to represent 'the world as it really is'.

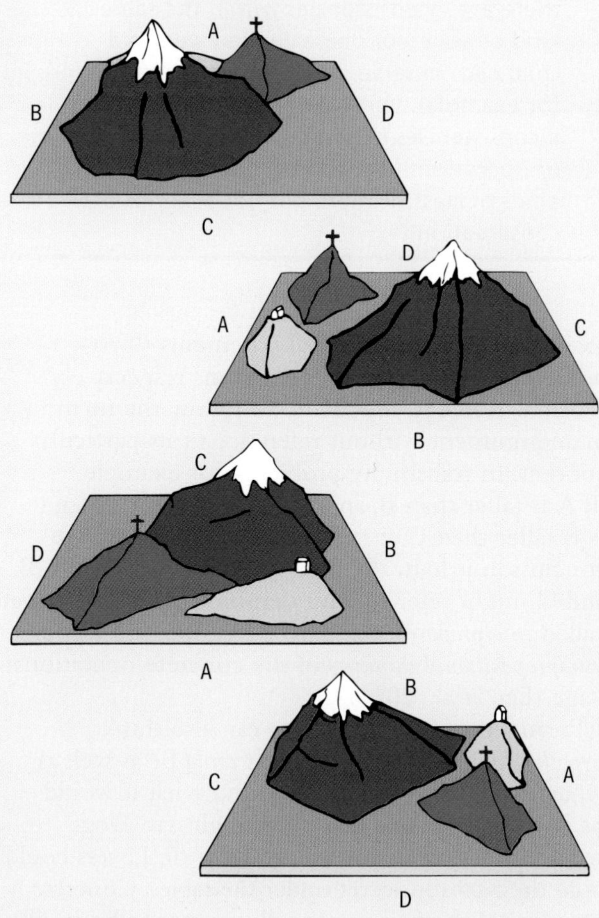

Figure 34.5 Piaget and Inhelder's three-mountain scene, seen from four different sides (from Smith and Cowie, 1988)

Conservation

Conservation is the understanding that any quantity (such as number, liquid quantity, length, or substance) remains the same despite physical changes in the arrangement of objects. Piaget believed that pre-operational children cannot conserve because their thinking is dominated by the perceptual nature of objects (their 'appearance').

The inability to conserve is another example of centration. With liquid quantity, for example, the child centres on just one dimension of the beaker, usually its height, and fails to take width into account (see Figure 34.6).

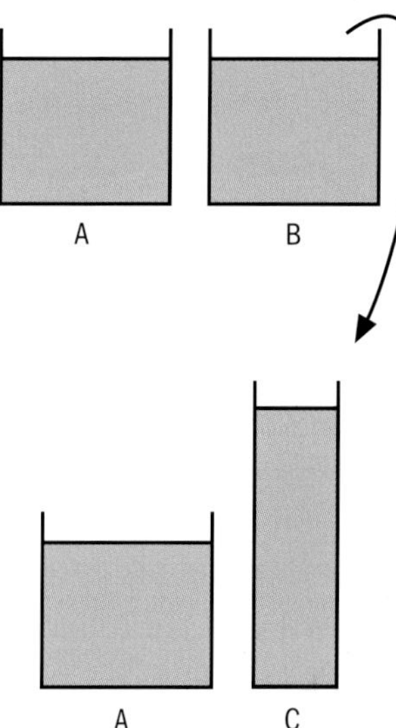

Figure 34.6 The conservation-of-liquid quantity. Although the child agrees that there's the same amount of liquid in A and B, when the content of B is poured into C, the appearance of C sways the child's judgement so that C is now judged to contain more liquid than A ('it looks more' or 'it's taller'). Although the child has seen the liquid poured from B into C and agrees that none has been spilled or added in the process (what Piaget calls 'identity'), the appearance of the higher level of liquid in the taller, thinner beaker C is compelling

Only in the concrete operational stage do children understand that 'getting taller' and 'getting narrower' tend to cancel each other out (*compensation*). If the contents of the taller beaker are poured back into the shorter one, the child will again say that the two shorter beakers contain the same amount. But it cannot perform this operation mentally and so lacks *reversibility* (understanding that what can be done can be undone without any gain or loss). These same limitations apply to other forms of conservation, such as number, and substance/quantity (see Figures 34.7 and 34.8).

Figure 34.7 Number conservation using counters. Two rows of counters are put in a one-to-one correspondence and then one row is pushed together. The pre-operational child usually thinks there are more counters in A than in C because A is 'longer', despite being able to count correctly and agreeing that A and B have equal numbers

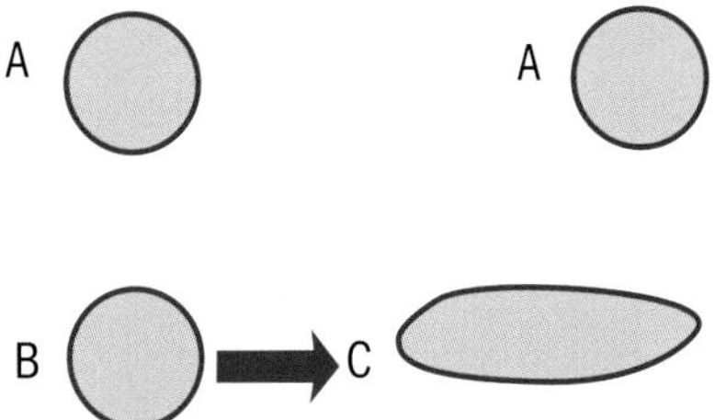

Figure 34.8 Substance or quantity conservation using modelling clay. Two equal-sized balls of modelling clay are used. B is rolled into a sausage shape (C); the pre-operational child typically thinks there's more in C than A, having originally agreed that A and B have the same amount

The concrete operational stage

The child is now capable of performing logical operations, but only in the presence of actual objects. S/he can conserve, and shows reversibility and more logical classification.

Further examples of the child's ability to decentre include its appreciation that objects can belong to more than one class (e.g. Andrew is Bob's brother *and* Charlie's best friend). There's also a significant *decline* in egocentrism (and the growing *relativism* of the child's viewpoint), plus the onset of *seriation* (arranging objects in order of size, etc.) and *reciprocity of relationships* (such as knowing that adding one to three produces the same amount as taking one from five).

One remaining problem for the concrete operational child is *transitivity tasks*. For example, if told that 'Alan is taller than Nigel, and Nigel is taller than Charlie' and asked whether Alan or Charlie is taller, children under 11 cannot solve this problem entirely in their heads. They can usually only solve it using real (or concrete) objects (such as dolls).

The formal operational stage

While the concrete operational child is still concerned with manipulating things (even if this is done mentally), the formal operational thinker can manipulate *ideas* or *propositions* and can reason solely on the basis of verbal statements ('first-order' and 'second order' operations respectively). 'Formal' refers to the ability to follow the form of an argument without reference to its particular content. In transitivity problems, for example, 'If A is taller than B, and B is taller than C, then A is taller than C', is a form of argument whose conclusion is logically true, regardless of what A, B, and C might refer to. This demonstrates what Piaget called *interpropositional thinking* (as opposed to the *intrapropositional thinking* of the concrete operational stage (Lee *et al.*, 2011).

Formal operational thinkers can also think *hypothetically*, that is, about what *could* be as well as what *actually* is. For example, asked what it would be like if people had tails, they might say 'Dogs would know when you were happy' or 'Lovers could hold their tails in secret under the table'. Concrete operational thinkers might tell you 'not to be so silly', or say where on the body the tail might be, showing

Box 34.3 Horizontal and vertical décalage

- Some types of conservation are mastered before others, and their order tends to be invariant. *Liquid quantity* is mastered by age 6–7, *substance/quantity* and *length* by 7–8, *weight* by 8–10, and *volume* by 11–12.
- This step-by-step acquisition of new operations is called *décalage* (displacement or 'slips in level of performance').
- In conservation, décalage is *horizontal* because there are inconsistencies *within* the same kind of ability or operation (a 7-year-old child can conserve number but not weight, for example). Vertical décalage refers to inconsistencies *between* different abilities or operations (a child may have mastered all kinds of classification, but not all kinds of conservation).

their dependence on what they've actually seen (Dworetzky, 1981). This ability to imagine and discuss things that have never been encountered is evidence of the continued *decentration* that occurs beyond concrete operations.

Formal operational thinkers also display *hypothetico-deductive reasoning*, as demonstrated in a series of tasks devised by Inhelder and Piaget, 1958 (see Key Study 34.2). Other examples include the balance-scale problem and the pendulum problem (see Lee *et al.*, 2011).

Key Study 34.2

A demonstration of formal operational thinking (Inhelder and Piaget, 1958)

- Inhelder and Piaget gave adolescents five containers filled with clear liquid. Four were 'test chemicals' and one an 'indicator'. When the correct combination of one or more test chemicals was added to the indicator, it turned yellow. The problem was to find this combination.
- *Pre-operational* children simply mixed the chemicals randomly, and *concrete operational* children, although more systematic, generally failed to test all possible combinations.
- Only *formal operational* thinkers considered all alternatives and systematically varied one factor at a time. Also, they often wrote down all the results and tried to draw general conclusions about each chemical.

An evaluation of Piaget's theory

As we noted in the Introduction and Overview Piaget's theory has had an enormous impact on our understanding of cognitive development. However, as Flavell (1982), and others (e.g. Siegal, 2003) have remarked:

> *Like all theories of great reach and significance ... it has problems that gradually come to light as years and years of thinking and research get done on it. Thus, some of us now think that the theory may in varying degrees be unclear, incorrect and incomplete.*

Object permanence

Piaget's claims about the sensorimotor stage have been criticised in both general and specific terms. Bower and Wishart (1972), for example, found that *how* an object is made to disappear influences the infant's response. If the infant is looking at an object and reaching for it and the lights are turned off, it will continue to search for up to one and a half minutes (as observed using infrared cameras). This suggests that it does remember the object is there (so, 'out of sight' isn't 'out of mind'). Baillargeon (1987) has shown that object permanence can occur as early as 3 and a half months, and that it isn't necessary for a baby younger than 6 months to see the whole object in order to respond to it.

Moore and Meltzoff (2008) found that the majority of the 32 8.75-month-old babies they tested were able to lift a cloth to reveal a *partially* hidden toy, but failed to lift a cloth to reveal a *completely* hidden toy. This shows that it's not a lack of coordination that prevents young babies from passing tests of object permanence. In a second experiment, they found that some 10-month-olds, but none of the 8.75-month-olds, were more likely to retrieve the completely hidden toy when it emitted a noise. This suggests that it's not a memory failure causing the younger babies to fail – the noise presumably would serve as a reminder. What might account for the failure (in younger and older babies) is suggested in an experiment by Topal *et al.* (2008) (see Key Study 34.3).

Key Study 34.3

Babies' social abilities can lead to cognitive errors (Topal *et al.*, 2008)

- Under standard testing conditions, when the experimenter hides a toy under the first cloth or cup (which is repeated several times), s/he looks at and chatters to the baby. This suggested to Topal *et al.* the hypothesis that the baby might infer from this communication that the toy is normally found under the (first) cloth or cup.
- To test this hypothesis, three groups of 10-month-old infants were tested under three conditions:
  - group I: as described above (the *standard* condition)
  - group II: the experimenter sat at right angles to the baby and made no eye contact (or communicated in any other way)
  - group III: the experimenter conducted the experiment from behind a curtain.
- Fourteen per cent of group I babies looked under the correct (second) cup, compared with 57 per cent for group II and 64 per cent for group III.
- This supports the hypothesis that human infants are highly social creatures who cannot help but interpret communicative signals.

Although such a disposition prepares them to efficiently learn from adults, in certain situations it can also misguide their performance. (Topal *et al.*, 2008).

Centration

One way to study centration (and classification) is through *class inclusion tasks*. If a pre-operational child is presented with several wooden beads, mostly brown but a few white, and asked 'Are they all wooden?', the child will respond correctly. If asked 'Are there more brown or more white beads?', the child will again respond correctly. But if asked 'Are there more brown beads or more beads?', the child will say there are more brown beads.

Ask Yourself

- Why do you think they say there are more brown beads?

The brown beads are more numerous than the white, and can be perceived in a more immediate and direct way than the wooden beads as a whole (despite the first question being answered correctly). For Piaget, the child fails to understand the relationship between the whole (the *superordinate* class of wooden beads) and the parts (the *subordinate* classes of brown and white beads). This is another example of the inability to decentre. However, Donaldson (1978) has asked if the difficulty the child experiences is to do with what's expected of it and how the task is presented (see Key Study 34.4).

Egocentrism

Gelman (1979) has shown that 4-year-olds adjust their explanations of things to make them clearer to a blindfold listener. This isn't what we'd expect if, as Piaget claims, children of this age are egocentric. Nor would we expect 4-year-olds to use simpler forms of speech when talking to 2-year-olds (Gelman, 1979) or choose appropriate birthday presents for their mothers (Marvin, 1975, in Morris, 1988).

Critics of the 'Swiss mountain scene' test (Key Study 34.1) see it as an unusually difficult way of presenting a problem to a young child. Borke (1975) and Hughes (cited in Donaldson, 1978) have shown that when the task is presented in a meaningful context (making what Donaldson calls 'human sense'), even 3 and a half-year-olds can appreciate the world as another person sees it. These are all examples of *perspective-taking* (P-T). According to Siegal (2003) young children aren't egocentric all of the time, but their perspective-taking skills clearly improve during childhood.

Baron-Cohen *et al.* (1985) make a distinction between *conceptual* and *perceptual* P-T. The former is what's being tested by their false-belief task for theory of mind (ToM) (see Key Study 40.2, p. 682), while the latter is tested by Piaget and Inhelder's 'three mountains' task (see above). In terms of this distinction, Piaget and Inhelder's task involves only *visuospatial skills* (seeing things from another's perspective), whereas ToM involves *attributing beliefs* to other people (including *false beliefs*). Evidence that autistic children are successful on perceptual perspective-taking tasks, but unsuccessful on the false-belief tasks, indicates very clearly that the two types of task are testing quite different abilities/skills (see Chapter 40). Flavell *et al.* (1990) make a similar distinction (see Box 34.4)

Key Study 34.4

Let sleeping cows lie (Donaldson, 1978)

- Donaldson describes a study with 6-year-olds using four toy cows, three black and one white. The cows were laid on their sides and the children told they were 'sleeping'. Of those asked 'Are there more black cows or more cows?', 25 per cent answered correctly. But of those asked 'Are there more black cows or more sleeping cows?', 48 per cent answered correctly.
- Chapman and McBride (1992) conducted a similar study with 4- to 10-year-olds involving sleeping horses. Although they replicated the results reported by Donaldson, most children couldn't effectively justify their answers. When this was taken into account, the difference in correct answers produced by the standard form of the task and the 'sleeping' form disappeared.
- In both studies, a majority of children still fail even under conditions where task demands are reduced.

This suggests a deep conceptual difficulty, as well as a linguistic one (Siegal, 2003).

Figure 34.9

- According to Gelman (1978), the word 'more' has a different meaning for children and adults. Adults use 'more' to mean 'containing a greater number'. But for children 'more' refers to the general concept of larger, longer, occupying more space, and so on.

Box 34.4 Perspective-taking, false beliefs and theory of mind

According to Flavell *et al.* (1990), there are two levels of P-T ability:

1. *level 1* (2- to 3-year-olds) – the child knows that some other person experiences something differently (*perceptual P-T*)
2. *level 2* (4- to 5-year-olds) – the child develops a whole series of complex rules for figuring out precisely what the other person sees or experiences (*affective and cognitive* P-T).

In a study of children's ability to distinguish between appearance and reality, Flavell (1986) showed children a sponge painted to look like a rock. They were asked what it looked like and what it 'really' was. Three-year-olds said either that it looked like a sponge and was a sponge, or that it looked like a rock and was a rock. However, 4- to 5-year-olds could say that it looked like a rock but was in fact a sponge.

Gopnik and Astington (1988) allowed children to feel the sponge before asking them the questions used in Flavell's study. The children were then told: 'Your friend John hasn't touched this, he hasn't squeezed it. If John just sees it over here like this, what will he think it is? Will he think it's a rock or a sponge?'

Ask Yourself

- How do you think the 3-year-olds answered?
- How do you think the 4- to 5-year-olds answered?

Typically, 3-year-olds said that John would think it was a sponge (which it is), while 4- to 5-year-olds said he'd think it was a rock (because he hadn't had the opportunity of touching/squeezing it). In other words, the older children were attributing John with a *false belief*, which they could do only by taking John's perspective.

Evidence like this has led several theorists (e.g. Gopnik and Wellman, 1994) to propose that 4- to 5-year-olds have developed a quite sophisticated *theory of mind* (Premack and Woodruff, 1978). This refers to the understanding that people (and not objects) have desires, beliefs and other mental states, some of which (such as beliefs) can be false (*cognitive* P-T). The older children in Gopnick and Astington's study understood that John wouldn't know something which *they did*.

Conservation

The ability to conserve also seems to occur earlier than Piaget believed. Rose and Blank (1974) showed that when the *pre-transformation question* (the question asked before one row of counters, say, is rearranged) was omitted, 6-year-olds often succeeded on the number conservation task. Importantly, they made fewer errors on the standard version of the task when tested a week later. These findings were replicated by Samuel and Bryant (1984) using conservation of number, liquid quantity and substance.

According to Donaldson (1978), the standard version of the task unwittingly 'forces' children to produce the wrong answer against their better judgement, by the mere fact that the same question is asked twice, before and after the transformation. Hence, *contextual cues* may override purely linguistic ones. Children may think the experimenter has rejected their first answer, so they feel they're required to give a *different* answer on the second question in order to please the adult questioner. This is the problem of a *clash of conversational worlds* between child and adult (Siegal, 2003).

Bruner (1966) argues that children's attention is so captured by the transformed state that they disregard the pre-transformed state and fail to attend to it when asked the second question.

Ask Yourself

- Apart from dropping the pre-transformation question, how else might conservation tasks be modified in order to prevent children from being distracted in this way?

Children can be asked to predict the outcome, without actually witnessing it. Under these conditions, those who'd normally 'fail' are more likely to give the correct answer (Siegal M, 2003).

According to Piaget, it shouldn't matter who, in the case of number conservation, rearranges the counters/Smarties or how this happens. Yet when 'Naughty Teddy', a glove puppet, causes the transformation 'accidentally', pre-operational children can conserve number and length (McGarrigle and Donaldson, 1974; Light *et al.*, 1979). This also applies when the transformation is made by someone other than the experimenter (Hargreaves *et al.*, 1982; Light, 1986).

Formal operations

Piaget's theory and research has stimulated a considerable number of follow-up studies and heated theoretical debates about exactly how adolescents think (Lee *et al.*, 2011). One of these debates concerns just what percentage of adolescents actually attain formal operational thought (using the types of task used by Inhelder and Piaget: see Key Study 34.2).

Research suggests that Piaget over-estimated adolescents' formal operational thinking. Only a third of adolescents and adults attain this level (e.g. Capon and Kuhn, 1979; Keating, 1980) and many adults may never attain it; nor are they necessarily used in all domains (as Piaget claimed). Many studies have also highlighted the importance of educational and cultural experiences, which Piaget believed played little or any role in the acquisition of formal operations (Lee *et al.*, 2011).

Cross-cultural tests of the stages

According to Schaffer (2004), Piaget's account gives the impression that the stages are an inevitable consequence of being human, and that external influences stemming from the social environment play no part. What evidence is there to support this?

The few cross-cultural studies of the sensorimotor stage have shown the substages to be universal. Overall, it seems that ecological or cultural factors *don't* influence the sequence of stages, but do affect the *rate* at which they're attained (Segall *et al.*, 1999).

Conservation experiments have also been conducted with Eskimo, African (Senegal and Rwande), Hong Kong and Papua New Guinea sample populations. Consistent with Dasen's findings (see Cross-Cultural Study 34.1), children from non-western cultures often show a considerable lag in acquiring operational thought. But this applies mainly to those having minimal contact with white culture. Where Aborigines, for example, live in white communities and attend school there, they perform at a similar level to whites. Even where there's a lag in development compared with whites, the stages still appear in the same order. So (as with the sensorimotor substages), cultural factors can affect rate of attainment, but they don't affect developmental sequence (Schaffer, 2004).

As Dasen (1994) puts it:

> *The deep structures, the basic cognitive processes, are indeed universal, while at the surface level, the way these basic processes are brought to bear on specific contents, in specific contexts, is influenced by culture. Universality and cultural diversity are not opposites, but are complementary aspects of all human behaviour and development.*

Cross-Cultural Study 34.1

Cultural influences on conservation and spatial relationships (Dasen, 1994)

- Dasen cites studies he conducted in remote parts of the central Australian desert with 8- to 14-year-old Aborigines. He gave them conservation-of-liquid, weight, and volume tasks, plus a task that tested understanding of spatial relationships. This involved either:
    - two landscape models, one of which could be turned round through 180° – the participants had to locate an object (doll or sheep) on one model and then find the same location on the second model, or
    - a bottle was half-filled with water, then tilted into various positions, with a screen hiding the water level – participants were shown outline drawings of the bottle and they had to draw in the water level.
- On *conservation tasks*, the same shift from pre-operational to concrete operational thought was found as with Swiss children – but it took place between 10–13 years of age (instead of 5–7). A fairly large proportion of adolescents and adults also gave non-conservation answers.
- On the *spatial tasks*, again there was the same shift from pre- to concrete operational thought as for Swiss children. But operational thinking develops *earlier* in the spatial domain; this is the *reverse* of what's found for Swiss (and other European) children.

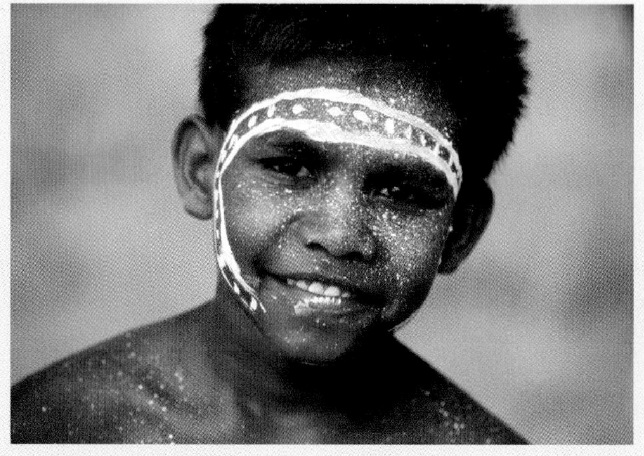

Figure 34.10

- According to Dasen, these findings make perfect sense in terms of Aboriginal culture, where things *aren't quantified*. Water is vital for survival, but the exact quantity is unimportant. Counting things is unusual, and number words only go up to five (after which everything is 'many'). By contrast, findings one's way around is crucial: water-holes must be found at the end of each journey and family members meet up at the end of the day after having split up in order to search for water. The acquisition of a vast array of spatial knowledge is helped by the mythology, such as the 'dream time' stories that attribute a meaning to each feature of the landscape and to routes travelled by ancestral spirits.

Applying Piaget's theory to education

Although Piaget wrote very little about the educational implications of his developmental theory (Davis, 2003), it has three main implications for education (Brainerd, 1983): the concept of *readiness*, the *curriculum* (what should be taught) and *teaching methods* (how the curriculum should be taught).

- *Readiness* relates to limits set on learning by a child's current stage of development (see Box 34.5). According to Schaffer (2004), Piaget's most relevant contribution to education (especially the teaching of maths and science: see below) is the recognition that careful thought must be given to the individual child's capacity for handling particular experiences. What's needed is a *child-centred approach*, whereby the tasks set by the teacher are adapted as precisely as possible to the child's cognitive level.
- Regarding the *curriculum*, the greatest impact of his theory has been on science and maths. Teaching materials should consist of concrete objects that children can easily manipulate. But rather than trying to base a curriculum on Piagetian stages, it would be more useful to modify the curriculum in line with what's known about them, and not allow them to limit teaching methods (Ginsberg, 1981). However, even today, an understanding of number conservation remains a criterion for an *attainment target* in the UK National Curriculum for maths (Davis, 2003; see below).
- Central to a Piagetian perspective is the view that children learn from actions rather than from passive observation (*active self-discovery/discovery learning*). As far as teaching methods are concerned, teachers must recognise that each child needs to construct knowledge for itself, and that deeper understanding is the product of active learning (Smith *et al.*, 1998). Piaget's account of development could be used by those involved in early education as a *formalisation* of many of the assumptions underlying child-centred education.

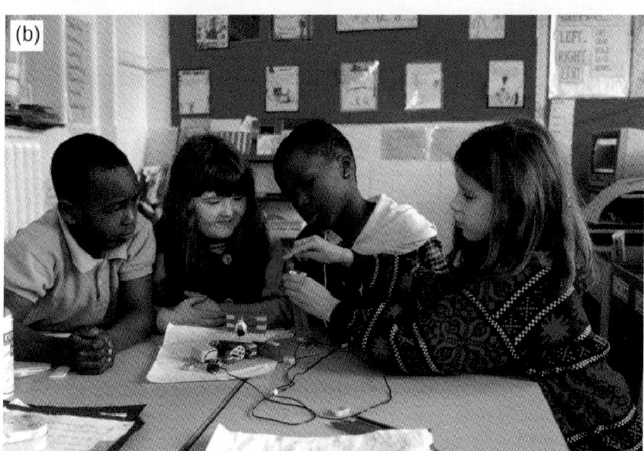

Figure 34.11 a and b In the traditional classroom (a), the teacher is at the centre of the learning process imparting ready-made ('academic'/'school') knowledge. By contrast, in the Piagetian classroom (b), the child actively discovers knowledge for him/herself, often through interaction with other children in small groups

VYGOTSKY'S THEORY: THE CHILD AS APPRENTICE

Vygotsky didn't produce a fully formed theory or coherent body of research, and many of his ideas weren't spelled out in detail. His works were published in the former Soviet Union in the 1920s and 1930s, but weren't translated into English until the early 1960s.

Vygotsky and Piaget agree that development doesn't occur in a vacuum: knowledge is constructed as a result of the child's active interaction with the environment. But, as we've seen, for Piaget that environment is essentially *asocial* (so his account is described as *constructivist*. But for Vygotsky:

> *... Human nature cannot be described in the abstract; whatever course children's mental growth takes is to a large extent a function of the cultural tools that are handed down to them by other people ... (Schaffer, 2004)*

So, cognitive development is a thoroughly *social* process (hence, Vygotsky is a *social constructivist*). His aim was to spell out and explain how the higher mental functions (reasoning, understanding, planning, remembering, and so on) arise out of children's social experiences. He did this by considering human development in terms of three levels: the *cultural*, *interpersonal* and *individual*. He had much more to say about the first two than the latter, so we'll concentrate on these here.

MEET THE RESEARCHER

Vasudevi Reddy

Studying how babies understand minds

I used to think babies were boring! As a student of Developmental Psychology, I had read a lot about the amazing skills and abilities of newborns and very young infants, but it did not really mean much to me. I changed my mind when I had my first baby. I could not believe the difference between seeing something 'with my own eyes' as it were and just reading about it! I have realised since then that it isn't just 'seeing' something that makes it most meaningful to us, it is engaging with that something that is crucial. It is when we 'engage' with them that the significance of phenomena strikes us most richly – whether psychological phenomena or chemical or astronomical! Although the psychological knowledge we gain from such engagements is less systematic and always based in our own emotional relations, it is fuller in background information, more sensitive to immediate nuances and contingencies, and more able to grasp subtle meanings precisely because we bring to such perceptions our own immediate emotional responses. Indeed, we could argue that unless Psychologists were people (rather than, say, aliens) we could never really understand people – a point beautifully made by philosopher John Macmurray, 'I can know another person as a person only by entering into personal relation with him. Without this I can know him only by observation and inference; only objectively' (Macmurray, 1961).

Most of the research I have done since I had my children has been inspired by observations I have made of them, which have then been studied further and more systematically with other children. Below are descriptions of my studies which began as tentative observations with my infants.

Video research into intentions

As a lecturer in early language development with a baby of 9 months in the house I started video-taping ordinary everyday interactions to show my students as examples of proto-language. One such video recording was of an interaction with her father a couple of weeks after she had learned to offer and give objects to people. In the video-taped interaction the baby was teasing her father – offering the object to him with a little wiggle to get his attention and then, as he reached forward, withdrawing it with a cheeky look, then doing it again. She seemed to be deliberately tricking him into reaching for the object before pulling it back. I was struck by the fact that this playing with her father's intentions and expectations did not fit with the dominant theory of the time which argued that children could not grasp others' intentions or expectations until something like their fourth birthday. I conducted two longitudinal studies with other infants using interviews and parental diaries as well as regular video-taped observations to check whether this phenomenon was peculiar to this baby or something more general (Reddy, 1991). And I found that before the end of the first year we see a blossoming of playfulness with a variety of different kinds of teasing – some quite ingenious – being displayed by babies. Although there were major individual differences, one of the most common kinds of teasing involved playfully provoking people through disobedience, sometimes acting as if they are about to touch something they know they shouldn't just for effect, sometimes deliberately pushing the boundaries of their parents' intentions and conventions. The idea that babies nearing the end of the first year are unaware of other people's intentions and expectations seemed an odd one and one that required some theoretical re-adjustment.

Babies and humour

Another 'phenomenon' that emerged from these studies was that of infant 'clowning' and 'showing off'. In addition to violating expectations and intentions, babies were also rapidly (from around 7 months) tuning in to the things that amused the people around them, or the things that brought them attention, and deliberately repeating them in order to re-elicit laughter or positive attention. While this may seem mundane and unexciting to anybody other than the parents, the striking thing about these behaviours was the acuteness of the infants' interest in others' emotional reactions and their ability to connect these reactions to their very specific eliciting behaviours. This was clever stuff for 8-month-olds! And although the motives for infant clowning are less complex, there is a remarkable similarity between the kinds of things babies do to make adults laugh and the kinds of things 'real' clowns do (Reddy, 2003). In a study with pre-school children with developmental disabilities, we found that these behaviours were differently distributed. In mental age matched children with Down syndrome, there was rich evidence of clowning, showing off and teasing. In mental age matched children with autism, however, there were significant deficits in all of these engagements, suggesting they may be important early indicators of the deficit in interpersonal awareness in autism (Reddy, *et al.*, 2002).

'Coy' smiling

One of the most intriguing studies I have done, also based on my initial puzzlement while chatting with my own babies, was of the very early presence of 'coy' smiling. In the same way that one might blush when one sees someone looking very positively at them, or that you might smile but turn away briefly when someone looks into your eyes and pays you a compliment, babies of 2 months also show such positive shyness or coyness in interaction with familiar people, and usually at the beginnings of interaction, turning head and eyes away with broad smiles and sometimes with arms rising up across their faces (Reddy, 2000). This response is both structurally and functionally similar to the embarrassed smiles that older children and adults show in these situations of unexpected positive attention and suggest that the earliest origins of self-conscious feelings might lie in these very simple but powerful engagements.

Deception

Another fun study that I did with my student Paul Newton was on early deception. Contrary to claims in Psychology that children cannot deceive people (and will not try to do so) until they are about 4 years old, we found that even when we limited the study to verbal fibs, children as young as 2½ years were being very creative in their representations of reality! While some of these fibs were rather formulaic in denying some wrongdoing with a 'I didn't do it' or claiming to have done some chore with a 'Yes, I did', many of them were elaborate and quite unique statements that could not have been learned in previous situations. Moreover, there was no substantial difference between the fibs of children who failed the key 'false-belief' tasks and those who passed them (Newton *et al.*, 2000; Reddy, 2007).

I have described these and other studies in my book *How Infants Know Minds* (Reddy, 2008), but I would like to emphasise one key point. As a student of Psychology (whether a young one like yourself or an old one like me), it is important to take one's own psychological observations and intuitions seriously, then to go that one step further, to test and study them in other contexts and with other people. Psychology needs you to be a person who engages with other 'persons' in order to be a good scientist!

Professor Vasudevi Reddy received her PhD at Edinburgh University (between 1977 and 1983). Returning to India, she taught Psychology at the University College for Women in Hyderabad for three years. She has been teaching at British universities since 1986.

The cultural level

Children don't need to 'reinvent the world anew' (as Piaget seemed to believe). They can benefit from the accumulated wisdom of previous generations; indeed, they cannot avoid doing so through interactions with caregivers. So each generation stands on the shoulders of the previous one, taking over the particular culture – including its intellectual, material, scientific and artistic achievements – in order to develop it further before handing it on, in turn, to the next generation (Schaffer, 2004).

Ask Yourself

- Can you think of examples of cultural tools that might be especially important for children's cognitive development?

Cultural tools are what the child 'inherits'. These can be:

- *technological* (clocks, bicycles and other physical devices)
- *psychological* (concepts and symbols, such as language, literacy, maths and scientific theories)
- *values* (such as speed, efficiency, and power).

It's through such tools that children learn to conduct their lives in socially effective and acceptable ways, as well as understanding how the world works.

Schaffer (2004) gives the example of *computers* as a major – and relatively recent – cultural tool:

> *There are few instances in history where a new technical invention has assumed such a dominant role in virtually all spheres of human activity as the computer ... in the space of just a few decades computing expertise is regarded as an essential skill for even quite young children to acquire ...*

The most essential cultural tool is language.

Box 34.5 The importance of language as a cultural tool

- Language is the pre-eminent means of passing on society's accumulated knowledge: how others speak and what they speak about is the main channel of communicating culture from adult to child.
- It enables children to regulate their own activities.
- At about age 7, speech becomes internalised to form internal thought: an essential social function thus becomes the major tool for cognitive functioning. (See Chapter 18.)

The interpersonal level

It's here that culture and the individual meet, and it's the level at which Vygotsky made his major contribution.

Figure 34.12 The computer: a powerful and pervasive cultural tool

Internalisation and the social nature of thinking

The ability to think and reason by and for ourselves (inner speech or verbal thought) is the result of a fundamentally *social* process. At birth, we're social beings capable of interacting with others, but able to do little either practically or intellectually, by or for ourselves. But gradually we move towards self-sufficiency and independence, and by participating in social activities our abilities become transformed. For Vygotsky, cognitive development involves an active *internalisation* of problem-solving processes that takes place as a result of mutual interaction between children and those with whom they have regular social contact (initially the parents, but later friends and classmates and teachers).

This is the reverse of how Piaget (at least initially) saw things. Piaget's idea of 'the child as a scientist' is replaced by the idea of 'the child as an apprentice', who acquires the culture's knowledge and skills through graded collaboration with those who already possess them (Rogoff, 1990). According to Vygotsky (1981):

> *Any function in the child's cultural development appears twice, or on two planes. First it appears on the social plane, and then on the psychological plane.*

So, cognitive development progresses from the *intermental* to the *intramental* (from joint regulation to self-regulation).

Box 34.6 Pointing: an example of cultural development from the physical to the social

- Initially, a baby's pointing is simply an unsuccessful attempt to grasp something beyond its reach.
- When the mother sees her baby pointing, she takes it as an 'indicatory gesture' that the baby wants something, and so helps it, probably making the gesture herself.
- Gradually, the baby comes to use the gesture deliberately. The 'reaching' becomes reduced to movements which couldn't themselves achieve the desired object even if it were in reach, and is accompanied by cries, looks at the mother and eventually words.
- The gesture is now directed towards the mother (it has become a gesture 'for others'), rather than towards the object (it's no longer a gesture 'in itself'; Meadows, 1995).

Scaffolding and the zone of proximal development (ZPD)

The *zone of proximal development* (ZPD) defines those functions that haven't yet matured but are in the process of maturing (Vygotsky, 1978). These could be called the 'buds' or 'flowers' rather than the 'fruits' of development. The actual developmental level characterises mental development *retrospectively*, while the ZPD characterises mental development *prospectively*.

Ask Yourself

- What do you understand by this distinction regarding level of mental development? (See Box 34.6.)

Scaffolding refers to the kind of guidance and support adults provide children in the ZPD by which children acquire their knowledge and skills (Wood *et al.*, 1976; Wood and Wood, 1996). As a task becomes more familiar to the child and more within its competence, those who provide the scaffold leave more and more for the child to do until it can perform the task successfully. In this way, the developing thinker doesn't have to create cognition 'from scratch': there are others available who've already 'served' their own apprenticeship. According to Meadows (1995), the internalised cognitive skills remain social in the sense that cognitive potential may be universal, but cognitive expertise is culturally determined.

Ask Yourself

- How does this distinction between cognitive potential and expertise relate to Dasen's (1994) assessment of Piaget's stages? (see Cross-Cultural Study 34.1.)

Since the 1980s, research has stressed the role of social interaction in language development, especially the facilitating effects of the use of child-contingent language by adults talking with children (Meadows, 1995; see Chapter 19). This 'fit' between adult and child language closely resembles the concept of 'scaffolding'.

Key Study 34.5

Scaffolding (or individual abilities are built on social support) (Wood *et al.*, 1976)

- Wood *et al.* found that on a construction task with 4- to 5-year-olds (fitting wooden blocks together with pegs to make a pyramid), different mothers used instructional strategies which varied in their levels of specificity. These ranged from general verbal encouragement to direct demonstration of a relevant action.
- No single strategy guaranteed learning, but the most efficient maternal instructors were those who combined general and specific interventions according to the child's progress.
- The most useful help is that which adapts itself to the learner's successes and failures (Bruner, 1983). An example would be using a general instruction initially until the child runs into difficulties. At this point, a more specific instruction or demonstration is given. This style allows the child considerable autonomy, but also provides carefully planned guidance in its ZPD.

Although 'scaffolding' doesn't actually explain how children internalise what the tutor provides, it draws attention to the conditions under which learning usually occurs. It also emphasises the essential social-interactive nature of these conditions (Schaffer, 2004).

According to Vygotsky, a more knowledgeable child can provide instruction and guidance for another, in order to bring the latter up to a similar level of competence (*peer tutoring*; Foot and Howe, 1998; Foot *et al.*, 1990).

As would be predicted from Vygotsky's theory, there is also evidence of scaffolding processes in everyday, naturalistic contexts. These are often linked to the transmission across generations of culturally valued skills, such as weaving among the Zinacauteco Mexicans and American mothers' involvement in their preschoolers' development of number (Durkin, 1995).

An evaluation of Vygotsky's theory

Ask Yourself

- What would you say is the key difference between Vygotsky's and Piaget's theories?

- Vygotsky's theory clearly 'compensates' for one of the central limitations of Piaget's theory. As Segall *et al.* (1999) put it:

  Piaget produced a theory of the development of an 'epistemic subject', an idealised, non-existent individual, completely divorced from the social environment.

  For Vygotsky, culture (and especially language) plays a key role in cognitive development: the development of the individual cannot be understood – and indeed cannot happen – outside the context of social interaction.
- While Vygotsky's theory hasn't been tested cross-culturally as Piaget's has, it has influenced Cross-cultural Psychology through the development of *Cultural Psychology* (e.g. Cole, 1990; see Chapter 47) and related approaches, such as *'socially shared cognition'* (Resnick *et al.*, 1991) and *'distributed cognition'* (Salomon, 1993). According to all these approaches, cognition isn't necessarily situated 'within the head' but is shared among people and settings (Segall *et al.*, 1999).
- Although Vygotsky didn't carry out much empirical research himself, the specific nature of many of his ideas has made it possible for others to follow them up. This has resulted in a substantial body of research on scaffolding, peer tutoring and other aspects of the educational process (see below).
- Schaffer (2004) believes that Vygotsky's neglect of emotional factors is a serious omission: he makes no reference to struggles, the frustrations of failure, the joys of success, or generally what motivates the child to achieve particular goals: Vygotsky's treatment of the child is as 'cold' as Piaget's (Schaffer, 2004).

Applying Vygotsky's theory to education

We've seen above that many of Vygotsky's most important ideas are related (directly or indirectly) to the learning process – and, hence, to education. Examples include the ZPD, scaffolding, and peer tutoring. According to Davis (2003):

By emphasising the social nature of development, Vygotsky's theory is not only a theory of learning, it also offers a theory of teaching, since language is the prime medium for sharing knowledge in formal contexts such as schools and informally in the home ...

Box 34.7 Applying the concept of the ZPD to education

Suppose a child is currently functioning at level 'x' in terms of attainment. Through innate/environmental means, the child has the potential to reach level 'x + 1'.

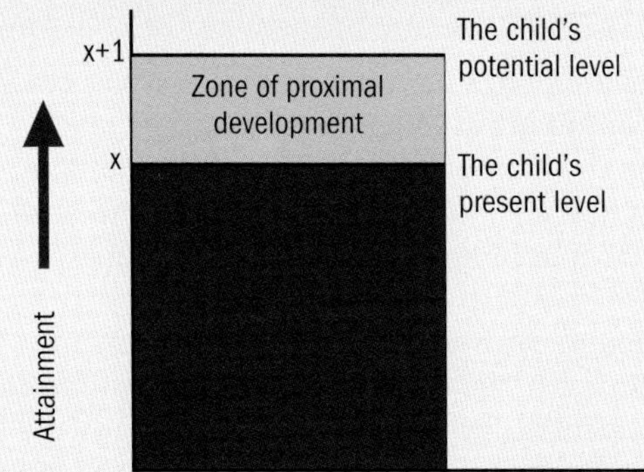

Figure 34.13 Vygotsky's zone of proximal development

The area between 'x' and 'x + 1' is the child's ZPD. The ZPD may be different for individual children, and children with large ZPDs will have a greater capacity to be helped than those with small ZPDs. Irrespective of the ZPD's size, Vygotsky saw the teacher as being responsible for giving children the cues they need or taking them through a series of steps towards the solution of a problem.
(Based on Sutherland, 1992)

In *collaborative learning*, children at similar levels of competence work together, either in pairs or groups. Slavin's (1990) Student Teams Achievement Divisions (STAD) involves small groups of varying ability, gender and ethnic background working on a topic. These groups show greater achievement than controls taught by more conventional methods. Educators now believe that both collaborative learning and *peer tutoring* can offer an effective environment for guiding a child through its ZPD. This may be because these settings encourage children to use language, provide explanations, and work cooperatively or competitively, all of which help produce cognitive change (Pine, 1999).

Vygotsky defines intelligence as the capacity to learn from instruction. Rather than teachers playing an *enabling* role, Vygotsky believes they should guide pupils in paying attention, concentrating, and learning effectively (a *didactic* role; Sutherland, 1992). By doing this, teachers scaffold children to competence.

BRUNER'S THEORY

Similarities and differences between Bruner, Piaget and Vygotsky

Bruner has helped to extend Vygotsky's ideas, and to apply them in the context of education (for example, the concept of scaffolding). Bruner has also been influenced by Piaget, and they share certain basic beliefs, in particular that:

- children's underlying cognitive structures mature over time, so that they can think about and organise their world in increasingly complex ways
- children are actively curious and explorative, capable of adapting to their environment through interacting with it. Abstract thinking grows out of action: competence in any area of knowledge is rooted in active experience and concrete mental operations.

Bruner places much greater emphasis than Piaget on the notion that humans actively construct *meaning* from the world. In *Actual Minds, Possible Worlds* (1986), Bruner states that:

> *Contrary to common sense there is no unique 'real world' that pre-exists and is independent of human mental activity and human symbolic language; that which we call the world is a product of some mind whose symbolic procedures construct the world.*

As such, the world we live in is 'created' by the mind. Bruner argues that the idea that we construct the world should be quite acceptable to Developmental or Clinical Psychologists, who find that people can attach quite different meanings to the 'same' event (Slee and Shute, 2003).

There are also some basic areas of disagreement between Bruner and Piaget, reflecting the influence of Vygoysky. In particular, Bruner (e.g. 1966) stresses the role of language and interpersonal communication, and the need for active involvement by expert adults (or more knowledgeable peers) in helping the child to develop as a thinker and problem-solver. Not only does language play a crucial role in the scaffolding process, but for Bruner language is intimately related to the child's cognitive growth. Indeed, thinking would be impossible without language.

Bruner (1987) also argued that children's competences are greater than Piaget's theory leads us to believe. Like Vygotsky, he places great emphasis on the child as a social being whose competences 'are interwoven with the competences of others'.

Bruner (1966) identified three major themes in understanding cognitive growth and the conditions that shape it. These relate to (i) *modes of representation* (*enactive, iconic,* and *symbolic*: see Gross and Rolls, 2009); (ii) the impact of *culture* on cognitive growth; Bruner notes that cognitive growth is shaped as much 'from the outside in as the inside out'; (iii) the *evolutionary* history of human beings: humans are particularly suited to adapting to their environment by *social* rather than *morphological* (bodily/physical) means (see Chapter 2). We shall say most about the first of these.

Figure 34.14 Jerome Bruner (born 1915)

Bruner was mainly interested in the *transition* from the iconic to the symbolic mode, where language comes into its own as an influence on thought. The child (of 6–7 years) is now freed from the immediate context and is beginning to be able to 'go beyond the information given' (Bruner, 1957). According to Bruner (1966):

> *The idea that there is a name that goes with things and that the name is arbitrary is generally taken as the essence of symbolism.*

Thus, a written sentence describing a beautiful landscape doesn't look like a landscape, whereas a picture of a landscape does. The landscape is symbolised in the language that describes it. Without the ability to symbolise, and in particular, to use language, the child would grow into adulthood dependent upon the enactive and iconic modes of representing and organising knowledge of the world.

The impact of culture

According to Bruner, development is culturally – and historically – embedded (Bruner, 1986; Bruner and Haste, 1987). In Bruner's (1986) words:

> *It can never be the case that there is a 'self' independent of one's cultural-historical context.*

In this way, Bruner's view is closely allied with Vygotsky's. Culture is the means by which 'instructions' about how humans should grow are carried from generation to generation (Bruner, 1987), that is, culture helps transmit knowledge and understanding.

Again in agreement with Vygotsky, Bruner and Haste (1987) emphasise that the child is a *social* operator, who through social life:

> *...acquires a framework for interpreting experience, and learns how to negotiate meaning in a manner congruent with the requirements of a culture.*

An evaluation of Bruner's theory

- As we've seen, Bruner has helped to build on some of Vygotsky's ideas and make them more widely known; scaffolding and the view of individual development as mediated through social and cultural influences are two important examples. His theory also represents an important alternative to Piaget's, although, as we've also seen, there's considerable overlap between them; arguably, they're more complementary than opposed theories.
- Slee and Shute (2003) believe that Bruner's work may not have received the attention it deserves in mainstream Developmental and Educational Psychology. Nonetheless, his research and writing have important implications for psychologists' understanding of the developing child:

> *... By emphasising the constructive nature of cognitive development and the influence of cultural factors, Bruner has added a richer dimension to our contemporary understanding of the nature of the child's thinking. (Slee and Shute, 2003)*

Applying Bruner's theory to education

Bruner's modes of representation lie at the heart of the '*spiral curriculum*', according to which the principles of a subject come to be understood at increasingly more complex levels of difficulty. Like Vygotsky, Bruner was unhappy with Piaget's concept of 'readiness', and proposed a much more active policy of intervention, based on the belief that:

> *...any subject can be taught effectively in some intellectually honest form to any child at any stage of development. (Bruner, 1966)*

This has contributed to the idea of the 'competent infant', that is, the belief that infants and young children, regardless of background, have much more capacity to learn academic skills than they actually display (Elkind, 1987). Elkind argues that Bruner, as well as other educators, may not have appreciated how sincerely parents and educators would take up this statement as a rallying call.

Educators need to provide learners with the means of grasping the structure of a discipline, that is, the underlying principles and concepts (rather than just mastering factual information). This enables learners to go beyond the information given, and develop ideas of their own. Teachers also need to encourage learners to make links, and to understand the relationships within and between subjects (Smith *et al.*, 1998).

THE INFORMATION-PROCESSING APPROACH

According to Bee (2000), it's more accurate to talk of the *information-processing* (IP) *approach* than a distinct IP theory of cognitive development. This approach grew out of, and in some ways represents a reaction to, Piaget's theory (Pine, 1999). Like Piaget, IP theorists believe there are psychological structures in people's minds that explain their behaviour, and which are essentially independent of the individual's social relationships, social practices, and cultural environment (Meadows, 1995).

Underlying the IP approach is the *computer analogy* (see Chapters 2, 17 and 20). This examines more closely than Piaget's theory how major cognitive processes, such as memory and attention, come into play when children deal with particular tasks and problems (Pine, 1999). To understand cognitive development, we need to discover what changes in any systematic way with age (Bee, 2000). Is it the system's basic storage capacity that increases (a 'hardware' difference), or do children become more efficient in using various processing strategies (a 'software' difference)? Of course, both types of change might be involved: brain growth occurs which, in turn, allows more functional development. But, at present, we know rather more about the *how* of change than the *why* (Schaffer, 2004).

One form of new strategy (new 'software') is the child's increasing awareness of its own mental processes (*metacognition*). This is part of a larger category of *executive processes* (planning what to do and considering alternative strategies). It may be precisely such metacognitive/executive skills that gradually emerge with age. Performance on a whole range of tasks will be better if the child can monitor its own performance, and recognise when a particular strategy is required or not. This self-monitoring improves fairly rapidly, beginning at school age (Bee, 2000).

CONCLUSIONS

Piaget's theory revolutionised the way that cognitive development has been investigated and understood. Both Vygotsky's theory and the IP approach challenge some of Piaget's basic assumptions, but they adopt radically different views from each other as to what cognitive development involves. While Vygotsky emphasises the *social* nature of cognitive change, both Piaget and the IP approach see development as occurring quite *independently* of social interaction. Bruner's theory reflects the influence of both Piaget and Vygotsky. All four theories have contributed to our understanding of the education of young children.

Chapter Summary

- Piaget sees **intelligence** as **adaptation to the environment,** and he was interested in how intelligence changes as children grow (**genetic epistemology**). Younger children's intelligence is **qualitatively different** from that of older children.
- **Cognitive development** occurs through the **interaction** between innate capacities and environmental events. It progresses through a series of **hierarchical, invariant** and **universal stages**: the **sensorimotor, pre-operational, concrete operational** and **formal operational**.
- Underlying cognitive changes are **functional invariants,** the most important being **assimilation, accommodation** (which together constitute **adaptation**), and **equilibration**. The major cognitive structures that change are **schemas/schemata**.
- During the sensorimotor stage, frequent interaction with objects ultimately leads to **object permanence,** which is fully developed when the child can infer invisible displacements.
- By the end of the sensorimotor stage, schemas have become '**interiorised**'. **Representational/make-believe play,** like **deferred imitation,** reflects the **general symbolic function.**
- Pre-operational children have difficulty in **seriation tasks** and also display **syncretic thought, transductive reasoning,** and **animism. Centration** is illustrated by the **inability to conserve**. Pre-operational children are also **egocentric.**
- During the concrete operational stage, logical operations can be performed only in the presence of actual or observable objects. Some types of conservation appear before others (**horizontal décalage**), and a child who's mastered all kinds of classification but not all kinds of conservation displays **vertical décalage.**
- Formal operational thinkers can manipulate ideas and propositions (**'second order' operations**) and think **hypothetically**.
- Four- and 5-year-olds are capable of **perspective-taking,** enabling them to attribute **false beliefs** to other people. This is a crucial feature of the child's **theory of mind (ToM).**
- Considerable **cross-cultural** support exists, especially for conservation, although cultural factors can affect the rate of attainment; much less support exists for formal operations.
- Central to Piagetian views of the **educational process** is **active self-discovery/discovery learning.** Teachers assess each individual child's current stage of cognitive development to set **intrinsically motivating** tasks, and provide learning opportunities that create **disequilibrium.**
- While Piaget's account is **constructivist,** Vygotsky's is **social constructivist**: human development proceeds at three levels, the cultural, interpersonal, and individual.
- At the **cultural level,** each child inherits a number of **cultural tools (technological, psychological** and **values**). For Vygotsky, the crucial cultural tool is **language**. This is the pre-eminent means of passing on society's accumulated knowledge and enables children to regulate their own activities.
- Culture and the individual meet at the **interpersonal level.** Cognitive development involves an active **internalisation** of problem-solving processes that occurs through mutual interaction between the child and parents, friends and teachers. Vygotsky's **the child as apprentice** replaces Piaget's **the child as scientist.**
- Cognitive development progresses from the **intermental** to the **intramental** (from joint regulation to self-regulation).
- **Joint collaboration** refers to active, shared participation for the purpose of solving a problem; through **scaffolding,** responsibility is gradually transferred from the adult/more advanced peer so that the child can perform the task independently. This all happens within the child's **zone of proximal development (ZPD).**
- Although Vygotsky's theory hasn't been tested cross-culturally, it has influenced Cross-cultural Psychology through the development of **Cultural Psychology** (and related approaches).
- Much of Vygotsky's theory is concerned, directly or indirectly, with formal **schooling.** Intelligence is the capacity to learn from instruction and teachers perform a **didactic** role, guiding pupils in paying attention, concentrating, and learning effectively. In this way, children are scaffolded.
- While Bruner was influenced by Piaget's ideas, he placed much greater emphasis on the notion that humans actively construct **meaning** from the world: the world we live in is 'created' by the mind.
- Like Vygotsky, Bruner stresses the role of culture and language as influences on cognitive growth; indeed, thinking would be impossible without language.
- Bruner identified three **modes of representation**: the **enactive, iconic** and **symbolic**. He was mainly interested in the **transition** from the iconic to the symbolic mode.
- Bruner's modes of representation lie at the heart of the **spiral curriculum**. This involves a rejection of Piaget's concept of readiness and has contributed to the idea of the 'competent infant'.
- Educators need to help learners grasp the underlying concepts and principles – rather than just mastering factual information.
- The **information-processing (IP)** approach is based on the **computer analogy**. Of crucial importance is **metacognition.**

Links with Other Topics/Chapters

Chapter 40 ⟶ The inability to engage in representational/make-believe play, and the general inability to use imagination, is a characteristic of children on the *autistic spectrum*

Chapter 47 ⟶ How children from *non-western cultures* perform on conservation tasks originally designed for Swiss samples will depend on the familiarity of the materials used, how the instructions are communicated, and the child's grasp of 'being tested' (Schaffer, 2004)

Chapter 38 ⟶ The issue of whether development is best understood in terms of stages is, arguably, most relevant and controversial in relation to *adulthood*

Chapter 32 ⟶ The related issue of *continuity/discontinuity* of development is especially relevant in understanding the *impact of early experience on later behaviour/personality*

Chapter 47 ⟶ According to Moghaddam (2002), stage models are compatible with, and supportive of, the ideal of *self-contained individualism* that's so central to US culture – and, through that, becoming so influential throughout the world. This makes them *culturally biased*

Chapter 35 ⟶ The reduction of egocentrism through peer interaction has major implications for children's *moral development*

Chapter 31 ⟶ Evidence exists to show that children's individual learning may be enhanced without direct interaction with peers, but simply having peers present in the same room performing the same task (Davis, 2003). This describes *social facilitation* through the *co-action effect*

Chapter 15 ⟶ Bruner's concept of 'going beyond the information given' is important for understanding *theories of perception* (such as Gregory's)

Chapter 40 ⟶ Impaired executive functioning is one proposed explanation of *autism*

Recommended Reading

Gross, R. (2008) *Key Studies in Psychology* (5th edn). London: Hodder Education. Chapter 25.

Lee, K. (2000) *Childhood Cognitive Development: The Essential Readings.* Oxford: Blackwell. Also relevant to Chapter 40.

Lee, K., Anzures, G. & Freire, A. (2011) Cognitive Development in Adolescence. In A. Slater & G. Bremner (eds) *An Introduction to Developmental Psychology* (2nd edn). BPS/Blackwell.

Meadows, S. (1993) *The Child As Thinker.* London: Routledge.

Piaget, J. (1973) *The Child's Conception of the World.* London: Paladin.

Schaffer, H.R. (2004) *Introducing Child Psychology.* Oxford: Blackwell Publishing. Especially Chapters 6, 7 and 8.

Useful Websites

http://tip.psychology.org/bruner.html (Constructivist Theory: Jerome Bruner)

www.piaget.org (The Jean Piaget Society)

http://tip.psychology.org/piaget.html (Genetic Epistemology: Jean Piaget)

www.bbc.co.uk/programmes/p00f8n1g (Programme 2: Piaget's Three Mountains experiment)

www.youtube.com/watch?V=4IXnxFw7ZEE (An egocentrism experiment with a difference, plus lots of other Piaget-related clips)

CHAPTER 35

MORAL DEVELOPMENT

Freud's psychoanalytic theory

Cognitive–developmental theories

Social learning theory

INTRODUCTION and OVERVIEW

At birth, we're *amoral,* lacking any system of personal values and judgements about right and wrong. By adulthood, though, most of us possess morality. Psychologists aren't interested in morality as such, but in the process by which it's acquired. The nature of that process is seen very differently by different psychological theories, which attempt to answer quite different questions.

According to Haste *et al.* (1998), historically four main questions have been asked about moral development.

1. How do conscience and guilt develop, acting as sanctions on our misdeeds? This relates to Freud's *psychoanalytic theory*.
2. How do we come to understand the basis of rules and moral principles, so that we can make judgements about our own and others' behaviour? This relates to the *cognitive–developmental theories* of Piaget, Kohlberg, and Eisenberg.
3. How do we learn the appropriate patterns of behaviour required by our culture? This relates to *learning theories,* including Bandura's *social learning theory*.
4. How do we develop the moral emotions that motivate our concern for others? Eisenberg's theory is also relevant here.

The relationship between morality and human nature has been debated by philosophers for thousands of years. According to Rousseau (1762), humans are 'naturally' good, but this natural goodness may be constrained and distorted by external factors. Only sociobiologists (such as Wilson, 1975; see Chapter 2) among modern-day scientists agree with this view of morality as innate. While we may like to believe that our actions are governed by higher moral principles, the reality is that 'The genes hold culture on a leash' (Wilson, 1975; see Chapter 30).

In contradiction of Wilson's claims, all the major theories to be discussed in this chapter share the assumption that the acquisition of morality is part of the wider process of *socialisation*. In other words, morality develops according to the same principles which govern the development of other aspects of socialised behaviour (see Chapter 2).

FREUD'S PSYCHOANALYTIC THEORY

Freud's account of moral development is closely related to other aspects of his *psychoanalytic theory*, in particular the *structure of the personality* and the *stages of psychosexual development.*

The psychic apparatus

Freud believed that the personality (or *psychic apparatus*) comprises three parts, the *id, ego* and *superego* (see Figure 35.1).

- The *id*:

> *... contains everything that is inherited, that is present at birth, that is laid down in the constitution – above all, therefore, the instincts ...*
> *(Freud, 1923)*

The wishes and impulses arising from the body's needs build up a pressure or tension (*excitation*), which demands immediate release or satisfaction. The id's sole aim is to reduce excitation to a minimum: it's governed by the *pleasure principle.* It is – and remains – the infantile, *presocialised* part of the personality. The two major id instincts are sexuality and aggression (see Chapter 29).

- The *ego* is:

> *... that part of the id which has been modified by the direct influence of the external world ...*
> *(Freud, 1923)*

It can be thought of as the 'executive' of the personality, the planning, decision making, rational, and logical part of us. It enables us to distinguish between a wish and reality (which the id cannot do), and is governed by the *reality principle*. While the id demands immediate gratification of our needs and impulses, the ego will postpone satisfaction until the appropriate time and place (*deferred gratification*):

> *The ego seeks to bring the influence of the external world to bear upon the id and its tendencies ... For the ego, perception plays the part which in the id falls to instinct. The ego represents ... reason and common sense, in contrast to the id, which contains the passions ...*
> *(Freud, 1923)*

- Not until the *superego* has developed can we be described as moral beings. It represents the *internalisation* of parental and social moral values:

> *It observes the ego, gives it orders, judges it and threatens it with punishment, exactly like the parents whose place it has taken ...*
> *(Freud, 1933)*

Strictly, it's the *conscience* which threatens the ego with punishment (in the form of guilt) for bad behaviour, while the *ego-ideal* promises the ego rewards (in the form of pride and high self-esteem) for good behaviour. These correspond to the punishing and rewarding parents respectively.

Psychosexual development

Although the id, ego and superego develop within the individual in that order, this isn't strictly part of Freud's developmental theory. According to his *theory of infantile sexuality*, sexuality isn't confined to physically mature adults, but is evident from the moment of birth. So, babies and young children have sexual experiences and are capable of sexual pleasure, which is derived from the rhythmical stroking or stimulation of any part of the body. However, different parts of the body (the *erogenous zones*) are particularly sensitive at different times during infancy and childhood, and become the focus of sexual pleasure (and frustration).

The sequence of these psychosexual stages is determined by *maturation* (it's biologically programmed), but how a child is treated by others (especially the parents) is crucial. Either excessive gratification or extreme frustration can result in an individual getting emotionally 'stuck' (*fixated*) at the particular stage at which this occurs, producing associated *adult* personality traits. For example, anal retentive traits include parsimony (miserliness) and obstinacy.

The Oedipus complex, identification and the superego

A boy, like a girl, takes his mother as his first love-object (see Chapter 32). Starting at about three, a boy's love for his mother becomes increasingly passionate, and he doesn't wish to share her with anyone. The boy is also jealous of his father,

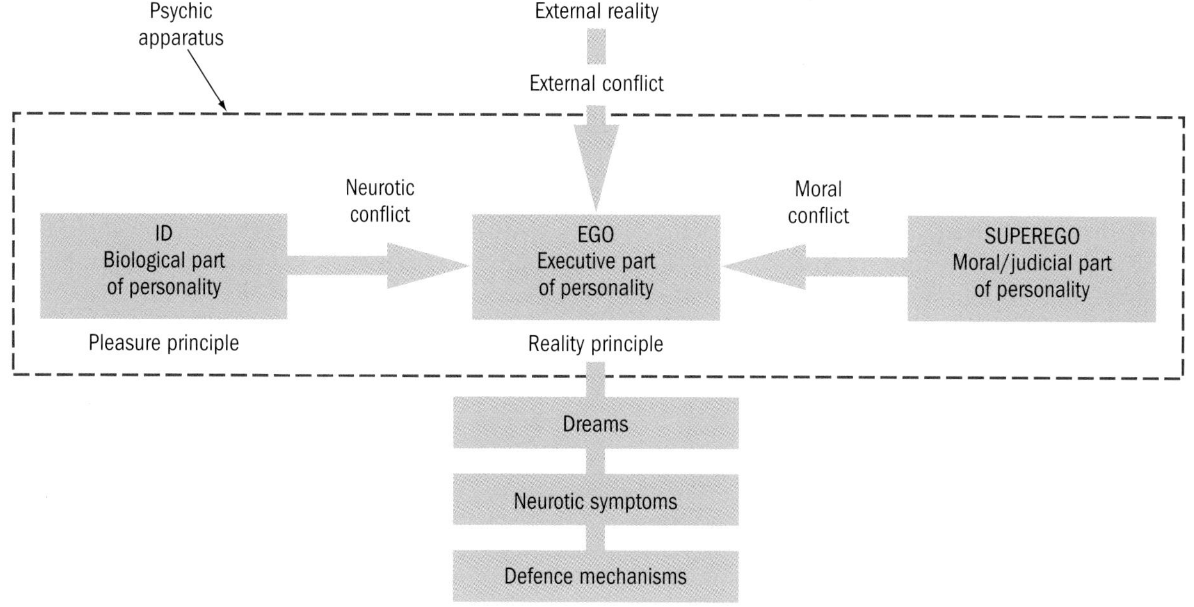

Figure 35.1 The psychic apparatus, showing sources of conflict and ways of resolving it

Box 35.1 Freud's stages of psychosexual development

- **Oral stage (0–1 year):** The nerve-endings in the mouth and lips are highly sensitive, and the baby derives pleasure from sucking for its own sake (*non-nutritive sucking*). In the earlier *incorporative substage*, the major oral activities are sucking, swallowing and mouthing. In the later *biting/aggressive substage*, hardening gums and erupting teeth make biting and chewing sources of pleasure.
- **Anal stage (1–3 years):** The anal cavity and sphincter muscles of the bowel are now the main sources of pleasure. In the earlier *expulsion substage*, the child undergoes potty-training and so has its first encounter with external restrictions on its wish to defecate where and when it pleases. Parental love is no longer unconditional, but now depends on what the child does. In the later *retention substage*, parents come to be seen for the first time as authority figures:

  > *By producing them [the contents of the bowels] ... [the infant] can express his active compliance with his environment, and by withholding them, his disobedience ... (Freud, 1905)*

- **Phallic stage (3–5/6 years):** Sensitivity is now concentrated in the genitals, and masturbation (in both sexes) becomes a new source of pleasure. The child becomes aware of anatomical sex differences ('*phallic*' comes from the Greek word *phallus* meaning penis), which marks the beginning of the Oedipus complex. The name derives from the classical Greek tragedy *Oedipus Rex*, in which Oedipus kills his father and marries his mother. Both boys and girls experience conflicting emotions in relation to their same- and opposite-sex parents, and how successfully these conflicts are resolved is crucial for future personality development. The child's superego and sex role are acquired through resolution of the Oedipus complex.

Figure 35.2 A scene from Pasolini's (1967) film of Sophocles' Greek tragedy, *Oedipus Rex,* who unknowingly kills his father and marries his mother

- **Latency period (5/6 to puberty):** The sexual preoccupations of the earlier years are *repressed* (made unconscious), which allows the child's energies to be channelled into developing new skills and acquiring new knowledge. The balance between the id, ego and superego is relatively greater than at any other time in the child's life.
- **Genital stage (puberty–maturity):** Latency represents the calm before the storm of puberty, which marks the beginning of adolescence. The relative harmony within the child's personality is disrupted by the id's powerful new demands in the form of heterosexual desires.

who already 'possesses' her, and wants him out of the way ('dead'), so that he can have his mother all to himself. However, his father is bigger and more powerful than he is, and he eventually becomes afraid that his father will punish him by cutting off his penis (*fear of castration/castration anxiety*). He reaches this conclusion partly as a result of previous punishments for masturbation, and partly based on his observation that females don't have a penis.

To resolve the dilemma, the boy represses his desire for his mother and his hostile feelings for his father, and identifies with his father (he comes to act, think and feel as if he were his father). Through this *identification with the aggressor*, a boy acquires the superego and the male sex role (see Chapter 36).

As for the girl, her Oedipus complex (sometimes referred to as the *Electra complex*) begins with the belief that she's already been castrated. She blames her mother for her lack of a penis, and experiences *penis envy* (she wants what males have). But she eventually realises that this is unrealistic, and substitutes the wish for a penis with the wish for a baby. This causes her to turn to her father as a love-object, in the hope that he'll provide her with a (preferably male) baby.

In order to identify with the mother, the girl must give up her father as a love-object and move

Figure 35.3 Norman Bates (Anthony Perkins), the main character in Hitchcock's *Psycho*, identifies very strongly with his dead mother. He attempts, unconsciously, to 'keep her alive' by, for example, dressing up in her clothes

back to her mother (while boys only have to make one 'move', from the mother to the father). However, Freud was much less sure about why the girl identifies with the mother than he was about the boy's motive for identifying with the father. The stronger the motive, the stronger (or more complete) the identification, which in turn makes for a stronger superego. So, boys' fear of castration is associated with a strong identification with the father (the 'aggressor') and a strong superego. As Freud (1924) says:

> *The fear of castration being thus excluded in a little girl, a powerful motive also drops out for the setting up of a superego.*

One suggestion Freud made was that the girl may fear loss of the mother's love. To keep the mother 'alive' inside her, she internalises her, becoming the 'good' child that her mother would want her to be (*anaclitic identification*). But what he was quite sure about was that identification with the mother is less complete. The girl's love for her father doesn't have to be as thoroughly abandoned as the boy's for his mother, and her Oedipus complex doesn't have to be so completely shattered (Mitchell, 1974). Consequently, females have a weaker superego and their identity as separate, independent persons is also less well developed.

Ask Yourself

- Do you agree with Freud regarding females' moral inferiority?

An evaluation of the Oedipus complex theory

- Freud assumed that the Oedipus complex was a universal phenomenon, but even if true for Western cultures, the Oedipus complex may not apply to every culture or to all historical periods (Segall *et al.*, 1990).

Cross-Cultural Study 35.1

Trobriand Island boys and their fathers (Malinowski, 1929)

- Among the Trobriand Islanders of Papua, New Guinea, boys were traditionally disciplined by their maternal uncle (their mother's brother), rather than by their own biological father. It was an uncle's role to guide his nephew through to adulthood. Such societies are described as *avuncular*.
- However, the father remained the mother's lover. Hence, the two roles (disciplinarian and mother's lover) were adopted by *different* men, whereas in Viennese society at the time that Freud was proposing his theories, the boy's father played both roles.
- By explaining the boy's hostility towards the father wholly in terms of sexual jealousy, Freud overlooked the possibility that he resented his father's *power* over him (Segall *et al.*, 1990).
- What Malinowski found was that a Trobriand Island boy's relationship with his father was very good, free of the love–hate ambivalence which is central to Freud's Oedipal theory. By comparison, the relationship with the uncle wasn't usually so good.
- However, this doesn't necessarily mean that Malinowski was right and Freud was wrong (Price and Crapo, 1999). Segall *et al.* (1990) suggest that more societies need to be examined, including both western and avuncular.

- Freud (1909) cited his case study of 'Little Hans' as supporting his Oedipal theory. This 5-year-old developed a phobia of being bitten by a horse, which Freud interpreted as a fear of castration (see Chapter 44). A common criticism made of Freud's developmental theory as a whole is that it was based largely on the study of his adult patients. This makes the case of Little Hans especially important, because he was Freud's only child patient.
- Freud saw Hans as a 'little Oedipus', having formulated his theory four years earlier (in *Three Essays on the Theory of Sexuality*, 1905). Hence, the case study is biased and provides no *independent* evidence to support Freud. In addition, Hans's therapy was conducted mainly by his own father, a supporter of Freud's ideas! Even more seriously, perhaps, other psychoanalytic theorists have provided alternative explanations of Hans's fear of horses, including Bowlby (1973) who reinterpreted the case in terms of attachment theory (see Chapter 32 and Gross, 2008).

Ask Yourself

- What kind of independent evidence might be considered valid?
- Why is it a problem that Hans's therapy was conducted by his own father?
- How do you think Bowlby might have reinterpreted Hans's fear of horses?

- Bee (2000) maintains that attachment research provides a good deal of support for the basic psychoanalytic hypothesis that the quality of the child's earliest relationships affects the whole course of later development. Both Bowlby (1973) and Erikson (1963; see Chapter 37) regard early relationships as prototypes of later relationships. Despite the considerable evidence showing that all types of early privation are reversible (see Chapter 32), and accepting all the criticisms of the Oedipal theory, belief in the impact of early experience is a lasting legacy of Freud's developmental theory.

COGNITIVE–DEVELOPMENTAL THEORIES

According to Haste *et al.* (1998), the question regarding moral rules, principles, and judgements (see *Introduction and overview*) has dominated research on moral development for 30 years, through work within the *cognitive–developmental theoretical framework*. While Kohlberg's theory has been the focus of research during this time, Piaget (1932) pioneered this approach to moral development. Cognitive–developmental theories maintain that it's the reason's *underlying* behaviour, rather than the behaviour itself, which make it right or wrong.

Piaget's theory

Piaget argued that morality develops gradually during childhood and adolescence. While these changes are usually referred to as qualitatively different stages of moral development, Piaget explicitly *didn't* use the concept of developmental stages in relation to moral development. Rather, he differentiated two types of *moral orientation*, namely *heteronomous* and *autonomous* (see Table 35.1). Instead of seeing morality as a form of cognition, Piaget discussed morality in the context of affects and feelings (Eckensberger, 1999).

Box 35.2 Heteronomous and autonomous morality

Piaget called the morality of young children *heteronomous* ('subject to another's laws or rules'). Older children possess *autonomous* morality ('subject to one's own laws or rules'), and see rules as the product of social agreements rather than sacred and unchangeable laws (the *morality of cooperation*).

Piaget believed that the change from heteronomous to autonomous morality occurred because of the shift at about 7 from egocentric to operational thought (see Chapter 34). This suggests that cognitive development is *necessary* for moral development, but since the latter lags at least two years behind the former, it cannot be *sufficient*.

Another important factor is the change from *unilateral respect* (the child's unconditional obedience of parents and other adults) to *mutual respect* within the peer group (where disagreements between equals have to be negotiated and resolved).

Understanding rules

To discover how moral knowledge and understanding change with age, Piaget began by looking at children's ideas about the rules of the game of marbles. He believed that the essence of morality lies in rules, and that marbles is a game in which children create and enforce their own rules free from adult influence. Piaget felt that in this way he could discover how children's moral knowledge in general develops. As he noted:

> *Children's games constitute the most admirable social institutions. The game of marbles, for instance, as played by boys, contains an extremely complex system of rules ... that is to say, a code of laws, a jurisprudence of its own ... All morality consists in a system of rules. (Piaget, 1932)*

Figure 35.4 According to Piaget, the rules of marbles could be used to study morality, since all morality consists of a system of rules

Moral judgement and punishment

Piaget also told children pairs of stories about (hypothetical) children who'd told lies, stolen or broken something. Piaget was more interested in the *reasons* children gave for their answers than the answers themselves.

An evaluation of Piaget's theory

- Piaget believed that popular girls' games (such as hop-scotch) were too simple compared with boys' most popular game (marbles) to be worthy of investigation. While girls eventually achieve similar moral levels to boys, they're less concerned with legal elaborations. This apparent *gender bias* is also evident in Kohlberg's theory (see below).
- Piaget argued that egocentrism could be overcome via *social interaction with peers.* Intellectually, and in terms of status, adults are too far removed from children, but peers provide the ideal potential source of *sociological conflict* necessary for development to take place. It's through resolution of conflict that cognitive development occurs, although there's no logical reason why it results in developmental advance (Bryant, 1990). Nevertheless, Piaget's claims have inspired some important research into the potential impact of peer interaction on *perspective-taking* (Davis, 2003; see Chapter 34).
- Children's understanding of *intention* is much more complex than Piaget believed, and children are able to bring this understanding to bear on moral decision making. The preschool child *isn't* amoral (Durkin, 1995).
- Piaget's stories make the *consequences* of behaviour explicit rather than the intentions behind it (Nelson, 1980). When 3-year-olds see people bringing about negative consequences, they assume that their intentions are also negative. But when information about intentions is made explicit, even 3-year-olds can make judgements about them, *regardless* of the consequences. This suggests they're only *less proficient* than older children at discriminating intentions from consequences, and in using these separate pieces of information to make moral judgements.
- According to some information-processing theorists (e.g. Gelman and Baillargeon, 1983; see Chapter 34), aspects of development which Piaget attributed to the increasing complexity and quality of thought, are actually the result of an increasing capacity for the storage and retrieval of information.

Cross-cultural validity

- Although evidence regarding the process of moral development is mixed, many of the age trends (not necessarily the actual ages) that Piaget described are supported by later research. This includes cross-cultural data, mainly from Africa (Eckensberger and Zimba, 1997).

Table 35.1 Summary of Piaget's theory of moral development

	Understanding rules	Moral judgement and punishment
5–9-year-olds: **Heteronomous moral orientation** ('subject to another's laws or rules')	*Rules represent an external law.* *Unilateral respect.*	*Objective/external responsibility.* Belief in: ● *Expiatory punishment* (paying the penalty for). ● *Moral realism* (punishment is accepted because it comes from an authority figure). ● *Collective punishment* (e.g. punishing whole class for misdeed of single child). ● *Immanent justice* (later mishap is punishment for an earlier misdeed that went unpunished).
10-year-olds and above: **Autonomous moral orientation** ('subject to one's own laws or rules')	*Mutual respect.*	*Internal responsibility.* Belief in: ● *Principle of reciprocity* (making good the loss/damage). ● *Moral relativism* (justice not tied to authority). No longer believe in *collective punishment/immanent justice.*

- Piaget *didn't* assume that the developmental changes he observed in his Swiss sample would necessarily be found in other cultures. On the contrary, he claimed that the essential issue was whether the cultural context would allow certain developmental changes to occur. This general orientation towards *contextualisation* is evident in current cross-cultural research (Eckensberger, 1999), and an interesting example is a study of lying and truth-telling by Lee *et al.* (1997).

Cross-Cultural Study 35.2

Lying and truth-telling in China and Canada (Lee *et al.*, 1997)

- Lee *et al.* tested the claim that the understanding of lying is greatly influenced by the cultural norms and values in which individuals are socialised.
- One hundred and twenty children from the People's Republic of China and 108 Canadian children (aged 7, 9 and 11) were presented with four brief stories, two involving a child who intentionally carried out a good deed (valued by adults in both cultures) and two involving a child who carried out a bad deed (viewed negatively by adults in both cultures).
- When the story characters were questioned by a teacher as to who performed the act, they either lied or told the truth. The children were asked to evaluate the story characters' deeds and their verbal statements as either 'naughty' or 'good'.
- Overall, the Chinese children rated truth-telling less positively and lie-telling more positively in prosocial settings compared with the Canadian children.
- This indicates that the emphasis on self-effacement and modesty in Chinese culture overrides Chinese children's evaluations of lying in some situations.
- Both groups rated truth-telling positively and lie-telling negatively in antisocial situations, reflecting the emphasis in both cultures on distinguishing between misdeed and truth/lie-telling.

Lee *et al.*'s results suggest a close link between sociocultural practices and moral judgement in relation to lying and truth-telling. China is a communist–collectivist society, which values the community over the individual and promotes personal sacrifice for the social good. Admitting a good deed is viewed as a violation of both traditional Chinese cultural norms and communist–collectivist doctrine. By contrast, in Western culture 'white lies' and deceptions to avoid embarrassment are tolerated, and concealing positive behaviour isn't explicitly encouraged (especially in the early school years).

Although cognitive development plays an undeniable role (as argued by Kohlberg: see below), cultural and social factors are also key determinants in children's moral development (Lee *et al.*, 1997).

Kohlberg's theory

As we noted earlier, Kohlberg's theory has dominated research in the field of moral reasoning for 30 years. Kohlberg was greatly influenced by Piaget, and, like him, believed that morality develops gradually during childhood and adolescence. Also like Piaget, he was more interested in people's *reasons* for their moral judgements than in the judgements themselves. For example, our reasons for upholding the law, as well as our views about whether there are circumstances in which breaking the law can be justified, might change as we develop.

Kohlberg assessed people's moral reasoning through the use of moral dilemmas. Typically, these involved a choice between two alternatives, both of which would be considered socially unacceptable. One of the most famous of these dilemmas concerns 'Heinz'.

Ask Yourself

- Read Box 35.3 and try answering the questions about Heinz.

Ask Yourself

In July 2004, a 100-year-old man, Bernard Heginbotham, who killed his 87-year-old wife by slitting her throat, avoided a prison sentence because the judge said he had acted out of love. Her health was failing and she'd been moved from one care home to another. He became very distressed and decided to end her suffering.

- Should he have killed his wife?
- Can slitting someone's throat be justified as an act of love?
- Should his age have been taken into account when passing sentence?
- Should he have been sent to prison?

Kohlberg's original study (beginning in 1956) involved 72 Chicago boys (10–16 years), 58 of whom were followed up at three-yearly intervals for 20 years (Kohlberg, 1984; Colby *et al.*, 1983; Colby and Kohlberg, 1987). Based on the answers given by this sample to the Heinz and other dilemmas, Kohlberg identified six qualitatively different stages of moral development, differing in complexity, with more complex types being used by older individuals. The six stages span three levels of moral reasoning (see Box 35.4).

Box 35.3 An example of a moral dilemma

In Europe, a woman was near death from a special kind of cancer. There was one drug that the doctors thought might save her. It was a form of radium that a druggist in the same town had recently discovered. The drug was expensive to make, but the druggist was charging ten times what the drug cost him to make. He paid $400 for the radium and charged $4000 for a small dose of the drug. The sick woman's husband, Heinz, went to everyone he knew to borrow the money, but he could only get together about $2000, which was half of what the drug cost. He told the druggist that his wife was dying and asked him to sell it cheaper or let him pay later. But the druggist said, 'No, I discovered the drug and I'm going to make money from it.' So Heinz got desperate and considered breaking into the man's store to steal the drug for his wife.

1. Should Heinz steal the drug? (Why or why not?)
2. If Heinz doesn't love his wife, should he steal the drug for her? (Why or why not?)
3. Suppose the person dying isn't his wife but a stranger. Should Heinz steal the drug for the stranger? (Why or why not?)
4. (If you favour stealing the drug for a stranger.) Suppose it's a pet animal he loves. Should Heinz steal to save the pet animal? (Why or why not?)
5. Is it important for people to do everything they can to save another's life? (Why or why not?)
6. Is it against the law for Heinz to steal? Does that make it morally wrong? (Why or why not?)
7. Should people try to do everything they can to obey the law? (Why or why not?)
8. How does this apply to what Heinz should do?

(From Kohlberg, 1984)

Box 35.4 Kohlberg's three levels and six stages of moral development and their application to the Heinz dilemma

Level 1: Preconventional morality

Stage 1 (punishment and obedience orientation): What's right and wrong are determined by what is and isn't punishable. If stealing is wrong, it's because authority figures say so and will punish such behaviour. Moral behaviour is essentially the avoidance of punishment.

- Heinz should steal the drug. If he lets his wife die, he'd get into trouble.
- Heinz shouldn't steal the drug. He'd get caught and sent to prison.

Stage 2 (instrumental relativist orientation): What's right and wrong are determined by what brings rewards and what people want. Other people's needs and wants are important, but only in a reciprocal sense ('If you scratch my back, I'll scratch yours').

- Heinz should steal the drug. His wife needs it to live and he needs her companionship.
- Heinz shouldn't steal the drug. He might get caught and his wife would probably die before he got out of prison, so it wouldn't do much good.

Level 2: Conventional morality

Stage 3 (interpersonal concordance or 'good boy–nice girl' orientation): Moral behaviour is whatever pleases and helps others and doing what they approve of. Being moral is 'being a good person in your own eyes and the eyes of others'. What the majority thinks is right by definition.

- Heinz should steal the drug. Society expects a loving husband to help his wife regardless of the consequences.
- Heinz shouldn't steal the drug. He'll bring dishonour on his family and they'll be ashamed of him.

Stage 4 (maintaining the social order orientation): Being good means doing one's duty – showing respect for authority and maintaining the social order for its own sake. This goes beyond the stage 3 concern for one's family: society protects the rights of individuals, so society must be protected by the individual. Laws are unquestioningly accepted and obeyed.

- Heinz should steal the drug. If people like the druggist are allowed to get away with being greedy and selfish, society would eventually break down.
- Heinz shouldn't steal the drug. If people are allowed to take the law into their own hands, regardless of how justified an act might be, the social order would soon break down.

Level 3: Post-conventional morality

Stage 5 (social contract–legalistic orientation): Since laws are established by mutual agreement, they can be changed by the same democratic process. Although laws and rules protect individual rights as well as those of society as a whole, individual rights can sometimes supersede these laws if they become destructive or restrictive. Life is more 'sacred' than any legal principle, and so the law shouldn't be obeyed at all costs.

- Heinz should steal the drug. The law isn't set up to deal with circumstances in which obeying it would cost a human life.

- Heinz shouldn't steal the drug. Even such extreme circumstances don't justify a person taking the law into his own hands. The ends don't always justify the means.

Stage 6 (universal ethical principles orientation): The ultimate judge of what's moral is a person's own conscience operating in accordance with certain universal principles. Society's rules are arbitrary and may be broken when they conflict with universal moral principles.

- Heinz should steal the drug. When a choice must be made between disobeying a law and saving a life, one must act in accordance with the higher principle of preserving and respecting life.
- Heinz shouldn't steal the drug. He must consider other people who need it just as much as his wife. By stealing the drug, he'd be acting in accordance with his own particular feelings with utter disregard for the values of all the lives involved.

(Based on Rest, 1983; Crooks and Stein, 1991)

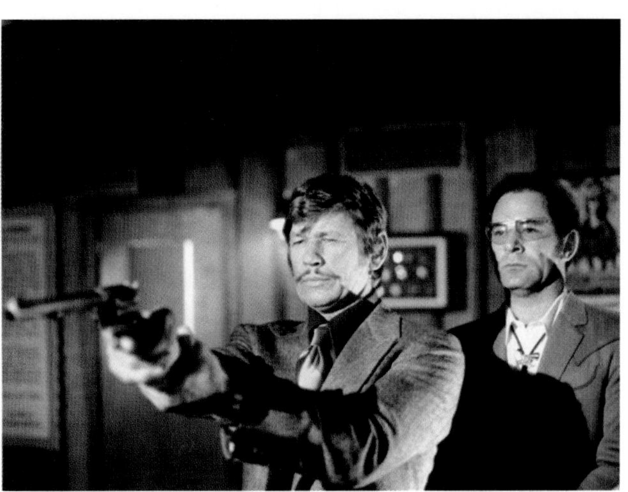

Figure 35.5 Charles Bronson in *Death Wish*: taking the law into his own hands in the most extreme way possible

Both Piaget and Kohlberg saw cognitive development as necessary for, and setting a limit on, the maturity of moral reasoning, with the latter usually lagging behind the former. So, for example, formal operational thought (see Chapter 34) is needed to achieve stages 5 and 6, but it cannot guarantee it. Because formal operational thought is achieved by a relatively small proportion of people, it's hardly surprising that only about 15 per cent of adults attain stages 5 and 6 (Colby *et al.*, 1983; see Table 35.2).

An evaluation of Kohlberg's theory

- Research has shown that young children's understanding of moral regulation is much more sophisticated than implied by Kohlberg's stage 1 (Hart *et al.*, 2003). Damon (1977) was one of the first to demonstrate that stage 1 children reason in thoughtful ways about sharing in peer contexts. (See Key Study 35.1.)

Key Study 35.1

Distributive justice (Damon, 1977)

- A typical *distributive justice task* involved children being asked to imagine that there's a school in desperate need of funds to buy essential writing materials (pens and notebooks). Teachers organise an open day and fair to raise funds.
- The art teacher asks the class to paint pictures for sale, the open day is a great success and more money is raised than needed. The teacher is given some of the surplus money, and the critical question is: How does she distribute the money to the children?
- The three possibilities are: *equality* (each child receives the same amount); *need* (poorer children receive more); and *merit* (those who worked hardest or whose paintings sold best are given more).
- Even 4-year-olds recognise the importance of sharing, and 8-year-olds can appreciate and discuss all three ways of sharing the money.

- Children have considerable experience of sharing food and toys with friends, which is translated into implicit principles. But they have little experience with the kinds of issues raised by Kohlberg's dilemmas, so their reasoning about theft and the importance of human life is rather muddled. Their moral understanding is, however, much more complex and sophisticated than was believed 30 years ago (Hart *et al.*, 2003).
- Findings from Kohlberg's longitudinal study showed that those who were initially at low stages had advanced to higher stages, suggesting 'moral progression' (Colby *et al.*, 1983). Based on these findings, he argued that the first five stages are *universal,* and that they occur in an *invariant sequence.* Similarly, Rest's (1983) 20-year longitudinal study of men from adolescence to their mid-30s showed that the developmental stages seem to occur in the order described by Kohlberg.

Is it gender biased?

- The claim that Kohlberg's theory is biased towards Western cultural ideals (*Eurocentrism)* mirrors a second major criticism, namely that it's biased in favour of males (*androcentrism*: see Chapter 47).

Table 35.2 The relationship between Kohlberg's stages and Piaget's types of moral development, and Piaget's stages of cognitive development

Kohlberg's levels of moral development	Age group included within Kohlberg's developmental levels	Corresponding type of morality (Piaget)	Corresponding stage of cognitive development (Piaget)
Preconventional (stages 1 and 2)	Most 9-year-olds and below Some over 9	Heteronomous (5–9/10)	Pre-operational (2–7)
Conventional (stages 3 and 4)	Most adolescents and adults	Heteronomous (e.g. respect for the law/ authority figures) plus autonomous (e.g. taking intentions into account)	Concrete operational (7–11)
Post-conventional (stages 5 and 6)	10–15% of adults, not before mid-30s	Autonomous (10 and above)	Formal operational (11 and above)

Gilligan (1982, 1993) has argued that because Kohlberg's theory was based on an all-male sample, the stages reflect a male definition of morality.

Ask Yourself

- What do you think Gilligan might mean by a 'male definition of morality'?
- How might this differ from a female definition of morality?

- While men's morality is based on abstract principles of law and justice, women's is based on principles of compassion and care. In turn, the different 'moral orientations' of men and women rest on a deeper issue, namely how we think about *selfhood*. An ethic of justice (male) is a natural outcome of thinking of people as separate beings, in continual conflict with each other, who make rules and contracts as a way of handling that conflict. A 'female' ethic of caring/ responsibility follows from regarding selves as being in connection with one another.
- However, the claim that women 'think differently' about moral issues has been challenged. According to Johnston (1988), each gender is competent in each mode, but there are gender-linked preferences. While boys tended to use a justice orientation, if pressed they'd also use the care orientation; similarly, girls preferred a care orientation, but also switched easily. According to Haste *et al.* (1998), these findings support Gilligan's argument that there's more than one moral 'voice', but *not* her claim that the 'caring' voice was more apparent among women. Several studies show that sex differences in moral orientations are less important than the kind of dilemmas being considered (see Key Study 35.2).
- The higher stages in Kohlberg's theory are associated with education and verbal ability (Shweder *et al.*, 1987). While 'college-educated' people give higher-level and more mature explanations of moral decisions, this doesn't make them more moral than the non-college-educated people: the former might simply be more sophisticated verbally. Nor is post-conventional morality necessarily superior to conventional morality (Shweder, 1991), and even Kohlberg (1978) acknowledges that there may not be a separate sixth stage.

Ask Yourself

- Do you always/necessarily act in accordance with your moral principles/beliefs?
- If not, can you account for the inconsistency?

Eisenberg's theory of prosocial moral reasoning

Kohlberg's concept of moral reasoning is *prohibition-oriented*. In the case of Heinz, for example, one prohibition (stealing) is pitted against another (allowing his wife to die). But not all 'moral conflicts' are like this. Eisenberg (1982, 1986; Eisenberg *et al.*, 1991) argues that if we want to understand developmental changes in helping or altruism (see Chapter 30), we need to examine children's reasoning when faced with a conflict between their own needs and those of others, in a context where the role of laws, rules, and the dictates of authority are minimal. This describes *prosocial moral reasoning*.

In a series of studies during the 1980s, Eisenberg presented children of different ages (sometimes

Key Study 35.2

Are males and females morally different? (Walker, 1989)

- Walker studied a large sample of males and females, aged 5–63. Participants were scored for both moral stage and orientation on both *hypothetical* and *personally generated, real-life dilemmas*. The only evidence of gender differences was for adults on real-life dilemmas.
- When asked to produce real-life dilemmas, females reported more *relational/personal* ones and males reported more *non-relational/impersonal* dilemmas (Walker *et al.*, 1987). A relational/personal conflict involves someone with whom the participant has a significant and continuing relationship (e.g. whether or not to tell a friend her husband was having an affair). A non-relational/impersonal conflict involves acquaintances or strangers (e.g. whether or not to correct a shop assistant's error in giving too much change).
- Regardless of gender, personal/relational dilemmas produced a higher level of response than impersonal/non-relational dilemmas. This is the *opposite* of what Gilligan claimed, namely that Kohlberg's stages are biased against an ethic of care (Walker, 1996). Both males and females tended to use the ethic of care mostly in personal dilemmas, and most people used both orientations to a significant degree, with no clear focus or preference. According to Walker (1996), the nature of the dilemma is a better predictor of moral orientation than is gender.
- Walker (1984, 1995) also refuted Gilligan's claim that Kohlberg's scoring system was biased against females, making them more likely to be rated at the conventional level, and men at the post-conventional level. Based on a review of all the available research evidence relating to gender differences (80 studies, 152 distinct samples, and over 10,000 participants), he found that, regardless of age category, the typical pattern was one of non-significant differences. Once any educational or occupational differences favouring men were controlled for, there was no evidence of a systematic gender difference in moral stage scores.

followed up into early adulthood) with illustrated hypothetical stories, in which the character can help another person, but at a personal cost.

Box 35.5 A hypothetical story used by Eisenberg to assess prosocial reasoning

A girl named Mary is going to a friend's birthday party. On her way, she sees a girl who has fallen down and hurt her leg. The girl asks Mary to go to her home and get her parents so the parents can take her to the doctor. But if Mary does run and get the child's parents, she will be late for the birthday party and miss the ice cream, cake and all the games.

- What should Mary do? Why?

Based on children's responses to this and other similar dilemmas, Eisenberg identified six stages of prosocial moral reasoning (see Table 35.3).

An evaluation of Eisenberg's theory

- In a review of her research, Eisenberg (1996) points out that, as predicted, children almost never said they'd help in order to avoid punishment or because of blind obedience to authority, such as adults. This would be expected, given that children are seldom punished for *not* acting in a prosocial way (but *are* often punished for wrongdoing). This differs greatly from what's been found for prohibition-oriented moral reasoning.
- For Kohlberg, other-oriented reasoning emerges relatively late, but Eisenberg expected to find it by the preschool years. Even 4- to 5-year-olds often appeared to orient to others' needs, showing what seemed to be primitive empathy. Also, references to empathy-related processes (such as taking the other's perspective and sympathising) are particularly common in prosocial moral reasoning.
- Contrary to Kohlberg's claims, even individuals who typically used higher-level reasoning occasionally reverted to lower-level reasoning (such as egotistic, hedonistic reasoning). This was especially likely when they chose not to help, suggesting the influence of situational variables. These are also implicated by some cross-cultural studies. For example, children raised on Israeli kibbutzim are especially likely to emphasise reciprocity between people, whereas city children (Israeli and from the USA) are more likely to be concerned with personal costs for helping others. If individuals' moral reasoning can vary across situations, then there's likely to be only a modest relationship between their typical level of moral reasoning and their actual prosocial behaviour. This is supported by Eisenberg's research.
- It's widely believed within Developmental Psychology that prosocial behaviours (such as helping, sharing, comforting and cooperating) *increase*

Table 35.3 Stages of prosocial moral reasoning (based on Eisenberg, 1982, 1986)

Level 1 (hedonistic, self-focused orientation): The individual is concerned with selfish, pragmatic consequences, rather than moral considerations. For example, 'She shouldn't help, because she might miss the party'. What's 'right' is whatever is instrumental in achieving the actor's own ends/desires. Reasons for helping/not helping include direct gain for the self, expectations of future reciprocity, and concern for others whom the individual needs and/or likes. [This is the predominant mode for preschoolers and younger primary-schoolers.]
Level 2 (needs of others orientation): The individual expresses concern for the physical, material and psychological needs of others, even though these conflict with his/her own needs. For example, 'She should help, because the girl's leg is bleeding and she needs to go to the doctor'. This concern is expressed in the simplest terms, without clear evidence of self-reflective role-taking, verbal expressions of sympathy, or reference to internalised affect, such as guilt. [This is the predominant mode for many preschoolers and primary-schoolers.]
Level 3 (approval and interpersonal orientation and/or stereotyped orientation): Stereotyped images of good and bad persons and behaviours and/or considerations of others' approval/acceptance are used in justifying prosocial or non-helping behaviours. For example, 'It's nice to help' or 'Her family would think she did the right thing'. [This is the predominant mode for some primary-schoolers and secondary-school students.]
Level 4a (self-reflective empathic orientation): The individual's judgements include evidence of self-reflective sympathetic responding, role-taking, concern with others' humanness, and/or guilt or positive affect related to the consequences of one's actions. For example, 'She cares about people', and 'She'd feel bad if she didn't help because she'd be in pain'. [This is the predominant mode for a few older primary-schoolers and many secondary-school students].
Level 4b (transitional level): The individual's justifications for helping/not helping involve internalised values, norms, duties or responsibilities, or refer to the need to protect the rights and dignity of others. But these aren't clearly or strongly stated. For example, 'It's just something she's learnt and feels'. [This is the predominant mode for a minority of people of secondary-school age and older.]
Level 5 (strongly internalised stage): As for 4b, but internalised values, norms etc. are much more strongly stated. Additional justifications for helping include the desire to honour individual and societal contractual obligations, improve the conditions of society, and belief in the dignity, rights and equality of all human beings. It's also characterised by the wish to maintain self-respect for living up to one's own values and accepted norms. For example, 'She'd feel bad if she didn't help because she'd know she didn't live up to her values'. [This is the predominant mode for a very small minority of secondary-school students and no primary-schoolers.]

in frequency as children grow older, reflecting the changes in prosocial reasoning (Eisenberg *et al.*, 2006). But Eisenberg herself (and others) also acknowledges that the developmental course of such behaviours is far from straightforward (e.g. Eisenberg, 2003; Eisenberg and Fabes, 1998). A recent study by Nantel-Vivier *et al.* (2009) adds further doubt to this widely held belief (see Key Study 35.3).

The role of emotion in prosocial behaviour

- One additional factor that's been implicated is emotion, in particular, *empathy*. Whether or not children help others depends on the *type* of emotional response that others' distress induces in them (rather than whether or not they respond emotionally). People who respond *sympathetically/empathically* (associated with, for instance, lowered heart rate) are more likely to help than those who experience *personal distress* (associated with accelerated heart rate).

Ask Yourself

- How are these findings related to the empathy–altruism hypothesis and universal egoism discussed in Chapter 30?

- A fundamental assumption of the *arousal: cost reward* (ACR) *model* of helping behaviour is that people are emotionally responsive to others' distress. Both adults and children not only report feeling empathy,

Key Study 35.3

The uneven path of prosocial behaviour (Nantel-Vivier *et al.*, 2009)

- Sample 1 comprised 1037 boys from low socio-economic backgrounds in Montreal, Canada. Mother and teacher reports were obtained at yearly intervals from age 10 to 15.
- Sample 2 consisted of 472 boys and girls from a variety of socio-economic backgrounds in Genzano, near Rome, Italy. Self and teacher ratings were obtained, also at yearly intervals, from age 10 to 14.
- For Sample 1, teachers and mothers were presented with a number of statements regarding prosocial behaviour (such as 'shows sympathy', 'helps hurt child', 'helps clean up mess'); these were rated on a 3-point scale (0 = never applies, to 2 = frequently applies).
- The results indicated stable or *declining* prosocial levels from late childhood to mid-adolescence. These findings don't support the common belief that prosocial behaviour increases over time.

they also become physiologically aroused by others' distress. Preschoolers also spontaneously show signs of facial concern and physiological arousal (Fabes *et al.*, 1993), and even one- to two-day-olds cry in response to another baby's distress (Sagi and Hoffman, 1976). Indeed, Bloom (2013) argues that human beings possess an innate (and universal) morality. This primitive morality may share features with the empathy displayed by chimps and even rats, and is then built on later. (See Critical Discussion 35.2.)

- There's a clear relationship between emotional regulation in parents and in their children, with sympathetic parents having sympathetic children (Eisenberg *et al.*, 1991). Democratic, warm and reasoning parenting is associated with an increased capacity for children's prosocial behaviour. Not surprisingly, autocratic, cold, harsh and inconsistent parenting predicts children's antisocial tendencies (Coie and Dodge, 1998).
- According to Eckensberger (1999), emotions (especially positive emotions) are increasingly being seen as the basis for moral development. This represents a move away from Kohlberg's theory and a return to Piaget's, in which feelings of mutual respect and empathy were seen as central.

Critical Discussion 35.1

When should children be held criminally responsible?

Using fMRI, Dosenbach *et al.* (2010) measured brain activity in 195 people aged 7–30 years. They tracked the changes which level off at around age 20 and after feeding the data into a computer, they were able to predict the chronological age of other individuals based on a five-minute scan. They claim 92 per cent accuracy as to whether a brain belongs to an adult (over 25) or a child.

Based on such evidence, could a scan, in theory, be used by a defendant to plead 'not guilty' on the grounds of 'immature brain'? Indeed, in the US, brain-based testimony is commonplace in murder trials: several convicted murderers have already appealed their death sentences on the grounds that their lawyers wrongly denied them brain-scan assessments (Satel and Lilienfeld, 2013).

The age of criminal responsibility (when an individual is considered 'fit to plead' and stand trial) is already a contentious issue. In the US alone, the age at which a person can be legally tried as an adult ranges from 7–18 depending on the State. In Europe it ranges from 10–18: 10 (England and Wales: raised from 8 in 1963); 12 (Scotland, Holland); 13 (France); 14 (Italy); 15 (Norway); 16 (Spain); and 18 (Belgium).

According to the Royal Society (2011), at age 10 parts of the brain related to decision making and judgement, impulse control and cognitive control – in particular, the prefrontal cortex (PFC) – are still developing. There's now indisputable evidence that the brain continues to develop throughout adolescence, with some regions not fully mature until 20 (see Chapter 37). While the PFC is the slowest brain region to mature, the amygdala develops during early adolescence.

While many psychiatrists, neuroscientists and legal professionals are campaigning for the age of responsibility to be raised, others argue that by age 10 a child understands the difference between right and wrong. Dosenbach *et al.*'s (2010) study suggests that 20 might be a reasonable cut-off point. But the *physical* maturity of the brain isn't necessarily correlated with *functional* maturity, which is what the legal system is concerned with (Hamzelou, 2014).

According to Satel and Lilienfeld (2013):

> *...the potential for functional brain imaging to mislead currently exceeds its capacity to inform...until neuroscientists and legal experts become able to translate information about brain function into the legal requirements for criminal responsibility, lawyers, jurors, and judges will still need to rely on traditional methods of assessing... the defendant's mental state...*

SOCIAL LEARNING THEORY

Social learning theories (SLTs), such as those of Bandura (1977a) and Mischel (1973), originated in the US in the 1940s and 1950s. They were an attempt to reinterpret certain aspects of Freud's psychoanalytic theory in terms of *learning theory* (classical and operant conditioning: see Chapter 11). In the 1960s and 1970s, Bandura and his colleagues tried to make Freud's concept of identification more objective by studying it experimentally in the form of *imitation*.

More specifically, many of these experiments were concerned with aggression (see Chapter 29). SLT has also been applied to many aspects of development, such as gender (see Chapter 36) and morality. This focus on *human social behaviour* is one feature that sets SLT apart from conditioning (or orthodox learning) theory.

The role of cognitive factors in observational learning

Observational learning takes place without any reinforcement – mere exposure to the model is sufficient for learning to occur (Bandura, 1965). However, whether the model's behaviour is imitated depends partly on the consequences of the behaviour, for both the model and the learner. Reinforcement is important only in so far as it affects *performance* (not the learning itself: see Chapter 11).

The learning process is much more complex for Bandura than it is for Skinner, for whom 'the mind' had no part to play in a scientific Psychology (see Chapter 2). In Bandura's (1974) view:

> *Contrary to mechanistic metaphors, outcomes change behaviour in humans through the intervening influence of thought.*

A demonstration of this more complex view of learning is Bandura's (1977a) challenge to Skinner's claim that reinforcements and punishments *automatically* strengthen and weaken behaviour (see Chapter 11). For Bandura:

> *Reinforcement serves principally as an informative and motivational operation rather than as a mechanical response strengthener.*

Reinforcement provides the learner with *information* about the likely consequences of certain behaviour under certain conditions: it improves our prediction of whether a given action will lead to pleasant (reinforcement) or unpleasant (punishment) outcomes in the *future*. It also *motivates* us by causing us to anticipate future outcomes. Our present behaviours are largely governed by the outcomes we expect them to have, and we're more likely to try to learn the modelled behaviour if we value its consequences.

Figure 35.6 After watching a film of an aggressive model who punched, kicked and hurled a Bobo doll, these children spontaneously imitated the model's aggression

Bandura identifies five major *cognitive mediating variables* which influence the likelihood of learning and/or performance: *attention, encoding into memory, long-term memory storage, reproducing the observed behaviour,* and *motivation* (including *self-reinforcement*).

An evaluation of Bandura's SLT

- The importance of cognitive factors is reflected in Bandura's (1986, 1989) renaming of SLT as *social cognitive theory* (SCT). Other important cognitive processes are those relating to the self (see Box 35.6).
- One of the strengths of Bandura's SLT (and other versions, such as that of Mischel, 1973) is the claim that behaviour can be understood only by taking the actor's self-concept, self-monitoring, self-efficacy, and other mediating variables into account. They make the theory far less mechanistic than

Skinner's, for example, which focuses entirely on external events. For Bandura (1973):

> *The environment is only a potentiality, not a fixed property that inevitably impinges upon individuals and to which their behaviour eventually adapts. Behaviour partly creates the environment and the resultant environment, in turn, influences the behaviour.*

This view is called *reciprocal determinism* (Bandura, 1977a, 1986). People are both products and producers of their environments.

Box 35.6 Self-evaluation, self-monitoring, and self-efficacy

- According to Bandura, children learn both overt behaviour/concrete skills and information, and also abstract skills and information through modelling. Indeed, *abstract modelling* is part of his SCT (1986, 1989). For example, the 'rule' underlying a model's behaviour can be extracted from observing the behaviour, without the rule being made explicit or articulated. In this way, the child can acquire attitudes, values, expectancies, ways of solving problems, and *standards of self-evaluation*.
- By incorporating (or internalising) societal standards into its self, the child can monitor its own behaviours in terms of these standards. This *self-monitoring* ensures that behaviour is regulated even in the absence of reinforcement. Indeed, according to Bandura (1971), 'There is no more devastating punishment than self-contempt' – we are our own harshest critics. This mirrors Freud's view of the young child's superego, which is often more punitive than the parents it has replaced (see text above, p. 590).
- *Self-efficacy* refers to our belief that we can act effectively and exercise some control over events that influence our lives (Bandura, 1977a, 1986). This is crucially important for motivation, since how we judge our own capabilities is likely to affect our expectations about future behaviour. For example, if we feel that a model's actions are within our capabilities, then we may attempt to imitate them, but a low sense of self-efficacy regarding the modelled skill is likely to inhibit us (Durkin, 1995).

Critical Discussion 35.2

The evolutionary function of morality

It's generally agreed that humans are unique in the animal kingdom in having a sense of right and wrong; the *universal* nature of morality in human culture suggests that it's part of our *human nature*.

But in terms of basic evolutionary principles (see Chapter 2), what possible advantage could a moral sense have for the individual and his/her genes to behave morally towards *non-kin*? Surely such behaviour could only be understood in terms of *group selection*: that is, moral behaviour is beneficial to the species as whole (see Chapter 30). According to Workman and Reader (2008), there are some clear advantages that a moral sense provides the individual.

Transgressing different *moral spheres* (*autonomy*: restricting individual freedom, protecting individual rights and property; *community*: disrespecting one's elders and the in-group's cultural traditions; *divinity*: defiling what's considered holy or sacrosanct) automatically triggers its own distinct emotional response (for example, *anger, contempt* and *disgust*, respectively); this occurs without first passing through conscious reasoning processes (Rozin *et al.*, 1999). Research using *f*MRI scans supports the role of emotions in moral decision making (e.g. Greene *et al.*, 2004).

Positive emotions are also associated with morality, such as the *esteem* in which we hold altruists or the *reverence* inspired by martyrs. Based on these considerations, Workman and Reader (2008) claim that

> *Morality might therefore be a system that protects the individual's sense of fairness, hierarchy and purity and enables us to thrive within our groups and engage in reciprocal altruism...*

But how can we account for the variability of moral values between – and within – cultures? Why didn't natural selection just 'wire in' the same set of values? One answer is provided by Wright (1994): when the environment is uncertain and unpredictable, it makes sense to build *flexibility* into the system rather than hard-wiring for particular moral values.

This 'ultimate reason' is complemented by a 'proximate' one (Haidt and Joseph, 2004). They propose that there are five moral domains (harm/care, fairness/reciprocity, in-group/loyalty, authority/respect, purity/sanctity) that are innate and universal, but which can be modified by cultural learning. While these domains are a kind of mental module, these are more flexible than those proposed by some Evolutionary Psychologists (e.g. Tooby and Cosmides, 1997; see Chapter 2) (Workman and Reader, 2008).

CONCLUSIONS

As we noted in the *Introduction and overview*, different psychological theories attempt to answer quite different questions about moral development. To the extent that all these questions are relevant to understanding the full complexity of moral development, psychoanalytic theory, cognitive developmental theories, and SLT all make significant contribution to our understanding of this critically important aspect of socialisation.

Chapter Summary

- According to Freud, the **psychic apparatus** consists of the **id**, **ego** and **superego**. The id and the ego are governed by the **pleasure principle** and **reality principle** respectively. The superego comprises the **conscience** and **ego-ideal**, representing the **punishing** and **rewarding parent** respectively.
- A boy's **Oedipus complex** ends when he identifies with his father (**identification with the aggressor**), motivated by his **fear of castration/castration anxiety.** Since a girl's Oedipus complex begins with her belief that she's already been castrated, Freud found it difficult to explain her identification with her mother. One suggestion was **anaclitic identification**.
- There's no evidence to support Freud's claim that females have weaker superegos than males, and **penis envy** has been reinterpreted as envy of men's superior **social status.**
- **Cognitive–developmental theories** are concerned with the **reasons** underlying moral judgements, rather than the judgements themselves.
- According to Piaget, the change from **heteronomous** to **autonomous** morality occurs due to the shifts from egocentric to operational thought, and from **unilateral respect** and adult constraint to **mutual respect** within the peer group.
- Although children's understanding of **intention** is much more complex than Piaget believed, many of the age trends he described have been supported by cross-cultural studies, mainly from Africa.
- Kohlberg identified six qualitatively different **stages** in moral development, spanning three basic levels of moral reasoning: **preconventional, conventional** and **post-conventional** morality.
- Despite extensive empirical support for the sequence and universality of the (first four) stages, the **sociocultural approach** maintains that cultural factors play a significant part in moral reasoning. For Kohlberg, the focus is on what takes place within the individual's head.
- Kohlberg's theory has been criticised for its **bias towards Western cultures**, and for being based on a **male definition of morality**. However, several studies show that gender differences in morality are less important than the **kind of dilemmas** being considered.
- Kohlberg has also been criticised for overemphasising moral thinking (rather than behaviour), and those who attain the highest stages may simply be more sophisticated verbally. A separate stage 6 may not even exist.
- While Kohlberg's theory is **prohibition-oriented**, Eisenberg concentrates on the development of **prosocial moral reasoning**. She identifies six **levels,** based on research using hypothetical stories in which the character can help another person – but at a personal cost.
- Many of the predictions derived from Eisenberg's theory have been supported, and her research has also indicated that situational variables influence moral reasoning. But **prosocial behaviour** may not go on increasing as children enter adolescence.
- Bandura's **social learning theory** (**SLT**) investigated Freud's concept of identification, largely through laboratory experiments of **imitative aggression**.
- Bandura emphasised **observational learning/ modelling**, distinguished between **learning** and **performance,** and identified several **cognitive variables** that **mediate** between observation of a model's behaviour and its imitation.
- **Reinforcement** is a source of both **information** and **motivation**. While not necessary for learning, reinforcement (**direct, vicarious** or **self-administered**) may be needed for performance.
- **Self-reinforcement** is related to **self-monitoring,** the SLT equivalent of Freud's superego. This represents an **internalised societal standard** or **expectancy**, another example being **self-efficacy**.

Links with Other Topics/Chapters

Chapter 42 ⟶ Through the concept of fixation, Freud was able to explain how *individual differences in personality* arise from common developmental patterns

Chapter 50 ⟶ Like Piaget, Freud saw both *biological* (e.g. maturation) and *experiential factors* contributing to personality development, especially individual differences

Chapter 47 ⟶ *Feminist Psychologists* have criticised the *androcentric* (male-centred) nature of Freud's and Kohlberg's theories

Chapter 23 ⟶ Taking credit for good deeds (part of the *self-serving bias*)

Chapter 22 ⟶ is an accepted part of *impression management*

Chapter 47 ⟶ in western *individualist* cultures, while in China (and other *collectivist* cultures) it's seen as a character flaw

Chapter 47 ⟶ *Cross-cultural* studies of, say, Kohlberg's theory, are more likely to look for the *universal* nature of the stages, while *Cultural Psychologists* are interested in *cultural diversity*

Chapter 47 ⟶ Gilligan's distinction between male and female moralities could be seen as the gender equivalent of the distinction between *individualis*t and *collectivist* cultures

Chapter 26 ⟶ The inconsistency between what people say and what they believe is demonstrated in Asch's *conformity experiments*

Chapter 27 ⟶ The inconsistency between what people say they'd do and what they'd probably do under particular conditions is demonstrated in studies of *obedience*

Chapter 46 ⟶ An inability to feel empathy for others may help explain (some cases of) *criminal behaviour*

Chapter 29 ⟶ Bandura's study of observational learning in relation to imitation of aggression represented the first wave of research into the *effects of media violence*

Chapter 45 ⟶ Bandura's concept of self-efficacy is important for understanding and evaluating the *effects of all forms of psychotherapy*

Chapter 49 ⟶ Reciprocal determinism is relevant to the debates concerning *free will and determinism*

Chapter 50 ⟶ and *nature–nurture*

Chapter 36 ⟶ Relevant to Eisenberg's theory and gender differences in moral development is Baron-Cohen's *empathising-systemising* (E-S) theory

Recommended Reading

Gilligan, C. (1993) *In A Different Voice: Psychological Theory and Women's Development* (revised edition). Cambridge, MA: Harvard University Press. Also relevant to Chapter 47.

Hart, D., Burock, D., London, B. & Atkins, R. (2003) Prosocial tendencies, Antisocial behaviour, and Moral Development. In A. Slater & G. Bremner (eds) *An Introduction to Developmental Psychology.* Oxford: Blackwell Publishing.

Haste, H., Diomedes, M. & Helkama, K. (1998) Morality, Wisdom, and the Life Span. In A. Demetriou, W. Doise & C. van Lieshout (eds) *Lifespan Developmental Psychology.* New York: Wiley.

Useful Websites

http://tigger.uic.edu/~lnucci/MoralEd/overview.html ('Moral Development and Moral Education: An Overview'. A discussion of the theories of Piaget, Kohlberg, Turiel and Gilligan)

www.xenodochy.org/ex/lists/moraldev.html (Stages of Moral Development – Kohlberg (1971), with a commentary and links embedded within it, including two to Gilligan's *In A Different Voice*)

CHAPTER 36

GENDER DEVELOPMENT

The 'vocabulary' of sex and gender

Gender stereotypes and gender differences

Theories of gender development

INTRODUCTION and OVERVIEW

Often the first thing we notice about other people is whether they're male or female. The importance of *sexual identity* to our self-concept and our interactions with others is a reflection of the fact that every known culture distinguishes between male and female (see Chapter 33). In turn, this distinction is accompanied by widely and deeply held beliefs (*stereotypes*) about the psychological make-up and behaviours belonging to each sex (see Chapter 22). The study of *psychological sex differences* is really an attempt to see how accurate these stereotypes are.

At the beginning of the twentieth century (especially in the USA), many of the first generation of scientifically trained women Psychologists channelled their research efforts into the extent and nature of sex differences. But Psychology's interest in this research area waned with the rise of behaviourism (Crawford and Unger, 1995). Interest was revived in the 1970s, driven largely by *Feminist Psychologists*. According to feminist interpretations of sex differences, social, political, economic, and cultural factors determine *gender*, our awareness and understanding of the differences that distinguish males from females. This view is directly opposed to those of sociobiologists and Evolutionary Psychologists, who argue that sex differences are 'natural', having evolved as a part of the more general adaptation of the human species to its environment (see Chapters 2 and 28).

Other theoretical accounts of gender and gender differences include *biological approaches*, *biosocial theory*, *psychoanalytic theory*, *social learning theory*, *cognitive–developmental theory*, and *gender schema theory*. All of these, with the exception of biological approaches, stress the *interaction* between biological and environmental influences, albeit in quite different ways.

THE 'VOCABULARY' OF SEX AND GENDER

Ask Yourself

- Excluding the act of sex (or sexual behaviour), can 'sex' mean different things?
- What's the difference between 'sex' and 'gender'?

Sex refers to the biological facts about us, usually summarised as 'male' and 'female'; it's a *multi-dimensional* variable, comprising (i) *chromosomal sex;* (ii) *gonadal sex*; (iii) *hormonal sex;* (iv) *sex of the internal reproductive structures;* and (v) *sex of the external genitals.*

Gender, by contrast, is what culture makes out of the 'raw material' of biological sex: it's the *social equivalent* or *social interpretation* of sex. As Maracek *et al.* (2004) put it :

> *...sex is to gender as nature is to nurture; that is, sex pertains to what is biological or natural, whereas gender pertains to what is learned or cultural...*

Sexual identity is an alternative way of referring to our biological status as male or female. Corresponding to gender is *gender identity*, our classification of ourselves (and others) as male or female, boy or girl, and so on.

For most people, their sexual and gender identities correspond. However, some individuals experience *gender dysphoria* (or dysmorphia), that is, anxiety, uncertainty or persistently uncomfortable feelings about their assigned gender (based on their anatomical sex). Gender dysphoria is the major symptom of *gender identity disorder*, in which individuals believe their gender identity is different from their sexual identity (their anatomical sex). These individuals usually become *transsexuals*, that is, they choose to undergo hormonal and surgical procedures that will 'correct' their sexual identity and bring it into line with their gender identity.

Figure 36.1 Nadia Almada, the Portuguese transsexual winner of Big Brother 2004

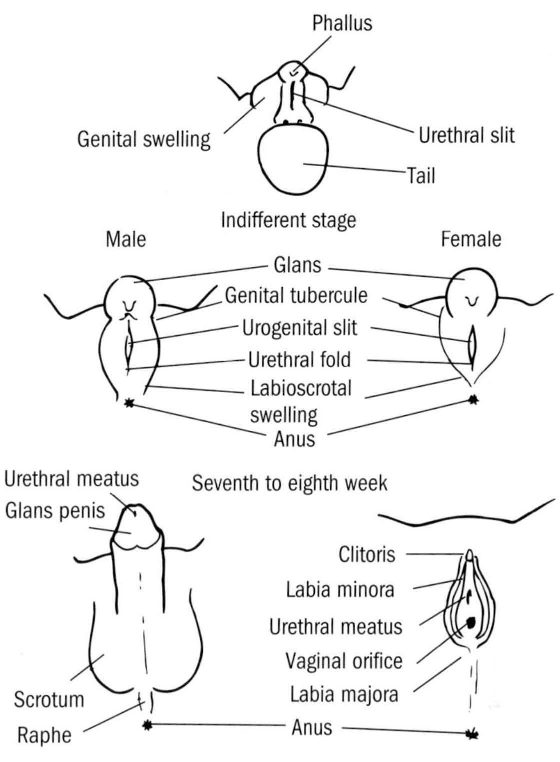

Figure 36.2 Prenatal differentiation of male and female genitalia. From a relatively undifferentiated state, development proceeds by means of the relative enlargement of structures that have analogues in members of the other sex (from Unger, R.K. (1979) *Female and Male,* New York: Harper & Row)

Gender (or *sex*) role refers to the behaviours, attitudes, values, beliefs and so on which a particular society either expects from, or considers appropriate to, males and females on the basis of their biological sex. To be *masculine* or *feminine*, then, requires males or females to conform to their respective gender roles. All societies have carefully defined gender roles, although their precise details differ between societies. *Gender* (or *sex*) *stereotypes* are widely held beliefs about psychological differences between males and females which often reflect gender roles (see pp. 609–11).

Sex typing is the process by which children acquire a sex or gender identity and learn gender-appropriate behaviours (adopt an appropriate sex role). Sex typing begins early in Western culture, with parents often dressing their new-born baby boy or girl in blue or pink, respectively. Even in the earliest days of infancy, our gender influences how people react to us (Condry and Ross, 1985). Indeed, usually the first question asked by friends and relatives of parents with a new-born baby is 'boy or girl?'.

Hermaphroditism

The categories of biological sex are usually highly correlated, so a person tends to be male (or female) in all respects. The categories also tend to be correlated with non-biological aspects of sex, including the sex the baby is assigned to at birth, how it's brought up, gender identity, gender-role identity, and so on. These facts help to explain why, whether we choose to focus on sex or gender, we assume that 'male' and 'female' are *dichotomous* categories; in other words, each of us can only be one *or* the other.

However, although estimates vary, it's been suggested that around 1 in 4500 live births involves an infant whose genitals are sufficiently ambiguous to make the immediate classification of male or female very difficult (Warne, 1998, in Liao and Boyle, 2004). Either pre- or postnatally, disorders can occur leading to an *inconsistency* or low correlation between the categories. These disorders can tell us a great deal about the development of gender identity, gender role, and gender-role identity. People with such disorders are collectively referred to as *hermaphrodites* (from the mythical Greek god/goddess Hermaphrodite, who had attributes of both sexes). *True hermaphrodites* have functioning organs of both sexes – either simultaneously or sequentially; they are very rare, and their external organs are often a mixture of male and female structures.

Case Study 36.1

Mr Blackwell: hermaphrodite (Goldwyn, 1979)

- In 'The fight to be male', Goldwyn cites the case of Mr Blackwell, only the 303rd true hermaphrodite in medical history.
- He's described as a handsome and rather shy 18-year-old Bantu. Although he had a small vaginal opening as well as a penis, he was taken to be a boy and brought up as such. But when he was 14 he developed breasts; it was also found that he had an active ovary on one side of his body and an active testicle on the other. He expressed the wish to remain male, and so his female parts were removed.
- If his internal ducts had been differently connected, Mr Blackwell could have actually fertilised himself without being able to control it.

Pseudohermaphrodites ('intersex' individuals') are more common. Although they too possess ambiguous internal and external reproductive structures, they're born with gonads that match their chromosomal sex (unlike true hermaphrodites).

- In *complete androgen insensitivity syndrome* (CAIS) (or *testicular feminising syndrome*), prenatal development in a chromosomally normal (XY) male is feminised. The internal reproductive structures of either sex fail to develop, and the external genitals fail to differentiate into a penis and scrotum. Normal-looking female external genitals and a shallow ('blind') vagina are present at birth. At puberty, breast development occurs, but the individual fails to menstruate. Very little or no surgery is needed for the adoption of a female appearance.
- *Congenital adrenal hyperplasia* (CAH) (or *adrenogenital syndrome*/AGS) is the most common and most studied intersex condition (Hines, 2004b), in which a chromosomally normal female (XX) is exposed to an excessive level of androgens during the critical period of prenatal sexual differentiation. While the internal reproductive structures are unaffected, girls with CAH are born with masculinised or ambiguous genitals: the androgens have caused phallic enlargement (the clitoris is larger than normal) and some degree of labial fusion (the outer lips of the vagina are joined together). These individuals are usually raised as females.
- In *DHT-deficient males* (or *5-alpha-reductase deficiency*), a genetic disorder prevents the normal prenatal conversion of testosterone into dihydrotestosterone (DHT). This hormone is necessary for the normal development of male external genitals. These males are usually incorrectly identified as females and raised as girls (but see Case Study 36.2).

Case Study 36.2

The Batista family: an overnight sex change? (Imperato-McGinley *et al.*, 1974)

- Imperato-McGinley *et al.* studied a remarkable family who live in Santo Domingo in the Dominican Republic. Of the ten children in the Batista family, four of the sons have changed from being born and growing up as girls into muscular men: they were born with normal female genitalia and body shape, but when they were 12, their vaginas healed over, two testicles descended, and they grew full-size penises.
- The Batistas are just one of 23 affected families in their village in which 37 children have undergone this change. All these families had a common ancestor, Attagracia Carrasco, who lived in the mid-eighteenth century. She passed on a mutant gene that shows only when carried by both parents.

- In *chromosome abnormalities*, there's a discrepancy between chromosomal sex and external appearance, including the genitalia. The most common examples are Turner's syndrome (where a female individual has a single sex chromosome: XO) and Klinefelter's syndrome (where a male individual has an extra X chromosome: XXY).

GENDER STEREOTYPES AND GENDER DIFFERENCES

Ask Yourself

- What do you consider to be 'typical' feminine and masculine characteristics?
- Are these merely stereotypes, or do you think there are real, actual differences between males and females?
- If there are real differences, how do they arise?

There appears to be a high degree of agreement across 30 countries regarding the characteristics associated with each gender group (Williams and Best, 1994). For example, male-associated terms included 'aggressive', 'determined' and 'sharp-witted', while female-associated terms included 'cautious', 'emotional' and 'warm'. However, as far as *actual* differences are concerned, many stereotypes about males and females have little empirical support.

Maccoby and Jacklin (1974) concluded that hardly any of the many psychological attributes they examined in their review (including aggression, verbal, mathematical and spatial ability) clearly differentiated the genders. This was subsequently confirmed by Ruble and Martin (1998).

According to Schaffer (2004), personality and cognitive differences are becoming less evident as society redefines the role of the sexes. Eliot (2012) maintains that most sex differences start out as small (mere biases in temperament and play style) but are amplified as children's brains meet our 'gender-infused' culture. While boys and girls are different, most psychological sex differences – as in verbal and mathematical abilities, empathy and most types of aggression – are modest and much smaller than the disparity in adult height (where the average 5 foot 10 inch man is taller than 98 per cent of women). In agreeing with Maccoby and Jacklin, Eliot argues that when it comes to mental abilities, males and females overlap much more than they differ.

THEORIES OF GENDER DEVELOPMENT

The biological approach

The influence of hormones

Although sexual differentiation *begins* with the sex chromosomes (XX or XY), their main job is to direct the gonads to develop as either testes (in males) or ovaries (in females). After that, hormones from the gonads, particularly androgens from the testes, provide the major biological influences on *sexual differentiation*.

The influence of hormones on sexual differentiation begins early in gestation (pregnancy) and involves the internal and external genitalia, as well as the brain and behaviour. According to Hines (2004a):

> *... Infants enter the world with some predispositions to 'masculinity' and 'femininity', and these predispositions appear to result largely from hormones to which they were exposed before birth.*

For many years, the accepted view was that the gonads are originally identical in both XX and XY embryos (see Figure 36. 2), i.e. *female* is the 'default' state. Then, in XY individuals, a gene called *sry* (for 'sex-determining region Y') switches on the development of the testes, which start pumping out testosterone (the primary androgen or male hormone). However, it's now known that there are 'pro-female' as well as 'pro-male' genes, and that sexual differentiation is controlled by a delicate balance between the two. For example, *r-spondin1* promotes the development of the ovaries; without it, genetic females grow up physically and psychologically male – although they have ambiguous external genitalia and are sterile (Spinney, 2011).

Between 24 weeks gestational age and birth, gonadal hormone levels are low in both sexes, but a surge of testicular hormones after birth makes testosterone once again higher in boys than in girls (for about the first six months).

Gonadal hormones, intersex conditions, and human behavioural development

Hormones clearly influence the human genitalia, but hormonal influences on behaviour are harder to establish; this is partly because behaviour is subject to social (and other) influences after birth. In addition, it's unethical to manipulate hormones experimentally in humans during early life as is done with non-humans (but even here, ethical issues arise). For this reason, the natural experiments represented by cases of intersex individuals are of particular importance.

According to Hines (2004a, 2004b), girls with CAH (compared with unaffected sisters/first cousins and girls matched for demographic background) are usually treated postnatally to normalise hormones, sex-assigned and raised as girls, and surgically feminised.

Play behaviour

These girls show increased preferences for male-typed toys (such as cars, trucks, and guns) and reduced preferences for female-typed toys (such as dolls, cosmetics, and kitchen equipment). These findings have been reported by researchers in several different countries (including the USA, Canada, the Netherlands, Germany, Sweden, and the UK), using interviews and questionnaires, as well as direct observation of children's toy choices. Girls with CAH also choose boys and other girls equally as favourite playmates, whereas their unaffected relatives choose other girls 80–90 per cent of the time (Hines and Kaufman, 1994). This male-typical behaviour occurs despite the girls having been surgically feminised and raised as girls, and despite their parents being encouraged to promote feminine behaviour in their daughters – which they do.

What does this imply for normal development? Normal variability in prenatal androgen appears to influence sex-typical play, without causing genital ambiguity. Testosterone levels during pregnancy have been found to be higher in mothers of healthy 3 and a half-year-old girls with extremely male-typical toy, playmate, and activity preferences (such as for rough-and-tumble play) than in mothers of girls with extremely female-typical behaviour (Hines *et al.*, 2002). Other evidence shows that levels of available testosterone in the maternal circulation during pregnancy, along with the daughters' own testosterone levels in adulthood, predict male-typical gender-role behaviour in daughters at the age of 27–30 years. Individual variability in testosterone during pregnancy could be genetic.

Core gender identity

Despite Money and Ehrhardt's (1972) claim that sex of rearing is more important than chromosomal or hormonal sex (see below), there's considerable evidence that points to the greater influence of biology.

Although for the vast majority of CAH individuals (or those with other intersex conditions), core gender identity *is* consistent with sex of rearing, some do experience gender dysphoria – and some express a desire to change sex. Although dysphoria is rare among intersex individuals, it's more frequent than in the general population (e.g. Zucker *et al.*, 1996).

Sexual orientation

Females with CAH are more likely than their sisters, or demographically matched controls, to report bisexual or homosexual erotic interests. These findings have been reported in the USA, the UK, Germany and Canada (Hines, 2004a, 2004b). Nevertheless, the majority of CAH women describe themselves as heterosexual. Women with CAH also report reduced erotic interest in general (i.e. in either males or females: Zucker *et al.*, 1996).

These outcomes for adult sexuality could be influenced by problems related to ambiguous genitalia and surgery. Feminising surgery doesn't usually produce genitalia that are identical to those of normal females, and surgery can make intercourse problematic. Individuals with CAIS almost always report a heterosexual orientation (i.e. towards men) and are just as likely as other women to form long-term heterosexual relationships or to marry (Hines *et al.*, 2003); this suggests that their inability to respond to androgens, or their feminine appearance and socialisation, is more important than the Y chromosome in determining sexual orientation (Hines, 2004b).

Gender and the brain

In the case of the Batista boys, the change that occurs at puberty is due to the flood of testosterone which, in turn, produces enough dihydrotestosterone to give the normal male appearance (which would normally happen 10–12 years earlier). Their ability to adopt a male gender identity and gender role suggests that their testosterone had pre-programmed masculinity into their *brains*.

Despite the complex interactions between hormones and genes prenatally and after birth, this isn't the end of sex determination – as was once thought.

> *Brain differences are indisputably biological, but they are not necessarily hard-wired. The crucial, often overlooked fact is that experience itself changes brain structure and function ... (Eliot, 2012)*

This *plasticity* of the brain could account for the claimed *structural differences* between male and female brains (based on imaging studies), such as larger amygdalae and parietal lobe in men, larger hippocampi, limbic cortex, and frontal lobe in women. Other anatomical evidence suggests that at least some sex differences in cognitive function don't result from cultural influences or the hormonal changes associated with puberty – but are there from birth (Cahill, 2012).

However, the evidence is far from conclusive (see Gross, 2008). Kimura (1999), for example, argues that overall, variation *between* men and women tends to be smaller than deviations *within* each sex. Also, neuroscientists still understand little about how they translate into behaviour. For example, Halpern *et al.* (2012) in discussing sex differences in mathematical and scientific abilities, conclude that:

> *It is important to emphasise ... that finding sex differences in brain structure and functions does not suggest these are the sole cause of observed cognitive differences between males and females. Because the brain reflects learning and other experiences, it is possible that sex differences in the brain are influenced by the differences in life experiences that are typical for men and women.*

However, see Box 36.1. Fine (2010), in *Delusions of Gender*, criticises much of the evidence on which Baron-Cohen bases his E-S theory.

Biosocial theory

According to Edley and Wetherell (1995), to ask 'What is the biological basis of masculinity (or femininity)?' is to pose a false question. In their view:

> *It requires us to separate what cannot be separated: men [and women] are the product of a complex system of factors and forces which combine in a variety of ways to produce a whole range of different masculinities [and femininities].*

For *biosocial theory*, it's the *interaction* between biological and social factors that's important, rather than biology's direct influence. From birth, the way adults respond to a child is influenced by the child's sex; as far as other people are concerned, the baby's sex is just as important as its temperament. Clearly, adults bring sexual stereotypes to their interactions with

Box 36.1 The empathising–systemising (E-S) theory of female and male brains (Baron-Cohen, 2003a, 2003b)

According to Baron-Cohen, the female brain is predominantly hardwired for *empathy*, while the male brain is predominantly hardwired for *understanding and building systems*. He calls this the *empathising–systemising* (E-S) *theory*, according to which a person (whether male or female) has a particular 'brain type'.

There are three common brain types:

1. for some individuals, empathising is stronger than systemising (the female brain/a brain of type E)
2. for others, systemising is stronger than empathising (the male brain/a brain of type S)
3. yet others are equally strong in their empathising and systemising ('balanced brain'/a brain of type B).

Anecdotal evidence for the theory comes in the form of typical male and female choices of reading material (magazines) and hobbies.

Scientific evidence shows that girls display more empathy and sensitivity towards others. For example, baby girls, as young as 12 months old, respond more empathically to others' distress, showing greater concern through more sad looks, sympathetic vocalisations and comforting. Similarly, more women report sharing their friends' emotional distress, and they also spend more time comforting people (see Chapter 35). Women are also more sensitive to facial expressions, better at decoding non-verbal communication, picking up subtle nuances from tone of voice or facial expression, or judging a person's character.

Boys, from toddlerhood onwards, are more interested in cars, trucks, planes, guns and swords, building blocks, constructional toys and mechanical toys (i.e. systems). They seem to love putting things together, and 'building' things, playing with toys that have clear functions, buttons to press, things that will light up, or devices that will cause another object to move. Males are also generally better at map-reading and mental rotation (both tests of systemising). Girls prefer dolls, soft toys and domestic articles (Golombok and Fivush, 1994).

All these differences are reflected in 'typical' male and female occupations, and hormonal factors are the most likely cause of this difference between male and female brains.

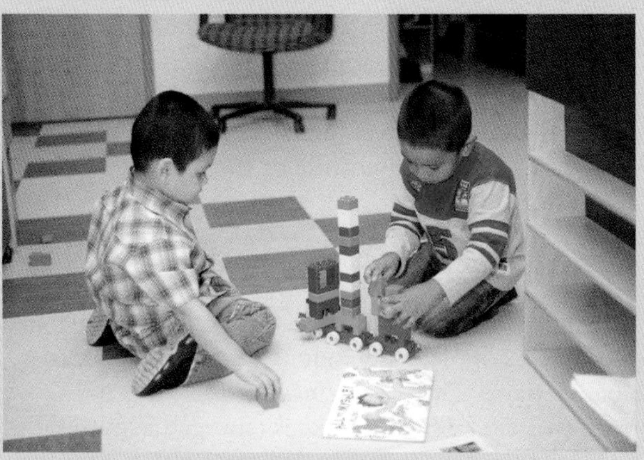

Figure 36.3 Boys 'systemising'

children, but are these expectations responsible for creating differences in the children or do adults react to differences that are already present? The 'Baby X' experiments tried to answer this question.

Key Study 36.1

The 'Baby X' experiments

- A series of studies, starting in the 1970s and collectively known as the 'Baby X' experiments, set out to answer the question regarding the direction of the influence between children's sex and the way they're typically treated by parents and other adults.
- One example is the study conducted by Condry and Condry (1976). A sample of over 200 adults, both men and women, were shown a videotape of a 9-month-old baby who was introduced to some as a boy ('David') and to others as a girl ('Dana'). Both in appearance and dress the baby was neither markedly masculine nor feminine. The baby was shown responding to various toys, such as a teddy and a doll, and to such stimuli as a jack-in-the-box and a sudden loud buzzer; for each of these the adults were asked to describe the emotion the baby displayed.
- The results clearly showed the influence of the baby's presumed gender. For example, when 'David' reacted to the jack-in-the-box by crying, most of the adults labelled this as *anger*; when 'Dana' showed exactly the same behaviour, it was identified as *fear*.
- Condry and Condry concluded that differences between male and female infants appear to be in the eye of the beholder.
- Smith and Lloyd (1978) dressed babies in unisex snowsuits and gave them names that were sometimes in line with their true gender, and sometimes not. When adults played with them, they treated the babies according to the gender they *believed* them to be. This indicates that a person's (perceived) biological make-up becomes part of his/her social environment through others' reactions to them.

However, not all such studies have obtained clear-cut results. For example, when adults were asked to rate the baby's personality characteristics (how friendly, cooperative etc.), few differences emerged according to gender labelling: the baby's *real* characteristics proved more important in determining how the child was perceived. Also, children asked to interact with a Baby X are more strongly influenced by beliefs about its gender than adults are (Stern and Karraker, 1989). According to Schaffer (2004):

> *... the gender-labelling effect is not as strong as originally thought. Whether a child is considered to be male or female is only one of several influences on the way others react. It is strongest when little other information is available about the child such as his or her real characteristics or when that information is ambiguous. However, when gender-label effects are found, they are almost invariably in keeping with cultural stereotypes of the sexes and may well therefore play a part in children's gender development.*

According to Money and Ehrhardt (1972), 'anatomy is destiny': how an infant is labelled sexually determines how it's raised or socialised. In turn, this determines the child's gender identity, and from this follow its gender role, gender-role identity, and sexual orientation. Psychologically, sexuality is *undifferentiated* at birth: it becomes differentiated as masculine or feminine in the course of the various experiences of growing up.

Much of the evidence for biosocial theory comes from studies of *intersex* individuals. These individuals represent a *natural experiment*: their gender of rearing is 'out-of-synch' with their chromosomal/hormonal/anatomical status, which makes it possible to assess the relative influence of environmental and biological factors on gender identity.

Money and Ehrhardt (1972) report their findings from CAH individuals, who were initially raised as boys. When the mistake was discovered, their genitals were surgically corrected; they were reassigned and raised as girls and showed a strong preference for the female role. Money and Ehrhardt also studied ten people with CAIS. They showed a strong preference for the female role, which also supports the view that gender of rearing is more important that biological sex.

Money and Ehrhardt claim that it's possible to change the gender of rearing without any undue psychological harm being done, provided this occurs within a 'critical' or 'sensitive' period of about 2 and a half to 3 years. After this, reassignment to the opposite gender can cause extreme psychological disturbance.

An evaluation of biosocial theory

- In addition to the study of intersex individuals, there are a few cases of XY infants with normally functioning testes who've been assigned and raised as girls, again with surgical feminisation. This can occur, for example, when the infant is born with a severely underdeveloped penis – or no penis at all (Hines, 2004b).

Case Study 36.3

The case of the penectomised twin (Money and Ehrhardt, 1972)

In 1966, at the age of 8 months, while undergoing a routine circumcision, Bruce Reimer's penis was accidentally burnt off (*penectomised*). After consulting with Money, his parents decided it was in Bruce's best interests to raise him as a girl (Brenda).

At 22 months, Brenda was surgically castrated (orchiectomy), he was given oestrogen injections, and a vaginal canal was constructed. He was subsequently raised as Joan.

At age 4, Joan preferred dresses to trousers, took pride in her long hair, and was cleaner than her twin brother, Brian. At age 9, although Joan had been the dominant twin since birth, she expressed this by being a 'fussy little mother' to Brian.

In *Man and Woman, Girl and Boy*, Money and Ehrhardt (1972) referred to Joan's 'tomboyish traits' in passing, focusing on the ways she conformed to female gender-role stereotypes. No mention was made of the rejection and teasing she'd encountered in school. Significantly, when she reached her teens she was an unhappy adolescent, with few friends, uncertain about her gender identity, and maintaining that boys 'had a better life'.

Aged 12, Joan (reluctantly) began taking oestrogen, and soon breast development and fat around her hips and waist began to appear. But she resisted any further (vaginal) surgery. By 14, the female hormones were now competing with her male hormonal system. She decided to stop living as a girl, changed her name (back to) John, and underwent sex reassignment surgery just before his sixteenth birthday. A rudimentary penis was constructed, but this neither resembled nor performed like the real thing. His popularity with girls caused him terrible distress and unhappiness, and at 18 he tried to commit suicide – on two separate occasions.

At 21, he had a second operation on his penis, which produced a significant improvement. Two years later, he met and fell in love with a single mother of three children – they married in 1990 (Colapinto, 2000). Colapinto met him in 1997 (he was then 31 and renamed David Reimer).

> The strongest impression I was left with was of John's intense, unequivocal masculinity. His gestures, walk, attitudes, vocabulary – none of them betrayed the least hint that he had been raised as a girl ... when conversation turns to his childhood ... his voice ... takes on a tone of aggrievement and anger, and he tends to drop the pronoun 'I' from his speech, replacing it with the distancing 'you' – almost as if he were speaking about someone else altogether. Which, in a sense, he is.

Tragically, he committed suicide in 2004.

Figure 36.4 David Reimer in 2000

- There are also a few cases where male infants have suffered accidental penile destruction (usually during surgery/circumcision) and have been reassigned as females. The most famous and well-documented case involves the twin boy whose penis was destroyed during circumcision. This has caused great controversy, partly because of Money's insistence that, despite blatant – and ultimately tragic – evidence to the contrary, that the findings support the view that gender identity (and gender role) is *learned*. This is described in Case Study 36.3
- Based on a re-examination of David Reimer's case, Diamond and Sigmundson (1997) challenged two basic assumptions ('postulates') of Money and Ehrhardt's biosocial theory, namely:
  - individuals are psychosexually neutral at birth
  - healthy psychosexual development is intimately related to the appearance of the genitals.
- They argue that cases of infant sex reassignment need to be reviewed after puberty: five- and ten-year post-sex reassignment follow-ups just aren't sufficient. No support exists for either of Money and Ehrhardt's postulates.
- In another case of a boy whose penis was destroyed (at 2 months), he was reassigned as a girl at 7 months, and now identifies as a bisexual woman; she shows no signs of gender dysphoria (Bradley *et al.*, 1998). It's difficult to account for the difference between the outcomes of this case and David Reimer's, but this second case is clearly consistent with biosocial theory.

- Just because some people appear to be flexible in their psychosexual development, doesn't in itself disprove that 'built-in' biases still have to be overcome (Diamond, 1978). Intersex individuals are, by definition, an *atypical* sample; this is the opposite side of the coin to the advantage that they allow the influence of environmental and biological factors to be separated. There's no evidence that people *in general* are as flexible in their psychosexual development. The first of Money and Ehrhardt's postulates was based on studies of intersex individuals (Diamond and Sigmundson, 1997).

Evolutionary approaches

Differential parental investment and sexual selection

Differential parental investment refers to the fact that males and females differ in the amount of resources they invest in offspring (Trivers, 1972). Eggs are generally more costly to produce than sperm, and in mammals this is compounded by a lengthy period of gestation, requiring a large amniotic sac which takes priority over the mother's own nutritional intake for several months. After birth, the female nurses the new-born, again sacrificing her own nutritional intake to feed her offspring. Human young need to be fed and cared for even after they're weaned. So, the minimum parental investment for female mammals is considerable.

Males can father young at much less investment: all it takes is one act of sexual intercourse. Kenrick *et al.* (2004) cite the example of the Xavante hunter-gatherer people: some Xavanate men had many offspring and others had few. Only one of 195 women was childless at age 20, but 6 per cent of men were still childless at age 40. One man fathered 23 children, whereas for a woman the highest number of children was 8. This pattern holds for most species.

This, in turn, is related to *sexual selection* (see Chapter 28). Because females invest more in any given offspring, a bad choice of mate would prove more costly for a female than for a male; thus, females, compared to males, tend to be more selective. However, human males, compared with other mammalian species, invest quite heavily in their offspring and exercise greater discrimination in mating.

Male parental investment

Without paternal investment, human offspring have lower survival rates, and sex differences tend to be smaller when males invest more in their offspring (Geary, 1998). Accordingly, men and women are relatively similar in size and decoration, in contrast to peacocks and peahens.

However, because men and women still contribute fundamentally different resources to produce offspring, the characteristics they desire in mates are also different. Women *directly* invest their bodily resources; their reproductive potential peaks in the mid-20s and ends with the menopause (Dunson *et al.*, 2002). Consistent with this, men's judgements of female attractiveness have been linked to indicators of youth and physical health (see Chapter 28). Men invest *indirect* resources (such as food, money, and protection) that don't necessarily diminish as they get older. So, women would be expected to value men's ability to provide those resources more than their youth.

Environmental influences on behaviour

According to Kenrick *et al.* (2004):

> *... an evolutionary perspective doesn't assume that human behaviour is based in rigid reflexes and closed instincts, but it does assume domain-specific biases relative to what is learned and how information is connected ...*

Research on humans and other animals has revealed different learning biases adapted to recurrent problems faced by the animals' ancestors.

For example, mothering is particularly sensitive to environmental constraints. Contrary to the belief that females are infinitely warm and nurturing, Hrdy (1999) argues that mothers are strategic actors that respond to environmental conditions in ways that enhance the chances of their own survival, as well as that of their offspring. This behaviour can appear ruthless at times. We all know that mothers will kill attackers to protect their offspring, but in rare circumstances, they might desert offspring to protect limited resources. Hrdy describes the South American Ache foragers, in which one mother's new-born was left behind because its father had died during the pregnancy and the mother's new husband wouldn't provide for the child. Also, when a close birth interval between two children threatened the older child's milk supply, the new-born was killed.

Infanticide has been documented on all continents. For example, in Denmark, all cases of female–female murder between 1933 and 1961 were infanticide (Daly and Wilson, 1988a, 1988b). These examples illustrate very real trade-offs that mothers must make between different offspring under particular environmental conditions.

Freud's psychoanalytic theory

Ask Yourself

- From what you know of Freud's theory of psychosexual development, try to outline his account of gender development (see Chapter 35).

Social learning theory (SLT)

> **Ask Yourself**
>
> - How do you think SLT tries to explain gender development? (See Chapter 35.)

According to Durkin (1995), early formulations of *social learning theory* (SLT) claimed that socialising agents, such as parents, teachers, peers, and the media, convey repetitive messages about the importance of gender role-appropriate behaviour.

The child is *positively reinforced* for behaving in gender-appropriate ways and *punished* for behaving in gender-inappropriate ways (based on the principles of *operant conditioning*). This is one means by which children *learn* their gender roles. But these socialising agents also *model* examples of appropriate and inappropriate behaviour and the consequences of conforming or not conforming with gender norms. Through *observational learning,* the child acquires knowledge regarding gender roles without actually 'doing' anything: the child sees *others* (the models) being reinforced or punished. Indeed, according to Perry and Bussey (1984), gender-role stereotypes are acquired mainly through observational learning.

The influence of parents

In one of the earliest versions of SLT, Bandura and Walters (1963) drew on examples of gender-role learning to illustrate that their theory could account for social learning in general. They pointed out that parents in many different cultures present their offspring with direct example (modelling) and instruction in appropriate gender-role behaviours; they also provide their children with toys and play materials that are stereotypically male or female.

So, one reason girls and boys learn to behave differently is that they're *treated differently* by their parents and others. As the 'Baby X' experiments show (see Key Study 36.1), when informed of a child's biological sex, parents and other adults often react to it according to their gender-role expectations. Thus, girls and boys are given different toys, have their rooms decorated differently, and are even spoken to in different terms (Rubin *et al.,* 1974). Boys tend to be positively reinforced more for behaviours reflecting independence, self-reliance, and emotional control, while girls are more likely to be reinforced for dependence, nurturance, empathy, and emotional expression (Block, 1979).

Fathers have been found to reinforce these sex-typed behaviours more than mothers do (Kerig *et al.,* 1993), especially in their sons (Siegal, 1987); in other words, fathers treat their children in a more *gendered* way (Maccoby, 1990). Typically, fathers interact in a more instrumental and achievement-oriented way, and give more attention to their sons; mothers attend equally to their sons and daughters (Quiery, 1998).

However, Karraker *et al.* (1995) found that this strong sex typing of infants at birth has declined, and that there were no differences between mothers and fathers in this respect.

Figure 36.5 Playing with dolls and displaying nurturant behaviour, and playing with guns and displaying assertive, even aggressive, behaviour, conform to female and male gender-role expectations/stereotypes, respectively. According to social learning theory, children receive parental reinforcement for displaying such gender-appropriate behaviours

An evaluation of SLT in relation to parental influence

Findings supporting SLT

- Sears *et al.* (1957) found that parents allowed sons to be more aggressive in their relationships with other children, and towards themselves, than daughters. For some mothers, 'being a boy' meant being aggressive, and boys were often encouraged to fight back. Although parents believe they respond in the same way to aggressive acts committed by sons and daughters, they actually intervene much more frequently and quickly when girls behave aggressively (Huston, 1983).
- Boys were more likely to imitate aggressive male models than were girls (Bandura *et al.*, 1961, 1963). Children are also more likely to imitate a same-gender model than an opposite-gender model, even if the behaviour is 'gender-inappropriate'.
- Parents tend to encourage their same-gender children to join them in traditionally gender-appropriate activities, such as cooking and shopping for mothers and daughters, and car washing and fishing for fathers and sons (Bandura and Walters, 1963; Huston, 1983; Lytton and Romney, 1991). Fathers begin to make themselves more available to their sons during the second year by talking to them more than to daughters (Lamb, 1977); by middle childhood, they tend to interact more with their sons than their daughters (Sears, 1965).
- Alongside this greater availability of different parental models, the child begins to attend selectively to models, taking into account both their gender and the gender-appropriateness of the model's behaviour (Bandura, 1977b, 1986). There's research evidence to support *both* claims (e.g. Bussey and Bandura, 1984).
- Further supporting evidence comes from studies of media portrayals of males and females (see Critical Discussion 36.1 below).

Findings not supporting SLT

- According to Maccoby and Jacklin (1974), there are no consistent differences in the extent to which boys and girls are reinforced for aggressiveness or autonomy. In fact, there appears to be remarkable *uniformity* in how the genders are socialised. This view is supported by Lytton and Romney (1991), who found very few gender differences in terms of parental warmth, overall amount of interaction, encouragement of achievement or dependency, restrictiveness and discipline, or clarity of communication. These findings are surprising, because most Psychologists would agree on the importance of parents as the major agents of socialisation. But perhaps the focus on reinforcement is misleading, since the main social learning mechanism might be modelling (Durkin, 1995).
- Although Bandura *et al.*'s research is often cited, the evidence concerning imitation and modelling is actually inconclusive, and some studies have failed to find that children are more likely to imitate same-gender than opposite-gender models. Barkley *et al.* (1977) reviewed 81 studies testing the prediction that children will imitate same-gender models; only 18 supported the prediction. Indeed, children have been shown to prefer imitating *behaviour* that's appropriate to their own gender *regardless* of the model's gender (Maccoby and Jacklin, 1974; Masters *et al.*, 1979).
- While modelling plays an important part in children's socialisation, there's no consistent preference for the same-gender parent's behaviour (Hetherington, 1967). Instead, children prefer to imitate the behaviour of those with whom they have most contact (usually the mother). Also, there's no significant correlation between the extent to which parents engage in sex-typed behaviours and the strength of sex typing in their children (Smith and Daglish, 1977). However, whether fathers adopt either traditional (sex-typed) or egalitarian attitudes has been found to correlate with 4-year-olds' perceptions of gender roles (Quiery, 1998).

Cognitive developmental theory

SLT implicitly assumes that the child already knows which gender s/he is, and proceeds accordingly to learn the appropriate role (Durkin, 1995). But where does that knowledge come from in the first place? According to *cognitive developmental theory* (CDT; Kohlberg, 1966; Kohlberg and Ullian, 1974), it arises in the same way as all knowledge, namely, from the child's *active construction* of an understanding of the world through interaction with it. This view of the child as 'discovering' the world through its exploration of it is a basic principle of Piaget's (e.g. 1950) *theory of cognitive development* on which Kohlberg's account was based (see Chapter 34).

Children's discovery that they're male or female *causes* them to identify with members of their own gender (*not* the other way round, as SLT and psychoanalytic theories suggest). While rewards and punishments influence children's choices of toys and activities, these don't mechanically strengthen stimulus-response connections, but provide children with *information* about when they're behaving in ways that other people deem appropriate (Bandura, 1977a).

According to Kohlberg, young children acquire an understanding of the concepts 'male' and 'female' in three stages (see Box 36.2).

Critical Discussion 36.1

The influence of the media on gender development

A large body of evidence suggests that gender-role stereotypes are portrayed by the media, as well as by parents and teachers (Wober *et al.*, 1987). In US TV programmes, males outnumber females by two or three to one on almost every kind of programme; in made-for-children programmes, it's more like five to one (Huston and Wright, 1997). Males are shown in more dominant roles with higher occupational status, while women are often presented in a narrow range of traditional feminine occupations, such as housewife, secretary, and nurse, or in a more subordinate role (Durkin, 1985, 1986).

In both commercials and regular programmes, men are shown solving problems and being more active, aggressive, powerful, and independent, whereas women are usually portrayed as submissive, passive, attractive, sensual, nurturing, emotional, and less able to deal with difficult situations (Golombok and Fivush, 1994; Huston and Wright, 1998). Bee (2000) cites research showing that commercials for boys' and girls' toys are produced differently: those for boys are fast, sharp, and loud ('action-packed'), while girls' are gradual, soft, and fuzzy. Even 6-year-olds notice these differences in style.

Children categorised as 'heavy' viewers of television hold stronger stereotyped beliefs than 'lighter' viewers (Gunter, 1986; Leaper and Friedman, 2007). This isn't too surprising perhaps, given that before starting school (at age 6), the average American child has already been exposed to thousands of hours of TV; by 18, the average child has spent more time in front of the TV than in a classroom (Huston *et al.*, 1990).

Other media, such as children's books, also perpetuate gender bias and stereotypes. Males still tend to be more common in titles and pictures, characters are still typically portrayed in terms of gender-stereotyped personality traits and activities (even in so-called 'non-sexist' books), and sexist language (such as the generic use of 'he') is common (Leaper and Friedman, 2008).

However, the fact that 'heavy' TV watchers hold stronger stereotyped beliefs doesn't, of course, mean that TV is responsible. These data are *correlational*: it's possible that highly sex-typed children like to watch lots of TV because it confirms their own limited world view. What's more, the correlations are generally weak at best, but they're often minimal or non-existent; one study actually found that 'heavy' viewers scored *lower* on a test of gender stereotype acceptance (Durkin, 1995). Durkin also cites studies showing that children sometimes change their stereotypes as a result of exposure to counter-stereotyped TV content.

The view that TV can impact upon a passively receptive child audience with messages about gender-role stereotyping, and mould young children's conceptions of gender, is over-simplistic (Gunter and McAleer, 1997). Gunter and McAleer maintain that children respond selectively to particular characters and events, and their perceptions, memories, and understanding of what they've seen may often be mediated by the dispositions they bring with them to the viewing situation.

Once children acquire gender constancy, they come to value the behaviours and attitudes associated with their gender. Only at this point do they identify with the adult figures who possess the qualities they see as being most central to their concepts of themselves as male or female (Perry and Bussey, 1979).

An evaluation of CDT

- Evidence suggests that the concepts of gender identity, stability and constancy occur in that order across many cultures (Munroe *et al.*, 1984). It's somewhat more advanced in children's understanding of their *own* as opposed to other people's gender (Leonard and Archer, 1989), presumably because parents and others draw a child's attention more to its own gender-specific characteristics than to others' (Schaffer, 1996a).
- Slaby and Frey (1975) divided 2- to 5-year-olds into 'high' and 'low' gender constancy. The children were then shown a silent film of adults simultaneously performing a series of simple activities. The screen was 'split', with males appearing on one side and females on the other. Children rated as high on gender constancy showed a marked same-sex bias, as measured by the amount of visual attention they gave to each side of the screen. (While this reached statistical significance in the case of boys, it didn't with the girls.) This supports Kohlberg's claim that gender constancy is a *cause* of the imitation of same-gender models, rather than an effect.
- Similarly, Ruble *et al.* (1981) found that high gender constancy preschoolers showed greater responsiveness to the implicit messages of television toy commercials compared with low constancy children. This affected both their tendency to play with the toys and their judgements as to which gender they were appropriate for.

Box 36.2 Stages in the development of gender identity

Stage 1 (Gender-labelling or basic gender identity): This occurs somewhere between 1 and a half and 3 years (Ruble, 1984) and refers to the child's recognition that it's male or female. According to Kohlberg, knowing one's gender is an achievement that allows us to understand and categorise the world. But this knowledge is fragile, with 'man', 'woman', 'boy' and 'girl' being used as little more than labels, equivalent to a personal name. Children sometimes choose the incorrect label and don't yet realise that boys invariably become men and girls always become women (Slaby and Frey, 1975).

Stage 2 (Gender stability): By age 3 to 5 years, most children recognise that people retain their genders for a lifetime. For example, if asked 'When you were a baby, were you a little boy or a little girl?' or 'Will you be a mummy or a daddy when you grow up?, children from age 4 onwards (but not before) can answer correctly (Slaby and Frey, 1975). But children still rely on superficial signs (such as the length of a person's hair) to determine their gender (Marcus and Overton, 1978). So, if someone is superficially transformed (for example, a woman has her long hair cut very short, or a man puts on women's clothes), children of this age are likely to infer that the person has changed gender (Emmerlich *et al.*, 1977). McConaghy (1979) found that if a doll was dressed in transparent clothing, so that its male or female genitals were visible, children of this age would judge its gender by its clothes (*not* its genitals).

Stage 3 (Gender constancy or consistency): At around age 6 to 7 years, children realise that gender is *immutable* (i.e. permanent): even if a woman has her head shaved, her gender remains female. Gender constancy represents a kind of *conservation* and, significantly, appears shortly after the child has mastered the conservation of quantity (Marcus and Overton, 1978; see Chapter 34).So, we can only conclude that gender understanding is complete when the child appreciates that gender is constant over time *and* situations.

Figure 36.6 Children of 4 to 5 years might be confused about this person's gender

- Several studies have found evidence for *self-socialisation* (Ruble, 1987; Slaby and Frey, 1975; Stangor and Ruble, 1987). Children actively construct their gender-role knowledge through purposeful monitoring of the social environment (Whyte, 1998).

Ask Yourself

- According to CDT, what is the relationship between gender constancy and the child's gender-appropriate behaviour?

- A major problem for CDT is that it predicts there should be little or no gender-specific behaviour before the child has acquired gender constancy. But even in infancy, both boys and girls show a marked preference for stereotypical male and female toys (Huston, 1983).As far as CDT is concerned, infants might have developed a sense of gender identity, but they're some years away from achieving gender stability and constancy (Fagot, 1985).
- *Gender-schematic processing theory* (GSPT) addresses the possibility that gender identity *alone* can provide children with sufficient motivation to assume sex-typed behaviour patterns (e.g. Bem, 1985; Martin, 1991). Like SLT, this approach suggests that children learn 'appropriate' patterns of behaviour by observation. However, consistent with CDT, children's active cognitive processing of information also contributes to their sex typing.

Cultural relativism

This really represents the most direct challenge to the biological approach. If gender differences reflect biological differences, then we'd expect to find the same differences occurring in different cultures. Any

Box 36.3 Are there more than two genders?

- Among the Sakalavas in Madagascar, boys who are thought to be pretty are raised as girls and readily adopt the female gender role. Similarly, the Alentian Islanders in Alaska raise handsome boys as girls; their beards are plucked and they're later married to rich men. They too seem to adapt quite readily to their assigned gender role.
- Studies of certain Native American peoples reveal the possibility of more than two basic gender roles. For example, the *berdache*, a biological male of the Crow tribe, simply chooses not to follow the ideal role of warrior. Instead, he might become the 'wife' of a warrior, but he's never scorned or ridiculed by his fellow Crows. (Little Horse in the film *Little Big Man*, starring Dustin Hoffman, was a berdache).
- Some *hijras* in India are physical hermaphrodites, others have male genitalia, and still others were born with male genitalia but opted to undergo castration. *Hijras* adopt female names and wear women's clothing – but they don't try to pass as women. Their heavy makeup, long, unbound hair, and sexualized gestures, set them apart from women in general (Nanda, 1990, in Maracek *et al.*, 2004).
- In Thailand, *kathoeys* have male genitalia but dress in women's clothing. But a *kathoey* isn't a man who wishes to be (or become) a woman, nor do they believe they have a 'woman's mind' trapped inside the 'wrong body' (in the way that transsexuals in Western countries describe themselves). Rather, they take some pride in their male genitals and they don't wish to pass as women; they act in dramatic, loud, brash ways that violate the norms of femininity in Thai culture.
- The Mohave Indians recognised *four* distinct gender roles : (i) traditional male; (ii) traditional female; (iii) *alyha*; and (iv) *hwame*. The *alyha* was the male who chose to live as a woman (mimicking menstruation by cutting his upper thigh and undergoing a ritualistic pregnancy); the *hwame* was a female who chose to become a man.

differences that exist between cultures with regard to gender roles (*cultural relativism*) support the view that gender role is culturally determined.

Are there cultural universals?

While most cultures distinguish between 'men's' and 'women's' work and while biological factors undoubtedly play some part in the sexual division of labour (see Box 36.3), the content of this work varies enormously between cultures. As Hargreaves (1986) observes, in some cultures:

> *... men weave and women make pots, whereas in others these roles are reversed; in some parts of the world women are the major agricultural producers, and in others they are prohibited from agricultural activity.*

Western culture has no formally recognised and accepted equivalent of the berdache. However, in recent times, as the economic lives of men and women have become more similar (see Chapter 38), we have at least informally developed some acceptance of berdache-like alternatives. For example, the concept of *androgyny* (Bem, 1974) refers to people who've developed both the 'masculine' and 'feminine' sides of themselves more fully than most (see Gross, 2008; Gross and Rolls, 2009). Similarly, the concept of sexual orientation implies an awareness that relationships aren't simply an expression of a single inborn norm (Price and Crapo, 1999).

CONCLUSIONS

While every known culture distinguishes between male and female, the evidence for the truth of sex stereotypes is inconclusive. Although anatomical sex is universal, *gender*, which refers to all the duties, rights and behaviours a culture considers appropriate for males and females, is a *social invention*. It's gender that gives us a sense of personal identity as male or female (Wade and Tavris, 1994). An even stronger argument for the *social construction* of gender comes from studies of societies where there are more than two genders.

All the perspectives discussed in this chapter have contributed to our understanding of that process, and they should be seen as *complementary* explanations (Whyte, 1998). According to Kenrick *et al.* (2004), that includes evolutionary explanations:

> *... The human brain was designed by the same natural forces that shaped other natural phenomena, but it is a brain designed to think, learn, and to construct cultures. To isolate or ignore any of these facets limits our understanding of human behaviour ...*

The Psychology of gender is perhaps the best area of research for integrating these different approaches and perspectives.

Chapter Summary

- Feminist Psychologists distinguish between **sex/sexual identity** and **gender/gender identity**.
- There's little empirical support for **actual gender differences** in terms of either aggression or verbal, spatial, or mathematical abilities.
- Biologically, sex is **multi-dimensional**. While the different categories are usually highly correlated with each other, in **pseudohermaphrodites (intersex** individuals) prenatal and postnatal disorders produce an **inconsistency** between them.
- Major types of pseudohermaphroditism include **complete androgen insensitivity syndrome (CAIS)** (or **testicular feminising syndrome**), **congenital adrenal hyperplasia (CAH)** (or **adrenogenital syndrome/AGS**), **DHT-deficient males** (or **5-alpha-reductase deficiency**), and **chromosome abnormalities**.
- According to the **biological approach**, males and females are biologically programmed for certain activities compatible with gender roles. The evidence for gender differences in **hemispheric specialisation** is inconclusive.
- The **empathising–systemising** (E-S) **theory** maintains that female brains are hardwired for **empathy** (E-type) while male brains are hardwired for **constructing systems** (S-type). These differences are reflected in male/female differences from birth, and in adult skills and occupations.
- Although **sexual differentiation** begins with the sex chromosomes (XX or XY), their main function is to direct the gonads to develop as either ovaries (female) or testes (male). After that, gonadal hormones – especially **androgens** from the testes – provide the major biological influences.
- Human behaviour is subject to both **prenatal** (biological) and **postnatal** (social and other) influences; this makes the natural experiments represented by cases of intersex individuals especially important.
- Money and Ehrhardt's **biosocial theory**, based on the study of intersex individuals, claims that it's the **interaction** between biological and social factors that determines a child's gender development.
- Social factors include adults' responses to the child, which are influenced by their gender stereotypes (as illustrated by the 'Baby X' experiments).
- Psychologically, gender identity is **undifferentiated** at birth; it becomes differentiated as masculine or feminine according to how the child is socialised during its first 2 and a half to 3 years. Gender reassignment after this **critical/sensitive period** can cause extreme psychological disturbance.
- From an **evolutionary** perspective, **differential parental investment** and **sexual selection** are two general principles used to explain the correlation between (i) sex differences in morphology and behaviour, and (ii) sex differences in mating strategies.
- Males and females differ in both the **amount** and **nature** of the resources they invest in offspring; this explains the different characteristics they desire in mates.
- According to **social learning theory (SLT)**, girls and boys learn to behave differently through being **treated differently** by parents and others. SLT also stresses the role of **observational learning** and **reinforcement** for imitating sex-appropriate behaviours.
- Evidence regarding the importance for imitation of the **sex-appropriateness** of a model's behaviour and the model's gender is inconclusive.
- A large body of evidence suggests that **gender-role stereotypes** are portrayed by the **media**, although much of this is **correlational**, and children aren't passive recipients of media content but respond selectively to what they see.
- According to the **cognitive–developmental approach**, children's discovery that they're male or female causes them to identify with and imitate same-sex models. Three stages in the development of gender identity are **gender-labelling/basic gender identity**, **gender stability**, and **gender constancy/consistency**.
- **Gender-schematic processing theory (GSPT)** maintains that gender identity **alone** can provide a child with sufficient motivation to assume sex-typed behaviour.
- According to **cultural relativism**, any differences in gender roles between cultures are likely to be **culturally determined**.
- The existence of more than two genders in some Native American and other non-Western peoples, strongly suggests that gender is **socially constructed**.

Links with Other Topics/Chapters

Chapter 50 ⟶ Feminist Psychology and (some versions of Evolutionary Psychology) fall at the two extremes of the continuum of the nature–nurture debate

Chapter 46 ⟶ The question of male/female differences in aggression/violence is relevant to understanding common reactions to female murderers and perpetrators of other violent crimes

Chapter 47 ⟶ According to Denmark *et al.* (1988), ignoring studies that fail to produce non-significant sex differences represents a form of *sexism* or *gender bias*

Chapter 48 ⟶ In turn, these constitute ethical issues, because of their potential consequences for females

Chapter 30 ⟶ Females' more empathic brains are relevant to understanding gender differences in relation to prosocial behaviour

Chapter 16 ⟶ Baron-Cohen (2003a, 2003b) has found that, at birth, girls look longer at a face, and boys look longer at a suspended mechanical mobile

Chapter 40 ⟶ According to Baron-Cohen (2003a, 2003b), people with autism may have an extreme male brain

Chapter 50 ⟶ The observation that adults prefer to spend time with babies who respond to them in 'rewarding' ways, and 'demanding' babies tend to receive more attention than 'passive' babies, illustrates the concept of a *reactive gene–environment correlation*

Chapter 50 ⟶ Cultural relativism, and the related cultural determinism, represent one extreme end of the *nature–nurture continuum*

Recommended Reading

Eagley, A., Beall, A.E. & Sternberg, R.J. (eds) (2004) *The Psychology of Gender* (2nd edn).

Edley, N. & Wetherell, M. (1995) *Men in Perspective: Practice, Power and Identity.* Hemel Hempstead: Prentice-Hall/Harvester Wheatsheaf.

Gergen, M.M. & Davis, S.N. (1997) *Toward a New Psychology of Gender: A Reader.* New York: Routledge. Also relevant to Chapters 2, 43, 44, 45 and 47.

Gross, R. (2008) *Key Studies in Psychology* (5th edn). London: Hodder Education. Chapter 41.

Gross, R. (2012) *Key Studies in Psychology* (6th edn). London: Hodder Education. Chapter 7.

Trew, K. & Kremer, J. (eds) (1998) *Gender and Psychology.* London: Arnold.

Unger, C.K. (1979) *Female and Male: Psychological Perspectives.* New York: Harper & Row.

Useful Websites

www.garysturt.free-online.co.uk/gender.htm (OCR Education Module: Gender. By Gary Sturt, 1998)

www.tripdatabase.com/search?criterion=gender+development+theories (Trip database: large number of articles dealing with various aspects of gender/gender development)

CHAPTER 37

ADOLESCENCE

Normative and non-normative shifts

Puberty: the social and psychological meaning of biological changes

Theories of adolescence

INTRODUCTION and OVERVIEW

The word 'adolescence' comes from the Latin *adolescere* meaning 'to grow into maturity'. As well as being a time of enormous physiological change, adolescence is also marked by changes in behaviour, expectations, and relationships with both parents and peers. In Western, industrialised societies, there's generally no single initiation rite signalling the passage into adulthood, making the transition more difficult than it appears to be in more traditional, non-industrialised societies. Relationships with adults in general, and parents in particular, must be renegotiated in a way that allows the adolescent to achieve greater independence. This process is aided by changing relationships with peers.

Figure 37.1 1950s films such as *Rebel Without A Cause*, starring James Dean (left), have been seen as helping to create the concept of the 'rebellious teenager'

Historically, adolescence has been seen as a period of transition between childhood and adulthood. But writers today are more likely to describe it as one of *multiple transitions*, involving education, training, employment and unemployment, as well as transitions from one set of living circumstances to another (Coleman and Roker, 1998).

This change in perspective in many ways reflects changes in the adolescent experience compared with those of previous generations: it starts five years earlier, marriage takes place six to seven years later than it did, and cohabitation is rapidly increasing (Coleman and Hendry, 1990).

Coupled with these 'adulthood-postponing' changes, in recent years adolescents have enjoyed greater self-determination at steadily younger ages. Yet this greater freedom carries with it more risks and greater costs when errors of judgement are made. As Hendry (1999) says:

> *... 'dropping out' of school, being out of work, teenage pregnancy, sexually transmitted diseases, being homeless, drug addiction and suicide, are powerful examples of the price that some young people pay for their extended freedom ...*

NORMATIVE AND NON-NORMATIVE SHIFTS

Ask Yourself

- What kinds of transitions do adolescents in Western societies experience?
- Are these necessarily the same for all adolescents?

One way of categorising the various transitions involved in adolescence is in terms of *normative* and *non-normative shifts* (Hendry and Kloep, 1999; Kloep and Hendry, 1999).

- *Normative, maturational shifts* include the growth spurt (both sexes), menarche (first menstruation), first nocturnal emissions ('wet dreams'), voice breaking (boys), changes in sexual organs, beginning of sexual arousal, changed romantic relationships, gender-role identity, changed relationships with adults, increasing autonomy and responsibility.

- *Normative, society-dependent shifts* include the change from primary to secondary school, leaving school, getting started in an occupation, acquiring legal rights for voting, sex, purchasing alcohol, driving licence, military service, and cohabitation.
- *Non-normative shifts* include parental divorce, family bereavement, illness, natural disasters, war, incest, emigration, disruption of peer network, risk-taking behaviours, 'disadvantage' (because of gender, class, regional or ethnic discrimination), physical and/or mental handicap.

According to Kloep and Hendry (1999):

> *Although all adolescents have to cope with the psychosocial challenges associated with their maturing body, new relationships with parents and peers, with school and the transitions toward employment, a growing number encounter additional problems like family disruption, economic deprivation or social or cultural changes ...*

A normative shift may become non-normative, if, say, there are other circumstances that cause a normal developmental 'task' to become more difficult. An example would be the unusually early or late onset of puberty.

PUBERTY: THE SOCIAL AND PSYCHOLOGICAL MEANING OF BIOLOGICAL CHANGES

Puberty and body image

Adjusting to puberty is one of the most important adjustments that adolescents have to make (Coleman and Hendry, 1990). Even as a purely biological phenomenon, puberty is far from being a simple, straightforward process. While all adolescents experience the same bodily changes (and usually in the order shown in Figure 37.2), this *may* vary within individuals (*intraindividual asynchronies*; Alsaker, 1996). For example, for some girls menstruation may occur very early on in puberty, while for others it may occur after most other changes (e.g. growth spurt, breast development) have taken place.

Major changes in puberty

Physiologically, puberty begins when the seminal vesicles and prostate gland enlarge in the male, and the ovaries enlarge in the female. Both males and females experience the *adolescent growth spurt*. Male *secondary sex characteristics* include growth of pubic and then chest and facial hair, and sperm production; in females, breast size increases, pubic hair grows and menstruation begins.

According to Davies and Furnham (1986), the average adolescent isn't only sensitive to, but also critical of, his or her changing physical self. Because

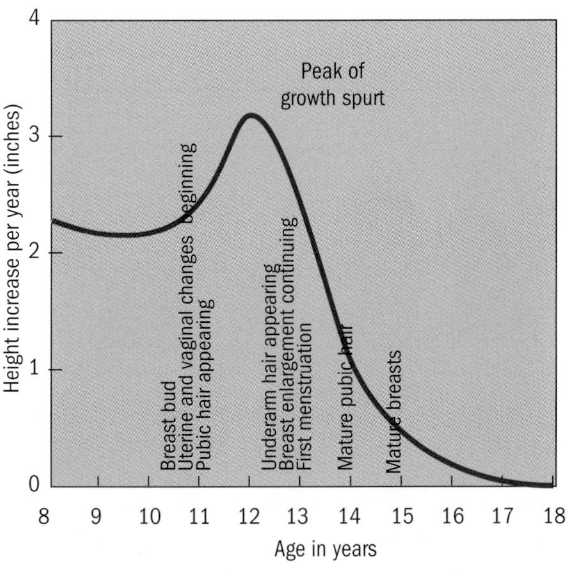

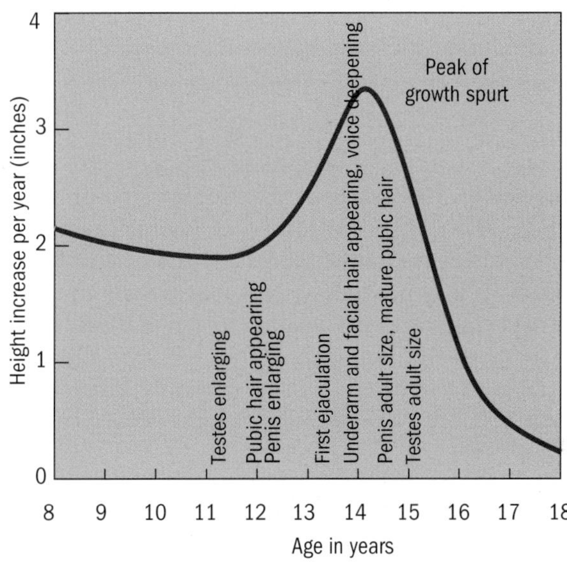

Figure 37.2 The development of secondary sex characteristics. The curved lines represent the average increase in height from 8 to 18 years of age. The characteristics shown may occur earlier or later in a person's development, but usually occur in the order shown. (Based on Tanner, 1978, and Tanner and Whitehouse, 1976. Reproduced with the permission of the copyright holders, Castlemead Publications.)

Box 37.1 Adolescents' brains

- While the plasticity of the infant's and young child's brain is widely accepted (see Chapter 4), this has traditionally been seen as stopping at puberty. However, several MRI studies, one longitudinal (which has followed up the same set of (almost) 400 youngsters from childhood to young adulthood: Giedd *et al.*, 1999; Gogtay *et al.*, 2009), others cross-sectional (e.g. Sowell *et al.* (2003), who compared 7- to 30-year-olds and 7- to 87-year-olds) suggest otherwise.
- Areas of the cortex that deal with more basic functions, such as sensory and motor processing, do indeed stabilise in early childhood. But the parietal and frontal lobes, which are specialised for visuospatial and 'executive functions' (e.g. planning and self-control), respectively, show a growth surge between the ages of 10 and 12. This sudden 'bulking up' is then followed by an equally dramatic *reduction* in size, which continues right through the teenage years and into the twenties ('*pruning*'). The grey matter density decreases (by about one per cent every year), indicating that the number of synaptic connections have become fewer. The pruning of connections in a mature brain strengthens those that remain.
- The connections that mature first are involved in basic sensory and motor areas, followed by regions involved in language and spatial orientation, and finally those involved in executive functions. Among the last to mature is the *dorsolateral prefrontal cortex* (DPFC) (at the very front of the frontal lobe), which is involved in impulse control, judgement and decision making. This area also controls and processes emotional information sent from the amygdala (Gogtay *et al.*, 2009).
- According to Sebastian *et al.* (2010), this 'developmental mismatch' between brain areas that process emotional and reward signals (such as the amygdala and ventral striatum) and those responsible for regulating these responses (e.g. parts of the PFC: see below) could interact with ongoing social cognitive development to account for social behaviours specific to adolescence; in particular, sensitivity to rejection (see Chapter 33).
- Another socially important, late-developing region is the *dorsomedial prefrontal cortex* (MPFC); this plays an important role in social emotions such as guilt and embarrassment, where other people (especially peers) are implicated. The MPFC is known to activate when adults think about themselves and other people (Burnett *et al.*, 2009).
- This lack of impulse control may produce risk-taking behaviours, such as drug and alcohol abuse, smoking and unprotected sex. According to Gosline (2009), imaging studies suggest that the motivation and reward circuitry in teen brains makes them almost hardwired for addiction (see Chapter 8).
- The data described above suggest that the neural basis of *theory of mind* (ToM) continues to develop well past early childhood (Blakemore, 2007; Zukerman and Purcell, 2011; see Chapter 40).

of gender and sexual development, young people are inevitably confronted, perhaps for the first time, by cultural standards of beauty in evaluating their own body images (via the media and the reactions of others). This may produce a *non-normative shift* in the form of dieting practices, leading to eating disorders (see Chapter 44). Young people may be especially vulnerable to teasing and exclusion if they're perceived by their peers as over- or under-weight (Kloep and Hendry, 1999).

Figure 37.3 The need to not be different

Gender differences

Ask Yourself

- Do you consider puberty to be a more difficult transition for boys or girls in general?
- Why?

While puberty may be a normative, maturational shift, it may be a more difficult transition for girls than boys. This is because of the *subjective meaning* of bodily change, which mirrors the *sociocultural significance* of puberty. According to the *cultural ideal hypothesis* (CIH) (Simmons and Blyth, 1987), puberty will bring boys *closer* to their physical ideal (an increase in muscle distribution and lung capacity produces greater stamina, strength and athletic capacities), while girls move *further away* from theirs.

For girls, who begin puberty on average two years ahead of boys, it's normal to experience an increase in body fat and rapid weight gain, thus making their bodies less like the Western cultural ideal of the thin, sylph-like supermodel. In addition, they have to deal with menstruation, which is negatively associated with blood and physical discomfort (Crawford and Unger, 1995).

The importance of timing

If the CIH is valid, it follows that early maturing boys will be at an advantage relative to their 'on-time' and late-maturing peers (they'll be moving faster towards the male ideal). By the same token, early maturing girls will be at a disadvantage (they'll be moving faster away from the female ideal). As Bergevin *et al.* (2003) put it:

> *... girls who enter puberty early relative to other girls are typically far ahead of virtually all boys. Likewise, boys who enter puberty late are far behind most boys and behind almost all girls. These two sets of adolescents, early maturing girls and late-maturing boys, are those who are clearly most out of step with their peers ...*

Indeed, according to Alsaker (1996) pubertal timing is generally regarded as a *more* crucial aspect of pubertal development than pubertal maturation itself: it's not the *fact* of puberty that matters as much as *when* it occurs, and it matters mainly in relation to body image and self-esteem.

Ask Yourself

- A common finding is that early maturing girls and late-maturing boys suffer lower self-esteem. Why do you think this might be?

According to Wichstrom (1998), the CIH is sensitive to changes in time and context. For example, in Norway there may be less emphasis on stereotypical male stature compared with the USA and UK. Perhaps also the embarrassment and negative affect experienced by American girls when starting their periods and becoming sexually responsive is less prevalent among Norwegian girls, due to relatively greater openness about adolescent sexuality (Wichstrom, 1998).

Box 37.2 The falling age of puberty onset

- The average age at menarche has plummeted over the last 150 years in Western societies from around 17 to under 12–13 (Macleod, 2007). Biro *et al.* (2010) reported that some girls in the USA were developing breast as young as 7, and other studies have revealed the same trend in girls all over the world (Harris, 2012).
- The average age of menarche has fallen below 13 in the UK for the first time; it's now 12 years, 10 months, compared with 13 years, 6 months in 1969. One in six girls reaches puberty by age 8, compared with one in 100 a generation ago (Peek, 2000).
- A study (Herman-Giddens *et al.*, 2012) of over 4000 boys (aged 6 to 16) in 41 US states has found that boys are showing signs of puberty six months to two years earlier than previously believed. African-Americans begin to show signs about a year earlier than white and Hispanic boys (9 and 10, respectively).
- While weight gain in girls is linked to oestrogen production, it is less clear what triggers puberty in boys. Pubic hair and testicle size are two important measures.

Box 37.3 Why do early maturing girls and late-maturing boys feel less good about themselves?

- One popular explanation is the *deviancy hypothesis* (DH), according to which those who are 'off time' in physical maturation are socially deviant compared with peers of the same age and gender (Wichstrom, 1998). Since girls begin puberty on average two years before boys, early maturing girls are the first to enter this deviant position, followed by late-maturing boys.
- An alternative explanation is the *developmental readiness hypothesis* (DRH) (Simmons and Blyth, 1987). In the case of early or sudden puberty, too little time will have been spent on ego development during latency, with early maturing girls once more being most affected. (This explanation is similar to Coleman's *focal theory*: see text below.)
- As far as the CIH is concerned, the suggestion that the pubertal girl moves further away from the Western stereotyped female ideal may not be true. Both boys and girls move closer to their ideals, provided they don't put on excessive weight (Wichstrom, 1998).

Critical Discussion 37.1

Puberty in girls, fathers and evolution

Maturing early for a girl isn't simply a vague matter of 'lost childhood' – it can have serious health repercussions, including an increased likelihood that she'll experience depression and breast cancer, indulge in substance abuse or risky sexual behaviour, become pregnant as a teenager, or suffer body-image dissatisfaction (Macleod, 2007; see text below).

One puzzle is that girls reach puberty at widely differing ages within Western countries that enjoy similarly high standards of nutrition and health care. Even more puzzling is the finding that girls who grow up without their biological father tend to mature *earlier.*

How can we account for this?

According to Belsky *et al.*'s (1991) *psychosocial acceleration theory*, girls who experience a lot of family stress will mature faster. If she grows up in a socially harsh environment, and so cannot expect much support in later life, she'll be better off if she adopts an accelerated reproductive strategy, including early onset of puberty and menarche, early first pregnancy, and less stable pair-bonding (short-term relationships) with less parental investment in each of her children.

Several studies have subsequently found that family stress can accelerate menarche by around four to six months. Although girls don't start ovulating immediately after menarche, full fertility is achieved far quicker if they mature earlier (Macleod, 2007).

Ellis *et al.* (2003) conducted the first *prospective* study designed to see if father absence predicts early sexual behaviour *independently* of other social variables (e.g. socio-economic status, academic performance, early behaviour problems, and other family stressors). This was in fact two longitudinal studies, one American (girls were followed up from kindergarten to age 18), the other involving a New Zealand sample (infancy to 18). In both countries, girls with absent fathers from early childhood were twice as likely to be sexually active before 16 (and three times more likely to get pregnant in their teens) compared with father-present girls. In both samples, father absence constituted a unique and independent path to early sexual activity and adolescent pregnancy.

Quite independently of father presence/absence, the closer and more affectionate the father-daughter relationship, the later her sexual development occurred. A supportive relationship between parents delayed puberty still further. The opposite applied if there was marital friction.

Ellis and Belsky both claim that girls have an evolved ability to adapt to their social environment: they adopt different reproductive strategies depending on the circumstances they grow up in. As to the exact *mechanism* involved, one possibility is that it involves the stress hormone *cortisol*. However, Ellis believes some additional factors are involved, such as *pheromones*. A study of over 2000 US college students (Matchock and Susman, 2006) not only confirmed Ellis *et al.*'s findings, but also found that the presence of half- and step-brothers accelerated menarche; that is, while biological fathers send out inhibitory chemical signals to their daughters, those produced by unrelated (or less closely related) males have the reverse effect.

While early puberty may represent a form of adaptation to a particular growing up environment, this creates a mismatch with the social and emotional competence needed to cope with being sexually active and – more significantly – with parenthood. This may apply to adolescents *in general*. (See discussion of Erikson's theory in text below.) Our Palaeolithic ancestors probably started having children at 12 or 14 – but by that age they were also fully mature members of society (Gluckman and Hanson, 2006).

THEORIES OF ADOLESCENCE

Hall's theory: adolescence as storm and stress

This is probably the earliest formal theory of adolescence. Influenced by Darwin's evolutionary theory, Hall (1904) argued that each person's psychological development *recapitulates* (repeats/recaptures) both the biological and cultural evolution of the human species. He saw adolescence as a time of 'storm and stress' (or *Sturm und Drang*), which mirrors the volatile history of the human race over the last 2000 years.

Some evidence suggests that emotional reactions are more intense and volatile during adolescence compared with other periods of life, such as Csikszentmihalyi and Larson's (1984) study of

Figure 37.4 Pre-teens are growing up faster than ever before, and early maturing girls are most at risk of mental disorder and delinquency

75 Chicago-area high-school students; they commonly displayed extreme mood swings, from extreme happiness to deep sadness (and vice versa) in less than an hour.

However, more important indicators of storm and stress are (a) mental disorder, and (b) delinquent behaviour.

Studies of mental disorder

Several studies have found that *early maturing girls* score higher on measures of depressive feelings and sadness (e.g. Alsaker, 1992; Stattin and Magnusson, 1990), although this was true only when the measures were taken before or simultaneously with changing schools (Petersen *et al.*, 1991). They've also been reported to have more psychophysiological symptoms (e.g. Stattin and Magnusson, 1990), to display greater concerns about eating (e.g. Brooks-Gunn *et al.*, 1989), and to score higher on Offer's psychopathology scale (e.g. Brooks-Gunn and Warren, 1985).

The evidence regarding *early maturing boys* is much more mixed (Alsaker, 1996). While early maturation is usually found to be advantageous, it's also been found to be associated with more psychopathology (e.g. Petersen and Crockett, 1985), depressive tendencies, and anxiety (e.g. Alsaker, 1992).

In Western societies, while some adolescents may display affective disturbances or disorders, it's a relatively small minority who'll show clinical depression or report 'inner turmoil' (Compas *et al.*, 1995). Instead, the majority worry about everyday issues, such as school and examination performance,

Key Study 37.1

The 'Isle of Wight' study (Rutter *et al.*, 1976)

- This involved a large, representative sample of 14- to 15-year-olds (more than 2000), whose parents and teachers completed a behaviour questionnaire about them.
- More detailed data were obtained from two subsamples: (i) 200 randomly selected from the total population; (ii) 304 with extreme scores on the teacher/parent questionnaires (suggesting 'deviant' behaviour).
- Those in both subsamples were given questionnaires and tests, and interviewed by psychiatrists. The major findings regarding rates of psychiatric disorder among the adolescents, compared with a sample of 10-year-olds and the adolescents' parents, are shown in Table 37.1.

Table 37.1 Percentage of 10-year-olds, 14–15-year-olds, and the latter's parents, displaying psychiatric disorder

	10-YEAR-OLDS	14- TO 15-YEAR-OLDS	ADULTS (PARENTS)
MALES	12.7	13.2	7.6
FEMALES	10.9	12.5	11.9

- According to Rutter *et al.* (1976):
  - there's a rather modest peak in psychiatric disorders in adolescence
  - although severe clinical depression is rare, some degree of inner turmoil may characterise a sizeable minority of adolescents. While it's not a myth, neither should it be exaggerated
  - a substantial proportion of those adolescents with psychiatric problems had had them since childhood; also, when problems did first appear during adolescence, they were mainly associated with stressful situations (such as parents' marital discord):

... adolescent turmoil is fact, not fiction, but its psychiatric importance has probably been overestimated in the past ... (Rutter *et al.*, 1976)

finding work, family and social relationships, self-image, conflicts with authority, and the future generally (Gallagher *et al.*, 1992).

Studies of delinquent behaviour

Caspi *et al.* (1993) studied all the children born in Dunedin, New Zealand between April 1972 and March 1973, following them up every two years from ages 3 to 15. Compared with on-time (menarche 12.5–13.5 years) and late maturers (after 13.5), early maturing girls were more at risk for:

- *early delinquency* (breaking windows, getting drunk, making prank phone calls, stealing from other pupils at school)
- *familiarity with delinquent peers* (having friends or knowing others who engaged in these activities), and
- *delinquency* (shoplifting, car theft, smoking marijuana, using weapons).

However, the risk for early delinquency was greater only in mixed-sex schools, and (as with a sample of Swedish girls studied by Magnusson *et al.*, 1985) early maturers were likely to mix with older peers. As for boys, off-time maturation (early and late) has been shown to be related to alcohol consumption, with late maturers also being at risk for later alcohol problems (Anderson and Magnusson, 1990).

Erikson's theory: identity crisis

Erikson (1963) believed that it's human nature to pass through a genetically determined sequence of *psychosocial stages*, spanning the whole lifespan. Each stage involves a struggle between two conflicting personality outcomes, one of which is positive (or *adaptive*), while the other is negative (or *maladaptive*). Healthy development involves the adaptive outweighing the maladaptive.

The major challenge of adolescence is to establish a strong sense of *personal identity*. The dramatic onset of puberty (combined with more sophisticated intellectual abilities: see Chapter 34) makes adolescents particularly concerned with finding their own personal place in adult society.

In Western societies adolescence is a *moratorium*, an authorised delay of adulthood, which frees adolescents from most responsibilities and helps them make the difficult transition from childhood to adulthood. Although this is meant to make the transition easier, it can also have the opposite effect. Most of the societies studied by cultural anthropologists have important public ceremonies to mark the transition from childhood to adulthood. This is in stark contrast to Western, industrialised nations, which leave children to their own devices in finding their identity. Without a clearly defined procedure to follow, this process can be difficult – for both adolescents and their parents (see section on the generation gap below).

Figure 37.5 The Jewish bar mitzvah marks the 13-year-old boy's entry into manhood. But to the rest of society, he's still just a teenager

Does society create identity crisis?

Ask Yourself

- Can you think of any inconsistencies or contradictions that adolescents face between different aspects of their development?
- How do they perceive their social status?

As well as the perceived absence of 'rites of passage' in Western society, a problem for both adolescents and their parents is the related lack of consensus as to where adolescence begins and ends, and precisely what adolescent rights, privileges and responsibilities are. For example, the question 'When do I become an adult?' elicits different responses from a teacher, doctor, parent and police officer (Coleman, 1995).

The 'maturity gap' refers to the incongruity of achieving biological maturity at adolescence without simultaneously being awarded adult status (Curry, 1998). According to Hendry and Kloep (1999):

> *... young people, as they grow up, find themselves in the trap of having to respond more and more to society's demands in a 'responsible' adult way while being treated as immature and not capable of holding sound opinions on a wide range of social matters.*

One possible escape route from this trap is *risk-taking behaviour* (see below). As well as having to deal with the question 'Who am I?', the adolescent must also ask 'Who will I be?'. Erikson saw the creation of an adult personality as achieved mainly through choosing and developing a commitment to an occupation or role in life. The development of ego identity (a firm sense of who one is and what one stands for) is positive, and can carry people through difficult times.

When working with psychiatrically disturbed soldiers in the Second World War, Erikson coined the term *identity crisis* to describe the loss of ego (personal) identity. These war veterans sensed that 'their lives no longer hung together – and never would again' (Friedman 1999). Some years later, he extended the use of the term to include severely conflicted young people whose sense of confusion is due 'to a war within themselves'.

Role confusion

Failure to integrate perceptions of the self into a coherent whole results in *role confusion*, which, according to Erikson, can affect several areas of life:

- *Intimacy:* a fear of commitment to, or involvement in, close relationships, arises from a fear of losing one's own identity. This may result in stereotyped and formalised relationships, or isolation.
- *Time perspective:* inability to plan for the future or retain any sense of time, reflecting anxieties about change and becoming an adult.
- *Industry:* difficulty in channelling resources in a realistic way into work or study, both of which require commitment. As a defence, the adolescent may find it impossible to concentrate, or becomes frenetically engaged in a single activity to the exclusion of all others.
- *Negative identity:* engaging in abnormal or delinquent behaviour (such as drug taking, or even suicide). This extreme position, which sets such adolescents apart from the crowd, is preferable to the loneliness and isolation that come with failing to achieve a distinct and more functional role in life ('a negative identity is better than no identity').

Related to Erikson's claims about negative identity is risk-taking behaviour. Hendry (1999) asks if risk-taking is part of the psychological make-up of youth – a 'necessary rite of passage *en route* to the acquisition of adult skills and self-esteem'. Many teenagers seek out excitement, thrills and risks as earnestly as in childhood, perhaps to escape a drab existence, or to exert some control over their own lives and to achieve *something*.

For some, delinquency may be the solution: it could actually be adaptive as a way of facilitating self-definition and expressing autonomy (Compas *et al.*, 1995).

According to Bergevin *et al.* (2003):

> *... One of the challenges of the self in adolescence is with identifying the ways that one is unique and how one is similar to others. Maintaining a sense of individuality while trying to fit into the group is an important task for adolescents. Emphasising differences can lead to loneliness and alienation, while emphasising similarities may impede the development of autonomy.*

Such conflict seems to be largely absent in societies where the complete transition to adulthood is officially approved and celebrated at a specific age, often through a particular ceremony. These enable both the individual and society to adjust to change and enjoy a sense of continuity (Price and Crapo, 1999) (see Cross-Cultural Study 37.1).

Ask Yourself

- Do you agree with Price and Crapo's comments about female circumcision?
- Is our condemnation of such practices simply a reflection of Western values, or are there universal principles and standards that apply regardless of who's being judged and who's doing the judging?

Segall *et al.* (1999) maintain that tension and some antisocial behaviour are only to be expected in Western societies, due to the much longer adolescent and youth period.

According to Coleman and Roker (1998), an important trend in adolescence research is a focus on identity development among ethnically diverse populations, such as young black women (e.g. Robinson, 1997) and mixed-race young people (Tizard and Phoenix, 1993).

Studies of self-esteem

Tests of Erikson's theory have typically used measures of *self-concept* (especially *self-esteem*) as indicators of crisis. Girls' dissatisfaction with their appearance begins during puberty, along with a decline in self-esteem (Crawford and Unger, 1995). Comparisons between early and late-maturing girls indicate that dissatisfaction with looks is associated with the rapid and normal weight gain that's part of growing up (Attie and Brooks-Gunn, 1989; Blyth *et al.*, 1981).

Early maturers have a less positive body image, despite the fact that they date more and earlier. Also, sexual activity is more problematic for adolescent girls (as it is for females in general): there are persisting double standards regarding sex (as reflected in the terms 'slag' and 'stud' for sexually active females

Cross-Cultural Study 37.1

Initiation into adulthood in non-western cultures

- Cohen (1964) looked at 45 non-industrialised societies that held adulthood ceremonies. In societies where adult skills were hard and dangerous, or where father–son relationships were weak but men had to co-operate in hard work, male initiation rituals were dramatic and painful. They allowed the boy to prove his manhood to the community – and to himself.
- Sometimes they're designed to give boys strength, often by associating them with animals or plants. For example, in the Merina of Madagascar, the boy is associated with the banana tree, which bears much fruit resembling the erect penis (an ideal symbol of virility and fertility). The to-be-initiated boy is removed from his mother's home (a symbol of his attachment to her), before being circumcised in the company of men.
- Brown (1963) described 'rites of passage' for girls in 43 societies from all major regions of the world. They most commonly occur where young girls continue to live and work in their mothers' home after marriage, but they also sometimes occur even when young women permanently leave home, and here they involve genital operations or extensive tattooing. These dramatically help the girl understand that she must make the transition from dependent child to a woman, who'll have to fend for herself in a male-dominated environment (Price and Crapo, 1999).
- In recent years, *infibulation* (the most extreme form of female circumcision) has become a global human rights issue. Its purpose is to preserve the virginity of young girls before marriage, and to tame the disturbing power of women. In many traditional Islamic countries, especially Sudan, Ethiopia and Somalia, millions of young girls continue to undergo painful and risky genital operations.
- Although the act of infibulation may, from a Western perspective, deindividualise and depersonalise women:

> ... it acts as a transition or a rite of passage to a greater female adult collective; one where women hold relatively few advantages in a male-dominated world. It may in fact be one of the few positive status markers for women in traditional Islamic societies ... (Price and Crapo, 1999)

Figure 37.6 Xhosa boys in Bisho, South Africa, singing traditional manhood songs as part of a six-week-long ceremony, which begins with circumcision

and males respectively), together with differential responsibility for contraception and pregnancy.

However, Offer *et al.* (1988) deny there's any increase in disturbance of the self-image during early adolescence. Although such disturbance is more likely in early than late adolescence, only a very small proportion of the total adolescent population is likely to have a negative self-image or very low self-esteem (Coleman and Hendry 1990).

By contrast, early maturing boys feel more attractive (Tobin-Richards *et al.*, 1983) and tend to be more satisfied with their bodies, looks, and muscle development (Blyth *et al.*, 1981; Simmons and Blyth, 1987). However, Alsaker (1996) refers to two studies, which have found a correlation between pubertal boys' dissatisfaction with their bodies and the development of pubic and body hair. She asks if this reflects some contemporary images of men in advertisements, and a new trend for men to shave their bodies and be *less* hairy.

Most of these (and other similar) studies have been conducted in the USA, UK, and other English-speaking countries. But a study of a very large, nationally representative Norwegian sample found that the global self-esteem of both late-maturing boys and girls suffered, while early and on-time maturers (of both sexes) enjoy equally high self-esteem (Wichstrom, 1998).

Sociological approaches: generation gap

Sociologists see *role change* as an integral aspect of adolescent development (Coleman, 1995). Changing school or college, leaving home, and beginning a job, all involve new sets of relationships, producing different and often greater expectations. These expectations themselves demand a substantial reassessment of the self-concept and speed up the socialisation process. Some adolescents find this problematic because of the wide variety of competing socialising agencies (such as the family, mass media and peer group), which often present conflicting values and demands (see discussion above of the identity crisis).

Sociologists also see socialisation as being more dependent on the adolescent's own generation than on the family or other social institutions (*auto-socialisation*; Marsland, 1987). As Marsland says, the crucial meaning of youth is withdrawal from adult control and influence compared with childhood. Young people withdraw into their peer groups, and this withdrawal is (within limits) accepted by adults. What Marsland is describing here is the *generation gap*.

Ask Yourself

- While adolescents and their parents are, by definition, different generations, does this necessarily and inevitably mean that there's a generation gap – that is, that there'll be conflict between them because they occupy 'different worlds'?

Parent–adolescent relationships

According to Hendry (1999), adolescence as a transition from childhood to adulthood requires changes from child–parent relationships to young adult–parent relationships.

Failure to negotiate new relationships with parents, or having highly critical or rejecting parents, is likely to make adolescents adopt a negative identity (Curry, 1998). Also, parents who rated their own adolescence as stormy and stressful reported more conflict in their relationships with adolescent children and were less satisfied with their family (Scheer and Unger, 1995). Parents of adolescents in general are often going through a time of transition themselves, reappraising their life goals, career and family ambitions, and assessing whether they've fulfilled their expectations as parents.

However, for most adolescents relationships with parents become more equal and reciprocal, and parental authority comes to be seen as open to discussion and negotiation (e.g. Coleman and Hendry, 1990; Hendry *et al.*, 1993). Hendry *et al.*'s (1993) findings also suggest that relationships with mothers and fathers don't necessarily change in the same ways and to the same extent. There seems to be a *disengagement* by fathers: girls tend to be very uncomfortable discussing pubertal issues with their fathers, and learn almost nothing from them about puberty. The mother's role in enforcing family rules brings her into conflict with the children more readily, but she's still seen as being supportive and caring, not 'distanced' like the father.

Studies conducted in several countries have found that young people get along well with their parents (e.g. Hendry *et al.*, 1993; Kloep and Tarifa, 1993), adopt their views and values, and perceive family members as the most important 'significant others' in their lives (McGlone *et al.*, 1996). Furthermore, most adolescents who had conflicts with their parents already had poor relationships with them before puberty (Stattin and Klackenberg, 1992).

Disagreements between young people and their parents are similar everywhere in Europe: Greece (Besevegis and Giannitsas, 1996), Italy (Jackson *et al.*, 1996), Scotland (Hendry *et al.*, 1993), Germany (Fischer *et al.*, 1985), Albania and Sweden (Kloep and Tarifa, 1993).

According to Jackson *et al.* (1996) disagreements can arise because:

- parents expect greater independence of action from their teenagers
- parents don't wish to grant as much autonomy as the adolescent demands (with young women experiencing more conflict than young men over independence)
- parents and adolescents have different personal tastes and preferences.

Despite this potential for conflict, evidence suggests that competence as an independent adult can best be achieved within the context of a secure family environment, where exploration of alternative ideas, identities and behaviour is allowed and actively encouraged (Barber and Buehler, 1996). So, while detachment and separation from the family are necessary and desirable, young people don't have to reject their parents in order to become adults in their own right (Ryan and Lynch, 1989; Hill, 1993; see Chapter 32). Indeed, Holmes *et al.* (2008) believe that one argument per day can actually be *beneficial* – to both the adolescent and his/her parent. Provided the conflict isn't too intense and the mother's understanding of the issues involved is sufficiently complex, rows can bring them closer together through the mutual sharing of opinions.

Figure 37.7 Generational harmony – not generation gap

MEET THE RESEARCHER

Jane Kroger

Identity in adolescence

Sometimes it is so incredibly difficult to know that it is only I who can be me! (22-year-old female university student)

In the 1970s, while living in the USA and searching for a topic for my doctoral dissertation, I came across the volume *A Nation of Strangers* (Packard, 1972). This volume characterised Packard's country as a 'nation of torn roots'; furthermore, data from the 1970 US census indicated that the average citizen would experience some 14 residential relocations in their lifetime. Residential moves that occurred between the ages of 18 and 24 years represented almost one-fourth of all residential relocations made by those aged 16 years and over. I found these very high rates of relocation among late adolescents to be a matter of concern.

During this same time period, I had also become familiar with the recently published volume *Identity, Youth and Crisis* (Erikson, 1968). Erikson, a psychoanalyst and himself German immigrant to the USA, had written of the importance of an average expectable continuity within the social environment to support the growing ego during childhood and adolescence:

> *Today, when rapid technological changes have taken the lead the world over, the matter of establishing and preserving in flexible forms an 'average expectable' continuity for child rearing and education everywhere has, in fact, become a matter of human survival (Erikson, 1968: 222).*

Successful identify formation vs identity confusion

Erikson (1968) had also written extensively about the primary psychosocial task of adolescence to be that of developing a sense of identity. By identifying with, or wanting to be like, important others during childhood, adolescents now faced the challenge of moving forward to develop their own identities. Successful identity formation is marked by a feeling of being at home in one's body, finding purpose and meaning in one's life directions, and feeling assured of recognition by important others in one's life. Identity confusion is the inability to synthesise childhood and present identifications into a coherent whole – where a sense of inner sameness and continuity with the past is not well integrated into present life directions and the individual may experience a deep sense of 'drifting' or 'centrelessness'.

With this background, I became curious about the development of adolescent identity, based on that sense of personal sameness and continuity so vital to its formation for those many adolescents who were experiencing such high levels of disruption in their social networks. Adolescent identity formation might be a far more difficult task for those highly residentially mobile youths (particularly for those moving greater distances) than for those who had experienced less frequent and/or dramatic changes of contexts. While the degree of family cohesion might play an important role in one's sense of inner coherence through family relocation, analyses did show that the greater the distance moved, the lower the acceptance of self among high school teens even when family cohesion levels were controlled. While other hypotheses tested did not show a strong relationship between residential mobility experiences and identity development in adolescence, I became very interested about the nature of adolescent identity development more generally.

Research into identity with the help of adolescents

As I finished my PhD and entered a university teaching career, I decided to pursue a number of questions related to Erikson's (1968) identity construct during both adolescent and adult development. While I began formulating a number of research questions and hypotheses for testing, my students always helped me to anchor these questions in the realities of their everyday lives. As I taught courses on adolescent and adult development, I started asking students anonymously to write down their answers to the question: 'How will you know (or how did you know) that you have your own sense of individual identity.' The responses they gave (one of which appears in the introduction to this section), have provided the impetus for many of the research questions that I have pursued over the years that followed.

Marcia's identity status model

By the mid-late 1970s, Marcia's (1966, 1967, 1976) identity status model was becoming a popular means of understanding different styles by which youth adopted vocational, ideological and sexual roles within their particular social contexts. Marcia had expanded upon some of Erikson's writings to propose that there are several different ways in which youth may adopt (or not) identity-defining such roles and values. The *identity achieved* individual has undertaken a thoughtful process of exploration prior to making identity-defining commitments on their own terms; the *foreclosed* individual has also made identity-defining commitments, but these commitments have been based on identifications with important others of childhood and not through a process of personal identity exploration. Both *moratorium* and *diffuse* individuals have not adopted identity-defining commitments; however, those in the moratorium identity status are very much in the process of trying to find some meaningful identity directions, while those in the diffusion status are not. Adolescent diffusions might be carefree in their drifting or, alternatively, very disturbed.

Many of the questions I have addressed over my career as a Developmental Psychologist have been based on issues of change and stability for those in Marcia's identity status positions. I have wondered, for example, how likely it is for one's identity status to change over the course of time, particularly from late adolescence through middle adulthood. I have been curious as to whether or not it is possible to predict those likely to move from a foreclosed or diffuse identity status in late adolescence to a moratorium or achieved position during young adulthood. Do men and women differ in their identity formation processes? Is the bulk of identity work undertaken in late adolescence, or is it possible for adults to undertake important identity development work as well? Can identity regress and, if so, what are the conditions under which regression may occur?

Recent studies

One of my most recent studies addresses some of these questions (Kroger *et al.*, 2010). Colleagues and I have systematically collected some 124 published studies or doctoral dissertations undertaken over the past 40 years that provide data on identity status change. Through a statistical process called meta-analysis, we have examined the most common identity status change patterns over the years of late adolescence and young adulthood in all of these studies. Among some of the very interesting findings has been the fact that relatively large average percentages of individuals were not identity achieved by young adulthood. In an analysis of cross-sectional studies (studies that examined identity status distributions for different individuals in various age groups), for example, only about one-third of participants were identity achieved, while a little over one-quarter were in the moratorium identity status. This finding was particularly striking, given that Erikson proposed identity formation to be the key psychosocial task of adolescence. The study also suggested that identity achievement was found more frequently among individuals in school or community settings that provided exposure to a diversity of individuals and ideas. And finally, regressive patterns of identity development appeared more frequently than measurement error alone might suggest. The study of adolescent and adult identity development has been rich, enjoyable, and rewarding for me, raising many new questions for future generations of identity researchers to explore.

Professor Jane Kroger is Professor of Developmental Psychology at University of Tromsø, Norway. She has been researching issues in both adolescent and adult identity development for some 40 years. Her most recent book is *Identity Development: Adolescence through Adulthood* (2007).

Coleman's focal theory: managing one change at a time

According to Coleman and Hendry (1990), most theories of adolescence help us to understand young people with serious problems and those belonging to minority or deviant groups: what's needed is a theory of normality. The research as a whole suggests that while adolescence is a difficult time for some, for the majority it appears to be a period of relative stability. Coleman's (1980) *focal theory* is an attempt to explain how this is achieved.

The theory is based on a study of 800 6-, 11-, 13-, 15- and 17-year-old boys and girls. Attitudes towards self-image, being alone, heterosexual and parental relationships, friendships and large-group situations, all changed as a function of age. More importantly, concerns about different issues reached a peak at different ages for both sexes.

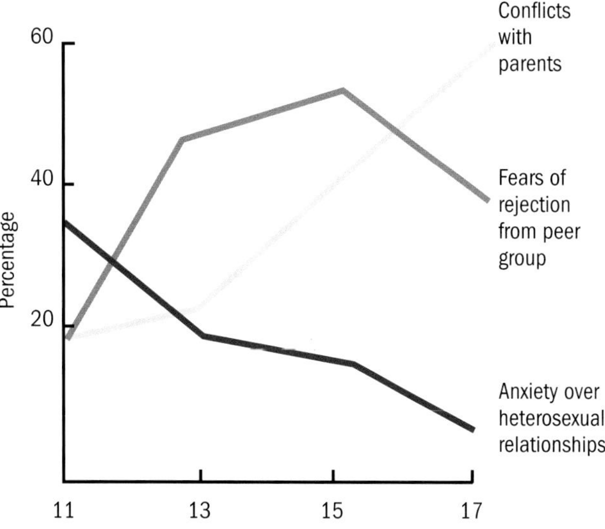

Figure 37.8 Peak ages of the expression of different themes. These data are for boys only (from Coleman and Hendry, 1990). Reproduced with permission of Taylor Francis.

Particular sorts of relationship pattern come into focus (are most prominent) at different ages, although no pattern is specific to one age. The patterns overlap and there are wide individual differences.

Coleman believes that adolescents are able to cope with the potentially stressful changes as well as they do by dealing with one issue at a time. They spread the process of adaptation over a span of years, attempting to resolve one issue first before addressing the next. Because different problems and relationships come into focus at different points during the adolescent years, the stresses resulting from the need to adapt don't all have to be dealt with together.

According to Coleman and Hendry (1990), adolescents who, for whatever reason, must deal with *more than one issue* (or normative shift) at a time, are those most likely to experience difficulties. If normative shifts coincide with non-normative ones, the situation is even more problematic (Hendry and Kloep, 1999).

Coleman's original findings have been successfully replicated by Kroger (1985) with large North American and New Zealand samples. Others have successfully tested hypotheses derived from the theory. For example, Simmons and Blyth (1987) predicted that, if change (such as puberty)

- occurred at too young an age (causing the individual to be developmentally 'off time')
- was marked by sharp discontinuity (i.e. sudden change) or
- involved accumulation of significant and temporally close issues (important shifts occurred together)

then adjustment would be more difficult. Their results strongly supported their predictions.

CONCLUSIONS

Adolescence involves a number of important transitions from childhood to adulthood, including puberty. The potential for storm and stress in Western societies is increased by the lack of clear definitions regarding when adulthood is reached. This makes the task of attaining an adult identity, as well as relationships with parents, more difficult compared with non-industrialised societies.

However, adolescence in Western societies isn't as problem-ridden as the popular stereotype would have it. If any serious problems do arise, they're directly linked to rapid social change (Dasen, 1999), with the associated extension of adolescence and youth. Young people aren't given a productive role to play when entering adult society (Segall *et al.*, 1999).

While most of the major theories of adolescence paint a picture of adolescence as an inherently difficult developmental stage, the evidence suggests that this isn't necessarily so. Certain groups may be more vulnerable than others (such as early maturing girls), but the majority seem to cope well. According to Coleman's focal theory, it isn't adolescence itself that's stressful, but the timing and combination of the transitions faced by young people.

Chapter Summary

- Adolescence involves **multiple transitions**. Compared with previous generations, it begins sooner and ends later. Various 'adulthood-postponing' changes have coincided with increased freedom at earlier ages.
- These transitions or shifts can be categorised as **normative maturational, normative society-dependent** and **non-normative**. Normative shifts can become non-normative, as when puberty begins unusually early or late.
- **Puberty** involves the **adolescent growth spurt** and the development of **secondary sex characteristics**. While girls typically enter puberty two years before boys, there are important individual differences within each sex (such as **intraindividual asynchronies**).
- According to the **cultural ideal hypothesis** (**CIH**), girls move further **away** from their physical ideal and early maturing girls will face a double disadvantage. Early maturing boys will move fastest **towards** their physical ideal.
- Hall's **recapitulation theory** saw adolescence as a time of **storm and stress**. While mood swings are more common during adolescence, rates of mental disorder (and delinquency rates) are higher only in early maturing girls and adolescents with problems prior to puberty. The evidence for off-time maturation in boys is more mixed.
- According to Erikson, adolescence involves a conflict between **ego identity** and **role confusion**. In Western societies, adolescence is a **moratorium**, intended to help ease the transition to adulthood. However, the lack of clear definitions of adulthood may contribute to the **adolescent identity crisis**.
- Role confusion can take the form of **negative identity**, related to which is **risk-taking behaviour**. These problems are largely absent in societies which mark the transition to adulthood by **initiation ceremonies**.
- While self-esteem may decline in early adolescence, especially in girls, this affects only a very small proportion of all adolescents. But research findings from English-speaking countries may not generalise to other cultures.
- **Sociological approaches** stress **role change**, the **conflicting** values and demands of different socialising agencies, and **auto-socialisation**, which produces the **generation gap**.
- Renegotiating relationships with parents is necessary, and while there are inevitable disagreements, adult status is probably best achieved within the context of a **secure family environment**.
- According to Coleman's **focal theory**, most adolescents cope as well as they do by dealing with **one issue at a time**. Having to deal with more than one issue simultaneously is stressful, especially if changes occur too early or suddenly.

Links with Other Topics/Chapters

Chapter 33 ⟶ The importance of puberty for changes in the adolescent's body image is mirrored by the fact that the *bodily self* is probably the first aspect of the *self-concept* to develop in the baby

Chapters 2 and 42 ⟶ Erikson's psychosocial theory is *psychodynamic*, but differs from Freud's *psychoanalytic theory* in fundamental ways

Chapters 38 and 39 ⟶ For Freud, the first five years are critical, while Erikson adopts a *lifespan developmental approach*

Chapters 38 and 47 ⟶ Marcia's admission that his theory only loosely applies to females (but much better to males) illustrates *androcentrism*. Erikson's theory has been criticised for similar reasons (Gilligan, 1982)

Chapter 38 ⟶ Adolescence coincides with parents experiencing their own transition, sometimes referred to as the *mid-life crisis*

Recommended Reading

Bergevin, T., Bukowski, W.M. & Miners, R. (2003) Social Development. In A. Slater & G. Bremner (eds) *An Introduction to Developmental Psychology.* Oxford: Blackwell Publishing.

Bukowski, W.M., Bergevin, T. & Miners, R. (2011) Social Development. In A. Slater & G. Bremner (eds) *An Introduction to Developmental Psychology* (2nd edn). BPS/Blackwell.

Coleman, J. & Hendry, L.B. (1990) *The Nature of Adolescence* (2nd edn). London: Routledge.

Coleman, J. & Roker, D. (1998) Adolescence. *The Psychologist, 11*(2), 593–6.

Gross, R. (2008) *Key Studies in Psychology* (5th edn). London: Hodder Education. Chapter 29.

Hendry, L.B. (1999) Adolescents in society. In D. Messer & F. Jones (eds) *Psychology and Social Care.* London: Jessica Kingsley Publishers.

Kroger, A. (2007) *Identity Development: Adolescence Through Adulthood* (2nd edn). Thousand Oaks, CA: Sage Publications. (Also relevant to Chapters 38 and 39.)

Useful Websites

www.youngpeopleinfocus.org.uk (Young People in Focus – formerly the Trust for the Study of Adolescence, whose Director was Coleman)

www.icn.ucl.ac.uk/research-groups/Developmental-Group/index.php (University College London Institute of Cognitive Neuroscience Developmental Group)

www.icn.ucl.ac.uk/sblakemore (Sarah-Jayne Blakemore's homepage, including The Learning Brain: Lessons for Education) Discussion of cognitive changes in adolescence (see textbook Chapter 34).

www.youngminds.org.uk (YoungMinds)

www.childdevelopmentinfo.com/development/teens_stages.shtml (Child Development Institute: Adolescence Stages of Development)

CHAPTER 38

ADULTHOOD

INTRODUCTION and OVERVIEW

Assuming that we enjoy a normal lifespan, the longest phase of the life cycle will be spent in adulthood. Until recently, however, personality changes in adulthood attracted little psychological research interest. Indeed, as Levinson *et al.* (1978) have observed, adulthood is:

> *... one of the best-kept secrets in our society and probably in human history generally.*

This chapter attempts to reveal this secret by examining what theory and research have told us about personality change in adulthood, including the occurrence of crises and transitions.

Many theorists believe that adult concerns and involvements are patterned in such a way that we can speak about *stages* of adult development. However, evidence concerning the predictability of changes in adult life (or what Levinson (1986) calls *psychobiosocial transitions*) is conflicting. Three kinds of influence can affect the way we develop in adulthood (Hetherington and Baltes, 1988):

1. *normative age-graded influences* are biological (such as the menopause) and social changes (such as marriage and parenting) that normally occur at fairly predictable ages
2. *normative history-graded influences* are historical events that affect whole generations (or *cohorts*) at about the same time (examples include wars, recessions, and epidemics)
3. *non-normative influences* are idiosyncratic transitions, such as divorce, unemployment, and illness.

Levinson's (1986) term *marker events* refers to age-graded and non-normative influences. Others prefer the term *critical life events* to describe such influences, although it's probably more accurate to describe them as *processes*. Some critical life events, such as divorce, unemployment, and bereavement, can occur at any time during adulthood (bereavement is discussed in Chapter 39). Others occur late in adulthood, such as retirement (also discussed in Chapter 39). Yet others tend to happen early in adulthood, such as marriage (or partnering) and parenting.

Ask Yourself

- What do you understand by the term adulthood?
- What does it mean to be an adult?

ERIKSON'S THEORY: INTIMACY AND GENERATIVITY

As we saw in Chapter 37, Erikson believes that human development occurs through a sequence of psychosocial stages. As far as early and middle adulthood are concerned, Erikson described two primary developmental crises (the sixth and seventh of his psychosocial stages: see Table 38.1).

The first involves the establishment of *intimacy*, which is a criterion of having attained the psychosocial state of adulthood. By intimacy, Erikson means the ability to form close, meaningful relationships with others without 'the fear of losing oneself in the process' (Elkind, 1970). As Erikson (1968) claims:

> *It is only when identity formation is well on its way that true intimacy ... is possible.*

Identity (the reconciliation of all our various roles into one enduring and stable personality: see Chapter 37) is necessary because we cannot know what it means to love someone and seek to share our life with them until we know who we are, and what we want to do with our lives. Thus, genuine intimacy requires us to give up some of our sense of separateness, and we must each have a firm identity to do this.

Since intimacy refers to the essential ability to relate our deepest hopes and fears to another person, and in turn to accept another's need for intimacy, it describes the relationship between friends just as much as that between sexual partners (Dacey, 1982). By sharing ourselves with others, our personal identity becomes fully realised and consolidated. Erikson believed that if a sense of intimacy isn't established with friends or a partner, then *isolation* (a sense of being alone without anyone to share with or care for) would result.

The relationship between identity and intimacy

Research into associations between identity and intimacy for both late adolescent men and women has produced mixed findings (Kroger, 2007). While those who are more advanced in terms of identity statuses tend to also be more advanced in terms of intimacy status, a meta-analysis by Årseth *et al.* (2005) showed that a more mature style of intimacy doesn't depend on attaining a more mature identity status for some women. For these women, identity and intimacy development seem to *co-develop*; they may be defining themselves through their close relationships.(See Evaluation of Erikson's theory below).

We normally achieve intimacy in young adulthood (our 20s and 30s), after which we enter middle age (our 40s and 50s). This involves the attainment of *generativity*, the positive outcome of the second developmental crisis.

An evaluation of Erikson's theory

- The sequence from identity to intimacy may not accurately reflect present-day realities. In recent years, the trend has been for adults to live together before marrying, so they tend to marry later in life than people did in the past.

Box 38.1 Generativity

- According to Erikson (1963):

  Generativity ... is primarily the concern in establishing and guiding the next generation, although there are individuals who, through misfortune or because of special and genuine gifts in other directions, do not apply this drive to their own offspring.

  So, while parenting is an important focus of generativity, it can be expressed in other ways, including productivity and the creation of works that contribute to the ongoing life of the community and society. Generativity is shown by anyone actively concerned with the welfare of young people and in making the world a better place for them to live and work.
- In a broader sense, generativity concerns leaving some kind of *legacy* for those that will follow us; this can include nurturing our life values, work and other creative projects, which will eventually outlive the self.
- People who successfully resolve this developmental crisis establish clear guidelines for their lives, and are generally productive and happy within this directive framework. Failure to attain generativity leads to *stagnation*, in which people become preoccupied with their personal needs and comforts. They indulge themselves as if they were their own (or another's) only child.

Many people struggle with identity issues (such as career choice) and intimacy issues *at the same time*.

- While Erikson's psychosocial stages were meant to be universal, applying to both genders in all cultures, he acknowledged that the sequence of stages is different for a woman, who suspends her identity as she prepares to attract the man who will marry her. As Gilligan (1982) has observed:

> *The female comes to know herself as she is known, through relationships with others.*

- The typical life course of women involves passing directly into a stage of intimacy *without* having achieved personal identity. Sangiuliano (1978)

Table 38.1 Comparison between Erikson's and Freud's stages of development (based on Thomas, 1985; Erikson, 1950)

No. of stage	Name of stage (psychosocial crisis)	Psychosocial modalities (dominant modes of being and acting)	Radius of significant relationships	Human virtues (qualities of strength)	Freud's psychosexual stages	Approx. ages
1	Basic trust vs basic mistrust	To get. To give in return	Mother or mother figure	Hope	Oral	0–1
2	Autonomy vs shame and doubt	To hold on. To let go	Parents	Willpower	Anal	1–3
3	Initiative vs guilt	To make (going after). To make 'like' (playing)	Basic family	Purpose	Phallic	3–6
4	Industry vs inferiority	To make things (completing). To make things together	Neighbourhood and school	Competence	Latency	6–12
5	Identity vs role confusion	To be oneself (or not to be). To share being oneself	Peer groups and out-groups. Models of leadership	Fidelity	Genital	12–18
6	Intimacy vs isolation	To lose and find oneself in another	Partners in friendship, sex, competition, cooperation	Love		20s
7	Generativity vs stagnation	To make be. To be taken care of	Divided labour and shared household	Care		Late 20s–50s
8	Ego integrity vs despair	To be, though having been. To face not being	'Humankind', 'my kind'	Wisdom		50s and beyond

argues that most women submerge their identities into those of their partners, and only in mid-life do they emerge from this and search for separate identities and full independence.

- To illustrate an interaction between gender and social class, working-class men see early marriage as a 'good' life pattern: early adulthood is a time for 'settling down', having a family and maintaining a steady job. By contrast, middle-class men and women see early adulthood as a time for exploration, in which different occupations are tried. Marriage tends to occur after this, and 'settling down' doesn't usually take place before 30 (Neugarten, 1975).

- There's also evidence of an interaction between gender, race and culture. In a study of over 1800 South African black and white men and women, Ochse and Plug (1986) found that 25- to 39-year-old white women appeared to develop a sense of identity *before* men: perhaps developing a true sense of intimacy must *precede* a sense of identity (not vice versa, as Erikson claimed). Not until this process is complete can a sense of identity be achieved. Due to prevailing social conditions in South Africa (including minority status, high poverty rates and fragmented living conditions), black women had a difficult time achieving a sense of intimacy and hence of identity. Black men also didn't achieve a sense of identity until late in life. In turn, this adversely affected black women, who still experienced a lack of self-definition, intimacy and well-being far into middle age:

  It appears that the experience of the 'adult years' was one thing for whites and something quite different for blacks. As social conditions change in South Africa, whole groups of blacks may expect to experience a completely different psychological development than they would have under apartheid ... (Price and Crapo, 1999)

- Just as achieving ego identity is a process that extends far beyond adolescence (see above), so several writers have pointed out that most adults will be starting families and raising children long *before* their 40s and 50s (as Erikson claims). If generativity is achieved by most people primarily through parenting, then generativity versus stagnation must be an important issue in the lives of *young* adults as well as those in mid-life.
- Bradley (1997) and Bradley and Marcia (1998a, 1998b) have developed a status approach to understanding different generativity *styles*; these are defined in terms of two variables, involvement and inclusivity, as they relate to (a) the self; and (b) others. *Involvement* is primarily a behavioural indicator of generativity: low involvement suggests little generative action; *inclusivity* concerns the scope of generative action (whether it includes or excludes both self and others). These five styles are shown in Table 38.2.

  Bradley and Marcia (1998a, 1998b) have found support for the predicted relationships between these statuses and other measures of generativity, as well as confirmation of predicted personality traits associated with each status. Kroger (2007) cites several other studies showing that generativity versus stagnation is an issue that concerns those in early – as well as middle – adulthood.

Table 38.2 Five styles of generativity in relation to involvement and inclusivity of self and others (based on Bradley, 1997; Bradley and Marcia, 1998a, 1998b)

Generativity style	Involvement		Inclusivity	
	Self	Others	Self	Others
Generative	High	High	High	High
Agentic	High	Low	High	Low
Communal	Low	High	Low	High
Conventional	High	Low	Low	Low

LEVENSON *ET AL.*'S 'SEASONS OF A MAN'S LIFE'

Perhaps the most systematic study of personality and life changes in adulthood began in 1969, when Levinson *et al.* interviewed 40 men aged 35 to 45. Transcripts were made of the five to ten tape-recorded interviews that each participant gave over several months. Levinson *et al.* looked at how adulthood is actually *experienced*.

In *The Seasons of a Man's Life*, Levinson *et al.* (1978) advanced a *life-structure theory*, defining life structure as the underlying pattern or design of a person's life at any given time. Life structure allows us to 'see how the self is in the world and how the world is in the self' and evolves through a series of *phases* or *periods*. Adult development comprises a sequence of *eras* which overlap in the form of *cross-era transitions*. These last about five years, ending the outgoing era and initiating the incoming one. The four eras are *pre-adulthood* (age 0–22), *early adulthood* (17–45), *middle adulthood* (40–65), and *late adulthood* (60 onwards).

The phases or periods alternate between those that are stable (or *structure-building*) and transitional (or *structure-changing*). Although each phase involves biological, psychological and social adjustments, family and work roles are seen as central to the life structure at any time, and individual development is interwoven with changes in these roles (see Figure 38.1).

The era of early adulthood

Early adult transition (17–22) is a developmental 'bridge' between adolescence and adulthood. (See Figure 38.2.)

Between ages 22 and 28, we *enter the adult world*. This is the first *structure-building* phase, and hence is referred to as the *entry life structure for early adulthood*. In it, we try to fashion 'a provisional structure that provides a workable link between the valued self and adult society'.

In the *novice phase*, we try to define ourselves as adults and live with the initial choices we make concerning jobs, relationships, lifestyles and values.

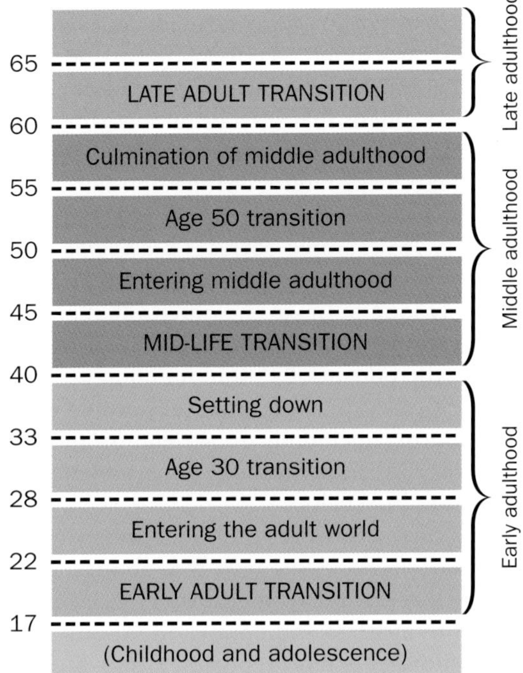

Figure 38.1 Levinson *et al.*'s theory of adult development. The life cycle is divided into four major eras that overlap in the form of cross-era transitions

Box 38.2 Separation and attachment

Two key themes of the early adult transition are *separation* and the formation of *attachments* to the adult world. There are two types of separation:

1. *External separation* involves moving out of the family home, increasing financial independence, and entering more independent and responsible roles and living arrangements.
2. *Internal separation* involves greater psychological distance from the family, less emotional dependence on the parents, and greater differentiation between the self and family. Although we separate from our parents, Levinson *et al.* argue that we never complete the process, which continues throughout life.

Attachment involves exploring the world's possibilities, imagining ourselves as part of it, and identifying and establishing changes for living in the world before we become 'full members' of it.

However, we need to create a balance between 'keeping our options open' and 'putting down roots' (or creating stable life structures).

Our decisions are made in the context of our *dreams*: the 'vague sense' we have of ourselves in the adult world and what we want to do with our lives. To help us in our efforts at self-definition, we look to *mentors*, older and more experienced others, for guidance and direction. *Formally,* mentors guide, teach, and help novices to define their dreams; *informally,* s/he may provide an advisory and emotionally supportive function (as a parent does).

Figure 38.2 Mentoring

The *age-30 transition* (28–33) provides an opportunity to work on the flaws and limitations of the first life structure, and to create the basis for a more satisfactory structure that will complete the era of young adulthood. Most of Levinson *et al.*'s participants experienced *age-30 crises* which involved stress, self-doubt, feelings that life was losing its 'provisional quality' and becoming more serious, and time pressure. Thus, the participants saw this as being the time for change, if change was needed. However, for a minority the age-30 transition was crisis-free. (See Box 38.3.)

The era of middle adulthood

Ask Yourself

- What do you think is meant by the 'mid-life crisis'?
- Do you think it's a real phenomenon?

Box 38.3 Settling down

The *settling down* (or *culminating life structure for early adulthood:* 33–40) phase represents consolidation of the second life structure. This involves a shift away from tentative choices regarding family and career towards a strong sense of commitment to a personal, familial, and occupational future: we see ourselves as responsible adults.

The settling down phase comprises two substages: *early settling down* (33–36) and *becoming one's own man* (BOOM) (36–40). In the latter, men strive to advance and succeed in building better lives, improve and use their skills, be creative, and in general contribute to society. A man wants recognition and affirmation from society, but he also wants to be self-sufficient and free of social pressure and control. This substage may also see him assume a mentor role for someone younger (see text above).

The *mid-life transition* (40–45) involves terminating one life structure, initiating another, and continuing the process of *individuation* started during the BOOM substage. This is a time of soul-searching, questioning, and assessing the real meaning of the life structure's achievement. It's sometimes referred to as the *mid-life crisis*, although Levinson *et al.* didn't actually use this term. For some people, the change is gradual and fairly painless. But for others, it's full of uncertainties. These difficulties stem from unconscious tensions between attachment and separation, the resurfacing of the need to be creative (which is often repressed in order to achieve a career), and retrospective comparisons between dreams and life's reality.

Most participants in Levinson *et al.*'s study hadn't reached age 45. Following interviews two years after the main study was concluded, some were chosen for more extensive study. But the evidence for the remaining phases is much less detailed than for the earlier ones.

Is there a 'mid-life crisis'?

Just as the 'identity crisis' is part of the popular stereotype of adolescence (see Chapter 37), Levinson *et al.* have helped to make the 'mid-life crisis' part of the common-sense understanding of adult development. Like Erikson, Levinson *et al.* see crisis as inevitable, claiming that it's not possible to get through middle adulthood without having at least a moderate crisis in either the mid-life transition or the age-50 transition. They also see crisis as *necessary*. If we don't engage in soul searching, we'll:

> *... pay the price in a later developmental crisis or in a progressive withering of the self and a life structure minimally connected to the self (Levinson et al., 1978)*

The view that crisis is both inevitable and necessary (or *normative*, to use Erikson's term) is controversial. People of all ages suffer occasional depression, self-doubt, sexual uncertainty, and concerns about the future. Indeed, there appear to be an increasingly wide age range and a growing number of people who decide to make radical changes in their lifestyle, both earlier and later than predicted by Levinson *et al.*'s theory. An example of this is *downshifting* – voluntarily opting out of a pressurised career and interminably long hours in the office, often giving up an exceptionally well-paid job in a high-profile industry in the pursuit of a more fulfilling way of life. Tredre (1996) identifies a number of possible reasons for downshifting, including anti-urbanism (fuelled by concerns over urban pollution), crime, violence and increasing job insecurity.

A large-scale, semistructured telephone survey by Wethington (2000) suggests that about 25 per cent of both men and women experience mid-life as a time of stress and confusion. About 20 per cent of respondents who reported a mid-life crisis indicated that awareness of ageing and time left to live running out were the source of the crisis (see Box 38.4). A further 13 per cent of both genders reporting a crisis described the experience as a major life review or time of re-evaluation. Thus, the experience of a major mid-life identity crisis doesn't appear to take place for the majority of mid-life adults (Kroger, 2007).

Box 38.4 Identity crisis and the life cycle

Marcia (1998) believes that the concept of a mid-life crisis is misleading and too narrow. *'Adolescing'* (making decisions about one's identity) occurs *throughout* the lifespan, whenever we review or reorganise our lives. At the very least, we might expect identity crises to accompany (in Erikson's terms) intimacy–isolation, generativity–stagnation, and integrity–despair (see Chapter 39).

Just as puberty and other changes in early adolescence disrupt the partial identities of childhood, so the demands of intimacy require a reformulation of the initial identity achieved at late adolescence. Similarly, the generative, caregiving requirements of middle age differ from those of being with an intimate partner. The virtues of fidelity, love and care (see Table 38.1), which derive from positive resolution of young and middle adulthood, don't emerge without a struggle. According to Marcia (1998), 'periods of adolescing are normal, expectable components of life cycle growth'.

Recent evidence that supports both Wethington's findings and Marcia's account comes from a structured retrospective autobiographical study of over 1000 UK-based adults (Robinson and Wright, 2013; see Key Study 38.1).

Key Study 38.1

Evidence for mid-life crisis in the UK (Robinson and Wright, 2013)

- Of the 20- to 29-year-olds, 39 per cent of men and 49 per cent of women reported having had crisis episodes during that decade; this compared with 47 and 51 per cent, respectively, for 30- to 39-year-old men and women, and 46 and 59 per cent for 40- to 49-year-olds.
- These crises were more likely to be work-related for men and relationship/family-related for women.
- However, across decades and genders, the most common crises were (i) divorce/relationship break-up and (ii) debt/financial problems, although for women in their 40s the death of a parent featured strongly.
- Of all age ranges and both genders, 40- to 44-year-old men were the least likely to display *post-crisis growth* (see Gross, 2014).

Figure 38.3 Kevin Spacey as a man experiencing a mid-life crisis in *American Beauty*. This becomes focused (literally) on his daughter's friend, played by Mena Suvari

Ask Yourself

- Who's 'more right', Levinson *et al*. or Marcia?
- Who would you prefer to be right?

The seasons of a woman's life

Levinson *et al*.'s research was carried out on an all-male sample. In *The Seasons of a Woman's Life*, Levinson and Levinson (1997) presented their findings for 45 women (aged 35 to 45), comprising 15 homemakers (full-time housewives/mothers), 15 businesswomen and 15 academics. The broad pattern of developmental periods based on the original male sample was confirmed. But men and women have been shown to differ in terms of their *dreams*.

Box 38.5 Women's dreams and 'gender-splitting'

Levinson (1986) argues that a *'gender-splitting'* phenomenon occurs in adult development. While men have fairly unified visions of their futures, which tend to be focused on their careers, women have 'dreams' which are more likely to be split between a career and marriage.

This was certainly true of academics and businesswomen, although the former were less ambitious and more likely to forego a career, whereas the latter wanted to maintain their careers but at a reduced level. Only the homemakers had unified dreams (to be full-time wives and mothers, as their own mothers had been).

Women's dreams were constructed around their relationships with their husbands and families, which subordinated their personal needs. So, part of her dream is his success. For Durkin (1995), this difference in women's and men's priorities may put women at greater risk '... of disappointment and developmental tension as their investment in others' goals conflict with their personal needs'.

Women who give marriage and motherhood top priority in their 20s tend to develop more individualistic goals for their 30s. However, those who are career-oriented early on in adulthood tend to focus on marriage and family concerns later. Generally, the transitory instability of the early 30s lasts longer for women than for men, and 'settling down' is much less clear-cut. Trying to integrate career and marriage/family responsibilities is very difficult for most women, who experience greater conflicts than their husbands are likely to.

Gender splitting is relevant to discussion of marriage/partnering and parenthood (see below).

HOW VALID ARE STAGE THEORIES OF ADULTHOOD?

Ask Yourself

- Do you think it's appropriate to describe adulthood in terms of distinct stages?

- Erikson's and Levinson *et al.*'s theories of adult development emphasise a 'ladder-like' progression through an inevitable and universal series of stages/phases. But this view underestimates the degree of *individual variability* (Rutter and Rutter, 1992).
- Stage theories also imply a *discontinuity* of development. But many Psychologists believe there's also considerable *continuity* of personality during adult life.
- Current views of adult development stress the transitions and milestones that mark adult life, rather than a rigid developmental sequence (Baltes, 1983; Schlossberg, 1984; *the life-events approach*). Yet, despite the growing unpredictability of changes in adult life, most people still unconsciously evaluate their transitions according to a social clock, which determines whether they're 'on time' with respect to particular life events (such as getting married; Schlossberg *et al.*, 1978). If they're 'off time', either early or late, they're *age-deviant*. Like other types of deviancy, this can result in social penalties, such as amusement, pity or rejection.
- While all cultures have social clocks that define the 'right' time to marry, begin work, have children, and so on, these clocks vary greatly between cultures (Wade and Tavris, 1999). Craig (1992) sees changes in adult thought, behaviour and personality as being less a result of chronological age or specific biological changes, and more a result of personal, social and cultural events or forces. Because of the sheer diversity of experiences in an adult's life, Craig doesn't believe it's possible to describe major 'milestones' that will apply to nearly everyone.

GOULD'S THEORY: THE EVOLUTION OF ADULT CONSCIOUSNESS

According to Gould (1978, 1980), adult consciousness evolves as '... we release ourselves from the constraints and ties of childhood consciousness'.

Gould sees the thrust of adult development as being towards the realisation and acceptance of ourselves as creators of our own lives, and away from the assumption that the rules and standards of childhood determine our destinies. We have to free ourselves of the *illusion of absolute safety*, which dominated childhood; this involves transformations, giving up the security of the past to form our own ideas. We have to replace the concept of parental dependency with a sense of autonomy, or owning ourselves. But this is difficult, because dependency on parents is a normal feature of childhood. As well as shedding childhood consciousness, Gould believes that our *sense of time* also changes (see Box 38.6).

MARRIAGE

Ask Yourself

- Identify some arguments for and against marriage, as compared with 'living together' (cohabitation).

Box 38.6 Our changing sense of time

- Up until age 18 or so, we feel both protected and constrained by our parents, and never quite believe that we'll escape the 'family world'. This is like being in a timeless capsule in which 'the future is a fantasy space that may possibly not exist'. But we begin to glimpse an endless future and see an infinite amount of time ahead of us.
- In our 20s, we become confident about being separated from the family. However, we haven't yet formed early adult life structures. Gould (1980) puts it like this:

  ... our time sense, when we're being successful, is one of movement along a chosen path that leads linearly to some obscure prize decades in the future. There is plenty of time, but we're still in a hurry once we've developed a clearer, often stereotyped, picture of where we want to be by then.

- At the end of our 20s, our sense of time incorporates our adult past as well as future. The future is neither infinite nor linear, and we must choose between different options because there isn't time to take them all.
- From our mid-30s to mid-40s, we develop a sense of urgency and that time is running out. We also become aware of our own mortality which, once attained, is never far from our consciousness: how we spend our time becomes a matter of great importance. Additionally, we begin to question whether our 'prize' (freedom from restrictions by those who have formed us – our parents) either exists or, if it does, whether it's been worth it (cf. Levinson *et al.*'s 'dream').

Since over 90 per cent of adults in western countries marry at least once, marriage is an example of a *normative age-graded influence*. Marriage is an important transition for young adults, because it involves a lasting personal commitment to another person (and, so is a means of achieving Erikson's intimacy), financial responsibilities and, perhaps, family responsibilities.

Cohabitation

Couples who live together (or *cohabit*) before marriage are more likely to divorce later, and be less satisfied with their marriages, than those who marry without having cohabited. Also, about 40 per cent of couples who cohabit don't marry. While this suggests that cohabitation may prevent some divorces, cohabitees who do marry are more likely to divorce.

As a group, cohabitees seem to be more willing to flout tradition in many ways (such as being less religious and disagreeing that one should stay with a marriage partner no matter what). Those who don't cohabit include a large proportion of 'more traditional' people (Bee, 1994).

The benefits of marriage

It's long been recognised that mortality is affected by marital status. Married people tend to live longer than unmarried people, are happier, healthier and have lower rates of various mental disorders than the single, widowed or divorced. The greater mortality of the unmarried relative to the married has generally been increasing over the past two to three decades, and it seems that divorced (and widowed) people in their 20s and 30s have particularly high risks of dying compared with other people of the same age (Cramer, 1995).

Figure 38.4 Being happily married protects against mental and physical illness

Ask Yourself

- Why – or how – might marriage produce these beneficial effects? Look back at your answers to the previous 'Ask Yourself' box. Did any of the arguments for marriage include its psychological/ emotional benefits?
- Are there any reasons for believing that either men or women derive greater benefits?

Critical Discussion 38.1

Do men get more from marriage than women?

Bee (1994) argues that the greatest beneficiaries of marriage are men, partly because they're less likely than women to have close confidants outside marriage, and partly because wives provide more emotional warmth and support for husbands than husbands do for wives.

Marriage is less obviously psychologically protective for women, not because a confiding and harmonious relationship is any less important for them (indeed, if anything it's more important), but because:

- many marriages don't provide such relationships, and
- other consequences of marriage differ between the sexes.

(The 'advantage' of marriage for men is reflected in the higher rates of men's re-marriage following divorce: see text below.)

Although our attitudes towards education and women's careers have changed, Rutter and Rutter (1992), echoing Levinson's concept of 'gender splitting', have proposed that:

The potential benefits of a harmonious relationship may, for a woman, be counterbalanced by the stresses involved in giving up a job or in being handicapped in a career progression or promotion through having to combine a career and parenthood.

DIVORCE

The average marriage in the USA lasts seven years; nine in the UK (Bedell, 2002). Divorce rates are highest during the first five years of marriage, and then peak again after couples have been married for 15–25 years (Turnbull, 1995).

Almost half of all marriages in England and Wales will end in divorce. Since 1997, the average age of divorce has risen from 40.2 to 43.7 years for men and from 37.7 to 41.2 years for women (partly due to the rise in age at marriage). The highest divorce rate is among men and women in their late 20s (Hill, 2009; http://www.statistics.gov.uk).

MEET THE RESEARCHER

Terri Apter

Pathways to adulthood

When does one become an adult? In 1970, the legal age of adulthood was lowered from 21 years of age to 18 in response to the apparent swiftness with which young people matured. Towards the end of the twentieth century, however, sociologists and Psychologists identified 'extended youth transitions', and the 'threshold' phase was added to the lifecourse model. This changing model shows how social context impacts on development.

Theories of adolescence

Until the 1990s, adolescence was seen as the direct pathway to adulthood. Anna Freud, one of the first Psychologists to focus on adolescence as a key developmental phase, called adolescence the psychological version of parent/child divorce (Freud, 1997). According to Anna Freud, a child's attachment to parents was replaced during the teenage years by attachments to friends and lovers; a child's idealisation of parents as all-knowing was overthrown as one exercised one's own power of thought. Peter Blos (Blos, 1979) developed this theory further and argued that the teen's irritability with parents arose from the effort to dismantle the child's love and idealisation of parents. Erik Erikson (Erikson, 1980) coined the now familiar term 'identity crisis' to describe the teenage challenge of distinguishing one's own goals and ideals from those of one's parents. Some Psychologists challenged the assumption that psychological separation from parents was a necessary step towards adult maturity (Apter, 1990, 2004; Gilligan, 1993), but the assumption that healthy adolescent development concluded with independence from one's family remained a staple cultural assumption.

Changing times for adolescents

Throughout the 1980s and 1990s, changes in employment opportunities for young adults upset social expectations as to the markers of maturity. Unskilled jobs were exported abroad, and expanding educational opportunities for young people raised employers' expectations for education qualifications, maturity and training of young employees. The changing employment market and expanding educational opportunities coincided with rapidly increasing costs of housing in the UK and United States, and these costs provided another impediment to leaving home. Increasing numbers of young people from all backgrounds remained financially dependent on their families; they also remained dependent on parents and teachers to help them weigh up goals and strategies for attaining those goals. The average age of marriage and parenthood rose from 23 years for women in 1961 to 29 years in 2000. Paradoxically, while there was much media attention on the rapidity with which young children matured physically, and took on the social and sexual savvy of teenagers, young people at the close of the teenage years were unlikely to meet the social expectations of adulthood.

The consequent delays in achieving adulthood conceptualised as psychological, financial and residential independence alarmed some social commentators. The sociologist Frank Furedi viewed contemporary culture as catering to 'a posse of Peter Pans', 'lost boys and girls hanging out on the edge of adulthood' (Furedi, 2003). He argued that parents who permitted their young adult sons and daughters to remain dependent on them 'infantilised' these young adults and undermined their capacity and motivation to achieve independence.

Troubled teens

Other research showed that young people were facing more stresses and hurdles in their lives. Since 1940, rates of suicide, eating disorders, depression, illicit drug use and alcoholism increased significantly for each subsequent cohort of 18- to 24-year-olds (Rutter and Smith, 1995). So, were young people 'spoiled' or were they confronting a new range of demands for which they needed special, extended support?

As a Psychologist who was working with young adults in an educational setting, I wanted to explore the experiences of young people in transition to adulthood. Between 1994 and 2000, I interviewed 32 young people whom I followed from the age of 18 to the age of 24 years. These case studies illustrate some of the ways young people make sense of their internal worlds, their responses to the confusions and disappointments along the pathway to adulthood, and the factors in their environment that facilitate this transition (Apter, 2002).

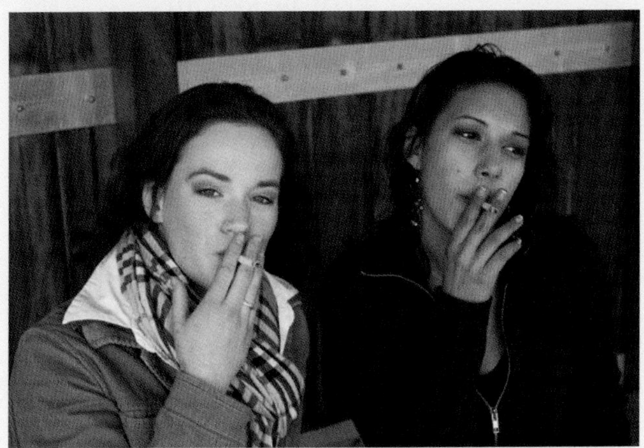

Research shows that adolescents today face more stresses and hurdles in their lives than young people did previously

'Thresholders'

A central experience shared by many young people in my study was of standing at the entrance to the adult world without feeling able to step across the threshold into that world. For this reason, I called these young people 'thresholders'. This term avoided the negative connotations of other terms given to such as parasitic singles (used in Japan) and 'bamboccioni' or 'big dummy boys' (used in Italy), and reflected their own experience. Young people were preparing for an increasingly complex adulthood in which they were likely to need extensive training before entering employment. Once in employment, they would require resilience and flexibility; they could expect to change jobs and to re-train several times throughout their twenties. Their social networks were likely to dissipate through the geographic mobility of their friends, and they often struggled with loneliness in a society that as a whole offered fewer social networks (Putnam, 2000). They developed independence in terms of competence and individual identity; nevertheless, most remained deeply attached to their parents and dependent upon parents' emotional, practical or financial support.

Immaturity

There were, however, some common 'pockets' or areas of immaturity. One 'pocket of immaturity' can be described as 'decision paralysis'. Making decisions about which course to take or which career to pursue could be daunting. Sometimes their high expectations and the wealth of choices, relative to those of previous generations, generated a reluctance to relinquish one pathway by choosing another. In this way, the benefits of having choice became an impediment to making a choice. Decision paralysis was likely to cause frustration for both the thresholder and the parents.

A second pocket of immaturity was the inability to plan and structure time realistically. During adolescence, when young people were working towards school qualifications, their days were highly structured and their discretionary time was limited. As thresholders, they often lacked experience in structuring their own time and in pacing their work. Some, accustomed to the very clear measures of school assessments, struggled to understand teachers' and employers' expectations. Many assumed that they were alone among their cohort in dealing with insecurity and uncertainty and a sense of inferiority.

The myth of maturity

While their social environment demanded a long transition period, thresholders themselves felt uneasy about their continued dependence. I concluded that maturity was a myth in two senses: it was a myth that adult maturity was achieved as soon as adolescence ended; and the underlying assumption that independence from one's family was necessary to adult competence, was also a myth. Moreover, the myth that maturity involved independence was itself harmful; it sometimes led parents to withdraw the support that helped their young adult sons and daughters navigate this transition, and it sometimes led thresholders to be dissatisfied with themselves and the rate at which they were achieving independence.

Continued parental support during this transition did not undermine the motivation to achieve greater independence. My study showed that thresholders benefited from parental support, and other large-scale studies confirm this finding (Catan, 2004). Family support comes in various forms. Emotional support provides comfort and reassurance and diffuses negative feelings such as anxiety and depression. Practical support involves help with decision-making and strategy. Financial support was provided even by low-income families as they allowed a thresholder to remain at home beyond the expected age of departure. With support from their families, young people were better placed to acquire the experience, training and confidence needed to thrive as adults.

Dr Terri Apter is a Psychologist, writer and Senior Tutor at Newnham College, Cambridge. Her research focuses on family dynamics and work/family balance. She explored young people's difficult transition to adulthood in *The Myth of Maturity: What Teenagers Need from Parents to Become Adults* in which she coined the now familiar term 'thresholders'.

In 1996, there were about 1,150,000 divorces in the USA, involving over 1 million children, 84 per cent of whom live with their mothers in single-parent homes. But this is usually only temporary, since 65 per cent of women and over 75 per cent of men remarry, and 40 per cent of all marriages are second-time arounders (Groskop, 2004). Rates of cohabitation are high in those who don't remarry. Divorce rates are even higher in remarriages than first marriages. Only 65 per cent of children in the UK live with both natural parents, and one in ten have a step-parent (1,284,000 children; Groskop, 2004).

So, in recent decades, the structure and stability of families in Western societies have undergone considerable changes. An increasing number of adults live in subsequent cohabiting or remarried relationships and, in turn, these changes have led to a marked rise in the number of children living in step-family situations (Nicholson *et al.*, 1999).

The stresses of divorce

As Key Study 38.2 testifies, divorce is a stressor for both men and women (see Chapter 12), since it involves the loss of one's major attachment figure and source of emotional support (see Chapter 32). But men appear to experience more stress than women, which is perhaps not altogether surprising given the greater benefits to men of marriage (see above).

PARENTHOOD

For most people, parenthood and child rearing represent key transitions. According to Bee (1994), 90 per cent of adults will become parents, mostly in their 20s and 30s (the average age of British women giving birth is a stable 29; Hill, 2007a). But parenthood varies in meaning and impact more than any other life transition. It may occur at any time from adolescence to middle age, and for some men, may even occur in late adulthood! Parenthood may also be planned or unplanned, wanted or unwanted, and there are many motives for having children.

Traditionally, parenthood is the domain of the married couple. However, it may involve a single woman, a homosexual couple, a cohabiting couple or couples who adopt or foster children. Increasingly, in recent decades there's been a marked rise in the number of teenage pregnancies (see Chapter 37), and even more recently, the phenomenon of 'minimal parenting' (as in donor insemination: see Chapter 32).

Equally, though, the increasing importance of work careers for women has also led to more and more couples postponing starting a family, so that the woman can become better established in her career. For example, women's average age at the birth of their first child was almost 30 in 2003 (compared with 23 in the 1960s; Groskop, 2004). In 2005, 10 times as many women in England and Wales had their first child between 35 and 39 as in 1975 and 13 times as many had their first child between 40 and 44 (Hill, 2007a). Consequently, there's a new class of middle-aged parents with young children (Turnbull, 1995). According to Wolf (2013), high-earning career 'alpha' women tend to have very few children.

Also, while in traditional and developing societies, reproductive rates rise with increasing wealth (i.e. more wealth, more children), this pattern is *reversed* in richer, industrialised countries (the *demographic transition*). For example, in the European Union, the average number of children per woman now stands at about 1.6, well below the 2.1 needed to maintain the population (Macleod, 2013).

Ask Yourself

- Assuming that they're planned, why do people have children? What are their motives?
- Is it 'natural' (at least for women) to want children?

Parenthood brings with it many psychological adaptations. For example, many women worry that their baby may be abnormal, about the changes in their body, and how well they'll cope with motherhood. Another concern is how the relationship with their husband or partner will be affected. While pregnancy brings many couples closer together, most men take longer than women to become emotionally involved in it – and some feel left out. This feeling of exclusion may continue after the baby is born, as the mother becomes preoccupied with it.

Figure 38.5 Being at the birth of his child can help counteract a father's feelings of being excluded during the pregnancy – and afterwards. It can also help him to form an emotional bond with the baby

Parents are, of course, attachment figures for their dependent children. Unlike the relationship with a partner, the relationship with a child is *asymmetrical* (the child isn't an attachment figure for its parents: see Chapter 32). This new form of responsibility can be very stressful, and has implications for how parents adapt to these new role demands, and the quality of their interactions with the child (Durkin, 1995). An unhappy couple may stay together not just 'for the kids' sake', but because the parental role has sufficient meaning and value for each partner to outweigh the dissatisfaction with their marriage (Levinson *et al.,* 1978).

Empty nest versus crowded nest

Regarding *empty-nest distress*, most parents don't find their children's departure from home to be a distressing time (Durkin, 1995). Indeed, many report that the end of child-rearing responsibilities is a 'liberating experience', and they welcome new opportunities for closer relationships with their partners, personal fulfilment through work, a return to education, and so on.

The *crowded nest* (Datan *et al.*, 1987), however, can be a source of stress. This occurs when grown-up children opt not to leave home, which defies the demands of the 'social clock' established by preceding generations. Middle-aged parents are increasingly sharing their homes with their *thresholder children* (see 'Meet the Researcher' pp. 346–7, and Figure 38.6).

Womanhood and motherhood

According to Kremer (1998), in the post-industrial/post-modern world of the twenty-first century we're still influenced by beliefs and attitudes regarding work and the sexes (or 'gendered employment profiles') inherited from an earlier time. For example, the *motherhood mystique/mandate* refers to the belief that women are born and reared to be, first and foremost, mothers (while the 'fatherhood mandate' is hardly, if ever, mentioned: see Chapter 32). Another example is the stereotype of men as inherently more committed to work than women, whose attitudes towards it are less positive than men's.

The motherhood mandate has at least three important implications.

1. Motherhood is 'natural'. Berryman (in Lacey, 1998) maintains that motherhood is still seen as synonymous with womanhood, a vital part of a

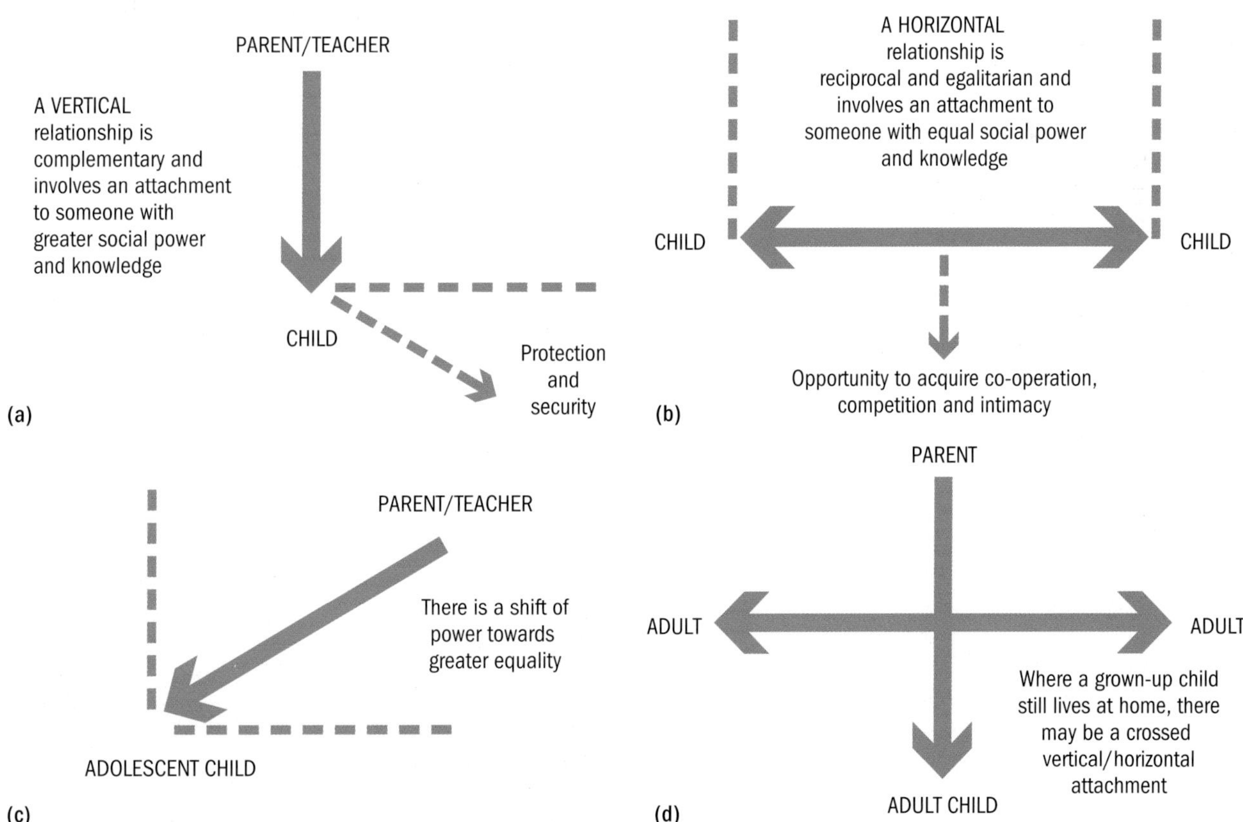

Figure 38.6 Different kinds of relationships based on Hartup's (1989) distinction between vertical and horizontal relationships. While (a) and (b) are clear-cut in terms of this distinction, (c) involves a change from vertical to horizontal, while (d) involves both dimensions simultaneously. Both (c) and (d) may involve conflict – but for different reasons

woman's life to such an extent that women who do not have children, or who do not find motherhood an innate skill, can be made to feel somehow inadequate in a way that men are not. But the reality is that, like many skills, motherhood is often learnt.

This belief that mothering comes 'naturally' is so deep-rooted that women who don't bond immediately with their babies feel inadequate or guilty, or perhaps both. However, there are indications that attitudes towards having children are changing.

2. Most people would probably consider it to be 'unnatural' (or 'wicked') for a mother to leave her children, even if they're left in the care of their father, whom she believes will look after them better than she could herself. However, the number of absent mothers targeted by the Child Support Agency trebled between 1995 and 1998, with over 37,000 being approached to pay child maintenance. One in 20 absent parents is a woman (Lacey, 1998). Either there are a lot more 'unnatural' or 'wicked' women out there than was previously thought, or the motherhood mandate needs serious revision.
3 It's 'unnatural' or simply 'wrong' for a mother of young children to go out to work. Related to this is the stereotype concerning women's attitudes towards paid employment. Is there any foundation for this stereotype?

The changing role of women in the workforce

At the end of the 1990s, employment profiles for both genders were changing rapidly. Women comprised about half the workforce (although a far higher proportion were part-time than men), and mothers were less likely to leave work to care for young children. Yet women were still more likely than men to interrupt their careers, at least temporarily, to take care of children, while men rarely did (Craig, 1992; Nicholson, 1993). (This relates to the 'gender-splitting' phenomenon identified by Levinson (1986).)

Kremer (1998) cites several surveys (conducted in the 1980s and 1990s) showing that, despite poorer working conditions, the overwhelming majority of working women prefer to be in paid employment. Additionally, most of those not in work (especially those under 50) would prefer to be. When asked to rate the importance of various factors at work, the differences between men and women are few, and usually only involve clashes between work commitments and domestic responsibilities. Men and women also tend to agree about the motivation for working, such as money, stimulation, and feeling useful. Ironically (given their poorer working

Box 38.7 Women, work and evolution

According to Hrdy (1999), these findings regarding women's attitudes towards work should come as no surprise. Arguing from an *evolutionary perspective*, Hrdy claims that being ambitious is just as natural for a mother as breastfeeding. It's a fallacy to believe that mothers who go out to work are in conflict with their natural instincts. She argues that there's nothing new about working mothers: for most of human existence, and for millions of years before that, primate mothers have combined productive lives with reproduction. This combination of work and motherhood has always entailed trade-offs.

Figure 38.7

What's new for modern mothers is the *compartmentalisation* of their productive and reproductive lives. The factories, laboratories and offices where women in post-industrial societies go to 'forage' are even less compatible with child care than jaguar-infested forests and distant groves of mongongo nuts.

Hrdy is especially interested in the Pleistocene period, which extends from about 1.6 million years ago (when humans emerged from apes) to the invention of agriculture (about 10,000 years ago). It was during this period that many human instincts – including mothering – evolved through natural selection. Pleistocene woman would have striven for status and 'local clout' among her female peers. Ambition was just as much the driving force for women as for men, serving the Darwinian purpose of producing offspring who survived to adulthood.

conditions), women consistently express higher job satisfaction (especially part-time workers and those working from home).

While the 1990s 'Superwoman' (who managed to juggle career, child care and household management successfully) may still exist, it seems she feels overworked and disillusioned. Contrary to the equation of womanhood with motherhood, many feel under pressure to go out to work and raise families, as they feel that society doesn't value mothers who stay at home (Brown, 1999).

A report ('Choosing to be Different') from the Centre for Policy Studies states that there's a general rejection of the 1980s and 1990s work ethic. Women want to fit their work round their home life (and not vice versa) (O'Kelly, 2004). Indeed, the 'Turning 30' report (published in *Elle* magazine in 2009), based on a survey of 1800 women, found that today's 30-year-olds are no longer the career-driven women of a decade ago; instead, they're looking for happiness in their personal lives ahead of fulfilment through work. Some 70 per cent of women considered it the age at which they put their relationships and personal lives before their careers, with more than 80 per cent thinking it was the perfect age to get married.

Rather than giving up on ambition, women seem to be widening their definition of it to include *all* the elements of their lives that bring them happiness, be that work, love, family or a combination of all of them – without the pressure to prove themselves in any one sphere (Hill and McVeigh, 2009).

Ask Yourself

- If women are having to juggle career and family, what does this tell us about the contribution of their husbands or partners?
- Does 'new man' exist?

Does 'new man' exist?

The phenomenon of 'dual-earner couples/marriages' (where the husband works full-time and the wife works at least 20 hours per week) has become quite common, both in the USA (Craig, 1992) and the UK (Nicholson, 1993). Compared with more 'traditional' couples, these husbands report more marital dissatisfaction and conflicts over family and work responsibilities, and the wives similarly report higher levels of conflict, as well as a very realistic work overload.

There's some evidence that domestic tasks (especially child care) are more evenly shared in some dual-earner families (for example, up to a third of all home child care is now done by men; Hinsliff, 2004). However, it's nearly always the woman who's still primarily responsible for both housework and child care, regardless of the age of the children and whether she works full- or part-time. Based on studies in eastern and western Europe, and North and South America, it seems that when there are no children, working wives do the bulk of the shopping, and so on. But when there are children, the husband's contribution to running the home actually *declines* (in relative terms) with each child: the wife's increases by 5–10 per cent with each child (Nicholson, 1993). While there are no apparent social-class differences in men's contributions to the domestic division of labour, there are cultural ones, with Swedish men doing much more than their North American counterparts (Durkin, 1995).

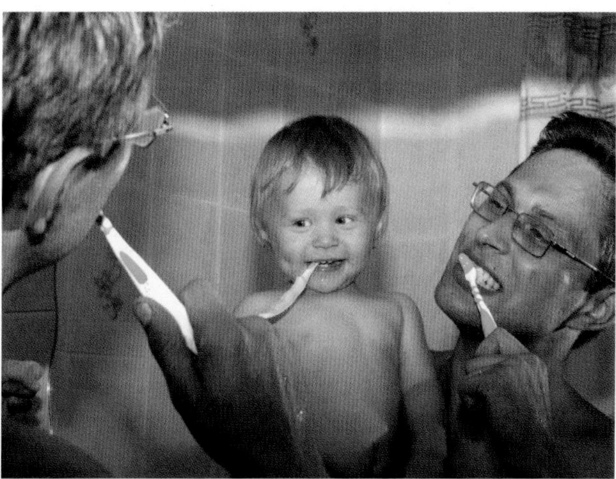

Figure 38.8 Fathers' involvement in child care, though on the increase, is still not seen as 'men's work', but is more of a bonus – for child and father alike. Nor does it seem to reduce any of the mother's burden of responsibility

According to Kremer (1998):

> *There is little evidence to suggest that domestic responsibilities have been lifted from the shoulders of women. Instead, women's dual roles (home carer and worker) persist. Indeed, even in situations where both partners are not in paid employment, or where the woman is the primary wage earner, then this pattern often still endures.*

Similarly, Quiery (1998) maintains that while there have been some changes in fathers' behaviour over the last 15–20 years, they're not dramatic and the burden of child rearing and home-making still falls on mothers. However, evidence from both the USA and the UK suggests that a rather more significant change is taking place (see Key Study 38.2).

Pleck (1999) concludes that although men still perform less child care than women, men's participation in family activities is increasing.

Figure 38.9 While child care is still regarded as predominantly 'woman's work', mothers are increasingly likely to have a 'second career' outside the home. Whether her paid employment is full- or part-time, this is likely to be additional to her domestic duties

However, most of the relevant data come from studies of *married* fathers, which excludes a substantial proportion of the adult male population. When these other groups are taken into account, the *opposite* picture emerges. Thus, it seems that American family life is changing in two *contradictory directions*: (i) in two-parent families, fathers' involvement with children and overall gender equality are increasing. Data for the UK mirror the US situation (Morgan, 2005); (ii) two-parent families have become a smaller proportion of all families, and families headed by single mothers have become more common. The overall effect of this is that more children don't have resident fathers (Pleck, 1999). In the UK, 70 per cent of non-resident fathers have contact with their children. In 10 per cent of families affected by divorce, the father is the main carer (Morgan, 2005).

Key Study 38.2

Are American men participating more in their children's activities? (Pleck, 1999)

- Pleck compared 11 studies dating from the mid-1960s to the early 1980s with 13 studies conducted between the mid-1980s and early 1990s. As shown in Figure 38.10, fathers' *engagement* with their children (as a percentage of the mothers' engagement) increased over that period from 34.3 to 43.5 per cent. Engagement refers to interaction with one's children, such as playing with them, reading to them, and helping them with their homework.

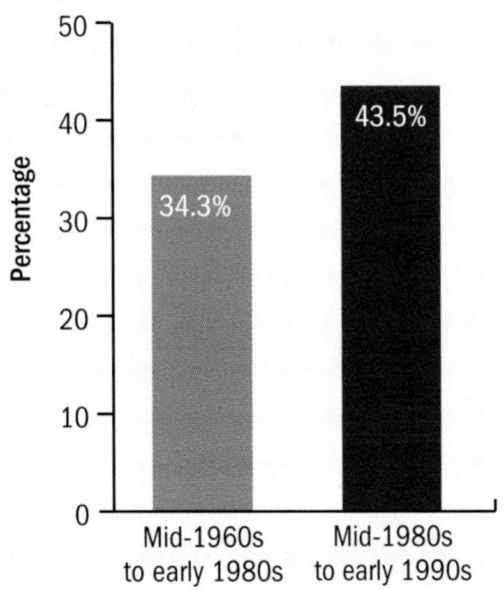

Figure 38.10 Amount of time fathers interact with their children as percentage of mothers' engagement (from Pleck, 1999)

- In that same period, fathers' *availability* also increased (again, as a percentage of the mothers') from 51.8 to 65.6 per cent (see Figure 38.11). Availability is a measure of how much time fathers spend near their children, either interacting with them or not (such as working on the computer while the children play video games).

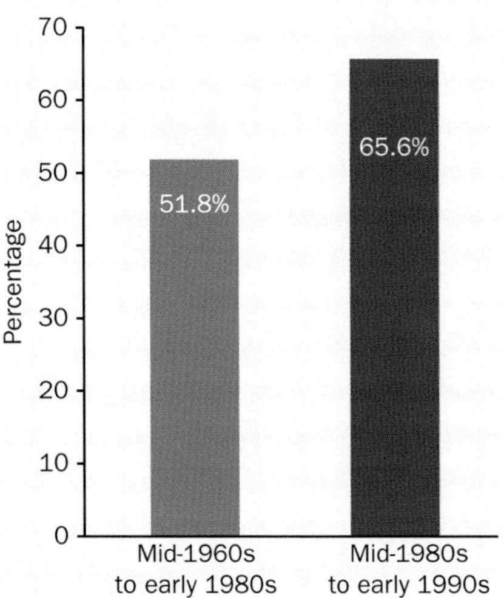

Figure 38.11 Amount of time fathers are near their children, either interacting or not, as percentage of mothers' availability (from Pleck, 1999)

Both Figures courtesy of Scientific American

Pleck also cites evidence (from both his own and others' research) showing that family is far more central psychologically to men than work, just as it is for women. This suggests that 'gender splitting' may not be such a clearly defined phenomenon as Levinson proposed. However, men are more likely to take workplace emotions home with them than are mothers, who keep these separate from their family experience.

Lesbian and gay parenting

In the context of advocating that Psychologists should study homosexual relationships in their own terms (and not by comparison with heterosexual ones), Kitzinger and Coyle (1995) suggest that we might want to ask how the children of lesbian/gay couples understand and talk about their parents' relationships, and how they can develop positive views about homosexuality in a heterosexual culture. Homosexual couples have always been involved in parenting through partners' previous heterosexual relationships. The recent increase in fostering/adoption of children by gay men, and the ongoing 'lesbian baby boom', means that many more homosexual couples are parents than used to be the case.

According to Kitzinger *et al.* (1998), research into lesbian/gay parenting was initially concerned with whether or how far the children of lesbians and (to a lesser extent) gay men could be distinguished psychologically from those of heterosexuals. On balance, this research suggested that these children were no more 'at risk' than children raised in heterosexual families.

For example, Taylor (1993) found no evidence that children reared in gay/lesbian families were more disturbed or had greater gender identity confusion than those reared in heterosexual families. Barrett and Robinson (1990) reviewed the impact of gay fathering on children. They stress the need to take into account that these children are likely to have experienced parental divorce and to show the psychological distress that often accompanies it (see Chapter 32). Although these children may be isolated, angry and in need of help sorting out their feelings about homosexuality in general, they're in little danger of being sexually abused, and adjust well to their family situations. While the relationships with their fathers may be stormy at first, they also have the potential for considerable honesty and openness.

Increasingly, Psychologists are researching areas directly rooted in the concerns of lesbian/gay parents themselves, including coming out to one's children, and managing different co-parenting arrangements (such as a lesbian mother with her female lover, her ex-husband, a gay male sperm donor, or a gay male co-parent; Kitzinger *et al.*, 1998).

CONCLUSIONS

Although some of the most influential and popular explanations of personality change in early and middle adulthood have adopted *stage approaches*, critics argue that adult development doesn't occur in predictable and ordered ways. An alternative, yet complementary, approach is to assess the impact of *critical life events*. These include two major *normative age-graded influences*, marriage/partnering and parenthood, and one *non-normative influence*, divorce.

In the case of parenthood, the changing roles of men and women have been shown to be crucial, especially women's participation in the labour market. This means that to appreciate the impact of various life events, they must be examined in the broader context of social norms, which, at least in Western countries, are constantly shifting. The chapter has also illustrated the mutual influence of different life events involving family and relationships.

Chapter Summary

- In Erikson's **psychosocial theory,** the task of **young adulthood** is to achieve **intimacy** and to avoid **isolation**. The central task of **middle adulthood** is the attainment of **generativity** and avoidance of **stagnation**.
- Many people struggle with issues of identity and intimacy **at the same time**, and women tend to achieve intimacy **before** 'occupational identity', submerging their identity into that of their partners. There are also important social-class, racial, and cultural differences in the timing of marriage and 'settling down'.
- Levinson *et al.* were concerned with how adulthood is actually **experienced**. Their **life-structure theory** identifies **phases/periods** that are either stable (**structure-building**) or transitional (**structure-changing**). A sequence of **eras** overlaps in the form of **cross-era transitions.**
- **Early adult transition** is a developmental bridge between adolescence and adulthood, and **entry life structure for early adulthood** is the first structure-building phase.
- Levinson *et al.* see **crisis** as both inevitable and necessary (**normative**). But people of all ages suffer crises (**'adolescing'**), and a growing number of people are deciding to make radical changes in their lifestyles (e.g. **downshifting**), both earlier and later than 'mid-life'.
- While men have fairly unified, career-focused visions of the future, women's **dreams** are split between career and marriage/family responsibilities (**gender-splitting**).

- The **age-30 transition** generally lasts longer for women than for men, and **'settling down'** is much less clear-cut. Trying to integrate career and marriage and family responsibilities is very difficult for most women.
- The view that adult development is **'stage-like'** has been criticised on the grounds that it underestimates **individual variability**. Stage theories also imply a **discontinuity** of development.
- According to Gould, the thrust of adult development is towards **adult consciousness** and freeing ourselves of the **illusion of absolute safety**. Adult development also involves a change in the **sense of time**.
- **Marriage** and **parenting** are **normative, age-graded influences**, while divorce is a **non-normative influence**. These are also called **marker events** or **critical life events**.
- Couples who **cohabit** before marriage are more likely to divorce later, or be less satisfied with their marriages, than those who don't cohabit.
- **Married people** tend to live longer, and are happier, healthier and have lower rates of mental disorder than unmarried people. Men benefit most from marriage, and the potential benefits of marriage for women may be counterbalanced by gender-splitting.
- **Parenthood** has greater variability in meaning and impact than any other life transition. While pregnancy can bring couples closer together, men can feel excluded, especially after their babies are born.
- There's little evidence for **empty-nest distress**, and marital satisfaction usually increases once children have left home. The **crowded nest** is more likely to be distressing.
- The **motherhood mystique/mandate** can make women who don't bond immediately with their babies feel inadequate. But women are increasingly postponing having children.
- The motherhood mandate also implies that it's unnatural for mothers to leave their children, and that it's wrong for a mother of young children to go out to work.
- Despite evidence that domestic duties are more evenly shared in some **dual-earner families**, it's invariably the woman who's still primarily responsible for both housework and child care.
- Although **married fathers** are **engaging** more with their children, many **divorced** fathers have little contact with their children. The overall effect is that more and more children are living without resident fathers.
- Many more **lesbian/gay couples** are parents than used to be the case. Early research examined whether the children of such parents were more 'at risk' than those raised in heterosexual families, but more recently the emphasis has shifted to issues such as co-parenting arrangements.

Links with Other Topics/Chapters

Chapter 12 ⟶ Normative age-graded influences and non-normative influences include many of the life events listed in Holmes and Rahe's *Social Readjustment Rating Scale* measure of *stress*

Chapter 47 ⟶ According to Gilligan, Erikson's theory is *androcentric* (male-centred), but is still meant to apply equally to males and females

Chapter 37 ⟶ Levinson *et al.*'s claim that separation from our parents is never complete is consistent with the evidence which shows that securely attached adolescents find it easier to achieve independence

Chapter 32 ⟶ Levinson *et al.* use 'attachment' differently from *attachment theorists*: attachment to 'the world', rather than to *attachment figures*

Chapter 34 ⟶ The debate regarding the validity of seeing adult development in terms of distinct stages mirrors that in relation to children's *cognitive development*

Chapter 32 ⟶ Gould's theory is really an extension of the Freudian idea of *separation anxiety*

Chapter 43 ⟶ Changing norms regarding the appropriate age to marry and have children illustrate the more general issue as to how *definitions of normality* can and do change over time

Chapter 28 ⟶ Marriage cannot be the same type of transition for everyone. In some cultures, for example, people have little choice as to who their partners will be (as in *arranged marriages*)

Chapter 28 ⟶ Much of the research into *interpersonal relationships* has focused on marriage and other forms of long-term partnering, including the reasons for the breakdown of relationships (e.g. divorce)

Chapter 32 ⟶ The psychological effects of divorce have been investigated mainly from the *child's* perspective. If the most damaging factor is *marital conflict*, then relief from this may be beneficial for both children and parents

Chapter 36 ⟶ The effects of being raised by gay or lesbian couples have been studied in relation to *gender identity* and *sexual orientation*

Recommended Reading

Gross, R. (2003) *Key Studies in Psychology* (4th edition). London: Hodder & Stoughton. Chapter 17.

Schaie, K.W. & Willis, S.L. (1999) *Adult Development and Ageing* (5th edition). New York: HarperCollins. Also relevant to Chapter 39.

Sheehy, G. (1996) *New Passages* (revised, UK edition). London: HarperCollins

Useful Website

http://midmac.med.harvard.edu/research.html (John D. & Catherine T. MacArthur Foundation: Research Network on Successful Midlife Development, 2006)

CHAPTER 39

OLD AGE

The meaning of 'old'

Ageism

Cognitive changes in old age

Social changes in old age

Retirement

Bereavement

INTRODUCTION and OVERVIEW

While 'growing up' is normally seen as desirable, 'growing old' usually has far more negative connotations. The negative view of ageing is based on the *decrement model*, which sees ageing as a process of decay or decline in physical and mental health, intellectual abilities and social relationships. According to Bond *et al.* (2007):

> *... The emphasis on decline rather than change underpins the almost universal negative stereotypes and attitudes of ageing and older people that appear to be held by most people of all ages and cultures ...*

An alternative to the decrement model is the *personal growth model*, which stresses the potential advantages of late adulthood (or 'old age'), such as increased leisure time, reduced responsibilities, and the ability to concentrate only on matters of high priority (Kalish, 1982). This much more positive view is how ageing has been studied within the *lifespan approach*.

In this chapter we consider some of the theories and research concerned with *adjustment to late adulthood*. It begins by looking at what's meant by the term 'old', which turns out to be more complex than it might seem. *Stereotyped beliefs* about what elderly people are like are an inherent part of prejudiced attitudes towards them. Research into some of the cognitive and social changes that occur in late adulthood bring these stereotypes and prejudice into sharp focus. The chapter also discusses the impact of two major life events, *retirement* (a *normative, age-graded influence*, often taken to mark the 'official' start of old age) and *bereavement* (a *non-normative influence*, although death of one's spouse becomes increasingly likely as we attain late adulthood).

THE MEANING OF 'OLD'

Ask Yourself

- How old is old?
- Is 'old' simply a matter of chronological age?

Since the Industrial Revolution in the middle of the nineteenth century, average female life expectancy has increased in Western societies from about 45 years to currently more than 80 (corresponding to an increase of 2.3 years per decade). Men's life expectancy has also risen, although more slowly: the gap between females and males has widened from two to six years (Westendorp and Kirkwood, 2007).

For the first time in 2009, the percentage of the UK population aged under 16 fell below the percentage of the population over 60. The fastest growing age group is now the over-80s (McVeigh, 2009). In the USA, men and women born in 1970 could expect to live to ages 67.1 and 74.7 years, respectively; for those born in 2000, the figures are 74.1 and 79.5. For those aged 50 in 2000, average life expectancy was 77.9 for men and 81.8 for women (Kroger, 2007).

In the UK, if the current trends continue, the number of people over 65 will triple from 4.6

million (2007) to 15.5 million (2074); the number of centenarians (people of 100 or more) will increase 100 times from 10,000 to 1 million (Brown, 2007).

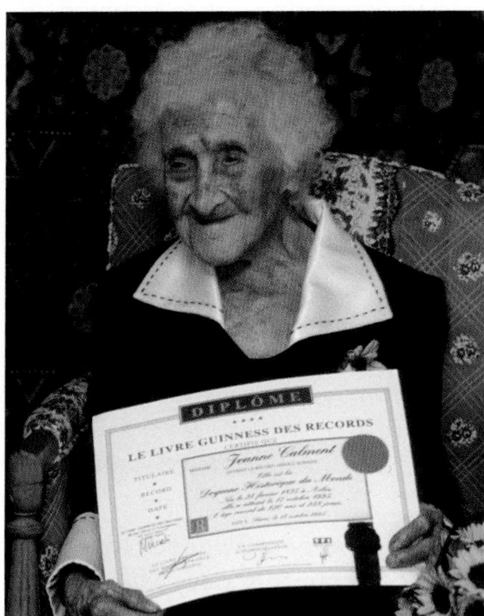

Figure 39.1 The oldest person who ever lived: Jeanne Calment died in 1997 at the age of 122

Because of this *demographic imperative* (Swensen, 1983), Developmental Psychologists have become increasingly interested in our later years. But what do we mean by 'old'? Kastenbaum's (1979) 'The ages of me' questionnaire assesses how people see themselves at the present moment in relation to their ages (see Box 39.1).

Ask Yourself

- How old are you according to Kastenbaum's questionnaire?

Few people, irrespective of their chronological age, describe themselves consistently (that is, they tend to give *different* responses to the different questionnaire items). For example, people over 20 (including those in their 70s and 80s) usually describe themselves as feeling younger than their chronological age. We also generally consider ourselves to be too old.

AGEISM

According to Comfort (1977), ageism is:

> *... the notion that people cease to be people, cease to be the same people or become people of a distinct and inferior kind by virtue of having lived a specified number of years ... Like racism, which it resembles, it is based on fear.*

Box 39.1 Kastenbaum's 'The Ages of Me' questionnaire

- My *chronological age* is my actual or official age, dated from my time of birth. My chronological age is ...
- My *biological age* refers to the state of my face and body. In other people's eyes, I look as though I am about ... years of age. In my own eyes, I look like someone of about ... years of age.
- My *subjective age* is indicated by how I feel. Deep down inside, I really feel like a person of about ... years of age.
- My *functional age*, which is closely related to my *social age*, refers to the kind of life I lead, what I am able to do, the status I believe I have, whether I work, have dependent children and live in my own home. My thoughts and interests are like those of a person of about ... years of age, and my position in society is like that of a person of about ... years of age.

Figure 39.2 While (c) might depict someone's chronological age, (a) might correspond to his biological age and (b) might represent his subjective age

(Adapted from Kastenbaum, 1979)

Similarly, Bromley (1977) argues that most people react adversely to the elderly because they seem to deviate from our concept of 'normal' human beings. As part of the 'welfarist approach' to understanding the problems of an ageing society (Fennell *et al.*, 1988), 'they' (i.e. the elderly) are designated as different, occupying another world from 'us' – a process that for all perceived minorities tends to be dehumanising and sets lower or different standards of social value or individual worth (Manthorpe, 1994).

Critical Discussion 39.1

The price we pay for a longer life

Until about 200 years ago, people died young and relatively quickly – mainly from infections. During the twentieth century, the average life expectancy in the world doubled, and people in developed countries now tend to die old and slowly – from degenerative diseases brought on by ageing (Brown, 2007).This increase in longevity and its accelerating rate has enormous implications for health and social service requirements of older adults in the coming years (Kroger, 2007).

The increased lifespan hasn't been matched by an extension of health: the years we gain are mostly spent with disability, disease and dementia. Between 1991 and 2001, life expectancy in the UK increased by 2.2 years, but healthy life expectancy increased by only 0.6 years: people experienced ill health for an extra 1.6 years of their lives. This is because we've not been able to slow the ageing process: the increased lifespan is accompanied by an increase in degenerative disease with age (the 'expansion of morbidity'), such as cancer and vascular and neurodegenerative disease (Brown, 2007).

For example, the prevalence of Alzheimer's disease is about 1 per cent at age 65 and roughly doubles every five years after that, to around 25 per cent for 85-year-olds. In the USA, 46 per cent of people over 85 are believed to have Alzheimer's (Brown, 2007). A report by the King's Fund health care charity found that the number of people in the UK with dementia will increase by 61 per cent – to more than 1.1 million – by 2026. Almost 80 per cent of people who live to be 95 already suffer some form of mild to severe dementia (McVeigh, 2009). According to Lees (2012), the single key risk factor for succumbing to dementia is a person's age. For a 65-year-old, that risk is one in 14; for someone over 80, it rises to one in six.

According to Brown (2007):

> *... It is tempting to think that ageing is 'natural', but the opposite is the case. Ageing is an artefact of culture. It is very rare in wild animals and was rare in humans until 200 years ago. As the population inexorably ages, maladies that were formerly rare or non-existent become commonplace ... we need a new attitude to death. Death is not the enemy; it is an integral part of life. It is ageing and its diseases that we should be fighting ...*

However, there's emerging evidence that dementia rates in developed countries have *fallen*: this conclusion is based on two recently published studies, one of which compared two UK surveys conducted 20 years apart (1994, 2014), the other a Danish study that compared the health of two groups of mid-90-year-olds born a decade apart (1905, 1915). While neither study was designed to account for this trend, rising prosperity, better health and education are the likely key factors (Drew, 2014). Other recent research has made it clear that poor physical fitness – including obesity and cardiovascular health – can be damaging to our brains, shrinking the hippocampus. So, the general decline in *physical* health as we age may also contribute to the gradual decrease in *mental* skills (Rabbitt, 2006; Robson, 2013) (see text below).

Research has begun to examine the nature and breadth of ageism throughout society. In the UK, the Research on Age Discrimination (ROAD) project, a partnership between Help the Aged (now part of Age UK) and the Open University, is beginning to identify the diversity of situations in which discrimination appears – from hairdressing to service delivery, from access to public toilets to 'what to wear', that is, facets of normal everyday life (Peace *et al.*, 2007).

The effects of stereotyping

Several studies by Levy and her colleagues have demonstrated that stereotypes can affect how the elderly think about themselves in ways that can be detrimental to their mental and physical health. For example, in Levy *et al.* (1999–2000), elderly participants spent a few minutes concentrating on a computer-based reaction-time test. Age-related words were subliminally presented on the screen (too quickly to be consciously registered), and were either negative (e.g. 'senile, 'forgetful', diseased'), or positive (e.g. 'wise', 'astute', 'accomplished').

The participants were subsequently asked if they'd request an expensive but potentially life-saving medical treatment, without which they'd die within a month. Most of those who'd 'seen' the positive words (evoking a positive stereotype) chose the life-saving treatment, but most of those who were exposed to negative words declined. As Levy *et al.* say, socially transmitted negative stereotypes of ageing weaken elderly people's will to live.

In another study, participants were challenged with a series of maths problems following ten minutes' exposure to positive or negative words. Those exposed to the latter showed increased cardiovascular response to stress – heart rate, systolic and diastolic blood pressure, and skin conductance all increased and stayed high for over 30 minutes. In contrast, those exposed to positive words sailed through the challenge stress-free (Levy *et al.*, 2000). So, not only may negative stereotypes contribute to adverse health outcomes in elderly persons without their awareness, but positive stereotypes could be used in interventions to reduce cardiovascular stress. (Levy's research is discussed further in Key Study 39.1.)

Box 39.2 Can stereotypes make you ill?

In April 2000, the charity Age Concern (now part of Age UK) highlighted the plight of Jill Baker, a cancer patient in her 60s. She was shocked to discover that, despite still being in a generally good state of health, a junior doctor she'd never met had put 'not for resuscitation' on her records. According to Ebrahim (in Payne, 2000):

> *Medical students still rejoice in their stereotypes of 'geriatric crumbly' and 'GOMER' (get out of my emergency room) patients.*

Ebrahim cites US evidence showing that 'do not resuscitate' orders are commonly used for people with HIV, blacks, alcohol misusers, and non-English speakers, suggesting that doctors have stereotypes of who isn't worth saving.

In the UK, one in 20 people aged over 65 had been refused treatment by the NHS, with one in ten over-50s believing they were treated differently (i.e. worse) because of their age (based on an Age UK survey).

Ask Yourself

- If you're being honest, do you stereotype elderly people ('the elderly')?
- If so, what characteristics do you attribute to them?

People are overwhelmingly unenthusiastic about becoming 'old' (Stuart-Hamilton, 1997). According to Jones (1993), everyone over retirement age is seen as forming a strange homogeneous mass, with limited abilities, few needs and few rights:

> *What other section of the population that spans more than 30 years in biological time is grouped together in such an illogical manner? ... As a consequence, older people suffer a great deal ... As for experience and wisdom, these qualities are no longer valued in this fast-moving high-technology world. They are devalued by the community, as well as by their owners ... (Jones, 1993)*

COGNITIVE CHANGES IN OLD AGE

Consistent with the decrement model, it's commonly believed that old age is associated with a decrease in cognitive abilities. Until recently, it was thought that intellectual capacity peaked in the late teens or early 20s, levelled off, and then began to decline fairly steadily during middle age and more rapidly in old age.

The evidence on which this claim was based came from *cross-sectional studies* (studying different age groups at the same time).

Ask Yourself

- Why can't we generalise from cross-sectional studies?

We cannot draw firm conclusions from such studies, because the age groups compared represent different generations with different experiences (the *cohort effect*). Unless we know how 60-year-olds, say, performed when they were 40 and 20, it's impossible to say whether or not intelligence declines with age.

An alternative methodology is the *longitudinal study*, in which the same people are tested and retested at various times during their lives. Several such studies have produced data contradicting the results of cross-sectional studies, indicating that at least some people retain their intellect well into middle age and beyond (Holahan and Sears, 1995). However, the evidence suggests that there are some age-related changes in different kinds of intelligence and aspects of memory.

Changes in intelligence

Although Psychologists have always disagreed about the definition of intelligence, there's general acceptance that it's *multi-dimensional* (composed of several different abilities). An important – and very relevant – distinction is that between crystallised and fluid intelligence (Horn, 1982; Horn and Cattell, 1967; see Chapter 41).

- *Crystallised intelligence* (what Baltes (1993) called the *pragmatics* of intelligence) refers to a largely culture- and education-related knowledge that involves general knowledge, vocabulary and application of knowledge. It's measured by tests of general information.

- *Fluid intelligence* (what Baltes (1993) called the *mechanics* of intelligence) consists of relatively culture-free types of information processing (such as pattern recognition, spatial orientation, memory, reasoning and abstraction). It's measured in terms of the ability to solve novel and unusual problems.

Crystallised intelligence increases with age, and people tend to continue improving their performance until near the end of their lives (Horn, 1982). Using the *cross-longitudinal method* (in which different age groups are retested over a long period of time), Schaie and Hertzog (1983) reported that fluid intelligence declines for all age groups over time, peaking between 20 and 30.

Explaining changes in intelligence

Intelligence tests are typically heavily loaded with fluid intelligence questions at the expense of crystallised intelligence, and they are also usually *timed*. This implies that tests of general intelligence are biased against older people (see below). But tests of crystallised intelligence are, arguably, biased *in favour* of older people (there's usually no time limit). However, removing the time limit from tests of fluid intelligence doesn't remove the age difference – but it does reduce it. So, the preservation of crystallised intelligence in later life is, in part, illusory (Stuart-Hamilton, 2000).

Physiological changes (such as cardiovascular and metabolic dysfunction) can have serious effects on physiological processes in the brain; in turn, these can lower intellectual performance. For example, response times (RTs) are a good indicator of how efficiently the nervous system operates. Not only do we get slower as we get older, but this slowing is strongly correlated with IQ test scores: the slower the RTs, the lower the test score (the *general slowing hypothesis*: Stuart-Hamilton, 2003). The prime cause of the decline in intelligence in elderly people is a slowing of nervous system processes (Stuart-Hamilton, 2003).

Some argue that an even better indication of change is the state of the sensory systems (as measured by vision and hearing). A composite index composed of measures of sensory efficiency correlates impressively with IQ test scores (Baltes and Lindenberger, 1997). Alternative measures of intellectual activity (such as problem-solving or memory: see below) are highly correlated with IQ (Rabbitt, 1993).

Box 39.3 Compensating for slowing down

- A proportion of older people never lose their youthful level of performance. For example, Rabbitt (1980) estimated that 15 per cent maintain their intellectual performance throughout life. This may be partly genetic and partly due to the level and type of their daily intellectual activity. Regular practice at intellectual skills means they're maintained at or near to a youthful level ('use it or lose it': Stuart-Hamilton, 2000).
- A longitudinal study by Schooler and Mulatu (2001) found that people who engage in intellectually demanding work or hobbies also tend to have 'better preserved' intellectual abilities. Such individuals have a lower incidence of dementia, or their symptoms may be less pronounced (Snowdon *et al.*, 2000; see text below).
- Older chess and bridge players perform at the same level as younger opponents (Charness, 1979, 1981). Although they had poorer memories, they could draw on a greater store of strategies and tactics. They compensated for the lowering of basic skills by calling on their higher level of experience.
- Such people are reversing the normal trend: we're less often challenged to use our fluid abilities in old age (Cavanaugh, 1995), whereas regular use of our crystallised abilities may help to maintain them (Denney and Palmer, 1981).
- Harrison *et al.* (2012) studied 12 'Super Agers', individuals over 80 who performed as well on memory tests as a group of 50- to 65-year-olds. Their average brain thickness matched the younger group's, which was significantly greater than typical 80-year-olds. The anterior cingulate (important for attention) was actually thicker in the Super Agers than the younger group. The older participants also had four times as many von Economo neurons (large cingulate brain cells involved in higher-level thinking: see Chapter 4) than typical 80-year-olds.

Changes in memory

Some aspects of memory appear to decline with age, possibly because we become less effective at processing information (which may underlie cognitive changes in general; Stuart-Hamilton, 1994). On *recall* tests, older adults generally perform more poorly than younger adults. But the reverse is sometimes true, as shown by Maylor's (1994) study of the performance of older contestants on *Mastermind*. On *recognition* tests, the differences between younger and older people are less apparent and may even disappear.

Key Study 39.1

The influence of stereotypes on memory (Levy and Langer, 1994)

- Levy and Langer investigated the memory capabilities of hearing Americans, members of the American deaf community, and people from mainland China. It was assumed that members of the deaf community were less likely to have been exposed to negative cultural stereotypes. People from mainland China were chosen because of the high esteem in which Chinese society holds its aged members.
- The older American deaf participants and the Chinese participants performed much better on memory tasks than the older American hearing participants.
- Also, younger hearing Americans held less positive views of ageing than any of the other groups. Among the older participants, attitudes towards ageing and memory performance were positively correlated.
- Levy and Langer believe that negative stereotypes about ageing may become *self-fulfilling prophecies*: low expectations mean that people are less likely to engage in activities that will help them maintain their memory abilities.
- The subliminal (below conscious awareness) presentation of negative self-stereotypes (e.g. 'Because of my age I am forgetful') tended to worsen memory performance, while positive self-stereotypes (e.g. 'Because of my age I have acquired wisdom') tended to improve it (Levy, 1996). Levy found no such effect with young participants, for whom stereotypes of ageing are obviously less salient.

Procedural memory is largely unaffected by ageing, as is *short-term memory*, although there are large age decrements in *working memory*. As far as *episodic memory* is concerned, there's a lot of evidence of an age-related decline in the ability to free recall, for example, previously presented words, sentences or pictures in an experimental setting, or names of people recently met, or issues read the previous day in a newspaper. Older people also tend to forget the *contextual* details of events of everyday experiences (e.g. repeating the same story to the same person several times). However, *semantic memory* remains almost intact from young adulthood to the mid-70s; after that, word-finding and name-retrieving become increasingly unreliable (Arkowitz and Lilienfeld, 2012b; Marcoen *et al.*, 2007; see Chapter 17).

Based on his conclusion that Alzheimer's is a disease process, which, while more likely to affect us as we get older (see Critical Discussion 39.1) *isn't* an acceleration of normal ageing, Smith (1998) argues that we must abandon the fatalistic view that mental decline is an inevitable accompaniment of ageing. Consistent with this conclusion is the belief that negative cultural stereotypes of ageing actually cause memory decline in the elderly (see Key Study 39.1).

SOCIAL CHANGES IN OLD AGE

Social disengagement theory (SDT)

According to Manthorpe (1994), Cumming and Henry's (1961) *social disengagement theory* (SDT) represented the first major theory about individuals' relationships with society. Based on a five-year study of 275 50- to 90-year-olds in Kansas City, USA, Cumming and Henry claimed that:

> *Many of the relationships between a person and other members of society are severed and those remaining are altered in quality.*

This social disengagement involves the mutual withdrawal of society from the individual (through compulsory retirement, children growing up and leaving home, the death of a spouse, and so on) and of the individual from society (Cumming, 1975). As people grow older, they become more solitary, retreat into the inner world of their memories, become emotionally quiescent, and engage in pensive self-reflection.

Cumming sees disengagement as having three components:

1. *shrinkage of life space*: the tendency to interact with fewer other people as we grow older, and to occupy fewer roles
2. *increased individuality*: in the roles that remain, older people are much less governed by strict rules and expectations
3. *acceptance* (even embrace) *of these changes*: withdrawal is a voluntary, natural, and inevitable process, and represents the most appropriate and successful way of growing old.

As far as society is concerned, the individual's withdrawal is part of an inevitable move towards death – the ultimate disengagement (Manthorpe, 1994). By replacing older individuals with younger people, society renews itself and the elderly are free to die (Bromley, 1988).

An evaluation of social disengagement theory

- Bee (1994) sees the first two components as difficult to dispute. However, the third is more controversial because of its view of disengagement as a natural, voluntary, and inevitable process, rather than an imposed one.
- Bromley (1988) argues that such a view of ageing has detrimental *practical* consequences for the elderly, such as encouraging a policy of segregation, even indifference, and the very destructive belief that old age has no value. For Bromley, an even more serious criticism concerns whether everyone actually does disengage.

Key Study 39.2

Do all older people disengage? (Havighurst *et al.*, 1968)

- Havighurst *et al.* followed up about half the sample originally studied by Cumming and Henry (1961).
- Although increasing age was accompanied by increasing disengagement, at least some remained active and engaged, and they tended to be the happiest. The fact that those who disengage the least are the happiest, have the highest morale and live the longest, contradicts SDT's view that withdrawal from mainstream society is a natural and inherent part of the ageing process (Bee, 1994).
- While some people may choose to lead socially isolated lives and find contentment in them, such disengagement doesn't appear to be necessary for overall mental health in old age.
- Havighurst *et al.* also identified several different personality types. These included:
  - *reorganisers*, who were involved in a wide range of activities and reorganised their lives to compensate for lost activities, and
  - the *disengaged*, who voluntarily moved away from role commitments.
- Consistent with SDT, the latter reported low levels of activity but high 'life satisfaction'. However, the disposition to disengage is a personality dimension as well as a characteristic of ageing (Bromley, 1988).

- SDT focuses on *quantitative* changes, such as the reduced number of relationships and roles in old age. But for Carstensen (1996), it's the *qualitative* changes that are crucial:

> *Although age is associated with many losses, including loss of power, social partners, physical health, cognitive efficiency, and, eventually, life itself – and although this list of losses encompasses the very things that younger people typically equate with happiness – research suggests that older people are at least as satisfied with their lives as their younger counterparts.*

Activity (or re-engagement) theory (AT)

The major alternative to SDT is *activity* (or *re-engagement*) *theory* (AT) (Havighurst, 1964; Maddox, 1964). Except for inevitable biological and health changes, older people are essentially the same as middle-aged people, with the same psychological and social needs. Decreased social interaction in old age is the result of the withdrawal of an inherently ageist society from the ageing person, and happens against the wishes of most elderly people. The withdrawal *isn't* mutual.

Optimal ageing involves staying active and managing to resist the 'shrinkage' of the social world. This can be achieved by maintaining the activities of middle age for as long as possible, and then finding substitutes for work or retirement (such as leisure or hobbies) and for spouses and friends upon their death (such as grandchildren). It's important for older adults to maintain their role counts, to ensure they always have several different roles to play.

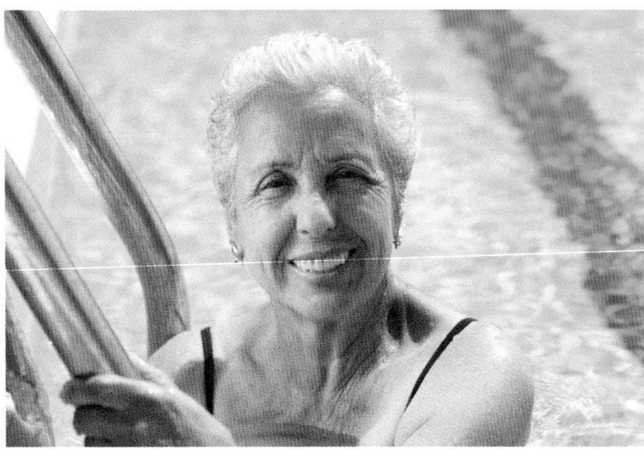

Figure 39.3 Activity theory personified

An evaluation of activity theory

Ask Yourself

- Can you think of any objections to activity theory?
- Is it realistic?
- Does it repeat any of the mistakes of SDT?

- According to Bond *et al.* (1993), activity theory can be criticised for being:

> *... unrealistic because the economic, political and social structure of society prevents the older worker from maintaining a major activity of middle age, namely, 'productive' employment.*

The implication seems to be that there really is no substitute for paid employment (at least for men: see below). According to Dex and Phillipson (1986), society appears to measure people's worth by their ability to undertake paid labour, and the more autonomous people are in their working practices, the more respect they seem to deserve. When someone retires, they not only lose their autonomy and right to work for money, but they also lose their *identity*: they cease to be a participant in society and their status is reduced to 'pensioner/senior citizen' or simply 'old person'.

- As noted in Key Study 39.2, some elderly people seem satisfied with disengagement, suggesting that AT alone cannot explain successful ageing. Nevertheless, activity or re-engagement prevents the consequences of disengagement from going too far in the direction of isolation, apathy, and inaction.
- Just as disengagement may be involuntary (as in the case of poor health), so we may face involuntarily high levels of activity (as in looking after grandchildren). SDT may actually *under*estimate, and AT *over*estimate, the degree of control people have over the 'reconstruction' of their lives.
- Additionally, both theories see ageing as essentially the same for everyone. They both refer to a legitimate process through which some people come to terms with the many changes that accompany ageing (they represent options; Hayslip and Panek, 1989). However, people will select styles of ageing best suited to their personalities and past experiences or lifestyles, and there's no single 'best way' to age (Neugarten and Neugarten, 1987). For Turner and Helms (1989), *personality* is the key factor, and neither theory can adequately explain successful ageing.

Social exchange theory (SET)

According to Dyson (1980), both SDT and AT fail to take sufficient account of the physical, social, and economic factors which might limit people's choices about how they age. Age robs people of the capacity to engage in the reciprocal give-and-take that is the hallmark of social relationships, and thus weakens their attachment to others. In addition, Dowd (1975) argues that unlike the aged in traditional societies, older people in industrialised societies have precious few power resources to exchange in daily social interaction. This inequality of power results in dependence on others and compliance with others' wishes.

However, for both Dyson and Dowd, there's a more positive aspect to this loss of power. Adjusting to old age in general, and retirement in particular, involves a sort of contract between the individual and society. The elderly give up their roles as economically active members of society, but in exchange they receive increased leisure time, take on fewer responsibilities, and so on. Although the contract is largely unwritten and not enforceable, most people will probably conform to the expectations about being old which are built into social institutions and stereotypes (see Key Study 39.1).

(a)

(b)

Figure 39.4 a and b The elderly couple in (a) seem to fit the stereotype of the withdrawn, isolated, 'disengaged' person, while the couple in (b) illustrate an alternative, but less common, stereotype, of the person who remains as active in old age as when s/he was middle-aged

Socio-emotional selectivity theory (SST)

According to *socio-emotional selectivity theory* (SST) (Carstensen, 1992, 1993, 1995; Carstensen and Turk-Charles, 1994; Lang and Carstensen, 2002), social contact is motivated by various goals, including basic survival, information-seeking, development of self-concept, and the regulation of emotion. While these all operate throughout life, the importance of specific goals varies, depending on one's place in the life cycle. For example, when emotional regulation is the major goal, people are highly selective in their choice of social partners, preferring familiar others. This selectivity is at its peak in infancy (see Chapter 32) and old age: elderly people turn increasingly to friends and adult children for emotional support (see above).

A major factor contributing to these changes in social motives is *construal of the future*, which is indicated by chronological age. When the future is perceived as largely open-ended, long-term goals assume great significance. But when the future is perceived as limited (see Gould's theory, p. 644), attention shifts to the *present*. Immediate needs, such as emotional states, become more salient. So, contrary to SDT (which sees reduced social contact as being caused by emotional states becoming diluted and dampened down), SST predicts that emotional concerns will become *more* important in old age. Reduced social activity in old age is deliberately and actively chosen, because it benefits the elderly person (and so can be considered 'successful').

Health is the other major factor that accounts for these changes. In many cases, healthy older people *don't* show these patterns of social activity (Carstensen, 1991).

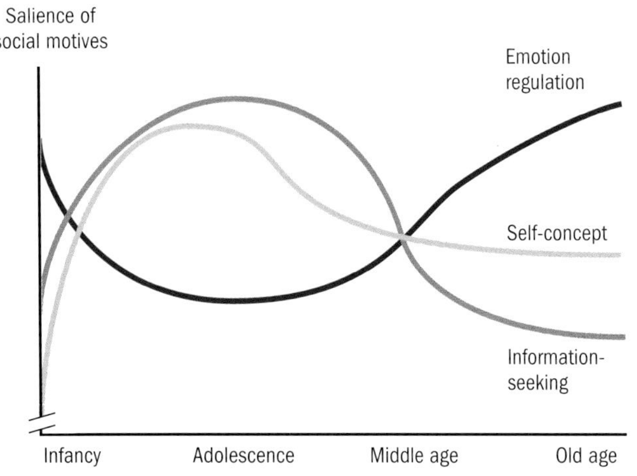

Figure 39.5 Idealised illustration of the lifespan trajectory (from Carstensen, Socioemotional selectivity: A lifespan developmental account of social behaviour. In M.R. Merrens and G.C. Brannigan (eds) *The Developmental Psychologists: Research Adventures across the Life-Span*. Copyright 1996, reproduced with permission of the McGraw-Hill Companies.)

Key Study 39.3

How a limited future can influence current concerns (Carstensen, 1996)

- Carstensen describes a study involving a group of healthy gay men, a group of HIV-positive, asymptomatic gay men, and a group of HIV-positive, symptomatic gay men. A group of young, middle-aged and old men representing the general population served as a control group.
- The social preferences of the healthy gay men were similar to those of the young men from the control group. Those of the asymptomatic group mimicked those of the middle-aged controls, while those of the symptomatic group were strikingly similar to those of the oldest control participants. In other words:

The closer the men were to the end of their lives, the greater weight they placed on affective qualities of prospective social partners ... changes in social preferences appear to be altered in much the same way when futures are limited by age as when futures are limited by disease ... (Carstensen, 1996)

An evaluation of SST

- If SST is correct, it would follow that when younger people hold expectations about the future which are similar to those of the elderly, they should make the same kinds of social choices as those typically made by older people (see Key Study 39.3).
- Lang and Carstensen (2002) found that older individuals in Germany perceived their time as more limited than younger adults and thus prioritized emotionally meaningful goals, such as being with close friends and family, rather than meeting new people. Adult children not only stay in contact with their elderly parents but also continue to share close emotional relationships with them (Lang and Carstensen, 1998).
- The findings relevant to SST taken together paint quite an optimistic picture. Age-related reduction in social contact appears to be highly selective (rather than reflecting a reduced capacity), such that interaction is limited to those people who are most familiar and can provide the greatest emotional security and comfort. This is an excellent strategy when time and social energy need to be invested wisely (Carstensen, 1996).
- The Australian Longitudinal Study of Ageing, begun in 1992 (Giles *et al.*, 2005) found that among those 70 and over, friendships actually increased life expectancy to a far greater extent than frequent contact with children and other relatives. This benefit held true even if the friends had moved away to another city and was independent of factors such as socio-economic status, health and lifestyle. The crucial ingredient seems to be the voluntary and pleasurable support given and received by friends, unlike the sense of duty that may underlie family support. Being able to choose our friends is, of course, consistent with SST.
- However, this optimism may reflect a context in which the older person is dealing with familiar situations and can rely on well-rehearsed solutions to emotional problems. But where they're having to deal with novel and demanding situations, older people may experience greater levels of disturbance

(Labouvie-Vief, 2005). Older people's continued positive functioning, therefore, may depend on control of environmental demands (Labouvie-Vief and Marquez Gonzales, 2004).

Psychosocial theory

Another alternative to SDT and AT is Erikson's *psychosocial theory* (see Chapter 38). A more valid and useful way of looking at what all elderly people have in common might be to examine the importance of old age as a stage of development, albeit the last (which is where its importance lies).

Erikson's theory suggests that in old age, there's a conflict between *ego integrity* (the positive force) and *despair* (the negative force). As with the other psychosocial stages, we cannot avoid the conflict altogether. The task is to end this stage, and hence life, with greater ego integrity than despair, and this requires us to take stock of our life, reflect on it, and assess how worthwhile and fulfilling it has been.

The characteristics of ego integrity

- We believe that life does have a purpose and makes sense.
- We accept that, within the context of our lives as a whole, what happened was somehow inevitable and could only have happened when and how it did.
- We believe that all life's experiences offer something of value, and that we can learn from everything that happens to us. Looking back, we can see how we have grown psychologically as a result of life's ups and downs, triumphs and failures, calms and crises.
- We see our parents in a new light and understand them better, because we've lived through our own adulthood and have probably raised children of our own.
- We realise that we share with all other human beings, past, present and future, the inevitable cycle of birth and death. Whatever the historical, cultural and other differences, we all have this much in common. In the light of this, death 'loses its sting'.

In *The Life Cycle Completed*, Erikson (1997) detailed some of the issues involved in the challenge of old age by pointing to the struggle for finding a sense of *integration* in one's identity; this occurs through such means as *reviewing* one's life to find threads of continuity and attempting to reconcile those elements that may have long been denied or abandoned. It also involves coming to terms with the many changes and losses that each one of us is likely to encounter.

Just as integrity's ultimate demand is facing death, ideally with some degree of acceptance, so *fear of death* is the most conspicuous symptom of *despair*. In despair, we express the belief that it's too late to undo the past and turn the clock back in order to right wrongs or do what hasn't been done. Life isn't a 'rehearsal'; this is the only chance we get.

An evaluation of psychosocial theory

- This last stage of Erikson's life cycle account is the least researched; only recently have researchers begun to explore and refine some of Erikson's constructs (such as how to *assess* integrity versus despair, *existential concerns*, the role and function of the *life review*, the phenomenon of *wisdom*, issues of *identity continuity/discontinuity*, dealing with *losses and physical decline*, and *coming to terms with death* (Kroger, 2007).
- The Self Examination Interview (SEI) (Hearn *et al.*, 2006) adopts a *status approach*, reconceptualising Erikson's bipolar task as one involving alternative styles of resolution (see Chapters 37 and 38).
- Joan Erikson (1997), Erik's wife, described a *ninth* stage, marking an extension of integrity versus despair issues into very old age.

RETIREMENT

Retirement has figured prominently in the discussion above of theories of social adjustment in old age. As a *normative, age-graded influence*, it's an inevitable and anticipated loss of work, which many people experience without undue psychological upheaval (Raphael, 1984). However, it may be unacceptable to those who, for example, see themselves as 'too young' to stop work.

However, while traditionally retirement was seen as the marker of entry into old age, now, thanks to government decree (in the UK and many other western European countries), the actual age of retirement can vary from middle age onward depending on individual circumstances.

> *... Nevertheless, the transition into being retired is still significant both for the individual and for their status in the eyes of other members of that society. (Kloep and Hendry, 2007)*

Different responses to retirement

According to Atchley (1982, 1985), retirement is a *process* and *social role* that unfolds through a series of six phases, each of which requires an adjustment to be made:

- pre-retirement phase
- honeymoon phase (immediate post-retirement)
- disenchantment phase
- reorientation phase
- stability phase
- termination phase.

The phases don't correspond with any particular chronological ages, occur in no fixed order, and not all of them are necessarily experienced by everyone.

In a Norwegian qualitative study of transitions into retirement, Kloep and Hendry (2006) identified three groups, with many psychosocial variations between them.

Figure 39.6 Victor Meldrew played by Richard Wilson (star of BBC TV's *One Foot in the Grave*) seems to personify the sense of frustration and uselessness that often sets in, especially for men, after the 'honeymoon period' of retirement

Box 39.4 Three different responses to being retired (Kloep and Hendry, 2006)

High distress: This describes a very small proportion of the sample. They hadn't liked their work, but neither did they adjust well to the experience of retirement; their problems didn't stem from the retirement transition as such, but were the result of accumulated negative life-course experiences and events (such as major health problems, loss of partner, lack of skills or hobbies, and family tragedies).
Work as a lifestyle: This group had achieved high administrative or academic posts in their careers, and most of their interests and social networks were linked to their professional positions: they were reluctant to give these up and accept the role and status of a retired person. If forced to do so, they had considerable adjustment problems and suffered quite badly from their perceived loss of social status.
Life beyond work: This describes the largest group. They'd enjoyed their jobs, but had retired willingly – and often earlier than required so as to enjoy activities, hobbies and commitments. They usually adapted well to retirement after an initial adjustment phase, and led busy, well-structured and active lives. Their hobbies and interests had been acquired much earlier in their lives and this helped facilitate the transition.

> *Clearly, retired people are a varied, heterogeneous group, who do not experience this life shift all in the same way. Retirement counselling should take this into account ... (Kloep and Hendry, 2007)*

BEREAVEMENT

Although the loss, through death, of loved ones (*bereavement*) can occur at any stage of the life cycle, it becomes more likely as we get older. The psychological and bodily reactions that occur in people who suffer bereavement are called *grief*. The 'observable expression of grief' (Parkes and Weiss, 1983) is called *mourning* (although this term is often used to refer to the social conventions surrounding death, such as funerals and wearing black clothes).

Approaches to the understanding of grief

According to Archer (1999), grief has been variously depicted as (a) a natural human reaction; (b) a psychiatric disorder; and (c) a disease process. All three approaches contain an element of truth. As far as (a) is concerned, grief is a *universal* feature of human existence, found in all cultures. But its form and the intensity of its expression vary considerably (see below). As far as (b) is concerned, although grief itself has never been classified as a mental disorder:

> *The psychiatric framework emphasises the human suffering grief involves, and therefore provides a useful balance to viewing it simply as a natural reaction ... (Archer, 1999)*

Regarding (c), although there may be increased rates of morbidity (health deterioration) or mortality (death) among bereaved people, these aren't necessarily directly caused by the grief process. For example, the effects of change in lifestyle (such as altered nutrition or drug intake), or increased attention to physical illness which predated the bereavement, might be mistaken for the effects of grief itself. However, there's substantial evidence that bereaved spouses are more at risk of dying themselves compared with matched non-bereaved controls. This is true mainly for widowers (Stroebe and Stroebe, 1993), and especially for younger widowers experiencing an unexpected bereavement (Smith and Zick, 1996).

Stage or phase accounts of grief

According to Archer (1999), a widely held assumption is that grief proceeds through an orderly series of stages or phases, with distinct features. While different accounts vary in the details of particular stages, the two most commonly cited are those of Bowlby (1980) (see Box 39.5) and Kübler-Ross (1969) (see Box 39.6).

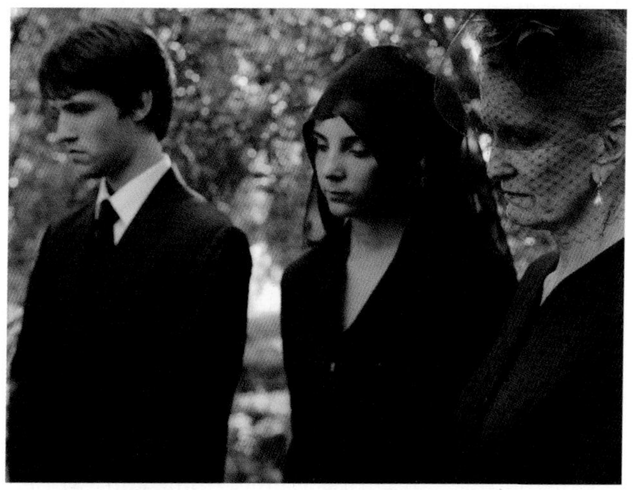

Figure 39.7 Mourners at a western funeral

Figure 39.8 Elizabeth Kübler-Ross (1926–2004)

Box 39.5 Bowlby's phase theory of grief

According to Bowlby (1980), adult grief is an extension of a general distress response to separation commonly observed in young children (see Chapter 32). Adult grief is a form of *separation anxiety* in response to the disruption of an attachment bond.

Phase of numbing: Numbness and disbelief, which can last from a few hours up to a week, may be punctuated by outbursts of extremely intense distress and/or anger.

Yearning and searching: These are accompanied by anxiety and intermittent periods of anger, and can last for months or even years.

Disorganisation and despair: Feelings of depression and apathy occur when old patterns have been discarded.

Reorganisation: There's a greater/lesser degree of recovery from bereavement and acceptance of what's occurred.

Box 39.6 Kübler-Ross' stages of dying

Denial ('No, not me'): This prevents the patient from being overwhelmed by the initial shock. It may take the form of seeking a second opinion, or holding contradictory beliefs.

Anger ('It's not fair – why me?'): This may be directed at medical staff and other healthy people who'll go on living.

Bargaining ('Please God let me ...'): This is an attempt to postpone death by 'doing a deal' with God (or fate, or the hospital), much as a child might bargain with its parents in order to get its own way.

Depression ('How can I leave all this behind?'): This is likely to arise when the patient realises that no bargain can be struck, and that death is inevitable. S/he grieves for all the losses that death represents.

Acceptance ('Leave me be, I am ready to die'): Almost devoid of feelings, the patient seems to have given up the struggle for life, sleeps more and withdraws from other people, as if preparing for 'the long journey'.

Kübler-Ross' stage theory: anticipatory grief

Kübler-Ross's (1969) stage view was based on her pioneering work with over 200 terminally ill patients. She was interested in how they prepared for their own imminent deaths (*anticipatory grief*), and so her stages describe the *process of dying*. But she was inspired by an earlier version of Bowlby's theory (Parkes, 1995) and her stages were later applied (by other researchers) to grief for others. Her theory remains very influential in nursing and counselling, both with dying patients and the bereaved (Archer, 1999).

Almost all the patients she interviewed initially denied they had life-threatening illnesses, although only three remained in a constant state of denial (the rest drifted in and out). Denial was more common when someone had been given the diagnosis in an abrupt or insensitive way, or if they were surrounded by family and/or staff who were also in denial (March and Doherty, 1999).

Depression is a common reaction in the dying. For example, Hinton (1975) reported that 18 per cent of those who committed suicide suffered from serious physical illnesses, with 4 per cent having illnesses that probably would have killed them within six months. Terminally ill patients suffer from what Kübler-Ross called *preparatory depression* (as opposed to *reactive*).

Elderly people who've lived full lives have relatively little to grieve for – they've gained much and lost few opportunities. But people who perceive lives full of mistakes and missed opportunities may, paradoxically, have more to grieve for as they begin to realise that these opportunities are now lost forever. This resembles Erikson's despair, as does *resignation*, which Kübler-Ross distinguishes from acceptance. The detachment and stillness of those who've achieved acceptance comes from calmness, while in those who've become resigned it comes from despair. The latter cannot accept death, nor can they deny its existence any longer (March and Doherty, 1999).

An evaluation of stage theories of grief

- Generally, stage models haven't been well supported by subsequent research. Both Bowlby's and Kübler-Ross's accounts were proposed before any prolonged, detailed follow-up studies of bereaved people had been undertaken (Archer, 1999).
- According to March and Doherty (1999), they represent generalisations from the experience of some individuals and lack the flexibility necessary to describe the range of individual reactions. Grief isn't a simple, universal process we all go through (Stroebe *et al.*, 1993).
- Some researchers prefer to talk about the *components of grief.* Ramsay and de Groot (1977), for example, have identified nine such components, some of which occur early and others late in the grieving process. The components are: *shock, disorganisation, denial, depression, guilt, anxiety, aggression, resolution* and *reintegration.*
- In fact, many stage theorists have explicitly denied that the stages are meant to apply equally and rigidly to everyone. For example, Bowlby (1980) himself said that the phases aren't clear-cut, and any one individual may oscillate for a time between any two of them.
- Yet stages provide us with a framework or guidelines for understanding the experiences of bereaved and dying individuals, while at the same recognising that there's a huge variability in the ways individuals react. Stages don't prescribe where an individual 'ought' to be in the grieving process (March and Doherty, 1999).

Becoming a widow(er): Loss of identity and intimacy

Becoming a widow(er) is one of the most stressful and emotionally demanding experiences that one can undergo (Kroger, 2007). The severity of the loss experience depends on a number of factors, such as the length of the relationship, the age of the partner and the children, whether the death was anticipated or sudden, the nature of the relationship itself, the existence of a support network, and socio-economic status (Kaslow, 2004).

In identity terms, becoming a widow(er) means coping not only with the emotional demands of the loss, but also the disruption of almost every aspect of one's life. Many identity-defining routines are lost and new roles must be performed. Over time, social relations may change as one is no longer part of a couple, participating in established networks. In Western society, unlike other cultures, the role of widow(er) beyond the funeral and early stages of widowhood isn't clearly defined (Kroger, 2007).

Widow(er)hood is a phenomenon most likely to affect older women, and the grief response to the loss of one's spouse has become the 'standard' against which other types of loss are measured (Parkes, 2006). Most of the research predicting risk following bereavement has been conducted with widow(er)s in the English-speaking world, and loss of spouse is the most frequent type of bereavement to lead to psychiatric referral.

Cultural influences on reactions to bereavement

Because of the huge individual variability, trying to distinguish 'normal' from 'abnormal' grief seems quite arbitrary (Schuchter and Zisook, 1993). According to Middleton *et al.* (1993), the validity of the concept of *pathological grief* must be considered in terms of *cultural norms*. Although grief is a universal response to major loss, its meaning, duration and how it's expressed, are all culturally prescribed. Grief, in turn, is related to cultural beliefs about death; for example, Laungani (2007) describes the *medicalisation, sanitization* and *secularization* of death in Western cultures.

Inter-cultural differences

According to Rosenblatt (1993):

> *Culture is such a crucial part of the context of bereavement that it is often impossible to separate an individual's grief from culturally required mourning.*

For example, in cultures that believe 'do not grieve because grief will cause the ghost of the deceased to take you away' or 'do not grieve because the deceased has gone to a better life', it's difficult to assess accurately what appears to be muted or restrained grief. Similarly, when the 'rules' say 'cry', and people cry, how do we know the grief is genuine, deeply felt and likely to occur in the absence of the cultural demands for crying?

The Jewish rites of mourning are believed to be of therapeutic benefit, enabling the expression, rather than the repression, of grief. For the first few days following a burial, mourners are expected to be distressed and their despair is recognised and supported by relatives and friends who come to pay their respects.

By contrast, the Hindu, Sikh, Muslim and Buddhist religions all discourage too much weeping (Firth, 1993). Hindus believe that weeping makes a river which the soul of the deceased has to cross, and Sikhs believe the deceased has gone to God. However, the expression of grief is less inhibited in villages on the Indian sub-continent compared with Sikhs and Hindus living in Britain. Similarly, wailing is still very common among Muslims in Muslim countries (Firth, 1993).

Compared with western women, Japanese women accept their husbands' death with composure and resignation. They believe strongly in an afterlife, and that their ancestors are always with them. Their beliefs mitigate feelings of complete loss and, to this extent, they have less to grieve about. The long-lasting grief and depression observed among the bereaved in the UK is partly a result of the lack of rituals and beliefs, as well as the lack of an externally based end to the grieving process (March and Doherty, 1999).

Figure 39.9 The degree to which weeping is acceptable or encouraged at funerals varies between religious and cultural groups

According to Firth (1993), all the major religions of the world teach that there's some sort of continuity or survival after death. They also comfort and reassure the bereaved by helping to make sense of death and personal loss, providing shape and meaning to the grieving process. Mourning lasts for a clearly defined period in different cultures, providing 'milestones'. These allow the bereaved a gradual time to let go of the deceased and adjust to the psychological and social changes in their lives.

CONCLUSIONS

The different meanings of 'old' suggest that chronological age is a poor indicator of what a particular elderly individual is like, either psychologically or socially. However, major theories of social adjustment to old age, such as SDT and AT, tend to regard the elderly as basically all the same. This implies that there's a particular way of ageing successfully, a view not shared by other theories and not supported by research evidence.

Similarly, the view that ageing inevitably involves rapid and generalised cognitive decline isn't supported by research evidence. Both intelligence and memory have many facets, which tend to decline at very different rates.

Retirement is a socially imposed loss of work, which has both social and psychological effects, as does bereavement. Attempts to identify stages of grief that apply equally to everyone have proved largely unsuccessful, partly because of individual variability and partly because of inter-cultural differences in how death and grief are understood and managed.

According to Voss (2002):

> *... Older people may not feel old; they may not feel any different than they did during their younger years. They simply face life from an angle that bears the shadow of death more acutely than before. This provides them with an insight unavailable to others and the wisdom not yet achieved by those trying to help them. Acknowledging this is an invaluable part of promoting the respect that older people deserve as fellow human beings ... we should ... help older adults to welcome integrity and wisdom, in whatever form, at the conclusion of their winter years.*

Chapter Summary

- While 'growing up' has positive connotations, 'growing old' has negative ones, reflecting the **decrement model.** An alternative, more positive view, is the **personal growth model**.
- One price we pay for greater **life expectancy (longevity)** is increased rates of age-related diseases, in particular **Alzheimer's disease.**
- One feature of **ageism** is the assumption that **chronological age** is an accurate indicator of **biological, subjective, functional** and **social age**.
- **Stereotypes** of the elderly are deeply rooted in rapidly changing Western societies, where their experience and wisdom are no longer valued. The aged are a collection of **subgroups**, each with its own problems and capabilities.
- The claim that intelligence declines fairly rapidly in old age is based on **cross-sectional studies**, which suffer from the problem of the **cohort effect**. **Longitudinal studies** indicate that while **crystallised intelligence** increases with age, **fluid intelligence** declines for all age groups over time.
- Some aspects of **memory** decline with age, perhaps due to less effective **information processing**. Older adults generally perform more poorly than younger adults on **recall** tests, but the differences are much smaller when **recognition** tests are used.
- **Negative cultural stereotypes** of ageing actually cause memory decline in older adults, and may become **self-fulfilling prophecies**.
- The most controversial claim made by **social disengagement theory** (**SDT**) is that elderly people accept and even welcome disengagement, and that this is a natural and inevitable process.
- SDT emphasises the **quantitative** changes to the exclusion of the **qualitative** changes, such as friendships, which are under the older person's control and provide essential informal support.
- **Activity** (or **re-engagement**) **theory** (**AT**) claims that the withdrawal of society and the individual isn't mutual, and **optimal ageing** involves maintaining the activities of middle age for as long as possible.
- According to **social exchange theory** (**SET**), older people in industrialised countries relinquish their roles as economically active members of society in exchange for increased leisure time and fewer responsibilities.
- **Socio-emotional selectivity theory** (**SST**) maintains that older adults are highly selective as regards social partners. This change in **emotional regulation** is largely determined by **construal of the future**.
- According to Erikson's **psychosocial theory**, old age involves a conflict between **ego integrity** and **despair**. The task of ageing is to assess and evaluate life's value and meaning; despair is characterised by a fear of death.
- While **retirement** is an **age-graded normative influence,** recent legislation in many countries means that people may retire from middle adulthood onwards. It's the **transition** between employment and retirement that causes adjustment problems.
- **Grief** has been portrayed as a natural, **universal** human reaction to bereavement, a **psychiatric disorder**, and a **disease process**.
- **Stage theories** have been criticised on the grounds that grief isn't a simple, universal process which is the same for everyone. However, stages provide a framework for understanding bereaved people's experiences, which display huge variability.
- Although grief is a universal response to major loss, its meaning, duration and expression are all **culturally prescribed**. Cultures differ in how they define death, and it's often impossible to separate an individual's grief from culturally required mourning.
- All the world's major religions teach that there's some kind of afterlife. They also comfort the bereaved by helping to make sense of death and by providing 'milestones', which allow a gradual time to adjust to life without the deceased.

Links with Other Topics/Chapters

Chapter 25 ⟶ Ageism is one of the '-isms' that refer to *prejudiced attitudes* and *discriminatory behaviour*

Chapter 41 ⟶ *IQ* (*intelligence quotient*) measures an individual's standing relative to some comparison group (such as people of a similar age). So, while *raw scores* on a test of general intelligence decline with age, one's IQ doesn't (Stuart-Hamilton, 2000, 2003)

Chapter 20 ⟶ *Expert chess players* show better memory than non-experts for actual (possible) chess positions, but there's no difference between them if the pieces are placed randomly. Based on their greater experience, elderly players may be displaying a similar superiority when they match the performance of younger opponents

Chapter 17 ⟶ The greater difference in *memory* capacity between younger and older participants on tests of *recall* compared with tests of *recognition* is what we'd predict from the greater *sensitivity* of recognition

Chapter 28 ⟶ SET in the context of ageing has a rather different meaning from the one it has in the context of *interpersonal relationships/attraction*, where individuals exchange rewards that will determine how much each partner wishes to stay in the relationship

Chapter 38 ⟶ The greater risk of death among widowers (compared with widows) is consistent with findings relating to the greater *benefits of marriage* for men and their greater difficulty in adjusting to *divorce*

Recommended Reading

Bond, J., Peace, S., Dittman-Kohli, F. & Westerhof, G. (eds) (2007) *Ageing in Society* (3rd edn). London: Sage/British Society of Gerontology. Especially Chapters 2, 3, 10 and 14.

Coleman, P.G. & O'Hanlon, A. (2004) *Ageing and Development.* London: Arnold.

Gross, R. (2008) *Key Studies in Psychology* (5th edn), London: Hodder Education. Chapter 32.

Scientific American Presents (2000) The quest to beat ageing. *Scientific American,11*(2) (Whole issue).

Useful Websites

www.youtube.com/watch?v=kmMVoltH6nE (A longitudinal study of 678 Catholic Sisters, aged 75–107, investigating the determinants of successful ageing)

www.growingolder.group.shef.ac.uk (Results from the Economic & Social Research Council/ESRC research programme 'Growing Older')

www.ageuk.org.uk (Age UK official website)

www.grandparenting.org (Foundation for Grandparenting official website)

CHAPTER 40

EXCEPTIONAL DEVELOPMENT

Giftedness

Autism

Learning difficulties (LDs)

INTRODUCTION and OVERVIEW

Sufiah Yusof began a maths degree at Oxford University in 1997 at the age of 13, becoming one of the youngest ever undergraduates in the UK. A few years earlier, Ruth Lawrence graduated with a first class degree from Oxford – she was also 13. At 14, Alexander Faludy became one of the youngest ever people to win a place at Cambridge University. With an IQ of 178, he can deliver verbal dissertations of enormous range and complexity, but he can write only two (illegible) words a minute: he's dyslexic (Martin, 2000).

The drawing above of Central Station, Amsterdam, was done by Stephen Wiltshire, who, as well as having extraordinary artistic skill, is autistic. Recent UK research suggests that a certain proportion of children with Down's syndrome may also be autistic.

What do all these cases have in common? They are all *exceptional*, in the sense of *atypical* (see Chapter 43). The average age for becoming an undergraduate is 18, most undergraduates don't have IQs anywhere close to 178, most people aren't dyslexic or autistic, nor do they have the artistic (or other exceptional) abilities demonstrated by Stephen Wiltshire and other *savants* (or *idiots savants* as they used to be called). Down's syndrome occurs in about 100 per 100,000 live births (Carpenter, 1997).

'Exceptional' usually implies 'exceptionally bright' or 'unusually gifted', but these various examples illustrate the more accurate sense of 'exceptionally different'. However:

> *It is very easy, when dealing with an atypical child, to be overwhelmed by the sense of differentness. But as Sroufe and Rutter and all the other developmental psychopathologists are beginning to say so persuasively, the same basic processes are involved (Bee, 2000).*

To emphasise the differences implies that 'ordinary' and 'exceptional' are *qualitatively different*, while to look for common processes implies that the differences are merely *quantitative*. The examples also illustrate that different types of exceptional abilities (e.g. very high IQ and dyslexia) can be found together *in the same individual*.

GIFTEDNESS

What do we mean by 'gifted'?

According to Smith *et al.* (1998):

> *A child may be described as 'gifted' who is outstanding in either a general domain (such as exceptional performance on an intelligence test) or a specific area of ability, such as music, or sport ...*

However, the borderline between gifted children and others isn't clearly defined, and different researchers have used different criteria. In Winner's (1998) view, gifted children and child *prodigies* (who are just extreme versions of gifted children) differ from average and bright children in three ways:

1. they're *precocious* – they master subjects earlier and learn more quickly
2. they 'march to their own drummers' – they make discoveries on their own and can often solve problems intuitively, without going through a series of logical, linear steps
3. they're driven by 'a rage to master' – they have an intense interest in the area or domain in which they excel, and can readily focus so intently on work in this domain that they lose sense of the outside world.

They also seem to have unusually good *metacognitive skills*: they know what they know and don't know, and spend more time than average IQ children planning how to go about solving a problem (Bee, 2000). They seem to teach themselves to read as toddlers, breeze through college maths in middle school, and draw more skilfully at age 7 than most adults (see Key Study 40.1).

Key Study 40.1

Gifted termites (Terman, 1925; Terman and Ogden, 1959; Holahan, 1988)

- The most famous study of giftedness is Terman's Stanford longitudinal study, which began in 1921.
- Based on his definition of giftedness as an IQ score of around 140 (on the Stanford–Binet test: see Chapter 41), 643 Californian 10-year-olds (the 'Termites') were first nominated by their teachers and then their intelligence was assessed. Their mean score was 151, with a range of 130–190 (only 22 scored below 140).
- They were followed up at various points for much of their lives.
- Their physical health and growth were superior from birth onwards, they walked and talked early, and excelled in reading (which they learnt to do before starting school), language, and general knowledge. Their parents described them as insatiably curious and having superb memories.
- By 1947 (average age 35), their initial level of intelligence had been maintained; 68 per cent had graduated from college, and many were already enjoying outstanding careers. By 1959, this occupational achievement continued. For example, 70 had been listed in the *American Men of Science,* and three were members of the highly prestigious National Academy of Science. In addition, 31 were listed in the *Who's Who* in America, and ten appeared in the *Directory of American Scholars.*

(Based on Smith *et al.*, 1998; Sternberg, 1990; Winner, 1998)

An evaluation of Terman's study

Terman's study showed that gifted children are, perhaps not surprisingly, highly likely to become successful adults. However, the sample of children was biased in at least two important ways (Winner, 1998).

1. Working-class and ethnic minority children were under-represented. Almost one-third of the children came from middle-class, professional families, so that at least some of their success may have been due to social-class factors as well as to their high IQs.
2. Children participated in the study only if nominated by their teachers, who probably overlooked those gifted children who were misfits, loners or difficult to teach. It was these same admiring teachers who gave such glowing evaluations of their social adjustment and personality.

Terman described the children as superior not just intellectually, but also in terms of their health, social adjustment and moral attitude. According to Winner, this helped create the myth that gifted children are happy, well-adjusted by nature, requiring little special attention, and easy-to-teach. The myth persists despite more recent evidence to the contrary.

Some disadvantages of giftedness

Children with exceptionally high abilities in any area (including the visual arts, music and athletics) are out of step socially with their peers. They tend to be highly driven, independent in their thinking and introverted. They spend an unusual amount of time alone and, although deriving pleasure and energy from their solitary mental lives, they also report feeling lonely. The more extreme the level of giftedness, the more isolated they feel (Winner, 1998).

It's been estimated that 20–25 per cent of profoundly gifted children have social and emotional problems (about twice the normal rate), while the moderately gifted show the average rate. By mid-childhood, they often try to hide their abilities in the hope of becoming more popular. One group particularly at risk for such underachievement is that of academically gifted girls, who report more depression, lower self-esteem and more psychosomatic symptoms than academically gifted boys.

Ask Yourself

- Why do you think this gender difference might occur?

While Sufiah's case may not be typical, it's not unique. There are some striking parallels between Sufiah's case and that of Ruth Lawrence (see *Introduction and overview*).

Gross (1993) describes the case of Ian. At age 5, he hated school, was uncontrollable in class, aggressive towards other children, and was referred to a special school for behaviourally disturbed children. He was found to have an IQ of over 170 (on the Stanford–

Case Study 40.1

Sufiah Yusof

As mentioned in the *Introduction and overview,* Sufiah Yusof became an Oxford University maths undergraduate at the age of 13.

She made the headlines in the summer of 2000, when she disappeared shortly after completing her final exams. After the police found her, they took the unusual step of revealing that Sufiah had requested that her whereabouts should remain secret – even (especially) from her parents. Earlier in the week that she was found, she sent her family an email, in which she declared: 'I've finally had enough of 15 years of physical and emotional abuse ...'

She vowed never to return to the 'living hell' of home. She accused her father of ruining his five children's lives by brainwashing and *hothousing* them; in her father's words: 'The goals were to prove that you can accelerate children's learning process ... one can nurture and accelerate learning programmes'.

At 11, she had twice attempted suicide.
(Based on Hattenstone and Brockes, 2000)

Figure 40.1 Sufiah Yusof pictured in Oxford in 1998 with her father, Farooq

Binet) and a reading age of 12. At age 9, his IQ was 200, but his school insisted that he follow the curriculum designed for 9-year-olds. This raises crucial questions regarding how gifted children in general should be educated (see Box 40.1).

Other researchers (e.g. Gottfried *et al.*, 1994), however, maintain that gifted children have about the same risk of social and emotional problems as normal-IQ children, so that most are well adjusted and socially adept. But the profoundly gifted (e.g. IQs over 180) are so different from their peers, they're likely to be seen as strange and disturbing. They have difficulty finding others who can play at their level (Bee, 2000).

The unevenness of giftedness

Certain gifted children can leap years ahead of their peers in one area, yet fall behind in another. These *unevenly gifted* children sometimes seem hopelessly out of sync. Terman promoted the view that gifted children were *globally gifted*, that is, evenly talented in all academic areas. While some children do fit this stereotype of the all-round high-achiever, many display giftedness in one area but are unremarkable, or even disabled, in others. These may be creative children who are difficult in school, and not immediately recognised as gifted.

This unevenness is quite common. For example, extraordinarily strong mathematical and spatial abilities often accompany average or even deficient verbal skills. A good example is Albert Einstein, who was sacked from two teaching jobs for terrible spelling, and once said: 'If I can't picture it, I can't understand it'. Similarly, Thomas Edison, inventor of the light bulb and phonograph, had spelling, grammar, and learning problems. Even Leonardo da Vinci had erratic spelling, and scribbled notes backwards (Martin, 2000).

Figure 40.2 Albert Einstein (1879–1955), unevenly gifted

Savants

Many children who struggle with language may have strong spatial skills, and the association between verbal deficits and spatial gifts seems especially strong among visual artists. The most unevenly gifted of all are the savants, such as Stephen Wiltshire.

The term 'idiots savants' was first used by Langdon Down (best known for having identified Down's syndrome) in 1887 to describe the coexistence in some individuals of low general cognitive functioning and above-average specific ability. They appear to be able to use processing strategies within a particular domain that seems independent of their general level of intelligence. While recognised for almost 200 years, savants were reported mainly in the form of descriptive case histories.

Savant syndrome and autism

Figure 40.3 Kim Peek

Savant syndrome is seen in about one in ten people with autism, and in approximately one in 2000 people with brain damage or mental retardation. Of the known savants, at least half are autistic, and the rest have some other kind of developmental disorder (Treffert and Wallace, 2004). The syndrome generally occurs in people with IQs between 40 and 70 – although it can occur in some with IQs up to 114 or over. It disproportionately affects males (four to six males for every female).

The skills involved in savant syndrome are rather limited in their range, restricted mainly to right-hemisphere non-symbolic, artistic, visual and motor abilities. They include music, art, maths and various forms of calculating (such as calendar-counting). For example, Kim Peek can tell you what day of the week you were born on and on what day you'll celebrate your 65th birthday. Despite being developmentally disabled, he knows more than 7600 books by heart, as well as every area code, highway, zip code and television station in the USA. He provided the inspiration for Dustin Hoffman's character Raymond Babbitt in *Rain Man* (1988) (Treffert and Wallace, 2004).

In 1983, O'Connor and Hermelin began a series of systematic, controlled experimental studies with groups of musical, calendar-calculating, and artistic savants. Their main aim was to find out why there was a marked frequency of individuals with autism in the savant population (O'Connor and Hermelin, 1988).

In discussing Stephen Wiltshire, Sacks (1995) asked whether one could speak of a 'distinctive autistic art'. He points to the concreteness, detailed perceptual accuracy, and the 'thisness' of Stephen's drawings of cars and buildings, with which he's preoccupied. At art school, he displayed an exceptional ability to depict space and distance in perspective (Pring and Hermelin, 1997). Such a remarkable focusing on perceptual details of a display, and on their accurate reproduction, are reminiscent of some of the characteristics considered to be typical of autism (Hermelin *et al.,* 1999; see below). However, Hermelin *et al.*'s study of several autistic artists strongly suggests that there's no stereotyped 'autistic art'; that is, their art reflects true artistic talent rather than being a manifestation of their autism.

A biological explanation: the left hemisphere hypothesis (LHH)

The most powerful currently available explanation of savant syndrome claims that some injury to the left hemisphere (LH) of the brain causes the right hemisphere (RH) to *compensate* for the loss. As we've seen, savant abilities are predominantly *right hemisphere*, which is consistent with the LHH. Also consistent with the LHH is Baron-Cohen's (2003a) *Empathising–Systemising* (E-S) *theory* of autism, according to which autistic individuals have *extreme male* brains (that is, brains that are hardwired for right-hemisphere skills and abilities: see below and Chapter 36).

Further support comes from the study of elderly patients with frontotemporal dementia (FTD), a form of pre-senile dementia (see Chapter 39). Some of these patients suddenly develop artistic skills they didn't previously possess, and all of them show damage on the left side of the brain. They become savant-like (visually creative: a right-hemisphere ability) as dementia takes hold in their left hemisphere (Treffert and Wallace, 2004) (see Critical Discussion 40.1).

While rTMS is non-invasive and the effects fade within an hour, preserving normal cognition, it is bulky and expensive. However, tDCS (*transcranial direct-current stimulation*) is a safe, simple way to alter the likelihood that networks of neurons near the surface of the brain will fire. A weak electric current passes between two electrodes placed on the scalp over the left and right anterior temporal lobes (just above the ears) (Snyder *et al.,* 2012). While the technique induces measurable changes in memory, language, mood, motor function, attention, and other cognitive domains, there's some debate concerning possible long-term neural changes (Hamilton and Zreik, 2014).

Critical Discussion 40.1

Are we all potential savants?

According to Snyder *et al.* (2012), we're all potential savants: savant brain processes occur in each of us, but they're overwhelmed by more sophisticated conceptual cognition (regulated for most of us by the LH).

In some autistic individuals and others with LH damage (savants), these (RH) abilities are 'released' because of abnormalities in the LH (as claimed by the LHH).

In addition to people suffering from FTD, there are cases of savant skills appearing suddenly in people following brain damage. For example, one 10-year-old child suddenly acquired spectacular calendar-calculating skills and an extraordinary memory for dates and music following an injury to the left side of the head. Another famous case is Alonzo Clemons, who developed a striking talent for animal sculpture following a childhood head injury (Phillips, 2004b).

Figure 40.4 Alonzo Clemons can create perfect wax replicas of any animals he sees, no matter how briefly

It follows that if you can reduce or stop electrical activity in the LH, it might be possible to unlock the 'little Rain Man in each of us' (Treffert and Wallace, 2004).

Snyder has attempted this, using a technique called *repetitive transcranial magnetic stimulation* (rTMS) (a 'creativity cap'). This is used routinely in neurology departments and hospitals as a research tool to test for side-effects of brain surgery, and to establish the function of different brain regions. A powerful magnet flicking on and off several times a second is held against the outside of the head; this induces an electrical current that penetrates 2 centimetres into brain tissue; this can either enhance or suppress activity in that area of the brain (Ainsworth, 2008).

By targeting specific areas of the brain involved in synthesising high-level concepts, Snyder and his colleagues are trying to reduce the influence of prior knowledge. They have successfully enhanced several skills in normal people, including drawing, proofreading, numerosity estimates (counting the number of items, such as matchsticks, in a group) and verbal memory (e.g. Chi and Snyder, 2012).

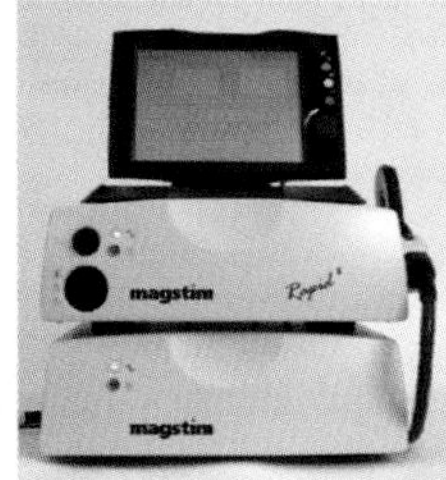

Figure 40.5 A TMS machine

Treffert and Wallace (2004) agree with Snyder's claims, concluding that:

> *... all of us have some of the same circuitry and pathways intrinsic to savant functioning but ... these are less accessible – in part because we tend to be a left-brain society. Sometimes, though, we can find elements of the savant in ourselves. At certain moments, we just 'get' something or discover a new ability ...*

Accounting for giftedness

Ask Yourself

- In light of the discussion above about the LHH, do you agree with Winner's conclusions?
- Does describing someone as talented help explain his/her exceptional ability?
- If so, where do you think this talent comes from?

In the case of savants' abilities it seems that both genetic and motivational factors are involved. The remaining mystery isn't so much how savants achieve their talents, but what drives them in the first place. Like giftedness in general, the savant skills are practised almost as if their lives depended on it (Biever, 2009) (see Box 40.1).

Giftedness and the brain

Neuroscientists assume that cognitive functions are realised by neuronal activity; it follows that complex skills should require additional neuronal resources (Hoppe and Stojanovic, 2009).

The neuronal resource account (NRA)

According to Geschwind and Galaburda's (1985a, 1985b, 1985c) NRA, talented people show less LH dominance and more pronounced interaction between the two hemispheres (the RH is more active). This was based on the observation that individuals with pronounced RH abilities (maths, music, and art) are disproportionately *non*-right-handed (they're either left-handed or ambidextrous). They also have higher than average rates of LH deficits (such as delayed speech onset, stuttering, or dyslexia), as well as higher prevalence of allergies and myopia.

Geschwind and Galaburda hypothesised that this association of gift and disorder ('the pathology of superiority') results from the effects of testosterone on the developing foetal brain. Raised levels can delay development of the LH ('testosterone poisoning'), which might in turn produce compensatory RH growth. This might also account for the larger number of males than females who display mathematical and spatial gifts, non-right-handedness, and language disorders.

However, recent evidence has challenged this almost 'classical dogma' regarding male superiority (Hoppe and Stojanovic, 2009). For example, Hyde *et al.* (2008) found no gender effects on maths skills at any level of performance (provided the test was compulsory for all children). Although research with musical experts provides evidence supporting the neuronal resource account, it also underlines the general role of years of practice (see discussion of the 'talent account' below).

The neural efficiency account (NEA)

While the NRA emphasises the neurophysiological basis of exceptional ability, the NEA addresses differences between talented (gifted) and non-gifted people while working on identical tasks. Obviously, a skilled cognitive system is more efficient (it achieves goals using fewer resources, such as time and subjective effort) – but how does cognitive efficiency translate to the neuronal level? (Hoppe and Stojanovic, 2009).

Neurocognitive efficiency has been investigated primarily through the use of task-related EEG recordings and advanced methods of EEG data analysis (see Chapters 4 and 7). Hoppe and Sojanovic cite research findings that talented individuals showed increased alpha-EEG power; this indicates that less cognitive effort is involved compared with non-talented individuals working on an identical task. It's been suggested that efficiency might reflect stronger *myelination* (again, see Chapter 4).

Taken together, these two accounts suggest that gifted people are *more efficient* in their particular domain because they can recruit more *neuronal resources* for automatic processing prior to frontal activation (i.e. before conscious/deliberate planning controlled by the prefrontal cortex comes into play). Gifted individuals may also have a more efficient working memory system (see Chapter 17) (Hoppe and Stojanovic, 2009).

The 'talent account': geniuses are born

According to the *'talent account' of giftedness*, the likelihood of becoming exceptionally competent depends on the presence or absence of inborn attributes ('talents', 'gifts', 'natural aptitudes'; Howe *et al.,* 1998). The judgement that someone is talented is believed to help *explain* (not merely describe) that person's success. According to Howe *et al.*, certain assumptions are made about talent:

- it originates in genetically transmitted structures, and so is at least partly innate
- its full effects may not be evident at an early age, but there will be some advance indications that allow trained people to spot its presence before exceptional levels of mature performance have been shown
- these early indications of talent provide the basis for predicting who's likely to excel
- only a minority is talented – if all children were, we couldn't predict or explain differential success
- talents are relatively domain specific.

For Gardner (1993), talent is a sign of precocious biopsychological potential in a particular domain, such as dance, chess, or maths (see his theory of *multiple intelligences:* Chapter 41). Similarly, Winner (1996) sees talents as unlearned, domain-specific traits that may develop or 'come to fruition' in favourable circumstances – but they cannot be manufactured.

Is the talent account valid?

According to Robinson (2011), hundreds of psychological studies have failed to provide conclusive evidence for the existence of innate talent. Not only have no genes 'for' domain-specific talents (such as musical ability) been located (see Chapter 49), but the 'indisputable and astonishing' improvement in performance standards observed in sports, music, chess and other fields during the past century, have occurred much too fast to be explained by genetic changes (which would require thousands of years) (Robinson, 2011).

According to Howe (1999), although it's widely accepted that innate talents can explain how genetic differences between people impact on their capabilities, there are good reasons for thinking that such talents are mythical rather than real.

Genetic contributions to human activities are complex and indirect (see Chapters 41 and 50). Also, it tends to be assumed that if there are qualities that make some people more capable than others and that have an inherited component, these will be closely related to a person's cognitive attributes (such as cleverness or creativity). But according to Howe (1999):

> *... it is just as likely that those – conceivably largely inherited – human qualities that make the larger contributions towards setting geniuses apart from other people are ones of temperament and personality rather than being narrowly intellectual ones ...*

Indeed, the qualities that contemporaries of geniuses such as Newton and Mozart most often remarked on were broadly temperamental: doggedness, persistence, capacity for fierce and sustained concentration, and intense curiosity. Several geniuses, including Darwin and Einstein, denied having any superior inherent intelligence (see above), but none has ever denied either possessing or relying on a capacity for diligence and healthy curiosity (Howe, 1999).

Figure 40.6 Portrait of Wolfgang Amadeus Mozart, aged 14 (Blanchet). Even this prodigy of prodigies had a composer–father who was also famously ambitious for his son and bullied him towards musical greatness

Box 40.1 If you want to be a genius, practise, practise, practise ...

Howe *et al.* (1998) found no evidence of innate attributes operating in the predictable and specific way implied by 'talent', and concluded that differences in early experiences, preferences, opportunities, habits, training and practice are the real determinants of excellence.

According to Gladwell (2008), what we think of as talent is actually a complicated combination of 'ability, opportunity and utterly arbitrary advantage'. Gladwell observes that the idea that excellence at a complex task requires a critical, minimum level of practice (the 'magical '10,000 hours, i.e. almost two hours per day between the ages of 3–17; Ericsson and Charness, 1994) surfaces again and again. Regardless of the area of expertise – musical geniuses, composers, basketball players, Olympic athletes, chess grand masters, fiction writers, ice-skaters , even master criminals – the same conclusion is reached (Gladwell, 2008):

> *... a key part of what it means to be talented is being able to practise for hours and hours – to the point where it is really hard to know where 'natural ability' stops and the simple willingness to work hard begins.*

According to the neurologist, Levitin (in Gladwell, 2008):

> *... No one has yet found a case in which true world-class expertise was accomplished in less time [than 10,000 hours]. It seems that it takes the brain this long to assimilate all that it needs to know to achieve true mastery.*

However, not everyone agrees. For example, Simonton (2012) observes that geniuses are more likely to have unusually wide interests and hobbies and to display exceptional versatility, often contributing to more than one domain of expertise. This is part of a wider argument that the role of genetic factors in creative genius has been underestimated.

AUTISM

Definition and classification

Autism was first identified by Kanner (1943) in the USA and Asperger (1944) in Austria, quite independently of each other. Kanner used the term 'early infantile autism' ('autos' is Greek for 'self') to describe individuals who had an 'aloneness', which involved the ignoring and shutting out of the world and living in an isolated, essentially asocial state. They were limited in language and obsessive about the need for sameness in particular aspects of their environment. Kanner speculated (incorrectly) that they fall within the average range of intelligence, and that any poor learning performance resulted from their difficulties with the social aspects of learning.

Asperger worked with an older age group, but his observations overlapped with Kanner's. He also used the term 'autistic', and there's an ongoing debate as to whether autism and what's now called Asperger's syndrome are distinct disorders, expressions of the same disorder, or both part of an *autistic spectrum* (with those displaying Asperger's constituting a high-IQ subgroup). According to Powell (1999), they aren't mutually exclusive – Asperger's individuals have a particular form of autism (see Box 40.2).

Later, ritualistic and compulsive dimensions were identified as crucial, resulting in the *triad of impairments* (see Box 40.3; Wing, 1976). Also, Wing and Gould (1979) found that learning disabilities (LDs) (IQ below 70) were clearly associated with the triad (see Table 40.1). Ninety per cent of those having 'full', typical autism had an IQ between 20 and 69 (see Box 40.2.)

Box 40.2 Autism Spectrum Disorder (ASD)

- As a result of Wing and Gould's (1979) findings, it became clear that there's a wide spectrum of autistic disorders, of which 'Kanner's autism' is only a part. They estimated that 20 children per 10,000 have AS disorders and mental retardation (learning disabilities), a figure that was revised by Wing (1997) to 9 per 1000. Does this reflect changes in diagnostic criteria or an increasing prevalence (Powell, 1999)?
- According to Scott (2004), the triad of impairments can be manifested in a wide variety of ways, such that no children with autism are alike – in fact, they can be extremely different. The latest edition of the most widely used manual of psychiatric classification of disorders (DSM-5, 2013; see Box 40.3) has replaced *autism, atypical autism, Asperger's syndrome* and *pervasive developmental disorder – not otherwise specified* (PPD-NOS) by *autistic spectrum disorder* (ASD).
- The notion of an ASD is no longer defined by any sharp distinction from normality (Wing, 1997). The clearest way of seeing this 'normal' distribution of autistic traits is using the autism spectrum quotient (AQ) (Baron-Cohen *et al.*, 2006), a screening instrument in the form of a questionnaire, either completed by a parent or by a 'high-functioning' individual him/herself. The AQ neatly separates the general population (93 per cent of which fall in the average range) from the autistic population (99 per cent of which fall in the extreme (high-end) of the scale) (Baron-Cohen, 2008).

Incidence and diagnosis

According to Mitchell (1997), the incidence of autism is one to two per 1000 live births. Classic autism occurs in four males for every one female, and Asperger's syndrome occurs in nine males for every one female (Baron-Cohen, 2008). Research conducted at the Autism Research Centre, University of Cambridge, shows that 6 per cent of siblings of children with autism will also have problems with all three kinds of impairment, 10–12 per cent will have problems with two or three areas, and a further 20 per cent in one area. If one identical (monozygotic/MZ) twin has autism, there's a 60 per cent chance the other twin will have problems in all three symptom areas, an 80 per cent chance of problems in any two areas, and a 90 per cent chance of problems in any one area. For non-identical (dizygotic/DZ) twins, the figures are the same as for ordinary siblings (Scott, 2004). These percentages are referred to as *concordance rates*.

Ask Yourself

- What do these figures suggest regarding the possible causes of autism?

Box 40.3 Criteria for diagnosing ASD (based on DSM-IV-TR, 2000)

Qualitative impairments in social interaction: impaired non-verbal behaviours (especially eye contact), failure to engage in genuinely social games (such as turn-taking), no attempt to share interests through *joint-attentional behaviours*, and a failure to develop any friendship beyond the most superficial acquaintance. A lack of empathy is often seen as the central feature of the social deficit (Baron-Cohen, 1988; Kanner, 1943).

Qualitative impairments in communication: failure to develop language and communication in the normal way (such as delayed and restricted language development, stereotyped and repetitive or idiosyncratic use of language), and failure to use gesture properly. Also, a lack of varied, spontaneous make-believe/symbolic play (Leslie, 1987), and engaging in play which is often lacking in creativity and imagination (Baron-Cohen, 1987).

Repetitive and stereotyped patterns of behaviour: an inflexible adherence to specific routines, becoming distressed if prevented from performing repetitive rituals, stereotyped and repetitive motor mannerisms, and persistent preoccupation with parts of objects.

ASD is typically very difficult to diagnose before about age 3 years. Many 'normal' children are slow to develop in their communication, for example, and complex social behaviours are hard to interpret before the child becomes capable of two-way social interactions (Scott, 2004). The CHAT (Checklist for Autism in Toddlers) has been developed by Baron-Cohen and his colleagues as a screening tool for ASD

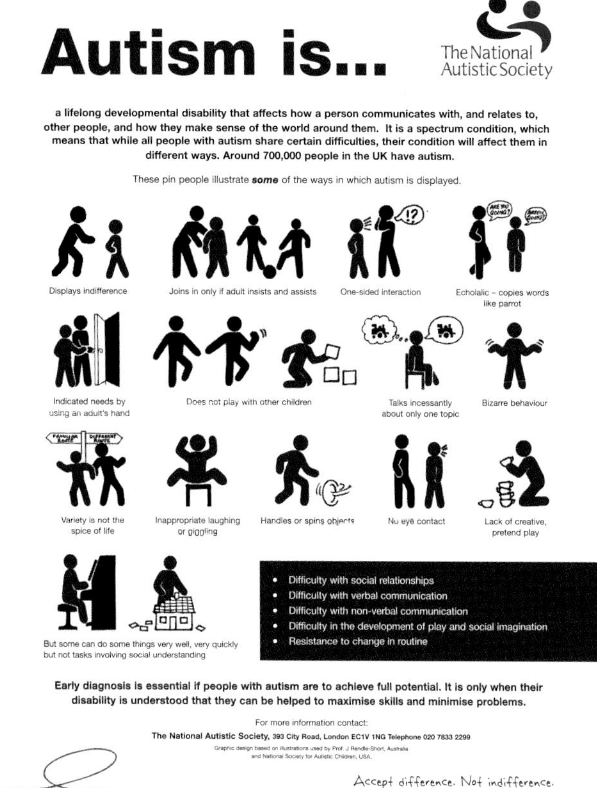

Autism is...
The National Autistic Society
a lifelong developmental disability that affects how a person communicates with, and relates to, other people, and how they make sense of the world around them. It is a spectrum condition, which means that while all people with autism share certain difficulties, their condition will affect them in different ways. Around 700,000 people in the UK have autism.
These pin people illustrate **some** of the ways in which autism is displayed.
Displays indifference
Joins in only if adult insists and assists
One-sided interaction
!?
Echolalic – copies words like parrot
Indicated needs by using an adult's hand
Does not play with other children
Talks incessantly about only one topic
Bizarre behaviour
Variety is not the spice of life
Inappropriate laughing or giggling
Handles or spins objects
No eye contact
Lack of creative, pretend play
But some can do some things very well, very quickly but not tasks involving social understanding
• Difficulty with social relationships
• Difficulty with verbal communication
• Difficulty with non-verbal communication
• Difficulty in the development of play and social imagination
• Resistance to change in routine
Early diagnosis is essential if people with autism are to achieve full potential. It is only when their disability is understood that they can be helped to maximise skills and minimise problems.
For more information contact:
The National Autistic Society, 393 City Road, London EC1V 1NG Telephone 020 7833 2299
Graphic design based on illustrations used by Prof. J Rendle-Short, Australia and National Society for Autistic Children, USA.
Accept difference. Not indifference.

Figure 40.7 From a National Autistic Society leaflet (reproduced by permission of the National Autistic Society)

at 18 months. It's designed to be used by GPs or health visitors, and involves a short series of parent questions and interviewer observations of the child. So far, the CHAT has been shown to have a 91.7 per cent success rate; the results suggest that absence of pretend play and joint-attention might be the clearest indicators of risk for ASD (Scott, 2004).

ASD and Down's syndrome

According to Lewis (2003), most children diagnosed as autistic have learning difficulties (LDs), with over half having IQs below 50. Typically, verbal ability is more seriously affected than non-verbal. Consequently, it's important to show that the characteristic behaviours are found across the ability range – otherwise there'd be a risk of confounding autism with LD. For this reason, much research has focused on relatively able autistic children, who are often compared with children with LDs but not autism (such as Down's syndrome children).

Mitchell (1997) identifies some important similarities and differences between ASD and Down's syndrome.

- Both conditions are present from birth. But whereas Down's is usually evident from the baby's facial appearance (and will often have been detected prenatally, especially with older mothers), autistic babies look perfectly normal and the diagnosis isn't made until the child is aged 4 or over. If the diagnosis is made later, this doesn't mean they've 'acquired' it at an older age; rather, a new label has been applied to existing behaviour patterns.
- Down's is classified as a chromosome abnormality (the child inherits an extra 21st chromosome) and is the most commonly occurring such abnormality (see Chapter 36). Diagnosis is based on the detection of this extra chromosome, while ASD is diagnosed on the basis of characteristic behaviours (see Box 40.2). Relatively little is known about its physiological basis.
- Neither condition can be 'cured', although adaptation and development can and do occur. For example, 50 years ago life expectancy among people with Down's was considerably lower than that of the general population. But the gap has narrowed significantly, mainly because of antibiotics and general improvements in diet, care, and living conditions (Moddia, 1996).
- However, some experts now claim that ASD *is* treatable: delivering therapy to 1- or 2-year-olds – instead of 4, as is more typical – can produce greater improvements in IQ, language and social skills (Gravotta, 2014). Also, some evidence suggests that improvements can occur spontaneously. For example, a study by Fein *et al.*, (2013) involving eight 21-year-olds suggests that some individuals with ASD as young children no longer had symptoms. According to Richler (2013), this well-controlled study represents a watershed moment in autism research. Nevertheless, the results should be treated cautiously, especially as the study used a *retrospective design*; what's needed is a *prospective, longitudinal design* (Richler, 2013). Early intervention programmes, such as the Early Start Denver Model (ESDM), are beginning to offer hope of improvement (Lange and McDougle, 2013).

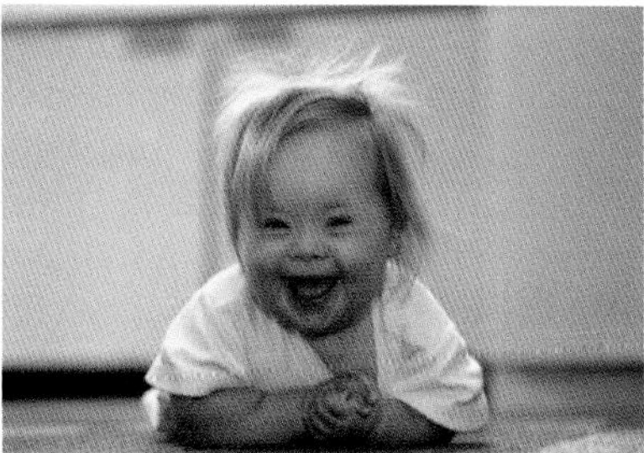

Figure 40.8 A child with Down's syndrome

- LDs are characteristic of Down's and common in autism (see above). But some autistic individuals have normal IQs, and some (5–30 per cent) may have above-average IQs. With increasing IQ, autism becomes more difficult to diagnose – and may escape diagnosis altogether.

- As we saw when discussing giftedness, many autistic individuals display outstanding musical or artistic abilities (savants). This doesn't occur in individuals with Down's syndrome.

Interestingly, about 7 per cent of children with Down's syndrome also have some level of autistic disorder (Kent *et al.*, 1999).

Theories of autism

According to Smith *et al.* (1998):

> *The challenge for any researcher investigating autism is trying to explain how one syndrome can lead to the specific combination of impairments which typify a person with autism (lack of socialisation, communication and imagination); how different people with autism can be affected in markedly different ways; and how it is that people with autism can sometimes have better than average abilities in one or two areas (the 'islets of ability').*

'Refrigerator-parenting' hypothesis

Kanner had originally suggested that autism was partly the result of 'cold', unemotional parenting, specifically by the mother. However, the prevailing current view is that parents' behaviour doesn't initiate or in any way provoke autism. Indeed, any difference in parents' behaviour towards their autistic child is more likely to be caused *by* the autism than vice versa (Powell, 1999).

Also, autism seems to strike indiscriminately. It's no respecter of social-class or family environment: it can affect a child with extremely warm and loving parents and where there are no autistic siblings (Mitchell, 1997).

Genetic theories

Kanner originally suggested that autism has a genetic component. According to Rutter *et al.* (1999), findings from several independent studies provide compelling evidence for a strong genetic component underlying autism:

- As we saw earlier, the rate of autism (involving all three problem areas) in siblings of children with autism is 6 per cent. This is many times the rate in the general population (ranging from 1 to 16 per 10,000). Rutter *et al.* maintain that:

> *Whatever the precise figure, it is clear that there is a very substantial degree of familial clustering of autism. Although this could reflect shared environmental factors, a loading as high as this points to the likelihood of a genetic component.*

- We also saw earlier that the concordance rate for MZ twins is far higher than for DZ twins. In other words, if one member of a twin pair is autistic, the probability that the other will also be autistic depends to a significant degree on whether they share all their genes (MZs) or only half their genes (DZs: the same as ordinary siblings). Rutter *et al.* (1999) believe that several different genes are involved, working in combination: the twin data indicate that autism is the most strongly genetically influenced of all *multifactorial* child psychiatric disorders.
- However, because autism is still rare (as are MZs) the prospects of finding autism in a member of an MZ pair is very remote. Hence, adding just one MZ pair either with or without concordance can radically shift the overall concordance rate (Mitchell, 1997).

If autism isn't caused solely by genetic factors, then there must be an environmental component. For example, Piven and Folstein (1994) found that about 30 per cent of parents with an autistic child show at least some autistic mannerisms, such as deficient turn-taking in conversation, misinterpreting or not noticing implied meanings of their conversational partner's utterances. Parents of Down's syndrome children, as controls, showed no such difficulties.

Ask Yourself

- Why was it necessary to have a control group at all?
- Why do parents of Down's children make a suitable control group?

Theory of mind (ToM) and mind-blindness

The most influential theory of autism in recent years maintains that what all autistic people have in common (the core deficit) is *mind-blindness* (Baron-Cohen, 1990), a severe impairment in their understanding of mental states and in their appreciation of how mental states govern behaviour (e.g. Baron-Cohen, 1993, 1995a, 1995b). They lack a 'theory of mind' (ToM), a term originally coined by Premack and Woodruff (1978) based on their work with chimps (see Gross, 2008).

Autistic individuals fail to develop the ability to attribute mental states to other people, and this has fundamental implications for communication, where making sense of others' intentions enables the listener to understand what's being said (Baron-Cohen, 1995a).

Ask Yourself

- Try to think of examples of 'mind reading', either from real-life interactions with others, or from TV programmes, films or literature.
- How vital is it that we take into account the fact that not everyone has access to the same information about a situation?

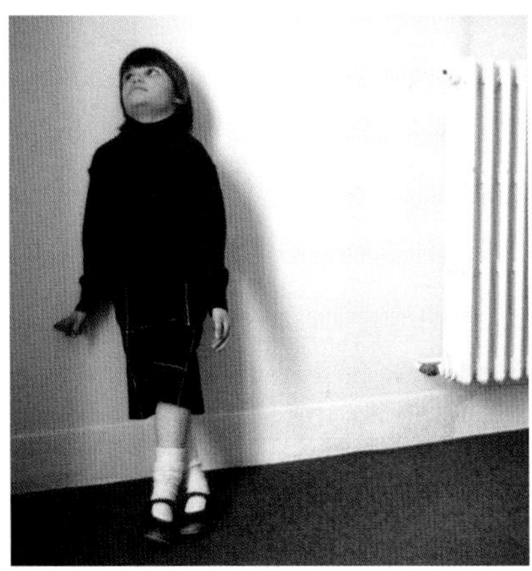

Figure 40.9 The self-absorption displayed by this autistic girl prevents her from developing a normal 'theory of mind'

Testing the ToM hypothesis

Wimmer and Perner (1983) devised a *false-belief task*, with 4-, 6- and 8-year-olds, involving two small dolls (Maxi and his mother). The dolls enact a story in which the mother moves Maxi's chocolate from a green drawer (put there by Maxi) to a blue drawer (while Maxi's outside playing). Children are asked *where Maxi would look for the chocolate* when he returned. A *correct answer* ('green drawer') involves attributing to Maxi a *false belief*: the children know the chocolate's in the blue drawer, but they also know that Maxi doesn't have this knowledge (so he thinks it's still in the green drawer). An *incorrect answer* ('blue drawer') indicates that children cannot distinguish between what they themselves know and what Maxi knows. A correct answer reflects a ToM (see Key Study 40.2).

Key Study 40.2

Has Sally lost her marbles? (Baron-Cohen *et al.*, 1985)

- This was a replication of the Wimmer and Perner 'Maxi' study, retaining the vital elements but adapted to make it shorter and simpler and more appropriate in content for older children (Mitchell, 1997). Sally and Anne replace Maxi and his mother, and the story involves transfer of a marble from a basket to a box.
- A crucial difference between Baron-Cohen *et al.*'s and the Wimmer and Perner study is that the latter involved only normal children. Baron-Cohen *et al.* tested:
  - 20 autistic children, chronological age (CA) 6–16 (mean 11.11), mean verbal mental age (vMA) 5.5
  - 14 Down's syndrome children, CA 6–17 (mean 10.11), mean vMA 2.11
  - 27 normal children, CA 3–5 (mean 4.5), assumed to have vMAs equivalent to their CAs.

Ask Yourself

- Why were these two other groups used?

- The dependent variable was success or failure on the Sally–Anne test, specifically, on the question: 'Where will Sally look for her marble?' (*belief question*).

Ask Yourself

- Assuming the autistic children don't possess a ToM, while normal children and those with Down's syndrome do, how would they have answered the question?

- The results for Down's syndrome and normal children were strikingly similar: 23 out of 27 normal children, and 12 out of 14 Down's syndrome children passed the belief question. By contrast, 16 of the 20 autistic children (80 per cent) failed. This difference between the groups was highly significant.

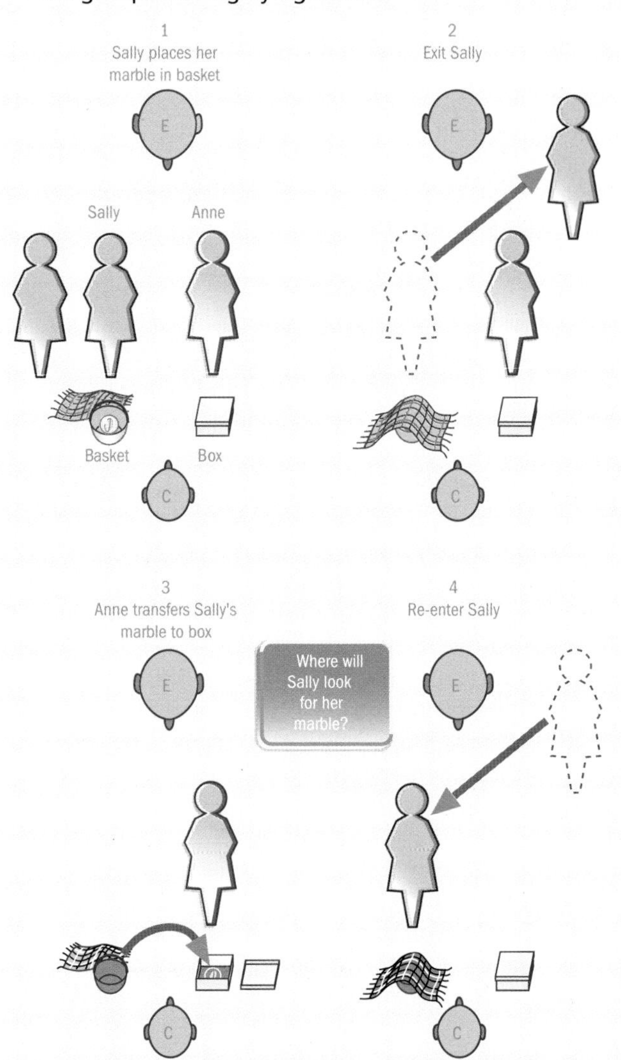

Figure 40.10 The experimental scenario used in Baron-Cohen *et al.*'s (1985) study

It was as if the autistic children had been asked: 'Where is Sally's marble?' They performed much like clinically normal young children do (i.e. below 4), but their average CA was just below 12 (Mitchell, 1997). They also performed far worse than the Down's children, despite having a higher mean verbal MA.

Baron-Cohen (1995a) proposed the existence of four modules involved in 'mindreading': the *intentionality detector* (ID), *eye-direction detector* (EDD), *shared-attention mechanism* (SAM), and the *theory of mind mechanism* (ToMM). ToMM is innately determined and begins to mature from about 12–18 months to 4 years. It processes information in the form of *metarepresentations* ('beliefs about beliefs') (Leslie, 1987, 1994; Leslie and Roth, 1993).

An evaluation of the ToM hypothesis

- Since Baron-Cohen *et al.*'s (1985) study, researchers from all over the world have replicated and extended the basic findings (see Happé, 1994). But despite the ToM hypothesis being both convincing and powerful, a substantial amount of evidence is accumulating that undermines it (Mitchell, 1997).
- For example, some autistic children *do* pass the Sally–Anne and other false-belief tasks, although often later than non-autistic children. Equally, it fails to address some of the apparent *strengths* of at least some autistic individuals, such as their excellent rote memory and the exceptional abilities (the 'islets of ability'), as demonstrated by Stephen Wiltshire and other savants (Frith, 1996; Mitchell, 1997; Powell, 1999; see above).
- Mind-blindness isn't unique to autism: patients with schizophrenia (Corcoran and Frith, 1997) or narcissistic and borderline personality disorders (Fonagy, 1989) or children with conduct disorder (Dodge, 1993) also display forms of mind-blindness.
- Also, the hypothesis doesn't account for all the impairments/difficulties associated with autism. While it can make sense of the social and communication difficulties common to all individuals on the autistic spectrum, it fails to account for the *non-social* features (Baron-Cohen, 2008), such as a restricted range of interest, the obsessive need for sameness and preoccupation with parts rather than the whole (the trees rather than the wood).
- Another shortcoming is that while mindreading is one component of *empathy*, true empathy also requires an *emotional response* to another person's state of mind (Davis, 1994).
- An attempt to remedy these last two limitations of the ToM hypothesis is in the shape of *empathising–systemising* (E-S) *theory* (Baron-Cohen, 2002, 2003a). This is discussed in Chapter 36 in relation to gender differences: male brains are 'hardwired' for systemising, while female brains are hardwired for empathising. According to Baron-Cohen, people with autism (male or female) have an extreme male brain, which means that they cannot empathise (*extreme male brain theory*). While mind-blindness might account for the *cognitive* component of empathy, it cannot explain *affective empathy*; and it's the discrepancy between E and S that determines whether you're likely to develop ASD (Baron-Cohen, 2008).
- Consistent with the E-S theory is the greater prevalence of both autism and Asperger's syndrome among males (see above); this suggests that the number of autistic traits is related to a sex-linked biological factor – genetic or hormonal (Baron-Cohen *et al.*, 2005).
- *Neurological findings* consistent with the extreme male brain theory include the following: (a) in brain areas that are normally smaller in males than females (e.g. the anterior cingulate, superior temporal gyrus, prefrontal cortex and thalamus), people with autism have *even smaller* areas than typical males; (b) in regions where male brains are, on average, larger than female brains (e.g. amygdala and cerebellum), people with autism have *even larger* regions than typical males; (c) the male brain, on average, is larger than in females, and people with autism have been found to have *even larger* brains than typical males. However, some studies have failed to produce such findings (Baron-Cohen, 2008) (see Critical Discussion 40.2).
- Other attempts to correct some of the limitations of the ToM hypothesis include (a) *weak central coherence* and (b) *impaired executive functioning*.

Weak central coherence

Frith (1989; Frith and Happé, 1994a, 1994b) proposed that the deficits and strengths described above stem from the same cognitive source involving how information is integrated. Specifically, they claimed that autism is at least partly the result of a 'weak drive for central coherence'.

Weak central coherence may help to explain at least some of the exceptional abilities shown by savants, where attention to detail is paramount. For example, Stephen Wiltshire's drawings seem to be built up from detail to the whole (not vice versa; Powell, 1999). This style of thinking may not be unique to people with autism.

Box 40.4 Central coherence

While we normally process information at a *global* (holistic or 'top-down') level, autistic individuals tend to do this at a *local* (segmental or 'bottom-up') level. This corresponds to 'the whole' and 'the parts' respectively (see Chapter 15). The former allows us to *disambiguate* ambiguous words (homographs) within the context of a sentence, something which autistic children couldn't do even if they did succeed at ToM tasks (Frith and Snowling, 1983; Happé, 1994).

These same children also tend to have difficulties in real-life situations where ToM is required, since they cannot extract information from its context:

> *Knowing the theory of how other minds work is simply not enough if that knowledge does not take account of context and in the social world context is all-important, ever-changing and often implicit ... (Powell, 1999)*

Impaired executive functioning

Executive functions refer to the ability to 'maintain an appropriate problem-solving set for the attainment of a future goal' (Ozonoff *et al.*, 1991) and include planning, impulse control, and working memory (WM; see Chapter 17). Autistic individuals may become distressed by changes in their immediate environment which interfere with their ritualised behaviours, they don't plan ahead well, and they often seem unable to anticipate the consequences of their actions.

Box 40.5 Executive functioning and the brain

Executive functioning is believed to depend on intact frontal lobes (see Chapter 4). There's increasing evidence for poor performance on many 'frontal' tasks in autism (Frith, 1996).

Rigidity and *perseveration* (ritualistic repetition of certain behaviours) are found both in patients with frontal lobe damage and individuals with autism, implying that autism may involve frontal lobe impairments. But patients with frontal lobe damage are strikingly *not* autistic (Frith, 1996).

One possible explanation for these apparently inconsistent findings is that brain damage from birth and in later life produce very different behavioural pictures – even if the same brain area is involved. The later damage would be expected to have more specific consequences.

So, although an executive function deficit isn't a sufficient explanation of the specific nature of autism (Lewis, 2003), it can potentially explain several features not tackled by ToM (Frith, 1996).

Critical Discussion 40.2

Might there be a two-tier ToM?

The first challenge to the ToM hypothesis came when Onishi *et al.* (2005) reported that ToM seemed to be present in babies just 15 months old. Then Kovacs *et al.* (2010) found evidence for ToM in 7-month-old infants. It was suggested that something about the Sally–Anne test must be confusing 3-year-olds (Weir, 2013).

However, another possibility is that we gain ToM *twice*: from very young, we possess a basic, implicit form of mentalising, which is automatic but limited in scope; then, at around age 4, we develop an explicit, more sophisticated version, which is what's required to pass the Sally–Anne test (Apperley and Butterfill, 2009). Apperley and Butterfill found evidence that adults still possess the implicit system.

Senju *et al.* (2009) found that people with Asperger's syndrome possess the explicit system while lacking the implicit form; this finding suggests that the capacity to understand others shouldn't be so easily dismissed in people with ASD. In other words, ToM isn't an all-or-nothing ability.

LEARNING DIFFICULTIES (LDs)

LDs and learning disabilities, and mental impairment

'*Learning difficulty*' is defined by the Education Act 1993 as:

> *A condition that exists if a child has significantly greater difficulty in learning than the majority of children of his age, or a disability which either prevents or hinders him from making use of educational facilities of a kind generally provided for children of his age in schools within the area of the local education authority.*

While the term 'learning disability' isn't used in any relevant legislation (Lyon, 1995), it's the generally accepted term in service provision in the UK (e.g. by social workers). But education authorities, and the Code of Practice for Special Educational Needs, use the legally defined term 'learning difficulties' to refer to preschool and school-age children who, as adults, would be identified as having 'learning disabilities' (Dockrell *et al.*, 1999).

LDs (children)/learning disabilities (adults) cover what have variously been called 'mental handicap', 'mental subnormality' and 'mental retardation'. DSM-5 (2013) now uses 'intellectual disability'. Another legally defined term is 'mental impairment'. According to the Mental Health Act (1983), mental impairment is:

> *A state of arrested or incomplete development of mind which includes significant impairment of intelligence and social functioning.*

Diagnosing LDs

People diagnosed with LDs don't all experience the same type or degree of problem. They come from all social-class and ethnic backgrounds, but black people with LDs experience two sorts of oppression at the same time (see Chapter 25). Assessment measures may be biased, either in terms of the materials used or the assessment situation itself. Many standard test procedures and equipment are based on white, middle-class values and experiences, producing an underestimation of an individual's level of competence (Chaudhury, 1988).

While IQ is still the main criterion used to diagnose LDs, the extent of impairment in children's ability to adapt to the demands of society is crucial for considering the likelihood of their successful integration into mainstream school (Dockrell *et al.*, 1999). Indeed, DSM-5 (2013) assesses severity in terms of *level of adaptive* functioning (rather than IQ). Also, a diagnosis of LD (or mental retardation) is made only if the individual is under 18 (Carpenter, 1997; see above). A distinction is commonly made between LDs which have known *organic* (genetic or brain-related) causes and those which don't, and this distinction is associated with different degrees of difficulty (see Table 40.1).

Prevalence (the proportion of the whole population affected) has changed little since the 1930s, because people with LDs are living longer. However, the *incidence* (the number of new cases) of severe mental retardation has fallen by one-third. Half of that fall is attributable to improved antenatal and neonatal care (Gelder *et al.*, 1999).

According to Cline (2008), in the past it would have been expected that a child whose IQ was under 50 would attend one type of school (for those with severe or profound LDs) and those with IQ in the 51–70 range would attend another type (for those with moderate LDs). However, studies conducted over an extended period of time showed that not all children within those IQ bands were required to attend the 'appropriate' type of school: those in the 51–70 range might continue to attend a mainstream school (if their reading attainment level was higher or if they showed relatively fewer behavioural difficulties).

Separate placement in a special school has become less and less common partly as a result of policies of *educational inclusion*, and partly due to dissatisfaction with *cultural bias* in IQ tests; this undermined confidence in the validity of such tests for educational purposes (Cline, 2008; see Chapter 41). More fundamentally, however, the categorisation of LDs by IQ was undermined by the finding that

Table 40.1 Different categories of mental retardation

Name	IQ range	Prevalence	Description
Mild	50–70	3% (80% of all cases)	Adults can be expected to acquire some independence in most self-care/domestic activities, and earn money from unskilled work. Main difficulties will be in reading, writing, monetary skills, emotional and social immaturity, and inability to adapt readily to social expectations and external stressors
Moderate	36–49	0.3% (12% of all cases)	Adults frequently have additional disabilities, such as epilepsy, and physical and sensory disabilities. Most need supervision with self-care
Severe	20–35	0.04% (7% of all cases)	As above
Profound	Below 20	0.05% (1% of all cases)	Adults usually need close supervision and care their whole life. Many can feed themselves with a spoon, most can understand and make simple statements and requests. Most have multiple disabilities

(Based on Carpenter, 1997; Gelder et al., 1999)

> *... there is no simple relationship between differences in measured intelligence and patterns of learning behaviour. Knowing the IQ of a child with moderate and severe learning difficulties does not give a teacher useful information about whether they are likely to learn in a particular way or to experience particular learning problems ... (Cline, 2008)*

Cline argues that more attention needs to be given to *motivational* and *attitudinal problems*.

The causes of LDs

People with *mild* LDs don't usually have clear aetiological diagnoses, that is, there's seldom an obvious, single cause. Most have family histories of low IQ, but it's unclear if this reflects a genetic influence, the effects of the environment, or the effects of undocumented specific causes. For example, it was traditionally assumed that mild LDs were caused by genetic and sociocultural factors. The discovery of *fragile X syndrome* and *foetal alcohol syndrome* (FAS; see Box 40.6) has suggested that (other) more specific causes will be discovered in time. However, it's rare for a child from a high socio-economic background to have either mild or severe LDs without some medical cause being apparent (Carpenter, 1997). As Dockrell *et al.* (1999) say:

> *The mild level of learning difficulty is viewed primarily as an academic dysfunction, or as a deficiency in learning ability with aetiology unknown ...*

People with *severe* or *profound* LDs are more likely to have an identifiable primary cause, usually genetic. The most common known autosomal chromosomal abnormality responsible for intellectual impairment is Down's syndrome (see above). This occurs in one-third of people with an IQ below 50 (Carpenter, 1997). The most common well-documented single-gene recessive defect is *phenylketonuria* (PKU), which affects 12 in 1,000,000 people. This is routinely tested for at birth in the UK, and a special diet can prevent LDs from developing. But an appreciable minority still isn't put on the special diet within three weeks of birth (Carpenter, 1997). (See Chapter 50.)

Secondary causes include the following.

- *Hypothyroidism*: in its severe form, this used to be called 'cretinism'. One cause is cerebral palsy (see below), but early detection and administering thyroxine within the first three months of life will prevent intellectual impairments. But many affected children will also be deaf, which can impair intellectual development.
- *Cerebral palsy*: this can be congenital (present at birth), as in congenital *rubella* (German measles) but may also result from postnatal events. About one-third of full-term infants with cerebral palsy have severe LDs, and it's much more common in low-birthweight (premature) babies (but only 20 per cent of the latter have severe LDs).
- *Neural tube abnormalities*: spina bifida is one example, affecting 70–150 per 100,000 live births. Up to 10 per cent will have LDs, and almost all of these will be multiply handicapped.
- *Foetal alcohol syndrome*.

Box 40.6 Foetal Alcohol Syndrome (FAS)

Children with FAS are typically smaller than normal and suffer from *microcephaly* (unusually small heads and brains). Such children often have heart defects, short noses and low nasal bridges. The eyes, too, have a distinctive appearance.

FAS children are generally mildly retarded, though some may be moderately retarded and others of average intelligence. But in those of average intelligence, there are significant academic and attentional difficulties (Sue *et al.*, 1994).

The syndrome is a consequence of the mother's excessive alcohol consumption during pregnancy. While there doesn't seem to be an agreed 'safe' level of maternal drinking during pregnancy, there appears to be a linear relationship between the amount of alcohol consumed and the risk of FAS. Binge drinking may be as dangerous as regular drinking. (See Chapter 8.)

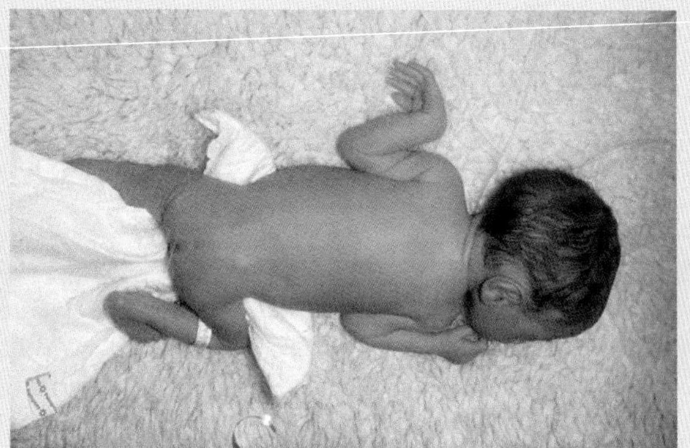

Figure 40.11 A child with FAS

CONCLUSIONS

Howe *et al.* (1998) conclude their review of giftedness by saying that if excelling is a consequence of possessing innate gifts, there's no point trying to nurture them in children without them:

> *... categorising some children as innately talented is discriminatory. The evidence suggests that such categorisation is unfair and wasteful, preventing young people from pursuing a goal because of*

the unjustified conviction of teachers or parents that certain children would not benefit from the superior opportunities given to those who are deemed to be talented.

According to Ross (2006):

The preponderance of psychological evidence indicates that experts are made, not born ... What is more, the demonstrated ability to turn a child quickly into an expert – in chess, music and a host of other subjects – sets a clear challenge before the schools ...

In relation to ASD, Frith (1996) concludes by saying:

It seems unlikely that one single cognitive abnormality can be identified that would explain all the abnormalities present in autism. The existence of multiple deficits ... might help us understand why autism can exist in many different forms ranging from mild to severe. The explanation of autism at the cognitive level needs to be complemented by the explanation at the biological level ...

Chapter Summary

- **Gifted children** tend to be **precocious**, make discoveries on their own, have an obsessive interest in their domain of giftedness, and have unusually good **metacognitive skills.**
- Cases like those of Sufiah Yusof and Ruth Lawrence illustrate the kinds of social and emotional problems gifted children are prone to.
- Terman's study of giftedness also created the myth that these children are **globally** gifted. In fact, the **unevenness** of gifted children's abilities is quite common and is also demonstrated in extreme form by savants such as Stephen Wiltshire.
- Both savants and non-savant gifted children appear to have **atypical brain organisation**, possibly caused by **'testosterone poisoning'**. This may account for the **'pathology of superiority'**.
- The belief that giftedness is hardwired in the infant brain is consistent with the **'talent account'**. But critics argue that **temperamental** and **personality qualities,** rather than cognitive ones, are what set geniuses apart from the rest of us, and that **practice from an early age** is the crucial environmental influence.
- The **autistic spectrum disorder** (ASD) has been defined in terms of the **triad of impairments**: **social relationships, language/communication** and **stereotyped/repetitive behaviour**. There's a wide **spectrum** of autistic disorders, which includes **Asperger's syndrome**.
- An early, unsuccessful, attempt to explain autism was the **'refrigerator-parenting'** hypothesis.
- Many researchers believe that there's compelling evidence for a strong **genetic component** underlying autism, based on studies of siblings of autistic individuals and of identical/non-identical twins.
- The strongest evidence for autistic children's lack of a **theory of mind (ToM)** and **mind-blindness** is their consistent failure on **false-belief tasks.** By comparison, Down's syndrome and normal children reliably pass them.
- Two alternative, complementary, cognitive explanations are **weak central coherence** and **impaired executive functioning.**
- Another complementary explanation is Baron-Cohen's **empathising–systemising (E-S)** theory, according to which the autistic individual has an **extreme male brain.**
- **Learning difficulty (LD)** is a legally defined term, synonymous with **learning disability**, and the internationally used term **mental retardation.** **Intellectual disability** and **mental impairment** are alternative terms.
- LDs are defined primarily in terms of **IQ (intelligence quotient)**, but the **level of adaptive functioning** is equally important. Mental retardation is usually subdivided into **mild, moderate, severe** and **profound.**
- **Primary (organic**: genetic or brain-related) **causes**, such as **Down's** and **fragile X syndromes,** are usually associated with severe and profound LDs.
- **Secondary (non-genetic)** causes include **foetal alcohol syndrome (FAS)** and **sociocultural** and other **environmental** factors.

Links with Other Topics/Chapters

Chapter 43 ⟶ Both exceptionally high achievers (such as Sufiah Yusof and Ruth Lawrence) and Down's syndrome children are *statistically abnormal*, but their behaviours/abilities are clearly very different, as are the *valuations* placed on them by society

Chapter 34 ⟶ *Metacognition* is an important feature of the *information-processing approach* to explaining *cognitive development*

Chapter 4 ⟶ The LHH explanation of savant syndrome rests on the assumption that the two hemispheres really are different in the kinds of abilities they control (*lateralisation of brain function*)

Chapters 4 and 41 ⟶ According to Treffert and Wallace (2004), savant syndrome provides a unique window into the brain regarding *general versus multiple forms of intelligence, plasticity, compensation* and *repair*

Chapter 39 ⟶ The latter are vital in understanding and treating conditions such as *Alzheimer's disease*

Chapter 50 ⟶ To say that talents cannot be manufactured is another way of claiming that they develop through *maturation*

Chapter 43 ⟶ Unlike other disorders, people with autism seem to be virtually cut off from other people ('in a world of their own'). This is why it's sometimes categorised as a *psychosis*, implying that it's unlike anything in the normal range of experience (Baron-Cohen, 1995a)

Chapters 41, 44 and 50 ⟶ *Twin studies* (comparing DZs with MZs, the latter both reared together and separately) is one of the major methods for assessing the influence of genetic factors involved in *intelligence differences, schizophrenia* and other *mental disorders,* and is crucial for the *nature–nurture debate* as a whole

Chapter 36 ⟶ Baron-Cohen's E-S theory is relevant to understanding psychological *gender differences*

Chapter 45 ⟶ All the *treatment approaches* used with autistic individuals are also used with adults with a wide range of *mental disorders*

Recommended Reading

Gross, R. (2008) *Key Studies in Psychology* (5th edn). London: Hodder Education. Chapter 8.

Gross, R. (2012) *Key Studies in Psychology* (6th edn). London: Hodder & Stoughton. Chapter 4.

Happé, F. (1999) Why success is more interesting than failure. *The Psychologist, 12*(11), 540–5.

Mitchell, P. (1997) *Introduction to Theory of Mind: Children, Autism and Apes.* London: Arnold.

Useful Websites

www.transporters.tv (The Transporters website: an attempt to teach ToM to autistic children)

www.autism-society.org (The US Autism Society)

www.autism.com (Autism Research Institute)

www.aspergersyndrome.org (Online Asperger's syndrome information and support)

http://apa.org/ed/schools/gifted/index.aspx (Centre for Gifted Education Policy – American Psychological Association)

CHAPTER 41

INTELLIGENCE

Defining intelligence

Theories of intelligence

Intelligence testing

Explaining individual differences: heredity and environment

INTRODUCTION and OVERVIEW

The concept of intelligence is one of the most elusive in the whole of Psychology; perhaps nowhere else does so much of the research and theory attempt to define the concept under investigation.

But intelligence isn't just of academic interest. The intelligence test (in one form or another) has impinged on the lives of most of us, whether in the context of educational or occupational selection, or even selection for Mensa, the high-IQ society.

How intelligence is conceptualised varies enormously. Biological definitions see intelligence as related to adaptation to the environment. For Piaget (1950), intelligence is:

> *... essentially a system of living and acting operations, i.e. a state of balance or equilibrium achieved by the person when he is able to deal adequately with the data before him. But it is not a static state, it is dynamic in that it continually adapts itself to new environmental stimuli.*

Piaget was interested in the *qualitative* aspects of intelligence, that is, the nature of intelligence itself.

By contrast, the *psychometric* ('mental measurement') approach is concerned with measuring individual differences in intelligence, through the use of intelligence (IQ) tests, and so emphasises the *quantitative* aspects of intelligence. This approach, associated with Psychologists such as Spearman, Burt, Vernon, Thurstone, and Guilford, has predominated until fairly recently. Important alternatives are Sternberg's *information-processing approach* and Gardner's *theory of multiple intelligences*.

The near-obsession of Western society with measuring and categorising people is emotionally charged and politically sensitive, especially in relation to the 'race and IQ' debate. This is one form of the *nature–nurture/heredity–environment debate*, which has become associated with extremes of political viewpoints. It highlights the impossibility of completely divorcing the social from the scientific functions of Psychology (see Chapter 3).

DEFINING INTELLIGENCE

Ask Yourself

- How would you define intelligence?

Most definitions reflect the *psychometric approach*. As we saw in the *Introduction and overview*, this is concerned with the measurement of intelligence in order to compare 'how much' of it different individuals possess (see Table 41.1).

Ask Yourself

- What similarities and differences are there between the different definitions in Table 41.1?

The definitions of Terman, Burt and Vernon all stress the purely cognitive/intellectual aspects of the concept, while those of Binet and Wechsler are much broader and perhaps closer to common-sense understanding. Heim objects to the use of intelligence as a noun, and believes that it should be regarded as part of personality as a whole. Consequently, she prefers to talk about 'intelligent activity' rather than 'intelligence'.

Table 41.1 Some definitions of intelligence

Definition
'It seems to us that in intelligence there is a fundamental faculty, the impairment of which is of the utmost importance for practical life. This faculty is called judgement, otherwise called good sense, practical sense, initiative, the faculty of adapting one's self to circumstances. To judge well, to comprehend well, to reason well ...' (Binet, 1905)
'An individual is intelligent in proportion as he is able to carry on abstract thinking.' (Terman, 1921)
'... innate, general, cognitive ability' (Burt, 1955)
'... the aggregate of the global capacity to act purposefully, think rationally, to deal effectively with the environment' (Wechsler, 1944)
'... the effective all-round cognitive abilities to comprehend, to grasp relations and reason' (Vernon, 1969)
'Intelligent activity consists in grasping the essentials in a situation and responding appropriately to them.' (Heim, 1970)
'... the ability to deal with cognitive complexity' (Gottfredson, 1998)

Other definitions

An *operational definition* defines intelligence in terms of tests designed to measure it, that is, 'Intelligence is what intelligence tests measure' (Boring, 1923). But this begs the question as to what intelligence tests measure and is *circular* (the concept being defined is part of the definition itself). Miles (1967) argues that if we substitute the names of particular tests, then we can break into the circle, but Heim points out that this merely decreases the circumference of the circle!

Like Heim, Ryle (1949) believes that 'intelligence' doesn't denote an entity or an engine inside us causing us to act in particular ways. Rather, any action can be performed more or less intelligently, so it should be used as an adjective and not as a noun.

THEORIES OF INTELLIGENCE

Psychometric (factor-analytic) theories

Psychometric theories are based upon analysis of scores of large numbers of individuals on various intelligence tests using a statistical technique called *factor analysis* (FA).

Box 41.1 Factor Analysis (FA)

This involves correlating the scores of a large sample of participants to determine whether scores on certain tests are related to scores on certain other tests (whether some, or any, of the tests have something in common).
The basic assumption is that the more similar the scores on two or more tests (the higher the correlation), the more likely it is that these tests are tapping the same basic ability (or factor).
For example, if we find that people's scores on tests A, B, C, D and E are highly positively correlated, then it could be inferred that (a) all five tests are measuring the same ability, and (b) individuals differ according to how much or how little of that particular ability they have.

The two hypothetical outcomes in Box 41.1 correspond roughly to two theories of intelligence: (i) the 'London line' is associated with Spearman (1904, 1967), Burt (1949, 1955), and Vernon (1950); (ii) the mainly American approach of Thurstone (1938) and Guilford (1959).

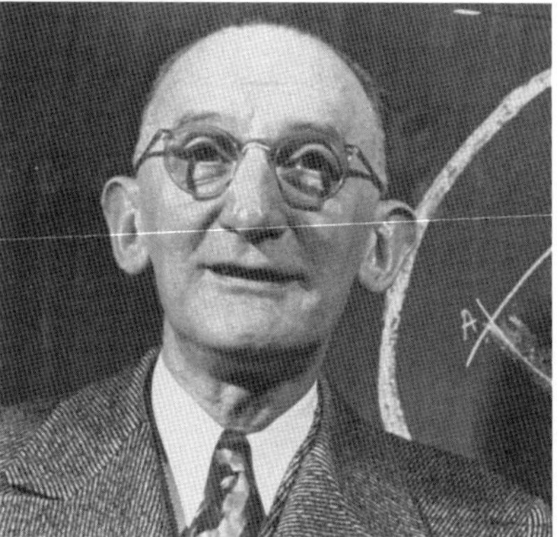

Figure 41.1 L.L. Thurstone (1887–1955)

Spearman's two-factor theory

Spearman factor-analysed the results of children's performance on various tests, and found that many tests were moderately positively correlated. He concluded that every intellectual activity involves both a general factor (*g* or general intelligence) and a specific factor (*s*), and differences between individuals are largely attributable to differences in their *g* factor (*g* is, in fact, an abbreviation for *neogenesis*, the ability to 'educe relations', as in a common kind of test item which asks 'A is to Y as B is to ?'). The *g* factor accounts for why people who perform well using one mental ability also tend to perform well in others, and is entirely innate.

Spearman himself believed that he'd discovered the elusive entity, the innate essence of intelligence, that would make Psychology a true science. As Gould (1981) puts it:

> *Spearman's g would be the philosopher's stone of psychology, its hard, quantifiable 'thing' – a fundamental particle that would pave the way for an exact science as firm and as basic as physics ...*

Although this proved to be a rather exaggerated claim, Guilford (1936, in Gould, 1981) believed that no single event in the history of mental testing has proved to be of such momentous importance as Spearman's proposal of his famous two-factor theory.

Burt and Vernon's hierarchical model

Burt (a student of Spearman) agreed that there's a *g* factor common to all tests, but also thought that the two-factor model was too simple. He and Vernon elaborated and extended Spearman's model by identifying a series of *group factors* (major and minor) in between *g* and *s* factors (see Figure 41.2). The *g* factor is what *all* tests measure, the *major group factors* (v:ed and k:m) are what *some* tests measure (some to a greater extent than others), the *minor group factors* are what *particular* tests measure whenever they're given, while *specific factors* are what *particular* tests measure on *specific occasions* (Vernon, 1971).

An important *educational* implication of this model is that, given the dominance of *g* in the hierarchy, each child can be ranked on a single scale of (innate) intelligence. The *g* factor can be measured early in life, and children sorted according to their intellectual promise. (This is the thinking behind the eleven-plus examination: see Box 41.3.)

Thurstone's primary mental abilities

Using 14-year-olds and college students as his participants, Thurstone (1935, 1938, 1947) found that not all mental tests correlate equally. Rather, they appear to form seven distinct factors or groupings, which he called *primary mental abilities* (PMAs), namely:

- *spatial* (S) – the ability to recognise spatial relationships
- *perceptual speed* (P) – the quick and accurate detection of visual detail
- *numerical reasoning* (N) – the ability to perform arithmetical operations quickly and accurately
- *verbal meaning* (V) – understanding the meaning of words and verbal concepts
- *word fluency* (W) – speed in recognising single and isolated words
- *memory* (M) – the ability to recall a list of words, numbers or other material
- *inductive reasoning* (I) – the ability to generate a rule or relationship that describes a set of observations.

Thurstone sometimes referred to these mental abilities as 'mental faculties' or 'the vectors of mind' (the title of his 1935 book). He saw *g* as a grand average of positive correlations for a particular battery of tests. This means that *g* can change according to the particular battery of tests used, and so it:

> *... has no fundamental psychological significance beyond the arbitrary collection of tests that anyone happens to put together ... We cannot be interested in a general factor which is only the average of any random collection of tests ... (Thurstone, 1940, in Gould, 1981)*

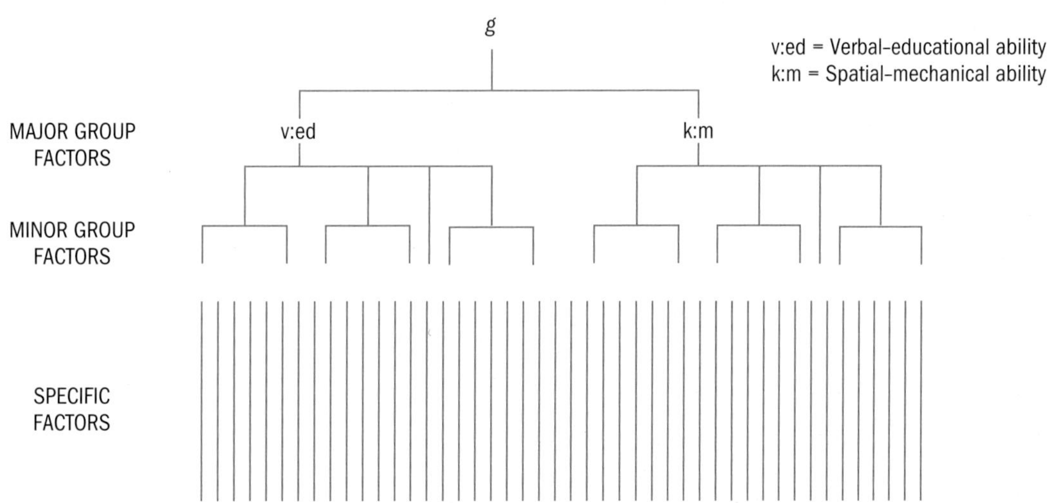

Figure 41.2 The hierarchical model of intelligence (after Vernon, 1950)

So the PMAs are independent and uncorrelated. They correspond to the group factors in the hierarchical model, but there's no general factor to which they're all related. As there's no general ability, the overall ranking of pupils is inappropriate: some children will be good at some things, others at other things. He advocated the use of individual profiles of all PMAs. However, Thurstone (1947) later admitted that *g does* seem to be involved in all PMAs (having carried out a 'second-order' factor analysis on the results of the first: see Chapter 42).

Jensen (1980), a major advocate of the view that intelligence differences are largely genetic, believes that this change of mind by Thurstone proves that Spearman and Burt were right all along. Jensen is a 'pure Spearman-ian' (Gould, 1981), who claims that 'To the extent that a test orders individuals on *g*, it can be said to be a test of intelligence'.

However, Gould (1981) argues that *g* was still of secondary importance to the PMAs. Even after admitting a second-order *g*, Thurstone continued to contrast himself with the 'London line'.

Guilford's 'structure of intellect' model

This represents the most extreme alternative to Spearman's two-factor theory, and totally rejects the notion of a general intelligence factor. Guilford first classified a cognitive task along three major dimensions:

1. *content* (what must the participant think about?)
2. *operations* (what kind of thinking is the participant being asked to perform?)
3. *products* (what kind of answer is required?).

He identified five kinds of content, five kinds of operation, and six kinds of product which, multiplied together, yield a total of 150 distinct mental abilities (see Figure 41.3). Guilford set out to construct tests to measure each of the 150 abilities, and tests have been devised to assess more than 70 (Shaffer, 1985). However, people's scores are often correlated, suggesting that the number of basic mental abilities is much smaller than Guilford assumed (Brody and Brody, 1976).

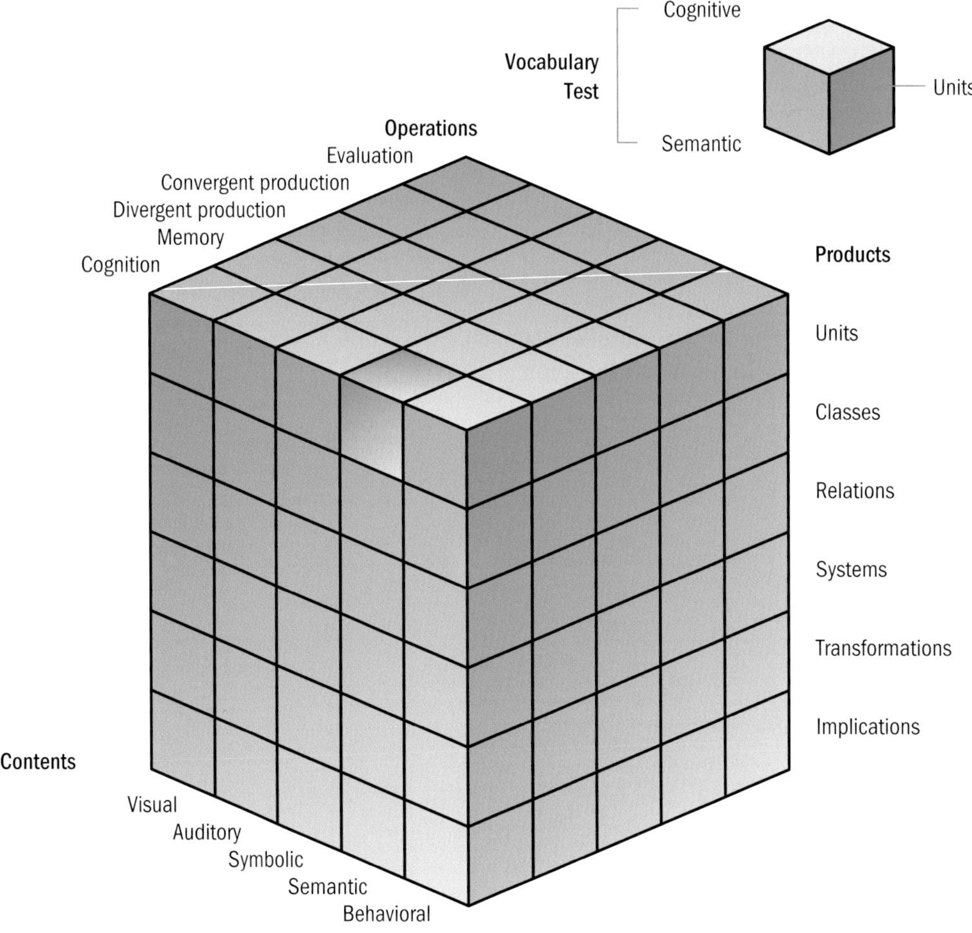

Figure 41.3 Guilford's (1967, 1982) structure of intellect model. (From Zimbardo, P.G., (1992) *Psychology and Life*, 13th ed. New York, HarperCollins Publishers.) (Originally, Guilford identified 120 abilities, but he later distinguished between visual and auditory content (previously included under 'figural') giving 5 x 5 x 6 = 150)

An evaluation of factor-analytic models

According to Vernon (1950, 1971), intelligence is neither a single general mental ability nor a number of more specific, independent abilities, but *both*. General intelligence plays a part in all mental activities, but more specific abilities are also involved in producing performance. Sternberg (1995) believes that this combined, hierarchical approach is probably the most widely accepted factorial description of intelligence. However:

- there's more than one way of factor-analysing a set of data, and there's no 'best' way. Thurstone originally used a form of FA which gives a 'simple structure' solution in contrast to the 'principal component' solutions resulting from Spearman's and Burt's analyses. These two alternatives are *mathematically equivalent*, and the same data from the same sample can produce a number of different patterns of factors depending on which alternative is used (Shackleton and Fletcher, 1984)
- FA produces a cluster of intercorrelations between different tests and subtests – it's then up to the researcher to scan these patterns of intercorrelations and to label them. As Radford (1980) says, factors don't come 'ready-labelled': clusters of intercorrelations are meaningless until they're given an interpretation by a Psychologist
- Once a factor has been labelled (e.g. 'verbal ability'), there's the danger of believing that it exists in some objective way (*reification*). But in reality, a factor is merely a statistic (or 'mathematical abstraction': Gould, 1981); it has no *intrinsic* psychological significance (Gillham, 1978).

Fluid and crystallised intelligence

Working within the FA approach, Cattell (1963) and Horn and Cattell (1967, 1982) proposed a model which can to some degree reconcile the different models discussed above. They argue that *g* can be subdivided into two major dimensions – fluid and crystallised intelligence (see Chapter 39).

- *Fluid intelligence* (*gf*) is the ability to solve abstract relational problems of the sort that aren't taught, and which are relatively free of cultural influences. It increases gradually throughout childhood and adolescence as the nervous system matures, then levels off during young adulthood, and after that begins a steady decline.
- *Crystallised intelligence* (*gc*) increases throughout the lifespan, and is primarily a reflection of one's cumulative learning experience. It involves understanding relations or solving problems which depend on knowledge acquired as a result of schooling and other life experiences (e.g. general knowledge, word comprehension and numerical abilities).

The information-processing approach

The *information-processing approach* sees intelligence as the steps or processes people go through in solving problems (Fishbein, 1984). One person may be more intelligent than another, because s/he moves through the same steps more quickly or efficiently, or is more familiar with the required steps.

Advocates of this view (e.g. Sternberg, 1979) focus on: (i) how information is internally represented; (ii) the kinds of strategies people use in processing that information; (iii) the nature of the components (e.g. memory, inference, comparison) used in carrying out those strategies; and (iv) how decisions are made as to which strategies to use. Regarding (iii), Sternberg (1987) identifies five major kinds of components: the *g* factor results from the operations of components, which are general across the range of tasks represented on IQ tests and are mainly *metacomponents* (i.e. higher-order control processes used in planning how a problem should be solved, in making decisions regarding alternative courses of action during problem-solving, and in monitoring one's progress during the course of problem solution).

Ask Yourself

- How do you think *cultural factors* might relate to these five kinds of components?

While the components involved in the solution of the 'same' problem would overlap regardless of the particular culture, the kinds of problems needing solution will differ widely from one culture to another. As Sternberg (1987) says:

> *... the kinds of persons who are considered intelligent may vary widely from one culture to another, as a function of the components that are important for adaptation to the requirements of living in the various cultures.*

Cultural context is central to Sternberg's *contextual subtheory*, part of his *triarchic theory* (1985, 1988a).

Figure 41.4 Robert Sternberg, born 1949

Information-processing theories are intended to be *universal* (like Piaget's), and at the same time explain *individual differences* (like factor-analytic theories). As Fishbein (1984) puts it, they see intelligence as neither an 'it' (for example *g*) nor a 'them' (for example, PMAs), but as everything the mind does in processing information.

Gardner's theory of multiple intelligences

Gardner's (1983, 1998) theory of multiple intelligences (MI theory) is based on three fundamental principles:

1. Intelligence isn't a single, unitary thing but a collection of multiple *intelligences*, each one a system in its own right (as opposed to merely separate aspects of a larger system, i.e. 'intelligence').
2. Each intelligence is independent of all the others.
3. The intelligences interact, otherwise nothing could be achieved.

MI theory also makes two strong claims:

1. All humans possess all these intelligences, and collectively they can be considered a cognitive definition of *Homo sapiens*.
2. Just as we all look different and have unique personalities and temperaments, so we also have different *profiles* of intelligences. No two individuals, not even identical twins, have exactly the same mix of intelligences, with the same strengths and weaknesses (see Chapter 42).

Gardner (1998) defines an intelligence as:

> *... a biopsychological potential to process information that can be activated in a cultural setting to solve problems or create products that are of value in a culture.*

Entire cultures may encourage the development of one or other intelligence. For example, the seafaring Puluwat of the Caroline Islands (in the South Pacific) cultivate spatial intelligence and excel at navigation. The Manus children of New Guinea learn the canoeing and swimming skills that elude the vast majority of western children (Gardner, 1998).

Figure 41.5 These boys from Papua New Guinea display how intelligence can be defined in terms of adaptations to the cultural environment

Gardner (1983) originally identified seven intelligences, and added an eighth, *naturalistic* (or 'the naturalist'), in 1995. Darwin is a good example. Gardner is currently considering the possibility of a ninth – *existential intelligence*, which captures the human tendency to raise and ponder fundamental questions about existence, life, death, and so on (e.g. the existential philosopher, Kierkegaard) (Gardner, 1998).

Gardner identifies eight different criteria for distinguishing an independent intelligence, including the following:

- *potential isolation by brain damage:* each intelligence resides in a separate region of the brain, so that a given intelligence should be isolable by studying brain-damaged patients. For example, naturalistic intelligence is based on evidence that certain parts of the temporal lobe are dedicated to naming and the recognition of natural things, while others are attuned to human-made objects. Brain-damaged people sometimes lose the capacity to identify living things, but can still name inanimate objects (Gardner, 1998; see Chapter 4)
- an identifiable core operation (or set of operations)
- support from psychometric findings (patterns of intercorrelations, based on FA: see Box 41.1)
- the existence of idiots savants, prodigies, and other exceptional individuals (see Chapter 40).

Table 41.2 Gardner's eight intelligences

Linguistic	Includes skills involved in reading, writing, listening and talking
Logical–mathematical	Involved in numerical computation, deriving proofs, solving logical puzzles, and most scientific thinking
Spatial	Used in marine navigation, piloting a plane, driving a car, working out how to get from A to B, figuring out one's orientation in space. Also important in the visual arts, playing chess, and recognising faces and scenes
Musical	Includes singing, playing an instrument, conducting, composing and, to some extent, musical appreciation
Bodily–kinaesthetic	Involves the use of one's whole body or parts of it, to solve problems, construct products and displays. Used in dance, athletics, acting and surgery
Interpersonal	Includes understanding and acting upon one's understanding of others – noticing differences between people, reading their moods, temperaments, intentions, and so on. Especially important in politics, sales, psychotherapy and teaching
Intrapersonal	Self-understanding – symbolised in the world of dreams
Naturalistic	Permits the recognition and categorisation of natural objects (as in biology, zoology, etc.)

Ask Yourself

- Explain how savant abilities suggest the existence of separate intelligences.

Figure 41.6 Musical intelligence in action

Box 41.2 Multiple intelligences and education

MI theory proved popular with educators, who saw it as egalitarian: everyone might have an intelligence through which they could demonstrate strengths, even if they didn't do well on tests of *g*. It highlighted the value of teaching outside the core academic skills of literacy and numeracy (Cline, 2008).

The theory stimulated experiments in teaching designed to draw on and enrich different intelligences. Different initiatives were implemented to develop assessments based on MI theory that would help teachers choose teaching methods and materials appropriate for each individual child (Chen and Gardner, 2005; see Chapter 34).

However, critics within education have argued that the theory is too broad to be useful for detailed curriculum planning and presents a static view of student competence (Klein, 1997). It's also been observed that Gardner's intelligences are positively correlated with *g*; so, like Thurstone's PMAs, they're best thought of as factors of general intelligence (Brand, 1996).

Goleman (1995) believes that Gardner's multifaceted view of intelligence offers a richer picture of a child's ability and potential for success than the standard IQ. Complementary to Gardner's MI theory is Goleman's concept of *emotional intelligence*, which he defines as:

> *... abilities such as being able to motivate oneself and persist in the face of frustrations; to control impulse and delay gratification; to regulate one's moods and keep distress from swamping the ability to think; to empathise and to hope ... (Goleman, 1995)*

INTELLIGENCE TESTING

A brief history of intelligence tests

The Stanford–Binet test

In 1904, Binet and Simon were commissioned by the French government to devise a test which would identify those children who wouldn't benefit from ordinary schooling because of their inferior intelligence. The result was the Simon–Binet test (1905), generally accepted as the first intelligence test. The sample of children used for the development of the test (the *standardisation sample*) was very small, and it was subsequently revised in 1908 and 1911, using much larger samples.

In 1910, Terman, at Stanford University in California, began adapting the Simon–Binet test for use in the USA. The test became known as the Stanford–Binet test, and is still referred to in this way. The first revision was published in 1916, followed by the Terman–Merrill revision (1937), which comprised two equivalent forms (L and M). In 1960, the most useful questions from the 1937 revision were combined into a single form (L–M) and an improved scoring system was used. Prior to 1960, the Stanford–Binet test was designed for individuals up to age 16 (starting at 2 and a half to 3), but this was extended to 18 in the 1960 revision.

A further revision was published in 1973, and the most recent in 1986, which is designed for people from age 2 years up to 23 years, 11 months. Subtests assess verbal reasoning, quantitative (mathematical) reasoning, abstract and visual reasoning, and memory. The testee is given a vocabulary test that serves as a routing test to determine the starting level for all the other scales (Sparrow and Davis, 2000).

In the 1986 revision, items are grouped into four broad areas of intellectual ability: (i) verbal reasoning; (ii) abstract/visual reasoning; (iii) quantitative reasoning; and (iv) short-term memory. A separate score is obtained for each area (whereas previously a single overall IQ score was given).

The Wechsler tests

Wechsler developed the most widely used test of adult intelligence, the *Wechsler adult intelligence scale* (WAIS, Wechsler, 1944), revised in 1958 and again in 1981 (WAIS-R). WAIS-III (1997) is designed for use with adults aged 16–89. Like WAIS-R, WAIS-III is constructed much like the *Wechsler intelligence scale for children* (WISC), first published in 1949 and revised in 1974 (WISC-R), and again in 1991 (WISC-III) and designed for 5- to 15-year-olds. Finally, the *Wechsler preschool primary scale of intelligence* (WPPSI, 1963; WPPSI-R, 1989) is designed for 4- to 6 and a half-year-olds.

The Wechsler tests produce three IQ scores: *verbal*, *performance*, and *full* (combined or general) IQs. Although there's much debate about the atheoretical nature of all the Wechsler tests, they're by far the most widely used cognitive assessment instruments today, both in the USA and around the world, having been translated into French, Greek, Japanese and Chinese (Sparrow and Davis, 2000) (see Table 41.3).

Army alpha and beta tests

The Stanford–Binet and Wechsler tests are *individual tests* (i.e. given to one person at a time). *Group tests* are administered to several people at once (as in written examinations). A major impetus to the development of group testing was America's involvement in the First World War. A quick and easy method of selecting over 1 million recruits was needed, and the result was the *army alpha* and *beta tests* (see Gould, 1981 and Gross, 2008).

The British ability scales (BAS)

The *British ability scales* (Elliot *et al.*, 1979) assesses five major 'mental processes', including retrieval and application of knowledge, and speed of information processing. The latter is meant to underlie performance on all the other subscales, and is one of the novel features of the test, reflecting the influence of the information-processing approach (see Chapter 34).

Like the Wechsler scales, the BAS gives three IQ scores – *verbal*, *visual*, and *overall/general* IQs. In keeping with Thurstone's PMA model, the aim was to construct an intelligence scale which would provide a profile of special abilities, rather than merely produce an overall IQ figure (Richardson, 1991).

The original British test was revised and standardised in the USA as the *Differential abilities scale* (Elliot, 1990), although it's used mainly in the UK. Its British revision (BASII, Elliot, 1996) was based on a new standardisation sample of 1700 British children, and the upper age limit is now 17 years, 11 months. Scales are now clearly divided into early years (2 years, 6 months to 5 years, 11 months) and school age (6 years to 17 years, 11 months). In consultation with applied Psychologists, Elliot established that the key issues that BASII should address were

> *... the need for the scales to reflect and embrace more contemporary theoretical models of intelligence, and ongoing concerns regarding the relevance of these tests for children and young people from diverse social, racial, linguistic and cultural backgrounds ... (Hill, 2005).*

It was considered crucial that the standardisation sample should reflect the current diversity of the UK population.

What do intelligence tests measure?

IQ tests represent one kind of *ability test*, designed to measure underlying constructs that aren't a direct result of training (Coolican *et al.*, 2007). This contrasts with *attainment* (or *achievement*) *tests* (such as tests of reading and comprehension, spelling, and numeracy)

Table 41.3 Some items from the Stanford–Binet (1973) and the two scales of the WAIS-R (1981)

Stanford-Binet	WAIS-R
Children of 3 should be able to: Point to objects that serve various functions (e.g. 'goes on your feet') Repeat a list of two words or digits (e.g. 'can', 'dog') **Children of 4 should be able to:** Discriminate visual forms (e.g. squares, circles, triangles) Define words (e.g. 'ball', 'bat') Repeat ten-word sentences, count up to four objects, solve problems (e.g. 'In daytime it is light, at night it is …') **Children of 9 should be able to:** Solve verbal problems (e.g. 'Tell me a number that rhymes with tree') Solve simple arithmetic problems and repeat four digits in reverse order **Children of 12 should be able to:** Define words (e.g. 'skill', 'muzzle') Repeat five digits in reverse order Solve verbal absurdities (e.g. 'One day we saw several icebergs that had been entirely melted by the warmth of the Gulf Stream. What's foolish about that?')	**Verbal scale** (none of the subtests is timed): ● **Information:** general knowledge ● **Comprehension:** ability to use knowledge in practical settings (e.g. 'What would you do if you were lost in a large, strange town?') ● **Arithmetic** ● **Similarities:** conceptual and analogical reasoning (e.g. 'In what ways are a book and TV alike?') ● **Digit span:** STM (e.g. repeating a string of digits in the same/reverse order) ● **Vocabulary:** word meaning **Performance scale** (all subtests are timed): ● **Picture completion:** assessment of visual efficiency and memory by spotting missing items in drawings ● **Picture arrangement:** assessment of sequential understanding by arranging a series of pictures to tell a story ● **Block design:** ability to perceive/analyse patterns by copying pictures using multi-coloured blocks ● **Object assembly:** jigsaw puzzles ● **Digit symbol:** ability to memorise and order abstract visual patterns

Box 41.3 Some differences between individual and group tests

- *Individual tests* are used primarily as *diagnostic tests* in a clinical setting (for example, to assess the ability of a child with learning difficulties (see Chapter 40). *Group tests* are used primarily for *selection* and *research* purposes. For example, until the mid-1960s the eleven-plus examination determined the kind of secondary schooling that every child in England and Wales would receive. It consisted largely of an intelligence test, designed largely to assess *g*.
- *Individual tests* usually involve some *performance items* (as in the Wechsler performance scale: see Table 41.3). *Group tests* are 'pencil-and-paper' tests, and in this way are much like other written examinations.

Ask Yourself

- Can you think of some advantages and disadvantages of individual and group tests?

- *Individual tests* are much more time-consuming than group tests, and can be administered only by specially trained testers – usually Educational or Clinical Psychologists (see Chapter 1). There's some degree of flexibility as to how the test is conducted (such as how long the child is allowed to relax before the test proper begins), and some room for interpreting the child's answers. *Group tests*, which are timed, can be administered by teachers, researchers, and other non-trained personnel. Marking is usually done using a special marking key or by computer; in this respect, they are more objective.

designed to assess specific school learning. *Aptitude tests* are aimed at measuring *potential* performance (such as a logic test aimed at predicting how good someone would be at computer programming). Gottfredson (1998) describes IQ tests as tests of 'mental aptitude rather than accumulated knowledge' or 'pure *g*'.

The relationship between intelligence and IQ

Ask Yourself

- Try to formulate some arguments for and against the claim that IQ is a valid measure of intelligence.

From the *psychometric perspective*, an individual's score on an intelligence test (his/her intelligence quotient or IQ) is an accurate measure of his/her intelligence. Effectively, and implicitly, this is based on an *operational definition* of intelligence. But this begs many fundamental questions, relating to the *meaning* of the IQ (first introduced by Stern in 1912).

What kind of concept is IQ? Ratio and deviation IQs

Before 1960, the Stanford–Binet test calculated IQ by expressing *mental age* (MA) as a ratio of *chronological age* (CA) and multiplying by 100 (so as to produce a whole number). Hence, the first IQ was a *ratio IQ*. The Wechsler tests have instead always used a *deviation IQ*: the test result is expressed as a *standard score*, that is how many standard deviations (SDs) above or below the mean of the testee's age group the score lies. Although all tests are designed in such a way as to produce a normal curve (a symmetrical distribution of IQ scores with a mean of 100), the SD (dispersal of the scores around the mean) can still differ from test to test (see Box 41.4).

This suggests that while intelligence is a *psychological* concept, IQ is a purely *statistical* concept. If it's possible for the same characteristic (intelligence) to be assigned different values according to which test is used to measure it, then instead of asking 'How intelligent is this individual?, we should ask 'How intelligent is this individual as measured by this particular test?'. Since the IQ score of the same individual can vary according to the SD of the particular test being used, we cannot equate 'IQ' with 'intelligence'.

How is IQ measured? Ordinal vs interval scales

While an operational definition of, say, someone's height is uncontroversial, in the case of intelligence there's a genuine debate concerning what it is – and unless we know what it is, we cannot be sure we're measuring it properly. In agreeing with Heim that to name the particular test used is merely to reduce the circumference of the circle represented by an operational definition, we could take this a step further by saying that for each separate test there exists a separate circle!

Box 41.4 Demonstrating the difference between intelligence and IQ

Imagine two tests, A and B. Test A has a standard deviation (SD) of 10, and test B has a SD of 20. In both cases, 68 per cent (approximately) of children would be expected to have scores one SD below or above the mean (i.e. between 90 and 110 in test A, and between 80 and 120 in test B).

So, a particular child might have a score of 110 on test A and 120 on test B, and yet the scores would be telling us the same thing.

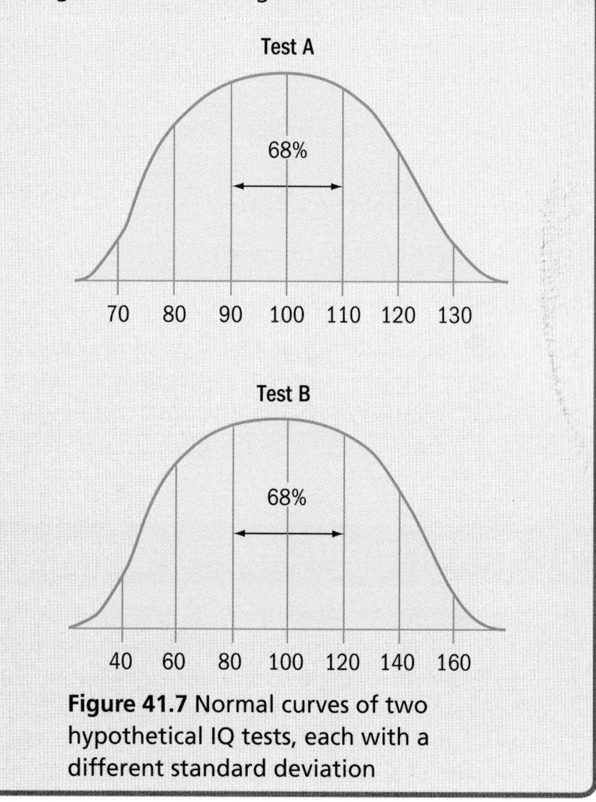

Figure 41.7 Normal curves of two hypothetical IQ tests, each with a different standard deviation

According to Ryan (1972), IQ creates the impression that we know in some absolute way what an individual's intellectual ability is. But unlike height, which is measured on an *interval* or *ratio* scale, IQ is measured on an *ordinal* scale: it tells us only whether one person is more or less intelligent than another (it's a *relative* measurement). We can measure one person's height accurately without knowing anyone else's, but the purpose of IQ tests is always to compare people's scores with those of others from the same population and of approximately the same age (Grigorenko and Sternberg, 2003; see below). (The BAS claims to give 'direct estimates of ability' – that is, it claims to use interval scaling as if by a dipstick or linear rule, but Richardson (1991) doubts that this claim is valid.) While IQ tests *appear* to be using an interval or ratio scale, 'the IQ scale is more like a piece of elastic, to be stretched to fit social expectations and adjusted accordingly' (Rose, 2013).

Are IQ tests properly standardised?

Standardisation requires testing a large, representative sample of the population for whom the test is intended, otherwise the resulting norms cannot be used legitimately for certain groups of individuals. In the 1960 revision of the Stanford–Binet test, Terman and Merrill took only the population included in the census as their reference group, which excluded many migrant and unemployed workers.

More seriously, both tests were standardised on whites only, and yet they were to be used with both black and white children. As Ryan (1972) says, these tests are therefore tests of white abilities. This means that any comparison between black and white children is really an assessment of 'how black people do on tests of white intelligence'. The 1973 revision of the Stanford–Binet did include black children in the 2100-strong standardisation sample.

Are IQ tests valid?

Ask Yourself

- What do you understand by the validity of a psychological test?
- What does it mean in the context of intelligence?

A test is valid if it measures what it claims to measure. In relation to intelligence tests, the question is 'Do they measure intelligence?'. There are different kinds of validity and ways of measuring it (see Coolican, 2004), but probably the most commonly used in relation to psychological tests in general, and IQ tests in particular, is *predictive validity* (or *efficiency*). This refers to the correlation of a test with some future criterion measure, and the most common and powerful external criterion is *educability* or *educational success*. Also important is occupational success.

Before 1937, the mean score of women on the Stanford–Binet was ten points lower than that of men, and it was decided to eliminate this discrepancy by modifying the items so that average scores for men and women were the same. Heather (1976) asks why this hasn't been done with black people. The answer lies in the test's predictive validity. Changing a test in order to eliminate racial differences, while not also changing social inequalities, would make the test a less efficient predictive tool. Removing the male–female bias did, in fact, make the test less efficient as a predictor of gender differences in educational and occupational success (Heather, 1976).

Do IQ tests predict educational success?

According to Gottfredson (1998):

> *Intelligence as measured by IQ tests is the single most effective predictor known of individual performance at school and on the job. It also predicts many other aspects of well-being, including a person's chances of divorcing, dropping out of high school, being unemployed or having illegitimate children.*

Typically, conventional IQ tests will correlate 0.4–0.6 with school grades. However, a test that predicts performance with a correlation of, say, 0.5, still accounts for only 25 per cent of the variation between the performance of different individuals (variation is calculated as the correlation squared = 0.5 squared = 0.25). This leaves 75 per cent of the variation unexplained, so there must be more to school performance than IQ! (Sternberg, 1998)

The predictive validity of tests declines when they're used to forecast outcomes in later life, such as job performance, salary, or obtaining the job in the first place (Rose, 2013). Generally, the correlations are just over 0.3, meaning that the tests account for roughly 10 per cent of the variation in people's performance. Also, the content of IQ tests has changed little from what it was at the beginning of the twentieth century (Sternberg, 1998).

Ceci and Liker (1986) claim that 'IQ is unrelated to real-world forms of cognitive complexity'. However, teachers, doctors, accountants, pharmacists, lawyers and other professionals have a mean IQ above 120, while people in semi-skilled and low-skilled occupations (such as barbers, farm hands and labourers) score below 100 (Grigorenko and Sternberg, 2003). So, does IQ genuinely measure something worthwhile after all?

According to Duckworth *et al.* (2011), people score higher on IQ tests when they're given an incentive, such as a small financial reward. This finding has major implications for the study of success. While IQ is traditionally regarded as the key to educational and occupational success, Duckworth's research suggests that IQ tests measure *more* than intelligence – and that *motivation* is a potent asset (Bond, 2014).

Motivation, in turn, is a major component of *grit*, which also includes the willpower to see something through to the end (see Chapter 40). Willpower is largely about having *self-control*, which is a better predictor of exam results among adolescents than IQ scores. Bond (2014) cites a study involving over 1000 children in New Zealand who were followed from birth to 32 years old. Those who displayed greater self-control in childhood grew into healthier, more emotionally stable adults; they were also more successful financially.

Can IQ tests measure potential?

As we noted above, IQ tests are designed as tests of mental aptitude or potential (underlying *competence*), rather than as tests of attainment/achievement (*performance*). But according to Ryan (1972), it's logically impossible to measure potential separately from some actual behaviour. In other words, some of the skills that individuals have developed during their lifetime must be used when they do intelligence tests: there's nothing extra 'behind' the behaviour corresponding to potential that could be observed independently of the behaviour itself. Ryan concludes that the notion of 'innate potential' itself makes no sense.

Each of us presumably has some upper limit of ability (what we could do under ideal conditions, when we're maximally motivated, well, and rested). But everyday conditions are rarely ideal, and we typically perform below this hypothetical ability. Bee (1994) agrees with Ryan that it's not possible to measure competence, and so we're always measuring 'today's' performance. All IQ tests are really achievement tests to some degree; the difference between tests called IQ tests and those called achievement tests is really a matter of degree (Bee, 1994).

Box 41.5 Do IQ tests measure rationality?

According to Stanovich (e.g. Stanovich, 2009; Stanovich and West, 2014), a fundamental limitation of IQ tests is that they overlook *rationality/irrationality*. This conclusion is based on the heuristics and biases identified by Kahneman and Tversky in the 1970s (see Chapter 20).

There are types of rationality: (i) taking the appropriate action given one's goals and beliefs (*instrumental rationality*); and (ii) holding beliefs that are consistent with available evidence (*epistemic rationality*).

Kahneman and Tversky showed how the basic architecture of human cognition makes us all prone to errors of judgement and decision making. But being prone to such errors doesn't mean that we always – and inevitably – make them. While we're all capable of overriding these reasoning errors and making the rational response, there are systematic individual differences in the tendency to make these errors (Stanovich and West, 2014). IQ tests fail to take account of such tendencies.

These tendencies are largely independent of IQ (Stanovich *et al.*, 2013). For example, undergraduates with higher IQs are no less likely to process information from an egocentric perspective (the 'Myside bias') than are those with relatively lower IQs. Your *rationality quotient* (RQ) is based on *metacognition* (Adee, 2013) (see Chapter 40).

Are IQ tests culturally biased?

Ask Yourself

- What do you understand by the terms 'culture-fair' and 'culture-free'?
- How do you think they might apply to IQ tests?
- Even without any written instructions, you can probably infer what you have to do.

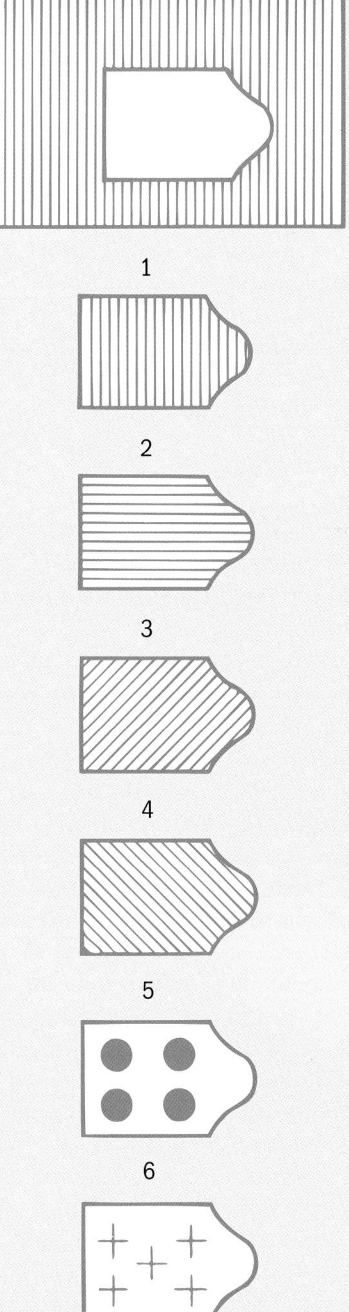

Figure 41.8 A sample item from Raven's progressive matrices test. This claims to be a *culture-free* test

Critical Discussion 41.1

Intelligence as a cultural phenomenon

A major reason that the construction of culture-fair tests has proved so problematical could be that the very notion of intelligence is itself culturally defined. For example, Bruner (in Gillham, 1975) maintains that:

The culture-free test is the intelligence-free test, for intelligence is a cultural concept.

Similarly, Gillham (1975) argues that any attempts to 'define' intelligence which don't involve identifying 'specially valued cultural attainments' must fail. The concept of intelligence derives its meaning only within a particular cultural and social context.

Something which can never be 'built-in' to a test's construction (or translation) is the meaning of the experience of taking an intelligence test. Taking tests of various kinds is a familiar experience for members of Western culture (both within and outside education), but what about cultures in which there's no generally available schooling? The very nature or form of the tasks involved in an IQ test (as distinct from the content) is something that has a cultural meaning.

For example, Glick (1975, in Rogoff and Morelli, 1989) asked members of the Kpelle people to sort 20 familiar objects into groups. They did this by using *functional groupings* (such as knife with orange, potato with hoe), rather than *taxonomic groups*, which the researcher thought more appropriate. When their way of classifying the objects was challenged, they often explained that this was how a wise man would do it. When the exasperated researcher finally asked 'How would a fool do it?', the objects were immediately arranged into four neat piles of foods, tools, clothing, and utensils (i.e. taxonomic groups!). The Kpelle participants and the American researcher differed in their beliefs about the intelligent way of doing things.

Different cultures may also promote the development of different abilities. For example, Serpell (1979) predicted that Zambian children would perform better than English children on a task in which they were required to copy objects using bits of wire. This was based on the observation that children all over central and southern Africa are very skilled at constructing wire cars from scraps of wire as a popular form of play. He also predicted that the English children would perform better when asked to draw the objects. Both predictions were supported, demonstrating that the abstract psychological function of pattern reproduction can be manifested in different ways according to the demands of the *ecocultural niche* to which participants' behaviour is adapted (Serpell, 1994).

EXPLAINING INDIVIDUAL DIFFERENCES: HEREDITY AND ENVIRONMENT

According to Sternberg and Grigorenko (1997), virtually all researchers accept that:

- both heredity and environment contribute to intelligence
- heredity and environment interact in various ways
- extremely poor, as well as highly enriched, environments can interfere with the realisation of a person's intelligence, regardless of his/her heredity.

Genetic influences

Studies of IQ stability

Since people's genetic inheritance is a constant, then if measured intelligence (an IQ test score) is largely determined by genetic factors, there should be a high degree of continuity in IQ throughout a person's lifespan (McGurk, 1975). IQ isn't normally used as a measure of intelligence below age 2; instead, a *developmental quotient* (DQ) is used, which assesses a child's developmental rate compared with an 'average' child of the same age (Bayley, 1969). The younger a child is when given a developmental test, the lower the correlation between its DQ and later IQ. Once IQ is measurable, it becomes a better predictor of adult IQ.

Although the *stability coefficients* reported by some researchers (e.g. Honzik *et al.*, 1948) are impressive, they're based on large numbers of people and tend to obscure individual differences. Others have reported very low stability coefficients. For example, McCall *et al.* (1973) found that in 140 middle-class children, the average IQ change between the ages of 2 and a half and 17 was 28 points. The most 'stable' children changed an average of 10 points, while 15 per cent shifted 50 points or more in either direction. One child's IQ increased by 74 points!

Even in studies where the correlation between IQ at different ages is statistically significant, the stability coefficients are low and suggest greater fluctuation in scores than a simple genetic theory predicts. So, there's a large amount of convincing evidence that a person's intelligence level can alter, sometimes substantially (Howe, 1997).

Family resemblance studies

Family resemblance studies examine the correlation in intelligence test scores among people who vary in genetic similarity. If genetic factors influence IQ, then the closer the genetic relationship between two people, the greater the correspondence (or *concordance*) between their IQs should be.

Monozygotic (MZ) or *identical twins* are unique in having exactly the same genetic inheritance, since they develop from the same single fertilised egg. *Dizygotic* (DZ) or *non-identical (fraternal) twins* develop from two fertilised eggs, and so are no more alike than ordinary siblings (they share about 50 per cent of their genes). If genes have any influence on the development of measured intelligence, then MZs should have the highest concordance rates; any difference between them would have to be attributed to environmental or experiential influences.

Many studies (e.g. Erlenmeyer-Kimling and Jarvik, 1963; Bouchard and McGue, 1981) have shown that the closer people's genetic similarity, the more strongly correlated are their IQs. Figure 41.9 presents a summary of Bouchard and McGue's worldwide review of 111 studies reporting IQ correlations between people of varying genetic similarity.

Ask Yourself

- **What conclusions can you draw from Figure 41.9 regarding the influence of genetic factors?**

Figure 41.9 shows that the closer the genetic relationship between two individuals, the stronger the correlation between their IQ scores. So, the correlation between cousins (who share roughly 12.5 per cent of their genes) is weaker than that for parents and their offspring (who share roughly 50 per cent of theirs). The strongest correlation of all is for MZs.

At first sight, these data suggest that heredity is a major influence on IQ test performance. However, as the genetic similarity between people increases, so does the similarity of their environments: parents and offspring usually live in the same households, whereas unrelated people don't. In other words, family resemblance studies *confound* genetic and environmental influences. In the case of comparisons between MZs and DZs, there's a unique problem regarding the role of environmental factors, namely the *equal environment assumption* (EEA) (see 'An evaluation of twin studies', second bullet).

Studies of separated twins

One way of overcoming the problem of family resemblance studies in general, and the EEA in particular, is to compare the IQs of MZs reared together in the same environments (MZsRT) with those raised separately in different environments (MZsRA). As Figure 41.9 shows, MZsRT show a greater similarity in IQ scores than MZsRA. However, the fact that MZsRA are still more similar than same-sex DZsRT suggests a strong genetic influence (Bouchard *et al.*, 1990).

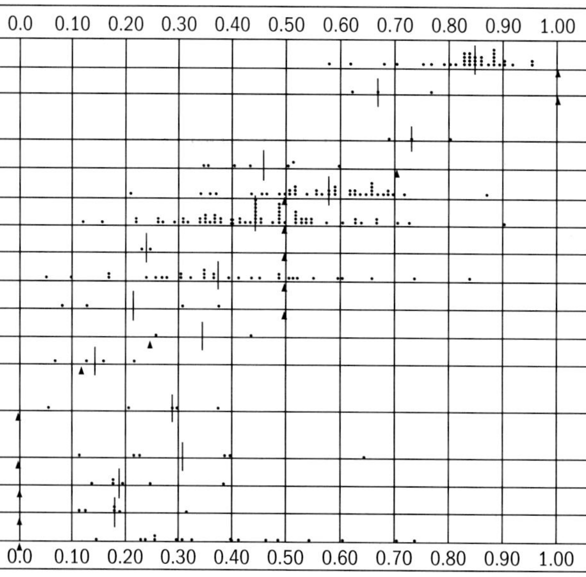

	No. of correlations	No. of pairings	Median correlation	Weighted average
Monozygotic twins reared together	34	4672	0.85	0.86
Monozygotic twins reared apart	3	65	0.67	0.72
Midparent-midoffspring reared together	3	410	0.73	0.72
Midparent-offspring reared together	8	992	0.475	0.50
Dizygotic twins reared together	41	5546	0.58	0.60
Siblings reared together	69	26 473	0.45	0.47
Siblings reared apart	2	203	0.24	0.24
Single parent-offspring reared together	32	8433	0.385	0.42
Single parent-offspring reared apart	4	814	0.22	0.22
Half-siblings	2	200	0.35	0.31
Cousins	4	1176	0.145	0.15
Non-biological sibling pairs (adopted/natural pairings)	5	345	0.29	0.29
Non-biological sibling pairs (adopted/adopted pairings)	6	369	0.31	0.34
Adopting midparent-offspring	6	758	0.19	0.24
Adopting parent-offspring	6	1397	0.18	0.19
Assortative mating	16	3817	0.365	0.33

Figure 41.9 Familial correlations for IQ. The vertical bar on each distribution indicates the median correlation. The arrow indicates the correlation predicted by a simple polygenic model (that is, the view that many pairs of genes are involved in the inheritance of intelligence) (Based on Bouchard and McGue, 1981)

Key Study 41.1

The Minnesota Study of Twins Reared Apart (MISTRA)

- This was started in 1979 by Bouchard and his colleagues at the University of Minnesota. Reports have been published since 1988. Each twin was given a Life History Interview, a Clinical Interview, a Sexual Life History Interview, a Life Stress Interview, a Child Rearing and Schooling Interview, and the Briggs Life History Questionnaire.
- As of 1998, Bouchard *et al.* had studied 71 pairs of MZsRA. They've been the subject of numerous articles, several books popularising the study of the influence of genetics on behaviour (*behaviour genetics research*), and TV programmes.
- A 1990 article compared MZsRA and MZsRT for physical variables, IQ and personality. Overall (combined) IQs on the WAIS showed correlations of 0.69 for MZsRA (48 pairs) and 0.88 for MZsRT (40 pairs). For personality, correlations were 0.49 for both groups. For other abilities, such as memory, the correlations are low or, as with spatial ability, inconsistent (Thompson *et al.,* 1991).
- Bouchard *et al.* concluded that psychological traits are strongly influenced by genetic factors. They were careful to test each twin separately and to have different testers administer the tests. They also vigorously recruited all twin pairs they became aware of, regardless of whether they were MZsRA or DZsRA.

Ask Yourself

- Why do you think they took these precautions?

- Using different testers to test the twins separately ensured that the testers were 'blind' to the twins' identity – that is, they couldn't be (unconsciously) influenced by knowledge of the co-twin's score (*experimenter bias*) when testing the other co-twin. If they'd selected twin pairs knowing they were MZs or DZs, results could again have been biased, based on the assumption that MZs are psychologically more similar (*ascertainment bias*; Joseph, 2003).
- According to Bouchard and Loehlin (2001), only 'the most extreme sceptic' would dispute the finding that virtually all human psychological traits are significantly influenced by genetic factors.

Figure 41.10 Barbara Herbert and Daphne Goodship, one of the pairs of (English) separated identical twins reunited through their participation in the Minnesota twin study

An evaluation of twin studies

- According to Joseph (2003), despite the 'safeguards' described in Key Study 41.1, in many ways the MISTRA is methodologically inferior to earlier studies. These include Newman *et al.* (1937), Shields (1962), Juel-Nielsen (1965) and Burt (e.g. 1966), and they share many of the same methodological shortcomings as the MISTRA.
- 'Separated' twins often turn out not to have been reared separately at all. In Shields' and Juel-Nielsen's studies, some of the twins were raised in related branches of the parents' families, attended the same schools and/or played together (Farber, 1981; Horgan, 1993). When these are excluded from analysis in Shields's study, for example, the correlation decreases from 0.77 to 0.51. Moreover, even if the twins are separated at birth, they've shared the same environment of the mother's womb for nine months. Their identical prenatal experiences may account for the observed similarities in IQ (Howe, 1997). The MISTRA MZsRA were recruited partly on the basis of their pre-exiting knowledge of their co-twin.
- Studies of MZsRA are also *adoption studies* (see below) and a critical assumption of all adoption studies is that children are placed *randomly* into available adoptive homes (see below). But when twins have to be separated, the agencies responsible for placing them generally try to match the respective families as closely as possible. Genetic inferences from such studies depend on the assumption that the twins' environments aren't systematically more similar than those of a group of randomly selected, biologically unrelated paired

individuals (an *unequal environment assumption*; Joseph, 2003). When the environments are substantially different, there are marked IQ differences between the twins (Newman *et al.*, 1937).

- In Newman *et al.*'s and Shields' studies, the experimenters knew which twins were identical and which had been separated. Participants in MISTRA were recruited by means of media appeals and 'self-referrals'. Kaprio (in Horgan, 1993) claims this has tended to attract people who enjoy publicity, and therefore constitute an atypical sample of MZsRA.
- Related to this is the fundamental question of whether MZs (whether reared together or apart) are *representative* of people in general. According to Joseph (2003), the only valid control group in a study involving MZsRA would be two randomly selected, biologically unrelated pairs of strangers matched on the same environmental variables shared by MZs. They are (by definition) exactly the same age, gender and (almost always) ethnicity, they're (usually) strikingly similar in appearance, which will probably elicit similar treatment, they're usually raised in the same socio-economic and cultural contexts, and so on. Plus, they've shared a womb for nine months before any of these postnatal factors begin to 'kick in'.
- Different studies have used different IQ tests, making comparisons between them difficult. Moreover, some of the tests used were inappropriate and/or not standardised on certain groups (see above).
- For a long time, the most widely cited and best-known studies of MZsRA were those reported by Burt (e.g. 1966), who found high correlations between the IQs of 53 pairs of twins supposedly reared in very different environments. After noticing several peculiarities in Burt's procedures and data, Kamin (1974) and Gillie (1976) questioned the genuineness of Burt's research. Even Burt's most loyal supporters have conceded that at least some of his data were fabricated (e.g. Hearnshaw, 1979).
- A problem unique to MISTRA is Bouchard *et al.*'s refusal to make the life history and tests score data available to other researchers (such as Kamin) for independent analysis. Yet during the 1980s, they provided information to journalists and others, which led to twins' stories appearing in leading US magazines and newspapers.

Adoption studies

Adopted children share half their genes but nothing of their environment with their biological parents, and they share at least some of their environment but none of their genes with their adoptive parents.

One research methodology involves comparing the correlations between the IQs of children adopted in infancy with those of (i) their biological parents and (ii) their adoptive parents: if the correlation involving (i) is greater than that involving (ii), then this is taken as strong support for the influence of genetic factors.

Munsinger (1975) found that the average correlation between adopted children and their biological parents was 0.48, compared with 0.19 for adopted children and their adoptive parents. Also, by the end of adolescence, adopted children's IQs are correlated only weakly with their adoptive siblings, who share the same environments but are biologically unrelated (Plomin, 1988).

An evaluation of adoption studies

- Munsinger's finding seems to be contradicted by the separate finding that the IQs of working-class children reared in middle- or upper-class families typically rise by 12-14 points. In general, supporters of the genetic theory focus on the former, while environmentalists emphasise the latter.
- According to Joseph (2003), the higher correlations between adopted children and their biological parents is an artefact of sampling, and can be explained in terms of the 'restrictive variance' of adoptive families (Kamin, 1981): they're similar in socio-economic status and have been carefully screened by the adoption agencies. So, while most adoptive parents are of above-average intelligence and provide above-average environments, adopted children will come from a range of backgrounds, many from below-average backgrounds. The inevitable statistical consequence of this restricted environmental variance of adoptive families is low correlations between the adoptive parents and adopted children.
- Kamin (1981) makes an analogy with boxing:

> *... in terms of the environment provided for their children almost all adoptive parents – unlike biological parents – are in the heavyweight division. That would account for the lower parent–child IQ correlation observed in adoptive families. The correlation would presumably be much higher if parents who would provide poor environments wanted to, and were allowed to, adopt more often.*

- According to Schiff and Lewontin (1986), even though adopted children may correlate *individually* with their *biological parents* more than with their adoptive parents, they're actually more similar *as a group* to the *adoptive parents* than to their biological ones.
- Plomin and DeFries's Colorado Adoption Project (begun in 1975) is an ongoing study involving over 200 adopted children. By middle childhood, natural (birth) mothers and their children who were adopted were just as similar as control parents and their children on measures of both verbal and spatial ability. In contrast, the adoptees' scores don't resemble their adoptive parents' at all.

- According to Plomin and DeFries (1998), these results are consistent with a growing body of evidence suggesting that the *shared family environment* doesn't contribute to similarities between family members. Rather, family resemblance on measures such as verbal and spatial ability seems to be controlled almost entirely by genetics; environmental factors often end up making family members *different*, not the same.

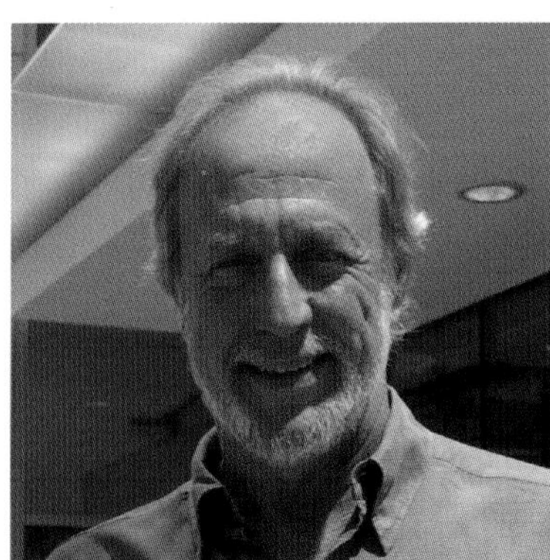

Figure 41.11 Robert Plomin, born 1948

Environmental influences

While not denying the role of genetic factors, those who believe that the environment influences IQ identify a whole range of (pre- and postnatal) environmental factors.

Prenatal environmental influences

Prenatal non-genetic factors account for the largest proportion of biologically caused learning difficulties and lowered IQ. Known prenatal *teratogens* (any agent causing abnormalities in the developing foetus) include certain infections (e.g. maternal rubella), toxic chemicals in the mother's body (e.g. drugs like heroin, cocaine, and alcohol; see Box 40.6, p. 686), radiation, and pollutants. Other toxins are produced by the mother's own faulty metabolism, or as a result of incompatibility between the rhesus factors in the mother's blood and that of her developing foetus (Frude, 1998).

Anxiety has also been found to lead to low birth-weight babies (due to impaired blood flow to the uterus: Teixeira, 1999). In turn, low birth weight is associated with neurological impairment, lower IQ, and greater problems in school (e.g. Hack *et al.*, 1994).

Postnatal environmental influences

Other studies suggest that periodic or chronic *subnutrition* can adversely affect cognitive development in its own right. For example, when children in developing countries are given high-quality nutritional supplements in infancy and early childhood, their later IQ and vocabulary scores are higher than those of non-supplemented children (Pollitt and Gorman, 1994).

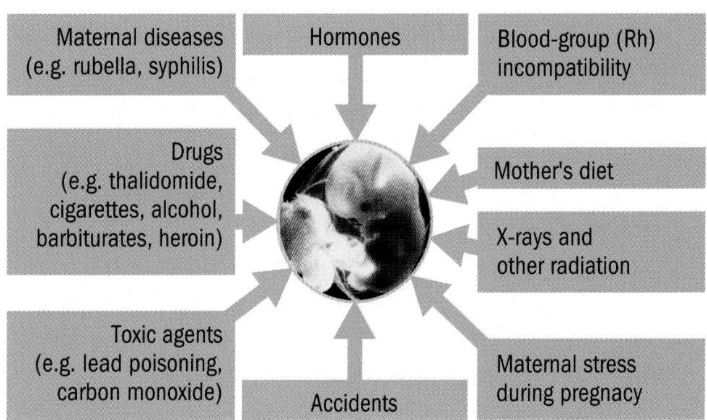

Figure 41.12 The prenatal, biological environment

Key Study 41.2

Romanian orphans (Rutter and the ERA study team, 1998)

- Rutter *et al.* studied 111 institutionalised Romanian children adopted into English families within 24 months of birth. The children had experienced extreme privation, both physically and psychologically, and were all severely malnourished.
- Compared with 42 English adoptees, the Romanian children showed developmental deficiencies in weight, height, and head circumference, as well as deficits in reaching developmental milestones.
- By age 4, they showed considerable physical and developmental catch-up (see Chapter 32), and 'spectacular' cognitive catch-up. Those who were adopted before 6 months had a clear advantage over the later-adopted children.
- Although their data don't allow a clear differentiation to be made, Rutter *et al.* conclude that the effects of malnutrition don't appear to be independent of the effects of the psychological privation.
- By age 6, they'd maintained their progress, but there was no evidence of any further recovery (O'Connor and the ERA Study Team, 2000).

Environmental enrichment studies

Operation Headstart (OH), begun in 1965, was an ambitious compensatory programme designed to give culturally disadvantaged preschoolers enriched opportunities in early life (as part of President Johnson's 'war on poverty'). It began as an eight-week summer programme, and shortly afterwards became a full year's preschool project. In 1967, two additional Follow Through programmes were initiated, in an attempt to involve parents and members of the wider community. Early findings indicated that there were significant short-term gains for the children. But when IQ gains did occur, they disappeared within a couple of years, and the children's educational improvement was minimal.

Key Study 41.3

The Milwaukee Project (Heber *et al.*, 1968)

- The Milwaukee Project is perhaps the most publicised of all the early intervention studies (Clarke and Clarke, 2000).
- Heber *et al.* found that mothers (living in the Milwaukee slum) with IQs under 80 (less than half the total of all mothers) accounted for almost 80 per cent of children with similarly low IQs.
- An intensive intervention programme involving 40 poor, mostly black families, began with the birth of their babies, and continued until the children started school at age 6. Twenty of the women were given job training and sent to school (the 'experimental group'), while the other 20 (the 'control group') received no job training or special education.
- At the point of starting school, the 'experimental group' children had an average IQ score of 120.7, compared with 87.2 for the control group. By age 10, these were 104 and 86, respectively. Educationally too, the experimental group was clearly superior.
- But after 10, both groups' performance fell below national norms, and over time the experimental group declined first to the lower levels of the city of Milwaukee, then still lower to the level of inner-city schools. When assessed at 12–14, mean IQs for the experimental and control groups were 100 and 90, respectively.
- Like OH, the Milwaukee project showed that vigorous and relatively prolonged intervention can make a difference to severely disadvantaged children's cognitive performances. But much of the gain is lost in the years following the end of the programme (Rutter and Rutter, 1992).

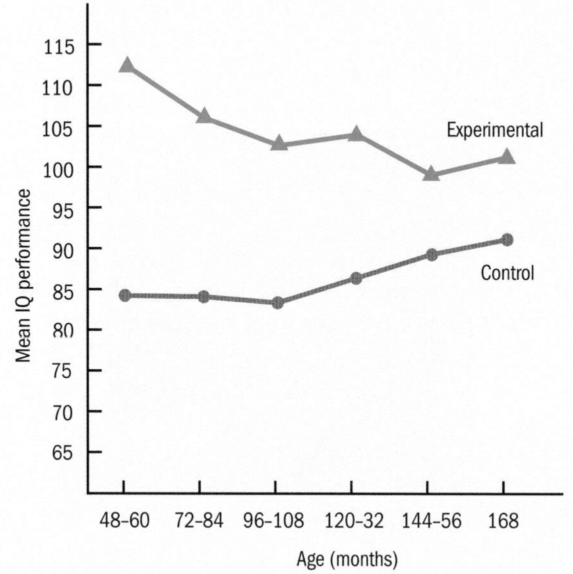

Figure 41.14 IQ performance with increasing age of severely disadvantaged children participating in a broad-ranging intensive intervention programme in the preschool years (data from Garber, 1988 and taken from Figure 6.5 (pp. 212–213) from *Developing Minds: Challenge and Continuity Across the Life Span*, by Michael Rutter and Marjorie Rutter (Penguin Books, 1992), copyright © Michael and Marjorie Rutter, 1992)

Figure 41.13 Children at the Bloomingdale Day Centre Headstart Program, New York City

An evaluation of early intervention studies

- As the Milwaukee project was one of the most ambitious preschool programmes ever attempted, it raises the fundamental question of whether there can be any lasting benefits unless early intervention radically alters the whole context of family and other social and school relationships. Once the programme ended, all the adversities associated with poor social conditions and poor schooling provided an antidote to the earlier intervention (Clarke and Clarke, 2000).
- Hunt (1969) argued that OH was inappropriate to the children's needs, and didn't provide them with the skills they'd failed to develop at home during their first four years (and which are developed by most middle-class children). Also, IQ changes were the main outcome measure used to evaluate its effectiveness. Measures which reflect social competence, adaptability, and emotional health are

much better criteria of success (Weinberg, 1989). According to Bee (2000), because children aren't randomly allocated to OH or non-OH, interpreting the differences becomes very difficult.

- However, the criticisms were apparently premature, and several reviews looking at OH's *long-term effects* have concluded that the programme has brought about lasting changes in children's cognitive abilities. The greatest gains are shown by children with the lowest initial IQs. There's also a *sleeper effect* at work: the impact of intervention programmes is *cumulative* (Collins, 1983).
- Enrolled children function better in school than non-enrolled children. When some kind of supportive intervention continues into the early years of elementary (primary) school, and when the school is of a reasonable quality, the beneficial effects on school performance are even more evident (e.g. as in the Abcedarian Project; Ramey and Ramey, 1992).
- Howe (1997, 1998) believes that it would be inconceivable if the improvements in IQ produced by intervention programmes didn't fade. In the case of OH schemes, for example, the urban environments where they've been set up have often involved squalor, addiction, violence, unemployment, poor housing and inadequate parenting. Together, these negative influences work to restrict a child's opportunities to practise and maintain recently acquired mental skills. This makes it highly likely that they'll fade (see Key Study 41.3).
- Even if the vast majority of intervention studies had failed to raise children's IQs at all, this wouldn't be conclusive evidence that intelligence is fixed. Before 1972, the total amount of time a child would have spent in a OH programme was 180 hours. This rose to 720 hours after 1972. But when compared with real-life exposure to language of children from different social-class backgrounds, 720 hours represents a rather modest intervention:

> *Regarded in that light, the finding that educational intervention programmes ... have nevertheless yielded large ... IQ gains would appear to provide rather conclusive evidence that IQ scores are highly changeable ... (Howe, 1998)*

The interaction between genetic and environmental factors

How much does each contribute?

Behaviour genetics attempts to determine the relative contributions made by genetic and environmental factors: *heritability* refers to the mathematical estimate of how much variability in a particular trait is a result of genetic variability (Carlson, 1988). Eye colour, for example, is affected almost entirely by heredity and little, if at all, by environmental factors. As a result, the heritability of eye colour is close to 100 per cent. Early *heritability estimates* for IQ of 80 per cent (Jensen, 1969) have been revised more recently down to around 50–60 per cent (Bouchard and Segal, 1988).

What does heritability really mean?

- To say that the heritability of measured intelligence is 50–60 per cent *doesn't* mean that 50–60 per cent of measured intelligence is determined by genetic factors. This is because heritability estimates apply only to a particular population or group of people at a particular time – not to a single individual. So, of the variation in intelligence test scores within a group of people, about 50–60 per cent can be attributed to genetic factors (assuming Bouchard and Segal's estimate is correct).
- However, heritability describes what *is* rather than what *could be* (Pike and Plomin, 1999). If environmental factors within a population change (e.g. educational opportunities), then the relative impact of genes and environment will change. Even for a highly heritable trait such as height, environmental changes could make a large difference. Indeed, the huge increase in height during the twentieth century is almost certainly the result of improved diet (Pike and Plomin, 1999). As far as intelligence is concerned, heritability of 50 per cent means that environmental factors account for as much variance as genes do (Plomin and DeFries, 1998; see Chapter 50).

Critical Discussion 41.2

Heritability – a measure of inheritance or inherently misleading? (Joseph, 2003)

Joseph argues that 'heritability' is perhaps the most misunderstood and misguided concept in the psychological (and psychiatric) literature.

The calculation of a heritability estimate is based on the assumption that genes and environment *don't* interact; but clearly they do (and most behaviour geneticists would agree). For example, in the USA and UK, a person who is genetically coded to have dark pigmentation will usually experience a far different (inferior) environment compared with someone born with light skin, and four-feet-tall adult males will experience different environments than six-foot males.

Even if the concept of heritability were valid and important for humans, the fact remains that heritability estimates are derived from family resemblance, twin and adoption studies, with all their associated problems and limitations (see text above).

Box 41.6 Are there IQ genes?

Since mass-analysis of DNA variations became possible, several genome-wide association studies have sought the genes 'for' intelligence, yet results have varied widely and none has been replicated.

Since it's generally accepted that a large number of genes is involved, each individual gene linked with IQ is likely to have only a tiny effect on overall intelligence (MacKenzie, 2013).

Rose (2013) cites one such 2013 study, based on 127,000 people, which tried to find genes associated with educational attainment. It concluded that the genes accounted for a mere 0.02 per cent of the variation in attainment.

Rose argues that, whatever intelligence is, the failures of these genome-wide association studies show that:

> *... to hunt for it [intelligence] in the genes is an endeavour driven more by ideological commitment than either biological or social scientific judgement. To suggest that identifying such genes will enable schools to develop personalised educational programmes to match them ... is sheer fantasy ... Heritability neither defines nor limits educability.*

Box 41.7 Why between-group differences cannot be inferred from within-group differences

Lewontin (1976) asks us to consider ten tomato plants grown in poor soil (see Figure 41.15 below). Their different heights are the result of genetic factors. If the same ten plants were grown in fertile soil, differences in height would again be due to genetic factors.

But the difference in the average height of the plants grown in poor and fertile soil is due to the *environmental* differences of the soils. So, even when the heritability of a trait is high within a particular group, differences in that trait between groups may have environmental causes (Myers, 1990).

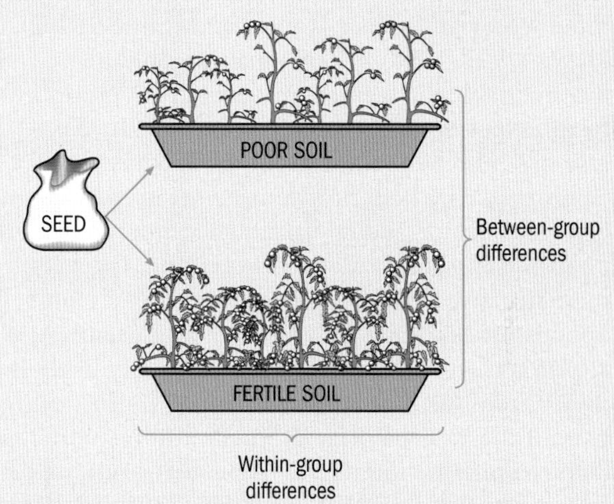

Figure 41.15 Although we can account for *within-group differences* in terms of genetic factors, *between-group differences* may be caused by environmental factors (i.e. poor/fertile soil)

How do heredity and environment contribute?

If we accept that genetic and environmental factors interact, then the focus shifts from *how much* they contribute to *how* they exert their influence. An example of how this might occur is *cumulative deficit*. Dozens of studies show that children from poor families, or families where the parents are relatively uneducated, have lower IQ scores than those from middle-class families (Bee, 2000). This could reflect either genetic or environmental factors, or both.

However, these social-class differences aren't found before the age of 2 and a half to 3, after which they widen steadily. This suggests that the longer a child lives in poverty, the more negative the effects on IQ test scores and other measures of cognitive functioning become (Duncan, 1993; Smith *et al.*, 1997). Hence, the effects of any genetic differences that may be involved to begin with are accentuated by environmental factors, especially poverty. Poverty has a significant effect on children's IQ scores over and above what the parents' own genes may have contributed (Bee, 2000).

The race and IQ debate

The false assumption that *between-group differences* can be inferred from *within-group differences* (see Box 41.7) forms a major part of the *hereditarian fallacy* (Gould, 1981). In turn, the fallacy is central to the claim that certain racial groups are genetically inferior to others.

Jensen (1969) published an article called 'How much can we boost IQ and scholastic achievement?', in which he reviewed all the literature which compared black and white IQ scores. The basic finding, that 'On average, Negroes test about one standard deviation (15 IQ points) below the average of the white population in IQ' is not itself a matter of dispute. What's controversial is Jensen's explanation of these findings:

> *Genetic factors are strongly implicated in the average Negro–white intelligence differences. The preponderance of the evidence is, in my opinion, less consistent with a strictly environmental hypothesis than with a genetic hypothesis ... (Jensen, 1969)*

Others, including Eysenck (1971) and Herrnstein (1971), agree with Jensen.

Some of the evidence on which Jensen based his genetic theory was the apparent failure of compensatory preschool programmes such as OH (see above). Perhaps the most fundamental criticism of Jensen is that he bases his view of black–white differences (between-group differences) on the heritability estimate (of 80:20) derived from studies of the white population (and so is based on within-group differences).

Ask Yourself

- If we apply the argument in Box 41.7 to Jensen's (1969) claim that 80 per cent of the differences between black and white people on IQ tests are due to black people's 'genetic inferiority', then his claim must be rejected.
- How else might you explain black–white differences?

Explaining race differences

IQ tests are biased

Environmental factors which could account for such differences include bias in the tests used to measure intelligence. According to Segall *et al.* (1999), IQ tests are biased against those (such as black people and other minorities) whose cultural backgrounds differ from that of the test's normative sample (white people). This relates to the issue regarding culture-fair/culture-free tests (see Critical Discussion 41.1 and Gross, 2014).

Unequal environments

It's perfectly possible, then, that *individual differences* in IQ (within-group differences) are heavily influenced by genetic factors, while *group differences* (between-group differences) are largely or entirely the result of environmental factors (such as test bias and other forms of discrimination). Jensen's response to this is to appeal to studies in which environmental factors are controlled.

For example, Shuey (1966) compared middle- and working-class black and white people and found the same average 15-point difference. But isn't there more to 'environment' than social class (measured largely in terms of occupation and income)? Given their history of slavery and continuing prejudice and discrimination, surely the experiences of working-class and middle-class black population cannot be considered equivalent to that of their white counterparts. According to Bodmer (1972):

> *Measuring the environment only by standard socio-economic parameters is … like trying to assess the character of an individual by his height, weight and eye colour.*

Critical Discussion 41.3

The political and racist nature of IQ tests

According to Richardson (1998), the gender difference that was found prior to the 1937 Stanford–Binet test (see text above) was accepted by Terman and Merrill as an undesirable artefact of the test items. The revision removed the gender differences because this was both possible and desirable.

But what about race (and social-class) differences? While these, too, could be eliminated, the reason they haven't been is that they're seen as real differences existing in nature. In other words, the belief that races (and classes) are genetically inferior is built into most standardised IQ tests (Joseph, 2003). As Joseph says, items on standardised IQ tests are carefully selected (out of a large pool of potential items) to produce results desired by the test creator. According to Sweet (2004):

> *… IQ tests remain a useful tool for racist ideologues … Go to the website of Richard Lynn, Professor Emeritus at the University of Ulster – a man who believes … not in 'genocide' but in the 'phasing out' of 'incompetent races' – and you'll find reams of … racist pseudoscience … His latest article … 'presents new evidence … [which] supports the theory that the proportion of white ancestry is a determinant of the intelligence of African-Americans …'*

Cumulative deficit and environmental disadvantage

Flynn (2008) takes a different approach to environmental differences, one which he acknowledges could itself be accused of being racist. It's been shown that African-American children lose ground on whites with age: at 10 months, they're just a single point behind, by 4 years the gap has widened to 4.6 points, and by the age of 25 it's a huge 16.6 points. This steady loss of about 0.6 points every year after age 4 suggests the role of non-genetic factors (Flynn, 2008). How can we explain this cumulative deficit?

Study after study shows that before they start school, African-American children are on average exposed to a smaller vocabulary than white children, partly due to socio-economic factors. But over and above this language difference, it's been claimed that many African-Americans haven't signed up for the 'great mission' of the white middle class – the constant quest to stimulate intellectual growth and get their children into a top university. Despite acknowledging the importance of education, many African-American males cannot resist the lure of the black teenage subculture. More African-American males go to prison than to university, and women are three times more likely to become single parents.

While Flynn's 'blaming' the African-American subculture is itself controversial, his intention is to counter the claims of genetic theorists.

CONCLUSIONS

By the late 1980s, the size of the black–white IQ gap had significantly narrowed – by about half to 7–8 points (Williams and Ceci, 1997) – although this trend didn't seem to continue into the 1990s. Closure of the gap seems to reflect increases in educational spending throughout the twentieth century, increased educational attainment by black parents, and reduction in the size of black families (Price and Crapo, 1999). This example of the 'Flynn effect' (the global rise in IQ over the last 100 years; Flynn, 1987) demonstrates that measured intelligence isn't set in 'genetic stone', a finding which Jensen, Eysenck and other believers in the genetic theory would find difficult to explain. Generational changes in IQ are unlikely to be caused by changes in the gene pool (Anderson, 2007).

However, as important as these socio-economic factors are, both genetic and environmental factors can influence the development of IQ. These factors are intertwined, not separate. According to Segall *et al.* (1999):

> *... For intelligence, as for any other human characteristic, biological factors provide a broad range of potential and the outer limits or constraints of that potential, but experience has much room to operate within those limits.*

According to Moghaddam (2002), intelligence isn't a single entity, but

> *... a social construct, with a multitude of different manifestations that can, and often do vary across groups and cultures ... As an alternative to viewing intelligence as ... something fixed, inherited, and independent of context – we should view it as ... a way of doing things (solving problems) that is intimately related to context ...*

Chapter Summary

- Piaget's **biological** definition of intelligence sees it as related to **adaptation to the environment.** In contrast with his emphasis on the **qualitative** aspects of intelligence, the **psychometric approach** is concerned with **individual differences** in measured intelligence (**quantitative** aspects).
- According to Spearman's **two-factor theory,** every intellectual activity involves both a general factor (***g***) and a specific factor (***s***). Burt and Vernon's **hierarchical model** extended this by identifying **major** and **minor group factors.**
- Thurstone identified seven distinct **primary mental abilities (PMAs)**. Instead of ranking individuals in terms of general intelligence, individuals should be profiled on all PMAs. Guilford's **'structure of intellect'** model also totally rejects the idea of *g*.
- Differences between British and American models reflect different forms of **factor analysis (FA)**. Factors have to be given a psychological interpretation, which isn't an objective process and involves **reification** of factors once they've been labelled.
- According to the **information-processing approach,** people differ according to how quickly or efficiently they move through the steps involved in solving problems.
- Sternberg's information-processing model comprises one part of his **triarchic theory,** namely the **componential subtheory**.
- According to Gardner's **theory of multiple intelligences,** intelligence is a collection of separate, independent but **interacting systems**. Criteria for distinguishing an independent intelligence include potential isolation by brain damage, an identifiable core operation, and the existence of idiots savants and other exceptional individuals.
- **Individual tests** of intelligence are used mainly as **diagnostic** tests in clinical settings, while **group tests** are used mainly for **educational selection** and **research.**
- Although all tests now use a **deviation IQ**, standard deviations (SDs) can still differ between tests. While intelligence is a **psychological** concept, IQ is a **statistical** concept.
- Both the **Stanford–Binet** and **Wechsler scales** were originally **standardised** on whites only, and the restandardisation of the former so as to equalise the mean scores of women and men reveals the **ideological significance** of IQ. This adjustment changes the test's **predictive validity** (or **efficiency**).
- Although several studies show high **stability coefficients** for IQ, these obscure sometimes very large individual differences, as well as many short-term fluctuations.
- As people's **genetic similarity** increases, generally so does the **similarity of their environments**. This can be overcome by comparing the IQs of MZs reared together (**MZsRT**) with those raised separately (**MZsRA**).
- MZsRA are still more similar than same-sex DZs reared together, suggesting a strong genetic influence. However, studies of MZsRA have been criticised on several important **methodological grounds**.

- Further support for the influence of genetic factors comes from **adoption studies**. But when children from disadvantaged parents are adopted into high socio-economic families, substantial gains in IQ can occur.
- **Intervention programmes** started with Operation Headstart (OH). Early findings indicated significant short-term IQ gains, but these were short-lived and the educational improvements were minimal. Similar results were reported for the Milwaukee Project.
- Studies of the longer-term effects have concluded that OH has lasting cognitive benefits, especially for those whose IQ scores were initially the lowest. There's also a **sleeper effect**.
- Even when **heritability** is high, differences in that trait between groups may have environmental causes.
- One assumption involved in the **hereditarian fallacy** is that heritability estimates based on **within-group differences** (such as are found in twin studies) can be applied to **between-group differences** (such as between blacks and whites).
- Trying to equate the environments of blacks and whites in terms of social class is invalid, and IQ tests are **racially biased**.

Links with Other Topics/Chapters

Chapter 34 ⟶ Piaget's view of intelligence as adaptation to the environment underlies his whole theory of *cognitive development*

Chapters 1 and 3 ⟶ Using the noun 'intelligence' rather than the adjective 'intelligent' is an example of *reification* – discussing a *hypothetical construct* as if it were real. Much of Psychology's subject matter ('the mind') can only be *inferred* from observable behaviour

Chapter 2 ⟶ One of the aims of *social constructionism* is to expose and highlight examples of reification

Chapter 42 ⟶ Factor analysis is just as important – and controversial – in relation to *theories of personality*

Chapter 39 ⟶ The distinction between fluid and crystallised intelligence is crucial for understanding cognitive changes in *old age*

Chapter 40 ⟶ The ability to deal with novelty (as in Sternberg's experiential subtheory) is a characteristic of *gifted children*

Chapter 50 ⟶ In relation to the equal environment assumption, the claim that twins create their own environment refers to *reactive gene–environment correlation*

Chapter 50 ⟶ The distinction between *shared* and *non-shared environments* illustrates the interaction between genetic and environmental factors

Chapter 50 ⟶ Cumulative deficit is one of many examples of *gene–environment interaction*

Chapter 48 ⟶ Bouchard *et al*. released selected information to journalists concerning separated MZs who'd signed an informed consent agreement. The researchers promised not to divulge information that could be traced to specific twin pairs, thus breaching the *confidentiality principle*

Chapters 44 and 49 ⟶ *Molecular genetic research* involves the search 'for' actual genes responsible for human characteristics, such a *schizophrenia* (what Rose (1997) calls *reductionism as ideology*)

Chapter 20 ⟶ The issue of whether or not IQ tests measure rationality relates to Kahneman's (2013) **Systems 1 and 2**.

Recommended Reading

Gould (1981) *The Mismeasure of Man*. New York: Norton. (A revised/expanded edition of this appeared in 1996 (Harmondsworth: Penguin).

Gross, R. (2008) *Key Studies in Psychology* (5th edn). London: Hodder Education. Chapters 34 and 35.

Howe, M.J.A. (1997) *IQ in Question: The Truth About Intelligence*. London: Sage.

Sternberg, R.J. (1990) *Metaphors of Mind: Conceptions of the Nature of Intelligence*. Cambridge: Cambridge University Press.

Sternberg, R.J. & Grigorenko, E. (eds)(1997) *Intelligence, Heredity and Environment*. New York: Cambridge University Press.

Useful Websites

www.psych.umn.edu/psylabs/mtfs (Minnesota Twin Family Study website)

www.iq-tests.eu/iq-test-Race-and-IQ-710.html (Race and IQ, including online IQ and other tests)

All the above recommendations are also relevant to Chapter 50.

CHAPTER 42

PERSONALITY

Classifying theories of personality

Nomothetic versus idiographic approaches

The psychometric approach

Kelly's personal construct theory

Humanistic theories

Psychodynamic theories

INTRODUCTION and OVERVIEW

However different they may be in other respects, most personality theories share the basic assumption that personality is something that 'belongs' to the individual: 'the appropriate unit of analysis for personality psychology is the person' (Hampson, 1995).

To the extent that each of us 'has' a personality that's stable and relatively permanent, our behaviour will be consistent from one situation to another. An alternative view is that behaviour is largely determined by situational factors and that it will vary considerably across situations. This is referred to as the *trait versus situation debate* or the *consistency controversy* (see Gross, 2009).

Personality theorists differ with respect to whether they're trying to compare individuals in terms of a specified number of traits or dimensions common to everyone (the *nomothetic approach*), or trying to identify individuals' unique characteristics and qualities (the *idiographic approach*).

According to the *constructionist approach* (Hampson, 1995), personality is constructed, in the course of social interaction, from three elements: a person's *self-presentation* (the *actor:* see Chapter 22), the *perception* of this presentation by an audience (the *observer:* see Chapter 22), and *self-awareness* (the *self-observer:* see Chapter 33). To this extent, personality isn't merely an abstraction which helps to explain people's behaviour (it's not something people 'have'), but it's to do with how we relate to other people and deal with the world in general.

CLASSIFYING THEORIES OF PERSONALITY

Ask Yourself

- Try to define 'personality'.

If we wish to identify some of the dimensions along which various theories differ, then a useful definition of personality would be:

> *... those relatively stable and enduring aspects of individuals which distinguish them from other people, making them unique, but which at the same time allow people to be compared with each other.*

This definition brings into focus two key questions.

- Does personality consist of *permanent traits* or characteristics?
- Is the study of personality the study of *unique individuals*, or is it aimed at comparing individuals and discovering the factors which constitute *personality in general*?

Psychologists who answer 'yes' to the first question, and who are interested in personality in general, belong to the *psychometric tradition* (*type* and *trait theorists*). The major figures are Eysenck and Cattell, who analyse the data from personality questionnaires using factor analysis (FA; see Chapter 41). In trying to establish factors in terms of which everyone can be compared, they adopt a *nomothetic approach.*

Psychologists who believe in the uniqueness of every individual adopt the *idiographic approach*, but beyond this it's difficult to say what else they have in common. For example, they may or may not see personality as permanent, or may differ as to how much or what kinds of change in personality are possible. But they're concerned with the *whole person*, whereas psychometric theorists want to rank or order individuals with respect to particular aspects of personality. Idiographic theorists include Allport, Kelly, and the *Humanistic* Psychologists

Table 42.1 A classification of personality theories

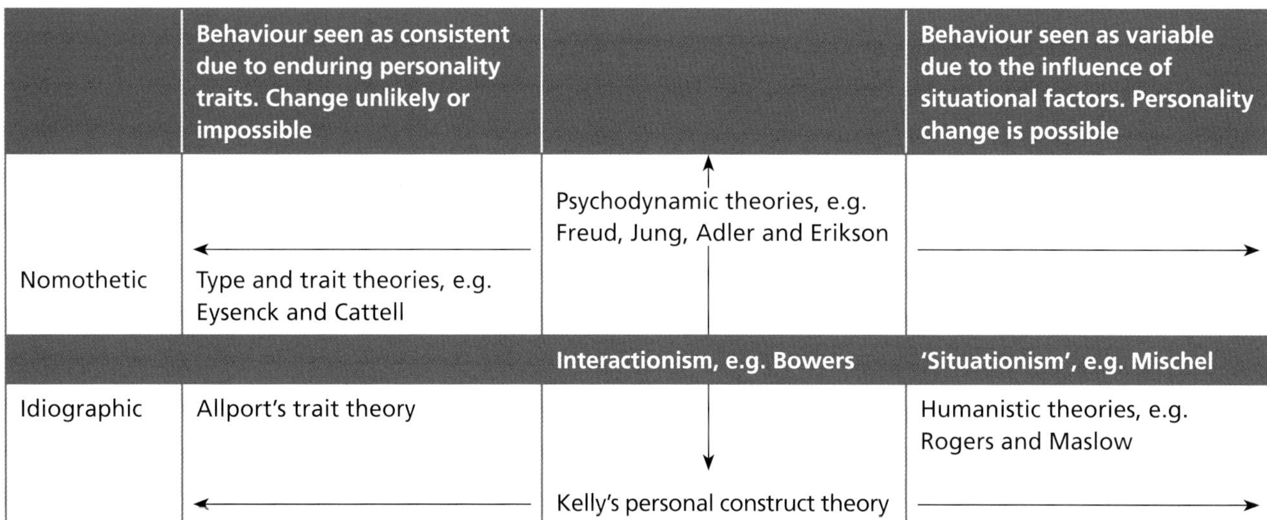

	Behaviour seen as consistent due to enduring personality traits. Change unlikely or impossible		Behaviour seen as variable due to the influence of situational factors. Personality change is possible
Nomothetic	Type and trait theories, e.g. Eysenck and Cattell	Psychodynamic theories, e.g. Freud, Jung, Adler and Erikson	
		Interactionism, e.g. Bowers	'Situationism', e.g. Mischel
Idiographic	Allport's trait theory	Kelly's personal construct theory	Humanistic theories, e.g. Rogers and Maslow

Maslow and Rogers. Humanistic theories share a concern for the characteristics which make us distinctively human, including our experience of ourselves as people.

The *psychodynamic* theories of Freud and Jung are clearly idiographic: they're based on case studies of patients in the clinical context of psychotherapy and aren't concerned with measuring personality. However, they're also concerned with the nature of personality and try to account for individual differences. For example, Jung was the first to distinguish between introverts and extroverts, which Eysenck later measured in his personality questionnaires. These theorists all allow for the possibility of personality change, primarily through psychotherapy.

NOMOTHETIC VERSUS IDIOGRAPHIC APPROACHES

Ask Yourself

- Do you believe that every person is unique, or are we all basically the same, differing only in the degree to which we display certain tendencies or characteristics?

According to Kluckhohn and Murray (1953):

> *Every man is in certain respects like all other men, like some other men and like no other men ...*

What we have in common with *all* other human beings is the subject of Experimental or 'General' Psychology, which includes the study of cognitive and physiological processes, and learning. Much of Developmental and Social Psychology is also concerned with discovering 'universal norms' which apply equally to all individuals. What we have in common with *some* other human beings is examined through the study of *individual differences*. Personality differences represent one kind of *group norm*, others being age, gender, ethnic and cultural background, and intelligence. It's the study of 'how and how much a particular individual is similar to or differs from others' (Shackleton and Fletcher, 1984) which constitutes the factor-analytic/psychometric approach. As we've seen, this is also a nomothetic approach.

Finally, what we have in common with *no* other human being are the qualities that make us unique. This is the idiographic approach, which attempts to discover *individual/idiosyncratic norms*.

Allport's trait theory

Allport (1961) defined personality as:

> *The dynamic organisation within the individual of those psychophysical systems that determine his characteristic behaviour and thoughts.*

He identified two basic kinds of traits:

1. *common traits*: basic modes of adjustment applicable to all members of a particular cultural, ethnic, or linguistic background (the subject matter of the *nomothetic* approach). For example, each of us can be placed somewhere along a scale of aggressiveness
2. *individual traits*: a unique set of personal dispositions and ways of organising the world, based on life

experiences (the focus of the *idiographic* approach). Individual traits can take one of three forms: *cardinal*, *central*, or *secondary*.

Figure 42.1 Gordon W. Allport (1897–1967) (UPI/ Bettmann Archive)

Box 42.1 Three kinds of individual traits

Cardinal traits are so all-pervading that they dictate and direct almost all of an individual's behaviour, such as someone who's consumed by greed, ambition or lust. However, such traits are quite rare, and most people don't have one predominant trait.

Central traits are the basic building blocks which make up the core of personality and which constitute the individual's characteristic ways of dealing with the world (e.g. honest, loving, happy-go-lucky). A surprisingly small number of these is usually sufficient to capture the essence of a person.

Secondary traits are less consistent and influential than central traits, and refer to tastes, preferences, political persuasions, reactions to particular situations, and so on.

The existence and nature of individual traits make it very difficult to compare people:

> *[Any given individual] is a unique creation of the forces of nature. There was never a person just like him and there never will be again ... (Allport, 1961)*

Comparing people in terms of a specified number of traits or dimensions is precisely what the nomothetic approach involves: traits have the same *psychological meaning* for everyone, so that people differ only in the extent to which each trait is present. For example, Eysenck maintains that everyone will score somewhere on the extroversion (E) scale, and the difference between individuals is one of degree only (i.e. a quantitative difference). For Allport (1961), people can be compared only in terms of *common* traits. The nomothetic approach can only portray human personality in an oversimplified, approximate way: even the traits that people apparently share with one another will always differ from individual to individual.

(For a discussion of the nomothetic/idiographic 'debate', and whether the wholly unique individual exists, see Gross, 2014.)

Traits versus situations

Most definitions of traits focus on their stability and permanency, which implies that an individual's behaviour is consistent over time and from one situation to another. Indeed, Baron and Byrne (1991) define personality as:

> *The combination of those relatively enduring traits which influence behaviour in a predictable way in a variety of situations.*

Ask Yourself

- According to the *fundamental attribution error* (FAE) and *actor–observer effect* (AOE), how are we likely to judge the consistency of our own and others' behaviour respectively? (See Chapter 23.)

The FAE involves attributing other people's behaviour primarily to their dispositional qualities (including personality traits). We're therefore likely to regard their behaviour as more consistent (and hence more predictable) than our own, which we see primarily as a response to the situation (AOE).

Seeing behaviour as being caused primarily by personality traits (the *trait approach*) is usually opposed to what has become known as *situationism* (Mischel, 1968) – the view that behaviour is largely determined by situational factors.

The consistency controversy

Mischel (1968), sparked the 'consistency controversy' by declaring that he could find very little evidence of *intraindividual* (or *cross-situation*) *consistency*. In other words, the same person tends to behave inconsistently in different situations – the opposite of what personality theorists would predict. He argued that the average correlation between different behavioural measures designed to tap the same personality trait was typically between 0.1 and 0.2, often lower. Correlations between scores on personality tests designed to measure a given trait and measures of behaviour in various situations meant to tap the same trait rarely exceeded 0.3 (see Box 42.2).

Figure 42.2 Walter Mischel (born 1930)

Box 42.2 Situationism

Mischel took these very low correlations to indicate the importance of the situation in determining behaviour (*situationism*).

If people behave inconsistently, the usefulness of the trait concept disappears and we're left only with situational influences to account for the inconsistency of individual behaviour. The same person behaves differently in different situations, because different situations require different behaviour and are associated with different kinds of reinforcements.

So, from this (rather extreme) situationist perspective, *intraindividual inconsistency* is exactly what we'd expect!

The psychological situation

Bowers (1973), Endler (1975), and Pervin and Lewis (1978) all advocate an *interactionist* position, which stresses the mutual influence of situational and dispositional variables:

Behaviour = Person × Situation

Ask Yourself

- Intuitively, does there seem to be anything wrong with situationism, at least in its extreme form?
- Surely different people behave differently even within the same situation and, conversely, aren't we recognisably the same person from one situation to another?

Mischel (1973) moved towards a more interactionist position. But, in preference to traits, he talked about *social cognitive units* (or *person variables*): these focus on what the person *does* (cognitively, affectively, and behaviourally), as opposed to what the person *has* in terms of traits, and include cognitive activities, encoding strategies, expectancies, values, preferences and goals.

Mischel believed that the same situation can have different *meanings* for different individuals, depending on past learning experiences. This determines how we select, evaluate, and interpret stimuli and, in turn, how particular stimuli affect our behaviour. It follows that situational factors on their own cannot account adequately for human behaviour, because they don't exist objectively, independent of the actor. Based on a study of children's ability to resist temptation when looking at attractive sweets, Mischel (1973) concluded that the results clearly show that what's in children's heads – not what's physically in front of them – determines their ability to delay.

So, the *psychological situation* constitutes a critical determinant of behaviour: the psychological meaning of a situation for the individual (how it's perceived) is a crucial factor in predicting behaviour and accounting for regularities in behaviour across situations (Krahé, 1992). Another sense in which the influence of situations cannot be defined objectively is that personality traits, in particular introversion–extroversion, dictate the choice of situations people expose themselves to (Eysenck and Eysenck, 1985).

According to Hampson (1999), contemporary Personality Psychology isn't so much concerned with consistency as with *coherence*. This acknowledges that people do show cross-situational variability in their behaviour, but that this can be understood when other factors are taken into account.

Figure 42.3 Different people are attracted to different kinds of situation, making it difficult to define their influence objectively

> **Box 42.3 A Cognitive-Affective Person System (Mischel and Shoda, 1995, 1998)**
>
> Mischel and Shoda's *cognitive–affective person system* accounts for both intraindividual consistency and predictable patterns of variability across situations.
>
> For example, a person may be shy in small groups but an excellent public speaker. Viewed in purely trait terms, this pattern of behaviour would be cross-situationally inconsistent, but if the differences in the psychological situation are taken into account, it becomes meaningful and predictable. Speaking to a large audience doesn't require engaging personally with any one individual, whereas making conversation in small groups does.
>
> Situational factors now represent a moderating influence on individual differences. This is a more sophisticated response to Mischel's critique of traits than pure situationism, or even 'mechanistic interactionism', in which behaviour is seen as a function of combined but independent situational and trait factors (Hampson, 1999).

THE PSYCHOMETRIC APPROACH

Factor analysis

As we saw in Chapter 41, *factor analysis* (FA) is a statistical technique, based on correlation, which attempts to reduce large amounts of data (such as scores on personality questionnaires) to much smaller amounts. Essentially, the aim is to discover which test items correlate with one another and which don't, and then to identify the resulting correlation clusters (or factors). A fundamental issue is: what's the smallest number of factors which can adequately account for the variance between participants on the measures in question?

Eysenck prefers an *orthogonal method* of FA, which aims to identify a small number of powerful, independent (*uncorrelated*) factors. Cattell's preference is for an *oblique method*, which aims to identify a larger number of less powerful factors, which aren't independent (they're *correlated* to some degree).

Since it's possible to carry out a further FA of oblique factors, they're referred to as *first-order factors* and the resultant regrouping of the oblique factors as *second-order factors*. In fact, Cattell identified a small number of second-order factors which correspond closely to Eysenck's three major second-order factors (see below). Eysenck's second-order factors are referred to as *types* (what Cattell calls *surface traits*) and Cattell's first-order factors as *traits* (or *source traits*).

Table 42.2 Differences between Eysenck and Cattell in their preferred method of factor analysis

	Eysenck	Cattell
Preferred method of FA	Orthogonal	Oblique
Level of analysis	Second order	First order
Description of factors	Types ('surface traits')	Traits ('source traits')

Both Cattell and Eysenck believe their own methods best reflect the psychological reality of personality, but there's no objective way of establishing that one is right and the other wrong. However, Kline (1981b) maintains that most factor analysts, in practice, prefer oblique factors.

Eysenck's type theory

What are 'types'?

The term 'type' was formerly used to describe people who belonged either to one *category* or another, so that it was impossible for a particular individual to be considered a member of both. For example, according to the ancient Greek theory of the 'Four Temperaments' or 'Four Humours' (Galen, second

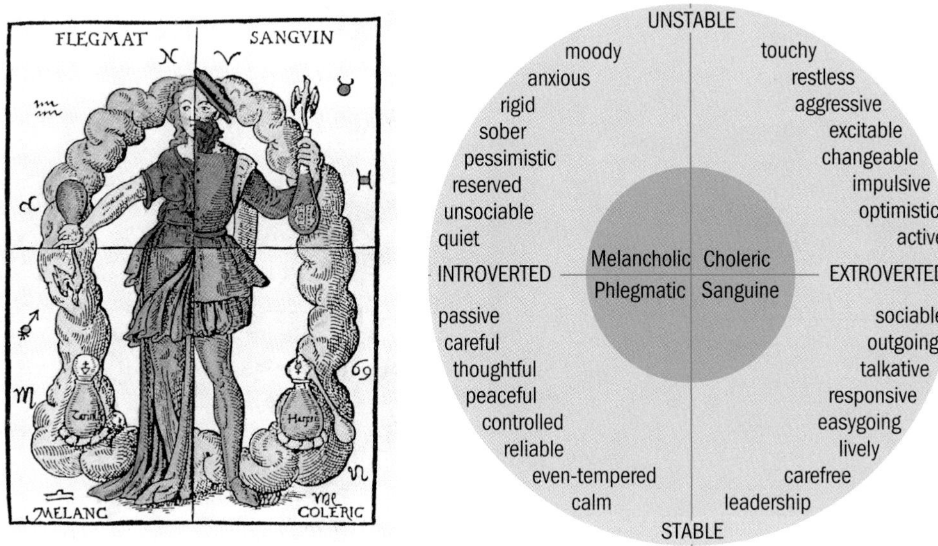

Figure 42.4 Personality has been dissected into component parts for thousands of years; what is interesting is how these ideas relate to the modern concept of personality traits, as shown by Eysenck's dimensions of personality (from Eysenck, 1965)

century AD), a person was either *choleric* (due to an excess of yellow bile), *sanguine* (due to an excess of blood), *melancholic* (due to an excess of black bile), or *phlegmatic* (due to an excess of phlegm).

These four humours are included in the inner circle of Eysenck's diagram, as shown in Figure 42.4.

According to Eysenck (1995), today the term 'type' is either not used at all, or reserved for combinations of traits that are found to correlate. For example, extroversion is a type concept based on the observed correlations of sociability, liveliness, activity, and so on. The search for a reliable and valid measurement of personality traits is only a first step: the traits we find aren't independent of each other but are correlated in certain patterns that suggest more complex entities that might be called types.

But unlike Galen's four humours, Eysenck's types are *personality dimensions,* which represent continua along which everyone can be placed.

Eysenck's dimensions in fact constitute the highest level of a hierarchy (Cattell's 'surface traits'), with a number of traits at the next level down (Cattell's 'source traits'). Below that is a set of habitual responses (typical ways of behaving) linked to a particular trait. At the lowest level is a specific response (a response on one particular occasion: see Figure 42.5).

Ask Yourself

- Which model of intelligence does Eysenck's personality theory remind you of (see Chapter 41)?

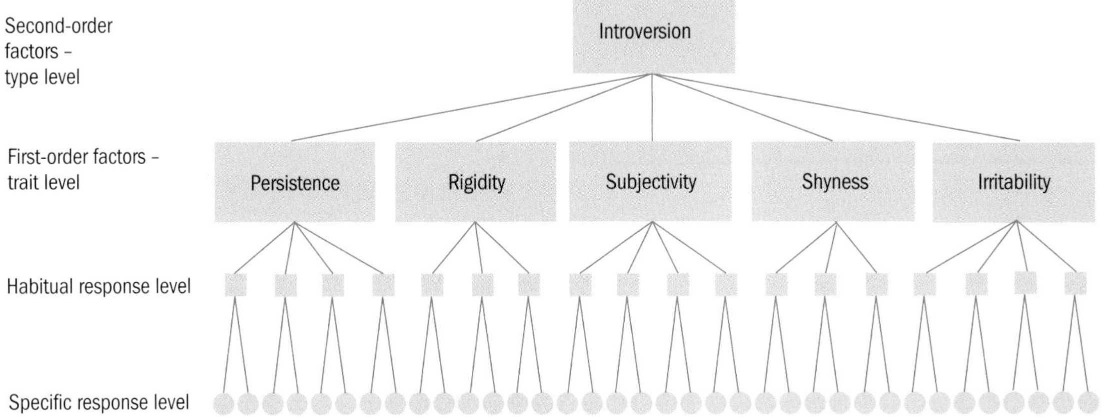

Figure 42.5 Eysenck's hierarchical model of personality in relation to the introversion dimension (after Eysenck, 1953)

Extroversion (E), neuroticism (N) and psychoticism (P)

Eysenck (1947) factor-analysed 39 items of personal data (including personality ratings) for each of 700 neurotic soldiers, screening them for brain damage and physical illness. Two orthogonal (uncorrelated) factors emerged: *introversion–extroversion* (E) and *neuroticism (emotionality)–stability* (N). These two dimensions are assumed to be normally distributed, so that most people will score somewhere in the middle of the scale, and very few at either extreme. 'Typical' introverts and extroverts are 'idealised extremes' (or ideal types).

Box 42.4 Typical introverts and extroverts (Eysenck, 1965)

- The *typical introvert* is a quiet, retiring sort of person, introspective, fond of books rather than people; he's reserved and distant except to intimate friends. He tends to plan ahead, 'looks before he leaps' and distrusts the impulse of the moment. He doesn't like excitement, takes matters of everyday life with proper seriousness, and likes a well-ordered mode of life. He keeps his feelings under close control, seldom behaves in an aggressive manner, and doesn't lose his temper easily. He's reliable, somewhat pessimistic, and places great importance on ethical standards.
- The *typical extrovert* is sociable, likes parties, has many friends, needs to have people to talk to, and doesn't like reading or studying by himself. He craves excitement, takes chances, often sticks his neck out, acts on the spur of the moment, and is generally an impulsive individual. He likes practical jokes, always has a ready answer, and generally likes change; he's carefree, easy-going, optimistic and likes to 'laugh and be merry'. He prefers to keep moving and doing things, tends to be aggressive and lose his temper quickly; altogether his feelings aren't kept under tight control and he's not always a reliable person.

As regards neuroticism, the *typical high N scorer* could be described as:

> *... an anxious, worrying individual, moody and frequently depressed; he is likely to sleep badly and to suffer from various psychosomatic disorders. He is overly emotional, reacting too strongly to all sorts of stimuli and finds it difficult to get back on an even keel after each emotionally arousing experience ... (Eysenck, 1965)*

By contrast, the *typical low N scorer* (stable) individual:

> *... tends to respond emotionally only slowly and generally weakly and to return to baseline quickly after emotional arousal; he is usually calm, even tempered, controlled and unworried ... (Eysenck, 1965)*

Since the original 1947 study, the existence of E and N has been supported by further research involving literally thousands of participants. Exhaustive research in many parts of the world, by many different researchers, has confirmed the existence of E and N, as well as a third dimension, *psychoticism* (P) (Eysenck and Eysenck, 1985). This was originally uncovered in a 1952 study of psychiatric patients, but is less well established than the other two dimensions. Just as E and N are unrelated to each other, so they are both unrelated to P. According to Eysenck and Eysenck (1975):

> *A high [P] scorer ... may be described as being solitary, not caring for people; he is often troublesome, not fitting in anywhere. He may be cruel and inhumane, lacking in feelings and empathy, and altogether insensitive. He is hostile to others, even his own kith and kin, and aggressive, even to loved ones. He has a liking for odd and unusual things, and a disregard for danger; he likes to make fools of other people, and to upset them.*

Unlike E and N, P isn't normally distributed – both normals and neurotics score low on P. Eysenck also believes that P overlaps with other psychiatric labels, in particular 'schizoid', 'psychopathic' and 'behaviour disorders'. The difference between normals and psychotics, as well as that between normals and neurotics, is one of degree only.

Personality questionnaires

The Maudsley Personality Inventory (MPI, 1959) measured both E and N. The Eysenck Personality Inventory (EPI) added a *lie scale*, which measures a person's tendency to give socially desirable answers (Eysenck and Eysenck, 1964). Finally, the Eysenck Personality Questionnaire (EPQ) added a P scale (Eysenck and Eysenck, 1975). There are also junior versions of these questionnaires for use with 9-year-olds and over.

The scales all comprise items of a 'yes/no' variety. They're intended primarily as research tools (as opposed to diagnostic tools for use in clinical settings) and, as such, they're generally regarded as acceptable, reliable, and valid (Kline, 1981a; Shackleton and Fletcher, 1984). The main exception is the P scale, which Eysenck himself admitted is psychometrically inferior to other scales.

A major way in which Eysenck has attempted to validate his scales is through *criterion analysis* – giving the questionnaires to groups of individuals known to differ on the dimensions in question. For example, although the EPQ isn't meant to diagnose neurosis, we'd expect diagnosed neurotics to score very high on N compared with non-neurotics – and generally this is found to be the case.

The biological basis of personality

Eysenck attempts to explain personality differences in terms of the kinds of nervous system individuals inherit.

- As far as E is concerned, what's crucial is the balance between excitation and inhibition processes in the central nervous system (CNS), specifically the *ascending reticular activating system* (ARAS: see Chapter 4). Its main function is to maintain an optimum level of alertness or 'arousal'. It does this by enhancing the incoming sensory data to the cortex through the excitation of neural impulses, or by 'dampening them down' through inhibition.
- Extroverts have a 'strong nervous system'. Their ARAS is biased towards the *inhibition* of impulses, with the effect of reducing the intensity of any sensory stimulation reaching the cortex (they're *chronically under-aroused*). For introverts, the bias is in the opposite direction: the intensity of any sensory stimulation reaching the cortex is *increased* (they're *chronically over-aroused*).
- As far as N is concerned, it's the *reactivity* (or *lability*) of the sympathetic branch of the autonomic nervous system (ANS) that's crucial, in particular, differences in the limbic system, which controls the ANS (see Chapter 4). The person who scores high on N has an ANS which reacts particularly strongly and quickly to stressful situations compared with less emotional or more stable individuals.
- The biological basis of P is much more uncertain, but Eysenck (1980) has suggested that it may be related to levels of the male hormone, androgen, and/or other hormones (see Chapter 36).

Drugs and personality

Ask Yourself

- **In terms of introverted and extroverted behaviour, what should be the effect of (a) stimulant and (b) depressant drugs (see Chapter 8)?**
- **Who should be easier to sedate – introverts or extroverts?**

According to Wilson (1976), we'd expect introverts to be more difficult to sedate using a drug such as sodium amytal, because they're supposed to be more aroused. A particularly powerful technique involves *sedation/sleep threshold*, in which a barbiturate (which depresses the CNS) is injected by continuous infusion until the participants either go to sleep or reach some specified level of drowsiness (defined behaviourally or physiologically). The amount of drug needed is a measure of tolerance of sedation (Claridge and Davis, 2003).

Using this method, it's been repeatedly shown that anxiety neurotics, and their 'normal' counterparts (introverted neurotics or *dysthymics*), show extremely high drug tolerance (resistance to sedation) (Claridge and Herrington, 1960, 1962). Both groups were much more difficult to sedate than extroverted neurotics (*hysterics*), who are more easily sedated than normal participants (who score in the middle ranges on E and N).

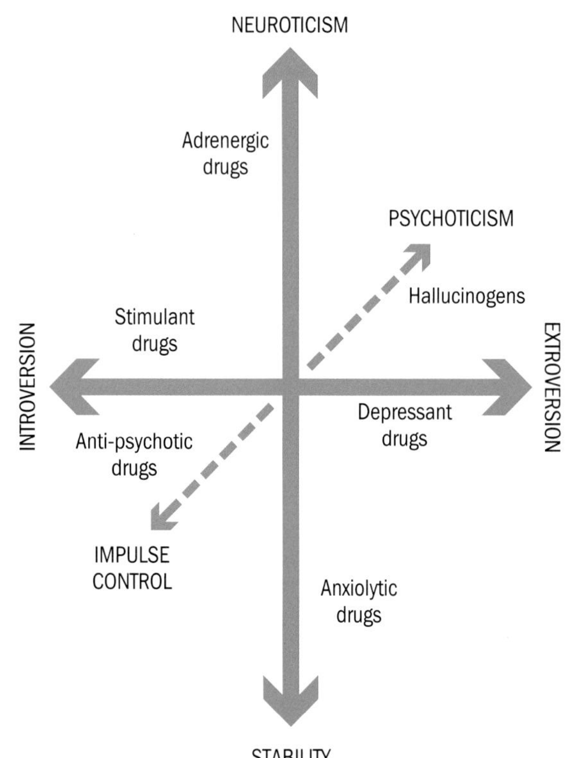

Figure 42.6 Drug addiction and personality (Eysenck, 1983). (Source Eysenck, H.J. (1995) 'Trait theories of personality'. In S.E. Hampson and A.M. Coleman (Eds) *Individual Differences and Personality.* London, Pearson Education.)

Although nearly 50 years old, these studies still represent a valid observation about biology and the pharmacology of personality and psychological disorders (Claridge and Davis, 2003).

For the same reasons, regardless of an individual's normal position on the scale:

- *stimulants* should shift behaviour in the direction of *introversion*
- *depressants* (such as alcohol) should have the opposite effect (see Chapter 8)

- *anxiolytics* (anti-anxiety drugs) should increase *emotional stability*
- *adrenergics* (those which mimic the effects of adrenaline) should *decrease* it
- *hallucinogens* should increase *psychotic behaviour*
- *antipsychotics* (*narcoleptics*) should *decrease* it.

According to Eysenck (1995), empirical studies have, on the whole, supported these causal hypotheses (see Figure 42.6).

In relation to the first claim, Smillie and Gokcen (2010) examined whether the effects of caffeine on working memory (WM) differed between those who self-reported as high or low E. They found that caffeine facilitated performance under high, but not low, WM load conditions and only for high E participants. Findings such as these highlight both the role that E plays in modulating basic cognitive processes, and the general robustness of Eysenck's causal approach (Pickering *et al.*, 2013).

Personality and conditionability

Ask Yourself...

- Given what we've said so far about Eysenck's theory, how would you expect introverts and extroverts to differ regarding how easily they can be (classically) conditioned? (See Chapter 11.)

From a strictly psychological point of view, the importance of the biological aspects of Eysenck's theory is how they're related to individual differences in *conditionability*. Because extroverts require a stronger stimulus to make an impact compared with the more easily stimulated introvert, and because the learning of S–R connections is best achieved by a strong and rapid build-up of excitation in the nervous system (which is characteristic of introverts), introverts should be more easily conditioned than extroverts.

Despite Eysenck's strong claims to the contrary, the evidence is inconclusive: only about one-half of the studies he reviewed in 1967 support his predictions. Eysenck seems to regard conditionability as a *unitary* trait: if introverts are easily conditioned to one kind of stimulus, they'll also condition easily to a range of other stimuli. But such a general trait has never been demonstrated, and the experimental evidence mainly involves three conditioned responses – the GSR (galvanic skin response), the eye blink, and simple verbal conditioning. According to Kline (1983), until such a general dimension is discovered, this part of the theory remains weak and, in addition, extrapolation from laboratory studies to real-life situations is dangerous.

An evaluation of Eysenck's theory

- Eysenck's theory has generated a vast amount of research (Shackleton and Fletcher, 1984) and E and N seem to have stood the test of time – they're both included in the 'Big Five' personality factors (see Table 42.3).
- While Eysenck's neurophysiological speculations were never entirely satisfactory, at the very least they stimulated research aiming at clarifying them. One of his students, Jeffrey Gray, proposed a more viable model of N. Gray's (1970, 1982) alternative account today forms the highly influential *reinforcement sensitivity theory* (RST) of personality. The most recent version of RST (Corr and McNaughton, 2008) proposes that one's level of N reflects sensitivity to punishment and threat in general. But, within N, there are two traits/emotions, each of which maps onto one of the two major systems for defensive behaviour:
  - *fear* and *trait fearfulness* arise from the functioning of the fight-flight-freeze system (FFFS) and are involved in active avoidance and escape behaviour; at the extreme end of the scale, this maps onto phobias, panic and OCD (see Chapter 44);
  - *anxiety* arises from variations in the sensitivity of the behavioural inhibition system (BIS), responsible for detecting and resolving goal conflict, and is involved in cautious behaviours in potentially dangerous situations; at the extreme end of the scale, this maps onto anxiety disorders (such as 'free-floating anxiety': see Chapter 44).
- Research into the psychobiological substrates of basic personality dimensions is currently flourishing in the UK and elsewhere. Eysenck's theoretical framework, which kick-started this field of research, is still strongly shaping the research agenda (Pickering *et al.*, 2013).
- One of its most serious weaknesses is the failure to produce any convincing evidence that introverts condition more easily than extroverts. Conditionability is a vital part of the overall theory, because it points 'inwards' towards the biological (including genetic) basis of personality and 'outwards' towards the socialisation experiences of different individuals (behaviour always being the product of an interaction between the nervous system and the environment).
- Heim (1970) has criticised the EPI (and, by implication, the EPQ) because of its *forced-choice* ('yes/no') format. She argues that a few, simple yes/no questions can hardly be expected to do justice to the complexities of human personality, and she has criticised the lie scale for its lack of subtlety.
- As we noted earlier, validation of the scales has involved the use of *criterion groups,* such as groups of neurotics, who tend to score at the extreme ends of the scale. But can we assume that the scale is 'valid'

for the majority of people who lie somewhere in the middle? This needs to be empirically tested rather than simply assumed. While Eysenck (1992) believed that P reflected a disposition towards psychotic illness ('psychosis-proneness'), high P scorers *don't* have a significantly increased risk of developing schizophrenia (Chapman *et al.*, 1994), nor do schizophrenic patients score high on P (Cochrane *et al.*, 2010). The clinical analogue is *psychopathy* and other antisocial behaviours (not psychosis) (Claridge and Davis, 2003).

- According to Claridge and Davis (2003), Eysenck can take most of the credit for the *dimensional approach* to understanding psychological disorders. In using FA to identify the basic dimensions of normal personality, he always had in mind the need to describe and explain the abnormal. He believed that the various psychological disorders recognised in psychiatry actually define the extremes of his personality dimensions (see Figure 42.7).

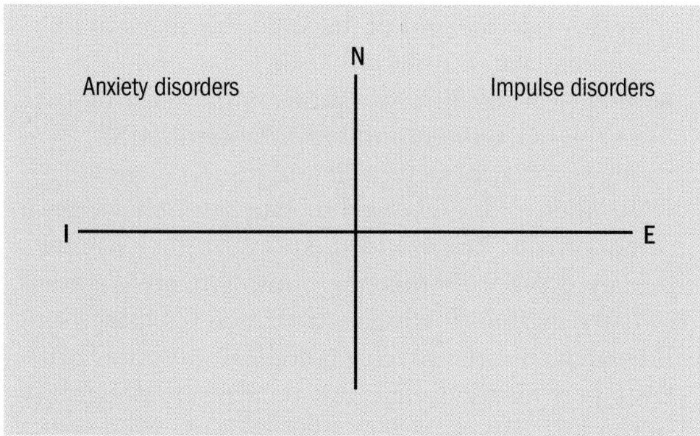

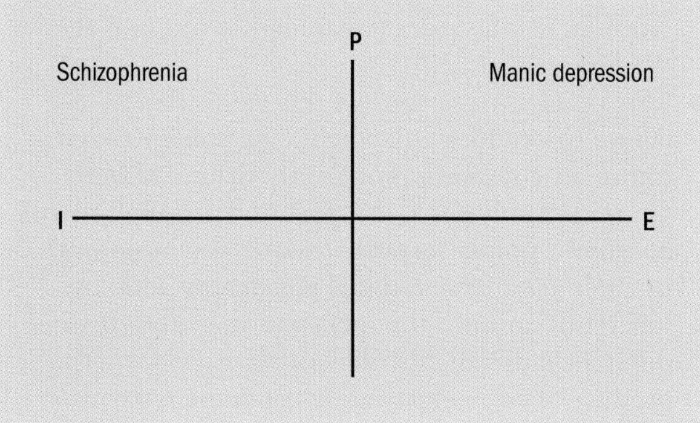

Figure 42.7 Eysenck's location of non-psychotic disorders in two dimensions of N/I-E (top) and psychotic disorders in two dimensions of P/I-E (bottom) (from Claridge and Davis, 2003)

Cattell's trait theory

Whereas surface traits may correspond to common-sense ways of describing behaviour and may sometimes be measured by simple observation, they're actually the result of interactions among the source traits. Valid explanations of behaviour must concentrate on source traits as the structural factors which determine personality (see Figure 42.9).

Figure 42.8 Raymond B. Cattell (1905–1998)

Differences between Cattell and Eysenck

- According to Cattell, some overlap between first-order (oblique) factors is to be expected. For example, an intelligent person (B-factor) is also likely to be shrewd and worldly (N-factor). Cattell conducted a second-order FA of his 16 primary factors, which produced a number of surface traits. The two most important were *exvia–invia* and *anxiety* (corresponding to Eysenck's E and N, respectively; see Figure 42.9). Others included *radicalism* (aggressive and independent), *tendermindedness* (sensitivity, frustration and emotionality), and *superego* (conscientious, conforming and preserving).
- Cattell believes there's a fundamental *discontinuity* between normals and, say, schizophrenics: there's a *qualitative* difference between them (and not merely a quantitative one, as Eysenck maintains). For example, Q-data used with psychiatric patients produce 12 factors which discriminate psychotics as a group (e.g. paranoia, suicidal disgust, schizophrenia and high general psychosis); they score highly on these factors compared with normals. A second-order FA of Q-data from psychiatric patients yields three factors, one of which resembles Eysenck's P.
- Cattell, much more than Eysenck, acknowledges how behaviour can fluctuate in response to *situational factors*. His definition of personality as that which 'determines behaviour in a defined situation and a defined mood' (Cattell, 1965) implies that behaviour is never totally determined by source traits. Although personality factors remain fairly stable over time, they constitute only one kind of variable influencing overt behaviour. Others include (a) *mood and state factors* (e.g. depression, arousal,

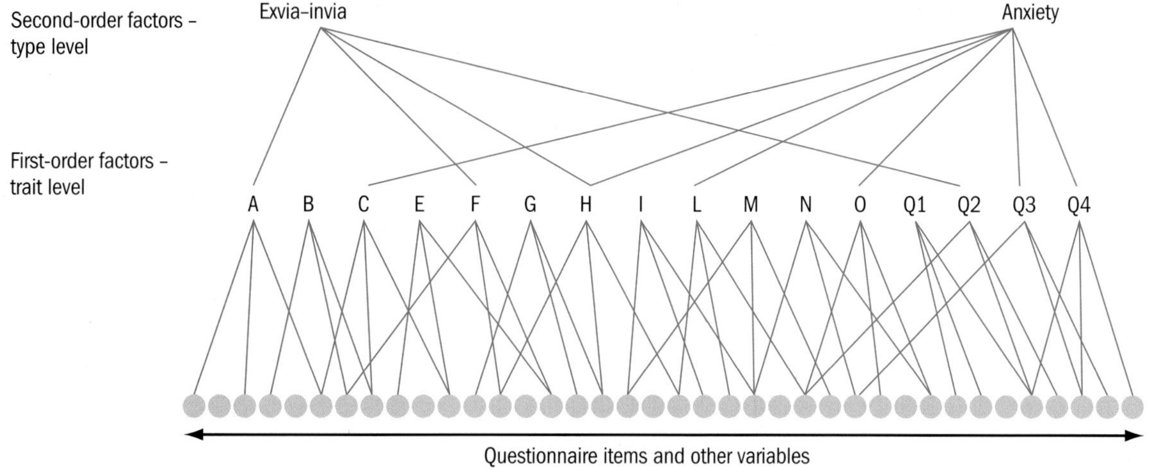

Figure 42.9 The hierarchical organisation of personality resulting from a second-order analysis of the first-order 'source traits' (after Cattell, 1965)

anxiety, fatigue and intoxication); and (b) *motivational factors* (innate, biological drives and culturally acquired drives).

Single- and multi-trait theories, and the Big Five

Eysenck's and Cattell's theories are *multi-trait* theories. (Eysenck's is sometimes called the *tripartite division* of personality, or the 'Giant Three' model). (Pickering *et al.,* 2013.) An influential *single-trait* theory is Rotter's (1966) *locus of control* (see Chapter 12). For a single-trait theory to be useful, it must identify a trait that determines a wide range of important behaviours (Hampson, 1995).

Multi-trait theories try to include all aspects of personality, and assume that individual differences can be described in terms of a particular profile on the same set of traits. Since the 1980s, there's been a vast amount of research to discover a small but comprehensive number of basic trait dimensions which can account for the structure of personality and individual differences.

There's a growing consensus that personality can be adequately described by five broad constructs or factors, the *five factor model* (often referred to as the *Big Five*) (Costa and McCrae, 1992; Digman, 1990; Goldberg, 1993; McCrae and Costa, 1989). As with Cattell's theory, the Big Five have their roots in the *lexical hypothesis:* the assumption that every aspect of an individual's personality can be described by existing English words (Chamorro-Premuzic, 2007).

The five major personality traits or factors (commonly abbreviated to NEOAC or OCEAN) are shown in Table 42.3. Note that Neuroticism and Extroversion correspond to Eysenck's constructs.

Table 42.3 The Big Five personality factors

	Desirable traits	Undesirable traits
(I) Neuroticism (or Emotional Stability)	Calm, even tempered, imperturbable	Anxious, moody, temperamental, impulsive
(II) Extroversion	Outgoing, sociable, assertive	Introverted, reserved, passive
(III) Openness to experience	Imaginative, intelligent, creative	Shallow, unsophisticated, unperceptive
(IV) Agreeableness	Kind, trusting, warm, altruistic, modest	Hostile, selfish, cold
(V) Conscientiousness	Organised, thorough, tidy, competent	Careless, unreliable, sloppy

An evaluation of the Big Five

- The Big Five model offers a *descriptive* (rather than causal) classification of individual differences; in other words, it lacks a theoretical account of the development and nature of the processes underlying (in particular) O, A and C. However, in recent years there's growing interest in possible genetic influences (Loehlin, 1992).
- Although Eysenck (1991) argues for his 'giant three' (E, N and P), the differences seem quite trivial now compared with, say, the disagreement between Eysenck and Cattell's 16 source traits (Hampson, 1995). Not only do E and N appear in Table 42.3, but the negative pole of Agreeableness is similar to P, with overtones of aggressiveness, impulsiveness and general 'nastiness' (Claridge and Davis, 2003).
- Nevertheless, there remains the fundamental problem of the *meaning* of the factors that are extracted (Kline, 1993; Krahé, 1992). Ultimately, personality factors, however many, must be identified from their correlations with external criteria (Kline, 1993).
- Although the Big Five are meant to be orthogonal (uncorrelated), when N is reversed and scored in terms of Emotional Stability several studies find that all five factors are positively and significantly intercorrelated. Despite being modest in size, the intercorrelations suggest that personality could be further simplified to more 'basic' underlying traits – perhaps even *one* general factor (Chamorro-Premuzic, 2007).
- Hampson (1999) believes that, at the end of the 1990s, the Big Five remain pre-eminent as a description of normal personality. The model has shown good reliability and validity (Chamorro-Premuzic, 2007).
- According to Moghaddam (2002), Big Five theorists claim to have uncovered *universal* traits, with the implication that the central features of personality are relatively fixed from birth. However, while he accepts that the disposition to have dispositions is universal:

> *... the particular dispositions one develops are to a large degree a result of interactions with the social and physical environment. The so-called Big Five have emerged through research with respondents from either Western societies or Westernized sections of other societies, typically students in modern universities modelled on Western universities.*

KELLY'S PERSONAL CONSTRUCT THEORY

Kelly's *personal construct theory* (PCT) is an *idiographic* approach, stressing the uniqueness of each individual. It's also a *phenomenological* approach, that is, a view of the world through a person's own eyes and not an observer's interpretation or analysis.

Figure 42.10 George A. Kelly (1905–1966)

Man the scientist

According to Kelly, we're all scientists in the sense that we put our own interpretation (or theories) on the world of events, and from these personal theories we produce hypotheses (predictions about future events). Every time we act, we're putting our hypotheses to the test and, in this sense, behaviour is the independent variable – it is the experiment. Depending on the outcome, our hypotheses are either validated or not, and this will determine the nature of our subsequent behavioural experiments (Fransella, 1981).

Constructive alternativism

Although a real world of physical objects and events does exist, no one individual has the privilege of 'knowing' it: all we can do is place our personal constructs upon it. The better our constructs 'fit' the world generally, the better our control over our own, personal world will be. According to Kelly (1955), there's no way of getting 'behind' our interpretation of the world to check if it matches what the world is really like. All we have are our own interpretations, and so we necessarily see the world 'through goggles', which cannot be removed. However, these goggles or constructs aren't fixed once and for all; the person as scientist is constantly engaged in testing, checking, modifying, and revising his/her unique set of constructs.

The repertory grid technique

The *repertory grid test* is an attempt to help individuals discover the fundamental constructs they use for perceiving and relating to others. It's used as a major research instrument, is very flexible, and can be used in different ways. It can be factor-analysed, which often reveals that many constructs overlap. Probably three to six major constructs cover most people's construct system.

Box 42.5 Constructing a repertory grid (rep grid) (Based on Kelly, 1955)

The basic method involves the following steps.

- Write a list of the most important people in your life (*elements*).
- Choose three of these elements.
- Ask yourself, how are two of these alike and different from the third?

The descriptions given (e.g. 'My mother and girlfriend are affectionate, my father is not') constitute a *construct*, which is expressed in a *bipolar way* ('affectionate–not affectionate').

- This *construct* is applied to all the remaining elements.
- Then another set of three elements is selected, and the whole process is repeated. It continues until either you've produced all the constructs you can (which is usually no more than 25 with one set of elements), or until a sufficient number has been produced as judged by the investigator.

All this information can be collated in the form of a grid, with the elements across the top and the constructs down the side, and a tick or cross indicating which pole of the construct is applicable (for example, a tick indicates 'affectionate' and a cross indicates 'not affectionate').

Ask Yourself

- Have a go at constructing your own repertory grid (see Box 42.5).

The rep grid can be used *nomothetically*, as Bannister and Fransella have done with thought-disordered schizophrenics. Their *grid test of thought disorder* (Bannister and Fransella, 1967) contains standardised elements and constructs (supplied by the researcher), so that an individual score can be compared with group norms. However, this is probably rather far removed from how Kelly intended the technique to be used.

The rep grid has also been used to study how patients participating in group psychotherapy change their perception of each other (and themselves) during the period of therapy: the group members themselves are the elements and a number of constructs are supplied (Fransella, 1970). Fransella (1972) has used this method extensively with people being treated for severe stuttering.

An evaluation of PCT

- Bannister and Fransella (1980) and Fransella (1981) point out that PCT is deliberately stated in very abstract terms to avoid the limitations of a particular time and culture. It's an attempt to redefine Psychology as a Psychology of people and is 'content free'. PCT isn't so much a personality theory, more a total Psychology. But Kelly isn't concerned with separate subdivisions of Psychology as dealt with in most textbooks. For example, the traditional concept of *motivation* can be dispensed with: we don't need concepts like drives, needs, or psychic energy to explain what makes people 'get up and go' – man is a form of motion and a basic assumption about life is that 'it goes on': 'It isn't that something makes you go on, the going on is the thing itself …' (Kelly, 1962).
- However, he implicitly assumes that we all seek a sense of order and predictability in our dealings with the external world – the overriding goal of anticipating the future represents a basic form of motivation. We achieve this through behaving much like a research scientist: 'The scientist's ultimate aim is to predict and control' (see Chapter 3).
- Various aspects of *emotion* are dealt with in terms of how an individual's construct system is organised and how it changes. For example, 'anxiety' is the awareness that what you're confronted with isn't within the framework of your existing construct system – you don't know how to construe it. For some, this approach is far too cognitive and rational, leaving the subjective experience (the 'gut feeling') that we call anxiety out of the picture (see Chapter 44).
- Peck and Whitlow (1975) believe that Kelly trivialises important aspects of behaviour, including learning, emotion and motivation, and neglects situational influences on behaviour. PCT appears to place the person in an 'empty world'.

HUMANISTIC THEORIES

Humanistic theories (and Kelly's PCT) have their philosophical roots in *phenomenology* and *existentialism*, and some would say they're more 'philosophical' than 'psychological'. They're concerned with characteristics that are distinctively and uniquely human, in particular experience, uniqueness, meaning, freedom, and choice. We have first-hand experience of ourselves as people, and Rogers' theory in particular is centred around the *self-concept*.

What Rogers and Maslow have in common is their positive evaluation of human nature, a belief in the individual's potential for personal growth (*self-actualisation*). But while Maslow's theory is commonly referred to as a 'Psychology of being' (self-actualisation is an end in itself and lies at the peak of his *hierarchy of needs*: see Chapter 9), Rogers' is a 'Psychology of becoming' (it's the process of becoming a 'fully functioning person' that's of major importance and interest).

Rogers' self theory

Rogers (like Maslow) rejected the deterministic approach of psychoanalytic theory (see below) and Behaviourism (see Chapter 2). Instead, Humanistic theorists see behaviour as a response to the individual's perception/interpretation of external stimuli. As no one else can know how we perceive, we're the best experts on understanding our own behaviour. Rogers also sees human nature in a very positive and optimistic light: 'There is no beast in man; there is only man in man'.

The self

The self is an 'organised, consistent set of perceptions and beliefs about oneself'. It includes a person's awareness of 'what they are and what they can do', influencing both their perception of the world and their behaviour. We evaluate every experience in terms of self, and most human behaviour can be understood as an attempt to maintain consistency between our self-image and our actions (see Chapter 33).

However, this consistency isn't always achieved and our self-image (and related self-esteem) may differ quite radically from our actual behaviour and from how others see us. For example, a person may be highly successful and respected by others, and yet regard him/herself as a failure! This illustrates what Rogers calls *incongruence*. Because incongruent experiences, feelings, actions, and so on conflict with our (conscious) self-image (and because we prefer to act and feel in ways that are consistent with our self-image), they can be threatening. Consequently, we may deny them access to awareness (they may remain *unsymbolised*) through actual denial, distortion or blocking.

These *defence mechanisms* prevent the self from growing and changing, and widen the gulf between our self-image and reality (our actual behaviour or our true feelings). As the self-image becomes more and more unrealistic, so the incongruent person becomes more and more confused, vulnerable, dissatisfied and, eventually, seriously maladjusted. By contrast, the self-image of the congruent person is flexible and changes realistically as new experiences occur. When your self-image matches what you really think and feel and do, you're in the best position to self-actualise.

(See Chapter 2 for an evaluation of Humanistic theories.)

PSYCHODYNAMIC THEORIES

As we saw in Chapter 2, 'psychodynamic' implies the active forces within the personality that motivate behaviour, in particular the unconscious conflict between the id, ego and superego. Freud's was the first of this kind of theory and all *psychodynamic* theories stem, more or less directly, from Freud's *psychoanalytic theory*.

Freud's psychoanalytic theory

Ask Yourself

- What do you already know about Freud's ideas?
- Psychoanalytic theory applies to *motivation* (Chapter 9), *forgetting* (Chapter 21), *prejudice* (Chapter 25), *aggression* (Chapter 29) and many aspects of *development* (see Chapters 35–38).

Freud believed that conflict within the personality is unavoidable, because the ego is being 'pulled' in two opposing directions by the id and the superego. The ego's solution comes in the form of three forms of 'compromise', namely *dreams, neurotic symptoms* and *defence mechanisms*.

Dreams

'A dream is a [disguised] fulfilment of a [suppressed or repressed] wish' (Freud, 1900/1976a). It represents a compromise between forbidden urges and their expression. What we dream about and are conscious of upon waking is called the *manifest content*, while the dream's meaning (the wish being fulfilled) is the *latent content*. The manifest content is often the product of the weaving together of certain fragments from that day's events (*day residues*) and the forbidden wish. *Dream interpretation* (a major technique involved in *psychoanalysis*) aims to make sense of the manifest content (which is often disjointed, sometimes bizarre and nonsensical) by 'translating' it into the underlying wish fulfilment (see Case Study 42.1).

Dreams come into being through *dream work* (controlled by the ego), which converts the underlying (latent) wish into the manifest content. It involves *displacement*, *condensation* and *concrete representation*.

- *Displacement* refers to the substitution of the real target of the dreamer's feelings by a person or object which then becomes the target for those feelings. The substitute is symbolically (unconsciously) linked to the true target, as in the case of one of Freud's patients who dreamt of strangling a little white dog which represented her sister-in-law, who had a very pale complexion and whom the dreamer had previously called 'a dog who bites' (Stevens, 1995). This is a crucial part of the *disguise* that conceals from the dreamer the true meaning of the dream. This example shows how certain symbols will be peculiar to individual dreamers. But many dream symbols have a conventional meaning within a culture, particularly those that represent the penis (e.g. snakes, trees, trains, daggers, umbrellas), the vagina (e.g. small boxes, cupboards, ships, and other vessels), and sexual intercourse (e.g. climbing ladders or stairs and entering tunnels).

Case Study 42.1

An Oedipal dream reported by one of Freud's patients (from *The Interpretation of Dreams,* 1900/1976a)

A man dreamt that he had a secret liaison with a lady whom someone else wanted to marry. He was worried in case this other man might discover the liaison and the proposed marriage come to nothing. He, therefore, behaved in a very affectionate way to the man. He embraced him and kissed him.

Ask Yourself

- How do you think Freud interpreted this 'typical' dream?

Figure 42.11 A symbol of sexual intercourse – or simply a train entering a tunnel?

- *Condensation* involves the same part of the manifest content representing different parts of the latent wish. For example, a king may represent not only the dreamer's father, but also authority figures or very wealthy and powerful people in general. So, more than one dream idea may be 'condensed' into a single manifest image.
- *Concrete representation* refers to the expression of an abstract idea in a very concrete way. For example, the concrete image of a king could represent the abstract notions of authority, power, or wealth. This is sometimes called 'dramatisation'.

Dream interpretation is what Freud called the 'royal road to the unconscious': reversing the dream work, and unravelling the wish from the manifest content, can provide invaluable information about the unconscious mind in general, and about the dreamer's in particular.

Neurotic symptoms

Like dreams, neurotic symptoms are essentially the expression of a repressed wish (or memory) that's become disguised in very similar ways to dream work. The symptom may symbolise the wish it's linked to, as in a patient who suffered from hysterical hand-twitching, which was related to her memories of being badly frightened while playing the piano (*displacement*). This same patient's hand-twitching was traced to two other memories (receiving a disciplinary strapping on the hands as a schoolgirl, and being forced to massage the back of a detested uncle: *condensation*). The symptom is often something 'physical', while the underlying cause is something 'mental' (*concrete representation*).

Defence mechanisms

The *ego defence mechanisms* are, by definition, unconscious, which is partly what makes them effective. They involve some degree of self-deception and distortion of reality; this prevents us from being overwhelmed by temporary threats or traumas and can provide 'breathing space' in which to come to terms with conflict or find alternative ways of coping. As short-term measures, they're advantageous, necessary and 'normal', but as long-term solutions to life's problems they're usually regarded as unhealthy (and, indeed, form the basis of a great deal of neurosis). Many of the defences described in Table 42.4 were originally proposed (or implied) by Freud and later elaborated by his daughter, Anna Freud (1936).

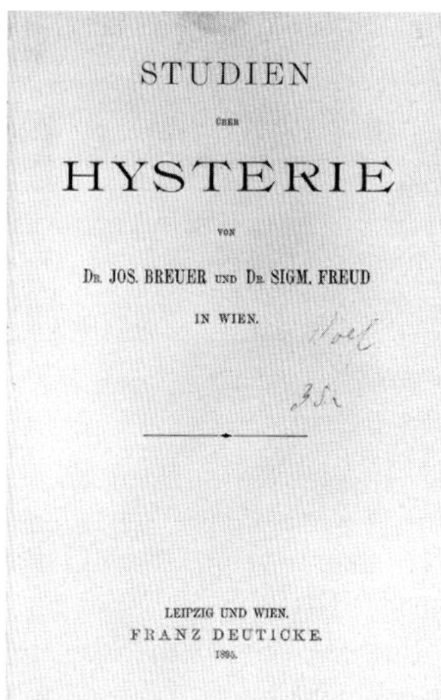

STUDIEN

ÜBER

HYSTERIE

VON

DR. JOS. BREUER UND DR. SIGM. FREUD

IN WIEN.

LEIPZIG UND WIEN.
FRANZ DEUTICKE.
1895.

Figure 42.12 Cover of the first edition of *Studies of Hysteria* (1895), by Breuer and Freud

An evaluation of Freud's theory

Empirical studies

- Fonagy (1981) believes that the most relevant kind of study are those which attempt to identify basic *underlying mechanisms*. Most recently, this has been attempted by *neuropsychoanalysis* (NP) (see Research Update 42.1).

Table 42.4 Some major ego defence mechanisms

Name of defence mechanism	Description	Example(s)
Repression	Forcing a threatening or distressing memory/feeling/wish out of consciousness and making it unconscious	Five-year-old child repressing its incestuous desire for the opposite-sex parent (see Chapter 35)
Displacement	Transferring our feelings from their true target onto a harmless, substitute target (e.g. 'kicking the cat')	Frustration caused by problems at work expressed as domestic violence (see Chapter 29); phobias (see Chapter 44)
Denial	Failing/refusing to acknowledge/perceive some aspect of reality	Refusing to accept that you have a serious illness or that your partner is going off you (see Chapter 28)
Rationalisation	Finding an acceptable excuse (a 'cover story') for some really quite unacceptable behaviour/situation	'Being cruel to be kind'; 'I only did it because I love you' (see Chapter 24)
Reaction formation	Consciously feeling/thinking the opposite of your true (unconscious) feelings/thoughts	Being considerate/polite to someone you strongly dislike – even going out of your way to be nice to them
Sublimation	A form of displacement in which a (socially positive) substitute activity is found for expressing some unacceptable impulse	Playing sport to redirect aggressive urges (see Chapter 29)
Identification	Incorporating/introjecting another person into one's own personality – making them part of oneself	Identification with the aggressor (boys); anaclitic identification (girls) (see Chapter 35)
Projection	Displacing your own unacceptable feelings/ characteristics onto someone else	'I hate you' becomes (through reversal of subject/object), 'You hate me' (see Chapter 44)
Regression	Reverting to behaviour characteristic of an earlier stage of development	Losing your temper, comfort-eating, sleeping more when depressed (see Chapter 44)
Isolation	Separating contradictory thoughts/feelings into 'logic tight' compartments	Talking about some traumatic experience without any show of emotion – or even giggling about it (see Chapter 44)

(For further discussion of empirical studies, see Chapter 2.)

Is the theory scientific?

Popper's criticism that Freud's theory is *unfalsifiable* and, therefore, unscientific, is discussed in Chapter 2. However, it would be a serious mistake to regard reaction formation (the example used by Popper) as typifying Freudian theory, and the sheer volume of research suggests that Freudian theory cannot be dismissed as lightly as Popper and Eysenck would like on the grounds of it being 'unscientific'. According to Kline (1989), the view adopted by almost all Experimental Psychologists involved in the study of Freud's theory is that it should be seen as a *collection of hypotheses*. As Fisher and Greenberg (1977) argue, some of these hypotheses will turn out to be true, others false, when put to Popper's test of falsifiability.

Some hypotheses are undoubtedly more critical to the overall theory than others. For example, if no evidence could be found for repression, this would alter considerably the nature of psychoanalysis (but see Research Update 42.1). But if it was found that the Oedipus complex was more pronounced in small as opposed to large families, the theory wouldn't be radically affected (Kline, 1989).

How valid is the case study method?

Although Freud often states or implies that his theories have been derived from his observations of his patients, he left no direct record of the original data. He deliberately made no notes during

Research Update 42.1

Freud and neuroscience

As we noted in Chapter 2, support for certain aspects of Freud's theories has been provided by the relatively new sub-discipline of *neuropsychoanalysis* (NP), one of the many spin-offs of neuroscientific research. NP aims to link psychodynamic concepts and neuroscientific mechanisms (Northoff, 2012).

According to Solms (2006), the simple aim of NP is to introduce the psyche into neuropsychology – to demonstrate that the brain cannot possibly be understood if the subjective aspect of its nature is neglected or even ignored. Solms and other leading figures in NP see their research as a continuation and completion of Freud's attempt to establish a scientifically-based account of the human mind (Northoff, 2012).

NP focuses primarily on linking psychodynamic concepts to specific psychological (e.g. cognitive and affective) functions, which, in turn, may be localised in particular brain regions (i.e. the *neural correlates* of psychodynamic concepts). Some of the major psychodynamic concepts that have been investigated are (i) unconscious motivation and memory; (ii) ego defence mechanisms; and (iii) dreams (see Chapter 7).

Unconscious motivation and memory

Research findings are confirming the existence and pivotal role of unconscious mental processing. For example, the behaviour of patients who are unable to consciously remember events that occurred after damage to certain memory-encoding structures of their brains is clearly influenced by the 'forgotten' events. Cognitive neuroscientists make sense of such cases by distinguishing between memory systems that process information 'explicitly' (i.e. consciously) and 'implicitly' (i.e. unconsciously). This is consistent with how Freud described memory (Solms, 2006)

Neuroscientists have also identified unconscious memory systems that mediate emotional learning. LeDoux (e.g. 1994) discovered, below the conscious cortex, a neuronal pathway that connects perceptual information with the primitive brain structures responsible for generating fear responses. Because this pathway bypasses the hippocampus – which generates conscious memories – current events routinely trigger unconscious memories of emotionally significant past events; this causes conscious feelings that may seem irrational (e.g. 'men with hairy arms make me feel young').

Research has also shown that the major brain structures essential for forming conscious (explicit) memories aren't functional during the first two years of life; this provides an elegant explanation of what Freud called *childhood amnesia*. Rather than forgetting our earliest memories, Freud proposed that we simply cannot recall them to consciousness. But this inability doesn't prevent them from affecting adult feelings and behaviour (Solms, 2006). Solms claims that most (if not all) developmental neurobiologists believe that early experiences, especially involving mother-infant interaction, influence the pattern of brain connections in ways that fundamentally shape our future personality and mental health. Yet none of these experiences can be consciously recalled.

Ego defence mechanisms

As Solms (2006) points out, even if we are mostly driven by unconscious thoughts, this doesn't in itself prove anything about Freud's claim that we actively 'forget' unacceptable information. However, case studies supporting his theory of repression are accumulating, most famously involving patients with *anosognosia* (Ramachandran, 1994, 2011).

- Damage to the right parietal region of patients' brains makes them unaware of gross physical defects, such as paralysis of a limb or *hemiplegia* (complete paralysis of one side of the body).
- After artificially activating the right hemisphere of one such patient, Ramachandran observed that she suddenly became aware that her left arm was paralysed – and that it had been paralysed continuously since her stroke eight days before. This demonstrated that she was capable of recognising her deficits and that she had unconsciously registered them for the previous eight days – despite her conscious *denials* that there was any problem.
- Significantly, once the effects of the stimulation wore off, the patient not only reverted to the belief that her arm was normal, she also forgot the part of the interview in which she'd acknowledged that her arm was paralysed – even though she could recall every other detail of the interview.

Ramachandran took this as evidence for the concept of *repression*. This woman is just one of many such cases that Ramachandran has seen; they bear a striking resemblance to the kinds of everyday denials and *rationalisations* that we all engage in (Ramachandran, 2011).

Suppression is the voluntary form of repression, in which the individual consciously pushes unwanted, anxiety-provoking thoughts, memories, emotions, etc. out of awareness. It's more amenable to controlled experiments than is repression (Berlin and Koch, 2009). Although some argue that suppression is a psychoanalytical myth with no scientific support, data from fMRI studies suggest otherwise (Wickelgren, 2012).

therapy sessions, since this might interfere with the therapeutic relationship (see Chapter 45); he wrote them up several hours later, so that his case studies are *reconstructions* of what happened. He also reported in depth on only 12 patients, and in some cases the details are incomplete (Stevens, 1995).

The case study relies on the reconstruction of childhood events, and, as used by Freud, is generally considered to be the least scientific of all empirical methods used by Psychologists. It's open to many types of distortion and uncontrolled influences. (But see Gross, 2014.)

How representative were Freud's patients?

One of the standard criticisms made of Freud's database is that his patients were mainly neurotic, wealthy, middle-class Jewish females, living in Vienna at the turn of the twentieth century. This makes them highly unrepresentative of the population to whom his theories were generalised

More serious, perhaps, is the criticism that Freud studied only adults (with the very dubious exception of Little Hans), and yet he put forward a theory of (child and adolescent) personality *development*. How many steps removed were his data from his theory? According to Thomas (1985), the analyst interprets, through his or her theoretical 'lens', ostensibly symbolic material derived from the reported dreams, memories, and so on of neurotics about apparent experiences stemming from their childhood one or more decades earlier. However, this in itself doesn't invalidate the theory; it merely makes the study of children all the more necessary.

Reification

Several writers have criticised terms like id, ego and superego as bad metaphors. They don't correspond to any aspect of psychology or neurophysiology, and they encourage *reification*, that is, treating metaphorical terms as if they were 'things' or entities.

However, Bettelheim (1985) points out that much of Freud's terminology was mistranslated, and this has led to a misrepresentation of those parts of his theory. For example, Freud used the German terms *das Es* ('the it'), *das Ich* ('the I') and *das Über-Ich* ('the over-I'), which were intended to capture how the individual relates to different aspects of the self. The Latin terms *id*, *ego*, and *superego* tend to depersonalise these, and give the impression that there are three separate 'selves' which we all possess! The Latin words (chosen by his American translator to give them greater scientific credibility) turn the concepts into cold technical terms which arouse no personal associations. Whereas 'the I' can only be studied from the inside (through introspection), the 'ego' can be studied from the outside (as behaviour). In translation, Freud's 'soul' became scientific Psychology's 'psyche' or 'personality' (Bettelheim, 1985).

The nature of Freudian theory

As noted in Chapter 2, Freud's theory has great *hermeneutic strength*, that is, it provides methods and concepts which enable us to interpret and 'unpack' underlying meanings (Stevens, 1995). Stevens claims that:

> *Although Freud wanted to create a nomothetic theory … in effect he finished up with a set of 'hermeneutic tools' – concepts and techniques that help us to interpret underlying meanings …*

There's no doubting the tremendous impact that Freud has had, both within Psychology and outside. The fertility of psychoanalytic theory, in terms of the debate, research, and theorising it has generated, makes it one of the richest in the whole of Psychology.

Jung's Analytical Psychology

Structure of the personality and levels of consciousness

For Jung, the person is a whole almost from the moment of birth. Personality isn't acquired piece by piece (the 'jigsaw' concept) through learning and experience, but is already there. So, instead of striving to achieve wholeness, our aim in life is to maintain it and to prevent the *splitting* (or *dissociation*) of the psyche into separate and conflicting parts. Jung saw the role of therapy as helping the patient recover this lost wholeness, and to strengthen the psyche so as to resist future dissociation.

The psyche comprises three major, interacting levels:

1. consciousness
2. the personal unconscious
3. the collective unconscious.

The distinction between 2 and 3 represents one of the major differences between Jung and Freud.

Consciousness

This is the only part of the mind known directly by the individual. It appears early in life through the operation of four basic functions: *thinking*, *feeling*, *sensing*, and *intuiting*. In addition, there are two attitudes which determine the orientation of the conscious mind: *extroversion* and *introversion* (see Box 42.6).

The development of consciousness is also the beginning of *individuation*, the process by which a person becomes psychologically 'in-dividual' (a separate, indivisible unit or whole). From this process emerges the *ego*, which provides a sense of identity and continuity, and is the *central core* of the personality.

Box 42.6 Extroversion and introversion, Jungian style

The *extrovert's* libido (Jung's term for psychic energy as a whole or life-force) is directed outwards towards the objective world of physical objects, people, customs and conventions, social institutions, and so on. Extroverts are preoccupied with *interpersonal* relationships, and are generally more active and outgoing.
The *introvert's* libido is directed inwards towards the subjective world of thoughts and feelings, and they're preoccupied with *intrapersonal* matters, are introspective and withdrawn, and may be seen by others as aloof, reserved, and antisocial.
For Jung, extroversion–introversion represents a *typology* of the 'either/or' variety.

The personal unconscious

The Freudian unconscious, in Jung's terms, is predominantly 'personal', that is, composed of the individual's particular and unique experiences which have been made unconscious through repression. For Jung, repressed material represents only one kind of unconscious content. The personal unconscious also includes things we've forgotten, as well as all those things we think of as being 'stored in memory' and which could become accessible by conscious recall (see Chapter 17).

Associated groups of feelings, thoughts and memories may cluster together to form a *complex*, a quite autonomous and powerful 'mini-personality' within the total psyche. Freud's Oedipus complex illustrates this constellation of thoughts and feelings. Complexes often prevent complete individuation from taking place, and one aim of therapy is to free the patient from their grip. In looking for the origin of complexes, Jung eventually turned to the *collective unconscious*.

The collective unconscious

This part of Jung's theory sets him apart from Freud probably more than any other. While Freud's id is part of each individual's personal unconscious and represents our biological inheritance, Jung believes that the mind (through the brain) has inherited characteristics which determine how a person will react to life experiences, and what type of experiences these will be. Unlike Freud, Jung attached relatively little importance to our individual past in relation to the personal unconscious, but saw the *evolutionary history of human beings as a species* as being all-important in relation to the collective (or racial) unconscious.

The collective unconscious can be thought of as a reservoir of *latent* (or *primordial*) images (also known as *archetypes* – a prototype or 'original model or pattern'). These relate to the 'first' or 'original' development of the psyche, stemming from our ancestral past, human, pre-human, and animal (Hall and Nordby, 1973). These images are predispositions or potentialities for experiencing and responding to the world in the same way that our ancestors did. For example, we don't have to learn to fear the dark or snakes through direct experience, because we're naturally predisposed to develop such fears through the inheritance of our ancestors' fears.

Jung identified a large number of archetypes, including birth, rebirth, death, power, magic, the hero, the child, the trickster, God, the demon, the wise old man, earth mother, and the giant. He gave special attention to the *persona,* the *anima/animus*, the *shadow*, and the *self*. (See Box 42.7.)

Ask Yourself

- Is there any evidence from the study of phobias that supports Jung's account of the collective unconscious? (See Box 42.7.)

According to Brown (1961), there are three major sources of evidence for the collective unconscious:

1. the 'extraordinary' similarity of themes in the mythologies of various cultures
2. the recurring appearance, in therapy, of symbols which have become divorced from any of the patient's personal experiences, and which become more and more like the primitive and universal symbols found in myths and legend
3. the content of fantasies of psychotics (especially schizophrenics), which are full of themes such as death and rebirth (similar to those found in mythology).

Brown argues that members of all cultures share certain common experiences, and so it's not surprising that they dream or create myths about archetypal themes. (See Figure 42.14.)

CONCLUSIONS: CAN WE TELL WHAT SOMEONE IS LIKE FROM THEIR FACE?

First impressions are highly influential (see Chapter 22); within a tenth of a second of seeing an unfamiliar face, we've already made a judgement about its owner's character. What's more, different people come to strikingly similar conclusions about a particular face (Highfield, 2009; Wiseman and Jenkins, 2009). But is there any substance to such snap judgements?

Box 42.7 The four major archetypes of the collective unconscious

The persona ('mask'): This is the outward face we present to the world, both revealing and concealing the real self. It allows us to play our part in social interaction, and to be accepted by others. It's the 'packaging' of the ego, the ego's PR man or woman, a kind of cloak between the ego and the objective world.
Anima/animus: This refers to the unconscious mirror image of our conscious ('official') gender. If we're male, our anima is our unconscious female side, and if we're female, our animus is our unconscious male side. We all have qualities of the opposite sex/gender – both biologically and psychologically – and in a well-adjusted person both sides must be allowed to express themselves in thought and behaviour. Repression of the anima/animus is very common in Western culture, where the persona predominates.
The shadow: This contains more of our basic animal nature than any other archetype. Like Freud's id, it must be kept in check if we're to live in society. But this isn't achieved easily, and is always at the expense of our creativity and spontaneity, depth of feeling and insight. So, the shadow represents the source of our creative impulses, but also of our destructive urges. The shadow of the highly creative person may occasionally overwhelm the ego, causing temporary insanity (confirming the popular belief that genius is akin to madness: see Chapter 44).
The self: This is the 'the archetype of archetypes', which unites the personality, giving it a sense of 'oneness' and firmness. The ultimate aim of every personality is to achieve a state of selfhood and individuation (similar to self-actualisation). This is a lifelong process, attained by very few individuals, Jesus and Buddha being notable exceptions. It's commonly represented as a *mandala*, an age-old symbol of wholeness and totality, found all over the world.

Figure 42.13 A mandala, the Buddha of the Golden Wheel (fourteenth century)

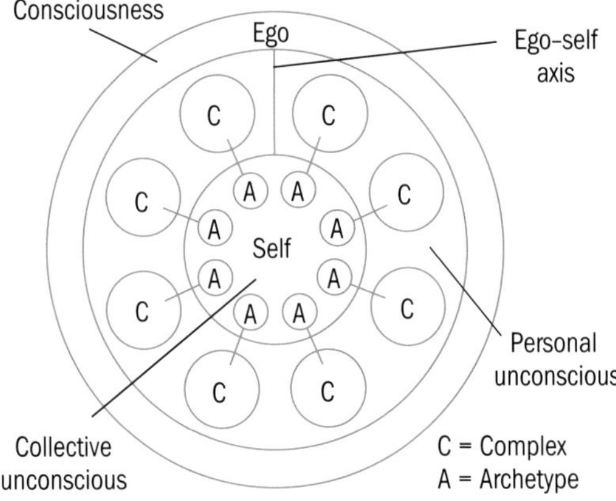

Figure 42.14 Schematic diagram of Jung's model of the psyche (based on Stevens, 1990)

Penton-Voak *et al.* (2006) investigated the relationship between self-report and perceived personality using both faces of individuals and computer graphic composites. Photographs were taken of 146 men and 148 women who each completed a self-report personality questionnaire from which scores on the Big Five personality factors were derived. In one study, the researchers found a relationship between self-reported E and perceived E in individual faces; for male faces only, they also found some accuracy in the perception of emotional stability and O. In a second study, Penton-Voak *et al.*, using composite faces made from individuals self-reporting high and low scores on each of the five factors, (and controlling for attractiveness) found evidence of raters' ability to discriminate between high and low A, E and, for male faces only, emotional stability.

Also using composite faces of those scoring high and low on self-ratings for the Big Five, Little and Perret (2007) found evidence for correct attributions of personality, particularly for C and E.

This basic method of deriving composite faces from photographs of people who gave extreme personality self-ratings has been used in an ongoing, online experiment by Wiseman and Jenkins for *New Scientist* (www.richardwiseman.com/faces2). Using personality dimensions not usually examined in this kind of research (lucky, humorous, religious and trustworthy), Wiseman and Jenkins (2009) conclude that:

Our findings ... raise the intriguing possibility that, among women at least, subtle aspects of an individual's personality may indeed be written all over her face.

Chapter Summary

- Experimental/'General' Psychology is concerned with psychological processes common to all human beings ('**universal norms**'). Personality differences represent one kind of '**group norm**' and reflect the **nomothetic** approach. The **idiographic** approach is concerned with discovering **individual/idiosyncratic norms**.
- Allport distinguished between **common** and **individual traits**. Individual traits can be **cardinal**, **central** and **secondary**. Most people possess a small number of central traits which compose the core of the personality.
- The nomothetic–idiographic approaches are increasingly being seen as **complementary** and **interdependent** and even Allport argued that both should be used together in order to achieve the aims of science.
- The **consistency controversy** was fuelled by Mischel, who rejected the **trait approach** in favour of **situationism**. **Interactionists** argue that all behaviour is the product of both personality and situational variables, and Mischel himself claims that it's the **psychological situation** that influences behaviour.
- **Orthogonal factor analysis (FA)** aims to identify a small number of powerful, **uncorrelated** factors (Eysenck's preferred method), while **oblique** FA aims to identify a larger number of less powerful, correlated factors (preferred by Cattell).
- Eysenck uses the term '**type**' for sets of correlated traits or personality dimensions, specifically **introversion–extroversion (E)**, **neuroticism–stability (N)**, which are both normally distributed, and **psychoticism (P)**, which isn't.
- E, N and P are measured by the **Eysenck Personality Questionnaire (EPQ)**. E and N are widely accepted as being reliable and valid, but there's much more doubt about P.
- Extroverts are chronically **under-aroused**, while introverts are chronically **over-aroused**. Compared with low N scorers, the sympathetic branch of the ANS reacts particularly strongly to stressful situations in high N scorers. The biological basis of P is much more uncertain, but male hormones may be involved.
- Introverts should be more easily **conditioned** than extroverts, but the evidence is inconclusive. Eysenck assumes that conditionability is a **unitary trait**, but this has never been demonstrated and represents a weakness of the theory.
- Cattell has identified a number of **second-order, surface traits**, including **exvia–invia** and **anxiety**, corresponding to E and N respectively. Cattell claims that with psychiatric patients, Q-data reveal a **qualitative** difference between normals and psychotics.
- Compared with Eysenck, Cattell acknowledges the influence of **situational factors** on behaviour, as well as mood and state factors and motivational factors.
- There's a growing consensus that personality can be adequately described by five broad constructs/factors (the **Big Five**), namely **openness to experience (O)**, **conscientiousness (C)**, **extroversion (E)**, **agreeableness (A)** and **neuroticism/emotional stability (N)**.
- Kelly's **personal construct theory (PCT)** is both idiographic and **phenomenological**. The underlying model is **man the scientist**. Personal constructs are designed to make the world more predictable and controllable.
- PCT is more a **total Psychology** than a personality theory. It's often called a **cognitive** theory of personality, and has been criticised for denying the subjective reality of emotional experience, as well as neglecting situational influences on behaviour.
- Like PCT, Humanistic theories are rooted in phenomenology and **existentialism** and are concerned with uniquely human characteristics, including **self-actualisation**.
- The central concept in Rogers' theory is the **self**. Failure to maintain consistency between our self-image and our actions produces **incongruence**. Defence mechanisms prevent the self from growing and changing, widening the gap between self-image and reality.
- Freud's **psychoanalytic theory** was the original **psychodynamic** theory, in which unconscious motivating forces play a central role. **Dreams, neurotic symptoms** and **defence mechanisms** represent three types of **compromise** through which the ego tries to meet the conflicting demands of the id and superego.

- Dreams consist of the **manifest content** and the **latent content** (the dream's meaning, namely, a disguised wish fulfilment). Dreams are created through **dream work**, with **symbols** playing a central role.
- **Neurotic symptoms** have a similar structure to dreams.
- **Defence mechanisms** involve some degree of **self-deception** and **distortion of reality** which, in the short term, prevent us from being overwhelmed by anxiety. But as long-term solutions, they're unhealthy and undesirable.
- The most relevant studies of Freud's theories are likely to be those which try to identify **underlying mechanisms**. Recently, **neuropsychoanalysis** (NP) has begun identifying the **neural correlates** of psychodynamic concepts.
- Freud's work can be thought of as a set of **hermeneutic tools** that help to interpret underlying meanings. Although this kind of theory is difficult to test empirically, it has influenced our everyday understanding of ourselves.
- In Jung's **Analytical Psychology**, the Freudian unconscious is largely **personal**. It comprises much more than repressed material, including **complexes**.
- Complexes originate in the **collective/racial unconscious**, a reservoir of primordial images or **archetypes**, stemming from our ancestral past. Most important are the **persona, anima/animus**, the **shadow** and the **self**.

Links with Other Topics/Chapters

Chapter 7 ⟶ Maslow's Humanistic theory is probably best known for his *hierarchy of needs*, which is often discussed in relation to *motivation*

Chapter 43 ⟶ Eysenck's claim that differences between normals and neurotics/psychotics are quantitative (as opposed to qualitative) represents the *dimensional view of abnormality* (as opposed to the *categorical* view)

Chapter 44 ⟶ Eysenck (1995) points out that N and P represent only a *predisposition* ('diathesis'), unlike *neurosis* and *psychosis* which are actual *psychological disorders*. Under extreme stress, however, the predisposition can become a psychiatric illness (Claridge, 1985)

Chapter 8 ⟶ The effects of *'recreational' drugs* are usually discussed without taking individual differences such as personality into account

Chapter 45 ⟶ In the case of *psychotropic drugs* (used for treating psychological disorders), the focus is on the *disorder* (rather than the individual with the disorder)

Chapter 46 ⟶ A way of testing the part of Eysenck's theory that deals with conditionability in the real world is through applying it to *criminality*

Chapter 49 ⟶ Assessing personality through the use of forced-choice items on a questionnaire is an example of *reductionism*

Chapter 39 ⟶ A major criticism of theories of *social changes in ageing* is their neglect of individual differences

Chapter 23 ⟶ Kelly's 'man the scientist' idea is consistent with Heider's *common-sense psychology*, which forms the basis of *attribution theory*

Chapter 36 ⟶ Jung's anima/animus archetype is related to Bem's concept of *psychological androgyny*

Recommended Reading

Carver, C.S. & Scheier, M.F. (1992) *Perspectives on Personality* (2nd edn). Boston: Allyn & Bacon.

Chamorro-Premuzic, T. (2007) *Personality and Individual Differences.* BPS/Blackwell. Chapters 2 and 3 deal specifically with personality. Chapter 4 discusses psychopathology (see Chapters 43 and 44), and Chapters 5, 6 and 8 discuss Intelligence (Chapter 41).

Cooper, C. (2002) *Individual Differences* (2nd edn). London: Arnold.

Freud, S. (1900/1976) *The Interpretation of Dreams.* Harmondsworth: Penguin (Pelican Freud Library).

Pennington, D. (2003) *Essential Personality.* London: Arnold.

Useful Websites

http://webspace.ship.edu/cgboer/perscontents.html (Personality Theories by C.G. Boeree)

www.outofservice.com/bigfive/ (The Big Five Personality Test)

www.bradley.edu/dotAsset/165904.pdf (Schmitt, D.P., Allik, J., McCrae, R.R. & Benet-Martinez, V. (2007) The Geographic Distribution of Big Five Personality Traits: Patterns and Profiles of Human Self-Description Across 56 Nations)

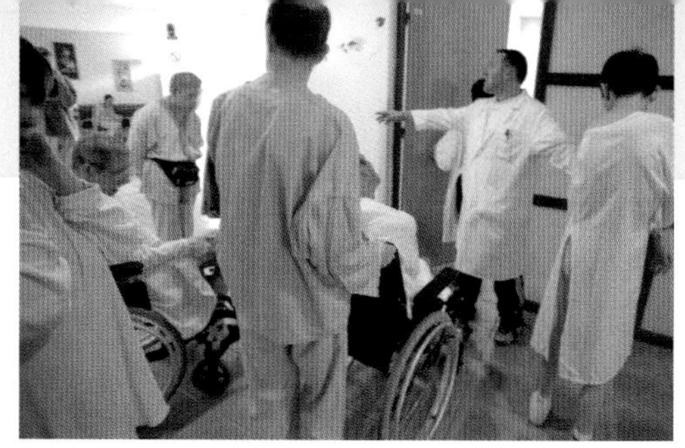

CHAPTER 43

PSYCHOLOGICAL ABNORMALITY: DEFINITIONS AND CLASSIFICATION

The concept of abnormality

The classification of mental disorders

INTRODUCTION and OVERVIEW

The emphasis in the preceding 42 chapters has been on normal psychological processes and development. However, we've also had occasion to qualify our discussion in two ways; first, by considering examples of abnormality (which also often serve to illuminate the normal); and second, by considering individual differences. This chapter brings these two issues together. Also, two whole earlier chapters have been devoted to discussing abnormality in different ways: *substance abuse* (Chapter 8) and *exceptional development* (Chapter 40).

Clearly, normality and abnormality are two sides of a coin: each can be defined only in relation to the other. Also, implicit within this statement is the assumption that it's possible, and meaningful, to draw the line between normal and abnormal. Different criteria for defining normality/abnormality propose how and where the line can be drawn.

As we saw in Chapter 2, each of the major theoretical approaches discussed throughout this book – especially the *biopsychological*, *psychodynamic*, *behavioural, humanistic*, and *cognitive* – defines psychological abnormality, and advocates ways of dealing with it, in its particular way. These will be discussed together in Chapter 45. By focusing here on the concept of abnormality itself, and how psychiatrists have attempted to classify mental disorders (*psychopathology*: see Chapter 44), we shall be discussing the *medical model*, which sees abnormality as *mental illness*.

THE CONCEPT OF ABNORMALITY

Abnormality as deviation from the average

This represents the *literal* sense of abnormality, whereby any behaviour which isn't typical or usual (that is, infrequent) is, by definition, abnormal: 'normal' is 'average'. However, this *statistical criterion* doesn't help to distinguish between atypical behaviour which is desirable (or, at least, acceptable) and that which is undesirable and unacceptable. For example, creative genius (such as Picasso's) and megalomania (such as Hitler's) are both statistically rare (and according to this criterion abnormal), but the former would be rated as much more desirable than the latter.

Ask Yourself

- Try to think of some examples of people behaving in 'odd' or 'strange' ways.
- What does 'odd' or 'strange' really mean here?
- Would this behaviour be sufficient grounds for labelling the person – or their behaviour – as 'abnormal'?

Conversely, there are certain types of behaviour and experience which are so common as to be normal in the statistical sense, but which are regarded as constituting psychological disorders (such as anxiety and depression). So, the statistical criterion appears to be neither necessary nor sufficient as a way of defining abnormality.

Abnormality as deviation from the norm

The statistical criterion is insufficient because it's essentially *neutral*; *deviation from the norm*, however, implies not behaving or feeling as one *should*. 'Norm' has an 'oughtness' about it: particular behaviours are expected from us at particular times and in particular situations, and if those expectations aren't met or are positively 'transgressed', we and/or our behaviour may be judged 'bad' or 'sick'.

For example, many people regard homosexuality as abnormal, not because it's statistically less common than heterosexuality, but because the 'normal' or 'natural' form of sexual behaviour in human beings is heterosexual. From a religious or moral perspective, homosexuality might be judged as 'bad', 'wicked' or 'sinful' (implying, perhaps, the element of choice). From a more biological or scientific perspective, it might be labelled 'sick', 'perverse' or 'deviant' (implying, perhaps, lack of choice).

Either way, even if it was found that a majority of men and women engaged in homosexual relationships (making *heterosexuality* abnormal according to the statistical criterion), these same people would still consider homosexuality a deviation from the norm and, therefore, abnormal. A further implication is that what's 'normal' is also 'desirable': unlike the statistical criterion, deviation from the norm doesn't allow for deviations which are also desirable.

Different kinds of norms

Within the same culture or society, a particular instance of behaviour may be considered normal or abnormal depending on the *situation* or *context*. For example, taking your clothes off is fine if you're about to step into a bath, but not if you're in the middle of a supermarket. However, situational norms aren't the only ones used to judge behaviour. *Developmental* (or *age*) *norms* dictate that, for instance, temper tantrums are perfectly normal in a 2-year-old regardless of where they occur, but decidedly abnormal in a 22-year-old (even in the privacy of his/her own home). *Cultural norms* are discussed below in relation to the ideal mental health criterion.

It's often far from obvious what norms are being broken when someone displays mental disorder: there's no law against being schizophrenic or having a panic attack, or being depressed, nor is it obvious what moral law or ethical principle is being broken in such cases. The kind of rule-breaking involved is discussed below in relation to the concept of mental illness.

Figure 43.1 Flagellants in the Philippines walk with bleeding wounds during an Easter re-enactment of Christ's crucifixion

Abnormality as deviation from ideal mental health

One way of 'fleshing out' the notion of desirability is to identify characteristics and abilities which people should possess for them to be considered normal. By implication, any lack or impoverishment of these characteristics and abilities constitutes abnormality or disorder.

Jahoda (1958) identified several ways in which mental health has been (or might be) defined, including:

- the absence of mental illness (clearly, a very negative definition)
- the ability to introspect, including the awareness of what we're doing and why
- the capacity for growth, development, and self-actualisation (as emphasised by Rogers and Maslow: see Chapters 9 and 42)
- integration of all the person's processes and attributes (e.g. balance between the id, ego and superego (Freud), and the achievement of ego identity (Erikson): see Chapters 37–39)
- the ability to cope with stress (see Chapter 12)
- autonomy (a concept that appears in many theories, including those of Erikson and Gould: see Chapter 38)
- seeing the world as it really is (part of Erikson's concept of ego identity)
- environmental mastery – the ability to love, work and play, to have satisfying interpersonal relationships, and to have the capacity for adaptation and adjustment (Erikson's ego identity again, and Freud's *lieben* und *arbeiten* – to love and to work).

Ask Yourself

- Is it possible to construct a list of ideals that everyone would agree with?
- What's wrong with this approach to defining normality?

While many or all these criteria of mental health may seem valid and are intuitively appealing, their claim to be universal and absolute raises serious problems.

- According to these criteria, most of us would be considered maladjusted or disordered. For example, according to Maslow most people don't achieve self-actualisation, so there's a fundamental discrepancy between these criteria and the statistical criterion (Mackay, 1975).
- Although many psychologists would accept these criteria, they're essentially *value judgements*, reflecting what's considered to be an *ideal state* of

being human. By contrast, there's little dispute as to the precise nature of physical health: according to Szasz (1962), 'The norm is the structural and functional integrity of the human body', and if there are no abnormalities present, the person is considered to be in good health. Judgements about physical health don't involve making moral or philosophical decisions. 'What health is can be stated in anatomical and physical terms' (Szasz, 1962): ideal and statistical criteria tend to be roughly equivalent (Mackay, 1975).

- It follows that what's considered to be psychologically normal (and, hence, abnormal) depends upon the culture in which a person lives. Psychological normality and abnormality are *culturally defined* (unlike physical normality and abnormality which, Szasz believes, can be defined in universally applicable ways).

Figure 43.2 Oscar Wilde (1854-1900), the Irish writer, was imprisoned for homosexuality in 1895 (see Critical Discussion 43.1)

Critical Discussion 43.1

Homosexuality – shifting definitions of abnormality

DSM-II (the second edition of the American Psychiatric Association's [APA] official classification of mental disorders, published in 1968) included homosexuality as a sexual deviation.

In 1973, the APA Nomenclature Committee, under pressure from many professionals and gay activist groups, recommended that the category should be removed and replaced with 'sexual orientation disturbance'. This was to be applied to gay men and women who are 'disturbed by, in conflict with, or wish to change their sexual orientation'. The change was approved, but not without fierce protests from several eminent psychiatrists who maintained the 'orthodox' view that homosexuality is inherently abnormal.

When DSM-III was published in 1980, another new term, *ego-dystonic homosexuality* (EDH) was used to refer to someone who is homosexually aroused, finds this arousal to be a persistent source of distress, and wishes to become heterosexual.

Since homosexuality itself was no longer a mental disorder, there was no inclusion in DSM-III of predisposing factors (as there was for all disorders). But they were included for EDH, namely, the individual homosexual's internalisation of society's negative attitudes (*homophobia* – fear of homosexuals – and *heterosexism* – anti-homosexual prejudice and discrimination). So, according to DSM-III, a homosexual is abnormal if s/he has been persuaded by society's prejudices that homosexuality is inherently abnormal, but at the same time it denied that homosexuality in itself is abnormal (Davison *et al.,* 2004).

Not surprisingly, no such category as 'ego-dystonic heterosexuality' has ever been used (Kitzinger, 1990). When DSM-III was revised (DSM-III-R, 1987), the APA decided to drop EDH (which was rarely used). However, one of the many 'dustbin' categories, 'sexual disorder not otherwise specified', included 'persistent and marked distress about one's sexual orientation'; this was retained in DSM-IV (1994) and DSM-IV-TR (2000).

ICD-10 (1992), the latest edition of the World Health Organization's classification of diseases, also includes 'ego-dystonic sexual orientation' under 'disorders of adult personality and behaviour'.

In the UK up until the 1960s, homosexuality among consenting adults was illegal; in 1995 the age of consent was lowered to 18. Clearly, nothing has happened to homosexuality itself during the last 30 years or so. What has changed are attitudes towards it, which then became reflected in its official psychiatric and legal status. Homosexuality *in itself* is neither normal nor abnormal, desirable nor undesirable, and this argument can be extended to behaviour in general.

Abnormality as personal distress

From the perspective of the individual, abnormality is the subjective experience of intense anxiety, unhappiness, depression, or a whole host of other forms that personal distress/suffering can take. While this may often be the only indication that anything is wrong (and may not necessarily be obvious to others), it may be a sufficient reason for seeking professional help. As Miller and Morley (1986) say:

> *People do not come to clinics because they feel they have met some abstract definition of abnormality. For the most part they come because their feelings or behaviour cause them distress ...*

However, the converse is also sometimes true: someone whose behaviour is obviously 'mad' as far as others are concerned may be oblivious of how others see them and may experience no subjective distress. This *lack of insight* is a feature of psychosis.

Abnormality as others' distress

If the person seen by others as behaving abnormally is the last to recognise there's a problem, then others' concern may act as a counterbalance to his/her lack of insight. This suggests, as with all behaviour, that abnormality is *interpersonal* and not simply *intrapersonal/intrapsychic*: it's something which takes place *between* people, in social situations, and isn't merely a reflection of an individual actor's personal qualities or characteristics (see Chapter 42).

Abnormality as maladaptiveness

Behaviour may be seen as abnormal if it prevents people from pursuing and achieving their goals, or doesn't contribute to their personal sense of well-being, or prevents them from functioning as they would wish in their personal, sexual, social, intellectual and occupational lives. For example, substance abuse is defined mainly by how it produces social and occupational disability, such as poor work performance and serious marital arguments. Similarly, a fear of flying might prevent someone from taking a job promotion (Davison and Neale, 1994).

Although the emphasis here is on the *consequences* of the behaviour, such behaviours may be very distressing in themselves for the person concerned. For example, phobias are negative experiences, because they involve intense fear, regardless of any practical effects brought about by the fear.

Abnormality as unexpected behaviour

According to Davison *et al.* (2004), it's abnormal to react to a situation or event in ways that couldn't be (reasonably) predicted, given what we know about human behaviour. For example, anxiety disorders are diagnosed when the anxiety is 'out of proportion to the situation'. The problem with this criterion is: who decides what's 'in proportion'? Is it just another form of deviation from the average, whereby what's reasonable or acceptable is simply how most people would be expected to behave? By this definition, *under-reacting* is just as abnormal as over-reacting, and yet only the latter is usually seen as a problem.

Abnormality as highly predictable/ unpredictable behaviour

Ask Yourself

- In light of the discussion of the consistency controversy in Chapter 42, how might abnormality be defined in terms of the consistency of behaviour?

If we have generalised expectations about people's typical reactions to particular kinds of situation, then a person's behaviour is predictable to the extent that we know about the situation. However, not all situations are equally powerful influences on behaviour, and so cannot be used equally to predict a person's behaviour. It follows that it's normal for any individual's behaviour to be only *partially* predictable or consistent and, in turn, that it's abnormal for a person to display either *extremely predictable* or *extremely unpredictable* behaviour.

If people act so consistently that they seem to be unaffected by situations (including the other people involved), it's almost as if they're *automata*. For example, someone suffering from paranoid delusions may see the world entirely in terms of others' harmful intentions.

This may, in turn, elicit certain kinds of responses in others, which may reinforce the delusions. According to Smith *et al.* (1986), people with behaviour disorders are unable to modify their behaviour in response to changing environmental requirements; their behaviour is maladaptive because it's inflexible and unrealistic. Equally, someone whose behaviour is very unpredictable is very difficult to interact with. People

Figure 43.3 Arnold Schwarzenegger in *Terminator*

with schizophrenia are often perceived as embodying this kind of unpredictability, which is unnerving and unsettling – for others!

Abnormality as mental illness

Many writers (e.g. Maher, 1966) have pointed out that the vocabulary we use to refer to psychological disorder is borrowed from medical terminology: deviant behaviour is referred to as *psychopathology*, is classified on the basis of *symptoms*, the classification being called a *diagnosis*, the methods used to try to change the behaviour are called *therapies*, and these are often carried out in *mental* or *psychiatric hospitals*. If the deviant behaviour ceases, the patient is described as *cured*.

Other related terms include *syndrome*, *prognosis*, and *in remission*. This way of talking about psychological abnormality reflects the pervasiveness of a 'sickness' (or medical) model. Whether we realise it or not, when we think about abnormal behaviour we tend to think about it as if it were indicative of some underlying illness.

How valid is the medical model?

Ask Yourself

- Try to formulate arguments for and against seeing abnormal behaviour as indicating mental illness.

Many defenders of the medical model have argued that it's more humane to regard a psychologically disturbed person as sick (or mad) than plain bad (it's more stigmatising to be regarded as morally defective; Blaney, 1975). However, when we label people as sick or ill, we're removing from them all responsibility for their behaviour. Just as we don't normally hold someone responsible for having cancer or a broken leg, so 'mental illness' implies that something has *happened* to the person. S/he is a victim who is, accordingly, put in the care (and often the custody) of doctors and nurses who'll take over responsibility.

The stigma attached to mental illness may actually be greater than that attached to labels of 'bad', because our fear of mental illness is even greater than our fear of becoming involved in crime or other immoral activities. This, in turn, is based on our belief that while illness 'just happens to people' (we've no control over it), at least there's some degree of *choice* involved in criminal activity.

Figure 43.4 During the Middle Ages, what we'd now call mental disorder was seen as possession by the devil or as witchcraft

Diagnostic labelling as a form of control

As we noted earlier, people considered to be 'mentally ill' are often unpredictable, something others find disturbing. Indeed, it's usually others who are disturbed by the patient's behaviour, rarely the patient (Laing, 1967). Attaching a diagnostic label represents a 'symbolic recapture' and this may be followed by a physical capture (hospitalisation, drugs, and so on; Szasz, 1974).

While medical diagnosis usually focuses only on the damaged or diseased parts of the body, psychiatric diagnosis describes the *whole person* – someone doesn't 'have' schizophrenia but *is* schizophrenic. This

Critical Discussion 43.2

Is psychiatry value-free?

As we saw in Critical Discussion 43.1, norms change within the same culture over time. Hence, the criteria used by psychiatry to judge abnormality must be seen in a *moral context*, not a medical one (Heather, 1976). Psychiatry's claim to be an orthodox part of medical science rests upon the concept of mental illness, but far from being another medical speciality, psychiatry is a 'quasi-medical illusion' (Heather, 1976).

Similarly, Szasz (1962) argues that the norms from which the mentally ill are thought to deviate have to be stated in psychological, ethical, and legal terms, and yet the remedy is sought in terms of medical measures. For this reason, Szasz believes that the concept of mental illness has replaced beliefs in demonology and witchcraft:

> *Mental illness thus exists or is 'real' in exactly the same sense in which witches existed or were real . . .*

It also serves the same *political* purposes. Whenever people wish to exclude others from their midst, they attach to them stigmatising labels (e.g. 'foreigner', 'criminal', 'mentally ill') (Littlewood and Lipsedge, 1997). Unlike people suffering from physical illness, most people considered to be mentally ill (especially those 'certified' or 'sectioned' and so legally mentally ill) are so defined by *others* (relatives, friends, employers, police, and so on). They've upset the social order (by violating or ignoring social laws and conventions), and so society labels them as mentally ill and (in many cases) 'punishes' them by committing them to a mental hospital (Szasz, 1974).

represents a new and total identity, which describes not only the person but also how s/he should be regarded and treated by others. Psychiatric diagnosis, therefore, is a form of *action*.

What are schizophrenics doing wrong?

In what ways are schizophrenics unpredictable, and what kinds of rules are they breaking? According to Scheff (1966), they're breaking *residual rules,* the 'unnameable' expectations we have regarding such things as 'decency' and 'reality'. These rules are themselves implicit, which makes behaviour that violates them difficult to understand and also difficult to articulate. This is what makes it seem strange and frightening.

According to Becker (1963), psychiatric intervention is based, generally speaking, on middle-class values regarding decent, reasonable, proper behaviour and experience. These are then applied to working-class patients, who constitute the vast majority of the inmates of psychiatric hospitals.

Mental illness or problems in living?

Szasz (e.g. 1962) is probably the most radical critic of the concept of mental illness. He argues that the basic assumption made by psychiatrists is that 'mental illness' is caused by diseases or disorders of the nervous system (in particular, the brain), which are revealed in abnormal thinking and behaviour. If this is the case, it would be better to call them 'diseases of the brain' or *neurophysiological disorders*; this would then get rid of any confusion between physical, organic defects (which must be seen in an anatomical and physiological context) and '*problems in living*' the person may have (which must be seen in an ethical and social context).

Figure 43.5 Thomas Szasz (1920–2012)

Szasz argues that the vast majority of cases of 'mental illness' are actually cases of problems of living. It's the exception rather than the rule to find a 'mentally ill' person who's actually suffering from some organic brain disease (such as in Alzheimer's disease, or alcohol poisoning). (See Table 43.1 and Critical Discussion 43.3.) This has traditionally been recognised by psychiatrists themselves, who distinguish between *organic* and *functional psychosis*. 'Functional' means that there's no demonstrable physical basis for the abnormal behaviour and that something has gone wrong with how the person functions in the network of relationships which make up their world (Bailey, 1979).

However, many psychiatrists believe that medical science will, in time, identify the physical causes of functional disorders (which include schizophrenia and psychotic depression); indeed, many claim that this point has already been reached (see Chapter 44). Yet according to Heather (1976), such evidence wouldn't cover all major categories of mental disorder (in particular, neurosis and personality disorder). Not even the most organically oriented psychiatrists would claim that these are bodily diseases in any sense! (But see Critical Discussion 43.3.)

While the views of Szasz and Heather are rather extreme, many other less radical critics of mainstream psychiatry have asked two related questions regarding psychiatric diagnosis:

1. Can mental health problems be 'created' through the *medicalisation* of everyday problems in living?
2. Is sadness – and even depression- a necessary – and even beneficial – part of human experience? (See Chapter 44.)

Diagnosis in general medicine and psychiatry

An important difference between diagnosis in general medicine and psychiatry is in the role of *signs* and *symptoms*. When doctors diagnose physical illnesses, they look for signs of disease (the results of objective tests, such as blood tests and X-rays, as well as physical examination) and symptoms (the patient's report of pain, and so on); they tend to attach more weight to the former. By contrast, psychiatrists are much more at the mercy of symptoms. Although psychological tests are the psychiatric equivalent of blood tests and X-rays, they're nothing like as reliable and valid (see Chapters 41 and 42) and, in practice, the psychiatrist will rely to a large extent on the patient's own description of the problem.

However, observation of the patient's behaviour, talking to relatives and others about the patient's behaviour and, increasingly, the use of brain-scanning techniques (such as CAT and PET: see below and Chapter 4) also contribute data regarding the signs of the illness (especially in the case of serious disorders, such as schizophrenia). Nevertheless, DSM and ICD are based largely on the abnormal experiences and beliefs reported by patients: we have no objective or biological markers for most neurotic or psychotic disorders (Frith and Cahill, 1995). (See Critical Discussion 43.3.)

A major change that took place in DSM-IV (1994) compared with DSM-III-R (1987) was the removal of the category 'organic mental disorders' and its replacement with 'delirium, dementia, amnesic and other cognitive disorders' (see Table 43.1). According to Davison and Neale (1994), this change was made because the term 'organic' implies that the other major categories don't have a biological basis; since research

Figure 43.6 A patient being assessed by a psychiatrist

has shown the influence of biological factors through a whole range of disorders, it's now considered misleading to use the term 'organic'. To this extent, the concept of psychological abnormality is even more *medicalised* than it's ever been. However, ICD retains a separate category for organic disorders.

THE CLASSIFICATION OF MENTAL DISORDERS

A brief history

An integral part of the medical model is the classification of mental disorder and the related process of diagnosis. All systems of classification stem from the work of Kraepelin, who published the first recognised textbook of psychiatry in 1883. Kraepelin claimed that certain groups of symptoms occur together sufficiently often for them to be called a 'disease' or syndrome. In other words, there's an underlying physical cause, just as a physical disease may be attributed to a physiological dysfunction (Davison *et al.*, 2004). He regarded each mental illness as distinct from all others, with its own origins, symptoms, course, and outcome.

Figure 43.7 Emil Kraepelin (1856–1926)

Kraepelin (1896) proposed two major groups of serious mental diseases: *dementia praecox* (the original term for schizophrenia) caused by a chemical imbalance, and *manic–depressive psychosis* caused by a faulty metabolism. His classification helped to establish the organic nature of mental disorders, and formed the basis for the *Diagnostic and Statistical Manual of Mental Disorders* (DSM), the APA's official classification system, and the *International Classification of Diseases* (ICD) (Chapter 5: 'Mental and behavioural disorders') published by the World Health Organization.

DSM-I was published in 1952, DSM-II in 1968, followed by DSM-III (1980), DSM-III-R (1987), DSM-IV (1994), and DSM-IV-TR (2000; TR stands for 'Text Revision'). The latest major revision is DSM-5 (2013). Mental disorders were included in ICD for the first time in 1948 (ICD-6) and ICD-10 was published in 1992. Table 43.1 shows the major categories of DSM-5 (including changes to DSM-IV-TR).

Kraepelin's classification is also embodied in the Mental Health Act 1983 (in England and Wales). The Act identifies three major categories of mental disturbance/disorder, namely, *mental illness* (neurosis and psychosis, the latter subdivided into organic and functional), *personality disorder* (including psychopathy), and *mental impairment.*

Table 43.1 Major categories of mental disorder in DSM-5 and category changes (based on Frances, 2013b; Reichenberg, 2014)

Major categories of mental disorder, with examples	Relationship to DSM-IV-TR and commentary
1. **NEURODEVELOPMENTAL DISORDERS**	
Attention-deficit/hyperactivity disorder (ADHD)	
Autism spectrum disorder (ASD)	'Autistic disorder' (severe classic autism) and 'Asperger's' now dropped
Intellectual developmental disorder	'Intellectual disability' replaces 'mental retardation'. Severity determined by level of adaptive functioning (rather than IQ)
Tic disorders (including Tourette's disorder)	
2. **SCHIZOPHRENIA SPECTRUM AND OTHER PSYCHOTIC DISORDERS**	
Schizophrenia	Subtypes removed
Schizophreniform disorder	
Schizoaffective disorder	
Delusional disorder	
Attenuated psychosis syndrome (APS)	Aimed at catching young people at risk before they develop full-blown psychosis. Appears in Section III of DSM-5*
Schizoptypal (personality) disorder	Also appears under 'Personality disorders'
3. **BIPOLAR AND RELATED DISORDERS**	
Bipolar I disorder	
Bipolar II disorder	
4. **DEPRESSIVE DISORDERS**	
Major depressive disorder (MDD)	
Chronic depressive disorders (dysthymic disorder)	
Disruptive mood dysregulation disorder (DMDD)	Applies to children up to age 18 with frequent temper tantrums. Justified by need to reduce overdiagnosis of childhood bipolar disorders
Premenstrual dysphoric disorder (PMDD)	Previously in DSM-IV-TR Appendix
Bereavement exclusion	This had 'protected' people in the early stages of 'normal' grief (first two months) from being diagnosed with mild MDD

Major categories of mental disorder, with examples	Relationship to DSM-IV-TR and commentary
Depressive episodes with short duration of hypomania	Section III*
Persistent complex bereavement disorder	Section III*
5. **ANXIETY DISORDERS**	
Panic disorder	
Agoraphobia	
Social anxiety disorder	Formerly 'social phobia'
Separation anxiety disorder (children and adults)	
Specific phobia	
Generalised anxiety disorder (GAD)	
6. **OBSESSIVE-COMPULSIVE AND RELATED DISORDERS**	
Obsessive-compulsive disorder (OCD)	Moved from anxiety disorders
Body dysmorphic disorder	Moved from somatoform disorders
Hoarding disorder	Previously a symptom of obsessive-compulsive personality disorder
Excoriation (skin-picking)	
Hair-pulling disorder (trichotillomaina)	Previously listed under 'Impulse-control disorder'
7. **TRAUMA- AND STRESSOR-RELATED DISORDERS**	
Post-traumatic stress disorder (PTSD)	Moved from anxiety disorders
Acute stress disorder	
Adjustment disorder	
8. **DISSOCIATIVE DISORDERS**	
Dissociative identity disorder (DID)	Formerly multiple personality disorder (MPD)
Depersonalisation/derealisation disorder	'Derealisation' previously considered a symptom of 'Depersonalisation'
9. **SOMATIC SYMPTOMS AND RELATED DISORDERS**	Formerly 'Somatoform disorders'
Somatic symptom disorder	
Factitious disorder	
Conversion disorder (Functional neurological symptom disorder)	
10. **FEEDING AND EATING DISORDERS**	
Anorexia nervosa (AN): (i) Restricting type; (ii) Binge-eating/purging type	Amenorrhea criterion dropped; severity (mild, moderate, severe, extreme) based on body-mass index (BMI)
Bulimia nervosa (BM)	Same severity criteria as for AN
Binge-eating disorder	Previously in Appendix
Avoidant/restrictive food intake disorder	Previously classified as a 'Feeding disorder of Infancy/Early Childhood'
Pica (children and adults)	Previously classified as 'Disorder usually first diagnosed in Childhood'

Major categories of mental disorder, with examples	Relationship to DSM-IV-TR and commentary
11. **ELIMINATION DISORDERS**	
Enuresis	
Encopresis	
12. **SLEEP-WAKE DISORDERS**	
Insomnia disorder	
Sleep apnea	
Narcolepsy	
13. **SEXUAL DYSFUNCTIONS**	
Female sexual desire and arousal disorder	
Premature (early) ejaculation	
14. **GENDER DYSPHORIA (ALL AGE GROUPS)**	Formerly 'Gender identity disorder'
15. **DISRUPTIVE, IMPULSE-CONTROL, AND CONDUCT DISORDERS**	
Kleptomania	
Pyromania	
Antisocial personality disorder	Also appears under 'Personality disorders'
16. **SUBSTANCE-RELATED AND ADDICTIVE DISORDERS**	
Substance use disorder (SUD)	Mild, moderate, severe
Alcohol; hallucinogen; opioid; tobacco; cannabis	There's a SUD linked to each of these: caffeine in Section III; 'substance abuse' and 'dependence' have been merged. 'Dependence' limited to *physiological* and 'craving' added (see Chapter 8)
Non-substance-related disorders	The first behaviour disorder to be included in this new category
Gambling disorder	Internet gaming disorder in Section III*
17. **NEUROCOGNITIVE DISORDERS (NCDs)**	
Delirium	
Major NCD (dementia)	Due to Alzheimer's disease, vascular dementia, traumatic brain injury, Parkinson's disease, HIV infection, Huntington's disease
Mild NCD	
18. **PERSONALITY DISORDERS**	
Paranoid, schizoid; antisocial; narcissistic; obsessive-compulsive	Unchanged
19. **PARAPHILIC DISORDERS**	
Paedophilic disorder	Previously 'paraphilias' (now regarded as a *prerequisite* for having a disorder – *not* a disorder in and of itself)
Sexual sadism/masochism disorder	
Fetishistic disorder	
Transvestic disorder	

*Section III is 'Conditions for Further Study' (there's insufficient evidence to warrant inclusion as an official disorder at the present time, but it does warrant further investigation).

Terms in bold in the first column denote either (a) completely new categories/categories of disorder ('chapters') or (b) a renamed category/disorder.

An evaluation of DSM-5

- Several of the changes shown in Table 43.1 and described below were intended to increase reliability and validity of diagnosis; this, in turn, would increase DSM's clinical utility and enhance its value for clinicians and researchers alike. They're also intended to make DSM more consistent with ICD (Reichenberg, 2014).
- Although the overall number of disorders has remained more or less the same, Frances (2013a) believes this is still a staggeringly large number.
- The order in which the mental disorders are listed (the 'chapters') is now *chronological*, i.e. it starts with 'Disorders Usually First Diagnosed in Childhood and Adolescence'. However, since the vast majority of disorders are 'adult', this isn't quite the 'lifespan' approach it claims. According to Frances (2013a), who led the DSM-IV revision, this is equivalent to rearranging deck chairs on the *Titanic*.
- The *multi-axial system* (originally introduced in DSM-III) has been dropped. The former Axis I (Clinical syndromes), II (Personality disorders; Mental retardation) and III (General medical condition) are combined, with separate notations for psychosocial and contextual factors (IV) (such as family separation/divorce) and Disability (V). The aim is to make DSM-5 more holistic and integrative.
- As genetic and neuroimaging studies improve our understanding of mental disorders, DSM will be able to respond to and incorporate this new understanding. It will be published both as a book and an electronic document that can be updated as necessary as version 5.1, 5.2 and so on. (This is why '5' was used instead of Roman numerals as in previous editions.)
- In an effort to improve diagnosis and care of people of all backgrounds, DSM-5 incorporates a greater cultural sensitivity throughout. Rather than a simple list of culture-bound syndromes (CBSs; see p. 747), DSM-5 updates criteria to reflect cross-cultural variations in how disorders are presented, gives more detailed and structured information about cultural concepts of distress, and includes a clinical interview tool to facilitate comprehensive, person-centred assessments. This *cultural formulation interview guide* includes questions about the patient's understanding of their symptoms and treatment options; it provides an opportunity for individuals to define their distress in their own words and then relate this to how others – who may not share their culture – perceive their problems (American Psychiatric Association, 2013).
- Different cultures and communities display or explain symptoms in various ways, which makes it important for clinicians to be aware of relevant contextual information stemming from a patient's culture, race, ethnicity, religion or geographical origin. For example, uncontrollable crying and headaches are symptoms of panic attacks in some cultures, while breathing difficulties may be the primary symptom in others. Attempts have been made to make the diagnostic criteria more applicable across different cultures. For example, the criteria for social anxiety disorder now include the fear of 'offending others' to reflect the Japanese concept in which avoiding harm to others is stressed rather than harm to oneself.
- According to Frances (2013a), 'there is no reason to believe that DSM-5 is safe or scientifically sound'. Disappointingly, 30 years of advancing knowledge has had no impact whatsoever on psychiatric diagnosis or treatment. *Translational research*, which bridges the gap between basic research and clinical application, has been distressingly slow in medicine as a whole, but is particularly difficult because the brain is so much more complex than any other organ. While we'll probably soon have accurate tests for Alzheimer's disease (which is included in DSM), there's nothing in the pipeline for any other mental disorder. It was hoped that DSM-5 would include such biomarkers, but mental disorders are too diverse and overlapping to be good research targets. This raises the fundamental question: Are mental disorders *real*? (See Critical Discussion 43.3.)

Figure 43.8 Bethlem Royal Hospital, London ('Bedlam'), the world's oldest institution for those with mental disorders

Cultural influences on mental disorder

Cooper (1994) asks whether the social consequences should be included among the defining features of a disorder itself, especially within an internationally used system such as ICD, since the social environment of individuals varies so widely between cultures:

Critical Discussion 43.3

The objective nature of mental disorders: do they exist?

According to Maddux *et al.* (2012), the single overriding question is: are psychopathology and related terms (such as mental disorder/mental illness) scientific terms that can be defined objectively and by scientific criteria, or are they *social constructions* (Gergen, 1985) that are defined largely or entirely by societal and cultural values? (See Gross, 2014.)

While the first two editions of DSM favoured a psychodynamic perspective, the definition of mental disorder in DSM-5 refers to a 'psychobiological dysfunction' in recognition that mental disorders, ultimately, reflect a *brain* dysfunction (Stein *et al.*, 2010).

Insel, 2009 (head of the US National Institute of Mental Health/NIMH) advocates a major shift away from the DSM's categorisation of mental disorders based on a person's symptoms. Instead, he wants mental disorders to be diagnosed more objectively using a combination of genetics, brain scans and cognitive testing. However, rapidly expanding knowledge about the genes and brain circuits underlying human behaviour is failing to generate major clinical advances.

The reason for this failure is that this knowledge doesn't readily map onto the disorders as described in DSM (Aldhous and Coghlan, 2013). Most mental disorders aren't 'real' in the way that what are now called *Neurocognitive disorders* are real; these include Alzheimer's disease and other dementias, traumatic brain injury, and Parkinson's disease. But this observation cuts two ways: it can either be interpreted in line with Szasz's rejection of the very concept of mental illness (see text above) or, as Insel advocates, supporting the view that *all* mental disorders are biological problems involving brain circuits underlying cognition, emotion and behaviour.

To speed up the shift to biologically based diagnosis, Insel favours an approach called the *Research Domain Criteria Project* (RDCP); this represents a biological alternative to DSM-5, with a strong focus on biological processes and neural circuits (Sanislow *et al.*, 2010). Priority for future research funding will be given to studies that formally adopt a 'clinical neuroscience' perspective (Insel, 2009).

Both DSM-5 and Insel's alternative approach are based on the assumption that each disorder has a specific and distinct cause. However, the considerable overlap between different disorders (*co-morbidities*) undermines this assumption (Kupfer *et al.*, 2002).

The BPS's Division of Clinical Psychology (DCP) issued a position statement in 2013; while not about DSM specifically, it was concerned with conceptual systems based on a 'disease' model (that would include ICD). The statement isn't a denial of the role of biology in mediating and enabling all forms of human experience, behaviour and distress and recognises the complex relationship between social, psychological and biological factors. It does, however, claim that it's neither accurate nor helpful to conceptualise the experiences that may lead to a 'functional' psychiatric diagnosis in terms of biological causal factors (such as genes and biochemistry). While the DCP doesn't object to classification *per se*, it does call for a 'paradigm shift' in the diagnosis of mental health problems, for an approach that's 'multifactorial, contextualises distress and behaviour, and acknowledges the complexity of the interactions involved in all human experience.'

The same symptoms and behaviour that are tolerated in one culture may cause severe social problems in another culture, and it is clearly undesirable for diagnostic decisions to be determined by cultural and social definitions.

Cooper seems to be saying that definitions of normality/abnormality are *culturally relative*. But he also implies that it's possible to diagnose mental disorders *independently* of cultural norms, values, and worldviews. This raises the fundamental question as to whether mental disorders exist in some objective sense (see Critical Discussion 43.3). Just as modern medicine is based on the assumption that physical illness is the same throughout the world, and that definition, classification, causation, and diagnosis are largely unaffected by cultural factors, so biologically-oriented psychiatrists argue that organic psychoses, in particular schizophrenia and depression, are also 'culture-free'. (See Critical Discussion 43.4.)

Several studies have found that, in a wide range of non-Western cultures, there are apparently unique ways of 'being mad' (Berry *et al.*, 1992) – that is, there are forms of abnormality that aren't easily accommodated by the categories of ICD or DSM. These *culture-bound syndromes* (CBSs) or 'exotic' disorders are first described in, and then closely or exclusively associated with, a particular population or

Critical Discussion 43.4

Is schizophrenia culture-free?

During the 1970s and 1980s, psychiatrists and Clinical Psychologists became increasingly interested in 'cultural psychiatry'. According to Berry *et al.* (1992), the central issue in the cross-cultural study of mental disorder is whether phenomena such as schizophrenia are:

- *absolute* – found in all cultures in precisely the same form
- *universal* – present in some form in all cultures, but subject to cultural influence
- *culturally relative* – unique to particular cultures and understandable only in terms of those cultures.

Of these three possibilities, only the first corresponds to a 'culture-free' view of abnormality. Berry *et al.* reject this view of abnormality, on the grounds that:

> *... cultural factors appear to affect at least some aspects of mental disorders, even those that are so closely linked to human biology.*

Universality is a more likely candidate for capturing the objective (biological) nature of mental disorder. Schizophrenia is the most commonly diagnosed mental disorder in the world, and of the major disorders, the largest number of culture-general symptoms has been reported for schizophrenia (WHO, 1973, 1979; Draguns, 1980, 1990).

However, according to Brislin (1993), there are at least three possible ways in which culture-specific factors can influence schizophrenia: (i) the form that symptoms will take, (ii) the precipitatory factor involved in the onset of the illness, and (iii) the prognosis.

1. When schizophrenics complain that their minds are being invaded by unseen forces, in North America and Europe these forces keep up to date with technological developments. So, in the 1920s, these were often voices from the radio; in the 1950s, they often came from TV, in the 1960s it was satellites in space, and in the 1970s and 1980s spirits were transmitted through microwave ovens. In cultures where witchcraft is considered common, the voices or spirits would be directed by unseen forces under the control of demons.
2. Day *et al.* (1987) studied schizophrenia in nine different locations in the USA, Asia, Europe, and South America. Acute schizophrenic attacks were associated with stressful events 'external' to the patients (such as losing one's job, unexpected death of spouse), which tended to cluster within a two- to three-week period before the onset of obvious symptoms. Some events could only be understood as stressful if the researchers had considerable information about the cultural background of the sample.
3. Lin and Kleinman (1988) found that the prognosis for successful treatment of schizophrenia was better in non-industrialised than industrialised societies. The former provide more structured, stable, predictable, and socially supportive environments that allow schizophrenic patients to recover at their own pace and to be reintegrated into society.

cultural area, with the local, indigenous name being used. DSM-IV-TR defines them as:

> *... locality-specific patterns of aberrant behaviour and troubling experience that may or may not be linked to a persistent DSM-IV diagnostic category ... (American Psychological Association, 2000)*

For example, *Koro, jinjin bemar, suk yeong, suo-yang* (usually just 'Koro') refers to an acute panic/anxiety reaction to the belief, in a man, that his penis will suddenly withdraw into his abdomen, or in a woman that her breasts, labia or vulva will retract into her body. This is reported in south-east Asia, south China and India. Other examples include *amok, brain fag, dhat*, and *ghost sickness*. These disorders are 'outside' the mainstream of abnormality as defined by, and 'enshrined' within, the classification systems of western psychiatry, which determines the 'standard'. The underlying assumption is that mental disorders in the West are *culturally neutral*, that they can be defined and diagnosed objectively, while only CBSs show the influence of culture (Fernando, 1991).

Figure 43.9 Amok – a culture-bound syndrome. But aren't western mental disorders also influenced by culture?

At the same time, these (and other) cross-cultural studies suggest that the concept of mental disorder isn't merely an expression of western values, but represents a basic human way of perceiving certain behaviour as evidence of abnormal psychological processes. According to Price and Crapo (1999):

> *... mental disorders occur in all cultures ... all cultures appear to label some specific behaviours in a way that is similar to the categories and definitions used by western psychiatry ...*

Problems with the classification of mental disorder

One of the most famous studies criticising basic psychiatric concepts and practices is that of Rosenhan (1973). The intention was to test the hypothesis that psychiatrists cannot reliably tell the difference between people who are genuinely mentally ill and those who aren't (see Key Study 43.1).

Ask Yourself

- What conclusions can you draw about psychiatric diagnosis from Rosenhan's study? Was his hypothesis supported?
- Are there any features of the study that would make generalisation difficult?

Since reliability is a necessary prerequisite for validity, the implications of Rosenhan's results for the traditional psychiatric classification of mental disorders are very serious indeed.

Reliability

Diagnosis is the process of identifying a disease and allocating it to a category on the basis of symptoms and signs. Clearly, any system of classification will be of little value unless psychiatrists can agree with one another when trying to reach a diagnosis (*inter-rater/ inter-judge reliability*) and represents a fundamental requirement of any classification system (Gelder *et al.*, 1989, 1999).

Studies conducted in the 1970s consistently showed poor diagnostic reliability. Since then, things have slowly improved. Much more attention is now paid to how symptoms of a given disorder may differ depending on the *culture* in which it appears (see Critical Discussion 43.4 and 'Evaluation of DSM-5').

Despite some DSM categories (still) having greater reliability than others, this is now quite acceptable for most of the major categories (Davison *et al.*, 2004). However, problems remain.

- Specifying a particular number of symptoms from a longer list that must be evident before a particular diagnosis can be made seems very arbitrary.
- There's still room for *subjective interpretation* on the part of the psychiatrist. For instance, the elevated mood must be 'abnormally and persistently elevated' in order to diagnose mania. This begs all sorts of questions.
- However, Falek and Moser (1975) found that agreement between doctors regarding angina, emphysema and tonsillitis (diagnosed without a definitive laboratory test) was no better (and sometimes actually worse) than that for schizophrenia. Clare (1980) argues that the nature of

Key Study 43.1

On being sane in insane places (Rosenhan, 1973)

- Eight psychiatrically 'normal' people (a Psychology student, three Psychologists, a paediatrician, a psychiatrist, a painter–decorator, and a housewife) presented themselves at the admissions offices of 12 different psychiatric hospitals in the USA, complaining of hearing voices saying 'empty', 'hollow' and 'thud' (auditory hallucinations).
- These symptoms, together with their names and occupations, were the only falsification of the truth involved at any stage of the study.
- All eight *pseudo-patients* were admitted (in 11 cases with a diagnosis of 'schizophrenia', in the other 'manic depression'), after which they stopped claiming to hear voices. They were eventually discharged with a diagnosis of 'schizophrenia (or manic depression) in remission' (i.e. without signs of illness).
- The only people to have been suspicious of their true identity were some of their 'fellow' patients. It took between 7 and 52 days (average 19) for them to convince the staff that they were well enough to be discharged.
- In a second experiment, members of a teaching hospital were told about the findings of the original study, and were warned that some pseudo-patients would be trying to gain admission during a particular three-month period. Each member of staff was asked to rate every new patient as an impostor or not. During the experimental period, 193 patients were admitted, of whom 41 were confidently alleged to be impostors by at least one member of staff, 23 were suspected by one psychiatrist, and a further 19 were suspected by one psychiatrist and one other staff member. All were genuine patients.

physical illness is not as clear-cut as the critics of the medical model claim. While agreeing with criticisms of psychiatric diagnosis, Clare believes these should be directed at psychiatrists and not the process of diagnosis in general.

Validity

This is much more difficult to assess than reliability, because for most disorders there's no absolute standard against which diagnosis can be compared. However much we improve reliability, this is no guarantee that the patient has received the 'correct' diagnosis (Holmes, 1994). (See Critical Discussion 43.3.)

Predictive validity

The primary purpose of making a diagnosis is to enable a suitable programme of treatment to be chosen. Treatment cannot be selected randomly, but is aimed at eliminating the underlying cause of the disorder (where it's known). But in psychiatry there's only a 50 per cent chance of predicting correctly what treatment a patient will receive on the basis of diagnosis (Heather, 1976). Bannister *et al.* (1964) found there was simply no clear-cut connection between diagnosis and treatment in 1000 cases. One reason for this seems to be that factors other than diagnosis may be equally important in deciding on a particular treatment.

For example, not only are black people in the UK more likely to be diagnosed as schizophrenic or compulsorily admitted to psychiatric hospital, they're also more likely to be given major tranquillisers or electroconvulsive therapy (ECT) than white people (Fernando, 1988). All ethnic minorities are less likely to be referred for psychotherapy than indigenous white people, and similar differences have been reported between working-class and middle-class groups. Women are also more likely to be diagnosed as psychiatrically ill than men (Winter, 1999; see Chapters 44 and 47). Winter (1999) believes that one viable explanation for these differences is that:

> *... general practitioners and psychiatrists, who are predominantly white, middle class and male, may be biased against, or insufficiently sensitive to the cultural and social situations of, black, working-class or female clients ...*

Response to treatment is also difficult to predict (Winter, 1999). (See Chapter 45).

Construct validity

This is the most relevant form of validity in relation to diagnosis. According to Davison *et al.* (2004), the categories are *constructs* because they're *inferred* – not proven – entities. For example, a diagnosis of schizophrenia doesn't have the same status as a diagnosis of, say, diabetes. With physical disease, there's a real sense in which patients 'have' it, and it's feasible to distinguish them from their disease. But even in the more extreme psychotic states, it's impossible to divorce the condition from the person (Marzillier, 2004).

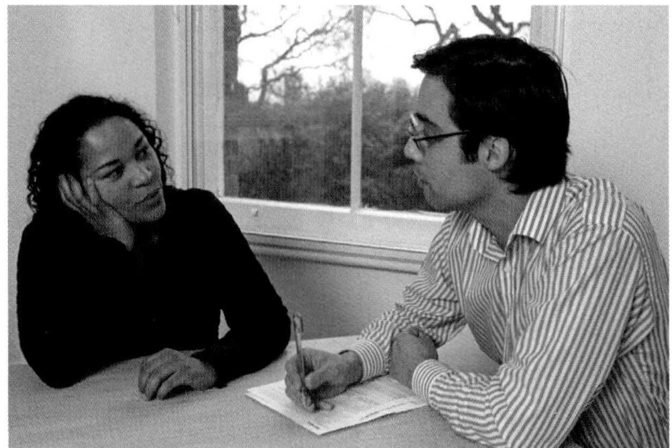

Figure 43.10 Culture plays a part in all aspects of psychiatric assessment and treatment

Construct validity is determined by evaluating the extent to which accurate statements and predictions can be made about a category. For example, to what extent does the construct form part of a network of lawful relationships? These relationships could concern:

- possible causes (such as genetic predisposition or biochemical imbalance: see Chapter 44)
- characteristics of the disorder that aren't symptoms as such, but are associated with the disorder (such as poor social skills in schizophrenia)
- predictions about the course of the disorder and probable response to particular treatments (see above).

Davison *et al.* (2004) believe that the DSM diagnostic categories do indeed possess some construct validity – some more than others. However, according to Mackay (1975):

> *The notion of illness implies a relatively discrete disease entity with associated signs and symptoms, which has a specific cause, a certain probability of recovery and its own treatments. The various states of unhappiness, anxiety and confusion which we term 'mental illness' fall far short of these criteria in most cases.*

Pilgrim (2000) argues that calling madness 'schizophrenia', or misery 'depression' merely *technicalises* ordinary judgements. What do we add by calling someone who communicates unintelligibly 'schizophrenic'? Similarly, Winter (1999) argues that diagnostic systems are only aids to understanding, not necessarily descriptions of real disease entities.

CONCLUSIONS: TO CLASSIFY OR NOT TO CLASSIFY?

Ask Yourself

- Do you think it's scientifically valid – and ethically acceptable – to categorise people in terms of mental disorders?

The case for

- Classifications are needed in psychiatry, as in medicine, to aid communication about the nature of patients' problems, prognosis and treatment. It obviously helps when exchanging information about individual cases if there's some agreed terminology available and if a label can be assigned that distinguishes one patient's disorder from another's (Aboraya, 2012; Claridge and Davis, 2003; Gelder *et al.*, 1989).
- Assuming that various types of abnormal behaviour do differ from one another, classifying them is essential: these differences may facilitate decision making regarding their causes and treatments (Aboraya, 2012; Claridge and Davis, 2003; Davison *et al.,* 2004).
- Classification allows research to be conducted with comparable groups of patients (Gelder *et al.*, 1989).

The case against

- The very fact that there are different classification schemes (DSM and ICD are the most commonly used and cited, but aren't the only ones) demonstrates that there's a certain degree of *arbitrariness* about how people are diagnosed. DSM-5 and ICD-10 merely represent the *current* (or most recent) beliefs of experts in the field about how psychological disorders should be classified (Claridge and Davis, 2003). These limitations relate to the validity of classification (see above).
- Similarly, the fact that DSM has undergone several revisions confirms the *constructive* nature of attempts to classify psychological disorders. As Critical Discussion 43.1 shows, psychiatrists can, and do, change their views regarding what should count as a disorder in response to wider social and cultural changes. Critical Discussion 43.2 shows, in addition, that psychiatry reflects fundamental social values. In both these ways, classification can never be completely objective or based on science alone.
- A central problem for DSM in particular, and classification of disorders in general, is the tendency for an individual to meet the diagnostic criteria for more than one disorder (*comorbidity*). This is well documented in medicine, but in these cases the two illnesses/conditions have quite separate aetiology and they *look* very different. But in psychiatry, comorbid disorders often seem surprisingly similar, as though they share a common cause and underlying mechanism (Claridge and Davis, 2003).
- Categorical models assess the presence or absence of a *disorder* and don't allow for evaluation of the *severity* of the disorder in question. For example, two patients, each diagnosed with schizophrenia, may present very different symptoms, and may be receiving quite different treatment regimens (Aboraya, 2012). Classifying patients in this way inevitably results in the loss of considerable detailed information about them as individuals.

Categories versus dimensions

As we've seen, the classification of mental disorders is *categorical*. Abnormality is assumed to differ *qualitatively* from normality, so that a person either belongs in a particular category or doesn't. But some researchers have argued that the most appropriate system for diagnosing and assessing mental disorders is *dimensional*: abnormality and normality are only *quantitatively* different (involving a *continuum* of severity; Lilienfeld, 1998; Maddux *et al.,* 2012; Widiger, 2012).

These two approaches mirror the important difference between psychiatry and Psychology. According to Pilgrim (2000), diagnosis is a medical task that creates a simple dichotomy between the sick and the well: 'Is this person suffering from a mental disorder or not?' (and by extension, if 'yes', 'which one?'). By contrast, Psychologists assume a *continuity* between normal and abnormal: 'How do we account for this person's actions and experience in this particular context?' The experiences that lead people to be diagnosed as 'mentally ill' are experiences that all of us can have in some form or at some stage (Marzillier, 2004).

According to Bentall (2003), many contemporary approaches to the problem of 'madness', 'although cloaked with the appearance of scientific rigour, have more in common with astrology than rational science'. Two serious misunderstandings are, first, that madness can be divided into a small number of diseases and, second, that the manifestation or 'symptoms' of madness cannot be understood in terms of the psychology of the person who suffers from them.

Gelder *et al.* (1989) believe that:

> *The use of classification can certainly be combined with consideration of a patient's unique qualities, indeed it is important to combine the two because these qualities can modify prognosis and need to be taken into account in treatment ...*

In other words, the categorical and dimensional approaches aren't necessarily incompatible. Figure 43.11c suggests how they might be combined.

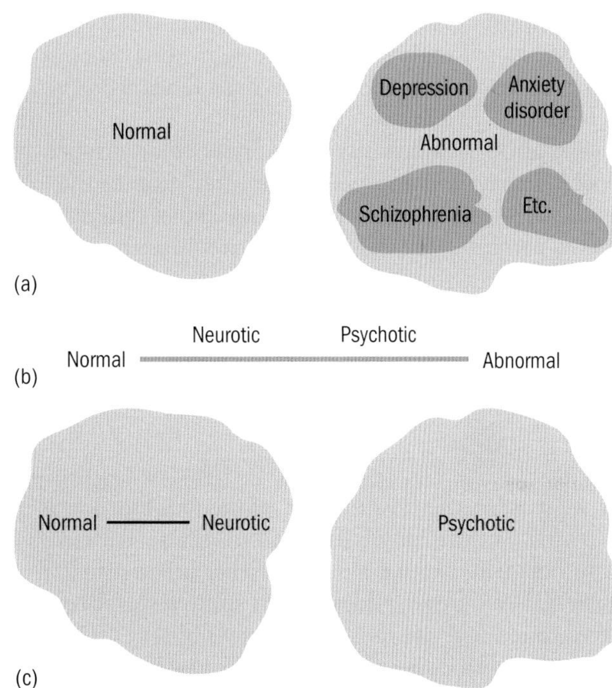

Figure 43.11 Representations of (a) the categorical and (b) the dimensional view of abnormality; (c) combines (a) and (b)

Indeed, DSM-5 requires psychiatrists to grade the *severity* of the patient's symptoms (see Table 43.1): this ideological shift signals a step away from the simplistic notion that mental disorders are discrete conditions wholly distinct from 'mental health' (Jabr, 2012). This incorporation of a *dimensional* approach should both increase the reliability of diagnosis and make treatments more tailored to patients' needs. (This combination of categorical and dimensional models within the same diagnostic system is called a *hybrid model*; Aboraya, 2012). The challenge for DSM-5 is to 'find ways to create dimensional measures that are compatible with categorical definitions and not overly disruptive to clinical practice' (Helzer *et al.*, 2008).

However, the proposed measures (including severity) are vague, complicated, not designed for clinical applications and insufficiently researched to justify their inclusion (Aboraya, 2012; Simonsen, 2010). For example, dimensional approaches don't solve the subjectivity problem: the decision regarding how far from the mean a person's thoughts, feelings or behaviour must be to be considered abnormal remains a subjective one.

While a primary goal of DSM-5 was to move towards a dimensional classification (Helzer *et al.*, 2008; Regier *et al.*, 2010), the move is neither fundamental nor significant. The dimensions serve as ancillary descriptions that lack any official status within a patient's medical records. Essentially, DSM-5 remains a categorical dimensional system (Widiger, 2012).

Chapter Summary

- Abnormality as **deviation from the average** (the **statistical criterion**) defines abnormality as not behaving in the way that most people do. But this fails to distinguish between atypical behaviour that's desirable and undesirable.
- **Deviation from the norm** defines abnormality as not behaving or feeling as one **should**. But it's not obvious what norms are being broken in the case of mental disorder.
- The **deviation from ideal mental health** criterion involves **value judgements** about ideal states that are culturally defined (unlike physical health).
- Abnormality as **personal distress/suffering** defines abnormality in terms of subjective experiences. **Other people's distress** may act as a counterbalance to the lack of insight shown by some people with a mental disorder.
- Abnormality as **maladaptiveness** focuses on the **consequences** of abnormal behaviour for the individual, especially being prevented from achieving one's goals.
- Abnormality as **unexpected behaviour** means over-reacting to something, but **under-reacting** could be considered just as abnormal. Behaviour that's highly **consistent/predictable** or highly **inconsistent/unpredictable** may be considered abnormal.
- The way we talk about psychological disorder reflects the **medical model.** Critics argue that the norms from which the mentally ill are thought to deviate are expressed in moral, psychological and legal terms, not medical ones, yet the solution takes the form of medical treatment.
- According to Scheff, schizophrenics are breaking **residual rules**, which tend to reflect middle-class values regarding 'decency' and 'reality'.
- According to Szasz, individuals diagnosed as mentally ill either have **neurophysiological disorders** (corresponding to **organic psychosis**) or, more often, **problems in living** (corresponding to **functional psychosis**).
- An integral part of the medical model is the **classification** of mental disorder and the related process of **diagnosis.** All systems of classification stem from Kraepelin's identification of **dementia praecox** (schizophrenia) and **manic–depressive psychosis.**

- In an effort to improve diagnosis and care of people of all backgrounds, DSM-5 incorporates greater **cultural sensitivity**.
- But it has also been criticised for its near total lack of biomarkers for mental disorders (except Alzheimer's disease). This calls into question the **objective nature** of mental disorders.
- Both DSM and ICD have dropped the traditional distinction between **neurosis** and **psychosis**. Psychosis is a much more serious form of mental disorder, due to loss of contact with reality, and is **qualitatively different** from 'normal' behaviour.
- The **cross-cultural** study of schizophrenia tries to determine whether it's **absolute** ('culture-free'), **universal** or **culturally relative**. Culture can influence the form of symptoms, precipitating events for the onset of symptoms, and prognosis.
- **Culture-bound syndromes (CBSs)** are seen as falling outside mainstream classifications of disorder, implying that Western mental disorders are objective and uninfluenced by cultural factors. However, all cultures seem to have the concept of mental disorder.
- **Inter-rater/judge reliability** has been improved in more recent versions of both DSM and ICD by the use of **standardised interview schedules** and **explicit diagnostic criteria**. But there's still room for **subjective interpretation**.
- **Validity** is more difficult to assess in the absence of absolute standards. For a diagnosis to be considered valid, it should allow prediction of treatment and recovery, as well as implying the cause(s) of the disorder.
- Mainstream psychiatry's **categorical** view of abnormality differs from Psychologists' preference for a **dimensional** approach. But these two approaches aren't mutually exclusive.

Links with Other Topics/Chapters

Chapter 12 ⟶ The concepts of *health*, *illness* and *disease* are central to *Health Psychology*

Chapter 30 ⟶ In the context of definitions of abnormality, *helping* the 'patient' could be motivated either by an *altruistic desire* to end his/her distress, or by an *egoistic desire* to end the helper's own distress. This distinction applies to *bystander intervention*

Chapters 23 and 30 ⟶ The *attribution of blame and responsibility* (denied to the mentally ill) is relevant to understanding why certain types of *victim* are more or less likely to be helped

Chapter 41 ⟶ The idea that schizophrenia might be found in all cultures in precisely the same form ('culture-free') corresponds to the belief that it's possible to construct *culture-free tests of intelligence*

Chapter 49 ⟶ Szasz's argument, that only the brain can literally be diseased, and not the mind, breaks down if we identify the mind with the brain

Chapter 47 ⟶ While *Cross-cultural Psychology* looks for *universal* aspects of human behaviour, *Cultural Psychology* focuses on how behaviour *differs* between cultures (*cultural relativism*)

Chapter 3 ⟶ Regular revisions of DSM and other classification systems have a parallel in the *scientific revolutions* (involving *paradigm shifts*) described by Kuhn. Both illustrate the *social nature* of scientific activity

Chapter 42 ⟶ Eysenck is largely responsible for introducing the *dimensional approach* to abnormality through his *theory of personality*

Chapter 42 ⟶ The categorical system adopts a *nomothetic approach* (e.g. what all schizophrenics have in common), while psychotherapists and Psychologists favour an *idiographic approach*

Recommended Reading

Bentall, R.P. (2003) *Madness Explained: Psychosis and Human Nature*. London: Penguin.

Gross, R. (2012) *Key Studies in Psychology* (6th edn). London: Hodder Education. Chapter 8.

Lilienfeld, S.O. (1995) *Seeing Both Sides: Classic Controversies in Abnormal Psychology*. Pacific Grove, CA: Brooks/Cole Publishing Company. Also relevant to Chapters 44 and 45.

Littlewood, R. & Lipsedge, M. (1997) *Aliens and Alienists: Ethnic Minorities and Psychiatry* (3rd edn). Oxford: Routledge.

Maddux, J.E. & Winstead, B.A. (eds) (2012) *Psychopathology: Foundations for Contemporary Understanding* (3rd edn). New York: Routledge. Chapters 1–6.

Reichenberg, L.W. (2014) *DSM-5 Essentials: The Savvy Clinician's Guide to the Changes in Criteria*. Hoboken, NJ: Wiley.

Useful Websites

www.sane.org.uk (SANE: Meeting the challenge of mental illness)

www.mind.org.uk (MIND: For better mental health)

www.who.int/mental_health/en/ (World Health Organization: Mental health)

www.mental-health-matters.com/index.php?option=com_content&view=category&id=83 (Mental Health Matters)

www.understandingpsychosis.com (British Psychological Society Division of Clinical Psychology report on psychosis, 2007)

www.critpsynet.freeuk.com/index.htm (Critical Psychiatry Network)

www.hearing-voices.org (Hearing Voices Network)

CHAPTER 44

PSYCHOPATHOLOGY

Anxiety disorders

Obsessive–compulsive and related disorders

Trauma and stress-related disorders

Depressive and bipolar disorders

Schizophrenic spectrum and other psychotic disorders

Feeding and eating disorders

INTRODUCTION and OVERVIEW

As we saw in Chapter 43, the classification of mental disorders is an integral part of the medical model. DSM-5 (2013) (and ICD-10, 2000) identify several general categories of mental disorder, within each of which are found a number of specific disorders. This chapter samples some of the disorders which, both historically and currently, have attracted most research interest, and often the most debate and controversy, both within and outside psychiatry.

Anxiety disorders in DSM include *phobic disorders* (such as agoraphobia and specific phobia). *Obsessive–compulsive disorder* (OCD) was reclassified from an anxiety disorder (in DSM-IV-TR) to an *Obsessive-compulsive and related disorder* (in DSM-5). Similarly, *post-traumatic stress disorder* (PTSD) was reclassified from an anxiety disorder to a *Trauma- and Stressor-related disorder'*. Two major *Feeding and Eating disorders* are *anorexia nervosa* (AN) and *bulimia nervosa* (BN).

Of all the disorders identified in DSM, *schizophrenia* is the most serious (now falling under the *schizophrenic spectrum and other psychotic disorders* category). Kraepelin (1913) called the disorder *dementia praecox* (senility of youth), believing that it occurred early in adult life and was characterised by a progressive deterioration or dementia. However, Bleuler (1911) observed that it also began in later life, and wasn't always characterised by dementia. Bleuler coined the word 'schizophrenia' to refer to a splitting of the mind's various functions, in which the personality loses its unity.

Depressive disorders and *Bipolar* and related *disorders* (two separate categories, previously classified as *Mood* (or *affective*) *disorders*: see Table 43.1) involve a prolonged and fundamental disturbance of mood and emotions. At one extreme is *manic disorder* (or *mania*), and at the other is *major depressive disorder* (MDD). Mania usually occurs in conjunction with depression (*bipolar disorder*). The term *unipolar* is reserved for the occurrence of depression on its own. (The term *manic–depressive* refers to both the unipolar and bipolar forms of affective disorder.)

ANXIETY DISORDERS

Of all forms of psychological distress, emotional disturbances are perhaps the most common (Lilienfeld, 1998), and 'fear is a core emotion in psychopathology' (LeDoux, 1998a, 1998b). While *anxiety* (a brooding fear of what might happen) was a central feature of Freud's psychoanalytic theory (LeDoux, 1998), many Psychologists have argued that *fear* is a fundamentally *adaptive* reaction to stressors (specifically, threat). It's generally considered abnormal only when it's disproportionate to objective circumstances. Fear probably evolved as an alarm signal to warn organisms of potential danger, but some people tend to feel afraid even when there's no (objective) threat present: these 'false alarms' are what we call anxiety disorders.

For example, people with *panic disorder* experience sudden surges of extreme terror, even in perfectly safe environments. As Lilienfeld (1998) says:

> *... it is this mismatch between the severity of individuals' emotional reactions and of objective stressors that makes panic disorder psychopathological ...*

> **Ask Yourself**
> - While this might seem like a perfectly reasonable way of distinguishing normal from abnormal anxiety, can you see any flaws in the argument?
> - How does it relate to the categorical/dimensional approaches discussed in Chapter 43?

Phobic disorders

A *phobia* is an extreme, irrational fear of some specific object or situation. Typically, the patient acknowledges that the object of fear is harmless, but the fear is experienced nonetheless (this is the irrational element). Trying to avoid the feared object or situation at all costs can interfere with the person's normal functioning, and distinguishes a phobia from a milder fear or mere dislike of something. Attempts to hide the phobia from others may induce further anxiety, guilt, and shame. Almost anything may become the object of a phobia, but some phobias are much more common than others.

Figure 44.1 Astraphobia

Agoraphobia

This is the most common of all phobias (accounting for about 60 per cent of all phobic patients), and occurs predominantly in women (while most other phobias tend to be fairly evenly divided between the genders). While agoraphobia is commonly defined as fear of open spaces, the *primary* fear is leaving the safety and security of home and/or companions. Fear of being in public places is *secondary* but, significantly, this is what the patient is usually aware of.

Figure 44.2 Having to make a speech in front of any kind of audience is likely to induce some degree of anxiety in most people. As a social phobia, anxiety over public speaking is an intense and excessive fear of being exposed to scrutiny by other people; it's an example of performance social phobia

Specific phobias

Most phobias fall into this category (see Box 44.1), and definitions of phobias usually relate to specific phobias. Generally, these are less disruptive than agoraphobia or social phobias. They can develop at any time of life, although some are quite common in childhood (such as cynophobia: fear of dogs; and nycotophobia: fear of the dark), while 'illness and injury' phobias (and thanatophobia: fear of death) tend to occur in middle age.

Explaining phobias

> **Ask Yourself**
> - How would Freud account for phobias (see Chapter 43)?
> - How would learning theory explain them (see Chapter 11)?

OBSESSIVE–COMPULSIVE AND RELATED DISORDERS

Obsessive–compulsive disorder (OCD)

Obsessions are recurrent, unwanted, intrusive thoughts or images that don't feel voluntarily controlled, and which are experienced as morally repugnant or intensely distressing. They mostly have sexual, blasphemous, or aggressive themes (see Case Study 44.1). For example, it's not uncommon for deeply religious people to have repeated

Box 44.1 Preparedness

Rosenhan and Seligman (1984) propose an interaction between biological and conditioning factors that predisposes us to acquire phobias of certain classes of stimuli.

According to the concept of *preparedness/ prepared conditioning*, we're genetically prepared to fear things that were sources of danger in our evolutionary past.

However, while certain animals that might have posed a danger to our ancestors tend to be those about which we're most likely to develop a phobia (such as snakes and spiders – both of which are poisonous in many parts of the world), whether or not we develop such a phobia depends very much on our early experience with them (Workman and Reader, 2008).

Hugdahl and Ohman (1977) have shown that in laboratory experiments, people without pre-existing phobias can be conditioned more easily to snakes than flowers.

However, snakes have a negative 'reputation' or social status, while flowers are generally viewed positively and are completely non-threatening. So, although preparedness as an explanation for direct conditioning may not be valid, preparedness for observational and instructional learning is possible (Murray and Foote, 1979; Rachman, 1977).

Figure 44.3

Case Study 44.1

Obsession without the compulsion (Sutherland, 1976)

An example of an obsession occurring without compulsive behaviour is sexual jealousy, an extreme case of which is described by Stuart Sutherland in *Breakdown* (1976).

Sutherland was a well-known British Experimental Psychologist who'd been happily married for several years when his wife suddenly revealed she'd been having an affair (but had no wish to end their marriage). At first, he was able to accept the situation, and found that the increased honesty and communication actually improved their marriage.

However, after asking his wife for further details of the affair, he became obsessed with vivid images of his wife in moments of sexual passion with her lover, and he couldn't remove these thoughts from his mind, day or night.

Finally, he had to leave his teaching and research duties, and it was only after several months of trying various forms of therapy that he managed to reduce the obsessive thoughts sufficiently to be able to return to work.

blasphemous thoughts, such as 'God doesn't exist', or for caring parents to have thoughts of harming their children. These obsessions are resisted by being ignored or suppressed, or by 'neutralising' them with some other thought or action (Shafran, 1999); these may include compulsions.

Compulsions are actions which the victim feels compelled to repeat over and over again, according to rituals or rules. Obsessions and compulsions are often related, the latter representing an attempt to counteract the former. For example, compulsive hand-washing may be an attempt to remove the obsessive preoccupation with contamination by dirt or germs, either as agent or victim. While the person recognises that the compulsive act is unreasonable and excessive, it's also seen as purposeful. The function of compulsive acts is to prevent a dreaded event and reduce distress. Many patients find the need to perform the compulsion distressing in itself, and are frustrated by the time it takes to complete it 'correctly' and how it interferes with normal social and work functioning.

Shafran (1999) gives the example of a man who was obsessed with the thought that he'd contracted AIDS from sitting next to someone who looked unkempt. In response to this, he repeatedly checked his body for signs of illness and washed his hands whenever he

Figure 44.4 Compulsive hand-washing is often an attempt to remove an obsessive preoccupation with contamination

had an intrusive image of this person. When outside, he'd continually check to see if there were any discarded tissues that might carry HIV. This became so laborious that he stayed indoors for much of the time; any interruption to the checking and washing resulted in the entire routine starting again.

Until quite recently, OCD was regarded as a rare disorder (affecting less than 0.5 per cent of the population). Now, however, it's the fourth most common disorder, and lifetime prevalence is at least 3 per cent in females and 2 per cent in males. In the UK, an estimated one to one and a half million people suffer from OCD. According to Claridge and Davis (2003), it's still often under-diagnosed and under-treated in most populations.

Explaining OCD

Behavioural explanations

Ask Yourself

- How might you explain OCD in terms of conditioning principles? (See Chapter 11.)

An evaluation of behavioural explanations

See Box 44.2.

Cognitive–behavioural explanations

One currently popular account is Rachman's (1993) *thought-action fusion* (TAF), which involves appraising intrusive thoughts as equivalent to actions. One of its great strengths is that it can explain OCD symptoms in terms of everyday, 'normal' cognition and behaviour. (For a more detailed account, see Claridge and Davis, 2003.)

Box 44.2 The Superstition Hypothesis

While *negative reinforcement* (e.g. Rachman and Hodgson, 1980) can account for the *maintenance* of OCD, it doesn't explain how it develops in the first place. Skinner (1948a) argued that what we call 'superstition' develops as a result of a chance association between some behaviour and a reinforcer. In Skinner's experiments, pigeons were given food at regular intervals regardless of their behaviour. After a while, they displayed idiosyncratic movements, presumably because these were the movements they happened to be making when the food was given.

This chance reinforcement of behaviour can account for many compulsive rituals (O'Leary and Wilson, 1975). For example, the rituals of soccer players may include being last on to the pitch, or wearing only a particular pair of boots. Such behaviours may occur because in the past they were associated with success. If such rituals aren't enacted, anxiety is aroused.

However, while such chance associations might explain how particular behaviours arise, the development of intrusive thoughts are much more difficult to explain by the behavioural model.

Figure 44.5 The 'lucky kiss', a common form of superstitious behaviour among sportsmen and women

TRAUMA- AND STRESSOR-RELATED DISORDERS

Post-traumatic stress disorder (PTSD)

During the First World War, many soldiers experienced *shell shock* (a shock-like state which followed the traumatic experiences of prolonged combat). In the Second World War, *combat fatigue* (or 'traumatic neurosis') was used to describe a similar reaction, characterised by terror, agitation or apathy, and insomnia.

Following the Vietnam War, the syndrome was renamed *post-traumatic stress disorder* (PTSD) and first appeared by that name in DSM-III (1980). The term describes an anxiety disorder which occurs in response to an extreme psychological or physical trauma outside the range of normal human experience (Thompson, 1997). Apart from war, such traumas include a physical threat to one's self or family, witnessing other people's deaths, and being involved in natural or human-made disasters. Examples include the Hillsborough football tragedy, the *Herald of Free Enterprise* cross-channel ferry disaster, and the 7/7 London bombings in 2005.

Figure 44.6 197 people died when the *Herald of Free Enterprise* ferry capsized off Zeebrugge, Belgium, in 1987

Box 44.3 The major characteristics of PTSD

Increased arousal: severe anxiety, irritability, insomnia, poor concentration. There may also be panic attacks and episodes of aggression.
Persistent defences of avoidance and repression: avoidance of reminders of the events, difficulty in recalling the events at will, detachment, inability to feel emotion ('numbness'), diminished interest in activities.

Intrusions: memories of the traumatic events break through the repression as repeated, intense imagery ('flashbacks'), and distressing dreams. Anxiety increases further during flashbacks and reminders of the event.

There may also be additional maladaptive coping responses, such as excessive use of alcohol and drugs. Some people with PTSD may even pose a risk of suicide or violence (Rana and Rana, 2013).

(Based on Gelder *et al.*, 1999)

PTSD may occur immediately following a traumatic experience or weeks, months and even years later. In the Vietnam War, there were relatively few cases of shell shock or combat fatigue, but on their return to the USA soldiers found it more difficult adjusting to civilian life than did those who fought in the two world wars.

As well as the symptoms described in Box 44.3, Vietnam veterans felt extreme *guilt* at having survived, while so many of their comrades hadn't. This is also common among survivors of disasters, as are exaggerated startle responses to unexpected stimuli.

Interestingly, a growing body of research is now finding that trauma may produce OCD. For example, Fontenelle *et al.* (2012) found evidence for a post-traumatic subtype of OCD based on a study of 1000 adults; this has major implications for how such patients should be treated (see Chapter 45).

Explaining PTSD

Psychological explanations

Unlike other anxiety disorders, the causes of PTSD are largely, if not exclusively, *environmental*. While phobias or OCD tend not to have common background factors, all PTSD sufferers share the experience of having been involved in a profoundly traumatising event.

Sufferers tend to show classically conditioned responses to stimuli present at the time of the event (e.g. Charney *et al.*, 1993). But since not everyone exposed to the traumatic event develops PTSD, other factors must be involved. This is well illustrated by a ground-breaking *prospective* study described in Key Study 44.1.

Consistent with these findings, the overall picture following the 9/11 attacks in New York and Washington was one of *resilience,* not breakdown (Lilienfeld and Arkowitz, 2012a). More broadly, Bonanno *et al.* (2011) concluded that only about 5 per cent of people typically develop PTSD after experiencing traumatic life events. The rare exception may occur with repeated trauma. But not only is trauma insufficient to trigger PTSD, it may not even be necessary: while PTSD can only be diagnosed if some major life-threatening event has occurred (even if only *observed*), significant PTSD symptoms *can* follow emotional upheavals resulting from divorce, work-related problems or loss of a close friendship (Rosen and Lilienfeld, 2008) and being a patient in intensive care (ICU) (Wake and Kitchener, 2013).

According to Brewin *et al.* (1996), the symptoms of PTSD may result from the *dissociation* between the two aspects of normal memory formation: (i) autobiographical memories (AMs) give context to an event; and (ii) 'snapshots' that capture a scene in a lot of detail but with little context. Without the 'anchor', the snapshot memories are more likely to return as involuntary flashbacks. Consistent with this *dual representation theory* of PTSD, research has shown that people who have more trouble constructing their AMs are also more at risk of PTSD, perhaps because the flashback scenes are not tied to the rest of their life story (Heaven, 2013).

Biological explanations

According to Butler (1996), PTSD can be seen as the breakdown of the normal stress response.

Ask Yourself

- Remind yourself how the normal stress response works (see Chapter 12). Why do you think Butler (1996) describes PTSD as 'too much of a good thing'? (See Critical Discussion 44.1.)

Key Study 44.1

Resisting PTSD in Afghanistan (Bernsten *et al.*, 2012)

- In a study of young Danish army recruits who hadn't yet gone off to fight in Afghanistan, Bernsten *et al.* concluded that (i) PTSD doesn't appear to be triggered by a traumatic battle experience; and (ii) there's no typical trajectory for PTSD symptoms.
- Instead, after following them during combat and then for several months after arriving home, the researchers found wide variation in both the causes and development of PTSD.
- The vast majority of soldiers were resilient – recovering quickly from mild symptoms – or totally impervious to psychological harm. The rest displayed two distinct and unexpected patterns: (i) one group only started showing symptoms several months after returning home; (ii) the other group's stress seemed to *decrease* during deployment, in between major anxiety and nightmares after signing up and a recurrence of these after they were safely home.
- What these two vulnerable groups had in common was emotional problems and exposure to traumatic events *before* even signing up, such as severe physical punishment as children, witnessing family violence, and physical attacks, stalking or death threats by a spouse.
- Army life – even combat – offered these young men more social support and life satisfaction than they'd ever known at home; these benefits diminished after returning to civilian life.

DEPRESSIVE AND BIPOLAR DISORDERS

Manic disorder (mania)

Mania is a sense of intense euphoria or elation. A characteristic symptom is a 'flight of ideas': ideas come rushing into the person's mind with little apparent logical connection, and there's a tendency to pun and play with words. Manics have a great deal of energy and rush around, usually achieving little and not putting their energies to good use. They need little sleep and may appear excessively conceited (having 'grandiose ideas' or delusions). They display

Critical Discussion 44.1

Is PTSD being over-diagnosed?

According to Dobbs (2009), a wide range of experts in psychiatry (including Spitzer and First, who oversaw DSM-III and DSM-IV), Psychology (notably McNally) and epidemiology, are claiming that the diagnostic criteria for PTSD are faulty and outdated; as a consequence, depression, anxiety, and even normal adjustment are routinely mistaken for PTSD.

Since the National Vietnam Veterans Readjustment Survey (NVVRS; Kulka *et al*., 1990) involving more than 1000 male Vietnam returnees, 31 per cent has become the standard estimate of PTSD incidence. But when the figures were reanalysed (Dohrenwend, 2006, in Dobbs, 2009), that figure was reduced to 9 per cent and the lifetime rate 18 per cent.

McNally, in turn, considered that Dohrenwend's figures were too high. By including just those showing 'clinically significant impairment', the rates fell further to 5.4 and 11 per cent, respectively.

PTSD is almost unique among DSM diagnostic categories in being defined by its (supposed) cause, namely, having experienced a traumatic incident. However, this also makes it uniquely problematic, because it assumes the reliability and accuracy of the patient's *memory* of the incident. But research since PTSD was first included in DSM (1980), including that of Loftus, has highlighted memory's unreliability and malleability (see Chapter 21). McNally (2003) believes that 'late-onset' PTSD veterans may be attributing symptoms of depression, anxiety and other subtle disorders to a memory that has been elaborated and given new significance – or even unconsciously fabricated.

Also, recent studies have shown that traumatic brain injuries from bomb blasts, common among soldiers serving in Iraq, produce symptoms almost identical to those of PTSD (Dobbs, 2009). In all these cases of overlapping symptoms/disorders, the concern is that individuals will be given inappropriate *treatment* (McNally, 2003). According to Dobbs (2009):

> *PTSD exists ... but our cultural obsession with PTSD has magnified and finally perhaps become the thing itself – a prolonged failure to contextualize and accept our own collective aggression. It may be our own post-war neurosis.*

disinhibition, which may take the form of a vastly increased sexual appetite (usually out of keeping with their 'normal' personality), or going on spending sprees and building up large debts.

As we noted in the *Introduction and overview*, mania usually occurs in conjunction with depression (*bipolar disorder*). But in the rare cases in which mania occurs alone, 'bipolar' is also used. Most patients with mania eventually develop a depressive disorder (Gelder *et al*., 1999).

Strictly, mania on its own, and mixed episodes of both mania and depression are called 'Bipolar 1'. 'Bipolar 2' refers to major depression combined with *hypomania* (less extreme than full-blown mania).

Bipolar disorder is much less common than unipolar, occurring in fewer than 10 per 1000, usually before age 50. Each episode lasts about three months (Gelder *et al*., 1999). Bipolar 1 (mixed episodes) is more common than either Bipolar 1 (mania alone) or Bipolar 2; it affects 1 per cent of the population and usually first appears in the 20s; it occurs equally often in men and women.

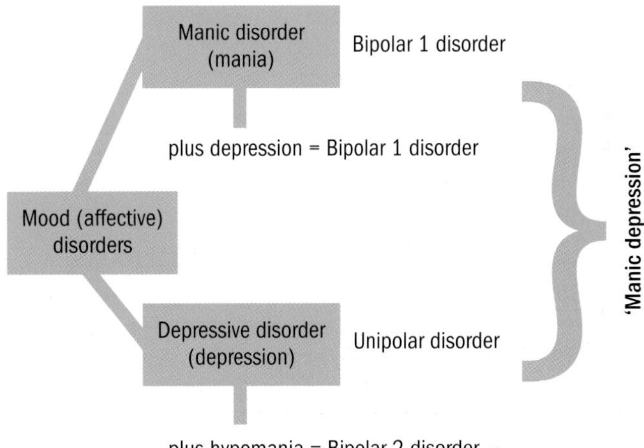

Figure 44.7 The relationship between manic and depressive disorders

Major (unipolar) depressive disorder (MDD)

Depression represents the complete reverse of mania. The depressed person experiences a general slowing down and loss of energy and enthusiasm for life. MDD may begin at any time from adolescence onwards, with the average age of onset being the late 20s. With treatment, each episode lasts two to three months; six months or longer if untreated. It affects up to twice as many women as men (Freeman and Freeman, 2014; Westly, 2012), but this is disputed by Seager *et al*. (2014). About 10 per cent of patients eventually commit suicide (Gelder *et al*., 1999). According to the WHO (2011), one person commits suicide every 40 seconds; by

Critical Discussion 44.2

Suicide and gender

While more women worldwide attempt suicide (*parasuicide*) each year, more men actually die from suicide. For example, in the Western hemisphere, twice as many men complete suicide compared with women. While this gender gap has existed for at least 120 years, it has widened in recent times: men now represent a large majority of all suicides across the world (WHO, 2011).

Until quite recently, the relationship between suicidal behaviour and men's gender (or *masculinities*) has largely been taken for granted or marginalised. But emerging evidence suggests that a more detailed examination of gender provides a powerful means of explaining the gender gap. More specifically, the construction of masculinities is believed to be one of the most important factors influencing how men discuss, contemplate and enact suicide (Swami *et al.*, 2008). (See Chapter 36.)

In the West, men experience considerable social pressure to aspire to dominant (*hegemonic*) gendered identities, such as being independent, strong and competitive, while also denying anxieties and insecurities (Golombok and Fivush, 1994). If all behaviours are an expression of gender, then perhaps 'doing masculinity' puts men at higher risk for suicidal behaviours compared with women's 'doing femininity'.

Payne *et al.* (2008) have documented the many ways in which the construction of masculinities impacts on men's greater rates of completed suicide. These include:

- In general, men are more likely to die through the use of violent methods, such as firearms and hanging. Such violent methods are consistent with the 'macho' construction of masculinity, as is men's greater familiarity with and ownership of shotguns and pistols, etc. It may also explain why women are so much more likely to survive suicide attempts.
- While most societies tend to stigmatise suicidal behaviours, surviving a suicidal act is more likely to be perceived as 'inappropriate' for men.
- Male suicides are less likely than female to have had contact with health services or to have been known to psychiatric services. This reflects the fact that men are less likely than women to consult for most conditions, especially mental health and emotional problems: men are supposed to deny pain, emotional sensitivity and anxiety. Asking for help, even in the face of possible suicide, may be viewed as feminine behaviour.
- Men's response to depression often involves social withdrawal (including hiding symptoms from others), unwillingness to consult health care professionals, and a denial of symptoms. Not surprisingly, alcohol and substance misuse more often precede suicide among men than among women.
- While the widowed, divorced/separated and single have higher suicide rates than married adults, non-married men are at higher risk than non-married women (see Chapter 36).
- Because men experience pressure to be successful and ambitious, being made redundant or his business going bust is likely to have a detrimental effect on a man's well-being; they're more sensitive to negative changes in their employment or socio-economic status than women. (See Chapter 36.)

2020 MDD is estimated to be the world's leading cause of disability. (See Critical Discussion 44.2.)

Consistent with these 'masculinities' is the gender difference in how depression is *experienced*: while for women, the primary emotion is usually sadness, for men it's more typically anger or irritability, often coupled with recklessness. Hormones are a major candidate for explaining this male–female difference (Westly, 2012). Given the widely accepted finding that men significantly underreport health problems (including mental health), relying only on men's disclosure of traditional symptoms could lead to an *under*-diagnosis of depression in men. Indeed, when this is allowed for, the prevalence of depression between men and women disappears (Martin *et al.*, 2013) (see above).

Explaining depression

All the major theoretical approaches have attempted to explain depression. Probably the most influential of these – both currently and in recent years – has been the cognitive model, especially Beck's (1963) *cognitive triad of depression*. Because his form of cognitive–behaviour therapy (CBT) is mainly intended to treat depression, this – and other cognitive explanations – will be discussed in Chapter 45.

Neurochemical explanations

According to the *monoamine hypothesis* (MAOH), a depletion of serotonin, noradrenaline and/or dopamine underlies the melancholic symptoms of depression. High levels induce mania. Serotonin (5-HT), norepinephrine (noradrenaline) and

Figure 44.8 Winston Churchill (1874–1965), famous British Prime Minister – and depressive

dopamine are collectively known as *monoamine oxidase* (MAO) *transmitters*. By far the greatest number of studies on these have involved 5-HT (Claridge and Davis, 2003).

The supporting evidence is based largely on working backwards from what's known about the mechanisms of drugs that either induce or reduce depressive symptoms.

It was discovered in the mid-1950s that depression was a common side-effect of one of the first effective drugs for treating high blood pressure, *reserpine*, which was known to reduce the levels of brain 5-HIAA (a chemical produced when 5-HT is broken down). Also in the 1950s, *tricyclics* and *monoamine oxidase inhibitors* (MAOIs) were found to be effective in relieving depression (see Chapter 45):

- *tricyclics* prevent some of the reuptake of both noradrenaline and serotonin; this leaves more of the transmitter in the synaptic gap, making transmission of the next nerve impulse easier (see Chapter 4)
- the newest antidepressants are called *serotonin reuptake inhibitors* (SRIs), because they act more selectively on serotonin (this is why they're sometimes called SSRIs – *specific* serotonin reuptake inhibitors). They raise levels of serotonin (5-HT) and have a well-established antidepressant effect; examples are fluoxetine (most familiarly marketed as Prozac). Because SSRIs are effective in treating MDD, a stronger link has been established between low levels of 5-HT and depression (Davison and Neale, 2001; Gelder *et al.*, 1999)
- *MAOIs* prevent the enzyme monoamine oxidase (MAO) from breaking down the neurotransmitters, increasing the levels of both 5-HT and noradrenaline in the brain. Like the tricyclics, this compensates for the abnormally low levels of these neurotransmitters in depressed people.

An evaluation of the MAOH

- The MAOH is the longest-standing and most persistent biological theory of depression (Claridge and Davis, 2003).
- It's known that all the main antidepressants have an immediate effect on the levels of 5-HT and noradrenaline in the brain. But it sometimes takes up to 7–14 days for them to have any noticeable effect on patients' symptoms; by the time the drugs begin to 'work', the neurotransmitter levels have returned to their previous state. So a simple increase in neurotransmitter levels isn't a sufficient explanation for why the drugs alleviate depression (Davison and Neale, 2001).
- An *indirect* way of testing the role of 5-HT is to measure concentrations of a particular *metabolite* (a by-product of the breakdown of the neurotransmitters, found in urine, blood serum and cerebrospinal fluid/CSF). These are found to be lower in patients with depression, especially in those who commit violent suicide (Claridge and Davis, 2003). This could, however, be the result of many different kinds of biochemical abnormality. Also, the lower concentrations probably aren't a direct indication of levels of either 5-HT or noradrenaline *in the brain*. Metabolites measured this way could reflect neurotransmitters anywhere in the body (Davison and Neale, 2001).
- A more *direct* test comes from *experimental depletion studies*: when normal participants are given drugs that *reduce* levels of 5-HT and noradrenaline in the brain, these people don't usually experience depressive symptoms (Claridge and Davis, 2003). Nor do the symptoms of unmedicated depressed patients become worse (Delgado, 2000).
- Research shows that men don't respond as well as women to SSRIs: they appear to work best in the presence of oestrogen, the female hormone. Men seem to respond better to antidepressants such as imipramine (Tofranil) that target dopamine and noradrenaline, rather than serotonin (Westly, 2012). While this is consistent with the MAOH, it also represents an important qualifying factor.

Learned helplessness theory (LHT)

Strictly, *learned helplessness theory* (LHT) is the original of three related cognitive theories of depression. (Only two will be discussed here.) The basic premise of LHT is that depression in humans is a form of *learned helplessness* (LH) (Seligman, 1974; see Chapter 11). On the basis of these observations, Seligman proposed that animals acquire a sense of helplessness when confronted with uncontrollable aversive stimulation. Later, this sense of helplessness impairs their performance in stressful situations which *can* be controlled. They seem to lose the ability and motivation to respond effectively to painful stimulation.

By extension, LH could provide an explanation for at least certain forms of depression in humans. Seligman believed that, like his dogs, many depressed people appear passive in the face of stress; they fail to initiate actions that might allow them to cope. Also, like depressed people, Seligman's dogs lost their appetite and lost weight, and showed reduced levels of noradrenaline.

By 1978, research with humans began to reveal several inadequacies of LHT. For example, many depressed people blame themselves for their failures, but this is incompatible with the claim that they see themselves as helpless. Also, the experience of being unable to control the outcome of one particular situation (helplessness) doesn't necessarily lead to clinical depression in most people. These and other findings suggest very strongly that LH cannot tell the whole story. LHT was revised by Abramson, Seligman and Teasdale in 1978. The major change they proposed was in terms of *attribution theory principles*.

Ask Yourself

- How do you think this modified LHT might have tried to explain depression? (See Chapter 23.)

An evaluation of the attributional theory of depression

- This clearly is an improvement on LHT, because it adds in the missing cognitive factors. The concept of attributional style represents a *diathesis,* a predisposition to develop a particular mental disorder under stressful conditions (see the discussion of schizophrenia below). A key assumption is that the DAS is a persistent part of the make-up of the depressed person: as a diathesis, it must be 'in place' before the person experiences some stressor. But Hamilton and Abramson (1983) showed that it disappears following a depressive episode.

Box 44.4 The Attributional Theory of Depression (Abramson *et al.,* 1978)

When we experience failure, for example, we try to explain it (just as we try to account for our successes); this is perfectly 'normal'. What's associated with depression is a particular *attributional style* – that is, a tendency to make particular kinds of causal inferences.

The 'depressed attributional style' (DAS) is based on three key dimensions, namely *locus* (whether the cause is internal or external, to do with the actor him/herself or some aspect of the situation), *stability* (whether the cause is stable or unstable, a permanent feature of the actor or something transient), and *global* or *specific* (whether the cause relates to the 'whole' person or just some particular feature or characteristic). The depressed person believes that his/her failure:

- is caused by *internal factors* ('I'm stupid')
- reflects *stable*, long-term, relatively permanent factors ('I never do well on tests or exams')
- reflects a *global,* pervasive deficiency – that is, failure applies to all or most aspects of his/her life ('I get everything wrong').

People diagnosed as clinically depressed are more likely to show this pattern when given, for example, the *Attributional Style Questionnaire* (ASQ) (Seligman *et al.,* 1979). Equally important, the person *prone* to depression may also display the DAS. It's believed to play a mediating role between negative life events and adverse physical and mental health outcomes. When such depression-prone people experience stressors, they're more likely to develop the symptoms of depression, and their self-esteem is shattered (Peterson and Seligman, 1984).

	Successes	Failures
Depressed	External Unstable Specific	Internal Stable Global
Non-depressed	Internal Stable Global	External Unstable Specific

Figure 44.9 Attributional styles for success and failure in depressed people (based on Abramson *et al.,* 1978; Abramson and Martin, 1981)

- Seligman *et al.* (1979) gave their ASQ to college students. As predicted by the theory, mildly depressed students more often attributed their failures to personal (internal), global and stable inadequacies than did non-depressed students.
- While some research has been conducted with clinical populations (people actually diagnosed as having a depressive disorder) (such as Abramson *et al.*, 1978), many studies have involved college students selected on the basis of the *Beck Depression Inventory* (BDI), or have simply tried to predict increases in BDI scores. But the BDI wasn't designed to diagnose depression, only to assess its severity among those already diagnosed. People selected on the basis of raised BDI scores aren't comparable to those with clinical depression. For example, high scorers have been found to score much lower when retested two to three weeks later. Also, the finding that the ASQ can predict BDI scores doesn't necessarily mean that it can predict the onset of actual clinical depression.
- A problem faced by most cognitive explanations of psychopathology is accounting for where the DAS comes from in the first place. It's thought to stem from childhood experiences, but there's little empirical support for this claim. However, Rose *et al.* (1994) found that DAS is related to sexual abuse in childhood, as well as to parental overprotectiveness, harsh discipline and perfectionistic standards.
- We've already noted the comorbidity of depression and anxiety. We need to be sure that the theories are truly about depression, rather than about negative affect in general. DAS seems to be related to anxiety and general distress, as well as depression.
- Despite these problems, attributional theories have clearly stimulated a great deal of research and theorising about depression; this is likely to continue for many years to come (Davison and Neale, 2001; Davison *et al.*, 2004).

Culture and depression

While there are an estimated 340 million people worldwide affected by depressive disorders (making it the most common of all mental disorders; Lyddy, 2000), Price and Crapo (1999) point out that various researchers have denied the presence of native concepts of depression among groups as diverse as the Nigerians, Chinese, Canadian Inuit, Japanese, Malaysians, and the Hopi Native Americans. Price and Crapo ask:

> *If depression, as currently defined in Western culture and psychiatric diagnosis, is not found in non-Western cultures, how do we know that 'depression' is not merely a Western folk concept, analogous to other culture-specific conditions such as koro, kayak-angst, amok or susto?*

Ask Yourself

- How does this discussion of cultural aspects of depression relate to the discussion in Chapter 43 of whether schizophrenia is culture-free? (See Critical Discussion 44.3.)

SCHIZOPHRENIC AND OTHER PSYCHOTIC DISORDERS

Schizophrenia

As we noted in the *Introduction and overview*, what we now call schizophrenia was originally called *dementia praecox* ('senility of youth') by Kraepelin (1896). Kraepelin believed that the typical symptoms (namely, delusions, hallucinations, attention deficits, and bizarre motor activity) were due to a form of mental deterioration which began in adolescence. But Bleuler (1911) observed that many patients displaying these symptoms didn't go on deteriorating, and that illness often began much later than adolescence. Consequently, he introduced the term 'schizophrenia' instead (literally 'split mind' or 'divided self').

According to Clare (1976), the diagnosis of schizophrenia in the UK relies greatly on Schneider's (1959) *first-rank symptoms* (FRSs) (see Table 44.1).

Schneider's FRSs are *subjective experiences,* which can only be inferred on the basis of the patient's verbal report. Slater and Roth (1969) regard hallucinations as the least important of all the major symptoms, because they aren't exclusive to schizophrenia (this is also true of delusions: see below). Slater and Roth identify four additional symptoms, which are *directly observable* from the patient's behaviour (see Table 44.2).

So who's right – Schneider or Slater and Roth?

According to Claridge and Davis (2003), 'first-rank symptoms' imply that:

> *... certain experiences of people clinically labelled 'schizophrenic' are so bizarre, incomprehensible, and distant from the normal that we are surely convinced that these must be central to the disorder.*

In other words, FRSs seem to describe the 'fundamental', core features of schizophrenia. But like Slater and Roth, Bleuler regarded hallucinations and delusions as *accessory* (secondary) symptoms – they're psychological consequences of a more primary, physical process that constitutes the *real* core. Claridge and Davis believe that the DSM and ICD criteria for diagnosing schizophrenia are a confused mix of these

Critical Discussion 44.3

The social construction of happiness and sadness

According to Moghaddam (2002):

... depression, as it is medically recognised and treated in Western societies, is fundamentally a social construction. This is not to say that people in other historical eras and in other societies have not experienced the same biological processes as do depressed people in Western societies today, but that the meanings and implications of experiences arising from such processes have been different in major ways ...

For example, in modern Western societies, especially the USA, greater and greater emphasis is being placed on presenting the self in a positive, happy way ('I'm doin' great'). But while this might be normative in the USA, it wouldn't be in most Eastern cultures, and someone displaying such a style would be regarded negatively.

Conversely, even in Western culture, 'negative' emotions (sadness, melancholy, depression) haven't always been shunned. They're a normal part of life and should be valued as an essential feature of human experience. The 'cult of melancholy' during the mid-eighteenth to late-nineteenth centuries was reflected in poetry and is still prominent in Farsi-speaking countries. For example, among Shi'ite Muslims (the religion of over 96 per cent of Iranians and 45 per cent of Iraqis) several important religious ceremonies involve participants weeping and wailing, self-flagellation, and expressing – and experiencing – misery.

The feelings of guilt and self-blame, loneliness and anxiety, commonly reported by depressed people in Western societies don't seem to be part of people's experience in non-Western societies. The latter typically look outside themselves, and refer to the rain, seasons, fate and various other external phenomena to explain their experiences (Moghaddam, 2002)

Figure 44.10 A flagellating Shi'ite Muslim

According to Horwitz and Wakefield (2007), the increasing tendency to treat normal sadness as if it were a disease is undermining a crucial part of our biology. Sadness undoubtedly serves an evolutionary purpose, which might be partly a form of self-protection and partly a way of learning from our mistakes.

Others have suggested that sadness may serve to communicate to others our need for support; even full-blown depression may save us from the effects of chronic stress (see Chapter 12). Negative feelings most likely aid in our survival by indicating that something needs our attention (Rodriguez, 2013). There's also biographical/autobiographical evidence that many great artists, writers and musicians have suffered from depression or bipolar disorders (Marshall, 2009).

Table 44.1 Schneider's (1959) first-rank symptoms of schizophrenia

Passivity experiences and thought disturbances: *thought insertion* (thoughts are inserted into one's mind from outside and are under external influence), *thought withdrawal* (thoughts are removed from one's mind and are externally controlled), and *thought broadcasting* (thoughts are broadcast to/otherwise made known to others). External forces may include the Martians, the Communists and the Government.
Auditory hallucinations (in the third person): hallucinatory voices are heard discussing one's thoughts or behaviour as they occur (a kind of running commentary), arguing about oneself (or using one's name), or repeating one's thoughts out loud/anticipating one's thoughts. They're often accusatory, obscene and derogatory, and may order the patient to commit extreme acts of violence. They're experienced as alien or under the influence of some external source, and also in the light of concurrent delusions (e.g. the voice of God or the devil: see below). The hallucinations of patients with *organic* psychoses are predominantly *visual*.
Primary delusions: false beliefs (incompatible with reality, usually of persecution or grandeur) held with extraordinary conviction, impervious to other experiences or compelling counter argument/contradictory evidence. The patient may be so convinced of their truth that they act on the strength of their belief, even if this involves murder and rape (as in the case of Peter Sutcliffe, the 'Yorkshire Ripper').

Table 44.2 Major symptoms of schizophrenia (based on Slater and Roth, 1969)

Thought process disorder: the inability to keep to the point, being easily distracted/side-tracked. In *clang associations* (e.g. 'big', 'pig', 'twig'), words are 'thrown together' based on their sound rather than their meaning; this produces an apparently incoherent jumble of words ('word salad'). Also the inability to finish a sentence, sometimes stopping in the middle of a word (*thought blocking*), inventing new words (*neologisms*) and interpreting language (e.g. proverbs) literally.
Disturbance of affect: events/situations don't elicit their usual emotional response (*blunting*), there's a more pervasive, generalised absence of emotional expression (as in minimal inflection in speech, and lack of normal variation in facial/bodily movements used to convey feelings: *flattening of affect*), loss of appropriate emotional responses (e.g. laughing/getting angry for no apparent reason, changing mood very suddenly, giggling when given some bad news: *incongruity of affect*).
Psychomotor disorders: muscles in a state of semi-rigidity (*catalepsy*), grimacing of facial muscles, limb twitching, stereotyped behaviours (such as constant pacing up and down), or assuming a fixed position for long periods of time, even several years in extreme cases (*catatonic stupor*).
Lack of volition: inability to make decisions or carry out a particular action, loss of will power or drive, loss of interest in what's going on and affection for friends/family.

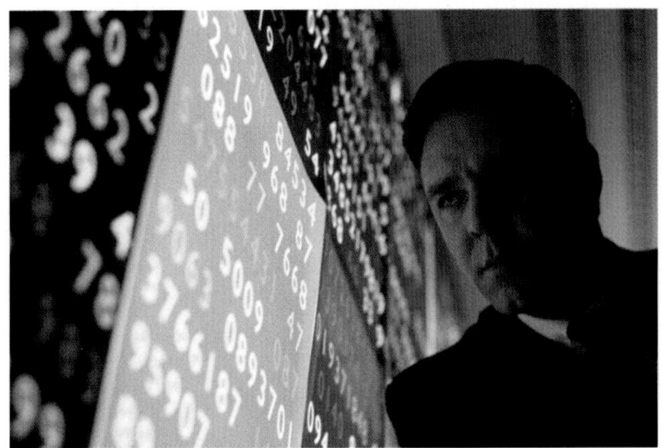

Figure 44.11 Russell Crowe as John Forbes Nash, mathematical genius who develops schizophrenia, in *A Beautiful Mind* (2001)

views – although there's a bias towards FRSs. This bias is understandable, since:

> *... Reporting that aliens in outer space are responsible for the thoughts in your head certainly seems more crazy than bemusing your neighbours with your stream of consciousness style of conversation! (Claridge and Davis, 2003)*

But, unlike most diagnostic categories, there's no essential symptom that must be present for a diagnosis of schizophrenia to be made (Davison and Neale, 2001).

Positive and negative symptoms

Most of Schneider's FRSs are what are known as *positive symptoms* (or Type I) – that is, excesses or distortions, the *presence of active symptomatology*. They're what define, for the most part, an acute episode, and are occurrences beyond normal experience (Javitt and Coyle, 2004). Typically, patients have several acute episodes, between which are less severe but still very debilitating symptoms.

Most of Slater and Roth's symptoms are *negative* (Type II) *symptoms*. They consist of behavioural deficits, *lack* of or *poverty* of behaviour. These symptoms tend to endure beyond the acute episodes, and have a profound effect on patients' lives. The presence of several negative symptoms is a strong predictor of a poor quality of life two years after leaving hospital (Davison *et al.*, 2004).

First rank symptoms (Schneider, 1959)

- Passivity experiences and thought disturbances
- Auditory hallucinations (in the third person)
- Primary delusions

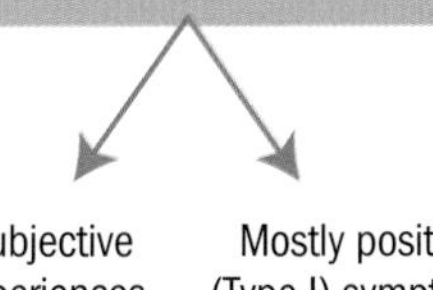

Subjective experiences of patient

Mostly positive (Type I) symptoms (presence of active symptomatology)

Major symptoms (Slater & Roth, 1969)

- Thought process disorder
- Disturbance of affect
- Psychomotor disorder
- Lack of volition

Mostly negative (Type II) symptoms (lack/poverty of behaviour)

Directly observable from patient's behaviour

Figure 44.12 Summary of different attempts to define the major characteristics of schizophrenia

A third group of symptoms (*disorganised* or *cognitive*) refer to difficulty in maintaining a logical, coherent flow of information, maintaining attention and thinking on an abstract level, and bizarre behaviour (Davison *et al.*, 2004; Javitt and Coyle, 2004).

The distinction between positive and negative symptoms is very important in relation to research into the causes of schizophrenia (see below). According to Claridge and Davis (2003), currently the most widely quoted research classification is based on this distinction.

Critical Discussion 44.4

Is hearing voices compatible with being mentally well?

- While 'auditory-verbal hallucinations' (AVH) are one of Schneider's FRSs of schizophrenia, 'hearing voices' is a common human experience that has a personal, interpretable meaning in relation to life history, often triggered and sustained by overwhelming, disempowering life events (Romme and Escher, 2000).
- Romme and Escher advocate a process of *normalising* voice-hearing, accepting and making sense of voice presence, and respecting the subjective reality of the voices for the voice-hearer.
- These initiatives have gained increasing popularity over the last 20 years and have led to the development of the Hearing Voices Movement (HVM), a social, clinical, and political collective in which groups of voice-hearers and professionals work together to support distressed individuals in respectful ways that promote recovery (Longden *et al.*,2013; Longden and Dillon, 2013).
- One way of challenging the disease model of schizophrenia is the observation that around two-thirds of people with complex AVHs either have other psychiatric diagnoses (such as personality disorder or PTSD), or are 'healthy voice-hearers' (i.e. they have no social/occupational dysfunction) (McCarthy-Jones, 2012).

Theories of schizophrenia

The biochemical theory of schizophrenia

According to the *dopamine hypothesis* (DH), the direct cause of schizophrenic symptoms is an excess of the neurotransmitter dopamine. The evidence for this hypothesis comes from three main sources:

- Postmortems on schizophrenics show unusually high levels of dopamine, especially in the limbic system (Iversen, 1979).
- Anti-schizophrenic drugs (such as chlorpromazine) are thought to work by binding to dopamine receptor sites, that is, they inhibit the ability of the dopamine (D2) receptors to respond to dopamine, thus reducing dopamine activity (see Chapter 45). These drugs produce side-effects similar to the symptoms of Parkinson's disease, which is known to be caused by low levels of dopamine in particular nerve tracts.
- High doses of L-Dopa (used in the treatment of Parkinson's disease) can sometimes produce symptoms very similar to the psychomotor disorders seen in some patients with schizophrenia. High doses of amphetamines induce *amphetamine psychosis* (AP), which closely resembles paranoid schizophrenia and can exacerbate the symptoms of a patient with schizophrenia (see Chapter 8). Both these drugs are believed to increase the activity of dopamine; dopamine-containing neurons are concentrated in the basal ganglia and frontal cortex, which are concerned with the initiation and control of movement. Degeneration of the dopamine system produces Parkinson's disease (see Chapter 4).

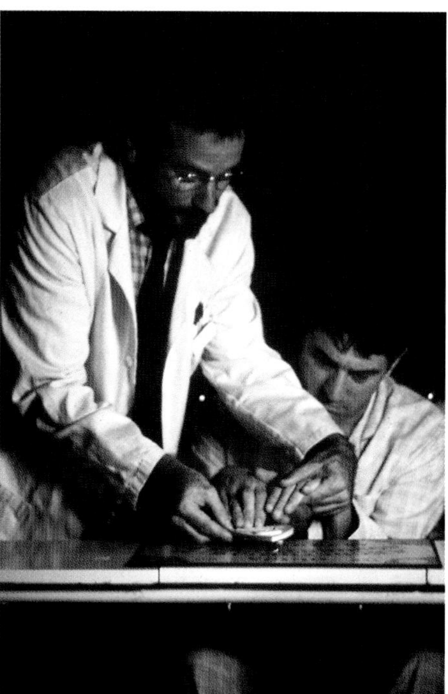

Figure 44.13 Robin Williams (left) in a scene from *Awakenings* (based on the book by Oliver Sacks). Patients with sleeping sickness (as portrayed in the film) have often been misdiagnosed with catatonic schizophrenia

An evaluation of the DH

- Overall, the evidence is inconclusive (Lavender, 2000). For example, there's no consistent difference in dopamine levels between drug-free schizophrenics and normals, nor is there any evidence of higher levels of other metabolites indicating greater dopamine activity (Jackson, 1986). Even if such evidence did exist, this could just as easily be an *effect* of schizophrenia as its cause. Even if dopamine were found to be a causative factor, this might only be *indirect* (for example, abnormal family circumstances give rise to high levels of dopamine which, in turn, trigger the symptoms (Lloyd *et al.*, 1984).

- This is consistent with evidence showing links between childhood treatment and trauma and adult psychosis, including – and especially – schizophrenia (Fisher, 2013; Varese *et al.*, 2012). While many individuals who suffer emotional, physical or sexual abuse don't develop any major difficulties, they are at higher risk of developing a range of adverse outcomes, including substance abuse (see Chapter 8), depression and anxiety, antisocial behaviour (see Chapter 46), PTSD, and personality disorders.
- While there's no conclusive evidence of a causal relationship between early abuse and adult psychosis, some children may have an almost immediate psychotic reaction to this maltreatment. Abuse may also have immediate *biological* consequences, such as brain injuries, which may then lead to psychotic symptoms (Fisher, 2013). Indirect pathways may include substance abuse that leads to psychosis, as can depression and anxiety (Fisher, 2013).
- It's unlikely that any problems with dopamine production/receptivity will prove to be the basic biochemical abnormality underlying all forms of schizophrenia – although it may play a crucial role in some forms (Jackson, 1990). According to Lavender (2000):

> *... if schizophrenia is not a clearly identifiable syndrome but an umbrella term covering a range of symptoms with unclear onset, course, and outcome, then it is obvious that much of the work investigating a specific biological basis will inevitably be inconclusive. So far, this appears to be the case.*

- As Bentall (1990) argues, perhaps the time has come to concentrate on specific symptoms, before trying to find the biochemical cause(s). (See discussion of the cognitive approach below.)
- The dopamine hypothesis cannot be a complete explanation. For example it takes several weeks for antipsychotics gradually to reduce positive symptoms, even though they begin blocking D2 receptors very quickly (Davis, 1978). Their eventual therapeutic effect may be due to the effect this blockade has on other brain areas and neurotransmitter systems (Cohen *et al.*, 1997).
- Antipsychotics seem to be effective in controlling *positive symptoms*, and where symptoms come on dramatically. But for patients whose symptoms appear gradually, and in whom negative or disorganised (cognitive) symptoms predominate, they're much less effective. The latter may stem from reduced dopamine levels in certain parts of the brain (such as the frontal lobes) and increased levels in others (such as the limbic system) (Javitt and Coyle, 2004).
- Newer anti-schizophrenic drugs implicate *serotonin*. Serotoninergic neurons are known to regulate dopaminergic neurons in the *mesolimbic pathway* (MLP; see Figure 44.14). The therapeutic effects of antipsychotic drugs on the positive symptoms occur by blocking D2 receptors there. The *mesocortical pathway* (MCP) begins in the same brain region as the MLP, but projects to the prefrontal cortex (PFC). So, dopamine may be just one piece in a much more complex jigsaw (Davison and Neale, 2001; Javitt and Coyle, 2004).

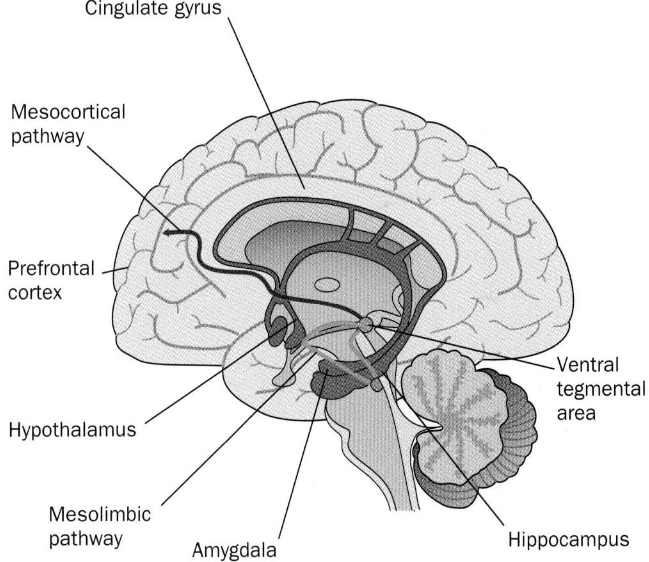

Figure 44.14 The brain and schizophrenia

- Focus has shifted recently to deficiencies in *glutamate*, a neurotransmitter found in almost every part of the human brain. It's known that angel dust (PCP, or phencyclidine) induces symptoms that resemble the full range of schizophrenic symptoms (see Chapter 8). At the molecular level, PCP impairs the function of the brain signalling systems that rely on glutamate, the brain's major excitatory neurotransmitter (see Chapter 4). More specifically, it blocks the action of a form of glutamate receptor called the NMDA receptor, which plays a crucial role in brain development, learning, memory and neural processing in general. It also plays a role in regulating dopamine. Blocking NMDA receptors produces the same disturbances of dopamine functioning as typically occur in schizophrenia. So, NMDA receptor dysfunction, by itself, can account for both negative and disorganised symptoms, and the dopamine abnormalities at the root of positive symptoms (Javitt and Coyle, 2004).

The genetic theory of schizophrenia

The nature and nurture of schizophrenia

Perhaps the most reasonable conclusion is that there's converging evidence, from multiple sources, implicating genetic factors in the aetiology of schizophrenia. Its heritability seems to be comparable to that of any medical condition known to have a major genetic component, such as diabetes, hypertension, coronary artery disease, and breast cancer (Lilienfeld, 1995). According to Claridge and Davis (2003):

> *... the contribution of genetic influences is one of the few factual certainties about schizophrenia. Even in the absence of the discovery of specific genes, this is clear from kinship data ...*

However, the precise mode of inheritance remains controversial (Frith and Cahill, 1995; Lilienfeld, 1995). The most popular current view is the 'multifactorial' (*polygenic*) model: a number of genes are involved which determine a predisposition, which then requires environmental factors to trigger the symptoms of the illness. This is referred to as a *diathesis* (i.e. predisposition) – *stress model.*

Zubin and Spring (1977), for example, claim that what we probably inherit is a degree of *vulnerability* to exhibiting schizophrenic symptoms. Whether or not we do depends on environmental stresses which may include viral infections during pregnancy (especially influenza A), severe malnourishment during pregnancy, birth injury or difficult birth, being born in winter, as well as 'critical life events' (see Chapter 12). So, any inherited factors don't *guarantee* that the vulnerable individual will actually become schizophrenic. Just as Claridge and Davis are certain that genetic factors are involved, they're equally certain that the genetic data tell us that environmental factors must also be important.

Tienari (1991) examined the rate of schizophrenia in Finnish people who'd been adopted and whose biological mothers were schizophrenic. As predicted, having a biological mother with schizophrenia increased the rate of schizophrenia in the adoptees, even if they were adopted by non-schizophrenic families. But the schizophrenia gene revealed itself only if the adoptive family was psychologically disturbed in some way. So even vulnerable individuals could be protected from schizophrenia if their family of rearing was healthy.

According to Claridge and Davis (2003), individual studies have reported concordance rates for monozygotic twins (MZs) ranging from zero to 90 per cent. Yet 50 per cent is often quoted. Heritabilities do vary in proportion to the judged severity among the cases sampled (Gottesman and Shields, 1982). More intriguing – and rather puzzling – is a finding relating to the same sets of twins diagnosed on two separate occasions: once according to FRSs, then again using broader criteria. On the broader criteria, the concordance rate for MZs was 50 per cent, but on FRSs, it was zero! (Farmer *et al.,* 1987; McGuffin *et al.*, 1987.) According to Claridge and Davis (2003):

> *... This tends to suggest that, despite their convincingly 'psychotic' appearance, first rank symptoms do not tap directly into whatever is inherited in schizophrenia; instead they may indeed be secondary elaborations of some more fundamental (inherited) cognitive processes, along the lines visualized by Bleuler.*

According to Joseph (2003):

> *... genetic theories aid the interests of the social and political elites, and the interests of the psychopharmaceutical industry ... Focusing attention on genetic research ... successfully diverts attention from the social factors that contribute to people exhibiting behaviours given the schizophrenia label.*

Laing and existential psychiatry

During the 1950s and 1960s, a group of British psychiatrists saw society as a problem for the individual. Laing, Cooper and Esterson were united in their rejection of the medical model of mental disorder, and, like Szasz, they denied the existence of schizophrenia as a disease entity; instead, they saw it as a *metaphor* for dealing with people whose behaviour and experience fail to conform to the dominant model of social reality. They thus spearheaded the *antipsychiatry movement* (Graham, 1986).

Heather (1976) identifies three major landmarks in the development of Laing's thought, corresponding to the publication of three major books.

- In *The Divided Self*, Laing (1959) tried to make sense of schizophrenia by 'getting inside the head' of a schizophrenic, trying to see the world as the schizophrenic sees it (the *psychoanalytic model*). This *existentialist analysis* retained the categories of classic psychiatry, but proceeded from the assumption that what the schizophrenic says and does are intelligible if you listen carefully enough. Laing found a split in the schizophrenic's relationship with the world and with the self: s/he experiences an intense form of *ontological insecurity*, making everyday events a threat to his/her very existence.

Figure 44.15 R.D. Laing (1927–1989)

- In *Self and Others*, Laing (1961) proposed the *family interaction model*. Schizophrenia can only be understood as something which takes place *between* people (*not* inside them). To understand individuals, we must study interactions between individuals, and this is the subject matter of *social phenomenology* (see Chapter 22).

The family interaction model was consistent with research in America, especially that of Bateson *et al.* (1956), which showed that schizophrenia arises within families which use 'pathological' forms of communication, in particular contradictory messages (*double-binds*). For example, a mother induces her son to give her a hug, but when he does she tells him 'not to be such a baby'. Laing and Esterson (1964) presented 11 family case histories (in all of which one member becomes a diagnosed schizophrenic), in order to make schizophrenia intelligible in the context of what happens within the patient's family and, in so doing, to undermine further the disease model of schizophrenia.

- In *The Politics of Experience* (Laing, 1967), two new models were presented. The *conspiratorial model* maintains that schizophrenia is a label, a form of violence perpetrated by some people on others. The family, GP, and psychiatrists conspire against schizophrenics in order to preserve their definition of reality (the *status quo*). They treat schizophrenics as if they were sick, imprisoning them in mental hospitals, where they're degraded and invalidated as human beings.

According to the *psychedelic model*, the schizophrenic is an exceptionally eloquent critic of society, and schizophrenia is 'itself a natural way of healing our own appalling state of alienation called normality'. Schizophrenia is seen as a voyage into 'inner space', a 'natural healing process'. Unfortunately, the 'natural sequence' of schizophrenia is very rarely allowed to occur because, says Laing, we're too busy treating the patient.

A cognitive approach: schizophrenia as psychological processes that go wrong

Bentall (2007) cites research into the psychological processes involved in psychotic disorders ('symptoms'), suggesting a very different view of schizophrenia itself.

In relation to auditory-verbal hallucinations, some researchers have attempted to directly measure *source monitoring* (the capacity to distinguish between self-generated thoughts and externally-presented stimuli). One idea is that hallucinating patients have *dysfunctional metacognitive beliefs* (beliefs about their own mental processes) that lead them to make self-defeating efforts to control their thoughts; this makes the thoughts seem *unintended* – and, therefore, *alien*.

Another example of dysfunctional metacognition is disabilities in predicting or recognising the consequences of their own actions, i.e. a poor perception of cause and effect (Metcalfe *et al.*, 2012).

A second proposal is that source monitoring errors reflect a general failure to monitor one's own intentional states, as demonstrated by voice-hearing psychotic patients' greater ability to *tickle themselves* compared with non-psychotic controls (Blakemore *et al.*, 2000). More direct evidence supporting this hypothesis comes from a series of electrophysiological studies which show that hallucinating patients don't display the same dampening in the auditory perception areas of the temporal lobe seen during talking and inner speech (Ford and Mathalon, 2004).

Patients with delusions seem to perform normally on conventional measures of reasoning (Bentall and Young, 1996; Corcoran *et al.*, 2006). The psychological abnormality that has been most reliably linked to delusional thinking is a tendency to 'jump to conclusions' when reasoning about probabilities: they request less information before reaching a decision compared with non-delusional controls. Deficits in *theory of mind* (ToM) skills have been specifically implicated in persecutory delusions (see Chapter 40).

Bentall (2003) argues that once these positive symptoms ('madness') have been adequately explained, there'll be no schizophrenia left behind to be explained.

FEEDING AND EATING DISORDERS

In the past 30 years, eating disorders (EDs) have become widespread in Western industrialised societies. This may be related to the overabundance of food, but it's likely to be influenced by societal norms that link attractiveness to being thin (American Psychological Association, 1994). Indeed, the popular and scientific assumption is that the preoccupation with thinness and dieting rampant in Western societies is a direct cause of eating disorders. However, it's well established that EDs are *multidetermined* and that culture is only one of many contributory factors (Fedoroff and McFarlane, 1998). Furthermore:

> *... cultural factors can only be understood as they interact with the psychology and biology of the vulnerable individual ... a culture cannot cause a disorder ... (Fedoroff and McFarlane, 1998)*

According to the *dimensional* view, the full-blown ED is the end-point along a continuum that begins with normal dieting, advances to excessive concern about weight and the emergence of some clinical symptoms, and finally a severe, pathological illness. In recent years, this viewpoint has become more popular – even in mainstream psychiatry. So, it's widely agreed that the EDs are most appropriately regarded as a 'spectrum of pathology', rather than discrete disease entities. Although we continue to use DSM diagnostic criteria and terminology for convenience, in practice assessment typically reflects the dimensional view, and patients with milder forms are treated alongside more serious cases (Claridge and Davis, 2003).

Anorexia nervosa

Anorexia nervosa (AN) (literally, 'nervous lack of appetite') usually begins in adolescence (16–17) after the patient (90–95 per cent of whom are female) has become over-concerned about 'puppy fat' and has begun to diet. This dieting often masquerades as 'vegetarianism' (Lipsedge, 1997) and progresses to a relentless attempt to achieve what is in fact an abnormally low body weight. AN affects 0.5–1 per cent of adolescent and young adult women (Claridge and Davis, 2003). Up to one-third also describe episodes of uncontrollable overeating (binge-eating/bulimia nervosa; see below). There's also evidence of an increase in cases of AN among males (Seligmann *et al.*, 1994). Where the age of onset is 8–14, about 25 per cent are boys (Frude, 1998).

DSM-IV-TR (2000) distinguished between the *restricting* and *binge-eating/purging* types of AN. The restricting type is what we most commonly associate with AN. Both the quantitative and qualitative value of food eaten is systematically reduced over time, producing an escalating state of malnutrition and loss of energy. But, as Claridge and Davis (2003) observe, the binge-eating/purging type sounds more like bulimia nervosa (BN) than it does the restricting type of AN. So, the DSM classification seems quite arbitrary, and some researchers have questioned whether these really are separate disorders (Mitchell and McCarthy, 2000). This has become even more of an issue with the addition of Binge-eating disorder in DSM-5 (see Chapter 43).

One difference between restricting type AN and BN is the patient's *body weight* (the latter's is either within normal limits or actually over). DSM-5 has chosen to use *body-mass index*/BMI) as the unifying characteristic for the AN subtypes, instead of classifying EDs according to their *psychobehavioural* similarities.

Probably the most useful marker of the distinction between AN restricting type and BN is *amenorrhoea* (cessation of menstruation); this often occurs early in the development of the disorder, preceding any obvious weight loss in about 20 per cent of cases. However, this criterion has been dropped from DSM-5. In AN restricting type, depression, lability of mood, social withdrawal and lack of sexual interest are all common. Some patients have signs that are secondary to the low food intake, including constipation, low blood pressure, brachycardia (slow heart rate), sensitivity to cold and hypothermia (Gelder *et al.*, 1999). Those whose dieting progresses to AN are more likely to have low self-esteem, and prevalence is increased among groups for whom weight and physical appearance are particularly relevant, such as ballet students and models (see Critical Discussion 44.5).

AN has the highest mortality rate of any psychiatric disorder (including depression and alcoholism). According to the Eating Disorders Association (EDA), mortality is 13–20 per cent (Waterhouse and Mayes, 2000), death arising from both the effects of starvation and suicide.

Among those with improved weight and menstrual function, some continue to have abnormal eating habits, some become overweight, and some develop BN. The most useful predictor of poor outcome is a long history of AN at the time the patient is first seen by a doctor (Gelder *et al.*, 1999).

Studies have found neuropsychological, behavioural and cognitive similarities in individuals with autistic spectrum disorder (ASD) and those with AN; this highlights the question of whether AN should be considered within the ASD spectrum (Allely, 2013) (see Chapter 40).

Figure 44.16 The much publicised English anorectic twins, Samantha and Michaela Kendall. Despite receiving treatment in the USA, Samantha eventually died. Michaela died three years later

Bulimia nervosa

While AN has been recognised in Europe and the USA since the 1870s, *bulimia nervosa* (BN) (from *bous* meaning 'ox' and *limos* meaning 'hunger') was virtually unknown before the 1970s. By the 1980s, however, it was widely agreed that BN was considerably more common than AN (Gordon, 2001).

BN sufferers tend to be older, less likely to come from middle- or upper-class backgrounds, more likely to have been overweight in the past and engage in self-destructive or antisocial, impulsive behaviours (such as shoplifting, drug abuse or deliberate self-harm). According to Russell (1979), BN is more intractable to treat, and patients have a poorer prognosis. It affects 2–3 per cent of adolescent and young adult women (Claridge and Davis, 2003).

Depression is common (mainly secondary to the ED), and there's considerable lability of mood. It's not uncommon for sufferers to contemplate suicide after binging, or to actually attempt suicide. While denial is a common feature of AN, BN sufferers are usually well aware that they have a serious problem and require help (Mitchell and McCarthy, 2000). However, the non-purging type is more likely to follow a binge with periods of fasting or excessive physical activity. This probably represents the most secretive and difficult to recognise type, since exercise is so highly valued in Western society. Because of all the known benefits of regular exercise, the exercising bulimic is likely to be seen by even close friends and family as the picture of health. By contrast, the anorectic who exercises obsessively will be conspicuous because of her emaciated appearance (Claridge and Davis, 2003). Unlike anorectics, bulimics don't 'look' bulimic.

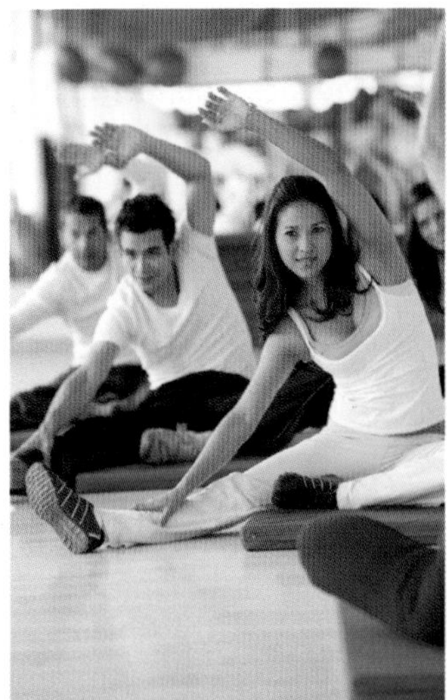

Figure 44.17 Regular exercise can be a way of concealing an eating disorder through a socially highly valued activity

It's the extreme lack of control over eating that distinguishes BN from AN. The binge initially provides pleasurable relief from the urge to eat and other kinds of tension, but this is soon followed by guilt and disgust. Repeated vomiting causes potassium depletion, which induces weakness, cardiac arrythmia (irregular heart rhythms), and renal damage. Urinary infections and epileptic seizures may also occur (Gelder *et al.*, 1999). Tooth enamel becomes eroded by the gastric acid brought up by vomiting.

Ask Yourself

- Based on these criteria for diagnosing AN and BN, do you think they represent exaggerations of 'normal' eating/dieting behaviours, or are they qualitatively different?

Explaining eating disorders

The quotes from Fedoroff and McFarlane (1998) at the beginning of this section imply that all the major theoretical perspectives have something to contribute to explaining the origins of both AN and BN. However, the recent – and ongoing – public debate about EDs, together with the claim that they may be a western *culture-bound syndrome* (CBS) (e.g. DiNicola, 1990), suggests that explanations at the cultural (rather than the individual) level may be the place to start. Since the 1980s, it's become clear that EDs are unique among psychiatric disorders in the degree to which social and cultural factors influence their epidemiology, development and perhaps even their aetiology (the *sociocultural hypothesis*) (Gordon, 2001).

Ask Yourself

- What kind of evidence would support the sociocultural hypothesis?
- What specific cultural factors would you expect to be particularly influential?

Are EDs universal? Are the causes universal?

While many studies have found evidence of common symptomatology as described by DSM and ICD in non-western societies, others have proposed that some symptoms don't appear in some non-western cultures. For example, an intense fear of fatness and body-image disturbance aren't typical of AN patients in Hong Kong and India, and their reasons for refusing food are more likely to be linked to somatic symptoms, such as abdominal bloating and fullness. They're also much less likely to display bulimic symptoms. In non-western countries, weight loss is often achieved purely by dietary restriction, rather than purging behaviours (Fedoroff and McFarlane, 1998). Although 'fat concern' has become a collective experience in the modern world (western and non-western), the experience of people with AN is extremely diverse (Lee, 2001).

Although emaciation, food refusal, and amenorrhoea are universal symptoms of AN, it's important to evaluate symptoms in their cultural context. For example, is fasting a culturally sanctioned expression of religious piety (as in Middle Eastern countries), or is it a symptom of an underlying disorder? All the screening and diagnostic instruments have been developed in Europe and North America, and are based directly on western concepts of abnormal eating. Consequently, patients who don't fit the model, but who may well be showing cultural diversity in the expression of a psychiatric disorder, will be ignored (Kleinman, 1987). Similarly, Lee (2001) argues that when the DSM approach is applied to AN, fat phobia becomes the 'core' symptom. This means that:

> *... patients who do not fit into this constructed (and constricted) template are conveniently discarded as unreal, atypical or simply dishonest deniers ...*

This makes the detection of reliable cross-cultural differences very difficult.

Critical Discussion 44.5

EDs and women's identity

The incidence of EDs appeared to rise sharply in the USA and UK, and many European countries, during the mid-to-late 1960s, then in accelerating fashion into the 1970s and through the late 1980s. Some have described this as a modern epidemic, which has coincided with a number of sweeping changes in Western societies during that period (Gordon, 2001). More specifically:

> *... because eating disorders affect mainly females and revolve around issues of identity and body image, it is not surprising that observers have linked the rise of eating disorders in the West with the crises of female identity and the forces impinging on women that followed the cultural upheavals of the 1960s ...* (Gordon, 2001)

According to Wolf (1991):

> *... As women have moved in increasing numbers into the spheres of education and work around the globe, expectations for achievement and performance have sometimes conflicted sharply with insistent demands for traditional postures of dependency and submissiveness ...*

These contradictory pressures have produced an increased sense of personal uncertainly, self-doubt and powerlessness. The thin body ideal de-emphasises traditional 'feminine' curvaceousness in a society still riddled with sexist stereotypes that associate 'curves' with low intelligence (Silverstein and Perlick, 1995).

All the evidence suggests that EDs are no longer unique to western societies. For example, Mumford *et al.* (1992) found that English-speaking girls in Lahore, Pakistan, showed similar rates of BN to white schoolgirls in England. Significantly, the Pakistani girls lived in an area where there were many advertisements for slimming clinics and 'keep fit' clubs. They were also from upper social classes, and were more likely to have adopted western lifestyles and values.

Crucially, there are contradictory pressures that emerge when women begin to have access on a mass scale to education and a more equal role in public life. This may be especially problematic in societies where the transition to a new female role is particularly sudden and conflicts sharply with traditional forces that demand deference to one's family and submissiveness to men (Gordon, 2001).

In post-apartheid South Africa, the evolving emancipation of women is part of profound changes in the sociocultural environment in general (Szabo and le Grange, 2001):

> *... If the central dynamic of an eating disorder is an identity struggle, then this struggle could be defined as a desire to become more 'western' while at the same time embracing a new found pride in being African, that is, to take pride in one's African culture, psychologically, and literally ...*

The conflict over gender roles may no longer be an exclusive issue for western women (Nasser, 1997), and EDs may be one way in which this search for identity in black South African women is expressed (Szabo and le Grange, 2001).

Anorexia and the brain

As powerful as cultural influences are, they cannot tell the whole story. Despite the fact that most women are exposed to pervasive media messages about attractiveness and thinness, the population incidence and prevalence of EDs are relatively low. As Claridge and Davis (2003) put it:

> *... If our glorification of the slender female body was the principal cause of eating disorders, we should find a far higher prevalence ... than we do. Whether media images of thinness play a causal role, or merely reflect wider cultural standards, is controversial, but it's unlikely that the relationship between the increasing demand for thinness and the rise of EDs is coincidental . . .*
> *(Gordon, 2001)*

According to Brewerton *et al.* (2009), SPECT and PET studies have consistently shown that in about 70 per cent of patients there's a reduction in blood flow (hypoperfusion) in the temporal region, in both early onset AN patients and in adults. Hypoperfusion seems to be positively correlated with severity of ED pathology and impaired visuospatial memory and executive functioning; it bears no relation to weight/body-mass index (BMI), mood, age at onset, or length of illness, nor does it appear to reverse with nutritional rehabilitation. It's possible that all these abnormalities are primary phenomena that pre-date the illness and so are probably *risk factors*; they may also represent a (neurodevelopmental) subtype of AN.

Box 44.5 AN and interoception

- As we saw in Chapter 33, the function of the *insula* is to integrate interoceptive signals from inside the body with exteroceptive signals; this integration forms our body image – what we think we look like.
- The *anterior* insula determines how we feel about our body and ourselves, helping to create a conscious feeling of 'being' (the *sentient self*) (Ananthaswamy, 2014).
- Research indicates that an unresponsive insula plays a crucial role in the development of AN, BN and body dysmorphic disorder (Arnold, 2012).
- For example, Sachdev *et al.* (2008) used fMRI to compare how female AN patients and female controls processed photographs of themselves and of other people. While both groups processed non-self-images in a similar way, their processing of self-images was quite discrepant: the AN participants showed no activation of the attentional system or the insula.
- Tsakiris *et al.* (2011) found that female students with lower bodily awareness (but without an ED) were more susceptible to the *rubber hand illusion* (being tricked into thinking that a rubber hand is actually part of their body).

CONCLUSIONS: A DIATHESIS-STRESS MODEL OF EATING DISORDERS

Ask Yourself

- Can you see any parallels between the vulnerability explanation of EDs and a particular explanation of schizophrenia (see p. 770)?

The findings of Brewerton *et al.* (2009) suggest another good example of a *diathesis-stress model* (as for schizophrenia): a defect in the insular cortex may represent the diathesis, with exposure to media pressures equating beauty with thinness constituting the (environmental) stress. Another, increasingly influential environmental stress is the existence of 'pro-ana' websites, which feature 'thin-spiration galleries' of emaciated women (including celebrities such as Victoria Beckham) and claim that 'being thin is more important than being healthy' (Goodchild, 2006) – or even 'It's better to be thin and dead than fat and living' (Atkins, 2002).

Cultural factors 'set the stage', provide the backdrop, heighten awareness and create, for many, the initial motive for dieting:

> *... the power and pervasiveness of advertising are primarily responsible for the normative discontent that many young women – and more recently men – feel about their physical appearance, and for the extraordinary methods they will use to improve their body image. The diet and fitness industries are dual conspirators in this process, and continue to make a fortune from the insecurities and dissatisfaction they have fostered in our society. (Claridge and Davis, 2003)*

External/environmental influences alone (here, cultural pressures towards thinness) cannot provide a complete explanation. A *complementary* approach is to regard only individuals who are vulnerable to these cultural pressures as likely to develop symptoms. As well as brain abnormalities, vulnerability may arise through pre-existing anxiety, depression, low self-esteem in childhood and history of weight preoccupation (Bulik, 2001). Other risk factors include *obsessionality*. Perhaps the most consistently reported association is between EDs (especially AN) and OCD (see above).

Another crucial finding is the comorbidity of EDs and *social anxiety*. Levinson and Rodebaugh (2012) identify five domains of social anxiety: (i) *social interaction anxiety;* (ii) *fear of scrutiny;* (iii) *fear of positive evaluation*; (iv) *fear of negative evaluation*; and (v) *social appearance anxiety*. They found that (v) predicted body dissatisfaction, bulimia symptoms, shape concern, weight concern, and eating concern over and above (i), (ii) and (iii). Fear of negative evaluation (iv) uniquely predicted drive for thinness and restraint; (iv) and (v) represent vulnerabilities for both social anxiety and eating disorder symptoms. Interventions that target these negative social evaluation fears may help prevent the development of EDs (Levinson and Rodebaugh, 2012).

Chapter Summary

- While **fear** evolved as an adaptive mechanism, **anxiety** often occurs in the absence of any external threat.
- A **phobia** is an extreme, irrational fear. Most common is **agoraphobia**, followed by **social** phobias and **specific** phobias. **Preparedness** may help explain why some phobias are more easily acquired than others.
- **Obsessions** are recurrent, intrusive thoughts and feelings, often accompanied by **compulsions,** which are repetitive, ritualised behaviours. Their function is to prevent a dreaded event and reduce distress.
- Skinner's **superstition hypothesis** tries to explain how **obsessive-compulsive disorder (OCD)** develops, but is more successful at explaining how it's **maintained**.
- **Cognitive** explanations include Rachman's **thought–action fusion (TAF)** interpretation.
- Symptoms of **post-traumatic stress disorder (PTSD)** include both defensive **avoidance/repression** and **flashbacks**. PTSD can be seen as a breakdown of the normal stress response.
- The traditional distinction between **endogenous/psychotic** and **reactive/neurotic depression** is controversial, and causation is no longer implied when a diagnosis of **major depressive disorder (MDD)** is made.
- The much higher (successful) **suicide rate** among males can be explained in terms of a number of factors related to the male **gender role ('masculinities')**.
- The **monoamine hypothesis (MAOH)** is based on the mechanisms of **tricyclics, monoamine oxidase inhibitors (MAOIs)** and **specific serotonin reuptake inhibitors (SSRIs)**.
- **Learned helplessness theory (LHT)** is the original of three **cognitive** explanations of depression. The realisation that there's more to depression than LH led to LHT's revision in terms of **attribution theory principles**.
- **Schizophrenia** is one of the most serious of all mental disorders. Schneider's **first-rank symptoms (FRSs)** are **subjective experiences,** while Slater and Roth's four additional symptoms are **directly observable** from the patient's behaviour.
- An important distinction is made between **positive (Type I)** symptoms (the presence of **active symptomatology), negative (Type II)** symptoms **(lack/poverty of behaviour)** and **disorganised** (or **cognitive) symptoms**.
- Differences between the brains of schizophrenics and non-schizophrenics aren't sufficient on their own to allow diagnosis, and evidence for the **dopamine hypothesis (DH)** is inconclusive.

- According to the **diathesis–stress model,** inherited factors can only increase the likelihood that **vulnerable** individuals will become schizophrenic. Environmental factors are needed to trigger the symptoms.
- **Anorexia nervosa** (**AN**) and **bulimia nervosa** (**BN**) have many symptoms in common. But bulimics are usually of normal weight, are older, are less likely to come from middle-/upper-class backgrounds, and more likely to engage in self-destructive or antisocial behaviours.
- AN and BN are occurring more frequently in developing cultures as they become more industrialised/westernised, which includes changes in diet and attitudes towards desirable physical appearance.
- Eating disorders (EDs) are now far too global to be considered Western culture-bound syndromes (CBSs).
- EDs may partially be the result of the **ambivalence** towards food in Western societies. The **thinness ideal** conflicts with the availability of food, and the promotion of cooking and general consumption of food.
- Research indicates that an unresponsive **insula** (that controls **interoception**) plays a crucial role in the development of AN and BN.
- While there's much support for the **sociocultural hypothesis,** other individual factors are needed to provide a complete account of EDs (including certain brain abnormalities, pre-existing social anxiety, depression, low self-esteem and obsessionality).

Links with Other Topics/Chapters

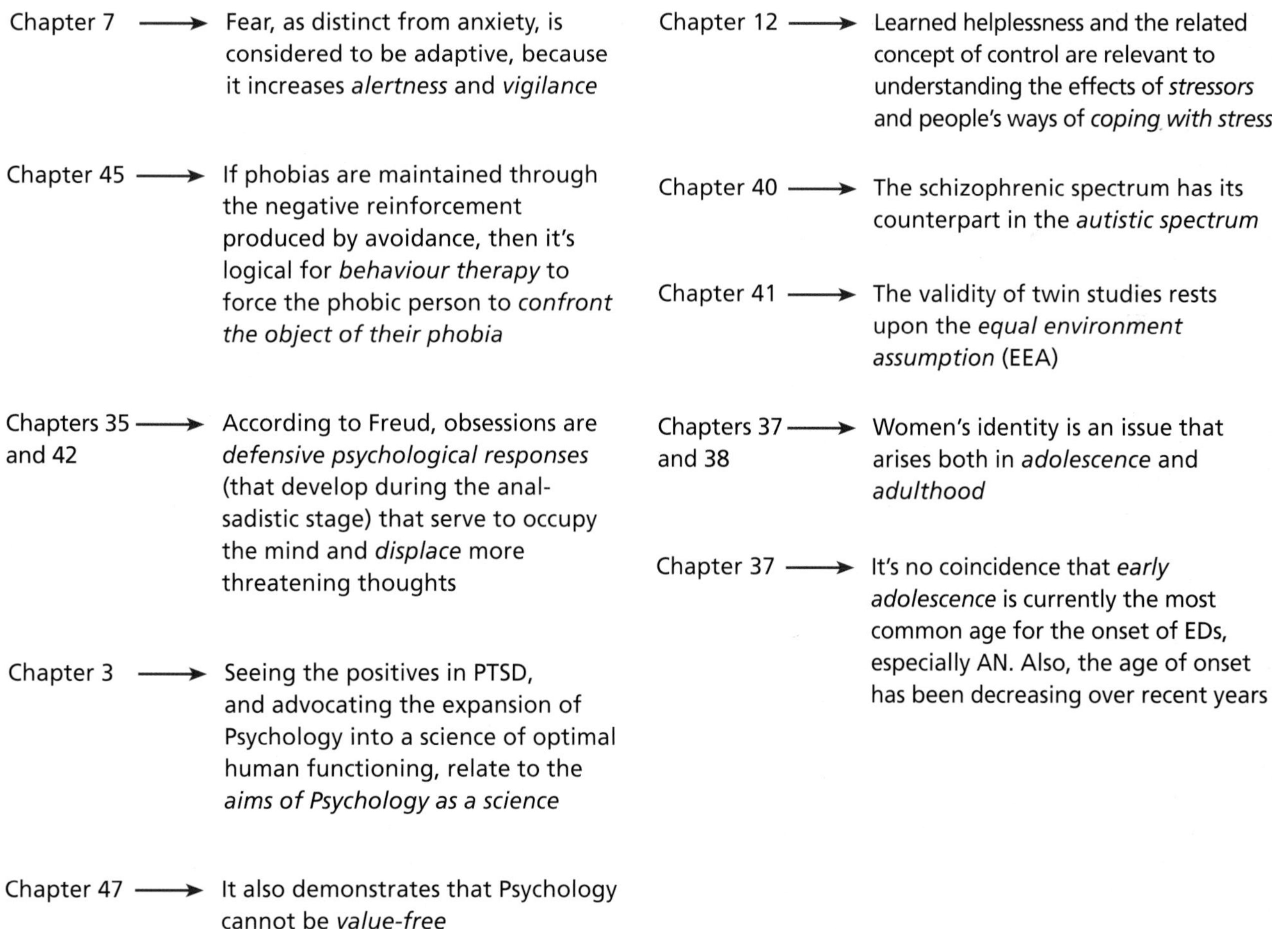

Chapter 7 ⟶ Fear, as distinct from anxiety, is considered to be adaptive, because it increases *alertness* and *vigilance*

Chapter 45 ⟶ If phobias are maintained through the negative reinforcement produced by avoidance, then it's logical for *behaviour therapy* to force the phobic person to *confront the object of their phobia*

Chapters 35 and 42 ⟶ According to Freud, obsessions are *defensive psychological responses* (that develop during the anal-sadistic stage) that serve to occupy the mind and *displace* more threatening thoughts

Chapter 3 ⟶ Seeing the positives in PTSD, and advocating the expansion of Psychology into a science of optimal human functioning, relate to the *aims of Psychology as a science*

Chapter 47 ⟶ It also demonstrates that Psychology cannot be *value-free*

Chapter 12 ⟶ Learned helplessness and the related concept of control are relevant to understanding the effects of *stressors* and people's ways of *coping with stress*

Chapter 40 ⟶ The schizophrenic spectrum has its counterpart in the *autistic spectrum*

Chapter 41 ⟶ The validity of twin studies rests upon the *equal environment assumption* (EEA)

Chapters 37 and 38 ⟶ Women's identity is an issue that arises both in *adolescence* and *adulthood*

Chapter 37 ⟶ It's no coincidence that *early adolescence* is currently the most common age for the onset of EDs, especially AN. Also, the age of onset has been decreasing over recent years

Recommended Reading

Chamption, L. & Power, M. (eds) (2000) *Adult Psychological Problems: An Introduction* (2nd edn). Hove: Psychology Press. Also relevant to Chapter 2.

Davey, G. (2008) *Psychopathology.* BPS/Blackwell.

Davison, G.C., Neale, J.M. & Kring, A.M. (2004) *Abnormal Psychology* (9th edn). New York: John Wiley & Sons.

Enoch, D. & Ball, H. (2001) *Uncommon Psychiatric Syndromes* (4th edn). London: Arnold.

Gross, R. (2012) *Key Studies in Psychology* (6th edn). London: Hodder Education. Chapter 8.

Maddux, J.E. & Winstead, B.A. (eds) (2012) *Psychopathology: Foundations for Contemporary Understanding* (3rd edn). New York: Routledge. Chapters 8–13.

Useful Websites

www.rcpsych.ac.uk (Royal College of Psychiatrists website)

www.edreferral.com/bulimia_nervosa.htm (Eating Disorder Referral and Information Center: International Eating Disorder Organization)

www.bbc.co.uk/radio4/science/allinthemind_20020410.shtml ('All in the Mind' presented by Raj Persaud)

www.psycom.net/depression.central (Dr Ivan's Depression Central: Huge resource for all aspects of the nature and treatment of depressive disorders)

CHAPTER 45

TREATMENTS AND THERAPIES

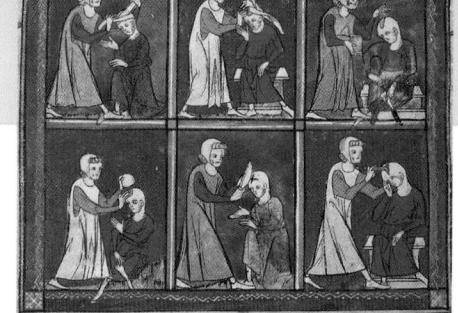

Classifying treatments and therapies

Biological (somatic) therapies

Psychoanalysis and other psychodynamic approaches

Behavioural approaches

Cognitive–behavioural therapy

An evaluation of therapy: is it effective?

INTRODUCTION and OVERVIEW

As Chapters 43 and 44 have shown, the study of psychological abnormality involves a convergence of *psychiatry* (a branch of medicine) and *Abnormal Psychology*, the latter defined as the scientific study of the causes of abnormal behaviour/mental disorders. In this chapter, the focus is on the application of what we know about abnormality in an attempt to help people with psychological problems. The two professional branches of Psychology whose goals are the maintenance and generation of mental health are *Clinical Psychology* and (the more recent) *Counselling Psychology* (Powell, 1995; see Chapter 1).

Both Clinical and Counselling Psychology draw on the same research findings and range of theoretical approaches that have recurred throughout this book. They also both adopt the *scientist–practitioner model* of helping: the professional helper is guided by, and operates within the framework of, general scientific methods when assessing alternative treatments/therapies (Dallos and Cullen, 1990; see Chapter 3).

While Clinical Psychologists have traditionally been more influenced by *behavioural approaches* (based on classical and operant conditioning), *cognitive-behavioural approaches* are now widely used (reflecting the dominance of the cognitive approach within Psychology generally). Counselling Psychologists (as well as trained counsellors, who may not be Psychologists) have been more influenced by the *Humanistic approach*. A third, overlapping, professional group are psychotherapists; their methods reflect (to varying degrees) the influence of Freud's *psychoanalysis*.

CLASSIFYING TREATMENTS AND THERAPIES

Dimensions along which treatments can be placed

- What most *psychological treatments* have in common is a *rejection of the medical model* (see Chapters 43 and 44). For example, although Freud distinguished between 'symptoms' and 'underlying pathology', the latter is conceived in psychological terms (not genetic or biochemical), and he was concerned with the individual and not the 'disorder'. Although he used diagnostic labels, he did so for linguistic convenience rather than as an integral part of his theories. He focused on understanding his patients' problems in their life context, rather than on clinical labelling (Mackay, 1975).
- One aspect of 'technique' which is profoundly important in the *therapeutic relationship* is whether or not the therapist makes suggestions and gives advice to the patient (or client). In *directive therapies*, concrete suggestions are made and clients are often instructed to do certain things (such as 'homework' in between sessions, or specific exercises under the therapist's supervision). For example, *behaviour therapy* concentrates directly upon changing people's behaviour (and any desired changes in thoughts and feelings will 'look after themselves'). By contrast, *cognitive–behaviour therapy* (CBT) is aimed directly at thoughts and feelings: clients are instructed to give themselves instructions for behaviour, to write down their distressing and negative thought patterns, and so on (and the *behaviour* will look after itself).

- *Non-directive therapies* concentrate on making sense of what's going on in the relationship between therapist and client, and on understanding the meanings of the client's experiences (as in *psychoanalysis* and *client-centred therapy*). These are more difficult to describe than directive therapies, because the therapist plays a more passive role:

  > *... listen[ing] and tak[ing] part with the client in exploring and experiencing what is going on between them ... (Oatley, 1984)*

- A major development in psychotherapy in the late 1970s and early 1980s was the emergence of *family therapies* and *marital/couple therapy*, reflecting the growing awareness by therapists of the important role played by the client's relationships in the development and maintenance of their problems (Dryden, 1984). Generally, where the problem is seen as *interpersonal*, family, marital/couple or group therapy is likely to be recommended. But where the problem is seen as 'residing' within the client (*intrapsychic*), individual therapy would be recommended.
- While most therapy is *face-to-face*, this is now increasingly conducted via the internet (*online therapy*) (Dunn, 2012). Leff *et al.* (2013) recently used *avatar therapy* with patients diagnosed with schizophrenia who hear voices; this involved a computer-generated embodiment (*avatar*) of their most troubling voice. Also, *brain-training* computer programs are being designed specifically to help memory, attention, and logical reasoning problems in people with schizophrenia (Wilson, 2014).

What is psychotherapy?

The term 'psychotherapy' is sometimes used to refer to all *psychological* treatments (as opposed to biological or somatic ones). For example, Holmes and Lindley (1989) define it as:

> *The systematic use of a relationship between therapist and patient – as opposed to pharmacological or social methods – to produce changes in cognition, feelings and behaviour.*

Similarly:

> *Psychotherapy is distinguished from such other forms of psychiatric treatment as the use of drugs, surgery, electric shock treatment and insulin coma treatment ... (Freedman* et al.*, 1975)*

'Psychotherapy' (or 'psychodynamic therapy': see Chapter 2) is also used to refer to those methods based, directly or indirectly, on Freud's psychoanalysis. This approach is also known as *insight therapies* ('talking cures').

In the UK, the tradition has been to contrast psychotherapy with behaviour therapy, while in the USA psychotherapy is used more broadly to include behavioural psychotherapy as well as 'psychodynamic therapy'. However, the *UK Council for Psychotherapy* (UKCP) has a behavioural psychotherapy section (members of which include the British Association for Behavioural and Cognitive Psychotherapy), as well as a psychoanalytic and psychodynamic psychotherapy section. Other sections include humanistic and integrative psychotherapy, and family, marital and sexual therapy. In 2009 there were over 80 member organisations of the UKCP, grouped together in modality sections and representing all the main traditions in the practice of psychotherapy in the UK. Two special members are the British Psychological Society (BPS) and the Royal College of Psychiatrists. The *British Association for Counselling and Psychotherapy* (BACP) is the largest and broadest body within the sector.

Ask Yourself

- Looking back at Chapter 44, try to identify (or infer) any principles (or specific details) that would be used by different theoretical approaches in the treatment of mental disorder. (You might find Chapter 2 useful too.)

BIOLOGICAL (SOMATIC) THERAPIES

Chemotherapy

This involves the use of *psychotropic drugs*, which are designed to affect mainly mental symptoms. Gelder *et al.* (1999) divide these into six groups, according to their primary actions (see Box 45.1). Several also have secondary actions (e.g. antidepressants also reduce anxiety). The focus here will be on the *antidepressants*, *anxiolytics*, and *antipsychotics*.

Antidepressants

The main difference between various kinds of antidepressants is in their *side-effects,* rather than their effectiveness or speed of action (Gelder *et al.*, 1999). They all increase 5-HT (serotonin) function, and many also increase noradrenaline function. Most can be

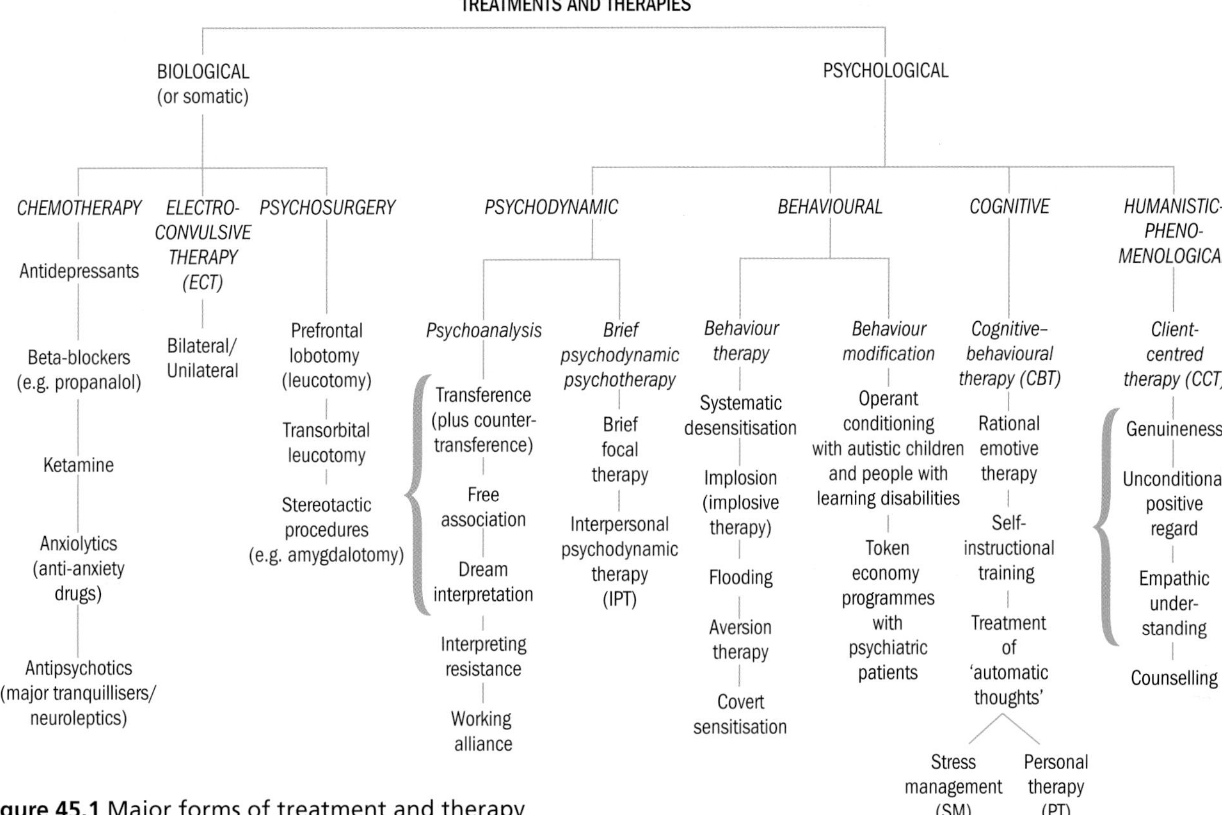

Figure 45.1 Major forms of treatment and therapy

Box 45.1 Major categories of psychotropic drugs (Based on Gelder *et al.*, 1999)

Anxiolytics reduce anxiety. Because they have a general calming effect, they're sometimes called *minor tranquillisers*. In larger doses, they cause drowsiness (and so are sometimes called *sedatives*).

Hypnotics promote sleep. Many are of the same type as drugs used as anxiolytics.

Antipsychotics control delusions, hallucinations, and psychomotor excitement in psychoses. They're sometimes called *major tranquillisers* because of their calming effect, and *neuroleptics*, because of their neurological side-effects, such as those resembling Parkinson's disease.

Mood-stabilising drugs are used to prevent the recurrence of affective disorders. One of these is *lithium carbonate* (Lithane or Lithonate), used to treat bipolar mood disorder.

Antidepressants relieve the symptoms of depressive disorders, but don't elevate the mood of non-depressed people. They're also used to treat anxiety disorders, including OCD.

Psychostimulants elevate mood, but are used mainly for treating hyperactivity in children.

given just once per day, but they usually 'kick in' only after 10–14 days. They should be withdrawn slowly: sudden cessation can cause restlessness, insomnia, anxiety, and nausea.

Monoamine oxidase inhibitors (MAOIs)

Iproniazid was originally used in 1952 as a treatment for tuberculosis – it elevated patient's mood (without, incidentally, affecting the disease). Iproniazid and related drugs (e.g. *phenelzine* or Nardil) inhibit the activity of an enzyme known as monoamine oxidase (MAO), and gradually increase the activity levels of neurons that utilise noradrenaline (a monoamine) and 5-HT.

These are generally less effective than tricyclics when used to treat severe depression, and no more effective for mild depression. They're seldom the first choice of treatment, because of their side-effects (including cerebral haemorrhage) and dangerous interactions with other drugs and foodstuffs (although *reversible* MAOIs are safer).

Tricyclics

These are so-named because their basic chemical structure includes three carbon rings. *Imipramine* (Tofranil) and *amitryptyline* were the first to be introduced and are still used as a standard for comparing other antidepressants. They seem to act by blocking the reuptake of dopamine and noradrenaline, but some also block the reuptake of serotonin, others block serotonin alone, and some have no known effect on any of these systems (Hamilton and Timmons, 1995). They're effective in the treatment of both mild and severe depression, and are the first choice of drug in the latter.

However, they have many side-effects, including toxic effects on the cardiovascular system. As a result, they're gradually being replaced by modified tricyclics (such as *lofepramine* and *trazedone*) which cause fewer side-effects (Gelder *et al.*, 1999).

Specific serotonin reuptake inhibitors (SSRIs)

These 'second generation' drugs selectively inhibit the reuptake of serotonin into presynaptic neurons, that is, they make more serotonin available (see Chapter 4). Examples include *paroxetine* and *fluoxetine* (Prozac). They seem to be as effective as tricyclics in treating mild depression, and they're safer for patients with glaucoma and in overdose. Prozac has rapidly become the most commonly prescribed antidepressant medication (Costello *et al.*, 1995), having been taken by more than 38 million people (Boseley, 1999) since its introduction in 1988.

Ask Yourself

- One aspect of the controversy surrounding Prozac is its use as a 'designer drug'. Kramer (1993) advocates that everyone could benefit from taking it, since it makes people more assertive and playful, and improves relationships. Kramer believes that in the near future, we'll be able to change our 'self' as easily as we change our clothes ('cosmetic psychopharmacology'). Even if this were possible, do you think it's right? (See Critical Discussion 45.1.)

How effective are antidepressants?

What this question usually means is: how much more effective are antidepressants than placebos ('dummy drugs', usually inert sugar pills). Fisher and Greenberg (1995) looked at 15 separate reviews of the literature relating to antidepressants, plus two large-scale meta-analyses (see Box 45.8). Overall,

Critical Discussion 45.1

The Prozac (and Seroxat) controversy: the 'safe' pill that can kill

According to Munro (2000):

Drugs like Prozac are firmly entrenched in both professional and public minds as the treatment of choice for depression. There is a growing concern that the widespread use of antidepressants is blocking the development of other forms of treatment, such as cognitive therapy. Such a trend could be exacerbated by the increased affordability of fluoxetine ...

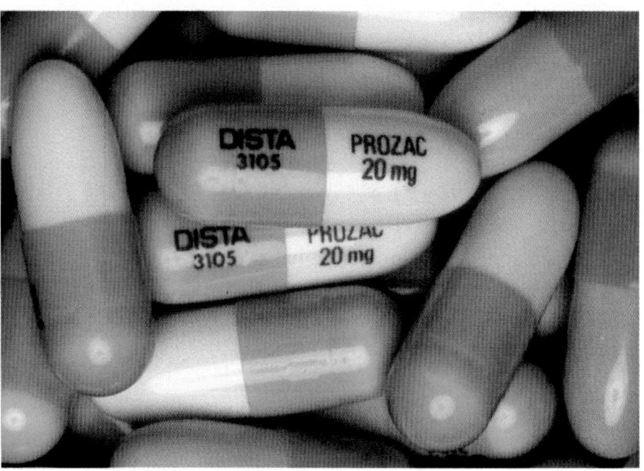

Figure 45.2 Prozac – the world's favourite antidepressant

Prozac was marketed as a wonder drug (Munro, 2000), and its biggest selling-pitch has been that it's almost impossible to kill yourself with an overdose. But since its launch in 1988 in the USA (and in the UK shortly afterwards), there's been a spate of disturbing accounts of violence and suicide committed by people prescribed the drug by their doctors. Victims and families of killers have sued Eli Lilly (see below) in 200 court cases (Boseley, 1999).

About 250,000 people worldwide taking Prozac have attempted suicide (because of the drug), and about 25,000 will have succeeded. Eli Lilly knew as long ago as 1979 that Prozac can produce in some people a strange, agitated state of mind that can trigger an unstoppable urge to commit murder or suicide. This is a recognised psychiatric disorder called *akathisia*, which has long been associated with antipsychotic drugs (such as chlorpromazine). But while these drugs take away the will to do anything about the suicidal/violent feelings, Prozac doesn't (Boseley, 1999).

Another SSRI, Seroxat, is proving at least as controversial. Seroxat is among the biggest-selling drugs in the world, and is taken by 600,000–800,000 people in the UK, of whom a significant proportion are under 30 (Laurance, 2004b).

In 2003, Seroxat was banned in the UK for under-18s because of an increased suicide risk. The ban applied to all other SSRIs – except Prozac. According to the Seroxat Users' Group, it's still being prescribed to children and under-18s despite the ban (Townsend, 2004).

the effectiveness of antidepressants appears to be modest, with a high relapse rate (over 60 per cent) among those who respond positively to the drugs but are then taken off them. Their benefits also tend to wane after a few months, even while they're still being taken.

Fisher and Greenberg also discuss the *methodology* of drug trials. In a classic *double-blind design*, neither the patient nor the researcher knows whether the patient is receiving a drug or a placebo. But when the (inactive) placebo doesn't produce as many bodily sensations as the drug, participants soon learn to discriminate between them. For example, imipramine causes dry mouth, tremor, sweating, and constipation. These side-effects could be used by those administering the drug/placebo to identify the 'ons' and the 'offs', and they might convey their resulting expectations as to the effects of the drug/placebo to the participants.

For these reasons, *active* placebos (such as *atropine*), which do produce side-effects, are sometimes used. In one review cited in Fisher and Greenberg (1995), 68 studies conducted between 1958 and 1972 which had used an inert placebo were compared with seven which had used atropine. The antidepressant was found to be superior to the placebo in 59 per cent of the former, but in only 14 per cent (one study) of the latter.

Kirsch *et al.* (2008) conducted a meta-analysis, which showed that while people got better on antidepressant medication, they also improved on placebos, and the difference was small; in fact, it fell below the criterion for clinical significance established by the UK's National Institute for Health and Clinical Excellence (NICE), which sets treatment guidelines for the NHS. Clinical significance was found only in a few, relatively small, studies involving extremely depressed patients.

A recent study conducted in New Zealand used an online questionnaire to survey the largest sample of antidepressant recipients to date (1829 adults prescribed the drugs during the previous five years) (Read *et al.*, 2014). Eight out of 20 adverse effects were reported by over half the participants: most frequent were *sexual difficulties* (62 per cent), and *feeling emotionally numb* (60 per cent). Other, less frequent, side-effects, included *suicidality* (39 per cent) and *feeling not like myself* (52 per cent). These side-effects may be more common than previously thought – indeed, they've been largely ignored or denied – and include both emotional and interpersonal effects (Read *et al.*, 2014).

According to Murphy (2013), there's been a steady rise in the past two decades of *treatment-resistant depression*. The effectiveness of some antidepressants has been overstated, to the extent that some drug companies have stopped researching them altogether; also, drugs such as Prozac seem to be getting less effective. Clinical trials in the 1980s and 1990s indicated that SSRIs would help 80-90 per cent of depressed people go into remission. But studies in the 2000s showed a decline to 60-70 per cent, and a huge, nationwide trial conducted by the US National Institute of Mental Health (NIMH) showed that few of the near 3000 participants fully recovered without switching to or adding other medications. (See Box 45.2.)

Box 45.2 Ketamine

- A major alternative treatment has recently emerged in the form of the drug *ketamine,* used primarily as an anaesthetic in veterinary medicine (especially horses) and as a short-acting anaesthetic and analgesic in surgery and other painful procedures.
- A randomised trial involving 18 patients with long-term, intractable (untreatable) depression found that a single dose of ketamine hydrochloride, given intravenously, lifted symptoms within two hours and this improvement was maintained one week later (Zarate *et al.*, 2006).
- One theory of how ketamine has its antidepressant effects relates to *glutamate*. Not only does it play a key role in learning, motivation, memory and plasticity, but it may help neurons to repair themselves. If, as some believe, depression causes some dendrites to shrivel, resulting in damaged synapses, then ketamine may be teaching a depressed brain how to repair itself (Murphy, 2013).
- However, serious side-effects include hallucinations and other psychotic symptoms. An alternative is *lanicemine,* a drug originally developed to treat epilepsy and which also targets glutamate receptors.
- Sanacora *et al.* (2013) gave 152 people with moderate to severe depression and a history of poor response to antidepressants, either lanicemine or a placebo three times a week for three weeks. The reduction in symptoms between the two groups was still statistically significant up to two weeks after treatment ended. However, unlike ketamine, it took this amount of time for the antidepressant effects to appear.

Gambling and SSRIs

Antidepressants aren't just used for treating depression. In one of the few evaluations of drug therapies in the treatment of gambling disorder, Hollander *et al.* (2000) evaluated the effectiveness of *fluvoxamine*, an SSRI, in a small study involving 15 people. They were first treated with a placebo drug before entering an eight-week period of active treatment. Although only ten people completed the study, the drug showed a significant benefit, with greater reduction in gambling and urges to gamble than in the placebo treatment phase. Bennett (2006) cites two other, more recent studies, which replicated these findings using other SSRIs.

Anxiolytics

Anxiolytics are used most appropriately to reduce severe anxiety. They should be prescribed for a short time only (usually a few days, seldom more than two to three weeks), because they can result in tolerance and dependence. Withdrawal effects are reported in people using them for more than six months: the withdrawal syndrome includes apprehension and anxiety, tremor, and muscle twitching (see Chapter 8). *Chlordiazepoxide* (marketed as Librium) and *diazepam* (Valium) appeared in the early 1960s, quickly becoming the most widely prescribed drugs of their time. In 1989, for example, there were 21 million prescriptions in the UK alone (Rassool and Winnington, 1993).

> **Box 45.3 Withdrawal from alcohol – detoxification**
>
> - When someone is dependent on alcohol, a sudden cessation of drinking may cause severe withdrawal symptoms, including *delirium tremens* or seizures. Since these complications may be dangerous, withdrawal (*detoxification*) should be carried out under medical supervision, whether at home or in hospital. In less severe cases, and where there's no significant physical illness or history of previous withdrawal seizures, detoxification can be carried out at home under the supervision of the GP.
> - Since dependent patients are unlikely to succeed in reducing alcohol gradually, it's usually best to stop the alcohol, replace it with a drug that will prevent delirium tremens or fits, and then withdraw this drug gradually. *Benzodiazepines* (such as *diazepam* and *chlordiazepoxide*) are the drugs of first choice (Gelder *et al.,* 1999). For most planned withdrawals, these drugs produce a smoother course of withdrawal, and are less likely to be abused (Gelder *et al.* 1999).

Chlordiazepoxide and diazepam are *benzodiazepines* (other examples being *temazepam* and *flurazepam*), which act by facilitating the activity of GABA (see Chapter 4). As well as anxiolytic, sedative, and hypnotic effects, they have muscle-relaxant and anticonvulsant properties (Gelder *et al.*, 1999).

Beta-blockers

Also used to treat anxiety are *beta-blockers*, developed for the treatment of high blood pressure and cardiac problems. A widely used example is *propanolol*, which works by blocking the effects of noradrenaline, one of the stress hormones (see Chapter 12). Brunet *et al.* (2011) compared 40 patients with PTSD who were given propanolol with 26 PTSD patients who weren't: on average, physiological symptoms of fear (such as racing heart and sweating) reduced by 50 per cent for the former and 7 per cent for the latter. Following the study, three-quarters of the treated patients no longer met the criteria for PTSD. Hamzelou (2014) reports on a study that is currently using propanolol in the treatment of arachnophobia.

Antipsychotics

Antipsychotics (or *major tranquillisers*) were originally developed to calm patients facing surgery, and they proved highly effective in reducing the incidence of death from surgical shock. *Chlorpromazine* (Largactil) and related *phenothiazines* were soon used with psychiatric patients (starting in the early 1950s). They revolutionised psychiatry by allowing the most disturbed schizophrenic patients to live outside a psychiatric hospital, or to reduce their average length of stay. However, many critics have called these drugs 'pharmacological straitjackets'.

They're effective in treating the acute, *positive* symptoms of schizophrenia, such as hallucinations, excitement, thought disorder, and delusions, and they seem to work by blocking the D2 receptor for dopamine. However, they don't touch the *negative* symptoms (see Tables 44.1 and 44.2).

The newer, 'atypical' antipsychotic drugs, such as *clozapine* and *riperidone*, are less likely to cause EP symptoms and may also treat the negative symptoms of schizophrenia. Clozapine is also the first atypical drug shown to be effective in treating patients who have failed to respond to 'typical' antipsychotics such as chlorpromazine (Effective Health Care, 1999; Gelder *et al.*, 1999).

Morrison *et al.* (2014) aimed to establish whether *cognitive therapy* (CBT) was effective in reducing psychiatric symptoms in people with schizophrenia spectrum disorders who'd chosen not to take

Box 45.4 Some side-effects of antipsychotic drugs

Extrapyramidal (EP): *acute dystonia* (involuntary muscle contraction), *akathisia* (inner restlessness, agitation and pacing), *Parkinsonism* (shuffling gait, tremor, expressionless face, etc.), and *tardive dyskinesia* (chewing and sucking movements, grimacing, akathisia).

Anticholinergic: dry mouth, blurred vision, low blood pressure (which may cause fainting attacks), constipation, glaucoma.

Neurolepticmalignant syndrome: fluctuating levels of consciousness, hyperthermia, muscular ('lead pipe') rigidity, autonomic disturbances (such as unstable blood pressure, urinary incontinence and tachycardia). While this is rare, it can be life-threatening, and can occur with any antipsychotic drug, at any dose, at any time (Hutton, 1998).

(Based on Gelder *et al.*, 1999)

antipsychotics. Using a single-blind randomised controlled trial, Morrison *et al.* found that, compared to 'treatment as usual', cognitive therapy significantly reduced psychotic symptoms (such as hearing voices and paranoia) and significantly improved everyday functioning; it seems to be a safe and acceptable alternative to antipsychotic drugs (see below, pp. 795–7).

Electroconvulsive therapy

In 1938, Cerletti and Bini, two Italian doctors, first gave an electric shock to the brain of a psychiatric patient, on the assumption that if a *grand mal* epileptic fit is induced (artificially), this should reduce or eliminate the symptoms of schizophrenia. *Electroconvulsive therapy* (ECT) started to be used widely in the USA from the early 1940s. Ironically, it was found to be more effective for severe depression than schizophrenia, and is now used mainly with depressive patients.

The procedure

The patient is made comfortable on a bed, clothes loosened and shoes and dentures removed. Atropine is given as a routine pre-anaesthetic medication (to dry up salivary and bronchial secretions) and then *thiopentone,* a quick-acting anaesthetic, followed by a muscle relaxant. A 70–150-volt shock lasting 0.04–1.00 second is then given through electrodes ('paddles') placed on the temples, producing a generalised convulsion lasting for up to a minute (detected by facial and limb twitching). Typically, two to three treatments per week are given for three to four weeks. Less commonly, treatment is given every two to four weeks for six months or longer to prevent relapse (*continuation* or *maintenance* ECT; Bennett, 2003).

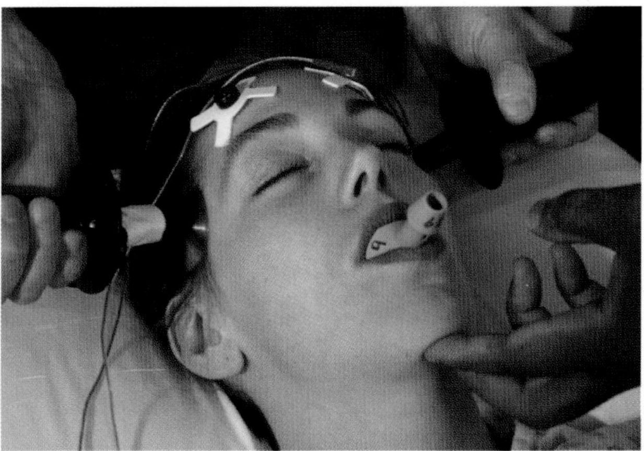

Figure 45.3 ECT as it is carried out today. Despite the technical improvements, ECT is a highly controversial treatment

Many psychiatrists believe that for severe depression, *bilateral* ECT (one electrode on each side of the head) is preferable, as it acts more quickly and fewer treatments are needed. (This was the common practice up until the 1950s.) In *unilateral* ECT, an electrode is applied to the non-dominant hemisphere side (the right side for most people) to reduce the side-effects, particularly memory disruption (Benton, 1981).

Contrary to popular belief, ECT is still widely used. Its use began to decline substantially during the 1950s with the introduction of psychotropic drugs, but it was given to 11,340 patients in England and Wales in 1999 (peaking at 28,000 in 1985). Of these, two-thirds were women, 41 per cent were over 65, and 15 per cent were in hospital under section (i.e. involuntarily). It's rarely used in Japan and many other European countries (Johnstone, 2003).

Side-effects

The question of the effectiveness of ECT is largely overshadowed by debate about its *ethics*. MIND (the National Association for Mental Health) and PROMPT (Protect the Rights of Mental Patients in Therapy) in the UK, and NAPA (Network Against Psychiatric Assault) in the USA, object to it primarily on ethical grounds. Some people describe it as a terrifying experience, and regard it as an abusive invasion of personal autonomy (Bennett, 2003). Some experience it as a damaging repeat of earlier traumas (such as physical/sexual abuse), undermining their trust in mental health professionals (Johnstone, 1999; MIND, 2001). Continuing to use ECT in the light of these accounts becomes an ethical issue. According to Szasz (1971),

> *... electricity as a form of treatment requires the sacrifice of the patient as a person,[and] of the psychiatrist as a clinical thinker and moral agent.*

The ethics of ECT are also related to its side-effects. *Short-term risks* are associated with being given an anaesthetic and having an epileptic fit. *Longer-term side-effects* involve memory disruption, such as *retrograde amnesia* (failure to remember what happened *before* the treatment) and impaired ability to acquire new memories. But because depression is associated with impaired memory function, it's unclear to what extent ECT itself is responsible (Benton, 1981). The patient is normally confused for up to 40 minutes following treatment, but recall of events prior to treatment gradually returns (although some degree of memory loss may persist for several weeks).

The shift from bilateral to unilateral ECT has reduced the amount of memory deficit (Bennett, 2003), but cognitive impairment seems to be unavoidable for an unknown number of patients. Contrary to the Royal College of Psychiatrists' (RCP, 1997) claim that ECT doesn't have any long-term effects on memory or intelligence, critics (e.g. Breggin, 1997) claim that ECT not only causes memory loss but general mental and emotional dysfunction.

According to Davison *et al.* (2004):

> *Given that suicide is a real possibility among depressed people and given a moral stance that values the preservation of life, the use of ECT, at least after other treatments have failed, is regarded by many as defensible and responsible.*

Consistent with this conclusion is the fact that ECT is increasingly used as a *second-line treatment* for those patients who don't respond to antidepressant medication, and perhaps psychological treatments; these 'treatment-resistant' individuals are also likely to be the greatest suicide-risks. (See Box 45.2.) However, there's hardly any evidence to suggest that ECT does actually prevent suicide (Read and Bentall, 2010; Read *et al.*, 2013).

How effective is ECT?

Current psychiatric opinion in the UK is represented by the RCP ECT *Handbook* (1995), according to which 'ECT ... is an effective treatment in severe depressive illness' and occasionally in other conditions, such as psychosis and mania. In support of ECT, the *Handbook* cites a study by Buchan *et al.* (1992), who compared sham (placebo) ECT with real ECT, following up patients four weeks and six months after treatment. They concluded that: (a) 'real ECT does not appear to be effective in non-retarded, non-deluded patients'; and (b) any benefits for retarded or delusional patients disappeared after six months.

Reviews of the research (e.g. Breggin, 1997) have generally been unable to find any controlled studies showing the benefits of ECT lasting longer than four weeks. According to Read *et al.* (2013), any benefits may last only a few days. Also, the relapse rate is high (RCP, 1995). According to Abrams (1997) author of the standard textbook *Electroconvulsive Therapy*:

> *Modern ECT researchers ... do not have any more of a clue to the relationship between brain biological events and treatment response in ECT than they did at the time of the first edition of this book – which is to say, none at all.*

Ask Yourself

- **Since we don't know how ECT works (and whether it works), should it be used at all?**

Benton (1981) argues that this isn't a reason for not using it: many medical treatments fall into this category (e.g. the use of aspirin in the treatment of headaches). But in other branches of medicine, a treatment with such an imbalance between risk and benefit would be deemed *unethical* (Andre, 2008; Breggin, 2008; Read and Bentall, 2010). Breggin (1991, 1997) claims that ECT 'works' by causing brain damage. Patients suffer *anosognosia*, a condition in which they deny their psychological and physical difficulties (rather like 'treating' prolonged depression by being permanently drunk). While loss of painful memories may be felt as a relief, this state is sometimes mistaken by staff and patients alike for improvement.

According to Lilienfeld and Arkowitz (2014), ECT is greatly misunderstood and misrepresented – in movies especially – as barbaric punishment. While acknowledging that the procedure should be improved and the side-effects reduced, Lilienfeld and Arkowitz believe that ECT is an option worth considering for unremitting psychological distress when all other interventions have failed.

Figure 45.4 Jack Nicholson as McMurphy and Louise Fletcher as Nurse Ratchet in *One Flew Over the Cuckoo's Nest*

PSYCHOANALYSIS AND OTHER PSYCHODYNAMIC APPROACHES

Freud's model of psychological disorder

In Chapter 42, neurotic symptoms were described as compromises between the opposing demands made on the ego by the id and the superego. Symptoms (along with dreams and defences) are expressions of the inevitable conflict which arises from these opposing demands and are, at the same time, attempts to deal with it.

When a person experiences anxiety, the ego is signalling that it fears being overwhelmed by an all-powerful id (*neurotic anxiety*) or superego (*moral anxiety*), and so must mobilise its defences. Anxiety is the hallmark of most neurotic disorders, but except in 'free-floating anxiety', it becomes redirected or transformed in some way (depending on which particular defence is used). Consequently, the resulting symptom makes it even less likely that the true nature of the problem (i.e. the underlying conflict) will be spotted. *Phobias*, for example, involve *repression* (as do all neuroses), plus *displacement* and *projection*.

Ask Yourself

- Try to explain Little Hans' phobia of being bitten by a horse in terms of these three ego defences (see Chapter 35).

Hans' horse phobia could be explained in terms of:

- repressing his jealous anger and hatred felt towards his father
- projecting these feelings onto his father, thus seeing him as a threatening, murderous figure, and
- displacing this perception of his father on to a 'safer' target, namely, horses.

As we noted in Chapter 42, Freud believed that phobic objects symbolically represent the object for which they're a substitute.

Box 45.5 Deep brain stimulation

- *Deep brain stimulation* (DBS) refers to the use of electric current to change brain function through the placing of electrodes deep inside the brain.
- Ainsworth (2008) cites research involving patients whose depression or OCD has resisted all other forms of treatment, leaving them suicidal and profoundly disabled; after receiving DBS, they've been able to go out, hold down jobs and form relationships.
- It's now being trialled with people suffering from drug addiction, AN, obesity stroke, Parkinson's disease, Tourette's, and Alzheimer's disease.
- In the case of depression, brain areas that have been targeted so far include the *subegenual cingulate*, and the *nucleus acumbens* (NA). Severely depressed people lose the ability to experience pleasure, suggesting that their reward systems are faulty.
- The NA was an attractive target for DBS because it's involved in processing reward and pleasure, as well as mediating motivational behaviour (see discussion of the 'addicted brain' in Chapter 8). The NA also receives input from, and sends output to, several different brain circuits, many of which are involved in processing emotions (including the subegenual cingulate). DBS produced immediate improvement (Ainsworth, 2008).
- Also, it's more precise: electrodes are guided to within a millimetre of their target. Not only is the procedure *reversible* (the electrical stimulation can be turned off), but the risks (including brain haemorrhage, infection or even death) are rare. However, some bioethicists argue that we don't yet know enough about DBS to broaden its use so quickly (Fisher, 2014).

Neuroses are *maladaptive solutions* to the individual's problems: they don't help resolve the conflict, but merely help to *avoid* it (both in thought and behaviour). The neurotic's behaviour usually creates its own distress and unhappiness – this is the *neurotic paradox*.

Ask Yourself

- Try to explain neurotic behaviours (and the neurotic paradox) in terms of learning theory (i.e. conditioning).

The aims of psychoanalysis

The goals of psychoanalysis can be stated in very broad, abstract terms, such as 'a far-reaching and radical restructuring of the personality' (Fonagy, 1995) and as attempts to provide the client with insight, self-knowledge and self-understanding. More specifically, the basic goal of psychoanalysis is to make 'the unconscious conscious', to undo unsatisfactory defences and, through a 'therapeutic regression' (Winnicott, 1958), to re-experience repressed feelings and wishes, which have been frustrated in childhood, in a safe context, and to express them, as an adult, in a more appropriate way, 'with a new ending' (Alexander and French, 1946).

In relation to the structure of personality model, Freud (1938) believed that the analyst and the patient's weakened ego needed to become allies against the instinctual demands of the id and the conscientious demands of the superego. Analysts who still subscribe to this model aim primarily to extend, through the psychoanalytic process, patients' knowledge of themselves (*insight*), in the hope that this may enable them to make choices that aren't exclusively ruled by neurotic needs – to explore new compromises and more adaptive solutions (Lemma, 2002).

Therapeutic techniques

The role of the analyst

In classical psychoanalysis, the analyst is meant to remain faceless and 'anonymous', not showing any emotion or revealing any personal information. Instead:

> *... The doctor should be opaque to his patients and, like a mirror, should show them nothing but what is shown to him ... (Freud, 1912, in Jacobs, 1992)*

With the analyst as an 'ambiguous object' or 'blank screen', the patient is able to project and displace repressed feelings, in particular those concerning parents (*transference*). This process is aided by the client lying on a couch, with the analyst sitting behind, out of the client's (*analysand's*) field of vision. Jacobs (1992) notes that, in practice, Freud often became personally involved in the therapeutic conversation and would explain his thinking to the patient (see below).

Transference and counter-transference

Transference typically goes through a positive phase of emotional attachment to the analyst, followed by a negative and critical phase. According to Freud, this reflects working through the ambivalence experienced in the patient's childhood relationship with his/her parents (Stevens, 1995). According to Thomas (1990), transference has become so central to the theory and practice of psychoanalysis that many analysts believe that making interpretations about transference is what distinguishes psychoanalysis from other forms of psychotherapy. When attention is focused on the transference and what's happening in the here and now, the historical reconstruction of childhood events and the search for the childhood origins of conflicts may take second place.

The related process of *counter-transference* refers to the therapist's feelings of irritation, dislike or sexual attraction towards the client. Thomas (1990) maintains that:

> *... In Freud's time, counter-transference feelings ... were considered to be a failing on the part of the analyst ... Now, counter-transference is considered an unavoidable outcome of the analytic process, irrespective of how well prepared the analyst is by analytic training and its years of required personal analysis ... most modern analysts are trained to observe their own counter-transference feelings and to use these to increase their understanding of the patients' transference and defences ...*

Interpretation and resistance

To enable the client to understand the transference and how it relates to childhood conflicts, the analyst must *interpret* it, that is, tell the client what it means in relation to what's already been revealed about the client's childhood experiences. Because this is likely to be painful and distressing, clients show *resistance*. This may take the form of 'drying up' when talking, changing the subject, dismissing some emotionally significant event in a very flippant way, even falling asleep or arriving late for therapy. All forms of resistance require interpretation.

Figure 45.5 Sigmund Freud's couch (Freud Museum Publications Ltd)

The working alliance, dream interpretation, and free association

As important as the analyst's anonymity may be, the '*working alliance*' with the client is just as crucial. According to Jacobs (1984), this consists of two adults cooperating to understand the 'child' in the client. The analyst adopts a quiet, reflective style, intervening when s/he judges the client to be ready to make use of a particular interpretation. This is an art, and doesn't involve fitting the client into psychoanalytic theory, as some critics suggest (Jacobs, 1984).

Two other major techniques used to reveal the client's unconscious mind are *dream interpretation* (see Chapter 42) and *free association*, in which the client says whatever comes to mind, no matter how silly, irrelevant or embarrassing it may seem. Free association is an *ideal* that patients strive towards – in practice, it's very difficult to share all the contents of our thoughts. Nevertheless, the principle of free association underpins all current psychoanalytic practice (Lemma, 2002). Both dream interpretation and free association may lead to resistance which, like transference, will in turn be interpreted by the analyst.

According to Fonagy (2000), evidence from a significant number of before–after studies suggests that psychoanalysis is consistently helpful to patients with milder (neurotic) disorders, and somewhat less consistently so for groups with more severe disorders. Other less well controlled studies suggest that longer intensive treatments tend to have better outcomes than shorter, non-intensive treatments. The impact of psychoanalysis is evident not just in relation to symptoms, but as measured by patient's work performance and reduction in health care costs.

Critical Discussion 45.2

The concept of cure: How do you know when to stop?

According to Jacobs (1984), the goals of therapy are limited by what clients consciously want to achieve and are capable of achieving, together with their motivation, ego strength, capacity for insight, ability to tolerate the frustration of gradual change, financial cost, and so on. These factors, in turn, determine how a cure is defined and assessed.

In practice, psychoanalysis ranges from *psychoanalytical first aid* (Guntrip, 1968) or symptom relief, to different levels of more intense work. However, Storr (1966) believes that symptom relief is an inappropriate way of perceiving 'cure', partly because symptom analysis is only the start of the analytic process, and also because a majority of clients don't have clear-cut symptoms anyway. Similarly, Fonagy (2000) says that:

> *... Symptom change as a sole indicator of therapeutic benefit must indeed be considered crude in relation to the complex interpersonal processes that evolve over the many hundreds of sessions ...*

Freud himself recognised that psychoanalysis was only likely to be successful if the patient is voluntary, open to change, acknowledges that there's a problem, and is neurotic rather than psychotic (the latter being unable to form a positive transference). Even if the patient possesses these characteristics, fresh neuroses or even the return of the original one cannot be ruled out. Analysis never really ends.

Indeed, Freud famously claimed that psychoanalysis could help transform 'hysterical misery' into 'common unhappiness'. This is as much as one could hope for, given that intrapsychic conflict is an inevitable part of human life.

Brief psychodynamic psychotherapy

According to Hoyt (2003), beginning with Freud, numerous theoreticians and clinicians have applied the psychoanalytic concepts of the unconscious, resistance, and transference to brief forms of treatment. Indeed, many of Freud's cases were 'brief', just a few sessions lasting weeks or months. By contrast, in the UK classic psychoanalysis requires the client to attend three to five sessions per week for several years (Fonagy, 2000); for many, this is far too expensive as well as too time-consuming. Early pioneers include Alexander and French (1946) and Ferenczi (1952).

Various short-term dynamic methods have been developed to 'bring the patient to a greater awareness of his or her maladaptive defences, warded-off feelings, and counterproductive relationship patterns' (Hoyt, 2003). What they all emphasise is increased therapist activity within a limited, central focus. There may be a 'contract' for a specified number of weeks as opposed to the open-ended arrangement of classic analysis. For example, Malan's (1976) *brief focal therapy* lasts for one session per week for about 30 weeks, targeting fairly specific psychological problems (such as a single area of conflict or relationship in the client's current life). Although all the basic techniques of psychoanalysis may be used, there's considerably less emphasis on the client's past, and client and therapist usually sit in armchairs facing each other.

This form of therapy is practised by many Clinical Psychologists (as well as psychiatrists and social workers), who haven't received a full-blown psychoanalytic training (Fonagy, 1995; Fonagy and Higgitt, 1984). Fonagy (2000) cites evidence for the effectiveness of brief dynamic psychotherapy.

Interpersonal psychodynamic therapy (IPT) is a variant of brief psychodynamic therapy that stresses the interactions between a client and his/her social environment. One of the pioneers was the American psychiatrist, Harry Stack Sullivan, who argued that patients' basic difficulty is misperceiving reality stemming from disorganised interpersonal relationships in childhood, in particular the relationship with the parents. In contrast with Freud's analyst-as-blank-screen, Sullivan advocated that the therapist was a 'participant observer' in the therapy process (cf Kelly's PCT; see Chapter 42).

IPT (Klerman *et al.*, 1984) concentrates on the client's current interpersonal difficulties and on discussing – even directly teaching – better ways of relating to others. The therapist combines empathic listening with suggestions for behavioural changes and how to implement them. The core of this approach is to help the depressed person examine the ways in which his/her interpersonal behaviour might interfere with obtaining pleasure from relationships. Clients are helped to improve their communication (verbal and non-verbal) and social skills, reality testing, and ability to meet their current social role obligations. The focus is on the person's *current* life, rather than exploring past – often repressed – causes of present-day problems.

In a review of depression treatment outcome studies (Leichsenring, 2001, in Davison *et al.*, 2004), the success rate of short-term psychodynamic treatment is comparable to that of CBT. One of the outcome studies included in this review is the Treatment of Depression Collaborative Research Program (Elkin *et al.*, 1989), which suggested that IPT is particularly effective for removing the symptoms of unipolar depression as well as for maintaining treatment gains (Frank *et al.*, 1990).

BEHAVIOURAL APPROACHES

Models of psychological disorder

According to the behavioural model, all behaviour, whether adaptive or maladaptive, is acquired by the same principles of classical and/or operant conditioning (see Chapter 11).

The medical model is completely rejected, including any distinction between 'symptoms' and underlying pathology. According to Eysenck (1960), if you 'get rid of the symptom … you have eliminated the neurosis'. But according to Freud, if treatment tackles only the symptoms and not the underlying conflict, new neurotic symptoms will replace those which are removed (*symptom substitution*).

However, this is increasingly being seen as an oversimplification and misunderstanding of what behaviour therapy involves. Wachtel (1989), for example, argues that in some ways all theories and therapies make assumptions about 'symptoms as manifestations of some underlying problem'. What distinguishes different approaches is the view taken of the *nature* of those underlying problems, and how much change is needed for the problem to be remedied. He calls for an *integration* between the two approaches which, in practice, is already happening.

Behavioural technology versus behavioural analysis

According to Mackay (1975), some behaviour therapists (e.g. Eysenck, Rachman, and Marks) try to discover which techniques are most effective with particular diagnostic groups. This *nomothetic* approach is called *behavioural technology*. Others (e.g. Yates and Meyer) believe that therapists should isolate the stimuli and consequences that are maintaining the inappropriate behaviour in each individual case, and that, accordingly, any treatment programme should be derived from such a 'behavioural analysis' (or 'functional analysis'). This *idiographic* approach is called *behavioural psychotherapy*.

Part of the functional analysis is an emphasis on current behaviour–environment contingencies, in contrast to the Freudian emphasis on past (particularly early childhood) events, and unconscious (and other internal) factors. *Psychological* problems are *behavioural* problems, which need to be *operationalised* (described in terms of observable behaviours) before we attempt to change them. According to Richards (2002), 'behavioural psychotherapy' is now the preferred term for describing all the techniques that have traditionally been called 'behaviour therapy' as well as those that are often discussed under the separate heading (as in this chapter) of *cognitive behaviour therapy* (CBT). For many Clinical Psychologists, the theoretical models of abnormality that behavioural techniques are derived from are less important than the fact that they are *evidence-based*.

Classical conditioning and phobias

Ask Yourself

- How, according to classical conditioning, do phobias arise? (See Chapter 11.)
- What are the limitations of this explanation?

According to Eysenck and Rachman (1965), the case of Little Albert exemplifies how *all* phobias are acquired (i.e. through classical conditioning):

> *Any neutral stimulus, simple or complex, that happens to make an impact on an individual at about the time a fear reaction is evoked, acquires the ability to evoke fear subsequently ... there will be generalisation of fear reactions to stimuli resembling the conditioned stimulus ... (Wolpe and Rachman, 1960)*

One of the problems with this explanation is that some phobias are easier to induce in the laboratory than others (in participants who don't already have them), and it's well known that certain naturally occurring phobias are more common than others. These findings are consistent with Seligman's (1970) concept of *preparedness.*

Even more difficult for the classical conditioning model to explain is the *persistence* of naturally occurring phobias (that is, their failure to extinguish).

Ask Yourself

- How can operant conditioning help to explain the persistence of phobias?

Mowrer's (1960) 'two-process' theory has been extremely influential in behavioural psychotherapy, much of which is aimed at helping clients to modify the reinforcers ('maintenance factors') that keep their problem behaviours going. People are helped to break the cycle of fear and avoidance (Richards, 2002; see below).

The persistence of neurotic behaviour may also be accounted for in terms of what Freud (1926) called *secondary gain*: the attention and sympathy the neurotic receives from other people, which (unintentionally) positively reinforces it.

Behaviour therapy

Behaviour therapy refers to techniques based (primarily) on *classical conditioning*, developed by Psychologists such as Eysenck and Wolpe. Wolpe (1958) defined behaviour therapy as 'the use of experimentally established principles of learning for the purpose of changing unadaptive behaviour'.

Systematic desensitisation

The case of Little Peter (see Chapter 11) represents the earliest example of any kind of behavioural treatment, and the methods used to remove his phobia of animals were later called *systematic desensitisation* (SD) by Wolpe (1958). It represents a form of *counter-conditioning*, and the key principle in SD is that of *reciprocal inhibition*, according to which:

> *... if a response inhibitory of anxiety can be made to occur in the presence of anxiety-evoking stimuli it will weaken the bond between these stimuli and the anxiety ... (Wolpe, 1969)*

In other words, it's impossible for someone to experience two opposite emotions (e.g. anxiety and relaxation) at the same time. Accordingly, a patient with a phobia is first taught to relax through deep muscle relaxation, in which different muscle groups are alternately relaxed and tensed (alternatively, hypnosis or tranquillisers might be used). So, relaxation and fear of the object or situation 'cancel each other out' (this is the '*desensitisation*' part of the procedure).

The '*systematic*' part of the procedure involves a graded series of contacts with the phobic object (usually by imagining it), based on a *hierarchy* of possible forms of contact from the least to the most frightening. Starting with the least frightening, the patient, while relaxing, imagines the object (e.g. the word 'spider' on a printed page) until this can be managed without feeling any anxiety at all. Then, and only then, the next most feared contact will be dealt with, in the same way, until the most frightening contact can be imagined with no anxiety (e.g. a large, hairy spider running all over your body).

Wolpe used imagination, because some of his patients' fears were so abstract (e.g. fear of criticism or failure) that it was impractical to confront them using real-life situations. He also believed that the ability to tolerate stressful imagery is generally followed by a reduction in anxiety in related real-life situations. Between sessions, patients are usually instructed to put themselves in progressively more frightening real-life situations. These 'homework assignments' help to move their adjustment from imagination to reality (Davison and Neale, 1994).

An evaluation of SD

- Rachman and Wilson (1980) and McGlynn *et al.* (1981) believe that SD is definitely effective, mostly for the treatment of specific phobias (e.g. animal phobias) as opposed to, say, agoraphobia (see Chapter 44), and for patients capable of learning relaxation skills and with sufficiently vivid imaginations to be able to conjure up the sources of their fear.
- There's some debate as to whether either relaxation or the use of a hierarchy of contact situations is actually necessary at all. According to Wilson and Davison (1971), for example, relaxation might be merely a useful way of encouraging a frightened person to confront what they're afraid of, which would otherwise be avoided.
- According to Marks (1973), SD works not because of reciprocal inhibition but because of the *exposure* to the feared situation; this seems to represent the generally accepted view among Psychologists. Exposure is especially effective if it allows the person to disprove his or her predictions that something awful will happen if they come into contact with the feared object or situation, and *graded exposure* helps to build up the person's confidence to cope with the exposure (Williams and Hargreaves, 1995).
- According to Richards (2002), graded exposure *in vivo* (that is, confronting real-life animals or situations) is the 'singularly most effective psychotherapeutic technique of modern times'.

Implosion (implosive therapy) and flooding

Implosion is essentially about exposing the patient to what, in SD, would be at the top of the hierarchy. Instead of gradual exposure accompanied by relaxation, the patient is 'thrown in at the deep end' right from the start. This is done by getting the patient to imagine their most terrifying form of contact (the big, hairy spider let loose, again) with vivid verbal descriptions by the therapist (*stimulus augmentation*) to supplement the patient's vivid imagery. How is it meant to work?

- The patient's anxiety is maintained at such a high level that eventually some process of *exhaustion* or *stimulus satiation* takes place – the anxiety level can only go down!
- Extinction occurs by preventing the patient from making the usual escape or avoidance response (Mowrer, 1960). Implosion (and flooding), therefore, represents a form of 'forced reality testing' (Yates, 1970).

Flooding is exposure that takes place *in vivo* (e.g. with an actual spider). Marks *et al.* (1971, cited in Marks, 1981a) compared SD with flooding, and found flooding to be superior. Gelder *et al.* (1973) compared SD with implosion and found no difference.

Ask Yourself

- What conclusions can you draw from these findings?

These findings suggest that *in vivo* exposure is what's crucial, and several researchers consider flooding to be more effective than implosion. Emmelkamp and Wessels (1975) and Marks (1981b) used flooding with agoraphobics very successfully, and other studies have reported continued improvement for up to nine years after treatment without the appearance of 'substitute' problems. Marks (1981a), in a review of flooding studies, found it to be the most universally effective of all the techniques used to treat phobias.

Ask Yourself

- Do you think that flooding is an ethically acceptable method of treating phobias?

Aversion therapy

In *aversion therapy*, some undesirable response to a particular stimulus is removed by associating the stimulus with another, *aversive*, stimulus. For example, alcohol is paired with an emetic drug (which induces severe nausea and vomiting), so that nausea and vomiting become a conditioned response to alcohol.

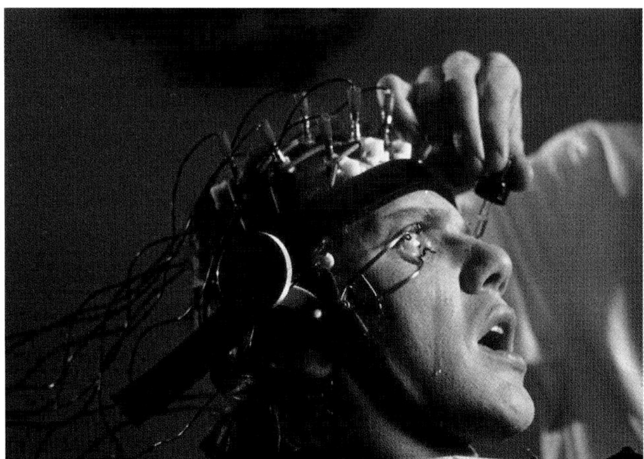

Figure 45.6 Malcolm McDowell in a scene from *A Clockwork Orange*. His eyes are clamped open, forcing him to watch a film portraying acts of violence and sadism, as part of aversion therapy. He'd earlier been given an emetic drug, so that extreme nausea and violence will become associated

Patients would, typically, be given warm saline solution containing the emetic drug. Immediately before the vomiting begins, they're given a four-ounce glass of whisky which they're required to smell, taste and swill around in the mouth before swallowing. (If vomiting hasn't occurred, another straight whisky is given and, to prolong nausea, a glass of beer containing emetic.) Subsequent treatments involve larger doses of injected emetic, or increases in the length of treatment time, or a widening range of hard liquors (Kleinmuntz, 1980). Between trials, the patient may sip soft drinks to prevent generalisation to all drinking behaviour and to promote the use of alcohol substitutes. Meyer and Chesser (1970) found that about half their alcoholic patients abstained for at least one year following treatment, and that aversion therapy is better than no treatment at all.

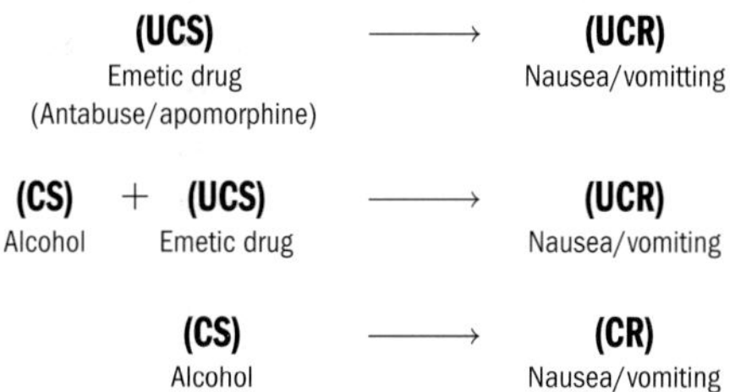

More controversially, aversion therapy has been used with homosexuals, fetishists, male transvestites, and sadomasochists. In a typical treatment, slides of nude males are presented to male homosexuals, and then quickly followed by electric shocks. The conditioned response to the slides is intended to generalise to homosexual fantasies and activities outside the treatment sessions. More recently, attempts have been made to replace homosexual responses with heterosexual ones, by showing slides of naked females: any sexual response will terminate the shock. Marks *et al.* (1970) reported desired changes for up to two years after treatment.

Behaviour modification

Behaviour modification refers to techniques based on *operant conditioning*, developed by Psychologists such as Ayllon and Azrin to build up appropriate behaviour (where it didn't previously exist), or to increase the frequency of certain responses and decrease the frequency of others.

According to Baddeley (1990), most behavioural programmes follow a broadly similar pattern involving a series of steps.

- **Step 1** Specify the behaviour to be changed. It's important to choose small, measurable, achievable goals.
- **Step 2** The goal should be stated as specifically as possible.
- **Step 3** A *baseline rate* should be measured over a period of several days, that is, how the person 'normally'

Critical Discussion 45.3

Aversion therapy as a form of heterosexism

Many Psychologists have argued that the social pressures on homosexuals to become 'straight' make it difficult to believe that the small minority of people who consult therapists for help in changing sexual preference are acting from choice (Davison and Neale, 1994).

The very fact that change-of-orientation treatments exist can be seen as condoning *heterosexism*. Clinicians work to develop procedures and study their effects only if they're concerned about the problem their techniques are intended to remedy; the therapeutic literature contains relatively little material on helping homosexuals develop as individuals without this involving a change of sexual orientation. This contrasts with the many books and articles on how best to discourage homosexual behaviour and replace it by heterosexuality.

One very radical proposal is that therapists shouldn't help homosexuals become straight, even when such treatment is requested. But this, in turn, raises basic questions about limiting the options available to clients and, in refusing such treatment, aren't therapists making value judgements, just as they are when they agree to it? Isn't it the professional responsibility of therapists to meet the needs expressed by their clients? However, a client's request for a certain kind of treatment has never been sufficient justification for providing it (Davison and Neale, 1994).

Bartlett *et al.* (2009) surveyed members of the BPS, BACP, UKCP, and RCP about their views regarding treatments to change homosexual desires. A significant minority (17 per cent) had attempted to 'help' lesbian, gay, and bisexual clients to reduce their sexual feelings – despite the lack of any evidence for the efficacy of such treatments and the potential harmful effects. The 'best' approach is to help people adjust to their situation, to value them as people and show them there's nothing pathological about their sexual orientation.

The Faculty of HIV and Sexual Health (part of the BPS) agrees with Bartlett *et al.* In fact, it believes that health care professionals who attempt to change sexual orientation may be committing human rights violations. Both the RCP and American Psychological Association (APA) argue that homosexuality is neither pathological nor deviant. When such clients do experience difficulties, it's as a result of prejudice and discrimination – not their sexual orientation itself (Kapp, 2010) (see Chapter 25).

behaves with respect to the selected behaviour. This may involve detailed observation, which can suggest hypotheses as to what's maintaining that behaviour.

- **Step 4** Decide on a *strategy*. For example, selectively reinforce non-yelling behaviour (through attention) and ensure that yelling behaviour is ignored.
- **Step 5** *Plan treatment*. It's essential that everyone coming into contact with the patient behaves in accordance with the chosen strategy.

A design that's commonly used to check the effectiveness of treatment is the *AB–AB design*, where A is the baseline condition and B is the experimental treatment. So, if treatment is working, the level of yelling should be reduced during the initial B-phase (compared with the initial A-phase), and should increase again when treatment is stopped (the second A-phase). When treatment is reintroduced (second B-phase), yelling should once more reduce.

- **Step 6** Begin treatment.
- **Step 7** Monitor progress.
- **Step 8** Change the programme if necessary.

Operant conditioning with special groups

Even under optimum conditions, *autistic children* never achieve the creative use of language and broad range of social skills of normal children (Thomas, 1985; see Chapter 40). However, Lovaas (1977) believes that many therapeutic gains can be retained at home (and even some modest improvements shown) if parents have been trained in the *shaping techniques* such as those described in Key Study 45.1.

Ask Yourself

- What do you understand by the term 'shaping'?
- What's a more technical term for shaping?
- How do you think shaping might be used to help autistic children develop language?

Key Study 45.1

Shaping speech in autistic children (Lovaas *et al*., 1967)

- Lovaas *et al*. pioneered operant conditioning with autistic children who normally had little or no normal speech. They used a *shaping* technique.
- Verbal approval was paired with a piece of food whenever the child made eye contact, or merely attended to the therapist's speech or behaviour (which is also unusual for autistic children). This reinforces attention and associates a positive social gesture with food, so that verbal approval eventually becomes a conditioned reinforcer.
- The child was reinforced with food and praise whenever it made any kind of speech sound, or even tried to imitate the therapist's actions.
- Once this occurred without prompting, the therapist gradually withheld reinforcement until the child successfully imitated complete actions or uttered particular vowel or consonant sounds, then syllables, then words and, finally, combinations of words.
- Sometimes, hundreds or even thousands of reinforcements were necessary before the child began to label objects appropriately or imitate simple phrases. Even when children have received extensive training, they're likely to regress if returned to a non-supportive institutional setting.

There are many striking examples of successful modification programmes involving people (both children and adults) with learning difficulties. In one large-scale study, Matson *et al*. (1980) reported substantial improvements in the eating behaviour of profoundly impaired adults. They used peer and therapist modelling (see below), social reinforcement, verbal prompts to shape eating, the use of utensils, table manners, and so on. Reinforcers included going to meals early, and having one's own table-mat. There was a significant improvement in the treated group even four months after the end of treatment, compared with an untreated control group.

Azrin and Foxx (1971) and Foxx and Azrin (1973) produced a toilet-training 'package' in which:

- the client is taken to the toilet every half hour and given extra fluids, sweets, biscuits, praise and attention when it's used successfully
- the client is strapped into a chair for half an hour, away from other people, if they have an accident; this isn't a punishment procedure, but 'time out', that is, a time away from positive reinforcement.

As with speech training in autistic children, there are problems of generalising from hospital-based improvement to the home situation. But if parents continue the programme at home, there can be short- and long-term benefits.

A form of behaviour often displayed by autistic and learning disabled individuals is *self-mutilation* by biting, scratching, head banging, and so on, all of which can be life-threatening. This has been treated successfully by using operant techniques (e.g. Bull and LaVecchio, 1978).

The token economy

The *token economy* (TE) is based on the principle of *secondary reinforcement*. Tokens (secondary or conditioned reinforcers) are given for socially desirable/acceptable behaviours as they occur, and can then be exchanged ('cashed in') later on for certain 'primary' reinforcers.

The TE was introduced by Ayllon and Azrin (1968), who set aside an entire ward of a psychiatric hospital for a series of experiments in which reinforcements were provided for activities such as face-washing, teeth-brushing, dressing properly, and making beds, and withheld for withdrawn or bizarre behaviour. The participants were 44 female chronic schizophrenic patients, with an average 16 years of hospitalisation. Some screamed for long periods, some were mute, many were incontinent, and a few were assaultive. Most no longer ate with cutlery, and some buried their faces in the food.

A baseline measure was made of how often socially desirable behaviours normally occurred. They were then systematically reinforced every time the desired behaviours occurred with plastic tokens that could later be exchanged for special privileges (e.g. listening to records, going to the cinema, renting a private room, extra visits to the canteen). The entire life of each patient was, as far as possible, controlled by this regime. Results showed that the patients significantly increased the frequency of the desired behaviours when they were reinforced.

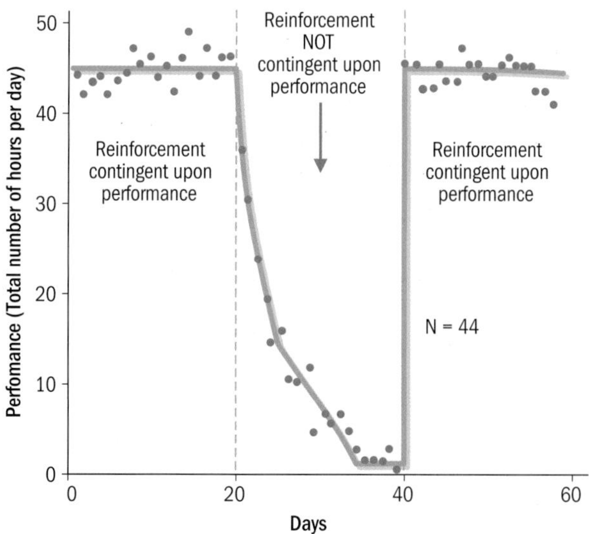

Figure 45.7 The effects of a token economy on the performance of 44 female hospitalised schizophrenics (from Ayllon and Azrin, 1968)

If the introduction of chlorpromazine and other antipsychotic drugs in the 1950s marked a revolution in psychiatry, the introduction of TE programmes during the 1960s was, in its way, equally revolutionary. This was partly because it drew attention to the ways in which nursing (and other) staff were inadvertently maintaining the psychotic ('mad') behaviour of many chronic schizophrenics by giving them attention, thus reinforcing unwanted behaviour.

An evaluation of the TE

Two main advantages of the TE are:

- tokens can be given immediately after some desirable behaviour occurs, thereby 'bridging' very long delays between the target response and the primary reinforcer; this is especially important when it's impractical or impossible to deliver the primary reinforcer immediately following the behaviour
- tokens make it easier to give consistent and effective reinforcers when dealing with a group of individuals.

According to Davison *et al.* (2004) these experiments demonstrated how even markedly regressed adult hospital patients can be significantly affected by systematic manipulation of reinforcement contingencies.

Since the 1960s, hundreds of carefully controlled experiments have shown that various psychiatric patient behaviours can be brought under control by manipulating reward and punishment contingencies. According to Holmes (1994), one of the most impressive tests of the effectiveness of the TE is a study by Paul and Lentz (1977).

However, there's been very little increase in the use of TEs, despite continuing evidence of their effectiveness (Paul and Menditto, 1992) (see Box 45.6).

COGNITIVE–BEHAVIOURAL THERAPY

Model of psychological disorder

According to Mahoney (1974) and Meichenbaum (1977), many (if not most) clinical problems are best described as disorders of thought and feeling. Since behaviour is to a large extent controlled by the way we think, the most logical and effective way of trying to change maladaptive behaviour is to change the maladaptive thinking which lies behind it. Beck (1993) defines *cognitive–behavioural therapy* (CBT) as:

> *the application of the cognitive model of a particular disorder with the use of a variety of techniques designed to modify the dysfunctional beliefs and faulty information processing characteristic of each disorder ...*

CBT is derived from various sources, including behaviour therapy and psychoanalysis, which define and operationalise cognition in different ways. However, the attempt to change cognition (*cognitive restructuring*) is always a means to an end, that end being 'lasting changes in target emotions and behaviour' (Wessler, 1986).

Major forms of CBT are *rational emotive therapy*/RET (Ellis, 1962, 1973), *self-instructional training*/SIT (Meichenbaum, 1977), and Beck's (1963, 1967, 1987) *treatment of 'automatic thoughts'*. The rest of this section will focus on Beck's contribution.

Box 45.6 Some problems with TEs

- The control of behaviours has to be transferred from tokens to social reinforcers, both within and, ultimately, outside the hospital. The former is normally achieved by gradually 'weaning' patients off the tokens, and the latter by transferring patients to halfway houses and other community live-in arrangements. But there tends to be a high re-hospitalisation rate for such patients.
- Tokens may work by encouraging staff to observe behaviour systematically – not because the tokens act as reinforcers of the patient's behaviour (Gelder *et al.*, 1989). Indeed, Burgio *et al.* (1983) found that selectively reinforcing *staff* for verbal interaction with residents produced a reliable improvement in the residents' behaviour. As with other successful behavioural interventions, the reason for the effectiveness of TE programmes may be quite unrelated to learning theory principles (Fonagy and Higgitt, 1984). This relates to process research (see text below).
- *Ethical problems* arise, because it's often necessary to deprive patients of some amenity before it can be earned with tokens. If this amenity is something the patient should have by right (e.g. food), there's clearly an ethical difficulty. With some amenities (e.g. watching TV), it's difficult to decide whether they're a right or a privilege (Gelder *et al.*, 1989).
- In some TEs, clients have the option of leaving the programme without penalty, and suggesting or negotiating changes in the contingencies used. Another precaution is to inform clients clearly of their legal and moral rights, and to instruct clients and staff to report any infringements of those rights. The ethics of a TE will ultimately be judged on the basis of how effectively and humanely the transfer to the natural environment is carried out (Martin and Pear, 1992).
- Baddeley (1990) argues that when used in an educational setting (e.g. in a home for emotionally disturbed children), a TE can instil a highly mercenary approach to learning (TEs lead to token learning). For example, children may only read or participate in any educational activity if directly rewarded for it. This may be effective within the confines of the TE itself, but will be inappropriate outside, where learning operates on a more indirect, long term, and less immediate reward system.

Treatment of 'automatic thoughts' (Beck, 1963, 1967, 1987)

In a reversal of Freud's view, Beck argues that our emotional reactions are essentially a function of how we *construe* the world (interpret and predict it). Depressed people see themselves as victims of their own illogical self-judgements. Beck's central idea is that depressed individuals feel as they do because their thinking is dominated by *negative schemas*. This is a tendency to see the world negatively, triggered whenever the person encounters new conditions that in some way resemble the conditions in which the schemas were originally learned (usually in childhood and adolescence). These negative schemas fuel and are fuelled by certain cognitive biases, which cause the person to mis-perceive reality. So:

1. an *ineptness schema* can make depressed people expect to fail most of the time
2. a *self-blame schema* makes them feel responsible for all misfortunes, and
3. a *negative self-evaluation schema* constantly reminds them of their worthlessness.

The main specific cognitive biases are described in Box 45.7.

Negative schemas, together with cognitive biases or distortions, maintain the *negative triad*: negative thoughts about the *self*, the *world* and the *future*.

Box 45.7 The main cognitive biases in Beck's Theory of Depression

Arbitrary inference: a conclusion drawn in the absence of sufficient evidence – or any evidence at all. For example, a man concludes that he's worthless because it's raining the day he's hosting an outdoor party.
Selective abstraction: a conclusion drawn on the basis of just one of many elements in a situation. For example, a worker feels worthless when a product doesn't work, even though she's only one of several people who contributed to making it.
Overgeneralisation: an overall sweeping conclusion drawn on the basis of a single, perhaps trivial, event. For example, a student regards his poor performance in a single class on one particular day as final proof of his worthlessness and stupidity.
Magnification and minimisation: exaggerations in evaluating performance. For example, a man believes he's completely ruined his car (*magnification*) when he sees a small scratch on the rear bumper. A woman believes herself to be worthless (*minimisation*) despite a succession of praiseworthy achievements.
(Based on Davison and Neale, 2001)

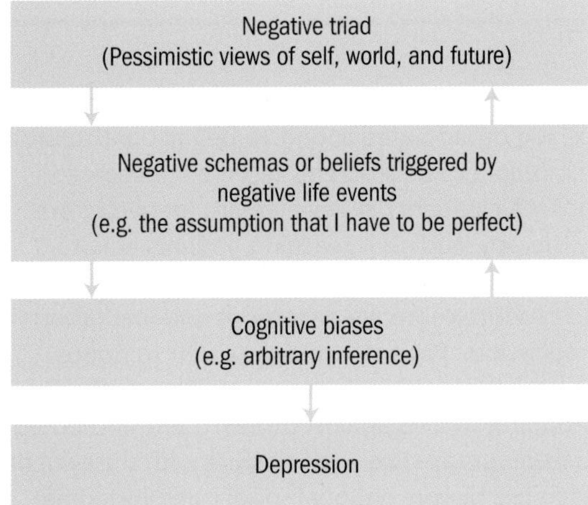

Figure 45.8 The interrelationship between different types of cognition in Beck's theory of depression

An evaluation of Beck's approach

- It's generally agreed that Beck's has been the most influential of the cognitive models of depression (Champion, 2000), although it's also been criticised for underemphasising social factors (Champion and Power, 1995).
- The evidence initially came from Beck's clinical observations (Beck, 1967). Further support comes from various sources, including self-report questionnaires, and laboratory studies of memory and other cognitive processes (Davison and Neale, 2001). Beck (1993) has reviewed the evidence concerning the effectiveness of his form of CBT in the treatment not just of MDD (for which it was originally designed), but also generalised anxiety disorder, panic disorder and EDs. These outcome studies show very clearly that CBT is highly effective. CBT is also being used in the treatment of drug abuse, bipolar disorder, patients with cancer, HIV, OCD, PTSD and schizophrenia, and it's also being applied in group and family therapy settings. Beck (1993) believes that:

  The very broad application of the theory and strategies bolsters the claim of cognitive therapy as a robust system of psychotherapy ...

- Perhaps the greatest challenge facing any cognitive theory of depression is to show that depressed people's thoughts are the cause of their depression rather than the effect. Probably, the relationship works both ways; in recent years, Beck himself has come to this more bidirectional position. There's certainly no unequivocal support for the claim that negative thinking causes depression (Davison and Neale, 2001).
- According to McCusker (2014), CBT has the largest evidence base of all forms of psychological therapy. NICE considers CBT the 'treatment of choice' for a number of mental health problems, including PTSD, anxiety, depression, and OCD.

(See Critical Discussion 45.4.)

Figure 45.9 Aaron T. Beck (born 1921)

AN EVALUATION OF THERAPY: IS IT EFFECTIVE?

This deceptively simple-sounding question really comprises two interrelated questions:

1. does it work? This is related to *outcome research.*
2. how does it work? This is related to *process research.*

Each question, in turn, comprises several other overlapping questions. *Outcome questions* include the following:

- is psychotherapy (in general) effective?
- is any one kind of psychotherapy more effective than another?
- what constitutes a satisfactory outcome?
- how should change be measured (and for how long after the end of treatment)?
- how much and what kind of change is necessary for a judgement of improvement to be made?

Process questions include the following:

- what are the necessary components of effective therapy?
- what are the mechanisms by which change is brought about (what are the 'active ingredients')?
- are different therapies effective because of the particular techniques and tools they use, or are there common factors that apply to all therapies?

Despite the close connection between them, researchers tend to focus on either outcome or process questions. Psychotherapy research began by concentrating on outcome, in the form of Eysenck's much-cited 1952 review article, in which he challenged what had up to that time been taken for granted about the effectiveness of psychoanalysis (see Key Study 45.2).

Critical Discussion 45.4

CBT and schizophrenia

It was once believed that it was futile to try to change the cognitive distortions of patients with schizophrenia. However, early attempts to change the *behaviour* of these patients, using behaviour modification techniques (such as the TE), exposure, and distraction, gradually gave way to cognitive-behavioural approaches. Although these vary in their emphasis and, to some degree, rationale, all interventions have the primary aim of modifying hallucinations and delusional beliefs (Roth and Fonagy, 2005). In fact, two major CBT approaches involving schizophrenic patients can be identified:

(i) *stress management* (SM) (Bennett, 2006) and is related to 'personal therapy' (PT) (Hogarty *et al.*, 1997)

(ii) *belief modification* or *reattribution therapy*, which is directly aimed at changing the patient's thinking.

SM approaches involve a detailed evaluation of the problems and experiences an individual is having, their triggers and consequences, and any strategies s/he may use to cope with them. Once the problems have been identified, the therapist and patient (client) work together to develop specific coping strategies to help the client cope more effectively with them. Potential strategies include cognitive techniques such as (a) distraction from intrusive thoughts or challenging their meaning; (b) increasing or decreasing social activity as a means of distraction from intrusive thoughts or low mood; and (c) using breathing or other relaxation techniques to help the client to relax (Bennett, 2006).

PT (which takes place both one-to-one and in small groups) is a broad-based cognitive-behavioural approach to the multiplicity of problems faced by discharged schizophrenic patients. A key element (derived from family therapy studies) is teaching patients how to recognise inappropriate affect; if ignored, this can build up and produce cognitive distortions and inappropriate social behaviour. Patients are also taught to notice small signs of relapse, such as social withdrawal or inappropriate threats against others. If left unchecked, such behaviours are likely to interfere with the patient's efforts to live by conventional social rules, including keeping a job and making and maintaining relationships.

Similar to reattribution therapy is *cognitive remediation* (CR). First developed to treat traumatic brain injury, CR is aimed at improving patients' ability to concentrate, remember, plan and solve problems, either by restoring skills through repetitive practice or by acquiring strategies for bypassing those deficits. CR therapies typically use computer software or pencil-and-paper exercises (Saperstein and Kurtz, 2013).

CR has been shown to increase activation in the medial prefrontal cortex, an area involved in decision making. This heightened brain activity is linked with schizophrenic patients' improved performance during 'reality monitoring', the ability to differentiate between internal experience and the outside world (Subramaniam *et al.*, 2012). Also, *social cognitive training* (SCT) helps people with schizophrenia identify emotional cues and take another person's perspective (Saperstein and Kurtz, 2013).

Key Study 45.2

The effectiveness of psychotherapy (Eysenck, 1952)

- Eysenck reviewed five studies of the effectiveness of psychoanalysis, and 19 studies of the effectiveness of 'eclectic' (mixed) psychotherapy.
- He concluded that only 44 per cent of psychoanalytic patients and 64 per cent of those who received the 'mixed' therapy improved.
- However, since roughly 66 per cent of patients improve without any treatment (*spontaneous remission*), Eysenck concluded that psychoanalysis in particular, and psychotherapy in general, simply don't work – they achieve nothing which wouldn't have happened anyway without therapy!

Outcome research

According to Eysenck (1992), the *outcome problem* had never been properly addressed by Clinical Psychologists prior to his article, which showed *only* that the available evidence wasn't sufficient to prove that psychoanalysis (and psychotherapy in general) was instrumental in bringing about recovery; it *didn't* suggest that it was ineffective (which is how many others interpreted his conclusions). Nevertheless, if it can be shown that psychoanalysis does no better than placebo treatments (see below) or no treatment at all (which the 1952 article showed):

> *... then clearly the theory on which it is based was wrong. Similarly, if there were no positive effects of psychoanalysis as a therapy, then it would be completely unethical to apply this method to patients, to charge them money for such treatment, or to train therapists in these unsuccessful methods ... (Eysenck, 1992)*

By 1960, Eysenck was arguing that behaviour therapy is the only kind of therapy worth rational consideration and he inspired an enormous amount of research on therapy outcomes (Oatley, 1984).

A reassessment of Eysenck's conclusions

- If the many patients who drop out of psychoanalysis are excluded from the 44 per cent quoted by Eysenck (they cannot legitimately be counted as 'failures' or 'not cured'), the figure rises to 66 per cent.
- Bergin (1971) reviewed some of the studies included in Eysenck's review and concluded that, by choosing different criteria of 'improvement', the success rate of psychoanalysis could be raised to 83 per cent. He also cited studies which showed only a 30 per cent spontaneous remission rate.
- One of the two studies which Eysenck used to establish his spontaneous remission rate of 66 per cent was conducted by Landis (1938). Landis compared patients who'd received psychotherapy ('experimental group') with a control group who'd been hospitalised for 'neurosis' in state mental hospitals. Landis himself pointed out a number of differences between his psychotherapy group and the hospital patient controls, concluding that the 66 per cent figure *shouldn't* be accepted as a baseline.
- Bergin and Lambert (1978) reviewed 17 studies of untreated 'neurotics' and found a median spontaneous remission rate of 43 per cent. They also found that the rate of spontaneous remission varies a great deal depending on the disorder: generalised anxiety and depression, for example, are much more likely to 'cure themselves' than phobias or OCD. Rachman and Wilson (1980) reached a similar conclusion.
- Garfield (1992) argued that both the quantity and quality of psychotherapy research had increased since Eysenck's 1952 article, especially since the 1970s, but Eysenck doesn't refer to this in his 1992 article.

Other outcome research

A review by Luborsky *et al.* (1975) concluded that all types of therapy are equally effective. Smith and Glass (1977) reviewed 400 studies of a wide variety of therapies (including psychodynamic, client-centred therapy (CCT), SD, and eclectic) and concluded that all were more effective than no treatment. For example, the 'average' client who'd received therapy scored more favourably on the outcome measures than 75 per cent of those in the untreated control groups.

Smith *et al.* (1980) extended the 1977 study to include 475 studies (an estimated 75 per cent of the published literature). Strict criteria for accepting a study included the comparison of a treated group (given a specified form of therapy) with a second group (drawn from the same population) that were either given no therapy, put on a waiting list, or given some alternative form of therapy. As with the 1977 results, the effectiveness of therapy was shown to be highly significant: the average client was better off than 80 per cent of the control groups on the outcome measures. Although different therapies had different kinds of effects, overall:

> *Different types of psychotherapy (verbal or behavioural, psychodynamic, client-centred, or systematic desensitisation) do not produce different types or degrees of benefit. (Smith et al., 1980)*

Box 45.8 Meta-analysis

A distinctive feature of the Smith and Glass (1977) and Smith *et al.* (1980) studies is their use of *meta-analysis* (MA). Lilienfeld (1995) defines MA as:

> *... a procedure for aggregating and averaging the results of a large number of studies. Unlike the 'voting' method, meta-analysis allows researchers to consider the magnitude of findings and yield an overall measure of effect size – that is, an index of the magnitude of the effects of a treatment ... averaged across all studies ...*

Effect size is essentially an indicator of the extent to which people who receive psychotherapy improve relative to those who don't: the greater the difference between these two groups, the greater the effect size. The 'voting method' (a term coined by Smith and Glass) simply involves adding up all the studies that support the effectiveness of psychotherapy and all those that don't – a result is counted as a 'hit' provided the difference between the two totals is statistically significant. But lumping together all the positive findings and all the negative findings obscures statistically very large and very small significant results; as a result, it provides only a crude and often misleading summary of a body of literature (Lilienfeld, 1995). All outcome studies prior to Smith and Glass (1977) used the 'voting method'. Another advantage of MA is that it allows researchers to examine whether certain variables are correlated with effect size, such as how experienced the therapist is and the age of clients. In this way, they can determine not only the overall effectiveness of psychotherapy (*outcome research*), but also what factors, if any, influence its effectiveness (*process research*).

Process research

Ask Yourself

- Based on the earlier discussion of specific treatment methods, try to formulate some questions relevant to process research (i.e. how the methods work).
- Do relaxation and graded exposure to the feared object/situation make SD an effective means of removing phobias?
- Are tokens an essential part of the TE, which successfully reduces the psychotic behaviour of schizophrenic patients?
- Are the three therapist attitudes identified by Rogers (see Chapter 2) necessary if clients are to develop positive self-regard and to achieve congruence?

According to Kazdin and Wilcoxin (1976), the crucial ingredients of therapy (whatever techniques are involved) are:

- the patient is influenced to expect success, and
- the patient's self-concept changes, whereby s/he comes to believe (through supervised practice) that the previously feared object or situation can be coped with.

The patient's expectations of success relate to the crucial and controversial issue of the *placebo effect*.

The placebo effect

A *placebo* denotes an inactive/inert substance, designed to take account of the psychological (as opposed to pharmacological) influences on physiological change (such as the expectation of improvement). So, in drug trials, the placebo condition is the *control* condition. In the case of antidepressants, about 80 per cent of their effect derives from people's faith that they'll work (Kirsch *et al.*, 2002).

In psychotherapy, the expectation that it will help is *part of the treatment* (Mair, 1992). Is it possible to devise a placebo control in psychotherapy research which is inactive in a way that's equivalent to taking a sugar pill? Even non-placebo controls (such as delayed treatment or no treatment conditions) will produce expectations specific to that particular condition (e.g. disappointment and rejection respectively) (Barkham and Shapiro, 1992).

If client expectations of success are one of the main 'active ingredients' or components involved in psychotherapy, then if a placebo has the capacity to inspire client expectations, making psychotherapy–placebo comparisons may underestimate the actual effectiveness of psychotherapy (Lilienfeld, 1995). Indeed, according to Frank (1989), if therapy effects don't exceed those of placebos (a conclusion drawn by, for example, Prioleau *et al.*, 1983), this is because the placebo *is* psychotherapy:

> *As a symbolic communication that combats demoralisation by inspiring the patient's hopes for relief, administration of a placebo is a form of psychotherapy. It is therefore not surprising that placebos can provide marked relief in patients who seek psychotherapy. (Mair, 1989, quoted in Mair, 1992)*

Whether in general medicine or psychiatry, the effect of expectation is often dismissed as a 'mere' placebo. But this is a very real, demonstrable biological effect involving endorphins (Zubieta *et al.*, 2005). Until recently it was claimed that belief in a drug's or procedure's effectiveness had to be conscious; now there's evidence that placebo effects can arise from *subconscious* associations between recovery and the experience of being treated. Such subliminal conditioning can control bodily processes we're unaware of, such as immune responses and the release of hormones (Niemi, 2009).

The role of non-specific factors

Cordray and Bootzin (1983) argue that one of the major ingredients involved in psychotherapy's effectiveness is the *non-specific* factors shared by most, or even all, therapies. The main proponent of this view is Frank (1973), who believes that the success of psychotherapy can be traced largely or entirely to four non-specific factors/components.

Box 45.9 Frank's (1973) four non-specific factors/components involved in therapy

According to Frank, all psychotherapies:

- prescribe clearly delineated roles for therapist and client, with the former defined as an 'expert' possessing unique healing skills. This raises the client's hopes that help will be forthcoming
- involve settings designed to be associated with the alleviation of psychological distress (a 'designated place of healing'), e.g. carpeted rooms with scholarly books and journals and prominently displayed diplomas
- provide a convincing theoretical rationale for making sense of the client's problems. This instils a sense of confidence in clients and reassures them that their problems aren't incomprehensible or unique
- include therapeutic rituals (prescribed tasks or procedures, such as SD and free association) that further enhance the client's faith in the therapist and the therapeutic rationale. These are akin to the ceremonial rituals of faith healers; they cultivate the impression that something deeply significant and mysterious is taking place.

Today, the view that these and other common factors are more powerful than those that distinguish one treatment approach from another is widely held (Lilienfeld and Arkowitz, 2012).

Most individuals who voluntarily seek treatment experience low self-esteem, despair, helplessness, alienation, and a profound sense of incompetence. All psychotherapies alleviate demoralisation by raising hopes and expectations of improvement, and by instilling feelings of confidence and self-worth (Mair, 1992).

Bandura (1977a) proposes that the central element in psychological therapy is the cognitive change towards *self-efficacy*, the 'conviction that one can successfully execute a behaviour to produce a specified outcome' (see Chapter 35). This is brought about best through actual experience in facing previously feared or avoided situations.

The results of studies like those of Smith and Glass (1977) and Smith *et al.* (1980), which claimed that differences in the effectiveness of various therapies are negligible, support Frank's argument. But other outcome studies have shown that the more active, structured, directive therapies work best (at least for certain types of disorder): they're more heavily 'saturated' with Frank's non-specific factors than are other psychotherapies (Lilienfeld, 1995).

CONCLUSIONS

There are different kinds of questions one can ask when trying to assess the effects of psychotherapy. Because Eysenck is interested in comparing recovery rates (measured statistically), his assessment of the effects of therapy is purely *quantitative*. Psychoanalysts and those practising CCT are likely to be much more concerned with the *qualitative* aspects of therapy (such as the nature of the therapeutic process, and the role of the relationship between client and therapist). These approaches aren't mutually exclusive, however. The interaction between experimental research (where hypotheses can be tested scientifically) and therapy (where they can be tried out clinically) can influence theory development and therapeutic practices (Marzillier, 2004).

According to Lilienfeld (1995), the question 'Is psychotherapy effective?', although remarkably complex in some respects, may actually be too simple in others. As Paul (1966) observes, what we need to ask is 'What treatment, by whom, is most effective for this individual, with that specific problem, and under which set of circumstances?' This is to do with matching client, therapy and setting and, according to Wilson and Barkham (1994), is a question that still haunts psychotherapy research and disturbs therapists.

Chapter Summary

- Both **Clinical** and **Counselling Psychology** adopt the **scientist–practitioner model** of helping, but they've been more influenced by behavioural and humanistic approaches respectively.
- Treatments and therapies differ according to whether they're **somatic** or **psychological, directive** or **non-directive, individual** or **group**.
- The term **'psychotherapy'** is sometimes used to refer to all non-somatic treatments, and sometimes to psychodynamic approaches/insight therapies.
- Major groups of **antidepressant drugs** include **MAOIs, tricyclics** and **SSRIs,** (including **fluoxetine** / Prozac). **Ketamine** is now used to treat depression.
- **Chlordiazepoxide** (Librium) and **diazepam** (Valium) are widely prescribed **anxiolytics**. They belong to the **benzodiazepines. Beta-blockers** are also used to treat anxiety.
- **Antipsychotic drugs (major tranquillisers/ neuroleptics)** revolutionised the treatment of **schizophrenia** and other psychotic disorders. But they only treat the **positive symptoms** and cause serious side-effects.
- **Electroconvulsive therapy (ECT)** is now used mainly with depressive patients. While it's probably more effective than antidepressants, its benefits are only short-term, and it may cause long-term cognitive and emotional deficits.
- According to Freud, **neuroses** involve the use of defences in an attempt to combat anxiety, but they're self-defeating, creating their own distress.
- The aims of **psychoanalysis** include **providing insight**. The analyst remains anonymous, which facilitates **transference**. Interpreting transference is a distinctive feature of psychoanalysis, as is the analyst's **counter-transference**.
- The client's **resistance** must itself be interpreted; **free association** and **dream interpretation** are other major techniques.
- **Brief psychodynamic psychotherapy** represents a modified form of psychoanalysis. **Brief focal therapy** deals with a specific area of difficulty in a much shorter period of time than classical psychoanalysis.
- **Behaviour therapy** and **modification** refer to techniques based on **classical** and **operant conditioning**, respectively. Both see adaptive and maladaptive behaviour as being acquired in the same way, and both reject the medical model.
- Eysenck and Rachman see the case of Little Albert as a model of how all **phobias** are acquired. But this can only account for the **initial learning** of

phobias (through classical conditioning), not for their **persistence** (which occurs through negative reinforcement).
- According to Wolpe, the key principle in **systematic desensitisation (SD)** is **reciprocal inhibition**. It appears that neither **relaxation** nor the use of a **hierarchy** is necessary, and the 'active ingredient' seems to be **exposure** to the feared object/situation.
- Both **implosion** and **flooding** represent forms of '**forced reality testing**'. Flooding is thought to be the most effective of all treatments for phobias.
- **Aversion therapy** is particularly controversial when used with homosexuals. **Covert sensitisation** is aversion therapy that takes place in the patient's imagination, and is preferable on humanitarian grounds.
- Lovaas pioneered the use of **operant conditioning** with autistic children in an attempt to teach them to use speech. **Behaviour modification** has been used successfully with adults and children with learning disabilities.
- Ayllon and Azrin pioneered the **token economy** (**TE**), based on the principle of **secondary reinforcement**. Tokens may be effective because of the way they change **staff** behaviour and attitudes, contrary to what learning theory principles would predict. TEs also raise some very important **ethical** issues.
- **Cognitive–behavioural therapy** (**CBT**) is based on the view that clinical disorders involve **faulty thoughts/cognitions**, which then produce maladaptive behaviour. **Cognitive restructuring** is a means to the end of changing emotions and behaviour.
- Beck's treatment of '**automatic thoughts**' aims to help clients understand the **cognitive triad of depression**. Therapy involves training in being more objective, separating fact from evaluation, and seeing things in less extreme ways.
- Evaluating the **effectiveness of therapy** involves both **outcome** and **process research**. Eysenck's landmark article claimed that recovery from neurosis following psychotherapy is no greater than the rate of **spontaneous remission**.
- Both the quantity and quality of subsequent outcome research have increased, one important improvement being the use of **meta-analysis**.
- Unlike drug trials it may be impossible in psychotherapy to devise an **inactive placebo control**.
- Frank identifies four **non-specific factors**, which help to combat demoralisation, the common factor shared by all those who seek therapeutic help. Related to this is Bandura's concept of **self-efficacy**.

Links with Other Topics/Chapters

Chapter 1 ⟶ The Psychologist as *counsellor* and as *agent for change* are two of the seven major skills used by Applied Psychologists (Hartley and Branthwaite, 2000)

Chapter 44 ⟶ Family and marital/couple therapy have been inspired by Laing's *family interaction model of schizophrenia*

Chapter 8 ⟶ *Alcoholics Anonymous* (AA), and other similar *self-help organisations* for drug abusers, victims of abuse etc. use group therapy

Chapter 43 ⟶ The ego defence mechanisms form an important part of Freud's theory of 'normal' personality (Chapter 42), as well as his account of phobias and other neurotic disorders. This demonstrates the *dimensional* (as opposed to the *categorical*) approach to mental disorder

Chapter 3 ⟶ Double-blind designs are used to prevent *experimenter effects/bias*

Chapter 49 ⟶ Freud's concept of free association is relevant to the discussion about *free will and determinism*

Chapter 3 ⟶ Criticisms of the use of therapy manuals in outcome research can be considered in terms of *internal versus external validity*. The better controlled the studies (thus increasing internal validity), the lower the external validity (relevance to actual therapy situations). This is a problem for psychological research in general

Recommended Reading

Bennett, P. (2006) *Abnormal and Clinical Psychology: An Introductory Textbook* (2nd edn). Maidenhead: Open University. Also relevant to Chapters 43 and 44.

Davey, G. (ed.) (2008) *Clinical Psychology.* London: Hodder Education. Especially Chapters 1 and 3.

Dryden, W. (ed.) (2002) *Handbook of Individual Therapy* (4th edn). London: Sage.

Dryden, W. & Feltham, C. (eds) (1992) *Psychotherapy and Its Discontents.* Buckingham: Open University Press.

Gross, R. (2008) *Key Studies in Psychology.* (5th edn). London: Hodder Education. Chapter 30.

Useful Websites

www.psychoanalysis.org.uk (The Institute of Psychoanalysis)

www.ect.org (ECT.ORG)

www.bapca.org.uk (The British Association for the Person-Centred Approach)

www.breggin.com (Psychiatric Drug Facts – P. Breggin)

www.mindstreet.com (Good Days Ahead : The Interactive Program for Depression and Anxiety)

CHAPTER 46

CRIMINOLOGICAL PSYCHOLOGY

Who commits crime?

Theories of criminal behaviour

Offender profiling

The treatment of offenders

INTRODUCTION and OVERVIEW

Psychology is just one of the several disciplines contributing to *criminology* (others being law, sociology, anthropology, economics, geography, politics, statistics, and psychiatry), and *Criminological* (or *Forensic*) *Psychology* attempts to apply psychological principles to the criminal justice system (Harrower, 1998).

While criminology is the study of *crime*, Criminological/Forensic Psychology is the study of *criminals* (Canter, 2010). Canter observes that although still a young discipline, Forensic Psychology has already spun off several sub-disciplines, notably *Prison Psychology, Investigative Psychology, Legal Psychology,* and forensic aspects of Clinical Psychology (see Chapter 1). Around the world, Forensic Psychology is the fastest-developing area of professional Psychology.

The present chapter clearly overlaps with, and complements Chapter 21, which looks specifically at aspects of *Cognitive Psychology* (in particular memory and face recognition) in relation to the law. By discussing research into eyewitness testimony and face recognition, Chapter 21 focuses on one-half of the 'crime–victim' equation. Here, the focus is on the person committing the crime, rather than on the witness (although witnesses aren't necessarily victims).

Because crime is a form of *social deviancy*, definitions and perceptions of crime overlap with the criteria discussed in Chapter 43 for defining psychological abnormality. Also, one theory of criminal behaviour holds that it reflects a particular type of *personality disorder* (see Chapter 44). Discussion of *moral development* (Chapter 35), *gender* (Chapter 36), *adolescence* (Chapter 37), and *personality* (Chapter 42) are all highly relevant to any attempt to understand and explain criminal behaviour.

WHO COMMITS CRIME?

Ask Yourself

- Think of a criminal and what comes to mind (i.e. what's your stereotype of a criminal)?
- Are different types of crime likely to be committed by different kinds of criminal (in terms of age, gender, social-class background etc.)?

One thing we can be certain about is that criminals aren't some distinct sub-species of human being; nor are all criminals alike (Canter, 2010). According to Hollin (1999), the strongest evidence relevant to predicting who'll commit crime comes from longitudinal studies. For example, Loeber *et al.* (1995) investigated predictive factors for the onset of conduct disorder, itself an established risk factor for later delinquency, in 177 males aged 8–17. They were followed up for six years, and data were collected on a range of psychological, psychiatric and social factors. Parental substance abuse, low socio-economic status (SES) and the child's resistance to discipline were important factors in eventual progression to diagnosed conduct disorder.

Longitudinal studies have helped illuminate our understanding of many criminological issues, including the relationship between age and crime, predictors of juvenile delinquency, and patterns of adult crime.

Age and offending

Two recurrent findings in all studies of criminality and delinquency that stand out above all others are (i) the great majority of crimes are committed by males (see below); and (ii) the great majority of these are in their mid-teens (Ioannou and Vettor, 2008)

'Crime rate' refers to prevalence, in terms of the percentage of people of specific ages who commit offences. As Figure 46.1 shows, about 20 per cent of 12-year-olds, 80 per cent of 16-year-olds, 20 per cent of 36-year-olds, and 8 per cent of 52-year-olds commit crime.

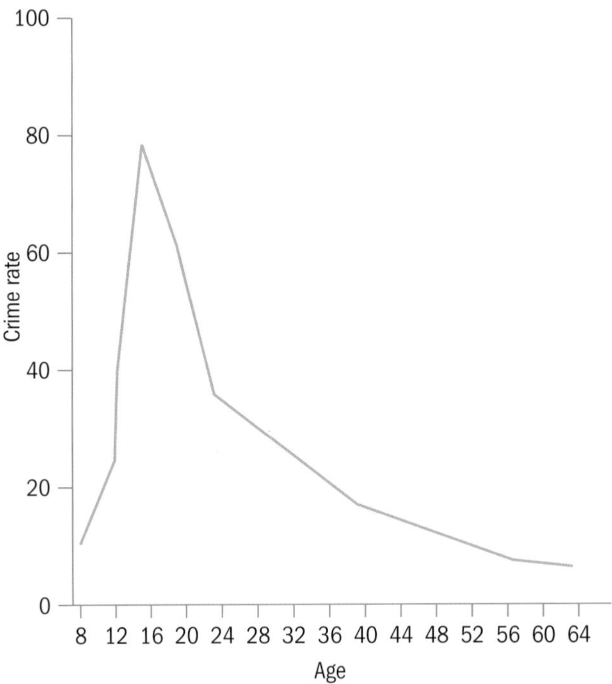

Figure 46.1 The relationship between age and crime (from Hollin, 1999)

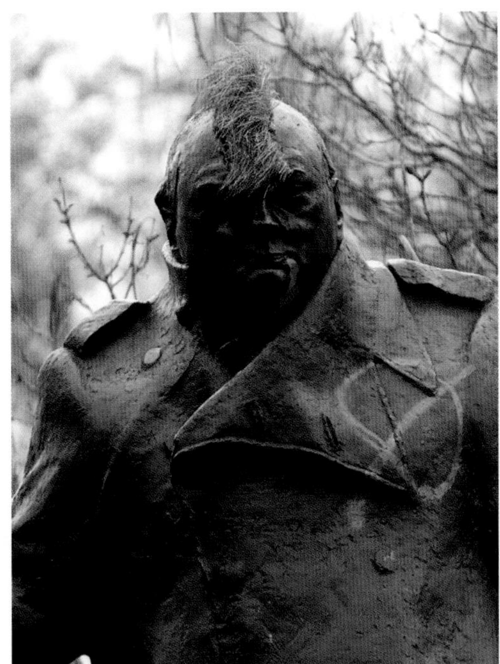

Figure 46.2 A defaced, graffitied statue of Winston Churchill

Although juveniles commit a lot of crime, most is relatively trivial, including a large number of *status offences* (which apply only to young people, such as truancy, under-age drinking, driving a motor vehicle under age) as opposed to *index* (or *notifiable*) *offences* (serious offences, such as murder, rape and sexual assault, burglary, arson and robbery, which are criminal acts regardless of age). Young people commit both types, but status offences are much more common (Hollin, 1999).

Figure 46.3 Car theft: a very young-male crime (posed by models)

The age–crime relationship has been demonstrated in longitudinal studies that explore the links between children's very early behaviour patterns and their subsequent offending. For example, the Dunedin study of children growing up in New Zealand has been used by Moffit *et al.* (1996) to identify developmental pathways for two distinguishable groups of male offenders: (i) 'life-course persistent'; and (ii) 'adolescence-limited'. Those who became chronic, serious or violent offenders tended to have histories of persistent, antisocial behaviour from an early age, unlike those (the large majority) who engaged in criminal behaviour for a relatively short time during adolescence. So, most young people 'grow out 'of delinquency by the time they're 18.

So, what is it about being a teenager that makes criminal behaviour so much more likely than at any other age? One answer is *risk-taking*.

Predictors of long-term offending

According to Hollin (1999), the most widely cited longitudinal study in the UK is the Cambridge Study in Delinquent Development. This is described in Key Study 46.1.

Key Study 46.1

The Cambridge Study in Delinquent Development (Farrington and West, 1990; Farrington, 1995; Farrington *et al.*, 2006)

This prospective, longitudinal study began in 1961 with 411 London males, aged 8–9; at age 48, 93 per cent of the participants who were still alive were interviewed. As well as interviews with the participants, parents, peers, and teachers have also been interviewed. A vast amount and range of data have been gathered, dealing with parental child-rearing practices, economic factors, school behaviour and much more.

The study is unique in (i) following up hundreds of children in a community sample for over 40 years; (ii) focusing on offending; (iii) including more than five personal interviews spanning the period from childhood to the late 40s; (iv) having a very low attrition (drop-out) rate (Farrington *et al*., 2006).

Between the ages of 10 and 50, 41 per cent of the males were convicted for standard list offences (excluding motoring offences). The average conviction career lasted from 19–28 and included five convictions. The chronic offenders (7 per cent) accounted for more than 50 per cent of all the officially recorded offences; each had at least ten convictions between the average ages of 14–35.

Those who were first convicted at the earliest ages tended to have the most convictions and the longest criminal careers. Self-reported delinquency matched official records reasonably well.

The most important distinguishing characteristics, observed at age 8 to 10, of later delinquents (measured by convictions and self-report) fell into six main categories:

- antisocial childhood behaviour, including troublesomeness in school, dishonesty and aggression
- hyperactivity/impulsivity/attention-deficit, including poor concentration, restlessness, psychomotor impulsivity and risk-taking
- low intelligence and poor academic record
- family criminal record, including convicted parents, delinquent older siblings and siblings with behavioural problems
- family poverty, including low family income, large family size and poor housing
- poor parental child-rearing behaviour, including harsh and authoritarian discipline, poor supervision, parental conflict and separation from parents.

The intensity and severity of these personal and social disadvantages in childhood appear to be predictive of chronic offending in adolescence and adulthood.

In addition to – but correlated with – some of the factors listed in Key Study 46.1, Sutton *et al.* (2006) identify a number of factors associated with antisocial behaviour. These include:

- low birth weight, which, in turn, is often associated with neurological impairment and cognitive difficulties
- maternal stress and anxiety during pregnancy, which, in turn, is often associated with smoking while pregnant (but which is a robust, independent risk factor for later conduct disorders in boys) and drinking alcohol and taking other drugs
- poor social support and antenatal (prenatal) care
- a secure attachment during the first two years of life as a *protective factor* (see Chapter 32); postnatal depression can make the development of secure attachment much more difficult.

In two independent studies, Elander *et al.* (2000a) confirmed that hyperactivity is a significant risk factor in boys, and Elander *et al.* (2000b) found that late-onset criminals (first conviction after age 22) were likely to have had a history of childhood and adolescent antisocial behaviour, major mental illness in adulthood, or both. Late-onset criminals are also more likely to be female.

By 18, the long-term offenders had adopted a lifestyle characterised by heavy drinking, sexual promiscuity, drug use, and minor crimes involving cars or group violence and vandalism. They were highly unlikely to have any formal qualifications, had unskilled manual jobs, and were often unemployed. By 32, they were likely to be residentially mobile, had low-paid jobs, tended to have physically assaulted their partners and used a wide range of drugs. They had an extensive list of fines, probation and prison sentences. Overall, this was a socially dysfunctional existence. They committed more crimes while unemployed, and these were for financial gain – theft, burglary and fraud.

Those who were married were less likely to offend than those who weren't, provided their partners weren't convicted offenders. But compared with non-offenders, they were more likely to have divorced or separated from their wives and children, and to have more conflict with their wives/partners (see Chapter 36).

However, there was still considerable overlap between offenders and non-offenders: not all the convicted men displayed these characteristics. Neither a disadvantaged background nor 'social failure' (Farrington, 1990) inevitably leads to crime, but it massively increases the risk of criminal behaviour (the 'good boys from bad backgrounds' phenomenon; Farrington and West, 1990).

Crime and gender

According to Harrower (1998):

> *Probably the most significant feature of both recorded and self-reported crime is that more males than females commit offences, particularly violent crimes, in spite of claims that women are becoming more violent in the 1990s ... or that, because of their inherent deviousness, they have always been more criminal but have simply been able to conceal it ...*

Until recently, the 'maleness' of crime was taken as an accepted fact. In contrast to the 'ordinariness' of male crime, the few early studies of female offenders focused on their extraordinariness, as odd or ill creatures deviating from the norm (Lyon, 1998). In the 1970s, feminist perspectives began to develop in criminology, and the neglect of gender (especially women) was highlighted.

Women and crime

According to Lloyd (1995) in a book called *Doubly Deviant, Doubly Damned:*

> *... when women commit violent crimes they are seen to have breached two laws: the law of the land which forbids violence and natural law which says women are passive carers not active aggressors.*

This applies especially in cases of maternal *filicide*, the murder by a biological parent of their biological child (see Critical Discussion 46.1).

Women and violence

Throughout the years of heated debate concerning Myra Hindley's release from prison, there seems to have been an implicit assumption that to have committed her crimes, she must be especially evil because ('ordinary') women don't commit (are incapable of) such crimes. Pearson (1998) tries to demolish the cherished myth that women aren't naturally aggressive; she blames feminists and society as a whole for refusing to see women as dangerous and destructive. We cannot bring ourselves to recognise the reality of female aggression and violence, so we find excuses for it, such as premenstrual tension, or we see female killers (including Hindley and Rose West) as always junior accomplices of violent men. Motz (2008) puts forward similar arguments in relation to *filicide* (see Critical Discussion 46.1).

But according to Smith (1998), the myth that Pearson tries to demolish tells only half the story. There's also a terror that women are innately *more cruel* than men, a sentiment summed up in Kipling's 'the female of the species is more deadly than the male'.

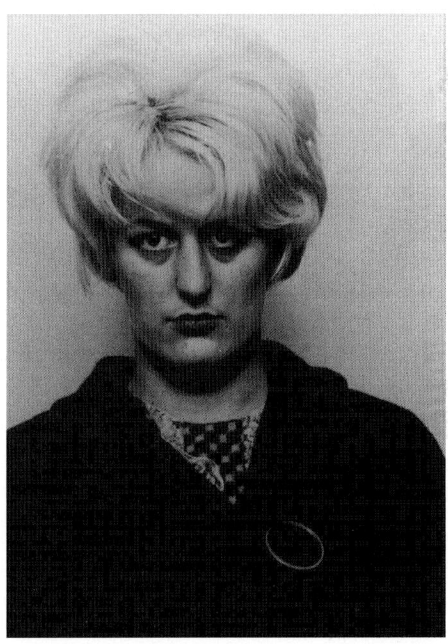

Figure 46.4 Myra Hindley, who died in prison in 2002

Men and crime

Feminist criminologists have helped to promote the view that 'masculinity' itself should be examined more closely in order to understand why so many young men commit offences – and are also the victims of crime. While at one time 'gender' was a 'code word' for women and femininity, it now refers to men and masculinity. Because of men's domination of all aspects of crime and the criminal justice system, it's only recently that their gender and the construction of their masculinity have been considered valid areas for study in their own right.

Critical Discussion 46.1

Women, homicide and filicide

The victim of a male murderer is highly likely to be another male; a significant proportion of male-on-male homicides take place among strangers or acquaintances and are the result of honour confrontations in response to fairly trivial arguments. When men kill women, it's often a current or former spouse or lover, with jealousy a common motive (Brookman, 2005).

While males comprised 90 per cent of the convicted murderers in England and Wales in 2001 (Brookman, 2005), this still leaves 10 per cent as females. However, when women do kill, it tends to be within a domestic context; specifically, they're most likely to kill their male intimate partner – or their own infant.

A common motive – and defence – is *battered woman syndrome* (BWS). An important distinction (both contextual and legal) is drawn between cases of homicide in which (i) the female perpetrator reacts immediately to a precipitating event (i.e. a particular occasion on which she's the victim of domestic violence) and (ii) where there's no specific trigger. In both cases, she's been the victim of violence over an extended period of time. In celebrated cases like that of Sara Thornton, who was initially convicted of her husband's murder, she successfully argued that the court should have taken into account the *cumulative effect* of her husband's violence towards her, and she was released from jail.

Filicide refers to (i) *neonaticide* (killing of a baby within its first 24 hours of life); (ii) *infanticide* (up to 12 months); and (iii) after 12 months and up to 16 years.

Neonaticide is almost exclusively perpetrated by the baby's mother, who is typically young, single, working class, immature but not suffering from any mental disorder; she's likely to have avoided antenatal care or medical help at the birth. The pregnancy may be unknown, certainly unplanned and concealed. The baby is usually killed immediately after birth.

Motz (2001) describes infanticide as:

> *... a tragic act of violence which can result from a tremendous fear of social stigma, feelings of total helplessness in relation to an unplanned baby, or a range of complex psychological factors, which result in an almost psychotic panic, in which killing seems the only solution*

Figure 46.5 Sara Thornton

She is often suffering from post-partum depression or psychosis (see Chapter 44).

Sometimes the mother is found guilty along with her partner (who may or may not be the biological father). In 2008, 16-month-old Amy Howson died at the hands of her parents (she had a broken spine, plus 40 other injuries); while he received a life sentence, she received a suspended sentence for 'allowing her child to die'. She was described as dominated by her partner, putting his needs above her child's.

Motz (2008) is appalled by our collective denial of what mothers are capable of: we cannot bear to believe that women are capable of such acts, so we blame the domineering male. Or we blame social workers and other agencies (as in cases involving Victoria Climbié, Baby 'P' and others). But this means we deny the woman her ability to act freely. Our first step in trying to understand maternal filicide must be to acknowledge the female capacity for aggression, violence and cruelty. Men and women share the same basic violent instincts, but they choose different targets: women's include their children and themselves (in the form of self-harm)

Ask Yourself

- Why is it that males are much more likely to commit crimes than females? (See Chapters 2, 36 and 50.)

As Wilson and Herrnstein (1985) point out:

> *Crime is an activity disproportionately carried out by young men living in large cities. There are old criminals, and female ones, and rural and small town ones, but*

to a much greater degree than would be expected by chance, criminals are young urban males.

According to Lyon (1998), two major explanations of the male domination of crime are *biological determinism* and *social constructionism*. Are men born to take risks, challenge authority, become violent and commit crimes? Or do they learn these behaviours, and is crime the context in which their masculine identity develops and is affirmed?

THEORIES OF CRIMINAL BEHAVIOUR

If, as we've seen, not all males commit crime and some females do, then there must be factors over and above gender that make people more likely to engage in this sort of behaviour. Similarly, not all boys growing up in disadvantaged circumstances become adolescent or adult offenders. So, although being an urban male significantly increases your chances of committing crime, Psychologists want to know what other influences are involved. In Hollin's (1997) terms:

... while the findings of the longitudinal surveys are important in describing the conditions associated with the onset of criminal behaviour, they also demand an explanation of how they cause delinquent behaviour. In other words, we still await a grand theory to explain the process by which the interaction between the young person and his or her environmental circumstances culminate in criminal behaviour.

In the meantime, we can draw on existing psychological theories, which may be applicable to criminal behaviour, without being theories of criminal behaviour as such.

Personality and criminality

According to Furnham and Heaven (1999), many studies have shown conclusively that personality factors are related to a wide range of antisocial, criminal, and delinquent behaviours. The vast majority of this research has been *cross-sectional* and has looked for links between criminal behaviour and introversion–extroversion (E), neuroticism–emotional stability (N), and psychoticism (P).

Eysenck's personality theory

E, N and conditionability

Ask Yourself

- How do you think Eysenck would explain criminal behaviour? (See Chapter 42.)

For Eysenck, the criminal is a neurotic extrovert (someone who scores high on both N and E). N is linked to crime through *anxiety* (Eysenck and Eysenck 1970). High anxiety functions very much like a drive, which multiplies with habit, so someone who engages in delinquent behaviour is likely to persist in that behaviour if they're also high N scorers. The high E scorer is *stimulus-hungry*, engages in thrill-enhancing behaviours, and is more difficult to *condition*. Because 'conscience' is nothing more than a series of conditioned anxiety responses, the neurotic extrovert is *undersocialised* and has an underdeveloped conscience.

Cochrane (1974) reviewed a number of studies in which prisoners and control groups were given EPI questionnaires. Although prisoners are generally higher on N, they're not higher on E and, indeed, several studies have shown criminals to be *less* extroverted than controls. However, Eysenck (1974) responded to these findings by claiming

Ask Yourself

- How would Freud explain criminal behaviour? (See Chapter 35.)
- How would Kohlberg explain criminal behaviour? (See Chapter 35.)
- How would social learning theorists (such as Bandura) explain criminal behaviour? (See Chapters 29 and 35.)
- How could Bowlby's maternal-deprivation hypothesis help to explain criminal behaviour? (See Chapter 32.)
- What methods would behaviour geneticists use to assess the influence of genetic factors on criminal behaviour? Based on studies of intelligence (see Chapter 41) and schizophrenia (see Chapter 44), what would you expect the relative influence of genetic and environmental factors to be?

that the EPI largely measures the 'sociability' component of extroversion rather than the 'impulsivity' component, which is more relevant to conditionability. This represents a change to his earlier position, in which he equated 'sociability' (the capacity for socialisation) and 'conditionability'. Cochrane concludes that, at least in its original form, the theory has been discredited.

Even if prisoners were uniformly more extroverted and neurotic than non-prisoners, factors other than personality could still be relevant. For example, offenders who are caught (or found guilty) might differ in certain significant ways from those who aren't, such as the nature of the offence and the 'offender's' social status.

Farrington (1992) argues that the exact role of N depends on whether we're referring to 'official' or self-reported delinquency. 'Official' offenders are most often characterised by high N and low E scores (agreeing with Cochrane's findings), whereas self-reported offenders are the reverse: low N and high E. However, both forms of delinquency are related to high P (see below). Either way, according to Heather (1976):

> *The notion that such a complex and meaningful social phenomenon as crime can ever be explained by appealing to the activity of individual nervous systems would be laughable were it not so insidious.*

What makes the theory insidious, he says, is that it 'places the fault inside individuals rather than in the social system where it almost always belongs'.

Psychoticism and crime

P is more strongly correlated with crime than either N or E (Eysenck and Eysenck, 1970, 1985; Eysenck and Gudjonsson, 1989). According to Furnham and Heaven (1999), it's well established that high P scorers are also aggressive, uncaring, troublesome, inhumane, insensitive to others' needs and feelings, tend to not experience guilt, prefer strange and unusual things, and appear foolhardy (Eysenck and Eysenck, 1970). Howarth (1986) found that high P scorers are impulsive, tend to be uncooperative, rigid, and lacking sensitivity, and Claridge (1981) found a close association between P and overt aggressiveness and impulsivity.

Not surprisingly, in view of all these findings, P scores are well able to discriminate between criminals and non-criminals (Eysenck and Gudjonsson, 1989).

According to Furnham and Heaven (1999), much more work needs to be done on assessing the *interaction* between personality and external factors such as family life, peer pressure, group norms and so on.

Key Study 46.2

A longitudinal study of delinquency and personality (Heaven, 1996b)

- Heaven studied 282 14-year-olds over a two-year period, measuring delinquency, E, P and self-esteem. The best longitudinal predictor of later delinquency was P, with E and low self-esteem both having little impact.
- Although the importance of P supports previous findings, the overall effect was quite small: the three factors accounted for just over 16 per cent of the variance in delinquency scores when first measured, and only 6 per cent two years later. So, over time, the impact of personality on the maintenance of delinquency scores seems to have been rather limited.
- Heaven suggests that factors (dimensions or domains) such as E are too broad and insensitive to capture the full subtlety of developmental change. Lower-order factors (or facets), such as excitement-seeking, trust, impulsiveness, and venturesomeness might capture these subtleties better. This conclusion was supported by a separate study involving delinquency and the Big Five personality factors (Heaven, 1996a; see Chapter 42).

Antisocial personality disorder (psychopathy)

Definitions and classification

'Psychopathy' was first included in the 1959 Mental Health Act, which defined it as:

> *... a persistent disorder or disability of mind (whether or not including subnormality of intelligence) which results in abnormally aggressive or seriously irresponsible conduct on the part of the patient and requires or is susceptible to medical treatment.*

According to the Mental Health Act 1983:

> *Psychopathy means a persistent disorder or disability of mind (whether or not including significant impairment of intelligence) which results in abnormally aggressive or seriously irresponsible conduct on the part of the person concerned.*

Because it was felt strongly that those with psychopathic disorder should only be compulsorily detained if there was a reasonable prospect of response to treatment, the diagnostic criteria in the definition were separated (in the 1983 Act) from the susceptibility to treatment clause (Prins, 1995). These are contained in other sections of the Act, which made compulsory admission for treatment available only if it can be stated that medical treatment is likely to alleviate or prevent a deterioration in the individual's condition. According to Prins (1995):

> *This was an important proviso because it recognised the difficulties involved in treating psychopaths, but kept the door open for therapeutic optimism ... It also serves to emphasise the fact that the term psychopathic disorder should be used sparingly and not as a 'dustbin' label for those clients or patients who are merely difficult, un-cooperative or unlikeable ...*

A report commissioned by the Department of Health and the Home Office (1994) recommended replacing the term 'psychopathic disorder' with 'personality disorder'. In fact, DSM–5 uses the term 'antisocial personality disorder' (APD) (see Box 46.1), and ICD–10 refers to 'dissocial personality disorder' (DPD).

The 2007 Mental Health Act includes changes that introduce an appropriate *treatment test*, which is meant to ensure that a person (regardless of their diagnosis) is detained only if appropriate medical treatment is available. The definition of medical treatment has been widened to include psychological intervention and specialist mental health habilitation, rehabilitation and care (Mental Health Network/NHS Confederation, 2007).

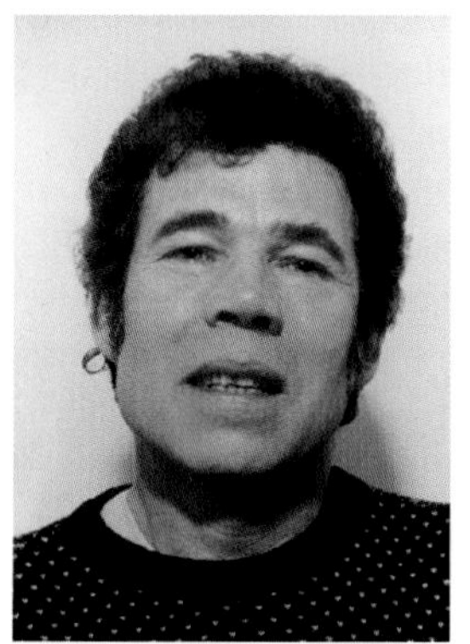

Figure 46.6 Fred and Rosemary West – husband and wife serial killers

The *Hare Psychopathy Checklist - Revised* (PCL-R; Hare, 1991) measures two distinct but correlated factors: *factor 1* describes a selfish, callous and remorseless use of others, and *factor 2*, a chronically unstable, antisocial and socially deviant lifestyle. Essentially, the psychopathic individual is someone with an emotional disorder who also has a high risk of antisocial behaviour.

Box 46.1 The major characteristics of antisocial personality disorder (APD)

Individuals diagnosed with APD:

- lack tender feelings and concern for others' feelings, so that relationships are shallow and unstable; sex is purely 'functional' (if male) and they're highly promiscuous
- appear to have no family loyalty and commit their crimes alone; they're basically loners
- have superficial charm and are often socially skilled; their charm can be very disarming and enables them to manipulate and exploit others for their own gain
- behave callously, as in inflicting pain or degradation or acting cruelly towards others
- act violently towards their marriage partners, and their children, whom they may also neglect, resulting in separation and divorce
- are impulsive and fail to strive consistently towards a goal, lacking a purpose in life; this may be reflected in an unstable employment record
- have low tolerance of frustration and a tendency towards violence, which often causes repeated criminal offences; this may begin with petty acts of delinquency, but progresses to callous, violent crimes; their lack of guilt and failure to learn from experience result in behaviour that persists despite serious consequences and legal penalties
- they commit a disproportionate number of violent crimes.

(Based on Gelder *et al.*, 1999; Prins, 1995)

Ioannou and Greenall (2008) describe PCL-R as the current gold standard for assessing psychopathy; it has proved very reliable and is extremely useful in risk assessment. For example, within three years of release, 80 per cent of those judged to be psychopathic (based on PCL–R) had violated the conditions of their release, compared with just 25 per cent of the non-psychopaths. A meta-analytic study by Hemphill *et al.* (1998) found that psychopathic offenders were three times more likely to re-offend and four times more likely to re-offend violently within a year of release, compared with non-psychopathic offenders.

What causes APD?

Display of the full disorder seems to involve a complex interaction between social environment and biological predispositions. In particular, social environment (such as socio-economic status/SES) influences factor 2, while factor 1 is unrelated to SES. This suggests that biological make-up determines whether individuals show emotional difficulties. But these emotional factors are only risk factors: an adverse social environment provides the conditions needed for the disorder to develop (Mitchell and Blair, 2000).

Ask Yourself

- Which explanation of schizophrenia mirrors this account of APD? (See Chapter 44.)

Like other forms of criminality (see Key Study 46.1), parental antisocial attitudes, inconsistent discipline, physical punishment, broken homes and childhood separations all predict high APD scores in adolescence (Forth, 1995). However, the quality of parenting doesn't influence the probability of conduct disorders in children who display the emotional difficulties associated with APD – but they do in most children (Wootton *et al.*, 1997).

APD and the brain

It appears that the amygdala functions atypically from an early age in people with APD. It's long been known that the amygdala plays a crucial role in the processing of emotion, especially fear. Just like people with APD, normal humans and non-humans suffering damage to this area don't show normal fear conditioning (Spence, 2004) or startle reflex potentiation/priming (LeDoux, 1998a). The amygdala has also been shown to be involved in human emotional response to sad facial expressions (Blair *et al.*, 1999). But this response is absent in individuals with APD.

Raine *et al.* (see Key Study 46.3) suggest that a bias towards activity in the right hemisphere might mean that processing of negative emotion (such as anger and aggression) might be subject to less inhibition from the left hemisphere: those emotions would be *less* controlled. Lower-than-normal activity in the PFC, parietal cortex and corpus callosum suggests a deficit in the integration of information needed to modify and inhibit behaviour. For example, increased blood flow to the PFC usually occurs when people are engaged in planning some future behaviour. People with PFC damage are often unable to plan ahead, and live in the 'here and now', controlled by currently physically present stimuli and situations (Luria, 1973). Abnormalities in the hippocampus and amygdala suggest deficiency in forming and utilising emotionally coloured perceptions and memories (Toates, 2001).

It's likely that at least some of the murderers in the Raine *et al.* study would be diagnosed as having APD. In a later study, Raine *et al.* (2000) used MRI to study the brains of 21 volunteers with APD. They were found to have 11 per cent less prefrontal grey matter than those without APD, the first evidence of a structural brain deficit in APD.

Key Study 46.3

Brain abnormalities in murderers (Raine *et al.*, 1997)

- Raine *et al.* wanted to provide direct evidence for the claim that murderers pleading not guilty by reason of insanity (NGRI) have brain dysfunction.
- Using PET scans, glucose metabolism (GM) was measured in a variety of brain regions and structures while participants engaged in a continuous performance challenge task. (Glucose is the principal type of fuel used by neurons when transmitting information, so, the lower the GM, the less the activity in any particular part of the brain.)
- The participants were 41 murderers pleading NGRI and controls matched for age and gender. Based on previous research (with both violent offenders and non-violent controls), Raine *et al.* expected to find differences between the two groups only in specific brain areas.
- As far as *cortical areas* are concerned, the murderers were expected to show lower GM in the *prefrontal cortex* (PFC), the *superior parietal gyrus* and the *left angular gyrus* (also an area within the parietal lobe). This prediction was supported. Also as expected, *no* differences were found in the *temporal lobe* or the *cingulate*.
- As far as *subcortical areas* are concerned, the murderers compared with the controls showed reduced GM in the *corpus callosum* and they also showed *abnormal asymmetries* in the *amygdala, thalamus* and the *medial temporal lobe* (including the *hippocampus*). The murderers showed a bias towards increased *right-hemisphere* activity. Also as expected, there were *no* differences found in the *basal ganglia*, *midbrain* or *cerebellum*.

In a later analysis of the Raine *et al.* data, murderers who killed on impulse were compared with those who'd planned their crime in detail and committed them in cold blood, apparently without conscience (Strueber *et al.*, 2006/2007). Only the former showed PFC abnormalities; this supports the claim that deficiencies in emotional control may fail to prevent impulsive violent offenders from acting (they don't stop to consider the consequences). In contrast, the cold, calculating criminal requires a largely intact PFC: long-term planning involves complex decision processes.

Decety *et al.* (2013) largely confirmed Raine *et al*'s. (1997) findings in their study of 121 male prison inmates using fMRI. When asked to imagine something painful happening to another person (such as stepping barefoot on a nail), the brains of those who scored highest on the PCL-R failed to show the usual connectivity between the amygdala and the ventromedial PFC (vital for emotion regulation, empathy and morality). In some cases, it seemed that brain areas associated with pleasure became active.

Raine *et al.* (2004) found that PFC deficits may have more to do with the criminal's chances of being caught than with serious, chronic violence. It's also unclear whether the PFC hypothesis applied to females; violent female offenders comparable to Raine's male participants are rare (see Critical Discussion 46.1) and so are less well studied. However, there's no apparent connection in females between a decreased PFC volume and psychopathological tendencies as demonstrated in males. Women have more effective impulse control, which tends to fail only when the functioning of the PFC is massively impaired in childhood (Strueber *et al.*, 2006/2007).

Can APD be treated?

Controversy surrounding APD rivals that which has always surrounded schizophrenia, and raises some of the same fundamental issues, such as reliability and validity (see Chapter 44). According to Smith (2000), 'Personality disorder is surely the greyest of grey areas', and the diagnosis, far from showing the way to treatment, is in fact extremely unhelpful for health care workers and patients alike. Believing that patients have a personality disorder can excuse us from trying to establish meaningful and helpful interactions with them.

While the general consensus is that APD – and personality disorder in general – is notoriously resistant to treatment, schizophrenia, for example, was also once thought to be untreatable. Mitchell and Blair (2000) are confident that research in the near future may allow us to treat APD too.

Critical Discussion 46.2

Do suicide bombers have APD?

According to Silke (2002), there are many myths surrounding terrorists and terrorism. One of the most common is that terrorists in general, and perhaps suicide bombers in particular, are crazed fanatics, psychopaths (i.e. they have APD), who are completely immune to the suffering of their victims (making the terrorists homicidal or suicidal maniacs).

It's comforting to think that suicide terrorists are different from the rest of us, either by virtue of a personality (and related brain) disorder, or because they're poor and ignorant, with little prospect of a decent future and are driven to act by unbearable political oppression and religious fanaticism (usually Islamic) (Bond, 2004). Although there are many cases which suggest that terrorists do possess a degree of callousness and fanaticism not usually found in 'normal' populations, these assumptions are wrong on almost every count.

Recent research by Psychologists and anthropologists suggests that suicide bombers are no less rational, no less sane, no worse educated, no poorer and no more religious than anyone else, and have none of the risk factors normally associated with suicide, such as depression and history of attempted suicides, schizophrenia or substance abuse (Bond, 2004).

The link with religion is complicated, because most Islamic terrorist groups use religious propaganda (largely the promise of paradise) to prepare recruits for suicide missions. But suicide terrorism isn't exclusive either to religious groups or Islamic culture. For example, the now destroyed Tamil Tigers, a Marxist-Leninist group came from Hindu families but were hostile to religion, and the

Figure 46.7 Reem Raiyshi, the first 'Martyr Mother' – a Palestinian suicide bomber who killed four Israelis in Gaza in 2004, leaving behind two young sons

Japanese kamikaze pilots flew their planes into enemy ships during the Second World War.

Suicide terrorism is an *organisational* phenomenon (not the act of a crazed individual). The decision to engage in it is political and strategic, and the aim is always to coerce a government into withdrawing from territory the group considers its homeland, sometimes by attacking fellow countrymen seen to be supporting them (as in ongoing attacks against police stations in Iraq).

Against this background of a sense of injustice and persecution, the move from being a 'disaffected individual' to a 'violent extremist' is usually facilitated by a catalyst (trigger) event. Most suicide bombers have had at least one relative or close friend killed, maimed or abused at the hands of enemies. They join terrorist groups in an angry and vengeful frame of mind, already intent on taking part in suicide attacks (Silke, 2002).

Some evidence suggests that suicide bombers are more 'marginal' people, more influenced by the group, more vulnerable, fragile, and narrow-minded (Merari, 2010). It's also been shown that 60 per cent of suicide bombers have anxious/dependent personalities, typical of avoidant and/or dependent attachment styles (Parkes, 2014) (see Chapter 32). However:

> *... in the vast majority of cases, individual psychology is not the determining factor ... All you need, it seems, is a peculiar mix of social, cultural and political conditions for a group to make the decision. After that, it could be anyone, school boys and mothers included ... (Bond, 2004)*

OFFENDER PROFILING

Ask Yourself

- What does offender profiling mean?
- Can you give any examples – fictional or real?

According to Harrower (2000), *offender profiling* (or *criminal personality*, *psychological*, or *behaviour profiling*) is seen as the sexy speciality of Forensic Psychology largely as a result of Fitz (Robbie Coltrane) in *Cracker*. But the poetic licence allowed in that TV series hasn't been particularly helpful to Psychology as a discipline.

Offender profiling and investigative psychology

Recognition of the potential contributions of scientific Psychology (Canter, 1989, 1994) has led to the development of *Investigative Psychology* (IP). Youngs (2008) defines IP as:

> *The scientific discipline concerned with ... the psychological principles, theories and empirical findings that may be applied to investigations and the legal process, with the aim of improving the effectiveness of criminal detection and the appropriateness of the work of the courts.*

IP is an overall approach to thinking about criminals and criminal behaviour that captures Canter's perspective on the psychology of his *laws of criminality* (Canter and Youngs, 2008). It has generated studies of diverse topics including the nature of the criminal emotional experience, the social networks of offenders, the identification of lying in insurance claims or false rape allegations, burglary *modus operandi* and the spatial behaviour of serial killers (Youngs, 2008).

Offender profiling (OP) represents the way that Psychologists can contribute to police investigations. As typically practised, OP is

> *... the process by which individuals, drawing on their clinical or other professional experience,*

Case Study 46.1

Adrian Babb, serial rapist

One Sunday afternoon in June 1987, a 75-year-old woman was returning to her flat in a tower block. As she entered the lift, a young man stepped in with her. Once the lift door had closed, he pinned her to the wall and forced her to the rooftop. There he raped her.

A few months later, Canter was given details of this and a number of related assaults, all against elderly and often frail victims in tower blocks in the same area of Birmingham. The information indicated a small area of the city in which the offender was likely to be living, his domestic circumstances and likely criminal record. It also pointed out his lack of experience in committing crimes, and the consequent likelihood that he'd have left forensic evidence at one or more of the crime scenes.

One of the principles on which *offender profiling* is based is that the details of exactly how the crime was committed (the stock-in-trade of detectives) is fundamental – there are many ways of raping and killing: the common themes of aggressive control and violent assault can be played out with many variations. For example, this serial rapist responded to aspects of his victims' discomfort. When one victim complained of the cold concrete on her bare flesh, he put some of the clothing he'd removed from her on the floor beneath her. This was typical of his style of assault. By contrast, other rapists delight in demeaning and degrading their victims.

These details suggested that he'd be known as helpful and considerate by those who didn't know of his violent assaults. He turned out to be Adrian Babb, a well-regarded, 20-year-old swimming pool attendant. His fingerprint was found at the scene of one of his crimes, he pleaded guilty to seven rapes, and was sentenced to 16 years in prison.

(Based on Canter, 1994)

make judgements about the personality traits or psychodynamics of the perpetrators of crimes ... (Youngs, 2008)

According to Harrower (1998), the overall aim of OP is to narrow the field of investigation, drawing inferences about the offender's motivation and personality from evidence left at the crime scene. OP is most useful when the scene reflects psychopathology, such as sadistic assaults. Ninety per cent of profiling involves murder and rape, although it's also used in arson, burglary, robbery, obscene phone calls and the new crime of stalking.

Canter's approach: profiling 'equations'

Youngs (2008) claims that there's been an overreliance on personal judgement, rather than the empirical analysis required by scientific Psychology. Similarly, the theories about criminals and their behaviour which much of OP has been based on are also open to question.

Canter was originally approached by the Metropolitan Police in 1985 to advise whether Psychology could contribute to criminal investigations. In 1986 he became involved in what was initially a serial rape investigation, but later developed into a notorious serial murder case. He helped secure the arrest of John Duffy, convicted in 1988 of two murders and five rapes, for which he was given seven life sentences. The accuracy of his description of Duffy astonished both the police and the media.

Figure 46.8 John Duffy, serial rapist-killer

Central to a more scientific approach are the Canter profiling 'equations' (Canter, 1994); these are hypothetical equations that capture the scientific approach to inferring associations between (i) what happens during the offence (when and where it happens and to whom) and (ii) the characteristics of the offender (including the offender's criminal history, background, base location, and relationships). They're also known as the actions (A) > characteristics (C) equations, where A denotes the actions involved in the crime and C the characteristics of typical offenders for such crimes; > is the theory or argument and the evidence for inferring one from the other.

Investigative Psychologists conduct a wide range of studies of different types of offences and the offenders who committed them, aimed at establishing solutions to these equations; the goal is to provide objective bases for the inferences that detectives make when investigating the perpetrator's likely characteristics.

According to the *differentiation hypothesis*, different sets of offenders should differ from each other: if every offender offended in the same way, then the A > C equations would provide characteristics that were the same for every offender (see Case Study 46.1). Consistent with the differentiation hypothesis, Canter claims that the criminal leaves 'psychological traces' or 'shadows' in committing a crime:

... tell-tale patterns of behaviour that indicate the sort of person he is. Gleaned from the crime scene and reports from witnesses, these traces are more ambiguous and subtle than those examined by the biologist or physicist ... They are more like shadows [which] ... can indicate where investigators should look and what sort of person they should be looking for ... (Canter, 1994)

In addition, we all operate within a social context, so there's an implicit social relationship between the offender and victim. This again will offer major clues to the pattern of the offender's life. Sensitive and detailed examination of victims' testimony can reveal speech patterns, interests, obsessions, and ways of behaving which will also have occurred in the offender's daily life. For example, rapists may treat their victims as they treat most of the women in their lives – in the case of Adrian Babb, he actually showed consideration for their feelings, which reflected a generally considerate attitude to other people.

Clearly, particular actions don't map onto particular characteristics in a simple or direct way. As Youngs (2008) points out, this may be because the same action can reflect more than one characteristic, and the same characteristic can be inferred from different actions. For example, extreme violence may be threatened in a robbery carried out by an inexperienced or a highly experienced offender. Conversely, both rapists and robbers tend to have a criminal record that included burglary convictions. The A-C relationship is further complicated by the finding that the same action can indicate different characteristics in different contexts and at different points in an offender's career.

Canter argues that differences in how offenders carry out their crimes relate to the role assigned to the victim (the offender's 'mode of interpersonal transaction'). These roles can be of three types:

1. *Victim as object:* the victim is regarded as something to be used and controlled through restraint and threat, often involving alternative gains in the form of other crimes (such as theft). Offenders have a complete lack of empathy; victims are chosen opportunistically and so tend to be vulnerable individuals.
2. *Victim as vehicle:* the victim is a means through which the offender can discharge his own emotional state (such as anger and frustration). There's some awareness of the victim as human, but this serves only to help the victim be used to express the offender's feelings and desires – typically through extreme violence and abuse.
3. *Victim as person:* The offender nurtures the confused belief that through the assault they achieve some sort of personal intimacy with the victim; offending actions will include attempts to create a degree of rapport or connection. Offenders believe they're heroes – one offender is quoted as saying to his victim, 'be more careful, next time someone nasty may attack you'.

Ask Yourself

- How would you describe the role assigned by Adrian Babb to his rape victims? (See Case Study 46.1.)

Studies have shown that this general model does help to understand the specific empirical differences in offending behaviour found within rape (Canter, 1994), paedophilia (Canter *et al.*, 1998) and stranger homicide (Salfati and Canter, 1999).

An evaluation of profiling

- According to Boon and Davies (1992), Canter and his colleagues have found five aspects of the criminal and his behaviour to be particularly revealing: residential location, criminal biography, personal characteristics, domestic and social characteristics, and occupational and educational history. Geography is especially important: offenders will operate in areas they know and feel comfortable in (a relatively short distance from their homes) ('geographical OP'/GOP; Canter, 2010).
- Canter's approach is much more rooted in *psychological principles* than the method used by the FBI. Criminals, like other people, act *consistently*, and analysis of their behaviour will reveal patterns which can offer clues as to how they live when they're not offending.
- OP has undoubted potential if used properly by trained professionals (Harrower, 1998). But how successful is it? Holmes (1989) cites FBI data claiming that 192 cases of profile construction (1981) resulted in 88 arrests, but OP was believed to have contributed to conviction in just 17 per cent of the arrests. Others (e.g. Oleson, 1996) point out that the FBI's methodology may be fundamentally flawed: there's no control group against which to compare the evidence obtained from offenders, no mention of the statistical techniques used to analyse the data, and much of the interview data is accepted at face value.
- In the UK, Copson and Holloway (1997) surveyed detectives who'd worked on 184 cases in which OP had been used. They believed it had produced identification of offenders in less than 3 per cent of cases, and 'helped to solve' the crime in 16 per cent. They conclude that:

> *Profiling can work very well, but certainly not in the way some practitioners, let alone dramatists, would have you believe. There is nothing in our findings to support the notion that complex offender characteristics can be predicted with any great accuracy. In fact, with some people you would be better off tossing a coin.*

- Youngs (2008) cites several studies which show that links between offending style and offender characteristics do exist and can be established.
- According to Harrower (2000), the phenomenon of serial murder and the development of OP have clearly captured the public imagination – and a growing number of Psychology students want to become Forensic Psychologists.

THE TREATMENT OF OFFENDERS

According to Honderich (1993), there are two distinct views (both implicit and explicit) as to why people commit crime:

- the individual is a rational agent with free will – an individual's circumstances reflect his/her choices (see Chapter 49)
- we're all, to a greater or lesser degree, products of our environments.

Related to the 'free will' viewpoint are two policies:

- provide as few opportunities as possible for choosing a criminal act
- when people are caught, make the consequences as painful as possible to deter them from future offending.

Based on the second view:

- if environmental conditions are implicated in the cause of the crime, then change is needed in the environment (primarily, the social structure)
- the adverse effects on individuals resulting from the environment need to be addressed.

According to Hollin (1999), in practice these viewpoints and policies crystallise into the debate about the relative effectiveness of punishment and treatment in crime prevention.

Situational crime prevention

If crimes are the end result of criminals seizing the opportunity to make a personal, usually financial, gain, then why not look at the opportunity as well as the criminal (Hollin, 1999)? This is exactly the approach of *situational crime prevention*: analysing and changing the environment in an effort to prevent crime.

Ask Yourself

- Try to think of some practical ways in which situational crime prevention could be achieved (see Chapter 21).

The most straightforward way is to reduce the opportunity for successful crime, by removing and protecting the target. For example, replacing phone coin boxes with cards, introducing night transport systems to ensure safety of late-night workers, and installing more car alarms, immobilisers and home security systems.

In addition, increasing the risk of detection can be achieved through formal surveillance in places where there's opportunity for crime. For example, increased police presence at football matches and city centres at pub-emptying times, CCTV, electronic 'tagging' of offenders, and neighbourhood watch schemes.

Box 46.2 Automated policing (Moskvitch, 2013)

- Over the past few years, law enforcement agencies have begun replacing human police officers with efficient, all-seeing *algorithms* (a form of artificial intelligence/AI: see Chapter 20). They look for crimes using sensors, cameras, facial-recognition software and intelligent computerised analysis.
- The scope of these devices has now widened beyond traffic offences (where they were first employed) to car theft. For example, in some UK car parks, the algorithms embedded in security cameras deduce that if you walk directly to a car and drive off, then you're the owner. But if someone hides in the shadows or zigzags through the parked cars checking out the cars, then they register that something suspicious is occurring.
- Algorithms are also being tested that can identify – in real time – faces in a crowd, people with a particular gait, or suspicious packages.

Figure 46.9 Increased police presence at football matches is a form of situational crime prevention, increasing the risk of detection

Ask Yourself

- Can you see any potential problems with situational crime prevention – both practical and ethical?

When offenders are deterred from committing a criminal act, is crime actually being reduced or merely *displaced* onto other victims, times and situations? There are also civil liberties issues relating to tagging, CCTV and other forms of surveillance.

Deterrence is also found in the harsh punishment approach (from fines to 'life sentences').

Punitive prison regimes

Ask Yourself...

- Do you believe that offenders should be punished rather than rehabilitated?
- Are your reasons moral, as opposed to pragmatic (such as what is most likely to prevent re-offending)?
- Are punishment and rehabilitation necessarily mutually exclusive?

Overall reconviction rate (*recidivism*) of people discharged from prisons in England and Wales for 2007 was 39 per cent (compared with 43 per cent in 2000), a decrease of 9.4 per cent. The proportion of offenders who reoffended fell by 9.2 per cent when controlling for changes in offender characteristics (Ministry of Justice, 2009).

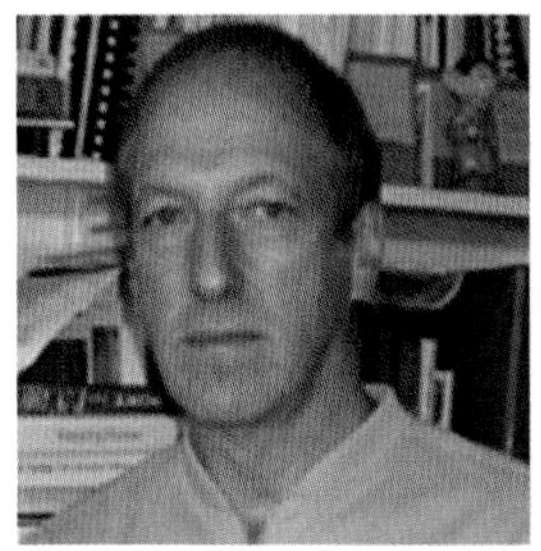

MEET THE RESEARCHER

David Canter

From Environmental to Investigative Psychology: the journey of a lifetime

In 1985, I found myself in an office at a police training college surrounded by senior police officers. They had just decided that a series of rapes and murders, committed across London and the southwest of England, were the acts of one man. That morning, they had set up a major enquiry linking together three large police forces to try to catch this serial killer. In a moment that would change my life, they turned to me and asked, 'Can you help us catch this man before he kills again?' My positive response set me on a path that eventually led to the development of the new field of Investigative Psychology.

Architectural Psychology

My willingness to take on such a daunting task was founded on 20 years of developing and applying Psychology in many different contexts. This had started in the unlikely context of studying the effects of open plan office size on worker performance, which grew out of my interest in the Psychology of art. I had been offered the opportunity to explore these matters in a School of Architecture as part of the growing emergence among all sorts of designers that some understanding of human actions and experiences was of direct value in making their designs more humanly effective. These studies were originally part of a field known as 'Architectural Psychology', which was soon embraced under the broader umbrella of 'Environmental Psychology'. Paradoxically, what emerged from these studies of the effects of the physical environment was the discovery that what people bring to the use of space and the sense they make of designs is far more powerful than how places influence people.

One fascinating consequence of this human agency is that people reveal something of themselves from the places they choose to be and how they modify those places. Indeed, one early finding from my study of teachers' satisfaction with school buildings was the counterintuitive result that the more they modified the building the happier they were with it. This also lays the groundwork for acknowledging that aspects of a person are reflected as much in what they do and where they do it as in how they may complete a personality inventory or answer questions in an interview. It was this awareness of how we all give away aspects of ourselves that led me to believe I may be able to help the police catch a serial killer.

Getting out of the lab

Before becoming involved with police investigations I had followed the implications of the earlier architectural research by seeking to develop a focus for research that took account of the important methodological implications of the significance of human agency. It means that many carefully controlled laboratory experiments are very unlikely to have any general applicability outside of the bounds of these sterile settings. It is almost impossible to simulate the reasons a person has for being in a location, so what is being explored in a laboratory is how people play the role of being an experimental subject. This may be relevant to analogous situations, like being a patient or a soldier under interrogation, but is more difficult to generalise to broader contexts. As a consequence, my research thereafter tended to focus on issues that were very difficult to simulate in a laboratory, such as users' reactions to and satisfaction with their physical surroundings, how people behave in emergencies and subsequently the actions of criminals.

The power of human agency

Beyond the methodological implications and the areas of research that I find of interest, the recognition of the power of human agency also has profound implications for the sorts of theoretical models that it is appropriate to develop. These are models of what people do and how they make sense of their context and act accordingly. George Kelly's Personal Construct Psychology is a powerful framework for considering many of these issues. This means that although my work has often focused on human actions, the underlying assumption is that these actions are not merely habitual responses but derive from the construct systems that give meaning to their interactions with others and the world around them.

Human responses to emergencies

The study of human actions in buildings on fire and other emergencies was greatly informed by this cognitive, behavioural perspective. Engineers seemed to think that human reactions could be understood by a very simple 'stimulus-response' system, e.g. smoke will cause people to panic. My research showed that people seek to make sense of the ambiguity of the early stages of an emergency and act in accordance with those interpretations. Furthermore, their understanding of the situation is strongly influenced by previous experience and the social processes in which they participate. It is only when cues build up to enable them to see that a radically different set of social rules are relevant that they change their normal actions and try to escape. This has significant implications for the management of emergencies, as well as for the development of emergency warning systems.

Would your escape plan be different if you'd already experienced a similar situation?

The development of these studies of human activity was further enhanced by the possibilities I perceived in the evolution of Kelly's Repertory Grid methodology for studying conceptual systems. This was rooted in the excitement generated in many areas of psychology by the possibility of large-scale, multivariate statistical analyses, especially the power of factor analysis, which emerged with availability of computers. It paralleled the seminal work of Charles Osgood with his 'measurement of meaning', but got its greatest impetus from applications in intelligence and personality testing. All of these explorations recognised the utility of conceptualising the vast array of human experiences and behaviour as points within some multidimensional space. With his 'facet approach', Louis Guttman took this work to the logical point where the relationships between variables are distances in a notional space between points that represent those variables. The visual strength of this makes it particularly powerful for demonstrating complex relationships to people who are not statistically sophisticated, such as architects. I had even used this approach in market research studies (cf. www.youtube.com/watch?v=KKlD6JS8Npk).

Transition to Investigative Psychology

The availability of these methodologies and the conceptualisations on which they were built, together with the experience of studying people outside of the laboratory, often in challenging and difficult situations, were all foundations for responding to the request to catch a killer before he killed again. I was able to think of the killer as a person trying to make sense of their surroundings and reduce the risk to themselves, who had a typical pattern of behaviour that would reveal aspects of his characteristics. The inferences I drew from this framework turned out to be of great help to the investigation, leading to an arrest and conviction.

Investigative Psychology tries to understand the motivations and behaviours of a killer in order to help to catch and convict them

I realised with this success that the problem-solving approach I had been developing for studying many aspects of human agency were of wide relevance across many areas of investigations. Therefore after contributions to a number of other police enquiries and a variety of studies of crimes and criminals, I realised that a new area of professional Psychology was emerging which I called 'Investigative Psychology' (cf. www.i-psy.com; www.ia-ip.org). This has now developed into a wide-ranging area of Psychology with its own theories and methods (Canter and Youngs, 2009), which is growing in reach week by week.

Professor David Canter is currently Director of the International Research Centre for Investigative Psychology at the University of Huddersfield. David has published 300 or more academic papers and 50 books, including his award-winning *Criminal Shadows*, and has contributed to many television documentary series.

Punishment-oriented regimes seek to reduce these figures by making the experience of prison so aversive as to deter ex-prisoners from re-offending. These include the 'short, sharp shock' (introduced in the UK in the 1980s) and 'boot camps', an American concept involving a short period of incarceration in a strict military environment, with a rigid daily schedule of hard labour, drill and ceremony, and physical training (Mackenzie and Souryal, 1995).

Mackenzie and Shaw (1990) found that compared with offenders sentenced to traditional prisons, those who went to boot camp were more positive about their prison experiences and their futures, and held more prosocial attitudes. Mackenzie and Souryal (1995) also reported a range of positive outcomes for the boot-camp group, such as being drug-free, physically healthy, believing that the regime had helped them, and an overall positive effect on their families. However, those sent to boot camp had been convicted of non-violent crimes, and had less serious criminal histories (Hollin, 1999).

There's little evidence that the military regime would successfully change future behaviour if the 'criminogenic needs of the offenders are not being addressed' (Mackenzie *et al.,* 1995).

According to Farrington (1995), findings from longitudinal studies point to the need for strategies to improve young people's academic achievement, interpersonal skills, parental child-rearing practices, and to reduce poverty (see Key Study 46.1).

Treatment programmes

There's a vast literature on therapeutic approaches, especially with young offenders (e.g. Hollin and Howells, 1996), but the principles apply to young and adult offenders alike. Most major therapeutic approaches discussed in Chapter 45 have been used with offenders including psychodynamic psychotherapy, behaviour therapy, social skills training and cognitive–behaviour therapy (CBT). This underlies many of the intervention programmes (such as *enhanced thinking skills*/ETS) used with sex offenders and addicts; it's also relevant to broader problems that offenders have to deal with, such as anger management (Canter, 2010).

Several *multimodal* (mixed or 'eclectic') programmes have also been used, in which several methods are combined. For example, aggression replacement training (Glick and Goldstein, 1987; Goldstein and Glick, 1996) combines structured learning training (including social skills and social problem-solving training), anger control and moral education (see Chapter 35).

Does treatment work?

There are hundreds of outcome studies, using different types of intervention, conducted in different settings, and using different measures of 'success'. As with outcome studies in the treatment of mental disorder, meta-analytic studies allow general conclusions to be drawn (see Chapter 45). According to Hollin (1999):

- Overall, there's a 10 per cent reduction in recidivism when treated offenders are compared with no-treatment controls; but this figure conceals tremendous variability between different programmes.
- The best results will be obtained with medium- to high-risk offenders, using structured/focused/directive approaches (in practice, this usually means behavioural methods that incorporate a cognitive component).
- Treatment in the community has a stronger effect on delinquency than residential programmes.
- Drug-dependency programmes eventually help to reduce acquisitive crime to one-third of what it was before participation, and the ETS courses also produce statistically significant improvements in behaviour, typically reducing recidivism by about 20 per cent (Canter, 2010).
- The key question, however, is whether this change would have happened anyway. There are real practical and ethical problems in randomly assigning participants to 'treatment'/'non-treatment' conditions, so comparisons have to be made with other groups that don't experience the interventions. In general, it's found that those who go through these carefully organised programmes do better than those who don't – but this is all relative: many offenders don't give up their drug habits and criminal lifestyles, but overall, fewer are involved in crime after these programmes and their drug habits tend to be milder (Canter, 2010).
- Byron (2014) cites evidence from both the USA and the UK showing that offenders with mental disorders released from special hospitals ('forensic hospitals' in the USA) (such as Broadmoor and Rampton) are less likely to re-offend and to turn to violence compared with those released from prisons. Treatment works, and yet we continue to put offenders with mental disorders in prison (Byron, 2014).

CONCLUSIONS: WHAT DO WE DO ABOUT PAEDOPHILES?

According to Ruszczynski (2008), it's easy to demonise paedophiles, such as Gary Glitter (see Figure 46.10). The media portray him as just a monster.

Perverse and violent acts locate inner pain, rage, fear and humiliation outside of the self by displacing them into the body and/or arousing it in the other person. Sex and sexuality are hijacked for the purposes of violation, humiliation and control. Probably the most difficult form of this to consider is the sexual abuse of children (Ruszczynski, 2008).

Figure 46.10 Gary Glitter (real name Paul Gadd), who was sentenced in 2015 to 16 years in prison for historical sex abuse, including attempting to rape a three-year old.

The paedophile (the person with *paedophilic disorder*) believes that a child is an appropriate sexual partner and that is very difficult for most of us to get our heads around. Whatever the unconscious motivation involved, what's required is a subtle balance between the criminal justice system (punishment) and the mental health services (help).

Regarding the former, paedophiles are increasingly targeting babies and children too young to speak in an orchestrated strategy to avoid being caught. While the true scale of paedophilia in the UK is impossible to quantify, it's believed that hundreds of online paedophile networks have yet to be uncovered; such is the size of the problem that as many as one in six children (1.9 million) might be a victim of abuse. The 30,000 Britons currently on the sex offenders register represent the tip of the iceberg (Townsend, 2008).

As far as helping/treating paedophiles, it's crucial to distinguish between paedophilia and sexual abuse. Not all abusers are paedophiles; some are attracted to children because they're weaker and more pliable than adults. Conversely, not everyone who's sexually attracted to children act on their tendencies or turn violent; remaining undercover, they may surround themselves with children while struggling with their secret desire. This separation of mental state and acts of child abuse might be the only way to bring into treatment the countless numbers of undetected paedophiles and reduce the chances of any particular child becoming a victim (Briken *et al.*, 2009).

Treatment (at least in the US) typically involves a combination of psychotherapy (psychodynamic or CBT) and SSRIs (see Chapter 45). However, not all paedophiles respond to psychotherapy (Brooks-Gordon and Bilby, 2006). Other promising medications target the hormonal regulatory system, which can block the sequence of events resulting in testosterone production ('chemical castration'). This makes patients significantly less likely to act on their sexual impulses and may enable them to unburden themselves to a therapist. Avoidance of child pornography is another tactic commonly used (Briken *et al.*, 2009).

According to Arkowitz and Lilienfeld (2009), research fails to support the common public perception that 'once a paedophile always a paedophile'. They also conclude that, although the development of treatment for sex offenders is still in its infancy, studies show that therapy can make a significant difference.

Chapter Summary

- **Longitudinal studies** help us understand the relationship between age and crime, with delinquency peaking at 16–17 years. This reflects a very high crime rate at this age.
- Most juvenile crimes are **status offences** (as opposed to **index/notifiable offences**). Also, most crime is 'adolescence-limited', which can be explained partly in terms of the greater **risk-taking** of adolescents, and partly in terms of **peer group pressure**.
- Several childhood factors have been shown to predict later offending, including **low intelligence/poor school record**, a **family criminal record, family poverty**, and **poor parental child-rearing practices.**
- Although neither a disadvantaged background nor 'social failure' inevitably leads to crime, they massively increase the risks of criminal behaviour.
- Most crimes, especially violent crimes, are committed by males. This has led to a view of women who commit murder as doubly deviant, breaking both the law of the land and the 'natural law' relating to women's 'nature'.
- Female homicide is usually directed either at an abusive partner or their own child (**filicide**); the latter may occur soon after birth (**neonaticide**) or within the first year (**infanticide**).
- Two extreme explanations of male domination of crime are **biological determinism** and **social constructionism**. All the major theoretical

perspectives within Psychology as a whole have been/can be applied to criminal behaviour.

- **Personality factors** (or **domains**), such as **N**, **E**, and especially **P** are related to a wide range of antisocial, criminal and delinquent behaviours. However, more specific **facets** may be more valid predictors of developmental change.
- **Antisocial personality disorder (APD)** or **psychopathy** has long been implicated in criminal behaviour, especially violent crimes. One very controversial aspect of APD is its **treatability**.
- At the heart of APD seems to lie an **emotional disorder**, which represents a **risk factor**; for the development of the full disorder, there needs to be an **adverse social environment**.
- There's growing evidence of **brain abnormalities** that are correlated with APD and murder, but this doesn't allow us to infer that the brain abnormalities actually **cause** the violent behaviour.
- A common perception of **terrorists** in general and suicide bombers in particular is that they're insane fanatics. But the evidence suggests that they're mainly quite ordinary individuals caught up in violent situations involving the occupation of their homeland by an invading enemy.
- **Offender profiling (OP)** is a major feature of **Investigative Psychology (IP)** . Canter's profiling **equations** and his identification of offender **modes of interpersonal transaction** have been extremely influential within the UK.
- **Situational crime prevention** involves both reducing the opportunity for successful crime and increasing the risk of detection. But criminals may simply **displace** their offences onto other victims, places and times.
- **Punitive prison regimes** may help to reduce **recidivism rates** among less serious criminals, while **treatment programmes** are most successful with medium- to high-risk offenders.
- A wide variety of treatments and therapies has been used, including **multimodal** approaches, **CBT** and **ETS**. **Structured methods** used in non-residential settings seem to be the most effective.
- An important distinction is that between **child sexual abuse** and **paedophilic disorder**. While those on the sex offenders register are probably a fraction of all paedophiles, research suggests that convicted offenders can respond to treatment and that recidivism isn't inevitable.

Links with Other Topics/Chapters

Chapter 37 ⟶ If risk-taking is a rite of passage into adulthood, it is so only for *adolescents* in Western culture, where *initiation ceremonies* are lacking

Chapter 47 ⟶ Criminology has notoriously ignored the fact of gender, preferring to offer *universal theories of crime* based on research with *males* (Harrower, 1998), (the *androcentric bias*)

Chapter 49 ⟶ Eysenck's attempt to explain crime in terms of high E and N scores on the EPI is an example of a *reductionist* explanation

Chapters 29 and 30 ⟶ APD individuals seem to lack the inborn sensitivity to *appeasement gestures* as well as the normal *empathic responses* to others' distress

Chapter 48 ⟶ The study of potential violent offenders, together with its practical implications, is an example of *socially sensitive research*

Chapter 42 ⟶ The idea that criminals act consistently assumes that *personality* is the major factor determining behaviour

Chapter 10 ⟶ Ekman is the 'guru of face reading', and has proposed a number of universal facial expressions related to particular *emotional states*

Chapters 11 and 44 ⟶ One characteristic of battered woman syndrome (BWS) is that the victim is actually taught by the offender to become *helpless*

Recommended Reading

Adler, J.R. (ed) (2004) *Forensic Psychology: Concepts, debates and practice.* Cullompton: Willan Publishing.

Brookman, F. (2005) *Understanding Homicide.* London: Sage.

Gross, R. (2008) *Key Studies in Psychology* (5th edn). London: Hodder Education. Chapter 36.

Canter, D. (Ed.) (2008) *Criminal Psychology.* London: Hodder Education.

Canter, D. (2010) *Forensic Psychology: A Very Short Introduction.* Oxford: Oxford University Press.

Harrower, J. (2001) *Psychology in Practice: Crime.* London: Hodder & Stoughton. Also relevant to Chapter 21.

Useful Websites

www.criminalprofiling.ch (The Swiss Criminal Profiling Scientific Research site)

www.hare.org ('Without Conscience', Robert Hare's website devoted to the study of psychopathy)

http://members.optushome.com.au/dwillsh/index.html (D. Willshire's Forensic Psychology, Psychiatry and Cycling Links)

www.davidcanter.com (David Canter's homepage)

CHAPTER 47

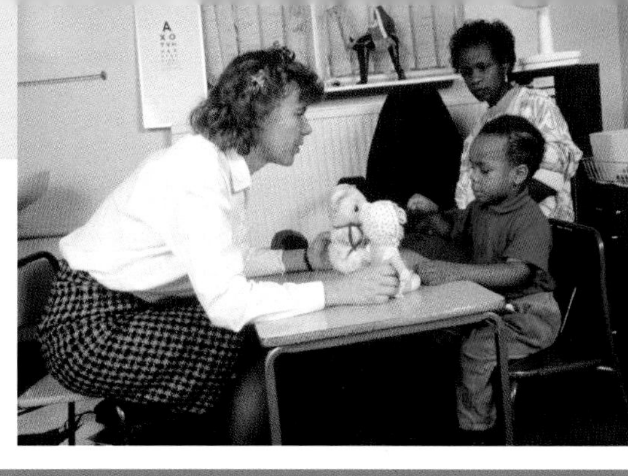

BIAS IN PSYCHOLOGICAL THEORY AND RESEARCH

INTRODUCTION and OVERVIEW

Mainstream academic Psychology, modelling itself on classical, orthodox, natural science (such as physics and chemistry), claims to be objective, unbiased, and value-free. Collectively, these aims form the *positivist* view of science (*positivism*) (see Chapter 3). As applied to the study of humans, this implies that it's possible to study people as they 'really are', without the Psychologist's characteristics influencing the outcome of the investigation in any way.

This chapter shows that a view of Psychology as unbiased and value-free is mistaken. Two major forms of bias, *sexism* and *ethnocentrism* (which relate to gender and culture, respectively) permeate much psychological theory and research.

Much of the chapter's content is relevant to the topic of prejudice and discrimination. As we saw in Chapter 25, prejudice and discrimination can be understood as characteristics of individuals or of social groups, institutions, and even whole societies. With bias in psychological theory and research, it's sometimes individual Psychologists, and sometimes 'Psychology as a whole', that are guilty.

GENDER BIAS: FEMINIST PSYCHOLOGY, SEXISM AND ANDROCENTRISM

Not surprisingly, most of the criticism of mainstream Psychology regarding its gender bias has come from Feminist Psychology (FP), which Wilkinson (1997) defines as:

> *... psychological theory and practice which is explicitly informed by the political goals of the feminist movement.*

While feminism and FP can take a variety of forms, two common themes are the valuation of women as worthy of study in their own right (not just in comparison with men), and recognition of the need for social change on behalf of women (Unger and Crawford, 1996).

FP is openly political and sets out to challenge the discipline of Psychology for its inadequate and damaging theories about women, and for its failure to see power relations as central to social life (Unger and Crawford, 1992). More specifically, it insists on exposing and challenging the operation of male power in Psychology:

> *Psychology's theories often exclude women, or distort our experience by assimilating it to male norms or man-made stereotypes, or by regarding 'women' as a unitary category, to be understood only in comparison with the unitary category 'men' ... Similarly, psychology [screens out] ... the existence and operation of social and structural inequalities between and within social groups ...*
> *(Wilkinson, 1991)*

Psychology obscures the social and structural operation of male power by concentrating its analysis on people as individuals (*individualism*): responsibility (and pathology) are located within the individual, to the total neglect of social and political oppression. By ignoring or minimising the social context, Psychology obscures the mechanisms of oppression. For example, the unhappiness of some women after childbirth is treated as a problem in individual functioning (with possible hormonal causes), thus distracting attention away from the difficult practical situation in which many new mothers find themselves (Wilkinson, 1997; see Chapters 44 and 46).

Box 47.1 Some major feminist criticisms of Psychology

- Much psychological research is conducted on all-male samples, but then either fails to make this clear or reports the findings as if they applied equally to women and men.
- Some of the most influential theories within Psychology as a whole are based on studies of males only, but are meant to apply equally to women and men.
- If women's behaviour differs from men's, the former is often judged to be pathological, abnormal, or deficient in some way (*sexism*). This is because the behaviour of men is, implicitly or explicitly, taken as the 'standard' or norm against which women's behaviour is compared (*androcentrism* – male-centredness, or the *masculinist bias*).
- Psychological explanations of behaviour tend to emphasise biological (and other internal) causes, as opposed to social (and other external) causes (*individualism*). This reinforces widely held *stereotypes* regarding the inevitability and unchangeability of *gender differences*; this contributes to the oppression of women (another form of sexism).
- Heterosexuality (both male and female) is taken, implicitly or explicitly, as the norm, so that homosexuality is seen as abnormal (*heterosexism*).

Ask Yourself

- Try to think of (at least) one example for each of the five major criticisms of psychological theory and research made in Box 47.1.
- Regarding the fourth point, how does this relate to attribution theory as discussed in Chapter 23?

The feminist critique of science

An even more fundamental criticism of Psychology than those listed in Box 47.1 is feminists' belief that scientific enquiry itself (whether this be within psychology or not) is biased. Psychology's claims to be a science are based on its methods (especially the experiment), and the belief that it's a value-free discipline. But can scientific enquiry be neutral, wholly independent of the value system of the human scientists involved? According to Prince and Hartnett (1993):

> *Decisions about what is, and what is not, to be measured, how this is done, and most importantly, what constitutes legitimate research are made by individual scientists within a sociopolitical context, and thus science is ideological.*

Many Feminist Psychologists argue that scientific method is gender biased. For example, Nicolson (1995) identifies two major problems associated with adherence to the 'objective' investigation of behaviour for the way claims are made about women and gender differences.

- The experimental environment takes the individual 'subject's *behaviour*', as distinct from the 'subject' herself, as the unit of study. Therefore, it becomes deliberately blind to the behaviour's *meaning*, including its social, personal, and cultural contexts. As a result, claims about gender differences in competence and behaviour are attributed to *intrinsic* qualities (either the product of 'gender-role socialisation' or biology) as opposed to *contextual qualities*. (This is another reference to individualism.)
- Experimental Psychology, far from being context-free, takes place in a very specific context which typically disadvantages women (Eagly, 1987). In an experiment, a woman becomes *anonymous*, stripped of her social roles and the accompanying power and knowledge she might have achieved in the outside world. She's placed in this 'strange' environment, and expected to respond to the needs of (almost inevitably) a male experimenter who's in charge of the situation, with all the social meaning ascribed to gender power relations.

The belief that it's possible to study people 'as they really are', removed from their usual sociocultural contexts (in a '*de-contextualised*' way), is completely invalid:

> *Psychology relies for its data on the practices of socialised and culture-bound individuals, so that to explore 'natural' or 'culture-free' behaviour (namely that behaviour unfettered by cultural, social structures and power relations) is by definition impossible ... (Nicolson, 1995)*

Feminist Psychologists offer a critical challenge to psychological knowledge on gender issues by drawing on other disciplines, such as sociology. According to Giddens (1979), for example:

There is no static knowledge about people to be 'discovered' or 'proved' through reductionist experimentation, and thus the researcher takes account of context, meaning and change over time.

Ask Yourself

- Do you agree with Nicolson's claim that all human behaviour is 'culture-bound'?
- What about 'instinctive' behaviours, such as eating, drinking and sex: does culture play a part here too? If so, in what ways?

(These questions are equally relevant to the section on culture bias.)

Some practical consequences of gender bias

According to Kitzinger (1998), questions about gender differences (and similarities) aren't just scientific questions, they're also highly *political*. Some answers to these questions have been used to keep women out of universities, or to put them in mental hospitals. Other answers have been used to encourage women to go on assertiveness training courses, or to argue that women should have all the same rights and opportunities as men. In other words, the science of gender differences research is always used for political reasons:

> *However much psychologists may think or hope or believe that they are doing objective research and discovering truths about the world they are always influenced ... by the social and political context in which they are doing their research ...* (Kitzinger, 1998)

Figure 47.1 Celia Kitzinger, lesbian Feminist Psychologist

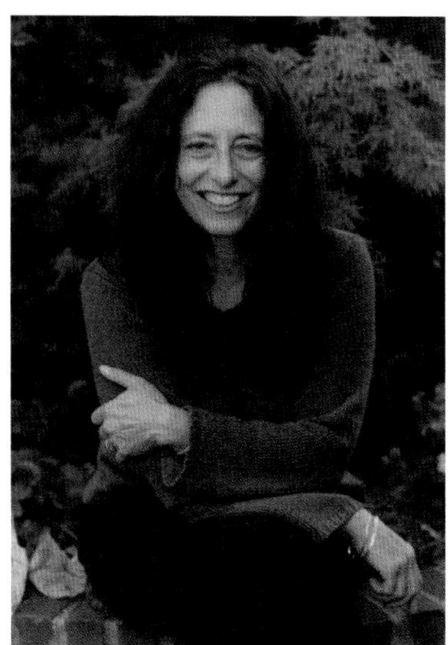

Figure 47.2 Carol Gilligan (born 1936)

In the 1993 preface to *In a Different Voice*, Gilligan (1982) says that at the core of her work on moral development in women and girls was the realisation that within Psychology, and in society at large, 'values were taken as facts'. She continues:

> *In the aftermath of the Holocaust ... it is not tenable for psychologists or social scientists to adopt a position of ethical neutrality or cultural relativism ... Such a hands-off stance in the face of atrocity amounts to a kind of complicity.*

While the example she gives is clearly extreme, it helps to illustrate the argument that not only do Psychologists (and other scientists) have a responsibility to make their values about important social and political issues explicit, but failure to do so may (unwittingly) contribute to prejudice, discrimination, and oppression. These considerations are as relevant to a discussion of the *ethics* of psychological research as they are to gender (and culture) bias, and are discussed in more detail in Chapter 48.

The masculinist bias and sexism: A closer look

The male norm as the standard

According to Tavris (1993):

> *In any domain of life in which men set the standard of normalcy, women will be considered abnormal, and society will debate woman's 'place' and her*

'nature'. Many women experience tremendous conflict in trying to decide whether to be 'like' men or 'opposite' from them, and this conflict is itself evidence of the implicit male standard against which they are measuring themselves. This is why it is normal for women to feel abnormal.

Tavris gives two examples of why it's normal for women to feel abnormal. First, in 1985, the American Psychiatric Association proposed two new categories of mental disorder for inclusion in DSM-III-R (see Chapter 43). One was *masochistic personality*. In DSM-II, this was described as one of the psychosexual disorders, in which sexual gratification requires being hurt or humiliated. The proposal was to extend the term so that it became a more pervasive personality disorder, in which one seeks failure at work, at home, and in relationships, rejects opportunities for pleasure, puts others first (thereby sacrificing one's own needs), plays the martyr, and so on.

While not intended to apply to women exclusively, these characteristics are associated predominantly with the female role. Indeed, according to Caplan (1991), it represented a way of calling psychopathological the behaviour of women who conform to social norms for a 'feminine woman' (the 'good wife syndrome'). In short, such a diagnostic label was biased against women, and perpetuated the myth of women's masochism. The label was eventually changed to 'self-defeating personality disorder', and was put in the appendix of DSM-III-R.

Ask Yourself

- If you were proposing a parallel diagnosis for men who conform to social norms for a 'masculine man', what characteristics would this have to include, and what would you call it?
- Could you justify including sadism in the diagnostic criteria for conformist men?

Tavris's second example of why it's normal for women to feel abnormal concerns *causal attributions* made about men's and women's behaviours. When men have problems, such as drug abuse, and behave in socially unacceptable ways, as in rape and other forms of violence, the causes are looked for in their upbringing. Women's problems, however, are seen as the result of their psyches or hormones (another form of individualism), with the further implication that it could have been different for men (they're the victims of their childhood, for example), but not for women ('that's what women are like'). (But see Chapter 46.)

Figure 47.3 Do women get into trouble with the law only for 'internal' reasons?

The 'mismeasure of woman' and alpha bias

According to Tavris, the view that man is the norm and woman is the opposite, lesser or deficient (the problem) constitutes one of three currently competing views regarding the 'mismeasure of woman' (meant to parallel Gould's (1981) *The Mismeasure of Man*, a renowned critique of intelligence testing: see Chapter 41). It's the view that underpins so much psychological research designed to discover why women aren't 'as something' (moral, intelligent, rational) as men (what Hare-Mustin and Maracek (1988) call *alpha bias*: see below). Alpha bias also underlies the enormous self-help industry: women consume millions of books and magazines advising them how to become more beautiful, independent, and so on. Men, being 'normal', feel no need to 'fix' themselves in corresponding ways (Tavris,1993).

Figure 47.4 Women are consumers of vast amounts of alpha bias

Box 47.2 A demonstration of alpha bias

- Wilson (1994) maintains that the reason 95 per cent of bank managers, company directors, judges, and university professors in Britain are men is that men are 'more competitive', and because 'dominance is a personality characteristic determined by male hormones'.
- Wilson also argues that women in academic jobs are less productive than men: 'objectively speaking, women may already be over-promoted'. Women who do achieve promotion to top management positions 'may have brains that are masculinised'.
- The research cited by Wilson to support these claims comes partly from the psychometric testing industries which provide 'scientific' evidence of women's inadequacies, such as (compared with men) their 'lack' of mathematical and spatial abilities. Even if women are considered to have the abilities to perform well in professional jobs, says Wilson, they have personality defects (in particular, low self-esteem and lack of assertiveness) which impede performance:

  These differences [in mental abilities, motivation, personality and values] are deep-rooted, based in biology, and not easily dismantled by social engineering. Because of them we are unlikely to see the day when the occupational profiles of men and women are the same.

(From Wilson, 1994; Wilkinson, 1997)

Ask Yourself

- Try to identify examples of individualism in Box 47.2.
- Can you formulate some arguments against Wilson's claims?

Wilson is combining alpha bias with individualism in order to argue that women are 'naturally' deficient in the 'male' qualities needed to achieve in certain occupations. He's also assuming that the research he draws on to make his claims isn't itself gender biased.

Sexism in research

The American Psychological Association's Board of Social and Ethical Responsibility set up a Committee on Nonsexist Research, which reported its findings as *Guidelines for Avoiding Sexism in Psychological Research* (Denmark *et al.*, 1988). This maintains that gender bias is found at all stages of the research process:

- question formulation
- research methods and design
- data analysis and interpretation, and
- conclusion formulation.

The principles set out in the *Guidelines* are meant to apply to other forms of bias too: those concerned with race, ethnicity, disability, sexual orientation and socio-economic status. (See Box 47.3.)

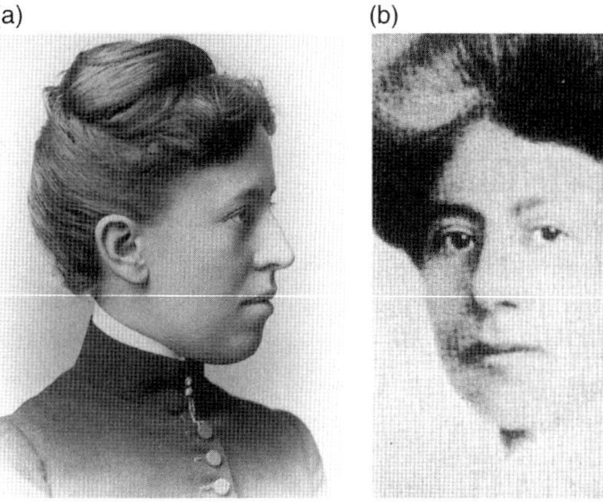

Figure 47.5 Margaret Washburn and Mary Calkins; if these women are not household names, it is because psychological literature's treatment of women Psychologists has kept them invisible (see Gross, 2014)

Sexism in theory: alpha and beta bias

Gilligan (1982) gives Erikson's theory of lifespan development (based on the study of males only) as one example of a sexist theory, which portrays women as 'deviants' (*alpha bias*). Erikson (1950) describes a series of eight universal stages: for both genders, in all cultures, the conflict between identity and role confusion (adolescence) precedes that between intimacy and isolation (young adulthood). But he acknowledges that the sequence is *different* for a female, who postpones her identity as she prepares to attract the man whose name she'll adopt, and by whose status she'll be defined (Erikson, 1968). For women, intimacy seems to go along with identity: they come to know themselves through their relationships with others (Gilligan, 1982). Despite this, the sequence of stages in Erikson's psychosocial theory remains unchanged (see Table 38.1).

As Gilligan (1982) points out:

> *Identity continues to precede intimacy as male experience continues to define his [Erikson's] life-cycle concept.*

Box 47.3 Examples of gender bias at each stage of the research process

Question formulation: It's assumed that topics relevant to white males are more important and 'basic' (e.g. the effects of TV violence on aggression in boys: see Chapter 29), while those relevant to white females, or ethnic minority females or males, are more marginal, specialised, or applied (e.g. the psychological correlates of pregnancy or the menopause).

Research methods and design: Surprisingly often, the gender and race of the participants, researchers, and any stooges/confederates who may be involved, aren't specified. Consequently, potential interactions between these variables aren't accounted for. For example, men tend to display more helping behaviour than women in studies involving a young, female confederate 'victim' (see Chapter 30). This could be a function of either the confederate's gender or an interaction between the confederate and the participant, rather than gender differences between the participants (which is the conclusion usually drawn).

Data analysis and interpretation: Significant gender differences may be reported in very misleading ways, because the wrong sorts of comparisons are made. For example:

'The spatial ability scores of women in our sample is significantly lower than those of men, at the 0.01 level'. You might conclude from this that women cannot or should not become architects or engineers. However, 'Successful architects score above 32 on our spatial ability test ... engineers score above 31 ... twelve per cent of women and 16 per cent of men in our sample score above 31; eleven per cent of women and 15 per cent of men score above 32'. What conclusions would you draw now? (Denmark et al., 1988)

Conclusion formulation: Results based on one gender only are then applied to both. This can be seen in some of the major theories within Developmental Psychology, notably Erikson's *psychosocial theory* of development (1950; see Chapters 37 and 38), Levinson *et al.*'s (1978) *Seasons of a Man's Life* (see Chapter 38), and Kohlberg's theory of moral development (1969; see Chapter 35). These all demonstrate *beta bias* (Hare-Mustin and Maracek, 1988), and are discussed further below.

(Based on Denmark *et al.*, 1988)

Similarly, Kohlberg's (1969) six-stage theory of moral development was based on a 20-year longitudinal study of 84 boys, but he claims that these stages are universal (see Chapter 35). Females rarely attain a level of moral reasoning above stage three ('Good boy–nice girl' orientation), which is supposed to be achieved by most adolescents and adults. This leaves females looking decidedly morally deficient (*alpha bias*).

Like other Feminist Psychologists, Gilligan argues that Psychology speaks with a 'male voice', describing the world from a male perspective and confusing this with absolute truth (*beta bias*). The task of FP is to listen to women and girls who speak in a 'different voice' (Gilligan, 1982; Brown and Gilligan, 1992). Gilligan's work with females has led her to argue that men and women have qualitatively different conceptions of morality. By stressing the *differences* between men and women (an *alpha-biased approach*), Gilligan is attempting to redress the balance created by Kohlberg's *beta-biased theory*.

Ask Yourself

- In what ways is Freud's psychoanalytic theory (especially the psychosexual stages of development) sexist (or what Grosz (1987) calls 'phallocentric')?
- Repeat this exercise for Levinson *et al.*'s theory of adult development, and any other theory you're familiar with.

CULTURE BIAS

As we noted earlier, Denmark *et al.*'s (1988) report on sexism is meant to apply equally to all other major forms of bias, including cultural (see Box 47.3). Ironically, many feminist critics of Gilligan's ideas have argued that women aren't a cohesive group who speak in a single voice, a view which imposes a false sameness upon the diversity of women's voices across differences of age, ethnicity, (dis)ability, class, and other social divisions (Wilkinson, 1997).

Ask Yourself

- Before reading on, ask yourself what's meant by the term 'culture'.
- How is it related to 'race', 'ethnicity' and 'subcultures'?

Box 47.4 Psychology's First, Second and Third Worlds

- The USA, the *First World* of Psychology, dominates the international arena and monopolises the manufacture of psychological knowledge, which it exports to other countries around the globe, through control over books and journals, test manufacture and distribution, training centres, and so on.
- The *Second World* countries comprise western European nations and Russia. They have far less influence in shaping Psychology around the world, although, ironically, it's in these countries that modern Psychology has its philosophical roots (see Chapter 3). Just as the countries of the Second World find themselves overpowered by American popular culture, they also find themselves overwhelmed by US-manufactured psychological knowledge.
- *Third World* countries are mostly importers of psychological knowledge, first from the USA but also from the Second World countries with which they historically had colonial ties (such as Pakistan and England). India is the most important Third World 'producer' of psychological knowledge, but even there most research follows the lines established by the USA and, to a lesser extent, western Europe.

(From Moghaddam and Studer, 1997)

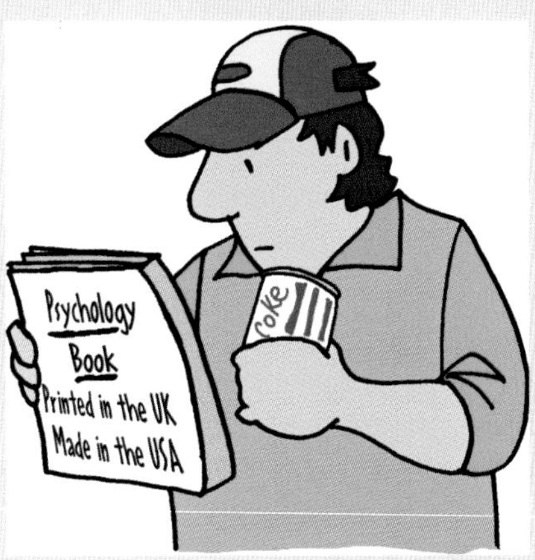

Figure 47.6

Cross-cultural Psychology and ethnocentrism

According to Smith and Bond (1998), Cross-cultural Psychology (CCP) studies *variability* in behaviour among the various societies and cultural groups around the world. For Jahoda (1978), its additional goal is to identify what's *similar* across different cultures, and thus likely to be our common human heritage (the *universals* of human behaviour).

CCP is important because it helps to correct *ethnocentrism*, the strong human tendency to use our own ethnic or cultural groups' norms and values to define what's 'natural' and 'correct' for everyone ('reality'; Triandis, 1990). Historically, Psychology has been dominated by white, middle-class males in the USA. Over the last century, they've enjoyed a monopoly as both the researchers and the 'subjects' of the discipline (Moghaddam and Studer, 1997). They constitute the core of Psychology's *First World* (Moghaddam, 1987). (See Box 47.4.)

According to Moghaddam *et al.* (1993), American researchers and participants:

> *... have shared a lifestyle and value system that differs not only from that of most other people in North America, such as ethnic minorities and women, but also the vast majority of people in the rest of the world.*

Yet the findings from this research, and the theories based upon it, have been applied to *people in general*, as if culture makes no difference. An implicit equation is made between 'human being' and 'human being from western culture' (the *Anglocentric* or *Eurocentric bias*).

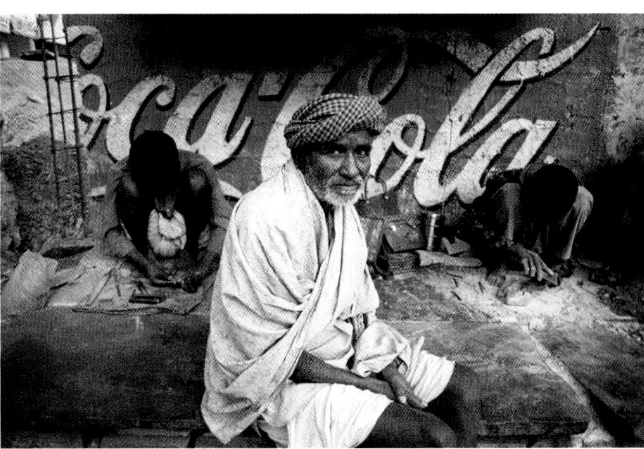

Figure 47.7 A symbol of western plenty in the midst of Third World poverty

When members of other cultural groups have been studied, they've usually been *compared* with western samples, using the behaviour and experience of the latter as the 'standard'. As with androcentrism, it's the failure to acknowledge this bias which creates the misleading and false impression that what's being said about behaviour can be generalised without qualification.

Cross-cultural Psychologists *don't* equate 'human being' with 'member of western culture', because for them, cultural background is the crucial *independent variable*. In view of the domination of First World Psychology, this distinction becomes crucial. At the same time, Cross-cultural Psychologists consider the search for universal principles of human behaviour (*absolutism*) as quite valid (and consistent with the 'classical' view of science: see above and Chapter 3).

What is culture?

Herskovits (1955) defines culture as 'the human-made part of the environment'. For Triandis (1994):

> *Culture is to society what memory is to individuals. In other words, culture includes the traditions that tell 'what has worked' in the past. It also encompasses the way people have learned to look at their environment and themselves, and their unstated assumptions about the way the world is and the way people should act.*

The 'human-made' part of the environment can be subdivided into:

1. *objective* aspects (such as tools, roads and radio stations)
2. *subjective* aspects (such as categorisations, associations, norms, roles and values). Value systems have a significant impact on various other aspects of culture, including child-rearing techniques, patterns of socialisation, identity development, kinship networks, work and leisure, religious beliefs and practices (Laungani, 2007).

This distinction allows us to examine how subjective culture influences behaviour (Triandis, 1994). While culture is made by humans, it also helps to 'make' them: humans have an interactive relationship with culture (Moghaddam *et al.*, 1993).

Much cross-cultural research is actually based on 'national cultures', often comprising a number of *subcultures*, which may be demarcated by religion (as in Northern Ireland), language (Belgium), or race (Malaysia and Singapore). However, such research often fails to provide any more details about the participants than the name of the country (national culture) in which the study was carried out. According to Smith and Bond (1998), when this happens, we pay two 'penalties':

- when we compare national cultures, we can lose track of the enormous diversity found *within* many of the major nations of the world, and differences found between any two countries might well also be found between carefully selected subcultures within those countries;
- there's the danger of implying that national cultures are unitary systems, free of conflict, confusion, and dissent; this is rarely the case.

Critical Discussion 47.1

The importance of studying black and minority ethnic (BME) participants

- In the context of mental health service provision (see Chapters 43–45), Farooq and Abbas (2013) point out that it's highly unlikely that a mental health practitioner won't encounter clients who differ from them in terms of religion, ethnicity and culture.
- Current treatments and interventions that are offered to BME service users may be seen as antagonistic and are often in conflict with their cultural values, mainly because the system of care is Eurocentric (Nadirshaw, 2009).
- Farooq and Abbas believe that this highlights the need to further understand the experiences of BME groups and to investigate possible interventions best suited for their specific needs.
- In addition, if Psychology as a profession is based on the scientist-practitioner model (see Chapter 45), then isn't it logical to move towards developing and implementing evidence-based interventions for diverse populations (Farooq and Abbas, 2013)?
- The best way to do this is by conducting innovative and culturally-informed research and clinical trials that will provide the evidence base that can then inform clinical practice. Excluding patients from a BME group in research is unethical (see Chapter 48) and introduces significant bias: the results are no longer representative of the population.

How do cultures differ?

Definitions of culture such as those above stress what different cultures have in common. To evaluate research findings and theory that are culturally biased, it's even more important to consider how cultures differ from each other. Triandis (1990) identifies several *cultural syndromes*, which he defines as:

> *... a pattern of values, attitudes, beliefs, norms and behaviours that can be used to contrast a group of cultures to another group of cultures.*

The emic–etic distinction

Research has to begin somewhere and, inevitably, this usually involves an instrument or observational technique rooted in the researcher's own culture (Berry, 1969). These can be used for studying both cross-cultural differences and universal aspects of human behaviour (or the 'psychic unity of mankind').

Box 47.5 Three major cultural syndromes used to contrast different cultures

- **Cultural complexity** refers to how much attention people must pay to time. This is related to the number and diversity of the roles that members of the culture typically play. More industrialised and technologically advanced cultures, such as Japan, Sweden and the USA, are more complex in this way.
- **Individualism–collectivism** refers to whether one's identity is defined by personal choices and achievements (the autonomous individual: *individualism*) or by characteristics of the collective group to which one is more or less permanently attached, such as the family, tribal or religious group, or country (*collectivism*). While people in every culture display both, the relative emphasis in the West is towards individualism, and in the East towards collectivism. Broadly, capitalist politico-economic systems are associated with individualism, while socialist societies are associated with collectivism.
- **Tight cultures** expect their members to behave according to clearly defined norms, and there's very little tolerance of deviation from those norms. Japan is a good example of a tight culture, and Thailand an example of a *loose culture*.

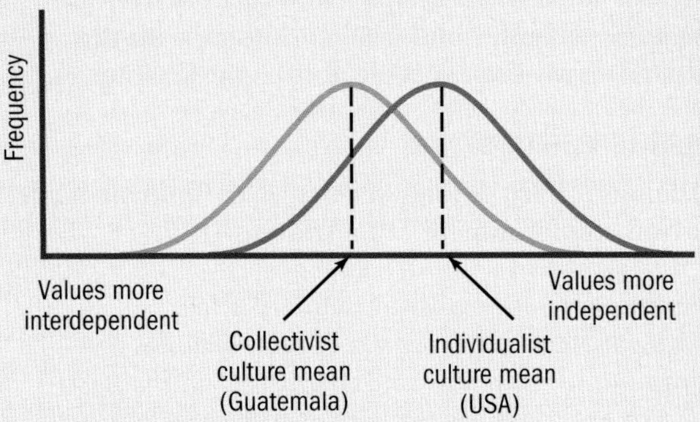

Figure 47.8 Hypothetical distributions of interdependent/ independent value scores in a collectivist and an individualist national culture

(Based on Smith and Bond, 1998; Triandis, 1990, 1994)

Ask Yourself

- Try to identify some behaviours (both normal and abnormal) that can be considered to have both universal (common to all cultures) and culture-specific features.

The distinction between culture-specific and universal behaviour is related to what Cross-cultural Psychologists call the *emic–etic distinction* (E-ED), first made by Pike (1954) to refer to two different approaches to the study of behaviour:

- the *etic* looks at behaviour from outside a particular cultural system
- the *emic* looks at behaviour from the inside.

This derives from the distinction made in linguistics between phon*etics* (the study of universal sounds, independently of their meaning) and phon*emics* (the study of universal sounds as they contribute to meaning: see Chapter 19). 'Etics' refers to *culturally general* concepts, which are easier to understand (because they're common to all cultures), while 'emics' refers to *culturally specific* concepts, which include all the ways that particular cultures deal with etics. It's the emics of another culture that are often so difficult to understand (Brislin, 1993).

The research tools that the 'visiting' Psychologist brings from 'home' are an emic for the home culture, but when they're assumed to be valid in the 'alien' culture and are used to compare them, they're said to be an *imposed etic* (Berry, 1969). Many attempts to replicate American studies in other parts of the world involve an imposed etic: they all assume that the situation being studied has the same meaning for members of the alien culture as it does for members of the researcher's own culture (Smith and Bond, 1998).

The danger of imposed etics is that they're likely to involve imposition of the researcher's own cultural biases and theoretical framework. These simply may not 'fit' the phenomena being studied, resulting in their distortion. A related danger is *ethnocentrism*. (See Critical Discussion 47.2.)

Psychologists need to adapt their methods so that they're studying the same processes in different cultures (Moghaddam *et al.*, 1993). But how do we know that we're studying the same processes? What does 'same' mean in this context? For Brislin (1993), this is the problem of *equivalence*. The very experience of participating in psychological testing will be strange and unfamiliar to members of non-Western cultures (Lonner, 1990). Even if measures are adapted for use in other cultures, Psychologists should be aware that simply being asked to do a test may be odd for some people (Howat, 1999). (See Gross, 2014; Laungani, 2007.)

Advantages of cross-cultural research

It may now seem obvious (almost 'common sense') to state that psychological theories must be based on the study of people's behaviours from all parts of the world. However, it's important to give specific reasons and examples in support of this argument.

Critical Discussion 47.2

Intelligence as an imposed etic

Brislin's (1993) example is the concept of intelligence. The etic is 'solving problems, the exact form of which hasn't been seen before', a definition which at least recognises that what constitutes a 'problem' differs between cultures.

However, is the emic of 'mental quickness' (as measured by IQ tests, for example) universally valid?

Among the Baganda people of Uganda, for example, intelligence is associated with slow, careful, deliberate thought (Wober, 1974). Nor is quick thinking necessarily a valid emic for all schoolchildren within a culturally diverse country like the USA (Brislin, 1993).

Figure 47.9 Village elders in Mali, assembled to make an important decision

Ask Yourself

- Can you identify other examples of imposed etics in relation to intelligence/intelligence tests? (See Chapter 41.)

Box 47.6 Major advantages of cross-cultural research (CCR)

- **Highlighting implicit assumptions**: CCR allows investigators to examine the influence of their own beliefs and assumptions, revealing how human behaviour cannot be separated from its cultural context.
- **Separating behaviour from context:** Being able to stand back from their own cultural experiences allows researchers to appreciate the impact of situational factors on behaviour. They're thus less likely to make the *fundamental attribution error* (see Chapter 23), or to use a 'deficit model' to explain the performances of minority group members.
- **Extending the range of variables:** CCR expands the range of variables and concepts that can be explored. For example, people in individualist and collectivist cultures tend to explain behaviour in different ways, with the latter less likely to make dispositional attributions (see Chapter 23).
- **Separating variables:** C-CR allows the separation of the effects of variables that may be confounded within a particular culture. For example, studying the effects of TV on school achievement is very difficult using just British or American samples, since the vast majority of these families owns (at least) one TV set!
- **Testing theories:** Only by conducting C-CR can Western psychologists be sure whether their theories and research findings are relevant outside their own cultural contexts. For example, Thibaut and Kelley's exchange theory of relationships (see Chapter 28), and Sherif *et al.*'s 'Robber's Cave' field experiment on intergroup conflict (see Key Study 25.1) have both failed the replication test outside North American settings.

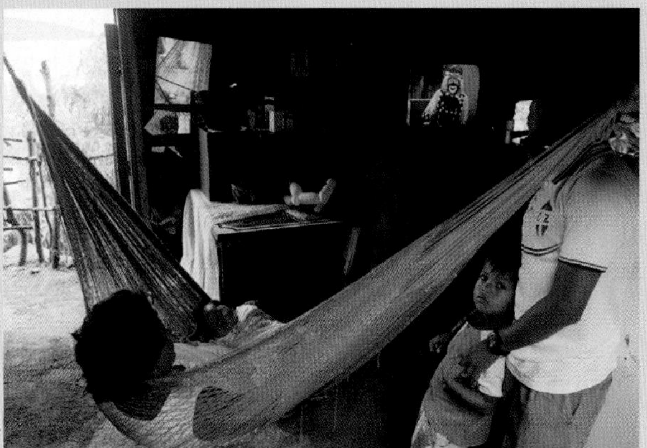

Figure 47.10 A researcher would have to go a long way to find a part of the world television hasn't reached

(Based on Brislin, 1993; Moghaddam *et al.*, 1993; Rogoff and Morelli, 1989; Smith and Bond, 1998)

CONCLUSIONS: CROSS-CULTURAL VERSUS CULTURAL PSYCHOLOGY

CCP is a branch of Experimental Social, Cognitive and Personality Psychology, and most of what's been known as CCP has presupposed the categories and models derived from (mostly experimental) research with (limited samples of) Euro-American populations. It has mostly either (i) 'tested the hypothesis' or 'validated the instrument' in other cultures, or (ii) 'measured' the social and psychological characteristics of members of other cultures with the methods and standards of western populations usually assumed as a valid norm. CCP is an outgrowth of 'mainstream' Psychology, with an emphasis on natural scientific methods.

The new *Cultural Psychology* (sometimes called *trans-cultural*; e.g. Bruner, 1990; Cole, 1990) can be seen as a rejection of mainstream Psychology, favouring the use of qualitative and ethnographic approaches (Martin, 1998). According to Cultural Psychologists, mind is embedded in a sociohistorical process that shapes and creates 'multiple realities' (Shweder, 1990). Instead of trying to identify universal 'laws' of psychological functioning (a major goal of CCP; Much, 1995), Cultural Psychologists adopt a *relativistic* approach and stress the *uniqueness* of different cultures.

An example of this alternative approach is *Indigenous* Psychology. Laungani (2007) prefers to talk of Indigenous *Psychologies*, given the vast number of countries that constitute eastern cultures and including those in Central America. According to Sinha (1993, in Laungani, 2007), *indigenisation* refers to the

> *... transformations of the scientific psychology that was borrowed from the West that would allow it to take on a character suited to the socio-cultural milieu of the country.*

Similarly, Kim and Berry (1993) define Indigenous Psychology as:

> *... the scientific study of human behaviour (or the mind) that is native, that is not transported from other regions, and that is designed for its people.*

Cole (1996) advocates a return to the early decades of Psychology, particularly Wundt's belief that the methods of natural science could be applied only to the most basic, universal and, therefore, timeless aspects of human behaviour. Culturally mediated and historically dependent 'higher psychological processes' need historical and developmental methods. What Wundt was advocating was a:

> *... road along which culture is placed on a level with biology and society in shaping individual human natures. The name correctly given to that enterprise is cultural psychology, a major late twentieth-century manifestation of the second psychology ... (Cole, 1996)*

Despite its shortcomings, Moghaddam and Studer (1997) believe that CCP is one of the avenues through which minorities have begun to have their voices heard in Psychology and that:

> *... there has been a demand that psychology make good its claim to being the science of humankind by including women and non-whites as research participants.*

Chapter Summary

- A **positivist** study of people implies an objective, value-free Psychology, in which the Psychologist's characteristics have no influence on the investigation's outcome. However, **sexism** and **ethnocentrism** pervade much psychological theory and research.
- **Feminist Psychologists** challenge mainstream Psychology's theories about women, who are either excluded from research studies or whose experiences are assimilated to/matched against male norms (**androcentrism**/the **masculinist bias**).
- Male power and social and political oppression are screened out through **individualism**, thus playing down the social context. This reinforces popular gender stereotypes, contributing to women's oppression.
- Feminist Psychologists also challenge Psychology's claim to be an objective, value-free science. Decisions about what constitutes legitimate research are made by individual scientists within a **sociopolitical context**, making science **ideological.**
- **Scientific method** itself is **gender biased,** concentrating on the 'subject's' behaviour, rather than its meaning, and ignoring contextual influences. These typically include a male experimenter who controls the situation.
- Using psychometric test results, Wilson argues that men and women differ in terms of mental abilities, motivation, personality, and values, which are based in biology. This demonstrates **alpha bias**.
- According to Denmark *et al*., gender bias is found at all stages of the **research process**. The last stage (**conclusion formulation**) is related to **theory construction**. Levinson *et al*.'s, Erikson's, and Kohlberg's theories are based on all-male samples and describe the world from male perspectives (**beta bias**).
- **Cross-cultural Psychology** (**CCP**) is concerned with both behavioural **variability** between cultural groups and behavioural **universals.** It also helps to correct ethnocentrism.
- American researchers and participants share lifestyles and value systems which differ from those of both most other North Americans and the rest of the world's population. Yet the research findings are applied to people in general, disregarding culture's relevance (the **Anglocentric/Eurocentric bias**).
- **Culture** is the human-made part of the environment, comprising both **objective** and **subjective** aspects.
- Different cultures can be assessed in terms of **cultural complexity, individualism–collectivism,** and considering whether they are **tight** or **loose.** The relative emphasis in the West is towards individualism, and in the East towards collectivism.
- The distinction between **culture-specific** and **culture-general** behaviour corresponds to the **emic–etic distinction (E-ED)**. When western Psychologists study non-Western cultures, they often use research tools which are emic for them but an **imposed etic** for the culture being studied.
- Only by doing cross-cultural research can western Psychologists be sure that their theories and research findings are relevant outside their own cultural contexts.
- CCP is an outgrowth of mainstream Psychology, adopting a natural scientific approach. **Cultural Psychologists** reject this approach in favour of qualitative and ethnographic methods, stressing the **uniqueness** of cultures (as in **Indigenous** Psychology).

Links with Other Topics/Chapters

Chapter 36 ⟶ Research into *psychological sex differences* is highly politicised, with a bias towards publishing only those studies that produce significant differences in the expected (i.e. stereotyped) direction

Chapter 44 ⟶ The *pathologising* of homosexuality – and the fact that it's no longer officially a mental disorder – demonstrates how psychiatry (like Psychology) isn't objective or value-free

Chapter 18 ⟶ The concept of time differs between cultures, as reflected in *language*

Chapter 43 ⟶ The tightness of cultures is relevant to the criteria for *defining normality/abnormality*

Chapters 2 and 3 ⟶ *Critical Psychologists* and *Discursive Psychologists* (sometimes both referred to as 'social constructionists'; Burr, 1995; Jones and Elcock, 2001) both reject many of the basic assumptions and practices of mainstream Experimental Psychology

Recommended Reading

Cole, M. (1996) *Cultural Psychology: A Once and Future Discipline.* Cambridge, MA: Harvard University Press.

Coyle, A. & Kitzinger, C. (eds) (2002) *Lesbian and Gay Psychology: New Perspectives.* Oxford: Blackwell/BPS.

Gross, R. (2014) *Themes, Issues and Debates in Psychology* (3rd edn). London: Hodder Education. Chapters 11 and 12.

Laungani, P.D. (2007) *Understanding Cross-Cultural Psychology.* London: Sage.

Magnusson, E. & Maracek, J. (2012) *Gender and Culture in Psychology: Theories and Practices.* Cambridge: Cambridge University Press.

Moghaddam, F.M. (2002) *The Individual and Society: A Cultural Integration.* New York: Worth Publishers.

Owusu-Bempah, K. & Howitt, D. (2000) *Psychology Beyond Western Perspectives.* Leicester: BPS Books.

Stevenson, A. (2010) *Cultural Issues in Psychology.* London: Routledge.

Useful Websites

www.webster.edu/~woolflm/sandrabem.html (Women's Intellectual Contributions to the Study of Mind and Society: Sandra Bem. By N. Bettis)

www.york.ac.uk/sociology/our-staff/academic/celia-kitzinger/ (Celia Kitzinger homepage, with some useful links)

www.wwu.edu/culture (Centre for Cross-Cultural Research, Western Washington University)

www.iaccp.org (International Association for Cross-Cultural Psychology)

www.apa.org/divisions/div45/resources.htm (American Psychological Association)

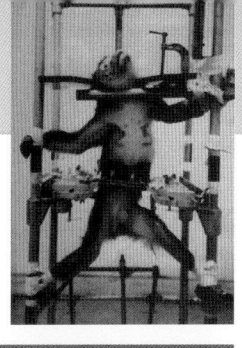

CHAPTER 48

ETHICAL ISSUES IN PSYCHOLOGY

Codes of conduct and ethical guidelines

Psychologists as scientists/investigators

Psychologists as practitioners

INTRODUCTION and OVERVIEW

One of Psychology's unique features is that people are both the investigators and the subject matter (see Chapter 3). This means that the 'things' studied in a psychological investigation are capable of thoughts and feelings. Biologists and medical researchers share this problem of subjecting living, *sentient* things to sometimes painful, stressful, or strange and unusual experiences in the name of furthering science.

Just as Orne (1962) regards the psychological experiment as primarily a *social situation* (which raises questions of objectivity; see Chapter 3), so every psychological investigation is an *ethical situation* (raising questions of propriety and responsibility). Similarly, just as methodological issues permeate psychological research, so do ethical issues. For example, the aims of Psychology as a science (see Chapters 1 and 3) concern what's *appropriate* as much as what's possible. Social Psychology's use of stooges to deceive naïve participants (Chapters 26, 27, 29 and 30), and the surgical manipulation of animals' brains in Physiological Psychology (Chapters 4 and 9) are further examples of the essential difference between the study of the physical world and that of living subjects. What Psychologists can and cannot do is determined by the effects of the research on those being studied, as much as by what they want to find out.

However, Psychologists are *practitioners* as well as scientists and investigators: they work in practical and clinical settings, where people with psychological problems require help (see Chapters 1 and 45). Whenever the possibility of changing people arises, ethical issues also arise, just as they do in medicine and psychiatry. This chapter looks at the ethical issues faced by Psychologists as scientists/investigators, both of humans and non-humans, and as practitioners.

CODES OF CONDUCT AND ETHICAL GUIDELINES

While there are responsibilities and obligations common to both the scientist and practitioner roles, there are also some important differences. These are reflected in the codes of conduct and ethical guidelines published by the major professional bodies for Psychologists, the British Psychological Society (BPS) and the American Psychiatric Association (APA).

As shown in Figure 48.1, the *Code of Conduct for Psychologists* (British Psychological Society, 1985a), the *Ethical Principles of Psychologists and the Code of Conduct* (American Psychiatric Association, 2002), the *Code of Conduct, Ethical Principles and Guidelines* (British Psychological Society, 2000), and the *Code of Ethics and Conduct* (British Psychological Society, 2006, 2009) apply to both the main areas of research and practice, while there are additional documents designed for the two areas separately.

The *Ethical Principles for Conducting Research with Human Participants* (British Psychological Society, 1992, which replaced the 1978 version and were incorporated into the *Code of Conduct*, 2000), the *Code of Human Research Ethics* (British Psychological Society, 2010), the *Guidelines for Ethical Conduct in the Care and Use of Animals* (American Psychiatric Association, 1985), and *Guidelines for Psychologists Working with Animals* (British Psychological Society, 2007a) all clearly relate to the scientist/investigator role. The *Code of Conduct* (2000) includes a section on 'Guidelines for Psychologists Working with Animals'. The BPS has also published *Guidelines for Ethical Practice in Psychological Research Online* (2007b).

In addition to the *Report of the Working Party on Behaviour Modification* (British Psychological Society, 1978b) and *Principles Governing the Employment*

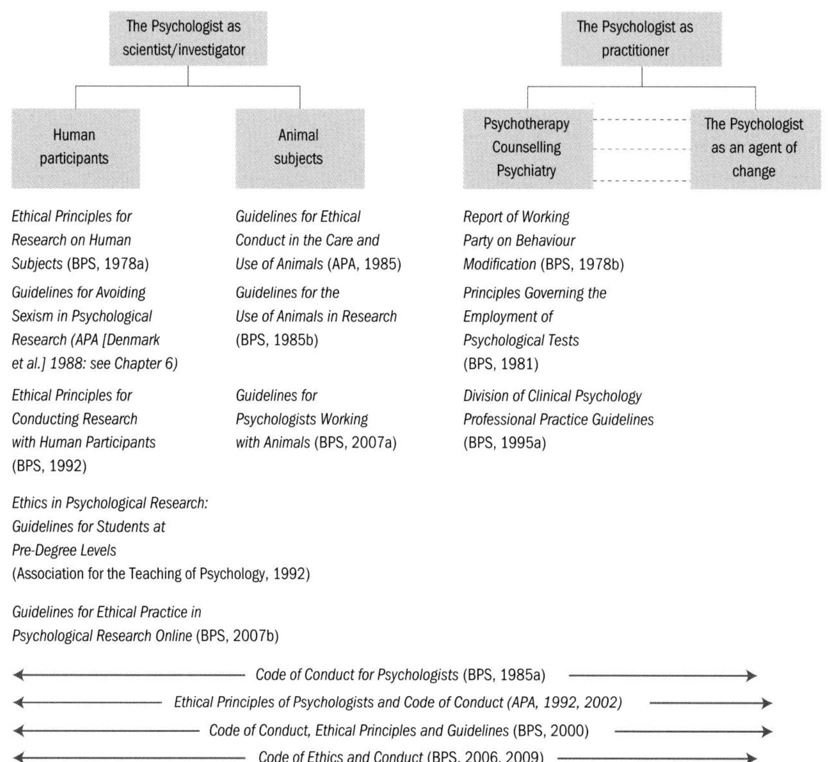

Figure 48.1 Major codes of conduct/ethical guidelines published by the British Psychological Society (BPS) and the American Psychological Association (APA)

of Psychological Tests (British Psychological Society, 1981), there exists the *Division of Clinical Psychology Professional Practice Guidelines* (British Psychological Society, 1995a); these all apply to the practitioner role.

Ask Yourself

- Do you think it's necessary for Psychologists to have written codes of conduct and ethical guidelines?
- What do you consider to be their major functions?

According to Gale (1995), the fact that both the BPS and APA codes are periodically reviewed and revised indicates that at least some aspects don't depend on absolute or universal ethical truths. Guidelines need to be updated in light of the changing social and political contexts in which psychological research takes place. For example, new issues, such as sexual behaviour in the context of AIDS, might highlight new ethical problems. Information revealed by participants can create conflict between the need to protect individuals and the protection of society at large. For instance, in spite of the confidentiality requirement, should a researcher inform the sexual partner of an HIV-infected participant? (See Critical Discussion 48.2.) As Gale (1995) points out:

> *One consequence of such breaches of confidentiality could be the withdrawal of consent by particular groups and the undermining of future research, demonstrating ... how one ethical principle fights against another.*

More importantly, changing views about the nature of individual rights will call into question the extent to which psychological research respects or is insensitive to such rights. (See Gross, 2014.)

PSYCHOLOGISTS AS SCIENTISTS/ INVESTIGATORS

Research with human participants

The *Ethical Principles for Conducting Research with Human Participants* (British Psychological Society, 1990, 1993, 2000, hereafter referred to as 'the *Principles*') identifies several guiding principles. Some of the most important issues addressed are:

- consent/informed consent
- deception

- debriefing
- protection of participants.

The introduction to the *Principles* states that:

> *Psychological investigators are potentially interested in all aspects of human behaviour and conscious experience. However, for ethical reasons, some areas of human experience and behaviour may be beyond the reach of experiment, observation or other forms of psychological investigation. Ethical guidelines are necessary to clarify the conditions under which psychological research is acceptable ... [paragraph 1.2]*

Psychologists are urged to encourage their colleagues to adopt the principles and ensure they're followed by all researchers whom they supervise (including GCSE, A/AS level, undergraduate and postgraduate students):

> *In all circumstances, investigators must consider the ethical implications and psychological consequences for the participants in their research. The essential principle is that the investigation should be considered from the standpoint of all participants; foreseeable threats to their psychological well-being, health, values or dignity should be eliminated ... [paragraph 2.1]*

Consent and informed consent

According to the *Principles*:

> *Participants should be informed of the objectives of the investigation and all other aspects of the research which might reasonably be expected to influence their willingness to participate – only such information allows informed consent to be given [paragraph 3.1] ... Special care needs to be taken when research is conducted with detained persons (those in prison, psychiatric hospital, etc.), whose ability to give free informed consent may be affected by their special circumstances ... [paragraph 3.5]*

Ask Yourself

- You may recall that in Perrin and Spencer's (1981) British replication of Asch's conformity experiment (see Chapter 26), some of the participants were young offenders on probation, with probation officers as stooges. According to paragraph 3.5, would this be acceptable today?

> *Investigators must realise that they often have influence over participants, who may be their students, employees or clients: this relationship must not be allowed to pressurise the participants to take part or remain in the investigation ... [paragraph 3.6]*

In relation to paragraph 3.6, it's standard practice in American universities for Psychology students to participate in research as part of their course requirements. So, while they're free to choose which research to participate in, they're not free to opt out altogether.

Box 48.1 Is there more to informed consent than being informed?

Although informed consent clearly requires being informed of the procedure, participants won't have full knowledge until they've actually experienced it. Indeed, there's no guarantee that the investigators fully appreciate the procedure without undergoing it themselves.

In this sense, it's difficult to argue that full prior knowledge can ever be guaranteed. How much information should be given beforehand? How much information can young children, elderly people, infirm or disabled people or those in emotional distress be expected to absorb?

However, there's more to informed consent than just this 'informational' criterion. The status of the experimenter, the desire to please others and not let them down, the desire not to look foolish by withdrawing after the experiment is already under way, all influence the participant and seem to detract from truly choosing freely in a way that is assumed by the *Principles*.

(Based on Gale, 1995)

Deception

The *Principles* states that:

> *Intentional deception of the participants over the purpose and general nature of the investigation should be avoided whenever possible. Participants should never be deliberately misled without extremely strong scientific or medical justification. Even then there should be strict controls and the disinterested approval of independent advisors ... [paragraph 4.2]*

The decision that deception is necessary should be taken only after determining that alternative procedures (which avoid deception) are unavailable. Participants must be debriefed at the earliest opportunity (see Critical Discussion 48.1).

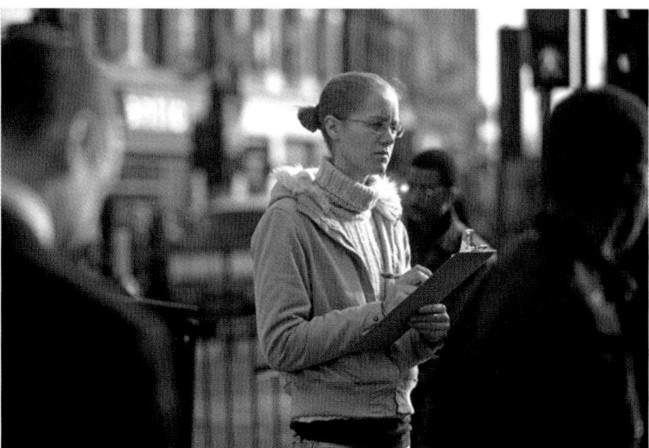

Figure 48.2 Observational research: are those being observed giving their consent?

Debriefing

According to Aronson (1988):

> *The experimenter must take steps to ensure that subjects leave the experimental situation in a frame of mind that is at least as sound as it was when they entered. This frequently requires post-experimental 'debriefing' procedures that require more time and effort than the main body of the experiment.*

Where no undue suffering is experienced, but participants are deceived regarding the real purpose of the experiment:

> *The investigator should provide the participant with any necessary information to complete their understanding of the nature of the research. The investigator should discuss with the participants their experience of the research in order to monitor any unforeseen negative effects or misconceptions ... [paragraph 5.1]*

However,

> *Some effects which may be produced by an experiment will not be negated by a verbal description following the research. Investigators have a responsibility to ensure that participants receive any necessary debriefing in the form of active intervention before they leave the research setting ... [paragraph 5.3]*

Ask Yourself

- Active intervention is more like a 'therapeutic' measure than just 'good manners'. Can you give examples of this second type of debriefing from both Milgram's and Zimbardo *et al.*'s experiments? (See Chapter 27.)

Protection of participants

> *Investigators have a primary responsibility to protect participants from physical and mental harm during the investigation ... participants should not be exposed to risks greater than or additional to those encountered in their normal life styles. [paragraph 8.1]*

Debriefing represents a major means of protecting participants where emotional suffering has occurred. They must also be protected from the stress that might be produced by disclosing confidential information without participants' permission. If participants have been seriously deceived, they have the right to witness destruction of any such records they don't wish to be kept. Results are usually made anonymous as early as possible by use of a letter/number instead of name (Coolican, 1994).

Figure 48.3 The US military prison for suspected terrorists at Guantanamo Bay employed teams of Psychologists to prepare psychological profiles for use by interrogators as well as to observe and provide them with feedback. Such a role may violate longstanding core clinical principles, such as 'do no harm' and 'respect confidentiality' (Seider *et al.*, 2007)

Ethical issues arising from the study of social influence

As we noted in Chapter 27, Milgram's obedience experiments have been criticised on ethical grounds, and they're often held up as examples of how psychological research with human participants *shouldn't* be done. They undoubtedly helped highlight the ethical dimension of psychological research, and to define specific principles, such as those discussed above. Milgram's and other experiments in the area of social influence are among the most controversial in the whole of Psychology, and for all these reasons are often cited in the context of the ethics of research.

> **Ask Yourself**
>
> - Are there any features of Milgram's experimental procedure that you'd consider unethical?
> - One way of approaching this is to ask yourself what you'd have found objectionable/ unacceptable, either during or after the experiment, if you'd been one of his participants.

Protection from harm

One of Milgram's fiercest critics was Baumrind (1964), who argued that the rights and feelings of Milgram's participants had been abused, and that inadequate measures had been taken to protect them from stress and emotional conflict. Milgram didn't deny that his participants did experience stress and conflict, but he argued that Baumrind's criticism assumes that the experimental outcome was expected. However, inducing stress *wasn't* an intended and deliberate effect of the experimental procedure. As Milgram (1974) noted, an experimenter cannot know what the results are going to be before the experiment is conducted.

We might accept Milgram's claim that there was no reason to believe that participants would need protection. However, once he observed the degree of distress in his first experiment, should he have continued with the research programme (17 more experiments)? To justify this, Milgram would have pointed out the following:

- At whatever shock level the experiment ended, the participant was reunited with the unharmed Mr Wallace, and informed that no shock had been delivered. In an extended discussion with Milgram, obedient participants were assured that their behaviour was entirely normal, and that the feelings of conflict and tension were shared by others. Disobedient participants were supported in their decision to disobey the experimenter. This was all part of a thorough debriefing or 'dehoaxing', which happened as a matter of course with every participant (see Critical Discussion 48.1).
- The experimenter didn't *make* the participant shock the learner (as Baumrind had claimed). Milgram began with the belief that every person who came to the laboratory was free to accept or reject the demands of authority. Far from being passive creatures, participants are active, choosing adults.

An APA ethics committee investigated Milgram's research shortly after its first publication in 1963 (during which time Milgram's APA membership was suspended). The committee eventually judged it to be ethically acceptable (Colman, 1987). In 1965, Milgram was awarded the prize for outstanding contribution to social psychological research by the American Association for the Advancement of Science.

According to Zimbardo (1973), the ethical concerns are even more pronounced in his own prison simulation experiment (see Chapter 27) than in Milgram's experiments:

> *Volunteer prisoners suffered physical and psychological abuse hour after hour for days, while volunteer guards were exposed to the new self-knowledge that they enjoyed being powerful and had abused this power to make other human beings suffer. The intensity and duration of this suffering uniquely qualify the Stanford prison experiment for careful scrutiny of violations of the ethics of human experimentation.*

Making a comparison with Milgram's experiments, Zimbardo (2007) maintains that the guards' realisation of their undeniably excessive abuse of the prisoners was much greater than the distress experienced by Milgram's participants. The latter's distress

> *... came from their awareness of what they might have done had the shocks been real. In contrast, the distress of our guards came from their awareness that their 'shocks' to the prisoners were all real, direct, and continual. (Zimbardo, 2007)*

Savin (1973) argued that the benefits resulting from Zimbardo *et al.*'s experiment didn't justify the distress, mistreatment and degradation suffered by the participants – the end didn't justify the means.

Ask Yourself

- How could Zimbardo *et al.* defend themselves against this criticism in a way that Milgram couldn't?

Their experiment was due to last for two weeks, but when it was realised just how intense and serious the distress, mistreatment and degradation were, it was ended after six days. However, it could be asked why it wasn't stopped even sooner!

Figure 48.4 Philip Zimbardo (born 1933)

Deception and informed consent

According to Vitelli (1988), almost all conformity and obedience experiments (and more than one-third of all social psychological studies) deceive participants over the purpose of the research, the accuracy of the information they're given, and/or the true identity of a person they believe to be another genuine participant (or experimenter). Deception is considered unethical for two main reasons:

1. It prevents the participant from giving informed consent.
2. The most potentially harmful deception is involved in studies, like those of Milgram and Zimbardo *et al.*, in which participants learn (unsettling) things about themselves as people.

Ask Yourself

- Given that it's important to understand the processes involved in conformity and obedience (the end), can deception be justified as a means of studying them?
- Identify the deceptions that were involved in the experiments of Asch (see Chapter 26), Milgram and Zimbardo *et al.* (See Gross, 2014.)
- Do you consider any of these to be more serious/ unethical than the others, and if so, why?

Critical Discussion 48.1

Can deception ever be justified?

Most participants deceived in Asch's conformity experiments were very enthusiastic, and expressed their admiration for the elegance and significance of the experimental procedure (Milgram, 1992).

In defence of his own obedience experiments, Milgram (1974) reported that his participants were all thoroughly debriefed. This included receiving a comprehensive report detailing the procedure and results of all the experiments, together with a follow-up questionnaire about their participation. More specifically, the 'technical illusions' (as Milgram calls deception) are justified because in the end they're accepted and approved of by those exposed to them. He saw this, in turn, as justifying the continuation of the experiments, which is relevant to the issue of protection from harm discussed above.

Christensen (1988) reviewed studies of the ethical acceptability of deception experiments and concluded that as long as deception isn't extreme, participants don't seem to mind. The widespread use of mild forms of deception is justified, first because no one is apparently harmed, and second, because there seem to be few, if any, acceptable alternatives.

Krupat and Garonzik (1994) reported that university Psychology students who'd been deceived at least once as research participants said they'd be less upset if they were lied to or misled again in the future (compared with those who hadn't been deceived).

Other researchers have defended Milgram on the grounds that without deception, he'd have found results which simply don't reflect how people behave when they're led to believe they're in real situations (Aronson, 1988). In some circumstances, then, deception may be the best (and perhaps the only) way to obtain useful information about how people behave in complex and important situations.

Widening the ethical debate: the ethics of socially sensitive research (SSR)

What is SSR?

According to Sieber and Stanley (1988), SSR refers to:

> *... studies in which there are potential social consequences or implications, either directly for the participants in the research or for the class of individuals represented by the research ...*

Two examples they give are:

1. a study that examines the relative merits of day care for infants versus full-time care by the mother can have broad social implications, and thus can be regarded as socially sensitive (see Chapter 32)
2. studies aimed at examining the relationship between gender and mathematical ability, which can also have significant social implications (see Chapter 47).

Sieber (2004) gives the further examples of domestic violence and teenagers and smoking. In research on domestic violence, the victim may experience severe distress at recounting being battered. The assailant may learn of the research and, in anger, harm the participant or the researcher – or the data may be subpoenaed in an investigation of the assailant. Most teenagers smoke without their parents' knowledge, yet research involving minors (usually under 16) should be done with parental permission.

Figure 48.5 Smoking teenagers: what should investigators do?

According to the APA's *Ethical Principles in The Conduct of Research* (1982), psychological research (like other scientific research) is a 'double-edged sword'. It can be used to benefit those being studied, or against their interests and for the benefit of those with social, economic and political power. There's nothing 'neutral' about research (see above and Chapters 3 and 47).

Protecting the individual versus harming the group

The debate about the ethics of psychological research usually focuses on the vulnerability of individual participants and the responsibility of Psychologists to ensure they don't suffer in any way from their participation. 'Protection of participants' is one of the specific principles included in the *Principles*, but the principles *as a whole* are designed to prevent any harm coming to the participant, or the avoidance of overt 'sins' (Brown, 1997).

However, Brown (1997) argues that formal codes focus too narrowly on risks to the individual participant, in the specific context of the investigation, neglecting broader questions about the risks to the group the participant belongs to. These groups can include women, ethnic minorities and other subcultural groups, as well as non-Western cultures (countries or national cultures). To the extent that gender and culture bias (and the underlying values and beliefs) are harmful to particular groups, they are *ethical* issues. In this sense, any comparison between women and men that is made from an alpha bias perspective is *socially sensitive*; equally, any comparison between blacks and whites is socially sensitive. A much-debated example is the study of racial differences in IQ (see Critical Discussion 48.2).

Ask Yourself

- Re-read Chapter 47. Try to identify some fundamental values and biases that are potentially damaging to particular social groups.
- In what ways are these values/biases harmful to these groups?

So, Psychologists might believe that (a) it's unethical to deceive individual black or female participants about the purposes of some particular study, but (b) it's ethically acceptable to use the results to support the claim that blacks or women are genetically inferior. This narrow view of ethics makes it an ineffective way of guiding SSR (Howitt, 1991). Formal codes continue to focus narrowly on risks to the individual participant, in the specific context of the investigation, but neglect questions about the risks to the group to which the participant belongs:

> *As long as research ethics avoid the matter of whether certain questions ethically cannot be asked, psychologists will conduct technically ethical research that violates a more general ethic of avoiding harm to vulnerable populations ... (Brown, 1997)*

Critical Discussion 48.2

The ethics of ethical codes: underlying assumptions

According to Brown (1997), a core assumption underlying ethical codes is that what Psychologists do as researchers, clinicians, teachers, and so on, is basically harmless and inherently valuable, because it's based on 'science' (defined as positivism; see Chapter 3). Consequently, it's possible for a Psychologist to conduct technically ethical research but still do great harm. For example, a researcher can adhere strictly to 'scientific' research methodologies, get technically adequate informed consent from participants (and not breach any of the other major prescribed principles), but still conduct research that claims to show the inferiority of a particular group. Because it's conducted according to 'the rules' (both methodological and ethical), the question of whether it's ethical in the broader sense to pursue such matters is ignored.

For example, neither Jensen (1969) nor Herrnstein (1971) was ever considered by mainstream Psychology to have violated Psychology's ethics by the questions they asked regarding the intellectual inferiority of African-Americans (see Chapter 41). Individual black participants weren't harmed by being given IQ tests, and may even have found them interesting and challenging. However, Brown (1997) argues that the way the findings were interpreted and used:

> *... weakened the available social supports for people of colour by stigmatising them as genetically inferior, thus strengthening the larger culture's racist attitudes. Research ethics as currently construed by mainstream ethics codes do not require researchers to put the potential for this sort of risk into their informed consent documents ...*

According to Anderson (2007), what might be harmless curiosity when applied to other topics can have profound and negative consequences on individual lives when the subject matter is racial differences. Nor does knowledge of racial differences add anything to our understanding of the underlying mechanisms involved in intelligence and its development. Jensen's and Herrnstein's research (highlighted by Herrnstein and Murray, in *The Bell Curve*, 1994) has profoundly harmed black Americans. Ironically, while the book has received much methodological criticism, only black Psychologists (such as Hilliard, 1995, and Sue, 1995) have raised the more fundamental question of whether simply conducting such studies might be ethically dubious.

Herrnstein and Murray, Rushton (1995), Brand (cited in Richards, 1996a) and others, like the Nazi scientists of the 1930s, claim that the study of race differences is a purely 'objective' and 'scientific' enterprise (Howe, 1997).

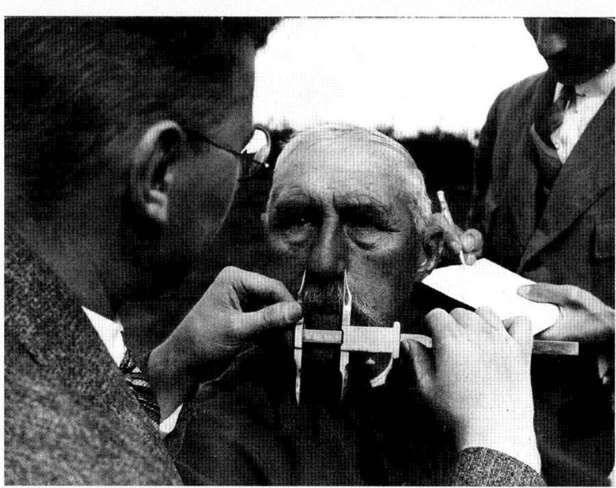

Figure 48.6 Nazi scientists conducting 'objective' scientific research

The *BPS Code of Conduct* (2000) comprises several sections (apart from the *Principles*). These include (a) 'Guidelines for Psychologists Working with Animals' (see below), and (b) 'Guidelines for Penile Plethysmography (PPG) usage'. The latter refers to the measurement of sexual arousal and involves apparatus being attached to the penis and sexual stimuli being presented. This might be used in the context of assessing paedophilia and sexual dysfunction – so its use is highly sensitive.

Protecting the individual versus benefiting society

As we've seen, the questions Psychologists ask are limited and shaped by the values and biases of individual researchers; the research they carry out is also constrained by ethical considerations. But it's also constrained by considerations of methodology (what it's possible to do, practically, when investigating human behaviour and experience). For example, in the context of intimate relationships, the laboratory experiment is, by its very nature, extremely limited in the kinds of questions it allows Psychologists to investigate (Brehm, 1992; see Chapter 28).

Conversely, and just as importantly, there are certain aspects of behaviour and experience that could be studied experimentally, although it would be unethical to do so (such as jealousy between partners). As Brehm says:

> *All types of research in this area involve important ethical dilemmas. Even if all we do is to ask subjects to fill out questionnaires describing their relationships, we need to think carefully about how this research experience might affect them and their partner.*

So, what it may be *possible* to do may be *unacceptable*, but equally, what may be *acceptable* may *not* be possible. As we saw earlier, focusing on protection of individual participants can work to the detriment of whole groups. But, by the same token, it may discourage Psychologists from carrying out socially *meaningful research* (what Brehm (1992) calls the *ethical imperative*) which may, potentially, improve the quality of people's lives. Social Psychologists in particular have a two-fold ethical obligation, to individual participants and to society at large (Myers, 1994). This relates to discussion of Psychology's aims as a science (see Chapters 1 and 3). Similarly, Aronson (1992) argues that Social Psychologists are:

> *... obligated to use their research skills to advance our knowledge and understanding of human behaviour for the ultimate aim of human betterment. In short, social psychologists have an ethical responsibility to the society as a whole.*

Ask Yourself

- Before reading on, try to think of some examples of how research findings you're familiar with might be used to benefit people in general. You may find it useful to focus on Social Psychology.

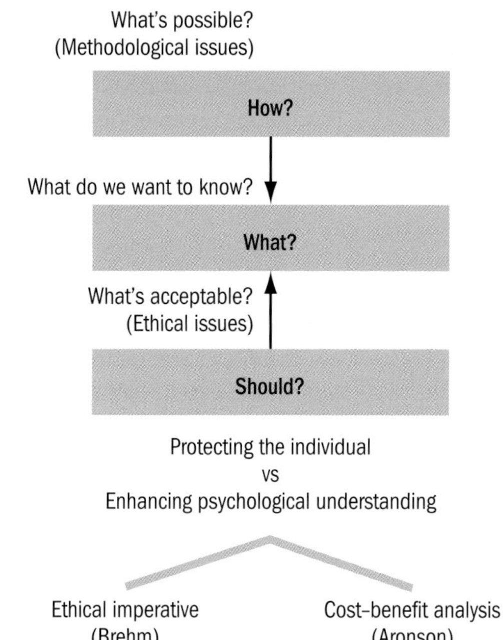

Figure 48.7 Ethical and methodological constraints on the questions that Psychologists can try to answer through the research process

Social Psychologists face a dilemma: the obligation to society (to achieve 'human betterment') can come into conflict with their more specific ethical responsibility to each individual research participant. Talking about the aim of 'human betterment' raises many important questions to do with basic values. This opens up the ethical debate in such a way that *values must be addressed and recognised* as part of the research process (something that Feminist Psychologists advocate very strongly).

Box 48.2 An example of the benefits of social psychological research

- In many bystander intervention studies (e.g. Latané and Darley, 1968; see Chapter 30), people are deceived into believing that an 'emergency' is taking place. Many of Latané and Darley's participants were very distressed by their experiences, especially those in the experiment in which they believed another participant was having an epileptic fit. Yet when asked to complete a post-experimental questionnaire (which followed a very careful debriefing), all said they believed the deception was justified and would be willing to participate in similar experiments again. None reported any feelings of anger towards the experimenter.
- Beaman *et al.* (1978) built on these earlier experiments. They used a lecture to inform students about how other bystanders' refusals to help can influence both one's own interpretation of an emergency and feelings of responsibility.
- Two other groups of students heard either a different lecture or no lecture at all. Two weeks later, as part of a different experiment in a different location, the participants found themselves (accompanied by an unresponsive stooge) walking past someone who was slumped over or sprawled under a bike. Of those who'd heard the lecture about helping behaviour, 50 per cent stopped to offer help compared with 25 per cent who hadn't.
- This suggests that the results of psychological research can be used to make us more aware of influences on behaviour, making it more likely that we'll act differently armed with that knowledge from how we might otherwise have done. In the case of bystander intervention, this 'consciousness-raising' is beneficial in a tangible way to the person who's helped. Being more sensitive to the needs of others, and feeling good about having helped another person, may also be seen as beneficial to the helper.

Table 48.1 Ethical principles and the related statement of values (BPS *Code of Ethics and Conduct,* 2006)

Ethical principle	Statement of values	Standards
Respect*	Psychologists value the dignity and worth of all persons, with sensitivity to the dynamics of perceived authority or influence over clients, and with particular regard to people's rights, including those of privacy and self-determination**	General respect Privacy and confidentiality Informed consent Self-determination
Competence	Psychologists value the continuing development and maintenance of high standards of competence in their professional work, and the importance of preserving their ability to function optimally within the recognised limits of their knowledge, skill, training, education, and experience	Awareness of professional ethics Ethical decision making Recognising limits of competence Recognising impairment
Responsibility	Psychologists value their responsibilities to clients, to the general public, and to the profession and science of psychology, including the avoidance of harm and the prevention of misuse or abuse of their contributions to society	General responsibility Termination and continuity of care Protection of research participants Debriefing of research participants
Integrity	Psychologists value honesty, accuracy, clarity and fairness in their interactions with all persons, and seek to promote integrity in all facets of their scientific and professional endeavours	Honesty and accuracy Avoiding exploitation and conflicts of interest Maintaining personal boundaries Addressing ethical misconduct

*This applies to '… culture and role differences, including (but not exclusively) those involving age, disability, education, ethnicity, gender, language, national origin, race, religion, sexual orientation, marital or family status, and socio-economic status'.

**Includes (i) the right to withdraw at any time from the receipt of professional services or from research participation; and (ii) the right of withdrawing clients to request destruction of any data by which they might be personally identified (including recordings).

The *Code of Ethics and Conduct* (British Psychological Society, 2006, 2009) includes a *Statement of Values* (which reflects fundamental beliefs that guide ethical reasoning, decision making and behaviour) together with a *Set of Standards* (which identifies the ethical conduct that the BPS expects of its members in relation to four major ethical principles: *respect*, *competence*, *responsibility* and *integrity*). These are summarised in Table 48.1.

Research with non-human (animal) subjects

Why do Psychologists study animals?

Putting ethics issues aside for the moment, there are very good practical/scientific reasons for the use of non-humans in psychological research (see Chapters 2 and 3). For example, there is an underlying *evolutionary continuity* between humans and other species, which gives rise to the assumption that differences between humans and other species are merely *quantitative* (as opposed to *qualitative*): other species may display more simple behaviour and have more primitive nervous systems than humans, but they are not of a different order from humans. In fact, the mammalian brain (which includes rats, cats, dogs, monkeys and humans) is built on similar lines in all these species, and neurons are the same in all species, and work in the same way. These similarities of biology are, in turn, linked to behavioural similarities. So, studying the more simple cases is a valid and valuable way of finding out about the more complex ones. Skinner's *analysis of behaviour* is a good example of this approach (see Chapter 3).

The *Guidelines for Psychologists Working with Animals* (British Psychological Society, 2007a) point out that research is not the only reason Psychologists work with animals, even though, not surprisingly, it's what has caused the most controversy and media attention. Animals are sometimes used in practical teaching within Psychology degree courses, and increasingly animals are being used in various forms of psychological therapy (including companion animal visiting schemes in hospitals or hospices, pet-keeping within prison rehabilitation schemes, and in behaviour therapy for the treatment of specific animal phobias). Psychologists may also be asked to advise on therapy for animals whose behaviour appears to de disordered in some way, as well as training animals for commercial purposes. (See Box 48.3.)

Figure 48.8 Kirby, a Pet Assisted Therapy (PAT programme) dog, visiting hospital patients in Los Angeles, California

The issue of animal suffering: do animals feel pain?

The case for: non-humans are sentient

The very existence of the guidelines described in Box 48.3 presupposes that animals are, like humans, *sentient*, roughly defined as the capacity for emotion, pleasure and pain (Boyle, 2009). Sentience may be applied to species which Regan (2006) calls 'subjects of a life', aware of what happens to them and that events affect their lives.

Boyle (2009) cites a range of evidence pointing to the belief that non-humans are sentient:

- Comparative neuroanatomical research emphasises continuity across species with regard to the central nervous system (CNS), which is found in all vertebrates from apes to bats to fish. The genes underlying NS development have been virtually

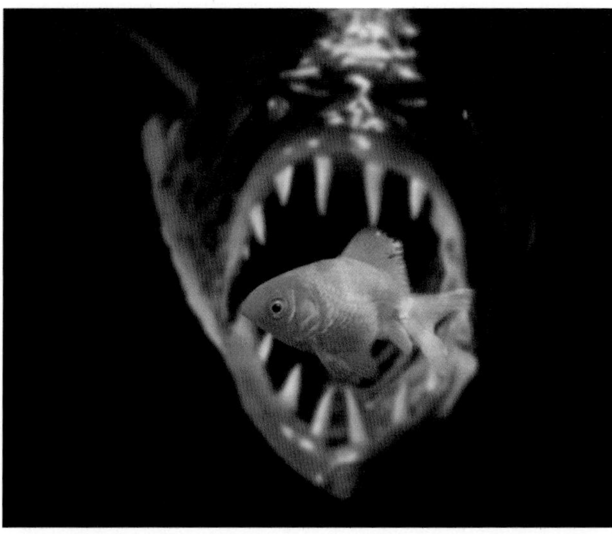

Figure 48.9 Is the unsuspecting goldfish going to feel pain?

  unchanged throughout evolution, and neurons are similar across species. The same is true for neurotransmitters, hormones and chemicals. Both the limbic system in general and the amygdala in particular (which mediate emotion) and the sensory input to it, are strikingly similar among vertebrates.
- Although most pain research has focused on mammals, other simpler vertebrates also have the neuroarchitecture to allow them to identify stimuli that hurt. But where do we draw the line? Recent research has focused on fish.
- According to Sneddon (Sneddon, 2006; Sneddon *et al.*, 2003), fish feel pain, implying that angling is cruel. They tested the neural responses of rainbow trout and injected the fish with mild poisons. Undoubtedly,
  - fish have specific neural receptors that respond to heat, mechanical pressure and acid; the neurons fire in a way very similar to the firing patterns of human neurons in response to aversive stimuli;
  - fish behave abnormally when their lips are injected with bee venom and vinegar, rocking from side to side and breathing very rapidly;
  - the abnormal behaviours and symptoms are not seen – or at least not to the same extent – either in fish that are simply handled or given an injection of a harmless substance.
- The degree to which invertebrates experience pain is less certain, but the inclusion of octopi as a 'protected' species in the Animals (Scientific Procedures) Act (1986) (see Box 48.3) suggests strongly that they do.
- Evidence is accumulating that birds display many remarkable skills once thought to be restricted to humans and/or other great apes. For example, European magpies display mirror self-recognition (Prior *et al.*, 2008) (see Chapter 33), New Caledonian crows make and use several types of tool (Chappell

Box 48.3 Guidelines for psychologists working with animals (British Psychological Society, 2007a)

Ten major areas that are covered as follows:

1 *Legislation*: The Animals (Scientific Procedures) Act (1986) governs any scientific procedure that may cause pain, suffering, distress or lasting harm to a 'protected' animal. Protected animals comprise all non-human vertebrates and a single invertebrate species (*Octopus vulgaris*). Psychologists working with animals in ways not covered by the Act should aim to maintain standards at least as high as those proposed in the guidelines for research use. In addition, Psychologists should be aware that they have a more general duty of care towards any protected animal under the Animal Welfare Act (2006).

2 *Replacing the use of animals*: Alternatives to intact behaving organisms, such as video records from previous work or computer simulations, may be useful – especially in a teaching context. Two specific examples are the 'Ratlife' project (video) and 'Sniffy the virtual rat' (computer simulation).

3 *Choice of species and strain*: Psychologists should choose a species that is scientifically and ethically suitable for the intended use: the species should be chosen for the least amount of suffering while still attaining the scientific objective. The choice must be justified as part of the application for a Project Licence (under the 1986 Act).

4 *Number of animals*: The 1986 Act requires use of the smallest number of animals sufficient to achieve the research goals.

5 *Procedures*: (See 'Legislation' above.) Permission to perform regulated procedures requires a *Project Licence,* which is granted only after weighing the benefits and costs (in welfare terms) to the animal subjects. In addition, the actual performance of a regulated procedure requires a *Personal Licence*, given only after successful completion of appropriate training. When applying for a licence, investigators must also discuss their proposal with a *Local Ethical Review Committee* (which must include a veterinary surgeon).

6 *Procurement of animals*: Common laboratory animals must come from Home Office Designated Breeding and Supply Establishments.

7 *Animal care*: The 1986 European Convention (Article 5) provides that:

> *Any animal used or intended for use in a procedure shall be provided with accommodation, and environment, at least a minimum of freedom of movement, food, water and care, appropriate to its health and well-being. Any restriction on the extent to which an animal can satisfy its physiological and ecological needs shall be limited as far as practicable.*

8 *Disposing of animals*: If animal subjects must be killed during or subsequent to the study, this must be done as humanely and painlessly as possible (as defined by the Act). A veterinary surgeon should be consulted regarding current methods of euthanasia.

9 *Animals in Psychology teaching*: Whoever the students are, ethical issues should be discussed with them. Only advanced undergraduates and postgraduate students would be eligible to apply for a Personal Licence, and any procedures would be carried out only under an existing Project Licence.

10 *The use of animals for therapeutic purposes*: In all cases, the same considerations concerning the general care and welfare as detailed for experimental animals apply. But there are also specific considerations, such as the individual animal's temperament and training being suitable for the planned task (e.g. a hospital visiting dog should be calm, placid and sociable with people). Contact with the client/patient needs to be carefully monitored.

and Kacelnik, 2002), and even chickens can be deceptive, and use sophisticated signals to convey their intentions (Smith and Zielinksi, 2014).

The case against: sentience doesn't equal consciousness

According to Robinson (2004):

> *To conclude that fish feel pain depends on a scientific definition of pain, of which there is none. We might define it with reference to the actions of neurons in response to aversive stimuli, but this is only the physiological cause: when we use the word we mean the* experience. *Even behavioural responses need not be correlated with an experiential mental state. An adequate definition must take in psychology as well as physiology and behaviour. (emphasis in original)*

So, perhaps we cannot proceed strictly by deduction from the scientific results to conclude that fish can feel pain. But isn't it reasonable to conclude that if another vertebrate species behaves in the same way as we do in response to a similar/equivalent stimulus, and if its physiological responses to that stimulus are the same as ours, that it feels what we feel?

DeGrazia (2002) defines *anxiety* in terms of four components, all of which have been scientifically observed in non-humans:

1. autonomic hyperactivity (rapid pulse and breathing, sweating, etc.)
2. motor tension (jumpiness)
3. inhibition of normal behaviours
4. hyperattentiveness (visual scanning, etc.).

These are the symptoms of anxiety that we see in humans. But as with pain, we usually use the word 'anxiety' to denote more than the physiological and behavioural components:

> *... When we say anxiety and mean an experience, we presume the thing that allows us to experience in the first place: consciousness of the self existing through time or* temporal self-awareness. *This is what allows us to be aware of what is happening to us ... (Robinson, 2004) (emphasis in original)*

DeGrazia *does* in fact assume this to be the context of the four components of anxiety, both in humans and non-humans. But as Robinson (2004) points out, this is a *circular* argument: he's asking us to assume what we're trying to prove, namely, that non-humans experience things as we do. In other words, 'anxiety' (and, by the same token, 'pain') comes pre-loaded with meanings that pertain to our subjective experience and emotions – the essence of being human.

Feelings versus emotions

After years of ignoring/discounting what pet lovers have long maintained, scientists are finally beginning to believe that mammals, at least, have some form of emotions (Wilhelm, 2006).

Damasio (2003) distinguishes between:

(a) primary, almost instinctive *emotions* that help an individual mesh with a group (including fear, anger, disgust, surprise, sadness and joy); they are physical signals of the body responding to stimuli; and

(b) *feelings*, which stem from self-reflection. They represent sensations that arise as the brain interprets (a). (See below.)

Damasio attributes (a) to many species. Even the primitive sea slug, *Aplysia*, shows fear: when its gills are touched, its blood pressure and pulse increase and it shrivels. These aren't reflexes, but elements of a fear response. However, such organisms *don't* have feelings.

Damasio also identifies *social emotions* (sympathy, embarrassment, shame, guilt, pride, envy, jealousy, gratitude, admiration, contempt and indignation). These aren't limited to humans (e.g. gorillas, wolves, dogs). Yet even in such cases, as with (a), some neuroscientists argue that these are largely automatic and innate responses and include them among the routinised survival mechanisms.

Are animals capable of self-reflection?

Extending Robinson's argument above regarding pain, we can say that, if non-humans are incapable of experiencing pain and feelings, then can they be said to 'suffer'? According to Robinson (2004):

> *Suffering depends upon our sense of ourselves, our sense of the passage of time and of the changing fortunes in our lives. When we are subjected to adverse stimuli we feel pain, anxiety and fear for the very reason that we are conscious of what is happening to us –* we experience *the stimuli, not only respond automatically to them. But because we share so much of our evolutionary history with animals, the outward signs of these responses are similar ... (emphasis in original)*

Fish don't have an area of the brain corresponding to our own neural pain-processor – the neocortex: although the same signals are sent to the brain, there's no recognisable pain-experience-producing region to go to when they arrive. There are no brain regions that produce the *unpleasantness* of pain; they have little more than a brainstem (no cerebral hemispheres).

While the 'sentience argument' helps us distinguish animals from physical objects, sentience on its own is insufficient to demonstrate that non-humans are capable of experiencing pain, feelings, suffering and so on. These experiences are part of what we mean by 'consciousness' (or, strictly, *self*-consciousness; see Chapter 33).

Do non-humans need consciousness?

It's difficult to prove that non-humans have self-reflection. Damasio argues that bonobos may be capable of displaying pity for other animals – but they don't realise they're displaying pity (could they without language?); he's reluctant to infer feelings from this.

Panskepp (e.g. Panskepp and Burgdorf, 2003) agrees that only humans can think about their feelings (thanks to their highly-developed neocortex).

> *In the end, it is not possible to prove through observation whether an animal possesses conscious feelings – no more than we can be sure about what another person is truly experiencing inside. We know from lab work that some animals, at least, are indeed self-aware, so it is not much of a stretch to think they could be cognisant of their emotions, too ... (Wilhelm, 2006)*

While sentience rests on the capacity to experience emotion, (self-)consciousness may not be necessary for sentience; much of the experience of emotion is generated *unconsciously* (Damasio, 2001). Also, when we talk about animal feelings, they don't have to be the *same* kind that people have. As Boyle (2009) observes, sentience involves the capacity for emotion and pain, whether or not the experience is cognitively sophisticated or human-like. If non-humans are capable of feeling emotion, then we have yet another reason to seriously consider how well we treat them.

Ask Yourself

- What do you think of the claim that particular non-human species, namely those that are closest to us in an evolutionary sense, should be given 'special consideration' in the context of animal experiments?

Research using great apes (gorillas, chimpanzees, bonobos and orang-utans) was banned in 1998 (Brown, 2004). But about 10,000 experiments, mainly on marmosets and macaques (and other primates), are carried out every year, with the UK leading the field (an annual total of almost 4000). Beginning in 2008, the European Union called for a ban on *all* experiments involving primates (McKie, 2008).

Speciesism

According to Gray (1991), most people (both experimenters and animal rights activists) would accept the ethical principle that inflicting pain is wrong. But we're sometimes faced with having to choose between different ethical principles, which may mean having to choose between human and non-human suffering. Gray believes that *speciesism* (discriminating against and exploiting animals because they belong to a particular [non-human] species) (Ryder, 1990) is justified, and argues that:

> *Not only is it not wrong to give preference to the interests of one's own species, one has a duty to do so.*

Such a moral choice involves establishing a calculus (Dawkins, 1980), which pits the suffering of non-humans against the human suffering which the former's use will alleviate. For Gray (1991):

> *In many cases the decision not to carry out certain experiments with animals (even if they would inflict pain or suffering) is likely to have the consequence that more people will undergo pain or suffering that might otherwise be avoided.*

One of the problems associated with the pro-speciesism argument is that medical advance may become possible only after extensive development of knowledge and scientific understanding in a particular field (Gray, 1991). In the meantime, scientific understanding may be the only specific objective that the experiment can readily attain. It's at this interim stage that the suffering imposed on experimental animals will far outweigh any (lesser) suffering eventually avoided by people, and this is at the core of the decisions that must be made by scientists and ethical committees.

PSYCHOLOGISTS AS PRACTITIONERS

Clinical Psychologists (as well as Educational Psychologists, psychotherapists, psychiatrists, social workers, nurses, counsellors and other professionals) are concerned with bringing about *psychological change.* It's in their capacity as agents of change that Clinical Psychologists face their greatest ethical challenges (see Chapter 1).

Ask Yourself

- Consider some of the ethical issues faced by Psychologists attempting to change other people's behaviour.
- Some are of a general nature, such as freedom and determinism (see Chapter 49), others will overlap with ethical principles governing research (such as confidentiality and informed consent), and yet others may be specific to particular therapeutic approaches (see Chapter 45).

Fairbairn and Fairbairn (1987) identify two quite common beliefs that are likely to detract from an explicit consideration of professional ethics and values in psychological practice: (a) Psychology is a value-free science, and (b) therapists should be value-neutral or 'non-directive'.

Psychology as value-free science

Central to Clinical (and Counselling) Psychology is the *scientist–practitioner model* of helping (Dallos and Cullen, 1990), according to which Clinical Psychology is guided by, and operates within, the framework of the general scientific method (see Chapters 3 and 45). This may discourage these practitioners from considering ethical issues, because these aren't amenable to objective consideration. But even if the psychological knowledge used in clinical practice was always the result of the application of an objective scientific method, *moral* questions of an interpersonal kind are bound to arise at the point at which it's *applied* (Fairbairn and Fairbairn, 1987).

This distinction between possession of knowledge and its application ('science' versus 'technology') is

Box 48.4 Criticisms of scientific behaviour therapy and modification

- Based on the scientist–practitioner model, behaviour therapy and modification tend to devalue and thereby dehumanise their clients by treating people, for 'scientific' purposes, as if they were 'organisms' as opposed to 'agents', helpless victims of forces outside their control.
- This criticism also applies to medical psychiatry and classical psychoanalysis, except that both see the controlling forces as being internal (organic abnormalities or intrapsychic forces, respectively) as opposed to environmental contingencies (see Chapters 2 and 45).
- Clients soon come to believe that they're abnormal, helpless, and also worthless, because this is part of the culture-wide stereotype of 'mental illness' (see Chapter 43). Negative self-evaluation and passivity characterise many, if not most, mental health clients, who think and behave like passive organisms. The solution lies in helping people recover, or discover, their *agency*.

(Based on Trower, 1987)

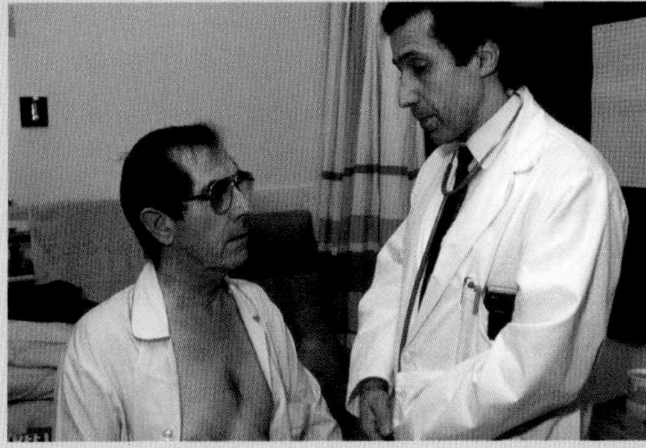

Figure 48.10 This passive patient looks vacantly at the doctor – the expert and authority figure

fundamental to any discussion of ethics, because it's related to the notion of *responsibility*. Presumably, Psychologists *choose* which techniques to use with clients and how to use them. The mere existence (and even the demonstrated effectiveness) of certain techniques doesn't in itself mean that they must be used. Similarly, the kind of research which Psychologists consider worth doing (and which then provides the scientific basis for the use of particular techniques) is a matter of choice, and reflects views regarding the nature of people and how they can be changed (see Chapters 1 and 2).

Therapists as value-neutral and non-directive

This second major issue is about the therapist or Psychologist functioning as something less than a complete person within the therapeutic situation. Providing help and support in a non-directive, value-free way is a tradition for psychotherapists and counsellors (Fairbairn and Fairbairn, 1987). However, such an approach may seem to require remaining aloof and distant from the client which, in turn, may entail not treating the client with respect as a person, since this requires the therapist to recognise that the client is a person like him- or herself.

Ask Yourself

- Is there a difference between, say, client-centred therapy and psychoanalysis in terms of this possible aloofness and failure to treat the client 'respectfully'? (See Chapter 45.)

Figure 48.11 Carl Rogers (right) in a group therapy session

Ask Yourself

- Do you believe that it's possible for therapists not to have any influence over their clients/patients?

The influence of the therapist

Adopting what's thought to be a value-free position in therapy may lead therapists to deny the importance or influence of their own moral values, which are often hidden in therapy. This kind of influence is much more subtle and covert than the coercion that can operate on hospitalised psychiatric patients, even voluntary ones. The in-patient is subjected to strong persuasion to accept the treatment recommendations of professional staff. As Davison and Neale (1994) observe, even a 'voluntary' and informed decision to take psychotropic medication or to participate in any other therapy regimen is often (maybe usually) less than free.

Critical Discussion 48.3

Therapist influence in psychodynamic and behaviour therapy

The issue of the therapist's influence on the patient/client has been central to a longstanding debate between traditional (psychodynamic) psychotherapists and behaviour therapists (who are usually Clinical Psychologists by training, see Chapter 45).

Psychotherapists regard behaviour therapy as unacceptable (even if it works), because it's manipulative and demeaning of human dignity. By contrast, they see their own methods as fostering the autonomous development of the patient's inherent potential, helping the patient to express his/her true self, and so on. Instead of influencers, they see themselves as 'psychological midwives', present during the 'birth', possessing useful skills, but there primarily to make sure that a natural process goes smoothly.

However, this is an exaggeration and misrepresentation of both approaches. For many patients, the 'birth' probably wouldn't happen at all without the therapist's intervention, and s/he undoubtedly influences the patient's behaviour. Conversely, behaviour therapists are at least partly successful because they establish active, cooperative relationships with their patients, who play much more active roles in the therapy than psychotherapists believe.

All therapists, of whatever persuasion, if they're at all effective, influence their patients. Both approaches comprise a situation in which one human being (the therapist) tries to act in a way that enables another human being to act and feel differently, and this is as true of psychoanalysis as it is of behaviour therapy.

(Based on Wachtel, 1977)

The crucial issue is the *nature* of the therapist's influence, rather than whether or not influence occurs. Therapist *neutrality* is a myth: therapists influence their clients in subtle yet powerful ways.

According to Davison *et al.* (2004), sometimes therapists' values are subtle and difficult to identify. Wachtel (1997) criticises both psychoanalysis and the humanistic-existential approaches for their overemphasis on people's need to change 'from within', rather than being assisted, even directed, in their efforts to change as happens in cognitive behaviour therapy (see Chapter 45). By concentrating on people gaining their own insights and making behavioural changes more or less on their own, and by discouraging therapists from influencing their clients by directly teaching them new skills, insight-oriented therapists unwittingly teach an *ethic of aloneness* devoid of social support. He asks whether this is an appropriate message to convey to patients and to society at large.

> *... many [insight] therapists who criticise behaviour therapy as an agent of cultural norms are themselves upholding one of the basic tenets of our capitalistic society, when they stress change based solely on autonomous action and deride the need for direct assistance from others ... It is, after all, just as human to be able to turn to others as it is to stand alone. (Wachtel, 1997)*

Freedom and behavioural control

While a behavioural technique such as *systematic desensitisation* (SD) is limited mainly to anxiety reduction, this can at least be seen as enhancing the patient's freedom, since anxiety is one of the greatest restrictions on freedom. By contrast, those who use methods based on *operant conditioning* (such as the *token economy* (TE)) often describe their work rather exclusively in terms of *behavioural control*, subscribing to Skinner's (1971) view of freedom as an illusion (see Chapter 49).

Wachtel (1977) believes that when used in institutional settings (such as with long-term schizophrenic patients in psychiatric hospitals), the TE is so subject to abuse that its use is highly questionable. It may be justifiable if it works, and if there's clearly no alternative way of rescuing a patient from an empty and destructive existence. But as a routine part of how society deals with deviant behaviour, this approach raises very serious ethical questions. One of these relates to the question of *power*. Like the experimental 'subject' relative to the experimenter, the patient is powerless relative to the institutional staff responsible for operating the token economy programme:

> *Reinforcement is viewed by many – proponents and opponents alike – as somehow having an inexorable controlling effect upon the person's behaviour and rendering him incapable of choice, reducing him to an automaton or duly wound mechanism ... (Wachtel, 1977)*

The alarming feature of the TE is the reinforcing agent's power to deprive unco-operative patients physically of 'privileges' (see Chapter 45).

CONCLUSIONS

This chapter has considered the ethics of psychological research, with both human participants and animal subjects, as well as ethical issues arising from the Psychologist's role as a professional involved in behaviour change. Discussion of ethical issues has, in various ways, struck at the heart of Psychology itself, requiring us to ask what Psychology is *for*. According to Hawks (1981), prevention rather than cure should be a primary aim of Psychology, enabling people to cope by themselves, without professional help, thus 'giving Psychology away' to people/clients. For Bakan (1967), the significant place in society of the Psychologist is more that of the teacher than expert or technician.

Chapter Summary

- Psychology's focus of study consists of **sentient** things. This makes every psychological investigation an **ethical situation**, with research determined as much by its effects on those being studied as by what Psychologists want to find out.
- The BPS's **Ethical Principles** identifies several issues relating to research with human participants, including **consent/informed consent, deception, protection of participants, debriefing** and **confidentiality**.
- Even if a participant has been fully informed about an experimental procedure, this doesn't guarantee **informed consent**.
- **Debriefing** must take place at the earliest opportunity, and an experimenter must ensure that participants leave the experimental situation in at least as positive a frame of mind as when they entered.
- The BPS and APA codes and guidelines are periodically revised in the light of changing social and political contexts. This indicates that there are **no absolute** or **universal ethical truths**.
- Ethical criticisms of Milgram's obedience experiments helped trigger the debate regarding the ethics of research within Psychology as a whole.
- While deception is unethical if it prevents participants from giving informed consent, those who've been deceived generally approve of it retrospectively. Deception may sometimes be the best/only way of obtaining valuable insights into human behaviour.
- **Socially sensitive research (SSR)** refers to studies with potential consequences or implications, either for the individual participants or for **the groups** they represent.
- While ethical codes serve to protect individual participants, underlying assumptions may harm the social groups they represent. Formal codes neglect wider issues regarding the ethical acceptability of SSR.
- Psychological research must be **socially meaningful** (the **ethical imperative**). This applies particularly to the work of Social Psychologists.
- A major reason for using non-human animals in research is the **evolutionary continuity** between humans and other species.
- Safeguards for animal subjects include the BPS's **guidelines** and the Animals (Scientific Procedures) Act. Animals are used for various purposes apart from research, which are also covered by the guidelines.
- The question of **animal suffering** centres around the distinction between **sentience** and **(self-) consciousness.** Without consciousness, animals may simply demonstrate **overt**, bodily signs of pain, anxiety, etc., without the accompanying **feelings**.
- According to **speciesism,** we're morally obliged to inflict pain on animals in order to reduce potential human suffering. The speciesism argument assumes a greater significance when the non-humans in question are chimpanzees and other **great apes**.
- Clinical Psychologists and other **agents of change** are likely to neglect professional ethics, because of the twin beliefs that Psychology is a **value-free science** (as embodied in the **scientist–practitioner model** of helping) and that therapists should be **value-neutral/'non-directive**'.
- However effective a particular technique may be, Psychologists still **choose** which techniques to use and what research is worth doing. **Behaviour therapy** and **modification** treat people as helpless organisms, resulting in low self-esteem and passivity.
- Psychiatric in-patients are subjected to subtle coercion to accept particular treatments, and therapists may exert an even more covert influence over their clients.
- All therapists, psychodynamic and behavioural alike, influence their clients/patients and there's a **power imbalance** between them. The crucial issue is the **nature** of that influence.

Links with Other Topics/Chapters

Chapter 47 ⟶ *Feminist Psychologists* have helped to bring about the removal of *sexist language* from BPS and APA journals as a matter of policy

Chapter 49 ⟶ Part of Milgram's justification of his obedience experiments is his belief in his participants' *free will*

Chapters 3, 26 and 27 ⟶ Crucial methodological issues raised by the double obligation dilemma include *experimental realism* and *external validity*/mundane realism

Chapter 26 ⟶ Traditionally, the most deeply informative experiments in Social Psychology include those examining how participants resolve conflicts, such as Asch's studies of *conformity* (truth versus conformity)

Chapters 27 and 30 ⟶ Latané and Darley's *bystander intervention studies* (getting involved in another's troubles versus not getting involved) and Milgram's *obedience experiments* (internal conscience versus external authority)

Recommended Reading

Banyard, P., Flanagan, C. (2011) *Ethical Issues in Psychology.* London: Routledge.

Brown, L. (1997) Ethics in Psychology: Cui Bono? In D. Fox & I. Prilleltensky (eds) *Critical Psychology: An Introduction.* London: Sage. Also relevant to Chapter 47.

Gross, R. (2014) *Themes, Issues and Debates in Psychology* (4th edn). London: Hodder Education. Chapter 5.

Milgram, S. (1992) *The Individual in a Social World: Essays and Experiments* (2nd edn). New York: McGraw-Hill. 'Subject Reactions: The Neglected Factor in the Ethics of Experimentation' (originally published 1977) and 'Ethics in the Conformity Experiment: An Empirical Study' (originally published 1960).

Sieber, J.E. & Stanley, B. (1988) Ethical and professional dimensions socially sensitive research. *American Psychologist, 43*(1), 49–55.

Wise, R. (2000) *Rattling the Cage: Towards Legal Rights for Animals.* London: Profile Books.

Useful Websites

www.mrmced.org/crit2.html (Medical Research Modernization Committee: A Critical Look at Animal Experimentation)

http://altweb.jhsph.edu/ (Johns Hopkins Bloomberg School of Public Health: Search for Alternatives [to animal testing])

http://goodworkproject.org (The Goodwork Project. This is concerned with all aspects of civic and institutional life, including research practice. A central principle relevant to psychology is responsibility.)

(See Chapter 1 for BPS and APA weblinks.)

CHAPTER 49

FREE WILL AND DETERMINISM, AND REDUCTIONISM

Free will and determinism

Reductionism

INTRODUCTION and OVERVIEW

Any discussion of Psychology's scientific status raises fundamental questions about the nature of the person (see Chapter 3) or, at least, the image of the person that underlies major psychological theories (see Chapter 2), and that is implicit in much of the study of human behaviour. This chapter discusses two of these fundamental questions.

One question, debated by western philosophers for centuries, is whether we choose to act as we do, or whether behaviours are caused by influences beyond our control (*free will versus determinism*). The other, which has a shorter history and is debated by philosophers of science, concerns the validity of attempts to explain complex wholes in terms of their constituent parts (*reductionism*). One example of this is the relationship between the mind (or consciousness) and the brain (the '*mind–body problem*').

FREE WILL AND DETERMINISM

What is free will?

One way of approaching this question is to consider examples of behaviour where 'free will' (however defined) is clearly absent.

Case Study 49.1

Tourette's syndrome

Tim is 14 and displays a variety of twitches and tics. His head sometimes jerks and he often blinks and grimaces. Occasionally, he blurts out words, usually vulgarities. He doesn't mean to do it and is embarrassed by it, but he cannot control it. Because of his strange behaviour, most other children avoid him. His isolation and embarrassment are interfering with his social development. Tim suffers from a rare condition called Tourette's syndrome.
(From Holmes, 1994)

Ask Yourself

- What specific aspects of Tim's disorder are relevant to understanding the concept of 'free will'?
- If you think Tim lacks free will, what led you to this conclusion?
- Think of other behaviours (normal or abnormal) that demonstrate a lack of free will.

Intuition tells us that people have the ability to choose what they do and how and when they do it; in other words, they have *free will*. However, this freedom is exercised only within certain physical, political, sociological, and other environmental constraints. Yet the positivistic, mechanistic nature of scientific Psychology (see Chapter 3) implies that behaviour is *determined* by external (or internal) events or stimuli, and that people are passive responders. To this extent, people aren't free. *Determinism* also implies that behaviour occurs in a regular, orderly manner which (in principle) is totally predictable. For Taylor (1963), determinism maintains that:

> *In the case of everything that exists, there are antecedent conditions, known or unknown, given which that thing could not be other than it is ... More loosely, it says that everything, including every cause, is the effect of some cause or causes; or that everything is not only determinate but causally determined.*

'Everything that exists' includes people and their thoughts and behaviours, so a 'strict determinist' believes that thought and behaviours are no different from (other) 'things' or events in the world. However, this begs the question as to whether thoughts and behaviours are the same kind of thing or event as, say, chemical reactions in a test tube, or neurons firing in the brain. We don't usually ask if the chemicals 'agreed' to combine in a certain way, or if the neurons 'decided' to fire. Unless we were trying to be witty, we'd be guilty of *anthropomorphism* (attributing human abilities and characteristics to non-humans, animals or objects).

Figure 49.1 This painting by Gustave Doré of the Old Testament story of Lot's wife being turned to stone (*The Rescue of Lot*) illustrates the human capacity for free will

It's only people who can agree and make decisions. These abilities and capacities form part of our concept of a person, which, in turn, forms an essential part of 'everyday' or common-sense Psychology (see Chapter 1). Agreeing and deciding are precisely the kinds of things we do *with our minds* (they're mental processes or events), and to be able to agree and make decisions, it's necessary to 'have a mind'. So free will implies having a mind. However, having a mind doesn't imply free will: it's possible that decisions and so on are themselves caused (determined), even though they seem to be freely chosen.

Ask Yourself

- Try to explain what someone means when s/he says 'I had no choice but to ...' or 'You leave me no choice ...'.
- Can you interpret this in a way that's consistent with a belief in free will?

Different meanings of 'free will'

Having a choice

If we have choice, then we could behave differently given the same circumstances. This contrasts sharply with a common definition of determinism, namely that things could only have happened as they did, given everything that happened previously (see above).

Not being coerced or constrained

If someone puts a loaded gun to your head and tells you to do something, your behaviour is clearly not free: you've been forced to act this way. This is usually where the philosophical debate about 'free will' begins, and is related to what James (1890) called *soft determinism* (see below).

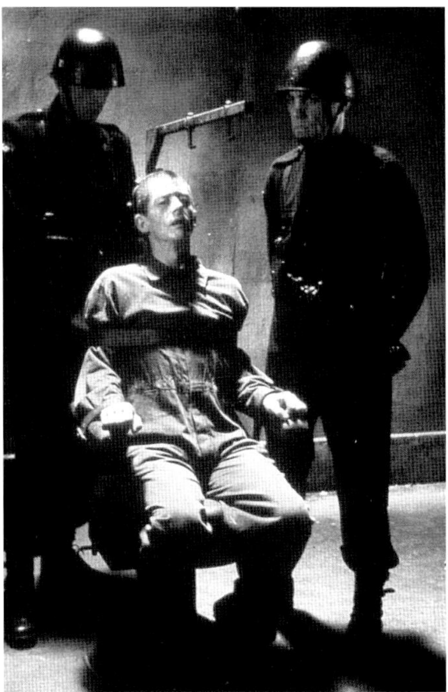

Figure 49.2 John Hurt as Winston Smith in the film of George Orwell's *1984*

Voluntary behaviour

If 'involuntary' conveys *reflex* behaviour (such as the eye-blink response to a puff of air directed at the eye), then 'voluntary' implies 'free' (the behaviour *isn't* automatic). By definition, most behaviour (human and non-human) isn't reflex, nor is it usually the result of coercion. So is most behaviour free?

One demonstration of people's belief in their free will is *psychological reactance* (Brehm, 1966; Brehm and Brehm, 1981; see Chapter 9). A common response to the feeling that our freedom is being threatened is the attempt to regain or reassert it, which is related to the need to be free from others' controls and not be dictated to. A good deal of contrary (resistant) behaviour, otherwise known as 'bloody-mindedness' ('Don't tell me what to do!') seems to reflect this process (Carver and Scheier, 1992).

Box 49.1 Evidence for the distinction between voluntary and involuntary behaviour

- Penfield's (1947) classic experiments involved stimulating the cortex of patients about to undergo brain surgery (see Chapter 4).
- Even though the cortical area being stimulated was the one involved in normal ('voluntary') limb movements, patients reported feeling that their arms and legs were being moved passively, quite a different experience from initiating the movement themselves.
- This demonstrates that the subjective experience (*phenomenology*) of the voluntary movement of one's limbs cannot be reduced to the stimulation of the appropriate brain region (otherwise Penfield's patients shouldn't have reported a difference). Doing things voluntarily simply *feels* different from the same things 'just happening'.
- Similarly, Delgado (1969) stimulated a part of the primary motor area in a patient's left hemisphere, causing the patient to form a clenched fist with his right hand. When asked to try to keep his fingers still during the next stimulation, the patient couldn't do it and commented, 'I guess, doctor, that your electricity is stronger than my will'.
- These examples support the claim that having free will is an undeniable part of our subjective experience of ourselves as people. The sense of self is most acute (and important and real for us) where moral decisions and feelings of responsibility for past actions are involved (Koestler, 1967). (See text below and Box 49.2 for further discussion of free will and moral responsibility.)

Related to this need to feel free from others' control is *intrinsic motivation* or *self-determination* (Deci, 1980; Deci and Ryan, 1987): people's intrinsic interest in things, such that they don't need to be offered extrinsic incentives for doing them. Engaging in such activities is motivated by the desire for competence and self-determination.

Deliberate control

Norman and Shallice (1986) define divided attention as an upper limit to the amount of processing that can be performed on incoming information at any one time. They propose three levels of functioning, namely *fully automatic processing*, *partially automatic processing* and *deliberate control*. Deliberate control corresponds to free will (see Chapter 13).

Why are Psychologists interested in the concept of free will?

As noted in the *Introduction and overview*, the philosophical debate about free will and determinism is centuries old. It can be traced back at least to the French philosopher Descartes (1596–1650), whose ideas had a great influence on both science in general and Psychology in particular. For much of its history as a separate, scientific discipline, Psychology has operated as if there were no difference between natural, physical phenomena and human thought and behaviour (see Chapter 3).

Ask Yourself

- Try to identify ways in which the issue of free will is relevant to psychological theory and practice. For example, how does the notion of free will relate to criteria for defining and diagnosing mental disorders? (See Chapter 43.)

Free will and psychological abnormality

Definitions of abnormality, and the diagnosis and treatment of mental disorders, often involve implicit or explicit judgements about free will and determinism. In a general sense, mental disorders can be seen as the partial or complete breakdown of the control people normally have over their thoughts, emotions and behaviours. For example, *compulsive* behaviour is, by definition, behaviour which a person cannot help but do (such as compulsive hand-washing). People are *attacked* by panic, *obsessed* by thoughts of germs, or become the *victims* of thoughts which are inserted into their brains from external sources. In all these examples, things are *happening to* the individual, both from his/her own perspective and that of a Psychologist or psychiatrist.

Being judged to have lost *control* (possession of which is usually thought of as a major feature of normality), either temporarily or permanently, is a legally acceptable defence in cases of criminal offences. (See Chapters 43 and 44.)

Free will and moral accountability

Underlying the whole question of legal (and moral) responsibility is the presupposition that people are, at least some of the time, able to control their behaviour and choose between different courses of action. How else could we ever be held responsible for any of our actions? In most everyday situations and interactions, we attribute responsibility, both to ourselves and others, unless we have reason to doubt it. According to Flanagan (1984):

> *It seems silly to have any expectations about how people ought to act, if everything we do is the result of some inexorable causal chain which began millennia ago. 'Ought', after all, seems to imply 'can', therefore, by employing a moral vocabulary filled with words like 'ought' and 'should', we assume that humans are capable of rising above the causal pressures presented by the material world, and, in assuming this we appear to be operating with some conception of freedom, some notion of free will.*

(See Critical Discussion 35.1, and Chapter 46.)

Ask Yourself

- Can you spot any weaknesses/inconsistencies in Zimbardo's argument? (See Critical Discussion 49.1.)

Critical Discussion 49.1

How powerful social situations can make us act against our will

The thrust of a great deal of social psychological research is to demonstrate the power of social situations to make individuals act in ways that are contrary to how they'd behave away from those situations. This may take the form of *conforming* with a peer group (or changing your opinion in line with a *minority*), *obeying* the orders of someone in authority, or taking others' behaviour as a guide to how you should act (as in *bystander intervention*). Perhaps the most blatant demonstration of this social power comes in the Stanford prison experiment (Zimbardo *et al.*, 1973, see Chapter 27).

Figure 49.3 Hooded prisoner in Abu Ghraib

As an iconic image of human rights abuse, the hooded prisoner (above) with electrodes attached to his fingers is hard to equal: he stands precariously on a small box and one slip will produce a numbing electric shock (Bond, 2007).

In April, 2004, this picture and others showing American soldiers mistreating Iraqi prisoners in Abu Ghraib prison were published all over the world. The electrode 'stunt' was the brainchild of a group of army reservists working as military policemen at the prison, one of whom was Ivan 'Chip' Frederick. This wasn't the only abuse he perpetrated. At his trial, the judge justified the severe punishment (eight years in prison, loss of salary and pension, etc.) on the grounds that Frederick was acting of his own free will: he was morally corrupt, the proverbial 'bad apple'.

However, Zimbardo, acting as an expert witness for the defence, argued that the judge was making a fundamental attribution error (FAE) (see Chapter 23) thereby underestimating the impact of environmental influences. Having ruled out mental disorder or sadistic tendencies, Zimbardo claimed that Frederick went from an 'American icon' (good husband, father, patriotic, religious, etc.) to a 'monster'.

Based on a meta-analysis of 25,000 Social Psychology studies, Fiske *et al.* (2004) concluded that almost everyone is capable of torture and other evil deeds if placed in the wrong social context. In addition, if we focus on individual 'bad apples', and overlook the power of the group, we'll never combat evils such as torture, suicide bombings (see Chapter 46) and genocide.

But doesn't this challenge our sense of being in control and our ability to exercise our free will? Perhaps. But Zimbardo (2007) also believes there's a positive side to this argument: our universal capacity to perform evil acts is matched by a universal capacity to resist peer pressure and become a 'hero'. Heroes are ordinary individuals who choose to do the right thing in a particular situation. Ordinary heroes, like ordinary monsters, are everywhere (Zimbardo, 2007).

Free will as an issue in major psychological theories

Most major theorists in Psychology have addressed the issue of free will and determinism, including James, Freud, Skinner and Rogers.

James and soft determinism

As we saw in Chapter 1, James pioneered Psychology as a separate, scientific discipline. In *The Principles of Psychology* (1890), he devoted a whole chapter to the 'will', which he related to attention:

> *The most essential achievement of the will ... when it is most 'voluntary' is to attend to a different object and hold it fast before the mind ... Effort of attention is thus the essential phenomenon of will.*

For James, there was a conflict. Belief in determinism seemed to fit best with the scientific view of the world, while belief in free will seemed to be required by our social, moral, political, and legal practices, as well as by our personal, subjective experience (see above). His solution to this conflict was two-fold.

1. He distinguished between the scientific and non-scientific worlds. Psychology as a science could progress only by assuming determinism, but this doesn't mean that belief in free will must be abandoned in other contexts. So, scientific explanation isn't the only useful kind of explanation.
2. He drew a further distinction between *soft* and *hard* determinism. According to *soft determinism*, the question of free will depends on the type(s) of cause(s) our behaviour has, not whether it's caused or not caused (the opposite of 'not caused' is 'random', not 'free'). If our actions have, as their immediate (proximate) cause, processing by a system such as *conscious mental life* (CML), which includes consciousness, purposefulness, personality and personal continuity, then they count as free, rational, voluntary, purposive actions. According to *hard determinism*, CML is itself caused, so that the immediate causes are only part of the total causal chain which results in the behaviour we're trying to explain. Therefore, as long as our behaviour is caused at all, there's no sense in which we can be described as acting freely.

Freud and psychic determinism

Although in most respects Freud's and Skinner's ideas about human behaviour are diametrically opposed, they shared the fundamental belief that free will is an illusion. However, in keeping with their theories as a whole, their reasons are radically different.

Ask Yourself

- Based on what you already know about Freud's psychoanalytic theory, try to identify those parts that are most relevant to his rejection of free will.

According to Strachey (1962–1977):

> *Behind all of Freud's work ... we should posit his belief in the universal validity of the law of determinism ... Freud extended the belief (derived from physical phenomena) uncompromisingly to the field of mental phenomena.*

Similarly, Sulloway (1979) maintains that all of Freud's work in science (and Freud saw himself very much as a scientist) was characterised by an abiding faith in the notion that all vital phenomena, including psychical (psychological) ones, are rigidly and lawfully determined by the principle of cause and effect. One major example of this was the extreme importance he attached to the technique of free association.

Box 49.2 How 'free' is Freud's 'free association'?

'Free association' is a misleading translation of the German *'freier Einfall'*, which conveys much more accurately the intended impression of an uncontrollable 'intrusion' (*Einfall*) by preconscious ideas into conscious thinking. In turn, this preconscious material reflects unconscious ideas, wishes, and memories (what Freud was really interested in), since here lie the principal causes of neurotic problems.

It's a great irony that 'free' association should refer to a technique used in psychoanalysis meant to reveal the *unconscious* causes of behaviour. It's because the causes of our thoughts, actions and supposed choices are unconscious (mostly *actively repressed*), that we *think* we're free.

Freud's application of this general philosophical belief in causation to mental phenomena is called *psychic determinism* (see Chapter 42).

(Based on Sulloway, 1979)

For Freud, part of what 'psychic determinism' conveyed was that in the universe of the mind, there are no 'accidents'. No matter how apparently random or irrational behaviour may be (such as '*parapraxes*' or 'Freudian slips'), unconscious causes can always account for them, and this also applies to hysterical symptoms and dreams. As Gay (1988) states, 'Freud's theory of the mind is … strictly and frankly deterministic'. However:

- Freud accepted that true accidents, in the sense of forces beyond the victim's control (e.g. being struck by lightning), can and do occur, and aren't unconsciously caused by the victim.
- One of the aims of psychoanalysis is to 'give the patient's ego *freedom* to decide one way or another' (Freud, quoted in Gay, 1988), so therapy rests on the belief that people *can* change. However, Freud saw the extent of possible change as being very limited (see Critical Discussion 45.2, p. 789).
- One aspect of psychic determinism is *overdetermination*: much of our behaviour has multiple causes, both conscious and unconscious. So although our conscious choices, decisions and intentions may genuinely influence behaviour, they never tell the whole story.
- Freud often explained his patients' choices, neurotic symptoms, and so on not in terms of causes (the *scientific* argument), but by trying to make sense of them and give them meaning (the *semantic* argument). Indeed, the latter is supported by the title of, arguably, his greatest book, *The Interpretation of Dreams* (1900) (as opposed to *The 'Cause' of Dreams*).

Skinner and the illusion of free will

While Skinner, like Freud, sees free will as an illusion, Skinner's *radical behaviourism* eliminates all reference to mental or private states as part of the explanation of behaviour (including theories like Freud's!).

Although Skinner doesn't deny that pain and other internal states exist, they have no 'causal teeth' and hence no part to play in scientific explanations of (human) behaviour (Garrett, 1996). Free will (and other 'explanatory fictions') cannot be defined or measured objectively, nor are they needed for successful prediction and control of behaviour (for Skinner, the primary aims of a *science of behaviour*).

Ask Yourself

- Given what you know about Skinner's theory of operant conditioning and his 'analysis of behaviour', try to identify the causes of human behaviour that he believes are often hidden from us in the environment. (See Chapters 2 and 11.)

It's only because the causes of human behaviour are often hidden from us in the environment, that the myth or illusion of free will survives.

Skinner argues that when what we do is dictated by force or punishment, or by their threat (negative reinforcement), it's obvious to everyone that we're not acting freely (such as when the possibility of prison stops us committing crimes). Similarly, it may sometimes be very obvious which positive reinforcers are shaping behaviour (a bonus for working overtime, for example).

However, most of the time we're unaware of environmental causes, and it looks (and feels) as if we're behaving freely. Yet all this means is that we're free of punishments or negative reinforcement; our behaviour is still determined by the pursuit of things that have been positively reinforced in the past. When we perceive others as behaving freely, we're simply unaware of their reinforcement histories (Fancher, 1996).

Box 49.3 The freedom myth and the rejection of punishment

In *Beyond Freedom and Dignity*, Skinner (1971) argued that the notion of 'autonomous man', upon which so many of western society's assumptions are based, is false and has many harmful consequences. In particular, the assumption that people are free requires that they're constantly exposed to punishment and its threat as a negative reinforcer (Fancher, 1996). In his novel *Walden Two*, Skinner describes a utopian society where only mutual reinforcement is used – never punishment or negative reinforcement (Skinner, 1948b).

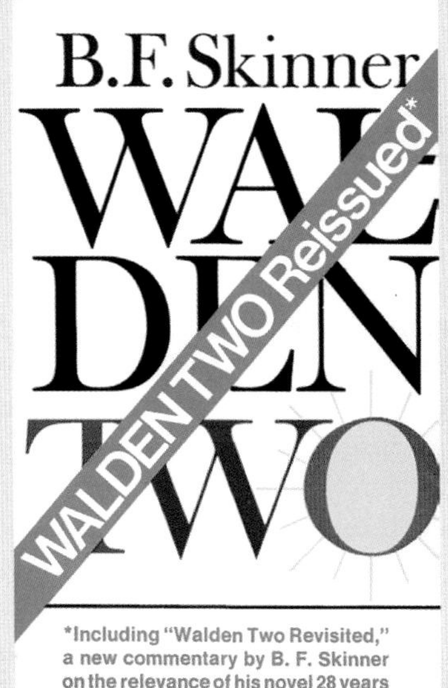

B.F. Skinner
WALDEN TWO
WALDEN TWO Reissued*
*Including "Walden Two Revisited," a new commentary by B. F. Skinner on the relevance of his novel 28 years after publication.

Figure 49.4 *Walden Two*

> **Ask Yourself**
>
> - What ethical issues are raised by Skinner's advocacy of a utopian society like *Walden Two*?
> - In what ways does this Utopia reflect Skinner's beliefs about the aims of a scientific Psychology?

Skinner's views on bettering society (through strict behavioural control or engineering) caused an enormous backlash from critical audiences and the general public. Rogers claimed that Skinner's utopian vision was indistinguishable from Orwell's *Nineteen Eighty-Four*, a nightmarish *dystopia*, which warns against a punitive society where people are treated as automatons by those in power (O'Donohue and Ferguson, 2001).

Clearly, Skinner's belief that free will is an illusion conflicts with the need to attribute people with free will if we're to hold them (and ourselves) morally (and legally) responsible for their behaviour. Skinner (1971) himself acknowledges that freedom and dignity are 'essential to practices in which a person is held responsible for his conduct and given credit for his achievements'.

However, he equates 'good' and 'bad' with 'beneficial to others' (what's rewarded) and 'harmful to others' (what's punished) respectively, thus removing morality from human behaviour. For Skinner, 'oughts' aren't 'moral imperatives': they reflect *practical*, rather than moral, guidelines and rules (Morea, 1990).

Figure 49.5 Afghan men in Kabul at a cockfighting match, very popular with gamblers in this war-torn country. Where activities like these are such a part of the culture, are individuals responsible for their behaviour?

Rogers, freedom and the fully functioning person

Rogers was perhaps the most influential *Humanistic, Phenomenological* Psychologist. As such, he stressed the process of self-actualisation and the necessity of adopting the other person's perspective if we're to understand that person, and in particular, his/her self-concept (see Chapter 42).

Understanding the self-concept is also central to Rogers' client-centred therapy (see Chapter 45). His experience as a therapist convinced him that real change does occur in therapy: people choose to see themselves and their life situations differently. Therapy and life are about free human beings struggling to become more free. Personal experience is important, but it doesn't imprison us: how we react to our experience is something we ourselves choose and decide (Morea, 1990).

> **Ask Yourself**
>
> - According to Rogers, in what ways are individuals prevented from recognising their true feelings and behaviour?
> - In what respect is Rogers' view of human beings a more optimistic one than, say, Freud's?

Rogers' deep and lasting trust in human nature didn't, however, blind him to the reality of evil behaviour:

> *In my experience, every person has the capacity for evil behaviour. I, and others, have had murderous and cruel impulses ... feelings of anger and rage, desires to impose our wills on others ... Whether I ... will translate these impulses into behaviour depends ... on two elements: social conditioning and voluntary choice ... (Rogers, 1982, cited in Thorne, 1992)*

By making the distinction between 'human nature' and behaviour, Rogers retains his optimistic view of human beings. However, this didn't exclude altogether a deterministic element in his later writings. In *Freedom to Learn for the Eighties* (Rogers, 1983), he states that it's becoming clear from science that human beings are complex machines and not free, and determinism 'is the foundation stone of present-day science'. So how can this be reconciled with self-actualisation, psychological growth and the freedom to choose?

One proposed solution is in the form of a version of soft determinism. Unlike neurotic and incongruent people whose defensiveness forces them to act in ways they'd prefer not to, the healthy, fully functioning person:

... not only experiences, but utilises, the most absolute freedom when he spontaneously, freely and voluntarily chooses and wills that which is absolutely determined.

He seemed to mean that at the same time as we choose our behaviour, it's also being *determined* by all the relevant conditions that exist. The open, responsive (fully functioning) person is fully aware of all that's going on inside, and has an accurate grasp of existing external factors. This individual is free, but s/he will take a particular course of action: in the presence of all available stimuli there are certain behaviours that are most productive both subjectively and objectively. In this sense, there's no contradiction between free will and determinism: they coincide (Nye, 2000).

Sociobiology: extreme biological determinism

Rose *et al.*'s *Not In Our Genes* (1984) is a critique of biological determinism in general. Here, we concentrate on those aspects that are most relevant to the issue of freedom and determinism.

The central claim of *sociobiology* is that all aspects of human culture and behaviour, like that of all animals, are coded in the genes and have been moulded by natural selection. Sociobiology is a reductionist, biological determinist explanation of human existence. Its adherents claim that:

- the details of present and past social arrangements are the inevitable manifestations of the specific action of genes
- the particular genes that lie at the basis of human society have been selected in evolution; therefore, the traits they determine result in higher reproductive fitness of the individuals that carry them (that is, they're more likely to survive to have offspring that will have genes for those traits: see Chapter 2).

If one accepts biological determinism, nothing needs to be changed:

... for what falls in the realm of necessity falls outside the realm of justice. The issue of justice arises only when there is choice ... To the extent that we are free to make ethical decisions that can be translated into practice, biology is irrelevant; to the extent that we are bound by our biology, ethical judgements are irrelevant ...

Biological determinism has such wide appeal because it removes guilt and responsibility: it's 'our biology' that's to blame, not *people*, either individually or collectively. But, according to Rose *et al.*, this involves a *false dichotomy* between biological and cultural/social, just as 'nature/nurture' (see Chapter 50) and 'mind/brain' (see below) are false dichotomies. 'Free will/determinism' is another. What characterises human development and actions is that they're the product of an immense array of interacting, intersecting causes:

... For biological determinists we are unfree because our lives are strongly constrained by a relatively small number of internal causes, the genes for specific behaviours or for predisposition to those behaviours. But this misses the essence of the difference between human biology and that of other organisms ... Our biology has made us into creatures who are constantly re-creating our own psychic and material environments, and whose individual lives are the outcomes of an extraordinary multiplicity of intersecting causal pathways. Thus, it is our biology that makes us free. (Rose et al., 1984)

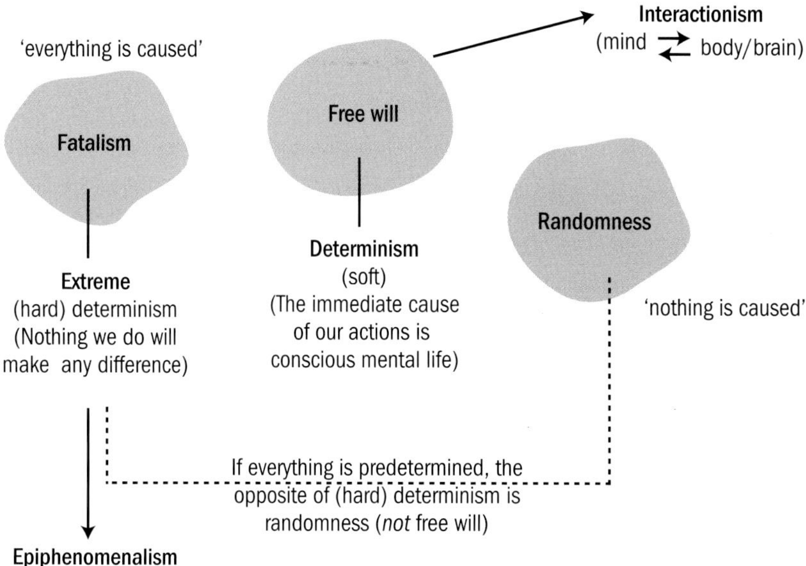

Figure 49.6 The relationship between free will and determinism, showing the link with theories of the mind–brain relationship

Critical Discussion 49.2

Freedom as an evolutionary reality

Belief in evolutionary forces and genetic influences may lead sociobiologists largely to deny free will, but it can also lead to the opposite conclusion. According to Dennett (2003):

> *Free will is an evolved creation of human activity and beliefs, and it is just as real as such other creations as music and money ... Recognising our uniqueness as reflective, communicating animals does not require any 'human exceptionalism' that must shake a defiant fist at Darwin ... We may thus concede that material forces ultimately govern behaviour, and yet at the same time reject the notion that people are always and everywhere motivated by material self-interest.*

Dennett believes that educated people are trapped in a strange kind of double-think. On the one hand, they believe that natural science implies determinism, which proves they have no control over their lives. But on the other hand, in their actual daily lives, they mostly assume they do have this control. The resulting conflict can create deep, underlying anxiety, confusion, guilt and a sense of futility.

This is basically the same dilemma faced by James (see text above). Consistent with James's position, Dennett argues that determinism *isn't* fatalism, which teaches that human effort makes no difference to what happens. Fatalism is another term for hard determinism, which reflects the view of the mind as mere *epiphenomenona* (i.e. by-products of brain activity without any causal influence). But fatalism is clearly false, based on an oversimplified, largely outdated scientific view of the world. All the sciences, including physics, now find complexity and variety of patterns everywhere; the more complex creatures become, the wider the range of activities open to them and with this increase goes a steadily increasing degree of freedom. According to Dennett:

> *The freedom of the bird to fly wherever it wants is definitely a kind of freedom, a distinct improvement on the freedom of the jellyfish to float wherever it floats, but a poor cousin of our human freedom ... Human freedom, in part a product of the revolution begat of language and culture, is about as different from bird freedom as language is different from birdsong. But to understand the richer phenomenon, one must first understand its more modest components and predecessors.*

This evolutionary view of human freedom is similar to that proposed by Rose (1997). Both make the central point that our conscious inner life isn't some sort of irrelevant supernatural intrusion on the working of our physical bodies (a 'ghost in the machine'), but a crucial feature of their design. We've evolved as beings that can feel and think in a way that makes us able to direct our actions. We operate as whole people, our minds and bodies are aspects of us, not separate items. They don't need to compete for the driving seat (Midgley, 2003).

REDUCTIONISM

What is reductionism?

Luria (1987) traces the origins of reductionism to the mid-nineteenth-century view within biology that an organism is a complex of organs, and the organs are complexes of cells. To explain the basic laws of the living organism, we have to study as carefully as possible the features of separate cells. From its biological origins, reductionism was extended to science in general. For example, the properties of a protein molecule could be uniquely determined or predicted in terms of properties of the electrons or protons making up its atoms. According to Ellis, himself a physicist, (2013):

> *There's a basic assumption that the things you see – be it humans, computers or trees – can ultimately be boiled down to the behavior of the particles they are composed of. Biology is determined by chemistry, which is in turn governed by the underlying physics ...*

Much of modern science is rooted in this *bottom-up, reductionist* view of cause-and-effect. While this has proved an excellent way of explaining many phenomena, Ellis (2013) asks if everything can be understood just by looking at their constituent parts?

Garnham (1991) defines reductionism as:

> *... the idea that psychological explanations can be replaced by explanations in terms of brain functioning or even in terms of physics and chemistry.*

Although reductionism's ultimate aim (according to its supporters) is to account for all phenomena in terms of microphysics, *any* attempt to explain something in terms of its components or constituent parts may be thought of as reductionist. A useful definition, which is consistent with this broader view, is that of Rose *et al.* (1984), for whom reductionism is:

> *... the name given to a set of general methods and modes of explanation both of the world of physical objects and of human societies. Broadly, reductionists try to explain the properties of complex wholes – molecules, say, or societies – in terms of the units of which those molecules or societies are composed.*

Rose (1997) identifies four major types of reductionism (or different meanings of the term in Box 49.4).

Box 49.4 Different meanings of reductionism

Reductionism as methodology: the attempt to isolate variables in the laboratory in order to simplify the living world's enormous complexity, flux and multitude of interacting processes. This is the basis of the experiment, which reflects natural science's attempt to identify cause-and-effect relationships (see Chapter 3).

Theory reduction: science's aim to capture as much of the world in as few laws or principles as possible. It's related to philosophical reductionism.

Philosophical reductionism: the belief that because science is unitary, and because physics is the most fundamental of the sciences, ultimately all currently separate disciplines (including Psychology) will be 'reduced' to physics.

Reductionism as ideology: the very marked tendency in recent years to identify genes responsible for a whole range of complex human behaviours, including stress, anxiety, depression, personality, homosexuality, intelligence, alcoholism, criminality and violence.

(Based on Rose, 1997)

Rose calls the claim that there's a direct causal link between genes and behaviour *neurogenetic determinism*. It involves a sequence of (false) assumptions and arguments, one of which is the dichotomy between genetic and environmental causes (or nature and nurture) (see Chapter 50).

Ask Yourself

- There are many examples of psychological theories and concepts that fit one or more of the definitions of reductionism above. These can be found in all areas of Psychology, but below are a few of the more 'obvious' examples. For each one, try to explain (a) why the theory or concept is reductionist, and (b) what the strengths and/or weaknesses of such an approach are.

(i) According to *structuralism* (e.g. Wundt), perception is simply a series of sensations (see Chapter 3).

(ii) According to Watson's *peripheralism*, thought consists of tiny movements of the vocal chords (see Chapter 18).

(iii) *Intelligence* is a person's performance on a standardised intelligence test (his/her IQ score (see Chapter 41).

(iv) *Psychological gender differences* are caused by biological factors (such as hormones; see Chapter 36).

(v) According to Freud, *personality development* involves progress through a series of *psychosexual stages* (see Chapter 35).

(vi) *Schizophrenia* is caused by an excess of the neurotransmitter *dopamine* (see Chapter 44).

(vii) According to Adorno *et al.* (1950), antisemitism (and other forms of *racism*) are symptomatic of the *authoritarian personality* (see Chapter 25).

The mind–body problem

Perhaps the oldest and most frequently debated example of reductionism is the *mind–body problem* (or the *problem of mind and brain*). Originally a philosophical issue, it continues to be discussed, often passionately, by neurophysiologists, biologists, Neuropsychologists and Psychologists in general. It's generally agreed that the mind (or consciousness) is a property of human beings (as is walking upright on two legs), and that without the human brain there'd be no consciousness. But a 'problem' remains (see Box 49.6.).

From an *evolutionary* perspective, could consciousness have equipped human beings with survival value unless it had causal properties (Gregory, 1981); that is, unless it could actually bring about changes in behaviour? Our subjective experiences tell us that our minds do affect behaviour, and that consciousness

Box 49.5 The reality of 'top-down' causation (based on Ellis, 2013)

- When you type a document on a computer keyboard, electrons in the transistors in the central processing unit flow in such a way as to make the letters you select appear on the screen. Far from the underlying physics controlling what happens (as reductionists would claim), the physics is dictated by your desired outcome. This is *top-down* causation from your brain to the fingers that press the keys, then down to the level of electrons flowing in the processor and onwards to the screen.
- If you're brought up in an English-speaking environment, society shapes your neural connections in such a way as to let you think in English. This is the result of *top-down* causation from the social environment to the synaptic connections in your brain.
- Physicists don't usually think in terms of top-down causation – they tend to assume that everything flows from *micro* to *macro* scales. But neuroscientists *must* think in terms of top-down causation in order to make sense of brain processes such as vision. As Frith (2007) explains, what we see is determined by what our brains predict we *ought* to see, rather than simply by the signals reaching our brain from the retina (see Chapters 5 and 15).

However, if we argue that our brains have causal powers in their own right (they direct and co-ordinate the way neurons – themselves composed of molecules, which, in turn, consist of protons, neutrons and electrons – work), isn't this, ultimately, nothing but *disguised* bottom-up causation? Reductionists argue that the physics at the bottom is causally closed – there's nothing but interactions between particles such as protons and electrons at that level, leaving no room for any other causal effect and no causal 'slack' to allow top-down effects to take place.
Ellis opposes this argument for two reasons:

1. It omits the crucial way in which a higher-level structure channels lower-level interactions. Paradoxically, when the wiring in a computer constrains the motion of electrons, this creates new possibilities that don't exist when the electron flow is unconstrained. While the physics *makes* things happen, the context *determines* what will happen (corresponding to *means* and *end,* respectively).
2. In biology and quantum physics, the lower-level entities aren't fixed, interacting with each other through deterministic laws; rather, context affects their nature and shapes how they behave.

Box 49.6 The problem of the mind–brain relationship

- How can two 'things' be related when one of them is physical (the brain has size, weight, shape, density, and exists in space and time) and the other apparently lacks all these characteristics?
- How can something non-physical/non-material (the mind) influence or produce changes in something physical (the brain/body)?
- The 'classic' example given by philosophers to illustrate the problem is the act of deciding to lift one's arm. From a strictly scientific perspective, this kind of causation should be impossible. Science (including Psychology and Neurophysiology) has traditionally rejected any brand of *philosophical dualism*: the belief in the existence of two essentially different kinds of 'substance', the physical body and the non-physical mind (see Box 49.7).

does have causal properties (just try lifting your arm). However, many philosophers and scientists from various disciplines haven't always shared the layperson's common-sense understanding.

Figure 49.7 Self-awareness/consciousness and the ability to understand and predict others' behaviour may be the characteristics of human beings which make us unique as a species

While there are many theories of the mind–brain relationship, most aren't strictly relevant to the debate about reductionism. Box 49.7 and Figure 49.8 summarise most of the major theories, but emphasis is given to reductionist approaches, especially as they impinge on psychological theories.

Box 49.7 Some major theories of the mind–brain relationship

- Theories fall into two main categories: *dualism* (which distinguishes between mind and brain) and *monism* (which claims that only mind or matter are real).
- According to Descartes' seventeenth-century dualist theory (which first introduced the mind–body problem into philosophy), the mind can influence the brain, but not vice versa. While *epiphenomenology* sees the mind as a kind of by-product of the brain (the mind has no influence on the brain), *interactionism* sees the influence as two-way.
- Most monist theories take one or other form of *materialism*.
- The *peripheralist* version of materialism is illustrated by Skinner's radical behaviourism. During the 1930s, Skinner denied the existence of mental phenomena (as had Watson). However, from 1945 he began to adopt a less extreme view, recognising their existence, but defining them as *covert/internal actions,* subject to the same laws of conditioning as overt behavioural events. This is a form of reductionism.
- *Centralist materialism* (or *mind–brain identity theory*) identifies mental processes with purely physical processes in the central nervous system. While it's logically possible that there might be separate, mental, non-physical phenomena, it just turns out, as a matter of fact, that mental states are identical with physical states of the brain. We are, simply, very complicated *physico-chemical mechanisms.*
- *Eliminative materialism* represents an extreme reductionist form of (centralist) materialism (see text below).

(Based on Flanagan, 1984; Gross, 2014; Teichman, 1988)

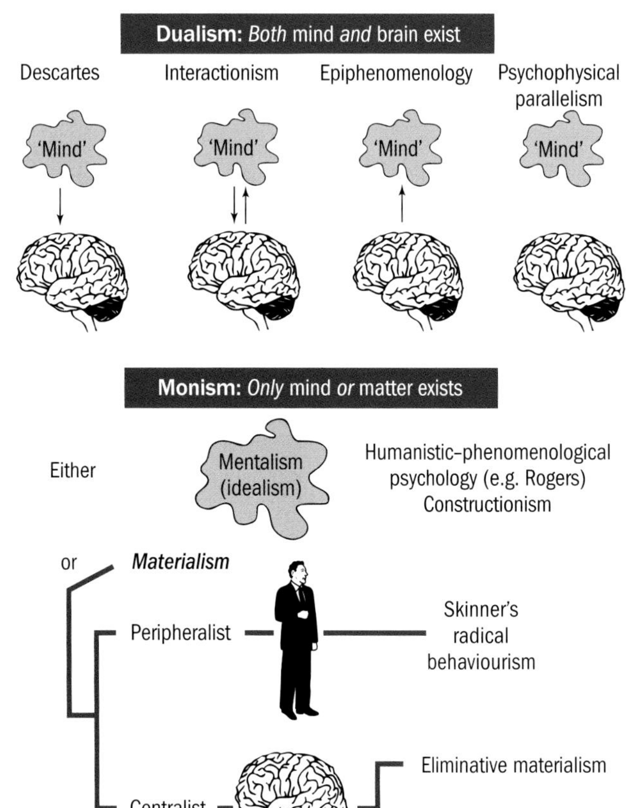

Figure 49.8 An outline of the major theories of the mind–brain relationship

Ask Yourself

- Using your knowledge of Biopsychology, try to relate the examples below to the theories outlined in Box 49.7 and Figure 49.8.
- Specifically, do these examples involve interactions between mind and brain, and, if so, in what direction is the influence taking place?
  - (a) the effects of psychoactive drugs (see Chapters 8 and 45)
  - (b) electrical stimulation of the brain (see Chapter 4)
  - (c) Sperry's study of split-brain patients (see Chapter 4)
  - (d) stress (see Chapter 12)
  - (e) placebo effects (see Chapter 45)

Reductionist theories of the mind–brain relationship

As Box 49.7 shows, *eliminative materialism* is an extreme form of reductionist materialism. What makes it reductionist is the attempt to *replace* a psychological account of behaviour with an account in terms of neurophysiology. An example of this approach is Crick's (1994) *The Astonishing Hypothesis: The Scientific Search for the Soul*. According to Crick:

You, your joys and your sorrows, your memories and your ambitions, your sense of personality and free will, are in fact no more than the behaviour of a vast assembly of nerve cells and their associated molecules.

But is this a valid equation to make?

Ironically, hard-line reductionists would question why Crick assigned causal powers to neurons. If you really believe in bottom-up causation, you cannot assign causal powers to an *intermediate level* like this – it's the electrons that are doing the real work (or perhaps even smaller particles). Higher levels like electrons and neurons are mere 'passengers' carried along by this underlying causation (Ellis, 2013).

But neuroscientists believe that neurons do indeed do real work. This is only possible if they act to channel and control the flow of electrons in neural axons – that is, if top-down causation takes place from the neuron to the electron level. And if that is so, the case for top-down causation is vindicated. (Ellis, 2013)

According to Smith (1994), the mind and brain problem is radically different from other cases of *contingent identity* (identical as a matter of fact) with which it's usually compared, such as 'a gene is a section of the DNA molecule'. What's different is reductionism, and the related issue of exactly what's meant by *identity* (see Box 49.8).

Box 49.8 Different meanings of 'identity' relevant to the mind–brain relationship

- While it's generally agreed that we cannot have a mind without a brain, mind states and brain states *aren't* systematically correlated, and the neurophysiological and neurological evidence points towards *token identity*. For example, we cannot just assume that the same neurophysiological mechanisms will be used by two different people both engaged in the 'same' activity of reading (Broadbent, 1981). There are many ways that 'the brain' can perform the same task.
- But it's precisely this kind of systematic correlation that mind–brain identity has been taken to imply, whereby whenever a mind state of a certain type occurs, a brain state of a certain type occurs (*type identity*).
- Token identity means that there must always be a place for an autonomous psychological account of human thought and action.

(Based on Harré *et al.*, 1985)

According to Penrose (1990), there's a built-in *indeterminacy* in the way individual neurons and their synaptic connections work (their responses are inherently unpredictable). Yet, despite this unpredictability at the level of the individual units or components, the system as a whole is predictable. The 'nervous system' (or subsystems within it) doesn't operate randomly, but in a highly organised, structured way.

Consciousness (Chapter 7), intelligence (Chapter 41), and memory (Chapter 17) are properties of the brain as a *system*, not properties of the individual units, and they couldn't possibly be predicted from analysing the units. Instead, they 'emerge' from interactions between the units that compose the system (and so are called *emergent properties*). The whole is greater than the sum of its parts (Rose, 1997; see Chapter 15).

Can you be a materialist without being a reductionist?

According to Rose (1992):

The mind is never replaced by the brain. Instead we have two distinct and legitimate languages, each describing the same unitary phenomena of the material world.

Rose speaks as a materialist and an anti-reductionist, who believes that we should learn how to translate between mind language and brain language (although this may be impossibly difficult). While most materialists are also reductionists, and vice versa, this isn't necessarily so. Freud, for example, was a materialist who believed that no single scientific vocabulary (such as anatomy) could adequately describe (let alone explain) all facets of the material world (the *autonomy of psychological explanation*).

The fact that there are different 'languages' for describing minds and brains (or different levels of description or *universes of discourse*) relates to the question of the relevance of knowing, say, what's going on inside our brains when we think or are aware. For Eiser (1994):

The firing of neurons stands to thought in the same relation as my walking across the room (etc.) stands to my getting some coffee. It is absolutely essential in a causal or physical sense, and absolutely superfluous ... to the logic of the higher-order description. In short, I can accept that it happens, and then happily ignore it.

This explains how it's possible to be simultaneously a materialist (the brain is necessarily implicated in everything we do and the mind doesn't represent a different kind of reality) and an anti-reductionist (we can describe and explain our thinking without having to 'bring my brain into it'). Two separate levels of description are involved.

CONCLUSIONS

Given Psychology's intellectual and historical roots in philosophy and natural science, it's hardly surprising that psychological theories have contributed to the debate about free will and determinism, and reductionism. The possession of free will is a fundamental aspect of our common-sense concept of a person. Therefore, any theory calling itself psychological must have something to say about this issue.

Equally, belief (or not) in the independence of psychological from neurophysiological explanations of behaviour is crucial to the survival of Psychology itself as a separate discipline. According to Hegarty (2000), *psychoneuroimmunology* (discussed in Chapter 12 in relation to stress) offers a:

> *... middle ground for mind–body monists and dualists to meet upon. Scientific research has given us insight into the complex realm of psychophysiology – the interface ... between body and mind and in which the emotions figure large ...*

Chapter Summary

- Our intuitive belief in **free will** conflicts with the scientific belief in **determinism**. While free will implies having a mind, the things we do with our minds may themselves be determined.
- Free will is an ambiguous concept and can denote **having a choice, not being coerced** or **constrained, voluntary behaviour** and **deliberate control**. The more automatic our behaviours, the weaker our subjective experience of freedom becomes.
- Stimulation of the brains of conscious patients supports the view that free will is part of our experience of being a person. This is demonstrated by **psychological reactance** and **intrinsic motivation/ self-determination.**
- Definitions of abnormality, and the diagnosis/ treatment of mental disorders, often involve judgements about free will. **Diminished responsibility** is a legally acceptable defence (for murder).
- James distinguished between **soft** and **hard determinism**, the former allowing **conscious mental life (CML)** to be the immediate cause of behaviour.
- Freud extended the law of determinism to mental phenomena (**psychic determinism**). His concept of **overdetermination** allows the conscious mind a role in influencing behaviour, and he often tried to interpret the **meaning** of patients' thoughts and behaviours (rather than looking for causes).
- Skinner's **radical behaviourism** involves a rejection of **explanatory fictions,** such as free will and other mentalistic terms. The **illusion of free will** survives because the environmental causes of behaviour are often hidden from us.
- Rogers stressed **self-actualisation, psychological growth** and the **freedom to choose**. But he also argued that science shows people to be complex machines and not free. The **fully functioning person** chooses to act the way s/he must.
- **Sociobiologists**, by explaining all individual and social behaviour in terms of genes selected through evolution, seem to deny guilt and responsibility. But this involves a **false dichotomy** between biological and cultural/social.
- According to Rose *et al.*, what makes humans unique is that our biology has made us into creatures who are constantly recreating our own psychic and material environments.
- According to Dennett, determinism isn't the same as **fatalism**, and conscious life is a crucial **design feature** of human beings.
- Although the ultimate aim of **reductionism** is to account for all phenomena (including psychological) in terms of microphysics, any attempt to explain something in terms of its components is reductionist.
- Rose identifies **reductionism as methodology, theory reduction, philosophical** and **ideology (neurogenetic determinism)**.
- From a strictly scientific perspective, it should be impossible for a non-physical mind to influence the physical brain. However, from an **evolutionary** perspective, consciousness should be able to produce behaviour change.
- Theories of the **mind–brain relationship** are either **dualist** or **monist**. Dualist theories include Descartes' original dualism, **epiphenomenology, interactionism** and **psychophysical parallelism**.
- Monist theories include **mentalism/idealism, peripheralist materialism** (such as Skinner's radical

behaviourism) and **centralist materialism/mind–brain identity theory**.

- Skinner's definition of mental phenomena as **covert/internal actions** is reductionist, as is **eliminative materialism**. The latter confuses **type** with **token identity.**
- **Emergent properties** (such as intelligence and consciousness) reflect the activity of the brain as a system and couldn't possibly be predicted from analysis of its components.
- While most materialists are also reductionists, some argue that Psychology and Neurophysiology constitute distinct **levels of description/universes of discourse,** which cannot replace each other. Freud, for example, believed in the **autonomy of psychological explanation**.

Links with Other Topics/Chapters

Chapter 13 ⟶ *Divided attention* is contrasted with *selective* (or *focused*) *attention*. These refer to the mechanisms that determine what we become consciously aware of at any one time, and how much information we can process at the same time, respectively

Chapter 46 ⟶ The issues of diminished responsibility and moral accountability are related to research showing brain abnormalities in *murderers* and other *offenders* with *antisocial personality disorder* (APD)

Chapter 45 ⟶ Free association is one of the therapeutic techniques involved in Freud's *psychoanalysis*

Chapters 45 and 48 ⟶ The behaviour therapist's dilemma is closely related to some of the most fundamental *ethical issues* faced by Psychologists as *agents of change*

Chapter 3 ⟶ Together with *positivism*, *mechanism*, *determinism* and *empiricism*, reductionism represents part of '*classical*' *science*

Recommended Reading

Gross, R. (2014) *Themes, Issues and Debates in Psychology* (4th edn). London: Hodder Education. Chapters 6 and 7.

Rose, S. (1997) *Lifelines: Biology, Freedom, Determinism.* Harmondsworth: Penguin Books.

Valentine, E.R. (1992) *Conceptual Issues in Psychology* (2nd edn). London: Routledge. Also useful for Chapter 3.

Useful Websites

http://serendip.brynmawr.edu/Mind/ ('Mind and Body: René Descartes to William James', by R.H. Wozniak, 1992)

www.leaderu.com/truth/2truth03.html ('Minds Are Simply What Brains Do'. By M. Minsky, *Truth Journal*, 2002)

http://carbon.ucdenver.edu/~mryder/itc_data/cogsci.html (Celebrities in Cognitive Science: links to large number of leading figures in Cognitive Psychology, philosophy and related fields. So relevant to many textbook chapters.)

CHAPTER 50

NATURE AND NURTURE

Nativism, empiricism and interactionism

INTRODUCTION and OVERVIEW

The debate concerning the influence of nature and nurture (or heredity and environment) on human behaviour is one of the longest-running, and most controversial, both inside and outside Psychology. It deals with some of the most fundamental questions that human beings (at least those from western cultures) ask about themselves, such as 'How do we come to be the way we are?' and 'What makes us develop in the way we do?'

These and similar questions have been posed (sometimes explicitly, sometimes implicitly) throughout this book in relation to a wide range of topics. These include perceptual abilities (Chapter 16), language acquisition (Chapter 19), aggression (Chapter 29), attachment (Chapter 32), gender development (Chapter 36), intelligence (Chapter 41), and schizophrenia and depression (Chapter 44). In some of these examples (such as language and perception), the focus of the debate is on an ability shared by *all human beings*, while in others (such as intelligence and schizophrenia) the focus is on *individual differences*.

In both cases, however, certain assumptions are made about the exact meaning of 'nature' and 'nurture', as well as about how they're related. By distinguishing different types of environment, such as shared and non-shared, it's easier to understand the relationship between nature and nurture, including *gene–environment correlation* and *gene–environment interaction*.

NATIVISM, EMPIRICISM AND INTERACTIONISM

Nativism is the philosophical theory according to which knowledge of the world is largely innate or inborn: nature (heredity) is seen as determining certain abilities and capacities. Descartes was a 17th-century nativist theorist who, as we noted in Chapter 3, had an enormous impact on science in general, including psychology. At the opposite philosophical extreme is *empiricism*, associated mainly with 17th-century British philosophers, and even more influential on the development of psychology. A key empiricist was Locke, who believed that at birth the human mind is a *tabula rasa* (or 'blank slate'), which is gradually 'filled in' by learning and experience.

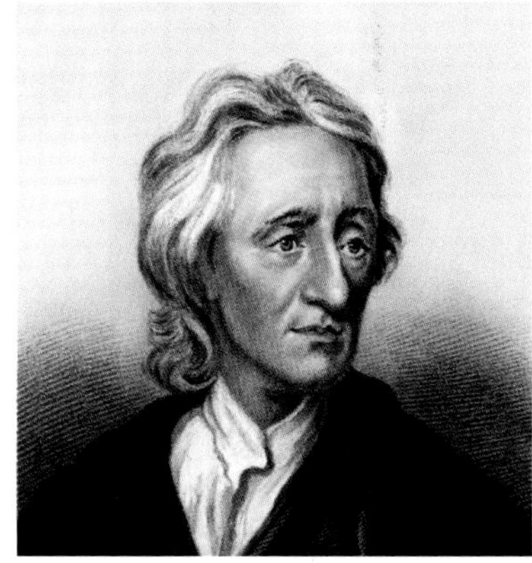

Figure 50.1 John Locke (1632–1704)

> **Ask Yourself**
>
> - Try to identify psychological (and other) theories that adopt an extreme position regarding the nature–nurture issue.
> - Which particular features of the theories made you classify them in this way?

Nativism and empiricism are *extreme* theories, trying to answer the question 'Is it nature or nurture?', as if only one or the other could be true. Early psychological theories tended to reflect these extremes, as in Gesell's concept of *maturation* and *Watson's behaviourism* (see Box 50.1).

> **Ask Yourself**
>
> - Try to identify psychological theories and areas of research in which the process of maturation plays an important role. Examples are most likely to be found in Developmental Psychology.

Box 50.1 Gesell and Watson: Two extreme viewpoints

- According to Gesell (1925), one of the American pioneers of Developmental Psychology, *maturation* refers to genetically programmed patterns of change. The instructions for these patterns are part of the specific hereditary information passed on at the moment of conception (Bee, 2000). All individuals will pass through the same series of changes, in the same order, making maturational patterns *universal* and *sequential*. They're also 'relatively impervious to environmental influence'.
- Gesell was mainly concerned with infants' psychomotor development (such as grasping and other manipulative skills), and locomotion (such as crawling and walking). These abilities are usually seen as 'developing by themselves', according to a genetically determined timetable. Provided the baby is physically normal, practice or training aren't needed – the abilities just 'unfold'.
- For Watson (1925), environmental influence is all-important (see Chapters 2 and 3), and human beings are completely malleable:

  Give me a dozen healthy infants, well-formed, and my own specialised world to bring them up in and I'll guarantee to take any one at random and train him to become any type of specialist I might select – a doctor, lawyer, artist, merchant-chief and, yes, even beggar-man and thief, regardless of his talents, penchants, abilities, vocations and race of his ancestors.
- Watson (1928) also claimed that there's no such thing as an inheritance of capacity, talent, temperament, mental constitution and character:

  The behaviourists believe that there is nothing from within to develop. If you start with the right number of fingers and toes, eyes, and a few elementary movements that are present at birth, you do not need anything else in the way of raw material to make a man, be that man genius, a cultured gentleman, a rowdy or a thug.

The concept of maturation continues to be influential within Psychology: not only does it explain major biological changes, such as puberty (see Chapter 37) and physical aspects of ageing (see Chapter 39), but all stage theories of development assume that maturation underpins the universal sequence of stages. Examples include Freud's *psychosexual theory* (see Chapter 35), Erikson's *psychosocial theory* (see Chapters 37, 38 and 39), and Piaget's *theory of cognitive development* (see Chapter 34). Watson's extreme empiricism (or *environmentalism*) was adopted in Skinner's *radical behaviourism*, which represents a major model of both normal and abnormal behaviour (see Chapters 2 and 45).

Are nativism and empiricism mutually exclusive?

As noted in Box 50.1, maturationally determined developmental sequences occur regardless of practice or training. However, as Bee (2000) points out:

> *These powerful, apparently automatic maturational patterns require at least some minimal environmental support, such as adequate diet and opportunity for movement and experimentation.*

At the very least, the environment must be *benign*, that is, it mustn't be harmful in any way, preventing the ability or characteristic from developing. More importantly, the ability or characteristic cannot develop without environmental 'input'. For example, the possession of a *language acquisition device* (LAD) (Chomsky, 1965, see Chapter 19) must be applied to the particular linguistic data provided by the child's linguistic community, so the child will acquire only *that* language (although it could just as easily have acquired *any* language).

Another example of the role of the environment involves vision. One of the proteins required for development of the visual system is controlled by a gene whose action is triggered only by visual experience (Greenough, 1991). So some visual experience is needed for the genetic programme to operate. Although every (sighted) child will have some such experience under normal circumstances, examples like these tell us that maturational sequences don't simply 'unfold'. The system appears to be 'ready' to develop along particular pathways, but it requires experience to trigger the movement (Bee, 2000).

Another way of considering the interplay between nature and nurture is to look at Freud's and Piaget's developmental theories. Although maturation underlies the sequence of stages in both theories, the role of experience is at least as important (see Box 50.2).

Both Freud's and Piaget's theories demonstrate that there's a trade-off in nature between *pre-specification*, on the one hand (e.g. maturation), and *plasticity*, on the other, leading ultimately to the kind of flexibility one finds in the human mind (Karmiloff-Smith, 1996).

Box 50.2 Nature and nurture in Freud's and Piaget's developmental theories

- For Freud, it's not the sexual instinct itself that matters, but rather the reactions of significant others (especially parents) to the child's attempts to satisfy its sexual needs. Both excessive frustration and satisfaction can produce long-term effects on the child's personality, such as fixation at particular stages of development (see Chapter 35). This makes him an *interactionist*:

  The constitutional factor must await experiences before it can make itself felt; the accidental factor must have a constitutional basis in order to come into operation ... (Freud, 1905b/1953b, cited in Miller, 2002)
- The demands of civilisation are as real as the demands of the body.
- Although Freud is commonly referred to as an instinct theorist (suggesting that he was a nativist), his concept of an instinct was very different from the earlier view of unlearned, largely automatic (pre-programmed) responses to specific stimuli (based on non-human species; see Chapters 2 and 9).
- As a biologist, Piaget stressed the role of adaptation to the environment. This involves the twin processes of *assimilation* and *accommodation*, which in turn are related to *(dis-) equilibration* (see Chapter 34). These mechanisms are part of the biological 'equipment' of human beings, without which their intelligence wouldn't change (the individual wouldn't progress through increasingly complex developmental stages).
- However, the infant actively explores its environment and constructs its own knowledge and understanding of the world (the child as scientist, Rogoff, 1990). According to Piaget (1970), intelligence consists:

  ... neither of a simple copy of external objects nor of a mere unfolding of structures preformed inside the subject, but rather ... a set of structures constructed by continuous interaction between the subject and the external world.

Another example of pre-specification is found in in-born biases. For example, very young babies already seem to understand that unsupported objects will fall (move downward), and that a moving object will continue to move in the same direction unless it encounters an obstacle (Spelke, 1991; see Chapter 16). However, these 'pre-existing conceptions' are merely the beginning of the story. What then develops is the result of experience filtered through these initial biases, which constrain the number of developmental pathways that are possible (Bee, 2000).

Figure 50.2 Annette Karmiloff-Smith (born 1938)

Both Freud and Piaget focused on interaction between biological maturation and experience with the physical world (especially Piaget) and the social world (especially Freud). Bandura's theory of *triadic reciprocal causation* (e.g. Bussey and Bandura, 1999) adds the person's *behaviour* to the interaction: one's behaviour can *change* the environment.

No Developmental Psychologists today would take the 'Is it nature or nurture?' form of the debate seriously. Essentially, every facet of a child's development is a product of some pattern of interaction between the two. Until fairly recently, however, the theoretical pendulum was well over towards the nurture/environmental end of the continuum. In the last decade or so, there's been a marked swing back towards the nature/biological end, partly because of the impact of sociobiology and its more recent off-shoot Evolutionary Psychology (see Chapter 2).

Ask Yourself

- Draw a diagram, representing a continuum, with 'extreme nativism' (nature) at one end and 'extreme empiricism' (nurture) at the other.
- Now place theories along the continuum to indicate the emphasis they give to either nature or nurture – or both.
- The theories can be drawn from any area of Psychology. They're likely to include those identified in the first 'Ask Yourself', but should also reflect the approaches discussed in Chapter 47. (Some examples are given in Figure 50.5.)

What do we mean by 'nature'?

In the *Introduction and overview*, we noted that some examples of the nature–nurture debate involve abilities or capacities common to all human beings (such as language and perception), while others involve individual differences (such as intelligence and schizophrenia). According to Plomin (1994), it's in the latter sense that the debate 'properly' takes place, and much of the rest of this chapter will reflect the 'individual differences' approach.

Within *genetics* (the science of heredity), 'nature' refers to what's typically thought of as inheritance, that is, differences in genetic material (chromosomes and genes) transmitted from parents to offspring. The 'father' of genetics, Gregor Mendel (1895), explained the difference between different genes in terms of smooth and wrinkled seeds in garden peas. Similarly, modern human genetics focuses on genetic differences between individuals, reflecting the use of the word 'nature' by Galton, who coined the phrase nature–nurture in 1883 as it's used in the scientific arena (Plomin, 1994).

Genes are the basic unit of hereditary transmission, consisting of large molecules of deoxyribonucleic acid (DNA). These are extremely complex chemical chains, comprising a ladder-like, double helix structure (discovered by Watson and Crick in 1953; see Figure 50.3). (For more details, see Gross 2012a and 2014.)

Neurogenetic determinism: are there genes 'for' anything?

Several claims have been made in recent years about the discovery of genes 'for' a wide range of complex human behaviours (*reductionism as ideology*: Rose, 1997). Related to this is what Rose calls *neurogenetic determinism*, the claim that there's a direct causal link between genes and behaviour. This involves the false assumption that causes can be classified as either genetic or environmental, and there are additional reasons for doubting the validity of neurogenetic determinism.

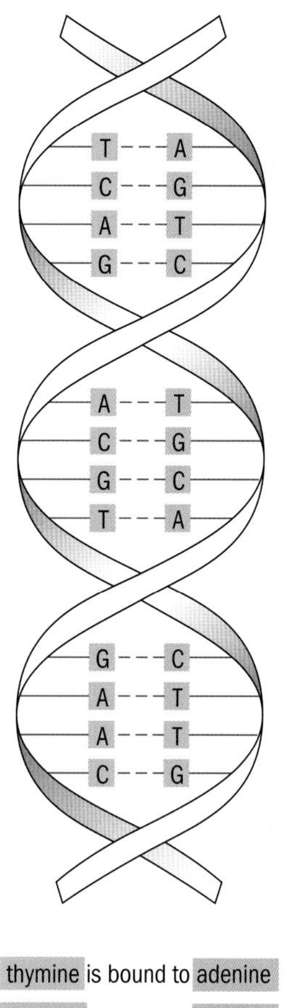

Figure 50.3 The structure of a DNA molecule represented schematically. This shows its double-stranded coiled structure and the complementary binding of nucleotide bases, guanine (G) to cytosine (C) and adenine (A) to thymine (T)

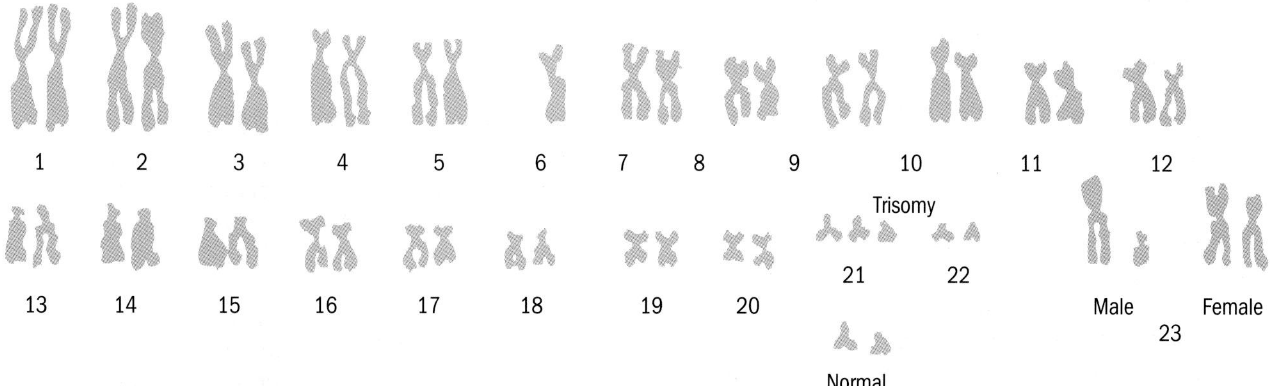

Figure 50.4 A sample karyotype. The 21st 'pair' has one too many chromosomes (trisomy: three instead of two). The 23rd chromosome pair is shown with both male and female versions (in a normal karyotype, only one such pair would be found)

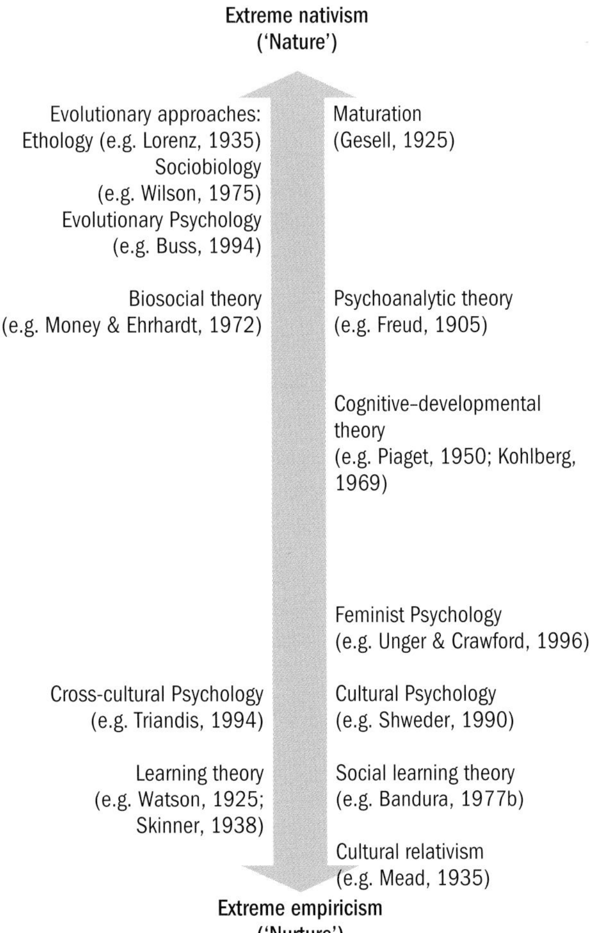

Figure 50.5 A continuum representing the position of various psychological (and other) theories on the nature–nurture debate

Objections to neurogenetic determinism

Ask Yourself

- Try to formulate some arguments against neurogenetic determinism.

- The phrase 'genes for' is a convenient, but misleading, shorthand used by geneticists. In the case of eye colour, for example (which, from a genetic point of view, is one of the more simple characteristics – or *phenotypes*), there's a difference in the biochemical pathways that lead to brown and to blue eyes. In blue-eyed people, the gene for a particular enzyme (which catalyses a chemical transformation en route to the synthesis of the pigment) is either missing or non-functional for some reason. A gene 'for blue eyes' now has to be reinterpreted as meaning 'one or more genes in whose absence the metabolic pathway that leads to pigmented eyes terminates at the blue-eye stage' (Rose, 1997).
- More generally, genes *don't* cause behaviour. They're chemical structures that have chemical effects on the body, and so influence behaviour through their effects on the body's response to the environment. So there are no genes 'for', say, neuroticism (N), although there's plenty of evidence that N is genetically influenced (such as inheriting a nervous system that's particularly sensitive to stress). Similarly, there are no genes 'for' alcoholism, but genetic factors may in some way affect the body's sensitivity to alcohol.
- Claridge and Davis (2003) make the point like this:

> *... Genes code for very precise, literally microscopic, bits of biological material (proteins) that are both physically and conceptually very distant from the complex behavioural and psychological characteristics which they are supposed to – and perhaps in some sense do – influence. But it is unlikely that there are genes, or sets of genes, 'for' impulsivity, the preference for gay relationships, religiosity, anxiety, or even serious mental disorders, such as schizophrenia. The route from genes to behaviour is likely to be much more tortuous than that and, for any particular characteristic, to involve a multitude of genes and interactions among them – as well as an interplay between genes and environmental factors ...*

- Ridley (2003) gives the example of the *FOXP2* gene (on chromosome 7); mutations in this gene cause specific language impairment, suggesting that it's necessary for the normal development of human speech and language. Yet nobody would dream of claiming that *FOXP2 determines* speech:

> *... Rather, it allows the human mind to absorb from its early experience the learning necessary for speaking. It allows nurture ... (Ridley, 2003)*

- The search for genes that 'cause' specific behaviours or characteristics is called *molecular genetic research* (MGR). According to Joseph (2003), there are two major reasons why we shouldn't expect MGR in psychiatry or Psychology to provide much useful information – now or in the future:
  1. It presupposes that family, twin and adoption studies have demonstrated the role of genetic factors; the serious limitations of these methods are discussed in Chapter 41.
  2. Proponents of MGR claim that techniques such as gene therapy can be used to prevent or cure

diseases influenced by identified genes; this is a commendable goal, but does society wish to use this technology to alter 'intelligence genes' or those associated with unpleasant personalities?

Critical Discussion 50.1

The ethics of MGR

It's understandable that researchers would want to alleviate the suffering of those with, say, schizophrenia to help restore them to productive lives. But even if we accept the behaviour genetic argument that genes exert an important influence on behaviour and IQ differences, we could still question the necessity of trying to identify the genes involved.

According to Plomin *et al.* (1977):

Psychology is at the dawn of a new era in which molecular genetic techniques will revolutionise genetic research in psychology by identifying specific genes that contribute to genetic variance for complex dimensions and disorders ... The breathtaking pace of molecular genetics ... leads us to predict that psychologists will routinely use DNA markers as a toll in their research to identify some of the relevant genetic differences among individuals.

But although behaviour genetic researchers continue to look for 'IQ genes', Joseph (2003) believes the search has been unsuccessful. Despite this failure, Plomin (1999) expects that he'll eventually succeed, and that he'll find genetic differences along race and social class lines. For Joseph:

... The point is not whether group differences in intelligence genes will be found – they won't – but rather the cavalier way in which investigators minimise the potential social impact of their research. Would Plomin have the same attitude if his research, for example, found that more Jews than non-Jews had ... [genes] ... associated with greed? Wouldn't there be a justifiable uproar that such research was even being done?

We've just identified another example of socially sensitive research (SSR) (see Chapter 48).

- MGR also presupposes that the phenotypes (whether mental disorders or intelligence) are 'real' and can be reliably and validly identified and measured. But how, for example, can 'schizophrenia susceptibility genes' (in reality, a mere association between 'schizophrenia' and genetic markers – not the same as finding an actual gene) be found when American psychiatrists cannot 'figure out who really is schizophrenic or what schizophrenia really is' (DeLisi *et al.* (2002), cited in Joseph, 2003)? (See Chapters 43 and 44.)

What do we mean by 'nurture'?

Ask Yourself

- What do you understand by the term 'environment'?
- Try to identify different uses of the term and different 'levels' at which the environment exists.

When the term 'environment' is used in a psychological context, it usually refers to all those *postnatal* influences (or potential sources of influence) lying *outside/external* to the individual's body. These include other people (both family and others), opportunities for intellectual stimulation, and the physical circumstances of the individual's life ('environs' or 'surroundings'). These influences are implicitly seen as impinging on a passive individual, who is *shaped* by them.

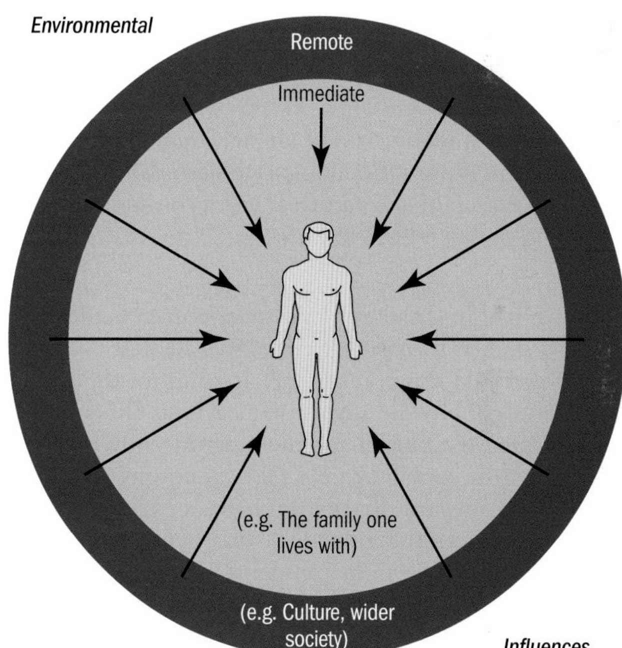

Figure 50.6 Traditional, extreme behaviourist/environmentalist view of the environment as a set of external, postnatal influences acting upon a purely passive individual

On all three counts, this view of the environment seems inadequate. It isn't just the individual person who's 'immersed in' or influenced by his/her environment, but during *mitosis* the specific location of any particular cell is constantly changing as the cluster of cells of which it's a part constantly grows. At an even more micro-level, the environment of the cell nucleus (which contains the DNA) is the cytoplasm (see Figure 50.7).

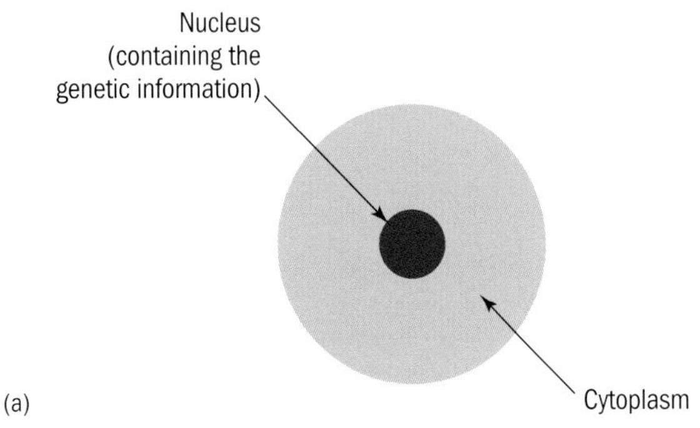

Nucleus
(containing the
genetic information)
Cytoplasm
(a)

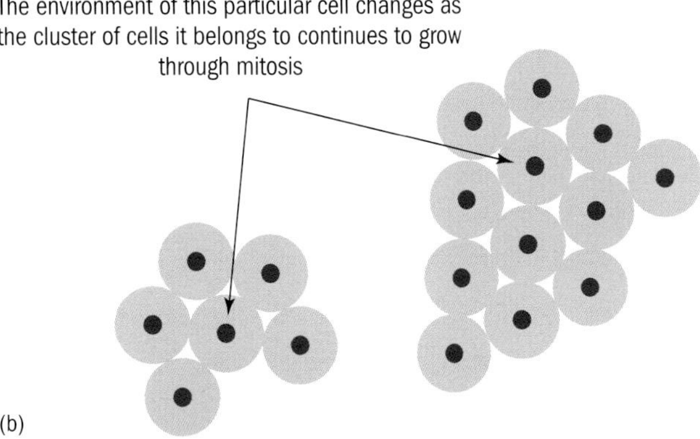

The environment of this particular cell changes as
the cluster of cells it belongs to continues to grow
through mitosis
(b)

Figure 50.7 For the nucleus of an individual cell, the environment is the surrounding cytoplasm (a). The specific location of any particular cell is constantly changing during mitosis (b)

As we noted in Chapter 41, prenatal non-genetic factors (such as the mother's excessive alcohol consumption during pregnancy) account for the largest proportion of biologically caused learning difficulties and lowered IQ. Finally, and most significantly, not only is 'nature' and 'nurture' a false dichotomy, but it's invalid to regard the environment as existing independently of the individual (that is, objectively). Not only do people's environments influence them, but people make their own environments (Scarr, 1992, see Box 50.3). A way of thinking about how people do this is through the concept of *non-shared environments*, which, in turn, is related to *gene–environment correlation*.

Shared and non-shared environments

When the environment is discussed as a set of (potential) influences that impinge on the individual, it's often broken down into factors such as overcrowding, poverty, socio-economic status (SES), family break-up, marital discord, and so on. In studies of intelligence, for example, children are often compared in terms of these environmental factors: children from low SES groups are commonly found to have lower IQs than those from high SES groups (see Chapter 41).

When families are compared in this way, it's assumed that children from the same family will all be similarly and equally affected by those environmental factors (*shared environment*). But for the majority of characteristics, most children within the same family aren't very similar; in fact, they're often extremely varied in personality, abilities and psychological disorders. This observation is most striking when two adopted children are brought up in the same family: they're usually no more alike than any two people chosen at random from the general population (Plomin, 1996; Rutter and Rutter, 1992).

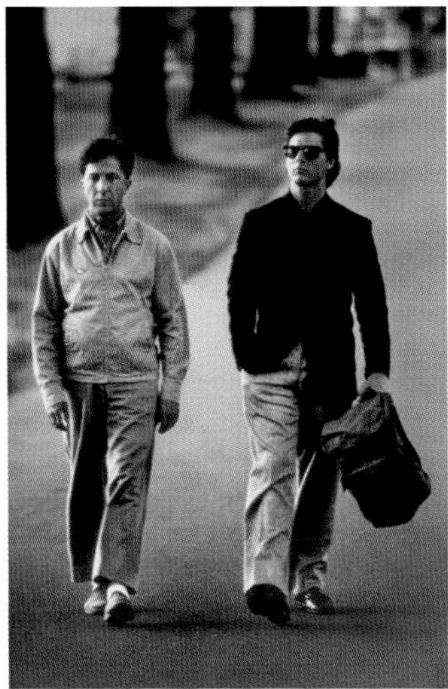

Figure 50.8 Dustin Hoffman as the autistic brother of Tom Cruise in *Rain Man*. Both genetic and non-shared environmental factors are likely to have contributed to their different characteristics and abilities

This substantial *within-family variation* doesn't mean that family environment is unimportant. Rather, as Plomin (1996) puts it, environmental influences in development are doled out on an *individual-by-individual* basis rather than on a *family-by-family basis*. In other words, differences between children growing up together is exactly what we'd expect to find, because it's the *non-shared environment* which has greater influence on development than the shared environment: different children in the same family have different experiences. For example, Dunn and Plomin (1990) found that the ways in which parents respond differently to their different children (*relative differences*) are likely to be much more influential than the overall characteristics of the family (*absolute differences*). So, it may matter very little whether children are brought up in a home that's less loving or more punitive than average, whereas it may matter considerably that one child receives less affection or more punishment than his/her sibling. These findings imply that:

> *... the unit of environmental transmission is not the family, but rather micro-environments within families ... (Plomin and Thompson, 1987)*

See Critical Discussion 50.2.

Figure 50.9 Differences within the same family may be more important than those between different families

Gene–environment correlations

The concept of non-shared environments helps explain how the environment influences development, which is far more sophisticated and useful than the original 'Is it nature or nurture?' question (see above). However, we need to understand the processes by which non-shared environments arise: why do parents treat their different children differently, and how do children in the same family come to have different experiences? In trying to answer these questions, Psychologists and behaviour geneticists (see below) have, paradoxically, stressed the role of *genetic differences*. A major example of this approach is the concept of *gene–environment* correlation.

Critical Discussion 50.2

Are shared environments really that unimportant?

Scarr (1992) acknowledges the influence of the environment on behaviour, but claims that, in reality, the environment is very similar for many individuals. According to the 'average expectable environment', assuming a 'normal' environment, genes will express their potential. Environmental variations within the normal range are *functionally equivalent*: provided the environment is 'normal', environmental changes (such as extra stimulation as provided by early enrichment programmes, see Chapter 41) will have no effect. Only if the environment is outside the range of normality (such as in abusive families), will such change significantly alter behavioural outcomes.

Scarr's theory implies that children could be reassigned to and brought up by different families, without significantly affecting how they turn out. For example, differences in parenting style make little difference, provided the parents are 'good enough'. But Scarr doesn't specify what she means by 'good enough' parenting, and 'All non-abusive environments above the poverty line are not equally facilitative of healthy development' (Baumrind, 1993).

Scarr accepted that her theory depends on children experiencing a broad range of environments, but she excluded individuals with disadvantaged circumstances and restricted life choices (Slee and Shute, 2003). For Baumrind (1993), such 'excluded' individuals are in fact the norm worldwide: the absence of disadvantage isn't the same as having a rich environment.

Also, what's 'normal 'or 'expectable' in one culture is totally unacceptable in another (Baumrind, 1993). (See Chapter 47.)

Box 50.3 Gene–environment correlations

Plomin *et al.* (1977) identified three types of gene–environment correlation.

Passive gene–environment correlations: Children passively inherit from their parents environments that are correlated with their genetic tendencies. For example, parents of above-average IQ are likely to provide a more intellectually stimulating environment than lower-IQ parents.

Reactive gene–environment correlations: Children's experiences derive from the reactions of other people to the children's genetic tendencies. For example, babies with a sunny, cheerful disposition/temperament are more likely to elicit friendly reactions from others than miserable or 'difficult' babies (see Key Study 50.1). It's widely accepted that some children are easier to love (Rutter and Rutter, 1992).

Active gene–environment correlations: Children construct and reconstruct experiences consistent with their genetic tendencies. Trying to define the environment independently of the person is futile, since every person's experience is different. According to Plomin (1994):

> *Socially, as well as cognitively, children select, modify and even create their experiences. Children select environments that are rewarding or at least comfortable, niche-picking. Children modify their environments by setting the background tone for interactions, by initiating behaviour, and by altering the impact of environments . . . they can create environments with their own propensities, niche-building.*

Gene–environment interactions

Another way of considering the environment's impact is to identify examples of *gene–environment interactions.*

Genetically speaking, *phenylketonuria* (PKU) is a simple characteristic: a bodily disorder caused by the inheritance of a single recessive gene from each parent. Normally, the body produces the amino acid phenylalanine hydroxylase, which converts phenylalanine (a substance found in many foods, particularly dairy products) into tyrosine. But in the presence of the two recessive PKU genes, this process fails and phenylalanine builds up in the blood, depressing the levels of other amino acids. Consequently, the developing nervous system is deprived of essential nutrients, leading to severe mental retardation and, without intervention, proves fatal (see Chapter 40).

The relationship between what the child inherits (the two PKU genes – the *genotype*) and the actual signs and symptoms of the disease (high levels of phenylalanine in the blood, and mental retardation – the *phenotype*) appears to be straightforward, direct, and inevitable: given the genotype, the phenotype will occur. However, a routine blood test soon after birth can detect the presence of the PKU genes, and an affected baby will be put on a low-phenylalanine diet. This prevents the disease from developing: an environmental intervention will prevent the phenotype from occurring. According to Jones (1993):

> *[The] nature [of children born with PKU genes] has been determined by careful nurturing and there is no simple answer to the question of whether their genes or their environment is more important to their well-being.*

Ask Yourself

- **Try to identify some examples of gene–environment interactions that involve behaviour, as distinct from bodily diseases, such as PKU. Two relevant areas are intelligence (Chapter 41) and schizophrenia (Chapter 44).**

If there's no one-to-one relationship between genotype and phenotype in the case of PKU, it's highly likely that there'll be an even more complex interaction in the case of intelligence, certain mental disorders, personality, and so on. One such example is *cumulative deficit* (discussed in Chapter 41). Another is the concept of *facilitativeness*.

According to Horowitz (1987, 1990), a highly *facilitative* environment is one in which the child has loving and responsive parents, and is provided with a rich array of stimulation. When different levels of facilitativeness are combined with a child's initial vulnerabilities/susceptibilities, there's an interaction effect. For example, a resilient child (one with many protective factors and a few vulnerabilities) may do quite well in a poor environment. Equally, a non-resilient child may do quite well in a highly facilitative environment. Only the non-resilient child in a poor environment will do really poorly (see Figure 50.6).

This *interactionist* view is supported by a 30-year longitudinal study that took place on the Hawaiian island of Kanuai.

Ask Yourself

- **In what ways can culture be thought of as an environmental influence on an individual's behaviour?**
- **Try to identify examples from different areas of Psychology, but Chapter 47 might be a good place to begin.**

Behaviour genetics and heritability

Behaviour genetics

According to Pike and Plomin (1999), behaviour geneticists attempt to quantify how much of the variability for any given trait (such as intelligence, aggressiveness, or schizophrenia) can be attributed to (a) genetic differences between people (*heritability*), (b) shared environments, and (c) non-shared environments. The heritability of intelligence was discussed in Chapter 41, as were the two major methods used by behaviour genetics, namely twin studies and adoption studies (also see Chapter 44).

If genetic factors are important for a trait, identical twins (MZs) will be more similar than non-identical twins (DZs). To the extent that twin similarity cannot be attributed to genetic factors, the shared environment is implicated. To the extent that MZs differ within pairs, non-shared environmental factors are implicated. Because adopted siblings are genetically unrelated to their adoptive family members, the degree of similarity between them is a direct measure of shared environmental influence (Pike and Plomin, 1999).

One interesting finding from behaviour genetic research is that the effects of a shared environment seem to *decrease* over time. In a 10-year longitudinal study of over 200 pairs of adoptive siblings, Loehlin *et al.* (1988) found that at an average age of 8 years, the correlation for IQ was 0.26. This is similar to other studies of young adoptive siblings, and suggests that shared environment makes an important contribution at this age. However, by age 18 the correlation was close to zero. According to Pike and Plomin (1999):

> *These results represent a dramatic example of the importance of genetic research for understanding the environment. Shared environment is important for [general intelligence] during childhood when children are living at home. However, its importance fades in adolescence as influences outside the family become more salient.*

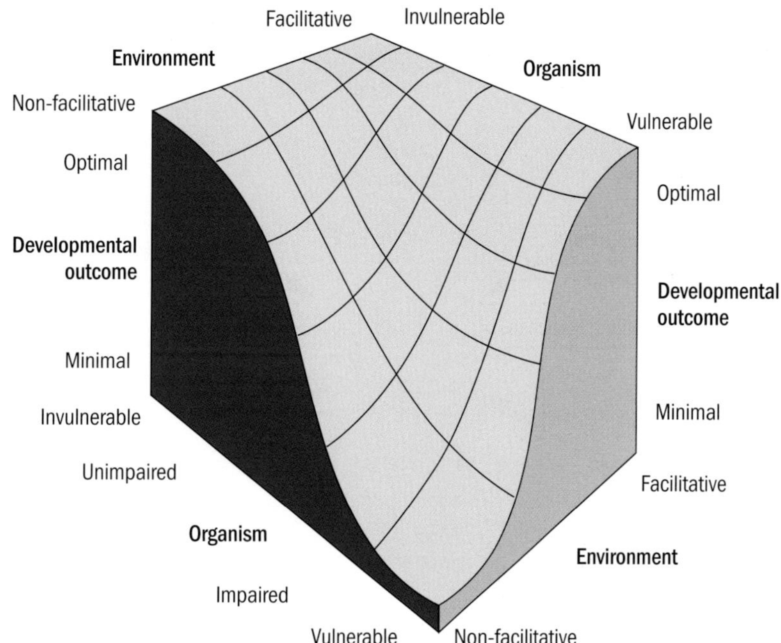

Figure 50.10 Horowitz's model of the interaction of a child's environment with protective factors and vulnerabilities. The surface of the curve illustrates the level of a developmental stage, such as IQ or social skills. If a low-birthweight child is reared in a poor environment, then it's likely to do less well than other children reared with a different combination of vulnerabilities and environment

Key Study 50.1

Werner's 'Children of the Garden Island'

- Starting in 1955, Werner and her colleagues studied all of the nearly 700 children born on Kanuai in a given period, and followed them up at the ages of 2, 10, 18 and 31–32.
- Werner became interested in 72 'high-risk'/'vulnerable' children. They'd been exposed before the age of 2 years to four or more of the following risk factors: reproductive stress (either difficulties during pregnancy and/or during labour and delivery), and discordant and impoverished home lives (including divorce, uneducated, alcoholic or mentally disturbed parents). Despite their early exposure to these risk factors, these children went on to develop healthy personalities, stable careers and strong interpersonal relationships.
- As babies, these resilient children were typically described as 'active', 'affectionate', 'cuddly', 'easy-going' and 'even tempered', with no eating or sleeping habits causing distress to their carers. These are all temperamental characteristics that elicit positive responses from both family members and strangers.
- There were also environmental differences between the resilient and non-resilient children, such as smaller family size, at least two years between themselves and the next child, and a close attachment to at least one carer (relative or regular babysitter). They also received considerable emotional support from outside the family, were popular with their peers, and had at least one close friend. School became a refuge from a disordered household.
- Sixty-two of the resilient children were studied after reaching their 30s. As a group, they seemed to be coping well with the demands of adult life. A total of 75 per cent had received some college education, nearly all had full-time jobs and were satisfied with their work. According to Werner (1989):

As long as the balance between stressful life events and protective factors is favourable, successful adaptation is possible. When stressful events outweigh the protective factors, however, even the most resilient child can have problems.

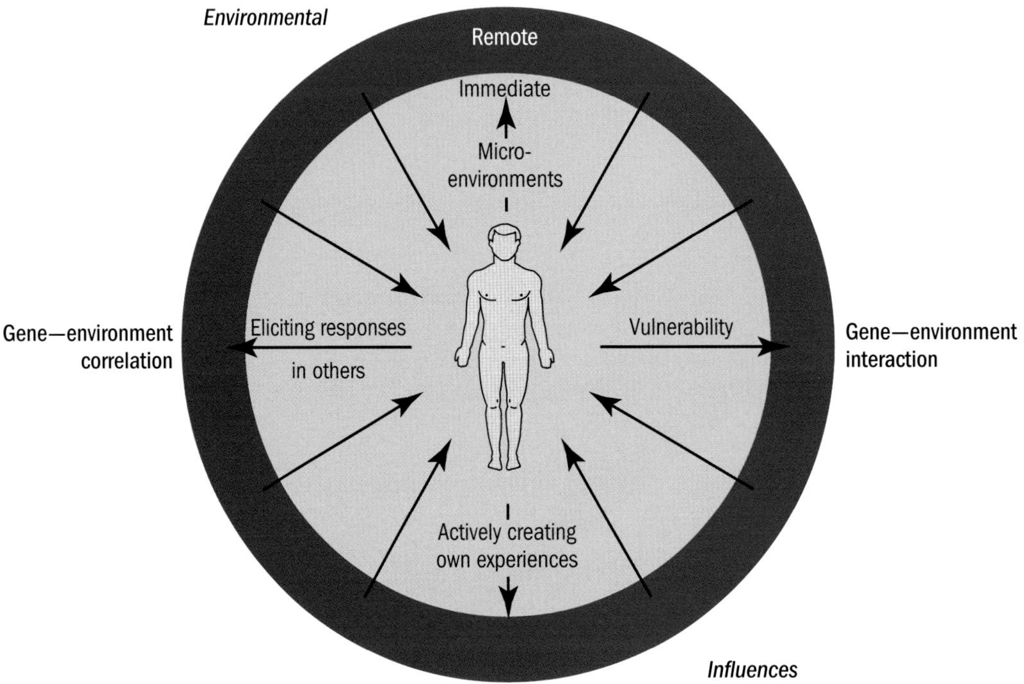

Figure 50.11 The postnatal, sociocultural environment, with the individual portrayed as actively influencing the environment as much as s/he is influenced by it

This conclusion might at first appear paradoxical, yet behaviour genetics provides the best available evidence for the importance of *non-genetic* factors in behavioural development (Plomin, 1995). For example, the concordance rate of MZs for schizophrenia is 40 per cent, which means that most pairs are discordant for diagnosed schizophrenia (see Chapter 44). While there can be no genetic explanation for this, 20 years ago the message from behaviour genetics research was that genetic factors play the major role. Today, the message is that these same data provide strong evidence for the importance of environmental factors as well as genetic factors (Plomin, 1995). Additionally, the data from twin studies are open to interpretation because not all MZs are equally identical. This is due to certain critical prenatal environmental factors (Ceci and Williams, 1999). (See Critical Discussion 50.3.)

Heritability

Heritability is one of the most controversial concepts in Psychology (Ceci and Williams, 1999). It tells us what proportion of individual differences within a population (*variance*) can be attributed to genes. However, this doesn't mean that 'biology is destiny'. Indeed, as also noted above, behaviour genetics has helped confirm the importance of environmental factors, which generally account for as much variance in human behaviour as do genes (Plomin and DeFries, 1998). Even when genetic factors do have an especially powerful effect, as in PKU, environmental interventions can often fully or partly overcome the genetic 'determinants'.

According to Ceci and Williams (1999):

> *Heritability estimates are highly situational: they are descriptions of the relative contributions of genes and environments to the expression of a trait in a specific group, place and time. Such estimates tell us nothing about the relative contributions if the group, place or time is changed.*

Ask Yourself

- Based on your reading of this chapter, what conclusions would you draw about the influence of nature and nurture?

CONCLUSIONS

According to Ceci and Williams (1999):

> *Nearly all responsible researchers agree that human traits are jointly determined by both nature and nurture, although they may disagree about the relative contributions of each.*

They also point out that not all biological influences on development are genetic: some are critical features of the intrauterine environment that are sometimes mistaken for genetic influences. So, 'biological' doesn't

Critical Discussion 50.3

Epigenetics: Beyond nature and nurture

Just when it seemed that a consensus was emerging regarding the inevitable – and necessary – interaction of genes and environment, twin research is showing that there's more to the debate than these two sets of factors. Similarly, the 'received wisdom' has been that identical twins (MZs) are, as the term conveys, genetically identical. However, evidence is emerging that challenges these twin beliefs (pun intended!).

Some of this evidence comes from the UK Adult Twin Registry, started in 1993 and comprising 10,000 white MZs and DZs, aged 16–85 years. The focus has been primarily on five areas of physical disease, plus the ageing process (Spector and Williams, 2006).

While twin studies have played an essential role in estimating phenotypic heritability (see Chapter 41 and text above), they now offer an opportunity to study *epigenetic variability* (EV) as a dynamic quantitative trait (Bell and Spector, 2011).

Basically, EV refers to differences between otherwise identical individuals, specifically, differences in the phenotypes of MZs. For example, there's only a 30 per cent chance that if one MZ develops heart disease the other one will as well. Trying to explain how these differences occur is throwing new light on how genes and environment interact. Put simply, environmental events can cause changes in genes, leading to phenotypic differences between MZs.

A key environmental process involved in epigenetics is *methylation:* methyl is a chemical which floats around inside our cells, attaching itself to our DNA. When it does so, it can inhibit or turn down the activity of a gene and block it from making a particular version of a protein. Crucially, all sorts of life events can affect DNA methylation levels in the body, including diet, illnesses, ageing, environmental chemicals, smoking, drugs and medications. So, MZs who inherit an identical *genome* can develop different *epigenomes*, which then produce different phenotypes, such as differences in pain tolerance and depression (McKie, 2013; Bell and Spector, 2011).

Perhaps even more intriguingly, differences in methylation are being linked to differences in *behaviour*. For example, one MZ sister was a danger-defying war journalist, while her co-twin was a risk-averse office manager; differences were found in a gene implicated in stress and anxiety (Pilcher, 2013). But since this evidence is only correlational, it's possible that methylation differences are the *result*, rather than the cause, of their different lifestyles. Indeed, much, if not most, EV is driven by all kinds of environmental factors both post- (see above) and *prenatal*. For example, Gordon *et al.* (2012) found unique methylation profiles in MZs born as early as 32 weeks; this could be due to subtle physical differences, such as variations in the size of their umbilical cords, or random events occurring during *mitosis* (for example, a small change in a single cell early in development could end up affecting many organs in adulthood).

mean 'genetic', and just as importantly, 'environment' can refer to biological, psychological, social and cultural influences.

In the 1950s, the extreme environmentalism of Behaviourism dominated thinking about nature–nurture, but the 1960s saw the adoption of a more balanced view. The 1980s and 1990s saw Psychology becoming much more accepting of genetic influence (Plomin, 1996). Plomin (1995) maintains that:

> *Research and theory in genetics (nature) and in environment (nurture) are beginning to converge ... the common ground is a model of active organism–environment interaction in which nature and nurture play a duet rather than one directing the performance of the other ... It is time to put the nature–nurture controversy behind us and to bring nature and nurture together in the study of development in order to understand the processes by which genotypes become phenotypes.*

For Ridley (2003), it's far more useful to think of genes as *mechanisms* of human nature rather than *causes* of it: they're cogs, not gods. Returning to the example of the *FOXP2* gene that allows us to learn language, rather than constraining our free will it *enhances* it (see Chapter 49):

> *... Even science itself expands free will. Knowing that you have an instinct makes it possible that you will decide to override that instinct. The more we learn about the genome, the more freedom we will find, and the more freedom we will gain. (Ridley, 2003)*

Chapter Summary

- The **nature–nurture debate** concerns fundamental questions about the causes of human behaviour, sometimes focusing on behaviours and abilities **shared by all human beings**, and sometimes on **individual differences**.
- **Nativists** see knowledge of the world as largely **innate**, while **empiricists** stress the role of **learning** and **experience**. These extreme viewpoints are reflected in early psychological theories, such as Gesell's **maturation** and Watson's **Behaviourism**, respectively.
- The concept of maturation continues to be influential in Psychology, as in **biological processes** such as puberty and ageing, and **stage theories** of development. Watson's **environmentalism** was adopted in Skinner's **radical behaviourism**.
- Nativism and empiricism aren't mutually exclusive. Not only must the environment be **benign**, but particular environmental input is often necessary. In both Freud's and Piaget's theories, experience is just as important as the underlying maturation. Both are **interactionists**.
- **Genetics** is the science of heredity; **genes** are the basic units of hereditary transmission.
- **Neurogenetic determinism** makes the false assumption that causes can be classified as either genetic or environmental. Also, the phrase 'genes for' is a convenient but misleading shorthand for complex biochemical processes.
- The term **'environment'** is commonly used to refer to **postnatal influences** lying outside the body of a passive individual who's shaped by them. However, people also make their own environments, and for most characteristics, the **shared environment** seems to have little impact on development compared with the **non-shared environment**.
- Two ways in which non-shared environments arise are **gene–environment correlations** and **gene–environment interactions**.
- PKU illustrates the lack of a one-to-one relationship between **genotype** and **phenotype**. Other examples include **cumulative deficit** and Horowitz's concept of **facilitativeness**.
- **Behaviour genetics** attempts to quantify how much of the **variability** for any particular trait is due to heritability, shared environments, and non-shared environments.
- **Heritability estimates** describe the relative contributions of genes and environment for particular traits, in a specific population, at a particular place and time.
- A key **environmental** process involved in **epigenetic variability** (EV) is **methylation**. This can account for different **epigenomes** between MZs.
- Human traits are determined by **both** nature and nurture. Where researchers may still disagree is over the **relative contributions** of each, and the specific genetic and environmental **mechanisms** involved.

Links with Other Topics/Chapters

Chapter 41 ⟶ Phenylketonuria (PKU) is especially relevant to discussion of individual differences in *intelligence*

Chapter 49 ⟶ Neurogenetic determinism is one of four major kinds of *determinism* identified by Rose

Chapters 42 and 49 ⟶ According to Claridge and Davis (2003), the reason for taking an interest in the genetic effects on individual differences *isn't* to *reduce* everything to heredity but to see where such influences fit into the larger picture about personality

Chapters 47 and 49 ⟶ According to Joseph (2003), in the MGR literature it's striking how little attention is paid to people's social environment as a cause of 'mental illness'. The causes are viewed as residing at the molecular level, epitomising the *reductionist view* of human problems and also illustrating *individualism*

Chapter 29 ⟶ An example of reactive gene–environment correlation is the observation that *aggressive children* tend to experience *aggressive environments* because they tend to evoke aggressive responses in others

Recommended Reading

Ceci, S.J. & Williams, W.M. (eds) (1999) *The Nature–Nurture Debate: The Essential Readings.* Oxford: Blackwell.

Grigorenko, E.L. & Sternberg, R.J. (2003) The nature–nurture issue. In A. Slater & G. Bremner (eds). *An Introduction to Developmental Psychology.* Oxford: Blackwell Publishing.

Pinker, S. (2002) *The Blank Slate.* London: Penguin.

Plomin, R. (1994) *Genetics and Experience: The Interplay Between Nature and Nurture.* Thousand Oaks, CA: Sage Publications.

Ridley, M. (2003) *Nature Via Nurture: Genes, Experience and What Makes Us Human.* London: Fourth Estate. Also relevant to Chapter 49.

Useful Websites

www.sanger.ac.uk (Wellcome Trust: Sanger Institute (genome project))

www.ucmp.berkeley.edu/history/evolution.html (University of California Museum of Palaeontology/ UCMP Exhibit Halls: Evolution. Also, useful link to 'Understanding Science': see textbook Chapter 3)

www.kumc.edu/gec (Genetics Education Center: University of Kansas Medical Center)

http://genetics.nature.com

www.guardian.co.uk/genes

http://en.wikipedia.org/wiki/Nature_versus_nurture

www.youtube.com/watch?v=F9EN0YbEoF8 (2014 documentary on feral/'wild' children)

ACKNOWLEDGEMENTS

I'd like to thank all those involved in the planning and production of this (very large) textbook. These include Francesca Naish, for whom this edition is her first commissioning task involving *The Science of Mind & Behaviour*, Hannah Ormiston, for her expert project management and all-round help and support, and all those copy editors who do such a vital job and spot things I think I have but haven't. Thanks too for another great cover design and the page design ain't half bad either!

Richard Gross

The author and publisher would like to thank the following for permission to reproduce material in this book:

Photo credits

p.1 *t* © Jon Berkeley/Getty Images; **p.4** © Zephyr/Science Photo Library; **p.6** *t* © Monkey Business – Fotolia.com, *b* © Ulrike Preuss/Photofusion; **p.7** © Sally & Richard Greenhill; **p.8** © Monkey Business – Fotolia.com; **p.9** *l* © Brian Lee/Corbis; **p.10** Courtesy of the British Psychological Society; **p.11** © Graham Waters/CartoonStock; **p.13** © Igor Mojzes – Fotolia; **p.16** © AP/Press Association Images; **p.18** *t* © George Disario/ Corbis, *b* © Bettmann/Corbis; *tl* © Bettmann/Corbis, *tr* © Bettmann/Corbis, *bl* © National Library Of Medicine/Science Photo Library, *br* © Bettmann/Corbis; **p.22** © Bettmann/Corbis; **p.23** *l* © Roger Ressmeyer/Corbis, *l* © Robert Lerich – Fotolia.com; **p.25** © Dr Debbie Joffe Ellis; **p.27** *t* © Sophie Bassouls/ Sygma/Corbis, *b* © REX/Adrian Brooks; **p.28** *t* © Viv Burr, *b* © Mat Hayward – Fotolia.com; **p.29** © William B. Plowman/Getty Images; **p.31** © akg-images; **p.32** *t* © Lance Workman, *b* © Pat Flanagan – Fotolia.com; **p.33** © ColorBlind/Getty Images; **p.34** © Rick Friedman/Corbis; **p.37** *t* © SSPL/Getty Images, *b* © Alfredo Dagli Orti/The Art Archive/Corbis; **p.38** © Bettmann/ Corbis; **p.39** *tl* © Bettmann/Corbis, *bl* © Bettmann/Corbis, *l* © Underwood & Underwood/Corbis; **p.45** © Stephen Ausmus/Us Department Of Agriculture/Science Photo Library; **p.47** Reproduced with permission © 2015 Scientific American, Inc. All rights reserved; **p.51** © pankajstock123 – Fotolia; **p.57** *bl* © 1947, The Royal Society, *l* © Aj Photo/Hop Americain/Science Photo Library; **p.58** (b) © Scott Camazine/Science Photo Library, (d) © Sovereign, ISM/Science Photo Library, (f) ©CNRI/Science Photo Library; **p.67** (a) © Kevin Peterson/ Photodisc/Getty Images, (b) © John Birdsall Photography; **p.74** © Eric Pearle/Getty Images; **p.79** *l* © Dario Principe – Fotolia.com, *l* © Susan Flashman – Fotolia.com; **p.89** © Donald Cooper/REX; **p.92** *all* © Susan Blackmore; **p.93** © Adam Hart-Davis/Science Photo Library; **p.96** © Jeremy Walker/ Science Photo Library; **p.105** © Salvador Dali, Fundació Gala-Salvador Dalí, DACS, 2015., Photo : Sleep, 1937 (oil on canvas) 88: Le Sommeil, Dali, Salvador (1904-89)/Ex-Edward James Foundation, Sussex, UK/Bridgeman Images; **p.107** © The Granger Collection/TopFoto; **p.112** © Charly – Fotolia.com; **p.113** © Bettmann/Corbis; **p.117** © Ed Young/Science Photo Library; **p.125** © bunyos – Fotolia; **p.127** © ShowBizIreland/ Getty Images; **p.128** © REX/Steve Richards; **p.130** *t* © Mark Griffiths; **p.130** *b* © ricky_68fr – Fotolia; **p.131** © Orlando Florin Rosu – Fotolia; **p.134** © Julian Smith/Corbis; **p.135** *l* © Mario Anzuoni/Reuters/Corbis, *r* © Douglas Kirkland/Corbis; **p.143** © Reuters/Corbis; **p.145** © Tyler Olson – Fotolia; **p.149** *t* © Joe Gough – Fotolia, *b* © Joe Gough – Fotolia; **p.150** From Crooks. Psychology Science, Behaviour, and Life, 2[e], 1991 Wadsworth, a part of Cengage Learning, Inc © Neal E. Miller; **p.154** *t* © University of Wisconsin, Harlow Primate Laboratory, *b* © Daryl Balfour/NHPA/Photoshot; **p.159** © Peter Barritt/ Alamy; **p.160** *tl* © iko – Fotolia, *tr* © Laurent Hamels – Fotolia; *cl* © olly – Fotolia, *cr* © Konstantin Shevtsov – Fotolia, *bl* © iko – Fotolia, *br* © olly – Fotolia; **p.161** © Louie Favorite/AP/Press Association Images; **p.162** © Brian Parkinson; **p.163** *l* © Brian Parkinson, *r* © Brian Parkinson; **p.170** © Richard Cummins/ Corbis; **p.175** © Universal History Archive/Getty Images; **p.181** © Nina Leen/The LIFE Picture Collection/Getty Images; **p.190** © Jodie Coston/Getty Images; **p.192** © Ronald Grant Archive; **p.196** © Jane Ogden; **p.197** *l* © Monkey Business - Fotolia, *r* © kmit - Fotolia; **p.202** © Bettmann/Corbis; **p.205** © Sam Tanner/ Photofusion; **p.209** © nazira_g – Fotolia.com; **p.217** © Kelly Harriger; **p.226** Courtesy of Ron Rensink, Department of Psychology, University of British Columbia; **p.229** © Monkey Business – Fotolia; **p.238** © Andy Young and Vicki Bruce; **p.239** © Peter Parks/AFP/Getty Images; **p.243** © Sara De Boer/Retna Ltd./Corbis; **p.246** © Dan Kitwood/Getty Images; **p.249** © Julius/Corbis; **p.252** *l* © Werner Nekes Collection, *l* © Werner Nekes Collection; **p.253** M.C. Escher's "Relativity" © 2015 The M.C. Escher Company-The Netherlands. All rights reserved. www.mcescher.com; **p.257** With kind permission by Richard L Gregory; **p.260** © Phil Schermeister/Corbis; **p.264** © Laura Dwight/Corbis; **p.273** *t* © Professor Mark Johnson, Centre for Brain and Cognitive Development; Reprinted from Cognition, 40, 1-19 : Johnson, M.H., Dziurawiec, S., Ellis H. & Morton, J. (1991) Newborns' preferential tracking of face-like stimuli and its subsequent decline; with permission from Elsevier, *b* © Pavel Losevsky – Fotolia.com; **p.281** © Philip James Corwin/Corbis; **p.285** © Charles Palle – Fotolia.com; **p.291** © Stefan Wermuth/ Reuters/Corbis; **p.302** © CM Dixon/HIP/TopFoto; **p.304** © Rob Howard/Corbis; **p.314** © Anna Clopet/Corbis; **p.315** © Mary Evans Picture Library/Thomas Philip Morgan; **p.320** © Rick Friedman/Corbis; **p.326** © Language Research Ctr., Georgia State University, Atlanta, GA; **p.329** © julien tromeur – Fotolia.com; **p.332** © 1925 Kegan Paul, Trench, Trubner & Co. Reproduced by permission of Taylor & Francis Books UK; **p.334** © Jerry Cooke/Corbis; **p.335** © ADE JOHNSON/epa/Corbis; **p.338** © Science Photo Library; **p.345** © Jonas Ginter – Fotolia; **p.346** © MBI/Alamy; **p.355** © Gavin Rodgers/REX; **p.356** © AP/Press Association Images; **p.358** *t* © Elizabeth F. Loftus, *b* © Nicole Hill/Getty Images; **p.363** © Ambrophoto – Fotolia; **p.366** © VALENTIN FLAURAUD/Reuters/Corbis; **p.368** © Michael Stephens/PA Archive/Press Association Images; **p.370** © Chris Frith; **p.374** © REX/Glyn Thomas; **p.383** © marko – Fotolia; **p.385** © 2002 Telegraph Media Group Ltd, Photo: © Reuters/Corbis; **p.394** © PA/PA Archive/Press Association Images; **p.399** © JEFF WIDENER/AP/Press Association Images; **p.403** © REX; **p.411** © Nathan Benn/Corbis; **p.412** © Arrow Studio – Fotolia.com; **p.413** *l* © REX, *r* © Anthony

Potter Collection/Getty Images; **p.415** © Bettmann/Corbis; **p.416** © Celia Kitzinger; **p.417** © Chris Jackson/Getty Images; **p.419** © Flip Schulke/Corbis; **p.420** © George Holliday/AP/Press Association Images; **p.423** © REX; **p.428** © Concord Video & Film Council; **p.431** © REX/Brian Rasic; **p.434** Reproduced with permission © 2015 Scientific American, Inc. All rights reserved; **p.442** © REX/Everett Collection; **p.446** © Ronald Grant Archive; **p.448** *l* From the film Obedience copyright 1968 by Stanley Milgram; copyright renewed by Alexandra Milgram 1993, and distributed by Penn State Media Sales/Photo: © The Granger Collection/TopFoto, *r* © Alexandra Milgram; **p.449** From the film Obedience © 1968 by Stanley Milgram; copyright renewed by Alexandra Milgram 1993, and distributed by Penn State Media Sales; **p.451** © Keystone/Hulton Archive/Getty Images; **p.452** © Barry Lewis/Corbis; **p.455** *l* With kind permission by Philip Zimbardo, Inc, *r* With kind permission by Philip Zimbardo, Inc; **p.456** *t* © Alex Haslam, *b* © Berliner Verlag/Archiv/dpa/Corbis; **p.457** © Daniel Berehulak/Getty Images; **p.461** © Imagno/Getty Images; **p.463** © Nik Wheeler/Corbis; **p.465** © Russell Underwood/Corbis; **p.467** © AF archive/Alamy; **p.469** © David Fisher/REX; **p.471** *t* © Alberto E. Rodriguez/Getty Images, *b* © The Barnes Foundation, Merion Station, Pennsylvania/Corbis; **p.472** *t* © Steve Duck, *b* © Pavel Losevsky – Fotolia.com; **p.474** © pressmaster – Fotolia.com; **p.474** © Dr Judith Langlois/Langlois Social Development Lab/Dept.of Psychology/The University of Texas at Austin; **p.475** © Bettmann/Corbis; **p.485** © Henrik Sorensen/Getty Images; **p.487** © Jeff Moore/Empics Entertainment/Press Association Photos; **p.491** © CalatheaPhoto/Alamy; **p.492** © Ronald Grant Archive; **p.497** With kind permission by Philip Zimbardo, Inc; **p.498** *t* © Barbara Krahé, *b* © attltibi – Fotolia.com; **p.503** © Comic Relief Limited; **p.507** © Brenda Prince/Photofusion; **p.511** © Ljupco Smokovski – Fotolia.com; **p.514** © Hans-Werner Bierhoff; **p.516** © Babu/Reuters/Corbis; **p.519** © John Gichigi/Getty Images; **p.521** *t* © Anion – Fotolia.com, *b* © Hulton-Deutsch Collection/Corbis; **p.525** © Phil Walter/EMPICS Sport/Press Association Images; **p.526** © Sue Colvil – Fotolia.com; **p.527** © Glyn Kirk/AFP/Getty Images; **p.531** © Hulton-Deutsch Collection/Corbis; **p.532** © Vladislav Gansovsky – Fotolia.com; **p.533** © University of Wisconsin, Harlow Primate Laboratory; **p.534** © Richard Bowlby; **p.536** *l* © microimages – Fotolia.com, *tr* Courtesy of University of Virginia Public Affairs; **p.539** © REX/Occidor Ltd/Robert Harding; **p.541** Robertson, J. & Robertson, J. (1967-73) Film Series Young Children in Brief Separation: No 3 (1969): John, 17 months, 9 days in a residential nursery. London: Tavistock © Robertson Films; **p.542** © Bubbles Photolibrary; **p.550** *t* © Susan Golombok, *b* © STR/AFP/Getty Images; **p.554** © Bridgeman/Getty Images; **p.556** © REX/Tim Rooke; **p.557** © James L. Stanfield/National Geographic/Getty Images; **p.558** © Steve Azzara/Corbis; **p.561** © Brian Mitchell/Photofusion; **p.563** © Pavel Losevsky – Fotolia.com; **p.564** © Biosphoto/SuperStock; **p.569** © *b* Christopher/Alamy; **p.570** © Farrell Grehan/Corbis; **p.576** © Bob Battersby/www.bdi-images.com; **p.578** © Paul Chesley/Getty Images; **p.579** *t* © Sally and Richard Greenhill, *b* © Sally and Richard Greenhill; **p.580** © Vasudevi Reddy; **p.581** © Alex Yeung – Fotolia.com; **p.582** © Art Directors & TRIP/Alamy; **p.589** © Pictorial Press Ltd/Alamy; **p.591** © Ronald Grant Archive; **p.592** © Ronald Grant Archive; **p.597** © Ronald Grant Archive; **p.602** With kind permission by Alfred Bandura; **p.606** © John Raffo/Science Photo Library; **p.607** © REX/Brian Rasic; **p.611** © Bob Ebbesen/Alamy; **p.613** © Reuters/Corbis; **p.615** *t* © Aliaksei Lasevich – Fotolia.com, *b* © Jose Manuel Gelpi – Fotolia.com; **p.618** © Jason Stitt – Fotolia.com; **p.622** *t* © Profimedia.CZ a.s./Alamy, *b* © Ronald Grant Archive; **p.627** © moodboard – Fotolia.com; **p.628** © David H. Wells/Corbis; **p.630** © Per-Anders Pettersson/Getty Images; **p.631** © Monkey Business – Fotolia.com; **p.632** *t* © Jane Kroger, *b* © Anton Vasilkovsky – Fotolia.com; **p.637** © Roger Ressmeyer/Corbis; **p.641** © Darama/Corbis; **p.643** © REX/Everett Collection; **p.645** © Papirazzi – Fotolia.com; **p.646** © Terri Apter; **p.647** © Simone van den Berg – Fotolia.com; **p.648** © Anthea Sieveking/Wellcome Images; **p.650** © Eric Baccega - www.robertharding.com; **p.651** © Andrei Vorobiev – Fotolia.com; **p.652** © Tatyana Gladskih – Fotolia.com; **p.656** © TopFoto; **p.657** © Parrot Pascal/Corbis Sygma; **p.662** © carmeta – Fotolia.com; **p.663** *t* © Topham Picturepoint/TopFoto, *b* © Glenda Powers – Fotolia.com; **p.666** © Moviestore Collection/REX; **p.667** *l* © Russell Underwood/Corbis, *r* © Ullsteinbild/TopFoto; **p.669** © NATI HARNIK/AP/Press Association Images; **p.672** © Stephen Wiltshire 2010; **p.674** *l* © REX/David Hartley, *r* © Bettmann/Corbis; **p.675** © REX/ITV; **p.676** *l* © Ed Andrieski/AP/Press Association Images, *r* Courtesy of The Magstim Company Ltd; **p.678** Portrait of Wolfgang Amadeus Mozart (1756-91) Aged 14, c.1770 (oil on canvas), Blanchet, Louis Gabriel (1705-72)/© Private Collection/Bridgeman Images; **p.680** © JOTI/Science Photo Library; **p.682** © Bernard Bisson/Sygma/Corbis; **p.686** © Wellcome Photo Library; **p.689** © Leemage/Getty Images; **p.690** © George Skadding/The LIFE Picture Collection/Getty Images; **p.694** *l* © Michelle McLoughlin/AP/Press Association Images, *r* © Rob Howard/Corbis; **p.695** © nsphotography – Fotolia.com; **p.703** © Barbara Herbert; **p.705** © Robert Plomin; **p.706** © James Leynse/Corbis; **p.713** © Ronald Grant Archive; **p.715** © Bettmann/Corbis; **p.716** © Dieter E. Hoppe; **p.717** © REX/Kim Ludbrook; **p.724** © Ohio State University Photo Archives; **p.727** *l* © Colin Garratt; Milepost 92 ½/CORBIS, *r* © Wellcome Library, London; **p.732** © Christie's Images/Corbis; **p.736** © REX/Sipa Press; **p.737** © Bettmann/Corbis; **p.738** © Bettmann/Corbis; **p.740** © Snap Stills/REX, *l* © Mary Evans Picture Library; **p.741** © David Lees/Corbis; **p.742** *t* © Dmytro Sidelnikov/Alamy, *b* © National Library of Medicine/Science Photo Library; **p.746** © Mary Evans Picture Library; **p.748** © Mathieu Garçon/Sygma/Corbis; **p.750** © Lucy Tizard/Bubbles Photolibrary; **p.755** © Art Media/HIP/TopFoto; **p.756** *l* © Iryna Petrenko – Fotolia.com; **p.757** © Aaron Horowitz/Corbis; **p.758** *t* © Marc Roche – Fotolia.com, *b* © Russell Underwood/Corbis; **p.759** © Reuters/Corbis; **p.763** © Hulton-Deutsch Collection/Corbis; **p.766** © GREG BAKER/AP/Press Association Images; **p.767** © REX/c.Universal/Everett; **p.768** © Moviestore Collection/REX; **p.771** © Allen Ginsberg/Corbis; **p.773** *l* © 1993 REX, *r* © Andres Rodriguez – Fotolia.com; **p.779** © The British Library; **p.782** © John Greim/Science Photo Library; **p.785** © Najlah Feanny/Corbis; **p.787** © Ronald Grant Archive; **p.789** © Peter Aprahamian/Corbis; **p.792** © REX/Everett Collection; **p.797** © Aaron Beck; **p.804** © United Archives GmbH/Alamy; **p.805** *l* © ADAM BUTLER/AP/Press Association Images, *r* © REX/Paul Brown; **p.807** Courtesy Greater Manchester Police; **p.808** © Topham/FNP-STAR/TopFoto; **p.811** *both* © Press Association Images; **p.813** © REX/Sipa Press; **p.815** © REX; **p.817** © REX; **p.818** © David Canter; **p.819** *l* © Remi Jakobsen – Fotolia.com, *r* © MSPhotographic – Fotolia.com; **p.821** © REX/South Coast Press; **p.824** © St Bartholomew's Hospital/Science Photo

Library; **p.826** *l* © Celia Kitzinger, *r* © Joyce Ravid; **p.827** *t* © REX/John Powell, *b* © Bob Battersby/www.bdi-images.com; **p.828** *l* © The Drs. Nicholas and Dorothy Cummings Center for the History of Psychology, The University of Akron, *r* © Wellesley College Archives; **p.830** *b* © Franck Metois - www.robertharding.com; **p.833** *t* © Black Star/Alamy, *b* © Gideon Mendel/Corbis; **p.837** © Bettmann/Corbis; **p.840** *l* © Lucy Tizard/Bubbles Photolibrary, *r* © Tomas van Houtryve/AP/Press Association Images; **p.842** © Philip Zimbardo Inc; **p.843** © Paul Baldesare/Photofusion; **p.844** © ullsteinbild/TopFoto; **p.847** *l* © David McNew/Getty Images, *r* © Aaron Horowitz/Corbis; **p.851** *t* © Mo Wilson/Photofusion, *b* © Michael Rougier/The LIFE Picture Collection/Getty Images; **p.855** © Otto Stadler – www.robertharding.com; **p.856** *l* © Prisma Archivo/Alamy, *r* © Ronald Grant Archive; **p.858** © REX; **p.860** Cover of Walden Two by B. F. Skinner. Copyright © 1948, 1976 by B. F. Skinner. Reprinted 2005 by Hackett Publishing Company Inc., by special arrangement with the B. F. Skinner Foundation. All rights reserved; **p.861** © Reuters/Corbis; **p.865** © Charles O'Rear/Corbis; **p.870** *t* © Tom & Dee Ann McCarthy/Corbis, *b* © Bettmann/Corbis; **p.872** © Dumbletons Photographers, Cambridge; **p.876** © REX/Everett Collection; **p.877** © Bubbles Photolibrary.

Text credits

p.16 © B.F. Skinner (1987), 'Skinner on behaviourism', 82 words from Chapter 2 in R.L. Gregory (ed.) *The Oxford Companion to the Mind*, Oxford University Press, reproduced by permission of Oxford University Press; **p.20** © R.E. Fancher (1996), *Pioneers of Psychology, 3rd edition*, Norton; **p.24** © A.J. Parkin (2000), *Essential Cognitive Psychology*, Psychology Press; **p.25** © R. Lachman, J.L. Lachman and E.C. Butterfield (1979), *Cognitive Psychology and Information Processing*, Lawrence Erlbaum Associates; **p.26** from *Social Constructionism, 2nd edition*, V. Burr, Copyright © 2003, Routledge, reproduced by permission of Taylor & Francis Books UK; **p.40** © J.B. Watson (1913), 'Psychology as the behaviourist views it', *Psychological Review*, 20, 158–177, content is in the public domain; **p.44** from *Putting Psychology in its Place*, G. Richards, Copyright © 1996, Routledge, reproduced by permission of Taylor & Francis Books UK; **p.75** from *Visual Perception, 2nd edition,* V. Bruce and P.R. Green, Copyright © 1990, Lawrence Erlbaum Associates, reproduced by permission of Taylor & Francis Books UK; **p.97** © H.J. Irwin and C.A. Watt (2007), *An Introduction to Parapsychology, 5th edition,* McFarland & Co. Inc.; **p.98** © K.R Rao and J. Palmer (1987), 'The anomaly called psi: Recent research and criticism', *Behaviour & Brain Sciences*, 10, 539–643; **p.105** © S. Greenfield (1998), 'How might the brain generate consciousness?' in S. Rose (ed.) *From Brains to Consciousness: Essays on the New Sciences of the Mind,* Penguin; **p.111** © C. Blakemore (1988), *The Mind Machine*, BBC Publications; **p.130** © G.A. Marlatt, J.S. Baer, D.M. Donovan and D.R. Kivlahan (1988), 'Addictive behaviours: Etiology and treatment', *Annual Review of Psychology*, 39, 223–252; **p.148** John P.J. Pinel, *Biopsychology, 2nd edition* © 1993. Reprinted by permission of Pearson Education, Inc., Upper Saddle River, N.J.; **p.149** © J.E. Blundell and A.J. Hill (1995), 'Hunger and appetite' in B. Parkinson and A.M. Colman (eds), *Emotion and Motivation*, Longman; **p.191** © C. Abraham, M. Connor, F. Jones and D. O'Connor (2008), *Health Psychology*, Hodder Education; **p.202** © V.S Ramachandran and S. Blakeslee (1998), *Phantoms in the Brain*, Fourth Estate, reproduced by permission of HarperCollins Publishers Ltd. © 1998 V.S Ramachandran and S. Blakeslee; reproduced in the USA, Canada and Philippines by permission of HarperCollins Publishers US; reproduced in the eBook edition by permission of Brockman, Inc. Literary Agency and the authors, V.S Ramachandran and S. Blakeslee; **p.203** © D. Bartlett (1998), *Stress: Perspectives and Processes*, Open University Press, reproduced with the kind permission of Open University Press. All rights reserved; **p.223** © J. Driver (1996), 'Attention and segmentation', *The Psychologist*, 9, 119–123; **p.270** © R. L. Fantz (1961), 'The origin of form perception', *Scientific American*, 204 (5), 66–72; **p.278** © Jan B. Deregowski (1972), 'Pictorial perception and culture', *Scientific American*, 227 (5), 82-88; **p.294** © D.M. Wegner and A.F. Ward (2013), 'How Google is Changing your Brain', *Scientific American*, 309 (6), 50-53; **p.306** © S. Newstead (1995), 'Language and thought: The Whorfian hypothesis', *Psychology Review*, 1, 5–7, reproduced by permission of Philip Allan (for Hodder Education); **p.333** © M.L. Ginsberg (1998), 'Computers, games and the real world', *Scientific American Presents*, 9 (4), 84–89; **p.339** © J.R. Searle (1980), 'Minds, brains and programs', *The Behaviour & Brain Sciences*, 3, 417–457; **p.340** © A.M. Turing (1950), 'Computing machinery and intelligence', *Mind*, 59, 433–460; **p.341** © K.M Ford and P.J. Hayes (1998), 'On computational wings: Rethinking the goals of artificial intelligence', *Scientific American Presents*, 9 (4), 78–83; **p.360** © A. Frankland and L. Cohen (1999), 'Working with recovered memories', *The Psychologist*, 12 (2), 82–83; **p.458** © P.G. Zimbardo (1973), 'On the ethics of intervention in human psychological research with special reference to the 'Stanford Prison Experiment'', *Cognition*, 2 (2), 243–255; **p.488** © E.I Megargee and G.A. Mendelsohn (1962), 'A cross validation of twelve MMPI indices of hostility and control', *Journal of Abnormal & Social Psychology*, 65, 431–438, content is in the public domain; **p.517** © Stanley Milgram, quoted in Maureen Dowd (1984), '20 years after the murder of Kitty Genovese, the question remains: Why?', *The New York Times*; **p.611** © D.F. Halpern, C.P. Benbow, D.C. Geary et al. (2012), 'Sex, math and scientific achievement', *Scientific American Mind*, 21(2), 26-33; **p.613** © Independent Print Limited, J. Colapinto (2000), 'What the doctor ordered' *Independent on Sunday Magazine*, 6 February, 8–13; **p.658** © G. Brown (2007), 'The bitter end', *New Scientist*, 196 (2625), 42–43; **p.659** © H. Jones (1993), 'Altered images', *Nursing Times*, 89 (5), 58–60, reproduced with permission from Emap Ltd.; **p.669** © S. Voss (2002), 'The winter years: Understanding ageing', *Psychology Review*, 8 (3), 26–28, reproduced by permission of Philip Allan (for Hodder Education); **p.676** © D.A. Treffert and G.L. Wallace (2004), 'Islands of Genius', *Scientific American Mind (Special Edition),* 14 (1), 14–23; **p.687** © U. Frith (1996), 'Cognitive explanations of autism', *Acta Paediatrica Supplement*, 416, 63–68; **p.709** © Independent Print Limited, M. Sweet (2004), 'The search for intelligent life', *Independent Review*, 2 June, 2–3; **p.782** © R. Munro (2000), 'Cheap and cheerful', *Nursing Times*, 96 (3), 16, reproduced with permission from Emap Ltd.; **p.809** © C.R. Hollin (1997), 'Adolescent predictors of adult offending', *Psychology Review*, 3 (4), 21–25, reproduced by permission of Philip Allan (for Hodder Education); **p.816** © G. Copson and K. Holloway (1997), 'Offender Profiling', Paper presented to the annual conference of the Division of Criminological & Legal Psychology, *British Psychological Society* (October); **p.827** © C. Tavris (1993), 'The mismeasure of woman', *Feminism & Psychology*, 3 (2), 149–168; **p.829** © F. Denmark, N.F. Russo, I.H. Frieze and J.A. Sechzer (1988), 'Guidelines for avoiding sexism in psychological research: A report of the ad hoc committee on nonsexist research', *American Psychologist*, 43 (7), 582–585.

REFERENCES

Abdulla, S. (1996) Illuminating our hardware. *The Times Higher*, 1 November, 18.

Abernathy, E.M. (1940) The effect of changed environmental conditions upon the results of college examinations. *Journal of Psychology, 10*, 293–301.

Aboraya, A. (2012) Coming Along with the DSM-5: Hybrid Models of Psychiatric Diagnosis. *Psychiatric Times*, 11 September.

Abraham, C., Connor, M., Jones, F. & O'Connor, D. (2008) *Health Psychology*. London: Hodder Education.

Abrahamson, D. (2014) Cognitive psychology, terrorism and cycles of violence. In C.M. Parkes (ed.) *Responses to Terrorism*. Hove, East Sussex: Routledge.

Abrams, D., Wetherell, M., Cochrane, S., Hogg, M.A. & Turner, J.C. (1990) Knowing what to think by knowing who you are: Self-categorisation and the nature of norm formation. *British Journal of Social Psychology, 29*, 97–119.

Abrams, R. (1997) *Electroconvulsive Therapy* (3rd edition revised). New York: Oxford University Press.

Abramson, L.Y. & Martin, D.J. (1981) Depression and the causal inference process. In J.M. Harvey, W. Ickes & R.F. Kidd (eds) *New Directions in Attribution Research, Volume 3*. Hillsdale, NJ: Erlbaum.

Abramson, L.Y., Seligman, M.E.P. & Teasdale, J.D. (1978) Learned helplessness in humans: Critique and reformulation. *Journal of Abnormal Psychology, 87*, 49–74.

Adam, B.D. (1987) *The Rise of a Gay and Lesbian Movement*. Boston: Twayne Publishers.

Adee, S. (2013) Stupid is as stupid does. *New Scientist, 217*(2910), 30–33.

Adler, A. (1927) *The Practice and Theory of Individual Psychology*. New York: Harcourt Brace Jovanovich.

Adler, R. (2000) Pigeonholed. *New Scientist, 167*(2258), 339–341.

Adorno, T.W., Frenkel-Brunswick, E., Levinson, J.D. & Sanford, R.N. (1950) *The Authoritarian Personality*. New York: Harper & Row.

Ahnert, L., Pinquart, M. & Lamb, M.E. (2006) Security of children's relationships with nonparental care providers. A meta-analysis. *Child Development, 77*, 664–679.

Ahuja, A. (2000) Drugs blow your mind. *The Times*, 15 June, 5.

Ainsworth, C. (2008) Wireheads. *New Scientist, 197*(2637), 36–39.

Ainsworth, M.D.S. (1967) *Infancy in Uganda: Infant Care and the Growth of Love*. Baltimore, MD: Johns Hopkins University Press.

Ainsworth, M.D.S. (1985) Attachments across the lifespan. *Bulletin of the New York Academy of Medicine, 61*, 792–812.

Ainsworth, M.D.S. & Wittig, B.A. (1969) Attachment and exploratory behaviour of 1-year-olds in a strange situation. In B.M. Foss (ed.) *Determinants of Infant Behaviour, Volume 4*. London: Methuen.

Ainsworth, M.D.S., Bell, S.M.V. & Stayton, D.J. (1971) Individual differences in Strange Situation behaviour of one-year-olds. In H.R. Schaffer (ed.) *The Origins of Human Social Relations*. New York: Academic Press.

Ainsworth, M.D.S., Blehar, M.C., Waters, E. & Wall, S. (1978) *Patterns of Attachment: A Psychological Study of the Strange Situation*. Hillsdale, NJ: Lawrence Erlbaum Associates Inc.

Aitchison, J. (1983) *The Articulate Mammal* (2nd edition). London: Hutchinson.

Aitchison, J. (1996) Wugs, woggles, and whatsits. *Independent*, Section 2, 28 February, 8.

Ajzen, I. & Fishbein, M. (1970) The prediction of behaviour from attitudinal and normative beliefs. *Journal of Personality & Social Psychology, 6*, 466–487.

Ajzen, I. (1988) *Attitudes, Personality and Behaviour*. Milton Keynes: Open University Press.

Ajzen, I. (1991) The theory of planned behaviour. *Organisational Behaviour & Human Decision Processes, 50*, 179–211.

Ajzen, I. & Fishbein, M. (1977) Attitude–behaviour relations: A theoretical analysis and review of empirical research. *Psychological Bulletin, 84*, 888–918.

Alcock, J.E. (1981) *Parapsychology: Science or Magic?* Oxford: Pergamon.

Aldhous, P. & Coghlan, A. (2013) A revolution in mental health. *New Scientist, 218*(2916), 8–9.

Alexander, F. & French, T.M. (1946) *Psychoanalytic Therapy*. New York: Ronald Press.

Alicke, M.D., LoSchiavo, F.M., Zerbst, J. & Zhang, S. (1997) The person who outperforms me is a genius: Maintaining perceived competence in upward social comparison. *Journal of Personality & Social Psychology, 73*, 781–789.

Allely, C. (2013) Anorexia nervosa – on the autistic spectrum? *The Psychologist, 26*(9), 656-658.

Allen, V. & Levine, J.M. (1968) Social support, dissent and conformity. *Sociometry, 31*, 138–149.

Allen, V. & Levine, J.M. (1971) Social support and conformity: The role of independent assessment of reality. *Journal of Experimental Social Psychology, 7*, 48–58.

Allport, D.A. (1980a) Patterns and actions: Cognitive mechanisms are content specific. In G. Claxton (ed.) *Cognitive Psychology: New Directions*. London: Routledge & Kegan Paul.

Allport, D.A. (1980b) Attention and performance. In G. Claxton (ed.) *Cognitive Psychology: New Directions*. London: Routledge & Kegan Paul.

Allport, D.A. (1989) Visual attention. In M. Posner (ed.) *Foundations of Cognitive Science*. Cambridge, MA: MIT Press.

Allport, D.A. (1993) Attention and control. Have we been asking the wrong questions? A critical review of twenty-five years. In D.E. Meyer & S.M. Kornblum (eds) *Attention and Performance, Volume XIV*. London: MIT Press.

Allport, D.A., Antonis, B. & Reynolds, P. (1972) On the division of attention: A disproof of the single-channel hypothesis. *Quarterly Journal of Experimental Psychology, 24*, 225–235.

Allport, F.H. (1924) *Social Psychology*. Boston: Houghton Mifflin.

Allport, G.W. (1935) Attitudes. In C.M. Murchison (ed.) *Handbook of Social Psychology*. Worchester, MA: Clark University Press.

Allport, G.W. (1947) *The Use of Personal Documents in Psychological Science*. London: Holt, Rinehart & Winston.

Allport, G.W. (1954) *The Nature of Prejudice*. Reading, MA: Addison-Wesley.

Allport, G.W. (1955) *Theories of Perception and the Concept of Structure*. New York: Wiley.

Allport, G.W. (1961) *Pattern and Growth in Personality*. New York: Holt, Rinehart & Winston.

Allport, G.W. (1968) The historical background of modern psychology. In G. Lindzey & E. Aronson (eds) *Handbook of Social Psychology, Volume 1* (2nd edition). Reading, MA: Addison-Wesley.

Allport, G.W. & Pettigrew, T.F. (1957) Cultural influences on the perception of movement: The trapezoidal illusion among Zulus. *Journal of Abnormal & Social Psychology, 55*, 104–113.

Allport, G.W. & Postman, L. (1947) *The Psychology of Rumour*. New York: Holt, Rinehart & Winston.

Almas, A.N., Degnan, A.K., Radulescu, A. et al. (2012) Effects of early intervention and the moderating effects of brain activity on institutionalised children's social skills at age 8. *Proceedings of the National Academy of Sciences USA, 109*, Supplement No. 2, 17,228-17,231.

Almeida, D.M. (2005) Resilience and vulnerability to daily stressors assessed via diary methods. *Current Directions in Psychological Science, 14*, 64–68.

Alsaker, F.D. (1992) Pubertal timing, overweight, and psychological adjustment. *Journal of Early Adolescence, 12*, 396–419.

Alsaker, F.D. (1996) The impact of puberty. *Journal of Child Psychology & Psychiatry, 37* (3), 249–258.

Alter, J. (2008) The tales Hillary tells. *Newsweek*, 37, 7 April.

Altman, I. & Taylor, D.A. (1973) *Social Penetration: The Development of Interpersonal Relationships*. New York: Holt, Rinehart & Winston.

Amato, P.R. (2000) The consequences of divorce for adults and children. *Journal of Marriage & The Family, 62*, 1269-1287.

American Psychiatric Association (1952) *Diagnostic and Statistical Manual of Mental Disorders*. Washington, DC: American Psychiatric Association.

American Psychiatric Association (1968) *Diagnostic and Statistical Manual of Mental Disorders* (2nd edition). Washington, DC: American Psychiatric Association.

American Psychiatric Association (1980) *Diagnostic and Statistical Manual of Mental Disorders* (3rd edition). Washington, DC: American Psychiatric Association.

American Psychiatric Association (1987) *Diagnostic and Statistical Manual of Mental Disorders* (3rd edition revised). Washington, DC: American Psychiatric Association.

American Psychiatric Association (1994) *Diagnostic and Statistical Manual of Mental Disorders* (4th edition). Washington, DC: American Psychiatric Association.

American Psychiatric Association (2000) *Diagnostic and Statistical Manual of Mental Disorders* (4th edition revised). Washington, DC: American Psychiatric Association.

American Psychiatric Association (2013) *Diagnostic and Statistical Manual of Mental Disorders* (5th edition). Arlington, VA: American Psychiatric Association.

American Psychological Association (1982) *Ethical Principles in the Conduct of Research with Human Participants*. Washington, DC: American Psychological Association.

American Psychological Association (1985) *Guidelines for Ethical Conduct in the Care and Use of Animals*. Washington, DC: American Psychological Association.

American Psychological Association (2002) *Ethical Principles of Psychologists and Code of Conduct*. Washington, DC: American Psychological Association.

American Psychological Association Council of Representatives (2004) Resolution on sexual orientation and marriage (www.apa.org/pi/families/resources/task-force/military-deployment.pdf).

Amir, Y. (1969) Contact hypothesis in ethnic relations. *Psychological Bulletin, 71*, 319–342.

Amir, Y. (1994) The contact hypothesis in intergroup relations. In W.J. Lonner & R.S. Malpass (eds) *Psychology and Culture*. Boston: Allyn & Bacon.

Ananthaswamy, A. (2014) Fits of rapture. *New Scientist, 221*(2953), 44-47.

Ancona, L. & Pareyson, R. (1968) Contributo allo studio della a aggressione: la diminica della obbedienza distructiva. *Archivo di Psichologia Neurologia e Psichiatra, 29*, 340–372.

Anderson, C.A. & Bushman, B.J. (2002) The effects of media violence on society. *Science, 295*, 2377–2379.

Anderson, C.A. & Ford, C.M. (1986) Affect of the game player: Short-term effects of highly and mildly aggressive video games. *Personality & Social Psychology Bulletin, 12*, 390–402.

Anderson, C.A., Benjamin, A.J. & Bartholow, B.D. (2002) Does the gun pull the trigger? Automatic priming effects of weapon pictures and weapon names. *Psychological Science, 9* (4), 308–314.

Anderson, C.A., Berkowitz, L., Donnerstein, E., Huesmann, L.R., Johnson, J.D., Linz, D., Malamuth, N.M. & Wartella, E. (2003) The influence of media violence on youth. *Psychological Science in the Public Interest, 4*, 81–110.

Anderson, J.R. (1983) *The Architecture of Cognition* (2nd edition). Cambridge, MA: Harvard University Press.

Anderson, J.R. (1985) *Cognitive Psychology and its Implications*. New York: Freeman.

Anderson, J.R. (1995a) *Learning and Memory: An Integrated Approach*. Chichester: Wiley.

Anderson, J.R. (1995b) *Cognitive Psychology and its Implications*. New York: W.H. Freeman & Company.

Anderson, M. (2007) Biology and intelligence – the race/IQ controversy. In S. Della Sala (ed.) *Tall Tales about the Mind & Brain: Separating Fact from Fiction*. Oxford: Oxford University Press.

Anderson, N.H. (1974) Cognitive algebra: Integration theory applied to social attribution. In L. Berkowitz (ed.) *Advances in Experimental Social Psychology, Volume* 7. New York: Academic Press.

Anderson, T. & Magnusson, D. (1990) Biological maturation and the development of drinking habits and alcohol abuse among young males. A prospective longitudinal study. *Journal of Youth & Adolescence, 19*, 33–41.

Andre, L. (2008) *Doctors of Deception: What they don't want you to know about Shock Treatment*. New Brunswick, NJ: Rutgers University Press.

Andreassen, C.S., Griffiths, M.D., Gjertsen, S.R. et al. (2013) The relationships between behavioural addictions and the five-factor model of personality. *Journal of Behavioural Addictions, 2*, 90–99.

Annett, M. (1991) Laterality and cerebral dominance. *Journal of Child Psychology & Psychiatry, 32*(2), 219–232.

Antaki, C. (1984) Core concepts in attribution theory. In J. Nicholson & H. Beloff (eds) *Psychology Survey 5*. Leicester: British Psychological Society.

Apperly, I.A. & Butterfill, S.A. (2009) Do humans have two systems to track beliefs and belief-like states? *Psychological Review, 116*(4), 953–970.

Apter, T. (1990) *Altered Loves: Mothers and Adolescent Daughters*. New York: Ballantine.

Apter, T. (2002) *The Myth of Maturity: What Teenagers Need from Parents to Become Adults*. New York: W.W. Norton.

Apter, T. (2004) *You Don't Really Know Me! Mothers and Teenage Daughters*. New York: W.W. Norton.

Archer, J. (1996) Evolutionary social psychology. In M. Hewstone, W. Stroebe & G.M. Stephenson (eds) *Introduction to Social Psychology* (2nd edition). Oxford: Blackwell.

Archer, J. (1999) *The Nature of Grief: The Evolution and Psychology of Reactions to Loss*. London: Routledge.

Arendt, H. (1965) *Eichmann in Jerusalem: A Report on the Banality of Evil*. New York: Viking.

Argyle, M. (1983) *The Psychology of Interpersonal Behaviour* (4th edition). Harmondsworth: Penguin.

Argyle, M. & Henderson, M. (1984) The rules of friendship. *Journal of Social & Personal Relationships, 1*, 211–237.

Argyle, M., Alkema, F. & Gilmour, R. (1972) The communication of friendly and hostile attitudes by verbal and non-verbal signals. *European Journal of Social Psychology*, 1, 385–402.

Argyle, M., Henderson, M. & Furnham, A. (1985) The rules of social relationships. *British Journal of Social Psychology, 24*, 125–129.

Arkes, H.R. & Blumer, C. (1985) The psychology of sunk cost. *Organisational Behaviour & Human Decision Processes, 35*, 124–140.

Arkowitz, H. & Lilienfeld, S.O. (2009) Misunderstood Crimes. *Scientific American Mind, 20*(3), 82–84.

Arkowitz, H. & Lilienfeld, S.O. (2012a) The truth about pot. *Scientific American Mind, 23*(1), 64-65.

Arkowitz, H. & Lilienfeld, S.O. (2012b) Memory in old age: Not a lost cause. *Scientific American Mind, 23*(5), 72–73.

Arnold, M.B. & Gasson, J.A. (1954) Feelings and emotions as dynamic factors in personality integration. In M.B. Arnold & J.A. Gasson (eds) *The Human Person*. New York: Ronald.

Arkowitz, H. & Lilienfeld, S.O. (2013) Is divorce bad for children? *Scientific American Mind, 24*(1), 68–69.

Arnold, C. (2012) Inside the wrong body. *Scientific American Mind, 23*(2), 36–41.

Aronson, E. (1980) *The Social Animal* (3rd edition). San Francisco: W.H. Freeman.

Arnsten, A., Majure, C.M. & Sinha, R. (2012) This is your brain meltdown. *Scientific American, 306*(40), 38–43.

Aronson, E. (1988) *The Social Animal* (5th edition). New York: Freeman.

Aronson, E. (1992) *The Social Animal* (6th edition). New York: Freeman.

Aronson, E. (2000) The jigsaw strategy: Reducing prejudice in the classroom. *Psychology Review*, 7(2), 2–5.

Aronson, E. & Carlsmith, J.M. (1963) Effect of the severity of threat on the devaluation of forbidden behaviour. *Journal of Abnormal & Social Psychology, 6*, 584–588.

Aronson, E. & Mills, J. (1959) The effect of severity of initiation on liking for a group. *Journal of Abnormal & Social Psychology, 59*, 177–81.

Aronson, E. & Osherow, N. (1980) Co-operation, prosocial behaviour and academic performance: Experiments in the desegregated classroom. In L. Bickman (ed.) *Applied Social Psychology Annual, Volume 1*. Beverly Hills, CA: Sage.

Aronson, E., Bridgeman, D.L. & Geffner, R. (1978) The effects of a co-operative classroom structure on student behaviour and attitudes. In D. Bar-Tal & L. Saxe (eds) *Social Psychology of Education*. New York: Wiley.

Årseth A., Kroger, J., Martinussen, M. & Marcia, J.E. (2009) Meta-analytic studies of identity status and the relational issues of attachment and intimacy. *Identity – An International Journal of Theory & Research, 9*, 1-32.

Arzi, A., Shedlesky, L., Ben-Shaul, M. et al. (2012) Humans can learn new information during sleep. *Nature Neuroscience, 15*, 1460-1465.

Asch, S.E. (1946) Forming impressions of personality. *Journal of Abnormal & Social Psychology, 41*, 258–290.

Asch, S.E. (1951) Effect of group pressure upon the modification and distortion of judgements. In H. Guetzkow (ed.) *Groups, Leadership and Men*. Pittsburgh, PA: Carnegie Press.

Asch, S.E. (1952) *Social Psychology*. Englewood Cliffs, NJ: Prentice-Hall.

Asch, S.E. (1955) Opinions and social pressure. *Scientific American, 193*, 31–35.

Aschoff, J. (1979) Circadian rhythms: General features and endocrinological aspects. In D.T. Krieger (ed.) *Endocrine Rhythms*. New York: Raven Press.

Aserinsky, E. & Kleitman, N. (1953) Regularly occurring periods of eye motility and concomitant phenomena during sleep. *Science, 118*, 273–274.

Aslin, R.N., Pisoni, D.B. & Jusczyk, P.W. (1983) Auditory development and speech perception in infancy. In P.H. Mussen (ed.) *Handbook of Child Psychology* (4th edition). New York: Wiley.

Asperger, H. (1944) Die 'Autistischen Psychopathen' in Kindesalten. *Archiv für Psychiatric und Nervenkrankheiter, 117*, 76–136.

Atchley, R.C. (1982) Retirement: Leaving the world of work. *Annals of the American Academy of Political & Social Science, 464*, 120–131.

Atchley, R.C. (1985) *Social Forces and Ageing: An Introduction to Social Gerontology*. Belmont, CA: Wadsworth.

Atkins, L. (2002) It's better to be thin and dead than fat and living. *Guardian*, 23 July, 10–11.

Atkinson, R.C., Hilgard, E.R. & Atkinson, R.L. (1983) *Introduction to Psychology* (8th edition). New York: Harcourt Brace Jovanovich.

Atkinson, R.L., Atkinson, R.C., Smith, E.E. & Bem, D.J. (1990) *Introduction to Psychology* (10th edition). New York: Harcourt Brace Jovanovich.

Attie, I. & Brooks-Gunn, J. (1989) Development of eating problems in adolescent girls: A longitudinal study. *Developmental Psychology, 25*, 70–79.

Attneave, F. (1954) Some informational aspects of visual perception. *Psychological Review, 61*, 183–193.

Averill, J.R. (1994) In the eyes of the beholder. In P. Ekman & R.J. Davidson (eds) *The Nature of Emotion: Fundamental Questions*. New York: Oxford University Press.

Ax, A.F. (1953) The physiological differentiation of fear and anger in humans. *Psychosomatic Medicine, 15*, 422–433.

Ayllon, T. & Azrin, N.H. (1968) *The Token Economy: A Motivational System for Therapy and Rehabilitation*. New York: Appleton-Century-Crofts.

Azrin, N.H. & Foxx, R.M. (1971) A rapid method of toilet training the institutionalised retarded. *Journal of Applied Behaviour Analysis, 4*, 89–99.

Azrin, N.H. & Holz, W.C. (1966) Punishment. In W.K. Honig (ed.) *Operant Behaviour: Areas of Research and Application*. New York: Appleton-Century-Crofts.

Baddeley, A. (2000) The episodic buffer: A new component of working memory? *Trends in Cognitive Sciences, 4* (11), 417–423.

Baddeley, A. (2008) What's new in working memory? *Psychology Review, 13* (3), 2–5.

Baddeley, A.D. (1966) The influence of acoustic and semantic similarity on long-term memory for word sequences. *Quarterly Journal of Experimental Psychology, 18*, 302–309.

Baddeley, A.D. (1976) *The Psychology of Memory*. New York: Basic Books.

Baddeley, A.D. (1981) The concept of working memory: A view of its current state and probable future development. *Cognition, 10*, 17–23.

Baddeley, A.D. (1986) *Working Memory*. Oxford: Oxford University Press.

Baddeley, A.D.(1990) *Human Memory*. Hove: Lawrence Erlbaum Associates.

Baddeley, A.D. (1995) Memory. In C.C. French & A.M. Colman (eds) *Cognitive Psychology*. London: Longman.

Baddeley, A.D. (1996) Exploring the central executive. *Quarterly Journal of Experimental Psychology, 49A*, 5–28.

Baddeley, A.D. (1997) *Human Memory: Theory and Practice* (revised edition). East Sussex: Psychology Press.

Baddeley, A.D. (1999) *Essentials of Human Memory*. Hove: Psychology Press.

Baddeley, A.D. & Hitch, G. (1974) Working memory. In G.H. Bower (ed.) *Recent Advances in Learning and Motivation, Volume 8*. New York: Academic Press.

Baddeley, A.D. & Warrington, E.H. (1970) Amnesia and the distinction between long- and short-term memory. *Journal of Verbal Learning & Verbal Behaviour, 9*, 176–189.

Bailey, C.L. (1979) Mental illness – a logical misrepresentation? *Nursing Times*, May, 761–762.

Bailey, S. (1993) Fast forward to violence. *Criminal Justice Matters, 3*, 6–7.

Baillargeon, R. (1987) Object permanence in 3½- and 4½-month-old infants. *Developmental Psychology, 33*, 655–664.

Balcetis, E. (2014) Wishful seeing. *The Psychologist, 27*(1), 22-25.

Balcetis, E. & Dunning, D. (2010) Wishful seeing: Desired objects are seen as closer. *Psychological Science, 21*, 147–152.

Baltes, P.B. (1983) Life-span developmental psychology: Observations on history and theory revisited. In R.M. Lerner (ed.) *Developmental Psychology: Historical and Philosophical Perspectives*. Hillsdale, NJ: Erlbaum.

Baltes, P.B. (1993) The ageing mind: Potential and limits. *Gerontologist, 33*, 580–594.

Baltes, P.B. & Lindenberger, U. (1997) Emergence of a powerful connection between sensory and cognitive functions across the adult life span: A new window to the study of cognitive ageing? *Psychology & Ageing, 12*, 12–21.

Bandura, A. (1965) Influence of model's reinforcement contingencies on the acquisition of imitative responses. *Journal of Personality & Social Psychology, 1*, 589–595.

Bandura, A. (1971) Vicarious and self-reinforcement processes. In A. Glass (ed.) *The Nature of Reinforcement*. New York: Academic Press.

Bandura, A. (1973) *Aggression: A Social Learning Analysis*. London: Prentice-Hall.

Bandura, A. (1974) Behaviour theory and models of man. *American Psychologist, 29*, 859–869.

Bandura, A. (1977a) Self-efficacy: Toward a unifying theory of behaviour change. *Psychological Review, 84*, 191–215.

Bandura, A. (1977b) *Social Learning Theory* (2nd edition). Englewood Cliffs, NJ: Prentice-Hall.

Bandura, A. (1986) *Social Foundations of Thought and Action*. Englewood Cliffs, NJ: Prentice-Hall.

Bandura, A. (1989) Social cognitive theory. In R. Vasta (ed.) *Six Theories of Child Development*. Greenwich, CT: JAI Press.

Bandura, A. (1994) Social cognitive theory of mass communication. In J. Bryant & D. Zillman (eds) *Media Effects: Advances in Theory and Research*. Hove: Erlbaum.

Bandura, A. (2002) Selective moral disengagement in the exercise of moral agency. *Journal of Moral Education, 31*, 101–119.

Bandura, A. & Walters, R.H. (1963) *Social Learning and Personality Development*. New York: Holt.

Bandura, A., Ross, D. & Ross, S.A. (1961) Transmission of aggression through imitation of aggressive models. *Journal of Abnormal & Social Psychology, 63*, 575–582.

Bandura, A., Ross, D. & Ross, S.A. (1963) Imitation of film-mediated aggressive models. *Journal of Abnormal & Social Psychology, 66*, 3–11.

Bannister, D. & Agnew, J. (1976) The child's construing of self. In J.K. Coal & A.W. Landfield (eds) *Nebraska Symposium on Motivation*. Lincoln: University of Nebraska Press.

Bannister, D. & Fransella, F. (1967) A grid test of schizophrenic thought disorder. *British Journal of Social & Clinical Psychology, 5*, 95–102.

Bannister, D. & Fransella, F. (1980) *Inquiring Man: The Psychology of Personal Constructs* (2nd edition). Harmondsworth: Penguin.

Bannister, D., Salmon, P. & Lieberman, D.M. (1964) Diagnosis–treatment relationships in psychiatry: A statistical analysis. *British Journal of Psychiatry, 110*, 726–732.

Banuazizi, A. & Mohavedi, S. (1975) Interpersonal dynamics in a simulated prison: A methodological analysis. *American Psychologist, 30*, 152–160.

Banyard, P. (1996) Psychology and advertising. *Psychology Review, 3* (1), 24–27.

Banyard, P. & Hayes, N. (1994) *Psychology: Theory and Applications*. London: Chapman & Hall.

Barber, B.K. & Buehler, C. (1996) Family cohesion and enmeshment: Different constructs, different effects. *Journal of Marriage & The Family, 58* (2), 433–441.

Bargh, J.A. (2014) Our Unconscious Minds. *Scientific American, 310*(1), 20-27.

Bargh, J.A., Chen, M. & Burrows, L. (1996) The automaticity of social behaviour: Direct effects of trait concept and stereotype activation on action. *Journal of Personality & Social Psychology, 71*, 230–244.

Barkham, M. & Shapiro, D. (1992) Response to Paul Kline. In W. Dryden & C. Feltham (eds) *Psychotherapy and its Discontents*. Buckingham: Open University Press.

Barkley, R.A., Ullman, D.G., Otto, L. & Brecht, A.M. (1977) The effects of sex typing and sex appropriateness of modelled behaviour on children's imitation. *Child Development, 48*, 721–725.

Barkow, J., Cosmides, L. & Tooby, J. (eds) (1992) *The Adapted Mind: Evolutionary Psychology and the Generation of Culture*. New York: Oxford University Press.

Barnes-Gutteridge, W. (1974) *Psychology*. London: Hamlyn.

Baron, R.A. (1977) *Human Aggression*. New York: Plenum.

Baron, R.A. & Byrne, D. (1991) *Social Psychology* (6th edition). Boston: Allyn & Bacon.

Baron, R.A. & Richardson, D.R. (1994) *Human Aggression* (2nd edition). New York: Plenum.

Baron, R.S. (1986) Distraction-conflict theory: Progress and problems. In L. Berkowitz (ed.) *Advances in Experimental Social Psychology, Volume 19*. New York: Academic Press.

Baron-Cohen, S. (1987) Autism and symbolic play. *British Journal of Developmental Psychology, 5*, 139–148.

Baron-Cohen, S. (1988) Social and pragmatic deficits in autism: Cognitive or affective? *Journal of Autism & Developmental Disorders, 18*, 379–402.

Baron-Cohen, S. (1990) Autism: A specific cognitive disorder of 'mindblindness'. *International Review of Psychiatry, 2*, 79–88.

Baron-Cohen, S. (1993) From attention–goal psychology to belief–desire psychology: The development of a theory of mind and its dysfunction. In S. Baron-Cohen, H. Tager-Flusberg & D.J. Cohen (eds) *Understanding Other Minds: Perspectives from Autism*. Oxford University Press.

Baron-Cohen, S. (1995a) Infantile autism. In A.A. Lazarus & A.M. Colman (eds) *Abnormal Psychology*. London: Longman.

Baron-Cohen, S. (1995b) *Mindblindness: An Essay on Autism and Theory of Mind*. Cambridge, MA: MIT Press.

Baron-Cohen, S. (2002) The extreme male brain theory of autism. *Trends in Cognitive Science, 6*(6), 248–254.

Baron-Cohen, S. (2003a) *The Essential Difference*. London: Penguin.

Baron-Cohen, S. (2003b) Sugar and spice. *New Scientist, 178* (2396), 54–55.

Baron-Cohen, S. (2008) Theories of the autistic mind. *The Psychologist, 21* (2), 112–114.

Baron-Cohen, S., Leslie, A.M. & Frith, U. (1985) Does the autistic child have a 'theory of mind'? *Cognition, 21*, 37–46.

Baron-Cohen, S., Knickmeyer, R. & Belmonte, M.K. (2005) Sex differences in the brain: Implications for explaining autism. *Science, 310*, 819–823.

Baron-Cohen, S., Hoekstra, R.A., Knickmeyer, R. & Wheelwright, S. (2006) The Autism-Spectrum Quotient (AQ) – Adolescent version. *Journal of Autism & Developmental Disorders, 36*, 343–350.

Barrett, D. (2011) Answers in your Dreams. *Scientific American Mind, 22*(5), 27–33.

Barrett, L.F. (2011) Was Darwin wrong about emotional expressions? *Current Directions in Psychological Science, 20*(6), 400–406.

Barrett, L.F., Mesquito, B. & Gendron, M. (2011) Context in emotional perception. *Current Directions in Psychological Science, 20*, 286.

Barrett, M.D. (1989) Early language development. In A. Slater & G. Bremner (eds) *Infant Development*. Hove: Erlbaum.

Bartlett, A., Smith, G. & King, M. (2009) The response of mental health professionals to clients seeking help to change or redirect same-sex sexual orientation. *BMC Psychiatry, 9*, 11.

Bartlett, D. (1998) *Stress: Perspectives and Processes*. Buckingham: Open University Press.

Bartlett, F.C. (1932) *Remembering*. Cambridge University Press.

Bartlett, J.C. & Searcy, J. (1993) Inversion and configuration of faces. *Cognitive Psychology, 25*, 281–316.

Barrett, J.L. (2004) *Why Would Anyone Believe in God?* London: AltaMira Press.

Barret, R.L. & Robinson, B.E. *Gay Fathers*. Lexington, MA: Lexington Books.

Bate, S. (2014) Face facts: Understanding prosopagnosia and face recognition. *Psychology Review, 19*(3), 18–20.

Bates, E., O'Connell, B. & Shore, C. (1987) Language and communication in infancy. In J.D. Osofsky (ed.) *Handbook of Infant Development* (2nd edition). New York: Wiley.

Bateson, G., Jackson, D., Haley, J. & Weakland, J. (1956) Toward a theory of schizophrenia. *Behavioural Science, 1*, 251–264.

Batson, C.D. (1991) *The Altruism Question: Toward a Social-Psychological Answer*. Hillsdale, NJ: Erlbaum.

Batson, C.D. (1998) Altruism and prosocial behaviour. In D.T. Gilbert, S.T. Fiske & G. Lindzey (eds) *The Handbook of Social Psychology, Volume 2* (4th edition). New York: McGraw-Hill.

Batson, C.D. (2000) Altruism: Why do we help others? *Psychology Review, 7* (1), 2–5.

Baumeister, R.F. (1982) A self-presentational view of social phenomena. *Psychological Bulletin, 91*, 3–26.

Baumeister, R.F. & Bratslavsky, E. (1999) Passion, intimacy and time: Passionate love as a function of change in intimacy. *Personality & Social Psychology Review, 3*, 49–67.

Baumeister, R.F., Campbell, J.D., Krueger, J.I. & Vohs, K.D. (2003) Does high self-esteem cause better performance, interpersonal success, happiness, or healthier lifestyles? *Psychological Science in the Public Interest, 4*, 1–44.

Baumrind, D. (1964) Some thoughts on ethics of research: After reading Milgram's behavioural study of obedience. *American Psychologist, 19*, 421–423.

Baumrind, D. (1993) The average expectable environment is not good enough: A response to Scarr. *Child Development, 64*, 1299–1317.

Bayley, N. (1969) *Bayley Scales of Infant Development*. New York: Psychological Corporation.

Bayne, T. (2013) Thought. *New Scientist, 219*(2935), 32–39.

Beaman, A.L., Barnes, P.J., Klentz, B. & Mcquirk, B. (1978) Increasing helping rates through information dissemination: Teaching pays. *Personality & Social Psychology Bulletin, 4*, 406–411.

Beaman, P. (2006) Attention and change. *Psychology Review, 12* (2), 18–20.

Beaumont, J.G. (1988) *Understanding Neuropsychology*. Oxford: Blackwell.

Beck, A.T. (1963) Thinking and depression. *Archives of General Psychiatry, 9*, 324–333.

Beck, A.T. (1967) *Depression: Causes and Treatment*. Philadelphia: University of Philadelphia Press.

Beck, A.T. (1987) Cognitive models of depression. *Journal of Cognitive Psychotherapy: An International Quarterly, 1*, 5–37.

Beck, A.T. (1993) Cognitive therapy: Past, present and future. *Journal of Consulting & Clinical Psychology, 61* (2), 194–198.

Becker, H.S. (1963) *Outsiders: Studies in the Sociology of Deviance*. New York: Free Press.

Becker, M.H. (ed.) (1974) The health belief model and personal health behaviour. *Health Education Monographs, 2*, 324–508.

Becker, M.H. & Rosenstock, I.M. (1984) Compliance with medical advice. In A. Steptoe & A. Mathews (eds) *Health Care and Human Behaviour*. London: Academic Press.

Becker, M.H. & Rosenstock, I.M. (1987) Comparing social learning theory and the health belief model. In W.B. Ward (ed.) *Advances in Health Education and Promotion*. Greenwich, CT: JAI Press.

Becker, M.H, Maiman, L.A., Kirscht, J.P., Haefner, D.P. & Drachman, R.H. (1977) The health belief model and prediction of dietary compliance: A field experiment. *Journal of Health & Social Behaviour, 18*, 348–366.

Bedell, G. (2002) Why don't we just grow up? *Observer Review*, 3 February, 4.

Bee, H. (1994) *Lifespan Development*. New York: HarperCollins.

Bee, H. (2000) *The Developing Child* (9th edition). Boston: Allyn & Bacon.

Beecher, H.K. (1956) Relationship of significance of wound to the pain experienced. *Journal of the American Medical Association, 161*, 1609–1613.

Bekerian, D.A. & Bowers, J.M. (1983) Eye-witness testimony: Were we misled? *Journal of Experimental Psychology: Learning, Memory & Cognition, 9*, 139–145.

Bekerian, D.A. & Dennett, J.L. (1993) The cognitive interview technique: Reviewing the issues. *Applied Cognitive Psychology*, 7, 275–298.

Bell, B.E. & Loftus, E.F. (1989) Trivial persuasion in the courtroom: The power of (a few) minor details. *Journal of Personality & Social Psychology, 56*, 669–679.

Bell, J.T. & Spector, T.D. (2011) A twin approach to unravelling epigenetics. *Trends in Genetics, 27*(3), 116–125.

Bellur, R. (1995) Interpersonal attraction revisited: Cross-cultural conceptions of love. *Psychology Review, 1*, 24–26.

Belsky, J. (1999) Modern evolutionary theory and patterns of attachment. In J. Cassidy & P.R. Shaver (eds) *Handbook of Attachment: Theory, Research, and Clinical Applications*. New York: Guilford Press.

Belsky, J. & Rovine, M.J. (1988) Nonmaternal care in the first year of life and the infant–parent attachment. *Child Development, 59*, 157–167.

Belsky, J., Steinberg, L.D. & Draper, P. (1991) Childhood experience, interpersonal development and reproductive strategy: An evolutionary theory of socialization. *Child Development, 62*, 647–670.

Bem, D.J. (1965) An experimental analysis of self-persuasion. *Journal of Experimental & Social Psychology, 1*, 199–218.

Bem, D.J. (1967) Self-perception: An alternative interpretation of cognitive dissonance phenomena. *Psychological Review, 74*, 183–200.

Bem, D.J. (1972) Self-perception theory. In L. Berkowitz (ed.) *Advances in Experimental Social Psychology, Volume 6*. New York: Academic Press.

Bem, S.L. (1974) The measurement of psychological androgyny. *Journal of Consulting & Clinical Psychology, 42* (2), 155–162.

Bem, S.L. (1985) Androgyny and gender schema theory: A conceptual and empirical integration. In T.B. Sonderegger (ed.) *Nebraska Symposium on Motivation*. Lincoln: University of Nebraska Press.

Bennett, M. (1993) Introduction. In M. Bennett (ed.) *The Child as Psychologist: An Introduction to the Development of Social Cognition*. Hemel Hempstead: Harvester Wheatsheaf.

Bennett, P. (2003) *Abnormal and Clinical Psychology: An Introductory Textbook*. Maidenhead: Open University Press.

Bennett, P. (2006) *Abnormal and Clinical Psychology: An Introductory Textbook* (2nd edition). Maidenhead: Open University Press.

Bennett, T. (2013) Leave those kids alone! *New Scientist, 219*(2932), 26–27.

Bentall, R.P. (ed.) (1990) *Reconstructing Schizophrenia*. London: Routledge.

Bentall, R.P. (2003) *Madness Explained: Psychosis and Human Nature*. London: Penguin.

Bentall, R.P. (2007) Researching psychotic complaints. *The Psychologist, 20* (5), 293–295.

Bentall, R.P. & Young, H.F. (1996) Sensible-hypothesis-testing in deluded, depressed and normal subjects. *British Journal of Psychiatry, 168*, 372–375.

Benton, D. (1981) ECT. Can the system take the shock? *Community Care, 12 March*, 15–17.

Bereiter, C. & Engelman, S. (1966) *Teaching Disadvantaged Children in the Pre-School*. Englewood Cliffs, NJ: Prentice-Hall.

Bergevin, T., Bukowski, W.M. & Miners, R. (2003) Social development. In A. Slater & G. Bremner (eds) *An Introduction to Developmental Psychology*. Oxford: Blackwell Publishing.

Bergin, A.E. (1971) The evaluation of therapeutic outcomes. In A.E. Bergin & S.L. Garfield (eds) *Handbook of Psychotherapy and Behaviour Change: An Empirical Analysis*. New York: Wiley.

Bergin, A.E. & Lambert, M.J. (1978) The evaluation of therapeutic outcomes. In A.E. Bergin & S.L. Garfield (eds) *Handbook of Psychotherapy and Behaviour Change: An Empirical Analysis* (2nd edition). New York: Wiley.

Berko, J. (1958) The child's learning of English morphology. *Word, 14*, 150–177.

Berkowitz, L. (1966) On not being able to aggress. *British Journal of Clinical & Social Psychology, 5*, 130–139.

Berkowitz, L. (1968) Impulse, aggression and the gun. *Psychology Today, September*, 18–22.

Berkowitz, L. (1993) *Aggression: Its Causes, Consequences and Control*. New York: McGraw-Hill.

Berkowitz, L. (1995) A career on aggression. In G.G. Brannigan & M.R. Merrens (eds) *The Social Psychologists: Research Adventures*. New York: McGraw-Hill.

Berkowitz, L. & Green, R.G. (1966) Film violence and the cue properties of available targets. *Journal of Personality & Social Psychology, 3*, 525–530.

Berkowitz, L. & LePage, A. (1967) Weapons as aggression-eliciting stimuli. *Journal of Personality & Social Psychology, 7*, 202–207.

Berlin, B. & Kay, P. (1969) *Basic Colour Terms: Their Universality and Evolution*. Berkeley: University of California Press.

Berlin, H.A. & Koch, C. (2009) Neuroscience meets psychoanalysis. *Scientific American Mind, 20*(2), 16-19.

Berlyne, D.E. (1960) *Conflict, Arousal and Curiosity*. London: McGraw-Hill.

Bermond, B., Fasotti, L., Nieuwenhuyse, B. & Schuerman, J. (1991) Spinal cord lesions, peripheral feedback and intensities of emotional feelings. *Cognition & Emotion, 5*, 201–220.

Bernstein, B. (1961) Social class and linguistic development: A theory of social learning. In A.H. Halsey, J. Floyd & C.A. Anderson (eds) *Education, Economy and Society*. London: Collier-Macmillan Ltd.

Bernsten, D., Johannessen, K.B., Thomsen, Y. et al. (2012) Peace and War: Trajectories of Posttraumatic Stress Disorder Symptoms before, during and after Military Deployment in Afghanistan. *Psychological Science, 23*(12), 1557–1565.

Bernstein, D.M., Laney, C., Morris, E.K. & Loftus, E.F. (2005) False beliefs about fattening foods can have healthy consequences. *Proceedings of the National Academy of Sciences, 102*, 13724–13731.

Berry, D.S. (2000) Attractiveness, attraction, and sexual selection: Evolutionary perspectives on the form and function of physical attractiveness. In M.P. Zanna (ed.) *Advances in Experimental Social Psychology, Volume 32*. New York: Academic Press.

Berry, D.S. & Willingham, J.K. (1997) Affective traits, responses to conflict, and satisfaction in romantic relationships. *Journal of Research in Personality, 31*, 564–576.

Berry, J.W. (1969) On cross-cultural compatibility. *International Journal of Psychology, 4*, 119–128.

Berry, J.W. (1998) Acculturation and health: Theory and research. In S.S. Kazarian & D.R. Evans (eds) *Cultural Clinical Psychology: Theory, Research, and Practice*. New York: Oxford University Press.

Berry, J.W., Poortinga, Y.H., Segall, M.H. & Dasen, P.R. (1992) *Cross Cultural Psychology*. Cambridge University Press.

Berscheid, E. (1985) Interpersonal attraction. In G. Lindzey & E. Aronson (eds) *Handbook of Social Psychology, Volume 2* (3rd edition). New York: Random House.

Berscheid, E. & Ammazzalorso, H. (2004) Emotional experience in close relationships. In M.B. Brewer & M. Hewstone (eds) *Emotion and Motivation*. Oxford: Blackwell Publishing.

Berscheid, E. & Reis, H.T. (1998) Attraction and close relationships. In D.T. Gilbert, S.T. Fiske & G. Lindzey (eds) *The Handbook of Social Psychology* (4th edition). Boston: McGraw-Hill.

Berscheid, E. & Walster, E.M. (1974) Physical attractiveness. In L. Berkowitz (ed.) *Advances in Experimental Social Psychology, Volume* 7. New York: Academic Press.

Berscheid, E. & Walster, E.M. (1978) *Interpersonal Attraction* (2nd edition). Reading, MA: Addison-Wesley.

Berscheid, E., Dion, K., Hatfield, E. & Walster, G.W. (1971) Physical attractiveness and dating choice: A test of the matching hypothesis. *Journal of Experimental & Social Psychology, 7*, 173–189.

Besevegis, E. & Giannitsas, N. (1996) Parent–adult relations and conflicts as perceived by adolescents. In L. Verhofstadt-Deneve, I. Kienhorst & C. Braet (eds) *Conflict and Development in Adolescence*. Leiden: DSWO Press.

Bettelheim, B. (1985) *Freud and Man's Soul*. London: Flamingo.

Bexton, W.H., Heron, W. & Scott, T.H. (1954) Effects of decreased variation in the sensory environment. *Canadian Journal of Psychology, 8*, 70.

Beyerstein, B.L. (2007) The neurology of the weird: Brain states and anomalous experience. In S. Della Sala (ed.) *Tall Tales about the Mind & Brain: Separating Fact from Fiction*. Oxford University Press.

Bickman, L. (1971) The effects of another bystander's ability to help on bystander intervention in an emergency. *Journal of Experimental Social Psychology, 7*, 367–379.

Biederman, I. (1987) Recognition-by-components: A theory of human image understanding. *Psychological Review, 94*, 115–147.

Bierhoff, H.W. (1983) Wie hilfreich ist der Mensch? *Bild der Wissenschaft, 12*, 118–126.

Bierhoff, H.W. (2002) Just world, social responsibility, and helping behaviour. In M. Ross & D.T. Miller (eds) *The Justice Motive in Everyday Life*. Cambridge University Press, 189–203.

Bierhoff, H.W. & Klein, R. (1988) Prosocial behaviour. In M. Hewstone, W. Stroebe, J.P. Codol & G.M. Stephenson (eds) *Introduction to Social Psychology*. Oxford: Blackwell.

Bierhoff, H.W. & Rohmann, E. (2004) Altruistic personality in the context of the empathy-altruism hypothesis. *European Journal of Personality, 18*, 351–365.

Bierhoff, H.W., Klein, R. & Kramp, P. (1991) Evidence for the altruistic personality from data on accident research. *Journal of Personality, 59*, 263–280.

Biever, C. (2009) The makings of a savant. *New Scientist, 202* (2711), 30–33.

Bilalic, M. & McLeod, P. (2014) Why good thoughts block better ones. *Scientific American, 310*(3), 58-63.

Billig, M. (1976) *Social Psychology and Intergroup Relations*. London: Academic Press.

Billig, M. (1978) *Fascists: A Social Psychological View of the National Front*. London: Harcourt Brave Jovanovich.

Billig, M. & Tajfel, H. (1973) Social categorisation and similarity in intergroup behaviour. *European Journal of Social Psychology, 3*, 27–52.

Binet, A. (1905) La science du temoignage [The science of testimony]. *Année Psychologique, 15*, v–vii.

Biro, F.M., Galvez, M.P., Greenspan, L.C.A et al. (2010) Pubertal assessment method and baseline characteristics in a mixed longitudinal study of girls. *Paediatrics, 126*, e583-e590.

Bivens, J.A. & Berk, L.A. (1990) A longitudinal study of the development of elementary school children's private speech. *Merrill-Palmer Quarterly, 36*, 443–463.

Blackman, D.E. (1980) Images of man in contemporary behaviourism. In A.J. Chapman & D.M. Jones (eds) *Models of Man*. Leicester: British Psychological Society.

Blackmore, S. (1995) Parapsychology. In A.M. Colman (ed.) *Controversies in Psychology*. London: Longman.

Blackmore, S. (2003) *Consciousness: An Introduction*. London: Hodder & Stoughton.

Blair, R.J.R., Morris, J.S., Frith, C.D., Perret, D.I. & Dolan, R.J. (1999) Dissociable neural responses to facial expressions of sadness and anger. *Brain, 122*, 883–893.

Blakemore, C. (1988) *The Mind Machine*. London: BBC Publications.

Blakemore, C. (2008) Hysteria over cannabis is getting in the way of truth. *Observer*, 4 May, 27.

Blakemore, C. & Cooper, G.F. (1970) Development of the brain depends on the visual environment. *Nature, 228*, 477–478.

Blakemore, S.-J. (2007) The social brain of a teenager. *The Psychologist, 20* (10), 600–602.

Blakemore, S.-J., Smith, J., Steel, R., Johnstone, E.C. & Frith, C.D. (2000) The perception of self-produced sensory stimuli in patients with auditory hallucinations and passivity experiences. *Psychological Medicine, 30*, 1130–1131.

Blaney, P. (1975) Implications of the medical model and its alternatives. *American Journal of Psychiatry, 132*, 911–914.

Blau, P.M. (1964) *Exchange and Power in Social Life*. New York: Wiley.

Bleicher, A. (2012) Edges of perception. *Scientific American Mind, 23*(1), 46–53.

Bleuler, E. (1911) *Dementia Praecox or the Group of Schizophrenias* (trans. J. Avikin). New York: International Universities Press.

Block, J. (1979) Another look at sex differentiation in the socialisation behaviours of mothers and fathers. In F. Denmark & J. Sherman (eds) *Psychology of Women: Future Directions of Research*. New York: Psychological Dimensions.

Bloom, P. (2013) *Just Babies: The origins of good and evil*. New York: Random House.

Blos, P. (1979) *The Adolescent Passage*. New York: International Universities Press.

Blundell, J.E. & Hill, A.J. (1995) Hunger and appetite. In Parkinson, B. & Colman, A.M. (eds) *Emotion and Motivation*. London: Longman.

Blyth, D.A., Simmons, R.G., Bulcroft, R., Felt, D., Vancleave, E.F. & Bush, D.M. (1981) The effects of physical development on self-image and satisfaction with body-image for early adolescent males. *Research in Community & Mental Health, 2*, 43–73.

Boden, M. (1980) Artificial intelligence and intellectual imperialism. In A.J. Chapman & D.M. Jones (eds) *Models of Man*. Leicester: British Psychological Society.

Boden, M. (1987a) *Artificial Intelligence and Natural Man* (2nd edition). Cambridge, MA: Harvard University Press.

Boden, M. (1987b) Artificial intelligence. In R. Gregory (ed.) *Oxford Companion to the Mind*. Oxford University Press.

Boden, M. (1993) The impact on philosophy. In D. Broadbent (ed.) *The Simulation of Human Intelligence*. Oxford: Blackwell.

Bodmer, W.F. (1972) Race and IQ: The genetic background. In K. Richardson & D. Spears (eds) *Race, Culture and Intelligence*. Harmondsworth: Penguin.

Bolles, R.C. (1980) Ethological learning theory. In G.M. Gazda & R.J. Corsini (eds) *Theories of Learning: A Comparative Approach*. Itaska, IL: Free Press.

Boly, M., Garrido, M.I., Gosseries, O. et al. (2011) Preserved Feedforward but Impaired Top-Down Processes in the VS. *Science, 332*(6031), 858–862.

Bonanno, G.A. (2009) *The Other Side of Sadness*. New York: Basic Books.

Bonanno, G.A., Westphal, M. & Mancini, A.D. (2011) Resilience to Loss and Potential Trauma. *Annual Review of Clinical Psychology, 7*, 511–535.

Bond, C.F., Jr. & Titus, L.J. (1983) Social facilitation: A meta-analysis of 241 studies. *Psychological Bulletin, 94*, 265–292.

Bond, J., Coleman, P. & Peace, S. (eds) (1993) *Ageing in Society: An Introduction to Social Gerontology*. London: Sage.

Bond, J., Dittmann-Kohli, F., Westerhof, G.J. & Peace, S. (2007) Ageing into the future. In J. Bond, S. Peace, F. Dittman-Kohli & G. Westerhof (eds) *Ageing in Society* (3rd edition). London: Sage Publications.

Bond, M. (2004) The making of a suicide bomber. *New Scientist, 182* (2447), 34–38.

Bond, M. (2007) They made me do it. *New Scientist, 194* (2599), 42–45.

Bond, M. (2014) The Secret of Success. *New Scientist, 221*(2959), 30–34.

Bond, R.A. & Smith, P.B. (1996) Culture and conformity: A metaanalysis of studies using Asch's (1952b, 1956) line judgement task. *Psychological Bulletin, 119*, 111–137.

Boon, J. & Davies, G. (1992) Fact and fiction in offender profiling. *Issues in Legal & Criminological Psychology, 32*, 3–9.

Booth-Kewby, S. & Friedman, H.S. (1987) Psychological predictors of heart disease: A quantitative review. *Psychological Bulletin, 101*, 343–362.

Boring, E.G. (1923) Intelligence as the tests test it. *New Republic*, 6 June, 35–37.

Boring, E.G. (1966) Introduction. In C.E.M. Hansel (ed.) *ESP: A Scientific Evaluation*. New York: Scribner.

Borke, H. (1975) Piaget's mountains revisited: Changes in the egocentric landscape. *Developmental Psychology, 11*, 240–243.

Bornstein, M.H. (1988) Perceptual development across the life-cycle. In M.H. Bornstein & M.E. Lamb (eds) *Perceptual, Cognitive and Linguistic Development*. Hove: Erlbaum.

Bornstein, M.H. (1989) Sensitive periods in development: Structural characteristics and causal interpretations. *Psychological Bulletin, 105*, 179–197.

Boseley, S. (1999) They said it was safe. *Guardian Weekend*, 30 October, 12–17.

Bouchard, T.J. & Loehlin, J.C. (2001) Genes, evolution, and personality. *Behaviour Genetics, 31*, 243–273.

Bouchard, T.J. & McGue, M. (1981) Familial studies of intelligence: A review. *Science, 212*, 1055–1059.

Bouchard, T.J. & Segal, N.L. (1988) Heredity, environment and IQ. In *Instructor's Resource Manual* to accompany G. Lindzay, R. Thompson & B. Spring, *Psychology* (3rd edition). New York: Worth Publishers.

Bouchard, T.J., Lykken, D.T., McGue, M., Segal, N.L. & Tellegen, A. (1990) Sources of human psychological differences: The Minnesota study of twins reared apart. *Science, 250*, 223–228.

Bower, G.H. (1975) Cognitive psychology: An introduction. In W. Estes (ed.) *Handbook of Learning and Cognitive Processes, Volume 1*. Hillsdale, NJ: Lawrence Erlbaum Associates Inc.

Bower, T.G.R. (1966) The visual world of infants. *Scientific American, 215*, 80–92.

Bower, T.G.R. (1977) *The Perceptual World of the Child*. London: Fontana Paperbacks.

Bower, T.G.R. & Wishart, J.G. (1972) The effects of motor skill on object permanence. *Cognition, 1*, 28–35.

Bowers, K. (1973) Situationism in psychology: An analysis and critique. *Psychological Review, 80*, 307–336.

Bowlby, J. (1951) *Maternal Care and Mental Health*. Geneva: World Health Organization.

Bowlby, J. (1969) *Attachment and Loss. Volume 1: Attachment*. Harmondsworth: Penguin.

Bowlby, J. (1973) *Attachment and Loss. Volume 2: Separation*. Harmondsworth: Penguin.

Bowlby, J. (1977) The making and breaking of affectional bonds: 1. Aetiology and psychopathology in the light of attachment theory. *British Journal of Psychiatry, 130*, 201–210.

Bowlby, J. (1980) *Attachment and Loss. Volume 3: Loss, Sadness and Depression*. London: Hogarth Press.

Bowlby, J. (1988) *A Secure Base: Clinical Applications of Attachment Theory*. London: Tavistock/Routledge.

Bowlby, J., Ainsworth, M., Boston, M. & Rosenbluth, D. (1956) The effects of mother–child separation: A follow-up study. *British Journal of Medical Psychology, 24* (3 & 4), 211–247.

Boyle, E. (2009) Neuroscience and Animal Sentience. www.animalsentience.com

Bradbury, T.N. & Fincham, F.D. (1990) Attributions in marriage: Review and critique. *Psychological Bulletin, 107*, 3–33.

Bradley, B.P. & Baddeley, A.D. (1990) Emotional factors in forgetting. *Psychological Medicine, 20*, 351–355.

Bradley, C.L. (1997) Generativity-stagnation: Development of a status model. *Developmental Review, 17*, 262–290.

Bradley, C.L. & Marcia, J.E. (1998a) Generativity-stagnation: A five category model. *Journal of Personality, 66*, 39–64.

Bradley, C.L. & Marcia, J.E. (1998b) The generativity status measure: Replication and extension in two adult samples. Unpublished manuscript, Simon Fraser University, British Columbia, Canada.

Bradley, L.A. (1995) Chronic benign pain. In D. Wedding (ed.) *Behaviour and Medicine* (2nd edition). St Louis, MO: Mosby-Year Book.

Bradley, S.J., Oliver, C.D., Chernick, A.B. & Zucker, K.J. (1998) Experiment of nurture: Ablatio penis at 2 months, sex reassignment at 7 months, and a psychosexual follow-up in young adulthood. *Paediatrics, 102*, 1–5.

Bradshaw, J.L. & Wallace, G. (1971) Models for the processing and identification of faces. *Perception & Psychophysics, 9*, 443–448.

Brainerd, C.J. (1983) Modifiability of cognitive development. In S. Meadows (ed.) *Development of Thinking*. London: Methuen.

Brand, C. (1996) *The g Factor: General Intelligence and its Implications*. New York: John Wiley.

Brandon, S., Boakes, J., Glaser, D. & Green, R. (1998) Recovered memories of childhood sexual abuse: Implications for clinical practice. *British Journal of Psychiatry, 172*, 293–307.

Breggin, P. (1991) *Toxic Psychiatry*. London: HarperCollins.

Breggin, P. (1997) *Brain-Disabling Treatments in Psychiatry*. New York: Springer.

Breggin, P. (2008) *Brain-disabling Treatments in Psychiatry*. New York: Springer.

Brehm, J.W. (1956) Post-decision changes in the desirability of alternatives. *Journal of Abnormal & Social Psychology, 52*, 384–389.

Brehm, J.W. (1966) *A Theory of Psychological Reactance*. New York: Academic Press.

Brehm, S.S. (1992) *Intimate Relationships* (2nd edition). New York: McGraw-Hill.

Brehm, S.S. & Brehm, J.W. (1981) *Psychological Reactance: A Theory of Freedom and Control*. New York: Academic Press.

Bremner, G. (2003) Perception, knowledge and action. In A. Slater & G. Bremner (eds) *An Introduction to Developmental Psychology*. Oxford: Blackwell Publishing.

Bremner, G. (2011) Perception, Knowledge, and Action in Infancy. In A. Slater & G. Bremner (eds) *An Introduction to Developmental Psychology* (2nd edition). BPS Blackwell.

Brewer, M.B. (1999) The psychology of prejudice: Ingroup love or outgroup hate? *Journal of Social Issues, 55*, 429–444.

Brewer, M.B. & Brown, R.J. (1998) Intergroup relations. In D.T. Gilbert, S.T. Fiske & G. Lindzey (eds) *Handbook of Social Psychology, Volume 2* (4th edition). New York: McGraw-Hill.

Brewer, N.T., Chapman, G.B., Brownlee, S. & Leventhal, E.A. (2002) Cholesterol control, medication adherence, and illness cognition. *British Journal of Health Psychology, 7*, 433–447.

Brewer, W.F. (1974) There is no convincing evidence for operant or classical conditioning in adult humans. In W.B. Weimar & D.S. Palermo (eds) *Cognition and the Symbolic Processes*. Hillsdale, NJ: Lawrence Erlbaum.

Brewerton, T.D., Frampton, I. & Lask, B. (2009) The neurobiology of anorexia nervosa. *US Psychiatry, 2*, 57–60.

Brewin, C.R., Dalgleish, T. & Jospeh, S. (1996) A Dual Representation Theory of Posttraumatic Stress Disorder. *Psychological Review, 103*(4), 670–686.

Brigham, J. & Malpass, R.S. (1985) The role of experience and contact in the recognition of faces of own- and other-race persons. *Journal of Social Issues, 41*, 139–155.

Briken, P., Hill, A. & Berner, W. (2009) Abnormal attraction. *Scientific American Mind: Special Collection on Sex, 20* (3), 76–81.

Brislin, R. (1981) *Cross-cultural encounters: Face-to-face interaction*. Elmsford, NY: Pergamon.

Brislin, R. (1993) *Understanding Culture's Influence on Behaviour*. Orlando, FL: Harcourt Brace Jovanovich.

British Psychological Society (1978a) Ethical principles for research on human subjects. *Bulletin of the British Psychological Society, 31*, 48–49.

British Psychological Society (1978b) *Report of the Working Party on Behaviour Modification*. Leicester: British Psychological Society.

British Psychological Society (1981) *Principles Governing the Employment of Psychological Tests*. Leicester: British Psychological Society.

British Psychological Society (1985a) The code of conduct for psychologists. *Bulletin of the British Psychological Society, 38*, 41–43.

British Psychological Society (1985b) *Division of Clinical Psychology Professional Practice Guidelines*. Leicester: British Psychological Society.

British Psychological Society (1990) Ethical principles for conducting research with human participants. *The Psychologist, 3* (6), 269–272.

British Psychological Society (1992) *Ethical Principles for Conducting Research with Human Participants* (revised). Leicester: British Psychological Society.

British Psychological Society (1993) Ethical Principles for conducting research with human participants (revised). *The Psychologist, 6* (1), 33–35.

British Psychological Society (1995a) *Division of Clinical Psychology Professional Practice Guidelines*. Leicester: British Psychological Society.

British Psychological Society (1995b) *Recovered Memories: The Report of the Working Party of the British Psychological Society*. Leicester: British Psychological Society.

British Psychological Society (2000) *Code of Conduct, Ethical Principles and Guidelines*. Leicester: British Psychological Society.

British Psychological Society (2004) *So You Want to be a Psychologist?* Leicester: British Psychological Society.

British Psychological Society (2006) *Code of Ethics and Conduct*. Leicester: British Psychological Society.

British Psychological Society (2007a) *Guidelines for Psychologists Working with Animals*. Leicester: British Psychological Society.

British Psychological Society (2007b) *Guidelines for Ethical Practice in Psychological Research Online*. Leicester: British Psychological Society.

British Psychological Society (2009) *The Code of Ethics and Conduct*. Leicester: BPS.

British Psychological Society (2010) *The Code of Human Research Ethics*. Leicester: BPS.

Broadbent, D.E. (1954) The role of auditory localisation and attention in memory span. *Journal of Experimental Psychology, 47*, 191–196.

Broadbent, D.E. (1958) *Perception and Communication*. Oxford: Pergamon.

Broadbent, D.E. (1961) *Behaviour*. London: Eyre and Spottiswoode.

Broadbent, D.E. (1975) The magic number seven after fifteen years. In A. Kennedy & A. Wilkes (eds) *Studies in Long-Term Memory*. New York: Wiley.

Broadbent, D.E. (1981) Non-corporeal explanations in psychology. In A.F. Heath (ed.) *Scientific Explanation*. Oxford: Clarendon Press.

Broadbent, D.E. (1982) Task combination and selective intake of information. *Acta Psychologica, 50*, 253–290.

Brodbeck, A. & Irwin, O. (1946) The speech behaviour of infants without families. *Child Development, 17*, 145–146.

Brody, E.B. & Brody, N. (1976) *Intelligence: Nature, Determinants and Consequences*. New York: Academic Press.

Bromley, D.B. (1977) Speculations in social and environmental gerontology. *Nursing Times (Occasional Papers)*, 21 April, 53–56.

Bromley, D.B. (1988) *Human Ageing: An Introduction to Gerontology* (3rd edition). Harmondsworth: Penguin.

Bronfenbrenner, U. (1960) Freudian theories of identification and their derivatives. *Child Development, 31*, 15–40.

Brookman, F. (2005) *Understanding Homicide*. London: Sage.

Brooks-Gordon, B. & Bilby, C. (2006) Psychological interventions for treatment of sex offenders. *British Medical Journal, 333*, 5–6.

Brooks-Gunn, J. & Warren, M.P. (1985) The effects of delayed menarche in different contexts. Dance and non-dance students. *Journal of Youth & Adolescence, 14*, 285–300.

Brooks-Gunn, J., Attie, H., Burrow, C., Rosso, J.T. & Warren, M.P. (1989) The impact of puberty on body and eating concerns in athletic and non-athletic contexts. *Journal of Early Adolescence, 9*, 269–290.

Brosschot, J.F., Gerin, W. & Thayer, J.F. (2006) Worry and health: the preserverative cognition hypothesis. *Journal of Psychosomatic Research, 60*, 113–124.

Brown, G. (2007) The bitter end. *New Scientist, 196* (2625), 42–43.

Brown, H. (1985) *People, Groups and Society*. Milton Keynes: Open University Press.

Brown, J. (1999) Superwoman is feeling overworked and fed up. *Oxford Times (Business Supplement)*, July/August, 11.

Brown, J.A.C. (1961) *Freud and the Post-Freudians*. Harmondsworth: Penguin.

Brown, J.A.C. (1963) *Techniques of Persuasion: From Propaganda to Brainwashing*. Harmondsworth: Penguin.

Brown, J.K. (1963) A cross-cultural study of female initiation rites. *American Anthropologist, 65*, 837–853.

Brown, L.M. & Gilligan, C. (1992) *Meeting at the Crossroads: Women's Psychology and Girls' Development*. Cambridge, MA: Harvard University Press.

Brown, L.S. (1997) Ethics in psychology: Cui bono? In D. Fox & I. Prilleltensky (eds) *Critical Psychology: An Introduction*. London: Sage.

Brown, R. (1958) *Words and Things*. Glencoe, IL: Free Press.

Brown, R. (1965) *Social Psychology*. New York: Free Press.

Brown, R. (1973) *A First Language: The Early Stages*. Cambridge, MA: Harvard University Press.

Brown, R. (1986) *Social Psychology: The Second Edition*. New York: Free Press.

Brown, R. & Kulik, J. (1977) Flashbulb memories. *Cognition, 5*, 73–99.

Brown, R. & Lenneberg, E.H. (1954) A study in language and cognition. *Journal of Abnormal & Clinical Psychology, 49*, 454–462.

Brown, R. & McNeill, D. (1966) The 'tip-of-the-tongue' phenomenon. *Journal of Verbal Learning & Verbal Behaviour, 5*, 325–337.

Brown, R.J. (1988) Intergroup relations. In M. Hewstone, W. Stroebe, J.P. Codol & G.M. Stephenson (eds) *Introduction to Social Psychology*. Oxford: Blackwell.

Brown, R.J. (1996) Intergroup relations. In M. Hewstone, W. Stroebe & G.M. Stephenson (eds) *Introduction to Social Psychology* (2nd edition). Oxford: Blackwell.

Brown, R.J., Marsas, P., Masser, B., Vivian, J. & Hewstone, M. (2001) Life on the ocean wave: Testing some intergroup hypotheses in a naturalistic setting. *Group Processes and Intergroup Relations, 4*, 81–98.

Brubaker, C. & Wickersham, D. (1990) Encouraging the practice of testicular self-examination: A field application of the theory of reasoned action. *Health Psychology, 9*, 154–163.

Bruce, V. (1995) Perceiving and recognising faces. In I. Roth & V. Bruce, *Perception and Representation: Current Issues* (2nd edition). Buckingham: Open University Press.

Bruce, V. & Green, P.R. (1990) *Visual Perception* (2nd edition). Hove: Erlbaum.

Bruce, V. & Young, A.W. (1986) Understanding face recognition. *British Journal of Psychology, 77*, 305–327.

Bruce, V. & Young, A. (1998) *In the Eye of the Beholder: The Science of Face Perception*. Oxford University Press.

Bruce, V., Henderson, Z., Greenwood, K., Hancock, P.J.B., Burton, A.M. & Miller, P. (1999) Verification of face identities from images captured on video. *Journal of Experimental Psychology: Applied, 5*, 339–360.

Brugger, P. & Funk, M. (2007) Out on a limb: Neglect and confabulation in the study of aplasic phantoms. In S. Della Sala (ed.) *Tall Tales about the Mind & Brain: Separating Fact from Fiction*. Oxford University Press.

Brugger, P. & Graves, R.E. (1997) Right hemispatial inattention and magical ideation. *European Archives of Psychiatry and Clinical Neuroscience, 247*, 55–57.

Bruner, J.S. (1957) On perceptual readiness. *Psychological Review, 64*, 123–152.

Bruner, J.S. (1966) *Towards a Theory of Instruction*. Cambridge, MA: Harvard University Press.

Bruner, J.S. (1975) The ontogenesis of speech acts. *Journal of Child Language, 2*, 1–21.

Bruner, J.S. (1978) Acquiring the uses of language. *Canadian Journal of Psychology, 32*, 204–218.

Bruner, J.S. (1983) *Child's Talk: Learning to Use Language*. Oxford University Press.

Bruner, J.S. (1986) *Actual Minds, Possible Worlds*. Cambridge, MA: Harvard University Press.

Bruner, J.S. (1987) *Child's Talk*. New York: Norton.

Bruner, J.S. (1990) *Acts of Meaning*. Cambridge, MA: Harvard University Press.

Bruner, J.S. & Goodman, C.C.(1947) Value and need as organising factors in perception. *Journal of Abnormal & Social Psychology, 42*, 33–44.

Bruner, J.S. & Haste, H. (1987) *Making Sense: The Child's Construction of the World*. London: Methuen.

Bruner, J.S. & Tagiuri, R. (1954) The perception of people. In G. Lindzey (ed.) *Handbook of Social Psychology, Volume 2*. London: Addison Wesley.

Bruner, J.S., Goodnow, J.J. & Austin, G.A. (1956) *A Study of Thinking*. New York: Wiley.

Brunet, A., Poundja, J., Tremblay, J. et al. (2011) Trauma reactivation under the influence of propranalol decreases posttraumatic stress symptoms and disorder: 3 Open-Label Trials. *Journal of Clinical Psychopharmacology, 31*(4), 547–550.

Bryant, P.E. (1990) Empirical evidence for causes in development. In G. Butterworth & P. Bryant (eds) *Causes of Development*. Brighton: Harvester Wheatsheaf.

Bublitz, N. (2008) A face in the crowd. *Scientific American Mind, 19* (2), 58–65.

Buchan, H., Johnstone, E., McPherson, K. Et al. (1992) Who benefits from electroconvulsive therapy? Combined results of the Leicester and Northwick Park trials. *British Journal of Psychiatry, 160*, 355–359.

Buchanan, M. (2007) Born prejudiced. *New Scientist, 193* (2595), 40–43.

Buckhout, R. (1974) Eyewitness testimony. *Scientific American, December*, 23–31.

Bulik, C.M. (2001) Eating disorders: Integrating nature and nurture through the study of twins. In M. Nasser, M.A. Katzman & R.A. Gordon (eds) *Eating Disorders and Cultures in Transition*. Hove: Brunner-Routledge.

Bull, M. & LaVecchio, F. (1978) Behaviour therapy for a child with Lesch–Nyhan syndrome. *Developmental Medicine & Child Neurology, 20*, 368–375.

Buller, D.J. (2009) Four fallacies of pop evolutionary psychology. *Scientific American, 300* (1), 60–67.

Buller, D.J. (2013) Four fallacies of pop evolutionary psychology. *Scientific American, 22*(1), 44–51.

Burger, J.M. (2009) Replicating Milgram: Would people still obey today? *American Psychologist, 64*(1), 1–11.

Burger, J.M. (2011) Alive and well after all these years. *The Psychologist, 24*(9), 654–657.

Burgio, L.D., Whitman, T.I. & Reid, D.H. (1983) A participative management approach for improving direct care staff performance in an institutional setting. *Journal of Applied Behaviour Analysis, 16*, 37–52.

Burley, P.M. & McGuiness, J. (1977) Effects of social intelligence on the Milgram paradigm. *Psychological Reports, 40*, 767–770.

Burnett, S., Bird, G., Moll, J., Frith, C. & Blakemore, S-J. (2009) Development during adolescence of the neural processing of social emotion. *Journal of Cognitive Neuroscience, 21*(9), 1736–1750.

Burns, R.B. (1980) *Essential Psychology*. Lancaster: MTP Press.

Burr, V. (1995) *An Introduction to Social Constructionism*. London: Routledge.

Burr, V. (2003) *Social Constructionism* (2nd edition). Hove: Routledge.

Burt, C. (1949) The structure of the mind: A review of the results of factor analysis. *British Journal of Educational Psychology, 19*, 110–11, 176–199.

Burt, C. (1955) The evidence for the concept of intelligence. *British Journal of Educational Psychology, 25*, 158–177.

Burt, C. (1966) The genetic determination of differences in intelligence: A study of monozygotic twins reared together and apart. *British Journal of Psychology, 57*, 137–153.

Bushman, B.J. (1998) Priming effects of media violence on the accessibility of aggressive constructs in memory. *Personality & Social Psychology Bulletin, 24*, 537–545.

Bushman, B.J. & Anderson, C.A. (2001a) Is it time to pull the plug on the hostile versus instrumental aggression dichotomy? *Psychological Review, 108*, 273–279.

Bushman, B.J. & Anderson, C.A. (2001b) Media violence and the American public. *American Psychologist, 56*, 477–489.

Bushnell, I.W.R. (2001) Mother's face recognition in newborn infants: Learning and memory. *Infant & Child Development, 10*, 67–74.

Bushnell, I.W.R., Sai, F. & Mullin, J.T. (1989) Neonatal recognition of the mother's face. *British Journal of Developmental Psychology, 7*, 3–15.

Buss, A.H. (1961) *The Psychology of Aggression*. New York: Wiley.

Buss, A.H. (1992) Personality: Primate heritage and human distinctiveness. In R.A. Zucker, A.I. Rabin, J. Aronoff & S.J. Frank (eds) *Personality Structure in the Life Course: Essays on Personality in the Murray Tradition*. New York: Springer.

Buss, D.M. (1989) Sex differences in human mate preferences: Evolutionary hypotheses tested in 37 cultures. *Behavioural & Brain Sciences, 12*, 1–49.

Buss, D.M. (1994) Mate preference in 37 cultures. In W.J. Lonner & R.S. Malpass (eds) *Psychology and Culture*. Boston: Allyn & Bacon.

Buss, D.M. (1995) Evolutionary psychology: A new paradigm for psychological science. *Psychological Inquiry, 6*, 1–49.

Buss, D.M. (1995) Evolutionary psychology: A new paradigm for psychological science. *Psychological Inquiry, 6*, 1–49.

Bussey, K. & Bandura, A. (1984) Influence of gender constancy and social power on sex-linked modelling. *Journal of Personality & Social Psychology, 47*, 1292–1302.

Bussey, K. & Bandura, A. (1999) Social cognitive theory of gender development and differentiation. *Psychological Review, 106*, 676–713.

Butler, K. (1996) The biology of fear. *Family Therapy Networker, 20*, 39–45.

Butler, R.A. (1954) Curiosity in monkeys. *Scientific American, February*, 70–75.

Buunk, A.P. & Dijkstra, P. (2008) Affiliation, Attraction and Close Relationships. In M. Hewstone, W. Stroebe & K. Jonas (eds) *Introduction to Social Psychology: A European Perspective* (4th edition). Oxford: BPS Blackwell.

Byrne, D. (1971) *The Attraction Paradigm*. New York: Academic Press.

Byron, R. (2014) Criminals need Mental Health Care. *Scientific American Mind, 25*(2), 20–23.

Cahill, L. (2012) His brain, her brain. *Scientific American Mind, 21*(2), 4–11.

Calder, A.J. & Young, A.W. (2005) Understanding the recognition of facial identity and facial expression. *Nature Reviews Neuroscience, 6*, 641–651.

Calvin, W.H. (1994) The emergence of language. *Scientific American, October*, 79–85.

Campbell, B.A. & Church, R.M. (1969) (eds) *Punishment and Aversive Behaviour*. New York: Appleton-Century-Crofts.

Campbell, J., Tyrell, D. & Zingaro, M. (1993) Sensation-seeking among water canoe and kayak paddlers. *Personality & Individual Differences, 14*, 489–491. 831

Campos, J.J., Langer, A. & Krowitz, A. (1970) Cardiac responses on the visual cliff in pre-locomotor human infants. *Science, 170*, 196–197.

Cannon, W.B. (1929*) Bodily Changes in Pain, Hunger, Fear, and Rage*. New York: Appleton.

Cannon, W.B. & Washburn, A.L. (1912) An explanation of hunger. *American Journal of Physiology, 29*, 441–454.

Canter, D. (1989) Offender profiling. *The Psychologist, January*, 12–16.

Canter, D. (1994) *Criminal Shadows*. London: HarperCollins.

Canter, D. (2010) *Forensic Psychology: A Very Short Introduction*. Oxford: Oxford University Press.

Canter, D. & Youngs, D. (2008) *Investigative Psychology: Offender Profiling and the Analysis of Criminal Action*. Chichester: Wiley.

Canter, D. & Youngs, D. (2009) *Investigative Psychology: Offender Profiling and the Analysis of Criminal Action*. Chichester: Wiley and Sons.

Canter, D., Hughes, D. & Kirby, S. (1998) Paedophilia: Pathology, criminality, or both? The development of a multivariate model of offence behaviour in child sexual abuse. *Journal of Forensic Psychiatry, 9*, 532–555.

Caplan, P.J. (1991) Delusional dominating personality disorder (DDPD). *Feminism & Psychology, 1* (1), 171–174.

Capon, N. & Kuhn, D. (1979) Logical reasoning in the supermarket: Adult females' use of a proportional reasoning strategy in an everyday context. *Developmental Psychology, 15*, 450–452.

Carlson, M., Marcus-Newhall, A. & Miller, N. (1990) Effects of situational aggression cues: A quantitative review. *Journal of Personality & Social Psychology, 58*, 622–633.

Carlson, N.R. (1988) *Foundations of Physiological Psychology*. Boston: Allyn & Bacon.

Carlson, N.R. (1992) *Foundations of Physiological Psychology* (2nd edition). Boston: Allyn & Bacon.

Carlson, N.R. & Buskist, W. (1997) *Psychology: The Science of Behaviour* (5th edition). Needham Heights, MA: Allyn & Bacon.

Carmichael, L., Hogan, P. & Walter, A. (1932) An experimental study of the effect of language on the reproduction of visually perceived forms. *Journal of Experimental Psychology, 15*, 1–22.

Carpenter, P. (1997) Learning disability. In L. Rees, M. Lipsedge & C. Ball (eds) *Textbook of Psychiatry*. London: Arnold.

Carroll, D.W. (1986) *Psychology of Language*. Monterey, CA: Brooks/Cole Publishing Co.

Carroll, J.B. & Casagrande, J.B. (1958) The function of language classifications in behaviour. In E.E. Maccoby, T.M. Newcombe & E.L. Hartley (eds*) Readings in Social Psychology* (3rd edition). New York: Holt, Rinehart & Winston.

Carstensen, L.L. (1991) Selectivity theory: Social activity in life-span context. In K.W. Schaie & M. Powell Lawton (eds) *Annual Review of Gerontology and Geriatrics: Behavioural Science and Ageing, Volume 11*. New York: Springer.

Carstensen, L.L. (1992) Social and emotional patterns in adulthood: Support for socioemotional selectivity theory. *Psychology & Ageing, 7*, 331–338.

Carstensen, L.L. (1993) Motivation for social contact across the life span: A theory of socioemotional selectivity. In J. Jacobs (ed.) *Nebraska Symposium on Motivation 1992, Developmental Perspectives on Motivation, Volume 40*. Lincoln: University of Nebraska Press.

Carstensen, L.L. (1995) Evidence for a life-span theory of socioemotional selectivity. *Current Directions in Psychological Science, 4*, 151–156.

Carstensen, L.L. (1996) Socioemotional selectivity: A life span developmental account of social behaviour. In M.R. Merrens & G.C. Brannigan (eds) *The Developmental Psychologists: Research Adventures across the Life Span*. New York: McGraw-Hill.

Carstensen, L.L. & Turk-Charles, S. (1994) The salience of emotion across the adult life course. *Psychology & Ageing, 9*, 259–264.

Carter, N.M. (2004) Implications for medicine in the 'post-genome era'. *Current Anaesthesia & Critical Care, 15*, 37–43.

Cartwright, J. (2000) *Evolution and Human Behaviour*. Basingstoke: Macmillan.

Carver, C.S. & Scheier, M.F. (1992) *Perspectives on Personality* (2nd edition). Boston: Allyn & Bacon.

Caspi, A., Lynam, T.E., Moffitt, T.E. & Silva, P.A. (1993) Unravelling girls' delinquency: Biological, dispositional and contextual contributions to adolescent misbehaviour. *Developmental Psychology, 29*, 19–30.

Castro, J. (2012) Sleep's secret repairs. *Scientific American Mind, 23*(2), 42–45.

Catan, L. (2004) *Becoming Adult: Changing Youth Transitions in the 21st Century*. Brighton: Trust for the Study of Adolescence.

Catania, J.A., Kegeles, S.M. & Coates, D.J. (1990) Towards an understanding of risk behaviour: an AIDS risk reduction model (ARRM). *Health Education Quarterly, 17*, 53–72.

Cattell, R.B. (1963) Theory of fluid and crystallised intelligence: A critical experiment. *Journal of Educational Psychology, 54*, 1–22.

Cattell, R.B. (1965) *The Scientific Analysis of Personality*. Harmondsworth: Penguin.

Cavanaugh, J.C. (1995) Ageing. In P.E. Bryant & A.M. Colman (eds) *Developmental Psychology*. London: Longman.

Ceci, S.J. & Liker, J.K. (1986) A day at the races: A study of IQ, expertise, and cognitive complexity. *Journal of Experimental Psychology, 115*, 255–266.

Ceci, S.J. & Williams, W.M. (eds) (1999) *The Nature–Nurture Debate: The Essential Readings*. Oxford: Blackwell.

Chaiken, S. (1987) The heuristic model of persuasion. In M.P. Zanna, J.M. Olsen & C.P. Herman (eds) *Social Influence: The Ontario Symposium, Volume 5*. Hillsdale, NJ: Lawrence Erlbaum Associates Inc.

Chaiken, S., Liberman, A. & Eagly, A.H. (1989) Heuristic and systematic information processing within and beyond the persuasion context. In J.S Uleman & J.A. Bargh (eds) *Unintended Thought*. New York: Guilford Press.

Chamorro-Premuzic, T. (2007) *Personality and Individual Differences*. Oxford: BPS Blackwell.

Champion, L.A. (2000) Depression. In L. Champion & M. Power (eds) *Adult Psychological Problems: An Introduction* (2nd edition). Hove: Psychology Press.

Champion, L.A. & Power, M.J. (1995) Social and cognitive approaches to depression: Towards a new synthesis. *British Journal of Clinical Psychology, 34*, 485–503.

Chapman, L.J., Chapman, J.P. & Kwapil, T.R. (1994) Does the Eysenck psychoticism scale predict psychosis? *Personality & Individual Differences, 17*, 369–375.

Chapman, M. & McBride, M. (1992) Beyond competence and performance: Children's class inclusion strategies, subordinate class cues, and verbal justifications. *Developmental Psychology, 28*, 319–327.

Chapman, R.S. (2000) Children's language learning: An interactionist perspective. *Journal of Child Psychology & Psychiatry, 41*(1), 33–54.

Chappel, J. & Kacelnik, A. (2002) Tool selectivity in a non-mammal, a New Caledonian crow (*corvus moneduloides*). *Animal Cognition, 5*, 71–78.

Charlton, T. & Hannan, A. (2005) *The St. Helena Project: Summary of Research Findings*. Economic & Social Research Council.

Charness, N. (1979) Components of skill in bridge. *Canadian Journal of Psychology, 133*, 1–16.

Charness, N. (1981) Ageing and skilled problem-solving. *Journal of Experimental Psychology: General, 110*, 21–38.

Charney, D.S., Deutsch, A.V., Krystal, J.H., Southwick, A.M. & Davis, M. (1993) Psychobiologic mechanisms of post-traumatic stress disorder. *Archives of General Psychiatry, 50*, 295–305.

Chaudhury, A. (1988) How special is special? *Issue*, Spring.

Chen, I. (2012) A feeling for the past. *Scientific American Mind, 22*(6), 24–31.

Chen, I. (2013) Hidden depths. *New Scientist, 220*(2939), 32–37.

Chen, J.-Q. & Gardner, H. (2005) Assessment based on multiple-intelligences theory. In D.P. Flanagan & P.L. Harrison (eds) *Contemporary Intellectual Assessment: Theories, Tests and Issues* (2nd edition). New York: Guilford Press.

Chen, S. & Chaiken, S. (1999) The heuristic-systematic model in its broader context. In S. Chaiken & Y. Trope (eds) *Dual-process Theories in Social Psychology*. New York: Guilford Press.

Cherry, E.C. (1953) Some experiments on the recognition of speech with one and two ears. *Journal of the Acoustical Society of America, 25*, 975–979.

Cherry, E.C. & Taylor, W.K. (1954) Some further experiments on the recognition of speech with one and two ears. *Journal of the Acoustical Society of America, 27*, 554–559.

Chi, R. & Snyder, A. (2012) Brain stimulation enables the solution of an inherently difficult problem. *Neuroscience Letters, 515*, 121–124.

Chisolm, K., Carter, M.C., Ames, E.W. & Morison, S.J. (1995) Attachment security and indiscriminately friendly behaviour in children adopted from Romanian orphanages. *Development & Psychopathology, 7*, 283–294.

Cho, K., Ennaceur, A., Cole, J.C. & Suh, C.K. (2000) Chronic jet-lag produces core defects. *Journal of Neuroscience, 20* (RC66), 1–5.

Chomsky, N. (1957) *Syntactic Structures*. The Hague: Mouton.

Chomsky, N. (1959) Review of Skinner's verbal behaviour. *Language, 35*, 26–58.

Chomsky, N. (1965) *Aspects of the Theory of Syntax*. Cambridge, MA: MIT Press.

Chomsky, N. (1968) *Language and Mind*. New York: Harcourt Brace Jovanovich.

Chomsky, N. (1979) *Language and Responsibility*. Sussex: Harvester Press.

Christenfeld, N. & Larsen, B. (2008) The name game. *The Psychologist, 21*(3), 210–213.

Christensen, L. (1988) Deception in psychological research: When is its use justified? *Personality & Social Psychology, 14*, 665–675.

Chwalisz, K., Diener, E. & Gallagher, D. (1988) Autonomic arousal feedback and emotional experience: Evidence from the spinal cord injured. *Journal of Personality & Social Psychology, 54*, 820–828.

Cialdini, R.B. (1988) *Influence: Science and Practice*. Glenview, IL: Scott, Foresman.

Cialdini, R.B. (2004) The science of persuasion. *Scientific American Special: Mind, 14*(1), 70–77.

Cialdini, R.B. & Trost, M.R. (1998) Social influence: Social norms, conformity, and compliance. In D.T. Gilbert, S.T. Fiske & G. Lindzey (eds) *Handbook of Social Psychology, Volume 2* (4th edition). New York: McGraw-Hill.

Cialdini, R.B., Kenrick, D.T. & Baumann, D.J. (1982) Effects of mood on prosocial behaviour in children and adults. In N. Eisenberg (ed.) *The Development of Prosocial Behaviour*. New York: Academic Press.

Cialdini, R.B., Schaller, M., Houlihan, D., Arps, K., Fultz, J. & Beaman, A.L. (1987) Empathy-based helping: Is it selflessly or selfishly motivated? *Journal of Personality & Social Psychology, 52*, 749–758.

Clare, A. (1976) What is schizophrenia? *New Society*, 20 May, 410–412.

Clare, A. (1980) *Psychiatry in Dissent*. London: Tavistock.

Claridge, G. (1981) Psychoticism. In R. Lynn (ed.) *Dimensions of Personality: Papers in Honour of H.J. Eysenck*. Oxford: Pergamon Press.

Claridge, G. (1985) *Origins of Mental Illness*. Oxford: Basil Blackwell.

Claridge, G. & Davis, C. (2003) *Personality and Psychological Disorders*. London: Arnold.

Claridge, G. & Herrington, R.N. (1960) Sedation threshold, personality, and the theory of neurosis. *Journal of Mental Science, 106*, 1568–1583.

Claridge, G.S. & Herrington, R.N. (1962) Excitation-inhibition and the theory of neurosis: A study of the sedation threshold. In H.J. Eysenck (ed.) *Experiments with Drugs*. New York: Pergamon Press.

Clark, K.E. & Miller, G.A. (1970) (eds) *Psychology: Behavioural and Social Sciences Survey Committee*. Englewood Cliffs, NJ: Prentice-Hall.

Clark, M. (1984) Record keeping in two types of relationships. *Journal of Personality & Social Psychology, 47*, 549–557.

Clark, M.S. & Grote, N.K. (1998) Why aren't indices of relationship costs always negatively related to indices of relationship quality? *Personality & Social Psychology Review, 2*, 2–17.

Clark, M.S. & Mills, J. (1979) Interpersonal attraction in exchange and communal relationships. *Journal of Personality & Social Psychology, 37*, 12–24.

Clark, M.S. & Mills, J. (1993) The difference between communal and exchange relationships: What it is and is not. *Personality & Social Psychology Bulletin, 19*, 684–691.

Clark, M.S., Mills, J. & Powell, M.C. (1986) Keeping track of needs in communal and exchange relationships. *Journal of Personality & Social Psychology, 51*, 333–338.

Clark, M.S., Millberg, S. & Erber, R. (1987) Arousal and state-dependent memory: Evidence and some implications for understanding social judgements and social behaviour. In K. Fiedler & J.P. Forgas (eds) *Affect, Cognition and Social Behaviour*. Toronto: Hogrefe.

Clarke, A. & Clarke, A. (2000) *Early Experience and the Life Path*. London: Jessica Kingsley.

Clarke, S.R. (2000) Home advantage in the Olympic Games. *Proceedings of the Fifth Australian Conference on Mathematics & Computers in Sport*, University of Technology, Sydney, 76–85.

Clarke, V., Burgoyne, C. & Burns, M. (2005) For love or money? *The Psychologist, 18*(6), 356–358.

Clarke, V., Ellis, S.J., Peel, E. & Riggs, D.W. (2010) *Lesbian, Gay, Bisexual, Trans and Queer Psychology: An Introduction*. Cambridge University Press.

Clarke-Stewart, K.A. (1989) Infant day care: Maligned or malignant? *American Psychologist, 44*, 266–273.

Clifasefi, S.L., Garry, M. & Loftus, E. (2007) Setting the record (or video camera) straight on memory: The video camera model of memory and other memory myths. In S. Della Sala (ed.) *Tall Tales about the Mind & Brain: Separating Fact from Fiction*. Oxford University Press.

Clifasefi, S.L., Bernstein, D.M., Mantonakis, A. & Loftusm E.F. (2013) "Queasy does it": False alcohol beliefs and memories may lead to diminished alcohol preferences. *Acta Psychologica, 143*, 14-19.

Cline, T. (2008) What use is 'intelligence'? In N. Frederickson, A. Miller & T. Cline (eds) *Educational Psychology*. London: Hodder Education.

Cloninger, C.R. (1987) Neurogenetic adaptive mechanisms in alcoholism. *Science, 236*, 410–416.

Clore, G.L. & Byrne, D.S. (1974) A reinforcement–affect model of attraction. In T.L. Huston (ed.) *Foundations of Interpersonal Attraction*. New York: Academic Press.

Cochrane, M., Petsch, M. & Pickering, A.D. (2010) Do measures of schizotypal personality provide non-clinical analogues of schizophrenic symptomatology? *Psychiatry Research, 176*, 150–154.

Cochrane, R. (1974) Crime and personality: Theory and evidence. *Bulletin of the British Psychological Society, 27*, 19–22.

Cochrane, R. (1983) *The Social Creation of Mental Illness*. London: Longman.

Cohen, F. & Lazarus, R.S. (1979) Coping with the stress of illness. In G.C. Stone, F. Cohen & N.E. Ader (eds) *Health Psychology: A Handbook*. Washington, DC: Jossey-Bass.

Cohen, G. (1975) Cerebral apartheid: A fanciful notion? *New Behaviour, 18*, 458–461.

Cohen, G. (1993) Everyday memory and memory systems: The experimental approach. In G. Cohen, G. Kiss & M. Levoi (eds) *Memory: Current Issues* (2nd edition). Buckingham: Open University Press.

Cohen, J. (2000) Primate education. *Sunday Times Magazine*, 13 August, 16–23.

Cohen, N.J. & Squire, L.R. (1980) Preserved learning and retention of pattern-analysing skills in amnesia: Dissociation of knowing how from knowing that. *Science, 210*, 207–210.

Cohen, R.M., Nordahl, T.E., Semple, W.E., Andreason, P., Litman, R.E. & Pickar, D. (1997) The brain metabolic patterns of clozapine and fluphenazine-treated patients with schizophrenia during a continuous performance task. *Archives of General Psychiatry, 54*, 481–486.

Cohen, S. & Taylor, L. (1972) *Psychological Survival: The Experience of Long-term Imprisonment*. Harmondsworth: Penguin.

Cohen, Y.A. (1964) *The Transition from Childhood to Adolescence: Cross-cultural Studies in Initiation Ceremonies, Legal Systems, and Incest Taboos*. Chicago: Aldine.

Coie, J.D. & Dodge, K.A. (1998) Aggression and antisocial behaviour. In N. Eisenberg (ed.) *Handbook of Child Psychology, Volume 3: Social, Emotional, and Personality Development* (5th edition). New York: Wiley.

Colapinto, J. (2000) What the doctor ordered. *Independent on Sunday Magazine*, 6 February, 8–13.

Colby, A. & Kohlberg, L. (eds) (1987) *The Measurement of Moral Judgement*. New York: Cambridge University Press.

Colby, A., Kohlberg, L., Gibbs, J. & Lieberman, M. (1983) A longitudinal study of moral development. *Monographs of the Society for Research in Child Development, 48*, (1–2, Serial No. 200).

Cole, M. (1990) Cultural psychology: A once and future discipline? In J.J. Berman (ed.) *Nebraska Symposium on Motivation: Cross-Cultural Perspectives*. Lincoln: University of Nebraska Press.

Cole, M. (1996) *Cultural Psychology: A Once and Future Discipline*. Cambridge, MA: Harvard University Press.

Cole, S., Balcetis, E. & Zhang, S. (2013) Visual perception and regulatory conflict: Motivational and physiological influences on distance perception. *Journal of Experimental Psychology, General, 142*, 18–22.

Coleman, J.C. (1980) *The Nature of Adolescence*. London: Methuen.

Coleman, J.C. (1995) Adolescence. In P.E. Bryant & A.M. Colman (eds) *Developmental Psychology*. London: Longman.

Coleman, J.C. & Hendry, L. (1990) *The Nature of Adolescence* (2nd edition). London: Routledge.

Coleman, J.C. & Roker, D. (1998) Adolescence. *The Psychologist, 11*(12), 593–596.

Collins, A.M. & Loftus, E.F. (1975) A spreading-activation theory of semantic processing. *Psychological Review, 82*, 407–428.

Collins, A.M. & Quillian, M. (1969) Retrieval time for semantic memory. *Journal of Verbal Learning & Verbal Behaviour, 8*, 240–247.

Collins, H. (1994) *Times Higher Education Supplement*, 30 September, 18.

Collins, J. (1994) What is pain? In J. Robbins (ed.) *Caring for the Dying Patient and the Family* (2nd edition). London: Chapman & Hall.

Collins, R.C. (1983) Headstart: An update on program effects. *Newsletter of the Society for Research in Child Development, Summer*, 1–2.

Collis, G.M. & Schaffer, H.R. (1975) Synchronisation of visual attention in mother–infant pairs. *Journal of Child Psychology & Psychiatry, 16*, 315–320.

Colman, A.M. (1987) *Facts, Fallacies and Frauds in Psychology*. London: Unwin Hyman.

Coltheart, M. (2006) What has functional neuroimaging told us about the mind (so far)? *Cortex, 42*, 323–331.

Colvin, M.K. & Gazzaniga, M.S. (2007) Split-brain cases. In M. Velmans & S. Schneider (eds) *The Blackwell Companion to Consciousness*. Malden, MA: Blackwell Publishing.

Comfort, A. (1977) *A Good Age*. London: Mitchell Beazley.

Compas, B.E., Hinden, B.R. & Gerhardt, C.A. (1995) Adolescent development: Pathways and processes of risk and resilience. *Annual Review of Psychology, 46*, 265–293.

Comstock, G. & Paik, H. (1991) *Television and the American Child*. New York: Academic Press.

Condry, J. & Condry, S. (1976) Sex differences: A study in the eye of the beholder. *Child Development, 47*, 812–819.

Condry, J.C. & Ross, D.F. (1985) Sex and aggression: The influence of gender label on the perception of aggression in children. *Child Development, 56*(1), 225–233.

Connor, S. (2004) Brain scans prove teenagers are children at heart. *Independent*, 18 May, 12.

Constandi, M. (2013) The Mind Minders. *New Scientist, 220*(2938), 44–47.

Cooley, C.H. (1902) *Human Nature and Social Order*. New York: Shocken.

Coolican, H. (1994) *Research Methods and Statistics in Psychology* (2nd edition). London: Hodder & Stoughton.

Coolican, H. (2004) *Research Methods and Statistics in Psychology* (4th edition). London: Hodder & Stoughton.

Coolican, H., Cassidy, T., Chercher, A., Harrower, J., Penny, G., Sharp, R., Walley, M. & Westbury, T. (1996) *Applied Psychology*. London: Hodder & Stoughton.

Coolican, H., Cassidy, T., Dunn, O., Sharp, R., Tudway, J., Simmonds, K., Westbury, T. & Harrower, J. (2007) *Applied Psychology* (2nd edition). London: Hodder & Stoughton.

Coon, D. (1983) *Introduction to Psychology* (3rd edition). St Paul, MN: West Publishing Co.

Cooper, C. & Faragher, B. (1993) Psychological stress and breast cancer: the interrelationship between stress events, coping strategies and personality. *Psychological Medicine, 23*, 653–662.

Cooper, G. (1994) Napoleon island to end TV exile. *Independent on Sunday*, 12 June, 7.

Cooper, J., Kelly, K.A. & Weaver, K. (2004) Attitudes, norms, and social groups. In M.B. Brewer & M. Hewstone (eds) *Social Cognition*. Oxford: Blackwell Publishing.

Cooper, P.J. (1995) Eating disorders. In A.A. Lazarus & A.M. Colman (eds) *Abnormal Psychology*. London: Longman.

Cooper, R.S., Rotimi, C.N. & Ward, R. (1999) The puzzle of hypertension in African-Americans. *Scientific American, 253*, 36–43.

Coopersmith, S. (1967) *The Antecedents of Self-Esteem*. San Francisco: Freeman.

Copson, G. & Holloway, K. (1997) *Offender Profiling*. Paper presented to the annual conference of the Division of Criminological & Legal Psychology, British Psychological Society (October).

Corcoran, R. & Frith, U. (1997) Conversational conduct and the symptoms of schizophrenia. *Cognitive Neuropsychiatry, 1*, 305–318.

Corcoran, R., Cummins, S., Rowse, G. et al. (2006) Reasoning under uncertainty. *Psychological Medicine, 36*, 1109–1118.

Cordray, D.S. & Bootzin, R.R. (1983) Placebo control conditions: Tests of theory or of effectiveness. *Behavioural & Brain Sciences, 6*, 286–287.

Coren, S. & Girgus, J.S. (1978) *Seeing Is Deceiving: The Psychology of Visual Illusions*. Hillsdale, NJ: Erlbaum.

Corr, P.J. & McNaughton, N. (2008) Reinforcement sensitivity theory and personality. In P.J. Corr (ed.) *The Reinforcement Sensitivity Theory of Personality*. Cambridge: Cambridge University Press.

Corteen, R.S. & Wood, B. (1972) Autonomic responses to shock-associated words in an unattended channel. *Journal of Experimental Psychology, 94*, 308–313.

Costa, P.T. & McCrae, R.R. (1992) *Revised NEO Personality Inventory (NEO-PI-R)*. Odessa, FL: Psychological Assessment Resources.

Costello, T.W., Costello, J.T. & Holmes, D.A. (adapting author) (1995) *Abnormal Psychology*. London: HarperCollins.

Cottrell, N.B. (1968) Performance in the presence of other human beings: Mere presence, audience, and affiliation effects. In E.C. Simmel, R.A. Hope & G.A. Milton (eds) *Social Facilitation and Imitative Behaviour*. Boston: Allyn & Bacon.

Cottrell, N.B., Wack, D.L., Sekerak, G.J. & Rittle, R.H. (1968) Social facilitation of dominant responses by the presence of others. *Journal of Personality & Social Psychology, 9*, 245–250.

Cowan, N. (2001) The magical number 4 in short-term memory: A reconsideration of mental storage capacity. *Behavioural & Brain Sciences, 24*, 87–185.

Cox, T. (1978) *Stress*. London: Macmillan Education.

Crago, M.B. & Gopnik, M. (1994) From families to phenotypes: Theoretical and clinical implications of research into the genetic basis of specific language impairment. In R. Watkins & M. Rice (eds) *Specific Language Impairments in Children*. Baltimore, MD: Paul H. Brookes.

Craig, G.J. (1992) *Human Development* (6th edition). Englewood Cliffs, NJ: Prentice-Hall.

Craik, F.I.M. & Lockhart, R. (1972) Levels of processing. *Journal of Verbal Learning & Verbal Behaviour, 11*, 671–684.

Craik, F.I.M. & Watkins, M.J. (1973) The role of rehearsal in short-term memory. *Journal of Verbal Learning & Verbal Behaviour, 12*, 599–607.

Cramer, D. (1995) Special issue on personal relationships. *The Psychologist, 8*, 58–59.

Crandall, J.E. (1985) Effects of favourable and unfavourable conditions on the psi-missing displacement effect. *Journal of the American Association for Psychical Research, 79*, 27–38.

Crano, W.D. (2000) Milestones in the psychological analysis of social influence. *Group Dynamics, 4*, 68–80.

Crawford, M. & Unger, R.K. (1995) Gender issues in psychology. In A.M. Colman (ed.) *Controversies in Psychology*. London: Longman.

Crick, F. (1994) *The Astonishing Hypothesis: The Scientific Search for the Soul*. London: Simon & Schuster.

Crick, F. & Mitchison, G. (1983) The function of dream sleep. *Nature, 304*, 111–114.

Crisp, A.H. (1980) *Anorexia Nervosa: Let Me Be*. London: Plenum Press.

Crisp, R.J. & Meleady, R. (2012) Adapting to a Multicultural Future. *Science, 336*(6083), 53–55 doi:10.1126/science.1219009

Crocker, J. & Carnevale, J.J. (2013) Letting go of self-esteem. *Scientific American Mind, 24*, 26–33.

Cromer, R.F. (1974) The development of language and cognition: The cognition hypothesis. In B.M. Foss (ed.) *New Perspectives in Child Development*. Harmondsworth: Penguin.

Crooks, R.L. & Stein, J. (1991) *Psychology: Science, Behaviour and Life* (2nd edition). London: Holt, Rinehart & Winston.

Crutchfield, R.S. (1954) A new technique for measuring individual differences in conformity to group judgement. *Proceedings of the Invitational Conference on Testing Problems*, 69–74.

Crutchfield, R.S. (1955) Conformity and character. *American Psychologist, 10*, 191–198.

Csikszentmihalyi, M. & Larson, R. (1984) *Being Adolescent: Conflict and Growth in the Teenage Years*. New York: Basic Books.

Cumberbatch, G. (1997) Media violence: Science and common sense. *Psychology Review, 3*, 2–7.

Cumming, E. (1975) Engagement with an old theory. *International Journal of Ageing & Human Development, 6*, 187–191.

Cumming, E. & Henry, W.E. (1961) *Growing Old: The Process of Disengagement*. New York: Basic Books.

Curry, C. (1998) Adolescence. In K. Trew & J. Kremer (eds) *Gender & Psychology*. London: Arnold.

Dacey, J.S. (1982) *Adolescents Today* (2nd edition). Glenview, IL: Scott, Foresman & Company.

Dahl, A., Campos, J.J., Anderson, D.I. et al. (2013) The Epigenesis of Wariness of Height. *Psychological Science, 24*(7), 1361–1367.

Dallos, R. & Cullen, C. (1990) Clinical psychology. In I. Roth (ed.) *Introduction to Psychology, Volume 2*. Hove/Milton Keynes: Open University Press/Lawrence Erlbaum Associates Ltd.

Dalton, K. (1997) Exploring the links: Creativity and psi in the Ganzfeld. *Proceedings of the 40th Annual Convention of the Parapsychological Association*. Hatfield: University of Hertfordshire Press.

Daly, M. & Wilson, M. (1988a) *Homicide*. New York: Aldine de Gruyter Hawthorne.

Daly, M. & Wilson, M. (1988b) Evolutionary social psychology and family homicide. *Science*, 28 October, 519–524.

Damasio, A.R. (2001) Fundamental feelings. *Nature, 413*, 781.

Damasio, A.R. (2003) *Looking for Spinoza: Joy, Sorrow and the Feeling Brain*. Orlando, FL: Harcourt.

Damon, W. (1977) *The Social World of the Child*. San Francisco: Jossey-Bass.

Damon, W. & Hart, D. (1988) *Self-understanding in Childhood and Adolescence*. Cambridge University Press.

Damrosch, S. (1995) Facilitating adherence to preventive and treatment regimes. In D. Wedding (ed.) *Behaviour and Medicine* (2nd edition). St Louis, MO: Mosby-Year Book.

Dana, C.L. (1921) The anatomic seat of the emotions: A discussion of the James–Lange theory. *Archives of Neurology & Psychiatry, 6*, 634.

Danelli, L., Cossu, G., Berlingeri, M. et al. (2013) Is a lone right hemisphere enough? Neurolinguistic architecture in a case with a very early left hemispherectomy. *Neurocase: The Neural Basis of Cognition, 19*(3), 209–231.

Darley, J.M. (1991) Altruism and prosocial behaviour research: Reflections and prospects. In M.S. Clark (ed.) Prosocial Behaviour: *Review of Personality & Social Psychology, 12*. Newbury Park: CA: Sage.

Darley, J.M. & Batson, C.D. (1973) From Jerusalem to Jericho: A study of situational and dispositional variables in helping behaviour. *Journal of Personality & Social Psychology, 27*, 100–108.

Darley, J.M. & Latané, B. (1968) Bystander intervention in emergencies: Diffusion of responsibility. *Journal of Personality & Social Psychology, 8*, 377–383.

Darley, J.M. & Latané, B. (1970) Norms and normative behaviour: Field studies of social interdependence. In J. Macaulay & L. Berkowitz (eds) *Altruism and Helping Behaviour*. New York: Academic Press, 83–101.

Darwin, C. (1859) *The Origin of Species by Means of Natural Selection*. London: John Murray.

Darwin, C. (1872) *The Expression of Emotion in Man and Animals*. London: John Murray.

Dasen, P.R. (1994) Culture and cognitive development from a Piagetian perspective. In W.J. Lonner & R.S. Malpass (eds) *Psychology and Culture*. Boston: Allyn & Bacon.

Dasen, P.R. (1999) Rapid social change and the turmoil of adolescence: A cross-cultural perspective. *International Journal of Group Tensions, 29* (1–2), 17–49.

Dashiell, J.F. (1935) Experimental studies of the influence of social situations on the behaviour of individual human adults. In C. Murchison (ed.) *Handbook of Social Psychology*. Worcester, MA: Clark University Press.

Datan, N., Rodeheaver, D. & Hughes, F. (1987) Adult development and ageing. *Annual Review of Psychology, 38*, 153–180.

Davey, G.C.L. (1983) An associative view of human classical conditioning. In G.C.L. Davey (ed.) *Animal Models of Human Behaviour: Conceptual, Evolutionary, and Neurobiological Perspectives*. Chichester: Wiley.

Davey, G.C.L. (2006) A mood-as-input account of perseverative worrying. In G.C.L. Davey & A. Wells (eds) *Worrying and its Psychological Disorders*. Chichester: Wiley.

Davidson, A.R. & Jaccard, J. (1979) Variables that moderate the attitude–behaviour relation: Results of a longitudinal survey. *Journal of Personality & Social Psychology, 37*, 1364–1376.

Davies, E. & Furnham, A. (1986) Body satisfaction in adolescent girls. *British Journal of Medical Psychology, 59*, 279–288.

Davies, G. (2008) Eyewitness testimony. *Psychology Review, 14* (1), 14–16.

Davies, J.C. (1969) The J-curve of rising and declining satisfactions as a cause of some great revolutions and a contained rebellion. In H.D. Graham & T.R. Gurr (eds) *The History of Violence in America: Historical and Comparative Perspectives*. New York: Praeger.

Davis, A. (2003) Educational Implications. In A. Slater & G. Bremner (eds) *An Introduction to Developmental Psychology*. Oxford: Blackwell Publishing.

Davis, J.P., Jansari, A. & Lander, K. (2013) 'I never forget a face!' *The Psychologist, 26*(10), 726–729.

Davis, J.A. (1959) A formal interpretation of the theory of relative deprivation. *Sociometry, 22*, 280–296.

Davis, J.M. (1978) Dopamine theory of schizophrenia: A two-factor theory. In L.C. Wynne, R.L. Cromwell & S. Matthysse (eds) *The Nature of Schizophrenia*. New York: Wiley.

Davis, M.H. (1994) *Empathy: A Social Psychological Approach*. Boulder, CO: Westview Press.

Davison, G. & Neale, J.M. (1994) *Abnormal Psychology* (6th edition). New York: Wiley.

Davison, G.C. & Neale, J.M. (2001) *Abnormal Psychology* (8th edition). New York: John Wiley & Sons.

Davison, G.C., Neale, J.M. & Kring, A.M. (2004) *Abnormal Psychology* (9th edition). New York: John Wiley & Sons, Inc.

Dawkins, M.S. (1980) The many faces of animal suffering. *New Scientist*, November 20.

Dawkins, R. (1976) *The Selfish Gene*. Oxford University Press.

Dawkins, R. (1989) *The Selfish Gene* (2nd edition). Oxford University Press.

Day, R., Nielsen, J.A., Korten, A., Ernberg, G., Dube, K.C., Gebhart, J., Jablensky, A., Leone, C., Marsella, A., Olatawura, M. et al. (1987) Stressful life events preceding the onset of schizophrenia: A cross-national study from the World Health Organization. *Culture, Medicine & Psychiatry, 11*, 123–205.

de Bono, E. (1967) *The Use of Lateral Thinking*. Harmondsworth: Penguin.

De Gelder, B. (2010) Uncanny sight in the blind. *Scientific American, 302*(5), 42–47.

de Groot, A.D. (1965) *Thought and Choice in Chess*. The Hague: Mouton.

de Groot, A.D. (1966) Perception and memory versus thought: Some old ideas and recent findings. In B. Kleinmuntz (ed.) *Problem-Solving: Research, Method and Theory*. New York: Wiley.

De Munck, V.C. (1998) Lust, love, and arranged marriages in Sri Lanka. In V.C. de Munck (ed.) *Romantic Love and Sexual Behavior: Perspectives from the Social Sciences*. Westport, CT: Praeger.

De Quervain, D.J.F., Roozendaal, B., Nitsch, R.M., McGaugh, J.L. & Hoch, C. (2000) Acute cortisone administration impairs retrieval of long-term declarative memory in humans. *Nature Neuroscience, 3*, 313–314.

de Ridder, D.T.D. (2000) Gender, stress and coping: Do women handle stress differently from men? In L. Sher & J.S. St. Lawrence (eds) *Women, Health and the Mind*. Chichester: John Wiley & Sons Ltd.

de Villiers, P.A. & de Villiers, J.G. (1979) *Early Language*. Cambridge, MA: Harvard University Press.

Decety, J., Chen, C. & Kiehl, K.A. (2013) An fMRI study of affective perspective taking in individuals with psychopathy: imagining another in pain does not evoke empathy. *Frontiers of Human Neuroscience, 7*, 489.

Deci, E.L. (1980) *The Psychology of Self-determination*. Lexington, MA: D.C. Heath.

Deci, E.L. & Ryan, R.M. (1987) The support of autonomy and the control of behaviour. *Journal of Personality & Social Psychology, 53*, 1024–1037.

Deese, J. (1972) *Psychology as Science and Art*. New York: Harcourt Brace Jovanovich.

DeGrazia, D. (2002) *Animal Rights: A Very Short Introduction*. Oxford: Oxford University Press.

Delboeuf, J.L.R. (1892) Sur une nouvelle illusion d'optique. *Bulletin de L'Academie Royale de Belgique, 24*, 545–558.

Delgado, J.M.R. (1969) *Physical Control of the Mind*. New York: Harper & Row.

Delgado, P.L. (2000) Depression: A case for a monoamine deficiency. *Journal of Clinical Psychiatry, 61* (Suppl. 6), 7–11.

Dement, W.C. (1960) The effects of dream deprivation. *Science, 131*, 1705–1707.

Dement, W.C. (2000) Tired of counting sheep? The world's greatest sleep expert on how to hit the snooze button. *Independent on Sunday, Real Life*, 16 January, 1–2.

Dement, W.C. & Kleitman, N. (1957) The relation of eye movements during sleep to dream activity: An objective method for the study of dreaming. *Journal of Experimental Psychology, 53* (5), 339–346.

Denmark, F., Russo, N.F., Frieze, I.H. & Sechzer, J.A. (1988) Guidelines for avoiding sexism in psychological research: A report of the ad hoc committee on nonsexist research. *American Psychologist, 43* (7), 582–585.

Dennett, D.C. (2003) *Freedom Evolves*. London: Allen Lane.

Denney, N. & Palmer, A. (1981) Adult age differences on traditional problem-solving measures. *Journal of Gerontology, 36*, 323–328.

Denzin, N.K. (1995) Symbolic interactionism. In J.A. Smith, R. Harré, & L.V. Langenhove (eds) *Rethinking Psychology*. London: Sage.

Department of Health & Home Office (1994) *Report of the Department of Health and Home Office Working Group on Psychopathic Disorder*. London: Department of Health & Home Office.

Department of Health & Social Security (1983) *Mental Health Act, 1983*. London: HMSO.

Deregowski, J. (1972) Pictorial perception and culture. *Scientific American, 227*, 82–88.

Dermer, M. & Thiel, D.L. (1975) When beauty may fail. *Journal of Personality & Social Psychology, 31*, 1168–1176.

Deutsch, M. & Collins, M.E. (1951) *Interracial Housing: A Psychological Evaluation of a Social Experiment*. Minneapolis: University of Minnesota Press.

Deutsch, J.A. & Deutsch, D. (1963) Attention: Some theoretical considerations. *Psychological Review, 70*, 80–90.

Deutsch, M. & Gerard, H.B. (1955) A study of normative and informational social influence upon individual judgement. *Journal of Abnormal & Social Psychology, 51*, 629–636.

DeValois, R.L. & Jacobs, G.H. (1984) Neural mechanisms of colour vision. In I. Davian-Smith (ed.) *Handbook of Physiology, Volume 3*. Bethseda, MD: American Physiological Society.

Devine, P.G. (1989) Stereotypes and prejudice: Their automatic and controlled components. *Journal of Personality & Social Psychology, 56*, 5–18.

Devine, P.G. & Zuwerink, J.R. (1994) Prejudice and guilt: The internal struggle to control prejudice. In W.J. Lonner & R.S. Malpass (eds) *Psychology and Culture*. Boston: Allyn & Bacon.

Devlin Report (1976) *Report to the Secretary of State for the Home Development of the Departmental Committee on Evidence of Identification in Criminal Cases*. London: HMSO.

Dex, S. & Phillipson, C. (1986) Social policy and the older worker. In C. Phillipson & A. Walker (eds) *Ageing and Social Policy: A Critical Assessment*. Aldershot: Gower.

Diagram Group (1982) *The Brain – A User's Manual*. New York: G.P. Putnam's Sons.

Diamond, L.M. (2006) How do I love thee? Implications of attachment theory for understanding same-sex love and desire. In M. Mikulincer & G.S. Goodman (eds) *Dynamics of Romantic Love: Attachment, Caregiving, and Sex*. New York: Guilford Press.

Diamond, M. (1978) Sexual identity and sex roles. *The Humanist, March/April*, 16–19.

Diamond, M. & Sigmundson, H.K. (1997) Sex reassignment at birth. *Paediatric & Adolescent Medicine, 151*, 298–304.

Diamond, R. & Carey, S. (1986) Why faces are and are not special: An effect of expertise. *Journal of Experimental Psychology: General, 115*, 107–117.

Dicks, L. (2000) All for one! *New Scientist, 167*(2246), 30–35.

Diener, E., Fraser, S.C., Beaman, A.L. & Kelem, R.T. (1976) Effects of deindividuation variables on stealing among Halloween trick-or-treaters. *Journal of Personality & Social Psychology, 33*, 178–183.

Digman, J.M. (1990) Personality structure: Emergence of the five-factor model. *Annual Review of Psychology, 41*, 417–440.

Dijksterhuis, A., Spears, R., Poatmes, T., Stapel, D.A., Koomen, W., van Knippenberg, A. & Scheppers, D. (1998) Seeing one thing and doing another: Contrast effects in automatic behaviour. *Journal of Personality & Social Psychology, 75*, 862–871.

DiNicola, V.F. (1990) Anorexia multiform: Self-starvation in historical and cultural context. *Transcultural Psychiatric Research Review, 27*, 245–286.

Dion, K.K. & Berscheid, E. (1974) Physical attractiveness and peer perception among children. *Sociometry, 37*, 1–12.

Dion, K.K. & Dion, K.L. (1995) On the love of beauty and the beauty of love: Two psychologists study attraction. In G.G. Brannigan & M.R. Merrens (eds) *The Social Psychologists: Research Adventures*. New York: McGraw-Hill.

Dion, K.K., Berscheid, E. & Walster, E. (1972) What is beautiful is good. *Journal of Personality & Social Psychology, 24*, 285–290.

Dobbs, D. (2009) The post-traumatic stress trap. *Scientific American, 300* (4), 48–53.

Dockrell, J., Grove, N. & Hasan, P. (1999) People with learning disabilities. In D. Messer & F. Jones (eds) *Psychology and Social Care*. London: Jessica Kingsley.

Dodge, K.A. (1993) Social-cognitive mechanisms in the development of conduct disorder and depression. *Annual Review of Psychology, 44*, 559–584.

Dodge, K.A. & Tomlin, A.M. (1987) Utilization of self-schemas as a mechanism of interpretational bias in aggressive children. *Social Cognition, 5*, 280–300.

Dodwell, P.C. (1995) Fundamental processes in vision. In R.L. Gregory & A.M. Colman (eds) *Sensation and Perception*. London: Longman.

Dohrenwend, B.P. (2006) Inventorying stressful life events as risk factors for psychopathology: Towards resolution of the problem of intracategory variability. *Psychological Bulletin, 132*, 477–495.

Dollard, J. & Miller, N.E. (1950) *Personality and Psychotherapy*. New York: McGraw-Hill.

Dollard, J., Doob, L.W., Mowrer, O.H. & Sears, R.R. (1939) *Frustration and Aggression*. New Haven, CT: Harvard University Press.

Donaldson, M. (1978) *Children's Minds*. London: Fontana.

Dosenbach, N.U., Nardos, B., Cohen, A.L. et al. (2010) Prediction of individual brain maturity using fMRI. *Science, 329*(5997), 1358–1361.

Dovidio, J.F. (1995) With a little help from my friends. In G.G. Brannigan & M.R. Merrens (eds) *The Social Psychologists: Research Adventures*. New York: McGraw-Hill.

Dovidio, J.F. & Penner, L.A. (2004) Helping and altruism. In M.B. Brewer & M. Hewstone (eds) *Emotion and Motivation*. Oxford: Blackwell Publishing.

Dovidio, J.F., Piliavin, J.A., Gaertner, S.L., Schroeder, D.A. & Clark, R.D. (1991) The arousal–cost–reward model and the process of intervention. In M.S. Clark (ed.) *Prosocial Behaviour: Review of Personality and Social Psychology, 12*. Newbury Park, CA: Sage.

Dovidio, J.F., Brigham, J.C., Johnson, B.T. & Gaertner, S.L. (1996). Stereotyping, prejudice, and discrimination: Another look. In C.N. Macrae, C. Stangor & M. Hewstone (eds) *Stereotypes and Stereotyping*. New York: McGraw-Hill.

Doward, J. & Templeton, T. (2008) Hippie dream, modern nightmare. *Observer*, 4 May, 4–6.

Dowd, J.J. (1975) Ageing as exchange: A preface to theory. *Journal of Gerontology, 30*, 584–594.

Downing, D. (1988) *Daylight Robbery*. London: Arrow Books.

Draguns, J. (1980) Psychological disorders of clinical severity. In H.C. Triandis & J. Draguns (eds) *Handbook of Cross-Cultural Psychology, Volume 6, Psychopathology*. Boston: Allyn & Bacon.

Draguns, J. (1990) Applications of cross-cultural psychology in the field of mental health. In R. Brislin (ed.) *Applied Cross-Cultural Psychology*. Newbury Park, CA: Sage.

Drew, L. (2014) Down with dementia. *New Scientist, 221*(2951), 32–35.

Drew, T., Vo, M.L.-H. & Wolfe, J.M. (2013) The invisible gorilla strikes again: Sustained inattentional blindness in expert observers. *Psychological Science, 20*(10), 1–6.

Driver, J. (1996) Attention and segmentation. *The Psychologist, 9*, 119–123.

Dryden, W. (1984) Therapeutic arenas. In W. Dryden (ed.) *Individual Therapy in Britain*. London: Harper & Row.

Dryer, D.C. & Horowitz, L.M. (1997) When do opposites attract? Interpersonal complementarity versus similarity. *Journal of Personality & Social Psychology, 34*, 590–598.

Dubois, D., Rucker, D.D. & Galinsky, A.D. (2010) The accentuation bias: Money literally looms larger (and sometimes smaller) to the powerless. *Social Psychological & Personality Science, 3*, 199–205.

Dubow, E.F., Huesmann, L.R. & Greenwood, D. (2007) Media and youth socialization: Underlying processes and moderators of effects. In J.E. Grusec & P.D. Hastings (eds) *Handbook of Socialization: Theory and Research*. New York: Guilford Press.

Duck, S. (1988) *Relating to Others*. Milton Keynes: Open University Press.

Duck, S. (1992) *Human Relationships* (2nd edition). London: Sage.

Duck, S. (1999) *Relating to Others* (2nd edition). Buckingham: Open University Press.

Duck, S. (2001) Breaking up: The dissolution of relationships. *Psychology Review,* 7 (3), 2–3.

Duck, S. (2005) How do you tell someone you're letting go? *The Psychologist, 18* (4), 210–213.

Duck, S.W. (2010) *Rethinking Relationships*. Thousand Oaks, CA: Sage.

Duck, S.W. & McMahan, D.T. (2010) *Communication in Everyday Life*. Thousand Oaks, CA: Sage.

Duck, S.W., Rutt, D.J., Hoy, M. & Strejc, H. (1991) Some evident truths about conversations in everyday relationships: All communication is not created equal. *Human Communication Research, 18*, 228–67.

Duckworth, A.L., Quinn, P.D., Lynam, D.R. et al. (2011) Role of test motivation in intelligence testing. *Proceedings of National Academy of Sciences, 108*(19), 7716.

Dugan, E. & Kivett, V.R. (1998) Implementing the Adams and Blieszner conceptual model: Predicting interactive friendship processes of older adults. *Journal of Social & Personal Relationships, 15*, 607–622.

Dugdale, N. & Lowe, C.F. (1990) Naming and stimulus equivalence. In D.E. Blackman & H. Lejeune (eds) *Behaviour Analysis in Theory and Practice: Contributions and Controversies*. Hillsdale, NJ: Lawrence Erlbaum.

Dunbar, G., Lewis, V. & Hill, R. (1999) Control processes and road-crossing skills. *The Psychologist, 12* (8), 398–399.

Dunbar, R. (2004) Can you guess what I'm thinking? *New Scientist, 182* (2451), 44–45.

Dunbar, R.I.M. (1993) Coevolution of neocortical size, group size, and language in humans. *Behavioural & Brain Science, 16*, 681–735.

Duncan, G. (1993) *Economic deprivation and child development*. Paper presented at annual meeting of the Society for Research in Child Development, New Orleans, LA.

Duncan, S.L. (1976) Differential social perception and attribution of intergroup violence: Testing the lower limits of stereotyping of blacks. *Journal of Personality & Social Psychology, 34*, 590–598.

Duncker, K. (1926) A qualitative (experimental and theoretical) study of productive thinking (solving of comprehensible problems). *Journal of Genetic Psychology, 68*, 97–116.

Duncker, K. (1945) On problem-solving. *Psychological Monographs, 58* (Whole No. 270).

Dunn, A.K. (2013) Understanding earwitness testimony. *Psychology Review, 19*(2), 13–15.

Dunn, J. & Plomin, R. (1990) *Separate Lives: Why Siblings Are So Different*. New York: Basic Books.

Dunn, K. (2012) A qualitative investigation into the online counselling relationship: To meet or not to meet, that is the question. *Counselling & Psychotherapy Research: Linking Research with practice, 12*(4), 316–326.

Dunn, O. (2007) Health psychology. In H. Coolican (ed.) *Applied Psychology* (2nd edition). London: Hodder Arnold.

Dunson, B.D., Colombo, B. & Baird, D.D. (2002) Changes with age in the level and duration of fertility in the menstrual cycle. *Human Reproduction, 17*, 1399–1403.

Durie, B. (2005) Doors of perception. *New Scientist, 185* (2484), 34–36.

Durkin, K. (1985) *Television, Sex Roles, and Children: A Developmental Social Psychological Account*. Milton Keynes: Open University Press.

Durkin, K. (1986) Sex roles and the mass media. In D.J. Hargreaves & A.M. Colley (eds) *The Psychology of Sex Roles*. London: Harper & Row.

Durkin, K. (1995) *Developmental Social Psychology: From Infancy to Old Age*. Oxford: Blackwell.

Dutton, D.C. & Aron, A.P. (1974) Some evidence for heightened sexual attraction under conditions of high anxiety. *Journal of Personality & Social Psychology, 30*, 510–517.

Dutton, D.C. & Aron, A.P. (1989) Romantic attraction and generalised liking for others who are sources of conflict-based arousal. *Canadian Journal of Behavioural Science, 21*, 246–257.

Dworetzky, J.P. (1981) *Introduction to Child Development*. St Paul, MN: West Publishing Co.

Dyson, J. (1980) Sociopolitical influences on retirement. *Bulletin of the British Psychological Society, 33*, 128–130.

Eagly, A.H. (1987) *Sex Differences in Social Behaviour: A Social Role Interpretation*. Hillsdale, NJ: Erlbaum.

Eagly, A.H. & Chaiken, S. (1993) *The Psychology of Attitudes*. Fort Worth, TX: Harcourt Brace Jovanovich.

Eagly, A.H. & Crowley, M. (1986) Gender and helping behaviour: A meta-analytic review of the social psychological literature. *Psychological Bulletin, 100*, 232–308.

Ebbinghaus, H. (1885) *On Memory*. Leipzig: Duncker.

Eboda, M. (2004) 'What I said was racist – but I'm not a racist. I am an idiot'. *Observer*, 25 April, 3.

Eckensberger, L.H. (1999) Socio-moral development. In D. Messer & S. Millar (eds) *Exploring Developmental Psychology: From Infancy to Adolescence*. London: Arnold.

Eckensberger, L.H. & Zimba, R. (1997) The development of moral judgement. In J.W. Berry, P.R. Dasen & T.S.

Saraswathi (eds) *Handbook of Cross-cultural Psychology, Volume 2: Basic Processes and Human Development.* Boston: Allyn & Bacon.

Edley, N. & Wetherell, M. (1995) *Men in Perspective: Practice, Power and Identity*. Hemel Hempstead: Harvester Wheatsheaf.

Edwards, D. & Potter, J. (1993) Language and causation: A discursive action model of description and attribution. *Psychological Review, 100*, 23–41.

Edwards, G. (1986) The alcohol dependence syndrome: A concept as stimulus to enquiry. *British Journal of Addiction, 81*, 71–84.

Effective Health Care (1999) Drug treatments for schizophrenia. *Effective Health Care, 5*, 6.

Ehrenfels, C. von (1890) Über Gestaltqualitäten. Vierteljahrschrift für wissenschaftliche *Philosophie und Soziologie, 14*, 249–292.

Eisenberg, N. (1982) The development of reasoning regarding prosocial behaviour. In N. Eisenberg (ed.) *The Development of Prosocial Behaviour*. New York: Academic Press.

Eisenberg, N. (1986) *Altruistic Emotion, Cognition and Behaviour*. Hillsdale, NJ: Erlbaum.

Eisenberg, N. (1996) In search of the good heart. In M.R. Merrens & G.C. Brannigan (eds) *The Developmental Psychologists: Research Adventures across the Life Span*. New York: McGraw-Hill.

Eisenberg, N. (2003) Prosocial behaviour, empathy, and sympathy. In M.H. Bornstein, L. Davidson, C.L.M. Keyes & K.A. Moore (eds*) Well-being: Positive Development Across the Life Course*. Mahwah, NJ: Lawrence Erlbaum Associates.

Eisenberg, N. & Fabes, R.A. (1998) Prosocial development. In W. Damon (series ed.) & N. Eisenberg (volume ed.) *Handbook of Child Psychology, Volume 3: Social, Emotional, and Personality Development* (5th edition). New York: Wiley.

Eisenberg, N. & Lennon, R. (1983) Sex differences in empathy and related capacities. *Psychological Bulletin, 94*, 100–131.

Eisenberg, N., Miller, R.A., Shell, R., McNalley, S. & Shea, C. (1991) Prosocial development in adolescence: A longitudinal study. *Developmental Psychology, 27* (5), 849–857.

Eisenberg, N., Gurthrie, I.K., Murphy, B.C., Shepard, S.A., Cumberland, A. & Carlo, G. (1999) Consistency and development of prosocial dispositions: A longitudinal study. *Child Development, 70*, 1360–1372.

Eisenberg, N., Fabes, R.A. & Spinard, T.L. (2006) Prosocial development. In W. Damon (series ed.), R.M. Lerner (series ed.) & N. Eisenberg (volume ed.) *Handbook of Child Psychology, Volume 3: Social, Emotional and Personality Development* (6th edition). New York: Wiley.

Eiser, J.R. (1983) From attributions to behaviour. In M. Hewstone (ed.*) Attribution Theory: Social and Functional Extensions*. Oxford: Blackwell.

Eiser, J.R. (1994) *Attitudes, Chaos and the Connectionist Mind*. Oxford: Blackwell.

Eiser, J.R. & van der Pligt, J. (1988) *Attitudes and Decisions*. London: Routledge.

Ekman, P. (1992) An argument for basic emotions. *Cognition & Emotion, 6*, 169–200.

Ekman, P. (1994) All emotions are basic. In P. Ekman & R.J. Davidson (eds) *The Nature of Emotion: Fundamental Questions*. New York: Oxford University Press.

Ekman, P. & Friesen, W.V. (1975) *Unmasking the Face*. Englewood Cliffs, NJ: Prentice-Hall.

Ekman, P., Friesen, W.V. & Ellsworth, P. (1972) *Emotion in the Human Face: Guidelines for Research and an Integration of Findings*. New York: Pergamon.

Elander, J., Simonoff, E., Pickles, A., Holmshaw, J. & Rutter, M. (2000a) A longitudinal study of adolescent and adult conviction rates among children referred to psychiatric services for behavioural and emotional problems. *Criminal Behaviour & Mental Health, 10*, 40–59.

Elander, J., Rutter, M., Simonoff, E. & Pickles, A. (2000b) Explanations for apparent late-onset criminality in a high-risk sample of children followed up in adult life. *British Journal of Criminality, 40*, 497–509.

Eliot, L. (2012) The truth about boys and girls. *Scientific American Mind, 21*(2), 22–29.

Elkin, I., Shea, T.M., Watkins, J.T., Imber, S.D., Sotsky, S.M., Collins, J.F., Glass, D.R., Pilkonis, P.A., Leber, W.R., Docherty, J.P., Fiester, S.J. & Parloff, M.B. (1989) NIMH Treatment of Depression Collaborative Research Program: 1. General effectiveness of treatments. *Archives of General Psychiatry, 46*, 971–983.

Elkind, D. (1970) Erik Erikson's eight ages of man. *New York Times Magazine*, 5 April.

Elkind, D. (1987) The child yesterday, today and tomorrow. *Young Children, May*, 6–11.

Elliot, C.D. (1990) *Differential Ability Scales: Introduction and Technical Handbook*. San Antonio, TX: The Psychological Corporation.

Elliot, C.D. (1996) *The British Ability Scales II*. Windsor, Berkshire: NFER-NELSON Publishing Company.

Elliot, C.D., Murray, D.J. & Pearson, L.S. (1979) *British Ability Scales*. Slough: National Foundation for Educational Research.

Ellis, A. (1962) *Reason and Emotion in Psychotherapy*. Secaucus, NJ: Lyle Stuart (Citadel Press).

Ellis, A. (1973) *Humanistic Psychotherapy*. New York: McGraw-Hill.

Ellis, A. (1987) The impossibility of achieving consistently good mental health. *American Psychologist, 42*, 364–375.

Ellis, B. J., Bates, J.E., Dodge, K.A., Fergusson, D.M., Horwood, L.J., Pettit, G.S. & Woodward, L. (2003) Does father absence place daughters at special risk for early sexual activity and teenage pregnancy? *Child Development, 74*, 801–821.

Ellis, G. (2013) View from the top. *New Scientist, 219*(2930), 28–29.

Ellis, H.D. & Young, A.W. (1990) Accounting for delusional misidentifications. *British Journal of Psychiatry, 157*, 239–248.

Ellis, H.D., Davies, G.M. & Shepherd, J.W. (1978) A critical examination of the Photofit system for recalling faces. *Ergonomics, 21*, 297–307.

Ellis, S.J. (2002) Student support for lesbian and gay human rights: Findings from a large-scale questionnaire study. In A. Coyle & C. Kitzinger (eds) *Lesbian and Gay Psychology*, Oxford: BPS/ Blackwell, 239–254.

Elms, A.C. (1995) Obedience in retrospect. *Journal of Social Issues, 51*, 21–31.

Emery, N, J, & Clayton, N.S. (2004) The mentality of crows: convergent evolution of intelligence in corvids and apes. *Science, 306*, 1903–1907.

Emmelkamp, P.M.G. & Wessels, H. (1975) Flooding in imagination versus flooding in vivo: A comparison with agoraphobics. *Behaviour Research & Therapy in Personality, 13*, 7–15.

Emmerlich, W., Goldman, K.S., Kirsch, B. & Sharabany, R. (1977) Evidence for a transitional phase in the development of gender constancy. *Child Development, 48*, 930–936.

Empson, J. (1993) *Sleep and Dreaming* (2nd, revised edition) Hemel Hempstead: Harvester Wheatsheaf.

Empson, J. (2001) *Sleep and Dreaming* (3rd edition). New York: Palgrave Macmillan.

Endler, N.S. (1975) A person–situation interaction model of anxiety. In C.D. Spielberger & I.G. Sarason (eds) *Stress and Anxiety, Volume 1*. Washington, DC: Hemisphere.

Engel, G.L. (1977) The need for a new medical model: A challenge for bio-medicine. *Science, 196*, 129–135.

Engel, G.L. (1980) The clinical application of the biopsychosocial model. *American Journal of Psychiatry, 137*, 535–544.

Enoch, D. & Ball, H. (2001) *Uncommon Psychiatric Syndromes* (4th edition). London: Arnold.

Ericsson, K.A. & Charness, N. (1994) Expert performance: Its structure and acquisition. *American Psychologist, 49*, 725–747.

Erikson, E.H. (1950) *Childhood and Society*. New York: Norton.

Erikson, E.H. (1963) *Childhood and Society* (2nd edition). New York: Norton.

Erikson, E.H. (1968) *Identity: Youth and Crisis*. New York: Norton.

Erikson, E.H. (1980) *Identity and the Life Cycle*. New York: W.W. Norton.

Erikson, E.H. (1997) *The Life Cycle Completed: Extended Version with New Chapters on the Ninth Stage of Development by Joan M. Erikson*. New York: W.W. Norton.

Erikson J. (1997) In E.H. Erikson *The Life Cycle Completed* (extended version). New York: Norton.

Erlenmeyer-Kimling, L. & Jarvik, L.F. (1963) Genetics and intelligence: A review. *Science, 142*, 1477–1479.

Eron, L.D. & Huesmann, L.R. (1985) The role of television in the development of prosocial and antisocial behaviour. In D. Olweus, M. Radke-Yarrow & J. Block (eds) *Development of Antisocial and Prosocial Behaviour*. Orlando, FL: Academic Press.

Ersche, K.D., Turton, A.J., Pradhan, S. et al. (2010) Drug addiction endophenotypes: Impulsive versus sensation-seeking personality traits. *Biological Psychiatry, 68*(8), 770–773.

Estes, W.K. (1970) *Learning Theory and Mental Development*. New York: Academic Press.

Evans, C. (1987a) Parapsychology: A history of research. In R.L. Gregory (ed.) *The Oxford Companion to the Mind*. Oxford University Press.

Evans, C. (1987b) Extra-sensory perception. In R.L. Gregory (ed.) *The Oxford Companion to the Mind*. Oxford University Press.

Evans, J. St. B.T. & Over, D.E. (1996) *Rationality and Reasoning*. Hove: Psychology Press.

Everett, D. (2009) *Don't Sleep, There are Snakes: Life and Language in the Amazonian Jungle*. London: Profile Books.

Eysenck, H.J. (1947) *Dimension of Personality*. London: RKP.

Eysenck, H.J. (1952) The effects of psychotherapy: An evaluation. *Journal of Consulting Psychology, 16*, 319–324.

Eysenck, H.J. (1953) The logical basis of factor analysis. In D.N. Jackson & S. Messick (eds) *Problems in Human Assessment*. New York: McGraw-Hill.

Eysenck, H.J. (ed.) (1960) *Behaviour Therapy and the Neuroses*. Oxford: Pergamon.

Eysenck, H.J. (1965) *Fact and Fiction in Psychology*. Harmondsworth: Penguin.

Eysenck, H.J. (1971) *Race, Intelligence and Education*. London: Temple-Smith.

Eysenck, H.J. (1974) Crime and personality reconsidered. *Bulletin of the British Psychological Society, 27*, 23–24.

Eysenck, H.J. (1980) The biosocial model of man and the unification of psychology. In A.J. Chapman & D.M. Jones (eds) *Models of Man*. Leicester: British Psychological Society.

Eysenck, H.J. (1985) *Decline and Fall of the Freudian Empire*. Harmondsworth: Penguin.

Eysenck, H.J. (1991) Dimensions of personality: 16, 5 or 3? Criteria for a taxonomic paradigm. *Personality & Individual Differences, 8*, 773–790.

Eysenck, H.J. (1992) The outcome problem in psychotherapy. In W. Dryden & C. Feltham (eds) *Psychotherapy and its Discontents*. Buckingham: Open University Press.

Eysenck, H.J. (1995) Trait theories of personality. In S.E. Hampson & A.M. Colman (eds) *Individual Differences and Personality*. London: Longman.

Eysenck, H.J. & Eysenck, M.W. (1985) *Personality and Individual Differences: A Natural Science Approach*. New York: Plenum.

Eysenck, H.J. & Eysenck, S.B.G. (1964) *EPI Manual*. London: University of London Press.

Eysenck, H.J. & Eysenck, S.B.G. (1975) *Manual of the Eysenck Personality Questionnaire*. London: Hodder & Stoughton.

Eysenck, H.J. & Gudjonsson, G. (1989) *The Causes and Cures of Criminality*. New York: Plenum Press.

Eysenck, H.J. & Rachman, S. (1965) *The Cause and Cure of Neurosis*. London: RKP.

Eysenck, H.J. & Wilson, G.D. (1973) (eds) *The Experimental Study of Freudian Theories*. London: Methuen.

Eysenck, M.W. (1982) *Attention and Arousal: Cognition and Performance*. Berlin: Springer.

Eysenck, M.W. (1984) *A Handbook of Cognitive Psychology*. London: Lawrence Erlbaum Associates.

Eysenck, M.W. (1986) Working memory. In G. Cohen, M.W. Eysenck & M.A. Le Voi (eds) *Memory: A Cognitive Approach*. Milton Keynes: Open University Press.

Eysenck, M.W. (1993) *Principles of Cognitive Psychology*. Hove: Erlbaum.

Eysenck, M.W. (1995) Attention. In C.C. French & A.M. Colman (eds) *Cognitive Psychology*. London: Longman.

Eysenck, M.W. (1997a) Doing two things at once. *Psychology Review, 4* (1), 10–12.

Eysenck, M.W. (1997b) Absent-mindedness. *Psychology Review, 3*, 16–18.

Eysenck, M.W. & Keane, M.J. (1990) *Cognitive Psychology: A Student's Handbook*. Hove: Lawrence Erlbaum Associates Ltd.

Eysenck, M.W. & Keane, M.J. (1995) *Cognitive Psychology: A Student's Handbook* (3rd edition). Hove: Erlbaum.

Eysenck, S. & Eysenck, H.J. (1970) Crime and personality: An empirical study of the three-factor theory. *British Journal of Criminology, 10*, 225–239.

Fabes, R.A., Eisenberg, N. & Eisenbud, L. (1993) Behavioural and physiological correlates of children's reactions to others in distress. *Developmental Psychology, 29*, 655–664.

Fagot, B.I. (1985) Beyond the reinforcement principle: Another step toward understanding sex-role development. *Developmental Psychology, 21*, 1091–1104.

Fairbairn, G. & Fairbairn, S. (1987) Introduction. In S. Fairbairn & G. Fairbairn (eds) *Psychology, Ethics and Change*. London: Routledge & Kegan Paul.

Fairbairn, R. (1952) *Psychoanalytical Studies of the Personality*. London: Tavistock.

Falek, A. & Moser, H.M. (1975) Classification in schizophrenia. *Archives of General Psychiatry, 32*, 59–67.

Fancher, R.E. (1979) *Pioneers of Psychology*. New York: Norton.

Fancher, R.E. (1996) *Pioneers of Psychology* (3rd edition). New York: Norton.

Fantz, R.L. (1961) The origin of form perception. *Scientific American, 204* (5), 66–72.

Farber, S.L. (1981) *Identical Twins Reared Apart*. New York: Basic Books.

Farooq, R. & Abbas, I. (2013) No voice, no choice. *The Psychologist, 26*(9), 660–663.

Farmer, A.E., McGuffin, P. & Gottesman, I.I. (1987) Twin concordance for DSM-III schizophrenia: Scrutinizing the validity of the definition. *Archives of General Psychiatry, 44*, 634–641.

Farr, R.M. & Moscovici, S. (eds) (1984) *Social Representations*. Cambridge University Press.

Farrar, M.J. (1992) Negative evidence and grammatical morpheme acquisition. *Developmental Psychology, 28*, 90–98.

Farrington, D.P. (1990) Implications of criminal career research for the prevention of offending. *Journal of Adolescence*, 13, 93–113.

Farrington, D.P. (1992) Juvenile delinquency. In J. Coleman (ed.) *The School Years: Current Issues in the Socialisation of Young People* (2nd edition). London: Routledge.

Farrington, D.P. (1995) The development of offending and antisocial behaviour from childhood: Key findings from the Cambridge Study in delinquent development. *Journal of Child Psychology & Psychiatry, 36*, 929–964.

Farrington, D.P. & West, D.J. (1990) The Cambridge Study in delinquent development: A long-term follow-up of 411 London males. In H.T. Kerner & G. Kaiser (eds) *Criminality: Personality, Behaviour, and Life History*. Berlin: Springer-Verlag.

Farrington, D.P., Coid, J.W., Harnett, L.M., Jolliffe, D., Soteriou, N., Turner, R.E. & West, D.J. (2006) *Criminal Careers up to Age 50 and Life Success up to Age 48: New Findings from the Cambridge Study in Delinquent Development* (2nd edition). Home Office Research, Development and Statistics Directorate (Research Study 299).

Fazio, R.H. (1986) How do attitudes guide behaviour? In R.M. Sorrentino & E.T. Higgins (eds) *Handbook of Motivation and Cognition: Foundations of Social Behaviour*. New York: Guilford.

Fazio, R.H. (1990) Multiple processes by which attitudes guide behaviour: The MODE model as an integrative framework. In M.P. Zanna (ed.) *Advances in Experimental Social Psychology (Volume 23)*. San Diego, CA: Academic Press.

Fazio, R.H. (1995) Attitudes as object-evaluation associations: Determinants, consequences, and correlates of attitude accessibility. In R.E. Petty & J.A. Krosnick (eds) *Attitude Strength: Antecedents and Consequences*. Hillsdale, NJ: Lawrence Erlbaum.

Fazio, R.H. & Olson, M.A. (2003) Implicit measures in social cognition research: Their meaning and use. *Annual Review of Psychology, 54*, 297–327.

Fazio, R.H. & Zanna, M.D. (1978) Attitudinal qualities relating to the strength of the attitude–behaviour relation. *Journal of Experimental Social Psychology, 14*, 398–408.

Fazio, R.H., Zanna, M.P. & Cooper, J. (1977) Dissonance and self-perception: An integrative view of each theory's major domain of application. *Journal of Experimental & Social Psychology, 13*, 464–479.

Fazio, R.H., Jackson, J.R., Dunton, B.C. & Williams, C.J. (1995) Variability in autonomic activation as an unobtrusive measure of racial attitudes: A bona fide pipeline? *Journal of Personality & Social Psychology, 69*, 1013–1027.

Fechner, G.T. (1860) *Elemente der Psychophysik*. Leipzig: Bretkopf und Hartel.

Fedoroff, I.C. & McFarlane, T. (1998) Cultural aspects of eating disorders. In S.S. Kazarian & D.R. Evans (eds) *Cultural Clinical Psychology: Theory, Research, and Practice*. New York: Oxford University Press.

Feeney, B.C. & Monin, J.K. (2008) An attachment-theoretical perspective on divorce. In J. Cassidy & P.R. Shaver (eds) *Handbook of Attachment: Theory, Research, and Clinical Applications*. New York: Guilford Press.

Fein, D., Barton, M., Eigst, I. et al. (2013) Optimal outcome in individuals with a history of autism. *Journal of Child Psychology & Psychiatry, 54*(2), 195–205.

Feist, G.J. (2013) The psychology of scientific thought and behaviour. *The Psychologist, 26*(12), 864–867.

Felmlee, D.H. (1998) 'Be careful what you wish for…' A quantitative and qualitative investigation of 'fatal attractions'. *Personal Relationships, 5*, 235–253.

Fennell, G., Phillipson, C. & Evers, H. (1988) *The Sociology of Old Age*. Milton Keynes: Open University Press.

Fenson, L., Dale, P.S., Reznick, J.S., Bates, E., Thal, D.J. & Pethick, S.J. (1994) Variability in early communicative development. *Monographs of the Society for Research in Child Development, 59* (5, Serial No. 242).

Ferenczi, S. (1952) *First Contributions to Psychoanalysis*. New York: Brunner/Mazel.

Ferguson, C.J. (2007) Evidence for publication bias in video violence effects literature: A meta-analytic review. *Aggression & Violent Behavior, 12*, 470–482.

Fernando, S. (1988) *Race and Culture in Psychiatry*. London: Croom Helm.

Fernando, S. (1991) *Mental Health, Race and Culture*. London: Macmillan, in conjunction with MIND.

Fernyhough, C. (2013) Life in the chatter box. *New Scientist, 218*(2919), 32–35.

Ferster, C.B. & Skinner, B.F. (1957) *Schedules of Reinforcement*. New York: Appleton-Century-Crofts.

Feshbach, S. (1964) The function of aggression and the regulation of aggressive drive. *Psychological Review, 71*, 257–272.

Festinger, L. (1950) Informal social communication. *Psychological Review, 57*, 271–282.

Festinger, L. (1954) A theory of social comparison processes. *Human Relations, 7*, 117–140.

Festinger, L. (1957) *A Theory of Cognitive Dissonance*. New York: Harper & Row.

Festinger, L., Schachter, S. & Back, K. (1950) *Social Pressures in Informal Groups: A Study of Human Factors in Housing*. Stanford University Press.

Festinger, L., Pepitone, A. & Newcomb, T. (1952) Some consequences of deindividuation in a group. *Journal of Abnormal & Social Psychology, 47*, 382–389.

Field, T., Cohen, D., Garcia, R. & Greenberg, R. (1984) Mother–stranger face discrimination by the newborn. *Infant Behaviour & Development, 7*, 19–26.

Fields, H.L. (2009) The psychology of pain. *Scientific American Mind, 20*(5), 42–49.

Fields, R.D. (2004) The other half of the brain. *Scientific American, 290* (4), 26–33.

Fincham, F.D. (2004) Attributions in close relationships: From Balkanization to integration. In M.B. Brewer & M. Hewstone (eds) *Social Cognition*. Oxford: Blackwell Publishing.

Fine, C. (2010) *Delusions of Gender: How our Minds, Society and Neurosexism Create Difference*. London: W.W. Norton & Co.

Finkel, E.J., Slotter, E.B., Luchies, L.B., Walton, G.M., Gross, J.J. (2013) A brief intervention to promote conflict reappraisal preserves marital quality over time. *Psychological Science, 24*(8), 1595–1601.

Finkel, E.J. & Duffy, C.W. (2013) The thin line between love and wrath. *Scientific American Mind, 24*(5), 50–55.

Firth, S. (1993) Cross-cultural perspectives on bereavement. In D. Dickenson & M. Johnson (eds) *Death, Dying and Bereavement*. London: Sage, in association with the Open University.

Fischer, A., Fuchs, W. & Zinnecker, J. (1985) Jugenliche und Erwachsene '85. In Jugenwerk der Deutschen Shell (ed.) *Arbeitsbericht und Dokumentation, Volume 5*. Leverskusen: Leske und Budrich.

Fishbein, H.D. (1984) *The Psychology of Infancy and Childhood: Evolutionary and Cross-cultural Perspectives*. Hillsdale, NJ: Lawrence Erlbaum.

Fishbein, M. (1967) Attitudes and the prediction of behaviour. In M. Fishbein (ed.) *Readings in Attitude Theory and Measurement*. New York: Wiley.

Fishbein, M. & Ajzen, I. (1974) Attitudes towards objects as predictors of single and multiple behavioural criteria. *Psychological Review, 81*, 59–74.

Fishbein, M. & Ajzen, I. (1975) *Belief, Attitude, Intention and Behaviour: An Introduction to Theory and Research*. Reading, MA: Addison-Wesley.

Fisher, C.E. (2014) Psychiatry's new surgeons. *Scientific American Mind, 25*(1), 24–25.

Fisher, H.L. (2013) Mind the gap – pathways to psychosis. *The Psychologist, 26*(11), 798–801.

Fisher, R. (2007) Focus, focus, focus. *New Scientist, 196* (2634), 30–33.

Fisher, R.P. & Geiselman, R.E. (1988) Enhancing eyewitness memory with the cognitive interview. In M.M. Gruneberg, P.E. Morris & R.N. Sykes (eds) *Practical Aspects of Memory: Current Research and Issues. Volume 1: Memory in Everyday Life*. Chichester: John Wiley & Sons.

Fisher, S. & Greenberg, R. (1977) *The Scientific Credibility of Freud's Theories*. New York: Basic Books.

Fisher, S. & Greenberg, R.P. (1995) Prescriptions for happiness? *Psychology Today, 28*, 32–37.

Fiske, A.P., Kitayama, S., Markus, H.R. & Nisbett, R.E. (1998) The cultural matrix of social psychology. In D.T. Gilbert, S.T. Fiske & G. Lindzey (eds) *Handbook of Social Psychology, Volume 2* (4th edition). New York: McGraw-Hill.

Fiske, S.T. (2004) *Social Beings: A Core Motives Approach to Social Psychology*. New York: John Wiley & Sons, Inc.

Fiske, S.T. & Neuberg, S.L. (1990) A continuum of impression formation, from category-based to individuating processes: Influences of information and motivation on attention and interpretation. In L. Berkowitz (ed.) *Advances in Experimental Social Psychology, Volume 23*. New York: Academic Press.

Fiske, S.T. & Taylor, S.E. (1991) *Social Cognition* (2nd edition). New York: McGraw-Hill.

Flanagan, O.J. (1984) *The Science of the Mind*. Cambridge, MA: MIT Press.

Flanagan, O.J. (2000) *Dreaming Souls: Sleep, Dreams, and the Evolution of the Conscious Mind*. New York: Oxford University Press.

Flavell, J.H. (1982) Structures, stages and sequences in cognitive development. In W.A. Collins (ed.) *The Concept of Development: The Minnesota Symposia on Child Development, Volume 15*. Hillsdale, NJ: Erlbaum.

Flavell, J.H. (1986) The development of children's knowledge about the appearance–reality distinction. *American Psychologist, 41*, 418–425.

Flavell, J.H., Shipstead, S.G. & Croft, K. (1978) What young children think you see when their eyes are closed. Unpublished report, Stanford University.

Flavell, J.H., Green, F.L. & Flavell, E.R. (1990) Developmental changes in young children's knowledge about the mind. *Cognitive Development, 5*, 1–27.

Fletcher, G. (2002) *The New Science of Intimate Relationships*. Oxford: Blackwell.

Flynn, J. (2008) A tough call. *New Scientist, 199*(2672), 48–50.

Flynn, J.R. (1987) Massive IQ gains in 14 nations: What IQ tests really measure. *Psychological Bulletin, 101*, 171–191.

Fodor, J.A. & Pylyshyn, Z.W. (1981) How direct is visual perception? Some reflections on Gibson's 'ecological approach'. *Cognition, 9*, 139–196.

Folkman, S. (1984) Personal control and stress and coping processes: A theoretical analysis. *Journal of Personality & Social Psychology, 46*, 839–852.

Folkman, S. & Lazarus, R.S. (1988) *Manual for the Ways of Coping Questionnaire*. Palo Alto, CA: Consulting Psychologists Press.

Fonagy, P. (1981) Research on psychoanalytic concepts. In F. Fransella (ed.) *Personality – Theory, Measurement and Research*. London: Methuen.

Fonagy, P. (1989) On tolerating mental states: Theory of mind in borderline personality. *Bulletin of the Anna Freud Centre, 12*, 91–115.

Fonagy, P. (1995) Psychoanalysis. In A.M. Colman (ed.) *Applications of Psychology*. London: Longman.

Fonagy, P. (2000) The outcome of psychoanalysis: The hope of a future. *The Psychologist, 13*(12), 620–623.

Fonagy, P. & Higgitt, A. (1984) *Personality, Theory and Clinical Practice*. London: Methuen.

Fonagy, P., Steele, H. & Steele, M. (1991) Maternal representations of attachment during pregnancy predict the organisation of infant–mother attachment at one year of age. *Child Development, 62*, 891–905.

Fonagy, P., Steele, M., Steele, H., Higgitt, A. & Target, M. (1994) The Emmanuel Miller Memorial Lecture, 1992: The theory and practice of resilience. *Journal of Child Psychology & Psychiatry, 35*, 321–257.

Fontenelle, L.F., Cocchi, L., Harrison, B.J. et al. (2012) Towards a post-traumatic subtype of OCD. *Journal of Anxiety Disorders, 26*(2), 377–383.

Foot, H. & Howe, C. (1998) The psycho-educational basis of peer-assisted learning. In K. Topping & S. Ehly (eds) *Peer-assisted Learning*. Mahwah, NJ: Erlbaum.

Foot, H. & Sanford, A. (2004) The use and abuse of student participants. *The Psychologist, 17*(5), 256–259.

Foot, H., Morgan, M.J. & Shute, R.H. (1990) *Children Helping Children*. Chichester: Wiley.

Ford, J.M. & Mathalon, D.H. (2004) Electrophysiological evidence of corollary discharge dysfunction in schizophrenia during talking and thinking. *Journal of Psychiatric Research, 38*, 37–46.

Ford, K.M. & Hayes, P.J. (1998) On computational wings: Rethinking the goals of artificial intelligence. *Scientific American Presents, 9*(4), 78–83.

Ford, R. (1998) Study fails to link film violence to crime. *The Times*, 8 January, 9.

Forshaw, M. (2002) *Essential Health Psychology*. London: Arnold.

Forster, S. & Lavie, N. (2007) High perceptual load makes everybody equal: Eliminating individual differences in distractability with load. *Psychological Science, 18*(5), 377–381.

Forth, A. (1995) Psychopathy in adolescent offenders: Assessment, family background and violence. *Issues in Criminololgical & Legal Psychology, 24*, 42–44.

Foxx, R. & Azrin, N. (1973) *Toilet Training the Retarded*. Champaign, IL: Research Press.

Frances, A. (2013a) Don't count on this manual. *New Scientist, 218*(2916), 5.

Frances, A. (2013b) *Saving Normal: An insider's revolt against out-of-control psychiatric diagnosis, DSM-5, big pharma, and the medicalisation of ordinary life*. New York: William Morrow.

Frank, E., Kupfer, D.J., Perel, J.M., Cornes, C., Jarrett, D.B., Mallinger, A.G., Thase, M.E., McEachran, A.B. & Grochocinski, V.J. (1990) Three-year outcomes for maintenance therapies in recurrent depression. *Archives of General Psychiatry, 47*, 1093–1099.

Frank, I.D. (1973) *Persuasion and Healing* (2nd edition). Baltimore, MD: Johns Hopkins University Press.

Frank, I.D. (1989) Non-specific aspects of treatment: The view of a psychotherapist. In M. Shepherd & N. Sartorius (eds) *Non-Specific Aspects of Treatment*. Toronto: Hans Huber.

Frankenhaeuser, F. (1975) Experimental approaches to the study of catecholamines and emotion. In L. Levi (ed.) *Emotions: The Parameters and Measurement*. New York: Raven Press.

Frankland, A. & Cohen, L. (1999) Working with recovered memories. *The Psychologist, 12* (2), 82–83.

Fransella, F. (1970) …And then there was one. In D. Bannister (ed.) *Perspectives in Personal Construct Theory*. London: Academic Press.

Fransella, F. (1972) *Personal Change and Reconstruction: Research on a Treatment of Stuttering*. London: Academic Press.

Fransella, F. (1981) Personal construct psychology and repertory grid technique. In F. Fransella (ed.) *Personality – Theory, Measurement and Research*. London: Methuen.

Frederickson, N. & Miller, A. (2008) What do educational psychologists do? In N. Frederickson, A. Miller & T. Cline (eds) *Educational Psychology*. London: Hodder Education.

Freedman, A.M., Kaplan. H.I. & Sadock, B.J. (1975) *Comprehensive Textbook of Psychiatry, Volume 2*. Baltimore, MD: Williams & Wilkins Co.

Freedman, J.L. (1963) Attidudinal effects of inadequate justification. *Journal of Personality, 31*, 371–385.

Freedman, J.L. (1965) Long-term behavioural effects of cognitive dissonance. *Journal of Experimental & Social Psychology, 1*, 145–155.

Freedman, J.L. & Fraser, S.C. (1966) Compliance without pressure: The foot-in-the-door technique. *Journal of Personality & Social Psychology, 4*, 195–202.

Freeman, D. & Freeman, J. (2014) The stressed sex? *The Psychologist, 27*(2), 84–87.

Freeman, E.D., Ipser, A., Palmbaha, A. et al. (2013) Sight and sound out of synch: Fragmentation and renormalisation of audiovisual integration and subjective timing. *Cortex, 49*(10), 2875–2877.

Freeman, T., Jadva, V., Kramer, W. & Golombok, S. (2009) Gamete donation: Parents' experiences of searching for their child's donor siblings and donor. *Human Reproduction, 24*(3), 505–516.

French, C. (2012) Peering into the future of peer review: A curious case from Parapsychology. *Psychology Review, 18*(2), 26–29.

Freud, A. (1936) *The Ego and the Mechanisms of Defence*. London: Chatto & Windus.

Freud, A., 1997, *Psychoanalytic Study of the Child: Anna Freud Anniversary Issue Volume 51*, New Haven: Yale University Press.

Freud, A. & Dann, S. (1951) An experiment in group upbringing. *Psychoanalytic Study of the Child, 6*, 127–168.

Freud, S. (1899) *Screen Memories: Standard Edition of the Complete Psychological Works of Sigmund Freud, Volume III*. London: Hogarth Press.

Freud, S. (1900/1976a) *The Interpretation of Dreams*. Pelican Freud Library (4). Harmondsworth: Penguin.

Freud, S. (1901/1976b) *The Psychopathology of Everyday Life*. Pelican Freud Library (5). Harmondsworth: Penguin.

Freud, S. (1905/1977a) *Three Essays on the Theory of Sexuality*. Pelican Freud Library (7). Harmondsworth: Penguin.

Freud, S. (1909/1977b) *Analysis of a Phobia in a Five-year-old Boy*. Pelican Freud Library (8). Harmondsworth: Penguin.

Freud, S. (1914) *Remembering, Repeating and Working Through. The Standard Edition of Complete Psychological Works of Sigmund Freud, Volume XII*. London: Hogarth Press.

Freud, S. (1915) *Repression. Standard Edition of the Complete Psychological Works of Sigmund Freud, Volume 14*. London: Hogarth Press.

Freud, S. (1920/1984) *Beyond the Pleasure Principle*. Pelican Freud Library (11). Harmondsworth: Penguin.

Freud, S. (1923/1984) *The Ego and the Id*. Pelican Freud Library (11). Harmondsworth: Penguin.

Freud, S. (1924) The passing of the Oedipus complex. In E. Jones (ed.) *Collected Papers of Sigmund Freud, Volume 5*. New York: Basic Books.

Freud, S. (1926) Inhibitions, symptoms and anxiety. In *Standard Edition of the Complete Psychological Works of Sigmund Freud, Volume XX*. London: Hogarth Press.

Freud, S. (1933) *New Introductory Lectures on Psychoanalysis*. New York: Norton.

Freud, S. (1938) *An Outline of Psychoanalysis*. Volume 15. London: Penguin.

Friedman, L.J. (1999) *Identity's Architect: A Biography of Erik H. Erikson*. London: Free Association Books.

Friedman, M. & Rosenman, R.H. (1974) *Type A Behaviour and Your Heart*. New York: Harper & Row.

Frijda, N.H. (1994) Varieties of affect: Emotions and episodes, moods, and sentiments. In P. Ekman & R.J. Davidson (eds) The *Nature of Emotion: Fundamental Questions*. New York: Oxford University Press.

Frith, C. (2007) *Making Up the Mind: How the Brain Creates Our Mental World*. Oxford: Blackwell Publishing.

Frith, C. & Cahill, C. (1995) Psychotic disorders: Schizophrenia, affective psychoses and paranoia. In A.A. Lazarus & A.M. Colman (eds) *Abnormal Psychology*. London: Longman.

Frith, C.D. (1992) *The Cognitive Neuropsychology of Schizophrenia*. Hove: Lawrence Erlbaum Associates.

Frith, M. (2005) 'Ethical sluts' develop new language of love for open relationships. *Independent*, 4 April, 16.

Frith, U. (1989) *Autism: Explaining the Enigma*. Oxford: Basil Blackwell.

Frith, U. (1996) Cognitive explanations of autism. *Acta Paediatrics Supplement, 416*, 63–68.

Frith, U. & Happé, F. (1994a) Autism: Beyond 'theory of mind'. *Cognition, 50*, 115–132.

Frith, U. & Happé, F. (1994b) Language and communication in the autistic disorders. *Philosophical Transactions of the Royal Society, Series B, 346*, 97–104.

Frith, U. & Snowling, M. (1983) Reading for meaning and reading for sound in autistic and dyslexic children. *Journal of Developmental Psychology, 1*, 329–342.

Frodi, A. (1975) The effect of exposure to weapons on aggressive behaviour from a cross-cultural perspective. *International Journal of Psychology, 10*, 283–292.

Fromm, E. (1962) *The Art of Loving*. London: Unwin Books.

Fromm, E. (1977) *The Anatomy of Human Destructiveness*. Harmondsworth: Penguin.

Frowd, C.D., Hancock, P.J.B. & Carson, D. (2004) EvoFIT: A holistic, evolutionary facial imaging technique for creating composites. *ACM Transactions on Applied Psychology (TAP), 1*, 1–21.

Frowd, C., Bruce, V. & Hancock, P.J.B. (2008) Changing the face of criminal identification. *The Psychologist, 21*(8), 668–672.

Frude, N. (1998) *Understanding Abnormal Psychology*. Oxford: Blackwell.

Fujino, D.C. (1997) The rates, patterns and reasons for forming heterosexual interracial dating relationships among Asian Americans. *Journal of Social & Personal Relationships, 14*, 809–828.

Funk, S.C. (1992) Hardiness: A review of theory and research. *Health Psychology, 11*(5), 335–345.

Furedi, F. (2003) The children who won't grow up. *Spiked-online.com*, 29 July.

Furnham, A. & Heaven, P. (1999) *Personality and Social Behaviour*. London: Arnold.

Furth, H.G. (1966) *Thinking Without Language*. New York: Free Press.

Gadow, J.D. & Sprafkin, J. (1989) Field experiments of television violence: Evidence for an environmental hazard? *Paediatrics, 83*, 399–405.

Gaertner, S.L. & Dovidio, J.F. (1977) The subtlety of white racism, arousal, and helping. *Journal of Personality & Social Psychology, 35*, 691–707.

Gaertner, S.L. & Dovidio, J.F. (2000) *Reducing Intergroup Bias: The Common In-group Identity Model*. Philadelphia, PA: Psychology Press.

Gahagan, J. (1984) *Social Interaction and its Management*. London: Methuen.

Gale, A. (1990) *Thinking about Psychology?* (2nd edition). Leicester: British Psychological Society.

Gale, A. (1995) Ethical issues in psychological research. In A.M. Colman (ed.) *Psychological Research Methods and Statistics*. London: Longman.

Gallagher, M., Millar, R., Hargie, O. & Ellis, R. (1992) The personal and social worries of adolescents in Northern Ireland: Results of a survey. *British Journal of Guidance & Counselling, 30*(3), 274–290.

Gallup, G.G. (1977) Self-recognition in primates. *American Psychologist, 32*, 329–338.

Gallup, G.G. (1998) Can animals empathise? Yes. *Scientific American Presents, 9*(4), 66, 68–71.

Gamble, J. (2013) Into darkness. *New Scientist, 220*(2945), 38–39.

Garcia, J. & Koelling, R.A. (1966) The relation of cue to consequence in avoidance learning. *Psychonomic Science, 4*, 123–124.

Garcia, J., Ervin, F.R. & Koelling, R.A. (1966) Learning with prolonged delay of reinforcement. *Psychonomic Science, 5*(3), 121–122.

Gardikotis, A. (2013) Minority Influence. *Psychology Review, 18*(4), 7–9.

Gardner, H. (1983) *Frames of Mind: The Theory of Multiple Intelligences*. New York: Basic Books.

Gardner, H. (1993) *Multiple Intelligences: The Theory in Practice*. New York: Basic Books.

Gardner, H. (1998) A multiplicity of intelligences. Scientific American Presents: *Exploring Intelligence, 9*(4), 18–23.

Gardner, R.A. & Gardner, B.T. (1969) Teaching sign language to a chimpanzee. *Science, 165*(3894), 664–672.

Garfield, S. (1992) Response to Hans Eysenck. In W. Dryden & C. Feltham (eds) *Psychotherapy and its Discontents*. Buckingham: Open University Press.

Garnham, A. (1988) *Artificial Intelligence: An Introduction*. London: Routledge & Kegan Paul.

Garnham, A. (1991) *The Mind in Action*. London: Routledge.

Garrett, R. (1996) Skinner's case for radical behaviourism. In W. O'Donohue & R.F. Kitchener (eds) *The Philosophy of Psychology*. London: Sage.

Gaschler, K. (2006) One person, one neuron? *Scientific American Mind, 17*(1), 76–82.

Gathercole, S.E. (2008) Working memory in the classroom. *The Psychologist, 21* (5), 382–385.

Gathercole, S.E. & Baddeley, A.D. (1990) Phonological memory deficits in language-disordered children: Is there a causal connection? *Journal of Memory & Language, 29*, 336–360.

Gathercole, S.E., Lamont, E. & Alloway, T.P. (2006) Working memory in the classroom. In S. Pickering (ed.) *Working Memory and Education*. London: Academic Press.

Gauker, C. (1990) How to learn language like a chimpanzee. *Philosophical Psychology, 3*, 31–53.

Gay, P. (1988) *Freud: A Life for Our Time*. London: J.M. Dent & Sons.

Gazzaniga, M.S. (1985) *The Social Brain: Discovering the Networks of the Mind*. New York: Basic Books.

Gazzaniga, M.S. (2000) Cerebral specialisation and interhemispheric communication: Does the corpus callosum enable the human condition? *Brain, 123*, 1293–1326.

Geary, D.C. (1998) *Male, Female: The Evolution of Human Sex Differences*. Washington, DC: American Psychological Association.

Geen, R.G. (1995) Social motivation. In Parkinson, B. & Colman, A.M. (eds) *Emotion and Motivation*. London: Longman.

Geiselman, R.E., Fisher, R.P., Mackinnon, D.P. & Holland, H.L. (1985) Eyewitness memory enhancement in the police interview: Cognitive retrieval, mnemonics versus hypnosis. *Journal of Applied Psychology, 70*, 401–412.

Gelder, M., Bancroft, J., Gath, D.H., Johnston, D.H., Matthews, A. M. & Shaw, P.M. (1973) Specific and non-specific factors in behaviour therapy. *British Journal of Psychiatry, 123*, 445–462.

Gelder, M., Gath, D. & Mayon, R. (1989) *The Oxford Textbook of Psychiatry* (2nd edition). Oxford University Press.

Gelder, M., Mayou, R. & Geddes, J. (1999) *Psychiatry* (2nd edition). Oxford University Press.

Gelman, R. (1978) Counting in the pre-schooler: What does and does not develop. In R.S. Siegler (ed.) *Children's Thinking: What Develops?* Hillsdale, NJ: Erlbaum.

Gelman, R. (1979) Preschool thought. *American Psychologist, 34*, 900–905.

Gelman, R. & Baillargeon, R. (1983) A review of some Piagetian concepts. In J.H. Flavell & E.M. Markman (eds) *Handbook of Child Psychology: Cognitive Development, Volume 3*. New York: Wiley.

Geraerts, E., Bernstein, D.M., Merckelbach, H., Linders, C., Raymaekers, L. & Loftus, E.F. (2008) Lasting false beliefs and their behavioral consequences. *Psychological Science, 19* (8), 749–753.

Gerard, H.B., Wilhelmy, R.A. & Connolly, E.S. (1968) Conformity and group size. *Journal of Personality & Social Psychology, 8*, 79–82.

Gergen, K.J. (1973) Social psychology as history. *Journal of Personality & Social Psychology, 26*, 309–320.

Gergen, K.J. (1985) The social constructionist movement in modern psychology. *American Psychologist, 40*, 266–275.

Gergen, K.J. & Gergen, M.M. (1981) *Social Psychology*. New York: Harcourt Brace Jovanovich.

Geschwind, N. & Galaburda, A.M. (1985a) Cerebral lateralisation. Biological mechanisms, associations and pathology: I. A hypothesis and a program for research. *Archives of Neurology, 42*, 428–459.

Geschwind, N. & Galaburda, A.M. (1985b) Cerebral lateralisation. Biological mechanism, associations and pathology: II. A hypothesis and program for research. *Archives of Neurology, 42*, 521–552.

Geschwind, N. & Galaburda, A.M. (1985c) Cerebral lateralisation. Biological mechanisms, associations and pathology: III. A hypothesis and program for research. *Archives of Neurology, 42*, 634–654.

Gesell, A. (1925) *The Mental Growth of the Preschool Child*. New York: Macmillan.

Gibson, E.J. & Walk, P.D. (1960) The visual cliff. *Scientific American, 202*, 64–71.

Gibson, E.J., Shapiro, F. & Yonas, A. (1968) Confusion matrices of graphic patterns obtained with a latency measure: A program of basic and applied research. Final Report Project No. 5–1213, Cornell University.

Gibson, J.J. (1950) *The Perception of the Visual World*. Boston: Houghton Mifflin.

Gibson, J.J. (1966) *The Senses Considered as Perceptual Systems*. Boston: Houghton Mifflin.

Gibson, J.J. (1979) *The Ecological Approach to Visual Perception*. Boston: Houghton Mifflin.

Giddens, A. (1979) *Central Problems in Social Theory*. Basingstoke: Macmillan.

Giedd, J.N., Blumenthal, J., Jeffries, N.O., Castellanos, F. X., Liu, H., Zijdenbos, A., Paus, T., Evans, A.C. & Rapoport, J.L. (1999) Brain development during childhood and adolescence: A longitudinal MRI study. *Nature Neuroscience, 2*, 861–863.

Gilbert, D.T. (1995) Attribution and interpersonal perception. In A. Tesser (ed.) *Advanced Social Psychology*. New York: McGraw-Hill.

Gilbert, D.T. (1998) Ordinary personology. In D.T. Gilbert, S.T. Fiske & G. Lindzey (eds) *The Handbook of Social Psychology, Volume 2* (4th edition). New York: McGraw-Hill.

Gilbert, D.T. & Malone, P.S. (1995) The correspondence bias. *Psychological Bulletin, 117*, 21–38.

Gilbert, G.M. (1951) Stereotype persistence and change among college students. *Journal of Abnormal & Social Psychology, 46*, 245–254.

Gilbert, S.J. (1981) Another look at the Milgram obedience studies: The role of the graduated series of shocks. *Personality & Social Psychology Bulletin, 7*, 690–695.

Giles, L.C., Glonek, G.F., Luszcz, M.A. & Andrews, G.R. (2005) Effects of Social Networks on 10-Year Survival in Very Old Australians. *Journal of Epidemiology & Community Health, 59*(7), 574–579.

Gilford, R. & Bengston, V. (1979) Measuring marital satisfaction in three generations: Positive and negative dimensions. *Journal of Marriage & The Family, 41*, 387–398.

Gillham, W.E.C. (1975) Intelligence: The persistent myth. *New Behaviour*, 26 June, 433–435.

Gillham, W.E.C. (1978) Measurement constructs and psychological structure: Psychometrics. In A. Burton & J. Radford (eds) *Thinking in Perspective*. London: Methuen.

Gillie, O. (1976) Pioneer of IQ fakes his research. *Sunday Times*, 29 October, H3.

Gilligan, C. (1982) In a Different Voice: Psychological Theory and Women's Development. Cambridge, MA: Harvard University Press.

Gilligan, C. (1993) Letter to Readers (Preface). *In a Different Voice*. Cambridge, MA: Harvard University Press.

Gilligan, C. (1993) *In A Different Voice: Psychological Theory and Women's Development* (revised edition). Cambridge, MA: Harvard University Press.

Gilling, D. & Brightwell, R. (1982) *The Human Brain*. London: Orbis Publishing.

Ginsberg, H.P. (1981) Piaget and education: The contributions and limits of genetic epistemology. In K. Richardson & S. Sheldon (eds) *Cognitive Development to Adolescence*. Milton Keynes: Open University Press.

Ginsberg, M.L. (1998) Computers, games and the real world. *Scientific American Presents, 9* (4), 84–89.

Gladwell, M. (2008) *Outliers: The Story of Success*. Harmondsworth: Allen Lane.

Glanzer, M. & Cunitz, A.R. (1966) Two storage mechanisms in free recall. *Journal of Verbal Learning & Verbal Behaviour, 5*, 928–935.

Glass, D.C. (1977) *Behavior Patterns, Stress and Coronary Disease*. Hillsdale, NJ: Lawrence Erlbaum Associates.

Glass, D.C. & Contrada, R.J. (2012) Bipolar disorder, Type A behaviour and coronary disease. *Health Psychology Review, 6*(2), 180–196.

Glassman, W.E. (1995) *Approaches to Psychology* (2nd edition). Buckingham: Open University.

Glick, B. & Goldstein, A.P. (1987) Aggression replacement training. *Journal of Counselling & Development, 65*, 356–367.

Gluckman, P.D. & Hanson, M.A. (2006) Evolutionary development and timing of puberty. *Trends in Endocrinology & Metabolism, 17*(1), 7–12.

Glucksberg, S. & Cowan, N. (1970) Memory for non-attended auditory material. *Cognitive Psychology, 1*, 149–156.

Glucksberg, S. & Weisberg, R. (1966) Verbal behaviour and problem-solving: Some effects of labelling upon availability of novel functions. *Journal of Experimental Psychology, 71*, 659–664.

Godden, D. & Baddeley, A.D. (1975) Context-dependent memory in two natural environments: On land and under water. *British Journal of Psychology, 66*, 325–331.

Godden, D. & Baddeley, A.D. (1980) When does context influence recognition memory? *British Journal of Psychology, 71*, 99–104.

Goetsch, V.I. & Fuller, M.G. (1995) Stress and stress management. In D. Wedding (ed.) *Behaviour and Medicine* (2nd edition). St. Louis, MO: Mosby-Year Book.

Goffman, E. (1968) *Asylums – Essay on the Social Situation of Mental Patients and Other Inmates*. Harmondsworth: Penguin.

Goffman, E. (1971) *The Presentation of Self in Everyday Life*. Harmondsworth: Penguin.

Gogtay, N., Giedd, J.N., Lusk, L., Hayashi, K.M., Greenstein, D., Vaituzis, A.C., Nugent, III, T.F., Herman, D.H., Clasen, L.S., Toga, A.W., Rapoport, J.L. & Thompson, P.M. (2009) Dynamic mapping of human cortical development during childhood through early adulthood. *Proceedings of the National Academy of Sciences, 101*(21), 8174–8179.

Goldberg, L.R (1993) The structure of phenotypic personality traits. *American Psychologist, 48*, 26–34.

Goldberg, S. (2000) *Attachment and Development*. London: Arnold.

Goldfarb, W. (1943) The effects of early institutional care on adult personality. *Journal of Experimental Education, 12*, 106–129.

Goldstein, A.P. & Glick, B. (1996) Aggression replacement training: Methods and outcome. In C.R. Hollin & K. Howells (eds) *Clinical Approaches to Working with Young Offenders*. Chichester: Wiley.

Goldwyn, E. (1979) The fight to be male. *The Listener*, 24 May, 709–712.

Goleman, D. (1995) *Emotional Intelligence*. London: Bloomsbury.

Gollwitzer, P.M. (1993) Goal achievement: The role of intentions. *European Review of Social Psychology, 4*, 141–185.

Gollwitzer, P.M. (1999) Implementing intentions: Strong effects of simple plans. *American Psychologist, 54*, 493–503.

Golombok, S. & Fivush, R. (1994) *Gender Development*. Cambridge University Press.

Golombok, S. & Tasker, F. (1996) Do parents influence the sexual orientation of their children? Findings from a longitudinal study of lesbian families. *Developmental Psychology, 32*(1), 3–11.

Golombok, S., Cook, R., Bish, A. & Murray, C. (1995) Families created by the new reproductive technologies: Quality of parenting and social and emotional development of the children. *Child Development, 66*, 285–289.

Golombok, S., Brewaeys, A., Cook, R., Giavazzi, M.T., Guerra, D., Mantovani, A., van Hall, E., Crosignani, P.G. & Dexeus, S. (1996) The European Study of Assisted Reproduction Families. *Human Reproduction, 11*(10), 2324–2331.

Golombok, S., Tasker, F. & Murray, C. (1997) Children raised in fatherless families from infancy: Family relationships and the socioemotional development of children of lesbian and single heterosexual mothers. *Journal of Child Psychology & Psychiatry, 38*(7), 83–92.

Golombok, S., Murray, C., Brinsden, P. & Addalla, H. (1999) Social versus biological parenting: Family functioning and socioemotional development of children conceived by egg or sperm donation. *Journal of Child Psychology and Psychiatry, 40*, 519–527.

Golombok, S., MacCallum, F. & Goodman, E. (2001) The 'test tube' generation: Parent–child relationships and the psychological well-being of in vitro fertilization children at adolescence. *Child Development, 72*, 599–608.

Golombok, S., MacCallum, F., Goodman, E. & Rutter, M. (2002a) Families with children conceived by donor insemination: A follow-up at age 12. *Child Development, 73* (3), 952–968.

Golombok, S., Brewaeys, A., Giavazzi, M.T., Guerra, D., MacCallum, F. & Rust, J. (2002b) The European Study of Assisted Reproduction Families: The transition to adolescence. *Human Reproduction, 17*(3), 830–840.

Golombok, S., Perry, B., Burston, A., Murray, C., Mooney-Somers, J., Stevens, M. & Golding, J. (2003) Children with lesbian parents: A community study. *Developmental Psychology, 39*(1), 20–33.

Golombok, S., Murray, C., Jadva, V., MacCallum, F. & Lycett, E. (2004a) Families created through a surrogacy arrangement: Parent–child relationships in the first year of life. *Developmental Psychology, 40*, 400–411.

Golombok, S., Lycett, E., MacCallum, F., Jadva, V., Murray, C., Rust, J., Abdalla, H., Jenkins, J. & Margara, R. (2004b) Parenting children conceived by gamete donation. *Journal of Family Psychology, 18*(3), 443–452.

Golombok, S., Jadva, V., Lycett, E., Murray, C. & MacCallum, F. (2005) Families created by gamete donation: Follow-up at age 2. *Human Reproduction, 20*(1), 286–293.

Golombok, S., MacCallum, F., Murray, C., Lycett, E. & Jadva, V. (2006) Surrogacy families: Parental functioning, parent–child relationships and children's psychological development at age 2. *Journal of Child Psychology & Psychiatry, 47*(2), 213–222.

Golombok, S., Owen, L., Blake, L., Murray, C. & Jadva, V. (2009) Parent–child relationships and the psychological well-being of 18-year-old adolescents conceived by in vitro fertilisation. *Human Fertility, 12*(2), 63–72.

Goodale, M.A. & Milner, A.D. (2004) *Sight Unseen*. Oxford University Press.

Goodale, M. & Milner, D. (2006) One brain – two visual systems. *The Psychologist, 19*(11), 660–663.

Goodale, M., Milner, A.D., Jakobson, L.S. & Carey, D.P. (1991) A neurological dissociation between perceiving objects and grasping them. *Nature, 349*, 154–156.

Goodchild, S. (2006) Dying to be thin. *Independent on Sunday*, 29 October, 8–9.

Gopnik, A. & Wellman, H.M. (1994) The theory theory. In L.A. Hirschfeld & S.A. Gelman (eds) *Mapping the Mind*. Cambridge University Press.

Gopnik, M. (1994) Impairments of tense in a familial language disorder. *Journal of Neurolinguistics, 8*, 109–133.

Gordon, I.E. (1989) *Theories of Visual Perception*. Chichester: Wiley.

Gordon, L., Joo, J.E., Powell, J.E. et al. (2012) Neonatal DNA methylation profile in human twins is specified by a complex interplay between intrauterine environmental and genetic factors, subject to tissue-specific influence. *Genome Research, 22*(8), 1395–1406.

Gordon, R.A. (2001) Eating disorders East and West: A culture-bound syndrome unbound. In M. Nasser, M.A. Katzman & R.A. Gordon (eds) *Eating Disorders and Cultures in Transition*. Hove: Brunner-Routledge.

Gosline, A. (2009) Five Ages of the Brain: 3. Adolescence. *New Scientist, 202*(2702), 29–30.

Gottesman, I.I. & Shields, J. (1982) *Schizophrenia: The Epigenetic Puzzle*. Cambridge University Press.

Gottfried, A.W., Gottfried, A.E., Bathurst, K. & Guerin, D.W. (1994) *Gifted IQ: Early Developmental Aspects*. New York: Plenum Press.

Gould, R.L. (1978) *Transformations: Growth and Change in Adult Life*. New York: Simon & Schuster.

Gould, R.L. (1980) Transformational tasks in adulthood. In S.I. Greenspan & G.H. Pollock (eds*) The Course of Life: Psychoanalytic Contributions Toward Understanding Personality Development, Volume 3*: Adulthood and the Ageing Process. Washington, DC: National Institute for Mental Health.

Gould, S.J. (1981) *The Mismeasure of Man*. Harmondsworth: Penguin.

Gouldner, A.W. (1960) The norm of reciprocity: A preliminary statement. *American Sociological Review, 25*, 161–178.

Graham, H. (1986) *The Human Face of Psychology*. Milton Keynes: Open University Press.

Gravotta, L. (2014) Taking early aim at autism. *Scientific American Mind, 25*(1), 52–57.

Gray, J.A. (1970) The psychophysiological basis of introversion-extraversion. *Behaviour Research & Therapy, 8*, 249–266.

Gray, J.A. (1982) *Neuropsychological theory of Anxiety* (2nd edition). Oxford: Oxford University Press.

Gray, J.A. (1991) On the morality of speciesism. *The Psychologist, 4* (5), 196–198.

Gray, J.A. & Wedderburn, A.A. (1960) Grouping strategies with simultaneous stimuli. *Quarterly Journal of Experimental Psychology, 12*, 180–184.

Graziano, W.G. & Eisenberg, N. (1997) Agreeableness: A dimension of personality. In R. Hogan, J. Johnson & S. Briggs (eds) *Handbook of Personality Psychology*. New York: Academic Press.

Green, S. (1980) Physiological studies I and II. In J. Radford & E. Govier (eds) *A Textbook of Psychology*. London: Sheldon Press.

Green, S. (1994) *Principles of Biopsychology*. Sussex: Lawrence Erlbaum Associates.

Greenberg, J., Solomon, S., Pyszczynski, T. et al. (1992) Assessing the terror management analysis of self-esteem: Converging evidence of an anxiety-buffering function. *Journal of Personality & Social Psychology, 63*, 913–922.

Greene, J. (1975) *Thinking and Language*. London: Methuen.

Greene, J. (1987) *Memory, Thinking and Language*. London: Methuen.

Greene, J. (1990) Perception. In I. Roth (ed.) *Introduction to Psychology, Volume 2*. Milton Keynes: Open University Press.

Greene, J.D., Nystrom, L.E., Engell, A.D., Darley, J.M. & Cohen, J.D. (2004) The neural bases of cognitive conflict and control in moral judgement. *Neuron, 44*, 389–400.

Greenfield, P.M. & Smith, J.H. (1976) *The Structure of Communication in Early Language Development*. New York: Academic Press.

Greenfield, S. (1998) How might the brain generate consciousness? In S. Rose (ed.) *From Brains to Consciousness? Essays on the New Sciences of the Mind*. Harmondsworth: Penguin.

Greenhaigh, T. (2000) 'Jigsaw' E-fit system helps ensure that the face fits. *The Times Higher*, 31 March, 14.

Greenough, W.T. (1991) Experience as a component of normal development: Evolutionary considerations. *Developmental Psychology, 27*, 11–27.

Greenwald, A.G. (1968) Cognitive learning, cognitive response to persuasion, and attitude change. In A.G. Greenwald, Brock, T.C. & Ostrom, T.M. (eds) *Psychological Foundations of Attitudes*. New York: Academic Press.

Greenwald, A.G. (1980) The totalitarian ego: Fabrication and revision of personal history. *American Psychologist, 35*, 603–613.

Greenwald, A., McGhee, D. & Schwartz, J. (1998) Measuring individual differences in implicit cognition: The Implicit Association Test. *Journal of Personality & Social Psychology, 74*, 1464–1480.

Greer, A., Morris, T. & Pettingdale, K.W. (1979) Psychological response to breast cancer: Effect on outcome. *The Lancet, 13*, 785–787.

Greer, S. & Morris, T. (1975) Psychological attributes of women who develop breast cancer: A controlled study. *Journal of Psychosomatic Research, 19*, 147–153.

Greer, S., Morris, T., Pettingale, K.W. & Haybittle, J.L. (1990) Psychological responses to breast cancer and fifteen year outcome. *The Lancet, 335*, 49–50.

Gregor, A.J. & McPherson, D. (1965) A study of susceptibility to geometric illusions among cultural outgroups of Australian aborigines. *Psychologia Africana*, 11, 490–499.

Gregory, R.L. (1966) *Eye and Brain*. London: Weidenfeld & Nicolson.

Gregory, R.L. (1972) Visual illusions. In B.M. Foss (ed.) *New Horizons in Psychology, 1*. Harmondsworth: Penguin.

Gregory, R.L. (1973) *Eye and Brain* (2nd edition). New York: World Universities Library.

Gregory, R.L. (1980) Perceptions as hypotheses. *Philosophical Transactions of the Royal Society of London, Series B, 290*, 181–197.

Gregory, R.L. (1981) *Mind in Science*. Harmondsworth: Penguin.

Gregory, R.L. (1983) Visual illusions. In J. Miller (ed.) *States of Mind*. London: BBC Productions.

Gregory, R.L. & Wallace, J. (1963) *Recovery from Early Blindness*. Cambridge: Heffer.

Griffit, W. & Veitch, R. (1974) Preacquaintance attitude similarity and attraction revisited: Ten days in a fallout shelter. *Sociometry, 37*, 163–173.

Griffiths, M. (1990) The cognitive psychology of gambling. *Journal of Gambling Studies, 6*, 31–42.

Griffiths, M. (1993) Are computer games bad for children? *The Psychologist, 6*, 401–407.

Griffiths, M. (1995) Technological addictions. *Clinical Psychology Forum, 76*, 14–19.

Griffiths, M. (1996) Behavioural addictions. *Psychology Review, 3*(2), 9–12.

Griffiths, M. (1997a) Video games and aggression. *The Psychologist, 10*, 397–401.

Griffiths, M. (1997b) Selling hope: The psychology of the National Lottery. *Psychology Review, 4* (1), 26–30.

Griffiths, M. (2005) A 'components' model of addiction within a biopsychosocial framework. *Journal of Substance Use, 10*(4), 191–197.

Griffiths, M. (2013) Addictive behaviour: What are the risk factors? *Psychology Review, 19*(1), 23–25.

Griffiths, M.D. (2000) Cyberaffairs: A new area for psychological research. *Psychology Review, 7*(1), 28–31.

Griffiths, M.D. (2005) A 'components' model of addiction within a biopsychosocial framework. *Journal of Substance Use, 10*, 191–197.

Grigorenko, E.L. & Sternberg, R.J. (2003) The nature–nurture issue. In A. Slater & G. Bremner (eds) *An Introduction to Developmental Psychology*. Oxford: Blackwell Publishing.

Grohol, J. (2013) DSM-5 Changes: Addiction, Substance-Related Disorders, and Alcoholism. http://pro.psychcentral.com/2013/dsm-5-changes-addiction-substance-related-disorders-alcoholism/004370.html.

Groome, D., Dewart, H., Esgate, A., Gurney, K., Kemp, R. & Towell, N. (1999) *An Introduction to Cognitive Psychology: Processes and Disorders*. London: Psychology Press.

Groskop, V. (2004) Minding the parent gap. *Observer*, 25 April, 4.

Gross, M.U.M. (1993) *Exceptionally Gifted Children*. London: Routledge.

Gross, R. (2008) *Key Studies in Psychology* (5th edition). London: Hodder Education.

Gross, R. (2009) *Themes, Issues and Debates in Psychology* (3rd edition). London: Hodder Education.

Gross, R. (2012a) *Being Human: Psychological and Philosophical Perspectives*. London: Routledge.

Gross, R. (2012b) *Key Studies in Psychology* (6th edition). London: Hodder Education.

Gross, R. (2014) *Themes, Issues and Debates in Psychology* (4th edition). London: Hodder Education.

Gross, R. & Kinnison, N. (2014) *Psychology for Nurses and Health Professionals* (2nd edition). Boca Raton, FL: CRC Press.

Gross, R. & Rolls, G. (2009) *A2 Psychology for AQA (A)*. London: Hodder Education.

Gross, R., McIlveen, R., Coolican, H., Clamp, A. & Russell, J. (2000) *Psychology: A New Introduction* (2nd edition). London: Hodder & Stoughton.

Grosz, E.A. (1987) Feminist theory and the challenge of knowledge. *Women's Studies International Forum, 10*, 475–480.

Gruendel, J.M. (1977) Referential overextension in early language development. *Child Development, 48*, 1567–1576.

Guilford, J.P. (1959) Three faces of intellect. *American Psychologist, 14*, 469–479.

Gunter, B. (1986) *Television and Sex-Role Stereotyping*. London: IBA and John Libbey.

Gunter, B. (1998) Telebuddies: Can watching TV make us more considerate? *Psychology Review, 4*, 6–9.

Gunter, B. (2000) Avoiding unsavoury television. *The Psychologist, 13*(4), 194–199.

Gunter, B. & McAleer, J.L. (1990) *Children and Television – The One-Eyed Monster?* London: Routledge.

Gunter, B. & McAleer, J.L. (1997) *Children and Television – The One-Eyed Monster?* (2nd edition) London: Routledge.

Guntrip, H. (1968) *Schizoid Phenomena: Object Relations and the Self*. London: Hogarth.

Gupta, U. & Singh, P. (1982) Exploratory study of love and liking and types of marriage. *Indian Journal of Applied Psychology, 19*, 92–97.

Gustafson, G. & Harris, K. (1990) Women's responses to young infants' cries. *Developmental Psychology, 26*, 144–152.

Guthrie, E.R. (1938) *Psychology of Human Conflict*. New York: Harper.

Hack, M., Taylor, C.B., Klein, N., Eiben, R., Schatschneider, C. & Mercuri-Minich, N. (1994) School-age outcomes in children with birth weight under 750 g. *New England Journal of Medicine, 331*, 753–759.

Hackel, L.M., Looser, C.E. & Van Bavel, J.J. (2014) Group membership alters the threshold for mind perception: The role of social identity, collective identification, and intergroup threat. *Journal of Experimental Social Psychology, 52*, 15–23.

Haddock, G. & Maio, G.R. (2012) Attitudes. In M. Hewstone, W. Stroebe & K. Jonas (eds) *Introduction to Social Psychology* (5th edition). BPS Blackwell.

Haidt, J. & Joseph, C. (2004) Intuitive ethics: How innately prepared intuitions generate culturally variable virtues. *Daedalus. Fall* (special issue on human nature), 55–66.

Haigh, J. (1995) Inferring gamblers' choice of combinations in the National Lottery. Bulletin – The Institute of *Mathematics and its Applications, 31*, 132–136.

Hall, C.S. (1966) *The Meaning of Dreams*. New York: McGraw-Hill.

Hall, C.S. & Nordby, V.J. (1973) *A Primer of Jungian Psychology*. New York: Mentor.

Hall, G.S. (1904) *Adolescence*. New York: Appleton & Co.

Halligan, P. (2007) Belief and illness. *The Psychologist, 20* (6), 358–361.

Halligan, P.W. (1995) Drawing attention to neglect: The contribution of line bisection. *The Psychologist, 8*, 257–264.

Halpern, D.F., Benbow, C.P., Geary, D.C. et al. (2012) Sex, Math and Scientific Achievement. *Scientific American Mind, 21*(2), 26–33.

Hamilton, E.W. & Abramson, L.Y. (1983) Cognitive patterns and major depressive disorder: A longitudinal study in a hospital setting. *Journal of Abnormal Psychology, 92*, 173–184.

Hamilton, L.W. & Timmons, C.R. (1995) Psychopharmacology. In D. Kimble & A. M. Colman (eds) *Biological Aspects of Behaviour*. London: Longman.

Hamilton, R.H. & Zreik, J. (2014) Wired for Thought. *Scientific American, 310*(2), 7.

Hamilton, V.L. (1978) Obedience and responsibility: A jury simulation. *Journal of Personality & Social Psychology, 36*, 126–146.

Hamilton, W.D. (1964) The genetical evolution of social behaviour, I, II. *Journal of Theoretical Biology, 7*, 1–52.

Hammersley, R. (1999) Substance use, abuse and dependence. In D. Messer & F. Jones (eds) *Psychology and Social Care*. London: Jessica Kingsley.

Hammond, L. & Thole, K. (2008) Interviewing and testimony. In D. Canter (ed.) *Criminal Psychology*. London: Hodder Education.

Hammond, L., Wagstaff, G.F. & Cole, J. (2006) Facilitating eyewitness memory in adults and children with context reinstatement and focused meditation. *Journal of Investigative Psychology and Offender Profiling, 3*, 117–130.

Hampson, P.J. & Morris, P.E. (1996) *Understanding Cognition*. Oxford: Blackwell.

Hampson, S. (1995) The construction of personality. In S.E. Hampson & A.M. Colman (eds) *Individual Differences and Personality*. London: Longman.

Hampson, S. (1999) Personality. *The Psychologist, 12*(6), 284–288.

Hamzelou, J. (2014) Erase your fear... *New Scientist, 221*(2960), 34–37.

Haney, C., Banks, C. & Zimbardo, P. (1973) A study of prisoners and guards in a simulated prison. *Naval Research Reviews*, September (1–17), Washington, DC: Office of Naval Research. Reprinted in E. Aronson (ed.) *Readings About the Social Animal* (3rd edition). San Francisco: W. H. Freeman, 52–67.

Hansel, C.E.M. (1980) ESP and Parapsychology: A Critical Evaluation. Buffalo, NY: Prometheus.

Happé, F. (1994) An advanced test of theory of mind: Understanding of story characters' thoughts and feelings by able autistic, mentally handicapped and normal children and adults. *Journal of Autism & Developmental Disorders, 24*, 129–154.

Harari, H. & McDavid, J.W. (1973) Teachers' expectations and name stereotypes. *Journal of Educational Psychology, 65*, 222–225.

Harcourt, D. & Rumsey, N. (2008) Psychology and visible difference. *The Psychologist, 21*(6), 486–489.

Hardy, L. (1989) Sport psychology. In A.M. Colman & J.G. Beaumont (eds) *Psychology Survey* 7. Leicester: British Psychological Society.

Hare, R.D. (1991) *Manual for the Hare Psychopathy Checklist* – Revised. Toronto: Multi-Health Systems.

Hare-Mustin, R. & Maracek, J. (1988) The meaning of difference: Gender theory, post-modernism and psychology. *American Psychologist, 43*, 455–464.

Hargreaves, D.J. (1986) Psychological theories of sex-role stereotyping. In D.J. Hargreaves & A.M. Colley (eds) *The Psychology of Sex Roles*. London: Harper & Row.

Hargreaves, D.J., Molloy, C. & Pratt, A. (1982) Social factors in conservation. *British Journal of Psychology, 73*, 231–234.

Harkins, S.G. & Jackson, J.M. (1985) The role of evaluation in eliminating social loafing. *Personality & Social Psychology Bulletin, 11*, 456–465.

Harlow, H.F. (1949) Formation of learning sets. *Psychological Review, 56*, 51–65.

Harlow, H.F. (1959) Love in infant monkeys. *Scientific American, 200*, 68–74.

Harlow, H.F. & Zimmerman, R.R. (1959) Affectional responses in the infant monkey. *Science, 130*, 421–432.

Harlow, H.F., Harlow, M.K. & Meyer, D.R. (1950) Learning motivated by a manipulation drive. *Journal of Experimental Psychology, 40*, 228–234.

Harré, R. (1985) The language game of self-ascription: A note. In K.J. Gergen & K.E. Davis (eds) *The Social Construction of the Person*. New York: Springer-Verlag.

Harré, R. (1989) Language games and the texts of identity. In J. Shotter & K.J. Gergen (eds) *Texts of Identity*. London: Sage.

Harré, R. (1999) Discourse and the embodied person. In D.J. Nightingale & J. Cromby (eds) *Social Constructionist Psychology: A Critical Analysis of Theory and Practice*. Buckingham: Open University Press.

Harré, R. & Finlay-Jones, R. (1986) Emotion talk across times. In R. Harre (ed.) *The Social Construction of Emotions*. Oxford: Blackwell.

Harré, R. & Secord, P.F. (1972) *The Explanation of Social Behaviour*. Oxford: Blackwell.

Harré, R., Clarke, D. & De Carlo, N. (1985) *Motives and Mechanisms: An Introduction to the Psychology of Action*. London: Methuen.

Harris, M. (1998) Perception. In P. Scott & C. Spencer (eds) *Psychology: A Contemporary Introduction*. Oxford: Blackwell.

Harris, P. (2012) Boys are hitting puberty up to two years earlier, reveals US study. *Observer*, 21 October, 24.

Harris, P. & Middleton, W. (1995) Social cognition and health behaviour. In D. Messer & C. Meldrum (eds) *Psychology for Nurses and Health Care Professionals*. Hemel Hempstead: Prentice-Hall/Harvester Wheatsheaf.

Harrison, T.M., Weintraub, S., Mesulam, M-M. & Rogalski, E. (2012) Super Memory and Higher Cortical Volumes in Unusually Successful Cognitive Ageing. *Journal of Epidemiology & Community Health, 59*(7), 574–579.

Harrower, J. (1998) *Applying Psychology to Crime*. London: Hodder & Stoughton.

Harrower, J. (2000) Cracker it ain't. *Psychology Review, 6* (3), 14–15.

Hart, D., Burock, D., London, B. & Atkins, R. (2003) Prosocial tendencies, antisocial behaviour, and moral development. In A. Slater & G. Bremner (eds) *An Introduction to Developmental Psychology*. Oxford: Blackwell Publishing.

Hartley, J. & Branthwaite, A. (1997) Earning a crust. *Psychology Review, 3* (3), 24–26.

Hartley, J. & Branthwaite, A. (2000) Prologue: The roles and skills of applied psychologists. In J. Hartley & A. Branthwaite (eds) *The Applied Psychologist* (2nd edition). Buckingham: Open University Press.

Hartung, B., Kauferstein, S., Ritz-Timme, S. & Daldrup, T. (2014) Sudden unexpected death under acute influence of cannabis. *Forensic Science International, 237*, e11–13.

Hartup, W.W. (1989) Social relationships and their developmental significance. *American Psychologist, 44*, 120–126.

Harwood, J., Hewstone, H., Paolini, S. & Hurd, R. (2003) Intergroup contact theory, the grandparent–grandchild relationship, and attitudes towards older adults. Manuscript submitted for publication (cited in Hewstone, 2003).

Haslam, S.A. & Reicher, S.D. (2007) Beyond the banality of evil: Three dynamics of an interactionist social psychology of tyranny. *Personality & Social Psychology Bulletin, 33*, 615–622.

Haste, H., Markoulis, D. & Helkama, K. (1998) Morality, wisdom and the life span. In A. Demetriou, W. Doise & C. van Lieshout (eds) *Life-Span Developmental Psychology*. Chichester: John Wiley & Sons Ltd.

Hastie, R. & Park, B. (1986) The relationship between memory and judgement depends on whether the judgement task is memory based or on-line. *Psychological Bulletin, 93*, 258–268.

Hattenstone, S. & Brockes, E. (2000) 'I'm not Crybaby Soo-Fi any more'. *Guardian*, 7 July, 2–3.

Hauser, M.D., Chomsky, N. & Fitch, W.T. (2002) The faculty of language: What is it, who has it, and how did it evolve? *Science, 298*, 1569–1579.

Havighurst, R.J. (1964) Stages of vocational development. In H. Borrow (ed.) *Man in a World of Work*. Boston: Houghton Mifflin.

Havighurst, R.J., Neugarten, B.L. & Tobin, S.S. (1968) Disengagement and patterns of ageing. In B.L. Neugarten (ed.) *Middle Age and Ageing*. University of Chicago Press.

Hawkins, L.H. & Armstrong-Esther, C.A. (1978) Circadian rhythms and night shift working in nurses. *Nursing Times*, 4 May, 49–52.

Hawks, D. (1981) The dilemma of clinical practice – Surviving as a clinical psychologist. In I. McPherson & M. Sutton (eds) *Reconstructing Psychological Practice*. London: Croom Helm.

Haxby, J.V., Hoffman, E.A. & Gobbini, M.I. (2000) The distributed human neural system for face perception. *Trends in Cognitive Sciences, 4*, 223–232.

Hayes, K.J. & Hayes, C. (1951) Intellectual development of a house-raised chimpanzee. *Proceedings of the American Philosophical Society, 95*, 105–109.

Haynes, R.B., Sackett, D.L. & Taylor, D.W. (eds) (1979) *Compliance in Health Care*. Baltimore, MD: Johns Hopkins University Press.

Hayslip, B. & Panek, P.E. (1989) *Adult Development and Ageing*. New York: Harper & Row.

Hazan, C. & Shaver, P.R. (1987) Romantic love conceptualised as an attachment process. *Journal of Personality & Social Psychology, 52* (3), 511–524.

Heard, D. & Lake, B. (1997) *The Challenge of Attachment for Caregivers*. London: Routledge.

Hearn, S., Glenham, M., Strayer, J., Koopman, R. & Marcia, J.E. (2006) Integrity, despair and in between: Toward construct validation of Erikson's eighth stage (cited in Kroger, 2007).

Hearnshaw, L.S. (1979) *Cyril Burt: Psychologist*. London: Hodder & Stoughton.

Heather, N. (1976) *Radical Perspectives in Psychology*. London: Methuen.

Heaven, D. (2013) Mirror, mirror. *New Scientist, 220*(2941), 39–41.

Heaven, P. (1996a) Personality and self-reported delinquency: A longitudinal analysis. *Journal of Child Psychology & Psychiatry, 37*, 747–751.

Heaven, P. (1996b) Personality and self-reported delinquency: analysis of the 'Big Five' personality dimensions. *Personality and Individual Differences, 20*, 47–54.

Hebb, D.O. (1949) *The Organisation of Behaviour*. New York: Wiley.

Heber, R., Dever, R.B. & Conry, R.J. (1968) The influence of environmental and genetic variables on intellectual development. In H.J. Prehm, L.J. Hamerlynck & J.E. Crosson (eds) *Behavioural Research in Mental Retardation*. Eugene: University of Oregon Press.

Hedge, A. & Yousif, Y.H. (1992) Effects of urban size, urgency, and cost of helpfulness: A cross-cultural comparison between the United Kingdom and the Sudan. *Journal of Cross-Cultural Psychology, 23*, 107–115.

Hegarty, J. (2000) Psychologists, doctors and cancer patients. In J. Hartley & A. Branthwaite (eds) *The Applied Psychologist* (2nd edition). Buckingham: Open University Press.

Hegarty, P., Barker, M. & McManus, J. (2006) On behalf of the Committee of the Lesbian and Gay Psychology Section of the British Psychological Society, March 2006. Public statement on the recognition of same-sex relationships. *Lesbian & Gay Psychology Review*, 7(2), 120–122.

Heider, E. & Oliver, D. (1972) The structure of the colour space in naming and memory for two languages. *Cognitive Psychology, 3*, 337–354.

Heider, F. (1958) *The Psychology of Interpersonal Relations*. New York: Wiley.

Heider, F. & Simmel, M. (1944) An experimental study of apparent behaviour. *American Journal of Psychology, 57*, 243–259.

Heim, A. (1970) *Intelligence and Personality – Their Assessment and Relationship*. Harmondsworth: Penguin.

Heine, S.J. & Lehman, D.R. (1997) Culture, dissonance, and self-affirmation. *Personality & Social Psychology Bulletin, 23*, 389–400.

Held, R. (1965) Plasticity in sensory-motor systems. *Scientific American, 213* (5), 84–94.

Held, R. & Hein, A. (1963) Movement-produced stimulation in the development of visually guided behaviour. *Journal of Comparative & Physiological Psychology, 56*, 607–613.

Helzer, J.E., Wittchen, H-U., Krueger, R.F. & Kraemer, H.C. (2008) Dimensional options for DSM-V: the way forward. In J.E. Helzer, H.C. Kraemer, R.F Krueger., H-U Wittchen, P.J. Sirovatka, & D.A. Regier (eds) *Dimensional approaches to diagnostic classification: Refining the research agenda for DSM-V.* Washington, DC: American Psychiatric Association.

Hemphill, J.F., Hare, R.D. & Wong, S. (1998) Psychopathy and recidivism: A review. *Legal & Criminological Psychology, 3*, 139–170.

Hendry, L.B. (1999) Adolescents and society. In D. Messer & F. Jones (eds) *Psychology and Social Care*. London: Jessica Kingsley.

Hendry, L.B. & Kloep, M. (1999) Adolescence in Europe – an important life phase? In D. Messer & S. Millar (eds) *Exploring Developmental Psychology: From Infancy to Adolescence*. London: Arnold.

Hendry, L.B., Shucksmith, J., Love, J.G. & Glendinning, A. (1993) *Young People's Leisure and Lifestyles*. London: Routledge.

Hennenlotter, A., Dresel, C., Castrop, F., Ceballos Baumann, A., Wohlschlager, A. & Haslinger, B. (2008) The link between facial feedback and neural activity with central circuitries of emotion – new insights from botulinum toxin-induced denervation of frown muscles. *Cortex, 19* (3), 537–542.

Hennessy, J. & West, M.A. (1999) Intergroup behaviour in organizations: A field test of social identity theory. *Small Group Research, 30*, 361–382.

Henry, J. (2005) Parapsychology. In J. Henry (ed.) *Parapsychology: Research on Exceptional Experiences*. Hove: Routledge.

Henry, P.J. & Sears, D.O. (2002) The symbolic racism 2000 scale. *Political Psychology, 23*, 253–283.

Hering, E. (1878) *Zur Lehre vom Lichtsinne*. Berlin: Springer.

Herman-Giddens, M.E., Steffes, J., Harris, D. et al. (2012) Secondary sexual characteristics in boys: data from the Paediatric Research in Office Settings Network. *Paediatrics, 130*(5), e1058–e1068.

Hermelin, B., Pring, L., Buhler, M., Wolff, S. & Heaton, P. (1999) A visually impaired savant artist: Interacting perceptual and memory representations. *Journal of Child Psychology & Psychiatry, 40* (7), 1129–1139.

Heron, W. (1957) The pathology of boredom. *Scientific American, 196*, 52–69.

Herrnstein, R.J. (1971) IQ. *Atlantic Monthly*, September, 43–64.

Herrnstein, R.J. & Murray, C. (1994) *The Bell Curve: Intelligence and Class Structure in American Life*. New York: Free Press.

Hershenson, M., Munsinger, H. & Kessen, W. (1965) Preference for shapes of intermediate variability in the newborn human. *Science, 147*, 630–631.

Herskovits, M.J. (1955) *Cultural Anthropology*. New York: Knopf.

Hess, E.H. (1956) Space perception in the chick. *Scientific American, July*, 71–80.

Hetherington, E.M. & Kelly, J. (2002) *For Better or for Worse: Divorce Reconsidered*. New York: Norton.

Hetherington, A.W. & Ranson, S.W. (1942) The relation of various hypothalamic lesions to adiposity in the rat. *Journal of Comparative Neurology, 76*, 475–499.

Hetherington, E.M. (1967) The effects of familial variables on sex-typing, on parent–child similarity, and on imitation in children. In J.P. Hill (ed.) *Minnesota Symposium on Child Psychology, Volume 1*. Minneapolis: University of Minnesota Press.

Hetherington, E.M. & Baltes, P.B. (1988) Child psychology and life-span development. In E.M. Hetherington, R. Lerner & M. Perlmutter (eds) *Child Development in Life-Span Perspective*. Hillsdale, NJ: Erlbaum.

Hetherington, E.M. & Stanley-Hagan, M. (1999) The adjustment of children with divorced parents: A risk and resiliency perspective. *Journal of Child Psychology & Psychiatry, 40* (1), 129–140.

Hewstone, M. (1996) Contact and categorization: Social psychological interventions to change intergroup relations. In C.N. Macrae, C. Stangor & M. Hewstone (eds) *Stereotypes and Stereotyping*. New York: Guilford Press.

Hewstone, M. (2003) Intergroup contact: Panacea for prejudice? *The Psychologist, 16* (7), 352–355.

Hewstone, M. & Brown, R.J. (1986) Contact is not enough: An intergroup perspective on the contact hypothesis. In M. Hewstone & R.J. Brown (eds) *Contact and Conflict in Inter-group Encounters*. Oxford: Blackwell.

Hewstone, M. & Fincham, F. (1996) Attribution theory and research: Basic issues and applications. In M. Hewstone, W. Stroebe & G.M. Stephenson (eds) *Introduction to Social Psychology* (2nd edition). Oxford: Blackwell.

Hewstone, M. & Martin, R. (2008) Social Influence. In M. Hewstone, W. Stroebe & K. Jonas (eds) *Introduction to Social Psychology: A European Perspective* (4th edition). Oxford: BPS Blackwell.

Hewstone, M. & Martin, R. (2012) Social Influence. In M. Hewstone, W. Stroebe & K. Jonas (eds) *Introduction to Social Psychology* (5th edition). BPS Blackwell.

Hewstone, M., Rubin, M. & Willis, H. (2002) Intergroup bias. *Annual Review of Psychology, 53*, 575–604.

Highfield, R. (2009) In your face. *New Scientist, 201* (2695), 28–32.

Hilgetag, C.C. & Barbas, H. (2009) Sculpting the brain. *Scientific American, 300* (2), 56–61.

Hill, A. (2007a) Women more stressed by insomnia. *Observer*, 7 July, 25.

Hill, A. (2007b) Cancer warning for stressed-out men. *Observer*, 2 September, 24.

Hill, A. (2009) Men become richer after divorce. *Observer*, 25 January.

Hill, A. & McVeigh, T. (2009) Women at 30 'putting careers second'. *Observer*, 29 March, 23.

Hill, E. & Williamson, J. (1998) Choose six numbers, any numbers. *The Psychologist, 11* (1), 17–21.

Hill H.M. & Kuczaj, S.A. (2011) The development of language. In A. Slater & G. Bremner (eds) *An Introduction to Developmental Psychology* (2nd edition). BPS Blackwell.

Hill, P. (1993) Recent advances in selected aspects of adolescent development. *Journal of Child Psychology & Psychiatry, 34* (1), 69–99.

Hill, V. (2005) Through the past darkly: A review of the British Ability Scales second edition. *Child & Adolescent Mental Health, 10* (2), 87–98.

Hilliard, A.G. (1995) The nonscience and nonsense of the bell curve. *Focus: Notes from the Society for the Psychological Study of Ethnic Minority Issues*, 10–12.

Hilton, D.J. & Slugoski, B.R. (1986) Knowledge-based causal attribution: The abnormal conditions focus model. *Psychological Review, 93*, 75–88.

Himmelbach, M., Boehme, R. & Karnath, H-O. (2012) 20 years later: A second look on DF's motor behaviour. *Neuropsychologia, 50*, 139–144.

Hines, M. (2004a) Androgen, oestrogen, and gender: Contributions of the early hormone environment to gender-related behaviour. In A.H. Eagly, A.E. Beall & R. Sternberg (eds) *The Psychology of Gender* (2nd edition). New York: Guilford Press.

Hines, M. (2004b) Neuroscience and intersex. *The Psychologist, 17* (8), 455–458.

Hines, M. & Kaufman, F.R. (1994) Androgen and the development of human sex-typical behaviour: Rough-and-tumble play and sex of preferred playmates in children with congenital adrenal hyperplasia (CAH). *Child Development, 65*, 1042–1053.

Hines, M., Ahmed, S.F. & Hughes, I. (2003) Psychological outcomes and gender-related development in complete androgen insensitivity syndrome. *Archives of Sexual Behaviour, 32*, 93–101.

Hines, M., Johnston, K., Golombok, S., Rust, J., Stevens, M. & Golding, J. (2002) Prenatal stress and gender role behaviour in girls and boys: A longitudinal, population study. *Hormones & Behaviour, 42*, 126–134.

Hinsliff, G. (2004) Baby, what shall I do? *Observer*, 9 May, 19.

Hinton, J. (1975) *Dying*. Harmondsworth: Penguin.

Hirsch, H. (1995) *Genocide and the Politics of Memory*. Chapel Hill: University of North Carolina Press.

Hirst, W., Phelps, E.A., Buckner, R.L. et al. (2009) Long-term memory for the terrorist attack of September 11: Flashbulb memories, event memories, and the factors that influence their retention. *Journal of Experimental Psychology: General, 138*(2), 161–176.

Hobara, M. (2003) Prevalence of transitional objects in young children in Tokyo and New York. *Infant Mental Health Journal, 24*(2), 174–191.

Hobbes, T. (1651/1914) *Leviathan*. London: Dent.

Hobson, J.A. (1995) Sleeping and dreaming. In D. Kimble & A.M. Colman (eds) *Biological Aspects of Behaviour*. London: Longman.

Hobson, J.A. (2002) *Dreaming: An Introduction to the Science of Sleep*. New York: Oxford University Press.

Hobson, J.A. & McCarley, R.W. (1977) The brain as a dream state generator: An activation–synthesis hypothesis of the dream process. *American Journal of Psychiatry, 134*, 1335–1348.

Hochberg, J.E. (1970) Attention, organisation and consciousness. In D.I. Mostofsky (ed.) *Attention: Contemporary Theory and Analysis*. New York: Appleton-Century-Crofts.

Hochberg, J.E. (1971) Perception. In J.W. Kling & L.A. Riggs (eds) *Experimental Psychology*. New York: Holt.

Hochberg, J.E. (1978) Art and perception. In E.C. Carterette & H. Friedman (eds) *Handbook of Perception, Volume 10*. London: Academic Press.

Hockett, C.D. (1960) The origins of speech. *Scientific American, 203*, 88–96.

Hodges, J. & Tizard, B. (1989) Social and family relationships of ex-institutional adolescents. Journal of Child *Psychology & Psychiatry, 30*, 77–97.

Hofling, K.C., Brotzman, E., Dalrymple, S., Graves, N. & Pierce, C.M. (1966) An experimental study in the nurse–physician relationships. *Journal of Nervous & Mental Disorders, 143*, 171–180.

Hogarty, G.E., Greenwald, D., Ulrich, R.F., Kornblith, S.J., DiBarry, A.L., Cooley, S., Carter, M. & Flesher, S. (1997) Three-year trials of personal therapy among schizophrenic patients living with or independently of family: II. Effects on adjustment of patients. *American Journal of Psychiatry, 154* (11), 1514–1524.

Hogg, M.A. (1992) *The Social Psychology of Group Cohesiveness: From Attraction to Social Identity*. London: Harvester Wheatsheaf.

Hogg, M.A. (1993) Group cohesiveness: A critical review and some new directions. *European Review of Social Psychology, 4*, 85–111.

Hogg, M.A. & Abrams, D. (1988) *Social Identifications: A Social Psychology of Intergroup Relations and Group Processes*. London: Routledge.

Hogg, M.A. & Abrams, D. (2000) Social psychology. In Carlson, N.R., Buskist, W. & Martin, G.N., *Psychology: The Science of Behaviour* (European adaptation). Harlow: Pearson Education Limited.

Hogg, M.A. & Hains, S.C. (1996) Intergroup relations and group solidarity: Effects of group identification and social beliefs on depersonalised attraction. *Journal of Personality & Social Psychology, 70*, 295–309.

Hogg, M.A. & Hardie, E.A. (1991) Social attraction, personal attraction, and self-categorization: A field study. *Personality & Social Psychology Bulletin, 17*, 175–180.

Hogg, M.A. & Vaughan, G.M. (1995) *Social Psychology: An Introduction*. Hemel Hempstead: Prentice-Hall/Harvester Wheatsheaf.

Hogg, M.A. & Vaughan, G.M. (1998) *Social Psychology: An Introduction* (2nd edition). Hemel Hempstead: Prentice-Hall/Harvester Wheatsheaf.

Hohmann, G.W. (1966) Some effects of spinal cord lesions on experienced emotional feelings. *Psychophysiology, 3*, 143–156.

Holahan, C.K. (1988) Relation of life goals at age 70 to activity participation and health and psychological well-being among Terman's gifted men and women. *Psychology & Ageing, 3*, 286–291.

Holahan, C.K. & Sears, R.R. (1995) *The Gifted Group in Later Maturity*. Stanford University Press.

Hollander, E., DeCaria, C.M., Finkell, J.M. et al. (2000) A randomised double-blind fluvoxamine/placebo crossover trial in pathologic gambling. *Biological Psychiatry, 47*, 813–817.

Hollin, C.R. (1997) Adolescent predictors of adult offending. *Psychology Review, 3* (4), 21–25.

Hollin, C.R. (1999) Crime and crime prevention. In D. Messer & F. Jones (eds) *Psychology and Social Care*. London: Jessica Kingsley.

Hollin, C.R. & Howells, K. (eds) (1996) *Clinical Approaches to Working with Young Offenders*. Chichester: Wiley.

Hollingham, R. (2004) In the realm of your senses. *New Scientist, 181* (2432), 40–43.

Holmes, B. (2009) The not-so-selfish gene. *New Scientist, 201* (2698), 36–39.

Holmes, D.S. (1994) *Abnormal Psychology* (2nd edition). New York: HarperCollins.

Holmes, J. & Lindley, R. (1989) *The Values of Psychotherapy*. Oxford University Press.

Holmes, R. (1989) *Profiling Violent Crimes*. Newbury Park, CA: Sage.

Holmes, T.H. & Masuda, M. (1974) Life change and illness susceptibility. In B.S. Dohrenwend & B.P. Dohrenwend (eds) *Stressful Life Events: Their Nature and Effects*. New York: Wiley.

Holmes, T.H. & Rahe, R.H. (1967) The social readjustment rating scale. *Journal of Psychosomatic Research, 11*, 213–218.

Holmes, T.R., Bond, L.A. & Byrne, C. (2008) Mothers' beliefs about knowledge and mother–adolescent conflict. *Journal of Social & Personal Relationships, 25* (4), 561–586.

Holowka, S. & Petitto, L.A. (2002) Left hemisphere cerebral specialization for babies while babbling. *Science, 297* (5586), 1515.

Holt, N.J., Simmonds-Moore, C., Luke, D. & French, C.C. (2012) *Anomalistic Psychology*. Basingstoke: Palgrave Macmillan.

Holtgraves, T. & Skeel, J. (1992) Cognitive biases in playing the lottery: Estimating the odds and choosing the numbers. *Journal of Applied Social Psychology, 22*, 934–952.

Homans, G.C. (1974) *Social Behaviour: Its Elementary Forms* (2nd edition). New York: Harcourt Brace Jovanovich.

Honderich, T. (1993) *How Free Are You? The Determinism Problem*. Oxford University Press.

Honorton, C. (1974) Psi-conducive states. In J. White (ed.) *Psychic Exploration*. New York: Putnam.

Honorton, C. (1985) Meta-analysis of psi Ganzfeld research: A response to Hyman. *Journal of Parapsychology, 49*, 51–91.

Honorton, C., Berger, R.E., Varvoglis, M.P., Quant, M., Derr, P. Schechter, E.I. & Ferrari, D.C. (1990) Psi communication in the Ganzfeld: Experiments with an automated testing system and a comparison with a meta-analysis of earlier studies. *Journal of Parapsychology, 54*, 99–139.

Honzik, M.P., MacFarlane, H.W. & Allen, L. (1948) The stability of mental test performance between two and eighteen years. *Journal of Experimental Education, 17*, 309–324.

Hood, B. (2012) Re-creating the real world. *Scientific American Mind, 23*(4), 42–45.

Hoppe, C. & Stojanovic, J. (2009) Giftedness and the brain. *The Psychologist, 22*(6), 498–501.

Hopson, J. (2013) Bad mix for the teen brain. *Scientific American Mind, 24*(3), 68–71.

Horgan, J. (1993) Eugenics revisited. *Scientific American, June*, 92–100.

Horn, J.L. (1982) The ageing of human abilities. In B. Wolman (ed.) *Handbook of Developmental Psychology*. Englewood Cliffs, NJ: Prentice-Hall.

Horn, J.L. & Cattell, R.B. (1967) Age differences in fluid and crystallised intelligence. *Acta Psychologica, 26*, 107–129.

Horn, J.L. & Cattell, R.B. (1982) Whimsy and misunderstanding of Gf–Gc theory: A comment on Guilford. *Psychology Bulletin, 91*, 623–633.

Horne, J. (1988) *Why We Sleep: The Functions of Sleep in Humans and Other Mammals*. Oxford University Press.

Horne, R. & Clatworthy, J. (2010) Adherence to Advice and Treatment. In D. French, K. Vedhara, A.A. Kaptein & J. Weinman (eds) *Health Psychology* (2nd edition). Oxford: BPS Blackwell.

Horowitz, F.D. (1987) *Exploring Developmental Theories: Towards a Structural/Behavioural Model of Development*. Hillsdale, NJ: Erlbaum.

Horowitz, F.D. (1990) Developmental models of individual differences. In J. Colombo & J. Fagan (eds) *Individual Differences in Infancy: Reliability, Stability, Predictability*. Hillsdale, NJ: Erlbaum.

Horton, M. (1999) Prejudice and discrimination: Group approaches. In D. Messer & F. Jones (eds) *Psychology and Social Care*. London: Jessica Kingsley.

Horwitz, A.V. & Wakefield, J.C. (2007) *The loss of sadness: How psychiatry transformed normal sorrow into depressive disorder.* New York: OUP.

Houston, J.P., Hammen, C., Padilla, A. & Bee, H. (1991) *Invitation to Psychology* (3rd edition). London: Harcourt Brace Jovanovich.

Hout, M.C. & Goldinger, S.D. (2013) To see or not to see. *Scientific American Mind, 24*(3), 60–67.

Hovland, C.I. & Janis, I.L. (1959) *Personality and Persuasibility*. New Haven, CT: Yale University Press.

Hovland, C.I. & Sears, R.R. (1940) Minor studies in aggression, VI: Correlation of lynchings with economic indices. *Journal of Psychology, 2*, 301–310.

Hovland, C.I., Janis, I.L. & Kelley, H.H. (1953) *Communication and Persuasion: Psychological Studies of Opinion Change*. New Haven, CT: Yale University Press.

Howard, J.W. & Rothbart, M. (1980) Social categorisation and memory for ingroup and outgroup behaviour. *Journal of Personality & Social Psychology, 38*, 301–310.

Howarth, E. (1986) What does Eysenck's psychoticism scale really measure? *British Journal of Psychology, 77*, 223–227.

Howat, D. (1999) Social and cultural diversity. *Psychology Review, 5*(3), 28–31.

Howe, M. (1980) *The Psychology of Human Learning*. London: Harper & Row.

Howe, M. (1997) *IQ in Question: The Truth about Intelligence*. London: Sage.

Howe, M. (1998) Can IQ change? *The Psychologist, 11* (2), 69–71.

Howe, M. (1999) *Genius Explained*. Cambridge University Press.

Howe, M., Davidson, J.W. & Sloboda, J.A. (1998) Innate talents: Reality or myth? *Behaviour & Brain Sciences, 21* (3), 399–407.

Howes, C. & Spieker, S. (2008) Attachment relationships in the context of multiple caregivers. In J. Cassidy & P. R. Shaver (eds) *Handbook of Attachment: Theory, Research and Clinical Applications*. New York: Guilford Press.

Howitt, D. (1991) *Concerning Psychology: Psychology Applied to Social Issues*. Milton Keynes: Open University Press.

Howitt, D. & Owusu-Bempah, J. (1994) *The Racism of Psychology: Time for Change*. Hemel Hempstead: Harvester Wheatsheaf.

Hoyt, M.F. (2003) Brief psychotherapies. In A.S. Gurman and S.B. Messer (eds) *Essential Psychotherapies: Theory and Practice* (2nd edition). New York: Guilford Press.

Hrdy, S.B. (1999) *Mother Nature*. London: Chatto & Windus.

Hubel, D.H. & Wiesel, T.N. (1959) Receptive fields of single neurons in the cat's striate cortex. *Journal of Physiology, 148*, 579–591.

Hubel, D.H. & Wiesel, T.N. (1962) Receptive fields, binocular interaction and functional architecture in the cat's visual cortex. *Journal of Physiology, 160*, 106–154.

Hubel, D.H. & Wiesel, T.N. (1968) Receptive fields and functional architecture of monkey striate cortex. *Journal of Physiology, 195*, 215–243.

Hubel, D.H. & Wiesel, T.N. (1977) Functional architecture of the macaque monkey visual cortex. *Proceedings of the Royal Society of London, Series B, 198*, 1–59.

Hudson, W. (1960) Pictorial depth perception in sub-cultural groups in Africa. *Journal of Social Psychology, 52*, 183–208.

Huesmann, L.R. & Eron, L.D. (eds) (1986) *Television and the Aggressive Child: A Cross National Perspective*. Hillsdale, NJ: Erlbaum.

Huesmann, L.R., Moise-Titus, J., Podolski, C. & Eron, L. (2003) Longitudinal relations between children's exposure to TV violence and their aggressive and violent behaviour in young adulthood: 1977–1992. *Developmental Psychology, 32* (2), 201–221.

Hugdahl, K. & Ohman, A. (1977) Effects of instruction on acquisition of electrodermal response to fear relevant stimuli. *Journal of Experimental Psychology, 3*, 608–618.

Hughes, V. (2011) Body conscious. *New Scientist, 211*(2826), 41–43.

Hull, C.L. (1943) *Principles of Behaviour*. New York: Appleton-Century-Crofts.

Humm, C. (2000) A hard day's night. *Nursing Times*, 96 (20), 28–31.

Humphrey, N. (1986) *The Inner Eye*. London: Faber & Faber.

Humphrey, N. (1993) *The Inner Eye* (new edition). London: Vintage.

Humphreys, G.W. & Riddoch, M.J. (1987) *To See But Not to See – A Case Study of Visual Agnosia*. London: Erlbaum.

Humphries, C. (2012) Not raving but frowning. *New Scientist, 215*(2874), 40–43.

Hunt, E. & Agnoli, A. (1991) The Whorfian hypothesis: A cognitive psychological perspective. *Psychological Review, 98*, 377–389.

Hunt, J. McVicker (1969) Has compensatory education failed? Has it been attempted? *Harvard Educational Review, 39*, 278–300.

Hunter, I.M.L. (1964) *Memory, Facts and Fallacies* (2nd edition). Harmondsworth: Penguin.

Huston, A.C. (1983) Sex-typing. In E.M. Hetherington (ed.) *Socialisation, Personality and Social Development*. New York: Wiley.

Huston, A.C. & Wright, J.C. (1997) Mass media and children's development. In W. Damon (series ed.), I. Sigel & A. Renniger (volume eds) *Handbook of Child Psychology, Volume 4: Child Psychology in Practice* (5th edition). New York: Wiley.

Huston, A.C., Wright, J.C., Rice, M.L., Kerkman, D. & St. Peters, M. (1990) Development of television viewing patterns in early childhood: A longitudinal investigation. *Developmental Psychology, 26*, 409–420.

Huston, M. & Schwartz, P. (1995) Lesbian and gay male relationships. In J.T. Wood & S. Duck (eds) *Understanding Relationship Processes 6: Under-studied Relationships: Off the Beaten Track*. Thousand Oaks, CA: Sage.

Hutton, A. (1998) Mental health: Drug update. *Nursing Times*, 11 February, 84.

Hyde, J., Lindberg, S.M., Linn, M.C., Ellis, A.B. & Williams, C.C. (2008) Gender similarities characterise math performance. *Science, 321*, 494–495.

Hyman, R. (1985) The Ganzfeld psi experiment: A critical appraisal. *Journal of Parapsychology, 49*, 3–49.

Hyman, R. & Honorton, C. (1986) A joint communique: The psi Ganzfeld controversy. *Journal of Parapsychology, 50*, 351–364.

IASP (International Association for the Study of Pain) (1986) Classification of chronic pain syndrome and definition of pain terms. *Pain, 3* (Supp.): S1–S226.

Ickes, W.J. & Barnes, R.D. (1977) The role of sex and self-monitoring in unstructured dyadic interactions. *Journal of Personality & Social Psychology, 35*, 315–330.

Idzikowski, C. (2013) Sleepwalking and the biology of sleep. *Psychology Review, 19*(2), 10–12.

Imperato-McGinley, J., Guemero, L., Gautier, T. & Peterson, R.E. (1974) Steroid 5 a-reductase deficiency in man: an inherited form of male pseudohermaphroditism. *Science, 186*, 1213–1215.

Inhelder, B. & Piaget, J. (1958) *The Growth of Logical Thinking*. London: Routledge & Kegan Paul.

Insel, T.R. (2009) Translating scientific opportunity into public health impact. A strategic plan for research on mental illness. *Archives of General Psychiatry, 66*, 128–133.

Insko, C.A., Drenan, S., Solomon, M.R., Smith, R. & Wade, T.G. (1983) Conformity as a function of the consistency of positive self-evaluation with being liked and being right. *Journal of Experimental Social Psychology, 19*, 341–358.

Ioannou, M. & Greenall, P.V. (2008) Mental disorder and crime. In D. Canter (ed.) *Criminal Psychology*. London: Hodder Education.

Ioannou, M. & Vettor, S. (2008) Social explanations of crime. In D. Canter (ed.) *Criminal Psychology*. London: Hodder Education.

Irwin, H.J. (2009) *The Psychology of Paranormal Belief: A Researcher's Handbook*. Hatfield: University of Hertfordshire Press.

Irwin, H.J. & Watt, C.A. (2007) *An Introduction to Parapsychology* (5th edition). Jefferson, NC: McFarland & Co. Inc.

Islam, M.R. & Hewstone, M. (1993) Dimensions of contact as predictors of outergroup anxiety, perceived out-group variability, and out-group attitude: An integrative model. *Personality and Social Psychology Bulletin, 19*, 700–710.

Ittel, A., Azmitia, M., Pfetsch, J.S. & Muller, C.R. (2014) Teasing, threats and texts: gender and the 'dark-side' of cyber-communication. In P.J. Leman & H.R. Tenenbaum (eds) *Gender and Development*. Hove, East Sussex: Psychology Press.

Ittelson, W.H. (1952) *The Ames Demonstrations in Perception*. Princeton University Press.

Iversen, L.L. (1979) The chemistry of the brain. *Scientific American, 241*, 134–149.

Iwao, S. (1993) *The Japanese Woman: Traditional Image and Changing Reality*. New York: Free Press.

Iyengar, S.S. & Lepper, M.R. (1999) Rethinking the value of choice: A cultural perspective on intrinsic motivation. *Journal of Personality & Social Psychology, 76*, 349–366.

Jabr, F. (2012) Redefining mental illness. *Scientific American Mind, 23*(2), 28–35.

Jabr, F. (2013) The Newest Edition of Psychiatry's "Bible", the *DSM-5,* IS Complete. *Scientific American,* 28 January, 9.

Jack, R.E., Garrod, O.G.B., Yu, H., Caldara, R., Schyns, P.G. (2012) Facial expressions of emotion are not culturally universal. *Proceedings of the National Academy of Sciences 109*(19), 7241–7244.

Jackendoff, R. (1993) *Patterns in the Mind: Language and Human Nature*. Hemel Hempstead: Harvester Wheatsheaf.

Jackendoff, R. & Pinker, S. (2005) The nature of the language faculty and its implications for evolution in language. (Reply to Fitch, Hauser and Chomsky). *Cognition, 97*(2), 211–225.

Jackson, H.F. (1986) Is there a schizotoxin? A critique of the evidence of the major contender – dopamine. In N. Eisenberg & D. Glasgow (eds) *Current Issues in Clinical Psychology (Volume 5)*. Aldershot: Gower.

Jackson, H.F. (1990) Biological markers in schizophrenia. In R.P. Bentall (ed.) *Reconstructing Schizophrenia*. London: Routledge.

Jackson, S., Cicogani, E. & Charman, L. (1996) The measurement of conflict in parent–adolescent relationships. In L. Verhofstadt-Deneve, I. Kienhorst & C. Braet (eds) *Conflict and Development in Adolescence*. Leiden: DSWO Press.

Jacobs, M. (1984) Psychodynamic therapy: The Freudian approach. In W. Dryden (ed.) *Individual Therapy in Britain*. London: Harper & Row.

Jacobs, M. (1992) Freud. London: Sage.

Jadva, V., Freeman, T., Kramer, W. & Golombok, S. (2009) The experiences of adolescents and adults conceived by sperm donation: Comparisons by age of disclosure and family type. *Human Reproduction, 24*(8), 1909–1919.

Jahoda, G. (1954) A note on Ashanti names and their relationship to personality. *British Journal of Psychology, 45*, 192–195.

Jahoda, G. (1966) Geometric illusions and environment: A study in Ghana. *British Journal of Psychology, 57*, 193–199.

Jahoda, G. (1978) Cross-cultural perspectives. In H. Tajfel & C. Fraser (eds) *Introducing Social Psychology*. Harmondsworth: Penguin.

Jahoda, M. (1958) *Current Concepts of Positive Mental Health*. New York: Basic Books.

James, W. (1890) *The Principles of Psychology*. New York: Henry Holt & Company.

James, W. (1902) *The Varieties of Religious Experience*. New York: Longmans Green.

Janis, I. (1971) *Stress and Frustration*. New York: Harcourt Brace.

Janis, I. (1982) *Groupthink: Psychological Studies of Policy Decisions and Fiascos* (2nd edition). Boston: Houghton Mifflin.

Janis, I. & Feshbach, S. (1953) Effects of fear-arousing communication. *Journal of Abnormal & Social Psychology, 48*, 78–92.

Janis, I. & Terwillinger, R.T. (1962) An experimental study of psychological resistance to fear-arousing communication. *Journal of Abnormal & Social Psychology, 65*, 403–410.

Janis, I., Kaye, D. & Kirschner, P. (1965) Facilitating effects of 'eating-while-reading' on responsiveness to persuasive communications. *Journal of Personality & Social Psychology, 1*, 181–186.

Janz, N.K. & Becker, M.H. (1984) The health belief model: A decade later. *Health Education Quarterly, 11*, 1–47.

Jaroff, L. (1993) Lies of the mind. *Time, 142*(23), 56–61.

Jarrett, C. (2011) Ouch! The different ways people experience pain. *The Psychologist, 24*(6), 416–420.

Jarrett, C. (2013a) 3D Brain Mapping. *The Psychologist, 26*(8), 552.

Jarrett, C. (2013b) Towards an activity map of the brain. *The Psychologist, 26*(4), 246.

Javitt, D.C. & Coyle, J.T. (2004) Decoding schizophrenia. *Scientific American, 290*(1), 38–45.

Jeffries, V. (1998) Virtue and the altruistic personality. *Sociological Perspectives, 41*, 151–166.

Jellinek, E.M. (1946) Phases in the drinking history of alcoholics. *Quarterly Journal of Studies on Alcohol, 7*, 1–88.

Jellinek, E.M. (1952) The phases of alcohol addiction. *Quarterly Journal of Studies on Alcohol, 13*, 673–684.

Jellinek, E.M. (1960) *The Disease Concept of Alcoholism*. New Haven, CT: Hillhouse Press.

Jenkins, J.G. & Dallenbach, K.M. (1924) Oblivescence during sleep and waking. *American Journal of Psychology, 35*, 605–612.

Jenkins, J.J. (1974) Remember that old theory of memory? Well, forget it! *American Psychologist, 29*, 785–795.

Jenness, A. (1932) The role of discussion in changing opinion regarding matter of fact. *Journal of Abnormal & Social Psychology, 27*, 279–296.

Jennet, B. & Plum, F. (1972) Persistent vegetative state after brain damage. RN, 35, ICU1–4.

Jensen, A.R. (1969) How much can we boost IQ and scholastic achievement? *Harvard Educational Review, 39*, 1–23.

Jensen, A.R. (1980) *Bias in Mental Testing*. London: Methuen.

Jodelet, D. (1980) Les fous mentales au village. Unpublished doctoral dissertation, Écoles des hautes études en sciences sociales, Paris.

Joffe, H. (1996) AIDS research and prevention: A social representation approach. *British Journal of Medical Psychology, 69*, 169–190.

Johnson, D.W. & Johnson, R. (1985) Classroom conflict: Controversy over debate in learning groups. *American Education Research Journal, 22*, 237–256.

Johnson, M.H. (2000) How babies' brains work. *The Psychologist, 13* (6), 298–301.

Johnson, M.H., Dziurawiec, S., Ellis, H. & Morton, J. (1991) Newborns' preferential tracking of face-like stimuli and its subsequent decline. *Cognition, 40*, 1–19.

Johnson, M.P. (2008) *A Typology of Domestic Violence: Intimate Terrorism, Violent Resistance and Situational Couple Violence*. Northeastern University Press.

Johnson, P.M. & Kenny, P.J. (2010) Addiction-like reward dysfunction and compulsive eating in obese rats: Role for dopamine D2 receptors. *Nature Neuroscience, 13*(5), 635–641.

Johnson, R.D. & Downing, L.E. (1979) Deindividuation and valence of cues: Effects on prosocial and antisocial behaviour. *Journal of Personality & Social Psychology, 37*, 1532–1538.

Johnston, D.K. (1988) Adolescents' solutions to dilemmas in fables: Two moral orientations – two problem-solving strategies. In C. Gilligan, J.V. Ward & J.M. Taylor (eds) *Mapping the Moral Domain*. Cambridge, MA: Harvard University Press.

Johnston, W.A. & Dark, V.J. (1986) Selective attention. *Annual Review of Psychology, 37*, 43–75.

Johnston, W.A. & Heinz, S.P. (1979) Depth of non-target processing in an attention task. *Journal of Experimental Psychology, 5*, 168–175.

Johnston, W.A. & Wilson, J. (1980) Perceptual processing of non-targets in an attention task. *Memory and Cognition, 8*, 372–377.

Johnston, W.M. & Davey, G.C.L. (1997) The psychological impact of negative TV news bulletins: The catastrophising of personal worries. *British Journal of Psychology, 88*, 85–91.

Johnstone, J. (1999) Adverse psychological effects of ECT. *Journal of Mental Health, 8* (1), 69–85.

Johnstone, L. (2003) A shocking treatment? *The Psychologist, 16* (5), 236–239.

Joinson, A.N. (1998) Causes and implications of disinhibited behaviour on the internet. In J, Gackenbach (ed.) *Psychology and the Internet: Intrapersonal, Interpersonal and Transpersonal Implications*. San Diego, CA: Academic Press.

Joinson, A.N. (2003) *Understanding the Psychology of Internet Behaviour*. Palgrave Macmillan.

Joinson, A.N. (2007) (ed.) *Oxford Handbook of Internet Psychology*. Oxford: Oxford University Press.

Jonas, K., Eagly, A.H. & Stroebe, W. (1995) Attitudes and persuasion. In M. Argyle & A.M. Colman (eds) *Social Psychology*. London: Longman.

Jones, D. & Elcock, J. (2001) *History and Theories of Psychology: A Critical Perspective*. London: Arnold.

Jones, E.E. & Davis, K.E. (1965) From acts to dispositions: The attribution process in person perception. In L. Berkowitz (ed.) *Advances in Experimental Social Psychology, Volume 2*. New York: Academic Press.

Jones, E.E. & Nisbett, R.E. (1971) *The Actor and the Observer: Divergent Perceptions of the Causes of Behaviour*. Morristown, NJ: General Learning Press.

Jones, E.E., Davis, K.E. & Gergen, K. (1961) Role playing variations and their informational value for person perception. *Journal of Abnormal & Social Psychology, 63*, 302–310.

Jones E.E., Rock, L., Shaver, K.G., Goethals, G.R. & Wand, L.M. (1968) Patterns of performance and ability attribution: An unexpected primacy effect. *Journal of Personality & Social Psychology, 10*, 317–340.

Jones, F. (1998) Risk taking and everyday tasks. *The Psychologist, 12*(2), 70–71.

Jones, H. (1993) Altered images. *Nursing Times*, 89 (5), 58–60.

Jones, J.G. & Hardy, L. (1990) *Stress and Performance in Sport*. Chichester: John Wiley & Sons.

Jones, M.C. (1924) The elimination of children's fears. *Journal of Experimental Psychology, 7*, 382–390.

Jones, S. (1993) *The Language of the Genes*. London: Flamingo.

Joseph, J. (2003) *The Gene Illusion: Genetic Research in Psychiatry and Psychology under the Microscope*. Ross-on-Wye: PCCS Books.

Jourard, S.M. (1971) *Self-disclosure: An Experimental Analysis of the Transparent Self*. New York: Wiley Interscience.

Jouvet, M. (1967) Mechanisms of the states of sleep: A neuropharmacological approach. *Research Publications of the Association for the Research in Nervous and Mental Diseases, 45*, 86–126.

Joynson, R.B. (1974) *Psychology and Common Sense*. London: RKP.

Joynson, R.B. (1980) Models of man: 1879–1979. In A.J. Chapman & D.M. Jones (eds) *Models of Man*. Leicester: British Psychological Society.

Juel-Nielsen, N. (1965) Individual and environment: A psychiatric and psychological investigation of monozygous twins raised apart. *Acta Psychiatrica et Neurologica Scandinavia* (Suppl. 183).

Jung, C.G. (ed.) (1964) *Man and his Symbols*. London: Aldus-Jupiter Books.

Jusczyk, P.W. (1997) *The Discovery of Spoken Language*. Cambridge, MA: MIT Press.

Kagan, J. (1971) *Change and Continuity in Infancy*. New York: Wiley.

Kagan, J., Kearsley, R.B. & Zelago, P.R. (1978) *Infancy: Its Place in Human Development*. Cambridge, MA: Harvard University Press.

Kahneman, D. (1973) *Attention and Effort*. Englewood Cliffs, NJ: Prentice-Hall.

Kahneman, D. (2013) *Thinking, Fast and Slow* (Reprinted edition). New York: Farrar, Strauss & Giroux.

Kalish, R.A. (1982) *Late Adulthood: Perspectives on Human Development* (2nd edition). Monterey, CA: Brooks-Cole Publishing Co.

Kamin, L.J. (1969) Predictability, surprise, attention and conditioning. In B.A. Campbell & R.M. Church (eds) *Punishment and Aversive Behaviour*. New York: Appleton-Century-Crofts.

Kamin, L.J. (1974) *The Science and Politics of IQ.* Potomac, MD: Lawrence Erlbaum Associates.

Kamin, L.J. (1981) *The Intelligence Controversy: H.J. Eysenck vs Leon Kamin.* New York: Wiley.

Kaminer, H. & Lavie, P. (1991) Sleep and dreaming in Holocaust survivors: Dramatic decrease in dream recall in well-adjusted survivors. *Journal of Nervous & Mental Diseases, 179,* 664–669.

Kanizsa, A. (1976) Subjective contours. *Scientific American, 234,* 48–52.

Kanner, A.D., Coyne, J.C., Schaefer, C. & Lazarus, R.S. (1981) Comparison of two modes of stress measurement: Daily hassles and uplifts versus major life events. *Journal of Behavioural Measurement, 4,* 1–39.

Kanner, L. (1943) Autistic disturbance of affective contact. *Nervous Child, 12,* 17–50.

Karau, S.J. & Williams, K.D. (1995) Social loafing: Research findings, implications, and future directions. *Current Directions in Psychological Science, 4,* 134–139.

Karlins, M., Coffman, T.L. & Walters, G. (1969) On the fading of social stereotypes: Studies in three generations of college students. *Journal of Personality & Social Psychology, 13,* 1–16.

Karmiloff-Smith, A. (1996) The connectionist infant: Would Piaget turn in his grave? *Society for Research in Child Development Newsletter, Fall,* 1–2 & 10.

Karney, B.R. & Bradbury, T.N. (2000) Attributions in marriage: State or trait? A growth curve analysis. *Journal of Personality & Social Psychology, 78,* 295–309.

Karraker, K.H., Vogel, D.A. & Lake, M.A. (1995) Parents' gender–stereotyped perceptions of newborns: The eye of the beholder revisited. *Sex Roles, 33* (9/10), 687–701.

Kaslow, F.W. (2004) Death of one's partner: The anticipation and the reality. *Professional Psychology: Research and Practice, 35,* 227–233.

Kastenbaum, R. (1979) *Growing Old – Years of Fulfilment.* London: Harper & Row.

Katz, D. (1960) The functional approach to the study of attitudes. *Public Opinion Quarterly, 24,* 163–204.

Katz, D. & Braly, K. (1933) Racial stereotypes of one hundred college students. *Journal of Abnormal & Social Psychology, 28,* 280–290.

Kaufman, H. (1967) The price of obedience and the price of knowledge. *American Psychologist, 22,* 231–232,

Kay, P. & Regier, T. (2007) Colour naming universals: The case of Berinmo. *Cognition, 102,* 289–298.

Kazdin, A.E. & Wilcoxin, L.A. (1976) Systematic desensitisation and nonspecific treatment effects: A methodological evaluation. *Psychological Bulletin, 83,* 729–758.

Keating, D.P. (1980) Thinking processes in adolescence. In J. Adelson (ed.) *Handbook of Adolescent Psychology.* New York: Wiley.

Kebbell, M.R. & Wagstaff, G.F. (1999) Face value? Evaluating the accuracy of eyewitness information. Police Research Series: Paper 102 (http://tna.europarchive.org/20071206133532/homeoffice.gov.uk/rds/prgpdfs/prg102bf.pdf).

Kellar, I. & Abraham, C. (2005) Randomised control trial of a brief research-based intervention promoting fruit and vegetable consumption. *British Journal of Health Psychology, 10*(4), 543–558.

Kelley, H.H. (1950) The warm–cold variable in first impressions of people. *Journal of Personality, 18,* 431–439.

Kelley, H.H. (1967) Attribution theory in social psychology. In D. Levine (ed.) *Nebraska Symposium on Motivation, Volume 15.* Lincoln: Nebraska University Press.

Kelley, H.H. (1972) Causal schemata and the attribution process. In E.E. Jones, D.E. Kanouse, H.H. Kelley, S. Valins & B. Weiner (eds) *Attribution: Perceiving the Causes of Behaviour.* Morristown, NJ: General Learning Press.

Kelley, H.H. (1983) Perceived causal structures. In J.M.F. Jaspars, F.D. Fincham & M. Hewstone (eds) *Attribution Theory and Research: Conceptual, Developmental and Social Dimensions.* London: Academic Press.

Kelley, H.H., Berscheid, E., Christensen, A., Harvey, J.H., Huston, T.L., Levinger, G., McClintock, E., Peplau, L.A. & Peterson, D.R. (1983) *Close Relationships.* New York: W.H. Freeman.

Kellogg, W.N. & Kellogg, L.A. (1933) *The Ape and the Child.* New York: McGraw-Hill.

Kelly, G.A. (1955) *A Theory of Personality – The Psychology of Personal Constructs.* New York: Norton.

Kelly, G.A. (1962) Europe's matrix of decision. In M.R. Jones (ed.) *Nebraska Symposium on Motivation.* Lincoln: University of Nebraska Press.

Kemp, R., Towell, N. & Pike, G. (1997) When seeing should not be believing: 'Photographs, credit cards and fraud'. *Applied Cognitive Psychology, 11,* 211–222.

Kennedy, J.E. & Taddonio, J.L. (1976) Experimenter effects in parapsychological research. *Journal of Parapsychology, 40,* 1–33.

Kenny, P.J. (2013) The food addiction. *Scientific American, 309*(3), 34–39.

Kenrick, D.T. (1994) Evolutionary social psychology: From sexual selection to social cognition. *Advances in Experimental Social Psychology, 26,* 75–121.

Kenrick, D.T., Trost, M.R. & Sundie, J.M. (2004) Sex roles as adaptations: An evolutionary perspective on gender differences and similarities. In A.H. Eagly, A.E. Beall and R. Sternberg (eds) *The Psychology of Gender* (2nd edition). New York: Guilford Press.

Kent, L., Evans, J., Paul, M. & Sharp, M. (1999) Comorbidity of autistic spectrum disorders in children with Down's syndrome. *Developmental Medical & Child Neurology, 41* (3), 154–158.

Kephart, W.M. (1967) Some correlates of romantic love. *Journal of Marriage & The Family, 29,* 470–474.

Kerckhoff, A.C. (1974) The social context of interpersonal attraction. In T.L. Huston (ed.) *Foundations of Interpersonal Attraction.* New York: Academic Press.

Kerckhoff, A.C. & Davis, K.E. (1962) Value consensus and need complementarity in mate selection. *American Sociological Review, 27,* 295–303.

Kerig, P.K., Cowan, P.A. & Cowan, C.P. (1993) Marital quality and gender differences in parent–child interaction. *Developmental Psychology, 29* (6), 931–939.

Kerr, N.L. (1983) Motivation losses in small groups: A social dilemma analysis. *Journal of Personality & Social Psychology, 45,* 819–828.

Kessler, T. & Mummendey, A. (2008) Prejudice and intergroup relations. In M. Hewstone, W. Stroebe & K. Jonas (eds) *Introduction to Social Psychology: A European Perspective* (4th edition). Oxford: BPS Blackwell.

Kestenbaum, G.I. & Weinstein, L. (1985) Personality, psychopathology and developmental issues in male adolescent video game use. *Journal of the American Academy of Child Psychiatry, 24*, 325–337.

Khan, S. (2003) New wave of heroin sucks in pre-teens. *Observer*, 6 July, 6.

Killham, W. & Mann, L. (1974) Level of destructive obedience as a function of transmitter and executant roles in the Milgram paradigm. *Journal of Personality & Social Psychology, 29*, 696–702.

Kim, U. & Berry, J.W. (eds) (1993) *Indigenous Psychologies: Research and Experience in Cultural Context, Volume 17: Cross-Cultural Research and Methodology Series*. Newbury Park, CA: Sage.

Kimura, D. (1999) Sex differences in the brain. *Scientific American Presents, 10*(2), 26–31.

Kirsch, I., Moore, T.J., Scoboria, A. & Nicholls, S.S (2002) The emperor's new drugs: An analysis of antidepressant medication data submitted to the US Food and Drug Administration. *Prevention and Treatment, 5*, 23–24.

Kirsch, I., Deacon, B.J., Huedo-Medina, T.B. et al. (2008) Initial severity and antidepressant benefits: A meta-analysis of data submitted to the Food and Drug Administration. *PLoSMed, 5*(2): e45.

Kitayama, S. & Markus, H.R. (1995) Culture and self: Implications for internationalizing psychology. In N.R. Goldberger & J.B. Veroff (eds) *The Culture and Psychology Reader*. New York University Press.

Kitzinger, C. (1987) *The Social Construction of Lesbianism*. London: Sage.

Kitzinger, C. (1990) Heterosexism in psychology. *The Psychologist, 3*(9), 391–392.

Kitzinger, C. (1998) Challenging gender biases: Feminist psychology at work. *Psychology Review, 4* (3), 18–20.

Kitzinger, C. (2005a) Heteronormativity in action: Reproducing the heterosexual nuclear family in 'after hours' medical calls. *Social Problems, 52*(4), 477–498.

Kitzinger, C. (2005b) Speaking as a heterosexual: (How) does sexuality matter for talk-in-interaction. *Research on Language & Social Interaction, 38*(3), 221–265.

Kitzinger, C. & Coyle, A. (1995) Lesbian and gay couples: Speaking of difference. *The Psychologist, 8*, 64–69.

Kitzinger, C. & Wilkinson, S. (2006) Gender, sexualities and equal marriage rights. *Lesbian & Gay Psychology Review*, 7(2), 174–179.

Kitzinger, C., Coyle, A., Wilkinson, S. & Milton, M. (1998) Towards lesbian and gay psychology. *The Psychologist, 11* (11), 529–533.

Klein, M. (1932) *The Psycho-Analysis of Children*. London: Hogarth.

Kleinman, A. (1987) Anthropology and psychiatry. The role of culture in cross-cultural research on illness. *British Journal of Psychiatry, 151*, 447–454.

Kleinmuntz, B. (1980) *Essentials of Abnormal Psychology* (2nd edition). London: Harper & Row.

Kleitman, N. (1927) Studies on the physiology of sleep: V. Some experiments on puppies. *American Journal of Physiology, 84*, 386–395.

Klerman, G.L., Weissman, M.M., Rounsaville, B.J. & Chevron, E.S. (1984) *Interpersonal Psychotherapy for Depression*. New York: Basic Books.

Kline, P. (1981a) The work of Eysenck and Cattell. In F. Fransella (ed.) *Personality Theory, Measurement and Research*. London: Methuen.

Kline, P. (1981b) Personality. In D. Fontana (ed.) *Psychology for Teachers*. London: British Psychological Society/ Macmillan Press.

Kline, P. (1983) *Personality – Measurement and Theory*. London: Hutchinson.

Kline, P. (1984) *Personality and Freudian Theory*. London: Methuen.

Kline, P. (1988) *Psychology Exposed*. London: Routledge.

Kline, P. (1989) Objective tests of Freud's theories. In A.M. Colman & J.G. Beaumont (eds) *Psychology Survey No. 7*. Leicester: British Psychological Society.

Kline, P. (1993) Comments on 'Personality traits are alive and well'. *The Psychologist, 6* (7), 304.

Kline, P. (1998) Psychoanalytic perspectives. *Psychology Review, 5*(1), 10–13.

Kloep, M. & Hendry, L.B. (1999) Challenges, risks and coping in adolescence. In D. Messer & S. Millar (eds) *Exploring Developmental Psychology: From Infancy to Adolescence*. London: Arnold.

Kloep, M. & Hendry, L.B. (2006) Entry or exit? Transitions into retirement. *Journal of Occupational & Organizational Psychology, 79*, 569–593.

Kloep, M. & Hendry, L.B. (2007) Retirement: A new beginning? *The Psychologist, 20* (12), 742–745.

Kloep, M. & Tarifa, F. (1993) Albanian children in the wind of change. In L.E. Wolven (ed.) *Human Resource Development*. Hogskolan: Ostersund.

Kluckhohn, C. & Murray, H.A. (1953) Personality formation: The determinants. In C. Kluckhohn, H.A. Murray & D.M. Schneider (eds) *Personality in Nature, Society and Culture* (2nd edition). New York: Knopf.

Kobasa, S. (1979) Stressful life events, personality, and health: An inquiry into hardiness. *Journal of Personality & Social Psychology, 37*, 1–11.

Kobasa, S., Maddi, S. & Kahn, S. (1982) Hardiness and health: A prospective study. *Journal of Personality & Social Psychology, 42*, 168–177.

Koch, C. (2012a) Movies in the cortical theatre. *Scientific American Mind, 22*(6), 20–21.

Koch, C. (2012b) Crystal clear on consciousness. *New Scientist, 214*(2860), 24–25.

Koestler, A. (1967) *The Ghost in the Machine*. London: Pan.

Koestler, A. (1970) *The Act of Creation*. London: Pan Books.

Koffka, K. (1935) *The Principles of Gestalt Psychology*. New York: Harcourt Brace and World.

Kohlberg, L. (1966) A cognitive developmental analysis of children's sex-role concepts and attitudes. In E.E. Maccoby (ed.) *The Development of Sex Differences*. Stanford University Press.

Kohlberg, L. (1969) Stage and sequence: The cognitive developmental approach to socialisation. In D.A. Goslin (ed.) *Handbook of Socialisation: Theory and Research*. Chicago: Rand McNally.

Kohlberg, L. (1978) Revisions in the theory and practice of moral development. *Directions for Child Development, 2*, 83–88.

Kohlberg, L. (1984) Essays on Moral Development: *The Psychology of Moral Development, Volume 2*. New York: Harper & Row.

Kohlberg, L. & Ullian, D.Z. (1974) Stages in the development of psychosexual concepts and attitudes. In R.C. Van Wiele (ed.) *Sex Differences in Behaviour*. New York: Wiley.

Köhler, W. (1925) *The Mentality of Apes*. New York: Harcourt Brace.

Koluchova, J. (1972) Severe deprivation in twins: A case study. *Journal of Child Psychology & Psychiatry, 13*, 107–114.

Koluchova, J. (1991) Severely deprived twins after 22 years' observation. *Studia Psychologica, 33*, 23–28.

Kovacs, A.M., Teglas, E. & Endress, A.D. (2010) The Social Sense: Susceptibility to Others' Beliefs in Human Infants and Adults. *Science, 330*(6012), 1830–1834.

Kowalski, R.M., Limber, R.M., Agatson, S.P. & Malden, P.W. (2008) *Cyberbullying: Bullying in the Digital Age*. New York: Blackwell.

Kraepelin, E. (1896) Dementia praecox. In J. Cutting & M. Shepherd (eds) (1987) *The Clinical Routes of the Schizophrenia Concept*. Cambridge University Press.

Kraepelin, E. (1913) *Clinical Psychiatry: A Textbook for Physicians* (trans. A. Diffendorf). New York: Macmillan.

Krahé, B. (1992) *Personality and Social Psychology: Towards a Synthesis*. London: Sage.

Krahé, B. (2008) Aggression. In M. Hewstone, W. Stroebe & K. Jonas (eds) *Introduction to Social Psychology: A European Perspective* (4th edition). Oxford: BPS Blackwell.

Krahé, B. & Möller, I. (2004) Playing violent electronic games, hostile attribution bias and aggression-related norms in German adolescents. *Journal of Adolescence, 27*, 53–69.

Kramer, P. (1993) *Listening to Prozac*. New York: Viking.

Krebs, D. & Blackman, R. (1988) *Psychology: A First Encounter*. New York: Harcourt Brace Jovanovich.

Kremer, J. (1998) Work. In K. Trew & J. Kremer (eds) *Gender & Psychology*. London: Arnold.

Kroger, J. (1985) Separation–individuation and ego identity status in New Zealand university students. *Journal of Youth & Adolescence, 14*, 133–147.

Kroger, J. (2007) *Identity Development: Adolescence Through Adulthood* (2nd edition). Thousand Oaks, CA: Sage.

Kroger, J., Martinussen, M. & Marcia, J.E. (2010) Identity status change during adolescence and young adulthood: A meta-analysis. *Journal of Adolescence, 33*(5), 683–698.

Kruglanski, A.W. (1977) The place of naive contents in a theory of attribution: Reflections on Calder and Zuckerman's critiques of the endogenous–exogenous partition. *Personality & Social Psychology Bulletin, 3*, 592–605.

Krull, D.S. (1993) Does the grist change the mill? The effect of the perceiver's inferential goal on the process of social inference. *Personality and Social Psychology Bulletin, 19*, 340–348.

Krupat, E. & Garonzik, R. (1994) Subjects' expectations and the search for alternatives to deception in social psychology. *British Journal of Social Psychology, 33*, 211–222.

Kubitschek, W.N. & Hallinan, M.T. (1998) Tracking and students' friendships. *Social Psychology Quarterly, 61*, 1–15.

Kübler-Ross, E. (1969) *On Death and Dying*. London: Tavistock/Routledge.

Kuczaj, S.A. & Hill, H.M. (2003) Development of language. In A. Slater & G. Bremner (eds) *An Introduction to Developmental Psychology*. Oxford: Blackwell Publishing.

Kuhl, P.K., Williams, K.A., Lacerda, F., Stevens, K.N. & Lindblom, B. (1992) Linguistic experience alters phonetic perception in infants by 6 months of age. *Science, 255*, 606–608.

Kuhn, H.H. (1960) Self attitudes by age, sex and professional training. *Sociology Quarterly, 1*, 39–55.

Kuhn, H.H. & McPartland, T.S. (1954) An empirical investigation of self attitudes. *American Sociological Review, 47*, 647–652.

Kuhn, T.S. (1962) *The Structure of Scientific Revolutions*. University of Chicago Press.

Kuhn, T.S. (1970) *The Structure of Scientific Revolutions* (2nd edition). Chicago University Press.

Kuhn, T.S. (2012) *The Structure of Scientific Revolutions* (50th Anniversary edition). Chicago, IL: University of Chicago Press.

Kulik, J.A. & Brown, R. (1979) Frustration, attribution of blame and aggression. *Journal of Experimental Social Psychology, 15*, 183–194.

Kulik, J.A. & Mahler, H.I.M. (1989) Stress and affiliation in a hospital setting: Pre-operative room-mate preferences. *Personality & Social Psychology Bulletin, 15*, 183–193.

Kulik, J.A., Mahler, H.I.M. & Moore, P.J. (2003) Social comparison affiliation under threat: Effects on recovery from major surgery. In P. Salovey & A. Rothman (eds) *Social Psychology of Health: Key Readings in Social Psychology*. New York: Psychology Press.

Kulka, R.A., Schlenger, W.E., Fairbank, J.A. et al. (1990) *Trauma and the Vietnam War Generation: Report of Findings From the National Vietnam Veterans Readjustment Study*. New York: Brunner/Mazel.

Kupfer, D.J., First, M.B. & Regier, D.A. (eds) Introduction. In D.J. Kupfer, M.B. First & D.A. Regier (eds) *A Research Agenda for DSM-V.* Washington, DC: American Psychiatric Association.

Kuppens, M., de Wit, J. & Stroebe, W. (1996) Angstaanjagenheid in gezondheids-voorlichting: Een dual process analyse. *Gedrag en Gezondheid, 24*, 241–248.

Kurdeck L. (1991) The dissolution of gay and lesbian relationships. *Journal of Social & Personal Relationships, 8*, 265–278.

Kurdeck, L. (1992) Relationship stability and relationship satisfaction in cohabiting gay and lesbian couples: A prospective longitudinal test of the contextual and interdependence models. *Journal of Social & Personal Relationships, 9*, 125–142.

Kurucz, J. & Feldmar, G. (1979) Prosopo-affective agnosia as a symptom of cerebral organic disease. *Journal of the American Geriatrics Society, 27*, 225–230.

Labouvie-Vief, G. (2005) The psychology of emotions and ageing. In M. Johnson, V.L. Bengston, P.G. Coleman & T. Kirkwood (eds) *The Cambridge Handbook of Age and Ageing*. Cambridge University Press.

Labouvie-Vief, G. & Marquez Gonzales, M. (2004) Dynamic integration: Affect optimization and differentiation in development. In D.Y. Dai & R.J. Sternberg (eds) *Motivation, Emotion, and Cognition: Integrative Perspectives on Intellectual Functioning and Development*. Mahwah, NJ: Erlbaum.

Labov, W. (1970) The logic of non-standard English. In F. Williams (ed.) *Language and Poverty*. Chicago: Markham.

Labov, W. (1973) The boundaries of words and their meanings. In C.J.N. Bailey & R.W. Shuy (eds) *New Ways of Analysing Variations in English*. Washington, DC: Georgetown University Press.

Lacey, H. (1998) She's leaving home. *Independent on Sunday*, Real Life, 31 May.

Lachman, R., Lachman, J.L. & Butterfield, E.C. (1979) *Cognitive Psychology and Information Processing*. Hillsdale, NJ: Lawrence Erlbaum Associates.

Laeng, B. & Sulutvedt, U. (2012) The eye pupil adjusts to imaginary light. *Psychological Science, 25*(1), 188–197.

Lai, C.S., Fisher, S.E., Hurst, J.A., Vargha-Khadem, F. & Monaco, A.P. (2001) A forkhead-domain gene is mutated in a severe speech and language disorder. *Nature, 413*(6855), 519–523.

Laing, R.D. (1959) *The Divided Self: An Existential Study of Sanity and Madness*. London: Tavistock.

Laing, R.D. (1961) *Self and Others*. London: Tavistock.

Laing, R.D. (1967) *The Politics of Experience and the Bird of Paradise*. Harmondsworth, Penguin.

Laing, R.D. (1970) *Knots*. London: Tavistock.

Laing, R.D. & Esterson, A. (1964) *Sanity, Madness and the Family*. London: Tavistock.

Laird, J.D. (1974) Self-attribution of emotion: The effects of facial expression on the quality of emotional experience. *Journal of Personality & Social Psychology, 29*, 475–486.

Lakoff, G. (1987) *Women, Fire and Dangerous Things: What Categories Reveal About the Mind*. University of Chicago Press.

Lamb, M.E. (1977) The development of mother–infant and father–infant attachments in the second year of life. *Developmental Psychology, 13*, 639–649.

Lamb, M.E., Sternberg, K.J. & Prodromidis, M. (1992) Nonmaternal care and the security of infant-mother attachment: A reanalysis of the data. *Infant Behaviour & Development, 15*, 71–83.

Lambie, J. (1991) The misuse of Kuhn in psychology. *The Psychologist, 4* (1), 6–11.

Land, V. & Kitzinger, C. (2005) Speaking as a lesbian: Correcting the heterosexist presumption. *Research on Language & Social Interaction, 38* (4), 371–416.

Lander, K. & Bruce, V. (2000) Recognizing famous faces: Exploring the benefits of facial motion. *Ecological Psychology, 12*, 259–272.

Landis, C. (1938) Statistical evaluation of psychotherapeutic methods. In S.E. Hinde (ed.) *Concepts and Problems of Psychotherapy*. London: Heineman.

Laney, C., Bowman Fowler, N., Nelson, K.J., Bernstein, D.M. & Loftus, E.F. (2008) The persistence of false beliefs. *Acta Psychologica, 129*(1), 190–197.

Lang, F.R. & Carstensen, L.L. (1998) Social relationships and adaptation in late life. In A.S. Bellack & M. Herson (eds) *Comprehensive Clinical Psychology, Volume 7*. Oxford: Pergamon.

Lang, F.R. & Carstensen, L.L. (2002) Time counts: Future time perspective, goals, and social relationships. *Psychology and Ageing, 17*, 125–139.

Lange, C. (1885) Om Sindsbevaegelser. et psychko. fysiolog. studie. English translation in K. Dunlap (ed.) (1967) *The Emotions*. London: Hafner.

Lange, N. & McDougle, C.J. (2013) Help for the child with autism. *Scientific American, 309*(4), 58–63.

Langer, E.J. (1975) The illusion of control. *Journal of Personality & Social Psychology, 32*, 311–328.

Langlois, J.H. & Roggman, L. (1990) Attractive faces are only average. *Psychological Science, 1*, 115–121.

Langlois, J.H., Roggman, L.A., Casey, R.J., Ritter, J.M., Rieser-Danner, L.A. & Jenkins, V.Y. (1987) Infant preferences for attractive faces: Rudiments of a stereotype. *Developmental Psychology, 23*, 363–369.

Lapidot-Lefler, N. & Barak, A. (2012) Effects of anonymity, invisibility, and lack of eye-contact on toxic online disinhibition. *Computers in Human Behaviour, 28*, 434–443.

LaPiere, R.T. (1934) Attitudes versus action. *Social Forces, 13*, 230–237.

Larsen, K.S. (1974) Conformity in the Asch experiment. *Journal of Social Psychology, 94*, 303–304.

Larsen, K.S., Triplett, J.S., Brant, W.D. & Langenberg, D. (1979) Collaborator status, subject characteristics and conformity in the Asch paradigm. *Journal of Social Psychology, 108*, 259–263.

Laswell, H.D. (1948) The structures and function of communication in society. In L. Bryson (ed.) *Communication of Ideas*. New York: Harper.

Latané, B. & Darley, J.M. (1968) Group inhibitions of bystander intervention in emergencies. Journal of *Personality & Social Psychology, 10*, 215–221.

Latané, B. & Darley, J.M. (1970) *The Unresponsive Bystander: Why Does He Not Help?* New York: Appleton-Century-Crofts.

Latané, B. & Nida, S. (1980) Social impact theory and group influence: A social engineering perspective. In P. Paulus (ed.) *The Psychology of Group Influence*. Hillsdale, NJ: Lawrence Erlbaum.

Latané, B. & Nida, S. (1981) Ten years of research on group size and helping. *Psychological Bulletin, 89*, 308–324.

Latané, B., Nida, S. & Williams, D.W. (1981) The effects of group size on helping behaviour. In J.P. Rushton & R.M. Sorrentino (eds) *Altruism and Helping Behaviour*. Hillsdale, NJ: Erlbaum.

Latané, B. & Rodin, J. (1969) A lady in distress: Inhibiting effects of friends and strangers on bystander intervention. *Journal of Experimental Social Psychology, 5*, 189–202.

Latané, B. & Wolf, S. (1981) The social impact of majorities and minorities. *Psychological Review, 88*, 438–453.

Latané, B., Williams, K. & Harkins, S.G. (1979) Many hands make light work: The causes and consequences of social loafing. *Journal of Personality & Social Psychology, 37*, 822–832.

Laungani, P.D. (2007) *Understanding Cross-Cultural Psychology*. London: Sage.

Laurance, J. (2000) Young cocaine users run higher risk of strokes. *Independent*, 13 May, 5.

Laurance, J. (2004a) Cannabis link to psychosis depends on age of first use. *Independent*, 2 December, 16.

Laurance, J. (2004b) Seroxat controversy deepens with Europe-wide warning on suicide. *Independent*, 26 July, 12.

Laurance, J. (2005) Stress can reduce breast cancer risk, researchers find. *Independent*, 9 September, 18.

Laureys, S. (2005) The neural correlates of (un)awareness: lessons from the vegetative state. *Trends in Cognitive Science, 9*(12), 556–559.

Lavender, T. (2000) Schizophrenia. In L. Champion & M. Power (eds) *Adult Psychological Problems: An Introduction* (2nd edition). Hove: Psychology Press.

Lawrence, C. (2011) On 'turning the other cheek'. *Proceedings of the International Society for the Study of Individual Differences*, July, 4.

Lawrence, C. , Ferguson, E. & Maltby, J. (2013) Personality and the pro-social context. *The Psychologist, 26*(1), 34–37.

Lawton, G. (2006) Get up and go. *New Scientist, 189* (2539), 34–38.

Lawton, G. (2011) What you see is not what you get. *New Scientist, 210*(2812), 36–37.

Lawton, G. (2013) Nudge in the right direction. *New Scientist, 218*(2922), 32–36.

Lazarus, R.S. (1966) *Psychological Stress and the Coping Process*. New York: McGraw-Hill.

Lazarus, R.S. (1982) Thoughts on the relations between emotion and cognition. *American Psychologist, 37,* 1019–1024.

Lazarus, R.S. (1991) *Emotion and Adaptation*. New York: Oxford University Press.

Lazarus, R.S. (1999) *Stress and Emotion: A New Synthesis*. London: Free Association Books.

Lazarus, R.S. & Folkman, S. (1984) *Stress, Appraisal, and Coping*. New York: Springer.

Le Bon, G. (1895) *The Crowd: A Study of the Popular Mind*. London: Unwin.

Leaper, C. & Friedman., C.K. (2007) The socialization of gender. In J.E. Grusec & P.D. Hastings (eds) *Handbook of Socialization: Theory and Research*. New York: Guilford Press.

Leary, M.R. (2004) The self we know and the self we show: Self-esteem, self-presentation, and the maintenance of interpersonal relationships. In M.B. Brewer & M. Hewstone (eds) *Emotion and Motivation*. Oxford: Blackwell Publishing.

Leary, M.R. & Kowalski, R.M. (1990) Impression management: A literature review and two-component model. *Psychological Bulletin, 107*, 34–47.

Leder, H. & Bruce, V. (1998) Local and relational aspects of face distinctiveness. *Quarterly Journal of Experimental Psychology: Human Experimental Psychology, 51A* (3), 449–473.

Leder, H. & Bruce, V. (2000) When inverted faces are recognized: The role of configural information in face recognition. *Quarterly Journal of Experimental Psychology: Human Experimental Psychology, 53A* (2), 513–516.

Leder, H. & Carbon, C.-C. (2006) Face-specific configural processing of relational information. *British Journal of Psychology, 97*, 19–29.

LeDoux, J.E. (1994) Emotion-specific physiological activity: Don't forget about CNS physiology. In P. Ekman & R.J. Davidson (eds) *The Nature of Emotion: Fundamental Questions*. New York: Oxford University Press.

LeDoux, J.E. (1998a) Fear and the brain: Where have we been, and where are we going? *Biological Psychiatry, 44,* 1229–1238.

LeDoux, J.E. (1998b) *The Emotional Brain: The Mysterious Underpinnings of Emotional Life*. New York: Simon & Schuster.

Lee, D.N. & Lishman, J.R. (1975) Visual proprioceptive control of stance. *Journal of Human Movement Studies, 1*, 87–95.

Lee, K., Cameron, C.A., Xu, F., Fu, G. & Board, J. (1997) Chinese and Canadian children's evaluations of lying and truth telling: Similarities and differences in the context of pro- and antisocial behaviours. *Child Development, 68*, 924–934.

Lee, K., Anzures, G. & Freire, A. (2011) Cognitive Development in Adolescence. In A. Slater & G. Bremner (eds) *An Introduction to Developmental Psychology* (2nd edition). BPS Blackwell.

Lee, S. (2001) Fat phobia in anorexia nervosa: Whose obsession is it? In M. Nasser, M.A. Katzman & R.A. Gordon (eds) *Eating Disorders and Cultures in Transition*. Hove: Brunner-Routledge.

Leekam, S. (1993) Children's understanding of mind. In M. Bennett (ed.) *The Child as Psychologist: An Introduction to the Development of Social Cognition*. Hemel Hempstead: Harvester Wheatsheaf.

Lees, A. (2012) *Alzheimer's: The Silent Plague*. Penguin E book.

Leff, J., Williams, G., Mark, A. et al. (2013) Computer-assisted therapy for medication-resistant auditory hallucinations: proof-of-concept study. *British Journal of Psychiatry, 202,* 428–433.

Lefkowitz, M.M., Eron, L.D., Walder, L.O. & Huesmann, L.R. (1972) Television violence and child aggression: A follow-up study. In G.A. Comstock & E.A. Rubenstein (eds) *Television and Social Behaviour, Volume 3. Television and Adolescent Aggressiveness*. Washington, DC: US Government Printing Office.

LeFrancois, G.R. (1983) *Psychology*. Belmont, CA: Wadsworth Publishing Co.

Legge, D. (1975) *An Introduction to Psychological Science*. London: Methuen.

Lemma, A. (2002) Psychodynamic therapy: The Freudian approach. In W. Dryden (ed.) *Handbook of Individual Therapy* (4th edition). London: Sage.

LeMoal, M.L. (2007) Historical approach and evolution of the stress concept: a personal account. *Psychoneuroendocrinology, 32*, S3–S9.

Leonard, S.P. & Archer, J. (1989) A naturalistic investigation of gender constancy in three- to four-year-old children. *British Journal of Developmental Psychology, 7*, 341–346.

Lerner, M.J. (1965) The effect of responsibility and choice on a partner's attractiveness following failure. *Journal of Personality, 33*, 178–187.

Lerner, M.J. (1980) *The Belief in a Just World: A Fundamental Delusion*. New York: Plenum.

Leslie, A.M. (1987) Pretence and representation: The origins of 'theory of mind'. *Psychological Review, 94*, 412–426.

Leslie, A.M. (1994) Pretending and believing: Issues in the theory of ToM. *Cognition, 50*, 211–238.

Leslie, A.M. & Roth, D. (1993) What autism teaches us about metarepresentation. In S. Baron-Cohen, H. Tager-Fusberg & D.J. Cohen (eds) *Understanding Other Minds: Perspectives from Autism*. Oxford University Press.

Leslie, J.C. (2002) *Essential Behaviour Analysis*. London: Arnold.

Leslie, L.M., Constantine, V.S. & Fiske, S.T. (2003) The Princeton quartet: How are stereotypes changing? Unpublished manuscript, Princeton University.

LeVay, S. (2006) Same sex, different rules. *New Scientist, 190*(2549), 42-45.

Levenson, R.W. (1994) The search for autonomic specificity. In P. Ekman & R.J. Davidson (eds) *The Nature of Emotion: Fundamental Questions*. New York: Oxford University Press.

Levenson, R.W., Ekman, P. & Friesen, W.V. (1990) Voluntary facial action generates emotion-specific autonomic nervous system activity. *Psychophysiology, 27*, 363–384.

Levine, D. (2012) Treating sleep improves psychiatric symptoms. *Scientific American Mind, 23*(5), 14.

Levine, J.M. & Moreland, R.L. (1998) Small groups. In D.T. Gilbert, S.T. Fiske & G. Lindzey (eds) *Handbook of Social Psychology* (4th edition). Boston: McGraw-Hill.

Levine, R., Sato, S., Hashimoto, T. & Verma, J. (1995) Love and marriage in 11 cultures. *Journal of Cross-Cultural Psychology, 26*, 554–571.

Levinger, G. & Clark, J. (1961) Emotional factors in the forgetting of word associations. *Journal of Abnormal & Social Psychology, 62*, 99–105.

Levinson, C.A. & Rodebaugh, T.L. (2012) Social anxiety and eating disorder comorbidity: The role of negative social evaluation fears. *Eating Behaviour, 13*(1), 27–35.

Levinson, D.J. (1986) A conception of adult development. *American Psychologist, 41*, 3–13.

Levinson, D.J. & Levinson, J.D. (1997) *The Seasons of a Woman's Life*. New York: Ballantine Books.

Levinson, D.J., Darrow, D.N., Klein, E.B., Levinson, M.H. & McKee, B. (1978) *The Seasons of a Man's Life*. New York: A.A. Knopf.

Levy, B. & Langer, E. (1994) Ageing free from negative stereotypes: Successful memory in China and among the American deaf. *Journal of Personality & Social Psychology, 66*, 989–997.

Levy, B., Ashman, O. & Dror, I. (1999–2000) To be or not to be: The effects of ageing stereotypes on the will to live. *Omega, 40* (3), 409–420.

Levy, B.R., Hausdorff, J.M., Hencke, R. & Wei, J.Y. (2000) Reducing cardiovascular stress with positive self-stereotypes of ageing. *Journals of Gerontology Series B: Psychological Sciences & Social Sciences, 55* (4), 205–213.

Levy, R. (1996) Improving memory in old age through implicit self-stereotyping. *Journal of Personality & Social Psychology, 71*, 1092–1107.

Levy-Agresti, J. & Sperry, R.W. (1968) Differential perceptual capacities in major and minor hemispheres. *Proceedings of the National Academy of Sciences, 61*, 1151.

Lewin, R. (1991) Look who's talking now. *New Scientist*, 27 April, 48–52.

Lewis, M. (1990) Social knowledge and social development. *Merrill-Palmer Quarterly, 36*, 93–116.

Lewis, M. & Brooks-Gunn, J. (1979) *Social Cognition and the Acquisition of Self*. New York: Plenum.

Lewis, V. (2003) Disorders of development. In A. Slater & G. Bremner (eds) *An Introduction to Developmental Psychology*. Oxford: Blackwell Publishing.

Lewontin, R. (1976) Race and intelligence. In N.J. Block & G. Dworkin (eds) *The IQ Controversy: Critical Readings*. New York: Pantheon.

Ley, P. (1988) *Communicating with Patients*. London: Croom Helm.

Leyens, J.-P. & Codol, J.P. (1988) Social cognition. In M. Hewstone, W. Stroebe, J.P. Codol & G.M. Stephenson (eds) *Introduction to Social Psychology*. Oxford: Blackwell.

Leyens, J.-P. & Corneille, O. (1999) Asch's social psychology: Not as social as you may think. *Personality & Social Psychology Review, 3*, 345–357.

Liao, L.-M. & Boyle, M. (2004) Surgical feminising. *The Psychologist, 17*(8), 459–462.

Liebert, R.M. & Baron, R.A. (1972) Some immediate effects of televised violence on children's behaviour. *Developmental Psychology, 6*, 469–475.

Light, P. (1986) Context, conservation and conversation. In M. Richards & P. Light (eds) *Children of Social Worlds*. Cambridge: Polity Press.

Light, P., Buckingham, N. & Robbins, A.H. (1979) The conservation task as an interactional setting. *British Journal of Educational Psychology, 49*, 304–310.

Lilienfeld, S.O. (1995) *Seeing Both Sides: Classic Controversies in Abnormal Psychology*. Pacific Grove, CA: Brooks/Cole Publishing Co.

Lilienfeld, S.O. (1998) *Looking into Abnormal Psychology: Contemporary Readings*. Pacific Grove, CA: Brooks/Cole Publishing Co.

Lilienfeld, S.O. & Arkowitz, H. (2012a) When coping fails. *Scientific American Mind, 23*(2), 64–65.

Lilienfeld, S.O. & Arkowitz, H. (2012b) Are all psychotherapies created equal? *Scientific American Mind, 23*(4), 68–69.

Lilienfeld, S.O. & Arkowitz, H. (2014) The truth about Shock Therapy. *Scientific American Mind, 25*(3), 70–71.

Lilienfeld, S.O., Wood, J.M. & Garb, H.N. (2005) What's wrong with this picture? *Scientific American Mind, 16*(1), 50–57.

Lin, E. & Kleinman, A. (1988) Psychopathology and clinical course of schizophrenia: A cross-cultural perspective. *Schizophrenia Bulletin, 14*, 555–567.

Lindsay, D.S., Read, J.D. & Sharma, K. (1998) Accuracy and confidence in person identification: the relationship is strong when witnessing conditions vary widely. *Psychological Science, 9*, 2215–2218.

Linville, P.W., Fischer, G.W. & Salovey, P. (1989) Perceived distributions of the characteristics of ingroup and outgroup members: empirical evidence and a computer simulation. *Journal of Personality & Social Psychology, 57*, 165–188.

Lippmann, W. (1922) *Public Opinion*. New York: Harcourt.

Lipsedge, M. (1997) Eating disorders. In L. Rees, M. Lipsedge & C. Ball (eds) *Textbook of Psychiatry*. London: Arnold.

Little, A.C. & Perrett, D.I. (2007) Using composite images to assess accuracy in personality attribution to faces. *British Journal of Psychology, 98*, 111–126.

Littlewood, R. & Lipsedge, M. (1989) *Aliens and Alienists: Ethnic Minorities and Psychiatry*. London: Unwin Hyman.

Littlewood, R. & Lipsedge, M. (1997) *Aliens and Alienists: Ethnic Minorities and Psychiatry* (3rd edition). London: Routledge.

Lloyd, A. (1995) *Doubly Deviant, Doubly Damned: Society's Treatment of Violent Women*. Harmondsworth: Penguin.

Lloyd, P., Mayes, A., Manstead, A.S.R., Meudell, P.R. & Wagner, H.L. (1984) *Introduction to Psychology – An Integrated Approach*. London: Fontana.

Locke, J. (1690) *An Essay Concerning Human Understanding*. New York: Mendon. (Reprinted 1964.)

Locksley, A., Ortiz, V. & Hepburn, C. (1980) Social categorisation and discriminatory behaviour: Extinguishing the minimal intergroup discrimination effect. *Journal of Personality & Social Psychology, 39*, 773–783.

Loeber, R., Green, S.M., Keenan, K. & Lahey, B.B. (1995) Which boys will fare worse? Early predictors on the onset of conduct disorder in a six-year longitudinal study. *Journal of the American Academy of Child & Adolescent Psychiatry, 34*, 499–509.

Loehlin, J.C. (1992) *Genes and Environment in Personality Development*. London: Sage.

Loehlin, J.C., Willerman, L. & Horn, J.M. (1988) Human behaviour genetics. *Annual Review of Psychology, 39*, 101–133.

Loftus, E.F. (1975) Leading questions and the eyewitness report. *Cognitive Psychology, 1*, 560–572.

Loftus, E.F. (1979) Reactions to blatantly contradictory information. *Memory & Cognition, 7*, 368–374.

Loftus, E.F. (1979/1996) *Eyewitness Testimony*. Cambridge, MA: Harvard University Press.

Loftus, E.F. (1997) Creating false memories. *Scientific American*, September, 50–55.

Loftus, E.F. (2005) A 30-year investigation of the malleability of memory. *Learning & Memory, 12*, 361–366.

Loftus, E.F. & Loftus, G. (1980) On the permanence of stored information in the human brain. *American Psychologist, 35*, 409–420.

Loftus, E.F. & Palmer, J.C. (1974) Reconstruction of automobile destruction: An example of the interaction between language and memory. *Journal of Verbal Learning & Verbal Behaviour, 13*, 585–589.

Loftus, E.F. & Zanni, G. (1975) Eyewitness testimony: The influence of wording on a question. *Bulletin of the Psychonomic Society, 5*, 86–88.

Loftus, G. (1974) Reconstructing memory: The incredible eyewitness. *Psychology Today, December*, 116–119.

Logan, G.D. (1988) Toward an instance theory of automatisation. *Psychological Review, 95*, 492–527.

Logie, R.H. (1995) *Visuo-Spatial Working Memory*. Hove: Lawrence Erlbaum.

Longden, E. & Dillon, J. (2013) The hearing voices movement. In J. Cromby, D. Harper & P. Reavey (eds) *Psychology, mental health and distress*. Basingstoke: Palgrave Macmillan.

Longden, E., Corstens, D. & Dillon, J. (2013) Recovery, discovery and revolution: The work of intervoice and the hearing voices movement. In S. Coles, S. Keenan & B. Diamond (eds) *Madness contested: Power and practice*. Ross-on-Wye: PCCS Books.

Lonner, W. (1990) An overview of cross-cultural testing and assessment. In R. Brislin (ed.) *Applied Cross-Cultural Psychology*. Newbury Park, CA: Sage.

Lorenz, K. (1935) The companion in the bird's world. *Auk, 54*, 245–273.

Lorenz, K.Z. (1966) *On Aggression*. London: Methuen.

Lott, A.J. & Lott, B.E. (1974) The role of reward in the formation of positive interpersonal attitudes. In T. Huston (ed.) *Foundations of Interpersonal Attraction*. New York: Academic Press.

Lovaas, O.I. (1977) *The Autistic Child: Language Development Through Behaviour Modification*. New York: Halste Press.

Lovaas, O.I. (1987) Behavioural treatment and normal educational and intellectual functioning in young autistic children. *Journal of Consulting & Clinical Psychology, 55*, 3–9.

Lovaas, O.I., Freitas, L., Nelson, K. & Whalen, C. (1967) The establishment of imitation and its use for the development of complex behaviour in schizophrenic children. *Behaviour Research & Therapy in Personality, 5*, 171–181.

Lowe, G. (1995) Alcohol and drug addiction. In A.A. Lazarus & A.M. Colman (eds) *Abnormal Psychology*. London: Longman.

Luborsky, L., Singer, B. & Luborsky, L. (1975) Comparative studies of psychotherapies: Is it true that 'everyone has won and all must have prizes'? *Archives of General Psychiatry, 32*, 995–1008.

Luca-Thompson, R.G., Goldberg, W.A. & Prause, J. (2010) Maternal work Early in the Lives of Children and Its Distal Associations with Achievement and Behaviour Problems: A Meta-Analysis. *Psychological Bulletin, 136*(6), 915–942.

Luchins, A.S. (1942) Mechanisation in problem-solving: The effect of Einstellung. *Psychological Monographs, 54* (Whole No. 248).

Luchins, A.S. (1957) Primacy–recency in impression formation. In C. Hovland (ed.) *The Order of Presentation in Persuasion*. New Haven, CT: Yale University Press.

Luchins, A.S. & Luchins, E.H. (1959) *Rigidity of Behaviour*. Eugene: University of Oregon Press.

Luria, A.R. (1961) *The Role of Speech in the Regulation of Normal and Abnormal Behaviour*. New York: Liveright.

Luria, A.R. (1968) *The Mind of a Mnemonist: A Little Book about a Vast Memory*. New York: Basic Books.

Luria, A.R. (1973) *The Working Brain: An Introduction to Neuropsychology* (trans. B. Haigh). New York: Basic Books.

Luria, A.R. (1987) Reductionism. In R.L. Gregory (ed.) *The Oxford Companion to the Mind*. Oxford University Press.

Luria, A.R. & Yudovich, F.I. (1971) *Speech and the Development of Mental Processes in the Child*. Harmondsworth: Penguin.

Lyddy, F. (2000) Depression: The state of the disorder. *The Psychologist, 13*(8), 414–415.

Lyon, C.M. (1995) Helping children with challenging behaviour. *Nursing Standard, 10*(1), 33–35.

Lyon, J. (1998) Crime. In K. Trew & J. Kremer (eds) *Gender & Psychology*. London: Arnold.

Lyons, J. (1970) *Chomsky*. London: Fontana.

Lyons-Ruth, K., Repacholi, B., McLeod, S. & Silva, E. (1991) Disorganized attachment behaviour in infancy: Short-term stability, maternal and infant correlates and risk-related subtypes. *Development & Psychopathology, 3*, 377–396.

Lytton, H. & Romney, D.M. (1991) Parents' differential socialisation of boys and girls: A meta-analysis. *Psychological Bulletin, 109*, 267–296.

MacCallum, F. & Golombok, S. (2004) Children raised in fatherless families from infancy: A follow-up of children of lesbian and single heterosexual mothers at early adolescence. *Journal of Child Psychology and Psychiatry, 45*(7), 1407–1419.

Maccoby, E.E. (1980) Social Development – Psychological Growth and the Parent–Child Relationship. New York: Harcourt Brace Jovanovich.

Maccoby, E.E. (1990) Gender and relationships: A developmental account. *American Psychologist, 45*, 513–520.

Maccoby, E.E. & Jacklin, C.N. (1974) *The Psychology of Sex Differences*. Stanford University Press.

Mackay, D. (1975) *Clinical Psychology: Theory and Therapy*. London: Methuen.

Mackay, D.G. (1973) Aspects of the theory of comprehension, memory and attention. *Quarterly Journal of Experimental Psychology, 25*, 22–40.

MacKay, D.G. (2014) The Engine of Memory. *Scientific American Mind, 25*(3), 30–38.

MacKay, D.G. & Johnson, L.W. (2013) Errors, error detection, error connection and hippocampal-region damage: Data and theories. *Neuropsychologia, 51*(13), 2633–2650.

MacKenzie, D. (2013) Finding the players in the symphony of IQ genes. *New Scientist, 218*(2920), 15.

Mackenzie, D.L. & Shaw, J.W (1990) Inmate adjustment and change during shock incarceration: The impact of correctional boot camp programs. *Justice Quarterly, 7*, 125–150.

Mackenzie, D.L. & Souryal, C. (1995) A 'Machiavellian' perspective on the development of boot camp prisons: A debate. Unpublished symposium presentation.

Mackenzie, D.L., Brame, R., McDowall, D. & Souryal, C. (1995) Boot camp prisons and recidivism in eight states. *Criminology, 33*, 327–357.

Mackie, D.M. (1987) Systematic and nonsystematic processing of minority and minority persuasive communications. *Journal of Personality & Social Psychology, 53*, 41–52.

Mackintosh, N.J. (1978) Cognitive or associative theories of conditioning: Implications of an analysis of blocking. In S.H. Hulse, M. Fowler & W.K. Honig (eds) *Cognitive Processes in Animal Behaviour*. Hillsdale, NJ: Lawrence Erlbaum.

Mackintosh, N.J. (1995) Classical and operant conditioning. In N.J. Mackintosh & A.M. Colman (eds) *Learning and Skills*. London: Longman.

Macknik, S.L. & Martinez-Londe, S. (2014) Filling in the _ _ _ _. *Scientific American Mind, 25*(1), 21–23.

Macleod, M. (2007) Her father's daughter. *New Scientist, 193* (2590), 38–41.

Macleod, M. (2013) Popualtion paradox. *New Scientist, 220*(2940), 46–49.

Macmurray, J. (1961/1991) *Persons in relation*. London: Faber & Faber.

MacNamara, J. (1982) *Names for Things*. Cambridge, MA: MIT Press.

Macrae, C.N., Bodenhausen, G.V., Milne, A.B., Thorn, T.M.J. & Castelli, I. (1997) On the activation of social stereotypes: The moderating role of processing objectives. *Journal of Experimental Social Psychology, 33*, 471–489.

Maddox, G.L. (1964) Disengagement theory: A critical evaluation. *The Gerontologist, 4*, 80–83.

Maddux, J.E., Gosselin, J.T. & Winstead, B.A. (2012) Conceptions of Psychopathology: A Social Constructionist Perspective. In J.E. Maddux & B.A. Winstead (eds) *Psychopathology: Foundations for a Contemporary Understanding* (3rd edition). New York: Routledge.

Maes, S. & van Elderen, T. (1998) Health psychology and stress. In M.W. Eysenck (ed.) *Psychology: An Integrated Approach*. London: Longman.

Magnusson, D., Stattin, H. & Allen, V.L. (1985) Biological maturation and social development: A longitudinal study of some adjustment processes from mid-adolescence to adulthood. *Journal of Youth and Adolescence, 14*, 267–283.

Maher, B.A. (1966) *Principles of Psychopathology: An Experimental Approach*. New York: McGraw-Hill.

Mahler, M. (1975) *The Psychological Birth of the Human Infant*. London: Hutchinson.

Mahoney, M.J. (1974) *Cognition and Behaviour Modification*. Cambridge, MA: Ballinger.

Maier, N.R.F. (1931) Reasoning in humans II: The solution of a problem and its appearance in consciousness. *Journal of Comparative Psychology, 12*, 181–194.

Maier, S.F. & Seligman, M.E.P. (1976) Learned helplessness: Theory and evidence. *Journal of Experimental Psychology: General, 105*, 3–46.

Main, M. (1991) Metacognitive knowledge, metacognitive monitoring, and singular (coherent) versus multiple (incoherent) models of attachment: Findings and directions for future research. In C.M. Murray Parkes, J.M. Stephenson-Hinde & P. Marris (eds) *Attachment Across the Life-Cycle*. London: Routledge.

Main, M. (1995) Recent studies in attachment. In S. Goldberg, R. Muir & J. Kerr (eds) *Attachment Theory: Social, Developmental, and Clinical Perspectives*. Hillsdale, NJ: The Analytic Press.

Main, M. & Hesse, E. (1990) Parents' unresolved traumatic experiences are related to infant disorganized attachment status: Is frightened and/or frightening parental behaviour the linking mechanism? In M.T. Greenberg, D. Cicchetti & E.M. Cummings (eds) *Attachment in the Preschool Years*. University of Chicago Press.

Main, M. & Weston, D.R. (1981) The quality of the toddler's relationship to mother and to father: Related to conflict behaviour and the readiness to establish new relationships. *Child Development, 52*, 932–940.

Main, M., Kaplan, N. & Cassidy, J. (1985) Security in infancy, childhood and adulthood: A move to the level of representation. In I. Bretherton & E. Waters (eds) *Growing Points of Attachment: Theory and Research*. University of Chicago Press.

Mair, K. (1992) The myth of therapist expertise. In W. Dryden & C. Feltham (eds) *Psychotherapy and its Discontents*. Buckingham: Open University Press.

Major, B. (1980) Information acquisition and attribution processes. *Journal of Personality & Social Psychology, 39*, 1010–1023.

Malan, D. (1976) *Toward the Validation of Dynamic Psychotherapy*. New York: Plenum.

Malinowski, B. (1929) *The Sexual Life of Savages*. New York: Harcourt Brace Jovanovich.

Mandela, N. (1995) *A Long Walk to Freedom: The Autobiography of Nelson Mandela*. London: Abacus.

Mandler, G. (1984) *Mind and Body: The Psychology of Emotion and Stress*. New York: Norton.

Mann, L. (1969) *Social Psychology*. New York: Wiley.

Manning, R., Levine, M. & Collins, A. (2007) The Kitty Genovese murder and the social psychology of helping: The parable of the 38 witnesses. *American Psychologist, 62*, 555–562.

Manstead, A.S.R. & Semin, G.R. (1980) Social facilitation effects: Mere enhancement of dominant responses? *British Journal of Social & Clinical Psychology, 19*, 19–36.

Manstead, T. (2005) The social dimension of emotion. *The Psychologist, 18*(8), 484–487.

Manthorpe, J. (1994) Life changes. *Nursing Times, 90* (18), 66–67.

Maracek, J, Crawford, M. & Popp, D. (2004) On the construction of gender, sex, and sexualities. In A.H. Eagly, A.E. Beall & R. Sternberg (eds) *The Psychology of Gender* (2nd edition). New York: Guilford Press.

Marañon, G. (1924) Contribution à l'etude de l'action emotive de l'adrenaline. *Revue Française d'Endocrinologie, 2,* 301–325.

March, P. & Doherty, C. (1999) Dying and bereavement. In D. Messer & F. Jones (eds) *Psychology and Social Care.* London: Jessica Kingsley.

Marcia, J.E. (1966) Development and validation of ego identity status. *Journal of Personality & Social Psychology, 3,* 551–558.

Marcia, J.E. (1967) Ego identity status: Relationship to change in self-esteem, 'general maladjustment,' and authoritarianism. *Journal of Personality, 35,* 118–133.

Marcia, J.E. (1976) Identity six years after: A follow-up study. *Journal of Youth & Adolescence, 5,* 145–150.

Marcia, J.E. (1998) Peer Gynt's life cycle. In E. Skoe & A. von der Lippe (eds) *Personality Development in Adolescence: A Cross National and Lifespan Perspective.* London: Routledge.

Marcoen, A., Coleman, P.G. & O'Hanlon, A. (2007) Psychological ageing. In J. Bond, S. Peace, F. Dittman-Kohli & G. Westerhof (eds) *Ageing in Society: European Perspectives on Gerontology* (3rd edition). London: Sage.

Marcus, D.E. & Overton, W.F. (1978) The development of cognitive gender constancy and sex-role preferences. *Child Development, 49,* 434–444.

Marcus-Newhall, A., Pedersen, W.C., Carlson, M. & Miller, N. (2000) Displaced aggression is alive and well: A meta-analytic review. *Journal of Personality & Social Psychology, 78,* 670–689.

Marks, I.M. (1973) The reduction of fear: Towards a unifying theory. *Journal of the Canadian Psychiatric Association, 18,* 9–12.

Marks, I.M. (1981a) *Cure and Care of Neurosis.* New York: Wiley.

Marks, I.M. (1981b) Space phobia: Pseudo-agoraphobic syndrome. *Journal of Neurology, Neurosurgery & Psychiatry, 44,* 387–391.

Marks, I.M., Gelder, M. & Bancroft, J. (1970) Sexual deviants two years after electric aversion. *British Journal of Psychiatry, 117,* 173–185.

Markus, H. (1978) The effect of mere presence on social facilitation: An unobtrusive test. *Journal of Experimental Social Psychology, 14,* 389–397.

Markus, H. & Nurius, P. (1986) Possible selves. *American Psychologist, 41,* 954–969.

Markus, H.R. & Kitayama, S. (1991) Culture and the self: Implications for cognition, emotion, and motivation. *Psychological Review, 98,* 224–253.

Marlatt, G.A., Baer, J.S., Donovan, D.M. & Kivlahan, D.R. (1988) Addictive behaviors: Etiology and treatment. *Annual Review of Psychology, 39,* 223–252.

Marr, D. (1982) *Vision: A Computational Investigation into the Human Representation and Processing of Visual Information.* San Francisco: W.H. Freeman.

Marrone, M (1998) *Attachment and Interaction.* London: Jessica Kingsley.

Marsh, P., Rosser, E. & Harré, R. (1978) *The Rules of Disorder.* London: RKP.

Marshall, G. & Zimbardo, P. (1979) Affective consequences of inadequately explaining physiological arousal. *Journal of Personality & Social Psychology, 37,* 970–988.

Marshall, J. (2008) Unforgettable. *New Scientist, 197* (2643), 30–33.

Marshall, J. (2009) Woes be gone. *New Scientist, 201* (2691), 36–39.

Marsland, D. (1987) *Education and Youth.* London: Falmer.

Martin, C.L. (1991) The role of cognition in understanding gender effects. *Advances in Child Development & Behaviour, 23,* 113–149.

Martin, G. (1998) Psychology and culture: Two major paradigms. *Psychology Teaching, New Series, No. 6,* 21–23.

Martin, G. & Pear, J. (1992) *Behaviour Modification: What It Is and How To Do It* (4th edition). Englewood Cliffs, NJ: Prentice-Hall.

Martin, L., Neighbors, H. & Griffith, D. (2013) The experience of symptoms of depression in men vs women. *JAMA Psychiatry, 70*(10), 1100–1106.

Martin, L.L. & Davies, B. (1998) Beyond hedonism and associationism: A configural view of the role of affect in evaluation, processing, and self-regulation. *Motivation and Emotion, 22,* 33–51.

Martin, P. (2000) Spell bound. *Sunday Times Magazine,* 23 July, 46–53.

Martin, R. & Hewstone, M. (2001) Conformity and independence in groups: Majorities and minorities. In M.A. Hogg & R.S. Tindale (eds) *Blackwell Handbook of Social Psychology: Group Processes.* Malden, MA: Blackwell.

Martin, R. & Hewstone, M. (2008) Majority versus minority influence, message processing and attitude change: The source context-elaboration model. In M.P. Zanna (ed.) *Advances in Experimental Social Psychology,* vol. 40. San Diego, CA: Academic Press.

Marzillier, J. (2004) The myth of evidence-based psychotherapy. *The Psychologist, 17*(7), 392–395.

Masheter, C. (1997) Former spouses who are friends: Three case studies. *Journal of Social & Personal Relationships, 14,* 207–222.

Maslach, C. (1979) Negative emotional biasing of unexplained arousal. *Journal of Personality & Social Psychology, 37,* 953–969.

Maslach, C., Stapp, J. & Santee, R.T. (1985) Individuation: Conceptual analysis and assessment. *Journal of Personality & Social Psychology, 49,* 729–738.

Maslow, A. (1954) *Motivation and Personality.* New York: Harper & Row.

Maslow, A. (1968) *Towards a Psychology of Being* (2nd edition). New York: Van Nostrand Reinhold.

Maslow, A. (1970) *Motivation and Personality* (2nd edition). New York: Harper & Row.

Massaro, D.W. (1989) *Experimental Psychology: An Information Processing Approach.* New York: Harcourt Brace Jovanovich.

Masters, J.C., Ford, M.E., Arend, R., Grotevant, H.D. & Clarke, L.V. (1979) Modelling and labelling as integrated determinants of children's sex-typed imitative behaviour. *Child Development, 50,* 364–371.

Matchock, R. & Susman, E.J. (2006) Family composition and menarachal age: Anti-inbreeding strategies. *American Journal of Human Biology, 18,* 481–491.

Matlin, M.W. & Stang, D.J. (1978) *The Pollyanna Principle.* Cambridge, MA: Schenkman.

Matson, J.L., Ollendick, T.H. & Adkins, J. (1980) A comprehensive dining program for mentally retarded adults. *Behaviour Research & Therapy, 18*, 107–112.

Matsumoto, D. & Willingham, B. (2009) Spontaneous facial expressions of emotion of congenitally and noncongenitally blind individuals. *Journal of Personality & Social Psychology, 96*(1), 1–10.

Matthews, K.A. (1982) Psychological perspectives on the Type A behaviour pattern. *Psychological Bulletin, 91*(2), 293–323.

Matthews, R. (2004) Parapsychology Special: Opposites detract. *New Scientist, 181*, 39–41.

Maunsell, J.H.R. & Newsome, W.T. (1987) Visual processing in monkey extrastriate cortex. *Annual Review of Neuroscience, 10*, 363–401.

Maurer, D. & Salapatek, P. (1976) Developmental changes in the scanning of faces by young infants. *Child Development, 47*, 523–527.

Maxwell, J.C. (1854) Some resolutions of problems 2. *Cambridge & Dublin Mathematics Journal, 8*, 188–195.

Maylor, E.A. (1994) Ageing and the retrieval of specialised and general knowledge: Performance of ageing masterminds. *British Journal of Psychology, 85*, 105–114.

McArthur, L.A. (1972) The how and why of why: Some determinants and consequences of causal attribution. *Journal of Personality & Social Psychology, 22*, 171–193.

McCall, R.B., Applebaum, M.I. & Hogarty, P.S. (1973) Developmental changes in mental test performance. *Monographs for the Society of Research in Child Development, 38* (3), (Whole No. 150).

McCann, J.J. (1987) Retinex theory and colour constancy. In R.L. Gregory (ed.) *Oxford Companion to the Mind.* Oxford University Press.

McCarley, R.M. (1983) REM dreams, REM sleep and their isomorphism. In M.H. Chase & E.D. Weitzman (eds) *Sleep Disorders: Basic and Clinical Research, Volume 8* (published as book). New York: Spectrum.

McCarthy-Jones, S. (2012) *Hearing voices: The histories, causes and meanings of auditory verbal hallucinations.* Cambridge: Cambridge University Press.

McCauley, C. & Stitt, C.L. (1978) An individual and quantitative measure of stereotypes. *Journal of Personality & Social Psychology, 36*, 929–940.

McCloskey, M. & Zaragoza, M. (1985) Misleading information and memory for events: Arguments and evidence against memory impairment hypothesis. *Journal of Experimental Psychology: General, 114*, 3–18.

McConaghy, M.J. (1979) Gender permanence and the genital basis of gender: stages in the development of constancy of gender identity. *Child Development, 50*, 1223–1226.

McCormick, L.J. & Mayer, J.D. (1991) *Mood-Congruent Recall and Natural Mood.* Poster presented at the annual meeting of the New England Psychological Association, Portland, ME.

McCrae, R.R. & Costa, P.T. (1989) More reasons to adopt the five-factor model. *American Psychologist, 44*, 451–452.

McCrone, J. (1999) Left brain, right brain. *New Scientist, 163*(2193), 26–30.

McCrone, J. (2004) The power of belief. *New Scientist, 181* (2438), 34–37.

McCusker, L. (2014) CBT in clinical practice. *Psychology Review, 19*(3), 25–27.

McDougall, W. (1908) *An Introduction to Social Psychology.* London: Methuen.

McEwan, B.S. & Seeman, T. (1999) Protective and damaging effects of mediators of stress: elaborating and testing the concepts of allostasis and allostatic load. *Annals of the New York Academy of Science, 896*, 30–47.

McGarrigle, J. & Donaldson, M. (1974) Conservation accidents. *Cognition, 3*, 341–350.

McGaugh, J.L. & Le Port, A. (2014) Remembrance of All Things Past. *Scientific American, 310*(2), 26–31.

McGinn, C. (1987) Could a machine be conscious? In C. Blakemore & S. Greenfield (eds) *Mindwaves.* Oxford: Blackwell.

McGlone, F., Park, A. & Roberts, C. (1996) *Relative Values.* Family Policy Studies Centre: BSA.

McGlynn, F.D., Mealiea, W.L. & Landau, D.L. (1981) The current status of systematic desensitisation. *Clinical Psychology Review, 1*, 149–179.

McGuffin, P., Farmer, A.E. & Gottesman, I.I. (1987) Is there really a split in schizophrenia? The genetic evidence. *British Journal of Psychiatry, 150*, 581–592.

McGuire, A.M. (1994) Helping behaviours in the natural environment: Dimensions and correlates of helping. *Personality & Social Psychology Bulletin, 20*, 45–56.

McGuire, W.J. (1968) Personality and susceptibility to social influence. In E.F. Borgatta & W.W. Lambert (eds) *Handbook of Personality: Theory and Research.* Chicago: Rand-McNally.

McGuire, W.J. (1969) The nature of attitudes and attitude change. In G. Lindzey & W. Aronson (eds) *Handbook of Social Psychology, Vol. 3* (2nd edition). Reading, MA: Addison-Wesley.

McGurk, H. (1975) *Growing and Changing.* London: Methuen.

McIlveen, R. (1995) 'Goofing off' in groups: The psychology of 'social loafing'. *Psychology Review, 1*(3), 16–18.

McKie, R. (2001) Whisper it quietly, but the power of language may all be in the genes. *Observer*, 7 October, 14.

McKie, R. (2002) How Ice Ages increased our brainpower. *Observer*, 14 April, 16.

McKie, R. (2008) Ban on primate experiments would be devastating, scientists warn. *Observer*, 2 November, 14.

McKie, R. (2013) Why do identical twins end up having different lives? *The Guardian New Review*, 2 June, 20–21.

McKnight, J. (1997) *Straight Science?: Homosexuality, Evolution, Adaptation.* London: Routledge.

McNally, R.J. (2003) Progress and controversy in the study of posttraumatic stress disorder. *Annual Review of Psychology, 54*, 229–252.

McNally, R.J. & Geraerts, E. (2009) A new solution to the recovered memory debate. *Perspectives on Psychological Science, 4*, 126–134.

McNeill, D. (1970) *The Acquisition of Language.* New York: Harper & Row.

McNeill, J.E. & Warrington, E.K. (1993) Prosopagnosia: A face-specific disorder. *Quarterly Journal of Experimental Psychology, 46A*, 1–10.

McVeigh, T. (2009) How Britain is coming to terms with growing old. *Observer*, 17 May.

Mead, G.H. (1934) *Mind, Self and Society.* University of Chicago Press.

Meadows, S. (1993) *The Child as Thinker: The Acquisition and Development of Cognition in Childhood.* London: Routledge.

Meadows, S. (1995) Cognitive development. In P.E. Bryant & A.M. Colman (eds) *Developmental Psychology.* London: Longman.

Medawar, P.B. (1963) *The Art of the Soluble*. Harmondsworth: Penguin.

Meddis, R. (1975) *The Sleep Instinct*. London: RKP.

Meeus, W.H.J. & Raajimakers, Q.A.W. (1986) Administrative obedience: Carrying out orders to use psychological-administrative violence. *European Journal of Social Psychology, 16*, 311–324.

Megargee, E.I. & Mendelsohn, G.A. (1962) A cross validation of twelve MMPI indices of hostility and control. *Journal of Abnormal & Social Psychology, 65*, 431–438.

Mehrabian, A. (1972) Nonverbal communication. In J. Cole (ed.) *Nebraska Symposium on Motivation, Volume 19*. Lincoln: University of Nebraska Press.

Meichenbaum, D. (1977) *Cognitive Behaviour Modification: An Integrative Approach*. New York: Plenum.

Meins, E. (2003) Emotional development and early attachment relationships. In A. Slater & G. Bremner (eds) *An Introduction to Developmental Psychology*. Oxford: Blackwell Publishing.

Meissner, C.A. & Brigham, J.C. (2001) Thirty years of investigating the own-race bias in memory for faces: A meta-analytic review. *Psychology, Public Policy, & Law, 7*, 3–35.

Meltzoff, A. & Moore, M. (1977) Imitation of facial and manual gestures by human neonates. *Science, 198*, 75–78.

Meltzoff, A. & Moore, M. (1983) Newborn infants imitate adult facial gestures. *Child Development, 54*, 702–709.

Meltzoff, A.N. & Moore, M.K. (2000) Imitation of facial and manual gestures by human neonates: Resolving the debate about early imitation. In D. Muir & A. Slater (eds) *Infant Development: The Essential Readings*. Malden, MA: Blackwell.

Melzack, R. & Wall, P.D. (1991) The Challenge of Pain (3rd edition). Harmondsworth, UK: Penguin.

Memon, A. & Thomson, D. (2007) The myth of the incredible eyewitness. In S. Della Sala (ed.) *Tall Tales About the Mind & Brain: Separating Fact from Fiction*. Oxford University Press.

Memon, A. & Wright, D.B. (1999) Eyewitness testimony and the Oklahoma bombing. *The Psychologist, 12*(6), 292–295.

Mendel, G. (1895) Versuche uber Pflanzenhybriden [Experiments in plant hybridisation]. *Verhandlungen des Naturs – Forschunden Vereines in Bruenn, 4*, 3–47.

Mental Health Network/The NHS Confederation (2007) *The Mental Health Act 2007*. Briefing, Issue 148, July.

Merari, A.(2010) *Driven to Death: Psychological and Social Aspects of Suicidal Terrorism*. Oxford: Oxford University Press.

Messer, D. (1995) Seeing and pulling faces. *The Psychologist, 8*, 77.

Metcalfe, J, Van Snellenberg, J.X., DeRose, P., Balsam, P. & Malhotra, A.K. (2012) Judgements of agency in schizophrenia: an impairment in autonoietic metacognition. *Transactions of the Royal Society B, 367*, 1391–1400.

Meyer, V. & Chesser, E.S. (1970) *Behaviour Therapy in Clinical Psychiatry*. Harmondsworth: Penguin.

Middleton, W., Moylan, A., Raphael, B., Burnett, P. & Martinek, N. (1993) An international perspective on bereavement-related concepts. *Australian & New Zealand Journal of Psychiatry, 27*, 457–463.

Midgley, M. (2003) Fate by fluke. *Guardian Review*, 1 March, 12.

Miell, D. (1990) Issues in social psychology. In I. Roth (ed.) *Introduction to Psychology, Volume 2*. Hove: Lawrence Erlbaum/Open University.

Milavsky, J.R., Kessler, R.C., Stipp, H. & Rubens, W.S. (1982) *Television and Aggression: A Panel Study*. New York: Academic Press.

Miles, T.R. (1967) On defining intelligence. In S. Wiseman (ed.) *Intelligence and Ability*. Harmondsworth: Penguin.

Milgram, S. (1963) Behavioural study of obedience. *Journal of Abnormal & Social Psychology, 67*, 391–398.

Milgram, S. (1965) Liberating effects of group pressure. *Journal of Personality & Social Psychology,* 1, 127–134.

Milgram, S. (1970) The experience of living in cities. *Science, 167*, 1461–1468.

Milgram, S. (1974) *Obedience to Authority*. New York: Harper & Row.

Milgram, S. (1992) *The Individual in a Social World* (2nd edition). New York: McGraw-Hill.

Miller, A.G. (1986) *The Obedience Experiment: A Case Study of Controversy in Social Science*. New York: Praeger.

Miller, D.T. & Ross, M. (1975) Self-serving biases in the attribution of causality: Fact or fiction? *Psychological Bulletin, 82*, 213–225.

Miller, E. & Morley, S. (1986) *Investigating Abnormal Behaviour*. London: Erlbaum.

Miller, G.A. (1956) The magical number seven, plus or minus two: Some limits on our capacity for processing information. *Psychological Review, 63*, 81–97.

Miller, G.A. (1962) *Psychology: The Science of Mental Life*. Harmondsworth: Penguin.

Miller, G.A. (1978) The acquisition of word meaning. *Child Development, 49*, 999–1004.

Miller, G.A. & Selfridge, J.A. (1950) Verbal context and the recall of meaningful material. *American Journal of Psychology, 63*, 176–185.

Miller, I. & Norman, W. (1979) Learned helplessness in humans: A review and attribution theory model. *Psychological Bulletin, 86*, 93–118.

Miller, N.E. (1941) The frustration–aggression hypothesis. *Psychological Review, 48*, 337–342.

Miller, N.E. (1948) Theory and experiment relating psychoanalytic displacement to stimulus-response generalisation. *Journal of Abnormal & Social Psychology, 43*, 155–178.

Miller, P.H. (2002) *Theories of Developmental Psychology* (4th edition). New York: Worth Publishers.

Miller, T.Q., Smith, T.W., Turner, C.W. et al. (1996) A meta-analytic review of research on hostility and physical health. *Psychological Bulletin, 119*, 322–348.

Milner, A.D., Perrett, D.I., Johnston, R.S. et al. (1991) Perception and action in visual form agnosia. *Brain, 114*, 405–428.

Milner, B., Corkin, S. & Teuber, H.L. (1968) Further analysis of the hippocampal amnesic syndrome: 14-year follow-up study of H.M. *Neuropsychologia, 6,* 215–234.

Milton, J. (1995) Issues in the adoption of methodological safeguards in parapsychological experiments. *The Parapsychological Association 38th Annual Convention Proceedings*. Fairhaven, MA: Parapsychological Association.

Milton, J. (1999) Should Ganzfeld research continue to be crucial in the search for a replicable psi effect? Part 1. Discussion Paper and introduction to an electronic-mail debate. *Journal of Parapsychology, 63*, 309–333.

Milton, J. (2005) Methodology. In J. Henry (ed.) *Parapsychology: Research on Exceptional Experiences*. Hove: Routledge.

Minard, R.D. (1952) Race relations in the Pocohontas coalfield. *Journal of Social Issues, 8*, 29–44.

MIND (2001) *Shock Treatment: A Survey of People's Experiences of ECT*. London: MIND.

Ministry of Justice (2009) *Reoffending of Adults: Results from the 2007 Cohort (England and Wales)*. Ministry of Justice Statistics Bulletin.

Minsky, M. (1975) A framework for representing knowledge. In P.H. Winston (ed.) *The Psychology of Computer Vision*. New York: McGraw-Hill.

Miranda, F.S.B., Caballero, R.B., Gómez, M.N.G. & Zamorano, M.A.M. (1981) Obedienca a la autoridad. *Pisquis, 2*, 212–221.

Mischel, W. (1968) *Personality and Assessment*. New York: Wiley.

Mischel, W. (1973) Toward a cognitive social learning reconceptualisation of personality. *Psychological Review, 80*, 252–283.

Mischel, W. & Shoda, Y. (1995) A cognitive-affective system theory of personality: Reconceptualising situations, dispositions, dynamics, and invariance in personality structure. *Psychological Review, 102*(2), 246–268.

Mischel, W. & Shoda, Y. (1998) Reconciling processing dynamics and personality dispositions. *Annual Review of Psychology, 49*, 229–258.

Misselbrook, D. & Armstrong, D. (2000) How do patients respond to presentation of risk information? A survey in general practice of willingness to accept treatment for hypertension (cited in Ogden, 2000).

Mistry, J. & Rogoff, B. (1994) Remembering in cultural context. In W.J. Lonner & R.S. Malpass (eds) *Psychology and Culture*. Boston: Allyn & Bacon.

Mitchell, A. (1999) Liquid genius. *New Scientist, 161* (2177), 26–30.

Mitchell, D. & Blair, J. (2000) Psychopathy. *The Psychologist, 13*(7), 356–360.

Mitchell, J. (1974) *Psychoanalysis and Feminism*. Harmondsworth: Penguin.

Mitchell, J. & McCarthy, H. (2000) Eating disorders. In L. Champion & M. Power (eds) *Adult Psychological Problems: An Introduction* (2nd edition). Hove: Psychology Press.

Mitchell, P. (1997) *Introduction to Theory of Mind: Children, Autism and Apes*. London: Arnold.

Moddia, B. (1996) Sold short. *Nursing Times, 92*(18), 26–30.

Moerk, E.L. (1989) The LAD was a lady, and the tasks were ill-defined. *Developmental Review, 9*, 21–57.

Moerk, E.L. & Moerk, C. (1979) Quotations, imitations and generalisations: Factual and methodological analyses. *International Journal of Behaviour Development, 2*, 43–72.

Moffit, T.E., Caspi, A., Dickson, N., Silva, P.A. & Stanton, W. (1996) Childhood-onset versus adolescent-onset antisocial conduct in males: Natural history from age 3 to 18. *Development & Psychopathology, 8*, 399–424.

Moghaddam, F.M. (1987) Psychology in the three worlds: As reflected by the crisis in social psychology and the move towards indigenous third world psychology. *American Psychologist, 42*, 912–920.

Moghaddam, F.M. (1998) *Social Psychology: Exploring Universals Across Cultures*. New York: W.H. Freeman & Co.

Moghaddam, F.M. (2002) *The Individual and Society: A Cultural Integration*. New York: Worth Publishers.

Moghaddam, F.M. & Studer, C. (1997) Cross-cultural psychology: The frustrated gadfly's promises, potentialities and failures. In D. Fox & D. Prilleltensky (eds) *Critical Psychology: An Introduction*. London: Sage.

Moghaddam, F.M., Taylor, D.M. & Wright, S.C. (1993) *Social Psychology in Cross-cultural Perspective*. New York: W.H. Freeman & Co.

Möller, I. & Krahé, B. (2009) Exposure to violent video games and aggression in German adolescents: a longitudinal analysis. *Aggressive Behavior, 35*, 75–89.

Mollon, P. (2000) *Freud and False Memory Syndrome*. Cambridge: Icon Books.

Money, J. & Erhardt, A. (1972) *Man and Woman, Boy and Girl*. Baltimore, MD: Johns Hopkins University Press.

Monti, M.M. & Owen, A.M. (2010) The aware mind in the motionless body. *The Psychologist, 23*(6), 478–481.

Monti, M.M., Coleman, M.R. & Owen, A.M. (2009) Executive functions in the absence of behaviour: Functional imaging of the minimally conscious state. *Progress in Brain Research, 117*, 249–260.

Moore, M. & Meltzoff, A. (2008) Factors affecting infants' manual search for occluded objects and the genesis of object permanence. *Infant Behaviour and Development, 31* (2), 168–180.

Moray, N. (1959) Attention in dichotic listening: Affective cues and the influence of instructions. *Quarterly Journal of Experimental Psychology, 11*, 56–60.

Morea, P. (1990) *Personality: An Introduction to the Theories of Psychology*. Harmondsworth: Penguin.

Moreno, J.L. (1953) *Who Shall Survive?* (2nd edition). New York: Beacon.

Morgan, C. & Averill, J.R. (1992) True feelings, the self, and authenticity: A psychosocial perspective. In D.D. Franks & V. Gecas (eds) *Social Perspectives on Emotion, Volume 1*. Greenwich, CT: JAI.

Morgan, C.D. & Murray, H.A. (1935) A method for investigating fantasies. *Archives of Neurological Psychiatry, 34*, 289–306.

Morgan, E. (2005) Father nature. *New Scientist, 187* (2514), 38–41.

Mori, K. & Arai, M. (2010) No need to fake it: Reproduction of the Asch experiment without confederates. *International Journal of Psychiatry, 45*(5), 390–397.

Morris, C.G. (1988) *Psychology: An Introduction* (6th edition). London: Prentice-Hall.

Morris, M.W. & Peng, K. (1994) Culture and cause: American and Chinese attributions for social and physical events. *Journal of Personality & Social Psychology, 67*, 949–971.

Morris, M.W., Menon, T. & Ames, D.R. (2001) Culturally conferred conceptions of agency: A key to social perceptions of persons, groups, and other actors. *Personality & Social Psychology Review, 5*, 169–182.

Morris, R.L. (1989) Parapsychology. In A.M. Colman & J.G. Beaumont (eds) *Psychology Survey, 7*. Leicester: British Psychological Society.

Morrison, A.P., Turkington, D., Pyle, M. et al. (2014) Cognitive therapy for people with schizophrenia spectrum disorders not taking antipsychotic drugs: a single-blind randomised controlled trial. *The Lancet*, Early Online Publication 6 February doi:10.1016/S0140-6736 (13)62246-1

Morrison, C. (2013) Would you want a super memory? *The Psychologist, 26*(10), 740–741.

Morselli, E. (1886) *Sulla dismorfofobia e sulla tafefobia*. Bolle Tino della R Accademia di Genova, 6, 110–119.

Moscovici, S. (1961) *La Psychoanalyse: Son Image et Son Public*. Paris: Presses Universitaires de France.

Moscovici, S. (1976) *Social Influence and Social Change*. London: Academic Press.

Moscovici, S. (1980) Towards a theory of conversion behaviour. In L. Berkowitz (ed.) *Advances in Experimental Social Psychology, 13*, 209–239.

Moscovici, S. (1981) On social representations. In J.P. Forgas (ed.) *Social Cognition: Perspectives on Everyday Understanding*. London: Academic Press.

Moscovici, S. (1982) The coming era of representations. In J.-P. Codol & J.P. Leyens (eds) *Cognitive Analysis of Social Behaviour*. The Hague: Martinus Nijhoff.

Moscovici, S. (1984) The phenomenon of social representations. In R.M. Farr & S. Moscovici (eds) *Social Representations*. Cambridge University Press.

Moscovici, S. (1985) Social influence and conformity. In G. Lindzey & E. Aronson (eds) *Handbook of Social Psychology* (3rd edition). New York: Random House.

Moscovici, S. & Faucheux, C. (1972) Social influence, conforming bias and the study of active minorities. In L. Berkowitz (ed.) *Advances in Experimental Social Psychology, Volume 6*. New York: Academic Press.

Moscovici, S. & Hewstone, M. (1983) Social representations and social explanations: From the 'näive' to the 'amateur' scientist. In M. Hewstone (ed.) *Attribution Theory: Social and Functional Extensions*. Oxford: Blackwell.

Moscovici, S. & Zavalonni, M. (1969) The group as a polariser of attitudes. *Journal of Personality & Social Psychology, 12*, 125–135.

Moscovici, S., Lage, E. & Naffrechoux, M. (1969) Influence of a consistent minority on the responses of a majority in a colour perception test. *Sociometry, 32*, 365–380.

Moskovitz, S. (1983) *Love Despite Hate – Child Survivors of the Holocaust and their Adult Lives*. New York: Schocken.

Moskovitz, S. (1985) Longitudinal follow-up of child survivors of the Holocaust. *American Academy of Child Psychiatry, 24*, 401–407.

Moskowitz, G.B., Gollwitzer, P.M., Wasel, W. & Schaal, B. (1999) Preconscious control of stereotype activation through chronic egalitarian goals. *Journal of Personality & Social Psychology, 77*, 167–184.

Moskvitch, K. (2013) Penal Code. *New Scientist, 219*(2933), 36–39.

Motluk, A. (1999) Jane behaving badly. *New Scientist, 164* (2214), 28–33.

Motz, A. (2001) *The Psychology of Female Violence: Crimes Against the Body*. Hove: Brunner-Routledge.

Motz, A. (2008) *The Psychology of Female Violence* (2nd edition). London: Routledge.

Mousseau, M.-C. (2003) Parapsychology: Science or pseudo-science? *Journal of Scientific Exploration, 17*, 271–282.

Mowrer, O.H. (1950) *Learning Theory and Personality Dynamics*. New York: Ronald Press.

Mowrer, O.H. (1960) *Learning Theory and Behaviour*. New York: John Wiley.

Moyer, K.E. (1976) *The Psychobiology of Aggression*. New York: Harper & Row.

Moyer, M.W. (2013a) Glia spark seizures. *Scientific American Mind, 24*(2), 16.

Moyer, M.W. (2013b) Without glia, the brain would starve. *Scientific American Mind, 24*(2), 17.

Much, N. (1995) Cultural psychology. In J.A. Smith, R. Harré & L.Van Langenhove (eds) *Rethinking Psychology*. London: Sage.

Mullainathan, S. & Shafir, E. (2014) Freeing up intelligence. *Scientific American Mind, 25*(1), 58–63.

Muller, H.J. & Maxwell, J. (1994) Perceptual integration of motion and form information: Is the movement filter involved in form discrimination? *Journal of Experimental Psychology: Human Perception & Performance, 20*, 397–420.

Mumford, D.B., Whitehouse, A.M. & Choudry, I.Y. (1992) Survey of eating disorders in English-medium schools in Lahore, Pakistan. *International Journal of Eating Disorders, 11*, 173–184.

Mummendey, A. (1996) Aggressive behaviour. In M. Hewstone, W. Stroebe & G.M. Stephenson (eds) *Introduction to Social Psychology* (2nd edition). Oxford: Blackwell.

Munro, R. (2000) Cheap and cheerful. *Nursing Times, 96* (3), 16.

Munroe, R.H., Shimmin, H.S. & Munroe, R.L. (1984) Gender understanding and sex-role preference in four cultures. *Developmental Psychology, 20*, 673–682.

Munsinger, H. (1975) The adopted child's IQ: A critical review. *Psychological Bulletin, 82*, 623–659.

Murdock, B.B. (1962) The serial position effect in free recall. *Journal of Experimental Psychology, 64*, 482–488.

Murphy, G. (1947) *Personality: A Bio-social Approach to Origins and Structure*. New York: Harper & Row.

Murphy, S. (2013) Rebuilding broken brains. *New Scientist, 219*(2927), 34–37.

Murray, E.J. & Foote, F. (1979) The origins of fear of snakes. *Behaviour Research & Therapy in Personality, 17*, 489–493.

Murray, H.A. (1938) *Explorations in Personality*. New York: Oxford University Press.

Murray, R. (2002) No smoke without fear. *Guardian*, 17 September, 8.

Murstein, B.I. (1972) Physical attractiveness and marital choice. *Journal of Personality & Social Psychology, 22*, 8–12.

Murstein, B.I. (1976) The stimulus–value–role theory of marital choice. In H. Grunebaum & J. Christ (eds) *Contemporary Marriage: Structures, Dynamics and Therapy*. Boston: Little, Brown.

Murstein, B.I. (1986) *Paths to Marriage*. Beverly Hills, CA: Sage.

Murstein, B.I. (1987) A clarification and extension of the SVR theory of dyadic pairing. *Journal of Marriage & The Family, 49*, 929–933.

Myers, D.G. (1990) *Exploring Psychology*. New York: Worth Publishers.

Myers, D.G. (1994) *Exploring Social Psychology*. New York: McGraw-Hill.

Myers, D.G. & Lamm, H. (1975) The group polarisation phenomenon. *Psychological Bulletin, 83*, 602–627.

Myers, L. & Abraham, C. (2005) Beyond 'doctor's orders'. *The Psychologist, 18* (11), 680–683.

Naci, L. & Owen, A.M. (2013) Making every word count for Nonresponsive Patients. *JAMA Neurology, 70*(10), 1235–1241.

Nagayama Hall, G.C. & Barongan, C. (2002) *Multicultural Psychology*. Upper Saddle River, NJ: Prentice-Hall.

Nakielska, A. & Goodwin, R. (2013) Cultural influence on relationships. *Psychology Review, 19*(2), 28–30.

Nantel-Vivier, A., Kokko, K., Caprara, G.V., Pastorelli, C., Gerbino, M.G., Paciello, M., Cote, S., Pihl, R.O., Vitaro, F. & Tremblay, R.E. (2009) Prosocial development from childhood to adolescence: A multi-informant perspective with Canadian and Italian longitudinal studies. *Journal of Child Psychology and Psychiatry, 50*(5), 590–598.

Nardishaw, Z. (2009) Race, culture and ethnicity in mental health care. In R. Newell & K. Gournay (eds) *Mental Health Nursing: An Evidence-based Approach*. London: Churchill Livingstone.

Nasby, W., Hayden, B. & DePaulo, B.M. (1979) Attributional bias among aggressive boys to interpret unambiguous social stimuli as displays of hostility. *Journal of Abnormal Psychology, 89*, 459–468.

Nasser, M. (1997) *Culture and Weight Consciousness*. London: Routledge.

National Institute of Child Health and Human Development (2010) *Study of Early Child Care*. Washington, DC: NICHD.

Naughton, J. (2012) Thomas Kuhn: the man who changed the way the world looked at science. *The Observer*, 19 August, 4.

Navon, D. (1984) Resources – A theoretical soup stone? *Psychological Review, 91*, 216–234.

Neave, N. & Wolfson, S. (2003) Testosterone, territoriality, and the 'home advantage'. *Physiology & Behaviour, 78*, 269–275.

Neisser, U. (1967) *Cognitive Psychology*. New York: Appleton-Century-Crofts.

Neisser, U. (1976) *Cognition and Reality*. San Francisco: W.H. Freeman.

Neisser, U. (1982) *Memory Observed*. San Francisco: W.H. Freeman.

Nelson, C, A, Zeanah, C.H. & Fox, N.A. (2007) Cognitive recovery in socially deprived young children: The Bucharest Early Intervention Project. *Science, 318*, 1937–1940.

Nelson, C, A, Fox, N.A. & Zeanah, C.H. (2013) Anguish of the Abandoned Child. *Scientific American, 308*(4), 44–49.

Nelson, K. (1977) Facilitating children's syntax acquisition. *Developmental Psychology, 13*, 101–107.

Nelson, S.A. (1980) Factors influencing young children's use of motives and outcomes as moral criteria. *Child Development, 51*, 823–829.

Nemeth, C., Swedund, M. & Kanki, G. (1974) Patterning of the minority's responses, and their influence on the majority. *European Journal of Social Psychology, 4*, 53–64.

Nestler, E.J. & Malenka, R.C. (2004) The addicted brain. *Scientific American, 290*(3), 50–57.

Neugarten, B.L. (1975) The future of the young-old. *The Gerontologist, 15*, 4–9.

Neugarten, B.L. & Neugarten, D.A. (1987) The changing meanings of age. *Psychology Today, 21*, 29–33.

New, R. (2013) The social psychology of prejudice. *Psychology Review, 19*(1), 2–4.

New Scientist (2004) On the edge of the known world. *New Scientist, 181*(2438), 32–33.

Newcomb, T.M. (1943) *Personality and Social Change*. New York: Holt, Rinehart & Winston.

Newell, A. & Simon, H.A. (1972) *Human Problem-Solving*. Englewood Cliffs, NJ: Prentice-Hall.

Newell, A., Shaw, J.C. & Simon, H.A. (1958) Elements of a theory of human problem-solving. *Psychological Review, 65*, 151–166.

Newitz, A. (2006) Love unlimited. *New Scientist, 191* (2559), 44–47.

Newman, H.H., Freeman, F.N. & Holzinger, K.J. (1937) *Twins: A Study of Heredity and the Environment*. University of Chicago Press.

Newstead, S. (1995) Language and thought: The Whorfian hypothesis. *Psychology Review, 1*, 5–7.

Newton, P., Reddy, V. & Bull, R. (2000) Children's everyday deception and performance on false-belief tasks. *British Journal of Developmental Psychology, 18*, 297–317.

NICE (2009) *Costing Statement: Medicines Adherence: Involving Patients in Decisions about Prescribed Medicines and Supporting Adherence*. London: National Institute for Health & Clinical Excellence.

Nicholson, J. (1993) *Men and Women: How Different Are They?* (2nd edition). Oxford University Press.

Nicholson, J.M., Fergusson, D.M. & Horwood, L.J. (1999) Effects on later adjustment of living in a stepfamily during childhood and adolescence. *Journal of Child Psychology & Psychiatry, 40*(3), 405–416.

Nicolson, P. (1995) Feminism and psychology. In J.A. Smith, R. Harré & L. Van Langenhove (eds) *Rethinking Psychology*. London: Sage.

Niemi, M.B. (2009) Cure in the mind. *Scientific American Mind, 20*(1), 42–49.

Nisbett, R.E. (1972) Hunger, obesity and the ventromedial hypothalamus. *Psychological Review, 79*, 433–453.

Nisbett, R.E. & Borgida, E. (1975) Attribution and the psychology of prediction. *Journal of Personality & Social Psychology, 32*, 923–943.

Nisbett, R.E, Caputo, C., Legant, P. & Maracek, J. (1973) Behaviour as seen by the actor and as seen by the observer. *Journal of Personality & Social Psychology*, *27*, 154–165.

Nisbett, R.E. & Ross, L. (1980) *Human Inference: Strategies and Shortcomings of Social Judgement*. Englewood Cliffs, New Jersey: Prentice-Hall.

Nisbett, R.E. & Wilson, T. (1977) Telling more than we can know: Verbal reports on mental processes. *Psychology Review, 84*, 231–259.

Nishida, M., Pearsall, J., Buckner, R.I. & Walker, M.P. (2009) REM sleep, prefrontal theta, and the consolidation of human emotional memory. *Cerebral Cortex, 19*, 1158–1166.

Nolan, J. & Markham, R. (1998) The accuracy–confidence relationship in an eyewitness task: Anxiety as a modifier. *Applied Cognitive Psychology*, *12*, 43–54.

Norman, D.A. (1968) Toward a theory of memory and attention. *Psychological Review, 75*, 522–536.

Norman, D.A. (1969) Memory while shadowing. *Quarterly Journal of Experimental Psychology, 21*, 85–93.

Norman, D.A. (1976) *Memory and Attention* (2nd edition). Chichester: Wiley.

Norman, D.A. & Bobrow, D.G. (1975) On data-limited and resource-limited processes. *Cognitive Psychology*, *7*, 44–64.

Norman, D.A. & Shallice, T. (1986) Attention to action: Willed and automatic control of behaviour. In R.J. Davidson, G.E. Schwartz & D. Shapiro (eds) *The Design of Everyday Things*. New York: Doubleday.

Northcote, J. (2007) *The Paranormal and the Politics of Truth: A Sociological Account*. Charlottesville, VA: Imprint Academic.

Northoff, G. (2012) Psychoanalysis and the brain – why did Freud abandon neuroscience? *Frontiers in Psychology, 3*, 1–11.

Nye, R.D. (2000) *Three Psychologies: Perspectives from Freud, Skinner, and Rogers* (6th edition). Belmont, CA: Wadsworth/Thomson Learning.

O'Connor, N. & Hermelin, B. (1988) Low intelligence and special abilities. *Journal of Child Psychology & Psychiatry, 29*(4), 391–396.

O'Connor, T.G. & the English and Romanian Adoptees Study Team (2000) The effects of global and severe privation on cognitive competence: Extension and longitudinal follow-up. *Child Development, 71*, 376–390.

O'Donohue, W. & Ferguson, K.E. (2001) *The Psychology of B.F. Skinner*. Thousand Oaks, CA: Sage Publications.

O'Keefe, D.J. & Hale, S.L. (2001) An odds-ratio-based meta-analysis of research on the door-in-the-face influence strategy. *Communication Reports, 14*, 31–38.

O'Kelly, L. (2004) It beats working. *Observer Review*, 6 June, 1–2.

O'Leary, K.D. & Wilson, G.T. (1975) *Behaviour Therapy: Application and Outcome*. Englewood Cliffs, NJ: Prentice-Hall.

O'Shea, M. (2013) The Human Brain. *New Scientist, Instant Expert 31,* (i)–(viii).

Oakes, P. (2004) The root of all evil in intergroup relations? Unearthing the categorization process. In M.B. Brewer & M. Hewstone (eds) *Social Cognition*. Oxford: Blackwell Publishing.

Oakes, P.J., Haslam, S.A. & Turner, J.C. (1994) *Stereotyping and Social Reality*. Oxford: Blackwell.

Oatley, K. (1984) *Selves in Relation: An Introduction to Psychotherapy and Groups*. London: Methuen.

Oatley, K., Keltner, D. & Jenkins, J. (2006) *Understanding Emotions* (2nd revised edition). Oxford: Blackwell.

Ochse, R. & Plug, C. (1986) Cross-cultural investigation of the validity of Erikson's theory of personality development. *Journal of Personality & Social Psychology, 50*, 1240–1252.

Offer, D., Ostrov, E., Howard, K.I. & Atkinson, R. (1988) *The Teenage World: Adolescents' Self-Image in Ten Countries*. New York: Plenum Press.

Ogden, J. (2000) *Health Psychobiology: A Textbook* (2nd edition). Buckingham: Open University Press.

Ogden, J. (2004) *Health Psychology: A Textbook* (3rd edition). Maidenhead: Open University Press/McGraw-Hill Education.

Ogden, J. (2007) *Health Psychology: A Textbook* (4th edition). Oxford: Open University Press.

Ogden, J. (2010) *The Psychology of Eating: From Healthy to Disordered Behaviour* (2nd edition). US/UK: Blackwell.

Ogden, J., Clementi, C. & Aylwin, S. (2006a) Having obesity surgery: A qualitative study and the paradox of control. *Psychology & Health, 21*, 273–293.

Ogden, J., Reynolds, R. & Smith, A. (2006b) Expanding the concept of parental control: A role for overt and covert control in children's snacking behaviour. *Appetite, 47*, 100–106.

Ohman, A., Erikkson, A. & Olofsson, C. (1975a) One-trial learning and superior resistance to extinction of autonomic responses conditioned to potentially phobic stimuli. *Journal of Comparative & Physiological Psychology, 88*, 619–627.

Ohman, A., Erixson, G. & Lofberg, L. (1975b) Phobias and preparedness: Phobic and neutral pictures as conditioned stimuli for human autonomic responses. *Journal of Abnormal Psychology, 84*, 41–45.

Olds, J. (1956) Pleasure centres in the brain. *Scientific American, October*, 105–106.

Olds, J. (1958) Self-stimulation of the brain. *Science, 127*, 315–23.

Olds, J. & Milner, P. (1954) Positive reinforcement produced by electrical stimulation of the septal area and other regions of the rat brain. *Journal of Comparative & Physiological Psychology, 47*, 419–427.

Oleson, J. (1996) Psychological profiling: Does it actually work? *Forensic Update, 46*, 11–14.

Oliner, S.P. & Oliner, P.M. (1988) *The Altruistic Personality. Rescuers of Jews in Nazi Europe*. New York: Free Press.

Olson, J.M. & Ross, M. (1988) False feedback about placebo effectiveness: Consequences for the misattribution of speech activity. *Journal of Experimental Social Psychology, 24*, 275–291.

Onishi, K.H. & Baillargeon, R. (2005) Do 15-month-old infants understand false beliefs? *Science, 308*(5719), 255–258.

Ono, T., Squire, L.R., Raichle, M.E., Perrett, D.I. & Fukuda, M. (eds) (1993) *Brain Mechanisms of Perception and Memory: From Neurons to Behaviour.* New York: Oxford University Press.

Operario, D. & Fiske, S.T. (2004) Stereotypes: Content, structures, processes, and context. In M.B. Brewer & M. Hewstone (eds) *Social Cognition*. Oxford: Blackwell Publishing.

Orne, M.T. (1962) On the social psychology of the psychological experiment: With particular reference to demand characteristics and their implications. *American Psychologist, 17*, 776–783.

Orne, M.T. & Holland, C.C. (1968) On the ecological validity of laboratory deceptions. *International Journal of Psychiatry, 6*, 282–293.

Ornstein, R. (1975) *The Psychology of Consciousness*. Harmondsworth: Penguin.

Ornstein, R. (1986) *The Psychology of Consciousness* (2nd revised edition). Harmondsworth: Penguin.

Osgood, C.E., Suci, G.J. & Tannenbaum, P.H. (1957) *The Measurement of Meaning*. Urbana: University of Illinois Press.

Oswald, I. (1966) *Sleep*. Harmondsworth: Penguin.

Oswald, I. (1974) *Sleep* (2nd edition). Harmondsworth: Penguin.

Oswald, K.D., Murdaugh, D.L., King, V.L. & Boqqiano, M.M. (2011) Motivation for palatable food despite consequences in an animal model of binge eating. *International Journal of Eating Disorders, 44*(3), 203–211.

Otten, C.A., Penner, L.A. & Waugh, G. (1988) That's what friends are for: The determinants of psychological helping. *Journal of Social & Clinical Psychology, 7*, 34–41.

Owen, A.M. & Coleman, M.R. (2008) Functional Neuroimaging of the vegetative state. *Nature Reviews Neuroscience, 9*, 235–243.

Owen, A.M., Coleman, M.R., Boly, M. et al. (2006) Detecting awareness in the vegetative state. *Science, 313*, 1402.

Owen, A.M., Coleman, M.R., Boly, M. et al. (2007) Response to comments on Owen et al. [as above]. *Science, 315*, 1221c.

Oxendine, J.B. (1970) Emotional arousal and motor performance. *Quest, 13*, 23–30.

Ozegovic, D., Carroll, L.J. & Cassidy, J.D. (2009) Does expecting mean achieving? The association between expecting to return to work and recovery in whiplash-associated disorders: a population-based prospective cohort study. *European Spine Journal, 18*(6), 893–899.

Ozonoff, S., Pennington, B.F. & Rogers, S.J. (1991) Executive function deficits in high-functioning autistic children: Relationship to the theory of mind. *Journal of Child Psychology & Psychiatry, 32*, 1081–1106.

Packard, V. (1972) *A Nation of Strangers*. New York: David McKay Co.

Pagel, M. (1995) Speaking your mind. *Times Higher*, 7 July, 17–18.

Paik, H. & Comstock, G. (1994) The effects of television violence on antisocial behaviour: A meta-analysis. *Communication Research, 21* (4), 516–546.

Palermo, D.S. (1971) Is a scientific revolution taking place in psychology? *Psychological Review, 76*, 241–263.

Palmer, B., Macfarlane, G., Afzal, C. et al. (2007) Acculturation and the prevalence of pain amongst South Asian minority ethnic groups in the UK. *Rheumatology, 46*, 1009–1014.

Panskepp, J. & Burgdorf, J. (2003) 'Laughing' rats and the evolutionary antecedents of human joy? *Physiological Behaviour, 79*(3), 533–547.

Papineau, D. (2007) Caveman conversations. *Independent*, 5 October, 23.

Parke, R.D., Berkowitz, L., Leyens, J.P., West, S.G. & Sebastian, R.J. (1977) Some effects of violent and non-violent movies on the behaviour of juvenile delinquents. In L. Berkowitz (ed.) *Advances in Experimental Social Psychology, Volume 10*. New York: Academic Press.

Parker, E.S., Cahill, L. & McGaugh, J.L. (2006) A case of unusual autobiographical remembering. *Neurocase, 12* (1), 35–49.

Parkes, C.M. (1993) Bereavement as a psychosocial transition: Processes of adaptation to change. In M.S. Stroebe, W. Stroebe & R.O. Hansson (eds) *Handbook of Bereavement: Theory, Research and Intervention*. New York: Cambridge University Press.

Parkes, C.M. (1995) Attachment and bereavement. In T. Lundin (ed.) *Grief and Bereavement: Proceedings from the Fourth International Conference on Grief and Bereavement in Contemporary Society, Stockholm, 1994*. Stockholm: Swedish Association for Mental Health.

Parkes, C.M. (2006) *Love and Loss: The Roots of Grief and its Complications*. London: Routledge.

Parkes, C.M. (2014) On the psychology of extremism. In C.M. Parkes (ed.) *Responses to Terrorism*. Hove, East Sussex: Routledge.

Parkes, C.M. & Weiss, R.S. (1983) *Recovery from Bereavement*. New York: Basic Books.

Parkin, A.J. (1987) *Memory and Amnesia: An Introduction*. Oxford: Blackwell.

Parkin, A.J. (1993) *Memory: Phenomena, Experiment and Theory*. Oxford: Blackwell.

Parkin, A.J. (2000) *Essential Cognitive Psychology*. Hove: Psychology Press.

Parkin, A.J., Lewinson, J. & Folkard, S. (1982) The influence of emotion on immediate and delayed retention: Levinger and Clark reconsidered. *British Journal of Psychology, 73*, 389–393.

Parkinson, B. (1987) Emotion – cognitive approaches. In H. Beloff & A.M. Colman (eds) *Psychology Survey, No. 6*. Leicester: British Psychological Society.

Parkinson, B. (2008) Social perception and attribution. In M. Hewstone, W. Stroebe & K. Jonas (eds) *Introduction to Social Psychology: A European Perspective* (4th edition). Oxford: BPS Blackwell.

Parkinson, B. (2012) Social perception and attribution. In M. Hewstone, W. Stroebe & K. Jonas (eds) *Introduction to Social Psychology* (5th edition). BPS Blackwell.

Parkinson, B. & Simons, G. (2009) Affecting others: Social appraisal and emotion contagion in everyday decision-making. *Personality & Social Psychology Bulletin, 35*, 1071–1084.

Parrott, A. (2008) Drug taking – for better or for worse? *The Psychologist, 21*(11), 924–927.

Parrott, W.G. (2004) The nature of emotion. In M.B. Brewer & M. Hewstone (eds) *Emotion and Motivation*. Oxford: Blackwell Publishing.

Patterson, C. (1995) Lesbian mothers, gay fathers, and their children. In A.R. D'Augelli & C.J. Patterson (eds) *Lesbian, Gay, and Bisexual Identities Over the Lifespan: Psychological Perspectives*. New York: Oxford University Press.

Patterson, F.G. (1978) The gestures of a gorilla: Language acquisition in another pongid. *Brain & Language, 5*, 72–97.

Patterson, F.G. (1980) Innovative uses of language by a gorilla: A case study. In K. Nelson (ed.) *Children's Language, Volume 2*. New York: Gardner Press.

Paul, G.L. (1966) *Insight Versus Desensitisation in Psychotherapy: An Experiment in Anxiety Reduction*. Stanford University Press.

Paul, G.L. & Lentz, R.J. (1977) *Psychosocial Treatment of Chronic Mental Patients: Milieu Versus Social Learning Programs*. Cambridge, MA: Harvard University Press.

Paul, G.L. & Menditto, A.A. (1992) Effectiveness of inpatient treatment programs for mentally ill adults in public psychiatric facilities. *Applied & Preventative Psychology: Current Scientific Perspectives, 1*, 41–63.

Pavlov, I.P. (1927) *Conditioned Reflexes*. Oxford University Press.

Payne, D. (2000) Shock study triggers call to ban ageist slur. *Nursing Times, 96* (18), 13.

Payne, S., Swami, V. & Stanistreet, D. (2008) The social construction of gender and its impact on suicidal behaviour. *Journal of Men's Health and Gender, 5*(1), 23–35.

Peace, S., Wahl, H.-W., Mollenkopf, H. & Oswald, F. (2007) Environment and ageing. In J. Bond, S. Peace, F. Dittmann-Kohli & G. Westerhof (eds) *Ageing in Society* (3rd edition). London: Sage.

Pearson, P. (1998) *When She Was Bad: How Women Get Away With Murder*. London: Virago.

Peck, D. & Whitlow, D. (1975) *Approaches to Personality Theory*. London: Methuen.

Peek, L. (2000) One in six girls now reaches puberty aged 8. *The Times*, 19 June, 3.

Peel, E. & Clarke, V. (eds) (2005) Critiquing psychology: A reappraisal of The Social Construction of Lesbianism. *Lesbian & Gay Psychology Review 6* (2), July (special issue).

Peele, S. (1989) *The Diseasing of America: Addiction Treatment Out of Control*. Lexington, MA: Lexington Books.

Pendry, L. (2008) Social cognition. In M. Hewstone, W. Stroebe & K. Jonas (eds) *Introduction to Social Psychology: A European Perspective* (4th edition). Oxford: BPS Blackwell.

Pendry, L. (2012) Social Cognition. In M. Hewstone, W. Stroebe & K. Jonas (eds) *Introduction to Social Psychology* (5th edition). BPS Blackwell.

Penfield, W. (1947) Some observations on the cerebral cortex of man. *Proceedings of the Royal Society, 134*, 349.

Penny, G. (1996) Health psychology. In H. Coolican (ed.) *Applied Psychology*. London: Hodder & Stoughton.

Penrose, R. (1987) Minds, machines and mathematics. In C. Blakemore & S. Greenfield (eds) *Mindwaves*. Oxford: Blackwell.

Penrose, R. (1990) *The Emperor's New Mind*. Oxford University Press.

Penton-Voak, I.S., Pound, N., Little, A.C. & Perrett, D.I. (2006) Personality judgements from natural and composite facial images: More evidence for a 'kernel of truth' in social perception. *Social Cognition, 24* (5), 607–640.

Perret, D.J., May, K.A. & Yoshikawa, S. (1994) Facial shape and judgements of female attractiveness. *Nature, 368*, 239–242.

Perrin, S. & Spencer, C. (1981) Independence or conformity in the Asch experiment as a reflection of cultural and situational factors. *British Journal of Social Psychology, 20*, 205–209.

Perry, D.G. & Bussey, K. (1979) The social learning theory of sex differences: Imitation is alive and well. *Journal of Personality & Social Psychology, 37*, 1699–1712.

Perry, D.G. & Bussey, K. (1984) *Social Development*. Englewood Cliffs, NJ: Prentice-Hall.

Pervin, L.A. & Lewis, M. (1978) *Perspectives in Interactional Psychology*. New York: Plenum Press.

Petersen, A.C., Sarigiani, P.A. & Kennedy, R.E. (1991) Adolescent depression: Why more girls? *Journal of Youth & Adolescence, 20*, 247–271.

Peterson, A.C. & Crockett, L. (1985) Pubertal timing and grade effects on adjustment. *Journal of Youth and Adolescence, 14*, 191–206.

Peterson, C. & Seligman, M.E.P. (1984) Causal explanations as a risk factor for depression: Theory and evidence. *Psychological Review, 91*, 347–374.

Peterson, L.R. & Peterson, M.J. (1959) Short-term retention of individual items. *Journal of Experimental Psychology, 58*, 193–198.

Petitto, L.A., Holowka, S., Sergio, L.E. & Ostry, D. (2001) Language rhythms in baby hand movements. *Nature, 413*, 35–36.

Petkova, B. (1995) New views on the self: Evil women – witchcraft or PMS? *Psychology Review, 2* (1), 16–19.

Pettigrew, T.F. (1959) Regional difference in antinegro prejudice. *Journal of Abnormal & Social Psychology, 59*, 28–56.

Pettigrew, T.F. (1971) *Racially Separate or Together*? New York: McGraw-Hill.

Pettigrew, T.F. (1997) Generalized intergroup contact effects on prejudice. *Personality & Social Psychology Bulletin, 23*, 173–185.

Pettigrew, T.F. (1998) Intergroup contact theory. In J.T. Spence, J.M. Darley & D.J. Foss (eds) *Annual Review of Psychology, Volume 49*. Palo Alto, CA: Annual Reviews.

Pettigrew, T.F. & Meertens, R.W. (1995) Subtle and blatant prejudice in western Europe. *European Journal of Social Psychology, 25*, 57–75.

Pettigrew, T.F. & Tropp, L.R. (2000) Does intergroup contact reduce prejudice? Recent meta-analytic findings. In S. Oskamp (ed.) *Reducing Prejudice and Discrimination: The Claremont Symposium on Applied Social Psychology*. Mahwah, NJ: Lawrence Erlbaum.

Pettigrew, T.F. & Tropp, L.R. (2006) A meta-analytic test of intergroup contact theory. *Journal of Personality & Social Psychology, 90*, 751–783.

Petty, R.E. & Cacioppo, J.T. (1981) *Attitudes and Persuasion: Classic and Contemporary Approaches*. Dubuque, IA: Brown.

Petty, R.E. & Cacioppo, J.T. (1986) The elaboration likelihood model of persuasion. In L. Berkowitz (ed.) *Advances in Experimental Social Psychology, Volume 19*. New York: Academic Press.

Petty, R.E., Cacioppo, J.T. & Goldmna, R. (1981) Personal involvement as a determinant of argument-based persuasion. *Journal of Personality & Social Psychology, 41*, 847–855.

Petty, R.E. & Wegener, D.T. (1999) The elaboration likelihood model: Current status and controversies. In S. Chaiken & Y. Trope (eds) *Dual-process Theories in Social Psychology*. New York: Guilford Press.

Phelps, E.A. & Thomas, L.A. (2003) Race, behaviour and the brain: The role of neuroimaging in understanding complex social behaviours. *Political Psychology, 24*, 747–758.

Phelps, E.A., O'Connor, K.J., Cunningham, W.A., Funayama, E.S., Gatenby, J.C., Gore, J.C. & Banaji, M.R. (2000) Performance on indirect measures of race evaluation predicts amygdala activation. *Journal of Cognitive Neuroscience, 12*, 729–738.

Phillips, D.P. (1986) Natural experiments on the effects of mass media violence on fatal aggression: Strengths and weaknesses of a new approach. In L. Berkowitz (ed.) *Advances in Experimental Social Psychology, Volume 19*. New York: Academic Press.

Phillips, H. (2000) They do it with mirrors. *New Scientist, 166*(2243), 26–29.

Phillips, H. (2004a) The cell that makes us human. *New Scientist, 182*(2452), 32–35.

Phillips, H. (2004b) The genius machine. *New Scientist, 182*(2441), 30–33.

Phillips, J.L. (1969) *The Origins of Intellect: Piaget's Theory*. San Francisco: W.H. Freeman.

Piaget, J. (1932) *The Moral Judgement of the Child*. London: Routledge & Kegan Paul.

Piaget, J. (1950) *The Psychology of Intelligence*. London: Routledge & Kegan Paul.

Piaget, J. (1951) *Play, Dreams and Imitation in Children*. London: RKP.

Piaget, J. (1952) *The Child's Conception of Number.* London: Routledge & Kegan Paul.

Piaget, J. (1970) Piaget's theory. In P.H. Mussen (ed.) *Carmichael's Manual of Child Psychology, Volume* 1 (3rd edition). New York: Wiley.

Piaget, J. (1973) *The Child's Conception of the World.* London: Paladin.

Piaget, J. & Inhelder, B. (1956) *The Child's Conception of Space.* London: RKP.

Piaget, J. & Inhelder, B. (1969) *The Psychology of the Child.* London: Routledge & Kegan Paul.

Picard, F. & Craig, A.D. (2009) Ecstatic epileptic seizures: A potential window on the neural basis for human self-awareness. *Epilepsy and Behaviour, 16*(3), 539–546.

Pickering. A.D., Cooper, A.J., Smillie, L.D. & Corr, P.J. et al. (2013) On the shoulders of giants. *The Psychologist, 26*(1), 22–25.

Pike, A. & Plomin, R. (1999) Genetics and development. In D. Messer & S. Millar (eds) *Exploring Developmental Psychology: From Infancy to Adolescence.* London: Arnold.

Pike, K.L. (1954) Emic and etic standpoints for the description of behaviour. In K.L. Pike (ed.) *Language in Relation to a Unified Theory of the Structure of Human Behaviour.* Glendale, CA: Summer Institute of Linguistics.

Pilcher, H. (2013) Beyond nature and nurture. *New Scientist, 219*(2932), 44–47.

Pilgrim, D. (2000) Psychiatric diagnosis: More questions than answers. *The Psychologist, 13* (6), 302–305.

Piliavin, J.A. & Charng, H.W. (1990) Altruism: A review of recent theory and research. *American Sociological Review, 16,* 27–65.

Piliavin, J.A. & Piliavin, I.M. (1972) Effects of blood on reactions to a victim. *Journal of Personality & Social Psychology, 23,* 353–362.

Piliavin, I.M., Rodin, J. & Piliavin, J.A. (1969) Good Samaritanism: An underground phenomenon? *Journal of Personality & Social Psychology, 13,* 289–299.

Piliavin, I.M., Piliavin, J.A. & Rodin, S. (1975) Costs, diffusion and the stigmatised victim. *Journal of Personality & Social Psychology, 32,* 429–438.

Piliavin, J.A., Dovidio, J.F., Gaertner, S.L. & Clark, R.D. (1981) *Emergency Intervention.* New York: Academic Press.

Pine, K. (1999) Theories of cognitive development. In D. Messer & S. Millar (eds) *Exploring Developmental Psychology: From Infancy to Adolescence.* London: Arnold.

Pinel, J.P.J. (1993) *Biopsychology* (2nd edition). Boston: Allyn & Bacon.

Pineo, P.C. (1961) Disenchantment in the later years of marriage. *Journal of Marriage & Family Living, 23,* 3–11.

Pinker, S. (1994) *The Language Instinct: How the Mind Creates Language.* New York: Morrow.

Pinker, S. (1997a) *How the Mind Works.* New York: Norton.

Pinker, S. (1997b) Why they kill their newborns. *New York Times Magazine,* 2 November, 52–54.

Piven, J. & Folstein, S. (1994) The genetics of autism. In M. Bauman & T. Kemper (eds) *The Neurobiology of Autism.* Baltimore, MD: Johns Hopkins University Press.

Pleck, J.H. (1999) Balancing work and family. *Scientific American Presents, 10*(2), 38–43.

Plomin, R. (1988) The nature and nurture of cognitive abilities. In R.J. Sternberg (ed.) *Advances in the Psychology of Human Intelligence, Volume 4.* Hillsdale, NJ: Erlbaum.

Plomin, R. (1994) *Genetics and Experience: The Interplay Between Nature and Nurture.* Thousand Oaks, CA: Sage.

Plomin, R. (1995) Genetics and children's experiences in the family. *Journal of Child Psychology & Psychiatry, 36,* 33–68.

Plomin, R. (1996) Nature and nurture. In M.R. Merrens & G.C. Brannigan (eds) *The Developmental Psychologists: Research Adventures across the Life Span.* New York: McGraw-Hill.

Plomin, R. (1999) Genetics and general cognitive ability. *Nature, 402,* C25–C29.

Plomin, R. & DeFries, J.C. (1998) The genetics of cognitive abilities and disabilities. *Scientific American, May,* 62–69.

Plomin, R. & Thompson, R. (1987) Life-span developmental behavioural genetics. In P.B. Baltes, D.L. Featherman & R.M. Lerner (eds) *Life-Span Development and Behaviour, Volume 8.* Hillsdale, NJ: Erlbaum.

Plomin, R., DeFries, J.C. & Loehlin, J.C. (1977) Genotype–environment interaction and correlation in the analysis of human behaviour. *Psychological Bulletin, 84,* 309–322.

Plutchik, R. & Ax, A.F. (1967) A critique of determinants of emotional state by Schachter and Singer (1962). *Psychophysiology, 4,* 79–82.

Pollitt, E. & Gorman, K.S. (1994) Nutritional deficiencies as developmental risk factors. In C.A. Nelson (ed.) *The Minnesota Symposia on Child Development, Volume 27.* Hillsdale, NJ: Erlbaum.

Popper, K. (1959) *The Logic of Scientific Discovery.* London: Hutchinson.

Popper, K. (1972) *Objective Knowledge: An Evolutionary Approach.* Oxford University Press.

Posner, M.I. (1980) Orienting of attention. *Quarterly Journal of Experimental Psychology, 32* (1), 3–25.

Posner, M.I. & Petersen, S.E. (1990) The attention system of the human brain. *Annual Review of Neuroscience, 13,* 25–42.

Posner, M.I., Nissen, M.J. & Ogden, W.C. (1978) Attended and unattended processing modes: The role of set for spatial location. In H.L. Pick & I.J. Saltzman (eds) *Modes of Perceiving and Processing Information.* Hillsdale, NJ: Erlbaum.

Posner, M.I., Snyder, C.R.R. & Davidson, B.J. (1980) Attention and the detection of signals. *Journal of Experimental Psychology: General, 109,* 160–174.

Potter, J. (1996) Attitudes, social representations and discursive psychology. In M. Wetherell (ed.) *Identities, Groups and Social Issues.* London: Sage, in association with the Open University.

Potter, J. & Wetherell, M.S. (1987) *Discourse and Social Psychology: Beyond Attitudes and Behaviour.* London: Sage.

Povinelli, D.J. (1998) …Maybe not. *Scientific American Presents, 9*(4), 67, 72–75.

Powell, G.E. (1995) Clinical and counselling psychology. In A.M. Colman (ed.) *Applications of Psychology.* London: Longman.

Powell, S.D. (1999) Autism. In D. Messer & S. Millar (eds) *Exploring Developmental Psychology: From Infancy to Adolescence.* London: Arnold.

Pratkanis, A. & Aronson, E. (2001) *Age of Propaganda: Everyday Uses and Abuses of Persuasion.* New York: Freeman.

Pratto, F. (1999) The puzzle of continuing group inequality: Piecing together psychological, social, and cultural forces in social dominance theory. In M. Zanna (ed.) *Advances in Experimental Social Psychology, Volume 31*. San Diego, CA: Academic Press.

Pratto, F., Sidanius, J., Stallworth, L.M. & Malle, B.F. (1994) Social dominance orientation: A personality variable predicting social and political attitudes. *Journal of Personality & Social Psychology*, *67*(4), 741–763.

Premack, D. (1971) Language in chimpanzee? *Science, 172*, 808–822.

Premack, D. & Woodruff, G. (1978) Does the chimpanzee have a theory of mind? *Behavioural & Brain Sciences, 4*, 515–526.

Price, R.A. & Vandenberg, S.G. (1979) Matching for physical attractiveness in married couples. *Personality & Social Psychology Bulletin, 5*, 398–400.

Price, W.F. & Crapo, R.H. (1999) *Cross-Cultural Perspectives in Introductory Psychology* (3rd edition). Belmont, CA: Wadsworth Publishing Company.

Price-Williams, D. (1966) Cross-cultural studies. In B.M. Foss (ed.) *New Horizons in Psychology, 1*. Harmondsworth: Penguin.

Prince, J. & Hartnett, O. (1993) From 'psychology constructs the female' to 'females construct psychology'. *Feminism & Psychology, 3* (2), 219–224.

Pring, L. & Hermelin, B. (1997) Naïve savant talent and acquired skill. *Autism, 1*, 199–214.

Pringle, Kellmer, M. (1986) *The Needs of Children* (3rd edition). London: Hutchinson.

Prins, H. (1995) *Offenders, Deviants or Patients?* (2nd edition). London: Routledge.

Prioleau, L., Murdock, M. & Brody, N. (1983) An analysis of psychotherapy versus placebo studies. *Behaviour & Brain Sciences, 6*, 273–310.

Prior, H., Schwarz, A. & Gunturkun, O. (2008) Mirror-induced behavior in the magpie (*Pica pica*): Evidence of self-recognition. *PLoS Biology, 6*(8):e202.

Putnam, R. (2000) *Bowling Alone: The Collapse and Revival of American Community*. New York: Simon & Schuster.

Quattrone, G.A. (1986) On the perception of a group's variability. In S. Worchel & W. Austin (eds) *The Psychology of Intergroup Relations, Volume 2*. New York: Nelson-Hall.

Quiery, N. (1998) Parenting and the family. In K. Trew & J. Kremer (eds) *Gender & Psychology*. London: Arnold.

Quinn, P.C., Uttley, L., Lee, K. et al. (2008) Infants' preference for female faces occurs for same – but not other – race faces. *British Journal of Neuropsychology, 2*, 15–26.

Quinton, D. & Rutter, M. (1988) *Parental Breakdown: The Making and Breaking of Intergenerational Links*. London: Gower.

Quiroga, R.Q., Kreiman, G., Koch, C. & Fried, I. (2008) Sparse but not 'Grandmother-cell' coding in the medial temporal lobe. *Trends in Cognitive Science, 12*(3), 87–91.

Rabbitt, P.M.A. (1967) Ignoring irrelevant information. *American Journal of Psychology, 80*, 1–13.

Rabbitt, P.M.A. (1980) A fresh look at reaction times in old age. In D.G. Stein (ed.) *The Psychology of Ageing: Problems and Perspectives*. London: Elsevier.

Rabbitt, P.M.A. (1993) Does it all go together when it goes? *Quarterly Journal of Experimental Psychology, 46A*, 385–434.

Rabbitt, P. (2006) Tales of the unexpected: 25 years of cognitive gerontology. *The Psychologist, 19*(11), 674–676.

Rachman, S. (1977) The conditioning theory of fear-acquisition: A critical examination. *Behaviour Research & Therapy in Personality, 15*, 375–387.

Rachman, S. (1993) Obsessions, responsibility and guilt. *Behaviour Research & Therapy, 31*, 793–802.

Rachman, S. & Hodgson, R. (1980) *Obsessions and Compulsions*. New York: Prentice-Hall.

Rachman, S. & Wilson, G. (1980) *The Effects of Psychological Therapy*. Oxford: Pergamon.

Radford, J. (1980) Intelligence. In J. Radford & E. Govier (eds) *A Textbook of Psychology*. London: Sheldon Press.

Radke-Yarrow, M., McCann, K., DeMulder, E., Belmont, B., Martinez, P. & Richardson, D.T. (1995) Attachment in the context of high-risk conditions. *Development and Psychopathology, 7*, 247–265.

Rafal, R.D. & Posner, M.I. (1987) Deficits in human visual spatial attention following thalamic lesions. *Proceedings of the National Academy of Sciences, 84*, 7349–7353.

Raine, A., Buchsbaum, M. & LaCasse, L. (1997) Brain abnormalities in murderers indicated by positron emission tomography. *Biological Psychiatry, 42*, 495–508.

Raine, A., Lencz, T., Bihrle, S., LaCasse, L. & Colletti, P. (2000) Reduced prefrontal grey matter violence and reduced autonomic activity in antisocial personality disorder. *Archives of General Psychiatry, 57*(2), 119–127.

Raine, I., Ishikawa, S.S., Arce, E., Lencz, T., Knuth, K.H., Bihrle, H., LaCasse, L. & Colletti, P. (2004) Hippocampal structural asymmetry in unsuccessful psychopaths. *Biological Psychiatry, 55*(2), 119–127.

Raley, Y. (2006) Electric thoughts? *Scientific American Mind, 17*(2), 76–81.

Ramachandran, V.S. (1985) Apparent motion of subjective surfaces. *Perception, 14*, 127–134.

Ramachandran, V.S. (1994) Phantom limbs, neglect syndromes, repressed memories, and Freudian psychology. *International Review of Neurobiology, 37*, 291–333.

Ramachandran, V.S (1998) The Unbearable Likeness of Being. *Independent on Sunday*, 22 November, 22–24.

Ramachandran, V.S. (2011) *The Tell-Tale Brain: Unlocking the Mystery of Human Nature*. London: Windmill Books.

Ramachandran, V.S. & Anstis, S.M. (1986) The perception of apparent motion. *Scientific American, 254*, 80–87.

Ramachandran, V.S & Blakeslee, S. (1998) *Phantoms in the Brain*. London: Fourth Estate.

Ramachandran, V.S. & Hubbard, E.M. (2003) Hearing colours, tasting shapes. *Scientific American, 288*(5), 42–49.

Ramachandran, V.S. & Rogers-Ramachandran, D. (2004) Illusions. *Scientific American Special: Mind, 14*(1), 100–C3.

Ramachandran, V.S. & Rogers-Ramachandran, D. (2009) Half a World. *Scientific American Mind, 20*(1), 18–20.

Ramachandran, V.S. & Rogers-Ramachandran, D. (2010) Hey, is that me over there? *Scientific American Mind, 21*(2), 18–20.

Ramey, C.T. & Ramey, S. (1992) Effective early intervention. *Mental Retardation, 30*, 337–345.

Ramsay, R. & de Groot, W. (1977) A further look at bereavement. Paper presented at EATI conference, Uppsala. Cited in P.E. Hodgkinson (1980) Treating abnormal grief in the bereaved. *Nursing Times*, 17 January, 126–128.

Rana, T.A. & Rana, A.W. (2013) Post-traumatic over-optimism? *The Psychologist, 26*(1), 5.

Rao, K.R. & Palmer, J. (1987) The anomaly called psi: Recent research and criticism. *Behaviour & Brain Sciences, 10*, 539–643.

Raphael, B. (1984) *The Anatomy of Bereavement*. London: Hutchinson.

Rassool, G.H. & Winnington, J. (1993) Using psychoactive drugs. *Nursing Times, 89*, 38–40.

Read, J., Cartwright, C. & Gibson, K. (2014) Adverse emotional and interpersonal effects reported by 1829 New Zealanders while taking antidepressants. *Psychiatry Research, 216*(1), 67–73.

Reason, J. (1979) Actions not as planned: The price of automatisation. In G. Underwood & R. Stevens (eds) *Aspects of Consciousness: Volume 1, Psychological Issues*. London: Academic Press.

Read, J.and Bentall, R. (2010) The effectiveness of ECT. *Epidemiology & Psychiatric Sciences, 19*, 333–347.

Read, J., Bentall, R., Johnstone, L., Fosse, R. & Bracken, P. (2013) Electroconvulsive therapy. In J. Read & J. Dillon (eds) *Psychological, Social and Biological Approaches to Psychosis*. London: ISPS/Routledge.

Reason, J. (1992) Cognitive underspecification: Its variety and consequences. In B.J. Baars (ed.) *Experimental Slips and Human Error: Exploring the Architecture of Volition*. New York: Plenum Press.

Reason, J. (2000) The Freudian slip revisited. *The Psychologist, 13*(12), 610–611.

Reason, J. & Mycielska, K. (1982) *Absentmindedness: The Psychology of Mental Lapses and Everyday Errors*. Englewood Cliffs, NJ: Prentice-Hall.

Rebok, G.W. (1987) *Life Span Cognitive Development*. New York: Holt, Rinehart & Winston.

Rechtschaffen, A., Bergmann, B.M., Everson, C.A., Kushida, C.A. & Gilliland, M.A. (1989a) Sleep deprivation in the rat: I. Conceptual issues. *Sleep, 12*, 1–4.

Rechtschaffen, A., Bergmann, B.M., Everson, C.A., Kushida, C.A. & Gilliland, M.A. (1989b) Sleep deprivation in the rat: X. Integration and discussion of the findings. *Sleep, 12*, 68–87.

Reddy, V. (1991) Playing with others' expectations: teasing and mucking about in the first year. In A. Whiten (ed.) *Natural Theories of Mind*. Oxford: Blackwell, 143–158.

Reddy, V. (2000) Coyness in early infancy. *Developmental Science, 3* (2), 186–192.

Reddy, V. (2003) On being the object of attention. *Trends in Cognitive Sciences, 7*, 397–402.

Reddy, V. (2007) Getting back to the rough ground: deception and social living. *Philosophical Transactions of the Royal Society of London B, 362*(1480), 621–637.

Reddy, V. (2008) *How Infants Know Minds*. Cambridge, MA: Harvard University Press.

Reddy, V., Williams, E. & Vaughan, A. (2002) Sharing humour and laughter in autism and Down's syndrome. *British Journal of Psychology, 93*, 219–42.

Regan, T. (2006) Sentience and rights. In J. Turner & J. D'Silva (eds) *Animals, Ethics and Trade: The Challenge of Animal Sentience*. London: Earthscan.

Regier, D.A., Narrow, W.E., Kuhl, E.A., & Kupfer, D.J. (2010) The conceptual development of DSM-V. *American Journal of Psychiatry, 166*, 645–655.

Reich, B. & Adcock, C. (1976) *Values, Attitudes and Behaviour Change*. London: Methuen.

Reichenberg, L.W. (2014) *DSM-5 Essentials: The Savvy Clinician's Guide to the Changes in Criteria*. Hoboken, NJ: Wiley.

Reicher, S.D. & Haslam, S.A. (2006) Rethinking the psychology of tyranny: The BBC prison experiment. *British Journal of Social Psychology, 45*, 1–40. (For further information about the BBC Prison Study, visit the official website at: www.bbcprisonstudy.org)

Reicher, S. & Haslam, S.A. (2011a) The shock of the old. *The Psychologist, 24*(9), 650–652.

Reicher, S. & Haslam, S.A. (2011b) After shock? Towards a social identity explanation of Milgram's 'obedience' studies. *British Journal of Social Psychology, 50*(1), 163–169.

Reicher, S.D., Haslam, S.A., Spears, R. & Reynolds, K.J. (2012) A social mind: The context of John Turner's work and its influence. *European Review of Social Psychology, 23*, 344–385.

Renzi, C., Schiavi, S., Carbon, C-C. et al (2013) Processing of featureal and configurational aspects of faces is lateralised in dorsolateral prefrontal cortex: A TMS study. *Neuroimage, 74*, 45–51.

Rescorla, R.A. (1968) Probability of shock in the presence and absence of CS in fear conditioning. *Journal of Comparative & Physiological Psychology, 66*, 1–5.

Resnick, L., Levine, J. & Teasley, S. (eds) (1991) *Perspectives on Socially Shared Cognition*. Washington, DC: American Psychological Association.

Rest, J. (1983) Morality. In J.H. Flavell & E. Markman (eds) *Handbook of Child Psychology, Volume* 3. New York: Wiley.

Restle, F. (1957) Discrimination of cues in mazes: A resolution of the 'place versus response' question. *Psychological Review, 64*, 217–228.

Revill, J. (2006) Sleep: Our new obsession. *Observer*, 9 April, 23–25.

Revonso, A. (2000) The reinterpretation of dreams: An evolutionary hypothesis of the function of dreaming. *Behavioural & Brain Sciences, 23*, 877–901, 914–1018, 1083–1121.

Rheingold, H.L. (1961) The effect of environmental stimulation upon social and exploratory behaviour in the human infant. In B.M. Foss (ed.) *Determinants of Infant Behaviour, Volume 1*. London: Methuen.

Rice, M. (1989) Children's language acquisition. *American Psychologist, 44*, 149–156.

Richards, D. (2002) Behaviour therapy. In W. Dryden (ed.) *Handbook of Individual Therapy* (4th edition). London: Sage.

Richards, G. (1996a) Arsenic and old race. *Observer Review*, 5 May, 4.

Richards, G. (1996b) *Putting Psychology in its Place*. London: Routledge.

Richardson, K. (1991) *Understanding Intelligence*. Milton Keynes: Open University Press.

Richardson, K. (1998) *The Origins of Human Potential*. New York: Routledge.

Richler, J. (2013) Is it possible to recover from autism? *Scientific American Mind, 24*(3), 26–27.

Ridley, M. (1993) *The Red Queen: Sex and the Evolution of Human Nature*. London: Penguin.

Ridley, M. (2003) Genes are so liberating. *New Scientist, 178* (2395), 38–39.

Riesen, A.H. (1947) The development of visual perception in man and chimpanzee. *Science, 106*, 107–108.

Riesen, A.H. (1965) Effects of early deprivation of photic stimulation. In S. Oster & R. Cook (eds) *The Biosocial Basis of Mental Retardation*. Baltimore, MD: Johns Hopkins University Press.

Rivers, I. (2001) The bullying of sexual minorities at school: Its nature and long-term correlates. *Educational & Child Psychology, 18* (1), 32–46.

Rivers, W.H.R. (1901) Vision. In A.C. Haddon (ed.) *Reports of the Cambridge Anthropological Expedition to the Torres Straits, Volume 2, Part 1*. Cambridge University Press.

Roberts, R. & Groome, D. (2001) *Parapsychology: The Science of Unusual Experience*. London: Arnold.

Robertson, D., Davies, I.R.L. & Davidoff, J. (2000) Colour categories are not universal: Replications & new evidence from a Stone-age culture. *Journal of Experimental Psychology: General, 129*, 369–398.

Robertson, D., Davidoff, J., Davies, I.R.L. & Shapiro, L.R. (2005) Colour categories: Evidence for the cultural relativity hypothesis. *Cognitive Psychology, 50*, 378–411.

Robertson, J. & Robertson J. (1967–73) *Film Series, Young Children in Brief Separation: No 3 (1969): John, 17 months, 9 days, in a Residential Nursery*. London: Tavistock.

Robinson, A. (2004) Animal rights, anthropomorphism and traumatised fish. *Philosophy Now, 46*, 20–22.

Robinson, A. (2011) *Genius: A Very Short Introduction*. Oxford: Oxford University Press.

Robinson, J.O. (1972) *The Psychology of Visual Illusions*. London: Hutchinson.

Robinson, L. (1997) Black adolescent identity and the inadequacies of western psychology. In J. Roche & S. Tucker (eds) *Youth in Society*. London: Sage.

Robinson, O.C. & Wright, G.R.T. (2013) The prevalence, types and perceived outcomes of crisis episodes in early adulthood and midlife: A structured retrospective-autobiographical study. *International Journal of Behavioural Development* doi:10.1177/0165025413492464

Robson, D. (2013) Old schooled. *New Scientist, 218*(2918), 32–35.

Rockman, H. (1994) Matchmaker matchmaker make me a match: The art and conventions of Jewish arranged marriages. *Sexual & Marital Therapy, 9*, 277–284.

Rodriguez, T. (2103) Taking the bad with the good. *Scientific American Mind, 24*(2), 26–27.

Rogers. C.R. (1951) *Client-centred Therapy – Its Current Practices, Implications and Theory*. Boston: Houghton Mifflin.

Rogers, C.R. (1959) A theory of therapy, personality and interpersonal relationships as developed in the client-centred framework. In S. Koch (ed.) *Psychology: A Study of Science, Volume III, Formulations of the Person and the Social Context*. New York: McGraw-Hill.

Rogers, C.R. (1983) *Freedom to Learn for the '80s*. Columbus, OH: Charles Merrill.

Rogers, L.J. & Andrew, R.J. (2002) *Comparative Vertebrate Lateralisation*. Cambridge: Cambridge University Press.

Rogoff, B. (1990) *Apprenticeship in Thinking: Cognitive Development in Social Context*. New York: Oxford University Press.

Rogoff, B. & Morelli, G. (1989) Perspectives on children's development from cultural psychology. *American Psychologist, 44*, 343–348.

Rokeach, M. (1960) *The Open and Closed Mind*. New York: Basic Books.

Rokeach, M. (1968) *Beliefs, Attitudes and Values*. San Francisco: Jossey-Bass.

Rollie, S.S. & Duck, S. (2005) Divorce and the dissolution of romantic relationships: Stage models and their limitations. In M.A. Fine & J.H. Harvey (eds) *Handbook of Divorce and Relationship Dissolution*. New York: Psychology Press.

Rollman, G.B. (1998) Culture and pain. In S.S. Kazarian & D.R. Evans (eds) *Cultural Clinical Psychology: Theory, Research, and Practice*. New York: Oxford University Press.

Rolls, E.T. & Rolls, B.J. (1982) Brain mechanisms involved in feeding. In L.M. Barker (ed.) *The Psychobiology of Human Food Selection*. Westport, CT: AVI Publishing Company.

Rolls, G. (2007) *Taking the Proverbial: The Psychology of Proverbs and Sayings*. London: Chambers Harrap.

Rolls, G. (2010) *Classic Case Studies in Psychology* (2nd edition). London: Hodder Education.

Romme, M. & Escher, S. (2000) *Making sense of voices*. London: Mind.

Rorer, L.G. (1998) Attacking arrant nonsense forthrightly. *Contemporary Psychology, 43*, 597–600.

Rose, D.T., Abramson, L.Y., Hodulik, C.J., Haslberstadt, L. & Gaye, L. (1994) Heterogeneity of cognitive style among depressed inpatients. *Journal of Abnormal Psychology, 103*, 419–429.

Rose, S. (1992) *The Making of Memory: From Molecule to Mind*. London: Bantam Books.

Rose, S. (1997) *Lifelines: Biology, Freedom, Determinism*. Harmondsworth: Penguin.

Rose, S. (2000) Escaping evolutionary psychology. In H. Rose & S. Rose (eds) *Alas, Poor Darwin: Arguments Against Evolutionary Psychology*. London: Jonathan Cape.

Rose, S. (2003) *The Making of Memory: From Molecules to Mind* (revised edition). London: Vintage.

Rose, S. (2011) Human evolution and human psychology. *Psychology Review, 16*(3), 16–18.

Rose, S. (2013) Back to the classroom. *New Scientist, 220*(2940), 28–29.

Rose, S., Lewontin, R.C. & Kamin, L.J. (1984) *Not in Our Genes: Biology, Ideology and Human Nature*. Harmondsworth: Penguin.

Rose, S.A. & Blank, M. (1974) The potency of context in children's cognition: An illustration through conservation. *Child Development, 45*, 499–502.

Rosen, G.M. & Lilienfeld, S.O. (2008) Post-traumatic stress disorder: An empirical evaluation of core assumptions. *Clinical Psychology Review, 28*(5), 837–868.

Rosenberg, M.J. & Hovland, C.I. (1960) Cognitive, affective, and behavioural components of attitude. In M.J. Rosenberg, C.I. Hovland, W.J. McGuire, R.P. Abelson & J.W. Brehm (eds) *Attitude Organisation and Change: An Analysis of Consistency Among Attitude Components*. New Haven, CT: Yale University Press.

Rosenblatt, P.C. (1993) The social context of private feelings. In M.S. Stroebe, W. Stroebe & R.O. Hansson (eds) *Handbook of Bereavement: Theory, Research and Intervention*. New York: Cambridge University Press.

Rosenman, R.H., Brand, R.J., Jenkins, C.D. et al. (1975) Coronary heart disease in the Western Collaborative Group Study: Final follow-up experience of 8.5 years. *Journal of American Medical Association, 22*, 872–877.

Rosenhan, D.L. (1973) On being sane in insane places. *Science, 179*, 365–369.

Rosenhan, D.L. & Seligman, M.E. (1984) *Abnormal Psychology*. New York: Norton.

Rosenthal, R. (1966) *Experimenter Effects in Behavioural Research*. New York: Appleton-Century-Crofts.

Rosenthal, R. & Fode, K.L. (1963) The effects of experimenter bias on the performance of the albino rat. *Behavioural Science, 8*, 183–189.

Rosenthal, R. & Jacobson, L. (1968) *Pygmalion in the Classroom: Teacher Expectation and Pupils' Intellectual Development*. New York: Holt.

Rosenthal, R. & Lawson, R. (1964) A longitudinal study of the effects of experimenter bias on the operant learning of laboratory rats. *Journal of Psychiatric Research, 2*, 61–72.

Rosenthal, R. & Rosnow, R.L. (1966) *The Volunteer Subject*. New York: Wiley.

Ross, L. (1977) The intuitive psychologist and his shortcomings. In L. Berkowitz (ed.) *Advances in Experimental Social Psychology, Volume 10*. New York: Academic Press.

Ross, L. & Nisbett, R.E. (1991) *The Person and the Situation: Perspectives of Social Psychology*. New York: McGraw-Hill.

Ross, M. & Fletcher, G.J.O. (1985) Attribution and social perception. In G. Lindzey & E. Aronson (eds) *Handbook of Social Psychology, Volume 2* (3rd edition). New York: Random House.

Ross, M. & Newby-Clark, I.R. (1998) Constructing the past and future. *Social Cognition, 16*, 133–150.

Ross, P.E. (2004) Draining the language out of colour. *Scientific American, 290* (4), 24–25.

Ross, P.E. (2006) The expert mind. *Scientific American, 295* (2), 46–53.

Roth, A. & Fonagy, P. (2005) *What Works for Whom? A Critical Review of Psychotherapy Research* (2nd edition). New York: Guilford Press.

Roth, I. (1986) An introduction to object perception. In I. Roth & J.P. Frisby (eds) *Perception and Representation*. Milton Keynes: Open University Press.

Roth, I. (1995) Object recognition. In I. Roth & V. Bruce (eds) *Perception and Representation: Current Issues* (2nd edition). Buckingham: Open University Press.

Rothbart, M. & Park, B. (1986) On the confirmability and disconfirmability of trait concepts. *Journal of Personality & Social Psychology, 50*, 131–142.

Rothbart, M., Evans, M. & Fulero, S. (1979) Recall for confirming events: Memory processes and the maintenance of social stereotyping. *Journal of Experimental Social Psychology, 15*, 343–355.

Rotter, J. (1966) Generalised expectancies for internal versus external control of reinforcement. *Psychological Monographs, 30* (1), 1–26.

Roughgarden, J. (2004) The in-crowd. *New Scientist, 181* (2430), 36–39.

Rousseau, J.J. (1762) *Emile*. New York: Dutton, Everyman's Library. (Republished 1955.)

Rowson, J. & McGilchrist, I. (2013) *Divided Brain, Divided World: Why the best part of us struggles to be heard*. London: RSA.

Royal College of Psychiatrists (1987) *Drug Scenes: A Report on Drugs and Drug Dependence by the Royal College of Psychiatrists*. London: Gaskell.

Royal College of Psychiatrists (1995) *The ECT Handbook*. London: Royal College of Psychiatrists.

Royal College of Psychiatrists (1997) *ECT (Electroconvulsive Therapy). Patient Information Factsheet No. 7*. London: Royal College of Psychiatrists.

Royal Society (2011) *Neuroscience and the Law*. London: Royal Society.

Rozin, P., Lowery, L., Imada, S. & Haidt, J. (1999) The moral-emotion triad hypothesis: A mapping between three moral emotions (contempt, anger, disgust) and three moral ethics (community, autonomy, divinity). *Journal of Personality & Social Psychology, 76*, 574–586.

Rubin, E. (1915) *Synsoplevede Figurer*. Kobenhaun: Gyldendalske Boghandel.

Rubin, J.Z., Provenzano, F.J. & Luria, Z. (1974) The eye of the beholder: Parents' views on sex of newborns. *American Journal of Orthopsychiatry, 44*, 512–519.

Rubin, Z. (1973) *Liking and Loving*. New York: Holt, Rinehart & Winston.

Rubin, Z. & McNeil, E.B. (1983) The *Psychology of Being Human* (3rd edition). London: Harper & Row.

Ruble, D.N. (1984) Sex-role development. In M.C. Bornstein & M.E. Lamb (eds) *Developmental Psychology: An Advanced Text*. Hillsdale, NJ: Erlbaum.

Ruble, D.N. (1987) The acquisition of self-knowledge: A self-socialization perspective. In N. Eisenberg (ed.) *Contemporary Topics in Developmental Psychology*. New York: Wiley.

Ruble, D.N. & Martin, C.L. (1998) Gender development. In W. Damon & N. Eisenberg (eds) *Handbook of Child Psychology*, Volume 3. New York: Wiley.

Ruble, D.N., Balaban, T. & Cooper, J. (1981) Gender constancy and the effects of sex-typed televised toy commercials. *Child Development, 52*, 667–673.

Ruch, J.C. (1984) *Psychology: The Personal Science*. Belmont, CA: Wadsworth Publishing Co.

Rumbaugh, D.M., Warner, H. & Von Glaserfeld, E. (1977) The Lana project: Origin and tactics. In D.M. Rumbaugh (ed.) *Language Learning by a Chimpanzee: The LANA Project*. New York: Academic Press.

Rumelhart, D.E. (1975) Notes on a schema for stories. In D.G. Bobrow & A. Collins (eds) *Representation and Understanding: Studies in Cognitive Science*. New York: Academic Press.

Rumelhart, D.E. & Norman, D.A. (1983) Representation in memory. In R.C. Atkinson, R.J. Herrstein, B. Lindzey & R.D. Luce (eds) *Handbook of Experimental Psychology*. Chichester: Wiley.

Rumelhart, D.E. & Norman, D.A. (1985) Representation of knowledge. In M.M. Aitkenhead & J.M. Slack (eds) *Issues in Cognitive Modelling*. London: Lawrence Erlbaum Associates Ltd.

Runciman, W.G. (1966) *Relative Deprivation and Social Justice*. London: Routledge & Kegan Paul.

Rushton, J.P. (1995) *Race, Evolution and Behaviour*. New Brunswick, NJ: Transaction Publishers.

Rushton, W.A.H. (1987) Colour vision: Eye mechanism. In R. Gregory (ed.) *The Oxford Companion to the Mind*. Oxford University Press.

Russell, G.F.M. (1979) Bulimia nervosa: An ominous variant of anorexia nervosa. *Psychological Medicine, 9*, 429–448.

Russell, R., Duchaine, B. & Nakayama, K. (2009) Super-recognisers: people with extraordinary face recognition ability. *Psychonomic Bulletin & Review, 16*, 252–257.

Ruszczynski, S. (2008) It's easy to demonise paedophiles. But it's not the answer. *Observer*, 24 August, 15.

Rutter, M. (1981) *Maternal Deprivation Reassessed* (2nd edition). Harmondsworth: Penguin.

Rutter, M. (1989) Pathways from childhood to adult life. *Journal of Child Psychology & Psychiatry, 30*, 23–25.

Rutter, M. (2006) The psychological effects of institutional rearing. In P. Marshall & N. Fox (eds) *The Development of Social Engagement: Neurobiological Perspectives*. New York: Oxford University Press.

Rutter, M. (2008) Implications of attachment theory and research for child care policies. In J. Cassidy & P.R. Shaver (eds) *Handbook of Attachment Theory: Theory, Research, and Clinical Applications* (2nd edition). New York: Guilford Press.

Rutter, M. & Rutter, M. (1992) *Developing Minds: Challenge and Continuity across the Life Span*. Harmondsworth: Penguin.

Rutter, M. & Smith, D. (1995) *Psychosocial Disorders in Young People: Time Trends and their Causes*. London: John Wiley.

Rutter, M. & the English and Romanian Adoptees (ERA) study team (1998) Developmental catch-up, and deficit following adoption after severe global early privation. *Journal of Child Psychology & Psychiatry, 39* (4), 465–476.

Rutter, M. & the English and Romanian Adoptees (ERA) study team (2004) Are there biological programming effects for psychological development? Findings from a study of Romanian adoptees. *Developmental Psychology, 40*, 81–94.

Rutter, M., Graham, P., Chadwick, D.F.D. & Yule, W. (1976) Adolescent turmoil: Fact or fiction? *Journal of Child Psychology & Psychiatry, 17*, 35–56.

Rutter, M., Silberg, J., O'Connor, T. & Siminoff, E. (1999) Genetics and child psychiatry, II: Empirical research findings. *Journal of Child Psychology & Psychiatry, 40* (1), 19–55.

Rutter, M., Colvert, E., Kreppner, J., Beckett, C., Castle, J., Groothues, C., Hawkins, A., O'Connor, T.G., Stevens, S.E. & Sonuga-Barke, E.J.S. (2007) Early adolescent outcomes for institutionally-deprived and non-deprived adoptees 1: Disinhibited attachment. *Journal of Child Psychology & Psychiatry, 48* (1), 17–30.

Rutter, M., Kreppner, J. & Sonuga-Barke, E. (2009) Emmanuel Miller Lecture: Attachment insecurity, disinhibited attachment, and attachment disorders: Where do research findings leave the concepts? *Journal of Child Psychology and Psychiatry, 50* (5), 529–543.

Ryan, J. (1972) IQ – the illusion of objectivity. In K. Richardson & D. Spears (eds) *Race, Culture and Intelligence*. Harmondsworth: Penguin.

Ryan, R.M. & Lynch, J.H. (1989) Emotional autonomy versus detachment: Revisiting the vicissitudes of adolescence and young adulthood. *Child Development, 60*, 340–356.

Ryder, R. (1990) Open reply to Jeffrey Gray. *The Psychologist, 3*, 403.

Ryle, G. (1949) *The Concept of Mind*. London: Hutchinson.

Sachdev, P., Mondraty, N., Wen, W. & Gulliford, K. (2008) Brains of anorexia nervosa patients process self-images differently from non-self-images: an fMRI study. *Neuropsychologia, 46*(8), 2161–2168.

Sacks, O. (1995) *An Anthropologist on Mars*. London: Picador.

Sagi, A. & Hoffman, M.L. (1976) Empathic distress in the newborn. *Developmental Psychology, 12*, 175–176.

Salapatek, P. (1975) Pattern perception in early infancy. In L.B. Cohen & P. Salapatek (eds) *Infant Perception: From Sensation to Cognition, Volume 1. Basic Visual Processes*. London: Academic Press.

Salfati, C.G. & Canter, D. (1999) Differentiating stranger murders. Profiling offender characteristics from behavioural styles. *Behavioural Sciences & the Law, 17*, 391–406.

Salomon, G. (ed.) (1993) *Distributed Cognitions: Psychological and Educational Considerations*. Cambridge University Press.

Samuel, J. & Bryant, P. (1984) Asking only one question in the conservation experiment. *Journal of Child Psychology & Psychiatry, 25*, 315–318.

Sanacora, G., Smith, M.A., Pathak, S. et al. (2013) Lanicemine: a low-trapping NMDA channel blocker produces sustained antidepressant efficacy with minimal psychotomimetic adverse effects. *Molecular Psychiatry*, doi:10.1038/mp.2013.130

Sanders, G.S., Baron, R.S. & Moore, D.L. (1978) Distraction and social competence as mediators of social facilitation. *Journal of Experimental Social Psychology, 14*, 291–303.

Sanislow, C.A., Pine, D.S., Quinn, K.J. et al. (2010) Developing constructs for psychopathology research: research domain criteria. *Journal of Abnormal Psychology, 119*(4), 631–639.

Sangiuliano, I. (1978) *In Her Time*. New York: Morrow.

Saperstein, A.M. & Kurtz, M.M (2013) Current trends in the empirical study of cognitive remediation for schizophrenia. *Canadian Journal of Psychiatry, 58*(6), 311–318.

Sapir, E. (1929) The study of linguistics as a science. *Language, 5*, 207–214.

Satel, S. & Lilienfeld, S.O. (2013) *Brainwashed: The Seductive Appeal of Mindless Neuroscience*. New York: Basic Books.

Savage-Rumbaugh, E.S. (1990) Language as a cause-effect communication system. *Philosophical Psychology, 3*, 55–76.

Savage-Rumbaugh, E.S., Rumbaugh, D.M. & Boysen, S.L. (1980) Do apes use language? *American Scientist, 68*, 49–61.

Savin, H.B. (1973) Professors and psychological researchers: Conflicting values in conflicting roles. *Cognition, 2* (1), 147–149.

Scarr, S. (1992) Developmental theories for the 1990s: Development and individual differences. *Child Development, 63*, 1–19.

Scarr, S. (1998) American child care today. *American Psychologist, 53* (2), 95–108.

Schachter, D.L. (2001) *The Seven Sins of Memory*. New York: Houghton Mifflin.

Schacter, D.L. (2002) *The Seven Sins of Memory: How the Mind Forgets and Remembers*. Houghton Mifflin.

Schachter, J. (1957) Pain, fear, and anger in hypertensives and normotensives: A psychophysiologic study. *Psychosomatic Medicine, 19*, 17–29.

Schachter, S. (1959) *The Psychology of Affiliation: Experimental Studies of the Sources of Gregariousness*. Stanford University Press.

Schachter, S. (1964) The interaction of cognitive and physiological determinants of emotional state. In L. Berkowitz (ed.) *Advances in Experimental Social Psychology, Volume 1*. New York: Academic Press.

Schachter, S. (1971) *Emotion, Obesity and Crime*. New York: Academic Press.

Schachter, S. & Singer, J.E. (1962) Cognitive, social and physiological determinants of emotional state. *Psychological Review, 69*, 379–399.

Schachter, S. & Wheeler, L. (1962) Epinephrine, chlorpromazine and amusement. *Journal of Abnormal & Social Psychology, 65*, 121–128.

Schachter, S., Goldman, R. & Gordon, A. (1968) The effects of fear, food deprivation, and obesity on eating. *Journal of Personality & Social Psychology, 10*, 107–116.

Schaffer, H.R. (1971) *The Growth of Sociability*. Harmondsworth: Penguin.

Schaffer, H.R. (1989) In A. Slater & G. Bremner (eds) *Infant Development*. Hove & London: Lawrence Erlbaum.

Schaffer, H.R. (1996a) *Social Development*. Oxford: Blackwell.

Schaffer, H.R. (1996b) Is the child father to the man? *Psychology Review, 2*(3), 2–5.

Schaffer, H.R. (1998) Deprivation and its effects on children. *Psychology Review, 5*(2), 2–5.

Schaffer, H.R. (2004) *Introducing Child Psychology*. Oxford: Blackwell Publishing.

Schaffer, H.R. & Emerson, P.E. (1964) The development of social attachments in infancy. *Monographs of the Society for Research in Child Development, 29* (Whole No. 3).

Schaie, K.W. & Hertzog, C. (1983) Fourteen-year cohort-sequential analysis of adult intellectual development. *Developmental Psychology, 19*, 531–543.

Schank, R.C. (1975) *Conceptual Information Processing*. Amsterdam: North-Holland.

Schank, R.C. & Abelson, R.P. (1977) *Scripts, Plans, Goals and Understanding*. Hillsdale, NJ: Lawrence Erlbaum Associates Inc.

Scheer, S.D. & Unger, D.G. (1995) Parents' perceptions of their adolescence – implications for parent–youth conflict and family satisfaction. *Psychological Reports, 76*(1), 131–136.

Scheerer, M. (1963) Problem solving. *Scientific American, 208* (4), 118–128.

Scheff, T.J. (1966) *Being Mentally Ill: A Sociological Theory*. Chicago: Aldine Press.

Schiff, M. & Lewontin, R.C. (1986) *Education and Class: The Irrelevance of IQ Genetic Studies*. Oxford: Clarendon Press.

Schiffman, R. & Wicklund, R.A. (1992) The minimal group paradigm and its minimal psychology. *Theory & Psychology, 2*, 29–50.

Schifter, D.E. & Ajzen, I. (1985) Intention, perceived control and weight loss: An application of the theory of planned behaviour. *Journal of Personality & Social Psychology, 49*, 843–851.

Schlenker, B.R. (1980) *Impression Management*. Monterey, CA: Brooks/Cole Publishing Co.

Schlenker, B.R. (1982) Translating action into attitudes: an identity-analytic approach to the explanation of social conduct. In L. Berkowitz (ed.) *Advances in Experimental Social Psychology, Volume 15*. New York: Academic Press.

Schlitz, M., Wiseman, R., Watt, C. & Radin, D. (2006) Of two minds: Sceptic-proponent collaboration within parapsychology. *British Journal of Psychology, 97*, 313–322.

Schlossberg, N.K. (1984) Exploring the adult years. In A.M. Rogers & C.J. Scheirer (eds) *The G. Stanley Hall Lecture Series, Volume 4*. Washington, DC: American Psychological Association.

Schlossberg, N.K., Troll, L.E. & Leibowitz, Z. (1978) *Perspectives on Counselling Adults: Issues and Skills*. Monterey, CA: Brooks/Cole Publishing Co.

Schmader, T. (2010) Stereotype threat deconstructed. *Current Directions in Psychological Science, 19*, 14.

Schmitt, B.H., Gilovich, T., Goore, N. & Joseph, L. (1986) Mere presence and socio-facilitation: One more time. *Journal of Experimental Social Psychology, 22*, 242–248.

Schneider, K. (1959) *Clinical Psychopathology*. New York: Grune & Stratton.

Schneider, W. & Fisk, A.D. (1982) Degree of consistent training: Improvements in search performance and automatic process development. *Perception & Psychophysics, 31*, 160–168.

Schneider, W. & Shiffrin, R.M. (1977) Controlled and automatic human information processing: I. Detection, search and attention. *Psychological Review, 84*, 1–66.

Schooler, C. & Mulatu, M.S. (2001) The reciprocal effects of leisure time activities and intellectual functioning in older people: A longitudinal analysis. *Psychology & Ageing, 16*, 466–482.

Schroeder, D.A., Penner, L.A., Dovidio, J.F. & Piliavin, J.A. (1995) *The Psychology of Helping and Altruism: Problems and Puzzles*. New York: McGraw-Hill.

Schroth, M. (1995) A comparison of sensation-seeking among different groups of athletes and non-athletes. *Personality & Individual Differences, 18*, 219–223.

Schuchter, S.R. & Zisook, S. (1993) The course of normal grief. In M.S. Stroebe, W. Stroebe & R.O. Hansson (eds) *Handbook of Bereavement: Theory, Research and Intervention*. New York: Cambridge University Press.

Schurz, G. (1985) Experimentelle überprufung des zusammenhangs zwischen persönlichkeitsmerkmalen und der bereitschaft der destruktiven gehorsam gegenüber autoritaten. *Zeitschrift für Experimentelle und Augewandte Psychologie, 32*, 160–177.

Scoboria, A., Mazzoni, G. & Jarry, J.L. (2008) Suggesting childhood food illness results in reduced eating behavior. *Acta Psychologica, 128* (2), 304–309.

Scodel, A. (1957) Heterosexual somatic preference and fantasy dependence. *Journal of Consulting Psychology, 21*, 371–374.

Scollon, R. (1976) *Conversations With a One-Year-Old*. Honolulu: University of Hawaii Press.

Scott, F.J. (2004) Research and theoretical developments in autism: An update on current thinking (Tim Gregson-Williams Memorial Lecture, ATP Annual Conference, Exeter University, July 2003). *Psychology Teaching*, Summer, 2–9.

Sebastian, C., Viding, E., Williams, K.D., Blakemore, S.-J. (2010). Social brain development and the affective consequences of ostracism in adolescence. *Brain and Cognition, 72*(1), 134–145.

Seager, M., Morison, L., Wilkins, D. et al. (2104) The hidden mental pain of men. *The Psychologist, 27*(3), 138–139.

Searle, J.R. (1980) Minds, brains and programs. *The Behaviour & Brain Sciences, 3*, 417–457.

Searle, J.R. (1987) Minds and brains without programs. In C. Blakemore & S. Greenfield (eds) *Mindwaves.* Oxford: Blackwell.

Sears, R.B. (1965) Development of gender role. In F.A. Beach (ed.) *Sex and Behaviour.* New York: Wiley.

Sears, R.R., Maccoby, E.E. & Levin, H. (1957) *Patterns of Child Rearing*. New York: Harper & Row.

Segall, M.H. (1994) A cross-cultural research contribution to unravelling the nativist–empiricist controversy. In W.J. Lonner & R.S. Malpass (eds) *Psychology and Culture*. Boston: Allyn & Bacon.

Segall, M.H., Campbell, D.T. & Herskovits, M.J. (1963) Cultural differences in the perception of geometrical illusions. *Science, 139*, 769–771.

Segall, M.H., Dasen, P.R., Berry, J.W. & Poortinga, Y.H. (1990) *Human Behaviour in Global Perspective: An Introduction to Cross-Cultural Psychology*. New York: Pergamon.

Segall, M.H., Dasen, P.R., Berry, J.W. & Poortinga, Y.H. (1999) *Human Behaviour in Global Perspective: An Introduction to Cross-Cultural Psychology* (2nd edition). Needham Heights, MA: Allyn & Bacon.

Seidenberg, M.S. & Petitto, L.A. (1987) Communication, symbolic communications and language: Comment on Savage-Rumbaugh, McDonald, Sevcik, Hopkins and Rupert (1986). *Journal of Experimental Psychology: General, 116*, 279–287.

Seider, S., Davis, K. & Gardner, H. (2007) Good work in psychology. *The Psychologist, 20*(11), 672–676.

Selfridge, O.G. (1959) Pandemonium: A paradigm for learning. *Symposium on the Mechanisation of Thought Processes*. London: HMSO.

Seligman, M.E.P. (1970) On the generality of the laws of learning. *Psychology Review,* 77, 406–418.

Seligman, M.E.P. (1972) *Biological Boundaries of Learning*. New York: Academic Press.

Seligman, M.E.P. (1974) Depression and learned helplessness. In R.J. Friedman & M.M. Katz (eds) *The Psychology of Depression: Contemporary Theory and Research*. Washington, DC: Winston-Wiley.

Seligman, M.E.P. (1975) *Helplessness: On Depression, Development and Death.* San Francisco: W.H. Freeman.

Seligman, M.E.P., Abramson, L.V., Semmel, A. & Von Beyer, C. (1979) Depressive attributional style. *Journal of Abnormal Psychology, 88*, 242–247.

Seligmann, J., Rogers, P. & Annin, P. (1994) The pressure to lose. *Newsweek*, 123, 60–61.

Sellen, A.J. & Norman, D.A. (1992) The psychology of slips. In B.J. Barrs (ed.) *Experimental Slips and Human Error: Exploring the Architecture of Volition*. New York: Plenum Press.

Selye, H. (1956) *The Stress of Life*. New York: McGraw-Hill.

Senju, A., Southgate, V., White, S. & Frith, U. (2009) Mindblind eyes: An absence of spontaneous theory of mind in asperger syndrome. *Science, 325*(5942), 883–885.

Sergent, J. (1984) An investigation into component and configurational processes underlying face recognition. *British Journal of Psychology*, *75*, 221–242.

Sergo, P. (2008) New weapons against cocaine addiction. *Scientific American Mind, 19*, 54–57.

Serpell, R.S. (1976) *Culture's Influence on Perception.* London: Methuen.

Serpell, R.S. (1979) How specific are perceptual skills? A cross-cultural study of pattern reproduction. *British Journal of Psychology, 70*, 365–380.

Serpell, R.S. (1994) The cultural construction of intelligence. In W.J. Lonner & R.S. Malpass (eds) *Psychology and Culture.* Boston: Allyn & Bacon.

Shackleton, V.J. & Fletcher, C.A. (1984*) Individual Differences – Theories and Applications*. London: Methuen.

Shaffer, D.R. (1985) *Developmental Psychology: Theory, Research, and Applications.* Monterey, CA: Brooks/Cole Publishing Co.

Shaffer, H.J., Stein, S.A., Gambino, B. & Cummings, T.N. (eds) *Compulsive Gambling: Theory, Research and Practice.* Lexington, MA: Lexington Books.

Shaffer, L.H. (1975) Control processes in typing. *Quarterly Journal of Experimental Psychology, 27*, 419–432.

Shafran, R. (1999) Obsessive compulsive disorder. *The Psychologist, 12* (12), 588–591.

Shanab, M.E. & Yahya, K.A. (1978) A cross-cultural study of obedience. *Bulletin of the Psychonomic Society, 11*, 267–269.

Shatz, M. (1994) *A Toddler's Life: Becoming a Person*. New York: Oxford University Press.

Shaver, P.R., Collins, N. & Clark, C.L. (1996) Attachment styles and internal working models of self and relationship patterns. In G.J.O. Fletcher & J. Fitness (eds) *Knowledge Structures in Close Relationships: A Social Psychological Approach*. Mahwah, NJ: Lawrence Erlbaum Associates.

Sheeran, P., Milne, S., Webb, T.L. & Gollwitzer, P.M. (2005) Implementation intentions and health behaviours. In M. Conner & P. Norman (eds) *Predicting Health Behaviour: Research and Practice with Social Cognition Models* (2nd edition). Maidenhead: Open University Press.

Sheridan, C.L. & King, R.G. (1972) Obedience to authority with an authentic victim. *Proceedings of the 80th Annual Convention, American Psychological Association,* 7 (1), 165–166.

Sherif, M. (1935) A study of social factors in perception. *Archives of Psychology, 27* (Whole No. 187).

Sherif, M. (1966) *Group Conflict and Co-operation: Their Social Psychology*. London: RKP.

Sherif, M., Harvey, O.J., White, B.J., Hood, W.R. & Sherif, C.W. (1961) *Intergroup Conflict and Co-operation: The Robber's Cave Experiment*. Norman: University of Oklahoma Press.

Sherrington, C.S. (1906) *The Integrative Action of the Nervous System*. London: Constable.

Shields, J. (1962) Monozygotic Twins Brought Up Apart and Brought Up Together. London: Oxford University Press.

Shiffrin, R.M. & Schneider, W. (1977) Controlled and automatic human information processing: II. Perceptual learning, automatic attending and a general theory. *Psychological Review, 84*, 127–190.

Shotland, R.L. & Straw, M.K. (1976) Bystander response to an assault: When a man attacks a woman. *Journal of Personality & Social Psychology, 34*, 990–999.

Shuey, A. (1966) *The Testing of Negro Intelligence*. New York: Social Science Press.

Shulman, H.G. (1970) Encoding and retention of semantic and phonemic information in short-term memory. *Journal of Verbal Learning & Verbal Behaviour, 9*, 499–508.

Shweder, R.A. (1990) Cultural psychology: What is it? In J.W. Stigler, R.A. Shweder & G. Herdt (eds) *Cultural Psychology*. Cambridge University Press.

Shweder, R.A. (1991) *Thinking Through Cultures: Expeditions in Cultural Psychology*. Cambridge, MA: Harvard University Press.

Shweder, R.A., Mahapatra, M. & Miller, J.G. (1987) Culture and moral development. In J. Kagan & S. Lamb (eds) *The Emergence of Morality in Young Children*. University of Chicago Press.

Sidanius, J. & Pratto, F. (1999) *Social Dominance: An Intergroup Theory of Social Hierarchy and Oppression*. New York: Cambridge University Press.

Sieber, J.E. (2004) Socially sensitive research. *Psychology Review, 11*(1), 6–9.

Sieber, J.E. & Stanley, B. (1988) Ethical and Professional Dimensions of Socially Sensitive Research. *American Psychologist, 43*(1), 49–55.

Siegal, M. (1987) Are sons and daughters treated more differently by fathers than by mothers? *Developmental Review,* 7, 183–209.

Siegal, M. (2003) Cognitive development. In A. Slater & G. Bremner (eds) *An Introduction to Developmental Psychology*. Oxford: Blackwell Publishing.

Siegel, J.M. (2003) Why We Sleep. *Scientific American, 289* (5), 72–77.

Siegler, R.S. (1998) *Children's Thinking* (3rd edition). Upper Saddle River, NJ: Prentice-Hall.

Silke, A. (2002) Understanding terrorism. *Psychology Review, 9*(1), 17–19.

Silverman, I. (1971) Physical attractiveness and courtship. *Sexual Behaviour, September*, 22–25.

Silverstein, B. & Perlick, D. (1995) *The Costs of Competence: Why Inequality Causes Depression, Eating Disorders and Illness in Women*. Oxford University Press.

Simmons, R.G. & Blyth, D.A. (1987) *Moving into Adolescence: The Impact of Pubertal Change and School Context*. New York: Aldine de Gruyter.

Simonsen, E. (2010) The integration of categorical and dimensional approaches in psychopathology. In T. Millon, R.F. Krueger, & E. Simonsen (eds) *Contemporary directions in psychopathology: Scientific foundations of the DSM-V and ICD-11*. New York: Guilford.

Simonton, D.K. (2012) The Science of Genius. *Scientific American Mind, 23*(5), 35–41.

Simpson, J.A., Campbell, B. & Berscheid, E. (1986) The association between romantic love and marriage: Kephart (1967) twice revisited. *Personality & Social Psychology Bulletin, 12*, 363–372.

Simring, K.S. (2013) Accidental Gluttons. *Scientific American Mind, 24*(5), 26–33.

Simpson, S.H., Eurich, D.T., Majumdar, S.R. et al. (2006) A meta analysis of the association between adherence to drug therapy and mortality. *British Medical Journal, 333*, 15.

Sims, A.C.P. & Gray, P. (1993) The media, violence and vulnerable viewers. Document presented to the Broadcasting Group, House of Lords.

Sinclair-de-Zwart, H. (1969) Developmental psycholinguistics. In D. Elkind & J. Flavell (eds) *Handbook of Learning and Cognitive Processes, Volume 5*. Hillsdale, NJ: Erlbaum.

Singer, D. (1989) Children, adolescents and television – 1989. *Paediatrics, 83*, 445–446.

Singer, W. (1998) Consciousness from a neurobiological perspective. In S. Rose (ed.) *From Brains to Consciousness: Essays on the New Sciences of the Mind*. Harmondsworth: Penguin.

Singh, D. (1993) Adaptive significance of female physical attractiveness: Role of waist-to-hip ratio. *Journal of Personality & Social Psychology, 65*, 293–307.

Singh, D. (2004) Mating strategies of young women: Role of physical attractiveness. *Journal of Sex Research, 41*, 43–54.

Sinha, D. (1997) Indigenising psychology. In J.W. Berry, Y.H. Poortinga & J. Pandey (eds) *Handbook of Cross-cultural, Psychology, Volume 1* (2nd edition). Boston: Allyn & Bacon.

Sinha, P. (2013) Once blind and now they see. *Scientific American, 309*(1), 36–43.

Sissons Joshi, M. (1995) Lay explanations of the causes of diabetes in India and the UK. In I. Markova & R.M. Farr (eds) *Representations of Health, Illness and Handicap*. Philadelphia: Harwood.

Skinner, B.F. (1938) *The Behaviour of Organisms*. New York: Appleton-Century-Crofts.

Skinner, B.F. (1948a) Superstition in the pigeon. *Journal of Experimental Psychology, 38*, 168–172.

Skinner, B.F. (1948b) *Walden Two*. New York: Macmillan.

Skinner, B.F. (1957) *Verbal Behaviour*. New York: Appleton-Century-Crofts.

Skinner, B.F. (1971) *Beyond Freedom and Dignity*. New York: Knopf.

Skinner, B.F. (1974) *About Behaviourism*. New York: Alfred Knopf.

Skinner, B.F. (1985) Cognitive science and behaviourism. Unpublished manuscript, Harvard University.

Skinner, B.F. (1987) Skinner on behaviourism. In R.L. Gregory (ed.) *The Oxford Companion to the Mind*. Oxford University Press.

Slaby, R.G. & Frey, K.S. (1975) Development of gender constancy and selective attention to same-sex models. *Child Development, 46*, 839–856.

Slater, A. (1989) Visual memory and perception in early infancy. In A. Slater & G. Bremner (eds) *Infant Development*. Hove: Erlbaum.

Slater, A. (1994) Perceptual development in infancy. *Psychology Review, 1*, 12–16.

Slater, A. & Morison, V. (1985) Shape constancy and slant perception at birth. *Perception, 14*, 337–344.

Slater, A., Mattock, A. & Brown, E. (1990) Size constancy at birth: Newborn infants' responses to retinal and real sizes. *Journal of Experimental Child Psychology, 49*, 314–322.

Slater, E. & Roth, M. (1969) *Clinical Psychiatry* (3rd edition). London, Ballière Tindall and Cassell.

Slater, A., Quinn, P.C., Kelly, D.J. et al. (2010) The shaping of the face space in early infancy: Becoming a native face processor. *Child Development Perspectives, 4*(3), 205–211.

Slater, M., Antley, A., Daviso, A. et al. (2006) A Virtual Reprise of the Stanley Milgram obedience Experiments. www.plosone.org/article/info%3Adoi%2F10.1371%2Fjournal.pone.0000039

Slavin, R.E. (1990) *Co-operative Learning: Theory, Research and Practice*. Englewood Cliffs, NJ: Prentice-Hall.

Slee, P. & Shute, R. (2003) *Child Development: Thinking About Theories*. London: Arnold.

Slobin, D.I. (1979) *Psycholinguistics* (2nd edition). Glenview, IL: Scott, Foresman and Company.

Sluckin, W. (1965) *Imprinting and Early Experiences*. London: Methuen.

Slugoski, B. & Hilton, D. (2000). Conversation. In W.P. Robinson & H. Giles (eds) *Handbook of Language and Social Psychology* (2nd edition). Chichester: Wiley.

Smillie, L.D. & Gökçen E. (2010) Caffeine enhances working memory for extraverts. *Biological Psychology, 85*, 496–498.

Smith, A.D. (1998) Ageing of the brain: Is mental decline inevitable? In S. Rose (ed.) *From Brains to Consciousness: Essays on the New Sciences of the Mind*. Harmondsworth: Penguin.

Smith, A.J. (1957) Similarity of values and its relation to acceptance and the projection of similarities. *Journal of Psychology, 43*, 251–260.

Smith, C. & Lloyd, B.B. (1978) Maternal behaviour and perceived sex of infant. *Child Development, 49*, 1263–1265.

Smith, C.L. & Zielinksi, S.L. (2014) Brainy Bird. *Scientific American, 310*(2), 46–51.

Smith, C.U.M. (1994) You are a group of neurons. *The Times Higher Educational Supplement*, 27 May, 20–21.

Smith, D. (2013) Beating the odds of addiction. *The Psychologist, 26*(8), 610–611.

Smith, E.M., Brown, H.O., Toman, J.E.P. & Goodman, L.S. (1947) The lack of cerebral effects of D-tubo-curarine. *Anaesthesiology, 8*, 1–14.

Smith, J. (1998) What happens when girl beats boy. *Independent on Sunday*, 30 August, 13.

Smith, J.A., Harré, R. & Van Langenhove, L. (1995) Introduction. In J.A.Smith, R. Harré, & L. Van Langenhove (eds) *Rethinking Psychology*. London: Sage.

Smith, J.R., Brooks-Gunn, J. & Klebanov, P.K. (1997) Consequences of living in poverty for young children's cognitive and verbal ability and early school achievement. In G.J. Duncan & J. Brooks-Gunn (eds) *Consequences of Growing Up Poor*. New York: Russell Sage Foundation.

Smith, K.R. & Zick, C.D. (1996) Risk of mortality following widowhood: Age and sex differences by mode of death. *Social Biology, 43*, 59–71.

Smith, M. (2000) Is there such a thing as a personality disorder? *Nursing Times, 96*(18), 16.

Smith, M.L. & Glass, G.V. (1977) Meta-analysis of psychotherapeutic outcome studies. *American Psychologist, 32*, 752–760.

Smith, M.L., Glass, G.V. & Miller, T.I. (1980) *The Benefits of Psychotherapy*. Baltimore, MD: Johns Hopkins University Press.

Smith, P.B. (1995) Social influence processes. In M. Argyle & A.M. Colman (eds) *Social Psychology*. London: Longman.

Smith, P.B. & Bond, M.H. (1993) *Social Psychology Across Cultures: Analysis and Perspectives*. Hemel Hempstead: Harvester Wheatsheaf.

Smith, P.B. & Bond, M.H. (1998) *Social Psychology Across Cultures* (2nd edition). Hemel Hempstead: Prentice-Hall Europe.

Smith, P.K. & Cowie, H. (1988) *Understanding Children's Development*. Oxford: Basil Blackwell.

Smith, P.K. & Daglish, L. (1977) Sex differences in parent and infant behaviour in the home. *Child Development, 48*, 1250–1254.

Smith, P.K., Cowie, H. & Blader, M. (1998) *Understanding Children's Development* (3rd edition). Oxford: Blackwell.

Smith, R.E., Sarason, I.G. & Sarason, B.R. (1986) *Psychology – The Frontiers of Behaviour* (3rd edition). New York: Harper & Row.

Smolak, L. (2012) Appearance in Childhood and Adolescence. In N. Rumsey & D. Harcourt (eds) *Oxford Handbook of The Psychology of Appearance*. Oxford: Oxford University Press.

Sneddon, L.U. (2006) Ethics and welfare: pain perception in fish. *Bulletin of the European Association of Fish Pathology, 26*(1), 6.

Sneddon, L.U., Braithwaite, A. & Gentle, M. (2003) Do fish have nociceptors: evidence for the evolution of a vertebrate sensory system. *Proceedings of the Royal Society: Biological Sciences, 270*(1520), 1115–1121.

Snow, C.E. (1977) Mother's speech research: From input to interaction. In C.E. Snow & C.A. Ferguson (eds) *Talking to Children: Language Input and Acquisition*. New York: Cambridge University Press.

Snow, C.E. (1983) Saying it again: The role of expanded and deferred imitations in language acquisition. In K.E. Nelson (ed.) *Children's Language, Volume 4*. New York: Gardner Press.

Snowdon, D., Greiner, L. & Markesbery, W. (2000) Linguistic ability in early life and the neuropathology of Alzheimer's disease and cerebrovascular disease: Findings from the Nun Study. In R.N. Kalaria & P. Ince (eds) *Vascular Factors in Alzheimer's Disease*. New York Academy of Sciences.

Snyder, A.W., Ellwood, S. & Chi, R.P. (2012) Switching on creativity. *Scientific American Mind, 23*(5), 58–62.

Snyder, M. (1974) Self-monitoring of expressive behaviour. *Journal of Personality & Social Behaviour, 30*, 526–537.

Snyder, M. (1979) Self-monitoring processes. In L. Berkowitz (ed.) *Advances in Experimental Social Psychology, Volume 18*. New York: Academic Press.

Snyder, M. (1987) *Public Appearances, Private Realities: The Psychology of Self-monitoring*. New York: Freeman.

Snyder, M. (1995) Self-monitoring: Public appearances versus private realities. In G.G. Brannigan & M.R. Merrens (eds) *The Social Psychologists: Research Adventures*. New York: McGraw-Hill.

Snyder, M., Tanke, E.D. & Berscheid, E. (1977) Social perception and interpersonal behaviour: On the self-fulfilling nature of social stereotypes. *Journal of Personality & Social Psychology, 35*, 656–666.

Snyder, S. (1977) Opiate receptors and internal opiates. *Scientific American, 236*, 44–56.

Sober, E. (1992) The evolution of altruism: Correlation, cost and benefit. *Biology & Philosophy, 7*, 177–188.

Solis, M. (2013) A lifeline for addicts. *Scientific American Mind, 24*(1), 40–43.

Solms, M. (2006) Putting the psyche into neuropsychology. *The Psychologist, 19*(9), 538–539.

Solms, M. & Turnbull, O. (2007) To sleep, perchance to REM? The rediscovered role of emotion and meaning in dreams. In S. Della Sala (ed.) *Tall Tales About the Mind & Brain: Separating Fact from Fiction*. Oxford University Press.

Solso, R.L. (1995) *Cognitive Psychology* (4th edition). Boston: Allyn & Bacon.

Southwick, S.M. & Charney, D.S. (2013) Ready for Anything. *Scientific American Mind, 24*(3), 32–41.

Sowell, E.R., Peterson, B.S., Thompson, P.M., Welcome, S.E., Henkenius, A.L. & Toga, A.W. (2003) Mapping cortical change across the life span. *Nature Neuroscience, 6*, 309–315.

Sparrow, B., Liu, J. & Wegner, D.M. (2011) Google effects on memory: Cognitive consequences of having information at your fingertips, *Science, 333*(6043), 776–778.

Sparrow, S.S. & Davis, S.M. (2000) Recent advances in the assessment of intelligence and cognition. *Journal of Child Psychology & Psychiatry, 41* (1), 117–131.

Spearman, C. (1904) General intelligence, objectively determined and measured. *American Journal of Psychology, 15*, 201–293.

Spearman, C. (1967) The doctrine of two factors. In S. Wiseman (ed.) *Intelligence and Ability*. Harmondsworth: Penguin. (Original work published 1927.)

Spector, T. D. & Williams, M. (2006) The UK Adult Twin Registry (TwinsUK). *Twin Research & Human Genetics, 9*(6), 899–906.

Speisman, J.C., Lazarus, R.S., Mordkoff, A.M. & Davidson, L.A. (1964) The experimental reduction of stress based on ego defence theory. *Journal of Abnormal & Social Psychology, 68*, 397–398.

Spelke, E.S. (1991) Physical knowledge in infancy: Reflections on Piaget's theory. In S. Carey & R. Gelman (eds) *The Epigenesis of Mind: Essays on Biology and Cognition*. Hillsdale, NJ: Erlbaum.

Spelke, E.S., Hirst, W.C. & Neisser, U. (1976) Skills of divided attention. *Cognition, 4*, 215–230.

Spence, S. (2004) Bad or mad? *New Scientist, 181*(2439), 38–41.

Spencer, C. & Perrin, S. (1998) Innovation and conformity. *Psychology Review, 5*(2), 23–26.

Sperling, H.G. (1946) An experimental study of some psychological factors in judgement. Master's thesis, New School for Social Research.

Sperry, R.W. (1943) The effect of 180 degree rotation in the retinal field of visuo-motor co-ordination. *Journal of Experimental Zoology, 92*, 263–279.

Sperry, R.W. (1964) The great cerebral commissure. *Scientific American, 210*, 42–52.

Sperry, R.W. (1968) Hemisphere deconnection and unity in conscious awareness. *American Psychologist, 23*, 723–733.

Spinney, L. (2011) Venus and Mars collide. *New Scientist, 209*(2802), 42–45.

Spitz, R.A. (1945) Hospitalism: An inquiry into the genesis of psychiatric conditions in early childhood. *Psychoanalytic Study of the Child, 1*, 53–74.

Spitz, R.A. (1946) Hospitalism: A follow-up report on investigation described in Volume 1, 1945. *Psychoanalytic Study of the Child, 2*, 113–117.

Spitz, R.A. & Wolf, K.M. (1946) Anaclitic depression. *Psychoanalytic Study of the Child, 2*, 313–342.

Sroufe, L.A. (1988) The role of infant-caregiver attachment in development. In J. Belsky & T. Nezworski (eds) *Clinical Implications of Attachment*. Hillsdale, NJ: Erlbaum.

Stahlberg, D. & Frey, D. (1988) Attitudes, 1: Structure, measurement and functions. In M. Hewstone, W. Stroebe, J.P. Codol & G.M. Stephenson (eds) *Introduction to Social Psychology*. Oxford: Blackwell.

Stainton Rogers, R., Stenner, P., Gleeson, K. & Stainton Rogers, W. (1995) *Social Psychology: A Critical Agenda*. Cambridge: Polity Press.

Standing, L. (1973) Remembering ten thousand pictures. *Quarterly Journal of Experimental Psychology, 25*, 207–222.

Stangor, C. & Ruble, D.N. (1987) Development of gender role knowledge and gender constancy. In L.S. Liben & M.L. Signorella (eds) *Children's Gender Schemata*. San Francisco: Jossey-Bass.

Stanovich, K.E. (2009) *What Intelligence Tests Miss: The Psychology of Rational Thought*. New Haven, CT: Yale University Press.

Stanovich, K.E. & West, R.F. (2014) What intelligence tests miss. *The Psychologist, 27*(2), 80–83.

Stanovich, K.E., West, R.F. & Toplak, M.E. (2013) Myside bias, rational thinking, and intelligence. *Current Directions in Psychological Science, 22*, 259–264.

Stanton, A.L., Danoff-Burg, S., Cameron, C.L. & Ellis, A.P. (1994) Coping through emotional approach: Problems of conceptualisation and confounding. *Journal of Personality & Social Psychology, 66*, 350–362.

Startup, H.M. & Davey, G.C.L. (2001) Mood-as-input and catastrophic worrying. *Journal of Abnormal Psychology, 110* (1), 83–96.

Stattin, H. & Klackenberg, G. (1992) Family discord in adolescence in the light of family discord in childhood. Paper presented at Conference Youth – TM, Utrecht.

Stattin, H. & Magnusson, D. (1990) *Pubertal Maturation in Female Development*. Hillsdale, NJ: Erlbaum.

Steele, C.M. (1997) A threat in the air: How stereotypes shape intellectual identity and performance. *American Psychologist, 52*(6), 613–629.

Steele, C.A. & Aronson, J. (1995) Stereotype threat and the intellectual test performance of African Americans. *Journal of Personality & Social Psychology, 69*(5), 797–811.

Steele, H., Steele, M. & Fonagy, P. (1995) Associations among attachment classifications of mothers, fathers, and their infants. *Child Development, 57*, 555–571.

Steele, H., Steele, M. & Fonagy, P. (1996) Associations among attachment classifications of mothers, fathers, and their infants. *Child Development, 67*, 541–555.

Stein, D.J., Phillips, K.A., Bolton, D. et al. (2010) What is a mental/psychiatric disorder? From DSM-IV to DSM-V. *Psychological Medicine, 40*(11), 1759–1765.

Steiner, I.D. (1972) *Group Processes and Productivity*. New York: Academic Press.

Stephan, W.G. (1978) School desegregation: An evaluation of predictions made in Brown vs. the Board of Education. *Psychological Bulletin, 85*, 217–238.

Stephan, W.G. & Stephan, C.W. (1985) Intergroup anxiety. *Journal of Social Issues, 41*, 157–175.

Stephenson, G.M. (1988) Applied social psychology. In M. Hewstone, W. Stroebe, J.P. Codol & G.M. Stephenson (eds) *Introduction to Social Psychology*. Oxford: Blackwell.

Sterling, P. & Eyer, J. (1988) Allostasis: a new paradigm to explain arousal pathology. In S. Fisher & J. Reason (eds) *Handbook of Life Stress, Cognition, and Health*. Oxford: John Wiley.

Stern, M. & Karraker, K.H. (1989) Sex stereotyping of infants: A review of gender labelling studies. *Sex Roles, 20*, 501–522.

Sternberg, E. (2000) *The Balance Within: The Science Connecting Health and Emotions*. New York: W.H. Freeman.
Sternberg, E. & Gold, P.W. (1997) The mind–body interaction in disease. *Scientific American Mysteries of the Mind, 7*(1), 8–15.
Sternberg, R.J. (1979) The nature of mental abilities. *American Psychologist, 34*, 214–230.
Sternberg, R.J. (1985) *Beyond IQ: A Triarchic Theory of Human Intelligence*. Cambridge University Press.
Sternberg, R.J. (1987) Intelligence. In R. Gregory (ed.) *The Oxford Companion to the Mind*. Oxford University Press.
Sternberg, R.J. (1988a) *The Triarchic Mind: A New Theory of Human Intelligence*. New York: Viking.
Sternberg, R.J. (1988b) Triangulating love. In R.J. Sternberg & M.L. Barnes (eds) *The Psychology of Love*. New Haven, CT: Yale University Press.
Sternberg, R.J. (1990) *Metaphors of Mind*. Cambridge University Press.
Sternberg, R.J. (1995) Intelligence and cognitive styles. In S.E. Hampson & A.M. Colman (eds) *Individual Differences and Personality*. London: Longman.
Sternberg, R.J. (1998) How intelligent is intelligence testing? *Scientific American Presents: Exploring Intelligence, 9* (4), 12–17.
Sternberg, R.J. & Grigorenko, E. (eds) (1997) *Intelligence, Heredity and Environment*. New York: Cambridge University Press.
Stevens, A. (1990) *On Jung*. London: Routledge.
Stevens, R. (1995) Freudian theories of personality. In S.E. Hampson & A.M. Colman (eds) *Individual Differences and Personality*. London: Longman.
Stewart, V.M. (1973) Tests of the 'carpentered world' hypothesis by race and environment in America and Africa. *International Journal of Psychology, 8*, 83–94.
Stix, G. (2011) The neuroscience of True Grit. *Scientific American, 304*(3), 20–25.
Stoet, G. & Snyder, L.H. (2003) Executive control and task-switching in monkeys. *Neuropsychologia, 41*, 1357–1364.
Stoet, G. & Snyder, L.H. (2007) Extensive practice does not eliminate human switch costs. *Cognitive, Affective and Behavioural Neuroscience, 7*(3), 192–197.
Stoner, J.A.F. (1961) A comparison of individual and group decisions involving risk. Unpublished master's thesis, Massachusetts Institute of Technology.
Storms, M.D. (1973) Videotape and the attribution process: Reversing actors' and observers' points of view. *Journal of Personality & Social Psychology, 27*, 165–175.
Storr, A. (1966) The concept of cure. In C. Rycroft (ed.) *Psychoanalysis Observed*. London: Constable.
Storr, A. (1968) *Human Aggression*. Harmondsworth: Penguin.
Stouffer, S.A., Suchman, E.A., DeVinney, L.C., Starr, S.A. & Williams, R.M. (1949) *The American Soldier: Adjustment During Army Life, Volume 1*. Princeton University Press.
Strachey, J. (1962–1977) Sigmund Freud: A sketch of his life and ideas. (This appears in each volume of the Pelican Freud Library.) Originally written for *the Standard Edition of the Complete Psychological Works of Sigmund Freud, 1953–1974*. London: Hogarth Press.
Stratton, G.M. (1896) Some preliminary experiments on vision. *Psychological Review, 3*, 611–617.
Strayer, D.L. & Watson, J.M. (2012) Supertaskers and the multitasking brain. *Scientific American Mind, 23*(1), 22–29.
Stroebe, M.S. (1998) New directions on bereavement research: explorations of gender differences. *Palliative Medicine, 12*, 5–12.
Stroebe, M.S. & Stroebe, M. (1993) The mortality of bereavement: A review. In M.S. Stroebe, W. Stroebe & R.O. Hansson (eds) *Handbook of Bereavement: Theory, Research and Intervention*. New York: Cambridge University Press.
Stroebe, M.S., Stroebe, W. & Hansson, R.O. (1993) Contemporary themes and controversies in bereavement research. In M.S. Stroebe, W. Stroebe & R.O. Hansson (eds) *Handbook of Bereavement: Theory, Research and Intervention*. New York: Cambridge University Press.
Stroebe, W. (2000) *Social Psychology and Health* (2nd edition). Buckingham: Open University Press.
Stroebe, W. (2008) Strategies of attitude and behaviour change. In M. Hewstone, W. Stroebe & K. Jonas (eds) *Introduction to Social Psychology: A European Perspective* (4th edition). Oxford: BPS Blackwell.
Stroebe, W. (2012a) The subtle power of hidden messages. *Scientific American Mind, 23*(2), 46–51.
Stroebe, W. (2012b) Strategies of Attitude and Behaviour Change. In M. Hewstone, W. Stroebe & K. Jonas (eds) *Introduction to Social Psychology* (5th edition). BPS Blackwell.
Stroebe, W., Hewstone, M. & Jonas, K. (2012) Introducing Social Psychology. In M. Hewstone, W. Stroebe & K. Jonas (eds) *Introduction to Social Psychology* (5th edition). BPS Blackwell.
Strueber, D., Lueck, N. & Roth, G. (2006/2007) The violent brain. *Scientific American Mind, 17*(6), 20–29.
Stuart-Hamilton, I. (1994) *The Psychology of Ageing: An Introduction* (2nd edition). London: Jessica Kingsley.
Stuart-Hamilton, I. (1997) Adjusting to later life. *Psychology Review, 4*(2), 20–23, November.
Stuart-Hamilton, I. (2000) Ageing and intelligence. *Psychology Review, 6*(4), 19–21.
Stuart-Hamilton, I. (2003) Intelligence and ageing: Is decline inevitable? *Psychology Review, 9*(3), 14–16.
Subramaniam, K.M., Luks, T.L., Fisher, M. et al. (2012) Computerised cognitive training restores neural activity within the reality monitoring network in schizophrenia. *Neuron, 73*, 842–853.
Suler, J. (2004) The online disinhibition effect. *CyberPsychology and Behaviour, 7*(3), 321–326.
Sue, D., Sue, D. & Sue, S. (1994) *Understanding Abnormal Behaviour* (4th edition). Boston: Houghton Mifflin.
Sue, S. (1995) Implications of the Bell curve: Whites are genetically inferior in intelligence? *Focus: Notes from the Society for the Psychological Study of Ethnic Minority Issues*, 16–17.
Sulloway, F.J. (1979) *Freud, Biologist of the Mind: Beyond the Psychoanalytic Legend*. New York: Basic Books.
Sumner, W.G. (1906) *Folkways*. Boston: Ginn.
Surrey, D. (1982) 'It's like good training for life'. *Natural History, 91*, 71–83.
Sussman, S. & Ames, S.L. (2001) *The Social Psychology of Drug Abuse*. Buckingham: Open University Press.
Sussman, S. & Ames, S.L. (2008) *Drug Abuse: Concepts, Prevention, and Cessation*. New York: Cambridge University Press.

Sutherland, P. (1992) *Cognitive Development Today: Piaget and his Critics*. London: Paul Chapman Publishing.

Sutherland, R., Strange, D. & Garry, M. (2007) We have got the whole child witness thing figured out, or have we? In S. Della Sala (ed.) *Tall Tales About the Mind & Brain: Separating Fact From Fiction*. New York: Oxford University Press.

Sutherland, S.N. (1976) *Breakdown*. London: Weidenfeld & Nicolson.

Sutton, C., Utting, D. & Farrington, D. (2006) Nipping criminality in the bud. *The Psychologist, 19* (8), 470–475.

Sutton, J. (2013) Memory matters. *The Psychologist, 26*(5), 326.

Swami, V. & Furnham, A. (2006) The science of attraction. *The Psychologist, 19* (6), 362–365.

Swami, V., Stanistreet, D. & Payne, S. (2008) Masculinities and suicide. *The Psychologist, 21* (4), 308–311.

Sweet, M. (2004) The search for intelligent life. *Independent Review*, 2 June, 2–3.

Swensen, C.H. (1983) A respectable old age. *American Psychologist, 46*, 1208–1221.

Szabo, C.P. & Le Grange, D. (2001) Eating disorders and the politics of identity: The South African experience. In M. Nasser, M.A. Katzman, & R.A. Gordon (eds) *Eating Disorders and Cultures in Transition*. Hove: Brunner-Routledge.

Szasz, T.S. (1962) *The Myth of Mental Illness*. New York: Harper & Row.

Szasz, T.S. (1971) From the slaughterhouse to the madhouse. *Psychotherapy Theory Research and Practice, 8*, 64–67.

Szasz, T.S. (1974) *Ideology and Insanity*. Harmondsworth: Penguin.

Szymanski, K. & Harkins, S.G. (1987) Social loafing and self-evaluation with a social standard. *Journal of Personality & Social Psychology, 53*, 891–897.

Taddonio, J.L. (1976) The relationship of experimenter expectancy to performance on ESP tasks. *Journal of Parapsychology, 40,* 107–114.

Tagiuri, R. (1969) Person perception. In G. Lindzey & E. Aronson (eds) *Handbook of Psychology, Volume 2*. Reading, MA: Addison-Wesley.

Tajfel, H. (1969) Social and cultural factors in perception. In G. Lindzey & E. Aronson (eds) *Handbook of Social Psychology, Volume 3*. Reading, MA: Addison-Wesley.

Tajfel, H. (1972) Experiments in a vacuum. In J. Israel & H. Tajfel (eds) *The Context of Social Psychology: A Critical Assessment*. London: Academic Press.

Tajfel, H. (ed.) (1978) *Differentiation Between Social Groups: Studies in the Social Psychology of Intergroup Relations*. London: Academic Press.

Tajfel, H. & Turner, J.C. (1986) The social identity theory of intergroup behaviour. In S. Worchel & W. Austin (eds) *Psychology of Intergoup Relations*. Chicago: Nelson-Hall.

Tajfel, H., Billig, M.G. & Bundy, R.P. (1971) Social categorisation and intergroup behaviour. *European Journal of Social Psychology, 1*, 149–178.

Talaska, C., Fiske, S.T. & Chaiken, S. (2003) Biases hot and cold: Emotional prejudices and cognitive stereotypes as predictors of discriminatory behaviour. Unpublished manuscript, Princeton University (cited in S.T. Fiske, 2004).

Tanaka, J.W. & Farah, M.J. (1993) Parts and wholes in face recognition. *Quarterly Journal of Experimental Psychology, 46A*, 225–246.

Tanner, J.M. (1978) *Fetus into Man: Physical Growth from Conception to Maturity*. Cambridge, MA: Harvard University Press.

Tanner, J.M. & Whitehouse, R.H. (1976) Clinical longitudinal standards for height, weight, velocity, weight velocity and stages of puberty. *Archives of Disease in Childhood, 51*, 170–179.

Tardif, T., Fletcher, P., Liang, W. et al. (2008) Baby's first 10 words. *Developmental Psychology 44*(4), 929–938.

Tasker, F. & Golombok, S. (1995) Adults raised as children in lesbian families. *American Journal of Orthopsychiatry, 65* (2), 203–215.

Tausch, N., Hewstone, M., Kenworthy, J.B. et al. (2010) Secondary transfer effects of intergroup contact: Alternative accounts and underlying processes. *Journal of Personality & Social Psychology, 99*. 282–302.

Tavris, N. (1993) The mismeasure of woman. *Feminism & Psychology, 3* (2), 149–168.

Taylor, D. (2002) One bad score. *Guardian*, 16 January, 6.

Taylor, D.M. & Porter, L.E. (1994) A multicultural view of stereotyping. In W.J. Lonner & R.S. Malpass (eds) *Psychology and Culture*. Boston: Allyn & Bacon.

Taylor, G. (1993) Challenges from the margins. In J. Clarke (ed.) *A Crisis in Care*. London: Sage.

Taylor, P.F. & Kopelman, M.D. (1984) Amnesia for criminal offences. *Psychological Medicine, 14*, 581–588.

Taylor, R. (1963) *Metaphysics*. Englewood Cliffs, NJ: Prentice-Hall.

Taylor, S.E. (1981) A categorisation approach to stereotyping. In D.L. Hamilton (ed.) *Cognitive Processes in Stereotyping and Intergroup Behaviour*. Hillsdale, NJ: Erlbaum.

Taylor, S.E., Peplau, L.A. & Sears, D.O. (1994) *Social Psychology* (8th edition). Englewood Cliffs, NJ: Prentice-Hall.

Tedeschi, R.G. & Calhoun, L.G. (1996) The posttraumatic growth inventory: measuring the positive legacy of trauma. *Journal of Traumatic Stress, 9*, 455–471.

Tedeschi, J.T. & Rosenfield, P. (1981) Impression management theory and the forced compliance situation. In J.T. Tedeschi (ed.) *Impression Management Theory and Social Psychological Research*. New York: Academic Press.

Teichman, J. (1988) *Philosophy and the Mind*. Oxford: Blackwell.

Teigen, K.H. (1994) Variants of subjective probabilities: Concepts, norms and biases. In G. Wright & P. Aytan (eds) *Subjective Probability*. Chichester: John Wiley.

Teitelbaum, P.H. (1955) Sensory control of hypothalamic hyperphagia. *Journal of Comparative & Physiological Psychology, 48*, 156–163.

Teitelbaum, P.H. (1967) Motivation and control of food intake. In C.F. Code (ed.) *Handbook of Physiology: Alimentary Canal, Volume 1*. Washington, DC: American Physiological Society.

Teixeira, J.M.A. (1999) Association between maternal anxiety in pregnancy and increased uterine resistance index: Cohort based study. *British Medical Journal, 318*(7177), 153–157.

Temoshok, L. (1987) Personality, coping style, emotions and cancer: Towards an integrative model. *Cancer Surveys, 6*, 545–567 (Supplement).

Terman, L. (1921) In symposium: Intelligence and its measurement. *Journal of Educational Psychology, 12*, 127–133.

Terman, L. (1925) *Genetic Studies of Genius, Volume 1: Mental and Physical Traits of a Thousand Gifted Children*. Stanford University Press.

Terman, L. & Ogden, M.H. (1959) *Genetic Studies of Genius, Volume 4: The Gifted Group at Midlife*. Stanford University Press.

Terrace, H.S. (1979) *Nim*. New York: Knopf.

Terrace, H.S. (1987) Thoughts without words. In C. Blakemore & S. Greenfield (eds) *Mindwaves*. Oxford: Basil Blackwell.

Tesser, A. (2004) Self-esteem. In M.B. Brewer & M. Hewstone (eds) *Emotion and Motivation*. Oxford: Blackwell Publishing.

Tey, S.L. et al. (2012) Long-term consumption of high energy-dense snack foods on sensory-specific satiety and intake. *American Journal of Clinical Nutrition, 95*(5), 1038–1047.

Thaler, L., Arnott, S.R. & Goodale, M.A. (2011) Neural correlates of natural human echolocation in early and late blind echolocation experts. *PLoS One 6*(5):e20162.

Thayer, J.F. & Brosschot, J.F. (2010) Stress, health and illness: The effects of prolonged physiological activity and perseverative cognition. In D. French, K. Vedhara, A.A. Kapstein & J. Weinman. *Health Psychology* (2nd edition). Oxford: BPS Blackwell.

Thibaut, J.W. & Kelley, H.H. (1959) *The Social Psychology of Groups*. New York: Wiley.

Thomas, K. (1990) Psychodynamics: The Freudian approach. In I. Roth (ed.) *Introduction to Psychology*. Hove: Lawrence Erlbaum Associates Ltd.

Thomas, R.M. (1985) *Comparing Theories of Child Development* (2nd edition). Belmont, CA: Wadsworth Publishing Company.

Thompson, L.A., Detterman, D.K. & Plomin, R. (1991) Associations between cognitive abilities and scholastic achievement: Genetic overlap but environmental differences. *Psychological Science*, 2, 158–165.

Thompson, P. (1980) Margaret Thatcher – a new illusion. *Perception, 9*, 483–484.

Thompson, S.B.N. (1997) War experiences and post-traumatic stress disorder. *The Psychologist, 10*, 349–350.

Thorndike, E.L. (1898) Animal intelligence: An experimental study of the associative processes in animals. *Psychological Review Monograph Supplement* 2 (Whole No. 8).

Thorndike, E.L. (1911) *Animal Intelligence*. New York: Macmillan.

Thorne, B. (1992) *Rogers*. London: Sage.

Thornhill, R. & Palmer, C.T. (2000) *A Natural History of Rape: Biological Bases of Sexual Coercion*. Cambridge, MA: MIT Press.

Thornhill, R. & Wilmsen-Thornhill, N. (1992) The evolutionary psychology of men's coercive sexuality. *Behaviour & Brain Sciences, 15*(2), 363–375.

Thurstone, L.L. (1935) *The Vectors of the Mind*. University of Chicago Press.

Thurstone, L.L. (1938) Primary mental abilities. *Psychometric Monographs, No. 1.*

Thurstone, L.L. (1947) *Multiple Factor Analysis*. University of Chicago Press.

Tienari, P. (1991) Interaction between genetic vulnerability and family environment: The Finnish adoptive family study of schizophrenia. *Acta Psychiatrica Scandinavia, 84*, 460–465.

Tipper, S. (2005) Memories of attention. *The Psychologist, 18*(6), 362–364.

Tipper, S.P. & Driver, J. (1988) Negative priming between pictures and words: Evidence for semantic analysis of ignored stimuli. *Memory & Cognition, 16*, 64–70.

Titchener, E.B. (1903) *Lectures on the Elementary Psychology of Feeling and Attention*. New York: Macmillan.

Tizard, B. (1977) *Adoption: A Second Chance*. London: Open Books.

Tizard, B. (1986) *The Care of Young Children*. London: Institute of Education.

Tizard, B. & Hodges, J. (1978) The effects of early institutional rearing on the development of eight-year-old children. *Journal of Child Psychology & Psychiatry, 19*, 99–118.

Tizard, B. & Phoenix, A. (1993) *Black, White or Mixed Race?* London: Routledge.

Toates, F. (2001) *Biological Psychology: An Integrative Approach*. Harlow: Pearson Education Ltd.

Tobin-Richards, M.H., Boxer, A.M. & Petersen, A.C. (1983) The psychological significance of pubertal change: Sex differences in perceptions of self during early adolescence. In J. Brooks-Gunn & A.C. Petersen (eds) *Girls at Puberty: Biological and Psychosocial Perspectives*. New York: Plenum.

Tolman, E.C. (1948) Cognitive maps in rats and man. *Psychological Review, 55*, 189–208.

Tolman, E.C. & Honzik, C.H. (1930) Introduction and removal of reward and maze-learning in rats. *University of California Publications in Psychology, 4*, 257–275.

Tolman, E.C., Ritchie, B.F. & Kalish, D. (1946) Studies in spatial learning, 1: Orientation and the short-cut. *Journal of Experimental Psychology, 36*, 13–25.

Tononi, G. & Cirelli, C. (2013) Perchance to prune. *Scientific American, 309*(2), 26–31.

Tooby, J. & Cosmides, L. (1990) The past explains the present: Emotional adaptations and the structure of ancestral environments. *Ethology & Sociobiology, 11*, 375–424.

Tooby, J. & Cosmides, L. (1997) Evolutionary psychology: A primer (www.psych.ucsb.edu/research/cep/primer.html).

Topal, J., Gergeley, G., Miklosi, A., Erdohegyi, A. & Csibra, G. (2008) Perseverative Search Errors are induced by Pragmatic Misinterpretation. *Science, 321* (5897), 1831–1834.

Tourangeau, R. (2004) Survey methodology. In S.T. Fiske, D.L. Schacter & C. Zahn-Waxler (eds) *Annual Review of Psychology (Volume 5)*. Palo Alto, CA: Annual Reviews.

Townsend, M. (2004) Exam fears driving teenagers to Prozac. *Observer*, 6 June, 1.

Townsend, M. (2008) Babies are new target Met warns as paedophile threat spirals. *Observer*, 24 August, 15.

Tredre, R. (1996) Untitled article. *Observer Life*, 12 May, 16–19.

Treffert, D.A. & Wallace, G.L. (2004) *Islands of Genius. Scientific American MIND* (Special Edition), *14*(1), 14–23.

Treisman, A.M. (1960) Contextual cues in selective listening. *Quarterly Journal of Experimental Psychology, 12*, 242–248.

Treisman, A.M. (1964) Verbal cues, language and meaning in selective attention. *American Journal of Psychology, 77*, 206–219.

Treisman, A.M. (1988) Features and objects: The fourteenth Bartlett memorial lecture. *Quarterly Journal of Experimental Psychology, 40A*, 201–237.

Treisman, A.M. & Geffen, G. (1967) Selective attention: Perception or response. *Quarterly Journal of Experimental Psychology, 19*, 1–18.

Treisman, A.M. & Gelade, G. (1980) A feature-integration theory of attention. *Cognitive Psychology, 12*, 97–136.

Treisman, A.M. & Riley, J.G.A. (1969) Is selective attention selective perception or selective response? A further test. *Journal of Experimental Psychology, 79*, 27–34.

Trevens, M. (2013) Your instinctive genius. *New Scientist, 220*(2938), 28–29.

Triandis, H. (1990) Theoretical concepts that are applicable to the analysis of ethnocentrism. In R.W. Brislin (ed.) *Applied Cross-Cultural Psychology*. Newbury Park, CA: Sage.

Triandis, H. (1994) *Culture and Social Behaviour*. New York: McGraw-Hill.

Triplett, N. (1898) The dynamogenic factors in pacemaking and competition. *American Journal of Psychology, 9*, 507–533.

Trivers, R.L. (1971) The evolution of reciprocal altruism. *Quarterly Review of Biology, 46*, 35–57.

Trivers, R.L. (1972) Parental investment and sexual selection. In B. Campbell (ed.) *Sexual Selection and the Descent of Man*. Chicago: Aldine.

Troscianko, T. (1987) Colour vision: Brain mechanisms. In R. Gregory (ed.) *The Oxford Companion to the Mind*. Oxford University Press.

Trower, P. (1987) On the ethical bases of 'scientific' behaviour therapy. In S. Fairbairn & G. Fairbairn (eds) *Psychology, Ethics and Change*. London: RKP.

Tsakiris, M., Tajadura-Jiminez, A. & Constantini, M. (2011) Just a heartbeat away from one's body: Interoceptive sensitivity predicts malleability of body-representations. *Proceedings of the Royal Society B, 278*, 2470–2476.

Tuckman, B.W. (1965) Developmental sequences in small groups. *Psychological Bulletin, 63*, 384–399.

Tulving, E. (1972) Episodic and semantic memory. In E. Tulving & W. Donaldson (eds) *Organisation of Memory*. London: Academic Press.

Tulving, E. (1985) How many memory systems are there? *American Psychologist, 40*, 385–398.

Turing, A.M. (1936) On computable numbers, with an application to the Entscheidungsproblem. *Proceedings of the London Mathematical Society, Series 2* (42), 230–265.

Turing, A.M. (1950) Computing machinery and intelligence. *Mind, 59*, 433–460.

Turnbull, C. (1961) *The Forest People*. New York: Simon & Schuster.

Turnbull, S.K. (1995) The middle years. In D. Wedding (ed.) *Behaviour and Medicine* (2nd edition). St Louis, MO: Mosby-Year Book.

Turner, J.C. (1991) *Social Influence*. Milton Keynes: Open University Press.

Turner, J.C. (2006) Tyranny, freedom and social structure: Escaping our theoretical prisons. *British Journal of Social Psychology, 45*, 41–46.

Turner, J.C., Hogg, M.A., Oakes, P.J., Reicher, D.S. & Wetherell, M.S. (1987) *Rediscovering the Social Group: A Self-categorisation Theory*. Oxford: Blackwell.

Turner, J.S. & Helms, D.B. (1989) *Contemporary Adulthood* (4th edition). Fort Worth, TX: Holt, Rinehart & Winston.

Turney, J. (1999) Human nature totally explained. *The Times Higher*, 12 March, 18.

Turpin, G. & Slade, P. (1998) Clinical and health psychology. In P. Scott & C. Spencer, *Psychology: A Contemporary Introduction*. Oxford: Blackwell.

Tversky, A. (1972) Elimination by aspects: A theory of choice. *Psychological Review, 79*, 281–299.

Tversky, A. & Kahneman, D. (1971) Belief in the law of small numbers. *Psychological Bulletin, 76*, 105–110.

Tversky, A. & Kahneman, D. (1973) Availability: A heuristic for judging frequency and probability. *Cognitive Psychology, 5*, 207–232.

Tversky, A. & Kahneman, D. (1974) Judgement under uncertainty: Heuristics and biases. *Science, 185*, 1124–1131.

Tversky, A. & Kahneman, D. (1980) Causal schemas in judgements under uncertainty. In M. Fishbein (ed.) *Progress in Social Psychology*. Hillsdale, NJ: Erlbaum.

Tyerman, A. & Spencer, C. (1983) A critical test of the Sherifs' Robber's Cave experiment: Intergroup competition and co-operation between groups of well-acquainted individuals. *Small Group Behaviour, 14*, 515–531.

Tyler, T.R. & Cook, F.L. (1984) The mass media and judgement of risk: Distinguishing impact on personal and societal level judgement. *Journal of Personality & Social Psychology, 47*, 693–708.

Underwood, G. (1974) Moray vs the rest: The effects of extended shadowing practice. *Quarterly Journal of Experimental Psychology, 26*, 368–372.

Unger, R. (1979) *Female and Male*. London: Harper & Row.

Unger, R. & Crawford, M. (1992) *Women and Gender: A Feminist Psychology*. New York: McGraw-Hill.

Unger, R. & Crawford, M. (1996) *Women and Gender: A Feminist Psychology* (2nd edition). New York: McGraw-Hill.

Ungerleider, L.G. & Mishkin, M. (1982) Two cortical visual systems. In D.J. Ingle, M.A. Goddale & R.J.W. Mansfield (eds) *Analysis of Visual Behaviour*. Cambridge, MA: MIT Press.

Uskul, A.K. (2010) Sociocultural aspects of health and illness. In D. French, K. Vedhara, A.A. Kaptein & J. Weinman (eds) *Health Psychology* (2nd edition). Oxford: BPS Blackwell.

Valentine, E.R. (1982) *Conceptual Issues in Psychology*. London: Routledge.

Valentine, E.R. (1992) *Conceptual Issues in Psychology* (2nd edition). London: Routledge.

Valentine, GT. & Bruce, V. (1986) The effects of distinctiveness, inversion and race in face recognition. *Perception, 15*, 525–535.

Valins, S. (1966) Cognitive effects of false heart-rate feedback. *Journal of Personality & Social Psychology, 4*, 400–408.

van Avermaet, E. (1996) Social influence in small groups. In M. Hewstone, W. Stroebe & G.M. Stephenson (eds) *Introduction to Social Psychology* (2nd edition). Oxford: Blackwell.

Van Bavel, J.J. & Cunningham, W.A. (2012) A social identity approach to person memory: Group membership, collective identification, and social role shape attention and memory. *Personality & Social Psychology Bulletin, 38*, 1566–1578.

Van Essen, D.C. (1985) Functional organisation of primate visual cortex. In A. Peters. & E.G. Jones (eds) *Cerebral Cortex, Volume 2: Visual Cortex*. New York: Plenum Press.

Van Ijzendoorn, M.H. & Bakjermans-Kranenburg, M.J. (1996) Attachment representations in mothers, fathers, adolescents and clinical groups: A meta-analytic search for normative data. *Journal of Consulting & Clinical Psychology, 64*, 8–21.

Van Ijzendoorn, M.H. & De Wolff, M.S. (1997) In search of the absent father: Meta analyses of infant–father attachment: A rejoinder to our discussants. *Child Development, 68*, 604–609.

Van Ijzendoorn, M.H. & Kroonenberg, P.M. (1988) Cross-cultural patterns of attachment: A meta-analysis of the Strange Situation. *Child Development, 59*, 147–156.

Van Ijzendoorn, M.H. & Schuengel, C. (1999) The development of attachment relationships: Infancy and beyond. In D. Messer & S. Millar (eds) *Exploring Developmental Psychology: From Infancy to Adolescence*. London: Arnold.

Van Langenhove, L. (1995) The theoretical foundations of experimental psychology and its alternatives. In J.A. Smith, R. Harré & L.Van Langenhove (eds) *Rethinking Psychology*. London: Sage.

Vanneman, R.D. & Pettigrew, T.F. (1972) Race and relative deprivation in the urban United States. *Race, 13*, 461–486.

Varese, F., Smeets, F., Drukker, M. et al. (2012) Childhood adversities increase the risk of psychosis. *Schizophrenia Bulletin, 38*, 661–671.

Vasey, M. & Borkovec, T.D. (1992) A catastrophising assessment of worrisome thoughts. *Cognitive Therapy & Research*, 16, 505–520.

Vaughn, B.E., Gove, F.L. & Egeland, B.R. (1980) The relationship between out-of-home care and the quality of infant–mother attachment in an economically disadvantaged population. *Child Development, 51*, 1203–1214.

Veitia, M.C. & McGahee, C.L. (1995) Ordinary addictions: Tobacco and alcohol. In D. Wedding (ed.) *Behaviour and Medicine* (2nd edition). St Louis. MO: Mosby-Year Book.

Veltkamp, M., Aarts, H. & Custers, R. (2008) Perception in the service of goal pursuit: Motivation to attain goals enhances the perceived size of goal-instrumental objects. *Social Cognition, 26*, 720–736.

Vernon, M.D. (1955) The functions of schemata in perceiving. *Psychological Review, 62*, 180–192.

Vernon, P.E. (1950) The hierarchy of ability. In S. Wiseman (ed.) *Intelligence and Ability*. Harmondsworth: Penguin.

Vernon, P.E. (1969) *Intelligence and Cultural Environment*. London: Methuen.

Vernon, P.E. (1971) *The Structure of Human Abilities*. London: Methuen.

Vitelli, R. (1988) The crisis issue reassessed: An empirical analysis. *Basic & Applied Social Psychology, 9*, 301–309.

Vivian, J. & Brown, R. (1995) Prejudice and intergroup conflict. In M. Argyle & A.M. Colman (eds) *Social Psychology*. London: Longman.

Von Senden, M. (1960) *Space and Sight: The Perception of Space and Shape in the Congenitally Blind Before and After Operations* (trans. P. Heath). London: Methuen. (Original work published 1932.)

Vogel, M., Monesson, A., Scott, L.S. (2012) Building biases in Infancy: The influence of race on face and voice emotional matching. *Developmental Science, 15*(3), 359.

Voss, S. (2002) The winter years: Understanding ageing. *Psychology Review, 8*(3), 26–28.

Vul, E., Harris, C., Winkelman, P. & Pashler, H. (2009) Puzzlingly high correlations in fMRI studies of emotion, personality and social cognition. *Perspectives in Psychological Science, 4*(3), 274–290.

Vygotsky, L.S. (1962) *Thought and Language*. Cambridge, MA: MIT Press. (Originally published 1934.)

Vygotsky, L.S. (1978) *Mind in Society*. Cambridge, MA: Harvard University Press.

Vygotsky, L.S. (1981) The genesis of higher mental functions. In J.V. Wertsch (ed.) *The Concept of Activity in Soviet Psychology*. Armonk, NY: Sharpe.

Wachtel, P.L. (1977) *Psychoanalysis and Behaviour Therapy: Toward an Integration*. New York: Basic Books.

Wachtel, P.L. (1989) Preface to the paperback edition. In *Psychoanalysis and Behaviour Therapy*. New York: Basic Books.

Wachtel, P.L. (1997) *Psychoanalysis, Behaviour Therapy, and the Relational World*. Washington, DC: American Psychological Association.

Wade, C. & Tavris, C. (1990) *Psychology* (2nd edition). New York: Harper & Row.

Wade, C. & Tavris, C. (1994) The longest war: Gender and culture. In W.J. Lonner & R.S. Malpass (eds) *Psychology and Culture*. Boston: Allyn & Bacon.

Wade, C. & Tavris, C. (1999) *Invitation to Psychology*. New York: Longman.

Wagenaar, W.A. (1988) *Paradoxes of Gambling Behaviour*. Hove: Lawrence Erlbaum.

Wake, S. & Kitchener, D. (2013) Post-traumatic stress disorder after intensive care. *BMJ, 346*, f3232.

Walker, L.J. (1984) Sex differences in the development of moral reasoning: A critical review. *Child Development, 55*, 677–691.

Walker, L.J. (1989) A longitudinal study of moral reasoning. *Child Development, 60*, 157–166.

Walker, L.J. (1995) Sexism in Kohlberg's moral psychology? In W.M. Kurtines & J. Gewirtz (eds) *Moral Development: An Introduction*. Needham Heights, MA: Allyn & Bacon.

Walker, L.J. (1996) Is one sex morally superior? In M.R. Merrens & G.C. Brannigan (eds) *The Developmental Psychologists: Research Adventures Across the Life Span*. New York: McGraw-Hill.

Walker, L.J., DeVries, B. & Trevathan, S.D. (1987) Moral stages and moral orientations in real-life and hypothetical dilemmas. *Child Development, 58*, 842–858.

Walker, M.B. (1992) *The Psychology of Gambling*. Oxford: Butterworth Heinemann.

Walley, M. & Westbury, T. (1996) Sport psychology. In H. Coolican (ed.) *Applied Psychology*. London: Hodder & Stoughton.

Walster, E., Aronson, E., Abrahams, D. & Rottman, L. (1966) Importance of physical attractiveness in dating behaviour. *Journal of Personality & Social Psychology, 4*, 508–516.

Walter, C. (2006/7) Why Do We Cry? *Scientific American Mind, 17*(6), 44–51.

Walters, G.D. (1999) *The Addiction Concept: Working Hypothesis or Self-Fulfilling Prophecy?* Needham Heights, MA: Allyn & Bacon.

Wamsley, E.J. & Stickgold, R. (2010) Dreaming and Offline Memory Processing. *Current Biology, 20*(23), R1010–R1013.

Wang, R., Li, J., Fang, H. et al. (2012) Individual differences in holistic processing predict face recognition ability. *Psychological Science, 23*(2), 169–177.

Ward, J. (2003) Synaesthesia. *The Psychologist, 16* (4), 196–199.

Warren, S. & Jahoda, M. (eds) (1973) *Attitudes* (2nd edition). Harmondsworth: Penguin.

Warrington, E.K. & Weiskrantz, L. (1968) New method of testing long-term retention with special reference to amnesic patients. *Nature, 217*, 972–974.

Warrington, E.K. & Weiskrantz, L. (1970) Amnesic syndrome: Consolidation or retrieval? *Nature, 228*, 628–630.

Warwick, I. & Aggleton, P. (2002) Gay men's physical and emotional wellbeing: Reorienting research and health promotion. In A. Coyle & C. Kitzinger (eds) *Lesbian and Gay Psychology*. Oxford: BPS Blackwell.

Waterhouse, R. & Mayes, T. (2000) Unhealthy obsession. *Sunday Times*, 25 June, 16.

Waters, E. (1978) The reliability and stability of individual differences in infant–mother attachments. *Child Development, 49*, 483–494.

Watkins, E.R. (2008) Constructive and unconstructive repetitive thought. *Psychological Bulletin, 134*(2), 163–206.

Watson, J.B. (1913) Psychology as the behaviourist views it. *Psychological Review, 20*, 158–177.

Watson, J.B. (1919) *Psychology from the Standpoint of a Behaviourist*. Philadelphia: J.B. Lippincott.

Watson, J.B. (1925) *Behaviourism*. New York: Norton.

Watson, J.B. (1928) *Psychological Care of Infant and Child*. New York: Norton.

Watson, J.B. & Rayner, R. (1920) Conditioned emotional reactions. *Journal of Experimental Psychology, 3*, 1–14.

Watt, C. & Wiseman, R. (2009) Foreword in Irwin, H.J. (2009) *The Psychology of Paranormal Belief: A Researcher's Handbook*. Hatfield: University of Hertfordshire Press.

Waugh, N.C. & Norman, D.A. (1965) Primary memory. *Psychological Review, 72*, 89–104.

Wearing, D. (2005) *Forever Today*. London: Corgi Books.

Webb, W.B. & Bonnett, M.H. (1979) Sleep and dreams. In M.E. Meyer (ed.) *Foundations of Contemporary Psychology*. New York: Oxford University Press.

Wechsler, D. (1944) *The Measurement of Adult Intelligence* (3rd edition). Baltimore, MD: Williams & Wilkins.

Wechsler, D. (1958) *The Measurement and Appraisal of Adult Intelligence* (4th edition). Baltimore, MD: Williams & Wilkins.

Wechsler, D. (1974) *Wechsler Intelligence Scale for Children*. New York: The Psychological Corporation.

Wechsler, D. (1981) *Manual for the Wechsler Adult Intelligence Scale – Revised*. New York: The Psychological Corporation.

Wechsler, D. (1989) *Wechsler Preschool and Primary Scale of Intelligence* (revised edition). San Antonio, TX: The Psychological Corporation.

Wechsler, D. (1991) *Wechsler Intelligence Scale for Children* (3rd edition) Manual. San Antonio, TX: The Psychological Corporation.

Wechsler, D. (1997) *Wechsler Adult Intelligence Scale* (3rd edition) Manual. San Antonio, TX: The Psychological Corporation.

Wegner, D.M. & Ward, A.F. (2013) How Google is Changing your Brain. *Scientific American, 309*(6), 50–53.

Weierstall, R., Schauer, M. & Elbert, T. (2013) An Appetite for Aggression. *Scientific American Mind, 24*(2), 46–49.

Weinberg, R. (1989) Intelligence and IQ: Landmark issues and great debates. *American Psychologist, 44*, 98–104.

Weiner, B. (1986) *An Attributional Theory of Motivation and Emotion*. New York: Springer-Verlag.

Weiner, B. (1992) *Human Motivation: Metaphors, Theories and Research*. Newbury Park, CA: Sage.

Weinman, J. (1995) Health psychology. In A.M. Colman (ed.) *Controversies in Psychology*. London: Longman.

Weinstein, N. (1983) Reducing unrealistic optimism about illness susceptibility. *Health Psychology, 2*, 11–20.

Weinstein, N. (1984) Why it won't happen to me: Perceptions of risk factors and susceptibility. *Health Psychology, 3*, 431–457.

Weir, K. (2013) Inside job. *New Scientist, 218*(2920), 32–35.

Weiskrantz, L. (1956) Behavioural changes associated with ablation of the amygdaloid complex in monkeys. *Journal of Comparative & Physiological Psychology, 49*, 381–391.

Weiskrantz, L. (1982) Comparative aspects of studies of amnesia. *Philosophical Transactions of the Royal Society. London B, 298*, 97–109.

Weiskrantz, L. (1986) *Blindsight: A Case Study and Implications*. Oxford University Press.

Weiss, R.S. (1982) Attachment in adult life. In C.M. Parkes & J. Stevenson-Hinde (eds) *The Place of Attachment in Human Behaviour*. New York: Basic Books.

Weisstein, N. (1993) Psychology constructs the female; or, The fantasy life of the male psychologist (with some attention to the fantasies of his friend, the male biologist and the male anthropologist). *Feminism & Psychology, 3*(2), 195–210.

Wellman, H.M. (1990) *The Child's Theory of Mind*. Cambridge, MA: MIT Press.

Wells, G.L. (1993) What do we know about eyewitness identification? *American Psychologist, 48*, 553–571.

Wells, G.L. & Harvey, J.H. (1977) Do people use consensus information in making causal attributions? *Journal of Personality & Social Psychology, 35*, 279–293.

Wells, G.L., Olson, E.A. & Charman, S.D. (2003) Distorted retrospective eyewitness reports as function of feedback delay. *Journal of Experimental Psychology: Applied, 9*, 42–52.

Wenner, M. (2009) The serious need for play. *Scientific American Mind, 20*(1), 22–29.

Werner, E.E. (1989) Children of the Garden Island. *Scientific American*, April, 106–111.

Wessler, R.L. (1986) Conceptualising cognitions in the cognitive behavioural therapies. In W. Dryden & W. Golden (eds) *Cognitive–Behavioural Approaches to Psychotherapy*. London: Harper & Row.

Westendorp, R.G.J. & Kirkwood, T.B.L. (2007) The biology of ageing. In J. Bond, S. Peace, F. Dittmann-Kohli & G. Westerhof (eds) *Ageing in Society* (3rd edition). London: Sage Publications.

Westly, E. (2012) Different shades of blue. *Scientific American Mind, 21*(2), 34–41.

Weston, K. (1991) *Families We Choose*. New York: Columbia University Press.

Wetherell, M. (1982) Cross-cultural studies of minimal groups: Implications for the social identity theory of intergroup relations. In H. Tajfel (ed.) *Social Psychology and Intergroup Relations*. Cambridge University Press.

Wetherell, M. (1987) Social identity and group polarisation. In J.C. Turner, M.A. Hogg, P.J. Oakes, S.D. Reicher & M. Wetherell (eds) *Rediscovering the Social Group: A Self-Categorisation Theory*. Oxford: Blackwell.

Wetherell, M. (1996) Group conflict and the social psychology of racism. In M. Wetherell (ed.) *Identities, Groups and Social Issues*. London: Sage, in association with the Open University.

Wethington, E. (2000) Expecting stress: Americans and the 'midlife crisis'. *Motivation & Emotion, 24*, 85–103.

White, R.A. (1976) The limits of experimenter influence on psi test results: can any be set? *Journal of American Society for Psychical Research, 70*, 333–369.

White, R.A. (1993) Working classification of EHEs. *Exceptional Human Experience, 11*(2), 149–150.

White, R.W. (1959) Motivation reconsidered: The concept of competence. *Psychological Review, 66*, 297–333.

Whorf, B.L. (1956) *Language, Thought and Reality*. Cambridge, MA: MIT Press.

Whyte, J. (1998) Childhood. In K. Trew & J. Kremer (eds) *Gender & Psychology*. London: Arnold.

Wichstrom, L. (1998) Self-concept development during adolescence: Do American truths hold for Norwegians? In E. Skoe & A. von der Lippe (eds) *Personality Development in Adolescence: A Cross National and Life Span Perspective*. London: Routledge.

Wickelgren, I. (2012) Trying to forget. *Scientific American Mind, 22*(6), 32–39.

Wickelgren, I. (2009) I do not feel your pain. *Scientific American Mind, 20*(5), 51–57.

Widiger, T.A. (2012) Classification and diagnosis: Historical development and contemporary issues. In J.E. Maddux & B.A. Winstead (eds) *Psychopathology: Foundations for a Contemporary Understanding* (3rd edition). New York: Routledge.

Wiemann, J.M. & Giles, H. (1988) Interpersonal communication. In M. Hewstone, W. Stroebe, J.P. Codol & G.M. Stephenson (eds) *Introduction to Social Psychology*. Oxford: Blackwell.

Wilding, J.M. (1982) *Perception: From Sense to Object*. London: Hutchinson.

Wilhelm, K. (2006) Do animals have feelings? *Scientific American Mind, 17*(1), 24–29.

Wilkinson, S. (1991) Feminism & psychology: From critique to reconstruction. *Feminism & Psychology, 1*(1), 5–18.

Wilkinson, S. (1997) Feminist psychology. In D. Fox & D. Prilleltensky (eds) *Critical Psychology: An Introduction*. London: Sage.

Wilkinson, S. & Kitzinger, C. (2005) Same sex marriage and equality. *The Psychologist, 18*(5), 290–293.

Wilkinson, S. & Kitzinger, C. (2006) In support of equal marriage: Why civil partnership is not enough. *Psychology of Women Section Review, 8*(1), 54–57.

Wilkinson, S. & Kitzinger, C. (2008) Conversation analysis. In C. Willig & W. Stainton Rogers (eds) *The Sage Handbook of Qualitative Research in Psychology*. London: Sage, 55–71.

Williams, C. (2006) Hello, strangers. *New Scientist, 192* (2579), 34–37.

Williams, C. (2012) The consciousness connection. *New Scientist, 215*(2874), 32–35.

Williams, J.E. & Best, D.L. (1994) Cross-cultural views of women and men. In W.J. Lonner & R.S. Malpass (eds) *Psychology and Culture*. Boston: Allyn & Bacon.

Williams, J.M.G. & Hargreaves, I.R. (1995) Neuroses: Depressive and anxiety disorders. In A.A. Lazarus & A.M. Colman (eds) *Abnormal Psychology*. London: Longman.

Williams, K., Harkins, S.G. & Latané, B. (1981) Identifiability as a deterrent to social loafing: Two cheering experiments. *Journal of Personality & Social Psychology, 40*, 303–311.

Williams, T.M. (ed.) (1986) *The Impact of Television: A National Experiment in Three Communities*. New York: Academic Press.

Williams, W.M. & Ceci, S.J. (1997) Are Americans becoming more or less alike? Trends in race, class, and ability differences in intelligence. *American Psychologist, 52*, 1226–1235.

Willis, R.H. (1963) Two dimensions of conformity–nonconformity. *Sociometry, 26*, 499–513.

Wilson, C. (2006) Glad to be gullible. *New Scientist, 189* (2536), 37–39.

Wilson, C. (2014) Out of the shadows. *New Scientist, 221*(2955), 32–35.

Wilson, E.O. (1975) Sociobiology – The New Synthesis. Cambridge, MA: Harvard University Press.

Wilson, G. (1994) Biology, sex roles and work. In C. Quest (ed.) *Liberating Women from Modern Feminism*. London: Institute of Economic Affairs, Health & Welfare Unit.

Wilson, G.D. (1976) Personality. In H.J. Eysenck & G.D. Wilson (eds) *A Textbook of Human Psychology*. Lancaster: MTP.

Wilson, G.T. & Davison, G.C. (1971) Processes of fear reduction in systematic desensitisation: Animal studies. *Psychological Bulletin, 76*, 1–14.

Wilson, G.T., O'Leary, K.D., Nathan, P.E. & Clark, L.A. (1996) *Abnormal Psychology: Integrating Perspectives*. Needham Heights, MA: Allyn & Bacon.

Wilson, J.E. & Barkham, M. (1994) A practitioner–scientist approach to psychotherapy process and outcome research. In P. Clarkson & M. Pokorny (eds) *The Handbook of Psychotherapy*. London: Routledge.

Wilson, J.Q. & Herrnstein, R.J. (1985) Crime and Human Nature. New York: Touchstone.

Wimmer, H. & Perner, J. (1983) Beliefs about beliefs: Representation and constraining function of wrong beliefs in young children's understanding of deception. *Cognition, 13*, 103–128.

Winch, R.F. (1958) *Mate Selections: A Study of Complementary Needs*. New York: Harper.

Wing, L. (1976) *Early Childhood Autism*. Oxford: Pergamon Press.

Wing, L. (1997) The history of ideas on autism: Legends, myths and reality. *Autism: The International Journal of Research & Practice, 1*, 13–23.

Wing, L. & Gould, J. (1979) Severe impairments of social interaction and associated abnormalities in children: Epidemiology and classification. *Journal of Autism & Developmental Disorders, 9*, 11–29.

Winner, E. (1996) The rage to master: The decisive role of talent in the visual arts. In K.A. Ericsson (ed.) *The Road to Excellence: The Acquisition of Expert Performance in their Arts and Sciences*. Hillsdale, NJ: Lawrence Erlbaum Associates.

Winner, E. (1998) Uncommon talents: Gifted children, prodigies and talents. *Scientific American Presents, 9* (4), 32–37.

Winnicott, D. (1965) *The Maturational Process and the Facilitating Environment*. London: Hogarth.

Winnicott, D.W. (1958) *Through Paediatrics to Psychoanalysis*. London: Hogarth Press.

Winson, J. (1997) The meaning of dreams. *Scientific American Mysteries of the Mind, Special Issues, 791*, 58–67. (Originally published November 1990.)

Winter, D.A. (1999) Psychological problems: Alternative perspectives on their explanation and treatment. In D. Messer & F. Jones (eds) *Psychology and Social Care*. London: Jessica Kingsley.

Wiseman, R. (2001) The psychology of psychic fraud. In R. Roberts & D. Groome (eds) *Parapsychology: The Science of Unusual Experience*. London: Arnold.

Wiseman, R. (2012) Wired for weird. *Scientific American Mind, 22*(6), 52–57.

Wiseman, R. & Jenkins, R. (2009) The New Scientist face experiment. *New Scientist, 201* (2695), 30–31.

Wittgenstein, L. (1921) *Tractatus Logico-Philosophicus*. London: Routledge.

Wober, J.M., Reardon, G. & Fazal, S. (1987) *Personality, Character Aspirations and Patterns of Viewing Among Children*. London: IBA Research Papers.

Wober, M. (1974) Towards an understanding of the Kiganda concept of intelligence. In J.W. Berry & P.R. Dasen (eds) *Culture and Cognition*. London: Methuen.

Wokke, M.E., van Gaal, S., Ridderinkhof, K.R. & Lamme, V.A.F. (2011) The flexible nature of unconscious cognition. *PLoS One, 6*(9): e25729.

Wolf, A. (2013) *The XX factor: How working women are creating a new society*. London: Profile.

Wolf, C.C. (2013) The Mystery of the Missed Connection. *Scientific American Mind, 23*(6), 54–57.

Wolf, N. (1991) *The Beauty Myth: How Images of Beauty are Used Against Women*. New York: Dutton.

Wolpe, J. (1958) *Psychotherapy by Reciprocal Inhibition*. Stanford University Press.

Wolpe, J. (1969) For phobia: A hair of the hound. *Psychology Today, 3*, 34–37.

Wolpe, J. & Rachman, S. (1960) Psychoanalytic evidence: A critique based on Freud's case of Little Hans. *Journal of Nervous & Mental Disease, 131*, 135–145.

Wood, D.J., Bruner, J.S. & Ross, G. (1976) The role of tutoring in problem-solving. *Journal of Child Psychology & Psychiatry, 17*, 89–100.

Wood, D.J. & Wood, H. (1996) Vygotsky, tutoring and learning. *Oxford Review of Education, 22*, 5–16.

Wood, J.T. & Duck, S. (1995) *Understanding Relationship Processes 6: Understudied Relationships: Off the Beaten Track*. Thousand Oaks, CA: Sage.

Wood, W. (2000) Attitude change: Persuasion and social influence. In S.T. Fiske, D.L. Schacter & C. Zahn-Waxler (eds) *Annual Review of Psychology, Volume 51*. Palo Alto, CA: Annual Reviews.

Wood, W., Lundgren, S., Ouellette, J.A., Busceme, S. & Blackstone, T. (1994) Minority influence: A meta-analytic review of social influence processes. *Psychological Bulletin, 115*, 323–345.

Woods, B. (1998) *Applying Psychology to Sport*. London: Hodder & Stoughton.

Woodworth, R.S. (1938) *Experimental Psychology*. New York: Holt.

Woolfson, S. (2012) Home advantage. *The Psychologist, 25*(7), 514–515.

Wootton, J.M., Frick, P.J., Shelton, K.K. & Silverthorn, P. (1997) Ineffective parenting and childhood conduct problems: The moderating role of callous-unemotional traits. *Journal of Consulting and Clinical Psychology, 65*, 301–308.

Workman, L. & Andrew, R.J. (1989) Simultaneous changes in behaviour and in lateralization. *Animal Behaviour, 38*: 596–605.

Workman, L. & Reader, W. (2008) *Evolutionary Psychology* (2nd edition). Cambridge University Press.

Workman, L., Chilvers, L., Yeomans, H. & Taylor, S. (2006) Development of cerebral lateralization for emotional processing of chimeric faces in children aged 5 to 11. *Laterality, 11*, 493–507.

World Health Organization (1973) *Report of the International Pilot Study of Schizophrenia, Volume 1*. Geneva: WHO.

World Health Organization (1979) *Schizophrenia: An Initial Follow-up*. Chichester: Wiley.

World Health Organization (1992) *The ICD-10 Classification of Mental and Behavioural Disorders: Clinical Descriptions and Diagnostic Guidelines*. Geneva: WHO.

World Health Organization (2011) *Suicide Rates Per 100,000 by Country, Year and Sex*. Geneva: WHO.

Wright, R. (1994) The Moral Animal. London: Abacus.

Wynn, V.E. & Logie, R.H. (1998) The veracity of long-term memory: Did Bartlett get it right? *Applied Cognitive Psychology, 12*, 1–20.

Yarbus, A.L. (1967) *Eye Movements and Vision* (trans. B. Haigh). New York: Plenum.

Yates, A.J. (1970) *Behaviour Therapy*. New York: Wiley.

Yin, R.K. (1969) Looking at upside-down faces. *Journal of Experimental Psychology, 81*, 141–145.

Yong, E. (2013) Armour against Prejudice. *Scientific American, 308*(6), 68–71.

Young, A.W. & Bruce, V. (1998) Pictures at an exhibition: The science of the face. *The Psychologist, 11*(3), 120–125.

Young, A.W., Hay, D.C. & Ellis, A.W. (1985) The faces that launched a thousand slips: Everyday difficulties and errors in recognising people. *British Journal of Psychology, 76*, 495–523.

Young, A.W., Hellawell, D.J. & Hay, D.C. (1987) Configurational information in face perception. *Perception, 16*, 747–759.

Young, A.W., Newcombe, F., De Haan, E.H.F., Small, M. & Hay, D.C. (1993) Face perception after brain injury: Selective impairments affecting identity and expression. *Brain, 116*, 941–959.

Young, E. (2008) Sleep tight. *New Scientist, 197*(2647), 30–34.

Young, E. (2009) Sleep well, stay sane. *New Scientist, 201* (2696), 34–37.

Young, T. (1801) On the mechanism of the eye. *Philosophical Transactions 91*, 23–28.

Youngs, D. (2008) Psychology and investigations. In D. Canter, *Criminal Psychology*. London: Hodder Education.

Yousif, Y. & Korte, C. (1995) Urbanization, culture, and helpfulness: Cross-cultural studies in England and the Sudan. *Journal of Cross-Cultural Psychology, 26*, 474–489.

Yuille, J.C. & Cutshall, J.L. (1986) A case study of eyewitness memory of a crime. *Journal of Applied Psychology, 71*, 291–301.

Zajonc, R.B. (1965) Social facilitation. *Science, 1429*, 269–274.

Zajonc, R.B. (1968) Attitudinal effects of mere exposure. *Journal of Personality & Social Psychology, Monograph Supplement 9*, Part 2, 1–27.

Zajonc, R.B. (1980a) Compresence. In P. Paulus (ed.) *Psychology of Group Influence*. Hillsdale, NJ: Lawrence Erlbaum.

Zajonc, R.B. (1980b) Feeling and thinking: Preferences need no inferences. *American Psychologist, 35*, 151–175.

Zajonc, R.B. (1984) On the primacy of affect. *American Psychologist, 39*, 117–123.

Zajonc, R.B. (1989) Styles of explanation in social psychology. *European Journal of Social Psychology, 19*, 345–368.

Zajonc, R.B. (1998) Emotion. In D.T. Gilbert, S.T. Fiske & G. Lindzey (eds) *Handbook of Social Psychology*. Boston: McGraw-Hill.

Zanna, M.P. & Cooper, J. (1974) Dissonance and the pill: An attribution approach to studying the arousal propensities of dissonance. *Journal of Personality & Social Psychology, 29*, 703–709.

Zarate, C.A., Singh, J.B., Carlson, P.J. et al. (2006) A randomised trial of an N-methyl-D-aspartate Antagonist in treatment of major depression. *Archives of General Psychiatry, 63*, 856–864.

Zautra, A.J. (2003) *Emotions, Stress and Health*. New York: Oxford University Press.

Zborowski, M. (1952) Cultural components in response to pain. *Journal of Social Issues, 8*, 16–30.

Zebrowitz, L.A. (1990) *Social Perception*. Milton Keynes: Open University Press.

Zeifman, D. & Hazan, C. (2000) A process model of adult attachment formation. In W. Ickes & S. Duck (eds) *The Social Psychology of Personal Relationships*. Chichester: John Wiley & Sons Ltd.

Zeldow, P.B. (1995) Psychodynamic formulations of human behaviour. In D. Wedding (ed.) *Behaviour and Medicine* (2nd edition). St Louis, MO: Mosby-Year Book.

Zillmann, D. (1988) Cognition-excitation interdependencies in aggressive behaviour. *Aggressive Behaviour, 14*, 51–64.

Zimbardo, P. (2007) *The Lucifer Effect – Understanding How Good People Turn Evil*. London: Ebury.

Zimbardo, P.G. (1969) The human choice: Individuation, reason, and order versus deindividuation, impulse, and chaos. In W.J. Arnold & D. Levine (eds) *Nebraska Symposium on Motivation*. Lincoln: University of Nebraska Press.

Zimbardo, P.G. (1973) On the ethics of intervention in human psychological research with special reference to the 'Stanford Prison Experiment'. *Cognition, 2*(2), 243–255.

Zimbardo, P.G. (1992) *Psychology and Life* (13th edition). New York: HarperCollins.

Zimbardo, P.G. & Leippe, M. (1991) *The Psychology of Attitude Change and Social Influence*. New York: McGraw-Hill.

Zimbardo, P.G., Banks, W.C., Craig, H. & Jaffe, D. (1973) A Pirandellian prison: The mind is a formidable jailor. *New York Times Magazine*, 8 April, 38–60.

Zubieta, J.-K., Bueller, J.A., Jackson, L.R., Scott, D.J., Xu, Y., Koeppe, R.A., Nichols, T.E. & Stohler, C.S. (2005) Placebo effects mediated by endogenous opioid activity on μ-opioid receptors. *Journal of Neuroscience, 25*(34), 7754–7762.

Zubin, J. & Spring, B. (1977) Vulnerability – a new view of schizophrenia. *Journal of Abnormal Psychology, 86*, 103–126.

Zucker, K.J., Bradley, S.J., Oliver, G., Blake, J., Fleming, S. & Hood, J. (1996) Psychosexual development of women with congenital adrenal hyperplasia. *Hormones & Behaviour, 30*, 300–318.

Zuckerman, A. (1979) *Sensation-seeking: Beyond the Optimal Level of Arousal*. New York: Wiley.

Zukerman, W. & Purcell, A. (2011) Brain pruning continues into early adulthood. *New Scientist, 211*(2826), 9.

INDEX

AUTHOR INDEX

SUBJECT INDEX